THE MIDDLE EAST AND NORTH AFRICA
1982-83

A survey and directory of Afghanistan, Algeria, Bahrain, Cyprus, Egypt, Iran, Iraq, Israel, Jordan, Kuwait, Lebanon, Libya, Morocco, Oman, Qatar, Saudi Arabia, Spanish North Africa, Sudan, Syria, Tunisia, Turkey, United Arab Emirates, Yemen Arab Republic and Yemen People's Democratic Republic.

THE
MIDDLE EAST
AND
NORTH AFRICA

1982-83

TWENTY-NINTH EDITION

EUROPA PUBLICATIONS LIMITED
18 BEDFORD SQUARE LONDON WC1B 3JN

29th Edition 1982

© EUROPA PUBLICATIONS LIMITED 1982

18 Bedford Square, London, WC1B 3JN

All rights reserved

AUSTRALIA AND NEW ZEALAND

James Bennett (Collaroy) Pty. Ltd., 4 Collaroy Street, Collaroy, N.S.W. 2097, Australia

INDIA

UBS Publishers' Distributors Ltd., P.O.B. 7015, 5 Ansari Road, New Delhi 110002

JAPAN

Maruzen Co. Ltd., P.O.B. 5050, Tokyo International 100-31

Library of Congress Catalog Card Number 48-3250

British Library Cataloguing in Publication Data

The Middle East and North Africa—29th ed. (1982–83)

1. Near East—Periodicals
2. Africa, North—Periodicals

956'. 04'05   DS 41

ISBN 0-905118-75-8
ISSN 0076-8502

Printed and bound in England by
Staples Printers Rochester Limited
at The Stanhope Press.

Foreword

AS THIS EDITION of *The Middle East and North Africa* has been going to press, the Middle East has been in turmoil with the move of Israeli forces into Lebanon. Casualties among Palestinians and Lebanese have been estimated as high as 10,000 killed, and the whole future of the Palestine Liberation Organization is in doubt as Israeli forces surround West Beirut. Every effort has been made to include the latest information on these developments wherever possible.

Once again we would like to thank the numerous individuals and organizations who have sent us both revised and new information for inclusion in this edition of *The Middle East and North Africa*. Without their assistance the book could not have become a recognized authority on the region.

July 1982.

Acknowledgements

We express our thanks for much help and information kindly supplied by many Foreign Ministries and National Statistical Offices and by the following embassies and other bodies.

Afghan Embassy, London

Algerian Embassy, London

Arab League

Arab World File (Fiches du Monde Arabe), Beirut

Arabian American Oil Company

Bahrain Embassy, London

Bank Markazi Iran

British Embassy, Kuwait

Central Bank of Yemen

Cyprus High Commission, London

Institute of Petroleum Information Service, London

Iranian Embassy, London

Iraqi Embassy, London

Israel Embassy, London

Jordan Embassy, London

Kuwait Embassy, London

Lebanese Embassy, London

London Representative, "Turkish Federated State of Cyprus".

Middle East Economic Digest

National Bank of Egypt, Cairo

National Iranian Oil Company

Moroccan Embassy, London

Oman Embassy, London

Organization of Arab Petroleum Exporting Countries (OAPEC)

Organization of Petroleum Exporting Countries (OPEC)

Palestine Liberation Organization, Beirut

Qatar Embassy, London

Regional Co-operation for Development

Saudi Arabian Embassy, London

Saudi Arabian Monetary Agency, Riyadh

Spanish Embassy, London

Sudanese Embassy, London

Syrian Embassy, London

Suez Canal Authority, Ismailia

Tunisian Embassy, London

Turkish Embassy, London

Embassy of the United Arab Emirates, London

United Nations Information Centre, London

United Nations Economic Commission for Africa

United Nations Economic Commission for Western Asia

United Nations Relief and Works Agency for Palestine Refugees in the Near East

Embassy of the Yemen Arab Republic, London

Embassy of the Yemen People's Democratic Republic, London

We also acknowledge with thanks the co-operation of the International Institute for Strategic Studies, 23 Tavistock Street, London, WC2E 7NQ, in permitting us to use data on defence manpower and finance from *The Military Balance 1981-1982*, and the Israel Embassy, London, for the use of two maps of the disengagement agreements between Israel and Egypt (1974) and Israel and Syria.

Contents

PART ONE
General Survey

PART TWO
Regional Organizations

CONTENTS

PART THREE

Country Surveys

CONTENTS

ix

CONTENTS

PART FOUR

Other Reference Material

Maps

Abbreviations

A ..	..	Ambassador
AAHO	..	Afro-Asian Housing Organization
AAPSO	..	Afro-Asian People's Solidarity Organization
Acad.	..	Academy
accred.	..	accredited
AD	..	Algerian Dinars
A.D.C.	..	Aide-de-camp
ADCO	..	Abu Dhabi Company for Onshore Oil Operations
ADMA-OPCO	..	Abu Dhabi Marine Areas Operating Company
Admin.	..	Administrative; Administration; Administrator
Admin.-Gen.		Administrator-General
ADMA	..	Abu Dhabi Marine Areas
ADOCO	..	Abu Dhabi Oil Company
ADPC	..	Abu Dhabi Petroleum Company
AfDB	..	African Development Bank
Afs...	..	Afghanis
Agric.	..	Agriculture
AIWO	..	Agudath Israel World Organization
ALF	..	Arab Liberation Front
ALN	..	Armée de Libération Nationale (National Liberation Army of Algeria)
Amb.	..	Ambassador
AMINOIL	..	American Independent Oil Company
AMOSEAS	..	American Overseas Petroleum Ltd.
AOC	..	Arabian Oil Company
AOF	..	Afrique Occidentale Française (French West Africa)
API ..	..	American Petroleum Institute
approx.	..	approximately
apptd.	..	appointed
A.R.	..	Arab Republic
Aramco	..	Arabian-American Oil Company
A.R.E.	..	Arab Republic of Egypt
Ass...	..	Assembly
Asscn.	..	Association
Assoc.	..	Associate
Asst.	..	Assistant
ATAS	..	Anatolian Refinery Company
ATUC	..	African Trade Union Confederation
AUA	..	Austrian Airlines
AUXERAP	..	Société Auxiliaire de la Régie du Pétrole
Ave.	..	Avenue
b. ..	..	born
B.A.	..	Bachelor of Arts
BADEA	..	Banque Arabe de Développement Economique en Afrique (Arab Bank for Economic Development in Africa)
BAPCO	..	The Bahrain Petroleum Company Ltd.
bbl(s).	..	barrel(s)
BD ..	..	Bahrain Dinars
Bd. ..	..	Board
Bde.	..	Brigade
B.Lit(t).	..	Bachelor of Letters
Blvd.	..	Boulevard
B.P.	..	Boîte Postale (Post Office Box)
BP ..	..	British Petroleum
BPC	..	Basrah Petroleum Company
br(s).	..	branch(es)
B.Sc.	..	Bachelor of Science
B.S.T.	..	British Standard Time
BUSHCO	..	Bushire Petroleum Company

CA ..	..	Chargé d'Affaires
CAFRAD	..	Centre Africain de Formation et de Recherches Administratives pour le Développement
CAMEL	..	Compagnie Algérienne du Méthane Liquide
cap...	..	capital
Capt.	..	Captain
CARE	..	Co-operative for American Relief Everywhere
CENTO	..	Central Treaty Organization
CEP	..	Compagnie d'Exploration Pétrolière
CEPT	..	Conférence Européenne des Administrations des Postes et des Télécommunications
CFP	..	Compagnie Française des Pétroles
Chair.	..	Chairman
Cie. ..	..	Compagnie (Company)
c.i.f...	..	cost, insurance, freight
C.-in-C.	..	Commander-in-Chief
Co. ..	..	Company
Comm.	..	Commission
Commdr.	..	Commander
Commdt.	..	Commandant
Commr.	..	Commissioner
Conf.	..	Conference
Contrib.	..	Contributor; Contribution
COPE	..	Compagnie Orientale des Pétroles
COPEFA	..	Compagnie des Pétroles France-Afrique
Corpn.	..	Corporation
CPA	..	Compagnie des Pétroles d'Algérie
CREPS	..	Compagnie de Recherches et d'Exploration de Pétrole du Sahara
CRNA	..	National Council of the Algerian Revolution
CRUA	..	Revolutionary Council for Unity and Action (now FLN)
ČSA..	..	Československé Aerolinie
Cttee.	..	Committee
Del...	..	Delegate; Delegation
D. en D.	..	Docteur en Droit
dep...	..	deposits
Dept.	..	Department
Devt.	..	Development
Dir. ..	..	Director
Div...	..	Division
DPA	..	Deutsche Presse-Agentur
DPC	..	Dubai Petroleum Company
DUP	..	Democratic Unionist Party (Sudan)
d.w...	..	dead weight
ECOSOC	..	Economic and Social Council (UN)
ECWA	..	Economic Commission for Western Asia
ed. ..	..	Educated
Edn.	..	Edition
Educ.	..	Education
EEC	..	European Economic Community
EFTA	..	European Free Trade Association
EOKA	..	National Organization of the Struggle for Freedom of Cyprus
ERAP	..	Entreprise des Recherches et d'Activités Pétrolières
est. ..	..	estimate(d)
excl.	..	excluded; excluding
Exec.	..	Executive
Extra.	..	Extraordinary

f. ..	..	founded
FAO	..	Food and Agriculture Organization
FCM	..	Federation of Muslim Councillors
Fed.	..	Federation; Federal
FFS..	..	Socialist Forces Front
FIDES	..	Fonds d'Investissement pour le Développement Economique et Sociale de la France d'Outre-Mer
FLN	..	Front de Libération Nationale (National Liberation Front)
FLOSY	..	Front for the Liberation of Occupied South Yemen
fmr...	..	former
f.o.b.	..	free on board
ft. ..	..	feet; foot
gal. ..	..	gallons
GDA	..	Gas Distribution Administration
G.D.P.	..	Gross Domestic Product
Gen. Man.	..	General Manager
G.H.Q.	..	General Headquarters
G.M.T.	..	Greenwich Mean Time
G.N.P.	..	Gross National Product
G.O.C.-in-C.	..	General Officer Commanding-in-Chief
Gov.	..	Governor
Govt.	..	Government
GPRA	..	Gouvernement Provisoire de la République Algérienne (Provisional Government of the Republic of Algeria)
GUPCO	..	Gulf of Suez Petroleum Company
ha. ..	..	hectares
H.E.	..	His Eminence; His Excellency
H.I.M.	..	His Imperial Majesty
H.M.	..	His (or Her) Majesty
Hon.	..	Honourable; Honorary
H.Q.	..	Headquarters
IAEA	..	International Atomic Energy Authority
IATA	..	International Air Transport Association
IBRD	..	International Bank for Reconstruction and Development
ICAO	..	International Civil Aviation Organization
ICATU	..	International Conference of Arab Trade Unions
ICFTU— AFRO	..	International Confederation of Free Trade Unions—African Regional Organization
ICOO	..	Iraqi Company for Oil Operations
IDA	..	International Development Association
IFC..	..	International Finance Corporation
ILO..	..	International Labour Organization
IMF	..	International Monetary Fund
IMINOCO..	..	Iranian Marine International Oil Company
Inc...	..	Incorporated
incl...	..	included; including
Ind...	..	Independent
Insp.	..	Inspector
Inst.	..	Institute; Institution
Int...	..	International
INOC	..	Iraq National Oil Company
IOP..	..	Iranian Oil Participants
IPAC	..	Iran-Pan American Oil Company
IPC..	..	Iraq Petroleum Company
ITU..	..	International Telecommunications Union
JAL	..	Japan Airlines
JAT	..	Jugoslovenski Aerotransport

kg. ..	..	kilogram
KFAED	..	Kuwait Fund for Arab Economic Development
kl. ..	..	kilolitre
KLM	..	Koninklijke Luchtvaart Maatschappij NV
km...	..	kilometres
KNPC	..	Kuwait National Petroleum Company
KOC	..	Kuwait Oil Company
KPC	..	Kuwait Petroleum Corporation
KSPC	..	Kuwait Spanish Petroleum Company
kWh.	..	kilowatt
L ..	..	Legation
lb. ...	..	pounds (weight)
LINOCO	..	Libyan National Oil Corporation
LL.B.	..	Bachelor of Laws
LN ..	..	League of Nations
LOT	..	Polskie Linie Lotnicze
Ltd...	..	Limited
M ..	..	Minister
m. ..	..	million
M.A.	..	Master of Arts
Maj.	..	Major
Maj.-Gen.	..	Major-General
Malev	..	Magyar Légyar Légiköz-lekedési Vállalat
Man.	..	Manager; Managing
M.B.E.	..	Member of the (Order of the) British Empire
M.D.	..	Doctor of Medicine
MEA	..	Middle Eastern Airlines
Mem(s).	..	Member(s)
MEOC	..	Middle East Oil Company
Mgr.	..	Monseigneur; Monsignor
Mil..	..	Military
Min.	..	Minister; Ministry
MNA	..	Mouvement National Algérien (Algerian National Movement)
M.P.	..	Member of Parliament
MRP	..	Mouvement Républicain Populaire
M.Sc.	..	Master of Science
MSS.	..	Manuscripts
MTA	..	Mineral Research and Exploration Institute of Turkey
MTLD	..	Mouvement au Triomphe des Libertés Démocratiques (Movement for the Triumph of Democratic Liberties in Algeria)
n.a. ..	..	not available
Nat.	..	National
NATO	..	North Atlantic Treaty Organization
NDRC	..	National Defence Research Council
NECCCRW	..	Near East Christian Council Committee for Refugee Work
n.e.s.	..	not elsewhere specified
n.i.e.	..	not included elsewhere
NIOC	..	National Iranian Oil Company
NLF	..	National Liberation Front (People's Democratic Republic of Yemen)
no. ..	..	number
NUP	..	National Unionist Party (Sudan)
N.Y.	..	New York (City)
OAPEC	..	Organization of Arab Petroleum Exporting Countries
OAS	..	Secret Army Organization (Algeria)
OAU	..	Organization for African Unity
O.B.E.	..	Officer of the (Order of the) British Empire
OCAM	..	Organisation Commune Africaine, Malgache et Mauricienne

OCRA	..	Clandestine Organization of the Algerian Revolution
OECD	..	Organisation for Economic Co-operation and Development
ORP	..	Organisation de la Résistance Populaire (Organization of Popular Resistance in Algeria)
OPEC	..	Organization of Petroleum Exporting Countries
Parl.	..	Parliament; Parliamentary
PDFLP	..	Popular Democratic Front for the Liberation of Palestine
PDO	..	Petroleum Development Oman
PDP	..	People's Democratic Party (Sudan)
PDR	..	People's Democratic Republic
Perm.	..	Permanent
Perm. Del.	..	Permanent Delegate
Perm. Rep	..	Permanent Representative
PFLO	..	Popular Front for the Liberation of Oman
PFLP	..	Popular Front for the Liberation of Palestine
Ph.D.	..	Doctor of Philosophy
PIA	..	Pakistan International Airlines
PLA	..	Palestine Liberation Army
PLO	..	Palestine Liberation Organization
P.O.B.	..	Post Office Box
Pres.	..	President
Prof.	..	Professor
Prop.	..	Proprietor
PSD	..	Parti Socialiste Destourien (Tunisia)
PPA	..	Parti des Peuples Algériens (Party of the Algerian People)
P.R.	..	People's Republic
p.u.	..	paid up
Publ(s).	..	Publication(s)
QGPC	..	Qatar General Petroleum Corporation
QPC	..	Qatar Petroleum Company
R.A.F.	..	Royal Air Force
RCC	..	Revolutionary Command Council (Libya)
RCD	..	Regional Co-operation for Development
Rd.	..	Road
RDA	..	Rassemblement Démocratique Africain
reg.	..	registered
Rep.	..	Representative; Represented
resgnd.	..	resigned
retd.	..	retired
R.P.	..	Révérend Père (Reverend Father)
RPP	..	Republican People's Party
Rt. Hon.	..	Right Honourable
Rt. Rev.	..	Right Reverend
SAS	..	Scandinavian Airlines System
SDF	..	Sudan Defence Force
Sec.	..	Secretary
Sec.-Gen.	..	Secretary-General
SEHR	..	Société d'Exploitation des Hydrocarbures de Hassi R'Mel
SIRIP	..	Société Irano-Italienne des Pétroles
SNPA	..	Société Nationale des Pétroles d'Aquitaine
SNREPAL	..	Société Nationale de Recherche et d'Exploitation des Pétroles en Algérie
Soc.	..	Society; Société
SOFIRAN	..	Société Française des Pétroles d'Iran
SONATRACH		Société Nationale pour la Recherche, la Production, la Transformation et la Commercialisation des Hydrocarbures

Sq.	..	Square
St.	..	Street
TAL	..	Trans-Alpine Line
Tapline	..	Trans-Arabian Pipeline Company
TAROM	..	Transporturile Aeriene Romậne
THY	..	Türk Hava Yollari
TMA	..	Trans Mediterranean Airways
TPAO	..	Turkish Petroleum Corporation
trans.	..	translated; translation
TRAPES	..	Société de Transport de Pétrole de l'Est Saharien
TRAPSA	..	Compagnie de Transport par Pipe-line au Sahara
TWA	..	Trans World Airlines
U.A.E.	..	United Arab Emirates
U.A.R.	..	United Arab Republic
UBAF	..	Union des Banques Arabes et Françaises
UDMA	..	Union Démocratique du Manifeste Algérien (Democratic Union of the Algerian Manifesto)
UGTA	..	Union Générale des Travailleurs Algériens (Algerian General Workers Union)
U.K.	..	United Kingdom
UN	..	United Nations
UNCTAD	..	United Nations Conference on Trade and Development
UNDOF	..	United Nations Disengagement Observation Force
UNDP	..	United Nations Development Programme
UNEA	..	Union Nationale des Etudiants Algériens (National Union of Algerian Students)
UNEF	..	United Nations Emergency Force
UNEP	..	United Nations Environment Programme
UNESCO	..	United Nations Educational, Scientific and Cultural Organization
UNFICYP	..	United Nations Peace-Keeping Force in Cyprus
UNFP	..	Union Nationale des Forces Populaires (National Union of Popular Forces in Morocco)
UNFPA	..	United Nations Fund for Population Activities
UNICEF	..	United Nations International Children's Emergency Fund
UNIDO	..	United Nations Industrial Development Organization
UNIFIL	..	United Nations Interim Force in Lebanon
Univ.	..	University
UNMEM	..	United Nations Middle East Mission
UNRWA	..	United Nations Relief and Works Agency for Palestine Refugees in the Near East
UNTSO	..	United Nations Truce Supervision Organization
UPAF	..	Union Postale Africaine (African Postal Union)
U.P.	..	University Press
UPI	..	United Press International
U.S.A. (U.S.)		United States of America (United States)
USIS	..	United States Information Services
U.S.S.R.	..	Union of Soviet Socialist Republics
UTA	..	Union de Transports Aériens
vols.	..	volumes
VSO	..	Voluntary Service Overseas Limited
WEPCO	..	Western Desert Petroleum Company
WFTU	..	World Federation of Trade Unions
WHO	..	World Health Organization

TRANSCRIPTION OF ARABIC NAMES

The Arabic language is used over a vast area. Though the written language and the script are standard throughout the Middle East, the spoken language and also the pronunciation of the written signs show wide variation from place to place. This is reflected, and even exaggerated, in the different transcriptions in use in different countries. The same words, names and even letters will be pronounced differently by an Egyptian, a Lebanese, or an Iraqi—they will be heard and transcribed differently by an Englishman, a Frenchman, or an Italian. There are several more or less scientific systems of transliteration in use, sponsored by learned societies and Middle Eastern governments, most of them requiring diacritical marks to indicate Arabic letters for which there are no Latin equivalents.

Arabic names occurring in the historical and geographical sections of this book have been rendered in the system most commonly used by British and American Orientalists, but with the omission of the diacritical signs. For the convenience of the reader, these are explained and annotated below. The system used is a transliteration—i.e. it is based on the writing, which is standard throughout the Arab world, and not on the pronunciation, which varies from place to place. In a few cases consistency has been sacrificed in order to avoid replacing a familiar and accepted form by another which, though more accurate, would be unrecognizable.

Consonants:

d represents two Arabic letters. The second, or emphatic *d*, is transliterated *ḍ*. It may also be represented, for some dialects, by *dh* and by *z*, e.g. Qāḍī, qadhi, qazi.

dh in literary Arabic and some dialects pronounced like English *th* in *this*. In many dialects pronounced *z* or *d*.

gh A strongly guttural *g*—sometimes written *g*, e.g. Baghdād, Bagdad.

h represents two Arabic letters. The second, more guttural *h*, is transliterated *ḥ*, e.g. Husain, Husein.

as English *j* in *John*, also represented by *dj* and *g*. In Egypt this letter is pronounced as a hard *g*, and may be thus transcribed (with *u* before *e* and *i*), e.g. Najib, Nadjib, Nagib, Naguib, Neguib.

kh as *ch* in Scottish *loch*, also sometimes represented by *ch* and *h*, e.g. Khalīl, Chalil, Halil.

q A guttural *k*, pronounced farther back in the throat. Also transcribed *ḳ*, *k*, and, for some dialects, *g*, e.g. Waqf, Wakf, Wakf, Wagf.

s represents two Arabic letters. The second, emphatic *s*, is transliterated *ṣ*. It may also be represented by *ç*, e.g. Sālih, Saleh, Çaleh.

t represents two Arabic letters. The second, emphatic *t*, is transliterated *ṭ*.

th in literary Arabic and some dialects pronounced as English *th* in *through*. In many dialects pronounced *t* or *s*, e.g. Thābit, Tabit, Sabit.

w as in English, but often represented by *ou* or *v*, e.g. Wādī, Vadi, Oued.

z represents two Arabic letters. The second, or emphatic *z*, is transliterated *ẓ*. It may also be represented, for some dialects, by *dh* or *d*, e.g. Ḥāfiz, Hafidh, Hafid.

A glottal stop, as in Cockney '*li'l bo'ls*'. May also represent the sound transliterated ', a deep guttural with no English equivalent.

Vowels

The Arabic script only indicates three short vowels, three long vowels, and two diphthongs, as follows:

a as in English *hat*, and often rendered *e*, e.g. balad, beled, emir, amir; with emphatics or gutturals usually pronounced as *u* in *but*, e.g. Khalīfa, Baghdād.

as in English *bit*. Sometimes rendered *e*, e.g. jihād, jehād.

u as in English *good*. Often pronounced and written *o*, e.g. Muhammad, Mohammad.

In some Arabic dialects, particularly those of North Africa, unaccented short vowels are often omitted altogether, and long vowels shortened, e.g. Oued for Wādī, bled for balad, etc.

ā Long *a*, variously pronounced as in *sand*, *dart* and *hall*.

ī As *ee* in *feet*. In early books often rendered *ee*.

ū As *oo* in *boot*. The French transcription *ou* is often met in English books, e.g. Mahmūd, Mahmood, Mahmoud.

ai Pronounced in classical Arabic as English *i* in *hide*, in colloquial Arabic as *a* in *take*. Variously transcribed as *ai, ay, ei, ey* and *ê*, e.g. sheikh, shaikh, shaykh, etc.

aw Pronounced in classical Arabic as English *ow* in *town*, in colloquial Arabic as in *grow*. Variously rendered *aw, ew, au, ô, av, ev*, e.g. Tawfīq, Taufiq, Tevfik, etc.

TURKISH ORTHOGRAPHY AND PRONUNCIATION

Turkish has been written in Roman characters since 1928. The following pronunciations are invariable:

c hard *j*, as in *majority*, *jam*.

ç *ch*, as in *church*.

g hard *g*, as in *go*, *big*.

ğ not voiced, or pronounced *y*; Ereğli is pronounced *erayly*.

short vowel, as the second vowel of '*centre*', or French '*le*'.

i *i* sound of *Iran*, *bitter* (NOT as in *bite*, *might*).

o *o*, as in *hot*, *boss*.

ö *i* sound of '*birth*', or French '*oeuvre*'.

u as in *do*, *too*, German '*um*'.

ü as in *burette*, German '*Hütte*'.

The Year in the Middle East—June 1981-82

W. B. Fisher

In broad, and probably over-simplified, summary, this twelve-month period could be regarded as one of reversals: a major break in the consistently upward sweep over 20 years in oil prices; the survival and revival, militarily, of Iran; the handing back of the Sinai; movement in Algeria towards privatization and the quiet dropping of many of the policies of former President Boumedienne, and major economic changes in Turkey towards greater openness in fiscal, if not political, action. At the same time, the level of disturbance and assassination continued; the killings of Presidents Sadat of Egypt and Rajai of Iran being only two in a long list of violent deaths; Libyan-U.S. relations deteriorating further; and the Israeli-Arab situation hardening, with tighter policies in the occupied territories producing stronger reaction—all these were prominent features of the year. Non-alignment, as between the U.S.A. and the U.S.S.R., was tentatively explored further by the Gulf States; slight easing of tension became apparent in Morocco's relations with its neighbours; and resistance to Soviet occupation of Afghanistan continued. Then, in the last days of May 1982, came the statement by the U.S. Secretary of State, Alexander Haig: "now is America's moment in the Middle East"—indicative for the first time of a serious attempt by the Reagan administration to develop a Middle East policy.

TURKEY

The beneficial effects of the Iran-Iraq war on the Turkish economy continued to be felt very strongly. Besides a considerable growth in transit traffic, due in part to the closure of the Gulf ports and later difficulties with Syria, the textile and consumer industries gained from contracts with both combatants. It is highly significant that the Middle East has now become Turkey's chief customer, taking 30–35 per cent of exports, compared with only 13 per cent in 1978. The EEC is hence no longer Turkey's main trading area. As well, with the banning of strikes, Turkish industry is more active and competitive, and has undertaken a number of construction contracts abroad, particularly in Libya, which now has some 50,000 Turkish workers. Remittances from these Middle Eastern workers are increasing significantly, not only because of the greater number of Turks working in these territories, but because a greater proportion of earnings, as compared with the *Gastarbeiter* of Western Europe, is remitted home. Further, a growing proportion of Turkish-made materials—cement, woodwork, etc.—is used in these foreign projects.

Improved economic prospects and improved internal stability, because of success against the terrorism which caused 200 deaths per month prior to the military takeover, now allow political moves on a more positive scale. On July 5th, 1981, the Turkish Government put forward a peace plan for Cyprus that represented some advance and concession, in that it proposed handing back to the Greek area 3 per cent of the territory at present occupied by Turkey. These small areas of land were chiefly to be around Larnaca and Famagusta. The idea of parity between the two communities in a federal constitution for the whole island was, however, retained. The proposals were not accepted, but have remained a significant move—the first since Turkey occupied northern Cyprus in 1974. As well, a more relaxed policy towards Greece became apparent; and steps were taken in October to go some slight way to a revival of democratic rule by the formation of a Consultative Assembly that could eventually, though by no means immediately, allow an elective system.

Even so, the severe problems of Turkey—in September 1981 it was calculated that Turkey's foreign indebtedness amounted to $20,000 million, of which $5,700 million comprised interest payments—together with the generally stagnant situation over Cyprus (an initiative by the UN Secretary-General, Dr. Kurt Waldheim, on November 18th brought no effective result) meant that there was reluctance on the part of international agencies to offer credits and aid or the rescheduling of existing loans. The strict censorship of news, suggestions of torture in prison, the imprisonment in November of a former Prime Minister, Bülent Ecevit (though only for a four-month term), did not dispose outside agencies in Turkey's favour. The EEC countries, particularly West Germany and France, declared reservations about the admission of Turkey to the Community, though Turkey itself stated in mid-1981 that eventual full membership was still its objective. The problems of continuing high population growth, low agricultural productivity, inefficient industry and political difficulties remained. A short visit to Turkey by Mr. Haig in mid-May 1982 gave some indication that the U.S.A. continues to value its strategic links with Turkey.

IRAN AND IRAQ

Following the dismissal in June 1981 of Abolhasan Bani-Sadr, first as Commander-in-Chief of the Iranian armed forces and then as President of Iran, he went into hiding until, on July 29th, he managed to arrange an escape by air, which took him eventually to France, despite efforts by the authorities to find him.

In the meantime, however, his supporters had struck back. On June 28th a major bomb explosion at the headquarters of the Islamic Republican Party (IRP) killed 74 persons, including Ayatollah Beheshti, leader of the IRP and well-known as a "hard-liner", together with four Cabinet Ministers and 27 members of the *Majlis*. This was clearly part of a wider campaign by the *Mujaheddin Khalq* ("Holy Fighters for the People"), supporters of ex-President Bani-Sadr, to assassinate political figures and senior governmental officials, accompanied by commercial and industrial disruption and acts of sabotage. The reply was a closer assumption of power by the Islamic clergy (the "Mullahs") at the beginning of August, with an extensive crack-down on opponents. Many hundreds of these are thought to have been arrested and many were later executed during the ensuing weeks—perhaps as many as 50 to 60 per day. Nature, meanwhile, had also taken a destructive hand since there were two earthquakes in South Kerman province during June and July, with the loss of more than 1,000 lives.

On August 30th a further bomb explosion took place at the Prime Minister's office, as the result of which the new President, Muhammad Ali Rajai, and his successor as Prime Minister, Hojatoleslam Muhammad Javad Bahonar, were both killed. A third President, Hojatoleslam Sayed Ali Khamenei, the new leader of the IRP, was elected on October 2nd, with what was described as well over 90 per cent of votes cast. Some observers questioned both the majority and the claim of a high turnout; but the result was clear, as also was the continuance of executions of opponents—more than 60 on the same day as the election itself. Amnesty International estimated that, since the 1979 revolution, some 1,700 Iranians had been executed for political offences up to June 1981, with a further 1,800 from June to October 1981.

Disturbance at home, which some saw as near-civil war, did not, however, destroy the military capability of Iran. On September 27th a surprise attempt was launched to relieve Abadan, closely but not totally besieged by Iraqi forces. This was partially successful, although the Iranian Commander-in-Chief was killed in an air crash. On October 2nd Iran undertook a major air strike against targets in Iraq. Extensive damage was done to electric power plants in the Baghdad area, resulting in prolonged black-outs, while at the same time a Kuwaiti oil refinery was also bombed. This plant, located some 40 km. inside Kuwait's territory, could hardly have been attacked by mistake: the point was taken that the raid was intended as a deliberate warning to Kuwait to avoid support for Iraq. Nevertheless, this support continued and large numbers of vehicles moved daily from Kuwait towards the Iraqi town of Basra. It has been said that there was also a daily, but not continuous, barrage of Iranian artillery directed against this traffic, with a known and regular period of quiet. Another significant incident occurred during October. On the 4th, Iranians participating in the *haj* (the Muslim pilgrimage to Mecca) attempted to organize a political demonstration in favour of Shi'a principles, actually within Mecca itself. A similar demonstration had occurred during the previous *haj* in 1980, without much reaction from the Saudi authorities; but this year it was broken up—religion only, and no politics during the pilgrimage, was the official view.

By the autumn of 1981 the situation in Iran was one of intensive terrorist campaigns, with severe retaliation by a Government increasingly dominated by religious "hard-liners"— the "Mullahs". Nevertheless, as shown by increasing military activity, the Government was able to maintain its power. After October efforts to overthrow it, and attacks on its officials, declined. In Paris Mr. Bani-Sadr was subject to restriction, and opposition groups remained divided: Royalist supporters of the late Shah's young son proved ineffective; the efforts of a few former military commanders secured the temporary hijacking of an Iranian gunboat built in France but had little final result; while the group round another exile, Mr. Shahpour Bakhtiar, had earlier lost credibility by its support of the Iraqis against Iran in the Gulf war.

After a quiet period during the winter, with the armies on both sides holding positions as altered by the autumn campaign, the ruling group in Iran had gained markedly in confidence. On February 6th, 1982, the headquarters of the *Mujaheddin* was stormed by government troops and the group's leader, Musa Khiabani (who had been, in effect, leader of the opposition to the ruling Mullahs within Iran), killed. Many of his supporters were imprisoned or executed, giving a total put by some as 25,000 now in prison and between 2,000 and 8,000 executed since the summer of 1981. In mid-March Iran opened a major offensive round the towns of Shush and Dezful. During several days' fighting, the Iraqis were forced to give up some 3,000 sq. km. of territory, and considerable casualties were incurred by both sides. Although not a rout, as the Iranians first claimed, this Iranian action could be said to have been a major turning point in the Iran-Iraq war; and some effects were soon clear. The mass of sophisticated weaponry available to the Iraqis was proving much less effective, and it was not always properly used, against the fervour of Iranian troops, some of whom—as the Iraqis protested—were extremely young. Initiative thence passed clearly to Iran, and the Iranians again took the Iraqis by surprise with a drive starting on April 30th over a front 100 km. further north. By mid-May Iran had succeeded in threatening the Iraqi hold on Khorramshahr by crossing the Karun river, and reaching points only 35 km. from the Iraqi frontier. On May 23rd Khorramshahr itself was captured.

Within Iraq, the shifting of military initiative to the Iranians has had notable effects. The twelve-month period had begun badly for Iraq, with the air attack by Israel on the Osirak nuclear reactor near Baghdad. Besides the loss of the reactor itself (for which the Saudi Arabian Government has promised to meet costs of replacement, with the French at first much less openly keen to undertake this but, later "softer" and more acquiescent), there was the demonstration of Israeli ability to undertake an undisputed air strike across hostile territory despite sophisticated warning and defence systems being operated within a country actually at war (another Entebbe)—a matter not lost on the Iranians, who later, as we have partly noted, undertook air raids as far west as the Iraq-Syria border. In May 1982 Israel's Defence Minister confirmed that Israel had regularly supplied arms to Iran.

A year of economic targets, with the greatest overall expenditure of any Middle Eastern country (more than that of Saudi Arabia), then led in Iraq to the imposition of austerity in the spring of 1982, with the curtailing of non-essential imports. Syria, friendly a year earlier, once more became difficult, and closed its frontier with Iraq on April 8th, thus inhibiting the flow of oil to the Lebanese port of Tripoli (between 50 and 60 per cent of Iraqi exports), resulting in a loss of $17 million per day to Iraq, and also cutting road and rail communications through Turkey. The development budget—by far the largest in Iraq's history—may well have to be reduced significantly; and loans from outside, negotiated with ease until 1981, are now distinctly more difficult to obtain. All this led to peace "feelers" by Iraq in mid-March; but the Foreign Minister of Algeria, Muhammad Benyahia (who was attempting to mediate between Iran and Iraq), was killed in an air crash during early May.

Nevertheless, despite Saudi Arabian calls on May 27th for a "holy war" against the rulers of Iran ("symbols of Satan"), appeals for a cease-fire and peace negotiations are now much stronger, especially from the smaller Gulf States.

SYRIA

Besides its involvement in Lebanon, which will be discussed later, other highly critical events also occurred in Syria. In addition to rising internal unrest, particularly in Aleppo and Hama, Syria has become increasingly isolated from most Arab States other than Libya and South Yemen. This was due, in part, to Syria's increasingly close ties with the U.S.S.R. (one aspect being support of the Soviet invasion of Afghanistan); the theoretical union with Libya; and markedly worsening relations with Jordan. Syria's stand against Israel during May–June 1981, in the matter of the missiles in Lebanon, gained it some temporary prestige and solidarity; but a month or so later the number of bomb incidents within the country had greatly increased, with a reported total of 150 killed in Hama during August, Then on January 10th, 1982, there was a bomb attempt on a meeting in Damascus of the ruling Baath Party. This appears to have involved about 150, mainly air force officers. A smaller army revolt occurred on the 24th. Both incidents seem to have arisen from discontent over the lack of success of Syria against better-armed and better-led Israelis, low morale generally, and perhaps also President Assad's action in sabotaging the Arab Summit Conference at Fez, in Morocco, some weeks earlier. In early February a much more serious revolt occurred in Hama. This continued well into March, by which time the larger part of the centre of the city had been destroyed, with considerable loss of life, put by later observers at between 8,000 and 30,000 persons. The ferocity of the fighting, with much wanton destruction, looting and violation of women, showed the strength and bitterness of fundamentalist feeling, which provoked savagery in return. Although the government troops were eventually successful, President Assad has been even further isolated and his power-base diminished. The tenuous links with Libya and South Yemen, and closer ties with Iran (the reason given for closing the pipeline through Iraq in 1982 was that the Syrian refinery at Banias would in future handle Iranian crude shipped in by tanker via Suez), have led to a considerable fall-off in aid from the Gulf States, and from Saudi Arabia especially.

ISRAEL, LEBANON, JORDAN

Following the high crisis period of early June 1981, a series of Israeli bomb attacks were launched during early July on the PLO in Damour, Sidon and Beirut—this last left 200 killed and 800 wounded, including 200 children. Then a gradual calming down began, with an eventual cease-fire on July 24th that was to last until the spring of 1982. The Maronite Christian's siege of Zahlé was lifted at this time—a considerable blow to the Phalangist Party, which saw its links with Israel diminish and the Lebanese Government generally weakened. The efforts of President Reagan's emissary, Philip Habib, were, after rebuffs, at last successful, at least for a short, limited term. There had been considerable efforts by the U.S.A. behind the scenes, to bring about this cease-fire. One of the more extreme political notes was struck at this time by Libyan claims that Egypt, in alliance with Israel, was preparing to invade Libya, following a remark made by President Sadat that Libya was the world's largest tank-park.

During August the U.S.A. resumed delivery to Israel of military supplies: these had been temporarily stopped during June–July as a mark of U.S. disapproval of Israeli actions and in order to give muscle to Mr. Habib's activities. The French Ambassador to Lebanon was assassinated on September 4th, 1981, and a further bomb attack on the French Embassy took place in May 1982. During November 1981 King Hussein of Jordan visited the U.S.A. in an attempt to improve relations that had become somewhat cool under President Carter; and in November the King also visited Moscow with the aim of negotiating arms sales.

One other important effect of the early summer crisis was to provide Menachem Begin's Likud Party (that had been expected earlier to lose the June general election in Israel) with a relative success that gave it a precarious majority in the new Knesset. Likud increased its membership from 43 (in 1977) to 48, while the main opposition group, the Labour Alignment, also gained, from 32 to 47. Mr. Begin was able to form a new government with the support of three National Religious Party members and others, bringing his support to 61 members in a Knesset of 120. One result of this was the introduction of legislation strengthening religious observance in Israel, especially on the Sabbath. Even so, demonstrations against Sabbath activities continued—for example a sporting fixture was stopped by the incursion of more than 1,000 zealots in May 1982, and El Al, the national airline, is virtually grounded internally during the Sabbath.

Religious feeling had also developed further during

the summer in Egypt, where riots between Muslim fundamentalists and Coptic Christians broke out, mainly in Cairo but also in Asyut and a few other towns. Some 150 Coptic officials were arrested and the Coptic Pope suspended from office; and on September 3rd a major purge of government appointees was undertaken by the President, Anwar Sadat: about 1,500 politicians, religious leaders (especially Muslim fundamentalists) and journalists were dismissed.

On October 6th came the assassination of President Sadat by six soldiers, during an army parade. In contrast to the fervent scenes of grief at the death of his predecessor, President Nasser, there was remarkably little public reaction: a quiet, almost private funeral was accompanied by a smooth assumption of the presidency by Vice-President Hosni Mubarak, who has deliberately followed a low-key, low-profile style of personal and governmental activity. In mid-November the deteriorating situation in the occupied West Bank region of Jordan—Palestinian protest and Israeli repression—led to a conference between Egypt and Israel, with little result. Bir Zeit Arab University and others were closed, and the destruction (as a deterrent) of Arab protestors' houses continued on a larger scale. Mr. Begin saw considerable difficulty, including at first the impossibility of the inclusion of European elements in the proposed peace-keeping force to be organized by the U.S.A. in the Sinai. In the latter part of December, starting on the 19th, co-incidentally with the major upheavals in Poland, that were attracting world attention, and the start of the Christmas season for many in the west, Israel declared the annexation to itself of the occupied Golan Heights area of Syria. Again there was wide reaction: the U.S.A. suspended U.S.-Israeli strategic cooperation, and there were movements of alarm, followed by reconciliation and solidarity, among Arab states. Libya and Saudi Arabia agreed to resume diplomatic relations; Syria opened its oil pipeline (closed for five years previously and to be closed again on April 8th, 1982) and expressed suitable regrets for its cold attitude toward the Arab Summit held in Fez. There were suggestions of reconvening an Arab Summit, which, however, did not materialize. In spite of all this, facts remained facts: the Golan was absorbed more fully into the Israeli polity with an announcement of new settlement plans for 20,000 Israelis. This led to a "strike" by Druze Arabs in mid-February, which, however, had little effect. In January a resolution of the UN Security Council, calling for voluntary sanctions against Israel for its action in the Golan, was vetoed by the U.S.A.; but a voluntary sanctions motion in the General Assembly was accepted on February 6th.

April saw the handover of the final agreed portion of territory by Israel to Egypt in the Sinai. Egypt had carefully maintained the lowest political activity possible—avoiding provocation and blandly negating vexatious rumours. Israel was troubled by disturbances, particularly in the town of Yamit, which was occupied for some weeks by Israeli zealots who had ultimately to be removed from the town by force. This was regarded by some Israelis as a warning of what must never be allowed to happen in the West Bank.

Conditions in the West Bank deteriorated considerably during the year. Throughout the autumn of 1981, the appointment of Menahem Milson as head of the "small village leagues" led to active pressure on Arab villages. The leagues were designed to counteract Arab intransigence and civil disobedience by providing an alternative civic structure, thus reducing the power of Arab mayors who, for some time, had been leaders of resistance to Israeli local rule. Some $12 million was made available by central government to provide infrastructures—roads, wells, etc.—and the effect of this beneficence on some Arabs was notable. The Government of Jordan warned West Bank Arabs that to accept these subsidies could amount to "treason". The Israeli counter was to impose restrictions on the transfer of money between the occupied Palestine territories; then in March came the suggestion that Arabs favouring the leagues might be armed by the Israeli Government against other Arabs.

Thus, by the spring of 1982, it could be said that relations within the West Bank had rarely been worse, short of actual warfare, and a high level of tension had built up. Arab-Jordanian moves to gain the loyalty of West Bankers had led to a marked escalation of violence: stone-throwing, demonstrations and sabotage by young Arabs; with shooting—by no means always in the air or as a last resort—and the destruction of Arab homes and wells by Israeli soldiers. An incident on April 11th, when an Israeli of U.S. origin attacked passers-by near the Al Aqsa Mosque in Jerusalem (killing two Arabs), led to a call by King Khalid of Saudi Arabia for a one-day strike throughout Arab countries that was largely, but not wholly, observed.

At the beginning of April another UN Security Council resolution, denouncing Israeli action in the West Bank and Gaza areas and the dismissal for "non-cooperation" of three Arab mayors, was vetoed by the U.S.A. Israel was accused of venting its frustration over the loss of the Sinai by repression within the remaining occupied territories. On May 16th the Israeli Chief of General Staff ordered an official inquiry into allegations of unnecessary violence against Palestinian Arabs by Israel's reserve troops.

Within days of the cession of the Sinai, the nine-month cease-fire was broken. Some 60 Israeli aircraft (in retaliation for provocation by PLO guerrilla sabotage and bomb attacks) mounted massive air raids once again on Beirut, Damour and Tyre, and a state of alert was declared in northern Israel. May saw massive reinforcement of Israeli troops, said to number 30,000, in northern Israel, to which the Syrians responded by building extensive defensive works further south, along the lower Bekaa valley, and increasing their own military concentrations. Once more there is a reminder of the crucial and central importance of Arab-Israeli relations, not only in the Middle East but as a highly significant and dangerous element in world affairs.

On May 27th Mr. Haig announced that the U.S.A. would supply a further 75 F-16 fighter aircraft to Israel, and six C-130 Hercules transport to Iraq.

EGYPT AND SUDAN

A distinctly new trend in Egyptian policy was opened with the demise of President Sadat, the man who had actually initiated relations with Israel. With the takeover by President Mubarak, it was possible to see the beginnings of political realignment—a quiet approach to the other Arab states while, at the same time, doing nothing to upset the fragile relationship with Israel (at least in the short term) which was soon to return the Sinai; a more even-handed "line" as regards the U.S.A. and the U.S.S.R. (one of Sadat's last acts had been to expel 1,500 Soviet advisers), with recognition that there could be important changes with the shift of fortunes in the Gulf War.

Yet the economy of Egypt continued to pose problems. On the credit side, remittances from abroad continued at a high level, due to the fact that possibly as many as 1.5 million Egyptians were working temporarily in Iraq: new discoveries of oil and, particularly, gas occurred; and aid from the West (chiefly from the U.S.A.) continued. On the other hand, the fall in the price of crude oil, the partial failure of Sadat's "open-door" policy on foreign economic links (which had led to much evasion and unnecessary luxury imports) and generally low agricultural productivity remained adverse factors. Overall, however, it is fair to say that there had been a distinct improvement in Egypt's economic position, and this has allowed a relatively quiet year—even with the assassination of President Sadat and the further growth in Islamic fundamentalism. The possibility of *rapprochement* with the other Arab countries became stronger during the year and there were the obvious gains from negotiation with Israel that could possibly go further, although recent difficulties, due to a stronger Israeli policy in the West Bank, have reduced this possibility considerably.

For Sudan, in sharp contrast, the last twelve-month period has seen mounting difficulties. Several years of declining cotton production have led to a real fall in living standards, and the yield of the 1981 cotton crop (less than 2 kantars per feddan, far below the average of a few years ago) meant that cotton ceased to be the country's largest single export item. Heavy indebtedness, with a record current deficit on the balance of payments of around $1,000 million in 1981, and the inability of the Kenana sugar scheme to achieve rapid self-sufficiency were important adverse factors.

In early October President Nimeri dissolved the National Assembly, and in the following month undertook a drastic government reshuffle, at the same time introducing austerity measures—ending the subsidy on petrol, and phasing out, by stages, subsidies on sugar and flour. These measures were designed to counter the expected $700 million budget deficit for the current year. Food riots occur-red in a number of towns, exacerbated by the growing number of refugees now temporarily settled in various frontier areas from Ethiopia, the Central African Republic and Chad. At the same time, however, the guerrilla war waged agross the frontiers of Chad by followers of Hissène Habré (who had earlier been driven from Chad) was brought to a possibly temporary end, partly, it is believed, as the result of U.S. influence. Sudan is seen as an area that must be retained for Western influence; and, now that there is some (though apparently limited) prospect of oil development (the Chevron Co. has announced significant discoveries), U.S. interest continues. It also became easier to secure the restructuring of Sudanese debts and $600 million of debt was handled in this way at the end of December.

Troubles developed over the status of the large, remote Southern Province. The regional assembly for the south was dissolved in October, and student riots in various towns during early January, mainly against the removal of the sugar subsidy, were particularly strong in the south, leading to temporary closure of the university at Juba. Uncertainty about the status of the south (a focus of pressure from the Islamic north) and the possibility of the domination by single local groups, such as the Dinka, have surfaced once more after several years of relative quiet and harmony. The building of a refinery at Kosti was taken as a political move that did not please many in the south.

THE GULF STATES

The main development was the announcement on August 8th, 1981, by Crown Prince (now King) Fahd of Saudi Arabia of an eight-point peace plan for Israel/Palestine. This plan was soon dismissed, both by the PLO (as inadequate) and by the Israeli Government (as demanding too much), but its points appeared to most outside observers as sound, if unexceptional, principles. Qualified support was expressed by the EEC, which, at the time, was experiencing lukewarm or hostile reaction to its own attempts (chiefly by Lord Carrington, then Britain's Foreign Secretary) to find a similar solution. A visit to Israel in November by the French Minister for Foreign Affairs disassociated France from the EEC initiative and, in effect, spelt the end of the EEC action.

In July 1981 Saudi Arabia announced a $34,000 million trading surplus for 1980, with the U.S.A. and Japan as its two principal partners. On September 1st it was announced that Saudi oil production would be cut back by 10 per cent in order to maintain a price of $34 per barrel. Because of the sag in world demand, oil prices on world markets had fallen below $30 per barrel. During the rest of the year, Saudi efforts were directed strongly to maintaining solidarity and united action among OPEC members in order to keep up this price level, if necessary, by reduced output. Saudi Arabia is thought to have cut back production even more during the spring of 1982, and by June of that year it was becoming clear that the strategy had probably succeeded—at least temporarily. Pressure has been put on purchasers of oil to buy from OPEC sources rather than from others —this by threats of curtailing OPEC purchases of manufactured goods, and by offering subsidies and loans to those OPEC partners that were in difficulty, such as Nigeria. At the end of October King Khalid visited President Mitterrand of France, the first foreign Head of State to do so.

On November 25th came the abortive Arab Summit Conference at Fez. The openly hostile absence of Syria, the bickering between other members and the inability of Saudi Arabia to push for positive action led the host, King Hassan of Morocco, to end the conference only a few hours after its opening—a considerable humiliation for Saudi Arabia, and a demonstration of Arab disarray that was not lost on Mr. Begin, who shortly afterwards annexed the Golan Heights to Israel.

In December, too, there was an attempt at a coup in Bahrain. Dissidents, supported from Iran, carried out a landing but were imprisoned by the Bahrain authorities, who maintained a quiet, low-key stance over the affair.

During 1982 the revival of Iranian fortunes in the Gulf War led to some nervousness in the region, especially among the smaller Gulf states, all of which had supported Iraq, to a greater or lesser extent, during the war. There is now growing interest in possible peace talks, and a Summit Conference has been proposed by certain "non-aligned" countries (including India and Yugoslavia), to be held in September 1982. In the meantime, as Iraqi reverses occur on a larger scale and casualties mount steeply, hopes are increasingly centred on these peace initiatives and on the Iranian declaration that it is intended only to recover Iranian sovereign territory, not to invade Iraq. (In June 1982 Saddam Hussein stated that Iraqi forces were withdrawing from Iranian territory—*Editor*).

On May 15th, as a result of Iran's military successes, an emergency meeting of the Gulf Co-operation Council (GCC) was held. The GCC had been formed a year previously, with a secretariat in Riyadh, and includes the Arab countries of the Gulf (Saudi Arabia, Bahrain, Kuwait, Qatar, the United Arab Emirates and Oman). When it met, the GCC did no more than postpone action to a later date, but its *raison d'être* is to assess the new situation in the Gulf and the possibility of Shi'a uprisings, perhaps in Iraq and south Lebanon, where there are sizeable Shi'a minorities, and possibly also in Bahrain, Dubai, Kuwait and Oman. Outside observers are beginning to regard the Gulf conflict as something of a sectarian, religious struggle, as well as the more apparent nationalist clash. It is perhaps indicative that the GCC meeting, having assembled amid feelings of emergency, immediately decided to adjourn.

LIBYA

The year began with Libyan withdrawal from Chad and the restoration of relations with Morocco—both of which strengthened Colonel Gaddafi's prestige in black Africa. Then, on August 19th, two Libyan but Soviet-made SU-22s were shot down over the Gulf of Sirte by American naval fighter aircraft, as the result of a territorial dispute. Libya had claimed a zone 300 miles wide in the Gulf as Libyan territory, but the U.S.A. deliberately disputed this and, when its aircraft were attacked by Libyan fighters, responded in kind but to greater effect. Expressions of solidarity and support, but little more, came from most Arab countries, including the conservative Arab states. Much of this sympathy evaporated, however, when, on September 1st, Libya threatened to ally formally with the U.S.S.R. and to attack U.S. and NATO nuclear installations in the Mediterranean area. In the meantime, because of Libyan complicity in an explosion in Khartoum, Sudan broke off relations with Libya, and Libya also continued to bomb villages in south-west Sudan in order to harass refugees from Chad who had taken refuge there. This led to a Sudanese protest in October to the UN Security Council. On November 4th Libya withdrew its troops from Chad. During the autumn, U.S.-Libyan relations remained very tense, with U.S. reminders of so-called "assassination squads" said to be directed even against President Reagan. This was denied in Libya, but in December President Reagan ordered a withdrawal of U.S. personnel from Libya. This was only partially obeyed: some oil companies merely reduced staffs, although Exxon had already withdrawn totally from Libya during November. By the end of 1981 Libya had begun to feel the severe effects of the drop in the oil price, which had reduced Libyan revenue by 50 to 60 per cent. Cash flow difficulties began to be apparent, as indicated by a delay in settling payments of local contracts and for development infrastructure projects. This produced some congestion in ports, particularly Tripoli, and led to Libyan attempts to barter oil for foreign goods. Overall, however, cash reserves are still considerable, but the increasing number of foreign workers (now about half of the total Libyan labour force) poses obvious problems.

NORTH AFRICA

The main feature here has been a prolonged drought, felt especially severely in Morocco, where it has lasted for two years. This has greatly depressed economic activity in Morocco, retarding the effective start of the Five Year Plan (1981–86) and perhaps helping to bring about a reorientation of policy by Algeria. June 1981 saw riots in Casablanca but, at the same time, Algeria showed some signs of softening its former opposition to Morocco over the Polisario Front, which was increasingly dominated by Libya. In July King Hassan proposed what he termed a controlled referendum in the disputed territory of the Western Sahara, but this came to nothing because of difficulties over defining the size of the population eligible to take part. In July diplomatic relations were restored between Libya and Morocco, after an earlier rupture due to Libya's support of Polisario. In early July President Chadli of Algeria dismissed two rivals, Abdelaziz Bouteflika (formerly Minister for Foreign Affairs) and Col. Muhammad Yahiaoui (an advocate of "Arab Socialism"), from the central committee of the ruling National Liberation Front. This enabled the President to move more rapidly towards privatization and to open the country rather more to foreign investment. At the end of September, Algeria claimed that Libya had been encroaching on a small enclave of its territory, and at the same time supplying Soviet-made light armaments to dissident Tuareg groups.

Much was made by Morocco of a clash on October 13th in the Western Sahara, which resulted in a local defeat of Polisario activists. However, the incident could be held to justify somewhat closer U.S. interest and assistance—especially as, at this time, relations with Libya were moving towards an extremely low ebb.

The visit of President Mitterrand of France to Algiers during the first few days of December marked an important turning point in policy for both countries, which had remained at odds since the successful assertion of Algerian independence, the friction exacerbated by the problem of Algerian workers in France. With the swing to the left in France in 1981 and the gradual shift to a more rightist stance in Algeria (as shown by a critical reassessment of the productivity of collective farming, and greater emphasis on the production of consumer goods), more amicable relations could be, and have since, developed. This, as was stated above, is one of the more significant changes during 1981–82. Algeria's involvement in Gulf oil development and its role as an intermediary in the U.S.–Iran hostage crisis have now been followed by a move towards slightly more moderate, pro-Western policies. The further growth of Muslim fundamentalism in Algeria, with demonstrations by zealots and the adoption of Islamic dress by women, is also a feature.

One further item of importance was the judgment of the International Court of Justice on February 24th which ended a four-year dispute between Libya and Tunisia, over off-shore oil rights. In effect, a compromise was proposed, with no alteration in existing oil concession limits. On April 3rd came an announcement of economic collaboration between Algeria and Libya, with a scheme for progressive integration of the two economies.

AFGHANISTAN

It is now estimated that some 3 to 4 million Afghans are living as refugees in neighbouring countries: 1.5 million in Iran, according to Sheikh Khalkli in the summer of 1981 and well over 2 million in Pakistan.

The efforts of the EEC (with, at the time, Lord Carrington as Chairman of the Council of Ministers) to solve the Afghan crisis were dismissed in early July as "unrealistic" by the U.S.S.R., and a similar initiative during August had no result either. During the summer of 1981 it became apparent that, under President Reagan, the U.S.A. had increased its supply of arms to groups resisting Soviet forces in Afghanistan and that Egypt and Saudi Arabia were involved in this supply (which included many Soviet-made weapons). In September it was reported that riots had occurred in Kabul over the issue of conscription. During October the level of fighting increased. It was claimed that 600 rebels had been killed in Herat. This led to proposals of a "Shi'a" solution from Iran, and a UN resolution on November 18th, calling for the withdrawal of all foreign troops from Afghanistan. Over the whole year it would seem that the pattern of confrontation between the two sides has changed to a marked extent. The pro-government troops, both Afghan and Soviet, are now using more helicopter gunships to attack tribesmen in mountain areas, with rapid and devastating action against rebel groups, irrespective of detailed allegiance, with, also, more action closer to frontier areas. On the other side, the lesson of the need for co-operation is gradually being learned and, despite an extraordinarily hard winter climatically, these groups are now somewhat better-armed and, apparently, still very resilient.

Despite friction over Afghanistan and Iranian attempts to influence, by broadcasts, the Muslim populations of Soviet Central Asia—matters of friction between Iran and the U.S.S.R.—it was apparent that trade between these two countries greatly increased over the last year. In April 1982 the opening of a new bridge over the Amu Darya (Oxus) river—the first between Afghanistan and the U.S.S.R.—was a visible indication of the closeness of relations between official Afghanistan and the U.S.S.R.

Editorial Note: The Israeli invasion of Lebanon took place after this article was written. A summary of the situation up to mid-July 1982 is given under *Late Information* on page xxiii.

LATE INFORMATION

THE ISRAELI MOVE INTO LEBANON

In the article on The Arab-Israeli Confrontation 1967–82 (p. 62), and in the History sections of the chapters on Israel and Lebanon, the picture presented is that of late June 1982, when approximately 6,000 Palestinian guerrillas were besieged in West Beirut by Israeli forces. By late July there had been no significant change in the disposition of forces. Negotiations had been in progress to secure the evacuation of the PLO fighters, but no conclusion had been reached on their destination. Syria had stated its unwillingness to receive them. By late July the sixth ceasefire in the fighting was in operation. The U.S. attitude towards the whole situation, which at the outset had been condemnatory of the Israeli move but lacking in positive action, became clearer after Secretary of State Alexander Haig's resignation at the end of June, ostensibly because he felt that U.S. foreign policy lacked a clear direction.

By July 19th, Phillip Habib, President Reagan's special Middle East envoy, had presented his "final" proposals to the Israelis, the Palestinians, the Syrians and the Lebanese. These called for a total Syrian and Palestinian evacuation of Lebanon and the withdrawal of Israeli forces to the port of Sidon. There was no suggestion, however, of an acceptable destination for the besieged Palestinians, and the Israelis refused to withdraw south of Damour.

On July 20th it appeared that the PLO had agreed in principle to accept UN Resolution 242 (see p. 76), which in effect recognizes Israel, in return for U.S. recognition of the PLO. This would not only help to solve the immediate PLO question in Lebanon, but would open up the possibility of far-reaching developments in reaching a solution to the whole Palestinian question. On the following day, however, Dean Fischer, the State Department spokesman, stated: "We will not recognize or negotiate with the PLO until that organization has accepted UN Security Council Resolutions 242 and 338 and recognized Israel's right to exist. In our view these conditions must be made clearly and unequivocally; in our view they have not been".

THE IRANIAN MOVE INTO IRAQ

In the middle of July 1982 Iranian forces moved into Iraq and at one time threatened the port of Basrah, but by July 22nd a lull had developed in the fighting. The Iranian advance had been on two fronts near Basrah. Iraqi communiqués stated that heavy losses had been inflicted on Iranian forces.

TURKEY

(Government reshuffle, July 14th, 1982)

Minister of State (replacing Deputy Prime Minister for Economic Affairs and Minister of State Turgut Özal): SERMET REFIK PASIN.

Minister of Finance: ADNAN BASER KAFAOGLU.

Minister of Housing and Reconstruction: Prof. AHMET SAMSUNLU.

PART ONE

General Survey

The Middle East and North Africa: An Introduction

W. B. Fisher

Definition of the Area

The term "Middle East and North Africa" is a cumbersome and, possibly to some, even a misleading description. Besides already embracing part of northern Africa, "Middle East" has the further objection of meaning different things to different people. Some would apply it to areas much farther east, and not to Africa at all—which is geographically more logical—but then Libya and Egypt would no longer be in the "Middle East", a nonsense for some others. Perhaps only when we come to consider alternatives do the merits, such as they are, of our present title begin to emerge. "Muslim World" is too extensive in that it could reach as far as Pakistan, Malaysia and Indonesia; whilst reference to "Arab" only would exclude Turkey, Iran, Cyprus (80 per cent Greek) and, logically to one way of thinking, the Berber areas of Tunisia, Algeria and Morocco.

We can trace popular use of "Middle East" back to the Second World War. It developed in a casual, almost haphazard, manner following the territorial expansion of a unified military command that was originally based on countries lying east of the Suez Canal. In this way, the British and American publics grew accustomed to the association of Jerusalem, Damascus, Cairo and then Benghazi and even Tripoli with the collective description "Middle East" (now increasingly shortened in America, to "Mid East"); and, in the writer's view, the expression has come to have a validity based on popular usage which it is now difficult to challenge. There are, however, numerous geographers and historians who are unwilling to abandon the older concept of southern Asia as divisible into a Near, Middle and Far East; and in 1946 the Royal Geographical Society protested against the British Government's continued official usage of "Middle East" to indicate Palestine, Egypt and countries further west. If we talk of a Middle East, the logical argument runs, there is also implied a Near East; and in fact this term was once in great vogue, as referring to the territories along the seaboard of the eastern Mediterranean. It was, moreover, a useful collective geographical description for the lands of the former Ottoman Empire.

However, usage of "Middle East" in the present volume may be justified on several grounds. (a) Few definitions of a Near East ever agreed—some authors extended it eastwards to include Afghanistan, others terminated it at the coastal ranges of Syria and Palestine; and some included Egypt, whilst others did not. (b) "Near East" is convenient to apply, in an historical sense only, to the now defunct Ottoman Empire. (c) Nowadays, for the English-speaking public at least, the term "Middle East" would have

no validity if applied, in a strictly logical sense, to Afghanistan, Pakistan and India. (d) The term can be taken as denoting a single geographical area in which occur broadly similar features of physical environment and ways of life.

We thus arrive at the definition of the Middle East as given on the title-page of earlier editions of this volume—the highland countries of Turkey and Iran; Cyprus; the Arab-speaking states of the eastern Mediterranean seaboard; Israel; the Arabian peninsula; the valley of the Tigris-Euphrates (chiefly but not entirely comprising Iraq), the Nile Valley (Egypt, and also Sudan); and Libya. This, in no sense an ideal or unassailable solution, has at least considerable sanction in popular usage and technical utility. Subsequently, the addition of chapters on north-western Africa and on Afghanistan has extended the range of the present volume beyond many but by no means all of the numerous definitions of the "Middle East" which have been proposed. North-western Africa (Tunisia, Algeria and Morocco) spoken of by Arab geographers as "Jeziret al Maghreb" ("island of the west", or "setting sun"), or usually nowadays just "Maghreb" ("west"), surrounded as it is to the south by deserts and on its remaining sides by sea, may be looked on in many ways as linked to the Middle East both by environment and culture, whilst retaining something of the separateness indicated by the term "island".

Physical Background

STRUCTURE

Geologically speaking, the entire area can be regarded as deriving from two distinct provinces. The south consists largely of continental massifs (increasingly spoken of today as "plates") that would appear once to have been joined in one large mass, known as Gondwanaland. To the north of this mass there has been throughout most geological time a trough or geosyncline. This, a zone of crustal weakness, has mostly been occupied by deep seas of varying extent (at some periods more extensive than now) and in these seas lived the immense numbers of living creatures whose bodies after death decayed to form the oil deposits now so characteristic of the central Middle East. Alternate periods of quiescence and geological disturbance occurred. During quiescent phases, material eroded from the neighbouring continental masses accumulated in the oceanic deeps of the geosyncline, rapidly covering the fatty bodies of dead sea organisms to allow petroleum formation; then periods of contraction occurred, heaving up marine sediments in enormous flexures or fold-structures to produce mountain chains. Sometimes the flexures were relatively simple, like hogs' backs; in other instances they were much more intense, giving rise to tightly packed, highly distorted folds, with extremes where shearing and total deformation of the structures produced an overthrust ("nappe") rather than a recognizable fold.

From various parts of the geosyncline has emerged a great series of fold-mountain chains that are traceable from Western Europe and North-West Africa as far as Northern India. This is the so-called "Alpine" or Tertiary fold system, since it is the latest in geological time of three major mountain-building periods. The Pyrenees and Sierra Nevada of Spain, the Alps, Appennines, and Carpathians in Europe, and the massive Atlas Mountains of Africa are all part of this system. Further east many of the mountain chains of Asia Minor, the Caucasus, the Zagros and Elburz Ranges of Iran, and the complex of ridges that form the Afghan Pamir are all part of this "Alpine" system—geologically young in age, and relatively uneroded and therefore high in altitude.

This is by no means the whole story. Besides the actual fold ranges, simple and complex, there are often embedded between them portions of older, more resistant structures. Some of these are remnants of the first two mountain building phases: Palaeozoic (or Caledonian) and Mesozoic (Hercynian), the latter now being found extensively in central Europe. Parts of these remnant structures, certainly of Hercynian age and possibly also Caledonian, are found in western Morocco, the central Atlas, Asia Minor, the interior of Iran, and western Afghanistan. One cannot trace any simple pattern in the arrangement of the folds, which may occur in straight parallel ranks, or sinuous arcs and garlands that may alter trend abruptly. Explanation of this is given later in this article, as part of the discussion of plate tectonics.

North Africa is a good example of the complexity of conditions. Generally speaking, the entire highland zone consists of a series of parallel-fold mountain chains of Tertiary age running east-west or north-east/south-west, and separated by tablelands or narrow trough-like valleys. In the extreme west, however, areas of Palaeozoic and Mesozoic remnant structures are prominent. The whole mountain system is higher and wider in the west (Morocco) and diminishes considerably in width towards the east (Tunisia), as well as declining in height. Much discussion centres on how far the Tertiary Atlas fold structures can be regarded as continuations of the fold mountains of southern Spain and Italy: whether there is in fact an almost continuous ring of folds enclosing the entire western Mediterranean basin, and breached only by the Straits of Gibraltar and the narrows between Tunis, Sicily and Italy. All this may sound highly academic and remote from everyday realities: but it is not. Geological and topographical structure form part of the basis to political claims to control offshore areas that are strongly put forward nowadays by various countries—especially round the Mediterranean and nearby Gulf zones. Besides the possible presence

of oil, strategic issues are involved—in 1981 we saw Libyan aircraft shot down by Americans over the definition of "a gulf".

Somewhat different conditions obtain in Asia Minor, where much larger interior plateaux, often eroded into sumps or basins, are surrounded by Tertiary fold ranges. Of this kind are the Taurus and Anti-Taurus Ranges of the south, and the coastal ranges of the north, which continue into the Caucasus and Iranian mountains. Within Iran the interior basins (composed in part of Hercynian nuclei) are even more developed, so that, with minor variations, the whole country can be regarded as saucer-shaped, a rim of Tertiary fold mountains very clearly framing and defining a series of interior basins—which are hardly plains, since most are above 2,000 ft. in altitude.

Further east still, in Afghanistan, the Tertiary folds again develop into enormous dominating ridges that bunch together eastwards and northwards to form a formidable, though relatively narrow, mountain complex that presents a major barrier between central and southern Asia. The first portion of it is the Pamir "knot"—a "swag" or bunch of mountain ranges enclosing tenuous and restricted valleys. Intervening blocks or interior plateaux, present in the west on a small scale, disappear entirely towards the east, with topography passing unbroken into the main Himalaya.

The southern geological province of the Middle East contrasts markedly with that of the north as just described. It consists essentially of the platform (or basement) of extremely ancient rocks, some amongst the oldest known in the world (Precambrian and Archaean). These—chiefly granites, schists and quartzites—most likely once made up the enormous Gondwana continent, which included much of Australia, southern India, Arabia, most of Africa, and parts of South America. Whilst generally rigid and resistant to the pressures that rucked up the sediments of the geosyncline, this ancient mass was from time to time, especially on its northern fringe, overrun by shallow seas, which deposited thin, often horizontal layers of limestones and sandstones. In addition, wind- and water-eroded silts and sands from the surface became consolidated in similar thin, level strata. Thus the basement area of the south, whilst generally flat and fairly uniform in character, is not wholly so, since much of its surface is covered by these deposits, which erode differentially, the harder bands standing out as ridges and the less resistant as vales. The whole aspect of this southern basement/platform is one of a vast open plateau diversified here and there by small-scale hill-systems and shallow valleys. Much is occupied by sand deposits in the form of major dunes or as irregular shifting masses—the "sand-seas" of the Sahara and inner Arabia.

One major feature of considerable importance, now accepted as part in fact of a world-wide process, is the drift apart of the two major platforms of Arabia and Africa, which until relatively recent geological time (mid-Tertiary) formed a single larger continent. Further east was another relatively large platform, which appears to have drifted north from a location

[*continued on p.* 6

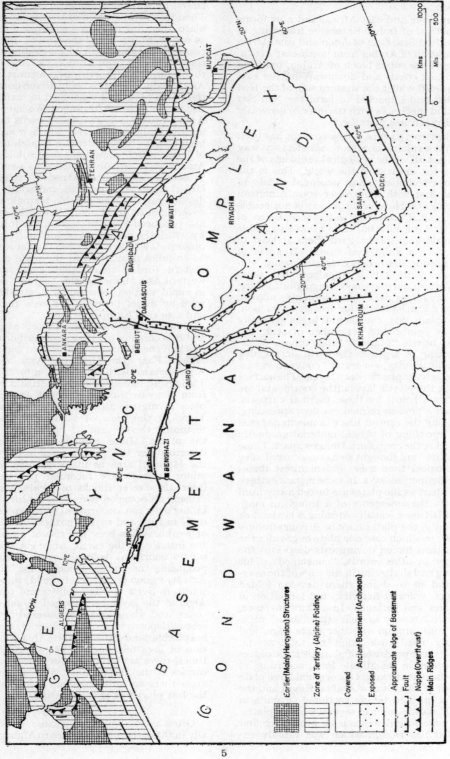

Sketch of structural elements.

Earlier (Mainly Hercynian) Structure

Zone of Tertiary (Alpine) Folding

Ancient Basement (Archaean)

Covered

Exposed

Approximate edge of Basement

Fault

Nappe (Overthrust)

Main Ridges

continued from p. 4]
close to Mozambique and east Africa, and now forms the Deccan Plateau of India. Extensive fracturing in the area of the Red Sea, Gulf of Aden and east Africa led to the separation of Arabia from north-east Africa, and the tilting of the entire block of Arabia, uplifting the west (Red Sea coast) and downwarping the east (Persian/Arab Gulf) whilst the western side of the Red Sea has buckled and impacted to form the Red Sea hills of Egypt and the Sudan with the interior generally horizontal and much less disturbed.

Within the last 10-15 years, a new concept has been worked out that explains in a more satisfactory way many, though not all, of the geological problems of the area—and also for the rest of the world. This is the theory of "plate tectonics", now accepted widely in Britain, but at first with more reserve by American and Soviet geologists. However, 1981 saw a noticeable shift in the U.S.S.R. towards wider acceptance of plate theories, and it is now fair to say that a probable majority of world geologists regard them at least in considerable part as valid and useful. If areas of tectonic and seismic disturbance (earthquakes, volcanoes, etc.) are plotted it is apparent that these occur only in certain narrow zones, ringing or forming boundaries to far larger near continental-size masses, where tectonic disturbance is far less or even non-existent. To explain this, continental areas generally are regarded as comprising a number of stiff, but rather shallow, brittle "plates". From time to time, differential heating at depth in the earth's crust, due to phases of radioactivity, generates "convection currents" in the relatively plastic, deep layers. The surface plates overlying the plastic layers (the continents) are then cracked from below by these thermal currents, and there occurs a process termed sea-floor spreading, where, often along the central line of some major seas or oceans, an upwelling of plastic material gradually takes place, forcing the continental masses apart. These "plate movements" are thought to have occurred very rapidly as geological time goes, and manifest themselves in three distinctive ways. In some instances there can be tearing apart as the plates are forced away from each other, with the emergence of a trough of magmatic material between, usually forming a lowland or sea floor. Secondly, the plates may be driven strongly against another; in which case one plate over-rides the other which is then forced downwards deep into the plastic layer, or in other words, "consumed". This leads to crushing and shattering in the edge of the over-riding plate and in so doing there develop folded mountain ranges, volcanic activity, and formation of mountainous arcs and garlands. In a third instance, plates may move laterally to each other (shear) without extensive consumption of either plate edge, and thus with only local dislocation of rock strata. Examples of all three processes of plate tectonic movement are to be seen in the Middle East, according to proponents of the plate theory. One original large plate comprising most of what is now Arabia, Egypt and the Sudan was first cracked by convectional currents in the lower earth mantle to form several smaller plates. Two of these were forced westwards, producing first the narrow Red Sea trough which was rapidly en-

larged by spreading along its floor to its present size. Then further migration of the second, more southerly plate, this time more in a southward direction as well as westward, produced the Gulf of Aden; and the process still continues with Africa continuing to drift away south and west from Arabia. The Arabian plate is held to be impinging northwards against an even larger Asian plate, where it is being driven downwards against the Asian plate and consumed in many places, giving rise to the Zagros fold ranges. We have noted that the Arabian plate is downtilted towards the east, producing the shallow Gulf area, which would seem to have been subject to considerable though minor oscillation of level, which sometimes made it almost dry land. Asia Minor is equally regarded as a smaller plate that is being pushed or "extruded" westward between larger plates to the north and south west with the development of considerable tectonic weakness zones covering most of the area. Part of the same process has also produced a lateral shear in the Jordan Valley area by which the plate west of Jordan (comprising mainly present-day Israel) has been displaced southwards by 60-80 miles in relation to the plate now forming the eastern Jordan area. Other, even smaller plates in western Asia Minor and the Aegean-Crete area may be in rapid motion westwards, "extruded" again as it were by major pressures between the larger African and also east European plates.

However one views the theory of plate tectonics, and it is emphasized that most authorities now accept much of the theory, it is clear that certain areas of the Middle East (the Maghreb, Asia Minor, Iran and Afghanistan, with offshoots into Syria, Lebanon, Jordan and Israel) are zones of crustal weakness, where from time to time adjustment and movement take place giving rise to earthquakes of varying severity. These in the view of those who accept the plate tectonics theory are of course the boundaries of the plates. Minor tremors are frequent (they are described for the Jordan area in the Bible), and in the Istanbul area as many as fifty to one hundred minor tremors are recorded per year. At longer intervals severer shocks of greater amplitude occur, causing on occasion severe loss of life. The two latest, killing over 200, occurred in southern and eastern Iran early in 1977 and 1978. Another feature of these zones of weakness has been the rise of liquid magma from the interior of the earth. Amongst the northern fold ranges enormous volcanic cones have been formed, producing the highest peaks in the Middle East (Mt. Ararat, 17,000 ft., Mt. Demavend, 19,000 ft.). Farther south, in Syria, Jordan, Libya and parts of southern Algeria, the lava has emerged in sheets rather than cones, and whole areas are covered by basalt of very recent deposition, giving a barren, desolate, and inhospitable landscape. Despite this widespread extension of lava outpourings in geologically very recent times, there are today, however, no really active volcanoes in the Middle East, although in a number of areas there are still emissions of hot gases and mud— the last phases of igneous activity.

Minerals
Often associated with volcanic outpourings, especially in the north, from Morocco to Afghanistan, are veins

of metallic minerals, antimony, cobalt, chromium, copper, iron, lead, molybdenum, silver and zinc—and also asbestos, barytes, coal, and emery, together with marble which is produced by the "baking" of strata by underground heat. These minerals are fairly widespread, and important new discoveries have been made over the last few years, so that the total reserves in some instances (copper at Chesmeh in Iran, iron in Egypt, Syria and Libya) are now much higher than once thought possible. Often, however, individual deposits tend to be of irregular occurrence, of varying quality, and sometimes in remote, difficult districts. The lack of fuel for treatment has also been a disadvantage, so that commercial exploitation has not always been possible. On the other hand, rises in world prices since 1940 and again in the 1970s have had a highly stimulating effect. World shortages, or threats of shortage, plus political attitudes (e.g., over Rhodesia and Chile) have led to increased interest in Middle Eastern minerals. Moreover, local governments will sometimes prefer to exploit national resources at higher cost rather than be dependent upon imports. Hence mineral exploitation has growing importance, with Turkey ranking second as a world producer of chromium and Cyprus a significant producer of asbestos, copper and iron ore. Egypt has recently begun to develop on an extensive scale the important iron deposits near Aswan, using hydro-electric power from the High Dam; and other iron deposits occur between the Nile Valley and the north-west coast of the Red Sea, and in the Behariya oasis due west of the Nile. Another important discovery of iron not yet producing is at Rajo, near Aleppo, in Syria, whilst it is now estimated that nearly four billion tons of mainly high-grade ore (some 5 per cent of world reserves) are located in the Wadi Shatty, in the Fezzan area of southern Libya. The region as a whole is now thought to have about 10 per cent of world reserves. North Africa is distinctly richer in minerals than most of the Middle East proper. Besides extensive deposits of phosphate (which make Morocco the second largest world producer), there are important deposits of iron ore, with smaller, but highly significant quantities of lead, zinc, antimony, cobalt, molybdenum and barytes. A mineralized zone (including uranium) occurs along the southern border of Libya—actually within the State of Chad; and this has led to military occupation of northern Chad by Libyan military forces, with attempts to annex the territory.

Elsewhere in the Middle East, other mineral resources are found, but on a scale somewhat smaller than in North Africa: phosphate in Egypt, Israel, Jordan and Syria—all of these deposits are exploited commercially; manganese in the Sinai peninsula; and small deposits of copper and natural gas in Israel. There is increasing use of soluble salts found in such lakes as the Dead Sea and the Wadi Natrun west of Cairo, chiefly (in the case of the Dead Sea) as sources of bromine. Very small quantities of alluvial gold are still produced, mainly from Saudi Arabia. During 1977 it was announced that extensive coal deposits have been discovered in south-central Iran.

On the southern flanks of the fold mountains, rock strata are tilted into great domes, in which have accumulated the vast deposits of petroleum that now make the Middle East the leading oil province in the world with some 60 per cent of proven world reserves. The vast bulk of this—about half the world's oil and much natural gas—lies around and under the shores of the Persian/Arabian Gulf. More will be said later about these deposits, but it may here be noted that the occurrence of oil is closely dependent upon a certain kind of geological structure. There must be first an alternation of porous and impermeable strata, with the latter uppermost so as to act as a seal, and prevent the oil from running away; and there must also be a slight degree of disturbance enough to produce domes and traps in which the oil can collect, but not sufficient to produce cracks which will allow oil to escape. Such factors can explain why oil is restricted in occurrence to a few zones, and why its discovery is such a chancy affair, with many disappointments—for every boring that produces oil, at least nine others are made without success.

CLIMATE

One basic reason for the distinctive character of the Middle East and North Africa is the special and unusual climate. Most parts of the world experience their rainfall either mostly during summer (the warm season) or distributed throughout the year. Only in a very few areas is there a maximum in winter (the cold season). This is the so-called "Mediterranean" climate, giving a long intensely hot summer, and a relatively mild, rainy winter, with occasional cold spells. The distinction may not seem very important, but it "conditions" plant life to a remarkable degree, and thus also agriculture and general ways of life. Native plants "rest" in the hot season, not in the cold one, which is the opposite to what happens in cooler temperate climates. Some indigenous plants, such as cereals, mature quickly in order to complete a rapid growth cycle before the onset of hot weather; others, chiefly bulbs, flower in spring or autumn; whilst some, such as the citrus, bear fruit in winter. All this has a marked effect on agricultural routines and general living habits. One obvious result is the summer "siesta", which involves breaking the day into two rest periods, with a very early morning start, and continuance of work well into the evening.

Weather conditions are dominated by the long, hot and dry summer, which then quickly gives way to a relatively rainy winter that is mild near the coast but can be surprisingly cold inland. Autumn is warm and sunny, and spring changeable and liable to cold spells —both are short, merely intermediate, seasons. Because of the absence of cloud during summer (away from the coast there can be days without any cloud whatever) the sun beats down uninterruptedly, and the temperatures reached are far higher than those at the Equator. Day maxima of 100° to 115° F. are usual, and a figure of over 125° F. is known. Parts of the interior of Arabia, Algeria, Libya and Iran may experience the highest temperatures occurring in the world.

In winter, though frost is uncommon actually at sea level, the land interior can be cold, especially at

[*continued on p.* 10

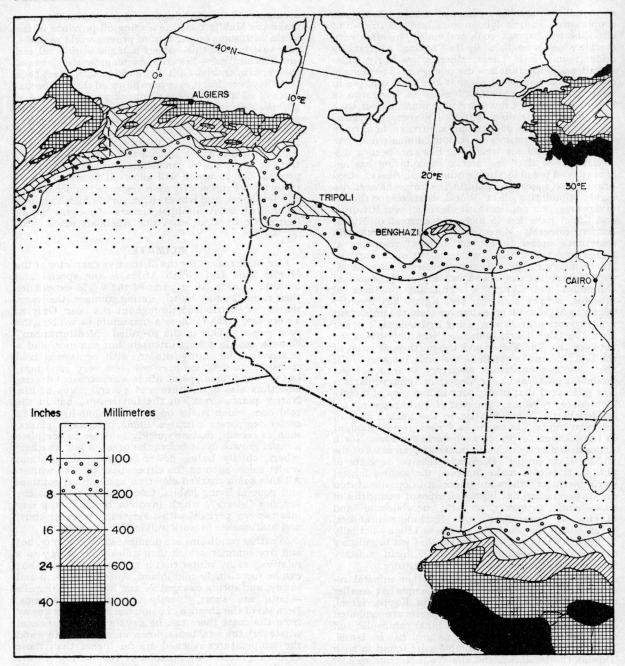

Annual rainfall: North Africa.

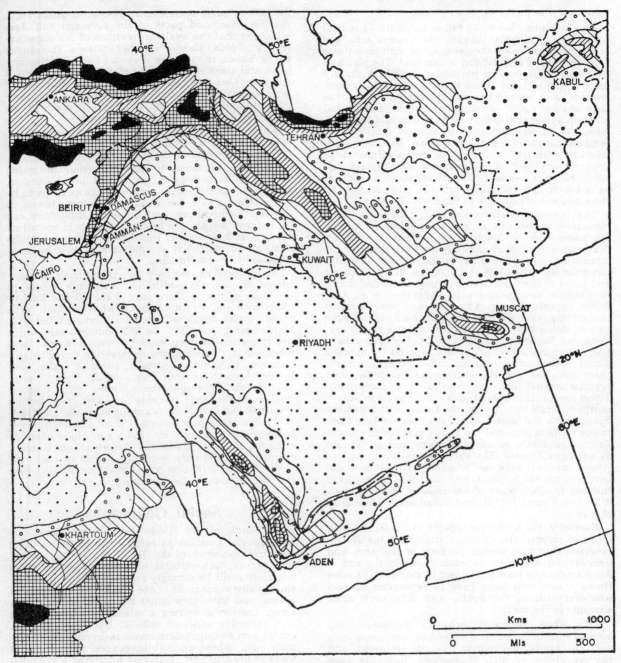

Annual rainfall: Middle East.

9

continued from p. 7]

higher altitudes. Snow can fall as far south as central Morocco and Algeria, Aswan, the Yemen A.R. and southern Iran, whilst the presence of high mountains has the effect of intensifying winter cold. The plateaux of Turkey and Iran in particular, and to a slightly lesser degree of the Atlas region, experience severe winters, with several months of frost, and up to 120 days of snow cover—a reminder of their geographical position adjacent respectively to Russia and to Spain, which is surprisingly cold in winter. Considerable seasonal change is thus the keynote of Middle Eastern climate, with 40° to 50° F of temperature range between one part of the year and another (cf. the 26° F. range in London). Wide changes of temperature as between day and night are also characteristic of the interior, but not close to the coast.

The second characteristic of Middle Eastern climate is the scantiness and irregularity of rainfall (*see* pages 8 and 9). Much of the entire region has less than 10 ins. (250 mm.) annually, and this deficiency is intensified by the highly sporadic and irregular nature of the actual fall—for instance, in 1972 Kuwait and parts of the Gulf coast had unprecedented floods that washed away parked cars, whilst the Yemen A.R. in the opposite corner of the Arabian peninsula was just ending seven years of drought. As much as three to four inches have been known to fall in a single day; there can be heavy rain in one locality and none a few kilometres away; and years may go by in some places without any substantial fall. On the other hand, there are a few regions where special circumstances produce annual totals of 30-40 ins. (750-1000 mm.). These are usually upland areas close to large seas— northern Israel and Jordan, the Lebanon and western Syria, south and west Turkey, the north of Iran close to the Caspian Sea, and the higher parts of the North African mountain zones, in Morocco and as far east as northern Tunisia. The extreme south and east of Arabia can, as it were, be "brushed" by the monsoonal current from the Indian Ocean, and thus have a local summer rainfall: parts of the interior of the Yemen A.R., the Yemen P.D.R. and Oman are influenced in this way.

Normally, the winter rains begin in October, with a series of storms (the "Former Rains" of the Bible) Heaviest rain falls during January in the west, and February or March in the east. Towards the end of April there may be a final onset of rain (the "Latter Rains"), and then from June to September no rain whatever falls in the south, and only very small amounts in the north.

Two other phenomena may be mentioned: the occurrence from time to time of hot, and sometimes dust- or sand-laden, winds from desert areas, and the prevalence of high atmospheric humidity near the coasts. The sand winds—known as *Khamsins*, *Simooms* (Iran) *Chehili* (Morocco) or *Ghibli* (Libya)— are unpleasant visitations that can last up to 48 hours, and their main effect, apart from personal inconvenience and mental irritation among humans, is to wither growing crops on a large scale. High humidity, especially in summer, makes living conditions

difficult in such areas as the Persian/Arabian Gulf, the Red Sea, and parts of the Lebanon and Asia Minor, so that the wealthier sections of the community try to pass this season in hill stations. Though, as we have seen, the summer is almost rainless, humidity in coastal areas may be highest at the hottest time of the year. One other effect is the intense evaporation from water surfaces, due not only to the high temperatures, but also to the windiness of much of the region, again more pronounced in summer.

Atmospheric pollution, with photo-synthesis of exhaust fumes to produce irritant "smog", is now becoming a feature of the larger cities.

The effects of climate are now increasingly mitigated by modern technology. Irrigation and, in a few places, large-scale distillation of sea water allows crops to be grown throughout the summer and new towns to develop. Temperature and humidity difficulties can be reduced by air conditioning, which is spreading rapidly, at least among the better-off classes. Public demand for electricity is now at a peak in summer because of air-conditioning.

At the present, we may be experiencing a minor phase of climatic oscillation, with the increased tendency of the northern part of the Middle East to experience slightly more unsettled conditions, with rather cooler temperatures, and increased but still highly sporadic rainfall. On the southern side, warm desert conditions have tended to intensify and creep southwards, producing the devastating droughts still occurring in Ethiopia, Somalia, parts of Sudan, and much of north central Africa (Mali, Upper Volta, Mauritania). This could be no more than a minor fluctuation that may last only for a few years, but its economic and social effects are considerable; and there is no sign that the fluctuation is at an end. Indeed, some researchers consider that we are in a phase of climatic extremes (in North America and Western Europe, we need only recall the winter of 1981–82), with sharp oscillation of actual conditions that statistically tend to be concealed.

Social Geography

The lands of the Middle East occupy a unique geographical position as lying between and linking the three continents of the Old World. We may therefore expect that cultural influences from all three continents will be strongly represented. At the same time, whilst some parts of the Middle East are easy of access, and have thus acted for centuries as transit zones, thereby acquiring a mixed culture, there are also extensive areas of difficult terrain—mountain, desert, and swamp, where invaders do not often penetrate, and where ancient languages, religions, and ways of life still persist, largely unaltered and undisturbed.

This contrast between seclusion and openness to outside influence is highly characteristic of the Middle East, and explains why in some parts the population is extremely mixed in racial origin (for example, the "Levantine" of the coasts), and why in other districts it is racially unmixed—(e.g. the Bedouin Arabs or

Armenians); and why in some regions there is a modernity of outlook existing alongside ways of life that have persisted with little change since Biblical days. Rapid transition from one way of life to another within a small region is thus a marked feature, and there can be groups of people with traditions, language, religion and racial origins radically different from those of near neighbours. The most outstanding example of this is to be found in the heart of Arabia, where a number of desert tribes living less than 500 miles from Mecca itself remained, until quite recently, only slightly affected by the Muslim faith, though Islam itself had reached out centuries before to overrun and influence countries as far away as Spain, India, and Central Africa. Now, with larger numbers and greatly improved and pervasive communications, old isolation declines year by year at an accelerating pace, producing local tensions from time to time.

RACIAL GROUPING

In recent years there has been a revaluation of ideas on racial questions. Previously the trend had been towards devising increasingly elaborate and subtle groupings based on finer and finer measurements of physical characteristics: bodily physique, hair and skin qualities, especially colour. But we are now aware that some, though not all of these, may be induced or modified by diet, upbringing as children, and social customs. At the same time, investigation of genetic differences, as partly evidenced by blood serum character, has demonstrated a whole new field of possible biological relationships that often bear little or no concordance with observed "racial" characters, but can be traceable in certain ways to geographical location and environment—for example, the perpetuation of certain physical traits and genetical characters through seclusion in a remote area with interbreeding, or the opposite in an "open" area subject to much human movement and interchange. Whilst it would be idle to deny that differences between various groups of the human race certainly exist—some are darker- or lighter-skinned, or with slight physical and anatomical differences—it would appear far less possible than was once thought to devise meaningful categories of racial groupings. Some authorities now speak only of a very few distinctive groups: "caucasoid" or white, "brown", "yellow" etc., and then distinguish minor variations as arising from the influences of genetical inheritance, geographical location, and cultural experience.

Thus, earlier typologies such as "Alpine", "Armenoid" or "Mediterranean" are now, in effect, wholly abandoned in favour of a more specific and detailed but, in one sense, restricted approach based on measurable elements such as blood grouping, or other qualities indicated directly as having an identifiable genetic basis, discarding what are now recognized as variable and partially subjective criteria such as bodily build.

The Middle East offers special difficulties partly because of its location, as just described, between major world zones, and partly owing to a dearth of information, for example, on blood groupings. At the present, given this unsatisfactory situation, it is perhaps best to limit our survey to noting that (a) there is, as might well be expected, evidence of considerable intermixture and variation, with African, Asian and other elements represented, alongside an indigenous "brown" racial type, from very dark to blond skin colour; and (b) there is evidence of persistence of special genetical factors (and hence of physical characters) in some groups, and much less in others. Variation of type is thus prominent.

LANGUAGE DISTRIBUTION

This is far clearer than the racial pattern. Arabic, the language of Muhammad, and of comparatively recent origin, was spread rapidly by the Islamic conquests of the seventh to ninth centuries A.D., and has now become universal in Egypt, the Sudan, Arabia, Jordan, Syria, Lebanon, and Iraq. There is a classical form, now understood with some difficulty and (as the language of the Koran) used for religious observance and broadcasting; and various regional dialects. Some of these latter are close to each other in syntax but differ in pronunciation (i.e. differences are of the order of those in English, spoken let us say, in London, Lancashire and Glasgow, or Massachusetts, Georgia and Nebraska). But in other instances the colloquial forms of Arabic can differ as widely, as say, French, Spanish or Italian, so that intercommunication is difficult.

Farther north, Turkish, a central Asiatic language brought in by the Turkish conquerors of the eleventh century A.D., is current over most of Asia Minor, with extensions into Iran and the U.S.S.R. Turkish was for many centuries written in Arabic characters, but as the sounds of Turkish are not easily adaptable to Arabic letters, Roman (i.e. European) characters were introduced by government decree in 1928. Persian is an Indo-Aryan language with affinities to some European forms of speech, but it is by no means universally spoken throughout Iran—probably by only one-half or at most two-thirds of the population. It is written in Arabic script. A variation known as Dari Persian is spoken in Afghanistan, as is the Pashtu language, another offshoot of the Persian language that is current both in Afghanistan and in neighbouring regions of Pakistan. The hill country from Asia Minor as far east as the Indian frontier is a mosaic of different dialects spoken by various tribal groups. Some of these dialects are remnants of ancient forms of speech that were once more widely current; some are of fairly recent origin; whilst some show relationships to languages of central and eastern Asia. Aramaic, the language of Palestine at the time of Christ, now persists in a modern and altered form only in a few villages near Damascus and Mosul; Kurdish, an Indo-Aryan language related to Persian (Farsi), has a fairly wide extension in the hills from central Turkey as far as south-west Iran; and Armenian, owing to the persecution and dispersal of Armenians from their homeland, is spoken in many large towns. Greek is the chief language of Cyprus. In Israel, Hebrew and Arabic are the two official languages, the former predominating. Berber is dominant in parts of the hill country and adjacent areas of Morocco, Algeria and Tunisia, with a few offshoots into Libya, and possibly even as far east as the Egyptian oasis of Siwa. Prior to invasion by the Arabs in the tenth and eleventh centuries, Berber was the major language in what is now Tripolitania, but it survives today in only a few towns —Aujila, Zuara and Garian.

Language and Educational Problems

Variation of language, as between written and spoken forms of the same dialect and as between families of languages, presents a serious problem at the present time, and is an important factor in the isolation and retarded economic level of several Middle Eastern states. In education, the problem is more complicated, because for a long time practically all modern scientific and technological works were written in English, French, German or Russian, with higher teaching often in the hands of foreigners. To the complication of having several indigenous languages within one country was thus added the difficulty of having higher instruction carried on by foreigners in their own tongue. Thus school and university teaching was frequently enmeshed in the toils of language, and timetables heavily weighted towards language teaching, as an essential preliminary to any other work. Because of the lack of contact, and the smallness of the potential market, which rarely made translation of serious works into Arabic, Turkish or Persian a commercial proposition, only a minority of standard texts from Europe or America could, until very recently, be read in the native languages of the Middle East. This has been a considerable, but not recognized, factor in the cultural and educational separation which has for long existed between the Middle East and other countries. Within the last few years certain governments, notably those of Egypt, Iran, Libya and Turkey, have tackled the problem, by sponsoring translation; and UNESCO has also been active in this connection. Another significant change is that with the expansion of general education, there is a greater flow of Middle Easterners abroad, and many of these have now returned as teachers, technicians and officials. In addition, locally-trained Arabic-speaking personnel, chiefly Egyptian, but also Palestinian and Syrian Arab, have tended to take up appointments in less developed Arab countries. Thus there is very much more specialist instruction in Arabic as compared with, say, twenty years ago. Nationalist feeling in itself, and the reduced openings for expatriates also foster this tendency. A very few universities still use English as the main medium of instruction, but opinion is divided as to whether this should continue. To some it appears that fuller use of Arabic will allow more effective teaching; to others, that it will reduce the reading of textbooks (a number of which are available only in a foreign language) and limit yet further the possibility of employing expatriate staff. Increasing segregation of male and female in schools and universities (especially in some of the Gulf states), in part as a response to an increasingly fundamentalist religious outlook, now means that women teachers (most of whom speak only Arabic) are increasingly employed. Radio and, to a lesser extent, television have been used with effect to overcome communication difficulties.

NOMADS

With much of the Middle East arid or semi-arid, animal rearing plays an important part in the life of the region, with numerous migratory tribes moving regularly in search of fresh pasture. Though the actual numbers of people who live as pastoral nomads are quite small and rapidly declining, their way of life, once of great significance but now less so, contrasts with that of the townspeople and peasant cultivators. The impact of desert life and ideas upon neighbouring peoples has from time to time been immense, through invasion and destruction, but also in more positive ways, often leading to cultural progress, particularly in the fields of religion and abstract thought. The Old Testament deals continually with the theme of desert against town; and we may also recall the words of T. E. Lawrence that the edge of the desert is littered with the relics of religions and ideas developed from the interaction of nomadic and sedentary ways of life. Many of these movements have perished, but a few have gained strength enough to affect the whole world.

The unit among nomads is the tribe—a group that ensures a certain advantage in numbers, yet is small enough to exist within the limits set by a hard environment. Tribal discipline is strong, and direction is in the hands of a leader whose right to rule is based partly on hereditary descent, and partly on personal merit. This system of rule may to some extent explain the general importance of leaders and persons, rather than principles and party doctrines, in the general political life of the present-day Middle East.

The mobility of the nomads, their predilection for raiding and skirmishing, and their scanty material possessions for long made them difficult subjects for any national government that attempted to impose its rule. An unusually vigorous head of state, such as Reza Shah in Iran, could from time to time successfully break or limit the power of the tribes; but a better policy (followed by the Ottomans, and by several present-day governments) has been to let the nomads go their way, with a minimum of interference. This was the situation until very recently, but the exploitation of oil has been a powerful solvent of ancient custom. Thus many former nomads have found sedentary occupations within oilfields, or in towns, or as semi-settled cultivators using irrigation water paid for or supplied largely by oil revenues. Now, nomadism and tribalism are in rapid decline, and it is the policy, stated or implicit, of most governments to bring about sedentarization. Twenty years or so ago, about 10 per cent of the population of the Middle East and North Africa was in the main nomadic, now the figure is about 1–2 per cent: half a million in Saudi Arabia, 400,000 in the rest of the Arabian Peninsula, 350,000 in Turkey, 300,000 in Iran and also in Iraq, 200,000 in Syria; 70,000 in Jordan, 50,000 in Egypt, and in Libya; and 18,000 in Israel. There are also uncertain numbers of nomads in the Sudan who move relatively short distances to escape annual floods.

One important feature in the sedentarization of nomads has been land-reform schemes by which plots of agricultural land, sometimes even with houses, have been made over to former pastoral nomads, e.g. in parts of the Nile valley, northern Syria and in north-east Iran; for such schemes to be successful, education in cultivation methods, and the provision of facilities and agricultural credit schemes are essentials.

RELIGIOUS DIVERSITY

Religious divisions are still strong within the Middle East; and for many persons religious and sectarian fidelity even replaces nationality, so that it is frequently possible, on asking an Arab to what country he belongs, to receive the answer, "I am a follower of Islam". A remarkable feature of the area, possibly connected with its geographical function as a meeting-place of peoples and ideas, is that three great religions of the modern world —Judaism, Christianity and Islam—have arisen within its limits; and that others, notably Zoroastrianism (now confined almost entirely to the Parsees of Bombay), Manichaeism, and Mithraism (of great influence in the later Roman Empire) should also be associated with the Middle East. The most recent example is the rise of Baha'i. Until recently, it seemed that the general awareness of religion in the Middle East was declining, but over the past few years, and especially since 1977, there has been renewal of religious and sectarian awareness, both as affecting everyday life, and in relation to politics. It would be true to say that this revival, manifested most strongly within Islam, is now one of the major features of the present-day Middle East, and affects almost all countries, whether conservative or radical in outlook. A bomb explosion in April 1981 in a Dubai "western" hotel which served alcohol to Muslims was just one indication of the growing tendency towards active fundamentalist expression within Islam; another (1982) is the tendency in some countries, such as Saudi Arabia, to avoid overt general use in commercial and social activities of religious symbols such as a cresecnt or a cross.

Judaism

All three of the modern religions have various branches or sects. Little need be mentioned concerning Judaism, except to note that one of the main social problems of the State of Israel is to absorb Jewish immigrants of widely differing backgrounds and religious traditions. Because of the dispersals of Jews in various continents, there have developed Hebrews of Oriental and African affinities, besides the two European groups of northern (Ashkenazim) and Southern (Sephardim) Jews. Since the establishment of the State of Israel divergence of view as to the part religion should play in everyday life, and its general relationship with politics have proved intractable questions in the Israel Parliament, and have led to several Cabinet crises. Because of greater levels of immigration and a generally higher birthrate Israelis of "Oriental" descent now outnumber those of "European" origin, and there are intense debates

from time to time as to how everyday life in Israel should respond to the situation. For example, civil riots occurred in Jerusalem during 1981 between "traditionalist" Jews, who wanted roads closed during the sabbath to prevent travel, and Jews of a more modernist, relaxed outlook.

Christianity

Christianity in the Middle East is even more widely divided. Geographical separation and the development of regional feeling during and after the end of the Roman Empire resulted in the rise of many cults that varied greatly in dogma, ritual and opinion; and despite the efforts of the early Fathers of Christianity, it proved impossible to reconcile all conflicting views, and maintain the unity of Christian peoples. There arose the Greek (or Orthodox) Church; the Roman Catholic Church (called the Latin Church in the Middle East); the Nestorians, who were once widespread from Mesopotamia and Asia Minor as far as India and China; the Armenians (or Gregorians); Copts; Abyssinians; Jacobites (or Syrian followers of Jacob Baradeus); and the Maronites (adherents of St. John Maroun). All of these sects came in time to possess complete autonomy, but following the rise of Islam in the seventh century A.D. the fortunes of many of them declined. Numbers of Armenians, Copts, Greeks, Jacobites, Nestorians and others (and the entire Maronite Church) were driven to accept aid from Rome, but at the price of recognizing the Pope as their titular Head. Thus we have what are termed the Uniate Churches—Armenian, Coptic, Nestorian Catholics, etc.—which further reduced the strength of the older autonomous groups, most of which managed to continue, though no longer of great importance. At present, therefore, we have more than twenty separate Christian sects, some powerful and world wide, others purely local in allegiance. The appearance of Protestant missionaries in the nineteenth century and after has added further to the religious bodies represented, although the number of converts is now very small.

Islam

Division in Islam began on the death of Muhammad. As the prophet designated no successor, most followers agreed that leadership of Islam could pass from any individual to another, according to merit and circumstance. This group came to be known as the *Sunni*, or Orthodox, and numbers about 90 per cent of all Muslims. A minority supported the claims of the next male relative of Muhammad, and these Muslims took the name of *Shi'a*, or Party. Shi'a adherents are dominant in Iran and the Yemen Arab Republic; in southern Iraq, where they form a large majority of the inhabitants; and as minorities in Syria, the Lebanon, and Turkey. Many sub-sects of the Shi'a are known, representing different forms of belief; and one such group was for a time a warlike military order, with much power in Syria and Iran. Its head was finally forced to take refuge in India, where his direct descendant is today the Aga Khan. Groups of his followers still remain in Iran and Syria. Many Muslims believe that there will one day arise a

Mahdi (Messiah) who will conquer the world for Islam, and this circumstance has led to the appearance at various times of leaders who have claimed to be the long-awaited incarnation—for example, the Mahdi in the Sudan in the late nineteenth century.

The revival during the present century of Wahhabi power may briefly be noticed. The Wahhabis, by reason of their dislike of ostentation in religious observance, and their desire to revive the earlier, simpler tenets of the Faith, have been termed the Puritans of Islam. Under the vigorous and skilled leadership of their late head, King Ibn Saud of Arabia, they rose from obscurity as a desert people to control of most of the Arabian peninsula, and hence domination of the holy cities of Mecca and Medina. One factor in the present Arab disunity is the division on general religious grounds between the Wahhabis, who tend to despise the Muslims of Egypt, Jordan and Syria as lax in observance, and as backsliders in the Faith, and who are in turn criticized as primitive reactionaries. There were also acute personal differences involving King Ibn Saud, who in conquering Mecca displaced the former ruler, Sharif Husain, a direct descendant of the Prophet. A descendant of the former Sharif rules in Jordan (as also until 1958 in Iraq), hence something of the animosity displayed between Saudi Arabia and its northern neighbours owed its origin to personal feuds. This particular issue has now declined; but other sharp issues with a religious basis have replaced them, notably in the Lebanon, but to some extent also in Turkey, where there is the National Salvation political party, of extreme Islamic views, that has come to have a significant voice in national affairs. The late 1970s and early 1980s have seen the emergence of pro-Shi'a movements among the populations of the Gulf States—particularly in the abortive attack on the Grand Mosque of Mecca. Some Shi'a insurgency has been incited and supported by the new republican leaders of Iran; and this is an important issue for Gulf States, since most have a Shi'a minority.

Political Complications

There are other questions of a general political nature that stem from religious differences within the Middle East. The willingness of outside nations to support various religious groups in their struggle against each other has from time to time led to large-scale intervention. France has championed the cause of the Latin and Uniate Churches, basing many of her claims to influence and territory within Syria and the Lebanon on her long connection with the Uniates, who form the largest single sect in the latter country.

Russia, under Tsarist and Soviet rule alike, has maintained a link with the Orthodox Church, and from time to time Russian bishops visit Jerusalem, where the larger part of Christian shrines are owned by the Orthodox Church. Within the last few years Russia has strongly supported, by means of legal and diplomatic action, Orthodox claims to ownership of property and privileges; and whatever the position within the U.S.S.R., Soviet policy is firmly directed to maintaining the rights and position of the Orthodox

Christians within the Middle East. Because of its territorial ownership within Old Jerusalem, Russia could in some respects make a good case for trusteeship of the Christian Holy Places. Britain, rather curiously, has at times supported Muslim groups—sometimes orthodox, sometimes dissident. American interest, though of long standing (as much as a century in one or two localities) has generally been much less direct, but over the last ten to fifteen years has greatly expanded. There are now within the Middle East a number of American educational institutions of great influence and standing (for example, the American University of Beirut and the American Colleges of Istanbul). Most of these were founded as Protestant missionary activities, but have since developed into secular institutions covering a wide range of subjects.

One other effect of religious differences may be noted. With the possibilities of appeal to outside assistance, and the internal vigorousness of religious feeling, it has happened that a political *modus vivendi* can be achieved only by a distribution of offices and appointments among the interested religious sects. This was for long particularly obvious in the Lebanon, where ever since independence the President of the Republic has been a Maronite Christian and the Prime Minister a Sunni Muslim—a precarious balance that in 1976 may well have ended for ever. Sunni Muslims have tended to have considerable influence in Iraq (especially up to 1958), though the majority of the population is Shi'a in adherence.

The last few years have however seen a remarkable change in the pattern of religious life in the Middle East. On the one hand there has been, usually among the better educated, a marked decline in religious beliefs—Christian, Muslim, and even Hebrew, with a parallel development of a growth in secular, materialist outlook that on occasion shows impatience over the prevailing close connection between religion and political and social life. But far more, there is an opposite tendency towards revival of a fundamentalism, most of all in Islam, though also recognisable (in a wholly different context) among extremist Jewish groups such as the *Gush Emunim*. Religious brotherhoods of an Islamic and extremist character have become prominent over the past few years, and a number of these—the *Ikhwan* of Egypt, *Fidaiyai* of Iran, and *Tijaniya* of Turkey—have demonstrably exerted growing and increasingly significant political influence. Moreover, there has been a general and rapid development of fundamentalist Islamic thinking throughout the Middle East and even beyond. The dramatic events of late 1978, when an exiled *Ayatollah* could bring down the Shah's Government are the most outstanding and compelling example of this new surge of fundamentalism; but it is by no means confined to the one state of Iran, and in slightly varied forms, but with a single clearly definable basic pattern, is clearly apparent in several countries, Sunni and Shi'a. President Sadat even felt it necessary in April 1979 to condemn this Islamic activism, saying that Islamic militancy was not desired in peaceful Egypt. The growth of Islamic fundamentalist fervour is now one of, if not first among, the principal social movements of the past ten or so years. It now affects many aspects of life—in education, civil justice (where "Islamic" penalties are increasingly applied) and in the general outlook of many people, who call for more specific "Islamic" ways of living—though it is not always easy to define precisely what these can be.

CITY LIFE IN THE MIDDLE EAST

From very early times, long before Plato commended the city-state as an ideal form of political organization, town life has exercised a predominant influence in lands of the Mediterranean; and this predominance, amounting to a marked disproportion, has been particularly characteristic of the Middle East. Here, towns stand out as islands of relative wealth, culture and progress in a poor and backward countryside; and it is significant that the two centres that dispute the title of the oldest continuously inhabited site in the world are Damascus and Aleppo, whilst the oldest undoubted port is Byblos (modern Jbeil, 20 miles north of Beirut), which from its trade in papyrus gave us the word Bible.

There have been several contributing factors in the precocious growth of Middle Eastern cities. Firstly, because of a wide variety in geographical environment —rich oasis or coastal plain, mountain, desert, steppe and forest—there soon arose a diversity of economic production, and hence a need for exchange and market centres. Then too, with frequent warfare and invasion, defence became a necessity, and strong points on mounds or peaks, commanding corridors, defiles and river passages soon developed and gathered around them a township. Examples of former simple tribal strongholds that have evolved into great cities are Aleppo, Ankara, Jerusalem, Mosul and Tabriz, the third city of Iran. Another feature of the Middle East is the number of "planted" towns—sites deliberately planned or designated to be important. Of this nature is Teheran, which before it was chosen as a new capital by the Qajar rulers in 1788 had few functions other than that of a wintering spot for pastoral nomads. Amman was largely uninhabited for several centuries previous to 1880, though the site (Philadelphia) had held importance in Roman times; and there are other towns whose origins can be clearly traced to planned development in early Arab, Roman or Classical Greek times. Alexander the Great, and especially his successors, fostered many new towns and extended others.

The City in Conquest

It is a feature of Middle Eastern history that, time and time again, small but energetic groups of people seized power, and for a limited period ruled a large territory. The Hyksos Kings of Egypt, the Medes, Assyrians, Macedonian Greeks, Romans, Arabs, and Ottomans can all be cited as examples; and for each conqueror there soon arose the acute problem of maintaining a hold on defeated but numerically superior subject races, and of spreading the language, religion and traditions of the minority ruling group.

Most conquerors found that it was usually easier

to dominate the cities, partly for the reason that military operations could be undertaken with more success against the inhabitants of a closely packed town, rather than against the nomads or peasants of trackless steppes, deserts, or mountains; partly because the towns with their trade could easily be taxed to support military rule; and partly because the population of the cities, polyglot in origin and in touch with outside conditions, could be more often induced to accept a new idea, a new language, or even a new religion. It is no accident that the great evangelical religions of the modern world should have extended from towns—that men first called themselves Christians in Antioch, or that Muhammad could feel that his cause had succeeded when Mecca and Medina acknowledged his rule, or that Jewish ritual should include the phrase "Next year in Jerusalem". We also have the curious position that the towns of the Middle East may often be strikingly different in wealth, in outlook and even in language and religion, as compared with the immediately surrounding countryside. The most famous example may be cited from the New Testament, as when the inscription on the Cross of Christ indicated the presence of a Latin-speaking ruling class, a Greek-speaking town and professional class, and an Aramaic-speaking peasantry. Such contrasts are apparent even today, though, of course, involving different languages.

Economic and Political Dominance

Another feature of Middle Eastern cities is their economic dominance, amounting almost to a stranglehold, in the life of each country. Town merchants are in touch with world markets and can control or "corner" the produce of the rural areas in their own district, for which, owing to the difficulties of transport, they are the only outlet. The strength of the merchants is indicated by the fact that in many Middle Eastern countries there is relatively little, or even in a few instances no, direct taxation, most governmental revenue being raised by indirect imposts. The merchant community of Iran, alienated by capricious regulations and arbitrarily imposed taxation, very clearly had an important role in the downfall of the Shah.

We also find that in many cities there are still, despite land reforms and nationalization, significant communities of wealthy absentee landlords. Unlike that of Europe, the Middle Eastern countryside does not attract resident "landed gentry"—because it is an area of few amenities, and still characterized by poverty, discomfort and disease: for example, two-thirds or even three-quarters of Middle East doctors practise in the larger towns. Hence landlords tend to remain in the towns, with rents collected in cash or kind by agents. The same is true of religious bodies, Muslim and Christian, many of which may possess landed estates or control the exploitation of land by tenant farmers. This means that there is in general a net flow of money derived from the countryside towards towns, and this provides a living not only for the wealthy but for others: artisans, domestic servants and shopkeepers. Though land reform and nationalization have of late years diminished the importance and wealth of some absentee landlords, these have by no means disappeared, partly because a new group of landlords has arisen as the result of the reform. Also, with depreciation of currencies and share prices, the ownership of land still remains a useful (though not now "gilt-edged") outlet for capital gains.

Another feature of town life in the Middle East until recently was the absence, or relatively slight development, of traditions of civic government and responsibility. There was little to parallel the growth of the burgher class that became so prominent in parts of Europe, and hence less of a corporate pride and pattern of local, as distinct from provincial or national, interest in problems of rule. The situation is changing markedly in some localities; but the absence of a bourgeois outlook (in its best sense) is still a feature.

Lastly, it is interesting to observe that towns have long tended to dominate Middle Eastern political life. The lure of greater wealth attracts the energetic, dissatisfied, and sometimes turbulent elements from the countryside. Many such immigrants, together with the occupants of city slums who become periodically unemployed because of trade slumps, and also a third element, inexperienced secondary school and university students, form a very dangerous combination—the Middle Eastern city mob. Mob violence, awakened at first over a political matter, sometimes assumes a religious complexion directed against minorities and foreigners, and among the demonstrators are often groups with few political or religious convictions, but whose aim is to spread disorder so that shops can be broken open and looted. Most Middle Eastern shops in the cities carry iron shutters that can cover the whole of the shop-front at the slightest sign of trouble. A restless, underfed proletariat, excited by political and religious issues, and inflamed by student agitators, can be very menacing in close, narrow streets. Even politicians themselves may ultimately go in fear of the tide of disorder that they themselves have had a hand in provoking. Over and over again in Middle Eastern affairs, demonstrators in the streets have swayed or brought about a total change of government: and, as in 1951 (Egypt), 1956 and 1976 (the Lebanon), 1958 (Iraq), 1960 (Turkey), 1963 (Iraq, Syria and Jordan), 1977 (Egypt) and 1978–80 (Iran), the dilemma of Pontius Pilate—how far to give way to turbulence in the streets—arises in an acute form at unhappily frequent intervals. The swift explosion of anti-American and anti-British feeling, expressed through mob violence in centres as far apart as Kuwait, Benghazi and Tunis, was a feature of June 1967, and again in 1980 in the Gulf states.

Urban Growth

A further considerable problem now arises from the exceedingly rapid physical growth of a few urban centres. Cairo, with a population of 8 to 9 million, is not only the capital of Egypt but the largest town of the Mediterranean area and by far the largest city in Africa. "Greater" Teheran is now near 5 million, and Baghdad 2–2½ million in population. Beirut and

Casablanca each (with their suburbs) have more than one million, Algiers about one million, and about one-fifth of the country's population live in Tunis. This rapid and accelerating growth—placed at six to ten per cent per annum for many large towns—is leading to a concentration of economic power, political influence, and social prestige which poses acute problems of two kinds. Besides the difficulties of providing adequate amenities and methods of administration—the demand for electricity is doubling every five years in many large cities, with severe traffic congestion also—there is something of a retrogression of provincial life, with near stagnation in a few distant parts. As well, with the "drift" to the towns, shanty areas pose increasing problems: well over one half of all the inhabitants of Ankara, for instance, live in houses that are officially regarded as "illegal". Regeneration of regional centres is now being taken up as an urgent matter in those countries that have oil revenues to support expansion plans or programmes. There has been a search for specifically "Islamic" patterns in city growth, partly in order to avoid some of the aesthetic and social problems which now characterize "Western" cities. The solution, however, remains elusive.

Economic Geography

By far the greater part of the land surface in the Middle East is either mountain, desert, or swamp, and cultivated areas are extremely small in extent, covering no more than 5 to 7½ per cent of the total area. Nevertheless, agriculture is the main occupation of a large majority of the inhabitants; and a further proportion of the people is employed in processing the products of agriculture, as cotton and tobacco packers, fruit driers, or canners of fruit, vegetables, and olive oil. It is obvious, therefore, that the remaining activities in the Middle East are of relatively restricted extent. Pastoral nomadism is found in many districts, as the only possible way of life in an arid or mountainous environment; but few people are involved, and the nomads live mainly a self-sufficient existence, so that their contribution to general economic activity is on the whole small. Because of this relatively low level, we have the apparent paradox that, whilst in many (though not all) countries of the Middle East most of the inhabitants are engaged in agriculture or pastoralism, the total contribution of these two activities to Gross National Product is often well under 50 per cent and even in some countries declining—with oil and mineral exports and transit trading accounting for the larger share. For some countries, therefore, agricultural progress remains the least successful sector of current National Development Plans—Iran is a case in point.

AGRICULTURE
Cereals

The chief food crops grown in the Middle East are wheat, barley and rye in the north, and millet, maize and rice in the south. Wheat, the chief crop of Turkey,

[*continued on p.* 18

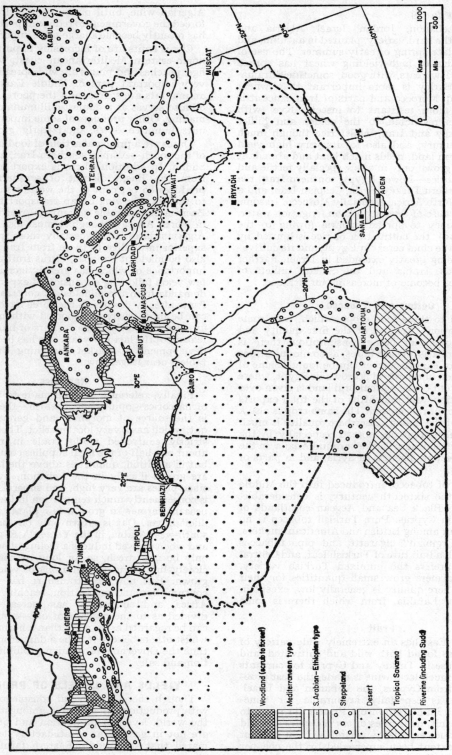

Natural vegetation.

Woodland (scrub to forest)

Mediterranean type

S. Arabian – Ethiopian type

Steppeland

Desert

Tropical Savanna

Riverine (including Sudd)

17

continued from p. 16]

Syria, the Lebanon, Jordan, Israel, Algeria and Tunisia, is of the hard variety, planted in autumn, and harvested in late spring or early summer. The use of Mexican strains of high-yielding wheat has spread over the past few years, with good, sometimes dramatic, results. Barley is more important than wheat in Libya, Iraq, Morocco and parts of Iran, since it is hardier and more resistant to insects. Rye (with some oats) is restricted to the colder and hillier parts of Turkey and Iran, whilst rice though much prized as a luxury, and also for its very high yield per unit of farm land, needs much heat and abundant water, and is grown only in a few specially fertile and favoured localities—Lower Egypt, southern Iraq, the valleys of southern Turkey, Syria, Caspian Iran, and a few parts of North Africa, especially Morocco. In some countries, because of its demands on irrigation water, and its tendency to spread malaria (owing to the flooded ground), the cultivation of rice is limited by law. Maize is the chief cereal in Egypt, and its cultivation is also being greatly extended in Israel. Farther south, towards Arabia and the Sudan, millets of various species become of increasing importance.

Cotton and Tobacco

In addition to these food crops, which, with some notable exceptions, are not of the first quality and thus are retained for home consumption, there is increasing emphasis on cash crops, as communications develop and an export market can be found. Some of the finest cotton in the world is grown in Egypt, where about 20 per cent of the agricultural land is given over to its production, and four-fifths of the total exports are in the form of raw cotton. The same crop is also a chief export of the Sudan. Elsewhere, quality is much lower, but cultivation has spread, especially in the Seyhan plain of southern Turkey around Adana, in the Aleppo and Jezireh districts of Syria, and in parts of Iran and Iraq.

Production of tobacco, introduced into the Middle East during the sixteenth century, is considerable, mainly in the Black Sea and Aegean coastlands of Turkey, and in Cyprus. Pure Turkish tobacco is no longer in favour among British and American smokers, but most "Virginian" cigarette and pipe tobaccos contain a small admixture of Turkish leaf; and Central Europe still prefers the unmixed Turkish variety. Many Arab farmers grow small quantities for their own use, but here quality is generally low, except in the district of Latakia, from which there is some export.

Fruit

The Middle East has an extremely wide variety of fruit. Vines are found both wild and cultivated, and besides their use in Turkey and Cyprus for currants and sultanas, much local wine is made, the best probably coming from Cyprus, the Lebanon and Israel. North Africa is especially favourable for wine-growing, which immigrants from France did much to foster. As a result, quantities of *vin ordinaire* are sold abroad, to France especially, where the local product had to some extent been superseded by the cheaper Algerian wine, until pressure from domestic growers forced the government to reduce imports. The U.S.S.R. has recently become a large-scale importer.

Citrus fruits are of increasing importance along the north-eastern Mediterranean coast, whilst apricots, figs, peaches and plums are widespread. Olives form a very important part of Middle Eastern diet, since animal fats are scarce, and the poorer fraction of the oil also serves as a domestic illuminant and for soap-making. Other products of some importance are hazel nuts, liquorice, dates, and latterly, groundnuts.

Dates are a principal article of food in the arid areas of the south—Arabia, southern Iran, and parts of the Sudan. In addition, there is export on a large scale from the Basra district of southern Iraq, which produces 80 per cent of the world's supply. Nearness to the sea, allowing cheap transport by water, gives Basra a considerable advantage over its competitors in North Africa—though it must also be stated that Algerian dates, and especially those from Biskra, are superior in quality to those from Iraq. Mention must also be made of bananas, citrus fruit and apples, the importance of which has greatly increased in the last few years following expansion of export markets, and demands from the oilfields. In contrast to the "soft" fruits already discussed, the three latter types of fruit can be more easily transported without damage, and are also less likely to be carriers of human disease. A feature of the last few years also has been considerable development of market gardening (fruit and vegetables) near larger towns.

Narcotics

Finally, reference may be made to the cultivation of narcotics—opium and hashish—the first of which is the source of morphine and heroin; and also of qat, which has a very local market. There is a legal and strictly controlled world trade in morphine, and about one-half of the legal supplies come from Turkey; but in addition, quantities above the legal maximum are grown illicitly in the Lebanon, Syria, and Iran, since prices are very high, and supervision lax. There is consequently much temptation in the way of a poor peasant farmer to grow a few plants for sale to the illicit buyer. Qat is grown only on the hill slopes of south-west Arabia, in the Yemen A.R. and near Aden, and when chewed induces a feeling of euphoria. It can only be used fresh, so for long its consumption was closely limited to the environs of where it could be grown. But now, air transport has allowed wider consumption and production, reaching as far as East Africa, and cultivation has increased. Opinion is divided as to the dangers of qat—some hold that it can be regarded as no more than a harmless addiction, whilst others believe it to be a dangerous drug. At one time the Government of Aden prohibited its production and sale.

YIELDS AND LEVELS OF PRODUCTION

Though there are several conspicuous exceptions, with production per unit area amongst the highest in the world, levels of production and quality of crops are not in general at a satisfactory level: it is estimated that the Middle Eastern farmer is no more than one-eighth to one-quarter as efficient a producer as his counterparts in Western Europe or the U.S.A. This is particularly true as regards basic food grains, and so despite much emphasis on farming and self-subsistence, some populations are among the poorest fed in the world.

Reasons for this situation are to be sought first in the obvious handicaps of heat and aridity, together with the resulting effects of this climatic regime upon soil character. Many Middle Eastern soils are lacking in humus; and another difficulty is that when watered copiously by artificial means (e.g. by irrigation) certain soils that would appear to be capable of bearing heavy crops can turn saline and sterile. This is at present a problem in the Nile Delta, where heavy irrigation is tending to induce soil salinity; and a number of large irrigation schemes, notably round Konya in Anatolia, and along the Karun River of south-west Iran, have failed to achieve success for the same reason. In 1949 it was estimated that for the whole of Iraq some 60 per cent of all irrigated land had become salinated to a certain degree; and that about 1 per cent of area is abandoned each year. Relatively little would appear to have been done to alter this general situation; though the development of the Wadi Tharthar drainage scheme could have some effect when it is fully in operation. The Tigris and Euphrates carry double the quantity of salts near their mouth as compared with upstream above Baghdad. The best remedy is to have extensive underground drains in the fields, to prevent accumulation of excess water. This is, however, expensive and adds greatly to the overall cost of irrigation schemes.

Another limiting factor is the unusually high soil temperature during summer—of the order of 130° to 180° F., which has the effect of destroying organic material within the soil itself, and of preventing the efficient use of fertilizers. There is a fundamental problem, as yet not solved, of maintaining soil fertility by artificial means, because the techniques successful in wetter and colder parts of the world do not always answer in the Middle East.

Pests and Diseases

One other source of agricultural loss occurs in the pests and diseases that affect both plants and man. As much as 60 per cent of a year's crops may be destroyed by locusts, which breed in the deserts of Arabia, Africa and Somalia, and move as swarms into cultivated areas. In Iraq and Iran the much smaller *sunna* fly causes periodic devastation—one reason for the emphasis on barley growing is that it ripens faster, and hence can be harvested before the arrival of the *sunna* insect in late summer. Scale diseases, rusts, and mildew are other handicaps. An encouraging feature is the expansion of activity on an international scale directed towards locust control. Faced with growing annual losses, Middle Eastern governments are now co-operating not only with neighbours but also with such organizations as FAO and UNESCO in preventive measures.

Equally severe, if not actually more damaging, are the diseases of man himself. In Egypt, rates of incidence of serious maladies were not long ago up to 70-75 per cent of the whole population, and there are still a few areas in districts of Iraq, Turkey, the Sudan and the Yemen A.R. where malaria affects over half the population. Plague was endemic, whilst Turkey, owing to its colder winter climate, has long been a stronghold of tuberculosis. Eye diseases, chiefly trachoma, are rife, and in some areas produce blindness in up to 20 per cent of the population. Typhoid and venereal diseases are still prevalent, and from time to time there are outbreaks of cholera, sometimes minimized or "played down" by local governments. On the other hand, smallpox has been brought under control and eliminated. However, the Sudan has a particularly poor level of public health, especially in the south, where diseases are not only endemic but spread easily from tropical Africa. The riverine areas of Egypt and Iraq are particularly notorious for parasitic infections—ankylostomiasis, bilharzia and hookworm—which, most unfortunately, tend to spread with the expansion of irrigation. Dysentery (usually of a relatively mild form) is an almost ubiduitous feature, especially affecting newcomers. Despite this depressing list, it is also true to say that very considerable changes have been brought about in many areas by better public health measures, control of insect and animal disease vectors, provision of cleaner drinking water, and improved medical care. In a few regions (e.g. Kuwait and central Saudi Arabia) hospital services are among the best in the world. Thus incidence of many diseases, especially in towns, has shown a marked drop generally over the past decade.

The high incidence of disease was for long, and still remains in some areas, an important contributing factor to low agricultural efficiency: besides reducing physical capacity, mental alertness may also be reduced, thus retarding the introduction of new techniques. Until recently, one could speak of a "vicious circle"—the peasant was diseased and could not work hard, yields were thus precarious leading to malnutrition which in turn pre-disposed to disease. Malaria alone has in the recent past been cited as a major cause of backwardness, including also the decay of the earlier brilliant Arab civilization. Over the past twenty years malaria has successfully been eradicated in most, though not all parts of the Middle East: down to the 1950s, mosquito nets were found in the better hotels of most cities, now they are rarely to be seen. However, it is now apparent, particularly in some parts of the south, that certain species of mosquito have developed higher resistance or even immunity to modern pesticides, and strains of the disease itself also appear less susceptible to eradication by drugs: this is becoming something of a new problem in the southern areas of the Middle East. It is also true that parasitic infections have become more widespread recently, due to the spread of irrigation and lack of sanitation and sewage disposal in new, poorly built settlements.

Land Tenure

Yet more factors in agricultural backwardness are the methods of land holding and forms of tenancy. Full ownership, with the possibility of applying long-term methods of improvement, is not frequent among Middle Eastern farmers. Instead, there are various forms of share-cropping or tribal ownership, which collectively tend to perpetuate old, wasteful methods, to emphasize conservatism in outlook, and to make it extremely difficult for an individual to introduce any innovation. Holdings are often small and scattered, so that modern ploughs, tractors, or reaping machinery cannot easily be introduced; and owing to extremely high rents and dues, amounting in some instances to 65 per cent of the total yield of the holding, the peasant farmer is entirely lacking in capital for improvements, and remains dependent on his landlord for seed and even implements. Land-reform schemes now in progress in several countries, notably Iran, Iraq, Syria and Egypt, are altering this picture, but they do not affect all areas. When they do become more widespread there is a risk that production will decline initially, owing to the lack of capital and knowledge of new techniques of the new owners.

A further feature of Middle Eastern farming has been the existence of numerous absentee landlords, who invest money in land purely as a safe outlet for surplus capital, and have no real interest in farming itself. Such owners live mainly in the towns, and delegate control of their agricultural estates to overseers, being satisfied if the same level of production is maintained from one year to another. Such owners are not often willing to sink capital in new methods or machines, but are content to perpetuate existing methods. Because of the lack of outlet for investment in most Middle Eastern countries—movable property may be stolen, paper securities may be repudiated, and foreign currency, particularly the franc, lira, pound sterling and even the dollar have depreciated—real property represents a fairly safe long-term investment that cannot easily depreciate.

In recent years, many Middle Eastern governments have made attempts to improve the position by redistribution of holdings, and enactments limiting the total area of land held by one individual. This has had some good effect, but in some cases the laws have been loosely applied, or even remained a dead-letter; and ways of ignoring or circumventing them have further reduced their efficiency. Extensive handing over of Crown land to peasant ownership in Iran, followed by the redistribution to peasant ownership on a national scale of all large estates, and the organization of Liberation Province in Egypt, mainly from expropriated and irrigated land, are outstanding but by no means the only large-scale examples of reallocation of big estates, which has also been energetically pursued in Iraq. In Iran, the process has been so fully pursued as to invite the description "White Revolution": during the period 1962–72 some 700,000 peasant families received land for the first time as full owners. Reform schemes have, however, demonstrated that for success, it is necessary to do far more than merely make over land to peasants; agricultural education, credit and co-operative schemes, and handling of water rights are essentials too.

It is also necessary to state that despite all the handicaps noted above considerable progress has been achieved in certain areas of the Middle East. In parts of the Nile Valley, yields per acre of one or two crops are among the highest in the world; and in Israel a remarkable development of mixed farming, based on cereals, vegetables and animal husbandry, has transformed conditions in many areas. Much the same could be said of parts of Cyprus, Syria and Lebanon. The influence of French and Italian settlers in North Africa and Libya respectively was to demonstrate what might be done to improve yields and methods. Iran and Turkey, too, have experienced considerable agricultural development in certain directions over the last twenty to thirty years. Such ameliorations stand, however, in sharp contrast to conditions elsewhere in the Middle East. Overall, there is now growing realization that food production may be insufficient for population numbers, and that a crisis, identified by increasing shortages and high prices, may be at hand. For example, all the substantial agricultural progress realized in Egypt over the past 25 years may have done little more than keep an increased population at stationary levels of living. Few Middle Eastern countries are self-sufficient in foodstuffs (at least, of the sort that more sophisticated consumers now expect) so large imports of cereals and meat have developed. Egypt alone now spends $4,000 to $5,000 million annually on food subsidies; and some estimates now suggest that, within a very few years, food imports into the Middle East could cost some $20,000 million. Besides the matter of actual food deficits, there is also growing concern that a situation of shortage could make the Arab oil producers politically vulnerable.

INDUSTRIAL ACTIVITIES

In medieval times Middle Eastern industrial products had a high reputation. Steelwork, silverware, pottery, leather, and above all, textiles (from Damascus and Mosul, giving the words damask and muslin) found their way into many parts of Europe. At the present time, however, the scale of Middle Eastern industries is small; lack of fuel (particularly of coal and hydro-electric power), scarcity of mineral ores and some other raw materials, and the poverty of local markets were once limiting factors. Over the last few years, however, oil has increasingly been used as prime fuel. There is only one coalfield of any great importance—this is in north-west Turkey, at Ereğli (Heraclea), and production is only 4–5 million tons per annum; whilst very much smaller amounts are produced from fields in the region of Teheran. New discoveries in the Kirman area of Iran and in Egypt may well, however, transform the situation.

In recent years a significant degree of industrial development has, however, taken place in Egypt, Turkey, Israel and Iran, with some industry on a smaller scale in Iraq, the Lebanon and Syria. Some industrial activity, on a smaller scale, and related chiefly to production of building materials, processing of agricultural produce, or the limited treatment of mineral ores for export, has developed in North Africa. Textiles—chiefly cotton, but also silk, wool and mohair

—are important, together with the transformation of agricultural products (sugar, tobacco, fruit processing and distilling) and the making of cement and bricks, for which there is a considerable local demand.

A further feature has been the growth of light consumer industries. Acute shortages during the Second World War impelled many Middle Eastern governments to try to develop local manufactures, even where local conditions were not outstandingly favourable; and over the last fifteen years there has been a marked growth of new power stations, factories and mills (detailed instances of which can be found in the economic surveys of the individual countries). Heavy capital goods such as machinery and vehicles are still imported on a large scale, though there are now assembly plants for motors and electrical machinery in Turkey, Iran, Israel and Egypt, with plans for similar plants, e.g. in the Lebanon, Syria and Iraq. Since 1960, however, there have been the beginnings of local manufacture of motors (in Egypt, Iran and Israel) and other machinery. Industrial expansion is marked in Egypt, Israel, Turkey and the Lebanon; and of late years particularly in Iran, Saudi Arabia and the Gulf States, where especially sophisticated industries based on petrochemicals and metals, with oil and natural gas as fuel and feedstocks, have recently developed. Restricted size of the potential market, competition of new nearby plants and of foreign produced goods are inhibiting factors, but the scale of actual and planned development (with the beginnings of exports in a few commodities such as fertilizers) is now impressive in a few countries.

The past few years have seen bold plans for raising steel production to some 15 million tons over the next decade, with possibilities even of 35 million. There are now 24 steel plants in the whole region, with a present capacity of about three million tons. Aluminium and copper smelting have also developed on a significant scale.

PETROLEUM RESOURCES

The general geological factors involved in the occurrence of petroleum have already been touched on; but it remains to add that there are a number of features special to the Middle East. Exploration was at first retarded by the presence of what may be described as misleading surface structures—in some places, the possibility of finding oil was at first entirely discounted (as in Saudi Arabia); whilst in others, leakages of oil to the surface have given rise to optimism that has not always been justified. Moreover, the oilfields are often of extraordinarily large size, and the oil is held under considerable pressure, so that very few wells need be sunk to tap a large area, and the crude oil often rises of itself without much pumping—factors that allow an unusually low cost of production. The open nature of the country, as compared with the jungle of the East Indies and the mangrove swamps of Venezuela, has been another favourable circumstance. Hence the cost of producing Middle Eastern oil is distinctly lower than that of oil from other parts of the world, both in terms of

actual production costs and as regards capital investment. This, together with high levels of production and proved reserves, has allowed Middle Eastern producers (especially Saudi Arabia) to assume, through OPEC, the dominant role in fixing world prices for oil. Within OPEC, Iran and Libya have tended to be "hawkish"—i.e. supporting moves towards higher prices; with a more 'moderate', cautious attitude pressed by Saudi Arabia and the United Arab Emirates. In 1981 Saudi Arabia reinforced its moderating policy by deliberately overproducing, with the aim of retarding price-rises. However, during 1981 world demand for petroleum fell sharply, due to conservation policies and a switch to alternative fuels, chiefly coal. This, the first "break" in general world demand, has led to considerable cut-backs in production and attempts to stabilize selling prices. (Petroleum development is discussed in more detail in a later chapter.)

One highly important element is the comparative cost of using pipelines to Mediterranean terminals in order to avoid the long journey by sea round the Cape of Good Hope. Generally speaking, movement of crude petroleum by pipeline offered lower costs, and hence countries through which the pipelines passed were able to demand substantial royalties. Libya, lying nearest to western markets, was also able to demand a higher price, reflecting shorter transport routes. However, the vulnerability of pipelines, owing to political troubles, has been more and more demonstrated since the 1960s; and the closure of the Suez Canal in 1967–75 led to rapid development of very large tankers using the Cape route. Alternatives are now possible: in 1972 Iraq, for example, began exploiting more intensively fields closer to the Persian Gulf, and exporting via the Cape. At the same time, a new pipeline was constructed from Kirkuk to the Mediterranean through Turkish rather than Syrian territory. Also, on re-opening the Suez Canal, Egypt undertook a programme of widening and deepening the Canal, even though a pipeline from Suez to Alexandria was in operation. One further element is the extreme vulnerability of very large tankers: a matter which has inhibited further growth in size.

Present-Day Problems

In the context of a rapid survey, it is possible to do no more than hint at a few acute issues which exert a profound influence on current trends in the Middle East. These issues may be summarized as population pressure, the question of finding a reasonably equitable basis for the distribution of wealth between social classes, political leadership, and the cultural crisis within Islam.

POPULATION PRESSURE

The population problem arises as the result of a high birth-rate, together with a fairly high death-rate which is now in some parts declining rapidly, as the result of improvements in public health. There is, in consequence, an increasing number of survivors, producing a population growth of the order of 2.3 per cent

(Egypt) to well over 3 per cent (Iran, Iraq, Jordan, Turkey, Gulf States). For the larger States (Egypt, Iran, Turkey) there is now the situation of an annual increase in each state of about one million, with the general prospect of a doubling of numbers for the Middle East as a whole within about 30 years or less. It has been noted above that the agricultural gains made in Egypt have been negated by larger human numbers; and there are now clear signs of severe population pressure on natural resources. In parts of the Nile valley there are substantial groups living by agriculture and concentrated at densities of 3–5,000 per square mile; whilst as regards Turkey, FAO reported some years ago that despite improvements since the 1940s, the situation calls for "a truly heroic" agricultural and livestock programme. The need for food imports grows yearly: one estimate is that consumption is rising by 12.5 per cent per annum, so that food imports in the Middle East, running at about $6,000 million in early 1981, could involve at east $10,000 million by the middle of the decade.

EXTREMES OF WEALTH

A second group of problems arises from the social inequality that is a feature of many Middle Eastern countries. There is the large mass of the poor, and a small number of wealthy families, with few of a "middle" class. At present it is fair to say that the gap between the groups is widening rather than closing, as the standard of living of the poor remains the same, or even falls, and that of the rich rises rapidly, owing to profits from high world prices in cotton, tobacco, and, above all, in petroleum. Equally significantly, the appearance of western luxuries—large automobiles, radios, refrigerators, furs, and luxury hotels—tends to increase the visible gap between rich and poor. Until 1918, an Arab who lived ostentatiously risked the vigorous attentions of the Ottoman tax-collector; today, the wealthy Arab is himself often closely connected with the government, and can manipulate its fiscal policy closely to his advantage. We have noted that the larger proportion of the revenues of Middle Eastern states is usually derived from indirect taxation of necessities such as food and clothing—a system that bears heaviest on the poorer classes. Even where oil wealth is available, there are few of the bureaucrats necessary for the imposition of direct taxation.

AUTHORITARIAN RULE

A third problem concerns the political organization in certain Middle East states. By temperament and experience, many Middle Easterners incline to personal and authoritarian forms of rule. Nomadic and pastoral ways of life tend to throw up individuals of much prestige and personal leadership; and even in religion —as indicated by the importance of prophetic revelation in Islam and Christianity—there is a tendency to respect the man equally with, if not more than, the principle. In consequence the idea of parliamentary democracy, introduced after 1920 partly in deference to the Western European views, has had a limited and

uncertain extension. The average man has tended to be impatient of rule by general consent, as expressed through Western democratic methods, preferring to follow a single individual of superior appeal and ability. Where such a figure has not been forthcoming, there has been acquiescence in rule by a caucus or oligarchy. In this situation, the importance of armed services is very great. As the final repository of physical power—only artillery, tanks, and aircraft can really control a large dissident mob—the army leaders especially come often to be the final arbiters in a struggle for power. Moreover, as something of a meritocracy in which able officers can most easily rise from humble origins to positions of power, the armed forces in the Middle East have often come to a centre of evolved middle-class, or even radical, opinion essentially different from the bourgeois attitude of the merchant groups.

Saudi Arabia and the Gulf states are ruled by absolute monarchs. For the twenty years preceding 1940 Turkey and Iran were ruled by despots. In more recent times, there has been a partial rejection of democracy on the Western pattern in countries where parliaments existed, and the last few years have seen a tendency towards a recrudescence of personal rule, the outstanding instances being in Egypt and Iraq. Parliamentary government seemed fairly strongly developed in Turkey until about 1955, but later events have suggested a reason for what, in some areas, is a normal pattern: military dictatorship. Moreover, a few years ago it seemed that eventually monarchy might be largely displaced by a rising tide of republicanism, as actually happened in Egypt, Iraq and Libya. During the 1970s, however, partly due to increased oil revenues, the monarchical principle showed distinct resilience, though, given the events in Iran in 1979, this could be only a temporary phase. Nevertheless, the Saudi Arabian monarchy has recently showed remarkable skill and energy in its attempts to lead Arab affairs.

MODERNIZING ISLAM

The widest problem of all concerns the cultural crisis within modern Islam. Until the end of the Middle Ages, Islamic culture was vigorous, and in many respects more advanced than that of Europe. Islamic thought greatly influenced the West, with a parallel superiority, or at least equality, in the political sphere. Since that time, however, there has been a considerable decline in power and intellectual strength: large-scale political penetration and domination from Europe began in the nineteenth century, and for several centuries material standards of life have no longer approximated to those of the West. There has, as a result, been much speculation in the Arab world upon the reasons for this decline. Three broad points of view can be discerned. There are those who see no good prospect in a continuance of Islamic traditions, and so wish to follow new ways of life— either Christian and western, or, less clearly, new materialistic doctrines, one ultimate expression of which may be Communism. At the opposite extreme are those, now more numerous, who suggest a return to a stricter form of Islam; and this policy is followed at the present time to a varying extent in Saudi Arabia, the Gulf States, Libya and Algeria. Then there is a third group of intermediates, whose position is perhaps the most difficult of all, since they wish to combine modernity with a maintenance of internal traditions. How far exactly can one go in this respect? And too often an attempt at combining widely diverse elements leads to superficiality, a rejection of fundamentals and a real understanding of neither aspect. We therefore have the phenomenon of the 'angry young Arab'—given more and more to rejection of existing ways and now actively critical of the failure of leadership over Palestine, and of inequalities in and lack of opportunity for economic advancement. He has an increasing sense of frustration which becomes more and more vocal with the spread of literacy. A further development, reflecting the special position of the Middle East between East and West, is the emergence of a specifically "Arab" socialism: neither Soviet nor Maoist communism, according to some Arab intellectuals, and certainly not "western" socialism, but reflecting the special social traditions of Islam. One aspect of this is the growth of Baathist ("Regeneration") movements of a socialist nature, in Syria and Iraq; the other, far wider in character, is, as we have seen, the rapid surge in fundamentalist Islam.

Summing Up

Having made a cursory survey of Middle Eastern lands and their resources, it is now possible to attempt a summary of conclusions. We may recall once again what was said concerning the geographical position of the Middle East as the land connexion between three continents; from this situation has arisen its main role in the world—as an intermediary between the nations of Europe, Asia, and Africa, both in the economic and cultural spheres. Sometimes this historic function has been discharged purely, so to speak, as an agent or middleman, without any indigenous contribution—as when, for example, silk, sugar, citrus fruit, paper, gunpowder, and the compass were introduced from Further Asia into Europe. At other times, a technique or an idea has been received or developed in the Middle East, expanded there into a great movement, and transmitted elsewhere. One may cite, for example, the system of garden irrigation brought by the Arabs to Spain, which is still a highly productive element in Spanish agriculture, or the religions of Christianity and Islam, or the scientific ideas of the Greeks and Hindus, which were preserved throughout the Dark Ages of Europe and later made available to the West through the works of Muslim commentators.

With the discovery of the sea route to India in the fifteenth century, the importance of the Middle East as a transit area greatly declined, but following the opening of the Suez Canal, and the later growth of air communications, the situation has once more altered. There has been a return to something of the ancient position, with air and sea routes now contributing again to outstanding prosperity, even though the Suez Canal, re-opened in 1975, has not so far recap-

tured all of its former trade. Nevertheless, as the result of recent enlargement, much medium-size tanker traffic has resumed use of the canal.

Beirut early emerged as a world centre for air traffic—it was one of the first airports to be designed for jet aircraft—and because of its central geographical location, a climate that is exceptionally favourable for air navigation, and the topographical and political difficulties in regions further north and south, the Middle East has become a world nodal centre of air traffic. In a broader sense still there has very recently been a major shift of political and economic influence within the world. For several centuries, wealth and hence power were concentrated in north-western Europe; but since about 1900 the rise of America and Russia, the independence of India and black Africa, revival of China, and growing dependence of Europe on foodstuffs and primary materials imported from Australasia and Africa brought about an expansion of global relations. The Middle East, situated at the cross-roads of the world, has increasingly profited from what is now a central geographical position. Over and above this have been the dramatic effects first from the fact of having more than half the world's proven reserves of oil and natural gas, and in 1974 awakening by Middle East governments to the implications of this commanding geopolitical situation. In only a few weeks during 1974 the dominance of Middle Eastern oil suppliers was demonstrated, with effects that will last for decades. A question anxiously debated since the quadrupling of oil revenues in 1973–74 is how far the Middle East will play a much greater financial and hence political role in world affairs. Concern, even alarm, in early 1974 over whether the new revenues would overturn or disrupt world markets has subsided, as it becomes clearer that Middle Eastern oil states are now using the largest proportion of their revenues for internal development (including heavy emphasis on defence), and the remainder more or less equally split between outside loans (often to other Arab countries), and investment in world stock and property markets (mainly but not entirely American). The political effects of this new wealth are becoming apparent: a principal one is certainly the tendency of the U.S.A. to push Israel more strongly towards seeking political accommodation with its Arab neighbours.

Returning to more modest horizons, it is useful to notice one other feature of the Middle East, due in large part to its geography: potential as a tourist centre. It is probable that currently north-west Europe is experiencing a small climatic oscillation towards cooler, rainier summers; hence with "guaranteed" sunshine, excellent beaches, and considerable archaeological and human interest, certain parts of the Middle East have been able to develop a growing tourist attraction. New hotels, amenities and sports stadia are under construction; and given stable political conditions, this activity could well develop much further in the next few years, not merely for one season, but through a large proportion of the whole year. Tunisia, especially, owes much to a tourist boom, as does Cyprus.

POLITICAL OUTLINE

Similarly, there have been shifts in political fortune since the First World War. In 1916 the allocation of almost the entire Middle East as spheres of influence for European powers—Britain, France, Russia, Italy and Greece—had been agreed on. Treaties were actually in existence envisaging a territorial division which would have left only a fraction of Asia Minor under autonomous local rule.

From that apparent high water mark of Western influence, there has been a considerable decline; but the interest of external powers in the Middle East continues, fostered by the petroleum resources and strategic geographical location of the area.

At the same time there has been a parallel rise in nationalist feeling, helped on partly by differences among interested European powers and the skill with which these were exploited by Middle Eastern governments, and partly by the growth of internal wealth in the states themselves. This process became particularly vigorous after 1940, when from being a small marginal producer of in the main low-quality commodities, the Middle East became an important world supplier of petroleum, cotton, tobacco, wool and cereals.

The main element in the present-day politics of the Middle East is the existence of the state of Israel. To most Arabs, the creation first of a National Home for Jews and later of a Jewish State was a clear demonstration of hostility toward the Arab world on the part of Britain, France and the U.S.A.—a view which the events of 1956, and then of 1967, seemed only to confirm. As the Arabs see it, Western patronage of Zionism was a Machiavellian device to disrupt the Arab Middle East; and there can be no real friendship or understanding with the West until support for Zionism is disavowed. Moreover, uncertain of their own strength, Arab governments have increasingly turned to the U.S.S.R. for support against Zionism and its patrons. At times too it has been possible to take advantage of American divergence in policy from that of Britain and/or France (e.g. over oil concessions, Algeria, Cyprus and Suez). Moreover, the Middle East may offer a counterpoise to the forces balanced within the other southern extremity of Asia. Thus the present situation in many ways resembles that of the pre-1914 Balkans, with a number of small and antagonistic states manoeuvring between independence and "protection" from a great power in the background. But the Balkans never possessed more than half the world's oil, or had large groups of their nationals as sympathetic, involved minorities living inside the antagonistic super-states.

ECONOMIC TRENDS

In the economic sphere, it is more difficult to present a clearly defined picture. There is the unique asset of petroleum, which has already transformed ways of life in areas where it is exploited, and brought unexpected wealth to port terminals such as Abadan, Bahrain, Tripoli (Lebanon), Baniyas, Sidon, Kuwait and Benghazi. A striking inequality has consequently developed between various countries. Those actually producing oil have substantial extra wealth, and can embark on schemes of improvement, with at some time the possibility of a relatively unfettered foreign policy. Next in order come the non-producers with locational advantages—pipelines, good harbours or oil refineries. These countries can profit in a minor way from petroleum exploitation, but a ceiling is set by the cost of alternative transport. If too much is demanded by way of transit dues, the oil traffic could be re-routed either via Suez (in relatively small tankers, or by the new SUMED pipeline), or the Cape of Good Hope, and by the alternative pipeline routes, such as that from Eilat on the Gulf of Aqaba to the Mediterranean, or from Iraq to the Mediterranean through Turkey.

The relationships of foreign exploiting companies have undergone dramatic changes since the 1920s and 30s, when approximately 16 per cent only of net oil revenue was paid over to local governments, and companies enjoyed almost extra-territorial legal and fiscal rights. Although the volume of oil produced has increased enormously, the position of the foreign companies has been steadily reduced, until, in the mid-1970s, they have been entirely expropriated and reduced at most to the position of agents for a nationalized industry. The effect of a change of price from $2 to $34 per barrel since 1973 has been enormous internally, where there is a leap forward in the commercial and industrial spheres, to be set against the corroding effect of sudden easy wealth on traditional outlook and ways of life. Externally, oil wealth is now being deployed with increasing vigour and sophistication as a political weapon: to create friends, extinguish enmities, and persuade countries such as the U.S.A. that Arabs, as well as Jews, may be entitled to a National Home in Israel/Palestine.

As regards agriculture, the position is less satisfactory. Though there are certainly richly endowed spots (especially parts of the Nile Valley), the Middle East is on the whole a poor area, condemned by aridity and scantiness of resources to a marginal place as a producer. Nevertheless, the last twenty years have seen highly significant increases, particularly in Egypt, Iran and Turkey, which are now undoubtedly in numbers if not wealth the leading states of the Middle East. But overall, as we have noted, it is now becoming apparent that, despite progress achieved, present levels of agriculture are becoming insufficient to support the population growth, and that imports of foodstuffs on an increasing scale are becoming necessary. The only area of the Middle East where there is still large potential for further sustained agricultural development may well be the Sudan.

Turkey

Though an agricultural country, Turkey in 1920 imported almost one-half of her foodstuffs: most of the few public utilities were foreign-owned; and modern industry could hardly be said to exist. Following several phases of development (the last of which from 1947 onwards amounting almost to an agricultural revolution) Turkey is almost self-sufficient in food, and in favourable years since 1950 has even exported wheat. Foreign ownership has been very greatly reduced, and a variety of light industry created. At first much of this activity was state-sponsored and owned, but since 1950 there has been a partial denationalization of industry. The last few years, however, have seen a marked fall-off in prosperity, with increasing shortage of development capital and a tense atmosphere of domestic shortages due to lack of foreign exchange to pay for imports. Repeated financial crises and the intervention of the World Bank have led to currency devaluations at closer and closer intervals. Since the inauguration of military government in 1980, however, the economic position has undoubtedly improved: the rate of inflation has declined, production increased somewhat, and a limited confidence has returned.

Egypt

Progress in Egypt has also been considerable. The careful use of river barrage systems has made the lower Nile valley one of the most productive agricultural areas in the world, with highest unit yields in maize and sugar, and highest quality in cotton. Intensity and quality of farming are unrivalled elsewhere in the Middle East, though there are ominous signs that future progress will be difficult—almost all the Nile water is now in use, and more and more fertilizers must be imported. Also, war periods greatly stimulated the growth of local industry, which, until the 1952 revolution, had always been on a capitalist, *laissez faire*, basis. Textiles are most important, but the increased wealth of the upper and middle classes has provided a market for light consumer goods that is now largely supplied within the country. An outstandingly important development is the full implementation of the Aswan High Dam project which, besides adding one-third to the present total of cultivated land in Egypt, provides electric power for heavy and light industry on a very considerable scale, at prices comparable with those of Europe. There are, however, certain criticisms now levelled against the Aswan concept, some of which are on technical grounds, some purely political. Egypt has massive debts, and her poor record over the last few decades has made outside investors cautious. In 1977, however, there was an attempt to improve the position by negotiating extensive outside loans for development and the re-scheduling of past debts. This would not so far appear to have had outstanding success; and the "open door" policy has not produced a massive inflow of capital. The rich may well be better off; but the poor are not. Loss of good arable land to housing, declining revenue from oil, and the inexorable need for more food imports are pressing problems. The "open door" fiscal policy has led to much smuggling; remittances from abroad are levelling out at about $3,000 million per year; and subsidies on food and fuel absorb about 10 per cent of gross domestic product.

Israel

Israel had certain advantages when it began the desperate task of attempting to support relatively large numbers in a poor environment at high standards of life. There were the energy and skill of its European-trained population; an overriding determination to make a success from unpromising beginnings, much machinery imported from Europe (Hitler allowed refugees from Nazi Germany to take plant, but not capital), and financial support from outside, chiefly the U.S.A. The country is not richly endowed—though mineral deposits (oil, natural gas, copper and phosphates) on a relatively small scale have recently been discovered—and transport is difficult. Moreover, most of the south is arid, and good agricultural land is everywhere severely restricted. A further handicap has been the determination to maintain high levels of wages—a matter in which powerful trade unions are involved. The advances achieved both in agriculture and industry have been very great but some restriction of consumption of food and clothing is still necessary, and there is a severe adverse balance of trade with exports amounting to only one-half or in some recent years, one-quarter of imports. In consequence, despite stringent controls, and great efforts to expand production, loans from abroad are still vital to the Israeli economy, and unemployment on a moderate scale had come to be a problem before the 1967 War. After that time, the Israeli economy experienced boom conditions until 1974, after which heavy defence costs began to affect economic life unfavourably, helped on by the world economic downturn. Inflation remains severe, running at 130–140 per cent during 1981—the fears of pessimists that it would be above 150 per cent were not realized—and Israel's debts are now approaching $6,000 per head of population.

Iran

Iran has a long tradition of craft industry, especially in wool; and there are varied mineral deposits, including coal. With the exception of petroleum, copper and, less certainly, coal, these deposits are scattered, small in amount, often of low grade. Within the last few years, however, there has been a considerable degree of industrial growth in Teheran City, which now has industrial quarters that produce a wide range of constructional and consumer products. Rapid development here of industrial capacity is now seen as excessive in that it is stultifying growth in other regions of Iran; and is in general too rapid a process for the installed capacity of electricity generation. Construction of a gas grid from the southern fields to Isfahan and northwards to the U.S.S.R. at Astara has been a great impetus to development, and a large steel-making plant has been constructed by Soviet technicians at Isfahan—this is already planned to be extended. Overall Iran has experienced considerable, at times spectacular development with annual growth-rates of between 15 and 24 per cent. Liquidity was a problem in 1976 and growth plans have in consequence since been trimmed, but Iran's industrial programme in absolute terms, and certainly in comparison with that of her neighbours, can only be described as impressive. However, the cutback in oil production that accompanied the change of government in 1978, together with frequent strikes and the withdrawal of most expatriate workers, has caused considerable fall-off both in levels of activity and expansion of new development projects. Imposition of sanctions (removed in 1981), the war with Iraq and uncertainties over agricultural production have all been highly adverse factors, so that production has greatly declined. Nevertheless, the economy has shown some resilience: more perhaps than might have been expected under the circumstances.

Iraq

Until recently there was hardly any industry of any kind in Iraq, in distinct contrast to many of its neighbours. But since 1945 oil revenues have been allocated to a national Development Board, which has fostered the development of communications and agriculture, and begun to plan some industrial activity. Now, in addition to the processing of agricultural products, there is some textile manufacturing (chiefly cotton and rayon), a little light engineering, and a small chemical industry. Plans are in hand to expand these, especially the last. Agriculture is less developed than in Egypt, owing in part to the difficult nature of the two rivers, which have been more difficult to control and develop for irrigation. Since 1954, however, with the completion of Wadi Tharthar and other flood control and irrigation projects, the situation has changed, and large areas of good land which have hitherto remained unused can now be developed.

Syria, Lebanon, Jordan

At one time, Syria was the most industrialized province of the Ottoman Empire, with Aleppo second only to Constantinople in size. Loss of markets since 1918 has hampered but not destroyed the textile and metal manufactures of Aleppo and Damascus, and there are a small number of other industrial activities. Agriculturally, Syria has developed greatly since 1945. The irrigated "Fertile Crescent" has been expanded, and parts of the Euphrates valley brought back into cultivation for the first time in many centuries. Syria is self-sufficient in cereals, and exports these, together with raw cotton, to her less well-placed neighbours, the Lebanon and Jordan. The cotton is used both in the Middle East and in central Europe and Japan. The building of a dam across the Euphrates at Tabqa east of Aleppo, is only the largest factor in a general programme of Syrian development, which, however, has been increasingly affected by a general downturn in the world economy and, more specifically, by the recurring military burden in the Lebanon and along the frontier with Israel.

The Lebanon, like Israel, has severe natural handicaps. The rugged nature of the hills, which occupy most of the country, and aridity in the east greatly limit cultivation, and there are no mineral resources. Dependent on the import of foodstuffs, the country nevertheless has a considerable transit traffic, with the intelligence, adaptability and highly developed commercial sense of its people as the chief assets of the country. There is an international trade in gold, and Beirut (with four universities) has become a major cultural centre for the entire Middle East.

Since 1975 civil war on an increasing scale has brought the country into a desperate position, but with the cessation of major warfare in 1977 and the formation of a Reconstruction and Development Council it is possible (given the resilience of Lebanese entrepreneurs) that some activities will re-develop.

Jordan, with almost no sea outlet, is in a very different situation. Most of the country is either arid or covered by bare sheets of lava—the only cultivable areas are west of the Jordan (Israeli-occupied since June 1967), in the Judaean uplands, and around Amman. Nomadic pastoralism is the only possible activity over much of the country—though the exploitation of substantial phosphate deposits provides a further source of occupation. An artificial territorial unit, with very few resources, Jordan was for long hardly viable and depended on outside subsidies provided by Britain, the U.S.A. and, for varying periods since 1967, by Saudi Arabia, Kuwait and Libya. At present, there is a period of very much improved conditions, partly due to fuller exploitation of mineral resources (chiefly phosphate), partly due to better political relations with Syria; and partly because of the shift of commercial activity from the Lebanon, which has produced boom conditions, especially in Amman. Foreign loan and development capital has become available on a much more extensive scale, and rapid growth has taken place, to an extent that would not have seemed possible a few years ago. Closer political links with Iraq have led to a considerable increase in transit traffic.

Libya

A somewhat similar situation obtained in Libya until very recently where, despite the imposing size of territory, cultivated land is restricted to certain districts near or along the coast, together with a few inland oasis settlements. Now, discoveries of oil on a large scale are rapidly transforming the situation, and there is marked growth, especially in towns such as Benghazi and Tripoli.

Arabia

The Arabian peninsula is, so to speak, a stage beyond Libya. Before 1940 the territory was possibly the poorest in all the Middle East—only scattered oases with a largely nomadic population. Now the economic situation has been completely transformed; Saudi Arabia and Kuwait are, with the United Arab Emirates, among the largest oil producers of the Middle East. Qatar and Oman have also developed as significant contributors; and in all these countries schemes for infrastructures and industrial development are being pushed ahead. The immense oil revenues have financed lavish public works and welfare programmes, but the ease with which all imports needed for the small population can be paid for has reduced the incentive to develop the peninsula's other resources. Nevertheless, a major central industrial axis is rapidly developing across the country, based on the Jeddah-Yanbo industrial zone and Jubail in the west, and the oil-steel complex around Dammam on the east.

Cyprus

Though small, Cyprus prior to the troubles of 1974 had a very sound agricultural system, with over 55 per cent of the total land area used—a figure far higher than in any other Middle Eastern country. There are also small but useful deposits of iron, copper and asbestos; with a growing tourist trade. Since 1974, however, agriculture has been disrupted by the exchange of populations, with crops in some areas untended. Despite all this, however, exports of fruit have picked up, from the south, and tourism has shown marked signs of revival. The arrival of Lebanese Christian refugees (many with some capital) has proved a stimulus; and the speed of reconstruction in the southern (Greek) sector is now very considerable. Political uncertainties remain, however, a major handicap.

The Maghreb

Lastly, North Africa is still suffering from the effects of colonial rule. The effects of prolonged and bitter warfare, the withdrawal of French "colons" who contributed in predominant measure to the more highly developed economic activities, and the resulting disequilibrium in an economy that until independence was strongly integrated with that of France—all these will take time to dissipate. Whilst over and above, there is the desperate need to provide for the rapidly growing numbers of inhabitants, with the concomitant problem of greater imbalance between urban and rural areas—a declining countryside, resulting in a fall-off in agricultural production, and congestion at declining levels of subsistence in the larger towns.

The most hopeful element is the presence of substantial mineral resources. Oil and gas could be used in part directly as fuel for industry; and revenues from exports might be directed to an expansion both of home manufacturing and improved agricultural techniques. Hydro-electricity is another possible source of energy, and this could foster *inter alia* more methodical exploitation and treatment of metallic mineral resources. At long term, the problem is also one of transferring the liability of an underemployed and growing population into the economic asset of a large pool of labour and consumer demand. A feature of the last few years has been the movement in Algeria towards closer economic links with the capitalist West rather than the socialist countries of Europe.

Tunisia, though small, has shown particularly steady development, based on increased exploitation of limited mineral resources, a thriving tourist trade, and improved agricultural yields.

The Religions of the Middle East and North Africa

Islam

R. B. Serjeant

Islam is a major world religion and the faith predominating throughout the Middle East (with the exception of Lebanon the population of which is approximately half Muslim and half Christian) and North Africa. There are substantial Christian minorities in some countries and communities of oriental Jews and other faiths, for centuries integrated with the Muslim majority. Islam is not only a highly developed religious system but an established and distinctive culture embracing every aspect of human activity from theology, philosophy, literature to the visual arts and even man's routine daily conduct. Its characteristic intellectual manifestation therefore is in the field of Islamic law, the *Shari'ah*. Though in origin a Semitic Arabian faith, Islam was also the inheritor of the legacy of classical Greek and Roman civilization and, in its major phase of intellectual, social and cultural development after its emergence from its Arabian womb, it was affected by Christian, Jewish and Persian civilization. In turn, Greek scientific and philosophical writings—direct translations into Arabic or forming a principal element in the books of Arab scholars—began to enter medieval Europe in Latin renderings about the early 12th century from the brilliant intellectual circles of Islamic Spain, and formed a potent factor in the little Renaissance of western Europe.

Islamic civilization had, by about the 18th century, clearly lost its initiative to the ascendant West and has not since regained it. Today, however, certain oil-rich Arab states, notably Saudi Arabia and Kuwait, have entered in a large way into the world of international finance and mercantilism, including banking, but such activities can scarcely be described as "Islamic".

HISTORY

The founder of the religion of Islam was the Prophet Muhammad b. 'Abdullah, born about A.D. 570, a member of the noble house of Hashim, belonging to the 'Abd Manaf clan, itself a part of the Quraish tribal confederation of Mecca. 'Abd Manaf may be described as semi-priestly since they had the privilege of certain functions during the annual pilgrimage to the Meccan Ka'bah, a cube-shaped temple set in the sacred enclave (*haram*). Quraish controlled this enclave which was maintained inviolate from war or killing, and they had established a pre-eminence and loose hegemony even over many Arabian tribes which they had induced to enter a trading alliance extending over the main Arabian land routes, north and south, east and west. With the powerful Quraish leaders in Mecca, temple guardians, chiefs, merchant adventurers, Muhammad clashed, when, aged about 40, he began to proclaim the worship of the one God, Allah, as against their multiplicity of gods. These Quraish leaders were contemptuous of his mission.

While his uncle Abu Talib, head of the house of Hashim, lived, he protected Muhammad from physical harm, but after his death Muhammad sought protection from tribes outside Mecca—they would not accept him even when he asked only to remain quietly without preaching—Thaqif of Taif drove him roughly away. Ultimately pilgrims of the Aws and Khazraj tribes of Yathrib (Medina), some 200 miles north of Mecca, agreed to protect him there, undertaking to associate no other god with Allah and accepting certain moral stipulations. Muhammad left Mecca with his Companion Abu Bakr in the year 622—this is the year of the *hijrah* or hegira.

Arriving in Yathrib, Muhammad formed a federation or community (*ummah*) of Aws and Khazraj, known as the "Supporters" (*Ansar*), followed by their Jewish client tribes, and the "Emigrants" (*Muhajirun*), his refugee Quraish adherents, with himself as the ultimate arbiter of the *ummah* as a whole, though there remained a local opposition covertly antagonistic to him, the *Munafiqun*, rendered as "Hypocrites". Two internal issues had now to be fought by Muhammad—the enforcement of his position as theocratic head of the federation, and the acquisition of revenue to maintain his position; externally he took an aggressive attitude to the Meccan Quraish.

In Yathrib his disposal of the Jewish tribes who made common cause with the "Hypocrites" improved his financial position. The Meccan Quraish he overcame more by skilful political manoeuvre than through the occasional armed clashes with them, and in year 8 he entered Mecca without fighting. Previously he had declared Yathrib a sacred enclave (*haram*), renaming it Medina, the City (of the Prophet)—the two cities known as al-Haraman have become the holy land of Islam. Muhammad was conciliatory to his defeated Quraish kinsmen, and after his success against Taif, south of Mecca, deputations came from the Arabian tribes to make terms with the new Prophet—the heritor of the influence of the Meccan Quraish.

Early Islam

The two main tenets of Islam are embodied in the formula of the creed, "There is no god but Allah and Muhammad is the Apostle of God." Unitarianism (*tawhid*), as opposed to polytheism (*shirk*) or making partners with God, is Islam's basic principle, coupled with Muhammad's authority conferred on him by God. Muhammad made little change to the ancient Arabian religion—he abolished idolatry but confirmed the pilgrimage to the Ka'bah; the Koran, the sacred Book in Arabic revealed to Muhammad for his people, lays down certain social and moral rules. Among these are the condemnation of usury or interest (*riba*) on loans and prohibition of wine (*khamr*)—both ordinances have always been difficult to enforce. On the whole the little change involved seems to have made it easy for Arabia to accept Islam. While there is incontrovertible evidence of Muhammad's contact with Judaism, and even with Christianity, and the Koran contains versions of narrative known to the sacred books of these faiths, yet these are used to point purely Arabian morals. The limited social law laid down by the Koran is supplemented by a body of law and precept derived from the *Hadith* or Tradition of Muhammad's practice (*Sunnah*) at Medina, and welded into the Islamic system, mainly in its second and third centuries.

Subsequent History

Immediately after Muhammad's death in 632, Abu Bakr, delegated by him to lead the prayer during his last indisposition, became his successor or Caliph. Some Medinan supporters had attempted a breakaway from Quraish overlordship but Abu Bakr adroitly persuaded them to accept himself to follow Muhammad. But office in Arabia, generally speaking, is hereditary within a family group, though elective within that group, and Abu Bakr's action had taken no account of the claims of 'Ali, the Prophet's cousin and son-in-law—the house of Hashim to which Muhammad and 'Ali belonged was plainly aggrieved that a member of a minor Quraish clan should have snatched supreme power. Muhammad's Arabian coalition also showed tendencies to dissolve, the tribes particularly objecting to paying taxes to Medina, but Abu Bakr's firm line held it together. The expansionist thrusts beyond Arabia during his Caliphate, continuing under his successor 'Umar and part of the reign of the third Caliph 'Uthman, diverted tribal energies to profitable warfare in Mesopotamia, Palestine-Syria, Egypt and Persia. Muslim armies were eventually to conquer North Africa, much of Spain, parts of France, and even besiege Rome, while in the east they later penetrated to Central Asia and India.

During 'Uthman's tenure of office the tide of conquest temporarily slackened and the turbulent tribes, now settled in southern Iraq and Egypt, began to dispute the Caliph's disposal of booty and revenue, maintaining that he unduly favoured members of his own house. A delegation of tribal malcontents from Egypt murdered 'Uthman in the holy city of Medina, and in the resultant confusion 'Ali, Muhammad's cousin, was elected Caliph with the support of the tribesmen responsible for murdering 'Uthman. This raised grave constitutional problems for the young Muslim state, and is regarded as the origin of the greatest schism in Islam.

If Legitimist arguments were the sole consideration 'Ali's claims to succession seem the best, but he had previously lost it to 'Uthman—whose father belonged to the Umaiyah clan which had opposed Muhammad, but whose mother was of Hashim. 'Uthman naturally appointed Umaiyah men loyal to him to commands in the Empire, notably Mu'awiyah as governor of Syria—the son of that very Abu Sufyan who headed Quraish opposition to Muhammad at Mecca—though later reconciled to him. Mu'awiyah demanded 'Uthman's murderers be brought to justice in accordance with the law, but 'Ali, unable to cope with the

murderers, his supporters, was driven by events to take up arms against Mu'awiyah. When they clashed at Siffin in Syria 'Ali was forced, against his better judgement, to submit to the arbitration of the Koran and Sunnah, thus automatically losing the position of supreme arbiter, inherited by the Caliphs from Muhammad. Though history is silent as to what the arbiters actually judged it was most likely as to whether 'Ali had broken the law established by Muhammad, and that he was held to have sheltered unprovoked murderers. The arbiters deposed him from the Caliphial office, though the historians allege trickery entered into their action.

'Ali shortly after was murdered by one of a group of his former supporters which had come out against the arbitration it had first urged upon him. This group, the Khawarij, is commonly held to be the forerunner of the Ibadis of Oman and elsewhere. Mu'awiyah became Caliph and founder of the Umaiyad dynasty with its capital at Damascus. The ambitions of the Hashim house were not however allayed, and when Umaiyad troops slew 'Ali's son Husain at Karbala' in south Iraq they created the greatest Shi'ah martyr.

The house of Hashim also included the descendants of 'Abbas the Prophet's uncle, a relative, in Arabian eyes, as close as 'Ali to him, but 'Abbas had opposed Muhammad till late in the day. The 'Abbasids made common cause with the 'Ali-id Shi'ah against the Umaiyads, but were evidently abler in the political field. In the Umaiyad empire the Arabian tribes formed a kind of military élite but were constantly at factious war with one another. The Hashimites rode to power on the back of a rebellion against the Umaiyads which broke out in Khurasan in east Persia, but it was the 'Abbasid branch of Hashim which assumed the Caliphate and ruled from the capital they founded at Baghdad.

The 'Abbasid Caliphate endured up to the destruction of Baghdad in 1258 by the devastating Mongol invaders of the eastern empire, but the Caliphs had long been mere puppets in the hands of Turkish and other mercenaries, and the unwieldy empire had fragmented into independent states which rose and fell, though they mostly conceded nominal allegiance to the 'Abbasid Caliphs.

The Mongol Ilkhanid sovereigns, now turned Muslim, were in turn displaced by the conquests of Tamberlane at the end of the 14th century. In fact the Islamic empire had largely been taken over by Turkic soldiery. The Mameluke or Slave rulers of medieval Egypt who followed the Aiyubid (Kurdish) dynasty of Saladin were mainly Turks or Circassians. It was they who checked the Mongol advance at 'Ain Jalut in Palestine (1260). The Ottoman Turks captured Constantinople in 1453, and took Egypt from the Mamelukes in 1516, following this up by occupying the Hejaz where the Ashraf, descendants of the Prophet, ruled in Mecca and Medina, under first Mameluke then Turkish suzerainty. In 1533 the Turks took Baghdad and Iraq became part of the Ottoman Empire. The Ottoman Sultans assumed the title of Caliph—though in Islamic constitutional theory it is not easy to justify this. The Ottoman Caliphs endured till the Caliphate was abolished by Mustafa Kamal in 1924. The Turks have always been characterized by their adherence to Sunni orthodoxy.

Throughout history the 'Ali-ids have constantly asserted their right to be the Imams or leaders of the Muslim community—this in the religious and political senses, since Islam is fundamentally theocratic. The Shi'ah or followers of 'Ali and his descendants were in constant rebellion against the 'Abbasids and came to form a distinct schismatic group of Legitimist sects—at one time the Fatimid Shi'ah rulers of Egypt were near to conquering the main part of the Islamic world. The main Shi'ah sects today are the Ithna-'asharis, the Isma'ilis, and the near-orthodox Zaidis of the Yemen. The Safavids who conquered Persia at the beginning of the 16th century brought it finally into the Shi'ah fold. Sunni Hashimite dynasties flourish today in Jordan and Morocco as they did till fairly recently in Iraq and Libya, and the Shi'ah Zaidi ruler of Yemen was only displaced in 1962. The main difference between Sunnis and Shi'ah is over the Imamate i.e. the temporal and spiritual leader of Islam, for whereas Sunnis, while they respect the Prophet's house, do not consider the Imam *must* be a member of it—the Shi'ah insist on an Imam of the descendants of 'Ali and Fatimah his wife, the Prophet's daughter.

It has been too readily assumed that, during the later Middle Ages and long Turkish domination, the Islamic Middle East was completely stagnant. The shift in economic patterns after the New World was discovered, and the Cape route to India, coupled with widening Western intellectual horizons and the development of science and technology did push European culture far ahead of the Muslim Middle East. It was confronted by a vigorous and hostile Christianity intent on proselytising in its very homelands. Muslims had to face the challenge of the ideas and attitudes of Christian missionaries. Muslim thinkers like Muhammad 'Abduh (1849–1905) of Egypt and his school asserted that Islam had become heavily overlaid with false notions—hence its decline; like earlier reformers they were convinced that present difficulties could be solved by reversion to an (idealized) pure primitive Islam. Sometimes, in effect, this meant re-interpreting religious literature to suit attitudes and ideas of modern times—as for instance when they saw the virtual prohibition of polygamy in the restrictions which hedge it about. Since the earlier modern days political leaders like Mustafa Kamal of Turkey have often taken drastic measures, secularizing the state itself even up to the sensitive field of education, and accusing the more conservative forms of Islam of blocking progress. Today the Islamic Middle East has regimes ranging from the strong supporters of traditional Islam—like Sa'udi Arabia and Libya—to the anti-religious Marxist group controlling Aden. In Libya, nevertheless, Colonel Gaddafi has published *The Green Book*, embodying his personal solution, very socialist in tone, of problems of democracy and economics.

ISLAMIC LAW

Orthodox Sunni Islam finds its main expression in *Shari'ah* law which it regards with great veneration. The Sunnis have crystallized into four "schools" (*madhhab*) or "rites", all of which are recognized as valid. Though in practice the adherents of one school can sometimes be at loggerheads with another, in modern times it is claimed that the law of any one of the rites can be applied to a case. The schools, named after their founders, are the Hanbali, regarded as the strictest, with adherents mainly in Sa'udi Arabia, the Shafi'is, the widest in extent with adherents in Egypt, Syria-Palestine, Egypt, South Arabia, and the Far East, the moderate Hanafi school which was the official rite of the Ottoman Turkish empire and to which most Muslims in the Indian sub-continent belong, and the Malikis of the North African states, Nigeria, and the Sudan. The Shi'ite sects have developed their own law, and give prominence to *ijtihad*, the forming of independent judgement, whereas the Sunnis are more bound by *taqlid* or following ancient models. However as the law of Sunnis, the moderate Shi'ah, and the Ibadis is basically derived from the same sources the differences are generally more of emphasis than principle.

The completely Islamic state as the theorists envisage it, run in conformity with the rules of the *Shari'ah* has probably never been achieved, and people's practice is often at variance with some or other requirements of *Shari'ah*. The imprint of Islam is nevertheless unmistakably evident on every country in this volume.

Civil Courts. In the modern states of the Islamic world there exists, side by side with the *Shari'ah* court (judging cases on personal status, marriage, divorce, etc.), the secular court which has a wide jurisdiction (based on Western codes of law) in civil and criminal matters. This court is competent to give judgment irrespective of the creed or race of the defendant.

Islamic Law as Applying to Minorities. In cases of minorities (Christian or Jewish) residing as a community in Muslim countries, spiritual councils are established where judgment is passed according to the law of the community, in matters concerning personal status, by the recognised head of that community.

Tribal Courts. In steppe and mountain areas of countries where a proportion of the population is still tribal, tribal courts administer law and justice in accordance with ancient custom and tribal procedure. There is, nonetheless, constant pressure to eliminate customary practices where they are unequivocally seen to be contrary to Islamic principles.

Awqaf. In Muslim countries the law of Awqaf is the law applied to religious and charitable endowments, trusts and settlements. This important Islamic institution, found in all Eastern countries, is administered by the *Shari'ah* courts. Awqaf, or endowments, are pious bequests made by Muslims for the upkeep of religious institutions, public benefits, etc.

SUFIS

As in other religions, many Muslims find their emotional needs are not satisfied by observing a code of law and morals alone, and turn to mysticism. From early times Islamic mystics existed, known as Sufis, allegedly from their wearing a woollen garment. They seek complete identification with the Supreme Being and annihilation of the self—the existence of which latter they call polytheism (*shirk*). The learned doctors of Islam often think ill of the Sufis, and indeed rogues and wandering mendicants found Sufism a convenient means of livelihood. Certain Sufi groups allowed themselves dispensations and as stimulants even used hashish and opium which are not sanctioned by the Islamic moral code. The Sufis became organized in what are loosely called brotherhoods (*tariqah*), and have to a large extent been incorporated into the structure of orthodox Islamic society. Some *tariqahs* induce ecstatic states by their performance of the *dhikr*, meaning, literally, the mentioning (of Allah). Today there is much disapproval of the more extravagant manifestations of the Sufis and in some places these have been banned entirely.

BELIEF AND PRACTICE

"Islam" means the act of submitting or resigning oneself to God, and a Muslim is one who resigns or submits himself to God. Muslims disapprove of the term "Muhammadan" for the faith of Islam, since they worship Allah, and Muhammad is only the Apostle of Allah whose duty it was to convey revelation, though he is regarded as the "Best of Mankind". He is the Seal (*Khatam*) of the Prophets, i.e. the ultimate Prophet in a long series in which both Moses and Jesus figure. They are revered, but, like Muhammad the Prophet, they are not worshipped.

Nearly all Muslims agree on acceptance of six articles of the faith of Islam: (i) Belief in God; (ii) in His angels; (iii) in His revealed books; (iv) in His Apostles; (v) in the Resurrection and Day of Judgement; and (vi) in His predestination of good and evil.

Faith includes works, and certain practices are obligatory on the believing Muslim. These are five in number:

1. The recital of the creed (*Shahadah*)—"There is no god but God (Allah) and Muhammad is the Apostle of God." This formula is embodied in the call to prayer made by the muezzin (announcer) from the minaret of the mosque before each of the five daily prayers.

2. The performance of the Prayer (*Salat*) at the five appointed canonical times—in the early dawn before the sun has risen above the horizon, in the early afternoon when the sun has begun to decline, later when the sun is about midway in its course towards setting, immediately after sunset, in the evening between the disappearance of the red glow in the west and bedtime. In prayer Muslims face towards the Ka'bah in Mecca. They unroll prayer mats and pray in a mosque (place of prostration), at home, or wherever they may be, bowing and prostrating themselves before God and reciting set verses in Arabic from the Koran. On Fridays it is obligatory for men to attend congregational Prayer in the central mosque of the quarter in which one lives—women do not normally attend. On this occasion formal prayers are preceded by a sermon.

3. The payment of the legal alms (*Zakat*). In early times this contribution was collected by officials of the Islamic state, and devoted to the relief of the poor, debtors, aid to travellers and other charitable and state purposes. Nowadays the fulfilment of this religious obligation is left to the conscience of the individual believer.

4. The thirty days of the fast in the month of Ramadan, the ninth month in the lunar year. As the lunar calendar is shorter by 11 days than the solar calendar Ramadan moves from the hottest to the coldest seasons of the solar year. It is observed as a fast from dawn to sunset each day by all adults in normal health, during which time no food or drink may be taken. The sick, pregnant women, travellers and children are exempt; some states exempt students, soldiers and factory workers. The fast ends with one of the two major Muslim festivals, 'Id al-Fitr.

5. The pilgrimage (*Hajj*) to Mecca. Every Muslim is obliged, circumstances permitting, to perform this at least once in his lifetime, and when accomplished he may assume the title, *Hajji*. Over a million pilgrims go each year to Mecca, but the holy cities of Mecca and Medina are prohibited to non-Muslims.

Before entering the sacred area around Mecca by the seventh day of Dhu'l-Hijjah, the twelfth month of the Muslim year, pilgrims must don the *ihram*, consisting of two unseamed lengths of white cloth, indicating that they are entering a state of consecration and casting off what is ritually impure. The pilgrims circumambulate the Ka'bah seven times, endeavouring to kiss the sacred Black Stone. Later they run seven times between the near-by twin hills of Safa and Marwa (now covered in by an immense hall), thus recalling Hagar's desperate search for water for her child Ishmael (from whom the Arabs claim descent). On the eighth day of the month the pilgrims leave the city for Mina, a small town six miles to the east. Then before sunrise of the next day all make for the plain below Mount 'Arafat some twelve miles east of Mecca where they pass the day in prayers and recitation until sunset. This point is the climax of the pilgrimage when the whole gathering returns, first to Muzdalifah where it spends the night, then to Mina where pilgrims stone the devil represented by three heaps of stones (*jamrah*). The devil is said to have appeared to Abraham here and to have been driven away by Abraham throwing stones at him. This day, the 10th of Dhu'l-Hijjah, is 'Id al-Adha, the Feast of the Sacrifices, and the pilgrims sacrifice an animal, usually a sheep, and have their heads shaved by one of the barbers at Mina. They return to Mecca that evening. For some years past the enormous and ever-increasing numbers of pilgrims arriving by air especially has presented the Sa'udi authorities, guardians of the Holy Places, with major problems of organization, supply and health.

The Holy War (*Jihad*) against the infidel was the means whereby Arab Muslim rule made its immense expansion in the first centuries of Islam, but despite pressures to do so, it has never been elevated to form a sixth Pillar of Islam. Today many theologians interpret *jihad* in a less literal sense as the combating of evil.

The Koran (*Qur'an*, "recital", "reading") is for Muslims the very Word of God. The Koran consists of 114 chapters (*surah*) of uneven length, the longest coming first after the brief opening chapter called *al-Fatihah*. (The Koran is about as long as the New Testament). *Al-Fatihah* (The Opener) commences with the words, "*Bismillahi 'l-Rahmani 'l-Rahim*, In the name of God, the Compassionate, the Merciful", and forms part of the ritual five prayers (*salat*). Other special verses and chapters are also used on a variety of occasions, and of course Muslim children are taught to recite by heart a portion of the Koran or, preferably, the whole of it. The Koran has been the subject of vast written commentaries, but translation into other languages is not much approved by Muslims, though inter-linear translations (a line of Koran underneath which is a line of translation) are used, and a number of modern translations into English exist. The earlier (Meccan) chapters of the Koran speak of the unity of God and his wonders, of the Day of Judgement and Paradise, while the Medinan chapters tend to be occupied more with social legislation for marriage, divorce, personal and communal behaviour. The definitive redaction of the Koran was ordered by the Caliph 'Uthman (644–56).

HOLY PLACES

Mecca: Hijaz province of Sa'udi Arabia. Mecca is centred around the Ka'bah, the most venerated building in Islam, traditionally held to have been founded by Abraham, recognized by Islam also as a Prophet. It stands in the centre of the vast courtyard of the Great Mosque and has the form of a cube; its construction is of local grey stone and its walls are draped with a black curtain embroidered with a strip of writing containing Koran verses. In the eastern corner is set the famous Black Stone. The enlarging of the Great Mosque commenced under the second Caliph 'Umar. Both the Ka'bah and Great Mosque have undergone many renovations, notably recently since 1952. Mecca is the centre of the annual pilgrimage from all Muslim countries.

Al-Medina (*The City*, i.e. of the Prophet): Hijaz province of Sa'udi Arabia. Medina, formerly called Yathrib, was created a sacred enclave (*haram*) by Muhammad who died there in the year 11 of the *hijrah* and was buried in the Mosque of the Prophet. Close to his tomb are those of Abu Bakr and 'Umar and a little further away that of his daughter Fatimah. Frequently damaged, restored and enlarged, the mosque building was extensively renovated by the Sa'udi Government in 1955.

Jerusalem (Arabic *al-Quds* or *Bait al-Maqdis*, *The Hallowed/Consecrated*): Jordan (currently annexed by Israel). Jerusalem is Islam's next most holy city after al-Haraman (Mecca and Medina), not only because it is associated with so many pre-Islamic prophets, but because Muhammad himself is popularly held to have made the "Night Journey" there. Jerusalem contains the magnificent Islamic shrine, the Dome of the Rock (688–91), built by the Caliph 'Abd al-Malik, and the famous al-Masjid al-Aqsa a few years ago severely damaged by arson.

Hebron (Habrun): Israel-occupied Jordan. The Mosque of Abraham, called al-Khalil, the "Friend of God" is built over the tomb of Abraham, the Cave of Machpelah; it also contains the tombs of Sarah, Isaac, Rebecca, Jacob, and Leah. The shrine is revered by Muslims and Jews, and is also important to Christians.

Qairawan: Tunisia. The city is regarded as a holy place for Muslims, seven pilgrimages to the Great Mosque of Sidi 'Uqbah b. Nafi' (an early Muslim general who founded Qairawan as a base for the Muslim invaders of North Africa) being considered equivalent of one pilgrimage to Mecca.

Muley Idris: Morocco. The shrine at the burial-place of the founder of the Idrisid dynasty in the year 687, at Walili.

* * *

Every Middle Eastern country has a multitude of shrines and saints' tombs held in veneration, except Wahhabi states which consider saint cults to be polytheism (*shirk*). In Turkey, however, the policy of secularization led to Aya Sofya Mosque (St. Sophia) being turned into a museum.

The following shrines are associated with the Shi'ah or Legitimist sects of Islam.

Mashhad (Meshed): Iran. The city is famous for the shrine of Imam 'Ali al-Rida/Riza, the eighth Imam of the Ithna'ashari group, which attracts some hundred thousand pilgrims each year. The shrine is surrounded by buildings with religious or historical associations.

Qom: Iran. A Shi'ah centre, it is venerated as having the tomb of Fatimah the sister of Imam al-Rida/Riza and hundreds of saints and kings including Imams 'Ali b. Ja'far and Ibrahim, Shah Safi and Shah 'Abbas II. Since the Iranian revolution it has become the centre favoured by Ayatollah Khomeini.

Najaf: Iraq. Mashhad 'Ali, reputed to be constructed over the place where 'Ali b. Abi Talib, the cousin and son-in-law of Muhammad is buried, is a most venerated Shi'ah shrine drawing many pilgrims.

Karbala': Iraq. The shrine of Husain b. 'Ali where, at Mashhad Husain, he was slain with most of his family, is today more venerated by the Shi'ah than the Mashhad 'Ali. 'Ashura Day (10th Muharram) when Husain was killed is commemorated by passion plays (*ta'ziyah*) and religious processions when the drama of his death is re-enacted with extravagant expressions of emotion.

Baghdad: Iraq. The Kazimain/Kadhimain Mosque is a celebrated Shi'ah shrine containing the tomb of Musa al-Kazim/Kadhim, the 7th Imam of the Ithna'asharis.

RELIGIOUS GROUPINGS

Sunnis

The great majority, probably over 80 per cent of Muslims, is Sunni, followers of the *Sunnah*, i.e. the way, course, rule or manner of conduct of the Prophet Muhammad; they are generally called "Orthodox". The Sunnis recognize the first four Caliphs (Abu Bakr, 'Umar, 'Uthman, 'Ali) as Rashidun, i.e. following the right course. They base their *Sunnah* upon the Koran and "Six Books" of Traditions, and are organized in four Orthodox schools or rites (*madhhab*), all of equal standing within the Orthodox fold. Many Muslims today prefer to avoid identification with any single school.

Wahhabis

The adherents of "Wahhabism" strongly disapprove of this title by which they are known outside their own group, for they call themselves Muwahhidun or Unitarians. In fact they belong to the strict Hanbali school following its noted exponent, the 13th/14th century Syrian reformer Ibn Taimiyah. The founder of "Wahhabism", Muhammad b. 'Abd al-Wahhab of Arabian Najd (1703–87), sought to return to the pristine purity of early Islam freed from all accretions and what he regarded as innovations contrary to its true spirit, such as saint worship, lax sexual practices, and superstition. His doctrine was accepted by the chief Muhammad b. Sa'ud of Dar'iyah (near al-Riyadh). Ibn Sa'ud and his son 'Abd al-'Aziz—who proved a capable general—conquered much of Arabia. Medina fell in 1804 and Mecca in 1806 to Sa'ud son of 'Abd al-'Aziz, but after his death in 1814 the Wahhabis were gradually broken by the armies of the Pasha of Egypt, Muhammad 'Ali acting nominally on behalf of the Ottoman Sultan of Turkey. After varying fortunes in the 19th century the Wahhabis emerged as an Arabian power in the opening years of the 20th century. By the close of 1925 they held the Holy Cities and Jeddah and are today the strongest power in the Arabian Peninsula. Though Wahhabism remains the strictest of the Orthodox groups, Sa'udi Arabia has made some accommodation to modern times.

The Tariqahs or Religious Orders

In many Middle Eastern countries the Religious Orders (*Tariqahs*) have important political cum religious roles in society. There are the widely spread Qadiriyah who with the Tijaniyah are found in North Africa, the Khatmiyah in the Sudan, the Rifa'iyah in Egypt and Syria to pick out a few at random. The West has no organizations exactly equivalent to these Sufi orders into which an individual has to be initiated, and in which, by dint of ascetic exercises and study he may attain degrees of mystical enlightenment—this can also bring moral influence over his fellow men. The Orders may be Sunni or Shi'ah; some few Orders are even so unconventional as to be hardly Islamic at all. It was the Orthodox reformist Sanusi Order that has played the most significant role in our time. The Grand Sanusi, Muhammad b. 'Ali, born at Mustaghanem in Algeria

of a Sharif family, founded the first *zawiyah* or lodge of the Sanusis in 1837. The Sanusi *Tariqah* is distinguished for its exacting standards of personal morality. The Sanusis set up a network of lodges in Cyrenaica (Libya) and put up strong resistance to Italian colonization. The Grand Sanusi was recognized as King Idris of Libya in 1951, but lost his throne at the military revolt led by Colonel Gaddafi in 1969.

Shi'ah

The Legitimist Shi'ah pay allegiance to 'Ali as mentioned above. 'Ali's posterity which must number at least hundreds of thousands, scattered all over the Muslim world, are customarily called Sharifs if they trace descent to his son al-Hasan, and Saiyids if descended from al-Husain, but while the Sharifs and Saiyids, the religious aristocracy of Islam, traditionally are accorded certain privileges in Islamic society, not all are Shi'ah, many being Sunnis. By the 9th century many strange sects and even pagan beliefs had become associated with the original Shi'ah or Party of 'Ali, but these extremist sects called *ghulat* have mostly vanished except a few, often practising a sort of quietism or dissimulation (*taqiyah*) for fear of persecution. All Shi'ah accord 'Ali an exalted position, the extreme (and heretical) Shi'ah at one time even according him a sort of divinity. Shi'ite Islam does not in the main differ on fundamental issues from the Sunni Orthodox since they draw from the same ultimate sources, but Shi'ah *mujtahids* have, certainly in theory, greater freedom to alter the application of law since they are regarded as spokesmen of the Hidden Imam.

The Ithna'asharis (Twelvers)

The largest Shi'ah school or rite is the Ithna'ashariyah or Twelvers, acknowledging twelve Imams. From 1502 Shi'ism became the established school in Iran under the Safavid ruler Sultan Shah Isma'il who claimed descent from Musa al-Kazim (see below). There are also Ithna'ashariyah in southern Iraq, al-Hasa, Bahrain and the Indian sub-continent.

The last Shi'ah Imam, Muhammad al-Mahdi, disappeared in 878, but the Ithna'asharis believe he is still alive and will re-appear in the last days before the Day of Judgement as the Mahdi (Guided One)—a sort of Messiah—who will rule personally by divine right.

The twelve Imams recognized by the Twelver, Ithna'ashari Shi'ah are:

(1) 'Ali b. Abi Talib, cousin and son-in-law of the Prophet Muhammad.

(2) Al-Hasan, son of 'Ali.

(3) Al-Husain, second son of 'Ali.

(4) 'Ali Zain al-'Abidin, son of Husain.

(5) Muhammad al-Baqir, son of 'Ali Zain al-'Abidin.

(6) Ja'far al-Sadiq, son of Muhammad al-Baqir.

(7) Musa al-Kazim, son of Ja'far al-Sadiq.

(8) 'Ali al-Rida, son of Musa al-Kazim.

(9) Muhammad al-Taqi, son of 'Ali al-Rida.

(10) 'Ali al-Naqi, son of Muhammad al-Taqi.

(11) Al-Hasan al-Zaki, son of 'Ali al-Naqi, al-'Askari.

(12) Muhammad al-Mahdi, son of al-Hasan b. 'Ali, al-'Askari, known as al-Hujjah, the Proof.

Isma'ilis

This group of the Shi'ah does not recognize Musa al-Kazim as seventh Imam, but holds that the last Imam visible on earth was Isma'il, the other son of Ja'far al-Sadiq. For this reason they are also called the Sab'iyah or Seveners. There is however much disagreement among the Seveners as to whether they recognized Isma'il himself as seventh Imam, or one of his several sons, and the Fatimids of Egypt (10th–12th centuries) in fact recognized a son of Isma'il's son Muhammad. Schismatic off-shoots from the Fatimid-Isma'ili group are the Druzes, the Musta'lians first settled in the Yemen but now with their main centre in Bombay—where the Daudi section is known as Bohoras, but who are properly called the Fatimi Taiyibi Da'wah, and the Nizari Isma'ilis of whom the Aga Khan is the spiritual head. These sects have a secret literature embodying their esoteric philosophies. Small groups of Isma'ilis are to be found in north-west Syria, Iran, Afghanistan, East Africa and Zanzibar, and larger numbers in India and Pakistan.

'Alawis (Nusairis)

The 'Alawis believe Muhammad was a mere forerunner of 'Ali and that the latter was an incarnation of Allah. This Shi'i extremist sect established in the ninth century has also adopted practices of both Christian and pagan origin. Most of its members today live in north-west Syria.

Druze

The Druze are heretics, an off-shoot of the Fatimid Isma'ilis (see above), established in Lebanon and Syria. Their name (Duruz) derives from al-Darazi, a missionary of Persian origin who brought about the conversion of these Syrian mountaineers to the belief of the divine origin of the Fatimid Caliph al-Hakim. The origins of this sect and its subsequent expansion are still obscure. Hamzah b. 'Ali, a Persian contemporary of al-Darazi is the author of several of the religious treatises of the Druze. This community acknowledges one God and believes that he has on many occasions become incarnate in man. His last appearance was in the person of the Fatimid Caliph al-Hakim (disappeared 1020). The Druze have played a distinctive role in the political and social life of their country and are renowned for their independence of character.

Zaidis

The Zaidis are a liberal and moderate sect of the Shi'ah close enough to the Sunnis to call themselves the "Fifth School" (*al-madhhab al-khamis*). Their name is derived from a grandson of al-Husain b. 'Ali called Zaid b. 'Ali whom they recognize as fifth Imam. They reject religious dissimulation (*taqiyah*) and are extremely warlike. Zaidism is the dominant school of Islam in the Yemen Arab Republic, but Shafi'is form roughly half the population.

Ibadis

The Ibadis are commonly held to have their origins in the Khawarij who disassociated themselves from 'Ali b. Abi Talib when he accepted arbitration in his quarrel with Mu'awiyah, but this is open to question. They broke off early from the main stream of Islam and are usually regarded as heretics though with little justification. Groups of the sect, which has often suffered persecution, are found in Oman where Ibadism is the state religion, Zanzibar, Libya and Algeria, mainly in the Mzab.

THE ISLAMIC REVIVAL

In a number of Muslim countries revivalist or reactionary Islamic movements are taking place. Islam makes no essential distinction between religion and politics so this affects not only the whole Muslim community but also those of other faiths residing in an Islamic state. In one sense it may be said that there is a common basis to the revival in all the Islamic states in that people believe that a reversion to an idealized Islamic community, or the substitution of the principles embodied in *shari'ah* law for the practice of a secular state, will resolve current problems and tensions. Each country however seems to differ as to against what it expects the Islamic revival to react.

Sa'udi Arabia, the heartland of Islam, has always maintained a strict formal adherence to traditional Islam. The late King Faisal, though tactfully curbing the extreme trends of Sa'udi Arabia's Mutawwa' "clergy", initiated and financed a policy of promoting Islam to counter President Nasser's alignment with socialist propaganda to subvert monarchic regimes elsewhere. King Faisal's initiative took the form of subsidising the building of mosques in Muslim countries, the publication of Islamic books and religious tracts, and the founding or support of such institutions as the Islamic Council of Europe. Links were made with groups like the Muslim Brothers, the well-established inter-state Islamic society which Nasser tried to crush, and which has become the bitter enemy of the present Syrian government.

In general the concept of a "permissive society" as promoted by certain Western elements, is rejected with distaste by all Muslim countries. Sa'udi Arabia's financial and moral strength has enabled it to take practical steps to pressure other Islamic states to conform, sometimes if they fear only to be out of line, to such Islamic prescriptions as the prohibition of liquor. On the other hand banks and insurance companies which depend on taking interest on loans, seem to be regarded as earning profit (*ribh*) which is lawful to a Muslim, not taking usury (*riba*) which is unlawful. Since the recent wide revivalist trend that has reasserted itself in Islamic countries, the ethics of banking have troubled the conscience of certain

Muslim states and an experiment is being made with an Islamic Bank which, formally at least, avoids interest. President Gaddafi has also been making highly original experiments in the monetary field which he would regard as Islamic. To the West certain Islamic laws are repugnant, such as amputation of a hand for persistent theft, but the benefit in Sa'udi Arabia in compelling a high standard of honesty is undeniable—the penalty is probably not frequently inflicted. Stoning for adultery can rarely be imposed for in Islamic law it is, theoretically at least, next to impossible to prove—nevertheless it does seem occasionally to take place.

In Iran the motivation of Islamic reaction as symbolized in the Ayatollah (a high religious office), Khomeini, is in part that of the conservative, even chauvinistic, provinces against a secular monarch who introduced foreigners bringing with them Western manners distasteful to Islamic society. This has found expression in the destruction of bars, cinemas, etc., and the attempt, by imposing the veil, to reverse the tide of female emancipation. Persecution of the inoffensive Baha'is puts the clock back to the late 19th century. To what extent the economic, as contrasted with the religious, factor, the concentration of great wealth in the hands of a very few families, motivated the revolution is as yet undetermined.

In Iran the Khomeini Government aims at returning to the ideal "Islamic" state as conceived of by the Shi'ah mullahs, but the actions and practice of the new State have often been of an extremity rejected by Muslims and non-Muslims alike. Yet if on the one hand some Muslim countries criticize the Khomeini regime for actions difficult to reconcile with the spirit of Islam, on the other there has been a widespread sentiment of sympathy among ordinary Muslims for the "Islamic" Government of Iran in its opposition to the Goliath U.S.A., supporter of Israel, etc. Within Iran itself, obscure as the internal situation is, the split between the reactionary type of Muslim and the liberal, often western-educated, is more open, but issues are not clear-cut and some fervent Muslims seem also to hold extreme left-wing views.

As the very existence of Pakistan lies in the conception of a "pure" Islamic community opposed to heathen Hindustan, this, coupled with its ever growing internal troubles, has encouraged the retreat into a more rigid Islamic state. There seem, however, signs that Pakistan and India may arrive at a greater degree of accommodation than heretofore. A very large minority of Muslims lives in India.

The Turkey of Mustafa Kemal Ataturk aimed at a complete separation of religion and state—in this secular state women were accorded equal rights with men. It is now clear that secularization did not penetrate deeply into the urban and particularly the rural population. Resentment of financial hardships after the Second World War against the Government was fanned by religious leaders, and ever-increasing religious freedom has had to be conceded within the secular state. Many women have, illegally, resumed the veil. The upper classes tend to favour a secular state,

but religious feeling combined with chauvinism are behind the popular revival of Islam.

In no way is the interdependence of religion and politics in Islam better illustrated than in the condemnation of Egypt by forty Islamic states, over the Jerusalem question, a city sacred to Muslims from which the Prophet made his celebrated Night Ascent to Heaven. Intensity of feeling over the Palestine issue varies in degree from one Islamic country to another and is often far over-shadowed by local issues, but it remains everywhere an obstacle to East-West understanding. Though the Israeli Premier's intransigence over the West Bank and his resolve to incorporate the Syrian Golan Heights remain an issue causing acute tensions throughout the Middle East, the return of Sinai to Egypt has rendered the latter's position some shades less unfavourable than formerly with certain Arab States, and probably the Islamic world at large.

Arabs and Iranians frequently complain of the "bad press" and distortion of their religion and politics in the West through ignorance or deliberate bias. A flagrant example was the film "Death of a Princess" (shown on British TV in April 1980) which, apart from being wildly untrue to fact, has highly offensive aspersions on the morals of society in the country which was the cradle of Islam.

A Muslim writer recently distinguished between "westernization" and "modernization", describing the latter as broadly acceptable, except to a reactionary minority. If the distinction between the two is a little blurred, the idea has some validity. In general, however, the Islamic revival among ordinary Muslims is bound up with factors, simple conservatism apart, varying from country to country and class to class, and it may oppose either governments run on a secular basis, or those claiming to be "Islamic".

Christianity

DEVELOPMENT IN THE MIDDLE EAST

Christianity was adopted as the official religion of the Roman empire in A.D. 313, and the Christian Church came to be based on the four leading cities, Rome, Constantinople (capital from A.D. 330), Alexandria and Antioch. From the divergent development of the four ecclesiastical provinces there soon emerged four separate churches: the Roman Catholic or Latin Church (from Rome), the Greek Orthodox Church (from Constantinople), the Syrian or Jacobite Church (from Antioch) and the Coptic Church (from Alexandria).

Later divisions resulted in the emergence of the Armenian (Gregorian) Church, which was founded in the fourth century, and the Nestorian Church, which grew up in the fifth century in Syria, Mesopotamia and Iran, following the teaching of Nestorius of Cilicia (d. 431). From the seventh century on followers of St. Maron began to establish themselves in northern Lebanon, laying the foundations of the Maronite Church.

Subsequently the Uniate Churches were brought into existence by the renunciation by formerly independent churches of doctrines regarded as heretical by the Roman Church and by the acknowledgement of Papal supremacy. These churches—the Armenian Catholic, the Chaldean (Nestorian) Catholic, Greek Catholic, the Coptic Catholic, the Syrian Catholic and the Maronite Church did, however, retain their Oriental customs and rites. The independent churches continued in existence alongside the Uniate Churches with the exception of the Maronites, all of whom reverted to Rome.

HOLY PLACES

Bethlehem: Israeli-occupied Jordan. The traditional birthplace of Jesus is enclosed in the Basilica of the Nativity, revered also by Muslims. Christmas is celebrated here by the Roman and Eastern Rite Churches on December 25th, by the Greek Orthodox, Coptic and Syrian Orthodox Churches on January 6th and 7th, by the Ethiopian Church on January 8th, and by the Armenian Church on January 19th. The tomb of Rachel, important to the three faiths, is just outside the town.

Jerusalem: Jordan (but annexed by Israel). The most holy city of Christianity has been a centre for pilgrims since the Middle Ages. It is the seat of the patriarchates of the Roman, Greek Orthodox and Armenian Churches, who share the custodianship of the Church of the Holy Sepulchre and who each own land and buildings in the neighbouring area.

The Church of the Holy Sepulchre stands on the hill of Golgotha in the higher north-western part of the Old City. In the central chamber of the church is the Byzantine Rotunda built by twelfth century crusaders, which shelters the small shrine on the traditional site of the tomb. Here the different patriarchates exercise their rights in turn. Close by is the Rock of Calvary, revered as the site of the Crucifixion.

Most pilgrims devoutly follow the Way of the Cross leading from the Roman Praetorium through several streets of the Old City to the Holy Sepulchre. Franciscan monks, commemorating the journey to the Crucifixion, follow the course of this traditional route each Friday; on Good Friday this procession marks a climax of the Easter celebrations of the Roman Church.

Outside the Old City stands the Mount of Olives, the scene of Jesus' Ascension. At the foot of its hill is the Garden of Gethsemane which is associated with the vigil on the eve of the Crucifixion. The Cenaculum or traditional room of the Last Supper is situated on Mount Zion in Israel.

Nazareth: Israel. This town, closely associated with the childhood of Jesus, has been a Christian centre since the fourth century A.D. The huge, domed Church of the Annunciation has recently been built on the site of numerous earlier churches to protect the underground Grotto of the Annunciation. Nearby the Church of St. Joseph marks the traditional site of Joseph's workshop.

Galilee: Israel. Many places by this lake are associated with the life of Jesus: Cana, scene of the miracle of water and wine, which is celebrated by an annual pilgrimage on the second Sunday after Epiphany; the Mount of Beatitudes; Tabgha, scene of the multiplication of the loaves and fish; and Capurneum, scene of the healing of the Centurion's servant.

Mount Tabor: Israel. The traditional site of the Transfiguration, which has drawn pilgrims since the fourth century, is commemorated by a Franciscan Monastery and a Greek Basilica, where the annual Festival of the Transfiguration is held.

Jericho: Israeli-occupied Jordan. The scene of the baptism of Jesus; nearby is the Greek Monastery of St. John the Baptist.

Nablus (*Samaria*): Israeli-occupied Jordan. This old town contains Jacob's Well, associated with Jesus, and the Tomb of Joseph.

Qubaibah (*Emmaus*): Israeli-occupied Jordan. It was near this town that two of the Disciples encountered Jesus after the Resurrection.

'Azariyyah (*Bethany*): Israeli-occupied Jordan. A town frequented by Jesus, the home of Mary and Martha, and the scene of the Raising of Lazarus.

Mount Carmel: Haifa, Israel. The Cave of Elijah draws many pilgrims, including Muslims and Druzes, who celebrate the Feast of Mar Elias on July 20th.

Ein Kerem: Israel. Traditional birthplace of John the Baptist, to whom a Franciscan church is dedicated; nearby is the Church of the Visitation.

Ephesus: Turkey. The city, formerly a great centre of pagan worship, where Paul founded the first of the seven Asian Churches. The recently restored Basilica, built by Justinian, is dedicated to John the Evangelist, who legend claims died here; a fourth century church on Aladag Mountain commemorating Mary's last years spent here now draws an annual pilgrimage in August.

Judaism

There are two main Jewish communities, the Ashkenazim and the Sephardim, the former from east, central and northern Europe, the latter from Spain, the Balkans, the Middle East and North Africa. The majority of immigrants into Israel were from the Ashkenazim, and their influence predominates there, though the Hebrew language follows Sephardim usage. There is no doctrinal difference between the two communities, but they observe distinct rituals.

HOLY PLACES

Wailing Wall: Jerusalem. This last remnant of the western part of the wall surrounding the courtyard of Herod's Temple, finally destroyed by the Romans in A.D. 70, is visited by devout Jews, particularly on the Fast Day of the 9th of Av, to grieve at the destruction of the First and Second Temples which had once stood on the same site.

Mount Zion: Israel. A hill south-west of the Old City of Jerusalem, venerated particularly for the tomb of David, acknowledged by Muslims as abi Dawud (The Jebuzite hill on which David founded his Holy City is now known as Mount Ophel, and is in Jordan, just to the east of the modern Mount Zion). Not far from the foot of the hill are the rock-cut tombs of the family of King Herod.

Cave of Machpelah: Hebron, Israeli-occupied Jordan. The grotto, over which was built a mosque, contains the tombs of Abraham and Sarah, Isaac and Rebecca, Jacob and Leah.

Bethlehem: Israeli-occupied Jordan. The traditional tomb of Rachel is in a small shrine outside the town, venerated also by Muslims and Christians.

Mount Carmel: Israel. The mountain is associated with Elijah, whose Cave in Haifa draws many pilgrims. (*See* Christianity section).

Safad: Israel. Centre of the medieval Cabbalist movement, this city contains several synagogues from the sixteenth century associated with these scholars, and many important tombs, notably that of Rabbi Isaac Louria.

Meiron: Israel. The town contains the tombs of Shimon bar Yohai, reputed founder in the second century of the medieval Cabbalist movement, and his son Eleazer. A yearly Hassidic pilgrimage is held to the tomb to celebrate Lag Ba'Omer with a night of traditional singing and dancing in which Muslims also participate.

Tiberias: Israel. An ancient city containing the tombs of Moses Maimonides and Rabbi Meir Baal Harness. Famous as an historical centre of Cabbalist scholarship, it is with Jerusalem, Safad and Hebron, one of the four sacred cities of Judaism, and once accommodated a university and the Sanhedrin.

Other Communities

ZOROASTRIANS

Zoroastrianism developed from the teaching of Zoroaster, or Zarathustra, who lived in Iran some time between 700 and 550 B.C. Later adopted as the official religion of the Persian empire, Zoroastrianism remained predominant in Iran until the rise of Islam.

Many adherents were forced by persecution to emigrate, and the main centre of the faith is now Bombay, where they are known as Parsees. Technically a monotheistic faith, Zoroastrianism retained some elements of polytheism. It later became associated with fire-worship.

Yazd: Iran. This city was the ancient centre of the Zoroastrian religion, and was later used as a retreat during the Arab conquest. It contains five fire temples and still remains a centre for this faith, of which some 35,000 adherents live in Iran.

BAHA'IS

Baha'ism made its appearance in Persia during the middle of the nineteenth century. It was founded by Baha'ullah, who, after a revelation in Baghdad in 1863, declared himself to be the "Promised One". A member of the Persian nobility, he devoted his life to preaching against the corruption endemic in Persian society and as a result spent many years in exile; he died at Acre in Palestine in 1892. The Sect was administered by his descendants until 1957; the 56 national branches now elect the present governing body, the Universal House of Justice.

Baha'ism claims complete independence from all other faiths. Its followers believe that the basic principles of the great religions of the world are in complete harmony and that their aims and functions are complementary. Other tenets include belief in the brotherhood of man, the abolition of racial and colour discrimination, the equality of the sexes, progress towards world government and the use of an international language, monogamy, chastity and the encouragement of family life. There is no Baha'i priesthood, and asceticism and monasticism are discouraged. Most of the Middle Eastern adherents of the faith live in Iran or Israel. The Bahai's in Iran claim that conditions have become very difficult for them since the Iranian Revolution.

Haifa: Israel. Shrine of the Bab and gardens, world centre of the Baha'i faith. Pilgrims visit this centre, and one in Acre where Baha'ullah was imprisoned, on the anniversaries of the birth and death of the Bab and Baha'ullah.

SAMARITANS

Mount Gerazim: Jordan. The mountain is sacred to this small sect, who celebrate Passover here. The Samaritan High Priest lives at Nablus.

The Arab-Israeli Confrontation 1967-82

Michael Adams

(Revised for this and the previous edition by DAVID GILMOUR)

Israel's decisive victory over the Arab states in the Six Day war of 1967 raised hopes that at last it would be possible to reach a definitive settlement of the Arab-Israeli conflict. Instead it soon became apparent that the conflict had merely been complicated by the occupation of further Arab territory, the displacement of still more refugees and the aggravation of the sense of grievance felt by the Palestinians and now shared more widely than ever in the rest of the Arab world.

The course of events after June 1967

As soon as a ceasefire had brought an end to the fighting in June 1967 a series of international consultations began with the aim of bringing to a final conclusion the nineteen year old conflict between Israel and her Arab neighbours.

Once the ceasefire was in operation, the Security Council's next step was to pass a resolution (No. 237, of June 14th, 1967), calling on Israel to facilitate the return of the new refugees who had fled (and were still fleeing) from the areas occupied by Israel during the war. The resolution also called on Israel to ensure the safety, welfare and security of the inhabitants of the "Occupied Areas".

An emergency meeting of the UN General Assembly reiterated on July 4th the Security Council's call for the return of the refugees and on the same day it declared "invalid" the Israeli decision to annex the Arab sector of Jerusalem; but the Assembly failed to produce an agreed resolution on the basis for a settlement. A plan put forward later in the month by President Tito of Yugoslavia, calling for an Israeli withdrawal to the pre-war frontiers and a guarantee of those frontiers by the international community, was rejected by Israel on the ground that to recreate the pre-war situation would endanger that country's security.

The deadlock became total when an Arab summit conference, held in Khartoum between August 29th and September 3rd, 1967, confirmed earlier decisions not to negotiate directly with Israel, not to accord her recognition and not to sign a peace treaty. The Israeli Government, for its part, announced its refusal to undertake any but direct negotiations; if no such negotiations developed, Israeli forces would maintain their occupation of the Arab territories conquered during the war.

RESOLUTION 242

It was against this background that the UN Security Council met in the autumn of 1967 to consider the situation. A number of draft resolutions were submitted but failed to gain approval, either because (in the eyes of the supporters of the Arabs) they condoned the acquisition or occupation of territory by military force, or because (in the eyes of the supporters of Israel) they contained no adequate guarantee for Israel's security.

Finally, on November 22nd, 1967, the Security Council unanimously adopted a resolution which was to remain the basis of all subsequent peace initiatives during the next five years.

This, the famous Resolution 242 of November 1967, (see Documents on Palestine, p. 76) precariously bridged the gap between the Arab and Israeli positions, which were also the positions adopted by their superpower supporters, the Soviet Union and the United States. By emphasizing the inadmissibility of the acquisition of territory by war, the resolution satisfied the demand of the Arabs and the Russians for an Israeli withdrawal. By being less than categorical about the extent of that withdrawal, it became acceptable to the Israelis and the Americans. All the subsequent arguments which developed centred around the question of whether the Israelis, in return for a definitive peace treaty, would have the right to retain parts of the Arab territories occupied during the war.

PALESTINIAN RESISTANCE

Even before these arguments developed, and during the interval of nearly six months which elapsed between the ceasefire and the adoption of the Security Council's resolution, events on the ground had hardened the positions of both sides. In the immediate aftermath of the fighting, despite the Israeli Prime Minister's declaration on the eve of the war that Israel had no intention of annexing "even one foot of Arab territory", the Israeli Knesset had legislated the "reunification" of Jerusalem,* which amounted in fact to the annexation of the Arab sector of the city. The Israelis had also destroyed a number of Arab villages, notably the three villages of Imwas, Beit Nuba and Yalu in the Latrun area, and had expelled their inhabitants. These actions, which appeared to confirm Arab accusations of Israeli expansionism, greatly encouraged the rise of a Palestinian resistance movement, already stimulated by the failure of the Arab governments and the humiliation which that failure had brought on the Arab world. When the Israelis began, as early as September 1967, to establish Jewish settlements in the occupied territories,† at a time when the stream of Arab refugees set in motion by the June war was still flowing eastward at the rate of several hundred a day, support for the resistance movement became

---

* For a discussion of the Jerusalem issue, see p. 63.

† Between June 1967 and June 1981 more than 130 of these settlements had been established by the Israelis in the occupied areas of the West Bank of Jordan, the Gaza Strip, the Golan Heights in south-west Syria, and Sinai.

widespread in the Arab world. It was strengthened when the Israelis, after agreeing in response to United Nations resolutions to allow the return of these new refugees, arbitrarily closed the border again after only 14,000 had been allowed to re-enter Palestine, out of 150,000 who had filed applications with the Red Cross to do so.

The situation, then, was deteriorating even before Dr. Gunnar Jarring, whom the Secretary-General had appointed as his Special Representative in accordance with Resolution 242, went to the Middle East to undertake his mission at the end of 1967. During the first half of 1968 there were increasingly frequent breaches of the ceasefire along the Suez Canal (which remained blocked to traffic), while Palestinian guerrilla raids led to heavy Israeli reprisal actions in the Jordan valley. After the first anniversary of the June war, and while Dr. Jarring was patiently pursuing his contacts with both sides, the trend towards violence accelerated. In July 1968 guerrillas of the Popular Front for the Liberation of Palestine carried out the first hijack operation in the Middle East, diverting an Israeli airliner to Algiers. President Nasser in the same month warned that another explosion in the area was inevitable if a stalemate which left Israel in occupation of territory belonging to three of its neighbours was allowed to continue indefinitely. In the course of artillery duels across the Canal the towns of Suez and Ismailia were virtually destroyed by the Israelis and their populations had to be evacuated into the interior of Egypt.

PHANTOMS FOR ISRAEL

The governments of Egypt and Jordan had accepted Resolution 242, while Syria rejected it. Israel, while not rejecting the resolution, said it could not be a substitute for specific agreements between the parties. When the UN General Assembly met in the autumn of 1968, Israel put forward a nine-point plan for a Middle East settlement which made no mention of withdrawal, speaking instead of "a boundary settlement compatible with the security of Israel and the honour of the Arab states". This produced no response from the Arab governments, which were shocked when President Johnson at the height of the American election campaign, announced that the United States was considering the sale of Phantom aircraft to Israel. A month later Richard Nixon was elected as President Johnson's successor and sent Governor William Scranton on a fact-finding mission to the Middle East. Mr. Scranton was reported as saying that the United States should adopt "a more even-handed policy in the Middle East", but the sale of fifty Phantoms to Israel was confirmed at the end of December and marked an important stage in the escalation of the arms race in the Middle East.

The day after the sale of Phantoms was announced, Israeli parachutists raided Beirut airport, in reprisal for an Arab guerrilla attack on an Israeli airliner in Athens, and destroyed thirteen aircraft. This incident, which for the first time directly involved the Lebanon in the Arab-Israeli confrontation, brought about renewed diplomatic activity to arrest the worsening

situation. After the Security Council had unanimously condemned Israel for the Beirut raid, the Soviet Government took up an earlier French proposal that there should be Four-Power talks between the Soviet Union, the United States, Britain and France to obtain agreement between the major powers over the implementation of Resolution 242.

FOUR-POWER TALKS

Dr. Jarring withdrew from the scene while the "Big Four" tried to reconcile the conflicting interpretations of the Security Council resolution. At first the prospects seemed encouraging, with President Nixon eager to register an initial success in the field of foreign affairs and with general agreement that the drift to war in the Middle East threatened the peace of the world. At the beginning of February 1969, President Nasser declared his willingness to enter into direct negotiations once Israeli forces had withdrawn from Arab territory. Mr. Eshkol, the Prime Minister of Israel, stated his readiness to meet President Nasser and declared that Israel was prepared to be flexible about all the occupied territories except Jerusalem and the Golan Heights (captured from Syria in 1967). But as the year wore on, spasmodic fighting continued along both the Suez Canal and the Jordan fronts, until in July 1969 President Nasser publicly gave up hope of a peaceful settlement, forecasting that a long "war of attrition" would be necessary to dislodge Israel from the occupied territories. A month later a severe fire at Al Aqsa mosque in the Old City of Jerusalem, for which an Australian immigrant to Israel was later blamed, caused a further dangerous increase in tension.

THE ROGERS PLAN

The Four-Power talks were suspended while Soviet and American representatives engaged in bilateral contacts. There was a moment of optimism when it appeared likely that a formula had been found for "Rhodes-style" negotiations (on the pattern of the talks conducted in Rhodes which led to the armistice agreements between Israel and the Arab states in 1949), but the optimism faded when an Israeli suggestion that this would amount to direct negotiations led the Arabs to reject the formula. Instead the American Secretary of State, Mr. William Rogers, produced on December 9th, 1969, a set of proposals which came to be known as the Rogers Plan. The proposals represented an attempt to steer a middle course between the Arab view, that the Security Council resolution should be implemented *in toto* and did not call for negotiation, and the Israeli preference for direct negotiations which would decide where the new borders should be drawn. The most important aspect of the plan was that it made clear the American view that there should only be minor rectifications of the pre-June 1967 boundaries. This ensured Israeli hostility to the plan, since despite the insistence of the Israeli Foreign Minister, Abba Eban, that "everything is negotiable", it had now become clear that his cabinet colleagues were deeply divided on this crucial question.

President Nasser, impatient with what he saw as the hypocritical attitude of the American Government, also rejected the plan, which in any case was presently swept aside by a serious renewal of hostilities in January 1970, when the Israelis initiated a series of deep penetration bombing raids (using the new American Phantom aircraft) on targets inside Egypt. General Dayan announced at the beginning of February that the Israeli bombing attacks had three aims: to force the Egyptians (who had been sustaining heavy casualties along the Canal front) to respect the ceasefire, to prevent Egyptian preparations for a new war and to weaken the Egyptian regime. In practice, the raids (which caused heavy civilian casualties) had three results: they strengthened Egyptian support for President Nasser; they damaged Israel's image in the outside world: and they drew the Russians into providing further assistance to Egypt.

International concern over these developments paved the way for a renewal of diplomatic efforts. In April 1970 the American Assistant Secretary of State, Joseph Sisco, visited the Middle East to explain the objectives of the Rogers Plan. Israeli requests for more Phantoms were not granted and it appeared that the immediate American objectives were to obtain a renewal of the ceasefire and to extract from the Israeli Government an undertaking to withdraw from the greater part of the occupied territories as part of an overall peace settlement. President Nasser, in a speech on May 1st said that "despite Phantoms and napalm" he was keeping the door open to the American initiative. The Israelis made no public commitment on withdrawal, but their response in private was sufficiently encouraging for Mr. Rogers to relaunch his proposals, with the backing of the four major powers. After a variety of bilateral contacts between the various parties, President Nasser announced in a speech on July 23rd, 1970, Egypt's acceptance of the American proposal for a renewal of the ceasefire, followed by negotiations through Dr. Jarring for the implementation of Resolution 242. A week later, the Israeli Government, after receiving assurances on the future supply of arms from the United States, also agreed to the American proposal, with the proviso that Israel would never return to the pre-war boundaries and that none of its troops would be withdrawn from the ceasefire lines until a binding peace agreement had been signed.

The renewed ceasefire along the Suez Canal front came into operation on the night of August 7th/8th, with a duration of ninety days, during which the two sides were to engage in indirect negotiations under the auspices of Dr. Jarring. Two fresh developments, however, frustrated the movement towards an overall settlement. After a single meeting with Dr. Jarring in New York, the Israeli representative was recalled to Jerusalem and the Israeli Government protested that the ceasefire had been violated by the movement of Soviet missiles behind the Egyptian lines. The confused American reaction suggested that there had been a genuine misunderstanding about the conditions agreed to, but the negotiations in New York had not been renewed when a serious crisis in Jordan distracted the attention of all the parties concerned.

KING HUSSEIN AND THE PALESTINE GUERRILLAS

On September 6th, 1970, Palestine guerrillas of the Popular Front for the Liberation of Palestine hijacked two airliners and flew them to a desert airfield in Jordan. A third airliner was taken to Cairo and destroyed on the airfield there. Three days later a fourth aircraft was hijacked and joined the two in the desert near Zerqa, where the guerrillas, after releasing a number of passengers, held some three hundred others as hostages, demanding in exchange for them the release of a substantial number of Palestinians held prisoner in Israel.

This episode, which marked the high point of guerrilla activity, proved also the last straw as far as the Government of Jordan was concerned. During the previous two years, as the strength of the guerrilla movement increased, the Jordan Government had faced a dilemma. If it allowed the guerrillas freedom of movement in Jordan, it invited retaliation from Israel—and the retaliation had been heavy, in the form of ground and air raids which had depopulated the East Bank of the Jordan river and caused severe casualties in Irbid, Salt and other towns and villages of east Jordan. If the Government tried to control or suppress the activities of the guerrillas, it faced the possibility of civil war in Jordan.

The relationship between the Government and the guerrillas was linked to the question of a political settlement with Israel. The Palestine resistance movement, whose declared objective was the reconstitution in Palestine of a democratic state open to Jews and Arabs alike, opposed the idea of a political settlement with Israel, since this would involve the recognition and the perpetuation of a Zionist state. King Hussein had followed the lead of President Nasser in accepting the Rogers Plan and was thus committed to the principle of a political settlement involving the recognition of Israel. So long as a political settlement was not in prospect, it had been possible for the King and the guerrillas to pursue their diverse objectives without coming into open conflict, but as soon as such a settlement became a serious possibility the uneasy coexistence between them was threatened. On several previous occasions in 1969 and 1970 the Jordan Government and the guerrillas had come close to a confrontation and after the renewal of the ceasefire in August 1970 and the acceptance by the Jordan Government of the Rogers Plan, a clash became inevitable.

The multiple hijack operation by the PFLP, which explicitly challenged the authority of the Jordan Government, provided the spark and on September 16th King Hussein appointed a military government in Jordan which next day set about the liquidation of the resistance movement. After ten days of heavy fighting in Amman, mediation efforts by other Arab governments, and in particular by President Nasser, brought about a truce, which was signed in Cairo on September 27th, 1970. On the following day President Nasser suffered a heart attack and died almost immediately.

As far as a settlement between Israel and the Arabs

was concerned, it looked as though the position so painstakingly established in August had been undermined. The ceasefire along the Suez Canal endured, though precariously; but the negotiations through Dr. Jarring were not renewed and until President Nasser's successor had had time to consolidate his position, it seemed unlikely that they would be. Jordan was faced with the task of overcoming the effects of an inconclusive civil war and only Israel, which had achieved its objective of a renewal of the ceasefire, had any reason to feel satisfied with the turn of events. Miraculously, all of the hostages held in Amman throughout the fighting were released unharmed (indeed, they praised their captors for the care they had taken to protect them), although the three airliners were blown up by the guerrillas.

PRESIDENT SADAT AND THE CEASEFIRE

There was both surprise and relief, therefore, when the new President of Egypt, Anwar Sadat, established himself without opposition and showed himself willing to take up the search for a settlement where it had been left by his predecessor. He agreed to renew the ceasefire for a further 90 days and, after intensive consultations between Israeli and American leaders and the extension to Israel of American credits worth $500 million, Israel agreed to return to the Jarring talks. Preliminary discussions took place in New York and in January 1971 Dr. Jarring visited Israel and Egypt, where both sides restated their positions to him on all the points at issue. When the ceasefire agreement was again coming to an end, on February 5th, 1971, President Sadat once more agreed to renew it, this time for 30 days, adding the proposal that Israel should begin to withdraw its forces from the east bank of the canal, in which case Egypt would be able to clear the canal for navigation.

On February 8th Dr. Jarring wrote to the Governments of Israel and Egypt, expressing his optimism about the desire of both parties for a settlement and inviting each of them to give firm commitments which would resolve the central deadlock. Israel, Dr. Jarring suggested, should agree on certain stated conditions (providing guarantees for security and freedom of navigation) to withdraw to the international boundary between Egypt and the Palestine of the British Mandate. Egypt should give a parallel undertaking to conclude a peace agreement explicitly ending the state of belligerency and recognizing Israel's right to exist in peace and security. In other words, both parties were asked formally to accept the principal obligations laid on them by Resolution 242.

The Egyptian reply gave the undertaking called for by Dr. Jarring, provided that Israel did the same and agreed to withdraw its forces to the international border. The Israeli reply stated firmly that, while Israel would be prepared to withdraw its forces to "secure, recognized and agreed boundaries to be established in the peace agreement", it would in no circumstances withdraw to the pre-June 1967 lines.

This official confirmation of Israel's insistence on territorial expansion as part of a peace settlement embarrassed the American Government, which had first withheld and then granted military and economic assistance to Israel, in the attempt to persuade the Israeli Government to accept only "minor rectifications" of the armistice lines. The Americans made one further attempt when Mr. Rogers, at a press conference on March 16th, 1971, urged the Israelis to accept international guarantees in place of territorial gains, adding that security did not "necessarily require additions of territory" and that in the American view "the 1967 boundary should be the boundary between Israel and Egypt".

PROPOSAL FOR A "PARTIAL SETTLEMENT"

When this too met with an Israeli refusal, the American Government took up instead President Sadat's suggestion of an Israeli withdrawal for some distance in Sinai to allow the reopening of the Suez Canal. But the opportunity had been lost and the new proposal for a partial settlement quickly became bogged down in arguments over the extent of the Israeli withdrawal and the question of whether it should be seen as the first step in a complete withdrawal or not. The arguments dragged on through most of 1971 until the proposal was finally dropped by the Americans in November.

In December the UN General Assembly, in a resolution reaffirming the "inadmissibility of the acquisition of territory by war" and calling for an Israeli withdrawal, also urged Israel to "respond favourably" to the proposals made by Dr. Jarring in February. Only seven states voted against the resolution (Israel and six Latin American states) and it was noted that the United States, which in the past had always voted in support of Israel on territorial questions, abstained, reflecting the American view that Israel should withdraw from all but insubstantial portions of the occupied territories. However, no action followed and the year ended with President Sadat in a dangerously weakened position. He had taken considerable risks in going so far in pursuit of a political settlement and had promised the Egyptian people that 1971 would be the "year of decision". He blamed the lack of progress on American "political manoeuvring", and when the American Government ushered in the new—election—year by promising Israel a further 42 Phantom and 90 Skyhawk aircraft, there was little likelihood that a fresh American suggestion of indirect talks between Israeli and Egyptian representatives in New York would come to anything.

In February 1972 the Israelis launched a large-scale incursion into the Lebanon, stating that its aim was the elimination of guerrilla bases near Israel's northern border. In June a further Israeli raid on the Lebanon, carried out after an attack on Lydda airport by Japanese gunmen on behalf of the PFLP, was condemned by the Security Council after more than 70 civilians had been killed or wounded by what the Israeli Deputy Prime Minister described as an "error".

An unexpected development followed when President Sadat, in July 1972, called for the withdrawal from Egypt of the large contingent of Soviet advisers engaged on the reorganization of Egypt's defence system. This surprise move, which gravely damaged Egypt's defensive capability, was interpreted as a final appeal to the American Government to bring pressure to bear on Israel to accept a settlement involving an Israeli withdrawal from Sinai. If this was its intention, the move was ill-timed, since the approach of the Presidential election made it virtually certain that no American politician would advocate a course of action so unwelcome to Zionist opinion in the United States.

In Europe, however, partly out of a feeling that an important opportunity was being allowed to slip and partly as a reflection of a sense of disillusionment with American leadership, a reappraisal of Middle Eastern policy was taking place. In preparation for Britain's entry into the European Community (which took place on January 1st, 1973) an attempt was being made to concert a European approach to important questions of foreign policy. The attempt found expression in the voting at the end of the annual Middle East debate in the General Assembly of the United Nations when, with the single exception of Denmark, all the members of the Community followed the lead of Britain and France in voting for a resolution strongly critical of Israel. (The United States again abstained.)

TERROR AND COUNTER-TERROR IN THE MIDDLE-EAST

The cease-fire along the Suez Canal was maintained, but along the northern borders of Israel and Israeli-held territory there was a renewal of violence in the second half of 1972, accompanied by a mounting series of terrorist attacks by both Israelis and Palestinians in various parts of the world. In July and August 1972, a number of Palestinian leaders were killed or seriously injured by explosive devices sent to them in Beirut. In September, during the Olympic Games in Munich, Palestinian guerrillas captured a number of Israeli athletes and held them hostage in an attempt to obtain the release of Palestinians held captive in Israel. The attempt failed when West German police, after promising the Palestinians safe conduct out of Germany, opened fire on them at Munich airport, whereupon the guerrillas killed the hostages and were themselves either killed or captured. (The three Palestinians who survived were later released when a West German airliner was hijacked and flown, with the guerrillas on board, to Libya.)

The Munich attack was followed by heavy Israeli ground and air raids into the Lebanon, which the Israeli Government held responsible for the activities of guerrillas whose bases (since their expulsion from Jordan in 1970 and 1971) were in the refugee camps of the Lebanon and in Beirut. The fact that many civilians were killed in these raids, among them women and children in the refugee camps, provoked a confused international response and a growing sense of alarm as the unsettled conflict in the Middle East sparked violence in countries far from the conflict itself. Letter bombs were posted to Israeli representatives in various countries—an attaché at the Israeli Embassy in London was killed by one in September 1972—and after the Israeli Prime Minister, Mrs. Meir, had announced that "we have no alternative but to strike at the terrorist organizations wherever we can locate them", representatives of the Palestine Liberation Organization were attacked by gunmen or with explosive devices in Rome, Stockholm, Paris and Nicosia.

For a brief period at the beginning of 1973 it looked as though an effort would be made to take the conflict out of the hands of the terrorists and return it to the political arena. In rapid succession Mr. Hafez Ismail (President Sadat's political adviser), King Hussein of Jordan and Mrs. Meir visited Washington for talks with President Nixon. But the frail hopes aroused by this diplomatic activity were dashed when, in February 1973, a heavy Israeli attack on guerrilla installations in a refugee camp in North Lebanon was followed immediately by the shooting down by Israeli fighters of a Libyan airliner whose French captain had strayed over occupied Sinai in a sandstorm. The two incidents caused the death of 150 people—almost all of them civilians—within twenty-four hours and provoked an unprecedented wave of criticism of the Israelis on the eve of Mrs. Meir's arrival in Washington. Before she left, however, Palestinian guerrillas had diverted international indignation onto themselves by attacking the Saudi Arabian Embassy in Khartoum, where they held hostage and eventually murdered the American Ambassador and two other diplomats, one American and the other Belgian. A month later, following an abortive Palestinian attack on the Israeli Embassy in Nicosia, Israeli commandos mounted a carefully planned and ruthlessly executed attack in Beirut, penetrating into a residential district in the heart of the Lebanese capital and killing, among a number of other people, three leading members of the PLO.

On May 7th, 1973, the twenty-fifth anniversary of the creation of the State of Israel was celebrated with a massive military parade in Jerusalem. The parade symbolized Israel's commanding military position but was widely criticized, both inside and outside Israel, as an indication of the Israeli Government's refusal to consider any compromise formula which might lead to peace with the Arabs.

STALEMATE

In the autumn of 1973, the Arab-Israeli conflict appeared to be further than ever from solution. The Israelis, confident that their military supremacy over the Arabs had if anything increased, remained in control of all the territories they had occupied in 1967 and had established in these territories some fifty civilian and paramilitary settlements. The Egyptian and Jordanian Governments—though not yet the Syrian—had long since modified their earlier refusal to negotiate a settlement and had clearly indicated their willingness to recognize the State of Israel; but they still refused to envisage a peace settlement which did not provide for the return of all the occupied territories. The United Nations, despite the passage every year of resolutions calling for an Israeli withdrawal, found all its efforts to devise a settlement blocked by Israel's refusal to relinquish its 1967 conquests. A dangerous mood of frustration enveloped the Middle East, while for the outside world anxiety over a possible renewal of the conflict was compounded by apprehensions about the maintenance of vital oil supplies.

More than ever, the key to the situation rested in the hands of the United States, which found itself isolated in support of Israel and yet faced with the prospect of becoming increasingly dependent on Arab oil. America's allies, for whom dependence on Arab oil was already a fact, were growing increasingly impatient with the American Government's Middle East policy, which seemed to be aimed at maintaining Israel's overall supremacy without seeking in return any concessions from the Israeli government over the occupied territories or the other necessary ingredients of a peace settlement. The Watergate scandal in Washington appeared to make it even less likely than before that the Nixon administration would risk unpopularity with the Zionist lobby by proposing any fresh initiative to break the deadlock in the Middle East. The isolation of the United States was emphasized during the debate in the Security Council in the summer of 1973. After prolonged discussion, the Council considered a resolution put forward by eight non-aligned members which was strongly critical of Israel's continued occupation of Arab territory. The United States found it necessary to use its veto to prevent the passage of the resolution, which obtained the affirmative votes of all the other Council members except China, which abstained.

This American decision played its part in convincing the Arabs that only by a renewal of the war could they hope to break the stalemate in the Middle East and look forward to the recovery of their lost territories. They had no illusions about their ability to recover them by defeating Israel; but they judged that, unless the superpowers were brought face to face with the danger of a fresh round of fighting which would threaten their own interests, they would not exert themselves to obtain a settlement. They were influenced in forming this judgment by the American decision (announced in March, shortly after President Sadat's special envoy had visited President Nixon) to furnish another forty-eight jet fighters to Israel, and by the progress towards détente between the United States and the Soviet Union (symbolized by the meeting between President Nixon and Mr. Brezhnev in June). From both it appeared plain to the Arabs that the stalemate in the Middle East was to be preserved at their expense.

RENEWAL OF THE WAR

The attack which was launched on two fronts by the Egyptian and Syrian forces on October 6th took everyone by surprise. Unusual activity behind the lines had been observed by Israeli and American intelligence agencies west of the Suez Canal and east

of the cease-fire line on the Golan Heights; but in each case its importance was discounted because of the Israeli conviction (shared by military experts elsewhere) that the Egyptian army was incapable of the elaborate operation required to cross the canal and breach the chain of Israeli fortifications known as the Bar-Lev line on the east bank. Their success in guarding the secret of the attack won for the Egyptian and Syrian forces on both fronts a substantial initial advantage, which was enhanced by the fact that October 6th was Yom Kippur, the Day of Atonement in the Jewish calendar, when all public services were suspended, which made it unusually difficult for the Israelis to mobilize their forces rapidly to meet the emergency. By midnight on the first day of the war, four hundred Egyptian tanks had crossed the canal, the Bar-Lev line had been outflanked and a massive Syrian tank attack beyond the Golan Heights had only been stemmed by a masterly rearguard action by greatly outnumbered Israeli armour, aided by costly air strikes.

During the fighting that followed and which continued for three weeks (despite a United Nations cease-fire on October 22nd) before all operations ceased, the Syrians were driven back beyond the old cease-fire line and Israeli forces counter-attacking on the Suez front effected a westward crossing of the canal, to establish a wide bridgehead on the edge of the Nile delta. At the end of the war, the military advantage lay with the Israelis, who had occupied a further area of Syrian territory and were threatening Damascus, while their units west of the canal had isolated an Egyptian army in Suez, cutting its communications with Cairo. Meanwhile, however, largely as a result of the intervention of the Arab oil-producing states, the political objectives of the Arabs had been achieved and the whole context of the confrontation with Israel had been decisively altered.

To begin with, the legend of Israeli invincibility had been shattered. Making unexpectedly efficient use of new weapons (especially portable anti-tank missiles) the Arab armies demonstrated that since 1967 they had significantly narrowed the technological gap between themselves and the Israelis. By doing so, they exposed the fallacy on which Israeli strategy had been based since the Six Day War: the fallacy that the control of wide buffer zones (in the shape of the territories occupied since 1967), together with the military supremacy of which they felt assured, rendered the Israelis immune to Arab attack. This assumption had encouraged in the Israeli leaders the dangerous conviction that since they were in no danger from the Arabs they could afford to disregard the mounting pressure of world opinion calling for an Israeli withdrawal as the essential condition for a negotiated settlement with the Arabs.

THE OIL WEAPON

Soon after the outbreak of the war, there were calls within the Arab world for measures to deny Middle East oil to the supporters of Israel. On October 17th a meeting in Kuwait of representatives of the Arab oil producers resulted in an agreement to reduce output; two days later Abu Dhabi took the lead in stopping altogether the export of oil to the United States. In adopting and presently intensifying these measures, the Arab oil-producing states showed an unexpectedly determined sense of solidarity. This had an evident effect on the Governments of Western Europe, conscious of their dependence on the free flow of oil from the Middle East. On November 6th the nine member states of the Common Market endorsed in Brussels a statement calling for an Israeli withdrawal from the territories occupied in 1967 and asserting that, while all states in the Middle East should enjoy the right to secure boundaries, the legitimate rights of the Palestinians should be taken into account in any settlement (*see* Documents on Palestine, page 79). This provoked accusations from the Israelis to the effect that the Europeans were giving in to Arab "blackmail", but these took too little account of the fact that for several years past (as shown by the yearly votes at the United Nations) the Europeans had been dissociating themselves from United States policy and registering their growing impatience with Israel's refusal to make any concession.

AMERICAN INITIATIVE

These developments underlined the central point which the Arabs had sought to make by their resort to war: the point that neither the Israelis nor those countries which were dependent on Middle East oil would be safe if they allowed a situation to continue in the Middle East which left large areas of Arab territory under Israeli occupation. The Americans, who alone possessed the influence that could induce the Israelis to withdraw—and who now found themselves inconvenienced much more by the oil embargo than they had anticipated—accepted the need to use their influence to bring about a settlement. The American Secretary of State, Dr. Kissinger, who had been active in obtaining Soviet co-operation over a cease-fire, now embarked on a dramatic series of visits to the capitals of the contestants in the Middle East, out of which there resulted disengagement agreements between Egypt and Israel (signed on January 18th 1974) and—after much more protracted and intricate exchanges—between Syria and Israel (signed on May 30th 1974). In the middle of June 1974 President Nixon, whose domestic position had become dangerously insecure on account of the protracted investigations into the Watergate scandal, embarked on a triumphant tour of the Middle East, forecasting a new era of co-operation between the United States and the Arab world, while reassuring the Israelis of continuing American support. Thanks largely to the personal success achieved by Dr. Kissinger with both Arab and Israeli leaders, this American initiative was generally well received, except by some Israelis who foresaw mounting pressure on Israel to make concessions inconsistent with her security, and by the extreme wing of the Palestinian resistance movement, which engaged in a series of terrorist attacks on targets in northern Israel in an effort to frustrate a settlement inconsistent with their aim of total liberation in Palestine.

Otherwise, Mr. Nixon's visit revealed a strong desire on the part of the Arab governments concerned to restore friendly relations between themselves and the United States. Diplomatic relations between Washington and Damascus were re-established and the embargo on the export of Arab oil to the United States was lifted in recognition of Dr. Kissinger's efforts to promote a satisfactory settlement in the Middle East.

CHANGE IN THE BALANCE OF POWER

This Arab-American reconciliation was one of the most striking results of the October war; it was a reminder of the greatly increased influence of the Arab states so long as they continued to act in concert. Conversely, Israel's international position had been much weakened by the failure of her pre-war policies and by the revelation of the extent to which the rest of the world was dependent on Arab goodwill. The Government headed by Mrs. Golda Meir, in which General Dayan had been the very influential defence minister, was widely blamed both for provoking the October war by its policy of "creeping annexation" and for being caught unawares when the war came. After winning a narrow victory in a general election at the end of 1973, Mrs. Meir finally abandoned the attempt to rebuild her coalition in April 1974. She was succeeded as leader of the Labour party and prime minister by General Itshak Rabin, who had been Chief of Staff at the time of the 1967 war and later Israeli ambassador in Washington. In the Arab world, the effect of the war was to strengthen the position of the regimes in Cairo and Damascus and to give new authority to King Faisal of Saudi Arabia, whose control of the greatest share of the oil reserves of the Middle East made him a dominant figure in Arab politics. The fact that the disengagement agreements arranged with the help of Dr. Kissinger involved small but significant Israeli withdrawals from Arab territory gave satisfaction throughout the Arab world; but the central problem of the future of the Palestinians remained unsolved. The difficulty of finding a solution to this problem which would prove acceptable both to the Israelis and to the Palestine Liberation Organization (which the Arab governments, meeting in Algiers in November 1973, had recognized as "the sole legitimate representative of the Palestinian people") posed a continuing threat to the stability of the disengagement agreements entered into in 1974.

Despite the general awareness of the new strength of the Arab world, the movement towards a settlement in the Middle East gradually lost momentum during the second half of 1974 and a mood of apprehension developed in which a further outbreak of war at times seemed imminent. The disengagement agreements were carried out and UN forces were inserted between the combatants in Sinai and on the Golan front, but mutual recriminations were exchanged between the Syrians and the Israelis over the ill-treatment of prisoners and the destruction of the Syrian town of Kuneitra, demolished by the Israelis on the eve of their withdrawal. The arms lost by both sides during the October war were rapidly replaced, although the Egyptians complained that the Soviet Government had restricted supplies to Egypt while making good all Syria's losses. During the year following the October war the United States Government committed $3,000 million of military aid to Israel, whose leaders claimed that the country was stronger at the end of 1974 than it had been before the Egyptians crossed the Suez Canal on October 6th, 1973.

While the optimism generated by the disengagement agreements was dissipated by the renewal of the stalemate between the Arab governments and Israel, the Palestinians saw their central role in the conflict strikingly endorsed. On September 21st, 1974, the UN General Assembly voted to include "the Palestine Question" on its agenda for the first time since the establishment of the state of Israel in 1948. (Only four governments opposed this decision: Israel, the United States, the Dominican Republic and Bolivia.) On October 14th the General Assembly invited the Palestine Liberation Organization to take part in the debate and a month later the Chairman of the PLO, Yasser Arafat, outlined to the Assembly the PLO's design for a "democratic, secular state" in Palestine in which Jews and Arabs would coexist on terms of equality, specifying that "all Jews now living in Palestine who choose to live with us there in peace and without discrimination" were included in this design. At the end of October a meeting of Arab Heads of State in Rabat confirmed that the PLO was the "sole legitimate representative of the Palestinian people", with the right to speak for the Palestinians at any future Middle East peace talks and to establish an independent national authority in any part of Palestine liberated from Israeli occupation.

These decisions greatly strengthened the hand of the Palestinians and of the PLO as their representative. However, they also deepened the impasse over movement towards a settlement because the Israeli Government adamantly refused to have any dealings with the PLO, dismissing it as a terrorist organization which Israel would meet, in Prime Minister Rabin's words, "only on the battlefield". The position of the PLO was also complicated by internal divisions over the objective which the organization should pursue. Although Yasser Arafat at the United Nations had spoken only of the PLO's goal of a unitary Palestine (whose achievement would mean the elimination of the state of Israel), he was under pressure from the Arab governments to accept the limited objective of a Palestinian state on the West Bank and the Gaza Strip, whose establishment could only be envisaged (if at all) in the context of a compromise settlement including the recognition of Israel within its pre-1967 borders. A majority within the PLO appeared at the end of 1974 to be moving towards acceptance of this formula, but the minority rejected any thought of compromising with the long-term goal of the total liberation of Palestine. This "rejection front", which had the backing of the governments of Iraq and Libya, made it difficult for the PLO openly to align itself with those Arab governments (notably the

government of President Sadat in Egypt) which were prepared to exchange recognition of Israel for an Israeli withdrawal from the territories occupied in 1967, including Arab Jerusalem, and the creation of a Palestinian state on the West Bank.

This was in effect the pattern for a settlement which had been envisaged in the Security Council's resolution 242 in November 1967 and which had provided the basis for all the international initiatives undertaken, with diminishing prospects of success, between 1967 and 1973. These initiatives had failed because the Israelis, before October 1973, had felt confident of their ability to retain control of at least substantial parts of the occupied territories and to hold off any Arab attempt to recover them by force. The October war, by undermining this confidence, had made more evident the Israelis' total dependence on American support; and the initial efforts of Dr. Kissinger immediately after the war had encouraged the Arabs to believe that American influence would at last be used to promote a settlement based on an Israeli withdrawal. It was this belief which had brought about the restoration of diplomatic relations between Washington and both Cairo and Damascus and the lifting of the Arab oil embargo.

ARAB IMPATIENCE

The Arab-American reconciliation, in which President Sadat had taken the lead and to which he totally committed himself during 1974, had failed by the end of the year to produce any results beyond the initial disengagement agreements. Apart from the tiny areas of territory conceded by Israel under those agreements, the Israeli occupation was maintained in Sinai, the Golan Heights (including the plateau up to the outskirts of Kuneitra), the West Bank (including the Old City of Jerusalem) and the Gaza Strip, with no relaxation of the ban on political activity by the Arab population or of the repressive measures enforced against that population by the occupation authorities. None of the fifty-odd Jewish settlements established in the occupied territories before October 1973 had been given up; indeed, the Israeli Government, under pressure from the right-wing opposition and the religious parties in the Knesset, continued to announce plans to extend the pattern of Jewish settlement. In the wake of Yasser Arafat's appearance at the United Nations in November 1974 there were demonstrations on the West Bank in support of the PLO, to which the Israelis responded by widespread arrests of Palestinians and the deportation of a number of leading citizens, among them the President of Bir Zeit College, Dr. Hanna Nasir.

These developments caused growing impatience in the Arab world, symbolized by rioting in Cairo in January 1975, over the lack of progress towards a settlement. The tension was heightened by a series of widely advertised statements by American leaders, including Secretary of State Kissinger, hinting at the possibility of armed intervention by American forces in the event of a fresh oil embargo by the Arab oil-producing states. Although these statements were later discounted as somewhat heavy-handed propaganda, those Arab leaders, like President Sadat, who had pinned their faith to American sincerity in the search for a settlement and had nothing to show for it, found themselves under heavy pressure. It was in these circumstances that Dr. Kissinger announced his intention to use his own brand of personal diplomacy to carry the process of disengagement between Israel and Egypt a stage further. When he returned to the Middle East in March it was widely assumed that Dr. Kissinger had obtained prior assurances from both sides of their willingness to conclude a bargain; but after two weeks of intensive "shuttle diplomacy" he had to admit failure when the Israelis refused to withdraw from the Mitla and Giddi passes in Sinai and from the oilfield at Abu Rudeis without an explicit undertaking of future non-belligerency from President Sadat. The latter demand was clearly unrealistic, since to satisfy it would have confirmed Arab suspicions that the Egyptians were prepared to abandon their allies and envisage a separate peace with Israel. There was therefore little surprise when the American Secretary of State (and later President Ford) let it be known that they blamed Israeli obstinacy for the breakdown of the negotiations and announced that the United States would embark on a "reassessment" of its Middle East policy. This was held to mean that the latest Israeli request for increased military and economic aid from the United States would not be granted until the Israelis showed a more conciliatory attitude.

The breakdown of Dr. Kissinger's mission coincided with the assassination in Riyadh of King Faisal of Saudi Arabia, whose prestige and authority had been greatly strengthened as a result of his support for the Arab war effort during and after the October war. Together, the two events brought renewed anxiety about the stability of the Middle East; and this anxiety was increased by the simultaneous and abrupt collapse of American policy in Indochina, where the capitals of Cambodia and South Viet-Nam fell in rapid succession to communist forces.

Two practical steps were taken on the Arab side which helped to allay the anxieties aroused by the breakdown of the peace-making mission of Dr. Kissinger. In May the Syrian Government unexpectedly agreed to renew for a further six months the mandate of the UN force separating the two sides on the Golan front; and on June 5th the Egyptian Government reopened the Suez Canal, eight years to the day after the outbreak of the June war which led to its closure in 1967.

At the time of his failure in March, Dr. Kissinger's critics had pointed to two weaknesses in his "step-by-step" approach to peace-making in the Middle East. In concentrating on limited territorial issues, they said, he had ignored the real heart of the problem, which was the future relationship between Israel and the Palestinians. And by using his personal style of diplomacy, he had excluded the Soviet Government from participation in the negotiations for a settlement which they too would eventually be expected to accept and endorse. When his mission broke down, the Soviet and Egyptian governments at once called for the resumption of the Geneva peace conference, which had met briefly at the time of the Egyptian-Israeli disengagement agreement at the end of 1973 but had been in abeyance ever since. In the absence, however, of any real prospects for progress at Geneva until the gap between the positions of the two sides had been narrowed, none of the parties showed real enthusiasm for reconvening the conference and the Soviet Government tacitly agreed to let the Americans make one more effort to break the deadlock.

FURTHER DISENGAGEMENT IN SINAI

On August 21st Dr. Kissinger flew to Israel to renew his attempt to promote a second disengagement agreement between Israel and Egypt. His return provoked violent demonstrations in Tel Aviv and Jerusalem among Israelis who opposed the idea of further concessions; and while the American Secretary of State was well received in Egypt, the resumption of his mission aroused hostility in other parts of the Arab world. Disregarding the critics on both sides, Dr. Kissinger succeeded after two weeks of intensive negotiations in persuading the Egyptians and Israelis to accept an agreement which was signed in Geneva on September 4th, 1975.

The new agreement provided for an Israeli withdrawal from the strategic Mitla and Giddi passes and the return to the Egyptians of the Abu Rudais oilfields, on which the Israelis had been dependent for some 50 per cent of their oil supplies since they had captured them in 1967. As in the first disengagement agreement signed in January 1974, a UN buffer zone was established separating the Egyptian and Israeli forces and the most important new element was the provision for five electronic listening posts in this zone, of which one was to be manned by Egyptians, one by Israelis and the other three by a team of 200 American civilians who would monitor troop movements both east and west of the passes. Both sides undertook to respect the ceasefire and to resolve the conflict between them by peaceful means rather than by the use of force. Non-military cargoes in ships sailing to or from Israel were to be allowed through the Suez Canal and the agreement was to remain in force "until superseded by a new agreement".

The conclusion of this second disengagement agreement was considered a triumph for American diplomacy and it had significant effects both on Egypt's relations with its Arab allies and on the pattern of international relationships with the various parties to the Middle East conflict. Within the Arab world, where only Saudi Arabia, Sudan and (with reservations) Kuwait expressed approval, the agreement was criticized—most vehemently by the Syrians and the PLO—as a surrender to American and Israeli interests. The united Arab front created during the October war and precariously maintained during the two succeeding years was now disrupted.

On the international plane, the second disengagement agreement marked a further stage in the

American-Egyptian rapprochement and the estrangement between Egypt and its former ally, the Soviet Union. In October 1975 President Sadat was well received on an official visit to Washington, but his repeated criticisms of the Soviet Union led to a steady deterioration of relations which culminated in Egypt's abrogation of the Soviet-Egyptian Treaty of Friendship in March 1976.

By refusing to follow the Egyptian example and agree to a further partial agreement with Israel, Syria now assumed the leadership of the Arab cause which Egypt appeared to have renounced. President Assad, who impressed foreign visitors (including Dr. Kissinger) as a skilful and determined politician, found his position in the Arab world greatly strengthened and even succeeded in restoring close relations with King Hussein of Jordan, with whom he established a joint Syrian-Jordanian Command Council. In October 1975 President Assad visited Moscow, where he had talks with President Podgorny and other leaders and gained a promise of further arms supplies to counter the very considerable deliveries reaching Israel from the United States. At the end of November Syria's already considerable prestige as the most consistent defender of the rights of the Palestinians was enhanced when President Assad agreed to renew the mandate of the UN Disengagement Observer Force (UNDOF) on the Golan Heights, extracting in return a promise that the Security Council would hold a special debate on the Palestine question in January with the PLO taking part.

PLO'S STANDING ENHANCED

This debate marked a further strengthening of the international position of the PLO. Already in November 1975 the UN General Assembly had adopted three resolutions concerning Palestine, of which the first had established a twenty-nation committee to work out plans for the implementation of the Palestinian right "to self-determination and national independence", the second invited the PLO to take part in all future UN debates on the Middle East, and the third denounced Zionism as "a form of racism and racial discrimination". (The last of these provoked an international storm of criticism in which the importance of the other two resolutions was widely overlooked.) A month later only an American veto saved Israel from censure by the Security Council for a series of severe air raids on targets in the Lebanon in which 75 people were killed and 150 wounded. When the Security Council, at Syria's request, debated the Palestine question in January 1976, the American delegate again found it necessary to use the veto to prevent the adoption of a resolution affirming the Palestinians' right to establish a state of their own and calling for an Israeli withdrawal from all the territories occupied since June 1967.

Despite America's continuing support for Israel, many Israelis were alarmed by indications that the attitude of the United States Government, despite the pressures of a presidential campaign, was moving in the direction of an acceptance of Palestinian rights as an essential ingredient in any Middle East settlement. In November 1975 the Ford administration had given wide publicity to the testimony given by Harold Saunders, deputy assistant Secretary of State, before a congressional sub-committee, in which Mr. Saunders had said that it was "obvious that thinking on the Palestinian aspects of the problem must evolve on all sides", adding that the American administration was "prepared to consider any reasonable proposal from any quarter and we will expect other parties to the negotiations to be equally open-minded". In January 1976 there had been reports in the Western press that American officials were already in secret contact with Palestinian representatives. The impression that a major change in American policy was in the making was reinforced in March when the UN Security Council debated the question of Israeli policies in the occupied territories. Although the American delegate again exercised the veto on Israel's behalf (for the third time in less than four months) to defeat a resolution which gained the affirmative votes of the other 14 members of the Security Council, he strongly condemned Israel's establishment of "illegal" settlements in Jerusalem and other occupied areas, emphasizing that "the presence of these settlements is seen by my Government as an obstacle to the success of the negotiations for a just and final peace between Israel and its neighbours".

The Israelis' persistence in establishing these settlements was a major factor in provoking serious rioting all over the occupied West Bank and in Gaza during the spring and summer of 1976. The riots, which found an echo inside Israel on March 30th (when a strike led to a confrontation with the Israeli security forces in which six Israeli Arabs were killed), had a decisive effect on the outcome of municipal elections organized by the Israeli occupation authorities on the West Bank in April. Instead of producing, as the Israelis had hoped, "moderate" Palestinian leaders who would be content with a measure of autonomy under a continuing Israeli occupation, the elections demonstrated the strength of Palestinian nationalism and the widespread support enjoyed by the PLO among the Palestinians living under occupation.

CIVIL WAR IN LEBANON

At the same time the lack of unity within the Arab camp was highlighted by events in the Lebanon, where armed clashes between Palestinian guerrillas and Christian militiamen in April 1975 touched off a civil war which threatened to destroy the Lebanese state and came near to provoking yet another Arab-Israeli confrontation. Attempts at mediation by the Arab League and by French and American emissaries failed to reconcile the warring parties in the Lebanon, which in turn were supported by rival interests in a divided Arab world, while the Israelis kept a close watch on events whose outcome was bound to affect the security of Israel's northern border. After nine months of heavy fighting, in which Palestinian guerrillas were drawn into a leftist alliance against the defenders of the conservative Christian establishment, the Syrian Government in January 1976 used Syrian-based units of the Palestine Liberation Army to impose a ceasefire which was to be followed by a reform of the Lebanese political system. However, the ceasefire broke down in March, like more than a score of others before it, when Christian extremists supporting President Frangieh prevaricated over the implementation of the reform programme and the Druze leader of the leftist alliance tried to seize the opportunity to force the president's resignation.

Faced with the prospect of an outright victory for the leftists and their Palestinian allies, which in turn might provoke the Israelis into military intervention in southern Lebanon, the Syrian Government used all its influence to restrain the leftists, eventually sending Syrian troops across the border at the end of May 1976. This move was made with tacit American approval and at the same time President Assad renewed the mandate of the UN force on the Golan front for a further six months. He thus reassured his opponents in Israel but found himself virtually isolated in the Arab world and facing a confrontation with the PLO.

The disastrous situation in the Lebanon and the recriminations it caused in the Arab world provided the Israelis with a breathing-space, temporarily obscuring the weakness of their position. Together with the suspension of almost all political activity in the United States during the 1976 presidential election campaign, it relieved the Israeli Government of the necessity to take any initiative to resolve the conflict with its Arab neighbours and left it free to press ahead with the colonization of the occupied territories, where fresh settlements were established in the Golan Heights, in Sinai and on the West Bank.

In the autumn of 1976, however, both of the factors which had prevented any movement towards an Arab-Israeli settlement were removed. After repeated failures on the part of the Arab League to play an effective mediating role in the Lebanon, determined efforts by the Saudi Arabian and Kuwaiti governments brought about a restricted Arab summit meeting in Riyadh in October, at which the leaders of Egypt, Syria, the Lebanon and the PLO agreed to the terms of a ceasefire. These were confirmed at a further meeting in Cairo on October 26th and provided for the creation of a substantial Arab peace-keeping force which within a month had put a stop to the savage fighting in Beirut, reopened the Beirut-Damascus road and occupied the main towns in the north and south of the country.

NEW ADMINISTRATION IN WASHINGTON

By this time the presidential election in the United States was over and the new President-elect, Jimmy Carter, had indicated his intention to take early action over the Middle East. Both from the Arabs, whose renewed solidarity was symbolized by a reconciliation between the presidents of Egypt and Syria, and from the Americans, freed at last from the handicap of a lame duck administration, the Israelis found themselves again under pressure. Even before

the Carter administration formally took office in January, a new tone was discernible in the pronouncements coming out of Washington and a clearer American voice began to be heard at the United Nations. On November 11th, 1976, the American delegate joined in approving a unanimous "consensus statement" by the Security Council which "strongly deplored" Israel's actions in establishing settlements in the occupied territories and attempting to alter the demographic balance in Jerusalem. On November 19th the American Ambassador to Israel, speaking to the annual convention of B'nai B'rith in Jerusalem, said that "unless Israel's professed willingness to return occupied territory is seen as more than mere rhetoric, the vicious circle of mutual mistrust cannot be broken". On November 24th the United States joined 117 other nations in voting in the UN General Assembly (against the opposition of Israel and Costa Rica) to deplore Israel's refusal to allow the return of the Palestinian refugees who had left their homes in 1967.

In the occupied West Bank intermittent unrest continued throughout 1976. Demonstrations in Nablus, Ramallah and the Old City of Jerusalem in May and June, in which Palestinian schoolchildren played a leading part, were subdued by the Israeli security forces with exceptional violence. In October there were serious riots in Hebron over the respective rights of Jews and Arabs to pray in the mosque built over the Tombs of the Patriarchs. In December a hunger strike by Arabs detained in the Israeli prison at Ashkelon focused attention on the grievances of Arab political prisoners and the lack of any prospect of ending an occupation which had been in existence for nearly ten years. Israel's occupation policy was again condemned by the UN General Assembly on December 20th, following the publication of a report by the UN Special Committee for the Investigation of Israeli Practices in the Occupied Territories, and on February 15th, 1977, the UN Human Rights Commission expressed "grave concern" over the deteriorating situation in the occupied territories and unanimously called on the Government of Israel to adhere to the terms of the Fourth Geneva Convention in its treatment of civilians in "all the occupied territories, including Jerusalem".

Conscious of the growing tension in the Middle East and of the steadily increasing dependence of the Western world on supplies of oil from the Arab world, the new American administration which took office in January 1977 moved with unexpected swiftness to reactivate the machinery for an Arab-Israeli settlement. In February President Carter despatched his new Secretary of State, Cyrus Vance, on a tour of the Middle East (where he followed in the footsteps of the Secretary-General of the United Nations, Dr. Waldheim) and invited Israeli and Arab leaders to visit him in Washington. In the course of a visit by the Israeli Prime Minister, Yitzhak Rabin, in March 1977, President Carter surprised all parties by speaking frankly about the nature of the settlement he envisaged. He pleased his Israeli guest by a reference to Israel's need for "defensible borders", but disconcerted him by making plain that in the American view an ultimate settlement should involve a return to the 1967 borders with only "minor adjustments". During an interim period and as the prelude to the conclusion of a final peace agreement, the American President indicated that arrangements might be made to extend Israel's defence capability beyond its eventual legal frontiers. A week later, speaking in a small New England town, President Carter confirmed the broad lines of his thinking about an Arab-Israeli settlement and added, again unexpectedly, that the final element in such a settlement should be the creation of a "homeland" for the dispossessed Palestinians.

ISRAELI GOVERNMENT RESIGNS

The renewed emphasis on the Palestinian aspect of the problem, which had been highlighted by the unrest on the West Bank and reflected in the repeated decisions of the United Nations and which was now echoed by President Carter, was unwelcome to the Israelis. The governing coalition was already under considerable internal pressure as a result of the difficult economic situation and the failure to devise any constructive policy for achieving peace with the Arabs; in addition, it had been undermined by a series of scandals involving leading figures in the Labour Party which had dominated this and every preceding government since the creation of the state. The most crucial issue facing the Government concerned the occupied territories and in particular the extent to which it should allow—or could control—Jewish settlement on the West Bank. Mr. Rabin's cabinet, already under pressure from the right-wing Likud party (which opposed any withdrawal from the West Bank), was divided within itself on this issue and in December 1976, following a dispute with one of his coalition partners, Mr. Rabin announced the Government's resignation. This necessitated a general election, which was fixed for May 17th, 1977. (The Israeli constitution required Mr. Rabin to stay in office as head of a caretaker government and it was in this capacity that he visited Washington in March).

ARAB GOVERNMENTS AND THE PLO

Once they had achieved a reconciliation between themselves and put an end to the war in the Lebanon in the autumn of 1976, the Arab Governments set about enlisting the help of the new American administration in working towards a peace settlement with Israel. Their common position was that the Geneva conference should be reconvened, with the Palestinians participating, and that an overall settlement should be negotiated on the basis of an Israeli withdrawal to the 1967 borders and the establishment of a Palestinian state on the West Bank and the Gaza Strip. Their efforts were complicated by the refusal of the PLO to agree explicitly to renounce its objective of the establishment of a unitary, "secular, democratic state" in the whole of Palestine (which would replace the existing state of Israel), although PLO spokesmen on a number of occasions did indicate their willingness to establish a state "on any part of Palestine" from which the Israelis would withdraw.

Since the Israelis refused either to entertain the idea of an independent Palestinian state or to negotiate under any circumstances with the PLO (whether or not the PLO agreed to recognize the state of Israel), no movement appeared possible unless the American Government brought pressure to bear on Israel. This the new administration in Washington was reluctant to do in the run-up to the Israeli general election, although the Israelis were uneasy over repeated indications that the Americans, like the Arab Governments, were in contact with the PLO in an effort to persuade the Palestinians to modify their attitude.

RIGHT-WING VICTORY IN ISRAEL

The prospects for a negotiated Arab-Israeli settlement received a severe setback in May, when the elections in Israel resulted in an unexpected victory for the right-wing Likud grouping at the expense of the Labour alignment. The elections were fought mainly over domestic issues and the defeat (for the first time in the history of the state) of the ruling Labour party was widely attributed to discontent over the failure to control the economic situation and over the series of scandals which had involved senior figures in the former administration. The result, largely unforeseen, was to put in power a party publicly committed to maintaining Israeli rule over the whole of the occupied West Bank, on the ground that it constituted part of Israel's divinely-ordained biblical inheritance, and led by the veteran politician, Mr. Menachem Begin, who had made his name in the pre-state period as the leader of the terrorist organization *Irgun Zvai Leumi*. This caused widespread apprehension in the Arab world and presented a challenge to President Carter, whose tentative ideas for a settlement presupposed an Israeli withdrawal from at least the greater part of the West Bank.

Faced with this difficulty, President Carter invited the new prime minister of Israel to visit Washington and before his arrival took steps to restate his own view of the essentials for a peace settlement in the Middle East and to obtain the endorsement of this view by America's allies in Europe. A statement published at the end of June by the U.S. State Department reaffirmed American adherence to Security Council resolution 242 and stressed that a settlement must involve Israeli withdrawal "on all three fronts of the Middle East—that is, Sinai, Golan, West Bank and Gaza—with the exact border and security arrangements being agreed in the negotiations". The State Department spokesman added that a Middle East settlement which was to be durable would have to deal with the Palestinian issue and that "in this connection the President has spoken of the need for a homeland for the Palestinians, whose exact nature should be negotiated between the parties".

The theme of a Palestinian "homeland" was taken up two days later at a meeting of the Heads of Government of the European Community in London.

In a Declaration published on June 29th, 1977, the leaders of the nine members of the European Community restated "their view that a peace settlement should be based on Security Council resolutions 242 and 338", adding that a solution to the Middle East conflict would be possible "only if the legitimate right of the Palestinian people to give expression to its national identity is translated into fact, which would take into account the need for a homeland for the Palestinians". The Declaration also said that representatives of "the Palestinian people" must be included among those taking part in negotiations to reach a peace agreement.

When Mr. Begin arrived in Washington in July 1977, he was warmly received by President Carter and achieved an unexpected success with the American public; but it was clear that no serious attempt had been made in the talks between the two leaders to examine the basic conditions for a peace settlement, on which there was an implicit divergence of views. In particular, the American administration was now intent on securing Palestinian participation in any peace negotiations, to which the Israeli Government was strenuously opposed. When the Secretary of State, Mr. Cyrus Vance, in the course of a tour of Middle East capitals in August, was told by the Saudi Arabian Government that the PLO would accept resolution 242 if it were amended to include provision for Palestinian self-determination, there was a moment of optimism in which Mr. Carter spoke of the possibility that acceptance by the PLO of resolution 242 might open the way to PLO participation in a reconvened Geneva peace conference. But the Secretary of State's visit ended discouragingly in Israel, where Mr. Vance encountered a categorical refusal on the part of Mr. Begin's government to negotiate under any circumstances with the PLO or to consider the idea of a Palestinian homeland. In any case, the PLO, sceptical about the terms of the proposed bargain, finally refused to amend its stand over resolution 242 without firm assurances that it would receive in return something more substantial than a vague offer to talk to the Americans.

Within a few days of Mr. Vance's departure from Jerusalem, it was announced that Israeli social services in the fields of education, health and welfare were to be extended to the Arab population of the West Bank and the Gaza Strip, which was widely interpreted as a step towards the annexation of these areas; and the same intention seemed to be implicit in the Israeli Government's decision to authorize three new Jewish settlements on the West Bank. Both decisions caused an immediate hardening of the PLO attitude and complicated still further the task which the Americans had set themselves of bringing the Israelis and the Arabs—including, if possible, the Palestinians—to the negotiating table.

When the Israeli Foreign Minister, Mr. Moshe Dayan, went to Washington in September 1977, he took with him draft proposals for a territorial settlement which envisaged the maintenance of the Israeli occupation throughout the West Bank and the Gaza Strip. These proposals, approved by the Israeli cabinet, expressed the continuing resolve of Mr.

Begin's government to agree to no step which in any conceivable circumstances could lead to the creation of an independent Palestinian state. The Americans, by contrast, were apprehensive that anything which appeared to extinguish all hope of that ill-defined Palestinian "homeland" to whose existence President Carter had committed himself would not merely ensure the continuation of Palestinian resistance but would also alienate those Arab governments on whose goodwill the United States was increasingly dependent.

Towards the end of September there was a fresh outbreak of fighting in south Lebanon, with Israeli troops openly intervening across the border in support of right-wing forces and against the Palestinians. This helped to prompt an American initiative, reluctantly accepted by the Israeli Government under considerable pressure from Washington, to include Palestinian representatives in a joint Arab delegation to the peace conference when it should be resumed in Geneva. Mr. Moshe Dayan emphasized on behalf of the Israeli Government that this did not mean that Israel was ready to abandon its attitude towards the PLO or its rejection of the idea of a Palestinian state; but the conviction of the Israelis that they were being driven in that direction was strengthened by the publication on October 1st, 1977, of a joint Soviet-American statement calling for a Middle East settlement that would ensure "the legitimate rights of the Palestinians". The use for the first time of this phrase by the American Government (whose representatives had previously spoken only of Palestinian "interests") alarmed the Israelis and was taken by the Arabs as an indication that President Carter was prepared for the confrontation that had long been threatening with the Israeli Government and its powerful supporters in the United States.

As the controversy over this aspect of the Soviet-American statement died down, its true significance as a symbol of superpower co-operation in the Middle East became apparent. The Soviet Union and the United States had been the joint Chairmen of the Geneva Conference at its first and only meeting at the end of 1973. After that Dr. Kissinger's ostentatiously personal style of diplomacy had numbered among its disadvantages the fact that it excluded the Soviet Union from any useful role in Middle East peacemaking. The prospect that the two superpowers were now prepared to collaborate again made a renewal of the Geneva Conference look less unlikely and encouraged a fresh outburst of diplomatic activity, with even the PLO expressing its qualified acceptance of the Soviet-American statement as the basis for a reconvened peace conference.

PRESIDENT SADAT'S VISIT TO JERUSALEM

Once again, however, the momentum was lost and as fresh procedural arguments developed which seemed likely to defer indefinitely the opening of serious negotiations, the Middle East settled back into an atmosphere of mistrust and intermittent violence. In October the Israeli Government announced its intention to establish six new settlements on the West Bank before the end of 1977 and on November 9th, in retaliation for a rocket attack by Palestinian guerrillas which killed three Israelis in a northern settlement, the Israeli air force attacked refugee camps in south Lebanon and completely destroyed the village of Azziye, killing more than 100 Lebanese civilians.

A few hours later, in the course of a speech to the Egyptian Parliament in which he expressed impatience with the endless debates over procedural questions, President Sadat said that he would be willing to go to Jerusalem and to the Knesset itself to negotiate a peace agreement with the Israelis. Despite widely expressed scepticism, the suggestion was immediately taken up by the Israeli Prime Minister and pursued through intermediaries in the American embassies in Cairo, Beirut and Jerusalem. Resisting a rising tide of Arab disapproval, and despite the last-minute resignation of his foreign minister and the minister's deputy, President Sadat flew to Jerusalem on November 19th, 1977, and the next day made a dramatic appeal for peace in the Knesset and before the television cameras of the world.

This altogether unexpected initiative took the world by storm. It was greeted with enthusiasm in the West, where it was regarded as a bold and constructive break with the sterile attitudes of the past, and with incredulous delight by the Israelis, who glimpsed the prospect of an end to their dangerous isolation. Among the Arabs, however, while there were scattered and mainly private expressions of approval and optimism, the general reaction of furious resentment left the Arab world in a state of unparalleled disunity, whose immediate effect was to make it harder than ever for the Arabs to achieve a common platform on which to negotiate a settlement with Israel.

Nor did the euphoria which surrounded President Sadat in Jerusalem long survive his return to Cairo after a series of meetings with Israeli political leaders. It soon became apparent that his Israeli hosts had assumed—like his Arab critics—that President Sadat had despaired of achieving an overall settlement between the Arabs and Israel and had set himself the more limited objective of an Egyptian-Israeli peace treaty. For this, the Israeli leaders were ready to withdraw from almost all Egyptian territory; they were not prepared to meet Mr. Sadat's other demands for a complete withdrawal from all Arab territory occupied in 1967 and recognition by the Israelis of the Palestinian right to self-determination.

In the conviction that his initiative must not be allowed to founder for lack of movement, President Sadat summoned a conference in Cairo to which he invited delegations from the United Nations, the two superpowers, Israel, the Arab confrontation states and the PLO. Of these, only Israel, the U.S.A. and the UN accepted the invitation, while the mutual recriminations between Egypt and the absentees widened still further the rift in the Arab world. Serious negotiations were postponed until December 25th, 1977, when Mr. Begin flew to Ismailia for a

much-advertised "summit" meeting with President Sadat, at which the Israeli Prime Minister produced a set of proposals for the future of Sinai, the West Bank and the Gaza Strip. On the crucial question of the future of the Palestinians, Mr. Begin offered only a limited form of self-rule for the population of the West Bank and the Gaza Strip, with Israel remaining in control of "security and public order", and this was criticized in the Arab world as being merely a formula for the maintenance of the Israeli occupation.

President Sadat's position was made more difficult, not only by his failure to win a more constructive response from the Israelis, but also by a statement from President Carter apparently approving the Begin proposal for Palestinian "self-rule". When Mr. Carter, in an evident attempt to repair the damage, altered the schedule of a foreign tour in order to spend an hour and a half with Mr. Sadat at Aswan on January 4th, he took the opportunity to reiterate the need to recognize "the legitimate rights of the Palestinian people" and to enable the Palestinians "to participate in the determination of their own future". This did something to restore relations between the United States and Egypt, but elsewhere in the Arab world cynicism about the prospects for an overall Arab-Israeli settlement was deepened by mistrust of President Sadat's motives and by the apparent inconsistency of American policy, especially where the rights of the Palestinians were concerned.

The Ismailia summit meeting produced a decision to institute bilateral talks on political and military questions affecting a settlement. The military talks opened in Cairo on January 11th and were at once complicated by a dispute over Israeli settlements in Sinai, which had been criticized as illegal by the International Commission of Jurists in Geneva on January 5th. This criticism was echoed in unusually categorical terms by President Carter a week later and when the political talks opened in Jerusalem on January 16th they were interrupted after only twenty-four hours when President Sadat recalled the Egyptian delegation, saying that in view of Israel's insistence on retaining the settlements he saw no hope of reaching agreement on a declaration of principles which might form the basis for negotiations.

When President Sadat visited Washington at the beginning of February for talks with President Carter and leading members of both houses of Congress, his claim that the Israelis had made no constructive response to his Jerusalem initiative was sympathetically received. The Israeli Prime Minister at the same time was encountering an unprecedented wave of criticism from American politicians and editorial writers, who found his policies incomprehensibly rigid, especially on the issue of the settlements in the occupied territories. When Mr. Begin chose this moment to assert that UN resolution 242, in the Israeli Government's opinion, did not require an Israeli withdrawal from the West Bank, American impatience was redoubled. The Israeli prime minister was invited to visit Washington in the middle of March 1978 and it was widely assumed that President Carter would take the opportunity to exert serious pressure on the Israeli Government to alter policies which were clearly frustrating President Sadat's peace initiative and weakening the position of the moderates in the Arab world.

ISRAELI INVASION OF SOUTH LEBANON

In the event, Mr. Begin's journey to Washington was delayed for a week by a fresh crisis arising out of a terrorist raid near Tel Aviv by Palestinian guerrillas operating from south Lebanon, in which 36 Israelis were killed, including a number of women and children, and 76 wounded.

The Israeli response was to mount a major attack across the border into south Lebanon, whose original purpose was to wipe out Palestinian guerrilla bases and establish a security belt some six miles wide along the Lebanese side of the frontier. When the United States hurriedly introduced a resolution in the UN Security Council calling for an Israeli withdrawal to be supervised by a UN force, the Israelis deepened their penetration and when a ceasefire finally came into effect on the evening of March 20th their forces were in occupation of the whole of south Lebanon as far as the Litani river, with the exception of the port of Tyre.

The terrorist raid by the PLO on March 11th had been very widely condemned; but the Israeli invasion, which was accompanied by heavy and indiscriminate land, sea and air bombardments in which most of the towns and villages of south Lebanon were destroyed, provoked even more severe denunciation, especially as it became clear that, while most of the guerrillas had escaped, an estimated 1,000 Lebanese civilians had been killed, in addition to some 200 guerrillas, and upwards of 200,000 refugees had been driven from their homes.

When Mr. Begin finally met President Carter on March 20th, the differences between them over the basic requirements of a Middle East peace settlement led to a confrontation which was barely masked by the niceties of diplomatic protocol. Relations between the United States and Israel had reached their lowest point since President Eisenhower ordered Mr. Ben Gurion to withdraw his forces from Sinai in 1957, and Mr. Begin returned from Washington to face a threat to his leadership in Israel, where there was dissension within the cabinet and a movement of ex-servicemen urged the prime minister not to press territorial claims at the cost of peace.

There was friction over the role of the UN Interim Force in Lebanon (UNIFIL), whose mandate was to supervise the withdrawal of the Israeli army from south Lebanon and to restore the authority of the Lebanese Government in the area. The Israelis carried out a partial withdrawal at the end of April but insisted that they would maintain an armed presence in Lebanon until the UN force could ensure the security of northern Israel against attacks by Palestinian guerrillas. The PLO, which was determined not to relinquish its last area of operations, promised to co-operate with UNIFIL but found it difficult to control the activities of some of its units in the area around Tyre, which remained in Palestinian hands.

At the beginning of May 1978 Mr. Begin again visited Washington, where President Carter assured him that "we will never waver in our absolute commitment to Israel's security". However, two weeks later, as the Israelis were celebrating the thirtieth anniversary of the birth of their state, the US Senate authorized the sale of advanced fighter aircraft to Saudi Arabia. The Senate's decision, which was taken despite a sustained attempt by the pro-Israeli lobby in Washington to prevent it, was the first of its kind and clearly reflected American impatience with Mr. Begin's stand on peace negotiations with the Arabs, as well as the importance attached by the United States to retaining the friendship of Saudi Arabia, the leading oil producer in the Middle East.

When the Israelis withdrew the last of their forces from South Lebanon on June 13th, they refused to hand over their positions to UNIFIL but left them in the hands of Christian Lebanese militia units which had been collaborating with the Israelis against the Lebanese Government. This helped to cause a crisis in Beirut at the beginning of July, when the Syrian-dominated Arab peace-keeping force attempted to impose its authority on the right-wing Christian militias.

The American Government, alarmed at the prospect of renewed Israeli intervention and of the final breakdown of the peace initiative launched by President Sadat in November 1977, exerted its influence to restrain both sides in the Lebanon and persuaded the Israeli and Egyptian Governments to send their foreign ministers to a meeting in England, which took place at Leeds Castle on July 18th. When this meeting failed to narrow the gap between the two sides, President Sadat announced that he would not engage in further negotiations with Israel unless the Israeli Government changed its position. Faced with a deteriorating situation, President Carter took the unexpected step of inviting the Egyptian and Israeli leaders to meet him in a final attempt to break the deadlock in the privacy of the presidential lodge at Camp David at the beginning of September 1978.

CAMP DAVID SUMMIT

There was little optimism in advance of the Camp David summit meeting, since the Egyptian and Israeli positions seemed to be as far apart as ever on the crucial questions of the future of the West Bank and Gaza. The atmosphere was worsened by continuing friction between the Israelis and UNIFIL in South Lebanon and by persistent though contradictory reports about the Israeli Government's intention to expand the number of Jewish settlements on the West Bank. On both issues the United States was critical of the Israeli stand and it was widely felt that President Sadat, by involving the Americans so closely in the search for a settlement, had put himself in an advantageous position for the approaching confrontation at the summit, especially since Mr. Begin continued to assert Israel's claim to sovereignty over the West Bank (and so, by implication, its refusal of Security Council resolution 242).

The Camp David meeting, which lasted for twelve days and appeared more than once to be on the point of breaking down, ended on September 17th when President Carter made a triumphant appearance on television to announce that Mr Begin and President Sadat had signed two documents which together provided a framework for peace in the Middle East. One of these dealt with the bilateral problems between Egypt and Israel, which the two leaders undertook to resolve by concluding within three months a peace treaty providing for an Israeli withdrawal from Sinai and the establishment of normal relations between the two countries The other dealt with the wider question of the future of the West Bank and Gaza and provided for the election of a Palestinian self-governing authority to replace the existing Israeli military government; once the authority was in being, there should be a transitional period of not more than five years, during which the inhabitants of the West Bank and Gaza would exercise autonomy; and finally, "as soon as possible, but not later than the third year after the beginning of the transitional period", there should be negotiations to determine the final status of the West Bank and Gaza and to conclude a peace treaty between Israel and Jordan.

The Camp David agreements were greeted with a very mixed reception by the different participants. President Carter's own standing was greatly enhanced in the United States, where it was felt that his daring personal diplomacy had forced the Israeli and Egyptian leaders to make the concessions without which no positive outcome was possible. In Israel the agreements were greeted with more cautious approval, in the belief that Mr Begin had realized Israel's long-standing ambition to conclude a separate peace with Egypt without making any substantive concessions over Israel's right to maintain control of the West Bank and Gaza. In the Arab world, however, the agreements were seen as confirmation of the charge that President Sadat had abandoned the Palestinians and his Arab allies in order to satisfy purely Egyptian interests. In the chorus of protest that followed, even the government of Saudi Arabia contributed the unusually outspoken comment that the Camp David agreements constituted "an unacceptable formula for a definitive peace", while the resignation of the Egyptian foreign minister (who was at Camp David with President Sadat) showed that not even Egyptian opinion was wholeheartedly in favour of the Camp David formula.

The controversy within the Arab world centred around the question of whether or not the agreements gave any real promise of eventual self-determination for the Palestinians. The advocates of the Camp David "framework for peace" argued that if the Palestinians co-operated in the arrangements for a transitional period of self-rule they would set in motion a process which would be irreversible; that the end result of this process would be, sooner or later, an independent Palestinian state; and that, if the Palestinians refused to co-operate, they would provide Israel with an excuse to perpetuate its occupation of the West Bank and Gaza. Against this the critics argued that it was futile for Egypt to negotiate on behalf of the Palestinians over an issue on which the Palestinians themselves had not been consulted; that the arrangements for Palestinian autonomy outlined at Camp David were so imprecise as to be useless; that in any case the Israelis would hold a power of veto over their implementation and over the eventual future of the West Bank; and that the Israelis had no intention of ending their occupation or of allowing any development which might lead in the end to Palestinian independence.

The last of these arguments was much strengthened in the immediate aftermath of the Camp David meeting by the actions of Mr. Begin. Even before he left the United States, the Israeli Prime Minister declared that Israeli forces would remain on the West Bank (which he refused to refer to as anything but "Judea and Samaria") and publicly challenged President Carter's assertion that he had agreed not to establish any more settlements there during the five-year transitional period. As soon as he was back in Israel, he declared emphatically in the Knesset that Israel would not allow "under any conditions or in any circumstances" the establishment of an independent Palestinian state, and that Israel would continue to create new settlements on the West Bank and would expect to maintain an armed presence there even after the end of the transitional period.

ARAB OPPOSITION HARDENS

In the circumstances it was not surprising that the U.S. Secretary of State, Mr. Vance, whom President Carter dispatched to the Middle East with the special assignment of trying to enlist Arab support for the Camp David agreements, met with a frosty reception even in the capitals normally most friendly to the United States. The governments of Jordan, whose co-operation would be necessary if the provisions for the West Bank were to be put into effect, and of Saudi Arabia, whose influence was likely to be decisive in shaping the Arab attitude, both expressed serious reservations, while the more radical Arab governments, led by Syria acting in cooperation with the PLO, declared their total rejection of the agreements.

So strong were the feelings aroused in the Arab world that they led to a reconciliation between the rival Baathist governments of Iraq and Syria, which had been at loggerheads for a decade, and to a summit conference of all the Arab states (apart from Egypt) which met in Baghdad at the beginning of November 1978 to consider means of preventing the implementation of the Camp David agreements. After a fiery debate in which various proposals were aired for isolating Egypt and denying it all forms of economic aid, the Arab leaders agreed, at the insistence of Saudi Arabia, to delay the implementation of any such measures until Egypt should actually sign a peace treaty with Israel.

In this way the door was left open for President Sadat to reconsider a policy which would leave him totally dependent on the support of the United States. Together with further decisions by the Israelis to press ahead with the expansion of their settlements on the West Bank, this led President Sadat to press for a revision of the Camp David agreements in order to link the provisions concerning the future of the West Bank more closely to those for a bilateral peace treaty between Egypt and Israel. This question of "linkage", to which President Sadat added the demand that a specific timetable should be adopted for the introduction of autonomy on the West Bank, brought the peace-making process once again to a standstill. Despite another hurried visit to the Middle East by U.S. Secretary of State Vance, which was cut short after five hours of inconclusive discussions with Prime Minister Begin in Jerusalem, the target date of December 18th (by which the two sides had agreed at Camp David to sign a peace treaty) came and went with the outstanding issues still unresolved.

REVOLUTION IN IRAN

During the final weeks of 1978 a fresh complication arose with the disintegration of the Shah's regime in Iran. This had important repercussions throughout the Middle East. The inability of the United States to do anything to prevent the collapse of its principal ally in the area struck a damaging blow at American prestige. The suspension of oil exports from Iran, as a result of a strike in the oilfields, threatened to provoke an international energy crisis and cut off the most important source of Israel's oil supplies. It also became clear, even before the Shah went into exile on January 16th, 1979, that whatever government might succeed him would give strong backing to the Palestinians in their struggle to achieve independent statehood.

These developments gave added urgency to the American desire to achieve at least a partial Arab-Israeli settlement, but stiffened the attitudes of all the possible participants in any such settlement. The Israelis now insisted on including a clause in the draft peace treaty with Egypt guaranteeing them access to oil from Sinai after their evacuation of the peninsula. For President Sadat, who could ill afford to seem less fervent a protector of Arab rights in Palestine than the non-Arab rulers of revolutionary Iran, it became more necessary than ever to obtain some concession over the West Bank. Without such a concession it was even more unlikely that Saudi Arabia or Jordan—let alone the other Arab states—would moderate their opposition to the Camp David peace formula.

In these circumstances President Carter embarked in February on a series of foreign policy initiatives which were designed to demonstrate the continuing usefulness of the United States as an ally in the Middle East. The U.S. Defense Secretary, Mr. Harold Brown, was sent on a tour of Saudi Arabia, Jordan, Egypt and Israel with the twin assignments of reassuring both Arabs and Israelis of American backing and enlisting the support—or at least the acquiescence—of the conservative Arab states in a fresh attempt to get the Egypt-Israel peace treaty signed. Both Mr. Brown and the U.S. Energy Secretary, Mr. Arthur Schlesinger, referred publicly to the determination of the United States to protect its interests and those of its allies in the Middle East, if necessary by force.

PRESIDENT CARTER VISITS THE MIDDLE EAST

These moves did little to lessen the tension and when a further meeting in Washington between the Egyptians and Israelis at ministerial level failed to remove the remaining obstacles in the way of the peace treaty, President Carter again took matters into his own hands. On March 7th, 1979 he flew to the Middle East to exert his personal influence in a final effort to persuade the Egyptian and Israeli leaders to sign the long-deferred peace treaty.

After a week of alternating optimism and pessimism, Mr. Carter returned to Washington to announce that "we have now defined the major components of a peace treaty"; but before the treaty could be signed there were further acrimonious arguments about Israeli settlements on the West Bank (which were again condemned by the UN Security Council on March 22nd, in a resolution which called for the establishment of a special commission to examine the position regarding the settlements and to report back to the Security Council by July 1st, 1979), while opposition to the peace treaty on the part of even the most moderate Arab governments emphasized the isolation of Egypt within the Arab world. The reaction of America's European allies was also unenthusiastic, especially as it became plain that the United States expected them to share the high cost of the treaty and that Arab resentment was likely to find expression in higher oil prices.

ARAB BOYCOTT OF EGYPT

The attitude of Saudi Arabia was crucial and the euphoria in the United States over the signing of the peace treaty—which finally took place in Washington on March 26th—was sharply reduced when Saudi Arabia made plain its opposition to the treaty by attending a meeting of the Arab League in Baghdad at which a decision was taken to impose a political and economic boycott against Egypt. Arab ambassadors were withdrawn from Cairo, economic aid to Egypt was suspended and it was announced that the headquarters of the Arab League would be transferred from Cairo to Tunis. In agreeing to these measures and in subsequently breaking off diplomatic relations with Egypt, the Government of Saudi Arabia in effect chose to maintain solidarity with the rest of the Arab world at the expense of an open breach with the United States.

The opposition to the peace treaty throughout the Arab world was due to the treaty's failure to make any clear provision for Palestinian self-determination. President Sadat maintained that the treaty was the first step towards a comprehensive settlement which would restore the rights of the Palestinians; but to the other Arabs it appeared to be a separate peace between Egypt and Israel which would restore Sinai to Egypt but would leave Israel in unfettered control of the rest of the occupied territories. That this was also the view of the Israeli Government seemed to be confirmed when Mr. Begin, in an outspoken broadcast on Israel's Independence Day on May 2nd, 1979, reiterated that no border would ever again be drawn through "the land of Israel" and that "We shall never withdraw from the Golan Heights''. Such statements embarrassed the United States and strengthened the conviction of the Arabs that President Carter, despite his earlier support for ''the legitimate rights of the Palestinians'' and their need for a ''homeland'', had been deflected by the opposition of the Zionist lobby in the United States from his pursuit of a comprehensive settlement in the Middle East.

THE AUTONOMY TALKS

Soon after the signing of the Egyptian-Israeli peace treaty in March 1979 the two countries began negotiations on the question of autonomy for the Palestinians in the occupied territories. From the outset these negotiations were difficult. The principal issue over which the two sides differed was the establishment of Israeli settlements in the occupied territories. While the Israeli Prime Minister, Mr. Begin, insisted that these were in no way contrary to the Camp David Accords, the Egyptians took the opposite view. When the Israeli Minister in charge of Settlements, Ariel Sharon, announced plans at the end of May to build new settlements on the West Bank and in the Gaza strip, the Egyptian Prime Minister, Mustapha Khalil, warned Israel that their establishment would jeopardize the peace process. Shortly afterwards, on June 12th, the second round of autonomy talks broke up with the two sides unable to agree on even the first principles of the autonomy plan.

On September 4th President Sadat of Egypt went to Haifa to begin new talks with Mr. Begin and announced that he was ''determined to spread the umbrella of peace to include the Palestinian people''. In the course of the talks a few minor matters were sorted out. Bilateral agreements were made on the issues of border patrols, oil sales from Egypt to Israel, and the return of the Santa Caterina monastery to the Egyptians. No progress was registered on the autonomy question.

The two countries drifted still further apart a week later when the Israeli Government withdrew its ban on the purchase of Arab land in the occupied territories by Israeli citizens. The United States Government immediately condemned the action as ''contrary to the spirit and intent of the peace process' and, at the sixth round of the autonomy talks in Alexandria on September 26th, Egypt declared that the lifting of the ban was an ''obstacle to peace'' which would discourage other parties from joining the peace process. On October 10th at the Parliamentary Assembly of the Council of Europe in Strasbourg, Egypt's acting Foreign Minister, Boutros Ghali, delivered a devastating attack on Israeli attitudes to the negotiations. He also outlined his government's position. Egypt, he declared, supported the rights of the Palestinians to an independent state, recognized the PLO as the representative of the Palestinians and deplored Israel's continued colonization of the areas under discussion.

ISRAEL'S INTERNAL DISPUTES

While Egyptian-Israeli negotiations were continuing, there was extensive debate inside Israel about the government's policy on settlements in the occupied territories. Although the opposition movement, Peace Now, organized demonstrations to protest against the establishment of more settlements, a parliamentary committee in July 1979 approved plans to build thirteen new ones during the next twelve months. The government and its supporters suffered a setback, however, when the Israeli Supreme Court ruled that the Elon Moreh settlement near Nablus was illegal and had to be dismantled. The ruling denied that the settlement served a necessary military function and ordered the expropriated land to be restored to its Arab owners. At the end of October an extremist nationalist party, Tehiya, was founded, its principal objective being the construction of Jewish settlements throughout the West Bank.

PALESTINIAN DIPLOMATIC GAINS

During the summer of 1979 there was speculation that the U.S.A. was making overtures to the PLO in order to bring the Palestinians into the peace process. Although this was repeatedly denied by President Carter, the American ambassador at the UN, Mr. Andrew Young, met with the PLO observer, Zehdi Labib Terzi, in September. After strong protests from the Israelis, Young resigned a few days later and declared that the American refusal to talk to the PLO was ridiculous.

While the Palestinians found themselves rebuffed by the United States, the PLO was making significant diplomatic headway among the countries of western Europe. In July Yasser Arafat held discussions with Chancellor Kreisky of Austria and in September he was officially received by King Juan Carlos of Spain and his Prime Minister, Adolfo Suárez. At the UN General Assembly meeting later in the month, the Irish Foreign Minister, Michael O'Kennedy, who was speaking on behalf of the EEC, voiced Europe's strong criticism of current Israeli policy and mentioned, for the first time, the role of the PLO. In the same debate the British Foreign Secretary, Lord Carrington, called for an end to Israel's policy of settlement in the occupied territories and for a reversal of the decision to allow Israeli citizens to buy land there. In the autumn the PLO achieved a number of further significant diplomatic successes. In November the PLO was accorded ''political recognition'' by the Italian Government and at the same time Arafat was received by the President and Prime Minister of Portugal. In addition, the PLO's spokesman on foreign affairs, Farouk Kaddoumi, held discussions with the Foreign Ministers of Belgium, Italy and Greece. Meanwhile, a minister at the Foreign Office in London declared that evidence of links between the PLO and the Irish Republican Army (IRA) was an obstacle to closer relations between Britain and the PLO.

FURTHER CRISES IN SOUTHERN LEBANON

The tension in southern Lebanon, which had seldom been relaxed since Israeli troops invaded the area in March 1978, continued throughout the summer of

1979. Between June and September Israel launched a dozen attacks by land, air and sea on Palestinian positions in the area. On two occasions a number of Syrian aircraft, sent up to defend Lebanese air space, were shot down.

The situation deteriorated still further in 1980 and in April supporters of Israel's Lebanese ally, Sa'ad Haddad, kidnapped and shot two Irish soldiers serving with UNIFIL. The Irish Government and the other countries contributing troops to the UN force quickly made it clear that they held Israel—which was arming and supplying Haddad—responsible for the murders.

UNREST ON THE WEST BANK

While Egypt and Israel continued to make little progress on the autonomy question, the Palestinian population of the West Bank grew increasingly restless and frustrated. In November 1979 Bassam Shaka, the Mayor of the Arab town of Nablus, was served with a deportation order for allegedly condoning terrorism in a conversation he had had with the head of the military government of the West Bank. While the Supreme Court considered Shaka's appeal the Mayor was imprisoned in Ramleh gaol. Protests throughout the West Bank followed immediately. The Nablus municipality resigned and the Mayors of all the major towns threatened to do so as well unless Shaka was released. On December 5th, however, Israel cancelled the deportation order and freed Shaka on condition that he thenceforth restricted himself to municipal affairs.

In February 1980 a new crisis erupted when the Israeli cabinet decided in principle to allow Jews to settle in the town of Hebron. This action, which was taken in response to the killing of an Israeli settler, was widely condemned in Israel and abroad and led to increased tension throughout the West Bank. Riots and demonstrations took place in a number of towns and in April a group of Jewish extremists caused havoc in Ramallah, destroying a large number of cars and other property. On May 1st a Palestinian youth was shot dead by an Israeli officer in Anabta, and the following day PLO guerrillas struck in Hebron and killed six Jewish settlers. The Israeli authorities reacted by blowing up a number of houses near the scene of the ambush and by deporting the Mayors of Hebron and Halhul and the Qadi (religious leader) of Hebron—a move which was immediately condemned by the UN Security Council.

NO PROGRESS TOWARDS REAL PEACE

The seizure of American embassy officials in Iran and the Soviet invasion of Afghanistan at the end of 1979 diverted international attention from the Arab-Israeli conflict. Although Arab and other Islamic leaders repeatedly warned the West that the question of Jerusalem and the rights of the Palestinians were at least of equal international significance as the events in Iran and Afghanistan, it became clear that the American administration was concentrating most of its attention on the recovery of the hostages in Teheran.

On March 1st, however, the Arab-Israeli conflict was again on the agenda when the UN Security Council unanimously adopted a resolution (465—*see* Documents on Palestine, p. 87) calling upon Israel to "dismantle the existing settlements" and "to cease, on an urgent basis, the establishment, construction and planning" of new ones. Two days later President Carter astonished the international community by retracting the affirmative American vote and announcing that it had been a mistake. The U.S. vote, he said, had been "approved with the understanding that all references to Jerusalem would be deleted", and he added: "While our opposition to the establishment of the Israeli settlements is long-standing and well-known . . . the call for dismantling was neither proper nor practical." This retraction, which was criticized even by America's allies, was widely seen as a surrender to the Zionist lobby by an American President needing votes in an election year.

As the autonomy negotiations continued to show little hope of success, the countries of the EEC began to look for new ways to break the deadlock. One idea that received support was the suggestion that Resolution 242 should be broadened in order to include a reference to the right of self-determination for the Palestinians. In February, during a visit to Bahrain, the Foreign Minister of Ireland recognized the PLO and called for the establishment of a Palestinian state. In the course of an important tour of the Middle East in the following month, President Giscard d'Estaing of France supported the principle of self-determination for the Palestinians and spoke of the need to include the PLO in peace negotiations. In April the PLO diplomatic success in Europe continued when Chancellor Kreisky of Austria officially recognized the PLO as the representative of the Palestinian people.

The United States, while still preoccupied with the Iran crisis, made it clear that it disapproved of European attempts to intervene in the peace process. In March President Carter, under attack from the other presidential candidates for his inept handling of the Security Council vote, decided to make yet another attempt to close the gap between Israel and Egypt. Although the two countries had exchanged ambassadors and some successes had been achieved on bilateral relations, their positions on the autonomy issue were still as far apart as ever. Determined to register some achievement on the matter before May 26th (the target date for the completion of the autonomy talks), Carter invited President Sadat and Mr. Begin to visit him separately in Washington during April. No progress was achieved and at the beginning of May President Sadat announced that Egypt was postponing the negotiations indefinitely. Later in the month Egyptian politicians declared that they were laying down no conditions for the resumption of talks except for one: the negotiations must be held in good faith. Israel, they claimed, was clearly not acting in good faith and, as examples, they pointed to Israel's new settlement plans (which this time included the Gaza Strip as well as the West Bank) and to a bill being debated by the Knesset which aimed to proclaim Jerusalem as Israel's indivisible capital. The Egyptians were further angered by Mr. Begin's announcement on June 23rd that he would be moving the Prime Minister's offices to East Jerusalem. Egypt's Vice-President, Hosni Mubarak, reacted by saying that the only thing Mr. Begin had managed to accomplish so far in implementing the peace treaty was to put up obstacles impeding a solution of the overall conflict in the Middle East.

THE EUROPEAN INITIATIVE

Despite the opposition of Israel, Egypt and the United States, the EEC countries finally produced their much-heralded Middle East statement at a meeting in Venice on June 13th. After criticism from the new American Secretary of State, Edmund Muskie, and a blunt warning from President Carter that the U.S. would not hesitate to use its veto in the Security Council, the Europeans decided to drop any attempt to introduce a new resolution on Palestinian rights at the UN. However, they did go further than ever before in their support of Palestinian aspirations.

The statement was inevitably a compromise between those countries, such as Denmark and the Netherlands, which merely wished to repeat previous EEC declarations on the Middle East and those, such as France and Italy, which would like to have called for the "participation" of the PLO in peace negotiations. In the event, the EEC broke new ground on two important issues. It declared, for the first time collectively, that the Palestinian people must be allowed "to exercise fully its right to self-determination", and it called for the PLO "to be associated with the negotiations". It also repeated its condemnations of Israeli settlements and any attempt to change the status of Jerusalem. Finally, the European leaders announced their intention of sending a fact-finding mission to the Middle East "to make the necessary contacts with all the parties concerned— and in the light of the results of this consultation process to determine the form which such an initiative on their part could take".

EGYPTIAN-ISRAELI RELATIONS

The negotiations over Palestinian autonomy, which President Sadat had postponed in May, were re-opened at the beginning of July in Washington. However, the optimism contained in the opening statements of the two countries was soon dispelled and the positions of the parties remained as far apart as ever. The Egyptians still vigorously opposed Mr. Begin's hardline policies on Jerusalem and the West Bank and it appears that President Sadat decided to resume the talks only in order to increase the chances of President Carter in the forthcoming American elections.

Meanwhile the so-called 'normalization' of relations between Egypt and Israel was moving forward at a slow pace. Although both countries had established embassies in each other's capitals and there were regular air-flights between the two, agreements on matters such as tourism, trade and communications were taking a long time to implement. The Israelis accused Egypt of causing delays and it seems probable that the Egyptians, irritated by the failure of the autonomy talks and by the behaviour of Israeli's hardline ambassador to Cairo, Eliahu ben Elissar, were consciously slowing down the process of 'normalization'.

WEST BANK NATIONALISM

Only a month after the Mayors of Hebron and Halhul had been deported by the Israeli authorities, Jewish extremists placed bombs in the cars of three other West Bank mayors. Two of them were severely injured, including Bassam Shaka, the Mayor of Nablus, who lost both his legs in the explosion. The outrage revealed the existence of a militant underground movement among the Jewish settlers in the West Bank. During the following weeks the movement emerged to issue death threats to Arabs and moderate Israelis, including Knesset members and prominent journalists. Tension in the area increased as leading Palestinians, including Mayor Shaka, accused the Israeli Government of having links with the extremists. The Government's failure to investigate the crime properly, and an Israeli journalist's allegation that the head of the Shin Beth (Israel's general security services) had resigned because Mr. Begin had refused to allow him to carry out an investigation of *Gush Emunim* members, gave some substance to these suspicions.

The consequent unrest in the West Bank was countered by an Israeli clampdown on Arab activities. In October the military governor confirmed the deportation orders on the Mayors of Hebron and Halhul, while 33 other mayors and political leaders were served with orders preventing them from leaving their towns. The military also closed down Ramallah's Orthodox Club and its art gallery and suspended its theatre group. In December, after Bir Zeit University (on the outskirts of Ramallah) had been closed down for holding a "Palestine Week", Palestinian students and schoolchildren took part in demonstrations in Ramallah, al-Bireh and Bethlehem. Israeli soldiers reacted by shooting at the legs of the demonstrators and causing ten of them to be treated in hospital for bullet wounds. When the demonstrations spread to Nablus and Jerusalem a few days later, a further six students were shot and wounded.

PARTY RIVALRY IN ISRAEL

Public opinion polls in Israel had long been predicting a disastrous defeat for Mr. Begin's Government at the next election and the only questions remaining seemed to concern the date of the election, which had to be held before November 1981, and the size of the Labour Party's victory. Likud's unpopularity stemmed largely from its failure to solve the country's economic problems, which now included an inflation rate of about 150 per cent, but during the early months of 1981 attention in Israel and abroad was focused on the parties' different policies towards the Occupied Territories.

For electoral and other reasons, the Labour Party refused to define too closely its policy towards the

West Bank but it emphasized that it did not plan to annex the area and its inhabitants. The Labour leader, Shimon Peres, seemed to favour the so-called "Jordanian option", involving the return of the populated areas to Jordan but the retention of the Jordan Valley and various blocks of settlements. Although King Hussein of Jordan repeatedly declared that the "Jordanian option" did not exist and that he was not empowered to speak for the Palestinians, Labour politicians continued to think in terms of a partition of the West Bank.

This policy, however, was totally opposed by the Likud Government, which was determined to make it impossible to implement. In the months before the election, now to be held in June 1981, the Likud decided to launch a vast new settlement programme which an incoming Labour government would be unable to dismantle. Despite criticism from the World Jewish Congress, which issued a document saying that Israel's settlement policy reflected "extremely parochial obtuseness", the Minister of Agriculture, Ariel Sharon, put forward plans to build ten new settlements in the West Bank and twelve smaller ones along the Israel-West Bank border, as well as to erect more permanent housing in the settlements that already existed. While these plans were being accepted by the Cabinet, thousands of acres of Arab land were being expropriated to cater for them.

THE EUROPEAN ROLE

As a consequence of the Venice Declaration, Mr. Gaston Thorn, the president-elect of the EEC Commission, was sent in August on a fact-finding tour of the Middle East. He visited eight Arab countries and Israel, where he had an acrimonious meeting with Mr. Begin, who claimed that the European initiative was a recipe for "the eventual destruction of Israel". Mr. Thorn received greater encouragement in the Arab countries, particularly in Jordan, Kuwait and Saudi Arabia, and in Beirut he met the PLO chairman, Yasser Arafat.

The outbreak of the Gulf war in September 1980 and the campaign for the American presidential election put a temporary break on European moves but at a summit meeting in Luxembourg in December the EEC heads of government discussed a secret document putting forward a number of possible solutions to the Arab-Israeli conflict. The Dutch Foreign Minister, Christoph van der Klaauw, was asked to discuss these proposals with the parties involved and in March 1981 he visited Syria, Jordan and Iraq. The European countries believed that the instability of the Middle East could be cured only by a just solution to the Palestinian question and remained pledged to try to bring this about. Nevertheless they found themselves increasingly hampered by the negative attitude of the new administration in Washington and by the deep divisions in the Arab world which followed the Iran-Iraq war.

REAGAN IN THE WHITE HOUSE

The election of Ronald Reagan as President of the United States was greeted enthusiastically in Israel but caused dismay in the Arab world, particularly in Egypt, where President Sadat had been hoping that a re-elected President Carter would be strong enough to pressure the Israelis into making concessions in the autonomy talks. During the campaign Mr. Reagan had been making pro-Israeli statements that seemed excessive even for an American presidential candidate and his early appointments reflected the influence of his team of Zionist advisers. Many of the new jobs in the State Department and elsewhere went to people who had little experience of the Middle East or else were known to have strong pro-Israeli inclinations. Nearly all of them shared the feelings of the new Secretary of State, Alexander Haig, and the National Security Adviser, Richard Allen, who judged the Arab-Israeli conflict not on its merits but in terms of the East-West confrontation. The gloom in the Arab world was increased by Dr. Henry Kissinger's return to the Middle East on an unofficial visit in January 1981, where he contemptuously dismissed the European initiative, and by the new President's own apparent ignorance of the issues. In an interview soon after taking office, Mr. Reagan declared that the Israeli settlements were "not illegal", thereby contradicting what had long been official American policy.

During its first months of office the administration made it clear that it regarded the European initiative as a hindrance to its own efforts in the Middle East. America's main preoccupation was not with the Palestinian question, which it regarded as rather peripheral, but with the threat which it believed the Soviet Union posed to the oil-rich Gulf. To counter this threat, the Americans busied themselves with the creation of a rapid deployment force able to intervene where necessary in the Gulf area. Although the Gulf Arabs denied that any such threat existed and declared that they opposed the establishment of such a force, the Americans went ahead with their plans for bases in Oman, Somalia and Kenya. In April Mr. Haig set off on a visit to Egypt, Israel, Jordan and Saudi Arabia, intent on convincing the conservative Arab regimes of the Soviet danger.

The Secretary of State's visit to the Middle East, which was somewhat overshadowed by the crisis in Poland, could not be counted as a major success from the American point of view. Both Jordan and Saudi Arabia, two of the United States' closest allies in the Arab world, showed themselves to be highly sceptical about the Reagan administration's new priorities in the area. Neither accepted the American thesis on the alleged Soviet threat and a Jordanian spokesman declared that King Hussein believed it was Israeli intransigence rather than Russian policy which "opened the door to turbulence, instability and other problems". Syria, the PLO and other forces in the region were even more outspoken in their criticism of American policies and Mr. Haig was left in no doubt that the Arabs were reluctant to listen to U.S. allegations about the intentions of the Soviet Union while nothing was being done to solve the problems caused by Israeli occupation of their lands.

THE LEBANESE ERUPTION

At the beginning of March 1981 the Syrian and Lebanese Governments made an important agreement to send regular units of the Lebanese army to join UNIFIL forces in southern Lebanon. This move was strongly opposed by the Israeli-backed Lebanese rebel leader, Sa'ad Haddad, whose troops subsequently opened fire on the UNIFIL positions, killing three Nigerian soldiers. It was in response to this action and to attempts by the Phalangist militia to strengthen its positions around the Lebanese town of Zahle that Syrian troops of the Arab Deterrent Force moved against the Maronite positions in central Lebanon.

In early April Lebanon saw its most serious fighting since the civil war had been "officially" terminated in 1976. The battles around Zahle were followed by fighting in Beirut and Baalbek and in the south between Haddad's forces and the Palestinians. Although a truce held during the week leading up to Easter, Israel launched a series of air-attacks, commando raids and long-range artillery barrages against the south. Renewed fighting broke out between the Syrians and the Phalangists on April 27th and the following day the Israeli air force intervened and shot down two Syrian helicopters. It was as a reaction to this attack that Syria deployed a number of Sam-6 anti-aircraft missiles to defend its positions in the Bekaa valley.

THE SYRIAN MISSILE CRISIS

Although the Syrian missiles were by definition defensive and were stationed deep inside Lebanon far from the Israeli border, the government in Jerusalem demanded their immediate removal. Mr. Begin, who was widely suspected of taking an extreme line in order to enhance his electoral prospects, said that the missiles would have to be withdrawn because they limited Israel's ability to fly over its northern neighbour. Later he admitted that he had planned to destroy the missile site but had been persuaded by the Americans to wait while they tried to defuse the crisis by diplomatic methods.

Mr. Philip Habib, who was accordingly despatched to the region by President Reagan, made a series of visits to Jerusalem and Damascus during May to try to work out a compromise formula that would satisfy both sides. He also attempted to persuade Saudi Arabia to encourage the Syrians to modify their position. The Saudis instead decided to begin a round of inter-Arab negotiations aimed at reaching agreement on the main points of a comprehensive Lebanese settlement which would then make it easier to solve the crisis caused by the missiles. The settlement envisaged would be based on the conclusions of the Beiteddine conference of 1978 with provisions for the future relations between the Lebanese factions, between Syria and Lebanon, and between the Palestinians and the Lebanese Government. Meanwhile, inter-Arab relations, which had deteriorated badly since the beginning of the Iraq-Iran war, improved and at a meeting of the Arab Foreign Ministers, in Tunis on May 23rd, Syria received the almost unanimous backing of the Arab world.

Any chance that the Syrians might climb down and accept some formula offered by the Americans was quickly destroyed by a new wave of Israeli attacks on Lebanon and by the further demands of Mr. Begin. The Israeli Prime Minister was now insisting on the removal of anti-aircraft missiles inside Syria itself and a Syrian promise not to fire at Israeli aeroplanes while they were "patrolling" Lebanon. As Mr. Habib returned once more to the Middle East in the middle of June, Mr. Begin warned that, if the Americans were unable to get the missiles withdrawn through diplomacy, the Israelis would get them out by force.

ISRAEL ATTACKS IRAQ

With the Syrian missile crisis still unresolved, the Israelis surprised the world, including their American allies, with an air attack on Iraq. On June 7th Israeli F-16 bombers destroyed the Iraqi nuclear plant near Baghdad, killing, among others, a French scientist. Mr. Begin immediately claimed that the attack was justified on grounds of self-defence and that Iraq would soon have had the capacity to produce nuclear bombs. However, the International Atomic Energy Agency (IAEA) in Vienna, which had recently inspected the plant, said that Iraq would not have had the means to make nuclear weapons for many years, a view that was also held by the Congressional research service in Washington. The IAEA pointed out that Iraq, unlike Israel, was a signatory of the Nuclear Non-Proliferation Treaty and that it had co-operated with the agency over safeguards.

The raid was criticized instantly by governments all over the world, including the administration of the newly-elected French president, François Mitterand. In the UN Security Council Britain and France demanded a "firm resolution" condemning Israel. Even the Israeli opposition leader, Shimon Peres, attacked Mr. Begin, accusing him of "acting out of electoral considerations which ignore the national interest". To this and other criticism, Mr. Begin merely replied that he would repeat the raid if and when it became necessary.

In the United States the action was immediately condemned by the State Department but it soon became clear that the American reaction was more ambivalent than the rest of the world's. As a gesture of official disapproval, President Reagan decided to suspend the delivery of four F-16 aircraft to Israel until the U.S. Congress had had time to consider whether or not Israel had violated an agreement whereby American weapons were sold on condition they were not used in "an act of aggression against any other state". Nevertheless, the President made clear that his own sympathies were with Israel when he stated, at his first press conference since an attempt on his life in March, that Israel had "reason for concern" about Iraq's nuclear capacity and that it "might have sincerely believed [the bombing] was a defensive move".

BEGIN RETAINS POWER

The Israeli general elections, which took place on June 30th, 1981, were the most violent in the country's history. The campaign was characterized by the Prime Minister's demagogic performances in front of huge crowds and by the physical attacks of his Likud supporters against members and property of the opposition Labour Party. Mr. Begin's vigorous and aggressive foreign policy managed to obscure his Government's failures on the domestic and economic fronts and, in the elections, the Labour Party failed to gain the huge victory which had earlier been predicted. The results showed the two main parties to be evenly balanced, but it was soon clear that the Prime Minister would remain in power if he was able to persuade the various religious parties to join him in a coalition. This was eventually achieved, after lengthy bargaining, and a new cabinet emerged that was more homogeneous and hard-line than its predecessor. The most significant appointment was that of Ariel Sharon, one of Israel's leading "hawks", to the Defence Ministry.

Ten days after the elections, Israel launched a series of air strikes against Palestinian targets in southern Lebanon. Guerrillas belonging to the PLO retaliated immediately with rocket and artillery attacks against settlements in Galilee and the Israelis responded with yet more air strikes and with raids by sea-borne commandos. This time the targets included urban areas and in one strike against Beirut on July 17th more than 150 people were killed and 600 wounded. The international community was shocked by the action and the United States reacted by suspending the delivery of F-16 aircraft to Israel and by making intensive attempts to bring about a ceasefire. While President Reagan's special envoy, Philip Habib, was trying to persuade the Israelis to accept a truce, Saudi Arabia was putting similar pressure on the Palestinians. A ceasefire finally came into effect on July 24th.

THE DEATH OF SADAT

At the beginning of August President Sadat of Egypt visited Washington for the first time since the beginning of the Reagan administration. Although the United States did not accept his suggestion that it was time for the Americans to talk to the PLO, the visit was considered to be a diplomatic success. Yet, for all his activity abroad and his popularity in the West, Sadat was facing major problems inside Egypt.

During the summer there had been serious clashes between Copts and Muslim fundamentalists in which several dozen people had been killed. Shortly after his return from Washington, Sadat decided on a massive clampdown. At the beginning of September some 1,700 people were arrested, a number of newspapers closed down and several foreign journalists expelled. Among those arrested were a large number of the President's political opponents who were neither Copts nor Muslim fundamentalists, and their arrest suggested that Sadat was using the religious clashes as an excuse to mount an intensive purge of the opposition. A month after the arrests, however, President Sadat was assassinated by Muslim extremists at a military parade in Cairo. The large Western attendance at the funeral, which included three former American Presidents, provided a strong contrast with the lack of grief shown on the streets of the capital and indicated how much Sadat's popularity in his own country had declined as a result of his pro-Western stance in foreign policy.

EUROPE AND THE FAHD PLAN

In July 1981 the British Foreign Secretary, Lord Carrington, became President of the EEC Council of Ministers and thus effectively in charge of Europe's peace initiative on the Middle East. He himself had clear ideas on the shape of a future settlement but his position was made difficult by the return of the Likud to power in Israel and by the fact that neither of the new administrations in Washington and Paris had yet revealed their own policies on the Middle East.

The major diplomatic initiative of the second half of 1981 came, in fact, not from Europe but from Saudi Arabia. This was contained in the "Fahd Plan", a programme of eight points put forward by Crown Prince Fahd. Although the United States reacted cautiously to the plan, European foreign ministers called it "extremely positive" and particularly welcomed Point Seven which, by guaranteeing "the right of all states in the region to live in peace", indicated that the Saudis were prepared to recognize Israel in return for a complete withdrawal from the occupied territories and the establishment of an independent Palestinian state.

Although Mr. Begin characteristically described the Fahd plan as a recipe for the destruction of Israel, the Europeans were quick to note the similarities between it and their own Venice Declaration of June 1980. At the beginning of November, Lord Carrington went to Saudi Arabia and said in Riyadh that the Fahd proposals, together with the European ideas, could form the basis for a comprehensive Middle East peace. By the end of the year, however, both plans had been virtually abandoned. Europe's initiative was wrecked when the French Foreign Minister, Claude Cheysson, dissociated his Government from it during a visit to Israel. The Saudi plan collapsed, along with the Arab League summit meeting in Fez, at the end of November.

Since its publication in August, the Fahd plan had received a general, if hesitant, welcome in the Arab world. Apart from Libya, no member of the Arab League had rejected it outright and even the PLO chairman, Yasser Arafat, had come out in support. The Saudi delegation went to the Fez summit confident, therefore, that it could win broad support for its proposals. However, a number of Arab states, led by Syria, had been moving against the plan, opposed not so much to its content as to its timing. At Fez the opposition hardened and, rather than indulge in a lengthy public quarrel before the whole world, King Hassan of Morocco acknowledged the summit's failure and closed the meeting only a few hours after its opening.

THE GOLAN ANNEXATION

While international attention was concentrated on the December crisis in Poland, the Israeli Government decided that it was an opportune moment to annex the Syrian Golan Heights. Overruling the more cautious minority in his cabinet, on December 14th Mr. Begin pushed through the Knesset a bill which extended Israeli laws, jurisdiction and administration to the territory Israel had occupied since 1967.

The UN Security Council unanimously condemned the action and gave Israel two weeks to rescind its decision. When the Israeli Government refused to comply, the Security Council reconvened at the beginning of January 1982 in order to study what measures should be taken against Israel. Syria advocated a tough resolution calling for mandatory sanctions under Chapter Seven of the UN Charter but, in a bid to attract wider international support, Jordan introduced a milder resolution calling merely for voluntary sanctions against Israel. However, even the Jordanian resolution was too strong for the U.S.A., which vetoed it, although at the same time it stressed its opposition to the annexation.

THE U.S.A. WITHOUT A POLICY

After more than a year in office, the Reagan administration was still unable to provide any clear outline of its Middle East policy. It had been lukewarm to the Fahd plan and hostile to the European initiative but it had not come up with any ideas of its own. While working somewhat fruitlessly towards a resumption of the autonomy talks between Egypt and Israel, and hoping that the Israeli withdrawal from Sinai in April would take place smoothly, the administration's main concern remained the so-called "Soviet threat". It was primarily for strategic reasons that the United States made its two most important moves in the autumn of 1981: the sale of sophisticated radar aircraft (AWACS) to Saudi Arabia, which was passed by Congress after strong opposition from the Zionist lobby in October, and the signing of a "memorandum of understanding" on defence co-operation with Israel on November 30th. However, this last agreement was short-lived since the U.S.A. suspended it a fortnight later to show its disapproval of Israel's annexation of the Golan Heights, and Mr. Begin reacted to the American move by verbally attacking the U.S.A. and repudiating the memorandum altogether.

The problems of understanding the American position on the Arab-Israeli conflict became more difficult in February 1982 after the U.S. Defence Secretary, Caspar Weinberger, visited Saudi Arabia, Oman and Jordan. After leaving Amman, a "senior official travelling with the Defence Secretary" told journalists that the United States' military policy would not be held "hostage" to Israel and said that Washington was going to "redirect" its military policy in the Middle East away from Israel and to-wards the Arabs. The uproar which these remarks created in Israel and among its supporters in Washington persuaded President Reagan to write to Mr. Begin, assuring him that his administration would maintain "Israel's qualitative technological edge" in military supplies.

ISRAEL WITHDRAWS FROM SINAI

Although President Mubarak of Egypt indicated soon after he succeeded his murdered predecessor that he wanted to improve his country's relations with the rest of the Arab world, it was clear that his immediate goal was the return of the last third of Sinai, which Israel was due to hand back in April 1982. Consequently, he was anxious not to do anything which might offer the Israelis a pretext to continue the occupation. Inside Israel there was much apprehension over the evacuation of Sinai and fears that it might lead to violence within the Jewish population. The right-wing nationalist parties were deeply divided on the issue and many people suspected that Mr. Begin and his Defence Minister, Ariel Sharon, would, in the last resort, refuse to order a withdrawal. From January two of Begin's own Ministers, Rabbi Haim Druckman and Mr. David Shifman, were actively campaigning against withdrawal and the relinquishment of the settlements.

In March, after months of hesitation, the Government finally ordered the army to move in to the Yamit area and evict illegal settlers who had recently entered it. In spite of last-minute problems over the exact positioning of the frontier, which were resolved only a few hours before the actual handover, the withdrawal took place on time on April 25th. In order not to embarrass the Israelis, the Egyptians took over the key points of Rafah and Sharm el-Sheikh with as little pomp as possible.

THE WEST BANK REVOLTS

For several months Israel had been trying to create an "alternative" leadership among the inhabitants of the West Bank which would collaborate in imposing some form of limited autonomy on the Palestinians. With financial aid and military protection from Israel, a small number of "village leagues" were established in a move to counter the radical nationalism of the urban leadership. Although the attempt was largely unsuccessful, it did provoke several of the West Bank's more radical mayors into refusing to collaborate with the Israeli administration. In response, on March 18th, the occupation authorities dismissed the Mayor of El-Bireh, Mr. Ibrahim Tawil, as well as the town's council.

The dismissals caused a three-day strike in East Jerusalem and the rest of the West Bank which was later extended as a result of the harsh manner in which the Israeli army dealt with Palestinian demonstrators. Rioting took place in most West Bank towns and spread to the Gaza Strip. A week after the action taken against the El-Bireh town council, Israel issued summary dismissal orders against the Mayor of Ramallah, Mr. Karim Khalaf, and the Mayor of

Nablus, Mr. Bassam Shaka, both of whom had been crippled in car-bomb attacks by Israeli extremists less than two years earlier. These further dismissals provoked more clashes in the Occupied Territories. After two weeks of the worst rioting the West Bank had yet seen, several Palestinians had been killed and about a hundred wounded.

ISRAEL'S INVASION OF LEBANON

On June 4th Arab gunmen in London shot and severely wounded the Israeli ambassador to the U.K. The Israeli Government blamed the PLO for the attack and ordered a massive air strike against Palestinian targets in Lebanon. On the first day there were several hundred casualties, most of them civilians. Palestinian forces reacted by rocket attacks against the settlements in northern Israel in which one person was killed.

In spite of an appeal from the U.S. State Department which urged all parties to refrain from further military action, Israel staged a second air attack on the following day and a few hours later embarked on a full-scale invasion of Lebanon. While the Israeli air force continued its strikes against Beirut and other towns, Israeli ground forces, numbering some 25,000 men, pushed through the UN zone in southern Lebanon and attacked Palestinian positions in Tyre, Sidon and Beaufort Castle. Simultaneously, Israeli units were landed by sea at different points along the Lebanese coast. After three days of fighting, in which several thousand civilians had been killed, the Israelis were within a few miles of Beirut. Most Palestinian positions in the south of the country had been captured but there were still some pockets of

resistance in the towns of Damour and Sidon. In Beirut the Israelis had bombed the PLO headquarters and destroyed much of the neighbouring area, although it had failed to eliminate the Palestinian leadership.

Syria, which had kept some 30,000 troops in Lebanon since its intervention in 1976, tried to avoid being drawn into the war but on the fourth day of the invasion its forces clashed with the advancing Israelis. Although the battles on the ground never became as serious as in the 1973 war, Syria committed its airforce against the Israelis and suffered a heavy defeat. Some sixty aeroplanes were shot down in three days and Syria's anti-aircraft system in the Beka'a valley destroyed. On June 11th, after some heavy diplomatic pressure from the United States, Israel agreed to a ceasefire with Syria. Fighting between the Palestinians and the Israelis, however, continued as Israeli forces tried to encircle PLO guerrillas in Beirut. On June 14th, after heavy fighting, Israeli units captured Beirut airport.

The extent of Israel's invasion even alarmed its major ally, the United States. President Reagan, who was in the middle of a European tour, sent two letters to Mr. Begin warning of "serious consequences" to U.S.-Israeli relations if there were not a prompt withdrawal from Lebanon, and Secretary of State Haig cancelled a visit to Jerusalem because of "insufficient flexibility in the Israeli position". However, the Americans were not prepared to agree to European calls for a formal condemnation of Israel at the NATO summit meeting in Bonn. Nor did they fail to veto a UN Security Council resolution which condemned Israel's failure to withdraw from Lebanon.

The Jerusalem Issue

Michael Adams

(Revised for this and previous editions by DAVID GILMOUR)

The Arab sector of Jerusalem, including the old walled city, was captured during the June War in 1967 by Israeli forces, which went on to occupy all the Jordanian territory lying west of the River Jordan. Theoretically, there was no difference in status between Jerusalem and the rest of the West Bank; both were occupied territory. In practice, the Israelis immediately removed the walls and barriers dividing the western (Israeli) and eastern (Arab) sectors of the city and at the end of June 1967 the Knesset passed legislation incorporating the Arab sector into a reunited Jerusalem under Israeli sovereignty. At the same time the boundaries of the municipal area of Jerusalem were greatly extended, reaching to near Bethlehem in the south and incorporating Kalandia airport (close to Ramallah) in the north.

Faced with Israel's effective annexation of the Arab sector, the General Assembly on July 4th, 1967, ruled, by 99 votes to none, that the annexation was invalid and called on Israel not to take any measures to alter the status of the city. Ten days later the Assembly adopted a second resolution "reiterating" the earlier one and "deploring" Israel's failure to implement it.

Before the first of these resolutions was passed, the Israeli authorities had embarked on a series of structural alterations and demolitions in the Old City of Jerusalem, which aroused strong Arab protests and whose continuation was to lead to considerable international controversy. In clearing the area in front of the Western (Wailing) Wall, they expropriated 50 Arab families at very short notice and demolished their houses, while in the Jewish Quarter they dispossessed a further 200 Arab families. In all, and before the end of June 1967, some 4,000 Arabs in Jerusalem had lost their homes. In some cases, but not all, they were provided with alternative accommodation.

In November 1967 the UN Security Council passed its unanimous resolution number 242 setting out the basis for an overall settlement between Israel and its Arab neighbours. However, it was not until May 1968 that the Security Council passed its first resolution dealing specifically with the Jerusalem issue.

The resolution (No. 252 of May 21st, 1968) deplored Israel's failure to comply with the two General Assembly resolutions of July 4th and 14th, 1967, confirmed that any measures taken by Israel to alter the status of Jerusalem were invalid and called on Israel to rescind all such measures and to refrain from similar action in the future. The effect was only to increase the haste with which the Israelis set about changing the face of the city. Bulldozers had been at work on Mount Scopus since February and soon the first of the new housing estates began to take shape beside the Nablus Road leading northwards out of Jerusalem. In the absence of any progress towards a peace settlement, it became clear that the Israeli Government intended to forestall, by establishing a physical presence in the Arab sector of Jerusalem, any future attempt to challenge their sovereignty over the whole of the municipal area.

Meeting again to consider the question in July 1969, the Security Council adopted, this time by a unanimous vote (in the previous year the United States had abstained from voting on the Jerusalem resolution), an even stronger resolution (No. 267 of July 3rd, 1969). Reaffirming its earlier stand and deploring "the failure of Israel to show any regard" for the previous resolutions both of the General Assembly and of the Security Council, the Council "censured in the strongest terms" all measures taken by Israel to change the status of Jerusalem, confirmed that all such measures were "invalid" and again called on Israel to desist from taking any further action of the same kind. The Israelis formally rejected the resolution and the Israeli Minister of Information stated in Jerusalem that it could not influence the "facts" which had been intentionally created by Israel "after due consideration of the political danger involved".

The situation in Jerusalem itself was further aggravated in August 1969 by a disastrous fire in Al Aqsa mosque, which at first sight appeared to confirm the fears of the Arabs for the safety of the Muslim and Christian shrines in the Old City. Israeli investigations showed that the fire had been caused by a deranged Australian religious fanatic and the Australian was later brought to trial; but from that moment the concern of Muslim communities throughout the world reinforced the Arab sense of grievance at the loss of the Holy city.

In the following year Christian concern also began to make itself felt, especially after the publication of an Israeli "master plan" for the future of Jerusalem. This plan envisaged the doubling of the Jewish population of the city by 1980 and an eventual total population of 900,000. An international conference of town planners, convoked by the Israeli municipal authorities at the end of 1970 to consider the plan, was almost unanimous in condemning its aesthetic implications. Early in 1971 a dispute also developed between the United Nations and the Israeli Government over the intention, announced in the master plan, to build another housing estate in the neighbourhood of Government House, the headquarters in Jerusalem of the United Nations. In March 1971 articles in the official Vatican newspaper *L'Osservatore Romano* and in the English Catholic weekly *The Tablet* revealed the strength of Catholic feeling over developments in the Holy City, and these feelings were strengthened when it became known that in the same month the Israelis had destroyed an Arab village on the hill of Nebi Samwil, north-west of Jerusalem, in preparation for the building on Arab land of yet another housing estate for immigrant Jews.

Israeli opinion was divided over the future of Jerusalem. Only a small minority of Israelis were in favour of relinquishing Israeli sovereignty over the Arab sector of the city, if negotiations for an overall settlement of the Arab-Israeli conflict should ever materialize. In the absence of any sign of such negotiations, the issue remained a hypothetical one and the Israeli Government made no secret of its determination to establish a hold on Jerusalem which would prove unbreakable. A further resolution by the Security Council (No. 298 of September 25th, 1971—*see* Documents on Palestine, p. 74) was rejected as brusquely as the previous ones and even the provision in the resolution that the Secretary-General, "using such instrumentalities as he may choose", should report to the Council within 60 days on the implementation of the resolution, failed to achieve any result since the Secretary-General eventually had to report that he had been unable to execute his mission, for lack of co-operation from the Israeli authorities.

On purely aesthetic grounds, however, many Israelis were disturbed by the physical changes overtaking Jerusalem. Within five years of the June War of 1967 the construction of large housing estates had transformed the appearance of Mount Scopus, where the Old City (and the whole of the Arab sector) was dominated by a row of apartment blocks breaking the historic skyline. There were acute disagreements between the Mayor of Jerusalem and the Ministers of Housing and of Tourism over some of the implications of this building programme, but continuing uncertainty over the prospects for a political settlement with the Arabs gave encouragement to the "activists" in Israel, and the creation of "facts" continued, in Jerusalem as in the rest of the occupied territories, throughout 1972 and most of 1973.

Anxiety over the future of Jerusalem and resentment at the Israelis' treatment both of the Arab population and of the physical fabric of the city played a part in provoking the Arab decision to resort to war in 1973. In particular, these feelings influenced King Faisal to throw Saudi Arabia's weight behind the attempt to enforce Israel's withdrawal from the occupied territories, including Arab Jerusalem. Henceforth the restoration to Arab sovereignty of the Old City became one of the principal conditions demanded by the Arabs for a comprehensive peace settlement with Israel.

Immediately after the October war political and economic conditions in Israel combined to slow down for a time the work of demolition and construction by which the face of the city was being transformed. In the course of 1974, however, the same general pattern as before was maintained, resulting in the steady eviction from the Old City of Arabs whose houses were demolished and replaced by dwellings for Jewish immigrants. Between 1967 and 1977 6,300 Arab residents of Jerusalem were evicted in this way from their homes in the Old City. Protests from the international community, stimulated by anxiety over the continuing exodus from Jerusalem of Christian Arabs, became more frequent but achieved only publicity.

Similar protests over excavations being conducted by the Israeli authorities in the vicinity of Muslim and Christian holy places in the Old City of Jerusalem brought to a head criticisms which had been voiced

for more than five years within UNESCO. Recalling that urgent appeals previously addressed to the Israeli Government to suspend these excavations had been ignored, the Executive Board of UNESCO, in June 1974, voted "to condemn the persistent violation by Israel of the resolutions and decisions adopted by the General Conference and the Executive Board". In its turn the General Conference of UNESCO, meeting in November 1974, condemned Israel's attitude as "contradictory to the aims of the Organization as laid down in its Constitution" and resolved to withhold assistance in the fields of education, science and culture until Israel agreed to respect previous Conference resolutions in the matter.

The attitude previously expressed by both the Security Council and the General Assembly of the United Nations was reaffirmed in subsequent years, despite the failure to obtain the compliance of the Government of Israel with existing resolutions. In a unanimous "consensus statement" adopted on November 11th, 1976, the Security Council "strongly deplored" Israel's actions in the occupied territories, including Jerusalem, required Israel once more to "desist forthwith from any action which tends to alter the status of Jerusalem", and called on her to comply with the terms of the Geneva Convention on the Protection of Civilians in Wartime.

Jerusalem once again became a controversial issue in May 1980, when the ultra-nationalist Israeli Knesset member, Mrs. Geula Cohen, tabled a bill in the Knesset with the object of confirming Jerusalem as Israel's indivisible capital. Despite strong protests from the Egyptian Government, which made it clear that it would not resume the peace negotiations on Palestinian autonomy (*see* The Arab-Israeli Confrontation 1967–81) unless the bill was rejected, it was sent to a Knesset committee. The Egyptians were further antagonized when, on June 23rd, the Israeli Prime Minister, Mr. Begin, announced that he was moving his offices to the Arab sector of Jerusalem. Hosni Mubarak, the Egyptian Vice-President, went so far as to say that the only thing Mr. Begin had managed to accomplish so far in implementing the Egyptian-Israeli peace treaty was to put up obstacles impeding a solution of the overall conflict in the Middle East.

At a time when the United States was desperately trying to produce some compromise on the Jerusalem issue which would enable Israel and Egypt to resume the negotiations, the Knesset's legal committee voted in favour of giving a first reading of the bill confirming the annexed status of the Arab sector of Jerusalem. As the authoress of the bill told *The Times* of London on June 30th: "This Bill is designed to ensure that there will never be any compromise over the sovereignty of Jerusalem."

Nevertheless, a debate taking place in the UN Security Council on the same day made it clear that this view would not be accepted by the international community. In a vote of fourteen to none, with only the United States abstaining, the Security Council passed a resolution denying Israel the right either to change the status of Jerusalem or to declare the city to be its capital.

The action of the Security Council was followed by an emergency resolution in the UN General Assembly on July 29th, which called upon Israel to withdraw completely and unconditionally from all territories occupied in 1967, including Jerusalem. The resolution (ES-7/2) was passed by 112 votes to 7, with 24 abstentions. The following day Israel enacted its "basic law" proclaiming Jerusalem as its eternal capital.

The Arab reaction to this law was swift and on August 6th Saudi Arabia and Iraq, the Middle East's two largest oil exporters, announced that they would break off economic and diplomatic relations with any country which recognized Jerusalem as Israel's capital. A fortnight later the Security Council adopted Resolution 478, which declared Israel's enactment of the "basic law" to be a violation of international law and urged "those states that have

established diplomatic missions in Jerusalem to withdraw such missions from the Holy City". The resolution was passed by 14 votes to none, with the United States abstaining. In his speech during the debate the American Secretary of State, Edmund Muskie, berated the council for passing a "series of unbalanced and unrealistic resolutions on Middle East issues".

Shortly afterwards those Latin American countries with embassies in Jerusalem announced that they would be moving them to Tel-Aviv. They were Venezuela, Uruguay, Chile, Ecuador, El Salvador, Costa Rica, Haiti, Panama, Colombia and Bolivia. The only European country which retained its ambassador in Jerusalem, the Netherlands, also decided to move to Tel-Aviv, a decision approved by an overwhelming majority in the Dutch parliament.

Documents on Palestine

DECLARATION OF FIRST WORLD ZIONIST CONGRESS

The Congress, convened in Basle by Dr. Theodor Herzl in August 1897, adopted the following programme:*

The aim of Zionism is to create for the Jewish people a home in Palestine secured by public law.

The Congress contemplates the following means to the attainment of this end:

1. The promotion on suitable lines, of the settlement of Palestine by Jewish agriculturists, artisans and tradesmen.

2. The organization and binding together of the whole of Jewry by means of appropriate institutions, local and general, in accordance with the laws of each country.

3. The strengthening of Jewish sentiment and national consciousness.

4. Preparatory steps towards obtaining government consent as are necessary, for the attainment of the aim of Zionism.

McMAHON CORRESPONDENCE†

Ten letters passed between Sir Henry McMahon, British High Commissioner in Cairo, and Sherif Husain of Mecca from July 1915 to March 1916. Husain offered Arab help in the war against the Turks if Britain would support the principle of an independent Arab state. The most important letter is that of October 24th, 1915, from McMahon to Husain:

. . . I regret that you should have received from my last letter the impression that I regarded the question of limits and boundaries with coldness and hesitation; such was not the case, but it appeared to me that the time had not yet come when that question could be discussed in a conclusive manner.

I have realized, however, from your last letter that you regard this question as one of vital and urgent importance. I have, therefore, lost no time in informing the Government of Great Britain of the contents of your letter, and it is with great pleasure that I communicate to you on their behalf the following statement, which I am confident you will receive with satisfaction:

The two districts of Mersina and Alexandretta and portions of Syria lying to the west of the districts of Damascus, Homs, Hama and Aleppo cannot be said to be purely Arab, and should be excluded from the limits demanded.

With the above modification, and without prejudice to our existing treaties with Arab chiefs, we accept those limits.

---

* Text supplied by courtesy of Josef Fraenkel.

† British White Paper, Cmd. 5957, 1939.

As for those regions lying within those frontiers wherein Great Britain is free to act without detriment to the interests of her ally, France, I am empowered in the name of the Government of Great Britain to give the following assurances and make the following reply to your letter:

(1) Subject to the above modifications, Great Britain is prepared to recognize and support the independence of the Arabs in all the regions within the limits demanded by the Sherif of Mecca.

(2) Great Britain will guarantee the Holy Places against all external aggression and will recognize their inviolability.

(3) When the situation admits, Great Britain will give to the Arabs her advice and will assist them to establish what may appear to be the most suitable forms of government in those various territories.

(4) On the other hand, it is understood that the Arabs have decided to seek the advice and guidance of Great Britain only, and that such European advisers and officials as may be required for the formation of a sound form of administration will be British.

(5) With regard to the *vilayets* of Bagdad and Basra, the Arabs will recognize that the established position and interests of Great Britain necessitate special administrative arrangements in order to secure these territories from foreign aggression, to promote the welfare of the local populations and to safeguard our mutual economic interests.

I am convinced that this declaration will assure you beyond all possible doubt of the sympathy of Great Britain towards the aspirations of her friends the Arabs and will result in a firm and lasting alliance, the immediate results of which will be the expulsion of the Turks from the Arab countries and the freeing of the Arab peoples from the Turkish yoke, which for so many years has pressed heavily upon them. . . .

ANGLO-FRANCO-RUSSIAN AGREEMENT (SYKES—PICOT AGREEMENT)

April-May 1916

The allocation of portions of the Ottoman empire by the three powers was decided between them in an exchange of diplomatic notes. The Anglo-French agreement‡ dealing with Arab territories became known to Sherif Husain only after publication by the new Bolshevik government of Russia in 1917:

1. That France and Great Britain are prepared to recognize and protect an independent Arab State or a Confederation of Arab States in the areas (A) and (B)

---

‡ E. L. Woodward and Rohan Butler (Eds.). *Documents on British Foreign Policy 1919–1939.* First Series, Vol. IV, 1919. London, H.M.S.O., 1952.

marked on the annexed map, under the suzerainty of an Arab Chief. That in area (A) France, and in area (B) Great Britain shall have priority of right of enterprises and local loans. France in area (A) and Great Britain in area (B) shall alone supply foreign advisers or officials on the request of the Arab State or the Confederation of Arab States.

2. France in the Blue area and Great Britain in the Red area shall be at liberty to establish direct or indirect administration or control as they may desire or as they may deem fit to establish after agreement with the Arab State or Confederation of Arab States.

3. In the Brown area there shall be established an international administration of which the form will be decided upon after consultation with Russia, and after subsequent agreement with the other Allies and the representatives of the Sherif of Mecca.

4. That Great Britain be accorded

    (a) The ports of Haifa and Acre;

    (b) Guarantee of a given supply of water from the Tigris and the Euphrates in area (A) for area (B).

His Majesty's Government, on their part, undertake that they will at no time enter into negotiations for the cession of Cyprus to any third Power without the previous consent of the French Government.

5. Alexandretta shall be a free port as regards the trade of the British Empire and there shall be no discrimination in treatment with regard to port dues or the extension of special privileges affecting British shipping and commerce; there shall be freedom of transit for British goods through Alexandretta and over railways through the Blue area, whether such goods are going to or coming from the Red area, area (A) or area (B); and there shall be no differentiation in treatment, direct or indirect, at the expense of British goods on any railway or of British goods and shipping in any port serving the areas in question.

Haifa shall be a free port as regards the trade of France, her colonies and protectorates, and there shall be no differentiation in treatment or privilege with regard to port dues against French shipping and commerce. There shall be freedom of transit through Haifa and over British railways through the Brown area, whether such goods are coming from or going to the Blue area, area (A) or area (B), and there shall be no differentiation in treatment, direct or indirect, at the expense of French goods on any railway or of French goods and shipping in any port serving the areas in question.

6. In area (A), the Baghdad Railway shall not be extended southwards beyond Mosul, and in area (B), it shall not be extended northwards beyond Samarra, until a railway connecting Baghdad with Aleppo along the basin of the Euphrates will have been completed, and then only with the concurrence of the two Governments.

7. Great Britain shall have the right to build, administer and be the sole owner of the railway connecting Haifa with area (B). She shall have, in addition, the right in perpetuity and at all times of carrying troops on that line. It is understood by both Governments that this railway is intended to facilitate communication between Baghdad and Haifa, and it is further understood that, in the event of technical difficulties and expenditure incurred in the maintenance of this line in the Brown area rendering the execution of the project impracticable, the French Government will be prepared to consider plans for enabling the line in question to traverse the polygon formed by Banias-Umm Qais-Salkhad-Tall 'Osda-Mismieh before reaching area (B).

8. For a period of twenty years, the Turkish customs tariff shall remain in force throughout the Blue and Red areas as well as in areas (A) and (B), and no increase in the rates of duties and no alteration of *ad valorem* duties into specific duties shall be made without the consent of the two Powers.

There shall be no internal customs barriers between any of the areas mentioned above. The customs duties to be levied on goods destined for the interior shall be collected at the ports of entry and remitted to the Administration of the area of destination.

9. It is understood that the French Government will at no time initiate any negotiations for the cession of their rights and will not cede their prospective rights in the Blue area to any third Power other than the Arab State or Confederation of Arab States, without the previous consent of His Majesty's Government who, on their part, give the French Government a similar undertaking in respect of the Red area.

10. The British and French Governments shall agree to abstain from acquiring and to withold their consent to a third Power acquiring territorial possessions in the Arabian Peninsula; nor shall they consent to the construction by a third Power of a naval base in the islands on the eastern seaboard of the Red Sea. This, however, will not prevent such rectification of the Aden boundary as might be found necessary in view of the recent Turkish attack.

11. The negotiations with the Arabs concerning the frontiers of the Arab State or Confederation of Arab States shall be pursued through the same channel as heretofore in the name of the two Powers.

12. It is understood, moreover, that measures for controlling the importation of arms into the Arab territory will be considered by the two Governments.

BALFOUR DECLARATION

November 2nd, 1917

Balfour was British Foreign Secretary, Rothschild the British Zionist leader.

Dear Lord Rothschild,

I have much pleasure in conveying to you on behalf of His Majesty's Government the following declaration of sympathy with Jewish Zionist aspirations, which has been submitted to and approved by the Cabinet.

"His Majesty's Government view with favour the establishment in Palestine of a national home for the Jewish people, and will use their best endeavours to facilitate the achievement of this object, it being clearly understood that nothing shall be done which may prejudice the civil and religious rights of existing non-Jewish communities in Palestine, or the rights and political status enjoyed by Jews in any other country."

I should be grateful if you would bring this declaration to the knowledge of the Zionist Federation.

Yours sincerely,

Arthur James Balfour.

HOGARTH MESSAGE*

January 4th, 1918

The following is the text of a message which Commander D. G. Hogarth, C.M.G., R.N.V.R., of the Arab Bureau in Cairo, was instructed on January 4th, 1918, to deliver to King Husain of the Hejaz at Jeddah:

1. The *Entente* Powers are determined that the Arab race shall be given full opportunity of once again forming a nation in the world. This can only be achieved by the Arabs themselves uniting, and Great Britain and her Allies will pursue a policy with this ultimate unity in view.

2. So far as Palestine is concerned, we are determined that no people shall be subject to another, but—

   (a) In view of the fact that there are in Palestine shrines, Wakfs and Holy places, sacred in some cases to Moslems alone, to Jews alone, to Christians alone, and in others to two or all three, and inasmuch as these places are of interest to vast masses of people outside Palestine and Arabia, there must be a special régime to deal with these places approved of by the world.

   (b) As regards the Mosque of Omar, it shall be considered as a Moslem concern alone, and shall not be subjected directly or indirectly to any non-Moslem authority.

3. Since the Jewish opinion of the world is in favour of a return of Jews to Palestine, and inasmuch as this opinion must remain a constant factor, and, further, as His Majesty's Government view with favour the realization of this aspiration, His Majesty's Government are determined that in so far as is compatible with the freedom of the existing population, both economic and political, no obstacle should be put in the way of the realization of this ideal.

In this connection the friendship of world Jewry to the Arab cause is equivalent to support in all States where Jews have political influence. The leaders of the movement are determined to bring about the success of Zionism by friendship and co-operation with the Arabs, and such an offer is not one to be lightly thrown aside.

ANGLO-FRENCH DECLARATION†

November 7th, 1918

The object aimed at by France and Great Britain in prosecuting in the East the war let loose by the ambition of Germany is the complete and definite emancipation of the peoples so long oppressed by the Turks and the establishment of national Governments and Administrations deriving their authority from the initiative and free choice of the indigenous populations.

In order to carry out these intentions France and Great Britain are at one in encouraging and assisting the establishments of indigenous Governments and Administrations in Syria and Mesopotamia, now liberated by the Allies, and in the territories the liberation of which they are engaged in securing and recognizing these as soon as they are actually established.

Far from wishing to impose on the populations of these regions any particular institutions they are only concerned to ensure by their support and by adequate assistance the regular working of Governments and Administrations freely chosen by the populations themselves. To secure impartial and equal justice for all, to facilitate the economic development of the country by inspiring and encouraging local initiative, to favour the diffusion of education, to put an end to dissensions that have too long been taken advantage of by Turkish policy, such is the policy which the two Allied Governments uphold in the liberated territories.

RECOMMENDATIONS OF THE KING—CRANE COMMISSION‡

August 28th, 1919

The Commission was set up by President Wilson of the U.S.A. to determine which power should receive the Mandate for Palestine. The following are extracts from their recommendations on Syria:

1. We recommend, as most important of all, and in strict harmony with our Instructions, that whatever foreign administration (whether of one or more Powers) is brought into Syria, should come in, not at all as a colonising Power in the old sense of that term, but as a Mandatory under the League of Nations with the clear consciousness that 'the well-being and development', of the Syrian people form for it a 'sacred trust'.

2. We recommend, in the second place, that the unity of Syria be preserved, in accordance with the earnest petition of the great majority of the people of Syria.

3. We recommend, in the third place, that Syria be placed under one mandatory Power, as the natural way to secure real and efficient unity.

4. We recommend, in the fourth place, that Amir Faisal be made the head of the new united Syrian State.

5. We recommend, in the fifth place, serious modification of the extreme Zionist programme for Palestine of unlimited immigration of Jews, looking finally to making Palestine distinctly a Jewish State.

---

* British White Paper, Cmd. 5964, 1939.

† Report of a Committee set up to consider Certain Correspondence between Sir Henry McMahon and the Sherif of Mecca in 1915 and 1916, March 16th, 1939 (British White Paper, Cmd. 5974).

‡ U.S. Department of State. *Papers Relating to the Foreign Relations of the United States. The Paris Peace Conference 1919.* Vol. XII. Washington, 1947.

(1) The Commissioners began their study of Zionism with minds predisposed in its favor, but the actual facts in Palestine, coupled with the force of the general principles proclaimed by the Allies and accepted by the Syrians have driven them to the recommendation here made.

(2) The Commission was abundantly supplied with literature on the Zionist program by the Zionist Commission to Palestine; heard in conferences much concerning the Zionist colonies and their claims; and personally saw something of what had been accomplished. They found much to approve in the aspirations and plans of the Zionists, and had warm appreciation for the devotion of many of the colonists, and for their success, by modern methods in overcoming great, natural obstacles.

(3) The Commission recognised also that definite encouragement had been given to the Zionists by the Allies in Mr. Balfour's often-quoted statement, in its approval by other representatives of the Allies. If, however, the strict terms of the Balfour Statement are adhered to—favoring 'the establishment in Palestine of a national home for the Jewish people', 'it being clearly understood that nothing shall be done which may prejudice the civil and religious rights of existing non-Jewish communities in Palestine'—it can hardly be doubted that the extreme Zionist program must be greatly modified. For 'a national home for the Jewish people' is not equivalent to making Palestine into a Jewish State; nor can the erection of such a Jewish State be accomplished without the gravest trespass upon the 'civil and religious rights of existing non-Jewish communities in Palestine'. The fact came out repeatedly in the Commission's conference with Jewish representatives, that the Zionists looked forward to a practically complete dispossession of the present non-Jewish inhabitants of Palestine, by various forms of purchase.

In his address of July 4th, 1918, President Wilson laid down the following principle as one of the four great 'ends for which the associated peoples of the world were fighting': 'The settlement of every question, whether of territory, of sovereignty, of economic arrangement, or of political relationship upon the basis of the free acceptance of that settlement by the people immediately concerned, and not upon the basis of the material interest or advantage of any other nation or people which may desire a different settlement for the sake of its own exterior influence or mastery.' If that principle is to rule, and so the wishes of Palestine's population are to be decisive as to what is to be done with Palestine, then it is to be remembered that the non-Jewish population of Palestine—nearly nine-tenths of the whole—are emphatically against the entire Zionist program. The tables show that there was no one thing upon which the population of Palestine were more agreed than upon this. To subject a people so minded to unlimited Jewish immigration, and to steady financial and social pressure to surrender the land, would be a gross violation of the principle just quoted, and of the people's rights, though it kept within the forms of law.

It is to be noted also that the feeling against the Zionist program is not confined to Palestine, but shared very generally by the people throughout Syria, as our conferences clearly showed. More than 72 per cent—1,350 in all—of all the petitions in the whole of Syria were directed against the Zionist program. Only two requests—those for a united Syria and for independence—had a larger support. This general feeling was duly voiced by the General Syrian Congress in the seventh, eighth and tenth resolutions of their statement.

The Peace Conference should not shut its eyes to the fact that the anti-Zionist feeling in Palestine and Syria is intense and not lightly to be flouted. No British officer, consulted by the Commissioners, believed that the Zionist program could be carried out except by force of arms. The officers generally thought that a force of not less than 50,000 soldiers would be required even to initiate the program. That of itself is evidence of a strong sense of the injustice of the Zionist program, on the part of the non-Jewish populations of Palestine and Syria. Decisions requiring armies to carry out are sometimes necessary, but they are surely not gratuitously to be taken in the interests of serious injustice. For the initial claim, often submitted by Zionist representatives, that they have a 'right' to Palestine, based on an occupation of 2,000 years ago, can hardly be seriously considered.

There is a further consideration that cannot justly be ignored, if the world is to look forward to Palestine becoming a definitely Jewish State, however gradually that may take place. That consideration grows out of the fact that Palestine is the Holy Land for Jews, Christians, and Moslems alike. Millions of Christians and Moslems all over the world are quite as much concerned as the Jews with conditions in Palestine, especially with those conditions which touch upon religious feelings and rights. The relations in these matters in Palestine are most delicate and difficult. With the best possible intentions, it may be doubted whether the Jews could possibly seem to either Christians or Moslems proper guardians of the holy places, or custodians of the Holy Land as a whole.

The reason is this: The places which are most sacred to Christians—those having to do with Jesus— and which are also sacred to Moslems, are not only not sacred to Jews, but abhorrent to them. It is simply impossible, under those circumstances, for Moslems and Christians to feel satisfied to have these places in Jewish hands, or under the custody of Jews. There are still other places about which Moslems must have the same feeling. In fact, from this point of view, the Moslems, just because the sacred places of all three religions are sacred to them, have made very naturally much more satisfactory custodians of the holy places than the Jews could be. It must be believed that the precise meaning in this respect of the complete Jewish occupation of Palestine has not been fully sensed by those who urge the extreme Zionist program. For it would intensify, with a certainty like fate, the anti-Jewish feeling both in Palestine and in all other portions of the world which look to Palestine as the Holy Land.

In view of all these considerations, and with a deep sense of sympathy for the Jewish cause, the Commissioners feel bound to recommend that only a greatly reduced Zionist program be attempted by the Peace Conference, and even that, only very gradually initiated. This would have to mean that Jewish immigration should be definitely limited, and that the project for making Palestine distinctly a Jewish commonwealth should be given up.

There would then be no reason why Palestine could not be included in a united Syrian State, just as other portions of the country, the holy places being cared for by an international and inter-religious commission, somewhat as at present, under the oversight and approval of the Mandatory and of the League of Nations. The Jews, of course, would have representation upon this commission.

ARTICLE 22 OF THE COVENANT OF THE LEAGUE OF NATIONS

1. To those colonies and territories which as a consequence of the late War have ceased to be under the sovereignty of the States which formerly governed them and which are inhabited by peoples not yet able to stand by themselves under the strenuous conditions of the modern world, there should be applied the principle that the well-being and development of such peoples form a sacred trust of civilization and that securities for the performance of this trust should be embodied in this Covenant.

2. The best method of giving practical effect to this principle is that the tutelage of such peoples should be entrusted to advanced nations who by reason of their resources, their experience or their geographical position can best undertake this responsibility, and who are willing to accept it, and that this tutelage should be exercised by them as Mandatories on behalf of the League.

3. The character of the Mandate must differ according to the stage of the development of the people, the geographical situation of the territory, its economic conditions and other similar circumstances.

4. Certain communities formerly belonging to the Turkish Empire have reached a stage of development where their existence as independent nations can be provisionally recognized subject to the rendering of administrative advice and assistance by a Mandatory until such time as they are able to stand alone. The wishes of these communities must be a principal consideration in the selection of the Mandatory.

7. In every case of Mandate, the Mandatory shall render to the Council an annual report in reference to the territory committed to its charge.

8. The degree of authority, control, or administration to be exercised by the Mandatory shall, if not previously agreed upon by the Members of the League, be explicitly defined in each case by the Council.

9. A permanent Commission shall be constituted to receive and examine the annual reports of the Mandatories and to advise the Council on all matters relating to the observance of the Mandates.

MANDATE FOR PALESTINE*
July 24th, 1922

The Council of the League of Nations:

Whereas the Principal Allied Powers have agreed, for the purpose of giving effect to the provisions of Article 22 of the Covenant of the League of Nations to entrust to a Mandatory selected by the said Powers the administration of the territory of Palestine, which formerly belonged to the Turkish Empire, within such boundaries as may be fixed by them; and

Whereas the Principal Allied Powers have also agreed that the Mandatory should be responsible for putting into effect the declaration originally made on November 2nd, 1917, by the Government of His Britannic Majesty, and adopted by the said Powers, in favour of the establishment in Palestine of a National Home for the Jewish people, it being clearly understood that nothing should be done which might prejudice the civil and religious rights of existing non-Jewish communities in Palestine, or the rights and political status enjoyed by Jews in any other country; and

Whereas recognition has thereby been given to the historical connection of the Jewish people with Palestine and to the grounds for reconstituting their National Home in that country; and

Whereas the Principal Allied Powers have selected His Britannic Majesty as the Mandatory for Palestine; and

Whereas the Mandate in respect of Palestine has been formulated in the following terms and submitted to the Council of the League for approval; and

Whereas His Britannic Majesty has accepted the Mandate in respect of Palestine and undertaken to exercise it on behalf of the League of Nations in conformity with the following provisions; and

Whereas by the afore-mentioned Article 22 (paragraph 8), it is provided that the degree of authority, control or administration to be exercised by the Mandatory, not having been previously agreed upon by the Members of the League, shall be explicitly defined by the Council of the League of Nations;

Confirming the said Mandate, defines its terms as follows:

ARTICLE 1. The Mandatory shall have full powers of legislation and of administration, save as they may be limited by the terms of this Mandate.

ARTICLE 2. The Mandatory shall be responsible for placing the country under such political, administrative and economic conditions as will secure the establishment of the Jewish National Home, as laid down in the preamble, and the development of self-governing institutions, and also for safeguarding the civil and religious rights of all the inhabitants of Palestine, irrespective of race and religion.

ARTICLE 3. The Mandatory shall, so far as circumstances permit, encourage local autonomy.

---

* British White Paper, Cmd. 1785.

ARTICLE 4. An appropriate Jewish Agency shall be recognized as a public body for the purpose of advising and co-operating with the Administration of Palestine in such economic, social and other matters as may affect the establishment of the Jewish National Home and the interests of the Jewish population in Palestine, and, subject always to the control of the Administration, to assist and take part in the development of the country.

The Zionist organization, so long as its organization and constitution are in the opinion of the Mandatory appropriate, shall be recognized as such agency. It shall take steps in consultation with His Britannic Majesty's Government to secure the co-operation of all Jews who are willing to assist in the establishment of the Jewish National Home.

ARTICLE 5. The Mandatory shall be responsible for seeing that no Palestine territory shall be ceded or leased to, or in any way placed under the control of, the Government of any foreign Power.

ARTICLE 6. The Administration of Palestine, while ensuring that the rights and position of other sections of the population are not prejudiced, shall facilitate Jewish immigration under suitable conditions and shall encourage, in co-operation with the Jewish Agency referred to in Article 4, close settlement by Jews on the land, including State lands and waste lands not required for public purposes.

ARTICLE 7. The Administration of Palestine shall be responsible for enacting a nationality law. There shall be included in this law provisions framed so as to facilitate the acquisition of Palestinian citizenship by Jews who take up their permanent residence in Palestine.

ARTICLE 13. All responsibility in connection with the Holy Places and religious buildings or sites in Palestine, including that of preserving existing rights and of securing free access to the Holy Places, religious buildings and sites and the free exercise of worship, while ensuring the requirements of public order and decorum, is assumed by the Mandatory, who shall be responsible solely to the League of Nations in all matters connected herewith, provided that nothing in this Article shall prevent the Mandatory from entering into such arrangements as he may deem reasonable with the Administration for the purpose of carrying the provisions of this Article into effect; and provided also that nothing in this Mandate shall be construed as conferring upon the Mandatory authority to interfere with the fabric of the management of purely Moslem sacred shrines, the immunities of which are guaranteed.

ARTICLE 14. A special Commission shall be appointed by the Mandatory to study, define and determine the rights and claims in connection with the Holy Places and the rights and claims relating to the different religious communities in Palestine. The method of nomination, the composition and the functions of this Commission shall be submitted to the Council of the League for its approval, and the Commission shall not be appointed or enter upon its functions without the approval of the Council.

ARTICLE 28. In the event of the termination of the Mandate hereby conferred upon the Mandatory, the Council of the League of Nations shall make such arrangements as may be deemed necessary for safeguarding in perpetuity, under guarantee of the League, the rights secured by Articles 13 and 14, and shall use its influence for securing, under the guarantee of the League, that the Government of Palestine will fully honour the financial obligations legitimately incurred by the Administration of Palestine during the period of the Mandate, including the rights of public servants to pensions or gratuities.

CHURCHILL MEMORANDUM*
June 3rd, 1922

The Secretary of State for the Colonies has given renewed consideration to the existing political situation in Palestine, with a very earnest desire to arrive at a settlement of the outstanding questions which have given rise to uncertainty and unrest among certain sections of the population. After consultation with the High Commissioner for Palestine the following statement has been drawn up. It summarizes the essential parts of the correspondence that has already taken place between the Secretary of State and a Delegation from the Moslem Christian Society of Palestine, which has been for some time in England, and it states the further conclusions which have since been reached.

The tension which has prevailed from time to time in Palestine is mainly due to apprehensions, which are entertained both by sections of the Arab and by sections of the Jewish population. These apprehensions, so far as the Arabs are concerned, are partly based upon exaggerated interpretations of the meaning of the Declaration favouring the establishment of a Jewish National Home in Palestine, made on behalf of His Majesty's Government on November 2nd, 1917. Unauthorized statements have been made to the effect that the purpose in view is to create a wholly Jewish Palestine. Phrases have been used such as that Palestine is to become "as Jewish as England is English." His Majesty's Government regard any such expectation as impracticable and have no such aim in view. Nor have they at any time contemplated, as appears to be feared by the Arab Delegation, the disappearance or the subordination of the Arabic population, language or culture in Palestine. They would draw attention to the fact that the terms of the Declaration referred to do not contemplate that Palestine as a whole should be converted into a Jewish National Home, but that such a Home should be founded *in Palestine*. In this connection it has been observed with satisfaction that at the meeting of the Zionist Congress, the supreme governing body of the Zionist Organization, held at Carlsbad in September 1921, a resolution was passed expressing as the official statement of Zionist aims "the determination of the Jewish people to live with the Arab people on terms

* Palestine, Correspondence with the Palestine Arab Delegation and the Zionist Organization (British White Paper, Cmd. 1700), pp. 17–21.

of unity and mutual respect, and together with them to make the common home into a flourishing community, the upbuilding of which may assure to each of its peoples an undisturbed national development."

It is also necessary to point out that the Zionist Commission in Palestine, now termed the Palestine Zionist Executive, has not desired to possess, and does not possess, any share in the general administration of the country. Nor does the special position assigned to the Zionist Organization in Article IV of the Draft Mandate for Palestine imply any such functions. That special position relates to the measures to be taken in Palestine affecting the Jewish population, and contemplates that the Organization may assist in the general development of the country, but does not entitle it to share in any degree in its Government.

Further, it is contemplated that the status of all citizens of Palestine in the eyes of the law shall be Palestinian, and it has never been intended that they, or any section of them, should possess any other juridical status.

So far as the Jewish population of Palestine are concerned, it appears that some among them are apprehensive that His Majesty's Government may depart from the policy embodied in the Declaration of 1917. It is necessary, therefore, once more to affirm that these fears are unfounded, and that that Declaration, re-affirmed by the Conference of the Principal Allied Powers at San Remo and again in the Treaty of Sèvres, is not susceptible of change.

During the last two or three generations the Jews have recreated in Palestine a community, now numbering 80,000, of whom about one-fourth are farmers or workers upon the land. This community has its own political organs; an elected assembly for the direction of its domestic concerns; elected councils in the towns; and an organization for the control of its schools. It has its elected Chief Rabbinate and Rabbinical Council for the direction of its religious affairs. Its business is conducted in Hebrew as a vernacular language, and a Hebrew Press serves its needs. It has its distinctive intellectual life and displays considerable economic activity. This community, then, with its town and country population, its political, religious and social organizations, its own language, its own customs, its own life, has in fact "national" characteristics. When it is asked what is meant by the development of the Jewish National Home in Palestine, it may be answered that it is not the imposition of a Jewish nationality upon the inhabitants of Palestine as a whole, but the further development of the existing Jewish community, with the assistance of Jews in other parts of the world, in order that it may become a centre in which the Jewish people as a whole may take, on grounds of religion and race, an interest and a pride. But in order that this community should have the best prospect of free development and provide a full opportunity for the Jewish people to display its capacities, it is essential that it should know that it is in Palestine as of right and not on sufferance. That is the reason why it is necessary that the existence of a Jewish National Home in

Palestine should be internationally guaranteed, and that it should be formally recognized to rest upon ancient historic connection.

This, then, is the interpretation which His Majesty's Government place upon the Declaration of 1917, and, so understood, the Secretary of State is of opinion that it does not contain or imply anything which need cause either alarm to the Arab population of Palestine or disappointment to the Jews.

For the fulfilment of this policy it is necessary that the Jewish community in Palestine should be able to increase its numbers by immigration. This immigration cannot be so great in volume as to exceed whatever may be the economic capacity of the country at the time to absorb new arrivals. It is essential to ensure that the immigrants should not be a burden upon the people of Palestine as a whole, and that they should not deprive any section of the present population of their employment. Hitherto the immigration has fulfilled these conditions. The number of immigrants since the British occupation has been about 25,000. . . .

REPORT OF PALESTINE ROYAL COMMISSION PEEL COMMISSION*

July 1937

The Commission under Lord Peel was appointed in 1936. The following are extracts from recommendations made in Ch. XXII:

Having reached the conclusion that there is no possibility of solving the Palestine problem under the existing Mandate (or even under a scheme of cantonization), the Commission recommend the termination of the present Mandate on the basis of Partition and put forward a definite scheme which they consider to be practicable, honourable and just. The scheme is as follows:

The Mandate for Palestine should terminate and be replaced by a Treaty System in accordance with the precedent set in Iraq and Syria.

Under Treaties to be negotiated by the Mandatory with the Government of Transjordan and representatives of the Arabs of Palestine on the one hand, and with the Zionist Organization on the other, it would be declared that two sovereign independent States would shortly be established—(1) an Arab State consisting of Transjordan united with that part of Palestine allotted to the Arabs, (2) a Jewish State consisting of that part of Palestine allotted to the Jews. The Mandatory would undertake to support any requests for admission to the League of Nations made by the Governments of the Arab and Jewish States. The Treaties would include strict guarantees for the protection of minorities. Military Conventions would be attached to the Treaties.

A new Mandate should be instituted to execute the trust of maintaining the sanctity of Jerusalem and Bethlehem and ensuring free and safe access to them

---

* *Palestine Royal Commission: Report*, 1937 (British Blue Book, Cmd. 5479).

for all the world. An enclave should be demarcated to which this Mandate should apply, extending from a point north of Jerusalem to a point south of Bethlehem, and access to the sea should be provided by a corridor extending from Jerusalem to Jaffa. The policy of the Balfour Declaration would not apply to the Mandated Area.

The Jewish State should pay a subvention to the Arab State. A Finance Commission should be appointed to advise as to its amount and as to the division of the public debt of Palestine and other financial questions.

In view of the backwardness of Transjordan, Parliament should be asked to make a grant of £2,000,000 to the Arab State.

WHITE PAPER*

May 1939

The main recommendations are extracted below:

10. . . . His Majesty's Government make the following declaration of their intentions regarding the future government of Palestine:

(i) The objective of His Majesty's Government is the establishment within ten years of an independent Palestine State in such treaty relations with the United Kingdom as will provide satisfactorily for the commercial and strategic requirements of both countries in the future. This proposal for the establishment of the independent State would involve consultation with the Council of the League of Nations with a view to the termination of the Mandate.

(ii) The independent State should be one in which Arabs and Jews share in government in such a way as to ensure that the essential interests of each community are safeguarded.

(iii) The establishment of the independent State will be preceded by a transitional period throughout which His Majesty's Government will retain responsibility for the government of the country. During the transitional period the people of Palestine will be given an increasing part in the government of their country. Both sections of the population will have an opportunity to participate in the machinery of government, and the process will be carried on whether or not they both avail themselves of it.

(iv) As soon as peace and order have been sufficiently restored in Palestine steps will be taken to carry out this policy of giving the people of Palestine an increasing part in the government of their country, the objective being to place Palestinians in charge of all the Departments of Government, with the assistance of British advisers and subject to the control of the High Commissioner. With this object in view His Majesty's Government will be prepared immediately to arrange that Palestinians shall be placed in charge of certain Departments, with British advisers. The Palestinian

heads of Departments will sit on the Executive Council, which advises the High Commissioner. Arab and Jewish representatives will be invited to serve as heads of Departments approximately in proportion to their respective populations. The number of Palestinians in charge of Departments will be increased as circumstances permit until all heads of Departments are Palestinians, exercising the administrative and advisory functions which are at present performed by British officials. When that stage is reached consideration will be given to the question of converting the Executive Council into a Council of Ministers with a consequential change in the status and functions of the Palestinian heads of Departments.

(v) His Majesty's Government make no proposals at this stage regarding the establishment of an elective legislature. Nevertheless they would regard this as an appropriate constitutional development, and, should public opinion in Palestine hereafter show itself in favour of such a development, they will be prepared, provided that local conditions permit, to establish the necessary machinery.

(vi) At the end of five years from the restoration of peace and order, an appropriate body representative of the people of Palestine and of His Majesty's Government will be set up to review the working of the constitutional arrangements during the transitional period and to consider and make recommendations regarding the Constitution of the independent Palestine State.

(vii) His Majesty's Government will require to be satisfied that in the treaty contemplated by sub-paragraph (i) or in the Constitution contemplated by sub-paragraph (vi) adequate provision has been made for:

(a) the security of, and freedom of access to, the Holy Places, and the protection of the interests and property of the various religious bodies;

(b) the protection of the different communities in Palestine in accordance with the obligations of His Majesty's Government to both Arabs and Jews and for the special position in Palestine of the Jewish National Home;

(c) such requirements to meet the strategic situation as may be regarded as necessary by His Majesty's Government in the light of the circumstances then existing.

His Majesty's Government will also require to be satisfied that the interests of certain foreign countries in Palestine, for the preservation of which they are at present responsible, are adequately safeguarded.

(viii) His Majesty's Government will do everything in their power to create conditions which will enable the independent Palestine State to come into being within ten years. If, at the end of ten years, it appears to His Majesty's Government that, contrary to their hope, circumstances require the postponement of the establishment of the independent State, they will consult with representatives

---

* British White Paper, Cmd. 6019.

of the people of Palestine, the Council of the League of Nations and the neighbouring Arab States before deciding on such a postponement. If His Majesty's Government come to the conclusion that postponement is unavoidable, they will invite the co-operation of these parties in framing plans for the future with a view to achieving the desired objective at the earliest possible date.

11. During the transitional period steps will be taken to increase the powers and responsibilities of municipal corporations and local councils.

14. ... they believe that they will be acting consistently with their Mandatory obligations to both Arabs and Jews, and in the manner best calculated to serve the interests of the whole people of Palestine by adopting the following proposals regarding immigration:

(i) Jewish immigration during the next five years will be at a rate which, if economic absorptive capacity permits, will bring the Jewish population up to approximately one-third of the total population of the country. Taking into account the expected natural increase of the Arab and Jewish populations, and the number of illegal Jewish immigrants now in the country, this would allow of the admission, as from the beginning of April this year, of some 75,000 immigrants over the next five years. These immigrants would, subject to the criterion of economic absorptive capacity, be admitted as follows:

(*a*) For each of the next five years a quota of 10,000 Jewish immigrants will be allowed, on the understanding that a shortage in any one year may be added to the quotas for subsequent years, within the five-year period, if economic absorptive capacity permits.

(*b*) In addition, as a contribution towards the solution of the Jewish refugee problem, 25,000 refugees will be admitted as soon as the High Commissioner is satisfied that adequate provision for their maintenance is ensured, special consideration being given to refugee children and dependants.

(ii) The existing machinery for ascertaining economic absorptive capacity will be retained, and the High Commissioner will have the ultimate responsibility for deciding the limits of economic capacity. Before each periodic decision is taken, Jewish and Arab representatives will be consulted.

(iii) After the period of five years no further Jewish immigration will be permitted unless the Arabs of Palestine are prepared to acquiesce in it.

(iv) His Majesty's Government are determined to check illegal immigration, and further preventive measures are being adopted. The numbers of any Jewish illegal immigrants who, despite these measures, may succeed in coming into the country and cannot be deported will be deducted from the yearly quotas.

15. His Majesty's Government are satisfied that, when the immigration over five years which is now contemplated has taken place, they will not be justified in facilitating, nor will they be under any obligation to facilitate, the further development of the Jewish National Home by immigration regardless of the wishes of the Arab population.

16. The Administration of Palestine is required, under Article 6 of the Mandate, "while ensuring that the rights and position of other sections of the population are not prejudiced," to encourage "close settlement by Jews on the land," and no restriction has been imposed hitherto on the transfer of land from Arabs to Jews. The Reports of several expert Commissions have indicated that, owing to the natural growth of the Arab population and the steady sale in recent years of Arab land to Jews, there is now in certain areas no room for further transfers of Arab land, whilst in some other areas such transfers of land must be restricted if Arab cultivators are to maintain their existing standard of life and a considerable landless Arab population is not soon to be created. In these circumstances, the High Commissioner will be given general powers to prohibit and regulate transfers of land. These powers will date from the publication of this statement of Policy and the High Commissioner will retain them throughout the transitional period.

17. The policy of the Government will be directed towards the development of the land and the improvement, where possible, of methods of cultivation. In the light of such development it will be open to the High Commissioner, should he be satisfied that the "rights and position" of the Arab population will be duly preserved, to review and modify any orders passed relating to the prohibition or restriction of the transfer of land.

BILTMORE PROGRAMME*

May 11th, 1942

The following programme was approved by a Zionist Conference held in the Biltmore Hotel, New York City:

1. American Zionists assembled in this Extraordinary Conference reaffirm their unequivocal devotion to the cause of democratic freedom and international justice to which the people of the United States, allied with the other United Nations, have dedicated themselves, and give expression to their faith in the ultimate victory of humanity and justice over lawlessness and brute force.

2. This Conference offers a message of hope and encouragement to their fellow Jews in the Ghettos and concentration camps of Hitler-dominated Europe and prays that their hour of liberation may not be far distant.

3. The Conference sends its warmest greetings to the Jewish Agency Executive in Jerusalem, to the Va'ad Leumi, and to the whole Yishuv in Palestine, and expresses its profound admiration for their steadfastness and achievements in the face of peril

---

* Text supplied by courtesy of Josef Fraenkel.

and great difficulties. The Jewish men and women in field and factory, and the thousands of Jewish soldiers of Palestine in the Near East who have acquitted themselves with honour and distinction in Greece, Ethiopia, Syria, Libya and on other battlefields, have shown themselves worthy of their people and ready to assume the rights and responsibilities of nationhood.

4. In our generation, and in particular in the course of the past twenty years, the Jewish people have awakened and transformed their ancient homeland; from 50,000 at the end of the last war their numbers have increased to more than 500,000. They have made the waste places to bear fruit and the desert to blossom. Their pioneering achievements in agriculture and in industry, embodying new patterns of cooperative endeavour, have written a notable page in the history of colonization.

5. In the new values thus created, their Arab neighbours in Palestine have shared. The Jewish people in its own work of national redemption welcomes the economic, agricultural and national development of the Arab peoples and states. The Conference reaffirms the stand previously adopted at Congresses of the World Zionist Organization, expressing the readiness and the desire of the Jewish people for full cooperation with their Arab neighbours.

6. The Conference calls for the fulfilment of the original purpose of the Balfour Declaration and the Mandate which *"recognizing the historical connexion of the Jewish people with Palestine"* was to afford them the opportunity, as stated by President Wilson, to found there a Jewish Commonwealth.

The Conference affirms its unalterable rejection of the White Paper of May 1939 and denies its moral or legal validity. The White Paper seeks to limit, and in fact to nullify Jewish rights to immigration and settlement in Palestine, and, as stated by Mr. Winston Churchill in the House of Commons in May 1939, constitutes "a breach and repudiation of the Balfour Declaration". The policy of the White Paper is cruel and indefensible in its denial of sanctuary to Jews fleeing from Nazi persecution; and at a time when Palestine has become a focal point in the war front of the United Nations, and Palestine Jewry must provide all available manpower for farm and factory and camp, it is in direct conflict with the interests of the allied war effort.

7. In the struggle against the forces of aggression and tyranny, of which Jews were the earliest victims, and which now menace the Jewish National Home, recognition must be given to the right of the Jews of Palestine to play their full part in the war effort and in the defence of their country, through a Jewish military force fighting under its own flag and under the high command of the United Nations.

8. The Conference declares that the new world order that will follow victory cannot be established on foundations of peace, justice and equality, unless the problem of Jewish homelessness is finally solved.

The Conference urges that the gates of Palestine be opened; that the Jewish Agency be vested with control of immigration into Palestine and with the necessary authority for upbuilding the country, including the development of its unoccupied and uncultivated lands; and that Palestine be established as a Jewish Commonwealth integrated in the structure of the new democratic world.

Then and only then will the age old wrong to the Jewish people be righted.

UN GENERAL ASSEMBLY RESOLUTION ON THE FUTURE GOVERNMENT OF PALESTINE (PARTITION RESOLUTION)
November 29th, 1947

The General Assembly,

Having met in special session at the request of the mandatory Power to constitute and instruct a special committee to prepare for the consideration of the question of the future government of Palestine at the second regular session;

Having constituted a Special Committee and instructed it to investigate all questions and issues relevant to the problem of Palestine, and to prepare proposals for the solution of the problem, and

Having received and examined the report of the Special Committee (document A/364) including a number of unanimous recommendations and a plan of partition with economic union approved by the majority of the Special Committee,

Considers that the present situation in Palestine is one which is likely to impair the general welfare and friendly relations among nations;

Takes note of the declaration by the mandatory Power that it plans to complete its evacuation of Palestine by August 1st, 1948;

Recommends to the United Kingdom, as the mandatory Power for Palestine, and to all other Members of the United Nations the adoption and implementation, with regard to the future government of Palestine, of the Plan of Partition with Economic Union set out below;

Requests that

(a) The Security Council take the necessary measures as provided for in the plan for its implementation;

(b) The Security Council consider, if circumstances during the transitional period require such consideration, whether the situation in Palestine constitutes a threat to the peace. If it decides that such a threat exists, and in order to maintain international peace and security, the Security Council should supplement the authorization of the General Assembly by taking measures, under Articles 39 and 41 of the Charter, to empower the United Nations Commission, as provided in this resolution, to exercise in Palestine the functions which are assigned to it by this resolution;

(c) The Security Council determine as a threat to the peace, breach of the peace or act of aggression, in accordance with Article 39 of the Charter, any attempt to alter by force the settlement envisaged by this resolution;

(*d*) The Trusteeship Council be informed of the responsibilities envisaged for it in this plan;

Calls upon the inhabitants of Palestine to take such steps as may be necessary on their part to put this plan into effect;

Appeals to all Governments and all peoples to refrain from taking any action which might hamper or delay the carrying out of these recommendations, and

Authorizes the Secretary-General to reimburse travel and subsistence expenses of the members of the Commission referred to in Part 1, Section B, paragraph 1 below, on such basis and in such form as he may determine most appropriate in the circumstances, and to provide the Commission with the necessary staff to assist in carrying out the functions assigned to the Commission by the General Assembly.

Official Records of the second session of the General¹ Assembly, Resolutions, p. 131.

UN GENERAL ASSEMBLY RESOLUTION 194 (III)

December 11th, 1948

The resolution's terms have been reaffirmed every year since 1948.

11. . . . the refugees wishing to return to their homes and live at peace with their neighbours should be permitted to do so at the earliest practicable date, and that compensation should be paid for the property of those choosing not to return and for the loss of or damage to property which, under principles of international law or in equity, should be made good by the Governments or authorities responsible;

Official Records of the third session of the General Assembly, Part 1, Resolutions, p. 21.

UN GENERAL ASSEMBLY RESOLUTION ON THE INTERNATIONALIZATION OF JERUSALEM

December 9th, 1949

The General Assembly,

Having regard to its resolution 181 (II) of November 29th, 1947 and 194 (III) of December 11th, 1948,

Having studied the reports of the United Nations Conciliation Commission for Palestine set up under the latter resolution,

I. Decides
In relation to Jerusalem,

Believing that the principles underlying its previous resolutions concerning this matter, and in particular its resolution of November 29th, 1947, represent a just and equitable settlement of the question,

1. To restate, therefore, its intention that Jerusalem should be placed under a permanent international

regime, which should envisage appropriate guarantees for the protection of the Holy Places, both within and outside Jerusalem, and to confirm specifically the following provisions of General Assembly resolution 181 (II): (1) The City of Jerusalem shall be established as a *corpus separatum* under a special international regime and shall be administered by the United Nations; (2) The Trusteeship Council shall be designated to discharge the responsibilities of the Administering Authority . . .; and (3) The City of Jerusalem shall include the present municipality of Jerusalem plus the surrounding villages and towns, the most eastern of which shall be Abu Dis; the most southern, Bethlehem; the most western, Ein Karim (including also the built-up area of Motsa); and the most northern, Shu'fat, as indicated on the attached sketchmap; . . . [*map not reproduced*: *Ed.*]

Official Records of the fourth session of the General Assembly, Resolutions, p. 25.

TEXT OF UN SECURITY COUNCIL RESOLUTION 242

November 22nd, 1967

The Security Council,

Expressing its continued concern with the grave situation in the Middle East,

Emphasizing the inadmissibility of the acquisition of territory by war and the need to work for a just and lasting peace in which every state in the area can live in security,

Emphasizing further that all Member States in their acceptance of the Charter of the United Nations have undertaken a commitment to act in accordance with Article 2 of the Charter

1. *Affirms* that the fulfilment of Charter principles requires the establishment of a just and lasting peace in the Middle East which should include the application of both the following principles:

(i) Withdrawal of Israel armed forces from territories occupied in the recent conflict;

(ii) Termination of all claims or states of belligerency and respect for and acknowledgement of the sovereignty, territorial integrity and political independence of every State in the area and their right to live in peace within secure and recognized boundaries free from threats or acts of force.

2. *Affirms further* the necessity

(*a*) For guaranteeing freedom of navigation through international waterways in the area;

(*b*) For achieving a just settlement of the refugee problem;

(*c*) For guaranteeing the territorial inviolability and political independence of every State in the area, through measures including the establishment of demilitarized zones;

3. *Requests* the Secretary-General to designate a Special Representative to proceed to the Middle East

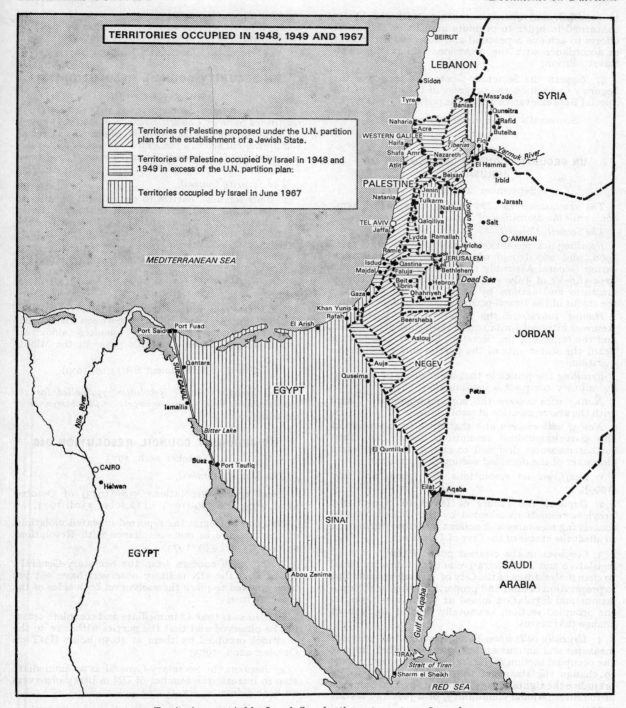

TERRITORIES OCCUPIED IN 1948, 1949 AND 1967

Territories of Palestine proposed under the U.N. partition plan for the establishment of a Jewish State.

Territories of Palestine occupied by Israel in 1948 and 1949 in excess of the U.N. partition plan:

Territories occupied by Israel in June 1967

Territories occupied by Israel. See also the maps on pages 81 and 90.

to establish and maintain contacts with the States concerned in order to promote agreement and assist efforts to achieve a peaceful and accepted settlement in accordance with the provisions and principles in this resolution;

4. *Requests* the Secretary-General to report to the Security Council on the progress of the efforts of the Special Representative as soon as possible.

Source: UN Document S/RES/242 (1967).

UN SECURITY COUNCIL RESOLUTION ON JERUSALEM

September 25th, 1971

The resolution, No. 298 (1971), was passed nem. con., *with the abstention of Syria.*

The Security Council,

Recalling its resolutions 252 (1968) of May 21st, 1968, and 267 (1969) of July 3rd, 1969, and the earlier General Assembly resolution 2253 (ES-V) and 2254 (ES-V) of July 4th and 14th, 1967, concerning measures and actions by Israel designed to change the status of the Israeli-occupied section of Jerusalem,

Having considered the letter of the Permanent Representative of Jordan on the situation in Jerusalem and the reports of the Secretary-General, and having heard the statements of the parties concerned in the question,

Recalling the principle that acquisition of territory by military conquest is inadmissible,

Noting with concern the non-compliance by Israel with the above-mentioned resolutions,

Noting with concern also that since the adoption of the above-mentioned resolutions Israel has taken further measures designed to change the status and character of the occupied section of Jerusalem.

1. *Reaffirms* its resolutions 252 (1968) and 267 (1969);

2. *Deplores* the failure of Israel to respect the previous resolutions adopted by the United Nations concerning measures and actions by Israel purporting to affect the status of the City of Jerusalem;

3. *Confirms* in the clearest possible terms that all legislative and administrative actions taken by Israel to change the status of the City of Jerusalem, including expropriation of land and properties, transfer of populations and legislation aimed at the incorporation of the occupied section, are totally invalid and cannot change that status;

4. *Urgently calls upon* Israel to rescind all previous measures and actions and to take no further steps in the occupied section of Jerusalem which may purport to change the status of the City, or which would prejudice the rights of the inhabitants and the interests of the international community, or a just and lasting peace;

5. *Requests* the Secretary-General, in consultation with the President of the Security Council and using such instrumentalities as he may choose, including a representative or a mission, to report to the Council as appropriate and in any event within 60 days on the implementation of the present resolution.

Source: UN Document S/RES/298 (1971).

UN SECURITY COUNCIL RESOLUTION 338

October 22nd, 1973

UN Resolutions between 1967 and October 1973 reaffirmed Security Council Resolution 242 (see above). In an attempt to end the fourth Middle East war, which had broken out between the Arabs and Israel on October 6th, 1973, the UN Security Council passed the following Resolution:

The Security Council,

1. *Calls upon* all parties to the present fighting to cease all firing and terminate all military activity immediately, not later than 12 hours after the moment of the adoption of the decision, in the positions they now occupy;

2. *Calls upon* the parties concerned to start immediately after the ceasefire the implementation of Security Council Resolution 242 (1967) in all of its parts;

3. *Decides that*, immediately and concurrently with the ceasefire negotiations start between the parties concerned under appropriate auspices aimed at establishing a just and durable peace in the Middle East.

Source: UN Document PR/73/29 (1973).

UN Security Council Resolution 339 called for the despatch of UN Observers to supervise the observance of the ceasefire.

UN SECURITY COUNCIL RESOLUTION 340

October 25th, 1973

The Security Council,

Recalling its Resolutions 338 (1973) of October 22nd, 1973 and 339 (1973) of October 23rd, 1973,

Noting with regret the reported repeated violations of the ceasefire in non-compliance with Resolutions 338 (1973) and 339 (1973),

Noting with concern from the Secretary-General's report that the UN military observers have not yet been enabled to place themselves on both sides of the ceasefire line,

1. *Demands* that an immediate and complete ceasefire be observed and that the parties withdraw to the positions occupied by them at 16.50 hours GMT on October 22nd, 1973;

2. *Requests* the Secretary-General as an immediate step to increase the number of UN military observers on both sides;

3. *Decides* to set up immediately under its authority a UN emergency force to be composed of personnel drawn from member states of the UN, except the permanent members of the Security Council, and

requests the Secretary-General to report within 24 hours on the steps taken to this effect; (*Details of the UN Emergency Force are given in the Chapter "United Nations in the Middle East and North Africa"— Editor*)

4. *Requests* the Secretary-General to report to the Council on an urgent and continuing basis on the state of implementation of this Resolution, as well as Resolutions 338 (1973) and 339 (1973);

5. *Requests* all member states to extend their full co-operation to the UN in the implementation of this Resolution, as well as Resolutions 338 (1973) and 339 (1973).

Source: UN Document PR/73/31 (1973).

DECLARATION OF EEC FOREIGN MINISTERS ON THE MIDDLE EAST SITUATION

November 6th, 1973

The Nine Governments of the European Community have exchanged views on the situation in the Middle East. While emphasizing that the views set out below are only a first contribution on their part to the search for a comprehensive solution to the problem, they have agreed on the following:

1. They strongly urge that the forces of both sides in the Middle East conflict should return immediately to the positions they occupied on October 22nd in accordance with Resolutions 339 and 340 of the Security Council. They believe that a return to these positions will facilitate a solution to other pressing problems concerning prisoners-of-war and the Egyptian Third Army.

2. They have the firm hope that, following the adoption by the Security Council of Resolution 338 of October 22nd, negotiations will at last begin for the restoration in the Middle East of a just and lasting peace through the application of Security Council Resolution 242 in all of its parts. They declare themselves ready to do all in their power to contribute to that peace. They believe that those negotiations must take place in the framework of the United Nations. They recall that the Charter has entrusted to the Security Council the principal responsibility for international peace and security. The Council and the Secretary-General have a special role to play in the making and keeping of peace through the application of Council Resolutions 242 and 338.

3. They consider that a peace agreement should be based particularly on the following points:

(i) the inadmissibility of the acquisition of territory by force;

(ii) the need for Israel to end the territorial occupation which it has maintained since the conflict of 1967;

(iii) respect for the sovereignty, territorial integrity and independence of every state in the area and their right to live in peace within secure and recognized boundaries;

(iv) recognition that in the establishment of a just and lasting peace account must be taken of the legitimate rights of the Palestinians.

Article 4 calls for the despatch of peace-keeping forces to the demilitarized zones.

Source: Bulletin of the European Communities Commission, No. 10, 1973, p. 106.

EGYPTIAN-ISRAELI AGREEMENT ON DISENGAGEMENT OF FORCES IN PURSUANCE OF THE GENEVA PEACE CONFERENCE

(signed by the Egyptian and Israeli Chiefs of Staff, January 18th, 1974)

This agreement was superseded by the second Egyptian-Israeli Disengagement Agreement signed in September 1975 (see p. 80 below) and then by the Peace Treaty between Egypt and Israel signed on March 26th, 1979 (see p. 84 below). A map showing the boundaries of the first agreement is reproduced in this edition (p. 81) and the terms can be found in the 1975–76 edition of The Middle East and North Africa.

DISENGAGEMENT AGREEMENT BETWEEN SYRIAN AND ISRAELI FORCES AND PROTOCOL TO AGREEMENT ON UNITED NATIONS DISENGAGEMENT OBSERVER FORCE (UNDOF)

(signed in Geneva, Friday, May 31st, 1974)

(*Annex A*)

A. Israel and Syria will scrupulously observe the cease-fire on land, sea and air and will refrain from all military actions against each other, from time of signing this document in implementation of the United Nations Security Council Resolution 338 dated October 22nd, 1973.

B. The military forces of Israel and Syria will be separated in accordance with the following principles:

1. All Israeli military forces will be west of a line designated line A on the map attached hereto (*reproduced below*), except in Quneitra (Kuneitra) area, where they will be west of a line A-1.

2. All territory east of line A will be under Syrian administration and Syrian civilians will return to this territory.

3. The area between line A and the line designated as line B on the attached map will be an area of separation. In this area will be stationed UNDOF established in accordance with the accompanying Protocol.

4. All Syrian military forces will be east of a line designated as line B on the attached map.

5. There will be two equal areas of limitation in armament and forces, one west of line A and one east of line B as agreed upon.

C. In the area between line A and line A-1 on the attached map there shall be no military forces.

D. *Paragraph D. deals with practical details of signing and implementation.*

E. Provisions of paragraphs A, B and C shall be inspected by personnel of the United Nations comprising UNDOF under the Agreement.

F. Within 24 hours after the signing of this Agreement in Geneva all wounded prisoners of war which each side holds of the other, as certified by the International Committee of the Red Cross, will be repatriated. The morning after the completion of the task of the Military Working Group, all remaining prisoners of war will be repatriated.

G. The bodies of all dead soldiers held by either side will be returned for burial in their respective countries within ten days after the signing of this Agreement.

H. This Agreement is not a peace agreement. It is a step towards a just and durable peace on the basis of the Security Council Resolution 338 dated October 22nd, 1973.

A. Protocol to the Disengagement Agreement outlined the functions of the United Nations Disengagement Observer Force (UNDOF).

RESOLUTION OF CONFERENCE OF ARAB HEADS OF STATE

Rabat, October 28th, 1974

The Conference of the Arab Heads of State:

1. *Affirms* the right of the Palestinian people to return to their homeland and to self-determination.

2. *Affirms* the right of the Palestinian people to establish an independent national authority, under the leadership of the PLO in its capacity as the sole legitimate representative of the Palestine people, over all liberated territory. The Arab States are pledged to uphold this authority, when it is established, in all spheres and at all levels.

3. *Supports* the PLO in the exercise of its national and international responsibilities, within the context of the principle of Arab solidarity.

4. *Invites* the kingdom of Jordan, Syria and Egypt to formalize their relations in the light of these decisions and in order that they be implemented.

5. *Affirms* the obligation of all Arab States to preserve Palestinian unity and not to interfere in Palestinian internal affairs.

Sources: Le Monde; Problèmes Politiques et Sociaux, March 7th, 1975; Arab Report and Record.

UN GENERAL ASSEMBLY RESOLUTION 3236 (XXIX)

November 22nd, 1974

The General Assembly,

Having considered the question of Palestine,

Having heard the statement of the Palestine Liberation Organization, the representative of the Palestinian people,

Having also heard other statements made during the debate,

Deeply concerned that no just solution to the problem of Palestine has yet been achieved and recognizing that the problem of Palestine continues to endanger international peace and security,

Recognizing that the Palestinian people is entitled to self-determination in accordance with the Charter of the United Nations,

Expressing its grave concern that the Palestinian people has been prevented from enjoying its inalienable rights, in particular its right to self-determination,

Guided by the purposes and principles of the Charter,

Recalling its relevant resolutions which affirm the right of the Palestinian people to self-determination,

1. *Reaffirms* the inalienable rights of the Palestinian people in Palestine, including:
   (a) The right to self-determination without external interference;
   (b) The right to national independence and sovereignty;

2. *Reaffirms also* the inalienable right of the Palestinians to return to their homes and property from which they have been displaced and uprooted, and calls for their return;

3. *Emphasizes* that full respect for and the realization of these inalienable rights of the Palestinian people are indispensable for the solution of the question of Palestine;

4. *Recognizes* that the Palestinian people is a principal party in the establishment of a just and durable peace in the Middle East;

5. *Further Recognizes* the right of the Palestinian people to regain its rights by all means in accordance with the purposes and principles of the Charter of the United Nations;

6. *Appeals* to all States and international organizations to extend their support to the Palestinian people in its struggle to restore its rights, in accordance with the Charter;

7. *Requests* the Secretary-General to establish contacts with the Palestine Liberation Organization on all matters concerning the question of Palestine;

8. *Requests* the Secretary-General to report to the General Assembly at its thirtieth session on the implementation of the present resolution;

9. *Decides* to include the item "Question of Palestine" in the provisional agenda of its thirtieth session.

Source: UN Document BR/74/55 (1974).

SECOND INTERIM PEACE AGREEMENT BETWEEN EGYPT AND ISRAEL

(signed September 4th, 1975)

This agreement has now been superseded by the Peace Treaty between Egypt and Israel signed on March 26th,

[continued on p. 82.

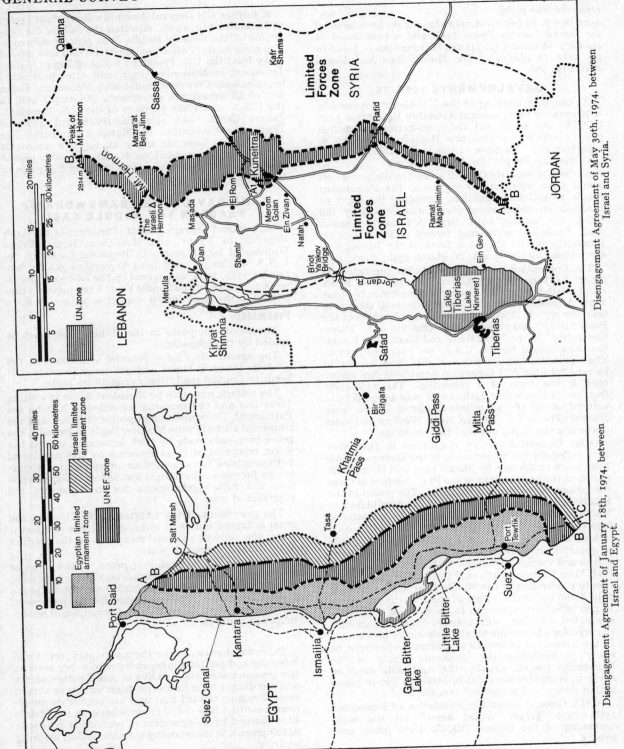

Disengagement Agreement of May 30th, 1974, between Israel and Syria.

Disengagement Agreement of January 18th, 1974, between Israel and Egypt.

continued from p. 80]

1979 (see *p. 84 below). A map showing the boundaries of the Second Interim Peace Agreement is reproduced in the 1979–80 edition* (p. 74) *and the terms can be found in the 1978–79 edition of* The Middle East and North Africa *(p. 70).*

DEVELOPMENTS 1975-78

At the 30th Meeting of the UN General Assembly in November 1975, General Assembly Resolution 3236 (XXIX) was reaffirmed and a 20-nation Committee (the Committee on Palestine Rights) was set up to report on the "Exercise of the Inalienable Rights of the Palestine People" by June 1st, 1976.

At the UN Security Council a draft resolution which would have affirmed the rights of the Palestinian people to self-determination, including the right to establish an independent state, was vetoed by the U.S.A. on January 26th, 1976. A Security Council draft resolution criticizing Israeli policies in East Jerusalem and on the West Bank of the Jordan was also vetoed by the U.S.A. on March 25th, 1976.

The Committee on Palestine Rights presented its report in June 1976 and recommended that Israel should withdraw from all occupied territories by June 1977. A resolution in the Security Council, stemming from the report, affirmed the "inalienable rights of the Palestinians" and called for the creation of a "Palestine entity" in the West Bank and Gaza. This resolution was vetoed by the U.S.A. on June 29th, 1976. The Committee on Palestine Rights then submitted its report to the UN General Assembly in November 1976 in the form of a resolution. The resolution (No. 20, of November 24th, 1976) was adopted by a vote of 90 to 16 (30 members abstained; 10 were absent). The U.S.A. and 10 other Western countries (including the U.K.) opposed the resolution.

Other General Assembly resolutions in December 1976 called for the reconvening of the Geneva Middle East peace conference by March 1977 and the participation in the negotiations of the PLO. Neither of these resolutions have been implemented. The policy of the Palestine Liberation Organization, as formulated in March 1977, is given in Palestine Organizations, pages 87–93.

After a meeting in London of the nine EEC heads of government at the end of June 1977, a statement was issued reaffirming earlier statements and stating that "The Nine have affirmed their belief that a solution to the conflict in the Middle East will be possible only if the legitimate rights of the Palestinian people to give effective expression to its national identity is translated into fact, which would take into account the need for a homeland for the Palestinian people. . . . In the context of an overall settlement Israel must be ready to recognize the legitimate rights of the Palestinian people; equally, the Arab side must be ready to recognize the right of Israel to live in peace within secure and recognized boundaries."

A UN General Assembly Resolution of November 25th, 1977 (32/30) "called anew" for the early convening of the Geneva Middle East peace conference.

A further UN General Assembly Resolution (33/29 of December 7th, 1978), repeated the call for the convening of the Geneva Middle East peace conference. The main focus of attention, however, had now moved away from the UN. President Sadat of Egypt visited Jerusalem in November 1977, and after protracted negotiations, President Sadat and Menachem Begin first of all signed two agreements at Camp David in the U.S.A. under the auspices of the U.S. President, Jimmy Carter, and subsequently signed a Peace Treaty in Washington on March 26th, 1979. The Arab League Council, angry at Egypt's unilateral action, met in Baghdad on March 27th and passed a series of resolutions aimed at isolating Egypt from the Arab world.

CAMP DAVID: THE FRAMEWORK OF PEACE IN THE MIDDLE EAST

Muhammad Anwar al-Sadat, President of the Arab Republic of Egypt, and Menachem Begin, Prime Minister of Israel, met with President Carter of the U.S.A. at Camp David from September 5th to September 17th, 1978, and agreed on the following framework for peace in the Middle East. They invited other parties to the Arab-Israeli conflict to adhere to it.

Preamble:

The search for peace in the Middle East must be guided by the following:

The agreed basis for a peaceful settlement of the conflict between Israel and its neighbours is UN Security Council resolution 242 in all its parts.

The historic initiative by President Sadat in visiting Jerusalem and the reception accorded to him by the Parliament, Government and people of Israel, and the reciprocal visit of Prime Minister Begin to Ismailia, the peace proposals made by both leaders, as well as the warm reception of these missions by the peoples of both countries, have created an unprecedented opportunity for peace which must not be lost if this generation and future generations are to be spared the tragedies of war.

The provisions of the Charter of the UN and the other accepted norms of international law and legitimacy now provide accepted standards for the conduct of relations between all states.

To achieve a relationship of peace, in the spirit of article 2 of the UN Charter, future negotiations between Israel and any neighbour prepared to negotiate peace and security with it, are necessary for the purpose of carrying out all the provisions and principles of resolutions 242 and 338.

*   *   *

Peace requires respect for the sovereignty, territorial integrity and political independence of every state in the area and their right to live in peace within secure and recognized boundaries free from threats or acts of force. Progress toward that goal can accelerate movement toward a new era of reconciliation in the Middle East marked by co-operation in promoting economic development, in maintaining stability and in assuring security. . . .

Framework

Taking these factors into account, the parties are determined to reach a just, comprehensive and durable settlement of the Middle East conflict through the conclusion of peace treaties based on Security Council resolutions 242 and 338 in all their parts. Their purpose is to achieve peace and good neighbourly relations. They recognize that, for peace to endure, it must involve all those who have been most deeply affected by the conflict. They therefore agree that this framework as appropriate is intended by them to constitute a basis for peace not only between Egypt and Israel but also between Israel and each of its other neighbours which is prepared to negotiate peace with Israel on this basis. With that objective in mind, they have agreed to proceed as follows:

A. West Bank and Gaza:

1. Egypt, Israel, Jordan and the representatives of the Palestinian people should participate in negotiations on the resolution of the Palestinian problem in all its aspects to achieve that objective, negotiations relating to the West Bank and Gaza should proceed in three stages.

(A) Egypt and Israel agree that, in order to ensure a peaceful and orderly transfer of authority, and taking into account the security concerns of all the parties, there should be transitional arrangements for the West Bank and Gaza for a period not exceeding five years. In order to provide full autonomy to the inhabitants, under these arrangements the Israeli military government and its civilian administration will be withdrawn as soon as a self-governing authority has been freely elected by the inhabitants of these areas to replace the existing military government.

To negotiate the details of transitional arrangement, the Government of Jordan will be invited to join the negotiations on the basis of this framework. These new arrangements should give due consideration to both the principle of self-government by the inhabitants of these territories and to the legitimate security concerns of the parties involved.

(B) Egypt, Israel and Jordan will agree on the modalities for establishing the elected self-governing authority in the West Bank and Gaza. The delegations of Egypt and Jordan may include Palestinians from the West Bank and Gaza or other Palestinians as mutually agreed. The parties will negotiate an agreement which will define the powers and responsibilities of the self-governing authority to be exercised in the West Bank and Gaza. A withdrawal of Israeli armed forces will take place and there will be a redeployment of the remaining Israeli forces into specified security locations.

The negotiations shall be based on all the provisions and principles of UN Security Council resolution 242. The negotiations will resolve, among other matters, the location of the boundaries and the nature of the security arrangements. The solution from the negotiations must also recognize the legitimate rights of the Palestinian people and their just requirements. In this way, the Palestinians will participate in the determination of their own future through:

(i) The negotiations among Egypt, Israel, Jordan and the representatives of the inhabitants of the West Bank and Gaza to agree on the final status of the West Bank and Gaza and other outstanding issues by the end of the transitional period.

(ii) Submitting their agreement to a vote by the elected representatives of the inhabitants of the West Bank and Gaza.

(iii) Providing for the elected representatives of the inhabitants of the West Bank and Gaza to decide how they shall govern themselves consistent with the provisions of their agreement.

(iv) Participating as stated above in the work of the committee negotiating the peace treaty between Israel and Jordan.

The agreement will also include arrangements for assuring internal and external security and public order. A strong local police force will be established, which may include Jordanian citizens. In addition, Israeli and Jordanian forces will participate in joint patrols and in the manning of control posts to assure the security of the borders.

(C) When the self-governing authority (administrative council) in the West Bank and Gaza is established and inaugurated, the transitional period of five years will begin. As soon as possible, but not later than the third year after the beginning of the transitional period, negotiations will take place to determine the final status of the West Bank and Gaza and its relationship with its neighbours, and to conclude a peace treaty between Israel and Jordan by the end of the transitional period. These negotiations will be conducted among Egypt, Israel, Jordan and the elected representatives of the inhabitants of the West Bank and Gaza.

Two separate but related committees will be convened, one committee, consisting of representatives of the four parties which will negotiate and agree on the final status of the West Bank and Gaza, and its relationship with its neighbours, and the second committee, consisting of representatives of Israel and representatives of Jordan to be joined by the elected representatives of the inhabitants of the West Bank and Gaza, to negotiate the peace treaty between Israel and Jordan, taking into account the agreement reached on the final status of the West Bank and Gaza.

2. All necessary measures will be taken and provisions made to assure the security of Israel and its neighbours during the transitional period and beyond. To assist in providing such security, a strong local police force will be constituted by the self-governing authority. It will be composed of inhabitants of the West Bank and Gaza. The police will maintain continuing liaison on internal security matters with the designated Israeli, Jordanian and Egyptian officers.

3. During the transitional period, the representatives of Egypt, Israel, Jordan and the self-governing authority will constitute a continuing committee to decide by agreement on the modalities of admission of persons displaced from the West Bank and Gaza in 1967, together with necessary measures to prevent dis-

ruption and disorder. Other matters of common concern may also be dealt with by this committee.

4. Egypt and Israel will work with each other and with other interested parties to establish agreed procedures for a prompt, just and permanent implementation of the resolution of the refugee problem.

B. Egypt-Israel

1. Egypt and Israel undertake not to resort to the threat or the use of force to settle disputes. Any disputes shall be settled by peaceful means in accordance with the provisions of article 33 of the Charter of the UN.

2. In order to achieve peace between them, the parties agree to negotiate in good faith with a goal of concluding within three months from the signing of this framework a peace treaty between them, while inviting the other parties to the conflict to proceed simultaneously to negotiate and conclude similar peace treaties with a view to achieving a comprehensive peace in the area. The framework for the conclusion of a peace treaty between Egypt and Israel will govern the peace negotiations between them. The parties will agree on the modalities and the timetable for the implementation of their obligations under the treaty.

Associated principles

1. Egypt and Israel state that the principles and provisions described below should apply to peace treaties between Israel and each of its neighbours—Egypt, Jordan, Syria and Lebanon.

2. Signatories shall establish among themselves relationships normal to states at peace with one another. To this end, they should undertake to abide by all the provisions of the Charter of the UN. Steps to be taken in this respect include:

(a) Full recognition.

(b) Abolishing economic boycotts.

(c) Guaranteeing that under their jurisdiction the citizens of the other parties shall enjoy the protection of the due process of law.

3. Signatories should explore possibilities for economic development in the context of final peace treaties, with the objective of contributing to the atmosphere of peace, co-operation, and friendship which is their common goal.

4. Claims commissions may be established for the mutual settlement of all financial claims.

5. The United States shall be invited to participate in the talks on matters related to the modalities of the implementation of the agreements and working out the time-table for the carrying out of the obligation of the parties.

6. The UN Security Council shall be requested to endorse the peace treaties and ensure that their provisions shall not be violated. The permanent members of the Security Council shall be requested to underwrite the peace treaties and ensure respect for their provisions. They shall also be requested to conform

their policies and actions with the undertakings contained in this framework.

The second agreement signed at Camp David was a framework for the conclusion of a peace treaty between Egypt and Israel. The actual Treaty was signed on March 26th, 1979, and is reproduced below.

THE PEACE TREATY BETWEEN EGYPT AND ISRAEL SIGNED IN WASHINGTON ON MARCH 26th, 1979

The Government of the Arab Republic of Egypt and the Government of the State of Israel:

Preamble

Convinced of the urgent necessity of the establishment of a just, comprehensive and lasting peace in the Middle East in accordance with Security Council Resolutions 242 and 338:

Reaffirming their adherence to the "Framework for Peace in the Middle East agreed at Camp David", dated September 17th, 1978:

Noting that the aforementioned framework as appropriate is intended to constitute a basis for peace not only between Egypt and Israel but also between Israel and each of the other Arab neighbours which is prepared to negotiate peace with it on this basis:

Desiring to bring to an end the state of war between them and to establish a peace in which every state in the area can live in security:

Convinced that the conclusion of a treaty of peace between Egypt and Israel is an important step in the search for comprehensive peace in the area and for the attainment of the settlement of the Arab-Israeli conflict in all its aspects:

Inviting the other Arab parties to this dispute to join the peace process with Israel guided by and based on the principles of the aforementioned framework:

Desiring as well to develop friendly relations and co-operation between themselves in accordance with the UN Charter and the principles of international law governing international relations in times of peace:

Agree to the following provisions in the free exercise of their sovereignty, in order to implement the "framework for the conclusion of a peace treaty between Egypt and Israel".

Article I

1. The state of war between the parties will be terminated and peace will be established between them upon the exchange of instruments of ratification of this treaty.

2. Israel will withdraw all its armed forces and civilians from the Sinai behind the international boundary between Egypt and Mandated Palestine, as provided in the annexed protocol (annexed), and Egypt will resume the exercise of its full sovereignty over the Sinai.

3. Upon completion of the interim withdrawal provided for in Annex 1, the parties will establish normal and friendly relations, in accordance with Article II (3).

Article II

The permanent boundary between Egypt and Israel is the recognized international boundary between Egypt and the former Mandated Territory of Palestine, as shown on the map at Annex 11, without prejudice to the issue of the status of the Gaza Strip. The parties recognize this boundary as inviolable. Each will respect the territorial integrity of the other, including their territorial waters and airspace.

Article III

1. The parties will apply between them the provisions of the Charter of the UN and the principles of international law governing relations among states in times of peace.

In particular:

A. They recognize and will respect each other's sovereignty, territorial integrity and political independence.

B. They recognize and will respect each other's right to live in peace within their secure and recognized boundaries.

C. They will refrain from the threat of use of force, directly or indirectly, against each other and will settle all disputes between them by peaceful means.

2. Each party undertakes to ensure that acts or threats of belligerency, hostility, or violence do not originate from and are not committed from within its territory, or by any forces subject to its control or by any other forces stationed on its territory, against the population, citizens or property of the other party. Each party also undertakes to refrain from organizing, instigating, inciting, assisting or participating in acts or threats of belligerency, hostility, subversion or violence against the other party, anywhere, and undertakes to ensure that perpetrators of such acts are brought to justice.

3. The parties agree that the normal relationship established between them will include full recognition, diplomatic, economic and cultural relations, termination of economic boycotts and discriminatory barriers to the free movement of people and goods, and will guarantee the mutual enjoyment by citizens of the due process of law. The process by which they undertake to achieve such a relationship parallel to the implementation of other provisions of this treaty is set out in the annexed protocol (Annex III).

Article IV

1. In order to provide maximum security for both parties on the basis of reciprocity, agreed security arrangements will be established including limited force zones in Egyptian and Israeli territory, and UN forces and observers, described in detail as to nature and timing in Annex 1, and other security arrangements the parties may agree upon.

2. The parties agree to the stationing of UN person-

nel in areas described in Annex 1, the parties agree not to request withdrawal of the UN personnel and that these personnel will not be removed unless such removal is approved by the Security Council of the UN, with the affirmative vote of the five members, unless the parties otherwise agree.

3. A joint commission will be established to facilitate the implementation of the treaty, as provided for in Annex 1.

4. The security arrangements provided for in paragraphs 1 and 2 of this article may at the request of either party be reviewed and amended by mutual agreement of the parties.

Article V

1. Ships of Israel, and cargoes destined for or coming from Israel, shall enjoy the right of free passage through the Suez Canal and its approaches through the Gulf of Suez and the Mediterranean Sea on the basis of the Constantinople Convention of 1888, applying to all nations. Israeli nationals, vessels and cargoes, as well as persons, vessels and cargoes destined for or coming from Israel, shall be accorded non-discriminatory treatment in all matters connected with usage of the canal.

2. The parties consider the Strait of Tiran and the Gulf of Aqaba to be international waterways open to all nations for unimpeded and non-suspendable freedom of navigation and overflight. The parties will respect each other's right to navigation and overflight for access to either country through the Strait of Tiran and the Gulf of Aqaba.

Article VI

1. This treaty does not affect and shall not be interpreted as affecting in any way the rights and obligations of the parties under the Charter of the UN.

2. The parties undertake to fulfil in good faith their obligations under this treaty, without regard to action or inaction of any other party and independently of any instrument external to this treaty.

3. They further undertake to take all the necessary measures for the application in their relations of the provisions of the multilateral conventions to which they are parties. Including the submission of appropriate notification to the Secretary-General of the UN and other depositories of such conventions.

4. The parties undertake not to enter into any obligation in conflict with this treaty.

5. Subject to Article 103 of the UN Charter, in the event of a conflict between the obligations of the parties under the present treaty and any of their other obligations, the obligations under this treaty will be binding and implemented.

Article VII

1. Disputes arising out of the application or interpretation of this treaty shall be resolved by negotiations.

2. Any such disputes which cannot be settled by negotiations shall be resolved by conciliation or submitted to arbitration.

Article VIII

The parties agree to establish a claims commission for the mutual settlement of all financial claims.

Article IX

1. This treaty shall enter into force upon exchange of instruments of ratification.

2. This treaty supersedes the agreement between Egypt and Israel of September 1975.

3. All protocols, annexes, and maps attached to this treaty shall be regarded as an integral part hereof.

4. The treaty shall be communicated to the Secretary-General of the UN for registration in accordance with the provisions of Article 102 of the Charter of the UN.

Annex 1—military and withdrawal arrangements:

Israel will complete withdrawal of all its armed forces and civilians from Sinai within three years of the date of exchange of instruments of ratification of the treaty. The withdrawal will be accomplished in two phases, the first, within nine months, to a line east of Al Arish and Ras Muhammad; the second to behind the international boundary. During the three-year period, Egypt and Israel will maintain a specified military presence in four delineated security zones, (see map), and the UN will continue its observation and supervisory functions. Egypt will exercise full sovereignty over evacuated territories in Sinai upon Israeli withdrawal. A joint commission will supervise the withdrawal, and security arrangements can be reviewed when either side asks but any change must be by mutual agreement.

Annex 2—maps.

Annex 3—normalization of relations:

Ambassadors will be exchanged upon completion of the interim withdrawal. All discriminatory barriers and economic boycotts will be lifted and, not later than six months after the completion of the interim withdrawal, negotiations for a trade and commerce agreement will begin. Free movement of each other's nationals and transport will be allowed and both sides agree to promote "good neighbourly relations". Egypt will use the airfields left by Israel near Al Arish, Rafah, Ras an-Naqb and Sharm ash-Shaikh, only for civilian aircraft. Road, rail, postal, telephone, wireless and other forms of communications will be opened between the two countries on completion of interim withdrawal.

Exchange of letters:

Negotiations on the West Bank and Gaza—Negotiations on autonomy for the West Bank and Gaza will begin within one month of the exchange of the instruments of ratification. Jordan will be invited to participate and the Egyptian and Jordanian delegations may include Palestinians from the West Bank and Gaza, or other Palestinians as mutually agreed. If Jordan decides not to take part, the negotiations will be held by Egypt and Israel. The objective of the negotiations is the establishment of a self-governing authority in the West Bank and Gaza "in order to provide full autonomy to the inhabitants".

Egypt and Israel hope to complete negotiations within one year so that elections can be held as soon as possible. The self-governing authority elected will be inaugurated within one month of the elections at which point the five year transitional period will begin. The Israeli military government and its civilian administration will be withdrawn, Israeli armed forces withdrawn and the remaining forces redeployed "into specified security locations".

MAIN POINTS OF THE RESOLUTIONS PASSED BY THE ARAB LEAGUE COUNCIL IN BAGHDAD ON MARCH 27th, 1979

—To withdraw the ambassadors of the Arab states from Egypt immediately.

—To recommend the severance of political and diplomatic relations with the Egyptian Government. The Arab governments will adopt the necessary measures to apply this recommendation within a maximum period of one month from the date of the issue of this decision, in accordance with the constitutional measures in force in each country.

—To consider the suspension of the Egyptian Government's membership in the Arab League as operative from the date of the Egyptian Government's signing of the peace treaty with the Zionist enemy. This means depriving it of all rights resulting from that membership.

—To make the city of Tunis, capital of the Tunisian Republic, the temporary headquarters of the Arab League, its general secretariat, the competent ministerial councils and the permanent technical committees, as of the date of the signing of the treaty between the Egyptian Government and the Zionist enemy. This shall be communicated to all international and regional organizations and bodies. They will also be informed that dealings with the Arab League will be conducted with its secretariat in its new temporary headquarters.

—To condemn the policy that the United States is practising regarding its role in concluding the Camp David agreements and the Egyptian-Israeli treaty.

The Arab League Council, at the level of Arab Foreign and Economy Ministers, has also decided the following:

—To halt all bank loans, deposits, guarantees or facilities, as well as all financial or technical contributions and aid by Arab governments or their establishments to the Egyptian Government and its establishments as of the treaty-signing date.

—To ban the extension of economic aid by the Arab funds, banks and financial establishments within the framework of the Arab League and the joint Arab cooperation to the Egyptian Government and its establishments.

—The Arab governments and institutions shall refrain from purchasing the bonds, shares, postal orders and public credit loans that are issued by the Egyptian Government and its financial foundations.

—Following the suspension of the Egyptian Government's membership in the Arab League, its membership will also be suspended from the institutions, funds and organisations deriving from the Arab League.

—In view of the fact that the ill-omened Egyptian-Israeli treaty and its appendices have demonstrated Egypt's commitment to sell oil to Israel, the Arab states shall refrain from providing Egypt with oil and its derivatives.

—Trade exchanges with the Egyptian state and with private establishments that deal with the Zionist enemy shall be prohibited.

Source: MEED Arab Report, April 11th, 1979, p. 9.

UN SECURITY COUNCIL RESOLUTION ON ISRAELI SETTLEMENTS

March 1st, 1980

The resolution, No. 465, was adopted unanimously by the fifteen members of the Council. The U.S.A. repudiated its vote in favour of the resolution on March 3rd, 1980 (see below).

The Security Council, taking note of the reports of the Commission of the Security Council established under resolution 446 (1979) to examine the situation relating to the settlements in the Arab territories occupied since 1967, including Jerusalem, contained in documents S/13450 and S/13679.

—Taking note also of letters from the permanent representative of Jordan (S/13801) and the permanent representative of Morocco, Chairman of the Islamic Group (S/13802),

—Strongly deploring the refusal by Israel to co-operate with the Commission and regretting its formal rejection of resolutions 446 (1979) and 452 (1979),

—Affirming once more that the fourth Geneva Convention relative to the protection of civilian persons in time of war of 12 August 1949 is applicable to the Arab territories occupied by Israel since 1967, including Jerusalem,

—Deploring the decision of the Government of Israel to officially support Israeli settlement in the Palestinian and other Arab territories occupied since 1967,

—Deeply concerned over the practices of the Israeli authorities in implementing that settlement policy in the occupied Arab territories, including Jerusalem, and its consequences for the local Arab and Palestinian population,

—Taking into account the need to consider measures for the impartial protection of private and public land and property, and water resources,

—Bearing in mind the specific status of Jerusalem and, in particular, the need for protection and preservation of the unique spiritual and religious dimension of the holy places in the city,

—Drawing attention to the grave consequences which the settlement policy is bound to have on any attempt to reach a comprehensive, just and lasting peace in the Middle East,

—Recalling pertinent Security Council resolutions, specifically resolutions 237 (1967) of 14 June 1967,

252 (1968) of 21 May 1968, 267 (1969) of 3 July 1969, 271 (1969) of 15 September 1969 and 298 (1971) of 25 September 1971, as well as the consensus statement made by the President of the Security Council on 11 November 1976,

—Having invited Mr. Fahd Qawasmah, Mayor of Al-Khalil (Hebron), in the occupied territories, to supply it with information pursuant to rule 39 of provisional rules of procedure,

1. Commends the work done by the Commission in preparing the report contained in document S/13679,

2. Accepts the conclusions and recommendations contained in the above-mentioned report of the Commission,

3. Calls upon all parties, particularly the Government of Israel, to co-operate with the Commission,

4. Strongly deplores the decision of Israel to prohibit the free travel of Mayor Fahd Qawasmah in order to appear before the Security Council, and requests Israel to permit his free travel to the United Nations headquarters for that purpose,

5. Determines that all measures taken by Israel to change the physical character, demographic composition, institutional structure or status of the Palestinian and other Arab territories occupied since 1967, including Jerusalem, or any part thereof, have no legal validity and that Israel's policy and practices of settling parts of its population and new immigrants in those territories constitute a flagrant violation of the Fourth Geneva Convention relative to the protection of civilian persons in time of war and also constitute a serious obstruction to achieving a comprehensive, just and lasting peace in the Middle East,

6. Strongly deplores the continuation and persistence of Israel in pursuing those policies and practices and calls upon the Government and people of Israel to rescind those measures, to dismantle the existing settlements and in particular to cease, on an urgent basis, the establishment, construction and planning of settlements in the Arab territories occupied since 1967, including Jerusalem,

7. Calls upon all states not to provide Israel with any assistance to be used specifically in connection with settlements in the occupied territories,

8. Requests the Commission to continue to examine the situation relating to settlements in the Arab territories occupied since 1967 including Jerusalem, to investigate the reported serious depletion of natural resources, particularly the water resources, with a view to ensuring the protection of those important natural resources of the territories under occupation, and to keep under close scrutiny the implementation of the present resolution,

9. Requests the Commission to report to the Security Council before 1st September, 1980, and decides to convene at the earliest possible date thereafter in order to consider the report and the full implementation of the present resolution.

PRESIDENT CARTER'S STATEMENT REPUDIATING U.S. VOTE IN SUPPORT OF UN SECURITY COUNCIL RESOLUTION 465

March 3rd, 1980

I want to make it clear that the vote of the U.S. in the Security Council of the UN does not represent a change in our position regarding the Israeli settlements in the occupied areas nor regarding the status of Jerusalem.

While our opposition to the establishment of the Israeli settlements is long-standing and well-known, we made strenuous efforts to eliminate the language with reference to the dismantling of settlements in the resolution. This call for dismantling was neither proper nor practical. We believe that the future disposition of the existing settlements must be determined during the current autonomy negotiations.

As to Jerusalem, we strongly believe that Jerusalem should be undivided with free access to the holy places for all faiths, and that its status should be determined in the negotiations for a comprehensive peace settlement.

The U.S. vote in the UN was approved with the understanding that all references to Jerusalem would be deleted. The failure to communicate this clearly resulted in a vote in favour of the resolution rather than abstention.

EEC STATEMENT ON THE MIDDLE EAST

Issued in Venice, June 13th, 1980

1. The heads of state and government and the ministers of foreign affairs held a comprehensive exchange of views on all aspects of the present situation in the Middle East, including the state of negotiations resulting from the agreements signed between Egypt and Israel in March 1979. They agreed that growing tensions affecting this region constitute a serious danger and render a comprehensive solution to the Israeli-Arab conflict more necessary and pressing than ever.

2. The nine member-states of the European Community consider that the traditional ties and common interests which link Europe to the Middle East oblige them to play a special role and now require them to work in a more concrete way towards peace.

3. In this regard, the nine countries of the Community base themselves on Security Council resolutions 242 and 338 and the positions which they have expressed on several occasions, notably in their declarations of June 29, 1977, September 19, 1978, March 26 and June 18, 1979, as well as the speech made on their behalf on September 25, 1979, by the Irish Minister of Foreign Affairs at the thirty-fourth United Nations General Assembly.

4. On the bases thus set out, the time has come to promote the recognition and implementation of the two principles universally accepted by the international community: the right to existence and to security of all the states in the region, including Israel, and justice for all the peoples which implies the recognition of the legitimate rights of the Palestinian people.

5. All of the countries in the area are entitled to live in peace within secure, recognised and guaranteed borders. The necessary guarantees for a peace settlement should be provided by the United Nations by a decision of the Security Council and, if necessary, on the basis of other mutually agreed procedures. The Nine declared that they are prepared to participate within the framework of a comprehensive settlement in a system of concrete and binding international guarantees, including (guarantees) on the ground.

6. A just solution must finally be found to the Palestinian problem, which is not simply one of refugees. The Palestinian people, which is conscious of existing as such, must be placed in a position, by an appropriate process defined within the framework of the comprehensive peace settlement, to exercise fully its right to self-determination.

7. The achievement of these objectives requires the involvement and support of all the parties concerned in the peace settlement which the Nine are endeavouring to promote in keeping with the principles formulated in the declaration referred to above. These principles apply to all the parties concerned, and thus the Palestinian people, and to the PLO, which will have to be associated with the negotiations.

8. The Nine recognise the special importance of the role played by the question of Jerusalem for all the parties concerned. The Nine stress that they will not accept any unilateral initiative designed to change the status of Jerusalem and that any agreement on the city's status should guarantee freedom of access for everyone to the holy places.

9. The Nine stress the need for Israel to put an end to the territorial occupation which it has maintained since the conflict of 1967, as it has done for part of Sinai. They are deeply convinced that the Israeli settlements constitute a serious obstacle to the peace process in the Middle East. The Nine consider that these settlements, as well as modifications in population and property in the occupied Arab territories, are illegal under international law.

10. Concerned as they are to put an end to violence, the Nine consider that only the renunciation of force or the threatened use of force by all the parties can create a climate of confidence in the area, and constitute a basic element for a comprehensive settlement of the conflict in the Middle East.

11. The Nine have decided to make the necessary contacts with all the parties concerned. The objective

of these contacts would be to ascertain the position of the various parties with respect to the principles set out in this declaration and in the light of the result of this consultation process to determine the form which such an initiative on their part could take.

Subsequent UN Resolutions (General Assembly Resolution ES-7/2, July 29th, 1980; Security Council Resolution 478, August 20th, 1980; General Assembly Resolutions 35-169 and 35-207 of December 15th and 16th, 1980) have reaffirmed earlier resolutions and condemned the Israeli "Jersualem Bill" of July 1980, which stated explicitly that Jerusalem should be for ever the undivided Israeli capital and seat of government, parliament and judiciary. A UN General Assembly Resolution of February 6th, 1982, condemned Israel's annexation of the Golan Heights. UN Resolutions in June 1982 condemned Israeli invasion of Lebanon, and called for the withdrawal of Israeli forces.

THE FAHD PLAN

In August 1981 Crown Prince Fahd of Saudi Arabia launched an 8-point peace plan for the Middle East. During the remainder of 1981 some Arab States showed their support, but failure to agree on the "Fahd Plan" caused the break-up of the Fez Arab Summit in November only a few hours after it had opened. The plan is as follows:

1.   Israel to withdraw from all Arab territory occupied in 1967, including Arab Jerusalem.

2.   Israeli settlements built on Arab land after 1967 to be dismantled.

3.   A guarantee of freedom of worship for all religions in holy places.

4.   An affirmation of the right of the Palestinian Arab people to return to their homes, and compensation for those who do not wish to return.

5.   The West Bank and the Gaza Strip to have a transitional period under the auspices of the United Nations for a period not exceeding several months.

6.   An independent Palestinian state should be set up with Jerusalem as its capital.

7.   All states in the region should be able to live in peace.

8.   The UN or member-states of the UN to guarantee carrying-out of these principles.

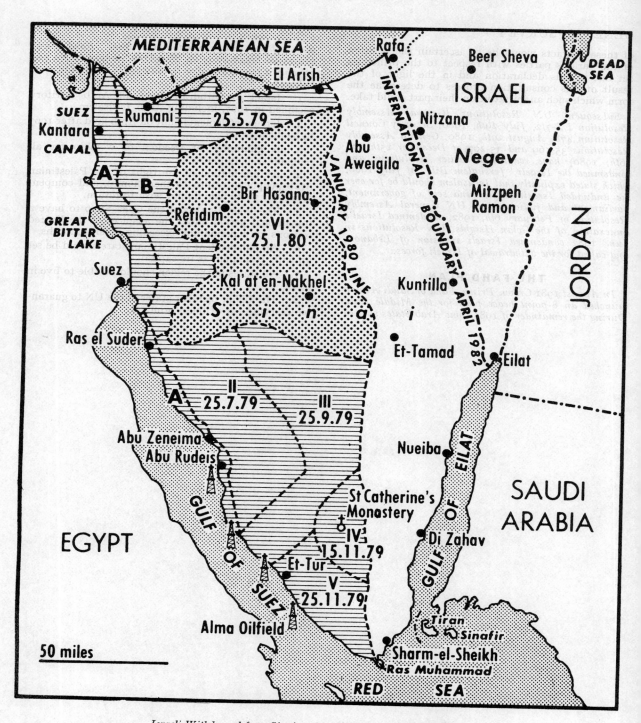

Israeli Withdrawal from Sinai under the Egyptian-Israeli Peace Treaty

Horizontal shading A includes areas already recovered by Egypt before the 1979 treaty, and B shows buffer zone under the 1975 agreement. Roman numerals I–VI indicate successive stages of withdrawal under the treaty, with dates. The final withdrawal took place as arranged, on April 25th, 1982.

© The Times, London

Palestine Organizations

Palestine Liberation Organization (PLO)

The Palestine Liberation Organization was founded in 1964 at the first Arab Summit Meeting, and the Palestine Liberation Army was established in the same year. The supreme organ of the PLO is the Palestine National Council (*see* below), while the Palestine Executive Committee, consisting of 15 members, deals with the day-to-day business. Fatah (the Palestine National Liberation Movement) joined the Palestine National Council in 1968, and all the guerrilla organizations joined the Council in 1969. The Palestine Executive Committee controls the following eight departments, and a member of the Executive Committee is at the head of each department:

(i) Military Department, which includes Palestine Liberation Army.

(ii) Cultural and Educational.

(iii) Political Department.

(iv) Palestine National Fund.

(v) Social Affairs (includes Palestine Red Crescent).

(vi) Occupied Territories.

(vii) Information and National Guidance.

(viii) Popular Organizations (Trade Unions, Students, Workers, Women, etc.).

The PLO has offices and representatives in every Arab country, as well as in non-Arab states such as U.S.A., U.S.S.R., China, Cuba, Yugoslavia, Switzerland and Britain. By early 1980 115 countries had recognized the PLO. The Rabat Arab Summit, in October 1974, affirmed the right of the Palestinian people to establish an independent national authority, under the leadership of the PLO in its capacity as the sole legitimate representative of the Palestine people, over all liberated territory (*see* Documents on Palestine, p. 80). In November 1974 Yasser Arafat addressed the UN General Assembly, and on November 22nd, 1974, the UN General Assembly passed a resolution acknowledging and reaffirming the PLO position (*see* Documents on Palestine, page 80). On the same day the PLO was granted permanent observer status at the General Assembly of the UN and at international conferences sponsored by the UN. A PLO Delegation was present at the Conference of the Inter-Parliamentary Union in London in September 1975, and also at the 30th Session of the UN General Assembly in November 1975. The PLO became a full member of the Arab League in September 1976.

The PLO condemned the Second Interim Egyptian-Israeli Disengagement Agreement as seriously weakening the united Arab effort to achieve the liberation of territories occupied by Israeli armed forces. In response Egypt closed the "Voice of Palestine" radio operating from Cairo. The general policy of the PLO was to remain aloof from the Lebanese civil war of 1975 and 1976, but after 1976 it became increasingly involved, particularly after the Syrian intervention.

Although many guerrilla units suffered heavy losses the PLO has not moderated its official policy, and when an enlarged Palestine National Council met in Cairo in March 1977, no changes were made in the Palestine National Charter (*see* below), and a 15-point political programme (*see* below) was adopted which set out in a forthright fashion the aims and principles of the PLO. The PLO has condemned the Camp David agreements of September 1978 (*see* p. 82) and the Peace Treaty between Egypt and Israel of March 1979 (*see* p. 84). See p. 97*.

Chairman: 1964-67   Ahmed Shukairi.

1967-68   Yahya Hammouda.

1968-   Yasser Arafat.

Main Regional Offices with Representatives:

Abu Dhabi: ANIS AL-KHATIB.

Aden: ABBAS ZAKI.

Addis Ababa: ABU NAYEL.

Algiers: ABU HASSAN.

Amman: ABDUL RAZZAQ AL-YAHYA.

Ankara: RIBHI HALLUM ("ABU FIRAS").

Athens: SHAWKI ARMALLI.

Beijing: TAYEB ABDER-RAHMAN.

Beirut: SHAFIQ HOUT.

Berlin: ISSAM KAMEL.

Bonn: ABDULLAH FRANGI.

Brussels: (vacant).

Budapest: ABDULLAH HIJAZI.

Damascus: MAHMOUD KHALIDI.

Dar es Salaam: FUAD BAYTAR.

Dublin: (vacant).

Geneva: DAOUD BARAKAT.

Islamabad: ABDUL RAHMAN ABU AL-KHAIR.

Khartoum: (vacant).

Kuwait: AUNI BATTASH.

London: NABIL RAMLAWI.

Maputo: HANI SHAWA.

Moscow: MUHAMMAD AL-SHAYER.

Nairobi: (vacant).

New York: SAA'DAT HASAN.

Nicosia: ABU AS-SAID QIRAWIYAH.

Paris: IBRAHIM SOUSS.

Qatar: YASIN SHARIF.

Rio de Janeiro: (vacant).

Riyadh: RAFIQ AN-NATSHAH.

Rome: NIMER HAMAD.

Teheran: SALAH AL-ZAWAWI.

Tokyo: FATHI ABDUL HAMID.

Tripoli: ABU TAREQ.

UNESCO: OMAR MASALHA.

Vienna: (vacant).

Washington: HATIM HUSSEINI.

Head of PLO Observer Mission at UN: Dr. ZEHDI LABIB TERZI.

PALESTINE NATIONAL COUNCIL

It has 301 members and meets once a year. Cairo has been the normal venue, but the 14th session in January 1979 was held in Damascus. As well as the guerrilla organizations, the other PLO bodies, trade and student unions, etc. are represented. The Council also includes Palestinian representatives from Jordan, the West Bank, the Gulf States and other countries. At the 14th session in Damascus in January 1979 a unity plan to reconcile the various elements in the PLO was adopted, but the PFLP did not rejoin the Executive Committee. The 15th PNC session was held in Damascus in April 1981 and voted to increase the number of members by between 30 and 40.

Chairman: KHALED FAHOUM.

Deputy Chairman: SALIM ZAANOUN ("ABU ADIB").

CENTRAL COUNCIL

It is appointed by the Palestine National Council; consists of the members of the Executive Committee, and other members, with a total possible membership of 55; acts as a steering group when the PNC is not in session. For affiliated organizations, *see* page 93.

EXECUTIVE COMMITTEE

(elected April 1981)

This is elected by the Palestine National Council and is responsible for the running of the PLO in between meetings of the Council. In September 1974 the PFLP withdrew from the Executive Committee and Central Council of the PLO because it rejected PLO policies which recognized the existence of Israel. This "rejectionist front" was later joined by the PFLP—General Command, the Arab Liberation Front and the Front for the Popular Palestinian Struggle, and in practice their members ceased to serve on the Executive Committee and Central Council listed below, although they remained members of the Palestine National Council. At the March 1977 meeting of the Palestine National Council, however, only the PFLP continued to boycott the work of the Executive Committee.

Chairman: YASSER ARAFAT (also known as "ABU AMMAR"—Fatah).

Members: FAROUK KADDOUMI (also known as "ABU LUTF"—Fatah—Head of Political Dept.), YASSER ABD-RABOU (PDFLP—Head of Information Dept.), AHMAD AL-YAMANI (also known as "ABU MAHER"—PFLP), ABDER-RAHIM AHMED (ALF), TALAL NAJI (PFLP—General Command—Head of Higher Education Dept.), AHMAD SIDQI AD-DAJANI (independent), MUHAMMAD ZUHDI NASHASHIBI (independent), ABDEL-MUHSEN ABU-MAIZER (independent—Official Spokesman), HAMED ABU-SITTA (independent), MAHMUD ABBAS (Fatah), MUHAMMAD KHALIFAH (Saiqa), JAMAL AS-SURANI (independent), Dr. HANNA NASIR (independent), Dr. SALAH AD-DABBAGH (independent—Chairman of Palestine National Fund).

PALESTINE LIBERATION ARMY (PLA)

The PLA was founded in 1964 and numbers between 6,000 and 10,000 men, mainly infantry; the commando wing (Popular Liberation Forces) was formed in 1968 but had only a short existence.

Commander-in-Chief: YASSER ARAFAT.

Head of Military Affairs Department: Maj.-Gen. MUHAMMAD AZZAM.

Chief of Staff: Brig.-Gen. TARIQ AL-KHADRA.

PALESTINE NATIONAL FUND

The fund is financed by a contribution of between 3 and 6 per cent from the income of every Palestinian and also aid from Arab and friendly countries.

Chairman: Dr. SALAH AD-DABBAGH.

Director: DARWICHE ABYAD.

PALESTINE PLANNING CENTRE

Director: Dr. NABIL SHAATH.

PALESTINE RED CRESCENT

P.O.B. 101, Ghoubiery, Lebanon;

President: Dr. FATHI ARAFAT; f. 1969; operates 7 hospitals, 4 emergency centres and several clinics.

PALESTINE RESEARCH CENTRE

Director: SABRI JERYES; f. 1965; library and archives; publ. *Shu'un Filastinaya* (Palestine Affairs, monthly).

PALESTINE MARTYRS' WORKS SOCIETY (SAMED)

P.O.B. 165024, Beirut; runs workshops making blankets, tents, uniforms, civilian clothes, toys, furniture, etc.

President: ABU ALA.

OTHER PLO BODIES

Palestine Trades Union Federation, General Union of Palestinian Women, General Union of Palestinian Journalists and Writers, Palestine Orphans' Trust, Palestine Youth Organization, General Union of Palestine Students, Palestine Medical Organization, Palestine Architects' Organization, Palestine Teachers' Organization, Palestine Artisans' Organization, Palestine Jurists' Union, Palestine Engineers' Union.

PRESS AND RADIO

Filastin Al-Thawra (*Palestine Revolution*): Beirut; weekly newspaper of the Palestine Liberation Organization.

Al Hadaf: Beirut; organ of the Popular Front for the Liberation of Palestine; weekly; Editor BASSAM ABU SHERIF.

Shu'un Filastinaya (*Palestine Affairs*): Palestine Research Centre, Beirut; monthly.

Voice of Palestine: official radio station of Palestine Liberation Organization; broadcasts from Baghdad and Algiers, and also from the Yemen Arab Republic.

Palestine News Agency (**WAFA**): Beirut; official PLO news agency; Editor ZIAD ABDEL FATTAH; Head of Foreign Information Office: MAHMOUD LABADI.

CENTRAL COUNCIL OF THE PALESTINE RESISTANCE MOVEMENT

It was created early in 1970 and represents all the guerrilla groups. The most important guerrilla organizations are:

Fatah (The Palestine National Liberation Movement): f. 1957; embraces a coalition of varying views from conservative to radical; leader YASSER ARAFAT; Sec.-Gen. FAROUK KADDOUMI; Central Cttee. elected by Fatah's 530-member Congress, May 31st, 1980): YASSER ARAFAT ("ABU AMMAR"), KHALIL WAZIR ("ABU JIHAD"), SALAH KHALAF ("ABU IYAD"), FAROUK KADDOUMI ("ABU LUTF" —also Sec. of Central Cttee.), NIMR SALIH ("ABU SALIH"), MAHMUD ABBAS ("ABU MAZIN"), KHALID al-HASSAN ("ABU as-SAID"), HAYIL ABDUL HAMID ("ABU al-HAWL"), MUHAMMAD GHUNAIM ("ABU MAHIR"), SALIM az-ZA'NUN ("ABU al-ADIB"), SAMIH QUWAYQ ("QADRI"), Col. SA'D SAYIL ("ABU al-WALID"), RAFIQ an-NATSHAH ("ABU SHAKIR"), HANI al-HASAN.

Al Asifah (*Fatah Forces*): Commdr. YASSER ARAFAT; Deputy Commdr. KHALIL WAZIR.

Popular Front for the Liberation of Palestine (PFLP): f. 1967; Marxist-Leninist; leader Dr. GEORGE HABASH; spokesman BASSAM ABU SHERIF.

Popular Front for the Liberation of Palestine— General Command: split from PFLP; pro-Syrian; leader AHMED JEBRIL.

Saiqa (Vanguard of the Popular Liberation War): f. 1967; Syrian-backed; leader SAMINI ATTARI.

Democratic Front for the Liberation of Palestine (DFLP): split from PFLP in 1969; Marxist; leader NAIF HAWATMEH.

Arab Liberation Front (ALF): Iraqi-backed; leader ABDEL RAHIM AHMED.

Popular Struggle Front (PSF): f. 1967; Sec.-Gen. SAMIR GHOUSHA.

Palestine Liberation Front (PLF): Pro-Iraqi; split from PFLP-GC in April 1977; Sec.-Gen. TALAAT YAQOUB.

"Black September" is a hard-core group which draws its support from a variety of organizations. "Black June" is the split from Fatah, the "Fatah Revolutionary Council" in Baghdad, and is headed by "ABU NIDAL". The "Rejectionist Front" consists of those who reject any settlement which recognizes Israel (*see* under Executive Committee, p. 92.)

THE PALESTINIAN NATIONAL CHARTER

(Palestine Liberation Organization)*

1. Palestine is the homeland of the Palestinian Arab people; it is an indivisible part of the Arab homeland, and the Palestinian people are an integral part of the Arab nation.

2. Palestine, with the boundaries it had during the British mandate, is an indivisible territorial unit.

3. The Palestinian Arab people possess the legal right to their homeland and have the right to determine their destiny after achieving the liberation of their country in accordance with their wishes and entirely of their own accord and will.

4. The Palestinian identity is a genuine, essential and inherent characteristic; it is transmitted from parents to children. The Zionist occupation and the dispersal of the Palestinian Arab people, through the disasters which befell them, do not make them lose their Palestinian identity and their membership of the Palestinian community, nor do they negate them.

5. The Palestinians are those Arab nationals who, until 1947, normally resided in Palestine regardless of whether they were evicted from it or have stayed there. Anyone born, after that date, of a Palestinian father—whether inside Palestine or outside it—is also a Palestinian.

6. The Jews who had normally resided in Palestine until the beginning of the Zionist invasion will be considered Palestinians.

---

* Decisions of the National Congress of the Palestine Liberation Organization held in Cairo July 1st–17th, 1968.

7. That there is a Palestinian community and that it has material, spiritual and historical connection with Palestine are indisputable facts. It is a national duty to bring up individual Palestinians in an Arab revolutionary manner. All means of information and education must be adopted in order to acquaint the Palestinian with his country in the most profound manner, both spiritual and material, that is possible. He must be prepared for the armed struggle and ready to sacrifice his wealth and his life in order to win back his homeland and bring about its liberation.

8. The phase in their history, through which the Palestinian people are now living, is that of national struggle for the liberation of Palestine. Thus the conflicts among the Palestinian national forces are secondary, and should be ended for the sake of the basic conflict that exists between the forces of Zionism and of imperialism on the one hand, and the Palestinian Arab people on the other. On this basis the Palestinian masses, regardless of whether they are residing in the national homeland or in diaspora, constitute—both their organizations and the indivi-duals—one national front working for the retrieval of Palestine and its liberation through armed struggle.

9. Armed struggle is the only way to liberate Palestine . . . . .

10. Commando action constitutes the nucleus of the Palestinian popular liberation war. This requires its escalation, comprehensiveness and the mobilization of all the Palestinian popular and educational efforts and their organization and involvement in the armed Palestinian revolution. It also requires the achieving of unity for the national struggle among the different

groupings of the Palestinian people, and between the Palestinian people and the Arab masses so as to secure the continuation of the revolution, its escalation and victory.

11. The Palestinians will have three mottoes: national unity, national mobilization and liberation.

12. The Palestinian people believe in Arab unity. In order to contribute their share towards the attainment of that objective, however, they must, at the present stage of their struggle, safeguard their Palestinian identity and develop their consciousness of that identity, and oppose any plan that may dissolve or impair it.

13. Arab unity and the liberation of Palestine are two complementary objectives, the attainment of either of which facilitates the attainment of the other. Thus, Arab unity leads to the liberation of Palestine; the liberation of Palestine leads to Arab unity; and work towards the realization of one objective proceeds side by side with work towards the realization of the other.

14. The destiny of the Arab nation, and indeed Arab existence itself, depends upon the destiny of the Palestine cause. From this interdependence springs the Arab nation's pursuit of, and striving for, the liberation of Palestine. The people of Palestine play the role of the vanguard in the realization of this sacred national goal.

15. The liberation of Palestine, from an Arab viewpoint, is a national duty and it attempts to repel the Zionist and imperialist aggression against the Arab homeland, and aims at the elimination of Zionism in Palestine. Absolute responsibility for this falls upon the Arab nation—peoples and governments —with the Arab people of Palestine in the vanguard. Accordingly the Arab nation must mobilize all its military, human, moral and spiritual capabilities to participate actively with the Palestinian people in the liberation of Palestine. It must, particularly in the phase of the armed Palestinian revolution, offer and furnish the Palestinian people with all possible help, and material and human support, and make available to them the means and opportunities that will enable them to continue to carry out their leading role in the armed revolution, until they liberate their homeland.

16. The liberation of Palestine, from a spiritual point of view, will provide the Holy Land with an atmosphere of safety and tranquillity, which in turn will safeguard the country's religious sanctuaries and guarantee freedom of worship and of visit to all, without discrimination of race, color, language, or religion. Accordingly, the people of Palestine look to all spiritual forces in the world for support.

17. The liberation of Palestine, from a human point of view, will restore to the Palestinian individual his dignity, pride and freedom. Accordingly the Palestinian Arab people look forward to the support of all those who believe in the dignity of man and his freedom in the world.

18. The liberation of Palestine, from an international point of view, is a defensive action necessitated by the demands of self-defence. Accordingly,

the Palestinian people, desirous as they are of the friendship of all people, look to freedom-loving, justice-loving and peace-loving states for support in order to restore their legitimate rights in Palestine, to re-establish peace and security in the country, and to enable its people to exercise national sovereignty and freedom.

19. The partition of Palestine in 1947 and the establishment of the state of Israel are entirely illegal, regardless of the passage of time, because they were contrary to the will of the Palestinian people and to their natural right in their homeland, and inconsistent with the principles embodied in the Charter of the United Nations, particularly the right to self-determination.

20. The Balfour Declaration, the mandate for Palestine and everything that has been based upon them, are deemed null and void. Claims of historical or religious ties of Jews with Palestine are incompatible with the facts of history and the true conception of what constitutes statehood. Judaism, being a religion, is not an independent nationality. Nor do Jews constitute a single nation with an identity of its own; they are citizens of the states to which they belong.

21. The Palestinian Arab people, expressing themselves by the armed Palestinian revolution, reject all solutions which are substitutes for the total liberation of Palestine and reject all proposals aiming at the liquidation of the Palestinian problem, or its internationalization.

22. Zionism is a political movement organically associated with international imperialism and antagonistic to all action for liberation and to progressive movements in the world. It is racist and fanatic in its nature, aggressive, expansionist and colonial in its aims, and fascist in its methods. Israel is the instrument of the Zionist movement, and a geographical base for world imperialism placed strategically in the midst of the Arab homeland to combat the hopes of the Arab nation for liberation, unity and progress. Israel is a constant source of threat *vis-à-vis* peace in the Middle East and the whole world. Since the liberation of Palestine will destroy the Zionist and imperialist presence and will contribute to the establishment of peace in the Middle East, the Palestinian people look for the support of all the progressive and peaceful forces and urge them all, irrespective of their affiliations and beliefs, to offer the Palestinian people all aid and support in their just struggle for the liberation of their homeland.

23. The demands of security and peace, as well as the demands of right and justice, require all states to consider Zionism an illegitimate movement, to outlaw its existence, and to ban its operations, in order that friendly relations among peoples may be preserved, and the loyalty of citizens to their respective homelands safeguarded.

24. The Palestinian people believe in the principles of justice, freedom, sovereignty, self-determination, human dignity, and in the right of all peoples to exercise them.

25. For the realization of the goals of this Charter and its principles, the Palestine Liberation Organization will perform its role in the liberation of Palestine in accordance with the Constitution of this Organization.

26. The Palestine Liberation Organization, representative of the Palestinian revolutionary forces, is responsible for the Palestinian Arab people's movement in its struggle—to retrieve its homeland, liberate and return to it and exercise the right to self-determination in it—in all military, political and financial fields and also for whatever may be required by the Palestine case on the inter-Arab and international levels.

27. The Palestine Liberation Organization shall cooperate with all Arab states, each according to its potentialities; and will adopt a neutral policy among them in the light of the requirements of the war of liberation; and on this basis it shall not interfere in the internal affairs of any Arab state.

28. The Palestinian Arab people assert the genuineness and independence of their national revolution and reject all forms of intervention, trusteeship and subordination.

29. The Palestinian people possess the fundamental and genuine legal right to liberate and retrieve their homeland. The Palestinian people determine their attitude towards all states and forces on the basis of the stands they adopt *vis-à-vis* the Palestinian case and the extent of the support they offer to the Palestinian revolution to fulfil the aims of the Palestinian people.

30. Fighters and carriers of arms in the war of liberation are the nucleus of the popular army which will be the protective force for the gains of the Palestinian Arab people.

31. The Organization shall have a flag, an oath of allegiance and an anthem. All this shall be decided upon in accordance with a special regulation.

32. Regulations, which shall be known as the Constitution of the Palestine Liberation Organization, shall be annexed to this Charter. It shall lay down the manner in which the Organization, and its organs and institutions, shall be constituted; the respective competence of each; and the requirements of its obligations under the Charter.

33. This Charter shall not be amended save by (vote of) a majority of two-thirds of the total membership of the National Council of the Palestine Liberation Organization (taken) at a special session convened for that purpose.

15-POINT POLITICAL PROGRAMME

(adopted by the Palestine National Council, March 20th, 1977 and reaffirmed by the PLO Central Council, August 25th, 1977)

Proceeding from the Palestine national charter and the previous national councils' resolutions; considering the decisions and political gains achieved by the PLO at the Arab and international levels during the period following the 12th session of the PNC; after studying and debating the latest developments in the Palestine issue; and stressing support for the Palestinian national struggle in the Arab and international forums, the PNC affirms the following:

1. The PNC affirms that the Palestine issue is the essence and the root of the Arab-Zionist conflict. Security Council Resolution 242 (*see* Documents on Palestine, p. 69) ignores the Palestinian people and their firm rights. The PNC therefore confirms its rejection of this Resolution, and rejects negotiations at the Arab and international levels based on this Resolution.

2. The PNC affirms the stand of the PLO in its determination to continue the armed struggle, and its concomitant forms of political and mass struggle, to achieve our inalienable national rights.

3. The PNC affirms that the struggle, in all its military, political and popular forms, in the occupied territory constitutes the central link in its programme of struggle. On this basis, the PLO will strive to escalate the armed struggle in the occupied territory, to escalate all other concomitant forms of struggle, and to give all kinds of moral support to the masses of our people in the occupied territory in order to escalate the struggle and to strengthen their steadfastness to defeat and liquidate the occupation.

4. The PNC affirms the PLO's stand which rejects all types of American capitulationist settlement and all liquidationist projects. The Council affirms the determination of the PLO to abort any settlement achieved at the expense of the firm national rights of our people. The PNC calls upon the Arab nation to shoulder its pan-Arab responsibilities and to pool all its energies to confront these imperialist and Zionist plans.

5. The Palestine National Council stresses the importance and necessity of national units, both political and military, among all the contingents of the Palestine Revolution within the framework of the PLO, because this is one of the basic conditions for victory. For this reason, it is necessary to co-ordinate national units at all levels and in all spheres on the basis of commitment to all these resolutions, and to draw up programmes which will ensure the implementation of this.

6. The Palestine National Council affirms the right of the Palestine Revolution to be present on the soil of fraternal Lebanon within the framework of the Cairo agreement and its appendices, concluded between the PLO and the Lebanese authorities. The Council also affirms adherence to the implementation of the Cairo agreement in letter and in spirit, including the preservation of the position of the

Revolution and the security of the camps. The Palestine National Council refuses to accept any interpretation of this agreement by one side only. Meanwhile, it affirms its eagerness for the maintenance of the sovereignty and security of Lebanon.

7. The Palestine National Council greets the heroic fraternal Lebanese people and affirms the eagerness of the PLO for the maintenance of the territorial integrity of Lebanon, the unity of its people and its security, independence, sovereignty and Arabism. The Palestine National Council affirms its pride in the support rendered by this heroic fraternal people to the PLO, which is struggling for our people to regain their national rights to their homeland and their right to return to this homeland. The PNC strongly affirms the need to deepen and consolidate cohesion between all Lebanese nationalist forces and the Palestine Revolution.

8. The Council affirms the need to strengthen the Arab front participating in the Palestine Revolution, and to deepen cohesion with all forces participating in it in all Arab countries, as well as to escalate the joint Arab struggle and to further strengthen the Palestine Revolution in order to contend with the imperialist and Zionist designs.

9. The Palestine National Council has decided to consolidate Arab struggle and solidarity on the basis of struggle against imperialism and Zionism, to work for the liberation of all the occupied Arab areas, and to adhere to the support for the Palestine Revolution in order to regain the constant national rights of the Palestinian Arab people without any conciliation or recognition.

10. The Palestine National Council affirms the right of the PLO to exercise its struggle responsibilities at the pan-Arab level and through any Arab land in the interest of liberating the occupied areas.

11. The Palestine National Council has decided to continue the struggle to regain the national rights of our people, in particular their rights of return, self-determination and establishing an independent national state on their national soil.

12. The Palestine National Council affirms the significance of co-operation and solidarity with socialist, non-aligned, Islamic and African countries, and with all the national liberation movements in the world.

13. The Palestine National Council hails the stands and struggles of all the democratic countries and forces against Zionism in its capacity as one form of racism, as well as against its aggressive practices.

14. The Palestine National Council affirms the significance of establishing relations and co-ordinating with the progressive and democratic Jewish forces inside and outside the occupied homeland, since these forces are struggling against Zionism as a doctrine and in practice. The Palestine National Council calls on all states and forces who love freedom, justice and peace in the world to end all forms of assistance to and co-operation with the racist Zionist regime, and to end contacts with it and its instruments.

15. Taking into consideration the important achievements in the Arab and international arenas since the conclusion of the PNC's 12th session, the Palestine National Council, which has reviewed the political report submitted by the PLO, has decided the following:

A. The Council confirms its wish for the PLO's right to participate independently and on an equal footing in all the conferences and international forums concerned with the Palestine issue and the Arab-Zionist conflict, with a view to achieving our inalienable national rights as approved by the United Nations General Assembly in 1974, namely in Resolution 3236 (*see* Documents on Palestine, page 80).

B. The Council declares that any settlement or agreement affecting the rights of our Palestinian people made in the absence of this people will be completely null and void.

Long live the Palestine Revolution. Long live Palestinian unity among the Revolution's contingents. Glory and immortality to our innocent martyrs. This Revolution will continue until victory.

RECOMMENDATIONS OF THE MILITARY COMMITTEE OF THE PALESTINE NATIONAL COUNCIL
(approved by the Council, March 20th, 1977)

1. Unification of the fighting forces of all the Palestinian revolutionary contingents, including the Palestinian armed struggle, the militia forces and the Palestine Liberation Army, in a united force to be named the army and the armed forces of the Palestine revolution that will be the military arm of the PLO.

2. The army and the armed forces of the Palestine revolution are to be composed of the following: (a) regular forces, to be named the Palestinian National Liberation Army, which will comprise all regular forces; (b) irregular forces; (c) the militia forces, including the youth and cubs organizations.

3. The Chairman of the PLO Executive Committee is the supreme commander of the army and the armed forces of the Palestine revolution; at the same time he will hold the position of general commander until someone is appointed to fill this post.

4. A supreme military council will be established under the leadership of the supreme commander, to include the military commanders of the organizations, the general commander and commanders of the three forces—the regular, irregular and militia forces. This council will pass the rules and regulations that are necessary to organize the army and the armed forces,

(service contractors should not be confused with ordinary foreign drilling contractors, such as Santa Fe and the South Eastern Drilling Company—SEDCO, which are employed on a straight fee basis by almost all oil companies and oil producing governments.)

Not dissimilar to service contracts are "production sharing" arrangements, of a type pioneered by Indonesia. Production sharing arrangements have been concluded by Egypt (which invited Western companies to bid for new acreage in 1973, following a period in which oil exploration had been given over to the Soviet Union), and by Libya in 1974. In the mid 1970s Syria signed a number of production sharing agreements, allowing Western companies into the country for the first time since 1964. There are considerable variations in this type of agreement, but in most cases the foreign company is compensated for its share of expenditure in cash or kind, or by favourable tax terms, while production is divided in a ratio of between 75-25 and 85-15 in favour of the state.

After the Iranian revolution the Government decided to end its four successful partnerships— SIRIP, IPAC (with Amoco), LAPCO (with Arco, Murphy, Sun and Unocal) and IMINOCO (with AGIP, Phillips and the Indian Oil and Natural Gas Commission). The Government took over the foreign partners' shareholdings and in August 1980 announced that their operations were to be run by a new Continental Shelf Oil Company. This was to be supervised by a directorate in the oil ministry.

The drive for participation, and Algerian takeovers

Parallel with the development of partnerships and contracts on new acreage, the 1960s saw a growing desire on the part of the producer governments for participation in existing concessions. This idea was originally put by Saudi Arabia to Aramco in 1964, and in 1968 it was given formal voice in OPEC's Declaratory Statement of Petroleum Policy. Apart from being satisfactory on nationalist grounds, and giving the producers a more direct say in such matters as the relinquishment of acreage, the employment of nationals, production rates and investment in new capacity, the governments felt that participation would give them a foothold in the oil industry, which would later enable them to mount their own crude oil sales operations, or expand their national companies downstream into the tankering, refining and marketing business. The producers, however, did not feel strong enough to press their claim until after the appearance of a seller's market and their success in the Teheran price negotiations of February 1971; and so it was not until OPEC's Twenty-fifth Conference in Vienna in July 1971 that the members decided to call the companies to formal talks on participation.

By this time a precedent had already been set by Algeria. For political reasons Algeria had nationalized its American concessionaires and Shell in 1967, without causing itself economic harm. This left the French companies, CFP and ERAP, which were responsible for most of the country's production, and were in a special position under the 1965 Franco-Algerian Evian

Agreement. Hopes of a satisfactory relationship under this agreement were not fulfilled, and in 1969, under the terms of the agreement, Algeria opened negotiations for higher prices. The talks were inconclusive, and in July 1970 Algeria increased its prices unilaterally. Then, after further fruitless discussions, it seized 51 per cent of the two French companies on February 24th, 1971. The French sponsored a highly effective boycott, but in June CFP settled its differences with the Government—Algeria agreeing to pay $60 million compensation, while CFP paid $40 million backpayments and accepted a higher price. Five months later ERAP also came to terms, agreeing that compensation and backpayments should cancel each other out and entering into a minority partnership with Sonatrach in the Hassi Messaoud South field. In 1975 CFP agreed to extend its partnership with Sonatrach for a further five years, but ERAP allowed its agreement to lapse at the end of the year.

The takeover of CFP and ERAP was not directly related to the formal OPEC participation demand, being very much a Franco-Algerian affair, having its roots in the colonial past and the aftermath of the country's independence—but it nevertheless increased the confidence of the other producers when they began negotiations with the companies in Geneva in January 1972. The countries concerned in these negotiations were just the five Arab producers in the Gulf (Venezuela and Indonesia having already achieved a degree of participation or close involvement in the running of their oil industries, and Iran, Libya and Nigeria having made it clear that they would pursue their own negotiations), and in practice the talks were conducted by Shaikh Ahmed Zaki Yamani of Saudi Arabia, representing the producers, and Aramco, representing the companies. Yamani's initial demand was for an immediate 25 per cent share rising to 51 per cent, with compensation to be at net book value, and that part of the government share of production sold back to the companies to be priced between the posted price and the tax paid cost (government revenue plus production cost). The companies' counter proposal, offering 50-50 joint ventures on new acreage, showed how big the gap between the two sides was at this point. In March, however, the companies agreed in principle to surrender 20 per cent of their operations, and in October, by which time Iraq, having nationalized IPC five months earlier, was no longer concerned in the negotiations, an outline agreement was reached in New York.

The General Agreement of 1972

The details of the General Agreement on Participation were finalized in December 1972, and ratified by Saudi Arabia, Qatar and Abu Dhabi at the turn of the year. Under the Agreement the producers took an immediate 25 per cent stake in the concessionaire companies. The earliest date for majority participation laid down was January 1st, 1982, with the initial shareholding rising by 5 per cent in 1978, 1979, 1980 and 1981 and by 6 per cent in 1982. This timetable was designed to make for a smooth transition and to

[continued on p. 103

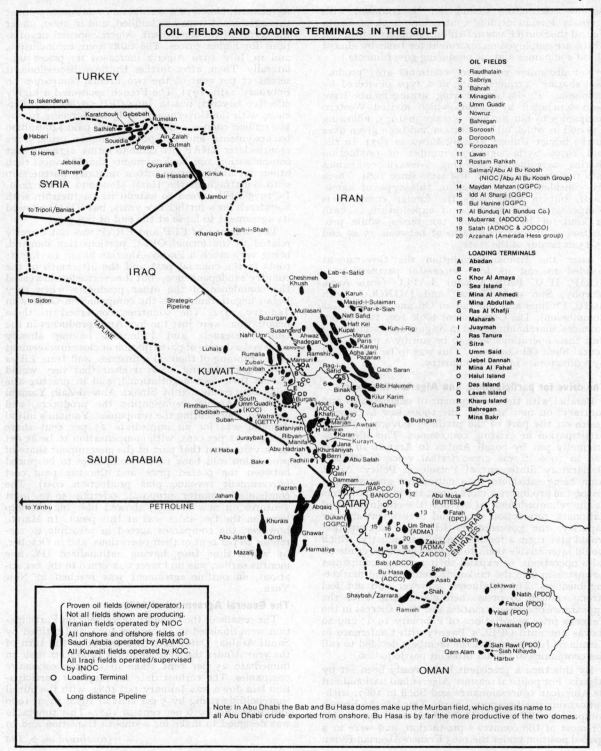

OIL FIELDS AND LOADING TERMINALS IN THE GULF

OIL FIELDS

1 Raudhatain
2 Sabriya
3 Bahrah
4 Minagish
5 Umm Guadir
6 Nowruz
7 Bahregan
8 Soroosh
9 Dorooch
10 Foroozan
11 Lavan
12 Rostam Rahksh
13 Salman/Abu Al Bu Koosh
   (NIOC/Abu Al Bu Koosh Group)
14 Maydan Mahzan (QGPC)
15 Idd Al Shargi (QGPC)
16 Bul Hanine (QGPC)
17 Al Bunduq (Al Bunduq Co.)
18 Mubarraz (ADOCO)
19 Satah (ADNOC & JODCO)
20 Arzanah (Amerada Hess group)

LOADING TERMINALS

A Abadan
B Fao
C Khor Al Amaya
D Sea Island
E Mina Al Ahmedi
F Mina Abdullah
G Ras Al Khafji
H Maharah
I Juaymah
J Ras Tanura
K Sitra
L Umm Said
M Jebel Dannah
N Mina Al Fahal
O Halul Island
P Das Island
Q Lavan Island
R Kharg Island
S Bahregan
T Mina Bakr

Note: In Abu Dhabi the Bab and Bu Hasa domes make up the Murban field, which gives its name to all Abu Dhabi crude exported from onshore. Bu Hasa is by far the more productive of the two domes.

Proven oil fields (owner/operator);
Not all fields shown are producing.
Iranian fields operated by NIOC
All onshore and offshore fields of
Saudi Arabia operated by ARAMCO
All Kuwaiti fields operated by KOC
All Iraqi fields operated/supervised
by INOC
○ Loading Terminal
Long distance Pipeline

continued from p. 101]

enable all the companies to adjust their supply arrangements over the following decade.

The need to ease company problems also accounted for the complex arrangements for pricing and disposing of the states' 25 per cent share of production. The 75 per cent companies entitlement, which became known as "equity crude" remained subject to the provisions of the Teheran Agreement of February 1971, but the balance belonging to the producing states was divided into three categories, each of them priced in a different way. A small proportion cf production (only 10 per cent of the states' share or 2.5 per cent of total output in 1973) the governments undertook to sell on the open market for whatever price they could get. The other two categories of crude were "bridging crude" and "phase in" crude, both priced at above the normal tax paid cost and both set to decline in volume as the states' direct sales were to increase. Within nine months of the General Agreement coming into effect, however, the Gulf producers decided that both bridging and phase-in crude should be treated on the same basis, and priced at 93 per cent of the posting—this being the price Saudi Arabia had obtained in the sale of its own 2.5 per cent crude entitlement in May.

For compensation under the General Agreement the criteria adopted was "updated book value" which took account of the cost of replacement of the companies' assets. This was a compromise between the producers' demand for compensation to be on a net book value basis (i.e. after depreciation) and the companies' efforts to obtain a formula which would repay them for some of the value of the proven reserves discovered in their concessions. In the event, the system adopted involved Saudi Arabia paying Aramco $500 million, Abu Dhabi paying $162 million in almost equal parts to Abu Dhabi Marine Areas and the Abu Dhabi Petroleum Company, and Qatar paying $28 million to the Qatar Petroleum Company and $43 million to Shell.

Iraqi nationalization

Iraq ceased to have any involvement with the participation negotiations in 1972, when it nationalized the Iraq Petroleum Company. For 20 years relations between the Government and the company had not been good. In the later 1950s, a dispute had arisen over the fact that IPC and its sisters, the Basrah Petroleum Company in the south and the Mosul Petroleum Company in the north, had developed only a very minor part of their 160,000 square mile concession. Combined with disagreements over the group's accounting procedures, this led to Law 80 of 1961 expropriating more than 99.5 per cent of the group's acreage. The companies never accepted the expropriation, and although several attempts were made to settle this and many other outstanding differences over the next 10 years, the two parties were forced to accept a position of stalemate, in which Iraqi production expanded very slowly.

In June 1971, as part of the agreement on Iraqi Mediterranean crude prices which followed the

Teheran pact in February, the IPC group gave commitments for increases in production, but in the following spring, the company found itself obliged to cut the throughput of its pipeline from Kirkuk to the Mediterranean terminals of Banias (Syria) and Tripoli (Lebanon). The company explained that in a period of low Gulf/Europe freight rates, the high prices negotiated for all Mediterranean crudes in the previous years made it uneconomic for its owners to run the pipe at more than half capacity. The Iraqi Government claimed that the cut-back was politically motivated, and presented IPC with alternatives: either the company was to restore Kirkuk production to normal levels and hand the extra production over to the Government, or it was to surrender the field entirely and concentrate production on BPC's acreage in the south. This conflict was further exacerbated by IPC's threats of legal action to prevent the sale of the Iraq National Oil Company's crude from North Rumaila (in expropriated BPC acreage), and by a number of old issues, including an Iraqi claim for royalty backpayments dating from 1964, which IPC had refused to pay until it received the compensation it was claiming for the acreage expropriated in 1971. On May 31st, IPC presented its answers to the Iraqi ultimatum. These did not satisfy the Government, and on the next day, IPC was nationalized. The affiliates, BPC and MPC, were not immediately affected.

In mid-July, negotiations got underway, with Nadim Pachachi, then Secretary-General of OPEC, and M. Jean Duroc-Danner of CFP, acting as mediators. IPC promptly announced that it would not pursue legal action against buyers of Kirkuk crude while mediation efforts were in progress, and the Iraqis were then able to sell substantial amounts of oil—including a deal in February 1973 under which CFP agreed to take 23.75 per cent of Kirkuk's output (equivalent to the company's stake in IPC) over ten years. On February 28th, 1973, IPC and the Government finally reached agreement. IPC accepted the expropriations of 1961 and the nationalization of the Kirkuk producing area, and at the same time handed over MPC and paid the Government $141 million of outstanding royalty backpayments. In return it was promised 15 million tons of oil in two batches in 1973 and 1974, and was given some assurance of the long-term security of its investment and growth of output from BPC's southern fields, where it agreed to more than double production from 640,000 b/d in 1972 to 1,626,000 b/d in 1976.

In the event, it was only seven months before BPC suffered the seizure, during the October war, of the holdings of Exxon and Mobil, and 60 per cent of Shell's share (a proportion relating to the Dutch-registered part of the group) as a political gesture against the U.S.A.'s and the Netherlands' association with Israel. Later the 5 per cent share of the Participations and Explorations Corporations (owned by the Gulbenkian family) was seized on the grounds that the company was registered in Portugal, which was pursuing racist policies in Africa. Thereafter the Government watched the progress of the takeover negotiations in Saudi Arabia and Kuwait, and a few days after a final agreement had been signed in Kuwait, it nationalized the remaining Western-owned share in BPC. It then held negotiations with the BPC partners over compensation and supply arrangements.

Iranian Sales and Purchase Agreement

Although it was clear from the beginning of the Saudi Arabian-Aramco negotiations in January 1972 that Iran was not interested in the type of participation envisaged by the Gulf states, the Shah did not decide exactly what Iran would demand instead until early 1973. On January 23rd the Shah gave the Consortium an ultimatum: under no circumstances would Iran extend its lease, and the companies could either continue under existing arrangements until the expiry of their lease in 1979 and then become ordinary buyers under contract, or they could negotiate an entirely new agency agreement immediately. The Consortium opted for the latter plan, and, under the Iranian Sales and Purchase Agreement, signed in Teheran in May, NIOC took formal control of the management of the Consortium's entire production operation and the Abadan refinery. The agreement laid down that NIOC would provide 60 per cent of the capital for expanding production and that the companies would contribute 40 per cent of the funds needed in the first five years (then expected to be the period of greatest expansion) in return for a 22 cents discount on their liftings.

Under the Sales and Purchase Agreement, though NIOC became owner/manager, the Consortium members established a service company, the Oil Service Company of Iran (OSCO), to carry out operations on NIOC's behalf for an initial period of five years, which could be renewed. NIOC undertook to raise total installed production capacity to 8 million b/d by October 1976. It was agreed that the national company would be entitled to take the oil needed for internal consumption and a "stated quantity" for export, which was to rise from 200,000 b/d in 1973 to 1.5 million b/d in 1981, and therefore, except in certain cases of *force majeure*, would remain in the same proportion to total crude available for export as 1.5 million b/d represented to oil available for export in 1981. The balance of crude production went to the Consortium members, which were guaranteed security of supply for 20 years.

Libya asserts 51 per cent control

It was only a matter of weeks after OPEC had made its formal call for participation in July 1971 that Libya, ever anxious to be first among the producers in militancy and to upstage any participation agreement negotiated by Saudi Arabia, let it be known that it would be interested in nothing less than an immediate 51 per cent share. Four months later, at the beginning of December 1971, Libya nationalized outright BP's half-share of the Sarir field, but this was a purely political gesture (against alleged British connivance in the Iranian invasion of the Tumbs Islands some 24 hours before Britain's withdrawal from the Gulf)—and for the next year the Libyan Government made no move while it awaited the outcome of the participation negotiations in the Gulf.

Talks on Libya's demand for majority control eventually began in early 1973, with the Government adopting its usual policy of negotiating on a company by company basis; but they made no progress. In June Libya nationalized outright the U.S. independent Nelson Bunker Hunt. This company had been BP's 50 per cent partner in the Sarir field, and the Government had chosen it for its first negotiations because it had no other source of oil outside the U.S. and seemed therefore to be especially vulnerable. Bunker Hunt, however, resisted hard. Being a private company it did not have shareholders to worry about and it was confident in the Libyan operators' secret agreement, under which the companies had promised to meet the supply commitments of any one of their number whose concession was expropriated. Colonel Gaddafi, the Libyan leader, correctly characterized the Bunker Hunt seizure as "a warning to the companies to respond to the demands of the Libyan Arab Republic". From circumstantial evidence it seems that Libya fully decided on nationalizing Bunker Hunt when it concluded that it would have no difficulty in selling the oil to markets apart from the East bloc. This followed the judgement of a local court in Sicily which dismissed a suit brought by BP against the importers and refiners of its expropriated Sarir oil.

Following its nationalization of Bunker Hunt, the Libyan Government proceeded in August to seize 51 per cent of Occidental's operations. Faced with the threat of having the rest of its assets seized and being deprived of its most vital source of oil outside the U.S., Occidental announced its "acquiescence" in the measure. For the other companies the significance of this "acquiescence" lay in the fiscal terms. The companies had in fact been prepared to offer Libya a nominal 51 per cent on the condition that the financial results gave parity with those deriving from the participation agreements with the Gulf producers and Nigeria—but this was not the case in the terms settled with Occidental. Compensation was agreed on at book value, rather than the updated book value formula used in the Gulf, and the buy-back price was set above the posting, rather than between the posting and the tax paid cost.

Five days after the Occidental seizure, three independent companies in the Oasis group, Continental, Marathon and Amerada Hess, accepted a majority takeover on similar terms, though Shell, the only major in Oasis, did not comply with the measure. Then in September the Government announced 51 per cent takeovers of all the other significant producing groups. Gelsenberg, a German concern in partnership with Mobil, and W. R. Grace, a small shareholder in the Esso Sirte venture, agreed to Libya's terms; but Atlantic Richfield (another partner in Esso Sirte) and the majors, Mobil, Esso (which held a concession on its own as well as the biggest share in Esso Sirte) and the Texaco-Socal company, Amoseas, joined Shell in resisting any sort of arrangement which might have undermined their participation agreements in the Gulf.

Libya's next move came in February 1974 when it seized all of the remaining assets of Texaco, Socal and Atlantic Richfield; and in the following month, Shell too was nationalized. Finally Mobil, in March, and

Esso, in April, accepted the 51 per cent seizure of the previous September.

Exxon and Mobil eventually withdrew from their concessions on their own initiative in November 1981 and April 1982. Exxon's liftings had stopped in the summer of 1981 and Mobil's liftings by the time of its withdrawal had fallen to only 10,000 b/d. Some months after its withdrawal Exxon negotiated an agreement with the Libyan Government under which it received compensation for the assets of its two former concessionaires—Esso Sirte and Esso Standard Libya—at about 70 per cent of net book value. The Libyans established the Sirte Oil Company, wholly owned by the National Oil Corporation, to run both operations formerly managed by Exxon. The W.R. Grace interest in the Sirte concession was unaffected.

Gulf States achieve 60 per cent participation

The General Agreement on Participation concluded at the end of 1972 had satisfied the Kuwaiti Government, and had been signed by the Minister of Finance and Oil, Mr. Abdel-Rahman Atiqi, at the beginning of January 1973; but the Kuwait National Assembly refused its approval. The determination of the handful of radicals lending opposition to the measure was strengthened by Iraq's success in settling its dispute with IPC in February and by the signature of Iran's Sales and Purchase Agreement in May; and by the summer of 1973, it had become clear that the Government would not, as it had originally hoped, be able to rally sufficient support to get the General Agreement accepted. On June 13th, the Ruler formally requested a revision of the accord, and during the autumn, when Libya announced its series of 51 per cent takeovers, the other Gulf producers followed Kuwait's example. In November Sheikh Ahmed Zaki Yamani announced that Saudi Arabia would not be satisfied with a simple majority holding, and it was subsequently made clear early in 1974 that the Saudi Government would be negotiating a complete takeover of Aramco's operations.

Negotiations between the Kuwait Government and the Kuwait Oil Company shareholders, BP and Gulf, during the winter, resulted at the end of January in the state gaining a holding of 60 per cent, which, after several months of further wrangling in the National Assembly, was ratified on May 14th, 1974. The new agreement was made valid from January 1st, meaning that the companies had given way on the principle of retroactivity on which they had held so firm in the past, and was to last for six years—though in explaining the terms, Mr. Atiqi was insistent about the Government's right to call fresh negotiations at any point before the end of 1974. The compensation formula agreed was net book value (giving KOC $112 million) rather than updated book value, but there was no settlement of buy-back terms, with the volume and price of oil being left for more hard bargaining over the summer. In fact Kuwait did not conclude a buy-back deal with BP and Gulf until after it had rejected all bids put in for its 60 per cent crude share at an auction in July. For the third quarter of the year, the Government then sold rather over 55 per cent of its entitlement to the two companies at 94.8 per cent of the posted price; and for the last quarter, BP and Gulf bought two-thirds of the state's crude at 93 per cent of the posting.

Three months before the ratification of the Kuwaiti participation agreement, Qatar concluded a similar accord with its concessionaires (the Qatar Petroleum Company and Shell) in February, and in April it settled buy-back arrangements for the following six months. These involved the two companies purchasing 60 per cent of the state entitlement (about 36 per cent of total output) at 93 per cent of the posted price—the same level as that agreed in September 1973 in the original modification of the terms of the General Agreement. Then in June, after the Kuwaiti ratification, Saudi Arabia concluded an "interim" 60 per cent participation agreement with Aramco though no details emerged about the buy-back arrangements. Finally, in September, Abu Dhabi negotiated a 60 per cent share in the Abu Dhabi Petroleum Company and Abu Dhabi Marine Areas, which like all the other revised participation agreements of 1974 was back-dated to the beginning of the year.

Aramco takeover negotiations

Although Saudi Arabia had decided that it would be asking for more than a simple majority stake in Aramco in November 1973, it was not until early 1974 (shortly before the government took 60 per cent of Aramco as an interim measure in June) that it finally became clear that the government was seeking a complete takeover. This, it was let known, was to be linked to sales and contracting arrangements similar to those concluded between Iran and the Consortium in May 1973. Within a matter of weeks the government and Aramco were reported to be close to clinching the deal, but over the next six years changing circumstances in the Middle East, in Saudi Arabia and in the world oil market continually postponed the conclusion of an agreement.

There was an initial breakthrough in November 1974 when Aramco conceded the principle of a complete takeover, and during the following 18 months in successive rounds of negotiations it was understood that general agreement was reached on all major practical issues. Indeed the two sides said as much in an announcement made after talks in Panama City, Florida, in March 1976. It was reported at this time that compensation was to be a little more than $1,500 million for 75 per cent of Aramco's assets (which had expanded considerably since 1973) at net book value. In due course part of this sum was transferred to the Aramco partners, bringing the compensation they had received for their assets up to the 60 per cent level. It was also reported from Florida that the companies would continue to take the bulk of Saudi production; that they would be paid a fee of 15 cents a barrel for production operations plus six cents a barrel for new reserves discovered; and that they would continue to put up part of the risk capital in exploration—only being refunded in the event of success.

During the four years that followed the announcement in Florida there were further rounds of negotiations, but an almost complete lack of news as to the substance of the talks. It was known that there were problems over the fees that Aramco would be paid: the four Aramco partners feared that under some of the formulae put forward their fees would not be big enough to cover their share of investment. On one occasion the companies were known to be objecting to a formula under which their fee would come out of a 75 cents per barrel margin allowed after deducting operating costs and payments to the government. This margin was supposed to cover exploration and the expansion of production capacity as well as the companies' fees.

Other problems centred on the companies' crude oil entitlements. The original understanding of 1976 and 1977 was that the Aramco partners should take up to 7.3 million barrels a day. But early in 1979 when Saudi Arabia's output was raised from the normal 8.5 million b/d to 9.5 million b/d in an attempt to stabilize the market in the aftermath of the Iranian revolution, the companies' entitlement was increased for a short time to 8.1 million b/d. In 1980 this figure was cut to 7.2 million b/d, at which level it was maintained through the early part of 1981. For short periods during the three years from 1977 to 1980 the government cut Aramco's entitlement to below 7 million b/d—for different reasons on each occasion.

The Aramco partners always argued against short term cuts in their entitlements, and for the longer term they were worried about their entitlements undergoing a progressive, permanent reduction. This seemed likely to be caused mainly by Saudi Arabia developing its own crude oil sales. It had long been Saudi policy to sell more oil directly to Third World countries and to the national oil companies of the industrial powers, rather than selling it through the integrated chains of the majors. (From just 190,000 b/d in 1973, Petromin's own sales by early 1981 had risen to some 2 million b/d.) At the same time it was clear that the amounts of crude available to Aramco would gradually be reduced further by three other developments. These were the rise in domestic consumption, supplies to new export refineries, and allocations of "incentive crude" being promised to foreign companies agreeing to invest in refineries and petrochemical plants in Saudi Arabia. An example of the volumes of crude involved in these deals—in this case applying to an Aramco partner—was provided by Mobil's commitment to invest in a petrochemical plant and a refinery at Yanbu. Over fifteen years, beginning at the time of the project's start-up, Mobil is to receive 1.4 thousand million barrels of oil, an average of 225,000 b/d. Although Exxon, Socal and Texaco were all involved in their own projects with the Saudi Government—albeit on a smaller scale than Mobil—most of the companies which concluded such deals in 1979 and 1980 were not Aramco partners. (In 1981 the Saudi Government announced that incentive crude would only be given to companies that had already signed agreements to participate in Saudi industrial projects. It was thought that the economics of Arabian industrialization had improved sufficiently since 1979 for prospective future partners not to need special incentives.)

In the background there was the further possibility of the Aramco partners' supplies being reduced by the government cutting production for internal or external political reasons—or because supplies from other producers had increased. A cutback was also thought likely to follow the government achieving its aim of stabilizing prices.

In 1980 the Aramco partners reckoned that if the Saudi Government were to return production to its "normal" 8.5 million b/d ceiling, they would be lucky to receive 5 million b/d. (In practice, when Saudi production was reduced to 8.5 million b/d in November 1981, it was thought that the Aramco partners were getting 5.4 million b/d. This compared with some 6.5–7.0 million b/d when the government was running production at 9 or 10 million b/d, or more.) A cutback in overall production to 5 million b/d, as advocated by the Saudi conservationists and mentioned on one or two occasions by Ahmed Zaki Yamani, the Saudi oil minister, would leave the Aramco partners with virtually no oil.

Both of the issues in dispute—the companies' fee and their crude entitlements—were apparently resolved early in 1980. In April the Saudi Government transferred to the companies the final instalment of compensation for their assets—$1.5 thousand million, in respect of the 40 per cent share in Aramco retained by the companies since the second participation accord was reached in 1974. At the same time the Government completed its takeover of the Ras Tanura refinery and natural gas liquids facilities, which had been excluded from the 60 per cent participation deal and for several years after 1974 had remained 100 per cent Aramco owned. The government then announced in April 1981 that it was taking 50 per cent of Tapline, in which the Aramco partners each had the same shares as they had in Aramco itself. Exports via Tapline had been suspended for economic reasons in February 1975 and the pipeline had been used only sporadically since.

Exactly what commitments the government had given the companies on crude oil entitlements were not revealed. However, it was known that as of 1980 the Aramco partners were receiving a fee of 27 cents per barrel produced—though again there was no announcement of the details of the formula on which the fee was based. Nor was there any announcement on the form of the new state oil corporation which would hold the government's production assets; only the Ras Tanura refinery had been handed over to the existing state oil company, Petromin. Likewise nothing official was said about what arrangements were to be made by the Aramco partners to form a service company to run the industry on behalf of the new state corporation. Despite the payment of the $1.5 thousand million, the takeover agreement was not signed in 1980 and still had not been signed by May 1981. It was thought the reason for the delay was that no decision had been taken on who should head the new state oil corporation.

In practice, while the negotiations with Aramco were in progress the oil industry in Saudi Arabia was already being run as if the government had total control—in other words the government made decisions but the day to day operations were managed by Aramco. The process of participation had involved the government's acquisition of the company's assets in Saudi Arabia and its decision-making powers over exploration, the development of production capacity and the volume and allocation of output. Technically Aramco remained (and remains) a wholly American-owned and American-registered company. Before the completion of the takeover it was part owner of the Saudi production operation; after the signing of the takeover agreement it was assumed in 1981 that its status would change to that of owner of a service company. For practical purposes within Saudi Arabia Aramco was seen both before and after the complete takeover as a giant foreign contractor and contract manager working for the government. In the mid-1970s the major projects entrusted to Aramco were a major expansion of production capacity and the installation of a huge sea water injection system, the supervision of the construction of a gas gathering system (the biggest industrial project ever undertaken anywhere), a gas liquids pipeline across the peninsula to Yanbu, and a unified electric grid for the Eastern Province.

Takeover in Kuwait

Over a year before Aramco and the Saudi Government reached even the general agreement in Panama City on the major issues of the takeover, the initiative in the movement towards complete ownership of oil producing operations in the Arabian Peninsula had been taken up by Kuwait, which announced on March 5th, 1975 that as of that date it had taken over all assets of the Kuwait Oil Company and would be beginning negotiations to settle the terms with BP and Gulf retroactively. The Kuwaitis made it clear that they wanted a continuing relationship with the KOC owners, but that they felt quite capable of running the production operations themselves. Given that geological and topographical conditions make Kuwaiti oil extremely cheap and easy to produce, and that the state has been fairly thoroughly explored and will not be requiring large-scale new exploration or development work, the continued presence of the major companies was very much less necessary for Kuwait than it was for Saudi Arabia and Abu Dhabi, where there are large potentially oil-bearing areas still to be opened up. For this reason it was felt at the time of the announcement that Kuwait might have decided on a complete take-over after consultation with the other Gulf producers —wanting to use Kuwait's negotiations to gauge what conditions the major companies might eventually be prepared to accept.

Successive rounds of negotiations, however, stuck on the problems of compensation, the service fee and credit terms, but at the beginning of December 1975 an agreement was announced. This involved: compensation of $66 million; a discount off the 93 per cent of postings third party selling price of 15 cents per barrel reflecting BP's and Gulf's continuing provision of technical services and technical personnel, the large size of their purchases and their undertakings

to buy Kuwait's bunker fuel and use Kuwaiti tankers; and commitments by BP to take an average of 450,000 b/d between January 1st, 1976 and April 1st, 1980 and by Gulf to take 500,000 b/d over the same period. The two companies were given an option on a further 400,000 b/d. All of these quantities are subject to the normal plus or minus 12.5 per cent variations.

Since the completion of the takeover the special relationship between Gulf and BP and the Kuwait oil industry has been reduced virtually to nothing. As the Kuwaitis have successfully Arabized many of the technical jobs in oil production and launched their own direct expatriate recruitment programmes to fill those jobs for which they have been unable to find experienced Arab personnel, the numbers seconded by BP and Gulf have fallen to a nominal level. The two companies' purchases of Kuwaiti crude were greatly reduced when their supply contracts were renegotiated in early 1980. Gulf took only 75,000 b/d at the official government selling price (GSP) under a two and a half year contract, while BP took 75,000 b/d at the GSP plus a further 75,000 b/d for one year (to April 1st, 1981) at a premium price. When these contracts were negotiated the original 15 cents discount of 1975 was eliminated.

Beginning in early 1981, the main traditional customers for Kuwaiti crude, Gulf, BP and Shell (which had bought much of Gulf's entitlement in the old concession days) began further to reduce their purchases of Kuwaiti crude. Shell and BP opted out of their contracts altogether in November 1981, and Gulf in January 1982 cut its liftings to just 35,000 b/d.

Takeovers in the Lower Gulf

The takeover in Kuwait in 1975 opened the way for other producers to take 100 per cent of their former concessionaires. Within days of the announcement in December 1975 Iraq nationalized the Basrah Petroleum Company, and in February 1976 Kuwait began negotiations for the takeover of Aminoil in its half of the Partitioned Zone (while stating that it did not intend to change the status of the Arabian Oil Company's operation offshore). Negotiations did not go well—becoming involved in a lot of financial issues related to the technical problems of Aminoil's operations—and in September 1977 the Kuwaitis nationalized the company. For a few months a Kuwaiti Wafra Oil Company was established to run operations, until in April 1978 it was decided that KOC should take over the production operation and KNPC the Mina Abdullah refinery, which had processed Aminoil's entire output.

Starting in June 1976 Qatar negotiated the complete takeover of its two concessionaires, signing broadly similar agreements with QPC in September that year and, after a somewhat tougher series of talks, with Shell in February 1977. Compensation was calculated on the basis of net book value, involving the payment of $14 million for Shell's remaining assets and $18 million for QPC's; both companies established new contracting subsidiaries (Dukan Oil Services and Qatar Shell Service Company) to second personnel to run the industry for the state oil corporation; and both companies accepted a fee of 15 cents per barrel of oil produced. This fee, which compared with the Kuwaiti terms of a 15 cents per barrel discount on just that part of production sold back to BP and Gulf, reflected the much bigger oil company presence retained in Qatar. (These fees, although invariably referred to as being 15 cents, were in fact tied to the official government selling prices, which meant that by mid-1980 the fee had risen to 42 cents.) Furthermore it was agreed that Shell should be paid an unspecified lump sum bonus as a condition of its undertaking further exploration (for gas) for QGPC on a contracting basis.

The five year operating agreements between the Qatar Government, the QPC group and Shell expired at the end of 1981 and early 1982. Dukan Oil Services and the Qatar Shell Service Company continued their work without interruption. It was assumed that the Government would renegotiate the onshore contract with just one of QPC's shareholders—probably B.P.

In Bahrain the Government announced the take-over of the production operations of BAPCO in April 1978, the arrangement being backdated to the beginning of January. The Sitra refinery was left in the hands of BAPCO (owned by Caltex—50–50 Texaco and Socal) until May 1980, when the government took a stake of 60 per cent.

In Abu Dhabi meanwhile the Government made it clear that it felt that its big potential for further discoveries and the technical problems involved in its offshore production made it very much in the state's interest for the companies to retain an equity participation and that the 60–40 agreement would be maintained. (Details of the main companies operating in Abu Dhabi are given in the company lists at the end of this chapter.) Payment for the companies' services in Abu Dhabi comes out of the margin between the GSP and the lower price, known as the tax paid cost, at which the companies get the 40 per cent of their supplies represented by their equity stakes. (See prices section below.) In 1978 the companies' margin of their 40 per cent crude entitlement worked out at 65 cents a barrel. With the oil price rises of 1979–80 this figure rose to $1.60, which the Abu Dhabi Government felt was excessive. It was therefore agreed in 1980 that the margin would be reduced to $1, which averaged over the full amount of production worked out at 40 cents a barrel.

The policy of retaining the concessionaire as a partner has also applied in Oman. There have been several reasons for this: the small size of the country's oil industry, its shortage of financial resources, the complexity of Oman's oil fields and the Sultanate's acute lack of trained manpower, which has made the government reluctant to undertake any inessential commitments. In practice the foreign company "presence" in Oman is considerably bigger than in Abu Dhabi. Shell not only provides virtually all of the staff and does the purchasing of equipment, it also seems to take many of the management decisions.

The end of the Iranian Consortium

In the true tradition of agreements of its type in the Middle East, it was not long before most of the Iranian Sales and Purchase Agreement became out of date. Whereas at one stage in 1973 the Shah had suggested that Iran's reserves might turn out to be more than 100,000 million barrels, in 1975 and 1976 it came to be realized quite suddenly that this was grossly over-optimistic. To add anything to the country's recoverable reserves beyond 65 billion barrels, or even to recover that volume of oil, the Iranians realized that they would have to invest huge sums in a gas re-injection secondary recovery system.

At the end of 1975 the Consortium stopped contributing the 40 per cent of development capital which it was supposed to invest under the Agreement, and in return NIOC reduced the Consortium's 22 cents a barrel discount to take account of interest accruing on the capital which NIOC saw itself as investing on the Consortium's behalf. Unsuccessful talks on a revision of the Agreement were held in late 1975 and early 1976. However, it was not until the beginning of 1978, after two years in which NIOC-Consortium relations had been further complicated by occasional big falls in Iranian production and by NIOC periodically lifting more than its share, that the two sides sat down to work out a complete replacement for the Agreement. After several rounds of difficult talks the negotiations were made irrelevant by the Iranian revolution of February 1979.

The disturbances of the autumn that preceeded the revolution had disrupted production (which normally ran at a bit below 6 million b/d) and in January and February 1979 exports stopped altogether. Production ran at only 235,000 b/d, not even enough to meet domestic demand of 700,000 b/d. At the end of February, soon after the Ayatollah Khomeini had appointed his Government, the NIOC Chairman, Hassan Nazih, announced that Iran was to have nothing to do with the Consortium ever again—though subsequently the company decided to employ directly (if it could) about 80 of OSCO's former 1,000 expatriate workers. It was reckoned that if Iran ran production at about two-thirds of its previous level, closing the more complex production areas and halting the development of its gas reinjection system, NIOC could carry out its work with minimal foreign assistance.

On March 5th exports started again, with production rising rapidly to over 4 million b/d, though this level was trimmed back by the beginning of May. It slowly emerged that government policy was not to allow production to exceed 4 million b/d, leaving about 3.3 million b/d for export. Later it was made known that the optimal production level was considered to be 3 million b/d, a figure which was still being quoted occasionally when the Iran-Iraq war broke out in the autumn of 1980. In practice during most of 1980 Iranian production ran at a level far below 3 million b/d.

Early sales contracts after the Revolution were with former direct customers of NIOC and the Consortium and former Consortium members, though by mid-May 1979 NIOC was talking to a number of entirely new companies. In total the Consortium members, who had been lifting 3.3 million b/d before the revolution, got 1.1 million b/d, of which BP took

450,000 b/d and Shell 235,000 b/d. Up to 1.9 million b/d was allocated for about 50 other companies— some 30 of which had signed by mid-May—including among the biggest buyers old NIOC and Consortium customers such as the Japanese, Ashland, Petrofina (of Belgium), Amerada Hess and Marathon. All buyers soon found their contracts subject to volume reductions, which NIOC made in order to have more crude available for new customers. As contracts came up for renewal the trend away from traditional custo- mers continued. For a long period in late 1979 and 1980 the major companies stopped liftings entirely— partly because the premiums being charged by Iran were too high and partly because it was the policy of the companies (acting under pressure from the U.S. Government) not to take Iranian oil while the Ameri- can diplomats in Teheran were held hostage. A further disruptive element was introduced by the outbreak of the Iran-Iraq war in the autumn of 1980, which led temporarily to a complete halt of production.

THE DEVELOPMENT OF PRICES

The 1940s and 1950s

In the years before the introduction of the 50-50 profit split in 1950 and 1951, when most of the pro- ducers received their revenues on the basis of the fixed royalty arrangements (22 cents a barrel) the development of prices was of only academic interest to the Middle Eastern governments. For all of the 1930s, and the first half of the 1940s, the pricing fo.mula applied was the "U.S. Gulf Plus" system, which was worked out by the chairmen of Shell, Standard of New Jersey and Anglo-Persian when they drew up their famous cartel agreement at Achnacarry House in 1928. The U.S. Gulf Plus system laid down that the price of oil in every export centre throughout the world should be the same as that obtaining in the Gulf of Mexico, but that the price at the point of delivery should˜be made up of the Gulf of Mexico price plus the cost of freight to that point from the Gulf of Mexico. It made no difference to the buyer where the oil actually came from. If a buyer in Bom- bay, for example, placed an order with a cartel company, the oil would probably be supplied from Persia, but he would still be charged the same freight cost as if the oil had been brought from the United States—and the saving, known as "phantom freight" would go to the cartel company. This system could also work in reverse. A shipment of Persian oil to London, which was nearer to the U.S. than to the Middle East, would still be priced at the Gulf of Mexico price plus freight from the Gulf of Mexico to London—leading to the company accepting an element of "freight absorption". The explanation for this peculiar system lay in the fact that the major com- panies, as a group, had their biggest and most valuable investments in the U.S., and therefore had an interest in maintaining the biggest possible market for American oil.

Given that all of the other major companies and most of the larger American independents joined the cartel, the U.S. Gulf Plus system continued to operate successfully until near the end of the Second World War, when the British Government objected to paying phantom freight for bunker fuel supplied to the navy in the Indian Ocean, and forced the com- panies to institute a Persian Gulf base. Under the new system, crudes f.o.b. the Persian Gulf were given the same price as similar crudes f.o.b. the Gulf of Mexico, and at the point of delivery only real freight was levied on top. This resulted in crude oils from the two producing areas finding their natural markets (which met in the Mediterranean near Italy)—though if Middle East oil was landed in north-west Europe, the company would, of course, still have to bear an element of freight absorption if its oil was to be competitive.

It was not long, however, before the Persian Gulf Base system itself began to come under attack from the governments of the importing countries. Immedi- ately after the war, the U.S.A. swung rapidly round from being a big net exporter to being a small net importer (a position it maintained for the next 25 years), and as soon as domestic price controls were removed in 1946, prices in the Gulf of Mexico climbed fast. Persian Gulf prices followed automatically, and because the production cost of Middle Eastern oil was very much lower than that of Texan oil, the com- panies made enormous profits. Despite the freight disadvantage they were able to import Middle Eastern oil into the U.S. and undercut domestic oil as far inland as the mid-West. In 1948 the companies, influenced in part by criticism from the U.S. Govern- ment, lowered their Persian Gulf prices so that the delivered prices of Middle Eastern and Texan oil equalized at London; and in 1949 the U.S. Government forced a further cut in the Persian Gulf so that the delivered prices of Texan and Middle Eastern oil were made to equalize at New York. This reduction, of course, affected only the profits of the companies in their sales to third parties, and made no difference to the profits down their integrated chain of affiliates.

The large profits made by the companies in this period were a major factor behind the Middle Eastern governments' demands in the late 1940s for better financial terms—demands which were met in 1950 and 1951 by the introduction of the 50-50 profit split (*see* "Concessions" above). The new financial terms (which increased government revenues on Saudi Arabian Light from some $0.22 a barrel to about $0.80—depending on the fluctuations of prices in Texas) served to make the producers price conscious. In retrospect they did not fail to notice that the price adjustments of the later 1940s had been to their considerable disadvantage.

The producers also noticed soon after the intro- duction of 50-50 that the profit split was not quite as even as it seemed, because the companies were always able to press them into giving discounts off the posted price—like volume discounts and the marketing allow- ance (which was hardly justified when almost all pro- duction was sold to affiliates of the operator or to major companies under long-term contracts). In fact, Abdullah Tariki, the radical Saudi Oil Minister during the 1950s, calculated soon after 50-50 came into force that the effective split of profits was 32-68 in favour of the companies.

Worse still, in the early 1950s, the price discrepancies between Texan, Venezuelan and Gulf crudes continued to expand, destroying the principle of the three crudes equalizing at New York. This ushered in a new era in which the price of Gulf crudes was to be determined by the supply and demand situation in Europe rather than in America—which directly or indirectly had been the basis for all quotations for Gulf crudes since 1929. In these new circumstances, the growing availability of production capacity in the Middle East, and increasing competition in the European market, led the companies to start giving their own discounts off the posted price for sales to third parties. It was at this stage that posted (or tax reference) prices and f.o.b. (or market) prices in the Gulf began to part company. Given that the 50-50 profit split was still worked out on the basis of the posting, this meant that the producer government's effective share of profits began to climb back towards the 50 per cent it was always supposed to have been.

Then in 1957, after the closure of the Suez Canal, all prices went up—and although in the Middle East the increase was smaller than in Texas or Venezuela, the new price of $2.12 represented the highest posting for Saudi Arabian Light since 1948. These levels were maintained until February 1959, when there was a general reduction, in which Gulf crudes fell by more than the others. Two months later, the Venezuelan price was lowered again, and in August 1960, the Gulf price was reduced without any parallel reduction being made elsewhere. Thus the discrepancy between Arabian Light and Texan crude had expanded from zero in 1948 (when both crudes were priced at $2.68) to $1.20 in 1960—when Texan crude stood at $3.00 and the Saudi Arabian Light posting at $1.80.

From the point of view of the governments in the Middle Eastern capitals and Caracas, the price cuts of 1959 and 1960 (about which they were never consulted) were very damaging—affecting the size of their budgets and their development prospects. In April 1959, at the first Arab Petroleum Congress in Cairo (to which Iranian and Venezuelan representatives were invited as observers), the oil ministers of Saudi Arabia and Venezuela, Abdullah Tariki and Perez Alfonso, sponsored the formation of the Oil Consultation Commission. Then in September 1960, a month after the further reduction of Middle Eastern prices, the ministers of Iran, Iraq, Saudi Arabia, Kuwait and Venezuela met again in an atmosphere of crisis in Baghdad. The Oil Consultation Commission was already defunct, having run into opposition from Iran and Iraq who objected to the inclusion of Egypt, and the ministers decided to create a permanent and stronger institution. The body that emerged was OPEC —the Organization of Petroleum Exporting Countries.

Since OPEC's formation, the original five members have been joined by Qatar in 1961, Libya and Indonesia in 1962, Abu Dhabi in 1967, Algeria in 1969, Nigeria in 1971, Ecuador in 1973 and Gabon—as an associate member in 1973 and a full member in 1975.

OPEC in the 1960s

At first the major companies ignored OPEC. In accordance with a resolution passed at the Organization's fourth conference in June 1962, the members addressed protests to the companies against the price cuts of August 1960, and demanded that prices be restored to their previous level. But the companies refused to enter into any collective negotiations, and in their individual replies they argued that the development of prices did not depend on their own will, but was determined by economic factors over which they had no control.

OPEC realized that the only way to achieve a restoration of posted prices would be to force up market prices, and this the producers decided would best be done by limiting the annual growth in their output. So over two years (from mid-1965 to mid-1967) the members worked out a joint production programme. In both years they over-estimated the overall growth in demand for their oil, and at the same time certain members, notably Libya and Saudi Arabia, and, to a lesser extent, Iran, made no effort to keep within their quotas. The obvious conclusion was that in a period when prices were low enough to cause a tight budgeting condition in some states, those countries which were either new exporters and/or had big oil reserves and expensive development programmes, would not be willing to make a temporary sacrifice and await an improvement in the unit price of their oil, but would be tempted to increase revenues by maximizing the volume of their output.

However, OPEC did manage to increase its members' effective share of profits during the 1960s. First in 1963 the companies accepted a cut in the marketing allowance (which they were able to deduct as an expense before making the profit split) from some $0.01–0.02, depending on arrangements in different states, to a uniform half-cent throughout the Gulf. Secondly, and more important, the Organization negotiated two agreements on the expensing of royalties. These agreements the Middle Eastern members saw as removing an anomaly in their fiscal arrangements, and as bringing their taxes into line with the system prevailing in Venezuela. Although the producers' revenues since 1950 had nominally been made up of a royalty of 12.5 per cent of the posted price (as payment for the oil itself) and income tax (representing the 50 per cent tax on the profits from the sale of this oil), payments made under the heading of royalties had always been totally deducted from tax. The producers, referring to the normal internationally accepted arrangements, under which the royalty payer was entitled to deduct the royalty only from his gross income when computing his tax liability, wanted royalties to be treated as an expense in their own countries also—and in 1964 this was what was agreed. As part of a package deal the companies received various further discounts off the posted price in respect of "royalty expensing" and "gravity differential". These discounts were set to be reduced each year—this process being accelerated by a second agreement in 1968, which arranged for the complete disappearance of the royalty expensing discount in

1972 and of the gravity allowance in 1975. Under the new system the companies deducted their production cost, the 12.5 per cent royalty, and the applicable allowances and discounts from the posted price, then split the remainder 50-50, and then added the royalty on to the government's share. For Arabian Light, the royalty expensing agreements and the reduction of the marketing allowance increased government take from $0.84 at the end of 1960 to about $0.90 in 1968.

The Independents in Libya

It was not, however, OPEC's achievements in improving its members' share of profits that were to be of the greatest long-term significance for the oil industry in the 1960s. In 1957, oil had been found in Libya. Unlike the governments in the Gulf, Libya had not awarded all its acreage to a single group, and as the discoveries were brought on stream in the early 1960s, it became clear that some of the largest fields lay in concessions held by American independent companies. These companies had originally ventured out of the U.S. in the late 1940s with the intention of finding new supplies for their marketing operations at home, but when the U.S. Government imposed import controls in 1959, they were forced either to launch themselves downstream in Europe, as Occidental (marketing as VIP or Oxy) and Continental (marketing as Conoco or Jet) did, or to sell their crude to others, as Marathon and Amerada Hess did.

Libya proved to be an ideal source of crude for such operations. Its oil yielded a high proportion of high value products such as gasoline and heating oils, and had a low sulphur content. The country's position gave its crude a big freight advantage over Gulf crudes (an advantage only enhanced by the closure of the Suez Canal in 1967), concession terms were uniquely generous, and for the first half of the decade the profit split was made not on posted prices, but on the much lower realized prices. In the mid-1960s these advantages were somewhat reduced when Libya seized the occasion of the first royalty expensing agreement as an opportunity to renegotiate its profit split on the basis of postings. The majors in Libya, who did not favour the independents having access to crude on terms so much more generous than those applying to their own production in the Gulf, agreed to Libya's request in 1965, but the independents only gave in in 1966, after a bitter struggle in which the Government threatened to stop exports or nationalize their assets. Even with these new terms, Libyan crude was still very competitive with Gulf crudes in Europe, because its posted prices, while higher than those in the Gulf, only partially reflected its freight advantage.

Given the relatively low price, Libyan production expanded extremely fast—from 20,000 b/d in 1962 to 3.3 million b/d in 1970—and throughout the decade prices in Europe fell. The majors' response to the independents' sales and marketing operations was to seek economies of scale in building ever larger tankers, refineries and storage and distribution facilities; but because larger units become most attractive when operated at near full capacity, this led the majors themselves to look for the highest possible market share, and led to an acceleration of price cutting. Although this process was most apparent at the downstream end of the industry, there was also an erosion of market prices in the Gulf, and because the existence of OPEC prevented a lowering of postings, the majors' margins were squeezed. The net earnings per barrel on the seven majors' eastern hemisphere operations dropped from $0.60 in 1958 to $0.33 in 1970, while the effective profit split in the Gulf climbed to something in the region of 70/30 in favour of the governments.

Teheran and Tripoli Agreements

In 1970 the marginal surpluses which had been so strong a feature of the previous decade suddenly disappeared. A combination of higher than expected demand as the Western economies entered a period of upturn, a shortage of tankers and a growing tightness of European refinery capacity, led to an unusually tight supply situation, which left the oil industry with very little flexibility to deal with any disruption which might occur in the Middle East.

These conditions coincided with a series of negotiations in Libya, where in January the new revolutionary regime of Colonel Gaddafi had started pursuing a claim, originally formulated by King Idris' government in 1969, for higher prices which would reflect the true freight advantage enjoyed by Libyan crude since the closure of the Suez Canal, and would incorporate a premium for the oil's high quality. During the early months of 1970, the Government took a notably moderate stance, but negotiations made rather slow progress, and although it seemed that they might still be brought to a satisfactory conclusion, by the beginning of the summer the Government's position had hardened. In part the regime's determination stemmed from an agreement in the spring to co-ordinate its efforts with the Algerians, who were engaged in similar negotiations with their French concessionaires, but at the same time, the Libyans could see that their bargaining position as a short-haul supplier was being considerably strengthened by events in the tanker market. The economic upturn in Europe was resulting in a rapid rise in demand for industrial fuel oils of the type derived from the heavier Gulf crudes, and this additional pull on long-haul supplies increased the demand for tanker charters. The strain was only made worse by the loss of several of the new class of mammoth tankers in mysterious explosions early in the year; and in May the situation deteriorated further when a Syrian bulldozer broke Tapline, running from Saudi Arabia to the Mediterranean port of Sidon, and deprived the industry of 480,000 b/d of short-haul crude.

In the same month, the Libyans ordered Occidental, a particularly vulnerable independent which derived nearly a third of its earnings from its Libyan concession, to cut back its production. Whether this decision was made for conservation reasons, or because the Government realized what chaos a further reduction in the supply of short-haul crude would cause, remains unclear—but either way the Libyans soon appreciated the value of production cuts as a lever in their price negotiations, and they quickly imposed further reductions on Occidental and on the other companies. By the beginning of September, the industry had lost about one million b/d of Libyan production, and freight rates soared as extra supplies had to be brought in from the Gulf. One by one the companies surrendered—led, naturally, by Occidental and followed by the other independents in the Oasis group. The majors held out a bit longer, but finally Texaco and Socal broke ranks, and then Esso, Mobil and, eventually, Shell gave in too. The Libyans achieved a price rise of $0.30, rising to $0.40 over the next five years, and their tax rate rose from 50 per cent to amounts varying from 54 to 58 per cent in payment for what the Government claimed should have been higher prices since 1965.

Although in theory these changes were made only to reflect the freight and quality advantages of Libyan crudes, the majors realized that they would be bound to result in higher prices in the Gulf, and they promptly decided to pay the Gulf producers a higher tax rate of 55 per cent and an extra $0.09 on heavier crudes (which although normally regarded as of lower quality, were in particularly high demand in 1970). Then in December 1970, at OPEC's Twenty-first Conference, in Caracas, the members decided that the Gulf countries should press for a further round of price increases.

The oil industry, with the support of the consumer governments, formed itself into a united front combining majors, independents and European national companies. When talks with the producers' representatives began in Teheran in January 1971, the companies agreed in principle to a price revision, but insisted that negotiations should cover all OPEC states, so as to avoid the leapfrogging of the past few months. The companies were forced to give in on this point and a parallel series of negotiations was begun in Libya. During the second half of January the gap between the Gulf producers and the companies was gradually narrowed, but on February 2nd the talks broke down. OPEC then held an extraordinary conference, and all members resolved to legislate a price increase if the companies did not respond to their minimum demands by February 15th. But none of the parties wanted a confrontation, and one day before the OPEC deadline, the companies gave in. The producers were given: an immediate $0.33 basic increase, $0.02 for freight disparities, half a cent for every degree API by which any crude fell below 40° API, the elimination of all remaining discounts and allowances, and provision for prices to increase by 2.5 per cent and $0.05 on June 1st, 1971, and January 1st, 1973, 1974 and 1975. This took 34° API Saudi Arabian Light from $1.80 to $2.18. In return, the companies were guaranteed that there would be no further claims until after December 31st, 1975, no more leapfrogging if the Mediterranean producers concluded better terms, and no embargoes.

Later, in March, negotiations were resumed in Libya, and on April 2nd an agreement was signed giving Libya $0.90, a uniform 55 per cent tax rate, and provision for annual price increases of 2.5 per cent

and $0.07. Subsequent negotiations secured similar terms for Iraqi and Saudi crude arriving at Mediterranean terminals through the IPC pipe and Tapline.

The price explosion

It was hoped that the Teheran and Tripoli Agreements would give a full five years of price stability—but it was only a matter of months before they began to come under strain. In August 1971, President Nixon's decision to float the dollar (leading to a formal devaluation in December) produced OPEC claims for compensation—though in a notably moderate tone. The claim was settled on January 20th, 1972, when the companies agreed in Geneva to an immediate price rise of 8.49 per cent in the Gulf; and later, in May, after rather tougher negotiations, the same was agreed for Libya.

In February 1973, the dollar was devalued a second time by 10 per cent, and under the terms of the Geneva Agreement, prices were duly raised by 5.8 per cent on April 1st. The OPEC states were disappointed by the time the adjustment mechanism took to operate, and by the small size of their compensation, and, after a further series of discussions with the companies, on June 1st a second dollar compensation agreement was signed in Geneva. The producers obtained an 11.9 per cent increase (which included the 5.8 per cent increase in April plus compensation for the further slide in the dollar's parity during May) and it was agreed that prices would in future be adjusted monthly according to a weighted average movement of 11 major currencies against the dollar. This formula resulted in further rises in August and September and a reduction in October.

The companies presented the Geneva Agreements as supplementary to the Teheran Agreement—although they both involved a significant rise in revenues, and could equally be characterized as a breach of the five-year price programme. Similarly, the participation arrangement negotiated in 1972 meant a significant increment in government receipts and a modification of the fiscal structure; and a still more drastic alteration came in September 1973 when Saudi Arabia agreed with Aramco that both categories of buy-back crude should be priced at 93 per cent of postings—this being the price obtained by the Saudis in May at the first auction of their own direct crude entitlement.

In the summer of 1973, there were, however, much more fundamental forces undermining the Teheran Agreement. As production in the U.S.A. began to fall after 1970, the world's biggest consumer began to look to the Eastern Hemisphere not only to make up for its declining domestic output, but also for an annual increment in supplies that was nearly as big as the annual increase demanded by the whole of Western Europe. United States imports from the Arab countries and Iran grew from 0.6 million b/d in 1971, to 1.0 million b/d in 1972, and to 1.7 million b/d in 1973. It was in 1973 that U.S. demand became really noticeable in the Middle East, and prices on the open market began to move up accordingly.

The OPEC states profited from this situation in as much as they received bids close to postings for the small amounts of crude they were selling on the market themselves; but, with the fiscal terms applied to the bulk of their production still tied to modified 1971 prices, they were for the most part excluded from sharing in the boom, and the main benefit went to the companies. The producers calculated that the effective profit split had changed from about 80-20 in their favour at the time of the Teheran Agreement to about 64-36, and they suggested that the companies were making excessive profits, and that the whole set of prices negotiated two years earlier had become out of date. These arguments were backed up by the producers pointing out that the small annual increments agreed at Teheran were not keeping up with the rate of world inflation.

At the OPEC conference in Vienna on September 15th–16th, the members agreed to call the companies to negotiations in the following month, and to seek a sizeable lump increase in posted prices to bring them sufficiently above market realizations to permit them to resume their function as a realistic tax reference, while establishing a mechanism whereby the desired differential between posted and realized prices could be maintained in future. The six Gulf members of the Organization began meetings with a company delegation in Vienna on October 8th, two days after the beginning of the Arab-Israeli October war, but the two sides' positions were far apart. The producers demanded an increase of some 70 per cent and the companies offered only 20 per cent. At the end of the week, the companies requested a fortnight's adjournment. The producers immediately held a meeting of their own, and decided to hold a conference in Kuwait four days later on October 16th "to decide on a course of collective action to determine the true value of the oil they produced".

When the producers met again, they quickly abandoned the idea of holding any further consultations with the companies, and raised their posted prices by 70 per cent. For the Arabian light "marker" crude, the posting rose from $3.01 to $5.12, while government take went up by a slightly larger proportion from $1.77 to $3.05. Subsequently, Libya raised its price by 94 per cent from $4.60 to $8.92, thereby widening further the differential between Gulf and Mediterranean crudes. The new prices were designed to be 40 per cent above the market price for any given crude as determined by the direct sales of governments to third parties, and OPEC gave notice that the movement of prices would in future be determined for each quarter by actual market realizations. Both the size of the October increase and the fact that it was made unilaterally were unprecedented, and signalled the final complete transfer of control over the price system, which until 1971 had been in the hands of the companies, into the hands of the producers—after a transitional three and a half year period of negotiated prices.

The price increase of October 16th was an important milestone in oil politics, but immediately, for the world economy, the meeting of Arab producers in Kuwait on the following day was far more cataclysmic. Gathering under the aegis of the Organization of Arab Petroleum Exporting Countries, they decided to use the "oil weapon" in support of Egypt and Syria in their war with Israel. With Iraq opting out, the other nine members of OAPEC decided upon a policy of 5 per cent cumulative monthly cuts in production from the levels of September—to continue until the political objective of Israeli withdrawal from the territories occupied in 1967 and the "restoration of the rights of the Palestinians" had been achieved. The meeting was far from being an occasion of complete unanimity, and the decision on 5 per cent cuts was taken with a degree of hesitancy on the part of some members and amounted to something of a compromise. But once the cuts had started, they escalated rapidly. Within days all of the Arab producers (including Iraq) placed embargoes on the U.S.A. and the Netherlands and reduced their production by equivalent additional amounts, while Saudi Arabia and Kuwait also incorporated the 5 per cent reduction scheduled for November in their initial cutback. Irritated by the lack of response from the West, the Arab producers then decided at a further meeting in Kuwait on November 4th to reduce output across the board by 25 per cent of the September level, and gave notice of a further 5 per cent cut in December. But in practice, the cutback again turned out to be rather larger than it appeared to be on paper, and by the middle of November, output in the two biggest Arab producers, Saudi Arabia and Kuwait, was down by between 30 per cent and 40 per cent.

With winter setting in, the Arab cuts had a dramatic effect on the market. Cargoes of Algerian and Nigerian short-haul crude fetched as much as $16 a barrel, and in December the National Iranian Oil Company in an auction of its crude entitlement under the Sales and Purchase Agreement got the staggering price of $17.40. In these conditions, the OPEC Economic Commission's search for a market price on which could be based the quarterly revision of postings became impossible, and the views of company representatives, who suggested in November in a brief exchange in Vienna that no changes should be made until the market had become more stable, were brushed aside. When the Gulf producers met in Teheran on December 22nd, the new price level set was an arbitrary one dictated largely by the Shah of Iran, who intervened directly in the ministers' deliberations. The Shah suggested a price of $14, while Sheikh Ahmed Zaki Yamani, the Saudi Oil Minister, argued for a price of about $7.50—though he did not, perhaps, put his plea for restraint as strongly as King Faisal would have wished. The other ministers gave Yamani little backing, although they resented the way in which the Shah took control of the meeting, and it was eventually decided that the posted price should be increased by nearly 130 per cent from $5.12 to $11.65—taking the government revenue from $3.05 to $7.00. The Libyan price rise which followed was rather more modest in percentage terms—from $8.92 to $15.76.

1974—changing the tax system

The OPEC conference at Geneva on January 17th–19th, 1974, revealed the full extent of Saudi Arabia's opposition to the price increase announced in the previous month—although in the conference chamber itself, Yamani did not raise a formal objection. As it was, members endorsed the new prices while deciding on a three-month freeze. This was extended for a further quarter, after a rather tougher argument, at the next meeting in March.

Coinciding with the OPEC conference in March, was another review by the Arabs of their embargo policy. In effect the cuts had come to an end in December, when the Arabs announced that they would not be imposing a further 5 per cent reduction in January, and reclassified most of the EEC and Japan as "favoured nations" for which they were prepared to run production as normal. But it was not until their meeting in March, by which time Dr. Kissinger had arranged the Egyptian-Israeli disengagement, that they lifted the embargo on the U.S. (with Libya and Iraq temporarily dissenting) and only in July was the embargo on the Netherlands lifted. The resumption of normal exports to the U.S. was accompanied by a decision to restore output to September 1973 levels, and Saudi Arabia, with an eye on the coming price battle within OPEC, which it saw would not be settled without reference to actual market realizations, let it be known that it would raise its output somewhat above September levels.

Inevitably, market prices weakened over the following months. After the failure of several participation crude auctions and price cuts of up to $3 by non-Gulf producers, in August, in the biggest single sale of 1974, the Kuwaitis failed to sell any of their 60 per cent of production at the 97 per cent of postings demanded. For the third quarter of the year they subsequently sold rather over 55 per cent of the oil on offer to BP and Gulf at 94.8 per cent of postings.

As the Saudis had hoped in March, the excess of supply assumed a critical importance in the struggle within OPEC over pricing policy. In June Yamani indicated the size of the reduction sought when he formally proposed that the marker crude posting should be lowered by $2.50. But when OPEC held its third meeting of the year at Quito in June, the other members argued for formulas which would have raised the cost of oil to the consumers by anything up to the region of $1.50. Saudi Arabia again threatened a unilateral lowering of prices, and a cheap auction of its participation crude entitlement, and the result was a stalemate in which it was decided (with the Saudis dissenting) to increase the royalty rate on the companies' 40 per cent crude entitlement (known as equity oil) from 12.5 to 14.5 per cent.

Although within OPEC in the summer of 1974 a major battle was being fought over the level of postings, there was at the same time a considerable (and unopposed) increase in government take (and therefore in the cost of oil to the consumers) coming about as a result of the 60 per cent participation agreements, concluded in the middle of the year but backdated to the beginning of 1974. In that the states' participation crude was either sold back to the companies at a level well above the governments' take on equity crude, or was sold on the open market at roughly similar prices, the average government revenue over their whole production was increased, even though on participation crude the governments had to bear the production cost themselves. In 1973, under the 25 per cent regime, the overall effect of participation was fairly small—increasing average government revenues by about $0.10 in the first nine months of the year and by $0.15/20 from September, when the 93 per cent of postings buy-back price came into force. But in mid-1974, under the 60 per cent participation regime, the weighted average revenue worked out, in theory, at some $2 above the government revenue on equity crude (which after the December 1973 increases was about $7.00). In practice, however, there were considerable variations between the different producers in the amount by which the weighted average revenue exceeded the take on equity crude, and in every case, the actual weighted average was lower than it appeared to be in theory. A relatively small factor in determining the variations between the states was the different percentages of postings (93 or 94.8 per cent) charged to the companies for buy-back crude. Much more important was that, following the failure of their auctions (or, in Saudi Arabia's case, in the event of their not holding an auction) the governments kept part of their crude entitlement in the ground, and thus lowered the proportion of participation crude in their overall output, and reduced their weighted average revenues. In Kuwait, for instance, during the third quarter of the year, the ratio of the two types of crude was 65 per cent equity and 35 per cent participation.

One of the consequences of this dual pricing system was that the companies got their crude on average at a price well below that demanded by governments for their direct sales. The OPEC states realized that the companies' own sales of this relatively cheap crude to third parties were not only undercutting state prices and causing the failure of the auctions, but were also giving the companies large windfall profits. It was these problems that the producers tackled during the latter part of 1974. When OPEC held its fourth meeting of the year in Vienna on September 12–13th the members decided on a further increase in the royalty rate on equity crude to 16.67 per cent, and an increase in the tax rate on equity crude from 55 per cent to 65.65 per cent. The Saudis argued that these tax increases should have been accompanied by a cut in postings, and again declined to implement the changes. It was only in the following month that the Saudis, increasingly irritated by the companies' profits, decided to call on Aramco for back-payments to cover the Quito and Vienna tax adjustments.

In November the Saudis took a more decisive step. A Saudi delegation held a meeting with the Qatar and Abu Dhabi oil ministers in Abu Dhabi and agreed with effect from the beginning of the month to raise the royalty rate on equity crude to 20 per cent and the tax rate to 85 per cent. At the same time $0.40 was cut off postings. This was intended to further narrow the gap between the weighted average cost of crude to the companies and the prices demanded at state sales—as well as reducing the impact of the changes on the consumers.

When OPEC met in Vienna for its fifth and final conference of 1974, on December 13th–14th, the other members endorsed the new arrangements. They also decided that from January 1st, 1975, (the date to which it was assumed the final takeover of Aramco would be backdated) all of the Gulf states would apply the new weighted average cost to all of their production exported by their concessionaire companies, and that the new price levels should be frozen for nine months. The distinction between equity and participation crude, and the possibility of variations in the weighted average cost being caused by alterations in the ratio between the two crudes, therefore ceased to exist—even though the notion of a 40:60 split was still used to work out the new cost, known afterwards as the "acquisition price". The new single price system involved a big jump in government revenue, not only because it was based in part on the higher tax and royalty rates agreed at Abu Dhabi but also because it was based on a 40:60 equity-participation crude ratio which in practice had not existed before. The government revenue on the "market" crude rose to $10.13, and the acquisition price for the companies to $10.25, reflecting the notional "marker" production cost of $0.12. The gap between the acquisition price and the 93 per cent of postings, $10.46, which remained the official state sale price, was narrowed to $0.21.

Over the following years the acquisition price applied only in countries where the companies retained a 40 per cent equity stake—which soon meant just Abu Dhabi and Saudi Arabia among the bigger producers. In Kuwait and Qatar the former concessionaires got their crude at the government selling price (93 per cent of postings) less a discount. This gave the companies a smaller margin than in Abu Dhabi and Saudi Arabia, which reflected the fact that in Kuwait and Qatar the companies were no longer investing capital. In Iran, where until the end of 1975 the companies did continue to invest capital, the discount off the state selling price was bigger. In practice it was the state selling prices, in all countries, that became henceforth the important prices for OPEC.

Differentials—1975-78

December 1974 marked the end of the oil price explosion; in the space of 15 months government revenues and the cost of oil to the consumer had multiplied almost exactly five times. From then until January 1st, 1979 there were only two OPEC price rises. One was in Vienna in September 1975, when it was agreed that the state selling price should be raised by 10 per cent, and the other was in Doha, in December 1976, when the majority of OPEC members raised their prices by a further 10 per cent—causing a split with Saudi Arabia and the U.A.E.

During much of the four year period 1975-8, there was rather weak demand. There was something of a revival in the market in 1976, but in late 1977 and most of 1978 there was a serious glut caused by the new Mexican fields, Alaska and the North Sea, which began to make a significant impact on the world market at the same time. In these conditions the OPEC members' attention became focused mainly on differentials —the different margins between crudes of different qualities in different locations. This problem was an important theme (sometimes the only theme) in at least half a dozen OPEC meetings: at Vienna in September and December 1975 (it was on the latter occasion that the ministers were kidnapped by the terrorist gang of Carlos Illych Ramirez), Geneva in April 1976, Bali in May 1976, Stockholm in July 1977 and Caracas in December 1977.

Differentials seems like a matter of technicalities, but in practice it had caused some of the most bitter arguments within OPEC, because indirectly agreement on differentials would imply agreement on different producers' production levels. Sometimes when demand has been buoyant, the members have been able to agree systems of differentials (see note 2 underneath the prices table for the workings of the system in 1974). The difficulties occur at times of slack demand when producers are competing for market shares and output is dropping in states whose crude is marginally overpriced. In January 1976, when Iranian heavy crude was over-priced by just 10 cents relative to Kuwaiti crude, output fell dramatically to a point where the light/heavy export ratio changed from the normal 52/48 to 72/28.

Although ministers reached a flexible understanding on differential adjustments at the Bali meeting in May 1976, and periodically referred the matter to special committees (at Geneva in April 1976 and Stockholm in July 1977), the Organization was not able to agree on any comprehensive new system. Generally adjustments were made unilaterally, sometimes in accordance with guidelines laid down by one of the committees. More often they took place when a state experienced a particularly embarrassing fall in demand, or when a price rise (in October 1975 or January 1977) produced an opportunity for producers to adjust their own crudes by implementing a fractionally bigger or smaller rise than that announced for the marker crude.

Apart from the differentials issue, OPEC meetings in 1975-8 were marked by quite frequent battles over price rises. Iraq and Libya were always in the hawks' camp (often with Iran, Algeria and Nigeria), and Saudi Arabia generally stood as the single dove—though sometimes it had the support of the U.A.E., Qatar and occasionally Kuwait. Although the Saudis were forced to compromise in September 1975 and before Stockholm in July 1977, they succeeded in preventing rises at Bali, at Caracas in December 1977 and at Geneva in June 1978.

Other recurrent issues were production programming (the artificial limiting of output so as to influence the state of the market) and the protection of oil prices against the dollar's fluctuations. The Saudis invariably refused to entertain the idea of production programming, or even discuss the level of their own output, on which any programme would have hinged. On the matter of dollar compensation mechanisms, which was an issue in early 1975 (at Vienna and Libreville) and late 1977–early 1978, the Saudis were less adamant, but still doubtful of the value of any of the formulae put forward.

OPEC split and reconciliation — December 1976– December 1977

The major event in OPEC—and the major confrontation over prices—in 1975–8 occurred at Doha in December 1976. Saudi Arabia, with the support of the U.A.E., flatly refused to countenance the increases demanded by other OPEC members, ranging upwards from 10 per cent, though it emerged later that had compromise been possible it would have been prepared to accept 7 per cent. The outcome was that Saudi Arabia and the U.A.E. opted for an immediate 5 per cent increase for the whole of 1977, while the other members decided on 10 per cent for the first six months of the year with an additional 5 per cent to come into effect on July 1st.

In part the Saudi policy at Doha stemmed from a hard-headed realization that the health of the OPEC economies is linked to that of the Western economies, and that inflation caused by oil price rises rebounds on to the OPEC members; but at the same time there is no doubt that the Saudis felt a genuine sense of responsibility for the West's economic well-being.

After the Doha meeting the Saudis announced that they were raising their production ceiling from 8.5 million b/d to 10 million b/d, and immediately there were big drops in the production of the other states. Yet for all the fuss there was no increase in Saudi production at the beginning of the year, indeed output in January and February fell from the record levels of late 1976 (9.2 million b/d in December) to only 8.2 million b/d and 8.7 b/d respectively. During the next four months, however, production picked up, reaching over 10 million b/d at one point. There was some mystery surrounding the reasons for this performance. On one hand it was suggested that the initial drop in output was caused either by the inevitable time lag that would elapse before the Saudis could sign up new customers or by the Saudis realizing that the expansion of production might be more effective as a threat than as something which had already come into operation. On the other hand, there was evidence that the Saudis had tried from the start to raise production to 10 million b/d but had been frustrated partly by bad weather preventing tankers loading, and partly by the realization that although they had rather over 10 million b/d of capacity installed in hardware terms and were planning on expanding this to some 12 million b/d by the end of the year, they did not have the personnel and management systems needed to maintain output at these levels. Certainly there was evidence in the frenetic activity visible in Dhahran early in the year that Aramco had been told to de-bottleneck its systems in a hurry.

Throughout the early months of 1977 there were attempts made to heal the rift in OPEC—notably by the President of Venezuela, Carlos Andrez Perez. At quite an early stage it became clear that the eleven upper tier countries would agree to a compromise involving Saudi Arabia and the U.A.E. raising their prices by 5 per cent in July and the rest at the same time forgoing their own scheduled 5 per cent increase, but it was not until sometime in June that it emerged that the Saudis would accept this formula. About a fortnight before the OPEC conference at Stockholm on July 12th, which it had been agreed should not be held unless a solution had been reached in advance, the two sides made their compromise public. The Stockholm meeting itself concentrated on the issue of differentials. At the later meeting in Caracas in December 1977 prices remained frozen, not because of a consensus, but because the Saudis managed to assemble behind them Iran, Kuwait, the U.A.E. and Qatar.

The second oil crisis—1979

Despite the oil glut of most of 1978, relations between OPEC members improved from the middle of the year. On May 6th and 7th the ministers held an informal exchange of ideas on long term strategy at the mountain resort of Taif in Saudi Arabia. Without the problems of decision-making or a fixed agenda, the meeting was relaxed and amicable, and one minister remarked that it was the most productive OPEC gathering he had attended. The good atmosphere was enhanced by the steps that Saudi Arabia was taking to cut its output. Late in 1977 it had reimposed its 8.5 million b/d ceiling, and in early 1978 it had decided to limit liftings of Arabian Light to not more than 65 per cent of total liftings (compared with 72–80 per cent in 1975–77). The market however was simply unable to absorb the extra amounts of heavy crude that this ratio implied at prevailing production rates, so for the first nine months of the year Saudi output fell sharply.

The broad drift of the ministers' discussions at Taif assumed that the glut would begin to come to an end in later 1978 or 1979, that there would then be a period of balance in the market—how long a period depending on the consumers' growth rates and their success or failure at developing alternatives and conserving energy—and that at some point in the 1980s the world would return to conditions of shortage. In these circumstances it was felt that the market itself would look after oil prices and that OPEC might possibly orientate itself to using its increased bargaining power for bringing about the new international economic order which had failed to emerge from the North-South dialogue in Paris. To study these questions the meeting established another ministerial committee composed of Saudi Arabia, Iran, Iraq, Kuwait, Venezuela (the five founders) and Algeria.

The turnaround in the market came much sooner than anyone had expected. At the end of October 1978 the strikes in Iran which were paralysing the Shah's regime began to affect oil production. During the next two months Iranian production fluctuated between its norm of about 5.8 million b/d and 1.2 million b/d, but at the end of December it fell to 235,000 b/d (insufficient to meet domestic demand), at which point it was to remain until March 1979.

Up to the end of the year the companies made up

the shortfall by increasing liftings elsewhere; Saudi output in December ran at a record 10 million b/d—it being permissible for Aramco to exceed the 8.5 million b/d limit for a month or so as long as it kept within it over the whole year. The Iranian crisis had no effect on the spot market. Nor did the crisis give much added impetus to the OPEC meeting at Abu Dhabi on 16-17th December, when it was decided to raise prices for 1979 by 10 per cent. This was to be done in instalments of 5 per cent for the first quarter, 3.8 per cent for the second, 2.3 per cent for the third and 2.7 per cent for the fourth. These would bring the marker crude selling price from $12.70 in December 1978 to $14.54 in October 1979—a rise of 14.5 per cent over nine months but an average increase for the year 1979 of 10 per cent. What was remarkable was the storm of protest with which this rise was greeted by Western governments, which seemed to ignore the fact that the rise was extremely modest and came after a long period of price stability.

In the month that followed the OPEC meeting, spot market prices began to climb at a rate which was to destroy the price programme agreed at Abu Dhabi and, by mid-May, to cause the Western world to talk of a "second oil crisis". With Iranian exports halted the international oil industry was short of some 5 million b/d, which was only partially made up by Saudi Arabia raising its production ceiling from 8.5 million b/d to 9.5 million b/d and by smaller increases in Kuwait, Iraq and other producers. By the middle of February, at which point OPEC announced an extraordinary meeting to be held in Geneva at the end of March, spot prices for light Gulf crudes had risen to $21 and higher, involving premiums of above $7.50.

On February 15th Abu Dhabi and Qatar imposed surcharges on their crudes of up to $1.02, promising an extra 18 cents at the beginning of April. A week later Libya followed with 68 cents and then Kuwait and Iraq with $1.20, Oman with $1.02, and the Soviet Union (for its Western customers) with $1.41.

On March 5th Iran resumed oil exports, building up over the next two months to a production level of some 4 million b/d (which meant exports of 1.5-2.0 million b/d less than before the revolution). This caused the spot premiums to fall from their end-February peak of $23, but the market pressure for a rise was still impossible for Saudi Arabia to resist when OPEC met at Geneva on March 26-27th. All producers agreed to bring forward their scheduled 1979 last quarter increase to the second quarter (raising the marker to $14.55), and it was decided that producers could impose whatever additional surcharges they deemed "justifiable in the light of their own circumstances". Saudi Arabia added no premiums to its Light, Medium and Heavy crudes, but $1.14 to its high quality Berri crude. All of the other Gulf producers increased the surcharges they had imposed in February (on top of the new price levels), while the African producers raised their selling prices to the $17.50–18.50 range.

In the middle of April it became known definitely that Saudi Arabia was not maintaining its extra one million b/d of output in the second quarter, partly because it argued that the resumption of Iranian exports made this unnecessary, and partly, it was thought, to show its displeasure with the United States over the Egypt–Israel peace treaty. Shortly after this the effects of the Iranian stoppage began finally to feed through to the market place, as oil companies cut back their deliveries and queues formed at petrol stations. Together these developments set off in May another jump in the spot market price for light crudes, taking the price back through the end-February level and then on to extraordinary levels in the region of $33 a barrel in mid-May. Nobody in the industry was surprised when the surge in the spot market was followed by two further rounds of leapfrogging increases—both led by Iran.

To try to alleviate some of the market pressures for higher prices, the Saudis let it be known before the OPEC meeting in Geneva on June 26th–28th 1979 that they were considering raising their output again. At the meeting the other members demanded further increases, which, if the Saudis had co-operated, would have raised the marker crude to at least $20. The Saudis, concerned at the recessionary influences that the oil price increases were having on the Western economies, sought to stabilize the price at a lower level of $17–$18. In the end the Organization reached an amicable compromise in which Saudi Arabia raised its marker price to $18 while the other members were allowed to impose surcharges up to $23.50. This figure was adopted for some of their crudes by Algeria, Libya, Nigeria and Venezuela. Soon after the meeting the Saudis announced that they were raising production for the third quarter of 1979 by 1 million b/d to 9.5 million b/d.

It was not until September 1979 that the Nigerians broke the $23.50 ceiling by imposing a further premium on the price of their crude—and so triggered yet another round of increases.

Saudi attempts to reunify prices—December 1979–September 1980

The Saudis made a major attempt to restore order to the situation in December 1979, when they raised their crude prices by $6 a barrel, taking Arabian Light from $18 to $24. In doing this the Saudis obviously hoped to set the stage for the unification of prices at the OPEC meeting in Caracas later in the month, but in the event, the Caracas meeting broke up in disarray. During January 1980 most OPEC members announced further increases backdated to the beginning of the year. The Saudis felt that there would be no point in allowing their prices to fall further out of line with other members and so raised their own crudes by $2 a barrel. For the future they were encouraged by a softening of the spot market, caused by the downturn in economic activity in the industrialized world. Other producers, however, were not deterred from asking for even larger premiums and bonuses over and above their official prices on new crude sales contracts.

The Saudis made another attempt to rationalize the price structure in May 1980. They raised their prices by a further $2, taking Arabian Light to $28, effective April 1st. This initiative failed as badly as its predecessor. Within a week or so all other OPEC members—except Iran, which had already increased its second quarter prices—had matched the Saudi increase. When OPEC met at Algiers in early June the best that could be managed was an agreement to accept a two-tier price system. A theoretical marker price was set at $32 a barrel and on this basis producers of light crudes were allowed to charge differentials of up to $5. This established a new ceiling for OPEC prices of $37. In the weeks that followed the meeting OPEC members waited for a move by the Saudis—but none came. The price charged for Arabian Light stayed at $28. When the other producers realized that no changes would come from Saudi Arabia, they gradually raised their prices in line with the new accord. The African producers put their best crudes at the $37 limit.

During the summer the market moved steadily in the Saudis' favour. The Kingdom's production had stayed at 9.5 million b/d since the middle of 1979. At the same time the oil companies had continued to pay high prices, with premiums, for other producers' crude in spite of the over-supply that had begun to be obvious in the winter of 1979–80. By mid-1980 stocks in the industrialized world had been raised to unprecedented levels, to the extent that the oil companies' storage facilities were simply unable to accommodate further crude. By September spot market prices for African crudes had fallen to some $5 below official levels, and OPEC production had dropped 1.5 million b/d below the 28.5 million b/d at which it had run during the early part of the year.

It was against this background that OPEC held two meetings in Vienna in September 1980—a regular oil ministers' meeting and a tri-ministerial meeting of oil, finance and foreign ministers. The latter group was convened to discuss the Organization's "Long Term Strategy". This involved a formula for future price increases, a wide-ranging programme of aid to the Third World, a revived North-South dialogue between the industrial powers and the developing countries, and a further bilateral dialogue between OPEC and the industrialized countries—all subjects which the Organization had begun to study at the meeting held in Taif in May 1978. Given the state of the market, the Saudi delegation in Vienna was able to make what seemed to be real progress towards a reunification of prices and agreement on a proper system of differentials. It was agreed that the actual Arabian Light price should be raised $2 to $30 a barrel and that this should be regarded as the official marker price. It was accepted that other OPEC crudes, aligned on the theoretical $32 marker, should not be reduced but would remain frozen until the next OPEC conference in December.

The Saudis argued strongly at the Vienna meeting that any price for Arabian Light of over $30 would be too high to serve as a starting point for the Organization's long term price formula, which members were hoping could be put into effect at the beginning of 1981. Noting that conservation and diversification measures in the industrialized world were at last beginning to bite, the Saudis were genuinely concerned that anything over $30 as the starting point

for escalation might lead to permanent damage to the world economy and an undesirably large drop in demand for OPEC crude. Arguing against the Saudis, the more militant OPEC members refused to accept the $30 starting point because it would have involved a reduction of their existing prices. The eventual compromise, lobbied most strongly by Kuwait, was based on the idea that if the majority of members agreed to freeze their prices, the escalation formula would quite quickly bring the Saudi price up to their desired $32 starting point—possibly as soon as the end of the first quarter of 1981.

There remained the question of the details of the price formula. The "draft plan" presented by the working group presided over by Ahmed Zaki Yamani envisaged quarterly price adjustments based on three indices: the exchange rates of the main industrial currencies, inflation in the industrial countries' consumer prices and export prices, and a GNP index reflecting the real rate of growth of the ten biggest industrial countries. The purpose of the last index was to bring the price of OPEC oil gradually up to the price of the "alternatives"—oil from tar sands, shales and coal. The plan also provided for the co-ordinated adjustment of production upwards and downwards to preserve the price structure in the face of serious glut or shortage, and for moderate one-off price increases in times of acute shortage.

Most of the OPEC members backed the draft plan and were broadly in sympathy with the Saudi stand. The dissenters were Algeria, Iran and Libya, which rejected the use of inflation and growth indices from the industrial nations in constructing the price escalation formula. They argued instead for an index based on the much higher growth rates of the OPEC members and on the inflation of OPEC's imports of industrial goods. As the tri-ministerial meeting proceeded there were indications that Algeria would be prepared to compromise with the majority—in which case it was thought that any further holding out by Libya or Iran would have little practical significance. This left only the issue of differentials. Here disagreements revolved around the Gulf producers' opinion that the $7 difference between African crudes and the new marker price of $30 were $4–$4.50 too high. As with the differences over the structure of the long term price formula there was some cautious optimism that the issue of differentials could be solved if there was the political will to do so. It was hoped that these issues could be tied up at three special meetings of the oil ministers and the finance ministers to be held before the OPEC summit, which was scheduled for Baghdad in November. The idea was that the heads of state might then endorse the long term pricing strategy in time for it to come into effect on 1st January.

Iran-Iraq War: renewed price discord

All of these hopes were destroyed at the end of September by the outbreak of the Iran-Iraq war, which soon led to the abandonment of the OPEC summit. The two countries' attacks on each others' loading terminals and refineries led to a complete halt in exports and the removal of 4 million b/d from the international market. Iraq asked other producers to increase their output to compensate for the loss. In October the oil ministers of the four Arabian OPEC members met in Taif and agreed on a programme of increases, though given the 2–2.5 million b/d surplus that had existed in the market before the war the amounts involved were modest. In all, the Arabian producers' output was raised by only some 1 million b/d of which some 7–800,000 b/d came from Saudi Arabia. This involved a new Saudi production level of 10.2–10.3 million b/d. The extra Saudi crude was sold to state-owned oil companies of industrialized and developing countries at a $2 premium over the official Arabian Light price of $30. The production increases were not big enough to prevent a gradual rise in spot market prices. In November the Rotterdam price for Arabian Light rose to $40, and by the end of the month there were a few examples of Arabian Light and African oils being traded for $42–3.

It was against this background that OPEC met again in Bali, Indonesia, in December 1980. The Iranians propped up in an empty chair at the head of their delegation a large photograph of their oil minister, Mr. Javad Tondguyan, who had been captured by the Iraqis. In view of the renewed discord and the more buoyant state of the market the more moderate OPEC members were pleased to achieve even a minimal degree of pricing order. The Conference saw a series of decisions very similar to those taken at the Algiers conference in June 1980. The Saudis agreed to raise the price of Arabian Light by $2 to $32, and the conference as a whole set a theoretical marker crude price of $36— this being intended as the basis for increases in the prices of other crudes. A differentials limit of $5 was set, making an OPEC ceiling price of $41. Somewhat to the oil industry's surprise, in early January 1981 Kuwait, Qatar and Iraq raised their prices by $4 aligning them either side of the "theoretical" marker price of $36. Abu Dhabi raised its price for Murban crude by just $3 to $36.56. The African producers moved the prices of their light crudes to the $40–41 range.

1981—Price reunification

During December 1980 both Iran and Iraq began exporting crude again. From the time lifting began both producers offered substantial discounts, nominally to offset the extra insurance premiums that tanker owners were obliged to pay for sailing their ships into a war zone. In response to the renewal of exports by the two countries, Abu Dhabi had promptly stopped its output of 80,000 b/d of war-relief crude, but Saudi Arabia resolutely maintained its output at 10.3 million b/d. This meant that the Kingdom was accounting for 43 per cent of total OPEC output—a figure which it had never attained in the 1970s and which gave it unprecedented power in OPEC. Certainly in 1980 the Saudis seemed much better equipped to dictate price levels to the other members of OPEC than they had been during the previous confrontation of 1977. (On that occasion Saudi attempts to raise output to 10 million b/d ran into difficulties for technical reasons.) In the circumstances it was inevitable that Iran's and Iraq's

return to the market would lead to a general erosion of prices elsewhere. In April and May several companies, including Atlantic Richfield in Nigeria, "walked away" from their contracts. Qatar dropped its $6.50 premium.

As they approached the next OPEC conference, scheduled for Geneva on May 25th, 1981, the Saudis felt confident of being able to persuade their fellow members, without too much difficulty, to accept a price freeze for the rest of the year. Ahmed Zaki Yamani made it known before the meeting that the Kingdom would like the freeze to be extended through 1982, to give the Western economies "time to breathe and recover". The Saudis also wanted to move towards a unified price structure and revive the Long-Term Strategy plan. This had been the subject of informal discussions which they had held with Kuwait, Nigeria, Algeria, Venezuela and Indonesia at a secret meeting in Geneva in February.

At the OPEC conference no progress at all was made towards reunification. A mooted compromise, which would have involved Saudi Arabia increasing its price by $2 to $34 and the other members lowering their theoretical marker price to the same figure proved unacceptable to the militants. Instead all members agreed to freeze the theoretical marker price at $36 and the maximum OPEC price at $41 until the end of the year.

Most of the members at the conference—the exceptions being Saudi Arabia, Iran and Iraq—also agreed to cut their output by 10 per cent in an attempt to reduce the surplus on world markets. This was important as the first occasion since the 1960s that OPEC had taken a decision on production levels. However, it was announced that the basis for the 10 per cent cut was to be the output levels obtaining at the beginning of the year and, as most producers' output was running at well below these levels in May 1981, the actual reductions that resulted from the decision were not very large.

There was another abortive attempt to reunify prices at $34 when OPEC held a consultative meeting in Geneva in August. Events in the period immediately after the meeting, however, had an important influence on OPEC attitudes. The Saudis in September reduced their production to 9–9.5 million b/d as a gesture of goodwill, while Nigeria, Indonesia, Gabon and Iraq all found that to maintain acceptable production levels they had unilaterally to cut their prices.

At the end of October, when OPEC gathered for its third Geneva meeting of 1981, the members were at least able to agree on reunification. As had been suggested at earlier meetings, the point of reunification was $34—a figure which involved the Saudis increasing their price by $2 and the other members of OPEC cutting their prices by $1–2. The Saudis agreed to underpin the new price structure by restoring their production level to their traditional ceiling of 8.5 million b/d. Various loose ends concerning differentials were tied up at a meeting in Abu Dhabi in December. On this occasion there was a general lowering of the prices of both light and heavy crudes, to be effective from the beginning of 1982, which cut the average cost of OPEC crudes to consumers by some 50 cents a barrel. The atmosphere of compromise that marked the autumn meetings of OPEC owed much to a new realism within the Organization, encouraged by the persistent mediatory efforts of the Kuwaiti Oil Minister, Sheikh Ali Khalifa al-Sabah.

OPEC crisis of early 1982

It was only a matter of weeks after the reunified price structure and the new, more realistic differentials had come into effect that OPEC found itself facing the worst crisis in its history. The continuing recession in the industrialized countries and a run-down of stocks at a rate believed to be 4 million b/d cut demand for OPEC oil in February to just 20.5 million b/d. This compared with a forecast of 23 million b/d made before the new year. In response to the pressure of the market Iran in February made three price cuts totalling $4; North Sea prices were reduced by similar amounts to around $31. The spot market price for Arabian Light fell to $28.50—$5.50 below the government selling price. There was speculation that OPEC might find itself riding a downwards price spiral similar to the upwards movement of two years previously.

Slightly to the surprise of many outside the Organization, OPEC rose to meet the challenge fairly effectively. On March 6th, 1982 the Saudis made a further cut in their production to 7.5 million b/d. On the same day informal discussion by some of the OPEC ministers, attending an Arab conference in Doha, resulted in a tentative agreement that the production of OPEC as a whole should be limited to 18.5 million b/d, and that a full, extraordinary meeting of the Organization should be called two weeks later in Vienna.

The extraordinary meeting, on March 19th and 20th, 1982, did not get off to a good start. Individual members produced a series of inflated figures for what they regarded as their minimum acceptable production quotas. By the end of the first morning the total of all quotas being insisted upon came to 21.9 million b/d. Striking a dire note of warning, Sheikh Yamani said that if the OPEC nations were not serious in their defence of the $34 marker price, and allowed the market to degenerate into a free for all, Saudi Arabia would have no alternative but to go it alone, which

would entail a whole barrage of competitive measures— reduction of the Arabian Light price to $24, an increase in output to 10 or 11 million b/d, and extensive sales of Saudi crude on the spot market. This glimpse of the abyss concentrated the minds of the other members wonderfully and caused them to agree on a realistic set of quotas involving an 18 million b/d ceiling. This was slightly below the ceiling which had been mentioned at Doha and some 1 million b/d below average first quarter production levels. The decision was accompanied by a further lowering of light crude prices in Africa and the Gulf, the establishment of a ministerial watchdog committee to monitor the market and the implementation of the quotas, and an agreement that the 18 million b/d ceiling should be reviewed at the next ordinary conference in Quito in May.

The quotas agreed at the Vienna meeting, in millions of b/d, were as follows: Iraq 1.2, Iran 1.2, Saudi Arabia 7.5, Kuwait 0.65, Neutral Zone 0.3, UAE 1.0, Qatar 0.3, Nigeria 1.3, Libya 0.75, Algeria 0.65, Venezuela 1.5, Indonesia 1.3, Ecuador 0.2, Gabon 0.15. Immediately after the meeting Sheikh Yamani announced yet another cut in the Saudi production ceiling to 7 million b/d in April—0.5 million b/d below its quota level.

In the two months that followed the Vienna meeting the OPEC quota system seemed to be working. The Saudis ran production at about 6.6 million b/d, well below even their self-imposed ceiling, and Iraq was faced with the physical impossibility of meeting its quota because of the closure of its Gulf terminals by war and one of its pipelines to the Mediterranean by Syrian political action. The drop in Iraqi output was offset by the Iranians making it clear that because of exceptional circumstances they did not feel bound by their quota, and would push their production to 2 million b/d or more. As OPEC output ran below the ceiling (at about 16.3 million b/d in April and 17.4 in May) and the rate of stock drawdown lessened—to 2–3 million b/d—spot market prices for OPEC crudes climbed back to official levels.

OPEC's ministerial watchdog committee met in Vienna in April. A month later an ordinary meeting of the Organization was held in Quito on May 20th and 21st. At both meetings ministers expressed themselves pleased with the success of their quota system. It was decided at Quito that a decision on the third quarter OPEC ceiling should be taken at an extraordinary meeting in early July.

Oil Statistics

(compiled by Michael Field)

CRUDE OIL PRODUCTION[1]

(million barrels per day)

	1971	1979	1980	1981	1980/81 % change
Middle East OPEC:					
Saudi Arabia	4.545	9.510	9.990	9.990	—
Kuwait	2.975	2.285	1.425	0.965	−32.3
Partitioned Zone[2]	0.545	0.560	0.535	0.370	−30.8
Iran	4.565	3.125	1.480	1.315	−11.1
Iraq	1.700	3.450	2.645	0.900	−66.0
U.A.E.—Abu Dhabi	0.935	1.460	1.345	1.140	−15.2
U.A.E.—Dubai	0.125	0.355	0.350	0.360	+2.9
U.A.E.—Sharjah		0.015	0.010	0.010	—
Qatar	0.430	0.505	0.470	0.405	−13.8
North Africa OPEC:					
Libya	2.765	2.070	1.790	1.120	−37.4
Algeria	0.780	1.215	1.040	1.010	−2.9
Other OPEC:					
Venezuela	3.620	2.425	2.240	2.170	−3.1
Nigeria	1.530	2.300	2.055	1.445	−29.7
Indonesia	0.890	1.590	1.580	1.605	+0.6
Ecuador	0.005	0.215	0.205	0.220	+7.3
Gabon	0.115	0.205	0.175	0.150	−14.3
Other Middle East and North Africa:					
Oman	0.285	0.295	0.285	0.315	+10.5
Bahrain	0.075	0.050	0.050	0.045	−10.0
Syria	0.100	0.170	0.165	0.165	—
Egypt[3]	0.415	0.505	0.635	0.690	+8.7
Tunisia	0.090	0.115	0.110	0.115	+4.5
Turkey	0.070	0.050	0.055	0.045	
Other producers:					
U.S.A.	11.160	10.210	10.155	10.150	−0.05
Canada	1.585	1.830	1.690	1.565	−7.4
Mexico	0.485	1.620	2.130	2.585	+21.4
Trinidad and Tobago	0.130	0.215	0.210	0.240	+14.3
Colombia	0.215	0.150	0.125	0.135	+8.0
Argentina	0.425	0.470	0.490	0.495	+1.0
Brazil	0.170	0.170	0.185	0.220	+18.9
Brunei	0.150	0.240	0.235	0.165	−29.8
Australia	0.310	0.455	0.395	0.415	+5.1
United Kingdom[4]	neg.	1.600	1.645	1.845	+12.2
Norway	0.005	0.385	0.525	0.505	−3.8
U.S.S.R.	7.630	11.870	12.215	12.370	+1.3
China	0.735	2.130	2.125	2.035	−4.2
Eastern Europe	0.365	0.410	0.385	0.355	−7.8
World Total	50.785	65.710	62.590	59.100	−9.9
Free World Total	42.055	51.300	47.865	44.340	−7.4
OPEC Total[5]	25.405	31.285	27.335	23.175	−15.2
OPEC % Free World Total[5]	60.4	61.0	57.1	52.3	−4.8
Middle East and North Africa Total	20.400	25.735	22.380	18.960	−15.3
Middle East and North Africa % Free World Total	48.5	50.1	46.8	42.8	−4.0

[1] Includes natural gas liquids.
[2] Partitioned Zone production is shared equally by Kuwait and Saudi Arabia.

[*Footnotes continued on next page*

CRUDE OIL PRODUCTION—*continued*]

[3] Includes output of fields occupied by Israel from 1967 to 1979.
[4] neg. = negligible = less than 5,000 b/d.
[5] OPEC total production and OPEC percentage contribution to total Free World production is based only on the production of countries which were members of the Organisation in the years in question. In 1971 Ecuador and Gabon were not members of OPEC. In 1974 Abu Dhabi asked that its membership in OPEC should be registered as United Arab Emirates, including Dubai and Sharjah.

Conversion factors based on world average crude oil gravity:

1 long ton = 7.42 barrels	1 short ton = 6.63 barrels	1 barrel = 35 imperial gallons
1 metric ton = 7.30 barrels		1 barrel = 42 U.S. gallons
To convert metric tons a year into b/d divide by 50.0		To convert long tons a year into b/d divide by 49.2

PROVEN PUBLISHED WORLD CRUDE OIL RESERVES AS AT JANUARY 1st, 1982

('000 million barrels)

MIDDLE EAST AND NORTH AFRICA	RESERVES	YEARS OF PRODUCTION AT 1981 LEVELS	OTHER LEADING PRODUCERS	RESERVES	YEARS OF PRODUCTION AT 1981 LEVELS
Saudi Arabia . . .	164.6	45	Other OPEC		
Kuwait : . . .	64.5	183	Venezuela . . .	20.3	26
Partitioned Zone . .	6.5	48	Nigeria . . .	16.5	31
Iran	57.0	119	Indonesia . . .	9.8	17
Iraq¹	29.7	90	Ecuador . . .	0.9	11
U.A.E.—Abu Dhabi .	30.6	74	Gabon . . .	0.5	9
U.A.E.—Dubai . .	1.3	10			
U.A.E.—Sharjah . .	0.3	82	TOTAL OPEC . .	436.6	*
Qatar	3.4	23			
Bahrain	0.2	12	Rest of World:		
Oman	2.6	23	U.S.A. . . .	29.8	8
Syria	1.9	32	Canada . . .	7.3	13
Algeria	8.1	22	Mexico . . .	56.0	59
Libya	22.6	55	United Kingdom . .	14.8	22
Egypt	2.9	12	Norway . . .	7.6	41
Tunisia	1.7	41	U.S.S.R. . . .	63.0	14
			Eastern Europe . .	2.9	*
			China . . .	19.9	27
MIDDLE EAST AND NORTH AFRICA TOTAL . .	397.9	*	WORLD TOTAL . .	670.7	31

* Not applicable.

Source: Oil and Gas Journal.

Note: Reserve figures are subject to wide margins of error, and there are considerable differences between sources—including oil companies and governments. Proven reserves do not denote "total oil in place", but only that proportion of the oil in a field that drilling has shown for certain to be there and to be recoverable with current technology and at present prices. Normally recoverable reserves amount to about a third of the oil in place. Because the potential of fields is continually being reassessed in the light of production experience and because the production characteristics of a field can (and often do) change as it gets older, proven reserves figures may sometimes be revised upwards or downwards by quite dramatic amounts without any new discoveries being made. Price rises tend inevitably to increase reserves figures by making small fields or more complex recovery techniques economic.

The only exception to the proven commercially recoverable reserves formula used in this table applies to the U.S.S.R. figure. The Soviet figures reported by *Oil and Gas Journal* are "explored reserves", which include proved, probable and some possible reserves.

RESERVES OF THE BIGGEST OIL FIELDS[1]
('ooo million barrels)

	YEAR OF DISCOVERY	CUMULATIVE PRODUCTION	ESTIMATED REMAINING RESERVES	DATES OF ESTIMATES
Middle East and North Africa[2]				
Saudi Arabia				
Ghawar	1948	23.1	54.0	July 1981
Safaniyah	1951	5.9	17.0	July 1981
Abqaiq	1940	6.5	12.0	July 1981
Manifa	1957	0.2	8.5	July 1981
Berri	1964	2.1	6.0	July 1981
Kuwait				
Burgan	1938	19.4	40.6	July 1979
Iran				
Gach Saran	1928	4.5	7.0	July 1979
Marun	1964	3.8	7.2	July 1979
Agha Jari	1938	6.9	3.1	July 1979
Ahwaz	1958	2.7	6.3	July 1979
Bibi Hakimeh . . .	1961	1.5	6.5	July 1979
Iraq				
Kirkuk	1929	7.6	8.9	January 1978
Rumaila	1953	2.9	11.1	January 1978
Libya				
Sarir	1961	1.1	6.9	January 1977
Other OPEC[3]				
Venezuela				
Langunillas	1926	9.8	1.0	July 1981
Bachaquero	1930	5.7	0.9	July 1981
Tia Juana	1928	3.3	1.2	July 1981
Lama	1937	2.2	2.0	July 1981
Indonesia				
Minas	1944	2.4	4.8	July 1979
Non-OPEC[4]				
United States				
Prudhoe Bay (Alaska) . .	1968	1.6	7.8	January 1981
East Texas	1930	4.6	1.4	January 1981
Wilmington (Cal.) . . .	1932	2.0	0.4	January 1981
U.S.S.R.				
Samotlor	1965	6.7	7.8	January 1981
Romashkino	1948	11.8	2.2	January 1981
Ust Balyk	1961	1.1	4.2	January 1981
Arlan	1955	2.2	2.4	January 1981
Novo-Elkhouskoye . . .	1951	1.6	1.4	January 1981
Uzen	1961	1.2	1.6	January 1981
United Kingdom				
Brent	1972	0.2	1.9	July 1981
Forties	1970	0.8	1.1	July 1981
Norway				
Statfjord	1973	0.05	3.9	July 1981
Ekofisk	1970	0.6	0.9	July 1981

[1] *Reserve figures:* By normal international standards a big field is considered to be one with reserves of more than one thousand million barrels. The figures in this table are even more speculative than the national reserve figures given in the table above. (See note following world reserves table.) The purpose of this table is to show: how few giant fields (containing over 5 billion barrels) there are in the world; what a large percentage of the world's total reserves these giant fields contain; and how many more of the biggest giant fields there are in the Middle East and elsewhere.

[FOOTNOTES—*continued on next page*

continued from p. 119]

  [2] *Other Middle Eastern and North African producers:* In Abu Dhabi there are four giant fields, though it is difficult to find precise figures for their reserves. Between them the onshore fields, Asab (discovered 1965) and the Bu Hasa dome of Murban (1962), are thought to have remaining reserves of up to 14 billion barrels. Offshore, Umm Shaif (1958) and Zakum (1964) together are thought to contain anything from 8 to 16 billion barrels. In Abu Dhabi it has been suggested that the upper strata of Zakum alone may contain as much as 10 billion barrels of recoverable reserves—though this is a highly complex field and there are wide differences of opinion on the amounts of oil that may be recoverable. In Qatar the Dukan field (1940), which is now ageing, was once estimated to have some 5–6 billion barrels. In Algeria, the Hassi Messaoud field (1956), divided between north and south domes, was said in the early 1970s to contain about 10 billion barrels, but in recent years this figure has been radically revised downwards. No up to date estimate of reserves has been published.

  [3] *Other OPEC producers:* There are no giant fields—or even very big fields in the 1–2 billion barrels range—in Nigeria, Ecuador or Gabon.

  [4] *Non-OPEC producers:* Prudhoe Bay, East Texas and Wilmington are by far the biggest fields ever discovered in the U.S.A. Few other U.S. fields have ever contained more than 300 million barrels of recoverable reserves. There are no reliable figures for reserves of the biggest fields of China, and figures for the new giant discoveries of Mexico are still speculative. Apart from the U.S.S.R., U.S.A., Mexico and, possibly, China, no producers outside OPEC contain giant fields, and only Britain and Norway have fields in the 1–3 billion barrels range.

GOVERNMENT OIL REVENUES†
(million U.S. dollars)

	1971	1972	1973	1974	1975	1976	1977	1978	1979	1980	1981
Iran	1,870	2,308	5,600	22,000	20,500	22,000	23,000	20,900	18,800	11,600	8,500
Saudi Arabia	2,160	3,107	7,200	29,000	27,000	33,500	38,000	36,700	59,200	104,200	113,300
Kuwait	1,395	1,657	2,800	8,000	7,500	8,500	8,500	9,500	16,300	18,300	14,800
Iraq	840	575	1,900	6,000	8,000	8,500	9,500	11,600	21,200	26,500	10,400
Abu Dhabi/ U.A.E.*	431	551	1,200	5,500	6,000	7,000	8,000	8,700	13,000	19,200	18,700
Qatar	198	255	600	1,650	1,700	2,000	1,900	2,200	3,100	5,200	5,300
Libya	1,766	1,598	3,000	6,000	6,000	7,500	9,400	9,300	15,200	23,200	15,700
Algeria	320	700	1,100	3,500	4,000	4,500	5,000	5,400	7,500	11,700	10,800

* Figures apply for Abu Dhabi from 1971 to 1973, and for U.A.E. from 1974 to 1981.
† Including income from refined products and natural gas liquids.

EVOLUTION OF PRICES AND GOVERNMENT REVENUES FOR THREE GULF CRUDE OILS
($ per barrel)

	Arabian Light		Kuwait		Abu Dhabi Murban	
Production Cost	1970-1 0.11		1970-3 0.06		1970-3 0.15	
	1972-3 0.10		1974-5 0.07		1974 0.165	
	1974 0.16				1975 0.20	
	1975 0.28					
API°	34°		31°		39°	
Percentage Sulphur Content	1.7		2.5		0.75	
	p.p.	g.r.	p.p.	g.r.	p.p.	g.r.
Pre-November 14th, 1970	1.80	0.91	1.59	0.83	1.88	0.92
January 1st, 1971	1.80	0.99	1.68	0.96	1.88	1.01
February 15th, 1971	2.18	1.26	2.09	1.23	2.24	1.27
January 20th, 1972	2.48	1.45	2.37	1.41	2.54	1.46
January 1st, 1973	2.59	1.62	2.48	1.57	2.65	1.66
June 1st, 1973	2.90	1.81	2.78	1.76	2.79	1.86
September 1st, 1973	3.07	2.01	2.94	1.96	3.14	2.04
October 16th, 1973	5.12	3.41	4.90	3.30	6.05	4.01
January 1st, 1974	11.65	9.27	11.55	9.25	12.64	10.07
July 1st, 1974	11.65	9.37	11.55	9.35	12.64	10.16

	Arabian Light		Kuwait		Abu Dhabi Murban	
	p.p.	g.r.	p.p.	g.r.	p.p.	g.r.
October 1st, 1974	11.65	9.69	11.55	9.68	12.64	10.52
January 1st, 1975	11.25	9.98	11.15	10.08	11.69	10.34
	g.s.p.		g.s.p.		g.s.p.	
October 1st, 1975	11.51		11.30		11.92	
July 1st, 1977	12.70		12.37		13.26	
January 1st, 1979	13.34		12.83		14.10	
July 1st, 1979	18.00		19.49		21.56	
January 1st, 1980	26.00		27.50		29.56	
July 1st, 1980	28.00		31.50		31.56	
January 1st, 1981	32.00		35.50		36.56	
January 1st, 1982	34.00		32.30		35.50	
March 20th, 1982	34.00		32.30		34.56	

NOTES

p.p. = posted price; g.r. = government revenue; g.s.p. = government selling price.

1. **The government selling prices** of other major Gulf crudes applying from March 20th, 1982, were as follows:
   Arabian Berri 39° API, 1.1 per cent sulphur, g.s.p. $34.52;
   Arabian Light ex-Yanbu 34° API, 1.7 per cent sulphur, g.s.p. $34.00;
   Arabian Medium 31° API, 2.4 per cent sulphur, g.s.p. $32.40;
   Arabian Heavy 27° API, 2.85 per cent sulphur, g.s.p. $31.00;
   Iranian Light 34° API, 1.3 per cent sulphur, g.s.p. $30.20;
   Iranian Heavy 31° API, 1.6 per cent sulphur, g.s.p. $28.30;
   Abu Dhabi Marine (Umm Shaif) 37° API, 1.3 per cent sulphur, g.s.p. $34.36;
   Abu Dhabi Zakum 40° API, 0.95 per cent sulphur, g.s.p. $34.46;
   Iraq Basrah Light 34° API, 1.95 per cent sulphur, g.s.p. $33.96 ($34.21 ex-Mediterranean ports);
   Iraq Kirkuk 36° API, 1.9 per cent sulphur, g.s.p. $34.08 ($34.83 ex-Mediterranean ports);
   Qatar Dukan 40° API, 1.17 per cent sulphur, g.s.p. $34.49;
   Qatar Marine 36° API, 1.4 per cent sulphur, g.s.p. $34.30.

2. **Differentials:** Arabian Light has been designated the "Marker" crude, forming the basis of the prices of all other Gulf crudes. During 1974 other Gulf crudes were priced at the Marker plus or minus set amounts for: (a) API Gravity Differential—added to the price of crudes lighter than the Marker and subtracted from crudes heavier than the Marker; (b) Sulphur Premium—for all crudes with a sulphur content lower than that of the Marker; and (c) Freight Differential—involving crudes loaded nearer the entrance of the Gulf (nearer the markets) being given a marginal price differential over those loaded at the top of the Gulf. Since the beginning of 1975, when the first unilateral adjustments to these set amounts were made, there has been no agreed system of differentials, and different producers have made their own adjustments on the occasions of price rises, or as and when they have felt that the prices of their crudes have got out of line with competing crudes. The result has been that during recent years there have often been anomalies in Gulf crudes' pricing.

3. **The dates in the table** denote changes in price and tax formulas (*see* text for details), excluding adjustments to differentials, as follows:
   (a) Pre-November 14th, 1970: before price increase for heavy crudes (27° and 31° API) and introduction of 55 per cent tax rate. Revenue calculation: posted price, minus expensed 12.5 per cent royalty, production cost and appropriate discounts; taxed at 50 per cent with royalty added.

continued from previous page]

(b) January 1st, 1971: after November 1970 tax and price increases and scheduled reduction of price discounts and gravity adjustment discounts at beginning of year. Revenue calculation as in item (a) except for 55 per cent tax rate.

(c) February 15th, 1971: after Teheran Agreement price increases and elimination of all discounts. Revenue calculation as in item (a) except for absence of discounts and 55 per cent tax rate.

(d) January 20th, 1972: after first inflation and escalation increments of Teheran Agreement (June 1971) and first Geneva Agreement for dollar compensation, January 1972. Revenue calculation as in item (c).

(e) January 1st, 1973: after second inflation and escalation increments of Teheran Agreement and introduction of 25 per cent participation regime. Revenue calculation: Weighted average of revenue on: 75 per cent of production known as equity crude (calculated as in item (c)), 18.75 per cent of production known as buy-back bridging crude and 3.75 per cent of production known as buy-back phase-in crude—*see* text. Note: These calculations are somewhat notional because they do not take account of the remaining 2.5 per cent of production which the producers sold directly on the open market—at prices only a little below the postings.

(f) June 1st, 1973: after compensation for second dollar devaluation under Second Geneva Agreement. Revenue calculation as in item (e).

(g) September 1st, 1973: after introduction of 93 per cent of postings price for all buy-back crude under 25 per cent participation regime, and price adjustments under terms of second Geneva Agreement on July 1st and August 1st. Revenue calculation: weighted average of revenue on 75 per cent of production known as equity crude, calculated as in item (c), and 93 per cent of postings less production costs, on 22.5 per cent of production known as buy-back crude. See note at end item (e).

(h) October 16th, 1973: after first OPEC unilateral increase and price adjustment under terms of second Geneva Agreement on October 1st. Revenue calculation: as in item (g).

(i) January 1st, 1974: after second OPEC unilateral increase, introduction of 60 per cent participation regime (back-dated to January 1st) and previous adjustments under terms of second Geneva Agreement on November 1st and December 1st, 1973. Revenue calculation: weighted average of revenue on 40 per cent of production known as equity crude, calculated as in item (c), and 94 per cent of postings less production cost on 60 per cent of production known as buy-back crude. Note: in practice the weighted average figures for revenues in 1974 are notional—partly because during the year the division between equity and buy-back crude was often nearer 60–40 or 50–50 than 40–60, and partly because, up to October, there were variations at different times and in different states in the percentage of postings charged to the companies for buy-back crude. This percentage varied from 93 to 94.8 per cent of postings.

(j) July 1st, 1974: after royalty rate adjustment by OPEC at Quito. Revenue calculation: as in (i) except that royalty rate used in equity crude calculation is 14.5 per cent, and the percentage of postings charged for buy-back crude is 94.8 per cent.

(k) October 1st, 1974: after royalty and tax rate adjustments by OPEC at Vienna. Revenue calculation as in (i) except that in equity crude calculation royalty rate used is 16.67 per cent and tax is 65.65 per cent, and in the buy-back crude calculation the buy-back price is 93 per cent of postings.

(l) January 1st, 1975: after royalty and tax rate adjustment and posted price reduction agreed in Abu Dhabi in November, and introduction of single price structure in Vienna in December. Also after change in ratio used in calculating Abu Dhabi acquisition price from 40–60 to 50–50 made retroactive to January 1st, and introduction of 10 cents discount by Abu Dhabi on the 93 per cent of postings applied to the now notional buy-back crude. Revenue calculation: weighted average of posted price minus expensed 20 per cent royalty and production cost taxed at 85 per cent with royalty added for 40 per cent (or in Abu Dhabi's case 50 per cent) of production treated as equity crude, and 93 per cent of postings (less 10 cents in Abu Dhabi's case) less production cost for 60 per cent (or in Abu Dhabi's case 50 per cent) of production treated as buy-back crude. As from January 1st, 1975, this formula was applied to 100 per cent of production, so in practice the price distinction between equity and buy-back crude ceased to exist even if the notions of equity and buy-back crude were still used in working out the single price level. Note: In some cases figures in the table for government take in 1975 and selling prices in later years are notional because of unofficial discounts given by producers wanting to increase their output.

(m) October 1st, 1975: after 10 per cent increase announced by OPEC in Vienna. Revenue calculation: By October 1975 OPEC was talking in terms of official government selling prices to third parties (93 per cent of postings) rather than of posted prices. On this basis it is not possible to give a uniform formula for determining government revenues in later 1975, 1976 and 1977 because each country's situation was different. Variations would occur depending on whether a country had taken over its concessionaires entirely or whether the foreign companies still held a 40 per cent equity stake. In the first case crude sold back to the former concessionaires went at the selling price less varying amounts of discounts (15 cents per barrel *taken* by the foreign companies in the case of Kuwait and 15 cents per barrel *produced* in the case of Qatar) with further variations being caused by the different percentages of total production sold back to the concessionaires or sold to third parties. In the second case crude sold back to concessionaires had its price calculated as in item (l), while the remaining volume of crude went at the selling price. For these reasons the figures given in the table for October 1975 onwards are government selling prices, rather than posted prices and government revenues with production costs.

(n) July 1st, 1977: after OPEC split at Doha in December 1976 and reconciliation in June 1977.

(o) January 1st, 1979: after OPEC meeting in Abu Dhabi in December 1978 and adjustments to the differential affecting Kuwaiti crude earlier in the year.

(p) July 1st, 1979: after OPEC meeting in Geneva in June, which set marker crude price of $18 and OPEC ceiling price of $23.50 in attempt to end leapfrogging of previous six months.

(q) January 1st, 1980: after further leapfrogging in second half of 1979 and Saudi $6 increase in November intended to help unify prices. Also after OPEC meeting in Caracas in December and subsequent price rises by most OPEC members (including $2 by Saudi Arabia) backdated to beginning of 1980.

(r) July 1st, 1980: after price rises by all OPEC members in April and May. Also after OPEC meeting at Algiers in June when members established a "theoretical" marker crude price of $32 ($4 above the actual Arabian Light price) and a ceiling price of $37 for the highest quality OPEC crudes. Increases announced later under these arrangements were backdated to July.

(s) January 1st, 1981: after Saudi price rise to $30 agreed at OPEC meeting in Vienna in September 1980 (when other members did not raise prices) and general increases for all members (announced during January 1981 and backdated to the beginning of the year) permitted by OPEC meeting in Bali in December. At this meeting "theoretical" marker crude price was established at $36 and OPEC ceiling at $41.

(t) January 1st, 1982: after price reunification at Geneva in October, involving increase in price of Arabian Light and reduction of most other crude prices. Also after reduction of prices of light and heavy crudes agreed as part of adjustment of differentials in Abu Dhabi in December.

(u) March 20th, 1982: after agreement on production quotas in Vienna in March, accompanied by reduction in differentials affecting light crudes. Also after Iran's unilateral price cuts in February 1982.

REFINERY CAPACITY AND OWNERSHIP[1]

('ooo barrels per day)

(on stream in 1982)

STATE	REFINERY	CAPACITY	STATE TOTAL	OWNERSHIP
Iran	Abadan[2]	nil		National Iranian Oil Co.
	Esfahan	200		,, ,, ,, ,,
	Kermanshah	15		,, ,, ,, ,,
	Shiraz	80		,, ,, ,, ,,
	Tabriz	80		,, ,, ,, ,,
	Teheran	225	600	,, ,, ,, ,,
Iraq	Daurah	73		State Establishment for Oil Refining and Gas Processing
	Basra	140		,, ,, ,, ,,
	Kirkuk	18		,, ,, ,, ,,
	Alwand (Khanaqin)	12		,, ,, ,, ,,
	Haditha/K3	6		,, ,, ,, ,,
	Muftiah (Basra)	4		,, ,, ,, ,,
	Qaiyera (Mosul)	2	255	,, ,, ,, ,,
Kuwait	Shuaiba	180		Kuwait National Petroleum Co.
	Mina al Ahmedi	250		,, ,, ,, ,,
	Mina Abdullah	110	540	,, ,, ,, ,,
Saudi Arabia	Ras Tanura	415		Petromin
	Riyadh	120		,,
	Jeddah	95	630	,,
Partitioned Zone	Mina Saud	50		Getty
	Ras al Khafji	27	77	Arabian Oil Co.
Bahrain	Sitra	250	250	Government and Caltex
Qatar	Umm Said	20	20	National Oil Distribution Co.
Abu Dhabi	Umm al Nar	15		Abu Dhabi National Oil Co.
	Ruwais	120	135	,, ,, ,, ,,
Yemen, P.D.R.	Aden	160	160	Government
Lebanon	Tripoli	30		Government
	Sidon	17	47	MEDRECO (Caltex & Mobil)
Jordan	Zerqa	60	60	Jordan Petroleum Refining Co.
Syria	Homs	100		General Petroleum Authority
	Banias	120	220	,, ,, ,,
Egypt	Mex-Alexandria	64		Alexandria Petroleum Co.
	Suez	100		Suez Oil Processing Co.
	Tanta (Nile Delta)	14		,, ,, ,,
	Al Amiriyah (Alexandria)	36	214	El Nasr Petroleum Co.
Sudan	Port Sudan	22	22	British Petroleum & Shell
Libya	Marsa el Brega	8		Esso Sirte
	Zavia	60		Libyan Government
	Tobruk	120	188	,, ,,
Algeria	Hassi Messaoud	8		Sonatrach
	Algiers	50		,,
	Arzew	53		,,
	Béjaia	175		,,
	Skikda	362	648	,,
Tunisia	Bizerta	25	25	Soc. Tunisio-Italienne de Raffinage

[continued on next page

STATE	REFINERY	CAPACITY	STATE TOTAL	OWNERSHIP
Morocco	Sidi Kacem	15		Soc. Chérifienne des Pétroles
	Mohammedia	115	130	Marocaine-Italienne de Raffinage
M.E. AND N.A. TOTAL			4,273	
Venezuela			1,323	
U.S.A.			18,700	
United Kingdom			2,482	
Italy			4,003	
France			3,291	
Germany, Fed. Rep.			2,937	
Japan			5,601	

Note: This table may not be complete or entirely accurate. It is less reliable in the Iraqi and North African entries than in the Gulf and other Middle Eastern entries.

In Iran the Abadan refinery was mostly destroyed during the autumn of 1980, in the early months of the Iran-Iraq war. In May 1981 the Iranian authorities said that they were thinking of demolishing the refinery and building a new plant elsewhere in the south-western province of Khuzestan. The war also caused damage to several of the Iraqi refineries.

A major expansion of Middle East refining capacity is partly underway and partly planned. Projects are as follows:
Iraq: new 220,000 b/d refinery at Baiji to be completed 1983.
Kuwait: major modernization and expansion programmes underway on old Ahmedi and Mina Abdullah refineries. Ahmedi refinery has been operating far below capacity in recent years.
Qatar: Umm Said refinery, geared to domestic market, undergoing expansion. There are plans for a separate export refinery at Umm Said with a capacity of 150,000 b/d.
Abu Dhabi: Umm al Nar domestic refinery undergoing expansion programme to increase its capacity to 75,000 b/d by the end of 1983.
Oman: 50,000 b/d domestic refinery being built at Mina Fahal.
Egypt: Capacity of Mex-Alexandria refinery being increased to 110,000 b/d.
Libya: new 220,000 b/d refinery at Ras Lanuf due on stream in 1982.
Algeria: Capacity of Hassi Messaoud refinery being raised to 30,000 b/d.
Saudi Arabian export refineries: Projects going ahead or planned in 1981 were as follows:
    Jubail: Petromin/Shell joint venture for 250,000 b/d export refinery.
    Jubail: Petromin/Texaco-Socal joint venture for 12,000 b/d lube oil export refinery.
    Yanbu: Petromin/Mobil joint venture for 250,000 b/d export refinery.
    Yanbu: Petromin/Ashland joint venture for 5,000 b/d lube oil export refinery.
    Rabigh: Petromin/Petrola joint venture for 325,000 b/d export refinery. This project is for a much less sophisticated refinery than the Shell and Mobil plants. Petrola is owned by the Greek shipowner John Latsis.
Saudi Arabian domestic refineries: A new 170,000 b/d domestic refinery is being built at Yanbu for completion in late 1982 and there are plans for another new refinery at Juaymah. Of the refineries shown in the chart above but not mentioned in these notes, Ras Tanura, formerly owned by Aramco, is export orientated, while Jeddah and Riyadh are domestic.
Source: Part of the information in this table is drawn from *The Petroleum Economist.*

OIL CONSUMPTION
(million barrels per day)

	1980	1981	OIL AS PERCENTAGE OF PRIMARY ENERGY CONSUMPTION IN 1981		1980	1981	OIL AS PERCENTAGE OF PRIMARY ENERGY CONSUMPTION IN 1981
U.S.A.*	16.4	15.5	41	Latin America	4.6	4.7	65
Canada	1.9	1.7	37	Middle East	1.6	1.7	70
Total N. America	18.2	17.2	41	Africa	1.5	1.6	43
				S. and S.E. Asia	3.2	3.4	47
Belgium/Lux'bourg	0.55	0.5	53	Japan	5.0	4.7	63
Netherlands	0.8	0.7	51	U.S.S.R.	8.8	9.0	37
France	2.3	2.1	53	E. Europe	2.1	2.1	23
W. Germany	2.7	2.5	45	China	1.8	1.7	17
Italy	2.0	1.9	66				
United Kingdom	1.7	1.6	38	World Total	61.7	59.8	42
Total W. Europe	14.0	13.0	51	Free World Total	49.0	47.0	48

* U.S. Processing gain has been deducted from total domestic product demand.
Source: BP Statistical Review of World Energy 1981.

GAS: RESERVES, PRODUCTION, TRADE AND CONSUMPTION

(b.c.m.=billion cu. metres; LNG=liquefied natural gas; LPG=liquefied petroleum gas; b/d=barrels a day)

Country	Reserves Jan. 1st, 1982 (b.c.m.)	Production 1981 Net —Excluding Gas Flared or Reinjected		Gas Flared 1980 (b.c.m.)	Gas Reinjected To Maintain Oil Field Pressure 1980 (b.c.m.)	Exports of Gas by Pipeline or as LNG 1980 (b.c.m.)	Production of Ethane, LPG and Other NGLs 1979 (b/d)	Consumption— Methane and LPG 1981	
		(b.c.m.)	(million b/d oil equivalent)					(b.c.m.)	(million b/d oil equivalent)
Saudi Arabia (inc. half N. Zone)	3,346	14.6	0.264	38.4	0.3	nil	31,000	Total M.E. inc. others 39.2	Total M.E. inc. others 0.706
Kuwait (inc. half N. Zone)	981	5.8	0.104	1.4	0.5	nil	99,000		
Iran	13,707	6.4	0.114	9.5	2.3	0.7 to U.S.S.R.	nil		
Iraq	773	0.6	0.010	9.6	nil	nil	nil		
Abu Dhabi	552	5.9	0.108	7.6	nil	2.7 LNG to Japan	14,500		
Qatar	1,699	5.0	0.081	1.2	nil	nil	nil		
Libya	657	3.3	0.058	4.6	10.7	2.3 LNG	147,000	Total Africa inc. others 0.368	Total Africa inc.
Algeria	3,707	21.8	0.392	9.7	14.4	6.1 LNG	145,000		
Nigeria	1,147	0.7	0.014	23.5	nil	nil	nil		
Gabon	14	0.1	0.002	1.7	nil	nil	nil		
Indonesia	776	18.7	0.338	6.7	4.4	12.0 LNG to Japan	18,000	18.0 S & SE Asia	0.324 S & SE Asia
Venezuela	1,131	17.1	0.310	2.2	16.5	nil	69,500	Total Latin America 60.4	Total Latin America 1.088
Ecuador	122	neg	neg	0.3	nil	nil	300		
U.S.A.	5,607	554.1	9.984			1.3 to Canada	1,565,000	565.9	10.188
Canada	2,546	75.5	1.360			23.0 to U.S.A.	339,000	53.4	0.962
Mexico	2,134	35.7	0.642			3.0 to U.S.A.	148,000	See Latin Amer. fig.	See Latin Amer. fig.
U.K.	736	35.4	0.638			nil	39,500	46.7	0.840
Norway	1,398	25.2	0.454			25.0 to Europe	nil	nil	nil
Netherlands	1,577	72.2	1.300			52.0 to Europe	170	32.0	0.576
France	77	7.3	0.132			0.2 to Belgium & Switzerland	nil	27.4	0.494
Italy	103	12.9	0.232			nil	26,900	25.3	0.456
W. Germany	175	18.6	0.334			4.5 to Netherlands	nil	45.8	0.824

[continued on page 130

continued from p. 129]

Country	Reserves Jan. 1st, 1982 (b.c.m.)	Production 1981 Net —Excluding Gas Flared or Reinjected		Gas Flared 1980 (b.c.m.)	Gas Reinjected To Maintain Oil Field Pressure 1980 (b.c.m.)	Exports of Gas by Pipeline or as LNG 1980 (b.c.m.)	Production of Ethane, LPG and Other NGLs 1979 (b/d)	Consumption— Methane and LPG 1981	
		(b.c.m.)	(million b/d oil equivalent)					(b.c.m.)	(million b/d oil equivalent)
Japan . .	23	2.0	0.036			nil	nil	29.6	0.484
Brunei . .	201	9.1	0.148			8.0 LNG to Japan	nil	See Asia figure	See Asia figure
U.S.S.R. .	32,851	457.2	8.236			57.0 to E & W Europe	n.a.	393.0	7.074
World . .	82,451	1,530.0	27.570			202.0	n.a.	1,479.9	17.970
OPEC . .	28,725	101.0	1.820	116.4	49.1	23.8	524,300	n.a.	n.a.
OPEC % World Total .	35	6.6	6.6			12	n.a.	n.a.	n.a.

Notes: Figures in the Reserves column, drawn from *Oil and Gas Journal*, are for gas recoverable with present technology and at present prices. The only exceptions apply to the U.S.S.R. and Canada. The U.S.S.R. figure is for "explored" reserves, which include proved, probable and some possible reserves. The Canadian figure includes proved and some probable reserves. Figures for reserves of gas—like reserves of oil—may be subject to wide margins of error.

The blanks in the gas flared and gas reinjected columns for countries outside OPEC do not indicate that no gas is flared or reinjected in these countries. In practice flaring outside OPEC takes place on a relatively small scale whereas reinjection is regarded as a normal procedure. Figures for gas flared and reinjected are published regularly by OPEC because the utilization of gas resources has been the subject of a major development effort in member states during the last ten years.

Definitions: Natural gas may be found on its own (unassociated gas) or with oil (associated gas). Associated gas exists partly as a gas cap above the oil and partly dissolved in oil—it is the presence of gas under pressure in new oil fields which drives the oil to the surface. Associated gas is unavoidably produced with oil and may be flared, reinjected or used as fuel.

Natural gas is a mixture of numerous hydrocarbons and varying amounts of inert gases, including nitrogen, carbon dioxide and sulphur compounds. (Gas containing large quantities of sulphur is known as *sour* gas; gas without sulphur is *sweet* gas.) By far the biggest component of all natural gas by volume (at least 75 per cent) is methane, CH_4. Other components are ethane—C_2H_6, propane—C_3H_8, and butane—C_4H_{10}. All of these hydrocarbons are gases at normal temperatures and pressures. Suspended in the gas are various heavier hydrocarbons, pentane (C_5H_{12}), octane etc., which are liquids at normal temperatures and pressures. Gas with a relatively high proportion of propane, butane and the heavier hydrocarbons is known as *wet* gas. Associated natural gas tends to be wetter than unassociated gas.

Methane is the normal pipeline natural gas used for domestic and industrial purposes. It liquifies at very low temperatures ($-160°C$) and very high pressures, and in this condition is known as *liquefied natural gas*, LNG.

Ethane is either kept with methane and used as a fuel, or is separated and used as a feedstock for petrochemicals production. Ethane is not traded on its own internationally.

Propane and Butane are used as cylinder gases for a large number of industrial and domestic purposes. (Camping gas and cigarette lighter gas is either propane or butane). The two gases liquify at higher temperatures and lower pressures than methane. In their liquid state they are known as *liquefied petroleum gases*—LPGs.

Pentane and other heavier liquids are used for a variety of purposes, including the spiking of heavy crude oils and as petrochemical feedstocks. These hydrocarbons, liquid at normal temperatures and pressures, are known as *natural gasolines* or *condensate.*

Together, liquefied petroleum gases and natural gasolines are referred to as *natural gas liquids*—NGLs.

Gas Development and Trade: The main development of natural gas in the Middle East has taken place since the 1973–74 oil price rises. In the Gulf the normal strategy has been to keep fields of unassociated gas as a reserve to be exploited in the future. Associated gas, produced with oil, is normally split into its component parts: methane is used to fuel local industries (though Abu Dhabi liquifies and exports some of its methane), ethane is to be used as a feedstock for petrochemical plants, and the NGLs are exported. In North Africa, Algeria produces large quantities of unassociated gas, which it exports as LNG.

The international trade in NGLs in some respects is not dissimilar to the crude oil trade. Cargoes of LPG and other NGLs may be switched from one destination to another and traded forward or on the spot market.

The trade in methane, however, works on a completely different basis. Where methane is traded in a gaseous form it moves by pipeline from seller to buyer under long term contract. Similar long term contracts apply when it is traded as a liquid (LNG). The trade in LNG requires the construction of extremely expensive liquifaction plants, cryogenic tankers and regasification terminals. To date the practice has been to operate particular tankers on fixed routes between liquifaction plants and terminals.

For most of the world, natural gas in any form is a very new fuel. Twenty years ago virtually the only country to use natural gas on a large scale was the U.S.A. The 1960s saw the development of the huge Groningen gas field in Holland, Britain's southern North Sea fields, and the world's first exports of LNG—from Algeria to Britain. The 1970s and early 1980s have seen the beginning of LNG exports from Brunei, Libya and Abu Dhabi. The U.S. share of the Free World's natural gas consumption has fallen from 75 per cent in 1971 to 57 per cent in 1981.

There has been a similar expansion of the trade in natural gas liquids. Kuwait's NGL plant came on stream in the late 1970s and the Saudi NGL system is being brought on stream in stages; Saudi LPG and NGL production rose from some 30,000 barrels a day in 1979 to 266,000 b/d in 1980. Other countries to have brought NGL plants on stream recently are Qatar (whose first NGL plant exploded in 1978), Nigeria and Norway.

Principal Oil Groups Producing or Refining in the Gulf

This list accounts for well over 90 per cent of oil exploring, producing and refining operations in the Middle East. But it is not a complete list. There are a large number of small operators either exploring or producing oil in minor quantities. Further details of the national takeovers of the Gulf oil industry are given in the text which precedes the oil statistics.

NATIONAL IRANIAN OIL COMPANY (NIOC)

NIOC is responsible for all oil operations in Iran. At the end of February 1979 it was announced that the company was taking over entirely the role of producing and marketing oil in the area of "the Consortium". The Consortium, officially Iranian Oil Participants, had originally been formed as a lesee following the settlement of the 1951–53 Mossadeq crisis in which the Anglo-Iranian Oil Company (BP) had been nationalized. Its members were BP with 40 per cent; Shell 14 per cent; Exxon, Mobil, Socal, Texaco and Gulf with 7 per cent each; CFP 6 per cent; and a group of U.S. independents with 5 per cent between them. In 1973 this group surrendered administration of the oil fields to NIOC, but remained as privileged buyers of Iranian crude. To help run the industry the Consortium members founded two service companies, wholly owned by themselves. These were the Oil Service Company of Iran (OSCO) which operated the fields for NIOC in Iran, and Iranian Oil Services (IROS) which was London based and had the job of procuring equipment, organizing the training of Iranians and recruiting some of the non-Iranian staff of OSCO. (Most of OSCO's expatriate staff were seconded by the company's shareholders.) The OSCO operation accounted for about 90 per cent of Iranian crude production, and OSCO shareholders took over half of the crude produced—the rest being marketed by NIOC. Well before the whole operation was terminated by the revolution in 1979, the financial and crude oil lifting terms of the agreement of 1973 were mainly inoperative following the failure of successive rounds to renegotiations.

After the revolution NIOC crude sales moved away from members of the Consortium. OSCO was suspended. Its expatriate employees left Iran and its Iranian employees were transferred to NIOC. IROS, however, continued to work for NIOC. Intermittent discussions were held in 1979 and 1980 between the company's shareholders and the Iranians on NIOC's taking over IROS, and these resulted in early 1981 in IROS being replaced by Kala Limited. The new company, whose name means *supplies*, is wholly owned by NIOC and has taken some of IROS's employees onto its payroll.

Before it took over operations in the Consortium area NIOC had for some years operated itself a small oil field at Naft-i-Shah. Beginning in 1959 it had also entered a number of partnerships and service contracts with foreign companies (see main text for details)—five of which were producing oil (mostly from offshore fields) at the time of the revolution. In 1979 NIOC terminated these agreements by taking over the foreign shareholdings. In August 1980 it was announced that a new company, the Continental Shelf Oil Company, was to be formed to operate the fields formerly run by the partnerships. The company was to be supervised by a directorate in the Oil Ministry.

NIOC owns all of Iran's refineries and the internal distribution business (before the revolution Iran was consuming some 700,000 b/d). It also owns a tanker fleet and before the revolution had a number of overseas investments in refineries. Most of these investments have now been sold or abandoned.

IRAQ NATIONAL OIL COMPANY (INOC)

The Iraqi state oil company is responsible for all exploration, production, pipeline operations and crude oil marketing. Part of its exploration and production operations it carries out itself, part is assigned to contractors. Within INOC the supervision of exploration and production is split between the Northern Petroleum Organization, in charge of the Kirkuk and Mosul fields, and the Southern Petroleum Organization, in charge of the Basrah fields.

Until the nationalization measures of the early 1970s Iraq's production and exports were run entirely by the Iraq Petroleum Company (operating around Kirkuk) and its affiliates, the Basrah Petroleum Company and the Mosul Petroleum Company. These companies (together with the Qatar Petroleum Company and the Abu Dhabi Petroleum Company) were known collectively as IPC. They were owned by a consortium of BP, Shell, CFP and an Exxon-Mobil partnership, with 23¾ per cent each, and the Participations and Explorations Corporation (Gulbenkian) with 5 per cent.

Other government oil organizations in Iraq are: the State Organization for Oil Projects, responsible for contracting work; the State Establishment for Oil Refining and Gas Processing; the State Establishment for Distribution of Oil Products and Gas, running domestic marketing operations; and the Iraqi Oil Tankers Enterprise.

KUWAIT PETROLEUM CORPORATION

KPC was formed in 1980 as part of a rationalization of the structure of the Kuwaiti oil industry. It took over the existing state oil companies, which had inherited different parts of the former concessionaires' operations, and assigned them specialist roles as producers, refiners etc. The companies that now form the operating arms of KPC are as follows:

Kuwait Oil Company: runs oil and gas production both in Kuwait itself and in the Kuwaiti part of the onshore Partitioned Zone. Before the takeovers of the 1970s Kuwaiti production was run by a BP-Gulf partnership, also known as KOC. Production in the northern half of the Partitioned Zone was run by an American independent group, Aminoil.

Kuwait National Petroleum Company: runs liquified petroleum gases processing, domestic products marketing and Kuwait's three refineries. Before the takeovers and subsequent rationalization of the Kuwaiti oil industry, KNPC was the "national oil company", concerned with internal products distribution, the Shuaiba refinery and several investments in oil operations abroad.

Petrochemicals Industries Company: main operation at present is Kuwait Chemical Fertiliser Company's plant at Shuaiba. Runs various minor plants and will run new petrochemical plants planned in Kuwait.

Kuwait Oil Tankers Company: crude oil and products shipping. KOTC was formerly a public company, in which the government held a large minority stake.

The Kuwait Petroleum Corporation also owns 70 per cent of the Kuwait International Petroleum Investments Company. The remaining 30 per cent of this company is owned by the Kuwaiti public.

ARAMCO

Aramco is responsible for all exploration and production onshore and offshore in the Eastern Province. It accounts for all Saudi production except that coming from the Partitioned Zone, where Getty operates onshore and the Japanese Arabian Oil Company offshore. In the mid-1970s Aramco was given charge of the construction of the government's gas gathering system, a natural gas liquids pipeline across the Kingdom to Yanbu and the unification of the Eastern Province electricity grid.

Until the beginning of the participation process in the early 1970s, Aramco was Saudi Arabia's concessionaire. The company was formed by Socal, Texaco and Exxon, with 30 per cent each, and Mobil with 10 per cent. After long negotiations it was announced in early 1980 that the Saudi Government had completed the takeover of Aramco's assets in the Kingdom (though Aramco itself remained an entirely American owned and American registered company). It was not made known what local service operation the Aramco owners would establish to continue to run the oil industry on the government's behalf; nor was there any announcement on the form of the new state oil corporation which would hold the assets of the production industry and supervise operations.

The only facility in which the Aramco owners together retain a direct equity stake in Saudi Arabia is Tapline, the Dhahran-Sidon crude oil pipeline. This pipeline, built in the late 1940s to facilitate the flow of oil to Europe at the time of reconstruction, was owned by Socal, Texaco, Exxon and Mobil through the Tapline Company, which was separate from Aramco. Tapline was shut for economic reasons in 1975 and has seldom been used since. The Saudi Government announced that it was taking a 50 per cent share in the line in April 1981.

PETROMIN

The Saudi state oil company is responsible for the sale of that part of crude oil production which is not assigned to the Aramco partners. Petromin also handles all internal distribution of petroleum products and domestic refining operations at Jeddah and Riyadh. It runs the processing and foreign sales of natural gas liquids, which have started to come on stream from the vast gas gathering system being built for the company by Aramco. Petromin now owns the export refinery at Ras Tanura, taken over from Aramco in 1980, and is the Saudi partner in the export refineries being built in the new industrial cities of Jubail and Yanbu (see notes after refinery table in the statistical section of this chapter).

As of May 1982 no announcement had been made on how Petromin's role might be affected by the complete takeover of Aramco by the Saudi Government.

QATAR GENERAL PETROLEUM CORPORATION

QGPC owns all production, refining and distribution operations in Qatar, and holds the Qatar Government's shares in the Qatar Fertiliser Company, the Qatar Gas Company and the Qatar Petrochemicals Company. It also holds the government's shares in oil industry ventures outside Qatar and pan-Arab oil operations, such as the Arab Shipbuilding and Repairs Yard in Bahrain.

Before the takeovers of the 1970s Qatar's territory and offshore areas were divided between two concessionaires: offshore was Shell Qatar, operating three relatively small fields (Idd al-Shargi, Maydan Mahzam and Bul Hanine), and onshore was the Qatar Petroleum Company, owned by the IPC shareholders. (See INOC notes above.) QPC operated the large Dukan field. After the takeovers of 1976 and 1977 the two production operations were vested in the state owned Qatar Petroleum Producing Authority (Onshore Operations) and the Qatar Petroleum Producing Authority (Offshore Operations). Both of these

operations were incorporated into the Qatar General Petroleum Corporation in 1980, becoming the corporation's oil production divisions. Personnel for the onshore operation is provided by the Dukan Service Company, owned by the IPC shareholders, and for the offshore operation by the Qatar Shell Service Company, owned by Shell.

ABU DHABI COMPANY FOR ONSHORE OIL OPERATIONS (ADCO)

Before "participation" the Abu Dhabi onshore oil operation was owned by the Abu Dhabi Petroleum Company (ADPC)—an IPC company (see Iraq notes above). This company had been given a concession covering all onshore areas and territorial waters for 75 years from 1939 to 2014, though subsequently large areas had been relinquished. In 1973 the government took a 25 per cent share in the operation, and in 1974 negotiated a 60 per cent participation. No attempt is being made to complete the takeover. In 1978 the owners of ADPC (which remains a London registered company) established a locally incorporated operating company, the Abu Dhabi Company for Onshore Oil Operations (ADCO). In the new company the state oil corporation, the Abu Dhabi National Oil Company (ADNOC) has a stake of 60 per cent. ADCO accounts for all of Abu Dhabi's onshore oil production—though there are other foreign groups exploring onshore on a partnership or carried interest basis. Local refining operations are owned by ADNOC.

ABU DHABI MARINE AREAS OPERATING COMPANY—(ADMA-OPCO)

In 1953 Abu Dhabi's offshore concession was awarded to Abu Dhabi Marine Areas, a company owned by BP (two thirds) and CFP (one third). The concession was to run to 2018 and covered areas of the continental shelf beyond the state's three mile limit. In December 1972 BP sold part of its stake to a large group of Japanese industrial companies which formed the Japan Oil Development Company. In 1973 the government took a 25 per cent stake, and in 1974 negotiated a 60 per cent participation. No attempt has been made since to complete the takeover.

Early in 1979 all the shareholders established a locally incorporated operating company (ADMA-OPCO) in which the shareholdings are: Abu Dhabi National Oil Company (ADNOC) 60 per cent, BP $14\frac{2}{3}$ per cent, CFP $13\frac{1}{3}$ per cent and Japan Oil Development Company (JODCO) 12 per cent. This company operates the Umm Shaif field and the lower strata of the Zakum field, which together account for most of Abu Dhabi's offshore production. Technical staff for the operation are provided mainly by BP, which also manages the procurement of equipment and owns the BP Project Group in Abu Dhabi. The Project Group acts as the project arm of ADMA-OPCO.

ZAKUM DEVELOPMENT COMPANY (ZADCO)

The Zakum Development Company has been formed to develop the upper strata of the giant Zakum field. The company is registered in Abu Dhabi and is purely an operating company, with its shares held 50/50 by ADNOC and CFP. In practice, development work is carried out entirely by CFP.

The Zakum development itself, however, is owned 88 per cent by ADNOC and 12 per cent by the Japan Oil Development Co., JODCO. These are the companies that pay for the development work and will own the oil produced. The ADNOC-JODCO partnership does not have a name and is not incorporated in Abu Dhabi. The partnership came about through CFP and BP, both shareholders in

ADMA-OPCO, declining to participate in the development of Upper Zakum and having their shares taken by ADNOC.

It is intended that by 1986 production from upper Zakum will reach 500,000 b/d, equivalent to the 1980 production of Umm Shaif and lower Zakum combined.

Four other groups of mixed foreign ownership operate four rather marginal fields in Abu Dhabi waters.

DUBAI PETROLEUM COMPANY (DPC) GROUP

In July 1976 Dubai announced that it had negotiated a 100 per cent takeover of the DPC group, though the terms of the takeover were very different from those applying anywhere else in the Middle East. Ownership of the DPC group's offshore concession, originally granted in 1952 for 60 years to BP and CFP as Dubai Marine Areas, had changed on a number of occasions before July 1976, but the government had not previously taken a 25 or 60 per cent holding. Under the terms of the July agreement DPC itself (Conoco) remained as operator, and the DPC group continued to market Dubai's oil, take the risks, make the investment and bear the costs. The group was, however, paid back by the state all of its previous investment, and was in future to be able to depreciate new investments over three years instead of ten, giving the government

ownership of the oil-producing assets. DPC accounts for all of Dubai's production.

OWNERSHIP:

Dubai Petroleum Company (Continental) [Operator]	30%
Dubai Marine Areas (50/50 Hispanoil and CFP)	50%
Deutsche Texaco	10%
Sun Oil	5%
Wintershall	5%

PETROLEUM DEVELOPMENT OMAN (PDO)

Originally a concession of 75 years from 1937, expiring 2012. Onshore areas, originally covering northern provinces, now including Dhofar. Government took a 25 per cent share in 1973, and increased this to 60 per cent in 1974. PDO accounts for all of Oman's oil production, though other foreign groups are exploring.

OWNERSHIP:

Oman Government	60%
Shell	34%
Compagnie Française des Pétroles	4%
Participations and Explorations Corpn. (Gulbenkian)	2%

The Arms Trade with the Middle East and North Africa

Hanns Maull

Nothing could highlight the volatility of the Middle East better than the Iran-Iraq war which erupted in September 1980. Only two years earlier, the trend towards peaceful resolution of conflicts in the Gulf region seemed to have made the danger of war remote—although the tremors in Iran were an ominous sign of the brittleness of the Imperial political system in Iran. Internal changes in Iran triggered off a series of regional and international shock waves which fundamentally transformed previous patterns of regional politics. Military power had been the principal element in the Shah's strategy of cementing not only his own rule but also Iranian hegemony in the Gulf—but the seemingly powerful Iranian armed forces disintegrated under the pressure of revolutionary forces. And yet Iraqi military power could not secure a decisive victory over the weakened army and air force of Iran—mostly because the destructive power of the advanced weapon systems held by both sides could not be mobilized fully. But while the war demonstrated the limits to rapid infusions of military power through large-scale arms transfers, it also sparked off a new sense of insecurity in the whole Gulf region, which accelerated the push towards stronger military forces.

The enormous oil wealth of the Middle East and North Africa gives the region a central strategic importance in East-West relations. At the same time, two geographical areas within the region have been major arenas of indigenous military and political conflict: Palestine and the Persian Gulf. In Palestine, the issue is the struggle between Jewish and Arab (Palestinian) nationalism over the same territory; in the Persian Gulf, there are various rivalries, conflicts and tensions which all appear at least connected with the main source of wealth in this zone: oil. Both areas have also seen an unparalleled military build-up in two major arms races: the Arab-Israeli arms race, dominated by Israel, Egypt and Syria, but also including other countries; and the arms race in the Persian Gulf in which Iran, Saudi Arabia and Iraq were the main participants. Here, as well, the arms race has shown a tendency to spill over into other countries in the area. There is also a certain link between the two zones: the financial, military and above all the political support (in the form of the oil weapon) which the Arab Gulf producers gave to the countries fighting against Israel is clear evidence of this now strongly established connection between the Persian Gulf and the Arab-Israeli zone. This connection has direct implications for the arms build-up in the Arab-Israeli conflict, since it provides Arab combatant States with a source of finance for their weapons procurement, and potentially widens the circle of countries directly involved in a potential future conflict.

The period 1974 to 1978 saw a distinct movement towards a peaceful management of conflict both in the Arab–Israeli zone and in the Persian Gulf. The disengagement agreements negotiated by Dr. Kissinger; the emphasis of the Carter administration on securing an overall solution to the Arab–Israeli conflict; its shift to direct and even-handed participation in the negotiating process; and finally President Sadat's peace initiative in late 1977—all this could be seen as part of a progression towards a satisfactory settlement of the conflict between Israel and the Arab world. The moderate Arab oil producers led by Saudi Arabia were during this period willing to support the search for an agreement, and to give the United States and Egypt the freedom of manoeuvre to do so. Their understanding was that such an agreement would have to be comprehensive, i.e. resolving all issues of contention between Israel and the Arab world, and notably the Palestinian question, in a way which would satisfy the majority of Arabs, as well as Palestinians. The meeting between Carter, Begin and Sadat at Camp David, however, seemed to confirm fears which had been aroused already by Sadat's visit to Jerusalem: that Israel and Egypt had embarked on the road to a separate peace agreement with at best tenuous links with other Arab–Israeli issues of contention.

During the same period 1974–78, the three major Gulf states Iraq, Iran and Saudi Arabia had managed to settle, at least temporarily, most issues under dispute between them (bilateral agreements were made between Iran and Iraq and Saudi Arabia and Iraq). Saudi Arabia and Iran had even developed a close partnership based on largely identical regional objectives. This helped to ensure stability in the Gulf and a predominance of moderate policies in the Middle East region as a whole.

Since early 1979 three major events have fundamentally transformed the situation. First, the Egyptian-Israeli treaty had reduced the probability of a full-scale war between Israel and its neighbours very considerably, but it had also led to a polarization of the Arab world, with Egypt largely isolated: at the Baghdad meeting in late March 1979, a large majority of the Arab world agreed to ostracize Egypt through the severance of diplomatic and economic relations. Saudi Arabia and the other moderate oil producers reluctantly followed this course—from their point of view, the Egyptian-Israeli agreement did not make sufficient provisions for an overall settlement of the conflict and notably of the Palestinian problem. This left the Gulf producers vulnerable to pressures from the PLO and from radical regimes and groups in the Arab world, and gave them little choice but to align themselves with the mainstream of Arab reaction to the peace treaty.

The second event was the revolution in Iran and the fall of the Shah. The new regime in Teheran was sympathetic to the PLO and thus gave a boost to radical forces in the Arab world; at the same time, the fall of the Shah meant that Saudi Arabia had lost a powerful conservative partner and therefore much of its ability to impose moderation on Arab politics. The precarious balance in the Gulf during the years 1974 to 1978 had thus been overthrown; the internal fragmentation of Iran and the struggle for power, renewed tensions along ethnic lines and the conflict with the U.S. over the hostages held in the U.S. Embassy in Teheran all contributed to weakening Iran severely. At the same time, the Iranian attacks on the traditional regimes in the Arab Gulf countries and in Iraq (and incidents which demonstrated that Khomeini's revolution reverberated on the other side of the Gulf) raised the spectre of contagion: Iraq sought to pre-empt this danger to its internal stability by causing the fall of the revolutionary regime in Teheran; at the same time, the weakness of Iran also offered an opportunity to reverse the concessions Iraq had to make in its previous settlement of disputed issues with the Shah. Thus, the Iraqi regime decided to attack Iran.

The third major event was the Soviet invasion of Afghanistan at the end of 1979. It was a direct consequence of the Iranian revolution—not only because of the internal turmoil and the weakness of this country, but also because of the American preoccupation with the hostages held in the U.S. Embassy in Teheran. The military intervention of the U.S.S.R., in a bid to gain full control over Afghanistan. dramatically accelerated the trend towards superpower competition in Southwest Asia. This had become increasingly evident since 1978 through the military coup in Afghanistan in April of that year, through the consolidation of the Soviet presence in the Horn of Africa and in the People's Democratic Republic of Yemen, and through Moscow's overtures to Pakistan and Turkey. The invasion of Afghanistan dramatically ended the near-exclusion of the Soviet Union from the Persian Gulf region in the period 1974–78. It created a situation of direct superpower competition with poorly defined rules and therefore a dangerous potential for conflict—not least over access to oil from the region, which in the 1980s will be of growing importance to an increasingly oil-short Eastern Europe. In the Arab countries of the region, the Soviet invasion heightened the sense of insecurity and stimulated not only an intensification of regional cooperation (notably between Iraq and Saudi Arabia), but also renewed efforts to build up the armed forces.

These two main centres of conflict in the region, however, are not the only sources of instability and tension: there are at least two epicentres, in North Africa, and at the Western coast of the Red Sea, where Middle Eastern and North African countries are directly or indirectly involved on opposite sides. The former relates to the Moroccan takeover of the Spanish Sahara, the Algerian support for *Polisario*, the movement for independence of the Sahrawi Arab Democratic Republic, which has mounted a guerrilla war against Moroccan forces, and to recurrent tensions between Libya and its neighbours, particularly Egypt. The other conflict, in the Horn of Africa, escalated considerably during 1977. The Ethiopian regime, weakened by internal differences within the ruling junta and an extremely bloody suppression of domestic opposition, found itself confronted with dramatic new advances by the liberation movements in Eritrea, and with what was *de facto* a major Somali offensive in Ogaden. The threats were successfully contained with the help of massive arms transfers from the Soviet Union and large troop contingents from Cuba. Soviet presence in the Horn of Africa is of obvious strategic importance and political significance for the Gulf region and, as in Afghanistan, Moscow has undoubtedly a great interest in consolidating and expanding its control over Ethiopia. The struggle over Eritrea remained undecided, however, and the provision of limited military facilities for the U.S. in Somalia also injected an additional element of superpower rivalry into the Horn of Africa.

While the intensity of international and regional conflict increased after 1978, several Middle Eastern countries exhibited growing internal tensions and fragmentation, largely along religious and ethnic lines. This process began in Lebanon, where the fragile balance between the various communities broke down in 1975 under the contradictory pressures from outside, which turned the country increasingly into a chessboard for Syrian and Israeli moves of controlled conflict. Centrifugal forces also quickly came to the fore in the Iranian revolution; a third country experiencing rising tensions between different communities has been Syria. Other countries also showed signs of increasing domestic instability, providing a temptation for external interference. Attempts at internal repression, civil strife or even open civil war all also provided a stimulus for increased military spending.

THE NATURE OF THE ARMS RACES

Arms races tend to develop quantitative and qualitative aspects, and both are strongly at work in the Middle Eastern arms races. The *quantitative* aspect is apparent in the rapid growth of the armed forces (in terms of manpower, tanks, aircraft, artillery, etc.). In the 1967 war Israel could muster some 1,050 tanks and 290 combat aircraft, while Egypt and Syria together had some 1,650 tanks and 550 aircraft. In 1977, two bitter and costly wars later, the military power of Israel stood at 2,765 tanks and 543 combat aircraft, while Egypt and Syria together possessed 4,375 tanks and 928 combat aircraft. In 1982 Israel had a total of 602 combat aircraft and 3,500 tanks, while Syria had 448 combat aircraft and 3,700 tanks and Egypt possessed 290 combat aircraft and about 1,700 tanks. The developments of the military strength in each case demonstrate that Egypt has "opted out" of the arms race with Israel, a result of the peace process. The attention of Egypt seemed to turn increasingly westward and southward, at least in terms of its defence posture, while Syria's arms build-up continued unabated as the country tried to match growing Israeli capabilities.

The *qualitative* aspect is reflected by the rapid growth in destructive power of each weapon system and the deployment of totally new systems which replace old, outdated systems. This qualitative change means that less complex and sophisticated weapons are replaced by more sophisticated and therefore more expensive weapons. Impressive as the quantitative arms build-up in the Middle East may be, it is surpassed by the speed of qualitative changes. The gap between the arms technology of the Great Powers and the Middle Eastern countries has been gradually closed, with important thresholds being the deployment of supersonic jet fighters (between 1956 and 1967) and the large-scale introduction of missiles and electronic warfare (between 1970 and 1973). As far as conventional warfare is concerned, the main participants in the two Middle Eastern arms races now command weapon systems which are the most modern available for the Great Powers themselves; a development strongly underlined by U.S. deliveries of advanced aircraft and equipment (F–14 *Tomcat*, *Phoenix* air-to-air missiles, P–3F *Orion* anti-submarine surveillance planes; F–15 and F–16 fighter aircraft) to Iran, Israel and Saudi Arabia, and by the appearance of the most advanced Soviet fighter aircraft (MiG–23 and MiG–25) in Syria and Iraq. The rapid advance of the arms importers in technological terms is best reflected in the fact that some weapon systems are specifically developed or redesigned in accordance with the specifications of the buyers (e.g. Saudi financial support for the development of a new generation of French *Mirage* fighters, or the Saudi version of the *Maverick* missile), who also share development costs with the producer. The qualitative arms race also took a new turn in recent years in the area of surface-to-surface missiles: Israel received the American *Lance* missile (with a range of 70 miles), while both Egypt and Syria have been supplied by the Soviet Union with *Frog* (range: 30 miles) and *Scud* missiles (range: 185 miles).

The Israeli destruction of the "Osirak" nuclear reactor in Iraq has once more dramatically focused attention on the last remaining qualitative difference between Middle Eastern and superpower weapon systems: the nuclear threshold. While Israel certainly has had a nuclear option for some years, and would be capable of assembling nuclear warheads within a relatively short period, should she desire to do so, the growing interest of other Middle Eastern countries in nuclear technology and reactors poses the question whether some of these countries might also eventually try to develop nuclear weapons. Nuclear reactors normally burn enriched uranium, and produce plutonium. Both can be used to manufacture nuclear warheads, provided a country has access to enrichment facilities geared to producing heavily enriched uranium, or reprocessing capacity. Countries to receive reactors and/or to develop some form of co-operation with nuclear powers or countries with considerable know-how and capabilities in nuclear technology (threshold powers such as Argentina or Germany) include at present Egypt, Iraq, Saudi Arabia and Libya. Of these countries, Libya has allegedly already tried to acquire nuclear weapons

and Iraq has signed a number of bilateral agreements about the provision of nuclear installations and technology, including "Osirak", a French research reactor fuelled with weapon-grade enriched uranium and an Italian "hot cell" for the handling of highly radio-active material. This has led to renewed speculation about a possible Iraqi nuclear weapons programme and the Israeli air attack on the reactor in June 1981.

Arms races of such dimensions in a third world area necessarily mean heavy reliance on imported weapons. True, some Middle Eastern countries have indigenous arms industries producing small arms and ammunition and four Arab countries tried to launch an enterprise to develop a large-scale, indigenous arms industry in a joint venture based on Saudi, Qatari and U.A.E. oil revenues and existing technology in Egypt. The Egyptian-Israeli peace treaty and the subsequent Arab boycott of Egypt destroyed this venture; but the Gulf states were trying to press ahead without Egypt. But, so far, only Israel's arms industry is of a military significance, and even she has to rely heavily on arms imports.* Table 1 shows the amount of arms imports by Middle Eastern countries and (by comparison with *total* expenditure on arms imports from 1974 to 1978) the financial implications of quantitatively and qualitatively rapidly expanding arms races.

THE MOTIVES FOR THE ARMS BUILD-UPS

Arms build-ups, and arms races (i.e. competitive build-ups) are predominantly fuelled by a feeling of insecurity and a (real or imagined) threat to vital foreign policy objectives among the participants. The threat may emanate from other countries in the region, or from a superpower: in the Gulf region, developments after the Iranian revolution and the beginning of the Iran-Iraq war, and after the Soviet invasion of Afghanistan and a growing military presence of the U.S.S.R. and its allies elsewhere in the region, accentuated fears of Iranian and Soviet expansionism. There are, however, other factors which make for higher military expenditures or facilitate military build-ups. Generally speaking, external objectives include not only the obvious one—military forces sufficient to guarantee the security of the state against a threat from outside. They may also include the intention to expand the influence of the state

---

* Today, Israel produces two light transport airplanes, the *Arava* and the *Westwind*, and recently also started production of a new fighter, *Kfir* (based on French *Mirage* design and an American engine, the General Electric J-79) in addition to the *Barak*, another indigenous, less powerful Israeli version of the *Mirage* which had been already used in combat in 1973. The most recent major weapons system presented by the Israeli arms industry is a new battle tank, the *Merkava*. Israel also manufactures air-to-air missiles (*Shafir*) and ship-to-ship missiles (*Gabriel*) as well as missile boats and (under concession) the *Sabra* medium tank. The country has become an exporter of a considerable range of arms, from the UZI submachine gun to *Gabriel* and *Shafir* missiles, and has reportedly also offered the *Kfir* fighter for sale; according to the London-based IISS, Israel supplies military equipment to several Central and South American countries.

beyond its boundaries by the explicit or implicit threat and the application of force to achieve certain objectives. Military power also serves as a symbol of national independence and status.

Another set of motives for increasing military strength is internal: some of the Middle Eastern and North African regimes are politically unstable and still have to enforce the central power of the Government against the return or threat of tribal and minority challenges. The guerrilla war in the Dhofar province of Oman is a typical example here; the bloody civil war in the Lebanon no doubt also had strong roots in internal contradictions and conflicts, although outside interference and the presence of a large Palestinian refugee group linked the civil war to intra-Arab rivalries and the Israeli-Arab dispute. The internal violence in the Lebanon has led to a massive influx of arms.

Many Middle Eastern and North African countries are ruled by military regimes or governments whose main source of support is the armed forces. Consequently, the armed forces form an influential pressure group, whose demands have to be taken into account. Since the rulers of these countries depend on the loyalty of the army they will try to keep this by dispensing various benefits and privileges. A good example here is Libya: in the last year of its existence, the monarchy embarked on a modernization programme for the armed forces in order to appease the growing discontent in the officer corps; after the coup, military expenditure rose dramatically, and it is difficult to say whether the Libyan interest in the Arab-Israeli conflict under the new leadership in fact caused this increase or was a justification for it.

These external and internal factors fuel the demand for higher military expenditure and consequently for increased arms imports. The various mechanisms of arms races (worst-case assumptions of defence planners and the trend towards over-insurance: Israel, for instance, will plan for a contingency of a large Arab coalition of armed forces and attempt to provide forces appropriate to it while Egypt might try to achieve parity with Israel by itself) actually cause these factors to interlock so that internally motivated arms purchases might induce the opponent to increase his force level as well.

Of crucial importance for the actual development of the arms race are factors of availability—the resources available for military expenditure, and the interest of Great Powers in particular countries or groups. High oil revenues enable the oil producers (and other Arab countries as well) to buy weapons, and the involvement of the United States and the Soviet Union in the Arab-Israeli zone and in the Persian Gulf allowed countries in the region to receive weapons even without the financial burden this would normally constitute (reduced or suspended payment, favourable conditions for repayment). Besides, Saudi Arabia has begun to use its importance as the principal oil producer in the Middle East, and its close relationship with the United States in oil price and production decisions, as a lever in its arms demands: the sale of F-15s to Riyadh was explicitly linked by Saudi Arabian officials to future price and production policies, and the agreement to sell sophisticated AWACS reconnaissance and control aircraft to Saudi Arabia was again turned into a demonstration of Riyadh's influence in Washington. Thus, oil power has become a contributory factor to the massive increases in arms transfers from industrialized countries to the Middle East and North Africa—first, because it implies availability of large amounts of cash, and secondly because of the political influence which oil power lends to producer countries.

Looking at the two principal areas of tension more closely, the Arab–Israeli conflict continues in a state of stalemate. The political momentum towards a comprehensive settlement has largely become dissipated, but a renewal of hostilities between Israelis and Arabs on a war-like scale also appears unlikely (this article was written before the Israeli invasion of Lebanon in June 1982—*Editor*). *Egypt*, which in the past relied on an offensive military strategy to break the stalemate, has now effectively removed itself from any military confrontation. The country continues, however, to rebuild its military strength in the pursuit of wider regional objectives such as the checking of Libya's military build-up and political expansionism, and the support of moderate forces in the Middle East and in Africa. *Syria* has been increasing its military efforts for a number of reasons: in the Arab–Israeli conflict, the peace treaty between Egypt and Israel has meant that the country can no longer count on Egyptian support in a confrontation with Israel; tensions with Iraq have been growing again after a brief interlude of reconciliatory gestures; and the military presence and indirect conflict with Israel in Lebanon as well as the embattled domestic position of the regime of President Assad undoubtedly also portend higher military expenditure and more arms imports. *Israel* continues to rely on superior military strength to deter any attack on its territory, and to induce the Arabs to comply with its political demands. The influx of arms into the *Gulf region* complicates this drive for superiority, and thus enhances the push for additional military equipment.

THE PERSIAN GULF

While the Arab–Israeli conflict is essentially clear-cut, the Persian Gulf is characterized by a much more complex structure of varied, partly overlapping tensions. The crucial country in the past and present has been Iran, although for different reasons. Until the revolution, the country had been committed to a rapid build-up of military power, thereby providing a powerful stimulus for other Gulf states to expand their forces, too. After the revolution, the disintegration of the imperial army, the cancellation of arms deals worth several billions of dollars, and the uncertainty of the domestic situation in the aftermath of the Shah's demise, created a power vacuum in the Gulf.

Under the Shah, Iran's main concern had been the establishment of a dominant influence in the Gulf as a means to secure her vital trade routes. These trade routes were, in the eyes of Iran, potentially threatened by countries and forces hostile to Iran, and possibly through a Soviet co-ordination of these hostile forces.

Iraq was viewed in Teheran as the main opponent to Persian hegemony in the Gulf; the two states were at loggerheads over a wide range of conflicting claims and issues such as the mutual support for dissident movements in Kurdistan (supplied by Iran), Khuzistan/Arabistan (which Iraq regarded as part of the Arab world and its own territory), off-shore demarcation lines, and the shipping rights in the Shatt al-Arab waterway. Iraq never fully accepted the Iranian bid for hegemony in the Gulf and tried to match growing Iranian military power through a parallel build-up. In March, 1975, the two states signed an agreement which settled the differences between them, and relations improved markedly; nevertheless, underlying suspicions lingered on, and the arms race between the two continued. In the case of Iraq, the military build-up drew further momentum from involvement in the Arab-Israeli region, and from the need to suppress the domestic challenge of Kurdish nationalism.

The Shah also saw the survival of conservative states and regimes on the other side of the Gulf as a vital security objective of Iran, and he tried to prevent the spreading of radical regimes in the sheikhdoms through military support to the Sultan of Oman. This also enabled Iran to exert *de facto* control over both sides of the Strait of Hormuz, strategically the most sensitive point in the Gulf. Ironically, the Shah also voiced concern over the stability of the Saudi monarchy, and tried to push Riyadh and other conservative Arab oil producers into domestic reforms to modernize their political systems in line with economic development.

Iran's rapidly evolving military power gave the country a clear superiority in the Gulf region, and an important role beyond it in the Indian Ocean. The Iraqi-Iranian agreement marked a reluctant and presumably tactical acceptance of this by Iraq, and other Gulf states also recognized the dominant position of Iran. Nevertheless, it was not only Baghdad which tried to challenge the Iranian military build-up by parallel measures of their own: Saudi Arabia also embarked on a massive programme of expansion and modernization of her armed forces. The external motivations for this were presumably a certain distrust of Iranian ambitions and a fear of the radical regime in Baghdad.

The revolution in Iran changed the situation in the Gulf fundamentally. The first aspect of this change was the erosion of Iranian power and dominance in Gulf affairs—a result of the rapid disintegration of the armed forces as the main pillar of support of the *ancien régime*, the cancellations of arms contracts with a total value of more than $10,000 million, and the selling back of some modern Western weapon systems such as the F-14. This not only affected Iran's military capabilities, but even more so other countries' perceptions of those capabilities. Such perceptions played a role in Iraq's decision to settle differences with Iran on the battlefield—the weakened Iranian armed forces were apparently seen as a "push-over". Secondly, the domestic situation in Iran remained undecided, and there were signs of disintegration and a splintering of the polity along ethnic and confessional lines, as well as a diffusion of power to power centres outside

the control of the government. Thirdly, the Iranian revolution led to a deterioration of regional stability and co-operation in the Gulf, as several leading representatives of the new regime in Iran stated their desire to see similar revolutions topple the established regimes on the Arabian peninsula and in Iraq. Relations deteriorated, particularly with Iraq, which renewed its support for the separatist movement in the Iranian oil province of Khuzestan and its demand that Iran evacuate the small islands in the Strait of Hormuz occupied by the Shah in 1971 and concede a new border line in the Shatt al-Arab. The growing tensions finally exploded into open war, when Iraq attacked Iranian forces along the southern front with the double objective of toppling the revolutionary regime (and thus removing a potential threat to the Iraqi regime's domestic position), and of securing a favourable resolution of controversial issues such as the border demarcation and shipping rights in the Shatt al-Arab.

That the Iranian revolution might be contagious was demonstrated by Shi'a-inspired riots and demonstrations in Saudi Arabia, Kuwait and Bahrain. In Saudi Arabia, in particular, the fall of the Shah created a heightened feeling of insecurity, which was not alleviated by the Mecca incident. This sign of domestic fermentation, plus the Soviet invasion of Afghanistan with its overtones of a Soviet strategy to encircle and control the oil-rich countries in the Gulf, and the loss of the powerful Iranian ally on the other shore of the Gulf, and finally the polarization in the Arab world resulting from the Egyptian/Israeli peace treaty reduced Saudi influence and leverage in the region. The U.S. role in the events leading to the fall of the Shah can also hardly have been comforting for the Saudi monarchy, although Washington publicly underlined through words and gestures its commitment to Saudi Arabian security.

The new situation in the Gulf region after the fall of the Shah and the Soviet invasion of Afghanistan created powerful additional pressures for arms transfers—the heightened sense of insecurity among the conservative states in the region led to new orders, but the accentuation of Superpower rivalry in the Gulf also contributed to a new twist in the arms race.

The Iran-Iraq war, which in 1982 seemed to turn badly for Iraq, could yet spill over into neighbouring countries, and a decisive Iranian victory would constitute a new danger for the conservative oil states on the peninsula. Soviet, Cuban and East German military presence in South Yemen, Ethiopia and, of course, in Afghanistan accentuated fears about encirclement. The two Yemens continued to talk about unification, while the southern-supported National Democratic Front guerrilla movement posed a growing threat to the North Yemen regime. The loss of Iranian protection and its replacement by a potential Iranian threat, and the desire to keep Superpower involvement at a minimum led to a new effort at closer co-operation between the conservative Sheikhdoms and monarchies of the Gulf—in 1981, these countries agreed on a new, institutionalized form of co-operation which eventually might also cover external security matters.

Finally, another arms race in the region has accelerated rapidly: the one between Algeria and Morocco. As a result of growing tensions between the two countries over the Sahara issue, Morocco has in recent years dramatically stepped up its imports of weapons to reduce its inferiority in military power to Algeria.

THE EFFECT OF INCREASED ARMS

The vast amount of highly sophisticated weapons flowing into the Middle East and North Africa often transcends the capacity of the armed forces to absorb these weapons. If proof were needed for this, it was supplied by the difficulties experienced both by Iraq and Iran in their war with each other. Highly skilled personnel are needed to man and to maintain them— but in most countries this is a valuable and desperately scarce resource. Long training periods will be needed to operate those weapons effectively, and training can to a large extent only be provided by foreigners. A country then has to send either a great number of soldiers abroad or alternatively provide for training teams. Already, foreign military advisers can be found in many Middle Eastern and North African countries (Americans in Saudi Arabia, Russians in Syria, Indians in Iraq, Pakistanis in Abu Dhabi and Libya).

These technical problems will prove a formidable and sometimes extremely difficult barrier on the way towards a highly effective military force. To overcome this barrier will mean a heavy drain on precious and scarce resources in terms of manpower and for the poor countries also in terms of capital. But the influx of modern weapons is also likely to have social and political consequences: it will strengthen the power of the military elites and increase their size. The officer classes in the Middle East and North Africa in many countries have proved themselves highly politicized, and their increased power could be accompanied by or lead to more involvement in politics.

THE ARMS SUPPLIERS

The international arms trade has become a competitive business; one could talk about a buyers' market. As table 2 shows, some countries have successfully attempted a degree of diversification in their sources of arms supply. The most important suppliers of arms to the Middle East and North Africa are the U.S.S.R., the United States, Great Britain and France. Italy has also made large inroads into the arms exports business, and West Germany witnessed an agonized debate as to whether she should and could maintain her traditionally restrictive policy on arms exports into "areas of tension", triggered by Saudi Arabian interest in a large purchase of German tanks and aircraft. Other developed countries also export weapons into this region, but on a lower scale. Table 2 gives a survey of the main suppliers of arms to the Middle East and North Africa, and the volume of sales in the period 1974–78. Needless to say, the situation of war between Iran and Iraq led to a substantial influx of weapons, whose

origins are difficult to trace. Iran for example, received supplies from, among others, Israel, while Iraq obtained equipment from other Arab states.

Two distinct sets of objectives and motivations can be discerned which induce the industrialized countries to encourage and even actively promote arms exports into the area: political and economic. The political objectives in arms sales to the third world aim at gaining influence in the importing country and in the area. Arms exports can be used to strengthen a ruling group vis-à-vis external or internal threats, and if an exporting and importing country pursue similar foreign policy objectives in the area the latter can fulfill certain strategic functions which otherwise might require some form of military presence of the supplier himself. The supplier might also try to gain access to ports and receive naval and air facilities in exchange for arms sales. The leverage obtained by the exporting country consists basically of two factors: first, the buyer becomes dependent on a continuous flow of spares and the threat to cut this flow and thereby eventually reduce the military strength of the importing country might provide some influence on his behaviour. Second, and more important, sophisticated weapon systems require large-scale training and assistance by the exporting countries which allows the seller to gain access to the officer corps and therefore to one very influential group within the political framework of most importing countries. But the example of Iran has shown again that expectations of increased influence and leverage can be quite unfounded; indeed, in the case of Iran the large previous arms transfers probably contributed to the weakening of the Shah's regime which they were intended to bolster. Political objectives have been predominant in the arms supply policies of the superpowers, the U.S. and the U.S.S.R., and also China, and often arms deals are concluded to pre-empt arms sales by the rival superpower (this gives the importing country some leverage to press for new supplies).Such political motivations appear behind the U.S. intention to supply modern weapons to Egypt: these arms sales are an expression of support for the pro-Western course followed by Cairo. Similar motives are behind Chinese deliveries of MiG engines to the same country in an effort to counteract the Soviet embargo on spares to Egypt. Another example is the military assistance agreement with Saudi Arabia. U.S.-Saudi deals comprise not only considerable arms sales but also demonstrate the desire to back up the present regime by providing for arms deliveries and training for the National Guard, a military body which predominantly serves to protect the present regime against internal threat and to guard oil installations. It is on the National Guard the monarchy relies domestically, rather than on the army which in the past was considered to have only limited reliability. Attempts to gain political influence through arms sales, however, are not necessarily limited to states—as Soviet support for the PLO and the PFLO has demonstrated.

Although political objectives such as privileged relations with key oil states are by no means absent, the arms export policies of France and Britain and other suppliers are dominated by economic considerations—considerations which are of growing importance even for the U.S.A. and the Soviet Union (for the U.S.S.R., weapons can either be bartered for oil or—if sold—contribute welcome foreign exchange earnings). For Western countries, including the United States, the prevailing economic reasons for arms exports is its positive impact on the balance of payments, which the recent oil price increases have worsened for almost all Western industrialized countries. Arms sales help to offset the balance of payments deficits vis-à-vis oil exporting countries either directly (if oil producers and arms importers are identical) or indirectly (through increased export earnings). Lastly, an important economic consideration in arms supply policies, which applies to the superpowers as well as to other suppliers, is secure access to oil: in the aftermath of the 1979 developments in the international oil market, there was a strong revival of bilateral deals exchanging oil against arms.

Arms exports, however, are also vital for the economic viability of sophisticated arms industries in smaller industrialized countries such as France and Britain. Advanced weapon systems, with their enormous research and development costs, can hardly be produced on an economic scale on the basis of the comparatively small domestic military requirements of these countries: the costs would be prohibitive. Exports enable longer production runs, which reduce the cost per unit, and they can also make up for fluctuations in domestic demand which would otherwise have to be rescheduled according to economic rather than military requirements (this is done by Sweden, for example). Exports mean that labour and capital can be kept fully employed. It is not surprising, therefore, that the Governments of both Britain and France actively support and encourage arms exports by providing official sales' assistance and credit facilities and also design their own military requirements partly with the export potential of certain weapon systems in mind.

There is, however, also a restrictive side to arms exports, stemming in principle from the desire of exporting countries not to become unintentionally involved in local or international conflicts through their role as arms suppliers. All suppliers have some form of governmental say in the export decisions and licensing systems, and some of them have made exports conditional upon certain requisites, e.g. not to re-sell the weapons. There have also been repeated attempts to control the flow of arms in crisis areas by embargoes against certain countries or regions (such as the British embargo on combatant states in the Middle East war in 1973, which was lifted in January 1974). The most comprehensive attempt to control and limit the arms trade with the Middle East was the Tripartite Declaration of the U.S., France and Britain in 1950 which broke down with large-scale French sales to Israel and the appearance of the Soviet Union as arms supplier for Egypt in 1955. Attempts to arrive at some mutual restraint in arms transfers to the Third World in general were made in a series of talks between the Soviet Union and the U.S.A. under the Carter administration. These efforts brought no concrete results, however, and are unlikely to be resumed in the present changed climate of East–West relations.

Table 1

MAJOR REPORTED ARMS DEALS, JULY 1980 TO JUNE 1981

Recipient	Value of Total Arms Imports 1974–78 (million current U.S. $)	Supplier, Date of Agreement	System	Approx. Value (million $)	Quantity	Comments
Algeria	1,500	U.S.S.R., 1980	*Nanuchka* corvette	n.a.	1	delivery Nov. 1980
Egypt	1,200	Austria, Mar. 1981	*Kuerassier* self-propelled anti-tank gun	230	100	delivery 1982
		France, Jan. 1981	*Alpha Jet* fighter/training aircraft	360	30	
		France, June 1981	*Mirage* 5 fighter aircraft	n.a.	16	
		Italy, Sept. 1980	CH-47 *Chinook* transport helicopter	140	15	delivery 1980–81
		U.S.A., July 1980	M-60 A tank	104	67	delivery 1981–82
		U.S.A., Sept. 1980	M-901 self-propelled armoured fighting vehicle equipped with TOW anti-tank guided weapon	31.9	52	delivery 1980–81
		U.S.A., June 1981	C-130 H transport aircraft	101	6	delivery 1982
			TOW launcher	} 28	} 73	delivery 1980–81
			TOW anti-tank guided weapon		1,282	delivery 1981–82
			TOW (practice)		362	delivery 1981–82

[*continued on p.* 142]

continued from p. 141]

Recipient	Value of Total Arms Imports 1974–78 (million current U.S. $)	Supplier, Date of Agreement	System	Approx. Value (million $)	Quantity	Comments
Iraq	5,300	Indonesia, Aug. 1980	Bo-105 helicopter	n.a.	n.a.	
		Switzerland, 1980	PC-7 turbo trainer aircraft	n.a.	4	
		U.S.S.R., Oct. 1980	T-62 tank	n.a.	145	delivery Oct. 1980
Jordan	575	Austria, March 1981	*Kuerassier*	n.a.	100	delivery 1981–82 possibly transferred to Iraq
		U.K., Nov. 1980	*Bulldog* training aircraft	n.a.	5	delivery 1981
		U.S.A., July 1980	M-60 A3 tank	159.5	100	delivery 1981
		U.S.A., Oct. 1980	Hughes 500 training helicopter	n.a.	8	delivery 1981
		U.S.A., Feb. 1981	AH-1Q anti-tank helicopter with TOW	114	24	delivery 1982–83
Kuwait	750	U.S.A., Oct. 1980	M-113 A 2 armoured personnel carrier	} 24	52	} delivery 1981–82
			M-113 Ambulance		29	
			M-113 self-propelled armoured fighting vehicle with TOW		6	
			M-577 A 2 command post		14	
			M-125 A 2 mortar carrier		2	
		U.S.A., June 1981	Improved HAWK surface-to-air-missile	50	60	delivery 1982
Libya	5,000	Turkey, Oct. 1980	Landing craft	n.a.	16	delivery 1981–83
			SAR-33 fast attack boat with missiles	n.a.	14	
		U.S.S.R., Oct. 1980	SS-12 *Scaleboard* surface-to-surface missile	n.a.	24	delivery 1980
			SS-12 *Scaleboard* launcher	n.a.	12	delivery 1980
Morocco	950	France, Jan. 1981	*Gazelle* helicopter	n.a.	24	
			AMX-10C armoured reconnaissance vehicle	n.a.	100	
		Italy, Nov. 1980	AB-206 *Jetranger* helicopter	n.a.	19	
			AB-212 helicopter	n.a.	6	delivery 1981
			CH-47 C *Chinook* helicopter	n.a.	5	delivery 1981
		South Africa, 1980	*Eland* armoured car	n.a.	n.a.	delivery 1980
		U.S.A., Mar. 1981	M-60 A tank	108	182	delivery 1980
		U.S.A., June 1981	C-130 *Hercules* transport aircraft	100	7	delivery 1982
Oman	380	U.K., July 1980	*Jaguar* ground attack aircraft	n.a.	12	delivery 1981–82
			Blindfire radar for *Rapier* surface-to-air missile	n.a.	28	delivery 1981–82
		U.K., Feb. 1981	*Providence* fast attack boat	19.2	2	
		Singapore, April 1981	25 m fast attack boat for patrol	n.a.	4	
			Medium landing craft	n.a.	1	
		U.S.A., Oct. 1980	C-130 *Hercules* transport aircraft	17	1	delivery 1981
			M-60 tank	n.a.	6	delivery 1980
		U.S.A., Mar. 1981	C-130 *Hercules* transport aircraft	1.3	1	delivery 1981

[*continued on p.* 143]

continued from p. 142]

Recipient	Value of Total Arms Imports 1974–78 (million current U.S. $)	Supplier, Date of Agreement	System	Approx. Value (million $)	Quantity	Comments
Qatar	40	France, Sept. 1980	*La Combattante* fast attack boat	362	3	
			MM-40 *Exocet* surface-to-surface missile		100	
			Exocet coastal defence system		n.a.	
		France, 1980	SA-330 *Puma* helicopter	n.a.	n.a.	
		France, Dec. 1980	*Mirage* F-1 fighter aircraft	200	14	
Saudi Arabia	3,000	France, Oct. 1980	Anti-submarine warfare frigate	3,450	4	
			Crotale naval surface-to-air missile		n.a.	
			Otomat surface-to-surface missile		n.a.	
			Dauphin 2 helicopter		24	
			AS-15 TT air-to-surface missile		200	
			Durance-class oiler	218	2	delivery 1984
		France, Dec. 1980	*Atlantic* II maritime reconnaissance aircraft	n.a.	2	delivery 1981
		U.S.A., Feb. 1981	V-150 *Commando* armoured fighting vehicle	117	579	delivery 1981–82
Sudan	110	France, 1980	Mk F-3 155mm self-propelled gun	n.a.	11	delivery 1981
		U.S.A., Aug. 1980	M-113 A 2 armoured personnel carrier	14.5	80	delivery 1981
			M-163 *Vulcan* self-propelled anti-aircraft gun	9.5	8	delivery 1981
Syria	3,300	U.S.S.R., Oct. 1980	Tu-126 airborne early warning aircraft	n.a.	2	delivery 1981
Tunisia	80	Germany (F.R.), 1980	Luerssen 57 m fast attack boat	n.a.	3	delivery 1981–82
		U.S.A., July 1980	C-130 *Hercules* transport aircraft	24.6	1	delivery 1981
			Bell 205 A 1 helicopter		8	delivery 1981
		U.S.A., Aug. 1980	Improved *Chaparral* surface-to-air missile	23.8	300	
		U.S.A., Mar. 1981	M-109 A 2 155mm self-propelled howitzer	15	19	delivery 1981
United Arab Emirates	370	Brazil, Oct. 1980	*Cascavel* Mk 2 armoured car	n.a.	n.a.	
		Spain, May 1981	C-212 *Aviocar* transport aircraft	n.a.	4	delivery 1981
		Switzerland, June 1981	PC-7 *Turbo Trainer* training aircraft	n.a.	14	delivery 1982
		U.S.A., June 1981	C-130 *Hercules* transport aircraft	n.a.	2	delivery June 1982

Note: data about arms transfers to the Middle East and North Africa are always to be taken with some caution; the Iran-Iraq war has complicated things further. Thus, the list given above does not claim to be complete, nor to be free from errors.

Source: International Institute for Strategic Studies, London.

Table 2

CUMULATIVE VALUE OF ARMS TRANSFERS TO THE MIDDLE EAST AND NORTH AFRICA
BY MAJOR SUPPLIERS, 1974–78

(in current U.S. $ million*)

	Total	U.S.A.	U.S.S.R.	France	U.K.	Germany, Federal Republic	Italy	China, People's Republic	Other
Afghanistan . . .	350	—	330	—	—	—	—	—	15
Algeria . . .	1,500	—	1,200	10	—	280	10	—	40
Bahrain . . .	10	—	—	5	—	—	—	—	—
Egypt . . .	1,200	60	430	260	110	170	10	40	80
Iran . . .	8,700	6,700	310	200	420	470	350	—	290
Iraq . . .	5,300	—	3,600	430	20	150	70	10	1,020
Israel . . .	4,800	4,600	—	20	60	—	30	—	5
Jordan . . .	575	450	—	5	30	5	—	—	85
Kuwait . . .	750	330	50	150	190	20	—	—	10
Lebanon . . .	50	20	—	10	10	5	—	—	15
Libya . . .	5,000	5	3,400	270	20	140	330	—	750
Mauritania . . .	80	—	—	40	—	—	—	—	40
Morocco . . .	950	170	20	470	5	50	40	—	205
Oman . . .	380	5	—	—	330	—	5	—	40
Qatar . . .	40	—	—	30	10	—	—	—	—
Saudi Arabia . . .	3,000	1,500	—	280	725	20	90	—	380
Sudan . . .	110	30	30	10	—	30	—	5	10
Syria . . .	3,300	—	2,700	150	30	90	—	—	330
Tunisia . . .	80	20	—	10	5	10	5	10	30
U.A.E. . . .	370	10	—	210	120	—	20	—	10
Yemen Arab Republic .	180	40	50	50	—	—	—	—	30
Yemen, People's Dem. Republic . . .	380	—	370	—	—	—	—	—	10
Total . . .	37,105	13,940	12,490	2,610	2,085	1,440	960	65	3,395

* Figures are rounded.

Source: U.S. Arms Control and Disarmament Agency.

The Suez Canal

The Suez Canal joins the Mediterranean and Red Seas between Port Said and Suez, in Egypt. It was closed during the Arab-Israeli war of June 1967 and was not re-opened until June 5th, 1975. Between June 1967 and October 1973 the canal formed the demarcation line between Egypt and the Israeli-occupied Sinai peninsula. After 13 months of clearing the canal of obstacles, it was re-opened by President Sadat on June 5th, 1975. Transit rates were fixed at a level which represented an increase of more than 90 per cent on the rates before the closure in June 1967. Rates were then only marginally altered until January 1981, when a new tariff scale came into force, meaning average rises of between 22 and 25 per cent, but with discounts for larger tankers.

PRINCIPAL FACTS

Length: 107 miles including approach fairways.
Maximum Depth: 50 ft.
Maximum Width: 660 ft.
Minimum Width: 600 ft.
Transit Time: Average transit time was fifteen hours in 1967.

ORGANIZATION

Suez Canal Authority (*Hay'at Canal Al-Suess*): Ismailia, Egypt; Chair. MASSHOUR AHMED MASHHOUR; Dir.-Gen. EZZAT ADEL; Chief Pilot KAMAL HAMZA. The Suez Canal Authority manages the Canal on behalf of the Government of Egypt.

CHRONOLOGY

1854　Ferdinand de Lesseps granted building concession.
1859　Excavation began.
1869　Canal opened.
1875　Ismail Pasha of Egypt sold his shares in the French Suez Canal Company (44% of total to the British Government for nearly £4m.).
1888　Convention of Constantinople declared Canal open to vessels of all nations.
1956　President Nasser of Egypt nationalized Canal. Canal closed following invasion of Egypt.
1957　Canal re-opened under the control of the Egyptian Suez Canal Authority (April).
1959　World Bank lend Authority U.S.$56.5m.
1961　UN surcharge of 3% on transit dues, levied in 1958 to pay for clearing the Canal, was lifted (March).
1964　Loan of £E9.8m. granted by Kuwait Fund for Arab Development for dredging and widening operations. Permissible draught increased to 38 ft.
1965　Transit rates increased 1%, July.
1966　Transit rates increased 1%, July.
1967　Canal closed (June) during war with Israel.
1975　Canal re-opened (June).
1979　First transit of Israeli ship (April).
1980　Maximum permissible draught raised to 53 ft. (December).
1981　The Suez Canal Vessel Traffic Management System (SCVTMS) inaugurated (October).

IMPROVEMENT SCHEMES

In the years following the opening of the Canal the depth of the channel was 26.2 ft. (8 m.) and its breadth at the bottom 72.2 ft. (22 m.), with a wet cross-sectional area of 3,272 sq. ft. (304 sq. m.). The average gross tonnage of transiting vessels was then 1,700 tons and the highest authorized draught was 24.6 ft. (7.5 m.). Navigation speed was 6.21 miles (10 km.) per hour.

NASSER PROJECT

Seven programmes of improvement were executed between 1876 and 1954. The eighth programme had started before nationalization, was modified thereafter to achieve better results and is now called the Nasser Project. Under this scheme the Canal was widened and deepened to take large tankers. New navigational aids and dockyard facilities were built and tug and salvage services improved. A Research Centre has been founded at Ismailia.

Under the first stage, finished in 1961, the Canal was widened and deepened to take vessels of 37 ft. draught. Under the second stage, finished in 1964, the Canal was widened and deepened to take vessels of 38 ft. draught. The installation of two salvage stations and a system of direct radio between vessels and the traffic control station at Ismailia were finished during 1962.

SUEZ AREA REDEVELOPMENT

After the war of October 1973 Egypt announced a plan to re-open the Suez Canal and generally develop the canal area. The canal was re-opened in June 1975 with a permissible draught of 33 ft., increased to 38 ft. in July 1975. A £558 million Japanese-aided widening and deepening scheme raised the maximum permissible draft to 53 ft. in December 1980, enabling the passage of vessels of 150,000 tons (fully laden), 200,000 tons (partly-loaded) and 370,000 tons (unloaded). The 36-km. Port Said by-pass was opened on December 16th, 1980, and the widening operations enabled 90 ships per day to transit the canal instead of the former 65. Other by-passes were constructed at Timsah and Deversoir. The Ahmed Hamdi Tunnel is the first of three to traverse the canal, and it went into service on October 1st, 1980. Further development plans, again Japanese-aided, aim to build a second canal, parallel to the existing one, by 1995.

STATISTICS

SUEZ CANAL TRAFFIC

Year	Ships		Merchandise ('000 tons)		Number of Passengers	Total Transit Receipts (E £'000)
	Number	Displacement ('000 net tons)	Northbound	Southbound		
1962 . . .	18,518	197,837	151,190	31,207	269,685	53,958
1963 . . .	19,146	210,498	159,482	34,050	297,955	71,294
1964 . . .	19,943	227,991	172,463	38,518	269,569	77,697
1965 . . .	20,289	246,817	183,441	42,001	291,085	85,792
1966 . . .	21,250	274,250	194,168	47,725	299,557	95,187
1976 . . .	16,806	187,759	72,020	45,633	n.a.	140,000
1977 . . .	19,703	220,477	72,630	56,063	n.a.	168,000
1978 . . .	21,266	248,260	69,597	80,182	n.a.	n.a.
1979 . . .	20,363	266,171	78,730	81,919	n.a.	407,794
1980 . . .	20,795	281,305	86,547	89,729	n.a.	660,000
1981 . . .	21,577	342,356	93,896	102,532	n.a.	900,000

NORTHBOUND GOODS TRAFFIC
('000 tons)

	1979	1980	1981
Cereals . .	2,461	4,745	3,350
Coal and coke .	2,201	2,676	3,370
Crude petroleum .	20,225	19,077	25,624
Fabricated metals .	3,154	2,513	1,817
Fertilizers . .	1,534	1,840	2,011
Machinery and parts	1,108	1,489	1,596
Oil seeds . .	1,109	1,098	1,585
Oil seed cake . .	1,480	1,313	1,192
Ores and metals .	9,906	11,989	10,377
Petroleum products .	7,059	9,397	10,942
Starch and farinas .	2,509	2,546	3,572
Vegetable oils .	1,566	1,195	1,131
Wood . . .	2,655	2,002	1,761
Others . . .	21,763	24,667	25,468
Total .	78,730	86,547	93,896

SOUTHBOUND GOODS TRAFFIC
('000 tons)

	1979	1980	1981
Cement . . .	9,517	11,797	12,569
Cereals . . .	4,985	6,066	8,825
Chemical products .	2,189	2,351	2,805
Crude petroleum .	839	2,541	4,269
Fabricated metals .	6,677	5,973	7,324
Fertilizers . .	8,982	11,204	11,013
Foodstuffs . .	1,790	1,883	2,017
Machinery and parts	926	1,155	1,156
Ores and metals .	916	571	735
Petroleum products .	8,131	11,453	13,942
Sugar . . .	1,482	1,485	1,300
Wood and lumber .	631	898	704
Wood-pulp and paper	807	865	835
Others . . .	34,047	31,487	35,035
Total .	81,919	89,729	102,532

DISTRIBUTION OF NORTHBOUND PETROLEUM AND PRODUCTS
('000 tons)

Unloading Country	1979	1980	1981
Egypt . . .	2,589	1,070	1,065
France . . .	733	914	1,433
Italy . . .	10,294	9,049	12,939
Morocco . . .	769	1,135	1,587
Netherlands . .	913	1,768	2,117
Romania . . .	5,030	6,571	5,154
Spain . . .	506	752	1,845
Turkey . . .	867	2,503	1,748
U.S.A. . . .	988	379	1,448
Others . . .	4,595	4,333	7,230
Total . .	27,284	28,474	36,566

FLAG DISTRIBUTION OF NET TONNAGE
('ooo tons)

	1979 Tankers	1979 All Vessels	1980 Tankers	1980 All Vessels	1981 Tankers	1981 All Vessels
China, People's Republic . .	748	6,806	760	7,196	234	7,094
Denmark	839	4,621	402	4,665	2,878	8,508
France	6,152	12,313	6,637	12,796	11,470	18,347
Germany, Federal Republic .	1,860	10,398	2,324	10,653	2,816	10,412
Greece	12,653	37,800	11,313	39,041	13,778	42,702
India	183	4,514	209	5,569	945	7,472
Italy	2,559	6,999	2,448	6,386	4,582	9,173
Japan	752	12,151	1,390	13,804	1,805	15,322
Kuwait	2,681	5,380	1,663	3,826	2,646	4,752
Liberia	19,658	33,330	19,105	34,052	29,196	45,730
Netherlands . . .	699	6,999	491	6,573	1,398	7,908
Norway	6,669	15,953	7,705	17,288	11,735	21,256
Panama	3,034	12,798	3,443	15,597	5,930	21,007
Poland	1,186	3,118	1,072	3,143	1,066	3,879
Romania	1,487	2,803	1,952	3,348	1,922	5,373
Saudi Arabia . . .	2,362	2,781	2,562	3,568	4,327	7,194
Singapore . . .	1,498	6,621	1,752	7,553	2,340	7,928
Spain	2,726	3,328	3,259	3,836	4,453	5,061
Sweden	88	5,536	365	5,458	2,417	8,886
U.S.S.R.	4,221	16,371	5,173	19,610	4,876	18,125
United Kingdom . .	4,490	19,391	5,260	18,162	12,971	24,638
U.S.A.	660	4,583	1,055	5,269	789	5,192
Yugoslavia . . .	598	3,553	964	4,061	1,160	4,209
Others	8,475	28,024	7,566	29,851	9,430	32,288
TOTAL . . .	86,278	266,171	88,870	281,305	135,164	342,356

GOODS TONNAGE IN BOTH DIRECTIONS BY REGIONS
('ooo tons)

North of the Canal:	1981	*South of the Canal:*	1981
N. and W. Europe and U.K. Ports .	65,155	Red Sea Ports	48,874
Baltic Sea Ports . . .	4,035	E. Africa and Aden	9,928
N. Mediterranean Ports . .	50,201	India, Pakistan, Sri Lanka and Burma .	32,090
E. and S.E. Mediterranean Ports .	10,698	Arabian Gulf Ports . . .	42,232
W. and S.W. Mediterranean Ports .	16,232	S.E. Asia and Sunda Islands . .	23,356
Black Sea Ports	31,030	Far East	29,980
American Ports	15,720	Australia	9,693
Others	3,357	Others	275
TOTAL	196,428	TOTAL	196,428

PART TWO

Regional Organizations

REGIONAL ORGANIZATIONS

The United Nations in the Middle East and North Africa

MEMBER STATES, WITH CONTRIBUTIONS AND YEAR OF ADMISSION

(assessments for percentage contributions to budget for 1980–82)

Afghanistan	. . .	0.01	1946
Algeria	. . .	0.12	1962
Bahrain	. . .	0.01	1971
Cyprus	. . .	0.01	1960
Egypt	. . .	0.07	1945
Iran	. . .	0.65	1945
Iraq	. . .	0.12	1945
Israel	. . .	0.25	1949
Jordan	. . .	0.01	1955
Kuwait	. . .	0.20	1963
Lebanon	. . .	0.03	1945
Libya	. . .	0.23	1955
Morocco	. . .	0.05	1956
Oman	. . .	0.01	1971
Qatar	. . .	0.03	1971
Saudi Arabia	. . .	0.58	1945
Sudan	. . .	0.01	1956
Syria	. . .	0.03	1945
Tunisia	. . .	0.03	1956
Turkey	. . .	0.30	1945
United Arab Emirates	.	0.10	1971
Yemen Arab Republic	.	0.01	1947
Yemen, People's Democratic Republic	. . .	0.01	1967

PERMANENT MISSIONS TO THE UNITED NATIONS

(with Permanent Representatives)

(May 1982)

Afghanistan: 866 United Nations Plaza, Suite 520, New York, N.Y. 10017; MOHAMMAD FARID ZARIF.

Algeria: 15 East 47th St., New York, N.Y. 10017; M. MOHAMMED BEDJAOUI.

Bahrain: 747 Third Ave., 19th Floor, New York, N.Y. 10017; Dr. WASFI NIMER.

Cyprus: 13 East 40th St., New York, N.Y. 10016; ANDREAS V. MAVROMMATIS.

Egypt: 36 East 67th St., New York, N.Y. 10021; Dr. AHMED ESMAT ABDEL MEGUID.

Iran: 622 Third Ave., 34th Floor, New York, N.Y. 10017; Dr. SAID RAJAIE-KHORASSANI.

Iraq: 14 East 79th St., New York, N.Y. 10021.

Israel: 800 Second Ave., New York, N.Y. 10017; YEHUDA Z. BLUM.

Jordan: 866 United Nations Plaza, Room 550–552, New York, N.Y. 10017; Dr. HAZEM NUSEIBEH.

Kuwait: 801 Second Ave., 5th Floor, New York, N.Y. 10017; MOHAMMAD A. ABULHASSAN.

Lebanon: 866 United Nations Plaza, Room 533–535, New York, N.Y. 10017; GHASSAN TUÉNI.

Libya: 866 United Nations Plaza, New York, N.Y. 10017; ALI SUNNI MUNTASSER.

Morocco: 767 Third Ave., 10th Floor, New York, N.Y. 10017; MEHDI MRANI ZENTAR.

Oman: 866 United Nations Plaza, Suite 540, New York, N.Y. 10017; MAHMOUD ABOUL-NASR.

Qatar: 747 Third Ave., 22nd Floor, New York, N.Y. 10017; JASIM YOUSIF JAMAL.

Saudi Arabia: 405 Lexington Ave., 56th Floor, New York, N.Y. 10017; GAAFAR M. ALLAGANY (alternate).

Sudan: 210 East 49th St., New York, N.Y. 10017; ABDEL-RAHMAN ABDALLA.

Syria: 150 East 58th St., Room 1500, New York, N.Y. 10022; DIA ALLAH al-FATTAL.

Tunisia: 40 East 71st St., New York, N.Y. 10021; TAIEB SLIM.

Turkey: 821 United Nations Plaza, 11th Floor, New York, N.Y. 10017; ÇOŞKUN KIRCA.

United Arab Emirates: 747 Third Ave., 36th Floor, New York, N.Y. 10017; FAHIM SULTAN al-QASIMI.

Yemen Arab Republic: 747 Third Ave., 8th Floor, New York, N.Y. 10017.

Yemen, People's Democratic Republic: 413 East 51st Street, New York, N.Y. 10022; ABDALLA SALEH ASHTAL.

OBSERVERS

Afro-Asian Legal Consultative Committee: 24 Manning Circle, Pelham, New York, N.Y. 10803; Dr. SOELEIMAN H. TAJIBNAPIS.

League of Arab States: 747 Third Ave., 25th Floor, New York, N.Y. 10017; Dr. CLOVIS MAKSOUD.

Organization of the Islamic Conference: 130 East 40th St., 5th Floor, New York, N.Y. 10016.

Palestine Liberation Organization: 115 East 65th St., New York, N.Y. 10012; ZEHDI LABIB TERZI.

GENERAL ASSEMBLY COMMITTEES CONCERNED WITH THE MIDDLE EAST

Committee on the Inalienable Rights of the Palestinian People: f. 1975; 23 members, elected by the General Assembly.

Special Committee to Investigate Israeli Practices affecting the Human Rights of the Population of the Occupied Territories: f. 1968; three members, nominated by the Assembly President.

ECONOMIC COMMISSION FOR AFRICA—ECA

Africa Hall, P.O.B. 3001, Addis Ababa, Ethiopia
Telephone: 447200.

ECA was founded in 1958 by a resolution of ECOSOC to initiate and take part in measures for facilitating Africa's economic development.

MEMBERS

Algeria	Equatorial Guinea	Madagascar	Sierra Leone
Angola	Ethiopia	Malawi	Somalia
Benin	Gabon	Mali	South Africa*
Botswana	The Gambia	Mauritania	Sudan
Burundi	Ghana	Mauritius	Swaziland
Cameroon	Guinea	Morocco	Tanzania
Cape Verde	Guinea-Bissau	Mozambique	Togo
Central African Republic	Ivory Coast	Niger	Tunisia
Chad	Kenya	Nigeria	Uganda
Comoros	Lesotho	Rwanda	Upper Volta
Congo	Liberia	São Tomé and Príncipe	Zaire
Djibouti	Libya	Senegal	Zambia
Egypt		Seychelles	Zimbabwe

* Suspended since 1963.

ORGANIZATION

(May 1982)

COMMISSION

The Commission may only act with the agreement of the Government of the country concerned. It is also empowered to make recommendations on any matter within its competence directly to the Government of the member or associate member concerned, to Governments admitted in a consultative capacity, and to the UN Specialized Agencies. The Commission is required to submit for prior consideration by ECOSOC any of its proposals for actions that would be likely to have important effects on the international economy.

THE CONFERENCE OF MINISTERS

The Conference is attended by Ministers responsible for economic or financial affairs, planning and development of governments of Member States, and is the main deliberative body of the Commission. It meets annually. A Technical Preparatory Committee of the Whole representing all Member States was established in 1980 to deal with matters submitted for the consideration of the Conference.

The Commission's responsibility to promote concerted action for the economic and social development of Africa is vested primarily in the Conference, which considers matters of general policy and the priorities to be assigned to the Commission's programmes, considers inter-African and international economic policy and makes recommendations to Member States in connection with such matters. It reviews the course of programmes being implemented in the preceding year and examines and approves the programmes proposed for the next.

OTHER POLICY-MAKING BODIES

Conference of African Ministers of Industry.

Conference of African Ministers of Social Affairs.

Conference of African Ministers of Trade.

Conference of African Ministers of Transport, Communications and Planning.

ECA/FAO Regional Conference of Ministers of Agriculture.
Councils of Ministers of the MULPOCS (*see* below).

REGIONAL ORGANIZATIONS

SECRETARIAT

The Secretariat provides the services necessary for the meeting of the Conference of Ministers and the meetings of the Commission's subsidiary bodies, carries out the resolutions and implements the programmes adopted there.

HEADQUARTERS

The Headquarters of the Secretariat is in Addis Ababa, Ethiopia. It comprises a Cabinet Office and ten Divisions.

Cabinet Office of the Executive Secretary:

Administration and Conference Services Division
Policy and Programme Co-ordination Office
Economic Co-operation Office
Office of the Secretary of the Commission
Technical Assistance Co-ordination and Operations Office
Information Service
Environment Co-ordination Office
Pan-African Documentation and Information System (PADIS)

Divisions:

Socio-Economic Research and Planning
International Trade and Finance
Joint ECA/FAO Agriculture
Joint ECA/UNIDO Industry
Social Development
Natural Resources
Transport, Communications and Tourism
Public Administration, Management and Manpower
Statistics
Population

Executive Secretary: ADEBAYO ADEDEJI (Nigeria).

SUBSIDIARY BODIES

Joint Conference of African Planners, Statisticians and Demographers.

Report of the Executive Secretary (every two years).

STATISTICS

African Statistical Yearbook.
Foreign Trade Statistics for Africa series.
  Series A: Direction of Trade (quarterly).
  Series B: Trade by Commodity (twice yearly).
  Series C: Summary Table (annual).
Statistical Information Bulletin for Africa (twice yearly).
Statistical Newsletter (quarterly).

ECONOMIC

African Economic Indicators (every two years).
Agricultural Economics Bulletin for Africa (twice yearly).
Investment Africa (quarterly).
Survey of Economic and Social Conditions in Africa (annual).

ECA LIBRARY SERIES

Series A: periodicals and serials, suspended.
Series B: New Acquisitions in the UN ECA Library (twice monthly).
Series C: subject bibliographies (irreg.).
Series D: directories, manuals, glossaries (irreg.).

Intergovernmental Committee of Experts for Science and Technology Development.

Intergovernmental Regional Committee on Human Settlements.

REGIONAL OPERATIONAL CENTRES

Multi-national Programming and Operational Centres (MULPOCs) act as "field agents" for the implementation of regional development programmes, replacing the former UN Multidisciplinary Development Advisory Teams (UNDATS). The Centres are located in Yaoundé, Cameroon (serving Central Africa), Gisenyi, Rwanda (Great Lakes Community), Lusaka, Zambia (East and Southern Africa), Niamey, Niger (West Africa) and Tangier, Morocco (North Africa). Each centre holds regular ministerial meetings.

CO-OPERATION WITH OTHER ORGANIZATIONS

The ECA co-operates closely with the Organization of African Unity (the memberships of the two organizations are the same) and many other African bodies, notably the Economic Community of West African States (ECOWAS) and the African Development Bank.

It also participates in the work of many UN bodies in Africa and operates two divisions jointly with the FAO and UNIDO.

BUDGET

ECA's share of the UN budget for 1980–81 was $29.7 million.

RECENT ACTIVITIES

An account of ECA's recent activities may be found in a companion volume, *Africa South of the Sahara* 1982–83.

PUBLICATIONS

Series E: Africa Index: Selected Articles on Socio-Economic Development (three times a year).
Series F: ECA Index: Bibliography of Selected ECA Documents (annual, issued since Dec. 1975).

PLANNING AND SOCIAL DEVELOPMENT

Social Welfare Services in Africa (twice yearly).
Directory of Activities of International Voluntary Agencies in Rural Development in Africa.

POPULATION AND CENSUS

African Census Programme Newsletter (irreg.).
African Directory of Demographers (irreg.).
African Population Newsletter (quarterly).
African Population Studies Series (irreg.).
Demographic Handbook for Africa (irreg.).

TRADE

African Trade (quarterly).
See also *Statistics* above.

MAGAZINES

African Target (quarterly).
Rural Progress (quarterly).

ECONOMIC COMMISSION FOR WESTERN ASIA—ECWA

P.O.B. 4656, Beirut, Lebanon

Established in 1974 by a resolution of ECOSOC to provide facilities of a wider scope for those countries previously served by the UN Economic and Social Office in Beirut (UNESOB).

MEMBERS

Bahrain	Lebanon	Saudi Arabia
Egypt	Oman	Syria
Iraq	Palestine Liberation	United Arab Emirates
Jordan	Organization (PLO)	Yemen Arab Republic
Kuwait	Qatar	Yemen, People's Democratic Republic

ORGANIZATION

(May 1982)

COMMISSION

The eighth session of the Commission was held in May 1981 in Sana'a, Yemen Arab Republic.

Chairman (Eighth session): FOUAD QAID MOHAMMAD (Yemen Arab Republic).

SECRETARIAT

In September 1974 it was decided at a special session of ECWA that the headquarters should be at Beirut until 1979. During the hostilities in Lebanon in 1976 the Commission took up temporary offices in Amman, Jordan, moving back to Beirut in 1977. At its sixth session in 1979, the Commission decided to commence its move to permanent headquarters in Baghdad, Iraq.

Executive Secretary (1980–82): MOHAMMED SAID AL-ATTAR (Yemen Arab Republic).

ACTIVITIES

ECWA's development plans for the 1980s comprise the following points: making the best use of natural resources; strengthening the regional economy so as to reduce dependence on external sources, such as food imports, and to cut trade imbalances; planned use of petroleum energy; development of human resources; regulation of the movement of workers between countries; integration of women in development.

Much of ECWA's work is carried out in co-operation with other UN bodies. It conducts industrial studies for individual countries in conjunction with UNIDO. It co-operates with FAO in regional planning, food security and management of agricultural resources; in 1980 joint FAO/ECWA missions were sent to prepare for technical co-operation projects in the Yemen Arab Republic and the People's Democratic Republic of Yemen. ECWA runs an Environmental Co-ordination Unit with assistance from UNEP. It co-operated with UNCTAD in preparations for the UN Conference on Least-Developed Countries held in 1981, and with the secretariat of the International Year of the Disabled in preparing a regional plan of action. Studies on potential use of solar, wind, biomass and geothermal energy in the region were prepared by ECWA for the UN Conference on New and Renewable Sources of Energy held in 1981. A feasibility study for a census of the Palestinian people was carried out in 1980 with financial assistance from UNFPA.

The 1982–83 programme of work and priorities comprises studies of various technical and socio-economic problems, particularly those demanding inter-country and sub-regional co-operation. The main areas are:

food and agriculture;

development planning (particularly in the least-developed countries in the region);

human settlement (particularly housing finance and city management);

industrial development (appraisal of potential, co-ordination of policies);

international trade (identification of intra-regional trade and integration opportunities);

labour, management and employment (making the best use of available manpower, development of required skills);

natural resources (energy planning, minerals and water development);

science and technology (problems of dependence on imported technology; training of manpower);

social development (welfare, participation in development, training and planning);

statistics (improvement of procedures, adopting uniform standards);

transport, communications and tourism (multinational shipping enterprises, railway networks, road construction and maintenance, and tourism development);

trans-national corporations.

BUDGET

Budget approved by the General Assembly for the two-year period 1980–81: U.S. $14,451,500.

FOOD AND AGRICULTURE ORGANIZATION—FAO

Via delle Terme di Caracalla, 00100 Rome, Italy
Telephone: 57971.

FAO, the first specialized agency of the UN to be founded, was established in Quebec in October 1945. The Organization fights malnutrition and hunger and serves as an organizing and co-ordinating agency which brings together representatives of national governments, scientific bodies, non-governmental organizations, industry and banking to plan and carry out development programmes in the whole range of food and agriculture, including forestry and fisheries. It helps developing countries to promote educational and training facilities and institution-building.

ORGANIZATION

(June 1982)

SECRETARIAT

Director-General (1976–87): EDOUARD SAOUMA (Lebanon).
Deputy Director-General: EDWARD M. WEST (United Kingdom).

REGIONAL OFFICE

FAO Regional Office for the Near East: c/o FAO Headquarters, Via delle Terme di Caracalla, 00100 Rome, Italy.

REGIONAL COUNCILS AND COMMISSIONS

(c/o FAO Headquarters, Rome)

Animal Production and Health Commission in the Near East: f. 1967 to provide a means of initiating and promoting agricultural development with special reference to the field of animal production and health. Mems.: 13 states.

Commission for Controlling the Desert Locust in the Near East: f. 1965 to carry out all possible measures to control desert locust plagues within the Middle East and to reduce crop damage. Mems.: 14 states.

Commission for Controlling the Desert Locust in North-West Africa: f. 1971 to promote research on control of the desert locust in N.W. Africa. Mems.: 4 states.

Commission on Horticultural Production in the Near East and North Africa: f. 1964 to promote international collaboration in the study of technical problems and the establishment of a balanced programme of horticultural research at an inter-regional level. Mems.: 19 states.

General Fisheries Council for the Mediterranean—GFCM (*Conseil général des pêches pour la Méditerranée—CGPM*): f. 1952 to formulate oceanographical and technical aspects of developing and utilizing aquatic resources, to encourage and co-ordinate research in the fishing and allied industries, to assemble and publish information, and to recommend the standardization of scientific equipment, techniques and nomenclature. Mems.: 19 states.

Near East Commission on Agricultural Planning: f. 1962 to review and exchange information and experience on agricultural plans and planning, and to make recommendations to members on means of improving their agricultural plans. Mems.: 20 states.

Near East Commission on Agricultural Statistics: f. 1963 to review the state of food and agricultural statistics in the region and advise member countries on the development and standardization of agricultural statistics. Regular sessions are held every two years; technical subsidiary bodies include seminars and expert working groups. Mems.: 20 states.

Near East Commission on Land and Water Use: f. 1967 to study land and water use in the region; to identify the main problems concerning the development of land and water resources which require research and to consider related matters. Mems.: 20 states.

Near East Forestry Commission: f. 1953 to advise on formulation of forest policy and to review and co-ordinate its implementation at the regional level; to exchange information and, generally through subsidiary bodies, advise on suitable practices and action in respect of technical problems, and to make appropriate recommendations. Mems.: 20 states.

Near East Plant Protection Commission: f. 1963 to advise member countries, through FAO Conference, on matters relating to the protection of plant resources in the region. Mems.: 17 states.

Regional Project on the Improvement and Production of Field Food Crops in the Near East and North Africa: f. 1971 (replacing the Technical Committee on Cereal Improvement and Production in the Near East); aims to increase overall crop production (cereals, some food legumes and oil seed crops) through research, co-operative investigations and other forms of international action.

ACTIVITIES IN THE MIDDLE EAST AND NORTH AFRICA

During 1981 FAO continued in the execution of approximately 283 field projects in 21 countries in the Near East and North Africa, with a total aid allocation of U.S. $331,678,000. Of this total, UNDP-assisted projects numbered 122, with allocations of $128,930,000. These were slightly outweighed by the Unilateral Trust Fund projects which are a notable characteristic of the Region, with 46 larger-scale projects amounting in value to $151,813,000. Most of these projects are funded by the more affluent countries in the region which reimburse FAO for carrying out assistance activities on their behalf. The Near East Co-operative Programme is another activity particular to the Near East and North Africa region, whereby the oil-producing countries of the region finance projects to assist their less wealthy neighbours. Twenty-seven such projects were in operation during 1981, at a total value of $23,149,000. FAO's Technical Co-operation Programme funded 68 small-scale projects at a cost of $4,667,000. The remaining 22 projects, at a cost of $13,327,000, were funded by such programmes as the Government Co-operative Programme, the Prevention of Food Losses Programme, and the Freedom from Hunger Campaign/Action for Development.

By the end of 1981 FAO had completed, under Trust Fund arrangements, 24 projects at a cost of $19,577,000, while another 100 projects, at a value of $212,819,000, were awaiting completion.

There were 319 specialists serving in the Near East and North Africa as FAO's regular field staff, together with 27 associate experts and 50 consultants, making a total of 396 in the field during 1981.

WORLD FOOD PROGRAMME—WFP

WFP is a joint UN-FAO effort to stimulate economic and social development through food aid and to provide emergency relief, using contributions of commodities, cash and services made by member governments of the UN and FAO. It became operational in 1963.

WFP development projects approved in 1981 for the Middle East and North Africa region included the rebuilding of houses in Algeria following the El Asnam earthquake (U.S. $1.9 million), a grant for silk-farmers in Lebanon ($1.5 million), food for workers on a soil conservation project in Morocco ($1.8 million) and for workers on a project to control water-related diseases in irrigation schemes in Sudan ($1.6 million). During the first nine months of the year, emergency supplies were given to Lebanon ($850,000 worth of food for displaced persons), Morocco (food worth $5.6 million to meet the deficit caused by drought and frost) and the People's Democratic Republic of Yemen ($1.3 million worth of food for flood victims).

INTERNATIONAL BANK FOR RECONSTRUCTION AND DEVELOPMENT—IBRD (WORLD BANK)

1818 H Street, N.W., Washington, D.C. 20433, U.S.A.

Telephone: (202) 477 1234.

The World Bank was established in 1945. It aims to assist the economic development of member nations by making loans, in cases where private capital is not available on reasonable terms, to finance productive investments. Loans are made either direct to governments, or to private enterprises with the guarantee of their governments.

LOANS TO COUNTRIES IN THE MIDDLE EAST AND NORTH AFRICA

TOTAL LOANS CUMULATIVE TO JUNE 1981 (U.S. $ million)

COUNTRY	NUMBER	AMOUNT
Algeria	25	1,201.0
Cyprus	18	157.6
Egypt	26	1,214.0
Iran	33	1,210.7
Iraq	6	156.2
Israel	11	284.5
Jordan	6	125.0
Lebanon	4	116.6
Morocco	45	1,660.3
Oman	5	47.0
Sudan	8	166.0
Syria	13	483.7
Tunisia	46	902.4
Turkey	56	3,129.4

APPROVED LOANS JULY 1980—JUNE 1981 (U.S. $ million)

COUNTRY	PURPOSE	AMOUNT
Algeria	Transportation	110.0
Cyprus	Agricultural and rural development	14.0
Egypt	Energy	25.0
(Guarantor)	Industry	64.0
Jordan	Urban development	21.0
	Energy	25.0
Morocco	Urban development	36.0
	Water supply and sewerage	87.0
Morocco (Guarantor)	Development finance companies	100.0
Syria	Education	15.6
Tunisia	Education	26.0
	Small-scale enterprises	30.0
	Agricultural and rural development	24.0
	Population, health and nutrition	12.5
	Industry	18.6
Tunisia (Guarantor)	Energy	41.5
Turkey	Non-project	375.0
	Energy	87.0
	Development finance companies	40.0
	Agriculture and rural development	40.0
	Industry	110.0
Turkey (Guarantor)	Development finance companies	70.0

Source: World Bank/IDA 1981 Annual Report.

INTERNATIONAL DEVELOPMENT ASSOCIATION—IDA

1818 H Street, N.W., Washington, D.C. 20433, U.S.A.

Telephone: (202) 477 1234.

The IDA began operations in 1960. An affiliate of the World Bank, it advances capital on more flexible terms to developing countries.

DEVELOPMENT CREDITS TO MIDDLE EASTERN AND NORTH AFRICAN COUNTRIES

TOTAL CREDITS CUMULATIVE TO JUNE 1981
(U.S. $ million)

COUNTRY	NUMBER	AMOUNT
Afghanistan	20	230.1
Egypt	26	981.2
Jordan	15	85.3
Morocco	3	50.8
Sudan	25	595.5
Syria	3	47.3
Tunisia	5	74.6
Turkey	10	178.5
Yemen Arab Republic	25	249.3
Yemen, People's Democratic Republic	17	110.0

APPROVED CREDITS JULY 1980–JUNE 1981
(U.S. $ million)

COUNTRY	PURPOSE	AMOUNT
Egypt . .	Education	40.1
	Agriculture and rural development	94.0
	Water supply and sewerage	56.6
	Technical assistance	6.9
Sudan . .	Agriculture and rural development	67.0
	Technical assistance	6.0
Yemen Arab Republic .	Agriculture and rural development	17.0
	Energy	12.0
	Development finance companies	12.0
Yemen, People's Democratic Republic . .	Agriculture and rural development	8.0
	Transportation	12.5
	Water supply and sewerage	3.5

Source: World Bank/IDA 1981 Annual Report.

INTERNATIONAL FINANCE CORPORATION—IFC

1818 H Street, N.W., Washington, D.C. 20433, U.S.A.

Founded in 1956 as an affiliate of the World Bank to encourage the growth of productive private enterprise in its member countries, particularly in the less-developed areas.

IFC INVESTMENTS IN MIDDLE EASTERN AND NORTH AFRICAN COUNTRIES
TOTAL CUMULATIVE INVESTMENT TO JUNE 1981 (U.S. $'000)

COUNTRY	NUMBER OF ENTERPRISES	CUMULATIVE GROSS COMMITMENTS (Including Syndications)
Afghanistan	1	322
Cyprus	2	3,620
Egypt	7	74,468
Iran	7	42,536
Israel	1	10,500
Jordan	4	82,203
Lebanon	4	9,105
Morocco	6	43,755
Oman	1	2,029
Tunisia	6	21,784
Turkey	18	225,584
Yemen Arab Republic	1	3,150

APPROVED INVESTMENTS, JULY 1980–JUNE 1981 (U.S. $'000)

COUNTRY	PURPOSE	AMOUNT (Including Syndications)
Egypt	Tourism	5,267
Jordan	Fertilizers	2,232
	Money and capital market	298
Morocco	Cement and construction material	15,800
Turkey	Glass tableware	13,547

Source: IFC 1981 Annual Report.

UNITED NATIONS DEVELOPMENT PROGRAMME—UNDP

One United Nations Plaza, New York, N.Y. 10017, U.S.A.

Telephone: 754 1234.

Established in 1965, through the merger of the Expanded Programme of Technical Assistance and the UN Special Fund, to help the developing countries increase the wealth-producing capabilities of their natural and human resources.

ORGANIZATION

(June 1982)

AGENCIES PARTICIPATING

The following act as executing agencies or otherwise participate in the work of the UNDP: the UN Department of Technical Co-operation, for Development and 24 of the UN agencies and organizations, three regional development banks, five regional economic commissions, the International Fund for Agricultural Development and the Arab Fund for Economic and Social Development.

The UNDP is responsible to the General Assembly, to which it reports through ECOSOC.

Governing Council: representatives of 48 countries; 27 seats filled by developing countries and 21 by economically more advanced countries; the policy-making body of the UNDP. Meets annually. One-third of the membership changes each year. President (1982): DOUGLAS LINDORES (Canada).

Administrator: F. BRADFORD MORSE (U.S.A.).

Secretariat: composed of an international staff from over 100 countries.

Inter-Agency Consultative Board (IACB): composed of the UN Secretary-General and the Executive Heads of the UNDP's participating and executing Agencies; provides guidance and advice.

REGIONAL BUREAUX

Headed by assistant administrators, the regional bureaux share the responsibility for implementing the programme with the Administrator's office. Within certain limitations, large-scale projects may be approved and funding allocated by the Administrator, and smaller-scale projects by the Resident Representatives, based in 114 countries.

The four regional bureaux, all at the Secretariat in New York, cover: Africa; Asia and the Pacific; the Arab states; and Latin America; there is also a Unit for Europe.

FIELD OFFICES

In almost every country receiving UNDP assistance there is a Country Office, headed by the UNDP Resident Representative, who advises the Government on formulating the country programme, sees that the field activities are carried out, and acts as the leader of the UN team of experts working in the country. Resident Representatives are normally designated as co-ordinators for all UN operational development activities; the field offices function as the primary presence of the UN in most developing countries.

UNDP REPRESENTATIVES IN THE MIDDLE EAST AND NORTH AFRICA

Afghanistan: P.O.B. 5, Kabul; I. SCHUETZ-MUELLER (acting).

Algeria: B.P. 823, Algiers; CHRISTOPH JAEGER.

Bahrain: P.O.B. 26814, Manama; A. KHUZAYIM.

Cyprus: P.O.B. 3521, Nicosia; KSHITINDRA DALAL.

Egypt: P.O.B. 982, Cairo; G. L. PENNACCHIO.

Iraq: P.O.B. 2048 (Alwiyah), Baghdad; ADNAN SOGHAIER.

Jordan: P.O.B. 35286, Amman; ADNAN ROAUF.

Kuwait: P.O.B. 2993, Kuwait City; KHALIL OTHMAN.

Lebanon: P.O.B. 3216, Beirut; GUY VAN DOOSSELAERE.

Libya: P.O.B. 358, Triploli; AHMED BASHIN (acting).

Morocco: Casier ONU, Rabat-Chellah, Rabat; LAURICE HLASS.

Oman: P.O.B. 5287, Ruwi, Greater Muscat; H. B. DANISMAN.

Qatar: Box 3233, Doha; GUIDO ORDÓÑEZ.

Saudi Arabia: P.O.B. 558, Riyadh; ZUHEIR AMIN.

Sudan: P.O.B. 913, Khartoum; GARTH AP REES.

Syria: P.O.B. 2317, Damascus; KHALED YASSIR.

Tunisia: B.P. 863, Tunis; ALEXANDER DAVIDSON (acting).

Turkey: P.K. 407, Ankara; SARFRAZ MALIK.

United Arab Emirates: P.O.B. 3490, Abu Dhabi; BASEM KHADER.

Yemen Arab Republic: P.O.B. 451, Sana'a; TOSHIYUKI NIWA.

Yemen, People's Democratic Republic: P.O.B. 1188, Tawahi, Aden; ROLAND REIFENRATH.

UNDP—ASSISTED PROJECTS

In 1980 12 per cent (U.S. $81.5 million) of UNDP expenditure went to Arab states, covering 612 projects. Project work covers five main areas: locating, assessing and activating latent natural resources and other development assets, stimulating capital investment to help realize these possibilities; support for professional and vocational training; expansion of scientific research and applied technology; and strengthening of national and regional development planning.

Assistance under the UNDP is planned with reference to the Indicative Planning Figure (IPF) for the country concerned. This is a projection of the total financial resources the UNDP can expect to have at its disposal for the country over a five-year period.

Individual countries submit to the Governing Council of the UNDP a programme outlining areas needing assistance. The programme sets out the various national priorities and takes into account aid from other sources. The IPF gives an indication of future assistance so that overall national development plans can be formulated with more certainty.

THE UNITED NATIONS SUDANO-SAHELIAN OFFICE (UNSO)

UNSO co-ordinates United Nations efforts to help the

drought-stricken Sudano-Sahelian countries carry out recovery and development plans. Programmes to develop agriculture and increase crop production through seed multiplication and the provision of fertilizers, pest controls, equipment and irrigation systems are an important part of UNSO's work. Projects are also devoted to the rehabilitation and expansion of livestock herds, feeder roads, forest and water resources, agro-meteorological and hydrological services, fisheries, food storage facilities, vocational training and health care.

By December 1980 the Office had mobilized $646 million of bilateral and multilateral financing for 88 national and 25 regional projects. UNSO has also been assigned responsibility for combating desertification.

UNDP INDICATIVE PLANNING FIGURES FOR PROJECTS IN THE MIDDLE EAST AND NORTH AFRICA*

($'000)

COUNTRY	IPF 1977–81	IPF (illustrative) 1982–86
Afghanistan	38,000	71,500
Algeria	20,000	20,000
Bahrain	2,500	2,500
Cyprus	5,000	5,000
Egypt	31,500	56,000
Iran	20,000	n.a.
Iraq	15,000	15,000
Jordan	15,000	15,000
Lebanon	10,000	n.a.
Libya	5,000	5,000
Morocco	20,000	27,000
Oman	4,000	4,000
Saudi Arabia	10,000	10,000
Sudan	33,000	58,500
Syria	15,000	15,000
Tunisia	15,000	15,000
Turkey	20,000	20,000
United Arab Emirates . .	1,000	1,000
Yemen Arab Republic . .	23,750	30,000
Yemen, People's Democratic Republic .	14,500	17,250
Regional (Arab states) . . .	n.a.	57,800

* Owing to the insufficient level of contributions by member governments, illustrative figures for 1982–86 are likely to exceed actual figures.

UNITED NATIONS EDUCATIONAL, SCIENTIFIC AND CULTURAL ORGANIZATION—UNESCO

7 place de Fontenoy, 75700 Paris, France

UNESCO was established in 1946 "for the purpose of advancing, through the educational, scientific and cultural relations of the peoples of the world, the objectives of international peace and the common welfare of mankind."

ORGANIZATION

(June 1982)

SECRETARIAT

Director-General: AMADOU MAHTAR M'BOW (Senegal).
Deputy Director-General: (vacant).

Director of the Executive Office: CHIKH BEKRI (Algeria).

Regional Representative for the Arab States of the Gulf: P.O.B. 3945, Doha, Qatar; MOHAMMED EL-SHIBINY.

REGIONAL OFFICES

Arab States Regional Centre for Functional Literacy in Rural Areas: Sirs-El-Layan, Menoufia, Egypt.

International Institute for Adult Literacy Methods: (see p. 202).

Regional Office for Education in the Arab States: B.P. 5244, ave. de la Cité Sportive, Beirut, Lebanon.

Regional Office for Science and Technology in the Arab States: c/o UNESCO Secretariat, 7 place de Fontenoy, 75700 Paris, France.

ACTIVITIES IN THE MIDDLE EAST AND NORTH AFRICA

Literacy continues to be an important concern in the region. The Regional Centre for Functional Literacy in Rural Areas sends out mobile teams of experts and organizes courses and seminars for specialists in literacy and adult education.

Besides the programme of aid for Palestinian refugees in collaboration with UNRWA, UNESCO gives assistance to the Palestine Liberation Organization.

UNESCO has been actively involved in the establishment of several engineering institutes in the region, in Syria, Saudi Arabia, Iraq, Lebanon, Libya and Morocco; with the support of the governments concerned, these institutes have developed into important university engineering faculties.

The Regional Office for Science and Technology has organized courses and studies on the teaching of basic science, hydrology, oceanography, geophysics, soil biology, geomorphology and seismology. As part of its programmes in arid zone research, UNESCO has helped to create research institutes in Iraq, Saudi Arabia and Sudan and given financial aid to Egypt's Desert Research Institute.

Many years of efforts by UNESCO, the Egyptian Government and the international community to save the monuments of Nubia culminated in spring 1980 with the ceremony marking the final rebuilding on the island of Agilkia of the temples whose previous site had been flooded after the building of the Aswan Dam. UNESCO is assisting in the exploration of prehistoric sites in Libya, and in the preservation of sites and monuments in other countries, for example Carthage and Al Qayrawan in Tunisia, Fez in Morocco, Tyre in Lebanon and the Casbah of Algiers in Algeria. UNESCO collaborates closely with the Arab League Educational, Cultural and Scientific Organization (ALECSO: *see* page 186). UNESCO has assisted Iraq in the establishment of a regional training centre for the conservation of cultural property in the Arab countries.

UNESCO has provided expert services, fellowships and equipment for the development of national press agencies, radio and television organizations and film production, particularly in Algeria, Jordan, Kuwait and Libya. It helped to establish the Arab States Broadcasting Union in 1966. UNESCO collaborates with member states in the setting-up of satellites, due to begin servicing the region in 1983.

Under the International Programme for the Development of Communications, launched in 1981, UNESCO supports a scheme for planning and exchange of information in the field of communications, and a regional training centre is also envisaged.

UNITED NATIONS RELIEF AND WORKS AGENCY FOR PALESTINE REFUGEES IN THE NEAR EAST—UNRWA

Headquarters (Vienna): P.O. Box 700, 1400 Vienna, Austria
Headquarters (Amman): P.O.B. 484, Amman, Jordan

Began operations in 1950 to provide relief, health, education and welfare services for Palestine refugees in the Near East.

ORGANIZATION

(June 1982)

Commissioner-General: OLOF RYDBECK (Sweden).

UNRWA is a subsidiary organ of the United Nations General Assembly, and began operations in May 1950; it employs an international staff of 120 and 17,100 local staff, mainly Palestine refugees. The Commissioner-General is assisted by an Advisory Commission consisting of representatives of the governments of:

Belgium	Jordan	Turkey
Egypt	Lebanon	United Kingdom
France	Syria	U.S.A.
Japan		

REGIONAL OFFICES

Gaza Strip: UNRWA Field Office, P.O.B. 61, Gaza.
East Jordan: UNRWA Field Office, P.O.B. 484, Amman.
West Bank: UNRWA Field Office, P.O.B. 19149, Jerusalem.
Lebanon: UNRWA Field Office, P.O.B. 947, Beirut.

Syria: UNRWA Field Office, P.O.B. 4313, Damascus.
Egypt: UNRWA Liaison Office, 2 Dar el Shifa, Garden City, P.O.B. 277, Cairo.
United States: UNRWA Liaison Office, Room 937, United Nations, New York, N.Y. 10017.

ACTIVITIES

SERVICES FOR PALESTINE REFUGEES

Since 1950, UNRWA has provided relief (including food), health and education services for the needy among the Palestine refugees in Lebanon, Syria, east Jordan, the West Bank and the Gaza Strip. For UNRWA's purposes, a Palestine refugee is one whose normal residence was in Palestine for a minimum of two years before the 1948 conflict and who, as a result of the Arab-Israeli hostilities, lost his home and means of livelihood. To be eligible for assistance, a refugee must reside in one of the "host" countries in which UNRWA operates and be in need. A refugee's children and grandchildren who fulfil certain criteria are also eligible for UNRWA assistance. On December 31st, 1981, the registered refugee population numbered 1,902,843, (about half the estimated total number of Palestinians), living in five areas administered by four governments. There were about 668,730 living in 61 camps, while the remaining refugees have settled in the towns and villages already existing.

UNRWA's activities fall into the categories of education and training; health services; and relief and welfare services.

Education (under the technical supervision of UNESCO) and training took up 53 per cent of UNRWA's expenditure in 1980; in 1981/82 there were 338,386 pupils in 643 UNRWA schools: in Lebanon (85 schools), Syria (111), Jordan (208), the West Bank (99) and the Gaza Strip (140). In 1980/81 there were 9,674 teachers. At three-quarters of the schools, morning and afternoon shifts are held in order to accommodate more pupils. UNRWA also runs seven vocational training centres and three teacher-training centres with 5,125 places. UNRWA awarded 351 scholarships for study at Arab universities in 1981/82.

Health services accounted for 15 per cent of UNRWA expenditure in 1980. On December 31st, 1981, a total of 1.6 million refugees were eligible for health services; there were 2,947 medical staff, 100 health units, 104 specialist clinics and 87 maternal and child health clinics. UNRWA also runs a supplementary feeding programme, mainly for children, to combat malnutrition: there are 96 feeding centres. Technical supervision for the health programme is provided by WHO.

Relief services (which accounted for 28 per cent of UNRWA expenditure in 1980) comprise the distribution of food rations, the provision of emergency shelter and the organization of welfare programmes. Rations (flour, cooking oil, sugar and rice) were distributed to about 44 per cent of the refugee population in 1980, although amounts have been cut owing to shortage of funds: for example the flour ration was cut from 10 kg. to 5 kg. per month in 1979.

AID TO DISPLACED PERSONS

After the renewal of Arab-Israeli hostilities in the Middle East in June 1967, hundreds of thousands of people fled from the fighting and Israeli-occupied areas to east Jordan, Syria and Egypt. UNRWA provided emergency relief for displaced refugees and was additionally empowered by a UN General Assembly resolution to provide "humanitarian assistance, as far as practicable, on an emergency basis and as a temporary measure" for those persons other than Palestine refugees who were newly displaced and in urgent need. In practice, UNRWA has lacked the funds to aid the other displaced persons and the main burden of supporting them has fallen on the Arab governments concerned. The Agency, as requested by the Government of Jordan in 1967 and on that Government's behalf, distributes rations to displaced persons in east Jordan who are not registered refugees of 1948.

With the agreement of the Israeli Government, UNRWA has continued to provide assistance for registered refugees living in the Israeli-occupied territories of the West Bank and the Gaza Strip.

RECENT DISTURBANCES

Palestine refugees have been affected, and UNRWA's services disrupted, by continuing disturbances in Lebanon and the Israeli invasion of the south in March 1978, which caused the temporary evacuation of most of the 60,000 refugees living there and the flight of 17,000 refugees in other areas. With the assistance of governments and voluntary groups, UNRWA launched an emergency relief programme to provide food, clothing and blankets and temporary shelter in school buildings. Damage to UNRWA's property and installations, such as schools and clinics recently repaired in the wake of the civil war in Lebanon of 1975–76, was estimated at $450,000. While most of the refugees returned to their home towns and villages by the end of April 1978, the devastated economy of the south left them in continued need of extra-budgetary relief supplies and services.

In 1979 UNRWA again launched an emergency appeal for aid to southern Lebanon because of continuing Israeli and other attacks. At August 15th there were more than 50,000 registered refugees displaced from the year's military activities in southern Lebanon.

In 1981 civil strife and later Israeli attacks disrupted UNRWA activities. The education programme was hardest hit with up to 50 school days lost in some schools during the 1980/81 school year.

FINANCE

BUDGET
(U.S. $'000)

Expenditure	1981* (revised)	1982
Education services . . .	129,063	115,075
General education . .	103,299	90,818
Vocational training . .	13,394	12,662
Common costs . . .	12,370	11,595
Health services . .	37,358	36,447
Medical services . .	14,860	14,277
Supplementary feeding .	9,095	9,272
Environmental sanitation .	6,309	6,259
Common costs . .	7,094	6,639
Relief services	56,447	52,661
Basic rations . . .	40,928	36,584
Shelter	991	1,206
Special hardship assistance .	3,312	4,407
Common costs . . .	11,211	10,464
Total (incl. other costs) .	238,667	250,302

* Actual expenditure in 1981 amounted to $180,728,868, owing to lack of funds.

For the most part, UNRWA's income is made up of voluntary contributions, almost entirely from govern-ments, the remainder being provided by voluntary agencies, business corporations and private sources. However, the cost of the Agency's 120 international staff is funded by the UN, WHO and UNESCO.

In recent years financial crises have posed serious threats of cuts in services. Devaluation of the dollar and incessant inflationary pressures, which have had an adverse effect on the price of supplies and the cost of living, seriously affected the Agency's ability to meet the higher cost of health, education and relief services with voluntary contributions. In March 1981, individually addressed notices of termination were prepared for all UNRWA teachers in Jordan and Syria, which would have meant the closing of the 314 UNRWA schools in these countries. Notices were withdrawn when the Agency's cash position improved slightly. However, the continued deficit in 1982 made it possible that cuts in the education programme would still be necessary. In November 1981, 43 countries pledged about $107 million to UNRWA for 1982. Other countries later made pledges and several special contributions were made early in 1982 to help save the Agency's education programme. Income for 1982 was expected to be about $186.6 million out of a planned budget of almost $250.3 million leaving a deficit of nearly $63.7 million, to be made up by using up cash balances, by eliminating all capital expenditure and by not paying cost-of-living allowances to 5,600 staff in Jordan.

STATISTICS
REFUGEES REGISTERED WITH UNRWA
(as at December 31st, 1981)

	In Camps*	Not in Camps	Total
Jordan (east) . .	190,580	549,274	739,854
West Bank . .	85,440	252,310	337,750
Gaza Strip . .	206,717	165,693	372,410
Lebanon . .	121,575	113,814	235,389
Syria . . .	64,418	153,022	217,440
Total . .	668,730	1,234,113	1,902,843

* Total camp population is 715,009, made up of 668,730 registered refugees; 32,232 persons displaced as a result of the June 1967 hostilities and subsequent fighting in the Jordan Valley in early 1968, who are not registered with the Agency; and 14,047 who are neither registered nor displaced persons.

DISPLACED PERSONS

Apart from the Palestine refugees of 1948 who are registered with UNRWA and who are UNRWA's main concern (see table above), considerable numbers of people have, since 1967, been displaced within the UNRWA areas of operations, and others have had to leave these areas. According to government estimates, there were 210,000 displaced persons in east Jordan and 125,000 in Syria in June 1980.

NUMBER OF REFUGEE PUPILS RECEIVING EDUCATION IN UNRWA/UNESCO SCHOOLS*
(September 1981)

FIELD	NUMBER OF SCHOOLS	PUPILS IN ELEMENTARY CLASSES			PUPILS IN PREPARATORY CLASSES			TOTAL NUMBER OF PUPILS
		Boys	Girls	Total	Boys	Girls	Total	
East Jordan . . .	208	49,770	46,933	96,703	20,559	17,962	38,521	135,224
West Bank . . .	99	13,365	15,206	28,571	5,361	5,485	10,846	39,417
Gaza	140	30,794	27,445	58,239	11,139	9,783	20,922	79,161
Lebanon . . .	85	13,412	12,839	26,251	5,249	5,360	10,609	36,860
Syria	111	17,324	16,010	33,334	7,683	6,707	14,390	47,724
TOTAL . .	643	124,665	118,433	243,098	49,991	45,297	95,288	338,386

* At the end of the 1980/81 school year there were also 81,071 refugee children receiving education in government schools and 8,901 in private schools in the host countries, partly with grants paid by UNRWA.

About 11,200 local staff, most of them teachers, work in the education programme.

PUBLICATIONS

Annual Report of the Commissioner-General of UNRWA.

UNRWA—a survey of United Nations Assistance to Palestine Refugees (every 2 years).

Palestine Refugees Today—the UNRWA Newsletter (quarterly).

UNITED NATIONS OBSERVER MISSION AND PEACE-KEEPING FORCES IN THE MIDDLE EAST

UNITED NATIONS TRUCE SUPERVISION ORGANIZATION—UNTSO
Headquarters at Government House, Jerusalem

Set up in 1948 to supervise the truce called for by the Security Council in Palestine.

Chief of Staff: Maj.-Gen. E. A. ERSKINE (Ghana).

COMPOSITION

As at April 1982 there were 293 Military Observers from the following countries:

Argentina	Denmark	New Zealand
Australia	Finland	Norway
Austria	France	Sweden
Belgium	Ireland	U.S.S.R.
Canada	Italy	U.S.A.
Chile	Netherlands	

FUNCTIONS

UNTSO was established initially to supervise the truce called by the Security Council in May 1948 and has assisted in the application of the 1949 Armistice Agreements. Its activities have changed over the years in response to the development of affairs in the Middle East and in accordance with the relevant resolutions of the Security Council.

UNTSO observers assist the UN peace-keeping forces in the Middle East (see below), UNIFIL as a separate group and UNDOF as an integral part of the force. After the expiry of the mandate of UNEF (United Nations Emergency Force) on July 24th, 1979, UNTSO established Observer Group Egypt to maintain a number of outposts in the Sinai.

FINANCE

UNTSO expenditures are covered by the regular budget of the United Nations. For the biennial period 1980–81, a sum of U.S. $29,066,500 was appropriated by the General Assembly, and for 1982–83 the figure was $33,436,800.

UNITED NATIONS
DISENGAGEMENT OBSERVER FORCE—UNDOF
Headquarters at Damascus, Syria

Established for an initial period of six months by a Security Council resolution on May 31st, 1974, following the signature in Geneva of a disengagement agreement between Syrian and Israeli forces. The mandate has since been extended by successive resolutions.

Commander: Maj.-Gen. CARL-GUSTAF STAHL (Sweden).

COMPOSITION OF FORCE

(April 1982)

Austria	526
Canada	221
Finland	389
Poland . . .	131
UNDOF military observers (detailed from UNTSO) .	12
	1,279

ACTIVITIES

The initial task of the Force was to take over territory evacuated in stages by the Israeli troops, in accordance with the disengagement agreement, to hand over territory to Syrian troops, and to establish an area of separation.

UNDOF continues to man the area of separation, from which Syrian and Israeli forces are excluded; it carries out inspections of the areas of limited armaments and forces, and it uses its best efforts to maintain the ceasefire. The area of separation has been placed under Syrian civil administration.

FINANCE

The General Assembly appropriated $16.0 million for UNDOF for the period from December 1st, 1981, to May 31st, 1982. In addition to this appropriation, it authorized the Secretary-General to enter into commitments at a rate not to exceed $2.66 million per month for the period from June 1st to November 30th, 1982.

UNITED NATIONS INTERIM FORCE IN LEBANON—UNIFIL
Headquarters at Naqoura, Lebanon

Set up in March 1978 by Security Council resolution, for a six-month period, subsequently extended by successive resolutions.

Commander: Lt.-Gen. WILLIAM CALLAGHAN (Ireland).

COMPOSITION OF FORCE

(April 1982)

Fiji	623
France . . .	731
Ghana . . .	490
Ireland . . .	642
Italy . . .	36
Nepal . . .	430
Netherlands . . .	813
Nigeria . . .	695
Norway . . .	823
Senegal . . .	561
Sweden . . .	148
TOTAL . . .	5,992

In February 1982 the UN Security Council agreed to increase the force by 1,000 men.

A group of 74 military observers of UNTSO assist UNIFIL in the performance of its tasks. They form the "Observer Group, Lebanon".

FUNCTIONS

The functions of the force are to confirm the withdrawal of Israeli forces, to restore international peace and security and to assist the Government of Lebanon in ensuring the return of its effective authority in southern Lebanon.

FINANCE

The General Assembly authorized the Secretary-General to enter into commitments for UNIFIL at a rate not to exceed $13.3 million per month for the period from December 19th, 1981, to December 18th, 1982.

UNITED NATIONS PEACE-KEEPING FORCE IN CYPRUS—UNFICYP
Headquarters at Nicosia, Cyprus

Set up in March 1964 by Security Council resolution, for a three-month period, subsequently extended by successive resolutions.

Special Representative of the Secretary-General: HUGO JUAN GOBBI (Argentina).

Commander: Maj.-Gen. GÜNTHER G. GREINDL (Austria).

COMPOSITION OF FORCE
(April 1982)

	Military	Police
Australia . . .	—	20
Austria . . .	294	—
Canada . . .	505	—
Denmark . . .	341	—
Finland . . .	11	—
Ireland . . .	7	—
Sweden . . .	379	14
United Kingdom	794	—
TOTAL . . .	2,331	34

FUNCTIONS

The purpose of the Force has been to keep the peace between the Greek and Turkish Cypriot communities pending a resolution of outstanding issues between them, to help maintain law and order, and to promote a return to normal conditions. UNFICYP now also performs functions in relation to the supervision of the ceasefire between the armed forces of Turkey and Cyprus, and in providing humanitarian assistance to refugees and to villages isolated behind military lines. The United Nations High Commissioner for Refugees acts as Co-ordinator of UN humanitarian assistance for Cyprus.

FINANCE

The estimated cost to the United Nations for maintaining the Force during the period from December 15th, 1981, to June 15th, 1982, was $14.6 million. The total costs from the beginning of the operation in March 1964 to December 15th, 1981, were estimated at $383.9 million, a sum covered entirely by voluntary contributions. In January 1982 the Secretary-General of the UN appealed for an increase in voluntary contributions to meet a budget deficit of over $92 million

UNITED NATIONS HIGH COMMISSIONER FOR REFUGEES— UNHCR

Palais des Nations, 1211 Geneva 10, Switzerland

Telephone: 31 02 61.

The Office of the High Commissioner was established in 1951 to provide international protection for refugees and to seek permanent solutions to their problems. In 1977 the mandate of UNHCR was extended until the end of 1983

ORGANIZATION
(June 1982)

HIGH COMMISSIONER

High Commissioner (1978–82): POUL HARTLING (Denmark).

Deputy High Commissioner: WILLIAM R. SMYSER (U.S.A.).

The High Commissioner is elected by the United Nations General Assembly on the nomination of the Secretary-General, and is responsible to the General Assembly and to ECOSOC.

EXECUTIVE COMMITTEE

The Executive Committee of the High Commissioner's Programme, established by ECOSOC, gives the High Commissioner policy directives in respect of material assistance programmes, and advice at his request in the field of international protection. It meets once a year, usually at Geneva. It includes representatives of 40 states, both members and non-members of the UN.

Chairman: OMAR BIRIDO (Sudan).

Vice-Chairman: P. H. R. MARSHALL (U.K.).

ADMINISTRATION

Headquarters includes the High Commissioner's Office, and the following divisions: External Affairs, Protection, Assistance, and Administration and Management. As at May 31st, 1981, there were 10 Regional Offices, 34 Branch Offices and 17 Sub-Offices, eight Chargés de Mission and seven Honorary Representatives, Correspondents or Consultants located in 61 countries.

ACTIVITIES IN THE MIDDLE EAST AND NORTH AFRICA

In the field of protection, UNHCR continued to encourage national practices and procedures benefiting refugees, and followed up the application of the provisions of the 1951 Convention and 1967 Protocol relating to the status of refugees, to which eight States in the region are parties.

Palestinian refugees in the region are under the care of UNRWA (*see* page 162).

In 1980 UNHCR was providing assistance to some 5,000 refugees in Egypt, mostly from Ethiopia, at a cost for the year of U.S. $1.3 million, chiefly spent on education. In addition, UNHCR continues to co-ordinate humanitarian assistance for Sahrawis in the Tindouf area of Algeria; there were 52,000 registered refugees in Algeria in December 1980. A further 3,000 refugees from Europe, Latin America and Africa are living in Algeria, Morocco and Tunisia: U.S. $150,000 was spent by UNHCR on assisting them in 1980.

The High Commissioner continues to act as Co-ordinator of United Nations Humanitarian Assistance for Cyprus, at the request of the Secretary-General of the United Nations. In accordance with the wishes of the Government of Cyprus, a

total of U.S. $5.98 million was channelled through UNHCR in 1979 to finance the United Nations programme in the island. This programme included food and medical supplies for the displaced and needy, low-cost housing to replace temporary accommodation, and the continuation of existing efforts aimed at reactivating farms, small businesses and local crafts.

In October 1979 UNHCR set up an assistance programme for 200,000 refugees from Afghanistan in Pakistan: by June 1981 the number of Afghan refugees had increased to over 2,000,000, and during 1980 UNHCR appealed to the international community for over U.S. $160 million of assistance for them.

In June 1981 there were an estimated 500,000 refugees in Sudan, where UNHCR's budget for 1980 was over U.S. $11 million, mainly used for the establishment of organized rural or semi-urban settlements where refugees would have the chance of regaining self-sufficiency.

Assistance on a smaller scale is provided for displaced persons and refugees in Lebanon, Turkey and other countries of the region.

WORLD HEALTH ORGANIZATION—WHO

Avenue Appia, 1211 Geneva 27, Switzerland

Telephone: 34 60 61.

Established in 1948 as the central agency directing international health work. Of its many activities, the most important single aspect is technical co-operation with national health administrations, particularly in the developing countries.

ORGANIZATION

(June 1982)

SECRETARIAT

Director-General: Dr. HALFDAN MAHLER (Denmark).

Deputy Director-General: Dr. ADEOYE T. LAMBO (Nigeria).

Assistant Directors-General: Dr. CHEN WENJIE (People's Republic of China), Dr. JACQUES HAMON (France), WARREN W. FURTH (U.S.A.), Dr. I. D. LADNYI (U.S.S.R.), Dr. DAVID TEJADA-DE-RIVERO (Peru).

Regional Office for Africa: P.O.B. 6, Brazzaville, Congo; Dir. Dr. COMLAN A. A. QUENUM.

Regional Office for the Eastern Mediterranean: P.O.B 1517, Alexandria, Egypt; Dir. Dr. HUSSEIN ABDUL-RAZZAQ GEZAIRY.

ACTIVITIES IN THE MIDDLE EAST AND NORTH AFRICA

The WHO Regional Office for the Eastern Mediterranean covers 23 countries, of which five are designated as Least-Developed Countries. In June 1981 there were 298 WHO staff members working in the region, with a further 297 short-term consultants. The 1980-81 budget for the region amounted to U.S. $39,650,000, of which about two-thirds was allotted to national programmes and a quarter to inter-country programmes. Income from all sources for 1982–83 was estimated at about $70 million, of which $46.5 million was to come from the WHO regular budget.

The Regional Office's main area of work is in the preparation of national and regional strategies for the achievement of Health For All by the year 2000 in the Eastern Mediterranean region, in accordance with the Global Strategy adopted by the World Health Assembly in May 1981. Primary Health Care (PHC) is seen as the key to "Health For All", with the following as minimum requirements:

Safe water in the home or within 15 minutes' walking distance, and adequate sanitary facilities in the home or immediate vicinity;

Immunization against diphtheria, pertussis, tetanus, poliomyelitis, measles and tuberculosis;

Local health care, including availability of at least 20 essential drugs, within one hour's travel;

Trained personnel to attend childbirth, and to care for pregnant mothers and children up to at least one year old.

The development of health manpower is given high priority in the region. Educational development and support forms a prominent feature of the Regional Office's work. During 1979–80, 1,007 fellowships in health-related subjects were awarded. The Regional Arabic Programme issued 24 publications. mainly training manuals and working guidelines, between 1979 and 1981, and a further 26 were being prepared.

Communicable diseases are still a matter of concern in the region, including outbreaks of so-called "new diseases", e.g. several types of viral haemorrhagic fevers. WHO attempts to develop the control of groups of diseases which have features in common, such as water-borne diseases, in an integrated way, which is often more effective than trying to deal with each disease separately. One of the programmes which is expanding in the region is that of diarrhoeal diseases control, using oral rehydration to reduce child mortality. The Expanded Programme of Immunization (1976–90) is active in the region, and

between 1974 and 1980 the proportion of children receiving immunizations against diphtheria, pertussis, tetanus, poliomyelitis and measles rose from about 4 per cent to 23 per cent.

The Regional Office has initiated a programme of nutritional research in some countries of the region, aimed at improving the nutrition of infants and young children affected by an unsuitable choice of foods and the lack of hygienic practices. In May 1981 the International Code of Marketing of Breastmilk Substitutes was adopted by the World Health Assembly, aiming to provide safe and adequate nutrition for infants by promoting breast-feeding and by ensuring the proper use of breastmilk substitutes, when necessary, with controls on production, storage and advertising.

The International Drinking Water Supply and Sanitation Decade (1981–90) aims to eradicate a major cause of ill-health by providing hygienic water supply and sewage facilities. In 1981 it was estimated that only 32 per cent of the region's rural population had access to safe drinking water. Egypt, Somalia, Sudan and the Yemen Arab Republic are among the countries which co-operate most closely with WHO in formulating national policies. Approaches involve community participation, the use of appropriate technology and on-site training of local health workers.

OTHER REGIONAL OFFICES OF THE UN SYSTEM

UNITED NATIONS CHILDREN'S FUND—UNICEF
866 United Nations Plaza, New York,
N.Y. 10017, U.S.A.

UNICEF Regional Office for the Eastern Mediterranean: P.O.B. 5902, Beirut, Lebanon.

UNICEF Regional Office for North Africa: B.P. 660, Alger-Gare, Algeria.

INTERNATIONAL CIVIL AVIATION ORGANIZA-TION—ICAO
1000 Sherbrooke St. West, Montreal, P.Q.H3A 2R2, Canada

ICAO Middle East and Eastern African Office: 16 Hassan Sabri, Zamalek, Cairo, Egypt.

ICAO African Office: P.O.B. 2356, 15 blvd. de la République, Dakar, Senegal.

INTERNATIONAL LABOUR ORGANISATION—ILO
1211 Geneva 22, Switzerland

ILO Regional Office for Africa: P.O.B. 2788, Addis Ababa, Ethiopia.

ILO Regional Office for the Middle East and Europe: 4 Route des Morillons, CH-1218, Grand Saconnex, Switzerland.

UNITED NATIONS INFORMATION CENTRES

Afghanistan: Shah Mahmoud Ghazi Watt, Kabul; P.O.B. 5.

Algeria: 19 avenue Chahid el-Waly Mustapha Sayed, Algiers; B.P. 823.

Bahrain: King Faisal Rd., Gufool; P.O. Box 26004, Manama (also covers *Qatar* and *United Arab Emirates*).

Egypt: Sh. Osiris, Tagher Bldg., Garden City, Cairo; P.O.B. 262 (also covers *Saudi Arabia* and *Yemen Arab Republic*).

Iran: Ave. Gandhi, 3rd Ave., No. 43, Teheran; P.O.B. 1555.

Iraq: House 167/1 Abu Nouwas St., Bataween, Baghdad; P.O.B. 2398, Alwiyah.

Lebanon: Fakhoury Bldg., Montée Bain Militaire, Beirut; P.O.B. 4656 (also covers *Jordan, Kuwait* and *Syria*).

Libya: c/o UNDP, 67/71 Turkiya St., Tripoli; P.O. Box 358.

Morocco: "Casier ONU", Angle Charia Moulay Hassan et Zankat Assafi, Rabat.

Sudan: Al Qasr Ave., Street No. 15, Block 3, House 3, Khartoum East; P.O.B. 1992 (also covers *Somalia*).

Tunisia: 61 blvd. Bab Benat, Tunis; P.O.B. 863 (also covers *Libya*).

Turkey: 197 Ataturk Bulvari, Ankara; P.K. 407.

Arab Bank for Economic Development in Africa—BADEA

(Banque Arabe pour le développement économique en Afrique)

Sayed Abdel Rahman El-Mahdi Ave., P.O.B. 2640, Khartoum, Sudan

Created by the Arab League at the Sixth Arab Summit Conference in Algiers, November 1973. Operations began in early 1975. The purpose of the Bank is to contribute to Africa's economic development by providing all or part of the financing required for development projects and by supplying technical assistance to African countries.

MEMBERS

Subscribing countries: all members of the Arab League except Djibouti, Somalia, the Yemen Arab Republic and the People's Democratic Republic of Yemen. Egypt's membership was suspended in April 1979.

Recipient countries: all member countries of the Organization of African Unity except the member countries of the Arab League. A total of 41 countries are eligible for BADEA aid.

ORGANIZATION

(June 1982)

BOARD OF GOVERNORS

Highest authority of the Bank, composed of Finance Ministers of Arab League member states; meets annually; examines the Bank's activities in the past year and provides the resources required for the tasks assigned to it in the coming year. Only the Board of Governors has the power to increase the Bank's capital.

Chairman: Mohamed Yalla (Algeria).

BOARD OF DIRECTORS

Meets three times a year to make recommendations concerning policy to the Board of Governors and supervises the implementation of their decisions; performs all the executive functions of the Bank. The Board comprises a Chairman, appointed by the Board of Governors for a five-year term, and eleven other members. Countries with 200 or more shares each have a permanent seat on the Board (Algeria, Iraq, Kuwait, Libya, Qatar, Saudi Arabia and the United Arab Emirates); appointments to the remaining four seats are made by the Governors for a four-year term.

President of the Bank and Chairman: Dr. Chedly Ayari (Tunisia).

SUBSCRIPTIONS TO CAPITAL STOCK

(at December 31st, 1981)

	U.S. $ MILLION		U.S. $ MILLION
Algeria	30	Morocco	11
Bahrain	1.5	Oman	11
Egypt	1.5	Palestine	1.5
Iraq	105	Qatar	60
Jordan	1.5	Saudi Arabia	180
Kuwait	110	Sudan	1.5
Lebanon	5	Syria	1
Libya	120	Tunisia	6.25
Mauritania	1.5	United Arab Emirates	90
		Total	738.25

Paid-up capital: $735.5 million.

ACTIVITIES

BADEA aid consists mainly of loans on concessional terms for development projects, not exceeding $10 million or 40 per cent of the total cost of each project. Technical assistance is also provided, and Arab investment in Africa is encouraged.

The Special Arab Assistance Fund for Africa (SAAFA), established in 1972 as the Arab Loan Fund for Africa, was integrated with BADEA in 1977 after disbursing aid to the total of U.S. $221,744,000 to 33 African countries.

The Declaration on Afro-Arab Economic and Financial Co-operation, adopted at the first summit conference of Arab and African Heads of State at Cairo, Egypt, in March 1977, sought to promote Arab investment in Africa by a system of guarantees for investment and co-ordination of aid provided by Arab financial institutions. A Standing

Commission of 24 Arab and African Foreign Ministers, set up to implement this programme, entrusted BADEA and the African Development Bank with the task of carrying out preliminary investigations of the projects submitted for Arab aid. Subsequently, BADEA was to forward such projects to the Arab development agencies. In April 1977 the agencies asked BADEA to co-ordinate Arab aid to Africa. Accordingly, the Bank drew up a programme of 410 African development projects awaiting finance for consideration by the Arab agencies. Of the 410 projects, there were 346 national and 13 regional development plans and 51 projects for technical co-operation.

By December 1981 BADEA had approved loans and grants amounting to U.S. $459.7 million (or $673.9 million when SAAFA operations are included) involving 71 projects for a total of 38 African countries. BADEA was instrumental in the participation of other Arab agencies whose contributions were worth $778.48 million. In the first year of operations, 1975, $71.6 million was approved for 10 projects. In 1976 $61.9 million was approved for nine projects, in 1977 $66.24 million for nine projects, in 1978 $67.87 million for 14 projects, in 1979 $44.07 million for eight projects, in 1980 $71.95 million for nine projects and in 1981 $76 million for 12 projects.

In regional terms, U.S. $259.2 million of total aid (up to the end of 1981) went to West Africa and $198.8 million to East Africa. Viewed against the total commitments of the Bank, participation was as in the table below. In terms of aid per caput these commitments represent a roughly even balance between the two regions.

The sectoral distribution of aid is determined by development priorities adopted by the African countries themselves. The average distribution has been weighted in favour of projects for infrastructural development, which received 45.44 per cent of total aid up to the end of 1981. Commitment in this sector, however, declined between 1975 (when 58.7 per cent of aid financed infrastructure) and 1978 when its share was 25.9 per cent. The commitments to agriculture, industrial and energy development projects to the end of 1981 were 25.06 per cent, 19.04 per cent and 10.46 per cent respectively.

The projects for which loans were approved in 1981 were: fisheries rehabilitation in Angola ($10 million); port extension in Benin ($2.7 million); road improvement in the Central African Republic ($5 million); airport modernization in the Congo ($10 million); forestry in Madagascar ($8 million); rural water supply in Niger ($5 million); electric power generation in São Tomé and Príncipe ($5 million); river and rail transport in Zaire ($10 million); and road reconstruction in Zimbabwe ($10 million). In addition a $10 million line of credit was extended to the Development Bank of Zambia, and grants were made for a study on aid to Sahelian countries from Arab development institutions ($280,000) and for a feasibility study on livestock development in Senegal ($46,000).

TOTAL COMMITMENTS BY REGION

	WEST AFRICA %	EAST AFRICA %
1975	72.1	27.9
1976	44.9	54.9
1977	60.7	39.3
1978	59.6	38.2
1979	76.2	23.8
1980	38.2	61.8
1981	50.0	50.0

Total commitments over the period 1975-81: West Africa 56.4 per cent, East Africa 43.3 per cent. Commitments not specified by region accounted for 0.2 per cent in 1976 and 2.2 per cent in 1978.

LOANS APPROVED BY BADEA*
(cumulative to December 31st, 1981)

	U.S. $ MILLION		U.S. $ MILLION		U.S. $ MILLION		U.S. $ MILLION
Angola	33.2	Congo	20.0	Liberia	10.7	Seychelles	1.2
Benin	17.7	Equatorial Guinea	0.5	Madagascar	29.7	Sierra Leone	17.1
Botswana	14.9	Ethiopia	14.7	Mali	39.7	Swaziland	4.2
Burundi	22	Gambia	9.8	Mauritius	12.7	Tanzania	37.2
Cameroon	31.9	Ghana	22.7	Mozambique	37.0	Togo	3.3
Cape Verde	13.9	Guinea	11.9	Niger	23.6	Uganda	16.2
Central African		Guinea-Bissau	1.4	Rwanda	13.0	Upper Volta	9.1
Republic	7.4	Ivory Coast	3.3	São Tomé and		Zaire	36.8
Chad	18.5	Kenya	13.6	Príncipe	15.5	Zambia	32.7
Comoros	20.1	Lesotho	12.7	Senegal	27.3	Zimbabwe	10.0

Grants totalling U.S. $1.88 million were given for a PANAFTEL (Pan-African Telecommunication Union) Seminar and study (1976 and 1978) and for a special programme to support three African pest-control organizations (1978). Two lines of credit of U.S. $5 million were opened for the Banque des états de l'Afrique centrale (1978) and for the Kenya Industrial Development Bank (1979) to help finance small and medium-size industries.

* Including grants made by the Special Arab Assistance Fund for Africa before 1977.

TOTAL BADEA COMMITMENTS BY SECTOR, 1975–81

Sector	Total Commitments (U.S. $ million)
Infrastructure	208.5
Transport and communications	166.3
Dams, bridges and public services	28.2
Water supply and drainage	14.0
Agriculture	100.2
Food production	24.5
Rural development	44.1
Forestry development	8.0
Livestock and fishing	23.6
Industry	87.5
Chemical industry	20.0
Small and medium industry	20.0
Building materials industry	42.8
Textiles	4.7
Energy infrastructure and electric power	48.1
Special programme (emergency aid)	15.0
Total	459.4*

* Not including a grant of $280,000 made in 1981 for a study of Arab aid to Sahel countries.

Arab Fund for Economic and Social Development-AFESD

P.O.B. 21923, Kuwait City, Kuwait

Telephone: 431870.

Established in 1968 by the Economic Council of the Arab League, the Fund began its operations in 1972.

MEMBERSHIP

21 countries and the Palestine Liberation Organization (*see* table of subscriptions below)

FUNCTIONS

The Fund participates in the financing of economic and social development projects in the Arab states and countries by:

1. Financing economic projects of an investment character by means of loans granted on easy terms to governments, and to public or private organizations and institutions, giving preference to economic projects of interest specifically to Arab peoples, and to joint Arab projects.

2. Encouraging, directly or indirectly, the investment of public and private capital in such a manner as to ensure the development and growth of the Arab economy.

3. Providing technical expertise and assistance in the various fields of economic development.

In November 1980 it was suggested at the summit conference of the Arab League (*q.v.*) that AFESD should administer the fund set up to aid the least-developed Arab countries.

ORGANIZATION

(June 1982)

BOARD OF GOVERNORS

The Board of Governors consists of a Governor and an Alternate Governor appointed by each member of the Fund. The Board of Governors is considered as the General Assembly of the Fund, and has all powers.

Director-General and Chairman of the Board of Directors:
Dr. MOHAMMAD IMADY (Syria).

BOARD OF DIRECTORS

The Board of Directors is composed of six full-time Directors elected by the Board of Governors from among Arab citizens of recognized experience and competence. They are elected for a renewable term of two years.

The Board of Directors is charged with all the activities of the Fund and exercises the powers delegated to it by the Board of Governors.

FINANCIAL STRUCTURE

The authorized capital at commencement of operations in April 1973 was 100 million Kuwaiti dinars. In 1975 the capital was increased to KD 400 million, divided into 40,000 shares having a value of 10,000 Kuwaiti dinars each (one Kuwaiti dinar being equal to 2.48828 grammes of gold). In April 1981 it was announced that the capital would be further increased, to KD 800 million.

SUBSCRIPTIONS (1980)

	MILLION KUWAITI DINARS		MILLION KUWAITI DINARS
Algeria	32.39	Qatar	4.5
Bahrain	1.08	Saudi Arabia	79.47
Djibouti	0.01	Somalia	0.21
Egypt*	40.5	Sudan	6.32
Iraq	31.76	Syria	12.0
Jordan	8.65	Tunisia	2.16
Kuwait	84.85	United Arab Emirates	21.6
Lebanon	2.0	Yemen Arab Republic	2.16
Libya	47.76	Yemen, People's Democratic Republic	0.1
Mauritania	0.41		
Morocco	8.0		
Oman	8.64		
Palestine Liberation Organization	0.55	TOTAL	395.12

* In April 1979 all aid to and economic relations with Egypt were suspended, but finance for projects already in progress is continuing.

LOANS BY SECTOR, 1981
(U.S. $ million)

Sector	Amount
Transport and telecommunications .	76.20
Water and sewerage . .	48.95
Power	17.01
Industry . . .	7.81
Total . .	149.97

LOANS BY COUNTRY, 1981
(U.S. $ million)

Country	Purpose of Loan	Amount
Algeria . .	Telecommunications*	15.97
Djibouti . .	Telecommunications*	3.55
	Rural engineering	0.43
Jordan . .	Telecommunications*	4.71
Somalia . .	Telecommunications*	6.04
	Water supply	17.75
Syria . .	Telecommunications*	9.77
	Sewerage	18.10
	Garbage disposal	7.81
Tunisia . .	Fisheries	13.49
	Telecommunications*	13.14
Yemen Arab Republic . .	Electric power	17.01
	Telecommunications*	4.94
Yemen, People's Democratic Republic . .	Water supply	12.67
	Telecommunications*	4.59

* Projects forming part of the Pan Arab Telecommunication Network.

Arab Monetary Fund

P.O.B. 2818, Abu Dhabi, United Arab Emirates

Telephone: 328500.

The Agreement establishing the Arab Monetary Fund was approved by the Economic Council of Arab States in Rabat, Morocco, in April 1976 and entered into force on February 2nd, 1977.

MEMBERS

Algeria	Kuwait	Palestine Liberation	Syria
Bahrain	Lebanon	Organization	Tunisia
Egypt*	Libya	Qatar	United Arab Emirates
Iraq	Mauritania	Saudi Arabia	Yemen Arab Republic
Jordan	Morocco	Somalia	Yemen, People's
	Oman	Sudan	Democratic Republic

* Egypt's membership was suspended in April 1979.

ORGANIZATION

(June 1982)

BOARD OF GOVERNORS

The Board of Governors is the highest authority of the Arab Monetary Fund. It formulates policies on Arab economic integration and liberalization of trade among member states. With certain exceptions, it may delegate to the Board of Executive Directors any of its powers. The Board of Governors is composed of a Governor and a Deputy Governor appointed by each member state for a term of five years. It meets at least once a year; meetings may also be convened at the request of half the members, or of members holding half of the total voting power, or of the Board of Executive Directors. Each member country has 75 votes regardless of the number of shares it holds and, in addition, one vote for each share held.

Chairman: MUHAMMAD ABA AL-KHAIL (Saudi Arabia).

BOARD OF EXECUTIVE DIRECTORS

The Board of Executive Directors exercises all powers vested in it by the Board of Governors and may delegate therefrom to the President such powers as it deems fit. It is composed of the President and eight resident Directors elected by the Board of Governors. Each Director holds office for three years and may be re-elected.

Algeria and Saudi Arabia are each represented by a Director, while the other members are grouped into six groups each represented by one Director. In 1981 the six directors were nationals of Bahrain, Iraq, Syria, Tunisia, the United Arab Emirates and the People's Democratic Republic of Yemen.

THE PRESIDENT

The President of the Fund is appointed by the Board of Governors for a renewable five-year term. He serves as Chairman of the Board of Executive Directors and as Managing Director of the Fund.

He supervises a Committee on Loans and a Committee on Investments to make recommendations on loan and investment policies to the Board of Executive Directors. He is required to submit an Annual Report to the Board of Governors.

President (1982–86): SAEED GHOBASH (United Arab Emirates).

FINANCE

The authorized capital of the Fund is 263 million Arab Accounting Dinars. The Arab Accounting Dinar (AAD) is a unit of account equivalent to 3 IMF Special Drawing Rights (SDR 1=U.S. $1.1131 at March 31st, 1982). The capital stock comprises 5,260 shares, each having the value of AAD 50,000.

Each member paid, in convertible currencies, 5 per cent of the value of its shares at the time of its ratification of the Agreement and another 20 per cent when the Agreement entered into force. In addition, each member paid 2 per cent of the value of its shares in its national currency regardless of whether it is convertible. The second 25 per

CAPITAL SUBSCRIPTIONS

(million Arab Accounting Dinars; AAD1=SDR 3)

	NUMBER OF SHARES	VALUE OF SHARES
Algeria	760	38.0
Bahrain	80	4.0
Egypt	500	25.0
Iraq	760	38.0
Jordan	80	4.0
Kuwait	500	25.0
Lebanon	100	5.0
Libya	186	9.3
Mauritania	80	4.0
Morocco	200	10.0
Oman	80	4.0
Palestine	34	1.7
Qatar	200	10.0
Saudi Arabia	760	38.0
Somalia	80	4.0
Sudan	200	10.0
Syria	80	4.0
Tunisia	100	5.0
United Arab Emirates	300	15.0
Yemen Arab Republic	100	5.0
Yemen, People's Democratic Republic	80	4.0
TOTAL . .	5,260	263.0

cent of the capital was to be subscribed by the end of September 1979, bringing the total paid-up capital in convertible currencies to AAD 131.5 million (SDR 394.5 million). An increase in requests for loans led to a resolution by the Board of Governors in April 1981, giving members the option of paying the balance of their subscribed capital. This payment became obligatory in July 1981, when total approved loans exceeded 50 per cent

of the already paid-up capital in convertible currencies. At the end of 1981 total paid-up capital was AAD 151,742,000 (SDR 455.2 million).

The Board of Governors, by a special majority and subject to prescribed conditions, may increase the capital of the Fund. The Articles of Agreement provide for the establishment of a general reserve fund and, if necessary, special reserve funds.

AIMS AND LENDING POLICIES

The creation of the Arab Monetary Fund was seen as a step towards the goal of Arab economic integration. Like the IMF, it assists member states in balance of payments difficulties but it has a broader range of aims.

The Articles of Agreement define the Fund's aims as follows:

(a) to correct disequilibria in the balance of payments of member states;

(b) to promote the stability of exchange rates among Arab currencies, the realization of their mutual convertibility, and the removal of restrictions on current payments between member states;

(c) to establish policies and modes of monetary co-operation to speed up Arab economic integration and economic development in the member states;

(d) to tender advice on the investment of member states' financial resources in foreign markets, whenever called upon to do so;

(e) to promote the development of Arab financial markets;

(f) to promote the use of the Arab dinar as a unit of account and to pave the way for the creation of a unified Arab currency;

(g) to co-ordinate the dealings of member states with international monetary and economic problems; and

(h) to provide a mechanism for the settlement of current payments between member states in order to promote trade among them.

The Arab Monetary Fund functions both as a fund and a bank. It is empowered:

(a) to provide short- and medium-term loans to finance balance of payments deficits of member states;

(b) to issue guarantees to member states to strengthen their borrowing capabilities;

(c) to act as intermediary in the issuance of loans in Arab and international markets for the account of member states and under their guarantees;

(d) to co-ordinate the monetary policies of member states;

(e) to manage any funds placed under its charge by member states;

(f) to hold periodic consultations with member states on their economic conditions; and

(g) to provide technical assistance to monetary institutions in member states.

Loans are intended to finance an overall balance of payments deficit and a member may draw up to 75 per cent of its paid-up capital, in convertible currencies, for this purpose unconditionally (automatic loans). A member may, however, obtain loans in excess of this limit subject to agreement with the Fund on a programme aimed at reducing its balance of payments deficit (ordinary and extended loans). In April 1981 the maximum permitted borrowing was raised from 300 per cent of each member's paid-up contribution to 400 per cent. In addition, a member has the right to borrow up to 100 per cent of its paid-up capital in order to cope with an unexpected deficit in its balance of payments resulting from a decrease in its exports of goods and services or a large increase in its imports of agricultural products following a poor harvest (compensatory loans). Such a loan was made to Sudan in November 1980 to compensate for a poor cotton crop.

Automatic and compensatory loans are repayable within three years, while ordinary and extended loans are repayable within five and seven years respectively.

In 1981 the Fund introduced an Inter-Arab Trade Facility, designed to encourage trade among member countries. A member may borrow an amount equivalent to as much as 100 per cent of its subscription paid in convertible currencies, but not exceeding the size of its trade deficit with other members. The loan is repayable within three years.

Loans are granted at concessionary and uniform rates of interest which increase with the length of the period of the loan.

The Fund has granted loans to Egypt, Mauritania, Morocco, Somalia, Sudan, Syria, the Yemen Arab Republic and the People's Democratic Republic of Yemen. At the end of 1981 total approved loans amounted to AAD 113.4 million, of which AAD 29.4 million were automatic, AAD 55.8 million were extended, AAD 13.3 million were ordinary and AAD 14.8 million were compensatory.

Co-operation Council for the Arab States of the Gulf

Riyadh, Saudi Arabia

More generally known as the Gulf Co-operation Council, the organization was established on May 25th, 1981, by six Arab states.

MEMBERS

Bahrain	Qatar
Kuwait	Saudi Arabia
Oman	United Arab Emirates

ORGANIZATION

(June 1982)

The Constitution of the Council provides for the establishment of the following bodies:

SUPREME COUNCIL

The Supreme Council comprises the heads of member states, meeting twice a year in ordinary session, and in emergency session if demanded by two or more members. The Presidency of the Council is undertaken by each state in turn, in alphabetical order. The Supreme Council draws up the overall policy of the organization and the basic lines it will follow; it discusses recommendations and laws presented to it by the Ministerial Council and the Secretariat General in preparation for endorsement. A body for resolving disputes is also to be attached to and formed by the Supreme Council.

MINISTERIAL COUNCIL

The Ministerial Council consists of the Foreign Ministers of member states, meeting every three months, and in emergency session if demanded by two or more members. It prepares for the meetings of the Supreme Council, and draws up policies, recommendations, studies and projects aimed at developing co-operation and co-ordination among member states in various spheres.

SECRETARIAT GENERAL

The Secretariat is to be established in Riyadh, Saudi Arabia, to implement recommendations by the Supreme and Ministerial Councils, prepare reports and studies, budgets and accounts. The Secretary-General is appointed by the Supreme Council for a renewable three-year term. All member states contribute in equal proportions towards the budget of the Secretariat.

Secretary-General: ABDULLAH YACOUB BISHARA (Kuwait).

Assistant Secretary-General: IBRAHIM HAMUD AS-SUBHI (Oman).

ACTIVITIES

The Council was set up following a series of meetings of Foreign Ministers of the states concerned, culminating in an agreement on the basic details of its constitution on March 10th, 1981. The Constitution was signed by the six heads of state on May 25th. Although all the countries concerned belong to the Arab League, and were criticized by Iraq for setting up a separate organization, the formation of the Council was apparently prompted by a feeling that membership of the Arab League was not enough to bring about unity among the Gulf states, while the various bilateral agreements between the countries were too piecemeal for effective regional co-operation. A desire to emulate the European Community was frequently expressed by spokesmen for the Council from its outset. The constitution describes the organization as providing "the means for realizing co-ordination, integration and co-operation" in all economic, social and cultural affairs. During the ensuing year a series of ministerial meetings began to put the proposals into effect.

Economic co-operation

In June 1981 Gulf Finance Ministers drew up an economic co-operation agreement covering investment, petroleum, the abolition of customs duties, harmonization of banking regulations and the eventual formation of a common currency. In January 1982 a further meeting agreed to set up a Gulf Investment Corporation with capital of U.S. $3,000 million, as the first stage in the creation of a common market.

Industry

In October 1981 Ministers of Industry met to discuss the protection of domestic products, and set up a committee to prepare a system for exchanging industrial information.

Energy

In February 1982 a meeting of energy ministers agreed to set up a ministerial committee to co-ordinate hydrocarbons policies and prices. Three sub-committees were also formed: the first was to devise a system for exchanging information on prices; the second was to study the expansion of the hydrocarbons industry in Oman, the least-developed of the Gulf states in this respect, and to consider the building of a pipeline from the Gulf oilfields to the coast of Oman, which would mean that petroleum no longer had to be carried by sea through the Straits of Hormuz; the third was to examine domestic energy consumption and subsidies. The meeting also adopted a petroleum security plan to safeguard individual members against a halt in their production, to form a stockpile of petroleum products, and to organize a boycott of any non-member country when appropriate. A unified policy on the acquisition of technology was also approved.

Defence

Although no mention of defence or security was made in the original constitution, the summit meeting which ratified the constitution also issued a statement condemning every foreign military presence in the region. The Supreme Council meeting in November 1981 agreed to include defence co-operation in the activities of the organization: as a result, Defence Ministers met in January 1982 to discuss a common security policy, including a joint air defence system and standardization of weapons. The Council jointly endorsed the Saudi Arabian "Fahd Plan" (*see* Arab League, p. 185) for peace in the Middle East.

accounting for 40 per cent of Turkey's exports to the EEC: unmanufactured tobacco, dried raisins and figs, and nuts.

The transitional phase began in 1973, aiming to introduce a customs union by gradual stages over 12 to 22 years, depending on the product. The EEC granted immediate duty and quota free access for industrial products, but placed restrictions on refined petroleum products and three textile products. The EEC's financial assistance during 1970–81 was fixed at EUA 567 million. EUA 600 million was to be provided for a five-year period from the end of 1981, mainly in the form of loans on special terms.

In June 1980 agreements were reached on the removal of customs duties on imports of Turkish agricultural products, over a six-year period beginning on January 1st, 1981. A grant aid package of EUA 75 million for co-operation in industry, energy, agriculture and training was also approved, together with provisions for the free movement of workers and social security measures.

EURO-ARAB DIALOGUE

The Euro-Arab Dialogue was begun in 1973, initially to provide a forum for discussion of economic issues: the principal organ was a General Committee, and about thirty working groups were set up to discuss specific issues and prepare projects, such as the creation of a Euro-Arab Centre for the Transfer of Technology. Although it was not originally intended to include political discussion, the Dialogue was inevitably affected by politics, and after the Egypt-Israel peace agreement in 1979 all activity was suspended at the request of the Arab League: after the fourth General Committee meeting, in December 1978, no more meetings were held until 1981 and working groups were suspended likewise.

At the Venice meeting of the European Council in June 1980, the Heads of Government of the Nine declared the "advisability" of discussion at political level, and also said that the Palestine Liberation Organization (PLO) would "have to be associated" with any negotiations for a peaceful settlement, although the European Community had not granted formal recognition to the PLO as the representative of the Palestinian people. A Middle East peace mission was approved by the Foreign Ministers of the Nine in July, and Gaston Thorn, as President of the Council of Ministers, held discussions in various Middle East countries, including talks with the PLO, in August and September. In November Community representatives held a meeting with an Arab League delegation, chaired by the PLO, to arrange for the resumption of the Dialogue at every level, in preparation for the first-ever Euro-Arab Foreign Ministers' meeting originally to be held the following summer. Owing to the lack of progress, however, in political, economic and technical fields of co-operation, the meeting was not held.

Islamic Development Bank

P.O.B. 5925, Jeddah, Saudi Arabia

An international financial institution established in pursuance of the Declaration of Intent issued by a Conference of Finance Ministers of member countries of the Organization of the Islamic Conference, held in Jeddah in December 1973. Its aim is to encourage economic development and social progress of member countries and Muslim communities, in accordance with the principles of the Islamic Shariah (sacred law). The Bank formally opened in October 1975.

MEMBERS

There are 40 members (*see* table of subscriptions below).

ORGANIZATION

(June 1982)

BOARD OF GOVERNORS

Each member country is represented by a Governor, usually its Finance Minister or his alternate. The Board of Governors is the Supreme Authority of the Bank, and meets annually.

President of the Bank and Chairman of the Board of Executive Directors: Dr. AHMAD MOHAMED ALI (Saudi Arabia).

EXECUTIVE BOARD OF DIRECTORS

Consists of 10 members, four of whom are appointed by the four largest subscribers to the capital stock of the Bank; the remaining six are elected by Governors representing the other subscribers. Members of the Executive Board of Directors are elected for three-year terms. Responsible for the direction of the general operations of the Bank.

FINANCIAL STRUCTURE

The authorized capital of the Bank is 2,000 million Islamic Dinars divided into 200,000 shares having a value of 100,000 Islamic Dinars each. The Islamic Dinar is the Bank's unit of account and is equivalent to the value of one Special Drawing Right of the IMF.

The subscribed capital stood at 790 million Islamic Dinars in December 1980.

In January 1981 paid-up capital was 750.5 million Islamic Dinars (U.S. $948.7 million). Saudi Arabia, at the summit meeting of the Organization of the Islamic Conference in January, proposed that this sum should be increased to 2,252 million Islamic Dinars, and itself pledged some 790 million.

SUBSCRIPTIONS

(as at December 1980)

	MILLION ISLAMIC DINARS		MILLION ISLAMIC DINARS
Afghanistan	2.5	Niger	2.5
Algeria	25.0	Oman	5.0
Bahrain	5.0	Pakistan	25.0
Bangladesh	10.0	Palestine Libera-	
Cameroon	2.5	tion Organization	2.5
Chad	2.5	Qatar	25.0
Comoros	2.5	Saudi Arabia	200.0
Djibouti	2.5	Senegal	2.5
Egypt	25.0	Somalia	2.5
Gambia	2.5	Sudan	10.0
Guinea	2.5	Syria	2.5
Guinea-Bissau	2.5	Tunisia	2.5
Indonesia	25.0	Turkey	10.0
Iraq	10.0	Uganda	2.5
Jordan	4.0	United Arab	
Kuwait	100.0	Emirates	110.0
Lebanon	2.5	Upper Volta	2.5
Libya	125.0	Yemen Arab	
Malaysia	16.0	Republic	2.5
Maldives	2.5	Yemen, People's	
Mali	2.5	Democratic	
Mauritania	2.5	Republic	2.5
Morocco	5.0		

ACTIVITIES

During 1975/76 the Islamic Development Bank concentrated on setting up its organization and formulating its policies; financial operations began in 1976. The Bank, which adheres to the Koranic principle forbidding usury, does not grant loans or credits for interest, preferring to help development projects by taking up equity participation in them, or by giving interest-free loans with a charge to cover administrative expenses. Funds not immediately needed for projects are used for foreign trade financing, particularly for importing commodities to be used in development (such as fertilizers and raw materials) rather than consumer goods. Priority is given to the import of goods from other member countries. By November 1980 total approvals by the Bank had reached 1,245 million Islamic Dinars (U.S. $1,575 million), of which 445 million was for project financing (covering 95 projects in 36 countries) and 799 million was for foreign trade financing (80 operations in 22 countries).

The 46 loans recorded for 1981 amounted to U.S. $392 million, of which about 79 per cent was for foreign trade financing, 10 per cent for industrial projects, 7 per cent for transport and telecommunications, 3 per cent for water and sewerage and 1 per cent for agriculture.

League of Arab States

37 avenue Khereddine Pacha, Tunis, Tunisia
Telephone: 890 100.

The League of Arab States (more generally known as the Arab League) is a voluntary association of sovereign Arab states designed to strengthen the close ties linking them and co-ordinate their policies and activities and direct them towards the common good of all the Arab countries. It was founded in March 1945.

MEMBERS

Algeria	Kuwait	Palestine (*see below*)	Tunisia
Bahrain	Lebanon	Qatar	United Arab Emirates
Djibouti	Libya	Saudi Arabia	Yemen Arab Republic
Egypt (*see below*)	Mauritania	Somalia	Yemen, People's Democratic
Iraq	Morocco	Sudan	Republic
Jordan	Oman	Syria	

MEMBERSHIP AND FUNCTIONS

While it is a prerequisite that members must be Arab states that are fully independent, the activities of the League also often include Arab countries which are not independent. Palestine is considered an independent state, as explained in the Charter Annex on Palestine, and therefore a full member of the League.

The status of Palestine as a full member of the League was confirmed at a meeting of the Arab League Council in September 1976.

In March 1979 Egypt's membership of the Arab League was suspended, and it was decided to make Tunis the temporary headquarters of the League, its Secretariat and its permanent committees.

The Arab League itself is an international body with its own independent statutory powers and general objectives.

ORGANIZATION

(June 1982)

COUNCIL

The supreme organ of the Arab League. Consists of representatives of the twenty-one member states, each of which has one vote, and a representative for Palestine. Unanimous decisions of the Council shall be binding upon all member states of the League; majority decisions shall be binding only on those states which have accepted them.

The Council may, if necessary, hold an extraordinary session at the request of two member states. Invitations to all sessions are extended by the Secretary-General. The ordinary sessions are presided over by representatives of the member states in turn.

Sixteen committees are attached to the Council:

Political Committee: studies political questions and reports to the Council meetings concerned with them. All member states are members of the Committee. It represents the Council in dealing with critical political matters when the Council is meeting. Usually composed of the Foreign Ministers.

Cultural Committee: in charge of following up the activities of the Cultural Department and the cultural affairs within the scope of the secretariat; co-ordinates the activities of the general secretariat and the various cultural bodies in member states.

Economic Committee: complemented by the Economic Council since 1953.

Communications Committee: supervises land, sea and air communications, together with weather forecasts and postal matters.

Social Committee: supports co-operation in such matters as family and child welfare.

Legal Committee: an extension of the Nationality and Passports Committee abolished in 1947; studies and legally formulates draft agreements, bills, regulations and official documents.

Arab Oil Experts Committee: for study of oil affairs; also investigates methods to prevent the smuggling of Arab oil into Israel; and for co-ordination of oil policies in general.

Information Committee: studies information projects, suggests plans and carries out the policies decided by the Council of Information Ministers.

Health Committee: for co-operation in health affairs.

Human Rights Committee: studies subjects concerning human rights, particularly violations by Israel; collaborates with the Information and Cultural Committees.

Permanent Committee for Administrative and Financial Affairs.

Permanent Committee for Meteorology.

Committee of Arab Experts on Co-operation.

Arab Women's Committee.

Organization of Youth Welfare.

Conference of Liaison Officers: co-ordinates trade activities among commercial attachés of various Arab embassies abroad.

GENERAL SECRETARIAT

The administrative and financial offices of the League. The Secretariat carries out the decisions of the Council, and provides financial and administrative services for the personnel of the League. There are a number of departments: economic, political, legal, cultural, social and labour affairs, petroleum, finance, Palestine, health, information, communications, protocol. The most recently formed department deals with African affairs.

The Secretary-General is appointed by the League Council by a two-thirds majority of the member states. He appoints the Assistant Secretaries and principal officials, with the approval of the Council. He has the rank of Ambassador, and the Assistant Secretaries have the rank of Ministers Plenipotentiary.

Secretary-General: CHEDLI KLIBI (Tunisia).

Assistant Secretaries-General:

Organizational Affairs: OTHMAN AL-AHMED (Saudi Arabia).
Social Affairs: ASSAAD EL-ASSAAD (Lebanon).
Economic Affairs: ABDUL HASSAN ZALZALAH (Iraq).
Legal Affairs: MOHAMED BEN SLAMA (Tunisia).
Political Affairs: ADNAN OMRAN (Syria).

Adviser, Head of Cabinet of the Secretary-General: MONGI EL-FEKIH (Tunisia).

Adviser, Head of Department for Palestinian Affairs: MONCEF EL-MAY (Tunisia).

Adviser for African Affairs: ABDULLAH ADAM (Somalia).

DEFENCE AND ECONOMIC CO-OPERATION

Groups established under the Treaty of Joint Defence and Economic Co-operation, concluded in 1950 to complement the Charter of the League:

Arab Unified Military Command: f. 1964 to co-ordinate military policies for the liberation of Palestine.

Economic Council: to compare and co-ordinate the economic policies of the member states; the Council is composed of Ministers of Economic Affairs or their deputies. Decisions are taken by majority vote. The first meeting was held in 1953.

Joint Defence Council: supervises implementation of those aspects of the treaty concerned with common defence. Composed of Foreign and Defence Ministers; decisions by a two-thirds majority vote of members are binding on all.

Permanent Military Commission: Established 1950; composed of representatives of army General Staffs; main purpose: to draw up plans of joint defence for submission to the Joint Defence Council.

ARAB DETERRENT FORCE

Set up in June 1976 by the Arab League Council to supervise successive attempts to cease hostilities in Lebanon, and afterwards to maintain the peace. The mandate of the Force has been successively renewed. The Arab League Summit Conference in October 1976 agreed that costs were to be paid in the following percentage contributions:

Saudi Arabia	20
Kuwait	20
United Arab Emirates	15
Qatar	10
Other Arab states	35
	100

Commanding Officer: Pres. ELIAS SARKIS (Lebanon).

OTHER INSTITUTIONS OF THE COUNCIL

Other bodies established by resolutions adopted by the Council of the League:

Academy of Arab Music: P.O.B. 6150, Baghdad, Iraq.

Administrative Tribunal of the Arab League: f. 1964; began operations 1966.

Special Bureau for Boycotting Israel: P.O.B. 437, Damascus, Syria.

SPECIALIZED AGENCIES

All member states of the Arab League are also members of the Specialized Agencies, which constitute an integral part of the Arab League.

Arab Academy of Maritime Transport: P.O.B. 1552, Sharjah, United Arab Emirates; f. 1975; Dir.-Gen. MOUSTAPHA WAJIH TAYARA.

Arab Centre for the Study of Dry Regions and Arid Territories: P.O.B. 2440, Damascus, Syria; Dir.-Gen. MOHAMED KHASHIN.

Arab Civil Aviation Council: P.O.B. 4410, 17 Alnasr St., Rabat, Morocco; created 1965, began operations 1967; aims to develop the principles, techniques and economics of air transport in the Arab World; to co-operate with the International Civil Aviation Organization and to attempt to standardize laws and technical terms; also deals with Arab air rates; Pres. N. AL-KHANI. Publs. *Air Transport Activities in Arab Countries, Lexicon of Civil Aviation Terminology* (Arabic); *Unified Air Law for Arab States* (Arabic and English).

Arab Industrial Development Organization: P.O.B. 3156, Al-Saadoon, Baghdad, Iraq; f. 1968 (fmrly. Industrial Development Centre for Arab States); at the beginning of 1982, the Organization was assisting sugar industry development in Somalia and the Yemen Arab Republic, leather processing in Djibouti, and studies on Palestinian industrial projects; plans for a packaging plant in Morocco and leather processing in Tunisia were also announced in March 1982; Dir.-Gen. AYYAD MUHAMMED AL-AZZABI.

Arab League Educational, Cultural and Scientific Organization (ALECSO): P.O.B. 1120, Al Qabadha, Al-Asleya, Tunis, Tunisia; f. 1964; aims to promote intellectual unity of the Arab countries by means of education; to raise cultural standards; to enable the Arab countries to participate in technical development; to establish specialized institutes; to train experts for research in Arab civilization. Each member submits an annual report on progress in education, cultural matters and science. The Arab League has a Permanent Delegation at UNESCO which may act on behalf of Arab states that are not members of the world body. The first session of the General Conference was held in Cairo in 1970. The sixth session was held in Tunis, December 1981; Dir.-Gen. MOHIEDDIN SABER (Sudan).

There are four institutions within the framework of the Arab League Educational, Cultural and Scientific Organization:

Institute for Arab Research and Studies: f. 1953 for specialization by graduates of Arab universities; provides for studies in contemporary Arab affairs, including national and international affairs, economics, social studies, history, geography, law, literature and linguistics. A special department of the Institute is devoted to Palestinian affairs, to research into the Arab cause; the Institute aims to develop the understanding of Arab nationalism.

Arab Literacy and Adult Education Organization: Baghdad; f. 1966 to assist in the establishment and development of national institutions for literacy and adult education; to assist in formulating national plans in these respects; to hold regional training courses, seminars and conferences; to co-ordinate research work; to grant scholarships and provide technical assistance; and to provide information.

Institute of Arab Manuscripts: Kuwait.

Permanent Bureau for Arabization: Rabat, Morocco.

Arab Institute of Petroleum Research: f. 1966 to contribute to development of petroleum production, refining, transport and marketing.

Arab Labour Organization: P.O.B. 6067, Al-Mansoura, Baghdad, Iraq; established in 1965 for co-operation between member states in labour problems; unification of labour legislation and general conditions of work wherever possible; research; technical assistance; social insurance; training, etc.; the organization has a tripartite structure: governments, employers and workers; Dir.-Gen. IBRAHIM MUHAMMAD AHMED. Publs. *Bulletin* (monthly), *Arab Labour Review* (quarterly).

Arab Organization of Administrative Sciences: P.O.B. 17159, Amman, Jordan; set up with the approval of the League Council in 1961, commencing activity in 1969 soon after ratification of the agreement by four Arab states (Egypt, Iraq, Syria, Kuwait); to ensure co-operation in promoting administrative science, to improve the standard of administrative staff in the Arab states; Dir.-Gen. Dr. ABDULLA ZAABI. Publ. Research series in administrative science.

Arab Organization for Agricultural Development: 4 El Jamea St., P.O.B. 474, Khartoum, Sudan; proposed in 1969 by a decision of Arab Ministers of Agriculture, which was approved by the Economic Council in 1970 and ratified by the League Council; to contribute to co-operation in agricultural activities, and in the development of natural and human resources for agriculture; includes Arab Institute of Forestry.

Arab Organization for Standardization and Metrology: P.O.B. 926161, Amman, Jordan; began activity in 1968 to unify technical terms and standard specifications for products such as food, cloth, fertilizers, building materials, oil, minerals, electrical products; also deals with technical drawing and packaging; assists in the establishment of national bodies and collaborates with international standards activities; Sec.-Gen. M. SAWAF. Publs. *Annual Report* (French and English), *Quarterly Bulletin* (Arabic and English), *Standard Specification* (Arabic, English and French) and information pamphlets.

Arab Postal Union: P.O.B. 7999, Dubai, United Arab Emirates; f. 1954; aims: to establish more strict postal relations between the Arab countries than those laid down by the Universal Postal Union, to pursue the development and modernization of postal services in member countries. Sec.-Gen. HUSSEIN AL-HANADAN. Publs. *Bulletin* (monthly), *Review* (quarterly), *News* (annually) and occasional studies.

Arab Satellite Communication Organization (ASCO): P.O.B. 1638, Riyadh, Saudi Arabia; plans ARABSAT project, a satellite to be launched in 1984 from the European Space Agency's launching site in French Guiana, for the improvement of telephone, telex, data transmission and radio and television in Arab countries; Dir.-Gen. Dr. ALI AL-MASSHAT.

Arab States Broadcasting Union (ASBU): P.O.B. 54, 62 Nahj Ibn Bassam, Tunis, Tunisia; f. 1955 to promote Arab fraternity, to acquaint the world with the Arab nations, co-ordinate and study broadcasting subjects, to exchange expertise and technical co-operation in broadcasting. Mems.: 21 Arab radio and TV stations and four foreign associates. Sec.-Gen. ABDALLAH SHAKROUN. Publs. *Arab Broadcasts* (monthly, in Arabic), *ASBU Review* (quarterly, in English), *Broadcasting Studies and Researches* (irregular), *Broadcast Reports* (irregular).

Arab Telecommunications Union: P.O.B. 28015, Baghdad, Iraq; f. 1958; to co-ordinate and develop telecommunications between member countries; to exchange technical aid and encourage research. Sec.-Gen. SALEM KALAF IBRAHIM AL-ANI. Publs. *Economic and Technical Studies*; *Arab Telecommunications Union Journal* (quarterly).

Arab Organization for Social Defence Against Crime: P.O.B. 1341, 13 Abu Anan St., Rabat, Morocco; f. 1960 to study causes and remedies for crime and the treatment of criminals; Sec.-Gen. Dr. MOHAMED SHADADI; the organization consists of three bureaux:

Arab Bureau for Narcotics.
Arab Bureau for Prevention of Crime.
Arab Bureau of Criminal Police.

EXTERNAL RELATIONS

Arab League Offices and Information Centres abroad.

Set up by the Arab League to co-ordinate work at all levels among Arab embassies abroad. The Arab League Office in New Delhi has been given full diplomatic status.

Argentina: Oficina de la Liga de los Estados Arabes, Callao 1319, Buenos Aires.

Belgium: Bureau de la Ligue des Etats Arabes, 106 Ave. F. D. Roosevelt, Brussels 1040.

Brazil: Missão de Liga dos Estados Arabes, Sqs. 105, Bloco K, Apt. 201, 70000 Brasília, D.F.

Canada: Arab Information Centre, 170 Laurier Ave., West, Suite 709, Ottawa, Ontario.

Chile: Representación de la Liga de los Estados Arabes, Avda. Eliodoro Yáñez 809, Dept. 88, Santiago de Chile.

France: Bureau de la Ligue des Etats Arabes, 138 blvd. Haussmann, Paris 8.

Federal Republic of Germany: Delegation von der Liga der Arabischen Staaten, Friedrich Wilhelm Strasse 2A, Bonn 53.

India: League of Arab States Mission, 62 Golf Links, New Delhi 110003.

Italy: Arab League Office, Piazzale Belle Arti no. 6, Rome.

Japan: Office of the League of Arab States, 1-1-12 Moto Azabu, Minato-ku 106, Tokyo.

Spain: Oficina de la Liga de los Estados Arabes, Alcala 89-20 Derecha, Madrid 9.

Switzerland: Délégation de la Ligue des Etats Arabes, 9 rue du Valais, 1202 Geneva.

United Kingdom: Arab Information Office, 52 Green St., London, W.1.

U.S.A.: Arab Information Center, 14 Third Ave., New York, N.Y. 10017.

Arab Information Center, 18 South Michigan Ave., Chicago, Ill. 60603.

Arab Information Center, Suite 1302, Hartford Bldg., Dallas, Tex. 75201.

Arab Information Center, Suite 666, 235 Montgomery Ave., San Francisco, Calif. 94104.

Arab Information Center, 1875 Connecticut Ave., N.W., Suite 1110, Washington, D.C. 20009.

Arab League Representatives:

Ethiopia: P.O.B. 5768, Addis Ababa.

Kenya: Ucini House, 10th Floor, P.O.B. 30770, Nairobi.

Nigeria: Post Box 6916, 55 Ademola St., Ikoyi, Lagos.

Senegal: 3 place de l'Indépendance, P.O.B. 3122, Dakar.

RECORD OF EVENTS

1945	Pact of the Arab League signed, March.
1946	Cultural Treaty signed.
1950	Joint Defence and Economic Co-operation Treaty.
1952	Agreements on extradition, writs and letters of request, nationality of Arabs outside their country of origin.
1953	Formation of Economic Council. Convention on the privileges and immunities of the League.
1954	Nationality Agreement.
1956	Agreement on the adoption of a Common Tariff Nomenclature. Sudan joins Arab League.
1957	Cultural Agreement with UNESCO signed, November.
1958	Co-operation Agreement between the Arab League and the International Labour Organisation.
1959	First Arab Oil Congress, Cairo, April.
1960	Inauguration of new Arab League HQ at Midan Al Tahrir, Cairo, March.
1961	Kuwait joins League. Syrian Arab Republic rejoins League as independent member. Agreement with WHO on exchange of medical information, May.

1962	Arab Economic Unity Agreement. U.A.R. announced intentions of leaving Arab League.
1963	U.A.R. resumes active membership of League, March.
1964	First Summit Conference of Arab Kings and Presidents, Cairo, January. First session of the Council of Arab Information Ministers, Cairo, March. First meeting of Economic Unity Council, June. Arab Common Market approved by Arab Economic Unity Council, August. Second Summit Conference welcomes establishment of Palestine Liberation Organization, September. First Conference of Arab Ministers of Communications, Beirut, November.
1965	Arab Common Market established, January.
1969	Fifth summit Conference, Rabat. Call for mobilization of all Arab Nations against Israel.
1971	Bahrain, Qatar and Oman admitted to Arab League, September.
1973	Mauritania admitted to Arab League, December.
1974	Somalia admitted to Arab League, February.
1977	Djibouti admitted to membership, September.

1977	Tripoli Declaration, December. Decision of Algeria, Iraq, Libya and Yemen P.D.R. to boycott League meetings in Egypt in response to President Sadat's visit to Israel.	

1978   69th meeting of Arab League Council in Cairo, March, boycotted by "rejectionist" states. Resolutions calling for an emergency summit to settle differences within the League and for the establishment of an Arab Solidarity Committee to be chaired by President Nimeri of Sudan. All members except Egypt were present at a Council meeting in Baghdad in November. A number of resolutions were adopted to be taken should Egypt sign a peace treaty with Israel of which the three principal ones were: diplomatic rupture with Egypt, transfer of the League's headquarters from Cairo, and the economic boycott of Sadat's government.

1979   Council meeting in Baghdad, March: various resolutions were adopted of which the main points were: to withdraw Arab ambassadors from Egypt; to recommend severance of political and diplomatic relations with Egypt; to suspend Egypt's membership of the League on the date of the signing of the peace treaty with Israel; to make the city of Tunis the temporary HQ of the League, its Secretariat, ministerial councils and permanent technical committees; to condemn United States' policy regarding its role in concluding the Camp David agreements and the peace treaty; to halt all bank loans, deposits, guarantees or facilities, as well as all financial or technical contributions and aid to Egypt; to prohibit trade exchanges with the Egyptian state and with private establishments dealing with Israel.

1980   Meeting of Arab Foreign and Economic Ministers (as the Arab Economic and Social Council), Amman, July. An Iraqi plan for investment of at least $10,000 million over ten years, to aid

development in poorer Arab states (particularly Djibouti, Mauritania, Somalia, Sudan and the two Yemens), was discussed. The November summit conference in Amman was boycotted by the Palestine Liberation Organization, Algeria, Lebanon, Libya, Syria and the People's Democratic Republic of Yemen, maintaining that the conference should have been postponed because of the serious differences in the Arab world over the Iran-Iraq war and the approach to negotiations on Israel. The summit conference agreed to set up a $5,000 million fund for the benefit of poorer Arab states, with Iraq, Kuwait, Qatar, Saudi Arabia and the United Arab Emirates as donors: assistance was to take the form of 20-year development loans, and the fund was to be administered by the Arab Fund for Social and Economic Development (*q.v.*). The conference also approved a wider "Strategy for Joint Arab Economic Action", covering pan-Arab development planning up to the year 2000.

1981   In March the Council of ministers set up a conciliation mission to try to improve relations between Morocco and Mauritania.

Extraordinary meeting of Arab Foreign Ministers in May (on Lebanon), and June (following the Israeli attack on an Iraqi nuclear reactor).

Twelfth summit conference, Fez, Morocco, November. The meeting was suspended after a few hours, following disagreement over a Saudi Arabian proposal known as the Fahd Plan, which includes not only the Arab demands on behalf of the Palestinians, as approved by the UN General Assembly, but also an implied *de facto* recognition of Israel.

1982   In February the conference of Arab Ministers set up a ministerial commission to consider retaliatory measures against states supporting Israel.

PUBLICATIONS

Information Department: *Information Bulletin* (Arabic and English); also bulletins of treaties and agreements concluded among the member states.

New York Office: *Arab World* (monthly), and *News and Views*.

Geneva Office: *Le Monde Arabe* (monthly), and *Nouvelles du Monde Arabe* (weekly).

Buenos Aires Office: *Arabia Review* (monthly).

Paris Office: *Actualités Arabes* (fortnightly).
Brasília Office: *Oriente Arabe* (monthly).
Rome Office: *Rassegna del Mondo Arabo* (monthly).
London Office: *The Arab* (monthly).
New Delhi Office: *Al Arab* (monthly).
Bonn Office: *Arabische Korrespondenz* (fortnightly).
Ottawa Office: *Spotlight on the Arab World* (fortnightly), *The Arab Case* (monthly).

THE PACT OF THE LEAGUE OF ARAB STATES
(March 22nd, 1945)

Article 1

The League of Arab States is composed of the independent Arab States which have signed this Pact.

Any independent Arab state has the right to become a member of the League. If it desires to do so, it shall submit a request which will be deposited with the Permanent Secretariat-General and submitted to the Council at the first meeting held after submission of the request.

Article 2

The League has as its purpose the strengthening of the relations between the member states; the co-ordination of their policies in order to achieve co-operation between them and to safeguard their independence and sovereignty; and a general concern with the affairs and interests of the Arab countries. It has also as its purpose the close co-operation of the member states, with due regard to the organization and circumstances of each state, on the following matters:

- (a) Economic and financial affairs, including commercial relations, customs, currency, and questions of agriculture and industry.
- (b) Communications: this includes railways, roads, aviation, navigation, telegraphs and posts.
- (c) Cultural affairs.
- (d) Nationality, passports, visas, execution of judgments, and extradition of criminals.
- (e) Social affairs.
- (f) Health problems.

Article 3

The League shall possess a Council composed of the representatives of the member states of the League; each state shall have a single vote, irrespective of the number of its representatives.

It shall be the task of the Council to achieve the realization of the objectives of the League and to supervise the execution of agreements which the member states have concluded on the questions enumerated in the preceding article, or on any other questions.

It likewise shall be the Council's task to decide upon the means by which the League is to co-operate with the international bodies to be created in the future in order to guarantee security and peace and regulate economic and social relations.

Article 4

For each of the questions listed in Article 2 there shall be set up a special committee in which the member states of the League shall be represented. These committees shall be charged with the task of laying down the principles and extent of co-operation. Such principles shall be formulated as draft agreements, to be presented to the Council for examination preparatory to their submission to the aforesaid states.

Representatives of the other Arab countries may take part in the work of the aforesaid committees. The Council shall determine the conditions under which these representatives may be permitted to participate and the rules governing such representation.

Article 5

Any resort to force in order to resolve disputes arising between two or more member states of the League is prohibited. If there should arise among them a difference which does not concern a state's independence, sovereignty, or territorial integrity, and if the parties to the dispute have recourse to the Council for the settlement of this difference, the decision of the Council shall then be enforceable and obligatory.

In such a case, the states between whom the difference has arisen shall not participate in the deliberations and decisions of the Council.

The Council shall mediate in all differences which threaten to lead to war between two member states, or a member state and a third state, with a view to bringing about their reconciliation.

Decisions of arbitration and mediation shall be taken by majority vote.

Article 6

In case of aggression or threat of aggression by one state against a member state, the state which has been attacked or threatened with aggression may demand the immediate convocation of the Council.

The Council shall by unanimous decision determine the measures necessary to repulse the aggression. If the aggressor is a member state, his vote shall not be counted in determining unanimity.

If, as a result of the attack, the government of the State attacked finds itself unable to communicate with the Council, that state's representative in the Council shall have the right to request the convocation of the Council for the purpose indicated in the foregoing paragraph. In the event that this representative is unable to communicate with the Council, any member state of the League shall have the right to request the convocation of the Council.

Article 7

Unanimous decisions of the Council shall be binding upon all member states of the League; majority decisions shall be binding only upon those states which have accepted them.

In either case the decisions of the Council shall be enforced in each member state according to its respective basic laws.

Article 8

Each member state shall respect the systems of government established in the other member states and regard them as exclusive concerns of those states. Each shall pledge to abstain from any action calculated to change established systems of government.

Article 9

States of the League which desire to establish closer co-operation and stronger bonds than are provided by this Pact may conclude agreements to that end.

Treaties and agreements already concluded or to be concluded in the future between a member state and another state shall not be binding or restrictive upon other members.

Article 10

The permanent seat of the League of Arab States is established in Cairo. The Council may, however, assemble at any other place it may designate.

Article 11

The Council of the League shall convene in ordinary session twice a year, in March and in September. It shall convene in extraordinary session upon the request of two member states of the League whenever the need arises.

Article 12

The League shall have a permanent Secretariat-General which shall consist of a Secretary-General, Assistant Secretaries, and an appropriate number of officials.

The Council of the League shall appoint the Secretary-General by a majority of two-thirds of the states of the League. The Secretary-General, with the approval of the Council, shall appoint the Assistant Secretaries and the principal officials of the League.

The Council of the League shall establish an administrative regulation for the functions of the Secretariat-General and matters relating to the Staff.

The Secretary-General shall have the rank of Ambassador and the Assistant Secretaries that of Ministers Plenipotentiary.

The first Secretary-General of the League is named in an Annex to this Pact.

Article 13

The Secretary-General shall prepare the draft of the budget of the League and shall submit it to the Council for approval before the beginning of each fiscal year.

The Council shall fix the share of the expenses to be borne by each state of the League. This share may be reconsidered if necessary.

Article 14

The members of the Council of the League as well as the members of the committees and the officials who are to be designated in the administrative regulation shall enjoy diplomatic privileges and immunity when engaged in the exercise of their functions.

The building occupied by the organs of the League shall be inviolable.

Article 15

The first meeting of the Council shall be convened at the invitation of the head of the Egyptian Government. Thereafter it shall be convened at the invitation of the Secretary-General.

The representatives of the member states of the League shall alternately assume the presidency of the Council at each of its ordinary sessions.

Article 16

Except in cases specifically indicated in this Pact, a majority vote of the Council shall be sufficient to make enforceable decisions on the following matters:

(a) Matters relating to personnel.

(b) Adoption of the budget of the League.

(c) Establishment of the administrative regulations for the Council, the Committees, and the Secretariat-General.

(d) Decisions to adjourn the sessions.

Article 17

Each member state of the League shall deposit with the Secretariat-General one copy of every treaty or agreement concluded or to be concluded in the future between itself and another member state of the League or a third state.

Article 18
(deals with withdrawal)

Article 19
(deals with amendment)

Article 20
(deals with ratification)

Annex Regarding Palestine

Since the termination of the last great war the rule of the Ottoman Empire over the Arab countries, among them Palestine, which had become detached from that Empire, has come to an end. She has come to be autonomous, not subordinate to any other state.

The Treaty of Lausanne proclaimed that her future was to be settled by the parties concerned.

However, even though she was as yet unable to control her own affairs, the Covenant of the League (of Nations) in 1919 made provision for a regime based upon recognition of her independence.

Her international existence and independence in the legal sense cannot, therefore, be questioned, any more than could the independence of the other Arab countries.

Although the outward manifestations of this independence have remained obscured for reasons beyond her control, this should not be allowed to interfere with her participation in the work of the Council of the League.

The states signatory to the Pact of the Arab League are therefore of the opinion that, considering the special circumstances of Palestine and until that Country can effectively exercise its independence, the Council of the League should take charge of the selection of an Arab representative from Palestine to take part in its work.

Annex Regarding Co-operation with Countries which are not Members of the Council of the League

Whereas the member states of the League will have to deal in the Council as well as in the committees with matters which will benefit and affect the Arab world at large;

And whereas the Council has to take into account the aspirations of the Arab countries which are not members of the Council and has to work toward their realization;

Now therefore, it particularly behoves the states signatory to the Pact of the Arab League to enjoin the Council of the League, when considering the admission of those countries to participation in the committees referred to in the Pact, that it should do its utmost to co-operate with them, and furthermore, that it should spare no effort to learn their needs and understand their aspirations and hopes; and that it should work thenceforth for their best interests and the safeguarding of their future with all the political means at its disposal.

Organization of Arab Petroleum Exporting Countries—OAPEC

P.O.B. 20501, Safat, Kuwait City, Kuwait

Telephone: 448200.

Established 1968 to safeguard the interests of members and determine ways and means for their co-operation in various forms of economic activity in the petroleum industry.

MEMBERS

Algeria	Kuwait	Syria
Bahrain	Libya	Tunisia
Egypt*	Qatar	United Arab Emirates
Iraq	Saudi Arabia	

* Egypt's membership was suspended from April 17th, 1979.

ORGANIZATION

(June 1982)

COUNCIL OF MINISTERS

Supreme authority of the Organization, responsible for drawing up its general policy, directing its activities and laying down its governing rules. The Council consists normally of the Ministers of Petroleum of the member states. Meets twice yearly as a minimum requirement and may hold extraordinary sessions. Chairmanship on annual rotation basis.

EXECUTIVE BUREAU

Assists the Council to direct the management of the Organization, approves staff regulations, reviews the budget, and refers it to the Council, considers matters relating to the Organization's agreements and activities and draws up the agenda for the Council. The Bureau consists of senior officials from each member state. Chairmanship is by rotation. The Bureau convenes four times a year as a minimum requirement.

Budget (1981 draft): 2,358,000 Kuwaiti dinars.

SECRETARIAT

Secretary-General: Dr. ALI AHMAD ATTIGA (Libya).

Assistant Secretaries-General: ABDUL AZIZ AL-WATTARI, Dr. ADNAN MUSTAPHA.

Besides the Office of the Secretary-General, which assists the Secretary-General in following up resolutions and recommendations of the Council, there are seven departments: Administration and Financial, Legal, Economic, Information and International Relations, Oil Projects, Exploration and Production, Library and Documentation. There is also a Training Unit.

JUDICIAL BOARD

The Board comprises 11 judges from Arab countries. Its task is to settle differences in interpretation of the OAPEC Charter and disputes among member countries over petroleum matters falling within the Organization's jurisdiction and not under the sovereignty of member countries.

Chairman: Shaikh ABDUL RAHMAN AL-MANSOURI.

JOINT UNDERTAKINGS

Arab Engineering and Consulting Company—AECC: Abu Dhabi; f. 1980 to give support to national engineering firms by providing Arab experts, organizing a common operational base and supervising the training of Arab engineers. Authorized capital $20 million; subscribed capital $12 million.

Chairman: MAHMOUD HAMRA KROUHA.

General Manager: AZIZ AMARA KORBA.

Arab Maritime Petroleum Transport Company—AMPTC: f. 1973 in Kuwait to undertake transport of crude oil gas, refined products and petrochemicals, and thus to increase Arab participation in the tanker transport industry; capital authorized and subscribed $500 million. In January 1979 the Chairman requested that Arab states should demand that 20 per cent of their oil exports be carried in Arab ships; at that time about one-third of the AMPTC fleet was lying idle. Mems.: Algeria, Bahrain, Iraq, Kuwait, Libya, Qatar, Saudi Arabia, United Arab Emirates.

Chairman: ABDUL AZIZ AL-TURKI.

Managing Director: ABDUL RAHMAN SULTAN.

Arab Petroleum Investments Corporation—APICORP: P.O.B. 448, Dhahran Airport, Saudi Arabia; f. 1975 to finance petroleum investments in the Arab world. Projects financed by 1980 included gas liquefaction plants, petrochemicals, tankers, oil refineries and fertilizers. Authorized capital: 3,600 million Saudi riyals; subscribed capital: 1,200 million Saudi riyals.

Chairman: JAMAL JAWA.

General Manager: Dr. NUREDDIN FARRAG.

Arab Petroleum Services Company—APSC: established January 1977 at Tripoli, Libya. The company provides petroleum services through the establishment of one or more companies specializing in various activities. Also concerned with training of specialized personnel. Authorized capital: 100 million Libyan dinars; subscribed capital: 15 million Libyan dinars.

Chairman: AYYAD AL-DALY.

General Manager: HOCINE MALTI.

Arab Drilling and Workover Company: established 1977 as a subsidiary of APSC.

Arab Petroleum Training Institute: f. 1979 in Baghdad.

Chairman of Board of Trustees: Dr. HASAN ALI AL-NAJI.

General Manager: BURHAN EDDIN DAGHESTANI.

Arab Shipbuilding and Repair Yard Company: f. 1974 in Bahrain to undertake all activities related to repairs, service and eventually construction of vessels for the transport of hydrocarbons. In December 1977 the company opened a dry dock in Bahrain. Capital authorized and subscribed $340 million.

Chairman: Sheikh DAIJ IBN KHALIFAH AL-KHALIFAH.

General Manager: ANTONIO MACHADOLOPES.

Organization of the Islamic Conference

Secretariat-General, Kilo 6, Mecca Rd., P.O.B. 178, Jeddah, Saudi Arabia

Telephone: 6873880.

Formally established in May 1971 following a summit meeting of Muslim Heads of State at Rabat, Morocco, in September 1969, and the Islamic Foreign Ministers' Conference in Jeddah in March 1970, and in Karachi, Pakistan in December 1970.

MEMBERS

Afghanistan*	Guinea	Mali	Somalia
Algeria	Guinea-Bissau	Mauritania	Sudan
Bahrain	Indonesia	Morocco	Syria
Bangladesh	Iran	Niger	Tunisia
Cameroon	Iraq	Oman	Turkey
Chad	Jordan	Pakistan	Uganda
The Comoros	Kuwait	Palestine Liberation	United Arab Emirates
Djibouti	Lebanon	Organization	Upper Volta
Egypt*	Libya	Qatar	Yemen Arab Republic
Gabon	Malaysia	Saudi Arabia	Yemen, People's Democratic
The Gambia	Maldives	Senegal	Republic

* Egypt's membership was suspended in May 1979 and Afghanistan's in January 1980.

Nigeria and the Turkish Federated State of Cyprus have observer status.

AIMS

(as set out in the Charter of the Organization, adopted in 1972)

1. To promote Islamic solidarity among member states;

2. To consolidate co-operation among member states in the economic, social, cultural, scientific and other vital fields, and to arrange consultations among member states belonging to international organizations;

3. To endeavour to eliminate racial segregation and discrimination and to eradicate colonialism in all its forms;

4. To take necessary measures to support international peace and security founded on justice;

5. To co-ordinate all efforts for the safeguard of the Holy Places and support of the struggle of the people of Palestine, and help them to regain their rights and liberate their land;

6. To strengthen the struggle of all Muslim people with a view to safeguarding their dignity, independence and national rights; and

7. To create a suitable atmosphere for the promotion of co-operation and understanding among member states and other countries.

ORGANIZATION

(June 1982)

SUMMIT CONFERENCES

The supreme body of the Organization is the Conference of Heads of State, which met in 1969 at Rabat, Morocco, in 1974 at Lahore, Pakistan, and in January 1981 at Mecca, Saudi Arabia, when it was decided that summit conferences would be held every three years in future.

CONFERENCES OF FOREIGN MINISTERS

Conferences take place annually. An extraordinary session was held for the first time in January 1980 to discuss the situation in Afghanistan: further extraordinary sessions were held in July, September and October.

SECRETARIAT

Secretary-General: HABIB CHATTI (Tunisia).

ISLAMIC COMMISSION FOR ECONOMIC, CULTURAL AND SOCIAL AFFAIRS

The Commission supervises the implementation of the resolutions of the Council of Foreign Ministers, and makes recommendations to the Council. The Commission meets twice a year.

ISLAMIC SOLIDARITY FUND

The Fund, administered by a permanent Council, was established in 1974 to meet the needs of Islamic unity. Expenditure (about $20 million in 1980/81) is allocated mainly to the following areas: emergency aid; mosques; hospitals and schools; Islamic centres and universities.

COMMITTEE OF ISLAMIC SOLIDARITY WITH THE PEOPLES OF THE SAHEL

The Committee's purpose is to provide emergency food aid to countries in the African Sahel region affected by persistent drought.

AL-QUDS (JERUSALEM) COMMITTEE

Established 1975 to implement the resolutions of the Islamic Conference on the status of Jerusalem; since 1979 has met at the level of Foreign Ministers under the chairmanship of King Hassan of Morocco. At its meeting in April 1981 the Committee decided to start a campaign to publicize the Islamic point of view on the status of Jerusalem and the rights of the Palestinians.

Other subsidiary bodies of the Organization include:

International Islamic News Agency: P.O. Box 5054, Prince Fahd St., Jeddah, Saudi Arabia; f. 1972. Mems.: 42 Islamic states. Dir.-Gen. SAFDAR ALI QURESHI; Editor-in-Charge SHAH ALAM. Publ. *News Bulletin* (3 a year).

Islamic Centre for the Development of Trade: Tangier, Morocco; f. 1981.

Islamic Centre for Statistical, Economic and Social Research: Ankara, Turkey; f. 1978.

Islamic Centre for Technical and Vocational Training and Research: Tongi, Dacca, Bangladesh; f. 1979, expected to be operational 1983, to provide skilled technicians for Islamic countries; the Centre aims to begin by training 650 students (including 250 teachers, 300 technicians and 100 craftsmen), later increasing to 1,150.

Islamic Economic Chamber: NBP Bldg., Kahkashan, Clifton Rd., Karachi, Pakistan; f. 1980; 41 mems.; Pres. Sheikh ISMAIL ABY DAWOOD; Sec.-Gen. SAMI CANSEN ONARAN.

Islamic Development Bank (*see* page 184).

Islamic States Broadcasting Organization: Jeddah, Saudi Arabia.

Research Centre for Islamic History, Art and Culture: Istanbul, Turkey; f. 1982.

World Centre for Islamic Education: P.O. Box 1034, King Abdulaziz University, Mecca, Saudi Arabia; f. 1980 to uphold Islamic principles in every branch of education; affiliated Islamic Education and Research Centres are to be set up in member states; Dir.-Gen. Dr. SYED ALI ASHRAF (Pakistan).

At the summit conference in January 1981 it was decided that an Islamic Court of Justice should be established.

ACTIVITIES

The first summit conference of Islamic leaders (representing 24 states) took place in 1969 following the burning of the Al Aqsa Mosque in Jerusalem. At this conference it was decided that Islamic governments should "consult together with a view to promoting close co-operation and mutual assistance in the economic, scientific, cultural and spiritual fields, inspired by the immortal teachings of Islam". Thereafter the Foreign Ministers of the countries concerned met annually, and adopted the Charter of the Organization of the Islamic Conference in 1972.

At the second Islamic summit conference (Lahore, 1974), the Islamic Solidarity Fund was established, together with a committee of representatives which later evolved into the Islamic Commission for Economic, Social and Cultural Affairs. Subsequently, numerous other subsidiary bodies have been set up (*see* above).

A meeting of Ministers of Industry was held in February 1982, and agreed to promote industrial co-operation, including joint ventures in agricultural machinery, engineering and other basic industries.

The Organization is also active at a political level. From the beginning it called for vacation of Arab territories by Israel, recognition of the rights of Palestinians and of the Palestine Liberation Organization as their sole legitimate representative, and the restoration of Jerusalem to Arab rule. The 1981 summit conference called for a *jihad* (holy war—though not necessarily in a military sense) "for the liberation of Jerusalem and the occupied territories"; this was to include an Islamic economic boycott of Israel.

The first extraordinary Conference of Foreign Ministers

was held in Islamabad, Pakistan, in January 1980. The member states called for the immediate and unconditional withdrawal of Soviet troops from Afghanistan and suspended Afghanistan's membership of the organization. The Conference also reaffirmed the importance of the Iranian Islamic Republic's sovereignty, territorial integrity and political independence, and adopted a resolution opposing any foreign pressures exerted on Islamic countries in general and Iran in particular. The Conference further asked members not to participate in the 1980 Olympics unless the Soviet troops had withdrawn from Afghanistan; and adopted a resolution condemning armed aggression against Somalia and denouncing the presence of military forces of the Soviet Union and some of its allies in the Horn of Africa.

The 11th Conference of Ministers took place in Islamabad in May 1980: the problems in Afghanistan and Iran continued to be major topics of discussion, and a special committee was set up to conduct consultations on Afghanistan. Mediation in the Gulf war between Iran and Iraq was also attempted: a "goodwill mission", headed by the Secretary General of the Organization, was established in September 1980 and suggested a ceasefire supervised by an observer force of troops drawn from Islamic countries, but the terms were rejected by the protagonists.

The Third Islamic summit conference (Taif, Saudi Arabia, January 1981) repeated the demand for Soviet withdrawal from Afghanistan and affirmed Afghanistan's political independence. It also decided to continue attempts at mediation between Iran and Iraq (*see* also chapters on Afghanistan, Iran and Iraq).

Organization of the Petroleum Exporting Countries—OPEC

Obere Donaustrasse 93, 1020 Vienna, Austria

Telephone: 26 55 11.

Established 1960 to unify and co-ordinate members' petroleum policies and to safeguard their interests generally

The OPEC Fund for International Development is described on page 199.

MEMBERS*

Algeria	Iraq	Qatar
Ecuador	Kuwait	Saudi Arabia
Gabon	Libya	United Arab Emirates
Indonesia	Nigeria	Venezuela
Iran		

* OPEC members produced 45 per cent of world petroleum in 1980 (compared with a peak of 55.5 per cent in 1973). In 1982 OPEC countries were estimated to possess 67 per cent of known petroleum reserves, and 32.8 per cent of known natural gas reserves.

ORGANIZATION

(June 1982)

THE CONFERENCE

Supreme authority of the Organization, responsible for the formulation of its general policy. It consists of representatives of member countries, decides upon reports and recommendations submitted by the Board of Governors. Meets at least twice a year. It approves the appointment of Governors from each country and elects the Chairman of the Board of Governors. It works on the unanimity principle.

THE BOARD OF GOVERNORS

Directs management of the Organization; implements resolutions of the Conference; draws up an annual Budget. It consists of one Governor for each member country, and meets at least twice a year.

THE ECONOMIC COMMISSION

A specialized body operating within the framework of the Secretariat, with a view to assisting the Organization in promoting stability in international oil prices at equitable levels; consists of a Board, national representatives and a commission staff; the Board meets at least twice a year.

SECRETARIAT

Secretary-General: Dr. MARC S. NAN NGUEMA (Gabon).

Deputy Secretary-General: Dr. FADHIL AL-CHALABI.

Office of the Secretary-General: Provides him with executive assistance in carrying out contacts with governments, organizations and delegations, in matters of protocol and in the preparation for and co-ordination of meetings.

Research Division:

Energy Studies Department: Conducts a continuous programme for research in energy and related matters; monitors, forecasts and analyses developments in the energy and petrochemical industries; and the evaluation of hydrocarbons and products and their non-energy uses.

Economics and Finance Department: Analyses economic and financial issues of significant interest; in particular those related to international financial and monetary matters, and to the international petroleum industry.

Data Services Department:

Computer Section: Maintains and expands information services to support the research activities of the Secretariat and those of member countries.

Statistics Unit: Collects, collates and analyses statistical information from both primary and secondary sources.

Personnel and Administration Department: Responsible for all organization methods, provision of administrative services for all meetings, personnel matters, budgets, accounting and internal control.

Public Information Department: Responsible for a central public relations programme; production and distribution of publications, films, slides and tapes; and communication of OPEC objectives and decisions to the world at large.

Legal Affairs Unit: Undertakes special and other in-house legal studies and reports to ascertain where the best interests of the Organization and member countries lie.

OPEC News Agency: f. 1980 to provide information on OPEC to about 70 countries and counteract inaccurate reporting by some other sources: covers member countries' petroleum and energy issues; co-operation with other developing countries; news on oil companies; technical and policy information on the upstream and downstream sectors of the industry; energy supply and demand.

Head: GONZALO PLAZA.

RECORD OF EVENTS

1960 First OPEC conference held in Baghdad, September; meetings to be held twice yearly, secretariat to be formed.

1961 Second conference, Caracas, January. Qatar admitted to membership; Board of Governors formed and statutes agreed.

1962 Fourth conference, Geneva, April and June. Protests addressed to oil companies against price cuts introduced in August 1960. Indonesia and Libya admitted to membership.

1964 Seventh conference, Jakarta, November. Settlement of the royalties issue negotiated, giving producers an increased share of profits. OPEC Economic Commission established.

1965 Ninth conference, Tripoli, July. Agreement on a two-year joint production programme, implemented from 1965 to 1967, to limit annual growth in output to secure adequate prices.

1967 Abu Dhabi admitted to membership.

1968 Fifteenth conference (extraordinary), Beirut, January. Accepted offer on elimination of discounts submitted by oil companies following negotiations in November 1967.

1969 Algeria admitted to membership.

1970 Twenty-first conference, Caracas, December. Tax on income of oil companies raised to 55 per cent.

1971 Negotiations between OPEC and oil companies on Gulf oil prices broke down, January; OPEC members prepared to legislate unilaterally to set posted prices and tax rates.
Twenty-second conference (extraordinary), Teheran, February. Five-year agreement between the six producing countries in the Gulf and 23 international oil companies (Teheran Agreement).

Twenty-fourth conference, Vienna, July. Nigeria admitted to membership.

1972 Meetings between OPEC and oil companies, Geneva, January. Companies agreed to adjust oil revenues of the largest producers after changes in currency exchange rates (Geneva Agreement).

1973 Meeting between OPEC and oil companies, Cairo, April, discussed OPEC's demand for compensation following 10 per cent devaluation of U.S. dollar in February.
Agreement with companies reached under which posted prices of crude oil were raised by 11.9 per cent and a mechanism installed to make monthly adjustments to prices in future (Second Geneva Agreement).
Thirty-fourth conference, Vienna, June. Ministerial Committee formed to review world energy situation. Thirty-fifth conference (extraordinary), Vienna, September. Gulf states proposed negotiations with

oil companies to revise the Teheran Agreement. Negotiations broke down on October 12th. On 16th, the Gulf states held a meeting and, refusing to negotiate further with the companies, unilaterally declared 70 per cent increases in posted prices, from $3.01 to $5.11 per barrel.
Thirty-sixth conference, Teheran, December. Posted price increased by nearly 130 per cent from $5.11 to $11.65 per barrel from January 1st, 1974. Ecuador admitted to full membership, Gabon became an associate member.

1974 Thirty-seventh conference (extraordinary), Geneva, January. As a result of Saudi opposition to the December price increase, prices were held at current level for first quarter (and subsequently for the remainder of 1974). Abu Dhabi's membership transferred to United Arab Emirates.
Meeting, Quito, June, increased royalties charged to oil companies from 12.5 to 14.5 per cent in all member states except Saudi Arabia.
Meeting, Vienna, September, increased governmental take by about 3.5 per cent through further increases in royalties on equity crude to 16.67 per cent and in taxes to 65.65 per cent, except in Saudi Arabia.

1975 OPEC's first summit conference was held in Algiers in March. Gabon admitted to full membership. Meeting in Gabon in June, Conference proposed that OPEC oil prices should be quoted in Special Drawing Rights (SDRs) of the IMF, instead of U.S. dollars. It was also proposed that prices should be indexed to world inflation rates.
A ministerial meeting in September agreed to raise prices by 10 per cent for the period until June 1976. It referred the question of pricing oil in SDRs to the committee of Finance Ministers. The year's second meeting of Conference, in Vienna in December, ended abruptly when a terrorist gang kidnapped some of the participants.

1976 The OPEC special fund for international development was created in May.
Meeting in Bali, Indonesia, in May, Conference allowed the prices agreed in September 1975 to continue.
At the year's second meeting of Conference, in Doha, Qatar, December, a general 15 per cent rise in basic prices was proposed and supported by eleven member states. This was to take place in two stages: a 10 per cent rise as of January 1st, 1977, and a further 5 per cent rise as of July 1st, 1977. However, Saudi Arabia and the United Arab Emirates decided to raise their prices by 5 per cent only.

1977 Forty-ninth conference, Saltsjöbaden, near Stockholm, Sweden, July.
Following an earlier waiver by 9 members of the 5 per cent second stage of the price rise agreed at Doha, Saudi Arabia and the United Arab Emirates

1977 **announced** that they would both raise their prices
(cont.) by 5 per cent. As a result, a single level of prices
throughout the organization was restored.

Because of continued disagreements between the
moderates, led by Saudi Arabia and Iran, and the
radicals, led by Algeria, Libya and Iraq, the year's
second conference at Caracas, December, was
unable to settle on an increase in prices.

1978 Informal Consultative Conference, Taif, Saudi
Arabia, May.
Ministerial Committee from six member states
established to draw up long-term pricing and
production strategy. Production ceilings of members
lowered.
Fifty-first conference, Geneva, June. Price levels to
remain stable until the end of 1978. Committee of
Experts, chaired by Kuwait, met in July to consider
ways of compensating for the effects of the depreciation of the U.S. dollar.
At the fifty-second Conference in December 1978 it
was decided to raise prices by instalments of 5 per
cent, 3.8 per cent, 2.3 per cent and 2.7 per cent.
These would bring a rise of 14.5 per cent over nine
months, but an average increase of 10 per cent for
1979.

1979 At an extraordinary meeting in Geneva at the end
of March it was decided to raise prices by 9 per cent.
Many members maintained surcharges they had
imposed in February after Iranian exports were
halted.
Fifty-fourth Conference, Geneva, June. Agreed
minimum and maximum prices which seemed
likely to add between 15 and 20 per cent to import
bills of consumer countries.
Fifty-fifth Conference, Caracas, December. Recommended replenishment of the Opec Fund and
agreed in principle to convert the Fund into a
development agency with its own legal personality.
Decided to set up OPEC News Agency based at the
Secretariat.

1980 Fifty-seventh Conference, Algiers, June. Decided to
set the price for a marker crude at U.S. $32.00 per
barrel, and that the value differentials which could
be added above this ceiling (on account of quality
and geographical location) should not exceed $5.00
per barrel.
It was decided to begin studies on the feasibility of
an OPEC Institute of Higher Education, for
technological research and training.
A Workshop on Energy and Development was held
in July, to discuss constraints on the development
process and the ways of dealing with them.

The planned OPEC summit meeting in Baghdad in
November was postponed indefinitely because of the
Iran-Iraq war; issues which were to have been discussed included the linking of petroleum prices to
growth rates and inflation in Western countries,
and a reappraisal of OPEC aid.
In spite of the war, and the capture of the Iranian
petroleum minister by Iraqis in October, the
scheduled price-fixing meeting of petroleum ministers went ahead in Bali in December, with both
Iranians and Iraqis present. A ceiling price of
U.S. $41.00 per barrel was fixed for premium
crudes.

1981 In May attempts to achieve price reunification were
made, but Saudi Arabia refused to increase its
$32.00 per barrel price unless the higher prices
charged by other countries were lowered. Saudi
Arabia declared that it had been over-producing in
order to bring about a glut and force prices down.
Most of the other OPEC countries agreed to cut
production by 10 per cent so as to reduce the
surplus. An emergency meeting in Geneva in August
again failed to unify prices, although Saudi Arabia
agreed to make a production cut of a million barrels
per day, to be reviewed monthly.

In October OPEC countries agreed to increase the
Saudi marker price by 6 per cent to $34 per barrel,
with a ceiling price of $38 per barrel. This price
structure was intended to remain in force until the
end of 1982. Saudi Arabia also announced that it
would keep its production below 8.5 million b/d.

1982 The continuing world oil glut (resulting from a fall
in demand to a predicted 46 million b/d in 1982,
compared with 52 million in 1979) forced prices
below the official mark of $34 per barrel in some
producer countries. In March an emergency
meeting of petroleum ministers was held in Vienna
and agreed (for the first time in OPEC's history) on
an overall production ceiling of 18 million b/d,
effectively 17.5 million b/d with Saudi Arabia's
separate announcement of a cut to 7 million b/d in
its own production. Measures were taken to support
Nigerian prices following a slump in production:
sanctions were threatened against companies
putting pressure on Nigeria to reduce its prices to
the level of North Sea petroleum.
In May petroleum ministers met in Quito, Ecuador,
and agreed (with the exception of Iran) to maintain the production ceiling for the time being.

FINANCE

1981 budget: 214.85 million Austrian schillings, contributed in equal parts by members.

PUBLICATIONS

OPEC Bulletin (monthly).
Annual Report.
OPEC Member Country Profiles.

OPEC National Oil Company Profiles.
Selected Documents of the International Petroleum Industry.
Annual Statistical Bulletin.

Opec Fund For International Development

P.O.B. 995, 1011 Vienna, Austria

Telephone: 31 55 36-0.

Established by virtue of an agreement signed by all OPEC member countries in Paris on January 28th, 1976.

MEMBERS

Member countries of OPEC (*see* page 196).

AIMS

The OPEC Fund for International Development is a multilateral agency for financial co-operation and assistance. Its objective is to reinforce financial co-operation between OPEC member countries and other developing countries through the provision of financial support to the latter on appropriate terms.

The Fund is empowered to engage in all functions necessary or incidental to the carrying out of its objective. In particular, it is empowered to:

(a) Provide concessional loans for balance-of-payments support;

(b) Provide concessional loans for the implementation of development projects and programmes;

(c) Make contributions and/or provide loans to eligible international agencies; and

(d) Finance technical assistance activities.

In the cases where collective action by OPEC member countries is deemed appropriate, the Fund may be entrusted by its members with the task of an agent acting on their behalf, in particular in their relations with other international financial institutions.

The eligible beneficiaries of the Fund's assistance are the governments of developing countries other than OPEC member countries, and international development agencies whose beneficiaries are developing countries.

ORGANIZATION

(June 1982)

ADMINISTRATION

The Fund is administered by a Ministerial Council and a Governing Board composed of one representative of each Contributing Party to the Fund.

Chairman, Ministerial Council: Cέsar Robalino (Ecuador).

Chairman, Governing Board: Dr. Mahsoun Jalal (Saudi Arabia).

Director-General of the Fund: Dr. Ibrahim Shihata (Kuwait).

FINANCIAL STRUCTURE

The resources of the Fund, whose unit of account is the U.S. dollar, consists of:

(a) contributions by OPEC member countries; and

(b) funds received from operations or otherwise accruing to the Fund.

The initial endowment of the Fund amounted to U.S. $800 million. It has subsequently been boosted by three replenishments which brought the total Fund's resources to about $4,000 million. Other contributions consisted of the profits accruing to some OPEC member countries through the sales of gold held by the International Monetary Fund, and additional payments made by the OPEC member countries through the Fund to the International Fund for Agricultural Development.

OPERATIONS

Requests for the Fund's assistance are to be submitted by eligible beneficiaries to the Director-General of the Fund for evaluation. Approval of such assistance is extended by the Governing Board.

The Fund may entrust an appropriate international development agency, an Executing National Agency of a member or any other qualified agency with the task of technical, economic and financial appraisal of the projects submitted to the Fund. Such appraisal is otherwise to be undertaken by the Fund. Furthermore, the Governing Board may entrust these same agencies or any other qualified agency of a member with the task of the administration of the loans approved by it. Such administration is otherwise to be undertaken by the Fund.

Each member of the Fund designates its Executing National Agency which will act as the channel of communications with the Fund. If required, each Executing National Agency establishes in its records a special account in the name of the Fund, separate from its own accounts.

Contributions to the Fund are voluntary. In June 1981 a meeting of OPEC finance ministers rejected a proposal by Venezuela to make contributions compulsory according to each country's financial position.

By the end of 1981 the Fund had committed a total of U.S. $1,941 million, of which $1,305 million was in 267 direct loans to 79 developing countries, and the remainder consisted of a $435.5 million contribution to the initial resources of the International Fund for Agricultural

Development (IFAD), transfers of $110.72 million to the IMF Trust Fund, and other grants of $89.57 million. Disbursements had reached $1,237 million by the end of 1981.

During 1981 the Fund approved 64 loans of $490 million, and 36 grants of $51 million. A further contribution of $450 million was made from the Fund's resources for the replenishment of IFAD.

OPEC FUND COMMITMENTS AND DISBURSEMENTS IN 1981
(U.S. $ million)

	COMMITMENTS	DISBURSEMENTS
Lending operations:		
Balance-of-payments support	184.10	162.30
Food purchases	117.80	
Petroleum purchases	35.00	
Project financing	206.78	95.91
Energy sector	103.50	
Transport	31.78	
Lines of credit to banks	28.00	
Agriculture and agro-industry	19.50	
Industry	14.00	
Public utilities	10.00	
Programme financing (manufacturing rehabilitation in Zimbabwe)	10.00	0.99
	400.88*	259.20
Grant programme:		
World Food Programme (International Emergency Food Reserve)	25.00	10.00
Common Fund for Commodities (to cover subscriptions of 12 Least Developed Countries)	13.28	—
Technical assistance	12.48	9.50
Research	0.42	0.25
TOTAL	452.06	278.95

* In addition, eight loans worth $88.6 million were approved in 1981 but were not due to be signed until 1982.

Source: OPEC Bulletin.

Other Regional Organizations

These organizations are arranged under the following sub-headings:

Agriculture
Defence
Development
Education and Arts
Finance and Economics
Industrial Relations
International Relations
Law

Medicine
Planning and Administration
Religion and Welfare
Science and Technology
Tourism
Trade and Industry
Transport

AGRICULTURE

Arab Authority for Agricultural Investment and Development (AAAID): P.O.B. 2102, Khartoum, Sudan; f. 1977 to accelerate agricultural development in the Arab world and to ensure food security; activities began in Sudan owing to its great unexplored agricultural potential; launched four companies in Sudan in 1981 dealing with poultry, starch and glucose, dairy produce and vegetables. Mems.: Algeria, Egypt, Iraq, Kuwait, Mauritania, Morocco, Qatar, Saudi Arabia, Somalia, Sudan, Syria, United Arab Emirates.
Chair. OSMAN BADRAN (Egypt).

International Olive Federation (*Fédération internationale d'oléiculture*): Via del Governo Vecchio 3, 00186 Rome, Italy; f. 1934 to promote the interests of olive growers and to effect international co-ordination of efforts to improve methods of growing and manufacturing and to promote the use of olive oil. Mems.: organizations and government departments in Algeria, Argentina, France, Greece, Israel, Italy, Lebanon, Libya, Morocco, Portugal, Spain, Syria, Tunisia; in process of reorganization, 1981.

DEFENCE

Islamic Institute of Defence Technology: 16 Grosvenor Crescent, London, S.W.1, England; f. 1978.
Pres. SALEM AZZAM (Saudi Arabia); Dir.-Gen. Group-Capt. MUKARRAM ALI (Pakistan).

DEVELOPMENT

Afro-Asian Housing Organization (AAHO): P.O.B. 523, 28 Ramses St., Cairo, Egypt; f. 1965 to promote co-operation between African and Asian countries in housing, reconstruction, physical planning and related matters.
Sec.-Gen. HASSAN M. HASSAN (Egypt).

Afro-Asian Rural Reconstruction Organization (AARRO): C/117-118 Defence Colony, New Delhi 110024, India; f. 1962 to restructure the economy of the rural populations of Africa and Asia, and to explore collectively opportunities for co-ordination of efforts for promoting welfare and eradicating hunger, thirst, disease, illiteracy and poverty amongst the rural people; activities include launching of Integrated Rural Development Pilot Projects, organizing international seminars at AARRO's own training centres in Japan and Egypt, and awarding individual fellowships; mems.: 12 African, 15 Asian countries and the Central Union of Agricultural Co-operatives, Japan.
Sec.-Gen. Dr. B. S. MINHAS; Dir. M. R. KAUSHAL (India). Publ. *Rural Reconstruction* (half-yearly).

Near East Foundation: 54 East 64th St., New York, N.Y. 10021, U.S.A.; f. 1930. Aims: to conduct agricultural and educational programmes and demonstrations in order to improve standards of living in underdeveloped areas of the world, primarily the Near East, with technicians at work in Asia and Africa.
Comptroller N. T. WALLIN. Publ. *Annual Report*.

Regional Cooperation for Development: 5 Los Angeles Ave., Blvd. Keshawarz, P.O.B. 3273, Teheran, Iran; f. 1964 as a tripartite arrangement aiming at closer economic, technical and cultural co-operation; mems. co-operate in certain industrial projects and standards, trade, tourism, transport (including the building of road and rail links), communications and cultural affairs. Mems.: Iran, Pakistan, Turkey.
Sec.-Gen. MUKHTAR MASOOD (Pakistan).

EDUCATION AND ARTS

Afro-Asian Writers' Permanent Bureau: c/o AAPSO, 89 Abdel Aziz al-Saoud St., Manial El-Roda, Cairo, Egypt; f. 1958 by Afro-Asian Peoples' Solidarity Organization; Mems.: 78 writers' organizations.
Sec.-Gen. ABDER RAHMAN SHARQAWI. Publs. *Lotus Magazine of Afro-Asian Writings* (quarterly in English, French and Arabic), *Afro-Asian Literature Series* (in English, French and Arabic).

Alliance israélite universelle: 45 rue La Bruyère, 75425 Paris Cedex 09, France; f. 1860 to work for the emancipation and moral progress of the Jews; maintains 39 schools in the Mediterranean area; library of 100,000 vols. Mems.: 12,000 in 25 countries; local committees in six countries.
Pres. JULES BRAUNSCHVIG; Dir. JACQUES LEVY (France). Publs. *Cahiers de l'Alliance Israélite Universelle, The Alliance Review, Les Nouveaux Cahiers, La Revista de l'Alliance Israélite Universelle.*

Association of Arab Universities: Scientific Computation Centre, Tharwat St., Orman P.O.-Giza, Egypt; f. 1964. Mems.: 52 universities.
Sec.-Gen. Dr. MOHAMMED MURSI AHMED. Publs. *Bulletin* (2 a year), *Directory of Arab Universities, Directory of Teaching Staff of Arab Universities,* proceedings of seminars.

European Union of Arabic and Islamic Scholars (*Union Européenne d'Arabisants et d'Islamisants—U.E.A.I.*): Limite 5, Madrid 3, Spain; f. 1970 to organize a Congress of Arabic and Islamic Studies; 1982 Congress: Evora, Portugal. Mems.: about 120.
Sec. Prof. F. M. PAREJA (Spain).

International Institute for Adult Literacy Methods: 52 Zartosht Ave., P.O.B. 1555, Teheran, Iran; f. 1968 by UNESCO and the Government of Iran; carries out comparative studies of the methods, media and techniques used in literacy programmes; maintains documentation service and library on literacy; arranges seminars.

Dir. Dr. JOHN W. RYAN. Publs. *Literacy Review* (quarterly, English), *Awareness List on Literacy*.

International Union for Oriental and Asian Studies: Institut d'Etudes Turques, 13 rue de Santeuil, 75005 Paris, France; f. 1951 by the 22nd International Congress of Orientalists under the auspices of UNESCO Object: to promote contacts between orientalists throughout the world, and to organize congresses, research and publications. Twenty-six member countries.

Pres. R. N. DANDEKAR; Sec.-Gen. LOUIS BAZIN (France). Publs. Four oriental bibliographies, *Philologiae Turcicae Fundamenta, Materialien zum Sumerischen Lexikon, Sanskrit Dictionary, Corpus Inscriptionum Iranicarum, Linguistic Atlas of Iran, Matériels des parlers iraniens, Turcica*.

FINANCE AND ECONOMICS

Arab Bankers Association: 1/2 Hanover St., London W1R 9WB; f. 1980 to co-ordinate interests of Arab banks, improve relations with other countries, prepare studies for development projects in the Arab world, administer a code for arbitration between financial institutions, and provide training for Arab bankers. Mems.: 300 (Dec. 1981).

Pres. BASHIR AL-ZUHEIRI.

Arab Latin American Bank (*Banco Arabe Latinoamericano*): Juan de Arona 830, San Isidro, P.O.B. 10070, Lima 1, Peru; f. 1977 as a multinational offshore bank to increase economic co-operation between Arab and Latin American countries by financing foreign trade and investment. Mems.: 11 Arab and 18 Latin American Banks.

Chair. ABDULWAHAB A. AL-TAMMAR (Kuwait); Vice-Chair. ABDULLA A. SAUDI (Bahrain), MANUEL BUSTAMENTE (Peru).

Inter-Arab Investment Guarantee Corporation: P.O.B. 23568, Safat, Kuwait; f. 1974 by the Council of Arab Economic Unity and the Arab League; insures Arab investors for non-commercial risks. Mems.: all Arab governments.

Sec.-Gen. M. I. HASSAN. Publs. *Magazine* (2 a year), *News Bulletin* (monthly).

International Association of Islamic Banks: P.O.B. 4992, Jeddah, Saudi Arabia; branches in Cairo, Egypt (P.O.B. 2838), and Karachi, Pakistan (P.O.B. 541); f. 1977 to link Islamic banks, which do not deal at interest but work on the principle of participation; activities include training and research.

Chair. Prince MOHAMED AL-FAISAL AL-SAUD; Sec.-Gen. Dr. AHMED AL-NAGGAR.

International Centre for Research in Islamic Economics: P.O.B. 1540, King Abdulaziz University, Jeddah, Saudi Arabia; f. 1977 on recommendation of First International Conference of Islamic Economics held in 1976, to conduct, co-ordinate and support international research in Islamic economics.

Maghreb Permanent Consultative Committee (*Comité permanent consultatif du Maghreb*): 14 rue Yahia Ibn Omar, Mutuelleville, Tunis, Tunisia; f. 1964 as a forum for inter-governmental consultation on economic co-operation. Mems.: Algeria, Mauritania, Morocco, Tunisia.

Union of French and Arab Banks (*Union de banques arabes et françaises—UBAF*): "Le France", 4 rue Ancelle, 92521 Neuilly/Seine Cédex, France; f. 1970 to group together 26 banks of 20 Arab countries (with 60 per cent of share capital), the Crédit Lyonnais of France (30 per cent share capital), the Banque Française du Commerce Extérieur (8 per cent share capital) and the Banque Générale du Phénix (2 per cent of share capital) with the aim of contributing primarily to the development of financial, commercial, industrial and economic relations between the Arab countries on the one hand and Europe, and in particular France, and the international financial markets on the other; cap. 250 million French francs, total deposits 14,828 million French francs (Jan. 1981).

Chair. MOHAMED MAHMOUD ABUSHADI; Gen. Man. GÉRARD GERVAIS. Publs. *Annual Report, Quarterly Economic Report*.

INDUSTRIAL RELATIONS

Arab Federation of Petroleum, Mining and Chemicals Workers: 5 Zaki St., Cairo, Egypt; f. 1961 to establish proper industrial relations policies and procedures for the guidance of all affiliated unions; owns and manages the Arab Petroleum Institute for Labour Studies, Cairo; 18 affiliated unions in 12 countries.

Sec.-Gen. ANWAR ASHMAWI MOHAMED (Egypt). Publs. *Arab Petroleum* (monthly); English, Arabic and French editions, specialized publications and statistics.

International Confederation of Arab Trade Unions (ICATU): Ramses Building, P.O.B. 1041, Cairo, Egypt; f. 1956; mems.: 15 unions in 13 countries.

Sec.-Gen. AHMED JALLOUD. Publs. *Arab Workers* (Arabic), *ICATU Review* (English), *La Revue de CISA* (French), *CISTA* (Spanish).

INTERNATIONAL RELATIONS

Afro-Asian Peoples' Solidarity Organization (AAPSO): 89 Abdel Aziz Al-Saoud St., Manial, Cairo, Egypt; f. 1957 as the Organization for Afro-Asian Peoples' Solidarity; acts as a permanent liaison body between the peoples of Africa and Asia and aims to ensure their economic, social and cultural development. The Board of Secretaries is composed of 19 mems. from Algeria, Angola, Congo, Egypt, Ethiopia, the German Democratic Republic, Guinea, India, Japan, Madagascar, Namibia (SWAPO), Palestine Liberation Organization, Somalia, South Africa (African National Congress), Sri Lanka, Sudan, U.S.S.R., Viet-Nam, People's Democratic Republic of Yemen and Zambia. Mems.: national committees and affiliated organizations in 75 countries.

Pres. ABDEL-RAHMAN EL-SHARKAWI (Egypt); Sec.-Gen. NOURI ABDEL RAZZAK (Iraq). Publ. *Development and Socio-Economic Progress* (quarterly), *Afro-Asian Publications* (series).

EURABIA (European Co-ordinating Committee of Friendship Societies with the Arab World): 5 rue Dupont des Loges, 75007 Paris, France; f. 1972 to achieve greater co-operation between European organizations working for friendship with the Arab world; sponsors meetings and seminars to improve understanding of political, social, economic and cultural aspects of the Arab world, including the need to recognize the national rights of the Palestinian people.

Chair. LUCIEN BITTERLIN (Association de Solidarité Franco-Arabe); Admin. Sec. ROBERT SWANN. Publs. *Fortnightly Bulletin* (in French), pamphlets.

Jewish Agency for Israel: P.O.B. 92, Jerusalem 91920, Israel; f. 1929; undertakes absorption of immigrants in Israel, including absorption in agricultural settlements; immigrant housing, social welfare and health services, education, youth care and training.

Chair. of Exec. LEON DULZIN; Chair. of Board of Govs. MAX M. FISHER.

Multinational Force and Observers: Sinai, Egypt; f. 1982 following Israeli withdrawal from the Sinai region, to act as peace-keeping force; about 2,600 soldiers, of whom half are American and the rest from Australia, Colombia, Fiji, France, Italy, the Netherlands and the United Kingdom.

Commanding Officer Lt.-Gen. FREDERIK BULL-HANSEN (Norway); Civilian Dir. LEAMON HUNT (U.S.A.).

Parliamentary Association for Euro-Arab Co-operation: 5 rue Dupont des Loges, 75007 Paris, France; f. March 1974 as an association of more than 350 parliamentarians of the European Community to promote friendship and co-operation between Europe and the Arab world; Executive Committee has held joint meetings with Arab Parliamentary Union; represented in Council of Europe, Western European Union and European Parliament; works for the progress of the Euro-Arab Dialogue and a settlement in the Middle East which takes into account the national rights of the Palestinian people.

Joint Chair. MICHELE ACHILLI (Italy), KLAAS DE VRIES (Netherlands); Gen. Sec. ROBERT SWANN.

Asian-African Legal Consultative Committee: 27 Ring Road, Lajpat Nagar-IV, New Delhi 110024, India; f. 1956 to consider legal problems referred to it by member countries and to serve as a forum for Asian-African co-operation in international law and economic relations; provides background material for conferences, prepares standard/model contract forms suited to the needs of the region; promotes arbitration as a means of settling international commercial disputes; trains officers of member states; has permanent UN observer status. Mems.: 40 states.

Pres. N. D. M. SAMARAKOON (Sri Lanka); Vice-Pres. YUSUF ELMI ROBLEH (Somalia); Sec.-Gen. B. SEN (India).

LAW

Union of Arab Jurists: P.O.B. 6026, Dimasq St., Baghdad, Iraq; to facilitate contacts between Arab lawyers, to safeguard and develop legislative and judicial language, to allow all Arab lawyers to take cases in any Arab country and to restore the study of Muslim law. Mems.: 16 Bar Asscns. in 16 countries.

Publs. *Al Haak* (The Law), Documents and Studies.

MEDICINE

Middle East Neurosurgical Society: Neurosurgical Department, American University Medical Centre, Beirut, Lebanon; f. 1958; 212 mems. in Egypt, Greece, India, Iraq, Jordan, Lebanon, Pakistan, Syria and Turkey.

Pres. Prof. FEYAZ BERKAY; Hon. Sec. Prof. FUAD S. HADDAD.

PLANNING AND ADMINISTRATION

African Training and Research Centre in Administration for Development (*Centre africain de formation et de recherches administratives pour le développement—CAFRAD*): 19 rue Abou Alla El Maari, B.P. 310, Tangier, Morocco; f. 1964 by agreement between Morocco and UNESCO, final agreement signed by 33 African states; undertakes research into administrative problems in Africa, documentation of results, provision of a consultation service for governments and organizations; holds frequent seminars; aided by UNESCO and the UN Development Programme; library of 16,000 vols.

Pres. MOHAMED TOUGANI; Dir.-Gen. Dr. ALLOU SAMBA DIALLO. Publs. *Cahiers Africains d'Administration Publique* (twice a year), *African Administrative Abstracts* (quarterly, also in French), *Information Bulletin* (4 times a year, also in French), *CAFRAD News* (irregularly in English, French and Arabic).

Arab Towns Organization: P.O. Box 4954, Safat, Kuwait; f. 1967 to help Arab towns in solving problems, preserving the natural environment and cultural heritage; runs a fund to provide soft loans for needy members, and an Institute for Urban Development (AUDI) based in Riyadh, Saudi Arabia. Mems.: 230 municipalities.

Dir.-Gen. TALEB T. AL-TAHER; Sec.-Gen. ABDUL AZIZ Y. AL-ADASANI.

International Planned Parenthood Federation: Middle East and North Africa Bureau, 18/20 Lower Regent Street, London SW1Y 4PW, England; field offices in Amman, Cairo and Tunis; aims to advance education in family planning, to promote the use of family planning services through local voluntary associations, and to organize the training of workers. Member associations in Afghanistan, Bahrain, Cyprus, Egypt, Iraq, Jordan, Lebanon, Morocco, Sudan, Syria, Tunisia, Yemen Arab Republic and the People's Democratic Republic of Yemen.

Regional Dir. Dr. MOHAMMED BOUZIDI.

RELIGION AND WELFARE

Bahá'í International Community: Bahá'í World Centre, P.O. Box 155, 31 001 Haifa, Israel; f. 1844 in Persia to promote the teachings of the Bahá'í religion; to promulgate the unity of the human race; to work for the elimination of all forms of prejudice and for equality of men and women; to establish basic education schools for children; to maintain adult programmes in basic literacy and community training; participates in many UN activities. Mems. in 100,000 centres in 340 countries and territories. Governing body: The Universal House of Justice, consisting of nine members elected by National Spiritual Assemblies.

Rep. to UN Dr. VICTOR DE ARAUJO (U.S.A.); Alternate Dr. WILL. C. VAN DEN HOONAARD (Canada). Publs. *The Bahá'í World* (world survey), *La Pensée Bahá'ie* (quarterly), *World Order* (quarterly), *Maailman-Kansalainen* (quarterly), *Opinioni Bahá'í* (quarterly); national and local house organs; 18 Bahá'í Publishing Trusts in countries throughout the world; publications in over 600 languages and dialects.

Co-ordinating Board of Jewish Organizations—CBJO: 1640 Rhode Island Ave., N.W., Washington, D.C. 20036, U.S.A.; f. 1947; consultants with the United Nations ECOSOC on problems concerning human rights, prevention of discrimination, refugees, etc. Regional offices in London and Johannesburg.

Dir. Dr. DANIEL THURSZ; Council Dir. WARREN EISENBERG.

Islamic Council of Europe: 16 Grosvenor Crescent, London S.W.1., England; f. 1973 as a co-ordinating body for Islamic centres and organizations in Europe; an autonomous Council collaborating with the Islamic Secretariat and other Islamic organizations; aims to develop a better understanding of Islam and Muslim culture in the West.

Sec.-Gen. SALEM AZZAM.

Women's International Zionist Organization: Box 33159, 38 David Hamelech Blvd., Tel-Aviv, Israel; f. 1920; purpose: to promote constructive social work and education facilities for women and children in Israel. Mems.: 260,000 in 50 countries. Represented on UNICEF and ECOSOC at the UN. Affiliated to several international women's organizations.
Chair. RUTH IZAKSON. Publs. *WIZO Review* (2 a month), *Bamat Haisha* (bi-monthly), *Annual Report of World WIZO Executive, Survey of World WIZO Executive Activities* (every 4 years), leaflets, booklets, cultural publications.

World Jewish Congress (*Congrès Juif Mondial*): 1 rue de Varembé, Geneva, Switzerland; f. 1936 as a voluntary association of representative Jewish bodies, communities and organizations throughout the world. Aims: to foster the unity of the Jewish people, strive for the fulfilment of its aspirations and ensure the continuity and development of its religious, spiritual, cultural and social heritage. Mems.: Jewish communities in over 60 countries.
Pres. EDGAR M. BRONFMAN; Sec.-Gen. Dr. GERHART M. RIEGNER. Publs. *News and Views* (monthly, New York), *Patterns of Prejudice* (quarterly, London), *Gesher* (Hebrew quarterly, Jerusalem), *Jewish Cultural News* (quarterly, Jerusalem), *Boletín Informativo OJI* (fortnightly, Buenos Aires), *Christian Jewish Relations* (quarterly, London).

World Muslim League (*Rabitat al-Alam al-Islami*): Mecca al-Mukarramah, P.O.B. 538, Mecca, Saudi Arabia; f. 1962 to advance Islamic unity and solidarity; provides financial assistance to Muslim institutions in 28 countries; organizes educational exchanges, conferences and seminars and provides study grants.
Sec.-Gen. Shaikh MUHAMMAD ALI AL-HARAKAN. Publs. *Majalla Rabitat al-Alam al Islami* (monthly, Arabic), *Akhbar al-Alam al Islami* (weekly, Arabic), *The Journal* (monthly, English).

SCIENCE AND TECHNOLOGY

Arab Engineering Union: Damascus, Syria; a regional body of the World Federation of Engineering Organizations; co-operates with the Arab League, UNESCO and the other regional engineering federations. Holds a Pan-Arab conference on engineering studies every three years and annual symposia and seminars in different Arab countries. Mems.: 13 Arab countries.

Middle Eastern Regional Radioisotope Centre for the Arab Countries: Sh. Malaeb El Gamaa, Dokki, Cairo, Egypt; f. 1963; trains specialists in the applications of radioisotopes, particularly in the medical, agricultural and industrial fields; conducts research in hydrology, tropical and subtropical diseases, fertilizers and entomology; promotes the use of radioisotopes in the Arab countries.

TOURISM

Arab Tourism Union: P.O.B. 2354, Amman, Jordan; f. 1954. Mems.: Nat. Tourist orgs. of 21 Arab states, and 4 allied mems. in private sector; 9 members form the Executive Committee for a term of two years.
Sec.-Gen. ABU RABAH (Jordan). Publs. *Arab Tourism Magazine* (bi-monthly, Arabic), *Press Bulletin* (monthly, Arabic and English).

Federation of Arab Travel Agents' Associations (**FATAA**): Malab Salam St., Salam Bldg., P.O.B. 165036, Beirut, Lebanon; f. 1970; sole Arab organization of travel agents; protects their interests and negotiates in their name with local, governmental and international tourist organizations; mems.: all Arab Travel Asscns. and over 250 Travel Agents; 8th Gen. Assembly, Tunis, Feb. 80.
Pres. YASSER ABU SO'OUD (Jordan).

TRADE AND INDUSTRY

Arab Iron and Steel Union (**AISU**): B.P. 4, Cheraga, Algiers, Algeria; f. 1972 to develop commercial and technical aspects of Arab steel production by helping member associations to commercialize their production in Arab markets, guaranteeing them high quality materials and intermediary products, informing them of recent developments in the industry and organizing training sessions. Mems.: 54 producers, whose production is worth not less than £1 million per year, in 15 Arab countries.
Gen. Sec. MOHAMED LAÎD LACHGAR. Publs. *Arab Steel Review* (monthly), *Information Bulletin* (two a month), *Directory* (annual).

General Union of Chambers of Commerce, Industry and Agriculture for Arab Countries (*Union générale des chambres de commerce, industrie et agriculture des pays arabes*): P.O.B. 11-2837, Beirut, Lebanon; f. 1951 to foster Arab economic collaboration, to increase and improve production and to facilitate the exchange of technical information in Arab countries. Mems.: 20 Chambers of Commerce in 20 countries.
Pres. BADRUDDINE SHALLAH; Vice-Pres. ADNAN KASSAR; Gen. Sec. BURHAN DAJANI. Publ. *Arab Economic Report* (Arabic and English).

Gulf Organization for Industrial Consulting: P.O.B. 5114, Doha, Qatar; f. 1976 by seven Gulf Arab states to pool industrial expertise and encourage joint development of projects.
Sec.-Gen. Dr. ABDULLAH AL-MOAJI (Saudi Arabia).

International Olive Oil Council: Juan Bravo 10–2°, Madrid 6, Spain; f. 1959; responsible for administration of the International Olive Oil Agreement, the objectives of which are as follows: to facilitate international co-operation on problems created by the world olive oil economy; to facilitate research, development and modernization of olive cultivation and the olive oil industry through exchange of technology as well as technical and scientific programming; to facilitate the implementation of measures to increase consumption of, and international trade in, olive oil; to reduce obstacles entailed by market supply fluctuations; to take action against any unfair competition practices in the international olive oil trade; to facilitate the co-ordination of olive oil production and marketing policies; to facilitate access to the markets and reliable supplies as well as information procedures; to facilitate implementation of measures required for the other olive products. Mems. of the Agreement: Algeria, Egypt, European Community, Libya, Morocco, Portugal, Spain, Tunisia, Turkey, Yugoslavia.
Dir. GABRIELE LUZI; First Deputy Dir., Head of the Admin. and External Relations Service LUIS F. DE RANERO; Second Deputy Dir., Head of Economic Service HEDI GUERBAA. Publs. *Survey of the International Olive Oil Council* (fortnightly, French and Spanish, with a quarterly Technical Supplement), *National Olive Oil Policies* (annual) and studies of an economic and technical nature, etc.

TRANSPORT

Arab Air Carriers' Organization (**AACO**): 707 South Block, Starco Bldg., P.O.B. 11-7349, Beirut, Lebanon; f. 1965 to co-ordinate and promote co-operation in the activities of Arab airline companies. Mems.: 18 Arab air carriers.
Pres. (1980–81) Sheikh AHMED MATTAR, Dir.-Gen. Saudia; Sec.-Gen. SALIM A. SALAAM. Publs. Monthly statistical bulletins and research documents on aviation in the Arab world.

Arab Maritime Transport Academy: P.O.B. 1552, Sharjah, United Arab Emirates; f. 1975; Gen. Dir. M. W. TAYARA. First Deputy Gen. Dir. Commodore ALPHONSE SADEK. Publs. *Journal of Arab Maritime Transport Academy* (2 a year), *News Bulletin* (monthly), *Arab Maritime Directory* (annual).

Arab Railways Federation: P.O.B. 6599, Aleppo, Syria; f. 1979 to co-ordinate the development of Arab railways, particularly international railway links. Mems.: Algeria, Iraq, Jordan, Lebanon, Libya, Morocco, Syria, Tunisia.

Pres. Board of Management HASHEM EL-TAHER (Jordan); Gen. Sec. ZAFER ATTAR.

Trans-Sahara Liaison Committee: c/o Ministère des Travaux Publiques, 135 rue Didouche Mourade, Algiers, Algeria; f. 1964; beginning the study and construction of the Trans-Saharan Road and obtaining the necessary finance with UNDP backing in 1972. A feasibility study has been completed and contact made with an international consortium for the design; estimated cost for the road, 4-7 metres wide and 2,800 km. in total length, is U.S. $700 million. In Algeria, the section from El Golea to In Salah was completed in 1973, and the next section, as far as Tamanrasset, was completed in June 1978. In Niger the Government began negotiations over finance and construction in 1977. The Tunisian section, from Nefta to Hazoua, was completed in 1976. Nigeria joined the Committee in June 1976. A new constitution for the Committee was drawn up in 1977, giving it full responsibility for implementing the project. Mems.: Algeria, Mali, Niger, Nigeria and Tunisia.

INDEX OF REGIONAL ORGANIZATIONS

(main reference only)

PART THREE

Country Surveys

Afghanistan

PHYSICAL AND SOCIAL GEOGRAPHY

W. B. Fisher

Occupying an area of approximately 650,000 square kilometres (estimates range between 620,000 and 700,000 square kilometres), Afghanistan has the shape of a very irregular oval with its major axis running N.E.-S.W. and extending over roughly 1,125 kilometres, and the minor axis at right angles to this, covering about 560 kilometres. The country is in the main a highland mass lying mostly at an altitude of 1,200 metres (4,000 ft.) or more, but it presents a highly variable pattern of extremely high and irregular mountain ridges, some of which exceed 6,000 metres (20,000 ft.), ravines and broader valleys, parts of which are very fertile, and an outer expanse of undulating plateau, wide river basins, and lake sumps.

Politically, Afghanistan has two frontiers of major length: one on the north with the Turkmen, Uzbek and Tadzhik Republics of the U.S.S.R., the other on the south and east with Pakistan.

This frontier follows what was once termed the Durand Line (after the representative of British India, Sir Mortimer Durand, who negotiated it in 1893 with the Ruler of Afghanistan). So long as the British occupied India, it was generally accepted as forming the Indo-Afghan frontier, but in 1947 with the recognition of Pakistan as a successor to the British, the Afghan government recalled that for much of the eighteenth century, Peshawar and other parts of the Indus Valley had formed part of a larger Afghan state, and were moreover occupied largely by Pashtuns, who are of closely similar ethnic character to many Afghans. Accordingly, the Durand Line frontier was denounced by Afghanistan, and claims were made that the territories as far as the line of the Indus, including Chitral, Swat, and Peshawar, and continuing as far as the Pashtun areas of the North-west Frontier Province and Baluchistan, ought to be recognized as an autonomous state, "Pashtunistan". This remains a topic of dispute between Afghanistan and Pakistan.

There are shorter but no less significant frontiers on the west with Iran and on the north-east with Kashmir and with China. This last was fully agreed only in 1963, and the precise location of others in the south and west has not been fully delimited: an indication of the extreme difficulties of terrain, and an explanation of the uncertainty regarding the actual area of Afghanistan. It is noteworthy that, in order to erect a "buffer" between the then competing empires of Russia and India, under the Durand treaty of 1893 the Wakhan district, a narrow strip of land 200 miles long and under 10 miles wide in its narrowest part, was attached to Afghanistan. This strip controls the Baroghil pass over the Pamir and avoids having a Soviet-Indian frontier.

PHYSICAL FEATURES

The main topographical feature of Afghanistan is a complex of irregular highlands that is relatively broad and low in the west, and very much higher and also narrower towards the east. In this eastern part the mountains form a group of well-defined chains that are known by the general name of the Hindu Kush (Hindu destroyer), and are linked further eastward first to the Pamirs and then to the main Himalaya system. The Eastern Hindu Kush ranges form the southern defining limit of the Wakhan strip whilst a short distance to the north and east, a small but high ridge, the Little Pamir, forms the topographic link between the Hindu Kush and the main Pamir. From maximum heights of 6,000–7,000 metres (20,000–24,000 ft.) the peaks decline in altitude westwards, attaining 4,500–6,000 metres (15,000–20,000 ft.) in the zone close to Kabul. Further west still, the ridges are no more than 3,500–4,500 metres (12,000–15,000 ft.) and in the extreme west they open out rather like the digits of a hand, with the much lower Parapamisus ridges (proto-Pamir) forming the last member of the mountain complex. The various ridges are distinguished by separate names. The Hindu Kush, which has a general altitude of about 4,500 metres, with peaks 2,000–3,000 metres (7,000–10,000 ft.) higher still, is, however, narrow and crossable by quite a number of passes, some of which are indirect and snow-bound for much of the year.

In geological structure, Afghanistan has close affinities both to Iran further west, and, as has just been stated, to the massive Himalayan system further east. Development of present-day land-forms has been greatly influenced by the existence of several large, stable masses of ancient rocks, which, by drifting northwards, have acted as cores or plates around which rock series of younger age first developed and were then closely wrapped as fold structures. Most important of these ancient massifs, or "plate" areas so far as Afghanistan is concerned, is the plateau of the Deccan, the effect of which was to "bunch" a series of tight folds in a double loop or garland on its northern side. In this way can be explained the existence of the "knot" or "bunch" of fold structures lying partly in Afghanistan, and comprising the Pamir which forms the eastern limb and the Hindu Kush that makes up the western segment of the "garland". The abrupt change of direction and swinging of the fold structures from an east-west to, in some places, a north-south direction are a direct result of the presence of the resistant mass of the Deccan. The fold ranges themselves are composed in part of sediments mainly laid down under water, and include limestones with some sandstones and are of Cretaceous and later age, Eocene especially. Extensive heat and pressure in some regions have metamorphosed original series into schists and gneiss, and there has been much shattering and cracking of the rock generally, with the consequent development of fault-lines and overthrust zones. A further feature in much of Afghanistan has been a good deal of differential earth movement, uptilting, downwarping and local adjustment, making the region particularly susceptible to earth tremors, which occur frequently, usually on a small scale. Occasionally, however, a major disaster occurs, such as that in the Uzbek Republic of the U.S.S.R., just north of Afghanistan, in 1976.

As a consequence of frequent crustal disturbance, the rise of magma from the earth's interior has produced lava-flows and minor volcanos. Most of these are in a stage of old age—being merely fissures from which emanate gas, steam and mud flows, and the presence of soft volcanic debris adds considerably in places to soil fertility.

As far as river drainage is concerned, Afghanistan forms a major watershed, from which rivers flow outward. The Amu-Dar'ya (Oxus) rises on the north side of the Hindu Kush and flows northwestwards into the U.S.S.R. Here, away from the mountains, the presence of loess (a yellowish soil of high fertility) in small pockets offers scope for agriculture. The Hari Rud rises a short distance only from the Amu-Dar'ya but flows westward through Herat to terminate in a salt, closed basin on the Iranian frontier. From the south and west of the Hindu Kush flow a number of streams that become tributaries of the Indus; and in the extreme south-west the Helmand river flows through to end like the Hari Rud in a closed basin that is partly within Iranian territory. The Helmand basin is of interest in that because of a curious balance in water-level at its lowest part, the river here reverses its flow seasonally, and remains for much of its length non-brackish instead of becoming progressively more saline, as is normal when there is no outlet to the sea. The Helmand basin thus offers distinct potential for agricultural improvement, and in fact schemes for irrigation are in process of development. But political difficulties (part of the lower basin is Iranian territory) and remoteness have been inhibiting factors.

The lower-lying areas, which are in the main more densely peopled, occur either as a series of peripheral zones to north and south, or as a series of interior valleys and basins between the main mountain ridges of the centre. Largest of these areas is the piedmont lying on the northern flanks of the mountains, and dropping northwards in altitude to merge into the steppelands of Soviet Central Asia. This is Bactria (Balkh), a region of, in places, light yellowish loessic soils. An interior situation, shut off from the sea by mountains, means that rainfall is deficient and falls mainly over the mountains. Streams fed partly by mountain snow-melt straggle across the plain, to lose themselves in the sand, feed salt swamps, or in a few cases, join others to form larger rivers such as the Hari Rud. Much of Bactria thus consists of semi or full desert with sheets of sand and gravel in many places, with, nearer the mountains, outwash of larger, coarser scree. Given stable political conditions this area with

its areas of highly fertile loess soils and moderate water supplies offers much scope for economic development. For long inhabited by pastoral nomads, and disputed politically between various claimants (Afghan, Iranian and Soviet), this northern zone is now developing rapidly with irrigated cotton growing as a main element. Links with the U.S.S.R. are considerable, and the two chief towns of Herat in the west and Mazar-i-Sharif in the north have grown considerably in size over the past few years.

On the south, towards the east, is the Kabul basin, which is a relatively flat zone hemmed in closely by steep mountain ridges. Some distance away to the north-west, and reachable through two major passes is the narrower Vale of Bamian; whilst south-east of Kabul occurs another fertile lowland zone around Jalalabad. Here lower elevation and southerly situation produce warmer conditions, especially in winter, as compared with most of the rest of Afghanistan.

In the south-west, extending through Ghazni as far as Qandahar, there is another series of cultivated zones; but the extent of this piedmont area is much smaller than the corresponding one we have just described as Bactria. To the west aridity, the price of declining altitude, increases, so the lowland passes into the desert areas of Registan and the Dasht-i-Mayo. Registan has seasonal flushes of grass, which support relatively large numbers of pastoral nomads, who, however, are becoming increasingly settled following irrigation development on the Helmand and Arghandab rivers.

Two other regional units may be mentioned. South of the Parapamisus and Kuh-i-Baba mountain ranges are a number of parallel but lower massifs, with narrow valleys between. Here because of altitude there is relatively abundant rainfall, but owing to topography, the region is one of remoteness and difficulty. This is the Hazarat, so called from the name of the Hazara inhabitants, and it still remains, despite a central position, one of the least known and visited parts of the country. Another equally remote highland, this time located north-east of Kabul, is Nuristan, again high and mountainous, but well-wooded in places, and supporting a small population of cultivators and pastoralists who use the summer pastures of the high hills and move to lower levels in winter.

CLIMATE

Climatically, Afghanistan demonstrates a very clear relationship with Iran and the Middle East, rather than with Monsoon Asia, in that it has an almost arid summer, a small amount of rainfall which is largely confined to the winter season, and considerable seasonal variation in temperature. The monsoonal condition of heavy summer rainfall does not occur, despite Afghanistan's nearness to India. Annual rainfall ranges from 100–150 mm. (4–6 in.) in the drier, lower areas of the west and north, to 250–400 mm. (10–15 in.) in the east; on the highest mountains there is more still. Kabul, with an average of 330 mm. (13 in.) per annum, is typical of conditions in the east, and Herat with 125 mm. typical of the west. Almost all this falls in the period December to April, though there can be a very occasional downpour at other times, even in summer, when a rare damp monsoonal current penetrates from the Indian lowlands. Temperatures are best described as extreme. In July, the lowlands experience temperatures of 43°C. (110°F.) with 49°C. not uncommon—this is true of Jalalabad on the edge of the Indus lowlands. But the effects of altitude are important, and Kabul, at an elevation of 1,800 m., does not often experience temperatures of over 38°C. (100°F.). Winter cold can be bitter, with minima of −22° to −26°C. (−10° to −15°F.) on the higher plateau areas, and as a result there are heavy blizzards in many mountain areas. The January mean at Kabul is −4°C. (25°F.). Generally speaking, a seasonal temperature range of 45–55°C. is characteristic of many areas (cf. 14°C. for London). A further difficulty is the prevalence of strong winds, especially in the west, where a persistent and regular wind blows almost daily from June to September and affects especially the Sistan area of the lower Helmand basin, where it is known as the *Wind of 120 Days*.

With highly varied topography and climate, Afghanistan has a wide range of plant life—a good deal of which is not yet fully recorded. Conditions range from Arctic and Alpine type flora on the highest parts to salt-tolerant arid zone species in the deserts. Woodland occurs in a few areas, but much has been used for fuel in a country that has cold winters.

PEOPLE AND ACTIVITIES

The considerable variation in the types of terrain, and the considerable obstacles imposed by high mountains and deserts, have given rise to marked ethnic and cultural differences, so that heterogeneity in human populations is most characteristic. The Pashtuns live mainly in the centre, south and east of the country, and are probably numerically the largest group. The Ghilzays, also of the areas adjacent to Pakistan, are thought to be of Turkish origin, like the Uzbeks who live in the north, mainly in the Amu-Dar'ya lowlands. Another important element are the Tadzhiks or Parziwans who are of Persian origin, and in the opinion of some represent the earliest inhabitants of the country. Other groups, such as the Hazara (who are reputed to have come in as followers of Genghis Khan) and the Chahar Aimak, may have Mongol ancestry, but they now speak Persian and the Hazara are Shi'a Muslims. In the north-east, the presence of fair-haired groups has suggested connection with Europe. Another possibly indigenous group of long-standing, is the Nuristani or Kafirs, now small in number. Most Afghans (the Hazara and Qizilbash of Kabul excepted) are Sunni. Pashtu, one of the Eastern group of Iranian languages, is spoken by about 30 per cent of the total population (another 1½–2 million Pashtu-speakers live across the frontier in Pakistan). Since 1936 Pashtu and Farsi (Iranian) have been the official languages of the country, using an augmented Arabic script.

For long a difficult topography, extreme climate with a generally deficient rainfall, and political instability inhibited economic progress. Small communities lived by cultivation where water and soil were available, and there were relatively numerous pastoralists, mostly nomads, who formed an important section of the community. Even today, it is estimated that about 15 per cent of the population is nomadic, and tribal organization is strong. In fact, only 12 per cent of the land area is cultivated.

Two major handicaps, arising directly from its geography, have long been the fragmented nature of the settlement pattern and the difficulties of physical communications between the various communities. Scale of production and size of markets have consequently been very limited: local standards often prevail and the central Government does not find it easy to develop full control. So inherently strong is this fact of regional subdivision and diversity that the improvement of infrastructure (roads, airfields, radio and telephonic communication), undertaken with vigour over the past few years, has largely resulted in the intensification of regionalism.

In common with other countries of south-west Asia, Afghanistan experienced severe drought between 1968–72. This is thought to have been due to a major cyclical climatic shift that is traceable over a very wide area of the Northern Hemisphere. The economic consequences of this drought have been considerable, though varied regionally within Afghanistan, not only for the 75 per cent or so of the population who still live directly by agriculture, but also through restriction on water supplies for developing manufacturing and other activities.

Because of Afghanistan's former location as a buffer between Russia and British India, railways approached from various sides, but none actually penetrated the country, and so Afghanistan is one of the few parts of the world still to be without railways. In the 1970s a programme of road development was undertaken, resulting in considerable improvements. Since Soviet occupation in 1979, vigorous attempts have been made to link Afghanistan with the Soviet economy. A national development plan, financed from Soviet and COMECON (CMEA) sources, has been undertaken, which has had the effect of diverting trade (already moving that way) strongly towards the Soviet bloc, and hence reducing traditional commercial links with India and Pakistan to 10 per cent or less of former levels. Prospecting for various minerals known to exist in some quantity—chrome, coal, iron, uranium, petroleum and especially gas—has increased and, where production has occurred, all are exported to the U.S.S.R. Opponents of the new regime declare that prices paid to Afghanistan for these are little more than half of current world prices; and these are offset against charges levied by the U.S.S.R. for military costs in Afghanistan, again stated by opponents of the regime as having reached $3–4,000 million by early 1982. In 1981 an attempt was made to popularize the regime by largely abandoning an earlier scheme of land reform aimed at reducing holdings by individuals. This hasty, badly planned agrarian reform, undertaken without necessary supporting measures (such as technical and financial assistance), together with military action against insurrection (including destruction of food stocks in villages), has greatly reduced overall living standards. Shortages of basic food have thus been a feature of the last few years.

HISTORY
Malcolm E. Yapp

The history of Afghanistan has been largely determined by its geography. It stands at the meeting place of three geographical and cultural regions: the Iranian plateau to the west, Turkestan to the north, and the Indian sub-continent to the south. Throughout its history Afghanistan has been subject to influences and invasions from these neighbouring regions and until the eighteenth century was commonly divided, politically, between regimes based on the more fertile and populous regions which surrounded it. At the same time the mountainous terrain and poor communications have enabled large parts of Afghanistan to enjoy local independence of any government and permitted widely differing ethnic and religious groups to retain their identities. The great variety of Afghan historical experience consequent upon this situation makes it difficult to construct an intelligible narrative of Afghan history prior to the emergence of something which may be termed an Afghan state during the second half of the eighteenth century.

PREHISTORY

Significant archaeological investigation in Afghanistan developed only after 1949. Flints and bones discovered indicate human occupation in northern Afghanistan as early as *c.* 30,000 B.C. and the northern slopes of the Hindu Kush may have been one of the earliest centres of the domestication of plants and animals during the Neolithic period (*c.* 10,000 B.C.). Further south, at Mundigak, north-west of Qandahar, excavations have revealed the development of a small village into an urban centre during the period 3000 to 1500 B.C. Archaeological evidence of nomadic occupation is less easy to find but there is some indication of the presence of pastoral peoples in northern Afghanistan during the Iron Age.

EARLY HISTORY
The Achaemenids

Although scholars have argued that references to Afghanistan exist in the early religious works of India (the *Rig Veda*) and Iran (the *Avesta*), this is uncertain and the existence of various tribal kingdoms during this early period can only be postulated. Afghanistan's first appearance in recorded history dates from the sixth century B.C., when parts of western Afghanistan were conquered by the Achaemenid ruler of Iran, Cyrus the Great (reigned 559–530 B.C.), and much of the remainder was incorporated as provinces in the empire of Darius the Great (522–486 B.C.).

The Greeks

In 330 B.C. Afghanistan was invaded by the Macedonian, Alexander the Great, following his defeat of the Achaemenids. Alexander fought several campaigns in Afghanistan and founded cities near Herat, on an unknown site between Qandahar and Ghazni, near Begram, and at Bactria (Balkh), before moving on to India in 327 B.C.

Alexander's empire disintegrated after his death in 323 B.C. Afghanistan fell to the share of his general Seleucus, but revolts led to the establishment of several independent "Greek" kingdoms (that is kingdoms in which the names of the rulers, the language of the inscriptions and the style of the architecture were Greek). The most notable of these kingdoms were those of Bactria (north of the Hindu Kush) and the so-called Indo-Greek kingdom south of the mountains. In 1963 the important remains of one Greek city were discovered at Ai Khanoum in northern Afghanistan. From the third century B.C. these kingdoms were subjected to attacks from the Parthians from the west and the Mauryas from the south; and from the second century they were assaulted by nomads from the north.

The Kushans

During the first century A.D. Afghanistan (with Turkestan) became part of the empire of the Kushans, a Central Asian people who employed an Indo-European language. Under the remarkable ruler Kanishka I (probably early second century A.D.), the Kushans also took control of much of northern India. The capital was moved from the vicinity of Bactria to that of Peshawar, while Begram (near Kabul) was used as a summer capital. The Kushan period saw two important developments in Afghanistan: a major increase in the trade of the region, which became an entrepôt for commerce between Rome, China and India; and the spread of Buddhism, which had been introduced to Afghanistan by the Mauryas and whose presence is witnessed by several remarkable monuments including the great stone statues of the Buddha at Bamian.

During the third century A.D. the Kushan empire broke up under attack from the Sasanian rulers of Iran and for the next two centuries Afghanistan appears to have been divided among semi-independent Sasanian or Kushan rulers. In the mid-fifth century these petty states crumbled before the invasion of the so-called White Huns, or Hephthalites, from Central Asia. The regime of the White Huns endured for approximately 100 years before submitting to the attacks of a Turkish people from the north and the Sasanians from the west.

THE EARLY ISLAMIC PERIOD

The final Arab defeat of the Sasanians in A.D. 642 left the fragmented Afghan kingdoms independent. Although the Arabs raided into Afghanistan, they did not establish a permanent government in the area, preferring to work through local rulers. With the decline of the power of the Abbasid Caliphs in Baghdad during the ninth century, new local Iranian Muslim dynasties established themselves in the east and at various times parts of Afghanistan were included in the dominions of the Tahirids, Samanids and Saffarids. At the end of the tenth century new dynasties of Turkish origin emerged, notably that of the Ghaznavids.

The Ghaznavids

The Ghaznavid dynasty was founded by a Turkish mercenary soldier named Alptegin who settled in Ghazni. His son-in-law, Subuktigin (reigned 977–997), developed the new state which reached its climax under Subuktigin's son, Mahmud of Ghazni (998–1030), who defeated the rival Ghurid dynasty in central Afghanistan, raided extensively into surrounding areas, especially northern India, and made his court a centre of scholarship and the arts. Mahmud's tomb and his two great towers of victory may still be seen in the vicinity of Ghazni. During the twelfth century the Ghaznavid state was eaten away by regimes based upon Iran (the Seljuks), Turkestan (the Qarakhanids) and India. The final blow was administered by the resurgent Ghurids in 1186, although the Ghurids were quickly replaced by another Turkestan-based dynasty, that of the Khwarazmshahs.

The Mongols, Timur and the Timurids

In 1220 the Mongol conqueror, Genghis Khan, smashed his way through Turkestan and invaded Afghanistan. Political authority was fragmented and a confused period followed in which predominance belonged to the descendants of Genghis in Central Asia (the Chaghatay Khans). At the end of the fourteenth century a new great eastern empire was created by Timur (Tamerlane; 1370–1405), which included Afghanistan. Timur's empire broke up after his death but his descendants continued to rule in various parts of the region and, under Shah Rukh (1405–47) and Husayn Bayqara (1470–1506), Herat became one of the most notable cultural centres in the eastern Muslim world. Evidence of its architectural splendour still survives. In Turkestan power passed to the Uzbek Turks who invaded from the north. One of Timur's descendants, Babur, fled to Kabul, from where he launched a campaign into India which resulted in the establishment of the great Mughal Empire in the sub-continent.

Mughals and Safavids

In the early fifteenth century Afghanistan was once more surrounded by three powerful states. In Turkestan the Uzbeks quickly became divided into a number of small states, although they retained influence in northern Afghanistan. In India and in Iran the powerful Mughal and Safavid states became established and laid claim to Afghanistan, for the possession of which they contended for much of the following two centuries. Broadly speaking, western Afghanistan, including Qandahar, usually fell into the Safavid orbit while eastern Afghanistan, including Kabul, was often under Mughal control, although when Mughal power declined during the seventeenth century the area enjoyed greater independence.

Although imposing in appearance, the Safavid state was in reality weak and unstable and in the early eighteenth century it was overthrown by a revolt of the western Ghilzay Afghans. Under their leader, Mir Wais (died 1715), the Ghilzays defeated the Safavids at Qandahar in 1711. In 1721–22 Mir Wais's son, Mahmud, led a raid into Iran which ended in the siege and capture of Isfahan and the effective destruc-

tion of the Safavid state. The Afghans lacked the resources to create a new empire and were eventually defeated and expelled from Iran in 1730 by another great Asian conqueror, Nadir Shah, who went on to create a vast eastern empire in which Afghanistan was included. Many Afghans served in his victorious armies.

THE DURRANI EMPIRE (1747–1818)

In 1747 Nadir Shah was assassinated and his empire dissolved in anarchy. In Qandahar power was seized by one of his Afghan officers, Ahmad Shah (1722–72) of the Abdali Afghans. Ahmad renamed his tribe the Durranis. He constructed a new empire based upon Afghanistan and resting primarily upon the military power of the Afghan tribes. For these achievements Ahmad Shah is usually acknowledged as the founder of the Afghan state. After winning the support of the Abdalis and gaining acceptance by the Ghilzay Afghans, Ahmad went on to consolidate his hold on Afghanistan by seizing Kabul in 1748, Herat in 1749 and the area of northern Afghanistan between the Hindu Kush and the Amu-Dar'ya (Oxus) in 1751. He also made Khurasan into a dependency. His main efforts, however, were directed towards northern India, whither he led a total of eight campaigns. At its peak in 1757 his authority extended over the Punjab, Kashmir and Sind, but in his later years Ahmad met increasing competition from the Marathas (whom he defeated in 1761 at Panipat) and from the Sikhs, who gradually loosened the Afghan hold on the Punjab. The Durrani Empire was essentially a military empire and Ahmad relied upon a constant series of victorious campaigns to provide the booty which purchased the allegiance of the Afghan tribal chiefs. His military skills, his piety and his normally good relations with the Afghan chiefs maintained Ahmad's authority until his death. He also patronized the arts and built the new city of Qandahar.

Ahmad Shah was succeeded by his second son, Timur (reigned 1772–93), who adopted a less belligerent policy and allowed some outlying dependencies to gain substantial independence. Nevertheless Timur held the core of the Durrani empire intact and it was only during the civil war which followed his death that Afghan power crumbled. Between 1793 and 1818 the sons of Timur, notably Zaman Shah (1793–1800), Mahmud Shah (1800–03; 1809–18) and Shah Shuja (1803–09), contended for power, enlisting the support of tribal groups. This resulted in Afghanistan's becoming divided into several states. Mahmud retained possession of Herat but the remainder of Afghanistan proper was divided among chiefs from the Barakzay section of the Durrani confederation. Of the dependencies, Bactria, Sind, Baluchistan and the Punjab all became independent and the ruler of the Sikh state of Lahore, Ranjit Singh, went on to take control of Kashmir, Peshawar and other Afghan districts west of the river Indus.

EVENTS LEADING TO INDEPENDENCE

Gradually the situation in Afghanistan crystallized and three states emerged based upon the principal towns. In the west, in Herat, Mahmud extended his

AFGHANISTAN

power into Sistan and amongst the petty states on the north slope of the Paropamisus mountains. The area between the Helmand river and Kalat-i Ghilzay fell under the control of the Barakzay Sirdars of Qandahar. In the east Dost Muhammad of Kabul took control of Ghazni and Jalalabad and enforced his authority in the region of the Hindu Kush. The dissensions of these three states, however, aided their external foes: the Qajar state of Iran in the west and the state of Lahore in the east. In 1837 Afghans and Sikhs fought in the Khaibar Pass and the Iranians beseiged Herat. In consequence two new actors were introduced to the scene: Russia and Britain.

The First Anglo-Afghan War, 1839–42

British interest in Afghanistan derived from the establishment of British power in India through the agency of the East India Company. In 1809, as part of a series of diplomatic arrangements designed to protect India from a possible French invasion, a treaty was negotiated with Shah Shuja in Afghanistan, but, because of the disappearance of the alleged French threat and the fall of Shah Shuja, the treaty remained a dead letter. British interest in Afghanistan languished, to be revived from 1830 onwards as a result of fears of the spread of Russian influence towards India. An attempt was made to develop commercial relations with the Barakzay states but the deteriorating Sikh-Afghan and Iranian-Afghan relations caused difficulties. In the event, in 1838, the Governor-General, Lord Auckland, abandoned hope of reaching agreement with the Barakzays and decided to replace them in Qandahar and Kabul with Shah Shuja and, through him, to establish a powerful British influence in Afghanistan as a counterpoise to Russian influence in Iran. In 1839 Shah Shuja was re-established on the throne with the aid of British and Company troops and a Sikh diversionary action. For various reasons it proved impossible to withdraw the British and Company troops. Hostility to British influence multiplied and in November 1841 a rising took place in Kabul which led to the withdrawal of the British garrison from Kabul and its massacre during its retreat to Jalalabad. At Jalalabad and Qandahar the British garrisons held out and were reinforced in 1842 when Kabul was recaptured. It was then decided to abandon Afghanistan. Shah Shuja had been murdered and the Barakzay rulers returned from exile in 1843 to resume their rule in Kabul and Qandahar.

The Unification of Afghanistan, 1843–63

Following his return to power, Dost Muhammad resumed his previous policy of extending his authority over the other Afghan states. In northern Afghanistan he established his power in Bactria and Khulm (1850), Shibarghan (1854), Maymana and Andkhuy (1855) and Kunduz (1859). In the west he took Qandahar (1855) and Herat (1863). At the same time he increased his power over the tribal chiefs, reduced the power of the Ghilzays, and developed a regular army to replace the feudal militia. By the time of his death in 1863 he had established the outlines of modern Afghanistan. He also restored good relations with Britain and signed agreements with her in 1855 and 1857.

The Civil War and the Reign of Shir Ali, 1863–78

After Dost Muhammad's death his sons, whom he had employed as provincial governors, contended for supreme power. After five years and many vicissitudes Shir Ali Khan emerged triumphant and resumed the policy of consolidating Afghanistan and developing a reliable regular army. Britain had abstained from intervention until the issue was settled but when Shir Ali emerged as the victor good relations were established with him in 1869. However, these good relations did not last.

The Second Anglo-Afghan War, 1878–80

British interest in Afghanistan, which had waned after 1842, was revived first by a new Iranian threat to Herat and then, during the 1860s and 1870s, by the Russian conquest of Turkestan and its apparent threat to the security of British India. One school of thought held that Britain should seek friendly but distant relations with Afghanistan and negotiate an agreement with Russia; another, represented by Lord Lytton (Viceroy 1876–80), believed that British influence should be firmly planted in Afghanistan through a British Resident in Kabul. Shir Ali's unwilling acceptance of a Russian mission during the Eastern Crisis of 1878 provided an excuse for insisting on the reception of a British mission and when this demand was refused Afghanistan was invaded, Shir Ali fled and died, and his son, Yaqub, was obliged to surrender certain lands to Britain and accept a British Resident under the Treaty of Gandamak of 1879. The murder of the British Resident in September 1879 led to a further expedition to Afghanistan and a decision by Lytton to break up Afghanistan giving Herat to Iran, dominating Qandahar, and leaving Kabul largely to its own devices. However before this policy could be implemented the British forces in western Afghanistan suffered a severe defeat in 1880 at Maiwand at the hands of Ayyub Khan, the second son of Shir Ali, and were beseiged in Qandahar. Although the troops were rescued by the famous march of a British column under Gen. Sir Frederick Roberts from Kabul to Qandahar, the new Liberal Government in London decided to withdraw from Afghanistan. Of the gains made by Britain at Gandamak the Khaibar Pass and the districts of Kurram, Pishin and Sibi were retained, and Britain retained control of Afghanistan's foreign relations.

The Amir Abd al-Rahman, 1880–1901

The British installed, as ruler of Kabul, a grandson of Dost Muhammad named Abd al-Rahman and in 1881 Abd al-Rahman took possession of Qandahar and Herat and so reunited Afghanistan. It was during his reign that the boundaries of Afghanistan assumed their present form. The western frontier with Iran had been delimited in 1872; the northern frontier with Russian-controlled Turkestan was demarcated in two stages, in 1885–87 and 1895; and the southern and eastern frontiers with British India and its dependencies were outlined in the Durand Agreement of 1893 and demarcated in 1894–96. Within these limits Abd al-Rahman established a strong autocratic government. He pacified eastern Afghanistan, defeating tribal opposition and extending his power over outlying areas, including Kafiristan (renamed Nuristan); suppressed a major Ghilzay rising (1886–88); crushed a major uprising in northern Afghanistan (1888); and brought the Hazaras of central Afghanistan under control in a long and bitter war (1891–93). He also made major reforms in local government, law and taxation, and established new industries and constructed roads and bridges. His principal instrument was his new, regular, disciplined, conscript army, a great development from the models of Dost Muhammad and Shir Ali. He was also aided by a British subsidy. Although obliged to accept British control of his foreign relations, Abd al-Rahman preserved Afghanistan's internal independence and established some of the main features of the modern state.

MODERN AFGHANISTAN, 1901–73

Abd al-Rahman was succeeded as Amir by his son, Habibullah, who maintained the absolutist system of his father, while making more concessions to tribal and religious leaders. Habibullah introduced educational reforms: the first secondary school was founded in 1904 and the curriculum of the traditional religious schools was broadened. During his reign a modernizing, nationalist movement of Afghan intellectuals developed around the newspaper *Siraj al-Akhbar* (1911–19), edited by Mahmud Tarzi (1866–1935). During the First World War Habibullah successfully resisted pressure to join the Central Powers; Afghanistan remained neutral.

On February 20th, 1919, Habibullah was assassinated and was succeeded by his youngest son, Amanullah, who immediately proclaimed the independence of Afghanistan. War with Britain broke out when Afghan forces entered British Indian territory. Afghan forces in the Khaibar Pass were quickly repulsed but those in Waziristan achieved some successes before an armistice was signed. By the treaty of Rawalpindi in August 1919, peace was established, the British subsidy ended and the Durand frontier confirmed. A separate letter effectively recognized Afghanistan's independence. In November 1921 a treaty between Britain and Afghanistan was signed.

Amanullah, 1919–29

Amanullah confirmed Afghanistan's independence by agreements with other countries. In September 1920 he signed an agreement with Soviet Russia, in March 1921 with Kemalist Turkey, and in June 1921 with Iran. Diplomatic relations were opened with other countries. His hopes of territorial expansion were ended when neighbouring regimes consolidated their power. Amanullah began an extensive programme of modernization. First he concentrated on improving the legal, judicial and administrative framework of government. The first Afghan constitution was promulgated in 1923 and the whole administrative system was reorganized; a system of legislative councils was established; a new system of courts was set up with secular codes of law; major reforms were made in taxation and budgeting (the first government budget was introduced in 1922); and efforts at economic modernization were made. After his visit to Europe in 1927–28 Amanullah became more ambitious

and announced a further series of reforms especially directed against traditional social customs, including the wearing of the veil. Without doubt Amanullah saw himself as a modernizer in the mould of Atatürk in Turkey and Reza Shah in Iran; his mistake was to allow his army to become weak. In the autumn of 1928 tribal risings began in eastern Afghanistan, culminating in the occupation of Kabul in January 1929 by a Tajik bandit, known as the Baccha-i Saqqaw, who proclaimed himself Habibullah II of Afghanistan. After vain efforts to recover his power Amanullah fled to India and thence to Europe.

Nadir Shah, 1929–33

Leadership of the opposition to Habibullah II fell to a group of able brothers, Nadir, Hashim, Aziz, Shah Wali and Shah Muhammad Khan, who were members of the Musahiban family and were descended from a brother of Dost Muhammad Khan. Political disagreements with Amanullah had driven them into self-imposed exile. In 1929 they returned to rally the Pathan tribes against the Tajik, Habibullah, and in October captured Kabul. Habibullah and some of his followers were executed. Nadir Khan was elected ruler and began a programme of pacification, conciliation and cautious reform, beginning with the reconstitution of the army. In 1931 he introduced a new constitution. In foreign policy he followed the traditional neutralist policy, seeking good relations with the U.S.S.R. and Britain, while attempting to win the support of other European countries and the U.S.A.

The replacement of Amanullah by the Musahiban deeply divided the Afghan élite. In 1933 first Aziz and then Nadir were assassinated. Nadir was succeeded by his only son, Zahir Shah, but real power resided with the family as a whole and especially with Hashim, who became Prime Minister.

Afghanistan, 1933–53

The policy of the Musahibans was to preserve national independence, foster nationalist feeling and pursue modernization with circumspection. In foreign affairs they sought correct relations with Britain and the U.S.S.R. and close connections with other Muslim countries, especially Turkey, Iran and Iraq, with whom Afghanistan had signed the Sa'adabad Pact in 1937. Attempts to form close links with the U.S.A. had little success but important economic and technical connections were made with Germany. Nevertheless, during the Second World War Afghanistan resisted invitations to identify with the Axis cause, preserved its neutrality, and expelled Axis subjects when the Allies demanded this. The growth of nationalism was encouraged by the adoption of Pashtu as the official language in 1937; by the development of education at all levels, leading up to various institutions of higher education which were eventually grouped together in the University of Kabul in 1946; by the improvement of communications; and by the spread of newspapers. Economic modernization concentrated on improving the infrastructure. A bank was founded in 1932 and roads were developed, including a major new route to northern Afghanistan, which became the scene of important developments in the cotton and textile industries. However, as in previous periods, all modernization projects were hampered by lack of money and during the Second World War the prevailing economic dislocation set back programmes still further and led to discontent and tribal risings in 1944 and 1945.

Hashim was succeeded as Prime Minister by his brother, Shah Mahmud Khan. Economic difficulties (which obliged Afghanistan to import grain in 1946) continued, but an improvement in 1947 enabled Afghanistan to contemplate major economic development centring on the massive Helmand Valley scheme designed to irrigate a large area of western Afghanistan. It was badly planned and failed to yield any results commensurate with the cost. Between 1951 and 1953 Afghanistan once again found itself in severe economic trouble. The post-war period also saw Afghanistan's first experiment with parliamentary democracy. In 1947 the "Awakened Youth" movement began to agitate for social reform and to criticize government policy. In 1949 relatively free elections were permitted and the seventh Afghan Parliament (1949–51) gave voice to criticisms of the Government and traditional institutions, and enacted some liberal reforms including laws providing for a free press. Outside Parliament, radical groups became stronger, especially among students. The critics belonged to a tiny middle-class group, without real support in the country, and were easily silenced when the Government abandoned conciliation and returned to a policy of strict control in the elections for the eighth Parliament in 1952. Several of the liberal leaders were imprisoned. The seeds of a new type of opposition, however, had been planted in Afghanistan.

In foreign affairs the most notable event was the end of British rule in India and the creation in 1947 of the new states of Pakistan and India. Afghanistan's former balancing role was no longer possible and the country inevitably inclined more towards the U.S.S.R. This new direction was increased by the re-opening of the question of the tribal lands on Pakistan's north-western frontier. The Afghans contended that the Pathan tribesmen should be given the choice of joining Pakistan or forming an independent Pashtunistan. The issue led to bad relations between Afghanistan and Pakistan and handicapped Afghanistan's transit trade through Pakistan.

Daud Khan, 1953–63

In September 1953 Shah Mahmud was replaced as Prime Minister by his nephew, Lt.-Gen. Muhammad Daud, son of Aziz. Under Daud, Afghanistan returned to the path of autocratic modernization, now pursued with greater determination and ruthlessness. Daud favoured state-directed economic development aimed at improving communications. Large-scale economic aid was obtained from the U.S.S.R. from 1955 onwards and also considerable help from the U.S.A. Afghanistan's first five-year plan began in 1956. Daud also obtained military assistance, arms and training facilities from the U.S.S.R. and greatly strengthened the army. Daud introduced important social reforms, especially improving the status of women. In 1959 a campaign against the wearing of the veil was launched

and opposition by tribal and religious leaders was crushed.

In foreign affairs Daud pressed more strongly the case for Pashtunistan, especially after West Pakistan's "one unit" scheme of 1955 threatened the considerable autonomy which the tribal areas had enjoyed since 1947. Daud denounced the 1921 Anglo-Afghan treaty, which had endorsed the frontier line, and summoned a national assembly to pass a resolution supporting Pashtunistan. Eventually Afghan-Pakistan relations deteriorated to the point where Afghan troops entered Pakistan tribal territory, and in 1961 diplomatic relations were broken off and the border closed. Afghanistan was obliged to make new arrangements with the U.S.S.R. for transit facilities for its exports. Grapes were airlifted to both the U.S.S.R. and India, while greater use was made of road links to Iran. Nevertheless, Afghanistan's economic development was disrupted. In December 1955 the Soviet leaders, Nikolay Bulganin and Nikita Khrushchev, visited Kabul and voiced limited support for Afghanistan's stand on the Pashtunistan issue.

The Constitutional Period, 1963–73

In March 1963 Daud resigned because of the failure of his foreign policy and the desire for a more liberal regime. A new Government was formed by Dr. Muhammad Yusuf, the first Prime Minister not of royal birth. With Iranian help, relations between Afghanistan and Pakistan were quickly restored and the border re-opened. Relations with the U.S.S.R. remained good and close economic and other links continued. Nevertheless, Afghanistan recovered greater freedom in its dealings with the outside world. The new Government's main concern was with a programme of liberal domestic reform, of which the centre-piece was a new constitution promulgated in October 1964. The constitution provided for an elected lower house and partially elected upper house of Parliament. Elections were held in September 1965, with women voting for the first time. The new constitutional system did not work easily. Factions within the lower house bitterly attacked the Government while students demonstrated. In October 1965 riots led to three deaths and the Government of Dr. Yusuf resigned. Further disturbances took place under the Government of Muhammad Hashim Maiwandwal, who resigned in November 1967. There were continued student riots and even fighting in Parliament. Apart from a reorganization of provincial administration, by which 27 provinces were created to replace the old system, and a new liberal Press Law which led to a mushrooming growth of unofficial newspapers, there was little legislative reform. Government and Parliament were usually deadlocked in opposition, with the result that political parties were not legalized and democracy was not extended downwards to provincial and municipal councils. Although numerically insignificant, the radical left was especially vocal and grouped itself around a succession of newspapers (*Khalq*, *Parcham* and *Shu'la-yi Jawed*). There was no improvement in the situation under the new Prime Minister, Nur Ahmad Etemadi (November 1967– June 1971). In the thirteenth Parliament, elected in

218

August 1969, there was a marked change as compared with the twelfth. The 1965 Parliament had been elected on a very small turn-out which had led to the vocal predominance of Kabuli radicals; the thirteenth Parliament attracted much greater attention from the traditional Afghan élite, the turn-out in the election was much higher, and the radicals were almost extinguished. Nevertheless, although the basis of their opposition was different, the traditional élite were just as loud in their denunciations of the Government as the radicals were. In June 1971 Etemadi's Government resigned, over a dispute concerning the manner in which Ministers should answer parliamentary questions, and a new Government was formed under Abd al-Zahir (June 1971–December 1972). The new Government did establish better relations with Parliament and managed to get some long-delayed bills passed.

In the early 1970s Afghanistan was severely afflicted by three successive seasons of drought in central and north-western regions, including, in 1971, the worst ever recorded. A very large proportion of the sheep stock was lost, there was starvation (with considerable loss of life in some provinces, especially Ghor) and a substantial emigration to Pakistan and Iran. International aid alleviated, but did not eliminate, the problems and there was serious criticism of the Government's handling of the problem. Abd al-Zahir attempted to resign in September 1972 but was persuaded to stay until December, when a massive vote of "no confidence" in Parliament led to the formation of a new Government under Muhammad Musa Shafiq.

THE REPUBLIC OF AFGHANISTAN, 1973–78

On July 17th, 1973, a virtually bloodless military coup resulted in the deposition of King Zahir Shah and the creation of a republic headed by the former Prime Minister, Lt.-Gen. Muhammad Daud. Daud created a dictatorship dominated by himself, his relations and intimates. The 1977 constitution provided for a single political party. Elections for a new parliament were scheduled for November 1979. Daud was elected President for a six year term.

Daud's main objective was rapid economic development, centred on the improvement of communications, including the construction of a railway to develop the extensive mineral resources of central Afghanistan. To finance this work he increased tax yields three-fold and sought foreign aid from traditional suppliers, including the Western and Eastern blocs, and, increasingly, from Iran and the oil-rich Arab states. Daud tightened state control over the economy; in 1975 the principal private bank, the Banke Milli Afghan, was nationalized; in 1976 a major seven-year plan was unveiled; and a modest measure of land reform was announced but not implemented. In foreign affairs Daud followed a traditional policy of neutrality, maintaining good relations with the U.S.A. and the U.S.S.R. In 1975 the Soviet-Afghan Treaty of Neutrality and Non-Aggression was renewed for a further ten years. Relations with Pakistan, which deteriorated when Daud revived the Pashtunistan dispute, improved after 1976 following Soviet and Iranian mediation.

THE REVOLUTION OF APRIL 1978

During the latter part of 1977 and in 1978 Daud increased his attacks on his political opponents of the right and left. Following leftist anti-government demonstrations in Kabul in April 1978, Daud arrested seven leaders of the People's Democratic Party of Afghanistan (PDPA, founded 1965, divided into Khalq and Parcham factions in 1967, reunited in 1976) and began a purge of army officers and civil servants. On April 27th the commanders of military and air force units in the Kabul area staged a coup, which became known as the Great Saur (April) Revolution and on the following day, after heavy fighting against troops loyal to Daud, the rebels gained the victory. Daud, nearly all his family, the leading ministers and the principal military commanders were killed. The military rebels released the imprisoned PDPA leaders and brought them to power. There is no good evidence of outside intervention; the revolution appears to have been a purely internal struggle. As a result of the revolution the 1977 constitution was abolished, the Republic of Afghanistan was renamed the Democratic Republic of Afghanistan (DRA), power was vested in a Revolutionary Council, and the PDPA became the only political party. The PDPA leader, Nur Muhammad Taraki, became President of the Revolutionary Council and Prime Minister.

AFGHANISTAN UNDER TARAKI AND AMIN 1978–79

The PDPA came to power without any previously-agreed programme of reform and their long-term strategy was not fully unveiled until the publication of the draft Five-Year Plan in August 1979. This plan envisaged a state socialist system: economic growth at 5 per cent per annum, universal primary education by 1984 and a major adult literacy programme. But the central element in the PDPA policy, land reform, had already been put into practice. This was contained in three edicts issued between July and November 1978. These edicts provided for the gradual reduction of rural indebtedness, the abolition of dowries, and a major distribution of land holdings in favour of landless peasants. The land redistribution programme began on January 1st, 1979, and after six months it was announced that it had been successfully completed. The object was political: to destroy the basis of the political power of the former landlord-backed regimes and to win for the PDPA the allegiance of the peasant masses. In the absence of an industrial proletariat in Afghanistan, PDPA support was drawn from a tiny urban intelligentsia and professional group. The programme failed in its aim and the land reform and adult literacy campaigns caused widespread opposition to the DRA Government which led to armed insurrection in almost all provinces, the flight of thousands of refugees to Pakistan and Iran, and great economic dislocation.

From the start the PDPA Government was torn by factional disputes. In July 1978 some leading Parchamis were dismissed and took refuge in eastern Europe; in August 1978 two of the coup leaders, Abdul Qader and Mohammad Rafie, were arrested. Purges of party and army and arrests of opponents of the regime became regular features. In March 1979 more Parchamis were arrested and the Government again reorganized. The Foreign Minister, Hafizullah Amin, already Secretary of the PDPA since July 1978, now replaced Taraki as Prime Minister. Amin's power continued to increase in subsequent months. In July 1979 he added the Ministry of Defence to his responsibilities and in September attempted to remove rivals from the Cabinet. This became the occasion for an armed showdown with Taraki. Amin won and on September 16th became President of the Revolutionary Council. Taraki was put under house arrest and apparently strangled on October 8th. The dispute between Taraki and Amin was partly one of personality and partly of policy; whether the DRA should proceed with its radical politics, as Amin wished, or whether it should pursue more moderate, conciliatory policies, as Taraki and his Soviet backers desired.

Amin now pursued a radical, uncompromising policy. Opponents were imprisoned and executed, a counter-coup was defeated in October, and, after the failure of an amnesty appeal, a new campaign against the rebels in the provinces was launched. To legalize his own position, in October 1979 he appointed a committee to draft a new constitution and he tried to set up a new broad front organization—the National Organization for the Defence of the Revolution in the DRA.

Amin failed either to win over the rebels or to suppress them, and the flight of refugees from Afghanistan increased rapidly. Guerrilla organizations were formed among the refugees in Pakistan. The greater part of rebel military activity was the work of local groups within Afghanistan. The DRA Government accused China, Pakistan, Iran, the U.S.A., Egypt and other countries of aiding the rebels. Relations between the DRA and the U.S.A. steadily deteriorated; in February 1979 U.S.Ambassador Dubbs was killed in a kidnap attempt and the U.S.A. cut aid to Afghanistan. The DRA leaned more heavily on the U.S.S.R. (with which a Treaty of Friendship and Co-operation was signed on November 7th, 1978) for civil and military advice and equipment and for financial aid.

THE SOVIET INVASION OF AFGHANISTAN

From the early summer of 1979 the U.S.S.R. pressed for the adoption of moderate policies and the formation of a broad-based government in Afghanistan. These demands led to increasing friction with the radical elements in the PDPA, which culminated in December 1979 in a Soviet invasion of Afghanistan and the overthrow and execution of Amin on December 27th. A new Government, under the leader of the Parcham faction, Babrak Karmal, was formed, an event described as the inauguration of the second, new developmental stage of the revolution. The Karmal regime announced a policy of conciliation, respect for Islam and for Afghan traditions, particularly tribal customs, and the formation of a broad-based national government. These policies were embodied in the new Provisional Basic Principles, forming an interim constitution, approved by the Revolutionary Council on April 14th, 1980. In subsequent months a number of organizations of religious leaders, young people, women, private businessmen and workers were set up or reinvigorated. In June 1981 a Supreme Council of Afghan Tribes was established. Finally, and after much delay, the promised National Fatherland Front, bringing all these organizations under PDPA leadership, was organized on June 15th, 1981, with Saleh Mohammad Zirai as chairman. This event was accompanied by the introduction of a new political structure: the Revolutionary Council was enlarged and its Presidium separated from the Council of Ministers. This involved ministerial changes, including the replacement of Karmal by Sultan Ali Kishtmand as Prime Minister, although Karmal retained power through the offices of Chairman of the Revolutionary Council and Secretary-General of the PDPA. Land reform remained a key element in the policies of the regime but mistakes in its implementation during the first stage were admitted. Under the revised plan, the system of land redistribution was maintained, although major exemptions were allowed for supporters of the regime. Its implementation, however, was now made subject to surveys, the solution of the water problem and the formation of agricultural co-operatives. The campaign against illiteracy was also maintained but concessions were announced in respect of the education of women. Continued efforts were made to check bureaucratic corruption by the creation of a General Inspectorate under the Prime Minister's Office. In an effort to involve the people in government, a major scheme of decentralized local government, with elected councils, was unveiled at the end of September 1981.

The Karmal regime failed to achieve its objectives. The first essential was the achievement of party unity but disputes between Khalq and Parcham factions continued and there were accusations of corruption, nepotism and tribalism. Efforts to heal the divisions culminated in the PDPA National Conference of March 14th–15th, 1982, at which the Party Charter was amended and a new programme of action adopted. These efforts were evidently unsuccessful. The regime also failed to rebuild the army. Weakened by purges, desertions and mutinies, the Afghan army shrank from about 90,000 in 1978 to about 30,000 in 1981. In attempts to increase its strength, the age of conscription was reduced from 22 to 20 in January 1981 and to 19 in April 1982. On August 30th, 1981, it was decided to recall all reservists under the age of 35 who were released prior to October 22nd, 1978. The regime also made use of other forces: police, security forces, revolutionary guards and social order brigades, formed from those too young for military service. The formation of local defence groups was also publicized. Changes in the command structure were announced in August 1981, when a DRA Defence Council was formed to control all state and military power and to work through a new system in which provinces were grouped into eight zones under party officials. The Minister of Defence, Mohammad Rafie, and other senior officers disappeared at this time to reappear much later in the U.S.S.R. After some delay, Maj.-Gen. Abdul Qader became acting Minister of Defence.

The major problem for the Soviet-backed Karmal regime was the continuing civil war in Afghanistan. This war, mounted by local resistance groups in most areas of Afghanistan and supported by guerrilla organizations operating from the Afghan refugee communities in Pakistan and Iran, caused widespread destruction of roads, bridges, schools and other public buildings, interrupted communications, deprived the Government of authority over large areas of countryside, caused disturbances in towns, dislocated production, and killed many supporters of the regime. Although the regime often proclaimed that it had broken the back of the resistance and frequently announced victories over groups of rebels, it is clear that opposition to its authority was not overcome and in the summers of 1980 and 1981 the Government was in very grave difficulties. Meanwhile the efflux of refugees from Afghanistan continued, the number rising to a reported 2.6 million in Pakistan in February 1982. Including those in Iran, about one in five Afghan citizens had left the country in three years.

INTERNATIONAL RELATIONS

The Soviet invasion was defended on the basis of the November 1978 treaty and Article 51 of the UN Charter. It was claimed that Afghanistan had been attacked by forces from outside, that Amin had requested Soviet aid, and the Karmal Government (after achieving power by its own efforts) had renewed that request. It was alleged that Amin had plotted with the U.S.A., China, Egypt, Pakistan, etc., to partition Afghanistan and that the U.S.S.R. had been obliged to protect its own southern frontier.

World opinion was sceptical and hostile to the Soviet and DRA arguments, and the presence of Soviet forces was opposed by the UN General Assembly, the Organization of the Islamic Conference, ASEAN and the non-aligned movement as well as the Western powers. The U.S.A. took a number of measures against the U.S.S.R., including postponing

ratification of SALT II and banning grain exports to the U.S.S.R. (ban lifted April 1981). A partial boycott of the Moscow Olympic Games was arranged. New defensive agreements were negotiated by the U.S.A. with Oman, Kenya and Somalia. In February 1980 attempts were made to persuade the U.S.S.R. to withdraw by neutralizing Afghanistan, but this was denounced by the U.S.S.R. and the DRA as interference in the internal affairs of Afghanistan. The Afghan revolution, it was asserted, was irreversible and on April 17th the DRA put forward its own peace plan, elaborated on May 14th and repeated in the joint DRA/U.S.S.R. announcement on October 16th, 1980. The plan involved bilateral talks with Iran and Pakistan, a regional conference and a U.S. promise not to interfere in Afghanistan *before* discussion of a Soviet withdrawal. Pakistan rejected the plan and offered talks *after* the withdrawal of Soviet troops. In May 1980 the Islamic Foreign Ministers set up a committee to hold talks but this initiative made little progress. Relations between Pakistan and the DRA Government continued to deteriorate, with mutual accusations of frontier violations. In January 1981 it was agreed to hold talks between Pakistan and the DRA through a special representative of the UN Secretary-General. In April and August 1981 Dr. Javier Pérez de Cuellar held talks with Pakistan and the DRA independently. On June 30th, 1981, the EEC also launched a plan for a two-stage international conference which was rejected by the DRA. On August 26th, in the light of these discussions, the DRA refurbished its proposals, agreeing to trilateral talks with Iran and Pakistan in the presence of the Secretary-General and offering some apparent concessions on the timing of the withdrawal of Soviet troops. In September talks were held between Pakistan and Soviet representatives. The talks under UN auspices were resumed in New York in November 1981, and in April 1982 the new special representative of the Secretary-General, Diego Cordovez, visited Afghanistan and Pakistan. As a result of these meetings, there appeared to be some lessening of the differences between Pakistan and the DRA although considerable problems remained: those relating to the withdrawal of Soviet troops, recognition of the DRA Government by Pakistan and the question of the representation of Afghan opposition groups at any talks. Judging by a plan unveiled on November 10th, 1981, the Iranian position, based on the establishment of a purely Islamic regime in Afghanistan, remained very far apart.

ECONOMIC SURVEY

Kevin Rafferty

The greatest problem in trying to present an accurate economic profile of Afghanistan used to be that it was a backward, underdeveloped country where information was hard to come by. That difficulty has now been compounded by the Soviet invasion and the cruel war of attrition that has gone on since 1980. There was always a gulf between the small number of educated urban élite and the majority of

traditional tribal Afghans living in close community with a harsh and testing environment. The Soviet invasion and occupying force have widened these divisions. About 20 per cent of the population (over 3 million Afghans by mid-1982) has been driven out of the country into wretched refugee exile in Pakistan; others have fled their homes because of bombing or strafing. There is frequently more than one way of looking at the economies of developing countries. There is the view of the government planners, accustomed to nicely rounded numbers and the assumption that the capital can pull the strings; on the other hand there are the harsher facts of life. In Afghanistan, perhaps more than anywhere else in the world, the lines of communication never ran straight between the capital and the countryside; the effectiveness of the Kabul government was always tested by the rugged terrain of steep mountains, high desert plateaux and narrow valleys and by tribal and feudal laws. The Soviet invasion and the unrest and turmoil which it brought in its wake have merely added to these problems. Even in calmer days, Afghanistan's official statistics gave grounds for scepticism.

That is only the start of the problems of dealing with Afghanistan's statistics. There is the difficulty that no one really knows the size of the population, except that it is somewhere between 12 and 18 million (late 1970s). The Government's own figures would have surpassed 20 million by 1976 were it not for the fact that a substantial downward revision was made in mid-1976 to bring the estimated population to 16,665,000 at mid-1975, of whom 2.4 million were estimated to be nomads. Afghanistan's first national census, conducted in June 1979, gave a population figure of 15,551,358. This includes a nomadic population of 2,500,000. In figures supplied to the Asian Development Bank, the Kabul regime ignored any exodus of refugees and put the mid-1981 population at 16,370,000, a steady 2.6 per cent increase each year, as if the refugees were still solid Afghan citizens. It did acknowledge a large decline in G.N.P. in 1979 but said that the economy picked up in the following year so that total G.N.P. was Afs. 159,700 million ($3,400 million or $220 per caput at the official exchange rates then prevailing). The 1981 *World Bank Atlas* was more cautious and gave no figures for 1979 or 1980 G.N.P. In the previous edition it estimated G.N.P. (in average 1977–79 prices) as $2,290 million in 1978 and $2,590 million ($170 per caput) in 1979.

For much of the period since 1960 Afghanistan's economy has been stagnant. During the 1960s and early 1970s the rate of growth in real terms was below the rate of population increase. The years 1970 and 1971 marked the nadir as the serious droughts caused a 20 per cent drop in wheat production and killed livestock in large numbers. Since then economic performance has picked up. Better rains pushed the annual wheat crop to about 3 million tons so that in a normal year Afghanistan should be self-sufficient in food production. Industrial performance improved. Capital inflows pushed the foreign exchange reserves from U.S. $22 million at the end of 1974 to $411 million at the end of 1979 and led to an appreciation in the value of the afghani to 43 per U.S. dollar by late 1979, compared with 80.50 in 1972/73. By the late 1970s the time had come for a serious attempt to be made at planning Afghanistan's future economic development, taking into account all the disadvantages imaginable in a poor, land-locked country. However, then came the foreign invasion to make a mockery of all these projects.

THE START OF ECONOMIC PLANNING

Prior to the 1930s Afghanistan was still in the Middle Ages as far as economic development was concerned. The great armies and trade caravans of ancient times had struggled over it, but modern development had ignored it because, with the coming of sea power from the fifteenth century onwards, there were less arduous ways to India and China. Even the railway age bypassed Afghanistan. Only in 1932 when the Banke Milli Afghan (National Bank) was established did modern economic development begin. Before that the only modern features were the Government's workshops in Kabul chiefly providing for the needs of the army, and one small hydroelectric station. The formation of the bank gave an impetus to the foundation of private companies. These were mainly dealing in trade for karakul and lamb skins and wool, but textile and sugar companies were also set up. However, progress was slow and even at the end of the Second World War, internal trade was carried by caravan and inter-city roads were not paved. Only about 20,000 kilowatts of power was produced and few consumer goods were made locally.

In 1946 the new Prime Minister, Shah Mahmud Khan, began what he wanted to develop as an ambitious economic development programme using Afghanistan's agricultural exports as its base. But he failed for lack of finance. The next attempt to start economic planning came when Muhammad Daud took over as Prime Minister in 1953. Again, he ran into problems in finding foreign finance, and Washington refused to lend general support to the first five-year plan which got under way in 1957. It was ready only to provide money for individual projects. However, the Prime Minister, Daud, neatly sidestepped that problem by improving relations with the Soviet Union and delicately playing off the U.S.S.R. and the U.S.A. so that the U.S.A. closely followed and almost matched Soviet aid to Afghanistan. Moscow was prepared to underwrite a general five-year exercise. In all, between 1957 and 1972 the Soviet Union offered more than $900 million to support these plans, that is nearly 60 per cent of foreign aid, although some Western experts say that the sums promised were larger than the money handed over. The U.S.A. provided the second largest amount of aid but it usually offered better terms.

The first three plans (from 1957 to 1961 for the first; 1962 to 1967 for the second; 1968 to 1972 for the third) cannot really be described as an attempt to control the whole economy, though the Government described the economy as its "guided economy" and later "mixed guided economy". The plans offered a series of projects basically to improve the infrastructure and bring Afghanistan at least closer to the twentieth century.

The first plan set the pattern by putting great emphasis on communications, particularly road building and the establishment of air links, both national and international. In addition, 32 industrial projects were due to begin, though not all were started. The achievements of the first plan were patchy. Its great merits were the attempt to establish planned economy development, to tap external sources of finance, and at the same time to realize the need for internal finance. The great drawback was that this daring in planning was not matched by daring or so much success in implementation.

By the time of the second plan, the difficulties of the planning were beginning to be apparent, at least to outsiders. Proper cost-benefit studies were neglected, and the impact of projects on income and job opportunities was virtually ignored. The second plan also attempted to expand the role of the public sector because private industry was not big enough to undertake developments in power, gas, supply and making of cement, chemicals, and other important capital intensive industry. One problem which was not properly examined beforehand was where to find competent operators and managers to run the plants. At the start of the third plan, the Government reviewed the achievements and the lessons of the first two plans and emphasized the need to turn to more quickly yielding projects. However, in practice this proved more difficult.

For all this, 16 years of planning and public investment of Afs. 53,000 million produced an impressive list of achievements. Before planning started there were no paved roads in Afghanistan, few permanent bridges and air transport was almost non-existent. By the end of the third plan, in 1972, the country had 2,780 kilometres of paved roads and two international and 29 local airports. Dams and bridges were constructed. Registration of motor vehicles in Kabul went up from 16,000 in 1962 to 52,000 in 1971. In industry, production of cotton cloth quadrupled to 62 million metres, cement making and shoe manufacturing began, and output of the soap, sugar and coal industries increased by between 100 and 300 per cent. Electricity production rose almost nine-fold to 422.6 million kilowatt hours. Natural gas production was started and reached 2,635 million cubic metres annually, much of which is exported to the Soviet Union. There were big achievements in education where the number of schools rose from 804 to nearly 4,000, teachers from 4,000 to 20,000, and students from 125,000 to 700,000. Industrial employment rose from 18,000 in 1962 to nearly 27,000 in 1971. More than 60 private enterprise industries were set up employing nearly 5,000 people.

The fourth plan was published in 1973 and looked again to Soviet help as its mainstay but the planning procedure was disrupted by the coup and actual planning was on an annual basis. By 1976 an ambitious seven-year plan was announced, but before it had time to take effect President Daud was overthrown in the April 1978 coup and the future of the plan became uncertain.

THE ECONOMY IN THE LATE 1970s
Agriculture

Agriculture is in normal times the most important contributor to Afghanistan's economy, providing half the national income and four-fifths of the country's exports. Of the total land area of about 65 million hectares, 8 million hectares are considered to be arable, only half of which are cultivated every year. Experts estimate that a mere 2.6 million hectares of irrigated land provide 85 per cent of the crops. Irrigation is often primitive but ingenious. The impact of lack of water was shown sharply in 1971 when there was severe drought as a result of which the production of wheat, the main crop, dropped from nearly 2.5 million tons to below 2 million tons and millions of important livestock were slaughtered. It took two years for the crops to recover. Because of the large migrations of people, it is foolish to try to give specific annual production figures, but Afghanistan is capable of producing over 3 million tons of wheat a year, 160,000 tons of cotton, 400,000 tons of rice, 800,000 tons of maize, up to 400,000 tons of barley, about 1 million tons of fruit, 100,000 tons of sugar beet and 65,000 tons of sugar cane.

The severe drought of 1970 and 1971 is estimated to have cost between 30 per cent and 50 per cent of Afghanistan's livestock which in 1970 were estimated at 6.5 million karakul sheep, 15 million ordinary sheep, 3.7 million cattle, 3.2 million goats and 500,000 horses. By 1975 they were estimated to have increased to the 1970 levels. There was a 9 per cent shortfall in the agricultural production plan for 1979/80. In particular, the number of livestock declined considerably and it has been estimated that it will take four or five years to restore the cattle herds to an adequate level.

Industry

Although its series of economic plans set up modern industry and took Afghanistan out of the handicraft age, the contribution of industry to the G.D.P. is small, less than 10 per cent. Handicrafts, especially carpet making and weaving, still contribute more to the G.D.P. than modern industry. Industrial employment has hardly changed since 1971 when it was estimated that 27,000 people had paid jobs out of the total working population of about 4 million. Even the oldest established and largest industry, cotton textiles, is not able yet to produce enough cloth—output was 43.3 million metres in 1980/81—to satisfy domestic demand. Cement production fell to 87,200 metric tons in 1980/81 which was higher than the 1971 trough of 73,000 tons, but well below the 1966 peak of 174,000 tons. Changes in construction activity are responsible for these fluctuations. In 1972, owing to government concern to expand new industries, an Industrial Development Bank was established. The Daud Government said that it was anxious to encourage private enterprise, but subject to government surveillance.

Mining

Afghanistan has extensive mining resources of coal, salt, chrome, iron ore, silver, gold, fluorite, talc, mica, copper and lapis lazuli, but the country's problems of access and transport have posed questions about whether it is worth mining them. The most successful find has been of natural gas, most of which is piped to the Soviet Union in payment for imports and debts.

The annual volume of these exports was projected to double when operations at the new Jarquduq field commence. Production may soon rise to 4,000 million cubic metres per year, compared with 2,790.3 million in 1980/81 but even gas prodution has had problems due to rebel activity. However, unless new gas finds are made the existing fields may be exhausted some time before the turn of the century.

Iron ore reserves at Hajigak in Bamian province, with 1,700 million tons of high-grade ore (62 per cent), are the most promising of recent discoveries. However, although the ore would fetch a good price, much of it is located at heights of 3,500 metres or more. Moreover, there would be high costs involved in exporting it from remote Afghanistan, which has no sea-port of its own, nor even rail lines. There were hopes that the iron and natural gas could be used to make steel, but this has not been realized. Another potentially important mineral is copper, with estimated reserves of 4.7 million tons of ore. Provision to open up these deposits has been made in the 1979–84 Five-Year Plan. Two small oil-fields with total estimated reserves of 12 million tons have also been discovered in the north of the country.

Trade

Afghanistan's trade is small and it has become increasingly dependent on the Soviet Union, its northern neighbour. This is because of the mounting difficulties of using land routes to Pakistan and India, Afghanistan's principal trade outlets, both for fresh fruit going to the sub-continent and for other goods going beyond. In addition, turmoil in Iran made trade via the west difficult, and, of course, any organized road traffic would have to run the risks of rebel attack.

Through the 1970s, the balance of payments showed a surplus, thanks to tourism and remittances from Afghans working abroad. The main export items are fresh fruit and vegetables to Pakistan and India, natural gas to the Soviet Union, karakul to the fur markets of Europe, and carpets and rugs, raw cotton and dried fruits and nuts, which are just beginning to make inroads into the developed country markets. Imports include machinery, petroleum, pharmaceuticals, textiles and other consumer goods. Afghanistan is in the happy position, practically unique to the poor non-oil-producing countries, in that its oil-producing neighbours, Iran and the Soviet Union, have provided it with oil at low prices. Exports of natural gas meant that Afghanistan used to have a surplus on its energy account, yet figures supplied to the ADB show petroleum imports worth $124 million but no figures for gas exports.

Before the Soviet involvement, Afghanistan's main trading partner was the Soviet Union, which in 1977/78 provided 26 per cent of imports and took 37 per cent of the country's exports. Trade turnover between the two countries increased by 44 per cent in 1979, compared with the previous year, and further huge increases were planned. According to Kabul Radio, trade with the U.S.S.R. was $670 million in 1980 and this was expected to increase to $2,000 million in 1981.

Thus dependence on the Soviet Union increased as other countries were either unable or unwilling to export their products, and as foreign aid from the West began to decrease and then to disappear.

Since 1978 the Afghan Chamber of Commerce and Industry had acted as the sole agent for the twenty-two importers' associations and had controlled all import business. However, in order to encourage the private sector, the Government returned these exclusive export rights to the private merchants in 1980.

Money and Finance

The slow growth of the economy has created difficulties in raising the Government's internal revenues and the budget deficit has risen steadily. Half of the ordinary revenues come from indirect taxes. The next largest contributor is revenue from natural gas (21 per cent in 1979 and expected to reach 34 per cent in 1980). Only 10 per cent of the revenues comes from direct taxes. In 1978/79 domestic revenues were estimated at Afs. 15,684 million, leaving a huge deficit of Afs. 9,196 million, a rise of Afs. 2,400 million. Highest expenditure was on defence, accounting for almost 40 per cent. Social services were allocated 34 per cent of the budget.

In 1975 the Government decreed that all banks in Afghanistan had been nationalized in an attempt to bring about a more organized banking system. The move was directed at the Banke Milli Afghan, as the other banks were already under Government control. The chief bank is the Da Afghanistan Bank, the central bank which also does commercial business.

Tourism

In the 1970s tourism was an important contributor to Afghanistan's earnings, raising up to $10 million a year from visitors who numbered between 90,000 and 100,000 a year. The peak was 117,000 in 1977. Afghanistan's location off the main air routes of the world and its poor hotel facilities (apart from two international hotels in Kabul) meant that it was not able to tap the lucrative Western package holiday market. Its main tourist visitors were travellers going overland to or from Pakistan and India. The development of tourism suffered from the change of regime and internal unrest, which caused the number of tourists almost to disappear, as overland travel was too dangerous and even Kabul became unsafe for visitors.

The Seven-year Plan and After

In 1976 President Daud inaugurated an ambitious Seven-Year Economic and Social Development Plan intended to make major strides towards solving the problems of poverty and underdevelopment. The Plan is academic now because of the change of governments. Given the political setbacks to the economy, its targets—to increase the G.N.P. by more than 50 per cent by 1983, with annual growth rates of 6.3 per cent or double those of the past—also seem hopelessly optimistic.

Two things about the Plan are still worth noting. It aimed to bring Afghanistan into the railway age, through a U.S. $2,000 million project to build a 1,800-kilometres system linking with Iran in the west and with Pakistan, at Spin Boldak, in the east. Economically, it was a doubtful venture; politically, it is now dead because of the distrust of Afghanistan's neighbours. The other factor was that Daud saw the main thrust of development effort coming from the public sector and the main assistance coming from the U.S.S.R.

Over the past half-century, governments in Kabul had tried hard to lay the foundation of a modern state. The now much-abused Daud had introduced the notion of planning and been instrumental in securing Moscow's help. Some 3,000 kilometres of properly metalled roads were built and air links were established. Of course, plenty of questions can be asked about the efficiency of the plan expenditure. For example, more than 30 per cent of the money from the first three plans went on building the giant highways which opened up the country—some of them truly magnificent works of engineering like the Salang tunnel—but what use were they in helping local people living in scattered villages to get their crops to market? Although 85 per cent of the Afghans live in rural areas, although agriculture contributes 50 per cent of G.N.P. and although 90 per cent of export earnings have traditionally come from agricultural products, a much smaller proportion of the plan expenditure went to help agriculture or livestock, and little of the money went to the smaller farmers. Of the Afs. 12,500 million spent on the agricultural sector, half went on two huge irrigation projects. More attention to feeder roads to get crops to market, to small irrigation schemes and to agricultural extension work might have been better to increase agricultural production and to bring the ordinary Afghans into the market economy.

In addition, a lot of money was poured into grandiose schemes which were out of place in a poor and sparsely populated country. Qandahar airport, an American-aided project, never had enough traffic even when tourists and others could move about freely. Other schemes, such as the French-assisted Balkh textile mill, exceeded their original budget. Sometimes this was because the Kabul planners were always working in an ideal world and tended to forget their own and the country's slow pace. Yet other ventures were based on out-of-date technology, including the Soviet built Mazar-i-Sharif fertilizer factory.

Nevertheless, by the end of the Daud era, economists who looked at Afghanistan made two points. Firstly, there was hope of building a twentieth-century country with the prospect of prosperity ahead of it. There was scope for greatly increased agricultural yields and export earnings. Tree and field crops and livestock all have potential that has not been realized. Cotton has proved competitive in world markets, fresh fruit from the orchards of Afghanistan was in demand around the Gulf, while dried fruits, such as raisins, could be marketed worldwide. Mineral reserves are yet to be opened up. Industry, especially that devoted to the processing of agricultural products, offered increased value-added as well as jobs in the modern sector.

Secondly, though, all these projects would take time. In spite of progress, Afghanistan has a long way to go. Simple statistics tell one side of the story. According to comparative figures published in 1982 by the Asian Development Bank, 77.8 per cent of Afghans in 1980 were employed in agriculture, the fourth highest figure of all Asian countries. In terms of adult literacy, Afghanistan was well behind with a literacy rate of 11 per cent. (The next most illiterate country in the Asian-Pacific region is Solomon Islands with literacy of 19 per cent.) School enrolment does not offer any early hope of a dramatic improvement. Only 28 per cent of Afghan children enrolled for primary school and only 5 per cent for secondary school. Other social indicators also present a grim picture. Average life at birth in 1975–80 was only 40.5 years, the lowest in Asia and the Pacific (except for the special case of Kampuchea), infant mortality is 185 per 1,000 live births, the highest in the region (having actually increased from 182 per 1,000 in 1970). Only 20 per cent of the Afghans in urban areas and only 3 per cent in rural areas have access to safe water.

The statistics do not tell the whole story of the struggle that will be necessary. Socially, in tribal and nomadic Afghanistan, the barriers to progress are as high as the Hindu Kush mountains which Babur the Mogul called "the theatre of Heaven".

THE ECONOMY AND SOCIAL BENEFITS

The pattern of society in Afghanistan is remarkably static. Though there is some marginal movement, the tendency is for a son, if he survives (since the child mortality rate up to the age of 5 is 50 per cent), to follow in his father's footsteps. Outside the cities, the chances are that he will not have any schooling and that he will not have any adolescence and hardly any childhood. As soon as he is big enough to walk and talk, a son can be usefully employed looking after sheep or other animals.

To make any breakthrough the authorities would have somehow to penetrate the traditional hostility to government. Officials are usually met by a "mud curtain" of the village because of the suspicion—justifiable in the past—that the officials have come to extract something from the village.

There is also the problem of the role of women. In 1959, Prime Minister Daud passed a law saying that women no longer had to veil themselves. Yet the status of women has hardly changed. When a boy is born, he is greeted with bonfires and pistol shots signifying rejoicing that another man, a warrior, has entered the world. Yet when a girl comes into the world, the reaction is more likely to be one of shame. Educational opportunities for girls have increased, although of the roll of 720,000 pupils in all educational institutions in 1970, only 96,000 were girls. In village schools, there were only 13,000 girls. Of an estimated 100,000 Afghan women who have finished some kind of schooling only about 5,000 are employed, mainly in the professions and the majority of these in teaching. There are hardly any women in industry—because of the high unemployment rate.

In many ways, the Afghanistan that entered the 1980s was ripe for a reform or revolution that would tip the balance towards the less privileged members of society, especially the poor, the landless and women. This was the stage onto which the Soviet Union and its soldiers stepped. Although Afghanistan in many ways seemed ripe for revolution, the established system had its strengths and posed difficulties. The Kabul Government and its Soviet masters made the most of them. The Soviet operation came in two stages: firstly, after the Saur Revolution in which Daud was overthrown, when the new ruler, Nur Mohammed Taraki, invited hosts of advisers from Moscow as he tried to remodel the economy and then, when Moscow invaded, to get rid of Hafizullah Amin and put in 85,000 soldiers to support Babrak Karmal.

The Taraki Government quickly formulated plans to tackle the problems of those people so far unaffected by economic change. A Five-Year Plan started in 1979. This proposed a total investment of Afs. 105,000 million, 25 per cent of which would be allocated to agriculture in order to triple output. Investment in industry (in 1979 employing only 12 per cent of the working population) and mining was to amount to Afs. 43,654 million and should increase the contribution of industry to G.N.P. from 23 per cent to 41 per cent. The Plan envisaged the comprehensive development of both heavy and light industry based on the effective utilization of natural resources. Towards the end of 1978 it decreed important new measures: a major land reform limiting families to 15 irrigated acres each; a decree remitting debts of peasants; and dowry rules outlawing payment of more than Afs. 300 (about U.S. $8) in dowries and raising the minimum age for marriage to 16 years for women and 18 years for men. These measures caused head-on conflict with the powers of the old village and tribal order. The wisdom of such a direct attack could clearly · be doubted. Given the distrust of officialdom it was not surprising that the reforms were ignored or circumvented. However, the Government claimed at the beginning of 1980 that there were already almost 1,200 agricultural co-operatives in the country. The Five-Year Plan aims for a total of 4,500, uniting over one million people.

The room for manoeuvre economically is likely to be reduced with the return of large numbers of Afghan workers from Iran. The remittances from these workers had allowed the country to run a growing trade deficit. Without this cushion of about U.S. $100 million each year Afghanistan will have to rely even more on foreign help to pursue its economic plans. Western protests over the presence of Soviet troops in the country have affected the amount of aid coming into Afghanistan. The 1979/80 budget called for a 15 per cent decrease in development spending, which seemed to indicate that previously pledged aid would not necessarily be forthcoming. In January 1980 the World Bank stopped disbursing funds for develop-

ment projects in Afghanistan as Bank representatives had been unable to supervise the projects. This decision affected the payment of U.S. $115 million out of a total $227 million which had been approved. Socialist countries are expected to contribute 66 per cent of the foreign aid needed for basic projects in the 1979–84 Plan.

The unreality of all the plans of the new regime and their Soviet advisers became apparent by the middle of 1981. Links with the West were almost completely cut. Bright Afghan students, who would in the past have gone to universities in the West, now went to Soviet universities. The whole education system had been remoulded to fit an Eastern European system, with much emphasis on the virtues of Communism. The judicial system was also reformed. Even Western planners and technical advisers, attached to the United Nations, were weeded out and replaced by East Europeans or Indians. Daily, reports appeared in 1980 and 1981 of new co-operation agreements signed between Kabul and Moscow.

For all that, however, the life and the economy actually controlled from the capital was limited. The rebels opposed to the Kabul–Moscow axis had a free run of the countryside, and even towns like Qandahar, the second largest city, had their "no go" areas as far as the Kabul regime was concerned. The traditional economy, however, did suffer, a fact which was marked by the outflow of refugees. Much of the money sent from abroad never reached the Afghan people. In addition, by early 1981 it was clear that the Soviet leaders were trying to use food as a weapon against the rebellion. Food shortages became acute as the tribal groups preferred fighting to farming and as the regime destroyed grain stores, cattle and crops to try to bring dissidents to heel. By the middle of 1981 this began to cause a drift from the countryside to the towns, bringing new upheaval and the deterioration of what little remained of the traditional ways.

In Manila in April 1982 Kabul pleaded for a resumption of aid. Fazl Haque Khaliqyar, First Deputy Minister of Finance, said: "We find it regrettable and unfair that the flow of aid to our country should remain suspended even by international financial institutions because of political considerations and pressures". He spoke of Democratic Afghanistan's righteous cause". However, the President of the Asian Development Bank, Masao Fujioka, said that aid to Afghanistan would have to wait until the situation was "more conducive".

Total aid fell from more than $100 million per year in the late 1970s to only $34 million in 1980, with the prospect of further falls. Flows of funds from the industrialized countries, from multilateral agencies such as the World Bank and from the oil producers also dropped. In 1977, before Daud was killed, Afghanistan received more than $20 million from OPEC; by 1980, such aid was only $1.5 million.

The various pressures on the economy were beginning to tell. Khaliqyar put a brave face on things and claimed that there had been a 1.6 per cent increase in G.N.P. in the Afghan year 1359 (1980/81). He said, however, that in that year agriculture had declined by about 1 per cent and industry had been "relatively stagnant", so his optimism may not have been justified. In 1360 (1981/82) he promised greater growth, with a rise of 9.5 per cent in industry and 3.5 per cent in agriculture. He mentioned the support which the Government had given, including provision of inputs, setting of remunerative prices and ensuring of bank credit. Yet he conceded that it was an uphill struggle because of recession and what he termed "the destructive activities of counter-revolutionaries supported by international imperialism and regional reactionaries".

The impact of these pressures showed in both the statistics and the policies. Figures supplied by the Asian Development Bank showed a trade deficit which reached $300 million in 1979 and was $200 million in the following year. In spite of increased sales to the Soviet Union, which took 95 per cent of Afghanistan's natural gas (though at lower prices than Moscow received for sales of its own gas to Western Europe), and in spite of increased Soviet aid—$240 million in 1980—the budget and balance-of-payments positions were strained. In addition, the interlock between Afghanistan and the Soviet Union meant that most of the new project aid was for

schemes, such as in coal and natural gas development which would benefit the Soviet Union.

The Prime Minister, Sultan Ali Kishtmand, admitted to the Kabul press that the financial position was "rather tough", with revenues down and expenditures up. Some sources said that revenue collection had come to a virtual standstill in some provinces because of rebel activity. If taxes were levied in such areas, they were levied by the rebels. Khaliqyar said that Afghanistan's convertible foreign exchange reserves had declined by 16 per cent in the first 10 months of the 1981/82 financial year. He also said that "in the 1361 (1982/83) Development Plan several concessions are also being provided for promoting greater investment in the private sector". It was a good sign that the attempts to foist Marxism on a traditional people were acknowledged to be failing. The Government had to abandon its efforts at rural reform. In August 1981 it reversed its programme of land reform, and in February 1982 it dropped other rural measures and promised local tribal leaders control over internal affairs. This they had had anyway, so the Government's move was an attempt to woo the tribes back within Kabul's framework.

STATISTICAL SURVEY

AREA AND POPULATION

AREA	ESTIMATED MID-YEAR POPULATION			DENSITY (per sq. km.) 1979
	1977	1978	1979	
652,090 sq. km.*	14,795,733	15,158,632	15,551,358†	23.8

* 251,773 sq. miles.
† Result of Afghanistan's first national census, conducted on June 23rd, 1979. It includes an estimated nomadic population of 2,500,000.

Population (official mid-year estimates): 15,950,000 in 1980; 16,360,000 in 1981.

Note: In February 1982 it was estimated that over 2,600,000 Afghan refugees were living in Pakistan.

PROVINCES*
(Census of June 23rd, 1979)

	AREA (sq. km.)	POPULATION	DENSITY (per sq. km.)	CAPITAL (with population)
Kabul . . .	17,548	1,864,000	106.2	Kabul (913,164)
Parwan . . .	11,269	755,285	67.0	Charikar (22,424)
Bamian . . .	17,411	268,517	15.4	Bamian (7,355)
Ghazni . . .	23,373	646,623	27.7	Ghazni (30,425)
Paktika . . .	19,333	245,229	12.7	Sharan (1,398)
Paktia . . .	10,286	497,503	48.4	Gardiz (9,550)
Nangarhar . . .	7,614	745,986	98.0	Jalalabad (53,915)
Laghman . . .	7,209	310,751	43.1	Meterlam (3,987)
Kunar . . .	10,477	250,132	23.9	Hasan Abad (2,089)
Badakhshan . . .	47,393	497,758	10.5	Faizabad (9,098)
Takhar . . .	12,373	519,752	42.0	Taluqan (19,925)
Baghlan . . .	17,106	493,882	28.9	Baghlan (39,228)
Kunduz . . .	7,825	555,437	71.0	Kunduz (53,251)
Samangan . . .	16,220	272,584	16.8	Uiback (4,938)
Balkh . . .	11,833	569,255	48.1	Mazar-i-Sharif (103,372)
Jawzjan . . .	25,548	588,609	23.0	Shibarghan (18,995)
Fariab . . .	22,274	582,705	26.2	Maymana (38,251)
Badghis . . .	21,854	233,613	10.7	Qala-i-nau (5,340)
Herat . . .	61,301	769,111	12.5	Herat (140,323)
Farah . . .	47,778	234,621	4.9	Farah (18,797)
Neemroze . . .	41,347	103,634	2.5	Zarunj (6,477)
Helmand . . .	61,816	517,645	8.4	Bost (21,600)
Qandahar . . .	47,666	567,204	11.9	Qandahar (178,409)
Zabul . . .	17,289	179,362	10.4	Qalat (5,946)
Uruzgan . . .	29,289	444,168	15.2	Tareenkoot (3,362)
Ghor . . .	38,658	337,992	8.7	Cheghcheran (2,974)
TOTAL . .	652,090	13,051,358	20.0	

* Population figures refer to settled inhabitants only, excluding kuchies (nomads), estimated at 2,500,000 for the whole country.

PRINCIPAL CITIES
(population at June 23rd, 1979)

Kabul (capital) .	. 913,164	Kunduz .	.	53,251
Qandahar .	. 178,409	Baghlan .	.	39,228
Herat .	. 140,323	Maymana .	.	38,251
Mazar-i-Sharif .	. 103,372	Pul-i-Khomri .	.	31,101
Jalalabad .	. 53,915	Ghazni .	.	30,425

Births and Deaths (1979): Birth rate 48.1 per 1,000; death rate 23.3 per 1,000.

ECONOMICALLY ACTIVE POPULATION*
(ISIC Major Divisions, persons aged 8 years and over)

	1979 CENSUS
Agriculture, forestry, hunting and fishing	2,369,481
Mining and quarrying . . .	59,339
Manufacturing	423,373
Electricity, gas and water . . .	11,354
Construction	51,086
Trade, restaurants and hotels . .	137,860
Transport, storage and communications	66,243
Other services	749,345
TOTAL . . .	3,868,081

* Figures refer to settled population only and exclude persons seeking work for the first time.

AGRICULTURE
LAND USE
('ooo hectares)

	1973	1976	1979
Arable land . . .	7,910*	7,910	7,910*
Land under permanent crops .	138*	138*	140*
Permanent meadows and pastures . . .	50,000*	50,000*	50,000*
Forest and woodland .	1,900	1,900	1,900*
Other land and inland water .	4,802	4,802	4,800
TOTAL . . .	64,750	64,750	64,750

* FAO estimate.

Source: FAO, *Production Yearbook.*

PRINCIPAL CROPS
(year ending March 20th)

	AREA ('ooo hectares)			PRODUCTION ('ooo metric tons)		
	1978/79	1979/80	1980/81	1978/79	1979/80	1980/81
Wheat . . .	2,348	2,162	2,192	2,813	2,663	2,750
Maize . . .	482	472.3	477	780	759.8	797
Rice (paddy) . .	210	205.8	212	428	439	461
Barley . . .	310	303.8	306	325	318.4	321
Seed cotton . .	112	84.1	45	132	105	65
Sugar beet . .	4.9	3.2	2	73	70	35
Sugar cane . .	3.8	3.7	4	64	63.7	70
Vegetables . .	94.0	130.3	95	766	1,069.2	828
Fruits . . .	140.2	139.2	142.6	824	836	891
Oil seeds . . .	50	59	59	35	42	43

LIVESTOCK
('000)

	1976/77*	1977/78	1978/79	1979/80	1980/81
Cattle	3,835	3,650	3,730	3,710	3,710
Sheep†	22,000	20,244	19,075	18,400	18,700
Goats	3,000	3,000	3,000	2,885	2,850
Horses	370	392*	400		1,730
Asses	1,250	1,300	1,300	} 1,730	
Mules	26	48	40		
Buffaloes	35	n.a.	n.a.	n.a.	n.a.
Camels	290	300	300	270	265
Poultry	19,690	6,000	6,200	6,400	6,400

* FAO estimate.
† Including Karakul sheep, numbering 4.4 million in 1979/80, and 4.5 million in 1980/81.

Sources: FAO, *Production Yearbook*, and Central Statistics Office, Kabul.

LIVESTOCK PRODUCTS
('000 metric tons)

	1978	1979*	1980*
Beef and veal	67	67	67
Mutton and lamb . . .	103	99	100
Goats' meat	25*	25	25
Poultry meat	11*	11	11
Cows' milk	533	640	640
Sheep's milk	225*	230	230
Goats' milk	48*	48	48
Butter	5.6*	5.8	5.8
Cheese	9.8*	9.9	9.9
Hen eggs	16.8*	16.9	16.9
Honey	3.6†	3.6†	3.6
Wool: greasy	26.5*	27.0	27.5
clean	14.3*	14.5	14.8
Cattle and buffalo hides . .	11.1*	11.2	11.4
Sheep skins	16.1*	16.8	17.1
Goat skins	3.8*	3.8	3.8

* FAO estimate.   † Unofficial figure.

Source: FAO, *Production Yearbook*.

FORESTRY
ROUNDWOOD REMOVALS
(FAO estimates, '000 cubic metres, excluding bark)

	CONIFEROUS (soft wood)			BROADLEAVED (hard wood)			TOTAL		
	1977	1978	1979	1977	1978	1979	1977	1978	1979
Sawlogs, veneer logs and logs for sleepers* . . .	820	820	820	36	36	36	856	856	856
Other industrial wood . . .	122	125	129	488	501	515	610	626	644
Fuel wood	1,830	1,879	1,931	4,381	4,500	4,622	6,211	6,379	6,553
TOTAL . . .	2,772	2,824	2,880	4,905	5,037	5,173	7,677	7,861	8,053

* Assumed to be unchanged from 1977.

Source: FAO, *Yearbook of Forest Products*.

SAWNWOOD PRODUCTION
('ooo cubic metres, including boxboards)

	1971	1972	1973	1974*	1975*	1976*
Coniferous . . .	345	305	360*	360	310	380
Broadleaved . . .	60	55	50	50	20	20
Total . . .	405	360	410	410	330	400

* FAO estimate.

1977-79: Annual production as in 1976 (FAO estimates).

Source: FAO, *Yearbook of Forest Products.*

Inland Fishing (1964–80): Total catch 1,500 metric tons each year (FAO estimate).

MINING
(Twelve months ending March 20th)

		1977/78	1978/79	1979/80	1980/81
Hard coal . . .	'ooo metric tons	170.3	218.2	131.9	118.7
Salt (unrefined) . . .	,, ,, ,,	77.7	81.1	67.6	37.1
Natural gas . . .	million cu. metres	2,548	2,461	2,327	2,790.3

INDUSTRY
SELECTED PRODUCTS
(Twelve months ending March 20th)

		1977/78	1978/79	1979/80	1980/81
Ginned cotton . . .	'ooo metric tons	41.5	45.3	29.4	22.9
Cotton fabrics . . .	million metres	76.8	76.6	63.3	43.3
Woollen fabrics* . . .	'ooo metres	400.0	405.2	401.0	405.3
Rayon fabrics . . .	,, ,,	29,700.6	23,100.0	21,300.0	14,800.0
Cement . . .	'ooo metric tons	149.7	126.5	99.3	87.2
Electricity† . . .	million kWh.	776.1	845.4	907.8	958.8
Wheat flour . . .	'ooo metric tons	80.9	97.0	122.6	113.1
Refined sugar . . .	,, ,, ,,	11.2	10.8	8.6	2.7
Vegetable oil . . .	,, ,, ,,	9.9	10.4	9.6	6.5
Nitrogenous fertilizers‡ . . .	,, ,, ,,	99.7	105.7	106.2	106.3

* Including blankets.

† Production for public use, excluding industrial establishments generating electricity for their own use.

‡ Production in terms of nitrogen.

FINANCE

100 puls (puli) = 2 krans = 1 afghani (Af.).
Coins: 25 and 50 puls; 1, 2 and 5 afghanis.
Notes: 10, 20, 50, 100, 500 and 1,000 afghanis.
Exchange rates (May 1982): £1 sterling = 125.48 afghanis; U.S. $1 = 68.25 afghanis.
1,000 afghanis = £7.97 = $14.65.

Note: Multiple exchange rates were in operation before March 1963. Between 1956 and 1963 the official base rate was U.S. $1 = 20.00 afghanis. In March 1963 a single official rate of $1 = 45.00 afghanis was introduced. This remained in force until May 1979. The year-end exchange rate (afghanis per U.S. dollar) was: 42.25 in 1979; 45.85 in 1980; 50.60 in 1981. In terms of sterling, the official rate was £1 = 108.00 afghanis from November 1967 to August 1971; and £1 = 117.26 afghanis from December 1971 to June 1972.

BUDGET
(million afghanis, twelve months ending September 21st)

REVENUE	1976/77	1977/78	1978/79	EXPENDITURE	1976/77	1977/78	1978/79
Direct taxes	1,713	2,428	2,535	Administration	1,223	1,255	1,690
Indirect taxes	6,159	6,830	6,913	Defence, Security	2,381	2,656	3,007
Revenue from monopolies				Social services	2,254	2,538	3,186
and other enterprises	887	1,316	1,192	Economic services	1,219	870	985
Natural gas revenue	2,336	1,510	2,637				
Revenue from other property				TOTAL MINISTRIES	7,077	7,319	8,868
and services	2,179	2,357	1,954				
Other revenue	676	480	1,224	Foreign debt service	1,320	2,087	2,493
				Subsidies (exchange, etc.)	2,771	2,532	1,024
				TOTAL ORDINARY	11,168	11,938	12,385
TOTAL REVENUE	13,950	14,921	16,455	Development Budget	5,060	5,200	6,845

1980/81 (estimates in million afghanis): Revenue: internal sources 23,478, grants-in-aid from U.S.S.R. 1,735, loans and project assistance 8,546, total revenue 33,759; Expenditure: ministries' allocation 19,213, development budget 14,546, total expenditure 33,759.

BANK OF AFGHANISTAN RESERVES
(U.S. $ million at December)

	1975	1976	1977	1978	1979	1980
Gold*	39.35	39.35	39.69	40.02	42.97	270.32
IMF Special Drawing Rights	6.23	5.95	6.90	7.01	17.68	15.46
Reserve Position in IMF	—	—	10.02	11.69	12.42	19.22
Foreign Exchange	80.32	124.97	258.90	371.86	411.11	336.49
TOTAL	125.90	170.27	315.51	430.58	484.18	641.49

* National valuation. In March 1980 gold was revalued at U.S. $300 per troy ounce (31.1 grammes).

Source: IMF, *International Financial Statistics.*

MONEY SUPPLY
(million afghanis at March 21st)

	1977	1978	1979	1980	1981
Currency outside banks	15,232	17,968	22,046	28,624	33,545
Private sector deposits at Bank of Afghanistan	3,412	5,179	5,596	5,993	5,512
Demand deposits at commercial banks	1,339	1,427	1,304	1,814	1,877
TOTAL MONEY	19,983	24,574	28,946	36,431	40,934

Source: IMF, *International Financial Statistics.*

COST OF LIVING
(twelve months ending March 20th. Base: 1961/62=100)

	1975/76	1976/77	1977/78	1978/79	1979/80*	1980/81
Cereals . . .	308.6	303.5	351.2	366.2	113.2	105.1
Meat	368.6	389.3	399.4	385.7	100.8	123.3
Fruits . . .	305.9	361.7	358.9	390.3	118.2	109.1
Vegetables . .	335.3	349.6	349.3	350.7	122.5	99.3
TOTAL (incl. others)	298.2	300.8	335.6	346.1	112.2	109.6

* Base: 1978/79=100.

NATIONAL ACCOUNTS
('000 million afghanis at 1978 prices, twelve months ending March 20th)
GROSS NATIONAL PRODUCT BY ECONOMIC ACTIVITY

	1976/77	1977/78	1978/79	1979/80
Agriculture, hunting, forestry and fishing .	86.6	77.3	82.1	84.3
Mining	} 29.3	30.4	33.2	30.7
Manufacturing				
Electricity, gas and water . . .	5.7	6.9	8.6	7.6
Construction	11.8	11.1	11.5	10.3
Trade, restaurants and hotels .	5.3	6.0	6.1	5.2
Transport, storage and communications .	2.1	2.0	} 18.2	19.5
Other services	6.7	14.2		
Foreign transactions . . .				
G.N.P. IN MARKET PRICES . .	147.5	147.9	159.7	157.6

BALANCE OF PAYMENTS
(U.S. $ million, year ending March 20th)

	1976/77	1977/78	1978/79	1979/80
Merchandise exports f.o.b. . .	282.5	326.7	336.7	481.2
Merchandise imports c.i.f. . .	−349.8	−521.3	−638.6	−681.1
TRADE BALANCE . .	−67.3	−194.6	−301.9	−199.9
Travel (net)	30.2	38.0	28.0	7.0
Service component of project aid .	−20.1	−18.9	−17.1	—
Official loans and grants: project .	120.8	198.1	204.3	264.5
other .	39.5	20.3	31.5	52.6
External public debt service . .	−28.2	−50.8	−58.0	−18.0
Other transactions (net)* . .	−10.0	163.4	212.0	17.5
CHANGES IN RESERVES, etc. .	64.7	155.5	98.8	60.7

*Including errors and omissions.

EXTERNAL TRADE

(million afghanis, year ending March 20th)

	1975/76	1976/77	1977/78	1978/79	1979/80	1980/81
Imports c.i.f.* . . .	20,442	18,313	24,214	32,021	29,860	23,482
Exports f.o.b. . . .	13,085	16,320	15,296	15,120	21,476	32,362

* Including imports under commodity loans and grants from foreign countries and international organizations.

PRINCIPAL COMMODITIES

(distribution by SITC, U.S. $'000, year ending March 20th)

IMPORTS c.i.f.*	1973/74	1974/75	1975/76	1976/77
Food and live animals	25,687	44,891	74,817	38,885
Sugar, sugar preparations and honey . .	13,139	26,285	39,494	12,790
Refined sugar	13,071	26,097	33,811	12,768
Coffee, tea, cocoa and spices . .	10,849	15,648	31,436	22,976
Tea	10,143	15,066	30,492	21,940
Crude materials (inedible) except fuels .	4,540	7,552	5,412	5,896
Mineral fuels, lubricants, etc.. . .	8,521	22,617	27,072	35,676
Petroleum and petroleum products .	8,507	22,582	27,060	35,624
Petroleum products . . .	8,386	22,510	27,000	35,597
Motor spirit (petrol), etc. . .	2,900	4,998	9,265	12,073
Lamp oil and white spirit (kerosene) .	533	9,504	1,693	5,022
Distillate fuels . . .	3,598	6,400	13,391	15,280
Animal and vegetable oils and fats .	3,725	6,676	8,618	13,746
Chemicals	10,819	23,268	23,941	30,447
Medicinal and pharmaceutical products .	4,998	6,353	6,704	9,062
Medicaments	n.a.	6,324	6,700	9,035
Manufactured fertilizers . . .	n.a.	8,754	7,850	8,533
Nitrogenous fertilizers . . .	n.a.	7,811	—	—
Phosphatic fertilizers . . .	n.a.	943	7,850	8,533
Basic manufactures	49,022	85,448	92,024	93,888
Rubber manufactures . . .	11,677	11,323	21,699	18,917
Tyres and tubes . . .	11,612	11,298	21,631	18,761
Textile yarn, fabrics, etc. . .	27,520	60,040	49,983	55,159
Textile yarn and thread. . .	14,730	13,276	10,661	10,422
Yarn of flax, ramie and true hemp .	13,428	10,947	7,868	7,068
Woven cotton fabrics† . . .	2,032	7,881	2,968	3,145
Other woven fabrics† . . .	11,209	38,883	36,353	40,070
Fabrics of linen, ramie and true hemp† .	4,940	11,927	8,998	6,353
Fabrics of synthetic fibres† . .	3,278	20,657	18,839	21,809
Machinery and transport equipment .	16,208	19,229	34,482	29,025
Electrical machinery, apparatus, etc. .	3,294	5,384	6,459	12,682
Transport equipment . . .	9,750	10,499	24,351	10,912
Road motor vehicles and parts‡ .	9,403	9,812	n.a.	10,025
Buses	876	1,236	13,228	924
Miscellaneous manufactured articles .	9,136	9,033	12,535	14,479
TOTAL (incl. others) . . .	127,560	223,794	268,313	264,183

* Excluding imports under commodity loans and grants for which the distribution by commodity is not known (U.S. $'000): 26 in 1973/74; 19,169 in 1974/75; 67,815 in 1975/76; 71,346 in 1976/77.

† Excluding narrow or special fabrics.

‡ Excluding tyres, engines and electrical parts.

1977/78 (U.S. $'000): Sugar 16,569; Tea 27,935; Edible oil 9,790; Medicaments 11,384; Tyres and tubes 19,308; Textile yarn and thread 18,199; Textile fabrics etc. 51,469; Road vehicles 10,760; Petroleum products 34,426; Total (incl. others) 321,347 (excl. project imports 143,789; other loans and grants 26,141).

[continued on following page]

PRINCIPAL COMMODITIES—*continued*]

EXPORTS f.o.b.	1973/74	1974/75	1975/76	1976/77
Food and live animals	72,633	95,612	n.a.	94,326
Fruit and vegetables	69,779	n.a.	77,007	92,328
Fresh fruit and nuts (excl. oil nuts)* .	29,310	44,423	29,746	46,684
Fresh grapes	8,808	18,488	13,235	15,108
Edible nuts	5,965	12,913	n.a.	23,480
Dried fruit*	47,134	n.a.	47,261	43,604
Dried grapes (raisins) . . .	n.a.	37,238	n.a.	41,844
Crude materials (inedible) except fuels .	n.a.	80,476	89,123	130,688
Hides, skins and fur skins . . .	29,902	19,326	22,099	33,402
Hides and skins (undressed) . .	5,668	7,053	11,748	11,524
Hides of cattle, etc. . . .	1,566	2,777	6,647	8,866
Fur skins (undressed) . .	18,239	12,273	10,351	21,878
Oil-seeds, oil nuts and oil kernels .	3,597	4,133	8,251	12,912
Textile fibres and waste . . .	13,640	40,876	39,538	68,728
Wool and other animal hair . .	n.a.	6,193	7,980	7,212
Cotton	7,221	34,883	31,558	60,758
Raw cotton (excl. linters) . .	7,221	34,883	31,558	60,706
Plants mainly for medicines, perfumes, etc..	2,395	8,980	10,436	5,814
Mineral fuels, lubricants, etc. . .	17,985	32,095	45,342	39,540
Natural gas	17,985	32,095	45,342	39,540
Basic manufactures	n.a.	n.a.	n.a.	30,654
Textile yarn, fabrics, etc. . . .	15,898	20,077	18,469	30,084
Floor coverings, tapestries, etc. .	14,474	19,900	16,785	24,024
Knotted carpets, carpeting and rugs .	14,474	19,900	16,738	23,528
TOTAL (incl. others) . . .	159,102	230,550	223,363	298,997

* Dried citrus fruit are included with "fresh fruit and nuts".

1977/78 (U.S. \$'000): Fresh fruit and nuts 22,874; Dried fruit 83,840; Hides and skins 11,448; Fur skins 18,443; Raw cotton 55,040; Natural gas 39,349; Carpets and rugs 38,408; Total (incl. others) 313,374.

PRINCIPAL TRADING PARTNERS
(U.S. \$ million)

IMPORTS	1977/78	1978/79	EXPORTS	1977/78	1978/79
France	7.1	10.6	Germany, Federal Republic .	17.4	22.5
Germany, Federal Republic .	31.9	46.6	India	24.0	37.5
India	24.5	39.1	Iran	2.4	2.1
Japan	101.5	123.5	Pakistan . . .	36.7	41.1
Pakistan	12.5	16.9	Switzerland . . .	7.8	8.9
United Kingdom . . .	15.6	21.9	United Kingdom . .	37.1	30.2
U.S.A.	16.8	30.9	U.S.A. . . .	15.0	11.3
TOTAL (incl. others) . .	497.7	681.7	TOTAL (incl. others) . .	314.4	321.8

1977/78 (U.S. \$ million): Imports from U.S.S.R. 108.1, Iran 62.2; Exports to U.S.S.R. 117.4.

TOURISM
INTERNATIONAL TOURIST ARRIVALS BY COUNTRY

	1975	1976	1977	1978	1979
Australia	1,094	1,055	4,397	3,070	967
France	9,431	7,794	6,779	4,781	1,153
Germany, Federal Republic .	8,649	8,907	9,085	7,496	1,817
India	8,717	8,521	11,158	9,744	4,350
Pakistan	13,648	20,213	35,105	23,663	10,126
United Kingdom . .	9,777	10,108	11,526	9,102	1,850
U.S.A.	9,501	8,950	9,011	6,389	1,039
Others	27,662	23,406	31,299	27,744	8,902
TOTAL . . .	85,479	88,954	118,360	91,989	30,204

Receipts from tourism: U.S. $11 million in 1973; $12 million in 1974; $12 million in 1975.

TRANSPORT
CIVIL AVIATION
(twelve months ending March 20th)

	1977/78	1978/79	1979/80	1980/81
Kilometres flown ('000) . .	4,514	3,931	3,765	3,012
Passengers carried . .	97,100	69,800	104,000	86,199
Passenger-km. ('000) . .	298,200	206,200	238,068	173,855
Freight ton-km. ('000) . .	40,300	32,600	19,084	21,366
Cargo	13,300	14,000	7,070	n.a.
Mail	174	153	n.a.	n.a.

ROAD TRAFFIC
(motor vehicles in use)

	1976/77	1977/78	1978/79	1979/80	1980/81
Passenger cars . .	28,098	31,471	34,772	34,192	34,080
Commercial vehicles .	19,298	29,737	34,435	27,555	28,714

COMMUNICATIONS MEDIA

Telephones in use: 20,831 in 1977/78.
Radio sets in use: *c.* 1,000,000 in 1977.
Television sets in use: 120,000 in January 1980.

EDUCATION
(1977/78)

	INSTITUTIONS	PUPILS
Primary schools . .	1,778	751,252
Village schools . .	1,593	121,070
Secondary schools (to Grade nine)	134	10,177
General high schools . .	199	99,563
Vocational high schools .	27	10,816
Universities and Polytechnics	3	9,352

Note: Teachers in all institutions totalled 12,399 in 1975/76.

Source (unless otherwise stated): Central Statistics Office, Kabul.

THE CONSTITUTION

Immediately after the coup of April 27th, 1978 (the Saur Revolution), the 1977 Constitution was abolished. Both Taraki and Amin promised new constitutions but were removed from power before special commissions appointed by them had prepared any drafts. On April 21st, 1980, the Revolutionary Council ratified the Basic Principles of the Democratic Republic of Afghanistan. These are to remain valid until the ratification of the Constitution by a Loya Jirgah (National Assembly). The following is a summary of the Basic Principles.

General Provisions. The role of the State is to serve the well-being and prosperity of the people, to safeguard their peaceful life and to protect their rights.

The People's Democratic Party of Afghanistan, the party of the workers and the working class, is the country's guiding force. It aims to realize the ideals of the Great Saur Revolution for the creation of a new, just society.

Muslims are free to practise religious rites, as are members of other religions provided they pose no threat to Afghan society.

All nationalities, tribes and ethnic groups are equal.

Foreign policy is based on the principle of peaceful co-existence and active and positive non-alignment. Friendship and co-operation is to be strengthened with the U.S.S.R. as it will be with all countries of the socialist community. Afghanistan abides by the UN Charter, professes its desire for peace between neighbouring countries of the region and supports the struggle against colonialism, imperialism, Zionism, racism and fascism. Afghanistan favours disarmament and the prevention of proliferation of nuclear weapons. War propaganda is prohibited.

The State protects private ownership and guarantees the law of inheritance of private ownership. Banks, mines, institutes, insurance, heavy industries, radio and television are state-owned. The establishment of agricultural and industrial co-operatives is encouraged.

One of the State's major duties is to provide adequate housing for the workers. Family, mother and child are given special protection by the State.

The capital is Kabul.

Rights and duties of the people. All subjects of Afghanistan are equal before the law. The following rights are guaranteed: the right to life and security, to observe the religious rites of Islam and of other religions, to work, to protection of health and social welfare, to education, to scientific, technical, cultural and artistic activities, to freedom of speech and thought, to security of residence and privacy of correspondence and to complain to the appropriate government organs.

In crime, the accused is considered innocent until guilt is recognized by the court. Nobody may be arrested, detained or punished except in accordance with the law.

The defence of the homeland and of the achievements of the Saur Revolution, loyalty to its aims and ideals and services to the people are the responsibilities of every subject.

Loya Jirgah. This is the highest organ of State power. Its composition and the election of its representatives will be regulated by law. Elections to the Loya Jirgah will be based on a general, secret, free, direct and equal vote. The Loya Jirgah will ratify the Constitution at its first session.

The Revolutionary Council is the highest organ of State power until the necessary conditions for elections to the Loya Jirgah are met.

The number and election or selection of new members is proposed by the Presidium of the Revolutionary Council and ratified by the Revolutionary Council. It is empowered to ratify laws, decrees, state economic and social development plans and to form the Presidium and the Council of Ministers. It also has the authority to call elections for the Loya Jirgah and to declare war. Laws and decrees are ratified by a majority vote of the members and are enforced after their publication in the official gazette. Sessions of the Revolutionary Council are held twice a year and they require a minimum attendance of two-thirds of the members.

The permanent organ of the Revolutionary Council is the Presidium. The Revolutionary Council elects the Presidium from amongst its members. The President of the Revolutionary Council is the Chairman of the Presidium. The Presidium's responsibilities include the interpretation and enforcement of laws, the granting of amnesty and the commuting of punishment. Between sessions all responsibilities of the Revolutionary Council are transferred to the Presidium.

Until the appointment or election of a Prime Minister, the President of the Revolutionary Council is the Prime Minister.

The Council of Ministers is the supreme executive organ of State power and is responsible to the Revolutionary Council and to the Presidium when the Revolutionary Council is in recess. It is vested with the authority to implement domestic and foreign policy and to submit draft laws to the Revolutionary Council (or Presidium) for consideration and ratification. It comprises the President of the Council of Ministers (also known as the Prime Minister), his deputy or deputies and ministers.

Local administrative organs. Local committees and councils are to be formed in the provinces, cities, sub-districts and villages for the solution of all questions relating to the locality. All matters of election and representation will be regulated by law. Local executive committees of State power are to be established too. Besides taking decisions within the limits of their authority, these local organs are authorized to implement the decisions of higher organs.

The Judiciary. (*see* Judicial System section).

The Public Prosecution Department. The Attorney-General guides the activities of the country's prosecution organs. The Department consists of the Prosecutor General and the prosecution department of the provinces, cities, districts and sub-districts. These organs are independent of local organs, answerable only to the Prosecutor General. The Attorney-General, who is responsible to the Revolutionary Council, and the prosecutors supervise the implementation and observance of all laws. Until the appointment of the Prosecutor General his authority and duties are vested in the Minister of Justice.

Final Orders. Any alteration of these Basic Principles may be implemented on the proposal of the Presidium and the ratification by two-thirds of the members of the Revolutionary Council. The Basic Principles will remain valid until the ratification of the Constitution of the Democratic Republic of Afghanistan. Decrees, laws and other documents issued prior to the enforcement of the Basic Principles remain valid provided they are not contradictory to the Basic Principles.

THE GOVERNMENT

HEAD OF STATE

President of the Revolutionary Council and General Secretary of the People's Democratic Party Central Committee:
BABRAK KARMAL (took office December 27th, 1979).

PRESIDIUM OF THE REVOLUTIONARY COUNCIL

President: BABRAK KARMAL.

Vice-Presidents: Maj.-Gen. ABDUL QADER, Lt.-Col. GUL AQA.

Secretary: MOHAMMAD ANWAR FARZAN.

Members: NOOR AHMAD NOOR, ABDURRASHID ARYAN, ANAHITA RATEBZAD, NEJMUDDIN KAWYANI, Lt.-Col. NASER MOHAMMAD, ABDUL GHAFFAR LAKANWAL, Dr. SALEH MOHAMMAD ZEARAI.

COUNCIL OF MINISTERS
(May 1982)

President of the Revolutionary Council: BABRAK KARMAL.

President of the Council of Ministers: SULTAN ALI KISHT-MAND.

Vice-President of the Council of Ministers and Minister of Information and Culture: ABDUL MAJID SARBULAND.

Vice-President of the Council of Ministers and Minister of Higher Education: GUL DAD.

Vice-President of the Council of Ministers and President of the State Planning Committee: Dr. KHALIL AHMAD ABAWI.

Minister of Justice: ABDUL WAHAB SAFI.

Minister of Defence: Maj.-Gen. MOHAMMAD RAFIE.

Minister of Foreign Affairs: SHAH MOHAMMAD DOST.

Minister of the Interior: SAYED MOHAMMAD GULABZOI.

Minister of Communications: Lt.-Col. MOHAMMAD ASLAM WATANJAR.

Minister of Education: FAQIR MOHAMMAD YAQUBI.

Minister of Nationalities and Tribes: SULIEMAN ALI LAIQ.

Minister of Agriculture and Land Reform: FAZUL RAHIM MOHMAND.

Minister of Finance: ABDUL WAKIL.

Minister of Commerce: MOHAMMAD KHAN JALALAR.

Minister of Mines and Industries: Eng. MOHAMMAD ESMA'IL DANESH.

Minister of Transport: Lt.-Col. SHERJAN MAZDOORYAR.

Minister of Public Works: Eng. NAZAR MOHAMMAD.

Minister of Power: Prof. RAS MOHAMMAD PAKTIN.

Minister of Irrigation: Eng. AHMAD SHAH SORKHABI.

Minister of Public Health: Dr. MOHAMMAD NABI KAMYAR.

POLITBURO OF THE CENTRAL COMMITTEE OF THE PEOPLE'S DEMOCRATIC PARTY OF AFGHANISTAN

General Secretary: BABRAK KARMAL.

Full Members: ANAHITA RATEBZAD, SULTAN ALI KISHT-MAND, Dr. SALEH MOHAMMAD ZEARAI, GHULAM DASTAGIR PANJSHERI, NOOR AHMAD NOOR, Maj.-Gen. MOHAMMAD RAFIE, Lt.-Col. MOHAMMAD ASLAM WATANJAR, MOHAMMAD NAJIBULLAH.

Alternate Members: MOHAMMAD ISMAIL DANESH, MAH-MOUD BARYALAI.

POLITICAL PARTY

People's Democratic Party of Afghanistan (PDPA): Kabul; f. 1965, split 1967; re-founded 1976, when the Khalq (Masses) Party and its splinter Parcham (Flag) Party re-united and annexed the Musawat Party; Communist; Secretariat of the Central Cttee. BABRAK KARMAL, Dr. SALEH MOHAMMAD ZEARAI, NOOR AHMAD NOOR, MAHMOUD BARIALAI, NEYAZ MOHD. MOHMAND; publ. *Haqiqat Enqelab Saur*.

National Fatherland Front: f. 1981 as union of PDPA representatives, national and tribal groups; aims to promote national unity under the leadership of the PDPA; Exec. Bd. of 23 mems.; Chair. National Committee Dr. SALEH MOHAMMAD ZEARAI; Vice-Chair. SULIEMAN ALI LAIQ, SAYED AFGHANI, NEJMUDDIN KAWYANI, SAYED EKRAM PAYGIR.

No other political parties are allowed to function. There are many insurgent groups (*Mujaheddin*) fighting against the Government in Afghanistan. The principal ones are the two factions of Hizb-i Islami (leaders: GULBUDDIN HIKMATYAR and YUNUS KHALIS), Jamiat-i Islami (leader: BURHANEDDIN RABBANI), Harakat-i Inqilab-i Islami (leader: MOHAMMAD NABI MOHAMMADI), the National Islamic Front (leader: SAYED AHMAD GAILANI) and the National Liberation Front (leader: SEBQATULLAH MOJAD-DEDI). The different groups co-operate to varying degrees; the last three groups joined forces in June 1981 to form the Islamic Unity of Mujaheddin of Afghanistan, but the alliance has been strained by rivalry and feuding. Efforts were being made in March 1982 to form a grand alliance of the six major groups.

DIPLOMATIC REPRESENTATION

EMBASSIES ACCREDITED TO AFGHANISTAN*

(In Kabul unless otherwise stated)

(E) Embassy.

Algeria: New Delhi, India (E).

Argentina: Teheran, Iran (E).

Australia: Islamabad, Pakistan (E).

Austria: P.O.B. 24, Zarghouna Wat (E); *Chargé d'affaires a.i.:* MAXIMILIAN FREISCHLAGER (Ambassador resident in Teheran, Iran).

Bahrain: Teheran, Iran (E).

Bangladesh: House no. 19, Sarak "H", Wazir Akbar Khan Mena, P.O.B. 510 (E); *Chargé d'affaires a.i.:* MD. MIZANUR RAHMAN.

Belgium: Teheran, Iran (E).

Brazil: Teheran, Iran (E).

Bulgaria: Wazir Akbar Khan Mena (E); *Ambassador:* MLADEN NIKOLOV MLADENOV.

Burma: New Delhi, India (E).

Canada: Islamabad, Pakistan (E).

China, People's Republic: Shah Mahmoud Ghazi Wat (E); *Chargé d'affaires a.i.:* JIN CHANGRU.

Cuba: Char Rahi Haji Yaqub, opp. Shar-e-Nau Park (E); *Ambassador:* MANUEL PENADO CASANOVA.

Czechoslovakia: Taimani Wat, Kala-i-Fatullah (E); *Ambassador:* Dr. VACLAV KOUBA.

Denmark: Teheran, Iran (E).

Egypt: c/o Yugoslav Embassy.

Finland: Moscow, U.S.S.R. (E).

France: Avenue Enqelab Saur (E); *Chargé d'affaires a.i.:* ROLAND BARRAUX.

German Democratic Republic: Ghazi Ayub Wat, Shar-e-Nau (E); *Ambassador:* KRAFT BUMBEL.

Germany, Federal Republic: P.O.B. 83, Wazir Akbar Khan Mena (E); *Chargé d'affaires a.i.:* JOHANNES BAUCH.

Ghana: New Delhi, India (E).

Greece: Baghdad, Iraq (E).

Hungary: sin 306–308, Wazir Akbar Khan Mena, P.O.B. 830 (E); *Ambassador:* DEZSŐ KISS.

India: Malalai Wat, Shar-e-Nau (E); *Ambassador:* J. N. DIXIT.

Indonesia: Wazir Akbar Khan Mena (E); *Chargé d'affaires a.i.:* HADI MARTOYO.

Iran: Malekyar Wat (E); *Chargé d'affaires a.i.:* SEYYED ALIREZA NIKUNIA.

Iraq: P.O.B. 523, Wazir Akbar Khan Mena (E); *Chargé d'affaires a.i.:* HASSAN IBRAHIM D. AL-ADHAMI.

Italy: Khoja Abdullah Ansari Wat (E); *Chargé d'affaires a.i.:* CESARE CAPITANI.

Japan: No. 240–241, Wazir Akbar Khan Mena (E); *Chargé d'affaires a.i.:* AKIHISA TANAKA.

Jordan: Teheran, Iran (E).

Korea, Democratic People's Republic: Wazir Akbar Khan Mena (E); *Ambassador:* LI CHONG-RIM.

Korea, Republic: New Delhi, India (E).

Kuwait: Teheran, Iran (E).

Lebanon: Teheran, Iran (E).

Libya: 103 Wazir Akbar Khan Mena (People's Bureau); *Secretary:* MOHD HASAN AL-BURKI.

Malaysia: Teheran, Iran (E).

Mexico: New Delhi, India (E).

Mongolia: Wazir Akbar Khan Mena (E); *Ambassador:* (vacant).

Morocco: Teheran, Iran (E).

Nepal: New Delhi, India (E).

Netherlands: Teheran, Iran (E).

Norway: Teheran, Iran (E).

Pakistan: Zarghouna Wat (E); *Chargé d'affaires a.i.:* FEDA YUNIS.

Philippines: New Delhi, India (E).

Poland: Gozargah St. (E); *Ambassador:* Dr. EDWARD BARADZIEJ.

Portugal: New Delhi, India (E).

Qatar: Teheran, Iran (E).

Romania: Teheran, Iran (E).

Saudi Arabia: c/o French Embassy.

Senegal: Teheran, Iran (E).

Spain: Teheran, Iran (E).

Sri Lanka: New Delhi, India (E).

Sudan: Teheran, Iran (E).

Sweden: Teheran, Iran (E).

Switzerland: Teheran, Iran (E).

Syria: New Delhi, India (E).

Thailand: New Delhi, India (E).

Turkey: Shah Mahmoud Ghazi Wat (E); *Chargé d'affaires a.i.:* ALTAN GÜVEN.

U.S.S.R.: Dar-ul-Aman Wat (E); *Ambassador:* FIKRYAT A. TABEYEV.

United Arab Emirates: Teheran, Iran (E).

United Kingdom: Karte Parwan (E); *Chargé d'affaires a.i.:* JOHN D. GARNER.

U.S.A.: Khwaja Abdullah Ansari Wat (E); *Chargé d'affaires a.i.:* CHARLES F. DUNBAR.

Viet-Nam: No. 3 Nijat St., Wazir Akbar Khan Mena (E); *Ambassador:* NGUYEN SI HOAT.

Yugoslavia: No. 923 Main Rd., Wazir Akbar Khan Mena (E); *Ambassador:* BOGDAN MALBASIĆ.

* Not all of the above mentioned countries recognize the administration of Babrak Karmal as the legitimate government of Afghanistan.

Afghanistan also has diplomatic relations with Chile, Laos, Tunisia and the People's Democratic Republic of Yemen.

JUDICIAL SYSTEM

The functions and structure of the judiciary are established in Articles 54–58 of the Basic Principles ratified by the Revolutionary Council in April 1980.

Judgment is made by the courts on the basis of democratic principles. The courts implement the laws of the Democratic Republic of Afghanistan and, in cases of ambivalence, will judge in accordance with the rules of *Shari'ah* (Islamic religious law). Trials are held in open session except when circumstances defined by law deem the trial to be held in closed session. Trials are conducted in Pashtu and Dari or in the language of the majority of the inhabitants of the locality. The right to speak in court in one's mother tongue is guaranteed to the two sides of the lawsuit.

The judiciary comprises the Supreme Court, provincial, city and district courts, the courts of the armed forces and other such special courts as are formed in accordance with the directives of the law.

The supreme judicial organ is the Supreme Court, which consists of a President, Vice-President and other members. It supervises the judicial activities of the courts and ensures the uniformity of law enforcement and interpretation by those courts.

The Presidium of the Revolutionary Council appoints all judges. Death sentences are carried out after ratification by the Presidium.

RELIGION

The official religion of Afghanistan is Islam. Ninety-nine per cent of Afghans are Muslims, approximately 80 per cent of them of the Sunni and the remainder of the Shi'ite sect. There are small minority groups of Hindus, Sikhs and Jews.

THE PRESS

PRINCIPAL DAILIES

The newspapers and periodicals marked * were reported to be the only ones appearing regularly in May 1982.

*Anis (*Friendship*): Kabul; f. 1927; evening; independent; Dari and Pashtu; news and literary articles; Chief Editor ZAMON MOMAND; circ. 1,717.

Badakhshan: Faizabad; f. 1944; Dari and Pashtu; Chief Editor HADI ROSTAQI; circ. 1,000.

Bedar: Mazar-i-Sharif; f. 1922; Dari and Pashtu; Chief Editor ROZEQ FANI; circ. 2,500.

Ettehadi-Baghlan: Baghlan; f. 1930; Dari and Pashtu; Chief Editor SHAFIQULLAH MOSHFEQ; circ. 1,200.

*Haqiqat Enqelab Saur (*Truth of the April Revolution*): Kabul; f. 1980; Dari and Pashtu; organ of the Government; Editor-in-Chief MAHMUD BARIALAY; circ. 50,000.

*Hewad: Kabul; f. 1959; Dari and Pashtu; Editor-in-Chief ABDULLAH BAKHTIANAE; circ. 12,200.

Jawzjan: Jawzjan; f. 1942; Dari and Pashtu; Chief Editor A. RAHEM HAMRO; circ. 1,500.

*Kabul New Times: Ansari Wat, Kabul; f. 1962 as Kabul Times, renamed 1980; State-owned; English; Editor-in-Chief DANESHYOR; circ. 2,200.

Nangarhor: Jalalabad; f. 1919; Pashtu; Chief Editor MORAD SANGARMAL; circ. 1,500.

Sanae: Parwan; f. 1953; Dari and Pashtu; Chief Editor G. SAKHI ESHANZADA; circ. 1,700.

Tulu-i-Afghan: Qandahar; f. 1922; Pashtu; Chief Editor TAHER SHAFEQ; circ. 1,200.

Wolanga: Paktia; f. 1943; Pashtu; Chief Editor M. ANWAR; circ. 1,500.

PERIODICALS

Afghan Journal of Public Health: Institute of Public Health, Ansari Wat, Kabul; quarterly; Pashtu and Dari; Editor-in-Chief A. W. LATIFI; circ. 500.

Afghan Standard: Kabul; f. 1979; quarterly; Dari and Pashtu; Editor-in-Chief TAJMOHAMAD YORMAND; circ. 1,000.

*Afghanistan: Historical Society of Afghanistan, Kabul; f. 1948; quarterly; English; historical and cultural; Editor MALIHA ZAFAR.

*Aryana: Historical Society of Afghanistan, Kabul; f. 1943; quarterly; Pashtu and Dari; cultural and historical; Editor FAQIR MUHAMMAD KHAIRKHAH.

Awaz: Kabul; f. 1940; radio and television programmes; Pashtu and Dari; twice a month; Editor NASIR TOHORI; circ. 20,000.

De Kano Aw Sanayo (*Mines and Industry*): Kabul; f. 1955; quarterly; Dari and Pashtu; Editor-in-Chief MESBA SABA; circ. 1,500.

Eqtesad (*Economist*): Afghan Chambers of Commerce and Industry, Darulaman Watt, Kabul; f. 1922; weekly; Dari and Pashtu; Editor MUHAMMAD TAHIR PAYAM.

Erfan: Ministry of Education, Mohd. Jan Khan Wat, Kabul; f. 1923; monthly; Dari and Pashtu; Chief Editor KUBRA MAZHARI MALORAW; circ. 2,500.

Foreign Affairs Bulletin: Directorate of Information and Publicity, Ministry of Foreign Affairs, Shar-e-Nau, Kabul; f. 1982; fortnightly; official documents on government foreign policy and international issues.

Geography: Kabul; f. 1965; monthly; Pashtu and Dari; Editor-in-Chief STANAMIR ZAHER; circ. 2,500.

Gorash: Ministry of Information and Culture, Mohd. Jan Khan Wat, Kabul; f. 1979; weekly; Turkmani; Chief Editor S. MISEDIQ AMINI; circ. 1,000.

*Haqiqat-e-Sarbaz: Ministry of Defence, Kabul; f. 1980; Dari and Pashtu; three times a week; Chief Editor MER JAMALUDIN FAKHR; circ. 18,370.

Helmand: Bost; f. 1954; weekly; Pashtu; Editor-in-Chief M. OMER FARHAT BALEGH; circ. 1,700.

Herat: Ministry of Information and Culture, Mohd. Jan Khan Wat, Kabul; f. 1923; monthly; Dari and Pashtu; Chief Editor JALIL SHABGER FOLADYON.

Kabul: Academy of Sciences, Scientific Research Centre for Languages and Literature, Kabul; f. 1931; monthly; Pashtu; literature and language research; Editor N. M. SAHEEM.

Kamkyono Anis: Ministry of Information and Culture, Mohd. Jan Khan Wat, Kabul; f. 1969; weekly; Dari and Pashtu; Chief Editor NADIA; circ. 1,500.

Karhana: Ministry of Agriculture, Jamal Mena, Kabul; f. 1953; monthly; Dari and Pashtu; Editor Dr. BABRAK ARGHAND; circ. 1,500.

Mairmun: Kabul; f. 1955; Dari and Pashtu; produced by the Women's Welfare Association.

Mojalae Rana (*Light*): Kabul; f. 1978; monthly; Dari and Pashtu; Editor-in-Chief RASHID ASHTI; circ. 1,000.

Nengarhar: Kabul; f. 1919; weekly; Pashtu; Editor-in-Chief KARIM HASHIMI; circ. 1,500.

Paim Haq: Kabul; f. 1953; monthly; Dari and Pashtu; Editor-in-Chief FARAH SHAH MOHIBI; circ. 1,000.

Pamir: Kabul; f. 1952; organ of the Municipality; weekly; Dari and Pashtu; Chief Editor ZIA ROSHAN; circ. 2,000.

Samangon: Aybak; f. 1978; weekly; Dari; Editor-in-Chief M. MOHSEN HASSAN; circ. 1,500.

Seistan: Fareh; f. 1944; weekly; Dari and Pashtu; Editor-in-Chief M. ANWAR MAHAL; circ. 2,500.

Seramiasht: Afghan Red Crescent Society, Afshar, Kabul; f. 1958; Dari and Pashtu; quarterly; Editor H. R. JADIR; circ. 1,500.

Sewad (*Literacy*): Kabul; f. 1954; monthly; Dari and Pashtu; Editor-in-Chief MALEM GOL ZADRON; circ. 1,000.

Sob: Kabul; f. 1979; weekly; Balochi; Editor-in-Chief WALIMOHAMAD ROKHSHONI; circ. 1,000.

Talim Wa Tarbia: Kabul; f. 1954; monthly; published by Institute of Education.

Tanzimi Khanawada (*Family Management*): Kabul; f. 1981; Dari and Pashtu; monthly; Editor-in-Chief Ms. SORAYA KOHISTANI; circ. 1,500.

Urdu (*Military*): Kabul; f. 1922; quarterly; military journal; issued by the Ministry of National Defence; Dari and Pashtu; Chief Editor KHALILULAH AKBARI; circ. 500.

Yoduz (*Star*): Ministry of Information and Culture, Mohd. Jan Khan Wat, Kabul; f. 1979; weekly; Uzbeki; Chief Editor EKHAN BAYONI; circ. 2,000.

Zeray: Academy of Sciences, Scientific Research Centre for Languages and Literature, Kabul; f. 1938; weekly; Pashtu; Pashtu folklore, literature and language; Editor A. W. WAJID; circ. 1,000.

Zhwandoon (*Life*): Kabul; f. 1944; weekly; Pashtu and Dari; illustrated; Editor ROHELA ROSEKH KHORAMI; circ. 1,400.

NEWS AGENCIES

Bakhtar News Agency: Ministry of Information and Culture, Mohd. Jan Khan Wat, Kabul; f. 1939; Pres. ABDOLQADER MAL; Dir. ABDOLQODDUS TANDER.

FOREIGN BUREAUX

The following foreign agencies are represented in Kabul: APN (U.S.S.R.), TASS (U.S.S.R.), Tanjug (Yugoslavia) and Xinhua (People's Republic of China).

PRESS ASSOCIATION

Union of Journalists of Afghanistan: Wazir Akbar Khan Mena, St. No. 13, Kabul.

PUBLISHERS

Afghan Book: P.O.B. 206, Kabul; f. 1969 by Kabir A. Ahang; books on various subjects, translations of foreign works on Afghanistan, books in English on Afghanistan and Dari language textbooks for foreigners; Man. Dir. JAMILA AHANG.

Afghanistan Publicity Department: c/o Kabul New Times, Ansari Wat, Kabul; publicity materials; answers enquiries about Afghanistan.

Baihaqi Book Publishing and Importing Institute: P.O.B. 2025, Kabul; f. 1971 by co-operation of the Government Printing House, Bakhtar News Agency and leading newspapers; publishers and importers of books; Pres. MOHAMMAD ANWAR NUMYALAI.

Book Publishing Institute: Herat; f. 1970 by co-operation of Government Printing House and citizens of Herat; books on literature, history and religion.

Book Publishing Institute: Qandahar; f. 1970 by citizens of Qandahar, supervised by Government Printing House; mainly books in Pashtu language.

Educational Publications: Ministry of Education, Char Rahi Malek Asghar, Kabul; textbooks for primary and secondary schools in the Pashtu and Dari languages; also three monthly magazines in Pashtu and in Dari.

Government Printing House: Kabul; f. 1870 under supervision of the Ministry of Information and Culture; four daily newspapers in Kabul, one in English; weekly, fortnightly and monthly magazines, one of them in English; books on Afghan history and literature, as well as textbooks for the Ministry of Education; thirteen daily newspapers in thirteen provincial centres and one journal and also magazines in three provincial centres; Dir. MUHAMMAD AYAN AYAN.

Historical Society of Afghanistan: Kabul; f. 1931; mainly historical and cultural works and two quarterly magazines: *Afghanistan* (English and French), *Aryana* (Dari and Pashtu); Pres. AHMAD ALI MOTAMEDI.

Institute of Geography: Kabul University, Kabul; geographical and related works.

Kabul University Press: Kabul; publishes textbooks for Kabul and Nangarhar Universities, College Journals, etc.

Pashtu Tolana (*Pashtu Academy*): Sher Alikhan St., Kabul; f. 1937 by the Department of Press and Information; research works on Pashtu language and literature; Pres. POHAND RSHTEENE; publs. *Zeray* (weekly), *Kabul* (monthly).

RADIO AND TELEVISION

National Radio-TV of Afghanistan: P.O.B. 544, Ansari Wat, Kabul; Pres. (Radio) ABDUL LATIF NAZEMI; Pres. (Television) ABDULLAH SHADAN; the Afghan Broadcasting station is under the supervision of the Ministry of Communications and Culture; Home service in Dari, Pashtu, Pashai, Nuristani, Uzbeki, Turkmani and Balochi; Foreign service in Urdu, Arabic, English, Russian, German, Dari and Pashtu.

Number of radio receivers: over 1m. (approx.) in 1981.

Television broadcasting began in August 1978 with a transmission range of 50 kilometres.

Number of television sets: 120,000 in January 1980.

FINANCE

BANKING

(cap. = capital; auth. = authorized; p.u. = paid up; res. = reserves; m. = million; brs. = branches; Afs. = Afghanis).

In June 1975 all banks were nationalized.

Da Afghanistan Bank (*Central Bank of Afghanistan*): Ibne Sina Wat, Kabul; f. 1939; main functions: banknote issue, foreign exchange regulation, credit extensions to banks and leading enterprises and companies, government and private depository, government fiscal agency; 67 local brs.; cap. Afs. 2,000m.; dep. Afs. 20,839m.; res. Afs. 1,210m. (March 1981); Gov. MEHRABUDDIN PAKTIAWAL; 65 brs.

Agricultural Development Bank of Afghanistan: P.O.B. 414, Kabul; f. 1955; makes available credits for farmers, co-operatives and agro-business; aid provided by IBRD and UNDP; auth. share cap. Afs. 1,000m.; Pres. Eng. ABDUL WAHAD ASSEFI.

Banke Milli Afghan (*Afghan National Bank*): Jada Ibn Sina, Kabul; f. 1932; brs. throughout Afghanistan; cap. Afs. 500m.; total resources Afs. 3,807m. (March 1980); Pres. MOHAMMAD AKRAM KHALIL.

Export Promotion Bank of Afghanistan: 24 Mohammed Jan Khan Wat, Kabul; provides financing for exports and export-oriented investments; cap. Afs. 100m.; Pres. Prof. Dr. ZABIOULLAH A. ELTEZAM.

Industrial Development Bank of Afghanistan: P.O.B. 14, Kabul; f. 1973; provides financing for industrial development; total financial resources including cap. Afs. 842m.; Pres. T. SURKHABI; Gen. Man. SUNIT GUPTA.

Mortgage and Construction Bank: 2 Jade' Maiwand, Kabul; f. 1955 to provide short and long term building loans; cap. Afs. 100m.; Pres. (vacant).

Pashtany Tejaraty Bank (*Afghan Commercial Bank*): Mohd. Jan Khan Wat, Kabul; f. 1954 to provide long- and short-term credits, forwarding facilities, opening letters of credit, purchase and sale of foreign exchange, transfer of capital; cap. p.u. Afs. 500m.; total assets Afs. 6,997m. (March 1981); Pres. and Chief Exec. MOHD. NAIM ASKARYAR; 20 brs. in Afghanistan and abroad.

There are no foreign banks operating in Afghanistan.

INSURANCE

There is one national insurance company:

Afghan National Insurance Co.: P.O.B. 329, Timore Shahi Park, Kabul; f. 1964; mem. of Asian Reinsurance Corp.; marine, aviation, fire, motor and accident insurance; cap. Afs. 75m.; Pres. M. Y. DEEN; Vice-Pres. SANAULLAH DARWISH.

No foreign insurance companies are permitted to operate in Afghanistan.

TRADE AND INDUSTRY
CHAMBER OF COMMERCE

Federation of Afghan Chambers of Commerce and Industry: Mohd. Jan Khan Wat, Kabul; includes chambers of commerce and industry at Ghazni, Qandahar, Herat, Mazar-i-Sharif, Fariab, Jawzjan, Kunduz, Jalalabad and Andkhoy; Pres. MEHR CHAND VERMA.

TRADING CORPORATIONS

Afghan Carpet Exporters' Guild: P.O.B. 3159, Darul Aman Rd., Kabul; f. 1968; a non-profit making association for carpet exporters; Pres. A RATEB; publs. catalogues and pamphlets in English, Dari and Pashtu.

Afghan Raisins Export Promotion Institute: P.O.B. 3034, Kabul; exporters of dried fruit.

Afghanistan Karakul Institute: P.O.B. 506, Mohammed Jan Khan Wat, Kabul; exporters of furs.

TRADE UNIONS

Central Council of Afghan Trade Unions: P.O.B. 756, Kabul; f. 1978 to establish and develop the trade union movement, including the setting up of provincial councils and organizational committees in the provinces; 41 mems. and 7 alt. mems.; Pres. ABDUL SATAR PORDELY; Vice-Pres. ABDUL GHANY KARGAR; publ. *Kar* (Labour). The provincial councils are as follows:

Kabul Province: 6,500 mems.; Pres. MAIRAM JAN.
Kabul City: 72,000 mems.; Pres. ABDUL RAZAQ.
Balkh Province: 17,000 mems.; Pres. SALIM KARGAR.
Jawzjan Province: 8,500 mems.; Pres. JANATH GOUL.
Baghlan Province: 10,000 mems.; Pres. SIDIQ.
Kunduz Province: 2,000 mems.; Pres. JABAR.
Parwan Province: 10,000 mems.; Pres. NAPEES.
Kapisa Province: 3,000 mems.
Nangarhar Province: 13,000 mems.; Vice-Pres. NAZEER KARGAR.
Kandahar Province: 6,000 mems.; Pres. HAJI SHAR-APUDIN.

Helmand Province: 8,000 mems.; Pres. MOHAMMAD SAPY.
Herat Province: 7,000 mems.; Pres. AZIZ KARGAR.
Badakhshan Province: 1,000 mems.; Pres. A. AHMAD ROWSHAN.
Bamian Province: 700 mems.; Pres. S. TAHER.
Samangan Province: 1,200 mems.; Pres. ZAHER.
Takhar Province: 700 mems.; Pres. HAFIZ.
Fariab Province: 1,000 mems.; Pres. MURTAZA.
Farah Province: 300 mems.; Pres. KARIM.
Neemroze Province: 700 mems.; Pres. FAKIRI.
Kunar Province: 300 mems.; Pres. SAIDAN GUL.
Laghman Province: 600 mems.; Pres. MASOOM.
Paktia Province: 1,200 mems.; Pres. SHAH JEHAN.

TRANSPORT
RAILWAYS

In 1977 the Government approved plans for a railway system. The proposed railway (1,815 km. long) was to connect Kabul to Qandahar and Herat, and to run through Islamqala and Mashed to join the Iranian railway network. Another branch was to run from Qandahar to link with Pakistan Railways at Quetta. By 1982 work had not yet begun on the proposed railway..

ROADS

Ministry of Communications and Ministry of Public Works: Kabul; in 1978 there were 2,812 kilometres of paved roads out of a total distance of 18,752 kilometres. All-weather highways now link Kabul with Qandahar and Herat in the south and west, Jalalabad in the east and Mazar-i-Sharif and the Amu-Dar'ya river in the north.

Land Transport Company: Khoshal Mena, Kabul; f. 1943; commercial transportation within Afghanistan.

Afghan International Transport Company: Wazir Akbar Khan Mena, behind American Embassy, P.O.B. 768, Kabul.

The Millie Bus Enterprise: Ministry of Transport and Tourism, Kabul; government-owned and run; Pres. Dip. Eng. AZIZ NAGHABAN.

INLAND WATERWAYS

River ports on the Amu-Dar'ya are linked by road to Kabul.

CIVIL AVIATION

Civil Aviation and Tourism Authority: Ansari Wat, P.O.B. 165, Kabul; Pres. NOOR MOHAMMAD DALILI; Dir.-Gen. of Air Operations ABDUL WASEH HAIDARI.

There are international airports at Kabul and Qandahar and there are plans to rebuild Kabul airport and construct six airports in the northeast, with Soviet help.

NATIONAL AIRLINES

Ariana Afghan Airlines Co. Ltd.: P.O.B. 76, Ansari Wat, Kabul; f. 1955; services to India, U.S.S.R. and Europe; services to Iran, Turkey and Pakistan temporarily suspended; Pres. Capt. SAYED BABA; 1 DC 10-30, 2 Boeing 727-100C.

Bakhtar Afghan Airlines: Ansari Wat, P.O.B. 3058, Kabul; f. 1968; internal services between Kabul and 12 regional locations; 3 DHC-6 Twin Otter projects, 2 YAK-40 jets, 2 Antonov-24 aircraft; Pres. NIAZ MUHAMMAD; Dir. of Operations Capt. R. NAWROZ; Gen. Dir. Lt.-Col. ABDOL LATIF.

FOREIGN AIRLINES

The following airlines also operate services to Afghanistan: Aeroflot (U.S.S.R.), Indian Airlines and PIA (Pakistan) (suspended Sept. 1981).

TOURISM

Afghan Tourist Organization: Shar-e-Nau, Kabul; f. 1958; Pres. H. KYANWAR; Vice-Pres. S. J. BARAKZAI; publ. *Statistical Bulletin* (quarterly).

Afghan Tour: Salang Wat, Kabul; official travel agency supervised by A.T.O.

ATOMIC ENERGY

Atomic Energy Commission: Faculty of Science, Kabul University, Kabul; Pres. of Commission and Dean of Faculty Dr. MOHAMMAD RASUL.

DEFENCE

Commander-in-Chief of the Army: Gen. BABAJAN.

Commander-in-Chief of the Air Force and Air Defence Force: Maj.-Gen. NAZAR MOHAMMAD.

Supreme Defence Council: Kabul; founded March 1979 to improve defence, supervise the armed forces, approve the Defence Budget and safeguard internal security.

Armed Forces (July 1981 estimates): Army 35,000; air force 8,000 and para-military forces comprise 30,000 gendarmes; military service lasting two years is compulsory for every able-bodied man, but conscription is difficult to enforce and desertions are frequent.

Equipment: The army's equipment and training are very largely provided by the Soviet Union. The air force is equipped with Soviet built combat aircraft.

Defence Expenditure: Estimated defence expenditure in 1978/79 was 2,870 million afghanis (U.S. $63.8 million).

EDUCATION

The traditional system of education in Afghanistan was religious instruction in Madrasas, or Mosque schools. These centres are still active, but a modern educational system has been built up since 1904.

Since 1933 primary, middle and secondary schools have been opened all over the country. In March 1980 it was announced that the education system would comprise primary schools (four classes), basic middle schools (eight classes), full middle schools (ten classes) and religious schools. Those children aged 10 to 14 with no previous opportunity to attend school can study in specially accelerated training classes covering the elementary school curriculum in two years. The development of education since 1961 has been rapid especially at the primary level. It is estimated that the proportion of children aged 6 to 11 years receiving primary education increased from 9 per cent in 1960 to 23 per cent in 1975. Only 7 per cent of girls in this age-group were enrolled and only 8 per cent of all children aged 12 to 16 attended secondary schools. In 1979 the Government announced the introduction of free and compulsory primary education for children over seven years of age. Competitive examinations for high-school entrance were abolished in 1978 and in 1980 the Government claimed that the total number of schools (excepting religious and vocational schools) had increased by 13 per cent compared with 1979 and that the number of students at these schools had increased by 21 per cent in the same period.

Under the Five-year Social and Economic Development Plan (1979–84), a massive programme to combat adult illiteracy has been launched. (It has been estimated that only 10 per cent of males and 2 per cent of females are literate.) The programme aims to reach over 8 million people by the end of the Plan.

Teacher training began on an organized scale in the early 1950s. The University of Kabul was founded in 1932 when the Faculty of Medicine was established. It now has 10 Faculties. In 1962 a second university was founded in Jalalabad, Nangarhar province; again the nucleus was provided by the Medical Faculty of Kabul University.

Progress is also being made in women's education, and girls' schools are now found in all major cities.

In 1980 it was reported that up to 80 per cent of university staff had fled their posts.

BIBLIOGRAPHY

GENERAL

AFGHAN TRANSPORT & TRAVEL SERVICE. Afghanistan—Ancient Land with Modern Ways (London, 1961).

CAROE, OLAF. The Pathans.

DUPREE, LOUIS. Afghanistan (Princeton University Press, Princeton, N.J., 1973).

GRASSMUCK, GEORGE, and ADAMEC, LUDWIG. (eds.) **Afghanistan: Some new approaches (Center for Near Eastern and North African Studies, University of Michigan, Ann Arbor, Mich., 1969).**

GRIFFITHS, JOHN C. Afghanistan (Pall Mall Press, London, 1967).

KESSEL, FLINKER and KLIMBURG. Afghanistan (photographs, 1959).

KING, PETER. Afghanistan, Cockpit in Asia (Bles, London, 1966, Taplinger, N.Y., 1967).

KLIMBURG, M. Afghanistan (Austrian UNESCO Commission, Vienna, 1966).

SHALISI, PRITA K. Here and There in Afghanistan.

WILBER, DONALD N. Afghanistan (New Haven, Conn., 1956).

Annotated Bibliography of Afghanistan (New Haven, Conn., 1962).

GEOGRAPHY AND TRAVELS

BURNES, **Sir ALEXANDER. Cabool (John Murray, London,** 1842, reprinted Lahore 1961).

BYRON, ROBERT. Road to Oxiana (Jonathan Cape, London, 1937).

ELPHINSTONE, M. An Account of the Kingdom of Caubul and its Dependencies in Persia, Tartary and India (John Murray, London, 1815, reprinted Oxford University Press, London, 1972).

FERRIER, J. P. Caravan Journeys (1857, reprinted Oxford University Press, London).

HAHN, H. Die Stadt Kabul und ihr Umland (2 vols., Bonn, 1964–65).

HAMILTON, ANGUS. Afghanistan (Heinemann, London, 1906).

HUMLUM, J. La Géographie de l'Afghanistan (Gyldendal, Copenhagen, 1959).

MASSON, CHARLES. Narrative of various journeys in Baluchistan, Afghanistan and the Punjab (Bentley, London, 1842, reprinted Oxford University Press, London).

WOLFE, N. H. Herat (Afghan Tourist Organization, Kabul, 1966).

WOOD, JOHN. A Personal Narrative of a Journey to the Source of the River Oxus by the Route of Indus, Kabul and Badakshan (John Murray, London, 1841, reprinted Oxford University Press, London, 1976).

HISTORY

ADAMEC, LUDWIG W. Afghanistan 1900–1923 (University of California, Berkeley, 1967).

Afghanistan's Foreign Affairs to the Mid-Twentieth Century (University of Arizona Press, Tucson, 1974).

AKHRAMOVICH, R. T. Outline History of Afghanistan after the Second World War (Moscow, 1966).

ALDER, G. J. British India's Northern Frontier, 1865–1895 (Longmans, London, 1963).

BOSWORTH, C. E. The Ghaznavids (Edinburgh University Press, 1963).

CAMBRIDGE HISTORY OF INDIA, Vols. I, III, IV, V, VI.

DOLLOT, RENÉ. Afghanistan (Payot, Paris, 1937).

DUPREE, LOUIS and LINNET, ALBERT (eds.). Afghanistan in the 1970s (Praeger, New York, 1974 and Pall Mall Press, London).

FLETCHER, ARNOLD. Afghanistan, Highway of Conquest (Cornell and Oxford University Presses, 1965).

FRASER-TYTLER, Sir W. KERR. Afghanistan (Oxford University Press, 1950, 3rd edn., 1967).

GREGORIAN, VARTAN. The Emergence of Modern Afghanistan (Stanford University Press, Stanford, Calif., 1969).

KAKAR, HASAN, Afghanistan, 1880–1896 (Karachi, 1971). Government and Society in Afghanistan (University of Arizona Press, Tucson, Ariz., 1979).

KHAN, M. M. S. M. (ed.) The Life of Abdur Rahman, Amir of Afghanistan (John Murray, London, 1900).

KOHZAD, A. A. Men and Events (Government Printing House, Kabul).

MACRORY, PATRICK. Signal Catastrophe (Hodder & Stoughton, London, 1966).

MASSON, V. M., and ROMODIN, V. A. Istoriya Afghanistana (Akad. Nauk, Moscow, 1964–65).

MOHUN LAL. Life of the Amir Dost Mohammed Khan of Kabul (Longmans, London, 1846, reprinted Oxford University Press, London, 1978).

NEWELL, RICHARD S. The Politics of Afghanistan (Cornell University Press, Ithaca, N.Y., 1972).

NORRIS, J. A. The First Afghan War, 1838–42 (Cambridge University Press, 1967).

POULLADA, LEON B. Reform and Rebellion in Afghanistan, 1919-1929 (Cornell University Press, Ithaca, N.Y., 1972).

SYKES, Sir PERCY. A History of Afghanistan (Macmillan, London, 1940).

ECONOMY

FRY, MAXWELL J. The Afghan Economy (Leiden, 1974).

MALEKYAR, ABDUL WAHED. Die Verkehrsentwicklung in Afghanistan (Cologne, 1966).

RHEIN, E. and GHAUSSY. A. GHANIE. Die wirtschaftliche Entwicklung Afghanistans, 1880–1965 (C. W. Leske Verlag, Hamburg, 1966).

Algeria

PHYSICAL AND SOCIAL GEOGRAPHY

Algeria is the largest of the three countries in north-west Africa that comprise the Maghreb, as the region of mountains, valleys and plateaux that lies between the sea and the Sahara desert is known. It is situated between Morocco and Tunisia with a Mediterranean coastline of nearly 1,000 km. and a total area of some 2,381,741 sq. km., over four-fifths of which lies south of the Maghreb proper and within the western Sahara. Its extent, both from north to south and west to east, exceeds 2,000 km. The Arabic name for the country, *al Jazair* (the Islands), is said to derive from the rocky islands along the coastline, which have always constituted a danger to ships approaching the harbours.

Based on the 1977 census, the estimated population at January 1st, 1978, was 18,250,000 (including about 828,000 Algerian nationals living abroad). The great majority of the inhabitants live in the northern part of the country, particularly along the Mediterranean coast where both the capital, Algiers or El Djazaïr (population, with suburbs, 1.8 million in 1977), and the second largest town, Oran or Ouahran (about 500,000), are located. Many settlements reverted to their Arabic names in 1981; for the principal changes, *see* Statistical Survey, p. 267. The population is almost wholly Muslim, of whom a majority speak Arabic and the remainder Berber, the language of the original inhabitants of the Maghreb. Most educated Algerians, however, speak French. Nearly all the Europeans settlers, who numbered about 1 million in 1960, have left the country since it attained its independence from France in 1962.

PHYSICAL FEATURES

The primary contrast in the physical geography of Algeria is between the mountainous, relatively humid terrain of the north, which forms part of the Atlas mountain system, and the vast expanse of lower, flatter desert to the south, which is part of the Saharan tableland. The Atlas Mountains trend from south-west to north-east across the whole of the Maghreb. Structurally they resemble the "Alpine" mountain chains of Europe north of the Mediterranean and, like them, they came into existence during the geologically recent Tertiary era. They are still unstable and liable to severe earthquakes, such as those which devastated El Asnam in 1954 and 1980. They consist of rocks, now uplifted, folded and fractured, that once accumulated as submarine deposits beneath an ancestral Mediterranean sea. Limestones and sandstones are particularly extensive and they often present a barren appearance in areas where a cover of soil and vegetation is only thin or absent altogether.

In Algeria the Atlas mountain system is made up of three broad zones running parallel to the coast: the Tell Atlas, the High Plateaux and the Saharan Atlas. In the north, and separated from the Mediterranean only by a narrow and discontinuous coastal plain, is the complex series of mountains and valleys that comprise the Tell Atlas. Here individual ranges, plateaux and massifs vary in height from about 500 to 2,500 metres, and are frequently separated from one another by deep valleys and gorges which divide the country into self-contained topographic and economic units. Most distinctive of these are the massifs of the Great and Little Kabyle between Algiers and the Tunisian frontier, which have acted as mountain retreats where Berber ways of village life persist.

South of the Tell Atlas lies a zone of featureless plains known as the High Plateaux of the Shotts. To the west, near the Moroccan frontier, they form a broad, monotonous expanse of level terrain about 160 km. across and over 1,000 metres high. They gradually narrow and fall in height eastward and end in the Hodna basin, a huge enclosed depression, the bottom of which is only 420 metres above sea-level. The surface of the plateaux consists of alluvial debris derived from erosion of the mountains to north and south, and only here and there do minor ridges project through the thick mantle of alluvium to break the monotony of the level horizons. The plateaux owe their name to the presence of several vast basins of internal drainage, known as shotts, the largest of which is the Hodna basin. During rainy periods water accumulates in the shotts to form extensive shallow lakes which give way, as the water is absorbed and evaporated, to saline mud flats and swamps.

The southern margin of the High Plateaux is marked by a series of mountain chains and massifs that form the Saharan Atlas. They are more broken than the Tell Atlas and present no serious barrier to communications between the High Plateaux and the Sahara. From west to east the chief mountain chains are the Ksour, Amour, Ouled Naïl, Ziban and Aurès. The latter is the most impressive massif in the whole Algerian Atlas system and includes the highest peak: Djebel Chelia, 2,328 metres. The relief of the Aurès is very bold, with narrow gorges cut between sheer cliffs surmounted by steep bare slopes, and to the east and north of the Hodna basin its ridges merge with the southernmost folds of the Tell Atlas. North-eastern Algeria forms, therefore, a compact block of high relief in which the two Atlas mountain systems cease to be clearly separated. Within it there are a number of high plains studded with salt flats but their size is insignificant compared with the enormous shotts to the west.

CLIMATE AND VEGETATION

The climate of northernmost Algeria, including the narrow coastal plain and the Tell Atlas southward to the margin of the High Plateaux, is of "Mediterranean" type with warm wet winters and hot dry summers. Rainfall varies in amount from over 1,000 mm. annually on some coastal mountains exposed to rain-bearing winds to less than 130 mm. in sheltered, lee situations, and most of it occurs during the winter when depressions pass across the western Mediterranean most frequently. Complete drought lasts for three to four months during the summer and at this time, too, the notorious sirocco occurs. It is a scorching, dry and dusty south wind blowing from the Sahara and is known locally as the Chehili. It blows on 40 or more days a year over the High Plateaux but nearer the coast its frequency is reduced to about 20 days. When it sets in, shade temperatures often rise rapidly to over 40°C. and vegetation and crops, unable to withstand the intensity of evaporation, may wither and die within a few hours. As a result of low and uneven rainfall combined with high rates of evaporation the rivers of the Tell tend to be short and to suffer large seasonal variations in flow. Many dry out completely during the summer and are only full for brief periods following heavy winter rains. The longest perennially flowing river is the Oued Chélif which rises in the High Plateaux and crosses the Tell to reach the Mediterranean east of Oran.

Along the northern margin of the High Plateaux, which approximately coincides with the limit of 400 mm. mean annual rainfall, "Mediterranean" conditions give way to a semi-arid or steppe climate in which summer drought lasts from five to six months and winters are colder and drier. Rainfall is reduced to between 200 and 400 mm. annually and tends to occur in spring and autumn rather than in winter. It is, moreover, very variable from year to year, and under these conditions the cultivation of cereal crops without irrigation becomes quite unreliable. South of the Saharan Atlas annual rainfall decreases to below 200 mm. and any regular cultivation without irrigation becomes impossible. There are no permanent rivers south of the Tell Atlas and any surface run-off following rain is carried by temporary watercourses towards local depressions, such as the shotts.

The soils and vegetation of northern Algeria reflect the climatic contrast between the humid Tell and the semi-arid lands farther south, but they have also suffered widely from the destructive effects of over-cultivation, over-grazing and deforestation. In the higher, wetter and more isolated parts of the Tell Atlas relatively thick soils support forests of Aleppo pine, cork-oak and evergreen oak, while the lower, drier, and more accessible slopes tend to be bare or covered only with thin soils and a scrub growth of thuya, juniper and various drought-resistant shrubs. Only a few remnants survive of the once extensive forests of Atlas cedar which have been exploited for timber and fuel since classical times. They are found chiefly above 1,500 metres in the eastern Tell Atlas. South of the Tell there is very little woodland except in the higher and wetter parts of the Saharan Atlas. The surface of the High Plateaux is bare or covered only with scattered bushes and clumps of esparto and other coarse grasses.

SAHARAN ALGERIA

South of the Saharan Atlas, Algeria extends for over 1,500 km. into the heart of the desert. Structurally, this huge area consists of a resistant platform of geologically ancient rocks against which the Atlas Mountains were folded. Over most of the area relief is slight, with occasional plateaux, such as those of Eglab, Tademaït and Tassili-n-Ajjer, rising above vast spreads of gravel such as the Tanezrouft plain and huge sand accumulations such as the Great Western and Eastern Ergs. In the south-east, however, the great massif of Ahaggar rises to a height of 2,918 metres. Here erosion of volcanic and crystalline rocks has produced a lunar landscape of extreme ruggedness. Southward from the Ahaggar the massifs of Adrar des Iforas and Aïr extend across the Algerian frontier into the neighbouring countries of Mali and Niger.

The climate of Saharan Algeria is characterized by extremes of temperature, wind and aridity. Daily temperature ranges reach 32°C. and maximum shade temperatures of over 55°C. have been recorded. Sometimes very high temperatures are associated with violent dust storms. Mean average rainfall is everywhere less than 130 mm., and in some of the central parts of the desert it falls to less than 10 mm. It is, however, extremely irregular and often torrential; a fall of several cm. in one day may be followed by several years of absolute drought. These rigorous conditions are reflected in the extreme sparseness of the vegetation and in a division of the population into settled cultivators, who occupy oases dependent on permanent supplies of underground water, and nomadic pastoralists who make use of temporary pastures which become available after rain.

D.R.H.

HISTORY

Algeria as a political entity is a phenomenon of the last four hundred years: the history of its peoples, however, is of considerably greater antiquity. Little is known of the origin of the Berber people who have comprised the majority of the population of this part of Africa since the earliest times, but they had long been established there in numerous nomadic tribes when, at the time of the Punic Wars, the first ephemeral state-organizations may be distinguished in the area. The most important of these states was Numidia (208–148 B.C.), established by the chieftain Masinissa, which occupied most of present-day Algeria north of the Sahara. With the destruction of Carthage in 146 B.C., Numidia, greatly reduced in extent, was transformed into a Roman vassal-state. By the time of Augustus, Numidia was merely a senatorial province of the empire, while the rest of the area formed a loose confederacy of more or less independent tribes. In the coastal centres of trade and culture a certain degree of assimilation to Roman ways took place, but in the mountains and deserts of the interior the Berber tribes maintained their independence by frequent revolt.

The adoption of Christianity as the official religion of the Roman Empire, in the early part of the fourth century, provided a convenient ideological framework for Berber separatism. Under the impact of barbarian invasions, the Roman Empire in the west slowly disintegrated in the course of the fifth century, towards the end of which its rule in North Africa was replaced by the transient dominion of the Vandals. A nomadic people of Germanic origin, they established themselves in the east of present-day Algeria, but failed to gain any real control over the Berber tribes of the hinterland. In A.D. 531, Roman, or rather Byzantine, rule was restored in North Africa, with the conquest by the emperor Justinian of the provinces of Africa (the modern Tunisia) and Numidia, and the establishment of a tenuous hold on the coast as far west as the region of modern Algiers. Elsewhere the Berber confederacies, centred in the Aurès and the Kabyle, maintained their independence.

The rise of Islam in Arabia, and its rapid expansion after the death of the Prophet (632), leading to the Arab conquest of Syria and Egypt, was quickly followed by the penetration of North Africa. The first Arab raids into North Africa (or the Maghreb, as the region comprising the present states of Morocco, Algeria, and Tunisia now came to be called) took place about the middle of the seventh century. The foundation of Kayrawan in 670 provided a permanent base for their operations, which remained for a time little more than raids. The towns remained under Byzantine control, while the Berber tribes, uniting against the invaders, set up a Berber state centred in the eastern Maghreb. Increasing Arab immigration towards the end of the seventh century finally put an end to Berber resistance, under its heroic and legendary warrior-queen Kahina (692). At the same time the last Byzantine garrisons were dislodged from

their coastal strongholds, and the whole of the area was incorporated into the Ummayad Empire. The Berbers, for their part, became converted *en masse* to Islam, and, enrolling in its armies, went on with them to the conquest of the western Maghreb and of Spain.

BERBER UNREST

This new-found Islamic unity did not last long. Dissatisfied with their inferior position as non-Arabs in an Arab empire, the Berbers adopted Muslim heresies as eagerly as they had previously embraced Christian ones. The first signs of unrest appeared early in the eighth century, part of a general movement of discontent among the non-Arab peoples of the empire, which in the course of the succeeding years was to bring about the downfall of the Ummayad dynasty (750). By this time the Berbers had become converted to Kharijism, an esoteric radical Muslim sect, and in 756 under its auspices they destroyed completely the authority of the recently-established Abbasid Caliphate throughout the Maghreb. In the east of the area imperial authority was restored in 761, ushering in a period of forty years' anarchy and civil war. In the centre and west of the Maghreb a number of small, mostly heretical states arose. Later, in the ninth century, the focal point of Berber Kharijism was transferred from Tlemcen to Tiaret. Meanwhile, in the west, the authority of the caliphs had been superseded by that of an independent dynasty, the Aghlabids, who, ruling from Kayrawan, attempted to extend their control into the central Maghreb. In opposition to their rule the Berbers of the Kabyle now embraced Shi'i doctrines, a move which led in 910 to the establishment of the Fatimid dynasty in the central Maghreb. Fatimid rule, however, was not undisputed. From 943 to 947 they were faced with the terrible revolt of Abu Yazid and from then on their authority declined. The capital of the dynasty was in 973 transferred to Egypt, while power in the Maghreb was again disputed between various Berber confederacies. In the centre and the east the Sinhaja tribes, the successors to the Kutama who had established the Fatimids, supported the minor dynasty of the Zirids; in the west the more nomadic Zenata established themselves under the remote suzerainty of the Spanish Ummayads. In the early eleventh century the Sinhaja Banu Hammad rose to the status of a local dynasty, ruling as neighbours of the kingdom of Kayrawan.

In *c.* 1050 the Banu Hilal, a confederation of Arab tribes dislodged from Egypt, invaded the Maghreb. These nomads severely damaged the economy of North Africa, and represent the only considerable Arab immigration into the Maghreb since the original Arab conquest of the area. A period of anarchy ensued, but some order was restored by the Berber dynasty of the Almoravids who, coming from Morocco, brought the area of modern Algiers and Oran under their rule. The Banu Hammad, meanwhile, had become established at Bougie. Almoravid power rapidly declined, and *c.* 1147 they were succeeded by the Almohads. This dynasty, perhaps the most important to rule in North Africa in the medieval Islamic period, unified the whole of the Maghreb together with Muslim Spain. This was a time of cultural and economic prosperity for North Africa and witnessed the expansion of trade with the northern shores of the Mediterranean, but the precarious unity of the Maghreb was short-lived. By 1250 the area was again in a condition of political chaos and instability, with the Zenata Banu 'Abd al-Wad exercising such power as existed. A general decline set in, which was to last for over two centuries, during which time the general prevalence of the Berber language gradually gave way to Arabic, a further legacy of the Hilali invasions.

Throughout this period the chief seat of political power was at Tlemcen. In the interior various minor princes asserted their independence, while the coastal towns organized themselves into independent republics, the chief support of which came from piracy. This state of affairs, which lasted throughout the fourteenth century, was terminated by the sudden involvement of Algiers in matters of more than local significance.

OTTOMAN RULE

The Spanish monarchy, bringing to completion its task of driving Muslim power from the Iberian peninsula with the reconquest of Granada in 1492, now carried its crusade to North Africa. The fragmented political state of that area offered little obstacle to its progress. Mers el-Kebir was captured in 1505, Oran in 1509, and Bougie in 1510, while Algiers, at that time a small port of little importance except as a centre for piracy, was reduced to submission in the same year. On the death of Ferdinand of Castile in 1516 the Algerines, in an attempt to throw off Spanish rule, sent envoys to the Turkish corsair Aruj, seeking his assistance. Aruj took possession of the town, together with other places on the littoral and Tlemcen in the interior, and was proclaimed sultan. In 1518 he was succeeded by his brother Khayr al-Din (Barbarossa), who, in order to consolidate his position, placed all the territories which he controlled under the protection of the Ottoman sultan. This decisive act, which brought together under a single jurisdiction the whole of the coast of North Africa and its immediate hinterland between Constantine and Oran, may be said to mark the emergence of Algeria as a political concept. Meanwhile, the struggle for North Africa continued. In 1529 Khayr al-Din drove the Spaniards from Algiers, while throughout the next decade constant Spanish efforts were made to re-establish their position in the area. Finally, in 1541, a great expedition led by the Emperor Charles V failed miserably, and after that Algeria was left for three centuries to the Muslims. Ottoman rule in Algiers had already been further strengthened. In 1533 Khayr al-Din had been summoned to Istanbul to take charge of the Ottoman fleet. In his place a more regular administration was set up, under a succession of *beylerbeys* responsible directly to the sultan. In 1587 their regime was replaced by a government headed by a series of *pashas*, who were appointed for a term of three years. These again were succeeded in power in 1659 by the *aghas* (or commanders) of the corps of janissaries, replaced later by the *deys*, who retained their power until the French occupation in 1830. All these changes were, however, superficial. From the mid-sixteenth century actual Ottoman super-vision of Algerian affairs became increasingly a convenient fiction, perpetuated in the interests of both the Algerines themselves and the imperial authorities at Istanbul. The real power in Algiers gradually came into the hands of two main bodies. One, the nominal representative of Ottoman power, was the janissary corps, who were for the most part of Anatolian origin; the other, the so-called *taife-i ruesa*, was the guild of corsair captains, men of widely differing origins, who for over three centuries were the main financial support of the state.

The Regency of Algiers reached the peak of its prosperity in the course of the seventeenth century. During this period the rulers of the state entered into diplomatic relations with the leading maritime states of western Europe. The profitable trade of piracy flourished throughout the century, bringing great wealth and notoriety as the centre of the North African slave trade. Throughout the seventeenth and eighteenth centuries Algiers looked outwards to the sea. Despite some early Turkish attempts to control the interior, many of the Berber tribes, especially in the Aurès and the Kabyle, maintained their independence; others, more accessible to Algiers, paid to the *dey* a grudging tribute, or unwillingly recognized his suzerainty. With the eighteenth century, and the growth of European seapower in the Mediterranean, a period of decline set in. From a former figure of 100,000, the population of the city itself dropped to less than 30,000 at the beginning of the nineteenth century, while in the interior the tribal chiefs extended their authority and a period of relative economic prosperity ensued.

In the period of the Napoleonic wars piracy and the economy of Algiers both underwent a certain revival, but this renewal of prosperity was shortlived. On the restoration of peace the European powers called upon the *dey* to abandon piracy, and in 1816 the British fleet bombarded Algiers. It was obvious that before long one of the European powers would take advantage of the growing anti-slavery movement in Europe, and the increasing weakness of Algiers itself, to go beyond naval demonstrations, and to land forces in the country. In the event, the conquest of Algiers was the work of France.

THE FRENCH CONQUEST

The excuse for intervention was an insult offered by the *dey* to the French consul in 1827: the real cause was the pressing need of Polignac, the chief minister under Charles X, to secure some credit for his administration in the eyes of the French public. On July 5th, 1830, Algiers fell to a French expedition, the *dey* and most of the Turkish officials being sent into exile. But the Polignac administration was unable to gather the fruits of its triumph, for before further plans for the consolidation of French rule, and its extension to other coastal towns, could be put into effect, the Bourbon dynasty and its government were overthrown by revolution. A further casualty in the revolution was Polignac's plan for handing over the rest of the country, and the decision on its future, to a European congress; instead, for four years, the problem was left to mark time. Away from Algiers itself the absence of any central authority strengthened still further the prestige of the tribal chiefs. Finally, in 1834, following the report of a special commission, the further conquest and annexation of Algeria was decided upon, and a governor-general appointed.

The history of Algeria for the next quarter of a century is mainly concerned with the gradual reduction of the country by France, against bitter and continuing opposition. Constantine, the last stronghold of Turkish rule, was captured in 1837, and by 1841 French rule had been consolidated in most of the ports and their immediate environs. By 1844 most of the eastern part of Algeria had been brought under French control, but in the west the conquerors were faced with the formidable power of Abd el-Kadir. This Berber leader, a skilful diplomat and a military commander of genius, had at first concluded treaties with the French, which consolidated his position as leader of the Berber confederacies in the west. But in 1839 he declared war on France, achieving widespread unity between Berbers and Arabs against the invaders. He held out until 1847, when he was finally defeated by the persistence and ruthless tactics of the French general Bugeaud, the real architect of French rule in Algeria. During the late 1840s and 1850s the tribes on the edge of the Sahara were pacified, while the virtual end of the conquest was achieved by the submission of the hitherto independent Berber confederacies of the Kabyle, in 1857. Further rebellion was to occur, however, throughout the nineteenth century, and especially after France's defeat at the hands of Prussia in the war of 1870–71.

Meanwhile, a policy of colonization, with widespread confiscation of land and its transference to settler groups, had been pushed forward. Bugeaud had at first encouraged colonization in the coastal plains; after 1848 the influx of colonists was much increased, with the approval of the governments of the Second Republic and, in its early years, the Second Empire. A further stimulus to colonization was provided by the widespread confiscation of lands resulting from the unsuccessful rebellion of 1871. By 1860 much of the best land in Algeria was in French hands, and was the scene of considerable subsequent agricultural development, while the French settlers themselves rapidly became the dominant power in the land. This was well seen some ten years later. Napoleon III had been favourably disposed towards the Algerian Muslim population, and had taken steps to protect tribal lands against settler encroachments, at the same time securing for Muslims the right to acquire French nationality. These measures had provoked strong opposition among the settlers, and in 1870, in the confusion of the Franco-Prussian War, the French colonists in Algeria expelled the imperial agents and set up a revolutionary commune.

After the confusion of the period of "commune" rule, and the subsequent Muslim revolt of 1871, the situation was regularized by the new French administration under Thiers. A civil administration with the status of a French *département* was set up for much of Algeria, while the amount of territory under military rule steadily declined. From then until the end of the nineteenth century Algeria was the scene of considerable economic progress, and increasing European immigration, especially from Italy. A feature of this period was the growth of large-scale agricultural and industrial enterprises, which concentrated still more power in the hands of the most powerful members of the settler groups. In 1900 Algeria secured administrative and financial autonomy, to be exercised through the so-called "Financial Delegations", composed of two-thirds European and one-third Muslim members, and empowered to fix the annual budget and to raise loans for further economic development.

In seventy years the Muslim people of Algeria had been reduced from relative prosperity to economic, social and cultural inferiority. Three million inhabitants had died, tribes had been broken up and the traditional economy altered during the prolonged "civilizing" campaigns. In particular, the production of wine for export had replaced the traditional production of cereals for home consumption. The settlers, however, experienced a high level of prosperity and economic progress in the years before the First World War. For the present, the French ascendancy seemed assured.

BIRTH OF NATIONALISM

The spirit of nationalism was spreading throughout the Middle East, however, and it emerged among the Algerian Muslims as a force to be reckoned with after the First World War. Nationalist aspirations began to be voiced not only by Algerian veterans of the war in Europe but also by Algerians who went to France to study or take up employment. In 1924 one of these students, Messali Hadj, founded in Paris the first Algerian nationalist newspaper, in collaboration with the French communist party; the link with the communists was severed in 1927, however. Messali Hadj and his movement were driven underground by the French Government, but reappeared in 1933 as sponsors of a congress on the future of Algeria which called for total independence, the recall of French troops, the establishment of a revolutionary government, large-scale reforms in land ownership and the nationalization of industrial enterprises.

More moderate doctrines were put forward in the post-war years by an influential body of French-educated Muslims, formalized in 1930 as the Federation of Muslim Councillors. Under the leadership of Ferhat Abbas, this group called for integration with France on a basis of complete equality. The victory of the Popular Front in the French elections of 1936 gave rise to the hope that at least some of these aspirations might be peaceably achieved. The Blum-

Viollet Plan, which would have granted full rights of citizenship to an increasing number of Algerian Muslims, was, however, dropped by the French Government in the face of fierce opposition from the French settlers and the Algerian civil service.

The years immediately prior to World War II were marked by growing nationalist discontent, in which Messali Hadj, released from prison in 1936, played a significant part with the formation of the Party of the Algerian People (PPA). The outbreak of war in 1939 temporarily put an end to the nationalists' activities, but the war greatly strengthened their hand for the future. Although the Vichy administration in Algeria, strongly supported by the French settlers, was antipathetic to nationalist sentiment, the Allied landings in North Africa in 1942 provided an opportunity for the Algerian nationalists to put forward constitutional demands. A group headed by Ferhat Abbas on December 22nd, 1942, presented to the French authorities and the Allied military command a memorandum calling for the post-war establishment of an Algerian constituent assembly, to be elected by universal suffrage. No demand was made for Algerian independence outside the French framework, however.

These proposals, to which the French authorities remained unresponsive, were followed early in 1943 by the "Manifesto of the Algerian People", which called for immediate reforms, including the introduction of Arabic as an official language. Further proposals submitted in May envisaged the post-war creation of an Algerian state with a constitution to be determined by a constituent assembly, and looked forward to an eventual North African Union, comprising Tunisia, Algeria and Morocco. The newly-established Free French administration in Algiers rejected the Manifesto and the subsequent proposals out of hand.

In the face of growing Muslim discontent, and following a visit to Algiers by General de Gaulle, a new statute for Algeria was put into effect in March 1944. It was an attempt at compromise which satisfied neither the Algerian nationalists nor the European settlers. Membership of the French electoral college was opened to 60,000 Muslims, but there were still 450,000 European voters, and in the event only 32,000 Muslims accepted inscription. The Muslim share of the seats in the *communes mixtes* was restricted to 40 per cent. All further discussion of Algeria's future relationship with France was ruled out.

Ferhat Abbas shortly afterwards founded the Friends of the Manifesto of Freedom (AML), to work for the foundation of an autonomous Algerian republic linked federally with France. The new movement was based mainly on the support of middle-class Muslims, though it also gained a certain following among the masses. At the same time, the PPA gained many followers among the masses during 1944 and 1945.

FRENCH INTRANSIGENCE

All possibility of an evolutionary settlement was destroyed by blunders of post-war French policy and the opposition of the French settlers to any concessions to Muslim aspirations. The ruthless suppression of the riots at Sétif in May 1945, which claimed the lives of some 15,000 Muslims, and the subsequent arrest of Ferhat Abbas and the dissolution of the AML drove many of the nationalist leaders to regard force as the only means of gaining their objective.

Nevertheless, attempts to reach a compromise solution continued for some time. In March 1946 Ferhat Abbas, released under an amnesty, launched the Democratic Union of the Algerian Manifesto (UDMA), with a programme providing for the creation of an autonomous, secular Algerian state within the French Union. Despite successes in elections to the French Assembly, the UDMA failed to achieve any of its objectives. It withdrew from the Assembly in September 1946 and refused to participate in the next elections. The breach was filled by the more radical Movement for the Triumph of Democratic Liberties (MTLD), the party formed by Messali Hadj at the end of the war, which demanded the creation of a sovereign constituent assembly and the evacuation of French troops—aims which stood no chance of adoption.

In another attempt at compromise the French Government introduced a new constitution which became law on September 20th, 1947. This gave French citizenship, and therefore the vote, to all Algerian citizens, including women, and recognized Arabic as equal in status to French. The proposed new Algerian Assembly, however, was to be divided into two colleges, each of 60 members, one to represent the 1½ million Europeans, the other the 9 million Muslims. Other provisions ruled out all possibility of anti-European legislation.

The new constitution was never brought fully into operation. Following MTLD successes in the municipal elections of October 1947, the elections to the Algerian Assembly were openly and clumsily interfered with, many candidates being arrested, election meetings forbidden and polling stations improperly operated. As a result only a quarter of the members returned to the second college in April 1948 were MTLD or UDMA; the remainder, nominally "independent", were nonentities. Such methods continued to be employed in local and national elections during the next six years, as well as in the Algerian elections to the French National Assembly in June 1951. Some of the ameliorative provisions of the 1947 constitution were never put into effect. The aim was to destroy, or at least render harmless, opposition to French rule; the result was to drive the main forces of nationalism underground.

As early as 1947 several of the younger members of the MTLD had formed the "Secret Organization" (OS), which collected arms and money from supporters and built up a network of cells throughout Algeria in preparation for armed insurrection and the establishment of a revolutionary government. Two years later the OS felt itself strong enough to launch a terrorist attack in Oran. The movement was subsequently discovered and most of its leaders were arrested. A nucleus survived, however, in the Kabyle region, ever a stronghold for dissident groups, and the organizer of the attack, Ben Bella, escaped in 1952 to Cairo.

A decisive split was taking place in the ranks of the MTLD, and the veteran Messali Hadj, now embracing nebulous doctrines of pan-Arabism, was gradually losing control of the party organization to more activist members. The first open breach occurred in 1953, and in March the following year nine former members of the OS set up the Revolutionary Council for Unity and Action (CRUA) to prepare for an immediate revolt against French rule.

WAR OF INDEPENDENCE

Plans for the insurrection were worked out at a series of CRUA meetings in Switzerland between March and October 1954. Algeria was divided into six *wilaya* (zones) and a military commander appointed for each. When the revolt was launched on November 1st the CRUA changed its name to the National Liberation Front (*Front de Libération Nationale—* FLN), its armed forces being known as the National Liberation Army (*Armée de Libération Nationale—* ALN). Beginning in the Aurès, the revolt had spread by early 1955 to the Constantine area, the Kabyle and the whole of the Moroccan frontiers west of Oran. By the end of 1956 the ALN was active throughout the settled areas of Algeria.

Ferhat Abbas and Ahmed Francis of the more bourgeois UDMA and the religious leaders of the Ulema joined the FLN in April 1956, making it representative of all shades of Algerian nationalist feeling apart from Messali Hadj's Algerian National Movement (MNA). In August a secret congress of the FLN, held at Soummam in the Kabyle, formed a central committee and the National Council of the Algerian Revolution; drew up a socialist programme for the future Algerian republic; and approved plans for the launching of a terrorist offensive in Algiers.

In the early stages of the war the French Government was convinced that only external support kept the FLN offensive going. The Foreign Minister was therefore despatched to Cairo in an attempt to persuade President Nasser to withdraw his support. This mission was in vain, and Guy Mollet, the French Prime Minister, then resorted to collusion with the Israelis and the British in the abortive invasion of Egypt at the end of October 1956. The Suez operation actually strengthened the FLN's position by increasing support from newly independent and non-aligned states.

Between September 1956 and June 1957 bomb explosions engineered by the FLN caused much loss of life. This terrorism was brought to a stop only by severe French repression of the Muslim population, including the use of torture and internment, measures which aroused condemnation of French policy both at home and abroad. Guerrilla activities continued but electrified barriers were set up along the Tunisian and Moroccan borders and ALN bands attempting to cross into Algeria met with heavy losses.

In June 1957 the new Bourgès-Manoury administration in France put forward legislation intended to link Algeria indissolubly with France, but the bill was never passed. Following the Soummam conference, a joint Moroccan-Tunisian plan had been put forward for the establishment of a North African federation linked with France. FLN leaders began negotiations in Morocco in October 1957. However, Ben Bella and his companions were kidnapped on their way from Morocco to Tunisia, when the French pilot of their plane landed it at Algiers. The French authorities could hardly reject this *fait accompli*, and the hijacked leaders were arrested and interned in France. Neither the internment of FLN leaders nor the bombing by French aircraft, in February 1958, of the Tunisian border village of Sakhiet, in which 79 villagers were killed, had any effect on the FLN's capacity to continue fighting, and the failure of these desperate measures only made the possibility of French negotiations with the FLN more likely. This in turn provoked a backlash from the Algerian Europeans (only half of whom were of French origin).

In May 1958 they rebelled and set up committees of public safety in the major Algerian towns. Supported by the army and exploiting the widespread fear of civil war, the colonists caused the overthrow of the discredited Fourth French Republic and General de Gaulle's return to power, believing that he would further their aim of complete integration of Algeria into France. They were very soon to be bitterly disappointed. Although de Gaulle did step up military action against the FLN, this was only at the cost of increased terrorism in Algiers and of growing tension on the Tunisian and Moroccan borders. The FLN responded in August 1958 by establishing in Tunis the Provisional Government of the Algerian Republic (GPRA), headed by Ferhat Abbas and including Ben Bella and the other leaders who had been interned in France. De Gaulle was already beginning to recognize the strength of Algerian nationalism and was moving cautiously towards accepting FLN demands.

NEGOTIATIONS AND THE COLONISTS' LAST STAND

Initially de Gaulle's public statements on Algeria were vague. When he did make an unequivocal pronouncement, in September 1959, and upheld the right of Algerians to determine their own future, the colonists did not take long to react. In January 1960 they rebelled again, this time against de Gaulle, and erected barricades in Algiers streets. However, without the support of the army the insurrection collapsed within nine days. The first exploratory talks between French and FLN delegates took place in secret near Paris in the summer of 1960 but were abortive.

In November de Gaulle announced that a referendum was to be held on the organization of government in Algeria, pending self-determination, and in December he visited Algeria himself to prepare the way. In the referendum the electorate were asked to approve a draft law providing for self-determination and immediate reforms to give Algerians the opportunity to participate in government. There were mass abstentions from voting in Algeria, however, and in February 1961 new French approaches to the FLN were made through the President of Tunisia. Secret talks led to direct negotiations between French and FLN representatives at Evian, on the Franco-Swiss border. These began in May but were finally broken off in August over the question of the Sahara and because of the French attack on Bizerta.

Europeans in Algeria and segments of the French army had meanwhile formed the Secret Army Organization (OAS) to resist a negotiated settlement and the transfer of power from European hands. On April 22nd, 1961, four generals, Challe, Zeller, Jouhaud and Salan, organized the seizure of Algiers, but this attempt at an army *putsch* proved abortive, most regular officers remaining loyal to de Gaulle. Offensive operations against the Algerian rebels, which had been suspended when the Evian talks began, were resumed by the French Government in response to rebel pressure, and fighting continued, though on a reduced scale. At the same time the OAS began its campaign of indiscriminate terrorism against native Algerians. The Mayor of Evian had already been killed by an OAS bomb, and attacks were now also mounted in Paris.

Secret contacts between the French government and the FLN were re-established in October. Negotiations were resumed in December 1961 and January 1962 in Geneva and Rome, the five members of the GPRA interned in France taking part through a representative of the King of Morocco. Meetings at ministerial level were held in strict secrecy in Paris in February and the final stage of the negotiations was concluded at Evian on March 18th with the signing of a ceasefire agreement and a declaration of future policy. The declaration provided for the establishment of an independent Algerian state after a transitional period, and for the safeguarding of individual rights and liberties. Other declarations issued the following day dealt with the rights of French citizens in Algeria and with future Franco-Algerian cooperation. In the military sphere, France was to retain the naval base at Mers el-Kebir for 15 years and the nuclear testing site in the Sahara, together with various landing rights, for five years.

In accordance with the Evian agreements a provisional government was formed on March 28th, with Abderrahman Farès as provisional President and an executive composed of FLN members, other Muslims and Europeans. The Soviet Union, the East European and many African and Asian countries quickly gave *de jure* recognition to the GPRA.

The signing of the Evian agreements was the signal for a final desperate fling by the OAS. A National Council of French Resistance in Algeria was set up, with General Salan as Commander-in-Chief, and OAS commando units attempted by attacks on the Muslim population and the destruction of public buildings to provoke a general breach of the ceasefire. After the failure of the OAS to establish an "insur-rectional zone" in the Orléansville (El Asnam) area and the capture of General Salan on April 20th, and with a renewal of FLN terrorist activity and reprisals, increasing numbers of Europeans began to leave Algeria for France. Abortive secret negotiations by OAS leaders with the FLN, aimed at securing guarantees for the European population, disclosed a split in the OAS which heralded the virtual end of European terrorist activity. By the end of June over half the European population of Algeria had left.

The final steps towards Algerian independence were now taken. In a referendum on July 1st, 91 per cent of the electorate voted for independence, which was proclaimed by General de Gaulle on July 3rd, 1962.

THE INDEPENDENT STATE

The achievement of power by the FLN revealed serious tensions and weaknesses within the government, while the problems facing the new state after eight years of civil war were formidable.

The dominant position in the GPRA of the "centralist" group, headed by Ben Khedda and consisting of former members of the MTLD, was threatened by the release in March 1962 of the five GPRA members who had been detained in France—Ben Bella, Mohammed Khider, Mohammed Boudiaf, Ait Ahmed and Rabah Bitat. Boudiaf and Ait Ahmed rallied temporarily to the support of Ben Khedda, while the others formed yet another opposition faction besides that of Ferhat Abbas, who had been dropped from the GPRA leadership in 1961.

The ALN leadership was also split. The commanders of the main armed forces in Tunisia and Morocco were opposed to the politicians of the GPRA, and the commanders of the internal guerrilla groups were opposed to all external and military factions.

Serious differences had appeared when the National Council of the Algerian Revolution (CRNA) met in Tripoli in May 1962 to consider policies for the new state. A commission headed by Ben Bella produced a programme which included large-scale agrarian reform, involving expropriation and the establishment of peasant cooperatives and state farms; a state monopoly of external trade; and a foreign policy aimed towards Maghreb unity, neutralism and anti-colonialism, especially in Africa. Despite the opposition of Ben Khedda's group, the Tripoli programme became the official FLN policy.

When independence came on July 3rd the GPRA cabinet, with the exception of Ben Bella, flew to Algiers, where they installed themselves alongside the official Provisional Executive, and Ben Khedda attempted to reassert control over the ALN by dismissing the Commander-in-Chief, Col. Boumedienne. Ben Bella, however, flew to Morocco to join Boumedienne and on July 11th they crossed into Algeria and established headquarters in Tlemcen. Here Ben Bella set up the Political Bureau as the chief executive organ of the FLN and a rival to the GPRA. After negotiations he was joined by some of the GPRA leaders; this left Ben Khedda isolated in Algiers, with Boudiaf and Ait Ahmed in opposition.

Several of the *wilaya* leaders, however, felt that, having provided the internal resistance, they represented the true current of the revolution, and they were opposed to the Political Bureau and Boumedienne. While ALN forces loyal to the Bureau occupied Constantine and Bône (Annaba) in the east on July 25th, Algiers remained in the hands of the leadership of *wilaya* IV, who refused the Bureau entry. When Boumedienne's forces marched on Algiers from Oran at the beginning of September there were serious clashes with *wilaya* IV troops. Total civil war was averted, however, partly because of mass demonstrations against the fighting which were organized by the Algerian General Workers' Union (UGTA).

The struggle for power had gone against Ben Khedda. Before the elections were held on September 20th, 1962, a third of the 180 candidates on the single list drawn up in August were purged, including Ben Khedda himself, and their places filled with lesser-known figures. Although the elections failed to produce much public enthusiasm, some 99 per cent of the electorate were declared to have voted in favour of the proposed powers of the Constituent Assembly. The functions of the GPRA were transferred to the Assembly when it met on September 25th, and Ferhat Abbas was elected its President. The Algerian Republic was proclaimed and the following day Ben Bella was elected Prime Minister, with a cabinet drawn from his personal associates and former ALN officers.

BEN BELLA IN POWER

The new government immediately set about consolidating its position. Messali Hadj's PPA (formerly the MNA), the Algerian Communist Party, largely discredited because of its role in the war, and Boudiaf's Party of the Socialist Revolution were all banned in November; the *wilaya* system was abolished the following month, and, apart from the UGTA, all organizations affiliated to the FLN were brought firmly under control.

The economic plight of the country was severe. Some 90 per cent (one million) of the Europeans, representing virtually all the entrepreneurs, technicians, administrators, teachers, doctors and skilled workers had left the country. Factories, farms and shops had closed, leaving 70 per cent of the population unemployed. Public buildings and records had been destroyed by the OAS. At the end of the war, in which over a million had died, there had been two million in internment camps and 500,000 refugees in Tunisia and Morocco. In December 1962 an emergency austerity plan was drawn up and the government was enabled to continue functioning by large loans and technical assistance from France and other emergency foreign aid.

By packing the first UGTA congress with FLN militants and unemployed, the FLN managed in January 1963 to gain control of the UGTA executive, which had been opposed to the dictatorial nature of the new government. The decrees of March legalized the workers' committees which, aided by the UGTA, had taken over the operation of many of the deserted European estates in the summer and autumn of 1962; the remaining estates were nationalized in 1963. The system of workers' management known as *autogestion*, under which the workers elected their own management board to work alongside a state-appointed director, became the basis of "Algerian socialism".

In April 1963 Ben Bella increased his powers by taking over the post of general secretary of the FLN. In August he secured the adoption by the Assembly of a draft constitution providing for a presidential regime, with the FLN as the sole political party. The new constitution was approved in a referendum and on September 13th Ben Bella was elected President for a period of five years, assuming the title of commander-in-chief as well as becoming head of state and head of government. These moves towards dictatorial government aroused opposition. Ferhat Abbas, the leading spokesman for a more liberal policy, resigned from the presidency of the Assembly and was subsequently expelled from the FLN. In the Kabyle, where discontent was accentuated by Berber regionalism, revolts had to be suppressed in 1963 and 1964.

Long-standing disputes between Algeria and Morocco over areas on their common frontiers deteriorated into open conflict in October 1963. The hostilities, near the strategic posts of Hassi-Beida and Tinjoub, were not on a large scale and were soon brought to an end through the mediation of interested African states, but they left a legacy of bitterness between the two countries.

BOUMEDIENNE TAKES OVER

On June 19th, 1965, Ben Bella was deposed and arrested in a swift and bloodless military *coup d'état*, led by the Minister of Defence, Col. Houari Boumedienne, whose army had brought Ben Bella to power in 1962. In the face of Algeria's poor economic situation and Ben Bella's dictatorial tendencies, many administrators and politicians were not averse to the coup, and his elimination of most of the traditional leaders, his repeated attacks on the UGTA and his failure to turn the FLN into a broadly-based party left him without organized support once the army had turned against him. Bereft of its leader, the FLN accepted the coup, and the UGTA, while expressing no real support for Boumedienne, did not oppose it.

Supreme political authority in Algeria was taken over by a Council of the Revolution, consisting mostly of military figures and presided over by Col. Boumedienne. Under the Council's authority a new Government of 20 members was announced on July 10th, with Boumedienne as Prime Minister and Minister of Defence, besides being President of the Council; Rabah Bitat as Minister of State; and Bouteflika continuing as Foreign Minister. Nine members of the Government, which included technocrats and members of the radical wing of the FLN, had held office under Ben Bella. To ensure a satisfactory relationship between the government and the FLN, a five-man party secretariat under Cherif Belkacem was set up on July 17th.

The aims of the new regime, as described by Boumedienne, were to re-establish the principles of the revolution, to remedy the abuses of personal power associated with Ben Bella, to end internal divisions, and to create an "authentic socialist society" based on a sound economy. In international relations a policy of non-alignment would be pursued and support for people struggling for freedom and independence would continue.

Apart from preparations for elections to the Communal Councils, the regime showed no signs of seeking a popular mandate and the Algerian National Assembly remained in abeyance. New penal and civil legal codes were promulgated in 1966, the judiciary was Algerianized and tribunals to try "economic crimes" with powers to impose the death penalty were set up in July. New conditions of service and training schemes for public employees were introduced with the aim of improving the standard of administration. In accordance with its socialist policies, the regime increased state participation during 1966 in fields previously left to private enterprise. A state-owned construction company was set up, and it was decided in March that the distribution of the income of the oil and gas industry, both inside and outside Algeria, should be subject to government supervision. In May the nationalization was announced of 11 foreign-owned mines and of property of absentee owners, and all insurance activities were placed under state control. A National Bank of Algeria, specializing in short-term credit for the nationalized sector of the economy, was inaugurated in July.

Industrial activity continued at a low level and the country remained heavily dependent on external aid for industrial development. A new investment code, designed to attract both domestic and foreign capital and promulgated in September, contained assurances of indemnification in the event of nationalization.

CAUTION IN FOREIGN POLICY

The need to consolidate and build up national strength which influenced its domestic policies also caused Boumedienne's Government to conduct Algeria's foreign relations with caution, although it remained committed to "anti-imperialism" and a militant stand on the Palestine question.

The relationship with France, Algeria's main customer and the source of substantial assistance, remained paramount. In 1966 agreements were signed which provided for French technical and educational assistance for 20 years, cancelled Algeria's pre-independence debts and reduced indebtedness to France to 400 million dinars. France was disturbed by the growing Soviet influence in Algeria. Soviet advisers were playing a leading role in the development of mining and industry, and the Algerian army was receiving training and equipment from the U.S.S.R. However, French fears that the Soviet navy might be allowed to use the Mers el-Kebir base, handed over by France in January 1968, proved groundless. The French cultural influence remained: there were still many French teachers, although the teaching

of Arabic was being extended in the schools; large numbers of Algerians worked in France; there was a preference for such French consumer goods as were still being imported; and France continued to give assistance, including training and equipment for Algeria's armed forces.

Algerian involvement in the six-day Palestine war in June 1967 was small. When the ceasefire came, however, there were street demonstrations against Nasser's "treason" and also against the U.S.S.R. for lack of support for the Arab countries. At the Khartoum conference and also at the UN, Algeria's voice was one of the most belligerent, calling for a people's war, and as a token of support detachments of Algerian troops were maintained in the Suez Canal area until August 1970.

A highly critical, often openly hostile attitude to the U.S.A. was maintained, and diplomatic relations were severed in 1967. Nevertheless, American oil expertise was respected and encouraged as was investment in Algeria's oil industry; a contract to sell liquefied natural gas to the United States was signed in 1969.

In Africa the Boumedienne Government took a consistently anti-colonial line, breaking relations with Britain over Rhodesia in 1965 (but restoring them in 1968), and providing training and other facilities for the liberation movements of southern Africa, as well as to the Eritrean Liberation Front and the National Liberation Front of Chad. A determined effort was made to improve relations with neighbouring countries in the Maghreb. In January 1969 President Boumedienne paid his first official visit to Morocco for talks with King Hassan, and the following June frontier posts were reopened for the first time since 1963. In May 1970 an agreement was signed, settling the long-standing border dispute and pledging mutual co-operation on the question of the Spanish presence in North Africa. Further agreements were signed between the two leaders in June 1972, one defining the Algerian—Moroccan border (ratified in May 1973), the other providing for joint exploitation of the Gara-Djebilet mines in the border regions. An agreement with Mauritania was signed in December 1969 and a friendship treaty with Tunisia agreeing on common borders in January 1970. Whilst Algeria welcomed the Libyan revolution in 1969, the subsequent orientation of the Libyan leaders towards Egypt and the Sudan rather than the Maghreb was not conducive to close relations between the two regimes; nevertheless, an agreement to co-ordinate oil policies was signed.

INTERNAL OPPOSITION OVERCOME

Opposition came from certain left-wing ministers, such as Ali Yahia and Abdelaziz Zerdani, the UGTA, the students, and some sections of the army, notably the former *wilaya* leaders. These feared the imposition of a technocratic and centralized form of socialism, different from the syndicalist concepts embodied in *autogestion*, and felt that collegial rule was being supplanted by the dictatorship of the small group round Boumedienne. An armed uprising in the Mitidja, launched in December 1967, failed because the key posts in the army were held by the younger professionals loyal to Boumedienne; it was followed by a wave of arrests in the unions and the administration, selective dismissals in the FLN and the army in order to secure his position, and the appointment of well-known supporters to vacant ministerial offices.

Opposition to Boumedienne was by no means crushed, however. FLN attempts in February 1968 to impose a new loyal student committee at Algiers University provoked a long strike by students and teachers, and in the spring there were numerous reports of guerrilla activity in the Aurès and the Kabyle. The Organization of Popular Resistance (ORP) appeared to be active both in these areas and among the students. An attempt to assassinate Boumedienne was made on April 25th in Algiers, but he escaped with only minor injuries.

In the latter part of 1968 there were signs that the Government's position had strengthened and President Boumedienne made several visits to the provinces without special security precautions. In March 1969 a number of secret trials were held and numbers of less important prisoners were subsequently released. The second stage of the reform of governmental institutions (the first being the 1967 communal elections) was put into operation in May 1969 when elections were held for the 15 administrative districts (*wilaya*) and 72 per cent of the electorate voted for candidates on a single FLN list. In June 1970, following the celebration of his first five years in power, Boumedienne undertook an extensive tour of western Algeria, and when cabinet changes were made in July, his key colleagues retained their places, a fact which served to emphasize the regime's stability. On the anniversary of the revolution in November 1970 he amnestied about 100 political prisoners. The release of these former enemies gave some indication of the weakness of the underground opposition.

Only among students did discontent remain in evidence. A school strike in December led to violent clashes with the police, and in January 1971 the arrest of eight Algiers university students resulted in a strike at the university and the dissolution by the government of the National Union of Algerian Students (UNEA). The attitude of many students otherwise sympathetic to the aims and achievements of the FLN was doubtless affected by poor employment prospects.

RELATIONS WITH FRANCE

The improvement in President Boumedienne's position at home enabled him to adopt a more militant attitude towards France. He could afford to demand more for Algerian oil, and the resultant dispute over the price to be paid by the French oil companies culminated in the decision to take control of them by nationalization.

The two companies concerned, the *Compagnie Française des Pétroles* (CFP) and the *Entreprise de Recherches et d'Activités Pétrolières* (ERAP), were responsible for some two-thirds of Algeria's total production. In the first half of 1970 the Algerian government pressed them to accept an increase in the posted price of petroleum, but negotiations broke down and in July the Government unilaterally fixed a new price level. Further discussions between the French and Algerian Governments proved futile, and in February 1971 Boumedienne announced the take-over by the Algerian government of a 51 per cent holding in CFP and ERAP and the complete nationalization of the companies' gas and pipeline interests.

The French Government regarded this move as a breach of the 1965 agreement but could only ask for fair compensation. The subsequent Algerian offer was found unacceptable and in April 1971 France discontinued negotiations. Relations appeared to have reached their lowest ebb. It was announced that many French technicians and teachers were to leave Algeria, and attacks were made on some of the 700,000 Algerians in France. The French Government applied a boycott against Algerian oil and tried to persuade other major consumers to do the same. Talks between the two French companies and SONATRACH, the Algerian state oil concern, were resumed, however, and agreements were reached in June and September under which the role of CFP and ERAP became that of minority partners of the Algerian state in return for guaranteed oil supplies. After approval by the two governments a final agreement, which also provided for compensation and reduced back claims of taxes, was signed on December 15th.

In April 1975, Valéry Giscard d'Estaing became the first French President to visit Algeria since independence. According to Boumedienne, this event marked the definitive reconciliation of the French and Algerian peoples. However, the goodwill generated by Giscard's visit was quickly dissipated. The Algerian Government resented French economic policies which maintained an imbalance in trade between the two countries and also regarded French support for Morocco over the Sahara dispute (*see* below) as a betrayal, especially when France began supplying large quantities of arms to Algeria's potential enemy.

PALESTINE AND THE SAHARA

The Boumedienne Government's stand on the Palestine question remained uncompromisingly militant. Algeria accepted neither the 1967 UN resolution nor the ceasefire, and when, after the hostilities along the Suez Canal in 1969 and 1970, a further ceasefire was agreed in August 1970, Algerian troops were withdrawn. Radio stations of Palestine liberation movements banished from Cairo in July 1970 were allowed to broadcast from Algiers and relations with Jordan were broken off in June 1971 after the final destruction of Palestinian guerrilla bases in Jordan by King Hussein's forces. During the October War in 1973 Algeria was active on the diplomatic front, encouraging African countries to break off relations with Israel. It participated fully with other Arab oil-producing states in cut-backs in production and boycotts aimed at countries regarded as hostile to the Arab cause. Relations with Jordan were restored after the dispatch of Jordanian troops to the Syrian front, but Algeria continued to support the Palestinians against any Jordanian territorial claims. In December 1977 Algeria was one of the signatories of the Declaration of Tripoli opposing President Sadat's attempts to negotiate with Israel; diplomatic relations with Egypt were broken off.

Despite Algeria's policy towards Palestine and the welcome accorded to almost any exiled foreign opposition group, it continued to co-operate in the economic field with any state willing to do so. Fears that Algeria might fall under Soviet dominance proved groundless, although the U.S.S.R. continued to be a major source of military equipment. Despite strong disagreements with the U.S.A. over Viet-Nam and the Palestinian question, full diplomatic relations were restored at the end of 1974 and trade between the two countries increased dramatically; by the end of 1977 the U.S.A. had replaced France as Algeria's leading trade partner.

From early 1975 a major confrontation developed with Morocco over the future of the Spanish Sahara. Algeria opposed Morocco's claim to the territory, advocating the founding of an independent Saharan state after decolonization. In May 1975, at the International Court of Justice, Algeria called for genuine self-determination for the Saharans and denied any self-interest in the matter. This was, however, disingenuous, since Algeria could clearly draw considerable political and economic advantage from the existence of a weak, friendly state on its western border. When, in November 1975, Spain agreed to hand over the territory to Morocco and Mauritania, Boumedienne protested vehemently and promised full support for Polisario, the Saharan liberation movement. As Moroccan troops moved into the Western Sahara, Algeria mobilized part of its armed forces, and in January and February 1976 there were heavy clashes between units of the two armies in the Sahara several hundred miles from the Algerian border. In March Algeria recognized the Sahrawi Arab Democratic Republic, proclaimed by Polisario, and both Morocco and Mauritania broke off diplomatic relations with Algeria. The prospect of a full-scale war in the Sahara quickly receded, especially as there was little enthusiasm for war amongst the Algerian population, but the Government continued to provide support and refuge for Polisario guerrillas. Morocco and Mauritania refused to recognize the independent existence of the guerrilla movement and interpreted all armed incursions into the Sahara as Algerian attacks against their national territory. French bombing raids on Polisario troops, beginning in December 1977, were strongly condemned by Algeria, although the French Government declared that its intervention was solely for the protection of French citizens working in the area.

In August 1979 diplomatic relations with Mauritania were resumed after Mauritania had withdrawn its claim to the Western Sahara. Relations with Morocco remained unfriendly while the military and diplomatic stalemate in the Sahara continued.

(For a more detailed account of the Western Sahara dispute, *see* chapter on Morocco.)

HOME AFFAIRS

By 1971 Boumedienne's Government felt strong enough to initiate a more active social policy. The choice of capital-intensive export industry as the basis for economic development and of centralized bureaucratic state-control as the mode of organization had saddled Algeria with many of the same problems as countries dominated by foreign capitalism. The lives of the majority of the population, especially in the rural areas and the backward regions of the country, were untouched by the economic progress. There was mass unemployment and considerable inequality in the distribution of wealth. In 1971 a programme of agrarian reform, known as the Agrarian Revolution, was initiated. The reform was to proceed in three phases, the redistribution of state-owned and foreign land, the redistribution of private estates, and the transformation of the lives of the pastoral nomads. At the same time the government resolved to develop workers' control in industry and to reanimate the FLN as a radical force. Elected workers' councils slowly spread through nationalized industries, but the reorganization of the FLN was a failure. In 1972 Kaid Ahmed, the leader of the party, resigned because of his lack of success. The initiative in promoting the Agrarian Revolution passed to a student *volontariat*, in which the more radical students participated enthusiastically. Boumedienne's determination to build a socialist society encountered resistance from conservative sectors of the population, especially after the redistribution of private estates and the nationalization of food distribution. Conflict came into the open in May 1975 when there were clashes at Algiers University between radical students devoted to the Agrarian Revolution and conservative students wishing to give priority to Arabization. Boumedienne came out strongly in favour of the radicals.

The personal authority of Boumedienne grew in the 1970s. The death of Ahmed Medeghri and Belkacem's dismissal from the cabinet in 1974 left only Bouteflika as a figure of comparable stature in the government. Encouraged by the success of local and provincial elections since 1967 and 1969 respectively, Boumedienne announced in June 1975 that national elections for an assembly and a president were to be held and that a National Charter would be drawn up to provide the state with a new constitution.

Boumedienne's decision to consolidate the regime and his personal power provoked a resurgence of opposition, including the circulation, in March 1976, of a manifesto signed by, among others, Ferhat Abbas and Ben Youssef Ben Khedda, both former presidents of the Algerian government-in-exile during the war of liberation. The manifesto criticized Boumedienne for totalitarian rule and the personality cult. The signatories were reportedly placed under house arrest. Boumedienne rejected these criticisms of his rule as the work of bourgeois reactionaries, and declared that the revolution had reached the point of no return.

In April 1976 the Algerian press began publication of the National Charter, which, after public discussion, received approval by 98.5 per cent of the voters in a referendum in June. It was a sign of the confidence of the regime that discussion of the Charter was encouraged to be vigorous and critical. The essence of the Charter was the irreversible commitment of Algeria to socialism, though a socialism specifically adapted to Third-World conditions. The dominant role of the FLN was reasserted but, as a concession to more conservative sentiment, Islam was recognized as the state religion. The following November a new Constitution embodying the principles of the Charter was also approved by referendum, and in December Boumedienne was elected President unopposed with 99 per cent of votes cast. To complete the new formal structure of power, a national assembly of 261 members was elected in February 1977 from among 783 candidates selected by a committee of the FLN. Next, steps were taken yet again to strengthen and enlarge the FLN, in order to make it the guiding political force envisaged in the National Charter. FLN officials were installed alongside local administrative officials to form the basis of a full party apparatus at all levels, and the mass organizations affiliated to the FLN (the unions of workers, peasants, war veterans, women and youth) held a series of congresses which was to culminate in a national FLN Congress (the first since 1964) early in 1979.

THE DEATH OF BOUMEDIENNE

In November 1978, however, a more urgent problem arose when it gradually became clear that President Boumedienne was seriously ill. At the end of the month he fell into a coma which lasted almost continuously until his death on December 27th. During his illness there was anxious speculation as to who should succeed him, particularly since he had nominated neither a Vice-President nor a Prime Minister and was himself Minister of Defence (a post which had included, from 1977 onwards, direct supervision of the police and secret service) and Chief of Staff. For the time being, government was taken over by the Council of the Revolution, which by now consisted of only eight members, apart from Boumedienne (five ministers, two senior army officers and the administrative head of the FLN); although it had been given no official status in the 1976 Constitution, the Council declared that it would maintain continuity and protect existing institutions, and succeeded in bringing about a smooth transfer of power.

After Boumedienne's death Rabah Bitat, the President of the National Assembly, was automatically sworn in as Head of State for a 45-day period. At the end of January the long-planned FLN Congress was held. It now had the double task of attempting to restore the party's vitality and of choosing a presidential candidate. New statutes on party structure were adopted, whereby a Central Committee of between 120 and 160 members and between 30 and 40 advisory members, meeting at least once every 6 months, was to be elected by Congress and form the highest policy-making body not only of the party but of the country as a whole. The Committee was to select a party Secretary-General who would automatically become the FLN's (and therefore the only) presidential candidate. A Political Bureau of between 17 and 21 members, nominated by the Secretary-General, would be elected by the Central Committee and responsible to it. These structures superseded the Council of the Revolution, which was formally disbanded on January 27th.

It was expected that the chosen presidential candidate would be a member of the now-disbanded Council, and the most likely choice appeared to be either Abdelaziz Bouteflika, the Minister for Foreign Affairs, regarded as a moderate, or Mohamed Salah Yahiaoui, the administrative head of the FLN, regarded as a more radical socialist and favoured by the youth and workers' organizations. The eventual choice, Col. Bendjedid Chadli, the commander of the Oran military district, was something of a compromise between the two. He was inaugurated as President on February 9th, after his candidature had been approved by 94 per cent of the electorate. He declared that he would continue to uphold the policies of Boumedienne, the "irreversible option" of socialism and "national independence" in both political and economic spheres. It soon became clear that Chadli did not intend to monopolize power to the extent that Boumedienne had. For the first time since independence, a Prime Minister was named: Col. Mohamed Ben Ahmed Abdelghani, who also kept his post as Minister of the Interior until January 1980. This action anticipated the constitutional changes adopted by the National Assembly in June 1979, which made the appointment of a Prime Minister obligatory, and also reduced the President's term of office from six to five years, in line with five-yearly party congresses. Although he made cabinet changes (which included the removal of Abdelaziz Bouteflika from the post of Foreign Minister, held by him for 15 years), Chadli was not expected to depart from his predecessor's policies to any great extent. Nevertheless there were some signs of reduced austerity during the first few months of his presidency. Some of Boumedienne's political opponents were released from prison, and it was announced that the former President, Ben Bella, had been freed, although it later appeared that he had merely been placed under a less stringent form of house arrest; he was finally freed from restrictions in October 1980. Exit visas for Algerians, compulsory since 1967, were abolished; income tax was reduced and restrictions on owning property eased. In September, however, greater severity became apparent when a "clean-up" campaign in Algiers and other cities, initially intended to improve the appearance of the streets in preparation for the 25th anniversary of the revolution, expanded to include the arrest and imprisonment of hundreds of "social parasites" and a campaign against inefficiency and corruption.

During 1980 and 1981 this campaign was extended to the highest levels of state organizations, and numerous senior officials were arrested and tried by the *Cour des Comptes* for financial mismanagement.

In 1979 the Government encountered criticism from students, who went on strike protesting that the policy of replacing French with Arabic was not being carried out quickly enough, particularly in scientific and technical education, the law and the civil service. The students' demands were partly met by measures intended to speed up the process of "Arabization" in education and 600 Arabic-speaking trainee magistrates were also appointed. In May 1980 the FLN Central Committee announced that a central co-ordinating body was to be set up to encourage the use of Arabic, and that official newspapers should be printed in Arabic only. A year later, many settlements reverted to their Arabic names.

Protests and demonstrations against the suppression of the Berber language and culture have continued in recent years, generally centred on the Kabyle, a region long regarded as having dangerously separatist intentions. Although some concessions have been made, including the creation of chairs in Berber languages at the universities of Tizi-Ouzou and Algiers and the provision of Berber radio programmes, President Chadli has made it clear that he regards the Berber demands as a threat to national unity. The problem flared up again in 1981 when proposals for a "cultural charter", making provisions for the Berber culture as part of Algeria's national heritage, met with little approval; the discussions were accompanied by outbreaks of violence and had to be abandoned. In September, however, the announcement that departments of popular literature and dialect were to be opened in Algiers, Constantine, Oran and Annaba (although not in Tizi-Ouzou) slightly relaxed the tension in the Kabyle. Another serious problem is the gradual emergence of Muslim fundamentalists in Algeria. Several disturbances were caused in 1981 by their activities.

A meeting of the FLN Central Committee in ·December 1979 resulted in some important decisions concerning economic and social development. The Committee reviewed the past ten years and listed various "unsettling factors", such as dependence on hydrocarbons (earning some 85 per cent of foreign currency in 1979), persistent shortages of raw materials and consumer goods, bureaucratic attitudes, reliance on foreign resources, and regional imbalances: in short, it admitted the country's failure to implement a coherent national economic policy. It announced that Algeria would reduce its dependence on foreign financial and technical assistance, diversify its economic partners, and cut down its petroleum and gas exports in order to conserve these resources. The massive industrialization programme was to be scaled down and the large State companies reorganized into smaller units. Details of these changes were given in a new five-year plan adopted in June 1980 (*see* Economic Survey). The emphasis of government policy was to shift from heavy industry to social areas, such as health, education and infrastructure, and raising agricultural production. The private sector was to be considerably liberalized.

During 1980 a general streamlining of the FLN took place, and the President's control over it was strengthened. In June, at an extraordinary congress of nearly 4,000 delegates, important changes in the party structure were initiated. The Political Bureau was now to consist of between seven and 11 members (having previously numbered between 17 and 21), and was to meet monthly instead of weekly. The President, as Secretary-General of the FLN, was empowered to select the members of the Political Bureau rather than merely to "propose" them, although the choice would still be subject to the Central Committee's approval; he was also given a free hand in making other changes in the party which he considered necessary. All this reinforced the President's position, and reduced the role of the Political Bureau to that of an advisory body. President Chadli immediately reduced its numbers to the new statutory minimum of seven. The Prime Minister, Col. Abdelghani, and several other ministers were dropped from the Bureau, but it still represented a wide range of opinion, from the liberal views of M. Bouteflika, the former Foreign Minister, to the strict Islamic socialism of M. Yahiaoui, FLN Party Co-ordinator until July, when the post was abolished. In addition, the number of party Committees was reduced from 12 to five (dealing with general organization, external relations, internal party discipline, economic and social affairs, and information and culture). Changes were also made in the wider membership of the FLN. The June congress laid down that all officials of the main workers union, the UGTA, and the other mass organizations would have to be paid-up members of the FLN. In this way members of "unofficial" parties, such as the communist *Parti de l'avant-garde socialiste*, would be excluded from official positions.

Further changes were made to the composition of the FLN's Political Bureau in July 1981, when its membership was increased to 10. Col. Abdelghani was reappointed, but Yahiaoui and Bouteflika, Chadli's rivals for the presidency in 1979, were removed, although they retained their membership of the Central Committee. By their elimination from power, President Chadli further consolidated his own authority. In the following December Bouteflika was dismissed from the FLN Central Committee, as were three other senior members who had held important portfolios under Boumedienne.

Legislative elections were held on March 5th, 1982, when 72.65 per cent of the electorate voted for FLN candidates. The National Assembly's membership was increased to 281, of whom 55 were permanent members of the FLN.

Algeria played an important part in the negotiations over the American hostages in Iran, leading to their release in January 1981. Any resulting improvement in relations with the U.S.A. was cancelled, however, by the announcement shortly afterwards that the Americans were to sell tanks to Morocco, while in February negotiations on gas sales to the U.S.A. broke down over Algeria's insistence that prices of liquefied natural gas should be increased to parity with those of petroleum.

In September 1980 an agreement was signed with France on a system of incentives to be provided by the French Government for repatriating Algerian workers and their dependants, of whom there were about 800,000 living in France. In return, Algeria was to release French bank accounts which had been "frozen" since independence. Other causes of dispute

remained, however: the continuing trade deficit with France, the price of Algerian gas exported to France, and the still-unresolved question of the Western Sahara. Relations improved, however, with the advent of a socialist Government in France in May 1981. Gaston Defferre, the French Interior Minister, visited Algeria to discuss the problem of illegal immigration, and President Mitterrand followed soon after. Agreement on the price of Algerian gas was finally reached in February 1982.

ECONOMIC SURVEY

Algeria covers an area of 2,381,741 sq. km., of which a large part is desert. At the census of 1966 the population (including Algerians abroad) was returned at 12,090,547. The great majority of Europeans had returned to France by the early 1960s. On the basis of a census taken in February 1977, the estimated population at January 1st, 1981, had reached 19,118,000 in addition to about 850,000 Algerians living abroad, mainly in France. About 56 per cent of the population still live in rural areas but about 100,000 peasants migrate every year to the towns in search of work. Between 1967 and 1977 some 1,700,000 people moved from the countryside to the towns. The largest towns are Algiers or El Djezaïr, the capital (estimated population 2,100,000, including the suburbs, in 1980), Oran (846,000 with its suburbs), Constantine (756,000), Annaba (597,000), Tizi-Ouzou (934,000) and Sidi-Bel-Abbès (548,000). The population is growing at an estimated annual rate of 3.3 per cent and the birth rate is 47 per 1,000. About 58 per cent of the population are under the age of 19. In an effort to reduce the flow of peasants to the towns, the Government has started to implement a series of measures to boost the rural economy and to speed up the agrarian revolution. According to World Bank estimates, the population of urban centres was growing at 6.6 per cent annually in the period 1960–70 but this rate had been reduced to 5.7 per cent in 1970–75.

Algeria has varied natural resources. In the coastal region are highly fertile plains and valleys, where profitable returns are made from cereals, wine, olives and fruit. However, the rest of the country serves little agricultural purpose, though in the mountains grazing and forestry bring a small income for the population, and dates are grown in the oases of the Sahara. Mineral resources are abundant and are now the mainstay of Algeria's foreign trade. Revenues from oil and gas are being used to finance ambitious industrialization plans.

GOVERNMENT STRATEGY

Since independence in 1962 Algerian governments have sought to promote economic growth as a foundation for a future socialist society. They have either taken over completely or taken a controlling interest in most foreign-owned companies. In 1966 the Government nationalized foreign-owned mines, unoccupied lands deserted by Europeans at independence, and insurance companies; and took over the hydrocarbon sector in 1971.

Heavy industries are all state-run, while the consumer-oriented light industries have an important private-sector participation. Some 4,500 firms employ a total of 60,000 people. About half of these are in the textiles and leather sectors. The need to increase production and distribution of consumer goods means that the Government is allowing a controlled expansion of the "non-exploitative" private sector. In March 1982 a new investment code was published to encourage private savings and business in "non-strategic" fields like shops, bars, restaurants, hotels, housing, small handicrafts and some light industry. In April a new law on private joint ventures included tax "holidays" for foreign partners. Some import procedures were simplified for urgent projects in 1982. These changes reflect a degree of economic liberalism being introduced slowly under President Chadli. To increase productivity and efficiency, more than 30 of Algeria's giant state corporations were in January 1982 split up into smaller units with decentralized management away from Algiers. Corporations in heavy and light industry, housing, public works, shipping, water supply, posts and telegraphs, and tourism were affected. SONATRACH (hydrocarbons) and SONACOME (mechanical engineering) had already been split up in 1981.

The Government's strategy for development has involved a high degree of austerity, with heavy restrictions placed on the importation of "luxury" goods. The first Four-Year Plan, 1970–73, emphasized the establishment of a capital-intensive sector, involving the hydrocarbon, iron and steel, chemical and engineering industries and a 9 per cent annual growth rate was achieved. About 34,000 million dinars were invested. The second Plan, for 1974–77, aimed at laying the foundations of a sound industrial base and also emphasized improved agricultural methods, housing, health, job-creation and training. However, there was a marked lack of effective government policy with regard to agriculture and housing. Industry was allocated 43.5 per cent of total investment, infrastructure 14 per cent, social services and housing 13.3 per cent and agriculture 10.9 per cent.

The high level of investment (40 per cent of G.D.P.) was maintained and an average annual growth rate of 10 per cent was aimed at. Total expenditure, originally put at 52,000 million dinars, was later increased to 110,000 million dinars, on the basis of the large increase in income resulting from oil price rises.

The country's G.D.P. grew by an average annual rate of 6.2 per cent in real terms in the period 1970–76 and was estimated to have reached 70,000 million dinars in 1977, about 100,000 million dinars in 1978 and above 120,000 million dinars in 1979. During 1980 it was estimated to have grown by a further 6.5 per cent. In 1979 agriculture accounted for only 7.5 per cent of G.D.P., against 21 per cent in 1960; industry and construction provided 55.5 per cent. Per caput income in 1979 was about 5,700 dinars.

The adoption of the 1980–84 Five-Year Plan in 1980 ended three years of debate caused partly by the need to evaluate achievements at the end of the second Plan, partly by the death of President Houari Boumedienne at the end of 1978. Projected investment in the plan totals 400,600 million dinars, almost four times that for 1974–77. The projected G.D.P. growth rate during the plan is 8.2 per cent. Growth rates of 12.3 per cent for manufacturing industries and 12.9 per cent for other industries reflect a determination to meet severe shortages of consumer goods and to take up the slack in existing productive capacity. Per caput G.D.P. is expected to reach about 7,500 dinars by 1984.

Though the breakdown of investment indicates that more emphasis will be given to meeting social needs, such as housing, health and education, industry remains the basis of the Government's long-term strategy. There will, however, be a shift in emphasis from heavy to light industries, particularly basic foods, construction materials and textiles. Much of the new investment will go into creating a second industrial axis along the central high plateaux north of the Sahara.

AGRICULTURE

Algeria is still mainly an agricultural country. Over nine-tenths of the land consists of arid plateaux, mountains or desert, supporting scattered herds of sheep, goats or camel. Only the northern coastal strip, 100–200 km. wide, can be used for arable purposes. There are about 6.8 million hectares of cultivable land, representing less than one hectare per rural inhabitant. Forests cover about 4.4 million hectares. Most of the Sahara is devoted to semi-desert pasturage. The most valuable crop is the grape harvest, which represents 66 per cent of total agricultural exports by value; whilst wheat, barley and oats, grown for local consumption, cover a large area. Other crops include maize, sorghum, millet, rye and rice, as well as citrus fruit, olives, figs and dates, and tobacco. Agricultural development is restricted by problems such as erosion, adverse weather conditions, especially drought and flood, primitive methods of production, and under-employment.

Although it employs some 42 per cent of the nation's workforce, agriculture accounts for only 7 per cent of G.D.P. Output fell by an average of 8.7 per cent annually in the period 1970–76; the average annual decline in 1960–70 was 1.6 per cent. Planned investment in agriculture in 1980–84, at 20,000 million dinars, is almost double the amount projected under the 1974–77 Plan. In relative terms, however, the allocation has shrunk from 11 per cent to about 5 per cent of total investment. It is nonetheless recognized that food scarcity is an acute problem. Algeria was only 30 per cent self-sufficient in food in 1980, compared with 73 per cent in 1969. The Government aims to achieve 80 per cent self-sufficiency by 2000, when the population is expected to be about 35 million. During the 1980–84 Plan the Government will try to recover 1.7 million hectares of abandoned cultivable land by raising agricultural wages and otherwise improving conditions for rural workers. A number of large dams and irrigation projects are under construction or planned.

LAND REFORM

The first regulations, introduced in October 1962, enabled the state to take over any settler's property declared vacant. Land occupied by settlers was still legally owned by them, while the state "used" it. However, in March 1963, another Government decree declared that the state was taking over ownership of abandoned land. In May 1966 all remaining unoccupied property which had been evacuated by settlers was finally taken over by the state. These expropriated lands were turned into State farms run by workers' committees (*comités de gestion*).

After the total nationalization of French land in October 1963, state farm land accounted for 2.7 million hectares, roughly half the cultivable land in Algeria. The modern, "self-managed" agricultural sector represents one-third of the total agricultural area, provides work for only about 135,000 in permanent employment and about 100,000 in seasonal work, but its revenue is twice that of the "traditional" private sector, which provides a living for more than 5 million people.

In July 1971 President Boumedienne announced an agrarian reform programme which provided for the break-up of large, Algerian-owned farms and their redistribution to families of landless peasants, or *fellahs*, who would be organized in co-operatives. By early 1979, over 6,000 agricultural co-operatives of various kinds had been set up.

A census begun in September 1972 showed that a quarter of cultivable land was in the hands of 16,500 large landowners who represented only 3 per cent of the total number of farmers. In 1973 the Agrarian Revolution entered its second phase, that of re-distributing over 650,000 hectares of private land to 60,000 *fellahs*. Those receiving land were to be granted permanent use of it but they must belong to one of the new co-operatives. Through these they were to be given state loans and assistance in the form of seed, fertilizers and equipment. By early 1979, 22,000 absentee landowners had been obliged either to cultivate their own land or to hand it over to peasant farmers. A programme for the construction of socialist villages was started and by early 1981 140 of these had been built, 203 were under construction, 156 were programmed and a further 50 were being studied. The long-term goal is 1,700 villages housing 140,000 farmers. Under the *volontariat* scheme, young people are encouraged to spend their vacations working and teaching in rural areas.

The third phase of the Agrarian Revolution, begun in 1980, aims at increasing livestock production in the steppe areas. About 20 million hectares of pasturage, mostly in southern Algeria, grazed by the animals of 170,000 nomadic herdsmen, are to be nationalized. At present over 50 per cent of the livestock is owned by only 5 per cent of the herdsmen. The 8 million grazing animals are to be redistributed and grouped into settled co-operative units.

CROPS

The coastal areas of the Mediterranean produce grapes. Vines have been grown in Algeria since antiquity merely for local consumption; however, after the coming of the French in 1830, vine growing received substantial encouragement and wines still represent the principal agricultural export. Nevertheless, the Government regards agricultural dependence on wine as incompatible with real political independence. Thus it is tearing up the least productive vines and converting the land to cereal and dairy farming, and to forestry. The target for 1980 was 140,000 hectares under vines, compared with the 1978 total of 200,000 hectares. Production, which in 1960 was 18.6 million hectolitres, was down to 2.7 million hectolitres by 1979. The tendency will be for better quality wines and dessert grapes to be produced.

Grown principally in the Constantine, Annaba, Sétif and Tiaret areas, production of cereals fluctuates considerably, largely as a result of drought, and grains have to be imported, particularly from Canada. Wheat and barley are the most important cereals. Yields are very low, at 26–32 cwt. of wheat per hectare, compared with U.S. average yields of 70 cwt. By 1984 the Government aims to increase annual cereals production to about 30 million quintals, compared with 16.2 million quintals in 1979 (according to government estimates). Annual meat and dairy production goals for 1984 are 930 million litres of milk and dairy products (30 per cent more than in 1979), 146,000 tons of red meat (17 per cent more), and 151,000 tons of table eggs (5.2 times as many as in 1979).

Olives are grown mainly in the western coastal belt and in the Kabyle. Production fluctuates because of the two-year flowering cycle of the olive. In the 1978/79 season 1,569,000 quintals of olives were produced.

The citrus crop, grown in the coastal districts, totals between 400,000 and 500,000 tons per year. Production of potatoes is between 400,000 and 600,000 tons. About 46,000 tons of dried vegetables are produced annually. Market gardening is being encouraged, with the aim of finding a ready export market in Western Europe. Algeria is the world's fifth largest date producer, with an average of 130,000–180,000

tons per year, but 80 per cent of this is consumed locally.

Tobacco is the main industrial crop, employing about 13,000 people. About 3,000 tons per year are produced.

LIVESTOCK, FORESTRY AND FISHING

Sheep, goats and cattle are raised but great improvements will have to be made in stock-raising methods, grassland, control of disease and water supply if the increasing demand for meat is to be met. At present, a large part of Algeria's requirements in dairy products have to be imported. By September 1980 there were about 1.4 million head of cattle, 12.5 million sheep and 2.9 million goats (according to government estimates).

The area covered by forests has fallen rapidly in the past two decades, and the Government plans to reafforest 600,000 hectares during the 1980–84 plan, partly to protect cultivable land against erosion. A vast "green wall" of pines and cypresses, 20 km. wide, is being planted along 1,500 km. on the northern edge of the Sahara from the Moroccan to the Tunisian frontier, to arrest the steady northward encroachment of the Sahara desert. Work began in 1975 and the project has involved the construction of roads, reservoirs and pilot plantations of fruit trees and vegetables. However, the scheme has encountered numerous problems.

The Government feels that Algeria is not exploiting its fishing potential and hopes to raise annual production to 80,000 metric tons by 1984. The total sea catch in 1979 was 38,678 metric tons.

MINERALS

Algeria has rich mineral resources and, since before the petroleum era, has mined and exported high-grade iron ore, phosphates, lead, zinc and antimony. Mining is controlled by the state enterprise SONAREM, which was being reorganized in 1982.

Iron ore is mined at Beni-Saf, Zaccar, Timezrit and near the eastern frontier at Ouenza and Bou Khadra. The average grade of ore is between 50 and 60 per cent. Production has fluctuated greatly since independence but reached 2,064,000 metric tons (metal content) in 1974, falling to an estimated 1,645,000 tons in 1979. The deposits at Ouenza represent 75 per cent of total production. Exploitation may begin by 1985/86 of deposits at Gara Djebelit in the west. These reserves, which are in territory claimed by Morocco, are estimated at 2,000 million tons of medium-grade ore. Important deposits were found in 1975 at Djebel Bouari in Batna *wilaya*. Italy is the biggest customer, followed by the United Kingdom. Production of bituminous coal, mined at Colomb Béhar-Kenadza and Ksiksou, dropped steadily from 153,000 tons in 1958 and was only about 5,000 tons in 1979.

The most important zinc deposit is found on the Algerian-Moroccan frontier at El-Abed-Oued Zounder, and is an extension of the Moroccan deposits. Production fell from 17,000 metric tons (metal content) in 1972 to only 2,700 tons in 1977, then rose again to 6,000 tons in 1979. Lead is mined at El Abed on the Moroccan border; production in 1979 was 2,300 tons (metal content). A lead and zinc mine is to be developed at Kherzet-Youssef in Sétif *wilaya*.

Exploitation of large phosphate deposits at Djebel-Onk, 340 km. from Annaba, began in 1960 and annual output reached up to 800,000 metric tons in the 1970s. The deposits are used to feed the Arzew fertilizer plant and the surplus is exported, mainly to France and Spain.

Other mineral resources include antimony, tungsten, manganese, mercury, copper and salt. A mercury mine and refinery are being developed at Ismail. Exploration has been concentrated in the mountainous Hoggar region in the south. There are plans to launch mining operations within the next few years for tungsten, gold and uranium. Algeria is thought to have about 50,000 metric tons of uranium oxide deposits, mostly in the Tingaouine area; mining is due to start in 1984–85 at the rate of 1,000 metric tons per year and all the output will be exported.

PETROLEUM AND NATURAL GAS

Production of crude oil in the Sahara on a commercial scale began in 1958. The original principal producing areas were at Hassi Messaoud in Central Algeria and round Edjeleh-Zarzaitine in the Polignac Basin near the Libyan frontier. From 1.2 million tons in 1959, Algerian production of crude oil rose to a ceiling of 26 million tons in 1964 and 1965, limited by the capacity of the two pipelines to the coast, one from the eastern fields through Tunisia to La Skhirra, and the other from Hassi Messaoud to Béjaia on the Algerian coast. The Government set up its own company, *Société Nationale pour la Recherche, la Production, le Transport, la Transformation et la Commercialisation des Hydrocarbures* (SONATRACH) to be responsible for the construction of a third pipeline from Hassi Messaoud to Arzew on the coast. This pipeline came into operation early in 1966, and its maximum capacity is 22 million tons per year. In 1966 production was boosted by substantial quantities of crude from fields at Gassi Touil, Rhourde el Baguel and Rhourde Nouss. Subsequent discoveries of oil have been made at Nezla, Hoaud Berkaoui, Ouargla, Mesdar and El Borma, and more recently at Hassi Keskessa, Guellala, Tin Fouyé and El Maharis. Algeria now has seven main oil pipeline systems, the others being Mesdar-Skikda, Ohanet-Haoud el Mahra, Mesdar-El Borma and Beni Mansour-Algiers.

By 1977 petroleum production had reached 51.7 million tons (average 1,110,000 barrels per day). Production was 54.3 million tons in 1978 and 54.5 million tons in 1979. Output fell in 1980 to 47.4 million tons, following the government's decision to cut production by more than 15 per cent to conserve resources. In 1981 oil production fell below 40 million tons, owing to dwindling international demand. By the end of the year several oil-for-goods exchanges had been agreed with Japanese exporters, mostly

involving cars. However, the exporters found Algeria's oil too highly priced and difficult to resell. The price of Algerian crude oil became increasingly competitive after 1975, in relation to other North African and Nigerian crudes, and this helped to boost output. Algeria, which produces the lighter types of crude, with a low sulphur content, is the seventh largest Middle East oil producer but accounts for only 4 per cent of the total output of OPEC, which it joined in 1969. Its reported reserves totalled 8,000 million barrels by the end of 1978. The U.S.A. is the most important customer for Algerian crude oil, followed by West Germany and Italy. In line with policy in OPEC, where it has traditionally argued for higher prices, Algeria has successively raised the price of its oil, except during the periods of slack world demand in 1977–78 and again in 1981–82. During 1979 the price of its highest grade crude was increased from $14.10 per barrel at the beginning of the year to $30 in December. Two further increases in 1980 and one in 1981 brought the price by May 1981 to $40, to which was added a $3 surcharge for oil exploration. The surcharge was introduced to encourage foreign oil companies to participate in the oil exploration programme and was to be abolished as soon as agreements on oil exploration were finalized. By early 1982, however, world oversupply of oil forced the Government to drop the surcharge and—in line with OPEC—charge $37.50 per barrel.

The Government has complete control of the Algiers refinery (capacity 2.7 million tons per year) and of the domestic distribution network. The expansion of a small refinery at Hassi Messaoud was completed in 1979, bringing its capacity to about 1.3 million tons per year. Refineries at Arzew (built by a Japanese consortium and completed in June 1973; annual capacity 2.5 million tons) and Skikda (built by Snamprogetti of Italy and completed in March 1980; annual capacity 15 million tons) bring the country's total refining capacity to about 21.8 million tons per year. Revenues from oil and gas exports were worth $6,200 million in 1978 and increased by more than 52 per cent to $9,300 million in 1979. They are expected to contribute only $5,050 million, or 25 per cent, to 1982's total budgetary receipts of $20,200 million. This compares with an estimated $13,100 million in 1981, 33 per cent of receipts.

Domestic consumption trends suggest that the overall importance of hydrocarbons as a revenue earner is due to decline markedly. Annual domestic consumption accounts for 16 million petroleum equivalent metric tons, or 21 per cent of total production of 75 million petroleum equivalent metric tons. By 2000 it is expected to account for 70 million petroleum equivalent metric tons, or 77 per cent of total projected annual production. The balance of domestic consumption is moreover expected to shift markedly in favour of natural gas as oil reserves decline. In 1979 gas accounted for 44 per cent and oil for 48 per cent of domestic energy requirements. By 2000 gas is expected to account for at least 60 per cent of consumption, while oil falls to a little more than 20 per cent.

As oil production begins to decline, its place as Algeria's most valuable export will be taken by natural gas, of which Algeria is likely to become one of the world's leading exporters. At 3,200,000 million cubic metres, proved recoverable gas reserves, mostly unassociated with the oil fields, are the world's fourth largest, accounting for 3.9 per cent of the world total in 1981. Probable and possible reserves amount to a further 3,000,000 million cubic metres. Most of the gas (2,300,000 million cubic metres) is in the Hassi R'Mel region, 400 kilometres south of Algiers, where a Japanese consortium is now building a $250 million liquefied petroleum gas (LPG) plant with a capacity of 1.2 million tons per year. Unassociated gas is also found near In Amenas, Alrar, Gassi Touil, Rhourde Nouss, Tin Fouye and In Salah. Gas is also produced in association with oil. Three international consortia—from Japan, France and Italy—bid in December 1981 for a $700 million contract to develop the Rhourd Nousse field. Complex negotiations were expected to take up to a year. Deposits at Zarzaitine, near the Libyan border, are also being developed. A pipeline from Hassi R'Mel to Arzew, Algiers and Oran was opened in 1961. Shipments of liquefied natural gas (LNG) in specially constructed tankers to the United Kingdom began in 1964 and to France in 1965. Gross natural gas production in 1980, according to figures issued by the Ministry of Energy and Petrochemical Industries, was 42,500 million cubic metres. Of this, 10,971 million cubic metres was converted into LNG for export, and the rest was either flared, re-injected in the oil and gas fields, consumed by the liquefaction plants or marketed locally.

Contracts for sales of natural gas to Western Europe and the U.S.A. have shown a spectacular increase in size in recent years and, if all of them do come on stream, Algeria will be exporting about 80,000 million cubic metres per year by the mid-1980s. By the beginning of 1979 the following contracts were operational: British Gas, Gaz de France (GDF) and Distrigas and El Paso of the U.S.A. Deliveries to El Paso, which was contracted for 10,000 million cubic metres a year, were halted in April 1980 because of a pricing dispute; negotiations failed and in 1981 El Paso wrote off LNG assets valued at about $365 million. In May 1981 El Paso's three former U.S. customers—Columbia Gas System, Consolidated Natural Gas Company and Southern Natural Gas Company—started direct negotiations with SONATRACH in a bid to replace the LNG formerly carried by El Paso. Negotiations were still continuing in May 1982, with the U.S. companies "confident" of eventual success. Algeria has sought substantial price increases for its LNG to bring it up to par, on energy value, with the price of crude oil. In April 1981 Belgium's Distrigas signed a contract for 100,000 million cubic metres at $4.80 per million British thermal units (BTUs), but with the price indexed to a basket of crude oils, half imported by Belgium, half by countries also exporting gas. However, the major breakthrough was final agreement with GDF in February 1982 which followed political talks between Presidents Chadli and Mitterrand in late 1981. GDF agreed to pay just over $5 per million

BTUs, with the price indexed to a basket of six crudes, for 9,000 million cubic metres per year; however, the price was one-fifth more than that of Soviet gas sold to France in January 1982. It is to be 13.5 per cent subsidized by the French Government—the price of political goodwill and a $2,130 million boost to trade, with new orders expected from French companies. Because of the political element, the price has not fully served as a precedent for outstanding negotiations with other buyers, notably with ENI, the Italian state oil concern, for natural gas in the Transmed pipeline. Various price negotiations are now likely to succeed eventually, however, and are expected to absorb all of Algeria's exporting capacity well into the 1980s and probably beyond. The countries with which deals have been concluded are Austria, Belgium, France, the Federal Republic of Germany, Greece, Italy, the Netherlands, Spain, Tunisia, the U.S.A. and Yugoslavia.

To fulfil these commitments, Algeria is investing heavily in pipelines, liquefaction plants and tankers, although there have been serious delays in the programme to date. The first liquefaction plant at Arzew, the Camel plant, was built in 1964 and is now wholly state-owned. Algeria's second LNG plant was completed at Skikda in 1972 and has suffered from considerable technical difficulties. The third plant, Arzew 1, began operating in February 1978 and will eventually have an annual capacity of 10,500 million cubic metres per year. A second LNG plant at Arzew, Arzew 2 (capacity 10,500 million cubic metres per year), being built by Pullman Kellog, was expected to come on stream in mid-1981, though shipments from it were delayed because of unfinished pipeline work. GDF is technically assisting operations. Contracts for a third plant, Arzew 3, were cancelled in June 1980. The government, however, argues that the price it gets for its gas ($4–5 per million BTUs) is too low and does not justify the huge investment needed to build the plant. The existing Skikda plant is currently being expanded but it is now unlikely that two other planned plants, Skikda 2 and Arzew 4, will ever be built. In 1972 the 40-in. pipeline from Hassi R'Mel to Skikda was opened. The pipeline, 577 km. long, has a capacity of 12,700 million cubic metres per year. A second 40-in. pipeline from Hassi R'Mel to Arzew went on stream in March 1978. Two further gas pipelines are to be built by the Italian company Saipem: one of 28 in., 520 km. long, from Hassi R'Mel to Arzew and the other of 40 in., 160 km. long, from the Gassi Touil field to Hassi Messaoud. Plans for a 2,400-km. trans-Mediterranean gas pipeline to Italy were revived in 1977 when contracts were signed with Tunisia and with ENI. A 48-in. pipeline, with an initial capacity of 12,500 million cubic metres per year, was built from Hassi R'Mel to the Tunisian border (550 km.) and from there across Tunisia to the coast opposite Sicily (380 km.); the submarine section is 160 km. long and is owned by a joint Italian-Algerian company. The pipeline extends across Sicily and the Straits of Messina to Minerbio, near Bologna, and this section is owned by ENI. Tunisia will receive 5.25 per cent of the gas and owns the section of pipeline crossing its territory.

Italy had lent $1,030 million towards financing Algeria's $1,400 million share of total construction costs ($2,500 million). Work on the submarine section was completed at the end of 1980, and the whole pipeline was completed in late 1981. The possibility of laying a second pipeline across the Mediterranean and parallel to the first is being considered, while a special company, Segamo, owned 50 per cent by Algeria and 25 per cent each by Enegas of Spain and GDF, has been set up to study the feasibility of laying a gasline to Spain. The first route suggested, through Morocco to the Strait of Gibraltar, is considered unsatisfactory by Algeria for political reasons. A new route from Western Algeria is being sought and, despite serious technical problems regarding depth, the U.S. consultant Bechtel reported in March 1982 that it would be feasible. By May 1981 the Algerian national shipping line CNAN owned seven LNG carriers.

In 1970 the local interests of Shell, Phillips, Elwerath and AMIF were nationalized, following protracted negotiations which failed to achieve agreement on tax reference prices, and SONATRACH thus became Algeria's largest producer. In 1971, Algeria nationalized the French oil companies operating in the country, as well as pipeline networks and natural gas deposits. Later in the year President Boumedienne issued a decree banning concession-type agreements and laying down the conditions under which foreign oil companies could operate in Algeria. SONATRACH now directly controls 77 per cent of Algeria's oil production, compared with only 31 per cent in 1970. Despite a law of April 1972 requiring companies wishing to explore in Algeria to form a joint company with SONATRACH, in which the latter should have a controlling interest, co-operation with foreign oil firms is increasing. Under the terms of the 1972 law, agreements have been signed with Getty Oil and Sun Oil of the U.S.A., Hispanoil of Spain, Petrobras of Brazil, Total-Algérie (a subsidiary of CFP), Copex of Poland, Elf-ERAP of France, Deminex of West Germany and Amoco of the U.S.A. In 1978 Shell signed a new type of agreement under which it will finance the exploration work, in return for a percentage of oil output in the event of a commercially viable discovery. By mid-1982 similar agreements had been signed with about 15 foreign companies. Since it was set up in 1963, SONATRACH grew to become the largest, most complex and economically most important state company in Algeria. To rationalize it, the Government decided in May 1980 to have some of its activities taken over by three new companies; the *Entreprise Nationale des Grands Travaux Pétroliers* (major hydrocarbons and petrochemical projects), the *Entreprise Nationale de Raffinage et de Distribution des Produits Pétroliers* (oil refining and gas processing for exports and international distribution of refined products) and the *Entreprise Nationale des Plastiques et de Caoutchouc* (production and marketing of plastics and rubber). SONATRACH retains its responsibilities for the exploration, exploitation and transport of hydrocarbons. Eventually it is to be split into a total of 13 companies.

MANUFACTURING

Industrialization is the keynote of the government's economic policy and the major investment effort in the 1970–73 Plan was devoted to this end. Under the 1974–77 Plan, industry received about 43.5 per cent of total allocations. In the 1980–84 plan it is allocated 154,500 million dinars, or 38.6 per cent of total investment.

At the time of independence the Algerian industrial sector was very small, being confined mainly to food processing, building materials, textiles and minerals. The departure of the French entailed loss of demand, capital and skill, thereby slowing down the industrialization process. Foreign firms became increasingly reluctant in the 1960s to invest in Algeria because of the danger of nationalization. By 1978 about 300 state-owned manufacturing plants had been set up but productivity is very low, with some factories operating at only 15–25 per cent of design capacity.

The iron and steel industry is basic to the development of other industries and very large investments have been made in the El Hadjar complex at Annaba. The smelter and tube-mill were opened in 1969 and the steelworks in 1972. The complex is currently operating far below its capacity of 400,000 tons per year, but it is being expanded with additional steel-rolling mills to produce up to 1.8 million tons per year. Studies for an integrated steelworks at Jijel in the north, with a capacity of 2 million tons per year, have been completed. Work is expected to take 5–6 years and a shortlist of bidders was drawn up in late 1981. The scheme also involves building a port, for which the World Bank has earmarked $80 million, and a railway. The works will supply four rolling mills each with a capacity of 300,000–400,000 tons per year. The present Plan's more measured approach to heavy industrial development means that a scheme to build a steelworks at La Macta in the west, with a capacity of 10 million tons per year, is not likely to go ahead before 1985/86 at the earliest. Also postponed are plans to start aluminium production. A 132,000 tons-per-year smelter at M'Sila, 200 km. south-east of Algiers, was to have started up in 1982, supplying a sheet and extrusion factory at Bordjbou Arreridj and using alumina from Jamaica and Guinea. Petroleum coke and carbon for electrodes are available as by-products from local refineries. The scheme is now unlikely to go ahead before the beginning of the next development plan. The state steel organization, *Société Nationale de Sidérurgie*, is being reorganized into smaller units.

A vast petrochemical complex built at Skikda produces polyethylene, PVC, caustic soda and chlorine. An 800,000 tons-per-year nitrogenous fertilizer plant utilizing natural gas was opened in 1970 at Arzew, where there is also a complex for the manufacture of intermediate petro-chemical products. At Annaba, a 550,000 tons-per-year plant for phosphate fertilizers was opened in 1972 but output in 1976 was only 300,000 tons. A new fertilizer complex began production in March 1980, also at Annaba. New units starting up at Arzew and Annaba in

1981 and 1982, together with efforts to take up the slack in existing productive capacity, should provide exportable surpluses of ammonium nitrate, phosphate fertilizers and urea.

Algeria suffers from a severe shortage of vehicles of all types but is expanding its vehicle and farm machinery industries rapidly. At Constantine there is a factory producing tractors and diesel engines. A large farm machinery complex was officially opened at Sidi Bel Abbès in 1976. An industrial vehicles plant at Rouiba, about 25 km. from Algiers, started production in 1974 under a product-in-hand contract with Berliet of France. Assembly capacity is 7,000–10,000 vehicles per year. Mechanical shop capacity is, however, sufficient to produce parts for only about 4,500 vehicles per year and the giant state mechanical engineering and equipment concern, SONACOME, has had to import kits to fill the gap. Of the 6,000 vehicles produced in 1979, only 3,850 were fitted with components of which 75 per cent were locally made; local content in the remaining 2,150 vehicles was only about 30 per cent. In its first expansion phase, SONACOME aims to produce 7,200–7,500 vehicles per year with a 60 per cent local content. A second phase should raise production to 10,000–11,000 vehicles per year and bring the rate of integration nearer to the original target of 75 per cent. Since 1970, when the Renault assembly plant at Algiers closed down, Algeria has had no automobile manufacturing industry. The Ministry of Heavy Industry is considering plans for a factory to produce 200,000–250,000 private cars per year. The initial aim is to assemble imported parts, gradually increasing the contribution of locally-made components. A decision on the scheme is likely to be taken by the end of the 1980–84 plan. At Guelma there is a plant manufacturing motorcycles, bicycles and small motors. Pumps and irrigation equipment are produced at Médéa. SONATRACH is preparing studies for a factory to produce heavy-duty tyres for industrial vehicles to begin construction in 1983. The new factory will supplement a pre-independence plant near Algiers. SONACOME is being split into three groups to improve efficiency and decentralize the bureaucracy.

Other growth areas are the paper industry, textiles, electrical goods (including radio and television sets), flour milling and building materials. Joinery capacity is to be doubled by 1984 from 8 million square metres per year at the end of the second four-year plan. Annual flat-glass capacity will be increased by 40,000 tons, and two paint factories with a capacity of 40,000 tons per year each are to be built at Sig and Souk Ahras. There are six cement works with a total installed capacity of 8 million tons. Two works at Constantine and Bouira, each with a capacity of 1 million tons per year, are being built by Denmark's F. L. Smidth and France's Creusat Loire respectively. Construction started in 1981 on a works at Batna, with a capacity of 1 million tons per year, and was due to begin in 1982 on a works at Tebessa, with a capacity of 500,000 tons per year. Finance has been allocated for a further 1.5 million tons' capacity to be added during the plan. The Government intends to establish a major shipyard at Oran, and OAPEC is considering plans for a two-berth dry dock.

TRADE

Algeria had a consistent foreign trade deficit, with the exception of small surpluses recorded in 1967 and 1968, until the huge increases in oil prices in 1973 began to reverse the situation, altering it dramatically by 1974. Oil and natural gas exports have transformed the pattern of Algerian exports, previously limited to agricultural products and some minerals. mainly wine, citrus fruit and iron ore. Hydrocarbons account for about 95 per cent of total export earnings. Other exports include vegetables, tobacco, hides and skins, dates and phosphates. Imports of consumer goods are severely restricted. Capital goods made up 34.4 per cent of the total value of imports in 1979; raw materials and semi-finished goods 38.6 per cent; food and tobacco 15.8 per cent; consumer goods 8.9 per cent.

Algeria's visible trade account showed a deficit of 1,397 million dinars in 1973, which turned into a surplus of 982 million dinars in 1974, mainly as a result of soaring oil revenues. However, in 1975 there was a deficit of 5,192 million dinars, due to the sharp decline of oil exports as well as to higher import costs. Government curbs on imports, together with the higher price and volume of oil exports, reversed this trend in 1976 but again in 1977 there was a deficit, of 5,444 million dinars, with oil exports falling in the second half of the year and a sharp rise in imports. As a result of the doubling of oil prices in 1979 the balance of trade showed a surplus of about 3,700 million dinars, rising to 10,870 million dinars in 1980. However, declining world crude oil demand in 1981 was expected to curb the surplus swing.

Before independence France took 81 per cent of Algeria's exports and provided 82 per cent of its imports. This dominance declined steadily, particularly at the time of the 1971 oil nationalization crisis, and France's share of Algerian trade in 1977 had dropped to only 12.7 per cent of exports and 24 per cent of imports. Continuing poor relations between France and Algeria led to a further decline in the volume of trade. Towards the end of 1977 France decided to take a larger share of its crude oil from Saudi Arabia rather than Algeria (having already cut its Algerian oil imports sharply in 1975) and Algeria retaliated by imposing a ban on the import of French goods early in 1978. Relations improved in 1979 and although Algeria still has a big trade deficit with France this has decreased to less than $800 million in the first 11 months of 1979. An economic co-operation protocol was expected for mid-1982, following final gas price agreement and a new political dialogue at presidential level. These agreements were expected to lead to orders for French business worth more than $2,000 million, which would reassert French dominance in Algeria. In 1979 the main suppliers after France were the Federal Republic of Germany, Italy, the U.S.A. and Japan. Main customers were the U.S.A., the Federal Republic of Germany, France, Italy and Spain.

Under a decree of January 1978, the State trading agencies, which operate on a commercial basis and are not backed by the automatic guarante of the Algerian Government, now have a monopoly on all foreign trade. However, the private sector may be given some leeway to import urgently needed goods such as construction materials. In early 1982 import procedures were eased for essential spare parts and for the special $1,700 million prefabricated housing, schools and polyclinic programme. Similar concessions were allowed for reconstruction after earthquake damage at El Asnam in October 1980. Thirteen months later 20,000 homes had been built. The 1980–84 Plan calls for rapid construction of 450,000 homes to ease Algeria's chronic housing shortage. Similar urgency was placed on plans for several hundred vocational training centres. European, Comecon, and North and South American countries have signed protocols to carry out and, in cases, soft-finance the work. However, negotiations have frequently faltered over price, especially since local construction autonomy was passed to the *wilayas* in 1981.

In January 1976 a preferential trade agreement was signed between Algeria and the EEC. Under the agreement, aid is promised to Algeria in the form of loans and grants; there is an 80 per cent reduction of the common tariff on Algerian wine; the quota of Algerian petroleum products allowed into EEC countries will be steadily raised and eventually lifted altogether; and the tariffs on imports into the EEC of Algerian agricultural products will be either lowered or abolished. A new co-operation agreement, continuing the main provisions of the trade agreement, came into force in November 1978. In April 1982 a large economic co-operation programme with Libya was announced, eventually aiming "to achieve gradual integration of the (two) economies". Joint water-well drilling, hydrocarbons research and production, and geophysics companies were to be formed in 1982, and existing joint banks and a shipping company to be expanded.

FINANCE

Until independence, Algeria was mostly dependent on France for its central banking and monetary system, though some of the usual central banking functions were carried out by the *Banque d'Algérie*. The *Banque Centrale d'Algérie* started its operations on January 1st, 1963; it issues currency, regulates and licenses banks and supervises all foreign transactions. The banking system has been largely taken over by the state. A state monopoly on all foreign financial transactions was imposed in November 1967; this followed a similar monopoly imposed on insurance in June 1966. There are only three commercial banks: the *Banque Extérieure d'Algérie* which specializes in foreign trade, the *Banque Nationale d'Algérie* which specializes in agricultural financing but now also shares in foreign trading, and the *Crédit Populaire d'Algérie* which specializes in loans to small and medium-size industries. Specialized banks include the *Banque Algérienne de Développement* which provides

long-term finance for public sector capital projects and to stimulate local economic development; the *Caisse Centrale de Coopération Economique*, and the *Caisse d'Epargne et de Prévoyance* which acts as a savings and mortgage bank. In 1974 an Algerian-Libyan bank, the *Banque Internationale Arabe*, was opened in Paris to finance trade and investment between France and Arab countries. Two Algerian and six French banks set up the *Union Méditerranéenne de Banques* in 1975 to finance international trade, especially between Algeria and France. In 1981 a joint commercial bank was created with Italy and a similar bank was expected to be set up with the Ivory Coast; possible joint financial institutions have been discussed with Kuwait.

The 1982 budget envisaged total government spending of 84,842 million dinars, 25 per cent more than in 1981. Of this, 42,238 million dinars was for the administrative budget. The biggest allocations in the 42,604 million dinars development budget include education (5,900 million dinars, compared with 4,800 million in 1981), housing (3,100 million dinars, including 2,900 million for rural areas, compared with 3,050 million for all housing in 1981), water (2,800 million dinars, compared with 2,700 million), industry (1,777 million dinars, compared with 1,240 million), communications (4,228 million dinars, compared with 2,300 million dinars) and agriculture (1,050 million dinars). Oil revenues accounted for 67.6 per cent of total revenues in 1981, compared with 62.02 per cent in 1980, indirect taxation for 7.5 per cent, customs duties 5.73 per cent, indirect taxation 5.6 per cent and business taxes 2 per cent.

Much of Algeria's investment is financed by domestic saving and not more than 25 per cent of finance for the 1974–77 Plan was expected to be borrowed abroad. However, Algeria's political stability and its oil revenues have made many countries and international financial institutions willing to lend it money.

In 1978 there was continued heavy borrowing abroad, in particular for financing gas development. Borrowing on the Euromarket during the year, mainly by SONATRACH, amounted to $2,515 million and $721 million was raised in Eurobonds. Algeria also obtained loans from a number of other sources, including $500 million from Eximbank of the U.S.A. and a $1,000 million line of credit from Canada to finance imports of Canadian goods and services. In 1979 total borrowing dropped by almost one third to around $2,000 million. Since the beginning of 1980 Algeria has stayed out of the international money market and has no plans to return before 1982 at the earliest. In December 1981, however, SONATRACH renegotiated an undrawn $500 million Euroloan to improve the terms. Transmediterranean Pipeline Company (partly-owned by Algeria) raised a $150 million Euroloan in early 1982. By early 1981 a $2,000 million line of credit had been negotiated but not yet signed with Austria, chiefly to finance railway work still being negotiated. A similar credit was negotiated with Japan in mid-1982 to finance the Hassi R'Mel LPG plant and Zarzaitine field development equipment, although both were arranged separately.

Export credit funding has been widely raised on other schemes, especially housing. The total borrowing requirement for the 1980–84 Plan is estimated at $10,000 million.

Algeria has been criticized for being too much in debt. Its public external debt by the end of 1977 totalled $12,300 million, of which $7,600 million had been disbursed, and by the end of 1979 it had risen to about $19,000 million. However, the huge increase in revenues from hydrocarbons exports enabled Algeria to reduce its debt service ratio from 25 per cent in 1978 to around 22 per cent in 1979, with good prospects that it will continue to decrease. This was in spite of the fact that, in absolute terms, the debt service rose from $1,551.2 million in 1978 to $2,125.9 million in 1979 and was expected to rise for another year or two. The OECD estimated that by the end of 1980 the disbursed portion of Algeria's debt had reached $17,800 million.

According to IMF statistics, a balance of payments deficit of SDR 283 million in 1977 turned into surpluses of SDR 59 million in 1978 and SDR 375 million in 1979. Despite a slight decline in the volume of exports in 1979, total export receipts increased by 45 per cent. Since imports rose by less than 4 per cent, an unprecedented trade surplus of SDR 701 million was recorded in 1979, compared with deficits of SDR 1,340 million in 1978 and SDR 765 million in 1977. Although the service deficit widened considerably in 1979, mainly because of higher interest payments, the current account deficit was more than halved to SDR 1,312 million. Net capital inflows declined to SDR 1,687 million in 1979 from SDR 2,885 million in 1978, reflecting lower gross disbursements and higher external debt amortization.

International reserves fell from U.S. $1,987 million at the end of 1976 to $1,268 million in July 1978 but by the end of the year they had risen sharply to $2,233 million. Reserves increased to $2,915 million by the end of 1979, rising to $3,811 million by March 1982.

STATISTICAL SURVEY
AREA AND POPULATION

AREA	POPULATION					
	Census	Mid-Year Estimates†				
	April 4th, 1966	1975	1976	1977	1978	1979
2,381,741 sq. km.*	11,821,679	16,776,000	17,304,000	17,910,000	18,515,000	19,129,000

* 919,595 square miles.
† Including Algerian nationals living abroad, numbering 268,868 at the 1966 census.

Note: A census began throughout the country on February 12th, 1977. Based on this census, the estimated population at January 1st, 1978, was 18,250,000 (including nationals abroad), but full census details are not yet available.

AREA AND POPULATION BY WILAYAS (DEPARTMENTS)

	AREA (sq. km.)	POPULATION* (estimates at Jan. 1st, 1978)		AREA (sq. km.)	POPULATION* (estimates at Jan. 1st, 1978)
Adrar	422,498.0	142,046	Djelfa (El-Djelfa)	22,904.8	330,406
El Asnam (Ech-Cheliff)	8,676.7	885,200	Jijel	3,704.5	506,488
Laghouat	112,052.0	307,977	Sétif (Stif)	10,350.4	990,157
Oum El Bouaghi (Oum El Bouagul)	8,123.0	400,182	Saida	106,777.4	373,366
Batna	14,881.5	589,146	Skikda	4,748.3	493,929
Béjaia	3,444.2	554,876	Sidi Bel Abbès	11,648.2	531,694
Biskra (Beskra)	109,728.0	544,798	Annaba	3,489.3	507,806
Béchar	306,000.0	148,101	Guelma	8,624.4	552,455
Blida (El Boulaïda)	3,703.8	909,930	Constantine (Qacentina)	3,561.7	686,671
Bouira	4,517.1	385,452	Médéa (Lemdiyya)	8,704.1	482,183
Tamanrasset (Tamenghest)	556,000.0	45,622	Mostaganem (Mestghanem)	7,023.6	766,167
Tébessa (Tbessa)	16,574.5	372,479	M'Sila	19,824.6	438,317
Tlemcen (Tilimsen)	9,283.7	596,677	Mascara (Mouaskar)	5,845.6	435,776
Tiaret (Tihert)	23,455.6	619,826	Ouargla (Wargla)	559,234.0	199,691
Tizi-Ouzou	3,756.3	875,075	Oran (Ouahran)	1,820.0	761,507
Algiers (El Djezaïr)	785.7	1,988,000			
			TOTAL	2,381,741.0	17,422,000

* Excluding Algerian nationals abroad, estimated to total 828,000 at January 1st, 1978.

PRINCIPAL TOWNS
(estimated population in 1977)

Algiers (El Djezaïr, capital)	1,800,000	Tizi-Ouzou . . 230,000	Tlemcen (Tilimsen) . 120,000
Oran (Ouahran) . 500,000		Blida (El Boulaïda) . 162,000	El Asnam (Ech-
Constantine (Qacen-		Sétif (Stif) . . 160,000	Cheliff) . . . 118,000
tina) . . . 430,000		Sidi Bel Abbès . . 158,000	Boufarik . . . 112,000
Annaba . . . 340,000		Skikda . . 132,000	Béjaia . . . 108,000
		Batna . . . 120,000	Médéa (Lemdiyya) . 106,000

Source: Commissariat National aux Recensements et Enquêtes Statistiques, Algiers.

BIRTHS, MARRIAGES AND DEATHS

	LIVE BIRTHS*		MARRIAGES		DEATHS*	
	Number	Rate (per 1,000)	Number	Rate (per 1,000)	Number	Rate (per 1,000)
1966 . . .	561,528	46.2	61,981	5.1	122,999	10.1
1967 . . .	534,904	42.7	59,549	4.7	118,325	9.4
1968 . . .	529,806	39.3	n.a.	n.a.	134,160	9.9

1975: Registered live births 801,720 (birth rate 47.8 per 1,000).

1979 (Algerian population only): Registered live births 711,961 (birth rate 39.1 per 1,000); Registered deaths 144,993 (death rate 8.0 per 1,000).

* Data exclude live-born infants dying before registration of birth. Birth registration was estimated to be 90 per cent complete in 1968. Death registration was estimated to be between 40 and 60 per cent complete. According to United Nations estimates, the average annual birth rate was 48.2 per 1,000 in 1965–70, 47.9 per 1,000 in 1970–75 and 47.4 per 1,000 in 1975–80, while the death rate was 17.9 per 1,000 in 1965–70, 15.5 per 1,000 in 1970–75 and 14.2 per 1,000 in 1975–80.

EMPLOYMENT
('000 wage-earning employees)

	1973	1974	1975	1976
Industry	225	242	269	303
Construction and public works .	190	207	228	261
Transport	77	85	93	100
Trade	195	217	235	256
Services	180	197	216	237
Handicrafts	40	41	42	44
Administration . . .	300	n.a.	340	365
Others*	251	276	308	346
TOTAL . . .	1,458	1,580	1,731	1,812

* Including students and armed forces.

Note: The total economically active population on January 1st, 1978, was estimated at 4,002,000, of whom 42.1 per cent were employed in agriculture.

Source: Secrétariat d'Etat au Plan, Algiers.

AGRICULTURE

LAND USE, 1979
('ooo hectares)

Arable Land	6,846
Under Permanent Crops . . .	651
Permanent Meadows and Pastures . .	36,323
Forest Land	4,384
Other Land	189,970
Total Area	238,174

Source: FAO, *Production Yearbook.*

PRINCIPAL CROPS
('ooo metric tons)

	1978	1979	1980
Wheat	1,083	1,080	1,301
Barley	397	457	791
Oats	56	80	110
Potatoes	473	501	500*
Pulses	66	53	55*
Sugar beets . . .	68	93	95*
Onions (dry) . . .	90	114	114*
Tomatoes	181	182	187*
Grapes	267†	386†	372*
Olives	157	92*	140*
Oranges	285	297	305*
Tangerines and mandarines .	150	144	149*
Dates	196	208	180*
Watermelons . . .	142	159	166*
Tobacco	3	3	3*

* FAO estimates. † Unofficial figure.

Source: FAO, *Production Yearbook.*

LIVESTOCK
('ooo head, year ending September)

	1978	1979	1980
Sheep . . .	10,863	12,223	12,500*
Goats . . .	2,592	2,818	2,850*
Cattle . . .	1,213	1,328	1,433*
Horses . . .	149	172	176*
Mules . . .	191	206	210*
Asses . . .	495	527	538*
Camels . . .	139	150	150*
Chickens . . .	17,400	17,711	18,000*

* FAO estimate.

LIVESTOCK PRODUCTS
('ooo metric tons—FAO estimates)

	1978	1979	1980
Beef and veal . .	30	31	33
Mutton and lamb .	55	56	56
Goats' meat . .	10	10	11
Poultry meat . .	42	44	46
Cows' milk . .	500	503	518
Sheep's milk . .	140	150	160
Goats' milk . .	135	130	135
Hen eggs . .	18.1	18.7	19.1
Wool (clean) . .	9.5	9.6	9.8

Source: FAO, *Production Yearbook.*

FORESTRY

ROUNDWOOD REMOVALS

('000 cubic metres, excluding bark—FAO estimates)

	CONIFEROUS (soft wood)			BROADLEAVED (hard wood)			TOTAL		
	1977	1978	1979	1977	1978	1979	1977	1978	1979
Sawlogs, veneer logs and logs for sleepers	15	15	15	5	5	5	20	20	20
Pitprops (Mine timber) . .	—	—	—	1	1	1	1	1	1
Other industrial wood . .	111	115	119	55	57	57	166	172	178
Fuel wood	863	892	992	415	429	443	1,278	1,321	1,365
TOTAL . . .	989	1,022	1,056	476	492	508	1,465	1,514	1,564

Source: FAO, *Yearbook of Forest Products.*

SEA FISHING

('000 metric tons)

	1971	1972	1973	1974	1975	1976	1977	1978	1979
Total catch (live weight) . .	23.8	28.3	31.2	35.7	37.7	35.1	43.5	34.1	38.7

Source: FAO, *Yearbook of Fishery Statistics.*

MINING

		1976	1977	1978	1979
Coal	'000 metric tons	8	6	5	n.a.
Iron ore: gross weight . .	" " "	2,760	3,180	2,750	2,870
metal content . .	" " "	1,490	1,721	1,641	1,645‡
Antimony	metric tons	60†	60†	60†	
Lead ore*	" "	1,700	900	1,800	2,300‡
Zinc ore*	" "	6,200	2,700†	4,800†	6,000†
Copper ore*	" "	400	300	200	500†
Mercury	" "	1,065	1,049	1,055	1,035‡
Phosphate rock . . .	'000 metric tons	818	721	997	n.a.
Crude petroleum . . .	" "	48,735	51,700	54,300	54,500‡
Natural gas	million cu. metres	8,005	5,777	9,615	n.a.

* Metal content of concentrates.   † Estimates of U.S. Bureau of Mines.   ‡ Estimates.

Source: UN, *Yearbook of Industrial Statistics.*

1980: Crude petroleum 47.4 million metric tons.

INDUSTRY

SELECTED PRODUCTS

		1976	1977	1978	1979
Olive oil (crude)	'000 metric tons	17	11	22	11†
Margarine	,, ,, ,,	8.5	8.4	11.6	12.9
Flour	,, ,, ,,	715	1,520†	1,483	1,418
Raw sugar	,, ,, ,,	20†	25†	15†	15†
Wine	'000 hectolitres	3,783	2,549	1,840	2,710
Beer	,, ,,	590	616	601	n.a.
Cigarettes	metric tons	10,217	8,500	8,600	8,750
Manufactured tobacco . . .	,, ,,	5,025	n.a.	n.a.	n.a.
Woven cotton fabrics . . .	million sq. metres	50†	n.a.	n.a.	n.a.
Nitrogenous fertilizers (a)* . .	'000 metric tons	33.0	41.8	42.2	20.7
Phosphate fertilizers (b)* . .	,, ,, ,,	63.7	70.3	96.6†	53.5†
Naphtha	,, ,, ,,	452	352	303	350
Motor spirit (petrol) . . .	,, ,, ,,	816	787	876	900†
Kerosene	,, ,, ,,	227†	195†	195†	202†
Jet fuel	,, ,, ,,	180†	200†	200†	210†
Distillate fuel oils . . .	,, ,, ,,	1,459	1,348	1,290	1,350†
Residual fuel oils . . .	,, ,, ,,	1,389	1,141	1,109	1,200†
Liquefied petroleum gas . .	,, ,, ,,	508	535	692	700†
Cement	,, ,, ,,	1,400	1,777	2,697	3,773
Pig-iron and ferro-alloys . .	,, ,, ,,	413	389	288	496
Crude steel	,, ,, ,,	206	213	241	462
Radio receivers	'000	21	n.a.	n.a.	n.a.
Television receivers . . .	,,	54	n.a.	24	58
Buses and coaches (assembly) .	number	143	—	450	464
Lorries (assembly) . . .	,,	3,918	3,515	5,850	6,151
Electric energy . . .	million kWh.	4,370†	4,801†	4,967†	5,040†

* Production in terms of (a) nitrogen or (b) phosphoric acid. Phosphate fertilizers include ground rock phosphate.
† Provisional or estimated figures.

Source: mainly UN, *Yearbook of Industrial Statistics.*

1980 (provisional): Olive oil 19,000 metric tons; Wine 2,600,000 litres (FAO estimate); Nitrogenous fertilizers 23,800 metric tons; Phosphate fertilizers 30,800 metric tons.

FINANCE

100 centimes = 1 Algerian dinar (AD).

Coins: 1, 2, 5, 10, 20 and 50 centimes; 1 and 5 dinars.

Notes: 5, 10 and 100 dinars.

Exchange rates (May 1982): £1 sterling = 8.35 dinars; U.S. $1 = 4.54 dinars.
100 Algerian dinars = £11.98 = $22.03.

Note: The Algerian dinar was introduced in April 1964, replacing (at par) the new Algerian franc. From January 1960 the Algerian franc (equal to the French franc) was valued at 180 milligrammes of gold. Until August 1971 the dinar was thus valued at 20.255 U.S. cents (U.S. $1 = 4.937 dinars). Between December 1971 and February 1973 the dinar's value was 21.991 U.S. cents ($1 = 4.537 dinars); from February 1973 to January 1974 it was 24.435 U.S. cents ($1 = 4.093 dinars). Since January 1974 the Algerian authorities have allowed the dinar to "float" on foreign exchange markets. The average exchange rate (dinars per U.S. dollar) was: 3.9591 in 1973; 4.1808 in 1974; 3.9494 in 1975; 4.1638 in 1976; 4.1468 in 1977; 3.9659 in 1978; 3.8533 in 1979; 3.8375 in 1980; 4.3158 in 1981. In terms of sterling, the exchange rate between November 1967 and June 1972 was £1 = 11.849 dinars.

BUDGET

ADMINISTRATIVE BUDGET ('000 AD)

Expenditure	1980	1981
Presidency . . .	111,000	216,272
National defence . .	2,702,516	3,481,419
Foreign affairs . .	331,680	351,598
Light industry . .	130,081	128,954
Housing and construction	146,584	194,163
Finance. . . .	540,000	592,120
Home affairs . . .	1,410,645	1,641,505
Commerce . . .	55,925	67,079
Youth and sport . .	278,338	296,510
Information and culture .	301,549	336,167
Ex-servicemen . .	1,280,260	1,764,240
Tourism . . .	33,925	37,501
Agriculture . . .	532,809	759,167
Health	1,564,100	2,044,200
Transport . . .	187,066	203,888*
Justice	252,500	285,592
Employment and Training	373,100	418,140
Religious affairs . .	143,200	219,639
Public works . . .	435,034	479,108
Education . . .	4,955,227	6,713,494
Higher education and scientific research . .	1,493,000	1,891,791
Heavy industry . .	65,638	63,630
Water	219,728	297,997
Energy and petrochemicals industries .	164,779	169,448
Rural planning and development . .	78,243	92,808
Fisheries . . .	9,175	n.a.
Forestry . . .	160,208	n.a.
Total (incl. others) .	27,775,837	36,195,250

* Including fisheries

EQUIPMENT BUDGET ('000 AD)

Expenditure	1980	1981
Industry . . .	630,000	1,240,000
Agriculture . . .	1,217,000	1,170,000
Water	2,000,000	2,700,000
Tourism . . .	150,000	190,000
Fisheries . . .	80,000	70,000
Economic sub-structure .	1,900,000	n.a.
Transport . . .	500,000	500,000
Urban development .	3,360,000	n.a.
Livestock distribution .	50,000	n.a.
Education . . .	3,500,000	4,800,000
Training . . .	1,615,000	1,700,000
Social Affairs . . .	1,180,000	n.a.
Housing . . .	2,350,000	3,050,000
Administrative structure .	820,000	920,000
Total (incl. others) .	23,122,000	31,593,000

Revenue (1981): 68,305 million dinars, of which 3,830 million is from direct contributions, 7,492 million from business taxes, 46,180 million from petroleum.

CENTRAL BANK RESERVES
(U.S. $ million at December 31st)

	1979	1980	1981
Gold	256	248	226
IMF Special Drawing Rights	100	97	138
Reserve position in IMF .	40	130	136
Foreign exchange . .	2,518	3,546	3,421
Total . . .	2,915	4,021	3,921

Source: IMF, *International Financial Statistics.*

MONEY SUPPLY
(million AD at December 31st)

	1978	1979	1980
Currency outside banks .	27,285	35,398	42,344
Demand deposits at deposit money banks .	27,342	28,700	32,255
Checking deposits at Post Office . . .	5,279	6,595	7,826
Private sector demand deposits at Treasury .	722	728	794
Total Money . .	60,628	71,421	83,219

Source: IMF, *International Financial Statistics.*

COST OF LIVING
RETAIL PRICE INDEX FOR ALGIERS
(Average of monthly figures; base: 1969=100)

	1974	1975	1976	1977	1979*	1980
Food	134.2	149.6	171.2	197.5	268.0	297.2
Clothing	137.1	142.9	148.6	168.2	226.8	243.3
Rent	102.3	106.6	107.1	109.6	121.6	125.0
Furniture	121.5	136.5	144.6	159.9	218.3	249.5
Medical services	112.7	114.8	114.9	115.4	130.8	143.1
Transport and communications . .	117.4	121.1	127.0	130.4	140.3	143.3
Leisure	112.2	117.9	120.4	129.4	153.2	170.7
Other goods and services . .	119.2	137.7	145.3	162.8	220.2	244.0
ALL ITEMS . . .	126.0	137.1	149.3	167.2	219.0	239.9

* 1978 figures not available.

Source: Direction des Statistiques et de la Comptabilité Nationale, Algiers.

BALANCE OF PAYMENTS
(U.S. $ million)

	1975	1976	1977	1978	1979	1980
Merchandise exports f.o.b. . . .	4,501	5,221	6,009	6,340	9,484	13,652
Merchandise imports f.o.b. . . .	−5,452	−4,693	−6,198	−7,293	−7,798	−9,596
TRADE BALANCE . . .	−951	528	−189	−953	1,686	4,056
Exports of services	356	316	375	395	611	798
Imports of services	−1,442	−2,134	−2,791	−3,295	−4,344	−4,955
BALANCE ON GOODS AND SERVICES .	−2,037	−1,290	−2,605	−3,853	−2,047	−101
Private unrequited transfers (net) . .	356	386	278	295	304	321
Government unrequited transfers (net) .	20	18	4	20	8	22
CURRENT BALANCE . .	−1,661	−886	−2,323	−3,538	−1,735	242
Direct capital investment (net) . .	85	184	173	135	72	315
Other long-term capital (net) . .	1,310	1,559	1,724	3,515	2,643	583
Short-term capital (net) . . .	1	−30	119	−160	−131	57
Net errors and omissions . . .	−69	−204	−39	141	−366	145
TOTAL (net monetary movements) .	−334	623	−346	93	484	1,342
Allocation of IMF Special Drawing Rights .	—	—	—	—	38	39
Valuation changes (net) . . .	8	14	246	224	157	−267
Official financing (net) . . .	—	—	20	−20	—	—
CHANGES IN RESERVES . .	−326	637	−80	297	679	1,114

Source: IMF, *International Financial Statistics.*

EXTERNAL TRADE
(million AD)

	1973	1974	1975	1976	1977	1978	1979
Imports c.i.f.	9,535	17,754	23,755	22,227	29,534	33,968	32,794
Exports f.o.b.	7,479	19,594	18,563	22,205	25,356	23,805	36,503

PRINCIPAL COMMODITIES
(million AD)

IMPORTS	1976	1977	1978	1979
Foodstuffs and tobacco . . .	3,593	4,398	5,011	5,190
Energy and lubricants .	351	400	567	637
Primary products and raw materials .	956	1,596	1,452	1,631
Semi-finished products . .	7,586	9,237	7,935	11,043
Capital goods	8,288	10,103	14,336	11,296
Consumer goods . . .	1,432	3,760	4,599	2,925
Others	20	40	68	72

EXPORTS	1976	1977	1978	1979
Foodstuffs and tobacco . . .	628	551	582	467
Energy and lubricants . . .	21,097	24,391	22,856*	35,578
Primary products and raw materials .	279	212	185	266
Semi-finished products . . .	173	170	167	183
Capital goods	11	19	6	5
Consumer goods	17	11	9	4

* Estimate.

Source: Secrétariat d'Etat au Commerce Extérieur, Algiers.

PRINCIPAL TRADING PARTNERS*
('ooo AD)

IMPORTS	1976	1977†	1978	1979†
Belgium-Luxembourg . . .	649,219	1,164,677	1,395,366	2,223,000
Brazil	681,876	911,530	825,449	253,000
Canada	415,385	1,100,542	837,624	274,000
France	6,014,083	7,115,033	6,142,693	6,015,000
Germany, Federal Republic . .	3,246,395	4,275,734	6,063,368	5,840,000
Italy	1,965,092	2,861,669	3,702,902	n.a.
Japan	1,188,584	1,805,289	3,089,300	1,712,000
Netherlands	311,609	588,728	742,610	764,000
Poland	214,315	310,070	185,423	n.a.
Romania	150,249	354,010	498,315	418,000
Spain	812,730	1,446,998	1,567,949	1,630,000
Sweden	552,517	552,563	425,660	398,000
Switzerland	358,499	586,815	748,263	662,000
U.S.S.R.	468,470	374,647	293,430	163,000
United Kingdom . . .	1,013,349	875,901	1,103,985	1,016,000
U.S.A.	2,632,137	2,561,608	2,287,764	2,035,000

EXPORTS	1976	1977†	1978	1979†
Belgium-Luxembourg . . .	337,836	390,031	305,451	425,000
Brazil	n.a.	n.a.	231,805	41,000
China, People's Republic . .	n.a.	90,627	86,114	—
France	3,010,625	3,057,257	2,654,641	4,810,000
Germany, Federal Republic . .	4,027,414	3,533,208	3,339,976	4,268,000
Italy	1,671,265	1,309,150	1,757,167	n.a.
Japan	14,156	76,051	131,230	126,000
Morocco	n.a.	n.a.	n.a.	n.a.
Netherlands	214,202	547,837	470,865	1,066,000
Paraguay	9,668	108,187	121,240	204,000
Romania	7,184	36,343	192,502	574,000
Senegal	42,295	138,324	84,461	109,000
Spain	653,104	584,943	607,459	255,000
Sweden	32,841	336,672	n.a.	155,000
Switzerland	80,297	144,008	72,844	252,000
U.S.S.R.	352,872	230,854	227,810	230,000
United Kingdom . . .	524,037	330,287	452,518	541,000
U.S.A.	9,784,857	2,480,586	12,129,253	17,809,000

* Imports by country of production; exports by country of consignment. † Provisional figures.

Source: Secrétariat d'Etat au Commerce Extérieur, Algiers.

TRANSPORT
RAILWAYS

	1975	1976	1977	1978
Passengers carried ('ooo) . . .	8,693	10,221	16,465	n.a.
Freight carried ('ooo metric tons) . .	7,178	6,425	7,038	n.a.
Passenger-km. (million) . . .	1,128	1,369	1,506	1,644
Freight ton-km. (million) . .	1,740	1,727	1,940	2,177

Source: Ministère de la Planification et de l'Aménagement du Territoire, Algiers.

ROAD TRAFFIC
(motor vehicles in use at December 31st)

	1973	1974	1975*	1978†
Passenger cars	176,898	204,137	286,100	396,782
Commercial vehicles . . .	96,676	103,147	154,700	206,492

* UN estimate.

† 1976–77 figures not available.

Source: IRF, *World Road Statistics*, and UN, *Statistical Yearbook.*

INTERNATIONAL SEA-BORNE SHIPPING

	Goods Loaded ('ooo metric tons)		Goods Unloaded ('ooo metric tons)	
	1977	1978	1977	1978
Algiers	1,563	1,050	3,967	4,361
Annaba	1,970	2,174	2,238	2,516
Arzew	21,610	24,074	391	399
Béjaia	10,775	12,365	1,116	1,192
Oran	199	240	2,261	2,203
Total (incl. others) .	45,493	49,829	12,822	13,498

Source: Ministère de la Planification et de l'Aménagement du Territoire, Algiers.

CIVIL AVIATION
Scheduled Services

	1974	1975	1976	1977	1978
Kilometres flown ('ooo) . .	19,200	27,600	24,700	24,000	25,300
Passengers carried ('ooo) . .	1,090	1,618	1,682	1,997	2,229
Passenger-km. (million) . .	997	1,795	1,429	1,723	1,795
Freight ton-km. ('ooo) . .	5,600	7,200	9,100	9,000	10,800
Mail ton-km. ('ooo) . .	800	1,100	1,300	1,400	1,400
Total ton-km. ('ooo) . .	95,000	171,000	147,000	162,000	174,000

Source: UN, *Statistical Yearbook.*

TOURISM

Country of Origin	1976	1977	1978	1979	1980
France	83,391	94,701	93,124	105,836	113,667
Federal Republic of Germany .	10,627	13,572	12,960	14,460	15,819
Italy	10,366	15,375	19,446	21,286	20,872
Morocco	9,740	1,462	1,298	n.a.	n.a.
Tunisia	18,422	44,788	50,311	39,522	64,754
United Kingdom . . .	6,495	8,167	7,814	10,541	8,302
U.S.A.	5,154	6,558	7,085	n.a.	n.a.
Total (incl. others) .	184,795	244,980	259,527	265,667	290,950

Hotel Capacity (1979): 127 hotels; 17,670 beds.

Source: Ministère du Tourisme, Algiers.

EDUCATION*

	SCHOOLS		PUPILS		TEACHERS	
	1977/78	1978/79	1977/78	1978/79	1977/78	1978/79
Primary	8,380	8,653	2,894,084	2,972,242	77,009	80,853
Middle and Secondary .	1,159	1,232	741,961	844,291	27,764	32,621
General . . .	1,103	1,170	718,122	821,168	25,882	30,614
Technical . . .	19	22	11,798	11,904	823	1,021
Teacher training .	37	40	12,041	11,219	1,059	986
Higher (Universities) .	10	12	51,983	51,510	n.a.	6,421

* State institutions only.

Source (for Education): Ministère de l'Enseignement Supérieur et de la Recherche Scientifique, Algiers.

Source (unless otherwise stated): Direction Générale du Plan des Etudes Economiques, Ministère des Finances, Algiers.

THE CONSTITUTION

(*Approved by popular referendum, November 19th, 1976; promulgated November 22nd, 1976; amended by the National Assembly, June 30th, 1979*).

SUMMARY

The preamble recalls that Algeria owes its independence to a war of liberation which will go down in history as one of the epic struggles in the resurrection of the peoples of the Third World. It emphasizes that the institutions established since June 1965 are intended to transform the progressive ideas of the revolution into real achievements, affecting daily life, and to develop the content of the revolution by thought and action towards a definitive commitment to socialism.

FUNDAMENTAL PRINCIPLES OF THE ORGANIZATION OF ALGERIAN SOCIETY

The Republic: The State is socialist. Islam is the state religion and Arabic is the official national language. National sovereignty resides in the people. The National Charter is the fundamental source of national policy and law. It is to be referred to on ideological questions and for the interpretation of the Constitution. The popular assemblies are the basic institution of the state.

Socialism: The irreversible option of socialism is the only path to complete national independence. The individual ownership of property for personal or family use is guaranteed. Non-exploitative private property is an integral part of the new social system. The cultural, agrarian and industrial revolutions and socialist management of enterprises are the bases for the building of socialism.

The State: The State is exclusively at the service of the people. Those holding positions of responsibility must live solely on their salaries and may not, directly or by the agency of others, engage in any remunerative activity.

Fundamental Freedoms and the Rights of Man and the Citizen: Fundamental rights and freedoms are guaranteed. All discrimination on grounds of sex, race or occupation is forbidden. Law cannot operate retrospectively and a person is presumed innocent until proved guilty. Victims of judicial error shall receive compensation from the State.

The State guarantees the inviolability of the home, of private life and of the person. The State also guarantees the secrecy of correspondence, the freedom of conscience and opinion, freedom of intellectual, artistic and scientific creation, and freedom of expression and assembly.

The State guarantees the right to join a trade union, the right to work, to protection, to security, to health, to leisure, to education, etc. It also guarantees the right to leave the national territory, within the limits set by law. The law lays down the conditions under which the fundamental rights and freedoms may be withdrawn from anyone who uses them to attack the Constitution, the essential interests of the nation, the unity of the people and of the national territory, the internal and external security of the State, and the socialist revolution.

Duties of citizens: Every citizen must protect public property and safeguard national independence. The law sanctions the duty of parents to educate and protect their children, as well as the duty of children to help and support their parents. Women must participate fully in the building of socialism and national development.

The National Popular Army: The Army safeguards national independence and sovereignty. It participates in the development of the country and the building of socialism.

Principles of foreign policy: Algeria subscribes to the objectives of the United Nations, the Organization of African Unity and the Arab League. It supports Arab, Maghreb and African unity, on a basis of popular liberation. It is non-aligned and advocates peace and non-interference in the internal affairs of states. It fights against colonialism, imperialism and racial discrimination and supports the peoples of Africa, Asia and Latin America in their liberation struggles.

POWER AND ITS ORGANIZATION

Political power: The Algerian institutional system rests on the principle of the single-party state. The Front de Libération Nationale (FLN) is a vanguard force, guiding and organizing the people for the building of socialism. Party and state organs work in different frameworks and with different means to attain the same objectives. The decisive posts in the state organization are held by members of the party leadership.

The Executive: The President of the Republic is Head of State, Head of the Armed Forces and responsible for national defence. He must be of Algerian origin, a Muslim and more than 40 years old. He is nominated by the FLN Congress and elected by universal, secret, direct suffrage. His mandate is for five years, and is indefinitely renewable. The President embodies the unity of the political leadership of the party and the state. The President presides over joint meetings of the party and the executive. Ministers are appointed by the President. The President presides over meetings of the Council of Ministers. He may appoint one or more Vice-Presidents, to whom he may delegate some of his powers, and must appoint a Prime Minister, who will co-ordinate government activity. Should the Presidency fall vacant, the President of the National Popular Assembly temporarily assumes the office (subject to the approval of two-thirds majorities in the FLN Central Committee and the National Assembly) and organizes presidential elections within 45 days. He may not himself be a candidate in the election. The President presides over a High Security Council which advises on all matters affecting national security.

The Legislature: The National Popular Assembly prepares and votes the law. Its members are nominated by the party leadership and elected by universal, direct, secret suffrage for a five-year term. The deputies enjoy parliamentary immunity. The Assembly sits for two ordinary sessions per year, each of not more than three months' duration. The commissions of the Assembly are in permanent session. Both the President and the Assembly may initiate legislation. The Assembly may legislate in all areas except national defence. In the periods between sessions of the Assembly the President may legislate by decree, but all such legislation must be submitted to the Assembly in the following session.

The Head of State is empowered to dissolve the Assembly or call premature elections, having consulted a joint meeting of the party leadership and the Government.

The Judiciary: Judges obey only the law. They defend the socialist revolution. The right of the accused to a defence is guaranteed. The Supreme Court regulates the activities of courts and tribunals. The Higher Court of the Magistrature is presided over by the President of the Republic; the Minister of Justice is Vice-President of the Court. All magistrates are answerable to the Higher Court for the manner in which they fulfil their functions.

Constitutional revision: The Constitution can be revised on the initiative of the President of the Republic by a two-thirds majority of the National Assembly. The basic principles of the Constitution may not be revised.

THE GOVERNMENT

HEAD OF STATE

President: Col. BENDJEDID CHADLI (elected February 7th, 1979)

COUNCIL OF MINISTERS
(May 1982)

President and Minister of Defence: Col. BENDJEDID CHADLI.

Prime Minister: Col. MOHAMED BEN AHMED ABDELGHANI.

Minister of the Interior: MOHAMED HADJ YALLA.

Minister of Foreign Affairs: AHMED TALEB IBRAHIMI.

Minister of Agriculture and the Agrarian Revolution: Lt.-Col. SELIM SAADI.

Minister of Hydraulics: BRAHIM BRAHIMIA.

Minister of Public Works: MOHAMED KORTEBI.

Minister of Energy and Petrochemical Industries: BELKACEM NABI.

Minister of Light Industry: SAÏD AÏT MESSAOUDÈNE.

Minister of Heavy Industry: Col. KASDI MERBAH.

Minister of Finance: BOUALEM BEN HAMOUDA.

Minister of Planning and Regional Development: ABDELHAMID BRAHIMI.

Minister of Health: ABDERRAZAK BOUHARA.

Minister of Higher Education and Scientific Research: ABDELHAQ BREHRI.

Minister of Basic and Secondary Education: MOHAMED CHERIF KHARROUBI.

Minister of Vocational Training: MOHAMED NABI.

Minister of Labour: MOULOUD OUMEZIANE.

Minister of Commerce: ABDELAZIZ KHELLEF.

Minister of Posts and Telecommunications: BACHIR ROUIS.

Minister of Housing and Construction: AHMED ALI GHOZALI.

Minister of War Veterans: BAKHTI NEMMICHE.

Minister of Religious Affairs: ABDELRAHMANE CHIBANE.

Minister of Youth and Sport: ABDENOUR BEKKA.

Minister of Tourism: ABDELMADJID ALLAOUM.

Minister of Transport: SALAH GOUDGIL.

Minister of Justice: BOUALEM BAKI.

Minister of Culture: ABDELMADJID MEZIANE.

Minister of Information: BOUALEM BESSAIAH.

NATIONAL ASSEMBLY

The National Assembly (*Assemblée nationale populaire*) consists of 281 deputies elected by universal suffrage for a five-year term. Elections were held in March 1982. A single-party list of candidates was presented by the FLN, but the electorate was offered a choice of candidates within the list. Electoral participation was 72.7 per cent.

President of the National Assembly: RABAH BITAT.

There are two subsidiary levels of assemblies in Algeria. The communal assemblies (*assemblées populaires communales*) were created in 1967. They are headed by an elected president and are renewed by democratic vote every four years. The provincial assemblies (*assemblées populaires de wilayas*) were created in 1969 and are renewed every five years. The chief of the executive, the wali, is a government appointee. As for the national assembly, representatives are elected from a single list presented by the FLN.

POLITICAL PARTY

Government is based on a one-party system.

Front de Libération Nationale (FLN): place Emir Abdelkader, Algiers; f. 1954; socialist in outlook, the party is divided into a Secretariat, a Central Committee, a Political Bureau, Federations, Dairas and Kasmas; according to party statutes adopted at the FLN Congress in January 1979, the Central Committee (elected by Congress and consisting of 120–160 full members and 30–40 alternate members, meeting twice yearly) chooses a party Secretary-General who automatically becomes the candidate for the Presidency of the Republic. Members of the Political Bureau (between seven and 11 who meet monthly) are chosen by the Secretary-General and endorsed by the Central Committee; Sec.-Gen. Col. BENDJEDID CHADLI; Head of Secretariat MOHAMED CHERIF MESSAADIA.

Political Bureau: Col. BENDJEDID CHADLI (President), RABAH BITAT, Col. ABDALLAH BELHOUCHET, Col. MOHAMED BEN AHMED ABDELGHANI, MOHAMED CHERIF MESSAADIA, AHMED TALEB IBRAHIMI, BOUALEM BAKI, MOHAMED HADJ YALA, BOUALEM BENHAMOUDA, MOHAMED SAID MAZOUZI.

Under the aegis of the FLN there exists a number of mass political organizations, including *Jeunesse du Front de Libération Nationale* (JFLN) and the *Union Nationale des Femmes Algériennes* (UNFA).

There are several small opposition groups including the *Parti de l'avant-garde socialiste*, successor to the Algerian Communist Party; all are officially proscribed and in exile in France or in other Arab countries.

Frente Popular para la Liberación de Saguia el Hamra y Rio de Oro—POLISARIO: B.P. 10, El Mouradia, Algiers; f. 1973 to gain independence for Western Sahara, first from Spain and then from Morocco and Mauritania; originally based in Mauritania but later moved to Algeria where it is supported by the Algerian Government; in February 1976 proclaimed the Sahrawi Arab Democratic Republic, since recognized by 45 countries in Africa, Asia and Latin America; its main organs are a nine-member executive committee, a 21-member Political Bureau and a 41-member Sahrawi National Council; Sec.-Gen. MOHAMED ABDELAZIZ; Deputy Sec.-Gen. BACHIR MUSTAPHA SAYED; President of Ministerial Council MOHAMED LAMINE OULD AHMED.

DIPLOMATIC REPRESENTATION

EMBASSIES ACCREDITED TO ALGERIA

(In Algiers unless otherwise stated)

Afghanistan: Cairo, Egypt.

Albania: 50 rue Oukil Mohammed, Birmandréis; *Ambassador:* NESIP KACI.

Angola: 34 chemin Abdelkader, El-Mouradia; *Ambassador:* JOÃO BATISTA MAWETE.

Argentina: 7 rue Hamani; *Ambassador:* NEREO I. MELO.

Australia: 60 blvd. Bouraga; *Ambassador:* JOHN BROOK.

Austria: 19 blvd. Mohamed V; *Ambassador:* RUDOLF TOROVSKY.

Bangladesh: 141 blvd. Salah Bouakouir; *Ambassador:* ABUL FATEH.

Belgium: 22 chemin Youcef Tayebi, El-Biar; *Ambassador:* ROBERT GUILLOT-PINGUE.

Benin: B.P. 103, Birmandreis; *Ambassador:* ANTOINE LALEYE.

Brazil: 48 blvd. Mohamed V; *Ambassador:* RONALD L. M. SMALL.

Bulgaria: 13 blvd. Colonel Bougara; *Ambassador:* STEFAN PETROV.

Burundi: 116 bis blvd. des Martyrs; *Ambassador:* ANDRÉ NADAYIRAGE.

Cameroon: 21 blvd. Col. Bougara; *Chargé d'affaires:* FRANÇOIS N'DINE EBAKISSE.

Canada: 25 rue d'Anjou, Hydra; *Ambassador:* LOUIS A. DELVOIE.

Cape Verde: 3 rue Wiasse; *Ambassador:* ADELINO NUNES CORREIA (also representing Guinea-Bissau).

Chad: 6 rue Sylvain Fourastier, Le Golf; *Ambassador:* MBAILAOU NAIMBAYE LOSSIMIAN.

China, People's Republic: 34 blvd. des Martyrs; *Ambassador:* MING XU.

Congo: Hydra; *Ambassador:* BENJAMIN BOUNKOULOU.

Cuba: 18 rue Ibn Batran, El-Mouradia; *Ambassador:* RAUL BARZAGA.

Czechoslovakia: Villa Malika, 7 chemin Ziryab, B.P. 999; *Ambassador:* VLADIMÍR BERGER.

Denmark: 29 blvd. Zirout Youcef; *Ambassador:* HOLCK COLDING.

Egypt: 10 chemin Abdelkader Gadouche, Hydra.

Finland: 4 blvd. Mohammed V; *Ambassador:* OSMO KOCK.

France: rue Larbi Alik, Hydra; *Ambassador:* GUY GEORGY.

Gabon: 136 *bis* blvd. Salah Bouakouir au 80 rue Allili, B.P. 85; *Ambassador:* PIERRE CLAVER EYEGUET.

Gambia: Tripoli, Libya.

German Democratic Republic: 16 rue Payen, Hydra; *Ambassador:* Dr. KARL-HEINZ VESPER.

Germany, Federal Republic: 165 chemin Sfindja, B.P. 664; *Ambassador:* GERD BERENDONCK.

Ghana: 62 rue Parmentier, Hydra; *Ambassador:* GEORGE AVI ENYONAM SEPENU.

Greece: 38 rue Didouche Mourad; *Ambassador:* EFSTAKHIOS KALAMIDAS.

Guinea: 43 blvd. Central Said Hamdine, Hydra; *Ambassador:* DIAO KANTE.

Guinea-Bissau: 3 rue Wiasse; *Ambassador:* ADELINO NUNES CORREIA (also representing Cape Verde).

Hungary: 18 ave. des Frères Oughlis; *Ambassador:* BÉLA HAVASI.

India: 119 *ter* rue Didouche Mourad; *Ambassador:* K. K. S. RANA.

Indonesia: 119 *ter* rue Didouche Mourad; *Chargé d'affaires:* SAGIRI KARTANEGARA.

Iran: 60 rue Didouche Mourad; *Ambassador:* KAZEM CHIVA.

Iraq: 4 rue Arezki Abri, Hydra; *Ambassador:* IBRAHIM SHUJAA SULTAN.

Ireland: 7 rue des Glycines, El-Mouradia.

Italy: 37 chemin Bachir Brahimi, El-Biar; *Ambassador:* RICARDO PIGNATELLI DELLA LEONESSA.

Ivory Coast: Immeuble "Le Bosquet", Le Paradou, Hydra; *Ambassador:* EDMOND ISSOUF KONÉ.

Japan: 3 rue du Dr. Lucien Reynaud; *Ambassador:* YASUSHI MIYAZAWA.

Jordan: 6 rue Chenoua; *Chargé d'affaires:* YASSINE ISTANBULI.

Kenya: Cairo, Egypt.

Korea, Democratic People's Republic: 49 rue Hamia Abderrazak; *Ambassador:* PAK UI-CHUN.

Kuwait: 1 *ter* rue Didouche Mourad; *Ambassador:* ABDELLATIF HAMAD AL-SALIH.

Laos: Paris, France.

Lebanon: 9 rue Kaïd Ahmed, El-Biar; *Ambassador:* SALHAD NASRI.

Libya: 15 chemin Bachir Brahimi; *Ambassador:* ABDUL-FATTAH NAAS.

Madagascar: 22 rue Aouis, Bologhine; *Ambassador:* MAURICE JEAN-JACQUES.

Mali: Villa no. 15, Cité DNC/ANP, Chemin du Kaddous; *Ambassador:* BOUBACAR KASSE.

Malta: Tripoli, Libya.

Mauritania: B.P. 276, El-Mouradia; *Ambassador:* OULD MOHAMED MAHMOUD MOHAMEDOU.

Mexico: 103 rue Didouche Mourad; *Ambassador:* OSCAR GONZÁLES CEZAR.

Mongolia: 4 rue Belkacem Amani, Hydra; *Ambassador:* SONOMYN LUVSAN.

Nepal: Cairo, Egypt.

Netherlands: 23 chemin Cheikh Bachir Ibrahimi, El-Biar; *Ambassador:* Dr. HERMAN A. H. SCHOUTEN.

Niger: 137 *ter* blvd. Salah Bouakouir; *Ambassador:* AMADOU MOUMOUNI.

Nigeria: 27 *bis* rue Blaise Pascal; *Ambassador:* OLA M. A. ABIOLA.

Norway: Rabat, Morocco.

Oman: 126 rue Didouche Mourad; *Ambassador:* SALEM ISMAIL SUWAID.

Pakistan: 14 ave. Souidani Boudjemâa; *Ambassador:* BIRJIS HASAN KHAN.

Panama: Madrid, Spain.

Peru: 127 rue Didouche Mourad; *Ambassador:* JAIME CACEREZ ENRIQUE.

Philippines: Hôtel St. George; *Ambassador:* PACIFICO CASTRO.

Poland: 37 ave. Mustafa Ali Khodja, El-Biar; *Ambassador:* STEFAN BOZYM.

Portugal: 14 ave. B. Soviclani; *Ambassador:* ANTÓNIO MANUEL DA VEIGA E MENEZES CORDEIRO.

Qatar: 155 blvd. Salah Bouakouir; *Chargé d'affaires:* SAAD MOHAMED AL-KOBAISI.

Romania: 24 rue Si Areski, Hydra; *Ambassador:* (vacant).

Rwanda: Cairo, Egypt.

Saudi Arabia: 4 rue Arezki Abri, Hydra; *Ambassador:* HASAN FAQQI.

Senegal: B.P. 689D, 50 ave. Souidani Boudjemâa; *Ambassador:* IBRA DÉGUENE KA.

Somalia: 11 impasse Tarting, blvd. des Martyrs; *Ambassador:* ABDELHAMID ALI YOUCEF.,

Spain: 10 rue Azil Ali; *Ambassador:* JOSÉ MARIA ULLRICH Y ROJAS.

Sri Lanka: Belgrade, Yugoslavia.

Sudan: 27 rue de Carthage, Hydra; *Ambassador:* AHMED HAMMEIDA EL-TAYEB.

Sweden: 4 blvd. Mohammed V; *Ambassador:* HARALD EDELSTAM.

Switzerland: 27 blvd. Zirout Youcef; *Ambassador:* ERNST ANDRES.

Syria: Domaine Tamzali, chemin A. Gadouche, Hydra; *Ambassador:* AHMAD MADANIYA.

Tanzania: Paris, France.

Trinidad and Tobago: Lagos, Nigeria.

Tunisia: 11 rue du Bois de Boulogne, Hydra; *Ambassador:* AMOR FEZZANI.

Turkey: Villa dar el Ouard, chemin de la Rochelle, blvd. Colonel Bougara; *Ambassador:* SELÇUK KORKUD.

Uganda: Cairo, Egypt.

U.S.S.R.: Impasse Boukhandoura, El-Biar; *Ambassador:* VASSILY NAZAROVICH RYKOV.

United Arab Emirates: 26 rue Haouis Mokrane, El-Mouradia; *Ambassador:* KHALED ABDELLAH AL KASSIMI.

United Kingdom: 7 chemin des Glycines, B.P. 43; *Ambassador:* BENJAMIN LECKIE STRACHAN.

U.S.A.: 4 chemin Bachir Brahimi; *Ambassador:* CHRISTOPHER ROSS.

Upper Volta: Cairo, Egypt.

Vatican City: 1 rue de la Basilique; *Pro-Nuncio:* Dr. GABRIEL MONTALVO.

Venezuela: 38 rue Jean Jaurès, El-Mouradia; *Ambassador:* JOSÉ LUIS PERNÍA.

Viet-Nam: 30 rue de Chenoua, Hydra; *Ambassador:* TRAN VAN HUNG.

Yemen Arab Republic: 74 rue Bouraba; *Ambassador:* HAMOD MOHAMED BAYDER.

Yemen, People's Democratic Republic: Cité DNC-ANP, villa 19, Hydra; *Ambassador:* ABDEL-WAKIL ISMAIL ESSAROURI.

Yugoslavia: 7 rue d'Anjou, B.P. 632, Hydra; *Ambassador:* NEDJELJKO ZORIC.

Zaire: 12 rue A, Les Crêtes, Hydra; *Ambassador:* IKOLO BOLELAMA W'OKONDOLA.

Zambia: Cairo, Egypt.

Zimbabwe: *Ambassador:* SEREMAN NKOMA.

Algeria also has diplomatic relations with Barbados, Bolivia, Burma, the Central African Republic, Chile, Colombia, Costa Rica, Cyprus, Djibouti, Ecuador, Ethiopia, Grenada, Guyana, Jamaica, Lesotho, Liberia, Luxembourg, Malawi, Malaysia, Mauritius, Mozambique, Nicaragua, Seychelles, Sierra Leone, Swaziland, Thailand, Togo and Uruguay.

JUDICIAL SYSTEM

Ministry of Justice: 6 rue Delcasse, El-Biar, Algiers.

The highest court of justice is the Supreme Court (*Cour suprême*) in Algiers. Justice is exercised through 183 courts (*tribunaux*) and 31 appeal courts (*cours d'appel*), grouped on a regional basis. Three special Criminal Courts were set up in Oran, Constantine and Algiers in 1966 to deal with economic crimes against the state. From these there is no appeal. In April 1975 a *Cour de sûreté de l'état*, composed of magistrates and high-ranking army officers, was established to try all cases involving state security. The *Cour des comptes* was established in the same year. A new penal code was adopted in January 1982, retaining the death penalty.

President of Supreme Court: M. GATY.

Procurator-General: M. MOSTEFAÏ.

RELIGION

Ministry of Religious Affairs: 4 rue de Timgad, Hydra, Algiers.

Islam is the official religion and the whole Algerian population, with a few rare exceptions, is Muslim.

President of the Superior Islamic Council: AHMED HAMANI; place Cheik Abdelhamid ibn Badis, Algiers.

The Europeans, and a few Arabs, are Christians, mostly Roman Catholics.

Archbishop of Algiers: H.E. Cardinal LÉON-ETIENNE DUVAL; 13 rue Khélifa Boukhalfa, Algiers.

Protestant Church of Algeria: Pres. Dr. HUGH G. JOHNSON; 31 rue Reda Houhou, Algiers; 3 parishes (Algiers, Constantine and Oran).

THE PRESS
DAILIES

al Chaab (*The People*): 1 place Maurice Audin, Algiers; f. 1962; national information journal in Arabic; Dir. MOHAMED SAID.

al Joumhouria (*The Republic*): 6 rue Bencenoussi Hamida, Oran; f. 1963; Arabic language; Editor AÏSSA ADJINA; circ. 30,000.

el Moudjahid: 20 rue de la Liberté, Algiers; f. 1965; FLN journal in French; Dir. ABDELAZIZ MORSLI; circ. 130,000.

an Nasr: 100 rue Larbi Ben M'Hidi, Constantine; f. 1963; Arabic language; Editor-in-Chief El Hadi BENYAKHLEF; circ. 60,000.

WEEKLIES

Algérie Actualité: 20 rue de la Liberté, Algiers; f. 1965; French language weekly; Dir. KAMEL BELKACEM.

el Hadef: 100 rue Larbi Ben M'Hidi, Constantine; f. 1972; sports; in French; Editor-in-Chief MUSTAPHA MANCERI; circ. 110,000.

Révolution Africaine: 7 rue du Stade, Hydra, Algiers; FLN journal in French; Socialist.

PERIODICALS

al Acala: rue Timgad, Hydra, Algiers; f. 1970; published by the Ministry of Religious Affairs.

Algérie Médicale: 3 blvd. Zirout Youcef, Algiers; f. 1964; publ. of *Union médicale algérienne*; twice a year; circ. 3,000.

Alger Réalités: rue Acela Hocine, Algiers; f. 1972; organ of the Popular Assembly of the Wilaya of Algiers; monthly; French.

Alouan: 119 rue Didouche Mourad, Algiers; f. 1973; cultural review published by the Ministry of Culture; monthly; Arabic.

Bibliographie de l'Algérie: Bibliothèque Nationale, 1 ave. Docteur Fanon, Algiers; f. 1964; lists books, theses, pamphlets and periodicals published in Algeria; twice a year; Arabic and French.

Bulletin Economique: 7 blvd. Ché Guévara, Algiers; summary of items issued by state news agency; monthly.

al Chaab al Thakafi: Algiers; f. 1972; cultural monthly; Arabic.

el Chabab: 2 rue Khélifa Boukhalfa; journal of the JFLN; bi-monthly; French and Arabic.

el Djazairia: Villa Joly, 24 ave. Franklin Roosevelt, Algiers; f. 1970; organ of the UNFA; monthly; French and Arabic.

el Djeich: Office de l'Armée Nationale Populaire, 3 chemin de Gascogne, Algiers; f. 1963; monthly; Algerian army review; Arabic and French.

Journal Officiel de la République Algérienne Démocratique et Populaire: 7, 9 and 13 ave. A. Benbarek; f. 1962; French and Arabic.

al Kitab: 3 blvd. Zirout Youcef, Algiers; f. 1972; bulletin of SNED; every two months; French and Arabic.

Libyca: 3 blvd. Zirout Youcef, Algiers; f. 1953; anthropology and ethnography; irregular; French; Dir. MOULOUD MAMMERI.

Nouvelles Economiques: 6 blvd. Amilcar Cabral, Algiers; f. 1969; publ. of Institut Algérien du Commerce Extérieur; monthly; French and Arabic.

Révolution et Travail: Maison du Peuple, place du Ier mai, Algiers; journal of UGTA (central trade union) with Arabic and French editions; monthly; Editor-in-Chief ZIANE FARRAH.

Revue Algérienne du Travail: 28 rue Hassiba Benbouali, Algiers; f. 1964; Ministry of Labour publication; quarterly; French.

Revue d'Histoire et de Civilisation du Maghreb: 3 blvd. Zirout Youcef, Algiers; f. 1966; history and civilization; irregular; French and Arabic; circ. 4,000; Dir. M. KADDACHE.

at Thakafa: 119 rue Didouche Mourad, Algiers; f. 1971; published by the Ministry of Culture; cultural review; circ. 10,000; Editor-in-Chief Dr. HANAFI BENAÏSSA.

PRESS AGENCIES

Algérie Presse Service (APS): 7 blvd. Ché Guévara, Algiers; f. 1961; Dir. MOHAMED MERZOUG.

FOREIGN BUREAUX
Algiers

Agence France-Presse (AFP): 6 rue Abdelkrim El Khettabi; Chief BJÖRN AUGOT.

Agencia EFE (*Spain*): 4 ave. Pasteur; Chief JOSÉ LUIS VIDAL-COY.

Agentstvo Pechati Novosti (APN) (*U.S.S.R.*): B.P. 24, Muradia; Chief Officer YURI S. BAGDASAROV.

Agenzia Nazionale Stampa Associata (ANSA) (*Italy*): 4 ave. Pasteur; Chief BRUNO CAMPANINI.

Allgemeiner Deutscher Nachrichtendienst (ADN) (*German Democratic Republic*): 38 rue Larbi Alik, Hydra-Alger; Chief KARLHEINZ STÖCKNER.

Associated Press (AP) (*U.S.A.*): 4 ave. Pasteur, B.P. 769; Chief MICHAEL GOLDSMITH.

Bulgarian Telegraph Agency (BTA): Zaatcha 5, Muradia; Chief GORAN GOTEV.

Middle East News Agency (*Egypt*): 10 ave. Pasteur, B.P. 800.

Reuters (*U.K.*): 4 ave. Pasteur.

The following are also represented: Prensa Latina (Cuba), TASS (U.S.S.R.), Wikalat al-Maghreb al-Arabi (Morocco).

PUBLISHING

All privately owned publishing firms have been replaced by a single national organization:

Société Nationale d'Edition et de Diffusion (SNED): 3 blvd. Zirout Youcef, Algiers; f. 1966; publishes books of all types, and is sole importer, exporter and distributor of all printed material, stationery, school and office supplies; also holds state monopoly for commercial advertising.

RADIO AND TELEVISION

Radiodiffusion Télévision Algérienne (R.T.A.): Imm. RTA, 21 blvd. des Martyrs, Algiers; Government controlled; Dir. ABDERRAHMANE LAGHOUATI.

RADIO
Arabic Network: stations at Aïn Beïda, Algiers, Batna, Bechar, Oran, Touggourt and Souk-Ahras.

French Network: stations at Algiers, Constantine, Oran and Tipaza.

Kabyle Network: stations at Algiers and Michelet.

There were approximately 3,230,000 radio receivers in 1981.

Dir. M. A. BOUREGHEDA.

TELEVISION

The main stations are at Algiers, Batna, Bel Abbès, Constantine, Souk-Ahras and Tlemcen. The national network was completed during 1970. Television is taking a major part in the national education programme.

There were 525,000 television receivers in 1981.

Dir. MADANI HAOUES.

FINANCE

BANKING

(cap. = capital; dep. = deposits; m. = million; AD = Algerian dinars; Fr. = French francs; brs. = branches)

CENTRAL BANK

Banque Centrale d'Algérie: 8 blvd. Zirout Youcef, Algiers; f. 1963; cap. 40m. AD; central bank of issue; Gov. MAHFOUD AOUFI.

NATIONALIZED BANKS

From November 1967 only the following nationalized banks were authorized to conduct exchange transactions and to deal with banks abroad, and by May 1972 these three banks had absorbed all foreign and private banks. The *Banque Extérieure* and the *Banque Nationale* enjoy a monopoly in the financing of the agricultural sector and most of the new industries.

Banque Extérieure d'Algérie: 11 blvd. Colonel Amirouche, Algiers; f. 1967; cap. 500m. AD (1979); chiefly concerned with foreign trade transactions and the financing of industrial development in Algeria; brs. in Algiers and 20 other principal cities in Algeria; Gen. Man. HABIB HAKIKI.

Banque Nationale d'Algérie: 8 blvd. Ernesto Ché Guévara, Algiers; f. 1966; cap. 1,000m. AD; dep. 12,810m. AD (Nov. 1980); 170 brs.; Pres. and Gen. Man. MOHAMED THAMINI.

Crédit Populaire d'Algérie: 2 blvd. Colonel Amirouche, Algiers; f. 1966; cap. 600m. AD (Dec. 1981); regrouping of former credit banks; finances private and public industrial and commercial enterprise; foreign trade transactions; 92 brs.; Dir.-Gen. MOHAMED TERBECHE.

DEVELOPMENT BANKS

Banque Algérienne de Développement: Villa Jolly, ave. Franklin Roosevelt, Algiers; f. 1963; a public establishment with fiscal sovereignty, to contribute to Algeria's economic development through long-term investment programmes; Gen. Man. BENMALEK FAOUZI.

Caisse Centrale de Coopération Economique (CCCE): 22 rue Larbi Alik, Hydra, Algiers; f. 1968; Dir. F. PEYREDIEU DU CHARLAT.

Caisse Nationale d'Epargne et de Prévoyance: 40-42 rue Larbi Ben M'Hidi, Algiers; extends loans to housing sector; Dir.-Gen. MAHFOUD ZEROUTA.

INSURANCE
Insurance is a state monopoly.

Caisse Algérienne d'Assurance et de Réassurance: 48 rue Didouche Mourad, Algiers; f. 1963 as a public corporation; Admin.-Gen. A. BELBAY.

Caisse Nationale de Mutualité Agricole: 24 blvd. Victor Hugo, Algiers; Dir. O. LARFAOUI.

Compagnie Centrale de Réassurance: 21 blvd. Zirout Youcef, Algiers; general.

Société Algérienne d'Assurances: 5 blvd. Ché Guévara, Algiers; f. 1963; state sponsored company; Dir.-Gen. FARID BENBOUZID.

TRADE AND INDUSTRY

EXPORT INSTITUTE

Institut National Algérien du Commerce Extérieur-COMEX: 6 blvd. Amilcar Cabral, Algiers; f. 1975; publs. *Annuaire des Exportateurs Algériens, Annuaire de l'Industrie Algérienne de l'Emballage.*

CHAMBERS OF COMMERCE

Chambre de Commerce de Béjaia: B.P. 105, Béjaia; f. 1892; 11 mems.; Pres. BENCHEIKH ABDERRAHMANE; Sec.-Gen. MAHDI YOUNÉS.

Chambre de Commerce et d'Industrie de Constantine: 2 ave. Zebane, Constantine; Pres. BEN MATTI ABDESSELAM.

Chambre de Commerce et d'Industrie de la Wilaya d'Annaba: Palais Consulaire, 4 rue du Cénra, Annaba; Pres. BENZEGOUTA MOHAMED SEDDIK.

Chambre de Commerce de la Wilaya d'Oran: Angle 8 blvd. de la Soummam et 1 rue Ampère, Oran; f. 1844; Sec.-Gen. NOR'EDDINE ABDELHAK; publs. *Rapport Economique Bimestriel, Statistiques Mensuelles des Produits Exportés, Rapport d'Activité Trimestriel.*

Chambre de Commerce et d'Industrie de Mostaganem: ave. Bénaïed Bendehiba, Mostaganem; f. 1901; 8 mems.; Pres. MOHAMED BELHADJ; Sec.-Gen. HARRAG BENBERNOU.

Chambre Française de Commerce et d'Industrie en Algérie: 1 rue du Languedoc, Algiers; Pres. JEAN GLEDEL; Dir. M. G. FAULX-BRIOLE; publs. *Rapport de synthèse annuel, Guide des entreprises étrangères en Algérie.*

Jeune Chambre Economique d'Alger: rue de Nîmes, Algiers; Pres. M. DONNEAUD.

There are also Chambers of Commerce at Colomb-Béchar, Ghordaia and Tlemcen.

PRINCIPAL TRADE UNIONS

Union Générale des Travailleurs Algériens—UGTA: Maison du Peuple, place du 1er Mai, Algiers; f. 1956; 1,000,000 mems.; Sec.-Gen. TAYEB BELAKHDAR; publ. *Révolution et Travail* (fortnightly, French and Arabic).

AFFILIATES

It was announced in April 1982 that the following federations were to be replaced by eight national "professional sectors".

Fédération du Bois, du Bâtiment, des Travaux Publics et des Activités Annexes (*Federation of Building Trades Workers*): Maison du Peuple, Algiers; f. 1964; 17,000 mems.; Gen. Sec. BELHADJ BUKIR.

Fédération Nationale des Cheminots (*National Federation of Railwaymen*): 3 rue Alexandre Dumas, Algiers; Sec.-Gen. AZZI ABDELMOUDJID.

Fédération Nationale de la Santé (*Federation of Hospital Workers*): Maison du Peuple, Algiers; f. 1962; 15,000 mems.; Gen. Sec. DJEFFAL ABDELAZIZ.

Fédération Nationale des Travailleurs Communaux (*Federation of Municipal Employees*): Maison du Peuple, Algiers; f. 1956; 100,000 mems.; Sec.-Gen. BELKHIR KHENNAF.

Fédération Nationale des Travailleurs du Pétrole, du Gaz et Assimilés (*Federation of Oil and Gas Workers*): 21 blvd. Colonel Amirouche, Algiers; f. 1964; 45,000 mems.; Gen. Sec. ALI LASFER.

Fédération Nationale des Travailleurs de la Terre—FNTT (*Federation of Farm Workers*): 4 rue Arago, Algiers; f. 1964; Gen. Sec. BENMEZIANE DAOUD.

Fédération des Ports, Docks et Aéroports (*Federation of Dock and Airport Workers*): Maison du Peuple, Algiers; f. 1964; 2,500 mems.; Gen. Sec. SAID OUKALI.

Fédération des Postes et Télécommunications (*Federation of Postal and Telecommunications Workers*): Maison du Peuple, Algiers; f. 1964; 6,000 mems.; Gen. Sec. YSSAAD ABDELKADAR.

Fédération Sonelgaz (*National Federation of Utility Workers*): 47 rue Khélifa Boukhalfa, Algiers; f. 1963; 5,000 mems.; Gen. Sec. CHABANE LABOU.

Fédération des Travailleurs de l'Alimentation et du Commerce (*Federation of Food and Commerce Workers*): Maison du Peuple, Algiers; f. 1965; 14,000 mems.; Gen. Sec. DJEBIENE MAHMOUD.

Fédération des Travailleurs de l'Education et de la Culture—FTEC (*Federation of Teachers*): Maison du Peuple, Algiers; f. 1962; 13,000 mems.; Gen. Sec. BOUAMRANE CHAIKH.

Fédération des Travailleurs de l'Energie, de la Chimie et des Mines (*Federation of Energy, Chemical and Mine Workers*): 17 rue de la Liberté, Algiers; Sec.-Gen. LOUNIS AMMAR.

Union nationale des paysans algériens (UNPA): f. 1973; 700,000 mems.; Sec.-Gen. NEDJEM AÏSSA.

DEVELOPMENT

Société Centrale pour l'Equipement du Territoire—SCET International: 8 rue Sergent Addoun, Algiers; Dir. A. GAMBRELLE.

Société Nationale d'Etudes de Gestion, de Réalisations et d'Exploitations Industrielles (SNERI): 50 rue Khélifa Boukhalfa, Algiers; f. 1968; consultants for industrial projects; Dir.-Gen. M. MISSOUM.

NATIONALIZED INDUSTRIES

A large part of Algerian industry is nationalized. The following are some of the most important nationalized industries, each controlled by the appropriate Ministry.

Entreprise Nationale de Commerce d'Outils de Quincaillerie et d'Equipements Ménagères: 6 rue Lamartine, Hussein Dey, Algiers; f. 1971; tools and ironmongery.

Entreprise Nationale de Construction et de Réparation de Bateaux de Pêches (ECOREP): Quai d'Aigues Mortes, Port d'Alger; f. 1979 to replace (with ENAPECHES) former Office Algérien des Pêches; fishing equipment.

Entreprise Nationale des Pêches (ENAPECHES): Quai d'Aigues Mortes, Port d'Alger; f. 1979 to replace (with ECOREP) former Office Algérien des Pêches; fish importers and exporters.

Office National des Produits Oléicoles (ONAPO): Domaine Caridi, rue Bag M. Kouba, Algiers; f. 1974; vegetable oil products.

Office National des Travaux Forestiers (ONTF): Immeuble des Forêts, Petit Atlas, Algiers; f. 1971; production of timber, care of forests.

Pharmacie Centrale Algérienne: 2 rue Bichat, Algiers; f. 1969; pharmaceutical products.

Société Nationale de l'Artisanat Traditionnel (SNAT): 1 blvd. du Front de Mer, Bab El Oued, Algiers; traditional crafts; Dir.-Gen. M. BAIRI.

Société Nationale de Constructions Mécaniques (SONACOME): 1 route Nationale, Birkhadem, Algiers; f. 1967; reorganized in 1982 into three smaller companies dealing with manufacture, distribution, import and export of vehicles of more than 1.5 tons; distribution of private vehicles; agricultural machinery and distribution.

Société Nationale de Constructions Métalliques (SN METAL): 38 rue Didouche Mourad, Algiers; f. 1968; production of metal goods.

Société Nationale des Eaux Minérales Algériennes (SN-EMA): 21 rue Bellouchat Mouloud, Hussein Dey, Algiers; mineral water; Dir.-Gen. M. DJACTA.

Société Nationale de Fabrication et de Montage du Matériel Electrique (SONELEC): 4 & 6 blvd. Mohamed V, Algiers; electrical equipment.

Société Nationale de Gestion et de Développement des Industries Alimentaires (SOGEDIA): 13 ave. Mustapha El Ouali Sayed, Algiers; food industry; Dir.-Gen. M. AICHOUR.

Société Nationale des Industries de la Cellulose (SONIC): 63 rue Ali Haddad, B.P. 32, El Mouradia, Algiers; Dir.-Gen. M. CHAIB CHÉRIF.

Société Nationale des Industries Chimiques (SNIC): 4 et 6 blvd. Mohammed V, Algiers; chemical products; Dir.-Gen. M. ABDENNEBI.

Société Nationale des Industries du Liège et du Bois (SNLB): 1 rue Kaddour Rahim, Hussein Dey, Algiers; f. 1973; production of cork and wooden goods; Dir.-Gen. M. KERAMANE.

Société Nationale des Industries des Peaux et Cuirs (SONIPEC): 100 rue de Tripoli, Hussein Dey, Algiers; f. 1967; hides and skins; Dir.-Gen. M. BEN YOUNES.

Société Nationale des Industries Textiles (SONITEX): 5 rue Abane Ramdane, Algiers; f. 1966; split in 1982 into separate cotton, wool, industrial textiles, silk, clothing and distribution companies; 22,000 employees; Dir.-Gen. KACI ABDALLAH.

Société Nationale des Matériaux de Construction (SNMC): 17 rue Hamani, Algiers; f. 1968; building materials; Dir.-Gen. M. BELLANI.

Société Nationale de Recherches et d'Exploitations Minières (SONAREM): f. 1967; 127 blvd. Salah Bouakouir, Algiers; mining and prospecting; Dir.-Gen. FERHAT OUBRAHAM.

Société Nationale pour la Recherche, la Production, le Transport, la Transformation et la Commercialisation des Hydrocarbures (SONATRACH): 46 blvd. Mohamed V, Algiers; f. 1963; state-owned organization for exploration, exploitation, transport, refining and marketing of petroleum, natural gas and their products. In 1978 it accounted for 79 per cent of output and 75.9 per cent of exports, operating through a number of subsidiary companies formed in association with foreign oil companies; Dir.-Gen. MOURAD KHALLEF.

In May 1980 it was announced that SONATRACH was to be split up and some of its functions taken over by new companies, including the following:

Entreprise Nationale des Grands Travaux Pétroliers (ENGTP): for exploration and major projects.

Entreprise Nationale des Plastiques et de Caoutchouc (ENCP): production and marketing of rubber and plastics.

Entreprise Nationale de Raffinage et de Distribution des Produits Pétroliers (ENRDP): ave. Ahmed Ghermoul, Algiers; refining, export and internal distribution of products.

Société Nationale de Semouleries, Meuneries, Fabriques de Pâtes Alimentaires et Couscous (SN SEMPAC): rue Ahmed Ait Mohamed-El-Harrach; f. 1965; semolina, pasta, flour and couscous; Dir.-Gen. MUSTAPHA MOKKRAOUI.

Société Nationale de la Sidérurgie (SNS): Ravin de Sidi-Yahia, Algiers; f. 1964; steel, cast iron, zinc and products.

Société Nationale des Tabacs et Alumettes (SNTA): rue Marquis de Montcalm, Algiers; monopoly of manufacture and trade in tobacco, cigarettes and matches; Dir.-Gen. M. BENGHERBA.

STATE TRADING ORGANIZATIONS

Since 1972 all international trading has been carried out by state organizations, of which the following are the most important:

Office Algérien Interprofessionel des Céréales (OAIC): 5 rue Ferhat Boussaad, Algiers; f. 1962; monopoly of trade in wheat, rice, maize, barley and products derived from these cereals.

Office des Fruits et Légumes d'Algérie (OFLA): 12 ave. des 3 Frères Bouadou, Birmandreis, Algiers; f. 1969; division of the Ministry of Agriculture and Agrarian Reform; fruit and vegetable marketing.

Office National de Commercialisation (ONACO): 29 rue Larbi Ben M'hidi, Algiers; f. 1963; monopoly of bulk trade in basic foodstuffs except cereals; brs. in over 40 towns.

Office National de la Commercialisation des Vins (ONCV): 112 Quai-Sud, Algiers; f. 1968; monopoly of importing and exporting products of the wine industry; Dir.-Gen. B. DOUAOURI.

Office National des Foires et Expositions (ONAFEX): Palais des Expositions, Pins Maritimes, El Harrach, B.P. 656 Alger Gare, Algiers; f. 1971; arranges trade fairs and exhibitions, including the annual Foire Internationale d'Alger (19th Fair, Aug. 25th to Sept. 10th, 1982); Dir.-Gen. MAHMOUD OKBI.

TRANSPORT

RAILWAYS

Under the 1980–84 Development Plan U.S. $1,250 million was allocated to extending and improving the rail network. Studies were carried out in 1982 for an underground railway in Algiers.

Société Nationale des Transports Ferroviaires (SNTF): 21–23 blvd. Mohamed V, Algiers; f. 1976 to replace Société Nationale des Chemins de Fer Algériens; 3,890 km. of track, of which 299 km. are electrified and 1,276 km. are narrow gauge; daily passenger services from Algiers to the principal provincial cities and a service to Tunis; Pres. M. BOUSBA; Dir.-Gen. SASSEK BENMEHDJOUBA.

ROADS

There are about 82,000 km. of roads and tracks, of which 18,500 km. are main roads and 19,000 km. are secondary roads. The total is made up of 55,000 km. in the north, including 24,000 km. of good roads, and 27,000 km. in the south, including 3,200 km. with asphalt surface. The French administration built a good road system, partly for military purposes, which since independence has been allowed to deteriorate in parts, and only a small percentage of roads are surfaced. New roads have been built linking the Sahara oil fields with the coast, and the trans-Saharan highway is a major project. Algeria is a member of the Trans-Sahara Road Committee, organizing the building of this road, now renamed the "Road of African Unity". The first 360-km. stretch, from Hassi Marroket to Aïn Salah, was opened in April 1973, and the next section, ending at Tamanrasset, was opened in June 1978.

Société Nationale des Transports Routiers (SNTR): 27 rue des 3 Frères Bouadou, Algiers; f. 1967; holds a monopoly of goods transport by road; Dir.-Gen. HAOUSSINE EL-HADJ.

Société Nationale pour le Transport des Voyageurs (SNTV): 19 rue Rabah Midat, Algiers; f. 1967; holds monopoly of long-distance passenger transport by road.

SHIPPING

Algiers is the main port, with 23–29 metres anchorage in the Bay of Algiers, and anchorage for the largest vessels in Agha Bay. The port has a total quayage of 8,380 metres. There are also important ports at Annaba, Arzew, Béjaia, Djidjelli, Ghazaouet, Mostaganem, Oran and Skikda. It was announced in May 1981 that a new port is to be built at Djen Djen. Petroleum and liquid gas are exported through Arzew, Béjaia and Skikda. Algerian crude petroleum is also exported through the Tunisian port of La Skhirra.

ALGERIA

Compagnie Nationale Algérienne de Navigation (CNAN):
Quai 9, Nouvelle Gare Maritime, Algiers; f. 1964;
state-owned company which has the monopoly of
conveyance, freight, chartering and transit facilities in
all Algerian ports; operates fleet of freight and passenger ships; office in Marseilles and reps. in Paris, all
French ports and the principal ports in many other
countries. In October 1980 it was announced that
CNAN was to be split into 3 units, dealing with
hydrocarbons, general freight and passenger transport;
Pres. AMAR BOUSBAA.

Office National des Ports (ONP): 2 rue d'Angkor, B.P. 830,
Algiers; f. 1971; responsible for management and
growth of port facilities and sea pilotage; Dir.-Gen.
M. HARRATI.

Société Nationale de Manutention (SONAMA): 6 rue de
Béziers, Algiers; monopoly of port handling.

CIVIL AVIATION

Algeria's main airport, Dar el Beïda, 20 km. from Algiers,
is a class A airport of international standing. At Constantine, Annaba, Tlemcen and Oran there are also airports
which meet international requirements. All five are to be
substantially improved during the 1980–84 development
plan. There are also 65 aerodromes of which 20 are public,
and a further 135 airstrips connected with the oil industry.

Air Algérie: 1 place Maurice Audin, B.P. 858, Algiers;
f. 1947; internal services and extensive services to
Europe, North, Central and West Africa, the Middle
East and Asia; fleet of 10 Boeing 727, 13 Boeing 737,
13 Grumman AG-CAT, 17 Beechcraft, 1 King Air;
Dir.-Gen. BELKACEM MOUSSINI; Admin. Dir. HACENE
CHERGUI; publ. *Interline.*

FOREIGN LINES

The following foreign airlines operate services to Algiers:
Aeroflot (U.S.S.R.), Air France, Air Niger, Alitalia,
Balkan (Bulgaria), British Caledonian, ČSA (Czechoslo-
vakia), EgyptAir, Iberia (Spain), Interflug (German Demo-
cratic Republic), Iraqi Airways, Libyan Arab Airlines,
LOT (Poland), Lufthansa (Federal Republic of Germany),
Sabena (Belgium), Saudia, Swissair, Syrian Arab Airlines,
TAROM (Romania) and Tunis Air.

TOURISM AND CULTURE

**Office National Algérien de l'Animation de la Promotion et
de l'Information Touristique:** 54 rue Ali Haddad, El
Mouradia, Algiers.

**Société Nationale Algérienne de Tourisme et d'Hôtellerie
(ALTOUR):** 8 rue du Dr. Saadane, Algiers (general
affairs); 5 blvd. Ben Boulaid, Algiers (commercial
affairs).

THEATRE

Théatre National Algérien: 10 rue Hadj Omar, Algiers;
f. 1963; performances in Arabic and French in Algiers
and all main cities; drama, folk-dancing, modern
dance.

ATOMIC ENERGY

Centre des Sciences et de la Technologie Nucléaires (CSTN):
B.P. 1017, Alger-Gare; f. 1958 as Institut d'Etudes
Nucléaires d'Alger; research into nuclear physics,
reactor technology, solid and electronic physics and ore
processing; two Van de Graaff accelerators, 3 MeV and
2 MeV; Dir. A. BENNINI.

DEFENCE

**Commander-in-Chief of the Armed Forces and Minister of
Defence:** Col. BENDJEDID CHADLI.

Inspector-General of the Armed Forces: Col. ABDALLAH
BELHOUCHET.

Defence Budget (1981): 3,500 million dinars.

Military Service: compulsory six-month national service
for both sexes since 1969.

Total Armed Forces (July 1981): 101,000; army 90,000;
navy 4,000; air force 7,000.

Paramilitary Forces: 10,000.

EDUCATION

At present, education in Algeria continues broadly to
follow the pattern laid down during the French administration, but reforms initiated in 1973 should transform the
system by the mid-1980s. When completed, the reformed
education system should provide nine years instruction
in the national language (Arabic) for all Algerian children,
and training in the varied skills required to satisfy the
economic and technical needs of the country. Over one-
sixth of the 1981 administrative budget was allotted to
education.

About 80 per cent of children of school age receive an
education. In 1978/79 there were 2,972,242 pupils at
primary schools, compared with about 800,000 in 1962.
Facilities for middle and secondary education are still very
limited, although they have greatly improved since independence, accommodating about 844,000 pupils in
1978/79 compared with 48,500 in 1962. In September 1978
the total number of primary, middle and secondary school
pupils was about 3,816,500, some 5 per cent more than the
previous year. Whereas before independence most teachers
were French, in 1975/76 over 95 per cent of primary
teachers were Algerian, as were about 65 per cent of
middle and secondary teachers. Most education at primary
level is in Arabic, but at higher levels French is still
widely used. The majority of foreign teachers in Algeria
come from Egypt, Syria, Tunisia and other Arab countries.

In 1978/79 the number of students receiving higher
education was 51,510. In addition to the ten main universities there are a number of other *centres universitaires* and
technical colleges. In 1980 it was announced that 18 more
universities, each accommodating 3,000–4,000 students,
would be opened by 1983. Several thousand students
go abroad to study. Adult illiteracy, which in 1966 averaged 81.2 per cent (males 70.1 per cent, females 92.1 per
cent), is being combated by a large-scale campaign, in
which instruction is sometimes given by young people who
have only recently left school, and in which the broadcasting services are widely used.

BIBLIOGRAPHY

ALAZARD, J. and others. Initiation à l'Algérie (Paris, 1957).

ALLAIS, M. Les Accords d'Evian, le référendum et la résistance algérienne (Paris 1962).

AMIN, SAMIR. The Maghreb in the Modern World: Algeria,
Tunisia, Morocco. (Penguin, Harmondsworth, 1970).

ARON, RAYMOND. La Tragédie Algérienne (Paris, 1957).

BALOUT, L. Algérie Préhistorique (Algiers, 1958).

BOURDIEU, PIERRE. The Algerians (Boston, 1962).
Sociologie de l'Algérie (Que Sais-je, Paris, 1958).

BRACE, R. and J. Ordeal in Algeria (New York, 1960).

CHALIAND, G. L'Algérie, est-elle Socialiste? (Maspéro, Paris, 1964).

DE GAULLE, CHARLES. Mémoires d'espoir: Le Renouveau 1958–1962 (Plon, Paris, 1970).

DE GRAMMONT, H. Histoire d'Alger sous la Domination Turque (Paris, 1887).

ENCYCLOPAEDIA OF ISLAM. Algeria (New Edition, Vol. I. London and Leiden, 1960).

FANON, FRANZ. Les Damnés de la Terre (Maspéro, Paris, 1961).

FAVROD, CH.-H. Le F.L.N. et l'Algérie (Paris, 1962).

FERAOUN, MOULOUD. Journal, 1955-1962 (Paris, 1963).

FIRST, RUTH. The Barrel of a Gun: Political Power in Africa and the Coup d'Etat (Allen Lane, The Penguin Press, London, 1970).

FISHER, G. Barbary Legend (Oxford, 1957).

FRANCOS, AVIA, and SÉRÉRI, J.-P. Un Algérien nommé Boumedienne (Paris, 1976).

GILLESPIE, JOAN. Algeria (Benn, London, 1960).

GORDON, DAVID. North Africa's French Legacy, 1954-1963 (London, 1963).

The Passing of French Algeria (Oxford, 1966).

HENISSART, PAUL. Wolves in the City: The Death of French Algeria (Hart-Davis, London, 1971).

HORNE, ALISTAIR. A Savage War of Peace: Algeria 1954–1962 (Macmillan, London, 1977).

HUMBARACI, ARSLAN. Algeria—A Revolution that Failed (Pall Mall, London, 1966).

IBRAHIMI, A. TALEB. De la Décolonisation à la Révolution Culturelle (1962–72) (S.N.E.D., Algiers, 1973).

JEANSON, C. and F. L'Algérie hors la Loi (Paris, 1955).

JEANSON, F. La Révolution Algérienne; Problèmes et Perspectives (Milan, 1962).

JOESTEN, JOACHIM. The New Algeria (New York, 1964).

JULIEN, CHARLES-ANDRÉ. Histoire de l'Algérie contemporaine, conquête et colonisation, 1827-1871 (Presses Universitaires de France, Paris, 1964).

LACHERAF, MOSTEPHA. L'Algérie Nation et Société (Maspéro, Paris, 1965).

LAFFONT, PIERRE. L'Expiation: De l'Algérie de papa à l'Algérie de Ben Bella (Plon, Paris, 1968).

LAMBOTTE, R. Algérie, naissance d'une société nouvelle (Editions Sociales, Paris, 1976).

LEBJAOUI, MOHAMED. Vérités sur la Révolution Algérienne (Gallimard, Paris, 1970).

LECA, JEAN and VATIN, JEAN-CLAUDE. L'Algérie politique, institutions et régime (Fondation nationale des sciences politiques, Paris, 1974).

LESCHI, L. Algérie Antique (Algiers, 1952).

MALLARDE, ETIENNE. L'Algérie depuis (Paris, La Table Ronde, 1977).

MANDOUZE, ANDRE. La Révolution Algérienne par les Textes (Paris, 1961).

MANSELL, GERARD. Tragedy in Algeria (Oxford, 1961).

MARÇAIS, G. Algérie Médiévale (Algiers, 1957).

MARTENS, JEAN-CLAUDE. Le modèle algérien de développement (1962–1972) (S.N.E.D., Algiers, 1973).

MARTIN, CLAUDE. Histoire de l'Algérie Française 1830–1962 (Paris, 1962).

MOUILLESEAUX, LOUIZ. Histoire de l'Algérie (Paris, 1962).

M'RABET, FADELA. Les Algériennes (Maspéro, Paris, 1967).

NYSSEN, HUBERT. L'Algérie en 1970 (1970).

O'BALLANCE, EDGAR. The Algerian Insurrection 1954–62. (Archon, Hamden, Conn., and Faber, London, 1967).

OTTAWAY, DAVID and MARINA. Algeria. The Politics of a Socialist Revolution (Berkeley, University of California Press, 1970).

OUZEGANE, AMAR. Le Meilleur Combat (Julliard, Paris, 1962).

QUANDT, WILLIAM B. Revolution and Political Leadership: Algeria, 1954–1968 (M.I.T. Press, 1970).

REUDY, JOHN D. Land Policy in Colonial Algeria: The Origins of the Rural Public Domain (University of California Press, Berkeley, 1967.).

ROBSON, P. and LURY, D. The Economies of Africa (Allen & Unwin, London, 1969).

SA'DALLAH, A. Q. Studies on Modern Algerian Literature (Al Adab, Beirut, 1966).

SIVAN, EMMANUEL. Communisme et Nationalisme en Algérie (1920–1962) (Paris, 1976).

SMITH, TONY. The French Stake in Algeria 1945–1962 (Cornell University Press, 1978).

SOUSTELLE, J. Le Drame Algérien et la Décadence Française: Réponse à Raymond Aron (Paris, 1957).

SULZBERGER, C. L. The Test, de Gaulle and Algeria (London and New York, 1962).

TALBOTT, JOHN. France in Algeria, 1954–1962 (Knopf, New York, 1980).

THOMAS, BENJAMIN E. Trade Routes of Algeria and the Sahara (London, 1958).

VATIN, JEAN-CLAUDE. L'Algérie politique, histoire et société (Fondation nationale des sciences politiques, Paris, 1974).

Bahrain

GEOGRAPHY

The State of Bahrain consists of a group of islands situated midway down the Arabian Gulf about 30 km. (18 miles) from the east coast of Saudi Arabia.

The total area of the Bahrain group of islands is 258 square miles. Bahrain itself, the principal island, is about 50 km. (30 miles) long and between 13 and 25 km. (8 and 15 miles) wide. To the north-east of Bahrain, and linked to it by a causeway and motor road, lies Muharraq island, which is approximately 6 km. (4 miles) long. The archipelago comprising the State of Bahrain consists of thirty-three islands, including Nabih Salih, Jeddah, Hawar and Umm Suban. A causeway linking Bahrain to Saudi Arabia is expected to be completed by 1984.

The total population of Bahrain at the census of April 1971 was 216,078. This increased to 358,857 in April 1981, of whom 242,596 were Bahrainis. About 80 per cent are thought to be of Arab ethnic origin and 20 per cent Iranian. The port of Manama, the capital and seat of government, had a population of 88,785 (including several hundred foreigners, mainly businessmen) in 1971. The town of Muharraq had a predominantly Arab population of 37,732. The population is estimated to consist of between 45 and 50 per cent Sunni Muslims and between 50 and 55 per cent Shi'ite Muslims. The Ruling Family are Sunnis.

HISTORY

After several centuries of independence Bahrain passed firstly under the rule of the Portuguese (1521 to 1602) and then it occasionally came under Iranian rule (1602 to 1782). The Iranians were expelled in 1783 by the Utub tribe from Arabia whose paramount family, the Al-Khalifas, became the independent Sheikhs of Bahrain and have ruled Bahrain ever since, except for a short break before 1810. Iranian claims based on the Iranian occupation of the islands in the seventeenth and eighteenth centuries nevertheless have continued to be made from time to time, although officially denied by Iran in April 1980.

In the nineteenth century European powers began to interest themselves in the Gulf area, and Britain was principally concerned to prevent French, Russian and German penetration towards India, and to suppress the slave and arms trades. In 1861, in consequence of political claims put forward by Iran and Turkey, the Sheikh of Bahrain undertook to abstain from the prosecution of war, piracy and slavery by sea in return for British support against aggression. In 1880 and 1892 the Sheikh further undertook not to cede, mortgage or otherwise dispose of parts of his territories to anyone except the British Government, nor to enter into any relationship with a foreign government other than the British without British consent.

Bahrain was naturally affected by the general post-war ferment in the Arab world. A tentative step towards democratic institutions was taken in February 1956, when elections were held for members of an Education and Health Council, the first election in Bahrain being held in 1919 for the Municipal Council. Shortly afterwards there was a strike in the oil refinery, said to be partly a protest against the paternalistic attitude of the British adviser to the Sheikh. There were further disturbances at the time of the Suez crisis. Meanwhile, further symbols of Bahrain's growing independence were the establishment of Bahraini as opposed to British legal jurisdiction over a wide range of

nationalities (1957), the issue of Bahrain's own stamps (1960), and the introduction of a separate currency (1965). A small-scale distribution of village lands was started in 1960, and among economic developments the construction of a new town, Isa Town built to Western standards of amenity, was prominent. Bahrain also pioneered free education and health services in the Gulf. There was another major strike in 1965 lasting from March 19th to April 30th, the principal cause being a fear of redundancies in the oil companies. In May 1966 Britain announced that her principal base in Arabia would be transferred from Aden to Bahrain in 1968, and a more realistic rent was agreed with the Bahrain Government for the military establishment. However, in 1968 the British government announced that all forces "East of Suez"—including those in the Gulf—would be withdrawn by the end of 1971, a decision which was subsequently implemented. In October 1973, at the time of the Arab-Israeli war, the Bahrain Government gave one year's notice to quit to the U.S. Navy whose ships had docking facilities in Bahrain. The evacuation was not carried out, but negotiations continued and Bahrain finally took over the base in July 1977.

Extensive administrative and political reforms came into effect in January 1970. A twelve-member Council of State became the State's supreme executive authority, this being the first formal delegation of the sheikh's powers. Only four of the initial twelve "Directors" were members of the royal family, but all were Bahrainis, and the British advisers were officially reduced to civil servant status. Equal numbers of Sunni and Shi'ite Muslims were included (the royal family apart) to represent Bahrain's religious balance. In August 1971 the Council of State became the Cabinet of the State of Bahrain, authorized to direct the internal and external affairs of the State.

After 1968 Bahrain was officially committed to membership of the embryonic Federation of Arab Emirates, but with over half the Federation's population and high educational and social welfare standards built up over 40 years, Bahrain disagreed with the richer but more backward sheikhdoms further down the Gulf over the terms of the federal constitution (especially those relating to method of government), the allocation of common finances, etc. Bahrain's position was strengthened in May 1970 when Iran accepted the United Nations' report on Bahrain's future. The UN representatives visited the island in April and found that popular opinion overwhelmingly favoured a complete independence rather than union with Iran.

In August 1971 full independence was proclaimed, a new treaty of friendship signed with the U.K., and Sheikh Isa took the title of Amir. In September Bahrain became a member of the Arab League and the UN. In December 1972 elections were held for a Constituent Assembly which produced a new Constitution, enabling elections to a National Assembly to be held in December 1973. In June 1974 industrial unrest occurred, and the delay in allowing trade unions to be set up, although provided for in the constitution, was thought to be responsible, together with a large increase in the cost of living. In August 1975 the Prime Minister resigned because, it was said, the National Assembly was preventing the Government from carrying out its functions. The Amir invited the Prime Minister to form a new government and two days later the National Assembly was dissolved by Amir's decree. Further arrests of "leftists" took place in December 1975. Sporadic unrest continued, however, but it is thought that the majority of Bahrainis feel little concern about the lack of a National Assembly.

Although Bahrain was hitherto regarded as a "moderate" Arab State, it joined other Arab States in condemning the Egyptian-Israeli peace treaty in March 1979, subsequently breaking off diplomatic relations with Egypt in April. Some anxiety has been caused by the revolution in Iran. In September 1979 Iranian Shi'ite interests called upon Bahraini Shi'ites, who are in the majority, to demonstrate against the Sunni Amir. Calm was soon restored, but it was apparent that the new Iranian regime was interested in the old Iranian policy of making claim to Bahrain, a policy which the Shah had not renounced until 1975. In December 1981 trouble flared up again when between 50 and 60 people, mainly Bahrainis, were arrested in Bahrain accused of supporting an Iranian-backed plot to overthrow the Bahrain Government. Bahrain's Minister of the Interior alleged that the plot was the work of Hojatoleslam Hadi Al Mudarasi, an Iranian clergyman in Teheran operating in the name of the Islamic Front for the Liberation of Bahrain. Concern about Iranian intentions had been one of the reasons why Bahrain had joined with five other Gulf States in March 1981 in forming the Gulf Co-operation Council.

ECONOMY

Bahrain's prosperity has been built on its petroleum reserves. Petroleum in commercial quantity was found in 1932. The Bahrain Petroleum Company (BAPCO), which has been the main concessionaire, was formerly owned jointly by the Standard Oil Company of California and Texaco Inc. In November 1974 an agreement giving 60 per cent participation to the Bahrain Government was reached, and in March 1975 the Bahrain Government announced that it intended to take over full ownership of BAPCO. The take-over was completed in December 1979, and the Bahrain Government secured a 60 per cent interest in the BAPCO refinery in July 1980.

In common with other Arab oil-producing countries, Bahrain cut back its oil production after the October 1973 war with Israel, but it is estimated that the known oil reserves can be exploited only until about 1995. Crude oil production is declining at the rate of 4–6 per cent per year. Production in 1980 averaged 48,300 barrels per day, compared with 76,000 b/d in 1970, and had fallen to 45,000 b/d by August 1981. Production from Abu Saafa, an offshore field between Bahrain and Saudi Arabia, began in 1968, and in 1976 output was 39.2 million barrels, split 50/50 between Bahrain and Saudi Arabia. The Abu Saafa field was providing about 54 per cent of Bahrain's oil revenue in 1980.

Bahrain possesses the second largest refinery in the Middle East. In 1980 its output was 87.7 million barrels (compared with 89.2 million barrels in 1979), of which about 80 per cent originated from Saudi Arabia. The Low Sulphur Fuel Oil Project, which was brought into commission in late 1973, has meant that the refinery can manufacture 50,000 barrels of oil daily with a sulphur content of 0.5 per cent.

Natural gas production in late 1980 was running at 360 million cubic feet per day, and a new plant near Awali was producing 280,000 metric tons per year of propane, butane and naphtha from associated gas which was previously flared.

In view of the decline in oil reserves, major adjust-ments are being made to the economy. Bahrain is now concentrating on oil refining and gas processing, rather than crude oil production, and is expanding trade, finance and shipping activities, being to some extent helped by the decline of Beirut. The world oil glut at the beginning of 1982 caused both the Bahrain Petroleum Co. and the Bahrain National Oil Co. to cut back on their expenditure. Gulf Petrochemicals Industries Co. (GPIC), with Bahrain, Saudi Arabia and Kuwait each having a one-third share, had begun construction of its petrochemical complex in 1981.

Foreign investors have found Bahrain attractive because of its freedom from taxation, its good cable, telex and air communications, and its large surplus of low-cost natural gas. Under a commercial law which came into effect in January 1976, all companies registered in Bahrain are now required to have a majority of shares owned by Bahraini nationals. This does not apply to banks.

In October 1975 the Bahrain Government launched a plan which made Bahrain a major commercial centre in its own right—comparable with the position Singapore holds in the Far East. The plan involved the creation of "Offshore Banking Units" (OBUs) in Bahrain. An offshore banking unit is not permitted to provide local banking services but is allowed to accept deposits from governments and large financial organizations in the area and make medium-term loans for local and regional capital projects. By December 1981 offshore banking assets were about $50,700 million and 67 offshore banks were operating. In February 1982, however, the Bahrain Monetary Agency announced a 12-month moratorium on the formation of new publicly-owned offshore banking units.

In December 1971 the new Bahrain International Airport terminal building was opened. The first terminal designed specifically for jumbo jets, this building can handle the passengers of two Boeing 747s simultaneously and has all the equipment required for the handling of the largest aircraft planned from now until the end of the century. Further expansion is planned and Gulf Air have in hand the building of a new headquarters in Manama.

The port of Mina Sulman has 16 alongside berths for ships up to 36 ft. draught. A container terminal opened in April 1979. The port also has storage and refrigeration facilities for the transit trade, and a free zone in which many British, American and local concerns have their headquarters. The island is a major entrepôt market for the neighbouring Gulf states, and has also become the telecommunications centre of the Gulf.

A four-lane causeway and bridge joins the two main islands of Bahrain. A causeway is also planned which will link Bahrain with Saudi Arabia and which could provide much-needed employment during the construction period. The causeway should be completed in 1985.

A dry dock project, backed by the Organization of Arab Petroleum Exporting Countries, and costing U.S. $340 million, was officially opened in 1977. Known as ASRY (Arab Shipbuilding and Repair

Yards), the ship repair centre and dry dock take tankers of up to 500,000 deadweight tons. Management is provided by the Portuguese company Lisnave, under a 10-year contract signed in 1974. The yard serviced more than 400 ships between December 1977 and July 1981.

Traditional occupations such as dhow building, fishing and pearling continue but on a much smaller scale than before. In recent years, several soft drink factories and brick-making plants have been established. The Bahrain Fishing Company was forced to close down in 1979 because of the virtual disappearance of shrimps from the Gulf. Companies are now established producing offshore oil wellhead structures, manufactured domestic and industrial plastic products and there are several assembly plants. The construction boom, which was so pronounced in 1975–77, began to ease off in 1978 but work on the Gulf Petrochemical Industries Co., being built on reclaimed land, and the Arab Iron and Steel Company's plant is stimulating construction.

Bahrain's most ambitious project, the aluminium smelter, which is fuelled by natural gas, started production in 1970 and in 1977 produced 120,000 tons using alumina from Australia. Ancillary industries are now being established—a factory to produce alu-minium powder (Bahrain Atomisers) is now in production and an aluminium extrusion plant (BALEXCO) began operating in 1977. A 50 per cent price rise for aluminium on the spot market (between July 1979 and February 1980) encouraged ALBA to embark on a BD 45 million expansion aimed at increasing production to 170,000 tons per annum in 1981. World metal prices, however, slumped in 1981, and net earnings at ALBA were cut by 87 per cent. A loss is expected for 1982. ALBA exports 90 per cent of its production.

A Swiss survey of 1977 and a World Bank report of 1978 urge the development of medium and small-scale industries such as furniture manufacture and welding. Bahrain relies heavily on expatriate labour, and therefore training programmes for Bahrainis are being given priority in industrial planning. A Four-Year Plan is to begin in 1982, geared to a steady rate of growth of 7–10 per cent in real terms, and will concentrate on development projects.

Agriculture and cattle breeding are practised throughout the islands, the main crops being vegetables, lucerne, fodder crops and some dates. Here, experiments in modern methods are taking place to enable Bahrain to produce more of its own food.

STATISTICAL SURVEY

AREA AND POPULATION

AREA	POPULATION (census results)								
	February 13th, 1965			April 3rd, 1971			April 1979 (estimate)		
	Males	Females	Total	Males	Females	Total	Males	Females	Total
669.3 sq. km.*	99,384	82,819	182,203	116,314	99,764	216,078	218,900	146,100	365,000

* 258.5 sq. miles

Population (Preliminary census figures, April 1981): 358,857, of whom 242,596 were Bahrainis.
Principal towns (1971 census): Manama (capital) 88,785; Muharraq Town 37,732.

EMPLOYMENT
(1971)

Agriculture and fishing	3,990
Mining and manufacturing . . .	4,152
Oil	4,312
Public utilities	1,705
Construction	10,404
Wholesale and retail trade, and catering .	7,706
Transport, storage and communications .	7,743
Finance, insurance, property and business services	1,084
Community, social and personal services .	13,182
Public administration and defence .	5,206
Other	817
TOTAL	60,301

CRUDE OIL PRODUCTION
('000 metric tons)

1976	1977	1978	1979	1980
2,916	2,909	2,766	2,567	2,412

REFINERY PRODUCTION
(Output in million barrels)

1976	1977	1978	1979	1980
77.8	93.0	88.0	89.2	87.7

Note: 1 metric ton equals approx. 7.3 barrels.

NATURAL GAS PRODUCTION
(million cubic feet)

1976	1977	1978	1979	1980
107,464	121,228	131,152	142,147	123,422

Industry: Building materials, clothing, soft drinks, plastic products, industrial gases, boat building, air conditioning manufacture, flour mills and an aluminium plant. Estimated production of primary aluminium (in '000 metric tons) was: 122.1 in 1976; 121.4 in 1977; 122.8 in 1978; 126.1 in 1979.

FINANCE

1,000 fils = 1 Bahrain dinar (BD).

Coins: 1, 5, 10, 25, 50, 100, 250 and 500 fils.

Notes: 500 fils; 1, 5, 10 and 20 dinars.

Exchange rates (May 1982): £1 sterling = 693.1 fils; U.S. $1 = 377.0 fils.

100 Bahrain dinars = £144.28 = $265.25.

Note: The Bahrain dinar was introduced in October 1965, replacing the Persian Gulf Indian rupee at the rate of 1 dinar = 10 rupees = 15 shillings sterling (£1 = 1.333 dinars). Until August 1971 the dinar was valued at U.S. $2.10 ($1 = 476.19 fils). Between December 1971 and February 1973 the dinar was worth U.S. $2.28 ($1 = 438.60 fils). In February 1973 the dinar's official parity was fixed at $2.5333 ($1 = 394.74 fils) but the market rate of exchange was 1 dinar = $2.5284 ($1 = 395.5 fils) from January 1975 to May 1976 and 1 dinar = $2.5275 ($1 = 395.6 fils) from May 1976 to January 1978. A rate of 1 dinar = $2.6525 ($1 = 377 fils) was introduced in November 1979. This was revised in November 1980 to 1 dinar = $2.6596 ($1 = 376 fils) and that rate was in force throughout 1981. The average value of the Bahrain dinar was $2.5278 in 1976; $2.5809 in 1978; $2.6214 in 1979; $2.6531 in 1980. In terms of sterling, the value of the Bahrain dinar between November 1967 and June 1972 was 17s. 6d. (87½ new pence), the exchange rate being £1 = 1.143 dinars.

BUDGET
(million Bahrain dinars)

REVENUE	1977	1978	1979	1980–81*	EXPENDITURE	1977	1978	1979	1980–81*
Oil revenue	150	170	161	476	Capital	138.5	145	130	303
Government fees and services	45	69	63	} 204	Recurrent	111.0	135	150	377
Grants, loans, bonds	40	41	56						
TOTAL	235.5	280	280	680	TOTAL	249.5	280	280	680

* Two-year budget; BD 64 million was added in 1981.

1982-83 Budget (Two-year): Revenue BD 1,206 million; Expenditure BD 1,206 million.

1982-85 Development Plan: Proposed expenditure BD 2,300 million.

MONEY SUPPLY
(million Bahrain dinars at December 31st)

	1973	1974	1975	1976	1977	1978	1979	1980
Currency outside banks	14.9	16.9	23.5	33.2	41.6	44.1	49.9	58.3
Demand deposits	44.5	44.4	53.8	93.7	108.7	127.2	136.2	133.9
TOTAL MONEY	59.4	61.3	77.3	126.9	150.3	171.3	186.1	192.2

EXTERNAL TRADE*
(million Bahrain dinars)

	1973	1974	1975	1976	1977	1978	1979	1980
Imports c.i.f.	212.6	473.3	458.1	659.9	802.8	792.3	945.3	1,383.3
Exports f.o.b.	162.4	459.0	453.7	620.3	729.7	733.1	949.5	1,336.7

* Figures include stores and bunkers for ships and aircraft but exclude trade in silver bullion and dust.

PRINCIPAL COMMODITIES
('ooo Bahrain dinars)

IMPORTS (excl. petroleum)	1977	1978	1980*
Food and live animals	42,823.8	51,189.1	67,462
Beverages and tobacco . . .	10,185.0	10,942.1	9,528
Inedible raw materials (not fuels) .	9,110.8	9,044.2	8,003
Mineral fuels, lubricants etc. . .	7,442.7	6,812.6	16,553
Animal and vegetable oils and fats .	626.6	1,189.4	1,917
Chemicals	30,879.9	38,987.2	44,370
Basic manufactured goods . .	106,304.7	101,734.6	98,677
Machinery and transport equipment .	161,031.7	171,326.8	130,748
Miscellaneous manufactured articles .	76,259.9	61,864.4	53,160
Unclassified groups and transactions .	187.6	270.2	1,593
TOTAL	444,852.7	453,360.6	432,011

Imports of crude petroleum (million dinars): 357.8 in 1977; 338.9 in 1978; 476.0 in 1979; 750.0 in 1980.

* Figures for 1979 not available. Data for 1980 exclude transit trade.

EXPORTS (excl. petroleum)	1977	1978	1979*	1980
Cereals and cereal preparations . . .	883.8	1,284.9	9,507.0	1,042
Coffee, tea, cocoa and spices . .	3,599.0	3,164.8	1,760.0	2,648
Textile yarn, fabrics, etc. . . .	8,655.2	3,365.4	2,599.0	3,092
Iron and steel	4,608.9	2,510.7	450.0	4,533
Non-ferrous metals . . .	43,178.7	67,625.3	52,077.6	38,983
Machinery, other than electric . .	27,381.3	17,713.6	24,070.0	6,602
Electric machinery, etc. . .	11,296.6	4,628.5	26,568.0	4,295
Transport equipment . . .	5,533.0	7,873.3	63,191.0	3,068
Clothing	13,363.4	4,858.4	30,356.0	932
Footwear	6,516.2	2,776.2	2,742.0	3,963
Scientific instruments, optical and photographic goods, watches and clocks . .	2,125.3	2,262.6	700.0	32
TOTAL (including others) . .	157,605.7	147,546.9	n.a.	105,670

* Includes re-exports. Exports of refined petroleum (million dinars); 572.5 in 1977; 585.5 in 1978; 772.5 in 1979; 1,206 in 1980.

PRINCIPAL TRADING PARTNERS
('ooo Bahrain dinars)

IMPORTS (excl. petroleum)	1976	1977	1978	1979	1980
Australia	20,336	22,988	25,592	38,631	41,079
China, People's Republic . .	15,204	24,590	8,141	4,843	5,773
France	9,460	11,313	10,827	17,595	16,350
Germany, Federal Republic . .	24,844	26,178	36,753	412	18,437
Hong Kong	7,277	10,230	9,045	5,254	4,453
India	13,349	13,836	14,785	7,920	13,887
Italy	8,808	14,610	17,589	19,330	15,744
Japan	53,736	68,943	65,256	6,865	80,201
Netherlands	10,589	9,968	9,357	11,002	7,518
Pakistan	5,093	3,037	3,357	2,283	9,824
United Kingdom	68,369	87,035	90,185	80,365	70,680
U.S.A.	57,395	53,268	53,166	66,212	54,129

EXPORTS (excl. petroleum)	1976	1977	1978	1980*
China, People's Republic . .	7,247	6,072	4	—
Iran	5,157	14,020	13,672	15,027
Iraq	n.a.	n.a.	n.a.	12,262
Japan	25,684	23,513	51,775	8,170
Kuwait	3,163	5,256	8,126	11,755
Qatar	2,884	3,559	1,572	3,023
Saudi Arabia . . .	68,219	80,511	31,930	22,873
United Arab Emirates . .	6,139	5,600	17,516	12,150

* 1979 figures unavailable.

TRANSPORT
ROAD TRAFFIC
(motor vehicles registered)

TYPE OF LICENCE	1977	1978	1979	1980
Private Cars	34,284	39,928	44,922	46,054
Taxi Cabs	1,178	1,228	1,259	900
Vans and Lorries . . .	11,618	11,693	12,629	16,604
Private Buses	1,305	1,466	1,613	1,625
Public Buses	283	293	294	200
Motor Cycles	3,925	4,189	4,325	2,447
TOTAL	52,593	58,797	65,042	67,830

EDUCATION
GOVERNMENT EDUCATION, 1980

	CLASSES	STUDENTS
Primary	1,227	44,109
Intermediate	437	16,430
Secondary (General and Commercial)	252	7,315
Industrial Secondary . .	45	1,071
Teacher Training Colleges .	4	61
Religious	8	97

Source: Statistical Bureau, Ministry of Finance and
National Economy, Bahrain Government.

THE CONSTITUTION

A 108-article constitution was ratified in June 1973. It states that "all citizens shall be equal before the law" and guarantees freedom of speech, of the Press, of conscience and religious beliefs. Other provisions include the outlawing of the compulsory repatriation of political refugees. The constitution also states that the country's financial comptroller should be responsible to Parliament and not to the Government, and allows for national trade unions "for legally justified causes and on peaceful lines". Compulsory free primary education and free medical care are also laid down in the constitution. The constitution provides for a National Assembly, composed of the members of the Cabinet and 30 members elected by popular vote, although this was dissolved in August 1975.

THE GOVERNMENT

HEAD OF STATE
Amir: Sheikh ISA BIN SULMAN AL-KHALIFA, G.C.M.G. (succeeded to the throne on November 2nd, 1961; took the title of Amir on August 16th, 1971).

THE CABINET
(May 1982)

Prime Minister: Sheikh KHALIFA BIN SULMAN AL-KHALIFA.

Minister of Defence: Sheikh HAMAD BIN ISA AL-KHALIFA, K.C.M.G. (Heir Apparent).

Minister of Finance and National Economy: IBRAHIM ABDEL KARIM MOHAMED.

Minister of Foreign Affairs: Sheikh MOHAMED BIN MUBARAK BIN HAMAD AL-KHALIFA.

Minister of Education: Dr. ALI MUHAMMAD FAKHRO.

Minister of Health: JAWAD SALIM AL-URAYYID.

Minister of Interior: Sheikh MOHAMED BIN KHALIFA BIN HAMAD AL-KHALIFA.

Minister of Information: TARIQ ABDAL-RAHMAN AL-MUAYYAD.

Minister of Justice and Islamic Affairs: Sheikh ABDULLAH BIN KHALID AL-KHALIFA.

Minister of Development and Industry and Acting Minister of State for Cabinet Affairs: YOUSEF AHMED AL-SHIRAWI.

Minister of Transport: IBRAHIM MOHAMED HOMEIDAN.

Minister of Labour and Social Affairs: Sheikh KHALIFA BIN SALMAN BIN MUHAMMAD AL-KHALIFA.

Minister of Housing: Sheikh KHALID BIN ABDULLAH BIN KHALID AL-KHALIFA.

Minister of Public Works, Electricity and Water: MAJID JAWAD AL-JISHI.

Minister of Commerce and Agriculture: HABIB AHMED QASSEM.

Minister of State for Legal Affairs: Dr. HUSSAIN MUHAMMAD AL-BAHARNA.

NATIONAL ASSEMBLY

In accordance with the 1973 constitution elections to a National Assembly took place in December 1973. About 30,000 electors elected 30 members for a four-year term. Since political parties are not allowed, all 114 candidates stood as independents, but in practice the National Assembly was divided about equally between conservative, moderate and more radical members. In addition to the 30 elected members, the National Assembly contained the members of the cabinet. In August 1975 the Prime Minister resigned because, it was said, the National Assembly was preventing the government from carrying out its functions. The Amir invited the Prime Minister to form a new government and two days later the National Assembly was dissolved by Amiri decree.

DIPLOMATIC REPRESENTATION

EMBASSIES ACCREDITED TO BAHRAIN

(in Manama unless otherwise stated)

Afghanistan: Baghdad, Iraq (E).
Bangladesh: Abu Dhabi, United Arab Emirates (E).
Belgium: Kuwait City, Kuwait (E).
Canada: Kuwait City, Kuwait (E).
Denmark: Jeddah, Saudi Arabia (E).
France: Mahooz 1785/7, P.O.B. 26134 (E); *Ambassador:* RENÉ MOLINARI.
Germany, Federal Republic: Kuwait City, Kuwait (E).
Guinea: Jeddah, Saudi Arabia (E).
India: Wolverhampton Building, 1736/7, Mahooz, P.O.B. 26106 (E); *Ambassador:* PREM SINGH.
Indonesia: Kuwait City, Kuwait (E).
Iran: Sh. Isa Rd. 1018/7 (E); *Ambassador:* (vacant).
Iraq: Almutanabi Road 911/8, Al-Mahouz (E); *Ambassador:* RAFI SHARIF TAQA.
Ireland: Jeddah, Saudi Arabia (E).
Italy: Kuwait City, Kuwait (E).
Japan: Kuwait City, Kuwait (E).
Jordan: Street No. 2727, House 1549, P.O.B. 5242 (E); *Ambassador:* AHMED AL-HANDAWI.
Korea, Republic: Mahooz-Kuwait Rd., P.O.B. 5564 (E); *Ambassador:* SUNG HAN SONG.
Kuwait: Diplomatic Area, 76 Road 1702, Manama 317 (E); *Ambassador:* MOUSA SULAIMAN AL-MOUSA AL-SAIF.
Lebanon: Kuwait City, Kuwait (E).
Libya: Jufair St., P.O.B. 26062 (E); *Ambassador:* RAMADAN AL ROUBI.
Morocco: Kuwait City, Kuwait (E).
Netherlands: Kuwait City, Kuwait (E).
Norway: Jeddah, Saudi Arabia (E).
Oman: Adlia, Kuwait Rd.; *Ambassador:* ABDULLA AL-DAHAB.
Pakistan: 2516/8 Kuwait Rd., Extension, Mahooz, P.O.B. 563 (E); *Ambassador:* (vacant).
Saudi Arabia: Bani-Otbah Rd., Qudhaibiya, P.O.B. 1085 (E); *Ambassador:* ABDER-RAHMAN AL-QADI.
Senegal: Teheran, Iran (E).
Somalia: Jeddah, Saudi Arabia (E).
Spain: Kuwait City, Kuwait (E).
Sudan: Kuwait City, Kuwait (E).
Switzerland: Amman, Jordan (E).
Thailand: Teheran, Iran (E).

Tunisia: Doha, Qatar (E).
Turkey: Kuwait City, Kuwait (E).
United Kingdom: 21 Government Ave., P.O.B. 114 (E); *Ambassador:* WILLIAM R. TOMKYS.
U.S.A.: Off Sh. Isa Rd., P.O.B. 26431 (E); *Ambassador:* PETER A. SUTHERLAND, Jr.
Yemen Arab Republic: Kuwait City, Kuwait (E).

Bahrain also has diplomatic relations with Australia, Austria, Brazil, Finland, Greece, Malaysia, Maldives, Mauritania, Mexico, New Zealand, Qatar, Sweden, Syria and the United Arab Emirates.

JUDICIAL SYSTEM

Minister of Justice: Sheikh ABDULLAH BIN KHALID AL-KHALIFA.

Since the termination of British legal jurisdiction in 1971, intensive work has been undertaken on the legislative requirements of Bahrain. The Criminal Law is at present contained in various Codes, Ordinances and Regulations.

All nationalities are subject to the jurisdiction of the Bahrain Courts which guarantee equality before the Law irrespective of nationality or creed.

RELIGION

The great majority of the people are Muslims of the Sunni and Shi'ite sects. The ruling family is Sunni, although the majority of the Muslim population (slightly over 50 per cent) are Shi'ite.

Religious affiliation (1971 Census):

Muslims	.	206,708
Christians	.	6,590
Others	.	2,780
TOTAL	.	216,078

THE PRESS

DAILIES

Akhbar Al Bahrain: Ministry of Information, Manama, daily news sheet.
Akhbar Al Khalij: P.O.B. 5300, Manama; Arabic.
Awali Daily News: Published by The Bahrain Petroleum Co.; Saturday to Wednesday inclusive; English; Editor MICHAEL EVERALL; circ. 1,000.
Gulf Daily News: P.O.B. 5300, Manama; f. 1978; English; Editor CLIVE S. JACQUES; circ. 10,000.

WEEKLIES

al Adhwaa Newspaper: P.O.B. 250, Manama; f. 1965; Arabic; Chief Editor MUHAMMAD QASSIM AL-SHIRAWI; circ. 14,500.
Akhbar Bapco: Bahrain Petroleum Co. B.S.C., Awali, P.O.B. 25149; f. 1981; Arabic; house journal; Editor KHALID MEHMAS; circ. 8,000.
Bapco News: Published by The Bahrain Petroleum Co. every Wednesday; English; Editor MICHAEL EVERALL; circ. 5,000.
Al Bahrain Al-Yom (*Bahrain Today*): P.O.B. 253, Manama; Arabic; published by the Ministry of Information; Editor SALMAN TAK; circ. 4,000.
Gulf Mirror: P.O.B. 455, Manama; f. 1971; English; also circulates in Kuwait, Oman, Qatar, United Arab Emirates and eastern Saudi Arabia; Man. Editor BRIAN PAINE; Business Man. ABDUL KARIM; circ. 16,000.

al Jarida al Rasmiya (*Official Gazette*): Information Department, Government of Bahrain, Manama; f. 1957; Arabic.

al Mawakif: P.O.B. 1083, Manama; f. 1973; Arabic; world news, politics, arts, religion.

al Najma al Asbuia (*Weekly Star*): Awali; Arabic; published by The Bahrain Petroleum Co. Ltd.; circ. 8,000; Editor KHALID MEHMAS.

The New Society: P.O.B. 590, Manama.

Sada Al Usbou: P.O.B. 549, Bahrain; f. 1969; Arabic; Owner and Editor-in-Chief ALI SAYAR; circ. 10,000 (in various Gulf States).

OTHER PERIODICALS

Commerce Review: P.O.B. 248, Manama; monthly; Arabic; published by Bahrain Chamber of Commerce and Industry; Editor ABDULHADI AHMED MARHOON; circ. 3,300.

Al-Mujtama Al-Jadid: P.O.B. 590.

al Murshid: Arabian Printing and Publishing House, P.O.B. 553, Bahrain; monthly guide, including "What's on in Bahrain"; English and Arabic; Editor M. SOLIMAN.

This is Bahrain: P.O.B. 726, Manama; English; quarterly; information; published by Gulf Public Relations; Editor NIGEL PERRY.

NEWS AGENCIES

Reuters (*U.K.*): P.O.B. 1030, Manama.

Agence France-Presse, Associated Press and Gulf News Agency also have offices in Bahrain.

RADIO AND TELEVISION

Bahrain Broadcasting Station: P.O.B. 253, Manama; f. 1955; state-owned and operated enterprise; two 10kW. transmitters; programmes are in Arabic only, and include news, plays and talks; Dir. of Broadcasting IBRAHIM KANOO.

Radio Bahrain: P.O.B. 702, Manama; f. 1977; commercial radio station in English language; Man. AHMED M. SULEIMAN.

Bahrain Television: P.O.B. 1075, Manama; commenced colour TV broadcasting in 1973; second channel in English began broadcasting in October 1981. The station takes advertising; covers Bahrain, eastern Saudi Arabia, Qatar and United Arab Emirates; Gen. Man. E. J. W. PAYNE.

English language programmes broadcast by the U.S. Air Force in Dhahran and by ARAMCO can be received in Bahrain, as can the television service provided by the latter.

In 1980 there were approximately 100,000 radio receiving sets and 80,000 TV receiving sets.

FINANCE
BANKING

(cap. = capital; p.u. = paid up; dep. = deposits; m. = millions; br. = branch; B.D. = Bahrain Dinars)

CENTRAL BANK

Bahrain Monetary Agency: P.O.B. 27, Manama; f. 1973 and became fully operative January 1975; controls issue of currency, organization and control of banking system and bank credit; cap. and res. B.D. 58m. (Jan. 1982); Chair. Sheikh KHALIFA BIN SALMAN AL-KHALIFAH Deputy Chair. EBRAHIM A. KARIM; Governor ABDULLA HASSAN SAIF.

LOCALLY INCORPORATED COMMERCIAL BANKS

Al-Ahli Commercial Bank, B.S.C.: P.O.B. 5941, Manama; f. 1978; private bank; cap. p.u. B.D. 6m.; Gen. Man. GREGORY KRIKORIAN.

National Bank of Bahrain: P.O.B. 106, Manama; f. 1957; commercial bank with Government of Bahrain as major shareholder; cap. p.u. B.D. 14m.; total assets (Dec. 1981) B.D. 390m.; Chair. AHMED ALI KANOO; Gen. Man. and Chief Exec. Officer N. A. NOORUDDIN.

Bank of Bahrain and Kuwait: P.O.B. 597, Manama; cap. and res. U.S. $180m. (May 1982); Gen. Man. PAUL H. FRANCIS.

Gulf International Bank B.S.C.: P.O.B. 1017, Manama; f. 1975; equally owned by Govts. of Saudi Arabia, Kuwait, U.A.E., Qatar, Oman, Bahrain and Iraq; cap. p.u. U.S. $180.4m.; dep. U.S. $1,832.8m. (April 1982); Chair. ABDULLAH H. SAIF; Gen. Man. Dr. KHALED AL-FAYEZ.

FOREIGN COMMERCIAL BANKS

Algemene Bank Nederland: Amsterdam; P.O.B. 350, Manama; Man. Jhr. M. C. VAN DE POLL.

Arab Bank Ltd.: Amman, Jordan; P.O.B. 813, Manama Centre, Manama; Regional Man. Dr. MAKRAM RAHAL.

Bank Melli Iran: Teheran; Sheik Mubarak Bldg., P.O.B. 785, Manama; Gen. Man. (Bahrain brs.) H. SARPASH.

Bank Saderat Iran: Teheran; P.O.B. 825, Manama; Man. B. HAJIZADEH.

Banque du Caire: Cairo; P.O.B. 815, Manama; Man. A. FARID.

Banque de Paris et des Pays-Bas, FCB: Paris; P.O.B. 5241, Manama; Man. J. BOURCELOT.

British Bank of the Middle East: Hong Kong; P.O.B. 57, Manama; Man. E. C. O'BRIEN.

The Chartered Bank: London; P.O.B. 29, Manama; Man. FRANK YULE.

Chase Manhattan Bank: New York; P.O.B. 368, Manama; Man. A. S. HAZZAH.

Citibank N.A.: New York; P.O.B. 548, Manama; 1 br.

Grindlays Bank Ltd.: London; M.E. Regional Office, P.O.B. 5793, Manama; Regional Dir. (Middle East) A. ANDERSON.

Habib Bank Ltd.: Karachi; Manama Centre, P.O.B. 566, Manama; Exec. Vice-Pres. and Gen.-Man. C. AHSANUL HAQ.

National Bank of Abu Dhabi: Abu Dhabi; P.O.B. 5247, Manama; Man. ABDUL AZIZ AL-ASSAR.

Rafidain Bank: Baghdad; P.O.B. 607, Manama; f. 1969; Man. ABBAS HADY AL-BAYATY.

United Bank Ltd.: Karachi; Government Rd., P.O.B. 546, Manama; Man. ABDUL AZIZ KHAN.

SPECIALIZED FINANCIAL INSTITUTIONS

Bahrain Islamic Bank: P.O.B. 5240, Manama; f. 1979; Gen. Man. ABDUL LATIF JANAHI.

Housing Bank: P.O.B. 5370, Manama; f. 1979; Chair. Sheikh KHALID BIN ABDULLA.

OFFSHORE BANKING UNITS

Bahrain has been encouraging the establishment of Offshore Banking Units (OBUs) since October 1975. An OBU is not allowed to provide local banking services but is allowed to accept deposits from governments and large financial organizations in the area and make medium-term loans for local and regional capital projects.

Cyprus

PHYSICAL AND SOCIAL GEOGRAPHY

W. B. Fisher

The island of Cyprus, some 3,572 sq. miles in area, is situated in the north-eastern corner of the Mediterranean Sea, closest to Turkey (which is easily visible from its northern coast), but also under 100 miles from the Syrian coast. Its greatest length, including the long, narrow peninsula of Cape Andreas, is 140 miles. The population at the census of April 1st, 1973, was 631,778. By mid-1974 the total had risen to 639,000, including 496,200 Greeks and 117,300 Turks, but considerable changes have taken place since the political upheavals of 1974 (see History). In 1976 another census was held, in Greek Cypriot areas only, and the provisional mid-1981 population is estimated at 637,100.

PHYSICAL FEATURES

Cyprus owes its peculiar shape to the occurrence of two ridges that were once part of two much greater arcs running from the mainland of Asia westwards towards Crete. The greater part of these arcs has disappeared, but remnants are found in Cyprus and on the eastern mainland, where they form the Amanus Range of Turkey. In Cyprus the arcs are visible as two mountain systems—the Kyrenia Range of the north, and the much larger and imposing Troödos Massif in the centre. Between the two mountain systems lies a flat lowland, open to the sea in the east and west and spoken of as the Mesaoria. Here also lies the chief town, Nicosia.

The mountain ranges are actually very different in structure and appearance. The Kyrenia Range is a single narrow fold of limestone, with occasional deposits of marble, and its maximum height is 3,000 ft. As it is mainly porous rock, rainfall soon seeps below ground; and so its appearance is rather arid, but very picturesque, with white crags and isolated pinnacles. The soil cover is thin. The Troödos, on the other hand, has been affected by folding in two separate directions,

so that the whole area has been fragmented, and large quantities of molten igneous rock have forced their way to the surface from the interior of the earth, giving rise to a great dome that reaches 6,000 ft. above sea-level. As it is impervious to water, there are some surface streams, rounder outlines, a thicker soil, especially on the lower slopes, and a covering of pine forest.

CLIMATE

The climate in Cyprus is strongly "Mediterranean" in character, with the usual hot dry summers and warm, wet winters. As an island with high mountains, Cyprus receives a fair amount of moisture, and up to 40 in. of rain falls in the mountains, with the minimum of 12 to 15 inches in the Mesaoria. Frost does not occur on the coast, but may be sharp in the higher districts, and snow can fall fairly heavily in regions over 3,000 ft. in altitude. In summer, despite the nearness of the sea, temperatures are surprisingly high, and the Mesaoria in particular can experience over 100° F. A feature of minor importance is the tendency for small depressions to form over the island, giving slightly greater degree of changeability in weather than is experienced elsewhere in the Middle East.

Cyprus is noteworthy in that between 50 and 60 per cent of the total area is under cultivation—a figure higher than that for most Middle Eastern countries. This is partly to be explained by the relatively abundant rainfall; the expanses of impervious rock that retain water near the surface; and the presence of rich soils derived from volcanic rocks which occur round the Troödos Mountains. The potential of the tourist trade and the export markets in wine and early vegetables add to the incentives to development. In the southern (Greek) part of the island economic recovery after partition has been considerable: far less so in the north.

HISTORY

EARLY HISTORY

Cyprus first became important in recorded history when the island fell under Egyptian control in the second millenium B.C. After a long period during which the Phoenicians and the people of Mycenae founded colonies there, Cyprus, in the eighth century B.C., became an Assyrian protectorate, at a time when the Greeks of the mainland were extending their settlements in the island. From the sixth century B.C. it was a province of the Persian empire and took part in the unsuccessful Ionian revolt against Persian rule in 502 B.C. Despite the Greek triumph over Xerxes in

480 B.C., subsequent efforts by the Greek city states of the mainland to free Cyprus from Persian control met with little success, largely because of dissension among the Greek cities of Cyprus itself. For more than two centuries after 295 B.C. the Ptolemies of Egypt ruled in Cyprus until it became part of the Roman Empire.

Under the enlightened rule of Augustus the island entered upon a long period of prosperity, for trade flourished while the Romans kept the seas clear of piracy. When Jerusalem fell to the Emperor Titus in A.D. 70, many Jews found refuge in Cyprus where they became numerous enough to undertake a serious revolt in A.D. 115. Christianity, apparently introduced into the island in the reign of Emperor Claudius (A.D. 41–54), grew steadily in the next three centuries, during which Cyprus, isolated from a continent frequently ravaged by barbarian inroads, continued to enjoy a relative degree of prosperity. From the time of Constantine the Great, Cyprus was a province governed by officials appointed from Antioch and formed part of the diocese of the East. In the reign of Theodosius I (379–395) the Greek Orthodox Church was firmly established there and in the fifth century proved strong enough to resist the attempts of the Patriarchs of Antioch to control the religious life of the island.

The Arab attack of 649 began a new period in the history of Cyprus which now became, for more than 300 years, the object of dispute between the Byzantines and the Muslims. Whenever the Byzantine fleet was weak, Cyprus remained a doubtful possession of the Empire. From the decisive Byzantine reconquest of 964–5 Cyprus enjoyed for more than two centuries a period of relative calm disturbed only by occasional revolts.

WESTERN RULE

Only with the Third Crusade did Cyprus begin a new chapter of its long story. In 1192 Richard Coeur-de-Lion, having conquered the island from the Greek usurper Comnenus, bestowed it on Guy de Lusignan, formerly King of Jerusalem. There now began almost four hundred years of Western rule, which saw the introduction of Western feudalism and of the Latin Church into a land which hitherto had been Greek in its institutions and Orthodox in its religious beliefs.

In the period from 1192 to 1267 (when the direct line of the Lusignan house became extinct) the new regime was gradually elaborated. The Lusignan monarchy was limited in character, for the royal power was effective only in the military sphere, all other important business of State being decided in a High Court which consisted of the nobles, the fief-holders, and the great officers of State. This Court applied to the island a highly developed code of feudal law derived from the Assizes of Jerusalem, the Cypriots being allowed to retain their own laws and customs in so far as these did not conflict with the feudal law. The period was also marked by the determined efforts of the Latin clergy, supported by the Papacy, to establish a complete control over the Orthodox Church, a policy carried out with much harshness which the Crown and the feudal nobility often sought to mitigate in order to keep the loyalty of the subject population. The dominance of the Latin Church was finally assured by the Bulla Cypria of Pope Alexander IV (1260).

During the second half of the thirteenth century the kingdom of Cyprus (now ruled by the house of Antioch-Lusignan) played an important role in the last struggle to maintain the Latin States in Syria against the Mamluk offensive. The influence of the monarchy was further strengthened in this period, and when in 1324 Hugues IV became king, the great age of feudal Cyprus had begun. Cyprus was now of great importance in the commerce which the Italian republics maintained with the East, and Famagusta became a

flourishing port. The Papacy, however, always anxious to weaken the power of Mamluk Egypt, placed on the trade of the Italian republics with that State severe limitations and charged Cyprus and Rhodes with their enforcement. Thus began a conflict between the kings of Cyprus and the great republics of Venice and Genoa which did not endanger Cyprus so long as the Papacy could mobilize sentiment in the West to support the crusading State of the Lusignans. When, as the fourteenth century advanced, the Papacy lost its power to command such support in the West, Cyprus was left to face unaided the ambitions of Genoa and Venice, which she was powerless to withstand.

Before this decline began Cyprus enjoyed, in the mid-fourteenth century, a brief period of great brilliance under her crusading King Peter I (1359–69). In 1361 he occupied the port of Adalia on the south coast of Asia Minor, then held by the Turkish emirate of Tekke; and in the years 1362–65 toured Europe in an effort to win adequate support for a new crusade. His most memorable exploit came in 1356 when he captured Alexandria in Egypt, sacking it so completely that even as late as the sixteenth century it had not recovered its former splendour. With his assassination in 1369 the great period of the Lusignan house was ended.

The reign of King Janus I (1398–1432) was a long struggle to drive out the Genoese, who had seized Famagusta during the war with Cyprus in 1372–74, and to repel the attacks of Mamluk Egypt, which had become weary of the repeated sea-raids undertaken from the ports of Cyprus. After plundering Larnaca and Limassol in 1425 the Mamluks crushed the army of Cyprus in a battle at Khoirakoitia in 1426, King Janus himself being captured, and his capital Nicosia sacked. The King was released in 1427, when he had promised the payment of a large ransom and of an annual tribute. The last years of Lusignan power were marked by dissension in the ruling house and by the increasing domination of Venice which, with the consent of Caterina Cornaro, the Venetian widow of the last Lusignan king, annexed Cyprus in 1489.

TURKISH RULE

Venice held Cyprus until 1570 when the Ottoman Turks began a campaign of conquest which led to the fall of Nicosia in September 1570 and of Famagusta in August 1571. The Turks now restored to the Orthodox Greek Church its independence and ended the former feudal status of the peasantry. The Cypriots paid a tax for their freedom to follow their own religion and were allowed to cultivate their land as their own and to hand it to their descendants on payment of a proportion of the produce, which varied from one-fifth to one-tenth according to the locality. About thirty thousand Turkish soldiers were also given land in the island, thus forming a Turkish element in the population which was later reinforced by a certain amount of immigration from Asia Minor.

The seventeenth and eighteenth centuries were a melancholy period in the history of Cyprus. Repeated droughts and ravages of locusts preceded a famine in 1640 and an outbreak of plague in 1641. In 1660 the

Ottoman government, in order to limit the extortions of its officials and of the tax-farmers, recognized the Orthodox Archbishop and his three suffragans as guardians of the Christian peasantry, but this step did not prevent revolts in 1665 and 1690. A great famine in 1757–58 and a severe attack of plague in 1760 reduced the numbers of the peasantry very considerably, causing a widespread distress which culminated in the revolt of 1764–66. Cyprus from 1702 had been a fief of the Grand Vizier who normally sold the governorship to the highest bidder, usually for a period of one year. This practice created opportunities of financial oppression which were rarely allowed to pass unused. Perhaps the most striking development of the period was the continued rise in the power of the Orthodox bishops whose influence was so great in the late eighteenth century that the Turkish administration depended on their support for the collection of the revenues. The Turkish elements in Cyprus, who resented the dominance of the Orthodox bishops, accused them in 1821 of having a secret understanding with the Greeks of the Morea who had revolted against Turkish rule, and carried out a massacre of the Christians at Nicosia and elsewhere, which brought the supremacy of the bishops to an end.

In 1833 the Sultan granted Cyprus to Muhammad Ali, Pasha of Egypt, who was forced, however, to renounce possession of it in 1840 at the demand of the Great Powers. During the period of reforms initiated by Sultan Mahmud II (1808–39) and continued by his immediate successors, efforts were made to improve the administration of the island. The practice of farming out of the taxes was abolished (although later partially reintroduced) and the Governor now became a salaried official ruling through a divan half-Turkish and half-Christian in composition.

BRITISH RULE

In 1878 the United Kingdom made an agreement with the Sultan by which Cyprus was put under British control, to be used as a base from which to protect the Ottoman Empire against the ambitions of Russia, a defence then all the more important in that the opening of the Suez Canal (1869) had made the East Mediterranean an area of great strategic importance. Under the agreement of 1878 Cyprus remained legally a part of the Ottoman Empire, to which a tribute was paid consisting of the surplus revenues of the island, calculated at a sum rather less than £93,000 per annum.

From 1882 until 1931 the island had a Legislative Council partly nominated and partly elected. Various reforms were carried out in this first period of British rule: the introduction of an efficient judicial system and of an effective police force, and considerable improvements in agriculture, roads, education and other public services.

Cyprus was offered to Greece in 1915 provided Greece joined the Allies in the war, but the offer was refused and did not remain open. In 1925 the island became a Crown Colony, at a time when the discontent of the Greek Cypriots was beginning to assume more serious proportions.

In the period since 1931 the desire to achieve self-government within the Commonwealth grew stronger, but the *Enosis* movement remained a strong influence in the political life of the island. Cypriot troops performed valuable services in the war of 1939–45, for example in Libya under Lord Wavell and in the Greek campaign of 1941. Later Cyprus was used as a place of detention for illegal Jewish immigrants into Palestine, the last of such detention camps being closed in 1949.

CONSTITUTIONAL PROPOSALS

In July 1954 the United Kingdom made known its intention to prepare a restricted form of constitution for Cyprus, with a legislature containing official, nominated and elected members. The Greek Cypriots, insisting that their ultimate goal was *Enosis*, viewed the proposed constitution with disfavour, whereas the Turkish Cypriots declared their readiness to accept it. The Greek Government at Athens now brought the problem of Cyprus before the UN. Great Britain, however, urged that the question was one with which she alone was competent to deal. The result was that, in December 1954, the UN resolved to take no immediate action in the matter.

The more extreme advocates of *Enosis*, grouped together in the EOKA (National Organization of the Struggle for the Freedom of Cyprus) now began a campaign of terrorist activities against the British administration. A conference including representatives from the United Kingdom, Greece and the Turkish Republic met in London in August 1955. The British offer of substantial autonomy for Cyprus failed to win the approval of Greece, since it held out no clear prospect of self-determination for the island, and the conference therefore ended in frustration.

A new and more violent wave of terrorism swept Cyprus in November 1955. A state of emergency was declared on November 27th whereby the death penalty was imposed for the bearing of arms, life imprisonment for sabotage and lesser sentences for looting and the harbouring of terrorists. All public assemblies of a political nature were forbidden; the British troops in Cyprus (about 10,000 in all) assumed the status of active service in war time. The Governor now ruled the island through an executive council consisting of four officials from the administration, two Greek Cypriots and one Turkish Cypriot.

At the beginning of 1956 the Governor, Sir John Harding, discussed the situation with Archbishop Makarios, head of the Greek Orthodox Church in the island. Since the United Kingdom was now willing to accept the principle of ultimate independence for Cyprus, agreement seemed to be within reach. In March 1956, however, the discussions were broken off and Archbishop Makarios, implicated in the activities of the EOKA, was deported to the Seychelles Islands.

THE RADCLIFFE PROPOSALS

The United Kingdom, confronted with a general strike in Cyprus, with a renewed and more intense campaign of terrorism and with the first ominous signs of strife between the Greek and Turkish communities in the island, now appointed Lord Radcliffe, in July 1956, as Commissioner for Constitutional Reform. His report, published in December of that year, proposed that defence, foreign affairs and internal security should be reserved to the Governor, other spheres of rule being under the control of a cabinet of Cypriot Ministers responsible to an elected legislature. Lord Radcliffe laid down careful safeguards for the Turks in Cyprus—no laws affecting the domestic affairs of the Turks would be valid without the consent of two-thirds of the Turkish members in the legislature.

Meanwhile, in June 1956, Greece appealed once more to the United Nations. The United Kingdom, asserting that the internal affairs of Cyprus fell solely within her own competence, complained to the UN in October about the aid forthcoming from Greece for the EOKA terrorists. There were, however, talks at Athens and Ankara in December 1956, but to no effective end, since Greece rejected the proposals of Lord Radcliffe for constitutional reform in Cyprus. The UN, in February 1957, adopted a resolution urging that a peaceful and democratic settlement be found for the Cyprus problem.

RELEASE OF MAKARIOS

In March 1957 Archbishop Makarios was released from detention in the Seychelles and, since he was not allowed to return to Cyprus, went in fact to Athens. The British authorities also relaxed some of the emergency laws—e.g. the press censorship and the mandatory death penalty for the bearing of arms. These measures facilitated the holding of further discussions, but the progress made by the end of the year was inconsiderable.

The tide of violence ran high in Cyprus during the first half of 1958. EOKA carried out an intensive campaign of sabotage, especially at Nicosia and Famagusta. At the same time strife between the Greek Cypriots and the Turkish Cypriots was becoming more frequent and severe, the outbreaks in June 1958 being particularly serious. There was increased tension, too, between the governments at Athens and at Ankara.

BRITAIN'S SEVEN-YEAR PLAN

It was in this situation that in June 1958 the United Kingdom made public a new scheme for Cyprus. The island was to remain under British control for seven years; full autonomy in communal affairs would be granted, under separate arrangements, to the Greek Cypriots and the Turkish Cypriots; internal administration was to be reserved for the Governor's Council which would include representatives of the Greek Cypriot and Turkish Cypriot communities and also of the Greek and Turkish governments at Athens and Ankara. This scheme came into force in October 1958.

THE ZURICH AND LONDON AGREEMENTS

Negotiations between Greece and the Turkish Republic soon carried the Cyprus problem towards an agreed solution. As the result of a conference held at Zürich, it was announced in February 1959, that the two states had devised a compromise settlement. A further conference at London led to a full and formal publication of the details.

Cyprus was to become an independent republic with a Greek Cypriot President and a Turkish Cypriot Vice-President. There would be a Council of Ministers (seven Greeks, three Turks) and a House of Representatives (70 per cent Greek, 30 per cent Turkish) elected by universal suffrage for a term of five years. Communal Chambers, one Greek, one Turkish, were to exercise control in matters of religion, culture and education. The Turkish inhabitants in five of the main towns would be allowed to establish separate municipalities for a period of four years.

Cyprus was not to be united with another state, nor was it to be subject to partition. The United Kingdom, Greece and the Turkish Republic guaranteed the independence, the territorial integrity and the constitution of Cyprus. Greece received the right to station a force of 950 men in the island and the Turkish Republic, a force of 650 men. The United Kingdom retained under her direct sovereignty two base areas in Cyprus—at Akrotiri and at Dhekelia.

In November 1959 agreement was attained in regard to the delimitation of the executive powers to be vested in the President and Vice-President of Cyprus. A further agreement defined the composition of the Supreme Constitutional Court. In December 1959 the state of emergency (in force since 1955) came to an end and Archbishop Makarios was elected to be the first President of Cyprus. After long negotiations concluded in July 1960, the United Kingdom and Cyprus reached agreement over the precise size and character of the two military bases to be assigned to British sovereignty.

INDEPENDENCE

Cyprus became formally an independent republic on August 16th, 1960, and, in September, a member of the United Nations. The Conference of Commonwealth Prime Ministers, meeting at London, resolved in March 1961 that Cyprus be admitted as a member of the Commonwealth.

A team of experts from the United Nations visited Cyprus in the autumn of 1960. Its official report was made public in April 1961. In August 1961 Archbishop Makarios submitted to the Cyprus House of Representatives the outline of a five year plan based on the UN report. The Archbishop laid particular emphasis on reform in land-tenure and agrarian methods, on the conservation of existing and the development of new water supplies and on the introduction of long-term loans to farmers.

CONSTITUTIONAL PROBLEMS

As Cyprus entered thus into its independence, serious problems began to arise over the interpretation and working of the constitution. There was divergence of opinion between Greek Cypriots and Turkish Cypriots over the formation of a national army, as laid down in the Zürich agreement of 1959 (2,000 men; 60 per cent Greek, 40 per cent Turkish) the main point of dispute being the degree of integration to be established between the two racial components. In October 1961 the Turkish Vice-President, Dr. Küçük, used his power of veto to ban full integration which President Makarios favoured at all levels of the armed forces.

Difficulties arose also over the implementation of the 70 per cent-30 per cent ratio of Greek Cypriot to Turkish Cypriot personnel in the public services. There was friction too in the House of Representatives, about financial affairs—e.g. customs duties and income tax laws.

The year 1962 saw the growth of a serious crisis over the system of separate Greek and Turkish municipalities in the five main towns of Cyprus—Nicosia, Famagusta, Limassol, Larnaca and Paphos. In December 1962 the Turkish Communal Chamber passed a law maintaining the Turkish municipalities in the five towns from January 1st, 1963, and also establishing a similar municipality in the predominantly Turkish town of Lefka. President Makarios now issued a decree stating that from January 1st, 1963, Government-appointed bodies would control municipal organizations throughout the island—a decree which the Turkish Cypriots denounced as an infringement of the constitution.

The Constitutional Court of Cyprus, sitting in judgement on the financial disputes, ruled in February 1963 that, in view of the veto exercised by the Turkish members of the House of Representatives since 1961, taxes could be imposed on the people of the island, but that no legal machinery existed for the collection of such taxes. In April the court declared that the Government had no power to control the municipalities through bodies of its own choosing and that the decision of the Turkish Communal Chamber to maintain the separate Turkish municipalities in defiance of the Cyprus Government was likewise invalid.

Negotiations between President Makarios and Vice-President Küçük to resolve the deadlock broke down in May. Accordingly in November Archbishop Makarios put forward proposals for a number of reforms—e.g. that the President and Vice-President of Cyprus should lose their right of veto over certain types of legislation; that separate Greek Cypriot and Turkish Cypriot majorities in the House of Representatives should not be required for financial legislation; and that single municipal councils, with both Greek and Turkish Cypriot members, should replace the separate municipalities in the five chief towns of Cyprus. These proposals proved to be unacceptable to the Turkish Cypriots.

CIVIL WAR

Meanwhile, underground organizations, prepared for violence, had come into being both among the Greek and the Turkish communities. In December 1963 serious conflict broke out. The United Kingdom suggested that a joint force composed of British, Greek and Turkish troops stationed in Cyprus should be established to restore order. The Governments at Nicosia, Athens and Ankara gave their assent to this scheme. At this same moment the forces of the Turkish

Republic serving in the island occupied, north of Nicosia, a strong position which gave them control of the important road to Kyrenia on the northern coast of Cyprus—a road which was to become the scene of much conflict in the future. As a result of the December crisis co-operation between the Greek Cypriots and the Turkish Cypriots in government and in other sectors of public life came almost to an end.

The general situation was now becoming extremely tense. There was renewed violence in February 1964, especially at Limassol. Arms in considerable quantities were being brought secretly into the island for both sides and the number of armed "irregulars" was increasing rapidly. These developments also gave rise to friction between Athens and Ankara.

ESTABLISHMENT OF
UN PEACE-KEEPING FORCE

Cyprus, in January 1964, had asked the UN to send a representative to the island. On January 16th U Thant, the Secretary-General of the United Nations, nominated Lieutenant-General Prem Gyani of India to act in this role. Later in the same month the Cyprus Government informed U Thant that it would be glad to see a UN force established in the island. The UN Security Council debated the Cyprus question in February finally adopting a resolution in March authorizing the creation of a United Nations peace-keeping force for Cyprus. U Thant appointed Lieutenant-General Gyani to command this force. Advance units of the Canadian contingent reached the island later in the month and by May the UN Headquarters at Nicosia controlled some 7,000 men.

In March U Thant announced the appointment of Mr. S. Tuomioja, the Finnish Ambassador to Sweden, as United Nations mediator in Cyprus. In May U Thant nominated Dr. Galo Plaza, of Ecuador, to be his special representative in the island. After the death of Mr. Tuomioja Dr. Galo Plaza was to become, in September 1964, the UN mediator in Cyprus, Senhor Carlos Bernardes, of Brazil, taking his place as U Thant's Special Representative. The exploratory consultations of the UN officials—at Nicosia, at Athens and at Ankara—failed to achieve real progress in the summer of 1964.

There was more fighting between Greek and Turkish Cypriots in March and April 1964. On June 1st the Cyprus House of Representatives passed a Bill establishing a National Guard and making all male Cypriots between the ages of 18 and 59 liable to six months of service in it. Only members of the National Guard, of the regular police and of the army forces would now have the right to bear arms. One purpose of the Bill was to suppress the irregular bands which, as extremist sentiment grew stronger, tended more and more to escape from the control of the established regime.

Under the agreements concluded for the independence of Cyprus in 1959–60 the Turkish Republic maintained a contingent of troops in the island, the personnel of this force being renewed from time to time on a system of regular rotation. A new crisis arose in August-September 1964 when the Government at Nicosia refused to allow such a rotation of personnel. After much negotiation through the UN officials in the island the Cyprus Government agreed to raise its existing blockade of the Turkish Cypriots entrenched in the Kokkina district and to allow the normal rotation of troops for the Turkish force stationed at Cyprus. The Government at Ankara now consented that this force should come under the United Nations command in Cyprus.

LEGISLATIVE MEASURES

Towards the end of 1964 the Cyprus House of Representatives passed a number of important measures—a Bill for the creation of unified municipalities in Nicosia, Larnaca, Limassol, Famagusta and Paphos; a law restoring to the Government the right to exact income tax (a right inoperative since 1961 as a result of the veto of the Turkish Cypriot members in the House); and a Bill extending compulsory service in the National Guard for Greek Cypriots from six to twelve months. In July 1965 a new law was approved for unified elections on the basis of a common electoral roll, the communal distinction between Greek Cypriots and Turkish Cypriots being thus abolished.

The UN mediator in Cyprus, Dr. Galo Plaza, resigned in December 1965. Little had been done towards mediation since Dr. Galo Plaza published a detailed report in March 1965. Moreover, no clear indication existed at this time as to where the funds would be found to continue the existence of the UN forces in the island. The United Nations was in fact to renew the mandate of these forces in June 1966 and again in December 1966. In addition the UN Secretary-General, U Thant, announced in January 1967 that he had chosen Señor Bibiano Osorio-Tafall, of Mexico, to be his personal representative in Cyprus, Senhor Carlos Bernardes, of Brazil, having resigned the appointment for personal reasons.

GENERAL GRIVAS

There was further tension in Cyprus during March 1966 over the position of General Grivas, the former head of EOKA. The General had returned to the island in June 1964 at a time when it was felt that he might be able, with his high personal prestige, to bring to order the small "private armies" and "irregular bands" which had emerged among the Greek Cypriots and which were violently defying the Cyprus Government.

In March 1966 President Makarios attempted to limit the functions of General Grivas in Cyprus and so to end a situation which saw political control vested in himself, while command of the armed forces, both the Greek Cypriot National Guard and also the "volunteer" Greek troops stationed in Cyprus, rested with the General, who took his orders from Athens. The President suggested that the National Guard should be transferred to the control of the Cyprus Minister of Defence—a proposal which found favour neither with General Grivas nor at Athens, where it

provoked a sharp political crisis. The whole affair underlined the distrust separating President Makarios and General Grivas and the doubts existing at Athens as to the ultimate intentions of the President.

In November 1966 the United Kingdom announced her intention to reduce her military establishment in Cyprus. Some 2,000 servicemen would be withdrawn by the summer of 1967. At the same time there was to be a scaling down in the amount of stores held at the Dhekelia base. The Royal Air Force station at Nicosia had already been run down to care and maintenance status, leaving Akrotiri to function still as a large R.A.F. headquarters.

The military *coup* in Greece in April 1967 was followed by a brief improvement in Greco-Turkish relations. The Prime Ministers and Foreign Ministers of Greece and Turkey met in Thrace in September 1967, but failed to come to an agreement on Cyprus, Greece rejecting any form of partition, which was implicit in the Turkish proposal to accept *Enosis* in return for military bases and ten per cent of the island's territory.

TURKISH CYPRIOT ADMINISTRATION

On December 29th, 1967 the Turkish Cypriot community announced the establishment of a "Transitional Administration" to administer their affairs until the provisions of the 1960 Constitution were implemented. Measures were approved to establish separate executive, legislative and judicial authorities, and Dr. Fazil Küçük, Vice-President of Cyprus, was appointed President of the Transitional Administration, with Rauf Denktaş as Vice-President. A legislative body was set up, consisting of the Turkish Cypriot members of the House of Representatives elected in 1960 and the members of the Turkish Communal Chamber. The Executive Council's nine members functioned as the administration. President Makarios described the Transitional Administration as "totally illegal", but it continued to function as the *de facto* government of the Turkish community in Cyprus.

INTER-COMMUNAL TALKS

Between January and April 1968 the Cypriot Government gradually relaxed the measures it had taken against the Turkish community. With the exception of the Turkish area in Nicosia, freedom of movement for Turkish Cypriots was restored, checkpoints were removed and unrestricted supplies to Turkish areas were allowed. In April Rauf Denktaş, the Vice-President of the Turkish Cypriot Administration, was permitted to return from exile, and in May he began talks with Glavcos Clerides, the President of the House of Representatives. These talks were intended to form the basis of a settlement of the constitutional differences between the Greek and Turkish communities, but very little progress was made. After years of intermittent discussion, there was still an impasse, the Turks demanding local autonomy, the Greeks rejecting any proposals tending towards a federal solution, fearing that it might lead to partition. In June 1972 Dr. Kurt Waldheim, the UN Secretary-

General, attended the talks, stressing the need for a peaceful settlement and expressing a hope that UNFICYP might be withdrawn in the near future. By the end of 1973 the Greek Cypriot representative seemed to have accepted the principle of local autonomy, but the talks still dragged on, with no acceptable compromise having been found on the scope of local autonomy or the degree of control to be exercised by the central government over local authorities. A statement by Mr. Ecevit, Prime Minister of Turkey, calling for a federal settlement of the constitutional problem, caused the talks to break down in April 1974. The Greek and Cypriot governments claimed that the talks had been conducted on the understanding that any solution would be in terms of a unitary state, Mr. Denktaş that federation would not necessarily mean partition. Mr. Dentkaş also feared that the Greek Government was giving support to the *Enosis* movement. Each side accused the other of trying to sabotage the talks.

TERRORISM AND ELECTIONS

While the talks between the Greek and Turkish communities were drifting on, there was a marked reduction in intercommunal violence, but the Greek population of the island was split between supporters of Makarios and his aim of an independent unitary state and those who demanded union with Greece. In 1969 the National Front, an organization calling for immediate *Enosis*, embarked on a campaign of terrorism, raiding police stations to steal arms, bombing British military buildings and vehicles, shooting and wounding the chief of police and making several unsuccessful bomb attacks on Government ministers. Mr. Papadopoulos, the Greek Prime Minister, denounced terrorism in Cyprus and the National Front in particular.

On March 8th, 1970 there was an attempt to assassinate President Makarios, attributed to the National Front. The President escaped unhurt. A week later, Polycarpos Georghadjis, a former Minister of the Interior, was found shot dead. At the trial of the President's would-be assassins, Georghadjis was named as a member of the conspiracy.

Despite the activities of the National Front, the Government decided to hold a general election on July 5th, 1970. The dissolved House of Representatives had been in existence since 1960, and the elections which should have been held in 1965 according to the Constitution had been postponed from year to year due to the continuing crisis. The continued absence of the 15 Turkish members, who met as part of the Turkish Legislative Assembly, meant that the Greek Cypriot House of Representatives contained only 35 members. Fifteen of the Greek Cypriot seats were won by the Unified Party, led by Glavcos Clerides, with a policy of support for President Makarios and a united independent Cyprus. The Communist party AKEL won nine seats, to become the second largest in the House. None of the candidates of DEK, the Democratic National Party, which stands for *Enosis*, won a seat. The elections held at the same time by the

Turkish Cypriots resulted in a victory for the National Solidarity Party, led by Rauf Denktaş.

RETURN OF GRIVAS AND EOKA-B

The ideal of *Enosis* was still very attractive to many Greek Cypriots, despite the lack of success for pro-*Enosis* candidates in the election. Greek Cypriot students condemned President Makarios' policy of an independent unitary state, and called for an end to the inter-communal talks. General Grivas attacked the President in an article in an Athens newspaper, calling for his resignation on the grounds that, by abandoning *Enosis*, the President had betrayed EOKA's struggle for freedom.

At the beginning of September 1971 General Grivas returned secretly to Cyprus and began to hold meetings with the leaders of the National Front and his followers in the EOKA movement of the 1950s. President Makarios threatened to arrest the General for setting up armed bands, and declared his opposition to the achievement of *Enosis* by violent means. His opponents, pro-*Enosis* Greek Cypriots, condemned the inter-communal talks and rejected the idea of a negotiated compromise with the Turkish community. The Cyprus Government imported a considerable quantity of arms from Czechoslovakia as a precautionary measure, but after protests from the Greek and Turkish Foreign Ministries that the distribution of these arms would serve only to aggravate an already tense situation, the consignment was placed under the custody of UNFICYP. In April 1972 President Makarios expressed his support for the Turkish Prime Minister's suggestion that each community should gradually disarm, but nothing came of this move.

The President had been under pressure from the Greek Government to dismiss ministers considered hostile to Athens for some time. In February 1972 it was suggested in Athens that a Cypriot government of national unity should be formed, including moderate representatives of General Grivas. For some months the President resisted this pressure, and it seemed that the Greek Government in alliance with dissident bishops and General Grivas, was intent on forcing his resignation. In May Spyros Kyprianou, the Foreign Minister who had been the main target of Greek hostility and one of the President's closest collaborators, resigned, and in June the President gave way and carried out an extensive reorganization of his cabinet.

General Grivas organized a new guerilla force, which became known as EOKA-B, and launched a series of attacks on the Makarios Government similar to those against British rule in the 1950s. While the Committee for the Co-ordination of the *Enosis* Struggle, his political front organization, demanded a plebiscite on *Enosis* and rejected inter-communal agreement as a means of settling the future of Cyprus, EOKA-B raided police stations, quarries and warehouses, stealing arms, ammunition, dynamite and radio transmitters.

PRESIDENTIAL ELECTIONS

The demand for a plebiscite from supporters of General Grivas was put forward as an alternative to the election for the presidency, called by President Makarios as a test of strength. The President's speech of February 8th, 1973 explained his position. While believing in *Enosis*, he considered that talks with the Turkish community on the basis of an independent Cyprus were the only practical possibility. He condemned terrorism and violence as counter-productive, likely to lead to Turkish intervention and unsupported by the Greek and Cypriot authorities. The Greek Government also repudiated terrorism and expressed its support for a constitutional solution.

On February 8th, 1973 Makarios was returned unopposed for a third five year term as President, and in the Turkish quarter of Nicosia Rauf Denktaş was declared elected Vice-President following the withdrawal of Ahmet Berberoğlu.

EOKA-B continued its terrorist activities throughout 1973, concentrating on bombings and raids on police stations. In July the Minister of Justice, Christos Vakis, was kidnapped, and there were over 80 bomb explosions throughout Cyprus on the three following nights. The President refused to give in to violence or to blackmail, rejecting the terms put forward by Grivas for the release of Mr. Vakis. Numerous police and National Guard officers, suspected of being Grivas sympathizers, were dismissed, and Mr. Vakis was released in August. Action by security forces against secret EOKA bases resulted in many arrests, the seizure of quantities of munitions and the discovery of plans to assassinate the President. President Papadopoulos of Greece publicly condemned the activities of "the illegal organization of General Grivas", which undermined the Greek policy of "support for the finding of a solution to the Cyprus problem through the enlarged local talks aimed at ensuring an independent, sovereign and unitary state."

MAKARIOS AND THE BISHOPS

In March 1972 the three bishops of the Orthodox Church of Cyprus—Anthimos of Kitium, Yennadios of Paphos and Kyprianos of Kyrenia—called on Archbishop Makarios to divest himself of the temporal power of the Presidency, on the ground that his political role was incompatible with his ecclesiastical position under the rules of the Church. This provoked massive popular demonstrations and a resolution in the House of Representatives in support of the President. It appeared that the bishops had the support and protection of General Grivas. When the President rejected their demand for his resignation, they charged him with abandoning the ideal of *Enosis*, tolerating the growth of Communism and permitting the rise of anti-Greek attitudes.

The clergy of the diocese of Paphos voted Bishop Yennadios out of office in June 1972, but he and the other two bishops refused to accept this decision and continued their campaign against Archbishop Makarios. In March 1973 they held what they called a Holy Synod of the Church of Cyprus, and announced that in view of the Archbishop's refusal to resign the presidency they would strip him of his episcopal titles. Makarios disregarded this move and the bishops' declaration in April that he had been reduced to the rank of layman. While the bishops were attempting to gain control of the administration and finances of the Church, claiming that Yennadios had been appointed to the vacant archiepiscopal throne, Makarios was taking counter-measures. He called an election for the diocese of Paphos in succession to Yennadios, and in July 1973 held a synod of the Orthodox Churches in Nicosia. The synod, presided over by the Patriarch of Alexandria, gave its support to Archbishop Makarios. It ruled that the Presidency and the Archbishopric were not incompatible under canon law, that the bishops' attempt to depose the Archbishop was invalid and that the bishops were guilty of schism. The dissident bishops were replaced.

MILITARY COUP

Following the deposition of the three bishops, and the demonstrations of popular support for the President which their actions provoked, the Cypriot Government was able to take strong measures against other supporters of General Grivas. Forces loyal to the President waged guerrilla war against EOKA-B, and carried out a purge of the armed forces and police, some of whose members had collaborated with EOKA and helped their raids on police stations in search of arms. The Grivas campaign of terrorism seemed to have been checked by the beginning of 1974, and when General Grivas died of a heart attack in January 1974 the President granted an amnesty to 100 of his imprisoned supporters, hoping to restore normality in Cyprus.

In June 1974 President Makarios ordered a purge of EOKA supporters in the police, civil service, schools and National Guard, and on July 2nd wrote to President Ghizikis of Greece, accusing the Greek military regime of giving arms and subsidies to EOKA and using the Greek army officers attached to the Cyprus National Guard as a centre of subversion. The President demanded that the Greek officers who had collaborated with EOKA should be withdrawn, and began to take steps to ensure that the Guard should be loyal to Cyprus rather than to Greece and *Enosis*. The National Guard, apparently with Greek support, then staged a coup. On July 15th former EOKA gunman Nicos Sampson was appointed President. Makarios fled to Britain, the resistance of his supporters was crushed, and Greece sent more officers to reinforce the National Guard.

Rauf Denktaş, the Turkish Cypriot leader, called for military action by the United Kingdom and Turkey, as guarantors of Cypriot independence, to prevent Greece imposing *Enosis*. Having failed to induce the United Kingdom to intervene, Turkey acted unilaterally. Turkish troops landed in Cyprus on July 20th, and seized the port of Kyrenia and a corridor connecting it to the Turkish sector in Nicosia. A ceasefire on July 22nd did not prevent further Turkish advances, and the UN Peace-keeping Force had little success in its efforts to interpose itself between the two Cypriot communities. Massacres and other atrocities were reported from many bi-communal villages, reinforcing the hostility between Greeks and Turks.

TURKEY OCCUPIES NORTHERN CYPRUS

The successful Turkish invasion had foiled Greek plans to take over Cyprus using the National Guard, and when the military government of Greece resigned on July 23rd, Nicos Sampson did likewise. Glavcos Clerides, the moderate Speaker of the House of Representatives who had led the Greek Cypriot delegation to the intercommunal talks, was appointed President, and began negotiations with Rauf Denktaş. In Geneva, Britain, Greece and Turkey also held talks, seeking a settlement, but negotiations broke down following Turkish demands for the establishment of a cantonal federation giving almost a third of the area of Cyprus to the Turkish Cypriots.

On August 14th, the day after the Geneva talks ended, the war was renewed. Turkish forces seized the whole of Cyprus north of the Attila Line, running from Morphou through Nicosia to Famagusta, and the new civilian government in Greece announced its inability to intervene. Turkey announced that, by this *fait accompli*, the boundaries of an autonomous

Turkish Cypriot administration had been established, while Mr. Denktaş spoke of establishing a completely independent Turkish Cypriot state north of Attila Line and of encouraging the immigration of Turkish Cypriots from areas still under Greek Cypriot control, to produce a permanent ethnic and political partition of the island. Dr. Kurt Waldheim, the UN Secretary-General, succeeded in arranging talks between Mr. Clerides and Mr. Denktaş, but was unable to bring about any constructive results from these negotiations. Possibly the most crucial round of peace talks on the Cyprus problem began in Vienna between Mr. Clerides and Mr. Denktaş in January 1975 under the aegis of Dr. Waldheim. The success of the talks hinged on whether the two sides could reach agreement on the political future of the island: the Turkish Cypriots wanting a Greek-Turkish bi-regional federation with strong regional governments, whereas the Greeks, whilst not ruling out a bi-zonal solution, favoured a multi-regional or cantonal federation with strong central government. Both parties stressed the need for an independent, non-aligned, demilitarized Cyprus.

On February 13th a "Turkish Federated State of Cyprus" was proclaimed in the part of the island under Turkish occupation. The new state was not proclaimed as an independent republic but as a restructuring of the Autonomous Turkish Cypriot Administration, a body established after the invasion, "on

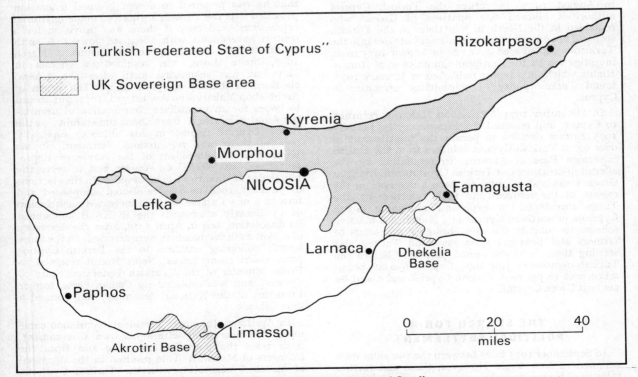

Cyprus, showing "Turkish Federated State".

the basis of a secular and federated state until such time as the 1960 Constitution of the Republic ... is amended in a similar manner to become the Constitution of the Federal Republic of Cyprus". Rauf Denktaş was appointed President of the new state. Greece denounced this move as a threat to peace and declared that the issue would be taken to the UN Security Council where a resolution was passed, on March 13th, regretting the unilateral decision to set up a Federated Turkish State. Talks were resumed in April and the foundation laid for intercommunal reconciliation and co-operation, when the Cypriot leaders agreed to form an expert committee, under the auspices of Dr. Luis Weckmann-Muñoz, Special Representative of the UN Secretary-General, to consider the powers and functions of a central government for Cyprus and present their findings in June to the Cypriot negotiators in Vienna.

The flight of Turkish Cypriots to British bases after the National Guard coup and the withdrawal of Greek Cypriot civilians before the advancing Turkish army had produced a major problem in Cyprus. In August 1974 the United Nations estimated that there were some 225,600 refugees in Cyprus, of whom 183,800 were Greek Cypriots. In the southern part of Cyprus, under Greek Cypriot control, were 198,800 of these refugees, of whom 35,000 were Turkish Cypriots, including prisoners of war. This problem remained unsolved in 1976, with an estimated 200,000 refugees on the island. However, 9,000 Turkish Cypriots were given the opportunity to move to the northern sector in August 1975. In return the Turkish Cypriot authorities allowed 800 relatives of Greeks who remained in the North to join them in the Turkish sector. The concern over the treatment of Greeks in the Turkish-occupied area gave rise in August 1975 to an investigation by the European Commission of Human Rights which, in a report published in January 1977, found Turkey guilty of committing atrocities in Cyprus.

In December 1974 Archbishop Makarios returned to Cyprus, and resumed the Presidency. In January 1975 Britain decided to permit the resettlement of over 9,000 Turkish Cypriot refugees from the British Sovereign Base at Akrotiri. In retaliation for the alleged ill-treatment of Turkish Cypriots still living in Greek areas and in order to force a decision on the release of the refugees and their resettlement, the Turks threatened to expel all remaining Greek Cypriots in northern Cyprus and launched a massive scheme to colonize the area, bringing thousands of farmers and peasants from mainland Turkey and settling them in Greek-owned property. Before the Turkish invasion of July 1974, Cyprus' 650,000 population was 18 per cent Turkish Cypriot and about 80 per cent Greek Cypriot.

THE SEARCH FOR A POLITICAL SETTLEMENT

In September 1975 talks between the two sides were resumed in New York. However, these and further talks in February 1976 were completely unproductive,

each side being unwilling to compromise on the major areas of dispute. In April 1976 the divergence in the policies of Archbishop Makarios and Glavkos Clerides, the Greek Cypriot negotiator, eventually led to the resignation of the latter and his replacement by Tassos Papadopoulos. At the same time the Turkish Cypriot negotiator, Rauf Denktaş, was replaced by Umit Suleyman Onan.

During 1976 general elections were held on both sides of the "Attila Line". In June Rauf Denktaş was elected President of the "Turkish Federated State of Cyprus". His election placed him constitutionally above party politics but in fact his position depends upon the support of the National Unity Party (NUP). Under the terms of the constitution promulgated by the Turkish Cypriot authorities, 40 deputies were elected to a legislative assembly, with the National Unity Party gaining a majority. Nejat Konut, the Secretary-General of the NUP, was appointed Prime Minister. In September general elections were held in the government-controlled area. A new party under Spyros Kyprianou, the Democratic Front, supporting the policies of Archbishop Makarios, won a decisive victory, gaining 21 of the 35 seats. The party of Glavcos Clerides, the Democratic Rally, did not win any seats.

In January 1977 Rauf Denktaş initiated a meeting with Archbishop Makarios to establish preliminaries for resuming inter-communal talks (suspended since February 1976); Archbishop Makarios made it clear that he was prepared to accept bi-zonal federation provided that the Turkish authorities made territorial concessions, and only if there was provision for a central government with adequate powers. A sixth round of talks, which opened in Vienna in March 1977, broke down, was resumed in Nicosia in May but was suspended until after the general elections in Turkey in June 1977. The death of Archbishop Makarios on August 3rd, 1977, put an end to hopes for an immediate continuation of negotiations and gave rise to fears about the stability of the Greek Cypriot regime in his absence, especially because there was no obvious successor. Spyros Kyprianou, the President of the House of Representatives, was elected on August 31st to serve the remainder of Makarios's term of office. In the elections of January 1978 he was re-elected unopposed and formed a new Cabinet with an increased membership of 13. Shortly afterwards the EOKA-B announced its dissolution, but in April 1978, after the discovery of a plot, 22 of its members were arrested. In the same month, following criticism in the Turkish Cypriot press about rising prices, Nejat Konut resigned as Prime Minister of the "Turkish Federated State of Cyprus" and was replaced by Osman Orek, former President of the National Assembly, who formed a new Cabinet.

In April and July 1978 President Kyprianou came under criticism from within his own Government, both from the powerful left wing and from the followers of Makarios. This resulted in the dismissal of his chief negotiator with the Turkish Cypriots, Tassos Papadopoulos. Little progress was made during 1978 in the attempt to find a solution to the problem of divided Cyprus. Proposals by both the U.S. Government and then by Dr. Waldheim produced no concrete results.

In December there was a crisis in the "Turkish Federated State" as a result of factional fighting in the NUP. In the midst of widespread rumours about the establishment of a multi-national company to which the Turkish Cypriot unions were opposed, all nine Cabinet Ministers resigned, followed by the Prime Minister. A new Cabinet was formed under Mustafa Çağatay, formerly Minister of Labour, Social Affairs and Health. In April 1979 a new party, the Democratic Party, was formed by former Premier Nejat Konut, as the NUP lost support in the Legislature.

On May 19th Kyprianou and Denktaş agreed a 10-point agenda based on the Makarios/Denktaş agreement. However, inter-communal talks in June were adjourned after a week over differences in the interpretation of the agreement, which Turkish Cypriots see as providing for bi-zonality on the island. In November Süleyman Demirel became Prime Minister of Turkey and in March 1980 Turkey signed a new defence agreement with the U.S.A. Meanwhile the mandate of the UN Peacekeeping Force (UNIFCYP) continued to be extended at 6-monthly intervals.

On September 9th, 1980, the Greek-Cypriot Government's reshuffle involved the appointment of seven new ministers. As a result, President Kyprianou was again attacked by AKEL and by the right-wing opposition under Clerides, thus losing his overall majority in the House of Representatives. During the next three months, three new political parties of the Centre were established: the Pan-Cypriot Revitalization Front (PAME), the new Democratic Party (DIKO) and the Centre Union.

On September 16th, 1980, in the shadow of the military coup in Turkey, the inter-communal peace-talks were resumed after a break of 15 months. These were to be held within the framework of a procedural formula proposed by Hugo Gobbi, the special UN representative for Cyprus. The negotiators for the Greek and Turkish sides were respectively George Ioannides and Umit Suleyman Onan. There were to be four main areas of discussion: the re-settlement of Varosha (the Greek area of Famagusta); constitutional aspects; territorial aspects; and "initial practical measures by both sides to promote good will, mutual confidence and the return to normal conditions". The talks continued intermittently, but by the spring of 1981 no concrete results had been achieved.

Negotiations with Britain re-opened in March 1981, and were still going on in May 1982, about outstanding development payments to Cyprus, which, according to the Cypriots, amounted to £150 million since 1960. In the same month the Foreign Minister, Nicos Rolandis, expressed his opposition to the possible use of the British airbases at Akrotiri and Dhekelia by the U.S.A.'s proposed Rapid Deployment Force.

Growing criticism of Kyprianou's Government for its failure to avert an economic crisis or to make any real progress in the inter-communal talks led the House of Representatives to vote almost unanimously on April 16th for the dissolution of the Government. In the subsequent parliamentary elections, held on May 24th, 1981, under a system of proportional representation, the Communist AKEL party and the Democratic Rally of Glavcos Clerides each gained 12 seats in the House of Representatives, while President Kyprianou's Democratic Party gained only eight seats. In the elections held in the "Turkish Federated State of Cyprus" in June 1981, President Rauf Denktaş was returned to office, but with only 52 per cent of the vote. His right-wing National Unity Party (NUP) won 18 out of 40 seats, compared with 23 at the previous elections.

The inter-communal talks continued throughout 1981, but little progress was made. In August there were signs of hope when fresh proposals were put forward by the Turkish Cypriots. These envisaged handing back 3 to 4 per cent of the 35.8 per cent of land now controlled by them, plus the buffer zone between the two communities, and allowing some 40,000 of the 200,000 Greek Cypriot refugees to return to the Famagusta area. The constitutional issue remained the main problem: the Greek Cypriots want a federation with a strong central government and freedom of movement throughout the island. The Turkish Cypriots favour something more like a partition within a confederation, with equal status for the two communities, equal representation in government and strong links with the mother country. The Greek Cypriots, although they agree to the principle of an alternating presidency, object to disproportionate representation of the Turkish community, who form less than 20 per cent of the population. The Turkish proposals were rejected by the Greek Cypriots, but it was agreed that the talks should continue.

In November 1981 the UN put forward a new peace plan, or "evaluation", for a federal, independent and non-aligned Cypriot state. Although more favourable to the Greek side than the Turkish Cypriot proposals had been, this was only accepted reluctantly as a basis for negotiation by the Greek Cypriots, in the face of opposition from the Church and some political groups. The Turkish Cypriots accepted the plan.

The new socialist government of Greece, elected in October 1981, pledged more active support for the Greek Cypriots than their predecessors. Andreas Papandreou, the Greek Prime Minister, who visited Cyprus early in 1982, would like to see the withdrawal of all Greek and Turkish troops from the island, and favours an international conference on Cyprus rather than the continuation of the inter-communal talks.

With presidential elections in view, President Kyprianou and his DIKO party formed an alliance with the communist AKEL party in April 1982. This put a strain on relations with the Greek government, as AKEL favours the continuation of the inter-communal talks, thus going against the policy recently laid down by Athens and Nicosia. The alliance with AKEL involved a Cabinet reshuffle in which all but three ministers were replaced.

In the presidential elections due early in 1983, two

candidates other than Spyros Kyprianou are likely to be Glavcos Clerides of the Democratic Rally, who made a remarkable come-back in the May 1981 elections, and George Ioannides, who resigned as Greek Cypriot negotiator in April 1982 through lack of confidence in the President. He was replaced by Andreas Mavrommatis, Director General of the Cyprus Foreign Ministry.

In the "Turkish Federated State of Cyprus" the

Cağatay Government resigned in December 1981, after a vote of "no confidence". A three-month crisis followed, in which the National Unity Party failed to form a coalition with the Communal Liberation Party. On March 16th, 1982, a coalition government, with a narrow majority in the Legislative Assembly, was formed between the National Unity Party, the Democratic People's Party and the Turkish Unity Party.

ECONOMIC SURVEY

Geographically, Cyprus may be divided into four regions, distinguished by their natural and climatic features. These are the north coastal belt, including the narrow Kyrenia mountain chain; the central plain, known as the Mesaoria, from Famagusta and Larnaca to Morphou Bay; the mountainous area of the south centre, dominated by the Troödos massif with its highest point of Mount Olympus (6,400 feet); and the coastal plain of the south running from a point west of Larnaca to Limassol and Paphos.

Since the middle of 1974, however, the most important geographical division on Cyprus has been that between the areas to the north and south of the Attila line (*see* map). The northern two-fifths of the country, under Turkish Cypriot control, is closely linked to the economy of Turkey, and has almost no economic contacts with the south of the island. Both areas suffered severe disruption as a result of the events of 1974. As well as the physical damage caused by the fighting, more than a third of the total population of around 640,000 became refugees, some 180,000 Greek Cypriots fleeing to the south and about 45,000 Turkish Cypriots moving to the north. The collapse of essential services in many places reduced economic activity to a low level. Crops were not harvested, tourism ceased, and industrial buildings and plant were destroyed or lost their workforce.

THE SOUTHERN ECONOMY

Since 1974 the economies to the north and the south of the Attila line have diverged. The economy of the south made a remarkable recovery, despite having lost 30 per cent of the island's factories, 60 per cent of the tourist installations, the main port (Famagusta) and 80 per cent of the citrus fruit groves, all of which were on the northern side of the line. In 1975 the GDP was only two-thirds of the 1973 level, but through 1976 and 1977 production rose at an average of 18 per cent a year. Even with the growth rate falling to an average 7 per cent annually during 1978 and 1979, at the end of that period production in the southern part of the island was 12 per cent higher than for the whole of Cyprus in 1973. Unemployment was reduced from almost 25 per cent in late 1974 to 1.8 per cent in 1979, partly by the emigration of workers, but largely through the promotion of labour-intensive industry and massive expansion of the construction sector, both for private housing and development projects.

By 1980, however, it was clear that the boom in the Cypriot economy was over. This was partly due to

the disappearance of short-term factors which had favoured growth: in 1977 market conditions in the Middle East and Europe were advantageous for Cypriot exports, and there was a lull in oil prices, whereas by 1979 it was becoming difficult for agricultural products from Cyprus to penetrate the European market and oil prices were once more rising sharply. However, there was also a deeper instability in the economy. Recovery was based on labour-intensive production by a low-wage workforce —wages in 1976 were lower than in 1973—but, with full employment from 1977, wage rises escalated. Between 1976 and 1979 real wages increased by an average 10 per cent annually, and in 1980 average wages rose by 20 per cent, not allowing for inflation, or by 6.5 per cent in real terms. Rising wages and the increasing cost of imported petroleum, among other factors, helped push up inflation from an annual average of 4 per cent in 1976–77 to 9.8 per cent in 1979 and 13.4 per cent in 1980. The Cyprus Government was also faced with a growing balance of payments deficit and a budgetary deficit. Economic growth had been stimulated by tax incentives and direct government investment in development projects. Consequently, revenue failed to keep pace with expenditure. Despite loans from international agencies and foreign governments and extensive borrowing abroad, Cyprus's reserves in 1980 were perilously low. The Government adopted a stabilisation programme designed to reduce imports, cut the budget deficit and limit inflation. As a result, inflation fell back to 11 per cent in 1981, but the trade deficit increased further to a record £C274 million and the budget was still not balanced.

Economic growth continued, however, if at a slower rate. GDP rose by 2.6 per cent in 1981, compared with 4.8 per cent in 1980 and 8.9 per cent in 1979. The rate of unemployment increased, but only from the low level of 1.8 per cent in 1979 to 2.9 per cent in 1981. Major development projects, such as expansion of the ports at Limassol and Larnaca ($51 million) and the Paphos irrigation project ($62 million), continued to progress.

THE NORTHERN ECONOMY

The economy of the area north of the "Attila line" has not recovered so quickly and an extensive programme of reconstruction, based on aid from Turkey, is under way. Turkish government aid provides roughly one-half of annual budget expenditure, set at about TL12,000 million in 1982. The Turkish

Agricultural Bank, which acts as a central bank, and various Turkish state enterprises also provide aid for corresponding areas of the Cypriot economy. The Five-Year Plan introduced in 1978 envisaged annual growth in G.D.P. of 7.5 per cent, but this has not been achieved: in 1980 G.D.P. actually fell slightly for the first time. Development priorities are the improvement of communications, irrigation and the restoration of damaged citrus groves. By 1980 fruit production in the Turkish-controlled area had recovered sufficiently for 96,637 metric tons to be exported, and in 1981 Turkey pledged TL2,000 million for irrigation work in the most important citrus region, Morphou. Turkey provides almost 50 per cent of the area's imports.

This reliance on Turkey, both as supplier and as a source of aid, has led to a rise in the cost of living, not helped by devaluations of the Turkish lira. Retail prices were reported to have risen by 60 per cent in 1980, leading to widespread labour unrest. The dependence on Turkey has been increased by the partial success of the Greek Cypriot Government's efforts to establish an international boycott of the "illegal" Turkish Cypriot state. The north's communications with th rest of the world have been severely disrupted, and little international aid has been made available.

AGRICULTURE

Agriculture is the most important single economic activity in Cyprus. In 1974 it employed 33 per cent of the labour force. Some 45 per cent of the northern population work in agriculture, compared with about 25 per cent in the south. The chief crops are citrus fruit, potatoes, carrots, grapes, carobs, tobacco, wheat and barley.

After the division of the island in mid-1974, the Greek Cypriot Government launched a series of emergency development plans in which agriculture and irrigation featured prominently. Loans were given to farmers and agricultural production responded rapidly. Most of the citrus trees were in the north, so they were replaced as the main agricultural product by potatoes and other vegetables. With good weather in Cyprus and favourable market conditions in the drought-ridden EEC, exports of vegetables flourished through 1976–77. Total exports of fruit and vegetables reached £C37.8 million in 1977, over one-third of all domestic exports by value. Exports of potatoes alone were worth £C19.4 million, well above pre-1974 levels. Neither production nor sales were as successful again in subsequent years, though, after a bad year in 1978, total fruit and vegetable exports recovered to £C36.2 million in 1979. This revival was not due to potatoes, which brought in £C13.6 million, well below the 1977 peak, but to the steady growth of citrus fruit and grape exports. Between 1976 and 1979, citrus exports rose from £C5.1 million to £C8.8 million, while exports of grapes increased from £C2.8 million to £C4.8 million. Wine production also grew substantially. This trend continued through to 1981, by which year citrus exports had risen to £C11.0 million and grape exports to £C6.3 million, although potatoes were

still the largest single agricultural export at £C16.1 million. Exports from the sector as a whole fell to £C33.8 million in 1980, but recovered to £C42.4 million in 1981. Underlying this pparent fluctuation was a steady decline in the relative importance of agricultural exports, from 28.4 per cent of total exports in 1979 to 21.9 per cent in 1981.

The largest irrigation scheme currently being implemented is the Paphos project, which will irrigate about 5,000 hectares along the coast at a cost of $62 million, of which the World Bank is contributing $23 million. Additional income from the development is expected to be $10 million a year. Crops planned for the area include tropical fruits such as mango, avocado and papaya as well as grapes and early vegetables.

The Turkish Cypriot north inherited about 80 per cent of the island's citrus groves, all the tobacco fields, 40 per cent of the carobs, 80 per cent of carrots and 10–15 per cent of potatoes. Yet since 1974 agriculture in the north has lagged behind that of the south. In the chaos which followed the fighting, many citrus trees were neglected and died, or contracted diseases. Production has very slowly been restarted, with exports of citrus fruit rising from 66,174 metric tons in 1976/77 to 96,637 tons in 1980. Quantities of potatoes, carobs and tobacco are also exported.

INDUSTRY

Industry, also, was severely affected by the war of 1974. It was estimated that the Greek Cypriots lost 70 per cent of gross domestic manufacturing output, yet the growth of this sector since 1975 has been spectacular. Government incentives for investment, combined with a drop in real wages, stimulated a rapid expansion of manufacturing industry, especially in small scale labour-intensive plants producing for export. The share of manufacturing exports in total exports increased from around 40 per cent in 1975 to over 62 per cent in 1981. The most striking success was in clothing and footwear, with exports by value rising from £C3.2 million in 1974 to £C55.8 million in 1981. Cement production rose from 338,000 metric tons in 1974 to 1.2 million metric tons in 1980. Cement exports increased from £C500,000 in 1974 to £C12.8 million in 1981. Other successful products include paperboard, transport equipment, cigarettes, processed foodstuffs and wine. Total manufactured exports for 1981 were worth £C121.1 million.

Construction expanded even more rapidly than manufacturing, with an average growth rate of 40 per cent annually from 1975 to 1979. This was largely a result of the need to house the influx of refugees and of government development projects, including the building of new tourist facilities. Manufacturing and construction together accounted for 28 per cent of GDP in 1979, compared with 21 per cent in 1975. Both continued to grow through 1980 despite the adverse effect of government measures to deflate the economy and the accumulated impact of several years' wage inflation.

Although the labour market has loosened somewhat since 1980, Cyprus still suffers from a shortage of skilled labour. In the early years after 1974, the Government encouraged the temporary emigration of workers as a solution to unemployment. Now the emphasis is more on encouraging workers to return, although their remittances are still vital to Cyprus's foreign reserves. At the end of 1981 about 10,500 Greek Cypriots were employed abroad, sending back some £C20 million per year.

The Turkish-occupied area has few industrial resources. It is estimated that 90 per cent of Cyprus's mining operations are in the Greek sector while the Turkish sector has no petroleum refinery and no power stations. The Cyprus Electrical Authority supplies to both sectors and the Turkish north's debt for unbilled consumption amounts to about £C8 million per year.

TRADE, TOURISM AND COMMUNICATIONS

Cyprus has experienced a trade deficit for many years, but in 1977 the trade deficit widened to £C124.3 million, 74 per cent up on the previous year, and in 1978 it grew to £C154.3 million. In 1979 both exports and imports exceeded the growth target of the Emergency Action Plan 1979–81 but the deficit increased further to £C196 million. Imports of fuel and raw materials increased, partly due to rising prices, but the value of imports of capital goods fell because of a slackening in investment.In 1981 a continuing increase in the value of petroleum imports (up 34 per cent to £C105 million) helped to produce a record visible deficit of £C274 million. The country's trade deficit is normally at least partly offset by a surplus in the invisible balance. Tourism is an especially important source of invisible earnings (£C102 million in 1981).

Since 1975 the Middle East has developed as the major market for Greek Cypriot exports, chiefly Lebanon, Syria, the Arabian peninsula and Libya. Between them, Arab countries took 51 per cent of the state's total exports in 1981, including by far the greater part of manufactured goods. The majority of agricultural exports go to the EEC (29 per cent of total exports in 1981), which is also Cyprus's main import supplier (49 per cent of total imports in 1981).

The United Kingdom is the single main trading partner of both the Government-controlled and the Turkish-occupied areas. In recent years, however, Cyprus's trade, notably in wine and fruit and vegetables, has been threatened by EEC regulations restricting their import into the United Kingdom. Cyprus's association agreement with the EEC, which came into force in 1973, did not prove altogether satisfactory from Cyprus's point of view. The EEC fixed a 28 per cent duty and an increase in the fixed price of the Cypriot grape crop. The situation was further aggravated in 1980 by Spain's proposed entry to the EEC, with attendant worries over the position of Cyprus sherry exports.

Cyprus is, however, pressing for easier access to the markets in developed countries, maintaining that the amounts involved would not seriously affect EEC trade. There has also been a dispute with the EEC over the recognition of the Turkish north in trade agreements. Customs union with the EEC was proposed for 1981 but this clearly cannot take place until the overall political question is settled. The Government in Nicosia is in a position to effect a boycott of the north by shipping lines and airlines so that the Turkish Cypriots cannot export the full EEC quota of produce. Meanwhile, Cyprus's association agreement with the EEC has been extended.

The Turkish sector's main exports are citrus fruit, potatoes and tobacco, the principal markets being the United Kingdom and Turkey. Exports in 1980 totalled TL 3,345 million, compared with TL 744 million in 1978. Imports were TL 7,086 million (TL 2,071 million in 1978). The foreign exchange deficit was expected to decrease in 1980 to TL 116.9 million from TL 315 million in 1979, due to encouragement of tourism and increasing exports to diversified markets.

Tourism was one of the areas of the economy hardest hit by the 1974 war as 90 per cent of the hotels fell into Turkish hands. Following the introduction of a government loan plan, however, the number of hotel beds increased from a low point of 3,880 in 1975 to 15,382 in 1981. Tourist receipts rose to £C50.1 million in 1979, with 297,013 visitors. In 1980 the sector continued to expand, 353,375 visitors providing receipts of £C71 million, but in 1981 all records were broken, with 429,810 visitors and receipts of £C102 million. Some 20 new hotels are planned, including five 500-bed hotels for Larnaca, as well as large-scale tourist development of the city and its surroundings. In addition, the proposed building of a civil airpot at Akhelia, near Paphos, would open up the west of the island to tourism and provide transport for local produce.

Tourism in the north has also expanded, giving rise to a shortage of hotel beds. The best hotels still exist in the Turkish sector but most remained unused and derelict after the invasion, although some were reported to have been taken over, much against the will of the Greek Cypriot owners. In 1979 income from tourism totalled TL 2,450 million, from 13,646 visitors. There were 14,703 tourist visits in 1980.

Famagusta used to handle 83 per cent of Cyprus's cargoes but, now that it is in Turkish hands, its place has been largely taken by Larnaca and Limassol. In 1977, 26,539 containers passed through Limassol, compared with 17,084 in 1976. Port development schemes for Larnaca and Limassol will cost $51 million, and a new port is also planned for Paphos. There has been a suggestion that Cyprus should be used as an entrepôt for distributing food supplies to Saudi Arabia and the Gulf states. Cyprus has to some extent benefited from the paralysis of Beirut, although none of its ports has the capacity of Beirut.

PROSPECTS

The political situation poses great problems for the future of the Cyprus economy. By April 1982 there were few indications of a political settlement being reached. One of the obstacles is the question of equal representation to the EEC. Another is Turkish anxiety over Greek Cypriot pressure on tour operators to prevent their booking holidays in northern Cyprus.

There have been some efforts to improve relations between the two communities. Pensions frozen since 1974 are to be paid to Turkish Cypriots. Turkish Cypriots will also be allowed to work in certain government-controlled areas and to attend state institutions. Meanwhile both sides are going ahead with their own plans for development.

STATISTICAL SURVEY

Note: The figures in this survey have been provided by the Department of Statistics and Research at the Ministry of Finance in Nicosia. Since July 1974 the northern part of Cyprus has been under Turkish occupation, so some of the statistics relating to subsequent periods may not cover the whole island. Some separate figures for the "TFSC" are given on page 318-9.

AREA AND POPULATION

AREA	POPULATION†						
	Census Results		Mid-Year Estimates				
	Dec. 11th, 1960	April 1st, 1973	1974	1977	1979†	1980	1981‡
9,251 sq. km.*	573,566	631,778	640,700	613,100	621,000	628,500	637,100

* 3,572 sq. miles.
† Excluding tourists and persons living in bases and other areas retained by the United Kingdom after independence.
‡ Provisional.

ETHNIC GROUPS
('000 persons at mid-year)

	1973	1979	1980
Greeks . . .	498.5	501.2	507.3
Turks . . .	116.0	116.5	117.9
Others . . .	17.3	3.3	3.3
TOTAL . .	631.8	621.0	628.5

PRINCIPAL TOWNS
(estimated population, December 31st, 1981)

Nicosia (capital)*	. 125,100	Larnaca	. 34,700
Limassol	. 105,200	Paphos	. 11,500
Famagusta†	. 39,400	Kyrenia†	. 3,900

* Excluding Turkish-occupied part of Nicosia.
† Estimated population at mid-1974.

BIRTHS AND DEATHS
(Government-controlled area only)

	BIRTH RATE (per '000)	DEATH RATE (per '000)
1977	18.4	9.0
1978	19.3	8.4
1979	20.5	8.3
1980	21.7	9.1
1981*	20.6	8.4

* Provisional.

ECONOMICALLY ACTIVE POPULATION
(Government-controlled area only)

	1978	1979	1980	1981
Agriculture, hunting, forestry and fishing .	44,483	44,660	44,541	44,400
Mining and quarrying	2,020	1,781	1,735	1,507
Manufacturing	36,795	38,330	38,514	38,912
Electricity, gas and water . . .	1,355	1,411	1,460	1,475
Construction	17,430	18,668	18,048	16,758
Commerce	21,311	22,135	23,178	23,400
Transport, storage and communications .	7,799	7,961	8,246	8,345
Community, social and personal services .	42,765	43,986	45,411	46,193
Others (unemployed, National Guard, working abroad)	28,380	27,368	26,986	28,437
TOTAL	202,338	206,300	208,119	209,419

AGRICULTURE

PRINCIPAL CROPS
(Government-controlled area, 'ooo tons)

	1979	1980	1981*
Wheat . . .	13	13	12
Barley . . .	63	80	71
Potatoes . . .	170	188	176
Carrots . . .	9	7	9
Carobs . . .	18	13	20
Olives . . .	10	15	10
Grapes . . .	200	205	210
Oranges . . .	36	32	39
Grapefruit . . .	46	47	50
Lemons . . .	16	17	17

* Provisional.

LIVESTOCK
('ooo head in December each year)

	1973	1979*	1980*	1981*
Cattle . .	33	22	24	26
Sheep . .	430	295	300	310
Goats . .	340	220	223	225
Pigs . .	163	148	173	180
Chickens . .	3,085	2,200	2,200	2,200

* Figures cover Government-controlled area only.

Fishing (Government-controlled area, metric tons, live weight): Total catch 1,083 in 1976; 1,190 in 1977; 1,245 in 1978; 1,283 in 1979; 1,306 in 1980.

MINING

EXPORTS
(Government-controlled area, metric tons)

	1978	1979	1980	1981
Asbestos	28,875	38,489	29,965	29,081
Chromite	10,972	10,530	7,382	10,689
Cupreous concentrates . . .	25,811	12,108	812	—
Iron pyrites	121,718	140,962	88,028	35,670
Gypsum, calcined . . .	2,646	4,394	5,519	5,185
Gypsum (stones) . . .	4,928	5,094	2,500	506
Terra umbra	10,189	9,943	5,919	8,085
Yellow ochre	305	276	189	217
Other minerals . . .	6,945	6,792	23,766	26,852

INDUSTRY

SELECTED PRODUCTS

(Government-controlled area only)

		1978	1979	1980	1981
Cement	'ooo metric tons	1,107.0	1,153.7	1,233.1	1,035.8
Bricks	million	35.7	47.9	52.8	48.2
Mosaic tiles	'ooo sq. metres	1,155	1,393	1,504.0	1,484.0
Cigarettes	million	2,896.0	2,855.2	2,901.0	3,320.4
Shoes*	'ooo pairs	4,730	5,153	5,725.0	6,800.0
Beer	million litres	15.2	17.4	18.1	19.8
Wines	,, ,,	39.4	41.6	37.4	42.3
Intoxicating liquors . . .	,, ,,	2.9	2.9	3.0	3.1

* Excluding plastic and semi-finished shoes.

FINANCE

1,000 mils = 1 Cyprus pound.

Coins: 1, 3, 5, 25, 50, 100 and 500 mils; 1 pound.

Notes: 250 and 500 mils; 1, 5 and 10 pounds.

Exchange rates (May 1982): £1 sterling = 840.7 mils; U.S. $1 = 457.3 mils.

Cyprus £100 = £118.94 sterling = $218.68.

Note: From November 1967 to August 1971 the par value of the Cyprus pound was U.S. $2.40 ($1 = 416.7 mils). Between December 1971 and February 1973 the Cyprus pound was valued at U.S. $2.6057 ($1 = 383.8 mils). From February to July 1973 the exchange rate was Cyprus £1 = U.S. $2.8952 ($1 = 345.4 mils). The Cyprus pound was at par with the pound sterling until the latter was allowed to "float" in June 1972; and it has itself been "floating" since July 1973. The average mid-point market value of the Cyprus pound was $2.861 in 1973; $2.743 in 1974; $2.716 in 1975; $2.437 in 1976; $2.451 in 1977; $2.680 in 1978; $2.822 in 1979; $2.834 in 1980; $2.383 in 1981.

BUDGET ESTIMATES, 1981

(Government-controlled area, Cyprus £)

REVENUE		EXPENDITURE	
Direct taxes	54,780,000	Agriculture and forests . . .	3,770,124
Indirect taxes	81,323,600	Water development	1,416,218
Sale of goods and services . .	9,719,355	Public works	1,649,041
Interest, dividends, rents and royalties .	9,899,100	Cyprus army and Tripartite Agreement	2,826,774
Transfers	7,648,400	Customs and excise . . .	7,588,248
Greek Government grants . .	10,100,000	Public debt charges . . .	20,692,492
Loan proceeds . . .	7,386,000	Pensions and grants . . .	6,068,030
Other	1,532,270	Medical	12,641,067
		Police	14,271,067
		Subsidies, subventions and contributions	30,433,088
		Education grants . . .	25,458,346
		Other	43,061,390
TOTAL	182,388,725	TOTAL	169,875,885

DEVELOPMENT BUDGET
(Government-controlled area, Cyprus £)

	1977	1978	1979	1980	1981
Water development . .	2,593,099	4,703,000	8,323,613	7,700,000	7,058,348
Road network . . .	1,648,196	1,988,163	4,949,659	5,800,000	6,910,000
Harbours . . .	3,157	39,974	5,263	5,000	10,000
Agriculture . . .	3,067,730	3,434,266	3,910,530	4,595,000	4,931,252
Commerce and industry . .	948,034	1,384,257	2,260,078	1,600,000	1,287,980
Airports . . .	704,508	908,836	589,492	800,000	3,267,700

1981 Development Budget: Total proposed expenditure £34,339,000.

INTERNATIONAL RESERVES
(U.S. $ million at December 31st)

	1975	1976	1977	1978	1979	1980	1981
Gold	15.9	15.2	16.8	19.0	20.8	19.7	16.7
IMF Special Drawing Rights	11.8	9.2	6.2	2.2	13.0	8.3	4.0
Reserve position in IMF	—	—	—	8.5	8.0	—	—
Foreign exchange . .	185.9	265.3	307.3	335.0	332.0	360.0	420.7
TOTAL . .	213.6	289.7	330.3	364.7	373.8	388.0	441.4

MONEY SUPPLY
(Government-controlled area, Cyprus £ million at December 31st)

	1975	1976	1977	1978	1979	1980	1981
Currency outside banks .	35.2	40.8	44.7	52.7	64.0	75.9	89.5
Demand deposits at deposit money banks . .	28.4	41.7	42.8	49.6	65.5	77.4	98.8
TOTAL MONEY .	63.6	82.5	87.5	102.3	129.5	153.3	188.3

COST OF LIVING
(Government-controlled area only)
RETAIL PRICE INDEX
(base: 1973 = 100)

	1977	1978	1979	1980	1981
All items . .	135.21	145.25	159.00	180.47	199.90
Food and drink .	145.95	154.21	164.62	188.60	210.24
Rent . .	104.52	113.32	125.49	138.70	148.98
Fuel and light . .	160.37	171.00	194.37	266.76	349.97
Household equipment .	137.65	149.75	162.69	178.21	189.93
Household operations .	162.08	165.96	175.06	199.82	223.65
Clothing and footwear .	127.56	138.49	152.28	166.00	178.76
Miscellaneous .	142.80	154.61	172.29	198.24	222.20

NATIONAL ACCOUNTS
(Government-controlled area, Cyprus £ million at current prices)

	1977	1978	1979	1980
GROSS DOMESTIC PRODUCT AT FACTOR COST .	390.2	464.8	576.0	695.0
of which:				
Agriculture, etc. .	56.4	56.2	65.7	74.3
Manufacturing .	70.3	85.4	102.0	124.6
Construction .	41.5	59.4	81.5	100.1
Wholesale and retail trade .	66.3	76.1	91.6	105.5
Income from abroad .	18.8	20.5	22.2	25.3
GROSS NATIONAL INCOME .	443.5	530.1	646.1	767.7
Less depreciation allowances .	44.4	53.0	64.6	76.8
NET NATIONAL INCOME .	399.1	477.1	581.5	690.9
Indirect taxes less subsidies .	34.5	44.8	47.9	47.4
NET NATIONAL PRODUCT AT FACTOR COST .	364.6	432.3	533.6	643.5
Depreciation allowances .	44.4	53.0	64.6	76.8
GROSS NATIONAL PRODUCT AT FACTOR COST .	409.0	485.3	598.2	720.3
Balance of exports and imports of goods and services, and borrowing .	84.4	104.3	120.2	132.1
AVAILABLE RESOURCES .	493.4	589.6	718.4	852.4
of which:				
Private consumption expenditure .	305.0	357.7	418.8	497.4
Government consumption expenditure .	62.2	68.1	87.8	107.6
Gross fixed capital formation .	122.6	170.9	219.8	255.4
Increase in stocks .	19.3	17.2	17.7	14.1

BALANCE OF PAYMENTS
(Government-controlled area, Cyprus £ million)

	1976	1977	1978	1979	1980
Exports f.o.b. .	102.7	124.2	122.0	149.5	172.7
Imports f.o.b. .	−163.3	−288.1	−255.4	−321.2	−381.0
TRADE BALANCE .	−60.6	−103.9	−133.4	−171.7	−208.3
Invisible Receipts .	112.1	137.5	150.4	195.1	241.9
Invisible Payments .	−55.7	−69.5	−75.6	−96.0	−114.7
Invisible Balance .	56.4	68.0	74.8	99.1	127.4
CURRENT ACCOUNT BALANCE .	−4.2	−35.9	−58.6	−72.6	−80.9
Short-term Capital .	−5.2	0.9	3.2	8.6	2.0
Long-term Loans .	12.4	17.9	32.5	20.2	47.2
Other Long-term Capital .	13.3	16.9	21.3	25.0	30.0
Net Capital Movement .	20.5	35.7	57.0	53.8	79.2
Net Errors and Omissions .	1.5	2.4	5.5	7.4	5.2
OVERALL BALANCE (minus=increase) .	−17.8	−2.2	−3.9	11.4	−3.5

EXTERNAL TRADE*
(Cyprus £'000)

	1974	1975	1976	1977	1978	1979	1980	1981
Imports c.i.f.† .	148,028	113,709	177,763	254,008	282,686	357,603	424,292	489,536
Exports f.o.b. .	55,287	56,012	106,332	129,751	128,370	161,871	188,036	234,773

* Since July 1974 figures cover the Government-controlled area only.

† Excluding NAAFI imports, imports of military stores and, beginning in 1979, imports by embassies and other foreign organizations. Figures include imports of non-monetary gold (Cyprus £'000): 213 in 1974; 684 in 1975; 905 in 1976; 1,200 in 1977; 1,845 in 1978; 2,707 in 1979; 2,355 in 1980; 3,440 in 1981.

PRINCIPAL COMMODITIES
(distribution by SITC, Cyprus £'000)

CIVIL IMPORTS c.i.f.	1978	1979	1980	1981
Food and live animals	34,777	42,435	50,507	66,581
Cereals and cereal preparations . .	11,845	15,967	17,965	30,540
Sorghum (unmilled) . . .	2,374	2,312	5,341	9,895
Crude materials (inedible) except fuels .	6,007	8,148	8,584	10,490
Mineral fuels, lubricants, etc. . .	30,979	44,464	78,540	105,360
Petroleum and petroleum products .	30,099	43,339	76,104	102,560
Crude petroleum oils, etc. . .	17,785	23,493	47,342	66,921
Refined petroleum products . .	12,314	19,590	28,438	35,335
Residual fuel oils . . .	8,524	10,639	19,634	24,423
Chemicals	19,193	28,843	31,012	34,460
Plastic materials, etc. . . .	6,014	10,334	10,077	10,747
Basic manufactures	76,329	105,011	113,953	127,443
Paper, paperboard and manufactures .	8,940	10,869	14,978	17,483
Textile yarn, fabrics, etc. . .	25,091	31,623	37,156	42,278
Woven textile fabrics (excl. narrow or special fabrics)	15,457	13,290	20,449	21,644
Non-metallic mineral manufactures .	7,167	9,104	10,429	12,836
Iron and steel	12,809	23,157	17,122	17,814
Bars, rods, angles, shapes, etc. .	7,004	14,289	9,006	8,503
Bars and rods (excl. wire rod) .	6,206	13,395	7,351	7,098
Machinery and transport equipment .	76,608	83,673	95,412	93,434
Specialized machinery . . .	14,673	14,752	16,039	11,726
General industrial machinery, etc. .	10,445	13,013	13,404	12,742
Telecommunications and recording equipment	4,281	8,783	10,252	17,097
Other electrical machinery, apparatus, etc. .	8,216	11,997	14,903	15,732
Transport equipment . . .	32,601	27,923	34,411	27,903
Road vehicles and parts . .	21,661	24,404	32,227	27,688
Passenger motor cars (excl. buses) .	11,914	13,589	15,182	11,482
Aircraft and parts . . .	10,872	3,184	1,896	16
Miscellaneous manufactured articles .	22,277	29,888	32,406	34,168
TOTAL (incl. others) . . .	282,686	357,603	424,292	489,536

EXPORTS f.o.b.*	1978	1979	1980	1981
Food and live animals	32,754	40,464	41,301	50,642
Vegetables and fruit . . .	29,283	36,208	34,767	41,812
Fresh or simply preserved vegetables .	15,071	18,317	17,103	20,838
Fresh potatoes . . .	10,772	13,624	12,686	16,064
Fresh or dried fruit and nuts . .	11,401	14,415	14,821	17,866
Citrus fruit	6,701	8,851	8,227	11,045
Grapes	4,005	4,887	5,947	6,257
Beverages and tobacco . . .	13,904	14,329	15,705	19,668
Beverages	7,945	8,567	8,692	10,809
Alcoholic beverages . . .	6,440	7,981	8,068	10,315
Wine (incl. grape must) . .	5,778	6,717	6,459	7,814
Wine of fresh grapes . .	4,982	4,958	4,850	6,303
Tobacco and tobacco manufactures .	5,959	5,762	7,013	8,860
Cigarettes	5,915	5,705	6,983	8,834
Crude materials (inedible) except fuels .	8,834	10,400	9,962	11,942
Crude fertilizers and crude minerals .	4,984	6,987	6,843	8,221
Basic manufactures	15,643	20,044	25,238	31,260
Paper, paperboard and manufactures .	2,959	5,218	6,767	9,788
Packaging containers . . .	2,823	5,046	6,503	9,074
Non-metallic mineral manufactures .	8,807	10,474	13,637	13,760
Lime, cement, etc. . . .	8,488	10,355	13,441	13,315
Cement	8,474	10,291	13,147	12,832
Machinery and transport equipment .	2,823	3,334	4,218	6,716
Miscellaneous manufactured articles .	26,738	36,340	46,203	64,678
Clothing (excl. footwear) . . .	16,322	22,111	27,937	39,507
Footwear	7,104	8,342	11,663	16,287
TOTAL (incl. others) . . .	103,575	127,644	148,485	193,298

* Excluding re-exports (Cyprus £'000): 20,071 in 1978; 23,723 in 1979; 25,916 in 1980; 22,934 in 1981. Also excluded are stores for ships and aircraft (Cyprus £'000): 4,724 in 1978; 10,504 in 1979; 13,634 in 1980; 18,541 in 1981.

PRINCIPAL TRADING PARTNERS*
(Cyprus £'000)

IMPORTS c.i.f.	1979	1980	1981	EXPORTS f.o.b.†	1979	1980	1981
Algeria . . .	3	328	11,380	Bahrain . . .	1,808	2,435	2,971
Austria . . .	6,039	5,552	9,775	Belgium/Luxembourg .	1,265	1,852	2,732
Belgium/Luxembourg .	8,014	6,454	7,033	Egypt . . .	2,697	3,110	5,679
Canada . . .	5,944	1,315	1,049	Germany, Fed. Republic	3,713	4,837	7,900
France . . .	17,979	18,817	24,305	Greece . . .	3,986	4,763	5,643
Germany, Fed. Republic	28,042	32,051	35,085	Iraq . . .	2,957	3,649	14,914
Greece . . .	26,655	29,831	38,179	Jordan . . .	2,938	3,423	4,825
Iraq . . .	23,495	42,998	32,479	Kuwait . . .	6,334	6,671	6,701
Israel . . .	6,226	9,225	8,695	Lebanon . . .	15,092	18,660	15,024
Italy . . .	41,783	45,807	47,324	Libya . . .	8,217	15,514	22,840
Japan . . .	18,330	29,885	33,701	Netherlands . .	2,013	2,523	3,033
Libya . . .	387	112	11,420	Nigeria . . .	4,587	2,106	1,533
Netherlands . .	7,346	8,914	12,500	Saudi Arabia . .	12,032	14,411	19,688
Saudi Arabia . .	15	4,349	8,959	Syria . . .	10,785	12,694	11,705
Spain . . .	9,211	7,243	7,515	U.S.S.R. . . .	3,483	7,163	9,979
Sweden . . .	4,961	4,958	5,963	United Arab Emirates .	3,539	5,001	7,476
U.S.S.R. . . .	12,411	16,883	16,138	United Kingdom . .	41,159	38,964	44,188
United Kingdom .	60,609	65,480	69,485	U.S.A. . . .	2,199	2,462	2,337
U.S.A. . . .	19,475	25,302	35,792	Yemen Arab Republic .	1,634	4,136	4,565
TOTAL (incl. others)	357,603	424,292	489,536	**TOTAL (incl. others)**	151,108	174,130	215,777

* Imports by country of production; exports by country of consignment.
† Excluding stores for ships and aircraft (Cyprus £'000): 10,504 in 1979; 13,634 in 1980; 18,541 in 1981. Also excluded are unspecified items sent by parcel post (Cyprus £'000): 259 in 1979; 271 in 1980; 455 in 1981.

TRANSPORT
ROAD TRAFFIC
(motor vehicles in use, Government-controlled area only*)

	1978	1979	1980	1981
Cars . . .	78,157	85,054	90,936	94,597
Taxis & self-drive cars . .	2,642	3,038	3,119	3,253
Lorries & buses .	20,033	22,404	25,894	28,532
Motor cycles .	14,243	19,562	31,173	35,905
Tractors, etc. . .	6,053	6,365	6,661	6,735
TOTAL .	121,128	136,423	157,783	169,022

* Including vehicles no longer in circulation.

SHIPPING
(Government-controlled area only)

	1978	1979	1980	1981
Vessels* entered ('000 net reg. tons) . .	5,675	6,168	5,743	6,489
Goods loaded ('000 tons)† . . .	1,343	1,463	1,592	1,544
Goods unloaded ('000 tons)† . . .	1,774	2,063	2,141	2,298

* Steam or motor vessels and sailing vessels.
† Excluding goods loaded and unloaded at Larnaca Airport.

CIVIL AVIATION
CYPRUS AIRWAYS

	1978	1979	1980	1981
Kilometres flown . . .	7,407,000	8,191,000	9,466,000	8,693,000
Passenger arrivals . . .	296,900	368,414	457,499	536,291
Passenger departures . .	294,656	381,428	454,504	533,677
Freight landed (tons) . .	4,049	6,000	5,213	4,401
Freight cleared (tons) . .	19,786	22,959	19,154	19,316

TOURISM
FOREIGN VISITORS BY COUNTRY OF ORIGIN*

	1977†	1978†	1979†	1980†	1981†
Greece	22,376	25,518	33,649	33,586	27,850
Israel	4,408	5,340	4,907	4,985	5,188
Lebanon	26,307	25,866	26,295	22,704	31,381
United Kingdom . .	55,565	74,593	106,287	111,359	129,051
U.S.A.	7,477	7,049	7,909	7,322	8,076
TOTAL (incl. others) .	178,185	216,679	297,013	353,375	429,313

* Excluding one-day visitors. † Excluding visitors to the Turkish-occupied zone.

Tourist earnings: (1978) C£33.3m.; (1979) C£50.1m.; (1980) C£70.5m.; (1981) C£102.4m.

Number of hotel beds: (1978) 6,032; (1979) 7,858; (1980) 8,571; (1981) 10,854.

Number of tourist nights: (1977) 677,709; (1978) 930,716; (1979) 1,369,839; (1980) 1,620,111.

EDUCATION
GREEK
(1981/82)

	ESTABLISH-MENTS	TEACHERS	PUPILS
Pre-Primary (state and private schools) .	281	451	11,541
Primary	438	2,192	46,095
Secondary (public) . . .	66	2,192	38,709
Secondary (private) . . .	20	320	4,629
Technical and vocational (public) .	12	495	5,543
Teacher training . . .	1	13	102
Other post-secondary . . .	12	186	1,875

Source: Department of Statistics and Research, Ministry of Finance, Nicosia.

"TURKISH FEDERATED STATE OF CYPRUS"

Population: 150,283 (1980 estimate, based on 1978 agricultural census).

Finance: Turkish currency (*q.v.*) is in use.

BUDGET, March 1st–December 31st, 1982
(Turkish liras)

REVENUE		EXPENDITURE	
Local taxes	4,600,000,000	Personnel	3,668,183,520
Local loans	3,027,452,581	Other current expenditure . .	1,077,678,000
Foreign aid	3,290,204,000	Investment	2,253,050,000
		Transfers	3,180,745,061
		Defence	738,000,000
TOTAL . .	10,917,656,581	TOTAL . .	10,917,656,581

EXTERNAL TRADE

Principal exports (**1980**)**:** Citrus fruit (first and second grade metric tons) 96,637; potatoes (first and second grade, metric tons) 10,354; carobs (first and second grade metric tons) 4,304; tobacco (first and second grade, metric tons) 106. Citrus fruit exports were 87,991 metric tons in 1977/78 and 92,000 metric tons in 1978/79.

1981 ('ooo Turkish liras): Imports 11,969,900; Exports 4,168,000.

PRINCIPAL TRADING PARTNERS
('ooo Turkish liras)

IMPORTS	1980	1981	EXPORTS	1980	1981
Germany, Federal Republic	484,692	482,200	Germany, Federal Republic	43,241	44,100
Italy	392,433	424,000	Italy	53,211	54,500
Turkey	3,115,159	2,796,700	Lebanon	38,116	67,400
United Kingdom .	1,608,860	1,389,900	Turkey	459,037	539,800
			United Kingdom .	2,469,568	1,526,500
TOTAL (incl. others) .	7,086,008	6,728,100	TOTAL (incl. others) .	3,345,262	2,774,000

Tourism: Visitors from mainland Turkey: (1978) 104,738; (1979) 95,115; (1980) 69,808; (1981) 62,660. Visitors from other countries: (1978) 8,172; (1979) 13,646; (1980) 14,703; (1981) 15,474.

EDUCATION
(1981/82)

	ESTABLISH-MENTS	TEACHERS	PUPILS
Nursery schools	6	20	668
Nursery classes	12	15	573
(attached to a primary school)			
TOTAL	18	35	1,241
Primary	166	670	18,179
Junior secondary (independent) .	9	112	2,140
Junior secondary (attached to a lyceé) .	10	458*	4,951
Junior secondary (attached to a technical school)	1	246†	370
Secondary education	11	458	3,407
Technical school	8	246	1,824
Adult education	51	82	1,981
Turkish teachers' training college .	1	7	135
Higher technical institute . .	1	25	266

Source: Office of the London Representative of the "Turkish Federated State of Cyprus".

* Including secondary school teachers.   † Including technical school teachers.

THE CONSTITUTION

The Constitution entered into force on August 16th, 1960, on which date Cyprus became an independent republic. In March 1961 Cyprus was accepted as a member of the Commonwealth.

ARTICLE I

The State of Cyprus is an independent and sovereign Republic with a presidential regime, the President being Greek and the Vice-President being Turkish, elected by the Greek and the Turkish Communities of Cyprus respectively as hereinafter in this Constitution provided.

ARTICLES 2–5

The Greek Community comprises all citizens of the Republic who are of Greek origin and whose mother tongue is Greek or who share the Greek cultural traditions or who are members of the Greek Orthodox Church.

The Turkish Community comprises all citizens of the Republic who are of Turkish origin and whose mother tongue is Turkish or who share the Turkish cultural traditions or who are Moslems.

Citizens of the Republic who do not come within the above provisions shall, within three months of the date of the coming into operation of this Constitution, opt to belong to either the Greek or the Turkish Community as individuals, but, if they belong to a religious group, shall opt as a religious group and upon such option they shall be deemed to be members of such Community.

The official languages of the Republic are Greek and Turkish.

The Republic shall have its own flag of neutral design and colour, chosen jointly by the President and the Vice-President of the Republic.

The Greek and the Turkish Communities shall have the right to celebrate respectively the Greek and the Turkish national holidays.

ARTICLES 6–35
Fundamental Rights and Liberties

ARTICLES 36–53
President and Vice-President

The President of the Republic as Head of the State represents the Republic in all its official functions; signs the credentials of diplomatic envoys and receives the credentials of foreign diplomatic envoys; signs the credentials of delegates for the negotiation of international treaties, conventions or other agreements; signs the letter relating to the transmission of the instruments of ratification of any international treaties, conventions or agreements; confers the honours of the Republic.

The Vice-President of the Republic as Vice-Head of the State has the right to be present at all official functions; at the presentation of the credentials of foreign diplomatic envoys; to recommend to the President the conferment of honours on members of the Turkish Community which recommendation the President shall accept unless there are grave reasons to the contrary. The honours so conferred will be presented to the recipient by the Vice-President if he so desires.

The election of the President and the Vice-President of the Republic shall be direct, by universal suffrage and secret ballot, and shall, except in the case of a by-election, take place on the same day but separately.

The office of the President and of the Vice-President shall be incompatible with that of a Minister or of a Representative or of a member of a Communal Chamber or of a member of any municipal council including a Mayor or of a member of the armed or security forces of the Republic or with a public or municipal office.

The President and Vice-President of the Republic are invested by the House of Representatives.

The President and the Vice-President shall hold office for a period of five years.

The Executive power is ensured by the President and the Vice-President of the Republic.

The President and the Vice-President of the Republic in order to ensure the executive power shall have a Council of Ministers composed of seven Greek Ministers and three Turkish Ministers. The Ministers shall be designated respectively by the President and the Vice-President of the Republic who shall appoint them by an instrument signed by them both.

The decisions of the Council of Ministers shall be taken by an absolute majority and shall, unless the right of final veto or return is exercised by the President or the Vice-President of the Republic or both, be promulgated immediately by them.

The executive power exercised by the President and the Vice-President of the Republic conjointly consists of:

Determining the design and colour of the flag.
Creation or establishment of honours.
Appointment of the members of the Council of Ministers.
Promulgation by publication of the decisions of the Council of Ministers.
Promulgation by publication of any law or decision passed by the House of Representatives.
Appointments and termination of appointments as in Articles provided.
Institution of compulsory military service.
Reduction or increase of the security forces.
Exercise of the prerogative of mercy in capital cases.
Remission, suspension and commutation of sentences.

Right of references to the Supreme Constitutional Court and publication of Court decisions.
Address of messages to the House of Representatives.

The executive power exercised by the President consists of:

Designation and termination of appointment of Greek Ministers.
Convening and presiding of the meetings of the Council of Ministers.
Right of final veto on Council decisions and on laws or decisions of the House of Representatives concerning foreign affairs, defence or security.
Right of recourse to the Supreme Constitutional Court.
Publication of the communal laws and decisions of the Greek Communal Chamber.
Prerogative of mercy in capital cases.
Addressing messages to the House of Representatives.

The executive power exercised by the Vice-President consists of:

Designation and termination of appointment of Turkish Ministers.
Asking the President for the convening of the Council of Ministers and being present and taking part in the discussions.
Right of final veto on Council decisions and on laws or decisions of the House of Representatives concerning foreign affairs, defence or security.
Right of recourse to the Supreme Constitutional Court.
Publication of the communal laws and decisions of the Turkish Communal Chamber.
Prerogative of mercy in capital cases.
Addressing messages to the House of Representatives.

ARTICLES 54–60
Council of Ministers

The Council of Ministers shall exercise executive power in all matters, other than those which are within the competence of a Communal Chamber, including the following:

General direction and control of the government of the Republic and the direction of general policy.
Foreign affairs, defence and security.
Co-ordination and supervision of all public services.
Supervision and disposition of property belonging to the Republic.
Consideration of Bills to be introduced to the House of Representatives by a Minister.
Making of any order or regulation for the carrying into effect of any law as provided by such law.
Consideration of the Budget of the Republic to be introduced to the House of Representatives.

ARTICLES 61–85
House of Representatives

The legislative power of the Republic shall be exercised by the House of Representatives in all matters except those expressly reserved to the Communal Chambers.

The number of Representatives shall be fifty:

Provided that such number may be altered by a resolution of the House of Representatives carried by a majority comprising two-thirds of the Representatives elected by the Greek Community and two-thirds of the Representatives elected by the Turkish Community.

Out of the number of Representatives 70 per cent shall be elected by the Greek Community and 30 per cent by the Turkish Community separately from amongst their members respectively, and, in the case of a contested election, by universal suffrage and by direct and secret ballot held on the same day.

The term of office of the House of Representatives shall be for a period of five years.

The President of the House of Representatives shall be a Greek, and shall be elected by the Representatives elected by the Greek Community, and the Vice-President shall be a Turk and shall be elected by the Representatives elected by the Turkish Community.

ARTICLES 86–111
Communal Chambers

The Greek and the Turkish Communities respectively shall elect from amongst their own members a Communal Chamber.

The Communal Chambers shall, in relation to their respective Community, have competence to exercise legislative power solely with regard to the following:

All religious, educational, cultural and teaching matters.
Personal status; composition and instances of courts dealing with civil disputes relating to personal status and to religious matters.
Imposition of personal taxes and fees on members of their respective Community in order to provide for their respective needs.

ARTICLES 112–121, 126–128
Officers of the Republic

ARTICLES 122–125
The Public Service

The public service shall be composed as to 70 per cent of Greeks and as to 30 per cent of Turks.

ARTICLES 129–132
The Forces of the Republic

The Republic shall have an army of two thousand men of whom 60 per cent shall be Greeks and 40 per cent shall be Turks.

The security forces of the Republic shall consist of the police and gendarmerie and shall have a contingent of two thousand men. The forces shall be composed as to 70 per cent of Greeks and as to 30 per cent of Turks.

ARTICLES 133–164
The Courts
(See section Judicial System)

ARTICLES 165–199
Financial, Miscellaneous, Final and Transitional Provisions

Note: The following measures have been passed by the House of Representatives since January 1964, when the Turkish members withdrew:

1. The amalgamation of the High Court and the Supreme Constitutional Court.
2. The abolition of the Greek Communal Chamber and the creation of a Ministry of Education.
3. The unification of the Municipalities.
4. The unification of the Police and the Gendarmerie.
5. The creation of a military force by providing that persons between the ages of eighteen and fifty can be called upon to serve in the National Guard.
6. The extension of the term of office of the President and the House of Representatives by one year intervals from July 1965 until elections in February 1968 and July 1970 respectively.
7. New electoral provisions; abolition of separate Greek and Turkish rolls; abolition of post of Vice-President, which was re-established in 1973.

THE GOVERNMENT*

HEAD OF STATE
President: SPYROS KYPRIANOU (took office August 3rd, 1977).

COUNCIL OF MINISTERS
(May 1982)

Minister of Foreign Affairs: NICOS A. ROLANDIS.
Minister of Finance: SIMOS VASSILIOU.
Minister to the President: STELIOS KATSELLIS.
Minister of the Interior and of Defence: CHRISTODOULOS VENIAMIN.
Minister of Agriculture and Natural Resources: DEMETRIOS CHRISTODOULOU.
Minister of Health: CHRISTOS PELEKANOS.

Minister of Education: PANOS IOANNOU.
Minister of Commerce and Industry: GEORGE ANDREOU.
Minister of Communication and Works: CHRISTOS MAVRELLIS.
Minister of Labour and Social Insurance: PAVLOS PAPAGEORGIOU.
Minister of Justice: PHEVOS CLERIDES.
Deputy Minister of the Interior: ELIAS ELIADES.

* Under the Constitution of 1960 the Vice-Presidency and three posts in the Council of Ministers are reserved for Turkish Cypriots. However, there has been no Turkish participation in the government since December 1963. In 1968 President Makarios announced that he considered the office of Vice-President in abeyance until Turkish participation in the government is resumed, but the Turkish community elected Rauf Denktaş Vice-President in February 1973.

HOUSE OF REPRESENTATIVES

The House of Representatives originally consisted of 50 members, 35 from the Greek community and 15 from the Turkish community, elected for a term of five years. In January 1964 the Turkish members withdrew and set up the "Turkish Legislative Assembly of the Turkish Cypriot Administration" (*see* pages 323–4).

President: GEORGE LADAS.

ELECTIONS FOR THE GREEK REPRESENTATIVES
(May 24th, 1981)

PARTY	SEATS	% OF VOTES
AKEL (Communist Party) .	12	32.79
Democratic Rally . . .	12	31.89
Democratic Party . .	8	19.50
EDEK (Socialist Party) .	3	8.17

Total number of seats: 35   Votes cast: 314,000.

POLITICAL PARTIES

Anorthotikon Komma Ergazomenou Laou (AKEL) (*Progressive Party of the Working People*): Akamantos St. 8, P.O.B. 1827, Nicosia; f. 1941; successor to the Communist Party of Cyprus (f. 1926); over 14,000 mems.; Gen. Sec. EZEKIAS PAPAIOANNOU; publs. *Haravghi* (daily), *Demokratia* (weekly).

Demokratiko Komma (DIKO) (*Democratic Party*): Nicosia; f. 1976; supports settlement of the Cyprus problem based on UN resolutions; Pres. SPYROS KYPRIANOU; publs. *I Eleftherotypia* (daily), *I Eleftherotypia Tis Defteras* (weekly).

Demokratikos Synagermos (DISY) (*Democratic Rally*): Nicosia; f. 1976; opposition party; absorbed Democratic National Party (DEK) in 1977; calls for more active involvement of the West in the settlement of the Cyprus problem; Pres. GLAVCOS CLERIDES.

Eniea Demokratiki Enosi Kyprou (EDEK)—Sosialistiko Komma (*Unified Democratic Union of Cyprus—Socialist Party*): Nicosia; f. 1969; the Socialist Party of Cyprus; supports independent, non-aligned, unitary, demilitarized Cyprus; stands for a socialist structure; Pres. Dr. VASSOS LYSSARIDES; publs. *Ta Nea* (daily), *O Anexartitos* (weekly).

Enosi Kentrou (E.K.) (*Centre Union*): Nicosia; f. 1981; Pres. TASSOS PAPADOPOULOS; publ. *O Kirykas* (daily).

Nea Demokratiki Parataxi (NEDIPA) (*New Democratic Camp*): Nicosia; f. 1981 by deputies from Democratic Party; Pres. ALECOS MICHAELIDES; publ. *To Vima* (weekly).

Pangiprion Ananeotikon Metopon (PAME) (*Pancyprian Renewal Front*): Nicosia; f. 1981; Pres. CHRYSOSTOMOS SOFIANOS; publ. *I Kypriaki* (weekly).

DIPLOMATIC REPRESENTATION

EMBASSIES AND HIGH COMMISSIONS ACCREDITED TO CYPRUS
(In Nicosia except where otherwise stated)
(E) Embassy; (HC) High Commission.

Algeria: Damascus, Syria (E).

Argentina: Beirut, Lebanon (E).

Australia: 4 Annis Komninis St., 2nd Floor (HC); *High Commissioner:* MARY MCPHERSON.

Austria: Athens, Greece (E).

Barbados: London, England (HC).

Belgium: Beirut, Lebanon (E).

Brazil: Tel-Aviv, Israel (E).

Bulgaria: 15 St. Paul St. (E); *Ambassador:* BOCHO V. BOCHEV.

Canada: Tel-Aviv, Israel (HC).

China, People's Republic: 27 Clementos St., P.O.B. 4531 (E); *Ambassador:* CAO ZHI.

Colombia: Tel-Aviv, Israel (E).

Cuba: 39 Regas Fereos St., Acropolis (E); *Ambassador:* FERMIN RODRÍGUEZ PAZ.

Czechoslovakia: 39 Agapinoros St. (E); *Ambassador:* JOSEF HEJC.

Denmark: Beirut, Lebanon (E).

Egypt: 3 Egypt Ave., P.O.B. 1752 (E); *Ambassador:* (vacant).

Finland: Tel-Aviv, Israel (E).

France: 6 Ploutarchou St., Engomi, P.O.B. 1671 (E); *Ambassador:* PHILIPPE OLIVIER.

German Democratic Republic: 115 Prodromos St. (E); *Ambassador:* GUENTER SCHURATH.

Germany, Federal Republic: 10 Nikitaras St., P.O.B. 1795 (E); *Ambassador:* Dr. HEINZ FRIEDRICH LANDAU.

Greece: 8/10 Byron Ave., P.O.B. 1799 (E); *Ambassador:* CHRISTOS G. ZACHARAKIS.

Hungary: Athens, Greece (E).

India: 3 Artemis St., Engomi (HC); *High Commissioner:* H. MAHAJAN.

Iraq: Beirut, Lebanon (E).

Israel: 44 Archbishop Makarios III Ave., P.O.B. 1049 (E); *Ambassador:* ZEEV Z. DOVER.

Italy: 15 Themistocli Dezvi St., P.O.B. 1452 (E); *Ambassador:* UGO TOSCANO.

Japan: Beirut, Lebanon (E).

Lebanon: 1 Queen Olga St., P.O.B. 1924 (E); *Chargé d'affaires a.i.:* ALEXANDER AMMOUN.

Libya: 9A Kypranoros St., P.O.B. 3669; *Secretary of People's Bureau:* Dr. A. ZUBEDI.

Malta: London, England (HC).

Mexico: Beirut, Lebanon (E).

Mongolia: Belgrade, Yugoslavia.

Netherlands: Beirut, Lebanon (E).

Nigeria: Athens, Greece (HC).

Norway: Tel-Aviv, Israel (E).

Pakistan: Beirut, Lebanon (E).

Poland: Athens, Greece (E).

Portugal: Beirut, Lebanon (E).

Romania: 10 Dramas St. (E); *Chargé d'affaires a.i.* MARIN ALEXIE.

Spain: Damascus, Syria (E).

Sweden: Tel-Aviv, Israel (E).

Switzerland: Tel-Aviv, Israel (E).

Syria: Corner Androcleous and Thoukidides Sts., P.O.B. 1891 (E); *Chargé d'affaires a.i.:* ANVAR SHEIKHOUNI.

Turkey: (vacant).

U.S.S.R.: 4 Gladstone St., P.O.B. 1845 (E); *Ambassador:* SERGEI T. ASTAVIN.

United Kingdom: Alexander Pallis St., P.O.B. 1978 (HC); *High Commissioner:* W. J. A. WILBERFORCE, C.M.G.

U.S.A.: Dositheon St. and Therissos St., Lycavitos (E); *Ambassador:* RAYMOND C. EWING.

Vatican: 2 Victoria Rd., P.O.B. 1964 (Apostolic Nunciature); *Apostolic Pro-Nuncio:* WILLIAM ALQUIN CAREW.

Viet-Nam: Tripoli, Libya.

Yugoslavia: 2 Vasilissis Olgas St. (E); *Ambassador:* CVIJETO JOB.

Cyprus also has diplomatic relations with the Bahamas, Burundi, Chile, Ecuador, Ethiopia, Fiji, Ghana, Grenada, Guyana, Iceland, the Ivory Coast, Kuwait, Malaysia, Morocco, Mozambique, Nepal, New Zealand, Oman, Panama, Papua New Guinea, Peru, the Philippines, Saint Lucia, Seychelles, Somalia, Sri Lanka, Sudan, Thailand, Trinidad and Tobago, Uganda, Uruguay, Zaire and Zambia.

JUDICIAL SYSTEM

Supreme Court: Nicosia.

President: Hon. Mr. Justice M. A. TRIANTAFYLLIDES.

Judges: Hon. Mr. Justice L. N. LOIZOU, Hon. Mr. Justice T. HADJIANASTASSIOU, Hon. Mr. Justice A. N. LOIZOU, Hon. Mr. Justice Y. CH. MALACHTOS, Hon. Mr. Justice D. GR. DEMETRIADES, Hon Mr. Justice L. G. SAVVIDES, Hon. Mr. Justice A. LORIS, Hon. Mr. Justice D. STYLIANIDES, Hon. Mr. Justice G. PIKIS.

The Constitution of 1960 provided for a separate Supreme Constitutional Court and High Court but in 1964, in view of the resignation of their neutral Presidents, these were amalgamated to form a single Supreme Court.

The Supreme Court is the final appellate court in the Republic and the final adjudicator in matters of constitutional and administrative law, including recourses on conflict of competence between state organs on questions of the constitutionality of laws, etc. It deals with appeals from Assize Courts and District Courts as well as from the decisions of its own judges when exercising original jurisdiction in certain matters such as prerogative orders of *habeas corpus, mandamus, certiorari*, etc., and in admiralty and certain matrimonial causes.

Assize Courts and District Courts:

As required by the Constitution a law was passed in 1960 providing for the establishment, jurisdiction and powers of courts of civil and criminal jurisdiction, i.e. of six District Courts and six Assize Courts.

Ecclesiastical Courts:

There are seven Orthodox Church tribunals having exclusive jurisdiction in matrimonial causes between members of the Greek Orthodox Church. Appeals go from these tribunals to the appellate tribunal of the Church.

Supreme Council of Judicature: Nicosia.

The Supreme Council of Judicature is composed of the Attorney-General, the President and Judges of the Supreme Court.

It is responsible for the appointment, promotion, transfer, etc., of the judges exercising civil and criminal jurisdiction in the District Courts and the Assize Courts.

"TURKISH FEDERATED STATE OF CYPRUS"

The Turkish intervention in Cyprus in July 1974 saw the establishment of a separate area in northern Cyprus under the control of the Autonomous Turkish Cypriot Administration with a Council of Ministers, and separate judicial, financial, military and educational machinery serving the Turkish community.

On February 13th, 1975, the Turkish-occupied zone of Cyprus was declared the "Turkish Federated State of Cyprus" and Rauf Denktaş elected President. At the second joint meeting held by the Executive Council and Legislative Assembly of the Autonomous Turkish Cypriot Administration it was decided to set up a Constituent Assembly which would prepare a Constitution for the "Turkish Federated State of Cyprus" within 45 days. This constitution, which was approved by the Turkish Cypriot population in a referendum held on June 8th, 1975, is regarded by the Turkish Cypriots as a first step towards a federal republic of Cyprus. The main provisions of the constitution are summarized below.

The "Turkish Federated State of Cyprus" is a democratic, secular republic based on the principles of social justice and the rule of law. It shall exercise only those functions which fall outside the powers and functions expressly given to the [proposed] Federal Republic of Cyprus. Necessary amendments shall be made to the constitution of the "Turkish Federated State of Cyprus" when the constitution of the Federal Republic comes into force. The official language is Turkish.

Legislative power is vested in a Legislative Assembly, composed of 40 deputies, elected by universal suffrage for a period of five years.

The President is Head of State and is elected by universal suffrage for a period of five years. No person may be elected President for more than two consecutive terms.

The Council of Ministers shall be composed of a Prime Minister and 10 Ministers.

Judicial power is exercised through independent courts.

Other provisions cover such matters as the rehabilitation of refugees, property rights outside the "Turkish Federated State", protection of coasts, social insurance, the rights and duties of citizens, etc.

The "Turkish Federated State of Cyprus" has neither sought nor received international recognition as an independent state, and in March 1975 the UN Security Council adopted a resolution regretting its creation.

Vice-President of the Republic and President of the "Turkish Federated State of Cyprus": RAUF R. DENKTAŞ.

CABINET

(April 1982)

Prime Minister: MUSTAFA ÇAĞATAY (NUP).

Minister of Foreign Affairs and Defence: Dr. KENAN ATAKOL (NUP).

Minister of Economy and Finance: SALIH COŞAR (NUP).

Minister of Industry and Cooperatives: İSMET KOTAK (DPP).

Minister of Agriculture, National Resources and Energy: İRSEN KÜÇÜK (NUP).

Minister of the Interior and Rehabilitation: EŞBER SERAKINCI (NUP).

Minister of Trade and Tourism: NAZIF BORMAN (NUP).

Minister of Education, Culture and Youth: AHMET ATAMSOY (DPP).

Minister of State and Social Insurance: İSMAIL TEZER (TUP).

Minister of Health and Labour: ÖZER TAHSIN (NUP).

Minister of Works and Communications: MEHMET BAYRAM (NUP).

PRESIDENTIAL ELECTION

(June 28th, 1981)

Candidates	Votes
Rauf R. Denktaş (National Unity Party) .	36,341
Ziya Rizki (Communal Liberation Party) .	21,367
Ösker Özgür (Republican Turkish Party) .	8,954
General Hüsamettin Tanyar (Democratic People's Party) .　　.　　.　　.　　.　　.	3,356

LEGISLATIVE ASSEMBLY

The forty-member Assembly replaced the former Constituent Assembly in June 1976. It is the only body empowered by the Constitution to exercise the Federated State's legislative functions. The 40 deputies are elected for a period of five years.

President: Nejat Konuk.

Vice-President: Ekrem Ural.

ELECTION (June 28th, 1981)

PARTY	SEATS
National Unity	18
Communal Liberation . . .	13
Republican Turkish . . .	6
Democratic People's . . .	2
Turkish Unity	1
TOTAL	40

POLITICAL PARTIES

Cumhuriyetçi Türk Partisi (*Republican Turkish Party*): 99A Şehit Salahi, Sevket Street, Nicosia; f. 1970 by members of the Turkish community in Cyprus; socialist principles with anti-imperialist stand; district organizations at Famagusta, Kyrenia, Morphou and Nicosia; Leader Özker Özgür.

Demokratik Halk Partisi (*Democratic People's Party*): Nicosia; f. 1979; based on social democratic principles; nationalist, revolutionist and secular; aims at bi-zonal bi-communal Federal Republic of Cyprus; Leader İsmet Kotak.

Toplumcu Kurtulus Partisi (*Communal Liberation Party*): Nicosia; f. 1976; main opposition, left of centre; based on Atatürk's reforms, social democratic principles, social justice; believes in leading role of organized labour for solution of Cyprus problem as an independent, non-aligned and bi-communal Federal state; Leader Alpay Durduran.

Türkiye Birlik Partisi (*Turkish Unity Party*): Extreme right-wing; Leader Ismail Tezer.

Ulusal Birlik Partisi (*National Unity Party*): Nicosia; f. 1975; party of Government; right of centre; based on Atatürk's reforms, social justice and peaceful coexistence in an independent, bi-zonal, federal state of Cyprus; Leader Mustafa Çaçatay; Gen. Sec. Hakki Atun.

JUDICIAL SYSTEM

Supreme Council of Judicature:

The Supreme Council of Judicature, composed of the President and Judges of the Supreme Court, a retired member of the Supreme Court, the Attorney-General of the "Turkish Federated State of Cyprus" and the elected President of the Cyprus Turkish Bar, is responsible for

the appointment, promotion, transfer, leave and discipline of all judges in accordance with the powers vested by the Constitution of the "Turkish Federated State of Cyprus". The appointment of the President and judges of the Supreme Court must be approved by the President of the "Turkish Federated State of Cyprus".

Supreme Court:

President: Hon. Mr. Justice Ülfet Emin.

Judges: Hon. Justices Şakir Sidki İlkay, Salih Dayioğlu, Ergin Salâhi, Niyazi F. Korkut, Aziz Altay.

In the areas governed by the "Turkish Federated State of Cyprus" the Supreme Court functions as the Constitutional Court, the Court of Appeal and the Supreme Administrative Court.

Subordinate Courts:

Judicial power other than that exercised by the Supreme Court is exercised by the Assize, District and Family Courts.

BRITISH SOVEREIGN BASE AREAS

AKROTIRI and DHEKELIA

Headquarters at Episkopi, British Forces Post Office 53.

Administrator: Air Vice-Marshal R. L. Davis.

Chief Officer of Administration: M. D. Tidy.

Senior Judge of Senior Judge's Court: D. M. Cowley, Q.C.

Resident Judge of Judge's Court: J. M. Long.

Under the Cyprus Act 1960, the United Kingdom retained sovereignty in two sovereign base areas and this was recognized in the Treaty of Establishment signed between the U.K., Greece, Turkey and the Republic of Cyprus in August 1960. The base areas cover 99 square miles. The Treaty also conferred on Britain certain rights within the Republic, including rights of movement and the use of specified training areas.

UNITED NATIONS PEACE-KEEPING FORCE IN CYPRUS

(UNFICYP)

Headquarters at P.O.B. 1642, Nicosia

Set up for three months in March 1964 (subsequently extended at intervals of three or six months) to keep the peace between the Greek and Turkish communities and help to solve outstanding issues between them.

Commander: Maj.-Gen. Günther G. Greindl (Austria).

Special Representative of the UN Secretary-General: Hugo Juan Gobbi (Argentina).

See page 167.

RELIGION

Greeks form 80 per cent of the population and most of them belong to the Orthodox Church. Most Turks (18 per cent of the population) are Muslims.

Greek Orthodox .	. .	449,000
Muslims .	. .	104,000
Armenian Apostolic	. .	3,500
Maronite .	. .	3,000
Anglican .	. . ⎫	
Roman Catholic .	. . ⎬	18,000
Other .	. . ⎭	

(1960 census)

The Orthodox Church of Cyprus: Archbishopric of Cyprus, P.O.B. 1130, Nicosia; f. 45 A.D.; the Autocephalous Orthodox Church of Cyprus is part of the Eastern Orthodox Church; the Church is independent, and the Archbishop, who is also the Ethnarch (national leader of the Greek community), is elected by universal suffrage; 500,000 members.

Archbishop of Nova Justiniana and all Cyprus: Archbishop CHRYSOSTOMOS.

Metropolitan of Paphos: Bishop CHRYSOSTOMOS.
Metropolitan of Kitium: Bishop CHRYSOSTOMOS.
Metropolitan of Kyrenia: Bishop GREGORIOS.
Metropolitan of Limassol: Bishop CHRYSANTHOS.
Metropolitan of Morphou: Bishop CHRYSANTHOS.
Suffragan Bishop of Salamis: Bishop BARNABAS.

Islam: Most of the adherents in Cyprus are Sunnis of the Hanafi Sect. The religious head of the Muslim community is the Mufti.

The Mufti of Cyprus: Dr. MUSTAFA RIFAT YUCELTEN, P.O.B. 142, Nicosia, Mersin 10, Turkey.

Roman Catholic Church: Archbishopric of Cyprus of the Maronite rite, subject to the Sacred Congregation for the Oriental Churches; 108 parishes, 54 educational institutes, 38 resident priests, 95,000 Catholics (1977).

Archbishop of Cyprus: Mgr. ELIE FARAH, Maronite Archbishopric, Antelias, Lebanon (winter); Cornet-Chahouane, Lebanon (summer).

Other Churches: Armenian Apostolic and Church of England.

THE PRESS

DAILIES

Adesmefti (*Impartial*): Vasiliou Voulkaroktonou 46, Nicosia; f. 1982; Greek; right of centre.

Agon (*Struggle*): Tryfon Bldg., Eleftheria Sq., P.O.B. 1417, Nicosia; f. 1964; morning; Greek; Independent, right-wing; Owner and Dir. N. KOSHIS; Chief Editor GEORGE A. LEONIDAS; circ. 7,500.

Apogevmatini (*Afternoon*): Grivas Dighenis Ave., P.O.B. 1094, Nicosia; f. 1972; afternoon; Greek; Independent; moderate; Co-owner and Chief Editor ANTHOS LYKAVGHIS; Editor M. HADJIEFTHYMIOU; circ. 11,000.

Birlik (*Unity*): 43 Yediler St., Nicosia, Mersin 10, Turkey; f. 1980; Turkish; organ of National Unity Party; Chief Editor ENVER EMIN.

Bozkurt (*Grey Wolf*): 142 Kyrenia St., Nicosia, Mersin 10, Turkey; f. 1951; morning; Turkish; Independent; Editor CEMAL TOGAN; circ. 5,000.

Cyprus Mail: P.O.B. 1144, 75 Vassiliou Voulgaroktonos St., Nicosia; f. 1945; English; Independent, conservative; Dir. IACOVOS IACOVIDES; Chief Editor PETER WILLIS; circ. 2,340.

Demokrasi: Turkish; f. 1982; Editor: BEKIR AZGIN.

Dilini (*Afternoon*): Solea Bldg., 4 Annis Komnenis St., Nicosia; f. 1981; Greek; afternoon; right-wing; supports DISY party.

Eleftherotypia (*Free Press*): P.O.B. 3821, Hadjisavvas Bldg., Eleftheria Sq., Nicosia; f. 1981; Greek; right of centre; organ of DIKO party; Chief Editor COSTAS YENNARIS.

Halkin Sesi (*Voice of the People*): 172 Kyrenia Ave., Nicosia, Mersin 10, Turkey; f. 1942; morning; Independent Turkish Nationalist; Editor AKAY CEMAL; circ. 5,000.

Haravghi (*Dawn*): P.O.B. 1556, Etak Bldg., 8 Akamas St., Nicosia; f. 1956; Greek; organ of AKEL (Communist Party); Dir. GEORGE SAVVIDES; Chief Editor ANDREAS KANNAOUROS; circ. 14,384.

Kirykas (*Herald*): Chanteclair Bldg., Nicosia; f. 1981; Greek; afternoon; right of centre; organ of Centre Union party.

Mesimvrini (*Noon*): 4 Costis Palamas St., Nicosia; afternoon; Greek; Independent; right-wing; Publisher and Dir. GEORGE HADJINICOLAOU.

Phileleftheros (*Liberal*): Tryfon Bldg., Eleftheria Sq., P.O.B. 1094, Nicosia; Independent, moderate; Greek; morning; Dir. MICHALAKIS HADJIEFTHYMIOU; Chief Editor CHR. KATSAMBAS; circ. 18,212.

Simerini (*Today*): Solea Bldg., 4 Annis Komnenis St., Nicosia; f. 1976; morning; Greek; right-wing; supports DISY party; Dir. COSTAS HADJICOSTIS; Chief Editor ALECOS CONSTANTINIDES.

Ta Nea (*The News*): 23B Constantine Palaelogos Ave., P.O.B. 1064, Nicosia; f. 1970; Greek; organ of EDEK party; morning; Editor TAKIS KOUNNAFIS; circ. 6,250.

WEEKLIES

Agrotiki Phoni (*Farmers' Voice*): A. Karyos St., Engomi Industrial Estate, Nicosia; Greek; organ of the Farmers' Union; affiliated to EDEK party; Chief Editor M. IERIDES.

Alithia (*Truth*): P.O.B. 1965, Hadjikyriakos Bldg., 121 Prodomos St., Nicosia; f. 1951; Greek; right-wing; supports DISY party; Dir. and Chief Editor GLAVKOS XENOS; circ. 5,692.

Ammochostos: 57 Ledra St., P.O.B. 3561, Nicosia; Greek; right-wing; reflects views of Famagusta refugees; Dir. and Chief Editor NICOS FALAS; circ. 3,152.

Anexartitos (*Independent*): Tryfon Bldg., Eleftheria Sq., Nicosia; f. 1974; Greek; organ of EDEK party; Dir. and Chief Editor RENOS PRENTZAS; circ. 4,820.

Cyprus Bulletin: Nicosia; f. 1964; Arabic, English, French, German, Greek, Russian, Spanish, Turkish; published by the Cyprus Public Information Office; circ. 53,000.

Cyprus Weekly: P.O.B. 1992, 216 Mitsis 3 Bldg., Archbishop Makarios Ave., Nicosia; f. 1979; English; Independent; conservative; Dirs. ALEX EFTHYVOULOU, ANDREAS HADJIPAPAS, GEORGE DER PARTHOG; Chief Editor STEVE MYLES; circ. 5,500.

Demokratiki (*Democratic*): P.O.B. 1074, Nicosia; Greek; Independent; left of centre; Dir. and Co-owner EFTHYMIOS HADJIEFTHYMIOU; Co-owner and Chief Editor ANTHOS LYKAVGHIS; circ. 18,000.

Demokratia (*Democracy*): P.O.B. 1963, Nicosia; f. 1975; Greek; pro-Government; organ of AKEL Party; Dir. GEORGE SAVVIDES; Chief Editor LYSSANDROS TSIMILLIS; circ. 9,231.

Eleftherotypia Tis Defteras (*Monday's Free Press*): P.O.B. 3821, Hadjisavvas Bldg., Eleftheria Sq., Nicosia; f. 1980; Greek; right of centre; organ of DIKO party.

Ergatiki Phoni (*Workers' Voice*): 35 Zenon St., Limassol; f. 1946; Greek; organ of Cyprus Workers' Confederation; Editor CHRISTODOULOS MICHAELIDES; circ. 5,500.

Ergatiko Vima (*Workers' Tribune*): P.O.B. 1885, Archermos St. 31–35, Nicosia; f. 1956; Greek; organ of the Pancyprian Federation of Labour; Editor-in-Chief ZAKHARIAS PHILIPPIDES; circ. 8,300.

Kibris: c/o T.F.S.C. Public Information Office, Mersin 10, Turkey; f. 1963 as *News Bulletin*; in English; published by Public Information Office of the "T.F.S.C."; circ. 5,000.

Kypriaki (*Cypriot*): Eiffel Bldg., 2 Chr. Sozou St., Nicosia; f. 1981; Greek; left of centre; organ of PAME party.

Kypros (*Cyprus*): P.O.B. 1491, 10 Apostolos Varnavas St., Nicosia; f. 1952; Greek; Independent, conservative; Dirs. MARIOS and HARIS KYRIAKIDES; circ. 6,127.

Listen Out: Listen Out Publications, P.O.B. 160, Larnaca; weekly programme guide for BFBS Cyprus; circ. 3,000.

Middle East Economic Survey: Middle East Research and Publishing Centre, P.O.B. 4940, Nicosia; f. 1957 (in Beirut); weekly review of petroleum and economic news; Editor and Publr. FUAD W. ITAYIM.

Northern Weekly Mail: P.O.B. 755, Nicosia, Mersin 10, Turkey; f. 1980; independent; English; Managing Ed. RAIF DENKTAS; circ. 750.

Official Gazette: Printing Office of the Republic of Cyprus, Nicosia; f. 1960; Greek; published by the Government of the Republic of Cyprus.

Phakos Tis Epikerotitos (*Mirror of Current Events*): 40 Sophoulis St., Chanteclair Bldg., 1st Floor, No. 116, P.O.B. 1999 Nicosia; Greek; independent; Editor PHAEDON KOTSONIS.

Satiriki (*Satirical*): 23 Bouboulina St., Strovolos, Nicosia; Greek; Independent; left-wing; Publisher and Dir. G. MAVROGENIS; circ. 4,025.

Synghroni Politiki (*Current Politics*): 306 Omirou 2B, Nicosia; f. 1981; Greek; Independent; political and economic review.

Tharros (*Courage*): P.O.B. 1105, Grivas Dighenis Ave.; Nicosia; f. 1961; Greek; Independent; circ. 9,200 (publication indefinitely suspended).

To Vima (*Tribune*): Nicosia; f. 1981; Greek; right of centre; organ of NEDIPA party; Chief Editor YIANNIS SPANOS.

PERIODICALS

Apostolos Varnavas: Archbishopric of Cyprus, Nicosia; Greek; monthly; organ of the Orthodox Church of Cyprus; Dir. Dr. ANDREAS N. MITSIDES; circ. 1,200.

Countryman: Nicosia; f. 1943; every two months; Greek; published by the Cyprus Public Information Office; circ. 6,000.

Cyprus Medical Journal: P.O.B. 1393, Nicosia; f. 1947; quarterly; English and Greek; Editor Dr. G. N. MARANGOS.

Cyprus Today: c/o Ministry of Education, Nicosia; f. 1963; every four months; cultural and informative review of the Ministry of Education; published and distributed by Press and Information Office; English; free of charge; Chair. Editorial Board P. SERGHIS; circ. 14,000.

Dimosios Ypallios (*Civil Servant*): 2 Andreas Demetriou St., Nicosia; fortnightly; published by the Cyprus Civil Servants' Trade Union; circ. 10,000.

Eğitim Bülteni (*Education Bulletin*): Nicosia; f. 1972; monthly; Turkish; published by Ministry of Education of the "Turkish Federated State of Cyprus"; circ. 3,000.

Eso-Etimos (*Ever Ready*): P.O.B. 4544, Nicosia; every three months; Greek; published by Boy Scouts of Cyprus; circ. 2,500.

International Crude Oil and Product Prices: Middle East Petroleum and Economic Publications, P.O.B. 4940, Nicosia; f. 1971 (in Beirut)); twice yearly review and analysis of oil price trends in world markets; Publisher FUAD W. ITAYIM.

Kooperatif (*Co-operative*): Nicosia; f. 1970; monthly; Turkish; published by Department of Co-operative Development of the "Turkish Federated State of Cyprus"; circ. 2,000.

Kypriakos Logos (*Cypriot Speech*): 10 Kimonos St., Engomi, Nicosia; f. 1969; Greek; every two months; philological, literary, historical and philosophical; Editor P. STYLIANOU; circ. 6,000.

Mathitiki Estia (*Student Hearth*): Pancyprian Gymnasium, Nicosia; f. 1950; annually; Greek; organ of the Pancyprian Gymnasium students; Editor GEORGE PRODROMOU.

Nea Epochi (*New Epoch*): P.O.B. 1581, Nicosia; f. 1959; every two months; Greek; literary; Editor ACHILLEAS PYLIOTIS; circ. 1,500.

Öğretmen (*Teacher*): Nicosia; f. 1972; monthly; Turkish; organ of Cyprus Turkish Secondary Schools' Teachers' Asscn.; circ. 1,200.

Paediki Hara (*Children's Joy*): 18 Archbishop Makarios III Ave., Nicosia; monthly; for students; published by the Pancyprian Union of Greek Teachers; Editor ELPIDOFOROS YIARGOU; circ. 13,000.

Pnevmatiki Kypros (*Cultural Cyprus*): Nicosia; f. 1960; monthly; Greek; literary; Owner Dr. KYPROS CHRYSANTHIS.

Radio Programme: Cyprus Broadcasting Corpn., P.O.B. 4824, Nicosia; fortnightly; Greek and English; published by the CBC; radio and TV programme news; circ. 25,000.

Synergatistis (*The Co-operator*): P.O.B. 4537, Nicosia; f. 1961; monthly magazine; Greek; official organ of the Pancyprian Confederation of Co-operatives; Editor G. I. PHOTIOU; circ. 4,300.

Trapezikos (*Bank Employee*): P.O.B. 1235, Nicosia; f. 1960; bank employees' magazine; Greek; monthly; Editor G. S. MICHAELIDES; circ. 17,500.

NEWS AGENCIES

Cyprus News Agency: c/o Director-General, Cyprus Broadcasting Corpn., P.O.B. 4824, Nicosia; f. 1976; Greek; Dir. ANDREAS CHRISTOFIDES.

FOREIGN BUREAUX

Agentstvo Pechati Novosti (APN) (*U.S.S.R.*): Kreontos 6, P.O.B. 4051, Nicosia; Rep. GAREGIN SHAHOUNIAN.

Associated Press (AP) (*U.S.A.*): P.O.B. 4853, Andreas Zakos St. 4, Engomi, Nicosia; Rep. A. EFTHYVOULOS.

Athinaikon Praktorion Eidision (*Greece*): Andreas Patsalides 10, Engomi; Rep. GEORGE LEONIDAS.

Československá tisková kancelář (ČTK) (*Czechoslovakia*): 30 Evagoros Pallikarides St., Strovolos; Rep. STAVROS ANGELIDES.

Deutsche Presse Agentur (dpa) (*Federal Republic of Germany*): Daidalou 9, Nicosia; Rep. ANDREAS LYKAVGIS.

Iraqi News Agency: P.O.B. 1098, Nicosia; Rep. CHRISTAKIS KATSAMBAS.

MEMO (Middle East Media Operations) Ltd. (*U.K. and U.S.A.*): P.O.B. 3779, Nicosia; representing BBC Radio and TV, Reuters (U.K.), *The Guardian* (U.K.), NBC Radio and TV (U.S.A.), *The Boston Globe* (U.S.A.), *Middle East Magazine* (U.K.), *Washington Post* and *Los Angeles Times* (U.S.A.), *Observer* (U.K.), *Campaign*

Mid-East (U.K.), *Christian Science Monitor* (U.S.A.), CBC Radio and TV (Canada), *International Herald Tribune* (Paris); Dir. CHRIS DRAKE, M.B.E.

Novinska Agencija Tanjug (*Yugoslavia*): Eleftheria Sq., Tryfon Bldg., Nicosia; Rep. MANO ALKOVIĆ.

Polska Agencja Prasowa (PAP) (*Poland*): Prodromos St. 24, P.O.B. 2373, Nicosia; Rep. MICHALAKIS PANTELIDES.

Prensa Latina (*Cuba*): Nicodemos Mylonas 21A, Nicosia; Rep. ANDREAS KANNAOUROS.

Telegrafnoye Agentstvo Sovietskogo Soyuza (TASS) (*U.S.S.R.*): 3 Philellinon St., Nicosia; Rep. VLADISLAV CHERTENKOV.

United Press International (UPI) (*U.S.A.*): Flat 42, 40 Nikis St., Nicosia; Rep. ANDREAS HADJIPAPAS.

PUBLISHER

MAM: P.O.B. 1722, Nicosia; f. 1965; specializes in publications on Cyprus and international organizations and by Cypriot authors.

RADIO AND TELEVISION

Cyprus Broadcasting Corporation: P.O.B. 4824, Nicosia; Chair. ANDREAS PHILIPPOU; Dir.-Gen. A. N. CHRISTOFIDES; Chief Engineer P. ASTREOS; Head of Radio Programmes P. IOANNIDES (acting); Head of Television Programmes CH. PAPADOPOULOS; Head of News Service L. KYTHREOTIS; publ. *Radio Programme*.

Radio: f. 1952; Programme I in Greek, Programme II in Greek, Turkish, English, Arabic and Armenian; two medium wave transmitters of 20 kW. in Nicosia with relay stations at Paphos and Limassol; two 30kW ERP VHF FM stereo transmitters on Mount Olympus; international service in English and Arabic; relays Radio Monte Carlo to the Middle East from a 600 kW. medium wave transmitter at Cape Greco.

Television: f. 1957; one Band III 40/4 kW transmitter on Mount Olympus with 26 transposer stations.

Bayrak Radio and TV: Atatürk Square, Nicosia, Mersin 10, Turkey; Dir. Gen. H. SUHA.

Radio Bayrak: f. 1963; Turkish Cypriot State Radio;

home service in Turkish, overseas services in Turkish, Greek and English; broadcasts 18 hours a day; Dir.-Gen. HAKKI SÜHA; Dir. of Programmes MEHMET FEHMİ; Tech. Dir. D. ÖZERBERKEM; Admin. Dir. HARİD FEDAİ.

Bayrak TV: f. 1976; transmits programmes in Turkish, Greek and Enlgish on three channels.

British Forces Broadcasting Service, Cyprus: British Forces Post Office 58; broa·casts continuously in English VHF and medium wave; alternative programme on M.W. 3 hours daily; Station Controller K. J. P. DOHERTY; Engineer-in-Charge M. E. TOWNLEY; publ. monthly programme guide.

Türkiye Radyo Televizyon (T.R.T.): Turkish television programmes are transmitted to the Turkish sector of Cyprus.

In December 1980, in the Government-controlled areas, it was estimated that there were 163,000 radio receivers and 86,000 television receivers.

FINANCE

(br.=branch; cap.=capital; p.u.=paid up; dep.=deposits; m.=million; amounts in Cyprus pounds)

BANKING
CENTRAL BANK

Central Bank of Cyprus: P.O.B. 5529, 36 Metochiou St. Nicosia; f. 1963; became the Bank of Issue in 1963; cap. p.u. £100,000; dep. £118.9m. (March 1981); Gov. C. C. STEPHANI; publs. *Report* (annual), *Bulletin* (quarterly).

CYPRIOT BANKS

Bank of Cyprus Ltd.: P.O.B. 1472, 86-90 Phaneromeni St., Nicosia; f. 1943 by the amalgamation of Bank of Cyprus, Larnaca Bank Ltd. and Famagusta Bank Ltd.; cap. p.u. £6m.; dep. £252.7m. (Dec. 1981); Gov. ANDREAS PATSALIDES; Chair. GEORGE C. CHRISTOFIDES; 73 branches throughout Cyprus.

Co-operative Central Bank Ltd.: P.O.B. 4537, Gregoris Afxentiou St., Nicosia; f. 1937 under the Co-operative Societies Law; banking and credit facilities to member societies; Sec.-Man. R. CLERIDES; 5 brs.

Cyprus Popular Bank Ltd.: Popular Bank Building, P.O.B. 2032, 39 Archbishop Makarios III Avenue, Nicosia; f. 1924 at Banque Populaire de Limassol Ltd.; cap. p.u. £4.5m.; dep. £100m. (Dec. 1981); Chair. EVAGORAS C. LANITIS; Gen. Man. KIKIS S. LAZARIDES; 50 brs.

Cyprus Turkish Co-operative Central Bank, Ltd.: P.O.B. 1861, Mahmout Pasha St., Nicosia; banking and credit facilities to member societies, bodies and individuals; Gen. Man. MEHMET ESHREF.

Hellenic Bank Ltd.: 92 Dhigenis Akritas Ave., P.O.B. 4747, Nicosia; f. 1974, began operations in 1976; affiliated to Bank of America N.T. and S.A.; cap. p.u. £1.5m.; dep. £39.76m. (Dec. 1981); Chair. P. L. PASCHALIDES; Gen. Man. P. C. GHALANOS; 25 brs.

Kibris Kredi Bankası (*Cyprus Credit Bank*): Nicosia, Mersin 10, Turkey; f. 1978; cap. p.u. £1m.; Chair. MACIT FERDI.

Mortgage Bank of Cyprus Ltd.: P.O.B. 1472, 86–90 Phaneromeni St., Nicosia; f. 1944; wholly owned subsidiary of Bank of Cyprus Ltd.; Chair. GEORGE C. CHRISTOFIDES; Gov. ANDREAS PATSALIDES; 47 brs.

Turkish Bank Ltd.: 92 Kyrenia St., Nicosia; f. 1901; cap. p.u. £800,000 (1981); dep. TL 4,855.4m. (Dec. 1981); Chair. UMIT S. ONAN; Gen. Man. KIAMOURAN M. JELÂLEDDIN; 11 brs.

DEVELOPMENT BANK

Cyprus Development Bank Ltd.: 50 Makarios III Avenue, Alpha House, P.O.B. 1415, Nicosia; f. 1963; cap. p.u. £2m.; reserves £410,000; provides medium and long term loans for productive projects, particularly in manufacturing and processing industries, tourism and agriculture, and technical, managerial and administrative assistance and advice; performs related economic and technical research; Chair. MIKIS N. TSIAKKAS; Gen. Man. JOHN G. JOANNIDES; Asst. Gen. Man. L. D. SPARSIS.

FOREIGN BANKS

Bank of Credit & Commerce International (BCCI): The first bank to receive an offshore banking licence from the Finance Ministry; due to open an office in Cyprus in May 1982.

Barclays Bank International Ltd.: P.O.B. 2081, Eleftheria Sq., Nicosia; Local Dir. J. D. PEPPER; 19 brs.

The Chartered Bank: P.O.B. 1047, Corner of Archbishop Makarios III and Evagoras Aves., Nicosia; Cyprus Man. J. L. BRADLEY; 12 brs.

Grindlays Bank PLC: 11-13 Archbishop Makarios III Ave., P.O.B. 2069, Nicosia; Gen. Man. in Cyprus J. M. MITCHELL; 31 brs.

Lombard Banking (Cyprus) Ltd.: P.O.B. 1661, Stylianos Lenas Sq., Nicosia; f. 1960; owns a subsidiary, Lombard (Cyprus) Ltd., specializing in hire purchase business; Chair. RONALD J. BARNES; Man. Dir. H. M. KEHEYAN; 5 brs.

National Bank of Greece, S.A.: P.O.B. 1191, 36 Archbishop Makarios III Ave., Nicosia; Regional Man. ARMANDOS KYRIAKIS; 12 brs.

Türkiye Cumhuriyeti Ziraat Bankası (*Agricultural Bank of Turkey*): Ankara, Turkey; Cyprus branch Kyrenia; Man. DOĞAN ERDOĞAN; acts as central bank for Turkish-occupied area of Cyprus.

Türkiye İş Bankası: 9 Kyrenia St., Nicosia; brs. at Famagusta and Kyrenia.

INSURANCE

Office of the Superintendent of Insurance: 3 Gregoris Afxentiou St., Nicosia; f. 1969 to control insurance companies and agents in Cyprus.

Allied Assurance & Reinsurance Co. Ltd.: 12 Themistoclis Dervis St., Ivory Tower, Office No. 201, P.O.B. 5509, Nicosia; f. 1982; Chair. HENRI J. CHALHOUB; Gen. Man. CONSTANTINOS AXIOTIS; offshore company operating outside Cyprus.

Commercial Union Assurance (Cyprus) Ltd.: Lavinia Building, Corner of Santa Rosa Ave. and Mykinon St., P.O.B. 1312, Nicosia; f. 1974; Chair. J. CHRISTOPHIDES; Gen. Man. G. GEORGALLIDES.

Compass Insurance Co. Ltd.: Corner Gladstonos and Olympion Sts., Themis Tower, 3rd Floor, P.O.B. 1183, Limassol; f. 1981; Chair. P. LOUCAIDES; Gen. Man. PHAEDON MAKRIS.

General Insurance Company of Cyprus Ltd.: 24–25 Lycourgus St., P.O.B. 1668, Nicosia; f. 1951; Chair. G. CH. CHRISTOFIDES; Gen. Man. S. SOPHOCLEOUS.

Hermes Insurance Co. Ltd.: 8 Michael Kazaoli St., 1st Floor, Office 101-103, P.O.B. 4828, Nicosia; f. 1980; Chair. and Man. Dir. P. VOYAZIANOS; Gen. Man. JOANNIS ALEXANDROU.

Laiki Insurance Co. Ltd.: 39 Arch. Makarios III Ave., Cyprus Popular Bank Buildings, P.O.B. 4515, Nicosia; f. 1981; Chair. E. K. LANITIS; Gen. Man. Y. E. SOLOMONIDES.

Minerva Insurance Co. Ltd.: 8 Epaminondas St., P.O.B. 3554, Nicosia; f. 1970; Chair. and Gen. Man. K. KOUTSOKOUMNIS.

Reliance Insurance Co. Ltd.: Avenue Court, Corner Severis Ave. and Katsonis St., First Floor, P.O.B. 3506, Nicosia; f. 1980; Chair. ZENON SEVERIS; Gen. Man. ALECOS POULCHERIOS.

Saudi Stars Insurance Co. Ltd.: Corner Makarios III Ave. and Methonis St., No. 2, P.O.B. 1493, Nicosia; f. 1979; Chair. M. F. AL-HAYRI; Sec. CHR. MITSIDES; offshore company operating outside Cyprus.

Universal Life Insurance Company Ltd.: Palace Princess Zena De Tyra, P.O.B. 1270, Nicosia; f. 1970; Chair. J. CHRISTOPHIDES; Gen. Man. ANDREAS GEORGHIOU; Life Man. ZENIOS DEMETRIOU.

About 40 foreign insurance companies operate in Cyprus.

TRADE AND INDUSTRY

CHAMBERS OF COMMERCE

Cyprus Chamber of Commerce and Industry: Evagoras Ave., Hadjisavvas Bldg. (6th Floor), P.O.B. 1455, Nicosia; Pres. ANDREAS AVRAAMIDES; Vice-Pres. GEORGE ROLOGIS, CHR. MAVROUDES; Sec.-Gen. P. LOIZIDES; 2,500 members, 35 affiliated trade associations; publ. *Directory, Monthly Information Bulletin.*

Famagusta Chamber of Commerce and Industry: P.O.B. 777, Famagusta; temporary address: P.O.B. 3124, Limassol; f. 1952; 300 mems.; Pres. PHANOS N. EPIPHANIOU; Vice-Pres. PHOTOS LORDOS; Sec.-Gen. IACOVOS HADJIVARNAVAS; publ. *Information Bulletin.*

Larnaca Chamber of Commerce and Industry: 33 Lord Byron St., 1st Floor, Popular Bank Bldg., P.O.B. 287, Larnaca; 300 mems.; Pres. Dr. A. FRANCIS; Vice-

Pres. KYPROS ECONOMIDES; Sec. OTHON THEODOULOU; publ. *Information Bulletin* (monthly).

Limassol Chamber of Commerce and Industry: 25 Spyros Araouzos St., P.O.B. 347, Limassol; Pres. KYRIACOS HAMBOULLAS; Vice-Pres. NICOS ROSSOS.

Nicosia Chamber of Commerce and Industry: Evagoras Ave., Hadjisavvas Building, 6th Floor, P.O.B. 1455, Nicosia; Pres. M. MICHAELIDES; Vice-Pres. C. CONSTANTINIDES.

Paphos Chamber of Commerce and Industry: 14–34 Nicolaou Ellina St., P.O.B. 61, Paphos; Pres. Loizos M. HAVOUZARIS; Vice-Pres. POLIDEFKIS GEORGIOU.

Turkish Cypriot Chamber of Commerce: 1 Cengiz St., Koskluciftlik, P.O.B. 718, Nicosia; Pres. MUSTAFA YILDIRIM; Sec.-Gen. TANER ATAER.

EMPLOYERS' ORGANIZATIONS

Cyprus Employers' & Industrialists' Federation: 30 Grivas-Dhigenis Ave., P.O.B. 1657, Nicosia; f. 1960; 14 member Trade Associations, 320 direct and 800 indirect members; Dir.-Gen. ANT. PIERIDES; Chair. MICHAEL COLOCASSIDES. The largest of the Trade Association members are: Cyprus Building Contractors' Association; Cyprus Hotel Keepers' Association; Clothing Manufacturers' Association; Cyprus Shipping Association; Shoe Makers' Association; Cyprus Metal Industries Association; Cyprus Bankers Employers' Association; Motor Cars, Tractors & Agricultural Machinery Importers' Association.

TRADE UNIONS

Pankypria Ergatiki Omospondia (*Pancyprian Federation of Labour*): P.O.B. 1885, 31-35 Archermos St., Nicosia; f. 1946, registered 1947; previously the Pancyprian Trade Union Committee f. 1941, dissolved 1946; 11 unions and 223 brs. with a total membership of 61,000; affiliated to the World Federation of Trade Unions; Gen. Sec. A. ZIARTIDES; publ. *Ergatiko Vima* (Workers' Forum), weekly.

Synomospondia Ergaton Kyprou (*Cyprus Workers' Confederation*): 23 Alkaiou St., P.O.B. 5018, Engomi, Nicosia; f. 1944, registered 1950; 7 Federations, 5 Labour Centres, 47 unions, 12 branches with a total membership of 40,444; affiliated to the Greek Confederation of Labour and the ICFTU; Gen. Sec. MICHAEL IOANNOU; publ. *Ergatiki Phoni* (Workers' Voice), weekly.

Pankyprios Omospondia Anexartition Syntechnion (*Pancyprian Federation of Independent Trade Unions*): 1 Menadrou St., Nicosia; f. 1956, registered 1957; has no political orientations; 8 unions with a total membership of 798; Pres. COSTAS ANTONIADES; Gen. Sec. KYRIACOS NATHANAEL.

Demokratiki Ergatiki Omospondia Kyprou (*Democratic Labour Federation of Cyprus*): 23 Constantinou Paleologou, Nicosia; f. 1962; 4 unions with a total membership of 272; Hon. Pres. PETROS STYLIANOU; Gen. Sec. IACOVOS KATSOUNATOS.

Kıbrıs Türk İşçi Sendikaları Federasionu (**TÜRK-SEN**) (*Turkish Cypriot Trade Union Federation*): Sehit Mehmet R. Hüseyin Sok., P.O.B. 829, Nicosia, Mersin 10, Turkey; f. 1954, registered 1955; 15 unions with a total membership of 15,000; affiliated to ICFTU, ETUC and the Confederation of Trade Unions of Turkey; Pres. NECATİ TAŞKIN; Gen. Sec. LÜTFİ ÖZTER.

Cyprus Civil Servants' Trade Union: 2 Andreas Demetriou St., Nicosia; f. 1949, registered 1966; restricted to persons in the civil employment of the Govt. and public authorities; 6 brs. with a total membership of 11,611; Pres. A. PAPANASTASSIOU; Gen. Sec. G. IACOVOU; publ. *Dimosios Ypallilos* (Public Servant), fortnightly.

Union of Cyprus Journalists: c/o A. Kannaouros, Haravghi, Nicosia.

On December 31st, 1980, there were 28 employers' associations, including 14 independent associations, with a total membership of 4,115. There were also 97 trade unions with 240 branches, 6 union federations and 5 confederations with 10 branches and a total membership of 118,281.

TRADE FAIRS

Cyprus International (State) Fair: P.O.B. 3551, Nicosia; eighth scheduled for May 28th–June 12th, 1983.

TRANSPORT

There are no railways in Cyprus.

ROADS

In 1980 there were 10,255 kilometres of roads, of which 5,095 kilometres were paved and 5,160 kilometres were earth or gravel roads. Bus and taxi services between Nicosia and the principal towns and villages were severely disrupted by the Turkish invasion. These have since been restored, but the north and south are now served by separate transport systems, and there are no services linking the two sectors.

SHIPPING

Until 1974 Famagusta was the island's most important harbour, handling about 83 per cent of the country's cargo. Famagusta is a natural port capable of receiving ships of a maximum draught of 9.2 metres. Since its capture by the Turkish army in August 1974 the port has been officially declared closed to international traffic. However, it continues to serve the Turkish-occupied region.

The ports which serve the island's maritime trade at present are Larnaca and Limassol, which were constructed in 1973 and 1974 respectively. Both ports have been expanded: the quay of the new Limassol port is 1,280 metres long and 11 metres deep, while the port of Larnaca has a quay length of 866 metres and a depth of of 9.5 metres.

In 1980, 4,066 ships entered and cleared at these two ports, loading 1,592,379 tons and unloading 2,140,663 tons. Limassol handled approximately two thirds of ships entered and cleared. Larnaca is the island's main petroleum port.

Both Kyrenia and Karavostassi are under Turkish occupation and have been declared closed to international traffic. Karavostassi used to be the country's major mineral port dealing with 76 per cent of the total mineral exports. However, since the war minerals are being passed through Vassiliko and Limni which are open roadsteads. In 1977 a hydrofoil service was started between Kyrenia and Mersin on the Turkish mainland.

The number of merchant vessels registered in Cyprus rose from 314 (1,575,702 g.r.t.) in 1970 to 1,233 (2,098,392 g.r.t.) in December 1980.

Brasal Offshore Services Ltd.: P.O.B. 1518, Limassol; one Z-craft, one cargo ship; Gen. Man. E. BRANCO.

A. Elias (overseas) Co. Ltd.: 104 Arch. Markarios III Ave., Limassol; four cargo ships; Gen. Man. T. ELIAS.

Eurointerlink Ltd.: 48-48A Omonia Ave., Limassol; four cargo ships; Gen. Man. I. THOMAIDES.

Fama Maritime Co. Ltd.: 124A Fr. Roosevelt Ave., Limassol; two cargo ships.

Hanseatic Shipping Co. Ltd.: 111 Sp. Araouzou, Limassol; 30 cargo ships; Gen. Man. Capt. J. MEYER.

Lefkaritis Bros. Marine Ltd.: 1 Kilkis St., Larnaca; four tankers.

Josef Roth (Cyprus) Shipping Co. Ltd.: 28 Arch. Makarios III Ave., 6th Floor, Limassol; six cargo ships.

Sol Lines: 140 Fr. Roosevelt Ave., Limassol; two passenger/ro-ro ferries, one ro-ro cargo ship; Gen. Man. T. SOLOMONIDES.

CIVIL AVIATION

There is an international airport at Nicosia, which can accommodate all types of aircraft, including jets. It has been closed since July 1974 following the Turkish invasion. A new international airport was constructed at Larnaca, from which flights operate to Europe and the Middle East.

In 1975 the Turkish authorities opened Ercan (formerly Tymbou) airport.

Cyprus Airways: 21 Alkeou St., P.O.B. 1903, Nicosia; f. 1946; jointly owned by Cyprus Government, British Airways and local interests; charter subsidiary Cyprair Tours; Chair. S. GALATARIOTIS; Man. Dir. S. NATHANAEL; services to Abu Dhabi, Amman, Athens, Bahrain, Birmingham, Beirut, Cairo, Cologne, Dhahran, Damascus, Dubai, Frankfurt, Jeddah, Kuwait, London, Manchester, Munich, Paris, Rhodes, Salonkia, Tel-Aviv and Zurich from Larnaca Airport; fleet of 4 Boeing 707, 3 BAC One-Eleven 500.

Cyprus Turkish Airlines Ltd.: Bedreddin Demirel Ave., Nicosia; f. 1974; jointly owned by "the Turkish Federated State of Cyprus" and Turkish Airlines; Gen. Man. I. DINCEL; Pres. P. TURGUD; routes from Ercan Airport, Nicosia, to Ankara, Adana and Istanbul; fleet of one Boeing 720B.

At present Cyprus is served by the following foreign airlines: Aeroflot (U.S.S.R.), Alia (Jordan), Alitalia (Italy), Austrian Airlines, Balkan (Bulgaria), British Airways, ČSA (Czechoslovakia), EgyptAir, Gulfair (Bahrain), Interflug (German Democratic Republic), Iraqi Airways, Kuwait Airways, Lufthansa (Federal Republic of Germany), MEA (Lebanon), MALÉV (Hungary), Olympic (Greece), Syrian Arab Airlines, TAROM (Romania), THY (Turkey) and Yemen Airways (Yemen Arab Republic).

TOURISM AND CULTURE

Cyprus Tourism Organization: Zena Building, 18 Th. Theodotou St., P.O.B. 4535, Nicosia; Chair. FRIXOS PETRIDES; Dir.-Gen. A. ANDRONICOU.

CULTURAL ORGANIZATIONS

E. Ka. Te: Pancyprian Chamber of Fine Arts, P.O.B. 2179, Nicosia; f. 1964; Pres. A. SAVVIDES; Sec.-Gen. A. LADOMMATOS; publ. *Bulletin* (monthly).

TH.O.C.: Cyprus Theatre Organization; 15 Heroon St., Nicosia; f. 1971; Dir. EVIS GABRIELIDES.

EDUCATION

Until March 31st, 1965, each community in Cyprus managed its own schooling through its respective Communal Chamber. Intercommunal education had been placed under the Minister of the Interior, assisted by a Board of Education for Intercommunal Schools of which the Minister was the Chairman. On March 31st, 1965, the Greek Communal Chamber was dissolved and a Ministry of Education was established to take its place. Intercommunal education has been placed under this Ministry.

Greek-Cypriot Education

Elementary education is compulsory and is provided free in six grades to children between 5½ and 14 years of age. In the towns and certain large villages there are separate junior schools consisting of the first three grades. Apart from schools for the deaf and blind, and the Lambousa

School for juvenile offenders there are also 7 schools for handicapped children. In 1981/82 there were 156 Kindergartens (5,405 pupils) run by the Ministry and 74 privately owned (3,600 children). There were 435 primary schools, including 9 privately run (46,000 pupils). In 96 primary schools there are children's clubs where pupils can spend their leisure time.

Secondary education is free for the first three years and is fee-paying for the rest, although senior pupils can be wholly or partially exempt from payment. Secondary schooling lasts six years, three years at the Gymnasion followed by three years at the Lykeion. There are three types of Lykeia: classical, science, and economic. Since 1977 a new type of upper secondary school has been operating: the Upper School of Options (*Lykeion Epilogis Mathemation*), which is expected to expand to all existing public secondary schools. There are also five-year vocational (trade) schools and six-year technical schools. In 1981/82 there were 98 secondary schools with 3,000 teachers and 48,881 pupils.

Post-Secondary education is provided at the Pedagogical Academy, which organizes three-year courses for the training of pre-primary and primary school teachers, and at the Higher Technical Institute, which provides three-year courses for technicians in civil, electrical and mechanical engineering. Specialized training is also provided at the Forestry College, the Hotel and Catering Institute, a Nurses' and Midwives' School and a School for Health Inspectors, all of which are State institutions. Adult education is conducted through Youth Centres in rural areas and Foreign Language Institutes in the towns, and in addition a number of private institutions offer courses in business administration, secretarial work etc. There are no universities in Cyprus, and in the academic year 1979–80 approximately 12,200 Cypriot students were studying in universities abroad, mainly in Greece and the United Kingdom, although fewer have been admitted to the United Kingdom in recent years.

Turkish-Cypriot Education

Education in the Turkish Cypriot zone is divided into two sections, formal and adult education. Formal education covers nursery, primary, secondary and higher education. Adult education caters for special training outside the school system.

Formal education is organized into three categories: basic, secondary and higher. Basic education caters for children from 6 to 15 years old and is free and compulsory. There are two stages of basic education, the first stage lasting six years and the second three years. Secondary education consists of a three-year course of one of three types: preparing for higher education; preparing for higher education and vocational training; preparing for vocational training only. All pupils who have completed their basic education are entitled to proceed to a course of secondary education according to their interest and ability. Secondary education is free for those who cannot afford the fees of a minimum of £18. It is not compulsory.

There are two higher education institutions in the Turkish Cypriot zone: the Teachers' Training College, which trains teachers for the elementary school stage, and the Higher Technical Institute, which trains engineers in three major fields: electrical, mechanical and civil.

BIBLIOGRAPHY

ALASTOS, D. Cyprus in History (London, 1955).

ARNOLD, PERCY. Cyprus Challenge (London: Hogarth Press, 1956).

BARKER, DUDLEY. Grivas (London, Cresset Press, 1960).

BYFORD-JONES, W. Grivas and the Story of EOKA (London, Robert Hale, 1960).

CASSON, S. Ancient Cyprus (London, 1937).

CRAWSHAW, NANCY. The Cyprus Revolt: An Account of the Struggle for Union with Greece (London, Allen & Unwin, 1978).

EMILIANIDES, ACHILLE. Histoire de Chypre (Paris, 1963).

ESIN, EMEL. Aspects of Turkish Civilization in Cyprus (Ankara University Press, Ankara, 1965).

FOLEY, CHARLES. Island in Revolt (London, Longmans Green, 1962).

Legacy of Strife (Penguin, London, 1964).

FOOT, SYLVIA. Emergency Exit (Chatto and Windus, London, 1960).

FOOT, Sir HUGH. A Start in Freedom (London, 1964).

GRIVAS (DIGHENIS), GEORGE. Guerilla Warfare and EOKA's Struggle (London, Longmans, 1964).
Memoirs of General Grivas (London, Longmans, 1964).

HARBOTTLE, MICHAEL. The Impartial Soldier (Oxford University Press, 1970).

HILL, Sir GEORGE. A History of Cyprus (4 vols., London, 1940-1952).

JENNES, D. The Economics of Cyprus (Montreal, 1962).

KYRIAKIDES, S. Cyprus—Constitutionalism and Crisis Government (Philadelphia, University of Pennsylvania Press, 1968).

LAVENDER, D. S. The Story of Cyprus Mines Corporation (San Marino, Calif., 1962).

LUKE, Sir H. C. Cyprus under the Turks 1571-1878 (Oxford, 1921).
Cyprus: A Portrait and an Appreciation (London, Harrap, 1965).

MEYER, A. J. (with S. VASSILIOU). The Economy of Cyprus (Harvard University Press, 1962).

NEWMAN, PHILIP. A Short History of Cyprus (1940).

PAPADOPOULLOS, T. The population of Cyprus (1570-1881) (Nicosia, 1965).

PURCELL, H. D. Cyprus (London, Benn, 1969).

RICHARD, J. Chypre Sous les Lusignan (Paris, 1962).

ROYAL COMMONWEALTH SOCIETY. Notes on Conditions in Cyprus (London, 1973).

SPYRIDAKIS, Dr. C. A. Brief History of Cyprus (Nicosia, 1964).

STORRS, Sir RONALD. A Chronology of Cyprus (Nicosia, 1930).

STYLIANOU, A. and J. Byzantine Cyprus (Nicosia, 1948).

XYDIS, S. G. Cyprus—Conflict and Conciliation 1945-58 (Ohio State University Press, Columbus, Ohio, 1967).

OFFICIAL BOOKS OF REFERENCE:

Cyprus: Documents relating to Independence of Cyprus and the Establishment of British Sovereign Base Areas (Cmnd. 1093, H.M.S.O., London, July 1960).

Cyprus: Treaty of Guarantee, Nicosia, August 16th, 1960.

Egypt

PHYSICAL AND SOCIAL GEOGRAPHY

W. B. Fisher

SITUATION

The Arab Republic of Egypt occupies the north-eastern corner of the African continent, with an extension across the Gulf of Suez into the Sinai region which is usually, but not always, regarded as lying in Asia. The area of Egypt is 997,738.5 sq. km. (385,229 sq. miles) but only 3.5 per cent can be said to be permanently settled, the remainder being desert or marsh. Egypt lies between Lat. 22° and 32° N.; and the greatest distance from north to south is about 674 miles (1024 km.), and from east to west 770 miles (1240 km.), giving the country a roughly square shape, with the Mediterranean and Red Seas forming respectively the northern and eastern boundaries. Egypt has political frontiers on the east with Israel, on the south with the Democratic Republic of Sudan, and on the west with the Socialist People's Libyan Arab Jamahiriya. The actual frontiers run in general as straight lines drawn directly between defined points and do not normally conform to geographical features. Between June 1967 and October 1973 the *de facto* frontier with Israel was the Suez Canal. Now, with the 1979 Peace Treaty, the frontier has reverted to much further east (*see* map on p. 90).

Egypt occupies an almost unique place in the world as a region where, in all probability, the earliest developments of civilization and organized government took place. Though many archaeologists would not wholly subscribe to the view of Egypt as actually the first civilized country, there can be no doubt that from very early times the lower Nile Valley has been prominent as possessing strongly marked unity, with a highly specialized and characteristic way of life. Empires with fluctuating boundaries and with varying racial composition have arisen in neighbouring lands of the Middle East, but Egypt has seemed able to stand relatively unchanged, with the facility of absorbing immigrants and outside ideas, of surviving military occupation and defeat, and of maintaining her own culture, finally shaking clear of foreign influence and rule.

PHYSICAL FEATURES

The reasons for this remarkable persistence of cultural cohesion amongst the Egyptian people may be found in the geography of the country. Egypt consists essentially of a narrow, trough-like valley, some 3 to 15 km. wide, cut by the River Nile in the plateau of north-east Africa. At an earlier geological period a gulf of the Mediterranean Sea probably extended as far south as Cairo, but deposition of silt by the Nile has entirely filled up this gulf, producing the fan-shaped Delta region (22,000 sq. km. in area), through which flow two main distributary branches of the Nile—the eastern, or Damietta branch (240 km. long), and the western, or Rosetta branch (235 km.), together with many other minor channels. As deposition of silt takes place large stretches of water are gradually impounded to form shallow lakes, which later became firm ground. At the present time there are four such stretches of water in the north of the Delta: from east to west, and, in order of size, Lakes Menzaleh, Brullos, Idku and Mariut.

Upstream from Cairo the Nile Valley is at first 10 to 15 km. in width, and, as the river tends to lie close to the eastern side, much of the cultivated land, and also most of the big towns and cities, lie on the western bank. Towards the south the river valley gradually narrows until, at about 400 km. from the frontier of Sudan, it is no more than 3 km. wide. Near Aswan there is an outcrop of resistant rock, chiefly granite, which the river has not been able to erode as quickly as the rest of the valley. This gives rise to a region of cascades and rapids which is known as the First Cataract. Four other similar regions occur on the Nile, but only the First Cataract lies within Egypt. The cataracts form a barrier to human movement upstream and serve to isolate the Egyptian Nile from territories farther south. In Ancient Egypt, when river communications were of chief importance, there was a traditional division of the Nile Valley into Lower Egypt (the Delta), Middle Egypt (the broader valley above the Delta), and Upper Egypt (the narrower valley as far as the cataracts). Nowadays it is usual to speak merely of Upper and Lower Egypt, with the division occurring at Cairo.

The fertile strip of the Nile Valley is isolated on the south by the cataracts and by the deserts and swamps of the Sudan; on the north by the Mediterranean Sea; and to east and west by desert plateaux, about which a little more must be said. The land immediately to the east of the Nile Valley, spoken of as the Eastern Highlands, is a complex region with peaks that rise 1,800 to 2,100 metres but also much broken up by deep valleys that make travel difficult. Owing to aridity the whole region is sparsely populated, with a few partly nomadic shepherds, one or two monasteries and a number of small towns associated chiefly with the exploitation of minerals—petroleum, iron, manganese and granite—that occur in this region. Difficult landward communications mean that contact is mostly by sea, except in the case of the ironfields. The Sinai, separated from the Eastern Highlands by the Gulf of Suez, is structurally very similar, but the general plateau level is tilted, giving the highest land (again nearly 2,100 metres in elevation) in the extreme south, where it rises in bold scarps from sea-level. Towards the north the land gradually slopes down, ultimately forming the low-lying sandy plain of the Sinai desert which fringes the Mediterranean Sea. Because of its low altitude and accessibility, the Sinai, in spite of its desert nature, has been for many centuries an important corridor linking Egypt with Asia. It is now crossed only by a motor road, the railway having been torn up in 1968 by occupying Israeli forces.

West of the Nile occur the vast expanses known as the Western Desert. Though by no means uniform in height, the land surface is much lower than that east of the Nile, and within Egypt rarely exceeds 300 metres above sea-level. Parts are covered by extensive masses of light shifting sand that often form dunes; but in addition there are a number of large depressions, some with the lowest parts actually below sea-level. These depressions seem to have been hollowed out by wind action, breaking up rock strata that were weakened by the presence of underground water, and most hollows still contain supplies of artesian water. In some instances (as for example, the Qattara depression, and the Wadi Natrun, respectively south-west and south-east of Alexandria) the subterranean water is highly saline and consequently useless for agriculture; but in others—notably the oases of the Fayyum, Siwa, Dakhla, Behariya, and Farafra—the water is sufficiently sweet to allow use for irrigation, and settlements have grown up within the desert. In the last few years, much attention has been given to irrigation development in these oases, which are sometimes spoken of as "the New Territories."

CLIMATE

The main feature of Egyptian climate is the almost uniform aridity. Alexandria, the wettest part, receives only 20 cm. of rain annually, and most of the south has 8 cm. or less. In many districts rain may fall in quantity only once in two or three years, and it is apposite to recall that throughout most of Egypt, and even in Cairo itself, the majority of the people live in houses of unbaked, sun-dried brick. During the summer temperatures are extremely high, reaching 38° to 43°C. at times and even 49°C. in the southern and western deserts. The Mediterranean coast has cooler conditions, with 32°C. as a maximum; hence the wealthier classes move to Alexandria for the three months of summer. Winters are generally warm, with very occasional rain; but cold spells occur from time to time, and light snow is not unknown. Owing to the large extent of desert, hot dry sand-winds (called *khamsin*) are fairly frequent particularly in spring, and much damage can be caused to crops; it has been known for the temperature to rise by 20°C. in two hours, and the wind to reach 150 km. per hour. Another unusual condition is the occurrence of early morning fog in Lower Egypt during spring and early summer. This, on the other hand, has a beneficial effect on plant growth in that it supplies moisture and is a partial substitute for rainfall.

IRRIGATION

With a deficient rainfall over the entire country, human existence in Egypt depends closely on irrigation from the Nile; in consequence it is now necessary to consider the regime of the river in some detail.

More detailed reference to conditions outside Egypt is made in the section on the geography of Sudan (below); but it may here be stated in summary that the river rises in the highlands of East Africa, with its main stream issuing from Lakes Victoria and Albert. In the southern Sudan it wanders sluggishly across a flat open plain, where the fall in level is only 1:100,000. Here the shallow waters become a vast swamp, full of dense masses of papyrus vegetation, and this section of the Nile is called the Sudd (Arabic for "blockage") Finally, in the north of the Sudan, the Nile flows in a well-defined channel and enters Egypt. In Upper Egypt the river is in process of cutting its bed deeper into the rock floor; but in the lower part of its course silt is deposited, and the level of the land is rising—in some places by as much as 10 cm. per century.

The salient feature of the Nile is, of course, its regular annual flood, which is caused by the onset of summer rains in East Africa and Ethiopia. The flood travels northward, reaching Egypt during August, and within Egypt the normal rise in river level was at first 6.4 metres, which had declined to 4.6 metres as irrigation works developed. This cycle of flood had been maintained for several thousand years until, in 1969, construction of the Aswan High Dam made it a feature of the past (see the section on the High Dam below) so far as Egypt is concerned.

Originally, the flood waters were simply retained in specially prepared basins with earthen banks, and the water could then be used for three to four months after the flood. Within the last century, building of large barrages held water all the year round, allowing cultivation at any season. The old (basin) system allowed one or two crops per holding per year, the newer (perennial) system, three or even four. In the past, barley and wheat were the main crops; under perennial irrigation maize and cotton, which can tolerate the great summer heat provided they are watered, take first and second place.

Changeover from basin to perennial irrigation allowed a considerable population increase in Egypt, from about 2½ million in 1800 to over 42 million in 1981, giving rural densities of over 2,500 per square km. in some areas; and, as 99 per cent of all Egyptians live within the Nile valley (only 4 per cent of its area), there is considerable pressure on the land.

With most Egyptians entirely dependent upon Nile water, the point has now been reached that almost all the water entering Egypt is fully utilized. However, there are enormous losses by evaporation which at present amount to some 70 per cent of the total flow. A political problem is concerned with the effects of devoting an increased area of the Nile Valley to the growing of commodities for export: cotton, rice and vegetables. Such a change from agricultural self-sufficiency to a cash economy involves the purchase abroad of fertilizers and even foodstuffs, and is inducing considerable social changes within the country. Moreover, so long as only one or two crops were taken per year, the silt laid down by the annual floods maintained soil fertility, but now that three or four crops are taken the import of fertilizer is essential. Hence Egypt has become increasingly sensitive to world trade prices. The position of the merchant and capitalist has greatly improved, often at the expense of the peasant farmer. This was to some extent true in Nasserist times and is certainly true of the situation since 1970.

Difficulties and opportunities over use of Nile water are exemplified in the High Dam scheme at Aswan, which has created a lake 350 miles (500 km.) in length and 6 miles (10 km.) wide that has extended southwards across the Sudanese frontier and inundated the town of Wadi Halfa, whose 55,000–60,000 inhabitants were re-settled at Kashm el Girba, a district lying south east of Khartoum, whilst displaced Egyptians were settled in 33 villages around Kom Ombo: total costs of re-settlement were about £14 million. Prior to 1959 technical and political objections delayed the High Dam scheme; and as the cost of the dam (estimated at £345–400 million) could not be met by the Egyptian Government alone, application was made to the World Bank, America and Britain for a loan. This was refused (Sudanese opposition being one, but only one, factor in this refusal), whereupon Egyptian reaction was to expropriate the Suez Canal Company, in order to finance part of the Aswan scheme.

Soviet offers to assist were made and accepted; and in 1959 a first Soviet credit of £33 million allowed preliminary work to begin in December of the same year. In 1960 further agreement was reached by which the U.S.S.R. supplied credits up to £81 million (making a total of £194 million) together with technical and material assistance; and in 1964 further proposals for credit and loans were made by Nikita Khrushchev, then the Soviet head of government. Egypt must thus find at least £200 million in addition to repayments at a later stage of the Soviet credits.

In May 1964 the first phase of the High Dam was inaugurated by President Nasser and Mr. Khrushchev. The High Dam is 3,600 metres across, with a girth of 980 metres at the river bed and 40 metres at the top. It holds back the largest artificial lake in the world, and makes possible large scale storing of water from year to year, and a regular planned use of all Nile water independently of the precise amount of annual flood. Its irrigation potential is 2 million feddans for Lower Egypt alone, and the total for the Nile valley (including Upper Egypt) is adding 30 per cent to the total cultivable area of Egypt. Twelve generator units incorporated in the dam give considerable quantities of low-cost electric power (lower than costs in much of Europe and less than 50 per cent of that of electricity in London). This power is already a most important aid to industrialization, especially for the new metal industries. Started in January 1960, the Dam was completed in July 1970 and officially inaugurated in January 1971.

Adverse effects have been noticed: scouring of the Nile bed below the dam; increased salinity in the lower stretches; reduced sedimentation below the dam and heavy deposition within the basin, resulting in the need for increasing use of artificial fertilizers, which must be imported; effects of blowing sand on the electric power lines; and, perhaps more seriously, the disappearance of fish (particularly sardines) off the Mediterranean coast of Egypt. It is hoped that this last can be compensated by new fishing within Lake Nasser.

Perhaps the most serious of all is a notable rise in the water-table in some areas, due to hydrostatic pressures, and all-the-year-round presence of water. Besides disturbing irrigation systems (which are adapted to pre-existing conditions), salinity and gleying of a more permanent nature are appearing; bilharzia and other parasitic diseases are spreading; and there is the appearance of the plant water hyacinth, which, if uncleared, can choke irrigation systems.

RACE

The racial origins of the Egyptian people present certain problems. In the deserts to east and west of the Nile Valley the population is of unmixed Mediterranean strains; but within the Nile Valley itself there is a special native Egyptian type that would seem to have developed partly from intermixture. The Egyptian peasant is more heavily built and muscular than the nomadic Bedouin, and his colouring is intermediate between the lighter brown of Syrian and Palestinian Arabs and the dark skins of the negroid peoples of the Sudan and Abyssinia. Facial features show some resemblance to those of other Arabs, but despite this there is often more than a hint of the features depicted in ancient monuments. It might thus be reasonable to suggest that there seems to have developed in Egypt a special racial sub-type, basically Mediterranean, with smaller elements both from the south and the north, but also greatly affected by local indigenous conditions which have given rise to a specific Egyptian racial type.

LANGUAGE

Arabic is the language of almost all Egyptians, though there are very small numbers of Berber-speaking villages in the western oases. Most educated Egyptians also speak either French or English, often with a preference for the former. This is a reflection of the traditional French interest in Egypt, which is reciprocated: governmental decrees are sometimes published in French, as well as Arabic, and newspapers in French have an important circulation in Cairo and Alexandria. Small colonies of Greeks and Armenians are also a feature of the larger Egyptian towns. It should perhaps be noted that the Arabic name for Egypt, Misr, is always used within the country itself.

HISTORY

Geography has influenced the history of Egypt from the earliest times. The narrow strip of cultivable land along the banks of the Nile between the First Cataract and the Delta is distinct from the extensive and fertile plain of the Delta itself, but the resultant tendency to separatism has been counterbalanced by the dependence of the people on the annual Nile flood: the control and exploitation of the water and silt have necessitated co-operation and obedience to routine and authority. The eastern and western deserts seal off the lower reaches of the Nile Valley from the neighbouring territories in Africa and Asia. Until recent times communication with the outside world was largely restricted to the route up the river into Nubia, the sea route across the Mediterranean to Syria and the land route to Palestine across the northern fringe of Sinai. The effect of Egypt's relative isolation has been to produce a high degree of cultural individuality.

PHARAONIC EGYPT TO 671 B.C.

Traditionally Egyptian history begins with the semi-legendary Menes, the first ruler of the united kingdom of Upper and Lower Egypt at the end of the fourth millenium B.C. But the flowering of the Old Kingdom came in the third millenium under the IVth Dynasty, which had its capital at Memphis, near the apex of the Delta. The technical and engineering progress of this period is witnessed by the pyramids. These and other works indicate a powerful monarchy commanding great resources.

This efflorescence was followed by a decline. Not until the XIth and XIIth Dynasties (c. 2000 B.C.) does the resurgence of a united Egypt in the Middle Kingdom become clear. The powerful provincial nobles were slowly brought under royal control. Improved conditions were reflected in reclamation works in the Fayyum and temple building at numerous sites. Egyptian armies penetrated into Nubia, a land at that time rich in gold, and the conquest of the region to a point above the Second Cataract was accomplished.

Another obscure period followed and the course of Egyptian history was interrupted by the invasion from Palestine of the Hyksos who established themselves as rulers in the Delta. Although they adopted Egyptian customs, they were never assimilated. About 1620 B.C. a revolt began under a southern prince and ultimately the Hyksos were expelled and Egypt was reunited.

Under the XVIIIth Dynasty, ancient Egypt reached her zenith. This period of the New Kingdom has left its mark up and down the land especially around the capital, Thebes, near the modern Luxor. Abroad the name of the pharaoh was feared in western Asia. The greatest of the conquerors was Thothmes III who established an Egyptian empire in Syria. Egyptian rule was restored and extended in Nubia.

The empire decayed during the reign of Akhenaten (c. 1380–1362), whose religious innovations antagonized the powerful priesthood of Thebes. On his death the old polytheism was restored. The outstanding figure of the XIXth Dynasty was Rameses II (c. 1300-1234). He fought the rising power of the Hittites in Syria for twenty years and was both a great builder and a usurper of other men's works.

After him Egypt passed into decline. The XXth Dynasty closed with a long series of insignificant pharaohs and under their successors Egypt was divided between a ruler in the Delta and a priest-king at Thebes. In the eighth century B.C. a dynasty originating from Nubia held Upper Egypt and even for a time the Delta. But Egypt was soon to pass under completely alien domination.

EGYPT UNDER FOREIGN RULERS: 671 B.C.-A.D. 640

In 671 the Assyrians conquered Egypt and drove out the Nubian pharaoh. The Assyrians, however, did not long maintain their hold and a native ruler succeeded in reuniting the country. The dynasty which he founded encouraged Greek traders and was supported by Greek mercenaries.

This last native dynasty came to an end in 525, when Persia conquered Egypt. The Persian kings patronized the religion of their subjects and were officially regarded as pharaohs. Darius I (522–485) completed the work of an Egyptian predecessor in cutting a canal linking the Nile and the Red Sea. His successors fought native pretenders to keep Egypt within their empire.

Under Alexander the Great another change of masters occurred. The Persian satrap surrendered in 332 and Alexander was recognized as pharaoh. His visit to the oracle at Siwa shows his fascinated interest in Egyptian religion, while by founding the city of Alexandria he conferred on Egypt a lasting benefit. After Alexander's death, Egypt fell to his general, Ptolemy. The Ptolemaic Dynasty was Greek in origin and outlook. Its capital was Alexandria, which was in effect a Greek rather than an Egyptian city. Egypt was the private estate of the Ptolemies, who taxed its people through a competent bureaucracy.

When Cleopatra committed suicide in 30 B.C., Egypt passed under Roman rule. Although the emperors were regarded as successors of the pharaohs the country sank into a mere province of a great Mediterranean empire. Egyptian Christianity had a distinctive doctrinal character and, by fostering monasticism, originated an important institution. In the dogmatic disputes of the Byzantine period, the adherence of the Coptic church of Egypt to monophysite beliefs in face of the official theology was a form of national self-assertion.

ARAB EGYPT: 640-969

In the early seventh century two great powers dominated the Middle East: the Byzantine empire and the Sasanian empire of the Persians. In 616 the Sasanian army invaded Egypt but Byzantine supremacy was soon restored. Meanwhile a third power was arising, the Arabs, summoned by Muhammad to belief in Islam.

The Prophet's death in 632 was followed by wars against the Byzantines and Sasanians. Egypt, the granary of the Byzantine Empire, soon attracted the Muslim warriors. In the reign of the Caliph Umar I an Arab army under 'Amr ibn al-As took the invasion route from Syria. The frontier towns fell after short sieges and in April 641 the key-fortress near the head of the Delta was captured. Alexandria, the capital, surrendered and was evacuated by the Byzantine garrison. A camp-city at Al-Fustat, again in the strategic position near the apex of the Delta, became the headquarters of the Muslim army and the new capital.

For some centuries Egypt remained an occupied rather than a Muslim country. The Copts, who disliked Byzantine rule, had not opposed the conquest. Under the Arabs they found less oppression and paid lower taxes at first than under Constantinople. In course of time, however, Egypt became an Arabic-speaking country with a Muslim majority. But to this day the Coptic Christian minority remains and uses the ancient language in its liturgy.

For over two centuries Egypt was administered as a province of the Arab Empire. By the middle of the ninth century the remoter territories were slipping from the grasp of the Abbasid caliphs of Baghdad. Egypt was obviously well-fitted to be the domain of an autonomous governor. Two short-lived Sunnite Dynasties, founded by men of central Asian origin, the Tulunids and the Ikhshidids, ruled in virtual independence of the caliph between 868 and 969. Each rapidly degenerated after the death of its founder. Ahmad ibn Tulun in 877 occupied Syria and thus once again created an empire based on Egypt.

THE FATIMIDS AND AYYUBIDS: 969-1250

Ikshidid rule was terminated in 969 by an invasion from Tunisia. Here the rival caliphate of the Fatimids had been set up by Muslims of the Shia sect, who believed that the caliphate could only pass through the direct descendants of 'Ali, the husband of Muhammad's daughter, Fatima. The fourth of these anti-caliphs, Al-Mu'izz, was made the master of Egypt by his general, Jawhar. Jawhar laid out a new capital, just outside Al-Fustat, which has developed into the modern city of Cairo, and was the founder of the mosque of Al-Azhar, the greatest centre of Islamic theological learning.

Under the early Fatimids Egypt enjoyed a golden age. The country was a well-administered absolute monarchy and it formed the central portion of an empire which at its height included North Africa, Sicily, Syria and western Arabia. Agriculture and industry were encouraged. Trade with Europe and India brought prosperity to the land and wealth to the ruler.

Soon, however, Fatimid rule began to decay. Ali Hakim (996-1021) departed from the tolerant policy towards Christians and Jews which was normal in Muslim states. The long reign of Al-Mustansir (1035-94) witnessed the break-up of the Fatimid Empire and the growing insubordination of the slave-soldiery. In 1073 the caliph was obliged to send for Badr al Jamali, the governor of Acre, to take control of the country. This he did and Egypt passed under the government of a military autocracy who kept the Fatimid caliphs under their tutelage. Thus the collapse of the Fatimid state was postponed for nearly a century but, after the death of Al-Mustansir, the six succeeding caliphs had no power.

Meanwhile a new enemy was on the threshold—the Crusaders who after 1098 established feudal, Christian states along the Syrian coast. Neither the Abbasids nor the Fatimids were capable of resisting them but in the later twelfth century the tide began to turn. The Muslim reconquest of Syria was largely due to the energy and ability of the Kurdish leader, Salah al-Din ibn Ayyub, known in European history as Saladin. In 1169 he became minister to the Fatimid caliph. In 1171 the last Fatimid was quietly deposed and Egypt restored to Sunni orthodoxy. The remainder of Saladin's life was a struggle against the crusading states but when he died in 1193 he was sultan over Egypt and practically the whole of the former Crusader territory.

Saladin's Empire was divided amongst his heirs, one branch of which, the Egyptian Ayyubids, reigned in Cairo. Dynastic struggles weakened the family and the Crusaders were able to recover some lost ground. Louis IX of France led an attack directly on Egypt. Damietta was occupied in 1249 but the advance of the Crusaders through the difficult and pestilential Delta was stopped at the battle of Al-Mansura in 1250. Louis was made prisoner but subsequently regained his liberty on paying a ransom and restoring Damietta.

THE MAMLUK SULTANATE: 1250-1517

During this Crusade the Ayyubid sultan, al-Malik al-Salih, died. This was virtually the end of the dynasty. After a short confused period the commander of the forces, a certain Aybak became the first of the Mamluk sultans who ruled Egypt from 1250 to 1517. These sultans were of slave origin. The Ayyubids had built up bodyguards of slave-troops, whose power increased as that of their masters declined. The earlier Mamluks, until 1390, were mainly of Turkish and Mongol origin, while their successors, originally the bodyguard of the former, were mostly Circassians. The Mamluk sultans did not form a dynasty in the hereditary sense but a caste from which successive rulers emerged after election or a struggle for power. The ranks of the Mamluks were replenished by fresh purchases.

The Mamluks were thus an alien element which was never fully assimilated in Egypt. They exploited the land for their own benefit and the Egyptians played a

On February 28th, 1922, the British Government issued a declaration unilaterally announcing the abolition of the protectorate and the recognition of Egypt as an independent sovereign state. Four matters were absolutely reserved to the discretion of the British Government, pending the conclusion of negotiated agreements. These were: the security of the communications of the British Empire in Egypt; the defence of Egypt; the protection of foreign interests and of minorities in Egypt; and the Sudan.

In March 1922 the Sultan, Fuad, took the title of King of Egypt and in April a committee was set up to draft a constitution.

THE TRIANGULAR STRUGGLE: 1922-39

The period after the declaration of independence saw a triangular struggle in Egypt between the King, the Wafd and the British Government. The Wafd was organized to carry out a revolution, not to direct affairs of state. The King owed his throne to the British and his presence guaranteed their interests, yet obvious subservience to them might have enabled the Wafd to rob him of his throne.

The new constitution, which made Egypt a parliamentary monarchy on the Belgian model, was promulgated in 1923. The Wafd triumphed in the elections which were then held and Saad Zaghlul became Prime Minister for a brief period in 1924. In the succeeding years political instability continued as the struggle for power between the Wafd and the throne went on. Elections usually gave the Wafd a majority but a Wafd ministry was unacceptable to King Fuad and in this he normally had the concurrence of the British Government. Hence Palace influence was predominant in the ministries appointed and at times legislation had to be enacted by decree. In 1928 the Parliament was suspended for three years, in 1930 modifications were made to the constitution which altered the electoral law, but in 1935 the original provisions were restored and in elections the following year the Wafd again obtained a majority. The month before the elections King Fuad had been succeeded by his son, Farouk, a minor. The new Prime Minister was Nahas Pasha, who had led the Wafd since Zaghlul's death in 1927.

Until 1936 negotiations for an Anglo-Egyptian treaty invariably broke down over questions of defence and the Sudan. The continued presence of British troops was regarded by Egyptians as denying the reality of independence. The Egyptians also felt that they had been ousted by Britain from dominion over the Sudan and control over their water supply. When the Governor-General of the Sudan was assassinated in Cairo in 1924, Allenby demanded the withdrawal of Egyptian troops from the Sudan, and also the unlimited extension of the irrigation of the Sudan Gezira. Although these demands were later modified, the Egyptian share in the Condominium was to remain nominal.

In 1929 the Nile Waters Agreement allotted the respective shares of Egypt and the Sudan, to Egypt's advantage. The deadlock over a treaty ended in 1936 when the rise of Italian power threatened British and Egyptian interests alike. On August 26th an Anglo-Egyptian treaty of twenty years duration was signed which formally terminated British occupation but empowered Britain to station forces in the Suez Canal zone until the Egyptian army was in a position to ensure the security of the Canal. The Sudan was to continue to be administered as in the past. The protection of foreign interests and of minorities in Egypt was recognized as the exclusive responsibility of the Egyptian Government. The abolition of the Capitulations was secured by the Convention of Montreux in May 1937. In the same month Egypt was admitted to the League of Nations.

THE SECOND WORLD WAR AND ITS CONSEQUENCES: 1939-52

In the Second World War Egypt was a vital strategic factor as the British base in the Middle East. Her treaty obligations were fulfilled but the ruling classes were by no means committed to the Allied cause and on occasions popular support for Germany became manifest. Nevertheless the presence of British forces ensured co-operation.

The young King Farouk, who had assumed full royal powers in 1937, was a popular national figure but as determined as his father to avoid domination by the Wafd. Although still the dominant political party, the Wafd was losing its revolutionary fervour and its appeal to youth was diminishing. Fascist influence appeared in the Greenshirt organization, while the Muslim Brotherhood, a puritanical religious body, developed a terrorist wing and threatened the established authorities.

The critical year was 1942. Alamein had not yet been fought, the King was disposed to appease the Axis powers and the government was under Palace influence. The Wafd, however, favoured co-operation with Britain. In February the British Ambassador, supported by an armed escort, entered the Palace and insisted on the formation of a Wafdist government. Threatened with deposition, Farouk acquiesced and Nahas Pasha became Prime Minister and Military Governor of Egypt.

Nahas held office until 1944. During this period Nuri al-Said, the Prime Minister of Iraq, and King Abdulla of Transjordan separately put forward proposals for a union of Arab states in the Fertile Crescent. These were opposed by Egypt as they seemed to favour Iraqi hegemony. Nahas took the initiative, proposing a broader league of Arab states, and a conference was held which in October 1944 produced the Alexandria Protocol. On this the Arab League was founded the following year. From the beginning Egypt held a position of leadership in the League, which was bitterly hostile to the idea of establishing a Jewish state in Palestine. Previously, preoccupied with her own national problems, Egypt had shown little interest in the Palestine problem.

By 1944 the danger to Egypt had passed. Nahas was no longer indispensable and his government fell, discredited by co-operation with the British and by the corruption which had flourished during its tenure of office. The struggle between the Wafd and the

Palace revived. Communism, made attractive, especially among students, by the Russian successes in the war, gained new adherents, and the Muslim Brotherhood continued its subversive activities. Negotiations in the immediate post-war years for a new treaty with Britain broke down over the questions of the British occupation of the Canal Zone and the future of the Sudan.

In Palestine Britain's renunciation of the Mandate on May 14th, 1948, was followed immediately by the declaration of the State of Israel and military action by Egypt, Iraq, Syria and Jordan. The Egyptian army was badly defeated. Although the fact was long concealed from the Egyptian public, it eventually recoiled on the ruling classes. The King's early popularity had vanished; military failure and the scandal of the supply of faulty arms, in which members of the Palace clique were implicated, undermined the loyalty of the army, which was his last support.

The fall of the discredited regime did not come immediately. The Communists, although widespread, lacked the means to capture the administration. A terrorist campaign by the Muslim Brotherhood was suppressed and the organization driven underground in 1949. Nahas, again in power, made a last bid for royal and popular support in 1951 by abrogating the Treaty of 1936 and the Condominium Agreement and proclaiming Farouk "King of Egypt and Sudan". New British proposals on the Sudan were rejected, as also were proposals on defence, involving the creation of an Allied Middle East Command with Egyptian participation, put forward jointly by Britain, France, Turkey and the United States. Terrorism and economic sanctions were then employed in an attempt to force the withdrawal of British forces from the Canal Zone. Clashes occurred, resulting in many deaths, and on January 26th, 1952, an anti-British demonstration in Cairo developed into rioting, looting and a conflagration, brought to an end only by army intervention.

THE REVOLUTION: 1952-56

On July 23rd, 1952, a group of young army officers, the "Free Officers", who had long been planning a *coup d'état*, seized power in Cairo. They invited the veteran politician, Ali Maher, to form a government under their control, and secured the abdication of King Farouk in favour of his infant son, Ahmed Fuad II, on July 26th. Farouk sailed to exile.

General Muhammad Neguib, an associate of the Free Officers who had incurred the enmity of King Farouk and who had earlier made himself popular by his condemnation of the British action in 1942, was made Commander-in-Chief of the armed forces and head of the military junta. A Council of Regency was formed in August. On September 7th, after an attempt by the Wafd and other parties to resume the political battle on their own terms, a new cabinet with General Neguib as Prime Minister was substituted for that of Ali Maher. Real power, however, lay with the nine officers who formed the Revolutionary Command Council.

The Revolution soon gained momentum. In September 1952 land ownership was limited to 300 acres in any one family and the power of the feudal class which had for so long dominated Egyptian political life was destroyed. Land owned by the royal family was confiscated. On December 10th the constitution was abolished and on January 16th, 1953, all political parties were dissolved. It was announced that there would be a three-year transition period before representative government was restored. On June 18th the monarchy was abolished and Egypt declared a republic, with Neguib as President and Prime Minister as well as Chairman of the Revolutionary Command Council. Colonel Gamal Abdel Nasser, who, although leader of the Free Officers, had hitherto remained in the background, became Deputy Prime Minister and Minister of the Interior, and Abdel Hakim Amer was appointed Commander-in-Chief of the armed forces.

A struggle for power soon developed between General Neguib, whose personal tendencies were Islamic and conservative, and Colonel Nasser. On February 25th, 1954, Neguib was relieved of his posts as President, Prime Minister and Chairman of the Revolutionary Command Council and accused of having attempted to concentrate power in his own hands. Nasser became Prime Minister and Chairman of the Revolutionary Command Council in his place for a few days but Neguib was restored as President and took back both the other posts, only to be ousted again as Prime Minister by Nasser in April. Neguib had suffered a defeat and his liberal measures were rescinded. When in October a member of the Muslim Brotherhood attempted to assassinate Nasser, its leaders and several thousand alleged supporters were arrested and in subsequent trials a number of death sentences were passed. On November 14th, 1954, General Neguib was relieved of the office of President and accused of being involved in a Muslim Brotherhood conspiracy against the regime. He was placed under house arrest and Colonel Nasser became acting head of state.

A settlement of the Sudan and Suez problems had been facilitated by the expulsion of King Farouk. The claim to the joint monarchy of Egypt and the Sudan was dropped and negotiations with Sudanese leaders were helped by the fact that Neguib himself was half-Sudanese and popular in the Sudan. An Anglo-Egyptian agreement, signed on February 12th, 1953, ended the Condominium and offered the Sudanese the choice of independence or union with Egypt. Egyptian expectation that they would choose the latter was disappointed; the overthrow of Neguib and the suppression of the Muslim Brotherhood fed the century-old suspicion of Egyptian motives.

An Anglo-Egyptian agreement on Suez was signed on October 19th, 1954; this provided for the withdrawal of British troops from the Canal Zone within twenty months. The agreement recognized the international importance of the Suez Canal (which was described as "an integral part of Egypt") and expressed the determination of both parties to uphold the 1888 convention.

Under Nasser Egypt began to assert her importance in world affairs. He sought influence in three circles: the Islamic, the African and the Arab, and his visit to the Bandung conference in 1955 added a fourth: the "non-aligned". Egypt led the opposition among certain Arab states to the Baghdad Pact (on which was founded the Central Treaty Organization). In October 1955 Egypt concluded defence agreements with Syria and with Saudi Arabia and in April 1956 a military pact was signed between Egypt, Saudi Arabia and the Yemen. Tension with Israel remained high, and raids and counter-raids across the border of the Gaza Strip called for unceasing vigilance on the part of the United Nations observers stationed on the frontier. In September 1955 Nasser announced an arms deal with Czechoslovakia which was to supply large quantities of military equipment, including Soviet tanks and aircraft, in return for cotton and rice.

In 1956 a constitutional basis for Colonel Nasser's authority was established. A new constitution providing for a strong presidency was proclaimed in January and on June 23rd approved in a plebiscite in which the citizens of the Egyptian Republic also elected Nasser as President.

THE SUEZ CRISIS AND ITS CONSEQUENCES: 1956-57

President Nasser's policy of non-alignment, which implied willingness to deal with both power blocs, was followed in the Egyptian attempt to obtain funds for the ambitious High Dam project at Aswan. By this project the Egyptian Government aimed to increase cultivable land and generate electricity for industrialization, which was seen as the main solution to Egypt's increasing population problem. Following offers of assistance from the United States and Britain and, separately, by the U.S.S.R., the International Bank for Reconstruction and Development offered a loan of $200 million in February 1956, on condition that the United States and Britain lent a total of $70 million and that the agreement of the riparian states to the scheme was obtained; Egypt was to provide local services and material.

The last British troops were withdrawn from Egypt in June 1956, in accordance with the 1954 agreement. Relations with the West were not helped, however, by Egyptian opposition to the Baghdad Pact and strong propaganda attacks on Britain, France and the United States. On July 20th the United States and Britain withdrew their offers of finance for the High Dam, pointing out that agreement between the riparian states had not been achieved and that Egypt's ability to devote adequate resources to the scheme was doubtful. The U.S.S.R. made no compensating move. On July 26th President Nasser announced that the Suez Canal Company had been nationalized and that revenue from the Canal would be used to finance the High Dam.

Britain, France and the United States protested strongly at this action and after an international conference had met in London in August a committee under the chairmanship of Mr. Menzies, the Prime Minister of Australia, went to Cairo to submit proposals for the operation of the Canal under an international system. These were rejected by the Egyptian Government. At a second London conference, in September, a Suez Canal Users' Association took shape and was later joined by sixteen states. On October 13th the UN Security Council voted on an Anglo-French resolution embodying basic principles for a settlement agreed earlier between the British, French and Egyptian Foreign Ministers in the presence of the UN Secretary-General. The first part of this, setting out the agreed principles, was adopted unanimously; the second, endorsing the proposals of the first London conference and inviting Egypt to make prompt proposals providing no less effective guarantees to users, was vetoed by the U.S.S.R.

Britain and France, thus frustrated in their attempts to retain some measure of control over the Suez Canal, at this stage reached a secret understanding with Israel involving military action. Following the disclosure on October 24th that a unified military command had been formed by Egypt, Jordan and Syria, Israeli forces on October 29th crossed into Sinai, ostensibly to attack Egyptian *fedayeen* bases, and advanced towards the Suez Canal. On October 30th France and Britain called on Israel and Egypt to cease warlike action and withdraw their forces from either side of the Canal; Egypt was requested to agree to an Anglo-French force moving temporarily into key positions at Port Said, Ismailia and Suez. Israel agreed but Egypt refused. The same day in the UN Security Council Britain and France vetoed United States and Soviet resolutions calling for an immediate Israeli withdrawal and calling on all UN members to refrain from the use of force or the threat of force.

Anglo-French air operations against Egypt began on October 31st but paratroops and seaborne forces landed in the Port Said area only on November 5th. Meanwhile, on November 2nd, the UN General Assembly called for a cease-fire and two days later adopted a Canadian proposal to create a United Nations Emergency Force to supervise the ending of the hostilities. On November 6th, following heavy United States pressure, the British Prime Minister, Sir Anthony Eden, announced that, subject to confirmation that Egypt and Israel had accepted an unconditional cease-fire, the armed conflict would end at midnight.

The organization of the UN force was rapidly put in hand and the first units reached Egypt on November 15th. The withdrawal of the Anglo-French forces was completed the following month. The Israelis, who had occupied the entire Sinai peninsula, withdrew from all areas except the Gaza strip, which they wished to prevent becoming a base for more raids, and Sharm el-Sheikh at the entrance to the Gulf of Aqaba, which commanded the seaway to the port of Eilat. These areas were returned to Egyptian control in March 1957 after pressure on Israel by the United States.

The Suez Canal, which had been blocked by the Egyptians, was cleared by a UN salvage fleet and reopened at the end of March 1957. The terms under which the canal reopened were full control by the

Egyptian Canal Authority and respect for the Constantinople Convention of 1888. Disputes would be settled in accordance with the UN Charter or referred to the International Court of Justice.

UNION OF EGYPT AND SYRIA

Elections to the Egyptian National Assembly, provided for in the 1956 constitution, were held in July 1957. Only candidates approved by President Nasser and his colleagues were permitted to stand and it was clear that the 350 members elected (who included women) were not expected to exert much influence on the government.

Following the defence agreement in 1955, discussions had been held in the following two years on union between Egypt and Syria. Both countries were aligned against the West and looked to the U.S.S.R. and other Communist states for support, and in Syria pro-Egyptian elements were in the ascendant. On February 1st, 1958 the union of Egypt and Syria under the title of the United Arab Republic (U.A.R.) was announced. The implementation of the union took time, and it was not until July 21st, 1960, that the first National Assembly of the U.A.R., consisting of deputies from both Egypt and Syria, was opened in Cairo by President Nasser.

EXTERNAL RELATIONS: 1958-61

During this period President Nasser was actively concerned with changes in the rest of the Arab world.

An invitation was extended to other Arab states to join the new Union and in March 1958 the U.A.R. and the Yemen entered into a loose association referred to as the United Arab States. This association did not prosper, however, and was terminated by the U.A.R. in December 1961.

The military revolution in Iraq in July, in which the royal family and the Prime Minister, Nuri al-Said, were murdered, destroyed the only Arab regime in the Middle East to have identified itself explicitly with the West. The immediate dispatch of American troops to the Lebanon and British forces to Jordan drew strong protests from the U.A.R. which were echoed by the U.S.S.R. The U.S.A. and Britain gave warning of the grave consequences of any conflict between their forces and those under the control of Egypt and Syria. President Nasser visited Moscow and on his return received in Damascus a delegation from the new republican regime in Baghdad. A joint communiqué on July 19th declared that the U.A.R. and Iraq would assist each other to repel any foreign aggression.

U.A.R. propaganda voiced support for a revolt which broke out at Mosul in Iraq in March 1959, and there were mass demonstrations in Cairo and Damascus in sympathy with the rebels. The Iraqi Government of General Kassem countered with the accusation that the revolt had been engineered from Syria. The political committee of the Arab League met at Beirut in April in an attempt to reduce the prevailing

tension but Iraq took no part in the principal activities of the League until 1960 when relations with the U.A.R. improved.

President Nasser's hostility to the West found favour with the U.S.S.R., with which the U.A.R. established closer ties during these years. Soviet military and industrial aid was granted and in December 1958 an agreement was concluded which ensured Soviet assistance for the building of the Aswan High Dam. Work on the first stage of the High Dam began in January 1960.

Relations with the West improved during 1959 and 1960. Through the mediation of the International Bank for Reconstruction and Development an agreement with Britain was signed on March 1st, 1959, providing for the payment by the U.A.R. of £27½ million as compensation for British private property taken over at the time of the Suez crisis in 1956. Diplomatic relations with Britain were resumed at chargé d'affaires level in December 1959 and raised to ambassadorial level early in 1961. A $56.5 million loan to improve the Suez Canal was obtained from the World Bank in 1959, and other aid came from the U.S.A. in 1960.

SYRIAN WITHDRAWAL FROM U.A.R.

President Nasser replaced the two Regional Executive Councils and the Central Cabinet of the U.A.R. with a single Central Government in August 1961. Syria had by now become dissatisfied with the union and on September 28th the Syrian army seized control in Damascus and Syria withdrew from the U.A.R. President Nasser at first called for resistance to the Syrian *coup d'état* but, when the rebels were seen to be in firm control, said on October 5th that he would not oppose recognition of Syria's independence. The loss of Syria was a bitter blow to President Nasser and his Egyptian colleagues who now set about a re-examination of their policies which resulted in a renewal of revolutionary fervour.

The U.A.R. Government (Egypt retained the full title) was re-formed on October 18th and a National Congress of Popular Forces, consisting of 1,750 delegates, representing not geographical areas but economic and professional interests and other social groups, met in Cairo on May 21st, 1962. President Nasser presented the National Congress with a draft National Charter outlining his programme for developing the U.A.R. on Arab socialist lines. A new democratic system of government was introduced, based on the Arab Socialist Union (replacing the National Union) and including popular councils at least half the members of which would be workers or *fellahin*.

MORE ATTEMPTS AT UNION

The Syrian *coup d'état* had been preceded by the overthrow in February 1963 of the regime of General Kassem in Iraq. These changes in power brought Syria and Iraq into closer alignment with Egypt and it was announced on April 17th that agreement had been reached on the formation of a federation of the three countries under the name of the United Arab

Republic. Rivalries, however, arose in both Baghdad and Damascus between supporters of the Baath Party and "Nasserists" and by August President Nasser had withdrawn from the agreement, claiming that the Baathists had set up one-party dictatorships in Syria and Iraq and ignored his insistence on wider nationalist representation.

A month later President Arif of Iraq called for a Baathist union of the three countries, but after the expulsion of Baath leaders from Iraq in November 1963 and the consolidation of power in Arif's hands the unity movement between Iraq and Syria fell apart and Iraq and Egypt again moved closer together. A Unified Political Command between Iraq and Egypt began work in early 1965, but progress towards unity was slow.

During 1964 President Nasser took an important initiative in Arab League affairs by calling two Arab summits in Egypt, which determined Arab policy on the use of water from the River Jordan and also strengthened the armies of Syria, Lebanon and Jordan. A further £E1 million was set aside for the formation of the Palestine Liberation Organization.

The Arab reconciliation and presentation of a united front lasted until the spring of 1965. Iraq, Kuwait, Yemen (Republic), Algeria and the Lebanon continued to follow President Nasser's lead, only Syrian critics complaining that U.A.R. policy was not sufficiently anti-Israeli. U.A.R. relations with Jordan improved strikingly and, after a conference of heads of Arab governments in Cairo in January 1965 to discuss co-ordination of Arab policies, King Hussein, previously the object of U.A.R. attacks and derision, himself paid a visit to Cairo.

In the Yemen, despite Egyptian support, the republican regime seemed no closer to victory over the royalists, who held the mountainous regions of the north-east and were assisted by Saudi Arabian finance and supplies of arms. This military stalemate and the financial burden of maintaining some 50,000 troops in the Yemen moved President Nasser to attempt to disengage, but negotiations ended in deadlock and Egyptian troops remained in the Yemen. On February 22nd, 1966, the day the British Government announced that British forces would leave Aden and South Arabia when that territory became independent in 1968, President Nasser stated that Egyptian troops would not be withdrawn until the revolution in the Yemen could "defend itself against the conspiracies of imperialism and reactionaries".

CHANGES OF INTERNATIONAL ALIGNMENT

The years 1964 and 1965 saw a deterioration of U.A.R. relations with the West and increasing dependence on the Soviet Union.

Relations with the United States were adversely affected by U.A.R. support for the Stanleyville rebels in the Congo during the winter of 1964–65. Diplomatic relations with Britain, already worsened by Egyptian encouragement of dissident elements in South Arabia, were severed by the U.A.R. in December 1965 over the Rhodesia issue, in common with eight other members of the Organization of African Unity.

Relations with the U.S.S.R. had been strengthened in May 1964 when the Soviet Premier, Nikita Khruschev, made a sixteen-day visit to Egypt to attend the ceremony marking the completion of the first stage of the Aswan High Dam, being built with Soviet aid. President Nasser paid his third visit to the U.S.S.R. in August 1965 and (Khruschev having been overthrown) the new Soviet Premier, Alexei Kosygin, visited the U.A.R. in May 1966, expressing support for U.A.R. policies and again demonstrating Soviet interest in the Middle East.

DOMESTIC TROUBLES

Although President Nasser obtained over 99 per cent of the votes cast in the presidential referendum in March 1965, there were subsequently more signs of discontent in the U.A.R. than at any time since he had come to power. In a speech to Arab students during his visit to Moscow in August 1965, he disclosed that a plot against his life had been discovered, in which the banned Muslim Brotherhood was thought to have been involved.

In September 1965 a new government headed by Zakaria Mohieddin replaced that of Ali Sabri, who became Secretary-General of the Arab Socialist Union. Thereafter, administrative changes were made and the security system was tightened up. Taxation was increased and measures of retrenchment were introduced because of increasing economic difficulties, particularly the acute shortage of foreign exchange. United States wheat supplies were continued, credits from France, Japan and Italy and a loan from Kuwait were obtained and there were increased drawings from the International Monetary Fund. Nevertheless the level of imports, particularly food to feed the growing population, and the debt service burden resulting from the first five-year plan caused a continuing drain on foreign exchange reserves and the U.A.R. faced a balance of payments crisis. The second five-year plan was revised and extended over seven years and President Nasser gave public warnings that sacrifices were necessary in every field as Egypt lacked the foreign currency to pay for imports. He refused, however, to abandon the expensive commitment in the Yemen. Zakaria Mohieddin's replacement in September 1966 by Sidki Soliman (a technocrat who retained his post as Minister of the High Dam) was seen as the outcome of disagreement over retrenchment measures. When the U.A.R. defaulted on repayments due to the International Monetary Fund in December 1966, the country was seen to be on the verge of bankruptcy.

WIDENING RIFT WITH SAUDI ARABIA

The rift between the U.A.R. and Saudi Arabia widened. President Nasser in February 1966 expressed opposition to an Islamic grouping which King Faisal was promoting, and in the succeeding months propaganda warfare between the two countries was intensified. In the middle of the year the President gave notice that he would not attend an Arab summit conference with Saudi Arabia and Jordan, both of whom he criticized for obtaining British and United States military aid, and called for the indefinite postponement of the conference planned for September. A majority of Arab states agreed, but in October Tunisia broke off relations with the U.A.R. over continued differences on Arab League policies.

In the Yemen Egyptian forces had been withdrawn from northern and eastern areas and concentrated in the triangle between Sana'a, Hodeida and Taiz. Egyptian control over the republican armed forces and administration was increased and when, in September 1966, after President Sallal had returned to the Yemen from a year's absence in Cairo, the republican Prime Minister, Hassan al-Amri, and seven senior members of his cabinet visited Egypt to make a plea for greater independence, they were arrested and detained there. The following month about 100 senior Yemen officials were dismissed and arrests and executions were carried out.

WAR WITH ISRAEL

The events of May 1967 were to transform the Middle East scene. There had been an increase of Syrian guerrilla activities in Israel during the previous six months and on April 7th the tension had led to fighting in the Tiberias area in which six Syrian aircraft had been shot down. Israeli warnings to the Syrian Government, culminating on May 12th in the threat by Premier Eshkol of severe reprisals if terrorist activities were not controlled, evoked Syrian allegations that Israel was about to mount a large scale attack on Syria. President Nasser, who had been reproached for not aiding Syria in the April fighting in accordance with the mutual defence agreement, responded immediately, moving large numbers of troops to the Israel border. He secured the dissolution of the UN Emergency Force, whose presence on the Egyptian side of the frontier depended on Egyptian permission, and re-occupied the gun emplacement at Sharm el Sheikh on the Straits of Tiran. He later justified these steps by claiming that he had received Syrian and Soviet warnings that Israeli troops were concentrated on the Syrian border (an allegation subsequently disproved by reports of UN truce observers) and an invasion of Syria was imminent.

When on May 23rd President Nasser closed the Straits of Tiran to Israeli shipping, thereby effectively blockading the Israeli port of Eilat, his prestige in the Arab world reached an unparalleled height. Britain and the United States protested that the Gulf of Aqaba was an international waterway; Israel regarded the blockade of the Straits as an unambiguous act of war. As tension increased, King Hussein of Jordan concluded a mutual defence pact with the U.A.R. and was immediately joined by Iraq. Gestures of support were made to Nasser by all Arab leaders, including President Bourguiba and King Faisal.

On the morning of June 5th Israel launched large-scale air attacks on Egyptian, Jordanian, Syrian and Iraqi airfields and Israeli ground forces made rapid advances into the Gaza Strip, Sinai and western Jordan; there was also fighting on the Israeli-Syrian border. The outcome was decided within hours by the air strikes, which destroyed the bulk of the Arab air forces, and the Israeli ground forces were everywhere successful. By June 10th, when all participants had accepted the UN Security Council's call for a cease-fire, Israeli troops were in control of the Sinai peninsula as far as the Suez Canal (including Sharm el Sheikh), the west bank of the Jordan (including the Old City of Jerusalem), the Gaza Strip and Syrian territory extending twelve miles from the Israel border. The Suez Canal was blocked by Egypt in the course of the fighting. President Nasser offered to resign, but popular support led him to withdraw his resignation. He dismissed a number of senior army officers and took over himself the duties of Prime Minister and Secretary-General of the Arab Socialist Union.

The implications of the catastrophe were only gradually realized. It was estimated that the loss of revenue from the Suez Canal, from oil produced in Sinai and from tourism amounted to some £12.5 million a month, or almost half Egypt's foreign currency earnings. Also, the withdrawal of a large part of the Egyptian force in the Yemen reduced Nasser's ability to influence affairs both in that country and in Aden and South Arabia (which became independent as the Republic of Southern Yemen on November 30th, 1967, after the withdrawal of British troops).

The Soviet Union, which had given the Arab cause strong verbal support throughout the crisis, continued to take a strong pro-Arab stand at the United Nations and President Podgorny paid a lengthy visit to Cairo to discuss future Egyptian policy. The U.S.S.R. replaced about half the lost Egyptian aircraft and provided other military supplies and instructors. Further economic assistance was also offered by the Soviet Union and in May 1968 an agreement was announced for the construction of a steel complex at Helwan.

Israel demanded direct negotiations with the Arab states for a peace settlement but the fourth conference of Arab heads of state, held in Khartoum at the end of August 1967, decided against recognition or negotiation with Israel. At this conference, in which Syria did not participate, it was agreed that the embargo on oil supplies to Western countries (applied the previous June) should be lifted, that the Suez Canal should remain closed until Israeli forces were withdrawn, and that Saudi Arabia, Kuwait and Libya should give special aid of £95 million a year to the U.A.R. (and also £40 million a year to Jordan) until the "effects of the aggression" were eliminated. King Faisal and President Nasser announced their agreement on a peace plan for the Yemen under which Egyptian troops were to be withdrawn within three months and Saudi Arabia was to stop supplying the royalists; the withdrawal was subsequently completed by December (President Sallal being deposed by republican leaders in November).

After repeated violations of the cease-fire by both

sides, the UN Security Council on November 22nd, 1967, adopted a British resolution laying down the principles for a just and lasting peace in the Middle East and authorizing the appointment of a special UN representative to assist in bringing about a settlement. This was Resolution 242 (*see* Documents on Palestine page 76) which later formed the basis of most attempts to restore peace to the Middle East. Dr. Gunnar Jarring was appointed special UN representative, and quickly began discussions with Arab and Israeli leaders which continued for a number of years.

U.A.R. AFTER THE JUNE WAR

Meanwhile President Nasser faced daunting economic difficulties and a disturbed political situation in Egypt. An austerity budget had been framed in July 1967. The cost of re-equipping the armed forces forced a cut in investment, in spite of Soviet aid and assistance from other Arab governments. Socialist policies were still followed, as was shown by the decision to nationalize the wholesale trade, announced in October. The continuing shortage of foreign exchange made desirable an improvement in the U.A.R.'s relations with the West and in December diplomatic relations with Britain were resumed. A bridging loan from British, West German and Italian banks, obtained in February 1968, enabled the U.A.R. to make the repayments to the International Monetary Fund which had been due since the end of 1966, and in March the IMF approved further drawings.

As a result of the military débâcle the Egyptian army was subjected to major reorganization, involving the dismissal of large numbers of officers and the reorganization of the armed forces supreme command.

Widespread demonstrations of students and workers took place in Cairo, Helwan and other centres, towards the end of February 1968. Initially in protest at the leniency of sentences on air force officers, they revealed widespread discontent. A number of persons were killed in clashes with police, and the universities were closed; nevertheless President Nasser realized the need for immediate conciliatory action. Re-trials were ordered and sweeping cabinet changes announced, a number of civilian experts in various fields being brought in. Ali Sabri, who had been reinstated as Secretary-General of the Arab Socialist Union in January, was also included but Zakaria Mohieddin left the government. President Nasser continued to exercise the functions of Prime Minister.

On March 30th President Nasser announced a new plan for building a modern state in Egypt based on democracy, science and technology. The single party would remain but there would be free elections from top to bottom of the Arab Socialist Union and changes were promised among leaders in all spheres. An announcement of the distribution of land taken over by the state or reclaimed was made on April 6th. In a plebiscite on May 2nd the "Declaration of March 30th" was overwhelmingly approved. The first Arab Socialist Union elections were held in

June; the 75,000 persons chosen then elected a national congress in July; this in turn chose a central committee which then chose the party's higher executive. These proceedings, however, did not appear to arouse much public interest. Further student riots in November 1968, and the closure of the universities left Nasser increasingly isolated and exposed.

Deprived of foreign exchange by the continued closure of the Canal and the drop in the tourist trade, the U.A.R. remained dependent on the regular aid payments from Saudi Arabia, Kuwait and Libya and on Soviet assistance, both humiliating to a people strongly nationalist in outlook. There were signs that the civilian economic ministers favoured some relaxation of over-rigid state control in industry and more encouragement of private enterprise and foreign investment. Military expenditure in 1968 and 1969 remained high. Soviet arms deliveries continued, as also did the presence of about 3,000 Russian military advisers and instructors.

The efforts of Dr. Jarring, the representative of the UN Secretary-General, to bring Israel, the U.A.R. and Jordan closer together had, by the end of 1968, yielded little success. In April 1969, following initiatives by the U.S.S.R. and France, those two countries together with Britain and the United States, as permanent members of the Security Council, began talks at the United Nations in New York in an unsuccessful attempt to promote a settlement.

A pattern of sporadic action, involving artillery duels across the Suez Canal, commando raids and air combat developed throughout 1969 and into 1970, with growing Soviet involvement in Egypt's defence. In the summer of 1970 the U.S. Secretary of State, Mr. William Rogers, put forward a set of proposals for solving the continuing Middle East crisis. An uneasy ceasefire, but no permanent solution, resulted.

EGYPT AFTER NASSER

Although President Nasser had had his differences with the Palestinian guerrillas over their rejection of the U.S. peace proposals and the hijackings of the western airliners at the beginning of September, one of his last acts was to secure agreement in Cairo between King Hussein and Yasser Arafat for an end to the fighting between the Jordanian army and the guerrillas.

Nasser's death on September 28th, 1970, came as a profound shock and it was feared by many that it would materially lessen chances of achieving peace in the Middle East. A close associate of Nasser, and Vice-President at the time of his death, Col. Anwar Sadat, was immediately appointed provisional President by the Cabinet and Party, being later elected President in a national referendum, and by mid-1971 he was firmly in control of the government of Egypt.

In November 1970 President Sadat had agreed to the federation of the U.A.R. with Sudan and Libya. Sudan, however, later postponed her membership of a union and it was Syria who in April became the third member of the Federation. The federation

proposals, together with Sadat's plan for the reopening of the Canal, precipitated a crisis in the leadership
which led to a comprehensive purge by Sadat of
opponents at all levels of the government, including
Ali Sabri, one of the two Vice-Presidents. In July
new elections were held, not only for all levels of the
Party, but also for trade unions and professional
bodies. A new constitution, the first permanent one
since the 1952 revolution, was voted in September. It
contained important clauses governing personal
freedoms and discarded at last the name of United
Arab Republic, the state being known henceforward
as the Arab Republic of Egypt.

The year 1971 was marked by repeated Egyptian
declarations of the intention to fight Israel—but only
when the time was ripe—and Egypt mounted an
extensive diplomatic campaign to state her case in
the West. In September 1971 came the first large-scale
military operations on the canal since the August 1970
ceasefire and in December the UN passed a resolution
calling for the resumption of the Jarring peace
mission.

Dr. Mahmoud Fawzi, who was appointed Prime
Minister in October 1970, resigned in January 1972
and was made a joint Vice-President. His successor
was Dr. Aziz Sidqi, who had been First Vice-Premier
since September 1971.

Egypt was becoming increasingly dependent on the
U.S.S.R., both militarily and economically. Student
riots at the beginning of 1972 brought assurances
from President Sadat that an armed confrontation with Israel was definitely intended. Against
this background of increasing internal uneasiness
Egypt intensified efforts to diversify sources of
development aid and armaments. The Suez-Alexand-
ria (Sumed) pipeline received promises of Western
backing and in May 1972 a five-year preferential
trade agreement was concluded with the EEC.

CRISIS IN EGYPTIAN-SOVIET RELATIONS

The most striking event of 1972 was the dismissal
of Soviet military advisers from Egypt in July and the
manning of installations by Egyptians. This did not
lead to a rupture in Egyptian-Soviet relations but
neither did it result in any significant rapprochement
with the West, anti-American feeling remaining very
strong. A new round of diplomatic visits to state
Egypt's case, particularly in the West and the Far
East, was embarked upon and arms supplies requested
from France and Britain. With the announcement on
August 2nd, 1972, of Egypt's plan to merge with
Libya, France stated that supplies of Mirage fighters
to Libya would continue, Libya not being in direct
conflict with Israel.

Contacts with the U.S.S.R. continued and economic
relations appeared unaffected by the events of July
but it was clear that the U.S.S.R. was looking elsewhere to maintain its presence in the Mediterranean.
It was unclear to what extent Sadat's hand had been
forced in ordering the Soviet withdrawal.

INTERNAL UNREST

A law passed in August 1972 provided for penalties
up to life imprisonment for offences endangering
national unity, including opposing the Government by
force and inciting violence between Muslims and the
Coptic minority. Clashes between these two communities were growing more frequent and, along with
increasing student unrest, were seen as an expression
of dissatisfaction with the state of "no-peace-no-war".
The Government resorted to repeated assurances of
military preparations. In December 1972, Sadat in
fact ordered preparations for fighting, after strong
criticism in the People's Assembly of the Government's policies. Another cause of uneasiness was the
proposed merger with Libya, which many people felt
might give Colonel Gaddafi too much control over
Egypt's destiny.

January 1973 saw violent clashes between police
and students and the universities had to be closed for
a short time. In February a number of left-wing
elements, among them many journalists, were expelled from the ASU, student unrest continued and in
March President Sadat took over from Aziz Sidqi as
Prime Minister. The new administration's policies
were approved by the People's Assembly but the
Government was criticized for failing to follow a
clear-cut economic policy, particularly with regard to
the five-year plan.

RELATIONS WITH LIBYA

Egypt and Libya had agreed on a programme of
full union by stages at a meeting between the two
Heads of State in Benghazi in August 1972, and a
merger of the two countries was planned to take
place on September 1st, 1973. The Libyan leader,
Colonel Gaddafi, showed more enthusiasm than
President Sadat for total union, and in July 1973
Gaddafi organized a march of 40,000 Libyans on
Cairo in order to bring pressure to bear on Egypt.
The march was turned back about 200 miles from
Cairo, however, and Sadat, although showing support
for eventual union, stated that "enthusiasm and
emotional impulses are not a sufficient basis for
unity." An agreement in principle was nevertheless
signed on August 29th, but few practical steps were
taken to implement the agreement.

Relations between Egypt and Libya have since
deteriorated. Gaddafi was very critical of Egypt's
strategy in the early days of the October war, and
when, in April 1974, a terrorist attack took place
on the Military Technical Academy at Heliopolis,
outside Cairo, it was suspected in Egyptian circles
that the attack was the beginning of an attempted
coup in which Libya was implicated. Throughout 1974
and early 1975 relations between the two countries
deteriorated to such an extent that President Sadat
asserted in a press interview in April 1975 that
Gaddafi was "100 per cent sick". At the time Libya
had been threatening to take action against Egyptians
working in Libya. In spite of the apparent temporary
success in May 1975 of attempts by a mission from
the National Assembly of the Federation of Arab
Republics to mediate between Sadat and Gaddafi,
relations soon worsened when a large Soviet-Libyan
arms deal was revealed later in the month. President
Sadat hastily accused Libya and the Soviet Union of

conducting an international campaign against him and his Middle East policy. Libya was among the Arab countries severely critical of the Second Interim Disengagement Agreement between Egypt and Israel in September 1975, and relations between Egypt and Libya showed little sign of improvement during 1976 and 1977. In fact, when severe riots against food prices took place in Cairo in January 1977, Gaddafi was among the people whom Sadat accused of being responsible. In July 1977 open warfare took place on the border between Egypt and Libya, and when Sadat visited Israel in November 1977 (*see* below), relations deteriorated even further, with Egypt breaking off diplomatic relations with Libya in December. Subsequent events have brought about a further deterioration in relations. Libya joined the rest of the Arab world in condemning the Egyptian-Israeli peace treaty in March 1979, and it was reported that renewed outbreaks of war on the Egyptian-Libyan border were prevented only by the intervention of the U.S.A. In March 1980 Libya constructed airfields and fortifications on the border with Egypt, and in June 1980 Egypt declared martial law in the border area with Libya for a period of one year.

THE OCTOBER WAR AND ITS AFTERMATH

Between the June 1967 war and October 1973 Egyptian leaders frequently stated that the war against Israel would be resumed, but when Egyptian forces crossed the Suez Canal on October 6th, 1973, it came as a surprise to Israel and to the rest of the world. The course of the war, and the political questions involved, are dealt with in the chapter "The Arab-Israeli Confrontation 1967–82", pages 43–44. For President Sadat the war was a considerable triumph. It appeared to end the years of stalemate with Israel, and his personal reputation was greatly enhanced. As a result of the Disengagement Agreement which Israel and Egypt signed on January 18th, 1974, Egyptian forces regained a strip of territory to the east of the Suez Canal (see map on page 81).

After the war extensive and far-reaching changes took place in Egypt. An amnesty was extended to many important political prisoners in January 1974, and in April an amnesty was extended to more than 2,000 persons who had been imprisoned for political or criminal offences. Press censorship was lifted in February, and in April about 8.5 million voters gave a 99.95 per cent endorsement to a programme of economic and social reform which concentrated on reconstruction, attracting foreign investment, limiting police interference in everyday life, and the introduction of a private enterprise sector in the economy while still maintaining the public sector (*see* Economic Survey).

One result of the October war was Egypt's improved relations with the U.S.A. Diplomatic relations between Egypt and the U.S.A. were restored in November 1973 and the U.S. Secretary of State, Dr. Henry Kissinger, had a cordial relationship with President Sadat during the disengagement talks. American

initiatives in peacemaking were generally welcomed by Egypt, while the Americans became more conscious of the extent of their dependence on Arab oil. It was therefore in an atmosphere of *rapprochement* that President Nixon visited Cairo in June 1974.

RETURN TO STALEMATE

The euphoria which the crossing of the Suez Canal had produced began to disappear during 1974. Increases in the cost of living, and the slowness with which the promised economic reform was proceeding, led to riots in Cairo on January 1st, 1975, and to further disturbances among textile workers in March 1975, when the textile complex at El Mahalla el Kubra was closed for several days after violent clashes over pay demands. Inflation was estimated at the time to be running at an annual rate of about 24 per cent.

As a result of these disturbances Dr. Abdel-Aziz Higazi, who had taken over the premiership from President Sadat in September 1974, resigned as Prime Minister and was replaced in April 1975 by Gen. Mamdouh Muhammad Salem, the former Minister of the Interior and Deputy Prime Minister. On May 1st, 1975, President Sadat announced that all lower-paid public-sector employees would receive additional cost-of-living allowances equal to 30 per cent of their pay, and later in May, in a speech to the People's Assembly, the new Prime Minister promised that steps would be taken to ensure that the economic programme of 1974 would be implemented and that foreign investors, whether from Western countries or from the Eastern bloc, would be given every facility.

During the first eight months of 1975 Dr. Kissinger engaged in considerable "shuttle diplomacy" and in September Egypt and Israel signed the Second Interim Disengagement Agreement. In brief, Israel withdrew from the Giddi and Mitla passes and Egypt recovered the Abu Rudais oilfield in Sinai, while Article I of the Agreement stated that Egypt and Israel have agreed that "the conflict between them and in the Middle East shall not be resolved by military force but by peaceful means." This agreement brought upon President Sadat the strong disapproval of other Arab interests, particularly Syria, Jordan, Iraq and the PLO, as it appeared to them that Egypt was seeking to commit the whole Arab world to a policy of peace with Israel. The position had also been complicated by the fact that, at the Arab Summit at Rabat in October 1974, the PLO had achieved the status of the sole legitimate representative of the Palestinian people. At the end of May 1976 Egypt attempted to consolidate an improvement in relations with the PLO by asking the Arab League to admit the PLO as a full member. Relations with Syria, at a particularly low ebb during the Lebanese civil war, improved after the Riyadh and Cairo summits in October 1976.

The rest of the Arab world was also aware that Egypt was drawing even closer to the United States. Certainly, Sadat was becoming disillusioned with the Soviet Union. In March 1976 he abrogated the Treaty of Friendship with the U.S.S.R. which Egypt had signed in 1971. In a speech to the Egyptian People's

Assembly Sadat accused the Soviet Union of exerting political, economic and military pressure on Egypt by criticizing his Middle East policies, refusing to reschedule Egypt's debts, and refusing supplies of weapons and spares. Sadat's disillusion with the U.S.S.R. was again in evidence when Egypt decided to expel about 40 Soviet diplomats in retaliation against the Soviet invasion of Afghanistan in December 1979.

POLITICAL ADVANCE AND DOMESTIC DIFFICULTIES

During 1976 and for most of 1977, President Sadat was forced to involve himself increasingly in domestic issues. In March 1976 three political "platforms" were allowed to form within the Arab Socialist Union, and in the November 1976 elections to the People's Assembly the "platforms" entered the contest as full-scale political parties. The Arab Socialists (a party of the centre, supporting Sadat) won 280 seats, while the Liberal Socialists (supporting political and economic liberalization) won 12 seats. The left-wing National Progressive Unionist Party won 2 seats. After the elections President Sadat announced that the Arab Socialist Union would fade into the background and would become merely a watchdog for the three parties' activities.

Egypt's economy, during 1976, was experiencing great difficulties (*see* Economic Survey), and when in January 1977 Sadat announced a budget which, because of the withdrawal of subsidies, meant large increases in food and other prices, severe riots broke out in Cairo and other centres.

In the face of this opposition Sadat had to revoke the price increases and in February he introduced a law which made a wide range of new offences punishable by hard labour for life. Among these offences were forming a political group other than the three legal parties; forming a group to destroy public or private property; failing to submit an accurate account of earnings and property; tax evasion; stirring up the people or impeding the Government, or public and private sectors, or the institutions of learning; and premeditated striking. These measures were put to a referendum in which 96.9 per cent of the enfranchised population voted, and 99.4 per cent of the votes cast approved of the measures.

By June 1977 Sadat considered the internal situation in Egypt to be sufficiently under control to regularize the current position on political parties. A law was adopted by the People's Assembly stating that each party must include at least 20 members of the People's Assembly (current parties excepted). This effectively excluded the Communist Party, the Muslim Brotherhood and the New Wafd Party.

PROGRESS TOWARDS A PEACE TREATY WITH ISRAEL

In November 1977, however, domestic questions were completely overshadowed by Sadat's visit to Israel and his address to the Knesset. It was by no means certain whether any tangible peace pro-

posals would result from Sadat's talks with Menachem Begin, the newly-elected Likud Premier of Israel whose hitherto "hawkish" attitude did not seem to augur well for the cause of peace, but who might use his newly-acquired power in putting forward a daring initiative. In the event, no significant breakthrough was made immediately. The status of any future Palestinian state presented the main obstacle. Talks continued in 1978 at various levels at several locations, in spite of the opposition of much of the Arab world, who regarded Egypt's unilateral bid for peace with Israel as detrimental to Arab unity. In September 1978 there came a somewhat unexpected breakthrough when, after talks at Camp David in the U.S.A. under the guidance of President Carter, Sadat and Begin signed two agreements. The first was a "framework of peace in the Middle East" (*see* p. 82) and the second was a "framework for the conclusion of a peace treaty between Egypt and Israel". The first agreement provided for a five-year transitional period during which the inhabitants of the Israeli-occupied West Bank of the Jordan and the Gaza Strip would obtain full autonomy and self-government, and the second agreement provided for the signing of a peace treaty within three months. In the event the signing of the peace treaty was delayed because of the question of whether there should be any linkage between the conclusion of the peace treaty and progress towards autonomy in the Israeli-occupied areas, but on March 27th, 1979, after another intervention by President Carter, the signing took place. The treaty (*see* p. 84) provided for a phased Israeli withdrawal from Sinai over a period of three years. This withdrawal has gone according to plan (*see* map on p. 90), and diplomatic relations between Egypt and Israel were established on February 26th, 1980.

Proposals for Palestinian autonomy were contained in a separate letter published with the treaty, and provided for both sides to attempt to complete negotiations within twelve months. There would then be elections of Palestinian local councils and a five-year transitional period would follow during which the final status of the West Bank and Gaza would be negotiated. The autonomy negotiations began in May 1979, but the deadline of May 26th, 1980, passed without agreement being reached. The main stumbling blocks have been the presence and growth of Israeli settlements on the West Bank, the strengthening of Israel's insistence that Jerusalem is its eternal indivisible capital, and a fundamental difference between Egyptian ideas of Palestinian autonomy (which are tantamount to an independent state) and those of Israel, which envisage a limited form of self-government. During 1980 the U.S.A. was preoccupied with Presidential elections. Indeed, U.S. support for the UN Security Council Resolution on Israeli settlements in March 1980 (*see* Documents on Palestine, p. 87) was later abrogated by President Carter, under pressure, some would say, to consider the Jewish vote. A European initiative to solve the deadlock produced the EEC Venice declaration in June 1980 (*see* p. 88), but this has achieved no practical advances.

The Camp David agreements and the subsequent

peace treaty resulted in Egypt's isolation in the Arab world. Syria, Algeria, Libya and the PLO had met in Damascus in September 1978 and strongly condemned the Camp David agreements, and in March 1979, after the signing of the peace treaty, the Arab League Council met in Baghdad and passed a series of resolutions (*see* p. 86) comprising the withdrawal of Arab ambassadors to Egypt, the severing of economic and political links with Egypt, the withdrawal of Arab aid and the removal of the headquarters of the Arab League from Cairo to Tunis. Egypt had already been threatened with these sanctions at an earlier Arab summit in Baghdad in November 1978. Some Arab States were reluctant to honour these decisions, but when Saudi Arabia broke off diplomatic relations with Egypt in late April, Egypt's isolation became potentially serious, although private Arab investment continued. As a result, Egypt came to rely even more heavily than before on financial and military aid from the U.S.A., although an arms agreement was also signed with the People's Republic of China. During 1980 it became evident that Egypt's isolation was having little practical effect. The economic measures taken against Egypt were softened by the growing strength of Egypt's own economy, and the exchange of Ambassadors between Egypt and Sudan in March 1981 was a recognition of this reduced isolation. Another sign of this was Egypt's sale of arms worth U.S. $25 million to Iraq in the same month.

INTERNAL POLITICAL CHANGE

Since 1976 President Sadat had been trying to allow the formation of political parties while at the same time ensuring that dangerous opposition did not achieve too much influence. In a law of June 1977 political parties were legalized. Disturbed by the revival of the Wafd Party (the New Wafd Party) and the criticisms of the National Progressive Unionist Party, Sadat won approval in a referendum for a new set of regulations on political parties which resulted in the disbanding of the New Wafd Party and the suspension of the National Progressive Unionist Party. In July Sadat announced the creation of a new political party, the National Democratic Party (NDP), with himself as leader, which in practice replaced the Arab Socialist Party. In September 1978 an official opposition party, the Socialist Labour Party, was formed.

The signing of the Camp David agreements in September 1978, although causing the resignation of the Egyptian Foreign Minister, Muhammad Ibrahim Kamel, was popular in Egypt and in October Sadat appointed a new government, specially geared to peace, with Mustapha Khalil as Prime Minister. Khalil also became Foreign Minister in February 1979. The signing of the peace treaty in March was followed by a referendum in April in which 99.95 per cent of the voters approved the treaty. A simultaneous referendum gave Sadat a mandate for fresh general elections and for future constitutional changes. The elections, held in June, resulted in a convincing win

for Sadat's National Democratic Party, who obtained 302 seats in the 392-seat People's Assembly. On April 30th, 1980, the People's Assembly passed a number of amendments to the constitution (*see* p. 371), the most important of which gave Sadat the power to serve further terms as President and which affirmed that Islamic jurisprudence was the basis of Egyptian law.

On May 12th, 1980, the Prime Minister, Mustafa Khalil, offered his resignation because Egypt was "on the threshold of a new stage of national construction" and a new government was called for. Two days later Sadat introduced a government in which he himself became Prime Minister. The constitutional amendments then received the approval of more than 98 per cent of the voters at yet another referendum. One of these amendments provided for the election of a 210-member *Shura* (Advisory Council), to replace the former Central Committee of the Arab Socialist Union. Elections took place in September 1980 and the NDP won all 140 elected seats. The remaining 70 members are appointed by the President. The NDP also gained more seats in the People's Assembly in 1980 and early 1981 as at least 13 members of the official opposition Socialist Labour Party defected to the NDP or became independents.

MUBARAK SUCCEEDS SADAT

Although political parties had been allowed by Sadat, power had remained with his own National Democratic Party, but latent opposition was never far beneath the surface. In the summer of 1981 there had been clashes between Copts and Islamic fundamentalists, resulting in numerous arrests and the closure of various newspapers. Sadat was trying to stifle the opposition, of whatever religious or political persuasion.

On October 6th, however, Sadat was assassinated at a military parade by a group of Islamic fundamentalists led by Lieut. Khald Islambouly, who was later executed on April 15th, 1982. An Islamic rebellion which broke out in Asyut immediately after the assassination was quickly suppressed, and Vice-President Muhammad Hosni Mubarak was confirmed as President at a referendum on October 13th.

Since his sudden rise to power, Mubarak has shown that he is not the nonentity which many believed him to be while he was Vice-President. He has released many of the political and religious detainees previously held by Sadat, and in a government reshuffle in early January 1982 he replaced Dr. Ali Abdel-Razzaq Abdel-Majid as Deputy Prime Minister for Finance and Economy by Muhammad Abdul-Fattah Ibrahim, the governor of the Central Bank of Egypt. Mubarak was anxious to improve the living conditions of the ordinary Egyptian, and felt that it was necessary to get rid of the architect of Egypt's "open door policy", which had resulted in wealth for the few and poverty for the many.

In foreign affairs, the early months of Mubarak's Presidency were preoccupied with the question of the return of Sinai by Israel under the "Camp David process". After many last-minute snags, the last section was returned to Egypt on April 25th, 1982. Prospects for settling the wider question of Palestinian autonomy, however, continue to look slim. Now that Sinai has been returned, it seems possible that Egypt may begin a process of returning to the Arab fold, from which she was ostracized after the Camp David agreements in late 1978. Iran's successes in the Gulf War against Iraq in the Spring of 1982, and the need for Iraq and the rest of the Arab world to band together against the rising tide of Islamic fundamentalism, could well mean the end of Egypt's isolation.

ECONOMIC SURVEY

INTRODUCTION

The assassination of President Sadat on October 6th, 1981, has, as yet, had little impact on the economy, and Egypt's GDP continues to rise at between 8 and 9 per cent per annum, which is slightly below the projected 10 per cent growth rate of the 1980–84 five-year plan. Inflation fell to between 25 and 30 per cent at the end of 1981, compared with 40 per cent in 1980. However, falling oil revenues in 1981 (resulting from the world oil glut), the continuing high levels of food subsidies and the disruption of the banking sector, following the devaluation of the Egyptian pound in August 1981, make Egypt's economic prospects look gloomier than they did at the end of 1980. The agricultural sector, employing 40 per cent of the labour force and contributing 25 per cent of the National Product, remains problematic.

Since 1973 great attempts have been made to repair the war damage, and Sadat's Law No. 43 of 1974 led to the replacement of Nasser's socialist planning by an "open door policy", encouraging foreign investment. The 1970s also saw a great increase in aid from the oil-rich Arab states. In 1967–73 Arab aid to Egypt was estimated at an annual average of U.S. $310 million. In 1973 this increased to $720 million, and in 1974 it rose to $1,260 million, while by 1977 it had risen to between $1,700 million and $2,000 million. Much of this aid was coming from the Gulf Organization for the Development of Egypt (GODE), set up by Saudi Arabia, Kuwait, the United Arab Emirates and Qatar in 1977. Saudi sources, in fact, claimed in May 1979 that Egypt had received more than U.S. $13,000 million from the four GODE countries in the past six years.

By signing the peace treaty with Israel in March 1979, however, Sadat undertook the risk of losing this Arab aid. The Arab League Council which met in Baghdad immediately after the signing of the peace treaty, agreed on a policy of economic and political isolation of Egypt (*see* p. 86). At first it seemed unlikely that the economic sanctions would be stringently carried out by some of the Arab countries but when in late April Saudi Arabia broke off diplomatic relations with Egypt, some of the more "moderate" Arab States gave effect to the boycott. The Arab Fund for Economic and Social Development suspended all future aid and credit relations with Egypt, although honouring transactions already in progress, and in May Saudi Arabia, Qatar and the United Arab Emirates withdrew from the Arab Organization for Industrialization, which was an Egypt-based Arab arms enterprise, causing its collapse and jeopardizing the employment of 15,000 Egyptians.

Egypt, however, responded by planning to set up its own arms industry with Western capital. While the loss of Saudi military aid, estimated at an annual rate of just under $2,000 million, is undoubtedly significant, the fact that only about 7 per cent of Egypt's total trade was with Arab countries implied that the Arab trade boycott would probably not be of major importance. Sadat hoped that Egypt's economic difficulties would be alleviated by the "Carter Plan", which he saw in the same light as the "Marshall Plan", by which Egypt would receive U.S. $12,250 million over a period of five years, mainly from the U.S.A., Western Europe and Japan. In December 1979 eleven Western nations, sponsored by the World Bank, promised Egypt $2,500 million in aid during 1980, and since then several other USAID and Japanese agreements have been signed. The return of multinationals such as Coca-Cola and Cadbury Schweppes, associated with the normalization of relations with Israel, clearly demonstrates the increased readiness of foreign capital to invest in Egypt.

Likewise, towards the end of 1980 Union Carbide announced that they were to build a battery plant near Alexandria, where a new gypsum plant is also being built, and Pepsi Cola also announced that they were to open a new bottling plant in 1981. France has greatly increased her trade and aid with Egypt, and in November 1980 replaced West Germany as Egypt's second most important unilateral aid giver after the U.S.A. The normalization of relations with Israel continues to progress slowly. During 1980 agricultural, trade, aviation and health agreements were signed, and the border was opened to commercial traffic towards the end of the year. With the replacement of Sadat by President Mubarak, it is possible that Egypt's economic links with other Arab countries may be re-established. Relations with the U.S.A. appear to have cooled slightly, and, although in October 1981 USAID agreed to provide $14 million credit for two new turbines for the Aswan 2 power station, at the end of the year the U.S.A. also put pressure on the IMF not to grant $670 million credit until Egypt had "put its house in order". During 1981 Sadat had expelled 1,000 Soviet advisers, but early in 1982 his successor reopened the doors to 66 Soviet technicians for the Helwan iron and steel plant, the Hamadi aluminium plant and the Aswan High Dam.

RECONSTRUCTION

After the October 1973 war, the most pressing need was to restore and reopen the Suez Canal and, at Sadat's initiative, the canal was reopened on June

5th, 1975, the eighth anniversary of the outbreak of war which led to its closure in 1967. Expansion has been made even more urgent because of the vast increase in oil-tanker sizes since June 1967 which the closure of the canal then helped provoke. A Japanese company, the Penta-Ocean Construction Company, was contracted to begin the work of widening and deepening the southern end of the canal at a cost of $172 million, backed by a Japanese Government loan. A new $113 million contract was given to Penta in November 1976 for expansion work in the Great Bitter Lake sector. The state of the tanker market means that the impact of the reopening on the oil trade is marginal for the moment, though for dry cargo the advantages of the shorter Suez route over the Cape route are much clearer. The Canal Authority set the dues for ships using the canal 90–100 per cent higher than in 1967, and revenue in the first year of operation was $230 million. In December 1980 the first phase of the work was completed at an estimated cost of $1,275 million, and at the beginning of the month a 145,000-ton oil tanker became the first boat to pass through the newly widened and deepened canal, which will allow ships of up to 53 ft. draught, or 350,000 tons, to pass through. In July 1979 there was a 50 per cent increase in charges on dry cargo ships, and in January 1981 there was a further restructuring of the prices by which 10,000-ton dry bulk carriers had a 53 per cent increase and tankers of 150,000 to 187,000 tons paid approximately 12.5 per cent less. The second phase of the development, beginning in 1982, is now to be carried out more slowly due to the uncertainty concerning oil supplies, and doubts about its economic viability. This second phase, when complete, will increase the draught from its present 53 ft. to 67 ft. The improvement already undertaken, though, saw a clear increase in revenue from the canal in 1981, when income reached $888 million, compared with $655 million in 1980.

Reconstruction of the canal cities, some of them up to 80 per cent destroyed, was put in hand and by 1979 more than a million Egyptians had returned to Port Said, Ismailia and Suez. In November 1979 construction of the Salem canal, to take water from the East Nile to Sinai, was started and in October 1980 the 1.64-km. Ahmad Hamdi tunnel was opened, thus providing the first road link under the Suez Canal.

GENERAL

The total area of Egypt is about 998,000 square km., but 96 per cent of the country is desert. With no forested land, and hardly any permanent meadows or pastures, the arable land available is greatly over-crowded. Relating the population, numbering 41 million in 1979, to the inhabited area, a density of over 1,000 persons per square kilometre gives 5.5 persons per acre of arable land, representing one of the highest man/land ratios in the world. At the root of Egypt's poverty lies the rapid rise in the population, of 2.58 per cent per annum for the period 1975–80, which is adding about a million people a year. The mid-1981 population was conservatively estimated at 43,465,000. Lack of employment opportuni-

ties has driven people from the country into already over-crowded cities, which have grown at a rate of 3.4 per cent per annum over the last five years, and hastened the emigration of qualified personnel the country can ill afford to lose. Many have gone to much better paid jobs in the rich Gulf states. Poor job prospects have also helped swell the bureaucracy, since the government is committed to giving a post to every Egyptian graduate who is unable to find other employment. In 1980 45 per cent of the population was estimated to be urban. Gross National Product per head was estimated at $500 in 1979.

Despite this low level of income, certain aspects of the Egyptian economy indicate a relative state of advance, notably communications, the irrigation system, public administration and education. In 1977/78 5,729,823 people, 14.7 per cent of the population, were receiving primary or preparatory education, 853,703 people secondary education, and there were 586,693 people in higher education or teacher training. Thus, while illiteracy rates remain high and the diet of the average inhabitant is poor, Egypt is a net exporter of skills, especially to other Arab countries, with remittances sent home from abroad amounting to $1,700 million in 1979. In an attempt to improve the educational basis, there were plans to build 161 primary, 6 secondary and 25 technical schools in 1980. In addition the government began a major campaign against illiteracy in May 1980.

From 1918–39, when the Egyptian pound was tied to sterling and a fairly free trade policy was being pursued, manufacturing industry had little chance of developing and agricultural production, though expanding, could not keep up with the rapidly rising population. A gradual deterioration of living standards set in. This trend did not change direction until the immediate post-war period, when cotton prices improved. These reached their greatest heights during the Korean boom of 1951–52, when "soft-currency cotton", including Egyptian cotton, enjoyed high premia over dollar-cotton. But the collapse of the boom, the easing up of the world dollar scarcity and the beginning of American subsidization of cotton exports in the mid-1950s, marked a turning point in raw cotton terms of trade which, until quite recently, showed a declining trend.

The regime which assumed power in 1952 and ended the monarchy gave urgent attention to Egypt's economic problems. Its policies included measures of agrarian reform, land reclamation, the High Dam, and a programme of industrialization which was accelerated in 1960 by the formation of a comprehensive social and economic development plan.

Egypt's first five-year plan aimed at increasing real national income by 40 per cent between 1960 and 1965. The five-year growth target was virtually fulfilled, so that the second plan was replaced by a more ambitious plan to double real income in seven years (i.e. by 1972). Lack of finance, however, frustrated this new plan, and after two years of uncertainty, a three-year "accomplishment" plan, beginning July 1967, was proclaimed. This was to aim at a target growth rate of 5 per cent per annum (compared with

7.2. per cent under the first five-year plan) with a total investment of £E1,085 million (against £E1,513 million in 1960–65), and would concentrate on completing projects already started, rather than initiating new ones. This plan was dropped as a result of the 1967 war and was substituted by annual development appropriations (£E320 million in 1968–69 and £E350 million in 1969–70). Apart from a few select new projects, the whole emphasis of Egyptian planning was turned towards rationalizing the existing industries, and introducing incentives to improve their performance.

This plan was, however, to be superseded by a more ambitious ten-year scheme under a Programme of National Action, proclaimed by President Sadat in July 1971, but the ten-year plan was never put into operation and the Government reverted to annual development appropriations until 1974.

The 1978–82 five-year plan foresaw total expenditure at some £E12,000 million ($17,000 million at the parallel rate), and its main objective was to achieve annual economic growth rates of 8 per cent. However, this was replaced by the 1980–84 five-year Peace Plan with planned investment of £E25,185 million, which aimed at average annual growth rates of over 10 per cent. It is intended that half of the investment for this restructured plan is to come from abroad. Within this new plan, agriculture is to grow at 3.2 per cent, with most other sectors at 11 per cent, apart from the Suez Canal's contributions which has a projected growth rate of 16.7 per cent. By 1984 it is hoped that agriculture will have fallen some 5 per cent in its sectoral importance to the economy, and that petroleum, industry, the Suez Canal and services will all have increased their relative contribution.

The end of 1981 saw the erosion of Egypt's traditional sources of income, namely tourism, workers' remittances, oil and the Suez Canal, but, despite the world oil glut, new oil finds do give some hope of relief from the country's problems, of which the spiralling food import bill remains paramount.

AGRICULTURE

Egyptian agriculture is dominated by the river Nile and the necessity for irrigation. During the 1970s agriculture's contribution to G.D.P. remained fairly constant at around 30 per cent, with industry accounting for 10–21 per cent. With the increasing importance of oil revenue in the next decade it is clear that agriculture will contribute less. In 1978 the agricultural sector accounted for approximately 60 per cent of total export earnings, but by 1979 this had fallen to 50 per cent, and it is likely to decrease further in the next few years. During the 1970s the increase in agricultural production was clearly outstripped by population growth, and this reflected a diminishing stress on agriculture in government plans. Between 1970 and 1976 food imports, in terms of weight, increased by over two and a half times, and exports of rice declined to one third of their former weight. Agricultural production has averaged an annual increase of only 3 per cent since 1977 and this has meant a continued dependence on substantial

imports of foodstuffs, which accounted for £E399.6 million in 1977. The difficulties in this sector are well illustrated by the food riots in Cairo in February 1980, and by the heavy subsidies on bread and flour. Although the riots were not as serious as those in January 1977, they emphasize the critical problem which the government faces in attempting to reduce basic subsidies.

These problems have resulted in increasing attention being paid to agriculture by the government. In an attempt to reduce prices President Sadat ordered a stop to all slaughtering of sheep and cattle during the month of September 1980, and in October of that year Egyptians were able to buy meat on only two days of the week. In addition total subsidies were raised in 1980 by $396.8 million, and the custom duties on imported food were lowered. In an agreement signed in May 1980 the U.S.A. provided a soft loan for Egypt to purchase a total of 1.6 million tons of wheat and 100,000 tons of maize from the U.S.A. In 1981 food subsidies cost 11 per cent of G.N.P., and the food bill of $4,400 million was up $1,000 million on the figure for 1980. By mid-1982, though, it is estimated that the food bill will be approximately 25 per cent of the country's G.N.P. While a reduction of the subsidies on energy is planned, past experience has shown that it is politically inadvisable to try to reduce food subsidies.

The arable area is 6 million feddans (one feddan = 1.038 acres) but not much more than a third of this is serviced by main and secondary drains. This deficiency is significant because an unforeseen effect of the high dam (*see* below) has been to make the water table rise (because of more abundant water and more intensive cropping) and lead to widespread waterlogging and high soil salinity. Insufficient attention to drainage has therefore been a serious problem with agricultural planning.

The extension of the cultivable area through reclamation has been slow, difficult and costly, but remains at the forefront of government policy. The increasing pressure of people on the land has led to an intensification of cultivation almost without parallel anywhere. Dams, barrages, pumps and an intricate network of canals and drains bring perennial irrigation to almost the whole area. The strict pursuit of crop rotation, lavish use of commercial fertilizer and pesticides, and the patient application of manual labour not only make multiple cropping possible, but also raise land yields to exceptionally high levels. Despite the difficulties concerning reclamation, early in 1981 the Government announced plans to reclaim 1.2 million hectares of land at a rate of 63,000 hectares per year over the next 20 years. In the 1980–84 plan land reclamation is to be the key to increases in output. The largest planned development is to take place at West Nuberiya near Alexandria where, in the first phase, 10,100 hectares of land will be irrigated and drained. Each family will be allocated a smallholding of 2.5 hectares, and there are also plans to create a large estate farm. The total cost of the scheme is estimated at $193 million, of which the International Development Association has pledged an $80 million loan. A second major agricultural reclamation project is in progress in the northern Tahriv region.

The bulk of agricultural production is intended for the market place and not for subsistence. Nearly three-quarters of agricultural income comes from field crops, the remainder deriving from fruit, vegetables, live-stock and dairy products. Long-staple cotton is the most important field crop but the area under culti-vation declined from two million acres in 1968 to just over one million acres in 1978. Peasants have been finding it unprofitable to grow.

Rice is another important crop and now, after cotton, is almost as important as fruit in the agri-cultural sector as a foreign currency earner. In an attempt to increase rice production, in May 1981 the Ministry of Agriculture increased the price which it paid for local paddy from £E75 to £E85 per ton. Other grain crops grown include wheat, maize, millet and barley. Population pressure has resulted in Egypt's becoming a net-importer of cereals, mostly wheat. Thus in 1980 £E452.9 million of cereals and milling products were imported, compared with exports of rice of only £E24.6 million. Recent agree-ments for 1982 allow for the U.S.A. to deliver 200,000 tons of wheat by mid-1982, to be paid for at 2 per cent interest with a grace period of 10 years. Pro-duction of wheat in 1979 and 1980, at 1,865,000 tons and 1,796,000 tons respectively, was below that of 1975 and 1976, but maize production does appear to have risen, with 3,231,000 tons produced in 1980, compared with 2,781,000 tons in 1975.

Another high-yielding crop is sugar-cane. It is nurtured by an expanding sugar industry, supplying the bulk of national requirements. Other crops include lucerne, a nitrogen-fixing fodder, beans, potatoes and onion and garlic.

The many kinds of fruit, vegetables and horti-cultural products grown are capable of great expansion and are potentially important as exports. Special efforts are being made to promote the production of these items, especially citrus fruit, and special areas are being allocated along the Mediterranean coast for their cultivation. Indeed, between 1974 and 1977 export earnings from edible fruit more than doubled although there was a marked fall off in earnings in 1978 and 1979. By 1980 edible fruit exports had recovered somewhat and were worth £E30.4 million. Recent attention has been given to animal hus-bandry in an attempt to raise diary and meat pro-duction, but there has so far been little increase in either number of livestock or productivity. Egypt has become a net importer of meats and meat-less days have been decreed to reduce consumption.

Egypt produces about a third of the world crop of long-staple cotton (1⅛ in. and longer). Many factors combine to give the high yields and excellent quality of Egyptian cotton. Among these should be mentioned climatic, soil and labour conditions, and a long experience with careful planting, watering and pick-ing. Government assistance and supervision has always been important. Fertilizers and pesticides are distributed through the government-sponsored agricultural credit banks, and agricultural co-operatives which are multiplying and expanding their area of activity. All the cotton ginning industry and the cotton exporting business had been nationa-lized by 1963. The cotton exchanges were closed, and the Government undertook to guarantee prices to regulate internal trade. A public organization for cotton was set up to regulate all aspects of cotton growing, marketing and manufacturing, but was abolished in 1976, being replaced by a loose super-visory council. The 1979–80 crop was 1,440,000 bales (each of 720 lb. or 326.6 kg.), which was an increase on the previous season, and achieved foreign currency earnings of $365 million. Increased spraying in 1978 and 1979 enabled the crop to escape serious insect damage and record yields were achieved. The 1980/81 cotton crop produced a further record, with output estimated at 1,589,000 bales, of which 465,489 bales were exported. This was produced on approx-imately 1.24 million feddans of land. The area under cotton in 1981/82 was only 1.18 million feddans and, although (despite a heavy leafworm infestation in the early summer) yields were higher than in 1980/81, the total production for the year was 1,554,000 bales. This reduction in output was exacerbated by a 20 per cent reduction in price compared with the previous year.

Demand for long-staple cotton has been shifting away towards man-made fibres, a fact which has tended to weaken Egypt's previous position of pre-eminence, and consequently the premia Egyptian cotton commanded over rival cottons. The shortage of land, however, together with the increasing require-ments of the domestic textile industry (874 million metres of cotton fabrics were produced in 1976) set a limit on the quantity available for export. About half of Egypt's cotton exports has gone to Communist countries in recent years under various bilateral agreements. Egyptian preference for trading with the Western countries, with which Egypt has a balance of payments deficit, has tended to be frustrated by a number of factors, including U.S. trade restrictions (on raw cotton imports), the decline of the high-grade sections of the European cotton industries, political considerations and shortage of finance. The avail-ability of credits (to finance imports) from the Com-munist countries has in the past tended to encourage Egyptian foreign trade with the Communist states, but the Soviet Union's share of Egypt's overall exports diminished from 43 per cent in 1975 to 23 per cent in 1977, 7.9 per cent in 1979 and 4.2 per cent in 1980.

AGRARIAN REFORM

Immediately after the Egyptian Revolution of 1952 an experiment in land reform was started. This has been among the more successful of such attempts, though only the very large estates were dismembered while medium-sized estates remained untouched. Among other measures, a limit of 200 feddans was imposed on individual ownership of land. This limit was lowered to 100 feddans in 1961 and again to 50 feddans in 1969. The primary aim of this reform was the destruction of the feudal power of the old politicians, an aim which was easily realized. In 1952, 5.8 per cent of all landowners held 64.5 per cent of the total area, but only a quarter of the national acreage (some 1.5 million feddans) was in plots of over 100 acres each. By 1961, however, this area had dwindled to about 1 million feddans, nearly all of which had been appropriated by the Ministry of Agrarian Reform and redistributed to landless peasants. The 1969 land reform affected a further 1.13 million feddans owned by 16,000 land-owners. By 1975 only 12.6 per cent of the total cultivated area was held by owners with 50 feddans or more.

Other measures of agrarian reform included rent control; the regulation of land tenure; consolidation of fragmented holdings for production purposes; and the drive to build co-operatives. By 1963 there were 4,897 agricultural co-operatives (compared with 1,727 in 1952) which offered more than £E46 millions in loans to 920,000 borrowers. However, co-operatives were open to corruption. Also in the process of dispossessing the large landowners and promoting co-operatives, the authorities unwittingly helped to eliminate many highly efficient medium-sized farmers. On balance, however, the redistribution of land was accompanied by improved land productivity and not the reverse.

Since land reform affected only about one-sixth of the total land, the main structure of land-ownership remained unaffected; in 1975, 5.4 per cent of the owners still held 42.9 per cent of the land while 94.6 per cent of the owners shared the remaining 57 per cent. The fundamental land tenure problem is not so much one of distribution but an overall scarcity.

Given the land shortage, special attention has naturally been paid to increasing the arable area. In view of the fact that the land to be reclaimed is often arid desert, reclamation is a costly process requiring substantial capital outlays, and the question has to be asked whether new investment should not be directed to the development of manufacturing industry instead, where returns to the scarce capital may well be higher. Between 1952 and 1976 912,000 feddans were reclaimed, 536,000 feddans being reclaimed during the 1960–65 Plan period. At the same time, however, some attention should also be paid to the high annual loss of arable land due to the expansion of towns and villages, which is currently approximating 20,000 feddans a year. Land is also being lost through increasing soil salinity, resulting from poor drainage. Consequently much remains to be done in the agricultural sector if Egypt's economy is to establish itself securely.

THE HIGH DAM

The decision to invest more than £E400 million in the High Dam project (including initial Russian credits of £E113 million, supported subsequently by another loan of £E81 million for the later stages) was, therefore, taken with an eye also on the development of cheap hydro-electric energy for industry. The official estimate of the dam's contribution to the increase in national production was £E234 million. By 1974 revenue from the dam had exceeded the cost of its construction. The project was started in January 1960, completed in July 1970, and officially inaugurated in January 1971. The power station's generating capacity, at 10,000 million kWh. exceeds by a considerable margin the 6,012 million kWh. produced in all Egypt in 1967 mostly from thermal stations with some hydro-electric energy from the old Aswan dam. Transmission lines carry the current from the Dam site to Cairo and further north, and a major scheme aiming at the complete electrification of Egypt's villages has already started. The storage lake behind the dam, which is 500 km. long and 10 km. wide, is the centre of a developing fishing industry which is expected to replace the sardine catch in the Mediterranean, lost as a result of building the dam.

When construction of the dam was agreed in 1958, a target of 1.2 million feddans was set for desert reclamation. However, costs have far outweighed returns and it has taken on average about ten years to raise any reclaimed area up to even marginal levels of production. Reclamation has started on some 900,000 feddans, but each year over the last 15 years or so the government has had to cover a deficit of around £E10 million on operations in reclaimed areas. In 1972 the Government stopped all new desert reclamation projects. But the country's very limited options in the face of acute pressure of population on the land have brought the idea of reclamation back into the Government plans. A figure of nearly 400,000 feddans has been mentioned in ministerial pronouncements on reclamation targets in the latest development plan, and other conservative ministerial estimates have put the amount to be reclaimed by the end of the century at 2–4 million feddans.

MANUFACTURING INDUSTRY

During the 1970s manufacturing industry suffered from a lack of foreign exchange, and some excess capacity resulting from shortages of spare parts and raw materials. Food processing and textiles have traditionally dominated the industrial sector, contributing 55–60 per cent of the total value of industrial output in the mid 1970s. With the growing importance of oil, though, this situation is likely to change. Employment data for 1978 indicate a work force of 1,554,900 in manufacturing and mining, 65,700 in electricity, gas and water and 448,500 in construction, totalling 20.6 per cent of employed labour, compared with 40 per cent for agriculture.

In manufacturing industry textiles still account for over a third of total output. The Government has embarked on a three-stage rehabilitation of the cotton-ginning industry costing $40.4 million and assisted by an $18.5 million loan from the IDA. The Arab Fund for Economic and Social Development (AFESD) is lending Egypt $40 million to finance a spinning and weaving project at Kafr al-Dawar and Bayda. Recent developments in the food processing industry are illustrated by the 75,000 tonne/year sugar refinery to be set up at Girga and the fact that in 1981 sugar production was expected to rise by 26 per cent.

Within heavy industry the development of projects established in the 1970s continues. The first stage of the expanded Helwan iron and steel complex was finished in 1973 and further growth up to 2 million tons is planned by 1982. The Nag Hammadi aluminium complex, using Australian and Guinean bauxite, was opened in 1975 with an initial capacity of 40,000 tons, and it is hoped to raise total aluminium production to 170,000 tons per year. In 1979 aluminium production was worth $140 million. A fertilizer project is taking shape at Talkha, costing $130 million and using $88 million in foreign loans. This was inaugurated in September 1981, three years late, and has a capacity of 570,000 tons of urea fertilizer per year, using gas from the Abu Madi field, in the Nile delta, as its feedstock. Other heavy industrial plans are concentrating on the iron and steel and construction industries, including sponge iron plants, a steel pipe plant, a glass factory and expanded cement output. A new steel pipe plant is to be constructed for the El-Nasr Company for Steel Pipes, using $13 million from USAID, and Japan is lending Egypt $180 million, mainly for industrial projects, of which $88 million is to be used for a steel reinforcing bar plant.

Partly due to surprisingly buoyant foreign exchange earnings and the freer availability of raw materials, there are now signs that the construction industry is beginning to take off. In this context Egypt signed an economic co-operation package with Romania in January 1980 in which 900,000 tons of cement and 1.5 million square metres of glass were ordered, and there were also plans to build 100,000 homes in 1980. The increasing interest of western investors in Egypt, associated with the relaxation of Egypt's boycott of Israel, is reflected in the government's achievement in late 1979 of persuading Siemens to undertake a $1,800 million renewal of the telephone network. Further evidence of increased foreign investment in Egyptian industry is provided by the World Bank's loan of $69 million towards the $109.3 million cost of the National Weaving and Spinning Company's building programme at Alexandria, the partly Japanese financed $520 million direct reduction steel plant at El Dikhelia to be completed in 1984, and the World Bank's $50 million loan towards the cost of expanding the National Paper Company.

Within the field of the motor industry a truck and diesel engine plant is to be built by Ford of the U.S. and American Motors is examining a jeep plant. In January 1979 it was announced that Egypt is to build Volkswagen "Beetle" cars under a licensing agreement. Volkswagen is to invest US $30 million in the project. In the same month Michelin announced plans to invest $81 million in a tyre factory near Alexandria.

The needs of heavy industry, and the plan to extend electric power to all Egypt's rural communities by 1982, has underlined the need for more power generation than that supplied by the High Dam. Hence, plans to implement the Qattara Depression scheme to generate energy by flooding the depression with waters from the Mediterranean have been speeded up and were given the final go-ahead late in 1980. The cost will be at least $2,600 million. In addition, Westinghouse of the U.S.A. is to build Egypt's first nuclear power station at Sidi-Krer, near Alexandria, and over the next five years power projects are to take 20 per cent of the development budget. In August 1980 the U.S.A. agreed to a $102 million loan to modernize the electricity grid, and plans for the implementation of complete rural electrification are in an advanced stage. In June 1981 the U.S.A. also signed the final agreement for nuclear co-operation with Egypt, which will lead to the construction of two nuclear power stations.

Egypt's mineral resources are now, though, being reappraised. Iron ore has traditionally been mined from the Aswan area, but new and better quality reserves have recently been discovered in the Baharia Oasis region. Similarly, manganese is being mined in the Eastern Desert and Sinai, and substantial new deposits of phosphates, estimated at 1,000 million tons, have recently been found at Abu Tartur in the Western Desert. When mined, these will add greatly to present phosphate production which comes mainly from the mines at Isna, Hamrawein and Safager.

OIL AND GAS

Production of crude petroleum at the end of 1980 was averaging approximately 600,000 barrels per day (b/d), compared with 420,000 b/d in 1977. Likewise the oil revenue for 1980 was $1,500 million compared with $960 million in 1979. In January 1981 Egypt raised the price of its Suez 33° API oil to $40.5 per barrel to increase oil revenues further. However, the first half of 1981 saw a drop of 10 per cent in oil production, with 661,000 b/d produced in the first quarter and 614,000 b/d in the second quarter, leading to a drop in the price of its top crude to $33 per barrel in July. Oil is thus clearly becoming of greater importance to Egypt's economy, as illustrated by its contribution to the G.D.P., which is expected to rise from £E1,874 million in 1980 to £E3,030 million in 1984. The current estimated revenue from oil sales in 1981/82 is $2,975 million. The most significant factors in explaining this great increase are the return of the Alma Oilfield, renamed the Sha'b Ali field, by Israel in November 1979, and the increase in concessions and finds, particularly in the Gulf of Suez. By the end of 1980 Egypt's proven oil reserves had risen to 3,068.6 million barrels, a rise of 47 per cent over the 1979 figures.

The main producing fields are Morgan, Ramadan and July in the Gulf of Suez. These are operated by the Gulf of Suez Petroleum Company (GUPCO), which accounted for 73.8 per cent of Egypt's total crude output in 1977. This was originally a joint venture between the Egyptian General Petroleum Corporation (EGPC) and Amoco of the U.S.A. In 1976 the relationship between the two companies was changed to a production-sharing basis, similar to nearly all the other agreements between Egypt and foreign oil companies—and the EGPC was converted into the Egyptian General Petroleum Authority (EGPA).

WEPCO's Alamein field, discovered at the end of 1966, got off to a promising start and early in 1970 was producing 43,000 barrels per day, but its output has since declined considerably.

The Abu Gharadeq field which came on stream in 1973 has been disappointing for oil but its operator, FAPCO, has struck it rich in gas. The Razzaq field, operated by NIPCO, the other Amoco-EGPA venture in the Western Desert, has more potential than Abu Gharadeq and estimates of eventual production range up to 60,000 barrels per day. The field is already linked to the Mediterranean by pipeline.

Apart from Phillips, Amoco and Hispanoil, the Italian state concern ENI and Conoco of the U.S. are involved in Egyptian oil through the International Egyptian Oil Company, which partners EGPA in the Delta Petroleum Company (Delpco), a joint venture operating company. Braspetro, the Brazilian state monopoly, is involved in several areas, notably in the Western Desert. Deminex of West Germany has a separate agreement with the EGPA covering 2,000 square kilometres in the Gulf of Suez, as well as a joint agreement with Shell and BP and the EGPA in the same area concluded in July 1974. Elf-Aquitaine of France and the Egyptian Petroleum Development Company, a Japanese company, both signed agreements with EGPC in 1975. Conoco and British Petroleum each signed agreements in 1978 for exploration in Sinai and further agreements were signed with other oil companies in 1979. Most of the other foreign participants with the EGPA are American.

In June 1979 oil concession agreements were signed with Murphy, Ultramar, Union Oil and Gulf Oil of the U.S.A., IEOC of Italy and OEMU of Austria. In July Total signed an agreement to prospect 400 sq. km. at Darag in the Gulf of Suez, and in November Exxon and Sedco signed concessions for further areas in the Gulf of Suez. In the first two months of 1980 EGPC signed six exploration agreements with U.S. firms and two others with the French company CFP-Total and the Italian IEOC. In addition, agreements with the Swiss-German group Aegypetco were altered. This increase in exploration is now beginning to produce rewards, with oil finds from three wells in the Gulf of Suez expected to yield 6,000 barrels a day reported in March 1979, a Japanese oil strike on the Red Sea coast in June, and production due to begin from the West Bakr area of the Eastern Desert in July 1980. In March 1980 huge oil reserves in the Western Desert were reported but, although this justifies Egyptian belief that the Western Desert could be an overlap of the giant Libyan field, there are as yet no details of its full extent. Twelve new finds were reported in the Gulf of Suez in 1980, leading to a doubling of Egypt's known oil reserves, and the most promising of these is that by Mobil seven miles offshore near the junction of the Red Sea and the Gulf of Suez. It is hoped that this discovery might eventually produced oil at a rate of 100,000 b/d. These rates of discovery continued in 1981, when 12 main new oil discoveries, 10 of which were in the Gulf of Suez, were made. In November 1981 the Suez Oil Company (SUCO), a joint venture between BP, Royal Dutch/Shell, Deminex and EGPC, announced a major find of between 50,000 and 100,000 b/d at Gemsa Bay in the Gulf of Suez. Similarly, Shell Winning has made a significant discovery in the Western Desert.

There are six oil refineries: at Suez (two), Musturud near Cairo, Amiriyah and Mex, both near Alexandria, and Tanta. Under the reconstruction plan, petroleum and petrochemical industries are to be established at Suez. The Mex refinery has been enlarged to a capacity of 75,000 barrels per day and the Amiriyah refinery, opened in 1972, has a capacity of 32,000 barrels per day. The Tanta refinery, designed to meet the needs of lower Egypt and with a capacity of only 15,000 barrels per day was opened in August 1973. There is a good network of product pipelines.

A major crude pipeline has been built between Ain-Sukhna on the Gulf of Suez and Sidi-Krer, west of Alexandria. Operations started initially on a test basis in December 1976 and the line was officially opened in July 1977. This Suez-Mediterranean pipeline (Sumed) had been under discussion for several years. At the end of 1973 Egypt formed with Saudi Arabia, Kuwait, Qatar and Abu Dhabi the Arab Company for Oil Pipelines-Sumed to finance the pipeline. Egypt's share in this is 50 per cent or $200 million.

The pipeline's capacity is 80 million tons per year and there is the possibility of expansion up to 120 million. However, use of the line has been lower than forecast, and the Government has had to reduce the original fee of $1.60 per ton to $1.52, with a sliding scale down to $1.00 per ton for large amounts. Some major oil companies use Sumed. The Sumed Company also purchases oil on its own behalf at the Suez end, and sells it off at the Mediterranean end. Sumed is not expected to compete with the Canal for oil shipments. The Government expects the two to be complementary. Despite the Arab boycott of Egypt in 1979, oil shipments to Western Europe through Sumed have not yet been affected. In June 1981 a further pipeline was opened, joining the town of Ras Shuqair on the Red Sea to the Musturud refinery near Cairo.

The first of Egypt's gas-fields to come on stream was Abu Madi, in the Nile Delta, in October 1974. Its capacity is 3.5 million cubic metres per day or 1 million tons of oil equivalent per year. Total gas reserves were estimated at the end of 1980 to be in the region of 85,000 million cubic metres. Abu Gharadeq, in the Western Desert, started production in April 1976; Abukir, offshore near Alexandria, was due to start in 1976/77 but operations were delayed. These two fields are said to have the same producing capacity and reserves as Abu Madi. Abu Madi is to be linked with the industrial centres of the Delta, in particular with the fertilizer plant to be built at Talkha, and Abu Gharadeq with the industrial centre of Helwan and notably the iron and steel complex. Abukir will eventually supply fertilizer and sponge iron plants in the Alexandria region (though these plans are a long way in the future). In 1981 a further gas find was made by Mobil in the Mediterranean, with a potential daily output of 25.9 million cubic feet.

BANKING

In late 1971 reorganization of the banking system resulted in the merger of three of the banks into others, with each of the rest being entrusted with specialized functions. The National Bank of Egypt was entrusted with foreign trade, the Bank of Port Said merged into Misr Bank which was to deal with home trade, including agricultural finance, the Industrial Bank merged into the Bank of Alexandria which was to deal with manufacturing, the Mortgage Credit Bank merged with the *Crédit Foncier Egyptian* and was to deal with construction and housing and the Bank of Cairo left to deal with operations of the public sector. In 1975, in line with the liberalization of the banking system, these restrictions on the sectoral operations of the major banks were removed. A new bank, the Nasser Social Bank, was created to deal with pensions and other forms of social security. The Egyptian International Bank for Foreign Trade and Development was also created in 1971 to promote foreign trade and attract foreign investment but was later transformed into the Arab International Bank for Foreign Trade and Development with Egypt, Libya and other Arab investors holding shares. These banks are additional to the Central Bank of Egypt, which was created from the issue department of the National Bank of Egypt in 1960, and the Public Organization for Agricultural Credit and Co-operatives, which the *Crédit Agricole* became in 1964.

Between 1977 and 1979 the money supply greatly increased, with currency outside banks rising from £E1,749.5 million to £E2,656.9 million. This figure had increased to £E3,407 million by the end of 1980. Similarly, demand deposits at commercial banks increased from £E1,193.5 million to £E1,697.3 million, although these had fallen to £E1,446 million by 1980. However, the Central Bank reserve also increased by 18 per cent over the same period, from $534 million to $635 million, largely through increases of foreign exchange.

Foreign banks are welcome in Egypt since it began liberalizing its economy in earnest in 1974. American Express, Citibank, Crédit Suisse and Lloyds Bank International are among those that have set up foreign currency branches. Manufacturers Hanover Trust Company has a "free zone" foreign currency branch. A number of other international banks have representative offices. The biggest impact on the Egyptian banking system from foreign banks, however, has come from the joint ventures established with Egyptian banks. These include Chase National Bank, which pairs Chase Manhattan and the National Bank of Egypt; Misr International Bank, which partners Misr Bank with First National Bank of Chicago, Banco di Roma and UBAF Bank (London); Egyptian-American Bank, which pairs American Express and Bank of Alexandria; Cairo Barclays International Bank, a venture between Banque du Caire and Barclays Bank International; Misr-America International Bank, owned 40 per cent by Bank of America, 4.5 per

cent by the Kuwait Real Estate Bank and 4.5 per cent by First Arabian Corporation on the foreign partners' side, and 26 per cent by the Development Industrial Bank (the former Industrial Bank recently hived off again from the Bank of Alexandria) and 25 per cent by Misr Insurance Company on the Egyptian side; and Banque du Caire et de Paris, a pairing of Banque Nationale de Paris and Banque du Caire. All these, with the exception of Cairo Barclays, are 51/49 ventures in favour of the Egyptian side; this allows them to act in domestic commercial operations, as well as foreign currency operations. Cairo Barclays, being a 50/50 venture, is not permitted domestic banking activity. Other developments include the opening in Cairo in July 1979 of the Faisal-Islamic bank, with 49 per cent Saudi and Gulf equity participation. This is the first bank to do business according to Sharia. In April 1980 interest rates were raised nationally by 1 per cent, and they were again raised by 1 per cent in June.

During 1980 a number of changes took place in the banking structure. In December Egypt's first international bank, the Egyptian International Bank, was opened with a capital of $100 million. 50 per cent of this capital was subscribed by the country's four main banks: the National Bank of Egypt, Bank of Alexandria, Banque de Caire, and Banque Misr, with the other half being provided by the Central Bank of Egypt. In addition a National Investment Bank was established earlier in the year to monitor public investment, and there were also plans to establish an import-export bank. The fiscal year was also changed in 1980 to begin in July and not January.

1981 saw confusion in Egypt's banking sector. On August 1st the Egyptian pound was devalued by 16.7 per cent, and the export of foreign currency banknotes was banned. In addition, banks were told to place up to 40 per cent deposit in local currency when opening most letters of credit. The devaluation led to a three-tier exchange rate, with an official rate for transactions on the government account of $1 = £E0.84, and a free market rate of $1 = £E0.88. It seems that this has led to a growth in the currency black market, and that the general confusion resulting from the changes caused a cutback in imports during the second half of the year.

BUDGET

Egypt draws up six budgets—the current services budget, the public authorities' current budget, the economic organizations' current budget, the special finance fund's current budget, the investment budget and the emergency fund—but in practice they can be grouped together,

In 1979, with inflation at 25–30 per cent and money supply growing at about 30 per cent, the question of subsidies was crucial for the government, and was one reason for the high projected net overall budget deficit of £E1,197 million. The 1980–81 budget aimed for a 10.8 per cent growth in G.D.P. within the year. The investment budget was £E3,200 million of which infrastructure and housing (22 per cent), agriculture and food processing (20 per cent), and transport and communications (17 per cent) took the highest shares. Over the year the average annual income was expected to rise 6.4 per cent to £E472.2. It was planned that the previous year's current budget deficit would be turned into a current expenditure surplus of £E218 million, largely through a revenue increase of 27 per cent to £E5,890.8 million. This increase is to be financed through increases in petroleum income, Suez Canal revenue, customs duties and tax. The June 1980 budget, however, has done little to stop inflation. Although it introduced lower prices for 77 commodities produced in the public sector, increased subsidies to £E1,555.2 million, and cut customs duties on such goods as foods and animal feedstuffs, it has not solved the fundamental problem of food provision.

FOREIGN TRADE AND PAYMENTS

The external trade deficit has persisted almost without interruption since before the Second World War. According to the I.M.F., the visible trade deficit rose from $357 million in 1972 to $2,844 million in 1978 and $3,589 million in 1979. In 1980, though, it fell slightly, to $3,074 million, largely as a result of oil exports. However, private and government unrequited transfers transformed a current account deficit into a surplus of $77 million in 1973, and transfers of $1,035 million in 1974 reduced the deficit to only $327 million. The current account deficit increased to $1,772 million in 1975, easing to $826 million in 1976. By 1979 the current deficit had again risen to $1,553 million. By 1980 the most significant change in the overall balance of payments position was an increase in Egypt's reserves of $664 million compared with a rise of $98 million in 1979 and a fall of $14 million in 1978. The Government keeps a constant vigil on all external payments, but the pressure of population on resources helps to keep the balance of payments in a critical state. The problem is unlikely to be solved without a breakthrough in the pattern of imports and exports which may be alleviated through the development of the petroleum sector. To be finally solved, though, the food import bill must be radically reduced.

Exports have traditionally been agricultural goods, with raw cotton accounting for almost one third of the value in 1977. However, by 1979 a change was apparent, with crude petroleum accounting for 30 per cent of the exports against raw cotton's 21 per cent. In 1976 crude petroleum had accounted for only 18 per cent of Egypt's exports. This trend is likely to be greatly increased in the next few years. The high import figures are mainly the result of the need to procure vital food supplies, particularly of wheat, and also machinery for a growing manufacturing industry.

There is also a geographical imbalance in Egypt's trade: in 1976 over half of exports went to the Eastern bloc, because of supply contracts to pay off debts, but most imports come from the West (with the U.S. recording a startling rise in sales to Egypt) and only 15 per cent of imports from the Eastern bloc. In 1977,

however, the proportion of exports going to the Eastern bloc had fallen to less than 50 per cent. While the Soviet Union remained Egypt's largest export market, by 1976 Italy had taken second place. In 1979 the U.S.A. was still the largest source of Egypt's imports, followed by West Germany, Italy, France and the United Kingdom, and these five countries supplied 51.2 per cent of Egypt's imports. In contrast, in 1979 Italy became Egypt's largest export market, receiving 27.4 per cent of Egypt's exports, relegating the U.S.S.R. to second place, and in 1980 the U.S.S.R. had fallen to fifth behind Italy, the U.S.A., the Netherlands and Switzerland. In terms of imports to Egypt, France has now become the second largest contributor, with 10.2 per cent, behind the U.S.A. with 19.3 per cent. It seems likely that France's share will increase further as its role as a military arms supplier increases.

ECONOMIC POLICY

According to the Permanent Constitution of 1971 the economy of Egypt is one based on socialism with the people controlling all means of production. In practice this means that the Government owns or controls practically every economic unit in the economy worth controlling. Although the doctrine of socialism was invoked from the first land reform in 1952, the economy remained largely in private hands until 1961, except for the nationalization of the Suez Canal company in 1956 and that of British and French property during the Suez attack. During 1961, all cotton exporting firms were nationalized, and the Alexandria futures market was closed; 275 industrial and trading concerns were taken over by the state in whole or in part; taxation was made so progressive that individual income was virtually limited to the official maximum of £E5,000; the maximum limit on land ownership was reduced from 200 to 100 feddans (before it was reduced again in 1969); individual shareholding was limited to £E10,000; 25 per cent of the net profits of industrial companies was to be distributed to the workers, who were to be represented on the boards of directors, and to work only a 42-hour week.

Other nationalization measures followed, so that the only sectors of the economy remaining outside complete government ownership are agriculture and urban real estate, but even these are overwhelmingly regulated by laws and decrees. Concerns are grouped under boards and boards under Chairmen and Ministers, and a constant stream of directives helps to bring the activities of all the controlled units in line with Government policies.

After 1967 the Government introduced yet more restrictive measures aimed at curbing consumer demand including a variety of taxes, forced savings and compulsory contributions out of wages and salaries. Since then, however, the trend has been towards "denasserization", the sequestrations of the 1960s have been ruled illegal, new laws are being passed to allow private-sector participation in former state preserves like exporting and importing and transport, and foreign investment is seen as the key to development. The latest development plan, the 1980–84 Peace Plan, also reflects the increased role of the private sector. Approximately one quarter of G.N.P. is to be invested in education, land reclamation and utilities, and by the end the growth in G.N.P. is expected to be 11.4 per cent a year.

In May 1980 there was a major Cabinet change with Ali Abdel-Razzaq Abdel-Majid becoming Deputy Prime Minister and Minister for Economic and Social Affairs. In the first six months of his appointment he introduced a large amount of economic legislation for debate in the House of Assembly, including bills covering the customs law, income tax, a conspicuous consumption bill, a bill to transform the stock exchange, and a joint-stock company bill. There were also plans to introduce several large holding companies to control industry in the public sector. Abdel-Majid's policies were not generally popular and, in a further Cabinet change in January 1982, he was replaced as Deputy Prime Minister for Economic Affairs by Muhammad Abdul-Fattah Ibrahim.

On February 20th, 1982, the Prime Minister addressed the People's Assembly with a major statement on the economic policy to be followed by the country under its new leader, President Mubarak. In general terms, this policy is to be based on a clear strategy for economic development aimed at increasing exports and employment, through the comprehensive planning of the public, private and co-operative sectors. Particular attention is to be paid to social problems. Investment resources are to be increased through new channels for private investment, increasing the contribution of the banking sector, improving the efficiency of the tax system, increasing indigenous financial resources, cutting government expenditure, and limiting the consumption of imported goods. The government aims to use the public sector as the main prop of production, and sees manpower as the real wealth of the country. The negative effects of subsidies are acknowledged, but the government sees the only way to remedy these problems being through increased rates of development and the promotion of productivity. Nevertheless, strenuous efforts are to be made to reduce the level of imports, and all import operations in the future are to be undertaken through the banks without the transfer of currency. In 1982 the government plans to achieve industrial production of £E4,000 million and to increase its export earnings, particularly through oil. The war production sector is also to be expanded. In agriculture, it envisages and reclamation as continuing to play an important role. Transport, communications, housing, tourism, health and education are also all to be boosted.

TRANSPORT

The Government is aiming to expand both the Mediterranean and Red Sea port capacities as well as reviving Port Said, Ismailia and Suez to cope with traffic passing through the reopened Suez Canal. Alexandria port is being expanded, aided by a $95 million loan from the World Bank, and a completely new port is planned, west of Alexandria, at Dakheila, with a capacity of 20 million tons per year, compared with Alexandria's present capacity of 13 million tons. Safaga on the Red Sea is also being developed but mainly to handle mineral imports and exports. There are also plans to build a port ten miles west of the Nile's Damietta tributary to handle between 10 million and 12 million tons of cargo per year by 2000.

River transport is being expanded to relieve the load on roads and railways for internal distribution. Navigable waterways total about 3,100 km., of which about half is the Nile and the rest canals. Canals such as the Nubariya canal in the delta and the Bahr Youssef between Fayoum and Asyut make it possible to link Alexandria with Upper Egypt through Cairo.

Egypt has over 4,000 km. of railway and modernization is urgently needed. A project using loans from various sources of up to $165 million is being undertaken to modernize the railway system and expand its carrying capacity, as well as to draw up a comprehensive national transport survey. A French consortium won a contract for 52 electric trains for the first stage of the Cairo metro system in January 1979. Earlier modernization plans have not been carried out, and, in an attempt to rectify these problems, it is intended that in 1982 all railway coaches will be remodelled. It is planned that, within the next three years, all the locomotives in the country will be replaced. Work has already begun on the Cairo underground metro system, using a French government "soft" loan of $176 million.

Good roads connect Cairo with Alexandria, the canal towns and Upper Egypt. There are plans to expand the output both of locally produced goods vehicles and of vehicles from joint-venture projects set up with foreign companies.

EgyptAir, the state airline, operates a network of domestic and international routes and since March 1980 commercial flights have begun to Tel-Aviv. At the end of 1980 EgyptAir doubled its capital to £E50 million, and it also put forward plans to establish the biggest aircraft servicing centre in the Middle East. Although in August 1980 it cancelled its option to buy 4 U.S. DC10/30 civilian aircraft, this expansion is seen as part of a concerted policy to further develop Egypt's expanding tourist trade. In the first six months of 1981 the total number of tourists was up 15.3 per cent on the same period in 1980, but since President Sadat's assassination these levels have fallen, so that in October and November there were 9 per cent fewer tourists than in the same period in the previous year, and in December 19 per cent fewer, thus reducing the anticipated level of income from tourism.

STATISTICAL SURVEY

AREA AND POPULATION

AREA	CENSUS POPULATION†		ESTIMATED MID-YEAR POPULATION†			
	Nov. 22nd-23rd, 1976	Jan. 24th, 1979 (Preliminary)	1978	1979	1980	1981
997,738.5 sq. km.*	38,198,204	40,500,000	39,767,000	40,983,000	42,289,000	43,465,000

* 385,229 sq. miles. Inhabited and cultivated territory accounts for 35,189 sq. km. (13,587 sq. miles).
† Including Egyptian nationals abroad (1,572,000 at the 1976 census).

GOVERNORATES*

GOVERNORATE	AREA (sq. km.)	CAPITAL	GOVERNORATE	AREA (sq. km.)	CAPITAL
Cairo . . .	214.2	Cairo	Menufia . . .	1,532.1	Shibin el-Kom
Alexandria . . .	2,679.4	Alexandria	Behera . . .	10,129.5	Damanhur
Port Said . . .	72.1	Port Said	Giza . . .	85,153.2	Giza
Ismailia . . .	1,441.6	Ismailia	Beni Suef . . .	1,321.7	Beni Suef
Suez . . .	17,840.4	Suez	Fayum . . .	1,827.2	Fayum
Damietta . . .	589.2	Damietta	Menia . . .	2,261.7	Menia
Dakahlia . . .	3,470.9	Mansura	Asyut . . .	1,553.0	Asyut
Sharkia . . .	4,179.6	Zagazig	Suhag . . .	1,547.2	Suhag
Kalyubia . . .	1,001.1	Benha	Kena . . .	1,850.7	Kena
Kafr el-Sheikh . . .	3,437.1	Kafr el-Sheikh	Aswan . . .	678.5	Aswan
Gharbia . . .	1,942.2	Tanta			

* Excluding the four sparsely-populated "frontier districts".

PRINCIPAL TOWNS

(final results of census of November 1976, excluding nationals abroad)

El Qahira (Cairo, the capital)	5,074,016	Zagazig . . .	202,575
El Iskandariyah (Alexandria)	2,317,705	El Suweis (Suez) . .	193,965
El Giza . . .	1,230,446	Damanhur . .	170,633
Subra-El Khema . .	394,223	El Faiyum . .	166,910
El Mahalla el Kubra .	292,114	El Minya (Menia) .	146,366
Tanta . . .	283,240	Kafr-El Dwar . .	146,248
Bur Sa'id (Port Said) .	262,760	Isma'ilia . .	145,930
El Mansura . .	259,387	Aswan . . .	144,654
Asyut . . .	213,751	Beni-Suef . .	117,910

Greater Cairo (November 1976): 6,818,318, (June 1979): 8,539,000.

CIVILIAN LABOUR FORCE
('ooo employed)

	1975	1977	1978	1979
Agriculture, forestry and fishing . . .	4,424.8	4,217.4	3,976.7	4,002.0
Mining and quarrying . . .	13.1	19.9	35.7	22.8
Manufacturing . . .	1,296.1	1,354.7	1,430.3	1,532.1
Electricity, gas and water . . .	46.0	52.4	68.9	65.7
Construction . . .	247.5	335.1	385.8	448.5
Commerce. . . .	842.0	915.2	913.1	918.4
Transport, storage and communications	420.4	428.4	467.5	488.4
Finance and insurance . . .	83.3	107.6	107.0	116.8
Social and personal services . . .	1,557.6	1,799.4	1,786.1	1,820.5
Other	333.3	264.2	631.4	608.3
TOTAL . . .	9,264.1	9,494.3	9,802.5	10,023.5

AGRICULTURE

AREA AND PRODUCTION OF LINT COTTON

	1977/78		1978/79		1979/80	
	'ooo feddans*	'ooo kantars†	'ooo feddans*	'ooo kantars†	'ooo feddans*	'ooo kantars†
Giza 70 . . .	334	1,945	358	2,525	366	2,921
Giza 45 . . .	29	150	25	133	25	153
Giza 68 . . .	156	774	39	222	45	291
Giza 69 . . .	156	1,032	128	1,060	121	1,097
Giza 67 . . .	241	1,643	184	1,359	176	1,395
Dandara . . .	145	860	193	1,335	194	1,394
Giza 66 . . .	263	843	118	696	54	344
Giza 72 . . .	16	51	20	75	—	—
TOTAL (incl. others) .	1,423	7,974	1,189	8,767	1,195	9,672

1980/81 Estimates: area 1.18 million feddans; production 10.33 million kantars.

* 1 feddan = 1.038 acres (0.42 hectare).   † 1 metric kantar = 50 kg.

OTHER PRINCIPAL CROPS

	AREA ('ooo feddans*)				PRODUCTION ('ooo metric tons)			
	1977	1978	1979	1980	1977	1978	1979	1980
Wheat . . .	1,207	1,380	1,391	1,326	1,697	1,933	1,856	1,736
Maize . . .	1,323	1,405	1,413	1,433	2,724	3,117	2,426	2,698
Millet . . .	393	413	394	398	648	681	619	640
Barley . . .	95	114	107	96	111	132	122	107
Rice . . .	1,040	1,025	1,037	970	2,272	2,351	2,507	2,382
Beans† . . .	325	272	250	245	270	231	236	213
Lentils . . .	48	36	22	15	24	16	9	7
Onions† . . .	31	27	27	35	723	599	560	611
Sugar cane . . .	250	248	249	253	8,379	8,296	8,791	8,544

* 1 feddan = 1.038 acres (0.42 hectare).
† Dry crop and the production of onions includes interplanted crop.
‡ Provisional.

LIVESTOCK PRODUCTS
('ooo metric tons)

	1978	1979	1980
Beef and veal .	122	122	124*
Buffalo meat . .	114	117	119*
Mutton and lamb .	24	23	25*
Goats' meat .	20*	20*	20*
Pig meat .	2	2	3
Poultry meat .	103	101	102*
Other meat .	42*	41*	42*
Edible offals .	55*	56*	57*
Cows' milk .	643	646	672*
Buffaloes' milk .	1,204	1,227	1,267*
Sheep's milk .	20*	20*	21*
Goats' milk .	8	8	8*
Butter . .	68.8*	66.7*	67.6*
Cow and buffalo cheese .	234.2*	238.0*	242.9*
Hen eggs .	82.5	89.0	90.2*
Honey . .	7.6	7.3	7.5*
Wool: greasy .	2.6	2.5	2.5*
clean .	2.2	2.3	2.3*
Cattle and Buffalo hides . .	35.7*	36.6*	36.8*
Sheep skins .	2.8*	2.7*	3.0*
Goat skins .	2.8*	2.9*	2.9*

* FAO estimates.

Source: FAO, mainly *Production Yearbook.*

LIVESTOCK
('ooo head, year ending September)

	1978	1979	1980*
Cattle . .	2,010	1,965	2,040
Buffaloes . .	2,295	2,321	2,379
Sheep . .	1,755	1,679	1,692
Goats . .	1,401	1,427	1,700
Pigs . .	15	15*	16
Horses . .	15	12	12
Asses . .	1,637	1,672	1,702
Camels . .	99	99	99
Chickens . .	26,986	27,292	27,457
Ducks . .	3,392	3,440	3,470
Turkeys . .	724	733	739

*FAO estimates.

Source: FAO, *Production Yearbook.*

FORESTRY

ROUNDWOOD REMOVALS
(FAO estimates, 'ooo cubic metres, all non-coniferous)

	1977	1978	1979
Industrial wood .	79	81	81
Fuel wood . .	1,587	1,630	1,673
TOTAL . .	1,666	1,711	1,754

Source: FAO, *Yearbook of Forest Products.*

FISHING
('ooo metric tons, live weight)

	1977	1978	1979
Marine . .	29.6	20.9	37.5
Freshwater . .	75.0	79.0	100.0
TOTAL CATCH .	104.5	99.9	137.5

Source: FAO, *Yearbook of Fishery Statistics.*

MINING

		1976	1977	1978	1979
Crude petroleum . .	'ooo metric tons	16,756	20,900	24,300	27,742
Iron ore* . . .	,, ,, ,,	1,243	1,308	1,468	1,435
Manganese ore* . .	,, ,, ,,	4	3	6	—
Salt (unrefined) . .	,, ,, ,,	606	741	755	728
Phosphate rock . .	,, ,, ,,	500	567	639	587
Natural gas . .	,, ,, ,,	115	405	750	1,365

Small quantities of lead and zinc are also mined.

* Figures refer to the metal content of ores.

1980 ('ooo metric tons): Crude petroleum 29,404; Natural gas 1,616.

INDUSTRY
SELECTED PRODUCTS

		1976	1977	1978	1979
Wheat flour[1] . .	'ooo metric tons	2,878	3,237	3,480	3,507
Raw sugar . .	,, ,, ,,	576	657	589	632
Margarine . .	,, ,, ,,	128.0	133.2	151.7	160.1
Cottonseed oil . .	,, ,, ,,	161	169	172	177
Wine	'ooo hectolitres	11	13	17	19*
Beer	,, ,,	302	388	423	340
Cigarettes . .	million	23,248	24,980	27,457	29,931
Manufactured tobacco .	metric tons	7,831	7,808	8,093	9,086
Cotton yarn (pure) .	'ooo metric tons	193.0	210.4	212.2	216.1
Woven cotton fabrics (pure and mixed) .	million metres	644	695	728	686
Flax yarn[2] . . .	'ooo metric tons	1.0	0.9	0.7	0.7
Jute yarn . .	,, ,, ,,	36.7	38.1	33.7	35.8
Wool yarn (pure and mixed) .	,, ,, ,,	12.9	13.4	10.2	11.0
Woven woollen fabrics (pure and mixed) .	'ooo metres	11,536	9,645	9,580	9,619
Woven rayon and acetate fabrics . .	'ooo metric tons	6.4	6.5	9.8	2.8
Paper and paperboard .	,, ,, ,,	118	118*	124	124*
Rubber tyres . .	'ooo	760	921	859	891
Ethyl alcohol . .	'ooo hectolitres	301	316	290	240
Sulphuric acid (100%) .	'ooo metric tons	27	30	33	32
Caustic soda (Sodium hydroxide) .	,, ,, ,,	27	28	31	37
Nitrogenous fertilizers (a)[3] .	,, ,, ,,	169.9	195.2	216.5	263.9
Phosphate fertilizers (b)[3] .	,, ,, ,,	73.7	88.4	97.8	93.0
Motor spirit (petrol)[4] .	,, ,, ,,	1,476	1,530	1,704	1,740
Kerosene . .	,, ,, ,,	1,320	1,379	1,508	1,540
Jet fuel . .	,, ,, ,,	117	123	136	140
Distillate fuel oils .	,, ,, ,,	1,717	1,961	2,180	2,220
Residual fuel oil (Mazout)	,, ,, ,,	5,056	5,264	5,462	5,570
Petroleum bitumen (asphalt) . .	,, ,, ,,	135	147	192	194
Coke-oven coke .	,, ,, ,,	628	694	691	855
Cement . .	,, ,, ,,	3,362	3,232	2,422	2,987
Pig-iron . .	,, ,, ,,	250	250	300	300
Crude steel . .	,, ,, ,,	457	263	600	635
Radio receivers .	'ooo	117	265	348	223
Television receivers .	,,	88	151	184	238
Passenger motor cars (assembly) . .	number	9,899	13,991	14,562	16,697
Electric energy . .	million kWh.	12,256	14,054	14,500	14,800

1980 ('ooo metric tons): Cotton yarn 232; Woven cotton fabrics 632 million metres; Jute yarn 36.2; Kerosene and jet fuel 1,714; Residual fuel oil 6,416; Cement 3,000.

* FAO estimate.

[1] *Source:* International Wheat Council, *World Wheat Statistics.*   [2] Including waste and yarn made from tow.
[3] Production in terms of (a) nitrogen or (b) phosphoric acid.   [4] Including naphtha (prior to 1978).

FINANCE

1,000 millièmes = 100 piastres = 5 tallaris = 1 Egyptian pound (£E).
Coins: 1, 2 and 5 millièmes; 1, 2, 5 and 10 piastres.
Notes: 5, 10, 25 and 50 piastres; 1, 5, 10 and 20 pounds.
Exchange rates (March 1982): £1 sterling = £E1.287; U.S. $1 = 700 millièmes.
£E100 = £77.70 sterling = $142.86.

Note: From September 1949 to May 1962 the Egyptian pound was valued at U.S. $2.87156 ($1 = 348.24 millièmes). Between May 1962 and February 1973 the pound's value was $2.30 ($1 = 434.783 millièmes). From February 1973 to December 1978 the official exchange rate was £E1 = $2.55556 ($1 = 391.304 millièmes) but there were other rates for tourism and since September 1975 a legal free currency market has operated in Port Said. Since May 1976 the "parallel" rate, previously fixed by the Government, has been subject to managed "floating". On January 1st, 1979, the official rate was abolished and the "parallel" rate came into use for all transactions. The unified rate was initially $1 = 700 millièmes (£E1 = $1.4286). From November 1967 to August 1971 the exchange rate was £1 sterling = £E1.0435; from December 1971 to June 1972 it was £1 sterling = £E1.1328.

BUDGET ESTIMATES
(£E million)
CURRENT BUDGETS

REVENUE		1978	1979	EXPENDITURE		1978	1979
Sovereignty revenue	. .	2,505.6	2,816.4	Wages	.	1,100.0	1,257.8
Current and transfer	. .	3,765.9	5,705.2	Current and transfer	. .	5,580.2	7,917.2
TOTAL	. .	6,271.5	8,521.6	TOTAL	.	6,680.2	9,175.0

CAPITAL BUDGETS

REVENUE		1978	1979	EXPENDITURE		1978	1979
Sundry	.	1,018.0	1,079.8	Investments .	.	1,421.1	1,684.9
Loans and credit facilities	.	547.0	634.9	Capital transfers	. .	1,832.7	2,064.6
TOTAL	. .	1,565.0	1,714.7	TOTAL	.	3,253.8	3,749.5

Source: National Bank of Egypt, *Economic Bulletin.*

G.D.P. GROWTH TARGETS UNDER 1980–84 PLAN
(at constant 1979 prices—£E million)

	REAL G.D.P.		AVERAGE ANNUAL GROWTH RATE (%)	SECTORAL STRUCTURE (%)	
	1980	1984	1980–84	1980	1984
Agriculture	2,670	3,023	3.2	23.7	18.3
Industry and mining	1,590	2,395	10.8	14.1	14.5
Petroleum	1,874	3,030	12.8	16.7	18.4
Power	110	163	10.3	1.0	1.0
Construction	540	840	11.7	4.8	5.1
Transport and communication . . .	475	740	11.7	4.2	4.5
Suez Canal	502	931	16.7	4.5	5.7
Trade and finance	1,170	1,773	11.0	10.4	10.8
Housing and utilities . . .	206	330	12.5	1.8	2.0
Other services	2,120	3,250	11.3	18.8	19.7
G.D.P. AT FACTOR COST . .	11,257	16,475	10.0	100.0	100.0

Source: Financial Times, July 23rd, 1980, derived from Ministry of Planning, Cairo.

CENTRAL BANK RESERVES
(U.S. $ million at December 31st)

	1978	1979	1980
Gold	104	104	103
IMF Special Drawing Rights	11	—	—
Foreign exchange . .	481	529	1,046
Total . .	596	633	1,149

Source: IMF, *International Financial Statistics.*

MONEY SUPPLY
(£E million at December 31st)

	1978	1979	1980
Currency outside banks	2,183.7	2,656.9	3,407
Demand deposits at commercial banks . .	1,369.1	1,697.3	1,446

Source: IMF, *International Financial Statistics.*

BALANCE OF PAYMENTS
(U.S. $ million)

	1975	1976	1977	1978	1979	1980
Merchandise exports f.o.b.	1,567	1,609	1,993	1,984	2,514	3,853
Merchandise imports f.o.b.	−3,941	−3,842	−4,123	−4,828	−6,103	−6,927
Trade Balance . . .	−2,374	−2,233	−2,130	−2,844	−3,589	−3,074
Exports of services	1,078	1,975	2,550	3,442	4,079	5,340
Imports of services	−566	−655	−1,682	−1,875	−2,097	−2,852
Balance on Goods and Services	−1,862	−913	−1,262	−1,277	−1,607	−586
Private unrequited transfers (net) . .	} 90	87 {	43	29	41	61
Government unrequited transfers (net) . .			18	23	13	35
Current Balance . . .	−1,772	−826	−1,201	−1,225	−1,553	−490
Long-term capital (net)	−231	428	335	509	1,508	1,004
Short-term capital (net)	−220	−272	−1,040	−531	−121	79
Net errors and omissions	−647	−636	8	180	190	71
Total (net monetary movements) .	−2,870	−1,306	−1,898	−1,067	24	664
Allocation of IMF Special Drawing Rights . .	—	—	—	—	31	31
Valuation changes (net) . .	−45	65	47	62	−19	−65
Intergovernmental grants received . .	986	623	386	297	36	1
Loans to Government and Central Bank . .	582	134	1,553	654	75	62
Official deposits in Central Bank (net) . .	1,323	403	—	40	−49	−29
Changes in Reserves . .	−24	−81	88	−14	98	664

Source: IMF, *International Financial Statistics.*

EXTERNAL TRADE
(£E million)

	1974	1975	1976	1977	1978	1979	1980
Imports c.i.f. . .	920.1	1,539.3	1,489.9	1,884.3	2,632.2	2,686.2	3,402.0
Exports f.o.b. .	593.3	548.6	595.4	668.5	679.8	1,287.8	2,132.2

PRINCIPAL COMMODITIES
(£E million)

IMPORTS c.i.f.	1977	1978	1979	1980
Foodstuffs	399.6	624.5	n.a.	n.a.
Cereals and milling products . .	208.0	283.0	274.6	452.9
Animal and vegetable oils . . .	35.1	69.2	94.7	152.6
Other consumer goods	209.5	283.8	n.a.	n.a.
Paper and paper products . . .	51.1	58.2	50.0	73.5
Tobacco	41.3	61.9	76.1	64.0
Raw materials and capital goods . . .	1,275.2	1,723.9	n.a.	n.a.
Mineral products	254.3	339.6	n.a.	n.a.
Chemical products	148.0	188.8	174.2	260.9
Wood, hides and rubber . . .	173.1	206.2	188.9	317.9
Machinery and electrical apparatus . .	389.5	575.4	548.3	575.8
Transport equipment	207.8	389.8	354.7	346.9
Watches, clocks, scientific apparatus .	27.4	47.5	n.a.	39.9
TOTAL	1,884.3	2,632.2	2,686.2	3,402.0

EXPORTS f.o.b.	1977	1978	1979	1980
Textile fibres and products	312.1	286.6	488.4	519.3
Raw cotton	182.3	131.5	267.3	296.4
Cotton yarn	68.6	89.6	130.1	135.9
Cotton fabrics	24.5	27.2	41.0	36.7
Other agricultural crops	103.0	87.5	n.a.	n.a.
Potatoes	16.4	5.8	18.8	22.7
Rice	23.4	19.9	22.1	24.6
Edible fruits	26.0	24.2	19.5	30.4
Manufactured products	49.7	45.2	n.a.	n.a.
Sugar and sugar confectionery . .	11.4	11.3	15.3	12.4
Raw hides, skins, footwear, etc. . .	10.1	10.7	18.3	3.4
Raw materials and capital goods . . .	203.7	260.5	n.a.	n.a.
Crude petroleum	119.1	140.7	396.5	1,233.3
Gasoline, kerosene and fuel oil . .	13.1	5.4	22.3	35.0
TOTAL	668.5	679.8	1,287.8	2,132.2

PRINCIPAL TRADING PARTNERS
(£E million)

IMPORTS c.i.f.	1978	1979	1980	EXPORTS f.o.b.	1978	1979	1980
Australia	53.8	38.2	58.1	China, People's Rep.	25.4	21.8	39.0
Belgium/Lux'bourg	42.1	42.4	73.7	Czechoslovakia	15.5	32.0	24.7
Czechoslovakia	31.8	23.7	35.5	France	31.9	35.8	36.9
Finland	28.8	38.6	60.9	German Dem. Rep.	24.4	30.8	13.5
France	194.4	206.9	347.9	Germany, Fed. Rep.	28.2	67.3	55.4
German Dem. Rep.	31.9	25.1	20.9	Greece	26.9	40.0	61.6
Germany, Fed. Rep.	289.3	288.0	321.0	India	12.4	3.0	—
Greece	48.6	50.8	75.6	Iraq	11.2	9.9	0.1
India	39.9	38.7	29.8	Italy	80.8	353.3	610.7
Italy	198.5	228.1	228.9	Japan	31.8	58.6	50.2
Japan	132.5	130.3	159.3	Lebanon	7.7	13.2	12.6
Netherlands	73.2	77.4	59.3	Netherlands	34.4	97.8	122.6
Romania	71.9	83.3	108.6	Poland	6.2	14.4	18.0
Saudi Arabia	21.2	23.7	33.0	Romania	10.2	34.4	77.8
Spain	56.0	55.2	83.3	Saudi Arabia	15.7	32.9	38.9
Sweden	35.4	41.1	66.1	Sudan	7.9	16.0	9.2
Switzerland	67.9	72.5	59.8	Switzerland	10.8	31.7	93.1
Turkey	41.0	30.7	11.7	Syria	11.0	5.6	0.2
U.S.S.R.	89.0	53.5	53.6	U.S.S.R.	115.2	101.8	89.5
United Kingdom	197.9	174.0	207.6	United Kingdom	27.0	63.1	67.7
U.S.A.	430.6	478.8	656.3	U.S.A.	37.0	44.2	163.8
Yugoslavia	74.5	43.0	74.3	Yugoslavia	23.6	37.9	44.3
TOTAL (incl. others)	2,632.7	2,686.6	3,402.0	TOTAL (incl. others)	679.8	1,287.8	2,132.2

TRANSPORT

RAILWAYS

	1977	1978
Total Freight (million ton km.)	2,415	2,302
Total Passengers (million passenger km.)	9,300	9,290
Track Length (km.)	4,385	4,385

ROAD TRAFFIC
(motor vehicle licences at December 31st)

	1978	1979	1980
Buses	12,737	14,825	16,689
Lorries	72,212	90,833	113,335
Cars	330,102	379,663	442,540
Motor Cycles	94,174	109,300	129,455

SHIPPING
SUEZ CANAL TRAFFIC

		1966	1977	1978	1979	1980
Transits	number	21,250	19,703	21,266	20,363	20,795
Net tonnage	'000	274,250	220,477	248,260	266,171	281,305
Goods traffic	'000 tons	241,913	128,693	149,779	160,649	176,276
Transiting tankers	number	n.a.	2,620	2,498	2,698	n.a.
Net tonnage of tankers	'000	n.a.	75,568	73,924	86,278	88,870

Source: Suez Canal Authority, *Yearly Report*, 1980 and monthly reports.

CIVIL AVIATION
(tons)

	1973	1974	1975	1976	1977	1978	1979
Cargo	18,760	22,036	25,572	30,409	39,781	37,993	44,293
Mail	1,437	1,276	1,236	1,238	1,461	1,365	1,394

TOURISM
TOURIST ARRIVALS BY REGION

	1977	1978	1979	1980
Arabs	474,946	455,418	396,872	480,282
Europeans . . .	330,810	358,519	415,400	492,494
Americans . . .	109,306	145,949	166,608	141,322
Others	88,874	91,962	85,196	138,999
TOTAL . .	1,003,936	1,051,848	1,064,076	1,253,097

EDUCATION
(1977/78)

	INSTITUTIONS		TEACHERS	PUPILS
	Public	Private		
Pre-primary	363*	—	n.a.	73,546
Primary	9,981	316	124,263	4,211,345
Preparatory . . .	1,689	246	40,401	1,518,478
Secondary general .	343	125	19,328	416,208
Secondary technical . .	381*	—	28,237	437,495
Teacher training . .	67	—	3,080	36,522
Higher	179*	—	23,390	550,171

* Includes Private.

Sources (unless otherwise stated): Central Agency for Public Mobilization and Statistics, Cairo; Research Department, National Bank of Egypt, Cairo; International Monetary Fund.

THE CONSTITUTION

The Permanent Constitution of the Arab Republic of Egypt was approved by referendum on September 11th, 1971. There are six chapters with 193 articles, many of them based on the 1964 Interim Constitution, but chapters 3 and 4 show a considerable degree of liberalization of the former statutes.

CHAPTER 1
The State

Egypt is an Arab Republic with a democratic, socialist system based on the alliance of the working people and derived from the country's historical heritage and the spirit of Islam.

The Egyptian people are part of the Arab nation, who work towards total Arab unity.

Islam is the religion of the State; Arabic is its official language and the Islamic code is a principal source of legislation. The State safeguards the freedom of worship and of performing rites for all religions.

Sovereignty is of the people alone which is the source of all powers.

The protection, consolidation and preservation of the socialist gains is a national duty: the sovereignty of law is the basis of the country's rule, and the independence of immunity of the judiciary are basic guarantees for the protection of rights and liberties.

The Arab Socialist Union is the political organization of the State which represents the alliance of the working forces of the people; the farmers, workers, soldiers, the intelligentsia and national capitalism.

CHAPTER 2
The Fundamental Elements of Society

Social solidarity is the basis of Egyptian society, and the family is its nucleus.

The State ensures the equality of men and women in both political and social rights in line with the provisions of Muslim legislation.

Work is a right, an honour and a duty which the State guarantees together with the services of social and health insurance, pensions for incapacity and unemployment.

The economic basis of the Republic is socialism based on sufficiency and justice. It is calculated to prevent exploitation and to level up differences between classes.

The people control all means of production and regulate the national economy according to a comprehensive development plan which determines the role of Arab and foreign capital.

Property is subject to the people's control.

Property shall be expropriated only by law and against fair compensation. Nationalization shall also be by law for public interest considerations or socialist objectives.

Agricultural holding may be limited by law.

The State follows a comprehensive central planning and compulsory planning approach based on quinquennial socio-economic and cultural development plans whereby the society's resources are mobilized and put to the best use.

The public Sector assumes the leading role in the development of the national economy. The State provides absolute protection of this Sector as well as the property of co-operative societies and trade unions against all attempts to tamper with them.

CHAPTER 3
Public Liberties, Rights and Duties

All citizens are equal before the law. Personal liberty is a natural right and no one may be arrested, searched, imprisoned or restricted in any way without a court order.

Houses have sanctity, and shall not be placed under surveillance or searched without a court order with reasons given for such action.

The law safeguards the sanctities of the private lives of all citizens; so have all postal, telegraphic telephonic and other means of communication which may not therefore be confiscated, or perused except by a court order giving the reasons, and only for a specified period.

Public rights and freedoms are also inviolate and all calls for atheism and anything that reflects adversely on divine religions is prohibited.

The freedom of opinion, the Press, printing and publications and all information media are safeguarded.

Press censorship is forbidden, so are warnings, suspensions or cancellations through administrative channels. Under exceptional circumstances as in cases of emergency or in war time, censorship may be imposed on information media for a definite period.

Egyptians have the right to permanent or provisional emigration and no Egyptian may be deported or prevented from returning to the country.

Citizens have the right to private meetings in peace provided they bear no arms. Egyptians also have the right to form societies which have no secret activities or are hostile to the government. Public meetings are also allowed within the limits of the law.

CHAPTER 4
Sovereignty of the Law

All acts of crime should be specified together with the penalties for the acts.

Recourse to justice, it says, is a right of all citizens, and those who are financially unable, will be assured of means to defend their rights.

Arrested persons may protest against their detention and their protests should be decided upon within a prescribed period otherwise they should be released.

CHAPTER 5
System of Government

The President, who must be at least 40 years old, is nominated by at least one-third of the members of the People's Assembly, approved by at least two-thirds, and elected by popular referendum. His term is for six years and he 'may be re-elected for another subsequent term.' He may take emergency measures in the interests of the state but these measures must be approved by referendum within 60 days.

The People's Assembly, elected for five years, is the legislative body and approves general policy, the budget and the development plan. It shall have 'not less than 350' elected members, at least half of whom shall be workers or farmers, and the President may appoint up to ten additional members. In exceptional circumstances the Assembly, by a two-thirds vote, may authorize the President to rule by decree for a specified period but these decrees must be approved by the Assembly at its next meeting. The law governing the composition of the People's Assembly was amended in May 1979 (*see* People's Assembly, below).

The Assembly may pass a vote of no confidence in a Deputy Prime Minister, a Minister or a Deputy Minister,

provided three days' notice of the vote is given, and the minister must then resign. In the case of the Prime Minister, the Assembly may "prescribe" his responsibility and submit a report to the President: if the President disagrees with the report but the Assembly persists, then the matter is put to a referendum: if the people support the President the Assembly is dissolved; if they support the Assembly the President must accept the resignation of the Government. The President may dissolve the Assembly prematurely, but his action must be approved by a referendum and elections must be held within 60 days.

Executive Authority is vested in the President, who may appoint one or more vice-presidents and appoints all ministers. He may also dismiss the vice-presidents and ministers. The President has 'the right to refer to the people in connection with important matters related to the country's higher interests.' The Government is described as 'the supreme executive and administrative organ of the state'. Its members, whether full ministers or deputy ministers, must be at least 35 years old. Further sections define the roles of Local Government, Specialized National Councils, the Judiciary, the Higher Constitutional Court, the Socialist Prosecutor General, the Armed Forces and National Defence Council and the Police.

CHAPTER 6
General and Transitional Provisions

No law shall normally have retroactive effect, but this may be changed, except in criminal matters, with the approval of a majority of the Assembly. Articles of the constitution may be revised, at the suggestion of the President or one-third of the Assembly, but the revision must be submitted for approval by a public referendum. The term of the present President shall date from his election as President of the United Arab Republic.

Political Parties

In June 1977 the People's Assembly adopted a new law on political parties, which, subject to certain conditions, permitted the formation of political parties for the first time since 1953. A new draft law was enacted in June 1978 by which the operation of political parties was made much more difficult but in July 1978 President Sadat announced the formation of his own political party, the National Democratic Party.

1980 Amendments

On April 30th, 1980, the People's Assembly passed a number of amendments, which were subsequently massively approved at a referendum the following month. A summary of the amendments follows:

(i)   the regime in Egypt is socialist-democratic, based on the alliance of working people's forces.

(ii) the political system depends on multiple political parties; the Arab Socialist Union is therefore abolished.

(iii) the President is elected for a six-year term and can be elected for "other terms".

(iv) the President shall appoint a Consultative Council to preserve the principles of the revolutions of July 23rd, 1952, and May 15th, 1971.

(v)   a Supreme Press Council shall safeguard the freedom of the press, check government censorship and look after the interests of journalists.

(vi) Egypt's adherence to Islamic jurisprudence is affirmed. Christians and Jews are subject to their own jurisdiction in personal status affairs.

(vii) there will be no distinction of race or religion.

THE GOVERNMENT
THE PRESIDENCY

President: Muhammad Hosni Mubarak (confirmed as President by referendum, October 13th, 1981, after assassination of President Sadat).

Vice-President: (vacant).

COUNCIL OF MINISTERS
(May 1982)

Prime Minister and Minister of Al-Azhar Affairs: Dr. Ahmad Fuad Mohieddin.

Deputy Prime Minister for People's Assembly and Consultative Council Affairs: Fikri Makram Obaid.

Deputy Prime Minister and Minister of Foreign Affairs: Gen. Kamaleddin Hassan Ali.

Deputy Prime Minister for Production and Minister of Petroleum: Eng. Ahmed Izzedin Hilal.

Deputy Prime Minister for Services and Minister of Local Government: Muhammad Nabawi Ismail.

Deputy Prime Minister for Economic and Financial Affairs and Minister for International Investment and co-operation: Muhammad Abdul Fattah Ibrahim.

Minister of Defence and War Production: Lieut.-Gen. Muhammad Abdul Halim Abu Ghazalah.

Minister of Finance: Dr. Muhammad Saliuddin Hamid.

Minister of Social Insurance and Minister of State for Social Affairs: Dr. Amal Abdul Rahim Othman.

Minister of Reconstruction and Minister of State for Housing and Land Reclamation: Eng. Hasaballah al-Kafrawi.

Minister of Transport, Communications and Maritime Transport: Eng. Sulayman Mutawalli Sulayman.

Minister of Irrigation and Minister of State for Sudan Affairs: Eng. Muhammad Abdul Hadi Samahah.

Minister of Electricity and Energy: Eng. Muhammad Mahir Muhammad Othman Abazah.

Minister of Supply and Internal Trade: Ahmad Ahmad Nuh.

Minister of Justice: Ahmad Samir Sami.

Minister of Cabinet Affairs and Minister of State for Administrative Development: Adil Mahmud Abdul-Baki.

Minister of Planning: Dr. Kamal Ahmad al-Janzuri.

Minister of Industry and Mineral Resources: Eng. Fuad Ibrahim Abu Zaglah.

Minister of Tourism and Civil Aviation: Adil Ibrahim Tahir.

Minister of Interior: Hasan Sulayman Abu Basha.

Minister of Economy and Foreign Trade: Dr. Fuad Hashim Awad.

Minister of State for Emigration and Egyptians Abroad Affairs: Albert Barsum Salamah.

Minister of State for Education and Scientific Research: Dr. Mustafa Kamal Hilmi.

Minister of State for Foreign Affairs: Dr. Butros Butros Ghali.

Minister of State for Manpower and Training: Sayed Muhammad Ahmed.

Minister of State for Military Production: Dr. Eng. Jamal as-Sayyid Ibrahim.

Minister of State for Popular Development: Sayed Muhammad as-Sayyid as-Shirbani.

Ministers of State for People's Assembly and Consultative Council Affairs: Muhammad Rashwan Mahmud, Mukhtar Hasan Salim Hani.

Minister of State for Culture: Muhammad Abdul Hamid Radwan.

Minister of State for Religious Trusts: Ibrahim ad-Dusuqi Abdul Hamid Mar'i.

Minister of State for Information: Muhammad Safwat Muhammad Yusuf as-Sharif.

Minister of State for Agriculture and Food Sufficiency: Dr. Yusuf Amin Wali.

LEGISLATURE
MAJLIS AL-SHA'AB
(People's Assembly)

The law governing the composition of the People's Assembly was amended on May 2nd, 1979. 176 constituencies now elect two members, at least one of whom must be from among the workers and peasants, and in 30 constituencies a third member, who must be a woman, is elected in addition to the other two members. Ten members are appointed by the President.

Speaker: Dr. Sufi Abu Talib.
Deputy Speakers: Muhammad Rashwan (workers), Mansour Hassan.
Leader of the Opposition: Ibrahim Shukri (Socialist Labour Party).

ELECTIONS, JUNE 7th and 14th, 1979

	Seats
National Democratic Party . . .	302
Socialist Labour Party	29*
Liberal Socialist Party	3
Independents	8
Women candidates (mostly NDP) . .	30
Copts (appointed)	10
Total (incl. others) . . .	392

* 17 of these have since become independent, defected to the National Democratic Party or won by the NDP at by-elections.

In September 1980 elections were held for a 210-member Shura (Advisory) Council, which replaced the former Central Committee of the Arab Socialist Union. The National Democratic Party won all 140 elected seats. The remaining 70 members were appointed by President Sadat. **Speaker:** Dr. Subhi Abdul Hakim.

POLITICAL PARTIES

Details of active and recently dissolved parties are given below:

Arab Socialist Party: f. 1976, but merged with National Democratic Party in October 1978; had been government party and Leader was MAMDUH MUHAMMAD SALEM.

Liberal Socialist Party: Cairo; f. 1976; advocates expansion of 'open door' economic policy and greater freedom for private enterprise; Leader MUSTAFA KAMEL MURAD.

Nasserite Party: Cairo; f. April 1979; Leaders MUHAMMAD HASSANEIN HEIKAL and Mrs. HODA NASSER.

National Democratic Party: Cairo; f. July 1978; government party founded by President Sadat; has absorbed Arab Socialist Party; Chair. MUHAMMAD HOSNI MUBARAK; Sec.-Gen. Dr. AHMAD FUAD MOHIEDDIN; Dir. of Sec.-Gen.'s Office KAMAL AS-SHADHILI; Deputy Chair. (Foreign Relations) Dr. MUSTAPHA KHALIL; Asst. Secs.-Gen. MUHAMMAD NABAWI ISMAIL, ALBERT BARSUM SALAMAH; Youth Sec.-Gen. Dr. AHMAD MURSI; Political Bureau: Chair. and Sec.-Gen. MUHAMMAD HOSNI MUBARAK; mems.: Dr. MUSTAPHA KHALIL, Dr. SUFI ABU TALIB, FIKRI MAKRAM OBAID, Gen. KAMA-LEDDIN HASSAN ALI, MUHAMMAD NABAWI ISMAIL, Dr.

AMAL UTHMAN, MANSUR HASAN, Dr. AHMAD FUAD MOHIEDDIN, Dr. SUBHI ABDUL HAKIM, Lieut.-Gen. MUHAMMAD ABDUL HALIM ABU GHAZALAH, MUKHTAR HANI, HILMI ABDU AKHIR, MUHAMMAD RADWAN, MUHAMMAD RASHWAN.

National Front Party: Cairo; f. Aug. 1978; Leader MUMTAZ NASSER and MAHMOUD QADI (formerly independent Deputies).

National Progressive Unionist Party: 1 Karim el Dawlah St., Cairo; f. 1976; left wing; Leader KHALED MOHIEDDIN; Sec. Dr. RIFAAT EL-SAID; 160,000 mems.

New Wafd Party: f. February 1978; Leader FUAD SERAGEDDIN; Sec.-Gen. HELMI MURAD; while active had 24 mems. in People's Assembly; disbanded June 1978.

Socialist Labour Party: 12 Awalie El-Ahd St., Cairo; f. September 1978; official opposition party; Leader IBRAHIM SHUKRY.

Arab Socialist Union: Cairo; f. 1961 as the alliance of all working people's forces; was sole legal political organization until People's Assembly elections of 1976, and henceforth fulfilled a "watchdog" role until its abolition by constitutional amendment in April 1980.

DIPLOMATIC REPRESENTATION

EMBASSIES ACCREDITED TO EGYPT

(In Cairo unless otherwise stated)

(E) Embassy.

Afghanistan: (*see* India).

Albania: 29 Sh. Ismail Muhammad (Zamalek) (E); *Ambassador:* MURAT ANGONI.

Algeria: *Interests served by India.*

Angola: 12 Midan El Nasr (Dokki) (E); *Ambassador:* JOAQUIM AUGUSTO DE LEMOS.

Argentina: 8 Sh. As-Saleh Ayoub (Zamalek) (E); *Ambassador:* LUIS JORGE WARCKMEISTER.

Australia: 1097 Corniche el Nil (Garden City) (E); *Ambassador:* FRANK MURRAY.

Austria: 21 Sh. Saad El-Aaly (Dokki) (E); *Ambassador:* Dr. CHRISTOPH CORNARO.

Bahrain: *Interests served by Pakistan.*

Bangladesh: 18 Souria St., Madinet El Mohamdessin (Dokki) (E); *Ambassador:* (vacant).

Belgium: 20 Kamel El Shnaoui St. (Garden City) (E); *Ambassador:* CLAUDE RUELLE.

Bolivia: 7 Rue El Nady (Heliopolis) (E); *Ambassador:* REINALDO DEL CARPO JUOREGIU.

Brazil: 1125 Corniche El Nil (Maspiro) (E); *Ambassador:* MARCUS ANTÔNIO DE SALVO COIMBRA.

Burma: 24 Rue Muhammad Mazhar (Zamalek) (E); *Ambassador:* U OHN MAUNG.

Burundi: 13 Rue El Israa, Madinet El Mohamdessin (Dokki) (E); *Ambassador:* GEDEON MAXJUSTI.

Cameroon: 42 Babel St. (Dokki) (E); *Ambassador:* El Hadj IBRAHIM MBOMBO NJOYA.

Canada: 6 Sh. Muhammad Fahmy El Sayed (Garden City) (E); *Ambassador:* R. ELLIOTT.

Central African Republic: 13 Rue Chehab, Madinet El Mohamdessin (Dokki) (E); *Ambassador:* JOSEPH HETMAN EL ROOSALEM.

Chad: 26 El Kurum St. (Dokki) (E); *Ambassador:* HOMSALA OUANGMOTCHING.

Chile: 5 Sh. Chagaret El-Dorr (Zamalek) (E); *Ambassador:* JORGE LEÓN V.

China, People's Republic: 14 Sh. Bahgat Aly (Zamalek) (E); *Ambassador:* LIU CHUN.

Colombia: 11 Rue Sad El Ali (Dokki) (E); *Ambassador:* JOSÉ JOAQUÍN BERNAL AREVALO.

Congo: (E); *Ambassador:* (vacant).

Costa Rica: Madrid, Spain (E).

Cuba: 2 Al Anab St. (Dokki) (E); *Ambassador:* DOMINGO GARCÍA RODRÍGUEZ.

Cyprus: (*see* United Kingdom).

Czechoslovakia: 4 Rue Dokki (Giza) (E); *Ambassador:* Dr. SLAVOMÍR NOVÁK.

Denmark: 12 Sh. Hassan Sabri (Zamalek) (E); *Ambassador:* J. KORSGAARD-PEDERSEN.

Ecuador: 8 Salamlek St. (Garden City) (E); *Ambassador:* Dr. ARMANDO PESANTES GARCÍA.

El Salvador: 20 Rue El Sad El Ali (Dokki) (E); *Ambassador:* JOSÉ LEONEL ARGUELLO.

Ethiopia: 12 Midan Bahlawi (Dokki) (E); *Ambassador:* Ato BETROU KIDANE MARIAM.

Finland: 10 El Kamel Muhammad St. (Zamalek) (E); *Ambassador:* OLLI AUERO.

France: 29 Sh. Giza (E); *Ambassador:* PHILIPPE CUVILLIER.

Gabon: 15 Rue Mosaddak (Dokki) (E); *Ambassador:* ETIENNE MBOUMBA MOUNDOUNGA.

Gambia: Jeddah, Saudi Arabia (E).

German Democratic Republic: 13 Sh. Hussein Wassef (Dokki) (E); *Ambassador:* HANS-JÜRGEN WEITZ.

Germany, Federal Republic: 20 Boulos Hanna St. (Dokki) (E); *Ambassador:* Dr. HANS-JOACHIM HILLE.

Ghana: Villa 24, Sh. 22 (Dokki) (E); *Ambassador:* GEORGE H. OSEKRE.

Greece: 18 Sh. Aïcha El-Taïmouria (Garden City) (E); *Ambassador:* JEAN YANNAKAKIS.

Guatemala: 29 Rue Dr. Mohamed Mandour Madinat Nasr (E); *Ambassador:* JULIO A. MERIDA.

Guinea: 46 Sh. Muhammad Mazhar (Zamalek) (E); *Ambassador:* SALIMOU SISSOKO.

Guinea-Bissau: (E); *Ambassador:* (vacant).

Honduras: Vatican City, Rome (E).

Hungary: 29 Sh. Muhammad Mazhar (Zamalek) (E); *Ambassador:* MIKLÓS NAGY.

India: 5 Aziz Abaza St. (Zamalek) (E); *Ambassador:* K. P. S. MENON (also looks after Afghanistan interests at 59 Sh. Orouba (Heliopolis), Algerian interests at 14 Brasil St. (Zamalek), Yemen Arab Republic interests at 28 Amin El Rifai (Dokki).

Indonesia: 13 Sh. Aicha El-Taimouria (Garden City) (E); *Ambassador:* FERDY SALIM.

Iran: *Interests served by Switzerland.*

Iraq: *Interests served by Yugoslavia.*

Ireland: 2 Maarouf St., Apt. 17 (E); *Ambassador:* BRIAN O CEALLAIGH.

Israel: 6 Ibn El-Malek (Giza) (E); *Ambassador:* MOSHE SASSON.

Italy: 15 Sh. Abdel Rahman Fahmi (Garden City) (E); *Ambassador:* ELIO GIUFFRIDA.

Ivory Coast: 39 Rue El Kods El Cherif, Madinet el Mohandessine (Dokki) (E); *Ambassador:* AKA MOISE.

Japan: 14 Sh. Ibrahim Naguib (Garden City) (E); *Ambassador:* TOSHIO YAMAZAKI.

Jordan: *Interests served by Pakistan.*

Kenya: 8 Madina El Munawara (Dokki) (E); *Ambassador:* RAPHAEL MULI KIILU.

Korea, Democratic People's Republic: 6 El Saleh Ayoub St. (Zamalek) (E); *Ambassador:* KANG MAN SU.

Kuwait: *Interests served by Malaysia.*

Lebanon: *Interests served by France.*

Lesotho: Nairobi, Kenya (E).

Liberia: 2 Rue El Batal Ahmed Abdel Aziz, Madinet El Awkaf (Dokki) (E); *Ambassador:* GABRIEL FARNGALA.

Malaysia: 7 Wadi El Nil St. (Agouza) (E); *Ambassador:* HASSAN ADLY ARSHAD.

Mali: 3 El-Kawsar St. (Dokki) (E); *Ambassador:* HALIDOU TOURÉ.

Malta: Tripoli, Libya (E).

Mauritania: *Interests served by Senegal.*

Mauritius: 47 Ahmed Hechmat (Zamalek) (E); *Ambassador:* MAHAMAD YOUSUF ABDUL RAZACK HAJEE.

Mexico: 5 Dar El Chifa (E); *Ambassador:* ARMANDO CANTU.

Mongolia: 3 Midan El Nasr (Dokki) (E); *Ambassador:* DALHYN LUVSANRINCHIN.

Morocco: *Interests served by Senegal.*

Nepal: 9 Rue Tiba (Madinet El Kodah) (E); *Ambassador:* Gen. SINGHA BAHADUR BASNYAT.

Netherlands: 18 Sh. Hassan Sabri (Zamalek) (E); *Ambassador:* PETRUS BUWALDA.

New Zealand: Rome, Italy (E).

Niger: 101 Rue les Pyramides, Giza (E); *Ambassador:* SORY MAMADOU DIALLO.

Nigeria: 13 Sh. Gabalaya (Zamalek) (E); *Ambassador:* A. M. S. IMAM.

Norway: 24 Hassan Assem St. (Zamalek) (E); *Ambassador:* BJØRN INGE KRISTVIK.

Oman: 30 Montaza St. (Zamalek) (E); *Ambassador:* ABDULLA GHAZALI.

Pakistan: 8 Sh. El Salouli (Dokki) (E); *Ambassador:* (vacant).

Panama: 8 Rue Abdul Rahman Fahmy, Apt. 41 (E); *Ambassador:* ALFREDO ALBERTO ARANGO.

Peru: 11 Brazil St. (Zamalek) (E); *Ambassador:* CARLOS JIMÉNEZ VÁSQUEZ DE VELASCO.

Philippines: 5 Sh. Ibn El-Walid (Dokki) (E); *Ambassador:* (vacant).

Poland: 5 Sh. Aziz Osman (Zamalek) (E); *Ambassador:* ANTONI PIERZCHALA.

Portugal: 15a Mansour Muhammad St. (Zamalek) (E); *Ambassador:* CONSTANTINO RIBEIRO VAZ.

Qatar: *Interests served by France.*

Romania: 6 Sh. El Kamel Muhammad (Zamalek) (E); *Ambassador:* ION IOSEFIDE.

Rwanda: 13 Midan Asswan Agouza (E); *Ambassador:* SIMON INSONERE.

Saudi Arabia: *Interests served by Pakistan.*

Senegal: 46 Rue Abdel Moneim Riad, Mohandessine (Dokki) (E); *Ambassador:* ABOUBACAR SY.

Sierra Leone: 70 Rue Ahmed Orabi (Embaba) (E); *Ambassador:* MUHAMMAD KEMOH FADIKA.

Singapore: 40 Babel St. (Dokki) (E); *Ambassador:* CHAN KENG HOWE.

Somalia: 38 Rue El Shahid Abdel Moneim Riad (Dokki) (E); *Ambassador:* ABDURRAHMAN FARAH ISMAIL.

Spain: 28 Ahmed Heshmat (Zamalek) (E); *Ambassador:* JOSÉ LUIS FLÓREZ-ESTRADA.

Sri Lanka: 8 Sh. Yehia Ibrahim (Zamalek) (E); *Ambassador:* E. B. SATTRUKALSINGE.

Sudan: 4 Sh. El Ibrahimi (Garden City) (E); *Ambassador:* ABDUL RAHMAN SALMAN NASR.

Swaziland: Nairobi, Kenya.

Sweden: 13 Sh. Muhammad Mazhar (Zamalek) (E); *Ambassador:* OLOV ARTHUR TERNESTROM.

Switzerland: 10 Sh. Abdel Khalek Saroit (E); *Ambassador:* JEAN CUENDET.

Tanzania: 9 Abdel Hamid Lotfi St. (Dokki) (E); *Ambassador:* ALI H. MWINYI.

Thailand: 2 Sh. El Malek El Afdal (Zamalek) (E); *Ambassador:* SUKRI GAJASENI.

Tunisia: *Interests served by Senegal.*

Turkey: Avenue El Nil (Giza) (E); *Ambassador:* BERDUK OLGACAY.

Uganda: 9 Midan El Missaha (Dokki) (E); *Ambassador:* SYLVANO K. BAGUMA.

U.S.S.R.: 95 Sh. Giza (Giza) (E); *Ambassador:* VLADIMIR POLIAKOV (*expelled September 1981*).

United Arab Emirates: *Interests served by Turkey.*

United Kingdom: Ahmed Raghab St. (Garden City) (E); *Ambassador:* Sir MICHAEL WEIR, K.C.M.G. (also looks after Cyprus interests at 23A Ismail Muhammad St. (Zamalek); Head of Section CONSTANTINOS MALLIOTIS).

U.S.A.: 5 America El Latinia St. (Garden City) (E); *Ambassador:* ALFRED ATHERTON.

Upper Volta: 40 Rue El Sawra, Medinat El Zobbat (Dokki) (E); *Ambassador:* (vacant).

Uruguay: 6 Sh. Loutfallah (Zamalek) (E); *Ambassador:* GASTÓN SCIARRA REBOLLO.

Vatican City: Apostolic Nunciature, 5 Sh. Muhammad Mazhar (Zamalek); *Pro-Nuncio:* Mgr. ACHILLE GLORIEUX.

Venezuela: 15A Sh. Mansour Muhammad (Zamalek) (E); *Ambassador:* (vacant).

Viet-Nam: 21 Rue El Madina El Mounawara (Dokki) (E); *Ambassador:* CHU DUC THANH.

Yemen Arab Republic: *Interests served by India.*

Yugoslavia: 33 Sh. El Mansour Muhammad (Zamalek) (E); *Ambassador:* ALEXANDER BOZOVIĆ.

Zaire: 5 Mansour Mohammad St. (Zamalek) (E); *Ambassador:* ATEMBINA TE BOMBO.

Zambia: 22 Rue El Nakhil (Dokki) (E); *Ambassador:* WINDSOR KAPALAKONJE.

Egypt also has diplomatic relations with Cape Verde, the Comoros, Djibouti, Equatorial Guinea, Fiji, Grenada, Guyana, Haiti, Iceland, Laos, Luxembourg, Madagascar, Malawi, Monaco, Mozambique, Nicaragua, Papua New Guinea, Paraguay, Seychelles, Suriname, Togo, Western Samoa and Zimbabwe.

JUDICIAL SYSTEM

The Courts of Law in Egypt are principally divided into two juridical court systems: Courts of General Jurisdiction and Administrative Courts. Since 1979 the Supreme Constitutional Court has been at the top of the Egyptian judicial structure.

I. THE SUPREME CONSTITUTIONAL COURT

Is the highest court in Egypt. It has jurisdiction over: (i) judicial review of the constitutionality of laws and regulations; (ii) resolution of positive and negative jurisdictional conflicts and determination of the competent court between the different juridical court systems, e.g. Courts of General Jurisdiction and Administrative Courts, as well as other bodies exercising judicial competence; (iii) determination of disputes over the enforcement of two final but contradictory judgments rendered by two courts each belonging to a different juridical court system; (iv) rendering binding interpretation of laws or decree laws in the event of a dispute in the application of said laws or decree laws, always provided that such a dispute is of a gravity requiring conformity of interpretation under the constitution. The Supreme Constitutional Court is composed of the Chief Justice and nine Justices.

Chief Justice: Hon. AHMED MAMDOUH ATTEYA.

II. COURTS OF GENERAL JURISDICTION

The Courts of General Jurisdiction in Egypt are basically divided into four categories, as follows: (i) The Court of Cassation (*Cour de Cassation*); (ii) The Courts of Appeal; (iii) The Tribunals of First Instance; (iv) The District Tribunals; each of the above courts is divided into Civil and Criminal Chambers.

(i) Court of Cassation: Is the highest court of general jurisdiction in Egypt. Its sessions are held in Cairo. Final judgments rendered by Courts of Appeal in criminal and civil litigation may be petitioned to the Court of Cassation by the Defendant or the Public Prosecutor in criminal litigation and by any of the parties in interest in civil litigation on grounds of defective application or interpretation of the law as stated in the challenged judgment, on grounds of irregularity of form or procedure, or violation of due process, and on grounds of defective reasoning of judgment rendered. The Court of Cassation is composed of the President, 15 Vice-Presidents and 80 Justices.

President: Hon. MOUSTAFA SELIM.

(ii) The Courts of Appeal: Each has geographical jurisdiction over one or more of the governorates of Egypt:

Cairo, Alexandria, Tanta, Asyut, Mansura, Ismailia and Beni-Suef. Each Court of Appeal is divided into Criminal and Civil Chambers. The Criminal Chambers try felonies, and the Civil Chambers hear appeals filed against such judgment rendered by the Tribunals of First Instance where the law so stipulates. Each Chamber is composed of three superior judges. Each Court of Appeal is composed of President, and sufficient numbers of Vice-Presidents and Superior Judges.

(iii) The Tribunals of First Instance: In each governorate there are one or more Tribunals of First Instance, each of which is divided into several Chambers for criminal and civil litigations. Each Chamber is composed of: (a) a presiding judge, and (b) two sitting judges. A Tribunal of First Instance hears, as an Appellate Court, certain litigations as provided under the law.

(iv) District Tribunals: Each is a one-judge ancillary Chamber of a Tribunal of First Instance, having jurisdiction over minor civil and criminal litigations in smaller districts within the jurisdiction of such Tribunal of First Instance.

PUBLIC PROSECUTION

Public prosecution is headed by the Attorney General, assisted by a number of Senior Deputy and Deputy Attorneys General, and a sufficient number of chief prosecutors, prosecutors and assistant prosecutors. Public prosecution is represented at all levels of the Courts of General Jurisdiction in all criminal litigations and also in certain civil litigations as required by the law. Public prosecution controls and supervises enforcement of criminal law judgments.

Attorney General: Hon. SALAH ELRASHEIDY.

III. ADMINISTRATIVE COURTS SYSTEM (CONSEIL D'ETAT)

The Administrative Courts have jurisdiction over litigations involving the State or any of its governmental agencies. The Administrative Courts system is divided into two courts: the Administrative Courts and the Judicial Administrative Courts, at the top of which is the High Administrative Court.

President of Conseil d'Etat: Hon. TAHER ABDEL-HAMID.

RELIGION

About 90 per cent of Egyptians are Muslims, and almost all of these follow Sunni tenets. A preparatory committee for a Supreme Islamic Council was set up in November 1979. There are about 4 million Copts, forming the largest religious minority. Besides the Copts there are other Christian minorities numbering about a quarter of a million and consisting of Greek Orthodox, Roman Catholics, Armenians and Protestants. There is also a small Jewish minority.

Grand Sheikh of Al Azhar: Sheikh JAD AL-HAQ ALI JAD AL-HAQ.

Grand Mufti of Egypt: Sheikh ABDUL LATIF ABDUL GHANI HAMZAH.

Coptic Orthodox Church: Anba Ruess Building, Ramses St., Abbasiya, Cairo; f. A.D. 61; Leader Pope SHENOUDA III; about 8 million followers in Egypt, Sudan, other African countries, the U.S.A., Canada, Australia; Europe and the Middle East. In September 1981 Pope Shenouda was banished to a monastery by President Sadat and a committee of five bishops was appointed to administer the Church.

Coptic Catholic Church: Patriarch Cardinal STEPHANOS I, SIDAROUSS, 34 Sh. Ibn Sandar, Koubbeh Bridge, Cairo; 4 dioceses; 150,000 mems.; publs. *Al Salah*, *Sadik el Kahen*, *Al Risalat*.

Greek Catholic Patriarchate: P.O.B. 50076 Beirut, Lebanon; 16 rue Daher, Cairo; Patriarch of Antioch, of Alexandria and of Jerusalem His Beatitude MAXIMOS V HAKIM; 500,000 mems. in the Middle East.

Greek Orthodox Church: Patriarch NIKOLAUS VI.

Armenian Apostolic Church: 179 Ramses Ave., Cairo P.O.B. 48-Faggala; Archbishop ZAVEN CHINCHINIAN; 12,000 mems.

Armenian Catholic Patriarchate: 36 Mohammed Sabri Abou Alam Street, Cairo; Archbishop RAPHAEL BAYAN.

Maronite Church: 15 Hamdi Street, Daher, Cairo; Archbishop JOSEPH MERHI.

Syrian Catholic Church: 46 rue Daher, Cairo; Bishop BASILE MOUSSA DAOUD.

Jewish Community: Office of the Chief Rabbi, Rabbi HAIM DOUEK; 13 Sebil-el-Khazindar St., Abbassia, Cairo.

THE PRESS

Despite a fairly high illiteracy rate, the Egyptian Press is well developed. Cairo is the biggest publishing centre in the Middle East.

Legally all newspapers and magazines come under the control of the Higher Press Council. The four big publishing houses of al-Ahram, Dar al-Hilal, Dar Akhbar al-Yom and Dar al-Gomhouriya, operate as separate entities and compete with each other commercially. Dar al-Hilal is concerned only with magazines and publishes *al-Mussawar*, *Hawa'a* and *al-Kawakeb*. Dar Akhbar al-Yom publishes the daily newspaper *al-Akhbar*, the weekly newspaper *Akhbar al-Yom* and the weekly magazine *Akher Saa*.

Dar al Gomhouriya publishes the daily *al-Gomhouriya*, the daily English language paper *Egyptian Gazette*, the daily French newspaper *Le Progrès Egyptien* and the afternoon paper *al-Misaa*.

The most authoritative daily newspaper is the very old established *al-Ahram*. Other popular large circulation magazines are *Rose al-Youssef*, *Sabah al-Kheir* and *al Izaw w'al Television*.

In February 1974 President Sadat ended press censorship, except on military matters, and foreign correspondents in Cairo were relieved of the duty of submitting their reports, except those on military matters, for censorship.

In May 1975 President Sadat set up the Supreme Press Council, under the Chairmanship of the First Secretary of the Arab Socialist Union, to supervise the Press.

In November 1978, however, President Sadat abolished the Ministry of Culture and Information, but major papers remained under government ownership. A Press Law of July 1980 liberalized the organization of the major papers and, while continuing to provide for 49 per cent ownership by the employees, arranged for the transfer of the remaining 51 per cent from the defunct Arab Socialist Union to the new Shura (Advisory) Council.

DAILIES

ALEXANDRIA

Barid al-Charikat: P.O.B. 813; f. 1952; Arabic; evening; commerce, finance, insurance and marine affairs, etc.; Editor S. BENEDUCCI; circ. 15,000.

al-Ittihad al-Misri: 13 Sharia Sidi Abdel Razzak; f. 1871; Arabic; evening; Propr. ANWAR MAHER FARAG; Dir. HASSAN MAHER FARAG.

Le Journal d'Alexandrie: 1 Sharia Rolo; French; evening; Editor CHARLES ARCACHE.

La Réforme: 8 Passage Sherif; f. 1895; French; noon; Propr. Comte AZIZ DE SAAB; circ. 7,000.

al-Safeer: 4 El-Sahafa St.; f. 1924; Arabic; evening; Editor MOSTAFA SHARAF.

Tachydromos-Egyptos: 4 Sharia Zangarol; f. 1879; Greek; morning; liberal; Publisher PENY COUTSOUMIS; Editor DINOS COUTSOUMIS; circ. 2,500.

CAIRO

al-Ahram (*The Pyramids*): Gallaa St.; f. 1875; Arabic; morning; Editor IBRAHIM NAFEH; circ. 400,000.

al-Akhbar: Dar Akhbar al-Yom, Sharia al-Sahafa; f. 1952; Arabic; Chair. and Editor MOUSA SABRY; Man. Editor AHMED ZEIN; circ. 695,000.

Arev: 3 Sharia Soliman Halaby; f. 1915; Armenian; evening; official organ of the Armenian Liberal Democratic Party; Editor AVEDIS YAPOUDJIAN.

Egyptian Gazette: 24 Sharia Galal; f. 1880; English daily; morning; Editor Dr. AMIN MOHAMED ABOUL-ENEIN; circ. 19,000.

al-Gomhouriya (*The Republic*): 24 Sharia Zakaria Ahmed; f. 1953; Arabic; morning; Chair. and Editor-in-Chief MOHSEN MOHAMED; circ. 400,000.

Journal d'Egypte, Le: 1 Borsa Guédida St.; f. 1936; French; morning; Propr. and Gen. Man. LITA GALLAD; Editor-in-Chief MOHAMED RACHAD; circ. 63,000.

May: organ of National Democratic Party; Supervisor MUHAMMAD SAFWAT AS-SHARIF.

al-Misaa (*The Evening*): 24 Sharia Zakaria Ahmed; Arabic; evening; Chief Editor SAMIR RAJAB ALI SHARAF; circ. 70,000.

Misr: f. 1977; organ of the Arab Socialist Party.

Phos: 14 Zakaria Ahmed St.; f. 1896; Greek; morning; Editor S. PATERAS; Man. BASILE A. PATERAS; circ. 20,000.

Le Progrès Egyptien: 24 Sharia Zakaria Ahmed; f. 1890; French; morning including Sundays; Chief Editor NAGUIB HENEIN; circ. 15,000.

PERIODICALS

ALEXANDRIA

al Ahad al Gedid: 88 Said M. Koraim St.; Editor-in-Chief and Publisher GALAL M. KORAITEM.

Alexandria Medical Journal: 4 G. Carducci; f. 1922; English, French and Arabic; quarterly; publ. by Alexandria Medical Asscn.; Editor AMIN RIDA; circ. 1,500.

Amitié Internationale: 59 Avenue Hourriya; f. 1957; publ. by Asscn. Egypt. d'Amitié Inter.; Arabic and French; quarterly; Editor Dr. ZAKI BADAOUI.

L'Annuaire des Sociétés Egyptiennes par Actions: 23 Midan Tahrir; f. 1930; annually in December; French; Propr. ELIE I. POLITI; Editor OMAR EL-SAYED MOURSI.

L'Echo Sportif: 7 rue de l'Archevêché; French; weekly; Propr. MICHEL BITTAR.

L'Economiste Egyptien: 11 rue de la Poste, Alexandria; P.O.B. 847; f. 1901; weekly; Propr. MARGUERITE and JOFFRE HOSNY.

Egypte-Sports-Cinéma: 7 Avenue Hourriya; French; weekly; Editor EMILE ASSAAD.

Egyptian Cotton Gazette: P.O.B. 433; organ of the Cotton Exporters Association; English twice yearly; Chief Editor AHMED H. YOUSSEF.

Egyptian Cotton Statistics: English; weekly.

Egyptian Customs Magazine: 2 Sharia Sinan; deals with invoicing, receipts, etc.; Man. MUHAMMAD ALY EL BADAWY.

La Gazette d'Orient: 5 rue de l'Ancienne Bourse; Propr. MAURICE BETITO.

Guide des Industries: 2 Sharia Adib; French; annual; Editor SIMON A. BARANIS.

Informateur des Assurances: 1 Sharia Adib; f. 1936; French; monthly; Propr. ELIE I. POLITI; Editor SIMON A. BARANIS.

La Réforme Illustrée: 8 Passage Sherif; f. 1925; French; weekly; Propr. Comte AZIZ DE SAAB; circ. 20,000.

Répertoire Permanent de Législation Egyptienne: 27 Ave. El Guesch, Chatby-les-Bains; f. 1932; French and Arabic; Editor V. SISTO.

Revue Economique Trimestrielle: c/o Banque de Port-Said, 18 Talaat Harb St., Alexandria; French (f. 1929) and Arabic (f. 1961) editions; quarterly; Editor MAHMOUD SAMY EL ADAWAY.

Sanaet El-Nassig (*L'Industrie Textile*): 5 rue de l'Archevêché; Arabic and French; monthly; Editor PHILIPPE COLAS.

Voce d'Italia: 90 Sharia Farahde; Italian; fortnightly; Editor R. AVELLINO.

CAIRO

Akhbar al-Yom: 6 Sharia al-Sahafa; f. 1944; Arabic; weekly (Saturday); Editor-in-Chief IBRAHIM ABU SADAH; Editing Man. SAID SONBOL; circ. 1,099,962.

Akher Saa: Dar Akhbar al-Yom, Sharia al-Sahafa; f. 1934; Arabic; weekly (Wednesday); independent; Editor-in-Chief MUHAMMAD WAJDI GANDIL; circ. 133,817.

al-Ahd al-Goumhouri: 132 Sharia Kalaa; Editor ABDEL-KHALEK TAKIA.

al-Ahra: f. 1977; weekly; published by Liberal Socialist Party; Chief Editor WAHID GHAZI.

al Ahram Iqtisadi: Gallaa St.; economic and political affairs; owned by *Al Ahram;* Chief Editor Dr. LOTFY ABDEL AZIM; circ. 20,000.

al-Azhar: Sharia al-Azhar; Arabic; Dir MUHAMMAD FARID WABDI.

al-Daoua: Arabic; monthly; organ of the Muslim Brotherhood.

al-Doctor: 8 Hoda Shaarawy St.; f. 1947; Arabic; monthly; Editor Dr. AHMAD M. KAMAL; circ. 30,000.

al-Fussoul: 17 Sharia Sherif Pasha; Arabic; monthly; Propr. and Chief Editor MUHAMMAD ZAKI ABDEL KADER.

al-Garida al-Togaria al-Misriya: 25 Sharia Nubar Pasha; f. 1921; Arabic; weekly; circ. 7,000.

al-Hilal Magazine: Dar al-Hilal, 16 Sharia Muhammad Ezz El-Arab; f. 1895; Arabic; literary monthly; Editor Dr. HUSSAIN MONES.

al-Hurriya: Arabic; weekly; published by Arab Socialist Union; Editor-in-Chief MUHAMMAD SUBAIH.

al-Izaa wal-Television: 13 Sharia Muhammad Ezz El-Arab; f. 1935; Arabic; weekly; Editor and Chair. AHMED BAHGAT; circ. 120,000.

al-Kawakeb (*The Stars*): Dar al-Hilal, 16 Sharia Muhammad Ezz El-Arab; f. 1952; Arabic; film magazine; Editor KAMAL EL-NAGMI; circ. 38,500.

al-Magalla al-Ziraia: monthly; agriculture; circ. 30,000.

al-Mussawar: Dar al-Hilal, 16 Sharia Muhammad Ezz El-Arab; f. 1924; Arabic weekly; Editors MORSI EL SHAFEE and SABRI ABDUL MAGD; circ. 162,000.

al-Sabah: 4 Sharia Muhammad Said Pasha; f. 1922; Arabic; weekly; Editor MOSTAFA EL-KACHACHI.

al-Shaab (*The People*): Corniche El Nil St., Cairo; organ of Socialist Labour Party; weekly; Editor-in-Chief HAMED ZAIDAN; circ. 50,000.

al-Tahrir: 5 Sharia Naguib-Rihani; Arabic; weekly; Editor ABDEL-AZIZ SADEK.

al-Tuqaddam (*Progress*): f. 1978; organ of National Progressive Unionist Party; replaced *Al-Ahali*.

Ana Wa Inta: Sharia Central; Arabic; monthly; Editor MOHAMED HASSAN.

Arab Observer: published by the Middle East News Agency, 11 Sh. Sahafa; f. 1960; weekly international news magazine; English; Editor-in-Chief Dr. ABDEL HAMID EL-BATRIK.

Contemporary Thought: University of Cairo; quarterly; Editor Dr. Z. N. MAHMOUD.

Echos: 1;5 Sharia Mahmoud Bassiouni; f. 1947; French; weekly; Dir. and Propr. GEORGES QRFALI.

Egyptian Mail: 24 Sharia Zakaria Ahmed; f. 1910; English; weekly; Editor Dr. AMIN ABOUL-ENEIN.

Études Médicales: Collège de la Ste. Familie Faggalah, Cairo; Editor HUBERT DE LEUSSE.

Études Scientifiques: Collège de la Ste. Familie Faggalah, Cairo; scientific and technical quarterly; Editor HUBERT DE LEUSSE.

La Femme Nouvelle: 48 Sharia Kasr-el-Nil; French; twice yearly.

Hawa'a (*Eve*): Dar al-Hilal, 16 Sharia Muhammad Ezz El-Arab; women's magazine; Arabic; weekly; Chief Editor SUAD AHMAD HILMI.

Industrial Egypt: P.O.B. 251, 26A Sharia Sherif Pasha, Cairo; f. 1924; Bulletin of the Federation of Egyptian Industries; English and Arabic; quarterly; Editor DARWISH M. DARWISH.

Industry and Trade Information: 13 Sharia Abdel Hamid Said; English; weekly; commercial and industrial bulletin; Dir. and Propr. NICOLAS STAVRI; Editor N. GHANEM.

Informateur Financier et Commercial: 24 Sharia Soliman Pasha; f. 1929; weekly; Dir. HENRI POLITI; circ. 15,000.

Kitab al-Hilal: Dar al-Hilal, 16 Sharia Muhammad Ezz El-Arab; monthly; Founders EMILE and CHOUKRI ZEIDAN; Editor Dr. HUSSAIN MONES.

Lewa al-Islam: 11 Sharia Sherif Pasha; Arabic; monthly; Propr. AHMED HAMZA; Editor MUHAMMAD ALY SHETA.

Lotus Magazine (*Afro-Asian Writings*): 104 Kasr El Eini St.; f. 1968; quarterly; English, French and Arabic.

Magalet al-Mohandeseen: 28 Avenue Ramses; f. 1945; published by The Engineers' Syndicate; Arabic and English; ten times a year; Editor and Sec. MAHMOUD SAMI ABDEL KAWI.

Medical Journal of Cairo University: Manyal University Hospital, Sharia Kasr el-Aini; f. 1933; Kasr el-Aini Clinical Society; English; quarterly.

The Middle East Observer: 8 Chawarby St.; f. 1954; weekly; English; specializing in economics of Middle East and African markets; also publishes supplements on law, foreign trade and tenders; Man. Owner AHMED FODA; Chief Editor AHMED SABRI; circ. 30,000.

October: Cairo; monthly; Chair. and Editor-in-Chief ANIS MANSUR.

Progrès Dimanche: 24 Sharia Zakaria Ahmed; French; weekly; Sunday edition of *Le Progrès Egyptien*.

Riwayat al-Hilal: Dar al-Hilal, 16 Sharia Muhammad Ezz El-Arab; Arabic; monthly; Proprs. EMILE and CHOUKRI ZEIDAN; Editor Dr. HUSSAIN MONES.

Rose el Youssef: 89A Kasr el Ainei St.; f. 1925; Arabic; weekly; political; circulates throughout all Arab countries, includes monthly English section; Chair. of Board and Editor-in-Chief ABDUL AZIZ KHAMIS; Editors FATHI GHANEM and SALAH HAFEZ; Editor English section IBRAHIM EZZAT; circ. 35,000.

Sabah al-Kheir: 18 Sharia Mohamed Said; Arabic; weekly; light entertainment; Chief Editor LOUIS JIRYIS.

Tchehreh Nema: 14 Sharia Hassan El-Akbar (Abdine); f. 1904; Iranian; monthly; political, literary and general; Editor MANUCHEHR TCHEHREH NEMA MOADEB ZADEH.

Up-to-Date International Industry: 10 Sharia Galal; Arabic and English; foreign trade journal.

NEWS AGENCIES

Middle East News Agency: 4 Sharia Sherrifin, Cairo; f. 1955; regular service in Arabic, English and French; Chair. MOHAMED ABDEL GAWAD MANSUR; Editors MOHAMED AL BIALI, KAMAL AMER and MUSTAFA NAGUIB.

FOREIGN BUREAUX

Agence France-Presse (AFP): 33 Kasr El Nil St., Cairo; Man. IGNACE DALLE.

Agencia EFE (*Spain*)*:* Nile Garden Hotel, Room 21; Correspondent FRANCISCO OSABA ARRANZ.

Agenzia Nazionale Stampa Associata (ANSA) (*Italy*): 19 Sh. Abdel Khalek Sarwat, Cairo; Chief ETTORE MENCACCI.

Allgemeiner Deutscher Nachrichtendienst (ADN) (*German Democratic Republic*): 17 Sharia el Brazil, Apt. 59, Cairo-Zamalek; Correspondents HARALD and BRIGITTA DITTMAR.

Associated Press (AP) (*U.S.A.*): 33 Kasr El Nil, Cairo; Chief ALEXANDER G. HIGGINS.

Bulgarian Telegraph Agency (BTA): 13 Sh. Muhammad Kamel Morsi, Aguza, Cairo; Chief DIMITER MASLAROV.

Deutsche Presse Agentur (dpa) (*Federal Republic of Germany*): 33 Kasr el Nil St., Apt. 13/4, Cairo; Chief Correspondent PETER W. FISCHER.

Kyodo Tsushin (*Japan*): 19 Gabalaya St., Flat 91, Zamalek, Cairo; Correspondent AKIRA TANI.

Reuters (*United Kingdom*): Apt. 43, Immobilia Bldgs., 26 Sh. Sherif Pasha, Cairo; P.O.B. 2040.

United Press International (UPI) (*U.S.A.*): 4 Sh. Eloui, P.O.B. 872, Cairo; Chief MAURICE GUINDI.

PUBLISHERS

Egyptian General Organization for Publishing and Printing: 117 Corniche el Nil St., Cairo; affil. to Min. of Culture.

ALEXANDRIA

Alexandria University Press: Shatby.

Artec: 10 Sharia Stamboul.

Dar Nashr ath-Thagata.

Egyptian Book Centre: A. D. Christodoulou and Co., 5 Sharia Adib; f. 1950.

Egyptian Printing and Publishing House: Ahmed El Sayed Marouf, 59, Safia Zaghoul; f. 1947.

Maison Egyptienne d'Editions: Ahmed El Sayed Marouf, Sharia Adib; f. 1950.

Maktab al-Misri al-Hadith li-t-Tiba wan-Nashr: 7 Nobar St.; also at 2 Sherif St., Cairo; Man. AHMAD YEHIA.

CAIRO

Al Ahram Establishment: Gallaa St., Cairo; f. 1875; publishes newspapers, magazines and books, inc. *Al-Ahram*; Chair. ABDALLA ABDEL BARI.

Akhbar El Yom Publishing House: 6 Sharia al-Sahafa; f. 1944; publishes *al-Akhbar* (daily), *Akhbar al-Yom* (weekly), and colour magazine *Akher Saa;* Pres. MOUSA SABRI; Dir.-Gen. AMIN ADLY.

Argus Press: 10 Zakaria Ahmad St., Cairo; Owners KARNIG HAGOPIAN and ABDEL MEGUID MUHAMMAD.

Dar al-Gomhouriya: 24 Sharia Zakaria Ahmad; publications include the dailies, *al-Gomhouriya, al-Misaa, Egyptian Gazette* and *Le Progrès Egyptien*; Pres. MOHSEN MOHAMED.

Dar al-Hilal Publishing Institution: 16 Muhammad Ezz El Arab St.; f. 1892; publishes *Al-Hilal, Riwayat al-Hilal, Kitab al-Hilal, Tabibak al-Khass* (monthlies); *Al-Mussawar, Al-Kawakeb, Hawaa, Samir, Mickey* (weeklies); Chair. MAKRAN MUHAMMAD AHMAD.

Dar al Kitab al Arabi: Misr Printing House, Sharia Noubar, Bab al Louk, Cairo; f. 1968; Man. Dir. Dr. SAHAIR AL KALAMAWI.

Dar al Maaref: 1119 Cornich El-Nil St.; f. 1890; publishing, printing and distribution of all kinds of books in

Arabic and other languages; publishers of *October* magazine; Chair. and Chief Editor ANIS MANSOUR.

Documentation and Research Centre for Education (Ministry of Education): 33 Falaky St.; f. 1956; Dir. Mrs. ZEINAB M. MEHREZ; bibliographies, directories, information and education bulletins.

Editions Horus: 1 Midan Soliman Pasha.

Editions le Progrès: 6 Sharia Sherif Pasha; Propr. WADI CHOUKRI.

Editions et Publications des Pères Jésuites: 1 rue Boustan al Maksi, Faggala; religious publications in Arabic.

Les Editions Universitaires d'Egypte: 41 Sharia Sherif Pasha.

Higher University Council for Arts, Letters and Sciences: University of Cairo.

Lagnat al Taalif Wal Targama Wal Nashr (*Committee for Writing, Translating and Publishing Books*): 9 Sharia El-Kerdassi (Abdine).

Librairie La Renaissance D'Egypte (Hassan Muhammad & Sons): 9 Adly St., P.O.B. 2172; f. 1930; Man. HASSAN MUHAMMAD; religion, history, geography, medicine, architecture, economics, politics, law, philosophy, psychology, children's books, atlases, dictionaries.

Maktabet Misr: P.O.B. 16, 3 Kamel Sidki St., Cairo; f. 1932; publ. wide variety of fiction, biographies and textbooks for schools and universities; Man. AMIR SAID GOUDA EL SAHHAR.

Mohamed Abbas Sid Ahmed: 55 Sharia Nubar.

National Library Press (*Dar al Kutub*): Midan Ahmed Maher; bibliographic works.

New Publications: J. Meshaka and Co., 5 Sharia Maspero.

The Public Organization for Books and Scientific Appliances: Cairo University, Orman, Ghiza; f. 1965; state organization publishing academic books for universities, higher institutes, etc.; also imports books, periodicals and scientific appliances; Chair. KAMIL SEDDIK; Vice-Chair. FATTHY LABIB.

Senouhy Publishers: 54 Sharia Abdel-Khalek Sarwat; f. 1956; Dirs. LEILA A. FADEL, OMAR RASHAD.

Other Cairo publishers include: *Dar al-Fikr al-Arabi, Dar al-Fikr al-Hadith Li-t-Tab wan-Nashr, Dar wa Matabi, Dar al-Nahda al-Arabiya, Dar al-Misriya Li-t-Talif wat-Tardjma, Dar al-Qalam, Dar ath-Thagapa, Majlis al-Ala Li-Riyyat al-Funun, Maktaba Ain Shams, Maktaba al-Andshilu al-Misriya, Maktabat al-Chandshi, Maktabat al-Nahira al-Hadith, Markaz Tasjil al-Athar al-Misriya, Matbaat ar-Risala, al-Qaumiya li-t-Tibaa wan-Nashr-Wizarat az-Ziraa Maslahat al-Basatin.*

RADIO AND TELEVISION

RADIO

Egyptian Radio and Television Federation (ERTV): Radio and TV Building, Corniche El Nil, P.O. Box 1186, Cairo; f. 1928; 300 hours daily; Pres. SAFWAT AL-SHERIF; Head of Eng. Section Eng. ABDEL AL-MUHAMMAD ABDEL AAL; Head of Int. and Public Relations and Liaison Officer Mrs. EFFAT SOUROR. Home Service programmes in Arabic, English, French, Armenian, German, Greek, Italian and Hebrew; foreign services in Arabic, English, Swahili, Hausa, Persian, Bengali, Urdu, German, Spanish, Indonesian, Thai, Hindi, Pushtu, Turkish, Somali, Portuguese, Fulani, Italian, Zulu, Shona, Sindebele, Nyanja, Lingala, Amharic, Yoruba, Wolof, Bambara, Dankali.

Middle East Radio: Société Egyptienne de Publicité, 24-26 Sharia Zakaria Ahmed, Cairo; f. 1964; commercial service with 500-kW. transmitter; U.K. Agents: Radio and Television Services (Middle East) Ltd., 21 Hertford St., London, W.1.

In 1978 there were 5.3 million radio receivers and 1.1 million television sets.

TELEVISION

Egyptian Television Organization: Corniche el Nil, Cairo; f. 1960; 19½ hours daily (two channels); Chair. Mrs. TOMADER TAWFIK.

FINANCE

BANKING

(cap.=capital; p.u.=paid up; dep.=deposits; res.= reserves; m.=million; amounts in £ Egyptian)

The whole banking system was nationalized in 1961.

CENTRAL BANK

Central Bank of Egypt: 31 Kasr-el-Nil St., Cairo; f. 1961; cap. 5.0m.; dep. £4,742m. (June 1981); Gov. MUHAMMAD SALEH AMIN SHALABY; publs. *Economic Review* (quarterly), *Annual Report*.

COMMERCIAL AND SPECIALIZED BANKS

Arab Land Bank: 33 Abdel-Khalek Sarwat St., Cairo; Pres. AHMED AMIN ALY FAHMI.

Bank of Alexandria, S.A.E.: 6 Salah Salem St., Alexandria; and 49 Kasr El-Nil St., Cairo; f. 1964; cap. p.u. 11m.; dep. 1,097m. (June 1981); 79 brs.; Chair. MOHAMED M. EL BAYOUMI.

Banque du Caire: 22 Adly St., P.O.B. 1495, Cairo; f. 1952; cap. 11m.; res. 44.2m.; dep. 1,400.9m. (June 1981); 88 brs.; Chair. MAHMOUD F. LABAN.

Banque Misr, S.A.E.: 151 Mohamed Farid St., Cairo; f. 1920; 300 brs.; cap. 15m., res. 50.7m., dep. 1,860m. (June 1981); Chair. AHMED FOUAD MAHMOUD FOUAD; publ. *Economic Bulletin*.

Crédit Foncier Egyptien: 11 El Mashadi St., Cairo; cap. 15m., res. 6.4m., dep. 18.2m.; Chair. Dr. ALI SABRI YASSIN.

Industrial Development Bank: 110 El-Gala St., Cairo; f. 1975; cap. 25m., dep. 7.4m. (Oct. 1981); Chair. ABDEL HAMID KABOODAN.

National Bank for Development: 48 Abdel Khalek Sarwat St., P.O.B. 647, Cairo; f. 1980; cap. p.u. 25m.; Chair. MUHAMMAD Z. EL ORABI; Dep. Chair. and Man. Dir. MUHAMMAD I. FARID; Man. Dir. IBRAHIM A. SIDKY.

National Bank of Egypt, S.E.A.: 24 Sherif St., Cairo; f. 1898; nationalized 1960; handles all commercial banking operations; cap. 11m.; res. 58.4m.; dep. 2,083.5m. (June 1981); 112 brs.; Chair. MOHAMED ABDEL MONEIM ROUSHDY; publ. *Quarterly Economic Bulletin*.

The Principal Bank for Development and Agricultural Credit: 110 El-Kasr El-Eini St., Cairo; f. 1976 to succeed

former Credit organizations; Chair. FATAHALLA RIFAAT
MOHAMED.

SOCIAL BANK

Nasser Social Bank: 35 Kasr El Nil St., Cairo; f. 1971;
interest-free savings and investment bank for social
and economic activities, participating in social insurance, specializing in financing co-operatives, craftsmen and social institutions; Chair. NASSEF TAHOUN.

MULTINATIONAL BANKS

Arab African International Bank: 5 Midan Al Saray Al
Koubra, Garden City, Cairo; f. 1964; cap. U.S. $112m.;
commercial investment bank; shareholders are Govern-
ments of Kuwait, Egypt, Iraq, Algeria, Jordan, Saudi
Arabia and Qatar; Chair. and Man. Dir. EBRAHIM
AL-EBRAHIM; Deputy Chair. MUHAMMAD SABEK; Chief
Gen. Man. ESSAM GABR; Gen. Man. MUHAMMAD A.
AZAB; brs. in Beirut, Al Hamra, Alexandria, Nassau,
Dubai and Abu Dhabi; Rep. Offices in Khartoum,
Amman, Tunis, and London; agency in New York.

Arab International Bank: 35 Abdel Khalek Sarwat St.,
Cairo; f. 1971; cap. U.S. $100m.; res. U.S. $95m. (June
1981); aims to promote trade and investment in
shareholders' countries and other Arab countries;
Chair. MUSTAPHA KHALIL.

COMMERCIAL FOREIGN VENTURE BANKS

El Ahram Bank: 14 El-Alfy St., Cairo; f. 1980; Chair. Dr.
MUHAMMAD ZAKI SHAFEI.

Alexandria-Kuwait International Bank: 110 Kasr El Eini
St., P.O.B. 1004, Cairo; Egyptian/Kuwaiti businessmen
have 55 per cent interest, Bank of Alexandria 25 per
cent, Sharjah Group 10 per cent, Principal Bank for
Development and Agric. Credit 5 per cent, Egyptian
Kuwait Real Estate Devt. Co. 5 per cent; Chair.
AHMED MARROUF; Man. Dir. S. M. F. EL KASRY.

Bank of Credit and Commerce (Misr) S.A.E.: Cairo Centre
Building, 106 Kasr El Aini St., Garden City, Cairo;
f. 1981; member of BCC Group.

Banque du Caire et de Paris: 14 El Saray El Kubra St.,
Garden City, P.O.B. 2441, Cairo; f. 1977; Banque du
Caire has 51 per cent interest and Banque Nationale de
Paris 49 per cent; Chair. MUHAMMAD ZAKI EL ORABI;
Gen. Man. A. F. SOLIMAN.

Cairo Far East Bank: 104 El Nil St., El Agoza, Cairo.

Chase National Bank (Egypt): 12 El Birgas St., Garden
City, P.O.B. 2430, Cairo; National Bank of Egypt has
51 per cent interest and Chase Manhattan Bank 49 per
cent; cap. 10m.; Chair. ALY DABBOUS.

Delta International Bank: Arab Socialist Union Building,
1113 Corniche El-Nil, Cairo.

Egyptian-American Bank: 4 Hassan Sabri St., Zamalek,
P.O.B. 1825, Cairo; f. 1976; Bank of Alexandria has
51 per cent interest and American Express Banking
Corporation 49 per cent; cap. 10m.; total resources
117.2m. (Dec. 1979); Chair. MOUSTAFA NOUR ELDIN;
Man. Dir. Dr. FARID W. SAAD.

Faisal Islamic Bank of Egypt: 1113 Corniche El-Nil, Cairo;
f. 1977; cap. U.S. $40m., dep. U.S. $469.2m. (April
1982); Chair. Prince MUHAMMAD AL-FAISAL AL-SAUD;
Gov. MUHAMMAD FOUAD EL-SARRAF.

Misr International Bank: 14 Alfy St., P.O.B. 631, Cairo;
Bank Misr has a 51 per cent interest and First National
Bank of Chicago, Banco di Roma, Europartners,
UBAF and Mitsui Bank hold 49 per cent.

Misr-America International Bank: 1 Behler Passage, Kasr
El Nil St., Cairo; Development Industrial Bank has
26 per cent interest, Misr Insurance Co. has 25 per
cent; while Bank of America has 40 per cent, Kuwait
Real Estate Bank 4.5 per cent and First Arabian
Corporation 4.5 per cent; Man. Dir. GEOFFREY MILTON.

Misr-Romanian Bank: P.O.B. 35, 15 Abu Elfida St.,
Zamalek, Cairo; f. 1977; Misr Bank has 51 per cent
interest, while Romanian Bank for Foreign Trade has
19 per cent, Romanian Bank for Agriculture and Food
Industries 15 per cent, and Romanian Investments
Bank 15 per cent; cap. U.S. $5m.; dep. U.S. $279.4m.
(Dec. 1981); Deputy Chair., Man. Dir. and Gen. Man.
GHEORGHE IDITOIU and BAHIR ABDEL KERIM FAHMI.

Mohandes Bank: 30 Ramses St., Cairo.

Nile Bank, S.A.E.: 35 Ramses St., Cairo; f. 1978; cap.
p.u. U.S. $15m. (June 1981).

Suez Canal Bank: 11 Muhammad Sabry Abu Alam St.,
Cairo; f. 1978; dep. 141m. (Dec. 1979); Chair. ZAKARIA
TAWFIK ABDEL FATAH; Gen. Man. MUHAMMAD HAMZA
EL ADAWI.

Al Watany Bank of Egypt: 1113 Corniche El-Nil St.,
Cairo.

NON-COMMERCIAL BANKS

**Arab Investment Bank (Federal Arab Bank for Develop-
ment and Investment):** 1113 Corniche El Nil, Cairo;
f. 1978; cap. p.u. U.S. $13m.; total assets U.S. $138.5m.
(Dec. 1981); Chair. and Man. Dir. Prof. Dr. WAGIH
SHINDY.

Cairo Barclays International Bank S.A.E.: 1 Latin America
St., P.O.B. 2335, Cairo; cap. U.S. $10m., dep. U.S.
$117m.; Chair. M. F. LABAN; Joint Gen. Mans. G. J. B.
GREEN, C.B.E., and A. H. FAIDY.

Crédit International d'Egypte: 2 Talaat Harb St., Cairo.

**Islamic International Bank for Investment and Develop-
ment:** 7 Marof St., Cairo.

Misr Iran Development Bank: 8 Adly St., Cairo; f. 1975;
cap. U.S. $40m.; dep. U.S. $252m. (August 1981);
Chair. FOUAD A. L. SULTAN; Gen. Man. AL-MOTAZ
MANSOUR.

National Société Générale Bank, S.A.E.: 4 Talaat Harb
St., 2nd Floor, P.O.B. 2664, Cairo; National Bank of
Egypt has 51 per cent interest, Société Générale, Paris
has 49 per cent; f. 1978; cap. £E7 million; Gen. Man.
ANDRE DOLEANS.

Reconstruction and Housing Bank: 9 Talaat Harb St., Cairo.

Société Arabe Internationale de Banque: 10 Abdel Salam
Aref St., P.O.B. 2673, Cairo; f. 1976; cap. U.S. $10m.;
dep. U.S. $119.1m. (March 1981).

BRANCHES OF PRINCIPAL FOREIGN BANKS

American Express International Banking Corporation,
Arab Bank Ltd., Banca Commerciale Italiana, Bank
Melli Iran, Bank of America, Bank of Credit and Com-
merce-International, Bank of Nova Scotia, Bank of Oman
Ltd., Bank Saderat Iran, Citibank, Crédit Lyonnais,
Gamal Trust Bank, Lloyds Bank International Ltd.,
National Bank of Abu Dhabi, National Bank of Greece,
National Bank of Oman Ltd., National Bank of Pakistan.

OFFSHORE BANK

Manufacturers Hanover Trust Co.

STOCK EXCHANGES

Capital Market Authority: Cairo; Chair. MAHMOUD FAHMI.

Cairo Stock Exchange: 4 El Sherifein St., Cairo; f. 1883;
Pres. MUHAMMAD ALY HASSAN.

Alexandria Stock Exchange: Pres. FOUAD SHAHEEN.

INSURANCE

Misr Insurance Company: Dokki Square, Giza, Cairo;
f. 1934; all classes of insurance and reinsurance; Chair.
FATHI MOHAMED IBRAHIM.

Arab International Insurance Co.: P.O.B. 2704, 28 Talaat
Harb Str., Cairo; a joint-stock free zone company

established by Egyptian and foreign insurance companies; Chair. GAMAL EL BOROLLOSSY; Man. Dir. HASSAN M. HAFEZ.

Al Chark Insurance Company, S.A.E.: Cairo; 15 Sharia Kasr-el-Nil; f. 1931; Chair. AMIN EL-HIZZAWI; general and life.

Commercial Insurance Company of Egypt, S.A.E.: 7 Midan E. Tahrir, Cairo; f. 1947; life, fire, marine, accident; Man. Dir. AHMED ZAKY HELMY.

The Egyptian Reinsurance Company, S.A.E.: 7 Dar el Shifa St., Garden City, P.O.B. 950, Cairo; f. 1957; Chair. FOUAD AHMED ABDEL RAHMAN.

L'Epargne, S.A.E.: Immeuble Chemla Sharia 26 July, P.O.B. 548, Cairo; all types of insurance.

Al Iktisad el Shabee, S.A.E.; 11 Sharia Emad El Dine, P.O.B. 1635, Cairo; f. 1948; Man. Dir. and Gen. Man. W. KHAYAT.

Al Mottahida: 9 Sharia Soliman Pasha, P.O.B. 804, Cairo; f. 1957.

National Insurance Company of Egypt, S.A.E.: 33 Sharia Nabi Danial, P.O.B. 446, Alexandria; f. 1900; Chair. ALI RAAFAT NAWITO.

Provident Association of Egypt, S.A.E.: 9 Sharia Sherif Pasha, P.O.B. 390, Alexandria; f. 1936; Man. Dir. G. C. VORLOOU.

TRADE AND INDUSTRY

CHAMBERS OF COMMERCE
ALEXANDRIA
Egyptian Chamber of Commerce, Alexandria: El-Ghorfa Eltegareia St.; Pres. ABDEL HAMIED SERRY; Sec. AHMED EL ALFI MUHAMMAD; Gen. Dir. MUHAMMED FATHY MAHMOUD.

CAIRO
Cairo Chamber of Commerce: 4 Midan El Falaki St.; f. 1913; Pres. MUHAMMAD ALI SHETA; Gen. Dir. SAID EL-BARRAD; publ. *Monthly Bulletin*.

OTHER TOWNS
Egyptian Chamber of Commerce for Aswan Governorate: Abtal El-Tahrir St., Aswan.

Egyptian Chamber of Commerce for Asyut Governorate: Asyut.

Egyptian Chamber of Commerce for Behera Governorate: Gomhouriya St., Damanhoru.

Egyptian Chamber of Commerce for Beni-Suef Governorate: Mamdouh St., Moqbel El-Guedid, Beni-Suef.

Egyptian Chamber of Commerce for Dakahlia Governorate, Mansura: El-Saleh Ayoub Square, Mansura.

Egyptian Chamber of Commerce for Damietta Governorate: Damietta.

Egyptian Chamber of Commerce for Fayum Governorate: Fayum.

Egyptian Chamber of Commerce for Gharbia Governorate: Tanta.

Egyptian Chamber of Commerce for Giza Governorate: El-Saa Square, Giza.

Egyptian Chamber of Commerce for Ismailia Governorate: Ismailia.

Egyptian Chamber of Commerce for Kafr-el-Sheika Governorate: Kafr-el-Sheikh.

Egyptian Chamber of Commerce for Kena Governorate: El-Gamil Street, Kena.

Egyptian Chamber of Commerce for Menia Governorate: Menia.

Egyptian Chamber of Commerce for Menufia Governorate: Sidi Fayed Street, Shibín-El-Kom.

Egyptian Chamber of Commerce for Port Said Governorate: Port Said.

Egyptian Chamber of Commerce for Kalyubia Governorate: Benha.

Egyptian Chamber of Commerce for Sharkia Governorate Zagazig.

Egyptian Chamber of Commerce for Suez Governorate: Suez.

Egyptian Chamber of Commerce for Suhag Governorate Suhag.

FOREIGN INVESTMENT ORGANIZATION
Investment and Free Zone Authority: 8 Adly St., P.O.B. 1007, Cairo; Man. Dir. ISMAEL H. GHANIM.

NATIONALIZED ORGANIZATIONS
In November 1975 a Presidential Decree ratified the establishment of Higher Councils for the various sectors of industry. During 1978, however, various Government Ministries took increasing control of industries. In 1980 it was estimated that the Government controlled about 350 companies.

PETROLEUM
Egyptian General Petroleum Corporation (EGPC): P.O.B. 2130, Cairo; State supervisory authority generally concerned with the planning of policies relating to petroleum activities in Egypt with the object of securing the development of the oil industry; has entered into 50-50 partnership agreements with a number of foreign companies; Pres. Eng. MOHAMED RAMZY EL-LEITHY; Gen. Man. Dr. MOSTAFA KAMAL EL AUOTY.

Belayim Petroleum Company (PETROBEL): 155 Sharia Mohamed Farid, Cairo; has absorbed Delta Petroleum Co.; capital equally shared between EGPC and International Egyptian Oil Co., which is a subsidiary of ENI of Italy; oil and gas exploration, drilling and production.

General Petroleum Company (GPC): P.O.B. 743, Cairo; f. 1962; wholly owned subsidiary of EGPC; operates mainly in Eastern Desert.

Gulf of Suez Petroleum Company (GUPCO): 1097 Sharia Corniche El Nil, Cairo; f. 1965; partnership between EGPC and Amoco-Egypt Co., U.S.A.; developed the El Morgan oilfield in the Gulf of Suez, also holds other exploration concessions in the Gulf of Suez and the Western Desert; output was averaging 600,000 b/d in April 1980; Chair. Dr. Eng. HAMDI EL BANBI.

Western Desert Petroleum Company (WEPCO): P.O.B. 412, Alexandria; f. 1967 as partnership between EGPC and Phillips Petroleum and later Hispanoil with 15 per cent interest; developed Alamein, Yidma and Umbarka fields in the Western Desert and later Abu Qir offshore gas field in 1978; Chair. Eng. HASSAN EL DEWY.

Arab Petroleum Pipelines Company (SUMED): 9 Amin Yehia St., Zizinia, P.O.B. 2056, Alexandria; f. 1974; Suez-Mediterranean crude oil transportation pipeline and oil terminal operators; Chair. and Man. Dir. Dr. MUHAMMAD RAMZY EL-LEITHY.

Numerous foreign oil companies are prospecting for oil in Egypt under agreements with EGPC.

EMPLOYERS' ORGANIZATIONS

Federation of Egyptian Industries: P.O.B. 251, 26A Sharia Sherif Pasha, Cairo, and P.O.B. 1658, 65 Horia Rd., Alexandria; f. 1922; Pres. Dr. Eng. MUHAMMAD EL SAYED EL KHOROURI; represents the industrial community in Egypt.

TRADE UNIONS

Egyptian Trade Union Federation (ETUF): 90 El Galaa St., Cairo; f. 1957; 21 affiliated unions; 2.5 million mems.; affiliated to the International Confederation of Arab Trade Unions and to the Organization of African Trade Union Unity; Pres. SAAD M. AHMED; Gen. Sec. IBRAHIM SHALABY; publ. *El Omal* (weekly, Arabic).

General Trade Union of Agriculture: 31 Mansour St., Bab el Louk, Cairo; 150,000 mems.; Pres. MOKHTAR ABDEL HAMIED; Gen. Sec. MOHAMED ABDEL KHALEK GOUDA.

General Trade Union of Air Transport: 5 Ahmed Sannan St., St. Fatima, Heliopolis, Cairo; 11,000 mems.; Pres. ABDEL MONEM FARAG EISA; Gen. Sec. SHEKATA ABDEL HAMEID.

General Trade Union of Banks and Insurance: 2 El Kady El Fadel St., Cairo; 56,000 mems.; Pres. MAHMOUD MOHAMED DABBOUR; Gen. Sec. ABDOU HASSAN MOHAMED ALI.

General Trade Union of Building Workers: 9 Emad El Din St., Cairo; 150,000 mems.; Pres. HAMID HASSAN BARAKAT; Gen. Sec. SALEM ABDEL RAZEK.

General Trade Union of Business and Management Services: 2 Mohamed Haggag St., Midan El Tahrir, Cairo; 100,000 mems.; Pres. ABDUL RAHMAN KHEDR; Gen. Sec. MAHMOUD MOHAMED.

General Trade Union of Commerce Workers: 70 El Gomhourria St., Cairo; 100,000 mems.; Pres. ABDEL RAZEK EL SHERBEENY; Gen. Sec. KAMEL HUSSEIN A. AWAD.

General Trade Union of Educational Services: 91 Magles El Shaab St., Cairo; 80,000 mems.; Pres. MOKHTAR YOUSIF MOHAMED; Gen. Sec. HALABI ABDEL HADI HALABI.

General Trade Union of Food Industries: 3 Housni St. Hadaek El Koba, Cairo; 111,000 mems.; Pres. SAAD M. AHMED; Gen. Sec. ADLY TANUS IBRAHIM.

General Trade Union of Health Services: 22 El Sheik Kamar St., El Sakakiny, Cairo; 56,000 mems.; Pres. IBRAHIM ABOU EL MOOTY IBRAHIM; Gen. Sec. AHMED ABDEL LATIF SALEM.

General Trade Union of Maritime Transport: 36 Sharif St., Cairo; 46,000 mems.; Pres. THABET MOHAMED EL SEFARY; Gen. Sec. MOHAMED RAMADAN ABOU TOR.

General Trade Union of Military Production: 90 El Galaa St., Cairo; 55,000 mems.; Pres. MOUSTAFA MOHAMED MOUNGY; Gen. Sec. IBRAHIM LOUTFY ZANATY.

General Trade Union of Mine Workers: 5 Ali Sharawi St., Hadaek El Koba, Cairo; 14,000 mems.; Pres. ABBAS MAHMOUD IBRAHIM; Gen. Sec. AMIN HASSAN AMER.

General Trade Union of Petroleum and Chemical Industries: 90 El Galaa St., Cairo; 103,000 mems.; Pres. AHMED AHMED EL AMAWI; Gen. Sec. ABDEL KADER HASSAN ABDEL KADER.

General Trade Union of Posts, Telegrams and Telephones: 90 E. Galaa St., Cairo; 80,000 mems.; Pres. MOHAMED KHAIRY HASHEM; Gen. Sec. MOHAMED ABDEL RAOOF DIRRAZ.

General Trade Union of Press, Printing and Information: 90 El Galaa St., Cairo; 43,100 mems.; Pres. MOHAMED ALI EL FIKKY; Gen. Sec. ABDEL AZIZ MOHAMED BASUNY.

General Trade Union of Public Utilities: 22 Sharif St., Cairo; 64,000 mems.; Pres. MANSOUR ABDEL MONEM MANSOUR; Gen. Sec. MOHAMED TALAAT HASSAN.

General Trade Union of Railways: 15 Emad El Din St., Cairo; 89,000 mems.; Pres. MAHMOUD ATITO; Gen. Sec. SAID MOUSTAFA ABOU EL ELA.

General Trade Union of Road Transport: 90 El Galaa St., Cairo; 243,000 mems.; Pres. MOHAMED MOHAMED AHMED EL OKALY; Gen. Sec. MOHAMED KAMAL LABIB.

General Trade Union of Textile Workers: 327 Shoubra St., Cairo; 244,000 mems.; Pres. ALI MOHAMED DOUFDAA; Gen. Sec. HASSAN TOULBA MARZOUK.

General Trade Union of Tourism and Hotels: 90 El Galaa St., Cairo; 21,400 mems.; Pres. AMIN MAWAD ALI; Gen. Sec. MOUSTAFA IBRAHIM MOUSTAFA.

General Trade Union of Workers in Engineering, Metal and Electrical Industries: 90 El Galaa St., Cairo; 130,000 mems.; Pres. SAID GOMAAA ALI; Gen. Sec. GAMAL TARABISHI.

TRANSPORT

RAILWAYS

Egyptian Railways: Midan Ramses, Cairo; f. 1851; length 4,882 km.; 2,327 km. auxiliary lines; 25 km. electrified; Chair. Eng. ABDEL MONEIM HESHMAT.

Alexandria Passenger Transport Authority: 21 Saad Zaghloul Square, P.O.B. 466, Alexandria; controls City Tramways (28 km.), Ramleh Electric Railway (16 km.), suburban buses (300 km.); Chair. Eng. MOHAMED ABDEL RAHMAN AMIN; Tech. Dir. Eng. MOHAMED AHMED BAYOUMY.

Heliopolis Company for Housing and Inhabiting: 28 Ibrahim El Lakkany St., Heliopolis, Cairo; 50 km., 148 railcars; Gen. Man. ABDEL MONEIM SEIF.

A 10-km. underground railway is under consideration in Cairo, and a 430 km. line to carry iron ore from the Bahariya mines to the Helwan iron and steel works was opened in August 1973.

ROADS

Egyptian General Organization of Inland Transport for Provinces Passengers: Sharia Kasr-el-Aini, Cairo; Pres. HASAN MOURAD KOTB.

There are good metalled main roads as follows: Cairo-Alexandria (desert road); Cairo-Benna-Tanta-Damanhur-Alexandria; Cairo-Suez (desert road); Cairo-Ismailia-Port Said or Suez; Cairo-Fayum (desert road); in 1980 there were over 90,000 km. of roads. The Ahmed Hamdi road tunnel beneath the Suez Canal was opened in October 1980.

SHIPPING

Alexandria Shipping and Navigation Co.: 557 El Horreya Ave., P.O.B. 812, Alexandria; services between Egypt; N. and W. Europe, U.S.A., Red Sea and Mediterranean, Chair. and Man. Dir. Eng. MAHMOUD ISMAIL.

Egyptian Navigation Co.: 2 Elnasr St., Alexandria; f. 1930; services Alexandria/Europe, U.S.A., Black Sea, Adriatic Sea, Mediterranean Sea, Indian Ocean and Red Sea; 48 vessels; Chair. H. Z. Yacout.

Pan Arab Shipping Co.: 13 Salah Salem St., P.O.B. 39, Alexandria; Arab League Company; Chair. Ezzeldin Rifaat.

THE SUEZ CANAL

Suez Canal Authority (*Hay'at Canal Al Suess*): Irshad Building, Ismailia; Cairo Office: 6 Lazokhli St., Garden City, Cairo; f. 1956; Pres. Eng. Mashhour Ahmed Mashhour.

Length of Canal 173 km.; maximum permissible draught: 38 ft. (increased to 53 ft. Dec. 1980); breadth of canal at water level 160–200m.; breadth between buoys defining the navigable channel 110m.

CIVIL AVIATION

EgyptAir: Cairo International Airport, Heliopolis, Cairo; f. 1932 as Misr Airwork; operates internal services in Egypt and external services throughout the Middle East, Far East, Africa and Europe; Chair. General Muhammad Rawan; fleet of 7 Boeing 707, 7 Boeing 737, 5 Airbus A300B4, 2 Beech Baron.

The following foreign airlines serve Egypt: Aeroflot (U.S.S.R.), Air France, Air India, Alia (Jordan), Austrian Airlines, British Airways, British Caledonian, ČSA (Czechoslovakia), Cyprus Airways, El Al (Israel), Ethiopian Air Lines, Finnair, Garuda (Indonesia), Ghana Airways, Interflug (German Democratic Republic), Iraqi Airways, JAL (Japan), JAT (Yugoslavia), Libyan Arab Airlines, KLM (Netherlands), Kuwait Airways, LOT (Poland), Lufthansa (Fed. Rep. of Germany), MALÉV (Hungary), MEA, Olympic Airways (Greece), Pan Am, PIA (Pakistan), Qantas (Australia), Sabena (Belgium), SAS (Sweden), Saudia, Sudan Airways, Swissair, TAROM (Romania), TWA (U.S.A.), and UTA (France).

TOURISM AND CULTURE

Ministry of Tourism: 110 Sh. Kasr-el-Aini, Cairo; f. 1965; branches at Alexandria, Port Said, Suez, Luxor and Aswan; Minister of Tourism and Civil Aviation Adil Ibrahim Tahir.

Egyptian General Company for Tourism and Hotels: 4 Latin America St., Garden City, Cairo; f. 1961; affiliated to the Ministry of Tourism.

Authorized foreign exchange dealers for tourists include the principal banks and the following:

American Express of Egypt Ltd.: 15 Kasr-el-Nil St., Cairo; f. 1919; 7 brs.

Thomas Cook Overseas Ltd.: 4 Sharia Champollion, Cairo.

CULTURAL ORGANIZATION

Ministry of Culture: Cairo; Minister of State for Culture Muhammad Abdul Hamid Radwan.

PRINCIPAL THEATRES AND ORCHESTRA

Egyptian General Organization of Cinema, Theatre and Music: Ministry of Culture.

Departments include the following: **Opera Lyric Troupe, Opera Ballet, Opera Chorale, Cairo Symphony Orchestra.**

Members frequently take part in performances with visiting opera companies.

National Puppet Theatre: Cairo.

ATOMIC ENERGY

A 32-man Higher Nuclear Council was formed in August 1975.

Atomic Energy Organization: 101 Kasr El-Eini Street, Cairo; f. 1955; Chair. Dr. Ibrahim Hamouda; Vice-Chair. Dr. Saleh Hashish; Dir. of Nuclear Research Centre Dr. E. Abdelaziz; Dir. of Nat. Centre for Radiation Research and Technology Dr. H. R. El-Kady.

DEFENCE

Supreme Commander of the Armed Forces: President Muhammad Hosni Mubarak.

Commander-in-Chief of the Armed Forces: Field-Marshal Muhammad Abdul-Karim Abu Ghazalah.

Chief of Staff of the Armed Forces: Maj.-Gen. Abdel-Rabb al-Nabi Hafiz.

Commander of the Air Force: Air Vice-Marshal Muhammad Abdel-Hamid Helmi.

Commander of Air Defence: Maj.-Gen. Hamdi Hasan Hamdi.

Commander of the Navy: Vice-Admiral Muhammad Ali Muhammad.

Defence Budget, 1979/80: U.S. $1,500 million.

Military service: One year, selective.

Total armed forces: (July 1981) 367,000; army 235,000; air defence command 85,000; navy 20,000; air force 27,000. Reserves 335,000. Paramilitary forces: about 139,000 (National Guard, etc.).

EDUCATION

It is estimated that 72 per cent of children aged 6 to 11 years were enrolled at primary schools in 1975, while 40 per cent of those aged 12 to 17 attended secondary schools.

Administration

Responsibility for education and training lies with the Ministry of Education and Scientific Research, except for the ministries which train manpower for their own specialized needs. The universities are outside ministerial jurisdiction.

The Ministry of Education is responsible for primary, preparatory, secondary general, secondary technical (commercial, agricultural and industrial), primary teacher training and Higher Education.

The universities, however, maintain their individual independence even though the President of the Supreme Council is the Minister of Education. The Council is a planning and co-ordinating body and comprises the Rectors, Vice-Rectors and some representatives of different disciplines of university education.

Structure

Education is compulsory for the primary level with entry allowed within the 6–8 years age range. The system has a four-tiered structure:

(i) Primary—Years 1–6 (Grades 1–6).

(ii) Preparatory—Years 1–3 (Grades 7–9).

(iii) Secondary—Years 1–3 (Grades 10–12).

(iv) Higher-Technician Training—Years 1 and 2. Higher Technical Institutes—Years 1–4 or 5. Universities—Years 1–4 or 5 or 6.

For the present, entry from one level into the next is based on success in a final year examination. Promotion from one grade to another in each level is also by final examination, except in primary education where promotion was until recently virtually automatic except for an examination at the ends of Grades 4 and 6.

At the end of the preparatory stage, students may enter:

(a) General Secondary Schools which after a common first-year divide into a humanities branch and a maths-science branch;

(b) Technical Schools—either industrial or commercial or agricultural;

(c) Training institutions administered by other ministries.

Numerical details or numbers of schools, teachers and pupils for the year 1976/77 can be found in the Statistical Survey.

BIBLIOGRAPHY

GENERAL

ABDEL-MALEK, ANWAR. Egypte, société militaire (Paris, 1962).
Idéologie et renaissance nationale/L'Egypte moderne (Paris, 1969).

AHMED, J. M. The Intellectual Origins of Egyptian Nationalism (London, Royal Institute of International Affairs, 1960).

ALDRIDGE, JAMES. Cairo: Biography of a City (Macmillan, London, 1970).

AYROUT, H. H. The Egyptian Peasant (Boston, 1963).

BADDOUR, ABD. Sudanese-Egyptian Relations. A Chronological and Analytical Study (Nijhoff, The Hague, 1960).

BADEAU, J. S. The Emergence of Modern Egypt (New York, 1953).

BAER, GABRIEL. A History of Landownership in Modern Egypt 1800–1950 (Oxford University Press, London, 1962).
The Evolution of Landownership in Egypt and the Fertile Crescent, the Economic History of the Middle East 1800–1914 (University of Chicago Press, Chicago and London, 1966).
Studies in the Social History of Modern Egypt (University of Chicago Press, Chicago and London, 1969).

BAKER, RAYMOND WILLIAM. Egypt's Uncertain Revolution under Nasser and Sadat (Harvard University Press, 1979).

BERGER, MORROE. Bureaucracy and Society in Modern Egypt: a Study of the Higher Civil Service (Princeton University Press, 1957).
Islam in Egypt Today: Social and Political Aspects of Popular Religion (Cambridge University Press, 1970).

BERQUE, JACQUES. Egypt: Imperialism and Revolution (Faber, London, 1972).

BOKTOR, AMIN. The Development and Expansion of Education in the U.A.R. (The American University, Cairo, 1963).

COULT, LYMAN H. An Annotated Bibliography of the Egyptian Fellah (University of Miami Press, 1958).

CROMER, EARL OF. Modern Egypt (2 vols., London, 1908).

DAWISHA, A. I. Egypt in the Arab World. (Macmillan, London, 1976).

DODWELL, H. The Founder of Modern Egypt (Cambridge, 1931, reprinted 1967).

DRIAULT, E. L'Egypte et l'Europe (5 vols., Cairo, 1935).

ELISOFAN, E. The Nile (New York, 1964).

GARZOUZI, EVA. Old Ills and New Remedies in Egypt (Dar al-Maaref, Cairo, 1958).

HARRIS, C. P. Nationalism and Revolution in Egypt: the Role of the Muslim Brotherhood (Mouton and Co., The Hague, 1964).

HARRIS, J. R. (Ed) The Legacy of Egypt (2nd ed. Oxford University Press, 1972).

HOLT, P. M. Egypt and the Fertile Crescent (Longmans, London, 1966).

HOPKINS, HARRY. Egypt, The Crucible (Secker and Warburg, London, 1969).

HURST, H. E. The Nile (London, 1952).
The Major Nile Projects (Cairo, 1966).

LACOUTURE, JEAN and SIMONNE. Egypt in Transition (London, Methuen, 1958).

LANDAU, JACOB M. Parliaments and Parties in Egypt (Israel Publishing House, Tel-Aviv, 1953).

LAUTERPACHT, E. (Editor). The Suez Canal Settlement (Stevens and Sons, London, 1960, under the auspices of the British Institute of International and Comparative Law).

LENGYE, EMIL. Egypt's Role in World Affairs (Public Affairs Press, Washington, D.C., 1957).

LITTLE, TOM. Modern Egypt (Ernest Benn, London, 1967, Praeger, New York 1967).

LLOYD, LORD. Egypt since Cromer (2 vols., London, 1933-34).

MAHMOUD, ZAKI NAGIB. Modern Egyptian Thought (London, 1946).

MARLOWE, J. Anglo-Egyptian Relations (London, 1954).

NASSER, ABDEL GAMAL. Egypt's Liberation: The Philosophy of the Revolution (Washington, 1955).

NEGUIB, MOHAMMED. Egypt's Destiny: A Personal Statement (New York, 1955).

OWEN, ROBERT and BLUNSUM, TERENCE. Egypt, United Arab Republic, The Country and its People (Queen Anne Press, London, 1966).

RIAD, HASSAN. L'Egypte Nassérienne (Editions de Minuit Paris, 1964).

RUSSELL PASHA, Sir THOMAS. Egyptian Service, 1902-1946 (London, 1949).

STEWART, DESMOND. Cairo (Phoenix House, London, 1965).

VAUCHER, G. Gamal Abdel Nasser et son Equipe, 2 vols. (Brill, Leiden, 1950).

VIOLLET, ROGER and DORESSE, JEAN. Egypt (New York, Cromwell, 1955).

WATERFIELD, GORDON. Egypt (Thames & Hudson, London, 1966).

WATT, D. C. Britain and the Suez Canal (London, Royal Institute of International Affairs, 1956).

WAVELL, W. H. A Short Account of the Copts (London, 1945).

WILBUR, D. N. The United Arab Republic (New York, 1969).

WILSON, JOHN A. The Burden of Egypt (Chicago, 1951).

WYNN, WILTON. Nasser of Egypt: The Search for Dignity (Cambridge, Mass., 1959).

ANCIENT EGYPT

ALDRED, CYRIL. Egypt to the End of the Old Kingdom (Thames and Hudson, London, 1965).

BERNARD, JEAN-LOUIS. Aux origines de l'Egypte (Laffont, Paris, 1976).

BREASTED, JAMES HENRY. A History of Egypt from the Earliest Times to the Persian Conquest (Harper and Row, New York, 1959).

DE LUBICZ, A. S. The Temples of Karnak (2 vols., London, 1961).

ERMAN, ADOLF. The Ancient Egyptians; a Sourcebook of their Writings (trans. A. M. BLACKMAN, Harper, New York, 1966).

FISCHEL, WALTER J. Ibn Khaldun in Egypt (University of California Press, 1967).

FORSTER, E. M. Alexandria: a History and a Guide (Doubleday, New York, 1961).

GARDINER, Sir ALAN HENDERSON. Egypt of the Pharaohs (Clarendon Press, Oxford, 1961).

GLANVILLE, S. R. K. (editor). The Legacy of Egypt (Oxford, 1942).

GREENER, L. The Discovery of Egypt (Cassell, London 1966, Viking Press, New York, 1967).

JOHNSON, ALLAN C. Egypt and the Roman Empire (Ann Arbor, 1951).

MEYER-RANKE, PETER. Der Rote Pharao (Christian Wegner Verlag, Hamburg, 1964).

MONTET, PIERRE. Das Leben der Pharaonen (Frankfurt/Berlin/Vienna, 1970).

PIRENNE, JACQUES. Histoire de la Civilization de l'Egypte antique (Neuchâtel, 1966).

La Religion et la Morale de l'Egypte antique (La Baconnière, Neuchâtel, 1966).

POSENER, G. (Ed.). A Dictionary of Egyptian Civilization (Methuen, London, 1962).

MODERN HISTORY

AVRAM, BENNO. The Evolution of the Suez Canal State 1869-1956. A Historico-Juridical Study (Librairie E. Droz, Libraire Minard, Geneva, Paris, 1958).

BARAWAY, RASHED EL. The Military Coup in Egypt (Cairo, Renaissance Bookshop, 1952).

BARRACLOUGH, GEOFFREY, Ed. Suez in History (London, 1962).

BLUNT, WILFRED SCAWEN. Secret History of the English Occupation of Egypt (Martin Secker, London, 1907).

CONNELL, JOHN. The Most Important Country. The Story of the Suez Crisis and the Events leading up to It (Cassell, London, 1957).

EFENDI, HUSEIN. Ottoman Egypt in the Age of the French Revolution (trans. and with introduction by Stanford J. Shaw) (Harvard Univ. Press, Cambridge, 1964).

FARNIE. D. A. East and West of Suez. The Suez Canal in history, 1854-1956 (Clarendon Press, Oxford, 1969).

HEIKAL, MUHAMMAD. The Road to Ramadan (Collins, London, 1975).

Sphinx and Commissar: The Rise and Fall of Soviet Influence in the Arab World (Collins, London, 1978).

HILL, R. Egypt in the Sudan 1820-1881 (Oxford University Press, London and New York, 1959).

HIRST, DAVID, and BEESON, IRENE. Sadat (Faber, London, 1981).

HOLT, P. M. Political and Social Change in Modern Egypt (Oxford University Press, 1967).

HUSSEIN, MAHMOUD. La Lutte de Classes en Egypte de 1945 à 1968 (Maspero, Paris, 1969).

ISSAWI, CHARLES. Egypt in Revolution (Oxford, 1963).

JOESTEN, JOACHIM. Nasser: The Rise to Power (London, Odhams, 1960).

KINROSS, LORD. Between Two Seas: The Creation of the Suez Canal (John Murray, London, 1968).

LACOUTURE, JEAN. Nasser: A Biography (Secker and Warburg, London, 1973).

LANE-POOLE, S. History of Egypt in the Middle Ages (4th edn., reprinted, Frank Cass, London, 1967).

LOVE, K. Suez: the Twice-fought War (Longman, 1970).

MANSFIELD, PETER. Nasser's Egypt (Penguin Books London, 1965).

Nasser (Methuen, London, 1969).

The British in Egypt (Weidenfeld and Nicolson, London, 1971).

MARLOWE, JOHN. Cromer in Egypt (Elek Books, London, 1970).

NUTTING, ANTHONY. No End of a Lesson; the Story of Suez (Constable, London, 1967).

Nasser (London, Constable, 1972).

O'BALLANCE, E. The Sinai Campaign 1956 (Faber, London, 1959).

RICHMOND, J. C. B. Egypt, 1798-1952: Her Advance towards a Modern Identity (Methuen, London, 1977).

SADAT, ANWAR AL. Revolt on the Nile (London, Allen Wingate, 1957).

SAFRAN, NADAV. Egypt in Search of Political Community. An analysis of the intellectual and political evolution of Egypt, 1804-1952 (Harvard University Press, Cambridge, Mass., Oxford University Press, London, 1961).

SAYYID, AFAF LUTFI AL. Egypt and Cromer: A Study in Anglo-Egyptian Relations (John Murray, London, Praeger, New York, 1968).

SCHONFIELD, HUGH A. The Suez Canal in Peace and War, 1869-1969 (Vallentine, Mitchell, London, 2nd revised edn., 1969).

SHAZLY, Gen. SAAD EL-. The Crossing of Suez: The October War (1973) (Third World Centre for Research and Publishing, London, 1980).

STEPHENS, R. Nasser (Allen Lane The Penguin Press, London, 1971).

TIGNOR, R. L. Modernization and British Colonial Rule in Egypt 1882-1914 (Princeton, 1966).

VATIKIOTIS, P. J. A Modern History of Egypt (Praeger, New York, 1966: Weidenfeld and Nicolson, London, 1969, Revised edition, 1980).

The Egyptian Army in Politics (Indiana University Press, Bloomington, 1961).

ZAKI, ABDEL RAHMAN. Histoire Militaire de l'Epoque de Mohammed Ali El-Kebir (Cairo, 1950).

ECONOMY

EL GHONEMY, M. RIAD. Economic and Industrial Organization of Egyptian Agriculture since 1952, Egypt since the Revolution (Allen and Unwin, London, 1968).

EL KAMMASH, M. M. Economic Development and Planning in Egypt (London, 1967).

HANSON, BENT, and MAZOUK, GIRGIS. Development and Economic Policy in the U.A.R. (Egypt) (North Holland Publishing Co., Amsterdam, 1965).

KARDOUCHE, G. S. The U.A.R. in Development (Praeger New York, 1967).

MABRO, ROBERT. The Egyptian Economy 1952-1972 (Oxford University Press, London, 1974).

MEAD, DONALD C. Growth and Structural Change in the Egyptian Economy (Irwin, Homwood, Ill., 1967).

O'BRIEN, PATRICK. The Revolution in Egypt's Economic System 1952-65 (Oxford, 1966).

RADWAN, SAMIR. Capital Formation in Egyptian Industry and Agriculture 1882-1967 (St. Antony's Middle East Monographs, published by Ithaca Press, London, 1975).

SAAB, GABRIEL S. The Egyptian Agrarian Reform 1952-1962 (Oxford University Press, London and New York, 1967).

WARRINER, DOREEN. Land Reform and Economic Development (Cairo, 1955).

Land Reform and Development in the Middle East—A Study of Egypt, Syria and Iraq (2nd ed. Oxford University Press, London, 1962).

Iran
(Persia)

PHYSICAL AND SOCIAL GEOGRAPHY

W. B. Fisher

SITUATION

The Islamic Republic of Iran is bounded on the north by the Caspian Sea and by the Transcaucasian and Turkistan territories of the U.S.S.R., on the east by Afghanistan and Pakistan, on the south by the Persian Gulf and Gulf of Oman, and on the west by Iraq and Turkey.

PHYSICAL FEATURES

Structurally, Iran is an extremely complex area; and owing partly to political difficulties and partly to the difficult nature of the country itself, complete exploration and investigation have not so far been achieved. In general, it can be stated that Iran consists of an interior plateau, 1,000 to 1,500 metres in height, that is ringed on almost all sides by mountain zones of varying height and extent. The largest mountain massif is that of the Zagros, which runs from the north-west of Iran, where the frontiers of Iran, Russia, Turkey and Iraq meet, first south-westwards to the eastern shores of the Persian Gulf, and then eastwards, fronting the Arabian Sea, and continuing into Baluchistan. Joining the Zagros in the north-west, and running along the southern edge of the Caspian Sea, is the narrower but equally high Elburz range; whilst along the eastern frontier of Iran are several scattered mountain chains, less continuous and imposing than either the Zagros or the Elburz, but sufficiently high to act as a barrier.

The Zagros range begins in north-west Iran as an alternation of high tablelands and lowland basins, the latter containing lakes, the largest of which is Lake Urmia. This lake, having no outlet, is saline. Further to the south-east the Zagros becomes much more imposing, consisting of a series of parallel hog's-back ridges, some of which reach over 4,000 metres in height. In its southern and eastern portions the Zagros becomes distinctly narrower, and its peaks much less high, though a few exceed 3,000 metres. The Elburz range is very much narrower than the Zagros, but equally, if not more abrupt, and one of its peaks, the volcanic cone of Mt. Damavand (5,601 metres), is the highest in the country. There is a sudden drop on the northern side to the flat plain occupied by the Caspian Sea, which lies about 27 metres below sea-level, and is shrinking rapidly in size. The eastern highlands of Iran consist of isolated massifs separated by lowland zones, some of which contain lakes from which there is no outlet, the largest being the Hirmand Basin, on the borders of Iran and Afghanistan.

The interior plateau of Iran is partly covered by a remarkable salt swamp (termed *kavir*) and partly by loose sand or stones (*dasht*), with stretches of better land mostly round the perimeter, near the foothills of the surrounding mountains. In these latter areas much of the cultivation of the country is carried on, but the lower-lying desert and swamp areas, towards the centre of the plateau, are largely uninhabited. The Kavir is an extremely forbidding region, consisting of a surface formed by thick plates of crystallized salt, which have sharp, upstanding edges. Below the salt lie patches of mud, with, here and there, deep drainage channels—all of which are very dangerous to travellers, and are hence unexplored. Because of this great handicap from the presence of an unusually intractable "dead heart", it has proved difficult to find a good central site for the capital of Iran—many towns, all peripheral to a greater or lesser degree, have in turn fulfilled this function, but none has proved completely satisfactory. The choice of the present capital, Teheran, dates only from the end of the eighteenth century.

Iran suffers from occasional earthquakes, which can cause severe loss of life, damage to property and disruption of communications. A particularly bad example occurred around Tabas in the north-eastern Khurasan province in September 1978; estimates placed the toll from this disaster at up to 20,000 deaths and severe damage over 2,000 square kilometres.

The climate of Iran is one of great extremes. Owing to its southerly position, adjacent to Arabia and near the Thar Desert, the summer is extremely hot, with temperatures in the interior rising possibly higher than anywhere else in the world—certainly over 55°C. has been recorded. In winter, however, the great altitude of much of the country and its continental situation result in far lower temperatures than one would expect to find for a country in such low latitudes. Minus 30°C. can be recorded in the north-west Zagros, and −20°C. is common in many places.

Another unfortunate feature is the prevalence of strong winds, which intensify the temperature contrasts. Eastern Iran in particular has a violent visitation in the so-called "Wind of 120 Days", which blows regularly throughout summer, reaching at times over 160 km. per hour and often raising sand to such an extent that the stone walls of buildings are sometimes scoured away and turn to ruins.

Most of Iran is arid; but in contrast, parts of the north-west and north receive considerable rainfall—up to 2,000 mm. along parts of the Caspian coast, producing very special climatic conditions in this small region, recalling conditions in the lower Himalayas. The Caspian shore has a hot, humid climate and this region is by far the most densely populated of the whole country. Next in order of population density comes the north-west Zagros area—the province of Azerbaizhan, with its capital, Tabriz, the fourth city of Iran. Then, reflecting the diminished rainfall, next in order come the central Zagros area, and adjacent parts of the interior plateau, round Isfahan, Hamadan, Shiraz, and Kermanshah, with an extension as far as Teheran. The extreme east and south, where rainfall is very scanty, were for long extremely lightly populated, except in the few parts where water is available, by nomadic groups. Over the past few years, however, a development programme has been initiated, and the effects are seen in the expansion of the towns, some of which have grown by 30-40 per cent since 1972.

ECONOMIC LIFE

Owing to the difficulties of climate and topography there are few districts, apart from the Caspian plain, that are continuously cultivated over a wide area. Settlement tends to occur in small clusters, close to water supplies, or where there are especially favourable conditions—a good soil, shelter from winds, or easy communications. Away from these cultivated areas, which stand out like oases among the barren expanses of desert or mountain, most of the population live as nomads, by the herding of animals. The nomadic tribesmen have had great influence on the life of Iran. Their principal territory is the central Zagros, where the tribal system is strongly developed; but nomads are found in all the mountain zones, though their numbers are very few in the south and east. Reza Shah (see "History") made considerable efforts to break the power of the nomadic tribes and to force them to settle as agriculturalists. Now, with the development of the economy, most nomads have moved into towns (though there are still a few remaining).

Economic activity has suffered from the handicaps of topography and climate, prolonged political and social insecurity (with constant pressure by foreign powers), and widespread devastation in the later Middle Ages by Mongol invaders, from which Iran has never fully recovered. Agricultural methods in particular are primitive, so that yields are low; but the drawbacks to efficient production mentioned in the general introduction to this volume—archaic systems of land tenure, absentee landlords, lack of education, and shortage of capital—are gradually being overcome. In the north and west, which are by far the most productive, a wide variety of cereals (including wheat, barley, and rice) and much fruit are grown, but in the south and east the date is the principal source of food. Some Iranian fruit is of remarkable quality (especially the apricots and grapes) and melons weighing more than 45 kg. are known.

Iran has a number of mineral resources, some of which are exploited on a commercial scale. The newly discovered copper deposits at Sar Cheshmeh could be among the largest in the world. Iran has the second largest natural gas deposits in the world; and during 1977 there was an announcement that large deposits of good quality coal had been discovered near Kirman. Iranians have always had a high reputation as craftsmen—particularly in metal work and in carpet making; and Reza Shah attempted to develop modern mechanized industry by placing state-owned factories in most of the big towns. Some of these have proved successful, others not, but bazaar manufactures still remain the more important. Teheran is now a major manufacturing centre, with a considerable spread of activities from processing of foodstuffs to manufacture of consumer and construction goods and an increasing range of more complex items: electronics, motor manufacturing and high-grade chemicals. Teheran is the headquarters of more than 90 per cent of all industrial firms in Iran; whilst a major industrial complex based on the steel mill at Isfahan is now taking shape. Carpet-making retains importance owing to considerable demand from the U.S.A. and Europe (West Germany especially), but major emphasis in Iran is now very much on modern manufacturing in metals, machinery, electronics and chemicals of an increasingly sophisticated kind, with the beginnings of attention to nuclear energy.

The adverse nature of geographical conditions has greatly restricted the growth of communications in Iran. The country is very large in relation to its size of population—it is 2,250 km. from north-west to south-west—and because of the interior deserts, many routes must follow a circuitous path instead of attempting a direct crossing. Then, too, the interior is shut off by ranges that are in parts as high as the Alps of Europe, but far less broken up by river valleys. Road construction is everywhere difficult, but since the mid-1960s increasing effort has gone into providing an all-weather surface set of trunk routes between major cities: special allocations are made in the Five-Year Plans. An important link is the railway constructed with great effort before the Second World War between the Caspian coast, Teheran and the Persian Gulf. Other rail links with bordering countries have already been and are still being built: from Teheran there are now direct links with the U.S.S.R., and more recently with Turkey, whilst a line is being pushed southeastwards that could one day link with Pakistan. Though there are mountain streams, many flowing in deep, inaccessible gorges, only one, the Karun river, is at all navigable. The Caspian ports are subject to silting, whilst in the south most harbours are either poorly sheltered or difficult of access from the interior. However, the last few years have seen a deliberate focusing of development on the Gulf, in response to the enhanced economic and political status of the region, now one of the wealthiest parts of the world. Development has occurred in the region of the Shatt al-Arab in the last years of the Shah's regime; but the outbreak of war between Iran and Iraq in 1980 has greatly set back any economic prospects both here and in the Persian Gulf. Overall, the effect of the Revolution of 1979 has been to reduce, though not entirely terminate, the sophisticated industrial developments initiated under the Shah, and to shift external trading more towards imports of basic raw materials and food, balanced (often by direct exchange approaching barter) by exports of oil which, though reduced (in part because of war in the Gulf), are still considerable. Even the U.S.A. has resumed (1982) purchases of Iranian oil.

RACE AND LANGUAGE

Iran has numerous ethnic groups of widely differing origin. In the central plateau there occurs a distinctive sub-race, termed by some anthropologists Iranian or Irano-Afghan. The distinguishing qualities are a moderate to rather tall stature, pronounced features, but less so than among neighbours, and a colouring generally lighter than that of many surrounding peoples. In the mountain districts there are many other smaller groups of separate racial composition. A number of nomads, including the Bakhtiari tribes, would seem to be of Kurdish stock; whilst Turki (Mongoloid) strains are apparent in others, such as the Qashqai tribes. Smaller groups from the Caucasus (Georgians and Circassians) are represented in Azerbaizhan and the Caspian provinces, whilst Turki influence is again apparent in the racial composition of the eastern districts of Iran, especially round Meshed. The Southern Zagros near the Arabian Sea

has a small population that tends to be of mixed Iranian, Afghan, and Hindu stock. Some observers have suggested that in this region there may also be representatives of a primitive nigrito race, related to the hill-tribes of India and of south-east Asia.

With so many differing ethnic groups, it is not surprising to find that several languages are current in Iran. Persian, an Indo-Aryan language related to the languages of western Europe, is spoken in the north and centre of the country, and is the one official language of the State. As the north is by far the most densely peopled region of Iran, the Persian language has an importance somewhat greater than its territorial extent would suggest. Various dialects of Kurdish are current in the north and central Zagros mountains, and alongside these are found several Turki-speaking tribes. Baluchi occurs in the extreme south-east. English and French are spoken by most of the educated classes.

HISTORY

EARLY HISTORY

The Achaemenid empire, the first Persian empire, was founded by Cyrus who revolted against the Median empire in 533 B.C. After the defeat of the Median empire Babylon was taken in 539 B.C., and in 525 B.C. under Cambyses, the successor of Cyrus, Egypt was conquered. The period of conquest was rounded off by Darius who reduced the tribes of the Pontic and Armenian mountains and extended Persian dominion to the Caucasus. The main work of Darius, however, lay not in the conquest but in the organization which he gave to the empire. During his reign wars with Greece broke out and in 490 B.C. the Persian army suffered a major defeat at Marathon; an expedition under Xerxes, the successor of Darius, which set out to avenge this defeat was, after initial successes, defeated at Salamis in 480 B.C. The empire was finally overthrown by Alexander who defeated the Persian army at Arbela in 331 B.C. and then burnt Persepolis, the Achaemenid capital; the last Darius fled and was killed in 330 B.C. Alexander thereafter regarded himself as the head of the Persian empire. The death of Alexander was followed by a struggle between his generals, one of whom, Seleucus, took the whole of Persia, apart from northern Media and founded the Seleucid empire. About the year 250 B.C. a reaction against Hellenism began with the rise of the Parthian empire of the Arsacids. Although by origin nomads from the Turanian steppe, the Arsacids became the wardens of the north-east marches and were largely preoccupied in defending themselves in the east against the Scythians who, with the Tocharians and Sacae, repeatedly attacked the Parthian empire, while in the west they were engaged in fending off attacks by the Romans.

The Arsacids were succeeded by the Sasanians, who, like the Achaemenids, came from Fars and, like them, were Zoroastrians. Ardashir b. Babak, after subduing the neighbouring states (c. A.D. 212), made war on the Arsacid, Artabanus V, whom he eventually defeated.

The empire which he founded largely continued the traditions of the Achaemenids, although it never equalled the Achaemenid empire in extent. The monarchy of the Sasanian period was a religious and civil institution. The monarch, who ruled by divine right, was absolute but his autocracy was limited by the powers of the Zoroastrian hierarchy and the feudal aristocracy. In the reign of Qubad (A.D. 488–531) a movement of revolt, partly social and partly religious, led by Mazdak, gained ground. Under Qubad's successor Anushiravan (531–579) orthodoxy was restored, but at the cost of the imposition of a military despotism. Like the Arsacids before them the Sasanians were occupied in the west with wars with Rome and in the east with repelling inroads of the nomads from Central Asia.

MUSLIM PERSIA

By the beginning of the seventh century A.D. Persia had been greatly weakened by these wars, and when the Muslim Arabs attacked, little effective resistance was offered. The decisive battles were fought at Qadisiyya (A.D. 637) and Nihavand (c. A.D. 641). Persia did not re-emerge as a political entity until the sixteenth century A.D., although with the decline of the Abbasid empire semi-independent and independent dynasties arose in different parts of Persia and at times even incorporated under their rule an area extending beyond the confines of present day Persia. As a result of the Arab conquest Persia became part of the Muslim world. Local administration remained largely in the hands of the indigenous population and many local customs continued to be observed. In due course a new civilization developed in Persia, the unifying force of which was Islam.

With the transfer of the capital of the Islamic empire from Damascus to Baghdad (c. A.D. 750) Persian influence began to be strongly felt in the life of the empire. Islam had already replaced Zoroastrianism and by the tenth century modern Persian, written in the Arabic script and including a large number of Arabic words in its vocabulary, had established itself. Its emergence was of immense importance; the literary tradition for which it became the vehicle has perhaps more than any other factor kept alive a national consciousness among the Persians and preserved the memory of the great Persian empires of the past, however much the details became blurred and even distorted in the course of transmission.

By the eighth century A.D. the Abbasid caliphate had begun to disintegrate and when in the eleventh century control of the north-eastern frontiers broke down, the Ghuzz Turks invaded Persia. This movement, of which the Seljuqs became the leaders, was ethnologically important since it altered the balance of population, the Turkish element from then on being second only to the Persian in numbers and influence. Secondly, it was in the Seljuq empire that the main lines of the politico-economic structure, which was to last in Persia in a modified form down to the twentieth century A.D., were worked out. The basis of this structure was the land assignment, the holder of which was often virtually a petty territorial ruler, who was required, when called upon to do so, to provide the ruler with a military contingent. This system was to some extent forced upon the Seljuqs and others after them, because they were unable to establish an effective system of direct administration or to exercise financial control over their military forces and because they could not integrate the settled and semi-settled elements of the population; the weakness of the system was that, whenever the central control slackened, the empire tended to split up into independent or semi-independent units.

The Seljuq empire itself broke up in the twelfth century into a number of succession states; the thirteenth century saw the Mongol invasion and in 1258 Hulagu, the grandson of Chinghiz (Jenghiz) Khan, sacked Baghdad and destroyed the caliphate. For some years the Ilkhan dynasty, founded by Hulagu, ruled Persia as vassals of the Great Khan in Qaraqorum, but from the reign of Abaqa (1265–1281) onwards they became virtually a Persian dynasty. Their empire, like that of the Seljuqs before them—and for very much the same reason—broke up at the beginning of the fourteenth century into a number of succession states. Towards the end of the century Persia again fell under the dominion of a military conqueror, when Timur, who had started his career as the Warden of the marches in the Oxus-Jaxartes basin against the nomads of Central Asia, undertook a series of military campaigns against Persia between 1381 and 1387. The kingdom founded by him was shortlived and rapidly disintegrated on the death of his son Shahrukh, the western part falling first to the Turkomans of the Black Sheep and then to the Turkomans of the White Sheep, while Transoxania passed into the hands of the Uzbegs.

THE PERSIAN MONARCHY

The sixteenth century saw the foundation of the Safavid empire, which was accompanied by an eastward movement of the Turkomans from Asia Minor back into Persia. For the first time since the Muslim conquest Persia re-emerged as a political unit; her frontiers became more or less fixed, although there was a general movement of contraction in the eighteenth and nineteenth centuries, notably in the north-west and north-east. The foundations of the Safavid empire were laid by Isma'il Safavi (1502–24). He deliberately fostered a sense of separateness and of national unity vis-à-vis the Ottoman Turks with whom the Safavids were engaged in a struggle for supremacy in the west, and the main weapon he used to accomplish his purpose was Shi'ism. Not only the Turks but the majority of his own subjects were at the time Sunni—nevertheless he imposed Shi'ism upon them by force and created among the population of his dominions, many of whom, especially among his immediate followers, were Turks, a sense of national unity as Persians. Apart from a brief interlude under Nadir Shah, Shi'ism has since then remained the majority rite in Persia and is the official rite of the country at the present day. Under Shah Abbas (1587–1629) the Safavid empire reached its zenith and Persia enjoyed a power and prosperity which she has not since achieved.

GREAT POWER RIVALRY

During the Safavid period, intercourse with Europe increased. Various foreign embassies interested mainly in the silk trade reached the Safavid court via Russia and via the Persian Gulf. In the latter area in the early years of the sixteenth century a struggle for supremacy developed between the British and the Dutch. "Factories" were established by the East India Company in the Gulf from the early sixteenth century.

Under the later Safavids internal decline set in and from 1722–30 Persia was subject to Afghan invasion and occupation while in the west and north she was threatened by Turkey and Russia. After the death of Peter the Great there was a temporary slackening of Russian pressure, but the Turks continued to advance and took Tabriz in 1725, peace being eventually made at Hamadan in 1727. The Afghans were finally evicted by Nadir Shah Afshar whose reign (1736–47) was remarkable chiefly for his military exploits. The Afsharids were succeeded by Karim Khan Zand (1750–79) whose relatively peaceful reign was followed by the rise of the Qajars who continued to reign until 1925. Under them the capital was transferred from Isfahan to Teheran. During the Qajar period events in Persia became increasingly affected by Great Power rivalry until not only Persia's foreign policy was dominated by this question, but her internal politics also.

With the growth of British influence in India in the late eighteenth and early nineteenth centuries the main emphasis in Anglo-Persian relations, which during the sixteenth and seventeenth centuries had been on commerce, began to shift to strategy. Persia and the Persian Gulf came to be regarded as one of the main bastions to India and the existence of an independent Persia as a major British interest. In the early nineteenth century fear of a French invasion of India through Persia exercised the mind of the British in India and Whitehall. French envoys were active in

Persia and Mesopotamia from 1796 to 1809, and to counter possible French activities Captain (afterwards Sir John) Malcolm was sent to Persia in 1800 by the Governor-General of India; he concluded a political and commercial treaty with Fath Ali Shah, the main purpose of which was to ensure that the Shah should not receive French agents and would do his utmost to prevent French forces entering Persia. With the defeat of Napoleon in Egypt the matter was no longer regarded as urgent and the agreement was not ratified. Subsequently the French made proposals to Persia for an alliance against Russia and in 1807 Persia concluded the Treaty of Finkenstein with France after which a military mission under General Gardanne came to Persia. In 1808 another British mission was sent under Malcolm. Its object was "first, to detach the Court of Persia from the French alliance and to prevail on that Court to refuse the passage of French troops through the territories subject to Persia, or the admission of French troops into the country. If that cannot be obtained, to admit English troops with a view of opposing the French army in its progress to India, to prevent the creation of any maritime post, and the establishment of French factories on the coast of Persia". Malcolm's task was complicated by the almost simultaneous arrival of a similar mission from Whitehall. In 1809 after the Treaty of Tilsit, which debarred the French from aiding the Shah against Russia, Gardanne was dismissed.

WARS WITH RUSSIA AND TURKEY

Meanwhile the formal annexation of Georgia by Russia in 1801 had been followed by a campaign against Russia. This proved disastrous to Persia and was temporarily brought to an end by the Treaty of Gulistan (1813) by which Persia ceded Georgia, Qara Bagh and seven other provinces. British policy continued to be exercised over the possibility of an invasion of India via Persia and in 1814 the Treaty of Teheran was concluded with Persia by which Great Britain undertook to provide troops or a subsidy in the event of unprovoked aggression on Persia. Although the treaty provided for defence against any European power it was primarily intended to provide against the designs of Russia. In fact it proved ineffective and when the Perso-Russian war recommenced in 1825 Great Britain did not interfere except as a peacemaker and discontinued the subsidy to Persia, who was technically the aggressor. The war was concluded in 1828 by the Treaty of Turkomanchai, under the terms of which Persia ceded Erivan and Nakhjivan and agreed to pay an indemnity; in addition, she was prohibited from having armed vessels on the Caspian.

During this period Persia was also engaged in hostilities with Turkey. Frontier disputes in 1821 culminated in the outbreak of war, which was concluded by the Treaty of Erzerum (1823).

By the nineteenth century the Persian Government had ceased to exercise effective control over the greater part of Khurasan. Russian policy, which became conciliatory towards Persia during the twenty-five years or so after the Treaty of Turko-

manchai, encouraged the Shah to reimpose Persian rule on the eastern provinces. British policy, on the other hand, having come to regard Afghanistan as an important link in the defence of India, urged moderation upon the Persian Government. Nevertheless a Persian expedition set out, took Quchan and Sarakhs and laid siege to Herat; on the death of Abbas Mirza, the heir apparent and commander of the Persian forces in the east at the time, the siege was raised. After the accession of Muhammad Shah in 1834, a new expedition was sent against Herat. The sending of this, too, was encouraged by Russia while the Barakzai chiefs of Kandahar also offered the Persians assistance against their Saduzai rivals in Herat. The siege of Herat began in 1837 but was raised when the Shah was threatened with British intervention. Subsequently local intrigues headed by Sa'id Muhammad had enabled the Persians to enter Herat, and when Muhammad Ysuf Saduzai seized Herat some years later in 1855 and put Sa'id Muhammad to death, relatives of the latter went to Teheran to enlist the support of the Shah who thereupon ordered the governor of Meshed to march on Herat. The seizure of the city by Persia led to the outbreak of the Anglo-Persian war in 1856, which was terminated by the Treaty of Paris (1857) after a British force had occupied the island of Kharg in the Persian Gulf.

In the second half of the century the subjection of the Turkoman tribes by Russia, her capture of Marv in 1854, and the occupation of the Panjeh, meant that Russian influence became dominant in Khurasan in the same way as the advance of Russia to the Araxes after the Persian wars in the early part of the nineteenth century had made Russian influence dominant in Azerbaizhan.

INCREASED FOREIGN INTERVENTION

Internally the second half of the nineteenth century was remarkable chiefly for the beginnings of the modernist movement, which was stimulated on the one hand by internal misgovernment and on the other by increased intervention in the internal affairs of the country by Russia and Britain. Towards the end of the century numerous concessions were granted to foreigners largely in order to pay for the extravagances of the court. The most fantastic of these was the Reuter concession. In 1872 a naturalized British subject, Baron de Reuter, was given by the Shah a monopoly for seventy years of railways and tramways in Persia, all the minerals except gold, silver and precious stones, irrigation, road, factory and telegraph enterprises, and the farm of customs dues for twenty-five years. Eventually this concession was cancelled and permission instead given for the foundation of a Persian state bank with British capital, which was to have the exclusive right to issue banknotes; and accordingly in September 1889 the Imperial Bank of Persia began business. In the same year Dolgoruki obtained for Russia the first option of a railway concession for five years. In November of the following year the railway agreement with Russia was changed into one interdicting all railways whatsoever in Persia. In 1889 after negotiations for foreign loans Belgian officials were put in charge of the customs administration. By the turn of the century there had been "a pronounced sharpening of Anglo-Russian hostility as a consequence of a whole series of Russian actions, not only in northern Persia where Russian ascendancy to a large extent had to be admitted, but as well in southern and eastern Persia which had hitherto been predominantly British preserves". In 1900 a Russian loan was given, to be followed by another in 1902 secured on the customs (excluding those of Fars and the Gulf). Subsequently various short-term advances and subsidies from the Russian treasury including advances to the heir apparent, Muhammad Ali, were made so that by 1906 some £7½ million were owing to the Russians. Under the 1891 Russo-Persian tariff treaty, trade between the two countries had increased, and when under the 1901 Russo-Persian commercial treaty a new customs tariff was announced in 1903, Russian exports to Persia were considerably aided and up to 1914 Russian commerce with Persia continued to grow.

The grant of these various concessions to foreigners and the raising of foreign loans gave rise to growing anxiety on the part of the Persian public. Further, large numbers of Persians had fled the country and were living in exile. When a tobacco monopoly was granted to a British subject in 1890, various elements of the population, including the intellectuals and the religious classes, combined to oppose it. Strikes and riots threatened and the monopoly was rescinded. No effective steps, however, were taken to allay popular discontent. In 1901 protests were made against the loans and mortgages from Russia which were being contracted to pay for Muzaffar ud-Din Shah's journeys to Europe. By 1905–6 the demand for reform had grown in strength and finally on August 5th, 1906, after 12,000 persons had taken sanctuary in the British legation, a constitution was granted. A long struggle then began between the constitutionalists and the Shah. The Cossack Brigade, formed during the reign of Nasir ud-Din Shah, which was under Russian officers and was the most effective military force in the country, played a major part in this struggle and was used by Muhammad Ali Shah to supress the National Assembly in 1908. Civil war ensued and Muhammad Ali Shah's abdication was forced in 1909.

Meanwhile in 1907 the Anglo-Russian convention had been signed. The convention, which included a mutual undertaking to respect the integrity and independence of Persia, divided the country into three areas, that lying to the north of a line passing from Qasri Shirin to Kakh where the Russian, Persian and Afghan frontiers meet in the east, that lying to the south of a line running from Qazik on the Perso-Afghan frontier through Birjand and Kerman to Bandar Abbas on the Persian Gulf, and that lying outside these two areas. Great Britain gave an undertaking not to seek or support others seeking political or economic concessions in the northern area; Russia gave a similar undertaking with reference to the southern area. In the central area the freedom of action of the two parties was not limited and their existing concessions (which included the oil concession granted to D'Arcy in 1901) were maintained. The

conclusion of this convention—which had taken place partly because of a change in the relative strength of the Great Powers and partly because the British Government hoped thereby to terminate Anglo-Russian rivalry in Persia and to prevent further Russian encroachments—came as a shock to Persian opinion which had hoped for much from the support which the British Government had given to the constitutional movement. It was felt that Persian interests had been bartered away by Great Britain for a promise of Russian support in the event of a European war. In fact, the convention failed in its object. Russian pressure continued to be exercised on Persia directly and indirectly. In 1909, 1911 and 1912 Russian troops occupied Tabriz and other towns in north Persia; and in 1911, as a result of Russian pressure, the National Assembly was suspended and the resignation forced of the American Administrator-General of the Finances, Shuster, who had been appointed in the hope of bringing order into the finances of Persia.

THE FIRST WORLD WAR

During the 1914–18 War Persia was nominally neutral but in fact Turkish; British and Russian forces and German agents were active in the country, and on the conclusion of the armistice between Russia and Turkey in 1917 two British expeditionary forces set out for Russia through Persia on what proved to be abortive missions. By the end of the war the internal condition of Persia was chaotic. To the British Government the restoration of order was desirable and with this end in view the Agreement of 1919 was drawn up whereby a number of men were to be lent to reorganize the Persian army and to reform the Ministry of Finance and a loan of £2 million was to be given. There was opposition to this agreement in the U.S.A. and France and in Persia, and the treaty was not ratified. A *coup d'état* took place in 1921, Reza Khan (later Reza Shah) becoming Minister of War. In February 1921 the Soviet-Persian Treaty was signed whereby the U.S.S.R. declared all treaties and conventions concluded with Persia by the Tsarist Government null and void. Under Article VI the U.S.S.R. was permitted "to advance her troops into the Persian interior for the purpose of carrying out the military operations necessary for its defence" in the event of a third party attempting "to carry out a policy of usurpation by means of armed intervention in Persia, or if such a Power should desire to use Persian territory as a base of operations against Russia. . . ." In a letter dated December 12th, 1921, from the Russian diplomatic representative at Teheran to the Persian Minister for Foreign Affairs, it was stated that this article was intended to apply "only to cases in which preparations have been made for a considerable armed attack upon Russia or the Soviet Republics allied to her, by the partisans of the régime which has been overthrown or by its supporters among those foreign Powers which are in a position to assist the enemies of the Workers' and Peasants' Republics and at the same time to possess themselves, by force or by underhand methods, of part of the Persian territory, thereby establishing a base of operations for any attacks—made either directly or through the counter-revolutionary forces—which they might meditate against Russia or the Soviet Republics allied to her".

REZA SHAH 1925-1941

In 1923 Reza Khan became Prime Minister and finally in 1925 the crown of Persia was conferred upon him. His first task was to restore the authority of the central government throughout the country, and the second to place Persia's relations with foreign countries on a basis of equality. All extra-territorial agreements were terminated from 1928. Lighterage and quarantine duties on the Persian littoral of the Persian Gulf, hitherto performed by Great Britain, were transferred to the Persian Government in 1930. The Indo-European Telegraph Company, which had been in operation since 1872, had almost entirely been withdrawn by 1931 and the British coaling stations were transferred from Basidu and Henjam to Bahrain in 1935.

In 1932 the cancellation of the Anglo-Persian Oil Company's concession was announced by Persia. The original concession obtained by D'Arcy in 1901 had been taken over by the Anglo-Persian Oil Company (later the Anglo-Iranian Oil Company) in 1909 and the British Government had acquired a controlling interest in the company in 1914. Thenceforward the main emphasis of British policy towards Persia had been on oil rather than strategy, though from 1941 onwards the strategic aspect again became important. The Persian Government's action in cancelling the concession was referred to the League of Nations. Eventually an agreement was concluded in 1933 for a new concession whereby the concession area was materially reduced and the royalty to be paid to the Persian Government increased. The concession was to run to 1993.

Internally Reza Shah's policy aimed at modernization and autarchy. In the later years of his reign the Government became increasingly totalitarian in its nature. Compulsory military service was introduced and the army much increased in size. Communications were greatly improved; the construction of a trans-Persian railway was begun. Education was remodelled on western lines. Women were no longer obliged to wear the veil after 1936. Foreign trade was made a state monopoly, currency and clearing restrictions were established. These arrangements fitted in with the economy of Germany and by the outbreak of World War II, Germany had acquired considerable commercial and political influence in Persia.

On the outbreak of war Persia declared her neutrality. In 1941 the Allies demanded a reduction in the number of Germans in the country, and when no satisfaction was obtained sent another communication demanding the expulsion of all German nationals, except such as were essential to Persian economy and harmless to the Allies. This demand was not complied with and on August 26th, 1941, Persia was invaded. Hostilities lasted some two days. On September 16th Reza Shah abdicated in favour of his son Muhammad Reza. In January 1942 a Tripartite Treaty of Alliance was concluded with Great Britain and the U.S.S.R.

whereby Great Britain and the U.S.S.R. undertook jointly and severally "to respect the territorial integrity, sovereignty and political independence of Persia" and "to defend Persia by all means in their command from aggression" and the Persian Government undertook to give the Allies for certain military purposes the unrestricted right to use, maintain and guard, and in the case of military necessity, to control, all means of communications in Persia. Allied forces were to be withdrawn not later than six months after the conclusion of hostilities between the Allied Powers and Germany and her associates. In so far as the establishment of communications with the U.S.S.R. was concerned the Treaty was effective; its operation in other respects was less satisfactory. In the Russian zone of occupation the Persian authorities were denied freedom of movement and effective administration made impossible. American advisers were appointed by the Persian Government in 1942 and 1943 in the hope of reorganizing certain aspects of the administration. Their efforts were for a variety of reasons in no case attended by more than a limited measure of success and in due course their services were terminated.

In 1943 a British company applied for an oil concession in south-east Persia and in 1944 the Socony Vacuum and Sinclair Oil Companies made various proposals to the Persian Government. In September the Persian Cabinet issued a decree deferring the grant of oil concessions till after the war. The U.S.S.R. meanwhile asked for an oil concession in the north and brought heavy, though unavailing, pressure to bear on the Persian Government to accede to this demand. Persian security forces were prevented by Soviet forces from entering Azerbaizhan or the Caspian Provinces and an autonomous government was set up in Azerbaizhan with Russian support in December 1945. In January 1946 the Persian Government had recourse to the Security Council. In March the Tripartite Treaty expired and British and American forces evacuated Persia, Soviet forces remaining. The Persian Government again presented a note to the Security Council. In April an oral understanding, confirmed by an exchange of letters between the Persian Prime Minister and the Soviet Ambassador, was arrived at whereby a joint Soviet-Persian company to exploit the oil in the northern provinces was to be formed. In May Soviet forces evacuated the country. Soviet pressure, however, continued to be exerted through the Tudeh party, the Democrat movement in Azerbaizhan, and the Kurdish autonomy movement, and the Persian Government was unable to re-enter Azerbaizhan until December. In the following October, the Soviet Oil Agreement was presented to the National Assembly but was not ratified. In October 1947 an agreement was signed with America, providing for a U.S. military mission in Persia to co-operate with the Persian ministry of war in "enhancing the efficiency of the Persian army".

NATIONALIZING THE OIL INDUSTRY

Meanwhile unrest and discontent at internal misgovernment increased, culminating in the Nationalist movement of 1950/51. In July 1949 a Supplemental Oil Agreement with the Anglo-Iranian Oil Company was initialled. Opposition to this agreement (whereby Persia was offered considerable financial gains) was strong. In November 1950 the oil commission of the National Assembly recommended its rejection. Meanwhile Persia had received a loan of $25 million from the Export & Import Bank of Washington and a grant of $500,000 under the Point IV allocation. Subsequently in 1952 the Point IV aid programme was expanded. In April 1951 the National Assembly passed a Bill for the nationalization of the oil industry, and in May Dr. Muhammad Musaddiq, who had led the campaign for nationalization of oil, became Prime Minister. In spite of efforts to involve the International Court of Justice, the *status quo* could not be maintained in Persia and the Anglo-Iranian Oil Company evacuated the country, being unable to continue operations.

On July 22nd, 1952, the International Court found that it had no jurisdiction in the oil dispute. This decision, however, was not a decision on the merits of the case. The Company accordingly maintained its claim to be entitled to all crude oil and oil products derived from the area covered by its concession agreement, and stated its intention to take such action as was necessary to protect its interests. American policy showed an increasing interest in Persian affairs. During the period August to October 1952, considerable correspondence passed between the British, American and Persian Governments in the oil dispute, culminating in a joint offer by Sir Winston Churchill and President Truman, making proposals concerning the assessment of the compensation to be paid to the Anglo-Iranian Oil Company and the re-starting of the flow of oil to world markets. The Persian Government rejected these proposals and put forward counter proposals which were unacceptable. On October 22nd the Persian Government broke off diplomatic relations with Great Britain. Further Anglo-American proposals for an oil settlement were put forward in February 1953, which the Persian Government rejected. Meanwhile dissension between Musaddiq and some of his supporters broke out, and a rift also developed between him and the Shah. The economic situation of the country began to deteriorate rapidly, culminating in the overthrow of Mussadiq by General Zahedi in August 1953. Musaddiq was tried and sentenced to three years solitary confinement for trying to overthrow the régime and illegally dissolving the *majlis*.

The new government resumed diplomatic relations with Great Britain in December 1953, and negotiations with British and American oil interests began for the solution of the oil problem. In September 1954 an agreement was signed, and ratified by the *majlis* and senate in October, granting a concession to a consortium of eight companies (subsequently increased to seventeen) on a percentage basis.

It was also agreed that the claims of the Anglo-Iranian Oil Company and the Persian Government against each other were to be settled by the payment of a lump sum to the Company, which was also to receive compensation from the other members of the consortium. The profits arising within Persia from the oil operations were to be equally shared between the Persian Government and the consortium. The agreement was for a period of twenty-five years with provision for three five-year extensions, conditional upon a progressive reduction of the original area. The National Iranian Oil Company was to operate the Naft-i Shah oilfield and the Kermanshah refinery to meet part of Persia's own needs and to handle the distribution of oil products in Persia and to be responsible for all facilities and services not directly part of the producing, refining, and transport operations of the two operating companies set up under the agreement. The greater part of the cost of these facilities and services, which would include industrial training, public transport, road maintenance, housing, medical care, and social welfare, would be recovered by the NIOC from the operating companies.

GROWING POWER OF THE SHAH

Internally order was restored. The Tudeh party was proscribed, but continued to exist underground, and in January and August 1954, Tudeh conspiracies were uncovered. The failure of the Government to push forward actively with reform, however, led in due course to a reappearance of unrest and discontent. In April 1955 Zahedi resigned and was succeeded by Ala, the Shah henceforward taking a more active part in the administration. In October, Persia joined the Baghdad Pact. The change of government, however, did not materially lessen the mounting discontent, and in November an attempt was made on the Prime Minister's life. Meanwhile, the country had not recovered from the financial difficulties brought on by the Musaddiq régime, in spite of the considerable financial aid granted to Persia by the U.S.A. to enable the country to carry on until oil revenues began to come in, and over 800 million U.S. dollars were poured into Iran between the end of the Second World War and September 1960. On March 5th, 1959, a bilateral defence agreement was signed in Ankara between the United States and Iran. Under the agreement the Government of the United States "will, in case of aggression, take such appropriate action, including the use of armed force, as may be mutually agreed, and as envisaged in the Joint Resolution to promote peace and security in the Middle East". (The Joint Resolution refers to the "Eisenhower Doctrine".)

Relations with the U.S.S.R. in the years following the fall of Musaddiq were not cordial, but in December 1954 an agreement providing for (1) the repayment by the U.S.S.R. of her war debts to Persia for goods supplied and services rendered, and (2) mapping of the revised frontiers was signed.

On April 3rd, 1957, Hussein Ala resigned and was succeeded as Prime Minister by Dr. Manoutchehr Egbal, who formed a new government. Immediately after taking office Dr. Egbal issued a decree ending martial law and declared his intention of forming a democratic two-party system, in accordance with the desires of the Shah. In February 1958, a pro-Government Nation Party was formed. An Opposition People's Party had been formed in 1957. Elections contested by both these political parties disclosed electoral irregularities, and in August 1960 Jaafar Sharif-Emami replaced Dr. Egbal as Prime Minister.

In May 1961, however, Dr. Emami resigned as a result of criticism of his handling of a teachers' strike, and the Shah called upon Dr. Ali Amini, the leader of the opposition, to form a new government.

Dr. Amini quickly took stern measures to halt the political and economic chaos in Iran. A drive against corruption in the Government and civil service was coupled with policies of land reform, decentralization of administration, control of government expenditure and limitation of luxury imports. Both Houses of Parliament were dissolved pending the passing of a new electoral law which would make free and fair elections possible. Postponement of elections, in July 1962, led to disorder in Teheran, and the added difficulty of producing a reasonably balanced budget led Dr. Amini to tender his resignation.

A new government was quickly formed by Mr. Assadollah Alam, the leader of the *Mardom* (People's) Party. Mr. Alam, one of Iran's largest landowners and administrator of the Pahlavi Foundation, had previously distributed much of his land voluntarily amongst the peasants. He stated that Iran would remain closely linked to the West, and that he would continue the land reform programme and the struggle against internal political corruption. A reform programme was approved by a national referendum held in January 1963.

REFORMS OF THE SHAH

In 1950 the Shah began distributing his estate amongst the peasants. By the end of 1963 he had disposed of all his Crown Properties. The Pahlavi Foundation was established in 1958 and received considerable gifts from the Shah for the purpose of improving standards of education, health and social welfare amongst the poorer classes. In October 1961 the Shah created the £40 million Pahlavi Dynasty Trust, the income of which was used for social, educational and health services for the Iranian people.

In January 1963 a referendum was held, as a result of which overwhelming approval was given to the Shah's six-point plan for the distribution of lands among the peasants, the promotion of literacy, the emancipation of women, etc. The break-up of great estates began almost immediately, and the programme was finally completed in September 1971; another important measure was the formation of the Literacy Corps (and later of the Health Corps), in which students could serve their period of national service as teachers, working in the villages.

The elections scheduled for July 1963 eventually took place in September of that year. The result was an overwhelming victory for the National Union of Mr. Alam; his party was in fact a coalition of several political groups, all pledged to support the reform programme of the Shah. The elections, in which for the first time women were allowed to vote, were held in the face of strenuous opposition from the left-wing parties of Iran, notably the National Front and the Communist Tudeh party, which called unsuccessfully for a boycott. The Shah called on the new Parliament to inaugurate a new 20-year programme of economic and social reform and political development and he also announced a second phase of the land reform programme, whereby it was hoped that another 20,000 villages would be added to the 10,000 already handed over to the tenants. The Alam government continued until March 1964, when without tendering any reason, Mr. Alam resigned. The new leader was Hassan Ali Mansur, a former Minister and founder of the Progressive Centre, which had played a prominent part in the coalition of Mr. Alam the previous year. In December 1963 he had formed the New Iran Party, which by now had the support of some 150 members of the *majlis*. The second stage of the land reform plan was placed before the *majlis* in May; this aimed to break down the great estates more thoroughly; the maximum permissible size was to be from 120 hectares in arid regions to 30 hectares in more fertile areas.

REGIONAL CO-OPERATION

In July 1964 the Heads of State of Iran, Turkey and Pakistan formed a new tri-partite scheme of collaboration known as "Regional Co-operation for Development". It involved close collaboration in the economic and technical spheres, and many projects were planned together in the fields of communications, agriculture, industry, education, health, tourism and regional development; cultural links, based on the common Islamic heritage of the three nations, were also strengthened.

On January 21st, 1965, Mr. Mansur was assassinated by members of the right-wing religious sect Fedayan Islam, but there was no suggestion that the murder was other than an internal affair. The assassins were reportedly followers of the Ayatollah Ruhollah Khomeini, a Shi'i Muslim religious leader exiled in 1964 for his opposition to the Shah's reforms.

Amir Abbas Hoveida, the Finance Minister, was immediately appointed Acting Premier, and became Prime Minister on the day following Mr. Mansur's death, retaining his post at the Finance Ministry. He pledged himself to the continuation of his predecessor's policies, and was given the massive support of the *majlis*. Although elections took place in 1967, 1971 and 1975, and there were several Cabinet reshuffles, Mr. Hoveida continued as Prime Minister until August 1977, when he was succeeded by Dr. Jamshid Amouzegar.

FOREIGN RELATIONS

Iran began a period of good relations with the U.S.S.R. in 1964/65 when various mutually beneficial trading and technical agreements were signed, and a regular air service between Teheran and Moscow was inaugurated. It had been an avowed part of Mr. Mansur's policy that Iran should be as much interested in maintaining links with the Soviet Union as with the West. In June 1965 the Shah visited Moscow, and in

October an agreement was signed for the construction by Soviet engineers of a steel mill. Relations with Iraq in early 1966 became strained when the long-standing disagreement over the Shatt-al-Arab erupted into a series of border incidents.

The magnificent coronation of the Shah in October 1967 seemed to augur forthcoming prosperity and the apparent stability of Iran was emphasized, not only by economic development and by the organization of international gatherings, but also by the formal ending in November of U.S. economic aid under the "Point Four" scheme. Iran, which had been the first country to accept this aid in 1951, was now the second (after the Republic of China) to find herself able to dispense with it. Military aid, however, was to continue. At the same time economic co-operation with the U.S.S.R. was developed, and an agreement was made for the purchase of £40,000,000 of munitions, the first time the Soviet Union had concluded an arms transaction with a member of the Western bloc.

In January 1968 the British Government announced its decision to withdraw all its forces from the Gulf by the end of 1971. Since these forces had apparently helped to preserve the local status quo, a revival of the ancient rivalry between Arabs and Persians over supremacy in the Gulf then seemed a likely prospect following their removal. The Iranian Government's reiteration of its claim to Bahrain in February 1968 did not help relations with the Arab world, but Iran cautiously welcomed the proposed Federation of Arab Emirates (which it was thought would incorporate Bahrain).

A UN Mission visiting Bahrain in early 1970 found that the large Arab majority overwhelmingly preferred full independence to joining Iran or remaining a British protectorate. Iran had previously agreed to accept the mission's findings, and it did so without complaint, though expressing concern for the future of Iranians in the Gulf states. In June 1970 a dispute with other Gulf states also arose over Iran's claim to the islands of Abu Musa and the Tumbs belonging to Sharjah and Ras al Khaimah respectively. The dispute was only settled at the beginning of December 1971. The Sheikh of Sharjah agreed to share his island of Abu Musa with Iran. The Sheikh of Ras al Khaimah was less accommodating, so Iran invaded his possessions of the Greater and Lesser Tumbs and took them by force. Since occupying Abu Musa and the Tumbs Iran has developed them as military bases to command the straits of Hormuz which lie at the neck of the Gulf. Iran regarded maintaining freedom of passage through the Straits of Hormuz as vital to her strategic and economic interests, and it is for this reason that she strengthened military forces in the region and also sent troops to help the Sultan of Oman in his struggle against the rebels of the Popular Front for the Liberation of Oman (PFLO). Iranian forces were finally withdrawn in early 1979, after the fall of the Shah.

Iran's relations with the more radical Arab states were less friendly under the Shah. These states had long been suspicious of Iran's close ties with the West, and especially of the generous American military aid to the powerful Iranian armed forces. Moreover, the Arab States distrusted Iran's attitude to Israel. Although no formal diplomatic links existed, trade, particularly in oil, was conducted with Israel, and one of the early acts of the Khomeini regime in early 1979 was to end any ties with Israel and to align Iran firmly behind the Arab cause, by allowing, for example, the opening of a PLO office in Teheran.

Iran's only frontier with an Arab state is with Iraq. Near the Gulf the border is delineated by the Shatt al-Arab waterway, and, by the terms of the 1937 treaty, it actually runs along the eastern, i.e. Iranian bank; thus Iraq legally has sovereignty over the whole waterway. Iran has long resented this position and in April 1969 it decided to abrogate the treaty by sending Iranian vessels flying the national flag through the waterway, whilst heavy naval forces stood by. The aim was apparently to force a re-negotiation of the treaty. In September 1969, there were further armed clashes on the border—reports differed as to the extent of the casualties. In January 1970, Iraq accused the Iranian Government of backing the abortive *coup* in Iraq, and diplomatic relations between the two countries were broken.

Relations between the two countries continued to be bad until diplomatic relations between Iran and Iraq were restored soon after the outbreak of the Arab-Israeli war in October 1973, but border incidents continued and it was therefore something of a surprise when, at the OPEC meeting in Algiers in March 1975, it was announced that the Shah and Sadam Hussein (then Vice-President of the Iraqi Revolution Command Council) had signed an agreement which "completely eliminated the conflict between the two brotherly countries". Not only did this agreement settle the outstanding border differences, but it also deprived the Kurds in Iraq of the help which they had been receiving from Iran in their struggle against the Iraqi Government, thus causing a Kurdish collapse and a virtual end to the Kurdish war.

The border agreement provided that Iran and Iraq would define their frontiers on the basis of the Protocol of Constantinople of 1913 and the verbal agreement on frontiers of 1914, and that the Shatt al-Arab frontier would be defined according to the Thalweg Line (i.e. the middle of the deepest shipping channel). The treaty giving effect to this agreement was signed on June 15th, 1975, and later became one of the key issues of the Gulf War with Iraq which broke out in September 1980 (*see* below).

INTERNAL PROBLEMS

Internally, signs of opposition to the Shah's régime, never far from the surface of Iranian life, became more and more evident as the celebrations for the 2,500th anniversary of the Persian monarchy were in preparation for October 1971. The combination of the very unequal distribution of the enormous earnings from oil and the suppression of any sign of dissent was made more politically explosive as the lavishness of the celebrations and the massiveness of the security precautions began to make their impact. From then, until the final fall of the Shah in early 1979, there were countless stories of the stifling of opposition by the ruthless activities of SAVAK, the Government security agency.

In March 1975 the Shah, dissatisfied with the current structure of party politics in Iran and wanting to weld together all those who supported the principles of his "White Revolution" policy (later known as the "Revolution of the Shah and People"), announced the formation of a single party system, the Iran National Resurgence Party (*Rastakhiz*), with the Prime Minister, Amir Abbas Hoveida, as Secretary-General. By 1978 it became clear that the single-party *Rastakhiz* system was not solving the problem of internal opposition in Iran, but few people in early 1978 would have forecast that, within a year, a completely new political system was to be introduced.

FALL OF THE SHAH

Demonstrations, particularly at the universities, and political violence built up during 1977 and 1978. All the Shah's attempts to control the situation, first by greater liberalization and then by firmer suppression, proved of little avail. In August 1977 Dr. Jamshid Amouzegar, Secretary-General of *Rastakhiz*, replaced the long-serving Amir Abbas Hoveida as Prime Minister but he resigned a year later. In August 1978 Jaafar Sharif-Emami was appointed Prime Minister (an office he had previously held in 1960–61) and, in response to the emerging mood of the country, promised that his government would observe Islamic tenets. Unrest continued, however. Martial law was introduced in September, and in November the Shah set up a military government headed by the Army Chief of Staff, General Gholamreza Azhari. Censorship was imposed, and strikes in the oil industry and public services presented the Shah with a desperate situation, and in early January 1979 he charged Dr. Shapour Bakhtiar, a former Deputy Leader of the National Front, with forming a "last-chance" government. Dr. Bakhtiar undertook to dissolve SAVAK (the security police), stop the export of oil to South Africa and Israel and support the Palestinians. However, opposition to the Shah continued to such an extent that he left the country on January 15th, never to return.

The opposition within Iran had stemmed from two main sources, with little in common except their desire to overthrow the Shah. By the time the Shah left Iran opposition from the left and the more liberal National Front had been overshadowed by the success of the opposition coming from the exiled religious leader Ayatollah Khomeini, who conducted his campaign from France where he had arrived in early October after 14 years of exile in Iraq for opposing the Shah's "White Revolution" because it conflicted with traditional Islamic values.

In January Khomeini formed an Islamic Revolutionary Council from near Paris and pressure in Iran grew for his return. The Bakhtiar Government tried to delay his return for as long as possible, but on February 1st Khomeini arrived in Teheran from Paris to a tumultuous welcome from the Iranian people. Bakhtiar refused to recognize Khomeini but, after several demonstrations and outbreaks of violence, the army withdrew its support from Dr. Bakhtiar and he resigned on February 11th. Dr. Mehdi Bazargan, who had been named "Provisional Prime Minister" by Khomeini on February 6th, formed a provisional government later in the month but it soon became clear that real power rested with Khomeini's 15-man Islamic Revolutionary Council.

IRAN UNDER AYATOLLAH KHOMEINI

Although Khomeini achieved his position as the *de facto* leader of Iran on the crest of a wave of public euphoria, the difficulties of putting into practice the ideals of the Islamic Revolution have severely tested the Revolutionary Government.

From the very outset there was conflict between the Islamic Revolutionary Council, which gave effect to its policies through a network of *Komitehs*, and the Prime Minister, Dr. Bazargan—an inheritance which President Bani-Sadr (*see* below) also found troublesome later.

Tension over Iran's ethnic minorities, either not in evidence or stifled under the Shah, has been a recurring problem since the revolution. Most serious has been the demand for autonomy from the Kurds in the west, which has often led to open warfare in that area. Other minorities have also demanded autonomy. These include the Baluchis in the south-east, the Turkomans in the north-east and the Azerbaijanis in the north-west. Conflict with the Arabs in the south-west has also interacted with hostile relations with Iraq, which later developed into the Gulf War in September 1980 (*see* below). It was also representatives of this minority who were responsible for the holding of Iranian and other hostages in the Iranian Embassy in London from April 30th to May 5th, 1980, in a siege which was dramatically broken by the storming of the Embassy by the British SAS. The position has been complicated by the fact that these minorities are Sunni Muslims, while the Khomeini regime and the majority of Iranians are Shi'ite.

Another major difficulty has been Iran's relations with the U.S.A. and, as an extension of that, with the Western world. Khomeini's regime from the outset had condemned previous American interference in Iranian affairs, and when on November 4th, 1979, Iranian students seized 53 hostages in the U.S. Embassy in Teheran, Khomeini was quite ready to offer his support to the students who demanded the return of the Shah (then in the U.S.A.) to Iran to face trial. This problem dominated relations with the U.S.A. for the next 14 months, and was not resolved by the death of the Shah in Egypt on July 27th, 1980. The *Majlis*, elected in March and May 1980, was slow to grapple with the problem of the hostages, who were not released until January 20th, 1981.

Another problem has been the range of Islamic fervour in Iran. Ayatollah Khalkhali, at one time Chief Justice of the Islamic Revolutionary Courts, set about his task with extraordinary fervour and by May

1980 claimed to have ordered more than 300 executions. Moreover, in May 1980 he destroyed the tomb of Reza Shah, an action which was later condemned by President Bani-Sadr who pointed out that such actions worked against the revolution. Not all Iranians approved of the ardour with which the "Bureau to Stop Bad Acts" set about cleaning up the moral lapses in Iranian society.

Khomeini's health presented a further problem. Bedridden in the early months of 1980, his statements were often read for him, mainly by his son Sayid Ahmed, and there was some speculation about who might succeed him as *faghih*, the religious leader who "carries the burden of leadership". The favourite seems to be Ayatollah Hussein Ali Montazeri, who succeeded Ayatollah Taleghani as leading Ayatollah of Teheran after the latter's death in the Autumn of 1979. Since 1981 there has been some apparent improvement in Khomeini's health.

CONSTITUTIONAL DEVELOPMENT

At the end of March 1979 Khomeini held a referendum on the question "Do you favour an Islamic Republic?". The result was an almost unanimous "yes" and on April 1st an Islamic Republic was declared. A draft constitution proposed that Iran be governed by a President, Prime Minister and a single-chamber Islamic Consultative Assembly (*Majlis*) of 270 deputies. Although there was pressure in Iran to submit the draft constitution to a newly-elected Constituent Assembly, Khomeini submitted it for revision to a "Council of Experts" consisting of 75 members who were elected on August 3rd. After prolonged deliberations the revised constitution was submitted to a referendum at the beginning of December 1979. The most important change from the draft constitution was provision for a *velayat faghih* (religious leader) who initially is Ayatollah Khomeini, who has the office for the rest of his natural life. The *faghih* has extensive powers (*see* The Constitution) which secure for him the most important levers of power in Iran. Votes against the constitution were negligible.

Presidential elections followed on January 25th, 1980, and resulted in a convincing win for Abolhasan Bani-Sadr, who polled about 75 per cent of the votes. All this time the Islamic Revolutionary Council had been taking the decisions on running the country, although there was a government headed by Dr. Mehdi Bazargan until his resignation in mid-November 1979 over Khomeini's support for the retention of the American hostages. Thereafter the Islamic Revolutionary Council, with President Bani-Sadr becoming its Chairman in February 1980, ruled more openly, appointing Ministers to run the country until elections to the *Majlis* in the Spring of 1980.

The elections took place in two rounds, on March 14th and May 9th, 1980. 3,300 candidates contested 270 seats, 30 of which were in Teheran. 98 deputies were elected outright at the first round, and the remainder were in contention for the second round. Disturbances in Kurdish areas and various allegations of fraud resulted in the fact that when the *Majlis*

began its first session on May 28th, 1980, only 234 deputies had been decided, and of those only 213 had received their credentials. It was clear, however, that the Islamic Republican Party, the party identified with the policies of Ayatollah Khomeini and led by Ayatollah Beheshti, was in a majority, claiming 130 seats. Ayatollah Beheshti presented a threat to the leadership of President Bani-Sadr. On May 7th Khomeini had given Bani-Sadr authority to appoint a Prime Minister until the *Majlis* met, but Beheshti successfully prevented this, insisting that this appointment be left to the *Majlis*.

Subsequent political development in Iran has been marked by faction-fighting and confusion. The Islamic Revolutionary Council was dissolved on July 18th, but there followed a delay in forming a government. Many of the Ministers proposed by the *Majlis* and backed by the Islamic Republican Party were unacceptable to President Bani-Sadr. He only agreed to the appointment of Muhammad Ali Rajai as Prime Minister with reluctance, doubting his competence. The Ministries of Finance and Economic Affairs, Commerce and Foreign Affairs were left without Ministers for some months, and a feud developed between President Bani-Sadr on the one hand and Rajai and the Islamic Republican Party on the other. An abortive three-man commission tried to resolve these differences in March 1981, but on June 10th Khomeini dismissed Bani-Sadr as Commander-in-Chief of the Armed Forces. A few days later he was deprived of the Presidency and later fled to France, where he formed a "National Council of Resistance" in alliance with Massoud Rajavi, the former leader of the Mujaheddin Khalq. A three-man Presidential Council replaced Bani-Sadr after his dismissal, until new Presidential elections could be held on July 24th. On June 28th, however, a bomb exploded at the Headquarters of the Islamic Republican Party, killing Ayatollah Beheshti (the Chief Justice and Head of the Islamic Republican Party), four Cabinet ministers, six deputy ministers and 20 parliamentary deputies.

On July 24th the Presidential elections took place as arranged and resulted in a win for the Prime Minister, Muhammad Ali Rajai. Muhammad Javad Bahonar then became Prime Minister of a Government introduced to the *Majlis* on August 13th. A further bomb outrage occurred on August 29th, this time killing both the President (Rajai) and the Prime Minister (Bahonar). Ayatollah Muhammad Reza Mahdavi Kani became Prime Minister in September, and another round of Presidential elections was held on October 2nd. Hojatoleslam Ali Khamenei, a leading figure of the Islamic Republican Party, was elected President, winning more than 16 million of the 16.8 million votes cast. At the end of October, after the resignation of Ayatollah Muhammad Reza Mahdavi Kani, Mir Hussein Moussavi was appointed Prime Minister.

THE GULF WAR

It was generally thought by outsiders at this time that the whole Iranian Islamic Revolution was about to crumble. In addition to internal troubles, Iran had been fighting "the Gulf War" with Iraq for over a year. Fighting between the two countries had begun after Iran ignored Iraqi demands for the withdrawal of Iranian forces from Zain ul Qos, on the border between the two countries. Iraq maintained that this territory should have been returned to Iraq under the 1975 agreement with Iraq. Iran therefore abrogated the 1975 Shatt al-Arab agreement and invaded Iran on September 22nd, 1980. Most observers now believe that this was no more than a pretext on Iraq's part: Saddam Hussein's real objective being to topple what he regarded as the threatening but vulnerable Iranian regime.

Iranian resistance was spirited, and a position of stalemate was soon reached along a 300-mile front. Various international peace missions all proved of no avail, and in the spring of 1982 the Iranian forces broke the stalemate by launching two offensives, the first in the Shush-Dezful area in March, and the second on a 60-mile front south of Susangerd to Khorramshahr at the end of April. Both offensives met with considerable success, with the Iranians recapturing Khorramshahr (Khuninshahr) in mid-May and the prospect of carrying the war into Iraqi territory.

These successes have indicated that the Iranian regime possesses greater resilience than was at one time

thought possible. To have even survived the bomb outrages of mid-1981 is no mean achievement. There are still numerous threats to the regime, however. In March 1982 Dr. Abdul-Rahman Qassemlou, the Secretary-General of the Democratic Party of Iranian Kurdistan, claimed that militant Kurds still controlled over 70,000 square kilometres of Iranian territory. An extended campaign of suppression was being waged against the Mujaheddin Khalq, and the government achieved some success in this respect when in February they killed Musa Khiabani, the Mujaheddin leader in Iran.

In April an anti-Government plot was uncovered in which Ayatollah Shariatmadari, one of Iran's leading *mullahs*, was at first thought to be implicated. He subsequently denied this, but admitted that he knew of the plot, in which former Foreign Minister Sadeq Ghotbzadeh was implicated deeply enough for him to have to stand trial.

By the end of June 1982 it seemed that the Gulf War was virtually over. On June 20th Saddam Hussein announced that Iraqi troops had started to withdraw from Iranian territory and would complete their pull-out within ten days. An Iraqi Government and party shake-up followed the withdrawal, and speculation continued about the stability of Saddam Hussein's regime.

ECONOMIC SURVEY

At the census of November 1966 the population was returned as 25,788,722. Of this total, some 9,800,000 were urban residents. The November 1976 census showed a total population of 33,591,875, and the mid-1980 estimate was 37,447,000. Since the mid-1930s there has been an accelerating migration from rural to urban areas. The population of Teheran and its suburbs reached an estimated 4,496,159 in 1976; one estimate put it at 7 million at the end of 1981. Much of the population is concentrated in the fertile northern areas of the country while the central desert lands are sparsely populated. The rate of population growth, 2.7 per cent annually in the late 1970s, is higher than in the past, owing to the reduction in deaths from malnutrition and famine and great advances in public health, particularly the virtual eradication of malaria over wide areas. The size of the nomadic population, now between 3 and 4 million, has declined since the 1940s, as a result of government attempts to settle the nomads in villages. These tribes are in fact semi-nomadic, moving between traditional winter quarters in the plains, and summer pastures in the mountains.

In 1978, the last year of the Shah's reign, per caput income was calculated at about U.S. $2,500, up from about $200 in 1963. During the period of the Fourth Plan (1968–73) Iran's Gross National Product (G.N.P.) rose at an annual average of 11.2 per cent in real terms. Over the period of the 1973–78 Plan G.N.P. rose in real terms from $17,000 million to $55,300 million. The growth rate of G.N.P., which was as much as 41 per cent in 1974/75, slowed down

to about 17 per cent the following year, due to declining oil revenues (which provided about 40 per cent of the total G.N.P.). In real terms the Gross Domestic Product (G.D.P.) was estimated to have grown by as little as 2.6 per cent in 1975/76. Iran's balance of payments difficulties during that year highlighted many problems connected with the rapid growth it had been experiencing, including the acute lack of skilled manpower at all levels which made ambitious development projects difficult to implement. In 1976/77 G.D.P. grew at over 14 per cent in real terms, but during 1977 the economy showed signs of further deceleration, partly as a result of very serious power shortages which hit the industrial sector. Total G.D.P. for 1977/78 was estimated at $56,500 million, representing growth in real terms of about 10 per cent over the previous year.

In the latter part of 1978 these trends continued and, combined with politically motivated industrial and business strikes, left the economy in near paralysis. The Shah felt forced to announce some cutbacks in industrial projects and military equipment purchases. By the time the Shah's last Prime Minister was ousted, announced cutbacks totalled over $15,000—mostly in U.S. and British-made military equipment.

The revolutionary government that followed the Shah's downfall reassessed nearly all Iran's economic and social strategies. The new leaders announced that priority would be given to low growth rates, a concentration on small-scale projects in industry, emphasis on traditional agriculture and stringent control of oil exports. Three years after the revolution Iran's economy remains in deep crisis. The war with Iraq, loss of forecast oil revenues in mid-1980 as the world went into recession, and failure of public utilities (mainly electricity) are among the problems advanced to account for a deteriorating economic situation. The war has taken its toll of physical damage in the south, with major settlements reduced to rubble and the destruction of oil installations and factories. However, political conflicts and confusion over the management of the economy have aggravated these problems and have resulted in contradictions in policy and economic mismanagement.

Early in 1981 President Bani-Sadr acknowledged that the economy was in deep recession, with national income falling steadily. He reported that agricultural output remained static, industrial production had fallen dramatically and even the minimum oil output required for national survival was not being attained. The poor returns to the major economic sectors had resulted in falls in G.D.P. of 13 per cent in 1979/80 and 10 per cent in 1980/81. At the same time, Ayatollah Khomeini warned Iranians that there would be ten years of austerity ahead before the country became productive enough to cover its needs from domestic sources.

The new government of Hojatoleslam Khamenei, which took office in October 1981, announced that it would implement a wide range of economic reforms, including radical reform of agriculture and worker participation in industrial management. If carried out, these changes could threaten further disruption to domestic agriculture and industry. The future looks bleak, with economic decline, growing oil dependence (despite a reduction in exports of crude oil), reliance on imports of vital commodities and a burgeoning and youthful population. Unemployment is already considerable—an estimated 2–3 million in 1981 out of a non-agricultural labour force of 7.5) million. The standard of living of many Iranians has, in fact, fallen since the Revolution.

AGRICULTURE

Out of a total surface area of 165 million hectares, 19 million (11.5 per cent) are under cultivation and over half is classified as uncultivable, non-agricultural land. About 5.3 million hectares of agricultural land are fed with perennial irrigation water supplies from modern water-storage systems or from the ancient system of qanats (underground water channels), although these fell into disrepair in recent years. Rain-fed agriculture is important in the western provinces of Kermanshah, Kurdestan and Azerbaizhan. Agriculture is the principal economic activity of the Iranian people. However, while agriculture employs over 35 per cent of the total labour force, it has accounted for less than 15 per cent of G.D.P., and as a result peasants' incomes remain generally low. The chief factors limiting the size of agricultural production are inadequate communications, limiting access to markets; poor seeds, implements and techniques of cultivation; lack of water and under-capitalization, chiefly the result of the low

income of the peasant. About four-fifths of all farms are of less than 11 hectares. Iran was self-sufficient in foodstuffs until the late 1960s but then began importing vast quantities, due to the failure of agricultural output to keep pace with increasing domestic consumption and the failure of the Government to produce a really sound agricultural policy. Although official figures gave a 7 per cent annual growth rate for the agricultural sector in the past few years (compared with the Fifth Plan target of 8 per cent), it was generally believed that the real rate was at most 2 per cent.

A large variety of crops is cultivated in the diverse climatic regions of Iran. Grains are the chief crops, including wheat (the major staple), barley and rice. Cotton, sugar beet, tea, almonds, pistachios and dates are of commercial importance, while olives and a variety of fruits and vegetables, as well as tobacco, are also grown. Cane sugar is being grown at Haft Teppeh, in the southern province of Khuzestan and a paper plant has been established in association with the plantation. Food requirements, as a result of improved living standards and increased population, have been growing at over 11.5 per cent a year.

Despite the early social and political benefits of land reform, which the Shah had vigorously pursued in the 1960s and 1970s, agriculture in general suffered under the Shah, to the point where it became one of the principal issues against him by his opponents. Typical of the Shah's grandiose projects were four joint ventures set up with foreign companies in 1970 on over 60,000 hectares of land in Khuzestan, in the south-west. Some 6,500 peasant families were moved out to make way for the agricultural business companies but, despite massive infusions of funds and government help, the projects began folding within half a dozen years for lack of proper planning, lack of skilled manpower and delays in irrigation schemes. By the time the revolution toppled the Shah the projects were in the process of being wound up.

Having made such an issue of agriculture in the political battle against the Shah, the victorious revolutionaries made its revival one of their priorities. Self-sufficiency in foodstuffs, above all else, became central to the economic philosophy of the new regime, and not inconsiderable resources have been allocated to the development of the agricultural sector. The new regime raised support prices for grains and other crops which are now purchased by the government, eliminating middlemen and allowing farm incomes to improve. Rural projects, such as the building of schools, mosques, public baths, silos, roads and irrigation networks and the extension of electricity to villages, have been undertaken by the Construction Crusade (*jihad-i-sazandaji*). However, the impact of the war, shortages of fuel, failure of government administration of credit, storage and marketing facilities, loss of educated officials and discontent in the provinces against the central government have had a generally deleterious effect on agricultural production. Production of oil-seeds, for example, fell to 150,000 tons in the year ending March 1981, compared with 249,000 tons in the previous year. Deliveries of sugar beet to refineries in Iran were estimated at 2.3 million tons by mid-December 1981, well below the 3.7 million tons attained in 1978/79 before the Revolution. There were reports of large-scale purchases of sugar from the EEC and the U.S.A. in 1981.

In a statement at the end of March 1981, the then President Bani-Sadr announced that during the first full Iranian year after the Revolution agricultural output declined by 3.5 per cent while the year 1980/81 would show a similar trend or stagnation. Although some reports indicate a slight improvement in agricultural production in 1981, the sharp rise in the levels of imports of agricultural items suggest that Bani-Sadr's estimate is close to the truth. Large-scale contracts for the supply of basic foodstuffs are still being given to overseas contractors. One estimate suggests that Iran's food imports could rise to between $4,500 million and $5,000 million in 1982, compared with $3,000 million in 1981 and $2,800 million in 1980. Australia reported that its exports to Iran in 1980 were valued at some $260 million, up threefold on 1979. Australian supplies included approximately 1 million tons of grain, 1.5 million live sheep and 22,000 tons of mutton. Total grain imports in 1980/81 were 1.94 million tons, compared with 1.44 million in 1979/80. Local grain purchases by the government fell to 437,000 tons—half the level of the preceding year. Paradoxically, the construction of increased storage capacity for foodstuffs, undertaken by the government as part of its campaign to free the country from import dependence, has enabled massive stockpiling of imported commodities, and there seems little chance that domestic output will provide a substitute in the near future.

Problems of land ownership and uncertainty about the new regime's land reform policies have added to the difficulties affecting the agricultural sector. After the fall of the Shah, when the authority of the central government was weak, land seizures began in many villages. The most dramatic examples occurred in Turkoman and Kurdish areas, where concentrations of large absentee land-holdings were especially pronounced, but other areas were also affected. In some cases the Government did not intervene but, where it did, it tended to oppose land seizures. The events were accompanied by mass migration from the countryside to the cities—nearly 1.5 million rural dwellers migrated to Teheran alone during the first year of the revolution. The regime recognized the economic disaster that this migration threatened. Some kind of land reform promised to keep people on the land and, at the same time, moderate land seizures and reassure small owners to encourage investment and production. A land reform programme prepared by the Ministry of Agriculture was submitted to the Revolutionary Council at the end of 1979. The programme planned to limit the size of holdings to three times the average in an area. The large landowners have been accused of influencing the clergy to oppose the new measures. The land reform bill was eventually introduced and passed by the *Majlis* in 1981, but later rejected by the Council of Guardians as un-Islamic. In late 1981 Khomeini

announced that he favoured land reform and that the *Majlis* alone should decide the question. A bill has gone back to the *Majlis* but has not yet been acted upon. Some observers have suggested that these delays reflect the continued close ties between the large landowners and the influential clergy of the Islamic Republican Party.

The Government has been accused of a total lack of perception of the problems affecting the agricultural sector. A programme for agricultural revival, introduced in May 1981, allocated a mere $100 million for reconstruction, all of which was to be devoted to the rehabilitation of the agro-industrial and farm corporation units set up under the Shah's regime and which had proved incapable of stimulating rural development. At the same time, the essential needs of farmers remain neglected. The merger of the Agricultural Development Bank and the Agricultural Co-operative Bank in May 1981 will enable an estimated $120 million to be made available to farmers adversely affected by the war and natural disasters. Final allocation of the $700 million earmarked for agriculture in the 1981/82 budget has not yet been decided.

Stability of land ownership, skilled management of the commodity market by the state and professional support systems for agriculture are essential if this section is to recover. They have been lacking for more than a decade and will not be easily remedied.

The principal products of the nomad sector of Iranian agriculture are livestock products—dairy produce, wool, hair and hides. About 40 per cent of sheep and goats are raised by semi-nomadic tribal herdsmen. Production is limited by the prevalence of animal pests and the apparently inevitable productivity of pastoral as compared with domestic stock breeding, although account must be taken of the fact that most of the land grazed by the nomads' herds is land which could not be made economically viable in any other way. During the reign of Reza Shah (1925–41) the Iranian Government tried to enforce settlement on the nomads but the tribes rebelled. Since the early 1960s, government "encouragement" and economic pressures resulted in significant settlement.

About 11.5 per cent of Iran is under forest or woodland, including the Caspian area—the main source of commercial timber—and the Zagros Mountains. Forestry in an economic sense is a recent activity and it is only since the nationalization of forest land in 1963 that effective attempts have been made, under the Forestry Commission, at protection, conservation and reafforestation. Total roundwood output in 1977 was estimated at 6.4 million cubic metres.

Although Iran has direct access to both the Caspian Sea and the Gulf, fishing remains poorly developed in both areas. Production in the Gulf amounts to about 14,000 tons per year. The Caspian fisheries are chiefly noted for an annual production of over 200 tons of caviar. In 1982 Iran is expected to export 195 tons of caviar, valued at $50 million, to Western Europe. Pollution and the steadily falling water-level of the Caspian Sea are two serious problems being tackled under a Soviet-Iranian agreement signed in 1973. One survey estimated that, if fully developed, Iran's southern fisheries could earn as much as U.S. \$200 million annually, chiefly from high-grade shrimps and prawns.

PETROLEUM

The major economic activity in Iran is the petroleum industry. The history of commercial exploitation dates back to 1901, when W. K. D'Arcy was granted a 60-year monopoly of the right to explore for and exploit oil in Iran, with the exception of the five northern provinces, which fell within the sphere of Russian influence. Oil was eventually discovered in commercial quantities at Masjid-i-Sulaiman in 1908 and the Anglo-Persian Oil Company was formed in 1909. The Company was renamed Anglo-Iranian in 1935. A long series of disputes between the Iranian Government and Anglo-Iranian ended with the nationalization of the oil industry by Iran in 1951 and the replacement in 1954 of Anglo-Iranian by what became known as the Consortium until it was dissolved in March 1979. The Consortium was an amalgam of interests (British Petroleum 40 per cent; Royal Dutch Shell 14 per cent; Gulf Oil, Socony, Mobil, Exxon, Standard Oil of California and Texaco each with 7 per cent; *Compagnie Française des Pétroles* 6 per cent; a group of independents under the umbrella of the Iricon Agency 5 per cent) formed to produce oil in the area of the old Anglo-Iranian concession as redefined in 1933. The Consortium's concession was to have lasted until 1979, with the possibility of a series of extensions under modified conditions for a further 15 years. Ownership of petroleum deposits throughout Iran and the right to exploit them, or to make arrangements for their exploitation, was vested in the National Iranian Oil Company (NIOC), an Iranian state enterprise.

Until 1973 Iran had a leasing agreement with the Consortium, but the Iranian Government then insisted that the companies should either continue under existing arrangements until 1979 and then become ordinary arm's-length buyers, or else negotiate an entirely new "agency" agreement immediately. The Consortium opted for the latter plan, and on July 31st, 1973, a contract was signed in Teheran under which NIOC formally took over ownership and control of the oil industry in the Consortium area, while the Consortium was to set up a new operating company, Oil Service Company of Iran, which would act as production contractor for NIOC. In return the western companies were granted a 20-year supply of crude as privileged buyers, which they would take in proportion to their shareholding in the Consortium.

Strikes at the oil installations, halting oil exports, constituted one of the difficulties which forced the Shah to leave Iran in January 1979. The strikers announced that exports would not resume until the Shah left the country. Iranian oil did not flow to the rest of the world until March 5th, 1979. The first shipments were sold on the "spot" market, fetching prices as high as \$20 per barrel, but NIOC said that this was a temporary measure. Within a matter of

weeks three dozen long-term contracts were signed with international companies for the supply of Iranian oil.

NIOC has cancelled the 1973 agreement to market Iranian oil through the Consortium and has since March 5th, 1979, been selling oil directly to individual companies and countries. After initial resistance the former members of the Consortium accepted the new arrangement and signed new nine-month supply agreements effective from April 1st. The role of the Consortium effectively came to an end on July 1st, 1981, when Kala Ltd., a subsidiary of NIOC established to undertake purchasing and service functions for the Iranian oil industry, replaced Iranian Oil Service Co. (IROS), one of the subsidiaries of the Consortium.

In order to conserve the country's oil resources, NIOC intends to keep average production as low as possible. After the capture on November 4th, 1979, of the U.S. embassy in Teheran and subsequent deterioration in relations with the U.S.A. and its allies, Iran began facing genuine problems in getting spare parts for the industry.

Iran's biggest difficulty after November 1979, however, was finding customers willing to pay its high prices. Supplies of about 900,000 b/d to the U.S.A. were stopped in November and by May 1980 deliveries of about 800,000 b/d to Japan and British Petroleum and Royal Dutch Shell were also halted. The U.S.A. stopped taking delivery for political reasons in order to put pressure on Iran for the release of its hostages; BP and Shell, themselves under pressure from the U.S.A., refused to buy Iranian oil from April 21st when the Oil Ministry raised the price of its lightest crude to \$35 per barrel, retroactive from April 1st. Including surcharges and other conditions Iran's oil was costing its customers closer to \$37.50 per barrel, perhaps the highest for any OPEC country. This price compared with \$17.17 per barrel less than a year earlier.

In early 1980 the Oil Ministry set the year's average production level at 3 million b/d, anticipating an annual revenue of about \$24,000 million, but in May was admitting that price disputes and the crisis with the West had forced production down to 2 million b/d. With at least temporary loss of its major western customers Iran began looking at the Eastern bloc and developing countries for its principal markets.

The Iran Government targeted crude oil exports for the Iranian year 1360 (March 1981–March 1982) at 2.5 million b/d. Such an export level would keep Iranian crude production within the 3 million b/d ceiling set after the revolution as the optimum production level. Before the revolution Iran was producing at 5 to 6 million b/d, of which around 800,000 b/d was required for domestic consumption. Political action in late 1978 brought production almost to a standstill but it built up to around 3 million b/d during the following 18 months. Average production in 1979 was just over 3 million b/d and in 1980 dropped to 1.5 million b/d, 49.5 per cent down on the 1979 level.

After the Prime Minister, Muhammad Ali Rajai,

presented his April 1981 budget, which was set at an ambitious U.S. $44,000 million, NIOC was apparently instructed to raise production to 2.5 million b/d to generate foreign exchange for the budget requirements. A special effort was made by NIOC to improve performance in oil exports by seeking contract customers as quickly as possible. By mid-1981 contract figures were as follows (in b/d): Shell (110,000), BP (65,000), Japan (194,000 with three companies still negotiating), India (100,000), Spain (95,000 of which Enpetrol 20,000, Rio Tinto Explosivos 15,000, Petroliber 15,000, CEPSA 30,000 with Petronor negotiating for 50,000), Romania (80,000), Turkey (70,000), South Korea (50,000), Belgium (50,000), the U.S.S.R. (40,000, in this case 1 million tons over 6 months), China (30,000), Portugal (20,000), Poland (20,000), Bulgaria (20,000), Finland (15,000), Sweden (15,000), Hungary (12,000), East Germany (15,000), Yugoslavia (10,000), Czechoslovakia (10,000), North Korea (10,000), Bangladesh (10,000) and Sri Lanka (10,000). Not all these contracts, however, produce Iran's much needed foreign exchange. Crude contracts with Comecon countries, including the U.S.S.R., are normally on a barter basis, with only the balance being made up in hard currency. In return for oil, these countries export industrial goods and services, plus some food. Iran and the Soviet Union, which have continued to wrangle for the last year over the price of natural gas through the Igat I gas trunkline, reached an agreement that Iran should export some oil in lieu of exporting gas. Iran and Romania have signed a barter deal worth $1,000 million. During 1982 Romania will buy 80,000 b/d of Iranian crude oil and $70 million worth of other non-oil goods while Iran will purchase 75,000 tractors and 50 rail locomotives, and will utilize Romanian services to help Iranian industry. 50 per cent of the agreement will be handled through direct barter, and the rest in a mix of hard and soft currencies. Turkey, with chronic payments problems, operates a barter arrangement with Iran, exporting mainly foodstuffs and cement.

These contracts may not be a full list since NIOC and the Iranian Oil Ministry no longer publish figures. Since the start of the Iraq-Iran war in September 1980, all information on oil—both production and exports—has been considered classified.

In October 1981, as a result of growing internal political violence and the war damage caused by the Iraqis, the main purchasers of Iranian oil announced that they would cease to lift Iranian crude. The contracts held by BP for 65,000 b/d, Mitsubishi for 40,000 b/d, Daikyo Oil for 10,000 b/d and Showa Oil for 18,000 b/d lapsed as from the end of September 1981. A group of nine Japanese firms also stopped purchases from Iran. Only Shell retained its contract. In September 1981 the Government announced that all agreements and contracts signed under the Shah's regime had been abrogated.

At the beginning of 1982 Japanese buyers re-entered the Iranian market. It was reported that a total of 230,000 b/d, formerly suspended by the Japanese in retaliation for high pricing of Iranian crudes, will be taken up. Mitsui signed an agreement in January 1982 to take 150,000 tons of fuel oil and also to purchase naphtha from NIOC at a cost of some $25 million. New contracts are needed to cover 1982 if Iran is to achieve its targets for export.

The pricing of Iranian crude has also had an adverse effect as both Iranian Light and Iranian Heavy have been priced towards the top of the market for similar API crudes. In April 1980 the price for Light was raised from $32.5 to $35 per barrel, with an additional premium of $2.5 per barrel. The Japanese, who had been lifting 520,000 b/d, suspended purchases and Shell and BP refused to buy until the price was below $35 per barrel. In July 1980 differentials between Iranian and similar Gulf crudes narrowed as Iraq and Kuwait raised prices up to the $32 benchmark agreed at the OPEC meeting in Algiers. In January 1981 prices were raised by $1.63 to $37 for Light and $36 for Heavy, with an additional premium of $1.8 per barrel. However, against this pricing policy, Iran was reported in early 1981 to have offered discounts of up to 20 per cent to offset the very high insurance rates of loading in the war zone of Kharg Island and to have offered 60 days' credit instead of 30 days.

In July and August 1981 Iran refused requests by its main customers for negotiations on prices of crude oil despite a difference of $5.50 per barrel between the Saudi reference price and the $37.50 per barrel charged by Iran. After the OPEC meeting in Abu Dhabi in December 1981, Iran dropped its prices to $34.20, just 20 cents above the reference price charged by Saudi Arabia, in February 1982, as part of its drive to increase oil exports, NIOC announced two price cuts. It was announced that prices per barrel were to be reduced by $1.00 as of February 5th and then again by another $1.00 as of February 12th. Taking into account 30 days' credit, the NIOC prices are now $32.20 for 34° API crude and $30.30 for 31° API crude. These reductions make Iran's oil the cheapest in the Middle East. However, given the high degree of competitiveness in the world market, Iran's plans for a rapid increase in exports may be difficult to achieve.

The period April 1980 to June 1981 was, in almost every way, very poor for the Iranian oil industry. Apart from factors already mentioned, the country was in a continuous state of political ferment, which spilled over into the hydrocarbon industry. Stoppages, strikes, go-slows and sabotage seriously hindered production .The loss of foreign personnel for oil field maintenance on the onshore fields was compounded by the May 1980 EEC sanctions, imposed in support of the U.S.A. over their hostages in Iran. This prevented Iran from purchasing some of the sophisticated spares and components required for repairs and maintenance. Secondary recovery systems on the onshore fields suffered, in particular the Gachsaran field, previously one of the most prolific. The offshore fields have had a better record, since foreign personnel remained longer, until threatened with nationalization in September 1979. Iran's response to the EEC sanctions deprived the country of some oil customers, since it cut off supplies to any country supporting the sanctions.

The Iraqi attack on Iran through the Shatt al-Arab in September 1980 and the consequent expanded and prolonged hostilities have further weakened the industry. Iraqi shelling of the 630,000 b/d Abadan refinery has permanently put it out of action. Spasmodic bombing of the main Kharg Island crude terminal has disrupted loadings. The effect of the war on tanker insurance in the Gulf has been an astronomic increase in charges. Iraqi action has disrupted the product lines running from Bandar Mahshahr up the country and the giant $3,500 million Iran-Japan Petro-chemical complex at Bandar Khomeini has been left uncompleted by the Mitsui-led consortium after five Iraqi attacks.

Oil production fluctuated considerably in 1980. In 1981 production is believed to have fluctuated at around 1–2 million b/d. Iranian sources put average output at 1,350,000 b/d. Exports were depressed but varied considerably—average exports for 1981 are put at 900,000 b/d. In December 1981 exports were estimated at between 700,000 and 950,000 b/d but in January 1982 they fell to between 600,000 and 700,000 b/d. The Gurreh pumping station, which handles the main-line crudes from Agha Jari and Gachsaran to the terminals at Kharg Island, was badly damaged by the Iraqis in late September 1981 and remains only partially usable.

The future direction of Iranian oil policies appears confused. Leading elements in the Islamic Republican Party remain committed to creating a new Iranian economy which does not depend on oil exports. According to this view, oil exports are seen as creating dependency on the outside world that could corrupt the state and undermine Islam. An opposite view, represented by former President Bani-Sadr, favoured continuing oil exports in order to finance future economic development, although this must be consistent with Islamic values. In the light of such contrary policies, Iran's future oil production must be open to many different interpretations. Muhammad Gharazi, the Minister of Oil, announced in January 1982 that oil production would be stepped up to between 2.0 and 2.5 million b/d in order to ensure adequate finance for the state budget from exports of 1.5–2.0 million b/d.

The loss of the Abadan refinery affected the already difficult situation in Iran for oil products. Iran has always imported some refined products, such as kerosene in winter, and has had shortages in the middle distillates range (diesel oil, kerosene and heating oil). The loss of Abadan denied Iran the flexibility of changing product volumes to meet market or seasonal variations of demand. Abadan was a highly sophisticated and flexible refinery, capable of substantial product conversion. It was also one of the main sources of aviation fuel and gasoline, though the Shiraz refinery, too, has some capacity. Iran has needed to import products so acutely that an immediate allocation of $200 million was earmarked in Premier Rajai's budget of 1981. However, any pro-

ducts imported through the safer southern Gulf port of Bandar Abbas have been subject to long delays, since Bandar Abbas has no railhead, little storage and no pipelines. To cut the expense of buying products for foreign currency, Iran has been negotiating oil-for-products barter arrangements with oil majors and North African producers.

NATURAL GAS

In January 1981 Iran announced that it was going ahead with the huge Kangan gas treatment plant, between Bushehr and Bandar Abbas, in the southern Gulf. The Kangan field is thought to have reserves of 820,000 million cubic metres and, when completed, the plant will have a daily production of 80 million cubic metres, coming on stream in two stages in 1983 and 1986. The treated gas will be used for gas reinjection programmes, for feedstock for the Iran-Japan Petrochemical works and for industrial and domestic uses. The basic design and engineering had almost been completed when the revolution stopped all work. Early in 1982 it was reported that Saipen of Italy, part of the state oil company ENI, had been asked to return to complete construction of the Kangan spur line to Igat I, which carries natural gas from the southern oilfields to northern Iran and, in the past, also to the U.S.S.R. Some 50 km. of the 560-km. line was laid before the Italians withdrew in 1979. The Iranian Government appears to be anxious to use gas to replace oil as feedstock and fuel for domestic industry and home consumption in order to raise the level of oil exports. Also planned for completion is the Sarrakhs gas treatment plant in northern Iran, planned to provide feedstock for the Neka power station in Mazandaran.

During the latter half of 1980 talks continued fruitlessly between the U.S.S.R. and Iran over pricing for natural gas exports to the U.S.S.R. via the Igat I gas trunkline. However, the discussions became somewhat academic since the Igat I gas is associated gas and, with declining oil production in Iran, there would have been, in any case, a gas shortfall. The natural gas reserves are enormous but the fields at Qeshm, Sarrakhs and Kangan have not been exploited. In 1981 an $11,000 million plan to extend the internal gas distribution system, begun before the Revolution, was announced in order to supply a further 220,000 consumers. It has been suggested that the scheme might utilize gas normally exported to the U.S.S.R.

OTHER MINERALS

The mineral resources of Iran have not been surveyed completely. Lead-zinc is mined at Bafq near Yazd, at Khomein, west of Isfahan, and at Ravanj near Qom, with a combined potential of 600 tons of concentrates daily, though current plans for development are limited to Bafq. Proposals for the construction of a smelting unit with an annual capacity of 400,000 tons of lead and 70,000 tons of zinc, supplied from domestic sources, have been made.

Chrome from the Elburz mountains and near Bandar Abbas, red oxide from Hormuz in the Persian Gulf and turquoise from Nishapur are all produced for export. Sulphur and salt are produced on the coast of the Gulf, near Bandar Abbas, and Iran is the leading sulphur exporter in the region. The major iron ore deposits are in the Kerman province in south-east Iran, in particular at Bafq, where proven reserves total 600 million tons, with probable reserves amounting to a further 400 million tons of ore. The ore from Bafq is carried 540 km. by a specially developed railway to the Isfahan steel plant. Reserves at Gol-e-Gohar are estimated at more than 200 million tons. Total coal reserves, at Kerman and in the Elburz Mountains, are estimated at more than 1,000 million tons but Iran has to import higher-grade coal for some purposes. Local production at Kerman has risen to 430,000 tons annually, according to a recent official report.

Deposits of copper ore have been found in Azerbaizhan, Kerman and in the Yazd and Anarak areas. A number of very important deposits have been discovered since 1967 in the Kerman area, the most important being at Sar Cheshmeh. Reserves are estimated at over 400 million tons, averaging 1.12 per cent copper content, with another 400 million tons of lower grade beneath. The giant project includes the construction of road and rail links to link the mine with Bandar Abbas 400 km. away on the Gulf, a training school, and a new town for the families of the 3,000 men who will work the mine. A large refinery and associated rolling mill and two continuous casting mills were to be built but construction was halted during the revolution. In late 1981 it was reported that East European specialists had been brought in to begin limited production, which it was planned to raise to half of the site's capacity of 60,000 tons per year. However, the project still faces serious problems of management and infrastructure. Exports will be expensive and domestic demand limited because of the rundown in Iranian industry.

A much smaller copper mine at Minakhan, developed in association with Japanese interests, has been brought under complete Iranian ownership.

In March 1976 it was announced that important uranium deposits had been found in Iran's northern and western regions and in 1978 agreements were signed with West German and French companies to carry out surveys. The scope and pace of exploration were reduced after the revolution. Long-term plans for a network of power stations were also abandoned because the project was too expensive, too dependent on Western technology and unnecessary in view of the availability of cheap natural gas. More recently, it was announced that Iran plans to resume imports of nuclear technology.

INDUSTRY

Three years after the Revolution, no clear policy has been formulated for the industrial sector. The modern manufacturing plants set up under the Shah's regime which have remained in production (estimated at only 20 per cent of the total by value of output) face serious difficulties. Raw materials are in short supply, as are spare parts and other inputs, and it is feared that many factories may soon close down. In March 1981 the then President Bani-Sadr estimated that in the period March 1979–March 1980 industrial and related output fell by 34 per cent and was still falling, possibly at a higher rate. Official thinking about the future of this sector appears confused. The stated policies of the Revolutionary Government favour small-scale, traditional or bazaar-related enterprises. Yet, in sharp contradiction, financial allocations to industry have followed the pattern laid down by the previous regime. In the 1981–82 budget most of the $2,000 million allocated to this sector was devoted to heavy industry. Some observers predict that Iran's industrial base will continue to decline, with only a few basic plants, using local raw materials and low-grade technology, surviving.

Steel, petrochemicals and copper remain the country's three basic industries. Other important branches are automobile manufacture, machine tools, construction materials, pharmaceuticals, textiles and food processing. With the exception of one major petrochemical plant and a number of textile and construction materials ventures, all these industries have been industrialized since the Revolution. A number of Japanese and West European firms have begun action against the Iranian Government for compensation following the nationalization of their plants in Iran.

Steel

The Government's target, like that of the Shah, is to achieve self-sufficiency in steel production and end dependence on imports. In 1980 steel accounted for almost one-sixth of total imports. Consumption was estimated at 6 million metric tons per year in mid-1981 and is expected to rise to 10 million tons by 1983. Domestic production and development plans have been badly hit by the revolution and the war with Iraq. Current output is now limited to 550,000 tons, produced by an old-fashioned coal-fired steel mill built by the U.S.S.R. in Isfahan (formerly known as the Aryamehr Steel Mill). Built under a $286 million credit agreement concluded with the Soviet Union in 1965, the mill went into operation in March 1973. Work is continuing on an extension to this mill which will bring production capacity up to 1.9 million tons per year by 1982/83. The extension, already five years behind schedule, is now expected to be completed in March 1982. No decision has been made on a planned second phase of expansion which would bring total capacity to 4 million tons. There are doubts about the ability of the local coal industry to supply sufficient feedstock and it seems likely that this project will be dropped in favour of development of gas-fired mills. The Italian state subsidiary Finsider was awarded a contract worth $3,000 million (at 1976 prices) to build a gas-fired steel plant with a capacity of 3 million tons per year, now relocated near Isfahan (originally to have been built at Bandar Abbas). Finsider have most of the equipment on site and the contracting firm of Italimpianti was poised to begin work in mid-1981, pending resolution of differences with the Iranian Government over escalation.

Other steel projects, located in Ahwaz in the province of Khuzestan, were all suspended following the outbreak of war with Iraq. They include a pipe mill and rolling mill, a sponge-iron plant and a direct reduction plant with a capacity of 3 million tons per year, started by the West German company of Korff and one-third completed when work was suspended just before the revolution. The future of these units is in doubt. Iran continues to be a major purchaser of steel on the world market, with imports increasing from South Korea and Japan. It has been reported that Japanese steel exports to Iran are expected to reach between 800,000 and 1 million metric tons in 1982/83, from a level of 55,000 tons in 1980/81.

Petrochemicals

The Shah had planned a huge petrochemical sector that would not only meet local demand but provide $2,000 million worth of exports by 1983. Development of the industry has been paralysed since the revolution, however. At present the sector comprises the following major ventures: the Iran Fertilizer Company, the Razi Chemical Company (formerly Shahpour), the Abadan Petrochemical Company, the Kharg Chemical Company, Iran Carbon Company, the Iran Nippon Chemical Company, Aliaf Company and Polyacryl Corporation. All these companies were nationalized in 1979 and are run by the National Petrochemical Company under the Ministry of Oil. The accumulated production of these companies supplies only a small percentage of Iran's needs. A major venture, to be the cornerstone of the petrochemical industry, was the $3,500 million Iran-Japan Petrochemical Complex at Bandar Khomeini. This is a joint 50–50 venture between the National Iranian Oil Company and a Mitsui-led consortium called Iran Chemical Development Company, and it is the only petrochemical company not nationalized. The mammoth 13-unit complex was 85 per cent finished at the time of the revolution. Work was resumed briefly in the summer of 1980 but halted again after Iraqi bombers hit the plant several times in late September and early October 1980. Despite the fact that an estimated $1,400 million has already been spent on the project, Mitsui and its Japanese partners appear anxious to withdraw. Costs have escalated and there have been changes in the international market for petrochemical goods and doubts about the availability of basic feedstocks since the destruction of the Abadan refinery and the decline in natural gas supplies from the oilfields. Projects for chemical sales in Iran are also poor. In January 1982 Mitsui demanded that Iran give firm guarantees that it would underwrite all additional costs of the scheme arising from the war and the effects of the Revolution. Iran has not given these guarantees and the Government appears undecided about the future of the project. Negotiations continue but agreement is still far off.

Work on extending the Shiraz petrochemical plant is to be completed by 1983. The plant's daily output is being increased nearly ten-fold to produce 1,200 tons of ammonia, 1,500 tons of urea, 100 tons of nitric acid and 750 tons of ammonium nitrate.

Copper

Completion of a multi-million dollar complex for the mining, refining and processing of copper at Sar Cheshmeh, near Kerman, is still hoped for, and is dealt with under "Other Minerals", above.

TRADE AND COMMUNICATIONS

Almost all of Iran's exports are crude petroleum or oil products. Non-oil exports account for only about 3 per cent of total export earnings. Traditional exports include cotton, carpets, fresh and dried fruit, hides and caviar. "New" industrial products include knitwear, textiles, clothes, metal ores, pharmaceuticals, chemicals, soaps, detergents and shoes. Processed foodstuffs and vehicles are also exported. Since the Revolution, the Government has declared that it seeks more trade with Islamic and Third World countries, even though it still needs Western goods and spare parts. New trading patterns have emerged but Iran remains heavily dependent on the advanced industrial economies.

Iran's imports in 1980 were valued at 863,300 million rials ($12,247 million), an increase of 25 per cent over 1979 despite six months of sanctions by the U.S.A., the EEC and Japan, and the outbreak of war with Iraq in September 1980. This compares with a total of $14,100 million in the Iranian calendar year 1357 (March 21st, 1978, to March 20th, 1979), the year immediately before the Revolution began to affect trade levels.

The major supplier to Iran, despite the imposition of official sanctions, was Japan, with total sales valued at 119,000 million rials or 13.8 per cent of the total. In the years before the revolution Japan was Iran's third most important supplier, with around 16 per cent of total imports, compared with the U.S.A. and West Germany which each accounted for about 18 per cent on average.

Following the taking of the U.S. hostages and the almost complete embargo on U.S. sales to Iran, imports from the U.S.A. plunged dramatically in 1980, falling to $25 million, compared with $2,200 million in 1977/78. A certain amount of U.S. goods, however, did come in "through the back door" in the guise of imports from European and Persian Gulf nations. West Germany is still an important supplier with sales of $1,600 million (13.2 per cent of Iran's imports) in 1980. In third place as an import source was the United Kingdom, with sales of $1,040 million. Although the value of British exports to Iran was slightly down from pre-revolution levels, its share of total imports increased from 6.9 per cent in 1977/78 to 8 per cent in 1980. As a result of the cutting off of U.S. imports and the EEC and Japanese sanctions,

Iran began to find new sources of supply in the third world and among non-aligned countries in Western Europe. Spain, Austria, Finland, Sweden and New Zealand all made significant gains in sales to Iran during 1980. There was also a considerable increase in imports from East European countries such as Romania and Bulgaria. No statistical breakdown of imports by commodity is available but major imports are known to be foodstuffs, equipment and raw materials for industry, and power transmission and generating equipment, with purchases of armaments and refined oil products increasing at the end of the year.

After the Revolution, the new Government declared itself in favour of the nationalization of foreign trade, but it was not until November 1981 that a law providing for the nationalization of trade was finally passed. There followed notification that, in future, all imports would be handled through state-controlled centres. The status of these centres remains unclear and traditional importers can still acquire import licences. Some merchants are convinced that they will be able to retain their links with foreign exporters, even if they have to become, in practice, agents of the Government. It would appear that the Government plans eventually to bring all imports under the control of state agencies. Corruption in the bureaucracy and the general inefficiency of state services suggest that a large volume of trade will remain within the traditional bazaar sector. Illegal imports continue to flourish across the eastern land border and via the smaller Gulf ports.

Imports rose rapidly during the first six months of 1981. The Iranian Customs Organization registered goods valued at $6,650 million, a rise of 20 per cent on the first half of 1980. In the Iranian month ending June 20th, 1981, imports were valued at $1,700 million, the highest level since the Revolution. West Germany became Iran's major supplier in the first half of 1981, with a total of $690 million worth of sales, followed by Japan with $555 million. Total OECD exports to Iran were estimated at $2,800 million for this period, a decline of over 50 per cent compared with 1980. U.S. exports improved considerably to $110 million, five times greater than in 1980. Bilateral trade with the U.S.S.R. increased rapidly during 1981.

In September 1981 the Central Bank of Iran stopped the issue of all letters of credit and imposed tighter controls on the activities of the new import centres. In January 1982 the Government, faced with a poor rate of foreign exchange earnings from oil exports and a deteriorating foreign reserves position, announced that restrictions on imports other than vital commodities would remain in force. Foodstuffs, medicines, agricultural goods and industrial supplies are permitted but all other items are classified as luxury goods and excluded. The aim is to reduce imports even further to below $600 million per month in line with reduced foreign exchange earnings.

The threat of a U.S. naval embargo in the Gulf at the time of the hostage crisis in 1980 focused attention on land supply lines through the Soviet Union and Turkey and air routes from Pakistan. A protocol with the Soviet Union, approved by the Islamic Revolutionary Council in May 1980, included arrangements for land supply lines through the Julfa and Astara border points, which were already becoming congested with heavy traffic.

Since the Revolution, there has been little investment in the transport and communications sector despite the problems caused by the war with Iraq. Few schemes have been introduced and only a limited number of existing projects are being completed. The only extension to the railway network has been the construction by the U.S.S.R. of the final section of the Tabriz-to-Julfa line, which has been electrified. In the ports sector a decision was taken in September 1981 to complete work on a major extension of Bandar Abbas, a project designed before the Revolution but scaled down after the fall of the Shah. Because of the war, capacity has been lost at the traditional seaports of Bandar Khomeini and Khorramshahr, and Iran has become heavily dependent on Bandar Abbas for its sea-borne imports. About 60 per cent of the new Bandar Abbas deep-water port has been completed. It has also been reported that the Islamic Republic of Iran Shipping Lines have been buying second-hand ships. This is partly a response to the steeply rising import costs, because of the war, and the rise in insurance. The line hopes to carry more of Iran's import trade and thus to cut costs.

FINANCE

The first post-revolutionary budget, for the Iranian year March 1979 to March 1980, was set at $34,000 million, just over half the target set the previous year by the Shah's regime. The following year's budget (1980/81) reached $40,000 million, including provisions for a $6,500 million deficit. In fact the deficit came to almost $12,000 million, mainly because of the drop in oil revenues from an estimated $23,000 million to $11,900 million. For the year March 1981 to March 1982 the Prime Minister, Muhammad Ali Rajai, drew up a $44,000 million budget which, he claimed, would be a non-deficit budget. The Prime Minister said that the entire expenditure plan would be financed through oil revenues and taxes, and that oil production would be boosted to the point where sufficient revenue was earned. He immediately came under fire from President Bani-Sadr and the Governor of the Central Bank, Ali Reza Nobari, who attacked the use of non-replenishable resources to finance excessive current expenditures as a matter of principle, and also pointed out that, with the present world glut of oil, it would be practically impossible to raise enough money from oil. Both Bani-Sadr and Nobari felt that such a budget would force the Government to print more money and aggravate the already serious inflation—officially 27 per cent but estimated by independent economists at over 40 per cent. Their vehement opposition to the budget was one of the key factors which led Islamic fundamentalists to push them out of power. Many other members of the *Majlis* also attacked the budget strongly. In July 1981 the *Majlis* reduced total allocations to $37,000 million. Some $2,500 million was cut from defence expenditure and $3,100 million from the development plan. An overall cut of 5 per cent in the expenditure by government departments was also demanded. Even so, a deficit fo $8,500 million was forecast. The final deficit may prove to be even higher as a result of increases in defence expenditure and a poor performance in oil exports.

For the year March 1982 to March 1983 the Government has proposed a $39,050 million budget to the *Majlis*. Revenues are estimated at $31,902 million, leaving a deficit of $7,150 million. As in the past, oil sector income, estimated at $19,000 million, is expected to finance the major part of the budget, but new domestic taxes are to be levied and savings made on administration. Priority for expenditure has been given to the reconstruction of the war damage in the south, and great emphasis is placed on restoring the existing agricultural and industrial base in order to create employment, reduce oil dependency and limit imports. The Government has been anxious to play down the costs of the war, estimated in mid-1981 at 600 million rials per day in cash outlay alone and widely believed to have risen substantially. The budget also assumes a high level of recovery in the oil sector; but, in spite of a return to competitive pricing, such a recovery seems far from guaranteed. In some months oil income has not covered the cost of imports, resulting in losses of foreign exchange from fragile reserves and the sale of gold at poor rates. With diminishing reserves of foreign exchange, official sources, including the Central Bank, have suggested that oil exports of 1,250,000 b/d would be necessary, at present prices, to start to pull the country out of its present financial crisis. Estimates of oil exports in January 1982 were only 600,000 to 700,000 b/d.

In May 1980, as part of its counter-measures and to fight inflation, estimated at about 30 per cent, Iran cut the rial's link to the dollar and pegged it to the IMF's Special Drawing Right (SDR). The rate on the first day of the changeover, May 22nd, was set at SDR1=IR92.3, deflating the rial marginally from IR70.60 to the dollar to IR70.75 to the dollar. The "black market" rate for the dollar after the Revolution hovered around 130 rials, necessitating continuation of foreign exchange controls first introduced in the last few months of the Shah's regime.

Inflation has become a persistent problem for the economy. Import controls have tended to feed inflation in a situation of growing shortages and especially in view of a policy favouring wage increases for the lower paid without increases in productivity. Official claims that the rate of inflation has been reduced to some 25 per cent appear to underestimate the problem, and unofficial sources suggest that a figure of 50 per cent is more realistic. The wholesale price index rose by 22.1 per cent in the first nine months of 1981. During the year ending August 1981, according to the Central Bank of Iran, food prices rose by 29 per cent, industrial raw materials by 19 per cent, mineral fuels and by-products by 3 per cent and construction materials by 17 per cent.

Following the June 1979 nationalization of banking and insurance, the Government announced in 1980 the official setting up of an Islamic banking system. Interest on loans was replaced by a commission—4 per cent, compared with the traditional 14 per cent—and interest on deposits was replaced with profits—estimated at a minimum 7–8.5 per cent. The banks would become temporary shareholders in big industries to which they lent money. The new banking system also merged the 20 or more banks into eight groups.

DEVELOPMENT PLANS

The five-year development planning concept, started in 1947 by the Shah's regime, was dropped after the Revolution. The fifth and last plan ended in March 1978 and the sixth plan, never published, was overtaken by the Revolution. A possibility was the enunciation of a 10- or 20-year economic framework within which future governments would work.

STATISTICAL SURVEY

(The Iranian year runs from March 21st to March 20th)

AREA AND POPULATION

AREA	POPULATION (census results)			
	November 1966	November 1976		
	Total	Males	Females	Total
1,648,000 sq. km.*	25,785,210	17,356,347	16,352,397	33,708,744

* 636,296 sq. miles.

Estimated population: 34,570,000 (July 1st, 1977); 35,504,000 (July 1st, 1978); 37,447,000 (July 1st, 1980).

PRINCIPAL TOWNS

(November 1976 census)

Tehran (Teheran)	4,530,223*	Imanshahr		Kerman	140,761
Mashad (Meshed)	667,770	(Kermanshah)	290,600	Khuninshahr	
Isfahan	661,510	Qom	247,219	(Khorramshahr)	140,490
Tabriz	597,976	Rasht	188,957	Qazvin	139,258
Shiraz	425,813	Hamedan	165,785	Karaj	139,019
Ahwaz	334,399	Rezaiyah	164,419	Yazd	135,925
Abadan	294,068	Ardebil	147,856		

* Including suburbs; Teheran's population was estimated at over 6,000,000 in May 1980.

Births and Deaths: Average annual birth rate 44.1 per 1,000 in 1970-75, 44.4 per 1,000 in 1975-80; death rate 15.4 per 1,000 in 1970-75, 13.6 per 1,000 in 1975-80 (UN estimates).

ECONOMICALLY ACTIVE POPULATION*

(November 1976 census)

	MALES	FEMALES	TOTAL
Agriculture, forestry, hunting and fishing	2,763,934	227,935	2,991,869
Mining and quarrying	86,604	3,284	89,888
Manufacturing	1,032,960	639,099	1,672,059
Construction	1,180,913	7,807	1,188,720
Electricity, gas, water supply.	59,716	1,917	61,633
Commerce	656,177	12,317	668,494
Transport, storage and communications	422,647	8,824	431,471
Services	1,324,586	296,011	1,620,597
Others (not adequately defined)	59,863	14,826	74,689
TOTAL IN EMPLOYMNET .	7,587,400	1,212,020	8,799,420
Unemployed	759,650	236,986	996,636
TOTAL .	8,347,050	1,449,006	9,796,056

* Including nomadic tribes and other unsettled population.

AGRICULTURE

PRINCIPAL CROPS
(FAO estimates, 'ooo metric tons)

	1978	1979	1980
Wheat . . .	5,700	5,800	6,000
Barley . . .	1,000	1,000	1,100
Rice (paddy) . .	1,280	1,420	1,150
Maize . . .	60	57	60
Sugar beet . .	3,900	3,900	3,000
Sugar cane . .	1,700	1,610	800
Tea (made) . .	27	28	29
Cotton (lint) . .	129	97	70
Tobacco. . .	15	15	15
Pulses . . .	199	212	213
Pistachios . .	60	10	40

LIVESTOCK
(FAO estimates, 'ooo head, year ending September)

	1978	1979	1980
Horses . . .	350	350	350
Mules . . .	122	123	124
Asses . . .	1,800	1,800	1,800
Cattle . . .	7,500	7,600	7,645
Buffaloes . .	220	220	220
Camels . . .	27	27	27
Pigs . . .	55	55	55
Sheep . . .	33,600	33,700	32,000
Goats . . .	13,500	13,500	13,627
Chickens . .	65,000	67,500	70,384
Ducks . . .	153	155	155

Source: FAO, *Production Yearbook.*

LIVESTOCK PRODUCTS
(FAO estimates, 'ooo metric tons)

	1978	1979	1980
Beef and veal .	160	161	163
Buffalo meat .	8	9	9
Mutton and lamb .	224	230	232
Goats' meat .	43	44	45
Pig meat .	2	2	2
Poultry meat . .	208	211	211
Other meat . .	16	16	16
Cows' milk . .	1,580	1,550	1,567
Buffaloes' milk .	37	39	39
Sheep's milk .	664	687	704
Goats' milk .	222	222	222
Cheese . .	98.4	98.5	99.5
Butter . .	66.4	66.4	67.4
Hen eggs . .	134	136	136
Honey . .	6.0	5.5	5.6
Wool: greasy .	17.0	16.0	16.1
clean .	9.5	8.9	8.9
Cattle and buffalo hides .	32.7	32.8	33.2
Sheep skins .	37.2	38.4	38.7
Goat skins .	6.9	7.1	7.2

Source: FAO, *Production Yearbook.*

FORESTRY

ROUNDWOOD REMOVALS
(FAO estimates, 'ooo cubic metres, all broadleaved)

	1974	1975	1977
Sawlogs, veneer logs and logs for sleepers . .	318	350	369
Pitprops (Mine timber) .	4	4	4
Other industrial wood .	4,003	4,003	4,003
Fuel wood . . .	1,997	1,997	1,997
TOTAL .	6,322	6,354	6,373

1976: Production as in 1975.
1978 and 1979: Production as in 1977.

SAWNWOOD PRODUCTION
('ooo cubic metres, all broadleaved)

	1975	1976	1977
Sawnwood (incl. boxboards)*	90	90	90
Railway sleepers . .	80	54	73
TOTAL . .	170	144	163

*FAO estimate.

1978 and 1979: Production as in 1977 (FAO estimate).

Source: FAO, *Yearbook of Forest Products.*

FISHING
('000 metric tons, live weight)

	1971	1972	1973
Inland waters . . .	6.3	3.0	3.1
Marine fishes . . .	13.3*	13.5*	13.5*
Marine crustaceans .	4.7*	3.0*	3.4*
TOTAL CATCH . .	24.3	19.5	20.0

* FAO estimate.

1974–80: Annual catch as in 1973 (FAO estimates).

Source: FAO, *Yearbook of Fishery Statistics*.

MINING
CRUDE PETROLEUM
(net production, '000 barrels per day)

	1975/76	1976/77	1977/78	1978/79	1979/80
Oil Service Company of Iran (OSCO)[1] . .	4,814	5,532	4,963	3,792	2,998
National Iranian Oil Company[2] . . .	16	19	17	13	12
Irano-Italian Oil Company (SIRIP) . .	49	47	42	32	35
Iran-Pan American Oil Company (IPAC) .	178	217	319	244	201
Lavan Petroleum Company (LAPCO) . .	170	156	188	132	130
Iranian Marine International Oil Company (IMINOCO)	52	48	46	31	37
TOTAL	5,279	6,019	5,585	4,252*	3,447*

[1] Now known as Southern Oil Fields.
[2] Now known as Naft Shah Oil Field.

* Including SOFIRAN.

Source: Bank Markazi Iran, *Bulletin*, No. 94.

NATURAL GAS
(million cubic metres)

	1975/76	1976/77	1977/78	1978/79	1979/80
Production . . .	44,600	52,300	59,500	44,300	41,600
Consumption (Domestic) .	12,300	14,000	23,900	16,600	21,200
Export . . .	9,600	9,300	9,200	5,200	3,500
Flared . . .	22,700	29,000	26,400	22,500	16,900

Source: Bank Markazi Iran, *Bulletin*, No. 94.

OTHER MINERALS*
('ooo metric tons, year ending March 20th)

	1975/76	1976/77	1977/78	1978/79	1979/80
Hard coal	1,000	900	900	900	900‡
Iron ore†	610	653	671	950	371
Copper ore† . . .	1.8	6.0	13.0	20.0	10.0
Lead ore†	53.0	35.0	40.0	30.0‡	28.0
Zinc ore†	66.0	72.0	61.5	45.0‡	40.0
Manganese ore† . .	13.7	13.0	13.0	10.0	7.0
Chromium ore† . .	84.0	78.2	114.2	96.9	66.7
Magnesite (crude) .	16.0‡	5.0‡	5.0	5.0‡	n.a.
Native sulphur . .	n.a.	188	188	150	175

* Based on data from the U.S. Bureau of Mines.
† Figures refer to the metal content of ores.   ‡ Estimated production.

Source: UN, *Yearbook of Industrial Statistics.*

INDUSTRY
PETROLEUM PRODUCTS
('ooo metric tons)

	1976	1977	1978	1979
Liquefied petroleum gas* . . .	359	375	370	310
Naphtha*	605	700	690	690
Motor spirit (Petrol)* . . .	3,468	4,402	4,000	3,400
Aviation gasoline* . . .	367	304	340	250
Kerosene*	4,223	4,401	4,074	4,000
White spirit*	94	100	100	90
Jet fuel*	1,140	1,545	1,421	1,360
Distillate fuel oils . . .	6,845	7,587	7,013*	7,000*
Residual fuel oil . . .	14,471	16,373	15,133*	15,100*
Lubricating oils* . . .	118	117	100	100
Petroleum bitumen (asphalt)* .	750	780	770	750

* Estimated production.
Source: UN, *Yearbook of Industrial Statistics.*

OTHER PRODUCTS
(twelve months ending March 20th)

		1975/76	1976/77	1977/78	1978/79
Vegetable ghee	'ooo metric tons	265	300	n.a.	n.a.
Refined sugar	,, ,, ,,	772	808	718	628
Cigarettes	million	15,314	15,591	13,456	10,565
Paints	'ooo metric tons	30	46	57	51
Cement	,, ,, ,,	5,421	5,955	6,323	6,228
Refrigerators	'ooo	459	513	536	320
Kitchen stoves	,,	335	434	449	349
Household ovens	,,	629	732	806	735
Radio receivers (sales) . . .	,,	345	242	194	80
Television receivers . . .	,,	344	296	264	277
Motor vehicles (assembled) . .	,,	140	168	189	88

FINANCE

100 dinars = 1 Iranian rial.
Coins: 50 dinars; 1, 2, 5, 10 and 20 rials.
Notes: 5, 10, 20, 50, 100, 200, 500, 1,000, 5,000 and 10,000 rials.

Exchange rates (May 1982): £1 sterling = 148.31 rials; U.S. $1 = 80.67 rials.
1,000 Iranian rials = £6.74 = $12.40.

Note: From December 1946 to May 1957 the official exchange rate was U.S. $1 = 32.25 rials (1 rial = 3.1008 U.S. cents) but other rates were in operation for certain commercial transactions. From 1956 the trade rate was $1 = 75.75 rials (1 rial = 1.3201 U.S. cents) and this was the official parity from May 1957 to February 1973, despite the devaluation of the U.S. dollar in December 1971. In terms of sterling, the exchange rate was £1 = 181.80 rials from November 1967 to August 1971; and £1 = 197.38 rials from December 1971 to June 1972. In February 1973 a new par value of $1 = 68.175 rials was established but the Iranian authorities introduced market rates of $1 = 67.50 rials (buying) or 67.75 rials (selling), with a mid-point of $1 = 67.625 rials. In February 1975 the direct link with the dollar was broken and until 1977 the rial was tied to the IMF Special Drawing Right (at a mid-point of 82.24 rials per SDR), whose value is determined by changes in a weighted "basket" of currencies. The market rate against the U.S. dollar was frequently adjusted. It was $1 = 66.641 rials from February to July 1975, $1 = 69.275 rials from October 1975 to March 1976, $1 = 70.625 rials from June 1976 to December 1977 and $1 = 70.475 rials from December 1977 to May 1980. The rial was again linked to the SDR in May 1980, with the exchange rate set at 1 SDR = 92.30 rials. The average exchange rate (rials per U.S. dollar) was: 67.639 in 1975; 70.222 in 1976; 70.617 in 1977; 70.615 in 1980; 78.328 in 1981.

GOVERNMENT BUDGET ESTIMATES

(million rials)

REVENUE	1980/81	EXPENDITURE	1980/81
Income from taxation . . .	418,187	Public services	263,990
Oil and gas . . .	1,754,000	Defence	365,165
Government enterprises . . .	36,063	Education	
Sale of goods and services . .	30,804	Health	
Miscellaneous	150,733	Welfare	} 521,175
Foreign borrowings . . .	} 37,146	Housing	
Domestic borrowings . . .		Agriculture	
Interest on loans to foreign countries .	55,600	Electricity	} 967,776
Other	240,000	Industry	
TOTAL	2,722,533	TOTAL	2,118,106

1981/82: Revenue and Expenditure 3,165,981 million rials.

1982/83: Current Expenditure 1,800,000 million rials; Development Expenditure 780,000 million rials; War Expenditure 400,000 million rials.

GOVERNMENT OIL REVENUES

Total oil revenues received by Iran, in U.S. $ million: (1972) 2,308, (1973) 5,600, (1974) 22,000, (1975) 20,500, (1976) 22,000 approx., (1977) 23,000 approx., (1978) 20,900 approx., (1979) 18,800 approx., (1980) 11,600 approx., (1981) 8,500 approx.

CENTRAL BANK RESERVES
(U.S. $ million at December 31st)

	1977	1978	1979
Gold	161	174	180
IMF Special Drawing Rights	85	125	220
Reserve position in IMF .	1,197	945	428
Foreign exchange . .	10,824	10,907	14,561
TOTAL .	12,267	12,151	15,389

Source: IMF, *International Financial Statistics.*

MONEY SUPPLY
('000 million rials at March 20th)

	1978	1979	1980
Currency outside banks . .	326.36	803.58	929.36
Official entities' deposits at Central Bank . .	143.49	154.72	205.34
Demand deposits at commercial banks	487.83	493.34	786.08
TOTAL . .	957.68	1,451.64	1,920.78

Source: IMF, *International Financial Statistics.*

BALANCE OF PAYMENTS
(U.S. $ million)

	1972	1973	1974	1975	1976	1977
Merchandise exports f.o.b. . .	3,966	6,122	21,356	20,432	23,959	24,356
Merchandise imports f.o.b. . .	−2,591	−3,985	−7,257	−12,898	−15,973	−15,823
TRADE BALANCE . . .	1,375	2,137	14,099	7,534	7,986	8,533
Exports of services . . .	318	649	1,354	2,472	2,886	3,629
Imports of services . . .	−2,086	−2,629	−3,153	−5,280	−6,139	−7,071
BALANCE ON GOODS AND SERVICES	−392	156	12,300	4,725	4,734	5,090
Unrequited transfers (net) . .	4	−2	−33	−18	−20	−9
CURRENT BALANCE . . .	−388	154	12,267	4,707	4,714	5,081
Direct capital investment (net) .	91	561	324	141	744	802
Other long-term capital (net) .	531	628	−2,263	−3,010	−2,580	−441
Short-term capital (net) . .	13	−730	−3,127	−1,079	−3,238	−2,961
Net errors and omissions . .	219	−547	−176	−648	800	925
TOTAL (net monetary movements)	467	66	7,026	110	440	3,406
Allocation of IMF Special Drawing Rights	22	—	—	—	—	—
CHANGES IN RESERVES, ETC. .	489	66	7,026	110	440	3,406

Source: IMF, *International Financial Statistics.*

EXTERNAL TRADE
('ooo million rials, year ending December 20th)

	1974	1975	1976	1977	1978	1979	1980
Imports c.i.f. . .	367.4	700.3	905.2	993.6	954.9	686.3	863.3
Exports f.o.b. . .	1,459.0	1,367.1	1,651.3	1,713.1	1,564.4	1,400.5	969.8

PRINCIPAL COMMODITIES
(U.S. $ million, year ending March 20th)

IMPORTS c.i.f.	1974/75	1975/76	1976/77	1977/78
Food and live animals . . .	852	1,555	1,232	1,486
Beverages and tobacco . .	13	26	77	130
Crude materials (inedible) except fuels .	344	369	365	437
Mineral fuels, lubricants, etc. . .	13	17	23	30
Animal and vegetable oils and fats . .	240	291	137	164
Chemicals	649	835	858	1,003
Basic manufactures . . .	2,198	3,342	4,202	4,316
Machinery and transport equipment .	2,109	4,973	5,526	6,063
Miscellaneous manufactured articles . .	195	286	345	494
Other commodities and transactions. .	1	2	1	1
TOTAL	6,614	11,696	12,766	14,124

[*continued on next page*

PRINCIPAL COMMODITIES—*continued*]

EXPORTS (excl. petroleum and gas)	1974/75	1975/76	1976/77	1977/78
Carpets	119.1	105.6	94.5	114.5
Cotton	85.3	136.2	122.3	92.6
Fresh and dried fruits . . .	71.8	74.7	70.3	90.4
Skins and leather . . .	27.8	28.3	31.9	39.9
Minerals and metal ores . .	32.8	32.8	10.2	1.1
Detergents and soap . . .	12.1	22.1	19.3	16.1
Glycerine and chemicals . .	22.0	18.5	31.6	12.1
Confectionery and biscuits . .	3.4	5.0	11.3	11.3
Clothing, knitwear and textiles .	44.2	28.7	26.7	23.9
Road vehicles	21.2	28.3	24.2	9.9
TOTAL (incl. others) . .	581.5	592.2	539.9	523.2

Crude petroleum (U.S. $ million): 15,724.2 in 1974/75; 17,470.6 in 1975/76.
Petroleum products (U.S. $ million): 1,367.9 in 1974/75; 966.6 in 1975/76.
Natural gas (U.S. $ million): 124.9 in 1974/75; 137.2 in 1975/76.

PETROLEUM EXPORTS
('ooo barrels per day, year ending March 20th)

	1975/76	1976/77	1977/78	1978/79	1979/80
Crude petroleum . .	4,617	5,278	4,817	3,455	2,613
Refined oil products . .	263	214	188	203	220

Value of crude petroleum exports ('ooo million rials—year ending December 20th): 1,245.1 in 1975; 1,539.3 in 1976; 1,593.4 in 1977; 1,470.3 in 1978; 1,227.7 in 1979; 745.2 in 1980. (*Source:* IMF, Inter-*national Financial Statistics*).

PRINCIPAL TRADING PARTNERS
(U.S. $ million, year ending March 20th)

IMPORTS c.i.f.	1975/76	1976/77	1977/78	EXPORTS f.o.b.*	1975/76	1976/77	1977/78
Australia . . .	192	172	209	Bahrain . . .	6.8	6.4	8.8
Austria . . .	77	98	142	China, People's Repub..	22.8	8.2	9.5
Belgium . . .	295	277	340	Czechoslovakia . .	10.5	9.7	8.9
France . . .	516	714	648	France . . .	17.1	14.4	13.1
Germany, Fed. Repub. .	2,024	2,273	2,747	Germany, Fed. Repub..	80.7	86.3	79.2
India	435	315	185	Hungary . . .	23.2	15.1	21.8
Italy	417	735	798	Iraq . . .	4.4	6.3	24.9
Japan . . .	1,853	2,201	2,215	Italy . . .	29.4	33.1	25.0
Netherlands . .	330	443	464	Kuwait . . .	25.8	16.9	19.4
Romania . . .	167	147	190	Saudi Arabia . .	17.0	25.0	23.1
South Africa . .	63	103	191	South Africa . .	6.4	1.6	19.9
Sweden . . .	151	143	191	Taiwan . . .	13.0	7.0	8.4
Switzerland . . .	271	473	444	U.S.S.R. . . .	110.4	79.3	87.8
U.S.S.R. . . .	168	117	271	United Arab Emirates .	11.7	10.4	10.4
United Kingdom . .	1,033	904	971	United Kingdom . .	14.3	16.2	15.3
U.S.A. . . .	2,287	1,972	2,205	U.S.A. . . .	46.4	35.6	44.2
TOTAL (incl. others) .	11,696	12,766	14,124	TOTAL (incl. others) .	592.2	539.9	523.2

* Excluding petroleum and gas exports.

PERCENTAGE GEOGRAPHICAL DISTRIBUTION OF CRUDE OIL EXPORTS
(companies affiliated with Oil Service Co. of Iran)

	1974*	1975*	1976	1977	1978
Western Europe . . .	44.5	46.6	52.8	43.3	44.4
Japan	26.9	27.1	23.1	22.7	24.5
Asia	5.0	2.3	1.8	2.6	2.6
Central and North America .	16.7	15.0	7.5	11.7	8.5
Africa	5.3	6.8	6.6	8.7	8.5
Australasia . . .	0.2	0.7	1.1	1.0	0.6
South America . .	0.5	0.4	6.4	9.1	8.0
Other regions . . .	0.9	1.1	0.7	0.9	2.9

* Consortium only.

Source: National Iranian Oil Company.

TRANSPORT

RAILWAYS

	1978/79	1979/80
Passenger journeys ('000) . .	5,419	6,101
Freight ('000 metric tons) . .	6,942	6,138

ROAD TRAFFIC
('000 vehicles in use)

	1977
Cars	1,162
Buses	38
Trucks . . .	218
Ambulances . . .	194
Motor cycles . . .	268

CIVIL AVIATION

	1976/77	1977/78	1978/79
Passenger-km. ('000) . .	3,059,225	4,115,981	4,754,063

MERCHANT SHIPPING FLEET
('000 gross registered tons at June 30th)

	1975	1976	1977	1978	1979	1980
Oil tankers . .	181	297	617	598	597	666
Other vessels .	299	386	385	597	610	618
TOTAL . .	480	683	1,002	1,195	1,207	1,284

INTERNATIONAL SHIPPING TRAFFIC*
('000 metric tons, year ending March 20th)

	1975/76	1976/77	1977/78	1978/79	1979/80
Goods loaded . . .	243,280	273,020	255,470	220,326	n.a.
Goods unloaded . .	10,964	13,642	15,046	14,536	8,773

* Including goods imported and exported other than by sea.

TOURISM

	1977/78	1978/79
Visitors . . .	502,278	147,532
Approximate Money Spent (million U.S. $) .	201	54

EDUCATION
(1977/78)

	SCHOOLS	PUPILS ('000)
Elementary . . .	24,814	4,314
Literacy Corps . . .	14,839	706
Orientation Course . .	5,142	1,446
Secondary . .	1,824	757
Technical and Vocational .	675	233
Primary Teacher Training .	228	54
Universities and Colleges .	224	146

Source (except where otherwise stated): **Statistical Centre of Iran**, Teheran.

THE CONSTITUTION

A draft Constitution was published in mid-June 1979 and a 75-member "Council of Experts" was elected to debate the various clauses and propose amendments. The amended Constitution was put to a referendum in early December 1979 and gained the approval of the electorate.

The Constitution states that the form of government of Iran is that of an Islamic Republic, and that the spirituality and ethics of Islam are to be the basis for political, social and economic relations. Persians, Turks, Kurds, Arabs, Baluchis, Turkomans and others will enjoy completely equal rights.

The Constitution provides for a popularly-elected President for a term of four years and a popularly-elected *Majlis* (Islamic Consultative Assembly) of 270 members for a term of four years. Provision is made for the representation of Zoroastrians, Jews and Christians.

All legislation passed by the Islamic Consultative Assembly must be sent to the Council for the Protection of the Constitution (Article 94), which will ensure that it is in accordance with the Constitution and Islamic legislation. The Council for the Protection of the Constitution consists of six religious lawyers appointed by the *faghih* (*see* below) and six lawyers appointed by the High Council of the Judiciary and approved by the Islamic Consultative Assembly. Articles 19–42 deal with the basic rights of individuals, and provide for equality of men and women before the law and for equal human, political, economic, social and cultural rights for both sexes.

The press is free, except in matters that are contrary to public morality or insult religious belief. The formation of religious, political and professional parties, associations and societies is free, provided they do not negate the principles of independence, freedom, sovereignty and national unity, or the basis of Islam.

The amended Constitution contains a significant change from the earlier draft. It provides for a *velayat faghih* (religious leader) who, in the absence of the Imam Mehdi (the hidden Twelfth Imam), carries the burden of leadership. Article 107 gives Ayatollah Khomeini these powers for the rest of his natural life. Thereafter, an elected council of experts will choose an individual or three or five people to form a council of leadership, and the choice must be "approved by the nation". According to Article 57 the executive, legislative and judicial branches of state power are under the authority of the *faghih*. Among the extensive powers reserved to the *faghih* is the right to appoint half the members of the Council for the Protection of the Constitution (*see* above). He is also Supreme Commander of the Armed Forces and can appoint the Joint Chiefs of Staff and the Head of the Revolutionary Guard. He appoints four of the seven members of the National Defence Council and, on their recommendation, appoints the senior commanders of the armed forces. He also has power to declare war and make peace on the recommendation of the National Defence Council. The first *faghih* has the right to vet all candidates for the Presidency (a right which was exercised by Ayatollah Khomeini). The *faghih* can also dismiss the President on the basis of a Supreme Court decision or a vote of no confidence by the Islamic Consultative Assembly.

PROVINCIAL DIVISIONS

According to the latest state division (May 1977), Iran is divided into 23 provinces (*Ostans*), 472 counties (*shahrestan*) and 499 municipalities (*bakhsh*).

THE GOVERNMENT

VELAYAT FAGHIH (RELIGIOUS LEADER)

Ayatollah RUHOLLAH KHOMEINI.

HEAD OF STATE

President: Hojatoleslam SAYED ALI KHAMENEI (took office October 13th, 1981).

COUNCIL OF MINISTERS

(May 1982)

Prime Minister: MIR HUSSEIN MOUSSAVI.

Minister of Foreign Affairs: ALI AKBAR VELAYATI.

Minister of Education and Training: ALI AKBAR PARVARESH.

Minister of Islamic Guidance: Hojatoleslam ABDOL MAJID MADIKHAH.

Minister of Commerce: HABIBOLLAH ASGAR-OWLADI-MOSALMAN.

Minister of Health: Dr. HADI MANAFI.

Minister of Posts, Telegraphs and Telephones: Eng. MORTEZA NABAVI.

Minister of Justice: SEYYED MUHAMMAD ASGHARI.

Minister of Defence: Col. MUHAMMAD SALIMI.

Minister of Roads and Transport: Eng. HADINEZHAD HOSEYNIYAN.

Minister of Industries: Eng. SEYYED MOSTAFA HASHEMI.

Minister of Higher Education and Culture: Dr. MUHAMMAD ALI NAJAFI.

Minister of Mines and Metals: SEYYED HUSSEIN MUSAVI-YANI.

Minister of Labour and Social Affairs: AHMED TAVAKOLI.

Minister of Interior: ALI AKBAR NATEGH NOURI.

Minister of Agriculture: MUHAMMAD SALAMATI.

Minister of Housing and Urban Development: Eng. MUHAMMAD SHAHAB GONABADI.

Minister of Energy: Dr. HASAN GHAFURI-FARD.

Minister of Oil: Eng. SEYYED MUHAMMAD GHARAZI.

Minister of Economic Affairs and Finance: Dr. HUSSEIN NAMAZI.

Minister of State for Plan and Budget Organization: Dr. MUHAMMAD TAQI BANKI.

Minister of State for Welfare Organizations: Dr. MAHMUD ROHANI.

Minister of State for Executive Affairs: Eng. BEHZAD NABAVI.

PRESIDENT AND LEGISLATURE

PRESIDENTIAL ELECTION

(October 2nd, 1981)

CANDIDATES		VOTES	%
Hojatoleslam Sayed Ali Khamenei		16,007,972	95.0
Ali Akbar Parvaresh	. .	341,841	2.0
Dr. Hasan Ghafuri-Fard	. .	78,658	0.5
Reza Zavarei	. . .	62,156	0.4
Invalid	. . . .	356,369	2.1
TOTAL	. . .	16,846,996	100.0

MAJLIS—ISLAMIC CONSULTATIVE ASSEMBLY

Elections took place in two rounds on March 14th and May 9th, 1980. 270 seats were contested by 3,300 candidates. The Islamic Republican Party won a clear majority of the seats.

Speaker: Hojatoleslam HASHEMI RAFSANJANI.

Deputy Speakers: Hojatoleslam MUHAMMAD MOUSSAVI KHOEINIHA, MUHAMMAD YAZDI.

POLITICAL PARTIES

Democratic Party of Iranian Kurdistan: Mahabad; wants autonomy for Kurdish area; f. 1945; 54,000 mems.; Sec.-Gen. Dr. ABDUL-RAHMAN QASSEMLOU; Publs. *Kurdistan, Tekoshar.*

Fedayeen-el-Khalq: urban Marxist guerrillas.

Hezb-e Komunist Iran: (*Communist Party of Iran*): f. 1979 on grounds that Tudeh Party was Moscow-controlled; Sec.-Gen. 'AZARYUN'.

Iran Liberation Movement: Islamic; Leader Dr. MEHDI BAZARGAN.

Islamic Republican Party: f. 1979; party founded to bring about the Islamic Revolution under the leadership of Ayatollah KHOMEINI; Sec.-Gen. Hojatoleslam SAYED ALI KHAMENEI; Principal Officers Ayatollah ABDOL-KARIM MUSAVI ARDEBILI and Hojatoleslam HASHEMI RAFSANJANI.

Mujaheddin Khalq: Islamic guerrilla group; Leader MASSOUD RAJAVI (in Paris); Leader (in Iran) Eng. ALI ZARKESH.

Muslim People's Republican Party: Tabriz; backed by Ayatollah SHARIATMADARI; over 3.5 million members (2.5 million in Azerbaizhan); Sec.-Gen. HOSSEIN FARSHI.

National Democratic Front: f. March 1979; Leader HEDAYATOLLAH MATINE-DAFTARI (in Paris, January 1982-).

National Front (*Union of National Front Forces*): comprises Iran Nationalist Party, Iranian Party, and Society of Iranian Students.

Pan Iranist Party: extreme right-wing; calls for a Greater Persia; Leader MOHSEN PEZESHKPOUR.

Sazmane Peykar dar Rahe Azadieh Tabaqe Kargar (*Organization Struggling for the Freedom of the Working Class*): Marxist-Leninist.

Tudeh Party (*Communist*): f. 1941; declared illegal 1949; pro-Moscow; First Sec. NUREDDIN KIANURI.

DIPLOMATIC REPRESENTATION

EMBASSIES ACCREDITED TO IRAN

(In Teheran unless otherwise stated)

Afghanistan: Ave. Dr. Beheshti, Pompe Benzine, Corner of 4th St.; *Chargé d'affaires a.i.:* Dr. BASSIR RANJBAR.

Albania: Ankara, Turkey.

Algeria: Ave. Mobarezan (Nord), 8th St., No. 13; *Ambassador:* ABDELKRIM GHRAIEB.

Argentina: North Bucharest Ave., Argentine Sq., Alitalia Building, 4th Floor, P.O.B. 98–164; *Ambassador:* ISVALDO GUILLERMO GARCÍA PINEIRO.

Australia: Ave. Somayye, P.O.B. 3408; *Chargé d'affaires a.i.:* K. J. BOREHAM.

Austria: Ave. Taleghani, Corner Forsat No. 140; *Ambassador:* Dr. JOHANN PLATTNER.

Bahrain: Ave. Park, 31st St., No. 16; *Ambassador:* HOSSEIN RASHED AL-SABAGH.

Bangladesh: Ave. Gandhi, 5th Street, Building No. 14; *Ambassador:* HUMAYUN KABIR.

Belgium: Ave. Ostad Motahari, 49 Ave. Daryaye Noor; *Ambassador:* ROGER MARTIN.

Brazil: Ave. Vali Asr, Alavi St. No. 61; *Chargé d'affaires a.i.:* JAYRO COELHO.

Bulgaria: Ave. Vali Asr, Place Dr. Hossein Fatemi, rue Shabnam No. 23; *Ambassador:* VELIKO VENCHEV.

Burma: Islamabad, Pakistan.

Cameroon: Jeddah, Saudi Arabia.

Chile: (*relations broken off Aug.* 1980).

China, People's Republic: Ave. Pasdaran, Ave. Golestan 1 No. 53; *Ambassador:* ZHUANG YAN.

Colombia: Ave. Bihaghi, 14th St., No. 15; *Ambassador:* ANTONIO BAYONA.

Cuba: Ave. North Gandhi, Amir Parviz St. No. 1/28; *Ambassador:* ALBERTO VELAZCO SAN JOSÉ.

Czechoslovakia: Ave. Enghelab, Sarshar No. 61; *Chargé d'affaires a.i.:* LADISLAV OPATRNY.

Denmark: Vejdani St. No. 40, P.O.B. 31; *Ambassador:* JØRGEN ADAMSEN.

Ethiopia: Ankara, Turkey.

Finland: Ave. Gandhi, corner of 25th St., No. 73; *Ambassador:* UNTO TANSKANEN.

France: France Ave. No. 85; *Chargé d'affaires a.i.:* JEAN-PIERRE GUINHUT.

Gabon: Ave. Darband, Ave. Khaliji, Sadr St., No. 6; *Ambassador:* MAMADOU DIOP.

Gambia: Jeddah, Saudi Arabia.

German Democratic Republic: Ave. Mirza-ye Shirazi, rue Afshin 15; *Ambassador:* WOLFGANG KONSCHEL.

Germany, Federal Republic: 324 Ferdowsi Ave.; *Ambassador:* Dr. JENS PETERSEN.

Ghana: Ave. Ghaem Magham Farahani, Rue Varahram No. 12; *Ambassador:* C. C. LOKKO.

Greece: Ave. Park, Rue 35 No. 20; *Chargé d'affaires a.i.:* SPYROS BACAS.

Hungary: Ave. Park, rue 13, No. 18; *Ambassador:* LAJOS NAGY.

India: Ave. Saba Shomali, No. 166; *Ambassador:* AKBAR MIRZA KHALILI.

Indonesia: Ave. Ghaem Magham Farahani, No. 210, P.O.B. 1559; *Ambassador:* IMAM SOEPOMO.

Iraq: Ave. Vali Asr No. 494; *Chargé d'affaires a.i.:* T. A. AL-MAROUF.

Ireland: Ave. Vali Asr, Ave. Razan Shomali No. 8; *Chargé d'affaires a.i.:* NIALL HOLOHAN.

Italy: France Ave. No. 81; *Ambassador:* FRANCESCO MEZZALAMA.

Ivory Coast: Africa Ave., Tour No. 3; *Chargé d'affaires a.i.:* EMMANUEL T. AMON.

Japan: Ave. Bucharest, N.W. Corner of 5th St.; *Ambassador:* SHOTARO TAKAHASHI.

Jordan: (*relations broken off February* 1981).

Korea, Democratic People's Republic: Ave. Fereshteh, Ave. Sarvestan, No. 11; *Ambassador:* CHA PYONG-OK.

Korea, Republic: 37 Ave. Bucharest; *Chargé d'affaires, a.i.:* SUNG KU KANG.

Kuwait: Dehkadeh Ave., 3–38 Sazman-Ab St.; *Ambassador:* AHMED ABDUL AZIZ AL-JASSIM.

Lebanon: Bucharest Ave., 16th St., No. 43; *Ambassador:* FOUAD TURK.

Liberia: Cairo, Egypt.

Libya: Ave. Motahari, No. 163; *Head of Committee of People's Bureau:* SAAD MOSTAPHA MOJBER.

Malaysia: Bucharest Ave., No. 8; *Chargé d'affaires a.i.:* ZAINUL ABIDIN BIN MUHAMMAD ZAIN.

Malta: London, U.K.

Mauritania: Ave. Africa Sayeh St., No. 78; *Ambassador:* ALI THIERNO BARO.

Mongolia: Prague, Czechoslovakia.

Morocco: (*relations broken off February* 1981).

Netherlands: Ave. Vali Asr, Ave. Ostad Motahari, Sarbederan St., Jahansouz Alley No. 36; *Ambassador:* EDUARD VAN DER PALS.

New Zealand: Ave. Mirza Sherazee, Ave. Afshin, No. 29; *Ambassador:* DONALD G. HARPER.

Niger: Cairo, Egypt.

Nigeria: Ave-Park, 31st St., No. 9; *Ambassador:* HARUNA BIN MUSA.

Norway: Bucharest Ave., 6th St., No. 23; *Ambassador:* T. P. SVENNEVIG.

Oman: Ave. Africa, Golnar St., No. 18–20; *Chargé d'affaires a.i.:* M. ABDULLAH AL-ASFOOR.

Pakistan: Ave. Dr. Fatemi, Jamshidabad Shomali, Ave. Khorshid No. 1; *Chargé d'affaires a.i.:* TARIQ MUHAMMAD MIR.

Philippines: Boulevard Keshavarz, rue Dehkadeh No. 19; *Chargé d'affaires a.i.:* RONALD ALLAREY.

Poland: Ave. Africa, Rue Piruz No. 1/3; *Ambassador:* JOZEF FILIPOWICZ.

Portugal: Ave. Vali Asr, Ave. Tavanir, Ave. Nezami, No. 30; *Chargé d'affaires a.i.:* LUIS MANUEL DIAS DA SILVEIRA.

Qatar: Ave. Africa, Ave. Golazin, Parke Davar No. 4; *Chargé d'affaires a.i.:* I. MUHAMMAD AL-QAYED.

Romania: Fakhrabad Ave. 12; *Ambassador:* NICOLAE STEFAN.

Saudi Arabia: Ave. Bucharest, No. 59, P.O.B. 2903; *Chargé d'affaires a.i.:* MARVAN BASHIR AL-ROOMI.

Singapore: New Delhi, India.

Somalia: Ave. Shariati, Ave. Soheyl No. 20; *Chargé d'affaires a.i.:* MUHAMMAD ALI SERAR.

Spain: Ave. Ghaem Magham Farahani, rue Varahram No. 14; *Ambassador:* JAVIER OYARZUN.

Sri Lanka: Islamabad, Pakistan.

Sudan: Ave. Bucharest, 10th St., No. 41; *Chargé d'affaires a.i.:* EL-TAYEB AHMED NASR.

Sweden: Taleghani Ave., Forsat Ave.; *Ambassador:* GORAN BUNDY.

Switzerland: Pasteur Ave.; *Chargé d'affaires a.i.:* FLAVIO MERONI.

Syria: Ave. Park, 27th St., No. 8; *Ambassador:* IBRAHIM YUNIS.

Thailand: Baharestan Ave., ParcAmin-ed-Doleh No. 14; *Ambassador:* ATAPORN CHARUBHAT.

Trinidad and Tobago: Beirut, Lebanon.

Tunisia: Embassy closed October 1981.

Turkey: Ferdowsi Ave. No. 314; *Ambassador:* TANSUG BLEDA.

U.S.S.R.: Neauphle-le-Château Ave.; *Ambassador:* VIL BOLDYREV

United Arab Emirates: Ave. Zafar, No. 355–7; *Chargé d'affaires a.i.:* T. AHMAD AL-HAIDAN.

United Kingdom: Ferdowsi Ave.; *Ambassador:* (vacant).

U.S.A.: Taleghani Ave., Mobarezan Ave.; diplomatic relations broken off April 7th, 1980.

Vatican: Razi Ave. 97 (Apostolic Nunciature) *Ambassador:* Mgr. ANNIBALE BUGNINI.

Venezuela: Ave. Bucharest, 9th St., No. 31; *Chargé d'affaires a.i.:* K. AREF KANSAO.

Viet-Nam: New Delhi, India.

Yemen Arab Republic: Ave. Bucharest, No. 26; *Chargé d'affaires a.i.:* HUSSAIN MOHSEN AL-JABRY.

Yemen, People's Democratic Republic: *Ambassador:* KHADIR SALIH AL-HAMZAH.

Yugoslavia: Ave. Pasdaran, Narenjestan St.; *Ambassador:* EDVARD KLJUN.

Zaire: Ave. Vali Asr, Chehrazi St., No. 68; *Chargé d'affaires a.i.:* ILANGWA E. YOKA.

Iran also has diplomatic relations with Albania, Barbados, Guinea, Guinea-Bissau, Madagascar, Maldives, Mozambique, Nepal, Senegal, Seychelles, Sierra Leone, Tanzania and Uruguay.

JUDICIAL SYSTEM

SUPREME COURT

President: Ayatollah ABDOLKARIM MUSAVI ARDEBILI.

Prosecutor-General: RABBANI AMLASHI.

ISLAMIC REVOLUTIONARY COURTS

Head of Military Revolutionary Courts and Head of Drug Offences Court: Hojatoleslam MOKHDAI.

These were introduced after the revolution and have tried and executed numerous people. Section 11 of the new Constitution outlines the new Judicial System. The *faghih* (religious leader) appoints the Head of the Supreme Court, the President of the Supreme Judicial Council and the Prosecutor-General. According to Article 167, judges must reach verdicts based on precedent or Islamic sources. In August 1980 talks were held on merging the Revolutionary Courts with the civil courts left from the Shah's regime. In September 1981 Ayatollah KHOMEINI delegated his power of appointment to the Supreme Judicial Council to Ayatollah MONTAZARI.

Administrative Tribunal: President MUHAMMAD YAZDI.

RELIGION

According to the new 1979 Constitution, the official religion is Islam and the Ja'fari Sect (Shi'ite), but other Islamic sects, including Zeydi, Hanafi, Maleki, Shafe'i and Hanbali, will be valid and respected. Zoroastrians, Jews and Christians will be recognized as official religious minorities. According to the 1976 census there were then 310,000 Christians (mainly Armenian), 80,000 Jews and 30,000 Zoroastrians.

MUSLIMS

The great majority of the Iranian people are Shi'i Muslims, but there is a minority of Sunni Muslims. Persians and Azerbaizhanis are mainly Shi'i, while the other national groups are mainly Sunni.

During 1978 there was a revival of the influence of the *Ayatollahs* (or senior Shi'ite divines). The Iranian people felt that a return to a closer observance of the tenets of Islam was necessary. Ayatollah Ruhollah Khomeini of Qom, who had been exiled to Iraq in 1964 and moved to near Paris in October 1978, conducted a campaign of opposition to the Shah, returning to Iran in February 1979 and bringing about the downfall of the Shah's regime. Other important Ayatollahs include Ayatollah ABDOL-KARIM MUSAVI ARDEBILI, Ayatollah HOSSEIN ALI MONTA-ZARI of Teheran and the Ayatollahs SHARIATMADARI, MARASHI-NAJANI and GOLPAYEGANI of Qom.

ZOROASTRIANS

There are about 30,000 Zoroastrians, a remnant of a once widespread sect. Their religious leader is MOUBAD.

OTHER COMMUNITIES

Communities of Armenians, and somewhat smaller numbers of Jews, Assyrians, Greek Orthodox, Uniates and Latin Christians are also found as officially recognized faiths. The Baha'i faith, which originated in Iran, has about 450,000 adherents.

Roman Catholic (Chaldean) Archbishop of Teheran: Ave. Forsat 91, Teheran; Most Rev. YOUHANNAN SEMAAN ISSAYI; 28,395 Catholics (1976).

Anglican Bishop in Iran and President-Bishop, Episcopal Church in Jerusalem and the Middle East: Rt. Rev.

H. B. DEHQANI-TAFTI, Bishop's House, P.O.B. 12, Isfahan; Diocese founded 1912.

Synod of the Evangelical (Presbyterian) Church in Iran: Assyrian Evangelical Church, Khiaban-i Hanifnejad, Khiaban-i Aramanch, Teheran; Moderator Rev. ADLE NAKHOSTEEN.

THE PRESS

Teheran dominates the press scene as many of the daily papers are published there and the bi-weekly, weekly and less frequent publications in the provinces generally depend on the major metropolitan dailies as a source of news. A press law which was announced in August 1979 required all newspapers and magazines to be licensed and imposed penalties of imprisonment for insulting senior religious figures. Offences against the Act will be tried in the criminal courts. In the new Constitution, approved in December 1979, the press will be free, except in matters that are contrary to public morality, insult religious belief or slander the honour and reputation of individuals. Many of the papers which were published under the Shah's regime ceased publication after the revolution. In August 1980 Ayatollah Khomeini issued directives which indicated that censorship would be tightened up, and several papers were closed down in 1981.

PRINCIPAL DAILIES

Alik: Naderi Ave., Teheran; f. 1931; morning; political and literary; Armenian; Propr. Dr. R. STEPANIAN; circ. 4,000.

Azadegan: Teheran; morning; Farsi.

Bahari: Khayaban Khayam, Shiraz.

Ettela'at (*Information*): Khayyam Ave., Teheran; f. 1925; evening; political and literary; Supervisor Hojatoleslam SEYYED MAHMUD DO'A'I; Editor H. BANIAHMAD; circ. 220,000.

Jomhouri Islami (*Islamic Republic*): Teheran; organ of Islamic Republican Party; Farsi.

Kayhan: Ferdowsi Ave., Teheran; f. 1941; evening; political; owned by Mostazafin Foundation October 1979; Supervisor: Hojatoleslam MUHAMMAD KHATAMI; circ. 350,000.

Khalqa-Musalman: Teheran; Farsi.

Khorassan: Meshed; Head Office: Khorassan Daily Newspapers, 14 Zohre St., Mobarezan Ave., Teheran; f. 1948; Propr. MUHAMMAD SADEGH TEHRANIAN; circ. 40,000.

Mojahed: P.O.B. 64-1551, Teheran; organ of the Mujaheddin Khalq.

Rahnejat: Darvazeh Dowlat, Isfahan; political and social; Propr. N. RAHNEJAT.

Teheran Times: Avenue Villa, Khusrow St. 52–54, Teheran; f. 1979; independent; English; Editor IRFAN PARVIZ.

PRINCIPAL PERIODICALS

Acta Medica Iranica: Faculty of Medicine, Teheran Univ., Teheran 14; f. 1958; English, French, German; quarterly; Editor Dr. H. AREFI; circ. 2,000.

Akhbare Pezeshki: 86 Ghaem Magham Farahani Ave., Teheran; weekly; medical; Prop. Dr. T. FORUZIN.

Al-Akha: Khayyam Ave., Tehran; f. 1960; Arabic; weekly; Editor NAZIR FENZA.

Armaghan: Baghe Saba, 127 Salim Street, Teheran;

literary and historical; Prop. Dr. MOHAMMAD VAHID-DASTGERDI.

Ashur: Ostad Motahari Ave., Teheran; Assyrian; Propr. Dr. V. BITMANSUR.

Auditor: Q. 77, Khayaban Firdowsi North, Teheran; financial and managerial studies.

Ayandeh: P.O.B. 98/811, Tajrish; literary, historical and book review journal; Editor IRAJ AFSHAR.

Daneshkadeh Pezeshki: Faculty of Medicine, Teheran University; medical magazine; ten issues per year; circ. 1,500.

Daneshmand: Baharestan St., Teheran 11; scientific and technical magazine; monthly; Editor Dr. N. SHIFTEH.

Dokhtaran and Pesaran: Khayyam Ave., Teheran; f. 1947; weekly teenage magazine; Editor NADER AKHAVAN HAYDARI.

Donaye Varzesh: Khayyam Ave., Ettela'at Bldg., Teheran; sport; Prop. M. FARZANAH.

Echo of Islam: P.O.B. 41-2334, Teheran; published by Ministry of Islamic Guidance; English; monthly.

Ettela'at Banovan: 11 Khayyam St., Teheran; women's weekly magazine; Editor Mrs. RAHNAWARD; circ. 85,000.

Ettela'at Haftegi: Akhavan Ave., Teheran; weekly; Editor RASOUL ANVANI KERMANI; circ. approx. 200,000.

Ettela'at Javanan: Khayyam Ave., Teheran; f. 1958; youth weekly; Editor R. ETTEMADI.

Farhang-e-Iran Zamin: P.O.B. 95/1642, Niyavaran; Iranian studies; Editor Prof. IRAJ AFSHAR.

Faza: Enghelab Ave., Teheran; aviation; Prop. H. KAMALI-TAQARI.

Film-Va-Honar: Mobarezan Ave., Teheran; weekly; Editor A. RAMAZANI.

Honar va Memar: Enghelab Ave. No. 256, Teheran; scientific and professional monthly; Propr. A. H. ECHRAGH.

Hoquqe Mardom: Villa Ave., 46 Damghan Street, Teheran; judicial; Prop. J. MANSURIAN.

Iran Economic Service: Hafiz Ave., 4 Kucheh Hurtab; P.O.B. 2008, Teheran; weekly, economic.

Iran Political Digest: Echo Bldg., Hafiz Ave., P.O.B. 2008; English; weekly; Editor J. BEHROUZ.

Jam: Jomhoori Islami Ave., Sabuhi Bldg., P.O.B. 1871, Teheran; arts; Prop. A. VAKILI.

Jame'e Dandan-Pezeshkan: 85 Hafez Ave., Teheran; medical; Prop. Dr. M. HASHEMI.

Kayhan Bacheha (*Children's World*): Kh. Ferdowsi, Teheran; weekly; Editor DJAAFAR BADII; circ. 150,000.

Kayhan Varzeshi (*World of Sport*): Kh. Ferdowsi, Teheran; weekly; Dir. MAHMAD MONSETI; circ. 125,000.

Khorak: 24 Esfand Square, Teheran; health and food; Prop. Dr. M. OLUMI.

Music Iran: 1029 Amiriye Ave., Teheran; f. 1951; monthly; Editor BAHMAN HIRBOD; circ. 7,000.

DEFENCE

Military service: 2 years.

Total armed forces: At the beginning of the Gulf War in September 1980 Iran's army was estimated to total between 120,000 and 150,000 men, and the navy to total 30,000.

Commander-in-Chief of the Armed Forces: Gen. QASEM ALI ZAHIRNEZHAD.

Commander of Army and Gendarmerie Overseer: Gen. ALI SAYYAD-SHIRAZI.

Commander of Air Force: Col. MO'INPUR.

Commander of Navy: KHALID BIN AL-WALID.

Commander of Islamic Revolution Guards Corps: MOHSEN REZAI.

EDUCATION

Primary and Secondary Education

When compulsory primary education was established by Reza Shah in the 1930s there were no more than 36,000 children attending school. In 1975/76 over six million children were attending many thousands of primary and secondary schools all over the country.

Primary education for five years is compulsory for all children and, along with a three years' guidance period, was declared free in 1974. An increasing number of children are now proceeding to secondary schools after obtaining their primary education certificate. It was reported in early 1979 that the government intended to abolish co-education.

Higher Education

Iran has 16 universities, including six in Teheran. There are several other institutes of higher education, four teachers' training colleges, a college of advanced technology in Abadan and colleges of agriculture in Karaj, Rezaiyah and Kerman. Vocational training schools also exist in Teheran, Shiraz, Tabriz, Rasht and other cities.

In recent years much emphasis has been put on improving higher education facilities as well as expanding research.

BIBLIOGRAPHY

GENERAL

ABDALIAN, S. Damavand (Iran) (Teheran, 1943).

BARTH, F. Nomads of South Persia (London, 1961).

CAMBRIDGE HISTORY OF IRAN.
Volume I: The Land of Iran.
Volume V: The Seljuq and Mongol Periods.
(Both Cambridge University Press, 1968).

CURZON, Lord. Persia and the Persian Question (2 vols., London, 1892).

DE PLANHOL, X. Recherches sur la Géographie humaine de l'Iran Septentrional (Paris, 1964).

ELWELL-SUTTON, L. P. Modern Iran (London, 1941).
A Guide to Iranian Area Study (Ann Arbor, 1952).
Persian Oil: A Study in Power Politics (London, 1955).

ENGLISH, P. W. City and Village in Iran (Wisconsin, 1967).

ESKELUND, KARL. Behind the Peacock Throne (Alvin Redman, New York, 1965).

FIELD, HENRY. Contributions to the Anthropology of Iran (Chicago, 1939).

FRYE, RICHARD N. Persia (Allen and Unwin, London, 3rd ed. 1969).

FURON, RAYMOND. L'Iran (Paris, 1952).
Géologie du Plateau iranien (Paris, 1941).
La Perse (Paris, 1938).

GAIL, MARZIEH. Persia and the Victorians (London, 1951).

GRAVES, PHILIP. The Life of Sir Percy Cox (1941).

HUOT, JEAN LOUIS. Persia Vol. I (Muller, London, 1966).

IQBAL, MUHAMMAD. Iran (London, 1946).
Iran Almanac (Echo of Iran, Teheran, annually).
Iran: A Selected and Annotated Bibliography (Washington, 1951).

KEDDIE, NIKKI R. Historical Obstacles to Agrarian Change in Iran (Claremont, 1960).
Iran. Religion, Politics and Society (London, Frank Cass, 1980).

KEMP, N. Abadan (London, 1954).

LAMBTON, A. K. S. Landlord and Peasant in Persia (New York, 1953).
Islamic Society in Persia (London, 1954).
A Persian Vocabulary (Cambridge, 1961).
The Persian Land Reform 1962-66 (Clarendon Press, Oxford, 1969).

MARLOWE, JOHN. Iran, a Short Political Guide (Pall Mall Press, London and New York, 1963).

MEHDEVI, A. S. Persian Adventure (New York, 1954).
Persia Revisited (London, 1965).

MILLSPAUGH, A. C. Americans in Persia (Washington, 1946).

MOTTER, T. H. VAIL. The Persian Corridor and Aid to Russia (Washington, 1952).

RAMAZANI, ROUHOLLAH K. The Persian Gulf: Iran's Role (Charlottesville, University Press of Virginia, 1972).

SANGHVI, RAMESH. Aryamehr: The Shah of Iran (Macmillan, London, 1968).

SAVORY, ROGER. Iran under the Safavids (Cambridge University Press, 1980).

SHAH OF IRAN. Mission for My Country (Hutchinson, London 1961).

SHEARMAN, I. Land and People of Iran (London, 1962).

SIRDAR, IKBAL ALI SHAH. Persia of the Persians (London, 1929).

STARK, FREYA. The Valleys of the Assassins (London, 1934).
East is West (London, 1945).

THARAUD, JÉRÔME. Vieille Perse et Jeune Iran (Paris, 1947).

VREELAND, H. H. Iran (Human Relations Area Files, 1957).

WICKENS, G. M. and SAVORY, R. M. Persia in Islamic Times, a practical bibliography of its history, culture and language (Institute of Islamic Studies, McGill University, Montreal, 1964).

WILBER, DONALD N. Iran: Past and Present (Princeton University Press, 1955, 8th edn. 1977).
Iran: Oasis of Stability in the Middle East (Foreign Political Association, Inc., New York, 1959).

ZABIH, SEPEHR. The Communist Movement in Iran (University of California Press 1967).

CIVILIZATION AND LITERATURE

ARBERRY, A. J. (ed.). The Legacy of Persia (London and New York, 1953).
Shiraz: The Persian City of Saints and Poets (Univ. of Oklahoma Press, 1960).
Tales from the Masnavi (London, 1961).
More Tales from the Masnavi (London, 1963).
(ed.). The Cambridge History of Iran (Cambridge University Press 1969).

BAUSANI, A. Der Perser: von den Anfängen bis zur Gegenwart (Kohlhammer, Stuttgart, 1965).

BELL, GERTRUDE L. Persian Pictures (London, 1928).

BROWNE, E. G. A Literary History of Persia (4 vols., Cambridge, 1928).

COLLEDGE, M.A.R. The Parthians (Thames and Hudson, London, 1968).

CULICAN, WILLIAM. The Medes and the Persians (1965).

DUCHESNE-GUILLEMIN, JACQUES. The Hymns of Zara-thustra (trans. with commentary) (Beacon, L. R., Boston, Mass., 1963).

GHIRSHMAN, R. L'Iran: des Origines à Islam (Paris, 1951).
Iran from the Earliest Times to the Islamic Conquest (London, 1954).
Arts of Ancient Persia from the Origins to Alexander the Great (London, 1963).
Iran (New York, 1964).

HERZFELD, E. Iran in the Ancient East (Oxford, 1941).

KAMSHAD, H. Modern Persian Prose Literature (Cambridge, 1966).

LEVY, REUBEN. The Persian Language (New York, 1952).
Persian Literature (1928).

LOCKHART, L. Famous Cities of Iran (London, 1939).
The Fall of the Safavi Dynasty and the Afghan Occupation of Persia (Cambridge University Press, 1958).

MONTEIL, V. Les Tribus du Fars et la sédentarisation des nomades (Mouton, Paris and The Hague, 1966).

OLMSTEAD, A. T. History of the Persian Empire, Achaemenid Period (Chicago, 1948).

POPE, ARTHUR. Survey of Persian Art from Prehistoric Times to the Present. Vols. 1-6 (Oxford University Press, 1938-58).

RICE, CYPRIAN. The Persian Sufis (Allen and Unwin, London, 1964).

ROSS, Sir DENISON. Eastern Art and Literature (London, 1928).
The Persians (London, 1931).

STOREY, C. A. Persian Literature (London, 1927).

SYKES, Sir PERCY. Persia (Oxford, 1922).
A History of Persia (2 vols.; 3rd edition, with supplementary essays) (London, 1930).

WIDENGREN. Die Religionen Irans (Kohlhammer, Stuttgart, 1965).

WULFF, H. E. The Traditional Crafts of Persia (M.I.T. Press, Cambridge, Mass., 1966).

RECENT HISTORY

AKHAVI, SHAHROUGH. Religion and Politics in Contemporary Iran (State University of New York Press, 1980).

BANANI, AMIN. The Modernization of Iran, 1921-1924 (Stanford, 1961).

BUNYA, ALI AKBAR. A Political and Diplomatic History of Persia (Teheran, 1955).

CHUBIN, SHARAM and ZABIH, SEPEHR. The Foreign Relations of Iran: A Developing State in the Zone of a Great-Power Conflict (University of California Press, 1975).

COTTAM, R. W. Nationalism in Iran (Pittsburgh University Press, 1964).

FATEMI, NASROLLAH S. Diplomatic History of Persia 1917-1923 (New York, 1952).

FISCHER, M. J. Iran: From Religious Dispute to Revolution (Harvard University Press, 1980).

HALLIDAY, FRED. Iran: Dictatorship and Development (London, 1978).

HAMZAVI, A. H. K. Persia and the Powers: An Account of Diplomatic Relations, 1941-46 (London, 1946).

HEIKAL, MOHAMED. The Return of the Ayatollah (London, André Deutsch, 1981).

HOVEYDA, FERYDOUN. The Fall of the Shah (Weidenfeld & Nicolson, London, 1979).

ISSAWI, CHARLES. The Economic History of Iran, 1800-1919 (University of Chicago Press, 1972).

KEDDIE, NIKKI. Roots of Revolution (Yale University Press, 1982).

KHOMEINI, Ayatollah RUHOLLAH. Islam and Revolution: Writings and Declarations of Imam Khomeini, trans. and ed. by Hamid Algar (Mizan Press, Berkeley, Calif., 1982).

LAING, MARGARET. The Shah (Sidgwick & Jackson, London, 1977).

LENCZOWSKI, GEORGE. Russia and the West in Iran (Cornell Univ. Press, 1949).

LENCZOWSCI, G. (Ed.). Iran under the Pahlavis (Stanford: Hoover Institution Press, 1978).

NAKHAI, M. L'Evolution Politique de l'Iran (Brussels, 1938).

RAMAZANI, ROUHOLLAH K. The Foreign Policy of Iran 1500-1941 (University Press of Virginia, Virginia, 1966).

ROOSEVELT, KERMIT. Countercoup: the Struggle for the Control of Iran (McGraw-Hill, 1980).

STEMPEL, JOHN D. Inside the Iranian Revolution (Indiana University Press, 1982).

STEPPAT, FRITZ. Iran zwischen den Grossmächten, 1941-48 (Oberursel, 1948).

UPTON, JOSEPH M. The History of Modern Iran: An Interpretation (Harvard University Press, 1960).

VILLIERS, GERARD DE. The Imperial Shah: An Informal
Biography (Weidenfeld and Nicolson, London, 1977).

ECONOMY AND OIL

AMUZEGAR, JAHANGIR. Technical Assistance in Theory and
Practice: the Case of Iran (Praeger Special Studies in
International Economics, New York, 1966).

AMUZEGAR, JAHANGIR and ALI FEKRAT, M. Iran: Economic
Development under Dualistic Conditions (University
of Chicago Press, 1971).

BALDWIN, GEORGE B. Planning and Development in Iran
(Johns Hopkins Press, Baltimore, 1967).

BHARIER, JULIAN. Economic Development in Iran 1900-
1970 (Oxford University Press, London, 1971).

GHOSH, SUNIL KANTI. The Anglo-Iranian Oil Dispute
(Calcutta, 1960).

GORELIKOV, SEMEN GERASIMOVICH IVAN. A study in the
Geography and Economics of Persia (Russian text),
(Moscow, 1961).

GUPTA, RAJ NARAIN. Iran: An Economic Study (New
Delhi, 1947).

MASON, F. C. Iran: Economic and Commercial Conditions
in Iran (H.M.S.O., London, 1957).

NAHAI, L. and KIBELL, C. L. The Petroleum Industry of
Iran (Washington: U.S. Department of the Interior,
Bureau of Mines, 1963).

NIRUMAND, BAHMAN. Persien, Modell eines Entwick-
lungslande, oder Die Diktatur der freien Welt (Rowohlt-
Verlag, Reinbek-bei-Hamburg, 1967).

SOTOUDEH, H. L'Evolution Economique de l'Iran et ses
Problèmes (Paris, 1957).

MODERN IRAN

AMIRSADEGHI, HOSSEIN. Twentieth Century Iran (Heinemann, London, 1977).

ARASTEH, REZA. Educational and Social Awakening in
Iran (E. J. Brill, Leiden, 1962).
Man and Society in Iran (Leiden, 1964).

AVERY, PETER. Modern Iran (Benn, London, 1967).

BINDER, LEONARD. Iran, Political Development in a
Changing Society (University of Calif. Press, 1962).

GRAEFE, A. VON. Iran, Das neue Persien (Berlin, 1937).

NIRUMAND, BAHMAN. Iran: the new imperialism in action
(Modern Reader Paperbacks, New York and London,
1971).

WOODSMALL, RUTH. Moslem Women Enter a New World
(London, 1936).

Iraq

PHYSICAL AND SOCIAL GEOGRAPHY

W. B. Fisher

Iraq is bounded on the north by Turkey, on the east by Iran, on the south by Kuwait and the Persian Gulf, on the south-west by Saudi Arabia and Jordan, and on the north-west by Syria. The actual frontier lines present one or two unusual features. In the first place, there exists between Iraq, Kuwait, and Saudi Arabia a "neutral zone", rhomboidal in shape, which was devised to facilitate the migrations of pastoral nomads, who cover great distances each year in search of pasture for their animals and who move regularly between several countries. Hence the stabilization or closing of a frontier could be for them a matter of life and death. Secondly, the frontier with Iran in its extreme southern portion below Basra follows the course of the Shatt al-Arab channel, but from 1936 until March 1975 the frontier was at the left (east) bank, placing the whole of the river within Iraq. This situation had become increasingly unacceptable to Iran, and in March 1975 the border was restored to the middle of the thalweg line in the middle of the deepest shipping channel in the Shatt al-Arab estuary. The position of this border is one of the key issues of the 1980–82 Gulf War with Iran. Thirdly, the inclusion of the northern province of Mosul within Iraq was agreed only in 1926. Because of its oil deposits, this territory was in dispute between Turkey, Syria and Iraq. Again the presence of large numbers of migratory nomads journeying each season between Iran, Turkey, Syria and Iraq was a further complicating factor.

PHYSICAL FEATURES

The old name of Iraq (Mesopotamia=land between the rivers) indicates the main physical aspect of the country—the presence of the two river valleys of the Tigris and Euphrates, which merge in their lower courses. On the eastern side of this double valley the Zagros Mountains of Persia appear as an abrupt wall, overhanging the riverine lowlands, particularly in the south, below Baghdad. North of the latitude of Baghdad the rise to the mountains is more gradual, with several intervening hill ranges, such as the Jebel Hamrin. These ranges are fairly low and narrow at first, with separating lowlands, but towards the main Zagros topography becomes more imposing, and summits over 3,000 metres in height occur. This region, lying north and east of Baghdad, is the ancient land of Assyria; and nowadays the higher hill ranges lying in the extreme east are called Iraqi Kurdistan, since many Kurdish tribes inhabit them.

On the western side of the river valley the land rises gradually to form the plateau which continues into Syria, Jordan, and Saudi Arabia, and its maximum height in Iraq is about 1,000 metres. In places it is possible to trace a cliff formation, where a more resistant bed of rock stands out prominently, and from this the name of the country is said to be derived

(Arabic *Iraq*=cliff). There is no sharp geographical break between Iraq and its western neighbours comparable with that between Iraq and Iran; the frontier lines are artificial.

THE RIVERS

It remains to describe the valley region itself and the two rivers. The Tigris, 1,150 miles (1,850 km.) in length, rises in Turkey, and is joined by numerous and often large tributaries both in Turkey and Iraq. The Euphrates, 1,460 miles (2,350 km.) in length, also rises in Turkey and flows first through Syria and then Iraq, joining the Tigris in its lower course at Qurna, to form the stream known as the Shatt al-Arab, which is 115 miles (185 km.) in length. Unlike the Tigris, the Euphrates receives no tributaries during its passage of Iraq. Above the region of Baghdad both rivers flow in well-defined channels, with retaining valley-walls. Below Baghdad, however, the vestiges of a retaining valley disappear, and the rivers meander over a vast open plain with only a slight drop in level—in places merely 1.5 or 2 metres in 100 km. Here the rivers are raised on great levees, or banks of silt and mud (which they themselves have laid down), and now lie several feet above the level of the surrounding plain. One remarkable feature is the change in relative level of the two river beds—water can be led from one to the other according to the actual district, and this possibility, utilized by irrigation engineers for many centuries, still remains the basic principle of present-day development. At the same time, the courses of both rivers can suddenly alter. A flood may breach the wall of the levee, and the water then pours out on to the lower-lying plain, inundating many square miles of territory. Ultimately, the river finds a new course and builds a fresh levee. Old river channels, fully or partially abandoned by the river, are thus a feature of the Mesopotamian lowland, associated with wide areas of swamp, lakes, and sandbars. The Tigris, though narrower than the Euphrates, is swifter, and carries far more water.

As the sources of both rivers lie in the mountains of Turkey, the current is very fast, and upstream navigation is difficult in the middle and upper reaches. In spring, following the melting of snows in Asia Minor, both rivers begin to rise, reaching a maximum in April (Tigris) and May (Euphrates). The spring is a very anxious time, since floods of 3.6 to 6.0 metres occur, and 10 metres is known—this in a region where the land may fall only 4 metres or less in level over 100 km. Immense areas are regularly inundated, levees often collapse, and villages and roads, where these exist, must be built on high embankments. The Tigris is particularly liable to sudden flooding, and can rise at the rate of one foot per hour. Contrasts with the Nile of Egypt will be noted. The latter river is confined in a steep-sided valley over most of its length, and floods do not spread far away from the river. In lower Iraq, on the other hand, wide expanses are inundated every year, e.g. as in early 1954 when a flood of 9 metres occurred and many thousands were rendered homeless. Construction of the Wadi Tharthar control scheme has, however, greatly reduced the incidence of severe flooding, particularly along the Tigris, and continued expansion of irrigation schemes (which has been a feature of Iraq since the late 1960s) is having a further effect.

Roads were formerly difficult to maintain because of floods, and the rail system was of different gauges. New standard-gauge rail links are planned: north-south from Mosul to Basra via Baghdad; various cross-country lines; and an extension along the Euphrates valley towards north-eastern Syria. Altogether, some 2,400 km. of new rail lines are envisaged in the 1981–85 Development Plan, and construction has begun. Also, two road "express ways" are under construction: one south from Baghdad to connect with Kuwait and Jordan, the other north towards Turkey. The first of these has taken on especial significance with the shift from Gulf ports, and the greater use of Jordan as an essential supply route during the present war with Iran.

Because of the former difficulties in communication, many communities of differing cultures and ways of life have persisted. Minority groups have thus been a feature in Iraq.

CLIMATE AND ECONOMIC ACTIVITY

The summers are overwhelmingly hot, with shade temperatures of over 43°C.; and many inhabitants retire during the heat of the day to underground rooms. Winters may be surprisingly cold: frost, though very rare at Basra, can be severe in the north. Sudden hot spells during winter are another feature in the centre and south of Iraq. Rainfall is scanty over all of the country, except for the north-east (Assyria), where 40 to 60 cm. occur—enough to grow crops without irrigation. Elsewhere farming is entirely dependent upon irrigation from river water. The great extent of standing water in many parts of Iraq leads to an unduly high air humidity, which explains the notorious reputation of the Mesopotamian summer.

The unusual physical conditions outlined present a number of obstacles to human activity. The flood waters are rather less "manageable" than in Egypt, and there is less of the regular deposition of thick, rich silt that is such a feature of the Nile. The effects of this are strikingly visible in the relatively small extent of land actually cultivated—at most, only one-sixth of the potentially cultivable territory and 3 per cent of the total area of the country. The population, of over 13 million, is about 30 per cent that of Egypt. Because of the easy availability of agricultural land, wasteful, "extensive" farming methods are often followed, giving a low yield. On the whole, Iraq is underpopulated, and could support larger numbers of inhabitants.

A feature of the last few years has been the use of oil royalties for development schemes, particularly in irrigation. Various Plans allocated up to £30 million annually, but this was not always used. Now, with much higher oil revenues, the figure has been revised upward, and far more extensive development is planned. A further favourable factor is the discovery in 1975 of a major new oilfield, which has now made Iraq the second largest Middle Eastern oil producer.

The unusual physical conditions have greatly restricted movement and the development of communications of all kinds. In the upper reaches of the rivers boat journeys can only be made downstream, whilst nearer the sea the rivers are wider and slower but often very shallow. Roads are difficult to maintain because of the floods, and the railways have two differing gauges—standard and metre; the latter is however in process of replacement and with decreasing risk of flooding, standard gauge has been laid between Baghdad and Basra via Kut. The effect has been to leave in isolation many communities that have differing ways of life and even differing languages and religious beliefs. Numerous minority groups are hence a feature of Iraq.

THE PEOPLE

In the marshes of the extreme south there are communities of Arabs who spend most of their lives in boats and rafts. Other important minorities live in, or close to, the hill country of the north: the Kurds, who number over one million and migrate extensively into Syria, Turkey and Iran (*see* History); the Yazidis of the Jebel Sinjar; the Assyrian Christians (the name refers to their geographical location, and has no historical connection); and various communities of Uniate and Orthodox Christians. As well, there were important groups of Jews—more than in most other Muslim countries—though since the establishment of the State of Israel much emigration has taken place. It should be noted that, while the majority of the Muslims follow Shi'a rites, the wealthier Muslims are of Sunni adherence.

Ethnically, the position is very complicated. The northern and eastern hill districts contain many racial elements—Turki, Persian, and proto-Nordic, with Armenoid strains predominating. The pastoral nomads of western Iraq are, as might be expected, of fairly unmixed Mediterranean ancestry, like the nomads of Syria, Jordan, and Saudi Arabia; but the population of the riverine districts of Iraq shows a mixture of Armenoid and Mediterranean elements. North of the Baghdad district the Armenoid strain is dominant, but to the south, it is less important, though still present.

Arabic is the official and most widely used language. Kurdish and dialects of Turkish are current in the north, whilst variants of Persian are spoken by tribesmen in the east. An estimate, probably over-generous to the Arabic speakers, puts the relative numbers at: Arabic 79 per cent, Kurdish 16 per cent, Persian 3 per cent, and Turkish 2 per cent of the total population.

HISTORY

Iraq was one of the earliest centres of civilization. Before 3000 B.C. the Sumerians, a people of problematical origin, had established a complete civilization in the marshy alluvial areas at the head of the Persian/Arabian Gulf. Here a number of city states developed, cities like Eridu, Uruk, Ur, Kish and Lagash. These states were supported by a highly developed agricultural economy, based on an intricate irrigation system.

Around 2500 B.C., Lagash gained ascendency over several other cities, until, not long afterwards, Lugalzaggisi, the governor of Umma, overran Uruk and embarked on a career of widespread conquest. Lugalzaggisi was in turn defeated by Sargon of Agade, who united the whole of Mesopotamia under Akkadian rule and conquered Elamite Susa, and whose armies penetrated as far as the Mediterranean. Akkadian dominions were extended even further under his successors, but the Sumerians of the south took every opportunity to revolt and attacks by Elamites and mountain tribesmen, the Gutians, caused the empire to collapse around 2200 B.C. After a period of chaos, a new Sumerian kingdom, centred at Ur (the Third Dynasty of Ur) established supremacy over the south, lasting through the twenty-first century B.C. It was finally sacked by invaders from Elam, and by the Amorites from the north-west, and was never again of great historical importance.

The Amorites were Semites, whose homeland was Arabia. They came into conflict with the Elamites in Sumer, and in the eighteenth century B.C. Hammurabi created an extensive empire famous for the splendour of its civilization. Pressure from the Caucasian tribes, Hurrians and Kassites, was increasing, but the empire finally crumbled before the onslaught of the Hittites, who sacked Babylon in the seventeenth century B.C.

In the north, new powers were emerging, notably the Mitanni, who occupied northern Iraq. At last their rule disintegrated under constant pressure from the Hittites of Asia Minor, whose influence, in the years following the reign of their great king Subbiluliuma (c. 1390–1350 B.C.), was advanced almost to the Persian/Arabian Gulf. Meanwhile, on the higher reaches of the Tigris, the warlike Assyrians, who hastened the decline of the Mitanni and the Hittite empire, embarked from time to time on a career of conquest destined to be of brief duration, as under Adad-nirari I (c. 1300 B.C.) and Tiglath-pileser I (c. 1200 B.C.). In the reign of Ashur-nasir-pal II (883–859 B.C.) Assyrian ambition burst forth once more, re-establishing control over northern Mesopotamia. Syria and Cilicia were subdued under Shalmaneser III (860–825 B.C.) and the Assyrian empire in its heyday comprised Van and other Armenian territories, Babylonia, Syria, Egypt and large areas of Persia. An army of unprecedented efficiency, mass deportations on a vast scale, relentless cruelty, a regime of rigid and despotic centralization—these features of Assyrian rule evoked the bitter enmity of the subject peoples, who, when the empire weakened as a result of incessant warfare and of Scythian

invasion from the north, rose in combined revolt and sacked Nineveh in 612 B.C. Iraq now became the centre of a neo-Babylonian state which, under Nebuchadnezzar (604–562 B.C.) included much of the Fertile Crescent, but was soon to fall before the Persians, who seized Babylon in 539–538 B.C.

Thereafter, Iraq was a mere province of the vast Achaemenid empire, which extended from Asia Minor to the Punjab in north-west India and from southern Russia to Egypt. Alexander the Great brought Persian rule to an end in a series of brilliant campaigns (334–327 B.C.). After his death in 323 B.C., one of his generals, Seleucus, controlled most of the Asiatic lands which the conqueror had dominated. The Seleucids maintained their hold on Iraq for more than a hundred years and then, in the course of prolonged warfare, lost it to the Parthians, who during the third and second centuries B.C. founded a powerful state in Persia.

Under the Parthians Iraq was a frontier province over against the might of Rome. To the north and west of Mesopotamia a line of strong fortresses, e.g., Carrhae (Harran), Edessa (modern Urfa), Diyarbakir, Dara, Nisibin, marked the ground where the rival armies fought. At Carrhae, in 54 B.C., the Parthian horsemen severely defeated the Romans but from the time of Augustus until the reign of the Emperor Trajan there was no major war between the two states. Between A.D. 113 and 117, Trajan conquered much of Iraq, yet his successor, Hadrian, felt that it would be too expensive to defend the new territories and so abandoned them. Rome resumed the offensive under Marcus Aurelius (162–166), Septimius Severus (195–199) and Caracalla (216–218), her rule being now extended from the middle Euphrates to the Khabur river.

The Parthian domination came to an end in 224 owing to internal revolt in Persia; the emergence of the Sasanid regime now began. In 260 Sapor I crushed the Romans in battle near Edessa and captured the Emperor Valerian. The endless frontier hostilities flared out once more into violent war under Diocletian, Constantius and Julian (third-fourth centuries), the Romans being forced back behind the line of the Euphrates. The conflict then died down for more than a hundred years and was not resumed on a large scale until the Sasanid state recovered much of its old vigour under Kobad I (488–531) and Khusran Anushirvan (531–579). The prolonged warfare of the sixth–seventh centuries came to an end with the brilliant campaigns of the Byzantine Emperor Heraclius in Armenia and Iraq (622–628). Byzantium and Persia were by now exhausted and in the meantime a formidable danger had arisen in the far south.

THE RISE OF ISLAM

The prophet Muhammad (d. 632) had created at Mecca and Medina a religious and political organization that aroused powerful forces long latent in Arabia.

The Arab nomads of the great desert, united within the community of Islam, were forbidden to pursue their ancient tribal feuds. The restless energy thus concentrated in the Muslim state found an outlet in war outside Arabia and the Arabs overran Syria and Egypt. By 634 the Arab warriors had begun the conquest of Iraq. The battle of Qadisiya in 635 led to the fall of the Persian capital, Ctesiphon, in June of that year. A further battle at Jalula in 637 marked the end of Sasanid power in Iraq, although resistance continued in the north until the Arabs took Mosul in 641. Kufa and Basra became the two great garrison cities on which Muslim rule in Iraq was to be based for the next hundred years.

The murder of the Caliph 'Uthman in 656 brought about a civil war between his successor, 'Ali, and Mu'awiya, a kinsman of 'Uthman, who had long been governor of Syria. After an indecisive battle at Siffin in 657 the two rivals had recourse to arbitration, as a result of which, at Adhruh in January 659, both men were deposed from their respective positions, a judgment which deprived 'Ali of his real status as Caliph and Mu'awiya of a pretension to that office which as yet he had not ventured openly to avow. The outcome of the conflict remained uncertain during the next two years, until at length the murder of 'Ali at Kufa in January 661 left the way clear for Mu'awiya to become Caliph. The war revealed that effective power within the new empire was passing from Mecca and Medina to the great garrison cities where the main Arab armies were stationed. 'Ali had been obliged to go from the Hijaz to Iraq, his chief support coming from Kufa. Mu'awiya relied for his success on the strength of Syria. The real issue had been whether Iraq or Syria should be the metropolitan province of the empire. With the emergence of Mu'awiya as Caliph in 661, the question was decided, for almost a hundred years, in favour of Syria.

During the period of the Umayyad dynasty (661–750) Iraq became the centre of the movement known as Shi'atu 'Ali, i.e. "the party of Ali". Born amongst the Arabs themselves, it assumed at first the form of a "legitimist" opposition to Umayyad rule, asserting that the Caliphate should of right belong to the descendants of 'Ali, the son-in-law of the Prophet. As a purely Arab and political faction, resting to a large degree on the bitter dislike of Iraq for the hegemony of Syria, it was to meet with failure, for the armies of Kufa and Basra could not overcome the military pre-eminence of the Syrians. At Karbala, in October 680, Husain, the son of 'Ali, fell in battle against the Umayyad forces in Iraq. This event, by giving to the Shi'a an illustrious martyr, inaugurated a new and rapid growth of the party, not on the political level but as a religious sect.

UMAYYAD RULE

The Umayyad state was based on the fundamental assumption that a vast subject population, non-Muslim and non-Arab, would continue indefinitely to yield tribute to a dominant Arab and Muslim warrior aristocracy, the revenues derived from the conquered territories and from the *jizya*, i.e. the poll-tax imposed on those who did not belong to the faith of the Prophet, being shared out amongst the members of that aristocracy. Whether from a genuine acceptance of the new religion or from motives of self-interest, e.g. to escape the poll-tax and to secure the financial, economic and social privileges of the Arab Muslims, the subject peoples began to adopt Islam. The revenues of the state fell and the decline could not be made good through the acquisition of rich new lands, for the age of rapid conquest was over. Since Muhammad had declared all Muslims to be equal, the new converts, or Mawali, demanded that the Arabs concede to them a due participation in the rewards of empire. When it became clear that the Arab aristocracy meant to defend its pensions, privileges and other exclusive rights—the available resources of the state were insufficient to meet the claims of the ever-increasing numbers of Mawali—a crisis of the first magnitude threatened the Umayyad regime.

The Mawali now gave their allegiance to the Shi'a, transforming the movement into a means for the expression of their social and economic grievances against the established order and, at the same time, remoulding it as a religious sect which embraced ideas not of Muslim origin but derived from their previous Christian, Jewish and Zoroastrian traditions. This radical change in the Shi'a was already visible in the years 685–687, when a serious revolt occurred at Kufa in the name of Muhammad ibn al-Hanafiya, a son of 'Ali by a wife other than Fatima, the daughter of the Prophet.

The Umayyad Caliph 'Umar II (717–720) introduced a series of financial reforms designed to conciliate the Mawali, a policy which met only with a transient success, for the ultimate effect of his measures was to increase the expenditure and lower the revenue of the state. Disillusionment grew apace amongst the non-Arab Muslims. An efficient propaganda machine, known under the name of the Hashimiya, made its appearance in Iraq, its task being to disseminate extreme Shi'i ideas. In 716 control of this organization fell into the hands of Muhammad ibn 'Ali ibn al-'Abbas, descended from an uncle of the Prophet. Its chief centre of activity was in the great frontier province of Khurasan, in north-east Persia, where Arab colonies from Basra and Kufa had settled in about 670. Abu Muslim, a Persian Mawla of Iraq, was sent to Khurasan as confidential agent of the Hashimiya in 743 and there raised the standard of revolt against the Umayyads. Syria, long since weakened by fierce tribal feuds amongst the Arabs, could not withstand the storm. In 750 Umayyad rule came to an end and was replaced by that of the 'Abbasid dynasty, while Iraq at last achieved her ambition of becoming the dominant province of the empire.

'ABBASID RULE

The 'Abbasid caliphs had now an immediate and urgent task to perform. It was impossible for them to govern as the representatives of the more advanced elements in the Shi'a, when most of their Muslim subjects were of the Sunni or orthodox faith. The second 'Abbasid, al-Mansur (754–775), the real founder of the new regime, therefore abandoned the extremists who had done so much to bring his house to power. He also built a new garrison city in Iraq for his main army, the hard core of which consisted largely of regiments from Khurasan. This capital of the 'Abbasid empire, Baghdad, soon developed into a great emporium of trade and a political centre of vast importance. An autocratic caliph, claiming divine authority for his power, which rested on regular armed forces and was exercised through a paid bureaucracy; a cosmopolitan ruling class of officials and landowners, of merchants and bankers; the 'Ulama, i.e. the hierarchy of religious scholars, jurists, teachers and dignitaries—these were the main characteristics of the 'Abbasid Caliphate, which for a time brought to Iraq and, indeed, to the Islamic state as a whole a splendid prosperity derived from a flourishing agriculture and industry and from the lucrative transit trade between India and the Mediterranean.

It was in regard to political unity that the 'Abbasid empire proved most vulnerable. The relative cohesion which the Muslim state had enjoyed owing to the dominance of the Arab warrior aristocracy did not survive the revolution of 750. The new dynasty sought to use the Muslim faith itself as a means of binding together the varied ethnic and social elements of the population, but the attempt was soon shown to be a failure. After the death of Harun ar-Rashid (786–809), whose reign marked the apogee of 'Abbasid power as well as fostering a great flowering of Arabic culture, civil war broke out between his sons Amin and Ma'mun, the former depending largely on the support of Iraq, the latter on the strength of Persia and, above all, on the troops of Khurasan. The conflict was, in one sense, a battle between Persia and Iraq for pre-eminence within the empire. Ma'mun conquered Baghdad in 813, but for a time considered the idea of making Marv in Khurasan his capital, a project which he abandoned only when he realized that it would lead to repeated revolt in Iraq. In August 819 he returned to Baghdad.

Persia, disappointed in its hopes, now began to break away from the caliphs of Baghdad. Local dynasties made their appearance in the east, the Tahirids in 820, the Saffarids in 867, the Samanids in c. 892. A similar process occurred in the west, Spain after 756, Morocco after 788, Tunisia after 800 being virtually independent of Baghdad. In 868 the dynasty of the Tulunids arose in Egypt. The more extreme elements of the Shi'a were also active, especially in Persia and the neighbouring regions, inspiring repeated insurrections against the 'Abbasid regime. Southern Iraq suffered heavily in the Zanj Rebellion (869–883), when one Ali ibn Muhammad founded a state of Negro slaves at Basra, which was sacked in 871. The Qarmatians, a religious movement of communistic and revolutionary tendencies, founded a strong regime of their own in the province of Bahrain (now called al-Hasa) and for most of the tenth century carried out frequent raids into Iraq. Meanwhile, at Baghdad, the power of the army was growing. The corps gathered for the Caliph's protection consisted

of slaves (Mamluks), mostly of Turkish origin, commanded by free officers. Since the reigns of al-Mu'tasim (833–842) and al-Wathiq (842–847), their officers had also been Mamluks. As power fell more and more into the hands of the army, the Mamluks were able to appoint and depose the caliphs at will. Iraq fell at length under the domination of Daylamite mountain dwellers from the region south of the Caspian Sea, Shi'i in religion and led by a family of *condottière* chieftains, the Buwaihids, who, after subduing most of western Persia, occupied Baghdad in 945. Buwaihid rule—a period of the deepest degradation for the Caliphate, since the Commander of the Faithful was now a mere puppet obedient to the orders of a Shi'i—lasted until 1055. It then collapsed before the assault of Turks from the steppe lands beyond the Oxus, who, led by the Seljuqs, a family also of *condottière* origin, overran Persia and then seized Baghdad under Tughril Beg. The Seljuq Turks were Sunni Muslims and their success was not unwelcome among the orthodox, who regarded it as a liberation from the yoke of the Shi'i Buwaihids. Yet the Caliph, although treated with deference, was still only in name the head of the state, all effective power being concentrated in the hands of the Seljuq Sultan.

After the death of Malik Shah in 1092, dynastic dissension and revolt amongst the Turkish tribesmen brought about a rapid decline of the new regime and the rise of succession states ruled by princes or by officers of the Seljuq house. In Iraq a series of nine Seljuq sultans ruled from 1118–94, almost all of them fated to die a violent death in conflict with rival claimants or with their Atabegs, i.e. amirs, who were the most powerful figures in the land. Some of these Atabegs established independent principalities of their own, e.g. the Zangid dynasty at Mosul, which played an important role in arousing the Muslims to defend Islam against the Christian Crusaders in Syria. The last Seljuq Sultan of Iraq, Tughril (1177–94), was defeated in battle with the Turkish ruler of Khwarizm (the region of Khiva, south of the Aral Sea). The victor, Takash (1172–1200), and his successor, 'Ala'ad-Din Muhammad (1200–20), sought to extend their rule over Iraq, but, before this ambition could be realized, the Mongols destroyed the power of the Khwarizm shahs.

THE MONGOL INVASIONS

By 1220 the great conqueror Genghis Khan had overrun all Transoxania and was threatening to invade Persia. His death in 1227 led to a long pause in the Mongol advance. In 1253 Hülakü, a grandson of Genghis Khan, moved westward in force, captured Baghdad in 1258 and thus made an end of the Abbasid Caliphate. Subordinated henceforth to the Mongol Khan of Persia, Iraq became a mere frontier province, bereft of all its former wealth and splendour and much neglected by its rulers. On the death of the Mongol Khan Abu Sa'id in 1335, Iraq, after a brief period of confusion, passed into the hands of a new dynasty, the Jala'irids, who ruled over the land until the early years of the fifteenth century. During this period Iraq was again overrun by Mongols and in

IRAQ

1401 Timur Beg sacked Baghdad with merciless severity. The Jala'irid regime did not long outlast the death of Timur in 1405.

To the north of Iraq, around Lake Van, a powerful Turcoman confederation, known as the Black Sheep (Kara Koyunlu) was rising into prominence. The Turcomans defeated the last Jala'irid, Ahmed, and created a new state which, under Jihan Shah (1444–67), extended from Tabriz to the Shatt al-'Arab. The power of the Kara Koyunlu soon collapsed in war with a rival Turcoman confederation, that of the Ak Koyunlu (White Sheep), who, led by their famous chieftain, Uzun Hasan (1423?–78), crushed Jihan Shah and took over the territories which he had ruled. Dynastic quarrels brought about a rapid disintegration of the White Sheep ascendancy.

In the years 1499–1508 the now crumbling Ak Koyunlu regime was destroyed by the Safavid, Isma'il. (His ancestors were hereditary masters of a powerful religious order notable for its advanced Shi'i teaching and, from their main centre at Ardabil near the Caspian Sea, had fashioned their numerous adherents amongst the Turcoman tribes of Asia Minor into a formidable military movement.) Isma'il made himself Shah of Persia and also conquered Iraq. To the Ottoman Sultan, the dissemination of Shi'i beliefs among the tribes of Anatolia was a menace which had to be eliminated, for it threatened to undermine his own control in that region, the Ottomans being Sunni, i.e. orthodox Muslims. Selim I made war on Shah Isma'il in 1514 and so began a protracted conflict between the Ottomans and the Safavids which was to last, with long intervals of precarious peace, until 1639. Sultan Suleyman, in the course of his first campaign against Persia, conquered Baghdad in 1534–35.

OTTOMAN IRAQ

The Ottomans were to find Iraq a most difficult and expensive province to administer. Religious animosities proved to be a constant source of trouble. Northern Iraq and Kurdistan followed largely the Sunni faith; Baghdad itself was divided in its allegiance between Sunni and Shi'i Islam; southern Iraq was a region under strong Shi'i influence. The task of restraining nomad tribes from raiding the settled lands was an endless and wearisome business. Moreover, the tribes of the delta marshlands and of the mountainous areas close to the frontier with Persia were ever liable to rise in revolt against the administration. From time to time Iraq was the scene of warfare between the Ottomans and the Safavids, e.g., in the years 1578–90, and indeed came once more under Persian control, when Shah Abbas (1587–1629) seized Baghdad in 1623 and retained it in the face of a determined Ottoman counter-offensive in 1625/26. After a second attempt at reconquest in 1629/30 had failed, the Ottomans at last recovered Baghdad in 1638 and in the next year made peace with the Safavids.

As the Ottoman state fell into decline, the Sultan at Istanbul became less able to dominate the course of events in so distant a province as Iraq. From about 1625 until 1668, Basra and the Delta marshlands were in the hands of local chieftains independent of the Ottoman administration at Baghdad, a state of affairs which recurred in the period 1694–1701. The appointment of Hasan Pasha to command at Baghdad in 1704 marked a new phase in the history of Ottoman Iraq. The pashalik was to pass from himself to his son, then to the husbands of his grand-daughters, and thereafter to a series of Mamluk governors raised and trained in the household of his immediate successors. From 1704 to 1831, therefore, the Sultan failed to enforce at Baghdad an appointment of his own choice.

Hasan Pasha died in 1723, just at the moment when the Ottomans had become involved in a new war against Persia. The last of the Safavids had been deposed in 1722 by the Afghan Mir Mahmud. Hasan Pasha's son, Ahmed Pasha, occupied Kermanshah, which Hasan himself had seized in the first stage of the conflict, and then overran Hamadan and Luristan, but these lands were lost once more to Persia when Nadir Shah, in the years after 1729, drove out the Afghans and invaded Iraq. Baghdad itself withstood a siege in 1733 and Mosul underwent the same experience in 1743. The war brought much suffering to Iraq, the province falling, as a result of frequent revolt amongst the restless tribesmen and the devastation caused by repeated campaigns, into a state of anarchy. None the less, Ahmed Pasha remained throughout this period in firm control of Baghdad and Basra and also exercised a strong influence over the affairs of Mosul and Kirkuk. He lived to see peace made with Persia in 1746 on terms which restored the general position to what it had been before the war. A few months later in 1747, he died, leaving no son to succeed him.

The palace household which his father had created and which he himself had further developed contained Mamluks recruited for the most part from Georgia, converted to Islam and trained in their youth for subsequent service in the administration of Iraq. After a brief interval of confusion, in which the Porte tried to impose its own nominee but soon had to admit failure, Suleyman Agha, one of the Mamluks whom Hasan Pasha had bought and educated, became the governor of Baghdad and Basra, an office which he held with great success for twelve years until his death in 1762. Yet another Mamluk, 'Umr Agha, ruled Iraq from 1764 to 1775. Internal strife and a frontier war which led to a Persian occupation of Basra marked the period immediately following his death.

At length, in 1780, the most famous of the Mamluk pashas, Suleyman the Great, assumed the government of Baghdad and Basra. Much of his time was spent in curbing the Kurdish chieftains in the north and the Arab tribes, above all the powerful Muntafiq confederation in the south of Iraq. From about 1790 he had to face the enmity of the formidable Wahhabi state recently founded in central Arabia. The raids of the Wahhabi tribesmen into Iraq intensified until in 1801 the great Shi'i sanctuary of Karbala was taken and sacked. The death of Suleyman in the next year threw Iraq into even greater confusion. There were further Wahhabi *razzias*, e.g. against Najaf in 1803 and Basra in 1804, and constant trouble with the tribes along the Persian border. It was only in 1817 that the last of the Mamluk pashas, Da'ud, secured control of the province and restored some semblance of order by repeated punitive campaigns against the Kurds and the nomads of the desert lands.

Meanwhile, reforms were being introduced at Istanbul which foreshadowed the end of the Mamluk regime in Iraq. Selim III (1789–1807) and Mahmud II (1808–39) sought to refashion the administration and the military forces of the empire on European lines. The moment when the Ottoman Sultan would attempt to end the Mamluk system and regain direct possession of Iraq was now at hand. Mahmud II sent 'Ali Ridha Pasha to perform this task in 1831. A severe outbreak of plague crippled the resistance of the Mamluks, Da'ud Pasha was deposed and the Mamluk regiments were at once exterminated. A new phase in the history of Iraq was about to begin.

WESTERN INFLUENCE

Although some of the European nations had long been in contact with Iraq through their commercial interests in the Persian/Arabian Gulf, western influences were slow to penetrate into the province. By 1800 there was a British Resident at Basra and two years later a British Consulate at Baghdad. France also maintained agents in these cities. French and Italian religious orders had settlements in the land. It was not, however, until after 1831 that signs of more rapid European penetration became visible, such as steam-boats on the rivers of Iraq in 1836, telegraph lines from 1861 and a number of proposals for railways, none of which was to materialize for a long time to come. The Ottoman government did much in the period between 1831 and 1850 to impose direct control over Kurdistan and the mountainous areas close to the Persian border, but the introduction of reforms was not, in fact, begun until in 1869 Midhat Pasha arrived at Baghdad. Much of his work, performed in the brief space of three years, proved to be superficial and ill-considered, yet he was able to set Iraq on a course from which there could be no retreat in the future. A newspaper, military factories, a hospital, an alms-house, schools, a tramway, conscription for the army, municipal and administrative councils, comparative security on the main routes and a reasoned policy of settling tribesmen on the land—these achievements, however imperfect, bear solid witness to the vigour of his rule. After his departure in 1872, reform and European influence continued to advance, although slowly. Postal services were much developed, a railway from Baghdad to Samarra was completed in 1914 (part of the projected *Baghdad-bahn*, which betokened the rapid growth of German interest in the Ottoman Empire) and the important Hindiya Barrage on the Euphrates was rebuilt between 1910 and 1913. The measures of reform and improvement introduced between 1831 and 1914 must indeed be judged as belated and inadequate—the Iraq of 1900 differed little from that of 1500—yet a process of fundamental change had begun, which no regime, however inept, could reverse.

In November 1914 Britain and the Ottoman Empire were at war. British troops occupied the Shatt al-Arab region and, under the pressure of war needs, transformed Basra into an efficient and well-equipped port. A premature advance on Baghdad in 1915 ended in the retreat of the British forces to Kut, their prolonged defence of that town and, when all attempts to relieve it had failed, the capitulation to the Ottomans in April 1916. A new offensive launched from Basra in the autumn of that year brought about the capture of Baghdad in March 1917. Kirkuk was taken in 1918, but, before the Allies could seize Mosul, the Ottoman government sought and obtained an armistice in October. For two years, until the winter of 1920, the Commander-in-Chief of the British Forces, acting through a civil commissioner, continued to be responsible for the administration of Iraq from Basra to Mosul, all the apparatus of a modern system of rule being created at Baghdad—e.g., departments of Land, Posts and Telegraphs, Agriculture, Irrigation, Police, Customs, Finance, etc. The new regime was Christian, foreign and strange, resented by reason of its very efficiency, feared and distrusted no less by those whose loyalties were Muslim and Ottoman than by important elements who desired self-determination for Iraq.

The last phase of Ottoman domination in Iraq, especially during the years after the Young Turk Revolution in 1908, had witnessed a marked growth of Arab nationalist sentiment. Local circles in Iraq now made contact with the Ottoman Decentralization Party at Cairo, founded in 1912, and with the Young Arab Society, which moved from Paris to Beirut in 1913. Basra, in particular, became a centre of Arab aspirations and took the lead in demanding from Istanbul a measure of autonomy for Iraq. A secret organization, al-'Ahd (the Covenant) included a number of Iraqi officers serving in the Ottoman armies. The prospect of independence which the Allies held out to the Arabs in the course of the war strengthened and extended the nationalist movement. In April 1920 Britain received from the conference at San Remo a mandate for Iraq. This news was soon followed by a serious insurrection amongst the tribesmen of the south. The revolt, caused partly by instinctive dislike of foreign rule but also by vigorous nationalist propaganda, was not wholly suppressed until early in the next year. In October 1920 military rule was formally terminated in Iraq. An Arab Council of State, advised by British officials and responsible for the administration, now came into being and in March 1921 the Amir Faisal ibn Husain agreed to rule as King at Baghdad. His ceremonial accession took place on August 23rd, 1921.

The Najdi (Saudi Arabian) frontier with Iraq was defined in the Treaty of Mohammara in May 1922. Saudi concern over loss of traditional grazing rights resulted in further talks between Ibn Saud and the U.K. Civil Commissioner in Iraq, and a Neutral Zone of 7,000 sq. km. was established adjacent to the western tip of the Kuwait frontier. No military or permanent buildings were to be erected in the zone and the nomads of both countries were to have unimpeded access to its pastures and wells. A further agreement concerning the administration of this zone was signed between Iraq and Saudi Arabia in May 1938.

MODERN IRAQ

Despite the opposition of the more extreme nationalists, an Anglo-Iraqi Treaty was signed on October 10th, 1922. It embodied the provisions of the mandate, safeguarded the judicial rights of foreigners and guaranteed the special interests of Britain in Iraq. An Electoral Law prepared the way for the choice of a constituent assembly, which met in March 1924 and, in the face of strong opposition by the nationalists, ratified the treaty with Britain. It accepted, too, an Organic Law declaring Iraq to be a sovereign state with a constitutional hereditary monarchy and a representative system of government. In 1925 the League of Nations recommended that the *vilayet* of Mosul, to which the Turks had laid claim, be incorporated into the new kingdom, a decision finally implemented in the treaty of July 1926 between the interested parties, Britain, Turkey and Iraq. By this year a fully constituted Parliament was in session at Baghdad and all the ministries, as well as most of the larger departments of the administration, were in effective control. In 1930 a new treaty was signed with Britain, which established between the two countries a close alliance for a period of 25 years and granted Britain the use of air bases at Shu'ayba and Habbaniya. On October 3rd, 1932, Iraq entered the League of Nations as an independent power, the mandate being now terminated.

The difficulties which confronted the Kingdom in the period after 1932 required much time and effort for their solution: e.g., the animosities between the Sunni Muslims and the powerful Shi'i tribes on the Euphrates, which tended to divide and embitter political life; the problem of relations with the Kurds, some of whom wanted a state of their own, and with other minorities like the Assyrians; the complicated task of reform in land tenure and of improvement in agriculture, irrigation, flood control, public services and communications. As yet the Government itself consisted of little more than a façade of democratic forms concealing a world of faction and intrigue. The realities of the political scene were a xenophobe press often ill-informed and irresponsible; "parties" better described as cliques gathered around prominent personalities; a small ruling class of tribal sheikhs; landowners; and the intelligentsia—lawyers, students, journalists, doctors, ex-officers—frequently torn by sharp rivalries. It is not surprising, therefore, that the first years of full independence showed a rather halting progress towards efficient rule. The dangerous nature of the tensions inside Iraq was revealed in the Assyrian massacre of 1933 carried out by troops of the Iraq army. Political intrigue from Baghdad had much to do with the outbreak of tribal revolt along the Euphrates in 1935/36. The army crushed the insurrection without much trouble and then, under the leadership of General Bakr Sidqi and in alliance with disappointed politicians and reformist elements, brought about a *coup d'état* in October 1936. The new regime failed to fulfil its assurances of reform, its policies alienated the tribal chieftains and gave rise to serious tensions even within the armed forces, tensions which led to the assassination of Bakr Sidqi in August 1937.

Of vast importance for Iraq was the rapid development of the oil industry during these years. Concessions were granted in 1925, 1932 and 1938 to the Iraq, Mosul and Basra Petroleum Companies. Oil had been discovered in the Kirkuk area in 1927 and by the end of 1934 the Iraq Petroleum Company was exporting crude oil through two 12-inch pipelines, one leading to Tripoli and the other to Haifa. Exploitation of the Mosul and Basra fields did not begin on a commercial scale until after World War II.

In 1937 Iraq joined Turkey, Persia and Afghanistan in the Sa'dabad Pact, which arranged for consultation in all disputes that might affect the common interests of the four states. A treaty signed with Persia in July 1937 and ratified in the following year provided for the specific acceptance of the boundary between the two countries as it had been defined in 1914. Relations with Britain deteriorated in the period after 1937, mainly because of the growth of anti-Zionist feeling and of resentment at British policy in Palestine. German influence increased very much at this time in Iraq, especially among those political and military circles associated with the army group later to be known as the Golden Square. Iraq severed her diplomatic connections with Germany at the beginning of World War II, but in 1941 the army commanders carried out a new *coup d'état*, establishing, under the nominal leadership of Rashid 'Ali al-Gaylani, a regime which announced its non-belligerent intentions. A disagreement over the passage of British troops through Iraq left no doubt of the pro-German sympathies of the Gaylani government and led to hostilities that ended with the occupation of Basra and Baghdad in May 1941. Thereafter Iraq co-operated with the Allies and declared war on the Axis powers in 1943.

Iraq, during the years after World War II, was to experience much internal tension and unrest. Negotiations with Britain led to the signing at Portsmouth in January 1948 of a new Anglo-Iraqi agreement designed to replace that of 1930 and incorporating substantial concessions, amongst them the British evacuation of the airbases at Shu'ayba and Habbaniya and the creation of a joint board for the co-ordination of all matters relating to mutual defence. The animosities arising from the situation in Palestine called forth riots at Baghdad directed against the new agreement with Britain, which were sufficiently disturbing to oblige the Iraqi Government to repudiate the Portsmouth settlement.

ARAB-ISRAEL WAR 1948

With anti-Jewish and anti-Western feeling so intense, it was inevitable that troops should be sent from Iraq to the Arab-Israeli war which began on May 15th, 1948. The Iraqi troops shared in the hostilities for a period of just over two months, their participation terminating in a truce operative from July 18th. Their final withdrawal from Palestine did not commence, however, until April 1949. Subsequently, there was a considerable emigration of Jews from Iraq to Israel, especially in the years 1951–52.

The expense of the war against Israel, bad harvests, the general indigence of the people—all contributed to bring about serious tensions resulting in rioting at Baghdad in November 1952 and the imposition of martial law until October 1953. None the less, there were some favourable prospects for the future— notably a large expansion of the oil industry. New pipelines were built to Tripoli in 1949 and to Banias in Syria in 1952; the oil-fields of Mosul and Basra were producing much crude petroleum by 1951–52. A National Development Board was created in 1950 and became later, in 1953, a national ministry. An agreement of February 1952 gave to the Iraq Government 50 per cent of the oil companies' profits before deductions for foreign taxes. Abundant resources were thus available for development projects of national benefit (e.g., the flood control and irrigation works opened in April 1956 on the Tigris at Samarra and on the Euphrates at Ramadi).

THE BAGHDAD PACT

Iraq, in the field of foreign relations, was confronted during these years with a choice between the Western powers, eager to establish in the Middle East an organized pattern of defence, and the Soviet Union, entering at this time into a diplomatic propaganda and economic drive to increase her influence in the Arab lands. Baghdad, in February 1955, made with Ankara an alliance for mutual co-operation and defence. Britain acceded to this pact in the following April, agreeing also to end the Anglo-Iraqi agreement of 1930 and to surrender her air bases at Shu'ayba and Habbaniya. With the adherence of Pakistan in September and of Iran in October 1955 the so-called Baghdad Pact was completed: a defensive cordon now existed along the southern fringe of the Soviet Union.

CONSEQUENCES OF THE SUEZ CRISIS

The outbreak of hostilities between Israel and Egypt on October 29th, 1956, and the armed intervention of British and French forces against Egypt (October 31st–November 6th) led to a delicate situation in Iraq, where strong elements were still opposed to all connections with the Western Powers. Iraq, indeed, broke off diplomatic relations with France on November 9th and announced that, for the immediate future at least, it could give no assurance of taking part in further sessions of the Council of the Baghdad Pact, if delegates from Britain were present.

The attitude of the Baghdad Government during the Suez crisis had provoked unrest in Iraq. Disturbances at Najaf and Mosul resulted in some loss of life. Student demonstrations against the Anglo-French intervention in Egypt and the Israeli campaign in Sinai led the Iraqi Government to close colleges and schools. Martial law, imposed on October 31st, 1956, was not raised until May 27th, 1957.

The tension born of the Suez crisis persisted for some time to come. President Eisenhower, concerned over the flow of Soviet arms to Syria and Egypt, sought from Congress permission to use the armed forces of the United States to defend nations exposed to danger from countries under the influence of international communism. He also secured authorization to disburse economic and military aid to the Middle East states prepared to co-operate with the West. This programme became known as the "Eisenhower Doctrine".

RELATIONS WITH SYRIA AND JORDAN

At the time of the Suez crisis there had been sharp tension between Iraq and Syria. Pumping-stations located inside Syria and belonging to the Iraq Petroleum Company were sabotaged in November 1956 with the result that Iraq suffered a large financial loss through the interruption in the flow of oil to the Mediterranean coast. Not until March 1957 did Syria allow the Iraq Petroleum Company to begin the repair of the pipelines.

Since the Suez crisis of 1956 troops of Iraq and Syria had been stationed in Jordan as a precaution against an Israeli advance to the east. Iraq, in December 1956, announced that her troops would be withdrawn; the Syrian forces, however, still remained in Jordan. The fear that Syria might intervene in favour of the elements in Jordan opposed to King Hussein brought about further recriminations between Baghdad and Damascus. The danger of an acute crisis receded in April 1957, when the U.S.A. declared that the independence of Jordan was a matter of vital concern and underlined this statement by sending its Sixth Fleet to the eastern Mediterranean. In February 1958 King Faisal of Iraq and King Hussein of Jordan joined together in an abortive Arab Federation.

OVERTHROW OF THE MONARCHY

King Faisal II, together with the Crown Prince of Iraq and General Nuri as-Sa'id, lost their lives in the course of a *coup d'état* begun on July 14th, 1958, by units of the Iraqi Army. Iraq was now to become a Republic. Power was placed in the hands of a council of sovereignty exercising presidential authority and of a cabinet led by Brigadier 'Abd al-Karim Kassem, with the rank of Prime Minister.

A struggle for power was now to develop between the two main architects of the July *coup d'état*— Brigadier (later General) Kassem, the Prime Minister, and Colonel (later Field-Marshal) Abd al-Salam Muhammad Aref, the Deputy Prime Minister and Minister of the Interior. Colonel Aref was associated with the influential Baath Party and had shown himself to be a supporter of union between Iraq and the United Arab Republic. Now, in September 1958, he was dismissed from his offices and, in November, was tried on a charge of plotting against the interests of Iraq. As reconstituted in February 1959 the new regime might be described as hostile to the United Arab Republic and inclined to favour a form of independent nationalism with left-wing tendencies.

General Kassem announced the withdrawal of Iraq from the Baghdad Pact on March 24th, 1959. Since the revolution of July 1958 Iraq's adherence to the Pact had been little more than nominal. One result of this withdrawal was the termination of the special agreement existing between Britain and Iraq since 1955 under the first article of the Baghdad Pact. On March 31st it was made known that the Royal Air Force contingent at Habbaniyah would be recalled.

PROBLEMS OF THE KASSEM REGIME

Earlier in 1959 the Communist elements in Iraq had been refused representation in the government. The Communists operated through a number of professional organizations and also through the so-called People's Resistance Force. Communist elements had infiltrated into the armed forces of Iraq and into the civil service. General Kassem now began to introduce measures which would limit Communist influence inside the government and administration of the country. In July 1959 fighting occurred at Kirkuk between the Kurds (supported by the People's Resistance Force) and the Turcomans, with the result that Kassem disbanded the People's Resistance Force. Much more important for the government at Baghdad was the fact that, in March 1961, a considerable section of the Kurdish population in northern Iraq rose in rebellion under Mustafa Barzani, the President of the Democratic Party of Kurdistan—a party established in 1958 after the return of Barzani from an exile occasioned by an earlier unsuccessful revolt in 1946. The refusal of the central regime at Baghdad to grant the reiterated Kurdish demands for an autonomous status had contributed greatly to bring about the new insurrection. Mustafa Barzani in March 1961 proclaimed an independent Kurdish state. By September 1961 the rebels controlled some 250 miles of mountainous territory along the Iraqi-Turkish and Iraqi-Persian frontiers, from Zakho in the west to Sulaimaniya in the east. The Kurds were able to consolidate their hold over much of northern Iraq during the course of 1962. The Kurds used guerrilla tactics with much success to isolate and deprive the government garrisons in the north of supplies. By December 1963 Kurdish forces had advanced south towards the Khanaqin area and the main road linking Iraq with Iran. The government troops found themselves in fact confined to the larger towns such as Kirkuk, Sulaimaniya and Khanaqin. Negotiations for peace began near Sulaimaniya in January 1964 and led to a cease-fire on February 10th. The national claims of the Kurds were to be recognized in a new provisional constitution for Iraq. Moreover, a general amnesty would be granted by the Iraqi Government. The Kurdish tribesmen, however, refused to lay aside their arms until their political demands had been given practical effect. Despite the negotiation of this settlement it was soon to become clear that no final solution of the Kurdish problem was as yet in sight.

FALL OF KASSEM

A military coup carried out in Baghdad on February 8th, 1963, overthrew the regime of General Kassem, the General himself being captured and shot. The coup arose out of an alliance between nationalist army officers and the Baath Party. Colonel Aref was now raised to the office of President and a new cabinet created under Brigadier Ahmed al-Bakr. The Baath Party, founded in 1941 (in Syria) and dedicated to the ideas of Arab unity, socialism and freedom, drew its main support from the military elements, the intellectuals and the middle classes. It was, however, divided in Iraq into a pro-Egyptian wing advocating union with the United Arab Republic and a more independent wing disinclined to accept authoritarian control from Egypt. The coup of February 1963 was followed by the arrest of pro-Kassem and of Communist elements, by mass trials and a number of executions, by confiscations of property and by a purge of the officer corps and of the civil service.

A number of efforts were made, during the years 1963–65, to further the cause of Arab unification, but agreements made between Syria and Iraq, and between Egypt, Syria and Iraq, had little practical effect.

MANOEUVRES OF THE BAATH PARTY

These same years saw in Iraq itself a conflict for control between the extremist and the more moderate Baath elements. At the end of September 1963 the extremists dominated the Baath Regional Council in Iraq. An international Baath Conference held at Damascus in October 1963 strengthened the position of the extremists through its support of a federal union between Syria and Iraq and its approval of more radical social and economic policies. A further Baathist conference at Baghdad in November 1963 enabled the moderates to elect a new Baath Regional Council in Iraq with their own adherents in control. At this juncture the extremists attempted a *coup d'état*, in the course of which air force elements attacked the Presidential Palace and the Ministry of Defence.

On November 18th, 1963, President Aref assumed full powers in Iraq, with the support of the armed forces, and a new Revolutionary Command was established at Baghdad. Sporadic fighting occurred (November 18th–20th) between the government troops and the pro-Baathist National Guard. A main factor in the sudden fall of the Baathists was the attitude of the professional officer class. Officers with Communist, Kassemite or pro-Nasser sympathies, or with no strong political views, or of Kurdish origin, had all been removed from important commands and offices. The privileged position of the National Guard caused further resentment in the army. The long drawn-out operations against the Kurds, the known dissensions within the Baathist ranks in Iraq and the intervention of Baath politicians from abroad in Iraqi affairs also contributed to discredit the extreme elements amongst the Baathists. On November 20th, 1963, a new Cabinet was formed at Baghdad, consisting of officers, moderate Baathists, independents and non-party experts.

THE ARAB SOCIALIST UNION

On July 14th, 1964, President Aref announced that all political parties would be merged in a new organization known as the "Iraqi Arab Socialist Union". At the same time it was revealed that all banks and insurance companies, together with thirty-two important industrial concerns, would undergo nationalization.

In July 1965 a number of pro-Nasser ministers handed in their resignations. At the beginning of September 1965 a new administration came into being with Brigadier Aref Abd al-Razzaq as Prime Minister. The Brigadier, reputed to be pro-Nasser in his sympathies, attempted to seize full power in Iraq, but his attempted *coup d'état* failed and, on September 16th, he himself, together with some of his supporters, found refuge in Cairo. On April 13th, 1966, President Abd al-Salam Aref of Iraq was killed in a helicopter crash. His brother Major-General Abd al-Rahman Aref succeeded him as President with the approval of the Cabinet and of the National Defence Council. In late June 1966 Brigadier Aref Abd al-Razzaq, who had staged the unsuccessful *coup d'état* of September 1965, led a second abortive coup, which was foiled by the prompt action of President Aref.

KURDISH NATIONALISM

The war against the Kurds, halted only for a short while by the cease-fire of February 1964, dragged out its inconclusive course during 1964–66. Some of the fighting in December 1965 occurred close to the Iraq-Iran border, leading to a number of frontier violations which gave rise to sharp tension between the two states during the first half of 1966. In June of 1966 Dr. Abd al-Rahman al-Bazzaz, Prime Minister of Iraq since September 1965, formulated new proposals for a settlement of the conflict with the Kurds. Kurdish nationalism and language would receive legal recognition; the administration was to be decentralized, allowing the Kurds to run educational, health and municipal affairs in their own districts; the Kurds would have proportional representation in Parliament and in the Cabinet and the various state services; the Kurdish armed forces (some 15,000 strong) were to be dissolved. Mustafa Barzani, the Kurdish leader, declared himself to be well disposed towards these proposals.

This entente was implemented only to a limited extent. The cabinet formed in May 1967 contained Kurdish elements, and President Aref, after a visit to the north in late 1967, reaffirmed his intention to make available to the Kurds appointments of ministerial rank, to help with the rehabilitation of the war-affected areas in Kurdistan, and to work towards effective co-operation with the Kurds in the Government of Iraq. This state of quiescence was, however, broken in the first half of 1968 by reports of dissension amongst the Kurds themselves, with open violence between the adherents of Mustafa Barzani and the supporters of Jalal Talabani, who had co-operated with the Government.

OIL DISPUTES AND THE JUNE WAR

Although the winter of 1966–67 brought an improvement in relations with Iran, it also witnessed a dispute between Syria and the Iraq Petroleum Company (IPC) over alleged losses of revenue on oil from Iraq passing through Syria by pipeline. The flow of oil was halted for a time and settlement was not reached until well into 1967.

When the Arab-Israeli war broke out in June 1967, the movement of Iraqi oil was again affected. Problems connected with its production and export constituted a major preoccupation of the Baghdad Government during the period immediately following the war. Iraq had at the outset severed diplomatic relations with the U.S.A. and Britain after Arab charges that the two states had aided Israel in the war and she also banned the export of oil to them. When, at the end of June, supplies of Iraqi oil began to be moved once more from the pipeline terminals on the Mediterranean, this embargo remained. In August Iraq, Syria and the Lebanon resolved to allow the export of Iraqi oil to most of the countries of Europe, the United Kingdom being still subject, however, to the embargo.

Relations with the West improved slightly during the autumn and winter of 1967. The remaining oil embargoes were gradually removed, and in December General Sabri led a military delegation to Paris. This was followed by President Aref's official visit to France in February 1968, and in April France agreed to supply Iraq with 54 Mirage aircraft over the period 1969–73. In May diplomatic relations with the United Kingdom were resumed.

THE 1968 COUP AND ITS AFTERMATH

Throughout the first half of 1968 the regime conspicuously lacked popular support, being commonly thought to be both corrupt and inefficient, and the sudden bloodless *coup d'état* of July 17th did not surprise many observers. General Ahmed Hassan al-Bakr, a former Prime Minister, became President; the deposed President Aref went into exile and his Prime Minister, Taher Yahya, was imprisoned on corruption charges. A new government was soon dismissed by the President, who accused it of "reactionary tendencies". He then appointed himself Prime Minister and Commander-in-Chief of the Armed Forces.

During the second half of 1968 the internal political situation deteriorated steadily. By November there were frequent reports of a purge directed against opponents of the new regime, and freedom of verbal political comment seemed to have disappeared. A former Foreign Minister, Dr. Nasser al-Hani, was found murdered, and a distinguished former Prime Minister, Dr. al-Bazzaz, and other members of former governments were arrested as "counter-revolutionary leaders"; most were later given long jail sentences. Open hostilities with the Kurds broke out in October 1968 for the first time since the June 1966 ceasefire, and continued on an extensive scale throughout the winter. Iraqi army and air force attempts to enforce the writ of the

Baghdad Government had little success; the regime claimed that the rebels were receiving aid from Iran and Israel. Fighting continued unabated through 1969, the Kurds demanding autonomy within the state and asking for UN mediation.

SETTLEMENT WITH THE KURDS

The most important event of 1970 was the settlement with the Kurds when, in March, a fifteen-article peace plan was announced by the Revolutionary Command Council and the Kurdish leaders. The plan conceded that the Kurds should participate fully in the Government; that Kurdish officials should be appointed in areas inhabited by a Kurdish majority; that Kurdish should be the official language, along with Arabic, in Kurdish areas; that development of Kurdish areas should be implemented; and that the provisional constitution should be amended to incorporate the rights of the Kurds.

The agreement was generally accepted by the Kurdish community and fighting ceased immediately. The war had been very expensive for Iraq and it had seriously delayed the national development programme. The Kurdish settlement, although not entirely satisfactory, did introduce an element of stability into life in Iraq and allowed a number of reforms to be initiated. In October 1970 the state of emergency, in operation almost continuously since July 1958, was lifted. Many political detainees, including former ministers, were released. Censorship of mail was abolished at the end of the year, having lasted for over thirteen years, and a month later the censorship of foreign correspondents' cables was brought to an end after a similar period.

Kurdish unity was boosted in February 1971 by the decision of the Kurdish Revolutionary Party to merge with the Kurdish Democratic Party of Mustafa Barzani and in July 1971 a new provisional constitution was announced, which embodied many of the points contained in the 1970 settlement. The Kurds were directed by the Supreme Committee for Kurdish Affairs to give up their arms by August 1971 and the situation in the north continued to be normal.

Evidence of unrest, however, was growing both in Kurdistan and in the Government itself. In July 1971 an attempted coup by army and air force officers was put down by the Government but dissatisfaction continued to be reported. The Kurds were beginning to show discontent with the delays in implementing the 1970 agreement. Their demand for participation in the Revolutionary Command Council was refused and in September 1971 an attempt was made on Barzani's life.

THE CONTINUING KURDISH PROBLEM

During 1972, possibly because of increasing preoccupation with foreign affairs, dissension within the Government was less in evidence. Clashes with the Kurds, however, became more frequent and there was another plot to assassinate Barzani in July. The Baath Party's deteriorating relations with the Kurds brought a threat from the Kurdish Democratic Party to renew the civil war. One of the main Kurdish grievances was that the census agreed upon in 1970 had still not taken place. The two sides met to discuss their differences, the Kurdish side pointing to the unfulfilled provisions of the 1970 agreement and the Baath reiterating the various development projects carried out in Kurdish areas. In December 1972, a break appeared in the Kurdish ranks when it was reported that a breakaway party was to be set up in opposition to Barzani's party.

FOREIGN RELATIONS 1968-71

The more radical section of the Arab world had initially greeted the July 1968 coup with disfavour and the new regime was at pains to prove itself as militant an exponent of Arab nationalism as its predecessor. The regime gradually became an accepted member of the nationalist group, but there was some Arab criticism of its policies, notably the public hangings and their effect on world opinion.

Like Algeria, on the opposite flank of the Arab world, Iraq took a hard line on the Palestinian problem. All peace proposals—American, Egyptian and Jordanian—were rejected. In theory total support was given to the Palestine liberation movement but, despite a threat to the Jordanian Government at the beginning of September 1970 to intervene in Jordan on behalf of the Palestinian guerrillas, the Iraqi forces stationed there did not take part in the fighting. In January 1971, most of Iraq's 20,000 troops were withdrawn from both Jordan and Syria. In March it was reported in Cairo that Iraq's monthly contribution to the Palestine Liberation Army had ceased. Iraq's attitude to Middle East peace proposals opened up a rift with Egypt even before President Nasser's death and her contempt for the proposed Egypt-Libya-Syria federation, as well as for any negotiated settlement with Israel, kept her well isolated from Egypt and almost all the other Arab states. In July 1971 there were signs that Iraq wished to reduce her isolation, offering to co-operate again with the Arab states if they abandoned attempts to negotiate with Israel, but the renewal of hostilities between the Jordanian Government and the guerrillas caused a break in relations with Jordan. Iraq closed the border, called for Jordan's expulsion from the Arab League and banned her from participating in the Eighth International Baghdad Fair.

Meanwhile, relations with Iran continued to be poor. Iraq frequently accused the Teheran Government of assisting the Kurdish rebellion and in April 1969 the Shatt al-Arab waterway again caused a minor confrontation. Iraq had benefited by a 1937 treaty which gave it control of the waterway. Iran tried to force a renegotiation of the treaty by illegally sending through vessels flying the Iranian flag. Being unwilling (or politically unable) to yield any of its sovereignty, and unable to challenge Iran militarily, Iraq was obliged to accept this situation. Iraq proposed referring the dispute to the International Court of Justice, but Iran rejected the suggestion. Minor border clashes between the two sides' forces continued to occur sporadically and both

Iran and Iraq accused each other of attempting to foment coups. Not surprisingly, the two countries were also divided on policy towards the Gulf States. Iraq broke off diplomatic relations with Iran (and Britain) after Iran's seizure of the Tumb Islands in the Persian/Arabian Gulf in November 1971.

Relations with the Western world, and the U.S.A. in particular, remained poor, several people arrested or expelled in late 1968 being accused of spying for the Americans. The friendship with the Soviet Union remained the major factor in Iraq's foreign policy, particularly since the U.S.S.R. was supplying the bulk of Iraq's military equipment.

THE PROBLEM OF OIL

In June 1972 Iraq nationalized IPC's interests and agreement on outstanding points of dispute was finally reached on February 28th, 1973. The company agreed to settle Iraqi claims for back royalties by paying £141 million, and to waive its objections to Law No. 80 under which the North Rumeila fields were seized in 1961. The Government agreed to deliver a total of 15 million tons of crude from Kirkuk, to be loaded at Eastern Mediterranean ports, to the companies as compensation. The Mosul Petroleum Company agreed to relinquish all its assets without compensation and the Basrah Petroleum Company, the only one of the group to remain operational in Iraq, undertook to increase output from 32 million tons in 1972 to 80 million tons in 1976. This agreement was regarded on the whole as a victory for the Iraqi Government, although the companies were by no means net losers by it.

With the IPC dispute out of the way, Iraq showed its unwillingness to continue indefinitely with exporting oil on a barter basis to the Eastern Bloc countries. The Government made it clear that it would press for a cash basis to future agreements.

FOREIGN RELATIONS 1972–73

The nationalization of IPC brought expressions of approval from a number of countries, including Arab States and the Soviet Union. The 15-year friendship treaty with the Soviet Union, signed in March 1972, was ratified in July and Iraq's relations with the Eastern Bloc states continued to be good. Despite this, however, the Government was well aware of the dangers of too close and exclusive a relationship with the Soviet Bloc. France was specifically singled out as the Western country most friendly towards the Arabs and the President's fourth anniversary speech in July revealed that Iraq would not be unwilling to open up friendly relations with Western countries. Although diplomatic relations with the United States were still severed, the U.S.A. established an "interests section" in Baghdad.

CONSTITUTIONAL CHANGE

In July 1973 an abortive coup took place, led by the Security chief, Nazim Kazzar, in which the Minister of Defence, General Hammad Shehab, was killed. It is thought that it was an attempt by a civilian faction within the Baath Party to get rid of President Bakr and the military faction. One result of the attempted coup was an amendment to the constitution giving more power to the President, and the formation of a National Front between the Baath Party and the Iraq Communist Party. There seemed a possibility at this time that the Kurdistan Democratic Party might be persuaded to join the National Front, but later events were to prove these hopes groundless.

CLIMAX AND END OF KURDISH WAR

According to the agreement made between the Iraqi Government and the Kurds in March 1970 the deadline for implementation of the agreement was March 11th, 1974. An uneasy peace between the Kurds and the Iraqis had existed between those two dates. When March 11th, 1974, arrived Saddam Hussain Takriti, the Vice-President of the Revolution Command Council and the "strong man" of the regime, announced the granting of autonomy to the Kurds. Barzani and his Kurdish Democratic Party felt that the Iraqi offer fell short of their demands for full government representation, which included membership of the Revolution Command Council. A minority of Kurds, who belonged to Abdel Satter Sharif's Kurdish Revolutionary Party welcomed the proposals, however. Barzani and his militia, the *Pesh Merga*, began armed resistance in north Iraq. In April 1974 the Iraqi Government replaced five Kurdish Ministers known to support Barzani by five other Kurds who supported the Government plan for giving the Kurds a measure of autonomy. Later in April the Iraqi Government appointed a Kurd, Taha Moheddin Marouf, as Vice-President of Iraq, but since he had long been a supporter of the Baghdad Government, it seemed unlikely that this would pacify the Kurds of the K.D.P.

By August 1974 the Kurdish war had reached a new level of intensity. The Baghdad Government was directing large military resources against the *Pesh Merga*, as Barzani's forces were called, and were deploying tanks, field guns and bombers. About 130,000 Kurds, mainly women, children and old men, took refuge in Iran. The *Pesh Merga* were able to keep up their resistance in Iraq only with the help of arms and other supplies from Iran. When, therefore, an agreement to end their border dispute was signed by Iraq and Iran at the OPEC meeting in Algiers on March 6th, 1975, both countries also agreed to end "infiltrations of a subversive character" and the Kurdish rebellion collapsed. Barzani felt that he could not continue his struggle without Iran's aid, and fled to Teheran. A ceasefire was arranged on March 13th, and a series of amnesties granted to Kurds who had fled to Iran encouraged most of them to return to Iraq. By February 1976, however, it was reported that the K.D.P. was secretly reorganizing inside Iraqi Kurdistan and preparing to resume its struggle. In March there were reports of clashes between Kurds and Iraqi security forces in the Rumanduz area, after Iraqi attempts to clear the frontier area with Iran and resettle Kurds in less sensitive areas of Iraq. A new political organization, the National

Union of Kurdistan, was also set up in Damascus quite separately from the K.D.P., which, in the opinion of the National Union of Kurdistan, had become discredited. Renewed Kurdish activity occurred in 1976 but was not serious enough to weaken the Iraqi claim that the Kurdish problem had been solved. Reconstruction and school-building was certainly undertaken in Kurdish areas in 1977, and in April 1977 the Iraqi authorities allowed 40,000 Kurds who had been compulsorily settled in the south in 1975 to return to their homes in the north. It was also decided in April 1977 by the Executive Council of the Kurdish Autonomous Region that Kurdish should become the official language to be used in all communications and by all government departments in the Kurdish Autonomous Region which had no connection with the central government.

FOREIGN AFFAIRS 1973-76

On the outbreak of the October 1973 war between the Arabs and Israel, Iraq sent considerable land forces to the Syrian front and took advantage of Iran's offer to resume diplomatic relations. The Iraqi Government, however, had taken offence because President Sadat had not consulted Iraq in advance, and because of this Iraqi forces were withdrawn from Syria as soon as the ceasefire went into effect, and Iraq boycotted the Arab summit meeting in Algiers in November.

Relations deteriorated with Iran in the early months of 1974, when frontier fighting broke out, and it was only after the appointment of a UN Mediator in March that "normal" relations on the frontier were restored, and they deteriorated again in August in spite of talks in Istanbul between Iraqi and Iranian diplomats. Further border clashes took place in December 1974, and secret talks in Istanbul between the Iraqi and Iranian Foreign Ministers in January 1975 failed to prevent the outbreak of fresh clashes in February. It was therefore something of a surprise when at the OPEC meeting at Algiers in March 1975 it was announced that Saddam Hussain Takriti, Vice-President of the Iraqi Revolutionary Command Council (RCC), and the Shah of Iran had signed an agreement which "completely eliminated the conflict between the two brotherly countries". This agreement also ended the Kurdish war (*see* above), and was embodied in a treaty signed between the two countries in June 1975. The frontiers were defined on the basis of the Protocol of Constantinople of 1913 and the verbal agreement on frontiers of 1914. The Shatt al-Arab frontier was defined according to the thalweg Line, which runs down the middle of the deepest shipping channel.

THE BAATH PARTY AND RELATIONS WITH SYRIA

Iraq was one of the many Arab states who were severely critical of the second interim disengagement agreement signed between Egypt and Israel in September 1975. Iraqi reaction to the agreement was similar to that of Syria, but this condemnation was perhaps the only thing upon which the two countries agreed upon between 1975 and 1978. Rivalry between the two wings of the Baath party in Baghdad and Damascus, and a dispute over the sharing of the water from the Euphrates were just two areas of contention. In February 1976 Iraq was reported to be diverting much of its oil from pipelines to the Mediterranean to terminals near Basra, thus depriving Syria of valuable pipeline revenues. Iraq was also very critical of Syria's intervention in the Lebanon. Syrian agents were also blamed for the violence which took place in the Shia holy cities of Najaf and Kerbala in February 1977. Rioting took place when Iraqi authorities banned a Shia procession. The secular wing of the Baath party are distrustful of Shia religious feelings and, on the other hand, the Shia element have always felt under-represented in Baghdad. Relations with Syria deteriorated even further in late 1977, and Iraq became somewhat isolated after President Sadat of Egypt's peace initiative in visiting Jerusalem in November 1977. At the Tripoli Conference, summoned by the States who disagreed with President Sadat's approach, Iraq wanted a specific rejection of UN Resolution 242. The stand taken by the other participants (Syria, Libya, Yemen P.D.R., Algeria and the Palestine Liberation Organization) seemed too moderate for Iraq, who walked out of the Conference. Iraq subsequently boycotted the Algiers conference of "rejectionist" States in February 1978, hoping unsuccessfully to form its own "steadfastness and liberation front" at a Baghdad conference.

NEW ALIGNMENTS

Iraq opposed the Camp David agreements made between Egypt and Israel in September 1978, but, continuing its attitude of boycott, it stayed away from the Damascus Arab summit which immediately followed the Camp David agreements. Iraq's period of isolation was almost at an end, however. In October President Assad of Syria visited Baghdad and, as a result, Iraq and Syria signed a Charter outlining plans for political and economic union between the two countries. Old rivalries and animosities were set aside in an effort to form a political and military power which would be a sizeable counterweight to Egypt in Middle Eastern affairs. In November Iraq successfully called a Pan-Arab summit which threatened sanctions against Egypt if a peace treaty with Israel should be signed, and in March 1979, when the peace treaty became a fact, Baghdad was the venue for the meeting of the Arab Foreign and Economic Ministers which resolved to put into practice the threats made to Egypt in the previous November.

The plans for complete political and economic union were pursued with enthusiasm but little real practical application by both countries until July 1979. On July 16th, 1979, Saddam Hussain replaced Bakr as President of Iraq and Chairman of the RCC. A few days later an attempted coup was reported and several members of the RCC were sentenced to death for their alleged part in the plot. Saddam Hussain believed Syria to be implicated, in spite of Syrian denials, and the newly-formed alliance foundered.

Another aspect of this political unrest in Iraq was the breakdown of the alliance between the Baath Party and the Communists. In the summer of 1978 21 army personnel were executed for conducting political activity in the army, and relations with the Communists have continued to deteriorate. They withdrew from the National Progressive Front in March 1979, and in early 1980 President Hussain referred to them in a speech as "a rotten, atheistic, yellow storm which has plagued Iraq". This has led to a decrease in dependence on the U.S.S.R. and to tentative moves to improve relations with the West. Hussain joined the general Arab condemnation of the Soviet invasion of Afghanistan at the end of 1979.

In February 1980 President Hussain announced his "National Charter", which reaffirmed the principles of non-alignment, rejecting "the existence of foreign armies, military forces, troops and bases in the Arab Homeland", and made a plea for Arab solidarity. With Sadat compromised by his *rapprochement* with Israel, Hussain saw himself in a position of virtual pre-eminence in the Arab world and, with the Non-Aligned Summit due to take place in Baghdad in 1982, he would be in a position to present himself as the responsible leader of the non-aligned world.

Domestically, Hussain has been engaged in restoring parliamentary government to Iraq. The intention had been announced for some years, but on March 16th, 1980, laws were adopted for the election of an Iraqi National Assembly of 250 deputies for a four-year session, and also for a Legislative Council for the Autonomous Region of Kurdistan, consisting of 50 members elected for a three-year session. Elections took place on June 20th, 1980, and deputies were elected by a direct, free and secret ballot. The first session of the National Assembly opened on June 30th, and one of the Deputy Premiers, Naim Haddad, was elected Chairman and Speaker. Elections to a 50-member Kurdish Legislative Council took place in September 1980.

WAR WITH IRAN

Although the 1975 peace agreement with Iran virtually ended the Kurdish rebellion, Iraq was dissatisfied and wanted a return to the Shatt al-Arab boundary whereby she controlled the whole water-way, and also the withdrawal of Iranian forces from Abu Musa and Tumb Islands, which Iran occupied in 1971. Conflict also became evident after the

Iranian Revolution over Arab demands for autonomy in Iran's Khuzestan (termed "Arabistan" by Arabs), which Iran accused Iraq of encouraging. In addition, Iraq's Sunni leadership was suspicious of Shi'ite Iran and fearful of trouble from her own Shi'ites, who are in the majority in Iraq. Border fighting between Iran and Iraq frequently occurred as 1980 progressed, and open warfare began on September 22nd when Iraqi forces advanced into Iran along a 300-mile front. Iran had ignored Iraqi diplomatic efforts demanding the withdrawal of Iranian forces from Zain ul Qos on the border. Iraq maintained that this territory should have been returned by Iran under the 1975 agreement. Iraq therefore abrogated the Shatt al-Arab agreement on September 16th.

Most commentators agree that Saddam Hussain's real intention was to topple the Iranian regime of the Ayatollahs when he invaded Iran. Resistance was fiercer than he expected, however, and stalemate was soon reached along a 300-mile front, while various international peace missions sought in vain for a solution. In the Spring of 1982 Iranian forces launched successful counter-offensives, one in the region of Deshful in March, and another in April which resulted in the recapture of Khorramshahr by the Iranians in May.

This setback put Saddam Hussain in a very vulnerable position. He faced threats from all quarters. In the previous summer an "Iraqi Front of Revolutionary, Islamic and National Forces", consisting of Kurds, exiled Shi'ites and disaffected Baath party members, was formed with Syrian backing. Syria supported Iran in the war with Iraq, and President Assad was as anxious as Ayatollah Khomeini to see the downfall of Saddam Hussain. The Shi'ite community in Iraq, who form a larger proportion of the population than the Sunnis (the sect of the Iraqi leadership), were always a potential threat, and now seemed even more likely to come to some effective arrangement with Iran. By late June 1982 Saddam Hussain had to acknowledge that the war against Iran had been a virtual failure. He arranged for the complete withdrawal of Iraqi troops from all Iranian territory and then appealed for a neutral peace-keeping force to monitor the cease-fire. Iran had been demanding Saddam Hussain's fall as a condition of peace, but by early July he was still in the saddle, having been re-elected Chairman of the Revolutionary Command Council and also Regional Secretary of the Arab Baath Socialist Party.

ECONOMIC SURVEY

In December 1981 foreign companies in Iraq were told that a moratorium was to be declared on contracts about to be signed, and that a number of projects were to be shelved. By April 1982 a clear list of priorities had been drawn up. First were projects that directly or indirectly supported the war effort; second were schemes related to the summit conference of non-aligned countries, scheduled for September 1982; and third were railways and roads. Once the war

has ended, reconstruction of oil and gas installations will be given priority status.

Iraqi economic planners must now substantially revise the present Five-Year Plan (1981–85), which forecast spending amounting to some ID 40,000 million. Initial outlines suggested that the most important sectors would be services, in particular housing, water and sewerage facilities, electricity and expansion of the health and education system; transport and communications—roads and bridges, railways, airports and telephones; and industry—expansion of brick and cement factories.

Since 1977 Iraq has shown a great appetite for economic development. Unlike other Arab Gulf states, Iraq has the advantage of a large population—an estimated 13.5 million in 1981—which gives it the labour force necessary for industrial development. The World Bank estimates that Iraq's population increased by an average 3.4 per cent annually in 1970–77 and that it should reach 23 million by the end of the century. About 51 per cent of the population is estimated to be of working age.

Agriculture was the mainstay of the economy until oil production began on a large scale. It still receives a large share of investment and took 20 per cent of socialist sector spending in 1981. Because of continued investment and Iraq's ample supply of irrigation water and fertile land, its agriculture is among the most developed in the region. The sector is not free from problems, however, and efforts have constantly to be made to control salinity and improve drainage.

In the two previous national development plans (1970–75 and 1976–80), priority was given to oil and other industries, the aim being to diversify sources of revenue (from different industrial exports). The country's increasing industrialization is reflected in the population distribution. About 64 per cent of the population was classed as urban in 1977, compared with 43 per cent in 1960. Similarly, only 30 per cent of the labour force was employed in agriculture, compared with 53 per cent in 1960.

Iraq has also put considerable emphasis on education, which has given it a big skilled workforce. This, with the country's natural resources and high revenues from oil exports, is helping to create a productive economy. Individual and national income have increased sharply in the last few years. Per capita income was estimated at ID 387 in 1976, compared with ID 135 in 1973, while national income rose to ID 4,478 million in 1976 from ID 1,412 million in 1973.

Since the Baath Socialist Party came to power in 1968, the Government has steadily expanded its control of the economy. Government organizations currently account for 78 per cent of Iraq's G.N.P. and purchase 90 per cent of imported goods. State companies own and operate all heavy industries and the Government, through the Industrial Bank, owns major shares of small "mixed" public sectors, which include electronics and several other light industries. The private sector, contributing about 20 per cent of G.N.P. and purchasing about 9 per cent of imports, is concentrated in food processing, textile manufacturing, tourism, services and retailing.

In 1974–79 the value of Iraq's oil exports increased from ID 1,921 million to ID 6,288 million. This rapid increase in wealth brought a corresponding rise in Gross Domestic Product (G.D.P.). According to the Central Statistical Organization of Iraq, G.D.P. amounted to ID 6,838 million in 1978, compared with ID 1,139 million in 1970. Per capita G.D.P. was ID 555 in 1978, compared with ID 120 in 1970.

AGRICULTURE

Agriculture employs about 30 per cent of the labour force and is, next to oil, the most important sector. Although the 1981–85 Development Plan gives high priority to other sectors, agriculture remains important. The aim is to produce an agricultural surplus for export by reducing dependence on weather conditions and solving the salinity problems which affect irrigated land.

Until 1958 agricultural improvement was often inhibited by the need for adequate land reform. In October 1958 the Government announced a new and more radical land reform project. This provided for the break-up of large estates whose owners were to be compelled to forfeit their "excess" land to the Government which would redistribute the land to new peasant owners. Under the terms of the reform the largest holding permitted on flow-irrigated land is 1,000 dunums (about 600 acres), and on land watered by rainfall 2,000 dunums. The estates broken up were to be allotted to farmers in holdings of a maximum of 60 or 120 dunums, according to the type of land, and the formation of agricultural co-operatives was planned to help the new owners with capital, machinery and technical advice. Landowners losing land were to be compensated in state bonds (in 1969 all the state's liabilities to recompense landowners were cancelled). It was hoped that the reform would take only five years to complete but the application of the law was initially mismanaged and the expropriation of land consistently ran ahead of the ability of the administration to distribute it. By the end of 1972 some 4.73 million dunums had been requisitioned from landlords and distributed to 100,646 families, but considerable areas of land remain awaiting distribution. The Government has been promoting the growth of co-operatives and collective farms since 1967.

The general system of cultivation is fallow farming and crop rotations are rare. Despite changes in recent years, the most common type of farm operation is by share tenancy, the farmer surrendering to the landowner a share of his crop, usually 50 per cent, in return for pump irrigation, water and other facilities. Other forms of operation are: (1) plantation farming, when the landowner or tenant of a rented farm employs paid labour; and (2) individual peasant proprietorships, when the farmer owns or rents his land and works it himself with his family.

The farm worker is concerned primarily with subsistence and grows crops and keeps animals to provide for himself and his family. Cash crops are grown by plantation farmers and peasant proprietors. A wide variety of crops is grown but the most important are barley and wheat. Production estimates vary considerably but, according to Iraq's Central Statistical Organization, about 910,000 metric tons of wheat and 617,000 tons of barley were produced in 1978. In the case of wheat, an estimated 1.2 million tons was produced in 1981, down from 1.3 million tons in 1980 and 1,492,000 metric tons in 1979. Normally Iraq produces an exportable surplus of barley, though in years of low rainfall barley exports are not possible.

Other crops are rice, vegetables, maize and millet, sugar cane and beet, oil seeds, pulses, dates and other fruits, fodder, tobacco and cotton. Rice production was 2.1 million tons in 1978, while maize output was 1.3 million tons. Vegetables grown include cabbages, spinach, carrots, tomatoes, okra, beans, cauliflowers and potatoes, while the main fruit is melon.

Dates are an important export and production in 1978 amounted to 389,000 tons. In 1980, some 209,000 tons were exported to 50 countries. Date production and marketing is the responsibility of the Iraqi Date Administration, which is expanding its storage capacity and cooling and processing systems to handle the expected increase in output. Dates are not only a lucrative export but are also being put to industrial use. The Ministry of Industry has started a major programme to produce sugar, dry sugar alcohol, vinegar and concentrated protein from dates. When in operation, these industries will need 175,000 tons of dates a year.

Aid to farmers is channelled through the Agricultural Co-operative Bank, which in 1981 lent ID 175 million. Of this, ID 72 million was for agricultural machinery and equipment. The remainder was lent mainly for poultry and livestock farming, for orchards and for agricultural buildings. To encourage farmers to use its services, the bank offers a low interest rate. A rural savings scheme and a rural property and life insurance scheme have also started.

The cost of food imports remains at a very high level having reached a total of U.S. $600 million in 1974, or 30 per cent of all imports, but dropping to $425 million, or 13 per cent of all imports, in 1976. Food subsidies in 1981 were covered by an allocation of ID 325 million, a 48 per cent increase from 1979. In the 1977 budget food subsidies amounted to ID 93 million. The main suppliers of cereals are the U.S.A., Australia and Argentina; rice is supplied by Pakistan and the U.S.A. Meat is imported mainly from Australia and New Zealand. Big improvements in cold storage and refrigeration in Iraq have made it much easier to buy meat from these countries and a big contract to purchase 30,000 tons of New Zealand lamb —more than twice the annual amount previously bought—was agreed for 1981. Cuba signed a contract in April 1975 to supply Iraq with 100,000 tons of sugar a year for five years and the Cubans are assisting in the development of Iraq's sugar cane production and refining. An Indian company was appointed in late 1981 to expand the Misan sugarcane plantation. All duties on raw sugar imports have been reduced. Self-sufficiency in food supplies, necessitating a 25 per cent increase in land under cultivation, is still a primary target under the 1981–85 Plan.

Investment in agriculture also includes expenditure on vocational training, to which Iraq gives high priority. In January 1981, for example, a DM535 million contract was awarded to the West German firm Ed Zublin for the construction of 16 agricultural colleges.

The livestock and poultry sector is also being developed. Dutch companies have provided technical assistance for cattle and dairy centres and poultry farming is being encouraged in the north as part of the Government's development drive in the predominantly Kurdish areas. Contracts to build and expand poultry farms have been awarded to British, West German and Hungarian companies.

Provision has also been made to develop a fishing industry and in early 1981 consultants were appointed to design a $160 million fisheries port complex near Basra. A committee has been set up to conserve domestic fish stocks.

RIVER CONTROL AND IRRIGATION

River control policy in Iraq has three main objects: the provision of water for irrigation, the prevention of devastating floods, and the creation of hydroelectric power. It is southern and central Iraq that are affected in all three cases, since northern Iraq is rainfed and for the most part the terrain is unsuitable for large-scale irrigation from the stored water of major dams. Minor local reservoirs and tube wells are enough to supplement the rain in the north.

At present the main systems providing flow irrigation are based on the Euphrates (serving nearly 3 million dunums), the Tigris (1.7 million dunums), the Diyalah River and the Lesser Zab River. Pumps are used extensively along both the Euphrates and the Tigris. Four dams, barrages or reservoirs (at Samarra, Dokan, Derbendi Khan and Habbaniyah) provide security against flood dangers. When the waters of the Euphrates and Tigris are fully utilized through dams and reservoirs, the area of cultivated land in Iraq will be almost doubled.

Great emphasis has been placed on the country's need for improved irrigation and an agreement has been signed with the U.S.S.R. for joint co-operation in irrigation affairs. Soviet experts are studying the Bakhma, Hindujah, Haditha and Fallujah irrigation projects. The current development plan envisages outlays on a number of major water storage and control schemes of which the most important are the Eski-Mosul dam and the Bakhma dam. The $1,500 million contract to build the Mosul dam was awarded to a consortium of West German and Italian companies in early 1981. Work is expected to take five years. Work on smaller-scale canal, drainage and diversion works will also form a continuing element in the overall water control programme. The first phase, 1975–80, of the Kirkuk irrigation project was under the supervision of a French company. Following phases will take a further seven years, with the ultimate objective of irrigating 1.5 million dunums. In all, more than ID 250 million will be spent at the Kirkuk site before the field level irrigation and reticulation system is complete. The Lower Khalis irrigation project, financed by the World Bank, will increase the irrigated area by 625,000 dunums. In addition, the Diwaniyah-Dalmaj scheme is due for completion soon and four other schemes—the Abu Ghraib, Al Ishaqi, Duja ila and Nahr Saad—will also increase irrigation facilities as well as being interlocked with general agricultural development. Consultants have been appointed to design irrigation schemes for Kifl-

IRAQ

Shinafiya, East Gharraf, Saba Nissan, New Rumaitha, Zubair, Bastora, Greater Musayyib and Makhmour. Work has also started on the ID 200 million second stage of the main outfall drain—Iraq's third river—which will collect excess water from more than 6 million dunums of irrigated land in central and southern Iraq, and drain it into the Gulf.

PETROLEUM

In the first nine months of 1980, before the outbreak of war with Iran, Iraq's oil exports had reached about 3.2 million barrels a day (b/d), making it the world's second largest crude oil supplier, after Saudi Arabia.

Following Iranian air raids on key installations in the early stages of the war, however, exports soon stopped from Iraq's major oil terminals at Mina al-Bakr and Khor al-Amaya on the Gulf. Refineries, pipelines, pumping stations and petrochemical plants were all damaged and it has been estimated that restoration of the pre-war export level will take at least a year from the end of hostilities.

Oil exports were at first diverted to Mediterranean ports via Iraq's reversible pipeline pumping network, but these were then brought to a halt by an explosion on the line through Turkey, reportedly the work of Kurdish guerrillas, and by Iranian bombing of the K-1 pumping station at the Kirkuk oilfield in the north.

By December 1980, however, oil exports through the Mediterranean ports had resumed and oil was being pumped through the pipeline across Turkey to Ceyhan at a rate of around 650,000 b/d. Not all of this was for worldwide exports, however, since Turkey was taking 250,000 b/d as its entitlement under the transit agreement. Preference in oil sales was given to countries which were major customers for Iraqi oil before the war and who had suffered most from the cessation of oil exports in the fourth quarter of 1980. These include Japan and France. Iraq's export quota was fixed at 1.2 million b/d at the March 1982 OPEC meeting in Vienna.

Despite tense political relations between Iraq and Syria, pumping through the trans-Syria pipeline to Banias resumed in early December at around 350,000 b/d but was soon halted and did not start again until the end of February. This pipeline, known as the strategic pipeline, can take crude from the Basra oilfields in the south as well as from Kirkuk in the north. It has a capacity of 1.4 million b/d but a great deal of maintenance work on the pumping stations and export terminals would be required to reach this level.

In February 1981, officials from Iraq, Syria and Lebanon met in Banias, Syria, to discuss reopening the Tripoli, Lebanon, branch of the Iraq-Syria pipeline. This branch was eventually opened. On April 10th, 1982, however, Syria closed the pipeline, depriving Iraq of a possible $17 million per day in lost revenues and leaving the Turkish pipeline as Iraq's only oil export outlet. The loss of the Gulf terminals and the vulnerability of the Turkish and Syrian pipelines have forced Iraq to look at alternative pipelines across Saudi Arabia, Kuwait and Jordan. The trans-Saudi line seems the most likely route; construction costs are estimated at $4,000 million.

Iraq is a major oil producer, with oil reserves estimated at 31,100 million million barrels, the third largest in OPEC. When war broke out in September 1980, many major oil and gas development projects were in progress. It is hard to assess how much war damage has been sustained. It is, however, known that the 140,000 b/d Basra oil refinery was bombed early in the war. Iraq was already short of oil refining capacity so the damage to the Basra refinery had a severe impact on domestic oil products supply. Some of the petrochemical and gas gathering related plants being built south of Basra were also damaged.

Projects in the Basra area include the construction of gas liquefaction and treating facilities by the French engineering contracting company Technip under a $239 million turnkey contract awarded in March 1980.

The plant, to be built at Zubair, near Basra, is to use as feedstock 6,000 million cubic metres of associated gas from the Rumaila oilfields to produce 4 million tons a year of propane and butane and 1.5 million tons a year of condensate. The plant was due for completion two and a half years from the date the contract was signed, but this date will now undoubtedly have been put back.

This plant is part of the southern gas project which entails gathering and compression facilities able to handle 16,000 million cubic metres a year of gas from the Rumaila oilfields. In April 1978 Snam Progetti—a subsidiary of Italy's Ente Nazionale Idrocarburi (ENI)—was awarded the engineering design contract. The following year, several other big contracts were awarded for the project. Mitsubishi Corporation and Chiyoda Chemical Engineering and Construction Company won a $138 million contract to build a natural gas liquids plant. Another ENI subsidiary, Nuovo Pignone, was awarded a $200 million contract for the supply of a complete gas processing system comprising 40 compressors, 10 gas turbines and other equipment. Toyo Engineering of Japan won a $63 million contract to build a liquefied petroleum gas (LPG) export terminal at Khor al-Zubair on the Gulf, and Hungary's Chemokomplex won a $8.8 million contract to build a pipeline network.

Apart from making use of the gas produced at the oilfields, Iraq is also expanding into downstream oil activities. A new refinery is being built at Baiji, on the Kirkuk-Mediterranean pipeline, mainly by two Czechoslovak companies, Technoexport and Chemoproject, which signed the contract in November 1978. Snam Progetti of Italy and Siemens of West Germany are also involved. The refinery was due to open in 1981 with a starting capacity of 70,000 b/d, rising to 150–220,000 b/d. The Basra refinery is also being expanded. Its capacity was raised from 70,000 to

140,000 b/d in 1979 and a 100,000 tons per year lube oil plant is being added.

A petrochemical complex is almost completed at Shuaiba in the Zubair area. The main contractors are a West German-U.S. group, Thyssen Rheinstahl Technik and C-E Lummus. The plant, on which work started in 1977, will produce 150,000 tons per year of low- and high-density polyethylene and PVC and 40,000 tons per year of caustic soda. Feedstock will be 90 million cubic feet a day of natural gas. Work has now started on the Baiji lubricants plant, part of the Baiji refinery complex.

The oil and gas industry is the responsibility of the Ministry of Oil and the Iraq National Oil Company (INOC), which came into being in 1964. Prior to the overthrow of the monarchy in 1958, oil exploration and production was carried out by the Iraq Petroleum Company (IPC), whose shareholders were Anglo-Persian Oil (later British Petroleum), Royal Dutch Shell, Compagnie Française des Pétroles, Near East Development Corporation (a U.S. consortium) and Sarkis Gulbenkian.

In 1967, all the rights taken from IPC in 1961 were formally granted to INOC. INOC then made a separate agreement with the French oil company ERAP (l'Entreprise de Recherches et d'Activités Pétrolières), to explore some 10,800 square kilometres of the North Rumaila field in the south. The experience it gained through this and other oil activities gave INOC the confidence to nationalize IPC. Negotiations started in 1972 and an agreement was signed the following year.

Subsidiaries of IPC were also nationalized. The Basrah Petroleum Company (BPC) was the last to be so, and the change took place in two stages in 1973 and 1975. After lengthy negotiations between the Government and the participants (BP, Shell, Compagnie Française des Pétroles, Exxon, Mobil and Partex) for compensation, the matter was finally settled in March 1979.

Meanwhile ERAP began drilling in 1968 near Basra, and discovered oil at Buzurgan, Abu Gharab and Siba. The development of these fields was delayed for some two years by disputes between ERAP and the Iraqi Government but in 1973 a contract was signed complementing the 1968 agreement and allowing for the export of 8 million tons of crude oil a year from the Abu Gharab and Buzurgan fields on completion of the Fao deepwater terminal. Under the original agreement, ERAP and a Japanese consortium (which took a 40 per cent share in 1973) were entitled to 15 per cent of production at a preferential price, and an option of 30 per cent more at market price. In July 1977, however, the Iraqi Government took over the operation and production sharing was no longer allowed. Foreign companies were then allowed to participate on straight fee contracts only.

Five major fields have been identified for future development—Majnoun, Nahr-Umr, Halfaya, East Baghdad and Qurnah. These fields are likely to increase production capacity by some 2 million b/d.

Iraq's oil industry is highly dependent on oil pipe-

lines which carry the oil through neighbouring territories or to the Gulf coast. The most recently built is a 40-inch line from Kirkuk through Turkey to Dortyol on the Mediterranean in the Gulf of Iskenderun. The line is 609 miles long, of which 212 miles are in Iraq and 397 miles in Turkey. It was finished in 1976. Total cost of the pipeline was $850 million, of which Iraq paid $250 million and Turkey $600 million. There have been several disputes with Turkey over transit fees.

Other pipelines go from Kirkuk and Haditha to Tripoli, Lebanon, from Kirkuk to Banias in Syria, from the Basra fields to the Gulf and from Kirkuk to Fao on the Gulf. In April 1976 the Iraqi Government decided to suspend Mediterranean deliveries through the Kirkuk pipeline across Syria to Tripoli because of a dispute with Syria over transit fees and other political issues. The dispute lasted for three years, until February 1979.

INOC's activities, too, extend beyond the exploration for and production of crude oil. In 1972 it established an autonomous company to be responsible for the operation and management of a tanker fleet.

Iraq, despite its reputation for being one of the OPEC "hawks", does not favour such high oil prices as some other oil producers. Though it wishes to get a good return for its natural resource, it nevertheless cannot afford to price itself out of the market. Unlike some other Gulf states, for example, Iraq urgently needs oil revenues for domestic development.

Just as Iraq has taken a more moderate line on oil prices, so it has opposed concerted oil production cuts. After the Arab-Israeli war of October 1973, Iraq opposed the restrictive oil sales policy of the Organization of Arab Petroleum Exporting Countries (OAPEC). Iraq even increased sales to favoured countries. But it did, however, follow OAPEC's policy in embargoing supplies to the U.S.A. and the Netherlands.

INDUSTRY

Until the 1970s Iraq had few large industries apart from oil. In greater Baghdad the larger enterprises were concerned with electricity and water supply and the building materials industry. In addition there was a large number of smaller-unit industries concerned with food and drink processing (date-packing, breweries, etc.), cigarette-making, textiles, chemicals, furniture, shoe-making, jewellery and various metal manufactures.

In recent years greater priority has been given to industrial developments and Iraq now has some major industrial plants, with others under construction. An iron and steel works has been completed by Creusot-Loire of France at Khor al-Zubair. It started production in the last quarter of 1978 and should eventually have a maximum annual output of 1.2 million tons of sponge iron and 400,000 tons of steel. Khor al-Zubair is also the site of a major petrochemicals complex (*see* section on Petroleum, above).

Iraq's mineral resources, besides oil, include sulphur and phosphate rock. The sulphur has been mined at Mishraq, near Mosul, since 1972. At present, much of the output is exported. In 1978 sulphur exports totalled 600,000 tons (up from 522,000 tons in 1977) and were sent mainly to India, China, Egypt and Bangladesh. The Japanese are now building a sulphuric acid plant which will use Mishraq sulphur. A considerable amount of sulphur will be later needed for sulphuric acid production at the phosphate processing plant now being built at Al-Qaim, but Iraq hopes to maintain sulphur exports by increasing the amount of sulphur recovered during hydrocarbon processing. A new recovery unit is being built at Kirkuk with completion scheduled for 1982/83.

The phosphate fertilizer plant at Al-Qaim is being built by Sybetra of Belgium, which also installed the phosphate mine in Akashat. The mine opened in April 1981 and will eventually produce 3.4 million metric tons a year of phosphate rock for the Al-Qaim plant. In July 1979, the Al-Qaim project was reported to be 22 months behind schedule and a new agreement, providing for an increase in the contract value, was reached in March 1980. Sybetra signed its original contract in the mid-1970s and the project cost was then estimated at $1,000 million. Another Belgian company, Mechim is to build a fertilizer by-product unit for Al-Qaim.

Major state factories also include a bitumen plant at Qaiyarah, south of Mosul; a textile factory at Mosul, producing calico from local cotton; brick and cement factories capable of covering domestic demand; three sugar refineries at Kerbala, Sulaimaniya and Mosul, with another four planned; a tractor assembly plant which produced 2,500 tractors in 1975; the Basra fertilizer plant which uses sulphur from Kirkuk and gas from the Rumaila field; a paper board factory at Basra, now in course of expansion; a synthetic fibres complex, also being extended, at Hindiyah; and a number of flour mills. Shoe and cigarette factories serve the domestic market. Seven cement factories were due to start operation in 1977/78, raising Iraq's cement production from 2.7 million tons per year to 7 million tons per year. Shortage of cement has delayed a number of construction projects. In 1980 local production stood at 6–7 million tons, and a further 3 million tons needed to be imported. Cement production is therefore being given priority and contracts to build five cement works, each with a capacity of 2 million tons per year, were awarded in early 1981. By 1985 local capacity is expected to reach an annual 25 million tons. The construction industry remains very important, particularly the building of schools and training establishments. Finnish concerns are building six agricultural colleges at a cost of $112 million, and smaller schemes using local contractors are under way to provide schools and colleges. The State Housing and Reconstruction Organization is to provide as many as 400,000 homes in 1979/80 and up to 4 million in the years 1981–2000.

The latest developments in the manufacturing sector have been in the production of pharmaceuticals, electrical goods, telephone cables and plastics. The food processing industries are being expanded with such projects as the vegetable oil plant planned for Baiji. Metalexport of Poland is to equip a bicycle factory at Mahmudiya which will produce 130,000 bicycles per year.

The Soviet Union has assisted with the construction of eleven factories, including a steel mill and an electrical equipment factory at Baghdad, a drug factory at Samarra and a tractor plant at Musayib. A large share of industrial development is taking place in co-operation with Eastern bloc countries and several agreements have been signed. These include loans from Bulgaria, to pay for complete industrial plants and technical aid in mineral exploration, which will be repaid in crude oil shipments, and a loan from Hungary, some two-thirds of which is also repayable in oil. The U.S.S.R. receives oil in return for services in connection with industrial projects. Other projects include the establishment of an electronics industry, by Thomson CSF of France, and domestic production of cars, lorries and tractors. The latter scheme is to produce 120,000 cars, 25,000 trucks and 15,000 tractors a year. Most of the parts would be manufactured, as well as assembled, locally. Weidle plan of West Germany was awarded a consultant planning contract for the project in 1981. Production is planned to start in 1985 and many West German and Japanese car industries have already expressed interest.

Two trade agreements have been completed with China. Under the terms of the first, Iraq will supply 100,000 tons of sulphur each year over a five-year period while China will make available ID 14 million to Iraq for the purchase by China of 250,000 tons a year of chemical fertilizer from the Basra fertilizer plant. Western countries, France, West Germany and Japan in particular, are making an equally large contribution to industrial development.

As far as local finance is concerned the commercial banks (which were nationalized in 1964) provide short-term credit, while longer term credit and aid for industry and agriculture is provided by several state-owned agencies—the Industrial, Agricultural, Mortgage and Co-operative banks. The Industrial Bank, whose board is appointed by the Council of Ministers, is a shareholder in several large plants and in the private Light Industries Company which is establishing plants for the manufacture or assembly of kerosene heaters, cookers, radio sets, animal fodder, bicycles and electric wire.

The electricity network is another sector which was severely disrupted by the war, when several power stations were bombed by Iranian aircraft. In 1981 a large number of contracts—worth more than $2,000 million—were awarded for additional generating facilities, as well as for the expansion and renovation of local and national networks. Yugoslav contractors won a $570 million contract to build a 600-MW power station at Haditha, and international companies have been invited to tender for three 1,200-MW power stations. Contracts were also awarded to Yugoslav, Swiss and Italian companies for further work on the 400-kV supergrid system.

By 1985, generating capacity is expected to double to 6,000 MW and almost all rural areas will have electricity. Some 2.5 million individual users have been connected to the network since 1977 and consumption is rising at an annual 30–40 per cent.

Iraq's nuclear plans were dashed when its experimental reactor was destroyed by an Israeli air-force bombing attack in June 1981. French technicians are now looking at alternative sites for a new reactor. Saudi Arabia is to help with development costs, Brazil and Portugal have agreed to supply uranium and Italy has also supplied nuclear technology.

COMMUNICATIONS

The communications sector is considered of major importance under the current Plan, and there was considerable activity in this sector during 1981. In May, a consortium of British consultants was awarded a $129 million contract to design an extensive underground public transport system for Baghdad. It was thought to be the biggest design contract ever awarded in Iraq and the full cost of constructing the metro was put at over $1,000 million. The consortium, known as the British Metro Consultants Group, consists of W. S. Atkins & Partners, Design Research Unit, Freeman Fox and Associates, Sir William Halcrow & Partners, Halcrow Fox & Associates, Charles Haswell & Partners, Henderson Busby Partnership, Kennedy & Donkin, Merz McLellan and Rendel Palmer & Tritton. The contract for soil investigation has been let and pre-qualification has been invited for detailed design work, and the supply and installation of electro-mechanical equipment.

Another major project is construction of the new Baghdad international airport. In April 1979 a $900 million contract was awarded to two French companies—Spie Batignolles and Fougerolle Construction—to build this airport for the State Organization for Roads and Bridges. Completion is due in time for the September 1982 non-aligned conference.

In preparation for the big increase in traffic that the opening of the new airport is expected to bring, Iraqi Airways began expanding its fleet and network. In May 1981, the U.S. Congress approved the sale of two Boeing 747s and three 727s to the airline at a cost of $183.6 million. The airline's director-general has said he expects the company's earnings to double by 1984, rising to about ID 8.7 million, from ID 4.5 million in 1978. Passenger traffic is expected to rise by 10 per cent a year. In 1978, 638,316 passengers were carried, compared with 130,520 in 1970. The airline flies to about 42 cities in Iraq and abroad.

Iraq's other international airport, at Basra, is also being extended, at a cost of $420 million. Expansion includes building a 4,000-metre runway able to take the biggest wide-bodied aircraft now available. Consultants have also been appointed to design airports at Mosul and Arbil. The latter is intended to form part of a domestic network which will also include Amara, Kirkuk and Najaf.

Iraq's main port is at Basra. A new port has been built at Um-Qasr with facilities for loading sulphur, and the oil terminals are at Khor al Amaya and Fao.

Iraq has been extremely anxious to secure the approaches to Um-Qasr, which lies at the head of a lagoon whose entrance is controlled by Kuwait. A scheme to build an industrial port complex at Khor al-Zubair was announced in 1976. The scheme was subsequently extended and estimates of its final cost range up to $500 million. The development of the port itself involves the digging of a canal to allow the passage of 60,000 d.w.t. ships through the Gulf and the construction of docks and warehouses. The port will also serve for the export of phosphate fertilizers from Al-Qaim and urea from the Khor al-Zubair plant, as well as iron ore imports. Entry to these ports has not been possible since the outbreak of war. Expansion work at Um-Qasr continues, although a $552 million contract awarded to a Yugoslav company to build 13 additional berths appears to have been frozen. Before using the ports again, the Shatt al-Arab waterway must be cleared of bombs and wreckage and then dredged, a process which may take up to six years.

River transport has been given increasing prominence. Dredging of several stretches of the Tigris between Baghdad and Basra has been completed, and navigation channels are being laid out. A French consultant has been appointed to study the navigation possibilities on the Euphrates between Haditha and Qurna, and the Iraqis have also asked consultants to bid for a navigation development study of the Tigris as a whole—from Mosul to Basra.

Some 3,000 kilometres of railways are due to be built in 1981–85. The principal railways run from Baghdad through Mosul to Tel Kotchek (529 km.) and from Basra to Baghdad (569 km.). Contractors have prequalified for two major lines—the track linking Baghdad with Um-Qasr via Basra and a line between Haditha and Kirkuk via Baiji. An Indian company has been appointed to build the third and fourth stages of the Musayyib-to-Samawa line. Other new projects include the 112-km. Baghdad loop line, which also includes building a new freight complex and three bridges, and a line from Baghdad to Mosul via Arbil and Kirkuk. A 550-km. line from Baghdad to Hussaibah and a link from that line to Akashat and Al-Qaim is being built by Mendes Junior (Construtora) of Brazil at a cost of $1,200 million. The Akashat to Al-Qaim section was due to open in October 1981, taking phosphate rock from the newly-opened mine at Akashat to the processing complex at Al-Qaim. Eventually the Government hopes to expand the system to provide links with Kuwait, Saudi Arabia and Lebanon. Negotiations for rail links with Saudi Arabia and Kuwait are under way.

Considerable emphasis is also being put on road construction. One of the biggest projects is a 1,200-kilometre six-lane expressway linking Iraq, Kuwait, Jordan and Syria. In 1980, several contracts were awarded for this road. Dragages & Travaux Publics of France, for example, is to build a 77-kilometre section between Hilla and Diwaniya, while Construction & Development Corporation of the Philippines has a $285 million contract for the 140-kilometre Baghdad to Basra section. Earlier contracts were awarded to Marubeni and Fujita Corporation of

Japan, to Yugoslavia's Union Engineering and to Poland's Dromex. The remaining sections are being built by Bilfinger & Berger and Dyckerhoff & Widmann, a West German joint venture; Brazil's Mendes Junior Construtoria; a West German–Austrian joint venture of Polensky & Zoellner, Strabag Bau and Universale; and South Korea's Hyundai Engineering & Construction Company.

A second expressway is intended to link Baghdad with the Turkish border via Samara, Kirkuk, Arbil, Mosul and Dohuk. Cowiconsult of Denmark is in charge of designs. There are also a number of urban expressway schemes planned and already under way in Baghdad. A three-stage programme to build 10,000 km. of rural roads is also being implemented.

Iraq has been modernizing its telecommunications system for some years and has introduced crossbar telephone switching, a telex system, a microwave link between major cities and an earth satellite connection for international communications. Early in 1980, Thomson CSF also signed a $150 million contract to supply 27 electronic exchanges providing 315,000 telephone lines in Baghdad and other towns. The same company is believed to have a contract to set up an electronics industry. In 1981 contracts were awarded for a mobile telephone system, a co-axial cable linking 38 northern towns and carrying some 2,400 lines, and a further cable carrying 225,000 lines and linking some 19 towns. By 1985 more than 1 million lines will have been added to the network and 10 out of every 100 people are expected to own a private telephone.

FINANCE

As a result of the war with Iran and reduced oil exports, Iraq's annual current account balance, which has been in substantial surplus in recent years, was estimated to be almost $10,000 million in deficit by the end of 1981. This contrasted with an estimated surplus of $9,100 million in 1980, accumulated in the first nine months of the year, and of around $9,250 million in 1979. The cost of financing the war, and Iraq's burgeoning economic development, has been heavy. As oil revenues have dropped, Iraq's reserves have been cut back from some $35,000 million to an estimated $18,000 million. Unlike other Arab surplus states, Iraq does not buy foreign government securities or take equity shares in foreign companies. It has, however, considerable gold holdings, some of which it was reported to have sold to help to finance the war with Iran.

In comparison with other Arab countries, Iraq has few banks and all are state-controlled. The Central Bank of Iraq, founded in 1947 as a successor to the National Bank of Iraq, was one of the first Arab monetary authorities. It has an authorized capital of ID 25 million and at the end of July 1980 its assets and liabilities balanced at ID 8,841 million.

The only commercial bank is Rafidain Bank, set up in 1941. Although its name is not well known in international financial circles, Rafidain is the biggest Arab commercial bank in terms of deposits and gross assets. In 1981 its capital was raised to ID 50 million;

deposits totalled ID 4,500 million and it had 205 local branches, and nine in Arab cities abroad and in London. It is a shareholder in several European-Arab consortia banks, such as the Paris-based Union de Banques Arabes et Françaises (UBAF), and development agencies. It is also one of the seven shareholders in Gulf International Bank, established in Bahrain in 1977 as a regional commercial bank. At the end of 1981, Rafidain established a joint venture bank with Banco do Brasil. Its capital was set at $28 million; each bank has an equal share.

The oldest specialized bank is the Agricultural Cooperative Bank, established in 1936, which provides medium- and long-term credits to farmers and agricultural development organizations. It has 21 local branches, including four in Baghdad. Its capital was increased to ID 150 million at the beginning of 1981. There are two other specialized banks. The Industrial Bank, set up in 1947, has nine branches and provides short-, medium- and long-term loans to public and private industrial companies. The Real Estate Bank, founded in 1948, now has 25 branches providing credits for housing, construction and tourism. Because of the high demand for housing, the bank has expanded rapidly in recent years, with loans amounting to ID 474 million in 1980.

Iraq is also a major aid donor, the third biggest among Arab states, after Saudi Arabia and Kuwait. In 1979, according to OECD figures, its disbursements totalled $861.5 million, representing about 3 per cent of G.N.P. Most of this is channelled through the Iraqi Fund for External Development (IFED) which has a capital of $677 million. In mid-1979, Iraq decided to compensate poorer customers for its oil for any future oil price increases by granting them long-term interest-free loans. Under this system, 12 developing countries (Bangladesh, India, Madagascar, Morocco, Mozambique, Pakistan, the Philippines, Senegal, Somalia, Sri Lanka, Tanzania and Viet-Nam) received over $200 million in the second half of 1979.

FOREIGN TRADE AND PAYMENTS

Oil exports have been by far Iraq's most important source of revenue. In 1980 they earned ID 7,719.7 million out of total export earnings of ID 7,781.9 million. Receipts from oil exports have risen sharply in the last few years, partly because of higher oil production but mainly because of the rise in prices. In 1979 Iraq's oil exports earned three times as much as in 1974. The main imports are capital equipment, raw materials, including iron and steel, and food. In 1978, the last year for which full trade statistics are available, imports totalled ID 1,244.1 million and exports ID 3,266.6 million, giving a trade surplus of ID 2,022.5 million.

Most trade is with Europe, the U.S.A. and Japan but Iraq also exports significant amounts of oil to Brazil, Yugoslavia, Romania, Turkey and Singapore. Trade with the Soviet Union consists mainly of Soviet military supplies. France has been Iraq's most important customer since 1976. In that year exports to France totalled $1,594 million. By 1978 they had risen to $2,115 million. The next most important customer in 1978 was Italy, with imports from Iraq worth $1,879 million. It was followed by the U.K., which bought only half as much ($953 million). Next came Japan, Spain, Yugoslavia, the Netherlands, Singapore and the U.S.A. in that order. West Germany is Iraq's most important supplier. Others are Japan, France, Italy, the United Kingdom and the U.S.A.

DEVELOPMENT AND PLANNING

Development is financed mainly from state oil revenues, supplemented by the net profits of government agencies and, in the years when oil revenues were low, by external loans. Any external loans have come mainly from the Soviet Union and other communist countries

Before the outbreak of war, high oil revenues

and the continued rise in oil prices gave Iraq a big opportunity to increase its development spending. Despite the heavy costs incurred by the war, the 1982 expenditure programme allocated ID 7,000 million to the ordinary budget and ID 7,000 million to investment spending. The import programme was allocated ID 5,000 million. The halting of oil exports through Iraq's Gulf oil terminals saw oil revenues drop from about $25,750 million in 1980 to about $9,500 million in 1981. Future earnings are likely to be further affected by the closure of the Syrian pipeline and the low price of oil.

At least $18,000 million is thought to have been committed in loans from Iraq's neighbours—Kuwait, Saudi Arabia, the United Arab Emirates and Qatar. They may well be called upon to pay more to fund reconstruction work—the full extent of which is still unclear—after the end of the war.

STATISTICAL SURVEY
AREA AND POPULATION

AREA	POPULATION (census results)†					DENSITY (per sq. km.)
	October 12th, 1957	October 14th, 1965	October 17th, 1977 (provisional)			1977
			Males	Females	Total	
434,924 sq. km.*	6,298,976	8,047,415	6,224,200	5,805,500	12,029,700	27.7

* 167,925 sq. miles. This figure includes 924 sq. km. (357 sq. miles) of territorial waters but excludes the Neutral Zone, of which Iraq's share is 3,522 sq. km. (1,360 sq. miles). The Zone lies between Iraq and Saudi Arabia, and is administered jointly by the two countries. Nomads move freely through it but there are no permanent inhabitants.

† Excluding Iraqis abroad, estimated at 141,720 in 1977.

GOVERNORATES
(estimated population at October 14th, 1976)

	AREA* (sq. km.)	POPULATION† ('000)	DENSITY (per sq. km.)
Nineveh	41,320	1,158	28.0
Salah al-Deen	21,326	356	16.7
Al-Ta'meem	9,426	439	46.6
Diala	19,047	663	34.8
Baghdad	5,023	3,036	604.4
Al-Anbar	89,540	405	4.5
Babylon	5,503	565	102.7
Kerbela	52,856	243	4.6
Al-Najaf	26,834	354	13.2
Al-Qadisiya	8,569	395	46.1
Al-Muthanna	49,206	184	3.7
Thi-Qar	13,668	617	45.1
Wasit	17,922	409	22.8
Maysan	16,774	419	25.0
Basrah	19,702	897	45.5
Autonomous Regions:			
D'hok	6,374	217	34.0
Arbil	14,428	492	34.1
Al-Sulaimaniya	16,482	656	39.8
TOTAL . . .	434,000	11,505	26.5

* Excluding territorial waters.
† Figures are projected from the 1965 census result and not revised in accordance with the 1977 census.

PRINCIPAL TOWNS
(population at 1965 census)

Baghdad (capital)	.	1,490,759	Kirkuk . . .	175,303
Basrah (Basra) .	.	310,850	Najaf . . .	134,027
Mosul .	.	264,146	Hillah . . .	84,704

Births, Marriages and Deaths (annual average rates per 1,000 in 1973–75): Births 42.6; Marriages 14.7; Deaths 10.9 (estimates based on results of a sample survey).

ECONOMICALLY ACTIVE POPULATION
(1977 census)

	MALES	FEMALES	TOTAL
Agriculture, forestry and fishing . . .	591,066	352,824	943,890
Mining and quarrying . . .	34,716	2,119	36,835
Manufacturing . . .	235,777	48,618	284,395
Electricity, gas and water . . .	22,241	949	23,190
Construction . . .	316,560	5,136	321,696
Trade, restaurants and hotels . .	207,949	16,155	224,104
Transport, storage and communications .	172,814	4,985	177,799
Financing, insurance, real estate and business services	26,023	5,066	31,089
Community, social and personal services .	871,879	86,100	957,979
Activities not adequately defined. . .	46,258	11,979	58,237
TOTAL EMPLOYED . . .	2,525,283	533,931	3,059,214
Unemployed	64,278	10,447	74,725
TOTAL LABOUR FORCE . .	2,589,561	544,378	3,133,939

AGRICULTURE

DATE CROP
(tons)

1976*	1977*	1978	1979†	1980†
371,980	578,310	389,000	389,000	395,000

* Official figure.   † Estimate.

Source: FAO, *Production Yearbook.*

AREA AND PRODUCTION OF COTTON

	1974	1975	1976	1977
Area (dunums) .	113,000	105,100	101,320	79,360
Production (tons) .	40,000	38,600	33,890	25,730

OTHER PRINCIPAL CROPS

	1975		1976		1977	
	Area ('ooo dunums)	Production ('ooo tons)	Area ('ooo dunums)	Production ('ooo tons)	Area ('ooo dunums)	Production ('ooo tons)
Winter crops						
Wheat	5,630.6	845.4	6,070.4	1,312.4	3,430.0	695.7
Barley	2,269.2	437.0	2,399.3	579.3	2,143.5	457.7
Linseed	9.2	1.3	4.0	0.7	3.9	0.1
Lentils	20.6	4.8	22.8	5.1	25.5	5.9
Vetch (Hurtman) . .	1.7	0.4	2.7	0.3	3.2	0.4
Broad beans . . .	45.6	80.0	72.3	97.1	69.5	93.9
Summer crops						
Rice	119.5	60.5	212.6	163.3	253.9	199.2
Sesame	46.7	7.6	53.6	7.0	36.7	4.6
Green grams . . .	52.3	7.0	56.4	7.6	45.3	7.6
Millet	n.a.	n.a.	n.a.	n.a.	n.a.	n.a.
Giant millet . . .	n.a.	n.a.	n.a.	n.a.	n.a.	n.a.
Maize	37.8	23.5	81.8	54.9	126.3	82.2

LIVESTOCK
('ooo head)

	1978*	1979*	1980*
Horses . .	65	65	65
Mules . .	28	28	28
Donkeys .	451	452	453
Cattle .	2,645	2,690	2,736
Buffaloes .	219	219	220
Camels .	235	241	246
Sheep .	11,420	11,440	11,460
Goats .	3,600	3,600	3,600
Poultry .	16,626	17,242	17,858

* FAO estimate.
Source: FAO, *Production Yearbook.*

FISHING
('ooo metric tons, live weight)

	1976	1977	1978*	1979	1980
Inland waters . .	19.0	17.5	17.5	17.5*	17.5*
Atlantic Ocean . .	—	—	—	29.2	27.3
Indian Ocean . .	9.3	8.6	8.6	8.6*	8.6*
TOTAL CATCH .	28.3	26.1	26.1	55.3*	53.4

* FAO estimates
Source: FAO, *Yearbook of Fishery Statistics.*

MINING
PRODUCTION OF CRUDE PETROLEUM
('ooo barrels per day)

	1976	1977	1978	1979	1980
Total production . .	2,280	2,210	2,600	3,450	2,645

PRODUCTION OF NATURAL GAS
(million standard cubic feet)

	1972	1973	1974	1975	1976
Total production . . .	262,000	308,253	328,963	368,921	468,476

Source: Ministry of Oil.

INDUSTRY
('000)

	1971	1972	1973	1974	1975
Leather tanning:					
Upper leather (sq. ft.) .	n.a.	n.a.	11,001.1	11,658.2	10,169.2
Toilet Soap (tons) . .	15.3	19.1	35.4	43.6	28.0
Vegetable oil (tons) . .	84.1	72.4	89.3	92.7	90.9
Woollen textiles:					
Cloth (metres) . .	1,001.1	n.a.	1,112.4	1,187.9	n.a.
Blankets (number) .	577.8	653.0	724.4	710.1	654.0
Cotton textiles (metres) .	59,326.1	71,000.0	76,031.8	71,844.9	n.a.
Beer (litres) . . .	8,983.8	10,238.0	12,723.1	12,321.4	19,297.0
Matches (gross) . .	1,629.3	1,861.0	2,101.3	2,253.1	n.a.
Cigarettes (million) . .	6.2	6.3	7.3	6.4	9.9
Shoes (pairs) . . .	n.a.	n.a.	4,597.4	5,820.6	8,321.3

FINANCE

1,000 fils = 20 dirhams = 1 Iraqi dinar (I.D.).

Coins: 1, 5, 10, 25, 50 and 100 fils.

Notes: 250 and 500 fils; 1, 5, and 10 dinars.

Exchange rates (May 1982): £1 sterling = 542.9 fils; U.S. $1 = 295.3 fils.

100 Iraqi dinars = £184.18 = $338.62.

Note: From September 1949 to August 1971 the par value of the Iraqi dinar was U.S. $2.80 ($1 = 357.14 fils). Between December 1971 and February 1973 the dinar's value was $3.04 ($1 = 328.95 fils). In February 1973 the par value of the dinar was fixed at $3.3778 ($1 = 296.05 fils), with a market rate of 1 dinar = $3.3862 ($1 = 295.31 fils). From 1976 the latter also became the rate for calculating the value of foreign trade transactions. The Iraqi dinar was at par with the pound sterling until November 1967, after which the exchange rate was £1 = 857.14 fils (1 dinar = £1.167) until June 1972.

BUDGET ESTIMATES
(1981—I.D. million)

Revenue		Expenditure	
Ordinary	5,025.0	Ordinary	5,025.0
Economic Development Plan .	6,742.8	Economic Development Plan . .	6,742.0
Autonomous Government Agencies . .	7,667.8	Autonomous Government Agencies . .	7,982.4
Total	19,434.9	Total	19,750.2

CENTRAL BANK RESERVES
(U.S. $ million at December 31st)

	1973	1974	1975	1976	1977
Gold	173.1	175.7	168.0	166.7	176.1
IMF Special Drawing Rights .	24.2	28.2	26.9	32.5	41.5
Reserve Position in IMF .	32.9	33.4	31.9	31.7	33.4
Foreign Exchange . .	1,322.9	3,035.9	2,500.5	4,369.8	6,744.7
TOTAL . . .	1,553.1	3,273.2	2,727.3	4,600.7	6,995.7

Source: IMF, *International Financial Statistics.*

CONSUMER PRICES INDEX (IFS)
(1975 = 100)

1973	1974	1975	1976	1977	1978
84.7	91.3	100.0	112.8	123.1	128.8

EXTERNAL TRADE
('ooo I.D.)

	1973	1974	1975	1976	1977
Imports .	270,317	773,432	1,426,858	1,150,898	1,151,268
Exports* .	32,523	28,129	35,565	46,530	42,670
Re-exports .	272	8.5	1.7	—	—
Transit .	56,095	89,724	118,141	121,947	150,075

* Excluding exports of crude petroleum (million I.D.): 555.3 in 1973; 1,921.0 in 1974; 2,414.6 in 1975; 2,691.6 in 1976; 2,806.9 in 1977; 3,204.2 in 1978; 6,287.0 in 1979; 7,718.3 in 1980.

PRINCIPAL COMMODITIES
('ooo I.D.)

IMPORTS	1973	1974	1975	EXPORTS	1973	1974	1975
Tea . . .	4,712	9,426	8,485	Crude oil .	621,100	2,031,300	2,457,000
Sugar . . .	14,599	18,839	35,649	Barley . . .	n.a.	n.a.	n.a.
Pharmaceutical				Dates . .	10,016	8,284	11,493
products .	1,270	9,027	15,503	Straw and fodder	371	60	4
Clothing. . .	191	679	1,746	Raw wool .	611	1,021	1,013
Boilers and engines .	47,898	84,536	202,315	Raw cotton .	84	77	20
Automobiles				Hides and skins	3,657	2,402	1,635
and parts .	10,867	39,689	174,382	Cement . .	3,402	1,292	597
Timber . .	2,235	3,741	5,074				

OIL REVENUES
(U.S. $ million)

1970	. .	521	1976	. .	8,500*
1971	. .	340	1977	. .	9,500*
1972	. .	575	1978	. .	11,600*
1973	. .	1,900*	1979	. .	21,200*
1974	. .	6,000*	1980	. .	26,500*
1975	. .	8,000*	1981	. .	10,400*

* Estimate.

PRINCIPAL TRADING PARTNERS
('ooo I.D.)

IMPORTS	1974	1975	1976	1977
Australia	26,139	15,230	29,006	24,085
Belgium	15,474	30,790	20,539	21,064
Brazil	n.a.	67,331	22,810	20,405
Canada	6,527	24,677	21,232	18,898
China, People's Republic	14,902	20,505	16,908	20,735
Czechoslovakia	16,789	20,027	20,329	13,782
Egypt	3,841	3,019	5,672	4,578
France	51,706	89,262	91,270	62,857
German Democratic Republic	8,312	8,219	14,337	14,462
Germany, Federal Republic	56,449	273,832	250,476	189,883
India	16,634	21,672	16,844	15,322
Italy	23,506	65,939	56,789	61,495
Japan	79,867	240,471	153,076	216,317
Lebanon	n.a.	16,293	4,863	5,922
Netherlands	11,343	20,787	22,139	48,373
Pakistan	—	4,810	14,374	13,196
Poland	10,495	14,279	12,694	13,507
Sweden	15,892	29,982	24,189	15,252
Switzerland	n.a.	15,676	11,855	22,911
U.S.S.R.	32,108	34,224	24,604	42,374
United Kingdom	37,378	83,008	80,620	82,872
U.S.A.	55,686	120,089	64,341	55,879

EXPORTS (excluding oil)	1974	1975	1976	1977
China, People's Republic	2,342	2,105	3,572	4,927
Egypt	2,331	2,409	778	1,920
India	3,361	1,897	5,456	6,931
Kuwait	2,542	1,565	2,490	3,360
Lebanon	3,502	2,059	293	700
Pakistan	n.a.	2,346	3,874	3,650
Switzerland	n.a.	1,678	3,020	1,463
Syria	2,792	2,068	2,250	1,362
U.S.S.R.	929	1,905	2,164	724
U.S.A.	415	1,615	1,077	541
Viet-Nam	n.a.	—	3,912	4,209

TRANSPORT

RAILWAYS

	1974/75	1975/76	1976/77
Passenger km. ('ooo)	644,816	634,919	797,315
Freight ton km. ('ooo)	1,871,138	1,883,580	2,254,119

ROAD TRAFFIC
('ooo licensed motor vehicles)

	1972	1973	1974	1975
Cars	75.5	77.3	85.7	118.3
Goods Vehicles	45.5	46.1	49.1	65.5
Buses	11.2	11.6	16.4	19.6
Motor Cycles	7.8	8.2	8.9	9.4

Source: International Road Federation.

SHIPPING
Movement of Cargo Vessels in Iraqi Ports.

	1975		1976		1977	
	Entered	Cleared	Entered	Cleared	Entered	Cleared
Number of vessels	828	827	891	892	984	977
Gross registered tonnage ('ooo)	8,343	8,305	8,861	9,393	11,855	11,872
Cargo ('ooo tons, excl. crude oil)	3,406	1,441	3,430	1,279	3,772	964

SHIPPING OF CRUDE OIL
Export by tankers from all ports.

	1971	1972	1973	1974	1975
Crude oil ('ooo tons) . .	19,288	21,955	26,669	35,710	37,052

CIVIL AVIATION
(Revenue traffic on Iraqi Airways)

	1975	1976	1977
Number of passengers . .	407,338	618,113	728,266
Cargo handled (tons) . .	3,034	7,523	10,090
Post handled (kg.) . .	468,229	688,842	790,596

TOURISM

	1974	1975	1976	1977
Visitors .	544,800	482,090	n.a.	593,611

EDUCATION
(1976/77)

	SCHOOLS	PUPILS
Primary . . .	8,156	1,947,182
Secondary (General) .	1,320	555,184
Vocational . .	82	28,365
Teacher Training .	43	21,186
Universities . .	6	71,536
Colleges and Technical Institutes . .	15	9,962

Source: Central Statistical Organization, Ministry of Planning, Baghdad, *Annual Abstract of Statistics.*

THE CONSTITUTION

The following are the principal features of the Provisional Constitution issued on September 22nd, 1968:

The Iraqi Republic is a popular democratic and sovereign state. Islam is the state religion.

The political economy of the state is founded on socialism.

The state will protect liberty of religion, freedom of speech and opinion. Public meetings are permitted under the law. All discrimination based on race, religion or language is forbidden. There shall be freedom of the Press, and the right to form societies and trade unions in conformity with the law is guaranteed.

The Iraqi people is composed of two main nationalities: Arab and Kurds. The Constitution confirms the nationalistic rights of the Kurdish people and the legitimate rights of all other minorities within the framework of Iraqi unity.

The highest authority in the country is the Council of Command of the Revolution (or Revolutionary Command Council—RCC), which will promulgate laws until the election of a National Assembly. Since September 1977 the membership of the RCC (17 in December 1980) and the Iraqi Command of the Arab Baath Socialist Party have been identical. The Council exercises its prerogatives and powers by a two-thirds majority.

Two amendments to the constitution were announced in November 1969. The President, already Chief of State and head of the government, also became the official Supreme Commander of the Armed Forces and President of the Command Council of the Revolution. Membership of the latter body was to increase from five to a larger number at the President's discretion.

Earlier, a Presidential decree replaced the 14 local government districts by 16 governorates, each headed by a governor with wide powers. In April 1976 Tekrit (Saladin) and Kerbala became separate governorates, bringing the number of governorates to 18, although three of these are designated Autonomous Regions.

The fifteen-article statement which aimed to end the Kurdish war was issued on March 11th, 1970. In accordance with this statement a form of autonomy was offered to the Kurds in March 1974, but some of the Kurds rejected the offer and fresh fighting broke out. The new Provisional Constitution was announced in July 1970. Two amendments were introduced in 1973 and 1974, the 1974 amendment stating that "the area whose majority of population is Kurdish shall enjoy autonomy in accordance with what is defined by the Law".

The President and Vice-President are elected by a two-thirds majority of the Council. The President, Vice-President and members of the Council will be responsible to the Council. Vice-Presidents and Ministers will be responsible to the President.

In July 1973, President Bakr announced a National Charter as a first step towards establishing the Progressive National Front. A National Assembly and People's Councils are features of the Charter. A law to set up a 250-member National Assembly and a 50-member Kurdish Legislative Council was adopted on March 16th, 1980, and the two Assemblies were elected in June and September 1980 respectively.

THE GOVERNMENT

HEAD OF STATE

President: SADDAM HUSSAIN (assumed power July 16th, 1979).

Vice-President: TAHA MOHEDDIN MARUF.

REVOLUTIONARY COMMAND COUNCIL

Chairman: SADDAM HUSSAIN.

Vice-Chairman: IZZAT IBRAHIM.

Members

TAHA YASIN RAMADAN   HASAN ALI NASSAR
ADNAN KHAIRALLAH   al-AMIRI
SAADOUN SHAKER MAHMUD   NAIM HAMID HADDAD
TARIQ AZIZ ISA   TAHA MOHEDDIN MARUF

COUNCIL OF MINISTERS

(June 1982)

First Deputy Prime Minister: TAHA YASIN RAMADAN.

Deputy Prime Minister: TAREQ AZIZ.

Deputy Prime Minister and Minister of Defence: Gen. ADNAN KHAIRALLAH.

Minister of Transport and Communications: ABDUL JABBAR ABDUL RAHIM AL-ASADI.

Head of Presidency Diwan: TARIQ HAMAD AL-ABDULLAH.

Minister of Foreign Affairs: Dr. SA'ADOUN HAMMADI.

Minister of the Interior: SAADOUN SHAKER.

Minister of Education: ABDUL QADIR IZILDIN.

Minister of Justice: Dr. MUNDHIR IBRAHIM.

Minister of Finance and Acting Minister of Planning: THAMIR RZOUQI.

Minister of Housing and Construction: MUHAMMAD FADHEL.

Minister of Planning: SAMAL MAJID FARAJ.

Minister of Health: Dr. SADIQ HAMID ALLUSH.

Minister of Industry and Minerals: SUBHI YASIN KHUDAYR.

Minister of Higher Education and Scientific Research: ABDUL RAZZAK QASIM AL-HASHIMI.

Minister of Oil: QASIM AHMAD TAQI.

Minister of Trade: HASSAN ALI.

Minister of Youth: AHMAD HUSAYN AS-SAMARRAI.

Minister of Agriculture and Agrarian Reform: SIDDIQ ABDUL LATIF YUNIS.

Minister of State for Foreign Affairs: HAMID ALWAN.

Minister of Culture and Information: LATIF NASEEF AL-JASIM.

Minister of Irrigation: ABDUL WAHAB MAHMOUD ABDULLA.

Minister of Labour and Social Affairs: BAKR MAHMOUD RASOUL.

Minister of Awqaf and Religious Affairs: ABDULLAH FADIL ABBAS.

Minister of Local Government: SADI AYYASH URAYM.

Minister of Light Industries: TARIQ HAMAD AL-ABDULLAH.

Advisers to President (with status of Minister): MUHAMMAD HAMZAH AZ-ZUBAYDI, ABDUL GHANI ABDUL GHAFUR, SAMIR MUHAMMAD ABDUL WAHHAB, ABDUL HASAN RAHI FIR'AWN, SAADI MAHDI SALIH, MAZBAN KADR HADI.

Ministers of State: HASHIM HASSAN, OBAIDULLA MUSTAFA, ABDULLA ISMAIL AHMED, ARSHAD AHMAD AZ-ZIBARI.

KURDISH AUTONOMOUS REGION

Executive Council: Chair. MUHAMMAD AMIN MUHAMMAD.

Legislative Council: Chair. AHMED ABDUL QADIR.

LEGISLATURE

NATIONAL ASSEMBLY

No form of National Assembly existed in Iraq between the 1958 revolution, which overthrew the monarchy, and June 1980. The existing provisional constitution contained provisions for the election of an assembly at a date to be determined by the Government. The members of the Assembly are to be elected from all political, social and economic sectors of the Iraqi people. In December 1979 the RCC invited political, trade union and popular organizations to debate a draft law for setting up a 250-member National Assembly and a 50-member Kurdish Legislative Council, both to be elected by direct, free and secret ballot. Elections for the National Assembly took place on June 20th, 1980, and for the Kurdish Legislative Council on September 11th, 1980. More than 75 per cent of those elected to the National Assembly are members of the ruling Baath Party.

Chairman and Speaker: NAIM HADDAD.

Speaker of Kurdish Legislative Council: AHMED ABDUL QADIR.

POLITICAL PARTIES

National Progressive Front: Baghdad; f. July 1973, when Arab Baath Socialist Party and Iraqi Communist Party signed a joint manifesto agreeing to establish a comprehensive progressive national and nationalistic front. In 1975 representatives of Kurdish parties and organizations and other national and independent forces joined the Front; the Iraqi Communist Party left the National Progressive Front in mid-March 1979; Sec.-Gen. NAIM HADDAD (Baath).

Arab Baath Socialist Party: Karkh, Baghdad; revolutionary Arab socialist movement founded in Damascus in 1947; has ruled Iraq since July 1968, and between July 1973 and March 1979 in alliance with the Iraqi Communist Party in the National Progressive Front; Sec.-Gen. MICHAEL AFLAQ; Regional Sec. SADDAM HUSSAIN; Deputy Regional Sec. IZZAT IBRAHIM; mems. of Regional Command: SAADOUN GHAIDAN, TAHA YASIN RAMADAN, NAIM HADDAD, HASSAN ALI, SAADOUN SHAKER, TAREQ AZIZ, ADNAN KHAIRALLAH, MUHAMMAD HAMZAH AZ-ZUBAYDI, ABDUL GHANI ABDUL GHAFUR,

SAMIR MUHAMMAD ABDUL WAHHAB, ABDUL HASAN RAHI FIR'AWN, SADI MAHDI SALIH, SAADOUN HAMMADI and MAZBAN KHADR HADI.

Iraqi Communist Party: Baghdad; f. 1934; became legally recognized in July 1973 on formation of National Progressive Front; left National Progressive Front March 1979; First Sec. AZIZ MOHAMMED.

Kurdistan Democratic Party: Aqaba Ben Nafia Square, Baghdad; f. 1946; Kurdish Party; supports the National Progressive Front; Sec.-Gen. AZIZ AQRAWI; publ. *Al-Iraq* (daily).

Kurdistan Revolutionary Party: f. 1972; succeeded Democratic Kurdistan Party; admitted to National Progressive Front 1974; Sec. Gen. ABDUL-SATTAR TAHER SHAREF.

There is also a Kurdish Democratic Party in opposition to the Iraqi Government; Leader MASOUD BARZANI.

DIPLOMATIC REPRESENTATION

EMBASSIES ACCREDITED TO IRAQ
(In Baghdad unless otherwise stated)
(E) Embassy.

Afghanistan: Maghrib St., al-Difa'ie, 27/1/12 Waziriyah (E); *Ambassador:* ABDOL HADI MOKAMMEL.

Algeria: Karradat Mariam (E); *Ambassador:* ABDER-RAHMAN SHARIF.

Argentina: Jadriya Al-Ziwiya St. No. 1/8/30 (E); *Ambassador:* A. H. PINEIRO.

Australia: Al Karada Al-Sharqiya Masbah 39B/35, P.O.B. 661 (E); *Ambassador:* A. L. VINCENT.

Austria: Hay Babil 929/2/5 Aqaba bin Nafi Square, Masbah (E); *Ambassador:* Dr. HEINRICH BIRNLEITNER.

Bahrain: 26/2/13 Deragh Quarter (E); *Ambassador:* SALIM BIN RASHID AL-ABSI.

Bangladesh: 38J/35 Al-Masbah, P.O.B. 3123 (E); *Ambassador:* (vacant).

Belgium: 25/27/929 Hay Babel (E); *Ambassador:* JAN HELLEMANS.

Belgium (U.S. Interest Section): Al Karada Al-Sharqiya Masbah 52/5/35; *Officer:* WILLIAM L. EAGLETON.

Brazil: 609/16 Al Mansour, Houses 62/62-1 (E); *Ambassador:* SAMUEL AUGUSTO ALVES CORRÊA.

Bulgaria: 9/12 Harthiya (E); *Ambassador:* ANGEL GEORGIEV ANGELOV.

Cameroon: Jeddah, Saudi Arabia (E).

Canada: Mansour, P.O.B. 323 (E); *Ambassador:* WITOLD WEYNEROWSKI.

Central African Republic: 208/406 Al Zawra, Harthiya (E); *Ambassador:* M. TSMAILA NIMAGA.

Chad: 97/4/4 Karradat Mariam (E); *Chargé d'affaires:* HAMID MUHAMMAD ISHAQ.

China, People's Republic: 82/1/1a Jadriya, P.O.B. 223 (E); *Ambassador:* HOU YEFENG.

Congo: 183/406 Harthiya (E); *Ambassador:* ALBERT FOUNGUI.

Cuba: Al Karada Al-Sharqiya 24/22 (E); *Ambassador:* JUAN CARRETERO IBAÑEZ.

Cyprus: Cairo, Egypt (E).

Czechoslovakia: Dijlaschool St., No. 37, Mansoor (E); *Ambassador:* JAN STRAKA.

Denmark: Zukak No. 34, Mahallat 902, Hay Al-Wahda, House No. 18/1, P.O.B. 2001, Alwiyah (E); *Ambassador:* FREDERIK KIAER.

Egypt: *see* Turkey.

Finland: P.O.B. 2041, Alwiyah (E); *Ambassador:* HAAKAN KROGIUS.

France: Kard el Pasha 9G/3/1 (E); *Ambassador:* PAUL DEPIS.

German Democratic Republic: Al Karada Al-Sharqiya Masbah 34/33/32 and 52/53/54/354 (E); *Ambassador:* KARL-HEINZ LUGENHEIM.

Germany, Federal Republic: Zukak 2, Mahala 929 Hay Babil (Masbah Square) (E); *Ambassador:* HERMANN HOLZHEIMER.

Greece: Jadrihah University Square No. 2H/2H2/2H3 (E); *Ambassador:* LEONIDES EVANGELIDIS.

Guinea: Cairo, Egypt (E).

Guyana: 61/1/609 Mansour (E); *Chargé d'affaires a.i.:* D. A. ABRAMS.

Hungary: Karradat Mariam 22/1/11 (E); *Ambassador:* ZOLTÁN PERESZLÉNYI.

India: Taha St., Najib Pasha, Adhamiya (E); *Ambassador:* P. L. SINAI.

Indonesia: 24/6/33 Alwiya, Wathiq Street (E); *Ambassador:* S. KARTANEGARA.

Ireland: Beirut, Lebanon (E).

Italy: 334/14 Al Jadryia Sq. (E); *Ambassador:* VALERIO BRIGANTE COLONNA.

Japan: 41/7/35 Al Karada Al-Sharqiya Masbah (E); *Ambassador:* HIDEO KAGAMI.

Jordan: Harthiyah; *Ambassador:* FALEH ABDEL-KARIM TAWIL.

Kenya: Cairo, Egypt (E).

Kuwait: 13/1/2 Al-Zuwiya, al Jadiriya, al-Karada al-Sharqiya (E); *Ambassador:* ABDUL AZIZ ABDULLAH AL-SAR'AWI.

Lebanon: 13/21/5D Husamuddin St. (E); *Ambassador:* BOUTROS ZIADE.

Malaysia: 61/2/35 Al Karada Al-Sharqiya Masbah (E); *Ambassador:* ANAITULLAH KARIM.

Mauritania: Mansour (E); *Ambassador:* MUHAMMAD ABDUL QADER WALAD DIDI.

Mexico: 1/36/903 Karrada (E); *Ambassador:* V. M. RODRÍGUEZ.

Mongolia: Prague, Czechoslovakia (E).

Morocco: Mansour Hay Dragh No. 13/1/69 (Almoutanbe) (E); *Ambassador:* ABDELESLAM ZNINED.

Nepal: Jeddah, Saudi Arabia (E).

Netherlands: Jadriyah 4/6/30 (E); *Ambassador:* D. M. SCHORER.

New Zealand: 2D/19 Zuwiyah, Jadriyah (E); *Chargé d'affaires:* D. L. SHROFF.

Niger: Cairo, Egypt (E).

Nigeria: Jadriyah (E); *Ambassador:* Haj HAMZA ABU BAKR.

Norway: (E); *Ambassador:* BJØRN BARTH.

Oman: al-Zaitoon St., Harithia, House No. 25B/406, Hay al-Zawra (E); *Ambassador:* MUHAMMAD SA'ID AL-MARHUM.

Pakistan: 4725/7 Opposite Mashtal Al-Mansour (E); *Ambassador:* SELIMUZ ZAMAN.

Philippines: Petra Hotel (E); *Ambassador:* J. V. CRUZ.

Poland: Al Karada Al-Sharqiya Masbah 2/1/27, P.O.B. 2051 (E); *Ambassador:* ANTONI CZARKOWSKI.

Portugal: P.O.B. 3014 (E); *Ambassador:* (vacant).

Qatar: 152/406 Harithia, Hay Al Kindi (E); *Ambassador:* ALI HUSAIN MUFTAH.

Romania: 303/7/19 Al Karada Al-Sharqiya Masbah (E); *Ambassador:* M. DIAMANDOPOL.

Saudi Arabia: Waziriyah (E); *Ambassador:* Sheikh AHMED AL-KUHAYIMI.

Senegal: Jadiriyah, 75G 31/15 (E); *Ambassador:* S. MBACKÉ.

Somalia: 49/5/35 Al Karada Al-Sharqiya Masbah (E); *Ambassador:* ABDULLA HAJ ABUBAKAR.

Spain: Babylon Quarter, Masbah District 929, Street No. 1, No. 4, P.O.B. 2072, Alwiyah (E); *Ambassador:* JOSÉ LUIS DE LA GUARDIA.

Sri Lanka: 10 B/6/12 Alwiyah (E); *Ambassador:* A. R. UDUGAMA.

Sweden: P.O.B. 2037, Alwiyah (E); *Ambassador:* LARS-OLOF BRILIOTH.

Switzerland: Al Karada Al-Sharqiya Masbah, House No. 41/2/35 (E); *Ambassador:* M. DISLER.

Thailand: (E); *Ambassader:* CHAMRAS CHOMHUBOL.

Tunisia: Mansour 34/2/4, P.O.B. 6057 (E); *Ambassador:* MARWAN BENLARBI.

Turkey: 2/8 Waziriya (E); *Ambassador:* (vacant); Egyptian interests section: *Head of Section:* AHMED KAMIL.

Uganda: 41/1/609 Mansour (E); *Ambassador:* SWAIB M. MUSOKE.

U.S.S.R.: 140 Mansour St., Karradat Mariam (E); *Ambassador:* VIKTOR I. MININ.

United Arab Emirates: Al-Mansour, al Mansour Main St. (E); *Ambassador:* MUHAMMAD ABDULLATEEF RASHED.

United Kingdom: Sharia Salah Ud-Din, Karkh (E); *Ambassador:* S. L. EGERTON, C.M.G.

U.S.A.: see Belgium.

Vatican: Abu Nawas St. 207/1, P.O.B. 2090 (Apostolic Nunciature); *Apostolic Pro-Nuncio:* Mgr. ANTONIO DEL GIUDICE.

Venezuela: Al-Mansour, House No. 4/4/56 (E); *Ambassador:* FREDDY RAFAEL ALVAREZ YANES.

Viet-Nam: Daoudi al-Mansour 71/7/17 (E); *Ambassador:* TRAN KY LONG.

Yemen Arab Republic: Al Karada Al-Sharqiya Masbah 19/935 (E); *Ambassador:* ABDALI UTHMAN MUHAMMAD.

Yemen, People's Democratic Republic: Al Karada Al-Sharqiya Masbah No. 1/9/21 (E); *Chargé d'affaires:* SHA'IR MUHSIN MUHAMMAD.

Yugoslavia: 16/35/923 Babil Area, Jadriyah, P.O.B. 2061 (E); *Ambassador:* Dr. VIDO KNEZEVIĆ.

Zambia: Cairo, Egypt (E).

Iraq also has diplomatic relations with Cape Verde, Colombia, the Comoros, Djibouti, Ecuador, El Salvador, Gabon, The Gambia, Grenada, Guatemala, Iceland, Jamaica, the Republic of Korea, Laos, Madagascar, Maldives, Mali, Malta, Mauritius, Mozambique, Nicaragua, Panama, Seychelles, Singapore, Sudan, Suriname, Tanzania, Uruguay, Zaire and Zimbabwe.

JUDICIAL SYSTEM

Courts in Iraq consist of the following: The Court of Cassation, Courts of Appeal, First Instance Courts, Peace Courts, Courts of Sessions, Shara' Courts and Penal Courts.

The Court of Cassation: This is the highest judicial bench of all the Civil Courts; it sits in Baghdad, and consists of the President and a number of Vice-Presidents and not fewer than fifteen permanent judges, delegated judges and reporters as necessity requires. There are four bodies in the Court of Cassation, these are: (a) The General body, (b) Civil and Commercial body, (c) Personal Status body, (d) The Penal body.

Courts of Appeal: The country is divided into five Districts of Appeal: Baghdad, Mosul, Basra, Hilla, and Kirkuk, each with its Court of Appeal consisting of a President, Vice-Presidents and not fewer than three members, who consider the objections against the decisions issued by the First Instance Courts of first grade.

Courts of First Instance: These courts are of two kinds: Limited and Unlimited in jurisdiction.

Limited Courts deal with Civil and Commercial suits, the value of which is five hundred Dinars and less; and suits, the value of which cannot be defined, and which are subject to fixed fees. Limited Courts consider these suits in the final stage and they are subject to Cassation.

Unlimited Courts consider the Civil and Commercial suits irrespective of their value, and suits the value of which exceeds five hundred Dinars with first grade subject to appeal.

First Instance Courts consist of one judge in the centre of each *Liwa*, some *Qadhas* and *Nahiyas*, as the Minister of Justice judges necessary.

Revolutionary Courts: These deal with major cases that would affect the security of the state in any sphere: political, financial or economic.

Courts of Sessions: There is in every District of Appeal a Court of Sessions which consists of three judges under the presidency of the President of the Court of Appeal or one of his Vice-Presidents. It considers the penal suits prescribed by Penal Proceedings Law and other laws. More than one Court of Sessions may be established in one District of Appeal by notification issued by the Minister of Justice mentioning therein its headquarters, jurisdiction and the manner of its establishment.

Shara' Courts: A Shara' Court is established wherever there is a First Instance Court; the Muslim judge of the First Instance Court may be a *Qadhi* to the Shara' Court if a special *Qadhi* has not been appointed thereto. The Shara' Court considers matters of personal status and religious matters in accordance with the provisions of the law supplement to the Civil and Commercial Proceedings Law.

Penal Courts: A Penal Court of first grade is established in every First Instance Court. The judge of the First Instance Court is considered as penal judge unless a special judge is appointed thereto. More than one Penal Court may be established to consider the suits prescribed by the Penal Proceedings Law and other laws.

One or more Investigation Court may be established in the centre of each *Liwa* and a judge is appointed thereto. They may be established in the centres of *Qadhas* and *Nahiyas* by order of the Minister of Justice. The judge carries out the investigation in accordance with the provisions of Penal Proceedings Law and the other laws.

There is in every First Instance Court a department for the execution of judgments presided over by the Judge of First Instance if a special President is not appointed thereto. It carries out its duties in accordance with the provisions of Execution Law.

RELIGION

ISLAM

About 95 per cent of the population are Muslims, more than 50 per cent of whom are Shi'ite. The Arabs of northern Iraq, the Bedouins, the Kurds, the Turkomans and some of the inhabitants of Baghdad and Basra are mainly of the Sunni sect, the remaining Arabs south of the Diyali belong to the Shi'i sect.

CHRISTIANITY

There are Christian communities in all the principal towns of Iraq, but their principal villages lie mostly in the Mosul district. The Christians of Iraq fall into three groups. (*a*) the free Churches, including the Nestorian, Gregorian, and Jacobite; (*b*) the churches known as Uniate, since they are in union with the Roman Catholic Church including the Armenian Uniates, Jacobite Uniates, and Chaldeans; (*c*) mixed bodies of Protestant converts, New Chaldeans, and Orthodox Armenians.

Catholic:

Latin Rite: Most Rev. ERNEST NYARY, Archbishop of Baghdad, Alwiyah 23/1/31, Baghdad; approx. 3,500 adherents.

Armenian Rite: Archbishop of Baghdad: P.O.B. 2344, Baghdad: Most Rev. JEAN KASPARIAN.

Chaldean Rite: Archbishop of Mosul, Most Rev. GEORGE GARMO; Patriarch of Babylon of the Chaldeans: His Beatitude PAUL II CHEIKHO, with 18 Archbishops and Bishops in Iraq, Iran, Syria, Turkey, Egypt, U.S.A. and Lebanon. Approx. 475,000 adherents.

Syrian Rite: Archbishop of Mosul: Most Rev. CYRIL EMANUEL BENNI; Archbishop of Baghdad: Most Rev. ATHANASE J. D. BAKOSE; approx. 35,000 adherents.

Orthodox Syrian Community: 12,000 adherents.

Armenian Orthodox (*Gregorian*) **Community:** 23,000 adherents, mainly in Baghdad; Primate: Bishop AVAK ASADOURIAN; Primate of the Armenian Diocese, Younis Al-Saba'awi Square, Baghdad.

JUDAISM

Unofficial estimates put the present size of the community at 2,500, almost all living in Baghdad.

OTHERS

About thirty thousand Yazidis and a smaller number of Turkomans, Sabeans, and Shebeks make up the rest of the population.

Sabean Community: 20,000 adherents; Head Sheikh DAKHIL, Nasiriyah; Mandeans, mostly in Nasiriyah.

Yazidis: 30,000 adherents; Leader TASHIN BAIK, Ainsifni.

THE PRESS

DAILIES

Baghdad Observer: P.O.B. 257, Karantina, Baghdad; f. 1967; state-sponsored; English; Editor-in-Chief NAJI AL HADITHI; circ. 12,000.

Al-Iraq: P.O.B. 5717, Baghdad; f. 1976; formerly *Al-Ta'akhi*; organ of the National Progressive Front; Editor-in-Chief HASHIM AKRAWI; circ. 30,000.

al-Jumhuriya (*The Republic*): Waziriya, Baghdad; f. 1963, re-founded 1967; Editor-in-Chief SAHIB HUSSEIN; circ. 25,000.

al Riyadhi (*Sportsman*): Baghdad; f. 1971; published by Ministry of Youth; circ. 30,000.

al Thawra (*Revolution*): Aqaba bin Nafi's Square, P.O.B. 2009, Baghdad; f. 1968; organ of Baath Party; Editor-in-Chief SAAD QASSEM HAMMOUDI; circ. 70,000.

WEEKLIES

Alif Baa (*Alphabet*): Karantina, Baghdad; Editor-in-Chief AMIR MA'ALA.

al-Mizmar: Ministry of Information, Baghdad; children's newspaper; Editor-in-Chief AMAL AL-SHARKI; circ. 50,000.

al-Rased (*The Observer*): Baghdad; general.

Sabaa Nisan: Baghdad; f. 1976; organ of the General Union of the Youth of Iraq.

Saut al Fallah (*Voice of the Peasant*): Karadat Mariam, Baghdad; f 1968; organ of the General Union of Farmers Societies; circ. 40,000.

Waee Ul-Omal (*The Workers' Consciousness*): Headquarters of General Federation of Trade Unions in Iraq, Gialani St., Senak, P.O.B. 2307, Baghdad; Iraq Trades Union organ; Chief Editor KHALID MAHMOUD HUSSEIN; circ. 25,000.

al-Idaa'h Wal-Television: Iraqi Broadcasting and Television Establishment, Karradat Maryam, Baghdad; radio and television programmes and articles; weekly; Editor-in-Chief KAMIL HAMDI AL-SHARKI; circ. 40,000.

PERIODICALS

Afaq Arabiya (*Arab Horizons*): Baghdad; literary and political; monthly; Editor-in-Chief SHAFEEK AL-KAMALI.

al Aqlam (*The Pen*): Ministry of Culture and Information, Baghdad; f. 1964; literary; monthly; circ. 20,000.

al-Funoon al-Ida'aiya: Iraqi Broadcasting and Television Establishment, Salihiya, Baghdad; supervised by Broadcasting and TV Training Institute; engineering and technical; quarterly.

L'Iraq Aujourd'hui: Ministry of Culture and Information, P.O.B. 4074, Baghdad; f. 1976; bi-monthly; cultural and political; French; Editor NADJI AL-HADITHI; circ. 12,000.

Iraq Oil News: P.O.B. 6118, Baghdad; f. 1973; publ. by the Dept. of Information and General Relations of the Ministry of Oil; monthly; English.

Journal of the Faculty of Medicine, The: College of Medicine, University of Baghdad, Baghdad; f. 1935; quarterly; Arabic and English; medical and technical; Editor Prof. YOUSIF D. AL NAAMAN, M.D., D.SC.

Majallat-al-Majma al-Ilmi al-Iraqi (*Iraq Academy Journal*): Iraqi Academy, Waziriyah, Baghdad; f. 1947; quarterly; scholarly magazine on Arabic Islamic culture; Gen. Sec. Dr. NURI HAMMODI AL QAISI.

Majallat al-Thawra al-Ziraia (*Magazine of Iraq Agriculture*): Baghdad; quarterly; agricultural; published by the Ministry of Agriculture.

al-Masrah Wal-Cinema: Iraqi Broadcasting, Television and Cinema Establishment, Salihiya, Baghdad; artistic, theatrical and cinema; monthly.

al-Mawrid: Ministry of Culture and Information, Dar-al-Jahiz, Baghdad; f. 1971; cultural quarterly.

al-Mu'allem al-Jadid: Ministry of Education, Baghdad; f. 1935; quarterly; educational, social, and general; Editor KHALIL AL-SAMARRAI; circ. 105,000.

Al Naft Wal Aalam (*Oil and the World*): publ. by the Ministry of Oil, P.O.B. 6118, Baghdad; f. 1973; Editor-in-Chief TAYEH ABDUL KARIM (Minister of Oil); monthly; Arabic.

Sawt al-Talaba (*The Voice of Students*): al-Maghreb St., Waziriya, Baghdad; f. 1968; organ of National Union of Iraqi Students; monthly; circ. 25,000.

al-Sina'a (*Industry*): P.O.B. 1166, Baghdad; publ. by Ministry of Industry and Minerals; Arabic and English; every two months; Editor-in-Chief ABDEL QADER ABDEL LATIF; circ. 16,000.

Sumer: Directorate-General of Antiquities, Jamal Abdul Nasr St., Baghdad; f. 1945; archaeological, historical journal; Chair. of Ed. Board Dr. M. SAID; annual.

al-Thaquafa (*Culture*): Place al-Tarir, Baghdad; f. 1970; Marxist; Editor-in-Chief SALAH KHALIS; monthly; circ. 5,000.

al-Thaquafa al-Jadida (*The New Culture*): Baghdad; f. 1969; pro-Communist; Editor-in-Chief SAFA AL-HAFIZ; monthly; circ. 3,000.

al-Turath al-Sha'abi (*Popular Heritage*): Dar Al-Jahidh, Ministry of Culture and Information, Baghdad; specializes in Iraqi and Arabic folklore; Editor-in-Chief LUTFI AL-KHOURI; monthly; circ. 15,000.

al-Waqai al-Iraqiya (*Official Gazette of Republic of Iraq*): Ministry of Justice, Baghdad; f. 1922; Dir. SABAH SALMAN; Arabic and English weekly editions; circ. Arabic 10,000, English 750.

NEWS AGENCIES

Iraqi News Agency (INA): Abu Nawwas St., P.O.B. 3084, Baghdad; f. 1959; Dir.-Gen. TAHA YASSIN HASSAN AL-BASRI.

FOREIGN BUREAUX

Allgemeiner Deutscher Nachrichtendienst (ADN) (*German Democratic Republic*): Zuqaq 24, Mahalla 906, Hai al-Wahda, Beit 4, Baghdad; Correspondent RAINER HÖHLING.

Deutsche Presse-Agentur (dpa) (*Federal Republic of Germany*): P.O.B. 5699, Baghdad; Correspondent NAJHAT KOTANI.

TASS (U.S.S.R.) and EFE (Spain) also have offices in Baghdad.

PUBLISHERS

al Hurriyah Printing Establishment: Baghdad; f. 1970; largest printing and publishing establishment in Iraq; state-owned; controls al-Jumhuriya (*see* below).

al-Jamaheer Press House: Sarrafia, Baghdad; f. 1963; publisher of a number of newspapers and magazines, *al-Jumhuriya, Baghdad Observer, Alif Baa, Yord Weekly*; Pres. SAAD QASSIM HAMMOUDI.

al Ma'arif Ltd.: Mutanabi St., Baghdad; f. 1929; publishes periodicals and books in Arabic, Kurdish, Turkish, French and English.

al-Muthanna Library: Mutanabi St., Baghdad; f. 1936; booksellers and publishers of books in Arabic and oriental languages; Man. MOHAMED K. M. AR-RAJAB.

al Nahdah: Mutanabi St., Baghdad; politics, Arab affairs.

Kurdish Culture Publishing House: Baghdad; f. 1976; attached to the Ministry of Information.

National House for Distributing and Advertising: Ministry of Information, P.O.B. 624, Al-Jumhuriyah St., Baghdad; f. 1972; importers, exporters and marketers of all kinds of books and periodicals; controls all advertising activities, inside Iraq as well as outside.

al-Thawra Printing and Publishing House: Baghdad; f. 1970; state-owned; Chair. SAAD QASSEM HAMMOUDI.

Thnayan Printing House: Baghdad.

RADIO AND TELEVISION

RADIO

Broadcasting Station of the Republic of Iraq: Iraqi Broadcasting and Television Establishment, Salihiya, Baghdad; home service broadcasts in Arabic, Kurdish, Syriac and Turkoman; foreign service in French, German, English, Russian, Persian, Swahili, Turkish and Urdu; there are 7 medium wave and 13 short wave transmitters; Dir.-Gen. HAMID SA'EED; Dir. of Engineering and Technical Affairs MUHAMMAD F. RASHEED.

Idaa'h Baghdad: f. 1936; 22 hours daily.

Idaa'h Sawt Al-Jamahir: f. 1970; 21 hours daily.

Other stations include **Idaa'h Al Kurdia, Idaa'h Al Syriania.**

Number of radio receivers (1980): 2.1 million.

TELEVISION

Baghdad Television: Ministry of Information, Iraq Broadcasting and Television Establishment, Salihiya, Karkh, Baghdad; f. 1956; government station operating 7 hours daily; Dir.-Gen. LATEEF AL-DELAIMY.

Kirkuk Television: f. 1967; government station; commercial; 6 hours daily.

Mosul Television: f. 1968; government station; commercial; 6 hours daily.

Basrah Television: f. 1968; government station; commercial; 6 hours daily.

Missan Television: f. 1974; government station; commercial; 6 hours daily.

Kurdish Television: f. 1974; government station; commercial; 6 hours daily.

Muthanna station opened in mid-1976 and Um Qasr station is under construction.

Number of TV receivers (1980): 625,000.

FINANCE

All banks and insurance companies, including all foreign companies, were nationalized in July 1964. The assets of foreign companies were taken over by the state.

BANKING

(cap. = capital; p.u. = paid up; dep. = deposits; res. = reserves; m. = million; amounts in Iraqi dinars.)

CENTRAL BANK

Central Bank of Iraq: Banks St., Baghdad; f. 1947 as National Bank of Iraq; brs. in Mosul and Basra; has the sole right of note issue; cap. and res. 125m., current and deposit accounts 7,132m. (Sept. 1980); Gov. HASSAN AL-NAJAFI.

COMMERCIAL BANK

Rafidain Bank: P.O.B. 11360 Massarif, New Banks St., Baghdad; f. 1941; 188 brs.; cap. p.u. 30m., res. 80.6m., dep. 2,308m. (Dec. 1979); Pres. and Chair. ADNAN AL-TAYYAR.

SPECIALIZED BANKS

Agricultural Bank of Iraq: Rashid St., Baghdad; 21 branches; cap. p.u. 6.4m.; Gen. Man. ABDUL RAZZAK AL-HILALI.

Estate Bank of Iraq: Hassan ibn Thabit St., Baghdad; f. 1949; 19 branches; gives loans to assist the building industry; cap. p.u. 34m.; acquired the Co-operative Bank in 1970; Dir.-Gen. LABEED AL-KARAGULLY.

Industrial Bank of Iraq: P.O.B. 5825, Al-Khullani Square, Baghdad; 9 brs.; f. 1940; cap. p.u. 50m.; Dir.-Gen. ABDUL SALAM ALLAWI.

INSURANCE

Iraqi Life Insurance Co.: 25 S/21 Curd Al-Pasha, Karadah Al-Sharqiah, P.O.B. 989, Baghdad; Chair. and Gen. Man. MEDHAT FADHIL AL-JARRAH.

Iraq Reinsurance Company: Khalid Ben Al-Waleed St., Aqaba Ben Nafe'e Square, P.O.B. 297, Baghdad; f. 1960; to transact reinsurance business on the international market; Chair and Gen. Man. K. M. AL-MUDERIES.

National Insurance Co.: Al-Aman Bldg., Al-Khullani St., P.O.B. 248, Baghdad; f. 1950; cap. p.u. 1m.; state monopoly for all direct non-life insurance; Chair. and Gen. Man. MOWAFAQ H. RIDHA.

OIL AND GAS

Ministry of Oil: P.O.B. 6118, Al-Mansour City, Baghdad; solely responsible for oil sector and activities relevant to it; Minister of Oil TAYEH ABDUL KARIM; controls the following:

Iraq National Oil Company (INOC): P.O.B. 476, Al-Khullani Sq., Baghdad; f. in 1964 to operate the oil

industry at home and abroad; when Iraq nationalized its oil, structural changes took place in INOC and it has become solely responsible for exploration, production, transportation and marketing of Iraqi crude oil and oil products. The Iraq Company for Oil Operations (ICOO) has become the Northern Petroleum Organization (NPO) and is under the control of INOC; Chair. TAYEH ABDUL KARIM (Minister of Oil).

Northern Petroleum Organization (NPO): P.O.B. 1, Al-Ta'ameem Governorate; established to carry out oil operations in northern area of Iraq; Chair. Dr. SAMI SHARIF.

Southern Petroleum Organization (SPO): P.O.B. 240, Basra; similar to the Northern Petroleum Organization, it was established to undertake oil operations in southern area of Iraq; Chair. RAFID ABDUL HALEEM.

State Organization for Oil Projects (SOOP): P.O.B. 198, Al-Sa'adoun St., Baghdad; responsible for construction of oil projects mostly inside Iraq through direct execution, and also for design supervision of the projects and contracting with foreign enterprises, etc.; Chair. RAJIH MOHIELDIN.

State Organization for Distribution of Oil Products and Gas: P.O.B. 302, South Gate, Baghdad; responsible for distribution, marketing and selling of all distillates, lubricating oils, greases, natural gas, liquid gas and others in Iraq. It supplies ships and tankers entering Iraqi waters and the Arabian Gulf with fuels by means of a special fleet of 6 tankers and 6 coasters. It also supplies aircraft in Iraqi airports; and has a network of pipelines, the most important of which is the pipeline for transporting oil products between Baghdad and Basra; Chair. HAZIM ALI AL-TALIB.

State Organization for Oil Refining and Gas Processing: P.O.B. 3069, Al-Sa'adoun St., Baghdad; responsible for oil refining and gas processing in Iraq. It operates 8 oil refineries (1981). A number of plants for gas production were established to use the gas as fuel, etc.; two major projects for exploitation of northern and southern gas are being executed; and after inauguration all the associated gas will no longer be flared; Chair. SA'AD ALLUH ALFATHI.

State Organization for Oil Marketing: Baghdad; is responsible for marketing of crude oil, negotiation and contracting with foreign enterprises; Chair Dr. RAMZI SALMAN.

State Establishment for Oil Tankers: P.O.B. 37, Basra; responsible for crude oil transportation; it owns and operates 15 tankers; Chair. ADNAN ABDUL HAMID NASIR.

State Establishment for Oil Training: P.O.B. 6073, Al-Mansoor, Baghdad; responsible for training and distribution of personnel to provide the oil sector with its specialist needs, in addition to those provided by the universities; Chair. MISHAAL M. HAMMODAT.

Middle Petroleum Establishment: P.O.B. 5271, Al-Khullani Sq., Baghdad; responsible for carrying out the oil operations in the middle area of the country; Chair. Dr. THAMIR AL-AUKAILI.

State Establishment for Oil Exploration and Gas: INOC Building, Al-Khullani Sq., Baghdad; responsible for exploration, operations at the marshes, swamps, deserts, valleys and on top of mountains; Chair. HASHIM AL-KHIRSAN.

TRADE AND INDUSTRY

CHAMBERS OF COMMERCE

Federation of Iraqi Chambers of Commerce: Mustansir St., Baghdad; f. 1969; all Iraqi Chambers of Commerce are affiliated to the Federation; Chair. HATEM ABDUL-RASHID; Sec.-Gen. FUAD H. ABDUL-HADI; publs. *Iraq Trade Directory, Annual Trade Report, Wholesale Price Bulletin*.

Amarah Chamber of Commerce: Al-Amarah; f. 1950; Pres. KAMAL LEFTA HASSAN; Sec. N. J. MANSHAMI.

Arbil Chamber of Commerce: Arbil; f. 1966; Pres. ANUAR SALIH IBRAHIM; Sec. JALAL K. KARIM.

Baghdad Chamber of Commerce: Mustansir St., Baghdad; f. 1926; 18,247 mems.; Pres. HATIM ABDUL RASHID; Sec. H. A. ABBAS; Dir.-Gen. F. A. AL-SALEH; publs. *Commercial Bulletin* (fortnightly), *Commerce* (quarterly).

Basrah Chamber of Commerce: Basrah; f. 1926; Pres. ABDUL KARIM AL-ATTAR; Sec. ABDUL RAZAK S. MAHDI; publ. *al Tajir* (monthly).

Dahok Chamber of Commerce: Dahok; Pres. K. D. MALKONIAN; Sec. T. A. AL-DAHER.

Diwaniya Chamber of Commerce: Diwaniya; f. 1961; Pres. HATEM HAMZA DHAHIR; Sec. AMIN A. MOSA.

Diyala Chamber of Commerce: Diyala; f. 1966; Pres. N. M. SALEH; Sec. TAHA H. HASSAN.

Hillah Chamber of Commerce: Hillah; f. 1949; Pres. KASSIM SAAD; Sec. A. H. SALMAN.

Karbala Chamber of Commerce: Karbala; f. 1952; 4,000 mems.; Pres. JAWAD R. ABULHAB; Sec. RASHEED ABDUL WAHAB; Dir. ALI A. DHIYAUDDIN.

Kut Chamber of Commerce: Kut; Pres. R. S. YOUNIS; Sec. A. H. ABDUL BARI.

Mosul Chamber of Commerce: Khalid ibn Al-Waleed, P.O.B. 35, Mosul; f. 1926; 7,350 mems.; Pres. MUDHAFAR A. AL-LAWAND; Sec. F. S. AL-MOULAH; publ. *Bulletin*.

Najaf Chamber of Commerce: Najaf; f. 1950; Pres. ABDUL ILAH I. LEFTA; Sec. N. H. HASSOWA.

Nasiriya Chamber of Commerce: Nasiriya; f. 1958; Sec. ABDUL HADI M. ALI.

Ramadi Chamber of Commerce: Ramadi; Pres. R. H. HMAYIM; Sec. R. SHOKER.

Sulaimaniya Chamber of Commerce: Sulaimaniya; f. 1967; Pres. N. I. AL-JAF; Sec. A. M. MOHAMMED.

EMPLOYERS' ORGANIZATION

Iraqi Federation of Industries: Iraqi Federation of Industries Bldg., Al-Khullani Square, Baghdad; f. 1956; 6,000 mems.; Pres. HATAM ABDUL RASHID; publs. *Al-Sina'a* (bi-monthly), Directory of Iraqi Industries and monthly reports.

INDUSTRIAL ORGANIZATIONS

General Establishment for Industry: Baghdad; state organization controlling most of Iraq's industry; organized into 5 departments covering (1) Clothing, Hides and Cigarettes, (2) Construction industries, (3) Weaving and Textiles, (4) Chemicals and Foodstuffs, (5) Engineering.

Iraqi Dates Administration: Museum Square, Jamel Abdul-Nasir St., Baghdad; responsible for date exports; Acting Dir. GEORGE BATTAH.

State Establishment for Phosphate: Al-Qaim; f. 1976; state organization responsible for all aspects of phosphate mining, treatment and marketing; also responsible for production of phosphatic fertilizers, etc.; initial cap. 350m. dinars.

State Organization for Minerals: P.O.B. 2330, Alwiyah, Baghdad; f. 1969; 1,210 mems.; responsible for exploiting all minerals in Iraq except oil; Pres. Dr. ABDUL RAZZAK AL-HASHIMI.

TRADE UNIONS

General Federation of Trade Unions of Iraq: P.O.B. 3049, Aleppo Square, Baghdad; f. 1959; 12 general unions and 18 local trade union federations in the governorates of Iraq. Number of workers in industry is 535,873, in agriculture 122,904 (excluding peasants) and in other services 376,917; GFTU is a member of the International Confederation of Arab Trade Unions and of the World Federation of Trade Unions; Pres. KHALID MUHSIN MAHMOOD; Sec.-Gen. FADHIL MAHMOOD GHAREB; publ. *Wai al-Ummal*.

Union of Teachers: Al-Mansour, Baghdad; Pres. Dr. ISSA SALMAN HAMID

Union of Palestinian Workers in Iraq: Baghdad; Sec.-Gen. SAMI AL-SHAWISH.

There are also unions of doctors, pharmacologists, jurists, artists, and a General Federation of Iraqi Women.

CO-OPERATIVES

By the end of 1977 there were 1,606 co-operatives with 287,672 members.

PEASANT SOCIETIES

General Federation of Peasant Societies: Baghdad; f. 1959; has 734 affiliated Peasant Societies.

TRADE FAIR

Baghdad International Fair: Damascus St., Al Mansour; Baghdad; administered by Iraqi Fairs Administration; held annually in October, although 1980 Fair was delayed until November; f. 1954.

TRANSPORT

RAILWAYS

Iraqi Republic Railways: Baghdad Central Station Building, Baghdad; total length of track (1975): 1,955 km., consisting of 1,130 km. of standard gauge, 825 km. of one-metre gauge; Dir.-Gen. SUHAIL M. SALEH.

The metre gauge line runs from Baghdad through Khanaqin, Kirkuk to Erbil and from Baghdad through Musayab to Kerbela. The standard gauge line covers the length of the country from Rabia on the Syrian border via Mosul to Baghdad and from Baghdad to Basra and Um-Qasr on the Arabian Gulf. A 550 km. line is planned, linking Baghdad to Hsaibah, near the Iraqi-Syrian frontier. All standard gauge trains are now hauled by diesel-electric locomotives. As well as the internal service, there is a regular international service between Baghdad and Istanbul.

ROADS

The most important roads are: Baghdad–Mosul–Tel Kotchuk (Syrian border), 521 km.; Baghdad–Kirkuk–Arbil–Zakho (border with Turkey), 544 km.; Kirkuk–Sulaimaniya, 109 km.; Baghdad–Amara–Basra–Safwan (Kuwaiti border), 595 km.; Baghdad–Rutba–Syrian border (to Damascus), 555 km.; Baghdad–Babylon–Diwaniya, 181 km. Work is in progress on the Baghdad–Babylon section of an Express Highway which will link Iraq with Syria, Jordan and Kuwait.

In 1975 there were 6,566 km. of main roads and 5,293 km. of secondary roads.

SHIPPING

State Organization of Iraqi Ports: Basra; Acting Pres. FALEH MAHMOUD EL MOOSA.

The Ports of Basra and Um Qasr are the commercial gateway of Iraq. They are connected by various ocean routes with all parts of the world, and constitute the natural distributing centre for overseas supplies. The Iraqi Maritime Company maintains a regular service between Basra, the Gulf and north European ports. The Port of Basra is closed because of the Gulf War (December 1981).

At Basra there is accommodation for 12 vessels at the Maqal Wharves and accommodation for 7 vessels at the buoys. There are 1 silo berth and 2 berths for oil products at Muftia and 1 berth for fertilizer products at Abu Flus. There is room for 8 vessels at Um Qasr.

There are deep-water tanker terminals at Fao and Khor Al-Amaya for 4 and 3 vessels respectively.

For the inland waterways, which are now under the control of the State Organization of Iraqi Ports, there are 1,036 registered river craft, 48 motor vessels and 105 motor boats.

Ministry of Oils and Minerals—Administration for Distribution of Oil Products and Gas: P.O.B. 302, South Gate, Baghdad; 8 tankers; Dir.-Gen. HAZIM T. A. AL TALIB.

Iraqi Oil Tankers Enterprise: P.O.B. 37, Basra; 15 tankers.

Iraqi State Enterprise for Maritime Transport (Iraqi Line): 14 July St., Basra; 15 general cargo vessels; Dir.-Gen. Dr. SALMAN D. SALMAN; Operations Man. M. A. ALI.

CIVIL AVIATION

There are international airports near Baghdad, at Bamerni, and at Basra. A new Baghdad International Airport is under construction. Internal flights connect Baghdad to Basra and Mosul.

Iraqi Airways: Al Kharkh, Baghdad; f. 1945; Dir.-Gen. MOHAMED TAHIR YASSIN; regular services from Baghdad to Abu Dhabi, Algiers, Amman, Amsterdam, Athens, Bahrain, Bangkok, Basra, Beirut, Belgrade, Berlin, Bombay, Bucharest, Budapest, Cairo, Casablanca, Copenhagen, Damascus, Dhahran, Doha, Dubai, Frankfurt, Geneva, Istanbul, Jeddah, Karachi, Khartoum, Kuala Lumpur, Kuwait, London, Madrid, Moscow, Mosul, Munich, New Delhi, Paris, Prague, Rome, Sofia, Teheran, Tripoli, Tunis, Vienna, Warsaw; fleet: 2 Boeing 747, 3 Boeing 707, 3 Boeing 727, 3 Boeing 737, 4 Ilyushin 76.

The following airlines also operate services to Iraq: Aeroflot (U.S.S.R.), Air France, Alitalia (Italy), Ariana Afghan, Balkan (Bulgaria), British Airways, ČSA (Czechoslovakia), Interflug (German Democratic Republic), JAL (Japan), KLM (Netherlands), Kuwait Airways, LOT (Poland), Lufthansa (Federal Republic of Germany), MALEV (Hungary), MEA (Lebanon), PIA (Pakistan), SAS (Sweden), Saudia (Saudi Arabia), Swissair, Syrian Arab.

TOURISM

Ministry of Information: Tourism and Resorts Administration: Ukba bin Nafi Sq., Baghdad; f. 1956; Dir.-Gen. Dr. ALI GHALIB AL-ANI; publs. *Tourism in Iraq* (bimonthly), guide books, posters, tourist maps and pamphlets.

DEFENCE

Military service: 2 years, but extended for the Gulf War.
Total armed forces (July 1981): 252,250: army 210,000; air force 38,000; navy 4,250; reserves 250,000. On the

outbreak of the Gulf War in September 1980, these forces were supplemented by a 250,000-strong popular army—a uniformed citizens' volunteer force.

Chief of the General Staff: General ABDEL-JABBAR SHANSHAL.

Deputy Commander of Armed Forces: Gen. ADNAM KHAIRALLA.

Commander of the Popular Army: TAHA YASSIN RAMADAN.

EDUCATION

Since the establishment of the Republic in 1958 there has been a marked expansion in education at all levels. Spending on education has increased substantially since 1958, reaching I.D. 211 million in the 1980 budget. During 1974-75 two decisions were promulgated which constitute a landmark in the history of the Iraqi educational System. The first was a decision of the Revolutionary Command Council announcing free education in all stages from pre-primary to higher. The second decision abolished private education and transferred all existing private schools into state schools. Pre-school education is expanding although as yet it reaches only a small proportion of children in this age group. Primary education, lasting six years, is now officially compulsory, and there are plans to extend full-time education to nine years as soon as possible. At present, secondary education, which is expanding rapidly, is available for six years. An anti-illiteracy campaign began during the 1978/79 academic year and it is hoped to wipe out illiteracy within three years.

Science, Medical and Engineering faculties of the universities have undergone considerable expansion, although technical training is less developed. Two branches of Baghdad University at Basra and Mosul became independent universities in 1967.

BIBLIOGRAPHY

GENERAL

BELL, Lady FLORENCE (Ed.). The Letters of Gertrude Lowthian Bell (2 vols., London, 1927).

BURGOYNE, ELIZABETH (Ed.). Gertrude Bell, from her personal papers, 1914-26 (London, 1961).

LLOYD, SETON F. H. Iraq: Oxford Pamphlet (Bombay, 1943).
Twin Rivers: A Brief History of Iraq from the Earliest Times to the Present Day (Oxford, 1943).
Foundations in the Dust (Oxford, 1949).

LONGRIGG, S. H. and STOAKES, F. Iraq (Ernest Benn, London, 1958).

QUBAIN, FAHIM I. The Reconstruction of Iraq 1950-57 (Atlantic Books, London, 1959).

SALTER, Lord, assisted by PAYTON, S. W. The Development of Iraq: A Plan of Action (Baghdad, 1955).

STARK, FREYA. Baghdad Sketches (John Murray, London, 1937).

STEWART, DESMOND, and HAYLOCK, JOHN. New Babylon: a Portrait of Iraq (London, Collins, 1956).

ANCIENT HISTORY

BRAIDWOOD, R. J. and HOWE, B. Prehistoric Investigation in Iraqi Kurdistan (Chicago, 1961).

CAMBRIDGE ANCIENT HISTORY (Vols. I and II, New Ed., Cambridge, 1962).

CHATERJI, S. Ancient History of Iraq (M. C. Sarkar Ltd., Calcutta, 1961).

FIEY, J. M. L'Assyrie Chrétienne (Imprimerie Catholique, Beirut, 1965).

FRANKFORT, H. Archaeology and the Sumerian Problem (Chicago, 1932).
The Birth of Civilization in the Near East (Anchor, New York, 1951).

LLOYD, SETON F. H. The Art of the Ancient Near East (London, 1961).
Ruined Cities of Iraq (Oxford, 1945).
Mesopotamia (London, 1936).
Mounds of the Near East (Edinburgh, 1964).

MALLOWAN, M. E. L. Early Mesopotamia and Iran (Thames and Hudson, London, 1965).

OATES, E. E. D. M. Studies in the Ancient History of Northern Iraq (British Academy, London, 1967).

OPPENHEIM, A. LEO. Ancient Mesopotamia (Chicago U.P., 1964).
Letters from Mesopotamia (Chicago U.P., 1967).

PARROT, A. Nineveh and Babylon (London, 1961).
Sumer (London, 1961).

PIGGOTT, S. (Ed.). The Dawn of Civilization (London, 1962).

ROUX, GEORGES. Ancient Iraq (London, 1964).

SAGGS, H. W. F. The Greatness that was Babylon (Sidgwick and Jackson, London, 1962).

STARK, FREYA. Rome on the Euphrates (John Murray, London, 1966).

WOOLLEY, Sir C. L. Abraham (London, 1936).
Mesopotamia and the Middle East (London, 1961).
The Sumerians (Oxford, 1928).
Ur of the Chaldees (London, 1950).
Ur Excavations. 8 vols. (Oxford, 1928-).

ISLAMIC PERIOD

CRESWELL, K. A. C. Early Muslim Architecture (3 vols., Oxford, 1932-50).

HITTI, P. K. A History of the Arabs (2nd ed., London, 1940).

LE STRANGE, GUY. The Lands of the Eastern Caliphate (Cambridge, 1905).

LOKKEGAARD, FREDE. Islamic Taxation in the Classical Period, with a Special Reference to Circumstances in Iraq (Copenhagen, 1950).

RECENT HISTORY

AL-MARAYATI, ABID A. A Diplomatic History of Modern Iraq (Speller, New York, 1961).

DANN, URIEL. Iraq under Qassem: A Political History 1958-63 (Praeger, New York, 1969).

EDITIONS DU MONDE ARABE. The Iraq-Iran Conflict (trans. from French, Paris, 1981).

FOSTER, H. A. The Making of Modern Iraq (London, 1936).

GALLMAN, W. J. Iraq under General Nuri (Johns Hopkins Press, 1964).

HALDANE, Sir J. A. L. The Insurrection in Mesopotamia, 1920 (Edinburgh, 1922).

KHADDURI, MAJID. Independent Iraq 1932-58, A Study in Iraqi Politics (2nd edition, Oxford University Press, 1960).
Republican Iraq: A study in Iraqi Politics since the Revolution of 1958 (Oxford University Press, 1970).
Socialist Iraq: A Study in Iraqi Politics since 1968 (Washington, The Middle East Institute, 1978).

KENT, MARIAN. Oil and Empire: British Policy and Mesopotamian Oil, 1900-1920 (Macmillan, London, 1976).

LONGRIGG, S. H. Four Centuries of Modern Iraq (Oxford, 1925).
Iraq 1900-1950: A Political, Social and Economic History (London, 1953).

MILLAR, RONALD. Kut: The Death of an Army (London, 1969).

MOBERLY, F. J. The Campaign in Mesopotamia, 1914-1918 (4 vols., London, 1923-27).

PAIFORCE: the official story of the Persia and Iraq Command, 1941-1946 (London, 1948).

PENROSE, EDITH and E. F. Iraq: International Relations and National Development (Benn, Tonbridge, 1978).

WILSON, Sir A. T. Loyalties: Mesopotamia, 1914-17 (London, 1930).
Mesopotamia, 1917-20: a Clash of Loyalties (London, University Press, 1931).

ZAKI, SALIH. Origins of British Influence in Mesopotamia (New York, 1941).

ECONOMY

AINSRAWY, ABBAS. Finance and Economic Development in Iraq (Praeger, New York, 1966).

GABBAY, R. Communism and Agrarian Reform in Iraq (Croom Helm, London, 1978).

JALAL, FERHANG. The Role of Government in the Industrialization of Iraq 1950-1965 (Frank Cass, London, 1972).

LANGLEY, KATHLEEN M. The Industrialisation of Iraq (Harvard University Press, 1961).

LONGRIGG, S. H. Oil in the Middle East (London, 1954).

MINORITIES

ARFA, HASSAN. The Kurds (Oxford University Press, Oxford, 1966).

BADGER, G. P. The Nestorians and their Rituals (2 vols., London, 1888).

BLUNT, A. T. N. Bedouin Tribes of the Euphrates (2 vols., London, 1879).

DAMLUJI, S. The Yezidis (Baghdad, 1948) (in Arabic).

DROWER, E. S. Peacock Angel (Being some account of Votaries of a Secret Cult and their Sanctuaries) (London, 1941).
The Mandeans of Iraq and Iran (Oxford, 1937).

EMPSON, R. H. W. The Cult of the Peacock Angel. (A Short Account of the Yezidi Tribes of Kurdistan) (London, 1928).

FIELD, H. Arabs of Central Iraq: Their History, Ethnology, and Physical Characters (Chicago, 1935).
The Anthropology of Iraq (4 vols., 1940, 1949, 1951, 1952, Chicago (first 2 vols.), Cambridge, Mass. (last 2 vols.).

KINNANE, DIRK. The Kurdish Problem (Oxford, 1964).
The Kurds and Kurdistan (Oxford, 1965).

LUKE, Sir H. C. Mosul and its Minorities (London, 1925).

O'BALLANCE, EDGAR. The Kurdish Revolt 1961-1970 (Faber and Faber, London, 1974).

SALIM, S. M. Marsh Dwellers of the Euphrates Delta (New York, 1961).

SHORT, MARTIN and McDERMOTT, ANTHONY. The Kurds (Minority Rights Group, London, 1975).

THESIGER, WILFRED. The Marsh Arabs (London, 1964).

Israel

PHYSICAL AND SOCIAL GEOGRAPHY

W. B. Fisher

The pre-1967 frontiers of Israel are defined by armistice agreements signed with neighbouring Arab states, and represent the stabilization of a military front as it existed in late 1948 and early 1949. These boundaries are thus in many respects fortuitous, and have little geographical basis. It may be pertinent to recall that prior to 1918 the whole area now partitioned between Syria, Israel and the kingdom of Jordan formed part of the Ottoman Empire, and was spoken of as "Syria". Then after 1918 came the establishment of the territories of the Lebanon, Syria, Palestine, and Transjordan—the frontier between the last two lying for the most part along the Jordan river.

The present State of Israel is bounded on the north by the Lebanon, on the north-east by Syria, on the east by the Hashemite Kingdom of Jordan, and on the south and south-west by the Gulf of Aqaba and the Sinai Desert, occupied in 1967 and returned in April 1982 to Egyptian sovereignty. The so-called "Gaza strip", a small piece of territory some 40 km. long, formed part of Palestine, but was, under the Armistice Agreement of February 1949, then left in Egyptian control. The territories occupied after the war of June 1967 are not recognized as forming part of the State of Israel, although it seems unlikely that she will give up her annexation of the Old City of Jerusalem. The geographical descriptions of these territories are, therefore, given in the chapters on the countries which controlled them before June 1967*.

Because of the nature of the frontiers, which partition natural geographical units, it is more convenient to discuss the geography of Israel partly in association with that of its neighbour, Jordan. The Jordan Valley itself, which is divided territorially between the two states, is dealt with in the chapter on Jordan, but the uplands of Samaria-Judaea, from Jenin to Hebron, and including Jerusalem, which form a single unit, will be discussed below, though a large part of this territory lies outside the frontiers of Israel.

PHYSICAL FEATURES

The physical geography of Israel is surprisingly complex and though the area of the state is small, a considerable number of regions are easily distinguished. In the extreme north the hills of the Lebanon range continue without break, though of lower altitude, to form the uplands of Galilee, where the maximum height is just over 1,200 metres. The Galilee hills fall

away steeply on three sides: on the east to the well-defined Jordan Valley (see Jordan), on the west to a narrow coastal plain, and to the south at the Vale of Esdraelon or "Emek Yezreel". This latter is a rather irregular trough formed by subsidence along faults, with a flat floor and steep sides, and it runs inland from the Mediterranean south-eastwards to reach the Jordan Valley. At its western end the vale opens into the wide Bay of Acre, 25 to 30 km. in breadth, but it narrows inland to only a mile or two before opening out once again where it joins the Jordan Valley. This lowland area has a very fertile soil and an annual rainfall of 40 cm., which is sufficient, with limited irrigation, for agriculture. Formerly highly malarial and largely uncultivated, the vale is now very productive. For centuries it has been a corridor of major importance linking the Mediterranean coast and Egypt with the interior of south-west Asia, and has thus been a passage-way for ethnic, cultural, and military invasions.

South of Esdraelon there is an upland plateau extending for about 150 km. This is a broad upfold of rock, consisting mainly of limestone and reaching 900 metres in altitude. In the north, where there is a moderate rainfall, the plateau has been eroded into valleys, some of which are fertile, though less so than those of Esdraelon or Galilee. This district, centred on Jenin and Nablus, is the ancient country of Samaria, until 1967 part of Jordan. Further south rainfall is reduced and erosion is far less prominent; hence this second region, Judaea proper, stands out as a more strongly defined ridge, with far fewer streams and a barer open landscape of a more arid and dusty character. Jerusalem, Bethlehem and Hebron are the main towns. Towards the south-east rainfall becomes scanty and we reach the Wilderness of Judaea, an area of semi-desert. In the extreme south the plateau begins to fall in altitude, passing finally into a second plateau only 300 to 450 metres above sea-level, but broader, and broken by occasional ranges of hills that reach 900 metres in height. This is the Negev, a territory comprising nearly half of the total area of Israel, and bounded on the east by the lower Jordan Valley and on the west by the Sinai Desert. Agriculture, entirely dependent on irrigation, is carried on in a few places in the north, but for the most part the Negev consists of steppe or semi-desert. Irrigation schemes are now being developed in those areas where soils are potentially productive.

Between the uplands of Samaria-Judaea and the Mediterranean Sea there occurs a low-lying coastal plain that stretches southwards from Haifa as far as the Egyptian frontier at Gaza. In the north the plain is closely hemmed in by the spur of Mount Carmel (550 metres), which almost reaches the sea; but the plain soon opens out to form a fertile lowland—the

---

* For the state of the *de facto* boundaries after the various agreements with Egypt and Syria, *see* maps, pp. 81 and 90.

Plain of Sharon. Further south still the plain becomes again broader, but with a more arid climate and a sandier soil—this is the ancient Philistia. Ultimately the plain becomes quite arid, with loose sand dunes, and it merges into the Sinai Desert.

One other area remains to be mentioned—the Shephelah, which is a shallow upland basin lying in the first foothills of the Judaean plateau, just east of the Plain of Sharon. This region, distinguished by a fertile soil and moister climate, is heavily cultivated, chiefly in cereals.

CLIMATE

Climatically Israel has the typical "Mediterranean" cycle of hot, dry summers, when the temperature reaches 32 to 38°C., and mild, rainy winters. Altitude has a considerable effect, in that though snow may fall on the hills, it is not frequent on the lowlands. Jerusalem can have several inches of snow in winter, and Upper Galilee several feet. The valleys, especially Esdraelon and adjacent parts of the upper Jordan, lying below sea-level, can become extremely hot (over 40°C.) and very humid.

Rainfall is very variable from one part of Israel to another. Parts of Galilee receive over 100 cm. annually, but the amount decreases rapidly southwards, until in the Negev and Plain of Gaza, it is 25 cm. or less. This is because the prevailing south-westerly winds blow off the sea to reach the north of Israel, but further south they come from Egypt, with only a short sea track, and are hence lacking in moisture.

RACE AND LANGUAGE

Discussion over the racial affinities of the Jewish people has continued over many years, but there has been no unanimity on the subject. One view is that the Jewish people, whatever their first origin, have now taken on many of the characteristics of the peoples among whom they have lived since the Dispersal—e.g., the Jews of Germany were often closely similar in anthropological character to the Germans; the Jews of Iraq resembled the Arabs; and the Jews of Abyssinia had a black skin. Upholders of such a view would largely deny the separateness of ethnic qualities amongst the Jews. On the other hand, it has been suggested that the Jews are really a particular and somewhat individual intermixture

of racial strains that are found over wider areas of the Middle East: a special genetic "mix" with ingredients by no means restricted to the Jews themselves. The correctness of either viewpoint is largely a matter of personal interpretation.

Under British mandatory rule there were three official languages in Palestine—Arabic, spoken by a majority of the inhabitants (all Arabs and a few Jews); Hebrew, the ancient language of the Jews; and English. This last was considered to be standard if doubt arose as to the meaning of translation from the other two.

Since the establishment of the State of Israel the relative importance of the languages has changed. Hebrew is now dominant, Arabic has greatly declined following the flight of Arab refugees, and English is also less important, though it remains the first foreign language of most Israelis.

Hebrew, once widely current in biblical days, underwent considerable eclipse after the dispersal of Jewish people by the Romans, and until fairly recently its use was largely restricted to scholarship, serious literature and religious observance. Most Jews of Eastern and Southern Europe did not employ Hebrew as their everyday speech, but spoke either Yiddish or Ladino, the former being a Jewish-German dialect current in East and Central Europe, and the latter a form of Spanish. Immigrants into Israel since 1890 have, however, been encouraged to use Hebrew as a normal everyday speech, and Hebrew is now the living tongue of most Israeli Jews. The revival has been a potent agent in the unification of the Israeli Jewish people because, in addition to the two widely different forms of speech, Yiddish and Ladino, most Jewish immigrants usually spoke yet another language according to their country of origin, and the census of 1931 recorded more than 60 such languages in habitual use within Palestine. Now, as the proportion of native born Israelis increases, Hebrew is dominant, and the spread of other languages diminishes.

It is only by a revival of Hebrew that the Jewish community has found a reasonable *modus vivendi*—yet this step was not easy, for some devout Jews opposed the use of Hebrew for secular speech. Furthermore, there was controversy as to the way Hebrew should be pronounced, but the Sephardic pronunciation was finally adopted.

HISTORY

Tom Little

(with subsequent revisions by the Editor)

For most Jews the creation of the State of Israel in 1948 was the fulfilment of Biblical prophecy; to some in this more secular age it is a country justifiably won by political skill and force of arms in a world that denied them one for nearly 2,000 years; but, however regarded, it is seen as the fulfilment of Jewish history.

Although clearly a more ancient people from east of the Euphrates, the Jews trace their descent from Abraham, the first of the Patriarchs, who departed from Ur, the centre of the ancient Chaldean civilization, about 2,000 years B.C. Oral tradition as recorded in the Old Testament states that he was instructed by God to leave Chaldea with his family and proceed to Canaan (Phoenicia), or Palestine, the land of the Philistines, where he would father a great nation which would play an important part in human history. The authors of the Old Testament were primarily concerned to establish the descent of the Jewish people from Abraham under the guidance of God but in so doing they preserved the ancient history of the Jews which archaeology has tended to confirm within a debateable chronology.

Abraham's nomad family eventually reached Canaan and grazed their flocks there for a time before crossing Sinai to the richer pastures of Egypt. They remained in Egypt probably about 400 years and multiplied greatly, but their separateness in race, religion and customs at last excited the fears of the pharaohs, who enslaved them. Moses, who had escaped this slavery because he was brought up an Egyptian, fled with the Jews from the country (c. 1,200 B.C.) and gave them his law (the Torah) proclaiming the absolute oneness of God and establishing the disciplines of His worship.

They wandered for some decades in the wilderness before reaching the river Jordan. Moses' successor, Joshua, led some of the families (or tribes) across it and conquered Canaan. It was a stormy occupation of constant conflict with the indigenous peoples until the warrior Saul triumphed and became the first 'king'. His successor, David, completed the subjugation of the Israelites' enemies and briefly united all the tribes. King Solomon, his son, raised the country to its peak and built the Temple of Jerusalem which came to be recognized as the temple of all the Jews and the focal point of worship. His magnificence burdened the people, and this and his tolerance of the worship of idols provoked a successful revolt of the ten northern tribes under Jereboam who established Israel as his own kingdom. This division into two parts, Israel and Judah (which contained Jerusalem), was disastrous, for Israel was soon overcome by the Assyrians and its people were taken into captivity and lost to history. About 100 years later Judah fell

victim to the Babylonians and its people were also taken captive, but their community endured to become an important element in the future of Judaism. The Babylonians destroyed Solomon's temple.

When the Persian leader Cyrus conquered Babylon he gave the Jews permission to return to Jerusalem, and some did so. There they set about rebuilding the Temple which was completed about 500 B.C. and in 200 years of relative tranquillity their religion was consolidated by a series of great teachers. Palestine was in turn conquered by Alexander the Great and it and the Jews became part of his empire; but Alexander was tolerant, as were his successors in Egypt, the Ptolemies, with the result that Alexandria became the centre of a learned school of Hellenic Judaism.

The results were tragic in the successor Roman empire. The Jews rebelled against the oppressive Roman rule and Nero sent his greatest general, Vespasian, and his son, Titus, to suppress them. The conquest was completed by Titus; Jerusalem and the second temple were destroyed (c. 70 A.D.), and the Diaspora which began with the Assyrian conquest of Israel was complete. A small community of Jews remained in Jerusalem and the surrounding countryside, and devoted themselves to their religion, producing their version of the Talmud, the repository of Judaic history, learning and interpretation which, with the Torah and the Old Testament, became the essence of the faith, but it was the version of the Talmud produced by the Babylonian scholars which became the accepted document.

Scattered across the world, throughout Arabia, Asia as far as China, North Africa and Europe as far as Poland and Russia, Jewish communities continued to exist, sometimes powerful, often persecuted, but held in their exclusiveness and survival by religion and certain central themes: their belief in the oneness of God, His promise to Abraham, the promise of the 'return', and the Temple as the temple of all Jews. In terms of time their occupation of Palestine was relatively short and for even less of that time did they hold or rule it all, but the scattered communities continued to look towards Jerusalem.

THE ZIONIST MOVEMENT

In the late nineteenth century there were affluent and even powerful groups of Jews in Europe but the people as a whole were usually treated as second-class citizens in the countries where they lived. The large, pious and orthodox groups in Eastern Europe, in particular, were subject intermittently to persecution, and in 1881 there was a series of pogroms in Russia which stirred the conscience of world Jewry into forming plans for their escape. For the eastern

Jews there could be only one destination: Palestine. The pogroms led directly to the formation in Russia of a movement called the Lovers of Zion (*Hovevei Zion*), and within that movement another was formed, called the *Bilu*, by a large community of young Jews in the Kharkov region. In 1882 a *Bilu* group in Constantinople issued a manifesto demanding a home in Palestine. They proposed that they should beg it from the Sultan of Turkey, in whose empire Palestine lay.

The word Zionism was coined by a Russian about a decade later as a spiritual-humanitarian concept but Theodor Herzl, who became the leader of the movement, defined its aim specifically at the Basle Congress of 1897 (*see* Documents on Palestine, p. 66): "Zionism", he said, "strives to create for the Jewish people a home in Palestine secured by public law." He wrote in his journal after the congress: 'At Basle I founded the Jewish State . . . perhaps in five years, and certainly fifty, everyone will know it." He is recognized as the founder of political Zionism.

He was concerned essentially with the creation of a safe refuge for the suffering communities of Eastern Europe and thought that their migration and settlement could and should be financed by prosperous Jews. When he failed to get help from the Sultan he considered other possible "homes" as far apart as Uganda and Latin America, but even safe places could never have the appeal to orthodox Jews as had Palestine, sanctioned in their scriptures and 'promised' to them by God. Some of the Jews of Russia and Poland escaped persecution to make their own way to Palestine and became the earliest immigrant communities there.

When the Turkish empire was destroyed by Allied forces in the 1914–18 war new possibilities of getting their 'home' or State in Palestine opened up before the Zionists. In the years 1915–16 Sir Mark Sykes for Britain and M. Charles Georges-Picot for France had, in fact, drafted an agreement (*see* Documents on Palestine, p. 66) in which, while undertaking 'to recognize and protect an independent Arab State or Confederation of Arab States', the two powers in effect carved the Middle East into their respective spheres of influence and authority pending the time of its liberation from Turkey. Influential Zionists, notably Dr. Chaim Weizmann, saw their opportunity to press Britain for a commitment to provide a home for the Jews in Palestine and secured the help of Judge Louis Brandeis, a leading United States Zionist and principal adviser to President Woodrow Wilson, in bringing the U.S. into the war on the side of the Allies in April 1917. The outcome was the Balfour Declaration (*see* Documents on Palestine, p. 67) which was contained in a letter from Arthur James Balfour to Lord Rothschild on behalf of the Zionist Federation, dated November 2nd, 1917. It stated:

"His Majesty's Government view with favour the establishment in Palestine of a national home for the Jewish people, and will use their best endeavours to facilitate the achievement of this object, it being clearly understood that nothing shall be done which may prejudice the existing civil and religious rights of existing non-Jewish communities in Palestine, or the rights and political status of Jews in other countries."

The San Remo Conference decided on April 24th, 1920, to give the Mandate under the newly formed League of Nations to Britain (the terms of which were approved by the United States, which was not a member of the League, before they were finally agreed by the League Council on July 24th, 1922). The terms (*see* Documents on Palestine, p. 70) included a restatement of the Balfour Declaration and provided that "an appropriate Jewish agency" should be established to advise and cooperate with the Palestine Administration in matters affecting the Jewish national home and to take part in the development of the country. This gave the Zionist Organization a special position because the Mandate stipulated that it should be recognized as such an agency if the mandatory authority thought it appropriate. Britain took over the Mandate in September 1923.

THE MANDATE

Herzl's first aim had thereby been achieved: the national home of the Jewish people had been "secured by public law"; but major obstacles were still to be overcome before the home, or State, became a reality. When the Mandate was granted, the Arabs constituted 92 per cent of the population and owned 98 per cent of the land in Palestine, and it could clearly not be a home unless the demography and land ownership were changed in favour of the Jews. It was to these ends that the Zionist movement now directed itself, but Britain and it had different views concerning what was meant by "favouring" the establishment of the home, both in the matter of boundaries and immigration, even though Britain was consistently sympathetic to the enterprise. This was important, for although she was nominally under the supervision of the Mandates Commission of the League, she was able to run Palestine very much as a Crown Colony and administered it through the Colonial Office.

The World Zionist Organization had presented a memorandum to the Paris Peace Conference in 1919 setting forth its territorial concept of the home, as follows:

The whole of Palestine, southern Lebanon, including the towns of Tyre and Sidon, the headwaters of the Jordan river on Mount Hermon and the southern portion of the Litani river; the Golan Heights in Syria, including the town of Quneitra, the Yarmuk river and Al-Himmeh hot springs; the whole of the Jordan valley, the Dead Sea, and the eastern highlands up to the outskirts of Amman, thence in a southerly direction along the Hedjaz railway to the Gulf of Aqaba; in Egypt, from El-Arish, on the Mediterranean coast, in a straight line in a southerly direction to Sharm as-Sheikh on the Gulf of Aqaba.

The League of Nations and the Peace settlement did not accept these boundaries but the mandate given to Britain included Transjordan, the territory east of the river and beyond Amman. Britain allotted Transjordan as an Emirate to Emir Abdullah in 1921 and with the grant of full independence in 1946 it became a kingdom.

The Arabs bitterly opposed the Balfour Declaration and Jewish immigration and called for the prohibition of land sales to Jews. Britain would neither accede to their demands nor to Jewish claims to a majority in Palestine. There were intermittent outbreaks of Arab violence, notably in 1922 and 1929, which brought the Arabs into conflict with the mandatory government and there were four British Commissions of Inquiry and two White Papers were issued (*see* Documents on Palestine, p. 70) on the situation before 1936, none of which envisaged a Jewish majority. In 1936 there was an effective six-months general strike of the Arab population followed by a large scale rebellion which lasted until the outbreak of the Second World War and in 1939 another Commission issued the third White Paper (*see* Documents on Palestine, p. 73) which stated that Britain would not continue to develop the Jewish national home beyond the point already reached, proposed that 75,000 more Jews should be admitted over five years and then Jewish immigration would cease. Finally, it proposed that self-governing institutions should be set-up at the end of the five years. This would have preserved the Arab majority in the country and its legislature.

THE BILTMORE PROGRAMME AND AFTER

The world emotional context at that time was conditioned by the horrifying Nazi policy of exterminating Jews—a policy which was to reach even more frightful proportions after the outbreak of war. Zionists and Jews generally regarded the White Paper as a betrayal of the terms of the Mandate and when David Ben Gurion, Chairman of the Jewish Agency Executive, was in New York in 1942 an Extraordinary Zionist Conference held at the Biltmore Hotel utterly rejected the White Paper and reformulated Zionist policy. The declaration of the conference (*see* Documents on Palestine, p. 74) issued on May 11th, 1942, concluded as follows:

> The conference urges that the gates of Palestine be opened; that the Jewish Agency be vested with control of immigration into Palestine and with the necessary authority for upbuilding the country, including the development of its unoccupied and uncultivated lands; and that Palestine be established as a Jewish Commonwealth integrated into the new structure of the democratic world.

This policy brought the Jews into head-on collision with the Palestine Government before the war was over. Those in Europe who escaped the Nazi holocaust were herded into refugee camps and some who could do so with organized Zionist help tried to reach Palestine, but the British authorities, in accordance with the 1939 policy, tried to prevent their entry.

The British failed. The Jewish population which had been 56,000 at the time of the Mandate was 608,000 in 1946 and was estimated to be 650,000 on the eve of the creation of Israel, or about two-fifths of the entire population. Further, the Jewish Agency had formed its own military organizations, the Haganah and its units of shock troops, the Palmach, which were strengthened by those Jews who had fought on the side of the British during the war, and supported by two smaller extremist groups, the Irgun Zvaei Leumi and the Stern Gang. Towards the end of the war they embarked on a policy of violence designed to impose the Biltmore programme. They successfully made the Mandate unworkable and Britain referred it to the United Nations (which had replaced the League) on April 2nd, 1947.

The UN General Assembly sent a Special Commission (UNSCOP) to Palestine to report on the situation and its report issued on August 31st, 1947 proposed two plans: a majority plan for the partition of Palestine into two States, one Jewish and one Arab, with economic union; and a minority plan for a federal State. The Assembly adopted the majority plan (*see* Documents on Palestine, p. 75) on November 29th by 33 votes for and 13 against, with ten abstentions. The plan divided Palestine into six principal parts, three of which, comprising 56 per cent of the total area, were reserved for the Jewish State and three, with the enclave of Jaffa, comprising 43 per cent of the area, for the Arab State. It provided that Jerusalem would be an international zone administered by the UN as the holy city for Jews, Moslems and Christians. The Arabs refused to accept this decision and in the subsequent disorders about 1,700 people were killed. In April 1948 the Jewish forces swung into full-scale attack and by the time the Mandate was terminated on May 14th, 400,000 Arabs had evacuated their homes to become refugees in neighbouring Arab countries.

THE STATE ESTABLISHED

The Mandate was relinquished by Britain at 6 p.m. Washington time; at 6.01 the State of Israel was officially declared by the Jewish authorities in Palestine; at 6.11 the United States accorded it recognition and immediately afterwards the Soviet Union did likewise. Thus Israel came into existence only one year late on Herzl's 50-year diary prophecy. The Arab States belatedly came to the help of the Palestinian Arabs but their attempt to overthrow the new state failed and Israel was left in possession of more territory than had been allotted to her under the UN partition plan, including new (non-Arab) Jerusalem. Israel rejected the proposed internationalization of the city, for the Jews considered the return to Jerusalem to be at the heart of the divine promise to them.

A provisional government was formed in Tel-Aviv the day before the Mandate ended, with Ben Gurion as Prime Minister and other members of the Jewish Agency Executive in leading ministerial posts. The constitution and electoral laws had already been prepared and the first general elections were held in January 1949 for a single-chamber Knesset (or parliament) elected by proportional representation. This enabled several parties to gain representation, with Mapai usually in the majority but never predominant. As a result, government has usually been conducted by uneasy coalitions.

After the war another 400,000 Arabs fled from the additional territory conquered by Israel and in the course of another year about 300,000 more left the impoverished Arab West Bank for Transjordan. (In 1950 King Abdullah held a referendum in which the West Bank Arabs agreed to be part of his kingdom which then became known as Jordan.) The Israeli Government maintained the mandatory military control, established in the earlier disorders, over those Arab populations which remained within its territory but allowed "co-operative" Arabs to be elected to the Knesset; four were elected to the first parliament.

A gigantic programme of immigration was launched immediately the Provisional Government took over and within three years the Jewish population was doubled. This result, unparalleled in history, was assisted by Iraq which expelled the larger part of its age-old Jewish communities. The 1961 census gave Israel's population as 2,260,700, of whom 230,000 were Arabs. The two-millionth Jew arrived in May 1962 and the three-millionth early in 1972. A massive plan for land development to provide for the new people was executed concomitantly with the early immigration programme; the Jewish National Fund took over 3,000,000 dunums of former Arab land and used heavy mechanical equipment to bring it rapidly back into production. This was made possible by the stupendous support from abroad which came in the form of private gifts from world Jewry, State loans and aid, and private Jewish investments. The United States was both privately and publicly the major contributor, but at the Hague in 1952 West Germany agreed to pay reparations for Nazi crimes, and these payments amounted to £216 million in Deutsche Marks before they were concluded in 1966. The effect of this influx of unearned money from all sources was to cause serious inflation which was still a grave problem in the 1980s (*see* Economic Survey).

Israel was admitted to the United Nations, albeit on conditions concerning Jerusalem and refugees which were contrary to her overall policy and were never fulfilled. Her relations with the Arab States were governed by a series of armistice agreements reached in Rhodes in 1949 which, in effect, established an unsteady truce without an Arab commitment to permanent peace. The Arabs continued to insist that the creation of Israel was a usurpation of Arab territory and right and a denial of UN principles. Defence policy therefore dominated Israel's political thinking and firmly established the principle that she would remain militarily superior to any combination of Arab States. In the early 1950s, however, it was the Palestinian refugees who caused intermittent frontier trouble, mainly from Syria and Jordan, but to some extent from the Gaza strip which, since the 1948 war, had been administered by Egypt.

Whenever one of the frontiers became too troublesome, Israel mounted a retaliatory raid *pour décourager les autres*. Acting on the principle that Nasser's Egypt was the only serious danger, Mr. Ben Gurion ordered a raid which on February 28th, 1955, wiped out the small Egyptian garrison at Gaza and the reinforcements travelling by road to its support. The result was contrary to Ben Gurion's intention; Nasser determined to secure adequate military strength and to that end entered in to the "Czech" arms agreement in August 1955, by which he bartered cotton and took credits from the U.S.S.R. for substantial quantities of arms and planes which began to arrive quickly. The threat to Israel was therefore increased.

SUEZ

On July 26th, 1956, Nasser nationalized the Suez Canal company of which Britain and France were the principal shareholders (*see* Egypt) and the two European powers prepared to retake control of it. Neither could expect any support from the two super-powers, or from world opinion in general, for open invasion, but in October Ben Gurion entered into a secret pact with them by which Israel would invade Sinai and thus justify Britain and France intervening to keep the combatants apart. The Israelis invaded on October 29th with powerful armoured columns and rapidly advanced towards the canal. The following day Britain and France issued their ultimatum that both sides should withdraw to 20 miles from the canal. Israel, which had by this time taken almost all of the Sinai, including the Gaza strip and Sharm as-Sheikh at the entrance to the Gulf of Aqaba, readily agreed to comply with the ultimatum, but Egypt refused on the grounds that she was being asked to withdraw from her own territory.

The Anglo-French force thereupon invaded the Port Said area and advanced some miles along the Suez Canal. There it was halted by Sir Anthony Eden, the British Prime Minister, in face of the forthright condemnation of the UN and financial sanctions threatened by the U.S.; a decision which the French Prime Minister, M. Guy Mollet, reluctantly accepted. Both countries withdrew their troops before the year was out. This was a severe blow to Mr. Ben Gurion who had counted on holding at least a security buffer zone on a line from El Arish, on the Mediterranean coast, to Sharm as-Sheikh (the Zionist 1919 frontier proposal). Therefore Israel delayed her final withdrawal from Egypt until January, and from the Gaza strip until March 1957 when a UN Emergency Force was safely established on the Sinai frontier and at Sharm as-Sheikh.

A development of great consequence to Israel at this time was the increasing involvement of the Soviet Union in the Middle East, especially in Egypt. The U.S.S.R. took no less than 50 per cent of Egyptian exports in 1957, and in 1958 agreed to finance and direct the building of the mammoth High Dam at Aswan. In keeping with this policy, the Soviet Union adopted a strongly pro-Arab and anti-Israeli line and steadily rearmed Nasser's forces.

Mr. Ben Gurion resigned "for personal reasons" in June 1963 and was succeeded by Levi Eshkol, his Finance Minister, who had been a minister continuously since joining the provisional government from the Jewish Agency in 1948. He was in modern terminology a "dove", inclined to a more conciliatory policy which he hoped would in time erode Arab enmity. This was opposed by many in the ruling hierarchy, notably the veteran Ben Gurion and Gen. Moshe Dayan, who had commanded the Israeli forces in their brilliant victory in 1956.

There was a notable increase in Arab guerrilla activity across the frontiers of Egypt, Jordan and Syria in the mid-1960s. The Palestinians formed a guerrilla organization called Al-Fatah for which the Syrian Prime Minister publicly declared his support in 1966. Mutual accusations of frontier violations followed, and President Nasser warned that he would have to activate the Egypt-Syrian Joint Defence Agreement if Israel's "aggression" did not cease. In May, King Hussein brought Jordan into the agreement and in that same month Nasser received information, which proved later to be untrue, that Israeli troops were massing on the Syrian frontier. In response Nasser ordered the withdrawal of the United Nations Emergency Force from the Gaza strip, the Sinai Desert and Sharm as-Sheikh. U Thant immediately obeyed, and Nasser then imposed a total blockade on Israeli shipping in the Straits of Tiran, although Israel had always made it plain that this would be considered a *casus belli*.

U Thant flew to Cairo on May 22nd, but by that time Nasser had already strengthened his forces in the Sinai and called up his reserves. Israel, Jordan and Syria had also mobilized. Israel formed a national government by bringing to the cabinet one representative of each of the three opposition parties. General Moshe Dayan, the victor of the 1956 Sinai campaign, was brought in as Defence Minister.

THE JUNE WAR

Israel made its pre-emptive strike in the early hours of June 5th when its armoured forces moved into Sinai. At 0600 hours GMT Israeli planes attacked 25 airfields in Egypt, Jordan, Syria and Iraq, destroying large numbers of planes on the ground and putting the runways out of action, thus effectively depriving the Egyptian and Jordanian ground forces of air cover. There were some fierce armoured battles in the Sinai but Israeli forces were in position along the Suez Canal on June 8th. They took Sharm as-Sheikh without a fight. On the eastern front, they reached the Jordan river on June 7th and entered and conquered Old (Arab) Jerusalem on the same day. Their main forces destroyed, President Nasser and King Hussein accepted a cease-fire on the 8th. Israel then turned its attention to the Syrian fortifications on the Golan Heights from which Israeli settlements were being shelled. In a brilliant but costly action, armour and infantry captured the heights. Syria accepted a

cease-fire on the 9th but Israel ignored it until the 10th, by which time her troops were in possession of Quneitra, on the road to Damascus. The "six-day war", as it became known, was over; Israel had achieved a victory more sweeping even than that of 1956.

Israel had recovered Jerusalem and access to the Western Wall of the Temples of Solomon and Herod, which were the most sacred places of worship for all Jews but to which they had been denied access since the division of the city between the Arabs and Israel in 1948. Israel immediately tore down the barriers, reunited the city, put the administration of Arab Jerusalem under her existing city administration, and effectively annexed it. The UN General Assembly passed a resolution on July 4th, which Israel disregarded, calling on her to rescind all the measures taken and to desist from any further action that would change the status of the holy city. Israel made it plain from the beginning that there could be no question of returning Old Jerusalem to Arab possession in any peace settlement.

The United Nations and the world powers busied themselves with the search for peace. On August 29th the heads of the Arab States began a Summit conference in Khartoum at which they decided to seek a political settlement but not to make peace with or recognize Israel or to negotiate directly with her, and meanwhile "to adopt necessary measures to strengthen military preparation to face all eventualities". On November 22nd, after many attempts, the UN Security Council agreed to Resolution 242, which stated that the establishment of a just and lasting peace in the Middle East should include the application of the following principles:

(i) withdrawal of Israeli armed forces from territories occupied in the recent conflict; and (ii) termination of all claims or states of belligerency and respect for and acknowledgement of the sovereignty, territorial integrity, and political independence of every State in the area, and their right to live in peace within secure and recognized boundaries free from threats or acts of force. The Council affirmed also the necessity for (a) guaranteeing freedom of navigation through international waterways in the area, and (b) achieving a just settlement of the refugee problem.

The Secretary-General designated Ambassador Gunnar Jarring of Sweden as Special Representative to assist the process of finding a peaceful settlement on this basis.

The essential ambiguity of the Council resolution was contained in the phrase "withdrawal . . . from territories occupied . . ." (which in the French translation became "les territoires"), and the Israeli Government has contended ever since that it meant an agreed withdrawal from some occupied territories "to secure and recognized boundaries". This was, in Israel's view, precluded by the Arab States' Khartoum resolution and their insistence that Resolution 242 meant total withdrawal from the 1967 occupied territories. Further, Israel insisted that she would only negotiate withdrawal directly with Egypt and the Arab States as part of a peace settlement and that the function of Jarring was to bring this about and not to initiate proposals of his own for a settlement.

UNEASY SECURITY

Meanwhile Israel based her policy on retention of the occupied territories as warranty of her security. The 1967 defeat had severely damaged the U.S.S.R.'s prestige in the Arab world, and to repair her position she began immediately to restore the Egyptian armed forces, including the air force. Meanwhile in 1967 President de Gaulle imposed an arms embargo on Israel and refused to deliver 50 supersonic Mirage IV fighters which Israel had ordered and paid for. Israel therefore turned to the United States, arguing that the balance of military power must, for her security, be maintained in her favour. This point was conceded by the U.S. in 1968 with a contract to deliver 50 Phantom jet fighter-bombers, which brought Cairo within range and were more powerful than any MiGs in Egypt.

Using powerful artillery installed by the U.S.S.R. west of the canal, Nasser began in 1968 a "war of attrition" in order to force Israel to accept his terms. Relatively heavy casualties were caused to the Israeli troops, notably in July and October, and throughout the period Israel retaliated punitively with air and artillery attacks which forced Egypt to evacuate the canal zone towns. Suez and its oil refineries were destroyed. The zone remained disturbed until 1970.

Israel's Prime Minister, Levi Eshkol, died on February 26th, 1969, and was succeeded in the following month by Mrs. Golda Meir, who had been Minister for Foreign Affairs from 1956 to 1966.

President Nixon, who had taken office in the United States, supported an initiative by his Secretary of State, William Rogers, "to encourage the parties to stop shooting and start talking". This was announced on June 25, 1970, and was unfavourably received in the Arab world. Nasser flew to Moscow with a proposal to accept it on condition that Russia supplied SAM-III missiles capable of destroying low-flying aircraft. He returned to Cairo and stunned Egypt and the Arab world with an unconditional acceptance of the Rogers plan and its related canal zone 90 day ceasefire. King Hussein immediately associated Jordan with Nasser's acceptance. Israel accepted the Rogers plan on August 7th but immediately complained that Egypt had broken the ceasefire agreement by moving SAM-III missile sites into the 30-mile wide standstill area along the canal.

President Nasser died suddenly on September 28th, 1970, but President Sadat, who succeeded him, sustained his policy. Although he only agreed to extend the ceasefire for another 90 days, it continued indefinitely. The American effort was directed towards securing an interim agreement by which Israel would withdraw from the Suez Canal and allow it to be reopened, but Israel, again on the basic principle of her security, would only consider a limited withdrawal and would not agree that Egyptian troops should cross the canal, terms which Egypt would not accept. U.S.-Israeli relations, vital to Israel, were uneasy during most of 1971 while the State Department pressed the Tel-Aviv Government to concede unacceptable terms of withdrawal from the canal. President Sadat gave the end of the year as a deadline for "peace or war", but before the year was out Mrs. Golda Meir secured a commitment to Israeli security from President Nixon firmer than any obtained in the past; the Rogers plan thereupon died, but 1972 dawned without the threatened outbreak of war from Egypt. Instead, there was a series of terrorist acts by various Palestinian groups, which in turn provoked punitive raids by Israeli forces.

The stated objective of Israeli punitive raids on Syria and Lebanon was to compel both countries to prevent the Palestinian resistance groups from mounting raids from within their borders, whether against Israel or in other countries. This objective seemed most successfully achieved in Lebanon on April 10th by a daring commando raid into the heart of Beirut, where the raiders killed three resistance leaders, while other commando units attacked two refugee camps outside the city and destroyed the PDFLP headquarters, killing one of its leaders. The Israeli authorities were able to make a number of arrests in the occupied territories from information gained in this raid.

THE OCCUPIED TERRITORIES

About 380,000 Arabs fled from the West Bank to Jordan, but nearly a million remained under Israeli occupation; of these, the 70,000 in East (Arab) Jerusalem, which was annexed, were treated as Israeli citizens and the remainder brought under military administration. This was of necessity strict for the first three years because of help given to Palestinian guerrillas by the Arabs in the occupied territories and, in some instances, in Israel proper. The Gaza strip was by far the most troublesome and it was not until the end of 1971 that Israeli security operations, including the clearance of one large refugee camp which had proved particularly difficult, brought the area under control. It was announced in March 1973 that the strip would be incorporated into Israel, that Jewish settlement in the strip would continue and that Arab inhabitants could circulate freely in Israel during the day. Higher living standards enjoyed by the Arabs under the occupation, 60,000 of whom found work in Israel itself, the inevitable growth of collaboration with the Israeli authorities and, finally, the disarray in which the Palestinian movement found itself by late 1970 rendered the security problem inside the country minimal during 1971. In March of the following year the Israeli military authorities successfully held elections for the mayors and municipalities in the main Arab towns, despite guerrilla threats of reprisals against any Arabs taking part.

Government policy was officially that in a peace settlement there would be substantial territories returned to the Arabs but there was no clear consensus in the Government or the country as to what they would amount to, except to the extent that Israel should have "secure frontiers". However, statements by Ministers made it clear that in addition to East Jerusalem and the Gaza strip, which had been effectively annexed, the Golan Heights of occupied Syria and parts of the Jordanian West Bank would not be returned. There was also increasing evidence on the ground. An extensive building programme to house immigrants was rapidly being executed in and around Jerusalem; 42 settlements had been established by January 1973 although, according to Israeli figures, only 3,150 Israeli civilians had been allowed to take up permanent residence in the areas.

Israel radio announced on August 18th, 1973 that another 35 settlements would be built in the occupied territories, bringing the total to 77. The Jewish National Fund and the Israeli Lands Administration had between them acquired 15,000 acres of Arab land and the army was in occupation of another 20,000 acres. A plan advanced by Deputy Prime Minister Yigal Allon, although not publicly approved by the Government, seemed to be in process of *de facto* execution. He proposed that a chain of Israeli settlements should be established along the Jordan river, which was effectively being done, a second chain along the Samarian Hills on the West bank, and a third along the road from Jerusalem to Jericho, in order to establish Israel's security. The rest of the West Bank and the main towns, excepting Jericho, would then be returned to Jordan.

The virtue of the Allon plan for most Israelis was that it would absorb few Arabs, for the core of the dispute within Israel remained the question of demographic balance between Arabs and Jews which would be changed in the Arabs' favour by the absorption of territory in which there were many of them resident. For that reason, the Government refused the request, submitted by the newly elected mayors of the Arab towns on the West Bank, that those Arabs who had fled the area after the 1967 war should be allowed to return. To restore the population balance the Jewish Agency, which was responsible for organizing immigration, concentrated upon Jews in Soviet Russia who were the largest reservoir of would-be immigrants. Russia began to relax its stringent opposition to Jewish emigration in 1971, with the result that thousands of Soviet Jews began to arrive in Israel. Of the 57,000 immigrants in the year 1972–73, 33,000 were from the Soviet Union.

THE YOM KIPPUR WAR

Although the Arab world had been urging Sadat to attack Israel, it was firmly believed that Egypt was afraid to go to war again and that the Bar-Lev defences along the eastern bank of the Suez Canal could not be overcome, but in fact Sadat was working steadily towards war, against the advice of his Soviet ally. He secured the financial support of King Faisal of Saudi Arabia to buy arms for hard currency, the agreement of Syrian President Hafez Assad to a limited war for the recovery of territories lost in 1967,

made his peace with King Hussein of Jordan and finally secured the arms required from the Soviet Union.

By the late Summer of 1973 he was ready for war on two fronts, Syria and Egypt, with King Hussein standing aside to tie-up a part of Israeli forces facing Jordan. At 2 p.m. on October 6th—the most important religious festival in Israel, Yom Kippur—the Egyptians launched their attack, breaking down the assumed impregnable sand banks of the Bar-Lev line with powerful water-jets, throwing pontoon bridges across the Suez Canal and breaking into Sinai. The line was undermanned. By midnight that day, the Egyptians had 500 tanks and missiles across the canal and destroyed 100 Israeli tanks. Almost simultaneously the Syrians had broken through the Israeli lines on the Golan heights.

Israel began the rapid mobilization of its reserve forces, the highly trained and numerically most important part of its defensive system, but before they could play an effective part the Egyptians had occupied the East bank of the canal to a depth of several miles and by the third day were advancing to the strategic Mitla pass in Sinai. The Syrian forces had by that time reached a point five miles from the Israeli frontier in Golan.

While fierce tank battles raged in Sinai, said to be bigger than any in the second World War, Israel halted the Syrians on its vulnerable northern frontier and counter-attacked successfully, driving the Syrians in a fighting retreat back over the 1967 cease-fire lines to within 20 miles of Damascus, where its forces were halted on the Syrian second line of defence. The Egyptians held their positions in Sinai but did not reach the Mitla pass.

The Egyptian High Command blundered on the twelfth day when it allowed a small Israeli commando force to cross to the West bank of the Suez Canal near Deversoir at the northern end of the Great Bitter Lake. The Israelis were able to reinforce the bridgehead with a force strong enough to swing southwards to Suez and endanger the Egyptian Third Army on the East bank. Losses were very heavy on both sides.

After three UN Security Council resolutions, a ceasefire became precariously effective on October 25th, but even then it was honoured more in the breach than observance until the end of the year. The U.S. Secretary of State, Dr. Henry Kissinger, did much to maintain a peace-making momentum by tours of the Arab countries to secure negotiations for a permanent settlement in Geneva on December 18th and in November Israel had accepted "in principle" the terms of an agreement Dr. Kissinger had reached with President Sadat for the "scrupulous" observance of the ceasefire.

Talks were soon adjourned to an unspecified date in order to allow time for the Israeli general elections, which had been postponed from October 30th to December 31st because of the war. Dr. Henry Kissinger returned to the Middle East in January and after days of intensive diplomatic activity, shuttling back and forward between Israel and Egypt, he secured the agreement of both countries to a disengagement of their forces which was announced on January 17th (*see* Documents on Palestine, p. 79). Israel agreed to withdraw its troops in Sinai to a line approximately 20 miles from the Suez Canal and Egypt to reduce its forces on the East bank. There was to be a neutral buffer zone between the two armies manned by troops of the UN Emergency Force.

Agreement for the disengagement of forces on the northern front was not signed until May 31st (*see* Documents on Palestine, p. 79), and then only after further shuttle diplomacy by Dr. Kissinger. Israel and Syria agreed to withdraw their troops to lines on each side of the 1967 cease-fire line, and the ruined town of Quneitra, capital of the Golan Heights, was handed back to Syria.

Two important factors weakened the Israeli position. In the last days of the war the Arab oil producing States banned the supply of oil to the United States and Holland and reduced supplies to Western Europe. (Britain and France were exempted but in fact were unable to get their full supplies.) This, combined with steep increases in oil prices which caused serious balance-of-payment problems for the European countries—although this had nothing to do with the war—led the EEC to issue a joint declaration in the Arab favour. Even more damaging to Israel was the confrontation which almost developed between the U.S.S.R. and the U.S.A. when they both began heavy supplies of war equipment to the Arabs and Israel respectively. Dr. Kissinger made it clear to Israel that the United States would continue to support Israel, but only within the limits imposed by détente with the U.S.S.R. It was unquestionably a form of pressure on Israel, although this was denied. President Nixon went on a peace-making mission to the Middle East in June, and shortly afterwards Israel's Finance Minister, Shimon Peres, visited Washington. The outcome was the conversion of a $500 million loan into a gift and an undertaking to supply a powerful force of warplanes to ensure Israel's security.

THE AFTERMATH

The war had a profoundly disturbing effect on Israeli public opinion. The country had never suffered such losses before: nearly 3,000 dead and missing, which was a substantial proportion of so small a population. The ease with which the Egyptians had crossed the canal and over-run the Bar-Lev line and the firmness with which the Syrians held the second line of defence 20 miles from Damascus were not off-set in Israeli eyes by the fact that Israeli troops had broken through and recrossed the canal and had made territorial gains in Syria; the Arab forces had fought with hitherto unknown determination and had used their sophisticated Soviet weaponry with great skill. The public's total confidence in the overwhelming superiority of their own army and air force was severely shaken, with the result that a sharp division of opinion occurred between those who thought the war emphasized the need to keep defen-

sible frontiers at all costs and those, less numerous, who viewed it as an argument for a more diligent search for a permanent peace. There was widespread dissatisfaction with the Government and a public debate ensued over the failure to anticipate the outbreak of war and the breakdown of military intelligence. There were mutual recriminations among the generals and Defence Minister Moshe Dayan's popularity in the country slumped. General Ariel Sharon, whose forces had made the breakthrough and canal crossing in Egypt, resigned from the army to join the right-wing Likud Party—the "hawks" of Israeli politics.

The elections of December 1973 reflected this confusion. The Labour alignment, led by Mapai, emerged as the strongest party with 51 seats. Likud, the main opposition, made substantial gains and won 39 seats. Mrs. Golda Meir reformed her coalition but resigned in April 1974 when the report on the 1973 war was published. She was succeeded in June by General Yitzhak Rabin, whose cabinet contained neither Moshe Dayan nor Abba Eban, who had been Foreign Minister since 1966. General Rabin, and his Foreign Minister, Yigal Allon, were both willing to make territorial sacrifices to achieve a settlement with the Arabs, and a Second Disengagement Agreement was signed with Egypt in September 1975 whereby Israel withdrew from some territory in the Sinai peninsula.

Meanwhile the PLO had achieved added status in 1974 by their recognition by the Arabs as "sole representative of the Palestinian people" at the Rabat summit of November 1974, but Mr. Rabin asserted Israeli policy, which he was to continue to hold throughout his premiership, of refusing to recognize a PLO delegation at any renewed Geneva peace talks.

Mr. Rabin was never able to command the support he needed as Prime Minister. The exact demarcation of functions between his role as Prime Minister and that of Shimon Peres, his Minister of Defence, and Yigal Allon, his Minister of Foreign Affairs, was never totally clear. Moreover, it soon became clear that, while Rabin was a "dove" in his attitude towards the Arabs, Peres was more of a "hawk". This became apparent over the question of Israeli settlements in the occupied territory on the West Bank of the Jordan. The settlement at Kaddum illustrates the problem. This was officially a "temporary" settlement, but there were considerable efforts by many groups in Israel, particularly the *Gush Emunim* movement, to make it permanent. Mr. Rabin, in 1976, announced that he would evict the rebels from Kaddum, but it was a decision that he never carried out, not least because of the opposition of Mr. Peres.

Moreover, Israel's economic difficulties (fully described in the Economic Survey) cost Mr. Rabin considerable popularity, and it seemed that the unpopular measures that he was forced to introduce to combat inflation won him few hearts, discouraged immigration, and made little visible progress towards a sounder economy.

In December 1976 the National Religious Party abstained in a confidence vote in the Knesset arising from charges that the Sabbath had been desecrated at a ceremony marking the arrival of three U.S. aircraft. Mr. Rabin subsequently dismissed two of the NRP ministers from his cabinet, and the consequent withdrawal of NRP support left the Government in a minority in the Knesset, thus precipitating Mr. Rabin's resignation.

Mr. Rabin carried on in a caretaker capacity until the election of May 1977, but in April 1977 he resigned as Leader of the Labour Party. On April 10th the Labour Party selected Shimon Peres as its new leader. Peres had earlier been narrowly defeated by Rabin in the February poll for the leadership of the Labour Party.

ISRAEL UNDER BEGIN

When the elections for the 9th Knesset took place on May 17th, 1977, the result was a surprise victory for the Likud, under Menachem Begin, who won 43 out of the 120 seats—the largest single total. The Likud victory removed the Labour Party from the predominant position it had held in Israel since 1949. With the support of the National Religious Party, Agudat Israel and Shlomzion, Mr. Begin was able to form a government on June 19th, and his position was strengthened in October 1977 when the Democratic Movement for Change (DMC) joined the Likud coalition. In September 1978, however, the DMC split into two factions, with seven Knesset members leaving Begin's coalition because they felt that his policy of announcing plans for further Israeli settlements on the West Bank was endangering prospects for peace.

A permanent peace settlement suddenly seemed possible when President Sadat of Egypt visited Jerusalem in November 1977 and addressed the Knesset. Talks between Sadat and Begin continued, and after various delays an unexpected breakthrough occurred in September 1978 after talks at Camp David in the U.S.A. under the guidance of President Carter, when Begin and Sadat signed two agreements. The first was a "framework of peace in the Middle East" (*see* p. 82) and the second was a "framework for the conclusion of a peace treaty between Egypt and Israel". The first agreement provided for a five-year transitional period during which the inhabitants of the Israeli-occupied West Bank and Gaza would obtain full autonomy and self-government, and the second agreement provided for the signing of a peace treaty between Egypt and Israel, which was finally signed on March 27th, 1979. The treaty provided for a phased withdrawal from Sinai which was successfully completed on April 25th, 1982 (*see* map on p. 90). Diplomatic relations between Israel and Egypt were opened on January 26th, 1980.

Proposals for Palestinian autonomy provided for negotiations to be completed by May 26th, 1980. That date passed with no agreement in sight. It became clear during the negotiations that Egypt and the Palestinians were considering "autonomy" in terms of an independent Palestinian State, whereas Israel had in mind only some form of administrative self-government for the Palestinian Arabs in the West Bank. The announcement of fresh Israeli settlements in the West Bank, and a Knesset Bill making East Jerusalem an integral part of the Jewish capital gave Arabs little ground for hope that their concept of Palestinian autonomy would ever emerge from the negotiations. No real progress had been made by June 1982, although both Israel and Egypt maintain their adherence to the "Camp David process."

BEGIN'S PROBLEMS

Since becoming Prime Minister, Mr. Begin has had to contend with two opposing factions in his Cabinet. Ariel Sharon, the Minister of Agriculture and the Minister responsible for Settlements, has followed the policy of the *Gush Emunim* movement, which has endeavoured to push the maximum number of Israeli settlements into the West Bank as quickly as possible. Sometimes voices calling for moderation have prevailed, but more often settlements have gone ahead unopposed. Particularly controversial was the Jewish settlement in the centre of Hebron, which the Israeli Cabinet agreed to in principle in February 1980. As the deadline for the autonomy talks (May 26th) approached, plans for more settlements were announced. Begin has prevaricated on the subject of the settlements, but more often than not supported them. The uncertainty of his exact position on many policy matters has led to strains in the Cabinet. Begin's health has also been a cause for concern at times. Moshe Dayan resigned as Foreign Minister in October 1979 because he considered the Israeli Government stand on Palestinian autonomy too hard-line, and at the end of May 1980 Ezer Weizman resigned as Minister of Defence, ostensibly because of defence cuts, but his dissatisfaction with the settlements position and with the autonomy talks was well-known. Begin encountered difficulty when trying to arrange the consequent Cabinet reshuffle. He was hoping to appoint the Foreign Minister, Yitzhak Shamir, to the post of Defence Minister but, when this met with opposition, Begin took over the Defence portfolio himself.

Begin's biggest problem, however, was the state of the Israeli economy (*see* Economic Survey). Rampant inflation called for austerity measures, and the Finance Minister, Yigael Horowitz, resigned in early January 1981 when the Knesset voted pay increases to teachers. Horowitz took his Rafi Party, with 3 Knesset members, out of the Likud coalition and the government could no longer command a majority. General elections were then called for June 30th. It was thought in early 1981 that Begin was certain of defeat in the forthcoming elections. But Begin's position grew stronger as the elections approached. The tax-cutting policies of the new Finance Minister, Yoram Aridor, proved popular. Begin's support for the Christians in the Lebanon, in their struggle with the Syrians, who had stationed SAM missiles on Lebanese soil, also proved electorally popular.

A SECOND TERM FOR BEGIN

Although the election results were close, Begin was able to present a new coalition to the Knesset in early August. This was possible only by making an agreement with the religious parties, in particular Agudat Israel, by which numerous undertakings on religious observance, affecting most aspects of everyday life, were guaranteed. Although these measures were welcomed by zealots, more secular elements in Israeli society found them unwelcome.

Begin's majority has always been precarious, and it is remarkable that this Government has survived as long as it has. In December he formally annexed the strategically-important Golan Heights, a step which pleased the "hawks" in Israel, but which angered the U.S.A. enough to cause it to suspend the strategic co-operation agreement which it had signed with Israel less than a month before.

As the time for withdrawal from Sinai drew nearer, there was increasing pressure from settlers in Sinai (particularly Yamit) to remain there. Squatters from the extreme right-wing Tehiya party took up a belligerent stance, but they were eventually removed and the withdrawal took place as planned on April 25th, 1982.

During the Spring of 1982 Arab disturbances on the West Bank became more severe (*see* Arab-Israeli Confrontation, p. 61). The event which produced another world-scale Middle East crisis, however, was Israel's "Operation Peace for Galilee", launched on June 6th. By the end of June, Israeli forces had advanced across Lebanon and surrounded West Beirut, where 6,000 PLO fighters had become trapped. Israel had declared a cease-fire and was demanding that the Palestinians lay down their heavy arms and leave Lebanon.

Israel's action met with disapproval from most of the world, and the support of the U.S.A. became questionable after Secretary of State Haig's resignation at the end of June, and his replacement by George Shultz. In Israel itself, fears were expressed that the casualties inflicted on Palestinians and Lebanese were out of proportion to the gain, and that the Minister of Defence, Ariel Sharon, had lost sight of the original objective of securing a line 25 miles north of the Israeli-Lebanese border (the Zahrani line) and had carried the Israeli army away in a vast military operation.

ECONOMIC SURVEY

Israel's gross national product (G.N.P.) rose during 1981 by 4.7 per cent to reach 8,943 million shekels, compared with 8,534 million shekels in 1980 (1975 prices). This record rise, the highest since the Yom Kippur war in 1973, contrasts sharply with the relative stagnation (a 1.2 per cent rise) which characterized 1980.

The year 1981 saw some decline in Israel's domestic inflation. The consumer price index rose by 101 per cent, equivalent to an average monthly rate of 6.0 per cent. A particularly sharp increase of 146 per cent was recorded in the price index for clothing and footwear. Housing prices went up by 132 per cent. In contrast, food prices increased by only 62 per cent.

The wholesale price index for industrial output rose by 105 per cent, the residential building inputs index increased by 109 per cent and the agricultural inputs price index rose by 96 per cent. One of the main factors behind this rise was the Government's economic policies, which included reductions in the rates of indirect taxes at the beginning of the year, as well as fairly heavy subsidizing of certain basic commodities for a prolonged period.

The Israeli currency's devaluation contributed to (and was influenced by) the consumer price index rise. The Israeli shekel (IS) depreciated in value by 45 per cent against the Bank of Israel's "basket" of five foreign currencies. Its devaluation was most pronounced *vis-à-vis* the U.S. dollar (52 per cent) and the Swiss franc (51 per cent). Its value fell by 40 per cent against the pound sterling and by 39 per cent *vis-à-vis* the French franc. On May 1st, 1982, the Israeli shekel was worth U.S. $0.048, £0.027 and DM 0.115.

Real wages rose during 1981 by approximately 8 per cent compared with 1980. Since a reduction of taxes ensued from a broadening of the income tax brackets, disposable income rose by about 12 per cent, while public consumption rose by nearly 8 per cent.

The general weakness in the labour market (although far from European levels), prevalent since the beginning of 1980, continued during the year under review. The unemployment rate rose during 1981 to reach 5.2 per cent, a proportion higher than in previous years. The fact that economic recovery and a rise in unemployment took place simultaneously suggests an improvement in productivity and more efficient use of capital assets.

Measured in current dollar terms, Israel's balance of payments deficit grew by about $500 million. The trade deficit, on the contrary, declined during 1981 by 2.6 per cent and totalled $2,517 million, compared with $2,385 million in the previous year.

The year 1981 witnessed a continuation of the slump in investment which characterized the previous year. Gross domestic fixed capital formation during 1981 declined by nearly 3 per cent and contributed only about 20 per cent of the G.N.P., compared with higher rates in the years following 1973. Investment in machinery and equipment of local manufacturers, however, picked up considerably during 1981.

AREA AND POPULATION

The total area of the State of Israel within its 1949 armistice frontiers amounts to 20,700 sq. km. This compares with the area of Palestine under British mandate which totalled 27,090 sq. km. By January 31st, 1982, the population of Israel proper was 3,980,900, 83.4 per cent of whom were Jews. In addition, there were about 1 million persons in the areas brought under Israeli administration as a result of the 1967 war, the Golan being annexed at the beginning of 1982 and Sinai evacuated at the end of April 1982.

The population density of Israel was 195.5 per square kilometre at the end of 1981. The population is heavily concentrated in the coastal strip, with about three-quarters of the Jewish and nearly two-thirds of the non-Jewish population located between Ashkelon and Naharia. The Tel-Aviv—Jaffa area, which had a population of 1,005,000 on December 31st, 1980, accounts for 25.6 per cent of the total population. A further 20.1 per cent live in the central area between Tel-Aviv and Jerusalem, 14.4 per cent around Haifa, 12.1 per cent in the southern district, 15 6 per cent in the northern area and 11.4 per cent around Jerusalem. Large desert areas are uninhabited except for nomadic Bedouin tribes numbering about 58,600 people in 1980. Approximately 87 per cent of the population was classified as urban in 1981, the urban population being made up of approximately 2,967,900 Jews and 433,600 non-Jews.

The main reason for the growth of the Jewish population was immigration, accounting for 58 per cent of the yearly increase in the Jewish population between 1948 and 1977. On December 31st, 1980, 41.0 per cent of the Jewish population had been born abroad. Of these, 55.7 per cent were born in Europe and America, 23.2 per cent in Africa and 20.1 per cent in Asia. Of the 1,835,300 Israeli-born Jews, 25 per cent were second generation Israelites. Immigration up to 1948 totalled 452,158 persons, of whom nearly 90 per cent came from Europe and America. The biggest wave of immigrants—over 576,000—arrived during the first six years of the new State. These were refugees from war-torn Europe, followed by Jews emigrating from the Arab States. Large numbers have come from North Africa as a result of political developments there and during 1955–64 a total of over 200,000 emigrated from Africa into Israel. Since 1956 immigration from Eastern Europe has been resumed. In the mid-1960s immigration declined, falling from 54,716 in 1964 to 14,327 in 1967, but the level of immigration picked up considerably after the 1967 war, bringing the total numbers of immigrants between 1965 and 1974 to over 300,000. Almost 70 per cent of these came from Europe and America. After the Yom Kippur war immigration dropped once more, falling from 54,886 in 1973 to 31,979 in 1974, and again to 19,754 in 1976. In 1981 immigrants totalled 12,600. With emigration running at about 18,000 per year, the decline of immigration posed a serious threat to the Israeli economy, which had always depended on an increasing supply of manpower to stimulate growth.

The Jewish birth rate was 21.2 per thousand in the first ten months of 1981, compared with a rate of 33.8 for non-Jews, but the infant mortality rate was much higher for the latter. The total yearly rate of increase (including immigration) of the Jewish population was only 2.0 per cent in 1975, compared with 3.1 per cent in 1973 and a peak annual rate of increase of 23.7 per cent during 1949–51.

The Israeli civilian labour force at the end of 1981 (seasonally adjusted) totalled 1,290,500 or 47.4 per cent of the population aged 14 years and over, and was made up of roughly 36 per cent women and 63 per cent men. The growth in the labour force from 735,800 in 1960 has been due chiefly to the rise in total population, since the participation rate has declined slightly.

An important characteristic is the relatively high proportion of dependants in the population, with one-third aged 14 years and under. As a result of this, the ratio of the labour force to total population—under 35 per cent—is low by European and American standards. Unemployment affected 5.1 per cent of the labour force in 1981, a 6 per cent rise over 1980, and totalled 46,000 individuals.

On December 31st, 1981, of 1,293,200 employees, some 75,000 were employed in agriculture, forestry and fishing; 301,200 in mining and manufacturing; 14,500 in electricity and water; 81,600 in construction; 151,200 in commerce, restaurants and hotels; 87,000 in transport, storage and communications; 112,000 were engaged in financing and business services; 384,200 in public and community service, and the rest (75,400) in personal and other services.

AGRICULTURE

The agriculture sector is relatively small, accounting for just under 6 per cent of domestic product and employing 6 per cent of the labour force. In spite of this, Israeli agriculture has attracted a great deal of international attention. Agriculture, more than any other sector of the economy, has been the focus of ideological pressure. For centuries Jews in the Diaspora were barred from owning land and the Zionist movement therefore saw land settlement as one of the chief objectives of Jewish colonization. Since the establishment of the State, government agricultural policy has centred chiefly on the attainment of self-sufficiency in foodstuffs, in view of military considerations and Israel's possible isolation from its chief foreign food supplies; on the saving of foreign exchange through import substitution and the promotion of agricultural exports; and on the absorption of the large numbers of immigrants in the agricultural sector. In line with these objectives, the promotion of mixed farming and of co-operative farming settlements has also been an important element in government policy. Although the increase in agricultural production has resulted in Israel becoming largely self-sufficient in foodstuffs—it is seriously deficient only in grains, oils and fats—and important savings have been made in foreign exchange, government intervention in the agricultural sector has been criticized as having resulted in a misallocation of resources and in impairment of the economic efficiency of agriculture.

Cultivation has undergone a profound transformation and from an extensive, primitive and mainly dry-farming structure it has developed into a modern intensive irrigated husbandry. A special feature of Israel's agriculture is its co-operative settlements which have been developed to meet the special needs and challenges encountered by a farming community new both to its surroundings and its profession. While there are a number of different forms of co-operative settlements, all are derived from two basic types: the *moshav* and the *kibbutz*. The *moshav* is a co-operative smallholders' village. Individual farms in any one village are of equal size and every farmer works his own land to the best of his ability. He is responsible for his own farm, but his economic and social security is ensured by the co-operative structure of the village, which handles the marketing of his produce, purchases his farm and household equipment, and provides him with credit and many other services. On December 31st, 1980, 143,700 people inhabited 400 *moshavim*.

The *kibbutz* is a collective settlement of a unique form developed in Israel. It is a collective enterprise based on common ownership of resources and on the pooling of labour, income and expenditure. Every member is expected to work to the best of his ability; he is paid no wages but is supplied by the *kibbutz* with all the goods and services he needs. The *kibbutz* is based on voluntary action and mutual liability, equal rights for all members, and assumes for them full material responsibility. On December 31st, 1980, 255 *kibbutzim* were inhabited by 111,200 people (2.8 per cent of the total population.)

During the years following the establishment of the State a large-scale expansion of the area under cultivation took place. This was caused by the heavy influx of immigrants and the recultivation and rehabilitation of the area from which the Arabs had been forced to flee. The cultivated area increased from 1.6 million dunums in the crop of 1948–49 to over 4.27 million dunums in 1977–78, of which some 1.90 million dunums are irrigated. Total water consumption at present amounts to 1,790 million cubic metres, of which 1,200 million cubic metres is consumed by agricultural users.

Without taking into consideration the cost or availability of irrigation water, it is estimated that the land potential ultimately available for farming under irrigation is 5.3 million dunums, while 4.1 million dunums is the figure given for the area potentially available for dry farming. There are also 8.5 million dunums available for natural pasture and 0.9 million dunums for afforestation.

The main factor limiting agricultural development is not land, but the availability of water. Since on average 800 cubic metres of water are needed per annum to irrigate one dunum of cultivated area, it is obvious that Israel must harness all water resources. For this reason, the Government established a special Water Administration headed by a Water Commissioner who has statutory powers to control and regulate both the supply and the consumption of water.

The Water Administration has been charged, among other tasks, with the implementation of the national water project. The purpose of this project is to convey a substantial part of the waters of the River Jordan and of other water sources from the north to southern Judea and to the Negev, to store excess supplies of water from winter to summer and from periods of heavy rainfall to periods of drought, and to serve as a regulator between the various regional water supply systems. The backbone of the national water project is the main conduit from Lake Tiberias to Rosh Haayin (near Tel-Aviv), known as the National Water Carrier, which has an annual capacity of 320 million cubic metres. Two other large schemes, also in operation, are the Western Galilee-Kishon and the Yarkon-Negev projects. Small desalination plants have been built at Eilat and elsewhere, and will be used more extensively if costs are eventually reduced. Desert farming in the Negev, using brackish water found underground, has achieved considerable success on an experimental basis.

The year from October 1980 to September 1981 (1980/81) witnessed some advance in agricultural production, which rose by 2 per cent in comparison with the previous year. This rise was accompanied by a stability in farmers' input, so that real net production rose by 4 per cent. The prices received by the farmers rose by 8 per cent, less than the rate of increase of farmers' costs and by 3 per cent less than the consumer price index.

In 1980/81 what production reached 176,200 metric tons, a 14 per cent decline in comparison with 1979/80, while potato crops increased by nearly 11 per cent to an output of 167,692 tons. Tomato production rose by 16 per cent and reached 274,340 tons. Avocado production declined by 70 per cent to 8,071 tons, 75 per cent of which was exported, earning $13,816,000; the apple harvest rose by 50 per cent to 131,342 tons; pear production rose even more sharply from 6,265 tons in 1979/80 to 18,500 tons, an increase of over 195 per cent; the banana harvest rose by 8 per cent to 54,450 tons.

Cultivation of citrus fruits is one of the principal agricultural branches and produces the main export crop (U.S. $236 million in 1980/81). The total crop during 1980/81 reached 1,389,673 tons, as in the previous years, but the composition in terms of varieties was modified: fewer "shamouti" oranges and more "late" oranges, grapefruit, lemons, tangerines, and citrons. A Citrus Marketing and Control Board supervises all aspects of the growing and marketing of the fruit, particularly exports. The area under cultivation continued to expand as a result of new plantings; the total fruitbearing area reached 374,300 dunums for the 1979/80 season, and with the stress laid on modern methods and techniques both in the groves and packing houses the yield increases each year.

Chief markets were West Germany, the United Kingdom and France. During the early part of 1978, exports were affected by a strike in the merchant navy, and by the panic caused after Palestinians injected mercury into some oranges in Europe.

Increasing emphasis is being laid on the growing of floral plants. During 1980/81, almost 750 million flowers (of which 420 million were spray carnations) were exported, earning $88.4 million. Today about 45,000 dunums are under glasshouse flower cultivation. The Flower Marketing Board is increasing the number of its packing houses and investing heavily in modern equipment.

Cotton plantations decreased in area by 1 per cent

and reached 621,900 dunums in 1980/81. Fibre lint and seed production rose by 8.7 per cent and totalled 246,600 tons, 26 per cent of which was exported. During 1980/81 Israel exported cotton to the value of $115.4 million, groundnuts to the value of $9.45 million, vegetables and potatoes estimated at $54.3 million and fruit with an estimated value of $21.6 million. This category included apples and stone-fruit (mainly avocado), sub-tropical fruits and grapes.

After a shortfall in milk production in 1973 (when production totalled 295 million litres against a demand of 550 million litres), production returned to normal. In 1980/81 it reached 657.5 million litres, a rise of 2 per cent in comparison with 1979/80 production, which was almost identical to that of the previous year.

In the poultry sector, egg production declined during 1980/81 by 11 per cent and totalled 1,073.7 million. In the same year poultry meat totalled 185,229 tons; this sector has been affected for two years by excess production because of the slight difference between the price of poultry meat and that of frozen imported cattle meat, resulting in a preference for the latter. The Ministry of Agriculture discouraged investment in the poultry sector in order to check too much accelerated development.

During 1980/81 beef meat production (live weight) totalled 29,059 tons, a decline of 13 per cent. Fish production reached 17,614 tons during that year.

CONSTRUCTION AND INDUSTRY

As a unit, construction is the leading sector in Israel since it constitutes 14 per cent of G.N.P., which totalled 233,933 million shekels in 1981, and 65.6 per cent of gross investment. Together with affiliated industries, (cement, wood, glass, ceramics), its part in the G.N.P. comes to 20 per cent. During 1981 there were 4,910,000 sq. metres of building area completed, of which 1,700,000 sq. metres were public buildings and 3,210,000 sq. metres private. These data mark a sharp decline since 1976, when total building reached a peak of 7,230,000 sq. metres of building area begun and completed. At the end of 1981, there were some 82,700 persons employed in this industry, a 4.1 per cent rise in comparison to 1980.

Israel derives more of its national income—some 30 per cent—from industry than does any other Middle Eastern country. In the period 1968–77 industrial production rose by 85 per cent. Gross domestic capital formation in machinery and equipment declined from IS824 million in 1970 to 743 million shekels at 1975 prices (17,210 million shekels in current prices), but constituted a rise of 11.7 per cent over 1980. Industrial growth was particularly vigorous after 1967. Output in the period 1968–72 in real terms rose by 80 per cent while exports rose over five years by 124 per cent. The expansion was particularly rapid in the more sophisticated industries—electrical and electronic equipment, transport equipment, machinery, metal and polished diamonds. Value of industrial exports rose by 26 per cent during 1974, but declined the following year.

In 1980 there were 11,199 establishments which engaged employees whose number totalled 275,800. Of these establishments 273 engaged between 100 and 300 persons and 154 more than 300 persons. In the latter category 127,800 were employed. On the other hand, 6,054 establishments engaged four or less persons, and 2,037 between five and nine persons; 10,815 establishments belonged in 1980 to the private sector, 314 to the Histadrut (Trade Union Syndicat) and 70 to the public sector (mainly Government companies). The main branches of these establishments were: metal products 2,471; wood and its products 1,783; clothing and made-up textiles 1,153; food, beverages and tobacco 1,044.

Israel's industry originally developed by supplying such basic needs as soap, oil and margarine, bread, ice, printing and electricity. It used raw materials available locally to produce citrus juices and other citrus by-products, canned fruit and vegetables, cement, glass and bricks. In order to save foreign exchange, imports of manufactured goods were curtailed, thus giving local industry the opportunity of adding local labour value to the semi-manufactures imported from abroad.

To stimulate investment and encourage the inflow of foreign capital the Law for the Encouragement of Capital Investments was enacted in 1950, broadened in 1959 and amended in 1967 and 1977. The Law sets up an Investment Centre and provides for the approval of projects contributing to the development of industrial potential, the exploitation of natural resources, the creation of new sources of employment —particularly in development areas—and to the absorption of new immigrants. Among the concessions granted to approved projects, particularly those financed in foreign currency, are remittance of profits and withdrawal of capital, and tax benefits in respect of income tax, indirect taxes and depreciation allowances.

Although most of Israel's industrial production still goes for home consumption, industrial exports (excluding diamonds) constituted about 68 per cent of total exports in 1981. Here again there has been a very rapid expansion as a result of tax and investment incentives from the Government. Israeli industrial exports, worth $18 million in 1950, had risen to $780 million by 1971, and by 1981 had reached $5,037.5 million.

Israel's most important industrial export product is diamonds, most of the expertise for the finishing of which was supplied by immigrants from the Low Countries. In 1980 Israel exported some $1,397.1 million worth of diamonds; the country's share of international trade in polished diamonds has risen to 30 per cent and as high as 80 per cent in medium-sized stones, in which she specializes. During 1980 precious stones and pearls earned $80 million.

Apart from diamonds (which account for 25 per cent of industrial exports, net exports constituting only 20 per cent), industrial exports were constituted of 6.7 per cent food stuffs; 8 per cent textiles, clothing and leather; 4.1 per cent mining and quarrying products; 17 per cent chemical and oil products;

ISRAEL

30 per cent metal products, machinery and electrical and electronic equipment. The figures show clearly the trend of an increase in metal and electrical products and a parallel decline in all other branches.

Israel Aircraft Industries, employing some 20,000, is Israel's largest single industrial enterprise. At its main plant adjacent to Lod Airport it produces the Kfir combat and multi-mission aircraft, the Arava, a twin-turboprop passenger/cargo transport, the Commodore Jet, a 10-place twin-jet executive aircraft, the Gabriel sea-to-sea missile, as well as other weapons.

The food, beverage and tobacco industries accounted in 1980 for about 13 per cent of manufactures. About 90 per cent of output is sold on the local market; the rest, such as juices, wines, chocolate and coffee, goes abroad. Exports totalled $337.8 million during 1981.

The textiles and clothing industry, which was developed chiefly because of its low capital-labour ratio, constituted 12 per cent of industrial production during 1981, when it exported goods worth some $395.4 million.

There is also a rapidly expanding electronics industry, specializing in equipment for military and communications purposes. Exports by this sector and by that of metal products and machinery rose from $12.8 million in 1970 to $1,494.8 million in 1981.

In view of the heavy power needs of irrigation and the water installations, agriculture as well as industry is a large-scale consumer of electricity. Total installed generating capacity at the end of 1980 was 2,737 megawatts, and generation in 1980 totalled 12,528.3 million kWh. Out of 10,796.1 million kWh total sales of electricity, industry used 3,772.6 million kWh. Total water production during 1979 reached 1,790 million cubic metres, of which industry used 6 per cent while agriculture consumed 74 per cent.

MINERALS

The Petroleum Law of 1952 regulates the conditions for the granting of licences for oil prospecting, divides the country into petroleum districts and fixes a basic royalty of 12.5 per cent. Oil was discovered in 1955 at the Heletz-Bror field on the coastal plain and later at Kokhav, Brur and Negba. Signs of .oil were also discovered near Ashdod. About 34 wells in Israel are now producing, and their output was 23,800,000 litres in 1979. From the time of the 1967 war to the 1975 disengagement agreement, Israel was able to exploit the oil resources of the Sinai and, during 1978–79, those of the Suez Gulf (Alma Fields).

Output of gas from Rosh-Zohar in the Dead Sea area, Kidod, Hakanaim and Barbur is transported through a 29 km. 6-inch pipeline to the Dead Sea potash works at Sodom and through a 49 km. 4-inch and 6-inch line to towns in the Negev and to the Oron phosphate plant. Production totalled 150.1 million cubic metres in the first nine months of 1981, a 59 per cent rise over the corresponding period in 1980.

Lacking large resources of fuel and power, Israel is very dependent on imports of petroleum and petro-

leum products, which rose in value from $210.6 million in 1973 to $597 million the following year, and reached $1,676 million in 1981, at current prices. During 1981 petroleum constituted 20 per cent of all goods imports (or 70 per cent of the trade deficit). Most imported crude oil is refined at the Haifa oil refinery, which has a capacity of over 6.0 million tons per year.

The Dead Sea, which contains .potash, bromides, magnesium and other salts in high concentration, is the country's chief source of mineral wealth. The potash works on the southern shore of the Dead Sea are owned by Dead Sea Works Ltd. The works are linked by road to Beersheba, from where a railway runs northward. Phosphates are mined at Oron in the Negev, and in the Arava. During the first nine months of 1981 Israel produced 23,173 tons of ammonium sulphate, 7,699 tons of potassium sulphate, 223,200 tons of sulphuric acid, 25,776 tons of chlorine, 41,882 tons of polyethylene, and 3,327 tons of potassium carbonate.

At Timna, in the southern Negev near Eilat, geological surveys have located proven reserves of 20 million tons of low-grade copper ore (about 1.5 per cent Cu). The building of a mill to make use of these ores and for producing copper-cement was completed in 1958. The ore was mined by open cast and underground methods until 1975 when copper production from the Timna complex totalled 8,000 tons. Due to the fall of the copper prices in the world markets, and following accumulated losses, the Government closed the mines in 1976 (copper imports during 1980 were worth $ 50.5 million).

FINANCE

Monetary expansion developed rapidly (10 per cent in real terms) during 1981, as in the previous year. The value of financial assets held by the public during the latter half of 1981 rose by about 8 per cent per month, while prices rose by 6.5 per cent, which meant a real gain of nearly 1 per cent per month, the same as in 1980 and in the first half of 1981.

Towards the end of the year, liquid financial assets contracted, in real terms, but this apparently did not imply a loss of purchasing power but rather a transfer of liquidity to foreign currency saving schemes and to shares whose liquidity increased. The rate of expansion of financial assets held by the public is influenced mainly by the following factors: government activity, increase of short-term bank credit, balance-of-payments differential payments on linked assets and banks' operations in the share market.

The excess demand in the public sector was paid for partially from the proceeds of special saving schemes launched during the year, by recourse to bank credit and from tax receipts, with a widening expenditure gap as a consequence. That gap reached its peak in June (during the election campaign). The real level of government excess demand in the latter half of 1981 was some 45 per cent higher than in the previous six months.

Bank credit made available for the financing of domestic economic activities during 1981 exceeded the guideline established by the Bank of Israel, following the real reduction in credit that occurred in 1980. The expansion of bank credit was especially prominent in the second quarter of the year, during which the U.S. dollar, to which certain of the credit ceilings had become linked, appreciated at an accelerated rate against the shekel. These developments led the Bank of Israel to establish lower ceilings for the volume of non-directed credit, and less favourable terms on which export credits were to be made available.

During the second half of 1981 the Bank of Israel maintained its policy of restricting the growth of short-term bank credit, setting a nominal expansion limit of 5.5 per cent per month, the intention being to curb anticipated inflation, since the government budget assumed a monthly price rise of 6 per cent. Credit restriction and the high real interest rates contributed to the limited demand by the business sector for stock renewal and investment.

The expansionary influences at work during 1981 manifested themselves in the rapid building up of financial assets held by the public, in general, and its share holding in particular. The value of share portfolios increased in real terms by some 6 per cent per month, and by the end of 1981 represented 32 per cent of aggregate financial assets. The increased weight of share holdings was due to a real rise in share values and to new issues.

Industrial shares rose from a level of 100 (base at December 31st, 1980) to 226.5 a year later; insurance company equities reached a level of 181.0, and mortgage banks and commercial banks attained levels of 203.7 and 268.4 respectively. General overall annual yield returned by equities totalled 153.8 per cent during 1981. Prominent among the factors behind the boom in the stock market was the public's substantial liquidity accumulation, resulting from the massive government infusion.

In 1981 imports of goods and services (worth U.S. $15,300 million) exceeded exports by U.S. $4,400 million (in 1980 the deficit totalled U.S. $3,900 million). The main reason for the deficit increase was the rise in defence imports (U.S. $2,200 million in 1981, compared with $1,700 million in 1980) and the rise in interest payments. About 76 per cent of the 1981 deficit was financed by transfer payments. These transfer payments were composed of compensation payments from Germany, other personal remittances, institutional remittances and, principally, intergovernmental transfer payments, and totalled $2,900 million. The remainder of the deficit was financed by an increase in liabilities. Thus, at the end of September 1981 the state's debt in foreign currency amounted to U.S. $22,712 million, compared with $21,339 million a year earlier.

TRADE

The performance of Israel's foreign trade during 1981 was influenced by several factors: a slowing down in the economic growth rates of the U.S.A. and of European countries, which resulted in declines in the prices which exports could fetch; continued crisis in the local diamond trade, as well as a reduction in the availability of credit—imports of rough diamonds declined by $590.6 million to reach $529.1 million and net exports of polished diamonds decreased $341.9 million to total $1,067 million during 1981; the depreciation of the major European currencies against the dollar meant an appreciation of the Israeli shekel in real terms (as mentioned above), which reduced the profitability of exports to, and encouraged imports from, Europe; the relatively low price of fuel that prevailed during the year under review.

Israel's net exports of merchandise in 1981 totalled $5,317 million, compared with $5,294 million in 1980. This nominal stability is explained by a 3 per cent growth in exports accompanied by an equal decrease in export prices. Excluding diamonds from the calculations, the value of Israel's total exports rose by 10 per cent. To alleviate the negative effect of other currencies' depreciation (in real terms) *vis-à-vis* the Israeli shekel, an exchange rate insurance scheme (abolished during the liberalization of 1977), designed to protect exporters, was introduced during 1981.

In 1981 the surplus of imports over exports totalled $2,517 million (in current prices), compared with $2,581 million in 1980 and $3,083 million in 1979. This stability in the trade deficit (a 2.6 per cent decrease) resulted from a $30 million decline in merchandise imports and a $37 million rise in exports. (Data do not include figures for the Administered Territories.) Net merchandise imports during 1981 totalled $7,845 million, compared with $7,875 million in 1980. Stability is due mainly to a sharp decline ($600 million) in imports of rough diamonds. In 1981 rough diamonds constituted 7 per cent of total merchandise imports, against a 14 per cent share in 1980. The value of fuel imports decreased by $60 million.

Imports of consumption goods in 1981 rose by 40 per cent in comparison with 1980. Excluding rough diamonds and fuel, imports rose by 11 per cent. Imports of investment goods (excluding ships and aircraft) remained unchanged. Net merchandise exports totalled $5,317 million in 1981, in comparison with $5,294 million in 1980 and $4,313 million in 1979. During 1981 industrial and agricultural exports (excluding polished diamonds) both rose by 9 per cent, while diamond exports declined by 24 per cent. Industrial exports (excluding diamonds) totalled $3,628 milloin in 1981 ($3,340 million in 1980). The 9 per cent increase is due to a 21 per cent rise in exports of electronics and machinery, a 21 per cent rise in mining products and a 13 per cent rise in food exports. On the other hand, textile exports declined by 17 per cent and sales of chemicals and plastics decreased by 2 per cent. Diamond exports totalled $5,037.5 million. Agricultural exports came to $606.1 million. Israel's trade deficit in 1981 thus attained $2,517 million (in current prices).

The focus of Israel's foreign trade is mainly the EEC and North America (during the first ten months of 1981, 57 per cent of total exports was destined for these countries), but efforts are being made to penetrate Central and South America. In November 1976 a financial and economic protocol was settled between Israel and the EEC, providing for the progressive dismantling of all tariff and quota barriers on industrial goods. On agricultural goods, the EEC agreed to cut tariffs on some 85 per cent of Israeli exports. In this domain, some difficulties (relative to agricultural exports) arise, following Greece's entry to the EEC in 1981 and the signing of a similar protocol with Spain and Portugal.

BANKING, TRANSPORT, COMMUNICATIONS AND TOURISM

Israel possesses a highly developed banking system, consisting of the central bank (Bank of Israel), 26 commercial banks and credit co-operatives, 16 mortgage banks, and other financial institutions. Nevertheless three bank-groups—namely Bank Leumi group, Bank Ha-Poalim and Bank Discount hold 92 per cent of the total assets of the banking system. Their subsidiaries are represented all over the world and enjoy a growing reputation; due to devaluation their share in the consolidated balance sheet is increasing markedly. Long-term credits are granted by mortgage banks, the Israel Agricultural Bank, the Industrial Development Bank and the Maritime Bank. In December 1981 the amount of outstanding credit allocated by the banks to the public reached the sum of 137,524.1 million shekels in Israeli and foreign currency.

The function of the Central Bank is to issue currency (and commemorative coins), to accept deposits from banking institutions and extend temporary advances to the Government, to act as the Government's sole fiscal and banking agent and to manage the public debt. Its Governor supervises the liquidity position of the commercial banks and regulates the volume of bank advances.

The continued severance of nearly all lines of communication with her Arab neighbours (except Egypt and the open bridges on the Jordan River) has not only intensified Israel's dependence on maritime and air communications, but has also given great impetus to the establishment of a national merchant marine and airline.

Since 1949, Israel has operated its own international air carrier—El-Al Israel National Airlines Ltd. Regular scheduled services to West Europe, U.S.A., Canada, Cyprus, Romania and parts of Africa and Asia are maintained. In 1976 a new private company—CAL, which specializes in cargo air transportation to Europe, was constituted. In addition some 14 international airlines call at Ben Gurion Airport, Lod (Lydda), near Tel-Aviv. The number of passengers carried in 1980/81 reached 2,849,000. Israel's merchant navy has been undergoing expansion, while the passenger fleet has been practically abolished. The number of ships under the Israeli flag in 1980 totalled 100. Their gross tonnage was 2,463,000. Israel Shipyards Ltd. at Haifa can build ships up to 10,000 dwt. In the north, the port of Haifa and its Kishon harbour extension provide Israel's main port facilities. The south is served by the port of Eilat—Israel's only non-Mediterranean port at the head of the Gulf of Aqaba, and mainly by the new deep water port at Ashdod, some 30 miles south of Tel-Aviv. Gaza port assures the needs of the Gaza Strip.

By 1980/81 Israeli railways operated some 516 km. of main lines and 314 km. of branch lines. The service extends from Nahariya, north of Haifa to Jerusalem and Tel-Aviv and then southwards through Beersheba. In 1965 it reached Dimona and in 1970 the phosphate works at Oron; the construction of a huge bridge over Tsin Valley will enable the extension to Eilat. Traction is wholly by diesel locomotives. In the budget year 1980/81 traffic consisted of 3.42 million passengers and 5.39 million tons of freight.

Roads are the chief means of transport. In 1980 there were some 11,810 km. of paved roads, of which 3,383 km. were inter-urban, out of which 250 km. were four or more lane motorways. Travelling them in 1980 were 405,007 private vehicles, about 10 per cent of the Israeli population, and 7,062 buses.

The drop in the number of tourists entering Israel which began in 1973 (a slowdown had already been recorded in the second half of 1972), continued in 1975, but at a more moderate rate of 0.8 per cent; 1976 witnessed a recovery, and the number of tourists rose, reaching 1,175,800 in 1980, although a slight drop to 1,137,055 was recorded in 1981.

Overall administration of Israeli tourism is sponsored by the Ministry of Tourism which maintains 20 offices abroad. It is also in charge of regulating tourist services in Israel, including arrangement of "package" tours and the provision of multilingual guides. In 1976 the Ministry promoted the inauguration of charter-flights from the U.S. and Europe to Israel. During 1980, 1,956 charter-flights landed in Israel, bringing some 585,051 passengers into the country. Telephone lines numbered 1,230,000 in 1980. They are connected to 143 exchanges, 36 of which are mobile.

STATISTICAL SURVEY

AREA AND POPULATION

Area	Population October 1981	Birth Rate (per '000) 1980	Marriage Rate (per '000) 1980	Death Rate (per '000) 1980
20,325 sq. km.*	3,968,300	24.3†	7.7†	6.7†

* 7,848 square miles.

† These figures include the population of the Old City of Jerusalem and the surrounding areas (area 70 sq. km.), which Israel annexed in 1967.

ADMINISTERED TERRITORIES*

	Area (sq. km.)	Population (June 1981)
Golan	1,150	n.a.
Judea and Samaria .	5,879	723,800
Gaza Strip (incl. El-Arish) .	378	} 452,900
Sinai	61,181	
Total . .	68,588	n.a.

* The area and population of the Administered Territories have changed as a result of the October 1973 war.

The area figures in this table refer to October 1st, 1973. No later figures are available.

POPULATION OF CHIEF TOWNS*

(January 1981)

Jerusalem (capital)	.	407,100	Ramat Gan .	120,300
Tel-Aviv—Jaffa	.	334,900	Petach-Tikva .	119,800
Haifa	.	230,000	Beersheba .	109,600
Holon	.	130,900	Bene Beraq .	91,400

*Provisional.

GROWTH OF POPULATION AND JEWISH IMMIGRATION, 1967–80

END OF YEAR	PERMANENT POPULATION	JEWS	OTHERS	IMMIGRATION
1967* . . .	2,773,900	2,383,600	390,300	14,327
1968* . . .	2,841,100	2,434,800	406,300	20,544
1969* . . .	2,929,500	2,506,800	422,700	23,510
1970* . . .	3,022,000	2,582,000	440,100	20,624
1971* . . .	3,120,500	2,662,000	458,700	41,930
1972* . . .	3,225,000	2,752,700	472,300	55,888
1973* . . .	3,338,200	2,845,000	493,200	54,886
1974* . . .	3,421,600	2,906,900	514,700	31,979
1975* . . .	3,493,400	2,959,400	533,800	20,028
1976* . . .	3,570,900	3,017,500	553,400	17,092
1977* . . .	3,653,000	3,077,300	575,900	18,641
1978* . . .	3,737,600	3,141,000	596,400	26,394
1979* . . .	3,836,200	3,218,400	617,800	37,222
1980* . . .	3,921,700	3,282,700	639,000	20,428

* These figures exclude the population of the areas administered by Israel since June 1967 (*see* above).

ECONOMICALLY ACTIVE POPULATION
(annual averages, '000 persons aged 14 and over)

	1977	1978	1979	1980
Agriculture, forestry and fishing . . .	72.6	73.9	72.1	79.2
Mining and quarrying	4.4	4.4	5.3	5.8
Manufacturing	273.2	280.6	293.0	288.5
Electricity, gas and water . . .	13.5	13.3	11.4	12.8
Construction	85.0	80.3	82.2	79.2
Trade, restaurants and hotels . .	140.9	143.4	144.7	145.5
Transport, storage and communications .	82.9	82.7	84.5	86.0
Financing and business services . .	83.0	91.4	96.5	102.5
Public and community services . .	322.5	349.9	361.9	367.9
Personal and other services . .	75.4	79.5	76.7	76.8
Activities not adequately defined . .	9.0	13.2	12.7	10.2
TOTAL EMPLOYED . . .	1,159.2	1,213.0	1,240.6	1,254.5
Unemployed	47.4	44.7	36.8	63.6
TOTAL CIVILIAN LABOUR FORCE .	1,206.6	1,257.7	1,277.4	1,318.1

AGRICULTURE
AGRICULTURAL LAND USAGE
('000 dunums)

	1974/75	1975/76	1976/77	1977/78	1978/79	1979/80
Field crops	2,624	2,595	2,662	2,549	2,536	2,593
Fruit incl. citrus . . .	861	870	885	856	876	886
Vegetables, potatoes, etc. . .	368	339	367	402	357	355
Nurseries, flowers, fish ponds, etc.	242	244	239	234	231	229
TOTAL CULTIVATED AREA .	4,095	4,048	4,153	4,041	4,000	4,270

PRINCIPAL CROPS
(production in metric tons, September to August)

	1974/75	1975/76	1976/77	1977/78	1978/79	1979/80
Wheat	243,300	205,500	220,000	169,000	133,200	253,200
Barley	20,600	18,200	16,600	8,000	6,000	29,900
Sorghum	32,200	12,600	13,500	3,000	4,100	32,500
Hay	148,400	140,100	111,100	97,000	87,000	110,000
Groundnuts . . .	18,800	23,500	22,500	21,500	20,500	19,500
Cotton lint . . .	48,800	53,650	64,000	79,200	75,100	79,100
Cottonseed . . .	82,000	87,000	108,000	132,600	124,100	125,000
Sugar beet . . .	259,000	323,600	320,000	116,700	146,700	n.a.
Melons and pumpkins .	134,800	134,800	132,000	144,800	123,300	117,100
Vegetables . . .	609,200	581,100	582,100	673,800	598,800	607,000
Potatoes	163,000	174,700	214,000	221,100	211,000	171,700
Citrus fruit . . .	1,506,000	1,513,350	1,528,100	1,473,800	1,568,700	1,542,700
Grapefruit . . .	416,800	456,450	497,200	461,400	500,400	508,800
Lemons	37,700	37,350	40,800	36,800	50,200	59,100
Oranges: Shamouti .	679,800	648,100	578,500	634,100	663,000	608,200
Lates .	299,700	298,250	329,000	267,700	268,500	277,000
Other varieties . . .	72,000	73,200	82,600	73,800	86,600	89,700
Other fruit	347,950	376,950	370,600	384,200	399,100	413,700
Milk (kl.) (incl. sheep and goat milk)	627,700	704,250	720,000	719,500	737,300	712,200

LIVESTOCK
('ooo head, in Jewish farms)

	1977/78	1978/79	1979/80
Cattle	303	304	294
Poultry*	15,950	15,250	14,750
Sheep	255	238	235
Goats	145	125	124

* Except broilers.

FISHING
(catch in metric tons)

1976/77	1977/78	1978/79	1979/80
24,500	24,500	24,100	24,700

MINING

		1977	1978	1979	1980
Crude petroleum . . .	million litres	31	28	24	23
Natural gas	million cu. metres	57	57	68	142
Phosphate rock . . .	'ooo metric tons	1,218	1,723	2,085.5	2,307

INDUSTRY
SELECTED PRODUCTS

		1977	1978	1979	1980
Wheat flour	'ooo metric tons	460	489	476	455
Refined sugar . . .	,, ,, ,,	33.6	12.4	13.5	n.a.
Margarine . . .	,, ,, ,,	30.6	33.3	34.2	33.6
Wine	'ooo litres	n.a.	20,939	18,479	18,896
Beer	,, ,,	35,347	38,926	40,652	39,437
Cigarettes . . .	metric tons	4,751	4,939	4,855	5,337
Cotton yarn . . .	,, ,,	22,370	20,604	20,182	20,013
Woven cotton fabrics* .	,, ,,	n.a.	n.a.	n.a.	n.a.
Newsprint . . .	,, ,,	16,051	12,443	4,676	4,548
Writing and printing paper .	,, ,,	50,369	56,729	66,689	59,894
Other paper . . .	,, ,,	29,201	31,496	32,421	23,541
Rubber tyres . . .	'ooo	1,720	1,538	1,317	1,242
Sulphuric acid . . .	'ooo metric tons	198	183	226	209
Caustic soda . . .	metric tons	26,836	21,626	25,919	35,268
Cement	'ooo metric tons	1,852	1,996	1,919	2,092
Passenger cars . . .	number	3,896	2,599	3,481	1,649
Commercial vehicles . .	,,	3,485	4,200	5,290	2,329
Electricity . . .	million kWh.	11,106	11,874	12,367	12,528

* Production was 11,640 metric tons in 1975.

FINANCE

100 new agorot (singular: agora) = 1 shekel.
Coins: 1, 5, 10 and 50 agorot.
Notes: 1, 5, 10 and 50 shekels.
Exchange rates (May 1982): £1 sterling = 38.28 shekels; U.S. $1 = 20.82 shekels.
1,000 shekels = £26.12 = $48.03.

Note: The shekel was introduced in February 1980, replacing the Israeli pound at the rate of 1 shekel = I£10. The Israeli pound had been introduced in August 1948, replacing (at par) the Palestine pound, equal to the pound sterling, then worth U.S. $4.03. In September 1949 the Israeli pound was devalued (in line with sterling) to $2.80 and this valuation remained in effect until February 1952. Multiple exchange rates were in operation between February 1952 and mid-1955. The official exchange rate was U.S. $1 = I£1.80 (I£1 = 55.56 U.S. cents) from July 1955 to February 1962; $1 = I£3.00 (I£1 = 33.33 U.S. cents) from February 1962 to November 1967; $1 = I£3.50 (I£1 = 28.57 U.S. cents) from November 1967 to August 1971; $1 = I£4.20 (I£1 = 23.81 U.S. cents) from August 1971 to November 1974; $1 = I£6.00 (I£1 = 16.67 U.S. cents) from November 1974 to June 1975. Since June 1975 the currency has been frequently devalued. In July 1976 the Israeli pound was linked to a "basket" of five currencies of the country's main trading partners, instead of being linked to the U.S. dollar alone, and since October 1977 the currency has been allowed to "float". The average market rate (I£ per U.S. $) was: 4.50 in 1974; 6.39 in 1975; 7.98 in 1976; 10.46 in 1977; 17.47 in 1978; 25.44 in 1979. At the time of the shekel's introduction the exchange rate was $1 = I£39, so the initial rate for the new currency was: $1 = 3.9 shekels. The average rate of shekels per U.S. dollar was: 5.124 in 1980; 11.431 in 1981. The exchange rate was £1 sterling = I£8.40 from February 1962 to August 1971; and £1 sterling = I£10.944 from December 1971 to June 1972.

CENTRAL GOVERNMENT BUDGET
(million shekels, twelve months ending March 31st)

REVENUE	1977/78	1978/79	1979/80	1980/81
Ordinary Budget	6,939.5	10,967.1	23,086.0	50,978.7
Income Tax and Property Tax . .	2,693.1	4,502.8	9,916.2	27,108.4
Customs and Excise . . .	1,248.7	966.2	1,874.9	3,633.5
Purchase Tax	723.8	1,230.5	2,010.8	4,133.3
Employers' Tax . . .	232.3	402.2	938.5	275.0
Value Added Tax . . .	943.4	2,319.4	4,494.4	8,846.1
Other Taxes . . .	253.4	316.8	598.8	1,053.1
Interest	268.5	406.9	1,047.1	1,793.4
Loans	214.2	371.7	654.3	n.a.
Other Receipts . . .	362.1	450.6	1,551.0	4,135.9
Development Budget . . .	6,368.1	9,352.9	19,908.0	46,424.7
Foreign Loans . . .	3,213.9	4,979.5	10,611.3	22,664.4
Internal Loans . . .	1,695.1	4,106.3	6,630.9	19,642.9
Other Receipts . . .	1,459.1	267.1	2,665.8	4,117.4
TOTAL . . .	13,307.6	20,320.0	42,994.0	97,403.4

[*continued on next page*

CENTRAL GOVERNMENT BUDGET—*continued*]

EXPENDITURE	1977/78	1978/79	1979/80	1980/81
Ordinary Budget	10,140.2	15,026.1	31,032.6	71,888.5
Ministry of Finance	71.8	127.8	233.2	548.8
Ministry of Defence	4,624.3	6,010.8	13,988.9	30,962.5
Ministry of Health	297.4	476.7	1,203.0	2,218.6
Ministry of Education and Culture .	858.5	1,426.7	3,021.0	7,026.8
Ministry of Police	173.8	291.9	630.7	1,433.1
Ministry of Labour and Social Welfare	191.2	362.3	666.2	1,652.8
Other Ministries	386.2	471.9	917.4	1,914.9
Interest	1,476.7	2,254.8	3,563.4	10,789.2
Pensions and Compensations . .	102.3	175.5	345.3	1,140.8
Transfer to National Insurance Institute .	473.8	615.9	1,084.4	1,627.6
Transfers to Local Authorities .	466.7	770.4	1,640.8	3,310.7
Subsidies	837.8	1,755.3	3,235.6	7,765.9
Other Expenditures . . .	179.7	285.9	502.8	1,496.8
Development Budget	3,119.7	5,247.3	10,257.4	27,591.2
Agriculture	105.4	259.5	327.2	832.3
Industry, Trade and Tourism . .	163.3	385.2	1,072.8	2,061.9
Housing	459.0	552.7	1,330.5	3,027.8
Public Buildings . . .	159.0	214.6	438.1	714.4
Development of Energy Resources .	42.8	96.9	200.8	349.4
Debt Repayment . . .	1,982.5	3,502.6	5,883.8	18,775.7
Other Expenditures . . .	207.6	235.7	1,004.2	1,829.7
TOTAL . . .	13,259.9	20,273.3	41,290.0	99,479.7

AVERAGE CONSUMER PRICE INDEX
(1970 = 100)

1976	1977	1978	1979	1980	1981
387.6	521.7	785.4	1,400.7	3,235.7	70,500

MONEY SUPPLY
(million shekels at year end)

	1976	1977	1978	1979	1980
Currency held by the public . . .	478	632	878	1,205	2,128
Current deposits	871	1,240	1,837	2,338	4,878
TOTAL MONEY SUPPLY . .	1,349	1,872	2,715	3,543	7,006

EXTERNAL TRADE
(U.S. $ million)
Excluding trade with the administered territories.

	1973	1974	1975	1976	1977	1978	1979	1980
Net imports c.i.f. . .	2,968.6	4,176.5	4,108.7	4,076.6	4,759.9	5,631.0	7,396.5	7,875.1
Net exports f.o.b. . .	1,391.8	1,737.4	1,834.6	2,305.9	2,962.7	3,716.1	4,313.4	5,294.4

PRINCIPAL COMMODITIES
(U.S. $'000)

IMPORTS	1977†	1978	1979	1980
Diamonds, rough . . .	1,011,723	1,246,141	937,602	1,067,723
Boilers, machinery and parts .	432,242	553,632	726,315	708,487
Electrical machinery . .	190,248	274,594	408,033	429,749
Iron and steel . . .	242,320	320,510	423,538	361,123
Vehicles	194,698	295,944	502,834	400,097
Chemicals . . .	291,904	353,293	456,567	425,794
Crude oil . . .	726,947	762,665	1,172,471	1,798,546
Cereals	217,422	221,645	276,351	299,421
Textiles and textile articles .	137,626	174,396	224,565	222,813
Ships, boats, aircraft, etc. . .	94,674	74,482	155,000	12,526

EXPORTS	1977†	1978	1979	1980
Diamonds, worked . . .	1,098,784	1,477,407	1,418,834	1,615,412
Edible fruits . . .	229,794	254,128	320,878	305,580
Textiles and textile articles .	242,945	270,454	404,535	538,598
Fruit and vegetable products .	101,888	119,900	151,134	165,770
Fertilizers . . .	76,549	92,197	123,070	202,670
Organic chemicals . .	80,072	92,364	141,790	184,373
Inorganic chemicals . .	45,614	64,079	90,390	123,553
Iron and steel . . .	261,887	356,863	345,549	390,284
Non-electric machinery .	76,853	92,279	121,445	243,243
Electrical machinery . .	105,128	105,964	129,482	196,902

† Revised.

PRINCIPAL TRADING PARTNERS
(U.S. $ '000)

IMPORTS	1978	1979	1980	EXPORTS	1978	1979	1980
Argentina . .	40,901	83,390	49,486	Australia . .	32,373	39,866	46,625
Austria . . .	29,645	35,471	33,377	Austria . . .	33,737	39,745	55,075
Belgium/Luxembourg	258,835	289,101	404,613	Belgium/Luxembourg	208,431	219,603	237,212
Brazil . . .	16,172	36,350	25,932	Canada . . .	39,967	n.a.	n.a.
Canada . . .	63,479	79,344	80,336	France . . .	180,150	247,140	300,602
Denmark . .	23,247	28,834	27,747	Germany, Fed. Rep.	340,386	n.a.	n.a.
Finland . . .	51,865	60,878	52,665	Greece . . .	43,350	47,786	55,720
France . . .	264,611	336,649	269,988	Hong Kong . .	307,986	247,195	251,099
Germany, Fed. Rep.	589,754	766,593	790,745	Iran . . .	97,078	3,285	n.a.
Italy . . .	282,951	378,800	314,885	Italy . . .	94,359	188,931	285,256
Japan . . .	123,527	169,606	120,380	Japan . . .	181,357	223,390	229,925
Netherlands . .	481,553	205,727	189,553	Netherlands . .	212,787	193,561	248,780
Romania . .	46,028	53,681	48,182	Romania . .	13,931	22,918	34,868
South Africa . .	80,398	152,691	116,922	Singapore . .	28,969	39,692	72,589
Spain . . .	35,200	47,829	39,564	South Africa . .	37,665	48,236	79,107
Sweden . . .	76,617	104,036	74,230	Sweden . . .	41,605	45,981	46,860
Switzerland . .	665,738	702,356	665,365	Switzerland . .	145,981	212,535	305,394
United Kingdom .	539,262	687,571	672,875	Turkey . . .	54,378	35,763	37,811
U.S.A. . . .	1,099,993	1,486,842	1,549,024	United Kingdom .	283,393	397,938	465,544
Uruguay . .	9,613	8,769	4,138	U.S.A. . . .	691,282	757,824	953,853
Yugoslavia . .	17,291	19,226	18,628	Yugoslavia . .	17,937	19,779	34,250

TRANSPORT

RAILWAYS

	1978	1979	1980
Passengers ('000) . .	2,720	2,959	3,300
Freight ('000 metric tons) .	4,559	4,935	5,326

ROAD TRAFFIC, 1980
MOTOR VEHICLES ('000)

Private Cars (incl. Station Wagons) . .	409.5
Trucks, Trailers	89.0
Buses	7.3
Taxis	5.1
Motorcycles, Motorscooters . .	25.4
Other Vehicles	3.2
TOTAL	539.5

SHIPPING
('000 tons)

	1978	1979	1980
Cargo Loaded .	5,200	5,658	6,257
Cargo Unloaded .	5,663	6,786	5,496

* Estimates.

CIVIL AVIATION
(El Al revenue flights only, '000)

	1978	1979	1980
Kilometres flown .	33,926	36,282	31,707
Revenue passenger-km.	5,001,000	5,678,000	5,297,000
Mail (tons) . .	808	814	720

TOURISM

	1976	1977	1978	1979	1980	1981
Tourist arrivals . .	796,598	986,534	1,070,813	1,138,622	1,175,819	1,137,200

COMMUNICATIONS MEDIA
(at December each year)

	1978	1979	1980
Telephones . .	1,035,000	1,100,000*	1,180,000
Daily newspapers . .	27	n.a.	n.a.

*Estimate.

Radio receivers: 750,000 in 1978/79.
TV receivers (number of households): 465,000 in 1978/79.

EDUCATION
(1980/81: provisional figures)

	SCHOOLS	PUPILS		SCHOOLS	PUPILS
JEWISH:			ARAB:		
Kindergarten . . .	n.a.	252,000	Kindergarten . .	n.a.	17,506
Primary schools . .	1,278	434,305	Primary schools . .	298	126,726
Secondary schools .	301	70,780	Secondary schools .	54	18,322
Vocational schools .	313	73,645	Vocational . .	34	3,093
Agricultural schools .	27	4,687	Agricultural schools .	2	748
Teachers' training .	47	11,955	Teachers' training .	2	424
Others (handicapped)	216	12,821	Others (handicapped)	16	889
Intermediate schools	251	76,772	Intermediate schools	45	15,220

Source: Central Bureau of Statistics, Jerusalem.

THE CONSTITUTION

There is no written Constitution. In June 1950, the Knesset voted to adopt a State Constitution by evolution over an unspecified period. A number of laws, including the Law of Return (1950), the Nationality Law (1952), the State President (Tenure) Law (1952), the Education Law (1953) and the "Yad-va-Shem" Memorial Law (1953) are considered as incorporated into the State Constitution. Other constitutional laws are: The Law and Administration Ordinance (1948), the Knesset Election Law (1951), the Law of Equal Rights for Women (1951), the Judges Act (1953), the National Service and National Insurance Acts (1953), and the Basic Law (The Knesset) (1958).

The President

The President is elected by the Knesset for five years.

Ten or more Knesset Members may propose a candidate for the Presidency.

Voting will be by secret ballot.

The President may not leave the country without the consent of the Government.

The President may resign by submitting his resignation in writing to the Speaker.

The President may be relieved of his duties by the Knesset for misdemeanour.

The Knesset is entitled to decide by a two-thirds majority that the President is incapacitated owing to ill-health to fulfil his duties permanently.

The Speaker of the Knesset will act for the President when the President leaves the country, or when he cannot perform his duties owing to ill-health.

The Knesset

The Knesset is the parliament of the State. There are 120 members.

It is elected by general, national, direct, equal, secret and proportional elections.

Every Israeli national of 18 years or over shall have the right to vote in elections to the Knesset unless a court has deprived him of that right by virtue of any law.

Every Israeli national of 21 and over shall have the right to be elected to the Knesset unless a court has deprived him of that right by virtue of any law.

The following shall not be candidates: the President of the State; the two Chief Rabbis; a judge (*shofet*) in office; a judge (*dayan*) of a religious court; the State Comptroller; the Chief of the General Staff of the Defence Army of Israel; rabbis and ministers of other religions in office; senior State employees and senior Army officers of such ranks and in such functions as shall be determined by law.

The term of office of the Knesset shall be four years.

The elections of the Knesset shall take place on the third Tuesday of the month of Cheshven in the year in which the tenure of the outgoing Knesset ends.

Election day shall be a day of rest, but transport and other public services shall function normally.

Results of the elections shall be published within fourteen days.

The Knesset shall elect from among its members a Chairman and Vice-Chairman.

The Knesset shall elect from among its members permanent committees, and may elect committees for specific matters.

The Knesset may appoint commissions of inquiry to investigate matters designated by the Knesset.

The Knesset shall hold two sessions a year; one of them shall open within four weeks after the Feast of the Tabernacles, the other within four weeks after Independence Day; the aggregate duration of the two sessions shall not be less than eight months.

The outgoing Knesset shall continue to hold office until the convening of the incoming Knesset.

The members of the Knesset shall receive a remuneration as provided by law.

The Government

The Government shall tender its resignation to the President immediately after his election, but shall continue with its duties until the formation of a new Government.

After consultation with representatives of the parties in the Knesset, the President shall charge one of the Members with the formation of a Government.

The Government shall be composed of a Prime Minister and a number of Ministers from among the Knesset Members or from outside the Knesset.

After it has been chosen, the Government shall appear before the Knesset and shall be considered as formed after having received a vote of confidence.

Within seven days of receiving a vote of confidence, the Prime Minister and the other Ministers shall swear allegiance to the State of Israel and its Laws and undertake to carry out the decisions of the Knesset.

THE GOVERNMENT

HEAD OF STATE

President: YITZHAK NAVON (took office May 29th, 1978).

THE CABINET
(June 1982)

Prime Minister: MENACHEM BEGIN (Likud-Herut).

Deputy Prime Minister and Minister of Agriculture: SIMCHA EHRLICH (Likud-Liberal).

Deputy Prime Minister and Minister of Housing and Construction: DAVID LEVI (Likud-Herut).

Minister of Foreign Affairs: ITZHAK SHAMIR (Likud-Herut).

Minister of Defence: ARIEL SHARON (Likud-Herut).

Minister of Finance: YORAM ARIDOR (Likud-Herut).

Chief Economic Co-ordinator: YAACOV MERIDOR (Likud-Herut).

Minister of Communications: MORDECHAI ZAPORI (Likud-Herut).

Minister of Transport: HAIM CORFU (Likud-Herut).

Minister without Portfolio: ITZHAK MODAI (Likud-Liberal).

Minister of Energy: ITZHAK BERMAN (Likud-Liberal).

Minister of Justice: MOSHE NISSIM (Likud-Liberal).

Minister of Industry and Trade: GIDEON PATT (Likud-Liberal).

Minister of Tourism: AVRAHAM SHARIR (Likud-Liberal).

Minister of Health: ELIEZER SHOSTAK (Likud-Laam).

Minister of Interior, Police and Religious Affairs: Dr. JOSEF BURG (National Religious Party).

Minister of Education and Culture: ZEVULAN HAMMER (National Religious Party).

Minister of Labour, Social Welfare and Integration of Immigrants: AHARON UZAN.

LEGISLATURE

KNESSET

Speaker: MENACHEM SAVIDOR.

The state of the parties in the 10th Knesset, following the General Election of June 1981, was as follows:

PARTY	VOTES	SEATS	PARTY	VOTES	SEATS
Likud	718,914	48	Techiya	44,700	3
Labour Alignment	708,536	47	Tami	44,466	3
National Religious Party	95,232	6	Telem	30,600	2
Agudat Israel	72,312	4	Change	29,837	2
Communist Party (RAKAH)	64,918	4	Citizens' Rights	27,921	1

POLITICAL PARTIES

Agudat Israel (f. 1912) and **Poalei Agudat Israel** (f. 1924) are Orthodox Judaist parties, the membership of the Poalei Agudat Israel being drawn largely from wage-earners. Agudat Israel supports the Likud-NRP coalition, but Poalei Agudat Israel was in opposition in the Ninth Knesset. Agudat Israel has 4 members in the Tenth Knesset. The official organ of Agudat Israel is the daily *Hamodia*, that of the Poalei Agudat Israel is the daily *Shearim*.

Citizens' Rights Party: breakaway movement from Labour Party; Leader MRS. SHULAMIT ALONI.

Communist Party of Israel (RAKAH): f. 1919; Jewish-Arab membership; favours full implementation of UN Security Council Resolutions 242 and 338, Israeli withdrawal from all Arab territories occupied since 1967, formation of a Palestinian Arab state in the West Bank and Gaza Strip, recognition of national rights of State of Israel

and Palestine people, democratic rights and defence of working class interests, and demands an end of discrimination against Arab minority in Israel and against oriental Jewish communities; publishes *Zo-Haderekh* (Hebrew); *Al-Ittihad* (Arabic); *Der Weg* (Yiddish).

Independent Liberal Party: P.O.B. 23076, Tel-Aviv; f. 1965 by 7 Liberal Party Knesset members after the formation of the Herut Movement and Liberal Party Bloc; 20,000 mems.; Chair. MOSHE KOL; Gen. Sec. NISSIM ELIAD; publs. *Temurot* (Hebrew, monthly), *Die Liberale Rundschau* (German, monthly), *Igeret* (Hebrew, quarterly).

Israel Labour Party: P.O.B. 3263, Tel-Aviv; f. 1968 as a merger of the three Labour groups, Mapai, Rafi and Achdut Ha'avoda; a Zionist democratic socialist party, was in government from 1948 to 1977; together with Mapam is forming the main opposition bloc under name of Labour-Mapam Alignment; Chair. of Israel Labour Party SHIMON PERES; Gen. Sec. HAIM BAR-LEV; Sec.-Gen. of Mapam VICTOR SHEM-TOV.

Likud: Tel-Aviv; f. September 1973; is a parliamentary bloc of Herut, the Liberal Party of Israel (Chair. AVRAHAM SHARIR), Laam (Leader YIGAEL HOROWITZ) and Ahdut (Leader HILLEL SEIDEL); aims: territorial integrity (advocates retention of all the territory of post-1922 mandatory Palestine); absorption of new-comers; a social order based on freedom and justice, elimination of poverty and want; development of an economy that will ensure a decent standard of living; improvement of the environment and the quality of life. Likud has been the government party since June 1977; Leader of Likud MENACHEM BEGIN.

Movement for Change: f. 1974 and restored 1978 when Democratic Movement for Change split into two parties; centrist party; left Begin's coalition in Sept. 1978 at time of split; Leaders AMNON RUBINSTEIN and MORDECAI VIRSHUBSKY.

National Religious Party: f. 1956; stands for strict adher-ence to Jewish religion and tradition, and strives to achieve the application of religious precepts of Judaism in everyday life; it is also endeavouring to establish the constitution of Israel on Jewish religious law; withdrew

from (Labour) government coalition in December 1976 and now supports the Likud coalition, occupying 2 cabinet posts.

Revival Movement: f. August 1979; also known as Renais-sance Party; against any territorial concessions; Leader YUVAL NEEMAN.

Shelli-Israel Peace and Equality Movement: 87 Dizingoff St., Tel-Aviv 64 332; f. 1977; an alliance of patriotic socialist peace groups, which included *Mokked* (Focus), the Independent Socialists, *Ha'olam Hazeh* party and others. In February 1979 these united. Leading per-sonalities in the Exec. Cttee.: Dr. YAAKOV ARNON, Dr. MATITYAHU PELED (Jerusalem), RAM COHEN, YONA-THAN PELED (Hakibbutz Haartzi), ARIEH ELIAV, URI AVNERI, Dr. MEIR PAIL (Tel-Aviv) and Dr. ZVI KULIKOVSKY (Haifa).

Tami: pressure group representing North African Jews; Leader AHARON ABU-HATZEIRA.

Techiya: break-away party from Likud; opposes Camp David agreement.

Telem: party founded by the late MOSHE DAYAN.

United Arab List: Arab party affiliated to Labour Party.

United Workers Party - Mapam: P.O.B. 1777, Tel-Aviv; f. 1948; left-wing Socialist-Zionist party; since January 1969 grouped in Labour-Mapam Alignment with Israel Labour Party.

DIPLOMATIC REPRESENTATION

EMBASSIES AND LEGATIONS ACCREDITED TO ISRAEL

(E) Embassy; (L) Legation.

Argentina: 112 Rehov Hayarkon, 2nd Floor, Tel-Aviv (E); *Ambassador:* ROBERTO TEMPORINI.

Australia: 185 Rehov Hayarkon, Tel-Aviv (E); *Ambassador:* DAVID GOSS.

Austria: 11 Rehov Herman Cohen, Tel-Aviv (E); *Ambas-sador:* Dr. OTTO PLEINERT.

Barbados: London, United Kingdom (E).

Belgium: 266 Rehov Hayarkon, Tel-Aviv (E); *Ambassador:* EDOUARD DECASTIAUX-HUGOT.

Bolivia: Tel-Aviv (E); *Ambassador:* Brig.-Gen. JOSÉ ANTONIO ZELAYA.

Brazil: 14 Hei Be'Yiar, Tel-Aviv (E); *Ambassador:* Dr. VASCO MARIZ.

Burma: 19 Rehov Yona, Ramat Gan (E); *Ambassador:* (vacant).

Canada: 220 Rehov Hayarkon, Tel-Aviv (E); *Ambassador:* JOSEPH STEPHEN STANFORD.

Chile: Tel-Aviv (E); *Ambassador:* Gen. JOSÉ BENDICKEW-SKY.

Colombia: Tel-Aviv (E); *Ambassador:* Dr. MIGUEL DURÁN ORDÓÑEZ.

Costa Rica: Jerusalem (E); *Chargé d'affaires:* FERNANDO GUARDIA ALVARADO.

Denmark: 23 Rehov Bnei Moshe, Tel-Aviv (E); *Ambas-sador:* SVEN A. NIELSEN.

Dominican Republic: Tel-Aviv (E); *Ambassador:* Dr. VÍCTOR RAÚL GIL BATLLE.

Ecuador: Tel-Aviv (E); *Ambassador:* Dr. WILSON VELA HERVAS.

Egypt: 12th Floor, Hilton Hotel, Tel-Aviv (E); *Ambas-sador:* SAAD MURTADA.

El Salvador: Tel-Aviv (E); *Ambassador:* Col. NAPOLEÓN ARMANDO GUERRA.

Finland: 224 Rehov Hayarkon, Tel-Aviv (E); *Ambassador:* (vacant).

France: 112 Tayelet Herbert Samuel, Tel-Aviv (E); *Ambassador:* MARC BONNEFOUS.

Germany, Federal Republic: 16 Rehov Soutine, Tel-Aviv (E); *Ambassador:* KLAUS SCHUETZ.

Greece: 35 Siderot Shaul Hamelech, Tel-Aviv (Diplomatic Representation); *Diplomatic Representative:* EMMANUEL S. SPYRIDAKIS.

Guatemala: Tel-Aviv (E); *Ambassador:* Col. RAMIRO GEREDA ASTURIAS.

Haiti: Tel-Aviv (E); *Ambassador:* ERNST M. REMY.

Honduras: Paris, France (E).

Iceland: Copenhagen, Denmark (E).

Ireland: Athens, Greece (E).

Italy: Asia House, 4 Rehov Weizman, Tel-Aviv (E); *Ambassador:* GIROLAMO NISIO.

Jamaica: Bonn-Bad Godesberg, Federal Republic of Germany (E).

Japan: Asia House, 4 Rehov Weizman, Tel-Aviv (E); *Ambassador:* KAGAO YOSHIDA.

Malawi: London, United Kingdom (E).

Malta: London, United Kingdom (E).

Mexico: 14 Rehov Hei Beiyar, Tel-Aviv (E); *Ambassador:* Dr. ALFONSO L. DE GARAY.

Nepal: Paris, France (E).

Netherlands: Shalom-Meyer Tower, 9 Ahad Ha'am, Floor 3, Tel-Aviv (E); *Ambassador:* CHRISTAAN BENJAMIN ARRIENS.

Nicaragua: Rome, Italy (E).

Norway: 10 Rehov Hei Beiyar, Tel-Aviv (E); *Ambassador:* KNUT AARS.

Panama: 17 Rehov Lipsky, Apt. 12, P.O.B. 21260, Tel-Aviv (E); *Ambassador:* Miss MARINA MAYO M.

Papua New Guinea: London, United Kingdom (E).

Paraguay: Rome, Italy (E).

Peru: 52 Rehov Pinkas, Apt. 31, 8th Floor, Tel-Aviv (E); *Ambassador:* BERNARDO ROCA REG.

Philippines: 14 Rehov Hei Beiyar, Tel-Aviv (E); *Ambassador:* Brig.-Gen. ERNESTO S. GIDAYA.

Romania: 24 Rehov Adam Hacohen, Tel-Aviv (E); *Ambassador:* CONSTANTIN VASILIU.

South Africa: 2 Rehov Kaplan, Tel-Aviv (E); *Ambassador:* DEREK STUART FRANKLIN.

Sweden: 198 Rehov Hayarkon, Tel-Aviv (E); *Ambassador:* TORSTEN ORN.

Switzerland: 228 Rehov Hayarkon, Tel-Aviv (E); *Ambassador:* ERNEST BAUERMEISTER.

Thailand: Rome, Italy (E).

Turkey: 34 Rehov Amos, Tel-Aviv (L); *Minister:* (vacant).

United Kingdom: 192 Rehov Hayarkon, Tel-Aviv (E); *Ambassador:* PATRICK MOBERLY, C.M.G.

U.S.A.: 71 Rehov Hayarkon, Tel-Aviv (E); *Ambassador:* SAMUEL LEWIS.

Uruguay: Tel-Aviv (E); *Ambassador:* Prof. BAUTISTA ETCHEVERRY BOGGIO.

Venezuela: Tel-Aviv (E); *Ambassador:* LUIS LA CORTE.

Israel also has diplomatic relations with the Bahamas, Cyprus, Dominica, Fiji, Grenada, the Republic of Korea, Lesotho, Luxembourg, Monaco, New Zealand, Portugal, Saint Lucia, San Marino, Singapore, Suriname, Swaziland, Tonga, Trinidad and Tobago, Western Samoa and Zaire.

THE JEWISH AGENCY FOR ISRAEL

P.O.B. 92, Jerusalem.

Organization:

The governing bodies are the Assembly which determines basic policy, the Board of Governors which sets policy for the Agency between Assembly meetings and the Executive responsible for the day to day running of the Agency.

Chairman of Executive: ARYE L. DULZIN.

Chairman of Board of Governors: MAX M. FISHER.

Director-General: SHMUEL LAHIS.

Secretary-General: HARRY M. ROSEN.

Functions:

According to the Agreement of 1971, the Jewish Agency undertakes the immigration and absorption of immigrants in Israel, including absorption in agricultural settlement and immigrant housing; social welfare and health services in connection with immigrants; education, youth care and training; neighbourhood rehabilitation through project renewal.

Budget (1979/80): U.S. $405 million.

JUDICIAL SYSTEM

The law of Israel is composed of Ottoman law, British law, Palestine law, applicable in Palestine on May 14th, 1948, when the independence of the State of Israel was declared, the substance of the common law and doctrines of equity in force in England, as modified to suit local conditions, and religious law of the various recognized religious communities as regards matters of personal status, in so far as there is nothing in any of the said laws repugnant to Israeli legislation and subject to such modifications as may have resulted from the establishment of the State of Israel and its authorities, and also of the laws enacted by the Israeli legislature. The pre-1948 law is increasingly being replaced by original local legislation.

CIVIL COURTS

The Supreme Court is the highest judicial instance in the State. It has jurisdiction as an Appellate Court from the District Courts in all matters, both civil and criminal (sitting as a Court of Civil Appeal or as a Court of Criminal Appeal), and as a Court of First Instance (sitting as a High Court of Justice) in matters in which it considers it necessary to grant relief in the interests of justice and which are not within the jurisdiction of any other court or tribunal. This includes applications for orders in the nature of *habeas corpus*, *mandamus*, prohibition and *certiorari*, and enables the court to review the legality of acts of administrative authorities of all kinds.

President of the Supreme Court: I. KAHAN.

Permanent Deputy President of the Supreme Court: M. SHAMGAR.

Justices of the Supreme Court: M. BEN-PORAT, M. EYLON, Y. COHEN, A. BARAK, M. BEISKI, SH. LEVIN, D. LEVIN.

Chief Registrar: Judge D. BARTOV (relieving president District Court).

The District Courts: Jerusalem, Tel-Aviv-Jaffa, Haifa, Beersheba, Nazareth. They have unlimited jurisdiction as Courts of First Instance in all civil and criminal matters not within the jurisdiction of a Magistrates' Court, all matters not within the exclusive jurisdiction of any other tribunal, and matters within the concurrent jurisdiction of any other tribunal so long as such tribunal does not deal with them, and as an Appellate Court in appeals from judgments and decisions of Magistrates' Courts and judgments of Municipal Courts and various administrative tribunals.

Magistrates' Courts: There are 26 Magistrates' Courts, having criminal jurisdiction to try contraventions and misdemeanours, and civil jurisdiction to try actions concerning possession or use of immovable property, or the partition thereof whatever may be the value of the subject matter of the action, and other civil actions where the amount of the claim, or the value of the subject matter, does not exceed I£150,000.

Labour Courts: Established in 1969. Regional Labour Courts in Jerusalem, Tel-Aviv, Haifa and Beersheba, composed of Judges and representatives of the Public. A National Labour Court in Jerusalem, presided over by Judge Z. Bar-Niv. The Courts have jurisdiction over all matters arising out of the relationship between employer and employee; between parties to a collective labour agreement; matters concerning the National Insurance Law and the Labour Law and Rules.

Municipal Courts: There are 5 Municipal Courts, having criminal jurisdiction over any offences against municipal regulations and by-laws and certain other offences, such as town planning offences, committed within the municipal area.

RELIGIOUS COURTS

The Religious Courts are the Courts of the recognized religious communities. They are competent in certain defined matters of personal status concerning members of their community. Where any action of personal status involves persons of different religious communities the President of the Supreme Court will decide which Court shall have jurisdiction. Whenever a question arises as to whether or not a case is one of personal status within the exclusive jurisdiction of a Religious Court, the matter must be referred to a Special Tribunal composed of two Justices of the Supreme Court and the President of the highest court of the religious community concerned in Israel.

The judgments of the Religious Courts are executed by the process and offices of the Civil Courts.

Jewish Rabbinical Courts: These Courts have exclusive jurisdiction in matters of marriage and divorce of Jews in Israel who are Israeli citizens or residents. In all other matters of personal status they have concurrent jurisdiction with the District Courts with the consent of all parties concerned.

Muslim Religious Courts: These Courts have exclusive jurisdiction in matters of marriage and divorce of Muslims who are not foreigners, or who are foreigners subject by their national law to the jurisdiction of Muslim Religious Courts in such matters. In all other matters of personal status they have concurrent jurisdiction with the District Courts with the consent of all parties concerned.

Christian Religious Courts: The Courts of the recognized Christian communities have exclusive jurisdiction in matters of marriage and divorce of members of their communities who are not foreigners. In all other matters of personal status they have concurrent jurisdiction with the District Courts with the consent of all parties concerned. But neither these Courts nor the Civil Courts have jurisdiction to dissolve the marriage of a foreign subject.

Druze Courts: These Courts, established in 1963, have exclusive jurisdiction in matters of marriage and divorce of Druze in Israel, who are Israeli citizens or residents, and concurrent jurisdiction with the District Courts in all other matters of personal status of Druze with the consent of all parties concerned.

MILITARY COURTS

Courts-Martial: A Court-Martial is competent to try a soldier within the meaning of the Military Justice Law, 1955, who has committed an act constituting a military offence, without prejudice to the power of any other Court in the State to try him for that act if it constitutes an offence under any other law. A Court-Martial is also competent to try a soldier for any offence which is not a military offence, but the Attorney General may order that he be tried by another Court if he is of the opinion that the offence was not committed within the framework of the Army or in consequence of the accused's belonging to the Army.

RELIGION

JUDAISM

Judaism, the religion evolved and followed by the Jews, is the faith of the great majority of the population. Its basis is a belief in an ethical monotheism.

There are two main Jewish communities: the Ashkenazim and the Sephardim. The former are the Jews from Eastern, Central, or Northern Europe, while the latter originate from the Balkan countries, North Africa and the Middle East.

The supreme religious authority is vested in the Chief Rabbinate, which consists of the Ashkenazi and Sephardi Chief Rabbis and the Supreme Rabbinical Council. It makes decisions on interpretation of the Jewish law, and supervises the Rabbinical Courts. There are 8 regional Rabbinical Courts, and a Rabbinical Court of Appeal presided over by the two Chief Rabbis.

According to the Rabbinical Courts Jurisdiction Law of 1953, marriage and divorce among Jews in Israel are exclusively within the jurisdiction of the Rabbinical Courts. Provided that all the parties concerned agree, other matters of personal status can also be decided by the Rabbinical Courts.

There are 195 Religious Councils, which maintain religious services and supply religious needs, and about 405 religious committees with similar functions in smaller settlements. Their expenses are borne jointly by the State and the local authorities. The Religious Councils are under the administrative control of the Ministry of Religious Affairs. In all matters of religion, the Religious Councils are subject to the authority of the Chief Rabbinate. There are 365 officially appointed rabbis. The total number of synagogues is about 7,000, most of which are organized within the framework of the Union of Israel Synagogues.

Head of the Ashkenazi Community: The Chief Rabbi SHLOMO GOREN.

Head of the Sephardic Community: The Chief Rabbi OVADIA YOSSEF.

Two Jewish sects still loyal to their distinctive customs are:

The Karaites, a sect which recognizes only the Jewish written law and not the oral law of the Mishna and Talmud. The community of about 12,000 many of whom live in or near Ramla, has been augmented by immigration from Egypt.

The Samaritans, an ancient sect mentioned in 2 Kings xvii, 24. They recognize only the Torah. The community in Israel numbers about 500; about half of them live in Holon, where a Samaritan synagogue has been built, and the remainder, including the High Priest live in Nablus, near Mt. Gerizim, which is sacred to the Samaritans.

ISLAM

The Muslims in Israel are in the main Sunnis, and are divided among the four rites of the Sunni school of Muslim thought: the Shafe'i, the Hanbali, the Hanafi, and the Maliki. Before June 1967 they numbered approximately 175,000; in 1971, approximately 343,900.

Mufti of Jerusalem: Sheikh SAAD ED-DIN AL-ALAMI.

CHRISTIAN COMMUNITIES

The Greek Melkite Church: P.O.B. 279, Haifa; numbers about 41,000 and Haifa is the seat of the Archbishop of Acre, Haifa, Nazareth and all Galilee; Archbishop MAXIMOS SALLOUM; publs. *Ar-Rabita* (Arabic monthly; circ.

4,000), *Message de Galilée* (3 a year in French and Flemish; circ. 2,000).

The Greek Orthodox Church in Israel has approximately 22,000 members. Patriarch of Jerusalem THEODOROS.

The Latin (Roman Catholic) Church has about 10,000 native members in Israel plus about 2,000 Polish and Hungarian Catholic refugees. The Latin Patriarch of Jerusalem is His Beatitude JAMES JOSEPH BELTRITTI; Representative in Israel H.E. Bishop HANNA KALDANY.

The Maronite Community, with 6,350 members, has communal centres in Isfyia, Haifa, Jaffa, Jish, Nazareth and Jerusalem. The Maronite Patriarch, Mgr. JOSEPH

KHOURY, resides in the Lebanon. The Vicar-General, Mgr. AUGUSTIN HARFOUCHE, is resident in Jaffa.

Episcopal Church in Jerusalem and the Middle East, belongs to the Anglican Communion; was reorganized in 1976; has Jerusalem Diocese and also Diocese of Iran, Egypt, Cyprus and the Gulf; Presiding Bishop Rt. Rev. HASSAN DEHQANI-TAFTI, P.O.B. 12, Isfahan, Iran (in exile in Winchester diocese, England).

Other denominations include the *Armenian Church* (900 members), the *Coptic Church* (700 members), the *Russian Orthodox Church*, which maintains an Ecclesiastical Mission, the *Ethiopian Church*, and the *Baptist Lutheran* and *Presbyterian Churches*.

THE PRESS

Tel-Aviv is the main publishing centre, only three dailies being published in Jerusalem. Largely for economic reasons there has developed no local press away from these cities; hence all papers regard themselves as national. Friday editions, Sabbath eve, are increased to up to twice the normal size by special weekend supplements, and experience a considerable rise in circulation. No newspapers appear on Saturday.

Most of the daily papers are in Hebrew, and others appear in Arabic, English, French, Polish, Yiddish, Hungarian and German. The total daily circulation is 500,000–600,000 copies, or twenty-one papers per hundred people, although most citizens read more than one daily paper.

Most Hebrew morning dailies have strong political or religious affiliations. *Al Hamishmar* is affiliated to Mapam, *Hatzofeh* to the National Religious Front—World Mizrahi. *Davar* is the long-established organ of the Histadrut. Mapai publishes the weekly *Ot*. Most newspapers depend on subsidies from political parties, religious organizations or public funds. The limiting effect on freedom of commentary entailed by this party press system has provoked repeated criticism.

The Jerusalem Arabic daily *Al Anba* has a small circulation (10,000) but an increasing number of Israeli Arabs are now reading Hebrew dailies. The daily, *Al Quds*, was founded in 1968 for Arabs in Jerusalem and the West Bank; the small indigenous press of occupied Jordan has largely ceased publication or transferred operations to Amman.

There are around 400 other newspapers and magazines including some 50 weekly and 150 fortnightly; over 250 of them are in Hebrew, the remainder in eleven other languages.

The most influential and respected dailies, for both quality of news coverage and commentary, are *Ha'aretz* and the trade union paper, *Davar*, which frequently has articles by government figures. These are the widest read of the morning papers, exceeded only by the popular afternoon press, *Ma'ariv* and *Yedioth Aharonoth*. The *Jerusalem Post* gives detailed and sound news coverage in English.

The Israeli Press Council, established in 1963, deals with matters of common interest to the Press such as drafting the code of professional ethics which is binding on all journalists.

The Daily Newspaper Publishers' Association represents publishers in negotiations with official and public bodies, negotiates contracts with employees and purchases and distributes newsprint, of which Israel now manufactures 75 per cent of her needs.

DAILIES

Al-Anba: P.O.B. 428, 3, Ohaleh Yossef St., Jerusalem; f. 1968; published by Jerusalem Publications Ltd.; Arabic; Editor OVADIA DANON; circ. 10,000.

Al Hamishmar (*The Guardian*): Al Hamishmar House, 4 Ben Avigdor St., Tel-Aviv; f. 1943; morning; organ of the United Workers' Party (Mapam); Editor MARK GEFEN; circ. 25,000.

Al Quds (*Jerusalem*): P.O.B. 19788, Jerusalem; f. 1968; Arabic; Editor ABU ZALAF.

Al Sha'ab: Jerusalem; Arabic; Editor ALI YA'ISH.

Chadshot Hasport: Tushia St., P.O.B. 20011, Tel-Aviv 61200; f. 1954; Hebrew; sports; independent; circ. 30,000.

Davar (*The Word*): P.O.B. 199, 45 Sheinkin St., Tel-Aviv; f. 1925; morning; official organ of the General Federation of Labour (Histadrut); Editor HANNAH ZEMER; circ. 50,000; there are also weekly magazine editions.

Ha'aretz (*The Land*): 21 Salman Schocken St., Tel-Aviv; f. 1918; morning; liberal, independent; Editor GERSHOM G. SCHOCKEN; circ. 55,000 (weekdays), 75,000 (weekends).

Hamodia: Kikar Hacheruth, P.O.B. 1306, Jerusalem; organ of Agudat Israel; morning; Editor YEHUDA L. LEVIN; circ. 8,000.

Hatzofeh: 66 Hamasger St., Tel-Aviv; f. 1938; morning; organ of the National Religious Front; Editor M. ISHON; circ. 16,000.

Israel Nachrichten: 52 Harakevet St., Tel-Aviv; f. 1974; morning; German; Editor S. HIMMELFARB; circ. 20,000.

Israelski Far Tribuna: 113 Givat Herzl St., Tel-Aviv; Bulgarian.

Jerusalem Post: P.O.B. 81, Romema, 91000, Jerusalem; f. 1932; morning; independent; English; Editor and Man. Dir. ARI RATH; Editor ERWIN FRENKEL; circ. 30,000 (weekdays), 47,000 (weekend edition); there is also a weekly international edition, circ. 55,000.

Le Journal d'Israel: 26 Agra St., P.O.B. 28330, Tel-Aviv; independent; French; Chief Editor J. RABIN; circ. 10,000; also overseas weekly selection; circ. 15,000.

Letzte Nyess (*Late News*): 52 Harakevet St., Tel-Aviv; f. 1949; Yiddish; morning; Editor S. HIMMELFARB; circ. 23,000.

Ma'ariv: Ma'ariv House, P.O.B. 20010, Tel-Aviv; f. 1948; mid-morning; independent; Editor SHMUEL SCHNITZER; circ. daily 147,000, Friday 245,000.

Nowiny i Kurier: 52 Harakevet St., Tel-Aviv; f. 1952; Polish; morning; Editor S. HIMMELFARB; circ. 15,000.

Omer: 45 Sheinkin St., Tel-Aviv; Histadrut popular vowelled Hebrew paper; f. 1951; Chief Editor MEIR BARELI; circ. 10,000.

Sha'ar: 52 Harakevet St., Tel-Aviv 64284; economy and finance; Hebrew and English; Editor J. KANSHAN.

Shearim: 64 Frishman St., Tel-Aviv; organ of Poalei Agudat Israel; Editor YEHUDA NACHSHONI; circ. 9,500.

Uj Kelet: 52 Harakevet St., Tel-Aviv; f. 1918; morning; Hungarian; independent; Editor S. HIMMELFARB; circ. 20,000.

Viata Noastra: 52 Harakevet St., Tel-Aviv; f. 1950; Romanian; morning; Editor ADRIAN ZAHAREANU; circ. 30,000.

Yedioth Aharonoth: 138 Petah-Tikva Rd., Tel-Aviv; f. 1939; evening; independent; Editor Dr. H. ROSENBLUM; circ. 180,000, Friday 280,000.

Yom Yom: P.O.B. 1194, Tel-Aviv; f. 1964; morning; economy and finance; Editor P. MERSTEN.

WEEKLIES AND FORTNIGHTLIES

Al Harriya: 38 King George St., Tel-Aviv; Arabic weekly of the Herut Party.

Al-Ittihad: P.O.B. 104, Haifa; f. 1944; Arabic; journal of the Israeli Communist Party; Chief Editor EMILE TOUMA.

Al-Mirsad: P.O.B. 736, 4 Ben Avigdor St., Tel-Aviv; Mapam; Arabic.

Bama'alah: P.O.B. 303, Tel-Aviv; journal of the young Histadrut Movement; Editor N. ANAELY.

Bamahane: Military P.O.B. 1013, Tel-Aviv; f. 1948; military, illustrated weekly of the Israel Armed Forces; Editor-in-Chief YOSSEF ESHKOL; circ. 70,000.

Bitaon Heyl Ha'avir (*Air Force Magazine*): Doar Zwai 1560, Zahal; f. 1948; Man. Editor D. MOLAD; Technical Editor U. AMIT; circ. 30,000.

Dvar Hashavua: 45 Sheinkin St., Tel-Aviv; f. 1946; popular illustrated; weekly; published by Histadrut, General Federation of Labour; Editor O. ZMORA; circ. 46,000.

Ethgar: 75 Einstein Street, Tel-Aviv; twice weekly; Editor NATHAN YALIN-MOR.

Glasul Populurui: Eilath St., P.O.B. 2675, Tel-Aviv; weekly of the Communist Party of Israel; Romanian; Editor MEIR SEMO.

Haolam Hazeh: P.O.B. 136, 3 Gordon St., Tel-Aviv; f. 1937; independent; illustrated news magazine; weekly; Editor-in-Chief URI AVNERY.

Harefuah: 39 Shaul Hamelech Blvd., Tel-Aviv 64928; f. 1920; with English summaries; fortnightly journal of the Israeli Medical Association; Editor I. SUM, M.D.; circ. 7,500.

Illustrirte Weltwoch: P.O.B. 2571, Tel-Aviv; f. 1956; Yiddish; weekly; Editor M. KARPINOVITZ.

Jerusalem Post International Edition: P.O.B. 81, Romema, Jerusalem; f. 1959; English; weekly; Overseas edition of the *Jerusalem Post* (*q.v.*); circ. 45,000 to 95 countries.

Kol Ha'am (*Voice of the People*): 37 Eilath St., P.O.B. 2675, Tel-Aviv; f. 1947; organ of the Communist Party of Israel; Editor B. BALTI.

Laisha: P.O.B. 28122, 7 Fin St., Tel-Aviv; f. 1946; Hebrew; women's magazine; Editor ZVI ELGAT.

Maariv Lanoar: 2 Carlebach St., Tel-Aviv; f. 1957; weekly for youth; Editor AMNON BEI-RAV; circ. 35,000.

Magallati: Arabic Publishing House, P.O.B. 28049, Tel-Aviv; f. 1960; young people's fortnightly; Editor-in-Chief IBRAHIM MUSA IBRAHIM; Editors GAMIL DAHLAN, MISHEL HADDAD; circ. 10,000.

MB (*Mitteilungsblatt*): P.O.B. 1480, Tel-Aviv; f. 1932; German weekly journal of the Irgun Olei Merkas Europa (Settlers from Central Europe); Editor Dr. HANS CAPELL.

Min Hayesod: Tel-Aviv; fortnightly; Hebrew; news and political commentary.

Reshumot: Ministry of Justice, Jerusalem; f. 1948; Hebrew, Arabic and English; official Government gazette.

Sada-A-Tarbia (*The Echo of Education*): published by the Histadrut and Teachers' Association, P.O.B. 2306, Rehovot; f. 1952; Arabic; educational; fortnightly; Editor TUVIA SHAMOSH.

OTHER PERIODICALS

Al-Bushra: P.O.B. 6088, Haifa; f. 1935; monthly; Arabic; organ of the Ahmadiyya movement; Editor and Manager FAZL ILAHI BASHIR.

Al Hamishmar: 20 Yehuda Halevy Street, Tel-Aviv; Bulgarian monthly of United Workers' Party.

Al Jadid: P.O.B. 104, Haifa; Arabic; literary monthly; Editor EMILE TOUMA.

Al Ta'awun: P.O.B. 303, Tel-Aviv; f. 1961; published by the Arab Workers' Dept. of the Histadrut and the Co-operatives Dept. of the Ministry of Labour; co-operatives quarterly; Editor TUVIA SHAMOSH.

Ariel: Cultural and Scientific Relations Division, Ministry for Foreign Affairs, Jerusalem; Publishers, Editorial and Distribution: La Semana Publishing Co. Ltd., P.O.B. 2427, 20 Kaf-tet Benovember St., Jerusalem 91023; f. 1962; quarterly review of the arts and letters in Israel; edns. in English, Spanish, French and German; Editor ASHER WEILL.

Avoda Ubituach Leumi: P.O.B. 915, Jerusalem; f. 1949; monthly review of the Ministry of Labour and Social Affairs, and the National Insurance Institute, Jerusalem; Editor AVNER MICHAELI; circ. 3,000.

Bekalkala Uvemis'har (*Economics and Trade*): P.O.B. 20027, Tel-Aviv; f. 1932; monthly; Hebrew; published by Federation of Israeli Chambers of Commerce; Editor J. SHOSTAK.

Business Digest Trade Lists: 37 Harbour St., Haifa; f. 1947; weekly; English, Hebrew; shipping movements, import licences, stock exchange listings, business failures, etc.; Editor G. ALON.

Christian News from Israel: 30 Jaffa Rd., Jerusalem; f. 1949; half-yearly; issued by the Ministry of Religious Affairs; in English, French, Spanish; Editor SHALOM BEN-ZAKKAI; circ. 10,000.

Di Goldene Keyt: 30 Weizmann St., Tel-Aviv; f. 1949; Yiddish; literary quarterly; published by the Histadrut; Editor A. SUTZKEVER; Co-Editor E. PINES; Man. Editor MOSHE MILLIS.

Divrei Haknesset: c/o The Knesset, Jerusalem; f. 1949; records of the proceedings of the Knesset, published by the Government Printer, Jerusalem; Editor ZIVIA KLEIN; circ. 300.

The Family Physician: 101 Arlosoroff St., P.O.B. 16250; Tel-Aviv; f. 1970; three times a year; medical; Hebrew with English summaries; Editor Prof. M. R. POLLIACK; circ. 4,500.

Folk un Zion: P.O.B. 92, Jerusalem; f. 1950; bi-monthly; current events relating to Israel and World Jewry; circ. 3,000; Editor EPHRAIM SHEDLETSKY.

Frei Israel: P.O.B. 8512, Tel-Aviv; Yiddish; progressive monthly, publ. by Asscn. for Popular Culture.

Gazit: 8 Zvi Brook St., P.O.B. 4190, Tel-Aviv; f. 1932; monthly; Hebrew and English; art, literature; Publisher G. TALPHIR.

Hameshek Hahaklai: 21 Melchett St., Tel-Aviv; f. 1929; agricultural; Editor ISRAEL INBARI.

Hamizrah Hehadash (*The New East*): The Hebrew University of Jerusalem; f. 1949; quarterly of the Israel Oriental Society; Hebrew with English summary; Middle Eastern, Asian and African Affairs; Editor AHARON LAYISH.

Hamlonai (*The Hotelier*): P.O.B. 11586, Tel-Aviv; f. 1962; monthly of the Israel Hotel Association; Hebrew and English; Editor Z. PELTZ.

Hapraklit: P.O.B. 14152, Tel-Aviv; f. 1943; quarterly; published by the Israel Bar Association; Editor-in-Chief A. POLONSKI; Editor ARNAN GAVRIELI; circ. 9,000.

Hassadeh: 8 Shaul Hamelech Blvd., P.O.B. 40044, Tel-Aviv 61400; f. 1920; monthly; review of agriculture; English summaries; Dir.-Gen. MARION R. COHN; Editor J. M. MARGALIT; circ. 10,000.

Hed Hagan: 8 Ben Saruk St., Tel-Aviv; f. 1935; educational; Editor Mrs. ESTHER RABINOWITZ; circ. 3,500.

Hed Hahinukh: 8 Ben-Saruk St., Tel-Aviv; f. 1926; monthly; educational; published by the Israeli Teachers' Union; Editor ORA GADELL; circ. 24,000.

Innovation: P.O.B. 8100, Jerusalem 91080; f. 1975; monthly; English; industrial research and development in Israel; Editor A. GREENFIELD.

Israel Business: P.O.B. 8100, Jerusalem 91080; f. 1961; monthly; English; business news and economic devt.; Editor A. GREENFIELD.

Israel Economist: P.O.B. 7052, 6 Hazanowitz St., Jerusalem; f. 1945; monthly; English; political and economic; independent; Editor J. KOLLEK, M.JUR. also publishes *The Tel-Aviv Stock Exchange Information Card Service*.

Israel Export and Trade Journal, The: P.O.B. 11586, Tel-Aviv; f. 1949; monthly; English; commercial and economic; published by Israel Periodicals Co. Ltd.; Man. Dir. ZALMAN PELTZ.

Israel Industry and Commerce and Export News: P.O.B. 1199, Tel-Aviv; English; monthly; serves Israeli exporters; Editor SHALOM YEDIDYAH.

Israel Journal of Medical Sciences: P.O.B. 1435, Jerusalem 91013; f. 1965; monthly; Editor-in-Chief Dr. M. PRYWES; Man. Mrs. S. TOLEDANO; circ. 5,500.

Israel Journal of Psychiatry and Related Sciences: Israel Science Publishers, P.O.B. 3115, Jerusalem 91030; f. 1963; quarterly; Editors-in-Chief H. Z. WINNIK, E. EDELSTEIN.

Israel Scene: P.O.B. 92, Jerusalem; f. 1957; World Zionist Organization news and analysis; monthly; circ. 22,000; Editor HELEN DAVIS.

Israel-South Africa Trade Journal: P.O.B. 11587, Tel-Aviv; f. 1973; bi-monthly; English; commercial and economic; published by Israel Publications Corpn. Ltd.; Man. Dir. Z. PELTZ.

Israels Aussenhandel: P.O.B. 11586, Tel-Aviv; f. 1967; monthly; German; commercial; Editor GABRIELA BLUM; Man. Dir. ZALMAN PELTZ.

Kalkalan: 8 Akiva St., P.O.B. 7052, Jerusalem; f. 1952; monthly; Hebrew commercial and economic; independent; Editor J. KOLLEK, M.JUR.

Kiryat Sefer: P.O.B. 503, Jerusalem; f. 1924; bibliographical quarterly of the Jewish National and University Library, Jerusalem; Editor Mrs. A. NEUBERG.

Labour in Israel: 93 Arlosoroff St., Tel-Aviv; periodic bulletin of the Histadrut; English, French, German and Spainish.

Leshonenu: Academy of the Hebrew Language, P.O.B. 3449, Jerusalem; f. 1929; quarterly; for the study of the Hebrew language and cognate subjects; Editor J. BLAU.

Leshonenu La'am: Academy of the Hebrew Language, P.O.B. 3449, Jerusalem; f. 1945; popular Hebrew philology; Editors E. ETAN, M. MEDAN.

Ma'arachot (*Campaigns*): Hakirya, 3 Mendler St., P.O.B. 7026, Tel-Aviv; f. 1939; military and political bi-monthly; periodical of Israel Defence Force; Editors Lt.-Col. Y. ZISKIND and Lt.-Col. Y. PORATH.

Mada: Weizmann Science Press of Israel, P.O.B. 801, Jerusalem 91007; f. 1956; popular scientific bi-monthly in Hebrew; Editor-in-Chief KAPAI PINES; circ. 11,000.

Melaha Vetaassiya (*Trade and Industry*): P.O.B. 11587, Tel-Aviv; f. 1969; bi-monthly review of the Union of Artisans and Small Manufacturers of Israel; Man. Dir. Z. PELTZ.

Mibifnim (*From Within*): 27 Sutin St., P.O.B. 16040, Tel-Aviv 61160; f. 1924; quarterly of the United Kibbutz Movement (T.K.M.); Editor ZERUBAVEL GILEAD; circ. 8,000.

Molad: P.O.B. 1165, Jerusalem; f. 1948; twice yearly; independent political and literary periodical; Hebrew; published by Miph'ale Molad Ltd.; Editor EPHRAIM BROIDO.

Monthly Bulletin of Statistics: Israel Central Bureau of Statistics, P.O.B. 13015, 91 130 Jerusalem; f. 1949.

Administered Territories Statistics Quarterly: f. 1971; Hebrew and English.

Foreign Trade Statistics: f. 1950; Hebrew and English; appears annually, 2 vols.; imports/exports.

Tourism and Hotel Services Statistics Quarterly: f. 1973; Hebrew and English.

Price Statistics Monthly: f. 1959; Hebrew.

Foreign Trade Statistics Quarterly: f. 1950; Hebrew and English.

Transport Statistics Quarterly.

Agricultural Statistics: quarterly and monthly pamphlet.

New Statistical Projects: quarterly.

Moznayim (*Balance*): P.O.B. 7098, Tel-Aviv; f. 1929; literature and culture; monthly; circ. 2,500; Editor B. Y. MICHALY.

Na'amat-Urim Lahorim: 5 Ben-Shaprut St., P.O.B. 303, Tel-Aviv; f. 1934; monthly journal of the Council of Women Workers of the Histadrut; Hebrew; Editor ZIVIA COHEN; circ. 16,500.

New Outlook: 2 Karl Netter St., Tel-Aviv 65202; f. 1957; Israeli and Middle Eastern Affairs; dedicated to Arab-Jewish *rapprochement;* monthly; circ. 10,000; Editor SIMHA FLAPAN.

Proche-Orient Chrétien: P.O.B. 19079, Jerusalem; f. 1951; quarterly on churches and religion in the Middle East.

Quarterly Review of the Israel Medical Association (*Mif'al Haverut Hutz*—World Fellowship of the Israel Medical Association): 39 Shaul Hamelekh Blvd., Tel-Aviv 64928; English; also published in French; quarterly; Editor Dr. S. ERDMAN.

Refuah Veterinarit: P.O.B. 3076, Rishon Le-Zion 13130; f. 1943; quarterly review of veterinary medicine; Editor Dr. I. DAFNI.

La Revue de l'A.M.I. (Mif'al Haverut Hutz—World Fellowship of the Israeli Medical Association): 39 Shaul Hamelekh Blvd., Tel-Aviv 64928; French and English; quarterly; Editor Dr. S. ERDMAN.

Scopus: Hebrew University of Jerusalem; f. 1946; published by Department of Information and Public Affairs, Hebrew University of Jerusalem; yearly; English; Editor E. GROSSBERG.

The Sea: Hane'emanim 8, Haifa; published by Israel Maritime League; review of marine problems; every two months; Pres. M. POMROCK; Man. Dir. ZADOK ESHEL; Chief Editor M. LITOVSKI; circ. 5,000.

Shedemot: 10 Dovnov, Tel-Aviv; journal of the Kibbutz Movement; quarterly.

Shituf (*Co-operation*): 24 Ha'arba St., Tel-Aviv, P.O.B. 7151; f. 1948; bi-monthly; economic, social and co-operative problems in Israel; published by the Central Union of Industrial, Transport and Service Co-operative Societies; Editor L. LOSH; circ. 12,000.

Sillages: P.O.B. 92, Jerusalem; f. 1980; published by Inf. Dept. of World Zionist Org.; literary and political; French; Editor-in-Chief KATY BISRAOR.

Sinai: P.O.B. 642, Jerusalem; f. 1937; Torah, science and literature; Editor Dr. YITZCHAK RAPHAEL.

Sindibad: P.O.B. 28049, Tel-Aviv; f. 1970; children's monthly; Editors WALID HUSSEIN, JAMIL DAHLAN; circ. 10,000.

Terra Santa: P.O.B. 186, Jerusalem; f. 1921; monthly; published by the Custody of the Holy Land (the official custodians of the Holy Shrines); Italian, Spanish, French, English and Arabic editions published in Jerusalem, by the Franciscan Printing Press, German edition in Vienna, Maltese edition in Valletta.

Tmuroth: 48 Hamelech George St., P.O.B. 23076, Tel-Aviv; f. 1960; organ of the Liberal Labour Movement; monthly; Editor S. MEIRI.

Trade and Economy: P.O.B. 20027, Tel-Aviv; f. 1979; bi-monthly; English; published by Federation of Israeli Chambers of Commerce; Editor NAOMI COHEN; circ. 5,000.

WIZO Review: Women's International Zionist Organization, 38 Sderoth David Hamelekh, Tel-Aviv; English, Spanish and German editions; Editor SYLVIA SATTEN BANIN; circ. 20,000.

Zion: P.O.B. 4179, Jerusalem; f. 1935; research in Jewish history; quarterly; Hebrew and English; Editors H. BEINART, S. ETTINGER, M. STERN.

Zraim: 7 Dubnov St., P.O.B. 40027, Tel-Aviv; f. 1953; journal of the Bnei Akiva (Youth of Hapoel Hamizrachi) Movement; Editor AMNON SHAPIRA.

Zrakor: 37 Harbour St., Haifa; f. 1947; monthly; Hebrew; news digest, trade, finance, economics, shipping; Editor G. ALON.

The following are all published by Weizmann Science Press Israel, P.O.B. 801, Jerusalem 91007; Exec. Editor L. LESTER.

Israel Journal of Botany: f. 1951; Editor Prof. MOSHE NEGBI; quarterly.

Israel Journal of Chemistry: f. 1951; Editor Prof. S. SAREL; quarterly.

Israel Journal of Earth-Sciences: f. 1951; Editor Y. WEILER; quarterly.

Israel Journal of Mathematics: f. 1951; Editors A. ZABRODSKY, H. FURSTENBERG; monthly, 3 vols. of 4 issues each per year.

Israel Journal of Technology: f. 1951; Editor Prof. D. ABIR; 6 issues per year.

Israel Journal of Zoology: f. 1951; Editor Prof. Y. L. WERNER; quarterly.

Journal d'Analyse Mathématique: f. 1955; Editor Prof. S. AGMON; 2 vols. per year.

PUBLISHERS' ASSOCIATION

Daily Newspaper Publishers' Association of Israel: P.O.B. 2251, 4 Kaplan St., Tel-Aviv; safeguards professional interests and maintains standards, supplies newsprint to dailies; negotiates with trade unions, etc.; mems. all daily papers; affiliated to International Federation of Newspaper Publishers.

NEWS AGENCIES

Jewish Telegraphic Agency (JTA): Israel Bureau, Jerusalem Post Building, Romema, Jerusalem; Dir. DAVID LANDAU.

ITIM, News Agency of the Associated Israel Press: 10 Tiomkin St., Tel-Aviv; f. 1950; co-operative news agency; Dir. and Editor ALTER WELNER.

FOREIGN BUREAUX

Agence France-Presse: 53 Hahashmonayin, Tel-Aviv; Chief EROL GUINEY; Jerusalem, P.O.B. 1507; Corresp. PIERRE LEMOINE.

Agencia EFE (*Spain*): P.O.B. 3279, Shderof Herzl 127/1, Jerusalem; Correspondent ELÍAS ZALDÍVAR.

Agenzia Nazionale Stampa Associata (ANSA) (*Italy*): P.O.B. 21342, Tel-Aviv; Bureau Chief VITTORIO FRENQUELLUCCI.

Associated Press (AP) (*U.S.A.*): 51 Petah Tikva Rd., Tel-Aviv; Chief of Bureau LARRY THORSON.

Deutsche Presse-Agentur (dpa) (*Federal Republic of Germany*): P.O.B. 33 189, Tel-Aviv; Correspondents GEORG SPIEKER and GIDEON BERLI.

Jiji Tsushin-Sha (*Japan*): 7/B/23 Etzel French Hill, Jerusalem; Corresp. HIROKAZU OIKAWA.

Kyodo Tsushin (*Japan*): 8 Bilu St., Tel-Aviv; Corresp. KO OGASAWARA.

Middle East Bureau: Jerusalem Post Bldg., Jerusalem 94467.

Reuters (*U.K.*): 8 Bilu Street, Tel-Aviv.

United Press International (UPI) (*U.S.A.*): 138 Petah Tikva Rd., Tel-Aviv; Bureau Man. BROOKE W. KROEGER.

The following are also represented: North American Newspaper Alliance and TASS (U.S.S.R.).

PUBLISHERS

Achiasaf Ltd.: 13 Yosef Hanassi St., Tel-Aviv; f. 1933; general; Man. Dir. SCHACHNA ACHIASAF.

Am Hassefer Ltd.: 9 Bialik St., Tel-Aviv; f. 1955; Man. Dir. DOV LIPETZ.

"Am Oved" Ltd.: 22 Mazah St., P.O.B. 470, Tel-Aviv; f. 1942; fiction, biography, history, social science; reference books, school and university textbooks, technical and professional works, juvenile, science fiction, crime; Man. Dir. DOV GORFUNG.

Amichai Publishing House Ltd.: 5 Yosef Hanassi St., Tel-Aviv; f. 1948; Man. Dir. YEHUDA ORLINSKY.

Arabic Publishing House: 17A Hagra St., P.O.B. 28049, Tel-Aviv; f. 1960; established by the Histadrut (trade union) organization; periodicals and books; Dir. JOSEF ELIAHU; Editor-in-Chief IBRAHIM M. IBRAHIM.

Carta, The Israel Map and Publishing Co. Ltd.: Yad Haruzim St., P.O.B. 2500, Jerusalem 91024; f. 1958; the principal cartographic publisher; Pres. EMANUEL HAUSMAN; Man. Dir. SHAY HAUSMAN.

Dvir Publishing Co. Ltd., The: 58 Mazah St., P.O.B. 149, Tel-Aviv; f. 1924; literature, science, art, education; Man. Dir. E. HAUSMAN.

Eked Publishing House: 29 Bar-Kochba St., Tel-Aviv; f. 1959; poetry; Dirs. ITAMAR YAOZ-KEST, MARITZA ROSMAN.

Encyclopedia Publishing Co.: Massada Press Ltd., 46 Beit Lehem Rd., Jerusalem; f. 1947; Hebrew Encyclopedia and other Encyclopedias; Chair. Mrs. BRACHA PELI; Pres. ALEXANDER PELI.

Rodney Franklin Agency: 5 Karl Netter St., P.O.B. 37727, Tel-Aviv; exclusive representative of various British and U.S.A. publishers; Dir. RODNEY FRANKLIN.

G.G. The Jerusalem Publishing House Ltd.: 39 Tchernechovski St., Jerusalem, P.O.B. 7147; f. 1967; history, encyclopaedias, archaeology, art and other reference books; Dir. SHLOMO S. GAFNI; Man. Editor RACHEL GILON.

Gazit: 8 Zvi Brook St., Tel-Aviv, P.O.B. 4190; art publishers; Editor GABRIEL TALPHIR.

Hakibbutz Hameuchad Publishing House Ltd.: P.O.B. 16040, 15 Nehardea St., Tel-Aviv; f. 1940; general; Dir. A. AVISHAI.

Israeli Music Publications Ltd.: 105 Ben Yehuda St., P.O.B. 6011, Tel-Aviv 61060; f. 1949; books on music and musical works; Dir. Dr. PETER E. GRADENWITZ.

Izre'el Publishing House Ltd.: 76 Dizengoff St., Tel-Aviv; f. 1933; Man. ALEXANDER IZREEL.

Jewish History Publications (Israel 1961) Ltd.: 46 Beit Lehem Rd., Jerusalem; f. 1961; encyclopedias, World History of the Jewish People series; Chair. ALEXANDER PELI; Pres. BRACHA PELI.

Jewish Agency Publishing Department: P.O.B. 704, Jerusalem; f. 1945; Palestinology, Judaism, scientific, classics, and publicity brochures; Dir. M. SPITZER.

Karni Publishers Ltd.: 58 Maze St., P.O.B. 149, Tel-Aviv; f. 1951; children's and educational books; Man. Dir. EMANUEL HAUSMAN.

Keter Publishing House Jerusalem Ltd.: P.O.B. 7145, Givat Shaul B, Jerusalem; f. 1959; original and translated works in all fields of science and humanities, published in English, French, German, other European languages and Hebrew; publishing imprints: Israel Program for Scientific Translations, Israel Universities Press, Keter Books, Encyclopedia Judaica; Man. Dir. ELIAV COHEN.

Kiryath Sepher: 15 Arlosorov St., Jerusalem; f. 1933; dictionaries, textbooks, maps, scientific books; Dir. SHALOM SIVAN (STEPANSKY).

Magnes Press, The: The Hebrew University, Jerusalem; f. 1929; biblical studies, judaica, and all academic fields; Dir. BEN-ZION D. YEHOSHUA.

Massada Press Ltd.: 46 Beit Lechem Rd., Jerusalem; f. 1961; encyclopaedias, judaica, the arts, educational material; Chair. ALEXANDER PELI.

Ministry of Defence Publishing House: Hakiriya, Tel-Aviv; f. 1939; military literature; Dir. SHALOM SERI.

M. Mizrachi Publishers: 67 Levinsky, Tel-Aviv; f. 1960; children's books, novels; Dir. MEIR MIZRACHI.

Mosad Harav Kook: P.O.B. 642, Jerusalem; editions of classical works, Torah and Jewish studies; Dir. Rabbi M. KATZENELENBOGEN.

Otsar Hamoreh: 8 Ben Saruk, Tel-Aviv; f. 1951; educational.

Alexander Peli Jerusalem Publishing Co. Ltd.: 46 Beit Lehem Rd., Jerusalem; f. 1977; encyclopedias, Judaica, the arts, educational material; Chair. ALEXANDER PELI.

I. L. Peretz: 31 Allenby Rd., Tel-Aviv; f. 1956; mainly books in Yiddish; Man. Dir. MOSHE GERSHONOWITZ.

Rubin Mass Ltd.: 11 Marcus St., P.O.B. 990, Jerusalem; f. 1927; Hebraica, Judaica; Dir. OREN MASS.

Schocken Publishing House Ltd.: P.O.B. 2316, Tel-Aviv 61022; f. 1938; general; Dir. Mrs. RACHELI EDELMAN.

Shikmona Publishing Co. Ltd.: P.O.B. 4044, Jerusalem; Zionism, archaeology, art, fiction and non-fiction.

Sifriat-Ma'ariv Ltd.: Derech Petach Tikva 72A, Tel-Aviv; f. 1954; Man. Dir. IZCHAK YACHIN; Editor-in-Chief NAFTALI ARBEL.

Sifriat Poalim Ltd.: 66 Achad Ha'am St., Tel-Aviv 65-171; f. 1939; general literature; Gen. Man. TSVI RAANAN.

Sinai Publishing Co.: 72 Allenby Rd., Tel-Aviv; Hebrew books and religious articles; Dir. AKNAH SCHLESINGER.

Weizmann Science Press of Israel: 8A Horkanya St., P.O.B. 801, Jerusalem 91007; f. 1955; publishes scientific books and periodicals; Man. Dir. RAMI MICHAELI; Exec. Editor L. LESTER.

Yachdav United Publishers Co. Ltd.: 29 Carlebach St., P.O.B. 20123, Tel-Aviv; f. 1960; educational; Chair. MORDECHAI BERNSTEIN; Dir. BENJAMIN SELLA.

Yavneh Ltd.: 4 Mazeh St., Tel-Aviv; f. 1932; general; Dir. AVSHALOM ORENSTEIN.

S. Zack and Co.: 2 King George St., Jerusalem; f. *c.* 1930; reference books, textbooks, dictionaries, judaica, children's books; Dirs. DAVID and MICHAEL ZACK.

Israel Book Publishers Association: 29 Carlebach St., P.O.B. 20123, Tel-Aviv; f. 1939; mems.: 79 publishing firms; Pres. MORDECHAI BERNSTEIN; Exec. Dir. BENJAMIN SELLA.

Jerusalem International Book Fair: 22 Jaffa Rd., Jerusalem 91000; f. 1961; takes place every two years; 45 countries were represented in 1981; Dir. ZEV BIRGER; Asst. to Dir. NAOMI SCHWAB.

RADIO AND TELEVISION

RADIO

Israel Broadcasting Authority (I.B.A.): 21 Heleni Hamalka, P.O.B. 7139, Jerusalem; f. 1948; station in Jerusalem with additional studios in Tel-Aviv and Haifa; Dir. JOSEPH LAPID. I.B.A. broadcasts five programmes for local and overseas listeners on medium, shortwave and VHF/FM in thirteen languages; Hebrew, Arabic, English, Yiddish, Ladino, Romanian, Hungarian, Moghrabit, Persian, French, Russian, Georgian and Spanish.

Number of radio receivers: 750,000 (1978/79).

Galei Zahal: A.P.O. 01005, Zahal; f. 1951; Army broadcasting station, Tel-Aviv with studios in Jerusalem; broadcasts music, news and other programmes on medium-wave and FM stereo in Hebrew.

TELEVISION

Israel Broadcasting Authority (I.B.A.): broadcasts began in 1968; station in Jerusalem with additional studios in Tel-Aviv; Dir. Gen. JOSEPH LAPID; one black and white network (VHF with UHF available in some areas); broadcasts in Hebrew and Arabic.

Instructional Television Centre: Ministry of Education and Culture, 14 Klausner St., Tel-Aviv; f. 1966 by Hanadiv (Rothschild Memorial Group) as Instructional Television Trust; began transmission in 1966; now broadcasts 44 hours a week; school programmes form an integral part of the syllabus in a wide range of subjects; also adult education; Gen. Man. YA'AKOV LORBERBAUM.

Number of TV receivers: 465,000 (1978/79).

FINANCE

BANKING

(cap. = capital; p.u. = paid up; dep. = deposits; m. = million; I£ = Israeli £; brs. = branches.)

CENTRAL BANK

Bank of Israel: Bank of Israel Bldg., Kiryat Ben Gurion, P.O.B. 780, Jerusalem 91007; f. 1954 as the Central Bank of the State of Israel; cap. 200m. shekels, reserves 800m. shekels, dep. 95,431m. shekels (Dec. 1981); Gov. Dr. MOSHE MANDELBAUM; Deputy Govs. Dr. E. SHEFFER, Dr. Z. SUSSMAN; Dir.-Gen. Y. SARIG; Mans. M. BENOUSILIO, S. BRONFELD, M. FRAENKEL, S. PELED, O. MESSER, M. LAHAV, A. H. LOZOWICK, V. MEDINA, F. WIEDER, S. BILITZKI; 2 brs.

ISRAELI BANKS

American Israel Bank Ltd.: 11 Rothschild Blvd., Tel-Aviv; f. 1975 as a result of a merger between Japhet Bank Ltd. and Exchange National Bank of Chicago; cap. and surplus 62m. shekels; dep. 5,258.167m. shekels (Dec. 1981); Chair. U. VARDY-ZER; Man. Dir. A. KROIZER; 27 brs.

Arab Israel Bank Ltd.: 53 Hameginim Ave., P.O.B. 442, Haifa; subsidiary of Bank Leumi le-Israel B.M.; f. 1959 to serve primarily the Arab sector of the economy; cap. p.u. I£14m., dep. I£1,011m. (Dec. 1981); Chair. S. TULCHINSKY; Gen. Man. E. ASHKENAZI; 30 brs.

Bank Hapoalim B.M.: 50 Rothschild Blvd., Tel-Aviv; f. 1921; cap. p.u., res. and convertible notes 2,673m. shekels, dep. 125,587m. shekels (June 1981); Chair. Bd. of Dirs. E. REINER; Chair. Bd. of Mans. G. GAZIT; Man. Dirs. H. BERGSTEIN, J. GEVA, G. GIL, M. OLENIK.

Bank Kupat-Am Le-Israel Ltd.: 13 Ahad Ha'am St., Tel-Aviv; f. 1918; subsidiary of Bank Leumi le-Israel B.M.; cap. I£4m.; reserves I£9.6m.; Chair B. YEKUTIELI; Man. Dir. M. OSTFELD; 17 brs.

Bank Lemelacha Ltd.: 18 Shoken St., Tel-Aviv; f. 1953; now assoc. with First International Bank of Israel; Chair. B. WINE; Man. Dir. Y. GAL'ON.

Bank Leumi le-Israel B.M.: 24–32 Yehuda Halevy St., Tel-Aviv; f. 1902; dep. 230m. shekels (Dec. 1981); Chair. and Chief Exec. E. I. JAPHET; 449 brs. and subs.; publ. *Economic Review* (quarterly).

First International Bank of Israel Ltd.: Shalom Mayer Tower, 9 Ahad Ha'am St., P.O.B. 29036, Tel-Aviv; f. 1972 as a result of a merger between The Foreign Trade

Bank Ltd. and Export Bank Ltd.; cap. p.u. 107.8m. shekels; dep. 9,665m. shekels (May 1981); Chair. M. MOSEVICS; Deputy Chair and Chief Exec. Officer DAVID GOLAN; Man. Dir. S. BINO; 83 brs.

Industrial Development Bank of Israel Ltd.: 2 Dafna St., Tel-Aviv 64928; f. 1957; share cap. 88.4m. shekels; total resources 5,006.7m. shekels (Dec. 1980); Chair. A. FRIEDMANN; Man. Dir. Y. GILL.

Israel Ampal Industrial Development Bank Ltd.: 111 Arlozorov St., Tel-Aviv; f. 1956; cap. p.u. 42.5m. shekels; dep. 1,587m. shekels (Dec. 1981); Chair. M. OLENIK; Man. Dirs. M. BACHAR, M. JAFFE.

Israel Bank of Agriculture Ltd.: 83 Hashmonayim St., Tel-Aviv; f. 1951; cap. p.u. I£1,945m., dep. I£11,233m.; Chair. A. BRUM; Man. Dir. D. CALDERON.

Israel Continental Bank Ltd.: 70 Ibn Gvirol St., Tel-Aviv; f. 1973; capital held jointly by Bank Hapoalim B.M. and Bank für Gemeinwirtschaft A.G.; cap. p.u. I£12.6m.; dep. I£3,349.8m. (Dec. 1981); Chair. Dr. WALTER HESSELBACH.

Israel Discount Bank Ltd.: 27–31 Yehuda Halevi St., Tel-Aviv 65546; f. 1935; cap. p.u. 181m. shekels; dep. 128.974m. shekels (Dec. 1981); Chair. RAPHAEL RECANATI; 257 brs. including sub-brs.

Israel General Bank Ltd.: 28 Achad Ha'am St., Tel-Aviv; f. 1964; cap. p.u. I£32.2m., dep. I£5,420.9m. (Dec. 1979); Chair. Baron EDMOND DE ROTHSCHILD; Man. Dir. DAVID SHOHAM; 3 brs.

Israel Loan and Savings Bank Ltd.: 21 Herzl St., Tel-Aviv; cap. I£10.3m.; Chair. E. AVEYNON; Man. Dir. I. GAFNI.

Mercantile Bank of Israel Ltd.: P.O.B. 512, 24 Rothschild Blvd., Tel-Aviv; f. 1924; subsidiary of Barclays Discount Bank; cap. p.u. 600,000 shekels; dep. 715m. shekels (Dec. 1981); Chair. and Gen. Man. SHLOMO MAGRISO.

Union Bank of Israel Ltd.: 6–8 Ahuzat Bayit St., P.O.B. 2428, Tel-Aviv; f. 1951; subsidiary of Bank Leumi le-Israel B.M.; cap. p.u. 180m. shekels; dep. 11,964m. shekels (Dec. 1980); Chiar. E. I. JAPHET; Man. Dir. M. M. MAYER; Gen. Man. S. SOROKER; 25 brs.

United Mizrahi Bank Ltd.: 48 Lilienblum St., Tel-Aviv; f. 1923; cap. p.u. 93m. shekels, dep. 8,240m. shekels (Dec. 1980); Chair. N. FEINGOLD; Man. Dir. A. MEIR; 71 brs.

MORTGAGE BANKS

Housing Mortgage Bank Ltd.: 2 Kaplan St., Tel-Aviv; f. 1950; subsidiary of Bank Hapoalim B.M.; cap. p.u. I£118.1m., dep. I£3,483m. (Dec. 1978); Chair. Y. RAVIN; Dir. and Gen. Man. D. TOMER.

Israel Development and Mortgage Bank Ltd.: 16 Simtat Beit Hashoeva, Tel-Aviv; f. 1959; subsidiary of Israel Discount Bank Ltd.; Chair. M. B. GITTER; Man. Dir. K. REICH.

Leumi Mortgage Bank Ltd.: 13 Ahad Ha'am St., Tel-Aviv; f. 1921; subsidiary of Bank Leumi le-Israel B.M.; cap. and res. 133.5m. shekels; dep. 2,076m. shekels (Dec. 1980); Chair. S. TULCHINSKY; Man. Dir. Z. BIRNBAUM.

Tefahot, Israel Mortgage Bank Ltd.: 9 Heleni Hamalka St., P.O.B. 93, Jerusalem; f. 1945; cap. and reserves I£401.1m.; total assets I£12,662.9m. (Dec. 1981); Man. Dir. MOSHE MANN. *Affiliated Bank:* **Carmel Mortgage and Investment Bank Ltd.,** 207 Hameginim Blvd., Haifa.

Unico Investment Co. Ltd.: 30 Yavneh St., Tel-Aviv; f. 1961.

FOREIGN BANKS

Barclays Discount Bank Ltd.: 103 Allenby Rd., Tel-Aviv 65 176; f. 1971 by Barclays Bank International Ltd. and Israel Discount Bank Ltd. to incorporate Israel brs. of Barclays; cap. and res. 90.3m. shekels; dep. 9,258m. shekels (Dec. 1981); Chair. GIDEON LAHAV; Gen. Man. MOSHE NEUDORFER; *Wholly owned subsidiary:* **Mercantile Bank of Israel Ltd.,** 24 Rothschild Blvd., Tel-Aviv.

STOCK EXCHANGE

Tel-Aviv Stock Exchange: 113 Allenby Rd.; Chair. Dr. M. HETH; Joint Gen. Mans. D. OTTENSOOSER, J. NITZANI; publs. *Official Quotations, Bond Guide* and *Stock Guide.*

INSURANCE

Ararat Insurance Company Ltd.: Ararat House, 13 Montefiore St., Tel-Aviv; f. 1949; Chair. PHILIP ZUCKERMAN; Gen. Man. A. RINOT.

Aryeh Insurance Co. Ltd.: Shalom Tower, Tel-Aviv; f. 1948; Chair. AVINOAM M. TOCATLY.

Clal Insurance Co. Ltd.: 42 Rothschild Blvd., P.O.B. 326, Tel-Aviv 61002; f. 1962; Man. Dir. M. SHANI.

Hassneh Insurance Co. of Israel Ltd.: 115 Allenby St., P.O.B. 805, Tel-Aviv; f. 1924; Man. Dir. EITAN AVNEYON.

Israel Phoenix Assurance Company Ltd., The: 30 Levontin St., Tel-Aviv; f. 1949; Chair. of Board DAVID J. HACKMEY; Man. Dir. JOSEPH D. HACKMEY.

Israel Reinsurance Company Ltd., The: 5 Drujanov St., P.O.B. 11589, Tel-Aviv; f. 1951; Chair. Board of Dirs. N. MISHOR; Gen. Man. S. JANNAI.

Maoz Insurance Co. Ltd.: 43 Brodetsky St., Ramat-Aviv; f. 1945; formerly Binyan Insurance Co. Ltd.; Chair. B. YEKUTIELI.

Mazada Insurance Service Ltd.: 3 Ahuzat Bait St., Tel-Aviv 65143; f. 1932; partly owned by Hassneh Insurance Co. Ltd.; Man. A. SPIGELMAN, M.A.

Menorah Insurance Company Ltd.: Menorah House, 73 Rothschild Blvd., Tel-Aviv; f. 1935; Gen. Man. DAVID HIRSCHFELD.

Migdal Insurance Co. Ltd.: 26 Sa'adiya Ga'on St., Tel-Aviv; part of Bank Leumi Group; f. 1934; Chair. B. YEKUTIELI; Gen. Mans. U. E. LEVY, M. ZANGEN.

Palglass Palestine Plate Glass Insurance Co. Ltd.: 30 Achad Ha'am St., Tel-Aviv; f. 1934; Gen. Man. AKIVA ZALZMAN.

Sahar Insurance Company Ltd.: Sahar House. 23 Ben-Yehuda St., Tel-Aviv 63806, P.O.B. 26222; f. 1949; Chair. A. SACHAROV; Man. Dir. AL. SACHAROV.

Samson Insurance Co. Ltd.: Asia House, 4 Weizman St., P.O.B. 33678, Tel-Aviv; f. 1933; Chair. A. AVNION; Gen. Man. D. SERR.

Sela Insurance Co. Ltd.: 13 Achad Haam St., Tel-Aviv; f. 1938; Man. Dir. E. SHANI.

Shiloah Company Ltd.: 2 Pinsker St., Tel-Aviv; f. 1933; Gen. Man. Dr. S. BAMIRAH; Man. Mme BAMIRAH.

Yardenia Insurance Company Ltd.: 22 Maze St., Tel-Aviv; f. 1948; Man. Dir. H. LEBANON.

Zion Insurance Company Ltd.: 120 Allenby Rd., Tel-Aviv; f. 1935; Chair. HAIM TAIBER.

THE HISTADRUT

Hahistadrut Haklalit shel Haovdim Beeretz Israel, 93 Arlosoroff St., Tel-Aviv

(GENERAL FEDERATION OF LABOUR IN ISRAEL)

Secretary-General: YERUHAM MESHEL.

The General Federation of Labour in Israel, usually known as the Histadrut, is the largest voluntary organization in Israel, and the most important economic body in the State. It is open to all workers, including members of co-operatives and of the liberal professions, who join directly as individuals. The Histadrut engages in four main fields of activity: trade union organization; economic development; social insurance based on mutual aid; and educational and cultural activities. Dues—3.9 per cent of wages (up to I£11,000 per month)—cover all its trade union, health and social services activities. The Histadrut was founded in 1920.

ORGANIZATION

In 1980 the Histadrut had a membership of 1,600,000, including over 160,000 in collective, co-operative and private villages (*kibbutzim* and *moshavim*) affiliated through the Agricultural Workers' Union, and 390,000 wives (who have membership status); 140,000 of the members were Arabs. In addition some 110,000 young people under 18 years of age belong to the Organization of Working and Student Youth, a direct affiliate of the Histadrut. The main religious labour organizations, *Histadrut Hapoel Hamizrahi* and *Histadrut Poalei Agudat Israel*, belong to the trade union section and welfare services, which thus extend to 90 per cent of all workers in Israel.

All members take part in elections to the Histadrut

Convention (*Veida*), which elects the General Council (*Moetsa*) and the Executive Committee (*Vaad Hapoel*). The latter elects the 36-member Executive Bureau (*Vaada Merakezet*), which is responsible for day-to-day implementation of policy. The Executive Committee also elects the Secretary-General, who acts as its chairman as well as head of the organization as a whole and chairman of the Executive Bureau. Nearly all political parties are represented on the Histadrut Executive Committee. Throughout Israel there are 68 local Labour Councils.

The Executive Committee has the following departments: Trade Union, Arab Affairs, Mutual Security Centre, Organization, International, Finance, Legal, Employment, Vocational Training, Absorption and Development, Academic Workers, Culture and Education, Institute of Economic and Social Research, Diaspora Communities, Youth and Sport, Consumers' Authority, Industrial Democracy, Religious Affairs and Higher Education.

TRADE UNION ACTIVITIES

Collective agreements with employers fix wage scales, which are linked with the retail price index; provide for social benefits, including paid sick leave and employers' contributions to sick and pension and provident funds; and regulate dismissals. Dismissal compensation is regulated by law. The Histadrut actively promotes productivity through labour management boards and the National Productivity Institute, and supports incentive pay schemes.

There are unions for the following groups: clerical workers, building workers, teachers, engineers, agricultural workers, technicians, textile workers, printing workers, diamond workers, metal workers, food and bakery workers, wood workers, government employees, seamen, nurses, civilian employees of the armed forces, actors, musicians and variety artists, social workers, watchmen, cinema technicians, institutional and school staffs, pharmacy employees, medical laboratory workers, X-ray technicians, physiotherapists, social scientists, microbiologists, psychologists, salaried lawyers, pharmacists, physicians, occupational therapists, truck and taxi drivers, hotel and restaurant workers, workers in Histadrut-owned industry, garment, shoe and leather workers, plastic and rubber workers, editors of periodicals, painters and sculptors and industrial workers.

ECONOMIC ACTIVITIES AND SOCIAL SERVICES

These include *Hevrat Ovdim* (Economic Sector, employing 260,000 workers in 1980), *Kupat Holim* (the Sick Fund, covering almost 75 per cent of Israel's population), seven pension funds, and *NA'AMAT* (women's organization which runs nursery homes and kindergartens, organizes vocational education and promotes legislation for the protection and benefit of working women).

TRADE AND INDUSTRY

CHAMBERS OF COMMERCE

Federation of Israeli Chambers of Commerce: P.O.B. 20027, Tel-Aviv; co-ordinates the Tel-Aviv, Jerusalem, Haifa and Beersheba Chambers of Commerce; Dir. ZVI AMIT.

Jerusalem Chamber of Commerce: P.O.B. 183, Jerusalem 91000; f. 1908; about 300 mems.; Pres. M. H. ELICHAR; Vice-Pres. CH. COHEN, A. DASKAL, SH. P. DORON, A. PEREZ, Y. PEARLMAN, M. ROIZMAN, M. YANOWSKI, A. TALBAR; publ. *Bulletin* (Hebrew and English).

Haifa Chamber of Commerce and Industry (*Haifa and District*): P.O.B. 33176, 53 Haatzmaut Rd., Haifa; f. 1921; 700 mems.; Pres. EMANUEL GORALI; Gen. Sec. A. MEHOULAL.

Chamber of Commerce, Tel-Aviv-Jaffa: P.O.B. 20027, 84 Hachashmonaim St., Tel-Aviv; f. 1919; 1,500 mems.; Pres. AVNER BEN-YAKAR; Dir.-Gen. ZVI AMIT; Secs. J. FEINER, Z. SEGAI, J. SHOSTAK, F. B. WAHLE; publs. *Bekalkala Uvemis'har, Economy and Trade.*

Federation of Bi-National Chambers of Commerce with and in Israel: 99 Ahad Haam St., Tel-Aviv, P.O.B. 1127; federates: Israel-America Chamber of Commerce and Industry; Anglo-Israel Chamber of Commerce; Australia-Israel Chamber of Commerce; Chamber of Commerce and Industry Israel-Africa; Chamber of Commerce Israel-Belgique-Luxembourg; Canada-Israel Chamber of Commerce and Industry; Israel-Danish Chamber of Commerce; Chambre de Commerce Israel-France; Chamber of Commerce and Industry Israel-Germany; Camera di Commercio Israeli-Italia; Israel-Japan Chamber of Commerce; Israel-Latin America, Spain and Portugal Chamber of Commerce; Netherlands-Israel Chamber of Commerce; Israel-Norway Chamber of Commerce; Handelskammer Israel-Schweiz; Israel-South Africa Chamber of Commerce; Israel-Sweden Chamber of Commerce; Pres. E. GOUSMAN; and also incorporates Bi-National Chamber of Commerce existing in 20 foreign countries with Israel.

Israel-British Chamber of Commerce: P.O.B. 3540, Tel-Aviv 61034; f. 1951; 440 mems.; Exec. Dir. NEHAMA RONEN; Chair. A. SACHAROV.

TRADE AND INDUSTRIAL ORGANIZATIONS

The Agricultural Union: Tchlenov 20, Tel-Aviv; consists of more than 50 agricultural settlements and is connected with marketing and supplying organizations, and Bahan Ltd., controllers and auditors.

Central Union of Artisans and Small Manufacturers: P.O.B. 4041, Tel-Aviv; f. 1907; has a membership of 40,000 divided into 70 groups according to trade; the union is led by a seventeen-man Presidium; Chair. JACOB FRANK; publ. *Hamlakha;* 30 brs.

Citrus Control and Marketing Boards: 6 Wissotzky St., P.O.B. 21371; Tel-Aviv 61213; the growers' institution for the control of the Israel citrus industry; Boards made up of representatives of the Government and the growers. Functions: control of plantations, supervision of picking and packing operations, marketing of the crop overseas and on the home markets; shipping; supply of fertilizers, insecticides, equipment for orchards and packing houses and of packing materials, technical research and extension work; long-term financial assistance to growers.

Farmers' Union of Israel: P.O.B. 209, Tel-Aviv; f. 1913; membership of 7,000 independent farmers, citrus and winegrape growers; Pres. E. IZAKSON; Chair. Council IZCHAK-ZIV-AV; Dir.-Gen. SHLOMO REISMAN; publ. *The Israeli Farmer* (bi-monthly).

General Association of Merchants in Israel: 6 Rothschild Boulevard, Tel-Aviv; the organization of retail traders; has a membership of 30,000 in 60 brs.

Israel Diamond Exchange Ltd.: P.O.B. 3222, Ramat-Gan; f. 1937; production, export, import and finance facilities; estimated exports (1980) U.S. $1,410m.

Israel Journalists' Association Ltd.: 4 Kaplan St., Tel-Aviv; Sec. MOSHE RON.

Manufacturers' Association of Israel: Industry House, 29 Hamered St., P.O.B. 29116, Tel-Aviv; Pres. AVRA-HAM (BUMA) SHAVIT; Dir. Gen. SHAUL ROSOLIO.

TRADE UNIONS

Histadrut Haovdim Haleumit (*National Labour Federation*); 23 Sprinczak St., Tel-Aviv; f. 1934; 144,000 mems.; publ. *Yaad*.

Histadrut Hapoel Hamizrahi (*National Religious Workers' Party*): 166 Even Gavirol St., Tel-Aviv; 125,000 mems. in 81 settlements.

Histadrut Poalei Agudat Israel (*Agudat Israel Workers' Organization*): Geula Quarter, Corner Yehezkel St., Jerusalem; has 19,000 members in 12 settlements.

TRANSPORT

RAILWAYS

Israel State Railways: Central Station, P.O.B. 44, Haifa; all lines are managed and operated from Haifa. The total length of main line is 550 km.; gauge 1,435 mm.

Freight traffic consists mainly of grain, phosphates, potash, containers, oil and building materials. Rail service serves Haifa and Ashdod, ports on the Mediterranean Sea, while a combined rail-road service extends to Eilat port on the Red Sea. A rail link from Dimona to Eilat is planned. Passenger services operate between the main towns: Nahariya, Haifa, Tel-Aviv and Jerusalem.

Gen. Man. ZVI TSAFRIRI; Deputy Gen. Man. I. BAR-ILAN; Deputy Gen. Man. (Admin.) L. HEYMAN.

UNDERGROUND RAILWAYS

Haifa Underground Funicular Railway: 12 Hanassi Ave., Haifa; opened 1959; 2 km. in operation; Man. D. SCHARF.

Tel-Aviv Metropolitan Area Rapid Transit: Ministry of Transport, 3 Eliashberg St., Tel-Aviv; a feasibility study has been made on the possibility of building a 60 km. rapid transit line (8 km. underground).

ROADS

Ministry of Construction and Housing: Public Works Dept., Jerusalem.

There are 4,600 km. of metalled inter-urban highways not including roads in towns and settlements.

Automobile and Touring Club of Israel (MEMSI): 19 Petah Tiqva Rd., P.O.B. 36144, Tel-Aviv 61630; f. 1949; over 35,000 mems.; Dir.-Gen. B. YACOBI; publ. Annual Year Book.

SHIPPING

The Israel Ports Authority: Maya Building, 74 Petah Tiqva Rd., P.O.B. 20121, Tel-Aviv; f. 1961; to plan, build, develop, administer, maintain and operate the ports. In 1981/82 investment amounted to I£258 million for the development budget in Haifa, Ashdod and Eilat ports. Cargo traffic April 1980–March 1981 amounted to 11.7m. tons (oil excluded).

ZIM Israel Navigation Co. Ltd.: 209 Hameginim Ave., P.O.B. 1723, Haifa; f. 1945; runs cargo services in the Mediterranean and to N. Europe, N. and S. America, Far East, Africa and Australia; operates 58 ships totalling 2.3m. d.w.t.; Chair. D. ELAZAR; Man. Dir. Y. ROTHEM.

Haifa and Ashdod are the main ports in Israel. The former is a natural harbour, enclosed by two main break-waters and dredged to 37 ft. below mean sea-level. In 1965 the new deep water port was completed at Ashdod which has a capacity of about 6 million tons per year.

In March 1980, Israel had a merchant fleet of 50 ships.

The port of Eilat is Israel's gate to the Red Sea. It is a natural harbour, operated from a wharf. A new port, to the south of the original one, started operating in 1965.

CIVIL AVIATION

El Al Israel Airlines Ltd.: P.O.B. 41, Ben Gurion Airport, Lod, Tel-Aviv; f. 1949; daily services to most capitals of Europe; over twenty flights weekly to New York; services to the U.S.A., Canada, Egypt, Greece, Kenya, Portugal, Romania, South Africa, Spain and Turkey; fleet of 4 Boeing 747-258B, 2 Boeing 747-258C, 2 Boeing 747-124F, 2 Boeing 707-458, 3 Boeing 707-358B, 2 Boeing 707-358C; (on order) 2 Boeing 737-200, 4 Boeing 767-200; Chair. NACHMAN PEREL; Pres. ITZHAK SHANDER.

Arka Israeli Airlines Ltd.: Sde-Dov Airport, P.O.B. 39301, Tel-Aviv; f. 1950; scheduled services from Tel-Aviv, Jerusalem and Haifa to Eilat, Ophira (Sharm-el, Sheikh), Santa Katarina (Mt. Sinai), Rosh Pina, etc.; fleet of 3 Boeing 737, 3 De Havilland Dash-7, 4 Metro II, 2 Metro III and 11 light aircraft.

The following airlines also serve Israel: Air France, Alitalia (Italy), Austrian Airlines, British Airways, Canadian Pacific, Cyprus Airways, KLM (Netherlands), Lufthansa (Federal Republic of Germany), Nile Valley Carriers (private Egyptian), Olympic Airways (Greece), Sabena (Belgium), SAS (Sweden), Swissair, Tarom (Romania), THY (Turkey), TWA (U.S.A.).

TOURISM AND CULTURE

Ministry of Tourism: P.O.B. 1018, Jerusalem; Minister of Tourism AVRAHAM SHARIR; Dir.-Gen. AVRAHAM ROZENMAN.

CULTURAL ORGANIZATIONS

The Israel Festival: 5th Floor, Binyaney Ha'ooma, P.O.B. 6001, 91060 Jerusalem; organizes the Israel Festival which takes place in September in Jerusalem, Tel-Aviv, Caesarea, Haifa and other sites; Chair. Board of

Dirs. A. GAFNI; Chair. Festival Council M. MUSHEVITZ; Dir.-Gen. G. PAZ.

Israel Music Institute: P.O.B. 11253, Tel-Aviv 61112; f. 1961; publishes and promotes Israeli music, educational music and musicological works abroad; member since 1969 of International Music Information Centres (IsMIC); Chair. MORDECHAI VIRSHUBSKY, M.K.; Dir.-Gen. and Editor-in-Chief WILLIAM Y. ELIAS.

The National Council of Culture and Art: Hadar Daphna Bldg., Shaul Hamelech Blvd., Tel-Aviv.

PRINCIPAL THEATRES

Cameri Theatre: Tel-Aviv; f. 1944; public trusteeship; repertory theatre; tours abroad.

Habimah National Theatre of Israel: P.O.B. 222, Tel-Aviv; f. 1918 in Russia, moved to Palestine 1928; Jewish, classical and modern drama.

Israel National Opera: 1 Allenby St., Tel-Aviv; f. 1947 by Edis de-Philippe (Dir.); classical and modern opera; open 50 weeks of the year.

PRINCIPAL ORCHESTRAS

Haifa Symphony Orchestra: 50 Pevsner St., P.O.B. 5210, Haifa; Music Dir. Mrs. ORA GILL.

Israel Chamber Orchestra: Asia House, Tel-Aviv; f. 1965; Musical Dir. URI SEGAL; Gen. Man. RONI ABRAMSON.

Israel Philharmonic Orchestra: Fredric R. Mann Auditorium, Tel-Aviv; f. 1936; Music Director ZUBIN MEHTA; Concertmasters CHAIM TAUB, URI PIANKA.

The Jerusalem Symphony Orchestra: Israel Broadcasting Authority, Binyaney Ha'ooma, Jerusalem; f. 1936; 96 mems.; Dir. YEHUDA FICKLER; Chief conductor and musical dir. GARY BERTINI.

DANCE TROUPES

Bat-Dor Dance Company: 30 Ibn Gvirol St., Tel-Aviv; contemporary repertory dance company; owns theatre in Tel-Aviv; frequent tours abroad; Producer BATSHEVA DE ROTHSCHILD; Artistic Dir. JEANNETTE ORDMAN; Gen. Man. BARRY SWERSKY.

Batsheva Dance Company: 9 Shderot Hahaskala, Tel-Aviv 67898.

Inbal Dance Theatre: 74 Arlosoroff St., Tel-Aviv; f. 1949; modern Israeli dance theatre specializing in their traditional folk art, with choreographic themes from the Bible; frequent tours abroad; Founder and Artistic Dir. SARA LEVI-TANAI.

FESTIVALS

Israel Festival: 5th Floor, Binyaney Ha'ooma, P.O.B. 6001, Jerusalem 91060; organizes the Israel Festival held annually in September in Jerusalem, Tel-Aviv, Haifa, Caesarea and other sites; Chair. Exec. Cttee. A. BEN-NATAN; Dir. J. BISTRITZKY.

Ein Gev Music Festival: Kibbutz Ein Gev, P.O. Ein-Gev 14 940; international festival; annually for one week at Passover.

Zimriya: P.O.B. 29334, Tel-Aviv 61292; World Assembly of Choirs, comprising Israeli and international choirs; f. 1952; every two years.

ATOMIC ENERGY

Israel Atomic Energy Commission: 26 Rehov Hauniversita, Ramat Aviv, P.O.B. 7061, Tel-Aviv; f. 1952; advises the Government on long term policies and priorities in the advancement of nuclear research and development; supervises the implementation of policies approved by the government; including the licensing of nuclear power plants; represents Israel in its relations with scientific institutions abroad and international organizations engaged in nuclear research and development (Israel is a member of IAEA); Chair. The PRIME MINISTER; Dir.-Gen. UZI EILAM.

The Atomic Energy Commission has two research and development centres: the Soreq Nuclear Research Centre and the Negev Nuclear Research Centre near Dimona. The main fields of research are: nuclear physics and chemistry, reactor physics, reactor engineering, radiation research and applications, application of isotopes, metallurgy, electronics, radiobiology, nuclear medicine, nuclear power and desalination. The centres also provide national services: health physics including film badge service, isotope production and molecule labelling, activation analysis, irradiation, advice to industry and institutions, training of personnel, technical courses, documentation.

Soreq Nuclear Research Centre: Yavne 70600; f. 1952; equipped with a swimming pool type research reactor IRR-1 of 5 MW thermal; Dir. S. FREIER.

Negev Nuclear Research Centre: Dimona; equipped with a natural uranium fuelled and heavy water moderated reactor IRR-2 of 26 MW thermal; Dir. ABRAHAM SEROUSSI.

Weizmann Institute of Science: Rehovot; Department of Nuclear Physics engaged in research and graduate teaching in experimental and theoretical nuclear structure and elementary particle physics, critical phenomena and theoretical astrophysics, as well as in applied physics; the department operates three electrostatic accelerators, the largest being a *14 MV Pelletron*; Head Prof. U. SMILANSKY.

Department of Isotope Research engaged in research and teaching in a broad area, ranging from environmental research to brain chemistry, using isotope techniques; it also operates a product on-scale plant for the separation of o^{17} and o^{18} from o^{16}; Head J. R. GAT.

Racah Institute of Physics: Faculty of Science, Hebrew University of Jerusalem, Givat Ram Campus, Jerusalem 91904; engages in research into atomic physics, microwaves, plasma and ionized gases, molecular, medical, solid state and theoretical physics.

Technion: Israel Institute of Technology: Haifa; the Dept. of Physics engages in undergraduate teaching in physics, as well as graduate teaching and research mainly in nuclear physics, high energy physics, foundations of quantum mechanics, atomic physics, relativity and astrophysics, solid state spectroscopy, very low temperature physics, phase transitions, semiconductor physics, magnetism and quantum optics; Chair. Dept. of Physics Prof. A. DAR; the Dept. of Nuclear Engineering undertakes teaching and graduate work in applied nuclear science and engineering; research groups work in the fields of theoretical and experimental nuclear reactor physics, neutron physics, nuclear desalination, heat transfer, nuclear radiations; Head, Nuclear Engineering Dept. Prof. A. NOTEA.

DEFENCE

The General Staff

This consists of the Chiefs of the General Staff, Manpower, Logistics and Intelligence Branches of the Defence Forces, the Commanders of the Air Force and the Navy, and the officers commanding the three Regional Commands (Northern, Central and Southern). It is headed by the Chief of Staff of the Armed Forces.

Chief of Staff of the Armed Forces: Maj.-Gen. RAFAEL EITAN.

Head of Ground Forces Command: Maj.-Gen. ISRAEL TAL.

Commander of the Air Force: Maj.-Gen. DAVID IVRI.

Commander of the Navy: Commodore ZEEV ALMOG.

Expenditure (1981): 62,940 million shekels.

Military Service (Jewish population only): Men under 29 and some unmarried women under 26 are called for regular service of up to 36 months for men and 24 months for women. Physicians may be called up to the age of 34.

Total Armed Forces: 172,000: including 120,300 conscripts; this can be raised to 400,000 by mobilizing reservists within 48–72 hours; army 135,000 (110,000 conscripts); navy 9,000 (3,300 conscripts); air force 28,000 (7,000 conscripts).

Paramilitary Forces: 4,500.

EDUCATION

The present-day school system is based on the Compulsory Education Law (1949), the State Education Law (1953), the School Inspection Law (1969) and on certain provisions of the 1933 Education Ordinance dating back to the British Mandatory Administration. The first of these introduced free compulsory primary education for all children aged between the ages of 5 and 13 (one year kindergarten, eight years' elementary schooling). This law was extended, with the school reform of 1968, to include the ninth and tenth grades. In the 1979/80 school year free, but not compulsory, education was extended up to and including the twelfth grade.

The State Education Law abolished the old complicated Trend Education System, and vested the responsibility for education in the Government, thus providing a unified State-controlled elementary school system. The law does, however, recognize two main forms of Primary Education—(a) State Education; (b) Recognized Non-State Education. State Education may be sub-divided into two distinct categories of schools—State Schools and State Religious Schools for Jews, and State Schools for Arabs. Schools and kindergartens of the State system are in the joint ownership of the State and the Local Authorities, while the recognized non-State institutions are essentially privately-owned and mainly religious, although they are subsidized, and supervised by the State and the Local Authorities.

The largest "recognized" school system is the Agudat Israel Schools (ultra-orthodox religious). The others are mainly Christian denominational schools.

State Primary Education is financed by a partnership of the Central Government and the Local Authorities. Since 1953 the salaries of all teachers of State Schools have been paid by the Central Government, whilst the cost of maintenance and of maintenance services, and the provision of new buildings and equipment have been the responsibility of the Local Authorities. The State does not impose an Education Tax but local authorities may, with the Ministry's approval, levy a rate on parents for special services.

The State provides schools in which the language of instruction is either Hebrew or Arabic according to the language spoken by the majority of the local population. Nevertheless, many Arab children attend Jewish primary, secondary, vocational, agricultural and even teacher-training colleges. In the Jewish sector there is a distinct line of division between the secular State schools and the Religious State schools, which are established

on the demand of parents in any locality, provided that a certain minimum number of pupils have first been enrolled. In the Arab Schools all instruction is in Arabic, and there is a special department for Arabic Education in the Ministry of Education and Culture. Some 90 per cent of the Arab children attend school regularly.

The law also provides schooling for working youth between the ages of 14 and 18 who have not completed their primary education, as well as special education for emotionally or physically handicapped children. In addition, special attention is given to those children who are culturally deprived and a great variety of methods is being devised to bring them up to the level of the other children.

Post-Primary Education is free, lasts six years, three of which are compulsory, and is divided into an intermediate and a higher level. The intermediate level provides general education and the higher level is roughly divided into academic; technical and vocational; and agricultural. The last two categories also have pre-academic streams lasting from one to two years and receive all the benefits of the regular post-primary schools. The pupils graduating from academic high school receive either a school leaving certificate or *bagrut* (matriculation). The *bagrut* certificate entitles the pupil to enter university, although the university is not obliged to accept him or her.

The frameworks offered by vocational and technical schools can be divided into three types: practical-technical; general-technical; and secondary technical. All three types are of three or four years' duration, depending on whether they are run under the Reform or under the old system. Very few of the practical-technical schools still offer a two-year course, i.e., a total of 11 years' schooling. The practical-technical schools train their pupils mainly for a profession and the ratio between general studies and vocational-technical studies is 40 : 60. The general-technical schools award a School Leaving Certificate to those pupils who complete the course successfully. This entitles them to continue their studies in the third level of education after some complementary examinations, either for one additional year to obtain a technician's certificate (*Techna'i*), or for two additional years to obtain the certificate of a practical engineer (*Handessa'i*). The ratio between general studies and vocational studies in these schools is 50 : 50. All graduates of the secondary technical schools may sit for the *bagrut* examinations. Even without achieving the *bagrut* certificate the pupils may continue their studies in the short-cycle post-secondary schools, described above, without further examination and obtain the technician or practical engineer certificate. The ratio between general studies and technical-vocational studies in these schools is 60 : 40.

Agricultural post-primary courses are of either three or four years' duration (again depending on the Reform) and some schools offer an additional year or year and a half (13th and 14th grade) leading to a practical engineer certificate. The holders of this certificate are eligible, without further examinations, for study in agricultural engineering or general agricultural higher studies in the Technion (the Israel Institute of Technology) at Haifa or the Faculty of Agriculture at the Hebrew University of Jerusalem. Unlike pupils at vocational-technical post-primary schools, all those completing agricultural courses may sit for the *bagrut* examinations. By and large, agricultural post-primary schools are boarding schools although some, mainly those of the *kibbutz* and the *moshav* movements, are regional day schools.

Adult Education. There is an extensive adult education programme. Programmes extend from literacy courses through primary and secondary level studies up to second-chance university facilities. There are post-army preparatory courses for entry into the university. High school courses may be completed in the army and in 1976 the Everyman's University began, based on the British model of Open University.

Teacher Training. Almost all kindergarten and primary school teachers are trained in three to three and a half year courses at post-secondary teacher training institutions (*Mossadot Le-Hakhsharat Morim Ve Gananot*). The Ministry's policy is to have only three-year teacher training colleges and to extend the training period to four years for a B.Ed. degree. Government regulations require that teachers for grades seven to 10 have a B.A. and a university teaching certificate, while for grades 11 and 12 they are required to have a master's degree and a university teaching certificate. The *bagrut* certificate is required for admittance to the above teacher training institutions.

BIBLIOGRAPHY

GENERAL

AVNERY, URI. Israel without Zionists (Collier-Macmillan, London, 1969).

GLUECK, NELSON. The River Jordan (Philadelphia, 1946.) Rivers in the Desert (London, 1959).

KOHN, HANS. Nationalism and Imperialism in the Hither East (London, 1932).

KOLLEK, TEDDY, and PEARLMAN, MOSHE. Jerusalem, Sacred City of Mankind (Weidenfeld and Nicolson, London, 1968).

MALLISON, W. T. (Jr.) The Zionist-Israel Juridical Claims to Constitute "The Jewish People" Nationality Entity and to Confer Membership of it. (*George Washington Law Review*, Vol. 32, No. 4-June 1964).

MARMORSTEIN, EMILE. Heaven at Bay: The Jewish Kulturkampf in the Holy Land (Oxford University Press, 1969).

ORNI, E. and EFRAT, E. The Geography of Israel (Darey, New York, 1965).

ORON, YITZHAK. Middle East Record, Vol. II (Daniel Davey and Co., New York, 1966).

PARKES, J. W. The Emergence of the Jewish Problem, 1878-1939 (Oxford, 1946).

A History of Palestine from A.D. 135 to Modern Times (Gollancz, London, 1949).

End of Exile (New York, 1954).

Whose Land? A History of the Peoples of Palestine (Pelican, Harmondsworth, 1970).

PATAI, R. Israel Between East and West (Philadelphia, 1953).

Culture and Conflict (New York, 1962).

SHAPIRO, HARRY L. The Jewish People: a biological history (UNESCO, 1960).

TUCHMAN, BARBARA W. Bible and Sword (Redman, London, 1957; Minerva, New York, 1968).

WEINGROD, ALEX. Reluctant Pioneers, Village Development in Israel (Cornell University Press, New York, 1966).

ZANDER, WALTER. Israel and the Holy Places of Christendom (Weidenfeld and Nicolson, 1972).

ANCIENT HISTORY

DE VAUX, R. Ancient Israel: Its Life and Institutions (New York, 1961).

ORLINSKY, H. M. Ancient Israel (Cornell University Press).

SMITH, Sir G. A. Historical Geography of the Holy Land (24th ed., London, 1931).

YADIN, YIGAEL. Message of the Scrolls (Grosset and Dunlap, New York).

Masada (Weidenfeld and Nicolson, London, 1966).

YEWIN, S. A Decade of Archaeology in Israel 1948-58 (Istanbul, 1960).

RECENT HISTORY

ALLON, YIGAL. The making of Israel's Army (Vallentine, Mitchell, London, 1970).

BARBOUR, NEVILL. Nisi Dominus: a survey of the Palestine Controversy (Harrap, London, 1946, reprinted by the Institute for Palestine Studies, Beirut, 1969).

BENTWICH, NORMAN and HELEN. Mandate Memories, 1918-1948 (Hogarth Press, London, 1965).

BERMANT, CHAIM. Israel (Thames and Hudson, London, 1967).

BERGER, EARL. The Covenant and the Sword, Arab-Israel Relations 1948–56 (University of Toronto Press, Toronto, 1965).

BETHELL, NICHOLAS. The Palestine Triangle: the Struggle between the British, the Jews and the Arabs, 1935–48 (André Deutsch, London, 1979).

CATTAN, HENRY. Palestine, the Arabs and Israel (Longmans Green, London, 1969).

CHURCHILL, RANDOLPH and WINSTON. The Six Day War (Heinemann/Penguin, London, 1967).

COHEN, MICHAEL J. Palestine, Retreat from the Mandate: The Making of British Policy (Elek, London, 1978).

CROSSMAN, R. H. S. Palestine Mission (London, 1947).

DRAPER, T. Israel and World Politics: Roots of the Third Arab-Israeli War (Secker and Warburg, London, 1968).

ESCO FOUNDATION FOR PALESTINE. Palestine: A Study of Jewish, Arab and British Policies (2 vols., New Haven, 1947).

ISRAEL

Bibliography

GABBAY, RONY E. A Political Study of the Arab-Jewish Conflict, the Arab Refugee Problem (Geneva and Paris, 1959).

HOWARD, M., and HUNTER, R. Israel and the Arab World (Institute of Palestine Studies, Beirut).

JIRYIS, SABRI. The Arabs in Israel (Institute for Palestine Studies, Beirut, 1968).

KADER, RAZZAK ABDEL. The Arab-Jewish Conflict (1961).

KHALIDI, WALID. From Haven to Conquest: Readings in Zionism and the Palestine Problem until 1948 (Institute for Palestine Studies, Beirut, 1971).

KIMCHE, JON. Palestine or Israel (Secker & Warburg, London, 1973).

KIMCHE, JON and DAVID. Both Sides of the Hill: Britain and the Palestine War (Secker and Warburg, London, 1960).

KOESTLER, ARTHUR. Promise and Fulfilment: Palestine, 1917-1949 (London, 1949).

Thieves in the Night (New York and London, 1946).

LANDAU, JACOB M. The Arabs in Israel (Oxford University Press, London, 1969).

LAQUEUR, WALTER. The Road to War 1967 (Weidenfeld and Nicolson, London, 1968).

The Israel-Arab Reader (Weidenfeld and Nicolson, London, 1969).

LILIENTHAL, ALFRED M. The Other Side of the Coin: An American Perspective of the Arab-Israeli Conflict (New York, 1965).

LORCH, N. The Edge of the Sword: Israel's War of Independence 1947-49 (Putnam, New York, 1961).

LUCAS, NOAH. The Modern History of Israel (Weidenfeld and Nicolson, London, 1974/75).

MARLOWE, JOHN. The Seat of Pilate, An Account of the Palestine Mandate (Cresset, London, 1959; Dufour, Philadelphia, 1958).

O'BALLANCE, E. The Arab-Israeli War (New York, Praeger, 1957).

The Third Arab-Israeli War (Faber & Faber, London, 1972).

PERETZ, DON. Israel and the Palestine Arabs (The Middle East Institute, Washington, 1958).

PERLMUTTER, AMOS. Military and Politics in Israel, 1948–1967 (2nd edition, Frank Cass, London, 1977).
Politics and the Military in Israel, 1967–1976 (Frank Cass, London, 1977).

RABIN, YITZHAK. The Rabin Memoirs (Weidenfeld and Nicolson, London, 1979).

RIZK, EDWARD. The Palestine Question, Seminar of Arab Jurists on Palestine, Algiers, 1967 (Institute for Palestine Studies, Beirut, 1968).

RODINSON, MAXIME. Israel and the Arabs (Penguin Books, Harmondsworth, 1968; Pantheon, New York, 1969).

ROULEAU, ERIC and HELD, JEAN-FRANCIS. Israël et les Arabes (Editions du Seuil, Paris, 1967).

ROYAL INSTITUTE OF INTERNATIONAL AFFAIRS. Great Britain and Palestine 1915-45 (London, 1946).

SHARABI, HISHAM B. Palestine and Israel: The Lethal Dilemma (Van Nostrand Reinhold, New York, 1969).

SYKES, CHRISTOPHER. Crossroads to Israel (Collins, London, 1965).

TEVETH, SHABTAI. Moshe Dayan (Weidenfeld and Nicolson, London, 1972).

WEIZMAN, EZER. The Battle for Peace (Bantam Books, New York, 1981).

THE STATE

AVI-HAI, AVRAHAM. Ben Gurion, State Builder (Israel Universities Press, 1974).

BADI, JOSEPH. Fundamental Laws of the State of Israel (New York, 1961).

BAR-ZOHAR, MICHAEL. Ben-Gurion: A Biography (London, Weidenfeld & Nicolson, 1978).

BARUTH, K. H. The Physical Planning of Israel (London, 1949).

BEN GURION, D. Rebirth and Destiny of Israel (New York, 1954).

Israel: A Personal History (London, New English Library, 1972).

BENTWICH, NORMAN. Fulfilment in the Promised Land 1917-37 (London, 1938).

Judæa Lives Again (London, 1944).

Israel Resurgent (Ernest Benn, 1960).

The New-old Land of Israel (Allen and Unwin, 1960).

Israel, Two Fateful Years 1967–69 (Elek, London, 1970).

BENTWICH, J. S. Education in Israel (Routledge and Kegan Paul, London, 1965).

BRECHER, MICHAEL. The Foreign Policy System of Israel (Oxford University Press, London, 1972).

COMAY, JOAN and PEARLMAN, MOSHE. Israel (New York, 1965).

CROSSMAN, R. H. S. A Nation Reborn (London, Hamish Hamilton, 1960).

DAVIS, MOSHE (Ed.). Israel: its Role in Civilisation (New York, 1956).

DAYAN, SHMUEL. The Promised Land (London, 1961).

DE GAURY, GERALD. The New State of Israel (New York, 1952).

EBAN, A. The Voice of Israel (New York, Horizon Press, 1957).

The Story of Modern Israel (Weidenfeld & Nicolson, London, 1973).

EDELMAN, MAURICE. Ben Gurion, a Political Biography (Hodder and Stoughton, London, 1964).

FRANKEL, WILLIAM. Israel Observed: an Anatomy of the State (Thames and Hudson, London, 1980).

HALPERIN, HAIM. Changing Patterns in Israel Agriculture (London, 1957).

JANOWSKY, OSCAR I. Foundations of Israel: Emergence of a Welfare State (Anvil Nostrand Co., Princeton, 1959).

KRAINES, O. Government and Politics in Israel (Allen and Unwin, London, 1961).

LIKHOVSKI, ELIAHU S. Israel's Parliament: The Law of the Knesset (Oxford, Clarendon Press, 1971).

MEDDING, PETER. Mapai in Israel: Political Organisation and Government in a New Society (Cambridge U.P., London, 1972).

MEIR, GOLDA. This is our Strength (New York, 1963).

MERHAV, PERETZ. The Israeli Left: History, Problems, Documents (Tantivy Press, 1981).

PREUSS, W. Co-operation in Israel and the World (Jerusalem, 1960).

SACHAR, H. M. ALIYAH. The Peoples of Israel (New York, 1962).

SAFRAN, NADAV. The United States and Israel (Harvard U.P., 1963).

SAMUEL, The Hon. EDWIN. Problems of Government in the State of Israel (Jerusalem, 1956).

SEGRE, V. D. Israel: A Society in Transition (Oxford U.P., London, 1971).

SHATIL, J. L'économie Collective du Kibboutz Israëlien (Paris, Les Editions de Minuit, 1960).

SITTON, SHLOMO. Israël: Immigration et Croissance 1948-58 (Editions Cujas, Paris, 1963).

ZIONISM

BEIN, ALEX. Theodor Herzl (East and West Library, London, 1957).

COHEN, ISRAEL. A Short History of Zionism (London, Frederick Muller, 1951).

FISCH, HAROLD. The Zionist Revolution: A New Perspective (London, Weidenfeld & Nicolson, 1978).

FRANKL, OSCAR BENJAMIN. Theodor Herzl: The Jew and Man (New York, 1949).

LAQUEUR, WALTER. A History of Zionism (Weidenfeld & Nicolson, London, 1972).

LIPSKY, L. A Gallery of Zionist Profiles (New York, Farrar, Straus and Cudahy, 1950).

LOWENTHAL, MARVIN (ed. and trans.). Diaries of Theodor Herzl (Grosset and Dunlap, New York, 1965).

PETUCHOWSKY, J. J. Zionism Reconsidered (Twayne, New York, 1966).

SCHAMA, SIMON. Two Rothschilds and the Land of Israel (London, Collins, 1978).

SCHECHTMAN, J. Rebel and Statesmen: the Jabotinsky Story (New York, Thomas Yoseloff, 1956).

SOKOLOW, NAHUM. History of Zionism (2 vols., Longmans, London, 1919; Ktav, New York, 1969).

STEIN, LEONARD and YOGEV, GEDILIA (Editors). The Letters and Papers of Chaim Weizmann; Volume I 1885-1902 (Oxford University Press, 1968).

VITAL, DAVID. The Origins of Zionism (Oxford University Press, 1975, re-issued 1980).
Zionism: The Formative Years (Oxford University Press, 1981).

WEISGAL, MEYER, and CARMICHAEL, JOEL. Chaim Weizmann—a Biography by Several Hands (London, Weidenfeld and Nicolson, 1962).

WEIZMANN, Dr. CHAIM. The Jewish People and Palestine (London, 1939).
Trial and Error: the Autobiography of Chaim Weizmann (Hamish Hamilton, London, 1949; Schocken, New York, 1966).

OFFICIAL PUBLICATIONS

Report of the Palestine Royal Commission, 1937 (Cmd. 5479), London.

Report of the Palestine Partition Commission, 1938 (Cmd. 5854), London.

Statement of Policy by His Majesty's Government in the United Kingdom (Cmd. 3692), London, 1930; (Cmd. 5893), London, 1938; (Cmd. 6019), London, 1939; (Cmd. 6180), London, 1940.

Government Survey of Palestine (2 vols., 1945-46), Jerusalem. Supplement, July 1947, Jerusalem.

Report of the Anglo-American Committee of Enquiry, Lausanne, 1946.

Report to the United Nations General Assembly by the UN Special Committee on Palestine, Geneva, 1947.

Report of the UN Economic Survey Mission for the Middle East, December 1949 (United Nations, Lake Success, N.Y.; H.M. Stationery Office).

Annual Yearbook of the Government of Israel.
Israel Government. The Arabs in Israel (1952).

Jewish Agency for Palestine. Documents Submitted to General Assembly of UN, relating to the National Home (1947).
The Jewish Plan for Palestine (Jerusalem, 1947).
Statistical Survey of the Middle East (1944).

Statistical Abstract of Israel. Central Bureau of Statistics (annual).

Jordan

PHYSICAL AND SOCIAL GEOGRAPHY

W. B. Fisher

The Hashemite Kingdom of Jordan (previously Trans-jordan) came officially into existence under its present name in 1947 and was enlarged in 1950 to include the districts of Samaria and part of Judaea that had previously formed part of Arab Palestine. The country is bounded on the north by Syria, on the north-east by Iraq, on the east and south by Saudi Arabia, and on the west by Israel. The total area of Jordan is approximately 37,500 sq. miles. The territory west of the Jordan river—some 2,165 sq. miles—has been occupied by Israel since June 1967.

PHYSICAL FEATURES

The greater part of the State of Jordan consists of a plateau lying some 2-3,000 ft. above sea-level, which forms the north-western corner of the great plateau of Arabia (see "Saudi Arabia"). There are no natural topographical frontiers between Jordan and its neighbours Syria, Iraq, and Saudi Arabia, and the plateau continues unbroken into all three countries, with the artificial frontier boundaries drawn as straight lines between defined points. Along its western edge, facing the Jordan Valley, the plateau is up-tilted to give a line of hills that rise 1-2,000 ft. above plateau-level. An old river course, the Wadi Sirhan, now almost dry with only occasional wells, breaks up the plateau surface on the south-east and continues into Saudi Arabia.

The Jordanian plateau consists of a core or table of ancient rocks, covered by layers of newer rock (chiefly limestone) lying almost horizontally. In a few places (e.g. on the southern edge of the Jordan Valley) these old rocks are exposed at the surface. On its western side the plateau has been fractured and dislocated by the development of strongly marked tear faults that run from the Red Sea via the Gulf of Aqaba northwards to the Lebanon and Syria. The narrow zone between the faults has sunk, to give the well-known Jordan rift valley, which is bordered both on the east and west by steep-sided walls, especially in the south near the Dead Sea, where the drop is often precipitous. The valley has a maximum width of 14 miles, and is now thought to have been produced by lateral shearing of two continental plates that on the east have been displaced by about 80 km. (50 miles).

The floor of the Jordan Valley varies considerably in level. At its northern end it is just above sea-level; the surface of Lake Tiberias (the Sea of Galilee) is 686 ft. below sea-level, with the deepest part of the lake 700 ft. lower still. Greatest depth of the valley is at the Dead Sea (surface 1,300 ft. below sea-level, maximum depth 1,298 ft.).

Dislocation of the rock strata in the region of the Jordan Valley has had two further effects: firstly, earth tremors are still frequent along the valley (Jerusalem has minor earthquakes from time to time); and secondly, considerable quantities of lava have welled up, forming enormous sheets that cover wide expanses of territory in the State of Jordan and southern Syria, and produce a desolate, forbidding landscape. One small lava flow, by forming a natural dam across the Jordan Valley, has impounded the waters to form Lake Tiberias.

The River Jordan rises just inside the frontiers of Syria and the Lebanon—a fruitful source of dispute between the two countries and Israel. The river is 157 miles long, and after first flowing for 60 miles in Israel it lies within Jordanian territory for the remaining 95 miles. Its main tributary, the Yarmuk, is 25 miles long, and close to its junction with the Jordan forms the boundary between Jordan State, Israel and Syria. A few miles from its source, the River Jordan used to open into Lake Huleh, a shallow, marsh-fringed expanse of water which was for long a breeding ground of malaria, but which has now been drained. Lake Tiberias, also, like Huleh, in Israel, covers an area of 122 sq. miles and measures 14 miles from north to south, and 16 miles from east to west. River water outflowing from the lake is used for the generation of hydro-electricity.

The river then flows through the barren, inhospitable country of its middle and lower valley, very little of which is actually, or potentially, cultivable, and finally enters the Dead Sea. This lake is 40 miles long and 10 miles wide. Owing to the very high air temperatures at most seasons of the year evaporation from the lake is intense, and has been estimated as equivalent to $8\frac{1}{2}$ million tons of water per day. At the surface the Dead Sea water contains about 250 grammes of dissolved salts per litre, and at a depth of 360 feet the water is chemically saturated (i.e. holds its maximum possible content). Magnesium chloride is the most abundant mineral, with sodium chloride next in importance; but commercial interest centres in the less abundant potash and bromide salts.

Climatically, Jordan shows close affinity to its neighbours. Summers are hot, especially on the plateau and in the Jordan Valley, where temperatures up to 120° F. have been recorded. Winters are fairly cold, and on the plateau frost and some snow are usual, though not in the lower Jordan Valley. The significant element of the climate of Jordan is rainfall. In the higher parts (i.e. the uplands of Samaria and Judaea and the hills overlooking the eastern Jordan Valley) 15 to 25 inches of rainfall occur, enough for agriculture; but elsewhere as little as 8 inches or less may fall, and pastoral nomadism is the only possible way of life. Only about 25 per cent of the total area of Jordan is sufficiently humid for cultivation.

Hence the main features of economic life in Jordan are subsistence agriculture of a marginal kind, carried on in Judaea-Samaria and on the north-eastern edge of the plateau, close to Amman, with migratory herding of animals—sheep, goats, cattle and camels—over the remaining and by far the larger portion of the country. As a result, the natural wealth of Jordan is small and tribal ways of life exist in parts. Before the June 1967 War tourism (with which must be included religious pilgrimage, mainly to the Holy Christian places of Jerusalem) had developed into a very important industry but this has been seriously jeopardized by the Israeli occupation of the West Bank territory and annexation of Jerusalem. However, civil war in the Lebanon and re-opening of the Suez Canal (which greatly affects the Jordanian port of Aqaba) have been very favourable factors. The war between Iran and Iraq has also had a very beneficial effect, since Aqaba, with the denial of Gulf ports to Iraq, has become a major supply base: Iraq is now Jordan's most important export market.

The shift of trade from the Lebanon, a very much better economic and political relationship with Iraq, continuing (though cool) relations with Syria, the inflow of remittances from Jordanians working abroad (now running at about U.S. $1,000 million annually), and subventions from Arab funds have together greatly improved the Jordanian economy. Foreign aid of various kinds, however, still accounts for more than 40 per cent of budgetary revenues, and workers in the service sector greatly outnumber those in directly productive activities. With so many Jordanians working abroad, local activities are hampered by lack of managerial and technical skills.

RACE AND LANGUAGE

A division must be drawn between the Jordanians living east of the River Jordan who, in the main, are ethnically similar to the desert populations of Syria and Saudi Arabia, and the Arabs of the Jordan Valley and Samaria-Judaea.

These latter are slightly taller, more heavily built, and have a broader head-form. Some authorities suggest that they are descendants of the Canaanites, who may have originated far to the north-east, in the Zagros area. An Iranian racial affinity is thus implied—but this must be of very ancient date, as the Arabs west of the Jordan Valley have been settled in their present home for many thousands of years. Besides the two groups of Arabs there are also small colonies of Circassians from the Caucasus of Russia, who settled in Jordan as refugees during the nineteenth and twentieth centuries A.D.

Arabic is spoken everywhere, except in a few Circassian villages, and, through the contacts with Britain, some English is understood in the towns.

HISTORY

Jordan, as an independent State, is a twentieth-century development. Before then it was seldom more than a rugged and backward appendage to more powerful kingdoms and empires, and indeed never had any separate existence. In Biblical times the area was covered roughly by Gilead, Ammon, Moab and Edom, and the western portions formed for a time part of the kingdom of Israel. During the sixth century B.C. the Arabian tribe of the Nabateans established their capital at Petra in the south and continued to preserve their independence when, during the fourth and third centuries, the northern half was incorporated into the Seleucid province of Syria. It was under Seleucid rule that cities like Philadelphia (the Biblical Rabbath Ammon and the modern Amman) and Gerasa (now Jerash) rose to prominence. During the first century B.C. the Nabateans extended their rule over the greater part of present-day Jordan and Syria; they then began to recede before the advance of Rome, and in A.D. 105–6 Petra was incorporated into the Roman Empire. The lands east of the Jordan shared in a brief blaze of glory under the Palmyrene sovereigns Odenathus (Udaynath) and Zenobia (al-Zabba') in the middle of the third century A.D., and during the fifth and sixth centuries formed part of the dominions of the Christian Ghassanid dynasty, vassals of the Byzantine Empire. Finally, after fifty years of anarchy in which Byzantine, Persian and local rulers intervened, Transjordania was conquered by the Arabs and absorbed into the Islamic Empire.

For centuries nothing more is heard of the country; it formed normally a part of Syria, and as such was generally governed from Egypt. From the beginning of the sixteenth century it was included in the Ottoman *vilayet* of Damascus, and remained in a condition of stagnation until the outbreak of the Great War in 1914. European travellers and explorers of the nineteenth century rediscovered the beauties of Petra and Gerasa, but otherwise the desert tribes were left undisturbed. Even the course of the war in its early stages gave little hint of the upheaval that was to take place in Jordan's fortunes. The area was included in the zone of influence allocated to Britain under the Sykes-Picot Treaty of May 1916 (*see* Documents on Palestine, p. 62), and Zionists held that it also came within the area designated as a Jewish National Home in the promise contained in the Balfour Declaration of November 1917. Apart from these somewhat remote political events the tide of war did not reach Jordanian territory until the capture of Aqaba by the Arab armies under Faisal, the third son of King Hussein of the Hijaz, in July 1917. A year later, in September 1918, they shared in the final push north by capturing Amman and Deraa.

The end of the war thus found a large area, which included almost the whole of present-day Jordan, in Arab hands under the leadership of Faisal. To begin with, the territory to the east of the River Jordan was not looked on as a separate unit. Faisal, with the assistance of British officers and Iraqi nationalists, set up an autonomous government in Damascus, a step encouraged by the Anglo-French Declaration of November 7th, 1918, favouring the establishment of indigenous governments in Syria and Iraq. Arab demands, however, as expressed by Faisal at the Paris Peace Conference in January 1919, went a good deal further in claiming independence throughout the Arab world. This brought them sharply up against both French and Zionist claims in the Near East, and when in March 1920 the General Syrian Congress in Damascus declared the independence of Syria and Iraq, with Faisal and Abdullah, Hussein's second son, as kings, the decisions were denounced by France and Britain. The following month the San Remo Conference awarded the Palestine Mandate to Britain, and thus separated it effectively from Syria proper, which fell within the French share. Faisal was forced out of Damascus by the French in July and left the country.

THE KINGDOM OF TRANSJORDAN

The position of Transjordania was not altogether clear under the new dispensation. After the withdrawal of Faisal the British High Commissioner informed a meeting of notables at Es Salt that the British Government favoured self-government for the territory with British advisers. In December 1920 the provisional frontiers of the Mandates were extended eastwards by Anglo-French agreement so as to include Transjordania within the Palestine Mandate, and therefore presumably within the provisions regarding the establishment of a Jewish National Home. Yet another twist of policy came as the result of a conference in Cairo in March 1921 attended by Winston Churchill, the new British Colonial Secretary, Abdullah, T. E. Lawrence and Sir Herbert Samuel, High Commissioner for Palestine. At this meeting it was recommended that Faisal should be proclaimed King of Iraq, while Abdullah was persuaded to stand down in his favour by the promise of an Arab administration in Transjordania. He had in fact been in effective control in Amman since his arrival the previous winter to organize a rising against the French in Syria. This project he now abandoned, and in April 1921 was officially recognized as *de facto* ruler of Transjordan. The final draft of the Palestine Mandate confirmed by the Council of the League of Nations in July 1922 contained a clause giving the Mandatory Power considerable latitude in the administration of the territory east of the Jordan (*see* Documents on Palestine, p. 70). On the basis of this clause a memorandum was approved in the following September expressly excluding Transjordan from the clauses relating to the establishment of the Jewish National Home, and although many Zionists continued to press for the reversal of this policy, the country thenceforth remained in practice separate from Palestine proper.

Like much of the post-war boundary delineation, the borders of the new state were somewhat arbitrary. Though they lay mainly in desert areas, they frequently cut across tribal areas and grazing grounds with small respect for tradition. Of the three or four hundred thousand inhabitants only about a fifth were town-dwellers, and these confined to four small cities ranging in population from 30,000 to 10,000. Nevertheless Transjordan's early years were destined to be comparatively peaceful. On May 15th, 1923, Britain formally recognized Transjordan as an independent constitutional State under the rule of the Amir Abdullah with British tutelage, and with the aid of a British subsidy it was possible to make some slow progress towards development and modernization. A small but efficient armed force, the Arab Legion, was built up under the guidance of Peake Pasha and later Glubb Pasha; this force distinguished itself particularly during the Iraqi rebellion of May 1941. It also played a significant role in the fighting with Israel during 1948. Other British advisers assisted in the development of health services and schools.

The Amir Abdullah very nearly became involved in the fall of his father, King Hussein, in 1924. It was in Amman on March 5th, 1924, that the latter proclaimed Caliph, and during the subsequent fighting with Ibn Sa'ud Wahhabi troops penetrated into Transjordanian territory. They subsequently withdrew to the south, and in June 1925, after the abdication of Hussein's eldest son Ali, Abdullah formally incorporated Ma'an and Aqaba within his dominions. The move was not disputed by the new ruler of the Hijaz and Najd, and thereafter the southern frontier of Transjordan has remained unaltered.

INDEPENDENCE

In February 1928 a treaty was signed with Great Britain granting a still larger measure of independence, though reserving for the advice of a British Resident such matters as financial policy and foreign relations. The same treaty provided for a constitution, and this was duly promulgated in April 1928, the first Legislative Council meeting a year later. In January 1934 a supplementary agreement was added permitting Transjordan to appoint consular representatives in Arab countries, and in May 1939 Britain agreed to the conversion of the Legislative Council into a regular Cabinet with ministers in charge of specified departments. The outbreak of war delayed further advances towards independence, but this was finally achieved in name at least by the Treaty of London of March 22nd, 1946. On the following May 25th Abdullah was proclaimed king and a new constitution replaced the now obsolete one of 1928.

Transjordan was not slow in taking her place in the community of nations. In 1947 King Abdullah signed treaties with Turkey and Iraq and applied for membership of the United Nations; this last, however, was thwarted by the Russian veto and by lack of American recognition of Transjordan's status as an independent nation. In March 1948 Britain agreed to the signing of a new treaty in which virtually the only restrictive clauses related to military and defence matters. Britain was to have certain peace-time military privileges, including the maintenance of airfields and communications, transit facilities and coordination of training methods. She was also to provide economic and social aid.

Transjordan had, however, not waited for independence before making her weight felt in Arab affairs in the Middle East. She had not been very active before the war, and, in fact her first appearance on the international scene was in May 1939, when Transjordanian delegates were invited to the Round Table Conference on Palestine in London. Transjordan took part in the preliminary discussions during 1943 and 1944 that led finally to the formation of the Arab League in March 1945, and was one of the original members of that League. During the immediately following years it seemed possible that political and dynastic differences would be forgotten in this common effort for unity. Under the stresses and strains of 1948 however, the old contradictions began to reappear. Abdullah had long favoured the project of a "Greater Syria", that is, the union of Transjordan, Syria, and Palestine, as a step towards the final unification of the Fertile Crescent by the inclusion of Iraq. This was favoured on dynastic grounds by various parties in Iraq, and also by some elements in Syria and Palestine. On the other hand it met with violent opposition from many Syrian nationalists, from the rulers of Egypt and Saudi Arabia—neither of whom were disposed to favour any strengthening of the Hashemite house—and of course from the Zionists and the French. It is in the light of these conflicts of interest that developments subsequent to the establishment of the State of Israel must be seen.

FORMATION OF ISRAEL

On May 14th–15th, 1948, British troops were withdrawn into the port of Haifa as a preliminary to the final evacuation of Palestine territory, the State of Israel was proclaimed, and Arab armies entered the former Palestinian territory from all sides. Only those from Transjordan played any significant part in the fighting, and by the time that major hostilities ceased in July they had succeeded in occupying a considerable area. The suspicion now inevitably arose that Abdullah was prepared to accept a *fait accompli* and to negotiate with the Israeli authorities for a formal recognition of the existing military boundaries. Moreover, whereas the other Arab countries refused to accept any other move that implied a tacit recognition of the *status quo*—such as the resettlement of refugees— Transjordan seemed to be following a different line. In September 1948 an Arab government was formed at Gaza under Egyptian tutelage, and this was answered from the Transjordanian side by the proclamation in December at Jericho of Abdullah as King of All-Palestine. In the following April the country's name was changed to Jordan and three Palestinians were included in the Cabinet. In the meantime armistices were being signed by all the Arab countries, including Jordan, and on January 31st, 1949, Jordan had at last been recognized by the United States.

On the three major problems confronting the Arab States in their dispute with Israel, Jordan continued to differ more or less openly with her colleagues. She refused to agree to the internationalization of Jerusalem, she initiated plans for the resettlement of the Arab refugees, and she showed a disposition to accept as permanent the armistice frontiers. In April 1950, after rumours of negotiations between Jordan and Israel, the Arab League Council in Cairo succeeded in getting Jordan's adherence to resolutions forbidding negotiations with Israel or annexation of Palestinian territory. Nevertheless, in the same month elections were held in Jordan and Arab Palestine, the results of which encouraged Abdullah formally to annex the latter territory on April 24th, 1950. This step was immediately recognized by Britain.

At the meeting of the Arab League that followed, Egypt led the opposition to Jordan, who found support, however, from Iraq. The decisions reached by the Council were inconclusive; but thereafter Jordan began to drift away from

Arab League policy. Jordan supported the United Nations policy over Korea, in contradistinction to the other Arab states, and signed a Point Four agreement with the United States in March 1951. Though there was at the same time constant friction between Jordan and Israel the unified opposition of the Arab States to the new Jewish State seemed to have ended, and inter-Arab differences were gaining the upper hand.

ABDULLAH ASSASSINATED

On July 20th, 1951, King Abdullah was assassinated in Jerusalem. Evidence brought out at the trial of those implicated in the plot showed that the murder was as much as anything a protest against his Greater Syria policy, and it was significant that Egypt refused to extradite some of those convicted. Nevertheless, the stability of the young Jordanian State revealed itself in the calm in which the King's eldest son Talal succeeded to the throne, and the peaceful elections held shortly afterwards. In January 1952 a new constitution was promulgated. Even more significant, perhaps, was the dignity with which, only a year after his accession, King Talal, whose mental condition had long been giving cause for anxiety, abdicated in favour of his son, Hussein, still a minor. In foreign policy Talal had shown some signs of a reaction against his father's ideas in favour of a *rapprochement* with Syria and Egypt, one step being Jordan's signature of the Arab Collective Security Pact which she had failed to join in the summer of 1950.

This policy was continued during the reign of his son, King Hussein, notably by the conclusion of an economic and financial agreement with Syria in February 1953, and a joint scheme for the construction of a dam across the Yarmuk River to supply irrigation and hydro-electric power. One problem which became pressing in 1954 was the elaborate scheme sponsored by the United States for the sharing of the Jordan waters between Jordan, Iraq, Syria and Israel, which could make no progress in the absence of political agreement.

During December a financial aid agreement was signed in London with the United Kingdom, and the opportunity was taken to discuss the revision of the Anglo-Jordanian Treaty of 1946. Agreement over this was not possible owing to British insistence that any new pact should fit into a general Middle East defence system. In May 1955 Premier Abu'l-Huda was replaced by Sa'id al-Mufti, while an exchange of state visits with King Sa'ud hinted at a *rapprochement* with Saudi Arabia. Nevertheless, in November Jordan declared its unwillingness to adhere either to the Egyptian-Syrian-Saudi Arabian bloc or to the Baghdad Pact.

DISMISSAL OF GLUBB PASHA

On December 15th, following a visit to General Sir. G. Templer, Chief of the Imperial General Staff, Sa'id al-Mufti resigned and was replaced by Hazza al-Majali, known to be in favour of the Baghdad Pact. The following day there were violent demonstrations in Amman, and on December 20th Ibrahim Hashim became Prime Minister, to be succeeded on January 9th by Samir Rifai. In February 1956 the new Prime Minister visited Syria, Lebanon, Iraq, Egypt and Saudi Arabia, and shortly after his return, on March 2nd, King Hussein announced the dismissal of Glubb Pasha, commander-in-chief of the Jordanian armed forces, and replaced him by Major-General Radi 'Annab. The Egyptian-Syrian-Saudi Arabian bloc at this juncture offered to replace the British financial subsidy to Jordan; but the latter was not in fact withdrawn, and King Hussein and the Jordanian government evidently felt that they had moved far enough in one direction, and committed

themselves to a policy of strict neutrality. In April, however, the King and the Prime Minister paid a visit to the Syrian President in Damascus, and in May Major-General Annab was replaced by his deputy, Lt.-Colonel Ali Abu Nuwar, generally regarded as the leader of the movement to eliminate foreign influence from the Jordanian army and government. This coincided with the reappointment of Sa'id al-Mufti as Prime Minister. During the same period discussions culminated in agreements for military co-operation between Jordan and Syria, Lebanon and Egypt, and in July Jordan and Syria formed an economic union. At the beginning of the same month al-Mufti was replaced by Ibrahim Hashim.

RELATIONS WITH ISRAEL AND WITH THE OTHER ARAB STATES

Meanwhile relations with Israel, including the problem of the Arab refugees, the use of Jordan waters, the definition of the frontier, and the status of Jerusalem, continued to provide a standing cause for anxiety. Tension between Jordan and Israel was further increased after the Israeli, British and French military action in Egypt. A new cabinet, headed by Suleiman Nabulsi, had taken office in October, and new elections were followed by the opening of negotiations for the abrogation of the Anglo-Jordan Treaty of 1948, and the substitution of financial aid from the Arab countries, notably Saudi Arabia, Egypt and Syria. Owing to subsequent political developments, however, the shares due from Egypt and Syria were not paid. On March 13th, 1957, an Anglo-Jordanian agreement was signed abrogating the 1948 treaty, and by July 2nd the last British troops had left. In the meantime Nabulsi's evident leanings towards the Soviet connection, clashing with the recently-enunciated Eisenhower doctrine, led to his breach with King Hussein and his resignation on April 10th, to be succeeded by Ibrahim Hashim. All political parties were suppressed, and plans to establish diplomatic relations with Russia were dropped. Gen. Ali Aby Nuwar was removed from the post of Commander-in-Chief, and the United States announced its determination to preserve Jordan's independence—a policy underlined by a major air-lift of arms to Amman in September in response to Syria's alignment with the Soviet Union. In May Syrian troops serving under the joint Syro-Egypto-Jordanian command were withdrawn from Jordanian territory at Jordan's request, and in June there was a partial rupture of diplomatic relations with Egypt.

On February 14th, 1958, the merger of the Kingdoms of Iraq and Jordan in a federal union to be called the Arab Federation was proclaimed in Amman by King Faisal of Iraq and King Hussein. This new federation proved abortive. Samir Rifai became Prime Minister of Jordan in May, on the resignation of Ibrahim Hashim who took up the appointment of Vice-Premier in the short-lived Arab Federation.

British troops were flown to Amman from Cyprus on July 17th, in response to an appeal by King Hussein. They had all been withdrawn by the beginning of November—under UN auspices—and in the two years that followed Jordan settled down to a period of comparative peace. Hazza' al-Majali succeeded Rifai as Prime Minister on May 6th, 1959. Firm measures were taken against communism and subversive activities and collaboration with the West was, if anything, encouraged by the country's isolation between Iraq, Israel and the two halves of the United Arab Republic. American loans continued to arrive at the rate of about $50,000,000 a year, and there was also technical aid of various kinds from Britain, Western Germany and other countries. An important development was the official opening of the port of Aqaba on the Red Sea, virtually Jordan's only outlet.

Relations with Jordan's Arab neighbours continued to be uneasy, though diplomatic relations with the United Arab Republic, broken off in July 1958, were resumed in August 1959. Incidents on the Syrian border were almost as frequent as on the Israeli, and there were no signs of a rapprochement with Iraq. In January 1960, both the King and the Prime Minister condemned the Arab leaders' approach to the Palestine problem, and in February Jordanian citizenship was offered to all Arab refugees who applied for it. On the other side of the balance sheet, King Hussein paid a flying visit to King Sa'ud in February, 1960, and in March strongly anti-Zionist statements appeared in the Jordanian press. Nevertheless there seemed to be no change in the general position that Jordan wished for formal recognition of her absorption of the Palestinian territory west of the Jordan, while the United Arab Republic and other Arab countries favoured the establishment of an independent Palestine Arab government.

On August 29th, 1960, the Jordanian Prime Minister, Hazza al-Majali, was assassinated and was followed by a succession of Prime Ministers during the next five years. In April 1965 a constitutional uncertainty was resolved, with the nomination of the King's brother Hassan as Crown Prince; the infant son of the formerly British Princess Muna was thus excluded.

WAR WITH ISRAEL

During the latter part of 1966 Jordan's foreign relations were increasingly worsened by the widening breach with Syria. Charges and counter-charges were made of plots to subvert each other's governments, and while the U.A.R. and the U.S.S.R. supported Syria, Jordan looked for backing to Saudi Arabia and the U.S. This situation made it increasingly difficult for Jordan's relations with Israel to be regularized. In July 1966 Jordan suspended support for the Palestine Liberation Organization, accusing its secretary Shukairy of pro-Communist activity. In November an Israeli reprisal raid aroused bitter feeling in Jordan and elsewhere. While Jordan introduced conscription and Saudi Arabia promised military aid, Syria and the Palestine Liberation Organization called on the Jordanians to revolt against King Hussein. Negotiations to implement the resolution of the Supreme Council for Arab Defence that Iraqi and Saudi troops should be sent to Jordan to assist in her defence broke down in December. This was followed by clashes on the Jordan/Syria frontier, by PLO-sponsored bomb outrages in Jordan (resulting in the closure of the PLO headquarters in Jerusalem), and by worsening relations between Jordan and the U.A.R. and a ban by the latter on aircraft carrying British and American arms to Jordan. In retaliation Jordan withdrew recognition of the Sallal régime in Yemen, and boycotted the next meeting of the Arab Defence Council. On March 5th Wasfi al-Tal resigned and was succeeded by Hussein bin Nasser at the head of an interim government.

As the prospect of war with Israel drew nearer, King Hussein composed his differences with Egypt, and personally flew to Cairo to sign a defence agreement. Jordanian troops, together with those of the U.A.R., Iraq and Saudi Arabia, went into action immediately on the outbreak of hostilities in June. By the end of the Six Days War, however, all Jordanian territory west of the River Jordan had been occupied by Israeli troops, and a steady stream of West Bank Jordanians began to cross the River Jordan to the East Bank. Estimated at between 150,000 and 250,000 persons, they swelled Jordan's refugee population and presented the government with intractable social and economic problems.

King Hussein formed a nine-man Consultative Council in August 1967, composed of former premiers and politicians of varying sympathies, to meet weekly and to participate in the "responsibility of power". Later a Senate was formed consisting of fifteen representatives from the inhabitants of the west bank area, and fifteen from eastern Jordan. Several changes of government took place and the King took over personal command of the country's armed forces.

Meanwhile the uneasy situation along the frontier with Israel persisted, aggravated by the deteriorating economic situation in the country. Reprisal actions by Israel after numerous commando raids directed against her authority in Jerusalem and the West Bank and operating from Jordanian territory provoked Jordan to appeal for UN intervention. In June 1969 Israeli commandos blew up the diversion system of the Ghor Canal, Jordan's principal irrigation project.

THE GUERRILLA CHALLENGE

The instability in Amman after the June War was reflected in the short life of Jordanian cabinets—it became rare for one to remain unchanged for more than three months. A careful balance had to be struck between the Palestinians and the King's traditional supporters. Thus, in the new cabinet announced after the June 1970 crisis, Palestinians were given more of the key ministries, including that of the Interior. Abdul Munem Rifai, Jordan's senior diplomat, became Prime Minister for the second time.

The main factor in Jordan's internal politics between June 1967 and 1971 was the rivalry between the official government and the guerrilla organizations, principally Al Fatah. These organizations gradually assumed effective control of the refugee camps and commanded widespread support amongst the Palestinian majority of Jordan's present population. They also received arms and training assistance from other Arab countries, particularly Syria, and finance from the oil-rich Gulf states. Some camps became commando training centres, the younger occupants of these, almost all unemployed, welcoming the sense of purpose and relief from idleness and boredom that recruitment into a guerrilla group offered. The fedayeen movement virtually became a state within a state. Its leadership has stated that "We have no wish to interfere in the internal affairs of Jordan provided it does not place any obstacles in the way of our struggle to liberate Palestine". In practice, however, its popularity and influence represented a challenge to the government, whilst its actions attracted Israeli reprisals that did serious damage to the east bank, now the only fertile part of Jordan, and generally reduced the possibilities of a peace settlement on which Jordan's long-term future depended.

A major confrontation between the two forces occurred in November 1968, after massive demonstrations in Amman on the anniversary of the Balfour Declaration. Extensive street fighting broke out between guerrillas and the army, and for a short period a civil war seemed possible, but both sides soon backed down. Similar confrontations followed in February and June 1970, and on both occasions the Government was forced to yield to Palestinian pressures. King Hussein and Yasser Arafat, the Al Fatah leader (whose own position was threatened by the rise of small extremist groups in Jordan), jointly drew up and signed an agreement redefining their respective spheres of influence. The guerrillas appeared to have granted little or nothing, but Hussein was forced to dismiss his Commander-in-Chief and a cabinet minister, both relatives. These were regarded as the leaders of the anti-fedayeen faction, which remained strong amongst the Bedouin sheikhs. Despite the agreement, the tension between the government and the guerrillas continued, aggravated by opposition to the government's concessions from hard-line army officers.

A new and dangerous stage in the relations between the two sides in Jordan was reached in July with the acceptance by the government of the American peace proposals for the Middle East. The guerrilla groups, with few exceptions, rejected these, and, as the cease-fire between the U.A.R. and Israel came into operation on August 7th, it was clear that the Jordanian Government was preparing for a full-scale confrontation with them.

CIVIL WAR

Bitter fighting between government and guerrilla forces broke out at the end of August. In the first part of September the violence was increased by two factors: the assassination attempt on King Hussein and the hijackings by PFLP of four Western Airliners. The threat of intervention on the side of the commandos by Iraq and Syria; the transference of Libyan aid from the Jordanian government to the guerrillas; a succession of cease-fire agreements between the two sides; the release of all but 54 hostages taken from the aircraft to secure the release of Palestinian commandos held by Western governments; none of these developments was enough to prevent the escalation into full civil war in the last half of the month, and thousands of deaths and injuries. The continued detention of any hostages by the PFLP was a direct challenge to the government's authority. On September 16th a military cabinet was formed under Brig. Muhammad Daoud—in any case martial law had been in force since the end of the June 1967 war—and immediately Field Marshal Habis Majali replaced as Commander-in-Chief Lt.-Gen. Mashour Haditha, who had been sympathetic to the commandos and had tried to restrain their severest opponents in the army.

In the fighting that followed, the guerrillas claimed full control in the north, aided by Syrian forces and, it was later revealed, three battalions of the Palestine Liberation Army sent back by President Nasser from the Suez front. The Arab states generally appealed for an end to the fighting. Libya threatened to intervene and later broke off diplomatic relations; Kuwait stopped its aid to the government; but the Iraqi troops stationed on the Eastern front against Israel notably failed to intervene. On the government side talks were held with the U.S.A. about direct military assistance. In the event such a dangerous widening of the Palestinian confrontation was avoided by the scale of the casualties in Jordan and by the diplomacy of Arab heads of state (reinforced by President Nasser's reported threat to intervene on the guerrillas' behalf) who prevailed upon King Hussein and Yasser Arafat to sign an agreement in Cairo on September 27th ending the war. The previous day a civilian cabinet had been restored under Ahmed Toukan. Five military members were retained.

A definitive agreement, very favourable to the liberation organizations, was signed by Hussein and Arafat on October 13th in Amman, but this proved to be simply the beginning of a phase of sporadic warfare between the two parties, punctuated by new agreements, during which the commandos were gradually forced out of Amman and driven from their positions in the north back towards the Syrian frontier. At the end of October a new government, still containing three army officers, was formed under Wasfi al-Tal. By January 1971 army moves against the Palestine guerrillas had become much more blatant, and the U.A.R., Syria and Algeria all issued strong protests at the Jordanian Government's attempt to "liquidate" the liberation movements. All but two brigades of Iraqi troops were, however, withdrawn from Jordan.

By April the Jordanian Government seemed strong enough to set a deadline for the guerrillas' withdrawal of their remaining men and heavy armaments from the capital. On July 13th a major government attack began on the guerrillas entrenched in the Jerash-Aljoun area. Four days later it was all over. The Government claimed that all the bases had been destroyed and that 2,300 ot 2,500 guerrillas in them had been captured. Most of the Palestinians taken prisoner by the Jordanian Government were released a few days later, either to leave for other Arab states or to return to normal life in Jordan.

The "solution" (in King Hussein's word) of the guerrilla "problem" provoked strong reaction from other Arab governments. Iraq and Syria closed their borders with Jordan; Algeria suspended diplomatic relations; and Egypt, Libya, Sudan and both Yemens voiced public criticism. Relations with Syria deteriorated fastest of all, but normal trading and diplomatic relations were restored by February 1972.

In the meantime, Saudi Arabia had been attempting to bring together guerrilla leaders and Jordanian Government representatives to work out a new version of the Cairo and Amman agreements. Meetings did take place in Jeddah but were fruitless, and the Palestinians responded in their own way to the events of July. Three unsuccessful attempts were made in September to hijack Jordanian airliners. Then, on September 28th, 1971, Wasfi al-Tal, the Prime Minister and Defence Minister, was assassinated by members of a secret Palestinian guerrilla group, the Black September Organization, and other assassination attempts were made.

HUSSEIN'S ANSWER

Throughout the period since the liquidation of the guerrillas in July 1971 Hussein had been seeking to strengthen his political position. In August he announced the creation of a tribal council—a body of sheikhs or other notables, appointed by him and chaired by the Crown Prince—which was to deal with the affairs of tribal areas. A month later the formation of the Jordanian National Union was announced. This (renamed Arab National Union in March 1972) was to be Jordan's only legal political organization. It was not a party in the usual sense; proponents of "imported ideologies" were debarred from membership; the King became President and the Crown Prince Vice-President; and appointed the 36 members of the Supreme Executive Committee.

However, the King's boldest political move, and an obvious attempt to regain his standing in the eyes of Palestinians, was his unfolding of plans for a United Arab Kingdom in March 1972. This kingdom was to federate a Jordanian region, with Amman as its capital and also federal capital, and a Palestinian region, with Jerusalem as its capital. Each region was to be virtually autonomous, though the King would rule both and there would be a federal council of ministers.

Outside Jordan there was almost universal criticism of this plan from interested parties—Israel, the Palestinian organizations and Egypt, which in the following month broke off diplomatic relations. Jordan's isolation in the Arab world had never been more complete.

Throughout the rest of 1972 and the first half of 1973 Hussein continued to stand by his original plans for a United Arab Kingdom, but at the same time insisting that peace with Israel can only come within the framework of UN Resolution 242 (*see* Documents on Palestine, page 76) and hotly denying suggestions from other Arab states that he was considering signing a separate peace treaty with Israel.

The internal security of Jordan was threatened in November 1972 when an attempted military coup in Amman by Major Rafeh Hindawi was thwarted. In February 1973 Abu Daoud, one of the leaders of Al Fatah, and 16 other guerrillas were arrested on charges of infiltrating into Jordan for the purpose of subversive activities.

The latter affair took place while King Hussein was on a visit to the U.S.A. requesting defence and financial aid. On his return he commuted the death sentences passed on the guerrillas by a Jordanian military court and previously confirmed by himself, to life imprisonment. In May 1973 Hussein's Prime Minister, Ahmed Lauzi, resigned for health reasons and a new government under Zaid-al Rifai, who was known to be against the Palestinian guerrillas, was formed.

In September 1973 Hussein attended a "reconciliation summit" with Presidents Sadat of Egypt and Assad of Syria. This was Jordan's first official contact with the two states since they had broken diplomatic relations, and they were restored after the summit. The meeting was condemned by Al Fatah, Libya and Iraq but Jordan regained some stature in the Arab world after Hussein's general amnesty for all political prisoners; among those released was Abu Daoud.

During the Middle East War in October 1973 Jordan sent troops to support Syria on the Golan Heights but was otherwise not actively involved, and did not open a third front against the Israelis as in the 1967 War. Jordan was represented at the Geneva talks in December 1973. During February 1974 there was considerable unrest among sections of the army though this was settled by increases in pay ordered by Hussein who was out of the country when the disturbances started. In April Hussein announced that the Arab National Union, which was then the sole political organization in Jordan, was to be reorganized with an executive and council of reduced numbers.

During most of 1974 the main characteristic of Hussein's policy towards the PLO and the status of the West Bank was extreme ambiguity. He continued to try to preserve the West Bank as part of his kingdom despite strong pressure from other Arab states and the increasing influence of the PLO. In September 1974 after a meeting between Egypt, Syria and the PLO expressing support for the PLO as the "only legitimate representative of the Palestinian people", Jordan refused to participate in further Middle East peace talks. However, in October 1974 at the Arab Summit Conference at Rabat (*see* Documents on Palestine, page 80), representatives of twenty Arab heads of state unanimously recognized the PLO as the sole legitimate representative of the Palestinians, and its right to establish a national authority over any liberated Palestinian territory. Effectively ceding Jordan's claim to represent the Palestinians and re-incorporate the West Bank, when recaptured, into the Hashemite Kingdom, Hussein reluctantly assented to the resolution. He said that Jordan would continue to strive for the liberation of the West Bank and recognize the full rights of citizenship of Palestinians in Jordan. The prospect of a separate, independently ruled Palestinian state was strongly condemned by Israel.

JORDAN AFTER THE RABAT SUMMIT

Following the Rabat Conference Hussein was given more extensive powers in revisions to the Jordanian constitution approved by parliament in November. He was allowed to rule without parliament for a year and reorganize his Kingdom in order to lessen the numbers of Palestinians in the executive and legislative branches of government, his 1972 plan for a United Arab Kingdom now being wholly defunct. Parliament was dissolved and a new government formed in November, with Zaid al-Rifai remaining Prime Minister. Palestinian representation was decreased, and the question of citizenship of the estimated 800,000 Palestinians on the East Bank became contentious. Elections in Jordan were postponed in March 1975 and when Parliament was briefly reconvened in February 1976 a constitutional amendment was enacted to suspend elections indefinitely.

The success of the PLO at the Rabat Conference had, despite internal feuds (*see* Palestine Organizations, page 80), considerably strengthened its position. This was further the case when the UN acknowledged the PLO as the legitimate representative of the Palestinians by an overwhelming majority in November. The PLO was also granted observer status at the UN.

One of the most notable results of the Rabat Summit Conference and Hussein's virtual abandonment of his claim to the West Bank was an improvement in relations with the Arab world in general, and with Syria in particular. During 1975 various links with Syria were forged and strengthened. Early in the year Hussein visited Damascus and President Assad visited Jordan in June. A supreme joint committee was set up to co-ordinate military and political planning, with the two prime ministers as Chairmen. In August a Supreme Command Council, headed by the King and President Assad, was formed to direct military and political action against Israel, and in December 1976 it was announced that a form of political union would be worked out between the two countries.

This close relationship, however, was put into jeopardy by President Sadat's visit to Israel in November 1977, and subsequently threatened by Syria's proposed *rapprochement* with Iraq. Since then closer economic links have been forged with Iraq. Jordan, unlike Syria, was anxious not to condemn Sadat's peace initiative, but did not want to destroy its growing relationship with Syria. King Hussein, therefore, "sat on the fence" and tried to act as a conciliator between Egypt on the one hand and the "rejectionist" States on the other (Algeria, Libya, Iraq, Syria and the People's Democratic Republic of Yemen). Jordan, however, emphatically rejected Israel's peace proposals which were put forward by Prime Minister Begin in December 1977, and maintained its policy of demanding an Israeli withdrawal from Gaza and the West Bank, including East Jerusalem, leaving no Jewish settlements. Jordan also wanted the creation of a Palestinian homeland, the nature of whose link with Jordan should be decided by a referendum.

It was these factors which helped to determine Jordan's attitude to the Camp David agreements (see p. 82) in September 1978 and the subsequent peace treaty between Egypt and Israel (see p. 84) in March 1979. Jordan refused to be drawn into the Camp David talks by the United States, and joined the other Arab States at the Baghdad Arab summit in drawing up a list of sanctions against Egypt.

Immediately prior to the signing of the peace treaty Jordan showed its commitment to the PLO by welcoming Yasser Arafat on an official visit, and after the treaty was signed Jordan was the first Arab country still having diplomatic relations with Egypt to break them off. In the months that followed the signing of the peace treaty, however, Jordan's hostility to Egypt subsided, and was replaced by the souring of relations with Syria. In spite of Jordanian denials, Syria was convinced that the Muslim Brotherhood (allowed limited freedom in Jordan) was fostering treachery inside Syria. Syria also disapproved of Jordan's support for Iraq in the Gulf War between Iran and Iraq. These factors led to a build-up of Syrian and Jordanian troops on the frontier in December 1980, and to mediation between the two sides by Saudi Arabia. Relations did not improve in February 1981 when the Jordanian Chargé d'affaires in Beirut was abducted (allegedly by Syrians), and Jordan responded by abrogating a six-year economic and customs agreement with Syria.

Throughout 1981 Jordan continued with her policy of supporting Iraq in the Gulf War, and in January 1982 Hussein announced that he was prepared to take charge of a special "Yarmuk Force" of Jordanians to give military help to Iraq. By April, however, as Iraq's position in the Gulf War grew weaker, Hussein was reportedly trying to encourage a negotiated settlement between Iran and Iraq and a revival of the Saudi Fahd Plan for a resolution of the Arab-Israeli question.

In domestic affairs, Hussein had dissolved the House of Representatives in 1974, but in April 1978 he formed a 60-member National Consultative Council (NCC) appointed by Royal Decree. The third term of the NCC began on April 20th, 1982. In December 1979 Sharif Abdulhamid Sharaf replaced Mudar Badran as Prime Minister. Sharaf, however, died of a heart attack on July 3rd, 1980, and was replaced as Prime Minister by the former Minister of Agriculture, Qassim al-Rimawi. In August, however, a new government under former Prime Minister Mudar Badran was introduced, although little change of policy resulted.

ECONOMIC SURVEY

Jordan's economy has twice been completely disrupted by war between the Arabs and the Israelis, first in 1948, and then in 1967. While Jordan in 1948 acquired some 2,165 square miles of new territory— the vast salient which juts out into Israel west of the River Jordan—the country's population also increased more than threefold. In 1948, before the war broke out, the country's population was perhaps 400,000. The number of those living on the West Bank of the River Jordan in the territory acquired in 1948 was well over 800,000. This territory was occupied by the Israelis in 1967, and perhaps 350,000 of the inhabitants fled to non-occupied Jordan. It is extremeley difficult to evaluate population estimates for the years between the census of 1961 and the most recent census, undertaken on November 11th, 1979. The latest figures give a total population for the East Bank of 2,152,273, which implies an annual growth rate between 1961 and 1979 of 4.8 per cent. Natural increase accounts for 3.8 per cent and immigration for 1.0 per cent. An estimated 700,000 people are refugees. Of the present population, 30 per cent live in the capital Amman, and a further 15 per cent in the cities of Zarqa and Irbid. A sample population survey in 1979 estimated that 60 per cent of the population lived in towns. There has been only a relatively small rise in crude birth rates, from 47.3 per 1,000 in 1960 to 50 per 1,000 in 1975, and most of the population increase results from the large drop in death rates, from 18 per 1,000 in 1961 to less than 12 per 1,000 at present. In February 1981 it was reported that there were 103,501 non-Jordanians working in the country and 80 per cent of those were Arab nationals. These levels of population increase are making themselves felt particularly in the major towns, where water shortages are becoming one of the most severe of the country's economic problems.

The absorption of the refugees of 1948 and of 1967 caused problems which were accentuated by ethnic, cultural and religious differences. Jordanians before 1948 were mainly Bedouin and mostly engaged in pastoral, and even nomadic, activities. They therefore had little in common with the Palestinians, many of whom established themselves in Jordan as traders and professional men. The vast majority of the country's original inhabitants were Sunni Muslims, but until 1967 at least there were also 180,000 Christians. Also in 1967 some 53 per cent of the population was classified as urban.

Again, the loss of the West Bank of the Jordan to Israel in the summer of 1967 created a whole series of new problems. The result was the loss not only of some efficiently farmed agricultural land, but also of the important and growing tourist industry, and the large sums in foreign exchange received from the people who annually visited the old city of Jerusalem and Bethlehem. Some of the immediate problems brought by the war of 1967 were met by aid from Arab countries, but Jordan's economic future in the long run will obviously depend on the nature of any settlement which may be reached with Israel.

During 1979 and the early part of 1980, Jordan moved closer to Iraq in both political and economic terms, and in May 1980 Iraq agreed to provide loans of $89.2 million to Jordan, together with grants of $58.3 million for construction and development. A further Iraqi loan of $100 million was announced in August 1980. The war between Iran and Iraq, which began in September 1980, further strengthened this alliance, and, in addition to increased trade for Iraq through Aqaba, Jordan is likely to benefit appreciably from Iraqi reconstruction after the cessation of hostilities. Towards the end of 1980, Iraq and Jordan signed agreements to confirm their tighter economic links, and, in practical terms, Iraq agreed to finance a new technical college at Mota. As 1981 progressed, Jordan began reaping the benefits from its support of Iraq. In April a trade protocol was signed through which Iraq agreed to give Jordan a grant of JD30 million for road construction. In October Iraq agreed to lend a further sum of JD58 million ($175 million) for development projects, and in November Iraq agreed to pay $200 million for a Soviet-built SAM-6 anti-aircraft missile system. In 1980 Jordan was active on other political fronts, signing trade agreements with Portugal, Turkey and Qatar, and an education agreement with the U.S.S.R. This political activity has continued, with an overland trade agreement signed with the United Kingdom in February 1981 and a labour agreement signed with Tunisia early in 1982.

AGRICULTURE

Between 1974 and 1978 agriculture accounted for approximately 10 per cent of the gross domestic product. Until the rains in November 1979, which were the heaviest for 35 years, Jordanian agriculture had, since 1974, been suffering from severe drought problems. With 92 per cent of its cultivable area rain-fed only, the vagaries of rainfall are still a crucial factor in Jordan's agriculture. Great improvements were achieved in the years prior to the 1967 war but the war and subsequent events on the East Bank resulted in almost complete disruption. In recent years, however, the economic situation on the East Bank has stabilized and agricultural production has begun to progress, although migration away from the agricultural sector suggests that possibly only 20 per cent of the total labour force now works in agriculture. The difficulties facing agriculture are illustrated by the fact that between 1974 and 1978 the value of net imports of food commodities rose from 52 to 66 per cent of the total value of consumption. In 1979 agriculture contributed 8.2 per cent to G.D.P. and employed approximately 18 per cent of the labour force. By 1980, although agriculture still employed 18 per cent of the workforce, its contribution to the G.D.P. had fallen to 7.6 per cent.

A contrast can be drawn between the rain-fed upland zone and the irrigated Jordan Valley, which, since 1973, has been subject to its own Development Plan. As a result of irrigation and the production of high-value crops, the productivity of the Jordan Valley is far higher than that of the uplands, where cultivation is concentrated mainly on wheat and barley. The development of irrigation in the Jordan Valley began in 1958, and between then and 1963 work on the East Ghor canal, carrying water from the Yarmuk river and running parallel to the Jordan, added 300,000 acres to the country's irrigated area. The installations were severely damaged by Israeli bombardment in 1967 and repairs were not carried out until after the 1970 civil war. Stage I of the Jordan Valley Development Plan, funded by a great variety of foreign aid bodies, finished at the end of 1979. Irrigation projects centred mainly on the extension of the East Ghor canal and the Zarqa river complex. The King Talal dam was constructed between 1972 and 1978, the East Ghor canal extended between 1975 and 1978, and the Zarqa Triangle Irrigation Project finished in 1978. Other irrigation works include the Hisban Kafrein project, constructed between 1976 and 1978, and the North-east Ghor complex. The Jordan Valley Development scheme is, however, more than just a complex of irrigation projects, and includes the development of transport links, grading, packing and marketing centres (which are only just beginning to be constructed), the development of schools and health centres, and also a housing programme. In 1981 the Jordan Valley Authority was responsible for 22,000 hectares of irrigated land. The use of plastic tunnels, greenhouses and drip-irrigation has greatly expanded within the valley and by 1978 6,000 dunums had plastic tunnels and 741 dunums had greenhouses. Most of the JD42 million earmarked for agricultural development in the 1976–80 Five-Year Plan was to be used for development of the valley. As well as irrigation, crop-raising has also been improved by the introduction of special strains of seed, inorganic fertilizers and mechanization.

The 1981–85 Five Year-Plan aims to invest JD 200 million in agriculture and to increase agricultural income by 40 per cent (an annual growth rate of 7 per cent), mainly through an expansion of the irrigated area in the Jordan Valley and the South Ghor region. During 1980 USAID agreed to provide a $9 million loan to Jordan for the construction of the Maqarin Dam on the Yarmuk river, which is due for completion in the late 1980s, and which will irrigate a further 10,000 hectares of land. At a cost of $1,000 million, this project, with its associated hydro-electric power station, is one of the major schemes planned for the 1980s in Jordan. Progress on it, though, is still blocked because of disputes with Syria and Israel. In April 1981 work was started on the Wadi al-Arab Dam, which, when completed in 1984 at a cost of JD 9.7 million, will irrigate 505 hectares in the Jordan Valley.

Cereals, fruit and vegetables are the mainstays of Jordan's agriculture. Since 1974 (a record year) yields of wheat and barley have been severely reduced owing to drought, so that by 1978, despite similar acreages being under cultivation, wheat production on the East Bank totalled only 53,300 metric tons and barley only 15,000 tons. In 1979 wheat production fell to an all-time low of only 16,000 tons, but the rains in November 1979 led to a great increase in the cultivated area. As a result of the excellent harvest produced in 1980, the Government banned imports of wheat, barley and lentils, and paid farmers almost double the normal price for imports. Wheat production in 1980 was 133,600 tons, barley 38,100 tons and lentils 6,300 tons. This was less than earlier estimates had predicted, but nevertheless provided a welcome respite from the previous five years of poor production. Field crop production rose appreciably from 32,400 tons in 1979 to 204,400 tons in 1980. In January 1980 the King Talal dam was full for the first time since its completion in 1978. In addition, the heavy rainfall has also replenished depleting groundwater resources. Towards the end of 1980 grain storage was also greatly improved with the opening of new silos at Aqaba, costing JD 13.6 million, which will have a storage capacity of 50,000 tons.

The loss of the West Bank had a serious effect on cereal production but its effect on fruit and vegetable cultivation was disastrous, lopping off some 80 per cent of the fruit-growing area and 45 per cent of the area under vegetables and depriving Jordan of an important and expanding source of some of its major export commodities. Production of fruit and vegetables on the East Bank has fluctuated violently, partly because of the weather and partly as a result of political instability in 1969 and 1970. However, vegetable production more than doubled from 204,400 tons to 410,000 tons between 1977 and 1978. Tomatoes showed the largest increase, rising from 85,700 tons to 208,800 tons, approaching the 1967 level of 259,700 tons. Total fruit production also rose from 103,600 tons in 1977 to 179,200 tons in 1978, with banana production showing the largest rise, from 3,400 tons to 21,000 tons, again approaching the 1967 total of 22,200 tons. Unfortunately, during 1979 fruit and vegetable production declined somewhat from previous years' levels: bananas and melons were particularly badly affected. In 1980 fruit production was up by 79.9 per cent on 1979, and vegetable production had increased by 6.3 per cent. During the five years to 1979, vegetable production in the Jordan Valley accounted for 56 per cent of the area cropped, field crops for 34 per cent and fruit trees for 10 per cent, but field crops contributed only 4–5 per cent of the gross value of produce in the valley. Freezing weather in January 1982 damaged 1,500 hectares of crops, and it is likely that production may, as a result, be down on 1980/81 levels. According to official estimates for 1979, the East Bank of Jordan had 924,000 sheep, 564,000 goats, 39,000 cattle and 11,000 camels.

INDUSTRY AND MINING

Industry, which is almost entirely of recent origin and accounted for approximately 18 per cent of the gross domestic product in the second half of the 1970s, is concentrated around Amman and in Nablus on the West Bank. During the 1976–80 Plan period, it experienced an average growth rate of 13.6 per cent per annum, which was only half the planned rate. About 65 per cent of all factories produce food products or clothing but the major industrial income derives from the three heavier industries—phosphate extraction, cement manufacture and petroleum refining.

The country's mineral wealth lies predominantly in its phosphate reserves, which are estimated at over 2,000 million tons, providing the country with its main export commodity. There are also known to be deposits of good-quality copper ore. Other minerals include gypsum, manganese ore, abundant quantities of glass sand and the clays and feldspar ore required for manufacturing ceramics. Foreign investors have been found to finance the establishment of companies to produce ceramics and sheet glass and also to exploit potash deposits in the Dead Sea. The Arab Potash Company (APC), formed in 1956 as one of the earliest Arab joint ventures, is 51 per cent owned by the Jordanian Government. Quantities of uranium and vanadium are now known to be mixed in with the phosphate reserves. Oil has not yet been commercially produced, but between 1981 and 1989 it is planned that oil exploration will cost approximately 1 per cent of the country's G.N.P.

Rich beds of phosphates exist at Rusaifa, a few miles north-east of Amman, and have been exploited since 1963 by a local company financed partly by the Government. Other deposits in the Wadi Hasa area, south of Amman, have been developed by American and Italian interests, and production is currently expanding. Phosphates are also found at Wadi Al Abyad and there are hopes for further expansion of resources at Shidiya, which are estimated to consist of more than 1,000 million tons. In 1968 the country's total production of natural phosphates was 1,162,000 tons, more than five times the production in 1956. Production fell, however, to 651,000 tons in 1971, mainly as a result of the closure of the Syrian borders to Jordanian traffic, but rose again to 715,000 tons in 1972 and 1,674,800 tons in 1974, surpassing for the first time the record set in 1968. Although in 1975 production fell slightly, 1976 was a record year with production exceeding 1.76 million tons. Export earnings from phosphates, constant in 1974 and 1975 at JD 19.5 million, dropped to JD 19.2 million in 1976. This was due to a fall in the international price of phosphate rock and prompted Jordan in 1976 to join with Morocco, Tunisia and Senegal in an association of phosphate exporters. Under the 1976–80 plan phosphate production was expected to increase to 6 million tons in 1980. Exports were slightly higher in 1977, at 1.8 million tons, but revenue, at JD 17.3 million, was 8 per cent lower than in 1976. In 1978 a record 2,159,000 tons were exported, and this was increased to approximately 3 million tons in 1979. Output in 1980 was 3,911,200 tons, and increased production of phosphate forms a major part of government policy for the 1981–85 Plan.

A phosphate fertilizer plant at Aqaba was initially due to start operations in 1980, but production has been delayed. When fully operational, it will have a daily capacity of 1,800 tons of sulphuric acid, 1,350 tons of phosphoric acid, and 1,200 tons of diammonium phosphate. The project, which is managed by the Jordanian Fertilizer Industry Company, will cost $320 million. Mitsui of Japan is providing technical advice. The Jordanian Government is the principal shareholder but much of its finance is coming from suppliers' credits, international organizations and bank loans. Full production is not expected to be achieved until 1983. In January 1980 plans were finalized by the APC for the construction of a solar evaporation plant to extract potash from the south end of the Dead Sea. The cost is estimated at $430 million and the scheme is expected to process 1.2 million metric tons of potash annually when it begins production by the end of 1982.

Output of petroleum products from Jordan's only oil refinery at Zarqa increased steadily from 445,800 tons in 1970 to 748,000 tons in 1974, and to 1,114,600 tons in 1976. Production capacity was scheduled to reach 3.5 million tons per year by the end of 1979. This would have been more than sufficient to meet Jordan's domestic requirements. In 1980, however, the refinery produced only 1,760,000 tons. In an attempt to reduce petroleum imports, attention is now being paid to the possibility of exploiting the estimated 800 million tons of shale oil deposits in the south of the country. Consequently in September 1980 an agreement was signed with Technopromexport of the U.S.S.R. for an oil-shale survey at Lajjoun. Similarly, at the beginning of 1981, a $1 million agreement to undertake seismic tests for oil was signed with the U.S. Geophysical Services. Intermediate Petrochemicals Industries is building a petrochemicals plant 15 km. from Amman on the Zarqa road. There are also long-term plans for a second cement plant in the south but in the meantime the existing plant at Fuheis, near Amman, is undergoing an expansion programme. It was hoped to increase output capacity from 620,000 tons per year in 1975 to 2.25 million tons by 1980. Cement production, badly hit by the troubles of 1970, rose to its peak in 1972 at 661,600 tons, but declined to 598,200 tons in 1975, to 533,000 tons in 1976 and again to 500,800 tons in 1977; the construction boom of 1976 and 1977 later levelled off. Output of cement reached 912,700 tons in 1980. Two sulphuric acid plants are also to be built, each with a daily production of 1,800 tons. There is also potential for the development of a flourishing fishing industry centred on the Gulf of Aqaba. The port of Aqaba itself is to undergo rapid expansion and there are plans to develop a $30 million container terminal, a $21 million fertilizer jetty and $50 million potash terminal. In August 1980 the Maritime Corporation banned all ships built more than 15 years ago from entering Aqaba, in an attempt to streamline operations. The 1980 figures for the port showed an increase in trade of 30 per cent over those of the previous year.

Early in 1982, in an attempt to increase industrial development, the government exempted six new industries, with a combined capital of $4.7 million, from government duties. These were a corn-chip plant, a stonecutting and ceramics company, the Jordan Valley crate plant, a textile company, a yoghurt company and a steel pipe firm. A new thermal power station is also planned for Aqaba. When completed in 1986, it will have two 130 MW oil-fired steam units.

In 1981 construction began on the 225-hectare Sahab industrial estate, 18 km. south east of Amman, which is being built at a cost of JD 18 million. Nevertheless, the main focus of the 1981–85 Plan would appear to be decentralization. The Plan, with a centrepiece in the construction of the $1,000 million Yarmuk University (which is due to receive its first students in 1985), concentrates on manpower, technology transfer and regional development. Export industries are also to be promoted. The industrial plans for the region around Irbid and the Maan-Aqaba area will form magnets for attracting benefits away from the industrial core of Amman. This industrial development is beginning to cause severe problems: in October 1980 an order was issued stating that all factories should install waste water treatment plants by January 1981.

A severe lack of water is rapidly becoming one of Jordan's most crucial problems. The latest scheme to resolve this situation is a project being discussed with Iraq to pipe water from the Euphrates River to Amman at a cost of $1,000 million. However, there are obvious strategic complications attached to being dependent for water on a pipeline from Iraq.

Four other schemes are outlined in the 1981–85 Five-Year Plan: the pumping of water to Amman and Irbid from the Jordan River; an increase in the search for groundwater; the expansion of the dam-building programme in the west; and the establishment of a central water authority. In the short term a 100-km. pipeline is planned to bring water to Amman from the eastern oasis of Azraq. A new $36 million water supply scheme for Aqaba was formally opened in February 1982. The allocation for water and irrigation in the 1981–85 Plan is JD 500 million, making this sector second only to industry in importance.

TRANSPORT

The development of the Jordanian economy has, in the past, been hampered by the difficulty of communication. Though there is a good road from Amman to

Beirut through Syria, transport costs on this route are heavy.

A vital railway link between Aqaba and the Al-Hasa phosphate mines has been built with financial backing from the Federal Republic of Germany. It was planned that by the end of 1980 29 locomotives and 350 lorries would be available to carry phosphate from the mines to Aqaba port, and the capacity of the railway system was expected to be 3 million tons by the end of 1981. A road between the port and the agricultural and mining installations of the southern Ghor is under construction. Cargo handled at Aqaba declined in the years immediately following 1967, falling from an average 100,000 tons a month in 1966 to 32,000 tons in 1970 but this figure rose again to 104,000 tons in 1973 although Aqaba was closed for a month during the Arab-Israeli war. It reached a monthly average of 250,000 tons in 1976 and by the end of 1977 annual unloading capacity had been increased to more than 2 million tons. Congestion had also been relieved by the use of a floating jetty while expansion of port facilities goes ahead at a cost of $54 million, with assistance of $25 million provided by Saudi Arabia. In addition the port has clearly benefited from increased trade with Iraq, resulting from the Gulf War. Future road schemes will include the construction of a network of roads inside Amman and a motorway from Rum, near Aqaba, through Ras al-Naq to Ma'an. The latter will be financed by a United States loan. There are also plans for a road link between Aqaba and Izraq, to be financed by Iraq. What was formerly Jordan's only railway, the single-track Hedjaz line, used to run through Ma'an northwards to Damascus and south to Mecca and Medina in Saudi Arabia. There are now plans to upgrade the whole length of the railway from Damascus to Medina.

Much of Jordan's port and road development is now being financed by Iraq, and the two countries are also discussing the expansion of the joint Iraqi-Jordanian Overland Transport Company.

The state airline is taking over a growing role in handling the country's freight and passenger transport. It made a net profit in 1973 for the first time in its 10-year existence, and increased this profit in subsequent years. The airline set up an air freight company in April 1975 to operate on routes to other Middle Eastern capitals, Europe and the Far East, and in 1981 Alia and Iraqi Airways set up another freight company as a joint venture. The new Queen Alia airport is planned to open in April 1982 at a cost of $300 million.

In the 1976–80 Plan the Government intended to invest JD 119.9 million, or 15.5 per cent of the total budget, on transport. This investment appears to have been worthwhile since the volume of freight carried on the railways rose from 12,329 tons in 1976 to 1,173,994 tons by 1978. Over the same period the number of registered motor vehicles increased from 60,455 to 97,402. By 1980 the number of registered vehicles had risen to 136,271. Freight carried by air rose from 19,067 tons in 1978 to 29,959 tons in 1980. In the first six months of 1979 over 1 million tons of goods passed through Aqaba port, compared with 547,255

FINANCE

1,000 fils = 1 Jordanian dinar (JD).
Coins: 1, 5, 10, 20, 25, 50, 100 and 250 fils.
Notes: 500 fils; 1, 5, 10 and 20 dinars.
Exchange rates (May 1982): £1 sterling = 627 fils; U.S. $1 = 341 fils.
100 Jordanian dinars = £159.51 = $293.26.

Note: The Jordanian dinar was introduced in July 1950, with a value of £1 sterling, then equal to U.S. $2.80 ($1 = 357.14 fils). This valuation in terms of U.S. currency remained in effect until February 1973, so that from December 1971 (when the U.S. dollar was devalued) the dinar became equivalent to 2.579 Special Drawing Rights (SDRs). In February 1973, when the dollar was again devalued, the dinar's par value was fixed at $3.111 ($1 = 321.43 fils), thus maintaining the exchange rate in terms of SDRs. Until the end of 1973 the market rate against the U.S. dollar was allowed to fluctuate above and below this valuation. During the first six months of 1974 the par value and market rate were unified. Since July 1974, when the fixed relationship between the SDR and the U.S. dollar was ended, the exchange rate has been maintained at a mid-point of 1 dinar = 2.579 SDRs. The average market value of the dinar was $3.0549 in 1973; $3.1198 in 1974; $3.1305 in 1975; $3.0115 in 1976; $3.0373 in 1977; $3.2620 in 1978; $3.3270 in 1979; $3.3478 in 1980; $3.0654 in 1981. The dinar was at par with the pound sterling until November 1967, after which the exchange rate was £1 = 857.14 fils (1 dinar = £1.167) until August 1971. The rate was £1 = 930.61 fils (1 dinar = £1.075) from December 1971 to June 1972.

BUDGET ESTIMATES*
(East Bank only)
(JD '000)

REVENUE	1978	1979	1980	EXPENDITURE	1978	1979	1980
Direct taxes	27,023	35,815	43,500	Education	24,360	33,094	36,647
Indirect taxes	68,506	85,289	92,400	Health and social welfare	10,025	13,028	14,350
Fees	30,239	29,944	31,750	Defence and police	95,300	132,328	136,700
Other internal receipts	33,049	247,149	143,250	Other current expenditure	71,839	142,885	113,603
				Development expenditure	170,289	194,329	227,932
	158,817	398,197	310,900				
Grants and loans	198,000	69,974	203,333				
TOTAL	356,817	468,171	514,233	TOTAL	371,813	515,664	529,233

* Total expenditure comprises regular, military and development budgets.

1981: Revenue JD 611.7 million; Expenditure JD 638.3 million.
1982: Revenue JD 729 million; Expenditure JD 765 million.

DEVELOPMENT EXPENDITURE ESTIMATES
Five-Year Plan, 1981-85
(U.S. $ million)

Industry and mining	1,993
Transport	1,527
Water and irrigation	1,115
Housing	1,115
Education, culture and information	709
Agriculture	706
Electrical power	537
Municipal and rural affairs	475
Communications	306
Health	224
Tourism	178
Labour and social development	138
Trade	108
Royal Scientific Society and Dept. of Statistics	33
Religious endowments	19
Other	49
TOTAL	9,233

Source: National Planning Council.

NATIONAL ACCOUNTS
(East Bank only)
(JD million)

	1977	1978	1979
Gross Domestic Product (at current prices) .	477.6	569.1	627.4

EXTERNAL TRADE
(JD '000)

	1977	1978	1979	1980	1981
Imports	454,518	458,943	585,666	715,977	1,048,000
Exports	60,289	64,136	82,559	120,107	169,000

PRINCIPAL COMMODITIES
(JD '000)

Imports	1978	1979	1980	Exports	1978	1979	1980
Animals and products .	22,903	24,884	29,917	Phosphates . . .	19,460	26,282	47,198
Grains and legumes .	19,916	32,079	27,449	Tomatoes . . .	3,699	5,258	5,394
Vegetables . . .	3,554	4,916	6,374	Lentils . . .	28	451	21
Fruits. . . .	9,369	11,731	12,475	Water Melons . .	6	5	31
Spices. . . .	5,621	5,141	5,405	Other vegetables and			
Other agriculture .	8,630	9,984	n.a.	fruit . . .	10,534	13,012	22,999
Forestry products .	6,139	8,806	12,825	Cigarettes . . .	1,227	3,382	5,107
Mining and quarrying .	44,747	71,731	12,097	Bananas . . .	2	—	2
Food manufactures .	27,283	27,961	37,797	Raw Hides and Skins .	313	373	170
Textiles . . .	19,349	21,937	17,733	Electric Accumulators .	33	257	691
Clothing . . .	10,599	12,454	15,480	Olive Oil and Prepared			
Wood and cork .	5,213	6,403	12,825	Olives . . .	733	414	n.a.
Paper and products .	6,025	8,597	10,982				
Printing and publishing.	1,697	2,075	2,183				
Rubber and products .	4,785	8,229	10,816				
Chemical products .	26,406	37,898	37,819				
Petroleum (refined) .	3,269	4,815	6,161				
Non-metallic minerals .	20,513	24,993	11,524				
Metallic minerals .	48,020	77,526	75,410				
Non-electric machines .	10,268	53,686	78,953				
Electric machines .	29,758	28,857	41,577				
Transport equipment .	53,000	70,239	78,302				

PRINCIPAL TRADING PARTNERS
(JD '000)

Imports	1978	1979	1980	Exports	1978	1979	1980
China, People's Repub. .	7,199.0	9,306.8	10,011.7	China, People's Repub. .	780.0	2,497.3	2,114.1
Egypt . . .	8,544.0	9,450.1	4,818.6	Czechoslovakia . .	301.0	128.2	847.6
France . . .	16,839.0	26,876.1	51,694.9	India . . .	3,531.0	6,135.7	8,037.2
Germany, Fed. Repub. .	60,125.0	58,218.5	71,162.4	Iraq . . .	3,446.0	12,719.0	28,347.3
India . . .	2,778.0	3,263.9	1,939.5	Kuwait . . .	4,211.0	4,436.6	5,342.8
Italy . . .	30,489.0	38,521.3	45,500.5	Lebanon . . .	1,824.0	2,273.2	2,182.9
Japan. . . .	30,819.0	37,312.2	51,337.0	Saudi Arabia . .	17,695.0	19,371.8	19,717.8
Lebanon . . .	18,782.0	16,679.3	14,590.4	Syria . . .	10,425.0	12,264.2	13,618.6
Netherlands . .	9,349.0	11,738.1	14,785.4	Turkey . . .	2,293.0	3,739.2	5,498.5
Romania . . .	22,871.0	13,677.9	13,844.2	Yugoslavia . . .	1,064.0	980.1	2,912.7
Saudi Arabia . .	43,449.0	69,141.4	114,123.7				
Syria . . .	11,930.0	11,427.5	10,475.5				
U.S.S.R. . . .	3,120.0	3,406.4	5,460.9				
United Kingdom .	36,549.0	45,065.8	55,685.0				
U.S.A. . . .	33,636.0	43,537.6	61,586.9				

TRANSPORT

RAILWAYS
(East Bank only)

	1978	1979	1980
Passengers carried .	53,135	45,400	47,200
Freight carried (tons) .	1,173,994	226,876	281,614

ROAD TRAFFIC
(motor vehicles registered, East Bank only)

	1978	1979	1980
Cars (private) . .	50,905	61,828	73,078
Taxis . . .	10,072	10,872	11,207
Buses . . .	918	1,170	1,415
Lorries and vans . .	20,033	25,464	29,528
TOTAL (incl. others) .	97,402	117,250	136,271

TOURISM
(East Bank only)

	1978	1979	1980
Visitors to Jordan .	1,184,000	1,311,700	1,624,200

SHIPPING
(East Bank only)
(Aqaba port)

	1978	1979	1980
Number of vessels calling .	1,197	997	1,466
Freight loaded ('ooo tons) .	1,551	2,708.7	3,574.5
Freight unloaded ('ooo tons)	2,108	2,301.4	3,024.1

CIVIL AVIATION
(East Bank only)

	1978	1979	1980
Passengers (number)	710,414	914,500	1,111,500
Freight ('ooo tons) .	19,067	27,012	29,959

COMMUNICATIONS MEDIA
(East Bank only)

Telephones (1980)		60,533
Radio sets (1974)		200,000

EDUCATION
(East Bank)

	SCHOOLS	TEACHERS	PUPILS
1978–79 . .	2,522	23,930	653,630
1979–80 . .	2,582	25,333	698,195
1980–81 . .	2,698	27,113	730,508

Source: Department of Statistics, Amman.

THE CONSTITUTION

(Revised Constitution approved by King Talal I on January 1st, 1952)

THE Hashemite Kingdom of Jordan is an independent, indivisible sovereign state. Its official religion is Islam; its official language Arabic.

Rights of the Individual. There is to be no discrimination between Jordanians on account of race, religion or language. Work, education and equal opportunities shall be afforded to all as far as is possible. The freedom of the individual is guaranteed, as are his dwelling and property. No Jordanian shall be exiled. Labour shall be made compulsory only in a national emergency, or as a result of a conviction; conditions, hours worked and allowances are under the protection of the State.

The Press, and all opinions, are free, except under martial law. Societies can be formed, within the law. Schools may be established freely, but they must follow a recognized curriculum and educational policy. Elementary

education is free and compulsory. All religions are tolerated. Every Jordanian is eligible to public office, and choices are to be made by merit only. Power belongs to the people.

The Legislative Power is vested in the National Assembly and the King. The National Assembly consists of two houses: the Senate and the House of Representatives.

The Senate. The number of Senators is one-half of the number of members of the House of Representatives. Senators must be unrelated to the King, over 40, and are chosen from present and past Prime Ministers and Ministers, past Ambassadors or Ministers Plenipotentiary, past Presidents of the House of Representatives, past Presidents and members of the Court of Cassation and of the Civil and Sharia Courts of Appeal, retired officers of the rank of General and above, former members of the House of Representatives who have been elected twice to that House, etc. .... They may not hold public office. Senators are appointed for four years. They may be re-appointed. The President of the Senate is appointed for two years.

The House of Representatives. The members of the House of Representatives are elected by secret ballot in a general direct election and retain their mandate for four years. General elections take place during the four months preceding the end of the term. The President of the House is elected by secret ballot each year by the Representatives. Representatives must be Jordanians of over 30, they must have a clean record, no active business interests, and are debarred from public office. Close relatives of the King are not eligible. If the House of Representatives is dissolved, the new House shall assemble in extraordinary session not more than four months after the date of dissolution. The new House cannot be dissolved for the same reason as the last. (Parliament was dissolved by Royal Decree in November 1974, and a National Consultative Council was formed in April 1978.)

General Provisions for the National Assembly. The King summons the National Assembly to its ordinary session on November 1st each year. This date can be postponed by the King for two months, or he can dissolve the Assembly before the end of its three months' session. Alternatively, he can extend the session up to a total period of six months. Each session is opened by a speech from the throne.

Decisions in the House of Representatives and the Senate are made by a majority vote. The quorum is two-thirds of the total number of members in each House. When the voting concerns the Constitution, or confidence in the Council of Ministers, "the votes shall be taken by calling the members by name in a loud voice". Sessions are public, though secret sessions can be held at the request of the Government or of five members. Complete freedom of speech, within the rules of either House, is allowed.

The Prime Minister places proposals before the House of Representatives; if accepted there, they are referred to the Senate and finally sent to the King for confirmation. If one house rejects a law while the other accepts it, a joint session of the House of Representatives and the Senate is called, and a decision made by a two-thirds majority. If the King withholds his approval from a law, he returns it to the Assembly within six months with the reasons for his dissent; a joint session of the Houses then makes a decision, and if the law is accepted by this decision it is promulgated. The Budget is submitted to the National Assembly one month before the beginning of the financial year.

The King. The throne of the Hashemite Kingdom devolves by male descent in the dynasty of King Abdullah Ibn al Hussein. The King attains his majority on his eighteenth lunar year; if the throne is inherited by a minor, the powers of the King are exercised by a Regent or a Council of Regency. If the King, through illness or absence, cannot perform his duties, his powers are given to a Deputy, or to a Council of the Throne. This Deputy, or Council, may be appointed by *Iradas* (decrees) by the King, or, if he is incapable, by the Council of Ministers.

On his accession, the King takes the oath to respect and observe the provisions of the Constitution and to be loyal to the nation. As head of the State he is immune from all liability or responsibility. He approves laws and promulgates them. He declares war, concludes peace and signs treaties; treaties, however, must be approved by the National Assembly. The King is Commander-in-Chief of the Navy, the Army and the Air Force. He orders the holding of elections; convenes, inaugurates, adjourns and prorogues the House of Representatives. The Prime Minister is appointed by him, as are the President and members of the Senate. Military and civil ranks are also granted, or withdrawn, by the King. No death sentence is carried out until he has confirmed it.

Ministers. The Council of Ministers consists of the Prime Minister, President of the Council, and of his Ministers. Ministers are forbidden to become members of any company, to receive a salary from any company, or to participate in any financial act of trade. The Council of Ministers is entrusted with the conduct of all affairs of State, internal and external.

The Council of Ministers is responsible to the House of Representatives for matters of general policy. Ministers may speak in either House, and, if they are members of one House, they may also vote in that House. Votes of confidence in the Council are cast in the House of Representatives, and decided by a two-thirds majority. If a vote of "no confidence" is returned, the Ministers are bound to resign. Every newly-formed Council of Ministers must present its programme to the House of Representatives and ask for a vote of confidence. The House of Representatives can impeach Ministers, as it impeaches its own members.

Amendments. Two amendments were passed in November 1974 giving the King the right to dissolve the Senate or to take away membership from any of its members, and to postpone general elections for a period not to exceed a year, if there are circumstances in which the Council of Ministers feels that it is impossible to hold elections. A further amendment in February 1976 enabled the King to postpone elections indefinitely.

THE GOVERNMENT

HEAD OF STATE

King HUSSEIN IBN TALAL; proclaimed King by a decree of the Jordan Parliament on August 11th, 1952; crowned on May 2nd, 1953.

Chief of Royal Court: AHMAD AL-LOUZI.

CABINET

(June 1982)

Prime Minister and Minister of Defence: MUDAR BADRAN.

Minister of Information: ADNAN ABU ODEH.

Minister of Finance: SALEM MUSADEH.

Minister of Culture, Youth, Tourism and Antiquities: MA'AN ABU NOWAR.

Minister of Justice: AHMAD ABDUL KARIM TARAWNEH.

Minister of Agriculture: MARWAN DODEEN.

Minister of Communications: Dr. MUHAMMAD ADOUB AL-ZABER.

Minister of Occupied Territories Affairs: HASAN IBRAHIM.

Minister of Awqaf and Religious Affairs: KAMEL SHARIF.

Minister of Foreign Affairs: MARWAN AL-KASIM.

JORDAN

Minister of the Interior: AHMED UTEIBAT.

Minister of Supply: IBRAHIM AYOUB.

Minister of Transport and Minister of State for the Prime Ministry: Eng. ALI SUHEIMAT.

Minister of State for the Prime Ministry: HIKMAT ALSAKET.

Minister of Education and Instruction: Dr. SAID AL-TAL.

Minister of Health: Dr. ZUHAIR MALHAS.

Minister of Social Development: Mrs. INAM AL-MUFTI.

Minister of Labour: Dr. JAWAD ANANI.

Minister of Industry and Commerce: WALEED ASFOUR.

Minister of Public Works: Eng. AWNI AL-MASRI.

Minister of Municipal and Rural Affairs: HASAN AL-MOMANI.

LEGISLATURE
MAJLIS AL-UMMA
(National Assembly)

THE SENATE
(HOUSE OF NOTABLES)

President: BAHJAT TALHOUNI.

The Senate consists of 30 members, appointed by the King. A new Senate was appointed by the King on January 20th, 1979.

HOUSE OF REPRESENTATIVES

Elections to the 60-seat House of Representatives took place in April 1967. There were no political parties. The House was dissolved by Royal Decree on November 23rd, 1974, but reconvened briefly on February 15th, 1976. Elections have been postponed indefinitely.

In April 1978 a National Consultative Council was formed by Royal Decree. It consists of 60 members appointed by the King, and serves for two years. The third term began on April 20th, 1982. The King has the right to dissolve the Council or dismiss members. The Speaker is SULAYMAN ARAR.

POLITICAL PARTIES

Political parties were banned before the elections of July 1963. In September 1971 King Hussein announced the formation of a Jordanian National Union. This was the only political organization allowed. Communists, Marxists and "other advocates of imported ideologies" were ineligible for membership. In March 1972 the organization was renamed the Arab National Union. In April 1974 King Hussein dissolved the executive committee of the Arab National Union, and accepted the resignation of the Secretary-General and in February 1976 the Cabinet approved a law abolishing the Union. Membership was estimated at about 100,000.

DIPLOMATIC REPRESENTATION

EMBASSIES ACCREDITED TO JORDAN
(E) Embassy.

Afghanistan: Jeddah, Saudi Arabia (E).

Algeria: Amman (E); *Ambassador:* AHMED LAIDI.

Argentina: Beirut, Lebanon (E).

Australia: Beirut, Lebanon (E).

Austria: Damascus, Syria (E).

Bahrain: Amman (E); *Ambassador:* ABDEL AZIZ HASSAN.

Bangladesh: Jeddah, Saudi Arabia (E).

Belgium: Amman (E); *Chargé d'affaires a.i.:* JEOPER BIOL.

Brazil: Beirut, Lebanon (E).

Bulgaria: Amman (E); *Chargé d'affaires:* FRANTISEK MATAI.

Canada: Beirut, Lebanon (E).

Chad: Beirut, Lebanon (E).

Chile: Amman (E); *Ambassador:* FERNANDO CONTRERAS TAPIA.

China, People's Republic: Amman (E); *Ambassador:* GU XIAOBO.

Czechoslovakia: P.O.B. 2213, Amman (E); *Ambassador:* FRANTIŠEK MATAL.

Denmark: Beirut, Lebanon (E).

Finland: Beirut, Lebanon (E).

France: Amman (E); *Ambassador:* (vacant).

German Democratic Republic: Amman (E); *Ambassador:* Dr. REINHARD ESCHERICH.

Germany, Federal Republic: Amman (E); *Ambassador:* Dr. HERMANN MUNZ.

Greece: P.O.B. 35069, Amman (E); *Ambassador:* CONSTANTINAS ELIOPOULOS.

Guinea: Cairo, Egypt (E).

Hungary: Damascus, Syria (E).

India: P.O.B. 2168 (E); *Ambassador:* ABDUL GHANI GONI.

Indonesia: Damascus, Syria (E).

Iran: Amman (E); Diplomatic relations broken off in Feb. 1981.

Iraq: Amman (E); *Ambassador:* IBRAHIM SHUJA' SULTAN.

Italy: Amman (E); *Ambassador:* FABRIZIO ROSSI LONGHI.

Japan: Amman (E); *Ambassador:* FUMIYA OKADA.

Korea, Democratic People's Republic: Amman (E); *Ambassador:* LI SOE RYONG.

Korea, Republic: Jabal Amman, 3rd Circle, Abu Tammam St., P.O.B. 3060, Amman (E); *Ambassador:* SOH JIN-CHUL.

Kuwait: Amman (E); *Ambassador:* IBRAHIM BAHD.

Lebanon: Amman (E); *Ambassador:* MARCEL NAMOUR.

Libya: Amman (E); *Ambassador:* AZIZ OMAR SHUNAIB.

Malaysia: Jeddah, Saudi Arabia (E).

Malta: Tripoli, Libya (E).

Mauritania: Jeddah, Saudi Arabia (E).

Morocco: Amman (E); *Chargé d'affaires:* MUHAMMAD EL-GUMARI.

Nepal: Jeddah, Saudi Arabia (E).

Netherlands: Beirut, Lebanon (E).

Nigeria: Jeddah, Saudi Arabia (E).

Norway: Cairo, Egypt (E).

Oman: Amman (E); *Ambassador:* NAZAR MUHAMMAD ALI.

Pakistan: Amman (E); *Ambassador:* Prof. EHSAN RASHID.

Philippines: Amman (E); *Chargé d'affaires a.i.:* EMMANUEL CONTRERAS.

Poland: Damascus, Syria (E).

Portugal: Beirut, Lebanon (E).

Qatar: Amman (E); *Ambassador:* Sheikh HAMAD BIN MOHAMMAD BIN JABER AL-THANI.

Romania: Amman (E); *Ambassador:* ANDREI CERVEN-COVICI.

Saudi Arabia: Um-Uthaina, Amman (E); *Ambassador:* Sheikh IBRAHIM MUHAMMAD AL-SULTAN.

Senegal: Jeddah, Saudi Arabia (E).

Somalia: Jeddah, Saudi Arabia (E).

Spain: Amman (E); *Ambassador:* LUIS DE PEDROSO.

Sri Lanka: Cairo, Egypt (E).

Sudan: Amman (E); *Ambassador:* AHMAD DIAB.

Sweden: Amman (E); *Ambassador:* STEN STROHOLM.

Switzerland: Amman (E); *Ambassador:* GUSTAV DUBOIS.

Syria: Amman (E); Ambassador recalled in Feb. 1981.

Thailand: Jeddah, Saudi Arabia (E).

Tunisia: Amman (E); *Ambassador:* MAHMOUD CHARCHOUR.

Turkey: Amman (E); *Ambassador:* RECHAT ARIM.

U.S.S.R.: Amman (E); *Ambassador:* RAFIK NISHANOVICH NISHANOV.

United Arab Emirates: Amman (E); *Chargé d'affaires a.i.:* JAMIL EL-RAMAHI.

United Kingdom: 3rd Circle, Jebel Amman, P.O.B. 87, Amman (E); *Ambassador:* ALAN URWICK, C.M.G.

U.S.A.: Amman (E); *Ambassador:* RICHARD N. VIETS.

Uruguay: Beirut, Lebanon (E).

Venezuela: Beirut, Lebanon (E).

Yemen Arab Republic: Amman (E); *Ambassador:* ALI ABDULLAH ABU LUHOUM.

Yugoslavia: Amman (E); *Ambassador:* DUŠAN ZAVASNIK.

Jordan also has diplomatic relations with Cuba, Ecuador, Maldives, Mexico, Mongolia, Viet-Nam and the People's Democratic Republic of Yemen.

JUDICIAL SYSTEM

With the exception of matters of purely personal nature concerning members of non-Muslim communities, the law of Jordan was based on Islamic Law for both civil and criminal matters. During the days of the Ottoman Empire, certain aspects of Continental law, especially French commercial law and civil and criminal procedure, were introduced. Due to British occupation of Palestine and Transjordan from 1917 to 1948, the Palestine territory has adopted, either by statute or case law, much of the English common law. Since the annexation of the non-occupied part of Palestine and the formation of the Hashemite Kingdom of Jordan, there has been a continuous effort to unify the law.

Court of Cassation. The Court of Cassation consists of seven judges, who sit in full panel for exceptionally important cases. In most appeals, however, only five members sit to hear the case. All cases involving amounts of more than JD 100 may be reviewed by this Court, as well as cases involving lesser amounts and cases which cannot be monetarily valued. However, for the latter types of cases, review is available only by leave of the Court of Appeal, or, upon refusal by the Court of Appeal, by leave of the President of the Court of Cassation. In addition to these functions as final and Supreme Court of Appeal, the Court of Cassation also sits as High Court of Justice to hear applications in the nature of habeas corpus, mandamus and certiorari dealing with complaints of a citizen against abuse of governmental authority.

Courts of Appeal. There are two Courts of Appeal, each of which is composed of three judges, whether for hearing of appeals or for dealing with Magistrates Courts' judgments in chambers. Jurisdiction of the two Courts is geographical, with the Court for the Western Region sitting in Jerusalem (which has not sat since June 1967) and the Court for the Eastern Region sitting in Amman. The regions are separated by the River Jordan. Appellate review of the Courts of Appeal extends to judgments rendered in the Courts of First Instance, the Magistrates' Courts, and Religious Courts.

Courts of First Instance. The Courts of First Instance are courts of general jurisdiction in all matters civil and criminal except those specifically allocated to the Magistrates' Courts. Three judges sit in all felony trials, while only two judges sit for misdemeanour and civil cases. Each of the seven Courts of First Instance also exercises appellate jurisdiction in cases involving judgments of less than JD 20 and fines of less than JD 10, rendered by the Magistrates' Courts.

Magistrates' Courts. There are fourteen Magistrates' Courts, which exercise jurisdiction in civil cases involving no more than JD 250 and in criminal cases involving maximum fines of JD 100 or maximum imprisonment of one year.

Religious Courts. There are two types of Religious Court: The Sharia Courts (Muslims): and the Ecclesiastical Courts (Eastern Orthodox, Greek Melkite, Roman Catholic and Protestant). Jurisdiction extends to personal (family) matters, such as marriage, divorce, alimony, inheritance, guardianship, wills, interdiction and, for the Muslim community, the constitution of Waqfs (Religious Endowments). When a dispute involves persons of different religious communities, the Civil Courts have jurisdiction in the matter unless the parties agree to submit to the jurisdiction of one or the other of the Religious Courts involved.

Each Sharia (Muslim) Court consists of one judge (Qadi), while most of the Ecclesiastical (Christian) Courts are normally composed of three judges, who are usually clerics. Sharia Courts apply the doctrines of Islamic Law, based on the Koran and the Hadith (Precepts of Muhammad), while the Ecclesiastical Courts base their law on various aspects of Canon Law. In the event of conflict between any two Religious Courts or between a Religious Court and a Civil Court, a Special Tribunal of three judges is appointed by the President of the Court of Cassation, to decide which court shall have jurisdiction. Upon the advice of experts on the law of the various communities, this Special Tribunal decides on the venue for the case at hand.

RELIGION

Over 80 per cent of the population are Sunni Muslims, and the King can trace unbroken descent from the Prophet Muhammad. There is a Christian minority, living mainly in the towns, and smaller numbers of non-Sunni Muslims.

Prominent religious leaders in Jordan are:

Sheikh IBRAHIM QATTAN (Chief Justice and President of the Supreme Muslim Secular Council).

Sheikh SUBHI AL-MUWQQAT (Director of Sharia Courts).

Sheikh MUHAMMAD ABDO HASHEM (Mufti of the Hashemite Kingdom of Jordan).

THE PRESS

DAILIES

Al-Dustour (*The Constitution*): P.O.B. 591, Amman; f. 1967; Arabic; publ. by the Jordan Press and Publishing Co.; owns commercial printing facilities; Dir.-Gen. and Editor-in-Chief MAHMOUD EL-SHERIF; Man. Dir. TAWFIQ KIWAN; circ. 55,000.

Al-Rai (*Opinion*): P.O.B. 6710, Amman; f. 1971; independent; published by Jordan Press Foundation; Gen. Man. JUMA'A HAMMAD; Editor-in-Chief MAHMOUD KAYED; circ. 70,000.

Al-Urdun: P.O.B. 6194, Amman; f. 1909; Editor Dr. HANNA NASR.

The Jordan Times: P.O.B. 6710, Amman; f. 1975; English; Managing Editor MOHAMMAD AMAD; Editor RAMI G. KHOUR; circ. 6,000.

Al-Akhbar (*News*): P.O.B. 62420, Amman; f. 1976; Arabic; publ. by the Arab Press Co.; Editor RACAN EL-MAJALI; circ. 15,000.

PERIODICALS

Akhbar al-Usbu: Amman; f. 1954; Arabic; weekly; Chief Editor ABDUL-HAFIZ MUHAMMAD.

Al Aqsa: Amman; armed forces magazine; weekly.

Huda El Islam: Amman; f. 1956; monthly; Islamic; scientific and literary; published by the Department of Islamic Affairs; Editor IZZIDIN AL-KHATIB.

Jordan: P.O.B. 224, Amman; f. 1969; published quarterly by Jordan Information Bureau, Washington; circ. 100,000.

Al-Liwa: Amman; f. 1972; Arabic; weekly; Chief Editor HASAN ATTEL.

Military Magazine: Army Headquarters, Amman; f. 1955; quarterly; dealing with military and literary subjects; published by Armed Forces.

Sharia: P.O.B. 585, Amman; f. 1959; fortnightly; Islamic affairs; published by Sharia College; circ. 5,000.

NEWS AGENCIES

Jordan News Agency (**PETRA**): P.O.B. 6845, Amman; f. 1965; government-controlled; Dir.-Gen. Y. ABULEIL.

FOREIGN NEWS BUREAUX

Agence France-Presse (**AFP**): P.O.B. 3340, Amman; Bureau Man. FOUAD NAIM.

Reuters (*U.K.*): P.O.B. 667, Amman.

ANSA (Italy), AP (U.S.A.), Central News Agency (Taiwan), dpa (Federal Republic of Germany), Iraqi News Agency, Qatar News Agency, Saudi Press Agency, TASS (U.S.S.R.), and UPI (U.S.A.) also maintain bureaux in Amman.

PUBLISHERS

Jordan Press and Publishing Co. Ltd.: Amman; f. 1967 by *al-Manar* and *Falastin*; cap. JD 250,000; publishes *al-Dustour* (daily); circ. 55,000.

Other publishers in Amman include: *Dairat al-Ihsaat al-Amman, George N. Kawar, al-Matbaat al-Hashmiya* and *The National Press.*

RADIO AND TELEVISION

The Hashemite Jordan Broadcasting Service (**H.B.S.**): P.O.B 909, Amman; f. 1959; station at Amman broadcasts daily 20 hours in Arabic to the Arab World, 15 hours in English regionally including 2½ hours in English to W. Europe and N. America; takes advertising; Dir.-Gen. NASHOU MAJALI.

Jordan Television Corporation: P.O.B. 1041, Amman; f. 1968; government station broadcasting for 80 hours weekly in Arabic and English; in colour; advertising accepted; Dir.-Gen. M. KAMAL; Chief Engineer R. ALKHAS.

Number of radio receivers 200,000, number of TV receivers 180,000 (East Bank only).

FINANCE

(cap. = capital; p.u. = paid up; dep. = deposits; m. = million; res. = reserves; JD = Jordanian dinars.)

BANKING

CENTRAL BANK

Central Bank of Jordan: P.O.B. 37, Amman; f. 1964; cap. JD 2m.; total resources JD 456.7m. (Dec. 1979); Gov. Dr. M. SAID NABULSI; Deputy Gov. HUSAYN EL-KASIM.

NATIONAL BANKS

Agricultural Credit Corporation: P.O.B. 77, Amman; f. 1960; cap. p.u. JD 6.5m.; total assets JD 11.3 m. (Dec. 1978); government-owned credit institution; Dir.-Gen. SAMI SUNAA.

Arab Bank Ltd.: King Faisal St., P.O.B. 68, Amman; f. 1930; cap. p.u. and reserves JD 72m.; dep. 1,700m.; total assets 2,700m. (June 1981); Chair. ABDUL MAJEED SHOMAN.

Bank of Jordan Ltd.: P.O.B. 2140, Jabal Amman on 3rd Circle, Amman; f. 1960; cap. p.u. JD 1,500,000; total assets 48.9m. (June 1981); 17 brs.; Chair. HUSNI SIDO AL-KURDI; Gen. Man. ZUHAIR IZZAT DARWAZA.

Cairo Amman Bank: P.O.B. 715, Prince Hassan St., Amman; f. 1960; cap. and res. JD 44m.; total assets 74.8m. (July 1980); 10 brs.; Chair. JAWDAT SHASHA'A; Gen. Man. HAIDAR CHUKRI; associated with Banque du Caire, Cairo, and succeeded their Amman Branch.

Jordan-Gulf Bank S.A.: P.O.B. 9989, Jabal Al-Hussein, Khalid Ben al-Waleed St., Amman; f. 1977; cap. p.u. JD 5m.; total assets JD 60.6m. (1981); 60 per cent Jordanian-owned and 40 per cent by Gulf businessmen; 14 brs.; Chair. H.E. MOHAMMED NAZZAL AL-ARMOUTI; Gen. Man. ADNAN DARWAZA.

Jordan Islamic Bank: P.O.B. 926225, Amman; f. 1979; cap. p.u. JD 2.6m. (Aug. 1981); total assets 15.5m. (Dec. 1980); 5 brs.; Chair. Sheikh SALEH KAMEL; Gen. Man. TAUFIQ MAREI.

Jordan Kuwait Bank: P.O.B. 9776, Amman; f. 1976; cap. p.u. JD 5m.; dep. JD 55m. (Dec. 1981); Chair. Sheikh NASSER AL-SABAH; Deputy Chair. and Gen. Man SUFIAN IBRAHIM YASSIN.

Jordan National Bank S.A.: P.O.B. 1578, Amman; f. 1956; cap. p.u. JD 3.3m.; dep. JD 52.5m. (Dec. 1979); 20 brs. in Jordan, 4 brs. in Lebanon; Chair. and Gen. Man. H.E. SULEIMAN SUKKAR; Deputy Gen. Mans. H.E. ABDUL-KADER TASH and Dr. ABDER RAHMAN S. TOUQAN.

Petra Bank: P.O.B. 6854, Amman; f. 1977; cap. p.u JD 3m.; dep. JD 48.6m. (Dec. 1980); 60 per cent owned by Jordanians and 40 per cent by other Arab interests; Chair. and Gen. Man. Dr. AHMAD CHALABI.

Syrian Jordanian Bank: P.O.B. 926636, Amman; f. 1979; cap. p.u. 1.6m.; total assets 12.3m. (Feb. 1982); Chair. FARUK AYASH; Deputy Chair. HUSSEIN KASSEM; Gen. Man. Dr. A. MURAD.

FOREIGN BANKS

British Bank of the Middle East: P.O.B. 925286, Amman; f. 1889; Chair. M. G. R. SANDBERG, O.B.E.; Area Man. A. D. E. DAWSON.

Chase Manhattan Bank (*U.S.A.*): P.O.B. 20191, On the First Circle, Jabal Amman; f. 1976; Gen. Man. RICHARD W. MOUNCE; Operations Man. A. SHANANIER.

Grindlays Bank (*United Kingdom*): P.O.B. 9997, Amman; acquired the Ottoman Bank interests in Jordan in 1969; brs. in Amman (8 brs.) Aqaba, Irbid (subbranch in Northern Shouneh), Zerak and Kerak; Gen. Man. in Jordan R. S. CORDINGLEY.

Rafidain Bank (*Iraq*): P.O.B. 11194, Amman; f. 1941; Area Man. MUHAMMAD F. AL-ALOOSY.

Other foreign banks include Arab Land Bank, Citibank, Bank Al Mashrek, Bank of Credit and Commerce International.

SPECIALIZED CREDIT INSTITUTIONS

Agricultural Credit Corporation: P.O.B. 77, Amman; cap. p.u. JD 6.9m.; total assets JD 14.5m. (July 1980); Chair. and Gen. Man. Dr. SAMI SUNA'A.

The Arab Jordan Investment Bank: P.O.B. 8797; Amman; f. 1978; cap. p.u. JD 5m.; Chair. and Gen. Man. ABDUL QADER QADI.

Cities and Villages Development Bank: P.O.B. 1572, Amman; cap. p.u. JD 6.5m.; total assets JD 23m. (Aug. 1981); Dir.-Gen. MUHAMMAD MAHDI FARHAN.

Housing Bank: Police College St., Abdali, P.O.B. 7693, Amman; f. 1973; cap. p.u. JD 12m.; total assets JD 203m. (Dec. 1981); Chair. and Dir.-Gen. ZUHAIR KHOURI.

Industrial Development Bank: P.O.B. 1982, Zahran St., Amman; f. 1965; cap. p.u. JD 4.5m.; total assets JD 29.8m. (Dec. 1981); Chair. ROUHI EL-KHATEEB; Gen. Man. ZIYAD ANNAB.

Jordan Co-operative Organization: P.O.B. 1343, Amman; cap. p.u. JD 1.9m.; total assets JD 11.7m. (July 1980); Gen. Man. Dr. HASSAN NABULSI.

Social Security Corporation: P.O.B. 926031, Amman; f. 1978; Dir.-Gen. FARHI AMER OBEID.

STOCK EXCHANGE

Amman Financial Market: P.O.B. 8802, Amman; Gen. Man. Dr. HASHIM SABAGH.

INSURANCE

Al-Ahlia Insurance Co. (Jordan) Ltd.: P.O.B. 2938, 2nd Circle, Jabal Amman; cap. p.u. JD 240,000.

Jordan Insurance Co. Ltd.: P.O.B. 279, King Hussein St., Amman; cap. p.u. JD 400,000; brs. in five Arab countries.

Middle East Insurance Co. Ltd.: P.O.B. 1802, Cairo Amman Bank Bldg., Shabsough St., Amman; cap. p.u. JD 200,000.

United Insurance Co. Ltd.: P.O.B. 7521, Abujaber Bldg., King Faisal St., Amman; cap. p.u. JD 250,000; all types of insurance.

Fourteen local and 14 foreign insurance companies operate in Jordan.

TRADE AND INDUSTRY

CHAMBERS OF COMMERCE AND INDUSTRY

Amman Chamber of Commerce: P.O.B. 287, Amman; f. 1923; Pres. MOHAMAD ALI BDEIR; Dr. RAJEH AMIN.

Amman Chamber of Industry: P.O.B. 1800, Amman; Pres. BANDAR TABBAA; Exec. Dir. ALI DAJANI.

Chamber of Commerce, Irbid: P.O.B. 13; f. 1950; Pres. MUFLEH HASSAN GHARAIBEH; Dir. HASSAN M. MURAD.

PUBLIC CORPORATION

Jordan Valley Authority: P.O.B. 2769, Amman; Stage I development projects now complete, and addition of 9,300 hectares to the irrigated land has been accomplished. Infrastructure projects also completed include 105 km. main highway, 300 km. secondary roads, 2,000 housing units, 48 schools, 13 health centres, 9 administration buildings. Electricity is now provided to 30 villages in the valley from the national network and domestic water is supplied to those villages from tube wells. Contributions to the cost of development came through loans from Kuwait Fund, Abu Dhabi Fund, U.S. A.I.D., Fed. Germany, World Bank, Netherlands, U.K., Japan and OPEC Special Fund. Further stages of development are the construction of Maqarin Dam on the Yarmouk River and projects to irrigate 17,000 hectares of land in the Jordan Valley and Southern Ghors.

TRADE UNIONS

The General Federation of Jordanian Trade Unions: Wadi as-Sir Rd., P.O.B. 1065, Amman; f. 1954; 33,000 mems.; member of Arab Trade Unions Confederation; Chair. SAMI HASAN MANSOUR; Gen. Sec. ABDER-RAZZAQ HAMAD.

There are also a number of independent unions, including:

Drivers' Union: P.O.B. 846, Amman; Sec.-Gen. SAMI MANSOUR.

Union of Petroleum Workers and Employees: P.O.B. 1346, Amman; Sec.-Gen. BRAHIM HADI.

PHOSPHATE

Jordan Phosphate Mines Co. Ltd.: P.O.B. 30, Amman; engaged in production and export of rock phosphates; Sec.-Gen. TAHASEEN KHREIS; production (1980) 3.9 million tons.

TRANSPORT

RAILWAYS

Hedjaz Jordan Railway (administered by the Ministry of Transport): P.O.B. 582, Amman; f. 1902; length of track 618 km.; Dir.-Gen. M. R. QOSEINI.

This was formerly a section of the Hedjaz railway (Damascus to Medina) for Muslim pilgrims to Medina and Mecca. It crosses the Syrian border and enters Jordanian territory south of Dera'a, and runs for approximately 366 km. to Naqb Ishtar, passing through Zarka, Amman,

Qatrana and Ma'an. Some 844 km. of the line, from Ma'an to Medina in Saudi Arabia, have been abandoned for the past sixty years. Reconstruction of the Medina line, begun in 1965, was scheduled to be completed in 1971 at a cost of £15 million, divided equally between Jordan, Saudi Arabia and Syria. However, the reconstruction work has been suspended at the request of the Arab States concerned, pending further studies on costs. The line between Ma'an and Saudi Arabia (114 km.) is now completed, as well as 15 km. in Saudi Arabia as far as Haret Ammar Station. A new 115 km. extension to Aqaba was financed by a JD 12 million loan from the Federal Republic of Germany; this line became operational in October 1975. It is used mainly for transporting phosphates and connects Aqaba to Beirut. On January 27th, 1980, an agreement was signed between the Supreme Commission of the Hedjaz Railway and Dorsch Consult (Federal Republic of Germany) for a feasibility study for construction of the Hedjaz Railway to high international specifications to connect Saudi Arabia, Jordan and Syria. The feasibility study is awaiting a decision (September 1981).

ROADS
Ministry of Public Works: Amman.

Amman is linked by road with all parts of the kingdom and with neighbouring countries. All cities and most towns are connected by a 2-lane paved road system. In addition, several thousand km. of tracks make all villages accessible to motor transport. In 1981, the latest inventory showed the East Bank of Jordan to have 1,943 km. of main roads, 820 km. of secondary roads and 2,187 km. of village roads, all of which are asphalted. There are also 1,950 km. of unsurfaced roads.

SHIPPING

The port of Aqaba is Jordan's only outlet to the sea and has two general berths of 340 metres and 215 metres, with seven main transit sheds, covered storage area of 4,150 sq. metres, an open area of 50,600 sq. metres and a phosphate berth 210 metres long and 10 metres deep. Ten new berths and storage facilities are being built, and a separate potash berth, a container terminal and a fertilizer jetty are planned.

Jordan National Line: Aqaba; f. 1979.

PIPELINES

Two oil pipelines cross Jordan. The former Iraq Petroleum Company pipeline, carrying petroleum from the oilfields in Iraq to Haifa, has not operated since 1967. The 1,717-km. (1,067-mile) pipeline, known as the Trans-Arabian Pipeline (Tapline) carries petroleum from the oilfields at Dhahran in Saudi Arabia to Sidon on the Mediterranean seaboard in Lebanon. It traverses Jordan for a distance of 177 km. (110 miles) and has frequently been cut by hostile action.

CIVIL AVIATION

There are international airports at Amman and Aqaba. Work is in progress on a new international airport, the Queen Alia International Airport, at Zizya, Amman. Inauguration is expected in August 1982.

Alia (The Royal Jordanian Airline): Head Office: P.O.B. 302, Arab Insurance Building, First Circle, Jabel Amman, Amman; f. 1963; government-owned; services to Middle East, Europe, Far East and U.S.A.; fleet of three Boeing 747-200, six Boeing 707-320C, six Boeing 727 200, one Boeing 720 B72, three Lockheed L-1011-500, four freighter Boeing 707 320C 70F; Chair. and Pres. ALI GHANDOUR.

Arab Wings Co. Ltd.: P.O.B. 39100, Amman; f. 1975; subsidiary of Alia; executive jet charter service, air ambulances, priority cargo; Chair. and Pres. ALI GHANDOUR; Exec. Vice-Pres. Captain R. K. JONES.

Jordan World Airlines: f. 1974; subsidiary of Alia; initial fleet: four Boeing 707; Chair. ALI GHANDOUR; Dir.-Gen. SALAH HUSSEIN ALI.

The following airlines also serve Jordan: Aeroflot (U.S.S.R.), Air France, British Airways, Cyprus Airways, EgyptAir, Gulf Air, Iraqi Airways, JAT (Yugoslavia), KLM (Netherlands), Kuwait Airways, Libyan Arab Airlines, Lufthansa (Federal Germany), MEA (Lebanon), PIA (Pakistan), SAS (Scandinavia), Saudia, Swissair, Tarom (Romania).

TOURISM

Ministry of Tourism and Antiquities: P.O.B. 224, Amman; f. 1952; Dir.-Gen. MICHEL HAMARNEH; publs. *Jordan* (quarterly), *Tourist Arrivals*, *Jordan Tourist News* (bi-monthly), Annual Report.

DEFENCE

Commander-in-Chief of the Armed Forces: Lieutenant-General ZAID BIN SHAKAR.

Assistant Commander-in-Chief of the Armed Forces and Commander of the Royal Jordanian Air Force: Brig. TAYSEER ZAROUR.

Chief of Staff of the Armed Forces: Gen. FATHI ABU TALIB.

Defence Expenditure (1979): JD 114 million.

Military Service: 2 years.

Total Armed Forces: 67,200: army 60,000; navy 200; air force 7,000.

Paramilitary Forces: 10,000 (3,000 Mobile Police Force, 7,000 Civil Militia).

EDUCATION

The Ministry of Education adopted the principle of decentralization from the beginning of 1980. It divided the East Bank into 18 districts, called Offices of Education, distributed over five Directorates of Education, each one run by a Director-General who is in charge of implementing educational policies and procedures in his own area. The Ministry of Education's Central Office is still responsible for all major educational decisions related to planning curricula, projects and examinations.

Education in Jordan is provided by public and private sectors. In 1980, 70.68 per cent of school enrolment was provided by the Ministry of Education, 0.84 per cent by other governmental agencies (such as the Ministries of Defence, Health, Labour and Islamic Affairs), 9.44 per cent by the private sector and 16.90 per cent by UNRWA, which offers educational facilities and services for Palestinian refugees in collaboration with UNESCO. The University of Jordan and Yarmouk University provided 2.94 per cent of total school enrolment.

A child is admitted to the first grade of the elementary school at the age of five years and eight months. The duration of this cycle is six years. Most of the students are promoted to the seventh grade, which makes, with the eighth and ninth grades, what are known as preparatory schools.

The secondary school course lasts three years, and is divided into three types: general school, vocational school and comprehensive school. At the end of this cycle all students sit the General Secondary Examination, and those who pass are entitled to continue their higher education by enrolling either in the three universities of Jordan or in Community Colleges—or in foreign universities and colleges.

Community Colleges, of two- or three-year post-secondary duration, include 12 colleges controlled by the Ministry, 20 colleges controlled by the private sector and 11 other colleges controlled by other governmental agencies such as the Ministries of Health and Social Development, the armed forces, the Department of Statistics and the Central Bank of Jordan.

For the year 1981, the budget of the Ministry of Education was JD 63 million. This was 8.0 per cent of the total government budget.

The Ministry of Education, in accordance with law No. 16 of 1964, provides free and compulsory education for nine years. It distributes textbooks free of charge for the compulsory cycle, and at cost price for the secondary cycle.

BIBLIOGRAPHY

ABDULLAH OF TRANSJORDAN, KING. Memoirs, trans. G. Khuri, ed. P. Graves (London and New York, 1950).

ABIDI, A. H. H. Jordan, a Political Study, 1948–1957 (Asia Publishing House, Delhi, 1966).

CROSS, FRANK M. (Jr.). Ancient Library of Qumran (Anchor Books, New York).

DEARDEN, ANN. Jordan (Hale, London, 1958).

FOREIGN AREA STUDIES. Jordan: A Country Study (American University, Washington, D.C., 1980).

GLUBB, J. B. The Story of the Arab Legion (London, 1948).
A Soldier with the Arabs (Hodder and Stoughton, 1957).
Britain and the Arabs: A Study of Fifty Years 1908–1958 (Hodder and Stoughton, London, 1959).
War in the Desert (London, 1960).
The Middle East Crisis—A Personal Interpretation (London, 1967).
Syria, Lebanon, Jordan (London, 1967).
Peace in the Holy Land (London, 1971).

GOICHON, A. M. L'Eau: Problème Vital de la Région du Jourdain (Brussels, Centre pour l'Etudes des Problèmes du Monde Musulmane Contemporain, 1964).

GRANQVIST, HILMA. Birth and Childhood among the Arabs: Studies in a Muhammadan Village in Palestine (Helsinki, 1947).
Family Life among the Arabs.
Marriage Conditions in a Palestinian Village.

HUSSEIN, HIS MAJESTY KING. Uneasy Lies the Head (London, 1962).

INTERNATIONAL BANK FOR RECONSTRUCTION AND DEVELOPMENT. The Economic Development of Jordan (Baltimore, Johns Hopkins Press, 1957).

JARVIS, C. S. Arab Command: the Biography of Lt.-Col. F. W. Peake Pasha (London, 1942).

JOHNSTON, CHARLES. The Brink of Jordan (London, Hamish Hamilton, 1972).

KENNEDY, Sir ALEXANDER. Petra: Its History and Monuments (London, 1925).

KOHN, HANS. Die staats- und verfassungsrechtliche Entwicklung des Emirats Transjordanien (Tübingen, 1929).

KONIKOF, A. Transjordan: An Economic Survey (2nd edn., Jerusalem, 1946).

LUKE, Sir HARRY C., and KEITH-ROACH, E. The Handbook of Palestine and Transjordan (London, 1934).

LYAUTEY, PIERRE. La Jordanie Nouvelle (Jiulliard, Paris, 1966).

MINISTRY OF FOREIGN AFFAIRS. Amman, Jordan: Some aspects of its growing importance in the Middle East (Amman, 1951).

MISHAL, SHAUL. West Bank/East Bank: The Palestinians in Jordan 1949–67 (Yale University Press, New Haven, London).

MORRIS, JAMES. The Hashemite Kings (Faber, London, 1959).

PALESTINE GOVERNMENT. Memorandum on the Water Resources of Palestine (Jerusalem, 1947).

PATAI, R. The Kingdom of Jordan (Princeton, 1958).

PEAKE, F. G. History of Jordan and Its Tribes (Univ. of Miami Press, 1958).

PEROWNE, STEWART. The One Remains (London, 1954). Jerusalem and Bethlehem (A. S. Barnes Ltd., South Brunswick, New Jersey, 1966).

PHILLIPS, PAUL G. The Hashemite Kingdom of Jordan: Prolegomena to a Technical Assistance Programme (Chicago, 1954).

SANGER, RICHARD H. Where the Jordan Flows (Middle East Institute, Washington, 1965).

SHWADRAN, B. Jordan: A State of Tension (Council for Middle Eastern Affairs, New York, 1959).

SMITH, Sir G. A. Historical Geography of the Holy Land (24th ed., London, 1931).

SNOW, PETER. Hussein: A Biography (London, Barrie and Jenkins, 1972).

SPARROW, GERALD. Hussein of Jordan (the authorized biography) (Harrap, London, 1961).
Modern Jordan (Allen and Unwin, 1961).

TOUKAN, BAHA UDDIN. A Short History of Transjordan (London, 1945).

U.S. GOVERNMENT PRINTING OFFICE. Area Handbook for the Hashemite Kindgom of Jordan (Washington, D.C., 1970).

VATIKIOTIS, P. J. Politics and the Military in Jordan 1921–57 (Praeger, New York, 1967).

VERDES, JACQUES MANSOUR. Pour les Fidayine (Paris, 1969).

Kuwait

PHYSICAL AND SOCIAL GEOGRAPHY

Kuwait lies at the head of the Persian Gulf, bordering Iraq and Saudi Arabia. The area of the State of Kuwait is 17,818 sq. km., including the Kuwaiti share of the Partitioned Zone (see below).

For long it was generally held that the Gulf extended much further north, but geological evidence suggests, first, that the coastline has remained broadly at its present position and, second, that the immense masses of silt brought down by the Tigris and Euphrates cause irregular downwarping at the head of the Gulf. Local variation in the coastline is therefore likely, with possible changes since ancient times. Kuwait grew up because it has a zone of slightly higher, firmer ground that gives access from the Gulf inland to Iraq, and because it has a reasonably good and sheltered harbour in an area that elsewhere has many sandbanks and, further south, coral reefs.

The territory of Kuwait is mainly almost flat desert with a few oases. With an annual rainfall of 1 to 37 centimetres, almost entirely between November and April, there is a spring "flush" of grass. Summer shade temperature may reach 120°F., though in January, the coldest month, temperatures range between 27° and 85°, with a rare frost. There is little drinking water within the state, and supplies are largely distilled from sea water, and brought by pipeline from the Shatt al-Arab.

Kuwait's population has increased very rapidly in recent years. It is unofficially estimated to have been 152,000 in 1950 but recent census results have produced totals of 206,473 (February 1957), 321,621 (May 1961), 467,339 (April 1965), 738,662 (April 1970), 994,837 (April 1975) and 1,355,827 (April 1980). Between 1963 and 1970 the average annual increase in Kuwait's population was 10.0 per cent, the highest growth rate recorded in any independent country. The average annual increase between 1970 and 1979 was 6.2 per cent.

Much of Kuwait's population growth has resulted from immigration, though the country also has one of the highest natural increase rates in the world. Between 1957 and 1980 the non-Kuwaiti population grew from less than 93,000 (45 per cent of the total) to more than 793,000 (58.5 per cent), most of them from other Arab states. In 1976 the natural increase of the population was 4.0 per cent, with 46,039 recorded births (44.1 per 1,000 inhabitants) and only 4,661 deaths (4.5 per 1,000). The high birth rate is particularly remarkable in view of the unequal distribution of the sexes, owing to the preponderance of males among the immigrant population. In 1980 the non-Kuwaitis comprised 497,609 males and 296,153 females. Among the 562,065 Kuwaiti citizens, by contrast, there were 278,516 males and 283,549 females. The birth rate for the Kuwaiti population alone exceeded 50 per 1,000 each year in 1973–76.

At the 1975 census Kuwait City, the capital and principal harbour, had a population of 78,116 (slightly less than in 1970), though the largest town was Hawalli, with 130,565 inhabitants. Other sizeable localities, all in Hawalli Governorate, were Salmiya (113,943), Abraq Kheetan (59,443) and Farawaniya (44,875). In all these towns, non-Kuwaitis formed a large majority. Kuwait City had only 11,777 Kuwaitis (15.1 per cent of the inhabitants), Hawalli had 9,816 Kuwaitis (7.5 per cent) and Salmiya had 16,764 (14.7 per cent).

Immediately to the south of Kuwait, along the Gulf, is a Partitioned Zone of 5,700 sq. km. which is divided between Kuwait and Saudi Arabia. Each country administers its own half, in practice as an integral part of the state. However, the oil wealth of the whole Zone remains undivided and production from the on-shore concessions in the Partitioned Zone is shared equally between the two States.

HISTORY

Although Kuwait is situated on the fringe of the Mesopotamian basin it has always belonged rather to the nomadic desert of Arabia than to the settled populations of the plains watered by the Euphrates and Tigris rivers. Thus the successive rule of the 'Abbasid Caliphate of Baghdad (750–1258), the Mongols (1258–1546) and the Ottoman Turks (1546–1918) had little direct influence on the area around Kuwait.

The origin of the present town of Kuwait is usually placed about the beginning of the 18th century, when a number of families of the famous Anaiza tribe migrated from the interior to the Arabian shore of the Gulf. These migrants included such important families as as-Sabah, al-Khalifa, az-Zayed, al-Jala-

hima and al-Ma'awida, from whom many of the present Kuwaitis are descended.

The foundation of the present Sabah ruling dynasty dates from about 1756, when the settlers of Kuwait decided to appoint a Sheikh to administer their affairs, provide them with security and represent them in their dealings with the Ottoman Government. The town prospered and in 1765 it was reported to contain some 10,000 inhabitants possessing 800 vessels and living by trading, fishing and pearling.

In 1776 war broke out between Persia and Turkey and the Persians captured Basra, which they held until 1779. During this time the East India Company moved the southern terminal of its overland mail route to Aleppo from Basra to Kuwait, and much of the trade of Basra was diverted to Kuwait. Sheikh Abdullah bin Sabah was reported to have been well disposed to the British, who for their part held him in high regard as being a man of his word.

About this time Kuwait was repeatedly threatened by raids from the Wahhabis, fanatical tribesmen from central Arabia, and the need for protection against these enemies led to closer contacts with the East India Company, who had a depot in the town. Ottoman dominion over the mainland was accepted in return for recognition of British trading interests over the route from the Mediterranean to India through the Gulf. The depredations of pirates and the threat from the Wahhabis caused Kuwait's prosperity to decline in the early years of the 19th century, but the British Navy restored peace to the Gulf, and by 1860 prosperity had returned.

In order to retain their autonomy the Kuwaitis had to maintain good relations with the Turks. Although not under direct Turkish administration the Sheikh of Kuwait recognized a general Ottoman suzerainty over the area by the payment of tribute and Sheikh Abdullah bin Sabah al-Jabir (1866–92) accepted the title of *Qa'immaqam* (Commandant) under the Turkish *Vali* (Governor) of Basra in 1871. His successor, Sheikh Mubarak "the Great", feared that the Turks would occupy Kuwait, and in 1899, in return for British protection, he signed an agreement with the British not to cede, mortgage or otherwise dispose of parts of his territories to anyone except the British Government, nor to enter into any relationship with a foreign government other than the British without British consent. This agreement prevented Germany from securing Kuwait as a terminal for the projected Berlin to Baghdad railway.

The reign of Sheikh Mubarak from 1896 to 1915 marked the rise of Kuwait from a Sheikhdom of undefined status to an autonomous state. In 1904 a British political agent was appointed, and in 1909 Great Britain and Turkey opened negotiations which, although never ratified because of the outbreak of the First World War, in practice secured the autonomy of Kuwait.

Sheikh Mubarak's second son, Sheikh Salim, who succeeded to the Sheikhdom in 1917, supported the Turks in the World War, thus incurring a blockade of Kuwait. Sheikh Salim was succeeded in 1921 by his nephew, Sheikh Ahmad al-Jabir. Kuwait prospered under his rule and by 1937 the population had risen to about 75,000.

Under Sheikh Ahmad the foundation of Kuwait's great oil industry was laid. After considerable prospecting, he granted a concession in 1934 jointly to the Gulf Oil Corporation of the U.S.A. and the Anglo-Persian Oil Co. of Great Britain who formed the Kuwait Oil Co. Ltd. Deep drilling started in 1936, and was just beginning to show promising results when war broke out in 1939. The oil wells were plugged in 1942 and drilling was suspended until the end of the war.

After the war the oil industry in Kuwait was resumed on an extensive scale (*see* Economic Survey)

and in a few years the character of Kuwait town was changed from an old-fashioned dhow port to a thriving modern city supported by the revenues of the oil industry. In 1950 Sheikh Ahmad died and was succeeded by Sheikh Abdullah as-Salim. His policy was to use the oil revenues substantially for the welfare of his people, and in 1951 he inaugurated a programme of public works and educational and medical developments which has turned Kuwait into a planned and well-equipped country.

THE MODERN STATE

The economic aspects of post-war development are dealt with in the survey following. Here it should be noted that Kuwait has gradually built up what are probably the most comprehensive welfare services in the world, very largely without charge, at least to native Kuwaitis. Education is completely free in Kuwait, and this includes free food and clothing for students. Medical attention is also free to all and the health service is generally considered to be of a very high standard. A heavily subsidized housing programme has now provided accommodation for most residents meeting the country's generous criteria of "poverty". Even local telephone calls are free.

In June 1961 the United Kingdom and Kuwait terminated the 1899 agreement which had given the U.K. responsibility for the conduct of Kuwait's foreign policy, and Kuwait therefore became a fully independent state. The ruling Sheikh took the new title of Amir. In July Kuwait was admitted as a member of the Arab League.

Shortly after attaining independence, Kuwait was threatened by an Iraqi claim to sovereignty over the territory. British troops landed in Kuwait in response to a request from the Amir for assistance. The Arab League met in July and agreed that an Arab League Force should be provided to replace the British troops as a guarantee of Kuwait's independence. This force, composed of contingents from Saudi Arabia, Jordan, the United Arab Republic and the Sudan, arrived in Kuwait in September 1961. The United Arab Republic contingent was withdrawn in December 1961, and those of Jordan, Saudi Arabia and the Sudan before the end of February 1963. On May 14th, 1963, Kuwait became the 111th member of the United Nations.

In December 1961, for the first time in Kuwait's history, an election was held to elect 20 members of the Constituent Assembly (the other members being Ministers). This Assembly drafted a new Constitution which was published on November 11th, 1962. Under the new Constitution a National Assembly of 50 members was elected in January 1963, and the first session was held on January 29th, with Sheikh Sabah as-Salim as-Sabah, brother of the Amir and Heir Apparent, as the Prime Minister of a new Council of Ministers.

In October 1963 the new Iraqi government announced that it had decided to recognize Kuwait's complete independence; Iraq wanted to clear her relations with Kuwait and remove the atmosphere created by the Kassem regime. Kuwait is thought to have made a substantial grant to Iraq to improve relations at this juncture, and relations certainly improved for a time.

In January 1965 a constitutional crisis, reflecting the tension between the paternalist ruling house and the democratically-minded National Assembly, resulted in the formation of a strengthened cabinet under the Heir Apparent, Sheikh Sabah as-Salim. In July 1965 Kuwait decided not to ratify the agreement to set up an Arab Common Market with Iraq, Jordan, Syria and the U.A.R. There was strong feeling in the National Assembly that such an association would be disadvantageous to Kuwait.

On November 24th, 1965, Sheikh Abdullah died and was succeeded by Sheikh Sabah. His post as Prime Minister was taken over by another member of the ruling family, Sheikh Jabir al-Ahmad, who became Heir Apparent in May 1966.

In the developments of 1966 and 1967 within the Arab community Kuwait continued to play a neutral role, and in particular tried to act as mediator in inter-Arab disputes such as the Yemen and South Arabian problems. Sheikh Sabah paid visits to Iraq and Lebanon, and Kuwait supported Syria in the dispute with the Iraq Petroleum Company.

Kuwait declared her support for the Arab countries in the 1967 war with Israel, and joined in the oil embargo on the U.S.A. and the United Kingdom. No Kuwaitis had, however, reached any theatre of war before the ceasefire was announced. The Government donated KD 25 million to the Arab war effort. At the Khartoum Conference in September 1967 Kuwait joined Saudi Arabia and Libya in offering financial aid to the U.A.R. and Jordan whilst their economies recovered from the June war. The Kuwaiti share of this amounted to KD 55 million annually.

On May 13th, 1968, it was announced that the agreement of June 1961—whereby Britain had undertaken to give military assistance to Kuwait if asked to do so by her ruler—would terminate on May 13th, 1971. This followed an earlier announcement that Britain would withdraw all troops from the Gulf region by the end of 1971. At this time, Kuwait continually encouraged the formation of a federation of Bahrain, Qatar and the Trucial States but her qualities as a go-between were insufficient to persuade the first two states to join what eventually became the United Arab Emirates.

Since the June 1967 war Kuwait has no longer been a frequent target of radical Arab criticism. Its financial support for the countries hit by the war and other generous economic assistance have no doubt contributed to this, while the lavish financing of the Palestinian guerrillas has been even more important. A factor behind this assistance is the large Palestinian community, said to be over 70,000 strong, in Kuwait; many of the most able and educated Palestinians have made a career in the country in recent years. Financial aid to Jordan, however, was cut off for a time in September 1970 following the war between government and guerrilla forces.

During the 1960s the Kuwaiti leadership's policies led to extensive redistribution of income, through the use of oil revenues in public expenditure and through the land compensation scheme. At the same time, however, there was popular discontent about corruption and inefficiency in public services and the manipulation of the Press and the National Assembly.

In response to public opinion, the ruling family permitted the Assembly elections of January 1971 to be held on the basis of a free vote, though women, illiterates and all non-Kuwaitis still have no voting rights. There was a lively election campaign, with 184 candidates contesting the 50 seats, despite the non-existence of political parties, which are still illegal. Several members and supporters of the Arab Nationalist Movement, founded in the 1950s by Dr. George Habash (now leader of the Popular Front for the Liberation of Palestine), were elected. This radical group, led by Dr. Ahmad al-Khatib, was generally regarded as the principal opposition to the Government.

After the 1971 elections the Crown Prince was re-appointed Prime Minister and formed a new Cabinet. The representation of the ruling family was reduced from five to three and, for the first time, the Cabinet included two Ministers drawn from the elected members of the National Assembly. After the elections in January 1975 a 16-member cabinet was appointed with the Crown Prince continuing as Prime Minister. Seven new Ministers were appointed, a new post of Deputy Prime Minister was created and the functions of the former Ministry of Oil and Finance were separated.

The main domestic problem is the difference in status between native-born Kuwaitis and immigrants, the latter comprising 58.5 per cent of the population in 1980. Whilst the living conditions of the immigrants are very good by Arabian standards, most senior positions are reserved for Kuwaitis, as is the suffrage and free use of some welfare services. The creation of sufficient employment opportunities to avoid the unsettling effects of idleness and boredom, a social problem even with generous unemployment benefits, is a major difficulty now confronting the Government.

In March 1973 Iraqi troops and tanks occupied a Kuwaiti outpost at Samtah, on the 100-mile border with Iraq. Iraq later withdrew its troops, but a source of potential dispute remains. Since the crisis in 1973 Kuwait has allocated large sums for the expansion of its armed forces and has announced intentions to establish its own navy. Legislation to introduce conscription was approved in 1975.

During the Arab-Israeli war of October 1973 Kuwaiti forces stationed along the Suez Canal were involved in fighting. Kuwait also contributed to the Arab cause by giving considerable financial aid, totalling KD 100 million, to other Arab states. While the war was still in progress, Kuwait called for a meeting of OAPEC to draw up a common Arab policy for the use of oil as a weapon to put pressure on Western countries, particularly the U.S.A., to force an Israeli withdrawal from occupied Arab territory.

This meeting took place in Kuwait, where OAPEC's ten member-states decided to reduce petroleum production by at least 5 per cent progressively each month. Kuwait was also one of the Arab countries which imposed a total embargo on oil shipments to the U.S.A. and, later, to the Netherlands.

Immediately before the OAPEC meeting, Kuwait joined other Gulf states in announcing a unilateral increase of 70 per cent in the posted price of crude petroleum (the reference price used for tax and royalty purposes) from November 1st, 1973. This followed similar moves by Algeria, Indonesia and Venezuela.

In November, at a further meeting in Kuwait, Oil Ministers from the Arab states agreed on an extra 5 per cent reduction in output for November, with the combined effect of the embargoes and production cutbacks expressed as an overall drop in supply of 25 per cent compared with September levels, to be followed by further reductions in the future. Later in November the Arab group in OPEC agreed on the next 5 per cent cut for December, but exempted EEC countries except the Netherlands.

At the next OAPEC meeting, held in Kuwait in December, an additional 5 per cent cut, without exemptions, was agreed for January 1974. A second December meeting, also in Kuwait, partly reversed earlier decisions to reduce oil production. Just before this, the Gulf states belonging to OPEC had agreed on a further sharp increase in the posted price of oil, effective from January 1st, 1974.

Kuwait played a leading part in all these moves and made considerable reductions in national oil output. Monthly production (in million metric tons) fell from 13.4 in September 1973 to 12.0 in October and 9.8 in November. There was later a reversal in this trend and monthly output was more than 10 million tons in the first half of 1974.

Following the conclusion in January of a disengagement agreement between Egypt and Israel and the consequent improvement in Arab relations with the U.S.A., seven of the Arab oil-producing states (including Kuwait) agreed in March to lift the embargo on supplies to the U.S.A. In July 1974 the Arab countries also lifted the oil embargo on the Netherlands. Kuwait's policy of conserving her oil reserves, and the fall in the world demand for oil, has meant that production fell from a peak of 3.3 million b/d in 1972 to an average of 1.5 million b/d in 1980, and a projected 1.25 million b/d in 1981. The recent world oil glut, however, forced production below 1 million b/d.

While the fuel crisis was developing, negotiations continued between the Government and KOC for new participation terms. Agreement was reached in January 1974 for the acquisition by the Government of a 60 per cent share, with the right to acquire the remaining 40 per cent in 1979. Although this gave Kuwait an immediate controlling interest in KOC, some members of the National Assembly, encouraged by the nationalization of foreign-owned oil companies in Iraq and Libya, demanded a third round of negotia-

tions to achieve 100 per cent ownership. In November 1975 after long negotiations agreement was reached with the oil companies. The take-over cost the Government $50.5 million in compensation on the basis of net book value backdated to March 1975. BP and Gulf Oil agreed to lift 950,000 b/d over the next five years, using Kuwaiti tankers.

After the National Assembly elections in January 1975 the Ministry of Finance and Oil was divided and oil affairs became the sole responsibility of the Ministry of Oil. In April 1975 the Government decided to take over the Kuwait National Petroleum Company, which was already 60 per cent government-owned. The KNPC came under the authority of the Supreme Oil Council and its Co-ordinating Committee and controlled all oil operations. KOC was therefore limited to production. Nationalization of the oil industry was almost complete when, in 1977, the Government acquired Aminoil and created the Kuwait Wafra Oil Company.

Until 1973 Kuwait's financial support for the leading Palestinian organizations had protected the country from active involvement in the guerrilla struggle. However, the activities of extremist groups, lacking such links with Kuwait, have resulted in incidents which embarrassed the Kuwait Government. In September 1973 Arab gunmen occupied the Saudi Arabian Embassy in Paris and later flew to Kuwait with five hostages. The gunmen surrendered to the Kuwaiti authorities, who later handed them over to the Palestine Liberation Organization (PLO), which had condemned the incident. Kuwait was later involved in two further terrorist incidents, in December 1973 and February 1974.

In August 1976 the Amir suspended the National Assembly for four years on the grounds that, amongst other things, it had been delaying legislation. A committee was ordered to be formed to review the constitution.

On December 31st, 1977, the Amir (Sheikh Sabah) died and was succeeded by his cousin, the Crown Prince, Sheikh Jaber al-Ahmad al-Sabah, who had been Prime Minister since 1966. The new heir apparent was Sheikh Saad al-Abdullah al-Sabah, who became Prime Minister as well as Crown Prince. In a Cabinet appointed in February 1978 Sheikh Ali al-Khalifa al-Sabah was introduced as Minister of Oil, and a policy of conservation of oil and a slow-down in the pace of new development has been introduced. Both the Amir and the Prime Minister publicly reaffirmed the Government's intention to restore the National Assembly and democratic government by August 1980. In response to increasing public pressure, a 50-member committee was set up in early 1980 to consider constitutional amendments and a revised form of legislature. Following its recommendations, an Amiri Decree issued in August 1980 provided for the holding of elections to a new Assembly before the end of February 1981. Despite the uncertainty generated by the Gulf War, the election campaign went ahead, with as many as 448 candidates contesting the 50 seats. The franchise was limited to 90,000 "first-class" Kuwaiti citizens and of these less than half (or about three per cent of the population) registered to vote. A moderate Assembly was returned, containing 23 conservative tribal leaders sympathetic to the ruling sheikhs and 13 young technocrats. The radical Arab nationalists, the fiercest opposition to the Government in the last Assembly, failed to win any seats and the Shia minority's representation was reduced to 4 seats. However, five Islamic fundamentalists of the Sunni sect were elected.

The Crown Prince was subsequently re-appointed Prime Minister and formed a new 15-member Cabinet in which the ruling family retained the key posts. There were seven new ministers, including the only member of the Cabinet to have been elected to the new Assembly, and the Finance and Planning Ministries were merged.

At the Baghdad summit in November 1978 Kuwait pressed for solidarity among the Arab nations in condemning the Egypt-Israeli peace agreement and supported the use of sanctions against Egypt. The Kuwaiti Ambassador has been recalled from Cairo

and all aid, except for specific development projects, has been withdrawn. Anxious to preserve Arab unity, Kuwait mediated successfully in the conflict between North and South Yemen in 1979, eventually bringing about a ceasefire, and was instrumental in resolving the crisis in the United Arab Emirates. Kuwait has supported Iraq in the Gulf War, allowing Iraqi troops access to its strategic ports, but, at the same time, relations with Iran have not been severed. In May 1981 Kuwait joined with Saudi Arabia, the U.A.E., Qatar, Oman and Bahrain to set up the Gulf Co-operation Council. By encouraging economic and social integration, it is hoped that the Council will increase the security of the small oil-producing states of the Gulf.

In September 1981 Kuwaiti oil installations at Umm al-Aish, near the Iraqi border, were bombed by Iran. Kuwait's ambassador to Iran was temporarily withdrawn, but in February 1982 Kuwait announced its willingness to mediate in the continuing conflict between Iran and Iraq.

ECONOMIC SURVEY

The State of Kuwait has an area of 17,818 square kilometres. Until petroleum was produced, the only town was the harbour of Kuwait on the Gulf. For about 150 years, however, this was a significant port because it was a centre for pearl fishing and the building of dhows or "booms", and several of the plans for building a railway across Mesopotamia envisaged Kuwait as the eastern terminus.

The rapid development of the oil industry since 1946 has dramatically changed all this. Kuwait has proven oil reserves of 67,930 million barrels and, at the May 1981 production level of 1.25 million barrels per day (b/d), this should last for 150 years. Since 1972, the year of Kuwait's peak oil production of 1,201.6 million barrels, the output has fluctuated, rising from 760.8 million barrels in 1975 to 911.2 million barrels in 1979, accounting for 4.5 per cent of the world's oil output, and falling to 607 million barrels in 1980, an average for that year of 1.65 million b/d, representing 3 per cent of world oil output. The recent oil glut and the March 1982 OPEC agreement on levels of oil prices and production led to a drop in production from 1.25 million b/d to 800,000 b/d, with a consequent loss of oil revenue. The World Bank estimated that in 1979 Kuwait had an average G.N.P. per head of $20,520, second only to the United Arab Emirates.

The population grew at the rate of 8.2 per cent per year between 1965 and 1973; it has been increasing at an annual rate of 6 per cent in recent years, and in April 1980 was 1,355,827, giving an overall density of 77 people per sq. km., the highest of the Gulf states. This growth is partly the result of immigration from the surrounding countries, arising from higher wages and better working conditions than anywhere else

in the Middle East. Of the total population in 1980, only 41.5 per cent (some 562,000) were Kuwatis. An important part of the annual revenue from oil has been spent on health, education and other social services. As a result, the standard of living in Kuwait is among the highest in the world. Most of the social services, such as education and health, are free for Kuwaiti citizens; it has been said that, as a welfare state, Kuwait now probably has no parallel. In recent years the Government has distributed some of its wealth to countries of the "Third World".

PETROLEUM

In 1933 the Anglo-Persian Oil Company, now the British Petroleum Company Limited, and Gulf Oil Corporation applied jointly to the Ruler of Kuwait for a concession to explore the territory. The two companies formed an operating unit, the Kuwait Oil Company, each holding 50 per cent of its share capital. A large oilfield was discovered at Burgan, about 25 miles south of the town of Kuwait, in 1938, but the onset of World War II delayed development until 1945. By 1948 six million tons were produced, but the main impetus to speed up development was supplied by the Abadan affair in 1951, which in effect denied Iranian production to the rest of the world for three years. By 1956 Kuwait's production had increased to 54 million tons, and was then the largest in the Middle East. Further fields were found by the company, notably at Raudhatain, north of Kuwait, and the company's production had reached over 148 million tons by 1972, although large areas of the original concession had been relinquished to the State in accordance with the Agreement. To handle this vast production, a huge tanker port has been constructed at Mina al-Ahmadi, not far from the Burgan field, which from a terminal some 10 miles offshore can now handle the largest tankers. Kuwait was the first Arab oil-producing nation to achieve complete control of its own oil output, buying out Gulf Oil and BP in March 1975 for approximately £32 million.

In addition to joining the Arab oil embargo of late 1973, Kuwait was the first OPEC state to restrict oil production for conservationist reasons. The production ceiling of 2 million barrels per day was lowered in April 1980 to 1.5 million b/d and in May 1981 to 1.25 million b/d. Despite the prescribed ceiling, Kuwait produced 2.37 million b/d in 1979 as it rushed to take advantage of high prices on the spot market. Until December 1976, when Kuwait was one of the 11 members of OPEC which decided to raise oil prices by 10 per cent (against 5 per cent implemented by Saudi Arabia and the U.A.E.), the country was generally regarded as a moderate with regard to oil pricing. Since then, however, Kuwait has become more and more "hawkish" and during 1979 and 1980 was one of the first to set still higher prices each time Saudi Arabia raised its prices to try and achieve some kind of unity within OPEC. In January 1981 Kuwait raised the price of its oil to U.S. $35.50 per barrel, which was, however, appreciably lower than the price of more "hawkish" countries such as Libya. In October 1981, however, the price of Kuwait's crude oil was lowered by $2.50 per barrel to $33, and again in December, in the face of the increasing world oil glut, it was lowered further to $32.30 per barrel.

Two other companies have been permitted by Kuwait and Saudi Arabia to operate in the Partitioned Zone, and produce oil. These were Aminoil, the American Independent Oil Company, owned by the U.S. firm Reynolds, which has a joint operating agreement with Getty Oil Co. under which Aminoil and Getty bear one-half of certain expenses such as drilling; and Arabian Oil Company in which Japanese interests own 50 per cent of the share capital, the governments of Kuwait and Saudi Arabia each holding 25 per cent. So far the production of these companies is small compared with that of the Kuwait Oil Company. However, at the end of 1980 Getty Oil announced plans for new exploration within the Neutral Zone. The Kuwait Government took over Aminoil in September 1977, when Aminoil's name was changed to the Wafra Kuwait Oil Company. The latter was dissolved in April 1978 and its operations merged with the Kuwait Oil Company and the KNPC. There are three oil refineries: one at Mina al-Ahmadi, built in 1946, with a capacity of 292,000 b/d, one at Mina Abdullah, built in 1958, with a capacity of 140,000 b/d, and the most recent at Shuaiba, built in 1966, with a capacity of 200,000 b/d. In 1980 and 1981 the Japan Gasoline Corporation (JGC) won contracts to modernize the al-Ahmadi refinery. In August 1981 a fire at the Shuaiba oil refinery destroyed nine oil storage tanks, halted production and caused damage estimated at $7 million. Kuwait intends to increase its "downstream" production and plans to raise the level of its refined oil products to one-half of the country's total exports by 1984, through the modernization of its oil refineries.

Reorganization of the oil industry took place in 1980 with the establishment of the Kuwait Petroleum Corporation (KPC), as an umbrella organization for the four companies involved in Kuwait's oil industry: Kuwait Oil Company, Kuwait National Petroleum Company, Petroleum Industries Company, and Kuwait Oil Tanker Company. This has led to the centralization of oil sales and should strengthen Kuwait's market competitiveness. A joint venture agreed with Pacific Resources of Honolulu in April 1981 to supply petroleum products to the Pacific area will give Kuwait a stake in a refinery in the U.S.A. and enable KPC to develop a marketing function. In 1980 a system of one-year contracts for oil production was introduced, and in March that year Kuwait levied a premium of $5.50 per barrel on oil sold to foreign companies for resale to third parties. In April 1981, when Shell, BP and Getty Oil's contracts were due for renewal, they refused to pay the premium on top of the official rate of $35.5 per barrel. Supplies of oil to these companies were suspended, but agreement was quickly reached. No premiums were to be charged, but Kuwait offered only 50,000 b/d to each company, compared with the 225,000 b/d sold to Shell and the 150,000 b/d sold to BP in the 1980/81 agreement.

A further development in Kuwait's oil industry has been the expansion of interests overseas. Thus, in the second half of 1981, the newly-formed Kuwait Overseas Exploration Company, a subsidiary of KPC, purchased from Elf Aquitaine a 22.5 per cent interest in a 22,000 sq. km. concession in Morocco.

NATURAL GAS

In November 1976 the Amir laid the foundation stone for the Kuwait Oil Company's Gas Project. The Gas Project is one of the largest development projects undertaken in Kuwait, and involves the construction of extensive facilities to utilize the gas associated with crude oil output for the production of liquefied natural gas (LNG) and such derivatives as propane and butane. Much of the gas associated with crude petroleum production is now being processed for export. New gas and oil deposits were found in the offshore Burgan field in late 1981.

A three-train LPG plant and a gas-gathering system, which came on stream in 1979, gather the gas produced with the oil at well-heads, remove LPG components and natural gasoline, treat them to conform to international standards and distribute them to fuel users and to pressure-maintenance facilities. A major contract was awarded to the Kuwait Metal Pipe Industries for the engineering, procurement and construction of a 300-mile network of gathering and transmission pipelines.

The plant, built at a cost of over U.S. $1,000 million, has a capacity of 2.2 million metric tons of LPG per year (60 per cent propane, 40 per cent butane) at a crude oil production rate of 1.5 million b/d. It was originally designed to take crude oil production of 3 million b/d. The Ahmadi refinery also has a capacity of 1.5 million tons of LPG per year. In March 1981 Kuwait reduced the price of her propane by U.S. $6 to U.S. $312 per ton, and for butane by $2 to $305 per ton. Most of this production is exported to Japan.

OTHER INDUSTRIES

The Government has done much to foster the growth of other industries in order to diversify the economy and to provide an alternative source of employment to oil, and during the course of the 1976–81 Five-Year Plan three industrial zones were set up: at Shuaiba, Shuwaikh and Ahmadi. Not surprisingly, however, oil-related activities still contribute an overwhelming proportion of Kuwait's total industrial output. Despite efforts at diversification, oil's share of G.D.P. rose from 61.1 per cent in 1977 to 72.3 per cent in 1979. An Industrial Development Committee existed for some years but was replaced in 1979 by a new body with far-reaching authority over regulating industry, issuing licences, imposing protective tariffs, etc. A Petrochemical Industries Company was formed in 1963 to manufacture fertilizers, and in 1964 a larger concern, Kuwait Chemical Fertilizer Company, was set up. With a new fertilizer plant at Shuaiba, owned by KNPC, Kuwait now has a potential production capacity of 1.65 million tons per year, mainly in the form of urea and ammonia products. The profitability of these products is proving difficult to maintain because of technical problems and weak market conditions.

PIC is planning a fourth ammonia line for its fertilizer plant, and there are also plans for an aromatics complex for the production of benzene and xylenes at a cost of approximately U.S. $500 million. Feasibility studies have been undertaken for an Olefin complex but this has been shelved, and Kuwait has hesitated to undertake other heavy industrial projects (such as iron and steel) because, unlike its neighbours in the area, it has had doubts about their viability and has been wary of increasing still further the number of foreign workers needed by the economy. It has favoured instead joint projects with Bahrain, Saudi Arabia and other Gulf countries. The latest of these include an agreement made in February 1981 to set up the Gulf Aluminium Rolling Mill Company, with a capital of BD 24 million in order to establish a 40,000 ton/year smelter at Bahrain, and the Gulf Petrochemical Industries Company in order to develop an ammonia plant and a dry methanol plant, also at Bahrain.

There are several factories in Kuwait supplying consumer requirements, such as processed food and soft drinks, and there is a flour mills company. The construction industry is of some importance, owing to the vast amount of house and office building there has been in the last decade, as well as roads, power stations, schools and hospitals. The major projects have been carried out by foreign contractors but in February 1981 the National Housing Authority announced that 80 per cent of future housing contracts would be given to local firms. Kuwait's main contribution has been in the building materials industry and related projects such as aluminium extrusion. Many of these smaller industrial projects have been promoted by the Industrial Bank of Kuwait (IBK), set up in 1973, which is 49 per cent government-owned. Industrial development, however, has been associated with a heavy reliance on foreign labour and in 1975 over 70 per cent of the labour force was non-Kuwaiti. In October 1980, in a departure from its traditional sources of labour (Jordan/Palestine and Iraq), Kuwait signed an agreement with China for the supply of migrant labour.

In addition to industrial diversification, Kuwait is also experimenting with alternative power sources, and in 1980 work was started by the Kuwait Institute for Scientific Research on an experimental solar energy station at Sulaibikhat, to be used for desalination when completed in 1981. At present there are two main power stations, at Shuwaikh and Shuaiba, and there are also plans for a 2,400 MW power station at Al-Zour. In 1981 Canada offered to help Kuwait to develop nuclear energy for peaceful purposes.

In 1981 KPC purchased the Santa Fe International Corporation and its subsidiary, C. F. Braun and Co., for $2,500 million. This represented a major new departure in the country's attempt to diversify the economy away from oil, and in the spring of 1982 the Kuwait-Santa Fe-Braun Engineering and Petroleum Projects Company was formed as a wholly-owned subsidiary of KPC. Also during 1981, a new private company, the Petroleum Contracting and Operations Company, was set up to undertake oil, gas, electricity and water construction work, with a capital of KD 2.5 million.

PUBLIC UTILITIES AND TRANSPORT

To support the increase of population brought about by the development of oil, a vast infrastructure of public works had to be created. There are desalination plants in Kuwait City, the Shuaiba industrial area, and at Doha. Important sources of fresh water have been found at Raudhatain and Al Shigaia but desalination provides 90 per cent of Kuwait's daily consumption. In 1979 Kuwait produced 8,617 million kWh of electric energy for public use. Another expansion of public services is the planned development of Sulaibikhat Bay as a recreation area, at a cost of KD 45 million. This project is expected to be completed in 1984.

The harbour of Kuwait City has been completely reconstructed to take account of the surge in imports after 1973. A new international airport was opened in 1979. There is a national airline with an international service, Kuwait Airways Corporation. All these facilities were created at the expense of the Government, the oil ports at Mina al-Ahmadi and nearby at Mina al-Abdullah having been made by the Kuwait Oil Company. The Kuwait Oil Tanker Company was fully nationalized in 1979. The Oil Ministry has started including the use of Kuwaiti tankers in the terms of

sale of its crude oil. There are plans to expand the
fleet to 27 vessels by 1982, and Shuwaikh port is also
undergoing expansion, due to be completed in 1983.
By 1985 it is planned that 70 per cent of Kuwait's
oil exports will be moved in Kuwaiti ships. The Iran-
Iraq conflict had recently brought increased transit
trade to Kuwait's ports of Shuaiba and Shuwaikh,
but during 1981 this increase led to severe congestion.
The Government is also undertaking a major expressway road development, the first phase of which
should be completed in 1983, at a cost of $2,000
million. The final network should be finished in 1987
or 1988.

AGRICULTURE AND FISHERIES

Owing to the present lack of water, little grain is
grown, and most of the food consumed in Kuwait has
to be imported. In 1978 the total cultivable area was
estimated at 17,800 dunums, of which vegetables and
crops occupy about 6,000 dunums, with another 1,000
dunums occupied by orchards and timber. The principal vegetable crops are tomatoes, melons and onions,
and production levels in the 1978/79 season reached
11,565 metric tons for tomatoes, 2,728 metric tons
for melons, and 1,570 metric tons for onions. The
Government plans to increase the overall level of
vegetable production from 42,000 tons in 1981
to 98,000 tons in 1986. This would, however, supply
only 40 per cent of projected local demand. However, the Government has done much to encourage animal husbandry, the main activity (before the
development of the oilfields) of the bedouin, who still
rear camels, sheep and goats. There is an experimental
farm of 90 acres owned by the Government, and in the
private sector there is a growing poultry and dairy
industry, and the growing of dates has also increased
in recent years. In January 1980 Kuwait Dairy Company opened a dairy with a capacity of 50 tons per
day, and an irrigation project covering 925 hectares
was started in association with a calf-raising unit at
Sulaibiyya. There is also investment in livestock
overseas, and in April 1982 plans were announced
by the Kuwait Livestock Transport and Trading
Company to invest in a $180 million sheep-rearing
scheme in the São Francisco Valley in Brazil. Fishing,
particularly of prawns and shrimps, is of some importance. There were four fishing companies based on the
abundance of fish in Kuwait's territorial waters, until
they were amalgamated into Kuwait United Fisheries
in 1972. The Government, however, is worried about
depletion of stocks, and in 1981 and 1982 shrimping
and the marketing of fresh shrimps were banned from
February to June.

FOREIGN TRADE AND BALANCE OF PAYMENTS

Total exports in 1979 were valued at KD 5,088.5
million, of which crude petroleum and petroleum
products accounted for KD 4,634.6 million (91.1 per
cent). In 1979 Japan took 25.4 per cent of Kuwait's
total exports while 11.2 per cent went to the Netherlands, 8.9 per cent to Italy and 6.4 per cent each to
the United Kingdom and Taiwan. South Korea took
6.2 per cent and Singapore 4.5 per cent. The value

of imports was KD 1,437.0 million in 1979 and KD
1,772.4 million in 1980. The most important item
is machinery and transport equipment, which in 1977
accounted for 45.5 per cent of total imports. By 1979,
however, its share had fallen to 35.5 per cent. Basic
manufactures rose from 21.6 per cent in 1977 to
24.9 per cent in 1979, and food and live animals
similarly increased slightly in importance from 10.6
per cent in 1977 to 13.5 per cent in 1979. Kuwait's
principal suppliers in 1979 were Japan (18.2 per cent),
the U.S.A. (14.5 per cent) and the United Kingdom
(10.0 per cent).

The current surplus on the balance of payments was
KD 1,923 million in 1978, KD 3,717 million in 1979
and KD 4,030 million in 1980. Official reserves
(excluding gold) rose from U.S. $2,871.3 million in
1979 to $3,928.4 million in 1980. At the end of 1981
it was estimated that Kuwait's foreign assets were
in the region of $76,000 million, compared with a level
of only $27,000 million in 1978, making the country
increasingly vulnerable to foreign financial policies.

BANKING AND FINANCE

No foreign banks are allowed to operate, except the
Bank of Bahrain and Kuwait, based in Bahrain and 50
per cent Kuwaiti-owned. The other main banking
institution, apart from the Central Bank of Kuwait
and the six commercial banks, is the Industrial Bank
of Kuwait (IBK), which, in addition to its promotion
of industry, has the objective of developing a capital
market in Kuwait.

Total assets of the commercial banks at the end of
February 1980 stood at KD 4,524.7 million, compared with KD 3,292.2 million a year earlier. Foreign
assets totalled KD 1,529.6 million, compared with
KD 1,193.3 million in February 1979. 1980 was a
good year for the banks, with the assets of the National
Bank of Kuwait, for example, rising to KD 1,373.9
million at the end of the year from KD 1,311 million
in 1979, making it the second biggest private Arab
bank (after the National Commercial Bank of Jeddah).
In 1981 the profits of the six commercial banks were
44 per cent up on 1980. The Central Bank has recently
been imposing tighter controls on the banks, and in
1979 ordered them to cut the proportion of overdrafts
to 55 per cent of total lending by the end of 1980.
Nevertheless, the increase in bank credits since 1977
has been over 25 per cent per annum. In 1981 the
country's only Islamic bank, the Kuwait Finance
House, doubled its balance-sheet footings to KD 351
million ($1,234 million). In 1980 Kuwait, Libya and
Abu Dhabi set up the Arab Banking Corporation and,
through this institution, Kuwaiti funds are being
channelled to numerous borrowers. At the end of
1980 its assets were $1,952 million, and by June 1981
these had risen to $2,457 million. Further banking
developments continued in 1982 when in April the
Cabinet agreed to set up the Kuwait International
Bank to act as a merchant bank with a capital of
KD 300 million, 25 per cent of the shares being
owned by the Government, 25 per cent by banks
and investment companies, and 50 per cent by the
public.

There are a number of investment companies, the most important of which are "the three Ks"—the Kuwait Investment Company (KIC), the Kuwait Foreign Trading, Contracting and Investing Company (KFTCIC) and the Kuwait International Investment Company (KIIC). KIC is government-owned, KFTCIC almost entirely government-owned, KIIC wholly private.

CAPITAL MARKET

A significant, though still minor (by international standards), capital market has been developed in Kuwait through the activities of the leading investment companies and the IBK, and with the encouragement of the Government. An active bond market developed after 1973, mostly for international borrowers from the Third World and Eastern Europe. Thirteen international public bond issues in Kuwaiti dinars, totalling KD 106 million, were floated in 1979, compared with 18 issues worth KD 154 million in 1978. The Central Bank closed the new-issue market in November 1979 as part of its efforts to boost liquidity in Kuwait's money market, but at the end of July 1981 the Kuwaiti dinar international bond market reopened, and since then a number of bonds have been issued. In 1981 two were issued above the usual 10 per cent ceiling: KD 6 million for the European Railway Rolling Stock Finance Company was issued at 11 per cent, and KD 7 million for the Union Pacific at 11.5 per cent. In March 1982 a new record was set with a KD 7 million bond issue for the U.S. pharmaceutical manufacturer Richardson-Merrell carrying a 12.5 per cent coupon.

The Kuwaiti stock market has traditionally been very active. In 1979 there were 39 Kuwaiti companies quoted. The amount of money looking for investment outlets in Kuwait and the innate entrepreneurial spirit of locals has generally pushed the values of shares to far beyond their real value. To stem this unhealthy trend, the Government in April 1978 sanctioned the reduction in nominal value of shares to one dinar, a move which resulted in a split of share values to 10–13 per cent of their current value. This broadened the base of the market. In 1981 247 million shares worth $6,854 million were traded in Kuwait's stockmarket, which represented a 72 per cent increase by volume, and a 47 per cent increase by value, over 1980's figures.

PUBLIC FINANCE

Since 1977/78 the Government has aimed to hold its spending steady in real terms in order to combat inflation. The 1981/82 budget was estimated at KD 5,279 million, a 13.7 per cent increase on the 1980/81 budget. Increasingly reduced oil income is beginning to cause financial problems. The 1982/83 budget allows for a deficit of KD 312.6 million ($1,097 million). The country's first budget deficit was in 1973 but, despite the fact that the 1982/83 allocation to the Reserve Fund for Future Generations at KD 320.6 million is larger that the predicted deficit, Kuwait's prospects for the 1980s, as with other oil-producing nations in the Gulf, look bleaker than they did in the late 1970s.

INVESTMENT

Kuwait's first priority for spending its oil income is the development of its own economy and the provision, through the investment of surplus funds, of an income for its citizens in the future when the oil wells have run dry. Of the budgetary surplus projected for 1979/80 of KD 991 million, KD 667 million was allocated to the state general reserve and KD 324 million to the Reserve Fund for Future Generations, set up at the end of 1976 to provide a more specific "pension fund" for the future than the general reserves. The KD 324 million represents the 10 per cent of total revenue that has to be added by law to the Reserve Fund. The State's concern for safeguarding the future of the economy was emphasised in the 1981/82 budget, when KD 2,196.3 million, over 40 per cent of expenditure, was allocated to the State General Reserve and the Reserve Fund for Future Generations. This was substantially more than the KD 1,665.1 million which those funds received in 1980/81.

Between 1972 and 1976 economic development was directed mainly through regular budget allocations. However, in 1976 the Ministry of Planning announced a Five-Year Plan to lay down guidelines for development. Housing, with 28.6 per cent of the proposed expenditure, was to receive the largest investment, followed by manufacturing (18.6 per cent), electricity and water (11 per cent) and transport (sea 6.8 per cent, land 6.3 per cent). Actual spending, however, has been less than that budgeted for. A further 1981/82–1985/86 Plan is in course of preparation.

Kuwait's financial assets at the end of 1979 totalled U.S. $48,700 million, and two-thirds of this was held abroad. Kuwait's official reserves, held by the Central Bank, usually total $2,000 million or less because the funds which are available for investment are held and managed by the Ministry of Finance, not the central bank, as in Saudi Arabia.

Kuwait had a budget surplus well before 1973 and therefore developed an investment strategy well ahead of the other oil states—and one which is considerably more sophisticated, though still quite conservative. The Kuwait Investment Office (KIO) in London, an arm of the Ministry of Finance, handles much of the State's investment in Europe and elsewhere too. Kuwait, through the KIO, owns up to 10 per cent of many of the leading companies quoted on the London stock exchange. In 1979 the KIO also started buying small stakes in leading Japanese electronics companies. The bulk of Kuwait's investments are in dollars, much of them in the U.S.A., but there has been considerable diversification since the dollar started to weaken against other currencies in 1977, and even more so since the U.S. Government froze Iranian assets in U.S. banks in November 1979. Even so, about 65 per cent of Kuwait's long-term investments are in the U.S.A., where the oil state has holdings up to a value of $50 million involving almost every one of the top 500 U.S. companies. Kuwait also has some major real estate projects there, including Kiwanah Island off the South Carolina coast, on which a tourist and office complex has been built. Exceptions to Kuwait's preference for small stakes in foreign companies include its outright purchase of the St. Martin's Property Corporation of the United Kingdom and its purchase of a 25 per cent holding in Daimler-Benz of West Germany and a 50 per cent holding in Korf Stahl, also German.

Kuwaiti private investment is also substantial. Again it is heavily geared to real estate and high-yielding equities. Although this investment is concentrated in the U.S.A., Europe and Japan, Kuwaitis have shown interest in investment in other non-Arab countries in Asia (South Korea, Hong Kong, Malaysia, etc.) and in Africa and South America, as well as in the Arab world, notably the United Arab Emirates, Bahrain, Sudan and Egypt. In 1980 KIO made an unsuccessful bid for a 14.6 per cent stake in Getty Oil, and it seems likely that it will continue to try to build up its interests in downstream oil activities. Successful 1980 bids in the United Kingdom brought KIO overall control of Proprietors of Hay's Wharf in London, and increased its holdings in the Savoy Hotel to 27 per cent. At the end of 1981 it was estimated that the KIO held at least £441 million worth of equity in companies in the United Kingdom.

After its own development, Kuwait's next priority

is that of the rest of the Arab and Muslim world, and then the Third World in general. It pioneered foreign aid in the Arab world, setting up the Kuwait Fund for Arab Economic Development (KFAED) in 1961 and, after 1974, raising its authorized capital from KD 200 million to KD 1,000 million and extending its operations to Africa and Asia. Kuwait also helped set up the Arab Fund for Economic and Social Development in Kuwait, and it is a member of various other Arab, Muslim and OPEC aid organizations, notably the Islamic Development Bank, the Arab Bank for Economic Development in Africa and the OPEC Special Fund. It has also contributed to IMF and World Bank facilities.

Total cumulative commitments by the KFAED at the end of 1979 were KD 700 million to 57 Arab, African and Asian countries. Kuwait's total foreign aid, which is substantially more than that given in projected aid by the KFAED, has ranged between about 8 and 15 per cent of Gross National Product since 1974. Early in 1981 the capital of the KFAED was increased to KD 2,000 million, and 1981 saw a sharp increase in the amount of loans given, which totalled $544 million in the first nine months, compared with $130 million in the same period of 1980.

STATISTICAL SURVEY

AREA AND POPULATION

AREA	CENSUS POPULATION†				ESTIMATED POPULATION (mid-year)		DENSITY (per sq. km.)
	April 19th, 1970	April 21st, 1975			1979	1980	1980
		Males	Females	Total			
17,818 sq. km.*	738,662	543,768	451,069	994,837	1,288,320	1,372,720	77.1

* 6,880 square miles.   † Including Kuwaiti nationals abroad: 754 in 1970; 636 (males 345, females 291) in 1975.

April 1980 Census (Preliminary results): total population 1,355,827, of whom 793,762 non-Kuwaitis and 562,065 Kuwaitis; males 776,125, females 579,702.

Principal Towns (1975 Census): Kuwait City (capital) 78,116; Hawalli 130,565; Salmiya 113,943; Abraq Kheetan 59,443; Farawaniya 44,875.

ECONOMICALLY ACTIVE POPULATION
(1975 Census)

	KUWAITIS	NON-KUWAITIS	TOTAL
Agriculture, hunting and fishing . .	3,983	3,531	7,514
Mining and quarrying	1,779	3,080	4,859
Manufacturing industries . . .	2,258	22,209	24,467
Electricity, gas and water . . .	2,034	5,237	7,271
Construction	1,756	30,500	32,256
Trade and restaurants	6,327	33,232	39,559
Transport, storage and communications .	4,567	11,118	15,685
Financial institutions, insurance . .	1,377	5,146	6,523
Services (including defence) . .	62,888	97,391	160,279
TOTAL*	86,971	211,444	298,415

* Including two Kuwaitis of unstated activity.

AGRICULTURE

LAND USE, 1979
('ooo hectares)

Arable land	1
Permanent meadows and pasture . .	134
Forests and woodlands	2
Other land	1,645
TOTAL	1,782

PRINCIPAL CROPS
(metric tons)

	1976/77	1977/78	1978/79
Tomatoes . .	6,531	10,957	11,562
Onions (dry) . .	917	1,343	1,570
Melons . .	4,633	4,466	2,728
Dates . .	647*	685*	n.a.

* Estimates.

LIVESTOCK
('ooo head)

	1977	1978	1979
Cattle . . .	6	6	5
Camels* . .	5	5	5
Sheep . .	28	15	21
Goats . . .	2	2	2
Poultry . .	1,378	1,146	1,540

* FAO estimates.

LIVESTOCK PRODUCTS

		1976/77	1977/78	1978/79
Beef and veal .	metric tons	2,240	3,266	5,729
Mutton and lamb .	,, ,,	12,140	13,718	18,871
Poultry meat .	,, ,,	9,000	10,000*	10,000*
Cows' milk .	,, ,,	15,584	22,585	24,497
Sheep's milk* .	,, ,,	5,000	5,000	5,000
Goats' milk .	,, ,,	5,323	10,725	19,117
Hen eggs .	'ooo	50,841	54,375	116,888
Sheep skins .	number	57,893	63,069	n.a.

* FAO estimates.

SEA FISHING
('ooo metric tons, live weight)

	1975	1976	1977	1978	1979	1980
TOTAL CATCH . .	5.1	4.7	5.3	6.4	5.0	5.8

Source: FAO, *Yearbook of Fishery Statistics.*

MINING
PETROLEUM PRODUCTION
(million barrels)

	1976	1977	1978	1979	1980
Kuwait*	700.0	650.8	691.2	807.9	508.2
Kuwait/Saudi Arabia Partitioned Zone:					
Onshore†	29.5	32.5	29.6	30.7	28.8
Offshore‡	55.7	34.8	56.3	72.6	70.2
TOTAL	785.2	718.1	777.1	911.2	607.2

* Kuwait Oil Co.   † Kuwait Wafra Oil Co. (Kuwait's share).   ‡ Arabian Oil Co. (Kuwait's share).

NATURAL GAS PRODUCTION
(million cu. ft.)

	Gas Produced	Used by Companies	Used for Injection	Used by State	Total Gas Used
1977 . .	362,624	92,107	34,092	118,863	245,062
1978 . .	392,828	84,500	20,186	136,562	241,248
1979 . .	460,376	131,356	30,208	172,807	339,371
1980 . .	310,066	93,818	16,545	149,676	260,039

INDUSTRY
SELECTED PRODUCTS

		1977	1978	1979	1980
Motor spirit (petrol)	'ooo barrels	6,218	7,458	8,834	7,947
Kerosene and jet fuel . . .	,, ,,	11,023	13,712	18,910	15,265
Distillate fuel oils . . .	,, ,,	31,419	31,711	32,786	28,561
Residual fuel oils . . .	,, ,,	60,179	58,334	66,095	53,109
Naphtha	,, ,,	18,891	18,581	23,034	17,045
Ammonium hydroxide . . .	metric tons	487,913	n.a.	n.a.	n.a.
Electricity generated . . .	million kWh.	6,018	6,990	8,617	9,023
Potable water	million gallons	17,321	20,753	23,086	23,480
Brackish water . . .	,, ,,	9,328	10,181	10,822	11,319
Sodium chloride . . .	tons	16,703	18,972	19,670	20,498
Chlorine	,,	5,759	7,009	8,170	8,041
Caustic soda	,,	6,499	8,009	9,219	9,112
Hydrochlorio acid . . .	gallons	333,430	344,810	291,885	240,240
Lime-sand bricks . . .	cubic metres	215,020	262,528	357,777	338,128
Flour (Kuwait Flour Mills Co.) .	tons	113,260	122,638	153,718	155,617

FINANCE

1,000 fils = 10 dirhams = 1 Kuwaiti dinar (KD).
Coins: 1, 5, 10, 20, 50 and 100 fils.
Notes: 250 and 500 fils; 1, 5 and 10 dinars.
Exchange rates (May 1982): £1 sterling = 523.5 fils; U.S. $1 = 284.7 fils.
100 Kuwaiti dinars = £191.04 = $351.22.

Note: The Kuwaiti dinar was introduced in April 1961, replacing the Persian Gulf Indian rupee. The dinar's initial value of U.S. $2.80 ($1 = 357.14 fils) remained in force until August 1971. Between December 1971 and February 1973 the dinar's par value was $3.04 ($1 = 328.95 fils). From February 1973 to March 1975 it was $3.3778 ($1 = 296.05 fils) but a fluctuating market rate was also in operation. The Kuwaiti dinar was at par with the pound sterling until November 1967, after which the exchange rate was £1 = 857.14 fils (1 dinar = £1.167) until June 1972. Since March 1975 the dinar's value has been determined in relation to a weighted group of currencies of the country's main trading partners. The average market value of the Kuwati dinar was $3.39 in 1973; $3.41 in 1974; $3.45 in 1975; $3.42 in 1976; $3.49 in 1977; $3.64 in 1978; $3.62 in 1979; $3.70 in 1980; $3.59 in 1981.

BUDGET
(KD million, year ending June 30th)

Revenue	1980/81	1981/82	1982/83	Expenditure	1980/81	1981/82	1982/83
Petroleum . . .	4,493	5,097	2,967	General	2,925	3,008	3,168
Other . . .	147	182	239	Salaries	499	591	630
				General running expenses	185	268	450
Total Revenues .	4,640	5,279	3,206	Development projects .	444	603	570
				Real estate acquisitions .	200	300	150
				Unclassified transfers and payments .	1,597	1,279	1,335
				Reserve Fund for Future Generations . . .	928	1,500	320.6
				KFAED* . . .	50	75	30
				State reserve . . .	737	696	—
				Total . . .	4,640	5,279	3,518.6

* Kuwait Fund for Arab Economic Development.

1976–81 DEVELOPMENT PLAN
PROPOSED EXPENDITURE
(KD million)

	PRIVATE SECTOR	TOTAL		PRIVATE SECTOR	TOTAL
Agriculture	20.7	33.2	Housing	695.4	1,400.8
Mining	4.9	88.7	Education	—	275.6
Manufacturing . . .	125.1	909.5	Health	—	133.4
Land transport . .	81.6	311.7	Social welfare . .	—	68.8
Sea transport . .	93.6	334.2	Religion . . .	—	16.4
Air transport . . .	—	29.2	Internal security . .	—	34.1
Communications . .	—	53.8	Information . . .	—	25.7
Transport contingency .	3.9	50.1	Public buildings and utilities .	—	104.1
Trade and finance. .	24.0	32.8	TOTAL . .	1,049.2	4,885.0
Electricity and water .	—	538.9			

CENTRAL BANK RESERVES
(U.S. $ million at December 31st)

	1979	1980	1981
Gold	116.1	116.8	112.6
IMF Special Drawing Rights	—	—	41.2
Reserve position in IMF	513.4	523.5	476.9
Foreign exchange. .	2,356.7	3,404.9	3,549.4
TOTAL . .	2,986.1	4,045.2	4,180.1

Source: IMF, *International Financial Statistics.*

MONEY SUPPLY
(KD million at December 31st)

	1979	1980	1981
Currency outside banks.	215.9	251.3	284.7
Demand deposits at commercial banks .	453.5	469.5	1,005.5
TOTAL MONEY	669.4	720.8	1,290.2

Source: IMF, *International Financial Statistics.*

EXTERNAL TRADE
(KD million)

	1972	1973	1974	1975	1976	1977	1978	1979	1980
Imports c.i.f. . .	262.2	310.6	455.1	693.2	972.0	1,387.0	1,263.9	1,437.0	1,772.4
Exports f.o.b. . .	1,005.4	1,128.2	3,212.7	2,663.0	2,874.4	2,792.6	2,864.1	5,088.5	5,484.7

PRINCIPAL COMMODITIES
(KD '000)

IMPORTS c.i.f.	1976	1977	1978	1979
Food and live animals . . .	121,236	147,674	162,659	194,157
Cereals and cereal preparations .	21,435	17,911	23,154	31,367
Fruit and vegetables . .	31,647	36,697	41,588	49,918
Coffee, tea, cocoa and spices . .	14,161	25,785	24,530	26,423
Chemicals	30,119	41,860	44,436	54,780
Basic manufactures . . .	214,691	299,755	290,333	357,897
Textile yarn, fabrics, etc. . .	61,577	84,089	77,755	90,035
Non-metallic mineral manufactures .	34,575	53,273	61,900	163,616
Iron and steel	56,587	62,747	60,155	85,333
Machinery and transport equipment .	406,705	631,195	500,295	510,427
Non-electric machinery . .	103,131	162,567	151,950	132,481
Electrical machinery, apparatus, etc. .	130,262	160,411	168,532	157,922
Transport equipment . .	173,313	308,217	179,763	228,584
Miscellaneous manufactured articles .	140,120	207,918	203,889	235,700
Clothing (excl. footwear) . .	51,212	76,055	67,835	78,323
Scientific instruments, watches, etc. .	23,070	33,538	38,320	39,451
TOTAL (incl. others) . .	971,993	1,387,036	1,263,948	1,437,023

[continued on next page

PRINCIPAL COMMODITIES—*continued*]

EXPORTS f.o.b.	1976	1977	1978	1979
Mineral fuels, lubricants, etc. . . .	2,658,738	2,557,082	2,628,688	4,780,999
Petroleum and petroleum products .	2,617,646	2,515,341	2,591,610	4,634,592
Crude petroleum . . .	2,151,667	2,080,847	2,155,019	3,770,184
Petroleum products . .	465,979	434,493	436,590	864,408
Gas (natural and manufactured) .	41,092	41,741	37,071	146,405
Chemicals	33,568	34,387	41,819	40,240
Manufactured fertilizers . .	18,498	20,407	28,988	27,891
Basic manufactures . . .	61,127	64,800	56,534	80,876
Machinery and transport equipment .	78,714	78,875	79,826	105,420
Electrical machinery, apparatus, etc. .	17,818	24,268	23,030	27,846
Transport equipment . . .	48,786	44,447	46,189	58,368
Miscellaneous manufactured articles .	21,683	35,873	34,166	43,568
TOTAL (incl. others) . . .	2,874,373	2,792,634	2,864,060	5,088,504

PRINCIPAL TRADING PARTNERS
(KD '000)

IMPORTS	1978	1979	1980
Australia . .	28,366	36,882	42,551
China, People's Republic .	26,437	36,394	39,552
France . . .	46,650	48,304	68,356
Germany, Federal Republic .	114,597	114,715	151,491
India . . .	43,165	47,098	41,203
Italy . . .	79,210	80,188	98,844
Japan . . .	247,098	262,374	370,556
Korea, Republic .	37,169	47,169	n.a.
Netherlands .	22,800	24,455	26,968
Spain . . .	24,349	24,363	28,787
Taiwan . . .	34,786	42,385	60,008
United Kingdom .	129,570	144,346	152,158
U.S.A. . . .	165,418	207,692	255,770
TOTAL (incl. others) .	1,263,948	1,437,023	1,772,400

EXPORTS	1978	1979	1980
Australia . .	46,370	78,341	93,877
Brazil . . .	87,522	91,682	216,765
France . . .	69,055	165,027	195,565
Iran . . .	24,456	33,086	73,935
Iraq . . .	28,573	65,417	113,337
Italy . . .	260,504	451,327	66,296
Japan . . .	710,257	1,295,014	1,105,327
Korea, Republic .	189,967	315,246	416,365
Netherlands .	258,156	567,914	640,213
Pakistan . .	49,515	81,818	118,318
Saudi Arabia .	114,665	122,231	136,688
Singapore . .	35,594	229,327	367,865
Taiwan . . .	315,594	323,123	484,800
United Kingdom .	248,043	323,458	378,709
TOTAL (incl. others) .	2,864,060	5,088,504	5,484,700

TRANSPORT
INTERNATIONAL SEA-BORNE SHIPPING
(freight traffic in '000 metric tons)

	1974	1975	1976*	1977*
Goods loaded .	122,142	107,233	106,822	95,890
Goods unloaded .	1,571	2,532	5,000	5,500

* Includes Kuwait's share of traffic in the Neutral Zone.

Road Traffic (motor vehicles in use): (1975) 272,232; (1976) 320,656; (1977) 397,101; (1978) 439,553; (1979) 496,584; (1980) 542,950.

Civil Aviation: Kuwait Airport, total aircraft movements (1975) 19,042; (1976) 23,625; (1977) 28,465; (1978) 30,408; (1979) 29,031; (1980) 27,805.

EDUCATION
(1980/81)*

	SCHOOLS	TEACHERS	STUDENTS
Kindergarten	61	1,269	17,770
Primary	180	6,936	125,114
Intermediate	135	7,879	100,618
Secondary	71	5,581	51,960
Commercial	2	127	1,710
Technological institute . .	1	156	708
Religious institutes . .	2	85	592
Special training institutes . .	24	433	1,985
Teacher training colleges . .	2	289	1,584
Institute of Public Health . .	1	36	141

* Data for government schools only; in 1980/81 there were 3,282 teachers and 64,964 pupils at 62 private schools.

Sources: Central Statistical Office, Planning Board, Kuwait; Ministry of Finance and Oil, Kuwait; Ministry of Education, Kuwait; National Bank of Kuwait, S.A.K.; Kuwait Oil Co. Ltd., Ahmadi, Kuwait.

THE CONSTITUTION
(Promulgated November 16th, 1962)

On August 29th, 1976, the Amir suspended four articles of the Constitution dealing with the National Assembly. In early 1980 a 35-member committee was appointed to debate a revised Constitution and presented its recommendation to the Amir. On August 24th, 1980, an Amiri Decree was issued, calling for an elected National Assembly before the end of February 1981. The new Assembly was elected on February 23rd, 1981.

The principal provisions of the 1962 Constitution are as follows:

SOVEREIGNTY

Kuwait is an independent sovereign Arab State; her sovereignty may not be surrendered, and no part of her territory may be relinquished. Offensive war is prohibited by the Constitution.

Succession as Amir is restricted to heirs of the late MUBARAK AL-SABAH, and an Heir Apparent must be appointed within one year of the accession of a new Amir.

EXECUTIVE AUTHORITY

Executive power is vested in the Amir, who exercises it through a Council of Ministers. The Amir will appoint the Prime Minister "after the traditional consultations", and will appoint and dismiss Ministers on the recommendation of the Prime Minister. Ministers need not be members of the National Assembly, though all Ministers who are not Assembly members assume membership *ex officio* in the Assembly for the duration of office. The Amir also lays down laws, which shall not be effective unless published in the *Official Gazette*. The Amir sets up public institutions. All decrees issued in these respects shall be conveyed to the Assembly. No law is issued unless it is approved by the Assembly.

LEGISLATURE

A National Assembly of 50 members will be elected for a four-year term by all natural-born literate Kuwait males over the age of 21, except servicemen and police, who may not vote. Candidates for election must possess the franchise and be over 30 years of age. The Assembly will sit for at least eight months in any year, and new elections shall be held within two months of the last dissolution of the outgoing Assembly.

Restrictions on the commercial activities of Ministers include an injunction forbidding them to sell property to the Government.

The Amir may ask for reconsideration of a Bill passed by the Assembly and sent to him for ratification, but the Bill would automatically become law if it were subsequently passed by a two-thirds majority at the next sitting, or by a simple majority at a subsequent sitting. The Amir may declare Martial Law, but only with the approval of the Assembly.

The Assembly may pass a vote of no confidence in a Minister, in which case the Minister must resign. Such a vote is not permissible in the case of the Prime Minister, but the Assembly may approach the Amir on the matter, and the Amir shall then either dismiss the Prime Minister or dissolve the Assembly.

An annual budget shall be presented, and there shall be an independent finance control commission.

CIVIL SERVICE

Entry to the Civil Service is confined to Kuwait citizens.

PUBLIC LIBERTIES

Kuwaitis are equal before the law in prestige, rights and duties. Individual freedom is guaranteed. No one shall be seized, arrested or exiled except within the rules of law.

No punishment shall be administered except for an act or abstaining from an act considered a crime in accordance with a law applicable at the time of committing it, and no penalty shall be imposed more severe than that which could have been imposed at the time of committing the crime.

Freedom of opinion is guaranteed to everyone, and each has the right to express himself through speech, writing or other means within the limits of the law.

The Press is free within the limits of the law, and it should not be suppressed except in accordance with the dictates of law.

Freedom of performing religious rites is protected by the State according to prevailing customs, provided it does not violate the public order and morality.

Trade unions will be permitted and property must be respected. An owner is not banned from managing his property except within the boundaries of law. No property should be taken from anyone, except within the prerogatives of law, unless a just compensation be given.

Houses may not be entered, except in cases provided by law. Every Kuwaiti has freedom of movement and choice of place of residence within the state. This right shall not be controlled except in cases stipulated by law.

Every person has the right to education and freedom to choose his type of work. Freedom to form peaceful societies is guaranteed within the limits of law.

THE GOVERNMENT

HEAD OF STATE

Amir of Kuwait: His Highness Sheikh JABER AL-AHMAD AL-SABAH (succeeded on the death of his cousin, December 31st, 1977).

COUNCIL OF MINISTERS

(May 1982)

Crown Prince and Prime Minister: Sheikh SAAD AL-ABDULLAH AL-SALEM AL-SABAH.

Deputy Prime Minister, Minister of Foreign Affairs and acting Minister of Information: Sheikh SABAH AL-AHMAD AL-JABER AL-SABAH.

Minister of the Interior: Sheikh NAWAF AL-AHMAD AL-JABIR.

Minister of Defence: Sheikh SALEM AL-SABAH AL-SALEM AL-SABAH.

Minister of Oil: Sheikh ALI AL-KHALIFA AL-SABAH.

Minister of Public Health: Dr. ABDEL-RAHMAN ABDULLAH AL-AWADI.

Minister of Social Affairs and Labour and Minister of Housing: HAMAD ISA AL-RUJAIB.

Minister of Public Works: ABDULLAH AL-DAKHAIL.

Minister of Electricity and Water: KHALAF AHMAD AL-KHALAF.

Minister of Justice, Legal and Administrative Affairs: Sheikh SULIMAN DUAIJ AL-SABAH.

Minister of Finance and Planning: ABDUL-LATIF YOUSEF AL-HAMAD.

Minister of Education: YACOUB YOUSEF AL-GHUNAIM.

Minister of Commerce and Industry: JASSIM AL-MARZOUK.

Minister of Communications: ISA IBRAHIM AL-MAZIDI.

Minister of Awqaf and Islamic Affairs: AHMAD SAAD AL-JASSER.

Minister of State for Cabinet Affairs: ABDEL-AZIZ HUSAIN.

Adviser to Amir with rank of Minister: ABDUL RAHMAN AL-ATEEQI.

PROVINCIAL GOVERNORATES

Ahmadi: Sheikh JABIR ABDULLAH JABIR AL-SABAH.

Hawalli: Sheikh JABER MUBARAK HAMAD AL-SABAH.

Jahra: Sheikh ABDUL RAHMAN AL-MIJHIM.

Kuwait: Sheikh SALEM SABAH AL-NASER.

LEGISLATURE

MAJLIS AL-UMMA

(National Assembly)

The National Assembly, suspended since August 1976, was reconstituted in 1981 after an Amiri Decree in August 1980 called for its restoration. In elections to the fifth National Assembly on February 23rd, 1981, 448 candidates were nominated for 50 seats (2 seats in each of 25 districts). The opposition groups of the 1976 assembly were all but eliminated in the 1981 elections although 5 Islamic fundamentalists were elected.

Speaker: MOHAMMAD YOUSEF AL-ADASANI.

DIPLOMATIC REPRESENTATION

EMBASSIES ACCREDITED TO KUWAIT

(In Kuwait City unless otherwise stated)

(E) Embassy.

Afghanistan: P.O.B. 22944, Rawdah (E); *Ambassador:* (vacant).

Albania: Cairo, Egypt (E).

Algeria: P.O.B. 578, Istiqlal St. (E); *Ambassador:* (vacant).

Argentina: Jeddah, Saudi Arabia (E).

Australia: Fahd Al Salem St., Al Rashed Bldg. (E); *Ambassador:* DOUGLAS STURKEY (resident in Jeddah, Saudi Arabia).

Austria: Rawdah, Villa 20, Street 35, Area 3 (E); *Chargé d'affaires a.i.:* Dr. HELMUT BAUER.

Bahrain: Riyadh St., Abdullah Salem District, Birgis Humoud Bldg. 9 (E); *Ambassador:* SAIF J. AL-MUSALAM.

Bangladesh: 19 Istiqlal St., Dasmah, Area No. 4 (E); *Ambassador:* MUHAMMAD A. BAREK.

Belgium: Mohammed Al-Ghunaiman Villa, Damascus St., P.O.B. 3280, Safat (E); *Ambassador:* PETER BERGHS.

Brazil: P.O.B. 21370, Istiqlal St. (E); *Ambassador:* PAULO H. PARANGUA.

Bulgaria: Mansuria, Parcel No. 1, 22 Cairo St., Naqi Bldg., P.O.B. 12090 (E); *Ambassador:* ASSEN I. ZLATONOV.

Cameroon: Jeddah, Saudi Arabia (E).

Canada: 28 Quraish St., Nuzha (E); *Ambassador:* F. IAN WOOD.

China, People's Republic: P.O.B. 2346, Safat (E); *Ambassador:* LU MING.

Colombia: Madrid, Spain (E).

Costa Rica: P.O.B. 26380, Kuwait (E); *Ambassador:* MIGUEL YAMUNI.

Cuba: P.O.B. 26385, Kuwait (E); *Ambassador:* JUAN C. IBÁÑEZ.

Czechoslovakia: Abdulla Salem Dist., No. 14, Abou Yousof St., Block 3, Plot 165, P.O.B. 1151, Safat (E); *Chargé d'affaires a.i.:* FRANTIŠEK MATĚJKA.

Denmark: Abdulla Al Salem District, Block No. 1, Parcel No. 175, P.O.B. 5452 (E); *Ambassador:* FRANTZ CENTURA.

Djibouti: Jeddah, Saudi Arabia (E).

Ecuador: Teheran, Iran (E).

Finland: Kuwait City (E); *Ambassador:* PERTI RIPATI.

France: Qabazard Bldg., Istiqlal St., P.O.B. 1037 (E); *Ambassador:* PIERRE BLOUIN.

Gambia: Jeddah, Saudi Arabia (E).

German Democratic Republic: P.O.B. 5930, Shuwaikh (E); *Ambassador:* Dr. GÜNTER DOBERENZ.

Germany, Federal Republic: Shamiya District, Al Mamoun St. Villa Shaikh, P.O.B. 805 (E); *Ambassador:* HEINRICH WERSDÖRFER.

Greece: 17 Al Mansour St., Shuwaikh "B" (E); *Ambassador:* LEONIDAS VRAILAS.

Guinea: Jeddah, Saudi Arabia (E).

Hungary: Dhahia District, Parcel No. 1 Villa 44 (E); *Ambassador:* ERNŐ HORVÁTH.

India: 34 Shara, Istiqlal St. (E); *Ambassador:* SURBIR JIT SINGH CHHATWAL.

Indonesia: Nuzha District, Block 3, Nuzha Main St. No. 32 (E); *Ambassador:* RADEN SAJOGO.

Iran: P.O.B. 4686, 2R, Istiqlal St. (E); *Ambassador:* Dr. ALI SHAMS ARDEKANI.

Iraq: 37, Istiqlal St., Al-Musa Bldg. (E); *Ambassador:* ABDEL-JABBAR OMAR GHANI.

Ireland: Jeddah, Saudi Arabia (E).

Italy: Villa No. 6, F. Omar Ben Al-Khatab St., Mulla Bldgs., Sharq (E); *Ambassador:* PAOLO TARONY.

Japan: House No. 5, Plot No. 1, Street No. 13, Rawdah Area (E); *Ambassador:* RYUKICHI IMAI.

Jordan: Mansour Qabazard Bldg., Istiqlal St. (E); *Ambassador:* SALEH AL SHARAA.

Kenya: Jeddah, Saudi Arabia (E).

Korea, Republic: Damascus St., Nuzha (E); *Ambassador:* IN-DU KIM.

Lebanon: 31 Istiqlal St., (E) *Ambassador:* FAISAL SULTAN.

Liberia: Cairo, Egypt (E).

Libya: Haroon Al Rashid St. (E); *Ambassador:* HUSNI S. AL-MUDEER.

Malaysia: Block 1, Parcel 2, Mansuria (E); *Ambassador:* MUHAMMAD KHATIB BIN ABDUL-HAMID.

Mali: Jeddah, Saudi Arabia (E).

Malta: Tripoli, Libya (E).

Mauritania: Rawdah, St. No. 34, Parcel No. 3, Villa No. 28 (E); *Ambassador:* LEMRABOTT OULD ISSELMOU.

Mexico: Beirut, Lebanon (E).

Morocco: Shuwaikh Area B (E); *Ambassador:* MOHAMED NASIRI.

Nepal: Cairo, Egypt (E).

Netherlands: Jabrieh Area No. 9, Plot No. 40A, P.O.B. 21822, Safat (E); *Ambassador:* Jhr. E. S. B. T. BEELAERTS VAN BLOKLAND.

Nigeria: Jeddah, Saudi Arabia (E).

Norway: Abdulla Salem St. No. 15 (E); *Ambassador:* JAN ØSTERN (resident in Jeddah, Saudi Arabia).

Oman: Istiqlal St. (E); *Ambassador:* SALEM MUHAMMAD AL-KHOSAIBI.

Pakistan: Sharah-i-Istiqial, P.O.B. 988 (E); *Ambassador:* MURAD KHAIRI.

Philippines: Rawdah, Street 33, Area 3, Villa 10 (E); *Ambassador:* FRANCISCO JOVES.

Poland: Al Rawdah, Block 4, 3rd Ring Road (E); *Chargé d'affaires a.i.:* TADEUSZ KOZAK.

Qatar: P.O.B. 1825, Istiqlal St. (E); *Ambassador:* MUHAMMAD M. AL-KHELAIFI.

Romania: 30, Istiqlal St. (E); *Ambassador:* (vacant).

Rwanda: Cairo, Egypt (E).

Saudi Arabia: P.O.B. 20498, Istiqlal St. (E); *Ambassador:* MUHAMMAD FAHD AL-EISA.

Senegal: P.O.B. 23892, Rawdah (E); *Ambassador:* SHAMSEDDINE NDOYE.

Sierra Leone: Jeddah, Saudi Arabia (E).

Somalia: Nasir St., Shuwaikh "B" (E); *Ambassador:* ALI H. HASHI.

Spain: 12, Abdullah Salem St. (E); *Ambassador:* EMILIO B. VILLAMIL.

Sudan: 34, Istiqlal St. (E); *Ambassador:* IZZEDDIN HAMID AL-HASSAN.

Sweden: Hilali St. (E); *Ambassador:* THORD BENGTSON.

Switzerland: House No. 12, Road No. 32, Adeliyah Area (E); *Ambassador:* (vacant).

Syria: No. 33, Rawdah (E); *Ambassador:* ISA DARWISH.

Thailand: Kuwait (E); *Ambassador:* SUVAT MIFUMIKI NATYA.

Tunisia: Sheikh Duaij Ibrahim Bldg., Istiqlal St. (E); *Ambassador:* MUHAMMAD MEGDICHE.

Turkey: Bneid Al-Gar (E); *Ambassador:* FAROUK CELILOGLU.

Uganda: Jeddah, Saudi Arabia (E).

U.S.S.R.: Baghdad St., House No. 6 (E); *Ambassador:* NIKOLAI N. SIKATCHEV.

United Arab Emirates: Istiqlal St. (E); *Ambassador:* MUHAMMAD SULTAN ABDULLA.

United Kingdom: P.O.B. 2, Al-Khalij Al Arabi St. (E); *Ambassador:* JOHN CAMBRIDGE, C.M.G.

U.S.A.: P.O.B. 1767, Bneid Al-Gar (E); *Ambassador:* FRANCOIS DICKMAN.

Upper Volta: Cairo, Egypt (E).

Venezuela: Dahiya Abdulla Salem, Parcel No. 1, Nossef El Yousef St. No. 72 (E); *Ambassador:* JESÚS GARCÍA-CORONADO.

Viet-Nam: Baghdad, Iraq (E).

Yemen Arab Republic: Abdullah Al-Salem Area, Riyadh St. (E); *Ambassador:* ABDULLAH ABDULSALEM SABRAH.

Yemen, People's Democratic Republic: Nuzha, Parcel No. 1, Second Ring Road, House 24 (E); *Ambassador:* ALI AYDARUS YAHYA.

Yugoslavia: Al-Mansour St., Shuwaikh "B" (E); *Ambassador:* JOZE INGOLIC.

Zambia: Cairo, Egypt (E).

Kuwait also has diplomatic relations with Burundi, Gabon, Grenada, Guinea-Bissau, Guyana, Jamaica, Lesotho, Madagascar, Maldives, Niger, São Tomé and Príncipe, Tanzania, Trinidad and Tobago and Uruguay.

JUDICIAL SYSTEM

There is a codified system of law based largely upon the Egyptian system. In criminal matters, minor contraventions are dealt with by Magistrates' Courts, felonies by Criminal Assize Courts. Appeal in the case of misdemeanours is to a Misdemeanours Court of Appeal.

Civil cases are heard by a General Court within which are separate chambers dealing with commercial cases, other civil cases and matters of personal status. Appeal is to a High Court of Appeal. Matters of personal status may go beyond the High Court of Appeal to a Court of Cassation.

In criminal cases, investigation of misdemeanours is the responsibility of the police, while responsibility for the investigation of felonies lies with the Attorney-General's Office.

Attorney-General: DHAR AL-UTHMAN.

RELIGION

MUSLIMS

The inhabitants are mainly Muslims of the Sunni and Shi'ite sects. The Shi'ites comprise between 15 and 20 per cent of the total.

CHRISTIANS

Roman Catholic: Right Rev. Mgr. FRANCIS MICALLEF, O.C.D., Vicar Apostolic of Kuwait, Bishop's House P.O.B. 266, Safat, Kuwait.

National Evangelical Church in Kuwait: Rev. HILMY HENAIN, Box 80, Kuwait; a United Protestant Church founded by the Reformed Church in America; services in Arabic, English and Malayalam.

There are also Armenian, Greek, Coptic and Syrian Orthodox Churches in Kuwait.

THE PRESS

DAILIES

Al-Anbaa: P.O.B. 23915, Kuwait; f. 1976; Arabic; general; Editor-in-Chief FAISAL YOUSEF AL-MARZOOQ; circ. 55,000.

Al-Qabas: P.O.B. 21800, Airport Rd., Shuwaikh, Kuwait; f. 1972; Arabic; Editor JASSIM AHMAD AL-NUSUF; Man. Editor R. CH'HOURI; circ. 75,000.

Al-Rai al-A'am (*Public Opinion*): P.O.B. 695, International Airport Rd., Shuwaikh Industrial Area, Kuwait; f. 1961; Arabic; political, social and cultural; circ. 50,000.

Al-Seyassa: P.O.B. 2270, Kuwait; f. 1967; Arabic; political; Editor AHMED AL-JARALLAH; circ. 80,000.

Al-Watan (*The Homeland*): P.O.B. 1142, Safat, Kuwait; f. 1974; Arabic; political; Editor-in-Chief JASIM AL-MUTAWA; circ. 58,000.

Arab Times: P.O.B. 2270, Kuwait; f. 1977 (formerly *Daily News*); English; Editor-in-Chief AHMED ABDULAZIZ AL-JARALLAH; Man. Editor R. MOHAN; circ. 42,000.

Kuwait Times: P.O.B. 1301, Safat, Kuwait; f. 1961; English; political; Owner and Editor-in-Chief YOUSUF ALYAN; Man. Editor CLEMENT MESENAS; circ. 28,000.

WEEKLIES AND PERIODICALS

Kuwait Al-Yawm (*Kuwait Today*): P.O.B. 193, Kuwait; f. 1954; Sunday; the "Official Gazette"; Amiri Decrees, Laws, Govt. announcements, decisions, invitations for tenders, etc.; published by the Ministry of Information; circ. 5,000.

Adhwa al-Kuwait: P.O.B. 1977, Kuwait; f. 1962; Arabic; literature and arts; weekly; free advertising magazine; Editor KHALID AL-HAMAD; circ. 5,000.

Al-Arabi: P.O.B. 748, Kuwait; f. 1958; Arabic; cultural; monthly; published by the Ministry of Information for distribution throughout the Arab world; Editor AHMAD BAHA-IDIN; circ. 250,000.

Al-Balagh: P.O.B. 4558, Safat, Kuwait; f. 1969; Arabic; political and Islamic; weekly; Editor ABDUL-RAHMAN RASHID AL-WALAYATI.

Al-Hadaf (*The Aim*): P.O.B. 1142, Safat, Kuwait; f. 1961; Arabic; political and cultural; weekly; Editor-in-Chief J. M. AL-MUTAWA; Chair. M. M. AL-SALEH; circ. 63,000.

Al Kuwaiti: Information Dept., Ahmadi 22; f. 1961; Arabic; weekly journal of the Kuwait Oil Co. (KSC); circ. 8,000.

Al-Mujtama'a: P.O.B. 4850, Kuwait; f. 1969; Arabic weekly issued by the Social Reform Society.

Al Nahdha (*The Renaissance*): P.O.B. 695, International Airport Rd., Shuwaikh Industrial Area, Kuwait; f. 1967; Arabic; weekly; social and political; Editor YOUSSUF AL-MASSAEED; circ. 45,000.

Arab Oil: P.O.B. 2270, Kuwait; f. 1977; international magazine for the oil industry; monthly; Editor DAVID LYNN PRICE; circ. 14,750.

Ar-Raid (*The Pioneer*): P.O.B. 11259, Cairo Rd., Kuwait; f. 1969; weekly; issued by Kuwaiti Teachers' Association; circ. 4,000.

Ar Ressaleh (*The Message*): P.O.B. 2490, Shuwaikh, Kuwait; f. 1961; Arabic; political, social and cultural; weekly; Editor JASSIM MUBARAK.

At-Tali'a: P.O.B. 1082, Mubarak al-Kabir St., Kuwait; f. 1962; Arabic; weekly; Editor SAMI AHMED AL-MUNAIS; circ. 10,000.

Al-Yaqza (*The Awakening*): P.O.B. 6000, Safat, Kuwait; f. 1966; political, economic, social and general; weekly; Editor-in-Chief AHMED YOUSUF BEHBEEANI; Gen. Man. NAKHLE I. BADER; circ. 72,000.

Hayatuna (*Our Life*): P.O.B. 1708, Kuwait; f. 1968; Arabic; medicine and hygiene; fortnightly; published by Al-Awadi Press Corporation; Editor Dr. ABDUL RAHMAN AL-AWADI; circ. 6,000.

Kuwaiti Digest: Information Dept., Ahmadi 22; English; quarterly; journal of Kuwait Oil Co.; circ. 8,000.

Mejallat al-Kuwait (*Kuwait Magazine*): P.O.B. 193, Kuwait; Arabic; news and literary articles; fortnightly illustrated magazine; published by Ministry of Information.

Osrati (*My Family*): P.O.B. 2995, Kuwait; Arabic; women's magazine; weekly; Editor GHANIMA F. AL-MARZOUK; published by Fahad al-Marzouk Establishment; circ. 65,000.

Sawt al-Khaleej (*Voice of the Gulf*): P.O.B. 659, Kuwait; f. 1962; political weekly; Editor BAQER KHRAIBITT; circ. 20,000.

NEWS AGENCIES

Kuwait News Agency (KUNA): P.O.B. 24063, Safat, Kuwait; f. 1976; Chair. and Dir.-Gen. BARGES HAMOUD AL-BARGES.

FOREIGN BUREAUX

ANSA (*Italy*): P.O.B. 24063, Kuwait; Corresp. MUHAMMAD AL-BARGES.

Middle East News Agency (MENA) (*Egypt*): P.O.B. 1927, Fahd El-Salem St., Kuwait; Dir. REDA SOLIMAN.

Reuters (*United Kingdom*): 4th Floor, al-Thuwaini Bldg., Ali as-Salem St., P.O.B. 5616, Safat, Kuwait.

Telegrafnoye Agentstvo Sovietskogo Soyuza (TASS) (*U.S.S.R.*): P.O.B. 1455, Kuwait.

Xinhua (*People's Republic of China*): P.O.B. 22168, nr. Dasman Palace, Kuwait.

The Iraqi News Agency, the Jamahiriya News Agency (Libya), Novosti (U.S.S.R.), Qatar News Agency and Syrian News Agency are also represented.

PUBLISHER

Ministry of Information: P.O.B. 193, Safat, Al-Sour St., Kuwait.

RADIO AND TELEVISION

RADIO

Kuwait Broadcasting Service: P.O.B. 193, Kuwait; f. 1951; broadcasts in Arabic, Farsi, English and Urdu, some in stereo; Asst. Under-Sec. for Broadcasting Affairs ABDUL AZIZ MOHAMED JA'FFER; Asst. Under-Sec. for Engineering Affairs ABDUL-RAHMAN IBRAHIM AL-HUTY.

Number of radio receivers (1981): 525,000.

TELEVISION

Television of Kuwait, Ministry of Information: P.O.B. 621, Kuwait; f. 1961; broadcasts in Arabic; colour television started in spring 1973; a second channel was opened in 1979. Asst. Under-Sec. of TV Affairs MUHAMMAD SANOUSSI; Dir. of Programmes RISA AL-FEELI.

Number of television receivers (1981): 542,000.

FINANCE

BANKING

(cap.=capital; p.u.=paid up; dep.=deposits; res.= reserves; m.=million; amounts in Kuwaiti dinars)

CENTRAL BANK

Central Bank of Kuwait: Abdulla Al-Salem St., P.O.B. 526, Kuwait; f. 1969; cap. 16.5m., reserves 67.7m.; Governor HAMZAH ABBAS HUSSAIN.

NATIONAL BANKS

Alahli Bank of Kuwait K.S.C.: Mubarak Al Kabir St., P.O.B. 1387, Kuwait; 10 brs.; cap. p.u. 16.5m.; dep. 1,168.1m.; res. 47.9m. (Dec. 1981); Chair. SAOUD AL ABDUL RAZZAK; Gen. Man. ABDUL KADIR ALSEESI.

Bank of Bahrain and Kuwait B.S.C.: Ahmad Al-Jaber St., P.O.B. 24396, Safat, Kuwait; Head Office in Bahrain; 50 per cent owned by Kuwaiti banks and financial institutions, 50 per cent by Bahraini individuals; cap. and res. BD 22m. (1980); Man. Dir. HAMAD M. AL-BAHAR; Gen. Man. DAVID W. STRECKER.

Bank of Kuwait and the Middle East K.S.C.: P.O.B. 71, Safat, Kuwait; 49 per cent owned by the Government; began operations in Dec. 1971 when it took over former branches of the British Bank of the Middle East; cap. p.u. 52.9m. (Dec. 1981); Chair. FAHAD AL-BAHAR; Gen. Man. SALEH MUBARAK AL-FALAH.

Burgan Bank, S.A.K.: P.O.B. 5389, Safat, Kuwait; f. 1975; 51 per cent owned by the Government, 49 per cent by Kuwaiti public; cap. and res. 26.9m.; dep. 511.5m.; total assets 551.1m. (Dec. 1981); 7 brs.; Chair. and Man. Dir. ABDULRASOOL ABULHASAN; Gen. Man. ABDUL-AZIZ AL-JASSAR.

Commercial Bank of Kuwait, S.A.K.: Mubarak Al Kabir St., P.O.B. 2861, Kuwait; total assets 1,444.2m. (Dec. 1981); 29 brs.; Chair. HAMAD A. A. AL-HAMAD; Gen. Man. ADOLF KNUL.

Gulf Bank K.S.C.: P.O.B. Safat 3200, Mubarak Al Kabir St., Kuwait; f. 1960; cap. p.u. 17.5m., res. 54m., dep. 963.3m. (1980); 20 brs.; Chair. MUSTAPHA SULTAN AL-ISSA; Gen. Man. S. WEBSTER.

Industrial Bank of Kuwait: P.O.B. 3146, Safat, Kuwait; 49 per cent owned by the Government; f. 1973; cap. p.u. 20m., res. 7.2m., dep. 384.2m. (Dec. 1980); Chair. and Man. ANWAR A. AL-NOURI; Exec. Mans. FAISAL S. KHADRA, LUCIEN S. TOUTOUNJI.

Kuwait Finance House S.A.K.: P.O.B. 24989 Safat, Kuwait; f. 1977; Islamic financial institution; cap. 10m. (49 per cent owned by Govt. of Kuwait); dep. 222.9m.; Chair. AHMED BAZIE AL-YASSIN; Deputy Chair. FAISUL A. AL-ALKHATRUSH; Man. Dir. and Gen. Man. BADR A. AL-MUKHAIZEEM.

Kuwait Real Estate Bank K.S.C.: P.O.B. 22822, Safat, Kuwait; f. 1973; total assets 310.2m. (Dec. 1980); Chair. and Man. Dir. SAAD ALI AL-NAHED; Gen. Man. ALI R. AL-BADER.

National Bank of Kuwait, S.A.K.: Abdulla Al-Salem St., P.O.B. 95, Kuwait; f. 1952; cap. and res. 96m., total assets 1,953m. (Dec. 1981); 40 brs.; Chair. MUHAMMAD ABDULMOHSIN AL-KHARAFI; Chief. Gen. Man. G. E. VENEMA.

Savings and Credit Bank: P.O.B. 1454, Kuwait; f. 1960; nominal cap. 500m. (1981); Chair. ABDUL RAZZAK AL-ASKAR; Dir.-Gen. YOUSEF M. SHAIJI.

INSURANCE

Al Ahleia Insurance Co., S.A.K.: P.O.B. 1602, Ali Al-Salim St., Kuwait; f. 1962; covers all classes of insurance; cap. 5m.; Chair. YOUSEF IBRAHIM AL-GHANIM; Man. Dir. ABDULLA A. AL-RIFAI; Gen. Man. Dr. RAOUF H. MAKAR.

Gulf Insurance Co. K.S.C.: P.O.B. 1040, Safat, Kuwait; f. 1961; cap. 8.7m.; Chair. and Man. Dir. KHALIL IBRAHIM AL-SHAMI.

Kuwait Insurance Co.: Abdullah As-Salim St., P.O.B. 769, Kuwait; f. 1960; cap. p.u. 9.18m.; Gen. Man. MAHMOUD S. GHUNAIM; Deputy Gen. Man. FOUAD A. AL-BAHAR.

Some 20 Arab and other foreign insurance companies are active in Kuwait.

STOCK EXCHANGE

Kuwait Stock Exchange: Safat, Kuwait.

TRADE AND INDUSTRY

PETROLEUM

Kuwait Petroleum Corporation: Kuwait; f. 1980; umbrella organization to run oil industry; controls companies listed below; Chair. Sheikh ALI AL-KHALIFA AL-SABAH (Minister of Oil).

Kuwait Foreign Petroleum Explorations Co. K.S.C.: Kuwait; f. 1981; state-owned; overseas oil exploration and development; Chair. ABDUL RAZZAK MULLA HUSSEIN.

Kuwait National Petroleum Co., K.S.C.: P.O.B. 70, Safat, Kuwait; f. 1961; oil refining and production of LPG; Chair. AHMAD ABDUL MUHSIN AL-MUTAIR; publ. *Al-Wataniah* (monthly).

Kuwait Oil Co., K.S.C.: Ahmadi 22, Kuwait; f. 1934; state-owned; 716 wells producing at end of December 1980; oil production in 1980 was 511,000,000 barrels, an average of 1.4 million barrels per day; Chair. and Man. Dir. AHMAD MOHAMED JA'AFAR.

Kuwait Oil Tankers Co. S.A.K. (*see* Transport).

Kuwait Petroleum Investment Co. (KPIC): f. 1981; petroleum related investments outside Kuwait; Chair. Sheikh ALI JABER AL-SABAH.

Petrochemical Industries Co. K.S.C. (*see* Development).

Arabian Oil Co.: Head Office Tokyo; Kuwait Office P.O.B. 1641, Kuwait; Field Office Ras Al-Khafji, Divided Zone, Saudi Arabia; a Japanese company which has concessions offshore of the Partitioned Zone; in 1980 crude oil production was 140,363,816 barrels (shared equally between Kuwait and Saudi Arabia).

CHAMBER OF COMMERCE

Kuwait Chamber of Commerce and Industry: P.O.B. 775, Chamber's Bldg., Ali Salem St., Kuwait State; f. 1959; 10,000 mems.; Pres. ABDUL AZIZ AL-SAGER; Vice-Pres YOUSEF AL FULEIJ and MOHAMAD A. AL-Kharafi; Adviser and Acting Sec.-Gen. MAJED JAMAL UD-DIN; publs. *The Kuwaiti Economist* (monthly) and annual economic and administrative reports.

DEVELOPMENT

Kuwait Foreign Trading, Contracting and Investment Co. (KFTCIC): P.O.B. 5665, Safat, Kuwait; f. 1965; overseas investment company; 80 per cent government holding; cap. and res. KD 78.8m., total assets KD 601.6m. (1981); Chair. and Man. Dir. ABDULWAHAB A. AL-TAMMAR.

Kuwait Fund for Arab Economic Development: cnr. Mubarak Al-Kabir St. and Al-Hilali St., P.O.B. 2921, Safat, Kuwait; f. 1961; cap. KD 2,000m.; wholly government owned; provides and administers financial and technical assistance to the countries of the developing world; cap. 19.2m.; Chair. ABDLATIF Y. AL-HAMAD; Dir.-Gen. FAISAL AL-KHALED.

Kuwait International Investment Co. (KIIC): Al-Salhia Commercial Complex, P.O.B. 22792, Safat, Kuwait; cap. and res. 33m.; total assets 180m.; domestic real estate and share markets.

Kuwait Investment Co. S.A.K. (KIC): P.O.B. 1005 Safat, Kuwait; f. 1961; total resources KD 294m. (December 1981); investment banking institution owned 50 per cent by the Government and 50 per cent by Kuwaiti nationals; international banking and investment; Chair. and Man. Dir. HAMAD MUHAMMAD AL-BAHAR; Gen. Man. HILAL MASHARI AL-MUTAIRI.

Kuwait Planning Board: Kuwait City; f. 1962; supervises long-term development plans; through its Central Statistical Office publishes information on Kuwait's economic activity; Dir.-Gen. AHMED ALI AL-DUAIJ.

National Industries Company: P.O.B. 417, Safat, Kuwait; f. 1961; 51 per cent government-owned company with controlling interest in various construction enterprises; Chair. and Man. Dir. MUFARREJ I. AL-MUFARREJ.

Petrochemical Industries Co. K.S.C.: P.O.B. 1084, Kuwait; owns and operates the Fertilizer Division which produces ammonia, urea, ammonium sulphate and concentrated sulphuric acid; also owns and operates the Salt and Chlorine Division, which produces salt, chlorine, caustic soda, hydrochloric acid, sodium hypochlorite, chlorsal and compressed hydrogen; Chair. and Man. Dir. ABDUL BAQI AL-NOURI.

Shuaiba Area Authority: P.O.B. 4690, Kuwait; f. 1964; an independent governmental authority to supervise and run the industrial area and Port of Shuaiba. It has powers and duties to develop the area and its industries which include an oil refinery, cement factory, fishing plant, power stations and distillation plants, chemical fertilizer and petrochemical industries, sanitary ware factory, asbestos plant and sand lime bricks plant; publs. (annual) *Statistical Abstract* and *Information Bulletin*.

TRADE UNIONS

General Confederation of Kuwaiti Workers: f. 1968; central authority to which all trade unions are affiliated.

KOC Workers Union: f. 1964; Chair. JASSIM ABDUL WAHAB AL-TOURA.

Federation of Petroleum and Petrochemical Workers: f. 1965; Chair. JASSIM ABDUL WAHAB AL-TOURA; publ. *The Worker*.

TRANSPORT

ROADS

Roads in the towns are metalled and the most important are dual carriageway. There are metalled roads to Ahmadi, Mina Al-Ahmadi and other centres of population in Kuwait, and to the Iraqi and Saudi Arabian borders, giving a total road network of 1,920 km. A four-lane trunk road to Dammam in Saudi Arabia is under construction and a motorway system is being developed.

Kuwait Transport Co. S.A.K.: Kuwait; provides internal bus service; regular service to Iraq.

SHIPPING

A modern port has been built at Shuwaikh, three km. west of Kuwait City. There are plans to increase the number of berths from the existing 21 to 30 by 1985. Ships of British and other lines make regular calls.

There is a second port at Shuaiba, 50 km. south of Kuwait, containing 15 berths and a liquid products pier with 4 berths. A further 5 berths are under construction.

The oil port at Mina Al-Ahmadi, 40 km. south of Kuwait City is capable of handling the largest oil tankers afloat, and the loading of over 2 million barrels of oil per day.

Arab Maritime Petroleum Transport Co.: Khalid al-Essa Bldg., P.O.B. 22525, Kuwait City; eight tankers and two LPG carriers; sponsored by OAPEC and financed by Algeria, Abu Dhabi, Bahrain, Iraq, Kuwait, Libya, Qatar and Saudi Arabia; Chair. Dr. A. H. TAHER; Vice-Chair. and Man. Dir. A. RAHMAD AL-SULTAN.

Kuwait Oil Tankers Co. S.A.K.: P.O.B. 810, Safat, Kuwait; f. 1957; state-owned; owns tankers totalling 1,971,051 d.w.t., and LPG carriers of 189,880 metric tons with 12 further LPG carriers on order; sole tanker agents for Mina al-Ahmadi, Shuaiba and Mina Abdulla and agents for other ports; LPG filling and distribution; Chair. and Man. Dir. FAISAL THUNYYAN AL-GHANEM.

United Arab Shipping Co. S.A.G.: P.O.B. 3636, Safat, Kuwait; f. 1976; the national company of six Arabian Gulf countries; services between Europe, U.K., Far East, Mediterranean ports, Japan and East Coast of U.S.A. and ports of participant States on Arabian Gulf and Red Sea; 62 vessels totalling 1.3 million tons; subsid. companies are Kuwait Shipping Agencies, Aratrans, and United Arab Chartering Company, London; cap. p.u. KD 280m.; Chair. EID ABDULLAH YOUSSOUF; Gen. Man. ABDUL AZIZ HUSSAIN SALATT.

CIVIL AVIATION

Kuwait Airways Corporation: B.P. 394, Kuwait International Airport, Kuwait; f. 1954; services to Abadan, Abu Dhabi, Aden, Amman, Amsterdam, Athens, Baghdad, Bahrain, Bangkok, Beirut, Belgrade, Bombay, Cairo, Casablanca, Copenhagen, Damascus, Delhi, Dhahran, Doha, Dubai, Frankfurt, Geneva, Istanbul, Jeddah, Karachi, Khartoum, London, Madrid, Muscat, New York, Nicosia, Paris, Prague, Ras al-Khaimah, Rome, Sana'a, Teheran, Tripoli, Tunis, Zurich; fleet of 8 Boeing 707, 3 Jumbo 747, 1 Boeing 737, 1 Jet Star, 3 Boeing 727 (on order), 11 Airbus (on order); Chair. and Man. Dir. GHASSAN AL-NISSIF; Gen. Man. AHMED AL-MISHARI; publs. *Al-Boraq* (magazine), *KAC News*.

Kuwait is also served by the following airlines: Air France, Air India, Alia (Jordan), Alitalia (Italy), British Airways, ČSA (Czechoslovakia), Cyprus Airways, Democratic Yemen Airlines, EgyptAir, Gulf Aviation, Iberia (Spain), Iranair, Iraqi Airways, Japan Air Lines, KLM (Netherlands), Korean Air Lines (Republic of Korea), LOT (Poland), Lufthansa (Federal Republic of Germany), Malév (Hungary), MAS (Malaysia), MEA (Lebanon), Olympic Airways (Greece), PIA (Pakistan), Saudia (Saudi Arabia), SIA (Singapore), Sudan Airways, Swissair, Syrian Arab Airlines, Thai International, TMA (Lebanon), Tunis Air, THY Turkish Airlines, Yemen Airways, Yugoslav Airlines.

DEFENCE

In July 1981 the armed forces numbered 12,400, and included 10,000 in the army and 1,900 in the air force. The navy consists of a coastguard force of 500 and there is a paramilitary force of 18,000. Defence expenditure amounted to KD 303 million in 1980. There is a period of Military Service lasting 18 months, compulsory since March 1979.

Chief of Staff of Armed Forces: Major-General ABDULLAH FARRAJ AL-GHANIM.

Commander of the Kuwait Navy: HABIB AL-MEEL.

EDUCATION

Within the last few years a comprehensive system of kindergarten, primary, intermediate and secondary schools has been built up, and compulsory education between the ages of 6 and 14 was introduced in 1966–67. However, many children spend two years before this in a kindergarten, and go on to complete their general education at the age of 18 years. In 1980/81 302,610 pupils attended 481 governments schools staffed by 22,755 teachers. In 1980/81 education was the largest item in the budget expenditure, at $600 million, or 8 per cent of the whole. The general policy of the Government is to provide free education to all Kuwaiti children from kindergarten stage to the University. Pupils are also provided, free of cost, with food, textbooks, clothing and medical treatment. In 1980/81 there were 64,964 pupils at private schools.

Primary education lasts four years, after which the pupils move on to an intermediate school for another four years. Secondary education, which is optional and lasts four more years, is given mainly in general schools. There are also commercial institutes, an Institute of Technology, a health institute, religious institutes (with intermediate and secondary stages) and eleven institutes for handicapped children.

Two-year courses at post-secondary teacher training institutes provide teachers for kindergartens and primary schools and the University provides for intermediate and secondary schools. The number of graduates is not enough to meet all the teaching staff requirements and so the Ministry of Education meets this shortage by recruiting teachers from other Arab countries.

Scholarships are granted to students to pursue courses which are not offered by Kuwait University. In 1978–79 there were 2,925 Kuwaiti scholarship students studying mainly in Egypt, Lebanon, U.K. and the U.S.A. There were also pupils from Arab, African and Asian states studying in Kuwait schools on Kuwait Government scholarships. Kuwait University has over 17,000 students, and also provides scholarships for a number of Arab, Asian and African students.

BIBLIOGRAPHY

BERREBY, JEAN-JACQUES. Le Golfe Persique; mer de légende—réservoir de pétrole (Payot, Paris 1959).

CHISHOLM, A. H. T. The First Kuwait Oil Concession: A Record of the Negotiations 1911–1934 (Cass, London).

DANIELS, JOHN. Kuwait Journey (White Crescent Press, Luton, England, 1972).

DEPARTMENT OF SOCIAL AFFAIRS. Annual Report (Kuwait).

DICKSON, H. R. P. Kuwait and her Neighbours (Allen and Unwin, London, 1956).

EL MALLAKH, RAGAEI. Economic Development and Regional Co-operation: Kuwait (University of Chicago Press, 1968).

FREETH, Z. Kuwait was my Home (Allen and Unwin, London, 1956).

GOVERNMENT PRINTING PRESS. Education and Development in Kuwait (Kuwait).

Port of Kuwait Annual Report (Kuwait).

HAKIMA, A. A. The Rise and Development of Bahrein and Kuwait (Beirut, 1964).

HAY, Sir RUPERT. The Persian Gulf States (Middle East Institute, Washington, 1959).

INTERNATIONAL BANK FOR RECONSTRUCTION AND DEVELOPMENT. The Economic Development of Kuwait (Johns Hopkins Press, Baltimore, 1965).

KHOUJA, M. W., and SADLER, P. G. The Energy of Kuwait: Development and Role in International Finance (Macmillan, London, 1978).

KOCHWASSER, FRIEDRICH H. Kuwait. Geschichte, Wesen und Funktion eines modernen Arabischen Staates (Tübingen, Eldmann, 1961).

KUWAIT OIL CO. LTD. The Story of Kuwait (London).

MARLOWE, JOHN. The Persian Gulf in the 20th Century (Cresset Press, London, 1962).

MEZERIK, AVRAHAM G. The Kuwait-Iraq Dispute, 1961 (New York, 1961).

WILSON, Sir A. T. The Persian Gulf (Oxford University Press, 1928).

WINSTONE, H. V. F., and FREETH, ZAHRA. Kuwait: Prospect and Reality (Allen and Unwin, London, 1972).

Lebanon

PHYSICAL AND SOCIAL GEOGRAPHY

W. B. Fisher

The creation, after 1918, of the modern State of the Lebanon, first under French Mandatory rule and then as an independent territory, was designed to recognize the nationalist aspirations of a number of Christian groups that had lived for many centuries under Muslim rule along the coast of the eastern Mediterranean and in the hills immediately adjacent. At least as early as the sixteenth century A.D. there had been particularist Christian feeling that ultimately resulted in the grant of autonomy, though not independence, to Christians living in the territory of "Mount Lebanon", which geographically was the hill region immediately inland and extending some 20–30 miles north and south of Beirut. The territory of Mount Lebanon was later expanded, owing to French interest, into the much larger area of "Greater Lebanon" with frontiers running along the crest of the Anti-Lebanon mountains, and reaching the sea some miles north of Tripoli to form the boundary with Syria. In the south there is a frontier with Israel, running inland from the promontory of Ras an-Nakura to the head of the Jordan Valley. In drawing the frontiers so as to give a measure of geographical unity to the new State, which now occupies an area of 10,400 sq. kilometres, large non-Christian elements of Muslims and Druzes were included, so that at the present day the Christians of the Lebanon form only about half the total population.

PHYSICAL FEATURES

Structurally, the Lebanon consists of an enormous simple upfold of rocks that runs parallel to the coast. There is, first, a very narrow and broken flat coastal strip —hardly a true plain—then the land rises steeply to a series of imposing crests and ridges. The highest crest of all is Qurnet as-Sauda, just over 10,000 ft. high, lying south-east of Tripoli; Mount Sannin, north-east of Beirut, is over 9,000 ft. A few miles east of the summits there is a precipitous drop along a sharp line to a broad, troughlike valley, known as the Beka'a (Biqa), about 10 miles wide and some 70 to 80 miles long. The eastern side of the Beka'a is formed by the Anti-Lebanon mountains, which rise to 9,000 ft., and their southern continuation, the Hermon Range, of about the same height. The floor of the Bekaa Valley, though much below the level of the surrounding mountain ranges, lies in places at 3,000 ft. above sea-level, with a low divide in the region of Baalbek. Two rivers rise in the Beka'a— the Orontes, which flows northwards into Syria and the Gharb depression, ultimately reaching the Mediterranean through the Turkish territory of Antioch; and the River Litani (Leontes). This latter river flows southwards, and then, at a short distance from the Israeli frontier, makes a sudden bend westwards and plunges through the Lebanon mountains by a deep gorge.

There exists in the Lebanon an unusual feature of geological structure which is not present in either of the adjacent regions of Syria and Israel. This is the occurrence of a layer of non-porous rocks within the upfold forming the Lebanon mountains; and, because of this layer, water is forced to the surface in considerable quantities, producing large springs at the unusually high level of 4,000 to 5,000 ft. Some of the springs have a flow of several thousand cu. ft. per second and emerge as small rivers; hence the western flanks of the Lebanon mountains, unlike those nearby in Syria and Israel, are relatively well watered and cultivation is possible up to a height of 4,000 or 5,000 ft.

With its great contrasts of relief, and the configuration of the main ranges, which lie across the path of the prevailing westerly winds, there is a wide variety in climatic conditions. The coastal lowlands are moderately hot in summer, and warm in winter, with complete absence of frost. But only 5 or 10 miles away in the hills there is a heavy winter snowfall, and the higher hills are covered from December to May, giving the unusual vista for the Middle East of snow-clad peaks. From this the name Lebanon (laban— Aramaic for "white") is said to originate. The Beka'a has a moderately cold winter with some frost and snow, and a distinctly hot summer, as it is shut off from the tempering effect of the sea.

Rainfall is on the whole abundant, but it decreases rapidly towards the east, so that the Beka'a and Anti-Lebanon are definitely drier than the west. On the coast, between 30 and 40 inches fall annually, with up to 50 inches in the mountains, but only 15 inches in the Beka'a. As almost all this annual total falls between October and April (there are three months of complete aridity each summer) rain is extremely heavy while it lasts, and storms of surprising intensity can occur. Beirut, for example, has slightly more rain than Manchester, but on half the number of rainy days. Another remarkable feature is the extremely high humidity of the coastal region during summer, when no rain falls. The sultry heat drives as many as can afford it to spend the summer in the hills.

ECONOMIC LIFE

The occurrence of high mountains near the sea, and the relatively abundant supplies of spring water have had a marked influence on economic development within the Lebanon. Owing to the successive levels of terrain, an unusually wide range of crops can be grown, from bananas and pineapples on the hot, damp coastlands, olives, vines and figs on the lowest foothills, cereals, apricots and peaches on the middle slopes, to apples and potatoes on the highest levels. These latter are the aristocrats of the Lebanese markets, since they are rarest, and, with the growing market in the oilfield areas of Arabia and the Persian Gulf, they fetch the highest price. Export of fruit is therefore an important item. Then, too, abundant natural water has led to the growth of pinewoods and evergreen groves, which add greatly to the already considerable scenic beauty of the western hill country. There has hence grown up an important tourist trade, centred in the small hill villages, some of which have casinos, luxury hotels, and cinemas. Main activity is during the summer months, when wealthy Middle Easterners and others arrive; but there is a smaller winter sports season, when ski-ing is carried on.

In addition, the geographical situation of the Lebanon, as a "façade" to the inland territories of Syria, Jordan, and even northern Iraq and southern Turkey, enables the Lebanese ports to act as the commercial outlet for a very wide region. The importance of Beirut as a commercial centre is due in large part to the fact that the Lebanon is a free market. Over half of the volume of Lebanese trade is transit traffic, and the Lebanon normally handles most of the trade of Jordan. Her own exports are mostly agricultural products. Byblos claims to be the oldest port in the world; Tyre and Sidon were for long world-famous, and the latter is now reviving as the Mediterranean terminal of the Tapline (Trans-Arabian Pipe Line) from Saudi Arabia. Another ancient centre, Tripoli, is also a terminal of the pipeline from Iraq (now closed). Beirut is now, however, the leading town of the country, and contains one-quarter of the total population. Though local resources are not in general very great (there are no minerals or important raw materials in the Lebanon) the city in normal times lives by commercial activity on a surprising scale, developed by the ingenuity and opportunism of its merchant class. The opening in 1951 of a commercial airport designed for jet airliners, before any such aircraft were actually in use in the world, is typical of the forward-looking attitude of many Lebanese.

Beirut has of recent years come to serve as a financial and holiday centre for the less attractive but oil-rich parts of the Middle East. Transfer of financial credit from the Middle East to Zürich, Paris, London, New York and Tokyo; a trade in gold and diamonds; and some connexion with the narcotic trade of the Middle East—all these give the city a very special function. In addition, the town provides discreet distraction for all types of visitor. Whether the traditional economic basis of the country—extreme individualism and "laisser-faire" for entrepreneurs—can revive is uncertain, but strenuous efforts began in 1977 to bring about reconstruction and redevelopment, assisted by loans from outside. During 1980 a large contribution of "front-line aid" was made by Arab League states, and this showed signs of producing marked economic recovery. However, the military flare-up that charac-

terized 1981–82 has negated these hopes. Production has fallen because of damage and disruption; the extreme south has been virtually cut off from the rest of the Lebanese state, and the impossibility of controlling customs and tax collection has greatly reduced governmental income. As well, aid promised by Arab states has not always been forthcoming.

RACE AND LANGUAGE

It is difficult to summarize the racial affinities of the Lebanese people. The western lowlands have an extremely mixed population possibly describable only as "Levantine". Basically Mediterranean, there are many other elements, including remarkably fair individuals—Arabs with blonde hair and grey eyes, who are possibly descendants of the Crusaders. The remaining parts of the country show a more decided tendency, with darker colouring and more pronounced facial features. In addition, small refugee groups, who came to the more inaccessible mountain zones in order to escape persecution, often have a different racial ancestry, so that parts of the Lebanon form a mosaic of highly varying racial and cultural elements. Almost all Middle Eastern countries are represented racially within the Lebanon.

Arabic is current over the whole country, but owing to the high level of education (probably the highest in any Middle Eastern country) and to the considerable volume of temporary emigration, English, French and even Spanish are widely understood. French is probably still the leading European language (though English is tending to replace it) and some of the higher schools and one university teach basically in this language. In addition, Aramaic is used by some religious sects, but only for ritual—there are no Aramaic speaking villages as in Syria.

HISTORY

ANCIENT AND MEDIEVAL HISTORY

In the Ancient World the Lebanon was important for its pine, fir, and cedarwood, which neighbouring powers, poorly supplied with timber resources, coveted so much that during the long period of Egyptian, Assyrian, Persian, and Seleucid rule, the exploitation of the forests of the Lebanon was normally a royal privilege. The area was also mined for its iron and copper in the time of the Ptolemies and the Romans. Gradually the Lebanon came to have a distinct history of its own, for the mountainous character of the region prevented any complete subjugation to outside authority. It is probable that the Arab conquest of Syria did not include the "Mountain", to which fled all those who, for one reason or another, were opposed to the Arab domination. The Caliph Mu'awiya (661–80) made some effort to assert a greater control, but the resistance of the native Aramaean Christians was reinforced by the arrival of the Mardaites from the fastnesses of the Taurus and the Amanus. These Christian nomads, led by Byzantine officers, made determined advances into the Lebanon, late in the seventh century, and seem to have united with the Maronite Christians who were later to become a Uniate Church of the Roman communion and to have a predominant role in the history of the Lebanon. The Caliph Abd al-Malik (685–705) paid tribute to Byzantium in return for a withdrawal of most of the Mardaite forces; but it is clear that the "Mountain" had begun to assume its historic function of providing a sure refuge for racial and religious minorities.

The Lebanon maintained its Christian character until the ninth century when, amongst other elements, the Arab

tribe of Tanukh established a principality in the region of al-Gharb, near Beirut, and acted as a counterpoise to the Maronites of the North Lebanon, and as a bulwark against Byzantine threats from the sea. Gradually, Islam and, more slowly still, the Arabic language penetrated the "Mountain" where, however, Syriac lingered on in the Maronite districts until the seventeenth century (it is still spoken in three villages of the Anti-Lebanon). In the ninth and tenth centuries Muslim sects began to take root in the "Mountain" as, for example, the Shi'i, known in the Lebanon under the name of Mitwali and, in the eleventh century, the Druze faith, which won a firm hold in the South Lebanon.

The Crusaders established in this area the County of Tripolis and the lordships of Gibelet and Batron which enjoyed considerable support from the Christian population of the North Lebanon and were protected by a network of fortresses, the most famous of which is Hisn al-Akrad (Crac des Chevaliers). In the Mamluk period the rulers of the Lebanon continued to practise the art of political manoeuvring, thus maintaining for themselves a considerable degree of autonomy. The Tanukhid Amirs, after a long period in which they had played off the Crusaders against the Muslim amirates, had eventually taken the Mamluk side. In the North Lebanon the Maronites, under their bishop, maintained contact with the Italian Republics and also with the Roman Curia. Less fortunate were the Druzes and the Mitwali who, in the last years of the thirteenth century, took advantage of the Mamluk preoccupation with the Mongol threat from Persia and began a protracted revolt which led to widespread devastation in the Central Lebanon.

THE OTTOMAN PERIOD

In the sixteenth century the Turcoman family of Assaf and, after them, the Banu Saifa rose to prominence in the area from Beirut to the north of Tripoli; while in the south the Druze house of Ma'an supplanted the Tanukhid Amirs. After the conquest of 1516–17, the Ottoman Sultan Selim I had confirmed the amirs of the Lebanon in their privileges and had imposed only a small tribute; yet not infrequently there was open conflict with the Ottomans, as in 1584–5 when, after an attack on a convoy bearing the tribute from Egypt to Constantinople, the Sultan Murad III sent a punitive expedition to ravage the lands of the Banu Saifa and of the Druzes.

The power of the House of Ma'an now reached its zenith in the person of Fakhr ad-din II (1586–1635), who by every possible means—bribery, intrigue, foreign alliance, and open force—set out to establish an independent power over the whole of the Lebanon and parts of Palestine to the south. To this end he entered into close relations with the Grand Duke of Tuscany, negotiating in 1608 a commercial agreement which contained a secret military clause directed against the Sultan. In 1613 a naval and military expedition sent from the Porte compelled Fakhr ad-din to seek refuge with his Tuscan ally; but, returning in 1618, he rapidly restored his power and within a few years was virtual ruler from Aleppo to the borders of Egypt. The Sultan, heavily engaged in repressing revolt in Anatolia, and in waging a long struggle with Persia, could do no more than recognize the *fait accompli*. Fakhr ad-din now embarked on an ambitious programme of development for the Lebanon. He sought to equip a standing army with arms imported from Tuscany. Italian engineers and agricultural experts were employed to promote a better cultivation of the land and to increase the production of silk and olives. The Christian peasantry were encouraged to move from the North to the South Lebanon. Beirut and Sidon flourished as a result of the favour he showed to commerce, and religious missions from Europe—Capuchins, Jesuits, Carmelites—were allowed to settle throughout Syria, a development of great importance for France which strove to assert a "protectorate" over all the Catholic and other Christian elements in the Ottoman Empire. However, the ambitions of Fakhr ad-din were doomed to failure when by 1632 the Sultan Murad IV assumed effective control at Constantinople. The Pasha of Damascus, supported by a naval squadron, began a campaign to end the independent power of the Lebanon, and in 1635 Fakhr ad-din was executed at Constantinople.

In 1697, the Ma'an family became extinct, and was succeeded by the House of Shihab, which maintained its predominance until 1840. In the course of the eighteenth century, the Shihab Amirs gradually consolidated their position against the other factions of the "Mountain" and for a while recovered control of Beirut. While normally they took care to remain on good terms with the Turkish Pashas of Tripoli, Sidon and Damascus, the Pashas, for their part, strove to exercise an indirect control by fomenting the family rivalries and religious differences which always marked the course of Lebanese politics. With the advent of Bashir II (1788–1840) the House of Shihab attained the height of its influence. Not until the death of Ahmed Jazzar, Pasha of Acre (1804), was he free to develop his power, which he maintained by the traditional methods of playing off one Pasha against the other, and by bribing the officials of the Porte whenever it seemed expedient. In 1810 he helped the Ottomans to repel an invasion by the Wahhabi power of Arabia; but in 1831 he sided openly with Muhammad Ali of Egypt, when that ruler invaded Syria. Holding the Lebanon as the vassal of Egypt, he was compelled, however, to apply to the "Mountain" the unpopular policy imposed by Ibrahim Pasha, the son of Muhammad Ali, with the result that a revolt broke out, which, after the Egyptian withdrawal of 1840, led to his exile. The age of the Lebanese Amirs was now at an end, for the Ottomans assumed control of the "Mountain", appointing two Kaimakams to rule there, one Druze and the other Maronite, under the supervision of the Pashas of Sidon and Beirut.

The period of direct Ottoman rule saw the rapid growth, between the Druzes and the Maronites, of a mistrust already visible during the time of the Egyptian dominance, and now fostered by the Ottomans as the only means of maintaining their influence over the Lebanon. As a result of social and economic discontent, due to the slow disintegration of the old feudal system which had existed in the Lebanon since the Middle Ages, the Maronite peasantry revolted in 1858 and destroyed the feudal privileges of the Maronite aristocracy, thus clearing the way for the creation of a system of independent smallholdings. The Druze aristocracy, fearing the consequences of a similar discontent among their own Maronite peasantry, made a series of attacks on the Maronites of the North Lebanon, who, owing to their own dissensions, could offer no effective resistance. The dubious attitude of the Turkish Pashas, in the face of these massacres of 1860, led to French intervention, and in 1864 to the formation of an organic statute for the Lebanon, which was now to become an autonomous province under a non-Lebanese Ottoman Christian governor, appointed by the Sultan and approved by the Great Powers. He was to be aided by an elected administrative council and a locally recruited police force. The statute also abolished legal feudalism in the area, thus consolidating the position won by the Maronite peasantry in 1858. The period from 1864 to 1914 was one of increasing prosperity, especially among the Christian elements, who also played an important role in the revival of Arab literature and Arab national feeling during the last years of the nineteenth century.

THE FRENCH MANDATE

The privileged position of the Lebanon ended when the Turks entered the war of 1914–18; and by 1918 the coastal areas of the Lebanon were occupied by British and French forces. In September 1920 the French created the State of the Greater Lebanon which included not only the former autonomous province but also Tripoli, Sidon, Tyre and Beirut, some of which had in earlier times been under the control of the Amirs of the Lebanon. The period from 1920–36 was for the Lebanon one of peaceful progress. A constitution was devised in 1926, which proved unworkable and was suspended in 1932, from which time the President of the Republic carried on the administration. He was, by convention, a Christian, while the Prime Minister was a Muslim, and both worked towards the achievement of a careful balance between the various religious communities of the new State. The Lebanon was not unaffected by the growth of the nationalist movement in Syria, some sections of which demanded the reduction of the Lebanon to its prewar limits and even the abolition of its existence as a separate State. These demands found some support amongst the Sunni Muslims of the areas added to the Lebanon proper in 1920, with the result that the Syrian revolt of 1925–26 spread to parts of the southern Lebanon. The Maronite Christians, on the whole, supported the idea of a separate Lebanon, but were not united in their attitude towards France on the one hand, and the Arab States on the other. The Franco-Lebanese Treaty of 1936 differed little from that which France negotiated at the same time with Syria, the chief difference being that the military convention gave France wider military powers in the Lebanon than in Syria. A reformed constitution was promulgated in 1937; but the French refusal to ratify the treaty in 1938, and the advent of war prolonged a situation which, if outwardly calm, concealed a considerable discontent beneath the surface. In November 1941 the Free French Commander, General Catroux, formally proclaimed the Lebanon a sovereign independent State. In September 1943 a new parliament which had a strong nationalist majority soon came into conflict with the French authorities over the transfer of the administrative services. When, in November 1943, the Lebanese Government insisted on passing legislation which removed from the constitution all provisions considered to be inconsistent with the independence of the Lebanon the French Delegate-General arrested the President and suspended the constitution. The other Arab States, together with Great Britain and America, supported the Lebanese demands and in 1944 France began to transfer to Lebanese control all important public services, save for the _Troupes Spéciales_, i.e. local levies under French command, whose transfer the French authorities at first made conditional on the signing of a Franco-Lebanese Treaty. But in 1945 the _Troupes Spéciales_ were handed over to the Lebanon without such conditions, and an agreement between France and the Lebanese Government in 1946 provided for the withdrawal of French troops.

MODERN HISTORY

Since 1946 the Lebanon has continued to view with great reserve all projects for a Greater Syria, or for the union of Syria and Iraq. Like the other Arab States, the Lebanon was at war with the new State of Israel from May 1948; but negotiated an armistice in March 1949. Just as in Syria the ill-success of the Arab arms had led eventually to the _coup d'état_ of March 1949, so in the Lebanon the widespread disillusionment of Arab nationalist hopes prepared the ground for a conspiracy against the Government. This conspiracy was easily suppressed in June 1949 and its leader, Antun Sa'ade, was executed.

In internal affairs, the Lebanese Government had to face considerable economic and financial difficulties soon after the end of the 1939-45 war. When, in January 1948, France devalued the franc (to which both the Lebanese and the Syrian currencies were linked) the Lebanon, economically weaker than Syria, felt obliged to sign a new agreement with France (February 1948). Syria refused to do so and began a long and complicated dispute with the Lebanon over the precise nature of the economic and financial arrangements which were to exist between the two States. In March 1950 the Lebanese Government refused a Syrian demand for full economic and financial union between Syria and the Lebanon. The severance of economic relations which now ensued did not end until the signing, in February 1952, of an agreement which arranged for the division of royalties due from oil companies, and for the status, for customs purposes, of agricultural and industrial products passing between the two states.

In September 1952 the Lebanon had to face a severe crisis in her internal affairs. Political and economic unrest brought about the fall of the Lebanese Government and the resignation of President al-Khuri, who had held office since 1943. Charges of corruption were made against the President. During his long tenure of power he had indeed used all the arts of political influence and manoeuvre in order to impose a real degree of unity on a state where the divergent interests of Maronites, Sunni and Shi'a Muslims, Druzes, and other religious communities underlined the need for firm and coherent rule.

To an even greater degree, however, the crisis was due to causes of an economic order. The Lebanon had attained its independence in the period of war-time prosperity. The end of the war meant a progressive dimunition of foreign

expenditure in the Lebanon, and the gradual disappearance of war shortages which had favoured Lebanese trade. The devaluation of the French franc, the unsuccessful war with Israel, and above all the economic rupture with Syria gave rise to further difficulties. The break with Syria hit the Lebanon hard, for Syria was the chief provider of agricultural goods to the Lebanon and the chief customer for Lebanese industrial products. By 1952 there was much discontent arising from the high cost of living and from considerable unemployment. It was in fact a loose coalition of all the elements of opposition, both political and economic, which brought about the fall of the al-Khuri regime.

CONSTITUTIONAL REFORM

As a result of the crisis Camille Chamoun became the new President of the Republic. The new administration, with the Amir Khalid Chehab as Prime Minister, bound itself to introduce reforms, including changes in the electoral laws, the grant of the vote to women, revision of the Press laws and the reorganization of justice. The elections held in July 1953 led to the formation of a Chamber of Deputies, 44 in number and divided as follows: 13 Maronites, 9 Sunni Muslims, 8 Shi'a Muslims, 5 Orthodox Christians, 3 Greek Catholics, 3 Druzes, 2 Orthodox Armenians and one member for other minorities.

The elections held in the Lebanon during the summer of 1953 were carried out under the provisions of the electoral law of November 1952. Since the foundation of the republic, all seats in the Chamber of Deputies had been distributed among the various religious communities in proportion to their numerical strength. Parliament was thus an institution reflecting in itself the religious and social structure of the state and capable of harmonious function, provided that the electoral system which maintained a delicate balance between the communities suffered no violent and prejudicial change. At the same time, it contained a strong "feudal" element—the tribal and religious leaders who, with their trusted retainers, formed powerful groups within the Parliament and were often criticised as being "anti-national" in their aims and methods. To end or at least weaken this "feudalization" of Lebanese political life, without, however, impairing the vital equilibrium between the Muslim and Christian communities, had long been the purpose of those who advocated a reasonable and well-considered policy of reform. The law of 1952 created 33 electoral districts (during the previous life of the republic the number had been, as a rule, five) and allotted to eleven of them two seats, and to the remainder one seat each. Of the sum-total of 44 seats the Maronites were now to receive 13, the Sunni Muslims 9, the Shi'a Muslims 8, the Greek Orthodox Christians 5, the Druzes 3, the Greek Catholics 3, the Armenian Catholics 2 and the other confessions (Protestant, Jewish, Nestorian, etc.) 1 seat.

FOREIGN RELATIONS 1953-56

In the period 1953–56 financial and economic relations with Syria remained on a provisional basis much the same as that which had prevailed in the years 1950–53, earlier short-term arrangements being renewed from time to time, as need arose. Discussions with Syria in November 1953 over problems of currency, loan policy, banks and exchange difficulties made no effective progress. The Lebanese Government was more successful, however, in its efforts to promote internal development. It was announced in August 1955 that the International Bank had granted to the Lebanon a loan of 27 million dollars for the Litani river scheme which, when completed, was expected to more than double the electric power available within the republic and also to irrigate a large acreage in the coastal region. The Lebanon signed a number of commercial treaties at this time, which bore witness to the growing penetration of the Eastern bloc into Arab lands.

At the Asian-African conference held at Bandung in April 1955 the Lebanese delegates expressed themselves in terms unfavourable to Communism. Since that time the Beirut government has not allowed its relations with Russia and her allies to pass beyond the limits of normal commercial intercourse.

THE EISENHOWER DOCTRINE

A state of emergency was declared in the Lebanon during the Sinai-Suez crisis at the end of October 1956. The Chamber of Deputies announced its support of Egypt, but the Lebanon did not break off diplomatic relations with Great Britain and France. In November there were disturbances, however, at Tripoli and Beirut against the attitude of the Government. Reports issued at this time intimated that the Egyptian military attaché at Beirut had been implicated in the recent disorders. The "Eisenhower Doctrine", a new programme, made known in January 1957, of financial, economic and military aid by the United States to those countries of the Middle East which were prepared to accept it, evoked a favourable response in Lebanese official circles. The Foreign Minister of the Lebanon declared that the Government was willing to collaborate closely with the U.S.A. in the implementation of the programme. During the visit to Beirut in March of Mr. Richards, special adviser to President Eisenhower on Middle Eastern affairs, it was announced that the Lebanon would co-operate with the United States in the task of opposing the growth of communist influence in the area and would receive, under the new programme, assistance to the amount of some 20 million dollars. The United States was also to help in the strengthening of the Lebanese armed forces. Some of the political groups in the Lebanon protested against this pro-Western alignment, asserting that it could not fail to isolate the Lebanon from the other Arab states and thus impair Arab solidarity. None the less, in April, the Government obtained from the Chamber of Deputies a vote of confidence in its policies.

The problem of electoral reform had been under consideration in the Lebanon in the course of 1956. The main proposal now to be given effect was that the number of seats in the Chamber of Deputies should be raised from 44 to 66. As election time drew near in the summer of 1957, riots occurred in Beirut, the government being compelled to call out troops for the maintenance of order. According to reports current at this time more than one hundred Communists were arrested for their share in the disturbances. The tense electoral campaign of June 1957 resulted in a marked triumph for the Government. A first provisional estimate suggested that it might count on the adherence of some three-quarters of the deputies in the new Chamber. Of the sum total of 66 seats the Maronites now received 20, the Sunni Muslims 14, the Shi'a Muslims 12, the Greek Orthodox Christians 7, the Druzes 4, the Greek Catholics 4, the Orthodox Armenians 3, the Armenian Catholics 1 and the other religious minorities (Protestants, Jews, etc.) also 1 seat.

It was announced in July 1957 that the Lebanon would receive from the United States, under the Eisenhower Doctrine, economic and military aid to the value of approximately 15 million dollars in the course of the fiscal year 1958. Military equipment granted under the Doctrine had in fact begun to reach Beirut in June 1957. The Lebanese Government reiterated in August 1957 its firm desire to continue co-operation with the United States.

There had been sharp disturbances in the Lebanon at the time of the elections held in June 1957. It became clear that unrest, especially among those elements of the population which opposed the pro-Western policies of the Lebanese Government and favoured an alignment with Egypt and Syria, was in no wise dead, when further incidents (bomb outrages, assassinations) occurred in November 1957. The Government, in its desire to halt these subversive activities, now imposed a close control over all Palestine refugees in the Lebanon. Indeed, after renewed outbreaks of violence in December, the northern area of the Lebanon was declared to be a military sector.

The Lebanese Government stated in March 1958 that it would not join the United Arab Republic (Egypt and Syria), the Arab Federation (Iraq and Jordan) or indeed any association which might limit its own independence and sovereignty. Large sections of the Muslim population, both in the north (at Tripoli) and in the south (at Tyre and Sidon), were inclined to be pro-Arab rather than pro-Lebanese in sentiment—a mood greatly stimulated by the emergence of the new United Arab Republic and by the propaganda emitted from Cairo and Damascus for the return to Syria of those predominantly Muslim areas which had been joined to the old Lebanon in the time of the French Mandate. There was conflict, too, between those who, although reluctant to see the Lebanon lose its separate political existence, were none the less strongly opposed to the pro-Western attitude of the Lebanese Government and those who, fearing the possible absorption of the Lebanon into the framework of a larger Arab state, felt themselves bound to support fully the policies of the Beirut regime. The danger was real that these complex tensions might explode in the form of a "confessional" conflict between Muslims and Christians, in which, if not the continued independence, then at least the entire political orientation of the Lebanon would be at stake.

THE CRISIS OF 1958

A reorganization of the Government, carried out in March 1958 and designed to remove certain members who were critical of the pro-Western policies of the Lebanon and favoured closer co-operation with the United Arab Republic, brought no relief to the grave situation then developing. Serious disturbances, originating in Tripoli and the northern areas adjacent to the Syrian border, broke out in the second week of May and spread rapidly to Beirut and also to Tyre and Sidon in the southern Lebanon. The Druze population in the south-east was involved, too, in the disorders, being sharply divided into pro- and anti-government factions. Hostile demonstrations led to the destruction of the United States Information Service centres at Tripoli and Beirut. At the request of the Lebanese Government, the United States agreed to dispatch in all haste supplies of arms and police equipment and decided at the same time to reinforce the American 6th Fleet stationed in the Mediterranean. The U.S.S.R. now accused the United States of interference in Lebanese affairs and declared that Western intervention might have grave consequences. The Lebanese Government itself charged the United Arab Republic with interference in its internal affairs and appealed for redress to the Arab League which, meeting at Benghazi in June, failed to agree on a course of action. The problem was now brought before the United Nations which resolved to send an Observer Corps to the Lebanon.

The Lebanese Government was now, in fact, confronted with a widespread insurrection, in which the Muslim elements in the population were ranged against the Christian elements. The forces opposed to the existing regime controlled parts of Beirut, Tripoli and Sidon, as well as large areas in the north and the south of the Lebanon. Attempts to negotiate a settlement led to no favourable result. The Prime Minister, Sami al-Sulh, gave an assurance that President Chamoun did not intend to ask

LEBANON

for a constitutional amendment which would enable him to seek re-election to his office in September 1958, the date when his present tenure of it was due to end. To this firm assurance the leaders of the insurrection replied with a firm demand for the immediate resignation of the President, who made it clear, however, that he would not relinquish his office until September.

On July 14th—the date of the *coup d'état* which led to a change of regime in Iraq—President Chamoun requested the United States to send American troops into the Lebanon to maintain security and preserve Lebanese independence. About 10,000 U.S. troops were sent to the Beirut area. The United States also made it known that action on the part of forces under the control of the United Arab Republic against American troops in the Lebanon might lead to most serious consequences. At this juncture, the U.S.S.R. and the Chinese People's Republic made strong protests against the American intervention and asked for the prompt withdrawal of the United States forces landed in the Lebanon. On August 18th, the United States gave a written undertaking to withdraw its troops, either at the request of the Lebanese Government, or in the event that the United Nations took appropriate measures to ensure the integrity and peace of the country. The UN General Assembly thereupon adopted a resolution, framed by its Arab members, which provided for the evacuation of American troops under the auspices of the United Nations and of the Arab League.

PRESIDENT CHEHAB, 1958-64

Meanwhile, the Lebanese Chamber of Deputies had, on July 31st, elected as the new President of State General Fuad Chehab, the Commander-in-Chief of the Lebanese Army—a choice supported by members from both sides involved in the internal conflict. He assumed office on September 23rd, in succession to President Chamoun and at once invited Rashid Karami, the leader of the insurgents at Tripoli, to become Prime Minister. An agreement was made on September 27th to the effect that the United States forces were to leave the Lebanon by the end of October.

In October 1959 the Lebanese Cabinet was increased from four to eight members, so that greater representation might be given to the various political groups. The Chamber of Deputies approved in April 1960 an Electoral Reform Bill, which imposed for the first time the principle of the secret ballot in Lebanese elections and also enlarged the Chamber itself from 66 to 99 deputies—a total figure that maintained the existing ratio (laid down in 1943) of six Christian to every five Muslim (including Druze) deputies in the Chamber. The Chamber was dissolved by the President of the Lebanon on May 5th, 1960, the government of Mr. Rashid Karami resigning nine days later. A general election was then held in four separate stages on June 12th, 19th and 26th and July 3rd, 1960.

The election took place in an atmosphere of complete calm, strict security measures being enforced throughout the various stages of the electoral process. In the new Chamber of Deputies there were 30 Maronite Christians, 20 Sunni Muslims, 19 Shi'a Muslims, 11 Greek Orthodox Christians, 6 Greek Catholics, 6 Druzes, 4 Armenian Orthodox Christians, 1 Armenian Catholic, 1 Protestant and 1 member representing other elements. A large number of the "rebel" personalities prominent in the events of 1958 and hitherto not seated in the Chamber were now returned as members.

A new government, under the leadership of Mr. Saeb Salam, took the oath of office on August 2nd, 1960. The Cabinet, which included several personalities active on one side or the other in the troubles of 1958, was prompt to reaffirm the traditional policies of non-expropriation, of minimal government intervention in private enterprise, of encouragement for private investment both foreign and domestic, and of currency convertibility. Economic trends during 1960 revealed that the Lebanon had recovered almost completely from the disturbances in 1958.

CABINET REFORM

It had come to be felt, since August 1960, that the Lebanese Cabinet, 18 members strong, was too large for the maintenance of an efficient administration and so, on May 22nd, 1961, the Prime Minister established a new Cabinet consisting of eight ministers only. Mr. Salam, as the result of a dispute with some members of his government, notable amongst them being Mr. Jumblatt, the Druze leader, who was Minister of Works and Planning, resigned his office on October 24th, 1961. Mr. Rashid Karami, a former Prime Minister, formed a new government on October 31st, 1961.

Military elements, acting in conjunction with civilians described as supporters of the extremist National Social Party, made an unsuccessful attempt, on December 31st, 1961, to overthrow the Lebanese government. The National Social Party was in fact the old Parti Populaire Syrien founded in the 1930s by Antoine Saadé with the aim of uniting several Arab States into a Greater Syria. Its current leader, Dr. Abdallah Saadé, was now arrested and the party itself dissolved by the Lebanese government on January 1st, 1962. The Lebanese government took firm action against all the elements suspected of implication in the revolt, and crushed it within a few days. During the next two years the Lebanese Government negotiated numerous commercial and economic agreements with both Eastern and Western countries.

On February 19th, 1964, the Cabinet led by Rashid Karami (which had held office for the last two years) resigned, after President Chehab had signed a decree dissolving the Chamber of Deputies (elected in 1960) and ordering elections to be held on four successive Sundays from April 5th, 1964 to May 3rd, 1964. A caretaker cabinet was appointed to supervise the elections for the new Chamber of Deputies.

PRESIDENT HÉLOU

General Chehab, whose six-year term of office as President of the Republic was due to end in September 1964, rejected all appeals that he should submit himself as a candidate for a second time. Even when the Chamber of Deputies passed a motion in favour of an amendment to the Constitution which would enable him to stand for a further term of office, General Chehab persisted (June 3rd, 1964) in his refusal. On August 18th, 1964, M. Charles Hélou, Minister of Education in the caretaker administration, succeeded General Chehab as President. M. Hélou pledged himself to follow the policies and reforms introduced under General Chehab.

On September 25th, 1964, Hussein Oweini, the Head of the caretaker Cabinet in office since February of that year, formed an administration at the request of President Hélou. The new administration aroused dissatisfaction, however, in the Chamber of Deputies, since, deriving from the Cabinet appointed originally to act as a caretaker during the period of the 1964 elections, it was in fact composed wholly of non-members of the Chamber. Having resigned on November 13th, 1964, Oweini now, on November 18th, 1964, gathered together a new cabinet which, save for himself and the Foreign Minister, consisted of members drawn from the Chamber of Deputies and reflected in itself all the main trends of opinion within the Chamber.

FOREIGN RELATIONS

On July 20th, 1965, the Prime Minister, Mr. Hussein Oweini, resigned. There had been much debate in the Chamber of Deputies about a proposed agreement to guarantee private American investment in the Lebanon against expropriation, war or revolution—an agreement construed in some political circles as giving to the United States a possible excuse for intervention, at need, in Lebanese affairs. On July 26th, Rashid Karami became the new Prime Minister, with nine Cabinet Ministers to assist him, all chosen from outside the Chamber of Deputies.

There was friction during the first months of 1965 between Federal Germany and the Arab States because of the decision by Bonn to enter into formal diplomatic relations with Israel. Anti-German demonstrations occurred at Tripoli and Beirut and on May 13th, 1965 the Lebanon broke off diplomatic relations with Federal Germany. In May 1965 Lebanon signed an agreement on trade and technical co-operation with the European Economic Community (EEC). There was some friction between Israel and the Lebanon over border incidents during the summer and autumn of 1965. Members of the Palestinian guerrilla organization, al-Fatah, raided into Israel, provoking Israeli reprisals against the Lebanese village of Noule.

FINANCIAL CRISIS

Rashid Karami modified his cabinet in December 1965 and January 1966, these changes arising from difficulties which hindered the full implementation of an administrative and judicial reform programme, one of the main advocates of which was President Hélou. Between December 1965 and March 1966 an estimated 150 officials including 100 civil servants were compelled to withdraw from public life. This sustained attempt to curb corruption and the abuse of office in government circles and to ensure efficient and honest administration inevitably caused considerable tension. There was strong pressure in the Chamber of Deputies for a return to a cabinet chosen mainly from the Chamber itself. This and other difficulties obliged Karami to offer his resignation to President Hélou who appointed Dr. Abdallah al-Yafi as the new Premier.

Dr. al-Yafi assembled a ten-man Cabinet drawn entirely from the Chamber of Deputies with the exception of himself and M. Philippe Takla, the new Foreign Minister. The constitution of the cabinet represented a balance between the various religious interests and, from the point of view of politics, between the left-wing and right-wing elements in the Chamber of Deputies.

In October 1966 the Intra Bank of the Lebanon was compelled to close its doors because of a run of withdrawals amounting to more than £11 million in the preceding month. One result of that financial crisis was that the Government resolved to discourage the creation of new commercial banks, foreign or Lebanese, for a period of five years. Hitherto there had been an almost complete freedom to establish new banks in the Lebanon and there had been a large expansion of the banking system based on the flow into the Lebanon of vast oil revenues from Saudi Arabia and from the states of the Persian Gulf.

On December 2nd the Prime Minister of the Lebanon Dr. Abdullah al-Yafi, offered the resignation of his government to President Hélou. Mr. Rashid Karami formed a new administration on December 7th, 1966. It was composed of men drawn from outside Parliament, six of whom held ministerial posts for the first time.

In June 1967 the Lebanese Government aligned itself with the Arab states then engaged in war against Israel. On June 8th the Government asked the Ambassadors of Britain and the U.S.A. to leave the Lebanon. Pro-Egyptian demonstrations at Beirut in June caused some damage to British and American properties there. Some trouble was also reported from Tripoli, where a West German cultural centre was subjected to attack. However, the months following the war witnessed a gradual easing of the tensions arising out of the conflict, and in September 1967 the Lebanese Cabinet agreed to reinstate its ambassadors in Washington and London.

POLITICAL INSTABILITY

Rashid Karami's Cabinet resigned from office in February 1968. President Hélou then asked Dr. Abdallah al-Yafi to form an interim administration, whose main task was to be the preparation and conduct of the general election in March 1968. The two most successful parties elected in the Chamber of Deputies were the Maronite-dominated Triple Alliance, of a right-wing complexion, and the Democratic Block aligned further to the left. However, Dr. al-Yafi's interim administration remained in office until October, when it was forced to resign, owing to bitter rivalry between the two main political groups, the "Chamounists" and the "Chehabists" (both named after former Presidents), disputes over sectional representation in the Cabinet, and the Government's inability to command a majority in the Chamber of Deputies. After a week of confusion, a new four-man government was announced on October 20th, still headed by Dr. al-Yafi.

THE GUERRILLAS AND ISRAEL

May 1968 had seen the first clash between Lebanese and Israeli forces on the border for over two years. But as the activities of the Palestinian guerrillas increased, so the Lebanon became more and more the scapegoat for Israel's grievances against the Palestinians. On December 26th an Israeli airliner was machine-gunned by Arab guerrillas at Athens airport. Two days later Israeli commandos raided Beirut airport and destroyed thirteen aircraft, all belonging to Lebanese lines. Israel said the raid should be seen as a reprisal for the Athens attack, a warning to the Arab world not to make any repetition of it, and a further warning to the Lebanon to police the activities of the *fedayeen* movement in the country more effectively. The financial cost to the Lebanon was relatively small as most were insured abroad. The major after-effects of the raid were, firstly, the widespread criticism it attracted even from countries normally favourable to Israel. The Lebanon was seen as a country which had taken little active part in the campaign against Israel, while the *fedayeen* within it were only enjoying the freedom available to them in Lebanon's open, tolerant society. The UN Security Council unanimously condemned Israel for the raid. The second effect was the fall of the Government on January 7th, 1969, its alleged lack of preparedness for Israeli aggression being the final blow to bring down a weak administration. After much political manoeuvring, a new ministry was formed on January 20th headed by Mr. Rashid Karami, Prime Minister for the seventh time.

This Government was immediately confronted with the basic problems underlying the Lebanese situation. Foremost among these is the Christian-Muslim balance; in theory both religions are equally represented in the Lebanon, but no census has been held since 1939 mainly because the authorities fear that the balance has shifted to a 60 per cent Muslim predominance, which would seriously affect the political situation. The Christian community has a disproportionate share of the wealth and important positions and is generally conservative by Arab standards and takes a moderate position on the Israel question. The less privileged Arab majority is more in favour of both domestic reform (Lebanon has, for example, only the beginnings of a welfare state) and of a more militant position towards Israel. Early in 1969 numbers of Syrian guerrillas entered the country and apparently spent as much time in action against the Lebanese army as against Israel. Unrest also appeared amongst the 260,000 Palestinian refugees in the Sidon camp; part of the frontier with Syria was eventually closed. Numerous strikes and demonstrations continued. The Karami Government felt unable to maintain the necessary coalition from the two communities and their various factions and resigned on April 25th, but it continued to function as a caretaker administration as no stronger government could be formed.

In the late summer of 1969 a number of guerrilla groups were reported to have moved to new bases better sited for attacks on Israel, which continued to raid these bases in reprisal; the combination of these factors created some friction between the guerrillas and the Lebanese army. In October the army apparently attacked some of these camps in an attempt to restrict or direct their activities. This triggered off a crisis in which the caretaker Government resigned, claiming that it had not authorized the army's actions, and the President and the armed forces administered the country directly. Radical elements and guerrillas took over Tripoli, the second largest city, for several days, and most of the Palestinian refugee camps became fully converted into military training and equipment centres. Militant support for the guerrillas was voiced throughout the Arab world, and there were threats of military intervention by Syria and Iraq.

On November 2nd the Lebanese Commander-in-Chief and Yasser Arafat, the leader of al-Fatah, signed a ceasefire agreement in Cairo. This limited the guerrilla freedom of movement to certain areas; as further defined in January 1970, it also provided that camps had to be set up some distance from towns, that military training must cease in refugee camps, and that guerrillas must enter Israel before starting to shoot. The intention was not to prevent guerrilla attacks, but to stop innocent Lebanese getting hurt, or their property being damaged, by Israeli counter-attacks.

The calmer atmosphere that followed the ceasefire enabled Mr. Karami to form another cabinet towards the end of November. There was much concern about the weakness of the country's southern defences, and in January 1970 the new ministry felt strong enough to fire the Commander-in-Chief, appointing instead Brigadier Jean Njeim. In March there was a series of street battles in the Beirut area between the Palestinian guerrillas and militant right wing Falangist groups, but the Government and the army managed to avoid becoming involved. In May, Israel launched a major air and ground attack on guerrilla positions in southern Lebanon, a substantial area being occupied for nearly two days. Syria sent air assistance for the small Lebanese air force.

POLITICAL CRISES

Sulaiman Franjiya was elected President in August 1970, and a new cabinet was formed by Saeb Salam. Some measures of political liberalization, such as the relaxation of press, radio and television censorship and the removal of the ban on extremist parties did little to curb domestic unrest. Strikes and demonstrations against unemployment and inflation, student disorders and fighting between Phalangists and the Parti Populaire Syrien continued throughout 1971. The parliamentary elections of April 1972 produced a marked swing towards left-wing political groups.

The Palestinian guerrillas remained Lebanon's major problem. Their bases in the refugee camps became more important following the expulsion of the guerrillas from Jordan in July 1971, and guerrilla operations against Israel produced violent Israeli reprisals in which both Palestinians and Lebanese suffered. The villages of southern Lebanon bore the brunt of Israeli raids, and their inhabitants secured a greater measure of Lebanese army control over guerrilla activities in March 1972. Arab terrorist actions still produced Israeli reprisals against Lebanon, even when there was little connection between the terrorists and Israel's vulnerable northern neighbour. The killing of Israeli athletes at the Olympic Games in Munich in September 1972 led to Israeli ground and air attacks on guerrilla bases, in which the Lebanese army suffered a number of casualties. The Lebanese Government was unable to persuade the guerrillas to suspend their activities against Israel, and several clashes between the Lebanese army and the guerrillas occurred.

In February 1973 Israeli commandos attacked guerrilla training bases in refugee camps about 100 miles north of the Lebanese frontier, and escaped virtually unopposed. A further Israeli raid, in which three guerrilla leaders were shot in their homes in the centre of Beirut, and an attempt to blow up oil storage tanks at the Zahrani terminal, attributed to Palestinian extremists, resulted in the fall of the Salam Government. Mr. Salam resigned, dissatisfied with the inability of the Lebanese armed forces to prevent an Israeli military action in the capital, and Dr. Amin Hafez formed a new government. Several members of the Salam cabinet remained in office, the new Government including representatives of most of the major political and religious groups.

Tension between the Lebanese army and the guerrillas culminated in May 1973 in Lebanese ground and air attacks on the refugee camps. An invasion by guerrillas based in Syria was repulsed and a ceasefire was brought about by the mediation of other Arab states. The guerrillas apparently agreed to remove heavy weapons from the refugee camps, to stop their terrorist activities within Lebanon and to cease using the camps as bases for training guerrillas.

The Hafez Government lasted only seven weeks. The Prime Minister resigned on June 14th, unable to settle the Sunni Muslim claim for a greater share in the allocation of government posts, and it was not until July 8th that Takieddin Solh was able to form a new ministry. A moderate, Mr. Solh enjoyed the support of many Sunni factions, and his cabinet included representatives of all the main religious blocs. Outside Parliament, however, violent disorders continued, with industrial disputes and the claims of tobacco growers, for instance, resulting in demonstrations and clashes with police. The Phalange party maintained training camps for its own militia, and the danger of the formation of private armies became apparent.

The potential religious hostility within Lebanon, and the political implications of the division of government and administrative posts on a confessional basis were again demonstrated in February 1974. Civil service reforms, intended to overcome the sectarian nature of certain appointments, were opposed by Maronites who feared that they would lose posts traditionally reserved to their community. The National Liberal Party threatened to withdraw its three cabinet members, and the proposed reforms were also condemned by the Phalange and the Bloc National. The Shi'a Muslims of southern Lebanon also made demands for increased representation and more investment and development in the south. The Shi'a leader, Imam Moussa as-Sadr, implied that he would organize his followers and arm them as protection against Israeli raids, which he later did.

Although Lebanon was not directly involved in the

October 1973 Arab-Israeli war, southern regions had continued to serve as a guerrilla base and to suffer Israeli reprisals. Southern villages were shelled intermittently, and small-scale raids across the border and acts of terrorism became commonplace. In the first six months of 1974 there were three notable Israeli attacks on Lebanese targets, each following guerrilla outrages in Israel, despite Lebanese denials that the terrorists involved came from Lebanon.

In July there were clashes between Palestinians and Phalangists who continued to demand more government controls on guerrilla activities. Throughout 1974 and into 1975 Israeli shelling, air raids and incursions into Lebanon continued, together with guerrilla attacks against the Israelis. Consequently the situation on the border remained tense. In September 1974, unable to curb internal sectarian violence by its ineffective ban on the possession of fire-arms, Takieddin Solh's cabinet resigned. In October a new government was formed under Rashid Solh though violence continued, finally erupting in a bloody clash between troops and citizens of the port of Sidon. The Cabinet split amid the granting of a Muslim demand to confer citizenship to long-time residents of the country. Letter bomb and dynamite explosions and further border fighting between the Israelis and guerrilla groups were followed by further fierce conflict between the Phalangists and Palestinians, in which over 150 died and 300 were wounded. Much damage was caused in Beirut and, after an agreement by Solh to normalize relations with the Palestinians and the fact that the security forces had not intervened in the fighting, the Phalangists appeared to be on the defensive.

CIVIL WAR

Intercommunal strife had never been far from the surface in Lebanon (*see* under The Guerrillas and Israel, p. 562). An incident in April 1975, when Palestinians made an attack on some Phalangists, led to the Phalangists killing the passengers of a bus, who were mainly Palestinians. From this incident inter-communal fighting between Christians and Muslims quickly spread, and continued, with short interruptions, until October 1976. At this point the official policy of the PLO under Yasser Arafat was to stand aloof from the conflict and Arafat himself was in fact instrumental in securing some of the many ceasefires.

In May 1975, shortly after the fighting began, Rashid Solh resigned as Prime Minister, and was replaced by Rashid Karami, who continued as Prime Minister through an exceedingly turbulent period until December 1976. In September 1975 a National Dialogue Committee was formed, consisting of 20 members from all political and confessional groups, to try to restore "normal life"—a task in which they were unsuccessful. By October 1975 there was evident dissatisfaction with President Franjiya and his inability to bring the fighting to an end, and it also became increasingly evident that in spite of the official policy of the PLO not to interfere in the internal affairs of the Lebanon, members of extremist Palestinian groups, particularly those of the "rejectionist front", were being drawn into the fighting on the side of the Muslims. It was also, at this point, the official policy of the Lebanese army not to intervene, although later, breakaway groups became involved in the fighting.

By the middle of January 1976 the PLO was becoming increasingly drawn into the conflict, and several Syrian-based units of the Palestine Liberation Army were in Lebanon fighting on the side of the Muslims. Under these increasingly ominous conditions the term of the Chamber of Deputies was extended by a year (later increased to two years) and the general elections scheduled for April 1976 were postponed for up to 26 months. In January 1978 the Chamber's term was extended until June 1980. In March

1979 the Chamber was renamed the National Assembly and in April 1980 its term was further extended to the middle of 1983.

A temporary ceasefire gave a brief respite in January 1976, but by March no agreement had been reached on political reforms, fighting had flared up again, and 70 deputies signed a petition asking President Franjiya to resign. Further weight was given to this request in April when a parliamentary session took place and 90 deputies voted unanimously to amend Article 73 of the Constitution to allow Presidential elections to be held up to 6 months before the expiry of the present incumbent's term of office. President Franjiya signed this amendment on April 23rd but, in spite of the election of his successor, refused to resign until the completion of his term of office in September 1976, when he was succeeded by Elias Sarkis, who had been Governor of the Central Bank.

INCREASED SYRIAN INTERVENTION

By May 1976 Syria was becoming increasingly involved in Lebanese affairs. By May 20th it was estimated that about 40,000 Syrian-controlled troops were in Lebanon. Yasser Arafat had ordered pro-Damascus Palestinian units to withdraw, and it now became clear that Arafat and the PLO had become entirely sympathetic to the Lebanese left wing. In early June Syria launched a full-scale invasion of Lebanon officially to end the civil war and restore peace, but unofficially, it became clear, to crush the Palestinians. The conflict threatened to grow to world proportions and an emergency meeting of the Arab foreign ministers met in Cairo under the sponsorship of the Arab League. It was agreed to send a joint Arab peace-keeping force to Lebanon and it was agreed that the introduction of the Arab peace-keeping force should be accompanied by a phased, but not complete, withdrawal of Syrian troops. The Arab peace-keeping force was to include participants from Syria, Libya, Algeria, Sudan, Saudi Arabia and the Palestine Liberation Organization, under an Egyptian Commander-in-Chief, General Muhammad Hassan Ghoneim, but by the end of June 1976 the 1,000-man force was made up of 500 Syrian troops merely under a different guise, and 500 Libyans. Meanwhile, fierce fighting broke out in the area of two Palestinian refugee camps, Tal al Zaatar and Jisr al Basha, and most of Beirut was without water or electricity. The Arab League took steps to hasten the arrival of further contingents of the peace-keeping force, and the Secretary-General, Mahmoud Riad, headed another mediation mission, but fighting continued unabated until October 1976, when Arab summit meetings in Riyadh and Cairo secured a lasting cease-fire. During the course of the fighting there had been more than 50 abortive cease-fires and it was estimated that up to 60,000 people had been killed and up to 100,000 injured.

The Riyadh and Cairo summits arranged for a 30,000-strong Arab Deterrent Force (mainly Syrians) to police the Lebanon, and a four-party disengagement committee was set up to attempt to implement the terms of the 1969 Cairo agreement between the Lebanese Government and the Palestine guerrillas, as this was considered to be one of the keys to a lasting peace. The disengagement committee consisted of Col. Muhammad Khouli (Syria), Abdel-Hamid Buaijan (the Kuwaiti Ambassador in Beirut), General Ali al-Shaer (Saudi Arabian Ambassador in Beirut), and Ahmad Loutfi Moutawalli, the Egyptian Ambassador in Beirut. The committee began by scaling down the level of heavy weapons allowed to the various factions, and then tried to find agreement on the proportion of armed men allowed in the Palestinian guerrilla camps. The Shtoura Agreement of July 1977 provided an attempted settlement of this problem, by endeavouring to regulate the Palestinian base camps and introduce a reconstituted Lebanese army into the border area.

In December 1976 President Sarkis appointed Dr. Selim Hoss as Prime Minister, who formed a cabinet of eight "technocrats" charged with rebuilding and reconstruction, and the Government was granted the power to rule by decree for six months, subsequently extended. A Reconstruction and Development Council was set up under the chairmanship of Muhammad Atalla, and this Council took over the functions of the former Ministry of Planning. In January 1977 censorship was imposed on the press, initially both on Lebanese and foreign journalists, but the restrictions on foreign despatches were soon lifted.

The Druze chief and leader of the Lebanese left, Kamal Jumblatt, was assassinated by unknown gunmen on March 16th, 1977. Although his murder was followed by a wave of "revenge" killings, it did not lead to any renewed outbreak of major fighting. The southern area of Lebanon, however, between the Litani river and the Israeli border, became the scene of renewed fighting during 1977. This area was largely spared during the civil war and fighting developed when the Palestinians moved to the hills of south Lebanon after being subdued by the Syrians in the civil war. A war "by proxy" developed, with Syria allied with the Palestine guerrillas and Israel supporting the Lebanese Government. The Shtoura Agreement in July 1977, and a later ceasefire in September 1977, arranged with the intervention of the U.S.A., was ineffective.

The precarious situation flared up in March 1978 as a result of a raid by Fatah guerrillas into Israel on March 11th, when a bus was attacked near Tel-Aviv in which more than 35 people were killed. As a retaliation, and to prevent further raids, Israeli forces advanced into southern Lebanon three days later. The UN Security Council called for an Israeli withdrawal and set up a United Nations Interim Force in Lebanon (UNIFIL) of 6,000 to maintain peace in the area. Israeli forces withdrew from southern Lebanon in June 1978 but handed over to a right-wing, mainly Christian Lebanese militia who maintained links with the Israelis.

In July 1978 fighting flared up again in Beirut between the Syrian troops of the Arab Deterrent Force and right-wing Christian militias. A ceasefire was proclaimed in early October and the Foreign Ministers of the Arab Deterrent Force states (Kuwait, Lebanon, Qatar, Saudi Arabia, Sudan, Syria and the U.A.E.) met at Beiteddin, near Beirut, and agreed on a Declaration which they hoped would bring peace to the area. It maintained that Lebanese central authority must be imposed, armed militias must be curbed and a truly national army must be formed.

LEBANON AFTER THE BEITEDDIN DECLARATION

The aims of the Beiteddin Declaration have not been realized. In April 1979 Major Saad Haddad, a right-wing Lebanese army officer, proclaimed "independent free Lebanon"—a 700 square mile slice of territory next to the Israeli border. Encouraged and supplied by Israel, he continues to maintain his independence. In July 1980 the Phalangist Commander, Bashir Gemayel, consolidated his power by overcoming the militia of the National Liberal Party. This led to a strengthening of the Phalangist militia, with the result that Phalangist forces occupied the town of Zahle in the Beka'a valley. In April 1981 fighting developed between Syrian troops and Christian militias in the Beirut area, and Syrian and Palestinian forces besieged Zahle. Syria maintained that Zahle and the Beka'a valley were essential for the security and defence of Syria against Israel, whereas the Phalangist forces would have liked the removal of Syrian forces from Lebanon.

During the remainder of April Israeli forces made frequent raids into southern Lebanon and Israeli aircraft strafed Palestinian guerrilla targets. When, at the beginning of May, two Syrian helicopters were destroyed by Israeli planes, Syria introduced SAM surface-to-air missiles into the Beka'a valley. Although it was thought that Israeli planes already had the capacity to withstand the outdated SAM missiles, the Israeli Prime Minister, Mr. Begin, took up a very belligerent stance and threatened to destroy the SAM missiles. An international crisis developed but on June 30th Syrian forces lifted the siege on Zahle, after mediation by the Saudi and Kuwaiti Ambassadors to the Lebanon. Regular troops of the Lebanese army then took up positions in the town, as the Phalangist militia move out. The U.S. Middle East peace envoy, Mr. Philip Habib, was able to arrange a ceasefire which became effective on July 24th, 1981.

The Lebanese Government has not been able to exert its authority. In July 1979 the Prime Minister, Dr. Hoss, introduced a Cabinet of 12 members, seven of whom were Deputies, to replace the government of eight technocrats which had been in office since December 1976. In April 1980 the National Assembly voted for its life to be extended by three years to June 30th, 1983, rather than the 18 months' extension which the Government would have preferred. President Sarkis has been trying to formulate a national accord. On March 5th he issued a message to the nation which reiterated his policy for the future: the unity, independence and sovereignty of the whole territory; total opposition to mini-states and militias; allegiance to parliamentary democracy; acknowledgement that Lebanon is an Arab country; rejection of the Camp David agreements; support for a future Palestinian State; co-operation with Syria; and support for UN Lebanon resolutions.

At the beginning of June 1980 the Prime Minister, Dr. Selim Hoss, offered his resignation on the grounds that no progress had been made towards this accord. He felt that a new Government was necessary to achieve national unity. The resignation was held in abeyance for more than a month, but on July 16th President Sarkis accepted Hoss's resignation, requesting him to stay on in a caretaker capacity. On July 20th Sarkis appointed Takieddin Solh as Prime Minister, but he soon resigned, being unable to form a government, and it was not until October 1980 that Chafic al-Wazzan was able to form a Cabinet.

In the spring of 1982, infringements of the ceasefire which had been imposed the previous July became more frequent, and Israeli air raids on Palestinian and Syrian targets in Lebanon gave rise to the view that a full-scale attack by Israel was imminent. It appeared that this course of action was being urged by the Israeli Minister of Defence, Ariel Sharon, and the Israeli Chief of Staff, Lt.-Gen. Rafael Eitan. It was certainly the wish of Major Saad Haddad in southern Lebanon, who in early June called for a quick decisive Israeli strike against what he claimed was a build-up of Palestinian forces. The attempted assassination of the Israeli Ambassador in London on June 3rd ended Israel's hesitation. Although the PLO officially denied responsibility for the attempted assassination, Israeli forces quickly moved into southern Lebanon.

By the beginning of July, Israeli forces had surrounded West Beirut, where approximately 6,000 PLO fighters were trapped. Negotiations were in progress between the PLO, Philip Habib, the Israelis and various Lebanese leaders for the departure of the PLO from Lebanon (for later details, see *Late Information* at the front of this volume). Prime Minister Chafic al-Wazzan had tendered his resignation.

ECONOMIC SURVEY

Lebanon, for long the commercial and financial centre of the Middle East, was brought to a standstill in 1975–76 by nineteen months of civil war. This was not the first civil war in Lebanon's recent history; indeed the events of 1975–76 were widely seen as the inevitable, if belated, outcome of the "no victor, no vanquished" situation in which the war of 1958 came to an end. However, in terms of loss of life and its effects on an economy so heavily dependent on the confidence of international business and banking circles, on tourism, transit trade and other services, the fighting that followed April 1975 caused unprecedented damage.

INTRODUCTION

Political and economic life since the civil war ended has been punctuated by violent episodes, including the Israeli invasion of the south in March 1978 and continuing clashes there, fighting between the Syrian Arab deterrent force and rightist militias, and more recently strife between supporters of Iran and Iraq. With no let-up in the violence, Lebanon in 1981 and the first months of 1982 remained far from the political stability that was essential if it was to recover its economic health. In 1980 there had been some hope that Lebanon could regain something of its former position as commercial and financial centre of the Middle East, for the economy had proved surprisingly resilient in some sectors. However, subsequent events dashed any hopes that the foreign business community might be persuaded to return in the near future. Indeed, in spring 1982 it became clear that the foreign diplomatic community was dwindling, with some Western embassies reducing the number of staff and certain Arab ambassadors no longer residing in Beirut.

In July 1980 the Phalangist Party was able to gain ascendancy over the rightist heartland when it crushed its rival, the National Liberal Party. The trend towards decentralization and economic autonomy of the rightist-controlled areas north of Beirut was hastened by the Phalangist victory, and a form of *de facto* partition has occurred. The Phalangists have set up a large computerized centre to help with their economic, social and political planning, and closely control functions such as taxation, public works, housing and development in the districts which they control.

Immediately after the civil war, it had looked as if reconstruction could get under way. The small Cabinet of technocrats formed under Dr. Selim Hoss in December 1976 set about implementing three overlapping programmes of action, dealing first with relief, then reconstruction and finally development. The Cabinet set up a 12-man Council for Development and Reconstruction (CDR), headed by economist Muhammad Atalla and, like the Cabinet, formed of economists and engineers. The Council, endowed with executive powers and authorized to negotiate loans, was intended to outlive the first stages of reconstruc-

tion. Its members were appointed for periods of three to five years.

During 1977 the Cabinet and Council set about providing relief for the homeless, orphaned and unemployed and organizing the reconstruction of the port, airport and other basic amenities. This process was interrupted by the hostilities of 1978, but early in 1979 a revised reconstruction plan, proposing expenditure of some £L22,000 million, was presented.

In practice, reconstruction and development plans have been frustrated both by political uncertainty and by shortage of funds. At the Tunis summit of November 1979, Arab heads of state pledged $2,000 million in aid to Lebanon over the next five years. In July 1980 the Cabinet approved a £L1,020 million reconstruction and development plan, to be funded by this aid. However, there was a serious shortfall, and by October 1981 only $236 million of the $400 million Tunis aid due for 1980 had been received. As a result of the disappointing results of the July 1980 plan, the CDR began in autumn 1981 to draw up an alternative 12-month plan, with the emphasis on key reconstruction projects.

A CDR progress report, released in late 1981, gave a grim assessment of the problems facing it. True, there had been some successes, including expanding Beirut port and airport and starting on programmes in the south. However, the report pointed out that, although the rebuilding of Beirut's commercial district had started on August 15th, 1978, outbreaks of violence had halted work. It estimated that the 3,500-km. road system was in danger of total collapse because there had been so little maintenance in the previous few years. It also said that, if Lebanon received the total $2,000 million pledged at Tunis, it could be rebuilt in five to eight years: without this aid, reconstruction could take 20 years or more.

Some steps to implement reconstruction programmes were taken, however. In October 1980, it was agreed that the UN Children's Fund (UNICEF) should carry out a £L150 million reconstruction programme in the south, funded by Arab aid. The following spring, UNICEF set up an office in the south to begin the programme, which included water supplies, health services and education.

The UNICEF scheme has been one of the brighter spots in the reconstruction programme, with projects launched in health, education and water. By early 1982 some 227 projects for the area had been put to tender, and 72 projects had been completed.

In the mid-1970s Lebanon signed a co-operation agreement with the EEC. Aid is given under the terms of five-year protocols. Under the 1977–81 protocol, Lebanon was allotted 30 million European Units of Account (EUAs) but by the end of 1981 EUA 7.5 million of these had not yet been allocated to specific projects.

Under the 1982–86 protocol, the EEC is to give a total of 50 million EUAs, 16 million of them in loans and grants from the EEC budget and 34 million from the European Investment Bank (EIB). Of the total, 40 per cent will be spent on infrastructure, 30 per cent on energy schemes, 21 per cent on health, housing and education, 5 per cent on agriculture, 2 per cent on commerce and industry and 2 per cent as aid to the CDR.

POPULATION

No proper census has been held in the country since 1932 for fear of upsetting the delicate political balance between the various sects or confessions. All political and administrative offices have been allocated on the basis of the 1932 census, which showed Christians in the majority by six to five over non-Christians. It has been thought for some time, however, that the Muslims compose about 60 per cent of the total population, in part because of the higher ratio of Muslims in the Palestinian population in Lebanon and in part because the Muslims have tended to have a higher birth rate and to emigrate less than Christians. Changes in the population make-up have strained to the limit the delicate system of allocating offices on a sectarian basis adopted under the National Pact of 1943. As a result, there have been demands in some quarters for taking a new census and for abandoning the National Pact altogether.

The effects of the civil war on the size, composition and geographical distribution of Lebanon's population have been dramatic. From an estimated 3.1 million inhabitants in 1974 (which made Lebanon one of the most densely-populated countries of the Middle East), the total is believed to have dropped to 2.6 million in 1979, or 2.26 million if non-Lebanese residents (mostly Palestinians) are excluded.

The total of those killed or disabled during 1975–76 has been put by the Lebanese Chamber of Commerce, Industry and Agriculture at 30,000 but other estimates run as high as 60,000, while thousands more were killed or wounded during the spring and autumn of 1978. Each round of violence tends to trigger a fresh wave of movement of population, whether within Lebanon, for example from the south into Beirut, or abroad. Those who went abroad often joined relatives or friends already there, for Lebanese emigration has been considerable for the past 90 years, and by 1960 an estimated 2.5 million Lebanese, or people of Lebanese descent, were living outside the country. The biggest migrant community has traditionally been in the U.S.A., and other favourite settling places were West Africa, Latin America and Australia.

A study carried out at the American University of Beirut (AUB) shows the impact of the civil war and its aftermath on the labour force. It states that in 1974 the non-agricultural labour force was 597,778, and had there been no civil war, the number would have reached 791,354 in 1979, instead of which it was only 426,239. The number of Lebanese working abroad in 1975 was 98,000, but by 1979 the number had jumped to 210,000. Of these, 73,400 were in Saudi Arabia, 15,800 in Kuwait, and smaller numbers in other Arab states. Outside the Arab world, 17,300 were in West Africa, 27,000 in Europe, 17,000 in

Latin America, 11,600 in North America and 14,000 in Australia. While Lebanon's recovery is being hampered by the drain of skills and brains, there is at the same time a pool of unemployed, estimated at more than 200,000 in 1979. The sectors in which there has been the greatest contraction of the work force between 1974 and 1979 are industry (from 138,359 to 86,941), construction (from 46,517 to 18,942) and transport and communications (from 47,113 to 25,256). Many of those not in regular employment are engaged in paramilitary activities, or are part of the thriving "black" economy.

AGRICULTURE

Of the total area of the country, about 52 per cent consists of mountain, swamp or desert, and a further 7 per cent of forest. Only 23 per cent of the area is cultivated, although a further 17 per cent is considered cultivable. The coastal strip enjoys a Mediterranean climate and is exceedingly fertile, producing mainly olives, citrus fruits and bananas. Many of the steep valleys leading up from the coastal plain are carefully terraced and very productive in olives and soft fruit. In the Zahlé and Shtaura regions there are vineyards, while cotton and onions are grown in the hinterland of Tripoli. The main cereal-growing district is the Beka'a, the fertile valley between the Lebanon and the Anti-Lebanon ranges, to the north of which lies the source of the river Orontes. The river Litani also flows southwards through the Beka'a before turning west near Marjayoun to flow into the Mediterranean just north of Tyre. This valley is particularly fertile and cotton is now grown there with some success. Throughout the country the size of the average holding is extremely small and, even so, a smallholding, particularly in the mountains, may be broken up into several fragments some distance apart. The agricultural sector contributed over 9 per cent of the Gross Domestic Product between 1972 and 1974 but this declined to 8.5 per cent after the war. Depopulation of the countryside and lack of both public and private investment led to a noticeable decline in farming activities in the immediate post-war years.

In 1963 the "Green Plan" government agency was established to carry out projects in land reclamation and agricultural development. Since its inception the plan has reclaimed more than 170,000 dunums of land, although this is less than has been swallowed up by urban development. In May 1980, the UN Food and Agricultural Organization (FAO) recommended a land and agricultural strategy to the Ministry of Agriculture. This involved preserving the 100,000 hectares of land under cultivation, protecting grazing lands, and halting the encroachment of housing on agricultural land. About 20,000 hectares of such land have been lost in the past 25 years. The FAO also recommended that afforestation be extended to cover 20 per cent of total land area.

In January 1982 a seminar was held in Beirut, chaired by Agriculture Minister Mustafa Durnaiqah, at which the programme of agricultural development for the next two decades was outlined. It was recommended that the ministry should be reorganized and a National Council for Agriculture created. It was agreed that there should be efforts to limit real estate development in agricultural areas and that funds for agricultural development and research should be made available. It was also decided that 45,000 hectares should be afforested and 96,000 hectares brought under cultivation.

The FAO has been active in Lebanon and since 1977 has been involved in 13 projects totalling $2.54 million. They range from vaccine production to marketing produce and encouraging silkworm cultivation. USAID has made a grant to small farmers of $1.2 million and the Save the Children Fund has donated $400,000 to allow 22,000 farmers to receive loans. Lebanon has applied to the International Fund for Agricultural Development for funds for four projects: construction or rehabilitation of roads in 48 rural areas, providing plastic boxes for apple farmers, supplying dairy farmers with cattle in the Akkar and Hermel areas and setting up goat-breeding centres, and providing credit for small farm co-operatives. The total cost of the projects is $32.2 million.

Lebanon's wheat crop, which occupied 65,000 hectares in 1974, can rise in good years to 75,000 metric tons or drop to 40,000 tons. Fruit-growing, however, has increased substantially since the early 1950s and has continued to play an important part in the economy since the war. The citrus fruit crop was 350,000 metric tons in 1980, compared with 340,000 tons the previous year. A rush to plant apple trees in the 1950s resulted in gluts, followed by a reduction in output in the late 1960s. Production of apples was 144,000 metric tons in 1980, compared with 90,000 tons in 1978. Production of grapes has been steady in recent years at between 130,000 and 140,000 metric tons.

In the first half of 1981 172,520 metric tons of fruit were exported—a drop from the 188,168 tons exported in the same months of 1980. The biggest market by far is Syria, which takes nearly 50 per cent. Saudi Arabia took 23 per cent, Kuwait 12 per cent, Iraq 5 per cent and Jordan 3 per cent of exports in the first half of 1981.

Other crops include sugar beet and tobacco, both of which have suffered decreases in cultivation in the past few years. The area planted with sugar beet was said in 1980 to have dropped by 50 per cent, with the harvest down to 50,000 metric tons. The Government was blamed for failing to solve problems between the growers and ministries, and for delaying announcement of an official price that would encourage production.

As a result of the Israeli invasion of March 1978, hundreds of domestic animals were killed, and thousands of hectares of orange, banana and tobacco groves left unharvested, causing an estimated $30 million loss. Banana exports fell from 2,393 metric tons in 1974 to only 709 tons in 1979. Exports of leaf tobacco were worth £L60 million in 1980. The crop was only 4.1 million kg., compared with 4.4 million kg. in 1979 and 9.3 million kg. in 1974. The decrease

was due both to continuing violence in the south, the main tobacco growing area, and to the fact that the state tobacco monopoly has raised tobacco prices by only 60 per cent since 1974 while inflation since then exceeded 100 per cent. In 1980, only 3,273 hectares were under tobacco cultivation, compared with about 8,000 hectares before the civil war.

One crop has been enabled to flourish by the lack of security in Lebanon: hemp (*cannabis sativa*), the source of hashish. About 80 per cent of the cultivated land in the northern Beka'a and hills of Hermel is planted with hemp, compared with 10 per cent before the war. It is estimated that the output of hashish in 1981 was 2,000 metric tons, whereas before the war it was 100 tons. The hashish is exported through the illegal ports dotted along the coast, and brings considerable wealth to the area where it is grown. All government attempts to introduce alternative crops have failed.

INDUSTRY

Until the time of the oil price explosion in 1973–74, the only minerals known to exist or exploited in Lebanon were lignite and some iron ore, smelted in Beirut. There have been hopes of oil discoveries for a number of years, but so far these hopes have been unfulfilled.

Even before hopes of an oil find were raised, Lebanon was of considerable importance to the oil industry. Two of the world's most important oil pipelines cross the country, one from the Kirkuk oil wells in Iraq to Tripoli and the other from Saudi Arabia to Zahrani near Sidon. At each terminal there is an important oil refinery. Both the pipelines and the refineries have, however, been the subject of disputes.

Revenues from the Kirkuk-Tripoli pipeline, which was run by the Iraq Petroleum Company (IPC), were reduced after both Iraq and Syria nationalized IPC assets in their countries on June 1st, 1972. Once the Iraqi Government and IPC had reached a settlement on the nationalization in 1973, a dispute over the ownership of the IPC refinery in Lebanon followed, as a result of which the Lebanese Government took over the refinery and agreed to compensate IPC. The Government started out with one considerable advantage in that Iraqi oil supplies were temporarily maintained at little over the pre-1974 price of $2.5 a barrel. But the cheap supplies ended when the financial clauses of the transit agreement expired in December 1975 and in April 1976 Iraq actually suspended pumping, choosing to direct its Kirkuk oil to the Gulf instead. The Lebanon was thus faced with a loss of around £L30 million a year in royalties as well as the loss of cheap oil. During the early part of 1977, as the economy was getting back in motion, the Tripoli refinery was processing only 5,000 barrels a day compared with an average 36,000 barrels a day in 1975. By 1978, however, it was operating at around 75 per cent of capacity on oil reaching Tripoli by sea or from nearby Zahrani. Iraq finally resumed pumping to Syria through the former IPC pipeline in early 1979 but throughput of Kirkuk crude via Lebanon remained dependent on conclusion of a new bilateral transit and supply agreement. It was reported in March 1981 that Iraq had agreed to start re-pumping, ending the five-year shut down. The initial rate of delivery was to be about 200,000 barrels a day, doubling after two months. Of this, 35,000 b/d were to be used domestically with the remainder exported. At the time of the agreement, the Tripoli refinery was running on 26,000 b/d of Saudi crude, which was pumped to Zahrani and then transported to Tripoli by tanker.

On December 24th, 1981, Iraqi oil started flowing through the pipeline, but within days it was damaged by a bomb blast. Although the pipeline was repaired, its vulnerability to sabotage was underlined when in March 1982 it was blown up again. Politics intervened when on April 10th the trans-Syria pipeline was closed and Iraqi deliveries to Tripoli were suspended.

Plans drawn up by Stone & Webster of the U.S.A. envisaged that the Tripoli oil refinery's capacity would be doubled to 70,000 barrels per day. The project, costing $300 million—$400 million, was planned to be carried out in two stages, 1982–85 and 1985–2000.

The Zahrani refinery is run by the Mediterranean Refinery Company (Medreco), jointly owned by Caltex and Mobil. Mobil, Caltex's two parent firms (Texaco and Standard Oil of California) and Exxon also own the Trans-Arabian Pipeline Company (Tapline), which in turn operates the Saudi-Lebanese pipeline. Tapline suspended its pumping operations in early February 1975, on the grounds that oil tankers found it cheaper to lift oil directly from the Saudi terminal at Ras Tanura in the Gulf. This shutdown cost the Lebanon more than £L20 million in royalties. Meanwhile the company also demanded that the Lebanese Government pay for the higher cost of Saudi oil (previously supplied to the Zahrani refinery at a price of $5 a barrel), claiming that it was owed $100 million in back payments. A settlement was reached in August 1975, but when the refinery, which had been put out of action for much of 1976, started up again at the end of November 1976, the question of back payments arose again. Accumulated debts over 1975/76 were estimated at $120 million, and in August 1977 it was finally agreed that these would be settled by the Saudi Government. However, it was not until early 1979, in the wake of the Iranian revolution and the drop in Iranian oil exports, that Tapline resumed operations on its former scale.

In early August 1981 Tapline suspended all crude deliveries to the Zahrani refinery because of non-payment of oil debts, but a few weeks later Saudi Arabia announced it was paying most of Lebanon's oil bill.

Manufacturing industry in the Lebanon has for many years been highly developed in comparison with other states in the area, although it suffered from political disruptions and strikes even before the 1975/76 civil war. Industrial exports increased by 90 per cent between 1973 and 1974 to reach just under £L846 million and the industrial sector in 1974 provided £L1,040 million, or 16 per cent of national income.

The number of workers employed in industry that year stood at over 120,000.

Coming immediately after the success of 1974, the effects of the war were all the more dramatic, leaving an estimated 200 factories damaged or destroyed. A study carried out by the Industrial Development Centre for Arab States during 1977 estimated that 15 per cent of total capital invested in industry had been lost and that war damage represented another 35–40 per cent. Industry was somewhat slow to pick up after the war. It was not until spring 1981 that the National Assembly (parliament) passed a law on the rescheduling of debts owed by industrialists and traders whose businesses were damaged in the war. Their total debts were put at £L12,000 million, £L8,000 million of which was borne by the commercial sector.

In spring 1980, the Association of Lebanese Industrialists presented the Government with a number of demands, including the creation of neutral industrial zones. They asked for reductions (of as much as 50 per cent) in the cost of electricity, fuel, gas oil, telephones and telexes to industry. They also urged that the Government curb smuggling, which was hitting the textile industry particularly badly. Smuggling also compounded the tobacco industry's problems, and the number of workers in the Régie des Tabac's four factories and three warehouses had by summer 1980 fallen to 2,300 from the pre-civil war level of 5,000. A study conducted by the Finance Ministry found that 90 per cent of the 5 million packets of cigarettes consumed daily were foreign, compared with 60 per cent in 1974.

A dispute erupted in spring 1982 between Lebanon's chambers of commerce and its industrialists over the problem of smuggling. While the industrialists demanded strict measures to curb smuggling, the merchants, who were prospering in the free market environment, were opposed to such a move.

Industry in the Lebanon has traditionally been a small-scale operation run by individuals employing a handful of people. Before the disruption of 1975, however, the number of limited liability companies was growing and had reached 44 in 1974 from only 18 the previous year. Food processing, yarn and textile firms accounted for about 44 per cent of industrial output and furniture and woodworking factories about 29 per cent. Mechanical industries accounted for only about 7 per cent of total production and the rest was divided among cement, ceramics, pharmaceutical and plastics industries. New factories licensed in 1980 showed a similar bias. Seventy-seven were licensed, most of them small: 12 for bottling oxygen and other substances, seven for food and drink processing, six for mineral water bottling, five for plastics and five for film manufacture and processing. Most of the others were in the production of construction materials. A marked feature of the new factories was their decentralized distribution. Before the civil war, 80 per cent of new factories were located in Beirut. But in 1980, Beirut was only the third most popular location, having nine of the new factories compared with Zahleh's 13 and the Shouf's ten.

Tripoli had seven, the western Beka'a seven and the north Metn six.

With the exception of the oil companies, the largest industrial employers in the pre-war period were probably the food-processing industries, followed by the well-developed textile industries. The inflow into real estate of funds from Lebanese abroad, mainly those whose property was sequestrated in West Africa, also helped to stimulate the building industry, bringing a sharp rise in land prices and construction activity in 1974. The production capacity of the country's cement factories has been sufficient to leave a surplus for export. In 1981, however, exports of black cement fell by 36.6 per cent, mainly because Syria became a major cement producer. Nevertheless, production of black cement in 1981 increased by 3.7 per cent to 2.2 million metric tons, and domestic sales rose by 127.8 per cent. Major construction projects went ahead despite the lack of security in the country, and absorbed much of the cement output.

In late 1981 the new cement plant at Sibline, in the south, was completed, with an initial daily output of 800 metric tons of clinker, expected to rise to 1,600 tons in 1982 with the introduction of another kiln. The plant was the brainchild of Kamal Jumblatt, the late Druze leader and founder of the Progressive Socialist Party, and is intended to bring employment to the area.

Several government-sponsored efforts aimed to promote industrial expansion. In March 1972, in a measure similar to one of 1954, all industries created between 1971 and 1976 were exempted from income tax for six years. Industries created before 1971 benefited from a partial tax holiday if they expanded their activities before the end of 1975.

As the reconstruction effort began to get under way in 1977 a series of fresh investment incentives was formulated, aimed at restoring confidence. A government-run body called the National Establishment for Investment Insurance was set up to provide investments taking the form of fixed assets with insurance cover at low premiums against hazards of civil war, revolutions, dissension and acts of violence. Legislation applying to foreign banks was amended to encourage them to contribute to the reconstruction programme by investing in the Housing Bank and the National Bank for the Development of Industry and Tourism. The Housing Bank in turn embarked on a large-scale lending programme, providing 15-year loans at an interest rate of only 2 per cent.

An indication that industry was slowly recovering was the gradual increase in industrial exports. In 1980 these were 15 per cent more than in 1979, although some observers argued that, with inflation estimated at 20 per cent, there had actually been a drop in exports in real terms. In 1981, however, there was a 25 per cent increase, to £L2,290 million. The major increases in exports in 1981 were in textiles, clothing and non-metallic minerals, but the value of exports of food, mineral water, cement, shoes and wood dropped. The major clients were Iraq, Syria, Saudi Arabia and Jordan, which between them accounted for 86 per cent of the total. Recorded

exports to Syria in 1981 were 26 per cent down on those in 1980, however, possibly because of an increased incidence of smuggling.

The lack of adequate sources of power hindered industrial development in the 1960s but Lebanon gradually achieved the position of having excess capacity. In 1972 it started supplying power through a 100 million kWh. line to southern Syria and in March 1976 the two countries agreed on the exchange of power through a similar line between Tripoli and Tartous. Work on implementing the power link-up project was given the go-ahead as part of moves to repair the country's badly damaged electricity network in 1977. A seven-year electrification scheme costing some £L1,260 million was drawn up, which was expected to be financed by the World Bank and the Arab Fund for Economic and Social Development. An important feature of the plan was the upgrading of the Zouk power station, and in 1980 the European Investment Bank (the EEC's long-term financing agency) lent around $4.3 million for two 125 MW generators for the station. The overall cost of the two units was $200.2 million. In early 1982 Electricité du Liban (EDL) obtained a loan of 7 million EUA to help finance the expansion of the Zouk power station. EDL had a difficult year in 1981 and lost £L250 million because of a combination of wage rises, increases in fuel prices, the high cost of equipment and the illegal "tapping" of the electricity network.

EXTERNAL TRADE

Lebanon has suffered from an adverse balance of visible trade for many years. Exports in 1974, for example, covered only 62 per cent of imports. Before the war, however, this deficit was generally amply covered by invisible earnings from services and tourism, transit trade and remittances from Lebanese working abroad. The war inevitably brought about a heavy drop in income from tourism and transit traffic but set against this was a parallel reduction in imports and an increase in remittances from the ever-growing numbers of Lebanese abroad. These remittances, together with other capital transfers, reached £L14,747 million in 1977, more than compensating for that year's £L2,963 million trade deficit. By 1978, however, the trade gap had widened to £L3,320 million and remittances had declined to £L3,145 million. With a surplus of £L720 million on the services account, the overall balance of payments in 1978 was only £L545 million in surplus, compared with a surplus of £L2,404 million the previous year. In 1979, however, there was a large balance of payments increase, to £L2,675 million. Exports in 1980 totalled £L4,160 million. This was 37.5 per cent more than the 1979 figure, but assuming an inflation rate of about 15 per cent, the real increase was 19.6 per cent. Imports were roughly the same as they were in 1979: £L7,500 million. Despite the large trade deficit there was a balance of payments surplus of £L2,675 million due largely to remittances and foreign aid.

In 1980, building materials accounted for about 26 per cent of total exports, agricultural produce for 20.2 per cent, chemicals for 8.2 per cent and textiles and clothing for 8 per cent. Arab countries took 82 per cent of the total exports, 32 per cent going to Saudi Arabia, 18 per cent to Iraq and 5 per cent to Jordan. In the first half of 1981 exports totalled £L2,567 million, of which £L965 million went to the Arab world. Iraq was the largest importer, taking £L362 million of goods. Saudi Arabia took £L344 million, Syria £L73 million and Libya and Jordan £L56 million each. The Government is concerned at its growing trade deficit with European countries. In 1981 the trade deficit with the EEC was estimated at over $1,000 million, compared with $580 million in 1978. Less than 6 per cent of exports go to the EEC. In February 1981 a Lebanese delegation held talks in Brussels with EEC officials to examine ways of lessening the deficit; a co-operation agreement signed with the EEC in May 1977 had already tried to effect this. The EEC package was to expire in October 1981, and covered $39 million in aid. Another package was due to come into effect subsequently.

As the reconstruction effort gets under way, the import bill, affected by heavy demand for both capital and consumer goods, is bound to rise, but it is still too early to say how its composition will compare with the pattern of pre-war years. Traditionally Lebanon's chief imports were precious metals, stones, jewellery and coins, machinery and electrical apparatus, transport equipment and industrial raw materials. In 1981 some 48,054 cars were bought, a 14.2 per cent drop from 1980. The greatest number were West German, then French and Japanese. With total sales of 13,503, Mercedes was the market leader.

CURRENCY AND FINANCE

The importance of Beirut as the commercial and financial centre of the Middle East derived, in the 1950s and onwards, from the almost complete absence of restriction on the free movement of goods and capital and from the transference of the Middle Eastern headquarters of many foreign concerns from Cairo to Beirut after 1952. Moreover, large sums were earned in the Gulf by Arabs who were seeking investment locally, especially in property, and for them Beirut was a convenient centre. Its dominance was further strengthened later by the massive increases in surplus oil revenues earned by the producing states, much of which was channelled through Lebanon.

By June 1975 the number of representative offices opened by foreign banks in Beirut had reached 72. But by February 1976, when a lull in the fighting encouraged the banks to open again after a two-month closure, 26 of these branches had been partially or totally destroyed. The calm was short-lived but was just long enough to quell fears of massive withdrawals as, even at the most active branches, the banks' reopening was believed to have resulted in withdrawals equivalent to only 7–8 per cent of total deposits and savings accounts. Another 10-month closure was to follow, however, before the banks formally reopened again in Beirut in mid-January 1977. By this time damage and losses through looting of vaults and safety deposit boxes were believed to amount to around $500 million, though even this

figure was thought to be conservative. But again fears of a flood of withdrawals proved unfounded. Instead, the liquidity accumulated outside the banking system during the war began to flow back to the extent that, by 1979, total bank deposits had reached more than £L19,000 million, far exceeding the previous peak of £L11,500 million recorded for February 1975. At the end of October 1980, bank deposits stood at £L23,300 million. Outstanding loans were £L29,200 million, an increase of 24.5 per cent from the end of 1979. At the end of June 1981 commercial bank deposits stood at £L31,583 million, having increased in local currency terms by 16 per cent since December 1980. In dollar terms, however, they had dropped by 1.4 per cent.

Private sector deposits moved increasingly out of Lebanese pounds and into foreign currencies. In 1974 deposits in Lebanese pounds were more than 70 per cent of the total but by 1981 they were only 55 per cent, largely because of high interest rates on foreign currencies. In an effort to stem the flow away from the pound, the Central Bank lifted the prime rate to 16.5 per cent in early 1982.

In 1981 commercial bank lending to the private sector lagged behind that to the public sector and lending overseas. Lending to the public sector and overseas rose by 57 per cent to £L24,774 million but private sector lending grew by only 29 per cent, to £L23,286 million—44 per cent of total lending.

The growing competitiveness of European and Gulf financial centres had, even before the disruption of 1975/76, led the Government to seek ways of enhancing Beirut's attractions as a banking centre. The need for such incentives is now infinitely greater. A banking free-zone law which came into effect in April 1977, exempting non-residents' foreign currency accounts from taxes on interest earned, from payment of a deposit guarantee tax and from reserve requirements was a step in this direction. Moreover, in June 1977 the Government decided to lift the moratorium on new bank licences which had been imposed in the wake of the Intra Bank crash of 1966. In 1977 a new specialized bank, the Banque de l'Habitat, was set up and in 1978 two new commercial banks, the International Commerce Bank and Universal Bank, were granted licences, bringing the total number of banks operating in Lebanon to 81 as of mid-1979. In April 1980 the American Express International Banking Corporation became the first foreign bank to open a new branch in Beirut since the war.

In 1981 the Central Bank made profits of £L855.9 million—37.6 per cent more than in 1980. However, the increase was offset by the relentless fall of the Lebanese pound and inflation of 20 per cent. By the end of 1981 the bank's reserves had risen to £L650.2 million but there was a fall in the relative value of foreign currency reserves. While these had been equivalent to 33 months' imports in 1974, by spring 1982 they equalled only 12 months' imports.

The remarkable resistance of the Lebanese pound to the pressures of the war can be attributed chiefly to the absence of restrictions on withdrawals or foreign exchange transactions, an increase in the supply of foreign currencies to finance the war, the pound's strong gold backing and the flow of remittances safeguarding the balance of payments. Shortly before the war, in October 1974, the pound had reached a record high, standing at £L2.22 against the U.S. dollar. It lost just over 30 per cent of this value during the war but quickly recovered to £L3 after the cease-fire.

Well before the civil war, inflationary pressures had been one of the country's most serious economic problems. The civil war removed all vestiges of price restraint, and inflation soared to 80–90 per cent a year. The minimum monthly wage was increased to £L310 in 1977, then to £L415 and from that to £L525 in 1979, but this did little to relieve the chronic postwar hardship afflicting much of the population.

Inflation has put intense pressure on the government to increase wages in recent years. In April 1982 the Cabinet approved a 17 per cent pay rise for private and public sector workers. The private sector rise was backdated to January 1st, and the public sector increase was due to take effect on July 1st.

Although the political situation dampened hopes that Lebanon would soon become a vital Middle East financial centre again, the domestic banking scene witnessed a series of important developments in 1980. One of these was the first ever issue of convertible bonds in Lebanon, for a winter sports company in Faraya. This issue, made in spring 1980, was followed by another convertible bond issue in the summer, for the Summerland Beach Complex in West Beirut. In August 1980 a syndicated loan was arranged for a company building a shopping complex in East Beirut, with interest based, for the first time ever, on the Beirut interbank offered rate. These innovations added to the sophistication of Beirut's repertoire of banking skills. Another significant development was the decision to set up a discount house to underwrite and deal in government bills and bonds.

There was a slump in stock exchange activity in 1981. In April that year the stock exchange was closed by violence, and in the summer only two sessions were held. The volume of shares traded fell by 62.5 per cent from 1980, to 7,047, and the value of dealings fell by 67 per cent to £L654,800.

TOURISM AND COMMUNICATIONS

Beirut's hotels, its port and airport as well as the Lebanon's largest non-government employer, Middle East Airlines (MEA), were all severely hit by the 1975–76 crisis. Tourism was just beginning to recover from the effects of the October 1973 war when the fighting broke out. The number of tourists arriving during the first quarter of 1975 exceeded the figure for the corresponding period of 1974 by 31 per cent but by the end of that year it had dropped by an overall 39 per cent.

As the war progressed the prosperous hotel district in the centre of Beirut became the scene of some of the fiercest fighting. According to the Lebanese Hotel Owners' Association, 145 hotels were damaged, incurring losses of some £L218 million. In Beirut alone

the number of hotels dwindled from 130 (with 10,486 beds) in 1975 to 44 (with 4,631 beds) by 1979. The contribution of tourism to G.N.P., which was 20 per cent in the pre-war period, shrank to 7.4 per cent in 1977. Visitors spent only 469,272 nights in Beirut in 1979, compared with 2,307,122 nights in 1974. In 1980 there was some improvement, with a 15 per cent rise in the number of visitors to 135,548, who spent a total of 585,531 nights in Beirut. Overall occupancy was only 27 per cent, however. The average length of stay rose from 3.9 to 4.3 nights.

The National Council for Tourism in Lebanon (NCTL) has undertaken a massive promotional campaign through its nine offices in Europe, the U.S.A. and the Middle East. The NCTL issues a glossy monthly bulletin and prepares brochures, books and other materials. The Ministry of Tourism and the Council for Development and Reconstruction have drawn up plans to rebuild the four international-class seaside hotels in Beirut at a cost of around $100 million. They have also outlined schemes to clean up the beaches. Although the security problem makes it difficult to move from area to area within Lebanon, inside those areas domestic tourism has boomed since the end of the war. In the areas controlled by the rightist militias north of Beirut, there are large beach complexes and clubs. In south-west Beirut the Summerland Beach Complex opened in 1978.

Middle East Airlines (MEA) suffered a loss of £L14 million in 1975, which rose to £L69.1 million in 1976. The following year saw some recovery, with over 1 million passengers carried and profits of £L22 million, but 1978 was again disappointing, with staff prevented by the fighting from reporting for duty and passenger traffic some 16 per cent below expectations. In 1979 MEA made a startling recovery, recording profits of £L51.14 million, its highest ever. This was despite a 59.7 per cent increase in the price of aviation fuel. The MEA Chairman, Asad Nasr, warned, however, that inflation and increases in fuel prices meant the airline must expect narrower profit margins in the future. Nasr's warning was proved right. In 1980 profits slumped to £L9 million, and in 1981 the airline's losses were £L88 million. In March 1982 Nasr predicted that MEA would again lose in 1982, but said there would be a return to profit within two years. MEA announced on November 24th, 1980, that it was to buy five Airbus A310 aircraft, with the option to purchase 14 more. The decision followed months of intense competition between the West European Airbus Industrie consortium and the U.S. Boeing Company to win the order. The order was valued at $350 million, of which $280 million was to be financed by the export credit guarantee departments of France, Britain and West Germany, and the remaining $70 million by a consortium of Arab and other banks. Crédit Lyonnais of France was responsible for arranging the latter loan, which involved some 40 banks. In April 1982 it was reported that the banks were considering a revision of its terms, and that the loan might be made conditional on MEA's obtaining the $280 million export credit. On May 6th, 1982, Asad Nasr resigned after a 27-year career with MEA but denied that his resignation had anything to do with the financing difficulties over the Airbus deal.

In October 1981 MEA increased its capital from £L100 million to £L150 million. Shortly beforehand, plans had been announced to introduce new routes. One of these was a twice-weekly service between Beirut and Manila via Dhahran and Bangkok, and its main customers were expected to be Filipinos working in Arab countries. A New York service was also announced, and another new route was to fly via west Africa (where there is a major Lebanese concentration) to Brazil.

There has been an increase in airfreight, due to companies' reluctance to store goods in Lebanon, which in turn necessitates a faster turnaround that can be provided only by air. Lebanon's chief cargo-carrier, Trans-Mediterranean Airways (TMA), in operation since 1953, is also likely to profit from this transport trend. Freight handled at Beirut International Airport in 1974 totalled 118,431 metric tons. Passengers passing through the airport reached 2,806,628 in 1974 but this dropped to 1,571,685 in 1979. This was predictable in view of the airport's vulnerability to attack and closure during the war. Because of this, Phalangist groups built their own independent airport in 1976–77, in the mountains north of Beirut.

Both MEA and the freight carrier Trans-Mediterranean Airways (TMA) were involved in 1980 and 1981 in a dispute with Britain, France and the Netherlands over the number of flights they operated. The U.K. Department of Trade was pressing for a reduction in MEA's flights between Beirut and London from seven to four a week, and for a reduction in TMA's flights from nine to five. British Airways had three flights a week on the route. The Lebanese argued that the U.K. was retaliating for the cessation of Concorde flights over Lebanon in late 1979, after complaints of damage to buildings and property.

Congestion at Beirut port was already chronic before the troubles, largely because of the volume of goods bound for Saudi Arabia, Kuwait and Iraq, where oil revenues were boosting development spending. A total of 3,972 ships called at Beirut port in 1974 and cargo handled, including cargo in transit, amounted to 5,057,545 tons. During the war, unloading was badly hindered by Muslim workers' reluctance to cross over into Christian areas and by a huge fire in April 1976 which destroyed a dozen major warehouses. Shortly before the civil war, British consultants Peat, Marwick Mitchell & Co. and consulting engineers Coode & Partners had carried out a major study of Beirut and Tripoli ports and drawn up a master plan. The plan for Beirut port included developing a fourth basin as a container terminal, and the possible creation of a fifth basin. In 1977, the British consultants revised their forecasts to include reconstruction, and the Council for Reconstruction and Development appointed a port committee in August 1977 to oversee the reconstruction and modernization process, whose total cost is put at more than $144 million. Although work on the port has continued, there have been frequent disruptions. In 1978, intense battles between Syrian troops and rightist forces closed the port from July to December, and in 1979 sniping frequently led to shut down. The port was again badly affected by the fighting in spring 1981.

There was some improvement in traffic at Beirut port in 1980, with the volume of traffic increasing by 11 per cent. Some 2.73 million tons of cargo were discharged and 248,056 tons loaded, compared with 2.37 million tons and 230,000 tons respectively in 1979. A total of 2,732 vessels called at the port. The fighting in spring 1981 took its economic toll, and in the first half of that year Beirut port's deficit was £L15 million. Only 310 vessels called at the port in the second quarter, compared with 713 in the first, and the volume of goods handled fell by 59.3 per cent.

Illegal ports have posed a great problem for the Government since the civil war. There are at least 17 such ports, which impose tariffs only a fraction of those payable at the official ports. The official ports have also been seriously hit by smuggling. The Council for Reconstruction and Development recommended to the Cabinet in late 1980 that the concession for a new port at Sidon should be given to Sidon businessman, Rafiq al-Hariri. The Council advised that al-Hariri should be granted the concession for 30 years, and should set up a joint company with the Council with capital of £L250 million. The decision aroused some controversy, as the U.K. consultants who had prepared the plans for Beirut port said that in a politically unified Lebanon only two ports, Beirut and Tripoli, were needed, and that if the South must have a port, then Tyre, further south, would be more suitable than Sidon.

PUBLIC FINANCE AND DEVELOPMENT

The effects of inflation are clearly seen in the evolution of Lebanon's budget expenditure. The overall state budget of 1977, the first to be adopted after the war, set spending at £L1,661.5 million and was already over 32 per cent higher than the budget for 1974. The 1982 draft budget was £L5,945 million, compared with £L4,489 million in 1981. The budget annexes—for telecommunications, the national lottery and the office for sugar beet and cereals—added another £L1,209 million. Announcing the budget to the National Assembly, the Minister of Finance, Dr. Ali al-Khalil, said that the government could fund only 55 per cent of the budget out of its own revenues because the precarious security situation made it impossible to collect a large portion of taxes. Smuggling has severely hit government revenues. While 47 per cent of government revenues came from customs in 1974, the proportion dropped to 14 per cent in the first half of 1981.

Government revenue was expected to be £L3,500 million in 1982, a large drop from the £L3,600 million realized in 1981 if one takes into account a possible 20 per cent inflation rate. The deficit was to be met by external borrowing and by short-term treasury bills. Some $190 million was expected to come from Arab sources in 1982—compared with the $400 million per year pledged at the Tunis summit of November 1979. Besides the respective deficits (also the result of repeated civil service salary increases), the post-war budgets have been characterized by large allocations to defence, education and public works. In keeping with the need to establish a credible army, the defence allocations of 1978, 1979 and 1980 accounted for approximately one-quarter of total spending—the defence budget for 1980 standing at £L80.4 million. In the 1982 budget, defence was allocated £L1,245.7 million. Education and fine arts received £L1,003.2 million, and public works and transport £L981.2 million.

The government's expanding role in directing economic activity in the country, where previously state interference had been minimal, was evident in

the breakdown of the £L22,000 million five-year reconstruction and development plan announced at the beginning of 1979. This plan, involving some 17 major projects, envisaged that £L10,000 million of total expenditure would be channelled through the public sector.

With the exception of the Palestinian refugee camps, the general standard of living in Lebanon before 1975/76 was relatively high. World Bank statistics put G.N.P. per caput at $1,070 in 1974, aligning Lebanon more closely with certain of the more populous oil-producers of the Middle East than with other non-oil states. Inevitably, since 1974 this lead has been undermined, though statistics to prove it are not available.

STATISTICAL SURVEY

AREA AND POPULATION

AREA	ESTIMATED POPULATION (November 15th, 1970)†		
	Males	Females	Total
10,400 sq. km.*	1,080,015	1,046,310	2,126,325

* 3,950 sq. miles.
† Figures are based on the results of a sample survey, excluding Palestinian refugees in camps. The total of registered Palestinian refugees was 187,529 at June 30th, 1973.

Total population (UN estimates, '000 at mid-year): 2,767 in 1975; 2,763 in 1976; 2,733 in 1977; 2,692 in 1978; 2,662 in 1979; 2,658 in 1980.

Principal towns (estimated population in 1972): Beirut (capital) 800,000; Tripoli 150,000.

Births and Deaths: Average annual birth rate 32.1 per 1,000 in 1970–75, 30.1 per 1,000 in 1975–80; death rate 9.3 per 1,000 in 1970–75, 8.7 per 1,000 in 1975–80 (UN estimates).

ECONOMICALLY ACTIVE POPULATION
(ISIC Major Divisions)

	1970 (sample survey)*			1975 (official estimate)†
	Males	Females	Total	
Agriculture, hunting, forestry and fishing . . .	80,535	21,225	101,760	127,000
Mining and quarrying	} 76,890	} 18,645	915	1,000
Manufacturing			94,620	135,000
Electricity, gas and water	5,550	60	5,610	8,000
Construction	34,800	255	35,055	50,000
Trade, restaurants and hotels . . .	85,845	5,775	91,620	130,000
Transport, storage and communications .	36,375	1,860	38,235	54,000
Financing, insurance, real estate and business services .	15,600	2,820	18,420	26,000
Community, social and personal services . .	106,605	43,185	149,790	213,000
Activities not adequately described . .	2,085	300	2,385	3,000
TOTAL	444,285	94,125	538,410	748,000

* Excluding unemployed persons, numbering 33,345 (males 28,335; females 5,010).
† Including unemployed.

AGRICULTURE
LAND USE
('ooo hectares)

	1973	1979
Arable land . . .	240	240*
Land under permanent crops	105	108*
Permanent meadows and pastures . . .	10	10†
Forests and woodlands .	95	74*
Other land . . .	573	591
Inland water . . .	17	17
TOTAL AREA . .	1,040	1,040

* FAO estimate.   † Unofficial estimate.

Source: FAO, *Production Yearbook.*

PRINCIPAL CROPS
(FAO estimates)

	AREA HARVESTED ('ooo hectares)			PRODUCTION ('ooo metric tons)		
	1978	1979	1980	1978	1979	1980
Wheat	45	45	45	45	40	40
Barley	7	5	8	8	5	8
Sugar Beet . . .	3	3	3	118	108	100
Potatoes . . .	7	7	7	70	112	145
Onions . . .	1	1	1	25	22	18
Tobacco . . .	8	8	8	4	5	5
Citrus Fruit . .	n.a.	n.a.	n.a.	335	340	350
Apples . . .	n.a.	n.a.	n.a.	90	135	144
Grapes . . .	18	19	20	130	135	140
Olives . . .	n.a.	n.a.	n.a.	65	15	60
Tomatoes . . .	6	6	6	75	75	75

Source: FAO, *Production Yearbook.*

LIVESTOCK
(FAO estimates, 'ooo head, year ending September)

	1978	1979	1980
Goats . . .	340	360	380
Sheep . . .	280	280	280
Cattle . . .	130	100	110
Donkeys . . .	37	37	37
Pigs . . .	75	75	70
Chickens . . .	6,400	6,900	6,976

Source: FAO, *Production Yearbook.*

INDUSTRY
CRUDE OIL PROCESSED
('ooo litres)

1974	1975	1976	1977	1978
2,756,534	2,415,047	832,639	1,994,665	2,008,390

PETROLEUM PRODUCTS
('000 litres)

	1974	1975	1976	1977	1978	1979
Petrol	740,404	597,085	187,846	450,187	641,663	563,171
Gas oil	505,442	518,707	186,073	394,735	390,572	410,603
Fuel oil	932,436	826,510	320,145	721,672	708,834	890,824
Kerosene . . .	27,289	31,529	37,513	27,160	25,194	92,214
Liquefied petroleum gas .	112,198	77,456	17,338	51,917	57,741	26,581

Source: Banque du Liban, *Bulletin Trimestriel*, March 1981.

OTHER PRODUCTS

		1971	1972	1973	1974
Tobacco manufactures .	metric tons	3,122	3,250	3,893	6,337
Timber	cu. metres	48,793	57,748	66,285	54,451
Cement	'000 metric tons	1,499	1,626	1,659	1,744
Electricity . . .	million kWh.	1,375	1,548	1,791	1,975

1977: Cement 1,172,000 metric tons; Electricity 1,839 million kWh.

Source: Conseil du Développement et de la Reconstruction, *Evaluation des Comptes Economiques de* 1977.

FINANCE

100 piastres = 1 Lebanese pound (£L).

Coins: 1, 2½, 5, 10, 25 and 50 piastres; 1 pound.

Notes: 1, 5, 10, 25, 50, 100 and 250 pounds.

Exchange rates (May 1982): £1 sterling = £L9.11; U.S. $1 = £L4.96.
£L100 = £10.97 sterling = $20.18.

Note: A basic official exchange rate of U.S. $1 = £L3.08 was introduced in January 1956. This remained in effect until February 1973, despite the devaluation of the U.S. dollar in December 1971. The official exchange rate was £1 sterling = £L7.392 from November 1967 to August 1971; and £1 sterling = £L8.026 from December 1971 to June 1972. However, the basic rate was used only for official exchange operations and for the valuation of official assets and customs duties. All commercial transactions take place on the basis of a fluctuating free market rate, established in November 1948. From 1954 to 1972 the exchange rate in the free market fluctuated between £L2.97 and £L3.37 per U.S. dollar. In February 1973, when the U.S. dollar was again devalued, the Lebanese pound appreciated considerably on the free market. At the same time a new official rate of $1 = £L2.772 was introduced but this became inoperative in March 1973, since when official valuations have been based on an "effective" rate whose parity is adjustable from month to month. The average market rates (£L per U.S. dollar) were: 3.2690 in 1970; 3.2277 in 1971; 3.0507 in 1972; 2.6104 in 1973; 2.3278 in 1974; 2.3095 in 1975; 2.9037 in 1976; 3.0690 in 1977; 2.9554 in 1978; 3.2428 in 1979; 3.4361 in 1980; 4.3139 in 1981.

ORDINARY BUDGET ESTIMATES
(Expenditure—million £L)

	1979	1980		1979	1980
President's Office . .	2.19	} 87.0	Ministry of National Economy .	14.54	156.9
Chamber of Deputies . .	10.27		Ministry of Posts and Telecommunications . .	26.22	26.5
Prime Minister's Office . .	64.55		Ministry of Planning . .	3.38	—
Ministry of Justice . .	26.26	27.5	Ministry of Hydraulic Resources	49.71	42.7
Ministry of Foreign Affairs .	48.59	62.0	Ministry of Tourism . . .	33.53	30.2
Ministry of Interior . .	209.93	217.6	Ministry of Industry and Oil .	2.61	2.8
Ministry of Finance . .	50.03	53.0	Ministry of Housing and Co-operatives . . .	7.11	6.5
Ministry of National Defence .	738.06	980.0	Payments on debt . . .	178.30	} 849.0
Ministry of National Education .	536.58	510.9	Reserves	141.21	
Ministry of Health . .	91.23	116.0			
Ministry of Social Affairs .	63.19	67.9			
Ministry of Information . .	14.56	14.7			
Ministry of Public Works .	450.28	571.2			
Ministry of Agriculture . .	43.65	46.1	Total . . .	2,806.00	3,868.5

1981 Budget: Expenditure £L5,200 million; **1982 Budget:** Expenditure £L5,945 million.

GROSS DOMESTIC PRODUCT BY ECONOMIC ACTIVITY
(£L million)

	1970	1971	1972	1973	1977†
Agriculture and livestock . .	445	466	631	664	700
Energy and water . . .	113	118	129	145	445
Industry	661	750	884	1,021	1,070
Construction . . .	218	239	290	310	280
Transport and communications .	401	438	478	526	630
Services*	1,078	1,214	1,469	1,632	1,920
Commerce. . . .	1,527	1,723	2,007	2,300	2,320
Administration . . .	423	451	477	505	835
Total . . .	4,866	5,399	6,365	7,103	8,200

* Including imputed rents of owner-occupied dwellings.
† Figures for 1974, 1975 and 1976 are not available.

EXTERNAL TRADE
(£L million)

	1975	1976	1977	1978	1979
Imports c.i.f. . . .	5,157	2,609	5,891	6,624	10,359
Exports f.o.b. . . .	2,663	1,610	2,267	2,402	2,863

Source: Conseil du Développement et de la Reconstruction.

1980: Exports £L4,160 million.

PRINCIPAL COMMODITIES
(£L '000)

Imports	1973	1977†	Exports*	1973	1977†
Precious Metals, Stones, Jewellery and Coins . . .	640,237	860,033	Vegetable Products . . .	145,354	193,455
Vegetable Products . . .	292,868	398,252	Precious Metals, Stones, Jewellery and Coins . . .	333,989	470,217
Machinery and Electrical Apparatus . . .	479,325	567,531	Animals and Animal Products .	51,874	20,084
Textiles and Products . .	413,261	442,057	Machinery and Electrical Apparatus . . .	168,238	118,354
Non-precious Metals and Products	346,365	414,069	Non-precious Metals and Products	114,037	181,914
Transport Vehicles . . .	322,734	423,982	Textiles and Products . .	172,662	123,019
Animals and Animal Products .	131,140	276,699	Manufactured food and Tobacco	87,559	148,861
Industrial Chemical Products .	259,480	353,484	Transport Vehicles . . .	150,162	26,548
Mineral Products . . .	187,469	492,386			
Manufactured food and Tobacco	150,428	311,219			

* Including re-exports.
† Estimated from sample survey.

PRINCIPAL TRADING PARTNERS
(£L '000)

IMPORTS	1972	1973	1977*	EXPORTS	1972	1973	1977*
Belgium . . .	70,149	91,941	132,000	France . . .	52,750	161,912	14,100
Czechoslovakia .	56,463	70,057	60,100	Germany, Fed. Rep.	12,039	19,315	4,700
France . . .	300,434	361,915	504,600	Greece . . .	1,739	6,388	16,800
Germany, Fed. Rep.	316,107	380,839	420,500	Iraq . . .	69,440	50,075	6,900
Iraq . . .	121,819	119,919	90,300	Italy . . .	16,875	22,695	4,400
Italy . . .	246,474	293,724	540,600	Jordan . . .	23,513	51,020	71,400
Japan . . .	120,785	126,233	165,300	Kuwait . . .	110,621	105,497	97,800
Jordan . . .	16,605	21,021	23,000	Libya . . .	n.a.	n.a.	167,500
Netherlands .	56,598	69,055	133,100	Saudi Arabia . .	190,284	260,910	446,000
Saudi Arabia . .	52,537	69,506	258,700	Spain . . .	3,023	5,294	200
Switzerland . .	189,587	141,886	874,600	Syria . . .	83,366	77,403	163,800
Syria . . .	69,125	51,544	60,400	U.S.S.R. . .	8,192	13,833	—
Turkey . . .	38,664	55,225	55,800	United Arab Emirates . .	n.a.	n.a.	60,000
United Kingdom .	239,685	261,409	333,300	United Kingdom .	44,962	148,288	45,900
U.S.A. . . .	322,355	377,542	336,200	U.S.A. . . .	71,636	72,069	50,100

* Estimated from sample survey.

TRANSPORT
RAILWAYS

	PASSENGERS ('000)		GOODS ('000)		REVENUE ('000 £L)		
	Journeys	Passenger-km.	Tons	Ton-km.	Passengers	Goods	Total
1969 .	78	7,278	313	24,455	178	2,018	2,196
1970 .	76	7,430	258	20,082	187	1,916	2,103
1971 .	71	7,187	325	26,789	184	2,236	2,420
1972 .	55	5,004	417	33,116	134	2,313	2,447
1973 .	36	2,829	512	35,063	81	2,446	2,527

ROAD TRAFFIC
(motor vehicles in use)

	1969	1970	1971	1972	1973	1974
Passenger cars (incl. taxis) .	129,674	136,016	146,270	164,790	185,935	220,204
Buses	1,763	1,794	1,905	2,067	2,258	2,397
Lorries	14,473	14,795	15,656	17,130	19,151	20,983
Motor cycles . . .	12,004	9,800	9,731	10,734	12,036	13,179

SHIPPING (Beirut)

	SHIPS ENTERED		MERCHANDISE (Metric Tons)	
	Number	Net Tons	Entered	Cleared
1977 .	2,783	3,120,365	2,047,239	140,151
1978 .	1,852	2,549,949	1,664,395	137,218
1979 .	2,257	2,833,349	2,373,851	225,935
1980 .	2,732	3,615,700	2,731,587	248,056
1981 .	2,095	2,804,079	2,195,499	287,531

CIVIL AVIATION
(revenue traffic on scheduled services)

	1977	1978	1979
Kilometres flown ('000)	42,608	44,499	45,585
Passengers carried ('000)	932	865	904
Passenger-kilometres (million)	1,564	1,398	1,505
Freight-tonne kilometres ('000)	540,227	510,474	645,431
Mail tonne-kilometres ('000)	3,035	3,935	4,247
Total tonne-kilometres (million)	687	644	789

TOURISM

	1971	1972	1973	1974
Total Foreign Visitors (except Syrians)	1,015,772	1,048,159	884,997	1,510,260
of which:				
Visitors from Arab countries	619,171	577,186	535,641	892,203
Visitors from Europe	213,698	250,932	171,338	316,080
Visitors from the Americas	94,076	102,281	75,606	143,000
Syrian Visitors	1,241,633	1,233,903	1,019,498	1,498,131
TOTAL	2,257,405	2,281,062	1,904,495	3,008,391

EDUCATION
(1972–73)

	SCHOOLS	PUPILS	TEACHERS
Public:			
Primary and kindergarten	740	202,913	
Upper primary	549	77,161	} 17,077
Secondary	65	18,240	
Private:			
Primary and kindergarten	742	} 366,987	16,168
Upper primary and secondary	390		

Sources (unless otherwise stated): Direction Centrale de la Statistique, Ministère du Plan, and Direction Générale des Douanes, Beirut.

THE CONSTITUTION

(Promulgated May 23rd, 1926; amended by the Constitutional Laws of 1927, 1929, 1943 and 1947.)

According to the Constitution, the Republic of the Lebanon is an independent and sovereign State, and no part of the territory may be alienated or ceded. Lebanon has no State religion. Arabic is the official language. Beirut is the capital.

All Lebanese are equal in the eyes of the law. Personal freedom and freedom of the Press are guaranteed and protected. The religious communities are entitled to maintain their own schools, provided they conform to the general requirements relating to public instruction as laid down by the State. Dwellings are inviolable; rights of ownership are protected by law. Every Lebanese citizen who has completed his twenty-first year is an elector and qualifies for the franchise.

Legislative Power

Legislative power is exercised by one house, the Chamber of Deputies, with 99 seats, 53 of which are allocated to Christians and 45 to Muslims (for full details of allocation, *see* Legislature, p. 794). Its members must be over 25 years of age, in possession of their full political and civil rights, and literate. They are considered representative of the whole nation, and are not bound to follow directives from their constituencies. They can be suspended only by a two-thirds majority of their fellow-members. Secret ballot was introduced in a new election law of April 1960.

The Chamber holds two sessions yearly, from the first Tuesday after March 15th to the end of May, and from the first Tuesday after October 15th to the end of the year. The normal term of the Chamber of Deputies is four years; general elections take place within sixty days before the end of this period. If the Chamber is dissolved before the end of its term, elections are held within three months of dissolution.

Voting in the Chamber is public—by acclamation, or by standing and sitting. A quorum of two-thirds and a majority vote is required for constitutional issues. The only exceptions to this occur when the Chamber becomes an electoral college, and chooses the President of the Republic, or Secretaries to the Chamber, or when the President is accused of treason or of violating the Constitution. In such cases voting is secret, and a two-thirds majority is needed.

Executive Power

The President of the Republic is elected for a term of six years, and is not immediately re-eligible. He and his ministers deal with the promulgation and execution of laws passed by the Chamber of Deputies. The Ministers and the Prime Minister are chosen by the President of the Republic. They are not necessarily members of the Chamber of Deputies, although they are responsible to it and have access to its debates. The President of the Republic must be a Maronite Christian and the Prime Minister a Sunni Muslim; and the choice of the other Ministers has to reflect the division between the communities in the Chamber.

The President himself can initiate laws. Alternatively, the President may demand an additional debate on laws already passed by the Chamber. He can adjourn the Chamber for up to a month, but not more than once in each session. In exceptional circumstances he can dissolve the Chamber and force an election. Ministers can be made to resign by a vote of no confidence.

Elections to the Chamber of Deputies, due in April 1976, were postponed for up to 26 months. In January 1978 the Chamber's term was further extended to June 1980. A further extension in April 1980 prolonged the life of the Chamber until June 1983.

In December 1976 the Chamber of Deputies gave the Government power to rule by decree for six months, subsequently extended until January 1978. In March 1979 the Chamber was renamed the National Assembly.

THE GOVERNMENT

HEAD OF STATE

President: ELIAS SARKIS (elected May 8th, 1976; took office September 23rd, 1976).

THE CABINET

(June 1982)

Prime Minister and Minister of the Interior: CHAFIC AL-WAZZAN.*

Deputy Prime Minister and Minister of Foreign Affairs: Dr. FUAD BOUTROS.

Minister of National Defence: JOSEPH SKAFF.

Minister of Public Health: Dr. NAZIH AL-BIZRI.

Minister of Justice: KHATCHIK BABIKIAN.

Minister of National Education and Fine Arts: RENÉ MOUAWWAD.

Minister of Information: MICHEL EDDÉ.

Minister of the Economy and Trade: KHALID JUNBLATT.

Minister of State: JOSEPH ABUKHATER.

Minister of Posts and Telecommunications: MICHEL AL-MURR.

Minister of Hydroelectric Resources: MAHMOUD AMMAR (acting).

Minister of Finance: Dr. ALI AL-KHALIL.

Minister of State: MAHMOUD ANMAR.

Minister of Public Works and Transport: ELIAS AL-HRAWI.

Minister of Industry and Oil: MUHAMMAD YUSIF BAIDOUN.

Minister of State: QAISAR NASR.

Minister of State: SAMI YOUNIS.

Minister of Housing and Co-operatives: SALIM AL-JAHEL.

Minister of Labour and Social Affairs: Dr. ABDURAHMAN LABBAN.

Minister of Agriculture: MUSTAFA DURNAIQAH.

Minister of Tourism: MARWAN HAMADE.

*tendered resignation, June 25th, 1982.

LEGISLATURE

MAJLIS AL-UMMA

(*National Assembly*)

The electoral reform bill of April 1960 maintained the existing ratio of 6 Christians to 5 Muslims in the Chamber of Deputies. It is the custom for the President of the Chamber of Deputies to be a Shi'a Muslim. The Chamber was renamed the "National Assembly" in March 1979.

    President: KAMAL ASAAD.
    Vice-President: MOUNIR ABU-FADEL.

There was a General Election in May 1972, but the diversity of allegiance in the Chamber makes a strict analysis by party groupings impossible. The distribution of seats among religious groups is laid down by law. The elections due in April 1976 were postponed for up to 26 months and in January 1978 the term of the Chamber of Deputies was further extended until June 1980. In April 1980 the term was extended until June 30th, 1983.

RELIGIOUS GROUPS					
Maronite Christians	.	.	.	.	30
Sunni Muslims	.	.	.	.	20
Shi'a Muslims	.	.	.	.	19
Greek Orthodox	.	.	.	.	11
Greek Catholics	.	.	.	.	6
Druzes	.	.	.	.	6
Armenian Orthodox	.	.	.	.	4
Armenian Catholics	.	.	.	.	1
Protestants	.	.	.	.	1
Others	.	.	.	.	1
TOTAL	.	.	.	.	99

POLITICAL PARTIES

Armenian Revolutionary Federation (ARF): Spears St., P.O.B. 11-587, Beirut; f. 1890; principal Armenian party; socialist ideology; collective leadership; 5 mems. in National Assembly.

al-Baath: f. in Syria, 1940, by MICHEL AFLAK; secular party with policy of Arab union, branches in several Middle Eastern countries; 2 mems. in National Assembly; Leader ASSEM QANSOU, Beirut.

al-Baath: pro-Iraqi wing of al-Baath party; Sec.-Gen. ABDEL-MAJID RAFEI.

Bloc National: f. 1943; policy of power-sharing and the exclusion of the military from politics; 5 mems. in the National Assembly; Leader RAYMOND EDDÉ (in self-imposed exile in Paris since 1976); Vice-Pres. SAYED AQL; Sec.-Gen. ANTOINE ABU-ZAID, Assemblée Nationale, Place de l'Étoile, Beirut.

ad-Dustour (*Constitutional Party*): f. 1943; led struggle against French mandate, established 1943 Constitution; party of the political and business élite; Leader MICHEL BECHARA AL-KHOURY, rue Michel Chiha, Kantari, Beirut.

al-Harakiyines al-Arab: Beirut; f. 1948 by GEORGES HABACHE; Arab nationalist party, with Marxist tendencies.

al-Hayat al-Wataniya: Beirut; f. 1964 by AMINE ARAYSSI.

al-Jabha al-Damukratiya al-Barlamaniya (*Parliamentary Democratic Front*): Beirut; mainly Muslim support; Leader RASHID ABDUL HAMID KARAMI, Assemblée Nationale, Place de l'Étoile, Beirut.

al-Kata'eb (*Phalanges Libanaises, Phalangist Party*): P.O.B. 992, Place Charles Hélou, Beirut; f. 1936; nationalist, reformist, democratic social party; 70,260 mems.; 7 mems. in National Assembly; announced merger with Parti National Liberal, May 1979; Leader PIERRE GEMAYEL; Vice-Pres. ELIE KARAME; Gen. Sec. JOSEPH SAADE; publs. *al-Amal* (Arabic daily), *Action— Proche Orient* (French political and scientific monthly).

Mouvement de l'Action Nationale: f. 1965; Founder and Leader OSMAN MOSBAH AD-DANA, P.O.B. 5890, Centre Starco, Bloc Sud, Beirut.

an-Najjadé: f. 1936; unionist; 3,000 mems.; Founder and Pres. ADNANE MOUSTAPHA AL-HAKIM, Sawt al-Uruba, P.O.B. 3537, Beirut; publ. *Sawt al-Uruba* (Arabic daily).

an-Nida' al-Kawmi: f. 1945; Founder and Leader KAZEM AS-SOLH, Ramlet al-Baïda, Imm. Chammat, Beirut.

Parti Communiste Libanais (*Lebanese Communist Party*): rue al-Hout, Imm. du Parti Communiste Libanais, P.O.B. 633, Beirut; f. 1924; officially dissolved 1948-71; Marxist, much support among intellectuals; 1 mem. in National Assembly; Leader and Sec.-Gen. GEORGE HAWI; publs. *an-Nida* (daily), *al-Akhbar* (weekly), *al-Tarik* (monthly), *Gantch* (Armenian weekly).

Parti Démocrate: f. 1969; supports a secular, democratic policy, private enterprise and social justice; Sec.-Gen. JOSEPH MUGHAIZEL; co-founder ÉMILE BITAR, rue Kantari, Imm. Labban, Beirut.

Parti National Liberal (*al-Wataniyin al-Ahrar*): f. 1958; liberal reformist party; 9 mems. and assocs. in National Assembly; announced merger with Phalanges Libanaises, May 1979; Founder and Pres. CAMILLE CHAMOUN, Assemblée Nationale, Place de l'Étoile, Beirut; Deputy Leader KAZEM KHALIL; Sec.-Gen. DORY CHAMOUN.

Parti Nationaliste Syrien: f. 1932, banned 1962-69; advocates a "Greater Syria", composed of Lebanon, Syria, Iraq, Jordan, Palestine and Cyprus; 1 supporter in National Assembly; Leader INAAM RAAD.

Parti Socialiste Progressiste (*al-Takadumi al-Ishteraki*): P.O.B. 2893, Zkak el-Blat, Beirut; f. 1949; progressive party, advocates constitutional road to socialism; over 16,000 mems.: 10 mems. in National Assembly; Pres. WALID JOUMBLATT; publ. *al-Anba'* (weekly).

Parti Socialiste Révolutionnaire: Beirut; f. 1964; Leader YOUSSEF MOUBARAK.

The *Lebanese Front* (Secretary DORY CHAMOUN) is a grouping of right-wing parties (mainly Christian) and the *National Front* (Sec.-Gen. KAMAL SHATILA) is a grouping of left-wing parties (mainly Muslim). Other parties include the *Independent Nasserite Movement* (Leader IBRAHIM QULAYAT) and the *Union of Working People's Forces* (Sec.-Gen. KAMAL SHATILA). *Amal* is a Shi'ite politico-military organization (Principal Controller of Command Council Sheikh MUHAMMAD MANDI SHAMS AD-DIN, Chair. SADR AD-DIN AS-SADR).

DIPLOMATIC REPRESENTATION

EMBASSIES AND LEGATIONS ACCREDITED TO LEBANON

(In Beirut unless otherwise stated)

(E) Embassy; (L) Legation.

Afghanistan: Cairo, Egypt (E).

Algeria: Jnah (opposite Coral Beach) (E); *Ambassador:* MUSTAPHA HACHMAOUI.

Argentina: 149 ave. Fouad 1er (E); *Ambassador:* LUIS RAUL DE LA VEGA.

Australia: rue Bliss (E); *Ambassador:* DAVID WILSON (no longer in Beirut).

Austria: Ras Beirut, rue Sadate, Imm. Sadate Tower (E); *Ambassador:* HERBERT AMRY.

Bahrain: Sami Fouad Hamzeh Bldg., Bir Hassan (E); *Chargé d'affaires:* ADEL YOUSSEF AL-AYADI.

Bangladesh: rue Tabet (Verdun), Imm. Said Jaafar (E); *Ambassador:* KHONDKER GOLAM MUSTAFA.

Belgium: 15th Floor, Centre Verdun, rue Dunant (E); *Ambassador:* HENRI DOUXCHAMPS SEGESSER DE BRUNEGG.

Bolivia: Dora, Imm. Tachjian (E); *Chargé d'affaires:* NAJIB BICHARA GHOSN.

Brazil: Baabda, Imm. Amin Helou (E); *Ambassador:* PAULO DA COSTA FRANCO.

Bulgaria: rue Australia, Imm. Hibri (E); *Chargé d'affaires a.i.:* TODOR DODEV.

Cameroon: Jeddah, Saudi Arabia (E).

Canada: rue Hamra, Centre Sabbagh (E); *Ambassador:* THÉODORE JEAN ARCAND.

Chad: blvd. Sami Solh, Forêt Kfoury, Imm. Kalot Frères (E); *Ambassador:* (vacant).

Chile: rue Taleb Hobeich, Quartier Badaro, Imm. Amine Cabbabe (E); *Ambassador:* ENRIQUE GUZMÁN.

China, People's Republic: rue 72, Nicolas Ibrahim Sursock, Ramlet El-Baida (E); *Ambassador:* (vacant)

Colombia: P.O.B. 1496, Chouran, Imm. Jaber al-Ahmad al-Sabbah (E); *Ambassador:* GUSTAVO DUARTE.

Congo: Cairo, Egypt (E).

Costa Rica: rue Hamra (E); *Chargé d'affaires:* RIAD ABDEL-BAKI.

Cuba: rue Abdel Sabbah between rue Sakiet el-Janzir and rue de Vienne, Imm. Ghazzal (E); *Ambassador:* (vacant).

Cyprus: Cairo, Egypt (E).

Czechoslovakia: ave. de 22 Novembre, B.P. 1529 (E); *Ambassador:* PAVEL LUKES.

Denmark: Imm. New Malas, rue California, P.O.B. 11-5190 (E); *Ambassador:* VILLADS VILLADSEN.

Ethiopia: Cairo, Egypt (E).

Finland: Centre Gefinor, rue Clemenceau (E); *Ambassador:* ARTO ENSIO TANNER.

France: rue Clemenceau (E); *Ambassador:* PAUL-MARC HENRY.

Gambia: Jeddah, Saudi Arabia (E).

German Democratic Republic: ave. de Paris (E); *Ambassador:* BRUNO SEDLACZEK.

Germany, Federal Republic: rue Mansour Jourdak, Imm. Daouk (E); *Ambassador:* HORST SCHMIDT-DORNEDDEN.

Ghana: Cairo, Egypt (E).

Greece: Sadat-Sadat Tower St. (E); *Ambassador:* (vacant).

Guinea: Cairo, Egypt (E).

Haiti: rue du Fleuve, Imm. Sarkis (E); *Ambassador:* (vacant).

Hungary: Jnah, Imm. Cheikh Salem Al-Sabah (E); *Ambassador:* IMRE SZTANKOVICS.

India: rue Kantari, Imm. Samharini (E); *Ambassador:* BENI PRASAD AGARWAL.

Indonesia: Damascus, Syria (E).

Iran: Jnah, Imm. Sakina Mattar (E); *Ambassador:* MUSA FAKHR RUHANI.

Iraq: (E); *Ambassador:* ABDEL RAZZAQ LAFTEH (no longer in Beirut).

Ireland: Sadat Tower Building, Third Floor, Sadat St., P.O.B. 113-5980 (E); *Ambassador:* GEARÓID Ó CLÉRIGH.

Italy: rue Makdissi, Imm. Cosmidis (E); *Ambassador:* STEFANO D'ANDREA.

Ivory Coast: rue Chouran, Imm. Kojok, P.O.B. 8160 (E); *Ambassador:* AMADOU BOCOUM.

Japan: Corniche Chouran, Imm. Olfat Nagib Salha (E); *Ambassador:* HIROJI YAMAGUCHI.

Jordan: rue Verdun, Imm. Belle-Vue (E); *Ambassador:* (vacant).

Kenya: Cairo, Egypt (E).

Korea, Democratic People's Republic: (E); *Ambassador:* YANG SONG-YONG.

Kuwait: Bir Hassan, The Stadium Roundabout (E); *Ambassador:* ABDEL-HAMID BUAIJAN (no longer in Beirut).

Liberia: rue Clemenceau, Imm. Alpha (E); *Ambassador:* WILMOT A. DAVID.

Libya: Jnah, Imm. Cheikh Abdallah Khalifé Al-Sabbah; *People's Bureau.*

Malaysia: Cairo, Egypt (E).

Mali: Cairo, Egypt (E).

Malta: Tripoli, Libya (E).

Mauritania: Damascus, Syria (E).

Mexico: P.O.B. 4332, rue Sadat, Sadat Tower, 6th Floor (E); *Ambassador:* VÍCTOR M. RODRÍGUEZ.

Morocco: Bir Hassan (E); *Chargé d'affaires a.i.:* MUHAMMAD ABDERRAHMAN EL ALAOUI.

Nepal: Cairo, Egypt (E).

Netherlands: rue Kantari, Imm. Sahmarani, B.P. 117 (E); *Ambassador:* AUGUST HYACINTH CROIN.

Nigeria: Cairo, Egypt (E).

Norway: Taher and Fakhry Bldg., Bliss St., Ras Beirut (E); *Chargé d'affaires a.i.:* OLA DORUM.

Oman: Bir Hassan (E); *Ambassador:* (vacant).

Pakistan: 2699 Lyon St. (E); *Ambassador:* Commodore KHATEEB MAQSOOD HUSSAIN.

Panama: (L).

Paraguay: rue Kantari, Imm. Muhammad El-Zeben (E); *Chargé d'affaires:* Dr. MAMDOUH H. AGHA.

Peru: Cairo, Egypt (E).

Poland: Ras Beirut, rue Sourati, Imm. Nassif (E); *Ambassador:* JANUSZ ZABLOCKI.

Portugal: rue Mme Curie, Green Building (E); *Ambassador:* Dr. JOÃO PERESTRELLO.

Qatar: Dibs Building, Chouran Street (E); *Ambassador:* (vacant).

Romania: Secteur 3G, Manara, rue 77, Imm. Khaled Abdo (E); *Ambassador:* FLOREA CHITU.

Saudi Arabia: rue Bliss, Manara (E); *Ambassador:* General ALI AL-SHAER (no longer in Beirut).

Singapore: Cairo, Egypt (E).

Spain: Ramlet el Baida, Imm. White Sands (E); *Ambassador:* LUIZ JORDANA DE POZAS.

Sri Lanka: Cairo, Egypt (E).

Sudan: rue Mme Curie, Imm. Minkara (E); *Ambassador:* Dr. ABDELLATIF ABDELHAMID (no longer in Beirut).

Sweden: rue Clemenceau, Imm. Moukarzel et Rubeiz (E); *Ambassador:* STEN STROMHÖLM.

Switzerland: rue John Kennedy, Imm. Achou (E); *Ambassador:* (vacant).

Thailand: Jeddah, Saudi Arabia (E).

Tunisia: Ramlet el-Baida, Imm. Rock and Marble (E); *Ambassador:* MUHAMMAD JENFAN (no longer in Beirut).

Turkey: Bir Hassan (E); *Ambassador:* NEJAT AYDIN.

U.S.S.R.: rue Mar Elias el-Tina (E); *Ambassador:* ALEXANDER SOLDATOV.

United Arab Emirates: Jnah, Face Eden Rock, Imm. Wafic Tanbara (E); *Ambassador:* ABDUL AZIZ HADEF AL-SHAMSI (no longer in Beirut).

United Kingdom: ave. de Paris, Ain el-Mreissé (E); *Ambassador:* D. A. ROBERTS, C.M.G.

U.S.A.: ave. de Paris (Corniche), Imm. Ali Reza (E); *Ambassador:* ROBERT DILLON.

Uruguay: rue Verdun, Fayoumé, Imm. Mohamad Hussein Ben Moutahar (E); *Ambassador:* (vacant).

Vatican: rue Hamara; *Apostolic Nuncio:* Mgr. CARLO FURNO.

Venezuela: rue Kantari, Imm. Sahmarani (E); *Ambassador:* José Miguel Quintana Guevara.

Viet-Nam: Damascus, Syria (E).

Yemen Arab Republic: blvd. Khaldé-Quzai, Imm. Ingénieur Ryad Amaiche (E); *Ambassador:* Ahmad Ahmad al-Moudwahi (no longer in Beirut).

Yemen, People's Democratic Republic: Bir Hassan, rue Ghubaïry (E); *Ambassador:* (vacant).

Yugoslavia: Imm. Daouk, Arts et Metiers Quarter (E); *Ambassador:* Radimilio Trojanović.

Zaire: Cairo, Egypt (E).

Zambia: Cairo, Egypt (E).

Lebanon also has diplomatic relations with Albania, Benin, the Central African Republic, Djibouti, the Dominican Republic, Ecuador, El Salvador, Gabon, Guatemala, Guinea-Bissau, Honduras, Iceland, the Republic of Korea, Luxembourg, Madagascar, Monaco, New Zealand, Nicaragua, Niger, the Philippines, Senegal, Sierra Leone, Togo, Trinidad and Tobago and Upper Volta.

JUDICIAL SYSTEM

Law and justice in the Lebanon are administered in accordance with the following codes, which are based upon modern theories of civil and criminal legislation:

(1) Code de la Propriété (1930).

(2) Code des Obligations et des Contrats (1932).

(3) Code de Procédure Civile (1933).

(4) Code Maritime (1947).

(5) Code de Procédure Pénale (Code Ottoman Modifié).

(6) Code Pénal (1943).

(7) Code Pénal Militaire (1946).

(8) Code d'Instruction Criminelle.

The following courts are now established:

(*a*) Fifty-six "Single-Judge Courts", each consisting of a single judge, and dealing in the first instance with both civil and criminal cases; there are seventeen such courts at Beirut and seven at Tripoli.

(*b*) Eleven Courts of Appeal, each consisting of three judges, including a President and a Public Prosecutor, and dealing with civil and criminal cases; there are five such courts at Beirut.

(*c*) Four Courts of Cassation, three dealing with civil and commercial cases and the fourth with criminal cases. A Court of Cassation, to be properly constituted, must have at least three judges, one being the President and the other two Councillors. The First Court consists of the First President of the Court of Cassation, a President and two Councillors. The other two civil courts each consist of a President and three Councillors. If the Court of Cassation reverses the judgment of a lower court it does not refer the case back but retries it itself.

First President of the Court of Cassation: Emile Aboukheir.

(*d*) The Council of State, which deals with administrative cases. It consists of a President, Vice-President and four Councillors. A Commissioner represents the Government.

President of the Court of the Council of State: Antoine Baroud.

(*e*) The Court of Justice, which is a special court consisting of a President and four judges, deals with matters affecting the security of the State.

In addition to the above, Islamic, Christian and Jewish religious courts deal with affairs of personal status (marriages, deaths, inheritances, etc.).

There is also a Press Tribunal.

RELIGION

PRINCIPAL COMMUNITIES

	1958	1974*
Christians	792,000	n.a.
Roman Catholics	529,500	1,141,740
Armenian Rite	14,500	24,500
Chaldean Rite	n.a.	6,459
Greek (Melkite) Rite	} 91,000 {	191,889
Latin Rite		20,000
Maronite Rite	424,000	878,892
Syrian Rite	n.a.	20,000
Orthodox	219,000	n.a.
Greek	150,000	n.a.
Armenian	69,000	n.a.
Protestant	14,000	n.a.
Muslims	624,000	n.a.
Sunni	286,000	n.a.
Shi'a	250,000	n.a.
Druzes	88,000	n.a.
Jews	6,600	n.a.

* The 1974 figures for members of the Roman Catholic churches are based on estimates by the curias of dioceses based in the Lebanon. National and diocesan boundaries do not necessarily correspond.

It will be seen that the largest single community in the Lebanon is the Maronite, a Uniate sect of the Roman Church. The Maronites inhabited the old territory of Mount Lebanon, i.e. immediately east of Beirut. In the south, towards the Israeli frontier, Shi'a villages are most common whilst between the Shi'a and the Maronites live the Druzes (divided between the Yazbakis and the Jumblatis). The Beka'a has many Greek Christians, while the Tripoli area is mainly Sunni Muslim. Altogether, of all the regions of the Middle East, the Lebanon probably presents the closest juxtaposition of sects and peoples within a small territory. As Lebanese political life is organized on a sectarian basis, the Maronites also enjoy much political influence, including a predominant voice in the nomination of the President of the Republic.

ROMAN CATHOLIC CHURCH

Armenian Rite

Patriarchate of Cilicia: Patriarcat Arménien Catholique, Jeitaoui, 2400 Beirut; includes Patriarchal Diocese of Beirut; 28 priests, 24,500 Catholics; Patriarch Hemaigh Pietro XVII Ghedighian.

Chaldean Rite

Diocese of Beirut: Evêché Chaldéen-Catholique, B.P. 8566, Beirut; 8 priests, 6,459 Catholics; Bishop Raphael Bidawid.

LATIN RITE

Apostolic Vicariate of Beirut: B.P. 11-4224, Beirut; 12 parishes, 20,000 Catholics; Vicar Apostolic PAUL BASSIM.

MARONITE RITE

Patriarchate of Antioch and all the East: Patriarcat Maronite, Bkerké (winter), Dimane (summer); includes Patriarchal Diocese of Gibail and Batrun; 203 priests, 197,266 Catholics; Patriarch ANTOINE KHORAICHE. The Maronite Rite includes the Archidioceses of Beirut, Cyprus, Tripoli, Aleppo, Saida and Tyre, and the Dioceses of Baalbeck-Zahlé, Jounieh, Latakia, Cairo, Australia, Brazil, U.S.A. and Sarba.

MELKITE RITE

Patriarchate of Antioch: Melkite-Greek-Catholic Patriarchate, P.O.B. 50076, Beirut; jurisdiction over one million Melkites throughout the world; publs. *Sophia* (English—in U.S.A.), *Le Lien* (French—Beirut); Patriarch of Antioch and all the East, of Alexandria and of Jerusalem MAXIMOS V HAKIM. The Melkite Rite includes the 3 Patriarchates of Damascus (Syria), Egypt, Sudan and Libya and Jerusalem; 7 Archdioceses in Lebanon (Tyre, Beirut, Baalbek, Baniyas, Saida, Tripoli and Zahleh); 4 Archdioceses in Syria (Aleppo, Latakia, Homs and Hauran); one in Jordan (Amman); one in Israel (Acre and Nazareth); also one in the U.S.A., one in Brazil and one in Canada.

SYRIAN RITE

Patriarchate of Antioch: Patriarcat Syrien-Catholique, rue de Damas, B.P. 116/5087, Beirut; jurisdiction over 100,000 Syrian Catholics in Palestine, Jordan, Lebanon, Syria, Iraq, Egypt and Turkey; publs.: *Revue pensée chrétienne* (monthly), *Revue Diocesonine d'Alebe* (quarterly); Patriarch IGNACE ANTOINE II HAYEK.

Patriarchal Vicariate of the Lebanon: Vicariat Patriarcal Syrien, rue de Syrie, Beirut; 12 priests, 18,000 Catholics; Vicar Patriarchal FLAVIEN ZACHARIE MELKI.

Note: The statistics of priests and Catholics are estimates by the diocesan curias for the situation on December 31st, 1974.

OTHER RELIGIOUS GROUPS

Armenian Apostolic Orthodox: Armenian Catholicosate of Cilicia, Antelias, Lebanon; f. 1441 in Cilicia (now in Turkey), transferred to Antelias, Lebanon, 1930; Leaders His Holiness KHOREN I (PAROYAN), Catholicos of Cilicia, His Holiness KAREKIN II (SARKISSIAN), Catholicos Coadjutor; one million mems. in Lebanon, Syria, Cyprus, Kuwait, Greece, Iran and U.S.A.; publs. *Hask* (monthly); *Hask Armenological Review* (yearly).

Greek Orthodox: Leader His Beatitude IGNATIUS IV, Patriarch of Antioch and All the East, Patriarcat Grec-Orthodoxe, P.O.B. 9, Damascus, Syria.

Syrian Orthodox: Leader IGNATIUS ZAKKA, Patriarch of Antioch and All the East, Patriarcat Syrien Orthodoxe, Damascus, Syria.

Shi'a Muslims: Leader Imam SAYED MOUSSA AS-SADR (missing since August 1978), President of the Supreme Islamic Council of the Shi'a Community of the Lebanon, Dar al-Iftaa al-Jaafari, Beirut.

Sunni Muslims: Leader S.G. Sheikh HASSAN KHALED, Grand Mufti of the Lebanon, Dar El-fatwa, Ilewi Rushed Street, Beirut.

Druzes: Leader S.G. Sheikh MUHAMMAD ABOUCHACRA, Supreme Spiritual Leader of the Druze Community, rue Abou Chacra, Beirut.

Jews: Leader CHAHOUD CHREIM, Beirut.

Protestants: Leader Rev. Dr. FARID AUDEH, Pres. of Nat. Evangelical Union of the Lebanon, P.O.B. 5224, rue Maurice Barrès, Beirut.

Union of the Armenian Evangelical Churches in the Near East: P.O.B. 377, Beirut; Moderator Prof. HOV P. AHARONIAN; the Union includes some thirty Armenian Evangelical Churches in Syria, Lebanon, Egypt, Cyprus, Greece, Iran and Turkey.

THE PRESS

The most important dailies are *al-Anwar* and *an-Nahar*, which have the highest circulations, *The Daily Star*, *al-Jarida* and *L'Orient-Le Jour*, the foremost French paper. The latter two are owned by Georges Naccashe, former Lebanese ambassador to France, and tend to take a pro-government line. In a country where most of the élite speak French the other French daily, *Le Soir*, is also influential, and, for the same reason, the twice-weekly publication *Le Commerce du Levant* occupies an important place in the periodical Press.

The civil war hindered the operation of the Press, but even at the height of the civil war about two dozen newspapers and magazines appeared, reflecting every shade of political opinion. In January 1977, however, censorship was imposed on all publications. Some papers ceased publication, if only temporarily. Before this, Lebanon enjoyed the reputation of having one of the freest presses in the Middle East and was an important base for foreign correspondents. Some Lebanese papers have since introduced London and Paris editions.

DAILIES

al-Amal: P.O.B. 959, rue Liberateur, Beirut; f. 1939; Phalangist Party; Arabic; circ. 45,000; Editor GEORGES OMEIRA.

al-Anba': P.O.B. 955, Beirut; f. 1948; Arabic.

al-Anwar: P.O.B. 1038, Beirut; f. 1959; independent; Arabic; Supplement, Sunday, cultural and social; published by Dar Assayad S.A.L.; circ. 75,200; Propr. SAID FREIHA; Editor ISSAM FREIHA.

Ararat: P.O.B. 756, Nor Hagin, Beirut; f. 1937; Communist; Armenian; circ. 5,000; Editor KRIKOR HAJENIAN.

Ayk: P.O.B. 2623, Beirut; f. 1953; English.

Aztag: P.O.B. 11-587, rue Selim Boustani, Beirut; f. 1927; Armenian; circ. 6,500.

al-Baïraq: P.O.B. 1800, rue Monot, Beirut; f. 1911; Arabic; published by Soc. Libanaise de Presse; Editor RAYMOND KAWASS; circ. 3,000.

Baïrut: P.O.B. 7944, Beirut; f. 1952; Arabic.

ach-Chaab (*The People*): P.O.B. 5140, Beirut; f. 1961; Arabic; Nationalist; Propr. and Editor MUHAMMAD AMIN DUGHAN; circ. 7,000.

ach-Chams: P.O.B. 7047, Beirut; f. 1925; Arabic.

ach-Charq: P.O.B. 838, rue de Verdun, Beirut; f. 1945; Arabic; Editor AOUNI AL-KAAKI.

Daily Star: P.O.B. 11-987, rue al-Hayat, Beirut; f. 1952; independent; English; Chief Editor JIHAD KHAZEN; circ. 19,220.

ad-Dastour (*The Constitution*): P.O.B. 886, Beirut; f. 1968; Arabic; Owner and Editor SHARIF AL-HINDI; temporarily published from London; circ. 53,400.

ad-Dunia: P.O.B. 4599, Beirut; f. 1943; Arabic; political; circ. 25,000; Chief Editor SULIMAN ABOU ZAID.

al-Hayat: P.O.B. 11-987, rue al-Hayat, Beirut; f. 1946; independent; Arabic; circ. 32,538.

al-Jarida: P.O.B. 220, place Tabaris, Beirut; f. 1953; independent; Arabic; Editor ABDULLA SKAFF; circ. 22,600.

al-Joumhouria (*The Republic*): P.O.B. 7111, Beirut; f. 1924; Arabic.

Journal al-Haddis: P.O.B. 5858, Jounieh; f. 1927; Arabic; political; Owner GEORGES ARÈGE-SAADÉ.

al-Khatib: P.O.B. 365, rue Georges Picot; Arabic.

al-Kifah al-Arabi: P.O.B. 5158-14, Chouran, rue Andalous, Beirut; f. 1950; Arabic; political, socialist, Pan-Arab; Publisher and Chief Editor WALID HUSSEINI.

Lissan-ul-Hal: P.O.B. 4619, rue Chateaubriand, Beirut; f. 1877; Arabic; Editor GEBRAN HAYEK; circ. 33,000.

al-Liwa': P.O.B. 2402, Beirut; f. 1970; Arabic; Propr. ABDEL GHANI SALAM; Editor AHMED SULEIMAN.

an-Nahar: P.O.B. 11-226, rue Banque du Liban—Hamra; Press Co-operative Bldg., Beirut; f. 1933; Arabic; independent; Publisher GHASSAN TUENI; Co-Editors MICHEL ABOU JAOUDÉ and LOUIS EL-HAJJ; Ed. Man. FRANÇOIS AKL; Pres. Man. Mrs. NADIA TUENI; circ. 85,000.

an-Nass: P.O.B. 4886, Fouad Shihab St., Beirut; f. 1959; Arabic; circ. 16,000; Editor HASSAN YAGHI.

an-Nida (*The Appeal*): P.O.B. 4744, Beirut; f. 1959; Arabic; published by the Lebanese Communist Party; Editor KARIM MROUÉ; circ. 10,000.

Nida' al-Watan: P.O.B. 6324, Beirut; f. 1937; Arabic.

an-Nidal: P.O.B. 1354, Beirut; f. 1939; Arabic.

L'Orient-Le Jour: P.O.B. 2488, rue Banque du Liban, Beirut; f. 1942; French; independent; Chair. PIERRE EDDÉ; Dir. CAMILLE MENASSA; Editorial Dir. AMINE ABOU-KHALED; Editor ISSA GORAIEB; circ. 23,000.

Raqib al-Ahwal: P.O.B. 467, rue Patriarche Hoyek, Beirut; f. 1937; Arabic; Editor SIMA'N FARAH SEIF.

Rayah: P.O.B. 4101, Beirut; Arabic.

Le Reveil: Beirut; French; Editor-in-Chief JEAN SHAMI; Dir. RAYMOND DAOU.

ar-Ruwwad: P.O.B. 2696, rue Mokhalsieh, Beirut; f. 1940; Arabic; Editor BESHARA MAROUN.

Sada Lubnan: P.O.B. 7884, Beirut; f. 1951; Lebanese Pan-Arab; Arabic; Editor MOHAMED BAALBAKI; circ. 25,000.

Sawt al-Uruba: P.O.B. 3537, Beirut; f. 1959; Arabic; an-Najjadé Party; Editor ADNANE AL-HAKIM.

Le Soir: P.O.B. 1470, rue de Syrie, Beirut; f. 1947; French; independent; Dir. DIKRAN TOSBATH; Editor ANDRÉ KECATI; circ. 16,500.

al-Tayyar: P.O.B. 1038, Beirut; Arabic; independent; issued weekly for the time being; circ. 75,000.

Telegraf—Bairut: P.O.B. 1061, rue Béehara el Khoury, Beirut; f. 1930; Arabic; political, economic and social; Editor TOUFIC ASSAD MATNI; circ. 15,500 (5,000 outside Lebanon).

al-Yawm: P.O.B. 1908, Beirut; f. 1937; Arabic; Editor WAFIC MUHAMMAD CHAKER AT-TIBY.

az-Zamane: P.O.B. 6060, rue Boutros Karameh, Beirut; f. 1947; Arabic.

Zartonk: P.O.B. 617, rue de l'Hôpital français, Beirut; f. 1937; Armenian; official organ of Armenian Liberal Democratic Party; Editor P. TOUMASSIAN.

WEEKLIES

al-Aalam al-Lobnani (*The Lebanese World*): Imm. Ministry of Foreign Affairs, P.O.B. 462, Beirut; f. 1964; Arabic, English, Spanish, French; politics, literature and social economy; Editor-in-Chief FAYEK KHOURY; Gen. Editor CHEIKH FADI GEMAYEL; circ. 45,000.

Achabaka: Dar Assayad, P.O.B. 1038, Beirut; f. 1956; society and features; Arabic; Founder SAID FREIHA; Editor GEORGE IBRAHIM EL-KHOURY; circ. 126,500.

al-Ahad: Quartier Chourah, rue Andalous, P.O.B. 1462, Beirut; Arabic; political; Editor RIAD TAHA; circ. 32,000.

al-Akhbar: Beirut; f. 1954; Arabic; published by the Lebanese Communist Party; circ. 21,000.

al-Anba': P.O.B. 2893, Beirut; Progressive Socialist Party; Arabic.

al-Anwar Supplement: P.O.B. 1038, Beirut; cultural-social; every Sunday; supplement to daily *al-Anwar*; Editor ISSAM FREIHA; circ. 90,000.

Argus: Bureau of Lebanese and Arab Documentation, P.O.B. 16-5403, Beirut; economic bulletin; Arabic and English; circ. 1,000.

Assayad: Dar Assayad, P.O.B. 1038, Beirut; f. 1943; Propr. SAID FREIHA; Editor RAFIQUE KHOURY; circ. 94,700.

Le Commerce du Levant: P.O.B. 687, Kantari St., Commerce and Finance Bldg., Beirut; f. 1929; weekly and special issue quarterly; commercial and financial; French; circ. 15,000; Editor: Société de la Presse Economique; Pres. MAROUN AKL.

Dabbour: Museum Square, Beirut; f. 1922; Arabic; Editors MICHEL RICHARD and FUAD MUKARZEL; circ. 12,000.

al-Dyar: P.O.B. 959, Verdun St., Bellevue Bldg., Beirut; f. 1941; Arabic; political; circ. 46,000.

al-Hadaf: P.O.B. 212, rue Béchir, Imm. Esseilé, Beirut; f. 1969; organ of Popular Front for the Liberation of Palestine (PFLO); Arabic.

al-Hawadess: P.O.B. 1281, Beirut; temporarily published from London (3 Harrington Gardens, S.W.7); f. 1911; Arabic; news; Chair. Mrs. OMAYA EL-LOZI; Gen. Man. SHAFIK JUME'AN; circ. 85,000.

al-Hurriya: P.O.B. 857, Beirut; f. 1960; voice of the Democratic Front for the Liberation of Palestine (DFLP) and the Organization for Communist Action in Lebanon (OCAL) 1969-81, of DFLP 1981-; Arabic; Editor DAOUD TALHAME; circ. 30,000.

al-Iza'a: rue Selim Jazaerly, P.O.B. 462, Beirut; f. 1938; politics, art, literature and broadcasting; Arabic; circ. 11,000; Editor FAYEK KHOURY.

al-Jamhour: Mussaïtbeh, P.O.B. 1834, Beirut; f. 1936; Arabic; illustrated weekly news magazine; Editor FARID ABU SHAHLA; circ. 45,000, of which over 30,000 outside Lebanon.

Kul Shay': rue Béchara el Khoury, P.O.B. 3250, Beirut; Arabic.

al-Liwa: rue Abdel Kaim Khalil, P.O.B. 2402, Beirut; Arabic; Propr. ABDEL GHANI SALAAM.

al-Moharrer: P.O.B. 5366, Beirut; f. 1962; Arabic; circ. 87,000; Gen. Man. WALID ABOU ZAHR.

Magazine: Quartier Sursock, Achrafieh, P.O.B. 1404, Beirut; f. 1956; in French; political and social; Publ.

Les Editions Orientales S.A.L.; Publisher GEORGES ABOU ADAL; Dir.-Gen. CHARLES ABOU ADAL; circ. 13,500.

Massis: place Debbas, Beirut; f. 1949; Armenian; Catholic; Editor F. VARTAN TEKEYAN; circ. 2,000.

Middle East Economic Survey: Middle East Research and Publishing Centre, P.O.B. 4940, Nicosia, Cyprus; f. 1957 (in Beirut); review of petroleum and economic news; Editor and Publr. FUAD W. ITAYIM.

al-Ousbou' al-Arabi (*Arab Week*): Quartier Sursock, Achrafieh, P.O.B. 1404, Beirut; f. 1959; Arabic; political and social; Publishers Les Editions Orientales, S.A.L.; Publisher GEORGE ABOU ADAL; Gen. Man. CHARLES ABOU ADAL; circ. 125,000 (circulates throughout the Arab World).

al-Rassed: P.O.B. 11-2808, Beirut; Arabic; Editor GEORGE RAJJI.

Revue du Liban: rue Issa Maalouf, Beirut; f. 1928; French; Publisher MELHEM KAREM; Gen. Man. MICHEL MISK; circ. 22,000.

Samar: P.O.B. 1038, Beirut; photorama magazine; circ. 50,000.

OTHER SELECTED PERIODICALS

Note: published monthly unless otherwise stated.

al-Adib: P.O.B. 11-878, Beirut; f. 1942; Arabic, artistic, literary, scientific and political; Editor ALBERT ADIB.

Alam Attijarat (*Business World*): Strand Bldg., Hamra St., Beirut; f. 1965 in association with Johnston International Publishing Corpn., New York; monthly; commercial; Editor NADIM MAKDISI; international circ. 17,500.

Arab Economist: Gefinor Tower, Clemenceau St., P.O.B. 11-6068, Beirut; monthly; published by Centre for Economic, Financial and Social Research and Documentation S.A.L.; Chair. Dr. CHAFIC AKHRAS.

L'Economie Arabe: P.O.B. 11-6068, Beirut; f. 1958; French; published by Centre d'Etudes et de Documentation Economiques Financières et Sociales S.A.L.; Chair. Dr. CHAFIC AKHRAS.

al-Idari: P.O.B. 1038, Beirut; f. 1975; business management; Arabic; Pres. and Gen. Man. BASSAM FREIHA; Chief Editor HASSAN EL-KHOURY; circ. 20,000.

International Crude Oil and Product Prices: Middle East Petroleum and Economic Publications, P.O.B. 4940, Nicosia, Cyprus; f. 1971 (in Beirut); twice yearly review and analysis of oil price trends in world markets; Publisher FUAD W. ITAYIM.

al-Intilak: c/o Michel Nehme, al-Intilak Printing and Publishing House, P.O.B. 4958, Beirut; f. 1960; literary; Arabic; Chief Editor MICHEL NEHME.

Lebanese and Arab Economy: Sanayeh, P.O.B. 11-1801, Beirut; f. 1951; Arabic and French; Publisher Beirut Chamber of Commerce and Industry.

Majallat al Izaat al Loubnaniat: Lebanese Broadcasting Corporation, Beirut; Arabic; broadcasting affairs.

al-Mouktataf: Quartier Chouran, rue Andalous, P.O.B. 11-1462; Arabic; general.

Naft al Arab: Beirut; f. 1965; monthly; Arabic; oil; Publisher ABDULLAH AL TARIQI.

Rijal al Amal (*Businessmen*): Gefinor Centre, Bloc C, 510, P.O.B. 6065, Beirut; f. 1966; Arabic; business; Publisher and Ed.-in-Chief MAHIBA AL-MALKI.

Tabibok: P.O.B. 4887, Beirut; f. 1956; medical, social, scientific; Arabic; Editor Dr. SAMI KABANI; circ. 90,000.

al-Tarik (*The Road*): Beirut; cultural and theoretical; published by the Lebanese Communist Party; circ. 5,000.

al-'Ulum: Dar al Ilm Lil Malayeen, rue de Syrie, P.O.B 1085, Beirut; scientific review.

Welcome to Lebanon and the Middle East: Tourist Information and Advertising Bureau; Starco Centre, North Block 711, P.O.B. 4204, Beirut; f. 1959; on entertainment, touring and travel; English; Editor SOUHAIL TOUFIK ABOU-JAMRA; circ. 6,000.

NEWS AGENCIES

FOREIGN BUREAUX

Agence France-Presse (**AFP**): B.P. 11-1461, Beirut; Dir. DAVID DAURE.

Agencia EFE (*Spain*): P.O.B. 113/5313, Beirut; Correspondent MARY ANGELES JUNQUERA.

Agentstvo Pechati Novosti (**APN**) (*U.S.S.R.*): Beirut Correspondent EDOUARD RIABTSEV.

Agenzia Nazionale Stampa Associata (**ANSA**) (*Italy*): rue Verdun, Immeuble Safieddine, B.P. 1525, Beirut; Correspondent BRUNO MAROLO.

Allgemeiner Deutscher Nachrichtendienst (**ADN**) (*German Democratic Republic*): P.O.B. 114/5100, Beirut; Correspondent PETER WENDT.

Československá tisková kancelář (**CTK**) (*Czechoslovakia*): P.O.B. 5069, Beirut; Chief Middle East Correspondent VLADIMIR OTRUBA.

Deutsche Presse-Agentur (**dpa**) (*Federal Republic of Germany*): P.O.B. 1266, Beirut; Correspondent HANS-ARMIN REINARTZ.

Jiji Tsushin-Sha (*Japan*): Jiji Press, Room 14, Dadis Bldg., 84 Colombani St., Ras Beirut; Correspondent KOJI MORITO.

Kyodo News Service (*Japan*): 2nd Floor, Manuelian Bldg., Shouran St., Ras Beirut; Correspondent NOBUO OSHIKA.

Middle East News Agency (**MENA**) (*Egypt*): 72 Al Geish St., P.O.B. 2268, Beirut.

United Press International (**UPI**) (*U.S.A.*): Press Co-operative Bldg., rue Hamra, Beirut; Bureau Man. VINCENT J. SCHODOLSKI.

Bulgarian Telegraph Agency, Iraq News Agency, Jamahiriya News Agency (Libya), Prensa Latina (Cuba), Reuters (United Kingdom) and TASS (U.S.S.R.) also have offices in Beirut.

PRESS ASSOCIATIONS

Lebanese Press Syndicate: P.O.B. 3084, Beirut; f. 1911; 18 mems.; Pres. MUHAMMAD AL-BAALBAKI; Vice-Pres. FADEL SAID AKL; Sec. BASSEM AL-SABEH.

PUBLISHERS

Arab Institute for Research and Publishing: Carlton Tower Building, Saqiat el-Janzeer, 3rd Floor, P.O.B. 11-5460, Beirut; Dir. MAHER KAYALI; works in Arabic and English.

Dar al Adab: Beirut; literary and general.

Dar El-Ilm Lilmalayin: Nassif Yazigi St., P.O.B. 1085, Beirut; f. 1945; dictionaries, textbooks, Islamic cultural books; Editorial Dir. MUNIR BA'ALBAKI; Man. Dir. BAHIJE OSMAN.

Dar-Alkashaf: P.O.B. 112091, A. Malhamee St., Beirut; f. 1930; publishers of *Alkashaf* (Arab Youth Magazine), maps and atlases; printers and distributors; Propr. M. A. FATHALLAH.

Dar al-Makshouf: rue Amir Beshir, Beirut; scientific, cultural and school books; owner: Sheikh FUAD HOBEISH.

Dar Al-Maaref Liban S.A.L.: P.O.B. 2320, Esseily Bldg., Riad Al-Solh Square, Beirut; f. 1959; children's books and textbooks in Arabic; Gen. Man. JOSEPH NASHOU.

Dar Al-Machreq S.A.R.L.: P.O.B. 946, Beirut; f. 1853; religion, art, literature, history, languages, science, philosophy, school books, dictionaries and periodicals; Dir. PAUL BROUWERS, S.J.

Dar An-Nahar S.A.L.: B.P. 11-226, Beirut; f. 1967; a pan-Arab publishing house; Pres. MOHAMED ALI HAMADÉ.

Dar Assayad S.A.L.: P.O.B. 1038, Beirut; f. 1943; publishes in Arabic *al-Anwar* (daily), *Assayad* (weekly), *al-*

Tayar (weekly), *Achabaka* (weekly), *Samar* (weekly), *Sahar* (weekly), and other publications; has offices and correspondents in Arab countries and most parts of the world; Chair. ISSAM FREIHA; Man. Dir. BASSAM FREIHA.

Institute for Palestine Studies, Publishing and Research Department: Nsouli-Verdun St., P.O.B. 11-7164, Beirut; f. 1963; independent non-profit Arab research organization; to promote better understanding of the Palestine problem and the Arab-Israeli conflict; publishes books, reprints research papers, etc.; Chair. Prof. CONSTANTINE ZURAYK; Exec. Sec. Prof. WALID KHALIDI.

The International Documentary Center of Arab Manuscripts: Maqdissi St., Ras Beirut Hanna Bldg., P.O.B. 2668, Beirut; f. 1965; publishes and reproduces ancient and rare Arabic texts; Propr. ZOUHAIR BAALBAKI.

Khayat Book and Publishing Co. S.A.L.: 90–94 rue Bliss, Beirut; Middle East, Islam, oil, Arab publications and reprints; Man. Dir. PAUL KHAYAT.

Librairie du Liban: Riad Solh Sq., P.O.B. 945, Beirut; f. 1944; dictionaries, Middle East, travel, Islam; Proprs. KHALIL and GEORGE SAYEGH.

Middle East Publishing Co.: Beirut, rue George Picot, Imm. El Kaissi; f. 1954; publishes *Medical Index* and *Revue Immobilière* (Real Estate); Man. Editor ELIE SAWAF.

New Book Publishing House: Beirut.

Rihani Printing and Publishing House: Jibb En Nakhl St., Beirut; f. 1963; Propr. ALBERT RIHANI; Man. DAOUD STEPHAN.

RADIO AND TELEVISION

RADIO

Lebanese Broadcasting Station: rue Arts et Métiers, Beirut; is a part of the Ministry of Information; f. 1937; Dir.-Gen. K. HAGE ALI; Technical Dir. J. ROUHAYEM; Dir. of Programmes N. MIKATI; Head of Administration A. AOUN; Public Relations FAOUZI FEHMY.

The Home Service broadcasts in Arabic on short wave, the Foreign Service broadcasts in Portuguese, Armenian, Arabic, Spanish, French and English.

Number of radio receivers: 605,000.

TELEVISION

Compagnie Libanaise de Télévision (C.L.T.): P.O.B. 4848, Beirut; f. 1959; commercial service; programmes in

Arabic, French and English on four channels; Dir.-Gen. PAUL TANNOUS; Technical Manager M. S. KARIMEH.

Télé-Liban S.A.L.: P.O.B. 11-5054, Beirut; f. 1978; commercial service; programmes in Arabic, French and English on three channels, and relays on three channels; Chair. and Dir.-Gen. Dr. CHARLES RIZK.

Télé-Management S.A.R.L.: P.O.B. 113-5310, Beirut; exclusive airtime sales and programmes sales contractor to Télé-Liban S.A.L. (channels 5, 7 and 9); Co. Dirs. WISSAM IZZEDDINE and RAMIZ RIZK; Gen. Man. CLAUDE SAWAYA.

Number of TV receivers: 425,000.

FINANCE

BANKING

Beirut has for long been the leading financial and commercial centre in the Middle East, as can be seen from the extensive list of banking organizations given below. However, public confidence in the banking system was strained by the closing of the Intra Bank, the largest domestic bank, late in 1966 when its liquid funds proved insufficient to cope with a run of withdrawals. The bank obtained enough guarantees to re-open in January 1968, though it is now an investment bank managed by a New York company. The civil disturbances between April 1975 and October 1976 considerably disrupted Beirut's banking and commercial facilities.

(cap. = capital; p.u. = paid up; dep. = deposits; m. = million; L£ = Lebanese £; res. = reserves)

CENTRAL BANK

Banque du Liban: Central Bank of Lebanon: P.O.B. 5544, rue Masraf Loubnane, Beirut; f. 1964; central bank; cap. L£15m.; dep. L£4,142m.; total assets L£10,989m. (Dec. 1980); Gov. MICHEL EL-KHOURY.

PRINCIPAL LEBANESE BANKS

Adcom Bank S.A.L.: P.O.B. 11-2431, Verdun St., Ammar Bldg., Beirut; f. 1960 as Advances and Commerce Bank; cap. p.u. £L20m.; dep. £L370m. (1981); Chair. and Gen. Man. HENRI R. SFEIR.

Arab Libyan Tunisian Bank S.A.L.: Riad Solh Sq., Shaker & Oueni Bldg., P.O.B. 11-9575, Beirut; f. 1973; subsid. of Libyan Arab Foreign Bank and Société Tunisienne de Banque; cap. p.u. L£10m.; Pres. MOHAMED ABDEL JAWAD; Gen. Man. AHMED SHERIF.

Bank Almashrek S.A.L.: Bank Almashrek Bldg., Riad Solh St. 52, Beirut, P.O.B. 1524; affil. with Morgan Guaranty Trust; brs. in Lebanon, Jordan and Qatar; cap. L£30m.; dep. L£1,311m. (1981); total assets L£1,608m. (1981); Chair. FAHD AL-BAHAR; Man. Dir. PETER DE ROOS.

Bank of Beirut S.A.L.: P.O.B. 11-7354, Gefinor Centre, rue Clemenceau, Beirut; cap. L£20m.; Chair. H.E. WILLIAM S. KAZAN; Man. Dir. RIDA ABUJAWDEH.

Bank of Beirut and the Arab Countries S.A.L.: 250, rue Clemenceau, P.O.B. 11-1536, Beirut; f. 1957; cap. L£25m.; dep. L£776.3m. (1980); Chair. TOUFIC S. ASSAF; Vice-Chair. NASHAT SHEIKH EL-ARD; Gen. Man. AMEEN M. ALAAMY.

Bank of Credit and Commerce International (Lebanon) S.A.L.: P.O.B. 11-1889, Piccadilly Bldg., 2nd Floor, Hamra St., Beirut; f. 1974; cap. p.u. L£10m.; Chair. SHAIKH MUHAMMAD FAYYAZ.

Bank Handlowy for the Middle East S.A.L.: P.O.B. 11-5508, Sehnaoui Bldg., Banque du Liban St., Beirut; f. 1974; cap. p.u. L£5m.; subsidiary of Bank Handlowy w Warszawie, Warsaw; Chair. JANUSZ MICHALSKI; Gen. Man. BOGDAN KOWALEWSKI.

Bank of Kuwait and the Arab World S.A.L.: P.O.B. 3846, Sehnaoui Bldg., Riad el-Solh St., Beirut; f. 1959; cap. p.u. L£12m.; dep. L£30m.; Chair. Dr. RAFIK A. NAJA; Gen. Man. ABDOU S. KARNABE.

Bank of Lebanon and Kuwait S.A.L.: P.O.B. 11-5556, Arab Bank Bldg., Riad el-Solh St., Beirut; f. 1974; cap. L£15m.; dep. L£68m.; Gen. Man. R. W. FREEMAN.

Banque al-Ahli (Banque Nationale) Foncière, Commerciale et Industrielle S.A.L.: rue Foch, P.O.B. 2868, Beirut; f. 1953; cap. L£10m.; res. L£3.16m.; Pres. and Gen. Man. BOUTROS EL KHOURY.

Banque Audi S.A.L.: ave. Fouad Chehab, St. Nicolas Area, P.O.B. 11-2560, Beirut; f. 1962; cap. p.u. L£50m.; dep. L£1,833m. (1981); Chair. and Gen. Man. GEORGES OIDIH AUDI.

Banque de la Bekaa, S.A.L.: Centre Fakhoury, Zahle; cap. p.u. L£3m.; Pres. and Gen. Man. E. W. FAKHOURY.

Banque Beyrouth pour le Commerce S.A.L.: P.O.B. 110-216, Arab Bank Bldg., Riad el-Solh St., Beirut; f. 1961; Chair. and Gen. Man. RIFAAT S. AL-NIMER.

Banque de Crédit Agricole, Industriel et Foncier: Oueini Bldg., Riad el-Solh St., Beirut; f. 1954; Dir.-Gen. Sheikh BOUTROS EL KHOURY; took over several banks in 1967–68, including Banque de l'Economie Arabe, Banque d'Epargne and Union National Bank.

Banque de Crédit National S.A.L.: Beirut Riyad Bank Bldg., Riad el-Solh St., P.O.B. 11-0204, Beirut; f. 1959; cap. and reserves L£5.8m.; dep. L£18.9m. (1979); Pres. and Gen. Man. EDMOND J. SAFRA; Deputy Gen. Man. HENRI KRAYEM.

Banque du Crédit Populaire, S.A.L.: P.O.B. 11-5292, Furn el Hayek St., Achrafieh, Beirut; f. 1963; cap. p.u. L£20m.; dep. L£764m. (December 1981); Chair. JOE I. KAIROUZ; Deputy Gen. Mans. HABIB L. RAHAL, IGNACE A. KAIROUZ.

Banque de l'Essor Economique Libanaise S.A.L.: Manassa Bldg., nr. Municipal Playground, Jounieh; cap. p.u. L£3m.

Banque de Financement S.A.L.: P.O.B. 5044, Intra Investment Company Bldg., Hamra, Beirut; Chair. and Gen. Man. ISSAM ASHOUR.

Banque de l'Industrie et du Travail, S.A.L.: B.P. 11-3948; rue Riad el-Solh, Beirut; f. 1961; cap. p.u. L£30m.; dep. L£834m. (1981); Chair. LAURA EMILE BUSTANI; Man. Dir. Dr. ASSAAD F. SAWAYA; Asst. Gen. Man. ALBERT I. TANNOUS.

Banque Joseph Lati et Fils S.A.L.: P.O.B. 1983, Bardawil Bldg., Adib Ishaq St., Beirut; f. 1924; Pres.-Dir.-Gen. ISAAC LATI; Asst. Dir.-Gen. JOSEPH LATI.

Banque du Liban et d'Outre-Mer (S.A.L.): P.O.B. 11-1912, Abdel-Aziz St., Hamra, Beirut; f. 1951; cap. p.u. L£50m.; dep. L£2,062m. (1980); Chair. and Gen. Man. Dr. NAAMAN AZHARI.

Banque Libanaise des Emigrés S.A.L.: Raouche, Beirut; cap. p.u. L£3m.; dep. L£4.3m.

Banque Libanaise pour le Commerce S.A.L.: P.O.B. 11-1126, rue Riad el-Solh, Beirut; f. 1950; cap. L£5m.; dep. L£1,089m. (Dec. 1980); Chair. and Gen. Man. JEAN F. S. ABOUJAOUDE.

Banque Libano-Française: 1 rue Riad el-Solh, Beirut; f. 1968; cap. p.u. L£15m.; dep. L£1,783.5m. (Dec. 1980); Chair. and Gen. Man. FARID RAPHAEL.

Banque Libano-Brésilienne S.A.L.: P.O.B. 11-3310, Banking Centre Bldg., Dora, Beirut; f. 1962; cap. L£10m.; res. L£3.5m. (Dec. 1979); Pres. J. A. GHOSN; Gen. Man. GEORGES N. GHOSN.

Banque de la Méditerranée S.A.L.: P.O.B. 348, Hadife Bldg., ave. Fouad Chehab, Beirut; f. 1944; cap. L£25m.; dep. L£1,100m. (Jan. 1981); Pres. and Gen. Man. JOSEPH A. EL-KHOURY; Asst. Gen. Man. SALIM SFEIR.

Banque Misr Liban, S.A.L.: Head Office: P.O.B. 7, Beirut.

Banque Nasr Libano-Africaine, S.A.L.: P.O.B. 798, Beydoun Bldg., Riad el-Solh St., Beirut; f. 1963; Pres. DIAB ISKANDAR NASR.

Banque Saradar S.A.L.: Sursock St., P.O.B. 11-1121, Beirut; f. 1948; cap. L£20m.; dep. L£1,399.9m. (Dec. 1981); Chair. and Gen. Man. JOE SARADAR; Asst. Gen. Man. ABDO I. JEFFI.

Banque Tohme S.A.L.: P.O.B. 11-837, Tabaris Square, Nicholas St., Beirut; f. 1919; cap. p.u. L£5m.; dep. L£118m.; Pres. and Gen. Man. ASSAD TOHME; Asst. Gen. Man. ROGER TOHME.

Banque G. Trad (Crédit Lyonnais) S.A.L.: P.O.B. 11-113, Beirut; f. 1951; cap. L£9m.; dep. L£477m. (Dec. 1978); Pres. G. A. TRAD.

Beirut-Riyad Bank S.A.L.: Beirut-Riyad Bank Bldg., Riad Solh St., P.O.B. 11-4668, Beirut; f. 1959; cap. L£24.8m.; dep. L£780.9m. (1979); Pres. and Gen. Man. HUSSEIN MANSOUR.

British Bank of the Lebanon S.A.L.: rue Trablos, P.O.B. 11-7048, Beirut; f. 1971; cap. p.u. L£5m.; dep. L£145.7m. (1980); subsidiary of British Bank of the Middle East; Chair. and Gen. Man. H. HAKIM.

Byblos Bank: P.O.B. 11-5605, Verdun St., Beirut; f. 1962; cap. L£44m.; res. L£44m.; dep. L£731m. (June 1980); Pres. Gen. Man. FRANÇOIS SEMAAN BASSIL.

Chemical Bank (Middle East) S.A.L.: P.O.B. 11-9506, Rabiya-Metn, Beirut; subsidiary of Chemical Bank, New York; Gen. Man. THEODORE E. AMSLEY.

Continental Development Bank, S.A.L.: Ghantous Bldg., Dora, P.O.B. 90263 Beirut; f. 1961; subsidiary of Continental Bank, Chicago; cap. L£8m.; total resources L£135m. (1979); Chair. JOHN D. BURN; Gen. Man. EDOUARD COZE.

Crédit Libanais S.A.L.: P.O.B. 11-1458, Riad el-Solh Square, Esseily Bldg., Beirut; f. 1961; cap. L£36m. dep. L£1,120m. (Nov. 1981); Chair. and Gen. Man. B. Y. OBÉGI; Gen. Man. H. Y. OBÉGI.

Federal Bank of Lebanon S.A.L.: Parliament Square, P.O.B. 11-2209, Beirut; f. 1952; cap. L£10m.; dep. L£190.6m. (Dec. 1980); Pres. and Gen. Man. MICHEL A. SAAB.

First National Bank of Chicago (Lebanon) S.A.L.: P.O.B. 11-1629, Riad el-Solh St., Beirut; f. 1968; wholly-owned subsidiary of First National Bank of Chicago, U.S.A.; cap. L£5m.; total resources L£226m. (Dec. 1980); Chair. MARTIN J. WHITE; Gen. Man. STEPHEN A. WAHMANN.

Fransabank (Banque Sabbag et Française pour le Moyen-Orient S.A.L.): P.O.B. 11-393, Imm. Centre Sabbag, rue Hamra, Beirut; f. 1978 as merger of Banque Sabbag and Banque Française pour le Moyen Orient S.A.L.; cap. L£40m.; dep. L£1,864m. (Dec. 1981); Chair. ADNAN KASSAR; Gen. Man. HABIB NAUPHAL.

Jammal Trust Bank, S.A.L.: Jallad Bldg., Riad el-Solh St., Beirut; f. 1963 as Investment Bank, S.A.L.; cap. p.u. L£60m. (1981); Chair. and Gen. Man. ALI A. JAMMAL.

MEBCO BANK—Middle East Banking Co. S.A.L.: P.O.B. 11-3540, Continental Center, Raouche, Beirut; f. 1959; cap. p.u. L£15m.; dep. L£677m. (Oct. 1981); Chair. JAWAD CHALABI; Gen. Man. HASSAN YAHYA.

Prosperity Bank of Lebanon S.A.L.: P.O.B. 11-5625, Acra Bldg., Place des Martyrs, Achrafieh, Beirut; f. 1963; cap. p.u. L£5m.; Gen. Man. S. S. WEHBE.

Rifbank S.A.L.: Head Office: P.O.B. 11-5727, rue Kantari, Beirut; f. 1965; in association with Commerzbank A.G., The National Bank of Kuwait S.A.K., Kuwait Foreign Trading Contracting and Investment Co. S.A.K., The Commercial Bank of Kuwait S.A.K.; cap. p.u. L£7m.; dep. L£204m. (1981); Chair. A. A. BASSAM; Vice-Chair. Dr. M. YOUNES; Acting Gen. Man. Dr. W. RELLECKE.

Royal Bank of Canada (Middle East) S.A.L.: Hanna Ghantous Bldg., Dora Blvd., P.O.B. 11-250, Beirut; f. 1959; cap. L£5m.; res. L£5.2m. (Dec. 1980); Pres. and Chair. W. C. C. MACKAY; Gen. Man. KHALIL KIKANO.

Société Bancaire du Liban S.A.L.: N. Sassine Bldg., Sassine Sq., P.O.B. 165–192, Beirut; f. 1899; cap. and res. L£32m.; total assets L£253m. (Dec. 1980); Chair. S. S. LEVY; Deputy Chair. A. BOULOS.

Société Générale Libano-Européenne de Banque S.A.L.: P.O.B. 11-2955, Beirut; f. 1953; cap. p.u. L£10m.; dep. L£650m. (Sept. 1980); Chair. A. M. SEHNAOUI; Gen. Man. JEAN-PIERRE LAFONTAINE.

Société Nouvelle de la Banque de Syrie et du Liban S.A.L.: P.O.B. 957, Beirut; f. 1963; cap. p.u. L£15m.; dep. L£710m. (1979); Pres. BERNARD DE MARGERIE; Gen. Man. ROLAND PRINGUEY.

Toronto Dominion Bank (Middle East) S.A.L.: P.O.B. 5580, Rue Banque du Liban, Beirut; f. 1964; cap. L£3m.; Chair. IBRAHIM AL-AHDAB; Man. Dir. E. ACHKAR.

Transorient Bank: P.O.B. 11-6260, Beirut; f. 1966; cap. p.u. L£14.6m.; dep. L£411m. (Sept. 1981); joint venture with the International Bank of Washington and Lebanese private investors; Chair. HAMED BAKI; Gen. Man. GABRIEL ATALLAH; Asst. Gen. Man. GEORGES E. SAYEGH.

United Bank of Lebanon & Pakistan, S.A.L.: P.O.B. 11-5600, Prince Fahed bin Abdel Saud Bldg., Chouran St., Raouche, Beirut; f. 1964; cap. L£7.5m.; dep. 474m. (Dec. 1981); Chair. ABDUS SAMI.

DEVELOPMENT BANKS

Banque Nationale pour le Développement Industriel et Touristique: Tabriz Sq., ave. Fouad Chehab, S.N.A. Bldg., 5th Floor, B.P. 8412, Beirut; f. 1973; cap. L£66m.; Chair. and Gen. Man. ABDUL RAHMAN AL-TAYYARAH.

Investment and Finance Bank S.A.L. (INFI): P.O.B; 16-5110, ave. Fouad Chehab, St. Nicolas Area, Beirut; f. 1974; medium- and long-term loans, 60 per cent from Lebanese sources; associated with Banque Audi (Lebanon), Banque Audi (France) S.A., Banque Audi (Suisse), AG (Zürich), Investbank (U.A.E.).

PRINCIPAL FOREIGN BANKS

Algemene Bank Nederland N.V. (*Netherlands*): P.O.B. 11-3012, Beirut; Man. Dir. W. U. HAZELHOFF ROELF-ZEMA; Man. M. CASSARD.

Arab African International Bank (*Egypt*): Riad el-Solh St., P.O.B. 11-6066, Beirut.

Arab Bank Ltd. (*Jordan*): Beirut Main Branch: Riad Solh Sq., P.O.B. 1015, Beirut; Asst. Gen. Man. SAMI ALAMI.

Banco Atlántico S.A. (*Spain*): P.O.B. 7376, Beirut; Rep. RAFAEL CASASUS ARBE.

Banco di Roma S.p.A. (*Italy*): Beirut, Saida and Tripoli; Dir.-Gen. MARCELLO CONTENTO.

Bank of America N.T. and S.A. (*U.S.A.*): P.O.B. 3965, Beirut; Vice-Pres. and Man. MARSHALL LEWIS JNR.

Bank of Nova Scotia (*Canada*): Riad el-Solh St., P.O.B. 4446, Beirut; Man. A. G. GALEA.

Bank Saderat Iran (*Iran*): Beirut Branch, P.O.B. 5126, Beirut.

Banque Nationale de Paris Intercontinentale S.A. (*France*): P.O.B. 1608, Beirut; Beirut Dir. HENRI TYAN.

British Bank of the Middle East (*Hong Kong*): Bab Edriss, Beirut; brs. at Ras Beirut, Dora, Mazra'a, Ashrafieh and Tripoli; Lebanon Area Man. A. L. GILLIBRAND.

The Chartered Bank (*United Kingdom*): P.O.B. 11-3996, Riad el-Solh St., Beirut; Man. in Beirut D. H. S. MOIR.

Chase Manhattan Bank, N.A. (*U.S.A.*): P.O.B. 11-3684, Beirut; Man. GUNTER NEUBERT.

Chemical Bank (*U.S.A.*): P.O.B. 11-9506, Beirut; Rep. THEODORE E. AMSLEY.

Citibank N.A. (*U.S.A.*): P.O.B. 11-3648, Zard Zard Bldg., Jounieh Rd., Jal El Dib; Resident Vice-Pres. L. A. MAESTRE.

Crédit Commercial de France S.A.: P.O.B. 11-6873, Port St., Beirut; Rep. M. HEMAYA.

Crédit Suisse: P.O.B. 11-35155, Mme Curie St., Beirut; cap. p.u. L£10m.; dep. L£77.3m.; Rep. MAJED DAJANI.

Deutsche Bank A.G. (*Federal Republic of Germany*): P.O.B. 11-710, Beirut; Rep. SIEGFRIED BRUNNEN-MILLER.

Habib Bank (Overseas) Ltd. (*Pakistan*): P.O.B. 5616, Beirut; Man. A. RASHID KHAN.

Jordan National Bank, S.A.: P.O.B. 5186, Beirut; Tripoli, Jdeideh and Saida.

Manufacturers Hanover Trust Co. (*U.S.A.*): P.O.B. 11-5133, Gefinor Center, Block C, Room 201, Clemenceau St., Ras Beirut, Beirut; Man. VAHAK T. TAHMAZIAN.

Morgan Guaranty Trust Co. (*U.S.A.*): P.O.B. 5752, Bank Almashrek Bldg., rue Riad el-Solh, Beirut; Rep. SELWA B. LORENZ (Vice-Pres.).

Moscow Narodny Bank Ltd. (*United Kingdom*): P.O.B. 5481, Beirut; Gen. Man. O. LAPOUSHKIN.

Rafidain Bank (*Iraq*): Hamra Branch: Sadat Tower Bldg., Sadat St., Beirut, P.O.B. 1891; f. 1941.

Saudi National Commercial Bank: P.O.B. 2355, Beirut; f. 1938.

State Bank of India: P.O.B. 7252, 5th Floor, Arab Bank Bldg., Riad el-Solh St., Beirut.

Union Bank of Switzerland: P.O.B. 11-5734, Starco South 1001-4, Beirut; Rep. G. E. SALAWI.

Numerous foreign banks have Representative Offices in Beirut.

BANKING ASSOCIATION

Association of Banks in Lebanon: P.O.B. 976, Riad el Solh Square, Beirut; f. 1959; serves and promotes the interests of the banking community in the Lebanon; mems.: 81 banks and 40 banking rep. offices; Pres. Dr. ASSAAD SAWAYA; Dep. Gen. Secs. ANTOINE OBEID, MAJID JOUMBLAT.

INSURANCE
NATIONAL COMPANIES

"La Phenicienne" (S.A.L.): H. Haddad Bldg., Amine Gemayel St., Sioufi, P.O.B. 5652, Beirut; f. 1964; Gen. Man. TANNOUS C. FEGHALI.

al-Ittihad al-Watani: Immeuble Fattal, P.O.B. 1270, Beirut; Chair. JOE I. KAIROUZ.

Arabia Insurance Co. Ltd. S.A.L.: Arabia House, Phoenicia St., P.O.B. 11-2172, Beirut; Vice-Chair. and Gen. Man. BADR S. FAHOUM.

Commercial Insurance Co. S.A.L.: St. Elie Sisters Building, Zouk Mikael, P.O.B. 84, Jounieh; f. 1962; Chair. MAX R. ZACCAR; Gen. Man. MYRIAM R. ZACCAR.

Compagnie Libanaise d'Assurances (S.A.L.): Riad el-Solh St., P.O.B. 3685, Beirut; f. 1951; Man. Dir. JEAN F. S. ABOUJAOUDÉ; Man. BAHJAT DAGHER.

Libano-Suisse Insurance Co. (S.A.L.): Centre Azzam, 4th Floor, Jdeideh; Pres. and Gen. Man. PIERRE J. SEHNAOUI; Man., Lebanon Branch NAJI HABIS.

Some twenty of the major European companies are also represented in Beirut.

TRADE AND INDUSTRY

DEVELOPMENT ORGANIZATION

Council of Development and Reconstruction: Beirut; f. 1976; aims to achieve reconstruction after civil war; Chair. Dr. MUHAMMAD ATALLAH.

CHAMBERS OF COMMERCE AND INDUSTRY

Beirut Chamber of Commerce and Industry: Justinian St., P.O.B. 111801, Beirut; f. 1898; 10,000 mems.; Pres. ADNAN KASSAR; Gen. Dir. WALID NAJA; publ. *The Lebanese and Arab Economy* (13 issues per annum).

Tripoli Chamber of Commerce and Industry: Tripoli.

Chamber of Commerce and Industry for Sidon and the South: P.O.B. 41, Sidon.

Zahlé Chamber of Commerce and Industry: Zahlé; f. 1939; 497 mems.; Pres. ALFRED SKAFF.

EMPLOYERS' ASSOCIATIONS

Association of Lebanese Industrialists: Chamber of Commerce and Industry Bldg., Justinian St., P.O.B. 1520, Beirut; Chair. FUAD ABI SALAH.

Conseil National du Patronat: Beirut; f. 1965.

TRADE UNION FEDERATION

Confédération Générale des Travailleurs du Liban (C.G.T.L.): P.O.B. 4381, Beirut; f. 1958; 200,000 mems.; only national labour centre in Lebanon and sole rep. of working classes; comprises 18 affiliated federations including all 150 unions in Lebanon; Pres. GEORGE SAKE; Vice-Pres. FARES DAGHER, HASSIB ABDUL JAWAD.

TRANSPORT

RAILWAYS

Office des Chemins de Fer de l'Etat Libanais et du Transport en Commun de Beyrouth et de sa Banlieue: P.O.B. 109, Souk el-Arwam, Beirut; since 1961 all railways in Lebanon have been state-owned. There are 335 km. of standard-gauge railway; Chair. ADEL HAMIÉ; Dir.-Gen. ANTOINE BAROUKI.

ROADS

Lebanon has 7,100 km. of roads, of which 1,990 km. are main roads. Most are generally good by Middle Eastern standards. The two international motorways are the north-south coastal road and the road connecting Beirut with Damascus in Syria. Among the major roads are that crossing the Beka'a and continuing south to Bent-Jbail and the Chtaura-Baalbek road. Hard-surfaced roads connect Jezzine with Moukhtara, Bzebdine with Metn, Meyroub with Afka and Tannourine. A Beirut-Tripoli Highway improvement scheme is being carried out with help from the World Bank and should be completed in 1983.

SHIPPING

Siège Provisoire de la Commission Portuaire: Immeuble de l'Electricité du Liban, Rue du Fleuve, Beirut.

Beirut is the principal port of call for the main shipping and forwarding business of the Levant; the port has frequently been closed by political disturbance. Tripoli, the northern Mediterranean terminus of the oil pipeline from Iraq (the other is Haifa), is also a busy port, with good equipment and facilities. Saida is still relatively unimportant as a port. Shipping was disrupted by the civil war.

There are many shipping companies and agents in Beirut. The following are some of the largest:

"Adriatica" S.p.A.N.: Rue du Port, Imm. du Port de Beyrouth, P.O.B. 1472; Gen. Man. J. WEHBE.

Ameaster Tanker Services: a division of American Lebanese Shipping Co. S.A.L., P.O.B. 113-5388, Beirut; Pres. PAUL PARATORE; Dir. M. SPITERI; Man. N. BALTAGI.

American Levant Shipping & Distributing Co.: P.O.B. 11-2736, Andalusia Bldg., Gouraud St., Gemmayzeh, Beirut; agents for: Holland America Line, Lykes Bros. Steamship Co.; correspondents throughout Middle East; Man. Dir. SAMIR ISHAK.

Arab Shipping and Chartering Co.: P.O.B. 1084; agents for China National Chartering Corpn., China Ocean Shipping Co., Kiu Lee Shipping Co. Ltd., Chinese-Tanzanian Joint Shipping Co.

Barrad Shipping Co. S.A.L.: P.O.B. 181, Beirut; refrigerated tramp services; 3 cargo reefer vessels; Chair. P. H. HELOU.

British Maritime Agencies (Levant) Ltd.: rue El Nahr, Karantina Bridge, Hafiz Hashem Bldg.; agents for Ellerman City Liners and Prince Line Ltd. (conventional ships), etc.

Catoni & Co. S.A.L.: P.O.B. 11-800, H. El Hashem Bldg., Karantina Bridge, Nahr, Beirut; agents for Royal Netherlands Steamship Co., Marseille-Fret, Lloyd's, O.C.L. (London) and A.C.T. Australia; Chair. HUGH BEARD; Gen. Man. GEORGE SAHYOUNI.

Ets. Derviche Y. Haddad: rue Derviche Haddad, P.O.B. 42; agents for: Armement Deppe, Antwerp and Compagnie Maritime Belge, Antwerp.

O. D. Debbas & Sons: Head Office: Sahmarani Bldg., Kantary St., P.O.B. 11-003, Beirut; Man. Dir. ELIE O. DEBBAS.

Fauzi Jemil Ghandour: P.O.B. 1084; agents for Denizçilik Bankasi T.A.O. (Denizyollari), D.B. Deniz Nakliyati T.A.Ş. (Dbcargo), Iraqi Maritime Transport Co., Kuwait Shipping Co. (S.A.K.)

T. Gargour & Fils: rue Foch, P.O.B. 11-0371; f. 1928; agents for: Assoc. Levant Lines S.A.L.; Dirs. NICOLAS T. GARGOUR, HABIB T. GARGOUR.

Henry Heald & Co. S.A.L.: P.O.B. 64; f. 1837; agents for: Nippon Yusen Kaisha, P. & O. Group, Scandinavian Near East Agency, Vanderzee Shipping Agency, Worms and Co.; Chair. J. L. JOLY; Dir. G. HANI.

Hitti Frères: rue de Phenicie, P.O.B. 511; airlines and shipping agents.

Mediterranean Maritime Co. S.A.L.: P.O.B. 1914, Bourse Bldg., Hoyek St., Beirut; managers for National Maritime Agencies Co. W.LL., Kuwait.

Mena Shipping and Tourist Agency: P.O.B. 11-884, Modern Bldg., El Arz St., Beirut; 5 cargo vessels; Man. Dir. W. LEHETA.

Messageries Maritimes: rue Allenby, P.O.B. 880.

Rudolphe Saadé & Co. S.A.L.: Freight Office: P.O.B. 2279; rue de la Marseillaise; Travel Office: ave. des Français. agents for American Export Lines, Rosade Lines and Syrian Arab Airlines; f. 1964; Pres. JACQUES R. SAADE.

Union Shipping & Chartering Agency S.A.L.: P.O.B. 2856; agents for Yugoslav vessels.

CIVIL AVIATION

MEA (*Middle East Airlines, Air Liban S.A.L.*): MEA Bldgs., Airport Blvd., Beirut, P.O.B. 206; f. 1945; regular services throughout Europe, the Middle East and Africa; fleet of 3 Boeing 747, 5 Boeing 707/320C, 12 Boeing 707/720, 4 Boeing 707/047; Chair. of Board and Pres. (vacant); Man. Dir. SALIM SALAAM.

Trans-Mediterranean Airways (TMA): Beirut International Airport, P.O.B. 11-3018, Beirut; f. 1953; world-wide cargo services between Europe, Middle East, S.-E. Asia, the Far East and U.S.A.; fleet of 11 Boeing 707/320C; Pres. and Chair. MUNIR ABU-HAIDAR.

The following foreign companies also operate services to Lebanon: Aeroflot (U.S.S.R.), Air Algérie, Air France, Air India, Air Maroc (Morocco), Alia (Jordan), Alitalia (Italy), Ariana Afghan Airlines, Austrian Airlines, British Airways, ČSA (Czechoslovakia), EgyptAir, Ethiopian Airlines, Garuda (Indonesia), Ghana Airways, Iberia, (Spain), Interflug (German Democratic Republic), Iranair, Iraqi Airways, JAL (Japan), JAT (Yugoslavia), KLM (Netherlands), Kuwait Airways, Libyan Arab Airlines, LOT (Poland), Lufthansa (Federal Republic of Germany), MALÉV (Hungary), Olympic Airways (Greece), PIA (Pakistan), Sabena (Belgium), SAS (Sweden), Saudia, Sudan Airways, Syrian Arab Airlines, TAROM (Romania), THY (Turkey), TWA (U.S.A.), UTA (France), Varig (Brazil), Viasa (Venezuela) and Yemen Republic Airlines.

TOURISM AND CULTURE

Ministry of Tourism: Beirut; f. 1966; official organization; Head of International Relations and Conventions Dept. ANTOINE ACCAOUI; Head Speleological Service SAMI KARKABI.

National Council of Tourism in Lebanon: P.O.B. 11-5344, Central Bank St., Beirut: government-sponsored autonomous organization; overseas offices in New York, Paris, London, Frankfurt, Stockholm, Brussels, Cairo,

Jeddah and Baghdad; Pres. CHEIKH HABIB KAYROUZ Vice-Pres. SELIM SALAM.

Baalbeck International Festival: Beirut; Dir. WAGIH GHOSSOUB.

THEATRE

Baalbeck Festival Modern Theatre Group: Baalbeck; Dir. MOUNIR ABU-DEBS.

DEFENCE

Commander of the Arab Deterrent Force: Maj.-Gen. SAAD TAYYAN.

Commander-in-Chief of the Armed Forces: Gen. VICTOR KHOURY.

Chief of Staff of Armed Forces: Brig.-Gen. MUNIR TERABAY.

Defence Budget (1981): L£1,000 million.

The 18,000 Lebanese army virtually disintegrated during the civil war, when it split up into factions, but a new 22,000-man army is being formed.

In March 1978 a 6,000-strong UN Interim Force in Lebanon (UNIFIL) took up positions to try to keep the peace near the border with Israel.

EDUCATION

Free primary education was introduced in 1960, but private institutions still provide the main facilities for secondary and university education. Private schools enjoy almost complete autonomy except for a certain number which receive government financial aid and are supervised by the Ministry's inspectors.

The primary course lasts for five years. It is followed either by the four-year intermediate course or the three-year secondary course. The baccalaureate examination is taken in two parts at the end of the second and third years of secondary education, and a public examination is taken at the end of the intermediate course. Technical education is provided mainly at the National School of Arts and Crafts, which offers four-year courses in elec-

tronics, mechanics, architectural and industrial drawing, and other subjects. There are also public Vocational schools providing courses for lower levels.

Higher education is provided by 12 institutions, including five universities. Teacher training is given at various levels. A three-year course which follows the intermediate course trains primary school teachers and another three-year course which follows the second part of the baccalaureate trains teachers for the intermediate school. Secondary school teachers are trained at the Higher Teachers' College at the Lebanese University. Two Agricultural Schools provide a three-year course for pupils holding the intermediate school degree.

BIBLIOGRAPHY

ABOUCHDID, E. E. Thirty Years of Lebanon and Syria (1917–47) (Beirut, 1948).

AGWANI, M. S. (Ed.). The Lebanese Crisis, 1958: a documentary study (Asia Publishing House, 1965).

ATIYAH, E. An Arab tells his Story (London, 1946).

BESOINS ET POSSIBILITÉS DE DÉVELOPPEMENT DU LIBAN, Étude Préliminaire, 2 Vols. (Lebanese Ministry of Planning, Beirut, 1964).

BINDER, LEONARD (Ed.). Politics in Lebanon (Wiley, New York, 1966).

BULLOCH, JOHN. Death of a Country: The Civil War in Lebanon (Weidenfeld and Nicolson, London, 1977).

BURCKHARD, C. Le Mandat Français en Syrie et au Liban (Paris, 1925).

CARDON, L. Le Régime de la propriété foncière en Syrie et au Liban (Paris, 1932).

CATROUX, G. Dans la Bataille de Méditerranée (Julliard, Paris, 1949).

CHAMOUN, C. Les Mémoires de Camille Chamoun (Beirut, 1949).

CORM, G. C. Politique Economique et Planification au Liban 1953–63 (Beirut, 1964).

EDDÉ, JACQUES. Géographie Liban-Syrie (Beirut, 1941).

FEDDEN, R. Syria (London, 1946) (also covers the Lebanon).

FRANCE, Ministère des Affaires Etrangères. Rapport sur la Situation de la Syrie et du Liban (Paris, annually, 1924–39).

GHATTAS, EMILE. The monetary system in the Lebanon (New York, 1961).

GULICK, JOHN. Social Structure and Culture Change in a Lebanese Village (New York, 1955).

HACHEM, NABIL. Liban: Sozio-ökenomische Groundlagen (Opladen, 1969).

HADDAD, J. Fifty Years of Modern Syria and Lebanon (Beirut, 1950).

HARDING, G. LANKESTER. Baalbek, a New Guide (Beirut, 1964).

HARIK, ILIYA F. Politics and Change in a Traditional Society—Lebanon 1711–1845 (Princeton University Press, 1968).

HEPBURN, A. H. Lebanon (New York, 1966).

HIMADEH, RAJA S. The Fiscal System of Lebanon (Khayat, Beirut, 1961).

HITTI, PHILIP K. Lebanon in History (3rd ed., Macmillan, London 1967).

HOURANI, ALBERT K. Syria and Lebanon (London, 1946).

HUDSON, MICHAEL C. The Precarious Republic: Political Modernization in the Lebanon (Random House, New York, 1968).

JIDEJIAN, NINA. Byblos Through the Ages (Dar El-Mashreq, Beirut, 1968).

LONGRIGG, S. H. Syria and Lebanon under French Mandate (Oxford University Press, 1958).

MILLS, ARTHUR E. Private Enterprise in Lebanon (American University of Beirut, 1959).

PENROSE, S. B. L. That They Have Life: the story of the American University of Beirut 1866–1941 (Princeton, New Jersey, U.P., 1941).

PUAUX, G. Deux Années au Levant; souvenirs de Syrie et du Liban (Hachette, Paris, 1952).

QUBAIN, FAHIM I. Crisis in Lebanon (Middle East Institute, Washington, D.C., 1961).

RONDOT, PIERRE. Les Institutions Politiques du Liban (Paris, 1947).

SABA, ELIAS S. The Foreign Exchange Systems of Lebanon and Syria (American University of Beirut, 1961).

SAFA, ELIE. L'Emigration Libanaise (Beirut, 1960).

SALIBI, K. S. The Modern History of Lebanon (Praeger, New York, and Weidenfeld & Nicolson, London, 1964); Cross Roads to Civil War: Lebanon 1958–76 (Caravan Books, New York, 1976).

SAYIGH, Y. A. Entrepreneurs of Lebanon (Cambridge, Mass., 1962).

STEWART, DESMOND. Trouble in Beirut (Wingate, London, 1959).

SULEIMAN, M. W. Political Parties in Lebanon (Cornell University Press, Ithaca, N.Y., 1967).

SYKES, JOHN. The Mountain Arabs (Hutchinson, London, 1968).

TIBAWI, A. L. A Modern History of Greater Syria, including Lebanon and Palestine (Macmillan, London, 1969).

VALLAUD, PIERRE. Le Liban au Bout du Fusil (Librairie Hachette, Paris, 1976).

WARD, PHILIP. Touring Lebanon (Faber and Faber, London, 1971).

ZIADEH, NICOLA. Syria and Lebanon (Praeger, New York, 1957).

Libya

(The Socialist People's Libyan Arab Jamahiriya)

PHYSICAL AND SOCIAL GEOGRAPHY

W. B. Fisher

The Socialist People's Libyan Arab Jamahiriya (Libya) is bounded on the north by the Mediterranean Sea, on the east by Egypt and the Sudan, on the south and south-west by Chad and Niger, on the west by Algeria, and on the north-west by Tunisia. The three component areas of Libya are: Tripolitania, in the west, with an area of 285,000 sq. km.; Cyrenaica, in the east, area 905,000 sq. km.; and the Fezzan, in the south, area 570,000 sq. km.—total for Libya, 1,760,000 sq. km. The independence of Libya was proclaimed in December 1951; before that date, following conquest from the Italians, Tripolitania and Cyrenaica had been ruled by a British administration, at first military, then civil; and the Fezzan had been administered by France. The revolutionary government which came to power in September 1969 has re-named the three regions: Tripolitania became known as the Western provinces, Cyrenaica the Eastern provinces, and the Fezzan the Southern provinces.

PHYSICAL FEATURES

The whole of Libya may be said to form part of the vast plateau of North Africa, which extends from the Atlantic Ocean to the Red Sea; but there are certain minor geographical features which give individuality to the three component areas of Libya. Tripolitania consists of a series of regions of different level, rising in the main towards the south, and thus broadly comparable with a flight of steps. In the extreme north, along the Mediterranean coast, there is a low-lying coastal plain called the Jefara. This is succeeded inland by a line of hills, or rather a scarp edge, that has several distinguishing local names, but is usually alluded to merely as the Jebel. Here and there in the Jebel occur evidences of former volcanic activity—old craters, and sheets of lava. The Jefara and adjacent parts of the Jebel are by far the most important parts of Tripolitania, since they are better watered and contain most of the population, together with the capital town, Tripoli.

South of the Jebel there is an upland plateau—a dreary desert landscape of sand, scrub, and scattered irregular masses of stone. After several hundred miles the plateau gives place to a series of east-west running depressions, where artesian water, and hence oases, are found. These depressions make up the region of the Fezzan, which is merely a collection of oases on a fairly large scale, interspersed with areas of desert. In the extreme south the land rises considerably to form the mountains of the central Sahara, where some peaks reach 3,500 metres in height.

Cyrenaica has a slightly different physical pattern. In the north, along the Mediterranean, there is an upland plateau that rises to 600 metres in two very narrow steps, each only a few miles wide. This gives a bold prominent coastline to much of Cyrenaica, and so there is a marked contrast with Tripolitania where the coast is low-lying, and in parts fringed by lagoons. The northern uplands of Cyrenaica are called the Jebel Akhdar (Green Mountain), and here, once again, are found the bulk of the population and the two main towns Benghazi and Derna. On its western side the Jebel Akhdar drops fairly steeply to the shores of the Gulf of Sirte; but on the east it falls more gradually, and is traceable as a series of ridges, only a few hundred feet in altitude, that extend as far as the Egyptian frontier. This eastern district, consisting of low ridges aligned parallel to the coast, is known as Marmarica, and its chief town is Tobruk.

South of the Jebel Akhdar the land falls in elevation, producing an extensive lowland, which except for its northern fringe, is mainly desert. Here and there occur a few oases—Aujila (or Ojila) Jalo, and Jaghbub in the north; and Jawf, Zighen, and Kufra (the largest of all) in the south. These oases support only a few thousand inhabitants and are of much less importance than those of the Fezzan. In the same region, and becoming more widespread towards the east, is the Sand Sea—an expanse of fine, mobile sand, easily lifted by the wind into dunes that can sometimes reach several hundred feet in height and over 100 miles in length. Finally, in the far south of Cyrenaica, lie the central Saharan mountains—the Tibesti Ranges, continuous with those to the south of the Fezzan.

The climate of Libya is characterized chiefly by its aridity and by its wide alternation of temperatures. Lacking mountain barriers, the country is open to influences both from the Sahara and from the Mediterranean Sea, and as a result there can be abrupt transitions from one kind of weather to another. In winter it can be fairly raw and cold in the north, with sleet and even light snow on the hills. In summer it is extremely hot in the Jefara of Tripolitania, reaching temperatures of 40°–45°C. In the southern deserts conditions are hotter still. Garian once (incorrectly) claimed the world record in temperature, but figures of over 49°C are known. Several feet of snow can also occur here in winter. Northern Cyrenaica has a markedly cooler summer of 27°–32°C, but with high air humidity near the coast. A special feature is the *ghibi*—a hot, very dry wind from the south that can raise temperatures in the north by 15°C or even 20°C in a few hours, sometimes giving figures of 20°C or 25°C in January. This sand-laden, dry wind may blow at any season of the year, but spring and autumn are the most usual seasons. Considerable damage is done to growing crops, and the effect even on human beings is often marked.

The hills of Tripolitania and Cyrenaica receive annually as much as 40 to 50 cm. of rainfall, but in the remainder of the country the amount is 20 cm. or less. A special difficulty is that once in every five or six years there is a pronounced drought, sometimes lasting for two successive seasons. Actual falls of rain can also be unreliable and erratic.

ECONOMIC LIFE

Such conditions impose severe restriction on all forms of economic activity. Although oil has been found in considerable quantities in Libya, physical and climatic conditions make exploitation difficult, and until the closing of the Suez Canal in 1967 the remote situation of the country, away from the currents of international trade, was a further handicap. But production of crude oil has increased rapidly and proximity to southern and central Europe presents a considerable advantage (no Suez dues) that can be reflected in the price charged for Libyan oil. The availability of oil revenues is transforming the economic situation of Libya. Plans for extensive development are in process of implementation, with the aim of improving housing, and the fostering of consumer goods industry. Roads, electricity, better water supplies and reorganized town planning are in process of being achieved, and a number of sizeable industrial plants are in construction.

In the better-watered areas of the Jafara, and to a smaller extent in northern Cyrenaica, there is cultivation of barley, wheat, olives, and Mediterranean fruit.

The Fezzan and the smaller oases in Cyrenaica are almost rainless, and cultivation depends entirely upon irrigation from wells. Millet is the chief crop, and there are several million date palms, which provide the bulk of the food. Small quantities of vegetables and fruit—figs, pomegranates, squashes, artichokes, and tubers—are produced from gardens. Along the northern coast, and especially on the lower slopes both of the Tripolitanian Jebel and the Jebel Akhdar, vines are widely grown, chiefly for wine-making. An edict imposing complete prohibition upon Libyan Muslims has, however, led to a restriction of production.

Over much of Libya pastoral nomadism, based on the rearing of sheep and goats, and some cattle and camels, is the only possible activity. In Cyrenaica nomads for long outnumbered the rest of the population, but in Tripolitania the main emphasis is on agriculture, though herding is still carried on. Within the last few years a number of industries have developed or are in prospect—refining, of course, plus some petrochemical activity and now iron and steel production. Overall the scale of industrial activity is still small, but growing. Major efforts have been made to improve agriculture, with debatable success. One increasing difficulty is the exodus of rural workers to jobs in the developing towns, and foreign labour has had to be introduced on some rural development schemes. Another limitation is over-use of artesian water in the Jefara. In certain areas near the coast, the water-table has fallen by 3–5 metres per year, resulting in invasion of the aquifers by sea-water.

The original population of Libya seems to have been Berber in origin, i.e. connected with many of the present-day inhabitants of Morocco, Algeria, and Tunis. The establishment of Greek colonies from about 650 B.C. onwards seems to have had little ethnic effect on the population; but in the ninth and tenth centuries A.D. there were large-scale immigrations by Arabic-speaking tribes from the Najd of Arabia. This latter group, of relatively unmixed Mediterranean racial type, is now entirely dominant, ethnically speaking, especially in Cyrenaica, of which it has been said that no other part of the world (central Arabia alone excepted) is more thoroughly "Arab".

A few Berber elements do, however, survive, mainly in the south and west of Libya; whilst the long-continued traffic in Negro slaves (which came to an end in the 1940s) has left a visible influence on peoples more especially in the south but also to some extent in the north.

Arabic, brought in by the tenth century invaders, is now current as the one official language of Libya, but a few Berber-speaking villages remain.

HISTORY

Until very modern times, the history of Libya consisted basically of a series of local histories of small cities, and it is difficult to obtain a clear conspectus of the history of the country as a whole.

Where harbours and roadsteads existed in Libya, which had more or less fertile immediate hinterlands, and which were conveniently sited with respect to the northern ends of caravan routes trading from the interior of Africa, those peoples of the Mediterranean who from time to time were active as seamen and traders, established, or maintained, "emporia"—small city colonies. These conditions existed in Libya only at the west and the east ends of the bleak and forbidding Gulf of Sirte where the desert reaches to the sea and separates the modern provinces of Tripolitania and Cyrenaica by a vacuum 250 miles across.

Where there was desert, there was nothing; where the semi-desert lay, and around the distant oases of the interior, there were the nomads and the semi-nomads, whose way of life changed little throughout the centuries and in whose history the main event was their conversion to Islam. Intolerant of all external controls, they seem perpetually to have resented the civilizing influences from without which clung to the two extremities of the Mediterranean coastline around Sabratha, Tripoli, Leptis at the west end, and ancient Cyrene, Barca, Berenice (now Benghazi) and Derna at the east. When the coastal cities were in strong hands, their civilizing influence was pushed inland to the limits of cultivable land. When they were in weak hands, their influence stopped at their city gates, and the very sands of the desert invaded what under stronger rulers of the cities bore crops of corn, olives and grapes.

From the evidence of Herodotus, and also from that of modern archaeological research, it appears that in the earliest historical times two races inhabited Libya—the "Libyans" and the "Ethiopians"—the former, of Mediterranean stock, inhabited the coastal areas; the latter, of negroid and African stock, inhabited the interior. They used neolithic stone instruments. They knew how to cultivate. The Garamantes of the Fezzan raised cattle over a thousand years before Christ, when Phoenician sailors from the cities of Tyre and Sidon in Syria began to visit Libya to trade for gold and silver, ivory, apes, and peacocks. The perils of their voyages in little ships and the advantages of having emporia at or near the northern ends of the caravan routes led the Phoenicians eventually to establish permanent colonies on the coast, at Leptis, Uai'at (Tripoli) and Sabratha, where more or less safe roadsteads existed. Their most famous colony, Carthage, lay to the west of the boundary of what is now called Libya. But this city, in its maritime and commercial struggle with the ancient Greeks, extended its influence eastward and by 517 B.C. had incorporated the three cities into its Empire.

By this time the Greeks had colonized Cyrene (about 600 B.C.) and raised it to be a powerful city. The Carthaginians, sensitive to competition in Libya, not only drove off an attempt by the son of a Spartan King to found a colony near Leptis, but advanced to contact with Cyrene, where, some time about the beginning of the fourth century B.C., a firm frontier was established against the Cyrenaicans at the Mounds of Philainos, where Mussolini placed his "Marble Arch". Cyrene herself fell under the domination of Alexander the Great, and although he was never able to carry out his threat of marching against Carthage, Ptolemy I Soter, heir to Alexander's Egyptian conquests, conquered Cyrenaica for Egypt and extended his empire westwards as far as Sirte.

By about 250 B.C. Carthage was at the height of her power. Her monopolistic policy in commercial and foreign relations reduced the three "emporia" to political non-entity, although their agriculture flourished.

By this time the Romans had substituted themselves for the Greeks as the most powerful Europeans in the Mediterranean. During the struggle between Rome and Carthage which followed, the Tripolitanian half of Libya fell into the power of the Numidians under Massinissa, who allied

LIBYA

himself with Rome. After the destruction of Carthage, the three emporia remained under nominal Numidian suzerainty, but in ever closer trading relationship with Italy, until Caesar's war against Pompey, when, after his victory at Thapsus over the Pompeians and their Numidian allies, Caecar created the Roman province of Africa Nova. Augustus set this province under a proconsul responsible to the Senate who also commanded the Legio III Augusta. Meanwhile Cyrenaica had passed under Roman sovereignty by the testament of the last of her Ptolemaic Kings—Ptolemy Apion—and was eventually created a province about 75 B.C.

The Pax Romana extended itself during the first century after Christ from the Mediterranean to the Fezzan. The second century was for Libya a period of prosperity, peace and civilization, the like of which she has never seen again. In particular under Septimius Severus, himself born in Leptis, and the successors of his family, the cities, and especially Leptis, attained the height of their splendour.

This condition did not last. Decline had set in by the middle of the fourth century. The general economic disease which was affecting Roman civilization affected also Africa. Christianity had challenged the spiritual values of the classical world but was itself too full of schisms to provide unity and strength. Libya itself was the scene of fierce internecine struggles caused by the Donatist heresy. Barbarians broke into the province, devastating the countryside, destroying its agricultural system, and spreading insecurity which caused depopulation through flight to the towns. In A.D. 431, Genseric and his Vandals appeared, overran the country, beat down the city walls, and brought ruin in their train. They were the first to introduce that piracy for which its harbours in a later age became notorious. A hundred years later the Emperor Justinian's general Belisarius found little difficulty in reconquering the country for the Byzantine Empire. There was a temporary revival of prosperity but continual rebellions by the Berber tribes soon reduced the country to anarchy.

THE MUSLIM PERIOD

In this condition the first Arab invaders found it. In the Caliphate of Omar, Amr ibn al-As, the conqueror of Egypt, overran the country as far as the Fezzan and Tripoli, the walls of which city he razed. This was in A.D. 643. There followed successive expeditions, mostly for booty, fiercely resisted by the Berbers, in the course of which Oqba ibn Nafi founded Qairawan (A.D. 670) and actually reached the Atlantic. The majority of the Berbers rapidly embraced Islam, but for the most part in its schismatic forms as Kharijites, Ibadites, and Shi'ites. An outlet for their turbulence was found in joining them with the Arabs in the invasion of Spain (A.D. 711).

Schism and continual rebellion induced the Caliph of Baghdad, Harun ar-Rashid, to appoint, in A.D. 800, Ibrahim ibn al-Aghlab as Governor with capital at Qairawan. He founded the Aghlabid dynasty, which became virtually independent of the Abbasid Caliph of Baghdad, but which brought little peace to Libya. A hundred years later a Shi'ite rising overthrew the Aghlabids and founded the Shi'ite Fatimid Dynasty, which from Tunisia conquered Egypt, transferred the seat of their Government to Cairo in A.D. 972, and made Bulukkin ibn Ziri Governor of Ifriqiya. He in turn set up a dynasty under which the land enjoyed considerable prosperity. But, at the beginning of the eleventh century, the Zirid Amir returned to orthodox Sunnism and acknowledged the sovereignty of the Caliph of Baghdad.

The Fatimid Caliph of Egypt, Al-Mustansir, reacted by sending against Libya two nomad Arab tribes which had been kept in Upper Egypt—the Banu Hilal and the Banu Suleim (A.D. 1049). This invasion was a final catastrophe for medieval Libya. The country was devastated, agriculture abandoned. The fortified cities, and in particular Tripoli, alone retained some vestiges of civilization. The next two centuries tell of little but intertribal wars, and the gradual fusion of the Arab and Berber races. Nor do the fourteenth and fifteenth centuries offer much more to record in "Ifriqiya". Murabit dynasts from Morocco contended with Muwahhid dynasts from the Balearic Islands. From these struggles emerged a dynasty in Tunisia called the Hafsids, whose power declined into a weak and anarchic state that attracted the attention of the new, crusading and imperialistic power of Christian Spain which could not overlook the fact that the cities of the northern coast of Africa had become dens of pirates.

Ferdinand the Catholic sent an expedition under Cardinal Ximenes and Don Pietro of Navarre which took Oran, Bugia, Algiers, and Tunis, and then, in 1510, Tripoli. These conquests produced a profound impression on the Muslim world, which at that time had become more united under the Ottoman Turks than it had been since the Abbasid Caliphs were at their zenith six hundred years earlier. The people outside the cities resisted the Spanish with Ottoman encouragement. Within the cities the Spanish were exposed to the dangers of conspiracy. Moreover they could make little effort to extend their power inland since, after the accession of the Emperor Charles V, Spain became heavily involved in European politics. The citizens of Tripoli intrigued unsuccessfully with the corsair Khair ad-Din, known as Barbarossa, who had made himself Lord of Algeria and had later become the Admiral of the Ottoman Sultan.

In these circumstances, the Emperor Charles V confided (A.D. 1530) the Lordship and the defence of Tripoli to the Knights Hospitallers of St. John (later to be known as the Knights of Malta) who had in A.D. 1522 lost Rhodes to the Ottoman Sultan, Suleyman the Magnificent. The Knights were able to maintain themselves there for only 21 years and then Sinan Pasha, who had been sent to reduce Malta but had failed in the attempt, invaded the town and forced the Knights to capitulate.

The Ottoman rulers of Constantinople now proceeded to organize their North African possessions into three Regencies—Algeria, Tunisia, and Tripoli, the last including also Cyrenaica and the Fezzan—each under a Pasha. But their organization contained from the first the germs of the disease to which it ultimately succumbed. The population of the interior was left almost unadministered. Tribute was levied and collected by a few regular troops, and by the "Maghzen" tribes from the remaining tribes, in return for the privilege of exemption from tithe and capitation tax. The system gave obvious opportunities for oppression and rebellion, and the division of the people into feudal lords and serfs. Worse still was the hardening of the professional soldiery of the garrisons, the Janissaries, of slave origin, into a military caste in which promotion was by seniority alone, and the retired officers of which had the right to a seat in the Pasha's Divan, or Council. The Janissaries became a power within the state. No less dangerous was the influence of the pirate captains—the corsairs. The Pashas subsidized them with arms and equipment and took their recognized share of their prizes. The Captains' Guild, called at-Ta'ifa, also became a power within the State. As early as A.D. 1595 the Divan was conceded by the Sultan the right of deciding foreign affairs and taxation. At the beginning of the seventeenth century the Janissaries introduced the custom of electing a "Dey" who sometimes reduced the Ottoman Pasha to a nonentity, sometimes shared with him the power, and sometimes was himself both Dey and Pasha. The history of the seventeenth and eighteenth centuries is one of intrigue, rebellion, sudden death, occasional outbreaks of pestilence, and of a country supported mainly by the depredations of the corsairs upon the merchant-fleets of Christian powers and the enslavement of their crews. In A.D. 1654 Admiral Blake was the first to bombard Tripoli in reprisal for such piracies. The great de Ruyter of Holland followed in 1669 and again in 1672.

In 1711 a local notable, Ahmed Karamanli, of Ottoman origin, and an officer of Janissaries, was proclaimed Dey. He succeeded not only in killing the former Dey and in defeating and killing the new Pasha sent from Constantinople, but also in persuading the Sultan Ahmed III to recognise him as Pasha. For the first time Libya had some sort of autonomous existence. The Karamanli dynasty lasted until 1835. Several of these rulers, and in particular the first and the last (Yusuf ibn Ali Karamanli, who was in power during the period of the Napoleonic wars) were men of strong personality, and capable statesmen who controlled the whole of Libya and improved the political and economic condition of the country. Like the former Pashas, they relied for much of their revenue on piracy. But the Karamanlis learned to make treaties with the maritime powers, bargaining with them to refrain from attacking their ships for a consideration, and for the most part restraining their Captains from breaking such treaties. When they failed to do so the powers would take strong action, as did the United States of America in 1805. The lesser powers naturally suffered most from the corsairs.

Such vast profits had the rulers of the Barbary coast made from piracy during the Napoleonic wars that the smaller powers made the abolition of piracy and of the enslavement of Christians points for discussion at the Congress of Vienna. England was entrusted with the suppression of these evils. It took ten years of naval and diplomatic action on the part of England and the Kingdom of the Two Sicilies to effect this. The suppression of piracy spelt the ruin of the Karamanlis. Yusuf Pasha fell into dire financial straits from which his expedients of adulterating the currency, of state trading, and of pledging in advance the already exorbitant taxes, so far from rescuing him served only to ruin both him and Libya. In 1830 French pressure compelled him to give up even the payments formerly exacted from Christian States for the right to maintain Consuls in Tripoli and for the right to unmolested navigation. In desperation, Yusuf demanded a special "aid" from both Jews and Muslims and this was the signal for revolt.

Probably through fear of the extension of French power in Algiers and Tunis, the Sultan decided to reoccupy Libya and to bring it once more under the direct rule of the Porte. This was in 1835. The rest of Libya's story in the nineteenth century is similar to that of most of the possessions of "The Sick Man of Europe"—corruption, oppression, revolts and their suppression—the towns alone being held by the Turks, with an occasional more energetic or more honest Governor. The period was, however, marked by the diffusion of Sanusi influence. The Sanusi were a religious brotherhood, founded by one Muhammad ibn Ali al Sanusi who settled in Cyrenaica on Jebel al Akhdar in 1834. From there the order spread, founding fraternities (*zawia*) throughout Libya and North Africa. In 1855 the Sanusi headquarters were transferred to Jaghbub to avoid opposition to the order of the Turks and, to some extent, Europeans. Al Sanusi was succeeded on his death in 1859 by his son Muhammad al Mahdi, who led the brotherhood until 1901.

ITALO-TURKISH CONFLICTS

On September 29th, 1911, Italy declared war on Turkey for causes more trivial than those which twenty-four years later led to her war with Ethiopia and her denunciation as an aggressor. After a short bombardment Italian troops

landed at Tripoli on October 3rd. Italy knew the Turks to be involved in the Balkans, and knew, through her commercial infiltration of Libya, their weakness in Africa. But her attack on Libya was not the easy exercise she expected. The Turks withdrew inland. But the Libyans organized themselves and joined the Turks, to whom the Porte sent assistance in the form of arms and of two senior officers, Ali Fethi Bey and Enver Pasha. The presence in the Italian army of Eritrean troops was a spur to the pride of the Libyans. In October and November a number of actions were fought around Tripoli in which the Italians had little success. A seaborne Italian force then descended on Misurata and seized it, but could make no progress inland. At Ar-Rumeila they suffered a considerable reverse. Turkey, however, defeated in the Balkan War, was anxious for a peace, which was signed on October 18th, 1912. One of the conditions of this peace was that the Libyans should be allowed "administrative autonomy". This was never realized.

Peace with Turkey did not, however, mean peace in Libya for the Italians. Although most of the Tripolitanians submitted and were disarmed within two years, the Sanusiya of Cyrenaica under Sayyid Ahmad ash-Sharif, and their adherents in the Fezzan and Tripolitania, refused to yield. The Sanusiya maintained a forward post at Sirte under Sayyid Ahmad's brother, Sayyid Safi ad-Din as-Sanusi. What contact there was between this Sayyid and one Ramadan as-Sueihli of Misurata is obscure. Ramadan had been in the resistance to the Italians and two years later had appeared to be submissive. At all events, he found himself commanding Libyans in an action started by the Italians at Al-Qaradabia in 1914, to push back Sayyid Safi ad-Din. Ramadan and his Misuratis changed sides in this action to the discomfiture of the Italians. By the time that the First World War had started, the Italians held only the coast towns of Tripoli, Benghazi, Derna and Tobruk, and a few coast villages near Tripoli.

The First World War gave Turkey and her German allies the opportunity of fermenting trouble against Italy in Libya. Arms and munitions were sent by submarine. Nuri Pasha from Turkey and Abdurrahman Azzam (late Secretary-General of the Arab League) from Egypt joined Sayyid Ahmad ash-Sharif in Cyrenaica. Ramadan as-Sueihli became head of a government at Misurata. The Sultan, to prevent quarrels, sent as Amir Osman Fu'ad, grandson of Sultan Murad; and Ishaq Pasha as commander in chief in Tripolitania. The strategical objective of these efforts was to tie up Italian forces in Libya and British forces in the Western Desert. The climax of Nuri Pasha's efforts with the Sanusi was their disastrous action in the Western Desert against the British, as a result of which Sayyid Ahmad ash-Sharif handed over the leadership to Sayyid Muhammad Idris. He was compelled to make the treaty of az-Zawiatna with the British and the Italians who recognised him as Amir of the interior of Cyrenaica, provided he desisted from attacks on the coastal towns and on Egypt.

The end of the war in 1918 left Italy weak and the Libyans, deserted by the Turks, weary. The Tripolitanians attempted to form a republic with headquarters at Gharian and with Abdurrahman Azzam as adviser. The Italians made a truce with them at Suaniibn Adam, permitting a delegation to go to Rome and entertaining the idea of "administrative independence". Ramadan as-Sueihli visited Tripoli. In Cyrenaica, Sayyid Muhammad Idris as-Sanusi likewise attempted to come to terms. In 1921 at Sirte the Tripolitanian leaders agreed with him to join forces to obtain Libya's rights and to do homage to him as Amir of all Libya. Meanwhile the delegation to Rome had returned empty-handed and Ramadan as-Sueihli had been slain in a tribal fight.

ITALIAN COLONIZATION

The advent of the Fascists to power in Italy (1922) coincided with the appointment in Tripoli of a vigorous Governor, Count Volpi. Thereafter, it took them until 1925 to occupy and pacify the province of Tripolitania and disarm the population. In Cyrenaica, however, the famous Sayyid Omar al-Mukhtar, representing the Amir Muhammad Idris, whose health had broken down, kept up the struggle. The Italians realized that the only effective policy was to deprive the Sanusiya of their bases, the oases of the South. Jaghbub was occupied in 1925, Zella, Ojila and Jalo in 1927. In 1928 Marshal Badoglio was appointed Governor General and in 1929 he occupied Mizda in the Fezzan. Omar Mukhtar still resisted. The Italians removed into concentration camps at al-Aqeila the tribes of the Jebel Akhdar. In 1930 Graziani was appointed to Cyrenaica, and the famous barbed-wire fence was erected along the frontier of Egypt. Finally, in 1931, cut off from all support, Omar Mukhtar, now an aged man, was surrounded, wounded, captured, and hanged.

Starting in the early 1920s, the Italians proceeded to colonize, in the sense of that word which is now in disrepute, those parts of Libya which they had occupied, and which geographical and ecological conditions rendered profitable for development. They enlarged and embellished the coastal towns. They extended throughout the cultivable areas a most excellent network of roads. They bored wells. They planted trees, and stabilized sand-dunes. But their civilizing policy was weighted heavily in favour of their own race. The object was clearly the settlement in Africa of as much as possible of Italy's surplus peasant population. These were encouraged to come in large numbers. Skilled cultivators of olives, vines, tobacco, barley, they needed the best lands and were provided with them. The priority given to the progress of the Libyans was a low one. Primary education for the Libyans was encouraged and schools provided for them. But the main medium of instruction was Italian. Very few Libyans were accepted into Italian secondary schools.

INDEPENDENCE

There followed the Second World War, and the occupation in 1942 of Cyrenaica and Tripolitania by a British Military Administration and of the Fezzan by French Forces. Thereafter until 1950 the country was administered with the greatest economy on a care and maintenance basis. Its final fate was long in doubt, until the United Nations decreed its independence by 1952. On December 24th, 1951, Libya was declared an independent United Kingdom with a federal constitution under King Idris, the former Amir Muhammad Idris, hero of the resistance.

According to the Constitution promulgated in October 1951, the state of Libya was a federal monarchy ruled by King Muhammad Idris al-Mahdi al-Sanusi and his heirs, and divided into the three provinces of Tripolitania, Cyrenaica and the Fezzan. The Federal Government consisted of a bicameral legislature, i.e., a Chamber of Deputies, to which was responsible a Council of Ministers appointed by the King, and a Senate of 24 members, 8 for each province. The King had the right to nominate half the total number of Senators, to introduce and to veto legislation, and to dissolve the Lower House at his discretion. The Constitution also provided that Provincial Legislatures should be created for the subordinate provinces of the new realm.

On the attainment of full independence serious political, financial and economic problems confronted Libya. Not the least of these was the task of fostering amongst the population a sense of national identity and unity. The loyalties of the people were still given to the village and the tribe, rather than to the new federal state.

These rivalries revealed themselves in the next two years. The Party of Independence, which supported the constitution, won control in the February 1952 elections for the Federal Chamber of Deputies. The National Congress Party of Tripolitania, however, was opposed to the federal principle and advocated a unitary state with proportional representation (which would have given Tripolitania the main voice). Disorders arising from this disagreement led to the outlawing of the Tripolitania party and the deportation of its leader al-Sa'adawi. A Legislative Council for Tripolitania was formed in 1952 but had to be dissolved in 1954 because of continued friction with the Federal Government and the King.

Efforts were undertaken, with Western technical aid, to increase the economic resources of Libya, e.g., to improve irrigation and initiate schemes for water catchments, to extend reafforestation, to teach better methods of farming, and to explore the possibilities of extending industries which could process local products and raw materials such as edible oils, fruits, vegetables, fish, etc.

FOREIGN RELATIONS IN THE 1950s

The first important development in the sphere of foreign relations was the admission of Libya to the Arab League in March 1953. The second development reflected the economic difficulties of the new state and its close links with Western Europe. In July 1953 Libya concluded a twenty-year treaty with Britain. In return for permission to maintain military bases in Libya, Britain undertook to grant the new state £1 million annually for economic development and a further annual sum of £2,750,000 to meet budgetary deficits.

In September 1954 a similar agreement was signed with the United States. A number of air bases were granted to the U.S. in return for economic aid amounting to $40 million over twenty years, which amount was later substantially increased. Libya also consolidated relations with France and Italy, signing a friendship pact with France in 1955 and a trade and financial agreement with Italy in 1956. In addition Libya was attempting to cement relations with her Arab neighbours. In May 1956 Libya concluded a trade and payments pact with Egypt, arranging the exchange of Libyan cattle for Egyptian foodstuffs.

The critical problem for Libya was to ensure that enough funds from abroad should be available to meet the normal expenses of the Government and to pay for much-needed improvements. At this time, her strategic position was all Libya had to sell, hence her involvement with the Western military alliance. The Libyan attitude to the Communist world was much more reserved. Reliance on income from foreign military bases continued, therefore, to dominate foreign policy, and in the late 1950s and early 1960s Libya received subsidies and military assistance from both the United Kingdom and the U.S.A. in return for the use of military bases.

OIL DISCOVERIES

After 1955–56, when Libya granted concessions for oil exploration to several American companies, the search for oil resources became one of the main interests of the Libyan Government. By the end of 1959 some fifteen companies held oil concessions in Libya. An oilfield at Zelten in Cyrenaica was discovered in June 1959. Before the year was out, six productive wells had been found in Tripolitania, four in Cyrenaica and one in the Fezzan. By the beginning of July 1960 there were thirty-five oil wells in production, yielding altogether a little less than 93,000

barrels of oil per day. The development of the oil fields is
dealt with in greater detail in the *Economic Survey* which
follows this history. Oil production showed a tremendous
increase in the 1962–66 period, with exports rising from
8 million tons in 1962 to over 70 million in 1966.

A UNITARY REALM

A general election was held in Libya on January 17th,
1960. Most of the 55 seats were contested, but there was
no party system in operation. The election was fought
mainly on a personal basis. Secret ballotting, limited in
earlier elections to the urban areas, was now extended to
the rural districts. The Prime Minister, Abd al Majid
Kubar, and the other members of his Cabinet retained
their seats.

Libya's increasing wealth was making the business of
government more complex and several changes of administration ensued between 1960 and 1963. Finally, in
March 1963, a new cabinet under the premiership of Dr.
Mohieddin Fekini was appointed.

Dr. Fekini stated in April 1963 that his government
intended to introduce legislation designed to transform
Libya from a federal into a unitary state—a change which
would mean increased efficiency and considerable economies
in administration. On April 15th the Prime Minister presented to the Chamber of Deputies a Bill which contained a
number of important reforms: (1) the franchise was to be
granted to women; (2) Libya would have (as before) a
bicameral parliamentary system, but henceforward the
King was to nominate all the 24 members of the Senate
(heretofore half nominated and half elected); (3) the Kingdom of Libya would cease to be a federal state comprising
three provinces (Tripolitania, Cyrenaica and Fezzan),
becoming instead a unitary realm divided into ten administrative areas; (4) the administrative councils established
in each of the three provinces were to be abolished, the
exercise of executive power residing now in the Council of
Ministers. Libya became a unitary state by royal proclamation on April 27th, 1963.

THE REALITY OF INDEPENDENCE

In the field of foreign relations, Libya was by now
helped by the prospect of financial independence and was
making her voice heard in international affairs, particularly in Africa. As a result of decisions taken at the
Addis Ababa conference of African Heads of State in
May 1963 Libya closed her air and sea ports to Portuguese
and South African ships. The signing of pacts with
Morocco (1962) and Algeria (1963) meant that Libya now
had closer links with all the Maghreb countries. Libya was
also showing signs of throwing off her dependence on the
West. The 1955 agreement with France had allowed France
to retain in Libya certain military facilities—notably in the
field of communications—for the defence of her African
territories, but Dr. Fekini felt that, with the coming of
independence to France's African territories in the early
1960s, the matter should be reconsidered.

The question of foreign military bases in Libya now came
to the fore. Dr. Fekini resigned in January 1964 and the
new Prime Minister was Mahmud Muntasser, hitherto
Minister of Justice. The Government issued a statement on
February 23rd to the effect that it did not propose to renew
or extend its military agreements with Great Britain and
the United States and that it supported the other governments of the Arab world in the resistance to imperialism.
Mr. Muntasser defined the aim of his government as the
termination of the existing agreements with Great Britain
and the United States and the fixing of a date for the
evacuation of the bases in Libya. The Chamber of Deputies

now passed a resolution calling for the achievement of this
aim and providing that, if negotiations were unsuccessful,
the Chamber would pass legislation to abrogate the treaties
and close the bases.

The Anglo-Libyan treaty of 1953 was due to expire in
1973. Under the treaty Great Britain maintained a Royal
Air Force staging post near Tobruk, an Air Force de-
tachment at Idris airport in Tripoli and Army District
Headquarters at Tripoli and Benghazi. The American-
Libyan agreement of 1954 was to expire in 1971. Near
Tripoli was situated the largest American air-base outside
the United States. Under the treaties Libya had received
large amounts of financial, economic and military aid
from the U.S. and from Great Britain. Oil revenues had
reduced Libyan dependence on such aid. Great Britain
withdrew the bulk of her forces in February and March
1966.

At elections for the Libyan Parliament held in October
1964 moderate candidates won most of the 103 seats.
Women received the right to vote in this election. King
Idris dissolved the Parliament, however, on February 13th,
1965, as the result of complaints about irregularities in
the election procedure of October 1964.

The Prime Minister resigned, to be succeeded by
Husayn Maziq, Minister for Foreign Affairs. A new election
for Parliament was held on May 8th, 1965, over two
hundred candidates contesting the 91 seats, 16 members
being returned unopposed.

The outbreak of the six-day Arab-Israeli war in June
1967 was followed by serious disturbances in Tripoli and
Benghazi, in which port and oil workers and students,
inflamed by Egyptian propaganda, played a prominent
part. The British and United States embassies were attacked
and the Jewish minorities were subjected to violence and
persecution which resulted in the greater part of them
emigrating to Italy, Malta and elsewhere. The Prime
Minister, Husayn Maziq, proved unable to control the
situation and was dismissed by the King on June 28th.
Firm measures by his successor, Abdul Qadir Badri,
brought a return to order but the antagonisms he aroused
forced him to resign in turn in October. He was succeeded
as Prime Minister on October 28th by the Minister of
Justice, Abdul Hamid Bakkush, a Tripoli lawyer.

An immediate result of the June war was a fall in the
Libyan output of crude oil of about 80 per cent because of
the boycott of oil supplies from Arab countries to Britain,
the United States and Federal Germany. There was a
gradual return to full production in the months following
the conflict, however, and the ban on the export of oil was
lifted in September. The closure of the Suez Canal brought
about a considerable increase in Libya's oil exports and
general prosperity, although the Libyan Government
agreed to make annual aid payments totalling £30 million
to the U.A.R. and Jordan to alleviate the consequences of
the war. Libya's oil output increased by about 50 per cent
in 1968 and the country became after only 7½ years the
second largest producer in the Arab world with the great
advantage, as a supplier to Europe, of being on the right
side of the Suez Canal.

The new Prime Minister, Abdul Hamid Bakkush, was
a progressive and he embarked on a programme of
rapid change, seeking to modernize Libya's administration,
reform the civil service and improve the educational
system. He also sought to provide the armed forces with
up-to-date equipment, and under a contract announced in
April 1968 the purchase from a British firm of a surface-to-
air missile defence system costing £100 million was
arranged. An agreement to buy British heavy arms,
followed, but in September 1968, Mr. Bakkush was
replaced as premier by Wanis el Qaddafi, the pace of his

reforms having apparently alienated some conservative elements. Both ministries enjoyed close relationships with the Western countries but played little part in Arab politics.

THE 1969 COUP

On September 1st, 1969, a military coup was staged in Tripoli whilst the King was in Turkey for medical treatment. Within a few days the new régime gained complete control of the entire country. The coup was remarkable for the absence of any opposition, relatively few arrests, virtually no fighting and no deaths at all being reported. A "Revolution Command Council" (RCC) took power and proclaimed the Libyan Arab Republic. The RCC initially remained anonymous but was soon revealed as a group of young army officers, the leader, Muammar Gaddafi, being only 27. The aged King refused to abdicate but accepted exile in Egypt when it became obvious that the revolution had been completely accepted by his people.

The provisional constitution announced in November stated that supreme power would remain in the hands of the RCC which appointed the cabinet; there was no mention of any future general election or of a National Assembly, and the royal ban on political parties continued. A largely civilian cabinet was appointed under close military supervision. The Ministers of Defence and of the Interior were accused of organizing an abortive counter-revolution in December, and were tried and sentenced in 1970. In January Col. Gaddafi himself became Prime Minister and several of his colleagues also joined the cabinet.

The principal force underlying the régime's policies was undoubtedly the professed one of Arab nationalism. Internally this led to the strict enforcement of the royal law requiring businesses operating in Libya to be controlled by Libyans—banks being particularly affected. The remaining British military establishment in Libya, requested to leave as soon as possible, was finally removed in March 1970, and the much larger U.S. presence at Wheelus Field followed suit in June. Most of the European and American managers, teachers, technicians and doctors were replaced by Arabs, mainly from Egypt. English translations disappeared from street signs, official stationery and publications, and most hoardings, the use of Arabic alone being permitted; similarly, the Islamic prohibitions on alcoholic drinks and certain Western clothes were officially revived. In July 1970 the property of all Jews and Italians still living in Libya—some 25,000 people—was sequestrated by the Government, and both communities were encouraged to leave without delay; some Jews were, however, offered compensation in government bonds. In the same month the three main oil marketing companies—Shell, Esso and an ENI subsidiary—had their distribution facilities nationalized.

Another anti-government plot was reported crushed in July 1970. In the autumn two ministers resigned and there were signs of a power struggle developing in the Revolution Command Council. The internal dissension apparently increased in the first part of 1970 over the proposed federation with the U.A.R., Syria and Sudan, and over President Gaddafi's promises of a constitution, and political institutions, including an elected president. A step towards introducing these was the announcement in June 1971 that an Arab Socialist Union was to be created as the state's sole party.

FOREIGN POLICY AFTER THE COUP

The new régime almost immediately received recognition—indeed acclaim—from the radical Arab countries and the U.S.S.R., and the rest of the world also granted recognition within a few days. As would be expected from the Arab nationalist inspiration behind the revolution, the monarchy's close ties with the Western powers were abandoned in favour of close relations with the Arab world and Egypt in particular; this friendship became the basis of a triple alliance announced late in 1969, the Sudan being the third member. The alliance was intended to develop both politically—as a strong bulwark against Israel and the West—and economically, in that the economies of the three countries complemented each other to a considerable extent. However, when a federation agreement was signed in April 1971, it was Syria which became the third member. Libya also adopted a militant position on the Palestine question, and this created some diplomatic problems regarding arms contracts, particularly with Britain.

Although in July 1970 the Libyan Government followed Egypt in accepting the American proposals for a cease-fire with Israel, it continued its militant statements on the Middle East problem. President Gaddafi stated that a peaceful solution was impossible and rejected the UN Security Council resolution on which the Rogers initiative was based. During the fighting between Palestine guerrillas and the Jordanian army in September 1970, Libya redirected its financial aid from the Government to the guerrillas and broke off diplomatic relations with Hussein's government.

Nearer home, the coup appeared to have reorientated Libya away from the Maghreb; in the summer of 1970 Libya withdrew from the Maghreb Permanent Consultative Committee. Relations with Tunisia improved in the last half of 1970, after initial concern in Tunis in 1969 at the radical leanings of the new régime, and President Gaddafi headed a delegation which visited Tunisia in February 1971. Relations with Morocco were severed in July 1971 after the Libyan Government prematurely gave its support to an attempt to overthrow King Hassan, which failed within twenty-four hours.

There was little evidence of any closer relationship with the communist powers, although China was recognized in June 1971 and the U.S.S.R. was given due credit for its Middle East policies. But communism was regarded in Libya as a "foreign" ideology, antipathetic to more "progressive" Arab socialism (as in Sudan). Hence, in July 1971, Gaddafi was ready to help President Nimeri of Sudan to regain power after a coup led by communists had ousted him. A regular BOAC flight from London to Khartoum was forced down over Libya and two leaders of the coup, one of whom, Major al-Nur, was travelling back to become head of state, were taken from the plane and handed over to Sudan. They were almost immediately executed by the restored regime.

OIL POWER

In April 1971 the negotiations with the oil companies operating in Libya, which had begun soon after the 1969 coup, finally ended in a new five-year agreement raising the total posted price for Libyan crude to $3.447 per barrel. In the last stage of the negotiations, conducted in Tripoli, the Libyan Government also represented the interests of the Algerian, Iraqi and Saudi Arabian Governments. Threats of an embargo on the export of crude oil were used as a lever in the negotiations.

In ten years Libya's position had changed from one of penury and dependence to one of power based entirely on her ability to cut off oil supplies. The pronouncements of President Gaddafi were, therefore, by now of great moment to the West. In July 1971, the Deputy Prime Minister, Major Abd al Salam Jalloud, visited West Germany, France and Britain. Germany, which buys a particularly large proportion of its crude oil from Libya, needed to maintain good relations. France was anxious over the use to which Libya would put the Mirage jet fighters being supplied under the 1970 agreement. The same anxiety was revealed in Britain over the supply of armaments, but none of these countries could afford to alienate Libya.

In December 1971, avowedly in retaliation for Britain's failure to prevent the Iranian occupation of the Tumb islands in the Gulf, Libya nationalized the assets of British Petroleum. This began the process of nationalizing the foreign oil companies which is described in more detail in the Economic Survey.

Relations with Britain became very much strained in the winter of 1971/72, not only because of the nationalization of BP but also because of Libyan intervention in the dispute with Malta over the British bases there. Libya had for some time been actively fostering relations with Malta, talks on possible Libyan aid being held in August 1971. In January 1972 the British naval training mission was ordered to leave Libya. And in February the 1954 agreement with the United States was abrogated.

Libya's attitude towards the Soviet Union had remained cool, and the Government was violently opposed to the Iraqi/Soviet treaty, signed in April 1972. Nevertheless, in February 1972, Major Jalloud visited Moscow and in March an agreement on oil co-operation was signed. It was also reported that the U.S.S.R. might supply arms to Libya.

At home, President Gaddafi continued to attempt to run the legislature and the Government entirely in accordance with Islamic principles. At the end of March 1972 the Arab Socialist Union held its first national congress. At subsequent sessions of the ASU resolutions were passed, clarifying its position and policies, and abolishing censorship of the Press, while at the same time maintaining financial control of newspapers.

In July 1972 disagreement within the RCC led to Maj. Jalloud taking over as Prime Minister from Gaddafi, a new cabinet being formed in which all but two of the ministers were civilians.

ARAB UNITY

A recurrent feature of President Gaddafi's foreign policy was the announcement of proposals for the union of Libya with neighbouring states, and their later collapse. The Tripoli Charter of December 1969 establishing a revolutionary alliance of Libya, Egypt (then the United Arab Republic) and Sudan was followed by gradual moves towards federation and the adhesion of Syria. Sudan withdrew, but in September 1971 referenda in Libya, Egypt and Syria approved the constitution of the Federation of Arab Republics, which officially came into existence on January 1st, 1972, but has had few practical consequences.

The Federation was not Gaddafi's only attempt to export his ideals by means of merger. At the time of Malta's dispute with Britain over the use of bases, in 1971, he proposed a union of Malta with Libya, but was rebuffed. In December 1972, in a speech in Tunis, he proposed the union of Libya and Tunisia, much to the surprise of his audience, not least President Bourguiba, who immediately rejected the idea, making some pointed remarks about Gaddafi's inexperience.

A merger of Libya and Egypt was agreed in principle in August 1972, but as the date when it should come into force approached, certain difficulties became apparent. Gaddafi, who had recently launched his Cultural Revolution of April 1973, was seen as a reactionary Islamic puritan in Egypt, and he was openly critical of Egyptian moral laxity. Some 40,000 Libyans attempted to stage a "march on Cairo" in July 1973, to bring pressure to bear on the Egyptian Government. The marchers destroyed an Egyptian border post, but were halted some 200 miles from Cairo. This incident served only to increase Egyptian suspicion of Libyan revolutionary enthusiasm, which was seen as unsuitable for Egypt's more advanced and cosmopolitan society. The union nevertheless came into effect on September 1st, 1973, with the establishment, on paper, of unified political leadership and economic policy and a constituent assembly. The union soon fell apart, wrecked by Gaddafi's opposition to Egypt's conduct of the October 1973 Arab-Israeli war.

President Gaddafi's attitude towards the Palestine problem had long been a source of discord between Libya and other Arab states. He gave financial support to the Palestinian guerrillas, and a number of Libyan volunteers were sent to assist them, Gaddafi's objective being the complete destruction of Israel. He was extremely critical of what he saw as the lack of total commitment to the Palestinian cause on the part of Egypt and Syria, and frequently expressed the opinion that the Arab states could not, and did not deserve to defeat Israel. He accused Egypt and Syria of being more interested in the recovery of territory lost in the 1967 war than in aiding the Palestinian resistance movement, which was being "destroyed by the Arabs in co-operation with Israel". Gaddafi was not informed of the Egyptian and Syrian plan to attack Israel in October 1973, was strongly critical of their battle plan, and refused to attend the Algiers meeting of Arab heads of state after the war, declaring that it would only ratify Arab capitulation. Libya was nevertheless an enthusiastic proponent of the use of the Arab oil embargo against countries considered to be pro-Israel. During the war, Libya's participation had been limited to the supply of arms and equipment, and its conclusion seemed only to complete Gaddafi's disillusionment with the union with Egypt.

Presidents Gaddafi and Bourguiba announced the union of Libya and Tunisia on January 12th, 1974, following two days of talks. A referendum to approve the decision was to be held on January 18th, but was almost immediately postponed. The decision had been taken in the absence of the Tunisian Prime Minister, Hedi Nouira. When he returned to Tunisia, the pro-merger foreign minister was dismissed, and Tunisia's attitude changed to one of indefinite deferment of the union. Gaddafi's impetuous action seemed to have produced a unified state, but Tunisia now treated the agreement as merely a declaration of principle, without any practical effect.

Gaddafi's enthusiasm for Arab unity continued unabated, but the failure of political mergers led him to propound a new course. His speeches attacked the Arab leaders who blocked unity and failed to "liberate" Palestine, and he spoke of Libyan aid for revolution and the achievement of Arab union by popular pressure on the governments of Tunisia, Egypt, Algeria and Morocco. Libya had for some time been providing money, arms and training for subversive or "liberation" organizations operating in Ireland, Eritrea, the Philippines, Rhodesia, Portuguese Guinea, Morocco and Chad, as well as providing aid for sympathetic countries such as Pakistan, Uganda, Zambia, Togo and, after May 1973, Chad. Now it appeared that Libya was supporting subversion in Egypt and Sudan. Attempted coups in Egypt in April and Sudan in May 1974 were believed to have had Libyan support, and relations between Libya and other Arab states became increasingly hostile. Gaddafi's failed mergers and his interference in the internal affairs of other countries were believed to have been major factors in his withdrawal from an active political role in April 1974, when it was seen that he had failed in his policy of exporting the ideals of the Libyan Cultural Revolution.

THE CULTURAL REVOLUTION

President Gaddafi's somewhat idiosyncratic political and social philosophy first obtained full expression in a speech in April 1973, when he called for the immediate launching of a "cultural revolution to destroy imported ideologies, whether they are eastern or western" and for the construction of a society based on the tenets of the Koran. The form which this revolution was to take was laid down in a five-point programme: "people's committees" would be set up to carry out the revolution, the "politically sick" would be purged, the revolutionary masses would be armed, a campaign would begin against bureaucracy and administrative abuses, and imported books which propagated Communism, atheism or capitalism would be burned. The people's committees set about their task of supervision of all aspects of social and economic life, criticizing and dismissing officials and business executives who failed to show the required revolutionary fervour, and offensive books and magazines were seized and destroyed.

In May 1973 Gaddafi presented his Third International Theory, "an alternative to capitalist materialism and communist atheism". In effect, it appeared to be a call for a return to Muslim fundamentalism (a call since echoed in other Middle Eastern countries), together with a rather confused combination of socialism and respect for private property, and much talk of tolerance and the rights of oppressed nationalities. Whilst the Cultural Revolution proceeded apace in Libya, Gaddafi seemed more concerned with foreign policy and his new-found role as revolutionary philosopher, who had put forward a universally applicable theory which would replace existing ideologies. Gaddafi concentrated on the formulation and propagation of his theory, and his erratic and unsuccessful attempts to export the Libyan revolution by merger or by subversion, while the mundane details of administration were increasingly left to Major Jalloud, the Prime Minister.

The return to the Koran and the rejection of external influences took several forms, some petty, such as the insistence upon the use of Arabic in foreigners' passports, some macabre, as in the revival of such features of Koranic law as the amputation of thieves' hands. The theory was also invoked in the disputes with foreign oil companies in 1973 (dealt with in detail in the Economic Survey), presented as an expression of Libyan independence.

On April 5th, 1974, it was announced that Gaddafi, while remaining head of state and commander-in-chief, had been relieved of political, administrative and ceremonial duties, and was to devote himself to ideological and mass organization work. It appeared that, willingly or otherwise, Gaddafi had effectively been replaced by Prime Minister Jalloud. After a five-month withdrawal from active direction of the Government, Gaddafi re-emerged in the autumn of 1974 and it soon became apparent that he was more than ever in command. Relations with Egypt deteriorated after Gaddafi boycotted the Rabat summit of Arab Heads of State in October. Gaddafi was unhappy about the decision to recognize the PLO, under Yasser Arafat, as the sole legitimate representative of the Palestinians, and Gaddafi has subsequently shown his support for the "rejectionist front"—the wing of the Palestine guerrilla movement which rejects the idea of a possible settlement of the Arab-Israeli conflict under terms acceptable to Arafat and Egypt.

The war of words with Egypt continued in 1975, with articles in the Libyan press containing bitter personal attacks on President Sadat and with the Egyptian press accusing Gaddafi of preparing to mount an invasion of Egypt. A delegation from the National Assembly of the Federation of Arab Republics, which visited Tripoli and Cairo in May, was able to bring about a temporary reconciliation, but at the end of May relations deteriorated

again after reports that Libya was to allow the establishment of Soviet military bases on its territory in return for huge supplies of Soviet weapons. It later appeared that the arms deal did not include the establishment of Soviet military bases in Libya, and was in fact smaller than at first reported. Relations with Egypt, however, have remained strained, and Libya was very critical of Egypt's part in the signing of the second interim disengagement between Egypt and Israel in September 1975. Relations with Egypt did not improve in 1976 or 1977, and in July 1977 relations were so bad that, for a while, frontier clashes had all the appearances of open war.

Relations with Egypt were not improved when in November 1977 President Sadat of Egypt launched his peace initiative by visiting Israel. Gaddafi condemned Sadat's move and was a leading instigator of the Tripoli summit of "rejectionist" States who formed a "front of steadfastness and confrontation" against Israel in December 1977. Gaddafi remained strongly opposed to Sadat's peace initiative throughout 1978 and, following the signing of the Egyptian-Israeli treaty in March 1979, there were reports of Libyan troop movements along the Egyptian border. Gaddafi subsequently walked out of the Baghdad summit meeting of Arab States on the grounds that the sanctions contemplated against Egypt were insufficiently far-reaching. In 1980 Libya was alleged to be building a 300-km. wall to defend its border with Egypt.

In early 1980 a serious rift developed between Gaddafi and Arafat, leader of the PLO, who was accused of having abandoned the armed struggle in favour of a strategy of diplomacy and moderation. In January relations were formally broken with Fatah, the largest component organization of the PLO, and all aid was suspended, although Libya continued to support other wings of the movement. The Libyan authorities began to organize Palestinians in the country into people's congresses to pursue war against Israel independently and by May about 27 were reported to have been set up. However, a summit of the steadfastness front in Tripoli in April seemed to restore a measure of solidarity and the PLO representative returned to Tripoli in May.

Relations with the U.S.A. were erratic throughout 1979 and the first half of 1980. In early 1979 Gaddafi threatened to cut off oil exports unless President Carter lifted a ban on sales to Libya of agricultural and electronic equipment and transport aircraft which was still in force in early 1980. The sacking of the American embassy in Tripoli by mobs protesting at the presence in the U.S.A. of the exiled Shah of Iran led to the withdrawal of the American ambassador in December 1979, at which Col. Gaddafi has expressed regret. In May 1980 Gaddafi announced that he was exacting compensation to the value of thousands of millions of dollars from the U.S.A., Britain and Italy for damage sustained by Libya during the North African campaigns of the Second World War. These countries were threatened with an oil embargo and the withdrawal of Libyan assets from their banking systems if the demands were not met. At mid-1979 Libyan oil accounted for an estimated 600,000 of the 8 million barrels per day imported by the U.S.A.

For many years Libya had been supporting the FROLINAT rebels in Chad in their struggle against the Chad Government. In 1973 Libya occupied the mineral-rich Aozou strip, a region of 114,000 sq. km. in the north of Chad, basing its action on a territorial agreement made between Italy and Vichy France during the Second World War. Chad raised this grievance at the OAU conference in Gabon in July 1977, and a committee of reconciliation was set up but without results. In March 1978 the FROLINAT rebels were achieving such success against the Chad army that General Malloum (the President of

Chad) was forced to appeal to Libya to arrest the progress of the rebels. A cease-fire was arranged at the end of March at reconciliation meetings held in Sebha and Benghazi in Libya. Sporadic fighting continued, however, amid allegations that certain factions of FROLINAT were still receiving substantial Libyan support. A series of military reverses brought down the Malloum government in March 1979 and, following an initiative by Nigeria, a ceasefire was signed at Kano by the four opposing Chadian factions. With the prospect of a share in the government of Chad at last, the mainstream of FROLINAT and, earlier, certain splinter groups broke with Libya over its annexation of the Aozou strip. Although a signatory of the Kano agreement, Libya carried out a series of retaliatory attacks deep inside the northern border in mid-April. In June a 2,500-strong Libyan army invaded northern Chad and was driven back after several days' fierce fighting by FROLINAT forces. A coalition government formed in late April was dominated by former FROLINAT insurgents and excluded the extreme factions of the south. The secessionist movement which subsequently appeared in the south was soon known to be receiving considerable support from Libya whilst Libyan military aid continued to certain guerrilla groups in the north. Dissent by the south and external pressure led to the disintegration of the coalition government but a second attempt to implement a "Government of National Unity" foundered as, parallel to the North-South conflict, the inter-Muslim conflict intensified between President Goukouni and his Defence Minister, Hissène Habré. By March 1980 N'Djamena was the site of a pitched battle between the armies of the President and his allies and Habré's forces and in May Libya responded to an appeal from President Goukouni (some of whose Muslim rivals Libya had been backing a year earlier) for reinforcements to help stem the rapid advance of Habré's forces in the capital.

Although Gaddafi has strenuously denied it, a guerrilla raid on the Tunisian mining town of Gafsa in January 1980, with the presumed intent to incite a popular rebellion, has been attributed to Libya. Relations between the two countries were subsequently strained. France sent military aid to back up the Tunisian government against this potential threat and in February the French embassy in Tripoli and consulate in Benghazi were burned as a demonstration of Libya's anger at this action. The incident prompted Gaddafi to pledge publicly his determination to counter French intervention in Africa by any means. In February 1982, however, relations between Libya and Tunisia improved when Gaddafi visited Tunisia and a co-operation agreement between the two countries was signed.

In March and April 1979 Libyan military presence in Uganda was unable to prevent the overthrow of Idi Amin and heavy losses were incurred. Morocco severed diplomatic relations in April 1980 following the decision by Libya to recognize the independence of the Western Sahara. During the latter half of 1980 more and more Libyan troops were engaged in Chad, eventually helping President Goukouni Oueddei to overcome the forces of Hissène Habré in December. In January 1981 it was announced that Libya and Chad had resolved to work for "complete unity". This could be interpreted either as an agreed merger or as an occupation imposed on Chad by Libya. Some Libyan units withdrew from Chad in May 1981, but others remained because of a supposed threat from Sudan, which distrusted Gaddafi's African intentions. Some observers considered that Gaddafi had plans for the creation of a vast "Saharan Republic", comprising Libya, Niger, Chad, Algeria, Tunisia and Mauritania, but, if so, this plan received a setback in October 1981 when President Goukouni of Chad

requested the removal of Libyan troops from Chad. They were subsequently replaced by an OAU peace-keeping force.

Gaddafi's alliances and alleged attempts at subversion in other countries led to Libya's being treated with suspicion by the great powers. During the Spring of 1981 there was a build-up of Soviet and East European military advisers in Libya, but Gaddafi failed to secure a Treaty of Friendship and Co-operation with the U.S.S.R. when he visited Moscow in April. His increased interest in the U.S.S.R. resulted in worsening relations with the U.S.A., and the American Embassy in Tripoli was closed down in May. Relations deteriorated further in August, when U.S. fighters shot down two Libyan jets which had intercepted them over the Gulf of Sirte, and in November President Reagan alleged that a Libyan hit-squad had been sent to assassinate him.

THE CREATION OF THE SOCIALIST PEOPLE'S LIBYAN ARAB JAMAHIRIYA

President Gaddafi's theories had, since 1973 when he presented his Third International Theory, shown a strong desire to foster people's assemblies at all levels of Libyan life. Under a decree promulgated by the ruling RCC in November 1975, provision was made for the creation of a 618-member General National Congress of the Arab Socialist Union (ASU), the country's only permitted political party. The Congress, which held its first session in January 1976, comprised members of the RCC, leaders of existing "people's congresses" and "popular committees", and trade unions and professional organizations. Subsequently the General National Congress of the ASU became the General People's Congress (GPC), which first met in November 1976. Gaddafi announced plans for radical constitutional changes and these were endorsed by the GPC in March 1977. The official name of the country was changed to The Socialist People's Libyan Arab Jamahiriya, and power was vested in the people through the GPC and the groups represented in it. The RCC disappeared and a General Secretariat of the GPC, with Gaddafi as Secretary General, was established. The Council of Ministers was replaced by the General People's Committee, with 26 members, each a Secretary of a Department. In early March 1979 Gaddafi resigned from his post of Secretary General of the General Secretariat of the GPC to devote more time to "revolutionary work". The General Secretariat was reorganized, as was the General People's Committee, which was reduced to 21 members.

In late 1979 Gaddafi urged Libyans living abroad to take over Libyan embassies; diplomats were ousted and "people's bureaux" established in most Western countries. At the fifth meeting of the GPC in January 1980 several government ministers were dismissed, notably the experienced Petroleum Secretary Izzedin Mabrouk, who was accused of inefficiency in nationalizing the petroleum industry. In February the third meeting of the revolutionary committees, bodies responsible for ensuring the progress of the revolution at popular level, called for the "physical liquidation" of opponents of the revolution living abroad and "elements obstructing change" inside Libya. A far-reaching anti-corruption campaign was launched the same month, ostensibly to eradicate "economic" crime. Between February and April over 2,000 people were arrested, mainly on charges of bribery, to be tried by members of the revolutionary committees. However, the arrests of several senior military officers have introduced political undertones. In April Gaddafi issued an ultimatum to Libyan exiles abroad to return to Libya by

June 10th, beyond which date he could not undertake to protect them from the revenge of the revolutionary committees. The killings in Western capitals of several Libyans known to be hostile to the regime since February 1980 have been linked with the purge, and were still an active part of Libyan policy in 1981.

The Sixth meeting of the GPC in January 1981 reshuffled several ministerial appointments, discussed the 1981–85 economic plan, and made further proposals for transforming Libyan society along the lines of Gaddafi's "Green Book". The Foreign Ministry was abolished and replaced by a Foreign Liaison Bureau.

ECONOMIC SURVEY

Oil has transformed Libya. Before its discovery in commercial quantities in the 1950s, agriculture was the basis of the economy and domestic revenue covered only about half of the Government's ordinary and development expenditure. But between 1962 and 1968, national income increased from LD 131 million to LD 798 million and gross national product (G.N.P.) increased from LD 163 million to LD 909 million. Oil exports during the period increased by 835 per cent, accounting for 51 per cent of gross domestic product (G.D.P.) in 1968. Since then, the country's G.N.P., according to official estimates, rose to LD 3,534 million in 1974 before falling slightly to LD 3,497 million in 1975, when oil exports accounted for 46.3 per cent of G.D.P., and subsequently rising strongly with a recovery in the price and volume of oil exports.

In foreign trade over 99 per cent of recorded exports between 1965 and the early 1970s consisted of crude petroleum, and a healthy trade surplus is being maintained. The merchandise trade surplus in 1977 was $5,476 million; the current account surplus in that year was $3,293 million. In 1978 the merchandise trade surplus and the current account surplus both fell, but in 1979 they rose again appreciably to $9,755 million and $7,365 million respectively.

Since the 1969 revolution, state intervention in the economy has increased, in line with Colonel Gaddafi's ideas of "Islamic socialism". The Government has at least a 51 per cent share in a number of sectors including banking and insurance, public transport, some sections of the construction industry and some manufacturing concerns. Apart, however, from the nationalization of distribution and marketing of oil in Libya in 1970, the Government refrained from directly taking over oil company assets until the dispute with BP in 1971. Nevertheless, in September 1978 and the first two months of 1979, a large number of private companies were taken over by workers' committees. Similarly, in 1979, all direct importing business was transferred to 62 public corporations, and the issuing of licences was stopped. In March 1981, it was announced that all licences for shops selling clothes, electrical goods, shoes, household appliances and spare parts were to be cancelled, and that by the end of the year all retail shops would have to close. Retail activity in the future will theoretically be controlled by state-administered supermarkets. The whole private sector was to be completely abolished by the end of 1981, to be replaced by People's Economic Committees, but by early 1982 this process had not been completed.

Until the country's oil resources began to be exploited not more than 25 per cent of the population lived in the towns. This is no longer true, and the drift to the towns has caused a serious problem. Something like half of the non-urban population is settled in rural communities, and the other half are semi-nomads, who follow a pastoral mode of life. According to the 1979 census the population was 3,245,000, compared with 2,290,734 in 1973. Of the 1979 total, 411,200 were foreigners and the work-force numbered 800,000. By 1982 it was estimated that 467,000 foreigners, 35 per cent of whom were Egyptians, were working in Libya.

In 1980 and 1981, Libya's political volatility came to the fore with the planned merger with Syria and the military adventure into Chad. These, on the whole, have had adverse effects on the economy: diplomatic relations were broken off with a number of West African countries. In the economic sphere, for example, Nigeria cut off uranium sales to Libya, which amounted to 500 tons in 1980. The purge on corruption in February 1980 increased payment delays and so deepened the reluctance of foreign companies to invest in Libya. By 1982 it seemed that little progress had been made in practical terms on the "merger" with Syria, although Libya had already paid off all Syria's debts to the U.S.S.R., and Libya itself appeared to be moving closer to the U.S.S.R. Worsening relations with the U.S.A. had also come to the fore, and in March 1982 President Reagan banned imports of Libyan oil to the U.S.A., and halted all exports to Libya other than food and medical supplies.

AGRICULTURE

Agriculture dominated the economy until the discovery of oil. Even now the oil industry gives direct employment to no more than a small fraction of the population and the present Government regards the agricultural sector as of the first importance, with Colonel Gaddafi himself regularly stating that more emphasis must be put on agriculture. Nevertheless, by 1978, the percentage of the population employed in agriculture had fallen to 17 per cent from around 50 per cent in the early 1970s. At present only a very small proportion of the total area of the country is cultivable and of this a high percentage is used for grazing in some regions, only 1.4 per cent is arable, and 0.1 per cent is irrigated. In mid-1970 all Italian-owned land and property in Libya, including 37,000 hectares of cultivated land, was confiscated and plans were made to distribute the expropriated lands to Libyan farmers, with government credits for seed, fertilizers and machinery. The area under irrigation is increasing and, according to 1976 figures, had reached 300,000 hectares. A number of very large contracts has been awarded for reclamation and irrigation work in various scheduled areas. The best-known schemes are the Kufra Oasis project to irrigate 10,000 hectares; the Tawurgha project to reclaim 3,000 hectares; the Sarir reclamation project; the Jebel el-Akhdar project; the Jefara plain project; and the Wadi Qattera reclamation project. The Wadi Jaref dam, one of the biggest in Libya, went into operation in 1976. In 1974 an allocation of LD 3.4 million was announced for six more agricultural projects, covering over 10,000 hectares. All projects are meant to be fully integrated, providing for the establishment of farms, the building of rural roads, irrigation and drainage facilities and, in some cases, the introduction of agro-industries. New ideas are: a scheme to turn unused oil tankers into water carriers to meet agricultural needs; and the construction of two refuse composting plants at Tripoli and Benghazi to produce fertilizer for desert areas. There are also plans to pipe water from natural reservoirs in the southern desert region to irrigate areas on the Mediterranean coast. In 1982 a five-year scheme to lay 1,600 km. of pipes to bring water from the Eastern Desert underground water reserve to the coast, at a cost of $7,000 million, was envisaged, and plans were being drawn up for a $1,000 million fertilizer complex at Sirte.

After a successful year in 1972–73, as far as the implementation of investment projects was concerned, the Government decided to make a great effort in agriculture, allocating to it a sum of LD 700 million over the 10-year period 1973–83 and it is now the major sector in Libya's development plan. The Three-Year Plan, as revised in February 1975, provided LD 566.9 million for agricultural development and agrarian reform. The revised 1976–80 Development Plan provided LD 498 million plus LD 977 million for integral developments. Indeed, an important feature of Libya's economic planning in the 1970s was the relatively high priority which was being given to agriculture. In 1975, agricultural development absorbed 21 per cent of total budget expenditure whilst in 1976 it had shot up to a corresponding 30 per cent. In the 1978 financial year, the agricultural sector was allocated 18.9 per cent of budgeted development expenditure and 14.6 per cent of overall budget spending. In most other oil-rich countries, agriculture hardly receives more than 10 per cent of development funds. In 1979, however, investment in agriculture decreased, receiving only 6.4 per cent of the general budget. This downward trend is likely to continue into the 1980s, as the new Five Year Plan is to give priority to industrial development rather than to agriculture. In the 1976–80 Development Plan, 21 per cent of expenditure was allocated to agriculture, whereas in the 1981–85 Plan the estimated expenditure is only 16 per cent or LD 3,000 million.

In spite of the money poured into the sector, however, results in terms of production were largely unsatisfactory, certainly up to 1973. Climatic and soil factors will, it is hoped, cease to play such a large part in fluctuations of output, once irrigation projects are under way and the distribution and use of fertilizers is well established. There have been signs in the production figures since 1973 that this is indeed happening; total foodstuffs production increased in each year from 1973 to 1976 when output, in aggregate, surpassed the previous record of 1970. Overall, agriculture has fared badly, declining by 3.6 per cent in the period of the 1976–80 Plan. The other problems, those of lack of trained technicians and administrators and poor education among the farming communities, are not so easily solved. Libya is obliged for the present to rely on foreign expertise.

Animal husbandry is the basis of farming in Libya and is likely to remain so until irrigation and reclamation measures really start to take effect. In recent years breeding of cattle for dairy produce has been expanded and milk production reached 62,000 tons in 1978. Livestock is being imported on an increasing scale from a number of sources. Breeding cattle have been supplied by the United Kingdom, and stock-raising co-operation agreements signed with Argentina, Romania and Australia. In 1974 contracts were awarded for fodder factories at Sebha, Zleiten and Zawia. Estimates of livestock numbers in 1978 showed a rise in the sheep, goat and cattle population as compared with 1970, but a drop in numbers of camels, reflecting the current emphasis on meat and dairy production. In 1979, though, the Department of Agriculture reported that there were 134,000 camels in the country, compared with their figure of 71,000 for 1978.

Of the cereal crops, barley, which is the staple diet of most of the population, is by far the most important. Yields fluctuate widely from year to year. In 1976 barley production was 184,000 metric tons, and in 1978 178,000 tons. In contrast, production of barley in 1977 was down at 58,000 tons, and in 1979 it was only 100,000 tons. In 1977 wheat production was less than half the 64,000 tons of 1976, but by 1979 it had risen to 110,000 tons.

Olives and citrus fruit are grown mainly in the west of the country, and other important food crops are tomatoes, almonds, castor beans, groundnuts and potatoes, also grown mainly in the west. Dates are produced in oases in the south and on the coastal belt. Esparto grass, which grows wild in the Jebel, is used for the manufacture of high quality paper and banknotes and was formerly Libya's most important article of export. The agricultural sector accounted for only 2.1 per cent of G.D.P. in 1976 and 1.5 per cent in 1977 and Libya still has to import over 80 per cent of its food requirements. The 1976–80 development plan envisaged an annual growth of 15.8 per cent in domestic production so that Libya would be self-sufficient in vegetables and dairy products by 1980 and would also be able to produce 92 per cent of its fruit requirements and 75 per cent of its meat and wheat consumption. However, these targets were too optimistic and were not achieved.

The Government is continuing to further land development and reform. Polish assistance is being used to open up new farms in eastern Libya and in March 1978 the Government transferred the ownership of 1,011 farms formerly owned by politicians to farmers at a subsidized price. An interesting new development, only possible in an oil-rich economy, is the development of hydroponic farming. A contract was signed with a U.S. firm in 1974 to develop a number of hydroponic farms.

Some attempts have been made by the Government at reafforestation, including a successful small-scale experiment in 1971 to stabilize the soil with a synthetic rubber spray and then plant eucalyptus saplings. Since then, a number of co-operation agreements signed with other countries have included schemes for dune stabilization. More widespread are projects involving large-scale rotating sprinklers, which are making circular green islands in the deserts.

The offshore waters abound in fish, especially tunny and sardines, but most of the fishing is done by Italians, Greeks or Maltese. Of special importance are the sponge-beds along the wide continental shelf. These are exploited by foreign fishermen and divers, mainly Greeks fron the Dodecanese.

OIL

That oil was present in both Tripolitania and Cyrenaica had long been suspected, and for several years after Libya became independent, a large number of the bigger oil companies carried out geological surveys of the country. In 1955 a petroleum law came into force setting up a petroleum commission, which was empowered to grant concessions on a fifty-fifty profit sharing basis, with parts of each concession being handed back to the Government after a given period. Under this law, concessions were granted to many American companies and to British, French and other foreign groups. By 1972 eleven groups, involving 21 companies, held concession rights.

Important oil strikes first began to be made in 1957, and ten years later Libya was already the fourth largest exporter in the world. The growth of the oil industry was particularly rapid after the closing of the Suez Canal in 1967.

Exports take place from five different ocean terminals connected to the various fields by pipelines built by the five groups which have made the major finds. The pipeline system and the terminals are, however, available to other groups. The first of the five terminals to be opened was at Mersa Brega on the Gulf of Sirte, in 1961. The pipeline was built to Bir Zelten, some 200 miles south of Benghazi, where Esso Standard (Libya) had found oil in 1959. This group also operates a refinery at Mersa Brega and a gas liquefaction plant to prepare gas for shipment to Italy and Spain. The terminal for the Oasis group's Hofra field is at Ras el Sidr, to the west of Mersa Brega. The Mobil/Gelsenberg group also found oil near Hofra, but built another pipeline to Ras Lanuf, just east of Ras el Sidr. From a fourth terminal at Mersa el-Hariga, near Tobruk, a pipeline some 320 miles long runs to Sarir, then the BP/Bunker Hunt concession. The most recent terminal is at Zuetina, and was opened in 1968 to serve the Augila and Idris fields. Here an American company, Occidental, which did not even obtain its concession until early in 1966,

had found oil in large quantities. The Amoseas group, which produces oil from the Nafoora field, not far from Augila, has a pipeline connected to the Ras Lanuf terminal.

Libya supports the general principle of higher world oil prices to meet inflation. Libya's policy of conserving its oil has also led to disputes with the companies. In October 1975 Occidental was ordered to reduce output to 210,000 b/d and a vigorous dispute ensued. It was finally settled in December 1975. Occidental was allowed an output of 300,000 b/d over three years with subsequent reductions.

Libya was a leader of those oil producers which demanded participation in oil company activities. In September 1972 it negotiated an agreement with ENI under which Libya received an immediate 50 per cent share in ENI's Libyan activities. ENI was induced to make this agreement by Libya's refusal to allow exports from Concession 100, the Italian company's first source of Libyan oil, and by the awarding of the Zawia refinery contract to an ENI subsidiary. Libya, for its part, reduced its initial demand, which was for a 51 per cent share.

Talks on participation began in earnest in January 1973. Agreements for 51 per cent participation were concluded with Occidental, Marathon, Continental and Amerada Hess, but the major oil companies, with interests elsewhere in the Arab world, proved recalcitrant, since any agreement concluded with Libya would inevitably affect those already made with, for example, the Arabian Gulf states. The result of a long round of negotiations was that the Government came to a 51 per cent share in the Libyan operations of Agip, Continental/Marathon/Amerada Hess, Exxon, Mobil and Occidental, while it has completely nationalized the holdings of Amoseas, BP/Bunker Hunt, Shell, Texaco, California Asiatic and Atlantic Richfield. Most outstanding claims by the companies were settled in 1977 following arbitration.

In fact, for some time the Government refrained from any general nationalization measures, apart from the takeover of distribution in 1970. But in December 1971 it took over BP's Libyan interests in retaliation for the British Government's failure to prevent the Iranian occupation of the Arabian Gulf islands of Abu Musa and the Tumbs. British Petroleum had operated the 400,000 barrels-a-day (b/d) Sarir field with Bunker Hunt and Libya set up the Arabian Gulf Exploration Company to operate BP's half of the field. Production dropped to a little over 200,000 b/d and BP warned that it would take legal action against any buyer of crude from AGEC. Meanwhile, talks with the other partner in the Sarir field, Bunker Hunt, dragged on until in June 1973 Libya nationalized the company's assets. Both BP and Bunker Hunt brought a number of actions against companies who bought Sarir crude after nationalization and the dispute lasted for many months. In 1974, however, following a compensation agreement between Shell and the Libyan Government, agreement was finally reached with BP and subsequently Bunker Hunt. It is perhaps significant that, at the beginning of 1980, the experienced Petroleum Secretary, Izzedin Mabrouk, was replaced by Abdul-Salam Mohammad Zagaar, for failing to speed up total Libyanization of the oil industry.

Following all the above upheavals production fell from 159.7 million metric tons in 1970 to 71.5 million metric tons in 1975. In 1976, however, output rose to 93.5 million tons under the influence of more reasonable prices and generally rising demand. This recovery in output continued in 1977, when production rose to 100 million metric tons but output fell by 3.5 per cent in 1978 in response to competition from North Sea oil and generally depressed market conditions. Although oil production fluctuated considerably in 1979, with the lowest level in 14 months reported in August, the annual average of 2.07 million b/d was the highest since 1973 and represented an increase of 4.7 per cent over 1978. In April 1980, however, oil production was cut by 16.8 per cent, reflecting a similar short-term cut in 1979. During 1979 Libya aligned itself with Iran as a hawk in terms of the international oil market, and at the beginning of 1980 raised its oil price by 28 per cent to $30 per barrel, only to raise it to $34.50 two weeks later. A further increase in May brought the price to $36.12 per barrel. This aggressive pricing policy continued into 1980, and in January 1981, the price of top-grade Zuetina was raised to $41 per barrel. In 1979, oil revenue totalled $16,000 million, and in 1980 was in the region of $20,000 million. However, the world oil glut has had serious repercussions in Libya. In 1979 oil exports reached 718 million barrels, but in 1980 the level was only 619 million barrels, a reduction of 13.7 per cent. Early in 1981 the production level was 1.75 million b/d, but this fell to 600,000 b/d before rising slightly to 700,000 b/d in August 1981. These low levels reflected Libya's high prices. In July 1981 the price of Zuetina and Brega crude was lowered to $39.9 per barrel from its earlier peak of $41 per barrel, but this was still higher than most other world oil prices. In the summer of 1981 BP suspended liftings of Libyan oil, owing to its high price, and the spot price of Libyan oil then fell rapidly to $33 per barrel. As a result of these problems, oil revenue for 1981, at approximately $11,000 million, was about half that of 1980. Although at the Abu Dhabi meeting of OPEC in December 1981 Libya stuck to its official price of $37–38 per barrel, by January 1982 the spot price of Zuetina crude was down to $36.25 per barrel, and production levels were up to 1.2 million b/d.

At present the Oasis group (comprising Continental, Marathon and Amerada) is responsible for over one-third of total crude oil output, while the NOC—including the production from the fully nationalized fields at Sarir (formerly BP/Hunt) and Nafoora (formerly Amoseas)—accounts for only about 21 per cent of overall production. The NOC is looking to the Sarir field in particular for increased production, since it has rarely produced at more than half its rate since being nationalized.

A new phase in exploration involving much greater Government participation is now under way in Libya. In particular, the Government is keen to maintain an active exploration campaign to evaluate the oil potential of parts of the country outside the Sirtica Basin in north-central Libya, where the currently commercial fields are grouped. There are two main areas of interest—western Libya (formerly Tripolitania) and the offshore, with particular stress on the Tripolitanian offshore. Indeed, exploration interest in areas off the Tripolitanian coast has been stimulated in recent years by the discovery of a series of commercial oil and gas fields—Ashtart, Miskar and Isis—in the Gulf of Gabès in the neighbouring Tunisian offshore. In 1976, the NOC announced the discovery of potentially the largest oilfield in Libya, about 100 kilometres north of the port of Zuara. The find was made by a consortium comprising Aquitaine, Elf, Austria's OMV and Wintershall. According to Elf-Aquitaine anhydrous oil has been tested at the bottom of a productive formation nearly 2,300 metres below the seabed.

Exploration also continues in other parts of the country, with some work being undertaken in the largely unexplored south. New finds continue to be made in the Sirtica Basin, despite the intensive exploration of previous years. In 1976, Occidental brought the new Almas field into production and the Libyan Umm-al-Jawaby company also has two commercial finds, one on the eastern side of the Sirtica Basin and one on the west, which it hopes to bring into production. At the end of 1978, Libya had 1,095 oil wells on stream: 375 were flowing and 738 were in various forms of artificial lift. By 1979 the total number of wells had risen to 1,492, of which 248 were flowing.

In 1979 it was estimated that Libya's oil reserves would last, at current rates of production, for 34 years. However, new agreements, such as those signed at the end of 1979 by Oxylibya and Deminex, and one in 1980 by Oasis, and the increase in the number of exploratory wells, such as the eight new wells planned for Agip in 1980, provide hope for increased reserves. Early in 1980 Braspetro reported finds of oil in the Mourzouk area but their extent was not known. Recent reductions in Libya's oil output have also meant that reserves will last longer. However, Libya's political activities in Africa in 1980 and 1981 led to some economic repercussions, and in January 1981, the French oil company Société Nationale Elf Aquitaine announced an indefinite postponement of exploration in Libya. The most significant factor in Libya's oil economy during 1981 was the decision by Exxon to withdraw from the country on November 10th. Exxon had been represented in Libya since 1955 by Esso Standard and Esso Sirte, and were owners of the Brega LNG plant which had been out of service since 1980. The company received 77 per cent of the net back value in cash compensation for the handing over of its Libyan rights and assets to the NOC.

On the marketing side, Libya has up to now tended to conclude agreements involving the exchange of crude oil for specific goods or services. Poland agreed to exchange oil for ships and machinery; a similar agreement was made with Yugoslavia to supply tankers; France signed a long-term agreement to barter technical assistance for oil; Italy is supplying industrial goods in return for oil; and, perhaps most controversial, co-operation agreements were signed in 1974 with the U.S.S.R. which provided for arms supplies and development assistance. Libya also has special oil arrangements with Brazil and Greece, and, together with Algeria, Nigeria and Gabon, has agreed to reserve 4 per cent of its output for delivery to African states at $37 a barrel.

Libya, however, in common with other large oil producers, would much prefer to refine and process its own oil, rather than export it in its crude state. Six oil refineries have been built since 1970, and three more are planned for completion in the mid-1980s to provide a total refining capacity of one million b/d. Zawia refinery was opened in 1974 and enlarged in 1977. The two other main refinery locations are at Tobruk and Misurata. Hitherto supplied by tanker with crude oil shipped from Marsa Brega, the Zawia refinery will eventually draw all of its materials from fields near the Algerian frontier through a new 400-km. pipeline (diameter 20 inches or 50 cm.) to be constructed by the Dutch company Protech International. Recent plans include a 220,000 b/d refinery to be built at Ras Lanuf by Italian contractors, and a pipeline from Saipem to Sarir.

In the petrochemical sphere, NOC have built one ammonia plant and one ethanol plant, each with a capacity of 1,000 tons per day, at Brega. These came on stream in September 1977. In 1978 NOC awarded a contract worth $150 million to an Italian company for the construction of a new 1,000 tons-per-day ammonia plant at Marsa al-Brega. A further $150 million contract has been granted at Marsa for a 1,000 tons-per-day urea plant. Sited near Exxon's liquefied natural gas (LNG) plant, the new units will process natural gas and are expected to make Marsa Brega the country's foremost petrochemical centre. The programme for the improvement of port facilities at Marsa Brega is also approaching completion. In 1980 an Italian firm received a contract worth $60 million for the construction of a 330,000 ton a year ethylene plant due to be completed in two years at the Ras Lanuf refinery and petrochemical complex. Similarly, an American firm has signed a contract for a monoethylene glycol plant at the same refinery. In addition, the contract for a 1,750 ton/day urea plant has been won by a joint West German/Italian venture. The Abu Kammash chemical complex was opened in September 1980.

The U.S.S.R. is to build a gas pipeline joining coastal centres to Brega and Misurata. There are also plans for a new $1,500 million refinery to be built at Misurata, with a capacity of 220,000 b/d.

Libya is also investing in refining ventures abroad, notably the refinery at Koper in Yugoslavia and the Adriatic pipeline from Libya to Eastern Europe. Clauses covering refining and petrochemicals development are now being included in new exploration agreements.

Despite the fact that most of Libya's oil is carried in foreign tankers, and there are vessels lying idle, the tanker fleet has been enlarged in recent years with three tankers ordered from Japan, two from Yugoslavia and four from Sweden. In fact, Libya's Grand National Maritime Transport Company (GNMTC) refused to take delivery of three of the Swedish vessels, which are 154,000 d.w.t. tankers, and has demanded repayment of almost $100 million in contract payments. The GNMTC argues that Sweden has violated Libya's regulations on boycotting Israel and that the tankers do not meet technical specifications. Libya rejected an international arbitration decision in April 1978 that it accept delivery of the tankers, which have been ready since late 1976 according to the Swedish builders, Gotaverken. By June 1981 they had eventually all been delivered, bringing the Libyan fleet to 13 tankers, eight cargo vessels and two passenger liners.

INDUSTRY

Manufacturing in Libya has been largely confined to the processing of local agricultural products and such traditional crafts as carpet weaving, tanning and leather working and shoe making. Plans were made several years ago for a whole range of factories to make such diverse articles as prefabricated construction materials, cables, glass, pharmaceuticals, woollen and synthetic textiles, among others. Most of these factories did not get past the tendering stage, but the Government is now settling down to getting Libyan development going again. In fact, during 1979 industrial production rose 15.7 per cent on the 1978 figure, largely due to increases in petrochemical output.

One critical problem facing Libya is the large number of foreign labourers necessary to complete the Libyan workforce. During 1979 official figures stated that 33 per cent of the total workforce of one million was foreign, but the real number of immigrant workers would appear to be far higher. The majority of these workers come from other parts of North Africa. In February 1980 it was stated that Libya plans to recruit 15,000 workers from Bangladesh, and a similar agreement was signed with the Philippines late in 1979.

Contracts for industrial plant have in the past been awarded mainly to Western European and U.S. companies, but Japanese firms are becoming more active in Libya and links with Eastern Europe, particularly Yugoslavia, are much closer. At the beginning of 1975 a joint venture agreement to manufacture carbon paper was signed with a Japanese firm and an aluminium plant is planned with Yugoslavian participation. Libya's first ready-made clothing factory at Derna, and a new tannery at Tajura, were opened in 1974. Other manufacturing projects planned are: a canning factory for Zawia; a tyre factory at Tajura; a hypodermic syringe plant; a soap factory, and a glass factory for Tripoli. President Gaddafi also said in January 1975 that Libya had plans for the establishment of a heavy industry sector involving vehicle and tractor assembly plants, shipbuilding and iron and steel works. A French firm won a contract in 1976 for the construction of two organic fertilizer plants at Tripoli and Benghazi. An Italian firm in 1977 won a contract for setting up a steel frame factory in Libya which will have an annual capacity of 35,000 tons. Also in 1977, a German company was awarded a $35 million contract to build a blanket factory, plans were announced for a joint venture with the United Kingdom to establish an electrical equipment plant, and an Italian company was awarded a contract to build refrigeration plants in Libya. Modest plans are under way to improve tourist facilities.

Notwithstanding its support for these smaller projects, the Government is giving more attention, and resources, to a few major ventures in heavy industry and in infrastructure development. In this context the master plan for the Misurata industrial city, due to house 180,000 people at a cost of $1,290 million, was submitted in September 1979. All new industry in the country is now planned by the General Public Organization for Industrialization.

Iron ore reserves estimated at over 700 million tons were discovered in 1974 at Wadi Shatti, in southern Libya and plans for their exploitation are under way. Work was initially planned to begin in November 1979 on the construction of a steelworks at Misurata for completion in 1985 at a cost of some $1,000 million. However, it was not until 1981 that Libya started awarding contracts for the Misurata steel works, the first phase of which having by then risen in cost to $3,500 million. The steel plant is expected to have an annual capacity of 1.2 million metric tons of steel by 1986. A 900-km. railway is also to be built, joining the iron ore mines in the south to Misurata. The contract for the port has been won by a Turkish company, and a Japanese/Mexican venture is to construct the rolling mills. Italian contracts totalling $300 million have been gained for a water purification plant, workshops and electricity transformer stations. There are plans to build a 120,000 metric tons-per-year aluminium smelter complex at Zuwara, 120 km. west of Tripoli, at a cost of $1,250 million. This is to be run by a joint company, Libal, formed by Yugoslavia's Energoinvest and Libya's Heavy Industries Secretariat. Eventually it is hoped that a petroleum coke plant and an industrial port will be built at Zuwara. A chemical complex is being built by the West German company Salzgitter at Abu Kammesh while a Belgian company, Tractionel, has prepared feasibility studies for a $300 million industrial complex at Murada.

The construction work now being carried out under the development programme has given rise to a rapidly increasing demand for cement, which is imported in large quantities. The existing cement plant at Homs is being expanded and two more are being built at Souk el-Khemis and Derna, with others planned. A new Benghazi cement factory was opened in August 1978. A completely new $150 million plant is being built at Homs by a French firm, and was due to go into operation in 1979. It is hoped that production will reach 4 million tons per year once all the plants are fully operational. Many of the recent construction contracts have been awarded to Turkish firms, and in 1981 there were 102 Turkish companies operating in Libya, with an estimated 80,000 Turkish

workers. One example of this new trend is the $140 million contract won in March 1982 by Turkey's Ozdemir Insaat to build 900 houses and infrastructure in Zlitin, 150 km. east of Tripoli. Falling oil revenues, though, forced Libya to tell Turkey early in 1982 that it wanted to deduct $70 million in oil debts from $100 million owed to various Turkish firms. South Korean companies, such as the Daewoo Corporation, are also carrying off many new contracts in Libya, and in May 1981 100 South Korean dockers were used to clear severe congestion at Benghazi port.

Infrastructure expenditure has put great emphasis on power generation. Since 1974 the Government has awarded several large contracts for power stations, some in association with desalination plants, and it was planned that national generating capacity would be raised to 4,000 MW by 1980. It had been hoped that this would include some use of nuclear power but, although Libya has received uranium yellow cake from Niger, the agreement on nuclear technology with India ran into difficulties in August 1979. Supplies of uranium oxide from Niger, though, resumed in 1981, and in the first half of the year reached 1,200 tons. Colonel Gaddafi has recently gone on record as saying that Libya is still seeking nuclear power, but only for peaceful purposes. Early in 1982 there were reports that plans were under way for a nuclear power station to be built on the Gulf of Sirte coast with Soviet assistance. Water shortages are also becoming critical, and in 1982 plans were announced for a 462,000 cubic metres-per-day desalination plant to provide Tripoli with drinking water.

As might be expected, the large and increasing volume of imports has led to severe congestion at the main ports of Tripoli and Benghazi. Worsening port conditions have led to increases in surcharges. In addition, Derna and Misurata ports are being reconstructed. Both Tripoli and Benghazi are undergoing large-scale expansion, the Tripoli project being, in fact, one of the larger projects in the 1976–80 Plan, involving an investment of LD 125 million. Port expansion is necessarily a long-term process and the development of rail, road and to some extent air freight is very important. There is an extensive road-building programme, and a number of large road-building contracts, such as the Sebha-Wadden road and the Mirzuk link, have gone to Egyptian companies. In 1980, an Indian company won a $129 million contract for the construction of desert roads at a variety of locations throughout the country. There have been no railways in Libya since 1964, when the Benghazi-Barce line was abandoned, but construction of a 170-km. line from Tripoli to the Tunisian border, based on Hungarian design, should get under way in 1982.

The telecommunications network is constantly being expanded; a new company was set up in 1976 to oversee all telecommunications contracts and imports of equipment. The first major contract awarded to a Japanese firm in Libya went to Nippon Electric for the installation of a microwave network. A number of contracts were awarded for telecommunications development in 1977; they included contracts with

Nippon Electric, the United Kingdom Post Office Consultancy Services and Marconi U.K. In March 1978 Plessey Telecommunications of the United Kingdom was awarded a $9 million contract to supply electronic automatic branch exchanges for Libya's National Telecommunications Company. During 1979 a 480-line, 1,650 km. telephone cable was opened between Tripoli and Marseilles, which will provide Libya with more international telephone links.

The estimated cost of the new international airport at Benghazi, on which construction work began in 1977, has risen to roughly $200 million; the airport was scheduled for completion in 1980. The contract for a new airport at Ghat went to an Indian company in 1976. The new Tripoli International Airport was opened in August 1978.

EXTERNAL TRADE

Until production of oil began, Libya's exports consisted almost entirely of agricultural products, and its imports of manufactured goods. In 1960, for instance, imports were valued at LD 60.4 million and exports at LD 4.0 million, leaving an adverse balance of LD 56.4 million (although LD 21 million of the total value of imports in 1960 was accounted for by goods imported for the account of the oil companies). Oil was first exported in the autumn of 1961, and by 1969, according to IMF data, imports totalled LD 241.3 million and exports LD 937.9 million, of which LD 936.5 million (or almost 100 per cent) was officially accounted for by crude petroleum. Oil exports in 1974 were worth LD 2,109.5 million (74 million tons), compared with LD 1,031.7 million (105 million tons) in 1973. In 1975 the value of oil exports fell to LD 1,786.8 million but there was a significant rise to LD 2,711.2 million in 1976 and to LD 3,189.6 million in 1977, when total recorded exports were worth LD 3,381.8 million. Oil exports in 1978 fell to LD 2,719.4 million, while total recorded exports were worth LD 2,933.0 million. By 1979 oil exports had risen to LD 4,419.2 million, 92 per cent of all Libyan exports by value. The minute proportion of remaining exports were mainly hides and skins, groundnuts, almonds, metal scrap and re-exports.

Imports now consist of a wide variety of manufactured goods, such as textiles, motor vehicles and luxury consumer goods. In the last few years imports of timber, chemicals and raw materials and, in particular, cement and building materials, have been stepped up. In addition, many foodstuffs have to be imported, for example tea, sugar, coffee and, in years of drought, wheat and flour. The value of imports increased more than six-fold between 1971 and 1979, from LD 250.4 million to LD 1,572 million, whereas over the same period exports by value grew only five-fold.

Since oil has been exported, Libya has experienced a considerable trade surplus. In 1971 exports f.o.b. (including re-exports) were valued at LD 962.5 million, and imports c.i.f. at LD 250.4 million, leaving a trade surplus of LD 712.1 million. In 1976 and 1977 the trade surpluses, measured on the same basis, were

LD 1,920.9 million and LD 2,264.7 million respectively. In 1978 the figure fell to LD 1,570.4 million, but in 1979 it reached a new peak of LD 3,189.6 million. Recent falls in oil exports suggest that Libya's balance-of-payments position will be much more hazardous over the next few years.

In 1978 and 1979 Libya's principal supplier was Italy, with 24 and 26 per cent of total imports. In 1978 West Germany supplied 11 per cent, France 8 per cent, Japan 7 per cent and the United Kingdom 7 per cent of total imports. Eastern Bloc countries are likely to take a larger share of the market as more trade and co-operation agreements are signed. In 1976, for example, Libya signed a trade and co-operation agreement with Yugoslavia and similar agreements have been signed with India and the U.S.S.R. During 1979 imports from France rose by 14 per cent compared with 1978, but, after France's military support of Chad and general French assistance of Tunisia at the time of the Gafsa attack early in 1980, relations have soured. Early in 1980 trade agreements were signed with Bangladesh and Seychelles, but economic relations with China have been severed, owing to its supply of fighter jets to Egypt. In February 1981, a new trade agreement was signed with Yugoslavia. Trade with Italy is experiencing an upturn, and the existence of a joint Libyan/Italian commission is one factor likely to ead to greater Italian participation in the latest Five-Year Plan.

Libya's best oil customers in 1975 were the United Kingdom, France, West Germany, Italy and the U.S.A. Sales to Italy were stimulated by the ENI settlement and to the U.S.A. by the much-publicized American fuel crisis. The events of 1973, and the embargo on sales to the U.S.A. and the Netherlands, altered the pattern somewhat, with sales to the U.S.A. later increasing rapidly. In 1977 the U.S.A. took 25 per cent of Libya's oil exports. The U.S.A. and Western Europe together accounted for almost 90 per cent of total oil exports from Libya. However, during 1979 and 1980 political relations with the U.S.A. varied greatly. Early in 1980 the U.S.A. refused export licences on Boeing 747 jumbo jets, since there had been no improvement in relations with Libya, and in 1982 all imports of Libyan oil to the U.S.A. were banned.

FINANCE

Before the 1969 coup most Libyan banks were subsidiaries of foreign banks. However, amongst the first decrees issued by the Revolutionary Council was one which required 51 per cent of the capital of all banks operating in Libya to be owned by Libyans; the majority of directors, including the chairman, of each bank had to be Libyan citizens. The royal Government had followed a similar policy without compulsion, and a number of foreign banks had accordingly already "Libyanized" themselves. In December 1970, all commercial banks were nationalized, with government participation set at 51 per cent. There are now only six commercial banks in the country.

The development of the oil industry has enabled Libya to maintain a high degree of stability in the external value of its currency. Indeed, the Libyan currency has maintained its dollar parity of $3.378 (or LD 0.296 per U.S. dollar) since it was established after the February 1973 U.S. dollar devaluation. The fact is that the Libyan authorities do not consider the country's exchange rate as an instrument of domestic economic policy which can be employed to counteract inflationary pressures. The dollar's weakness during 1974 and again in early 1977 undoubtedly has raised the cost of imported goods when converted into dinars at the official rate of exchange; but in respect of important items, such as food, the Government has tended to prefer introducing subsidies in order to dampen the impact of increased costs on local consumers. Since subsidies can be applied to specific goods, whereas a change in the exchange rate necessarily affects all commodities, the authorities have felt that relying on subsidies would be more equitable as well as simple. Further, the authorities have felt that pursuance of a neutral exchange rate policy made economic sense in endeavouring to diversify the country's export industries away from almost total reliance on foreign sales of crude petroleum to include exports of refined products, plastics, fertilizers and many other goods. Clearly, had the Libyan currency been allowed to appreciate against the dollar and other major currencies, this would have adversely affected prospects for domestic industries in international markets.

The massive growth in oil revenue has also allowed the Government to devote about half its income to development expenditure. It has even been able to give generous aid abroad, in particular to the Yemen P.D.R., Egypt, Syria and Jordan, although the Government is somewhat capricious in implementing aid agreements. Aid was cut off from the Jordanian Government in September 1970 when it attacked the Palestinian guerrillas. Egypt was criticized over its conduct of the war with Israel and in 1974 Libya demanded the return of a loan to the Sudan. Future aid to Egypt is suspended as a result of Egypt's signing the peace treaty with Israel in March 1979. There is no comparable organization in Libya to the Kuwait Fund for Arab Economic Development, but in 1974 Libya made a contribution to the Islamic Development Bank. In 1980 Libyan aid to developing countries was $281 million or 0.92 per cent of G.N.P. This compares with the $261 million given in 1975, which then represented 2.3 per cent of G.N.P.

Recent developments in the Libyan banking sector include the establishment of joint development banks with Algeria and Turkey and an agreement to establish a joint Libyan-Mali bank. In March 1977 the Libyan Arab Foreign Bank (LAFB) took up a 9.6 per cent stake in the equity of Fiat, the Italian motor car company. The deal is backed by a loan to Fiat from the LAFB of $105 million repayable over ten years (with two years grace). Until this purchase the LAFB had pursued a cautious and selective policy of putting Libyan capital into banking, hotel and tourism in many countries, as well as joint-stock ventures in

agriculture, fishing and forestry projects in some African countries. It seems clear that the Libyans regarded the Fiat purchase as the vanguard of Libyan investment into industrial countries' manufacturing base. Libya's holdings in Italy were enlarged at the end of 1981 when the LAFB bought up the bankrupt Italian sugar and steel concern Malradi for $450 million. In December 1979 Kuwait and Libya signed a $1,000 million agreement to set up an Arab investment company, and in April 1980 Libya, together with Kuwait and the United Arab Emirates, decided to establish a new international insurance company. This was finally established with a capital of $3,000 million in October 1981.

Although Libya enjoys a substantial trade surplus, it also experiences a substantial deficit on "invisibles" (services and transfer payments). This "invisible" deficit increased from $1,450 million in 1973 to $2,265 million in 1977. In most years it partly offsets the trade surplus, leaving a fluctuating surplus on current account, but in 1975 (when the trade surplus was reduced) the current account was pushed into deficit. Aid payments and arms purchases tend to bring about a substantial outflow on capital account— so that Libya's basic balance of payments often yields a deficit. International reserves totalled $4,208 million at December 31st, 1978, compared with $2,131 million at the end of 1973, and by the end of 1979 the figure rose to $6,449 million. At mid-1981 foreign exchange reserves stood at $13,444 million, but by March 1982 they had fallen to $7,499 million.

Libyan planning dates back to the 1960s, with the First Development Plan running from 1963/64 to 1967/68. The Second Plan ran from 1969/70 to 1973/74, and the Third Plan, with an investment of LD 2,200 million (of which 34 per cent was for industry, petroleum and electricity), from 1973 to 1975. Development budgets in the 1970s favoured agriculture, and the 1976–80 Development Plan, known as the Economic and Social Transformation Plan, involved a total investment of LD 9,250 million, with priority again given to agriculture, although industrial and communications sectors also received large allocations. The Plan aimed at an annual increase of 10.5 per cent in G.N.P. and a 26 per cent rise in industrial production. Industry received an allocation of LD 1,205 million, transport and communications LD 930 million and oil and gas exploitation LD 670 million. Housing allocations were LD 1,131 million.

In 1978 G.D.P. increased by 11 per cent, which was above the planned rate of 10.7 per cent, but the average growth for the period 1976–79 was only 9.5 per cent a year. In 1978 the allocations of most sectors of the budget were increased, but it appears that by the end of the plan it was greatly underspent, with only 80 per cent of the planned expenditure used. The overall aims of the plan were to achieve diversity of production, thus lessening the dependence on oil, to develop the economic and social infrastructure and to achieve a more equitable distribution of income and wealth. In 1980 development spending was raised by 40 per cent to LD

2,400 million and during 1980 the administrative budget was LD 900 million, which is similar in value to the 1979 figure.

The latest (1981–85) Five-Year Plan is seen as part of a major 20-year development programme, which aims at structural change in the economy to reduce its dependence on oil. Expenditure is to be LD 18,500 million, more than double the allocation for the previous Plan, and it is hoped that by 1985 the non-oil sector will contribute 53 per cent of national income, compared with 35 per cent in 1980. 23 per cent of investment is to be allocated to industry, and rapid growth is planned for electricity, transport, communications and housing. Agriculture

is to receive 16 per cent. The overall annual growth rate is set at 9.4 per cent, compared with the last Plan's 7 per cent, but industry's annual growth rate over the next five years is projected at 21.6 per cent. Agriculture's annual growth rate, on the other hand, is forecast at 7.4 per cent.

For 1982 the administrative budget was endorsed at LD 1,255 million, and the development budget at LD 2,600 million. 1982's development spending is thus 5 per cent down on that of 1981 and, of this, heavy industry has been allocated LD 493 million (19 per cent), communications and marine transport LD 355 million (14 per cent), and land reclamation and agrarian reform LD 347 million (13 per cent).

STATISTICAL SURVEY
AREA AND POPULATION

AREA (sq. km.)	POPULATION (census results)	
	July 1973	1979
1,775,500	2,249,237	3,245,000

POPULATION BY MOHAFDA (DISTRICT)
(1973 Census)

Tripoli	. . .	707,438
Benghazi	. . .	332,333
Zawia (Zavia)	. .	244,456
Misurata	. . .	178,129
Khoms	. . .	160,882
Gharian	. . .	154,297
Jebel Akhdar	. .	132,366
Derna	. . .	122,984
Sebha	. . .	111,303
Kalig	. . .	105,049

PRINCIPAL TOWNS
(population at 1973 census)

Tripoli (capital)	. .	481,295
Benghazi	. . .	219,317
Misurata	. . .	42,815
Zawia	. . .	39,382
El-Beida	. . .	31,796
Agedabia	. . .	31,047
Derna	. . .	30,241
Sebha	. . .	28,714
Tubruq (Tobruk)	.	28,061
El Marj	. . .	25,166
Zeleiten	. . .	21,340

AGRICULTURE

LAND USE, 1979
(FAO estimates, 'ooo hectares)

Arable land	2,420
Land under permanent crops . . .	144
Permanent meadows and pastures . .	6,700
Forests and woodlands	534
Other land	166,156
TOTAL	175,954

PRINCIPAL CROPS
('ooo metric tons)

	1977	1978	1979
Barley . .	58	178	100
Wheat . .	27	45	110
Olives . .	42	143	100
Citrus fruits .	47	37	48
Groundnuts .	13	13	n.a.
Almonds . .	4.7	5.3	5.5
Tomatoes . .	175	193	198
Dates . .	100	86	98
Potatoes . .	99	89	90
Grapes . .	16	15	16

Source: Department of Agriculture, Tripoli.

LIVESTOCK
('ooo head)

	1977	1978	1979
Horses . . .	14	14	14
Asses . . .	73	73	73
Cattle . . .	179	183	181
Camels . . .	69	71	134
Sheep . . .	3,826	3,982	5,445
Goats . . .	1,514	1,617	1,463
Foultry . . .	4,545	4,557	5,099

Source: Department of Agriculture, Tripoli.

LIVESTOCK PRODUCTS
('ooo metric tons)

	1976	1977	1978
Sheep's meat . .	19.7	20.3	17.5
Goats' meat . .	0.7	0.9	0.4
Cattle meat . .	22.2	24.7	30.6
Camels' meat . .	5.8	6.7	5.5
Milk . . .	93.5	81.9	86.9
Wool . . .	6.6	5.7	6.0
Cattle hides . .	1.4	2.2	2.5
Sheep skins . .	2.0	2.0	1.7
Goat skins . .	0.1	0.2	0.1
Camel hides . .	0.3	0.4	0.3
Eggs (million) . .	220.0	204.0	239.0

Source: Department of Agriculture, Tripoli.

FORESTRY
ROUNDWOOD REMOVALS
('ooo cubic metres, all non-coniferous)

	1971	1972	1973	1974	1975	1976	1977*	1978*
Industrial wood	44	34	70	62	39	43	68	90
Fuel wood*	416	434	452	470	488	504	520	536
TOTAL . . .	460	468	522	532	527	547	588	626

* FAO estimate.

1979: Production as in 1978.

Source: FAO, *Yearbook of Forest Products.*

SEA FISHING
('ooo metric tons)

	1968	1969	1970	1971	1972	1973	1974	1975
Total catch	5.5	11.3	5.5	5.7	2.4	2.9	3.8	4.8

1976–80: Annual catch as in 1975 (FAO estimates).

Source: FAO, *Yearbook of Fishery Statistics.*

MINING

		1975	1976	1977	1978	1979	1980
Crude petroleum . .	'ooo metric tons	71,533	93,452	99,503	95,606	100,879	88,324
Natural gas* . .	million cu. metres	n.a.	17,946	20,008	21,244	23,470	18,552

* Estimated production.

INDUSTRY
(Value of output in LD'ooo—Large establishments only)

	1973	1974	1975	1976
Food manufacturing . . .	12,823	20,806	26,066	32,541
Beverage industries . . .	4,265	5,301	5,590	6,744
Tobacco manufactures . . .	17,077	21,146	30,070	33,065
Chemicals and products . . .	7,294	10,535	13,661	14,458
Textiles	2,004	2,400	3,622	5,459
Cement and products . .	5,701	11,752	13,989	14,629
Fabricated metal products . .	3,487	4,096	5,022	3,704
TOTAL (incl. others) . .	58,799	84,978	110,579	127,079

FINANCE
1,000 dirhams=1 Libyan dinar (LD).

Coins: 1, 5, 10, 20, 50 and 100 dirhams.

Notes: 250 and 500 dirhams; 1, 5 and 10 dinars.

Exchange rates (May 1982): £1 sterling=544.29 dirhams; U.S. $1=296.05 dirhams.
100 Libyan dinars=£183.72=$337.78.

Note: The dinar is equivalent to the former Libyan pound (of 1,000 millièmes), which it replaced in September 1971. The Libyan pound had been introduced in March 1952, with a value of U.S. $2.80 ($1=357.14 millièmes). This valuation remained in effect until August 1971. Between December 1971 and February 1973 the new Libyan dinar (replacing the pound) was worth $3.04 ($1=328.95 dirhams). The present dollar valuation became effective in February 1973. The Libyan pound was at par with the pound sterling until November 1967, after which the exchange rate was £1 sterling=857.14 millièmes or dirhams (Lib£1 or 1 dinar=£1.167 sterling) until June 1972.

Administrative Budget, 1982: LD 1,255 million.

Development Budget, 1982: LD 2,600 million.

Development Plan 1981–85: Total LD 18,500 million, of which Industry LD 4,000 million, Agriculture LD 3,000 million.

CENTRAL BANK RESERVES
(U.S. $ million at December 31st)

	1978	1979	1980
Gold . . .	103	105	141
IMF Special Drawing Rights . . .	—	40	59
Reserve position in IMF	8	56	189
Foreign exchange .	4,097	6,248	12,842
TOTAL . .	4,208	6,449	13,231

Source: IMF, *International Financial Statistics.*

MONEY SUPPLY
(LD million at December 31st)

	1977	1978	1979
Currency held by public	540.4	834.1	1,053.7
Demand deposits held by public . .	914.6	935.5	1,196.9
TOTAL MONEY .	1,455.0	1,769.6	2,250.6

Source: Central Bank of Libya.

BALANCE OF PAYMENTS
(U.S. $ million)

	1973	1974	1975	1976	1977	1978	1979
Merchandise exports f.o.b. . .	3,528	7,803	6,418	8,748	10,405	9,900	15,915
Merchandise imports f.o.b. . .	−2,011	−3,746	−4,424	−4,277	−4,929	−5,764	−6,160
TRADE BALANCE . . .	1,516	4,057	1,994	4,470	5,476	4,135	9,755
Exports of services . . .	216	434	375	349	379	468	559
Imports of services . . .	−1,237	−1,372	−1,553	−1,574	−1,607	−1,815	−2,102
BALANCE ON GOODS AND SERVICES	495	3,119	816	3,245	4,248	2,789	8,212
Private unrequited transfers (net) .	−273	−350	−260	−257	−857	−577	−669
Government unrequited transfers (net)	−156	−69	−164	−144	−98	−91	−178
CURRENT BALANCE . .	66	2,700	392	2,844	3,293	2,121	7,365
Direct capital investment (net) .	−148	−241	−616	−521	−411	−557	−319
Other long-term capital (net) . .	−362	−182	−908	−987	−1,085	−817	−708
Short-term capital (net) . .	485	388	305	348	211	−212	185
Net errors and omissions . .	−1,023	−927	−823	−571	−67	−980	−3,955
TOTAL (net monetary movements) .	−982	1,739	−1,650	1,112	1,942	−445	2,567
Allocation of IMF Special Drawing Rights . . .	—	—	—	—	—	—	25
Valuation changes (net) . .	248	−236	245	−40	−209	−232	−193
CHANGES IN RESERVES . .	−734	1,503	−1,405	1,072	1,733	−677	2,399

Source: IMF, *International Financial Statistics.*

EXTERNAL TRADE
(LD million)

	1972	1973	1974	1975	1976	1977	1978	1979	1980
Imports c.i.f. . .	343.2	539.9	817.8	1,048.7	950.8	1,117.1	1,362.6	1,572.4	2,006.2
Exports f.o.b.* . .	968.1	1,197.1	2,446.2	2,025.1	2,871.7	3,381.8	2,933.0	4,762.0	6,489.2

* Including re-exports.

SELECTED COMMODITIES
(LD'ooo)

IMPORTS	1978	1979	1980	EXPORTS*	1978	1979	1980
Food and live animals .	205,330	238,067	338,638	Crude petroleum . .	2,719,481	4,419,237	4,486,378
Beverages and tobacco .	5,807	7,517	10,711				
Mineral fuels, etc. .	10,567	10,363	13,062				
Animal and vegetable oils and fats .	15,150	17,591	37,572				
Inedible crude materials excl. fuel . .	27,119	29,366	36,910				
Chemicals . .	42,206	64,149	107,760				
Basic manufactures .	296,896	366,710	484,473				
Machinery and transport equipment . .	567,528	668,248	762,194				
Miscellaneous manufactured articles .	191,864	170,401	214,831				

* Excluding re-exports.

PRINCIPAL TRADING PARTNERS
(U.S. $ million)

	IMPORTS c.i.f.			EXPORTS f.o.b.		
	1978	1979	1980	1978	1979	1980
Argentina	5	1	—	n.a.	n.a.	—
Bahamas	n.a.	—	—	62	522	1,097
Belgium	56	66	86	n.a.	81	50
Brazil	5	4	1	73	40	178
China, People's Republic .	58	32	11	n.a.	—	—
France	383	436	458	539	946	604
Germany, Federal Republic .	507	761	903	1,063	2,375	2,764
Greece	158	157	137	45	273	722
Hong Kong . . .	40	34	54	n.a.	—	—
Italy	1,109	1,402	2,002	2,158	2,896	4,061
Japan	343	474	511	15	74	297
Netherlands . . .	n.a.	—	—	n.a.	—	—
Romania	96	75	52	214	315	427
Spain	149	148	298	617	845	1,079
Turkey	58	52	53	247	304	699
United Kingdom . .	326	365	472	175	172	35
U.S.A.	288	284	426	3,912	5,543	7,765
Yugoslavia	72	67	82	44	128	275
TOTAL (incl. others)	4,602	5,311	6,776	9,906	16,076	21,919

TRANSPORT
ROAD TRAFFIC
(motor vehicles in use)

	1977	1978	1979
Private Cars . .	315,411	298,516	308,746
Taxis . . .	13,888	13,265	10,398
Lorries . . .	168,678	154,138	167,748
Buses . . .	2,116	1,571	2,835

INTERNATIONAL SEA-BORNE SHIPPING

	Ships ('ooo N.R.T.)		Cargo ('ooo metric tons)	
	Entered	Cleared	Loaded	Unloaded
1977 .	6,169	n.a.	93,845	7,569
1978 .	4,948	n.a.	89,458	6,626
1979 .	n.a.	n.a.	93,017	7,360
1980 .	n.a.	n.a.	81,896	6,519

CIVIL AVIATION

	1978	1979	1980
Number of Passengers			
Entering . . .	466,366	494,906	469,861
Leaving . . .	455,592	516,413	426,612
Cargo Unloaded (tons) .	39,936	34,756	31,361
Cargo Loaded (tons) .	2,824	3,147	2.689

EDUCATION
(1979/80)

State Schools	Schools	Students	Teachers
Primary . .	2,594	674,960	34,557
Preparatory . .	1,135	222,690	17,369
Secondary . .	160	49,449	3,330
Teacher Training .	104	27,827	2,113
Technical . .	581	13,847	1,004

Source (unless otherwise stated): Census and Statistical Dept., Ministry of Planning, Tripoli.

THE CONSTITUTION

The Libyan Arab People, meeting in the General People's Congress in Sebha from March 2nd to March 28th, 1977, proclaimed its adherence to freedom and its readiness to defend it on its own land and anywhere else in the world. It also announced its adherence to socialism and its commitment to achieving total Arab Unity; its adherence to the moral human values, and confirmed the march of the revolution led by Col. Muammar al-Gaddafi, the revolutionary leader, towards complete People's Authority.

The Libyan Arab People announced the following:

(i) The official name of Libya is henceforth *The Socialist People's Libyan Arab Jamahiriya.*

(ii) The Holy Koran is the social code in The Socialist People's Libyan Arab Jamahiriya.

(iii) The Direct People's Authority is the basis for the political order in The Socialist People's Libyan Arab Jamahiriya. The People shall practise its authority through People's Congresses, Popular Committees, Trade Unions, Vocational Syndicates, and The General People's Congress, in the presence of the law.

(iv) The defence of our homeland is the responsibility of every citizen. The whole people shall be trained militarily and armed by general military training, the preparation of which shall be specified by the law.

The General People's Congress in its extraordinary session held in Sebha issued four decrees:

The first decree announced the establishment of The People's Authority in compliance with the resolutions and recommendations of the People's Congresses and Trade Unions.

The second decree stipulated the choice of Col. Muammar al-Gaddafi, the Revolutionary Leader, as Secretary General of the General People's Congress.

The third decree stipulated the formation of the General Secretariat of the General People's Congress (*see* The Government, below).

The fourth decree stipulated the formation of the General People's Committee which comprises 26 Secretaries (reduced to 21 in March 1979) to carry out the tasks of the various former ministries (*see* The Government, below).

In February 1979 it was announced that the Secretariats were to be reorganized and their functions delimited. In March 1979, when Col. Gaddafi resigned from the post of Secretary General of the General People's Congress, the number of Secretaries of the General People's Committee was reduced to 21. Since 1979 progress has been made in furthering the spread of People's Committees in political and economic life.

THE GOVERNMENT

HEAD OF STATE

Revolutionary Leader: Col. MUAMMAR AL-GADDAFI (took office as Chairman of the Revolution Command Council September 8th, 1969).

GENERAL SECRETARIAT OF THE GENERAL PEOPLE'S CONGRESS

Secretary General: MUHAMMAD AZ-ZARROUK RAGAB.

Assistant Secretary General: ALI ABU AL-KHAYIR.

Secretary for Affairs of the Congress: MUHAMMAD ALI BA'WASH.

Secretary for Affairs of the People's Committees: ABDULLAH ZAHMUL.

Secretary for Trade Unions, Federations and Vocational Affairs: MUKHTAR QURBU.

GENERAL PEOPLE'S COMMITTEE

(June 1982)

Secretary-General of the General People's Committee: Eng. JADALLAH AZZUZ AT-TALHI.

Secretary of the General People's Committee (GPC) for Justice: MOHAMMED ABDUL-QASSIM AL-ZUWAI.

Secretary of the GPC for Health: MOURAD ALI LANKI.

Secretary for Petroleum: KAMEL HASSAN MABHUR.

Secretary of the GPC for Housing: Eng. MUHAMMAD AL-MANQUSH.

Secretary of the GPC for Economy and Light Industry: MUSA ABU FURAYWA.

Secretary of the GPC for the Treasury: MUHAMMAD KASSEM CHALALA.

Secretary of the GPC for Education: ABDEL HAFEZ ZLITNI.

Secretary of the GPC for Electricity: Eng. JUMAH AL-ARBASH.

Secretary of the GPC for Communications and Maritime Transport: SALEM AL-BUKHARI HOUDA.

Secretary of the GPC for Public Utilities: MUHAMMAD OBEID SHUKRI.

Secretary of the GPC for Planning: FAWZI SHAKSHUKI.

Secretary of the GPC for Land Reclamation and Land Reform: ABU ZAID OMAR DURDA.

Secretary for Heavy Industries: UMAR MUSTAFA AL-MUNTASIR.

Secretary of the GPC for Public Services: MUHAMMAD ABDULLAH AL-MABRUK.

Secretary of the GPC for Social Security: IBRAHIM AL-FAQIH HASAN.

Secretary of the Bureau for External Relations: ABDUL ATI AL-OBEIDI.

Secretary of the GPC for Atomic Energy: ABDUL MAJID AL-GOUD.

LEGISLATURE

GENERAL PEOPLE'S CONGRESS

The Senate and House of Representatives were dissolved after the *coup d'état* of September 1969, and the provisional constitution issued in December 1969 made no mention of elections or a return to Parliamentary procedure. However, in January 1971 Col. Gaddafi announced that a new Parliament would be appointed, not elected; no date was mentioned. All political parties other than the Arab Socialist Union were banned. In November 1975 provision was made for the creation of the General National Congress of the Arab Socialist Union, which met officially in January 1976. This later became the General People's Congress, which met for the first time in November 1976 and in March 1977 began introducing the wide-ranging changes outlined in "The Constitution" (above).

Secretary General: MUHAMMAD AZ-ZARROUK RAGAB.

DIPLOMATIC REPRESENTATION

EMBASSIES ACCREDITED TO LIBYA

(In Tripoli unless otherwise stated)

(E) Embassy.

Afghanistan: Sharia Moher Aftas (E); *Ambassador:* (vacant).

Algeria: Sharia Qayrouan 12 (E); *Ambassador:* SALEH BIN QUBY.

Argentina: Sharia Ibn Mufarrej, P.O.B. 932 (E); *Ambassador:* JULIO FREIXAS.

Australia: Beach Hotel, P.O.B. 5121 (E); *Chargé d'affaires:* RICHARD FLETCHER.

Austria: Sharia Khalid Ben Walid/corner (former) Sharia Arismondi, Dahra Area, Garden City (E); *Ambassador:* ERWIN MATSCH.

Bangladesh: Hadaba Al Khadra (E); *Ambassador:* MUHAMMAD MOHSIN.

Belgium: Abu Ubaida Ibn Al Jarah (E); *Ambassador:* FERDINAND DE WILDE.

Benin: (E); *Ambassador:* HASAN ABOUDO.

Brazil: Sharia Bin Ashur (E); *Ambassador:* CARLOS F. LECKIE LOBO.

Bulgaria: Sharia Murad Agha (E); *Ambassador:* VLADIMIR MEDAROV.

Burundi: Sharia Ras Hassan (E); *Ambassador:* MANGONA IBRAHIM.

Canada: Cairo, Egypt (E).

Chad: Sharia Muhammad Mussadeq (E); *Ambassador:* MUHAMMAD SENOUSSI.

Chile: Cairo, Egypt (E).

China, People's Republic: (E) *Ambassador:* PEI JIANZHANG.

Cuba: Sharia Ben Ashur y Shara Essagah (E); *Ambassador:* Dr. JOSÉ L. AVALO PINA.

Czechoslovakia: Ahmed Lutfi Street, Ben Ashour Area (E); *Ambassador:* VÁCLAV JUMR.

Denmark: Sharia Abdul Khader 38-40 (E); *Ambassador:* K. W. RASMUSSEN.

Ethiopia: Libya Palace Hotel (E); *Ambassador:* MOHAMMED ABDUL RAHMAN.

Finland: Garden City (E); *Ambassador:* JYRKI AIMONEN.

France: Sharia Ahmad Lutfi Said (E); *Ambassador:* CHRISTIAN GRAEFF.

Gambia: Maidan At-Tahrir, P.O.B. 10972 (E); (*Relations broken off November 1st, 1980*).

German Democratic Republic: Sharia Jumhuriya (E); *Ambassador:* Dr. WOLFGANG BATOR.

Germany, Federal Republic: Sharia Hassan al-Mashai (E); *Ambassador:* Dr. GÜNTHER HILD.

Greece: Sharia Jalal Bayar, 18 (E); *Ambassador:* EMMANUEL E. MEGALOKONOMOS.

Guinea: Sharia Bin 'Ashur (E); *Chargé d'affaires:* ABOUBACAR WAGUE.

Hungary: Sharia Talha Bin Abdullah (E); *Ambassador:* BÁLINT GÁL.

India: Sharia Mahmud Shaltut (E); *Ambassador:* A. G. ASRANI.

Iran: Tunis, Tunisia (E).

Iraq: Sharia Ben Ashur (E); (*Relations broken off October 1980*).

Italy: Sharia 'Oran 1 (E); *Ambassador:* ALESSANDRO QUARONI.

Japan: 37 Sharia Ubei Ben Ka'ab (E); *Chargé d'affaires a.i.:* MASAO WADA.

Jordan: Sharia Ali ibn Uloff (E); *Ambassador:* HISHAM SHEWA.

Kuwait: Sharia Bin Yassir (E); *Ambassador:* ABDUL HAJJI AL-MAHMID.

Lebanon: Sharia Bin Yassir (E); *Ambassador:* (vacant).

Malaysia (E); *Ambassador:* ABDUL BIN MUHAMMAD.

Malta: Sharia Ubei Ben Ka'ab (E); *Chargé d'affaires:* MAURICE J. LUBRANO.

Mauritania: Sharia Aissa Wokwak (E); *Ambassador:* MUHAMMAD MAHMUD OULD WADDADI.

Morocco: (E); *Ambassador:* MAATI JORIO.

Nepal: Jeddah, Saudi Arabia (E).

Netherlands: Sharia Jelal Bayar 20 (E); *Chargé d'affaires a.i.:* J. J. JONKER ROELANTS.

Niger: Tantawy Gohari No. 3 (E); *Ambassador:* Al Hadji ABU-BAKR BELLO.

Nigeria: Sharia Ammar Ben Yaser (E); *Ambassador:* ZUBEIRY KAZURE.

Norway: Athens, Greece (E).

Pakistan: Sharia al-Khitabi (E); *Ambassador:* SHAHID M. AMIN.

Philippines: (E); *Ambassador:* RODOLFO G. TUPAS.

Poland: Sharia Ben Ashur (E); *Ambassador:* SYKSTUS OLESIK.

Qatar: Garden City (E); *Ambassador:* (vacant).

Romania: Sharia Ben Ashur (E); *Ambassador:* ANDREI PACURA.

Rwanda: Hay al Andalus (E); *Ambassador:* NDUWAYEZU AUGUSTIN.

Saudi Arabia: Sharia al-Qayrounan 2 (E); *Ambassador:* (to be appointed).

Somalia: Sharia Khalid Ben Elwalid (E); (*Relations broken off August 1981*).

Spain: Sharia al-Jazayri (E); *Ambassador:* FRANCESCO JAVIR.

Sri Lanka: Cairo, Egypt (E).

Sudan: (E); *Ambassador:* ABDUL MAGID BASHIR EL-AHMADI.

Sweden: Sharia Mugaryef (E); *Ambassador:* B. H. HOLMQUIST.

Switzerland: Sharia Jeraba (E); *Chargé d'affaires:* HENNING RIEDER.

Syria: Sharia Muhammed Rashid Rida 4 (Relations Office); *Acting Head:* 'ALY HASAN.

Togo: Fashloum (E); *Ambassador:* Al Hadji KASSIM MENSAH.

Tunisia: Sharia Bashir al-Ibrahimi (E); *Ambassador:* HAMED AMMAR.

Turkey: Sharia Gamal Abdel Nasser 36 (E); *Ambassador:* MUSTAFA ASHULA.

Uganda: Ben Ashura-Jeraba St., P.O.B. 10978 (E); *Ambassador:* AMIN MUTYABA.

U.S.S.R.: Sharia Mustapha Kamel (E); *Ambassador:* ANATOLY ANISSIMOV.

United Arab Emirates: Sharia Ben Ashur (E); *Ambassador:* (vacant).

United Kingdom: Sharia Gamal Abdul Nasser (E); *Ambassador:* J. M. EDES, C.M.G.

U.S.A.: Sharia al-Nasr (E); (*Relations suspended*).

Venezuela: Sharia Abdulrahman Kwakby (E); *Ambassador:* JOSÉ GREGORIO GONZÁLES RODRÍGUES.

Viet-Nam: Sharia Ben Abdullah (E); *Ambassador:* NGUYEN VAN SAO.

Yemen Arab Republic: Sharia Ubei Ben Ka'ab 36 (E); *Ambassador:* AHMED TAIFELLAH AL-AZEIB.

Yemen, People's Democratic Republic: Sharia Bin 'Ashur (E); *Ambassador:* IBRAHIM ABDULLA SAIDI.

Yugoslavia: Sharia Turkia No. 14 (E); *Ambassador:* SAFET SERIFOVIĆ.

Zaire: Aziz al Masri (E); (*Relations broken off May 1982*).

Libya also has diplomatic relations with Botswana, Costa Rica, Cyprus, Djibouti, Gabon, Ghana, Grenada, Guinea-Bissau, Ireland, Jamaica, the Democratic People's Republic of Korea, the Republic of Korea, Laos, Liberia, Madagascar, Mali, Mauritius, Mexico, Nicaragua, Panama, São Tomé and Príncipe, Seychelles, Suriname, Thailand, Tonga and Zimbabwe.

JUDICIAL SYSTEM

President of the Supreme Court: MUHAMMAD ALI AL-JADI.

The law of the Judicial System of 1954 established the following courts: the Federal Supreme Court, the Courts of Appeal, the Courts of First Instance and the Summary Courts. Sittings are in public, unless the court decides to hold them *in camera* in the interests of decency or public order. Judgment is in all cases given in public. The language of the courts is Arabic, but there is a translation office attached to each Court to help non-Arabic speaking parties or lawyers.

In October 1971 the Revolution Command Council decreed that all legislation should conform with the basic principles of Islamic Law and set up committees to carry this out. In April 1973 Colonel Gaddafi declared that any legislation likely to impede the progress of the revolution or to defeat public interest must be repealed. In September 1979 Colonel Gaddafi announced that judicial power was to be put in the hands of People's Committees for Justice.

The **Supreme Court** consists at present of a Chief Justice and ten justices.

Courts of Appeal exist in Tripoli, Benghazi and Misurata, consisting of a President, Vice-President and three judges; judgments must be given by three judges. Each Court of Appeal includes a Court of Assize consisting of three judges.

Courts of First Instance are set up in the provinces, consisting of a President, Vice-President and a number of judges; judgment in these courts is given by one judge.

Summary Courts, composed of one judge, exist within the territorial jurisdiction of every Court of First Instance.

The People's Court is a special court set up by decree in October 1969 and is particularly concerned with cases of political and administrative corruption.

RELIGION

Islam: The Libyan Arabs, practically without exception, follow Sunni Muslim rites.

Chief Mufti of Libya: Sheikh TAHER AHMED AL-ZAWI.

Roman Catholic Church: Apostolic Vicariates of Benghazi (15,000 Catholics, 1978) and Tripoli (30,000 Catholics, 1981).

THE PRESS

Newspapers and periodicals are published either by the Jamahiriya News Agency (JANA), or by the Press Service or by Trade Unions.

DAILIES

TRIPOLI

Al-Fajr al-Jadid: P.O.B. 2303; f. 1969; since January 1978 published by JANA; circ. 40,000.

PERIODICALS

TRIPOLI

Al Amal: weekly; social, for children; published by the Press Service.

Al Ardh: weekly; published by Agricultural Trade Union.

Al Bait: fortnightly; social; published by the Press Service.

Economic Bulletin: monthly; published by JANA.

Al Jarida Al Rasmiya: irregular; official State Gazette.

Al Mishal: weekly; published by General Union of Petroleum, Petrochemicals and Mining.

Al Muallim: fortnightly; published by General Teachers' Congress.

Al Muwathaf: fortnightly; published by General Employees' Congress.

Scientific Bulletin: monthly; published by JANA.

Al Shurti: weekly; security and social; published by Secretariat of Justice.

Al Taleb: fortnightly; published by General Students' Union.

Al Thaqafa al Arabiya: P.O.B. 4587; f. 1973; cultural; monthly; circ. 25,000.

Al Usbu Al Assiyasi: weekly (Fridays); political; published by the Press Service.

Al Usbu Al Thaqafiy: P.O.B. 4845; weekly (Mondays); cultural; published by the Press Service; Editor MUSTAFA AL-MISULLATI.

NEWS AGENCIES

Jamahiriya News Agency (JANA): P.O.B. 2303, Tripoli; branches and correspondents throughout Libya; main foreign bureaux: London, Paris, Rome, Beirut, Nairobi, Nouakchott and Kuwait; serves Libyan and foreign subscribers; Dir.-Gen. IBRAHIM MUHAMMAD AL-BISHARI; publs. *Al Fajr al-Jadid* (daily), *Economic Bulletin* (monthly), *Scientific Bulletin* (monthly).

FOREIGN BUREAUX

Tass (U.S.S.R.) and ANSA (Italy) have offices in Tripoli.

PUBLISHER

Maison Arabe du Livre: P.O.B. 3185, Tripoli.

RADIO AND TELEVISION

Socialist People's Libyan Arab Jamahiriya Broadcasting Corporation: P.O.B. 333, Tripoli; P.O.B. 274, Benghazi; f. 1957 (TV 1968); broadcasts in Arabic and English from Tripoli and Benghazi; from September 1971 special daily broadcasts to Gaza and other Israeli-occupied territory were begun; under the direction of the Information Secretary; Dir.-Gen. N. DHAW EL-HOMIDE.

Number of radio receivers: 131,000 (1980).

A national television service in Arabic was inaugurated in December 1968. Channels transmitting for limited hours in English, Italian and French have since been added. Number of TV receivers: 160,000 (1980).

FINANCE

(br.=branch; cap.=capital; p.u.=paid up; dep.=deposits; LD=Libyan Dinar; m.=million; res.=reserves)

BANKING

CENTRAL BANK

Central Bank of Libya: Sharia al Malik Seoud, P.O.B. 1103, Tripoli; f. 1955; bank of issue and central bank carrying government accounts and operating exchange control; commercial operations transferred to National Commercial Bank 1970; publs. *Economic Bulletin, Annual Report*; cap. LD 1m.; res. LD 7m.; dep. LD 155.5m. (Dec. 1975); Governor RAJAB AL-MISALLATI.

OTHER BANKS

Jamahiriya Bank: P.O.B. 3224, Sharia Emhamed El Megarief, Tripoli; f. 1969 as successor to Barclays Bank International in Libya; known as Masraf al Gumhouria until March 1977; government-owned; 27 brs. throughout Libya; cap. LD 750,000; res. LD 17.5m.; dep. LD 192.8m. (Dec. 1978); Chair. SHTEWI K. ETTIR.

Libyan Arab Foreign Bank: 1st September St., P.O.B. 2542, Tripoli; offshore bank wholly owned by Central Bank of Libya; cap. p.u. and res. LD 61.5m. (Dec. 1980); Chair. and Gen. Man. ABOUBAKER ALI AL-SHERIF.

National Commercial Bank S.A.L.: Shuhada Square, P.O.B. 4647, Tripoli; f. 1970 to take over commercial banking division of Central Bank and brs. of Aruba Bank and Istiklal Bank; 22 brs.; cap. LD 2.5m.; dep. LD 461.1m.; res. LD 46.2m. (Dec. 1978); Chair. and Gen. Man. MUHAMMAD MUSTAFA GHADBAN.

Sahara Bank: Sharia 1st September, P.O.B. 270, Tripoli; f. 1964 to take over br. of Banco di Sicilia; 16 brs.; Chair. and Gen. Man. FARAG A. GAMRA.

Umma Bank S.A.L.: 1 Giaddat Omar Mukhtar, P.O.B. 685; Tripoli; f. 1969 to take over brs. of Banco di Roma, 24 brs.; cap. LD 500,000; res. LD 62m.; dep. LD 234m. (Dec. 1979); Chair. and Gen. Man. ALI M. EL-REMALI.

Wahda Bank: Jamal Abdul Naser St., P.O.B. 452, Benghazi; f. 1970 to take over Bank of North Africa, Commercial Bank, S.A.L., Nahda Arabia Bank, Société Africaine de Banque, Kafila Ahly Bank; 26 brs.; cap. and res. LD 33.2m.; dep. LD 649.6m. (Dec. 1980); Chair. and Gen. Man. YOUSSEF A. HASSADI.

INSURANCE

Libya Insurance Co.: 1st September St., P.O.B. 2438, Tripoli; P.O.B. 643, Benghazi; f. 1964; cap. LD1m.; all classes of insurance.

Al Mukhtar Insurance Co.: 230 Muhammad Lemgarief St., P.O.B. 2548, Tripoli; all classes of insurance; Chair. and Gen. Man. IBRAHIM FELFEL.

OIL

Petroleum affairs in Libya are dealt with primarily by the Secretariat of Petroleum. Since 1973 Libya has been entering into participation agreements with some of the foreign oil companies (concession holders), and nationalizing others. It has concluded 85–15 per cent production sharing agreements with various oil companies.

Secretariat of Petroleum: P.O.B. 256, Tripoli.

NATIONAL COMPANIES

National Oil Corporation (NOC): P.O.B. 2655, Tripoli; f. 1970 as successor to the Libyan General Petroleum Corporation, to undertake joint ventures with foreign companies; to build and operate refineries, storage tanks, petrochemical facilities, pipelines and tankers; to take part in arranging specifications for local and imported petroleum products; to participate in general planning of oil installations in Libya; to market crude oil and to establish and operate oil terminals; Chair. WAHID OMAR BUGHAIGIS.

Agip (N.A.M.E.) Libyan Branch: P.O.B. 346, Tripoli; Sec. of the People's Committee Dr. M. EL AGELI.

Arabian Gulf Oil Co.: P.O.B. 263, Benghazi; Sec. of People's Committee H. A. LAYASS.

Brega Oil Marketing Co.: P.O.B. 402, Nars St., Tripoli; f. 1971; Chair. of People's Committee D. B. MEGHARIEF.

Mobil Oil Libya: P.O.B. 690, Tripoli; Chair. SALEM A. FARKASH.

National Drilling Co.: P.O.B. 1454, Tripoli; Chair. and Gen. Man. MUHAMMAD AHMED ATTIGA.

Oasis Oil Co.: P.O.B. 395, Tripoli; Sec. of People's Committee ABDULLA S. EL-BADRI.

Occidental of Libya: P.O.B. 2134, Tripoli; Chair. and Gen. Man. MASSAOUD JARNAZ.

Sirte Oil Co.: P.O.B. 385, Tripoli; Sec. of People's Committee MANSOUR M. BENNIRAN.

Umm Al-Jawaby Petroleum Co.: P.O.B. 693, Tripoli; Chair. and Gen. Man. MUHAMMAD TENTTOUSH.

Zawiya Oil Refining Co.: affiliated with NOC, P.O.B. 6451, Tripoli, and P.O.B. 15715, Azzawiya; Chair. and Gen. Man. ALI HABBOUNI.

FOREIGN COMPANIES

Aquitaine Libya: P.O.B. 282, Tripoli; Man. JEAN LE BRETON.

Wintershall-Libya: P.O.B. 469 and 905, Tripoli; Man. JOBST KLEMME.

TRADE AND INDUSTRY

CHAMBERS OF COMMERCE

Chamber of Commerce and Industry for the Western Province: Al-Jomhourieh St., P.O.B. 2321, Tripoli; f. 1952; Pres. SALEM EL-SAGHIR GADDAH; Sec.-Gen. BASHIR K. EL-GENAYYEN; 40,000 mems.; publs. *Quarterly Bulletin, Trade Acquaintance* (bi-weekly) and *Commercial Directory* (annual, English and Arabic).

Chamber of Commerce, Trade, Industry and Agriculture for the Eastern Province: P.O.B. 208–1286, Benghazi; f. 1953; Pres. HASAN H. MATAR; Sec.-Gen. YOUSEF EL GIAMI; 5,400 mems.

DEVELOPMENT

General National Organization for Industrialization: P.O.B. 4388, Tripoli; f. March 1970; a public organization controlling various heavy and light industries.

Kufrah and Serir Authority: Council of Agricultural Development, Benghazi; f. 1972 to develop the Kufrah Oasis and Serir area in south-east Libya.

TRADE UNIONS

National Trade Unions' Federation: (affiliated to ICFTU); P.O.B. 734, 2 Sharia Istanbul, Tripoli; f. 1952; Sec.-Gen. HAMIED ABUBAKER JALLUD; 18 trade unions with 275,000 members; Publ. *Attalia* (weekly).

General Union for Oil and Petrochemicals: Tripoli; Chair. MUHAMMAD MITHNANI.

TRADE FAIR

Tripoli International Fair: P.O.B. 891, Tripoli; under control of Dept. of Tourism and Fairs, Secretariat of the General People's Committee for Economy; annual fair March 5th–25th, 1982; Chair. AYAD ETAHER AYAD.

TRANSPORT

ROADS

The most important road is the 1,822 km. national coast road from the Tunisian to the Egyptian border, passing through Tripoli and Benghazi. It has a second link between Barce and Lamluda, 141 km. long. The other national road runs from a point on the coastal road 120 km. south of Misurata through Sebha to Ghat near the Algerian border (total length 1,250 km.). There is a branch 260 km. long running from Vaddan to Sirte. There is a road crossing the desert from Sebha to the frontiers of Chad and Niger.

In addition to the national highways, the west of Libya has about 1,200 km. of black-top and macadamized roads and the east about 500 km. All the towns and villages of Libya, including the desert oases, are accessible by motor vehicle.

SHIPPING

Principal ports are Tripoli, Benghazi, Port Brega and the Oasis Marine Terminal at Es-Sider. Port Brega was opened to oil tankers in 1961. A 30-inch crude oil pipeline connects the Zelten oilfields with Marsa El Brega. Another pipeline joins the Sarir oilfield with Marsa Hariga, the port of Tobruk, and a pipeline from the Sarir field to Zuetina was opened in 1968. There is another oil port at Ras Lunuf, and a port is being developed at Darna. Libya also has the use of Tunisian port facilities at Sfax and Gabès, to alleviate congestion at Tripoli.

Libyan General Maritime Transport Organization: 10 Garnaia St., P.O.B. 4673, Tripoli; f. 1970 to handle all projects dealing with maritime trade; in June 1981 Libya's merchant fleet consisted of 23 vessels, 13 of which were tankers.

CIVIL AVIATION

There are four civil airports: Tripoli International Airport, situated at Ben Gashir, 34 km. (21 miles) from Tripoli; Benina Airport 19 km. (12 miles) from Benghazi; Sebha Airport; Misurata Airport (domestic flights only).

Libyan Arab Airlines: P.O.B. 2555, Tripoli; f. 1965; passenger and cargo services from Tripoli and Benghazi to London, Paris, Zürich, Frankfurt, Warsaw, Rome, Belgrade, Istanbul, Amman, Athens, Madrid, Malta, Beirut, Damascus, Jeddah, Tunis, Algiers, Casablanca, Niamey, Cotonou, Moscow and Sofia; domestic services throughout Libya; fleet of 10 Boeing 727-2000, 8 F-27; Chair. of People's Committee ALI AGHILA HANNOUSHI; Vice-Chair. MUHAMMAD M. ABREBISH.

Libya is also served by the following foreign airlines: Aeroflot (U.S.S.R.), Air Algérie, Alitalia (Italy), Biman (Bangladesh), British Caledonian, ČSA (Czechoslovakia), Interflug (German Democratic Republic), JAT (Yugoslavia), KLM (Netherlands), Korean Air Lines (Republic of Korea), LOT (Poland), Lufthansa (Federal Republic of Germany), MALÉV (Hungary), Malta Airlines, PIA (Pakistan), Saudia (Saudi Arabia), Sudan Airways, Swissair, Syrian Arab, TAROM (Romania), Tunis Air, UTA (France).

TOURISM

Department of Tourism and Fairs: Tripoli; f. 1964.

DEFENCE

Commander-in-Chief of Armed Forces: Brig. ABU-BAKR YOUNES JABIR.

Defence Budget (1978): LD 130 million.

Military Service: 3 years for ground forces, 4 years for air and naval forces (since May 1978).

Total Armed Forces: 55,000: army 45,000; navy 5,000; air force 5,000; Libya possesses over 2,500 tanks.

EDUCATION

By 1939 there were in Tripolitania 70 Italo-Arab primary schools with 6,884 Arab and 170 Italian pupils, 13 girls' trades schools with 944 pupils, a secondary school, and an arts and crafts school with 85 students. In addition, evening classes were started for adult Arab illiterates, and in 1928 Arabs were permitted to join Italian secondary schools. Small numbers of Arabs also gained admittance to Italian and Egyptian universities. Koranic schools also increased in numbers from 52 with 1,792 pupils in 1921 to 496 schools with 10,165 pupils in 1939. For Jews there were 19 primary schools (2,645 students), 2 trade secondary schools with 101 pupils, and 15 private schools catering for 1,939 pupils.

Up to the year 1939 the educational system for Arabs in Cyrenaica was similarly under-developed. At that time not more than 37 elementary schools were in existence with a total of 2,600 Arab pupils, and for Jews there were 5 elementary schools with 621 students.

A steady increase in educational facilities took place after 1943 and the numbers attending kindergarten, primary and secondary schools increased from a total of 6,808 in 1943/44 to 819,380 in 1978/79. The number of teachers rose similarly, from 219 in 1943/44 to 43,569 in 1978/79. Elementary education is compulsory for children of both sexes. The above statistics do not include "Kuttabs"—self-efforts at small groups of children being educated collectively in villages. By January 1982 the total number of students at all educational establishments was 1,089,953.

In 1958 the University of Libya opened in Benghazi with Faculties of Arts and Commerce, followed the next year by the Faculty of Science near Tripoli. Faculties of Law, Agriculture, Engineering, Teacher Training, and Arabic Language and Islamic Studies have since been added to the University. In 1973 the University was divided into two parts, to form the Universities of Tripoli and Benghazi, later renamed Alfateh and Ghar Yunis Universities.

In the 1976–80 Development Plan LD 122 million was allocated to education.

BIBLIOGRAPHY

ANSELL, MEREDITH O. and AL-ARIF, IBRAHIM M. The Libyan Revolution (The Oleander Press, London, 1972).

DI AGOSTINI, Col. ENRICO. La popolazione della Tripolitania (2 vols.; Tripoli, 1917).

La popolazione della Cirenaica (Benghazi, 1922-23).

Amministrazione Fiduciaria all'Italia in Africa (Florence, 1948).

Archivio bibliografico Coloniale (Libia) (Florence, 1915-21).

BARUNI, OMAR. Spaniards and Knights of St. John of Jerusalem in Tripoli (Arabic) (Tripoli, 1952).

BERLARDINELLI, ARSENIO. La Ghibla (Tripoli, 1935).

BLUNSUM, T. Libya: the Country and its People (Queen Anne Press, London, 1968).

CACHIA, ANTHONY J. Libya under the Second Ottoman Occupation, 1835-1911 (Tripoli, 1945).

CECCHERINI, UGO. Bibliografia della Libia in continuazione .... de F. Minutilli (Rome, 1915).

COLUCCI, MASSIMO. Il Regime della Proprieta Fondiaria nell'Africa Italiana: Vol. I. Libia (Bologna, 1942).

CORÒ, FRANCESCO. Settantasei Anni di Dominazione Turca in Libia (Tripoli, 1937).

CUROTTI, TORQUATO. Gente di Libia (Tripoli, 1928).

DESPOIS, JEAN. Géographie Humaine (Paris, 1946).
Le Djebel Nefousa (Paris, 1935).
La Colonisation italienne en Libye; Problèmes et Méthodes (Larose-Editeurs, Paris, 1935).

EPTON, NINA. Oasis Kingdom: The Libyan Story (New York, 1953).

EVANS-PRITCHARD, E. E. The Sanusi of Cyrenaica (London, 1949).

FARLEY, RAWLE. Planning for Development in Libya (Pall Mall, London, 1971).

FIRST, RUTH. Libya—the Elusive Revolution (Penguin, London, 1974).

FISHER, W. B. Problems of Modern Libya (*Geographical Journal*, June 1953).

FORBES, ROSITA. The Secret of the Sahara: Kufara (London, 1921).

FRANCA, PIETRO, and others. L'Italia in Africa: Incivilimento e Sviluppo dell'Eritrea, della Somalia, e della Libia (Rome, 1947).

GADDAFI, Col. MUAMMAR AL-. The Green Book (3 vols., Tripoli, 1976-79; Vol. I: The Solution of the Problem of Democracy, Vol. II: The Solution of the Economic Problem, Vol. III: The Social Basis of the Third Universal Theory).

HAJJAJI, S. A. The New Libya (Tripoli, 1967).

HERRMANN, GERHARD. Italiens Weg zum Imperium (Goldman, Leipzig, 1938).

HESELTINE, NIGEL. From Libyan Sands to Chad (Museum Press, London, 1960).

HILL, R. W. A Bibliography of Libya (University of Durham, 1959).

JONGMANS, D. G. Libie-land van de dorst (Boom, Meppel, 1964).

JUIN, A-P. Le Maghreb en Feu (French) (Paris, Librairie Plon, 1957).

KHADDURI, MAJID. Modern Libya, a Study in Political Development (Johns Hopkins Press, 1963).

KHALIDI, I. R. Constitutional Developments in Libya (Beirut, Khayat's Book Co-operative, 1956).

KUBBAH, ABDUL AMIR Q. Libya, Its Oil Industry and Economic System (The Arab Petro-Economic Research Centre, Baghdad, 1964).

LEBLANC, M. E. Anthropologie et Ethnologie (du Fezzan) (1944-45).

LEGG, H. J. Libya: Economic and General Conditions in Libya (London, 1952).

LETHIELLEUX, J. Le Fezzan, ses Jardins, ses Palmiers: Notes d'Ethnographie et d'Histoire (Tunis, 1948).

LINDBERG, J. A General Economic Appraisal of Libya (New York, 1952).

MICACCHI, RODOLFO. La Tripolitania sotto il dominio dei Caramanli (Intra, 1936).

MINUTILLI, FEDERICO. Bibliografia della Libia (Turin, 1903).

MURABET, MOHAMMED. Tripolitania: the Country and its People (Tripoli, 1952).

NORMAN, JOHN. Labour and Politics in Libya and Arab Africa (Bookman, New York, 1965).

OWEN, R. Libya: a Brief Political and Economic Survey (London, 1961).

PELT, ADRIAN. Libyan Independence and the United Nations (Yale U.P., 1970).

PICHOU, JEAN. La Question de Libye dans le règlement de la paix (Paris, 1945).

Lord RENNELL. British Military Administration of Occupied Territories in Africa during the years 1941-47 (London, H.M.S.O., 1948).

RIVLIN, BENJAMIN. The United Nations and the Italian Colonies (New York, 1950).

ROYAL INSTITUTE OF INTERNATIONAL AFFAIRS. The Italian Colonial Empire (London, 1940).

ROSSI, P. Libya (Lausanne, 1965).

RUSHDI, MUHAMMAD RASIM. Trablus al Gharb (Arabic) (Tripoli, 1953).

SCARIN, Prof. La Giofra e Zella (Florence, 1938).
L'Insediamento Umano nella Libia Occidentale (Rome, 1940).
Le Oasi Cirenaiche del 29° Parallelo (Florence, 1937).
Le Oasi del Fezzan (2 vols.; Florence, 1934).

SCHLUETER, HANS. Index Libycus (G. K. Hall, Boston, 1972).

SCHMEIDER, OSKAR and WILHELMY, HERBERT. Die faschistische Kolonisation in Nordafrika (Quelle and Meyer, Leipzig, 1939).

STEELE-GREIG, A. J. History of Education in Tripolitania from the Time of the Ottoman Occupation to the Fifth Year under British Military Occupation (Tripoli, 1948).

VILLARD, HENRY S. Libya: The New Arab Kingdom of North Africa (Ithaca, 1956).

WARD, PHILIP. Touring Libya. 3 vols. (1967-69).
Tripoli: Portrait of a City (1970).

WILLIAMS, G. Green Mountain, an Informal Guide to Cyrenaica and its Jebel Akhdar (London, 1963).

WILLIMOTT, S. G. and CLARKE, J. I. Field Studies in Libya (Durham, 1960).

WRIGHT, JOHN. Libya: a Modern History (Croom Helm, London, 1982).

Morocco

PHYSICAL AND SOCIAL GEOGRAPHY

The Kingdom of Morocco is the westernmost of the three North African countries known to the Arabs as Jeziret al Maghreb or "Island of the West". Intermediate in size between Algeria and Tunisia, it occupies an area of 458,730 sq. km. (excluding the portion of the former Spanish Sahara annexed in 1976, covering some 200,000 sq. km.), and has an extensive coastline facing both the Atlantic and the Mediterranean. However, as a result of both its position and the existence of massive mountain ranges within its borders, Morocco has remained relatively isolated from the rest of the Maghreb and has served as a refuge for descendants of the original Berber-speaking occupants of north-west Africa.

The population at mid-1980 was estimated to be 20,242,000. About 35 per cent of the total are Berber-speaking peoples, living mainly in mountain villages, while the Arabic-speaking majority is concentrated in towns in the lowlands, particularly in Casablanca, which is the largest city in the Maghreb, in Marrakesh, the old southern capital, and in Rabat (population 435,510, including Salé, in 1971), the modern administrative capital. There were some 450,000 Europeans living in Morocco before the country attained its independence from the French in 1956 but since then their number has greatly diminished.

PHYSICAL FEATURES

The physical geography of Morocco is dominated by the highest and most rugged ranges in the Atlas Mountain system of north-west Africa. They are the result of a phase of mountain-building that took place in the geologically recent Tertiary era when sediments deposited beneath an ancestral Mediterranean Sea were uplifted, folded and fractured. The mountains remain geologically unstable and Morocco is liable to severe earthquakes, such as the appallingly destructive one that took place at the port of Agadir in 1960.

In Morocco the Atlas Mountains form four distinct massifs which are surrounded and partially separated by lowland plains and plateaux. In the north, in the zone of the former Spanish Protectorate, the Rif Atlas comprise a rugged arc of mountains that rise steeply from the Mediterranean coast to heights of over 2,200 metres. There limestone and sandstone ranges are difficult to penetrate and have functioned as an effective barrier to east-west communications. They are inhabited by Berber farmers who live in isolated mountain villages and have little contact with the Arabs of Tétouan (population 137,080 in 1971) and Tangier (185,850) at the north-western end of the Rif chain.

The Middle Atlas lie immediately south of the Rif from which they are separated by the Col of Taza, a narrow gap which affords the only easy route between western Algeria and Atlantic Morocco. They rise to about 3,000 metres and form a broad barrier between the two countries. They also function as a major drainage divide and are flanked by the basins of Morocco's two principal rivers, the Oum er Rbia which flows west to the Atlantic and the Moulouya which flows north-east to the Mediterranean. Much of the Middle Atlas consists of a limestone plateau dissected by river gorges and capped here and there by volcanic craters and lava flows. Semi-nomadic Berber tribesmen spend the winter in valley villages and move to the higher slopes in summer to pasture their flocks.

Southward the Middle Atlas chain merges into the High Atlas, the most formidable of the mountain massifs, which rises to about 4,000 metres and is heavily snow-clad in winter. The mountains are aligned in a chain from south-west to north-east, and they rise precipitously from both the Atlantic lowland to the north and the desert plain of Saharan Morocco to the south. The contrast between the two sides is very striking; the northern slopes are covered by forest and scrub while the southern slopes consist of bare, sunbaked rock. Eastward the chain loses height and continues into Algeria as the Saharan Atlas. The central part of the massif is made up of resistant crystalline rocks which have been eroded by former glaciers and present streams into a wilderness of sharp peaks and steep-sided valleys, but elsewhere limestones and sandstones give rise to more subdued topography. There are no easily accessible routes across the High Atlas, but numerous mountain tracks make possible the exchange of goods by pack animal between Atlantic and Saharan Morocco. A considerable Berber population lives in the mountain valleys in compact, fortified villages.

The Anti Atlas is the lowest and most southerly of the mountain massifs. Structurally it forms an elevated edge of the Saharan platform which was uplifted when the High Atlas were formed. It consists largely of crystalline rocks and is joined to the southern margin of the High Atlas by a mass of volcanic lavas which separates the valley from the river Sous, draining west to the Atlantic at Agadir, from that of the upper Draa, draining south-east towards the Sahara. On the southern side of the chain barren slopes are trenched by gorges from which cultivated palm groves extend like green tongues out into the desert.

Stretching inland from the Atlantic coast is an extensive area of lowland, enclosed on the north, east and south by the Rif, Middle and High Atlas. It consists of the Gharb plain and the wide valley of the River Sebou in the north and of the plateaux and plains of the Meseta, the Tadla, the Rehamna, the Djebilet and the Haouz farther south. Most of the Arabic-speaking people of Morocco live in this region.

CLIMATE AND VEGETATION

Northern and central Morocco experiences a "Mediterranean" type of climate, with warm wet winters and hot dry summers, but this gives way southward to semi-arid and eventually to desert conditions. In the Rif and the northern parts of the Middle Atlas mean annual rainfall exceeds 75 cm. and the summer drought lasts only 3 months, but in the rest of the Middle Atlas, in the High Atlas and over the northern half of the Atlantic lowland rainfall is reduced to between 40 and 75 cm. and the summer drought lasts for 4 months or more. During the summer intensely hot winds from the Sahara, known as the Sirocco or Chergui, occasionally cross the mountains and sweep across the lowland desiccating all that lies in their path. Summer heat on the Atlantic coastal plain is tempered, however, by breezes that blow inland after they have been cooled over the cold waters of the Canaries current offshore.

Over the southern half of the Atlantic lowland and the Anti Atlas semi-arid conditions prevail and rainfall decreases to between 20 and 40 cm. per year. It also becomes very variable and is generally insufficient for the regular cultivation of cereal crops without irrigation. East and south of the Atlas Mountains, which act as a barrier to rain-bearing winds from the Atlantic, rainfall is reduced still further and regular cultivation becomes entirely dependent on irrigation.

The chief contrast in the vegetation of Morocco is between the mountain massifs, which support forest or open woodland, and the surrounding lowlands which, when uncultivated, tend to be covered only by scrub growth of low, drought-resistant bushes. The natural vegetation has, however, been widely altered, and in many places actually destroyed, by excessive cutting, burning and grazing. This is particularly evident in the lowlands and on the lower mountain slopes where such scrub species as juniper, thuya, dwarf palm and gorse are common. There is little doubt that cork oak covered a large part of the Atlantic lowland but today only the "forest" of Mamora remains to suggest the former abundance of this valuable tree. The middle and upper slopes of the mountains are often quite well wooded, with evergreen oak dominant at the lower and cedar at the higher elevations. The lowlands to the east and south of the Atlas Mountains support distinctive types of steppe and desert vegetation, in which esparto grass and the argan tree (which is unique to south-western Morocco) are conspicuous.

NEWLY-ANNEXED TERRITORY

After independence the Moroccan Government claimed a right to control a large area of the western Sahara, including territory in Algeria and Mauritania and the whole of the Spanish Sahara. The claim was based on the extent of Moroccan rule in medieval times. The existence of considerable deposits of phosphates in the Spanish Sahara and of iron ore in the Algeria-Morocco border region further excited Moroccan interest in expansion. After Spanish withdrawal from the Sahara in 1976 Morocco and Mauritania divided the former Spanish Sahara (now

known as Western Sahara) between them, Morocco annexing the northern part of the territory, including the phosphate mines of Bou Craa. In August 1979 Mauritania renounced its share, which was at once claimed by Morocco as a new province.

The Western Sahara has an area of about 266,000 sq. km. The population of the territory are mostly nomadic pastoralists, of Moorish or mixed Arab-Berber descent with some negro admixture, who depend for their existence on herds of sheep, camels and goats which they move seasonally from one pasture to another. The main tribes are the R'gibat, Uld Delim, Izargien and Arosien. In July 1975 the population of the Spanish Sahara was estimated at 117,000, but since annexation a considerable number of the former inhabitants have fled to refugee camps in Algeria. The principal towns in the area are El Aaiún, Essmara (formerly Smara) and Dakhla (Villa Cisneros).

The relief of most of the area is gentle. The coast is backed by a wide alluvial plain overlain in the south by extensive sand dunes aligned from south-west to north-east and extending inland over 250 km. Behind the coastal plain the land rises gradually to a plateau surface diversified by sandstone ridges that reach 300 m. in height. In the north-east, close to the Mauritanian frontier, isolated mountain ranges, such as the Massif de la Guelta, rise to over 600 m. There are no permanent streams and the only considerable valley is that of the Sekia el Hamra which crosses the northernmost part of the area to reach the coast at El Aaiún north of Cape Bojador. The whole of the region experiences an extreme desert climate. Nowhere does mean annual rainfall exceed 10 cm. and over most of the territory it is less than 5 cm. Vegetation is restricted to scattered desert shrubs and occasional patches of coarse grass in most depressions. Along the coast summer heat is tempered by air moving inland after it has been cooled over the waters of the cold Canaries current which flows off shore from north to south.

HISTORY

The Phoenicians and Carthaginians established staging posts and trading factories on the coasts of Morocco. Still later, the Romans established in what is now northern Morocco the province of Mauritania Tingitana, the frontier passing a little to the south of Rabat, Meknès and Fez. Muslim warriors raided into Morocco under Uqba ibn Nafi in A.D. 684–85. It was not, however, until the first years of the eighth century that the Muslims began to bring Morocco under durable control, their forces, under Musa b. Nusair, reaching the Tafilalet and the Wadi Draa. The Berber tribesmen of Morocco rallied to the cause of Islam and had a large share in the Muslim conquest of Spain after A.D. 711. Religious ideas of a heterodox character— i.e., the ideas of the Khawarij, who constituted the first of the great schismatic movements inside Islam—won much support among the Berbers of Morocco. The spread of Kharijite beliefs, the fierce particularism of the Berbers and their refractoriness towards all forms of political control, led to a great rebellion in 739–40, whoch had as its chief consequences the fragmentation of Morocco into a number of small Muslim principalities.

It was Idris, a descendant of the Prophet Muhammad, who, fleeing westward after an unsuccessful revolt against the Abbasid Caliph in Iraq, founded the first of the great Muslim dynasties ruling in Morocco. The Idrisid regime lasted from 788–89 to 985–86. Idris, the founder of the new state, died in 792–93, after reducing most of Morocco and also Tlemcen to obedience with the aid of Berber

tribesmen. His son, Idris II, founded Fez, the capital of the Idrisids and a notable centre of Muslim life and civilization. After the death of Idris II (d. 828–29) the regime fell into decline. Morocco now endured for some two hundred years a long period of internecine conflict, of tribal revolt and of warring principalities. At the same time it had to face external danger in the form of pressures from the Umayad Caliphate of Cordoba in Spain (at the apogee of its power and splendour in the reigns of Abd al-Rahman III (912–61) and al-Hakam II (961–76)) and also from the Fatimid Caliphate established and consolidated in Ifriqiya (i.e. modern Tunisia and eastern Algeria) during the years 908–69.

It was after this long period of turmoil and fragmentation that Morocco entered into the most splendid phase of its medieval history. There now arose, amongst Berbers of Sanhaja descent who followed a nomadic mode of life in the regions near the Senegal, the religious movement of "Frontiersmen", i.e. al-Murabitun or Almoravids. The chieftain of these Berbers, Yahya ibn Ibrahim, brought back from Mecca Abd Allah ibn Yasin to spread the true doctrine of Islam among his people. The Almoravids soon passed over from the pursuit of the ascetic life to war on behalf of the true faith. The tide of conquest in Morocco gathered momentum under the amir Abu Bakr and led, after his death, to the establishment of a vast Almoravid state in the time of Yusef ibn Tashufin (d. 1106), who in 1062 founded Marrakesh and extended the domination of

MOROCCO

the Almoravids over all Morocco and much of Algeria. In 1086 he halted the southward advance of the Christian *reconquista* in Spain and then annexed the Muslim lands there to the Almoravid territories in North Africa. His successor Ali ibn Yusuf (d. 1142) consolidated and maintained the empire, but thereafter the power of the Almoravids fell into a rapid decline. The Saharan nomads who had been the dynamic force behind the movement became absorbed, as it were, into the rich milieu of Andalusian Muslim civilization. Dynastic discord and incompetence among the Almoravid amirs hastened the collapse of the regime. The Christians in Spain took Saragossa in 1118 and began a new phase of their *reconquista*. And in the Atlas mountains of Morocco a new religious force was preparing to burst out over the Moroccan scene.

A religious leader, Muhammad ibn Tumart (d. 1130), taught amongst the Masmuda Berbers of the High Atlas doctrines of a strict unitarian character and assumed for himself the designation of al-Mahdi, "the rightly guided one". Amongst the Masmuda he gathered around himself a nucleus of Berber adherents—the "Unitarians", i.e. al-Muwahhidun or Almohads. After the death of Ibn Tumart in 1130, one of his ardent disciples, a Berber of the Kumiya tribe named Abd al-Mumin, became the Khalifa of the Mahdi. Under the guidance of Abd al-Mumin (d. 1163) the Almohads took Marrakesh in 1147, after 22 years of conflict, and then in the years 1151–59 overran the rest of Morocco and the North African lands as far east as Tripolitania and Cyrenaica. The Almohads reached the summit of their splendour in the reign of al-Mansur (1184–98), who brought Muslim Spain under Almohad control and checked the menacing advance of the Christians at the battle of Alarcos (1196). Under his successor Muhammad al-Nasir (1199–1214) the Almohads suffered a serious defeat in battle against the Christians of Spain at Las Navas de Tolosa (1212). Thereafter the Almohad empire began to decline. The Hafsids made themselves independent in Ifriqiya (1235–56). Much of the Central Maghreb came under the control of the Abd al-Wadid amirs ruling at Tlemcen. At the same time a new Berber house—the Merinids, of Zenata Berber origin—rose into prominence, conquering Fez in 1248 and Marrakesh in 1269 and thus bringing to an end the last remnants of Almohad rule.

THE MERINIDS

The Merinids, whose effective power lasted for about one hundred years, came from eastern Morocco, overran first the northern regions of Morocco and then the lands in the South. Their attempts to reconstitute the empire of the Almohads met with no durable success. Revolt against their domination was not infrequent in the southern regions of Morocco. Several campaigns undertaken to regain control of the eastern Maghreb brought no more than transient gains, both Ifriqiya and Tlemcen escaping from their domination. Nor could the Merinids establish themselves in Spain, although their interventions there did hinder the Christian *reconquista* and gave the Muslim state of Granada enough time to consolidate its resources and thus gain the strength to resist the Christians until 1492. The decline of the Merinid regime saw the culmination of a process long since in train. Nomadic tribes of Arab origin—the Hilal and the Sulaym—penetrated into the Maghreb during the course of the 11th and 12th centuries. Other Badawi elements infiltrated through the northern reaches of the Sahara during the later phases of Almohad rule. With the gradual disintegration of the Merinid state the Badawi tribes thrust westward through the Atlas mountains and penetrated into the heart-lands of Morocco. These Badawi invasions, although causing widespread disruption and confusion, contributed much to the

Arabization of Morocco and the neighbouring lands. During the years of Merinid decline, dynastic quarrels led to political disintegration, with the result that rival states came into being at Fez and Marrakesh. Morocco, until 1465, was a prey to prolonged internal discords, which ended, at least in part, only with the emergence of another regime of Zenata Berber origin—the Wattasid regime (1465–1549). The Wattasids had no long pre-eminence, their failure to halt the progress of the Portuguese and the Spaniards, who had begun to establish themselves along the Atlantic and the Mediterranean shores of Morocco, being one of the main reasons for their rapid decline.

THE LINE OF SHARIFS

A new movement of resistance to the intrusions of the Spaniards, and, above all, of the Portuguese (by 1500 the masters of Ceuta, Tangier, Arcila, Agadir, Mazagan and Safi on the western coast of Morocco) was born amongst the religious confraternities, amongst the *marabouts* and the "shorfa" (descendants of the Prophet) in Morocco, who now led the Jihad, or war on behalf of the Muslim faith, against the Christians. Out of this situation arose the Saadian regime, originating in a line of Sharifs from the region of the Wadi Draa on the Saharan side of the Atlas mountains. The Saadians took Fez in 1520 and Marrakesh in 1548. Their prestige was due to their status as descendants of the Prophet and to their success in driving the Portuguese from most of their possessions on the Atlantic littoral of Morocco. The most famous of the Sharifs, Ahmad al-Mansur (1578–1603), resisted the pressure of the Ottoman Turks on his eastern frontier with Algeria and in 1591 sent out a large expedition, which seized Timbuktu and Gao in the Western Sudan (now Mali), returning with rich plunder in the form of slaves and gold. Al-Mansur, realizing that his house had no strong tribal support, organized the Saadian regime on a new foundation (the Makhzan)—a system under which various Arab tribes enjoyed exemption from taxes in return for armed service to the state. Much depended, in such a system, on the character of the Sultan. The tribal rivalries would break out anew, the endless tensions between the nomadic and the settled elements in the population became intensified whenever the central government was weak or ill-directed. At such times the "Bled as-Siba" (the areas of dissidence—in particular the Atlas Mountains) set their tribal autonomies against the forces of the "Bled al-Makhzan" (the controlled areas). The period of Saadian rule, which ended in 1668, was, however, one of considerable prosperity for Morocco. Sugar cane culture was encouraged; gold brought by caravan from the Sudan added to the resources of the regime; close commercial contact was made with the lands of southern and western Europe.

Yet another wave of popular religious sentiment brought to power a new house—known under the designations Alawi, Hasani or Filali—which still reigns in Morocco. The Alawi Sharifs had their origin amongst the Berbers located in the oases of Tafilalet, i.e., Saharan Morocco. Under the guidance of the Alawi house Berber forces took Fez in 1644 and Marrakesh in 1668. The reigns of Rashid II (1664–72) and, above all, of Mulai Ismail (1672–1727) established the Alawi regime on a firm basis and saw Morocco more thoroughly pacified and more solidly united than it was ever to be again until the time of the French occupation. Ismail used as one of his main instruments of rule a powerful corps of negro troops, some stationed close to his capital, Meknès, others established in a network of Qasbahs (fortresses) which covered most of the land. He also had at his command a strong force of European renegades. Among the main achievements of Mulai Ismail must be numbered the occupation, in 1684, of Tangier (English since 1662) and the capture, in 1689, of

Larache (Spanish since 1610). Mulai Ismail concluded with France in 1682 a commercial agreement, which was confirmed later in 1787, precedence being then accorded to the consuls of France over the consuls of all other nations.

Mulai Ismail had managed to thrust back the pressure of the Sanhaja Berbers, who were beginning to move down from the Middle Atlas into the lowland areas of Morocco. His successors did not win the same degree of success, with the result that, after the death of Ismail in 1727, a period of confusion ensued in Morocco until the rise of yet another able prince, Sharif Muhammad Ibn Abdallah (1757–1790). Muhammad founded Mogador in 1765 and drove the Portuguese from Mazagan in 1769. He entered into a pact of friendship and commerce with Spain in 1767. A brief period of conflict with Spain followed in 1774, but a new agreement was negotiated between Morocco and Spain in 1780.

Muhammad ibn Abdallah and his immediate successors, Mulai Sulaiman (1792–1822) and Mulai Abd al-Rahman (1822–59) made strenuous efforts to maintain the control of the central regime in the face of tribal dissidence, and to ward off the possibilities of foreign intervention in the affairs of Morocco. The French conquest of Algiers in 1830 was bound, however, to have repercussions in Morocco. Mulai Abd al-Rahman gave assistance to Abd al-Qadir, the amir who led the Muslim resistance to France in Algeria during the years 1832–47. During the course of their campaigns against Abd al-Qadir the French met and defeated a Moroccan force at Wadi Isly in 1844.

A dispute over the limits of the Ceuta enclave, which was under Spanish rule, led in 1860 to a brief war between Morocco and Spain. Spanish troops under General O'Donnell defeated the Moroccans at Los Castillejos and seized Tetuan. A further engagement at Wadi Ras in March 1860 brought the war to a close. A peace settlement followed, under the terms of which the Ceuta enclave was enlarged and Spain was given indemnities amounting to 100 million pesetas. Morocco also granted to Spain a territorial enclave on the Atlantic coast opposite the Canaries (Santa Cruz de Mar Pequeña, now Ifni). In 1884 Spain claimed a protectorate over the coastal zone to the south of Morocco, from Cape Bojador to Cape Blanco, the future Spanish Sahara. The borders between this territory, known as the Río de Oro, and the French possessions to the south and east were agreed between France and Spain in June 1900.

FRENCH RULE

France, with her hold on Algeria secure, had begun to turn her eyes towards the Western Maghreb, but the rivalries among the Great Powers long hindered the establishment of a French protectorate over Morocco. In April 1904, however, Great Britain agreed to recognize the preeminence of French interests in Morocco in return for a similar recognition of English interests in Egypt. A convention between France and Spain in October 1904 assigned to Spain two zones of influence, one in northern and the other in southern Morocco. The southern border of Morocco was set at 27° 40′N., beyond which latitude Spain's Saharan territories were deemed to begin. The Germans now sought to intervene in Moroccan affairs and at the conference of Algeciras in 1906 secured the adherence of the Great Powers to the economic "internationalization" of Morocco. A sharp crisis in 1911, when the German gunboat *Panther* appeared at Agadir, ended in a Franco-German settlement, the Germans now recognizing Morocco as a French sphere of influence in return for territorial concessions in the Congo. In March 1912 Morocco became a Protectorate of France, with a French Resident-General empowered to direct foreign affairs, to control defence and also to introduce internal reforms. A new convention of

1912 between France and Spain revised the earlier agreement of 1904: Spain now received her zones of influence in Morocco (though somewhat diminished in extent)—but from France as the protecting power and *not* from the Sultan.

The first French Resident-General in Morocco was General Lyautey (1912–25). He established effective control, before 1914, over the plains and lower plateaux of Morocco from Fez to the Atlas mountains south of Marrakesh; then, before 1918, over the western Atlas, the Taza corridor connecting with Algeria and some areas of the northern highlands. French troops helped Spain to subdue the formidable rebellion (1921–26) of the Rif tribesmen under Abd al-Krim. This success meant the subjugation of the northern mountains and allowed the French to turn with unimpeded vigour to the reduction of the Middle Atlas and the Tafilalet—a task accomplished by 1934, when the pacification of the whole of Morocco could be regarded as complete.

It was at this time that nationalist sentiment began to make itself felt in Morocco. A "Comité d'Action Marocaine" now asked for a limitation of the protectorate. This "Comité" was dissolved in 1937, but nationalist propaganda continued against the French regime. Morocco rallied to the cause of France in 1939 and to the Free French movement in 1942. A Party of Independence (Istiqlal), formed in 1943, demanded full freedom for Morocco, with a constitutional form of government under Sultan Muhammad Ibn Yusuf, who supported the nationalist movement. Istiqlal, strong in the towns, did not find great favour at this time among the conservative tribesmen of Morocco, who tended to concentrate their resistance to reform on western lines around Thami al-Glawi, the Pasha of Marrakesh. The tensions between the new and the old ideas in Morocco became much sharper in 1953. Sultan Muhammad ibn Yusuf had fallen into disagreement with the French administration, refusing to issue *dahirs* (decrees) authorising various measures that the French desired to see in force. In May 1953 a number of Pashas and Caids, with al-Glawi, the Pasha of Marrakesh, at their head, asked for the removal of the Sultan. Berber tribesmen began to converge in force towards the main urban centres in Morocco. On August 20th, 1953, the Sultan agreed to go into exile in Europe, but not to abdicate. Muhammad ibn Arafa, a prince of the Alawi house, was now recognized as Sultan. The situation continued to be tense, with assassination attempts on the Sultan in 1953 and 1954, outbreaks of violence throughout Morocco in 1954–55 and nationalist fervour running high.

INDEPENDENCE—1956

Sultan Muhammad ibn Arafa renounced the throne and withdrew to Tangier in 1955. Muhammad ibn Yusuf, on November 5th in that year, was recognized once more as the legitimate Sultan. A joint Franco-Moroccan declaration of March 2nd, 1956, stated that the Protectorate agreement of 1912 was obsolete and that the French Government now recognized the independence of Morocco. A Protocol of the same date covered the transitional phase before new agreements could come into effect. The Sultan would now have full legislative powers in Morocco. Henceforward a High Commissioner was to represent France in the new state. France undertook also to aid Morocco with the organization of its armed forces and to assist in the re-assertion of Moroccan control over the zones of Spanish influence, the sole legal basis for which was the Franco-Spanish convention of 1912. On November 12th, 1956, Morocco became a member of the United Nations.

In August 1956 the Istiqlal proclaimed the need to abrogate the Convention of Algeciras (1906), which had

MOROCCO

"internationalized" the economic life of Morocco, and also to secure the withdrawal of all foreign troops from the land. Following an international conference in October 1956 Tangier was restored to Morocco. A Royal Charter of August 1957 maintained in general the former economic and financial system in force at Tangier, including a free money market, quota-free trade with foreign countries and a low level of taxation. In 1959 Tangier lost its special status and was integrated financially and economically with Morocco, but a Royal decree of January 1962 made it once more a free port. The Istiqlal, in 1956, had envisaged the creation of a "Great Morocco" which, according to a map published in July of that year, would include certain areas in South-West Algeria, the Spanish territories in North-West Africa and also Mauritania, together with the French Sudan (i.e., the Republic of Mali). Morocco reiterated these claims in the years which followed independence, beginning in 1960 an intensive propaganda and diplomatic campaign against Mauritania.

The problem of the Spanish territories in North-West Africa also came to the fore at this time. Spain had recognized the independence of Morocco, renouncing also the northern zone of the protectorate assigned to her in Morocco under the terms of the Franco-Spanish convention of 1912. No agreement was reached, however, on the enclaves of Ceuta and Melilla in the north, the enclave of Ifni in the south, or the Spanish territories to the south of Morocco. These territories had since 1934 been divided in two parts, the northern Seguia el Hamra and the southern Río de Oro, both administered jointly with Ifni, and separately from the contiguous southern zone of Spain's protectorate in Morocco. Raids on Ifni and the western Sahara by Moroccan irregular forces (the "Armée de Libération du Grand Sahara"), reputed to have some connection with the Istiqlal, caused serious trouble between 1956 and 1958, although the Moroccan Government denied responsibility. Negotiations between Morocco and Spain, held at Cintra in Portugal, led in April 1958 to an agreement under which Spain, in accordance with the settlement reached in April 1956, relinquished to Morocco the southern zone of her former protectorate. Spain retained possession of the enclaves and of Seguia el Hamra and Río de Oro, which were renamed the Spanish Sahara and separated from Ifni.

KING HASSAN II AND ROYAL DOMINANCE OF GOVERNMENT

The dominant political force after independence remained the Istiqlal, which obtained a majority in the Government. At the same time Sultan Muhammad strengthened the position of the monarchy. In July 1957 Prince Moulai Hassan was proclaimed heir to the throne and in August the Sultan assumed the title of king. Istiqlal's efforts to reduce the power of the monarch were hampered by divisions within the party itself. Tension between the conservative and radical wings reached breaking-point in December 1958 when a government was formed by Abdullah Ibrahim, a leader of the radical tendency. In the following months Ben Barka led a movement to establish a radical party organization independent of the conservative Istiqlal leadership of Allal El Fassi. In September 1959 this new organization became an independent party, the National Union of Popular Forces (UNFP). Although the UNFP supported Ibrahim's government, it became the object of repressive measures by the police and the army who were under the control of the king or of "king's men" in the cabinet. In May 1960 a new government was formed with the King himself as Prime Minister and Prince Hassan as his deputy, and the UNFP went into opposition. On the death of King Muhammad in February 1961 the prince ascended the throne as King Hassan II, and also

became Prime Minister. In December 1962 a new constitution was approved by referendum, establishing a constitutional monarchy with guaranteed personal and political freedoms. In January 1963 a cabinet reshuffle deprived the Istiqlal leaders of their posts in the Government, and when elections for the House of Representatives were held in May both Istiqlal and the UNFP appeared as opposition parties. The King was represented by the newly-formed Front for the Defence of Constitutional Institutions (FDIC). The election, by universal direct suffrage, failed to produce the expected clear majority for the government party, the results being: FDIC 69 seats; Istiqlal 41 seats; UNFP 28 seats; Independents 6 seats. In the following months repressive action was taken against both opposition parties. Several Istiqlal deputies were arrested for protesting against corruption and mismanagement of the election, leading the party to boycott further elections later in the year. Almost all the leaders of the UNFP were arrested in July 1963 in connection with an alleged coup attempt. Many of them were held in solitary confinement, tortured and eventually sentenced to death. In November the King gave up the post of Prime Minister, installing a Government of FDIC men devoted to his interests.

RELATIONS IN THE MAGHREB

In July 1962 Moroccan troops entered the region south of Colomb-Béchar in Algeria—a region never officially demarcated. The Moroccan press also launched a strong campaign in support of the view that the Tindouf area in the extreme south-west of Algeria should belong to Morocco—a claim of some importance, since the area contains large deposits of high-grade (57 per cent) iron ore and also considerable resources of oil and natural gas.

An arbitration commission was established by the OAU, and Algeria and Morocco submitted evidence in support of their respective territorial claims. On February 20th, 1964, an agreement was reached on the establishment of a demilitarized zone. A swift improvement in relations between the two countries followed.

A more amicable relationship also became evident between Morocco and Mauritania. The Ministers of Information of these two states met at Cairo in July 1964 during the course of an African Summit Conference. An understanding was reached to bring an end to the "war" of radio propaganda and criticism hitherto active between Morocco and Mauritania.

INTERNAL UNREST

In August 1964 the Moroccan Government was reorganized, although it remained composed largely of FDIC members. The reshuffle was the preparation for an attempt to attract the opposition parties back into a coalition government, since the FDIC had an inadequate majority in the House of Representatives and was itself split into two factions, the Democratic Socialist Party (PSD) and the People's Movement (MP). The weakness of the Government contributed to the tense political situation which developed in the first half of 1965 as unemployment and rising prices generated discontent among the urban working class. In June King Hassan proclaimed a state of emergency, under which he himself assumed full legislative and executive power. New elections, it was stated, would be held after the constitution had been revised and submitted to a referendum. In October 1965 the UNFP leader Ben Barka disappeared in France never to be seen again. Gen. Oufkir, one of the King's sturdiest supporters, was found guilty in France in his absence of complicity in Ben Barka's disappearance. Relations between Morocco and France became very strained and there were anti-government protest strikes in Morocco.

In July 1967, King Hassan relinquished the post of Prime Minister to Dr. Mohammed Benhima, and in 1967 and 1968 there were eight major cabinet reshuffles. Considerable student and trade union unrest continued during this period, but the King won some popularity by extensive nationalization measures and a degree of land redistribution.

There was a gradual return to full political activity in 1969, though still under royal direction. Municipal and rural communal elections were held in October, although these were boycotted by opposition parties and the successful candidates mostly stood as independents. Following this Dr. Mohammed Benhima was replaced as Prime Minister by Dr. Ahmed Laraki, formerly Foreign Minister. A national referendum on a new constitution was at last held in July 1970; official figures claimed that over 98 per cent of the votes were affirmative, despite general opposition from the main political parties, trade unions and student organizations. Elections for a new single-chamber legislature were held in August. Of the 240 members, 90 were elected by direct suffrage, 90 by local councils and 60 by an electoral college. The results were that 158 elected members were Independents, 60 were MP members and 22 from opposition parties.

In July 1971 there was an unsuccessful attempt to overthrow the King and establish a republic, apparently engineered by right-wing army officers, angered by the level of corruption in the royal administration and by the King's too lenient treatment of dissent on the left. During the months following the attempted coup, a series of conciliatory talks was held between the Government and members of Istiqlal and the UNFP who had united to form a National Front in July 1970, but they refused to compromise with government policies.

In March 1972 a new Constitution was promulgated, under which executive power is vested in the King. Legislative power lies with the Chamber of Representatives, with two-thirds of its members elected by universal suffrage, compared with one-half under the previous constitution. On April 30th, however, King Hassan announced that the Chamber, which was due to be reopened, would remain dissolved, and that elections for a new Chamber were being postponed until new electoral lists had been drawn up. In July a split occurred in the UNFP which separated the Rabat section from the rest of the party. As a consequence the National Front became a dead letter.

In August 1972 King Hassan survived another attempt on his life, which had apparently been planned by General Oufkir, the Minister of Defence and Army Chief of Staff, whose death occurred immediately afterwards. The King himself took over the command of the armed forces and defence matters and did not appoint a new Defence Minister until March 1973. He approached the opposition parties again, asking for their co-operation in supervising general elections and collaboration with the Government. However, both Istiqlal and the UNFP demanded that a number of far-reaching reforms be introduced, which were unacceptable to the King, as they included curtailing the King's powers and guaranteeing political freedom. The elections were postponed indefinitely, and a new cabinet was formed in November without opposition participation.

FOREIGN RELATIONS 1967-72

In the Arab-Israeli war in June 1967, the Moroccan Government gave voice to its support of the Arabs' anti-Zionist cause, but did not commit its troops to the fighting.

Morocco continued to press her claim to Spanish-held territories in north-west Africa. In December 1967 the UN passed a resolution urging Spain to hold a referendum in the Spanish Sahara to allow the population to determine its future; the referendum should be held in consultation with Morocco and Mauritania, which had also asserted a claim to the territory. Spain accepted the principle of self-determination, but positions hardened in June 1970 after riots in the major Sahara town, El Aaiún, were quelled with loss of life. Further UN resolutions were passed in support of decolonization, and Morocco, Mauritania and Algeria each gave some backing to three rival Saharan liberation movements. In contrast, the question of Ifni was settled amicably in June 1969, when Spain handed over the small coastal enclave to Morocco.

Morocco's claim to Mauritania was dropped in 1969. Full diplomatic recognition and an exchange of ambassadors followed in 1970 and a treaty of solidarity and co-operation was signed. Relations with France improved following the general pattern in the Arab world, and the diplomatic missions in Paris and Rabat were returned to full ambassadorial status for the first time since the Ben Barka affair in 1966.

In May 1970 final agreement was reached in the frontier dispute with Algeria, and a joint commission mapped out a delineation maintaining the boundaries of the colonial period. The disputed region of Gara-Djebilet, rich in iron ore deposits, thus became the property of Algeria, but Morocco was to have a share in a joint company to be established to exploit these deposits. The agreement was ratified on May 17th, 1973.

HASSAN IN CONTROL

At the end of 1972 King Hassan's position appeared precarious. He was politically isolated since the main political parties continued in opposition and the armed forces could no longer be relied upon to support him. Many observers doubted his ability to survive. However, the King took strong measures against dissidents and won support by adopting nationalist policies.

In March 1973 the King announced plans for the Moroccanization of parts of the economy in the course of the next two years. At the same time he reinforced his traditional support in the rural areas by ordering the confiscation of foreign-owned lands and their distribution among the peasantry. Since most of the landowners were French, relations between France and Morocco cooled and French aid was suspended pending an agreement on compensation. In the same month relations with Spain became strained when Morocco announced the extension of its territorial waters from 12 to 70 nautical miles; an agreement was reached between the two governments in January 1974 allowing a limited number of Spanish vessels to fish in Moroccan waters. The new nationalist policy also led Morocco to take a more active part than previously in the Arab-Israeli conflict. In February troops were despatched to the Syrian front and during the October War further detachments were sent to Egypt. The common cause produced a degree of rapprochement between Morocco and the more revolutionary Arab states.

In the early months of 1974 political trials continued. Another round of arrests followed the announcement in February of the discovery of a plot to free prisoners in Kenitra jail. The King, however, made some conciliatory gestures. In March he announced plans for university and judicial reforms, and in April several imprisoned UNFP leaders were released. Relations with France improved and French aid was resumed in February, but relations with Spain remained bad, since Morocco continued to press her claim to the Spanish Sahara. The growth of phosphate mining in the territory posed a threat to the Moroccan economy which was itself dependent on revenue from phosphate exports. The opposition parties, motivated by a mixture of anti-colonialism and nationalism, urged the Government to take action. In July 1974 the King held consultations with military leaders, ministers and leaders of all the political parties to prepare an international campaign for the annexation of the Sahara. An extraordinary degree of national unity was achieved, opposition leaders agreeing to act as government envoys to foreign capitals. Discussions with Spain in August produced no result. The Spanish pursued their own plan for the decolonization of the Sahara, involving the establishment of an independent state closely linked with Spain. This project was contested not only by Morocco but also by Mauritania which reasserted its old claim to the area. Both countries rejected Spain's plan to hold a referendum in the Sahara under UN supervision. In October the issue was debated in the UN General Assembly at the initiative of Morocco. Two months later the Assembly formally approved Morocco's suggestion that the matter be brought before the International Court of Justice at the Hague, and the UN Special Committee on Colonialism was instructed to send a mission to the territory. The referendum proposed by Spain was to be postponed for the time being.

In the atmosphere of national unity produced by the Sahara issue in the second half of 1974 there was an effervescence of political activity. New parties were formed and existing parties reorganized. Most notably the split in the UNFP was confirmed, as the Rabat section of the party became the *Union Socialiste des Forces Populaires* (USFP). King Hassan once more promised elections for the following year, and once more postponed them indefinitely, but even the opposition were not enthusiastic about elections before the settlement of the Sahara dispute. Harassment of opposition parties did not cease and no opposition figures were invited into the Government, but some political prisoners were released.

SAHARAN TAKEOVER

The situation in the Western Sahara developed rapidly. Since Spain reiterated its readiness to withdraw from the Sahara, it became clear that the chief conflict was between the rival North African countries and liberation movements. After Morocco and Mauritania reached some agreement on the future division of the territory Algeria became the main butt of Moroccan invective, because of its support for *Frente Popular para la Liberación de Saguia el Hamra y Rio de Oro* (Polisario), a Saharan liberation movement hostile to Moroccan claims.

On October 15th, 1975, a UN investigative mission reported that the majority of Saharans favoured independence, and the following day the World Court ruled in favour of self-determination. King Hassan responded immediately by ordering a march of 350,000 unarmed civilians to take possession of the Spanish Sahara. The Green March, as it was called, began on November 6th. The Spanish authorities allowed the marchers to progress a few miles across the border before halting their advance. On November 9th Hassan called off the march, declaring that it had achieved its objective, and on November 14th a tripartite agreement was signed in Madrid, by which Spain agreed to withdraw from the Sahara in 1976 and hand over to a joint Morocco-Mauritanian administration. Algeria reacted angrily to this agreement, stepping up its support for Polisario and making veiled threats of direct military intervention. Moroccan armed forces quickly moved into the territory, entering the capital, El Aaiún, on December 11th. They met sharp resistance from Polisario guerrillas, and many Saharans fled towards the Algerian border to avoid the Moroccan advance. The last

Spanish troops left in January 1976, a month before they were due to go under the terms of the tripartite agreement.

The Moroccan Prime Minister, Ahmed Osman, visited France in January and French arms supplies to Morocco were stepped up. On January 27th Algerian and Moroccan forces clashed at Amgalla, inside the Western Sahara, and there was further fighting in February. On February 27th the Sahrawi Arab Democratic Republic (SADR) was proclaimed, a Saharan government-in-exile was formed in Algeria and on March 7th Morocco broke off diplomatic relations with Algeria. The prospect of general war between the two countries faded, however, as Algeria contented itself with arming and training Polisario guerrillas for raids into the Sahara and providing camps for civilian refugees from the area, believed to number some 60,000.

In April 1976 Morocco and Mauritania reached agreement on the division of the Saharan territory, of which the greater part, containing most of the known mineral wealth, was allotted to Morocco, which then set about absorbing the new territory as three new provinces of the Kingdom. By placing strong army garrisons in the territory's few scattered urban settlements the Moroccans were able to secure them against guerrilla attacks, but Polisario incursions into the surrounding desert areas could not be checked. The conveyor belt from the important Bou Craa phosphate mines to the sea was sabotaged, and clashes between the Moroccan army and guerrillas caused heavy casualties on both sides. Polisario proved too strong for Mauritania's very limited armed forces in the south and Morocco took increasing responsibility for the defence of the region. The two countries formed a joint defence committee in May 1977 after a successful Polisario raid on the Mauritanian mining town of Zouérate, in which two French nationals were killed and six captured. In November King Hassan warned Algeria that Moroccan troops would pursue Polisario forces into Algerian territory if necessary; the Algerian Government retorted that any such incursion would mean war. Tension was increased by the direct intervention of France, following the release of the French captives in December, with three air attacks on the Polisario; although the French Government maintained that its action was for the protection of the French nationals working at the Saharan mines, and had been undertaken at the request of Mauritania, it was also clear that France favoured the expansion of Moroccan interests in the area rather than those of Algeria, for both economic and strategic reasons. During 1978 the situation of stalemate continued, with intermittent fighting and a further French air-raid in April. Proposed meetings of the OAU to discuss the issue were postponed on three occasions, revealing an apparent unwillingness on the part of many African leaders to commit themselves. The intransigence of both Morocco and Algeria was at least partly due to the fact that their governments relied to a great extent on their respective Saharan policies for popular support at home; in Morocco, the various opposition parties were still united in support of the King in this respect, despite the enormous expense of the war, which accounted for at least a quarter of the 1979 budget, and the cost of confirming Morocco's hold on the Saharan provinces by installing facilities such as schools, hospitals and housing for those inhabitants remaining in the area. In January 1978 a $292 million Sahara Development Programme had been announced, providing for the settlement of the nomads and the creation of a sedentary economy.

The war was having a still worse effect on the economy of Mauritania, and this was the chief reason for the coup which took place there in July 1978. Polisario at once announced a ceasefire in its hostilities against Mauritania; it was soon clear that the new President, Col. Moustapha

Ould Salek, would be willing to renounce the Saharan province altogether, were it not for the 10,000 Moroccan troops still stationed in Mauritania who might be used against the new regime if it antagonized Morocco. The coup was followed by renewed diplomatic activity, in which France played an important role. President Houphouët-Boigny of the Ivory Coast also offered to act as mediator, proposing the creation of a Saharan Republic in the Mauritanian sector of Western Sahara alone, a suggestion which was unacceptable to all parties. In September King Hassan accepted the proposal by the President of the OAU, President Nimeri of Sudan, that the Heads of State of six African countries (Guinea, the Ivory Coast, Mali, Nigeria, Tanzania and Sudan) should form a committee of "wise men" to mediate in the dispute. Spain, too, became increasingly involved, evidently uneasy about its role in the partition of the area, and anxious, too, to maintain good relations with Algeria and avoid provoking it into increasing its support for the independence movement in the Canary Islands; on the other hand, Spain also needed to avoid offending Morocco if it was to safeguard its fishing rights in Moroccan waters and, still more, its claim to the enclaves of Ceuta and Melilla. Nevertheless, in December 1980, following harassment of Spanish fishing boats by Polisario, the Spanish Government gave official recognition to Polisario (though not to the SADR itself) and stated its support for Saharan self-determination.

Meanwhile, the death of President Boumedienne in December 1978 had not led to a softening of Algeria's attitude. Fighting continued, and in January 1979 Polisario made an attack on the town of Tan-Tan, well within Morocco's pre-1975 borders. In March the Chamber of Representatives approved the formation of a National Defence Council to formulate defence policy. This Council comprised members of all the main political groups (independents, Istiqlal, Mouvement Populaire, USFP, Mouvement Populaire Constitutionnel et Démocratique, and Parti du Progrès et du Socialisme), a composition which suggested that the King was seeking to strengthen support for the war by enlarging the number and the political range of those responsible for its direction. At the same time the Chamber of Representatives showed that its attitude was still belligerent by reaffirming Morocco's right to its Saharan territory and recommended that the right of pursuit into foreign (i.e. Algerian) territory should be exercised.

In July 1979 Polisario broke their ceasefire with Mauritania, and the OAU summit conference passed a resolution calling for a referendum on self-determination in the Western Sahara. Prompted by these events, Mauritania at last withdrew from the war altogether, signing a peace treaty with Polisario in August and renouncing its territorial ambitions in the Western Sahara. King Hassan lost no time in claiming the former Mauritanian share of the area, declaring it a Moroccan province, to be known as Oued Addahab, and preparations were begun for the election of representatives from the province to the Moroccan Chamber of Representatives, which took place in May 1981. In spite of these measures, however, little of the area apart from the towns could strictly be said to be under Moroccan control, and the takeover meant that Morocco's military resources were considerably stretched. Polisario were not slow to retaliate. Over the next eighteen months numerous battles took place, often within Morocco's original borders and particularly around the garrison of Zak; although it is difficult to assess results because of the conflicting accounts coming from each side, it appears that Morocco came off worse in some of these encounters, in spite of the fact that, beginning with "Operation Ouhoud" in November 1979, it had adopted Polisario's tactics of using swiftly-moving armoured columns to seek out the enemy, instead of merely defending fortified bases. In 1980

Morocco again resorted to defensive tactics, concentrating on the *triangle utile* between the towns of El Aaiún, Bou Craa and Essmara. This area, containing most of the population and the chief phosphate mines, was to be protected by a line of defences about 600 km. long; work on this line was completed in May 1982.

Early in 1981 there were reports that Polisario, previously based only in Algeria, had set up bases in Mauritania, while in March the Mauritanians blamed Morocco for an attempted coup and temporarily broke off diplomatic relations. In April Col. Gaddafi, the Libyan leader, proposed that Mauritania and the Western Sahara should unite, and the two countries issued a joint condemnation of Morocco's "occupation" of the Sahara territory.

Meanwhile, international recognition of the SADR was slowly increasing. In November 1979 the UN General Assembly passed a resolution confirming the legitimacy of Polisario's struggle for independence, and a year later it called for Morocco to end its "occupation" of the Western Sahara. By February 1981, the fifth anniversary of the declaration of the republic, the SADR had been recognized by about 45 governments. It applied to join the OAU in July 1980 when, at the annual summit meeting, a majority (26 out of 50 countries) approved the admission of the SADR. Morocco, however, argued that a two-thirds majority was necessary, and threatened to leave the OAU if the SADR was admitted. The decision was postponed and referred once again to the committee of "wise men", who recommended in September that a ceasefire should be established by December, followed by a referendum to be supervised jointly by the OAU and UN. In June 1981, at the OAU summit conference, King Hassan agreed for the first time to a referendum, to be held according to OAU recommendations. The actual conditions of the referendum posed a serious problem. Morocco still refused to negotiate directly with Polisario, claiming that its members were simply Algeria's mercenaries, and insisted that the proposed referendum be based on the 1974 Spanish census of the area, which enumerated only 74,000 inhabitants. Polisario stipulated that, before the poll could take place, Morocco must withdraw its troops and administration to well within its original borders; allow refugees living in Algeria to return and participate in the referendum; and that an interim international administration be set up. In August the OAU implementation committee put forward proposals which would give the electorate a choice between independence or integration with Morocco. The referendum was to be carried out under the auspices of an OAU/UN peace-keeping force and administration, all other troops were to be confined to base and the 300,000 refugees living in Algeria and registered with the UNHCR were to be allowed to participate.

Fighting continued, however, and a new dimension was added to the conflict in October, when Moroccan aircraft were shot down near Guelta Zemmour by what Morocco claimed were sophisticated Soviet-built SAM-6 surface-to-air missiles. Mauritania was accused of allowing Polisario to establish bases on its soil, and of taking part in the attack itself. In response, King Hassan asked the U.S.A. for increased military assistance; under President Reagan, equipment had already been forthcoming, as the U.S.A. was evidently worried about the threat posed to the stability of the Maghreb and of a moderate pro-Western regime. Several visits by high-ranking U.S. officials culminated in talks in February 1982 between the Moroccan Government and Alexander Haig, the U.S. Secretary of State, as a result of which U.S. military aid to Morocco was to be tripled, and the establishment of U.S. transit bases on Moroccan soil was to be discussed.

The situation worsened still further that month when,

at the OAU Council of Ministers held in Addis Ababa, the SADR delegation was seated. Morocco immediately left the meeting in protest, and was followed by representatives of 18 other countries. Observers considered this to be the most serious crisis within the OAU since its inception and it was feared that the organization's very future might be at risk. Consequent OAU meetings often had to be postponed, since no quorum could be reached. By May 1982 the situation had still not been resolved.

PROGRESS TOWARDS DEMOCRACY

Despite the fighting, there is no doubt that King Hassan benefited greatly in prestige and popularity at home from the Saharan takeover. The staging of the Green March had particularly appealed to the Moroccan imagination. The King at last felt secure enough to hold the long-awaited elections. With the exception of the UNFP, the opposition parties agreed to participate, despite the continuation of political trials connected with the March 1973 uprising which resulted in heavy prison sentences for many of the accused in early 1977. Municipal elections were held in November 1976, and these were followed by provincial elections in January 1977 and elections for professional and vocational chambers the following March. At each stage, "independents", mostly pro-government and conservative, won over 60 per cent of the seats. Istiqlal and the USFP protested against electoral irregularities and administrative interference. On March 1st four party leaders, including M'Hamed Boucetta of Istiqlal and Abderrahim Bouabid of the USFP, agreed to join the Government as Ministers of State without Portfolio, in the hope of ensuring that the national elections would be fairly conducted. Press censorship was also abolished. Of the 264 members in the new Chamber of Representatives, 176 were directly elected on June 3rd and 88 chosen by an electoral college on June 21st. Independents won 141 seats (including 60 by indirect election), while Istiqlal and the MP won 49 and 44 respectively, the USFP won 16 and other opposition parties 14. The new Government, announced in October, included former opposition members, notably M'Hamed Boucetta as Foreign Minister, with seven other members of Istiqlal, four members of the MP and Maati Bouabid of the UNFP, whose party, however, subsequently disowned him. Thus the King won over the major part of the opposition, and appeared to have succeeded in his plan to combine the forms of democracy with strong royal authority.

Among the Moroccan people as a whole, support for the war appeared to be almost universal, but there were signs of discontent which could at least be partly attributed to the heavy cost of the fighting. During the first few months of 1979 there were strikes by many different sections of the work-force demanding higher wages, while the visit of the deposed Shah of Iran in March provided an excuse for the expression of discontent, particularly among students and the unemployed. On March 21st the Prime Minister, Ahmed Osman, resigned, ostensibly to devote himself to the organization of the newly formed Independents' party (RNI; in 1980 the rural branch of this party broke away to form the Independent Democrats Party, which included several cabinet ministers). He was replaced by Maati Bouabid, the Minister of Justice and a former trade union leader. The new Prime Minister held talks with union leaders, after which wage rises were announced, including an increase of 40 per cent in the minimum wage. Although this provided a short-term answer to social unrest, it could only add to the burden on the economy.

During 1980, attempts were made to cut spending on education, which accounted for nearly a quarter of the current budget, by reducing student grants and limiting university places, previously available to all who had passed the *baccalauréat* examination. Student strikes ensued, supported by the USFP and *Parti du Progrès et du Socialisme* (PPS) and unrest continued in 1981 and 1982. In June 1981 at least 66 people were killed during a general strike in Casablanca, protesting at increases in the price of subsidized food. The USFP and the CDT were accused of creating this unrest and all CDT offices were closed down. Following USFP criticism of government Saharan policy in September, Abderrahim Bouabid, its leader, and other senior officials were arrested and given prison sentences; the two USFP newspapers were suspended.

Further opposition was aroused in October by the implementation of the constitutional changes approved by referendum in May 1980, particularly the clause extending the maximum period between elections to the Chamber of Representatives from four to six years: the next parliamentary elections were thus postponed until 1983. The opposition parties were angered by the prolonged life of a body which, they maintained, had been irregularly elected in the first place, and in which the majority parties were guilty of absenteeism and passivity. Consequently, all 14 USFP deputies withdrew temporarily from the Chamber of Representatives. This was followed in November by a cabinet reshuffle which eliminated all former RNI ministers.

Abderrahim Bouabid was pardoned in March 1982, and CDT and USFP offices were allowed to reopen in April. Many trade union activists, including Amawi, remained in prison, however, and the ban on USFP newspapers was not lifted.

ECONOMIC SURVEY

Morocco, although a potentially rich developing country, has suffered since 1975 from the combined effects of the costly Saharan war, low world prices of phosphate rock—its main export—and a high population growth rate. These pressures on the economy started to have a severe impact by 1978 and the Government in that year introduced a series of austerity measures to check them, including a 25 per cent cut in imports and a shortening of the development plan from five to three years. By 1980 the balance of trade had improved and state expenditure, particularly on administration, had been reduced. But the cost of maintaining and equipping troops in the Sahara, especially at a time of deep world recession, largely undermined any salutary results of the austerity programme. In April 1981, however, Morocco announced an economic development plan for 1980-85 which set total expenditure at an ambitious 111,000 million dirhams, equivalent to almost twice as much outlay a year as in the 1978-80 plan. At the same time, the Secretary of State for Planning and Regional Development, Tayeb Bencheikh, who had formulated the two previous plans (1973–77 and 1978–80), was promoted to the rank of Minister, in a move which indicated the Government's confidence in his choice of priorities: the development of natural resources (phosphate rock, other minerals, agriculture and fisheries) and education and training.

Morocco is especially rich in natural resources. It has two-thirds of the world's phosphate rock reserves, many other minerals, most of which are as yet undeveloped, fertile agricultural land, rich fishing grounds off the Atlantic coast and many attractions for European tourists who bring in foreign exchange. Considerable investment has been put into developing a phosphate-processing industry at Safi, south of Casablanca, with a view to increasing exports of phosphate products, which yield a higher return than the raw rock. Some success in this direction has been achieved and Morocco is finding a ready market for its phosphoric acid, but progress is slow because of the high costs involved in establishing such industries. Substantial investment has also been put into developing agriculture. Agricultural produce is the second most important export after phosphate rock and about half the population is employed in agriculture, which makes its role in the economy crucial. The agricultural programme has centred mainly on the construction of dams, both to retain water and to prevent floods. Until its completion, Morocco remains extremely vulnerable to abrupt changes in the weather.

The difficulties which Morocco is experiencing stem partly from its high population growth rate (which has averaged 3 per cent a year since 1977). The population was estimated at 20,242,000 in mid-1980 and is expected to reach 36.5 million by the year 2000. The high birth rate (45 per 1,000) means that 56 per cent of the population is under the age of 20 and therefore not productive. Only about one-half of the population was estimated to be in active employment in 1977. More than one-third of the population live in the main towns, which are often overcrowded. The rural exodus has created pressures on all public services, especially housing, education, water and power supply and transport.

Pressures on the economy have resulted in a high inflation rate. Officially this was 12.6 per cent in 1981, compared with an average annual increase of 9 per cent in 1978–80. But prices of some commodities, such as food, have risen much more than that. Reduction of food subsidies in May 1981—causing the price of some basic items to rise by as much as 40 per cent—led to widespread unrest. Government price subsidies for 1982 were 2,000 million dirhams, compared with 1,400 million dirhams in 1981.

AGRICULTURE AND FISHERIES

Agriculture is the key to the economy of Morocco. Nearly 60 per cent of Morocco's population live in the countryside, and 53 per cent of the working population are engaged in agriculture, livestock-raising and fishing. Thus agriculture provides the means of livelihood of the majority of the population, supplies a high proportion of the country's food requirements and about 30 per cent of the country's total exports. In 1980, agriculture contributed about 18 per cent of total G.D.P. Changing climatic conditions cause substantial year-to-year variations in agricultural output. Severe drought in 1981—the worst for 35 years—caused estimated cereal production to fall by 50 per cent from 4.5 million tons in 1980, while overall agricultural production dropped by 25 per cent.

The principal crops are cereals (especially wheat, barley and maize), citrus fruit, potatoes, tomatoes, beans, chick peas and olives. Canary seed, cumin, coriander, linseed and almonds are also grown, and tea cultivation has started in the Loukkos. Sugar cane and beet are also being planted on a large scale to substitute for imports; sugar is one of Morocco's main food imports since per caput consumption is very high. The main suppliers are Brazil and Thailand. Sugar beet production amounted to 332,900 metric tons in 1977/78 but dropped to 239,555 metric tons in 1978/79 because of drought. Sugar cane production nearly doubled to 33,950 metric tons in 1978 but fell to 29,200 metric tons in 1979. Production rose again—by nearly 30 per cent—in 1980 to 37,516 tons.

Livestock numbers have been declining and the quality of herds is generally poor. In 1980, there were an estimated 25.9 million head of livestock, including 16.1 million sheep and 3.7 million cattle. Milk production falls far short of domestic demand, estimated at 1,000 million litres in 1979, and some 42,600 metric tons of dairy products had to be imported in that year, at a cost of about 200 million dirhams.

In the past, Morocco has been largely self-sufficient in foodstuffs, but population growth is fast outpacing increases in agricultural production. Food imports, particularly cereals, sugar and dairy products, have become substantial. Until 1973, agricultural produce accounted for by far the largest proportion of total exports, but its importance has declined since the sharp rise in phosphate prices in 1974. In 1980, sales of foodstuffs accounted for about 27 per cent of total exports. The main agricultural exports are citrus fruits (mostly oranges), tomatoes, processed fish and vegetables. Morocco is one of the world's largest exporters of citrus fruits: exports in 1980 were worth 1,160 million dirhams and amounted to 771,000 metric tons. A fruit processing industry is being developed, and preserved fruit, jam and fruit juice exports now contribute substantially to earnings. A separate Fisheries Ministry, formerly the responsibility of the Commerce, Industry and Tourism Ministry, was set up in April 1981.

MINING

Morocco has about two-thirds of the world's phosphate rock reserves. Known reserves are 10,600 million metric tons and probable reserves are 57,200 million metric tons. There are an estimated 3,700 million cubic metres at Khouribga, 1,600 million cubic metres at Youssoufia and 1,000 million cubic metres at Ben Guerir. Some 1,700 million cubic metres of reserves at Bou Craa in the former Spanish Sahara are now also administered by Morocco. Morocco is the world's third producer of phosphate rock, after the U.S.A. and the U.S.S.R., and the biggest exporter. In 1980 it produced 19.2 million metric tons, of which 16.5 million was exported, mainly to Spain, Poland, Romania, Mexico and Japan. Exports in 1981 were estimated to have fallen slightly to 15.6 million metric tons. Production is planned to increase considerably in the next 30 years. Total production capacity is now 25–26 million metric tons but this should increase to 37 million tons per year by 1985, according to the *Office Chérifien des Phosphates* (OCP). The expansion will be mainly at Khouribga. The new Ben Guerir mine has an initial capacity of 3 million metric tons per year, and a further mine is planned at Sidi Hajjaj. The Meskala mine, to be developed with Soviet help, is not expected to open until 1987/88. Its production will be almost entirely for the U.S.S.R., to meet that country's commitments to other members of the CMEA (COMECON).

Morocco is investing heavily in the "downstream" phosphates industry in order to increase the value of its exports. Three phosphate processing plants are already in operation at Safi and a fourth, Maroc Phosphore II, opened in 1981. Maroc Chimie I produces phosphoric acid and fertilizers, Maroc Chimie II produces phosphoric acid, and Maroc Phosphore I—a much bigger plant opened in June 1976—produces phosphoric acid and mono-ammonium phosphate. Since the opening of this plant, Morocco's phosphoric acid exports have increased substantially, reaching 409,374 metric tons in 1980 and earning 793 million dirhams, three times as much as in 1977. The main customers in 1980 were India, Brazil, Italy and the U.S.S.R. Plans to develop the industry further are far-reaching. Work has started, for example, on a phosphates port at Jorf Lasfar where further phosphate-processing plants may be sited. Framatome of France has also been contracted to carry out studies on the establishment of a nuclear power plant which might use uranium extracted from phosphate rock.

Morocco has many other minerals, most of which are untapped. They include coal, iron ore, lead and zinc, fluorspar, manganese, cobalt, silver, antimony, barytes and copper. About 750,000 metric tons of coal, in the form of anthracite, was produced in 1981, compared with 680,000 tons in 1980 and 710,000 tons in 1979. The deposit is estimated at 100 million metric tons and agreement has been reached with a Polish company on further development of the mine. Iron ore pellets are produced by SEFERIF from deposits in the north east near Nador where a steelworks is planned. Production of iron ore pellets rose to 444,000 metric tons in 1977, but in 1978 output was affected by the slump in the world iron ore market and production fell considerably. In 1980 Morocco's gross output of iron ore (about 55 to 60 per cent iron) was 78,000 metric tons, compared with only 61,700 tons in 1979. Production of lead ore rose to 172,200 metric tons (gross weight) in 1980, compared with 165,000 metric tons in 1979. The capacity of the lead

smelter at Oued Heimer, operated by the *Société des Mines de Zellidja*, is to be expanded, following studies which have indicated a high lead content in nearby deposits. Mine production of zinc, which is all exported, rose to 13,100 metric tons (gross) in 1980 from 12,900 tons in 1979. Output of copper ore increased to 24,000 metric tons (gross) in 1980 from 23,500 tons in 1979 and only 12,200 tons in 1978. Production of fluorspar at El Hammam near Meknès, and of barytes and cobalt concentrate has also increased. Interest has recently been shown in the possibility of recovering uranium from the phosphate rock reserves, and exploration by the *Bureau de Recherches et de Participations Minières* (BRPM) has recently revealed traces of uranium in the upper Moulouya valley, east of Zeida, in the High Atlas.

Production of crude petroleum is almost negligible. It fell in 1980 to 13,800 metric tons, from 18,600 tons in 1979 and 24,350 tons in 1978 (from the Sidi Ghalem field). Morocco is therefore almost entirely dependent on outside supplies. In 1980 the main suppliers were Iraq, Saudi Arabia, the U.S.S.R. and the United Arab Emirates, in that order. A total of 4 million metric tons of crude oil was imported at a cost of 3,600 million dirhams. Exploration efforts have been increased in recent years, especially offshore in the Atlantic. Phillips Petroleum of the U.S.A. started drilling in October 1978 in the offshore Cap Sim concession. Phillips is the operator for the concession, which is held jointly with Agip of Italy, Getty Oil and British Petroleum. The same consortium has other offshore concessions, one at Simmou in the same area, and another off the Saharan coast. Phillips is sole operator for an onshore concession, near Tafrata and Ksabi about 200 miles east of Rabat. In 1980 Elf Aquitaine of France and the Franco-Moroccan *Société Chérifienne des Pétroles* were awarded five oil prospection permits covering 8,416 square miles in north Morocco; their search is part of an intensive three-year exploration programme funded by a £50 million World Bank loan. However, despite the efforts of these companies and of others before them, no petroleum had been found in commercially exploitable quantities by early 1982. More promising, however, are efforts to extract oil from oil shale deposits at Timahdid in the Atlas mountains. An agreement was signed in 1978 with Occidental Petroleum of the U.S.A. for co-operation in the development of these deposits, with the aim of producing 3 million metric tons of oil a year.

INDUSTRY

Since 1973, the Government has made special efforts to increase industrial development, in order to reduce the country's dependence on agriculture and phosphate mining, to create jobs and to substitute for imports. Part of the strategy has been to encourage the development of industry away from Casablanca, where it is most concentrated. The main industry, in terms of investment, is the production of phosphates. Other important industries include oil refining, cement, food, textiles, chemicals, paper and timber, metals, rubber and plastics. The biggest project outside the phosphates industry in the 1973–77 development plan was the Nador steelworks, intended to produce 1 million metric tons per year, as a joint project with Algeria. A decision has still not been taken to go ahead with the entire steelworks project, which would be very expensive, but in April 1981 Davy Loewy of the U.K. signed a £75 million contract to build a steel rolling mill at Nador. The mill is considered the first phase of the Nador project and will initially produce about 420,000 metric tons of long products. As part of the agreement, the U.K. Government is making an outright grant of £13.5 million to Morocco to finance the purchase of equipment in the U.K., while the U.K.'s Export Credits Guarantee Department (ECGD) has guaranteed a 345 million dirham loan from Morgan Grenfell & Company to Morocco's state steel company *Société Nationale de Sidérurgie* (SONASID).

Oil refining is another major industry and the capacity of Morocco's biggest refinery, at Mohammedia, has recently been increased to 5 million metric tons a year. Morocco's other refinery is at Sidi Kacem. A third has been under consideration for Jorf Lasfar where more phosphate-processing plants may be built and discussions were reported to have been held with Gulf oil-producing states on joint financing for the project, but no decision has yet been reached. Oil refining is given priority because it substitutes for imports. Other import substitution industries are cement and sugar manufacturing; projects include a 1.2 million metric tons-a-year cement works south of Casablanca for which a contract was awarded to Fives-Cail Babcock of France in March 1981. At the same time, FCB was awarded a contract to build a sugar beet refinery at Zemamra. Altogether, 12 sugar refineries are planned in addition to six already operating. The new refineries should bring total refined sugar production to 1,165,000 metric tons a year by 1985, compared with about 370,000 in 1978. Other food industries include fruit and vegetable processing and canning—mainly for export—and fish canning. Fruit and vegetable development is planned in the agricultural areas of the Loukkos, Tadla, Doukkala and Lower Moulouya, date packing in Ouarzazate, fodder plants in the Souss-Massa, Haouz, Gharb and Oriental regions.

The textiles industry has also expanded in recent years. It is particularly favoured because it is labour-intensive but requires relatively little investment. At the beginning of 1980, projects in this sector included a textile spinning mill at Tensift, wool spinning mills at Oued Zem and Ben Guerir and a synthetic fibre plant. This industry suffered in 1977 from the introduction of EEC quotas on textiles imports, but a compromise agreement was reached for 1979–81, which set more flexible limits.

Metal industries are being developed to use raw materials from Morocco's extensive mineral deposits. A 70,000 metric tons-a-year lead smelter is to be built at Meknès and a 30,000 metric tons-a-year copper smelter at Agadir. Another plant at Mohammedia will produce 500,000 metric tons a year of sodium carbonate from rock salt.

A car industry is also being developed with the launching, by the French car manufacturer Citroën, of two new assembly lines, in Casablanca and Tangier. Both lines were in operation by the end of 1981, producing small-engined cars and a diesel-engine saloon. Two new companies have been set up to operate the ventures: Citroën Construction, with a capital of about £1 million, equally shared by France and Morocco, will operate the assembly lines, while Citroën Outillage will make spare parts and components. Both ventures will compete with the *Société Marocaine de Constructions Automobiles* (SOMACA) which assembles Fiat, Renault, Opel and Simca-Talbot cars.

A new investment code was approved by the Council of Ministers in December 1981, replacing the 1973 Moroccanization Law which required 50 per cent Moroccan ownership of local firms. Under the new code, full ownership of Moroccan companies by foreign investors is allowed. The code also liberalizes repatriation of capital and profits.

BALANCE OF PAYMENTS

Morocco's main sources of revenue are earnings from phosphate rock and agricultural exports, receipts from tourism and workers' remittances. Its main expenditure is on capital equipment, food and crude oil imports. Since 1976 the balance of payments deficit has widened as export earnings have increased only marginally, while the cost of capital equipment and crude oil imports in particular has soared. The trade deficit widened to 8,542 million dirhams in 1977, from 4,594 million dirhams in 1976, and seemed set to deteriorate further until, in June of that year, measures were announced to cut imports and improve receipts from Moroccan workers abroad. The package included a 25 per cent cut in imports which affected mainly consumer goods but also items of capital equipment, and a premium on remittances to encourage Moroccan emigrant workers to repatriate their earnings. These measures had some impact and the trade deficit was narrowed in 1978. At the same time, workers' remittances and tourism receipts were higher, so that the balance of payments looked much healthier.

However, because of high inflation in the West, from where Morocco's capital equipment and food is imported, and higher oil prices, the trade deficit widened again in 1979 to 6,706 million dirhams; it reached 7,148 million dirhams in 1980 and 10,309 million in 1981. Tourism receipts grew by only 1.2 per cent in 1979, to 1,670 million dirhams. Workers' remittances increased by 17.5 per cent in that year to 3,983 million dirhams but were not enough to compensate for the trade deficit. The balance of payments worsened as a result, foreign borrowing increased to cover the deficit and the foreign debt reached $7,000 million. By mid-1981, foreign exchange reserves were sufficient to cover 12 days' imports, compared with 35 days' imports in 1980.

TRADE

As stated above (*see* balance of payments), the trade deficit widened in 1980. Export earnings

MOROCCO

amounted to 9,645 million dirhams in that year, which was a 26.5 per cent improvement on 1979 but not enough to compensate for higher imports. The world price of phosphate rock—Morocco's main export—rose in 1980 for the first time in several years. Despite a drop in the volume exported, receipts therefore rose to 3,000 million dirhams, from 2,300 million dirhams in 1979. The main customers for phosphate rock in 1980 were Spain, Poland, Romania, Mexico and Japan. Morocco also now exports small quantities of phosphoric acid for which it is finding a ready market: in 1980 it sold 409,374 metric tons, mainly to India, Indonesia, Brazil, Italy and the U.S.S.R. Revenues from sales of citrus fruit, Morocco's second main export, have increased steadily in the last few years, reaching 1,160 million dirhams in 1980, compared with 859 million dirhams in 1979. The main customers in 1980 were France, the U.S.S.R., West Germany, Saudi Arabia, the Netherlands and the United Kingdom; Saudi Arabia, which imports almost all its food, was a new customer and the fruit may have been sold as part of a trade arrangement in exchange for crude oil.

The value of imports increased by 17.2 per cent in 1980 to 16,793 million dirhams. The main imports were capital equipment and semi-finished goods (6,712 million dirhams), energy and lubricants (3,961 million), food (2,833 million) and consumer goods (1,170 million).

France is Morocco's main trading partner. In 1980, French exports to Morocco were worth 4,168 million dirhams, representing about one-quarter of Morocco's total imports. Moroccan exports to France totalled 2,428 million dirhams in 1980, giving Morocco a deficit of 1,740 million. Spain was the second main supplier, with exports worth 1,388 million dirhams. Other important suppliers in 1980 were the U.S.A., the Federal Republic of Germany and Italy, in that order. Morocco's main customers, after France, were the Federal Republic of Germany, the Netherlands, Spain and Italy.

A co-operation agreement with the EEC was formally ratified on November 1st, 1978. It provided for tariff reductions on some Moroccan exports to the EEC (mainly citrus fruit) and for loans and grants worth 130 million European units of account (EUA) in 1978–81. This included a 40 million EUA loan from the European Investment Bank for the Jorf Lasfar phosphates port. The agreement's provisions on trade have been in force since 1976. They included an 80 per cent tariff reduction on EEC imports of Moroccan oranges, mandarins, clementines, lemons and grapefruit and a 60 per cent reduction, from November 15th to April 30th, of duty on tomatoes. The agreement will benefit Morocco, although in the long term competition from potential EEC members, like Spain, is bound to increase.

TRANSPORT

Morocco's infrastructure, that is roads, railways and ports, is fairly well developed in the north and in the west near Casablanca, although some of the facilities are overloaded. There are seven main ports: Casablanca, Safi, Mohammedia, Agadir, Tangier, Kénitra and Nador, which was recently completed by a Romanian firm. An eighth major port, at Jorf Lasfar, was inaugurated in 1982 and Casablanca port is being extended. Total cargo handled by these ports amounted to 31.3 million metric tons in 1978, of which 17.8 million was phosphates exports, 1.1 million exports and imports of other minerals and 3.5 million fuel imports. Total cargo in 1979 was 33.2 million metric tons.

The railways are operated by the *Office National des Chemins de Fer Marocains* (ONCFM). In 1977, they carried 22.9 million metric tons of freight. This figure was expected to increase by 12.5 per cent a year to 47 million metric tons in 1985, of which 34 million will be phosphate rock. Passenger traffic is also expected to increase, by about 12 per cent a year to 1985, from 5.9 million in 1977 to 10 million in 1985. One of the biggest railway projects started in the 1973–77 development plan was complete renewal of 100 km. of track between Casablanca and Marrakesh. Other major works carried out or started included: track renewal of part of the Tangier—Fès line, partial renewal of the Khouribga to Sidi Daoui track, installation of an internal railway at Maroc Phosphore I at Safi. Major projects include a 90-km. railway to be built with Soviet finance from the Meskala phosphate mine to Essaouira port, and a 850-km. railway from Marrakesh to El Aaiún in the former Spanish Sahara, begun in April 1981. Rolling stock is also being renewed and increased. From 1973–77, a total of 73 locomotives were bought, together with 124 passenger coaches, and 717 phosphate wagons.

There are thirty commercial airfields, of which eight are open to international traffic, the most important being Tangier-Boakhalf, Casablanca-Nouasseur and Rabat-Salé. Moroccan air transport is provided by Royal Air Maroc, which was formed in 1953 and is 90 per cent owned by the government. The airline carried 1.2 million passengers in 1978, up from 849,018 in 1976.

The road network of Morocco is well developed, consisting of 29,301 kilometres of roads (84 per cent paved) at the end of 1978. Most of Morocco's roads are built to design standards well in advance of the traffic which they are currently carrying. Many were built by the French army, primarily for strategic purposes. In 1979 there were 590,917 vehicles in Morocco. The amount of freight transported on Moroccan roads in 1975 was 6.8 million tons.

BANKING AND FINANCE

Strains on the economy resulting from the war, the high population growth rate, costly food and oil imports have led Morocco to resort increasingly to foreign borrowing. Until 1976 the foreign debt was very small, but since then it has risen sharply, reaching an estimated $7,000 million at the end of 1980. In that year, borrowing rose very sharply: in October, for example, Morocco negotiated a three-year loan of 817 million special drawing rights, equivalent to about $1,000 million, from the IMF, the biggest loan to a developing country that the IMF had ever granted. In 1980, too, Morocco was reported to have received $1,000 million from Saudi Arabia. It is also an important recipient of aid from other sources, such as the World Bank and Arab aid funds. Iraq has been lending on soft terms to cover Morocco's oil purchases.

Various Moroccan institutions, such as the *Banque Nationale pour le Développement Economique* (BNDE) and the *Office Chérifien des Phosphates* (OCP), have also borrowed on the Euromarket. In 1980, for example, the BNDE borrowed 38 million Swiss francs, while the OCP borrowed $170 million. The Government borrowed $250 million in its own right from a consortium of mainly Arab banks. A $40 million loan, in conjunction with a 344 million dirham export credit, was also raised early in 1981 for the *Société Nationale de Sidérurgie* for the first phase of the Nador steel complex.

Morocco has 15 commercial banks, all majority Moroccan-owned, and six specialized financial institutions. These include the BNDE, which finances industry; the *Caisse de Dépôt et de Gestion*, which finances small local projects; the *Crédit Immobilier et Hôtelier*, which finances tourism and property; the *Caisse Marocaine des Marchés*, which finances domestic trade; the *Caisse Nationale de Crédit Agricole*, which finances agricultural projects, and the *Société Nationale d'Investissement*. After credit restrictions had been imposed by the Government in 1978, as part of the effort to control spending, bank credit expanded by only 14 per cent in 1978 and 1979, compared with an average of 20 per cent a year from 1974 to 1977. Total credit in 1979 amounted to 17,029 million dirhams, of which 6,224 million came from the commercial banks and 10,287 million from the specialized institutions, the remainder being new money. Two-thirds of the total was short-term credit.

National savings increased by an estimated 16 per cent in 1978, after having declined steadily since 1975. The growth was attributed to an increase in the capital assets of private and mixed sector companies and to import deposits—in some cases amounting to 25 per cent of the value of the imported goods and held by the banks for six months, in conformity with regulations introduced in mid-1978.

DEVELOPMENT

The 1973–77 development plan aimed to stimulate investment in six sectors: industry (especially export-oriented and labour-intensive industry), mining, tourism, fisheries, handicrafts and agriculture. It was accompanied by an Investment Code which gave incentives, such as tax holidays and the right to repatriate all profits, to foreign companies setting up businesses in all these sectors, except agriculture. The

original investment target for the five-year period was 26,000 million Moroccan dirhams, of which 11,000 million dirhams was to come from the state and the remainder from private investors. These targets were revised in 1975, after receipts from phosphate rock exports increased. Total investment was then planned to reach 50,000 million dirhams, of which 35,000 million dirhams was to come from the state. In the event, about 45,000 million dirhams appears to have been invested.

G.D.P., measured at constant 1969 prices, was projected to grow by an average 7.5 per cent annually in the five years. The growth rate achieved was only 6.8 per cent, mainly because the strains of the war had begun to tell on the economy and because poor harvests substantially reduced agriculture's contribution to G.D.P. In 1977, for example, agriculture contributed only 3,538 million dirhams to G.D.P., representing only 13.9 per cent of total G.D.P., compared with 19.3 per cent in 1973. Industry's contribution to total G.D.P. increased during the five years but still amounted to only 34.9 per cent of the total in 1977. The main contribution came from the tertiary sector—services, trade, transport and tourism.

As part of a series of austerity measures introduced in June 1978, it was announced that the following development plan would span only three years, instead of five. A total of 36,894 million dirhams was to be invested, but the state's share of the total was to be much less than in the 1973–77 plan. The target for annual G.D.P. growth was set at a modest 4.6 per cent. Only 3 per cent annual growth, however, was attained in 1978 and 1979. Figures provided by the *Secretariat d'Etat au Plan et du Développement Régional* showed that about 16 per cent of total investment was for industry, about 16 per cent for rural development and hydroelectric schemes, 9 per cent for mining and 9 per cent for energy, the remaining 50 per cent being divided between transport, tourism, communications, trade, infrastructure, education, social sectors, administration and regional development.

In April 1981 a five-year development plan for 1980–85 was announced which seemed set to reverse the austere policies of the three-year plan. Investment was put at 111,000 million dirhams, which observers consider ambitious. The plan envisages increased investment from the private sector and parastatal organizations—notably the OCP and the BRPM. Together, they are expected to provide 76,000 million dirhams, or 68 per cent, of planned investment. One promising sign, however, is that the plan aims to encourage small and medium-sized industries, which are better fitted to the country's requirements. They involve less heavy outlay and can employ more people. They can also be set up more quickly and distributed evenly throughout the country, so helping to relieve pressure on Casablanca, the main industrial and commercial centre.

STATISTICAL SURVEY

Statistics for Morocco exclude the former Spanish Sahara unless otherwise stated.

AREA AND POPULATION

AREA (sq. km.)	POPULATION (Census of July 20th, 1971)		
	Total	Moroccans	Aliens
458,730	15,379,259	15,233,584	145,675

Estimated mid-year population: 18,245,000 in 1977; 18,906,000 in 1978; 19,470,000 in 1979; 20,242,000 in 1980.

ADMINISTRATIVE DISTRICTS*
(July 1st, 1979)

	AREA (sq. km.)	POPULATION (estimates)	DENSITY (per sq. km.)
Provinces:			
Agadir . . .	17,460	933,300	53.5
Al-Hocima . .	3,550	306,400	86.3
Azizal . . .	10,050	395,500	39.4
Beni Mellal . .	7,075	572,600	80.9
Boujdour . .	100,120	n.a.	n.a.
Boulemane . .	14,395	127,800	8.9
Chaouen . .	4,350	300,200	69.0
El Aaiún . .	39,360	n.a.	n.a.
El Jadida . .	6,000	703,200	117.2
El Kellaa Srarhna . .	10,070	559,100	55.5
Essaouira . .	6,335	456,300	72.0
Essmara . .	61,760	n.a.	n.a.
Fès . . .	5,400	744,900	137.9
Figuig . . .	55,990	107,800	1.9
Kemisset . .	8,305	427,700	51.5
Kénitra . . .	8,805	1,192,200	135.4
Khenifra . .	11,115	299,100	26.9
Khouribga . .	4,250	424,800	100.0
Marrakech . .	14,755	1,224,100	83.0
Meknès . . .	8,510	774,100	91.0
Nador . . .	6,130	609,400	99.4
Ouarzazate . .	46,460	587,900	12.7
Oujda . . .	20,700	769,100	37.2
Rachidia . .	59,585	405,000	6.8
Safi . . .	7,285	652,200	89.5
Settat . . .	9,750	694,100	71.2
Tanger . . .	1,195	377,600	316.0
Tan-Tan . .	17,295	26,500	1.5
Taounate . .	5,585	560,800	100.4
Tata . . .	25,925	106,100	4.1
Taza . . .	15,020	618,000	41.1
Tétouan . .	6,025	682,100	113.2
Tiznit . . .	6,960	336,400	48.3
Prefectures:			
Casablanca† . .	1,615	2,357,200	1,459.6
Rabat-Salé . .	1,275	865,100	678.5
TOTAL . .	659,970	19,470,000	42.4

*Area figures include 201,240 sq. km. annexed from Western Sahara in 1976 (Boujdour, Essmara and El Aaiún); the Mauritanian portion, about 104,000 sq. km., was claimed by Morocco as the province of Oued Addahab in 1979. Population figures exclude the new Saharan provinces. The estimated population of Western Sahara (including the then Mauritanian-held portion) was 165,000 at July 1st, 1979.

† It was announced in July 1981 that Casablanca was to be divided into five prefectures. Casablanca–Anfa (1,600,000 inhabitants), Hay-Mohamed–Aïn–Sebaa (600,000), Aïn–Chock–Hay–Hassani (500,000), Ben–Msik–Sidi–Othmane (800,000) and Mohamedia (250,000).

PRINCIPAL TOWNS
(1971 census)

Rabat (capital)*	.	435,510	Tanger (Tangier) . .	185,850
Casablanca . .	.	1,371,330	Oujda . . .	155,800
Marrakech (Marrakesh)	330,400		Tétouan . . .	137,080
Fès (Fez) . .	.	321,460	Kénitra . . .	135,960
Meknès . .	.	244,520	Safi . . .	129,100

* Including Salé.

Births and Deaths: Average annual birth rate 47.0 per 1,000 in 1970–75, 45.4 per 1,000 in 1975–80; death rate 15.8 per 1,000 in 1970–75, 13.6 per 1,000 in 1975–80 (UN estimates).

ECONOMICALLY ACTIVE POPULATION*
(1971 census)

Agriculture, hunting, forestry and fishing .	1,988,060
Mining and quarrying . . .	44,540
Manufacturing . . .	369,264
Electricity, gas and water . . .	10,810
Construction . . .	171,695
Trade, restaurants and hotels . .	289,082
Transport, storage and communications .	100,425
Financing, insurance, real estate and business services	5,602
Community, social and personal services .	501,728
Activities not adequately described . .	155,412
TOTAL IN EMPLOYMENT . .	3,636,618
Unemployed	343,900
TOTAL LABOUR FORCE . .	3,980,518
of which:	
Males	3,375,363
Females	605,155

* Figures are based on a 10 per cent sample tabulation of census returns. The figure for females excludes unreported family helpers in agriculture.

AGRICULTURE

LAND USE
('000 hectares)

	1973	1979
Arable land . . .	7,195*	7,269
Land under permanent crops	430*	450*
Permanent pastures .	12,500†	12,500†
Forests and woodland .	5,172†	5,195*
Other land . .	19,333	19,216
Inland water . .	25	25
TOTAL AREA . .	44,655	44,655

* FAO estimate.
† Unofficial figure.

Source: FAO, *Production Yearbook.*

PRINCIPAL CROPS
('000 metric tons)

			1978	1979	1980
Wheat .	.	.	1,876	1,796	1,811†
Barley .	.	.	2,328	1,888	2,212†
Maize .	.	.	390	312	333†
Olives .	.	.	200†	390†	300*
Dates .	.	.	97*	102*	104*
Pulses .	.	.	296	299	231
Tomatoes .	.	.	465†	413†	413*
Oranges .	.	.	785	645	720†
Tangerines .	.	.	272	247	267†
Potatoes .	.	.	250*	340†	390†
Sugar beet .	.	.	2,395	2,175	2,200*
Seed cotton .	.	.	11	15	17
Grapes .	.	.	230	239*	250*

* FAO estimate.
† Unofficial figure.

Source: FAO, *Production Yearbook.*

LIVESTOCK
('ooo head, year ending September)

	1978	1979	1980
Cattle . . .	2,907*	3,174*	3,680†
Sheep . . .	15,272*	14,146*	16,100‡
Goats . . .	5,972*	5,081*	6,070‡
Camels . . .	96*	95*	230‡
Horses . . .	320†	320†	320†
Mules . . .	370‡	380‡	390‡
Asses . . .	1,300‡	1,350‡	1,400‡
Chickens . . .	22,000‡	23,000‡	24,000‡

† Unofficial figure.
‡ FAO estimate.

Sources: * Banque du Maroc, *Annual Report* 1979, quoting Ministry of Agriculture, Rabat; FAO, *Production Yearbook.*

LIVESTOCK PRODUCTS
('ooo metric tons)

	1978	1979	1980
Beef and veal . .	76†	77†	77†
Mutton and lamb .	44†	40†	43†
Goats' meat . .	15†	15†	15†
Poultry meat . .	80†	90†	100*
Cows' milk . .	590*	600†	650*
Sheep's milk . .	23*	25*	26*
Goats' milk . .	26*	26*	26*
Hen eggs . .	72.3*	75.0*	78.0*
Wool (greasy) . .	12.0†	12.6†	12.7†

* FAO estimate.
† Unofficial figure.

Source: FAO, *Production Yearbook.*

FORESTRY
ROUNDWOOD REMOVALS
('ooo cubic metres)

	CONIFEROUS (soft wood)			BROADLEAVED (hard wood)			TOTAL		
	1977	1978	1979	1977	1978	1979	1977	1978	1979
Sawlogs and veneer logs . .	85	68	55	—	5	11	85	73	66
Pitprops (Mine timber) . .	—	—	—	20	24	17	20	24	17
Pulpwood	—	—	—	200	318	221	200	318	221
Other industrial wood . .	19*	19*	19*	167*	173*	177*	186*	192*	196*
Fuel wood	558*	575*	575*	687*	710*	733*	1,245*	1,285*	1,308*
TOTAL . . .	662	662	649	1,074	1,230	1,159	1,736	1,892	1,808

* FAO estimate.

Source: FAO, *Yearbook of Forest Products.*

FISHING
('ooo metric tons, live weight)

	1975	1976	1977	1978	1979	1980
Jack and horse mackerels . .	24.2	18.6	44.4	57.7	24.2	20.1
European pilchard (sardine) .	167.4	225.1	129.6	148.4	199.6	211.9
European anchovy . . .	1.8	5.7	10.4	9.0	11.3	9.5
Chub (Spanish) mackerel . .	12.3	16.1	40.3	46.1	14.8	24.2
TOTAL CATCH (incl. others) .	223.9	281.4	255.5	287.1	279.9	297.7

Aquatic plants ('ooo metric tons): 5.1 in 1975.

Source: FAO, *Yearbook of Fishery Statistics.*

MINING

('ooo metric tons)

	1976	1977	1978	1979	1980†
Coal	702	707	720	710	680
Crude petroleum . .	8.1	22.0	24.3	18.6	13.8
Iron ore* . . .	342.8	407.4	62.9	61.7	78.0
Antimony ore* . .	3.7	3.4	5.3	2.0	1.3
Cobalt ore* . .	7.2	7.8	8.7	8.0	6.7
Copper concentrates* .	16.4	12.1	12.2	23.5	24.1
Lead concentrates* .	98.7	155.7	165.9	165.3	172.1
Manganese ore* . .	117.3	113.5	126.2	135.7	132.1
Zinc concentrates* .	29.6	22.2	10.5	12.9	13.1
Phosphate rock . .	15,656.2	17,572.3	20,156.1	20,030.8	18,824.2
Fluorspar . . .	51.4	40.0	59.2	63.2	64.4
Barytes . . .	139.1	149.9	174.4	286.5	318.1
Pyrrhotite . . .	76.2	150.0	190.4	197.1	136.1
Salt (unrefined) . .	15	12	17	18	n.a.

* Figures refer to the gross weight of ores and concentrates. The metal content (in 'ooo metric tons) was: Iron 202 in 1976, 240 in 1977, 36 in 1978, 36 in 1979; Antimony 1.7 in 1976, 1.5 in 1977, 2.4 in 1978, 0.9 in 1979; Cobalt 0.8 in 1976, 0.9 in 1977, 1.0 in 1978, 0.9 in 1979; Copper 4.6 in 1976, 3.4 in 1977, 3.4 in 1978, 3.6 in 1979; Lead 68.1 in 1976, 107.4 in 1977, 115.3 in 1978, 114.1 in 1979; Manganese 60.1 in 1976, 58.2 in 1977, 64.7 in 1978, 69.5 in 1979; Zinc 15.4 in 1976, n.a. in 1977, 5.4 in 1978, 6.7 in 1979.
† Preliminary figures.

Natural gas (million cubic metres): 79.1 in 1976; 86.2 in 1977; 84.5 in 1978; 75.0 in 1979 (preliminary figure).

Source: Banque du Maroc, *Annual Report* 1980, quoting Ministry of Energy and Mines.

INDUSTRY
SELECTED PRODUCTS*

		1975	1976	1977	1978	1979
Cement	'ooo metric tons	2,028	2,140	2,604	2,819	3,317
Refined sugar . .	,, ,, ,,	466	445	n.a.	n.a.	n.a.
Textiles . . .	metric tons	45,644	50,393	n.a.	n.a.	n.a.
Electricity . . .	million kWh.	3,042	3,329	3,679	3,940	4,372
Cars† . . .	number	24,969	25,154	n.a.	n.a.	n.a.
Tyres . . .	,,	286,000	379,000	n.a.	n.a.	n.a.
Shoes . . .	'ooo pairs	17,173	15,209	n.a.	n.a.	n.a.
Phosphate fertilizers‡ .	'ooo metric tons	113.2	110.0	184.8	242.0	157.4
Carpets . . .	number	311,192	393,967	n.a.	1,827§	2,036§
Wine . . .	'ooo hl.	1,000	770	810	1,137	1,069
Olive oil . . .	metric tons	44,000	41,000	32,000	24,000	55,000
Beer . . .	'ooo hl.	254	316	n.a.	n.a.	n.a.
Cigarettes . . .	million	9,339	9,043	10,620	11,266	11,820
Sulphuric acid . .	'ooo metric tons	284	357	n.a.	n.a.	n.a.
Motor spirit (petrol) .	,, ,, ,,	366	356	380	391	400
Kerosene . . .	,, ,, ,,	77	94	54	96	90
Distillate fuel oils .	,, ,, ,,	654	734	659	682	700
Residual fuel oil . .	,, ,, ,,	1,035	1,153	1,180	1,266	1,300
Jet fuel . . .	,, ,, ,,	155	171	154	150	155
Petroleum bitumen (asphalt)	,, ,, ,,	72	83	85	90	95

* Major industrial establishments only.   † Assembly only.
‡ In terms of phosphoric acid.   § Amounts in 'ooo sq metres.

FINANCE

100 Moroccan francs (centimes) = 1 Moroccan dirham.
Coins: 1, 2, 5, 10, 20 and 50 francs; 1 and 5 dirhams.
Notes: 5, 10, 50 and 100 dirhams.

Exchange rates (May 1982): £1 sterling = 10.562 dirhams; U.S. $1 = 5.745 dirhams.
100 Moroccan dirhams = £9.47 = $17.41.

Note: The dirham was introduced in October 1959, replacing the Moroccan franc (at par with the old French franc until December 1958) at the rate of 1 dirham = 100 francs. At the same time the currency was devalued by 17.0 per cent, with the former exchange rate (U.S. $1 = 420 Moroccan francs) being replaced by a new rate based on a relationship with French currency, initially fixed at 1 French franc = 1.025 Moroccan francs (1 French franc = 1.025 dirhams after the introduction of the new French franc in January 1960). In terms of U.S. currency, the rate was $1 = 5.0605 dirhams (1 dirham = 19.761 U.S. cents), which remained in operation until August 1971, while the relationship to French currency became 1 French franc = 91.111 Moroccan francs after August 1969. From December 1971 to February 1973 the official exchange rate was $1 = 4.661 dirhams (1 dirham = 21.455 U.S. cents). A new par value of $1 = 4.195 dirhams (1 dirham = 23.84 U.S. cents) was established in February 1973 but in March 1973 the French authorities ceased to maintain the franc-dollar rate within previously agreed margins. Morocco maintained a link with the French franc, although the fixed relationship was ended in May 1973. As a result of these changes, the market exchange rate since March 1973 has fluctuated widely above and below the par value, although the latter continued to be the basis for calculating the value of foreign trade transactions until the end of 1974. In June 1978 it was announced that the dirham would be treated as being at par with the French franc for remittances from Moroccan workers in France. The average market rates (dirhams per U.S. dollar) were: 4.5959 in 1972; 4.1069 in 1973; 4.3698 in 1974; 4.0525 in 1975; 4.4193 in 1976; 4.5034 in 1977; 4.1667 in 1978; 3.8991 in 1979; 3.9367 in 1980; 5.1723 in 1981. In terms of sterling, the exchange rate between November 1967 and June 1972 was £1 = 12.145 dirhams.

BUDGET
(estimates, million dirhams)

REVENUE	1980	1981	EXPENDITURE	1980	1981
Direct taxes	4,403	4,769	Current expenditure	15,135	18,177
Customs duties	2,960	4,049	*of which:*		
Indirect taxes	5,243	6,157	Education	3,529	3,976
Registration fees and stamp duties	1,259	1,555	Defence	2,617	3,014
Government property	60	50	Interior	1,625	1,766
State monopolies	895	1,362	Health	630	701
Other income	311	439	Agriculture	601	680
Income carried in from adjusted expenditure	135	153	Debt servicing	2,500	2,821
Gross borrowings	6,350	7,068	Other	3,633	5,219
Transfers from other public sectors	—	46	Capital expenditure	8,428	9,997
Nominal receipts	50	50			
TOTAL	21,666	25,698	TOTAL	23,563	28,174

Source: Ministère des Finances, Rabat.

1982: Budget estimates (million dirhams): Revenue 39,900; Expenditure 46,765.

MONEY SUPPLY
(million dirhams at December 31st)

	1978	1979	1980
Currency outside banks	7,676	9,020	9,807
Private sector deposits at Bank of Morocco	265	262	324
Demand deposits at deposit money banks	10,873	11,897	13,149
Demand deposits at Post Office	912	1,118	1,169
Private sector demand deposits at Treasury	1,182	1,211	1,042
TOTAL MONEY	20,908	23,508	25,491

CENTRAL BANK RESERVES
(U.S. $ million at December 31st)

	1978	1979	1980
Gold	31	33	29
IMF Special Drawing Rights	16	20	1
Foreign exchange	602	537	398
TOTAL	649	590	428

Source: IMF, *International Financial Statistics.*

Statistical Survey

BALANCE OF PAYMENTS
(U.S.$ million)

	1975	1976	1977	1978	1979	1980
Merchandise exports f.o.b. . . .	1,530	1,247	1,284	1,487	1,937	2,414
Merchandise imports f.o.b. . . .	−2,266	−2,308	−2,821	−2,630	−3,244	−3,771
TRADE BALANCE	−736	−1,061	−1,537	−1,143	−1,307	−1,357
Exports of services	497	471	586	675	775	855
Imports of services	−804	−1,315	−1,465	−1,634	−1,924	−2,036
BALANCE ON GOODS AND SERVICES	−1,043	−1,905	−2,417	−2,099	−2,456	−2,538
Private unrequited transfers (net) .	482	499	545	702	891	1,003
Government unrequited transfers (net) .	33	6	14	58	44	115
CURRENT BALANCE . . .	−528	−1,400	−1,858	−1,339	−1,521	−1,420
Direct capital investment (net) . .	−1	38	57	48	39	90
Other long-term capital (net) . .	385	1,260	1,679	1,362	1,348	1,294
Short-term capital (net) . . .	159	76	146	−44	221	−331
Net errors and omissions . . .	−44	9	−40	−97	−199	77
TOTAL (net monetary movements) .	−29	−17	−16	−70	−112	−290

Source: IMF, *International Financial Statistics.*

EXTERNAL TRADE
(million dirhams)

	1974	1975	1976	1977	1978	1979	1980
Imports c.i.f. . .	8,292	10,394	11,555	14,401	12,361	14,328	16,793
Exports f.o.b. . .	7,440	6,238	5,579	5,860	6,261	7,622	9,645

PRINCIPAL COMMODITIES
(million dirhams)

IMPORTS	1978	1979	1980	EXPORTS	1978	1979	1980
Food, drink and tobacco	2,005	2,143	2,833	Food, drink and tobacco	2,022	2,283	2,599
Wheat . . .	856	973	1,255	Citrus fruit . .	810	859	1,160
Sugar . . .	305	269	627	Fresh tomatoes .			
Tea . . .	156	190	153	Potatoes . .	215	384	392
Dairy products . .	156	200	252	Fresh vegetables .			
Energy and lubricants .	1,782	2,769	3,961	Canned fruit and vege-			
Crude petroleum .	1,254	2,437	3,578	tables . . .	234	270	265
Animal and vegetable				Wine . . .	28	36	40
products . . .	1,022	1,332	1,397	Preserved fish . .	225	300	342
Crude vegetable oils .	360	531	481	Energy and lubricants .	88	176	467
Timber . . .	254	307	434	Animal and vegetable			
Minerals . . .	155	335	574	raw materials . .	203	218	399
Semi-finished products .	2,814	3,287	3,542	Olive oil . . .	0.5	0.8	106
Iron and steel goods .	696	880	911	Cotton . . .	55	1.6	34
Chemical products .	358	444	552	Pulp for paper . .	52	90	122
Fertilizers . .	83	198	232	Minerals . . .	2,449	2,542	3,711
Plastics . . .	192	265	316	Phosphates . .	2,034	2,213	3,012
Paper and cardboard .	125	191	228	Lead ore . . .	173	282	281
Synthetic textile fibres .	153	205	228	Cobalt . . .	54	119	138
Agricultural equipment .	128	161	119	Manganese ore . .	60	62	59
Industrial equipment .	3,259	3,130	3,052	Semi-finished products .	623	972	1,354
Consumer goods .	1,197	1,170	1,315	Phosphoric acid .	269	504	793
Passenger cars and				Fertilizers . .	134	120	153
spares . .	286	261	308	Refined lead . .	58	137	120
Pharmaceuticals .	113	131	153	Agricultural and indus-			
				trial equipment .	33	27	28
				Consumer goods .	843	997	1,087
				Carpets . .	247	283	286
				Clothing . .	196	261	296
				Hosiery . .	59	101	113
TOTAL .	12,361	14,328	16,793	TOTAL .	6,261	7,622	9,645

Source: Banque du Maroc, *Annual Report,* quoting Office des Changes and Ministère des Finances, Rabat.

PRINCIPAL TRADING PARTNERS
(million dirhams)

IMPORTS	1978	1979	1980*
Belgium/Luxembourg .	271	380	354
France . . .	3,227	3,965	4,168
Germany, Fed. Republic	849	887	982
Iraq . . .	n.a.	1,326	n.a.
Italy . . .	821	844	958
Japan . . .	277	239	221
Netherlands . .	417	373	402
Poland . . .	113	148	209
Saudi Arabia . .	n.a.	515	n.a.
Spain . . .	1,273	1,343	1,388
U.S.S.R. . .	332	393	599
United Kingdom .	414	409	496
U.S.A. . .	1,038	827	1,089

EXPORTS	1978	1979	1980*
Belgium/Luxembourg .	295	357	468
France . . .	1,661	2,086	2,428
Germany, Fed. Republic	667	806	788
Italy . . .	374	394	542
Japan . . .	109	120	141
Netherlands . .	275	426	570
Poland . . .	150	181	191
Spain . . .	415	474	565
U.S.S.R. . .	264	276	486
United Kingdom .	250	291	399
U.S.A. . .	178	179	131

* Provisional.

Source: Banque du Maroc, *Annual Report*, 1980, quoting Office des Changes.

TRANSPORT

RAILWAYS

	1977	1979*	1980
Passenger-kilometres (million)	835	803	946
Freight ton-kilometres (million)	3,474	3,854	3,760

* 1978 figures not available.

ROAD TRAFFIC
(motor vehicles in use)

	1978	1979
Cars . .	403,631	413,736
Buses and coaches .	6,420	6,947
Lorries and vans .	157,322	157,471
Motor cycles .	12,638	12,763

SHIPPING*

		1976	1979
Passenger arrivals .	number	392,845	445,992
Passenger departures .	„	451,997	381,295
Freight loaded .	'ooo tons	17,340	21,931
Freight unloaded .	„ „	7,902	11,303

* 1977–78 figures not available.

CIVIL AVIATION

	1979
Passenger arrivals .	1,340,011
Passenger departures .	1,413,135
Freight loaded and unloaded (metric tons)	27,202

TOURISM

COUNTRY OF ORIGIN	1976	1977	1978	1979	1980
Algeria	1,234	n.a.	n.a.	n.a.	n.a.
Belgium	25,080	27,531	30,581	34,597	28,263
Canada	18,424	20,119	30,697	18,146	11,417
France	225,413	284,029	315,962	323,057	340,380
Germany, Federal Republic	95,125	98,392	109,721	100,393	118,359
Italy	25,774	29,765	28,536	32,018	34,155
Netherlands	24,119	30,223	24,717	28,114	29,046
Scandinavia	57,926	56,933	49,430	63,720	60,162
Spain	115,714	141,665	142,678	134,879	122,912
Switzerland	18,699	22,715	22,023	24,383	22,103
United Kingdom	96,634	104,848	111,867	108,336	131,937
U.S.A.	97,071	108,542	110,984	84,732	62,179
Moroccans living abroad	204,974	364,670	364,485	357,318	327,492
Cruise visitors (short-term)	110,757	74,423	68,667	113,458	92,495
TOTAL (incl. others)	1,218,473	1,501,890	1,545,760	1,549,454	1,517,228

Source: Banque du Maroc, *Annual Report*, quoting Ministère d'Etat chargé du tourisme.

1981: Total 1,567,000.

EDUCATION

	1977/78	1978/79	1979/80	1980/81	1981/82
Primary school pupils	1,793,772	1,925,187	2,051,862	2,106,102	2,331,000
Secondary school pupils	582,197	650,796	726,595	754,542	826,500
University students	53,200	62,117	74,465	86,844	98,513
Student teachers	15,898	20,167	17,769	14,466	16,148
Students abroad	13,228	16,062	23,100	n.a.	n.a.

Source: Ministère de l'Education Nationale, Rabat.

Source (unless otherwise stated): Secrétariat d'Etat au Plan et au Développement Régional, Direction de la Statistique, Rabat.

THE CONSTITUTION

(Promulgated March 10th, 1972, after having been approved by national referendum.)*

Preamble: The Kingdom of Morocco, a sovereign Muslim State, shall be a part of the Great Maghreb. As an African State one of its aims shall be the realization of African unity. It will adhere to the principles, rights and obligations of those international organizations of which it is a member and will work for the preservation of peace and security in the world.

General Principles: Morocco shall be a constitutional, democratic and social monarchy. Sovereignty shall pertain to the nation and be exercised directly by means of the referendum and indirectly by the constitutional institutions. All Moroccans shall be equal before the law, and all adults shall enjoy equal political rights including the franchise. Freedoms of movement, opinion and speech and the right of assembly shall be guaranteed. Islam shall be the state religion.

The Monarchy: The Crown of Morocco and its attendant constitutional rights shall be hereditary in the line of H.M. King Hassan II, and shall be transmitted to the oldest son, unless during his lifetime the King has appointed as his successor another of his sons. The King is the symbol of unity, guarantees the continuity of the state, and safeguards respect for Islam and the Constitution. The King shall have the power to appoint and dismiss the Prime Minister and Cabinet Ministers and shall preside over the Cabinet. He shall promulgate legislation passed by the Chamber of Representatives and have the power to dissolve the Chamber; is empowered to declare a state of emergency and to initiate revisions to the Constitution. The Sovereign is the Commander-in-Chief of the Armed Forces; makes appointments to civil and military posts; appoints Ambassadors; signs and ratifies treaties; presides over the Council for National Development Planning and the Supreme Judiciary Council; and exercises the right of pardon.

Legislature: This shall consist of a single assembly, the Chamber of Representatives, whose members are to be elected for a six-year term. Two-thirds of the members shall be elected by direct universal suffrage, and one-third by an electoral college composed of councillors in local government and employers' and employees' representatives. The Chamber shall pass legislation, which may be initiated by its members or by the Prime Minister; authorize any declaration of war; and approve any extension beyond thirty days of a state of emergency.

Government: The Government shall be responsible to the King and the Chamber of Representatives and shall ensure the execution of laws. The Prime Minister shall be empowered to initiate legislation and to exercise statutory powers except where these are reserved to the King. He shall put before the Chamber the Government's intended programme and shall be responsible for co-ordinating ministerial work.

Relations between the Authorities: The King may request further consideration of legislation by the Chamber of Representatives before giving his assent; submit proposed legislation to a referendum by decree; and dissolve the Chamber if a Bill rejected by it is approved by referendum. He may also dissolve the Chamber by decree, but the succeeding Chamber may not be dissolved within a year of its election. The Chamber of Representatives may defeat the Government either by refusing a vote of confidence moved by the Prime Minister or by passing a censure motion; either eventuality shall involve the Government's collective resignation.

Judiciary: The Judiciary shall be independent. Judges shall be appointed on the recommendation of the Supreme Council of the Judiciary presided over by the King.

* For the most part the Constitution is unchanged from the one drawn up by King Hassan II and promulgated in 1962. This provided for two houses of parliament, one elected by universal suffrage and one by electoral colleges, and was superseded by that of July 1970, which introduced a unicameral Chamber of Representatives, of which two-thirds of the members were to be elected by universal suffrage, and increased the powers of the monarch. In May 1980 a national referendum approved a constitutional amendment allowing the duration of the Chamber's term to be extended from four to six years.

THE GOVERNMENT

HEAD OF STATE

H.M. King Hassan II (acceded March 3rd, 1961).

CABINET

(May 1982)

Prime Minister: Maati Bouabid.

Minister of State for Foreign Affairs: M'Hamed Boucetta.

Minister of State for Co-operation: Mahjoubi Aherdan.

Ministers of State without Portfolio: M'Hamed Bahnini, Moulay Ahmed Alaoui.

Minister of Posts and Telecommunications: Mohamed El-Ansar.

Minister of Culture: Said Belbachir.

Minister of State for the Interior: Driss Basri.

Minister of Equipment: Mohamed Kabbaj.

Minister of Finance: Abdellatif Jouhari.

Minister of Agriculture: Othman Demnati.

Minister of Information, Youth and Sports: Abdelouahed Belkaziz.

Minister of Religious Endowments (Waqfs) and Islamic Affairs: Hachemi Filali.

Minister of Planning and Vocational Training: M'Hamed Douiri.

Minister for Relations with Parliament: Ahmed Belhaj.

Minister of National Education: Dr. Azzedine Laraki.

Minister of Housing, Development and Environment: Lamfaddel Lahlou.

Minister of Handicrafts and Social Affairs: Abbes al-Fasi.

Minister of Transport: Mansouri ben Ali.

Minister of Trade, Industry and Tourism: Azzedine Gussous.

Minister of Maritime Fishing: Bensalem Smili.

Minister of Health: Dr. Rahal Rahhali.

Minister of Energy: Moussa Saadi.

Minister of Justice: Mustapha Benlarbi Alaoui.

Minister of Labour and National Revival: Arsalane el-Jadidi.

Minister to Prime Minister's Office: Abdelkrim Ghallab.

Minister Delegate, attached to Prime Minister, in charge of Economic Affairs: Taieb Bencheikh.

Secretary-General of Government: Abbes el Kaisi.

There are also five Secretaries of State.

LEGISLATURE

MAJLIS AL-NUWAB

Elections for the Chamber of Representatives, provided for under the 1972 Constitution, took place for the first time in June 1977. Two-thirds of the Chamber's members are elected by universal suffrage and one-third by an electoral college comprising representatives of commune and municipal councils, professional bodies and employees.

President: Dey Ould Sidi Baba.

1977 Elections (direct voting on June 3rd; electoral college voting on June 21st).

	Votes in Direct Election	Seats by Direct Election	Seats by Indirect Election	Total Seats
Independents* . . .	2,254,297	81	60	141
Istiqlal . . .	1,090,960	45	4	49
Mouvement Populaire . .	625,786	29	15	44
USFP	738,541	16	—	16
MPCD	102,358	2	1	3
Parti de l'Action . .	90,840	2	—	2
PPS	116,470	1	—	1
Others	26,111	—	8†	8†
Total . . .	5,045,363	176	88	264

* Candidates of a pro-Government, monarchist tendency.
† Includes six members of the Union marocaine du travail (UMT), one member of the Union générale des travailleurs marocains (UGMT) and one non-party member.

Note: Elections were held on May 29th, 1981, for two additional members of the Chamber, representing the province of Oued Eddahab, the former Mauritanian-held part of Western Sahara.

POLITICAL PARTIES

Istiqlal: f. 1944; aims to raise living standards, to confer equal rights on all, stresses the Moroccan claim to the Western Sahara; Sec.-Gen. M'Hamed Boucetta; publs. *Al Alam* (daily), and *L'Opinion* (daily).

Mouvement Populaire—MP: f. 1959; conservative; Leader Mahjoubi Aherdan.

Mouvement Populaire Constitutionnel et Démocratique—MPCD: breakaway party from *Mouvement Populaire*; Leader Abdelkrim Khatib.

Parti de l'Action: Rabat; f. 1974; advocates democracy and progress; Sec.-Gen. Abdallah Senhaji.

Parti Démocratique Constitutionnel: Leader (vacant).

Parti des Indépendants démocrates: f. 1981 from split within RNI; Leader Abdelhamid Kacemi.

Parti Libéral Progressiste—PLP: Casablanca; f. 1974; advocates individual freedom and free enterprise; Leader Aknoush Ahmadou Belhaj.

Parti du Progrès et du Socialisme—PPS: B.P. 152, Casablanca; f. 1974; successor to the Parti Communiste Marocain banned in 1952, and the Parti de la Libération et du Socialisme banned in 1969; left-wing; advocates nationalization and democracy; Sec.-Gen. Ali Yata; publ. *Al Bayane* (Arabic and French daily).

Rassemblement National des Indépendants—RNI: 20 ave. Prince Moulay Abdallah, Rabat; f. 1978 from the pro-Government independents' group forming the majority in the Chamber of Representatives; Pres. Ahmed Osman.

Union Nationale des Forces Populaires—UNFP: B.P. 747, Casablanca; f. 1959 by Mehdi Ben Barka from a group within Istiqlal; left-wing; opposition party; in July 1972 a split occurred between the Casablanca and Rabat sections of the party; Leader Abdullah Ibrahim.

Union Socialiste des Forces Populaires—USFP: 17 rue Oued Souss, Agdal, Rabat; f. 1959 as UNFP, Rabat section of UNFP became USFP in 1974; left-wing opposition party, 100,000 mems.; First Sec. Abderrahim Bouabid; publs. *Al Mouharir* (Arabic daily), *Libération* (French weekly), both suspended; *Al Machrou* (Arabic, 3 a year).

DIPLOMATIC REPRESENTATION

EMBASSIES ACCREDITED TO MOROCCO
(In Rabat unless otherwise stated)

Algeria: interests served by Embassy of the United Arab Emirates.

Argentina: 12 rue Mekki Bitaouri, Souissi; *Ambassador:* Enrique Quintana.

Australia: Paris, France.

Austria: 2 Zankat Tiddas, B.P. 135; *Ambassador:* Emil Staffelmayr.

Bangladesh: Paris, France.

Belgium: 6 ave. de Marrakech, B.P. 163; *Ambassador:* Luc Smolderen.

Brazil: 1 ave. Marrakech; *Ambassador:* Carlos Jacyntho de Barros.

Bulgaria: 4 ave. de Meknès; *Ambassador:* Stoyan Vladimirov Zaimov.

Burma: Cairo, Egypt.

Cameroon: Paris, France.

Canada: 13 *bis* rue Jaâfar As-Sadik, B.P. 709, Agdal; *Ambassador:* Gilles Duguay.

Central African Republic: 2 rue Oued El Makhazine, B.P. 770, Agdal; *Ambassador:* Claude Bernard Beloum.

Chile: 141 route des Zaërs; *Ambassador:* Carlos Valenzuela Montenegro.

China, People's Republic: 1 Zankat Ibn Al Abbar; *Ambassador:* Mi Yong.

Colombia: Lisbon, Portugal.

Costa Rica: Madrid, Spain.

Cuba: interests served by Embassy of Bulgaria.

Cyprus: Bonn, Federal Republic of Germany.

Czechoslovakia: Villa Merzaâ, Km. 4,500-Souissi, Zankat Zerhoune; *Ambassador:* JAN JUDA.

Denmark: 4 rue de Khémisset, B.P. 203; *Ambassador:* KARL-FREDERIK HASLE.

Dominican Republic: Madrid, Spain.

Egypt: interests served by Embassy of Senegal.

Equatorial Guinea: 30 ave. des Nations Unies, Agdal; *Ambassador:* SISIMIO MBANA NSORO.

Finland: Madrid, Spain.

France: 6 ave. Mohamed V; *Ambassador:* JACQUES MORIZET.

Gabon: 56 ave. de France, B.P. 1239, Agdal; *Ambassador:* BRUNO MÉTHODE NGOKAMA AWASSI.

Gambia: Dakar, Senegal.

German Democratic Republic: route des Zaërs, Km. 5.6, B.P. 463; *Ambassador:* ELEONORA SCHMID.

Germany, Federal Republic: 7 Zankat Madina, B.P. 235; *Ambassador:* Dr. WALTER JESSER.

Greece: 23 rue d'Oujda; *Ambassador:* EFTHYMIOS TZAFERIS.

Guinea: 12 Zankat ibn Molka, Orangers; *Ambassador:* Dr. KEKOURA CAMARA.

Hungary: 12 rue d'Agadir; *Ambassador:* SÁNDOR PAMUK.

India: 13 charia Michlifen, Agdal; *Ambassador:* ONKAR NATH SHEOPURI.

Indonesia: Tunis, Tunisia.

Iraq: 39 rue Béni Snassen, Souissi; *Ambassador:* IHSSANE ALI HOUCINE AL-KASSAB.

Ireland: Paris, France.

Italy: 2 Zankat Idriss El Azhar, B.P. 111; *Ambassador:* ALBERTO RAMASSO VALACCA.

Ivory Coast: 21 rue de Tedders, B.P. 192; *Ambassador:* KOUASSI EMMANUEL ALEXANDRE NOUAMA.

Japan: 70 blvd. des Nations Unies, Agdal; *Ambassador:* SONO UCHUIDA.

Jordan: 21 ave. de France, Agdal; *Ambassador:* MOHIEDDINE AL-HUSSEINI.

Kenya: Cairo, Egypt.

Korea, Republic: 19 ave. de Meknès; *Ambassador:* WOO YOUNG CHUNG.

Kuwait: 44 ave. Pasteur, Orangers; *Ambassador:* ABDALLAH AHMED HOSSEIN AL ROUMI.

Lebanon: 19 ave. de Fès; *Ambassador:* Dr. ADEL ISMAIL.

Libya: 1 rue Chouaïb Doukkali; *Chargé d'affaires a.i.:* ALI TAHER AL-MARMOURI.

Malaysia: Paris, France.

Mali: Dakar, Senegal.

Mauritania: 6 rue Thami Lamdouar, Souissi; *Ambassador:* (vacant).

Nepal: Cairo, Egypt.

Netherlands: 40 rue de Tunis, B.P. 329; *Ambassador:* Baron W. H. COLLOT D'ESCURY.

Niger: Dakar, Senegal.

Nigeria: 70 ave. Omar Ibn Al Khattab, B.P. 347, Agdal; *Ambassador:* Alhaji UMAR FAROUK KA'OJE.

Norway: 20 charia As-Saouira, B.P. 551; *Ambassador:* OLAV LYDVO.

Oman: 21 rue Hamza, Agdal; *Ambassador:* (vacant).

Pakistan: 20 ave. d'Alger; *Ambassador:* Dr. ALI MASOOD AKRAM.

Paraguay: Madrid, Spain.

Peru: Cairo, Egypt.

Philippines: 6 ave. Pasteur; *Chargé d'affaires:* HERMENEGLIDO B. GARCIA.

Poland: 23 Zankat Oqbah, Agdal, B.P. 425; *Ambassador:* CZESŁAW CIAPA.

Portugal: 45 rue Al Mansour Ad-Dahbi, B.P. 36; *Ambassador:* FERNANDO DELFIM MARIA LOPES VIEIRA.

Qatar: 4 charia Tarik Ibn Ziad; *Ambassador:* ABDALLAH YOUSSEF AL JIDA.

Romania: 10 rue d'Ouezzane; *Ambassador:* Dr. OVIDIU CORNELIU POPESCU.

Rwanda: Cairo, Egypt.

Saudi Arabia: 43 place de l'Unité Africaine; *Ambassador:* MAJED ALI KABBANI.

Senegal: 17 rue Cadi Ben Hamadi Senhaji, Souissi; *Ambassador:* ALY DIOUM.

Somalia: Paris, France.

Spain: 3 Zankat Madnine; *Ambassador:* ALFONSO DE LA SERNA.

Sudan: 29 Zankat Hamza, Agdal; *Ambassador:* ABBES MOUSSA MUSTAPHA.

Sweden: 157 ave. John Kennedy; *Ambassador:* KNUT JOHN RICHARD BERNSTROM.

Switzerland: Square de Berkane, B.P. 169; *Ambassador:* MAX CASANOVA.

Syria: 25 rue d'Oqbah, Agdal; *Ambassador:* AHMED AÏSSA.

Tunisia: 6 ave. de Fès; *Ambassador:* SALADDIN ABDULLAH.

Turkey: 19 ave. Tarik Ibn Ziad; *Ambassador:* NECDEK ILCI.

U.S.S.R.: Km. 4, route des Zaërs; *Ambassador:* YEVGENIY NERSESOV.

United Arab Emirates: 11 ave. des Alaouines; *Ambassador:* MOHAMED FAHD AL-DUHAIM.

United Kingdom: 17 blvd. de la Tour Hassan, B.P. 45; *Ambassador:* JOHN CAMBRIDGE.

U.S.A.: 2 Charia Marrakech, B.P. 120; *Ambassador:* JOSEPH VERNER REED, Jr.

Upper Volta: Paris, France.

Venezuela: Tunis, Tunisia.

Yemen Arab Republic: 113 ave. Houmane El Fetwaki, Mabella; *Ambassador:* GJHALIB ALI GAMIL.

Yugoslavia: 23 ave. Bani Iznassen, Souissi, B.P. 5014; *Ambassador:* SONJA ORESCANIN.

Zaire: 34 ave. de la Victoire, B.P. 537, Rabat-Chellah; *Ambassador:* KALENGA WA BELABELA.

Zambia: Cairo, Egypt.

Morocco also has diplomatic relations with Afghanistan, Albania, the Bahamas, Chad, Djibouti, Guatemala, Guinea-Bissau, Jamaica, Malta, Mauritius, Mexico, Monaco, Mongolia, Panama, Sierra Leone, Sri Lanka, Uganda, Uruguay and the Vatican City.

JUDICIAL SYSTEM

The **Supreme Court** (*Majlis el Aala*) is responsible for the interpretation of the law and regulates the jurisprudence of the courts and tribunals of the Kingdom. The Supreme Court sits at Rabat and is divided into five Chambers.

First President: MOHAMED LARBI MAJBOUB.

Attorney-General: AHMED ZEGHARI.

The nine **Courts of Appeal** hear appeals from lower courts and also comprise a criminal division.

The **Sadad Tribunals** pass judgment, without possibility of appeal, in personal, civil and commercial cases involving up to 300 dirhams. These tribunals also pass judgment, subject to appeal before the Regional Tribunals, in the same cases up to 900 dirhams, in disputes related to the personal and successional statutes of Moroccan Muslims and Jews, and in penal cases involving misdemeanours or infringements of the law.

The **Regional Tribunals** deal with appeals against judgments made by the Sadad Tribunals; and pass judgment in the first and last resort in cases of personal property of 900 to 1,200 dirhams or property producing a yield of up to 80 dirhams. The Regional Tribunals also pass judgment, subject to appeal before the Court of Appeal, in actions brought against public administrations in administrative affairs, and in cases of minor offences in penal matters.

Labour Tribunals settle, by means of conciliation, disputes arising from rental contracts or services between employers and employees engaged in private industry. There are 14 labour tribunals in the Kingdom.

A special court was created in 1965 in Rabat to deal with corruption among public officials.

RELIGION

ISLAM

Most Moroccans are Muslims and Islam is the state religion.

CHRISTIANITY

There are about 70,000 Christians, mostly Roman Catholics.

Archbishop of Rabat: JEAN MARCEL CHABBERT, 1 rue Abou Inane, B.P. 258, Rabat.

Archbishop of Tangier: CARLOS AMIGO VALLEJO; 55 Sidi Bouabid, B.P. 2116, Tangier.

Evangelical Church: 33 rue d'Azilal, Casablanca; f. 1920; established in 9 towns; Pastor GILBERT SCHMID; publ. *Vie Nouvelle* (monthly).

JUDAISM

There are about 30,000 Jews.

Grand Rabbi of Casablanca: 167 blvd. Ziraoui, Casablanca; CHALOM MESSAS, President of the Rabbinical Court of Casablanca, Palais de Justice, Place des Nations Unies.

THE PRESS

DAILIES

Casablanca

Al Bayane: 32 rue Ledru-Rollin, B.P. 152, Casablanca; Arabic and French; organ of PPS; Dir. ALI YATA.

Maroc Soir: 34 rue Mohammed Smiha; f. Nov. 1971 to replace *La Vigie Marocaine*, closed down by the Government; French; Pres. Dir.-Gen. MOULAY AHMED ALAOUI; circ. 35,000.

Le Matin du Sahara: 34 rue Mohammed Smiha; f. Nov. 1971 to replace *Le Petit Marocain*, closed down by the Government; French; Pres. Dir.-Gen. MOULAY AHMED ALAOUI; circ. 50,000.

Al Mouharir: 11 rue Soldat Roch; Arabic; organ of USFP; suspended; Editor MUSTAPHA KARCHAOUI; circ. 17,000.

Rabat

Al Alam (*The Flag*): 11 ave. Allal Ben Abdullah; organ of the Istiqlal Party; f. 1946; Arabic; Dir. MOHAMED LARBI MESSARI; Editor ABDELJABBAR SIHIMI; circ. 45,000; literary supplement on Fridays; weekly edition on Mondays.

Al Anba'a (*Information*): Zankat Al Medina, B.P. 65; Arabic; Dir. AHMED AL YAAKOUBI; circ. 15,000.

Al Maghreb: f. 1977; French; organ of RNI; Dir. HASSAN MOUTAHIR; circ. 30,000.

Al Maghreb al Arabi: 16 rue Al Abral, Agdal; Arabic; Dir. AMR ALOIQUOUTI; circ. 10,000.

L'Opinion: 11 ave. Allal Ben Abdullah; f. 1965; Istiqlal party newspaper; French; Dir. MOHAMED IDRISSI KAITOUNI; circ. 35,000.

PERIODICALS

Casablanca

Annidal: 10 rue Cols Bleus, Sidi Bousmara, Médina Kédima; f. 1973; weekly; Dir. IBRAHIMI AHMED.

CAF Omnisports: ave. Jean Mermoz; f. 1955; monthly; French; Dir. LÉON VERRAX.

Cedies Informations: 23 blvd. Mohamed Abdouh; weekly; French; Admin. MOHAMED AMOR.

Construire: 25 rue d'Azilal, Immeuble Ortiba; f. 1946; weekly; French; Dir. BOUCHAIB TALLAL.

Le Courrier Economique: 28 ave. de l'Armée Royale; weekly; French; Dir. BETOUL TAHIRI.

Les Echos Africains: B.P. 140, 27 ave. des F.A.R.; f. 1972; monthly; news, economics; French; Dir. MOHAMED CHOUFFANI EL FASSI; Editor Mme SOODIA FARIDI.

L'Espoir: 167 ave. Hassan; twice monthly; French; Dir. IDRIS CHARAF.

Al-Ittihad ul Watani: 46 rue de la Garon; organ of UNFP; weekly; Arabic; Dir. AHMED SHAKUR.

Lamalif: 27 rue d'Epinal; f. 1966; French; monthly; economic, social and cultural magazine; Dir. MOHAMED LOGHLAM.

Al Mabadie: rue Caporal Paul; monthly; Arabic; Dir. ABDESLAM BOURKIA.

Maroc-Fruits: 22 rue Al Messaoudi; f 1958; 2 a month; Arabic, French; organ of ASPAM; Dir AHMED BEN MANSOUR NEJJAI; circ 6,000.

Al-Oummal: 9 rue Rif; weekly; French and Arabic; organ of the U.G.T.M.; Dir. ABDERRAZAK AFILAL.

La Quinzaine du Maroc: 8 rue Voltaire; twice monthly; French; Dir. GABRIEL GAUTHEY.

Réalités Maghrebines: 69 rue Mohamed Smiha; f. 1965; monthly; French; general economic review; Dir. MOHAMED ELMERGAOUI.

Revue Automobile Africaine: 39 blvd. de la Gironde; monthly; French; Dir. ROBERT PERRIER.

Revue Fiduciaire Marocaine: 81 rue Colbert; twice monthly; French; Dir. MAURICE BERNARD.

Revue Marocaine de Droit: 70 rue Allal ben Abdullah; monthly; Arabic; Dir. MEYLAN BENCHALEL.

Revue Mensuelle de la Chambre de Commerce et d'Industrie de Casablanca: B.P. 423; monthly; French; Dir. ABDELLAH SOUIRI.

Télé Sport: 8 rue Voltaire; weekly; French; Dir. GABRIEL GAUTHEY.

La Tribune Economique: f. 1977; weekly; Editor ABDELHAFID ROUISSI.

La Vie Economique: 5 blvd. Ben Yacine; f. 1921; French; weekly; Dir. MARCEL HERZOG.

La Vie Industrielle et Agricole: 142 blvd. Mohamed V; twice monthly; French; Dir. AHMED ZGHARI.

La Vie Touristique: 142 blvd. Mohamed V; weekly; French; Dir. AHMED ZGHARI.

Vie Nouvelle: 33 rue d'Azilal; f. 1930; monthly; French; journal of the Protestant churches of the Maghreb; Dir. ROGER CHATAIGNÉ.

Rabat

Al Aamak: 291 ave. Mohamed V; monthly; Arabic; Dir. EL WAKILI THAMI.

Achaab (*The People*): 2 rue Parmentier, B.P. 364; independent; twice weekly; Arabic; Founder and Editor M. MEKKI NACIRI; Dir. MUSTAPHA BELHAJ; circ. 25,000.

Achorta: B.P. 437; monthly; Arabic; Dir. Directeur de la Sûreté Nationale.

Al Aklam: B.P. 2229; monthly; Arabic; Dir. ABDERRAHMANE BEN AMAR.

Asdae: 10 rue Port Said; weekly; Arabic; Dir. HASSAN ARABI.

Attadamoun: 23 ave. Allal ben Abdellah; monthly; Arabic; Dir. ABDELMAJID SEMLALI EL HASANI.

Barid el Maghreb: 281 ave. Mohamed V; monthly; Arabic; Dir. MUSTAPHA ALAOUI.

Daouat Elhak: Ministry of Waqfs; f. 1957; monthly; Arabic.

Al Iman: B.P. 356, rue Akenssous; f. 1963; monthly; Arabic; Dir. ELKADIRI BOUBKER.

Al Irchad: Ministry of Waqfs; f. 1967; monthly; Arabic.

Al Khansa: 154 ave. Souss Mohamedia; monthly; Arabic; Dir. ABOUZAL AICHA.

Tangier

Actualités Touristiques: 80 rue de la Liberté; monthly; French; Dir. TAYEB ALAMI.

Le Journal de Tanger: 11 ave. de Rabat, B.P. 2002; f. 1905; French, English, Spanish and Arabic; weekly; Dir. AHMED BENCHEKROUNE; circ. 6,500.

Tanjah: 8 place de France, B.P. 1055; f. 1956; French and Arabic; weekly; Dir. MOHAMMED MEHDI ZAHDI.

NEWS AGENCIES

Wikalat al-Maghreb al Arabi (WMA): 10 rue Al-Yamama, B.P. 1049, Rabat; f. 1959 as *Maghreb Arabe Presse*; Arabic, French and English; government-owned; Man. Dir. ABDULJALIL FENJIRO.

FOREIGN BUREAUX

Agence France-Presse (AFP): 2 bis rue Alkahira, B.P. 118, Rabat; f. 1920; Dir. HUBERT LAVERNE.

Agencia EFE (*Spain*): Cité O.L.M., No. 322, Souissi 2, Rabat; Bureau Chief ANTONIO CASTILLO DE URBERUAGA.

Agenzia Nazionale Stampa Associata (ANSA) (*Italy*): 10 rue Al Yamama, Rabat; Dir. RAFFA HOUCINE.

Reuters (*United Kingdom*): 17 rue de Baghdad, Rabat.

TASS (U.S.S.R.) and Xinhua (People's Republic of China) also have bureaux in Rabat.

PUBLISHERS

Dar El Kitab: place de la Mosquée, B.P. 4018, Casablanca; f. 1948; philosophy, law, novels, educational books; Arabic and French; Dir. BOUTALEB ABDOU ABDELHAY.

Editions La Porte: 281 ave. Mohammed V; Rabat; law, guides, educational books; Man. Dir. PAUL SOUCHON.

Editions Maghrébines: 5–13 rue Soldat Roch, Casablanca; f. 1962; general non-fiction.

Imprimerie Artistique: 31 ave. Es-Sellaoui, Fez.

RADIO AND TELEVISION

Radiodiffusion Télévision Marocaine: 1 Zenkat Al Brihi, B.P. 1042, Rabat; government station; *Radio:* Network 1 in Arabic, Network 2 in French, Network 3 in Berber, Spanish and English; Foreign Service in Arabic, French and English; *Television:* began 1962; 60½ hours weekly; French and Arabic; carries commercial advertising; Dir.-Gen. BENNACER DRISSI QEYTONI; Dir. Television SEDDIK MAANINOU; Dir. Radio MOHAMED BENDEDDOUCH; Dir. Foreign Service AHMED RAYANE; publ. *Al Idaa wa Talvaza al Maghribia.*

Voice of America Radio Station in Tangier: c/o U.S. Consulate General, Chemin des Amoureux, Tangier.

Number of radios (1981): 2,500,000.

Number of televisions (1981): 750,000.

FINANCE

(cap. = capital; p.u. = paid up; dep. = deposits; m. = million; brs. = branches; amounts in dirhams unless otherwise indicated)

BANKING

CENTRAL BANK

Banque du Maroc: P.O.B. 445, 277 ave. Mohammed V, Rabat; f. 1959; Gov. Prince MOULAY HASSAN BEN MEHDI; Vice-Gov. AHMED BENNANI.

Algemene Bank Marokko S.A.: place du 16 Novembre, Casablanca; f. 1948; 50 per cent participation of Algemene Bank Nederland N.V., Amsterdam, Netherlands; cap. 10m.; Pres. M. KASSIDI; Gen. Man. J. M. H. VAN T'HOFF, A. LAHLOU; 8 brs.

Arab Bank Maroc: 174 blvd. Mohammed V, B.P. 810, Casablanca; f. 1975; cap. 10m.; Pres. Hadj OMAR ABDELJALIL; Gen. Man. FAROUK ABDELMAJEED.

Banque Commerciale du Maroc S.A.: 2 blvd. Moulay Youssef, Casablanca; f. 1911; affiliated to Crédit Industriel et Commercial, Paris, France; cap. 32.5m.; Pres. ABDELAZIZ ALAMI; Vice-Pres. R. BELIN; 77 brs.

Banque Marocaine du Commerce Exterieur: 241 boulevard Mohammed V, Casablanca; f. 1959; partly state-owned; cap. 80m.; dep. 4,076m.; res. 75m. (Dec. 1979); Chair. and Chief Exec. Hadj ABDELMAJID BENGELLOUN; Man. Dir. DRISS GUEDDARI; Gen. Man. MOHAMED JOUAHRI; 90 brs.

Banque Marocaine pour l'Afrique et l'Orient: 80 ave. Lalla Yacout, B.P. 880, Casablanca; f. 1975 to take over British Bank of the Middle East (Morocco); cap. 10m.; Pres., Dir.-Gen. NAJEM ABAAKIL; 16 brs.

Banque Marocaine pour le Commerce et l'Industrie: 26 place Mohammed V, Casablanca, P.O.B. 573; f. 1964; cap. 65m.; res. 34m. (Dec. 1980); Pres. Hadj AHMED BARGACH; Gen. Man. MOHAMED BENKIRANE; 57 brs.

Banque Nationale pour le Développement Economique: B.P. 407, place des Alaouites, Rabat; f. 1959; cap. 70m.; Chair. and Gen. Man. ABDELKADER BENSLIMANE.

Compagnie Marocaine de Crédit et de Banque S.A.: 1 ave. Hassan II, Casablanca; f. 1964; cap. 35m.; Pres. ALI KETTANI; 50 brs.

Crédit du Maroc S.A.: B.P. 579, 48–58 blvd. Mohammed V, Casablanca; f. 1963; cap. 51.7m.; res. 33m.; dep. 870m. (Dec. 1980); Pres. M. KARIM-LAMRANI; Dir.-Gen. JAWAD BEN BRAHIM.

Société de Banque et de Crédit: 26 ave. de l'Armée Royale, B.P. 972, Casablanca; f. 1951; affil. to Swiss Bank Corporation and Crédit Commercial de France; cap. 9m.; Pres. IZARAB OUAZZANI; Dir.-Gen. TAYEB RHAFES; 7 brs.

Société Générale Marocaine de Banques: 55 blvd. Abdelmoumen, B.P. 90, Casablanca; f. 1962; cap. 51m.; res. 26.4m. (Dec. 1980); Chair. HAMED BARGACH; Man. Dir. ABDELAZIZ TAZI; 48 brs.

Société Marocaine de Dépôt et Crédit: 79 ave. Hassan II, Casablanca; cap. 18.144m. (Dec. 1980); Pres. ABDELKADER BENSALAH; Gen. Man. OMAR AKALAY.

Unión Bancaria Hispano Marroqui: 69 rue du Prince Moulay Abdullah, Casablanca; f. 1958; cap. 16m.; res. 10.5m. (Dec. 1978); Pres. MOHAMED BEN AHMED BENABUD; Gen. Man. PEDRO LANDRA VELON; 15 brs.

BANK ORGANIZATIONS

Groupement Professionnel des Banques du Maroc: 71 ave. de l'Armée Royale, Casablanca; f. 1967; groups all commercial banks for organization, studies, inquiries of general interest, and contacts with official authorities; 17 mems.; Pres. Hadj ABDELMAJID BENGELLOUN.

Association Professionnelle des Intermédiaires de Bourse: 71 ave. de l'Armée Royale, Casablanca; f. 1967; groups all banks and brokers in the stock exchange of Casablanca, for organization, studies, inquiries of general interest and connection with official authorities; 11 mems.; Pres. Hadj ABDELMAJID BENGELLOUN.

STOCK EXCHANGE

Bourse des Valeurs de Casablanca: Chamber of Commerce Building, 98 blvd. Mohammed V, Casablanca; f. 1929; Dir. ABDERRAZAK LARAQUI; publ. *Bulletin de la Cote.*

INSURANCE
(In Casablanca unless otherwise stated)

Al Amane: 298 blvd. Mohamed V; Dir.-Gen. M. BOUGHALEB.

Al Wataniya: 83 ave. de l'Armée Royale; Dir.-Gen. M. BAUDOIN.

Alliance Africaine: Tour Atlas, place Zallaqa; Pres., Dir.-Gen. M. CHERKAOUI.

Arabia Insurance: 30 rue de Foucauld; Dir.-Gen. Dr. HOURANI.

Atlanta: 49 angle rues Lafuente et Longwy; f. 1947; cap. 4.3m.; Dir. OMAR BENNANI.

Cie. Africaine d'Assurances: 120 ave. Hassan II; Dir.-Gen. M. SEKKAT.

Cie. Atlantique d'Assurances: 11 ave. de l'Armée Royale; f. 1931; cap. 1.6m.; Pres., Dir.-Gen. NAJEM ABAAKIL; Dir. MOHAMED DEFALOUI.

Cie. d'Assurances SANAD: 3 blvd. Mohammed V; Dir.-Gen. ANDRÉ HERNANDEZ.

Cie. Nordafricaine et Intercontinentale d'Assurances (C.N.I.A.): 157 ave. Hassan II; cap. 7m.; Pres. M'FADEL LAHLOU; Dir.-Gen. SAÏD AZMI.

L'Entente: 2 rue Mohammed Smiha; f. 1960; Pres. ABDELKADER BEN SALEH; Dir.-Gen. MOHAMED CHERKAOUI.

Garantie Générale Marocaine: 106 rue Abderrahman Sehraoui; Dir.-Gen. JACQUES GUILLON.

La Marocaine Vie: 392 rue Mustafa el Maani; Dir.-Gen. M. KETTANI.

Mutuelle Centrale Marocaine d'Assurances: B.P. 27, 14 rue Abou Inane, Rabat; Dir.-Gen. YACOUBI SOUSSANE.

Remar: 61 ave. de l'Armée Royale; Dir.-Gen. M. IBANEZ.

La Renaissance: 123 blvd. Rahal El Meskini; Pres., Dir.-Gen. M. ZAHRAOUI.

La Royale Marocaine d'Assurances: 67 ave. de l'Armée Royale; cap. 1.1m.; Pres., Dir.-Gen. M'HAMED BEN JILALI BENNANI.

Es Saada, Cie. Générale d'Assurances et de Réassurances: 123 ave. Hassan II; f. 1961; cap. 5m.; Pres. MEHDI OUAZZANI.

Société Centrale de Réassurance: B.P. 183, Tour Atlas, place Zallaqa; f. 1960; cap. 7m.; Pres. FAROUK BENNIS.

Société Nouvelle d'Assurances: 10 rue Mohamed Diouri; f. 1972; Chair. A. KETTANI; Gen. Man. J. KETTANI.

Fédération Marocaine des Sociétés d'Assurances et de Réassurances: 300 rue Mustafa el Maani, Casablanca; f. 1958; 19 member companies; Pres. MOHAMED CHERKAOUI; Dir. DRISS BEKKAYE.

TRADE AND INDUSTRY

CHAMBERS OF COMMERCE

La Fédération des Chambres de Commerce et d'Industrie du Maroc: B.P. 218, 11 ave. Allal Ben Abdullah, Rabat; f. 1962; groups the 15 Chambers of Commerce and Industry; Pres. ABDELLAH SOUIRA; publ. *Revue Trimestrielle.*

British Chamber of Commerce for Morocco: 291 blvd. Mohammed V, Casablanca; f. 1923; Exec. Sec. Mrs. C. A. LEBRUN.

Chambre de Commerce et d'Industrie de Casablanca: 98 blvd. Mohammed V, B.P. 423, Casablanca; Pres. MOHAMED DRISSI.

Chambre Française de Commerce et d'Industrie du Maroc (CFI): 15 avenue Mers-Sultan, B.P. 73, Casablanca; Pres. PIERRE PARDIGON; Dir. ALAIN ANDRÉ.

DEVELOPMENT ORGANIZATIONS

Bureau de Recherches et de Participations Minières (BRPM): 5–7 Charia Moulay Hassan, B.P. 99, Rabat; f. 1928; a state agency conducting exploration, exploitation and marketing of mineral resources; Gen. Man. MOHAMED CHAHID.

Caisse de Dépôt et de Gestion: place Moulay Hassan, B.P. 408, Rabat; f. 1959; finances small-scale projects; Dir.-Gen. M'FADEL LAHLOU.

Caisse Marocaine des Marchés (*Marketing Fund*): 52 ave. Hassan II, Casablanca; f. 1950; cap. 10m.; dep. 5m.; Pres. Dir.-Gen. ABDELKADER BENSLIMANE; Man. HASSAN KISSI.

Caisse Nationale de Crédit Agricole (*Agricultural Credit Fund*): B.P. 49, Rabat.

Centre Marocain de Promotions et des Exportations: 23 blvd. Giradot, Immeuble Pignal, Casablanca; f. 1980; seeks new export markets.

Crédit Immobilier et Hôtelier: 68 rue de Reims, Casablanca; f. 1920; cap. 160m. dirhams; financing of investments in the building and tourist industries; Pres. Dir.-Gen. OTHMANE SLIMANI.

Office National Interprofessionnel des Céréales et des Légumineuses: 3 ave. Hassan I, B.P. 154, Rabat; f. 1937; Dir. MOHAMED BRICK.

Office de Commercialisation et d'Exportation (OCE): 45 ave. des F.A.R., Casablanca; f. 1932 (nationalized 1965); turnover (1980/81) 3,230m. dirhams; takes part in productivity planning, industrialization, local marketing and overseas trade; deals with exports of foodstuffs and agricultural produce; Dir. ABDALLAH LAHLOU; Sec.-Gen. MOHAMMED GUESSOUS; publ. *Bulletin d'information de l'OCE* (4 a year).

Office pour le Développement Industriel (ODI): 8 rue Ghandi, Rabat; f. 1973; a state agency to develop industry; Man. Dir. MOHAMED BELKHAYAT.

Société de Développement Agricole (SODEA): 12 Zankat Tanja, Rabat; state agricultural development organization.

Société de Gestion des Terres Agricoles (SOGETA): 11 rue de Salé, Rabat; oversees use of agricultural land.

Société Nationale d'Investissement (SNI): 6 rue Omar Slaoui, Casablanca; Pres. M'HAMMED BARGACH; Dir.-Gen. ABDELLAH BELKZIZ.

PRINCIPAL STATE ENTERPRISES

Complexe Textile de Fès (COTEF): B.P. 267, Fez; f. 1967; 99 per cent state participation; started full activity in Jan. 1972; Dir.-Gen. MAHROUCH ABDESLAM.

Office Chérifien des Phosphates (OCP): 305 ave. Mohammed V, Rabat; f. 1921; a state company to produce and market rock phosphates and derivatives; Dir.-Gen. MOHAMMED KARIM LAMRANI.

Office National de l'Eau Potable (ONEP): 6 *bis* rue Patrice Lumumba, Rabat; responsible for drinking-water supply; Dir. HOUCINE TIJANI.

Office National de l'Electricité: B.P. 498, Casablanca; state electricity authority.

Office National des Pêches: 13/15 rue Chevalier Bayard, Casablanca; f. 1969; state fishing organization.

Société d'Exploitation du Fer du Rif (SEFERIF): B.P. 14, Nador; mines began production 1914, nationalized 1967; open and underground mines produce iron ore for export and for the projected Nador iron and steel complex.

Société Nationale de Sidérurgie (SONASID): 110 rue Ameziane Riffi, Nador, B.P. 151; f. 1974; iron and steel projects; cap. 390m.; Dir.-Gen. LARBI MOULINE.

EMPLOYERS' ORGANIZATIONS

Association Marocaine des Industries Textiles: 58 rue Lughérini, Casablanca; f. 1958; mems. 550 textile and ready-made factories; Pres. MOHAMED DRISSI; Sec.-Gen. A. MIKOU.

Association des Producteurs d'Agrumes du Maroc (ASPAM): 22 rue Al Messaoudi, Casablanca 02; f. 1958; links Moroccan citrus and vegetable growers; has its own processing plants; publ. *Maroc-Fruits* (2 a month).

Association Professionnelle des Cimentiers: 239 blvd. Moulay Ismail, B.P. 3096, Casablanca; cement manufacturers.

Association Professionnelle Sucrière: 14 blvd. Zerktouni, Casablanca; sugar manufacturers.

Confédération Générale Economique Marocaine (C.G.E.M.): 23 blvd. Mohammed Abdouh, Casablanca; Pres. MOHAMED AMOR; Sec.-Gen. ABDERRAHMANE OUALI.

Union Marocaine de l'Agriculture (U.M.A.): rue Gandhi, Rabat; Pres. M. NEJJAI.

TRADE UNIONS

Confédération Démocratique du Travail (CDT): Rabat; f. 1978; associated with USFP; Sec.-Gen. MOHAMED NOUBIR AMAWI.

Union Générale des Travailleurs du Maroc (UGTM): 9 rue du Rif, angle Route de Médiouna, Casablanca; f. 1960; associated with Istiqlal; supported by unions not affiliated to UMT; 673,000 mems.; Sec.-Gen. ABDERRAZZAQ AFILAL; publ. *Al Oummal* (weekly).

Union Marocaine du Travail (UMT): Bourse du Travail, 222 avenue de l'Armée Royale, Casablanca; left wing and associated with UNFP; most unions are affiliated; 700,000 mems.; Sec. MAHJOUB BEN SEDDIQ.

Union Syndicale Agricole (USA): agricultural section of UMT.

Union Marocaine du Travail Autonome: Rabat; breakaway union from UMT.

Syndicat National Libre: blvd. Hanasli (prolongé), Casablanca; f. 1958; 69,000 mems., Sec.-Gen. MEEKI IBRAHIMY.

TRADE FAIRS

Foire Internationale de Casablanca: 11 rue Jules Mauran, Casablanca; f. 1950; international trade fair; every two years for 18 days in April-May.

Salon des Textiles et Cuirs: 11 rue Jules Mauran, Casablanca.

TRANSPORT

Office National des Transports: 10 rue Annaba, B.P. Rabat-Chellah.

RAILWAYS

Railways cover over 1,756 km. of which 161 km. are double track; 708 km. of lines are electrified and diesel locomotives are used on the rest. All services are nationalized.

Office National des Chemins de Fer du Maroc (ONCFM): rue Abderrahman Alghafiki, Rabat-Agdal; f. 1963; runs all Morocco's railways; Pres. MANSOURI BENALI; Dir. MOUSSA MOUSSAOUI.

ROADS

In 1980 there were 57,634 km. of roads, of which 44 per cent were paved. There were 58 km. of modern motorway and 11,008 km. of main roads.

Compagnie de Transports au Maroc "Lignes Nationales" (CTM-LN): 303 blvd. Brahim Roudani, Casablanca; agencies in Tangier, Rabat, Meknes, Oujda, Marrakesh, Agadir, El Jadida, Safi, Essouira, Ksar-Es-Souk, Fez and Ouarzazate.

SHIPPING

The chief ports of Morocco are Casablanca, Safi, Mohammedia, Tangier, Kenitra and Agadir. In January 1962 the port of Tangier became an International Free Zone. Tangier is the principal port for passenger services. Casablanca is the principal freight port, handling 70 per cent of Morocco's trade. New ports have recently been completed at Nador and Jorf Lasfar.

Agence Gibmar S.A.: 3 rue Henri Regnault, Tangier; also at Casablanca; regular sea services from Tangier to Gibraltar.

Atlas S.A., Société Marocaine de Navigation: 81 ave. Houmane Elfatouaki, Casablanca; Pres. H. CHAMBI.

Compagnie Chérifienne d'Armement: 5 ave. de l'Armée Royale, Casablanca; f. 1929; Pres. BENNANI SMIRES; regular lines to North France and Europe.

Compagnie Marocaine d'Agences Maritimes (COMARINE): 65 ave. de l'Armée Royale, B.P. 60, Casablanca; f. 1969; Dir.-Gen. ABDELKRIM MOUTAOUKIL.

Compagnie Marocaine de Navigation (COMANAV): 7 blvd. de la Résistance, B.P. 628, Casablanca; f. 1946; Pres. Dir.-Gen. A. BOUAYAD; regular lines to Mediterranean, North-west European, Middle Eastern and West African ports; tramping.

Limadet-ferry: 3 rue Henri Regnault, Tangier; f. 1966; operates between Algeciras and Tangier; Dir.-Gen. AZIZ BOUZOUBAA.

Messageries Marocaines: B.P. 69, 65 ave. de l'Armée Royale, Casablanca; Dir.-Gen. ABDELKRIM MOUTAOUKIL.

Société Marocaine de Navigation Fruitière: 27 ave. de l'Armée Royale, Casablanca; Pres. M. SAGUENI; Gen. Man. HAMID KHAMMAL.

Société de Navigation Maghrebine: B.P. 746, 15 rue de Foucauld, Casablanca; f. 1974; oil and chemicals; Dir. Gen. ABDELWAHAB BENKIRANE.

Transmediterranea S.A. (Intercona): 31 rue Quévédo, Tangier; daily services Algeciras to Tangier.

Voyages Paquet: 65 ave. de l'Armée Royale, Casablanca, B.P. 60; f. 1970; Dir.-Gen. MICHEL BOUKHTIAROFF.

CIVIL AVIATION

The main international airports are at Casablanca (King Mohammed V), Rabat, Tangier, Marrakesh, Agadir and Fez.

NATIONAL AIRLINE

Royal Air Maroc: Aéroport International Casablanca-Anfa; f. 1953; 90 per cent owned by the Government; domestic flights and services to Western Europe, the U.S.A., Canada, Brazil, Argentina, North and West Africa, the Canary Islands and the Middle East; fleet of 4 Boeing 737, 8 Boeing 727, 2 Boeing 707, 1 Boeing 747; Chair. Gen. DRISS BEN AOMAR EL ALAMI; Man. Dir. SAID BEN ALI YAALA.

Casablanca is served by the following foreign airlines: Aeroflot (U.S.S.R.), Air Afrique (Ivory Coast), Air France, Balkan (Bulgaria), British Caledonian, Iberia (Spain), KLM (Netherlands), Kuwait Airways, Libyan Arab Airlines, Lufthansa (Federal Republic of Germany), Sabena (Belgium), Saudia (Saudi Arabia), Swissair, TAROM (Romania) and Tunis Air. In addition, ČSA (Czechoslovakia) flies to Rabat, British Airways to Marrakesh and Agadir, and Gibair (Gibraltar) to Tangier.

TOURISM AND CULTURE

Office National Marocain de Tourisme: B.P. 19, 22 ave. d'Alger, Rabat; f. 1946; Dir. ABDELLATIF AMOR; publ. *Maroc-Tourisme* (quarterly).

CULTURAL ORGANIZATIONS

Ministry of Cultural Affairs: rue Gandhi, Rabat; consists of departments of Cultural Activities and Art Education, Museums and Historic Monuments, together with administrative and legal divisions; publs. *Bulletin d'Archéologie Marocaine*, *Etudes et Travaux d'Archéologie*, etc.

Associations des Amateurs de la Musique Andalouse: 26 rue de Strasbourg, Casablanca; f. 1957; centres in 13 Moroccan towns; Dir. Hadj DRISS BENJELLOUN.

PRINCIPAL THEATRES

Théâtre National Mohammed V: Rabat; f. 1961; Morocco's national theatre with its own troupe, subsidized by the state; Dir. AZIZ SEGHROUCHNI; publ. *Le 246-91*.

Théâtre Municipal de Casablanca: blvd. de Paris, Casablanca; f. 1922, reorganized 1934 and 1949; presents a large number of foreign and national productions; maintained by the Casablanca Municipality; Dir. TAIB SASSIKI; Gen. Administrator ALI KADIRI.

PRINCIPAL ORCHESTRAS

Orchestre Symphonique du Conservatoire National de Musique: Rabat; European classical music and Andalusian (Arabic) music; chamber orchestra.

Orchestre du Conservatoire de Tétouan: Tetuan; specializes in Andalusian (Arabic) music; Dir. M. TEMSEMANI.

Orchestre du Conservatoire Dar Adyel: Fez; specializing in traditional music; Dir. Hadj ABDELKRIM RAIS.

DEFENCE

Defence Budget (1981): 4,700 million dirhams.

Military Service: 18 months.

Total Armed Forces (July 1981): 120,000; army 107,000; navy 5,000; air force 8,000. Paramilitary forces: 30,000.

EDUCATION

Since independence in 1956 Morocco has had to tackle a number of educational problems: a youthful and fast-growing population, an urgent need for skilled workers and executives, a great diversity of teaching methods between French, Spanish, Muslim and Moroccan Government schools, and, above all, a high degree of adult illiteracy. Morocco spends about 25 per cent of the national budget on education, of which a considerable proportion is devoted to constructing buildings for higher studies and technical education. In many small towns and villages, local craftsmen have co-operated in the building of elementary schools.

In 1981/82 there were 2,331,000 pupils in primary schools. At this level most instruction is given in government schools, where syllabuses have been standardized since 1967. Great progress was made in providing new schools between 1957 and 1964, but since then the increase in the number of places has slowed down. A decree of November 1963 made education compulsory for children between the ages of seven and thirteen, and this has now been applied in most urban areas, but throughout the country only 65 per cent of the age-group attended school in 1979/80. All primary teachers are Moroccan. Instruction is given in Arabic for the first two years and in Arabic and French for the next three years, with English as the first additional language.

Secondary education lasts for three or four years, depending on the type of course, and in 1981/82 provided for 826,500 pupils. Approximately a quarter of these pupils attended technical schools, where reforms have taken place since 1970 to attract more pupils and to provide relevant training to meet the country's need for technical manpower. Most secondary teachers are Moroccan, but in 1980/81 there were 4,082 from abroad, chiefly from France.

Higher education has a long history in Morocco. The Islamic University of Al Quarawiyin at Fez celebrated its eleventh centenary in 1959-60. The Mohammed V University opened in Rabat in 1957 and now has over 30,000 students in six faculties. In addition there are two other universities at Fez and Casablanca, and institutes of higher education in business studies, agriculture, mining, law, and statistics and advanced economics. In 1980/81 there were 98,513 university students and 16,148 at teacher-training college. In addition, there were 23,100 studying abroad and 48,241 at other institutions for higher education (1979/80).

Adult education is being tackled through the means of radio, simplified type, a special newspaper for the newly literate, and the co-operation of every teacher in the country. Another notable development in recent years has been the increasing attention given to education for girls. In 1980/81 about 37.5 pre cent of secondary school pupils were girls. There are now a number of mixed and girls' schools, and the proportion is growing every year, especially in urban areas.

BIBLIOGRAPHY

ABU-LUGHOD, JANET L. Rabat: Urban Apartheid in Morocco (Princeton University Press, Guildford, England, 1981).

AMIN, SAMIR. The Maghreb in the Modern World (Penguin, Harmondsworth, 1971).

ASHFORD, D. E. Political Change in Morocco (Princeton U.P., 1961).
Perspectives of a Moroccan Nationalist (New York, 1964).

AYACHE, A. Le Maroc (Editions Sociales, Paris, 1956).

BARBOUR, NEVILL. Morocco (Thames and Hudson, London, 1964).

BELAL, ABDEL AZIZ. L'investissement au Maroc (1912–1964) et ses enseignements en matière de développement économique (Mouton, Paris, 1968).

BEN BARKA, MEHDI. Problèmes de l'édification du Maroc et du Maghreb (Plon, Paris, 1959).
Option Révolutionnaire en Maroc (Maspéro, Paris, 1966).

BENNETT, NORMAN ROBERT. A study guide for Morocco (Boston, 1970).

BERNARD, STÉPHANE. Le Conflit Franco-Marocain 1943–1956, 3 vols. (Brussels, 1963; English translation, Yale University Press, 1968).

BERQUE, JAQUES. Le Maghreb entre deux guerres (Eds. du Seuil, Paris, 1962).

BIDWELL, ROBIN. Morocco under Colonial Rule: French Administration of Tribal Areas 1912–56 (Frank Cass, London, 1973).

CLASEN, DIRK. Stauffacher-Reiseführer Marokko (Stauffacher Verlag, Zürich, 1964).

COHEN, M. I., and HAHN, LORNA. Morocco: Old Land. New Nation (Praeger, New York, 1964).

COULAU, JULIEN. La paysannerie marocaine (Paris, 1968).

HALL, L. J. The United States and Morocco, 1776–1956 (Scarecrow Press, Metuchen, N.J., 1971).

HALSTEAD, JOHN P. Rebirth of a Nation: the Origins and Rise of Moroccan Nationalism (Harvard University Press, 1967).

HASSAN II, King of Morocco. Le Défi (Albin Michel, Paris, 1976).

JULIEN, CHARLES-ANDRÉ. Le Maroc face aux Impérialismes (1415–1956) (Editions Jeune Afrique, Paris, 1978).

KAY, SHIRLEY. Morocco (Namara Publications, London, 1980).

KININMONTH, C. The Travellers' Guide to Morocco (Jonathan Cape, London, 1972).

LACOUTURE, J. and S. Le Maroc à l'épreuve (du Seuil, Paris, 1958).

LANDAU, ROM. The Moroccan Drama 1900–1955 (Hale, London, 1956).
Morocco Independent under Mohammed V (Allen and Unwin, London, 1961).
Hassan II, King of Morocco (Allen and Unwin, London, 1962).
The Moroccans—Yesterday and Today (London, 1963).
Morocco (Allen & Unwin, London, 1967).

LANDAU, ROM, and SWANN, WIM. Marokko (Cologne, 1970).

LE TOURNEAU, ROGER. Evolution politique de l'Afrique du Nord musulmane (Armand Colin, Paris, 1962).

MAXWELL, GAVIN. Lords of the Atlas (Longmans, London, 1966).

METCALF, JOHN. Morocco—an Economic Study (First National City Bank, New York, 1966).

PERROUX, F. and BARRE, R. Développement, croissance, progrès—Maroc-Tunisie (Paris, 1961).

ROBERT, J. La monarchie marocaine (Librairie générale de droit et de jurisprudence, Paris, 1963).

SEHIMI, MUSTAPHA. Citations de S.M. Hassan II (Société marocaine des éditeurs réunis, Rabat, 1981).

STEWART, CHARLES F. The Economy of Morocco 1912-1962 (Oxford Univ. Press, 1965).

TERRASSE, H. Histoire du Maroc des origines à l'établissement du protectorat français, 2 vols. (Casablanca, 1949–50) (English trans. by H. Tee, London, 1952).

THOMPSON, VIRGINIA, and ADLOFF, RICHARD. The Western Saharans (Croom Helm, London/Barnes and Noble, Totowa, N.J., 1980).

TIANO, ANDRÉ. La politique économique et financière du Maroc indépendant (Presses universitaires de France, Paris, 1963).

TROUT, FRANK E. Morocco's Saharan Frontiers (Geneva, 1969).

WATERSON, ALBERT. Planning in Morocco (Johns Hopkins, Baltimore, 1963).

WATERBURY, JOHN. The commander of the Faithful. The Moroccan political élite (London, 1970).

WORLD BANK. The Economic Development of Morocco (Johns Hopkins Press, Baltimore, 1966).

ZARTMAN, I. W. Morocco: Problems of New Power (Atherton Press, New York, 1964).

Oman

GEOGRAPHY

The Sultanate of Oman lies on the east of the Arabian Peninsula and is flanked by the United Arab Emirates on the north and west, by Saudi Arabia on the west and by Southern Yemen on the south-west. Its sea coast extends for over 1,600 km. and its total area, including Dhofar, is about 120,000 square miles (300,000 sq. km.). The country's frontiers with its neighbours have never been clearly demarcated on the ground but agreement exists on their general lines.

No census has ever been held in Oman and estimates of the country's population are based on conjecture. Official estimates placed the mid-year total at 550,000 for each year between 1949 and 1958; at 565,000 between 1959 and 1966; and at 600,000 in 1972. Based on a mid-1965 estimate of 571,000, the UN Population Division has projected a total of 654,000 for mid-1970, 766,000 for mid-1975 and 891,000 for mid-1980. Preliminary surveys for a census were taken in 1975, and an estimate of 850,000 has been given for 1978.

At Muscat the mean rainfall is 10 cm. and the average mean temperature varies between 69°F. and 110°F. Rainfall on the hills of the interior is somewhat heavier and the south-western province of Dhofar is the only part of Arabia to benefit from the summer monsoon. Although most of the country is arid, there is cultivation on the coastal plain of the Batinah and in a number of valleys in the interior irrigation has been developed. The *Rub Al Khali* (or empty quarter) on Oman's western border is a rainless unrelieved wilderness of shifting sand almost entirely without human habitation.

HISTORY

Oman was probably the land of Magan mentioned in Sumerian tablets with which cities like Ur of the Chaldees traded in the third millenium B.C. The province of Dhofar also produced frankincense in vast quantities which was shipped to markets in Iraq, Syria, Egypt and the West. Roman geographers mention the city of Omana, although its precise location has not been identified, and Portus Moschus, conceivably Muscat. Masirah was also known to Pliny as the Island of Turtles. Oman at various times came under the influence of the Himyaritic kingdoms of South Arabia and of Iran, to which the introduction of the falaj irrigation systems is probably attributable, though legend attributes it to Sulaiman bin Daoud (Solomon).

The people of Oman come from two main stocks, the Qahtan who immigrated from South Arabia, and the Nizar who came in from the North. Tradition attributes the first important invasion from South Arabia to the leadership of Malik ibn Faham after the final collapse of the Marib dam in the Yemen in the first or second century A.D. Oman was one of the first countries to be converted to Islam by Amr ibn al As, who later converted Egypt to Islam. Omanis of the tribe of al Azd played an important part in the early days of Islam in Iraq. They subsequently embraced the Ibadhi doctrine which holds that the caliphate in Islam should not be hereditary or confined to any one family and established their own independent Imamate in Oman in the eighth century A.D. Subsequently, though subject to various invasions from time to time by the Caliphate, Iranians, Moguls and others, Oman has largely maintained its independence.

During the 10th century Sohar became probably the largest and most important city in the Arab world and Omani mariners, together with those from Basrah and other Gulf ports, went as far afield as China. Sohar, though subject to decline and recovery, remained an important port until, and indeed after, the Portuguese conquests. When the Portuguese under Albuquerque arrived in 1507 on their way to India, they found the Omani seaport under the suzerainty of the King of Hormus, himself of Omani stock. The towns of Qalhat, Quryat, Muscat and Sohar were all then thriving and prosperous.

The arrival of the Portuguese in the Indian Ocean changed the balance of power in the area radically. Previously the Omanis had been ubiquitous on the seas and it was an Omani pilot who guided Vasco da Gama across from Malindi to Calicut in India. The Portuguese established themselves in the Omani ports, concentrating principally on Sohar and Muscat, where they built the two great forts, Merani (1587) and Jalali (1588). British and Dutch traders followed in the wake of the Portuguese, though they did not establish themselves by force of arms in Oman in the same way. In 1650 the Imam Nasir bin Murshid of the Yaariba dynasty, who also inaugurated a period of Omani renaissance during which learning flourished, effectively turned the Portuguese out of Muscat and the rest of Oman. The country's external power grew and by 1730 the Omanis had conquered the Portuguese settlements on the coast of East Africa, including Mogadishu, Mombasa and Zanzibar.

The country was, however, ravaged by civil war in the first half of the eighteenth century when the strength and authority of the Imam diminished. During this period the Iranians were called in to assist one of the contenders for the Imamate, but they were finally expelled by Ahmad bin Said who was elected Imam in 1749 and was the founder of the Al Bu Said dynasty, which still rules Oman. The Al Bu Said is thus one of the oldest dynasties in the Middle East. The country prospered under the new dynasty and its maritime importance again grew. In about 1786 the capital of the country was moved from Rostaq to Muscat, a move which led to a dichotomy between the coast and the interior, creating political problems between the two regions at various times.

The Imam Said bin Sultan ruled Oman from 1804 until 1856. He was a strong and much beloved ruler, who also gained the respect and friendship of European nations, in particular the British. Treaties providing for the exchange of consular relations were negotiated with the British in 1839 (there had been earlier treaties of friendship in 1798 and 1800), the United States in 1833, France in 1844 and the Netherlands in 1877. British relations with Oman were maintained for the greater part of the period from the early eighteenth century until the present day, whilst the relations of the other states concerned were somewhat spasmodic.

Said bin Sultan revived Omani interest in Zanzibar and during the latter part of his reign spent an increasing amount of his time there. He started the clove plantations which were later to bring the territory great wealth and was the founder of the dynasty which ruled in Zanzibar until the revolution in 1964. When he died, his dominions were split between two of his sons, one of whom became Sultan of Oman and the other of Zanzibar. Following British mediation Zanzibar, which was the richer part of the heritage, agreed to pay Oman an annual subsidy of $6,400. During Said's time, Omani dominions reached their greatest extent in modern times. Dhofar became one of the constituent parts of the Sultanate in 1829, which it has remained ever since.

The next half of the century was one of some difficulty for the Sultanate on account of the erosion of the basis of its former prosperity. Not only had it lost its East African possessions but the series of treaties with Britain by which the slave trade was curbed also assisted the decline as Muscat had been an important port for this lucrative traffic.

Britain's only formal links with the Sultanate have been a series of Treaties of Friendship, Commerce and Navigation signed in 1891, 1939 and 1951. Britain has, however, given military assistance to Oman on a number of occasions in the past and is continuing to do so, though this is not based on any treaty obligation.

Several insurrections took place towards the end of the nineteenth century and in 1913 a new Imam was elected in the Interior, the Sultan who ruled from Muscat not having been elected. This led to the expulsion of the Sultan's garrisons from Nizwa, Izki and Sumail. In the same year Sultan Faisal bin Turki, who had ruled since 1888, died and he was succeeded by his son Taimur. Efforts to come to terms with the rebels failed but in 1920 an agreement between the Sultan and the principal dissidents, led by Isa bin Salih, was reached providing for peace, free movement of persons between the interior and the coast, limitation of customs duty and non-interference by the Government of the Sultan in the internal affairs of the signatory tribes. Relations between the Imam,

Mohammad bin Abdullah al Khalili, and the Sultan remained good until the Imam died in 1954 when rebellion again broke out under the Imam's successor Ghalib bin Ali, who sought foreign help to establish a separate principality. In December 1955, forces under the Sultan's control entered the main inhabited centres of Oman without resistance. The former Imam was allowed by the Sultan to retire to his village but his brother, Talib, escaped to Saudi Arabia and thence to Cairo. An "Oman Imamate" office was set up there and the cause of the Imam was supported by Egyptian propaganda. In the summer of 1957 Talib returned and established himself with followers in the mountain areas north-west of Niswa. The Sultan appealed for British help and fighting continued until early 1959 when the Sultan's authority was fully re-established. In October 1960 ten Arab countries secured the placing of the "question of Oman" on the agenda of the General Assembly of the United Nations, despite British objections. In 1961 a resolution calling for the independence of Oman failed to get the necessary majority, and in 1963 a UN Commission of Inquiry refuted the Imamate charges of oppressive government and strong public feeling against the Sultan. Nevertheless, a Committee was set up to study the "question of Oman" and, after its report had been submitted to the General Assembly in 1965, a resolution was adopted which, among other things, demanded the elimination of British domination in any form. The question was raised again in the United Nations on several occasions until, more than a year after Sultan Qaboos's accession, Oman became a member of the UN in October 1971.

THE SULTANATE SINCE 1970

By 1970 Sultan Said's government had come to be regarded as the most reactionary and isolationist in the area, if not the world—slavery was still common, and many mediaeval prohibitions were in force. The Sultan's refusal to use the oil revenues for any purpose other than the building up of his armed forces had particularly embarrassed Britain, the oil companies and most neighbouring states, and this attitude had provided ideal conditions for the rebellion which broke out in Dhofar province in 1964. On July 24th, 1970, the Sultan was deposed by a coup led by his son, Qaboos bin Said, at the royal palace in Salalah. Qaboos, aged 29 and trained at Sandhurst, thus became Sultan to general acclaim both within the Sultanate and abroad, including support from the army; reports of British complicity in the coup were strongly denied by London. The new Sultan announced his intention to transform the country by using the oil revenues for development, following the example of the Gulf sheikhdoms to the north. He asked the rebels for their co-operation in developing the country, but only the Dhofar Liberation Front reacted favourably. The Popular Front for the Liberation of the Occupied Arabian Gulf (reported to control much of Dhofar, and to be receiving Chinese aid through the Yemen P.D.R.) and its ally the National Democratic Front for the Liberation of the Occupied Arab Gulf appeared to think that the palace coup changed little. In August 1970 "Muscat" was dropped from the title of the country, which became simply the "Sultanate of Oman". Sultan Qaboos appointed his uncle, Tariq bin Taimur, as Prime Minister, but he resigned his office in December 1971, since when the Sultan has himself presided over cabinet meetings and acted as his own Prime Minister, Minister of Defence and Minister of Foreign Affairs. Government policy is aimed at providing the basic social and economic infrastructure which the former Sultan was rigidly opposed to—housing, education, communications, health services, etc. (Before the coup there were only three primary schools and one hospital). In addition, restrictions on travel have been lifted, many prisoners released, and many Omanis have returned from abroad. However, a substantial proportion of the annual budget has been devoted to defence and to quelling the Dhofar insurgency.

Oman's admission to the UN was achieved in face of opposition from the Yemen P.D.R., which supported the Popular Front for the Liberation of Oman and the Arab Gulf (PFLOAG), formed in 1972 by the unification of the two nationalist liberation fronts. The name of this organization was changed in July 1974 to People's Front for the Liberation of Oman. Oman's relationship with Britain also compromised Oman's candidature for UN membership. Britain still supplies arms and ammunition to the Oman Government and officers on secondment or contract. The progress achieved since the palace coup of 1970 did have some impact on the insurgents' following, with a number of defections to the Sultan's forces, but fighting continued until December 1975. Omani forces attacked the border area of the Yemen P.D.R. for the first time in May 1972, the guerrillas having increasingly operated from beyond the border as the Sultan's forces advanced into Dhofar. In 1973 Iranian troops entered the conflict on the side of the Sultan, who also received assistance from Jordan, Saudi Arabia, the U.A.E., Pakistan and India. The Sultan's forces gradually came to have the upper hand and development in the Jebel area of Dhofar has been considerable. The war turned out to be prolonged, however, and during October 1975 the rebels used sophisticated weapons such as SAM-7 missiles. In December 1975, after an offensive, the Sultan claimed a complete victory over the insurgents. On March 11th, 1976, a ceasefire between Oman and the Yemen P.D.R. was negotiated by Saudi Arabia, and Sultan Qaboos granted an amnesty to Omanis who had been fighting for the PFLO. Since then only desultory conflicts have taken place and many rebels have returned to their homes in Oman. In January 1977 Iran decided to withdraw the bulk of her forces who had been engaged in Dhofar, but a token force remained until the revolution in Iran in early 1979. A renewal of the insurrection against Sultan Qaboos occurred in June 1978, when a party of British engineers were attacked in the Salalah region of Dhofar. Reports from South Yemeni exiles would seem to indicate that there has been an increase in support for the PFLO from the Cubans. The PFLO has become largely an external force, however, and has achieved little success in attracting adherents within Oman, although the Governor of Dhofar was assassinated at the beginning of June 1979 and renewed insurgency from the PFLO was reported. In January 1981 Oman closed the border with South Yemen and more British officers were seconded to the Oman forces, as the frontier defences were put on the alert.

Oman's relations with her Arab neighbours have improved rapidly over the last few years. During the reign of Sultan Said the Omani dependence on British military forces was viewed with disfavour by her neighbours and this suspicion served only to deepen the isolation of Oman from the rest of the Arab world. However since the accession of Sultan Qaboos, and more especially since the defeat of the Dhofar insurgents, relations have improved considerably. Both Kuwait and the U.A.E. have supplied much-needed financial support to Oman, while Iraq, formerly a supporter of the PFLO, has established diplomatic relations. The establishment of close economic and diplomatic links with Saudi Arabia was an important step in the full emergence of Oman from her former isolated position in the Arab world. Oman's support of the Israeli-Egyptian peace treaty, however, could result in the distancing of relations with some of the "hard-line" members of the Arab League, and in closer ties with the U.S.A. and with Egypt, which has promised to respond to any request from Oman for military aid. Concern over regional security prompted Oman to join the Gulf Co-operation Council, set up in May 1981.

The strategic importance of military bases in Oman has long been recognized. The United Kingdom withdrew its forces from Masirah Island in the spring of 1977, and since then the U.S.A. has shown keen interest. In February 1980 Oman began negotiating with the U.S.A. concerning a defence alliance whereby, in exchange for U.S. military and economic aid and a commitment to Oman's security, Oman is to grant the U.S.A. use of port and air base facilities in the Gulf (including Masirah Island). The agreement was finalized in June, and was bitterly condemned by the Arab People's Congress in Libya as being a concession to "U.S. imperialism". The outbreak of the Gulf War in September 1980 only served to underline Oman's strategic importance, particularly with regard to the Strait of Hormuz.

Early in 1981 the U.S. set up a communications centre in Oman and President Reagan has pledged over U.S. $200 million in 1981–83 for developing port and airport facilities in return for the right to stockpile supplies in Oman for possible use by the Rapid Deployment Force. U.S. forces were permitted to make landings in Oman during the massive "Bright Star" military exercises, held in the region in December 1981.

A 45-member Consultative Assembly (consisting of 17 representatives of the Government, 17 representatives of the private sector and 11 regional representatives) was created in October 1981 in response to suggestions that Sultan Qaboos was not being made sufficiently aware of public opinion. However, its role will be confined to comment on economic and social development and recommendations on future policy.

ECONOMIC SURVEY

AGRICULTURE AND FISHERIES

About 70 per cent of the working population is engaged in agriculture and the Sultanate's long-term plans for development foresee a considerable increase in agricultural production. At present subsistence farming dominates Oman's agriculture: because of the very wide variations in rainfall from one year to another farming is heavily dependent on irrigation. The oases of the interior rely on a system of underground water channels, known as *falaj* (plural *aflaj*), to tap water tables. On the Batinah coast irrigation is by pump from wells. About half of the estimated 36,000 hectares under cultivation are planted with dates. Other crops include lucerne, limes, mangoes, melons, bananas and onions. Local tomatoes and cucumbers are also coming onto the town markets. Some wheat is grown in the interior around Nizwa. Agriculture and fishing contributed RO 32 million (2.8 per cent of the total) to the Gross Domestic Product in 1979, compared with RO 16.6 million (15 per cent of the total) in 1970.

In encouraging agricultural development the Department of Agriculture (which is a part of the Ministry of Development) hopes to increase production of traditional export crops and to reduce the level of food imports by producing more for the home market. The Department has five experimental and production farms and 22 extension centres throughout the country. A series of 5 surveys of water resources in Northern Oman by international consultants will provide the basis for future agricultural planning. The Government has provided for improvement and reactivation of the *falaj* systems.

Agriculture in Dhofar is the responsibility of the Dhofar Development Department. Because the province enjoys monsoon rains from June to September, the agricultural scene differs markedly from that in Northern Oman. Cattle are raised on the hills north of Salalah and coconut palms and a wide variety of vegetables are grown on the coastal plain. Although the insurgency delayed development on the hills, the Government is now establishing administrative centres and drilling for water.

Livestock farming in Dhofar is also under study. Among existing projects is the Garziaz cattle station, originally managed by a British company. A Swiss firm then took it over as a joint venture known as Sun Farms of Oman. Sun Farms will control livestock projects in Dhofar, Sahnut, Sohar and Saham, and will take over a vegetable farm and nursery in Salalah. The region also contains one of the most advanced dairy farms in the world, which has been jointly financed by the Government and a private concern. The constraints on agricultural development in Dhofar are the shortage of labour and the distance from markets, rather than any lack of water.

Fishing is a traditional industry in Oman and employs about 10 per cent of the working population. In 1979 the National Fishing Corporation was formed to be responsible for concession agreements, government trawlers and land facilities. The inshore waters are rich in fish which is the main source of protein in the diet of many Omanis. Most fishing is done from canoes equipped with outboard motors, but the Government has signed two agreements with the U.S. firm Mardela to develop commercial fishing in the Gulf of Oman. Other fisheries projects are being planned in co-operation with Kuwait, and freezing and processing facilities are being developed.

PETROLEUM AND NATURAL GAS

The economy of Oman is dominated by the oil industry, which provides almost all Government revenue. In 1937 Petroleum Concessions (Oman) Ltd., a subsidiary of the Iraq Petroleum Co., was granted a 75-year oil concession extending over the whole area except the district of Dhofar. A concession covering Dhofar was granted in 1953 to Dhofar Cities Service Petroleum Corporation, but the Dhofar fields are now operated by Petroleum Development Oman.

In 1964 Petroleum Development (Oman) Ltd., re-formed in 1967 as a subsidiary of Royal Dutch/Shell (with an 85 per cent interest), Compagnie Française des Pétroles (with 10 per cent) and Gulbenkian interests (with 5 per cent), announced that drilling had proved sufficient reserves for the company to go into commercial production. Production began in 1967 at a rate of 200,000 barrels per day and expanded to 360,000 barrels per day by the end of 1969. However, during late 1970 and early 1971 technical difficulties affected production and the 1971 production of 105.56 million barrels was 15 million down on 1970. Total oil exports in 1972 were 103.2 million barrels. By 1977 they had risen to 122 million barrels but continued falling from just under 116 million barrels in 1978 to 101.8 million in 1980. Total oil production in 1980 was 103.3 million barrels. Oman's oil reserves were estimated at about 2,484 million barrels in late 1981, representing over 20 more years of production at 1980 levels.

In 1973 the four connected oil fields at Fahud, Natih, Yibal and Al-Huwaisah together produced at an average rate of 293,000 barrels per day. The average rose to about 340,000 barrels per day in 1975, and increased to 385,900 b/d in December 1975, when the three Ghaba fields started production. The 1976 average rate of 368,000 b/d began a decline, and production in late 1981 was running at around 328,000 b/d from northern, central and southern fields. Oil fields in the south have been developed to compensate for lower production from northern fields, although recent investment by Petroleum Development (Oman) has succeeded in pushing up production from these.

Natural gas reserves in Oman are estimated at 6,300,000 million cubic feet. The Yibal gas fields are expected to be capable of a daily yield of 140 million cubic feet although the 1979 production rate was only about 60 million cubic feet. A pipeline to the power/desalination plant at Ghubra was completed in 1978 and gas liquefaction plants have been built at Yibal. There are plans to link all main towns into a national gas grid in order to free more oil for export.

Petroleum Development (Oman) is currently exploiting the Marmul and Amal fields in southern Dhofar. Development will prove to be costly because the oil is very heavy. The extra production amounted to some 20,000 b/d in 1981.

Amoco heads a group exploring in offshore areas south of the Masirah Island, and, in 1975 a concession was granted to Elf/Sumitomo to explore in the Butabul region. This was later changed to a production-sharing agreement and in 1978 20 per cent of the area was assigned to the West German Wintershall company. Exploration resulted in the discovery of several fields, which were yielding about 75,000 b/d in late 1981.

Oman's first oil refinery was due to come on stream at Mina al Fahal, near Muscat, in late 1981; at present all refined products are imported at high cost, and it is hoped that the proposed refinery, with a capacity of 50,000 barrels per day, will meet domestic demand for petrol.

In December 1973 the Oman Government purchased a 25 per cent share in Petroleum Development (Oman), and increased this to 60 per cent in July 1974. The present distribution of the remaining shares is Royal Dutch/Shell 34 per cent, Compagnie Française des Pétroles 4 per cent and Gulbenkian 2 per cent. Oman is not a member of the Organization of Petroleum Exporting Companies (OPEC), nor of the Organization of Arab Petroleum Exporting Countries (OAPEC), but under the terms of the concessions the Government of the Sultanate is assured of treatment equal to that received by members of OPEC.

INDUSTRY AND MINERALS

Before 1964 industry in Oman was confined to small traditional handicrafts. The development of oil generated activity in the construction sector, but it was not until the change of regime in 1970 that Government investment in infrastructure projects and private spending on housing started a boom in construction. Some of the new projects were not well conceived, resulting in the drain of resources abroad to foreign contractors. With oil revenues declining and a chronic shortage of manpower, Oman is not well placed to develop heavy industry or manufacturing on a large scale. The Government is, accordingly, turning more towards the development of agriculture and fisheries, and encouraging building in the rural areas with the emphasis on social projects and roads. Some industrial projects have been completed. A paint factory was opened in 1977 under Danish supervision. A large proportion of the workforce is Indian and Pakistani, illustrating Oman's dependence on foreign labour. A cement works in Muscat, built as a joint venture with Kuwait, will have a capacity of 350,000 tons per year.

Geological surveys are being carried out to locate mineral deposits. So far, sizeable reserves of copper and chromite have been found. Chromite reserves, estimated at 2 million tons of medium grade ore, exist on the coastal side of the Jebel Akhdar. The concession is held by a Canadian-based company and mining is due to start soon. The government-owned Oman Mining Company is developing three copper mines at Sohar, north-west of Muscat, where drilling has indicated about 12 million metric tons of ore. Production will be an estimated 20,000 tons per year and will begin in the first half of 1982. The project is to cost a conservative U.S. $120 million, to which Saudi Arabia has contributed $100 million, and the Japanese have also shown an interest. Construction of a complex for the smelting and refining of the copper ore is planned to the east of the mining compound, within reach of port facilities. A large cement factory is also proposed for this area and is to produce one million metric tons per year for the Oman Cement Company; Kuwait will have a 40 per cent stake in the latter project. There are plans to extend the Yibal – Ghubra gas pipeline out to the Sohar region, thus providing fuel for both projects. Another cement factory project is under way in Dhofar and should be completed in 1983.

FINANCE AND DEVELOPMENT

With the expected decline in revenue from oil, the Government has had to tailor its development programme accordingly, although the oil exploration programme is to continue. Expenditure on defence, however, continues to be a heavy burden. In 1980 the budget allocation was RO 304 million, compared with RO 238 million in 1979, when $15 million in defence aid was requested from the U.S.A. Infrastructural and communications projects are gradually being completed. Radar was installed at Salalah airport in 1978; previously Thumrait airport had to be used in bad weather and the monsoon season. The opening of twelve new berths at Mina Qaboos has improved port facilities and a West German firm is engaged on harbour expansion at Mina Raysut. Roads between Seeb and Nizwa and Salalah and Thumrait have been completed.

The targets of the 1976–80 development plan were relatively modest, concentrating on establishing a workable basis for light industry and agriculture. The Omani Development Bank was established in December 1977 to encourage private sector investment. The 1981–85 development plan envisaged a total expenditure of RO 7,400 million, of which RO 2,200 million was to be allocated to development projects. The general aim is to reduce economic dependence on oil, with special emphasis on private sector industry. The plan includes development of tourism and education, health, welfare, housing and road development. A much larger than anticipated drop in oil prices during 1981 forced the government to revise its budgeting for the plan and revised projections were to be published in 1983.

STATISTICAL SURVEY

Area: 300,000 sq. km. (120,000 sq. miles).

Population: for planning purposes the population is assumed to be 1,500,000 (1981); Capital area (Muscat to Seeb) estimated 50,000. Estimated number of gainfully employed 150,000: agriculture 109,000; fisheries 15,000; government 10,000; construction 6,000; oil, banking, services 5,000; others 5,000 (1972).

Agriculture: Total area under cultivation 1978/79 (hectares): 41,156 (Batinah and Capital Area 20,842, Oman interior 5,169, Sharqiya and Ja'alan 4,285). Crops include dates, lucerne, limes, onions, wheat, bananas, mangoes, tobacco, sorghum, sweet potatoes, chickpeas and coconuts.

Livestock (1978/79 Agriculture Census result, 'ooo head): goats 1,165, cattle 319.5, sheep 138.3, camels 229.3, donkeys 43.0.

PETROLEUM

	1976	1977	1978	1979	1980
Production (million barrels)	134.7	124.1	114.7	107.7	103.3
Exports (million barrels)	134.3	122.0	115.6	107.5	101.8
Value of exports (RO million) . . .	543.8	545.9	521.8	745.7	n.a.

FINANCE

1,000 baiza = 1 rial Omani (RO).

Coins: 2, 5, 10, 25, 50 and 100 baiza.

Notes: 100, 250 and 500 baiza; 1, 5, 10 and 20 rials.

Exchange rates (May 1982): £1 sterling = 635.0 baiza; U.S. $1 = 345.4 baiza.

100 rials Omani = £157.48 = $289.52.

Note: The rial Saidi (renamed the rial Omani in 1972) was introduced in May 1970, replacing the Persian Gulf Indian rupee at the rate of 1 rial = 21 rupees = £1 sterling. The initial value of the rial was U.S. $2.40 ($1 = 416.7 baiza), which remained in operation until August 1971. From December 1971 to February 1973 the rial's value was $2.6057 ($1 = 383.8 baiza). The present dollar valuation has been effective since February 1973. The rial was at par with the pound sterling until the latter was allowed to "float" in June 1972.

BUDGET ESTIMATES
(RO million)

REVENUE	1978	1979	1980	EXPENDITURE	1978	1979	1980
Oil revenues . .	457.7	634.6	831.2	Defence . . .	264.5	269.0	406.8
Other receipts .	44.6	57.6	92.5	Other current expenditure	172.9	188.3	271.2
Balance on grants and loans . .	26.1	10.3	36.5	Capital expenditure .	147.7	204.9	271.5
TOTAL .	528.4	702.5	960.2	TOTAL .	585.1	662.2	949.5

1981 Budget: Revenue RO 1,399 million; Expenditure RO 1,410 million.

1981–85 Development Plan: Expenditure RO 7,365 million.

EXTERNAL TRADE
(RO million)

	1973	1974	1975	1976	1977	1978	1979
Imports							
Recorded . . .	40.7	135.6	264.3	250.5	302.1	327.2	430.5
Unrecorded estimate .	45.1	78.5	120.0	155.0	104.0	108.3	n.a.
TOTAL . . .	85.8	214.1	371.3	405.5	406.2	435.5	n.a.
Exports							
Petroleum . . .	114.3	418.7	488.1	543.8	545.9	521.8	745.7
Other . . .	0.6	0.4	1.1	1.4	1.5	6.5	} 43.2
Re-exports	—	—	—	6.0	12.0	24.0	
TOTAL . . .	114.9	419.1	489.2	551.2	559.4	552.3	788.9

Source: Central Bank of Oman.

1980: Imports RO 598 million; Exports (excluding petroleum) RO 49.8 million.

Petroleum Exports (RO million): 1,133.2 in 1980; 1,523.1 in 1981 (*Source:* IMF, *International Financial Statistics*).

RECORDED IMPORTS
(RO '000)

PRINCIPAL COMMODITIES

	1979	1980
Food and live animals .	56,314	72,904
Beverages and tobacco .	18,761	14,843
Crude materials (inedible) except fuels .	5,068	9,863
Mineral fuels and lubricants	29,953	64,574
Animal and vegetable oils and fats . .	2,927	3,222
Chemicals . . .	16,348	20,820
Basic manufactures .	68,272	96,310
Machinery and transport equipment . .	171,433	235,726
Miscellaneous manufactured articles . . .	32,318	45,147
TOTAL .	430,517	598,245

PRINCIPAL TRADING PARTNERS

	1979	1980
Australia . . .	10,389	11,424
Bahrain . . .	10,216	26,575
Belgium . . .	4,273	9,740
China, People's Republic	5,187	6,200
France . . .	15,390	11,095
Germany, Fed. Repub. .	26,983	33,435
India . . .	15,825	17,235
Italy . . .	9,277	10,519
Japan . . .	66,342	117,630
Netherlands . .	33,745	33,508
Singapore . .	11,252	20,010
Sweden . . .	5,825	4,626
United Arab Emirates .	64,934	103,470
United Kingdom .	72,255	93,331
U.S.A. . . .	34,586	34,071
TOTAL (incl. others) .	430,517	598,245

EXPORTS
Non-oil exports consist mainly of limes, dates, fish and tobacco: 1974 RO 430,300; 1975 RO 1,078,231; 1976 RO 1,409,500; 1977 RO 1,527,900; 1978 RO 3,322,900; RO 4,717,200; 1980 RO 4,563,500.

TRANSPORT

ROAD TRAFFIC
(vehicles in use)

	1980
Private cars	42,596
Taxis	3,114
Public service	928
Commercial	43,941
Government	9,142
Motor-cycles	7,459
Private hire	87
Diplomatic	360
Total	107,627

CIVIL AVIATION
(Seeb International Airport)

	1978	1979	1980
Passengers ('ooo) . .	527.0	636.0	694.4
Cargo handled ('ooo tons)	11.1	10.8	11.9

EDUCATION

	PRIMARY		PREPARATORY		SECONDARY	
	Boys	Girls	Boys	Girls	Boys	Girls
1976/77 . .	44,668	17,962	1,609	406	233	97
1977/78 . .	49,294	21,377	3,819	861	397	139
1978/79 . .	53,025	24,949	5,765	1,513	529	156
1979/80 . .	56,409	27,294	7,838	2,339	708	235
1980/81 . .	60,290	31,362	10,284	3,445	1,168	383

THE GOVERNMENT

Head of State, Premier and Minister of Foreign Affairs, Defence and Finance:
Sultan QABOOS BIN SAID (assumed power July 24th, 1970).

CABINET

(June 1982)

Deputy Premier for Security and Defence: Sayyid FAHAR BIN TAIMOUR AL-SAID.

Deputy Premier for Legal Affairs: Sayyid FAHAD BIN MAHMOUD AL-SAID.

Deputy Prime Minister for Financial and Economic Affairs: QAIS ABDUL MUNIM AL-ZAWAWI.

Personal Adviser to the Sultan and Governor of Muscat: Sayyid THUWAINI BIN SHIHAB AL-SAID.

Minister of Diwan Affairs: Sayyid HAMAD BIN HAMUD AL-SAID.

Minister of Justice and of Awkaf and Islamic Affairs: Sayyid HILAL BIN HAMAD AL-SAMMAR.

Minister of State for Foreign Affairs: YOUSEF AL-ALAWI ABDULLAH.

Minister of Information: ABDULAZIZ AL-ROWASS.

Minister of Electricity and Water: HAMOUD ABDULLA AL-HARTHY.

Minister of Posts, Telegraphs and Telephones: KARIM AHMED AL-HAREMY.

Minister of Civil Aviation, Ports and Roads: SALIM BIN NASSIR AL-BUSAIDY.

Minister of Education and Youth Affairs and Acting Minister of Social Affairs and Labour: YAHYA MAHFOODH AL-MANDHRI.

Minister of Land Affairs and Municipalities (also Public Works): AHMAD ABDULLA AL-GHAZALI.

Minister of National Heritage and Culture: Sayyid FAISAL BIN ALI AL-SAID.

Minister of the Interior: Sayyid BADR BIN SAYD BIN HAREB.

Minister of Commerce and Industry: MUHAMMAD ZUBAIR.

Minister of Petroleum and Minerals: SAID AHMED AL-SHANFARI.

Minister of Agriculture and Fisheries: ABDEL HAFIZ SALEM RAJAB.

Minister of Health: Dr. MUBAREK AL-KHADDURI.

Governor of Dhofar and Minister of State: HILAL BIN SAID BIN HAREB.

Secretary to Council of Ministers: SALEM AL-GHAZALI.

Minister of State and Special Envoy for the Sultan: SHAHIB BIN TAIMOUR AL-SAID.

CONSULTATIVE ASSEMBLY

In October 1981 Sultan Qaboos issued a decree setting up a Consultative Assembly of 45 nominated members, 17 of whom are government officials. Members are nominated for a term of two years. The Assembly meets four times a year.

Speaker: KHALFAN BIN NASSIR AL-WAHAIBI.

DIPLOMATIC REPRESENTATION

EMBASSIES ACCREDITED TO OMAN
(In Muscat unless otherwise stated)

Argentina: Jeddah, Saudi Arabia.

Australia: Jeddah, Saudi Arabia.

Austria: Jeddah, Saudi Arabia.

Bangladesh: Jeddah, Saudi Arabia.

Belgium: Jeddah, Saudi Arabia.

Brazil: Jeddah, Saudi Arabia.

Canada: Teheran, Iran.

Chile: Amman, Jordan.

China, People's Republic: P.O.B. 3315; *Ambassador:* YUAN LOULIN.

Denmark: Jeddah, Saudi Arabia.

Egypt: P.O.B. 5252; *Ambassador:* MUHAMMAD SAID AL-DESOUKEY.

Finland: Jeddah, Saudi Arabia.

France: P.O.B. 591; *Ambassador:* PIERRE MORIZOT.

Gambia: Jeddah, Saudi Arabia.

Germany, Federal Republic: P.O.B. 3128, Ruwi; *Ambassador:* Dr. HEINRICH REINERS.

Greece: Jeddah, Saudi Arabia.

Guinea: Jeddah, Saudi Arabia.

India: P.O.B. 4727; *Ambassador:* KHIANGITE C. LALVUNGA.

Indonesia: Teheran, Iran.

Iran: P.O.B. 702; *Chargé d'affaires:* SAHIB SHASHTARY ZADA.

Iraq: P.O.B. 4848; *Ambassador:* YASEEN AL-WAAN ABOUD.

Italy: Islamabad, Pakistan.

Japan: P.O.B. 6511, Ruwi; *Chargé d'affaires:* KEISABURO YAMASHITA.

Jordan: P.O.B. 528; *Ambassador:* RIAD SELORI.

Korea, Republic: P.O.B. 5220; *Ambassador:* KYUNG HOON LEE.

Kuwait: P.O.B. 4798; *Ambassador:* ABDUL AZIZ ABDUL WAHAB AL-OSMAN.

Mali: Jeddah, Saudi Arabia.

Mauritania: Jeddah, Saudi Arabia.

Mexico: Teheran, Iran.

Morocco: P.O.B. 6125; *Ambassador:* AHMED BEN AL-BASHIR AL-HASSANI.

Nepal: Jeddah, Saudi Arabia.

Netherlands: Teheran, Iran.

Niger: Jeddah, Saudi Arabia.

Norway: Jeddah, Saudi Arabia.

Pakistan: P.O.B. 4302; *Ambassador:* ANWAR SAID.

Portugal: Jeddah, Saudi Arabia.

Qatar: P.O.B. 802; *Ambassador:* ALI ABDUL REHMAN AL-MIFTAH.

Romania: Teheran, Iran.

Saudi Arabia: P.O.B. 4411; *Ambassador:* MUHAMMAD AL-MUTLAQ.

Somalia: P.O.B. 4767, Ruwi; *Ambassador:* HASSAN KID ABDULA.

Spain: Jeddah, Saudi Arabia.

Sudan: P.O.B. 5205; *Ambassador:* ALI ABDEL RAHMAN NIMEIRI.

Sweden: Jeddah, Saudi Arabia.

Switzerland: Jeddah, Saudi Arabia.

Tunisia: P.O.B. 5755; *Ambassador:* ABDUL MALIK AL-ARIF.

Turkey: Jeddah, Saudi Arabia.

United Arab Emirates: P.O.B. 335; *Chargé d'affaires a.i.:* ABDUL ALI ABDULLAH AL-HUMAIDAN.

United Kingdom: P.O.B. 300; *Ambassador:* DUNCAN SLATER.

U.S.A.: P.O.B. 966; *Ambassador:* J. COUNTRYMAN.

Yemen Arab Republic: P.O.B. 3701; *Ambassador:* AHMED MUHAMMAD ANARWDA.

Yugoslavia: Islamabad, Pakistan.

Zaire: Jeddah, Saudi Arabia.

Oman also has diplomatic relations with Algeria, the Comoros, Cyprus, Djibouti, Gabon, Lebanon, Luxembourg, Kenya, Malaysia, Maldives, Malta, Nigeria, the Philippines, Sri Lanka, Tanzania, Thailand, Togo and Upper Volta.

JUDICIAL SYSTEM

Jurisdiction is exercised by the Sharia Courts, applying Islamic Law. Local courts are officered by *Qadhis* appointed by the Minister of Justice. The Chief Court is at Muscat. Appeals from local courts, including the court in the capital, go to the Court of Appeal at Muscat.

RELIGION

The majority of the population are Ibadhi Muslims; about a quarter are Sunni Muslims.

THE PRESS
NEWSPAPERS

Al Watan (*The Nation*): P.O.B. 463, Muscat; f. 1971; weekly; circ. 10,000.

Oman: P.O.B. 6002, Ruwi; daily; Arabic; published by Oman Newspaper House.

ENGLISH LANGUAGE

Akhbar Oman: P.O.B. 5884, Ruwi; f. 1977; weekly; Chief Editor R. D. NAIR; circ. 10,000.

Gulf Mirror: P.O.B. 455, Manama, Bahrain; f. 1971; weekly; Man. Editor ALAN G. BROWN; circ. 16,000 in Bahrain, Oman, Qatar, U.A.E., Kuwait and eastern Saudi Arabia.

Oman Daily Observer: P.O.B. 6002, Ruwi; f. 1981; daily; Editor-in-Chief G. REID-ANDERSON.

Times of Oman: P.O.B. 3770, Ruwi, Muscat; weekly; Editor-in-Chief ARTHUR CUSHING.

PERIODICALS

Al-Akidah (*The Faith*): P.O.B. 691, Ruwi; weekly illustrated magazine; Editor SAID AL-SAMHAN AL-KATHIRI; circ. 18,000.

Al Mawared Al Tabeiah: Ministry of Agriculture, Fisheries, Petroleum and Minerals, P.O.B. 551, Muscat; English and Arabic; Editor KHALID AL-ZUBAIDI.

Al Nahda (*The Renaissance*): P.O.B. 1178, Mutrah; fortnightly illustrated magazine; Editor TALEB SAID AL-MEAWALY.

Al Usra (*The Family*): P.O.B. 7440, Mutrah; socio-economic; fortnightly illustrated magazine; Chief Editor SADEK ABDOWANI.

Jund Oman (*Soldiers of Oman*): P.O.B. 113, Muscat; monthly illustrated magazine of the Department of Defence; Supervisor: Deputy Minister for Defence.

RADIO AND TELEVISION

Radio Oman: Muscat; f. 1970; transmits in Arabic 13 hours daily, English 2 hours daily; Acting Dir.-Gen. of Radio ABDUL RAHIM ESSA.

Radio Salalah: f. 1970; transmits daily programmes in Arabic and the Dhofari languages; Director: HAMMAD AL-GHAFRY.

A colour television station built at Qurm outside Muscat by the German Company Siemens A.G. was opened in November 1974. A colour television system for Dhofar opened in late 1975.

The British Broadcasting Corporation has built a powerful medium-wave relay station on Masirah Island. It is used to expand and improve the reception of the B.B.C.'s Arabic, Farsi and Urdu services.

There were an estimated 35,000 TV receivers in use in 1980.

FINANCE

BANKING

(cap.=capital; p.u.=paid up; dep.=deposits; m.=million; br.=branch; RO=rials Omani)

CENTRAL BANK

Central Bank of Oman: P.O.B. 4161 Ruwi, Muscat; f. 1975; cap. RO 50m.; dep. RO 28m.; Chair. (vacant); Deputy Chair. and Pres. Dr. ABDUL WAHAB KHAYATA.

COMMERCIAL BANKS

Al Bank al-Ahli al-Omani S.A.O.: P.O.B. 3134, Ruwi, Muscat; f. 1976; cap. and res. RO 3m.; 20 per cent Société Générale (France), 80 per cent Omani; Chair. Sheikh ZAHER AL-HARTHY; Gen. Man. DEREK J. FLETCHER.

Bank of Oman, Bahrain and Kuwait S.A.O.: P.O.B. 4708, Ruwi; f. 1974; cap. p.u. RO 2m.; dep. RO 38.5m. (April 1982); 11 brs.; Chair. MOHSIN HAIDER DARWISH; Gen. Man. MICHAEL McKINLAY.

Commercial Bank of Oman Ltd.: P.O.B. 4696, Ruwi, Muscat; Gen. Man. SAJID ALI ABBASI.

National Bank of Oman Ltd.: P.O.B. 3751, Ruwi, Muscat; f. 1973; cap. RO 4m.; dep. RO 166m. (Dec. 1981); 36 brs.; Dir. and Gen. Man. S. M. SHAFI.

Oman Arab African Bank: P.O.B. 484, Muscat; Man. BASEM R. NAJJAR.

Union Bank of Oman: P.O.B. 4565, Ruwi, Muscat; f. 1976; cap. p.u. RO 4m., dep. RO 13m. (November 1981); 4 brs.; Gen. Man. R. S. D. FRANK.

FOREIGN BANKS

Arab Bank Ltd. (*Jordan*): P.O.B. 991, Muscat; Man. ABDUL QADER ASKALAN.

Bank of Baroda (*India*): P.O.B. 7231, Mutrah; Man. S. N. AMIN; P.O.B. 4610, Ruwi.

Bank of Credit and Commerce International (Overseas) Ltd. (*Cayman Islands*): P.O.B. 840, Muscat; Country Man. M. ASHRAF KHAN.

Bank Melli Iran: P.O.B. 410, Muscat; Man. MOHSEN PIRZADEH.

Bank Saderat Iran: Muscat; Man. MASOOD AHMED.

Banque de Paris et des Pays-Bas (*France*): P.O.B. 425, Muscat.

British Bank of the Middle East: London; f. 1889; P.O.B. 234, Muscat; 15 brs.; Area Man. F. X. PAUL.

The Chartered Bank (*U.K.*): P.O.B. 5353, Ruwi; Man. A. R. HOLDEN; brs. in Mutrah, Ruwi, Birka and Salalah.

Citibank NA (*U.S.A.*): P.O.B. 918, Muscat.

Grindlays Bank Ltd. (*U.K.*): P.O.B. 91, Muscat; Gen. Man. I. G. McINTOSH; 5 brs. in Muscat, Mutrah, Seeb and Salalah.

Habib Bank AG-Zürich (*Switzerland*): P.O.B. 7338, Mutrah; f. 1969.

Habib Bank Ltd. (*Pakistan*): P.O.B. 7326, Mutrah; br. in Greater Mutrah; Man. S. M. BIRJEES ZAIDI.

National Bank of Abu Dhabi: P.O.B. 303, Muscat; Man. ALI ABDEL SADEQ.

DEVELOPMENT BANKS

Oman Bank for Agriculture and Fisheries: Muscat; f. 1981; short-term finance for private sector projects.

Oman Development Bank S.A.O.: P.O. 309, Muscat; f. 1976; cap. RO 10m.; 40 per cent Oman Government, 40 per cent foreign, 20 per cent Omani private; Chair. MUHAMMAD MUSA ABDULLAH.

Oman Housing Bank: Muscat; f. 1977; cap. RO 20m.; 60.9 per cent Oman Government, 39 per cent Government of Kuwait, 0.1 per cent Oman Development Bank; Gen. Man. MAHMOUD ABUTEEN.

INSURANCE

Oman National Insurance Co. S.A.O.: P.O.B. 5254, Ruwi.

Oman United Agencies Ltd: Muscat; representatives of several British insurance companies; subsidiary of Gray, MacKenzie and Co. Ltd.

TRADE AND INDUSTRY

Oman Chamber of Commerce and Industry: P.O.B. 4400, Ruwi-Muscat; Pres. Sheikh AHMAD MUHAMMAD BIN OMAIR; Dir.-Gen. ALI AL-DAHAB.

PETROLEUM

Petroleum Development Oman: P.O. Box 81, Muscat; incorporated in Sultanate of Oman since 1980 by Royal Decree as limited liability company; 60 per cent owned by Oman Government, 34 per cent by Shell, 4 per cent by CFP and 2 per cent by Partex; current production (November 1981) approximately 328,000 b/d from 12 fields situated in N., Central and S. Oman linked by a pipeline system to terminal at Mina al-Fahal, nr. Muscat; Man. Dir. H. M. BRINKHORST.

Amoco: holds concession area of 13,560 square km. south of Masirah Island; consortium composed of Amoco, Sun Oil, Home Oil of Canada, Canadian Superior, Deutsche Schachtbau and three others; exploration is in progress.

Elf/Sumitomo: concession granted in 1975 for exploration in the onshore region of Butabul; area of 7,000 square km.; converted to a production sharing agreement in October 1976; 48 per cent owned by Elf, 32 per cent by Sumitomo and 20 per cent by Wintershall.

The Government is hoping that more oil will be found in Dhofar and has granted exploration rights over a large area of western and south-western Dhofar to BP, Deminex, AGIP, Hispanoil, Elf/Aquitaine I, Quintana/Gulf and Cluff Oil.

TRANSPORT

ROADS

A network of adequate graded roads links all the main centres of population and only a few mountain villages are not accessible by Land Rover. A rapid road construction programme began in 1970 and by 1977 there were 1,447 km. of asphalt road and 10,500 km. of graded roads. The final link in the 362 km. Dubai-Oman highway was finished in November 1977. A new coastal highway between Muscat and Mutrah was opened in November 1978. In Dhofar tarmac roads have been completed from Raysut through Salalah to Taqa. Roads between Seeb and Nizwa and Salalah and Thumrait have been completed. 1,590 km. of asphalt road are to be built during the 1981–85 plan.

SHIPPING

Port Services Corporation Ltd.: Mina Qaboos, P.O.B. 133, Muscat; Chair. Sayed Salim bin Nasser al-Busaidi; Gen. Man. Awad Salim Shanfari.

The port of Mina Qaboos, at the entrance to the Gulf, was built in 1974 and provides nine deep-water berths varying in length from 250 to 750 feet (76 to 228 metres), with draughts of up to 34 feet (10.4 metres), and three berths for shallow-draught vessels drawing 12 to 16 feet (3.7 to 4.9 metres) of water. Two of the existing berths have been up-graded to a container terminal and equipped with two 35-ton capacity gantry cranes. By 1981 about 1,115 ships were calling at the port, which was handling about 1.5 million tons of cargo (about one-half of its capacity).

The oil terminal at Mina al Fahal can also accommodate the largest super-tankers on off-shore loading buoys. Similar facilities for the import of refined petroleum products exist at Mina al Fahal and Riyam (near Muscat).

Mina Raysut, near Salalah, has four deep-water berths and two shallow berths. Loading facilities for smaller craft exist at Sohar, Khaboura, Sur, Marbet and Salalah.

CIVIL AVIATION

Domestic and international flights operate from Seeb International Airport, whose extended runway was opened in December 1979. Oman's second international airport at Salalah was completed in 1978. Most towns of any size have small air strips.

Gulf Aviation Ltd (Gulf Air): P.O.B. 138, Bahrain; f. 1950; jointly owned by the Governments of Bahrain, Qatar, the United Arab Emirates and Oman; services linking Bahrain, Doha, Abu Dhabi, Dubai, Sharjah, Salalah and Muscat with London, Amsterdam, Paris, Larnaca, Beirut, Cairo, Kuwait, Dhahran, Ras-al-Khaimah, Shiraz, Karachi, Bombay, Baghdad, Amman, Bangkok, Hong Kong and Manila; fleet consists of nine Boeing 737-200, eight L-1011 TriStars.

Other airlines using Seeb for passenger flights include Alia (Jordan), Air India, Air Tanzania, British Airways, EgyptAir, Kuwait Airlines, MEA (Lebanon), PIA (Pakistan), Saudia, Somali Airlines and UTA (France). Cargo flights are operated by TMA (Lebanon) and Tradewinds Airways (United Kingdom).

DEFENCE

Defence Expenditure, 1980: 304 million Omani rials.

Military service: voluntary.

Total armed forces: (July 1981) 14,500: army 11,500; navy 1,000; air force 2,000.

Paramilitary forces: 3,300: tribal Home Guard.

EDUCATION

Until 1970 there were only three primary schools, offering a six-year course of basic education for boys only. There were no schools for girls. In the years since the accession of Sultan Qaboos emphasis has been placed on the expansion of education horizontally as well as vertically all over the Sultanate. From the three primary schools, with a total enrolment of 909 and 30 teachers, the enrolment rose in 1981 to a total of 106,932, of whom 67 per cent were boys and 33 per cent were girls. The number of schools increased to 373, with 5,265 teachers. More than 90 per cent of the teachers are seconded from other countries, primarily from Egypt, Jordan and Sudan. A new Teacher Training Institute was opened in 1978 and has been training Omani teachers for the primary levels at an annual rate of 100 graduates per year. Special institutions have also been established to train students at the preparatory level in technical skills and in agriculture. Plans are under way to found a national university, with the first class of students due to enter in 1986.

BIBLIOGRAPHY

Admiralty. A Handbook of Arabia (London, 1916).

Aitchison, C. V. (Ed.). Government of India Foreign Department—Collection of Treaties Relating to India and Neighbouring Countries. Volume XII (Calcutta 1932).

Badger, G. P. The History of the Imams and Sayyids of Oman, by Salilbin-Razik, from AD 661 to 1856 (Hakluyt Society 1871).

Busch, B. C. Great Britain and the Persian Gulf 1894–1914 (University of California Press, 1967).

Department of Information, Muscat. Oman (London, 1972).

Fact Sheets on Eastern Arabia (Information Center on Eastern Arabia, Brussels, Belgium).

Gibb, H. A. R. Ibn Battuta—Travels in Asia and Africa 1325–1354 (London, 1929).

Hawley, Donald. Oman and its Renaissance (Stacey International, London, 1977).

Holden, D. Farewell to Arabia (London, 1966).

Hopwood, D. (Ed.). The Arabian Peninsula: Society and Politics (London, 1972).

Kelly, J. B. Great Britain and the Persian Gulf, 1793–1880 (London).

Kelly, J. B. Eastern Arabia Frontier (Faber and Faber, London).

Landen, R. G. Oman Since 1856 (Princeton University Press, 1967).

Lorimer, J. C. Gazeteer of the Persian Gulf, Oman and Central Arabia, 2 vols. (Calcutta 1908 and 1915).

Miles, S. B. The Countries and Tribes of the Persian Gulf (3rd edition, Frank Cass, London, 1966).

Morris, James. Sultan in Oman (Faber, London, 1957).

Peterson, J. E. Oman in the Twentieth Century (Croom Helm, London, 1978).

Phillips, Wendell. Unknown Oman (Longmans, London, 1966).

Oman. A History (Longmans, London, 1967).

Royal Institute of International Affairs. Sultanate and Imamate in Oman (Oxford University Press, 1959).

Rubinacci, R. Religion in the Middle East (Ed. Arberry, A. J.) Vol. 2, Chapter 16 (Cambridge).

Skeet, Ian, Muscat and Oman: The End of an Era (Faber and Faber, 1974).

Thesiger, Wilfred. Arabian Sands (Longmans, London, 1959).

Townsend, John. Oman: The Making of the Modern State (Croom Helm, London, 1977).

Wilson, Sir A. T. The Persian Gulf (London, 1928).

Qatar

GEOGRAPHY

The Emirate of Qatar is a peninsula roughly 100 miles in length, with a breadth varying between 35 and 50 miles, on the west coast of the Persian Gulf. The total area is 11,400 sq. km. and in January 1980 the estimated population was 250,000, two-thirds of whom are concentrated in the town of Doha, on the east coast. Two other ports, Zakrit on the west coast and Umm Said on the east, owe their existence to the discovery of petroleum. Zakrit is a convenient, if shallow, harbour for the import of goods from Bahrain, while Umm Said affords anchorage to deep-sea tankers and freighters.

Qatar is stony, sandy and barren; limited supplies of underground water are unsuitable for drinking or agriculture because of high mineral content. Over half the water supply is now provided by sea water distillation processes. The inhabitants have traditionally lived from pearl-diving, fishing and nomadic herding.

HISTORY

Owing to the aridity of the peninsula the early history of Qatar is of little interest, though archaeological expeditions have found evidence of inhabitation in the Stone and Iron ages and as early as 4,000 B.C. In 1916 Great Britain, in order to exclude other powers from the area, made an agreement with the Sheikh of Qatar, who undertook not to cede, mortgage or otherwise dispose of parts of his territories to anyone except the British Government, nor to enter into any relationship with a foreign government other than the British without British consent. Similar agreements had been concluded with Bahrain in 1880 and 1892, with the Trucial States in 1892 and with Kuwait in 1899. In return Britain undertook to protect Qatar from all aggression by sea, and to lend her good offices in case of an overland attack.

The discovery of oil in the 1930s promised greater prosperity for Qatar, but because of the Second World War production did not begin on a commercial scale until 1949 (see below). An ambitious development programme has now been put into operation with the revenues from the production and export of oil. The Sheikhdom took a leading part in moves towards the formation of a Gulf Federation. In January 1961 Qatar joined the Organization of Petroleum Exporting Countries, and in May 1970 it also became a member of OAPEC (the Organization of Arab Petroleum Exporting Countries).

In April 1970 a provisional constitution was announced which, it was said, would assist Qatar's entry into the Federation of Arab Emirates. The first cabinet was formed in May; the Ruler became Prime Minister with responsibility for oil, and six of the other nine members were also members of the Royal Family. However, Qatar decided to remain outside a Gulf Federation and became independent on September 1st, 1971, joining the UN and the Arab League.

Qatar, however, still feels enthusiastic about the idea of some form of enlarged Gulf Federation in the future. Qatar and the United Kingdom immediately signed a new treaty of friendship. Sheikh Ahmad bin Ali al-Thani became Amir on September 4th, but apparently took little interest in affairs of the State. He was deposed on February 22nd, 1972, in a bloodless coup staged by his cousin Sheikh Khalifa bin Hamad al-Thani. Sheikh Khalifa seized power with the support of the ruling al-Thani family, although his avowed purpose included the curtailment of some of the family's long-held privileges. The coup also thwarted the ambitions of the deposed Amir's son, Sheikh Abdul Aziz, who went into exile. Qatar is closely allied with Saudi Arabia and is usually considered as one of the more moderate Arab states. It opposed the Camp David agreements between Egypt, Israel and the U.S.A. and the subsequent Egyptian-Israeli treaty signed in March 1979. In early 1981 Qatar joined the newly-established Gulf Co-operation Council (GCC).

Since his accession in 1972 the Amir has introduced discreet changes, but has preserved the Islamic pattern of life. In accordance with the 1970 constitution, Sheikh Khalifa decreed the first Advisory Council, to complement the ministerial government. Its 20 members, selected from representatives elected by limited suffrage, were increased to 30 in December 1975. The term of the Consultative Assembly was extended for four years in May 1978 and for a further four years in 1982. The Advisory Council's constitutional entitlements include power to debate legislation drafted by the Council of Ministers before ratification and promulgation. It also has power to request ministerial statements on matters of general and specific policy inclusive of the draft budget.

ECONOMIC SURVEY

Agriculture is still developing but outside the capital most of the population is employed in the oil industry, which is the state's principal source of wealth. Fishing, apart from shrimp fishing and processing, is carried on to supply local demands and employs about 2,000 people. Unlike many of the other Sheikhdoms, Qatar has no entrepôt trade.

Interest in the petroleum possibilities of Qatar was first stimulated by the entry of Standard Oil of California into Bahrain in 1930. Shortly afterwards the Anglo-Iranian Company received permission from the ruler to make a surface survey of his territories, and in 1935 they were granted a concession. This gave exclusive petroleum rights in the Sheikhdom and its territorial waters for 75 years. The concession was later transferred to Petroleum Concessions Ltd., which formed an operating company, Petroleum Development (Qatar) Ltd.

Petroleum Development started exploration in 1937 and oil was discovered in 1939. Field activities were interrupted during the war, but resumed in 1947.

By 1949 the company had completed a drilling programme, the laying of a pipeline system from the field of Dukhan, on the west coast, to Umm Said, and the construction of terminal facilities. At the end of that year the first shipment was made from the Umm Said offshore berths. In 1953 the name of the company was changed to Qatar Petroleum Company (QPC). From 1963 to 1970 production remained steady at about 9 million tons per year but expanded rapidly during 1971 to reach 10.3 million tons. The increase was maintained when production reached 11.4 million tons in 1972 and 11.7 million tons in 1973. As demand fell in 1974, production was reduced to 10.3 million tons and fell yet further to 8.0 million tons in 1975. It recovered in 1976 to 11.9 million tons.

An offshore grant, awarded to the Shell Overseas Exploration Company in 1952, covered an area of approximately 10,000 square miles and was due to expire in 2027. Exploration started in 1953. Completion of facilities on Halul Island, some 60 miles off the coast of Qatar, in 1966 catered for production from the offshore field of Idd el Shargi and Shell's second field in Maydam Mazam. Shell Qatar began commercial production of oil in 1966 at an annual rate of more than 5 million long tons, increasing to 15.4 million tons by 1973 but falling to 13.9 million tons in 1974 and 12.1 million tons in 1976. Production from a third field, Bul Hanine, began in 1972. In 1963 the Continental Oil Company of Qatar was granted a concession over land and offshore areas relinquished by the Qatar Petroleum Company and the Shell Company of Qatar, and over a strip of territory in the south of the peninsula not previously included in any concession. In 1969 Qatar and Abu Dhabi agreed on the joint exploration of the al-Bunduq field, which is shared by the two countries. This is being developed by the al-Bunduq Co. Ltd., which is owned by British Petroleum, Compagnie Française des Pétroles and Qatar Oil Japan. Production began in 1976.

By the 1970s the relationships between state and oil companies in the oil-producing countries were radically different from those existing 20 years earlier. In April 1972 the Amir signed a law to create the Qatar National Petroleum Co., with power to carry out a comprehensive range of production, refining and marketing functions. In January 1973 the Qatar Government signed participation agreements with both local crude-producing companies—Qatar Petroleum Co. Ltd. and Shell Company of Qatar Ltd.—whereby it acquired a 25 per cent share in the operations of each company, this to rise to a controlling interest by 1982. Following the Arab-Israeli war of October 1973, however, a movement developed in all the Arab oil-producing states towards increased participation in the operations of the western-owned oil companies (*see* chapter *Oil in the Middle East and North Africa*). Accordingly, the Qatar Government held negotiations with QPC and Shell Company of Qatar in February 1974 and reached agreement on the immediate acquisition by the Government of a 60 per cent interest in each of the companies. Two months later it was further agreed that the companies should buy back at least 60 per cent of the Government's 60 per cent share of production at an average price of 93 per cent of posted prices. After the first six months the price was to be subject to quarterly review. The Government retained its option to sell its remaining 40 per cent of production on world markets or to sell it to the two companies at the price agreed. In September 1976 an agreement was signed for the take-over of the remaining 40 per cent in QPC, and in February 1977 the process was completed when Qatar General Petroleum Corporation (QGPC) signed an agreement for the take-over of the concession originally held by Shell Qatar.

Equally significant results of the Arab-Israeli conflict were severe but temporary cut-backs in oil production among Arab states and sharp but sustained increases in oil prices. Between October 1973 and January 1974 the "take" of the governments of the Gulf producer states (which include Qatar) rose from $3 per barrel to $7. The series of oil price rises has enabled Qatar to contain oil production (reserves are calculated at 5,600 million barrels with little expectation of further discoveries) while increasing revenue. Oil production reached a high of 610,000 b/d in December 1976, was cut in 1977 and 1978 (462,000 b/d in 1978) and was held at around 500,000 b/d until 1981, when it dropped to an average of 404,887 b/d, owing to a surplus of oil on the world market. The Government aimed to export 400,000 b/d but it was doubtful whether this rate could be maintained. Oil revenues rose from $254.8 million in 1972 to $5,200 million in 1980.

In order to avoid complete dependence on oil, the Government has used oil revenues to encourage the growth of other industries. The industrialization programme is centred at Umm Said, employing 2,500 people by 1980. The steel works, built by Japanese firms at a cost of $250 million, opened in April 1978. The complex processes iron ore imported from Australia and the United States and local scrap iron to produce mainly round bars for export to the neighbouring Gulf States. Feasibility studies indicated that prices would be lower than those for European or Japanese products because of lower transport costs but a temporary tariff was introduced on imported steel bars to protect the new industry. Proposals for expansion were shelved in early 1981, but production that year reached 455,000 metric tons. The plant uses natural gas for smelting. The Qatar Fertilizer Company, recovering after initial technical problems, produced 705,906 metric tons of ammonia and 627,630 tons of urea in 1980. Two French companies have constructed a polyethylene plant at Umm Said as the first part of a petro-chemical complex of QPC which went into production in November 1980. An export refinery is planned by the QGPC, with a capacity of 150,000 barrels per day.

The natural gas industry received a setback in 1977 when the liquefaction plant NGL-1 at Umm Said was destroyed by fire, but the plant was rebuilt by the end of 1980 and produces 1,200 tons per day (t.p.d.) of propane, 750 t.p.d. of butane and 450 t.p.d. of gas distillate. NGL-2, when it is opened, will provide ethane for the Qatar Petrochemical Company

(QAPCO) and gas liquids for export. Studies are under way in the NW Dome gasfield, where proven reserves of 100 million million cubic feet exist, and reserves of about 300 million million cubic feet are estimated. By February 1982 five companies had submitted proposals for this project.

Other developments have been in diverse fields. The Qatar Flour Mills Co., which, though privately owned, was set up at the prompting of the Government, operates a mill which can process 100 tons of flour per day. The Qatar National Fishing Co., originally formed in 1966 as an extension of the local shrimp-fishing industry, now has refrigeration and processing plant near Doha harbour capable of handling seven tons of shrimps daily. The Qatar National Cement Manufacturing Co. at Umm Bab began production at a rate of 100,000 tons per year early in 1969; its capacity has since been expanded. A ready-mixed concrete factory, a joint venture with a British firm, started production in 1978. There is a sand-processing plant at Hofuf, and a plastics factory, making pipes, hoses and plastic bags; a paint factory opened in April 1982.

To meet the rising demand for electrical power made by a growing population and industrial expansion, the Government allocated QR 1,300 million to the electricity sector in 1981. The largest electrical project to date is the station at Ras Abu Fontas, built at a cost of $242 million. Completion of this station in 1980 raised total national capacity to 828 MW. The Ras Laffan steam turbine power station is expected to open by 1985, with an initial capacity of 600 MW. It will be fuelled by natural gas from the NW Dome field, and its eventual capacity should reach 1,500 MW. The station will also incorporate a desalination plant with a capacity of 40 million gallons per day.

The Department of Agriculture has already succeeded in making the country self-sufficient in vegetables, production of which was negligible as recently as 1960; fruit production and the planting of trees are making rapid progress. Some vegetables, mainly tomatoes, marrows and cucumbers, are now exported to other Gulf states.

The 1981 budget expenditure represents a 21.6 per cent increase over that of 1980. About QR 2,971 million of the total of QR 8,955 million goes to industry and agriculture, QR 2,366 million being earmarked for QGPC schemes. There has been a new stress on the development of private sector light industry. The benefits of oil revenue have resulted in increased allocations for social services and, in particular, education. Construction of the planned second airport, costing QR900 million, has been postponed, but work has begun on the new university which was expected to open in 1983.

Considerable sums have, of course, been invested in large projects. There is an international airport at Doha, the Doha earth satellite station is to be expanded and Doha port has been much improved with a consequent reduction in delays. Hospitals and other health services have, in the past, received large allocations in the development budget. Allocations for housing projects reached a peak of $257.5 million in 1980. Part of Qatar's oil income has been used to provide foreign aid through various agencies such as the United Nations and the OPEC Special Fund.

The volume of trade has been increasing, particularly with Japan, now Qatar's major trading partner, providing 19.7 per cent of imports in 1980. Imports in 1979 amounted to QR 5,400 million, compared with QR 4,590 million in 1978; the rise was accounted for by the decline in the 1978 figure over the previous year and by inflation and was not, therefore, a rise in real terms. There was a sharp fall in the volume of total imports in 1980, the value dropping less steeply to QR5,267.9 million. Qatar's non-oil export and re-export trade is conducted mainly with the neighbouring Arab states.

STATISTICAL SURVEY

AREA AND POPULATION

AREA	ESTIMATED POPULATION†			
	March 1976			Jan. 1980
	Males	Females	Total	
11,400 sq. km.*	129,518	54,082	183,600	250,000

* 4,402 sq. miles.

† Inclusive of immigrant communities. Native Qataris were estimated to number about 40,000 in 1978.

Capital: Doha (estimated population 180,000 at January 1980).

Labour force (March 1976): 86,727 (males 84,834; females 1,893).

AGRICULTURE
VEGETABLES

	1974	1975	1976	1977	1978
Area (dunums*) . .	9,703	9,812	10,767	13,167	13,840
Production (tons)	18,342	18,644	20,284	24,369	25,727

* 1 dunum = 4,201 sq. metres (1.038 acres).

LIVESTOCK
('ooo head)

	1977	1978	1979	1980
Cattle . .	9.9	7.4	7.5	9.9
Camels . .	10.5	10.9	10.9	10.0
Sheep . .	38.6	35.8	49.9	45.9
Goats . .	39.0	39.1	55.5	55.5
Horses . .	1.2	1.2	1.5	2.5

Livestock products (FAO estimates, 'ooo metric tons, 1980):
Meat 4; Cows' milk 6; Sheep's milk 2; Goats' milk 10.

Source: FAO, Production Yearbook.

Sea fishing ('ooo metric tons): 2.3 in 1974; 2.3 in 1975;
2.7 in 1976; 2.7 in 1977 (all FAO estimates).

MINING

		1974	1975	1976	1977	1978	1979
Crude petroleum .	'ooo metric tons	24,698	21,102	24,018	21,414	23,555	24,500
Natural gas .	million cu. ft./day	n.a.	n.a.	457.7	416.1	502.0	637.1

Sources: OPEC, *Annual Statistical Bulletin,* and *Qatar: Achievements in Industrial Development,* 1981.

CRUDE OIL PRODUCTION
(annual averages, barrels per day)

	1977	1978	1979	1980
Offshore	232,000	249,000	278,000	240,648
Onshore	200,000	234,000	230,000	230,777
Bunduq	10,000	2,500	negligible	n.a.
TOTAL . . .	442,000	485,000	508,000	471,425

Source: Financial Times, February 22nd, 1979 and 1980, February 16th, 1981.

INDUSTRY
SELECTED PRODUCTS

		1976	1977	1978	1979
Nitrogenous fertilizers* . . .	'ooo metric tons	87.0	95.2	75.9	104.0
Motor spirit (petrol)	,, ,, ,,	78	90	94	96
Jet fuel	,, ,, ,,	52	58	59	61
Distillate fuel oils	,, ,, ,,	116	128	126	132
Natural gasolene†	,, ,, ,,	73	20	—	—
Liquefied petroleum gas† . . .	,, ,, ,,	230	25	—	—
Cement	,, ,, ,,	172	167	208	237
Electric energy	million kWh.	816	1,026	1,364	1,400

* Estimated production in terms of nitrogen; figures refer to the 12 months ending June 30th of the year stated.

† Produced at natural gas processing plants.

Source: mainly UN, *Yearbook of Industrial Statistics.*

Nitrogenous fertilizers ('ooo metric tons): 228.6 in 1979/80; 286.1 in 1980/81.

FINANCE
100 dirhams = 1 Qatar riyal (QR).

Coins: 1, 5, 10, 25 and 50 dirhams.

Notes: 1, 5, 10, 50, 100 and 500 riyals.

Exchange rates (May 1982): £1 sterling = 6.69 riyals; U.S. $1 = 3.64 riyals.
100 Qatar riyals = £14.94 = $27.47.

Note: Before June 1966 Qatar's currency was the Persian Gulf Indian rupee, valued at 1s. 6d. sterling (£1 = 13.33 rupees). When the Indian rupee was devalued in June 1966 Qatar adopted Saudi Arabian currency prior to the introduction of the Qatar/Dubai riyal (at par with the old rupee) in September 1966. This new currency was also used in the states of Trucial Oman (now the United Arab Emirates) except Abu Dhabi. The Q/D riyal was valued at 21 U.S. cents ($1 = 4.762 riyals) until August 1971. The riyal's value was 22.8 U.S. cents ($1 = 4.386 riyals) from December 1971 to February 1973; and 25.333 U.S. cents ($1 = 3.947 riyals) from February 1973 to March 1975. In terms of sterling, the value of the Q/D riyal between November 1967 and June 1972 was 1s. 9d. (8.75 new pence), the exchange rate being £1 = 11.429 riyals. When the United Arab Emirates adopted a national currency in May 1973 the Q/D riyal was superseded by the Qatar riyal, with the same value as the old currency. Since March 1975 the value of the Qatar riyal has been frequently adjusted. The average exchange rate (riyals per U.S. dollar) was: 3.931 in 1975; 3.962 in 1976; 3.959 in 1977; 3.877 in 1978; 3.773 in 1979; 3.657 in 1980. Since June 1980 the rate has been $1 = 3.64 riyals.

GOVERNMENT FINANCE
(million Qatar riyals—Fiscal year)

	1978	1979	1980
Revenue . . .	8,225.1	11,743.0	13,744.6
Oil and gas . . .	7,420.8	11,000.0	12,621.3
Other . .	804.3	743.0	1,123.4
Expenditure . .	6,517.7	8,345.0	12,174.2
Foreign grants .	291.3	1,070.0	1,025.2
Other . .	6,226.4	7,275.0	11,149.0

OIL REVENUES
(million U.S. dollars)

1976	1977	1978	1979	1980
2,000	1,900	2,200	3,100	5,200

1980/81 Budget: Expenditure QR 8,955 million.

1981/83 Budget (18 months): Expenditure QR 8,362.6 million.

EXTERNAL TRADE
(million Qatar riyals)

	1974	1975	1976	1977	1978	1979	1980
Imports c.i.f. . .	1,068.9	1,609.8	3,300.3	4,850.1	4,589.7	5,377.7	5,267.9
Exports f.o.b. . .	7,321.0	7,133.0	8,723.0	8,274.0	9,249.0	14,655.0	21,208.0

Exports of crude petroleum (million Qatar riyals): 7,813.8 in 1974; 6,906.0 in 1975; 8,466.7 in 1976; 8,130.0 in 1977; 8,936.0 in 1978; 13,933 in 1979; 19,423 in 1980.

PRINCIPAL COMMODITIES
('ooo Qatar riyals)

IMPORTS	1977	1978	1979	1980
Food and live animals	346,301	456,181	564,576	704,001
Beverages and tobacco	46,845	46,491	55,142	59,992
Crude materials (inedible) except fuels .	62,367	25,977	31,651	74,657
Mineral fuels, lubricants, etc. . .	31,154	19,719	35,534	63,854
Animal and vegetable oils, fats and waxes	6,690	8,269	11,231	20,160
Chemicals and related products . .	145,486	179,931	216,762	281,165
Basic manufactures	982,923	735,723	1,027,443	1,151,080
Machinery and transport equipment .	2,773,464	2,697,573	2,865,636	2,331,540
Miscellaneous manufactured articles .	454,865	419,859	569,725	581,473
TOTAL	4,850,095	4,589,723	5,377,700	5,267,922

PRINCIPAL TRADING PARTNERS
('ooo Qatar riyals)

IMPORTS	1977	1978	1979	1980
Australia	39,660	54,372	106,200	115,549
China, People's Republic . . .	55,880	57,846	71,600	81,174
France	277,462	333,831	535,800	283,343
Germany, Federal Republic . .	344,138	851,364	903,500	323,042
India	106,709	98,980	91,300	109,372
Italy	135,490	213,326	309,600	277,301
Japan	1,293,864	906,473	998,900	964,852
Kuwait	102,760	44,369	38,800	54,738
Lebanon	42,124	41,905	40,200	51,926
Netherlands	167,223	188,392	130,300	154,134
Saudi Arabia	20,055	10,897	20,800	36,193
Switzerland	156,264	48,204	40,900	58,618
United Arab Emirates . . .	224,551	59,471	84,400	153,917
United Kingdom	915,338	721,270	832,400	934,093
U.S.A.	463,816	460,879	465,800	595,070

EXPORTS OF UREA AND AMMONIA

Urea: Total exports in 1977: QR 60.3 million, of which India received QR 19.0 million and Viet-Nam QR 12.3 million; total exports in 1978: QR 166.8 million, of which Pakistan received QR 72.6 million and India QR 66.7 million; total exports in 1979: QR 234.0 million, of which India received QR 108.3 million and China QR 52.2 million; total exports in 1980: QR 514.1 million, of which India received QR 309.1 million and China QR 124.2 million.

Ammonia: Total exports in 1977: QR 10.3 million, of which India received QR 8.1 million and Kuwait QR 2.2 million; total exports in 1978: QR 20.5 million, of which India received QR 15.6 million and Italy QR 3.2 million; total exports in 1979: QR 33.6 million of which India received QR 26.5 million and Italy QR 3.5 million; total exports in 1980: QR 77.4 million, of which India received QR 50.0 million, Denmark QR 6.8 million, France QR 6.1 million and the Philippines QR 5.2 million.

EDUCATION
(1975/76)

	PUPILS		SCHOOLS	TEACHERS
	Boys	Girls		
Primary . .	11,658	10,543	87	⎫
Preparatory . .	3,014	2,631	11	⎬ 1,912
Secondary . .	1,959	1,311	10	⎭
TOTAL . .	16,631	14,535	108	1,912

1980/81: Pupils: 40,000 (25,000 primary, 10,000 preparatory, 5,000 secondary); schools: 141; teachers: 3,486.

THE CONSTITUTION

A provisional constitution came into effect in July 1970. Executive power is put in the hands of the Council of Ministers, appointed by the Head of State, and assisted by an Advisory Council of 20 members (increased to 30 in December 1975), whose term was extended for six years in May 1975, for a further four years in May 1978, and for a further four years in 1982. All fundamental democratic rights are guaranteed. In December 1975 the Advisory Council was granted power to summon individual ministers to answer questions on legislation before promulgation. Previously the Advisory Council was restricted to debating draft bills and regulations before framing recommendations to the Council of Ministers.

THE GOVERNMENT

HEAD OF STATE

Amir: Sheikh KHALIFA BIN HAMAD AL-THANI (assumed power February 22nd, 1972).

COUNCIL OF MINISTERS

(June 1982)

Prime Minister: Sheikh KHALIFA BIN HAMAD AL-THANI.

Heir Apparent, Minister of Defence and Commander-in-Chief of the Armed Forces: Maj.-Gen. Sheikh HAMAD BIN KHALIFA AL-THANI.

Minister of Finance and Petroleum: Sheikh ABDUL-AZIZ BIN KHALIFA AL-THANI.

Minister of Foreign Affairs: Sheikh SUHAIM BIN HAMAD AL-THANI.

Minister of Education, Culture and Youth Care: Sheikh MUHAMMAD BIN HAMAD AL-THANI.

Minister of Public Health: KHALED BIN MUHAMMAD AL-MANA.

Minister of the Economy and Commerce: Sheikh NASSIR BIN KHALID AL-THANI.

Minister of Electricity and Water: Sheikh JASSIM BIN MUHAMMAD AL-THANI.

Minister of Justice: (vacant).

Minister of the Interior: Sheikh KHALID BIN HAMAD AL-THANI.

Minister of Industry and Agriculture: Sheikh FAISAL BIN THANI AL-THANI.

Minister of Public Works: KHALID BIN ABDULLAH AL-ATIYYAH.

Minister of Information: ISSA GHANIM AL-KAWARI.

Minister of Municipal Affairs: Sheikh MUHAMMAD BIN JABR AL-THANI.

Minister of Labour and Social Affairs: ALI BIN AHMAD AL ANSARI.

Minister of Communications and Transport: ABDULLAH BIN NASSIR AL-SUWAIDI.

Minister of State for Foreign Affairs: Sheikh AHMED BIN SAIF AL-THANI.

Adviser to the Amir: Dr. HASAN KAMEL.

ADVISORY COUNCIL

Founded 1972; *see* under Constitution.

Chairman: ABDEL AZIZ AL-GHANEM.

DIPLOMATIC REPRESENTATION

EMBASSIES ACCREDITED TO QATAR

(In Doha unless otherwise stated)

Afghanistan: Baghdad, Iraq.

Argentina: Jeddah, Saudi Arabia.

Australia: Jeddah, Saudi Arabia.

Austria: Jeddah, Saudi Arabia.

Bangladesh: P.O.B. 2080; *Ambassador:* ABDUL HAMEED CHOWDHURY.

Belgium: Kuwait City, Kuwait.

Brazil: Jeddah, Saudi Arabia.

Cameroon: Jeddah, Saudi Arabia.

Canada: Kuwait City, Kuwait.

Czechoslovakia: Kuwait City, Kuwait.

Denmark: Abu Dhabi, United Arab Emirates.

Djibouti: *Ambassador:* ADNAN AL-SHEIKH HASSAN.

Finland: Jeddah, Saudi Arabia.

France: P.O.B. 2669; *Ambassador:* HENRI PIOT.

Gabon: P.O.B. 3566; *Ambassador:* DENIS DANGUI-REWAKA.

Gambia: Jeddah, Saudi Arabia.

Germany, Federal Republic: P.O.B. 3064; *Ambassador:* Dr. THEODER MEZ.

Greece: Kuwait City, Kuwait.

Guinea: Jeddah, Saudi Arabia.

India: P.O.B. 2788; *Ambassador:* JAGANNATH DODDAMANI.

Indonesia: Kuwait City, Kuwait.

Iran: P.O.B. 1633; *Ambassador:* (vacant).

Iraq: P.O.B. 1526; *Ambassador:* TARIQ ABDEL JABBAR JAWAD.

Ireland: Jeddah, Saudi Arabia.

Italy: Kuwait City, Kuwait.

Japan: P.O.B. 2208; *Ambassador:* SHIGEMOTO NOGUSA.

Jordan: P.O.B. 2366; *Ambassador:* KHALID OBAIDAT.

Korea, Republic: P.O.B. 3727; *Ambassador:* WISSING KUSSING.

Kuwait: P.O.B. 1177; *Ambassador:* ABDUL RAHMAN AHMED AL-BAKR.

Lebanon: P.O.B. 2411; *Ambassador:* MUHAMMAD TOUFIK CHATILA.

Libya: P.O.B. 3361; *Secretary of People's Bureau:* MOHIDDIN AL-SADIQ AL-MASSOUDI.

Malaysia: Kuwait City, Kuwait.

Mali: Jeddah, Saudi Arabia.

Malta: Tripoli, Libya.

Mauritania: P.O.B. 3132; *Ambassador:* SEDNA ALI WELD SAHIRI.

Morocco: P.O.B. 3242; *Ambassador:* ABDUL HADI GALOON AL-ANDALUSSI.

Nepal: Jeddah, Saudi Arabia.

Netherlands: Kuwait City, Kuwait.

Norway: Jeddah, Saudi Arabia.

Oman: P.O.B. 1525; *Ambassador:* ABDULLAH ALI AL-NAJJAR.

Pakistan: P.O.B. 334; *Ambassador:* JAHANSIB ARBAB.

Saudi Arabia: P.O.B. 1255; *Ambassador:* ABDUL MOHSEN SOLEIMAN AL-ZAID.

Senegal: Cairo, Egypt.

Sierra Leone: Jeddah, Saudi Arabia.

Somalia: P.O.B. 1948; *Ambassador:* ABDINUR ALI YUSUF.

Spain: Abu Dhabi, United Arab Emirates.

Sudan: P.O.B. 2999; *Ambassador:* HAMAD AL-NIL.

Sweden: Kuwait City, Kuwait.

Switzerland: Amman, Jordan.

Syria: P.O.B. 1257; *Ambassador:* ABDUL AZIZ AL-REFA'AI.

Tunisia: P.O.B. 2707; *Ambassador:* MUHAMMAD EL-MAHERZI.

Turkey: P.O.B. 1911; *Ambassador:* HASSAN HALIS ONAR.

Uganda: Jeddah, Saudi Arabia.

United Kingdom: P.O.B. 3; *Ambassador:* STEPHEN DAY.

U.S.A.: P.O.B. 2399; *Ambassador:* CHARLES E. MARTHINSEN.

Venezuela: Kuwait City, Kuwait.

Yemen Arab Republic: P.O.B. 3318; *Ambassador:* YELNA ABDEL RAHMAN EL-ERIANI.

Zaire: Jeddah, Saudi Arabia (*diplomatic relations broken off in May* 1982).

Qatar also has diplomatic relations with Algeria, Bahrain, Burundi, Chad, Ecuador, Ethiopia, Ghana, Luxembourg, Mexico, Niger, the Philippines, Portugal, Rwanda, Sri Lanka, Thailand, the United Arab Emirates and Yugoslavia.

JUDICIAL SYSTEM

Justice is administered by five courts (Higher Criminal, Lower Criminal, Civil, Labour and the Court of Appeal) on the basis of codified laws. In addition the Sharia Court decides on all issues regarding the personal affairs of Muslims by recourse to Islamic Law of the Holy Quran and the Prophet's Sunna or tradition. Non-Muslims are invariably tried by a court operating codified law. Independence of the judiciary is guaranteed by the provisional Constitution.

Chief Justice: AL-FATEH AWOUDA.

RELIGION

The indigenous population are Muslims of the Sunni sect, most being of the strict Wahhabi persuasion.

THE PRESS

Al-Ahad: P.O.B. 2531, Doha; weekly magazine; Arabic; published by KHALIFA ABDULLAH AL-HUSSAINI.

Al-Dawri: P.O.B. 310, Doha; weekly; sport; published by RASHID BY WAIDAH AL-THANI.

Al-Doha Magazine: Ministry of Information, P.O.B. 1968, Doha; f. 1969; monthly; Arabic; circ. 40,000.

Al-Jawhara: P.O.B. 2531, Doha; monthly; women's magazine; Arabic; published by ABDULLA AL-HUSSAINI.

Al-Khalij al-Jadeed: P.O.B. 1836, Doha; monthly magazine; Arabic; published by Ministry of Information.

Al Mash'al: Qatar Petroleum Producing Authority, P.O.B. 47; Doha; monthly; English and Arabic.

Al-Ouroba: P.O.B. 52, Doha; Newspaper Printing and Publishing, Doha; f. 1957; publ. daily Arabic newspaper *Al-Arab*, circ. 10,000; weekly Arabic magazine *Al-Ouroba*, circ. 15,000; Proprietor and Editor-in-Chief ABDULLA HUSSAIN NAAMA.

Al-Saqer: P.O.B. 4925, Doha; sports magazine; weekly; Arabic.

Al-Tarbbia: P.O.B. 80, Doha; every 2 months; published by Qatar National Commission for Education, Culture and Science.

Al-Umma: Doha; monthly magazine.

Arrayah: P.O.B. 3464, Doha; political; daily; Arabic; published by Gulf Publishing and Printing Organization; circ. 7,000; Editor NASSER AL-OTHMAN.

Daily News Bulletin: P.O.B. 3299, Doha; daily; English and Arabic editions; Dir. and Chief Editor ALI SAEED AL-KAWARI.

Diaruna Wal Alam: Ministry of Finance and Petroleum, P.O.B. 3322, Doha; monthly; English and Arabic.

Gulf Times: P.O.B. 2888, Doha; daily and weekly editions; English; f. 1978; circ. 10,000; Editor BRIAN NICHOLLS.

NEWS AGENCY

Qatar News Agency: P.O.B. 3299, Doha; f. 1975; Dir. and Chief Editor ALI SAEED AL-KAWARI.

RADIO AND TELEVISION

Radio Qatar: P.O.B. 1414, Doha; f. 1968; government service transmitting for 18 hours daily in Arabic, 18 hours daily in English, 3 hours daily in local language and 1 hour daily in Urdu; Dir. ABDUL RAHMAN AL-MADHADI.

Qatar Television: P.O.B. 1944, Doha; f. 1970; 200 kW transmitters began transmissions throughout the Gulf in 1972. Colour transmissions began in 1974. Channel 11, with two 5 kW transmitters, began to operate in June 1980, and Channel 37 (UHF) was launched in February 1982. Dir. MANE ABDULHADI AL-HAJIRI. There were an estimated 100,000 TV receivers in use in 1982.

FINANCE

BANKING

Qatar Monetary Agency: P.O.B. 3144, Doha; f. 1966 as Qatar and Dubai Currency Board; became Qatar Monetary Agency 1973 when Qatar issued its own currency, the Qatar riyal; currency in circulation (first quarter of 1982) QR 1,186m.; Dir. MAJED AL-MAJED.

Qatar National Bank, S.A.Q.: P.O.B. 1002, Doha; f. 1965; cap. and res. QR 407m.; dep. QR 5,085m. (1981); Chair. Sheikh ABDUL AZIZ BIN KHALIFA AL-THANI; Gen. Man. H. A. ALAMI.

Bank Al-Mashrek, S.A.L.: P.O.B. 388, Doha.

Commercial Bank of Qatar Ltd.: P.O.B. 3232, Doha; f. 1975; cap. QR 30m., dep. QR 360m. (Dec. 1980); Gen. Man. FINALY MOODIE.

FOREIGN BANKS

Arab Bank Ltd. (*Jordan*): P.O.B. 172, Doha; Man. Dr. MUHAMMAD M. ABDUL HADI.

Bank of Oman: P.O.B. 173, Doha.

Bank Saderat Iran: P.O.B. 2256, Doha.

Banque de Paris et des Pays-Bas (*France*): P.O.B. 2636, Doha; Man. F. CAZE.

British Bank of the Middle East (*Hong Kong*): Sheikh Ali Rd., P.O.B. 57, Doha; Man. G. W. BARROW.

Chartered Bank (*U.K.*): P.O.B. 29, Doha; Gen. Man. JAMES KENT.

Citibank N.A. (*U.S.A.*): Citibank Bldg., Salwa Rd., P.O.B. 2309, Doha,

Doha Bank: P.O.B. 3818, Doha, and P.O.B. 2822, Doha.

Grindlays Bank Ltd. (*U.K.*): Rayyan Rd., P.O.B. 2001, Doha; Gen. Man. L. B. CANT.

United Bank of Pakistan: P.O.B. 242, Doha.

INSURANCE

Alkhaleej Insurance Co. S.A.Q.: Sheikh Abdul Aziz bin Ahmed al-Ahmed al-Thani St., P.O.B. 4555, Doha; f. 1978; authorized capital QR 3m. (1982); all classes.

Qatar General Insurance and Reinsurance Co. S.A.Q.: Ras Abu Aboud St., P.O.B. 4500, Doha; cap. QR 5m.; all classes.

Qatar Insurance Co.: P.O.B. 666, Doha; f. 1964; assets and reserves QR 160m. (1979); branches in Dubai and Riyadh; Man. FATHI I. GABR.

COMMERCE

Qatar Chamber of Commerce: P.O.B. 402, Doha; f. 1963; 13 mems. appointed by decree; Pres. AHMED MUHAMMAD AL-SOWAIDI; Dir.-Gen. KAMAL ALI SALEH.

TRADE AND INDUSTRY

STATE ENTERPRISES

Qatar General Petroleum Corporation (QGPC): P.O.B. 3212, Doha; capital QR 4,000 million; the State of Qatar's interest in companies active in petroleum and related industries has passed to the Corporation. In line with OPEC policy, the Government agreed a participation agreement with the Qatar Petroleum Company and Shell Company of Qatar in 1974 to secure Qatar's interest and obtained a 60 per cent interest in both. In late 1976, under two separate agreements, the Government secured a 100 per cent interest in both companies.

The Qatar Petroleum Producing Authority (QPPA) was established in 1976 as a subsidiary wholly owned by the Corporation to carry out all operations previously carried out by the two companies. In February 1980 the QPPA was merged with the Corporation.

Qatar General Petroleum Corporation wholly or partly owns: National Oil Distribution Co. (NODCO), Qatar Fertilizer Co. Ltd. (QAFCO), Qatar Petrochemical Co. Ltd. (QAPCO), Qatar Gas Co. (QGC), Compagnie Petrochemique du Nord (COPENOR), Arab Maritime Petroleum Transport Co. Ltd., Arab Pipelines Co. (SUMED), Arab Shipbuilding and Repair Yard Co., Arab Petroleum Services Co. and Arab Petroleum Investments Corp. (APICORP); Chair. Sheikh ABDUL AZIZ BIN KHALIFA AL-THANI (Minister of Finance and Petroleum); Dir.-Gen. ALI MUHAMMAD JAIDAH; Deputy Man. Dir. Sheikh RASHID O. AL-THANI.

Qatar General Petroleum Corporation (Onshore Operations): Doha; produces and exports crude oil and natural gas liquids from the Dukhan oilfield (onshore). The operation is now run by personnel seconded by the Dukhan Service Co. and by hired personnel; production in 1980 was 84.2 million barrels.

Qatar General Petroleum Corporation (Offshore Operations): P.O.B. 47, Doha; state-owned organization for offshore oil/gas exploration and production; Man. Dir. ALI M. JAIDAH; Exec. Man. MENNO SCHEPERS; Deputy Exec. Man. AHMED HASSAN BILAL; production in 1980 was 88 million barrels.

Qatar Gas Company: Doha; f. 1974; natural gas; Qatar Government owns 70 per cent and Shell the remaining 30 per cent; capital QR 400 million.

Wintershall: leads a consortium of five companies carrying out exploration.

TRANSPORT

ROADS

There are some 965 km. (600 miles) of surfaced road linking Doha and the oil centres of Dukhan and Umm Said with the northern end of the peninsula. A 105-km. (65-mile) long road from Doha to Salwa was completed in 1970, and joins one leading from Al Hufuf in Saudi Arabia, giving Qatar land access to the Mediterranean. A 418-km. (260-mile) highway, built in conjunction with Abu Dhabi, links both states with the Gulf network. Road construction is a continual process.

PIPELINES

Oil is transported by pipeline from the oilfields at Dukhan to the loading terminal at Umm Said. Natural gas is brought by pipeline from Dukhan to Doha where it is used as fuel for a power station and water distillation plant.

SHIPPING

Qatar National Navigation and Transport Co. Ltd.: P.O.B. 153, Doha; f. 1957; sole shipping agents for all dry cargo and passenger vessels.

Director of Ports: ABDULREHMAN JABER MUFTAH, P.O.B. 313, Doha.

Doha Port: In 1981 there were 4 berths of 9.1 metres depth and 5 berths of 7.5 metres depth. Total length of berths is 1,699 metres.

Umm Said Harbour: The Northern Deep Water Wharves consist of a deep-water quay 730m. long with a dredged depth alongside of 15.5m.; and a quay 570m. long with a dredged depth alongside of 13.0m. The General Cargo Wharves consist of a quay 400m. long with a dredged depth alongside of 10.0m. The Southern Deep Water Wharves consist of a deep water quay 508m. long with a dredged depth alongside of 13.0m.

CIVIL AVIATION

Doha international airport is equipped to receive jumbo jets; its runway was extended to 15,000 ft. in 1970. Plans for a new civil airport, to have one of the longest runways in the world (14,993 ft.), were postponed in early 1980.

Gulf Air Co. Ltd.: jointly owned by Bahrain, Qatar, the U.A.E. and Oman (*see* Oman—Civil Aviation).

Gulf Helicopters: P.O.B. 811, Doha; owned by Gulf Air Co. GSC; fleet of six Bell 212; Chair. ABDULLA AL-ATTIVA.

Doha is also served by the following airlines: Air France, Air India, Alia (Jordan), British Airways, Cathay Pacific Airlines (Hong Kong), EgyptAir, Iran Air, Iraqi Airways, KLM (Netherlands), Korean Air Lines (Republic of Korea), Kuwait Airways, MEA (Lebanon), PIA (Pakistan), Sabena (Belgium), Saudia, SIA (Singapore), Sudan Airways, Syrian Arab Airlines, TWA (U.S.A.), Yemen Airways (Yemen Arab Republic).

DEFENCE

Defence Expenditure, 1980: 2,200 million Qatar riyals.

Total armed forces: 9,700: army 9,000; navy 400; air force 300.

EDUCATION

All education within Qatar is free and numerous scholarships are awarded for study overseas. The state education system was inaugurated in 1956, when 1,388 boys attended 17 primary schools: by 1981/82 some 26,802 children (13,911 boys and 12,891 girls) attended primary school. The six-year primary stage is followed by a three-year preparatory stage (4,811 boys and 4,851 girls in 1981/82) and a further three-year secondary stage. In 1981/82 there were 3,797 teachers (1,704 males and 2,093 females) and about 42,610 pupils in all schools. General secondary education facilities are complemented by a National Training Institute, a technical school, a school of commerce and an institute of religious studies. An institute of administration and a language teaching institute help to raise the standard of government officials. In 1981/82 2,724 boys and 2,960 girls received general secondary education. In 1980/81 some 1,300 Qataris were sent on scholarships to higher education institutions abroad, in other Arab countries, Britain, France or the U.S.A. The number of schools (149 in 1981/82) and of teachers (3,797), together with budget expenditure of about £3,000 per pupil indicates the importance given to education in Qatar. In October 1973 the first two Higher Teacher Training Colleges were opened providing education to university level. In 1980/81 the University of Qatar comprised the faculties of education, science, social sciences and engineering. Faculties of administration and economics, and of communications and information were to be opened in 1983. A total of 2,642 students were enrolled (875 boys and 1,767 girls).

BIBLIOGRAPHY

See Bibliography on Bahrain, p. 296, and United Arab Emirates, p. 873.

Saudi Arabia

PHYSICAL AND SOCIAL GEOGRAPHY OF THE ARABIAN PENINSULA

The Arabian peninsula is a strongly marked geographical unit, being delimited on three sides by sea—on the east by the Persian Gulf and Gulf of Oman, on the south by the Indian Ocean, and on the west by the Red Sea—and its remaining (northern) side is occupied by the deserts of Jordan and Iraq. This isolated territory, extending over more than one million square miles, is, however, divided politically into several states. The largest of these is Saudi Arabia, which occupies over 2,000,000 sq. km.; to the east and south lie much smaller territories where suzerainty and even actual frontiers are in some instances a matter of doubt. Along the shores of the Persian Gulf and Gulf of Oman there are first the State of Kuwait, with two adjacent patches of "neutral" territory; then, after a stretch of Saudi coast, the island of Bahrain and the Qatar peninsula, followed by the United Arab Emirates and the much larger state of Oman. The People's Democratic Republic of Yemen occupies most of the southern coastline of the peninsula. To the north of it, facing the Red Sea, lies the Yemen Arab Republic. The precise location of frontiers between these states and Saudi Arabia, which adjoins them all, is still in some doubt, and atlases show varying positions. The granting of oil concessions and continued discoveries of oil may ultimately lead to a more accurate delimitation.

PHYSICAL FEATURES

Structurally, the whole of Arabia is a vast platform of ancient rocks, once continuous with north-east Africa. In relatively recent geological time a series of great fissures opened, as the result of which a large trough, or rift valley, was formed and later occupied by the sea, to produce the Red Sea and Gulf of Aden. The Arabian platform is tilted, having its highest part in the extreme west, along the Red Sea; and it slopes gradually down from west to east. Thus the Red Sea coast is often bold and mountainous, whereas the Persian Gulf coast is flat and low-lying, being fringed with extensive coral reefs that make it difficult to approach the shore in many places.

Dislocation of the rock strata in the west of Arabia has led to the upwelling of much lava, which has solidified into vast barren expanses known as *harras*. Volcanic cones and flows are also prominent along the whole length of the western coast as far as Aden, giving peaks that rise well above 3,000 metres. The maximum height of the mountains is attained in the south, in the Yemen Arab Republic, where summits reach 4,000 metres; and the lowest part of this mountain wall occurs roughly half-way along its course, in the region of Jeddah, Mecca, and Medina. One main reason for the presence of these three towns is the

geographical fact that they offer the easiest route inland from the coast, and one of the shortest routes across Arabia.

Further to the east the ancient platform is covered by relatively thin layers of younger rocks. Some of the strata have weathered away to form shallow depressions; others have proved more resistant, and now stand out as ridges. This central area, diversified by shallow vales and upstanding ridges and covered in many places by desert sand, is called the Najd, and is spoken of as the homeland of the Wahhabi sect, which now rules the whole of Saudi Arabia. Farther east still, practically all the land lies well below 300 metres in altitude, and both to north and south lie desert areas. The Nefud in the north has some wells, and even a slight rainfall, so life is possible for a few oasis cultivators and pastoral nomads. But south of the Najd lies the Rub' al-Khali, or Empty Quarter, a rainless, unrelieved wilderness of shifting sand, too difficult for occupation even by nomads.

Though most of the east coast of Arabia (termed al-Hasa) is low-lying, there is an exception in the imposing ridge of the Jebel Akhdar of Oman, which also produces a fjord-like coastline along the Gulf of Oman. One other feature of importance is the presence of several large river valleys, or *wadis*, cut by river action at an earlier geological period, but now almost, or entirely, dry and partly covered in sand. The largest is the Wadi Hadhramaut, which runs parallel to the southern coast for several hundred miles; another is the Wadi Sirhan, which stretches from the Nefud north-westwards into Jordan.

CLIMATE

Because of its land-locked nature, the winds reaching Arabia are generally dry, and almost all the area is arid. In the north there is a rainfall of 10 to 20 cm. annually; further south, except near the coast, even this fails. The higher parts of the west and south do, however, experience appreciable falls—rather sporadic in some parts, but copious and reliable in the Yemen Arab Republic. There are even small, regularly flowing streams in the higher parts of the Yemeni mountains, but none manages to reach the sea. The Jebel Akhdar (Green Mountain) of Oman, as its name indicates, also has more rainfall than the surrounding districts.

Because of aridity, and hence relatively cloudless skies, there are great extremes of temperature. The summer is overwhelmingly hot, with maxima of over 50°C., which are intensified by the dark rocks, whilst in winter there can be general severe frost and even weeks of snow in the mountains—sheepskins are worn in the Yemen Arab Republic. Another feature, due to wide alternations of temperature, is the prevalence of violent local winds. Also, near the coast, atmospheric humidity is very high, and this makes living conditions extremely unpleasant. The coasts of both the Red Sea and Persian Gulf are notorious for their humidity.

Owing to the tilt of the strata eastwards, and their great elevation in the west, rainfall occurring in the hills near the Red Sea apparently percolates gradually eastwards, to emerge as springs along the Persian Gulf coast. This phenomenon, borne out by the fact that the flow of water in the springs greatly exceeds the total rainfall in the same district, would appear to indicate that water may be present underground over much of the interior. Hence irrigation schemes to tap these supplies have been developed, notably in Najd at al-Kharj. Results are, however, fairly limited.

ECONOMIC LIFE

Over much of Arabia, life is dependent on the occurrence of oases. Many wells are used solely by nomads for watering their animals, but in some parts, more especially the south, there is some regular cultivation. The Yemen Arab Republic, in particular, has a well-developed agriculture, showing a gradation of crops according to altitude, with cereals, fruit, coffee and *qat* (a narcotic) as the chief products. Other agricultural districts occur in Aden and the Hadhramaut (in Yemen P.D.R.), in Oman, and in the large oases of the Hijaz (including Medina and Mecca).

Despite this, however, it must be emphasized that in the main, conditions in Arabia are harsh, and human life depends for existence partly on resources brought in from outside—the revenues from pilgrimage, etc. A major change in the economy of Saudi Arabia and the Gulf states has taken place following the exploitation of oil, the revenues from which have transformed those states.

RACE

The inhabitants of the centre, north, and west are of almost unmixed Mediterranean stock—lightly built, long-headed, and dark. In coastal districts of the east, south, and south-west intermixture of broader-headed and slightly heavier peoples of Armenoid descent is a prominent feature; and there has been some exchange of racial type with the populations on the Persian shores of the Persian Gulf and Gulf of Oman. Owing to the long-continued slave trade, negroid influences from Africa are also widespread. On this basis it is possible to delimit two ethnic zones within Arabia: a northern, central and western area, geographically arid and in isolation, with a relatively unmixed racial composition; and the coastlands of the south, south-west, and east, showing a mixed population.

LANGUAGE

Arabic is the only language of Arabia. Unlike many other parts of the Middle East, European languages are not current.

HISTORY

ANCIENT AND MEDIEVAL HISTORY

Although there is some support for the belief that Arabia was at one time a land of great fertility, there is little evidence of this in historical times. For the most part Arabian history has been the account of small pockets of settled civilization, subsisting mainly on trade, in the midst of an ocean of nomadic tribes whose livelihood was derived mainly from camel-breeding and raiding. The earliest urban settlements developed in the south-west, where the flourishing Minaean kingdom is believed to have been established as early as the twelfth century B.C. This was followed by the Sabaean and Himyarite kingdoms, which lasted with varying degrees of power until the sixth century A.D. The term "kingdom" in this connection implies rather a loose federation of city states than a centralized monarchy. As an important trading station between east and west, southern Arabia was brought into early contact with the Persian and Roman empires, whence spread the influence of Judaism, Zoroastrianism, and later Christianity. Politically, however, the south Arabian principalities remained independent, though there was an abortive Roman expedition in A.D. 24, and two brief periods of Abyssinian rule in the fourth and sixth centuries A.D.

By the end of the sixth century the centre of gravity had shifted to the west coast, to the Hijaz cities of at-Ta'if, Mecca and Medina. While the southern regions fell under the somewhat spasmodic control of the Sasanid rulers of Persia, the Hijaz grew in independence and importance as a trade route between the Byzantine Empire, Egypt, and the East. From the fifth century onwards Mecca was dominated by the tribe of Quraish, through whose extensive commercial activities influences from Byzantine, Persian, Aramaic and Judaic sources began to make themselves felt. Meanwhile the central deserts remained obstinately nomadic, and the inhospitable east coast formed for the most part a corner of the Persian sphere of influence.

It is not necessary here to relate in detail the events that led to the spectacular outbreak of the Arabs from the Arabian peninsula and their political and social domination within a century of an area extending from Spain to northern India. Ostensibly the driving force behind this great movement was the Islamic religion preached by Muhammad, a humble member of the Quraish tribe; and so powerful was its appeal that not only was the faith itself widely adopted, but even the language of its holy book, the Koran, has left an indelible impression on the speech of all the peoples it reached.

But this flowering and development of Arabism was to proceed for the most part outside the confines of the Arabian peninsula itself. The Islamic unification of the Near and Middle East reduced the importance of the Hijaz as a trade route. Mecca retained a unique status as a centre of pilgrimage for the whole Muslim world, but Arabia as a whole, temporarily united under Muhammad and his successors, soon drifted back into disunity. The Yemen was the first to break away from the weakening Abbasid Caliphate in Baghdad, and from the ninth century onwards a variety of small dynasties established themselves in Sana'a, Zabid, and other towns. Mecca also had its semi-independent governors, though their proximity to Egypt made them more cautious in their attitude towards the Caliphs and the later rulers of that country, particularly the Fatimids of the tenth to twelfth centuries. In Oman in the south-east a line of spiritual Imams arose who before long were exercising temporal power; to the north the Arabian shores of the Persian Gulf provided a home for the fanatical Carmathian sect whose influence at times extended as far as Iraq, Syria, Mecca, and the Yemen.

THE OTTOMAN PERIOD

Arabia continued to be restless and unsettled until the beginning of the sixteenth century, when the whole peninsula came nominally under the suzerainty of the Ottoman Sultans at Istanbul. It was a hold that was never very strong, even in the Hijaz, while in Oman and the Yemen native lines of Imams were once again exercising unfettered authority before the end of the century. More important for the future of the peninsula was the appearance of European merchant adventurers in the Indian Ocean and the Persian/Arabian Gulf. The Portuguese were the first to arrive in the sixteenth century, and they were succeeded in the seventeenth and eighteenth centuries by the English, Dutch and French. By the beginning of the nineteenth century Britain had eliminated her European rivals and had established her influence firmly in the Gulf and to a lesser extent along the southern coast.

The political structure of Arabia was now beginning to take the shape it has today. The Yemen was already a virtually independent Imamate; Lahej broke away in the middle of the eighteenth century, only to lose Aden to Britain in 1839 and to become the nucleus of the Aden Protectorate. To the north of the Yemen was the principality of the Asir, generally independent, though both countries were occupied by the Turks from 1850 to the outbreak of the Great War. The Hijaz continued to be a province of the Ottoman Empire. In 1793 the Sultanate of Oman was established with its capital at Muscat, and during the nineteenth century all the rulers and chieftains along the Persian Gulf coast, including Oman, the sheikhdoms of the Trucial Coast, Bahrain and Kuwait, entered into close and "exclusive" treaty relations with the British Government. Britain was principally concerned to prevent French, Russian and German penetration towards India and to suppress the slave and arms trades.

Meanwhile the Najd in the centre of Arabia was the scene of another upheaval with religious inspirations. The puritanical and reforming Wahhabi movement, launched in the middle of the eighteenth century, had by 1800 reached such strength that its followers were able to capture Kerbela and Najaf in Iraq, Damascus in Syria, and Mecca and Medina in the Hijaz. They were defeated by Muhammad Ali of Egypt, acting in the name of the Ottoman Sultan, in 1811–1818 and again in 1838; but the Wahhabi ruling house of Sa'ud continued to rule in the interior. Towards the end of the century they were in danger of being eclipsed by the Shammar line of Rashid to the north, who had Turkish support; but in 1902 Abd al-Aziz ibn Sa'ud, the late ruler of Saudi Arabia, succeeded in recapturing the Wahhabi capital of Riyadh, and by the outbreak of the Great War was master of the whole of central Arabia, including the Hasa coast of the Persian Gulf. In 1910, with the aim of reviving the ideals of the Wahhabi movement, he established the *Ikhwan* or Brethren and proceeded to settle them in colonies throughout the Najd, thus forming the basis of a centralized organization that was to prove a powerful instrument in later years.

MODERN HISTORY

When Turkey entered the war on the side of Germany in October 1914 Arabia inevitably became a centre of intrigue, if not necessarily of military action. British influence was paramount along the eastern and southern coasts, where the various sheikhs and tribal chiefs from Kuwait to the Hadhramaut lost no time in severing their last slender connections with the Ottoman Empire. On the other hand, the Turks had faithful allies in Ibn Rashid of the Shammar to the north of the Najd, and in Imam Yahya of the Yemen; they also retained their garrisons along the west coast, both in the Asir, whose Idrisi ruler was impelled by his long-standing enmity with the Imam of the Yemen to intrigue against them, and in the Hijaz, where Sharif Hussein of Mecca still acknowledged Ottoman suzerainty. In the centre Ibn Sa'ud, who had accepted Turkish recognition in 1913 of his occupation of the Hasa coast, was in close and friendly relations with the Government of India.

British military strategy developed as the war dragged on into a two-pronged thrust against the Turks from both Egypt and the Persian Gulf. In the implementation of this plan opinions were divided on the extent to which use could be made of the Arab population. The Indian Government on the eastern wing, while favouring the pretensions of Ibn Sa'ud, preferred to see the problem in purely military terms, and opposed any suggestion of an Arab revolt. This, however, was the scheme favoured by the Arab Bureau in Cairo, whose views eventually prevailed in London. They were alarmed at the Ottoman declaration of a *Jihad* (Holy War) and possible repercussions in Egypt and North Africa. Negotiations were started at a very early stage with Arab nationalist movements in Syria and Egypt, but these met with comparatively little success. More progress was made when the British negotiators turned their attentions to the Sharif of Mecca, Hussein, member of the Hashimi family that had ruled in Mecca since the eleventh century A.D. The support of such a religious dignitary would be an effective counter to Turkish claims. Hussein was inclined to favour the Allied cause, but was reluctant to act independently, and it was only after he had elicited from the British (in the Mac-Mahon correspondence—*see* DOCUMENTS ON PALESTINE, p. 66) promises which he believed would meet Arab nationalist aspirations that he decided to move. On June 5th, 1916, he proclaimed Arab independence and declared war on the Turks. By November things had gone so well that he felt able to claim the title of King of the Hijaz. Military operations continued throughout the winter, and in July 1917 the port of Aqaba was captured and the Hijaz cleared of Turkish troops except for a beleaguered and helpless garrison in Medina.

Arabia thereafter remained comparatively peaceful, and was not even greatly disturbed by the complicated post-war political manoeuvres in the Middle East. Hussein played a somewhat ineffectual role in maintaining the Arab point of view at the peace conferences and over the allocation of mandates, and as a result forfeited the favour of the British Government. When, therefore, he was unwise enough to challenge the growing power of his old enemy Ibn Sa'ud, he found himself entirely without support. Ibn Sa'ud's stature had been steadily growing since the end of the war. In November 1921 he had succeeded in eliminating the house of Ibn Rashid and annexing the Shammar, and a year later he was recognized by the Government of India as overlord of Ha'il, Shammar and Jawf. On March 5th, 1924, King Hussein laid claim to the title of Caliph, vacant by the deposition of the Ottoman Sultan. His claims were nowhere recognized, and Ibn Sa'ud, declaring him a traitor, overran the Hijaz in a campaign of a few months, captured Mecca and forced Hussein's abdication. Hussein's eldest son, Ali, continued to hold Jeddah for another year, but was then driven out, and on January 8th, 1926, Ibn Sa'ud proclaimed himself King of the Hijaz, so formally marking the establishment of the Saudi Arabian kingdom.

THE KINGDOM OF SAUDI ARABIA*

Ibn Sa'ud's new status was recognized by Britain in the Treaty of Jeddah of 1927, while Ibn Sa'ud in his turn acknowledged his rival Hussein's sons, Abdallah and Faisal, as rulers of Transjordan and Iraq, and also the special status of the British-protected sheikhdoms along the Gulf coast. The northern frontier of his domains had previously been established by the Hadda and Bahra agreements of November 1925, which set the Mandate boundaries as the limit of his expansion; while the border war with Yemen

* For subsequent developments in the rest of the Arabian Peninsula, *see* separate chapters on Bahrain, Kuwait, Oman, Qatar, United Arab Emirates, Yemen Arab Republic and Yemen People's Democratic Republic.

was, after protracted negotiations and a brief war, settled in 1934. (For a fuller account of this, *see* the Yemen Arab Republic chapter, History.)

During the years that followed, the new king continued to be absorbed in his primary task of unifying and developing his country. The colonization policy begun in 1910 was pursued vigorously; land settlements were established and Bedouin unruliness was suppressed. A start was made at the modernization of communications, and the need for economic development along modern lines was emphasized by the falling-off in the pilgrimage during the early 1930s. The serious crisis that this produced might indeed never have been averted had it not been for the discovery of oil in Bahrain in 1932 and the subsequent extension of prospecting to the mainland.

Saudia Arabia's chief sufferings during the Second World War were economic, though there was an Italian air raid on Dhahran in October 1940. The pilgrimage traffic dropped away almost to extinction, and in April 1943 it was found necessary to include Saudi Arabia in the benefits of Lease-Lend. By 1948 the oil industry alone was enough to establish the Saudi Arabian economy firmly on its feet.

In January 1944 the California Arabian Standard Oil Company, owned jointly by the Standard Oil Company of California and the Texas Company, was re-formed as the Arabian American Oil Company. This was reconstructed once more in December 1948 to include the Standard Oil Company of New Jersey and Socony Vacuum—a move that brought protests from the French Government. Under an agreement of 1928 shareholders in the Iraq Petroleum Company, who included the latter two American companies as well as French and British interests, had agreed not to secure rival concessions within an area including the Arabian peninsula. A settlement was finally reached at the end of 1948, by which this so-called "Red Line" clause was abandoned. Meanwhile production had been mounting steadily as new fields were developed; a refinery was opened at Ras Tanura in October 1945, and two years later work was started on a pipeline to connect the Arabian fields with the Mediterranean. In spite of a year's suspension owing to events in Palestine, the task was completed before the end of 1950, and oil first reached the Lebanese port of Sidon on December 2nd of that year. In the same month a new "fifty-fifty" agreement was signed with the Arabian American Oil Company which was to set an interesting example to other foreign oil interests in December 1951. In 1956 a government-owned National Oil Company was formed to exploit areas not covered by the Aramco concession.

Saudi Arabia was an original member of the Arab League formed in 1945, and to begin with played a loyal and comparatively inconspicuous part. Ibn Sa'ud sent a small force to join the fighting against Israel in the summer of 1948. When the solidarity of the League began to show signs of cracking, it was natural that he should side with Egypt and Syria rather than with his old dynastic enemies, the rulers of Iraq and Jordan. In course of time, however, he began to turn once more to internal development, and to forget his political quarrel with the United States in his need for economic advice and aid. The $15,000,000 Export-Import Bank loan was finally taken up in August 1950; in January 1951 a Point Four Agreement was signed, and in June a Mutual Assistance Pact. But the real basis of development was the revenue from the ever-expanding oil industry. This was sufficient to justify the announcement in July 1949 of a $270,000,000 Four Year Plan, in which an ambitious programme of railway development was the main item. A railway now links the oilfields in the east with Riyadh in the centre, and extends to the port of Dammam. For the rest the King's policy was one of cautious modernization at home, and the enhancement of Saudi Arabian prestige and influence in the Middle East and in world affairs generally.

AFTER IBN SA'UD

On November 9th, 1953, King Ibn Sa'ud died at the age of 71, and was succeeded peacefully by the Crown Prince, Sa'ud. It was assumed that there would be no major changes, but the policy already adopted of strengthening the governmental machine and of relying less on one-man rule was continued by the formation of new ministries and of a regular cabinet. In March 1958 King Sa'ud conferred upon his brother, the Amir Faisal, full powers over the foreign, internal and economic affairs of Saudi Arabia, with the professed aim of strengthening the machinery of government and centralizing responsibilities. In December 1960, however, the Amir Faisal resigned, and the King took over the office of Prime Minister himself. In the following month a High Planning Council, with a team of international experts, was set up to survey the country's resources, and thereafter there has been slow but steady progress in the modernization of the country.

Throughout his reign the King regarded his role as that of a mediator between the conflicting national and foreign interests in the Arab Middle East. He refused to join either the United Arab Republic or the rival Arab Federation. Relations with Egypt ranged from the mutual defence pacts between Egypt, Syria and Saudi Arabia in October 1955 (to which Yemen and Jordan adhered the following year) to the open quarrel in March 1958 over an alleged plot to assassinate President Nasser. Subsequently, relations improved, and the King visited Cairo in September 1959. Contacts with the United States have always been close, owing to the extensive American oil interests. The Saudi Arabian Government also played a leading role in bringing the Arab governments together after Egypt's nationalization of the Suez Canal in July 1956 and the Israeli, British and French military action in the Sinai peninsula in November. In 1961 Saudi Arabia supported the Syrians in their break with the United Arab Republic, and in general relations with the U.A.R. deteriorated. By 1964, however, in spite of the tensions over the Yemen revolution, there were signs of improved relations. King Sa'ud attended the Cairo conference on the Jordan waters dispute in January, and in March,

after a meeting in Riyadh, diplomatic relations with the U.A.R. were resumed. In September Prince Faisal attended the Arab Summit Conference in Alexandria, and afterwards had talks with President Nasser on the Yemen situation.

THE REIGN OF KING FAISAL

Meanwhile, in March 1964 King Sa'ud had relinquished all real power over the affairs of the country to his brother, Crown Prince Faisal, who had again acted as Prime Minister intermittently during 1962, and continuously since the middle of 1963. The rule of Prince Faisal was expected to result in many concessions to "Westernization" such as more cinemas and television, with more profound social and economic reforms to follow. The division of the country into provinces, each with a thirty-man council, was under study early in 1964. The change of power, by which King Sa'ud retired as active monarch, was supported in a statement by the *ulema* council of religious leaders "in the light of developments, the King's condition of health, and his inability to attend to state affairs". In November 1964 Sa'ud was formally deposed, and Faisal became King, as well as head of the Council of Ministers with the exclusive power of appointing and dismissing Ministers. His younger brother Khalid was appointed Crown Prince. On August 24th, 1965, King Faisal confirmed his stature as an important Arab leader, when he concluded an agreement at Jeddah with President Nasser of the U.A.R. on a peace plan for the Yemen.

Although the Yemen problem remained unsolved, there was evidence of Saudi Arabia's genuine anxiety that a solution should be found, even though in April 1966 the construction of a military airfield near the frontier brought protests from the Yemeni Republican Government and the U.A.R. Representatives of Saudi Arabia and the U.A.R. met in Kuwait in August 1966 in an attempt to implement the Jeddah agreement. But relations with both the U.A.R. and the Arab League continued to be tense, and no progress was evident. Matters were not improved by the appearance in Cairo of ex-King Sa'ud, with a public declaration of his support for U.A.R. policy in Yemen.

During 1966 and 1967 King Faisal made extensive visits abroad. In the June 1967 Arab-Israeli war, Saudi forces collaborated with Jordanian and Iraqi forces in action against Israel. At a summit conference of Arab leaders held in Khartoum at the end of August 1967 Saudi Arabia agreed to put up £50 million of a total £135 million fund to assist Jordan and the U.A.R. in restoring their economic strength after the hostilities with Israel. At the same time an agreement was concluded with President Nasser on the withdrawal of U.A.R. and Saudi military support for the warring parties in the Yemen. By way of recompense for these concessions the Saudi Arabian Government persuaded the other Arab states that it was in their best interests to resume production of oil, shipments of which to western countries had been suspended for political reasons after the war with Israel.

EVENTS SINCE THE 1967 WAR

Though outwardly calm, the internal political situation was apparently disturbed by abortive coups in June and September 1969. Plans for both are presumed to have been discovered in advance, the only visible evidence of the attempts being the arrests of numbers of army and air force officers. A flight of private capital abroad was also reported. In the Yemen the Royalist cause which the Saudi Government had strongly supported appeared to be within sight of victory early in 1968, but by mid-1969 its remaining adherents had largely been driven into exile and the civil war seemed to have come to an end, although further hostilities were reported during the 1969–70 winter. Dissension amongst the Royalists, which led to the withdrawal of Saudi assistance, was a principal factor in this decline. Discussions between Sana'a representatives and Saudi officials took place at Jeddah in March 1970, and the Yemen Republic was officially recognized in July. Relations with Southern Yemen deteriorated, however, and an extensive battle on the disputed frontier took place in December 1969, with Saudi Arabia apparently winning easily owing mainly to its superior air power.

Relations with Sudan improved after the communist-inspired coup attempt there in July 1971, and President Nimeri visited Saudia Arabia in November 1971 and April 1972. Saudia Arabia also played an important role in attempting to bring about agreement between the Palestinian guerrillas and the Jordanian Government after the final confrontation between them in north Jordan in July 1971.

The growing tension in the Gulf area generally was illustrated by an agreement with the U.S.A. in May 1973 for the supply of Phantom jets to Saudi Arabia, and the signing of a £250 million contract in June 1973 for British Aircraft Corporation to supply Saudi Arabia with air defence support systems. Saudi Arabia, however, warned the United States that she might be prepared to withhold oil supplies unless the U.S.A. changed her attitude in the Arab-Israeli dispute.

The warning was prophetic but went unheeded. When the Arab-Israeli war of October 1973 broke out, therefore, and when United States aid to Israel continued, Saudi Arabia, despite her traditionally good relationship with the West, led a movement by all the Arab oil-producing countries to exert political pressure by cuts in oil production. Since there was no immediate response from the U.S.A., OPEC members placed an embargo on oil supplies to that country and to several other developed western countries as well. Supplies to the western world were not cut off entirely, but it was announced that production would be progressively reduced until attitudes towards support for Israel changed. The Arab states having thus made clear the strength of their determination to achieve a Middle East settlement more favourable to the Palestinian cause, there then began, in the closing months of 1973 and the first months of 1974, a period of extremely active negotiating for a settlement that would mean more than simply an end to Arab-Israeli hostilities.

On the one hand the western nations attempted to repair their links with the oil-producing countries; on the other hand these latter debated among themselves how far they should wield the "oil weapon" to achieve their ends.

As the possessor of 40 per cent of Middle East oil reserves, and one quarter of world reserves, Saudi Arabia, together with Egypt, was in the very forefront of these negotiations. It soon became apparent, however, that the Saudis held views that differed from those of other producer nations (notably Libya, Algeria and Iran) on the extent to which oil could be safely used to put pressure on the West. It was feared in Riyadh that too much of this pressure would have economic repercussions that nobody wanted. The more radical OPEC members wanted to retain the oil embargo until a satisfactory outcome to the October hostilities was reached. At a meeting in March 1974, though, Saudi Arabia pressed for a resumption of supplies to the U.S.A. and, when this was agreed, resisted any moves to increase oil prices, which, by January 1974, had risen to nearly four times the pre-hostilities level. It was reported that, in order to achieve their aim, the Saudis threatened to leave OPEC and lower prices unilaterally. Reluctantly, therefore, the radical OPEC members agreed to a freeze on oil prices.

Meanwhile, in negotiations with consumer countries, the Saudis made it clear that the continued supply of oil was dependent not only on a change in attitudes towards supporting Israel but on assistance to Saudi Arabia itself in industrializing and diversifying its economy against the day when oil reserves become depleted. The U.S.A. in particular showed itself eager to satisfy these conditions and an important economic and military co-operation agreement was signed in May 1974.

On March 25th, 1975, King Faisal was assassinated by one of his nephews, Prince Faisal ibn Masaed ibn Abdul Aziz. Although at first it was feared that the assassination was a deep-seated plot it soon became clear that the assassin, although not mentally deranged, had acted on his own. King Faisal was succeeded by his half-brother, Khalid, the Crown Prince, and Khalid's brother Prince Fahd became Crown Prince, retaining his post as Minister of the Interior. Prince Fahd also became First Deputy Prime Minister.

No major change of policy resulted from Khalid's succession. He quickly announced that Saudi Arabia would follow the late King Faisal's policies involving Islamic solidarity and the strengthening of Arab unity, and that the objectives remained "the recovery of occupied Arab territories" and the "liberation of the City of Jerusalem from the claws of Zionism".

In March 1976 Saudi Arabia established diplomatic relations with the Yemen People's Democratic Republic. Although both countries have been ideological enemies since Aden achieved independence from Britain in 1967, both also were concerned about the presence of Iranian forces in Oman. A Saudi loan was made to the needy Yemen P.D.R. and it was expected that in return the Yemenis would abandon their support for the PFLO.

An indication of the growth in stature of Saudi Arabia in Arab affairs in the late 1970s was the key role she played in October 1976 in bringing about the Riyadh summit—a meeting which was instrumental in ending the civil war in the Lebanon and also brought about reconciliation between Egypt and Syria. Saudi Arabia also asserted herself at the OPEC summit in Doha in December 1976 when she, along with the United Arab Emirates, showed herself firmly committed to only a 5 per cent increase in oil prices while the other OPEC countries insisted on a 10 per cent rise (*see* Economic Survey for further details).

Saudia Arabia traditionally supported President Sadat of Egypt, fearing that his fall from power would result in Egypt's moving to the left. When Sadat visited Israel in November 1977 Saudi Arabia gave him discreet support in his peace initiative. This position, however, was abandoned following the signing of the Egyptian–Israeli treaty in the following spring. At the Arab Summit meeting held in April 1979 Saudi Arabia aligned itself with the "moderate" states in supporting the sanctions against Egypt which had been outlined at the Arab League meeting the previous November. In July 1979 the Saudi Government withdrew from its arms manufacturing consortium with Egypt. Nevertheless, flights between Egypt and Saudia Arabia continued, and there was no ban on the employment of Egyptian workers in Saudi Arabia.

THE SIEGE OF THE MECCA MOSQUE

In domestic affairs the Saudi Government had for long been content to allow social change to unfold organically, even though the vast oil wealth and the development plans of 1975–80 and 1980–85 had brought about a great improvement in communications, welfare services and the standard of living in general. Saudi Arabia still remains the most conservative of the Arab countries; the ancient restrictions on alcohol, dress, etc., have been continuously observed, and help to explain why the screening of the TV film "Death of a Princess" (about the execution for adultery of a Saudi princess) in April 1980 so deeply offended Saudi opinion and led to the withdrawal of the British Ambassador until August.

The Saudi royal family, who provide the basis for life in Saudi Arabia, had received a severe shock the previous November, when the Mosque at Mecca was occupied by about 250 followers of Juhaiman ibn Seif al-Oteibi, a Sunni extremist who had come to proclaim a Mahdi on the first day of the Islamic year 1400. The siege continued for two weeks, until the extremists were defeated; 102 insurgents died in the siege, or shortly afterwards, together with 127 Saudi soldiers. At the same time, but quite separately, the Shi'a minority in the Eastern Provinces rioted, as they did again in February 1980.

The siege has revealed unease in Saudi Arabia.

Although the royal family is firmly in control, for the most part with the support of the people, there have been murmurings against Royal conspicuous consumption and privilege. The creation of a Consultative Assembly (*Majless Al-Shoura*) of 50–70 nominated members has been promised and an eight-man committee under the Chairmanship of Prince Nayef, Minister of the Interior, was appointed in March 1980 to draw up a 200-article "system of rule" based on Islamic principles.

Saudi Arabia's geo-political position has added to the unease. With the Yemen People's Democratic Republic already in the Soviet orbit, and with the Yemen Arab Republic concluding an arms deal with Moscow in November 1979, and the Soviet invasion of Afghanistan in December 1979, Saudi Arabia came to feel increasingly threatened. This feeling was intensified by the outbreak of the Gulf War between Iran and Iraq in September 1980, causing further instability in the region. Saudi Arabia initially supported Iraq with enthusiasm, but later came to fear that Iranian retaliation might take the form of stirring up Saudi Arabia's Shi'a minority. Saudi Arabia therefore concentrated on securing her position in the early 1980s. Militarily this has meant the acquisition of F.15 fighters from the U.S.A. and in March 1981 President Reagan, in spite of Congressional Zionist lobby opposition, agreed to sell to Saudi Arabia five AWACS (airborne warning and control systems) aircraft in addition to the four that were supplied under U.S. control after the outbreak of the Gulf War. Saudi Arabia is also seeking arms from the United Kingdom, France and West Germany.

In May 1981 Saudi Arabia joined five other Gulf States in setting up the Gulf Co-operation Council, ostensibly a pact for economic co-operation, but also carrying the potential of a military alliance and collective security pact. In spite of her preoccupation with security, however, Saudi Arabia was one of the leading mediators in negotiations which ended the 1981 missile crisis in the Lebanon, and has beome increasingly involved in trying to find a solution to the whole Arab-Israeli question.

The basis of this policy has been the 8-point "Fahd Plan" first publicized by Prince Fahd in August 1981. The plan is reproduced on page 89, and caused concern in the remainder of the Arab world by recognizing Israel by implication, although Saudi Arabia was reluctant to admit this. The plan was due to be discused at the Arab summit meeting at Fez, in Morocco, in November, but there was disagreement over the implications of the plan and the summit quickly broke up in disarray.

King Khalid died suddenly on June 13th, 1982, and was succeeded by his younger brother, Crown Prince Fahd. Owing to Khalid's ill-health, Fahd had already exercised considerable power, and previous Saudi policy of attempting to take a positive role in seeking a solution of the Palestine question, inflamed still further by the Israeli move into Lebanon in July, is expected to continue.

ECONOMIC SURVEY

AREA AND POPULATION

The area of Saudi Arabia has been estimated at 2,149,690 square kilometres but the borders have not all been defined and therefore no precise figure can be arrived at. Estimates of the kingdom's population have been a subject of dispute for some years. An official estimate for January 1st, 1956, put the figure at 6,036,400. A census was held in 1962–63 but the results were officially repudiated. The UN Population Division estimated the mid-1965 population at 6,750,000 and projected figures of 7,740,000 for mid-1970 and 8,966,000 for mid-1975. Meanwhile, Saudi officials were still quoting figures of 5–6 million in 1975. A census was held in September 1974, a necessary preliminary to the ambitious second five-year development plan (1975–80), but even then the facts were not made clear. First reports put the census total for Saudis at 4.3 million. Later a figure of 7,012,642 was announced, though many observers still believe the lower figure to be more realistic. On the basis of the census total, the UN estimates that the population rose from 7,251,000 at mid-1975 to 8,960,000 at mid-1980. About 70 per cent of the population are thought to be urban by now, with the other 30 per cent composed of settled farmers, clustered around oases, and the Bedouin.

Foreigners working in Saudi Arabia probably total around 1.5 million and outnumber the native workforce. Regarding immigrants as a political and moral threat to Saudi society, the Government is attempting to restrict their numbers, but present development policies demand a far higher input of both skilled and unskilled labour than native sources can possibly provide. The almost total ban on the employment of women further restricts the Saudis' capacity to staff their own economy. The immigrant workers come mostly from the poorer Arab states, such as Egypt and the Yemens, from the Indian subcontinent, and from the Far East (especially Taiwan and South Korea). A large number of managerial and skilled posts are occupied by Westerners.

The population of Riyadh, the royal capital, was 666,840 at the 1974 census and that of Jeddah, the leading port and commercial centre, 561,104. The other main towns were the holy cities of Mecca (366,801) and Medina (198,186), the summer capital, Ta'if (204,857), the east coast commercial centre, Dammam (127,844), the agricultural centre, Hufuf (101,271), Tabouk (74,825), Buraidah (69,940) and Al-Mobarraz (54,325). Urban growth in Saudi Arabia is very rapid: according to some estimates, the population of Riyadh was approaching 1 million in 1980.

DEVELOPMENT PLANS

Since 1970 the development of the Saudi economy has been guided by a series of five-year plans. The first plan (1970–75) was a relatively modest programme costing 56,223 million riyals, of which 32,762 million riyals was allotted to economic and social development. After the rise in oil revenues in 1973–74 (*see* Petroleum below), however, the Government found itself in possession of vast financial resources and determined to embark on a massive programme of industrialization and modernization. Hence the second five-year plan (1975–80) provided for expenditure of no less than 498,230 million riyals (about $142,000 million). It was described by the Saudi Minister of Planning, Hisham Nazer, as an "experiment in social transformation". The largest single investment item in the second plan was defence, put at 78,157 million riyals, followed by education at 74,161 million riyals, urban development at 53,328 million riyals and industrial and mineral production at 45,058 million riyals.

A major feature of the second plan was the intention to create two completely new industrial cities, one at Jubail on the Gulf coast and the other at Yanbu on the Red Sea. Development of the two sites would take ten years and cost around $70,000 million. Jubail was to have three oil refineries, six petrochemical plants, an aluminium smelter and a steel mill, as well as support industries, an industrial port and large-scale urban development. Yanbu was planned on a slightly smaller scale: two oil refineries, a natural gas processing plant, a petrochemical complex, other lighter industries, an industrial port and a new urban area. The Yanbu industries would be fed by an oil pipeline and a gas pipeline across the Arabian peninsula from the Eastern province.

Despite the pessimism of most foreign commentators, the Saudis pursued the goals of the second plan with great determination, and the results have been, on the whole, successful. Although the main industrial projects fell behind schedule, infrastructure grew apace, endowing the country with the basic transport and communications facilities required by a modern industrial state.

Consequently, the third five-year plan (1980–85) is intended to shift the emphasis away from infrastructure projects onto the productive sectors, with a particular importance accorded to agriculture. The plan stresses the need for manpower training to reduce reliance on foreign labour and for Saudi private investors to be encouraged to play a more prominent role in the economy. Planned investment for the five-year period is set at 782,000 million riyals (about $235,000 million). However, actual spending under the plan can be expected to rise well above that figure, as real investment during the second plan period is estimated to have totalled about 700,000 million riyals, 40 per cent more than intended. It should also be noted that the third plan figure of 782,000 million riyals does not include defence spending, the largest item of expenditure under the previous plan.

AGRICULTURE

Agriculture contributed 2.4 per cent of non-oil G.D.P. in 1978 although it employs 30 per cent of the population. Cultivation is confined to oases and to irrigated regions, comprising a mere 0.2 per cent of the total land area: the remaining agricultural land is used for low-grade grazing. The chief crops cultivated on irrigated or cultivated soil are wheat, sorghum, maize, millet, barley and lucerne, while fruits of many varieties, particularly dates, grow in abundance in oases. Sheep and goats are bred extensively, both for meat and for wool. Both dairy and poultry farming are on the increase.

The Government has recognized the importance of developing agriculture as a means of reducing the dependence on imported food, and as a means of diversifying the economy and of raising rural living standards. Since scarcity of water constitutes the chief factor limiting the development of agriculture, the Government has launched an ambitious programme to overcome this obstacle. Execution of this programme—which includes surveys for underground water resources, construction of dams, irrigation and drainage networks, combined with distribution of fallow land, settlement of Bedouin and the introduction of mechanization—is aimed at eventually raising agricultural production to the level of near self-sufficiency in food. Consequently, budgetary allocations for the agricultural sector have increased considerably in recent years and the third five-year plan (1980–85) projects spending on agriculture at 7,975 million riyals and on water (mainly desalination plants) at no less than 52,979 million, although much of this is for developing urban water supplies. Surveys carried out in the 1960s indicated a potential for greatly increasing agricultural output by means of irrigation.

Important projects which have been undertaken by the Government include the al-Hasa irrigation scheme, the Faisal Model Settlement scheme, the Wadi Jizan and Najran dam projects and the Abha dam. The al-Hasa irrigation and drainage scheme, inaugurated in December 1971, was completed over five years at a cost of 260 million riyals. It is the country's biggest agricultural scheme and about 50,000 persons will benefit from it. The Faisal Model Settlement scheme, which cost 100 million riyals, has involved extensive land reclamation and irrigation and has provided permanent farmland and housing for 1,000 Bedouin families. The Wadi Jizan dam, which was inaugurated in March 1971, has a reservoir with a capacity of 71 million cubic metres of water and was built at a cost of 42 million riyals. A second dam at Wadi Najran, completed in 1980, has added a further 68 million cubic meters to water storage capacity in the Jizan-Najran area. The Abha dam in the Asir region was opened in April 1974 with a reservoir capacity of 2.4 million cubic metres. Under the third five-year plan, some 37 new dams are to be built.

Apart from lack of water, the major constraint on Saudi agriculture is the shortage of labour as the population is drawn away from rural areas by the attractions of urban development. The Government is countering the drift to the towns by improving rural facilities, but the future of Saudi agriculture must lie in capital-intensive, large-scale farming which is highly mechanized and requires only a small workforce. Already a successful start has been made with dairy farming, using the most modern foreign technical expertise from Sweden, Denmark and Ireland.

Government encouragement to farmers is substantial. Interest-free loans are available through the Agricultural Bank, set up in 1963, and chemical fertilizer, domestic or imported, is distributed at half-price. There are also large subsidies or incentives for irrigation pumps, farm machinery or imported rearing stock.

PETROLEUM

The most important industry in Saudi Arabia is the production of crude petroleum and petroleum products. Saudi Arabia is the biggest oil producer within OPEC, with around 40 per cent of the organization's output in 1981, and is the second or third biggest producer in the world (its rank varies with fluctuations in production), with about 17 per cent of world output. Saudi proven reserves were given as 165,000 million barrels at January 1st, 1981, allowing 45 more years of production at 1980 levels.

In 1933 a Saudi concession was granted to Standard Oil Company of California to explore for oil. The operating company, the Arabian American Oil Company (Aramco), began explorations for oil in 1933 and was soon drilling. It discovered oil in commercial quantities in 1938. By the end of the Second World War it had discovered four oil fields and had established the necessary facilities, including a large refinery, to meet post-war demands for crude oil and refined products. In 1936 Texaco bought a 50 per cent share in Aramco, and in 1948 it was joined by Exxon and Mobil; the ownership structure was then Standard Oil 30 per cent, Texaco 30 per cent, Exxon 30 per cent, and Mobil 10 per cent.

At the end of 1980, Aramco's proven reserves of crude oil were estimated to be 113,491 million barrels. Probable reserves are estimated at 178,070 million barrels. Production comes from 14 major oilfields: Ghawar, Abqaiq, Safaniya, Berri, Abu Hadriya, Abu Sa'fah, Qatif, Fadhili, Manifa, Khursaniyah, Dammam, Marjan, Zuluf and Khurais. Of these the four first-named are by far the most important. Ghawar is generally accepted as the world's largest oilfield and Safaniya is the world's largest offshore field. In 1979 Aramco initiated a major project to increase exploitation of the Marjan, Zuluf, Manifa and Safaniya offshore fields. It will involve installation of new capacity for producing and handling crude oil, a separate gas-gathering network and construction of an operations complex at Ras Tanajib, 200 km. north-east of the existing centre at Ras Tanura.

The area of Aramco's concession was about 1,285,000 square kilometres in 1939. The company has, however, agreed to relinquish progressively parts of its concession areas. Following relinquishments in 1960, 1963, 1968 and 1973, its concession has been reduced to 220,000 square kilometres (189,000 square kilometres onshore and 31,000 square kilometres offshore). Aramco produced 3,513 million barrels of petroleum in 1981, about 97 per cent of total Saudi output.

In line with moves by other Arab oil-producing states, the Saudi Government took a 25 per cent share in Aramco in January 1973, increased to 60 per cent from January 1974. After protracted negotiations, a 100 per cent takeover of the company was agreed in 1980, backdated to January 1st, 1976. State participation does not affect Aramco's Ras Tanura refinery, which remains the property of the original four Aramco partners. The state control over Aramco is exercised by the General Petroleum and Mineral Organization (Petromin), which also has wide responsibilities in exploration, refining and marketing of petroleum.

In 1949 the Saudi Arabian government granted the Getty Oil Corporation a 60-year exclusive concession covering its undivided half interest in the Saudi Arabian-Kuwait Neutral Zone, now called the Partitioned Zone. Getty's production in 1981 amounted to 27.2 million barrels. In 1969 Japanese interests, which had obtained concessions from Saudi Arabia and Kuwait in 1957 and 1958 covering an offshore area of the neutral zone of the Gulf, found oil which is now being exploited by the Arabian Oil Co. Production in 1981 was 45.6 million barrels.

The growth of Saudi Arabia's oil output in the first half of the 1970s was spectacular. Production rose from 1,387 million barrels in 1970 (3.8 million barrels per day) to 2,202 million barrels in 1972 (6 million b/d) and 3,095 million barrels in 1974 (8.5 million b/d). This growth in output was accompanied by rising oil prices, culminating in the huge increases of October and December 1973 which almost quadrupled the cost per barrel. Oil revenues shot up from $1,214 million in 1970 to $4,340 million in 1973, followed by a breath-taking leap to $22,573 million in 1974. The price rises reflected OPEC's collective will to exploit a favourable market situation; the industrialized countries' fears of a shortfall in oil supplies put them completely in OPEC's hands.

After the events of 1973–74, however, Saudi Arabia emerged as a powerful conservative and pro-Western influence in OPEC, using its high potential output to hold down prices. In the depressed market of 1975, Saudi production fell to 2,582 million barrels (7.1 million b/d), but it rose through 1976 to a new peak of 3,358 million barrels in 1977 (9.2 million b/d), with revenues at $36,540 million. The high output for 1977 was associated with an OPEC squabble over prices: eleven OPEC members had agreed in December 1976 to raise their prices by 10 per cent at the start of 1977 and by a further five per cent the following July, but Saudi Arabia and the U.A.E. would only increase their prices by five per cent for the whole year. By raising output, Saudi Arabia put pressure on the market to depress prices, for those states charging higher rates might find it difficult to sell their oil. In July 1977 a compromise was reached: Saudi Arabia and the U.A.E. increased their prices by another five per cent, the rest of OPEC forwent its proposed extra increase, and a unified price was restored.

At one stage in the early-1977 drive to lift production, levels rose above 10 million b/d; the unexpected consequence was damage to the oilfields and harm to future prospects of retrieval. As a result, the Government declared a ceiling on desirable output levels at 8.5 million b/d. For the first three quarters of 1978 world supply was plentiful, prices remained steady, and Saudi Arabia kept production below the declared limit. With the outbreak of the Iranian revolution, however, the situation was transformed. To cover the Iranian shortfall, Saudi Arabia once more pushed up production past the 10 million b/d mark. Total output for 1978 was 3,038 million barrels (8.32 million b/d), with revenue at $32,234 million, but 919 million barrels came in the last quarter. In the event, Saudi Arabia proved incapable of exercising the influence it had previously enjoyed. Although output was maintained at around 9.5 million b/d throughout 1979, apart from in the second quarter, prices shot up as paranoia over oil supplies seized the industrialized West. The Saudi Government held its own prices below those being asked by other OPEC members, but the only result was huge profits for the Aramco companies who bought cheap from the Saudis and sold dear to the West. When the Saudis tried to restore the OPEC unified pricing system by raising their prices, other oil producers simply preserved the differential by making equal increases in their own rates. Saudi light crude rose in price from $13.3 a barrel at the start of 1979 to $28 a barrel in May 1980, the fastest increase since 1973–74. Since total output for 1979 was 3,479 million barrels (9.1 million b/d) and prices doubled in the course of the year, revenue reached a new peak of $48,435 million.

Production was maintained at about 9.5 million b/d through the first nine months of 1980, but in the last quarter the Saudi Government raised production to 10.3 million b/d to compensate for lost output from warring Iraq and Iran, giving a record total production for the year of 3,634 million barrels. Prices continued to drift upwards, Saudi light crude reaching $32 per barrel by the end of 1980, and total revenue in that year was $84,466 million. an increase of 74 per cent over the previous year's figure. However, in the first three quarters of 1981 Saudi efforts to hold down prices at last began to have real effect. Slack demand in the West, combined with the continued high level of Saudi output (maintained at over 10 million b/d), made it difficult to sell oil at the official level and impossible for prices to rise any further. In October 1981, in an attempt to restore a unified price structure, Saudi Arabia induced OPEC to accept a package involving a $2 rise in the market price to $34 per barrel, accompanied by a cut in Saudi output to a ceiling of 8.5 million b/d. Total Saudi output for 1981 was 3,586 million barrels. In February 1982, as demand continued to fall, Saudi output dropped to 7.2 million b/d, and after a further OPEC meeting in March the Government declared a new upper limit of 7.5 million b/d.

Most of Saudi Arabia's oil goes to Western Europe (worth $13,961 million in 1978), Japan ($7,620 million) and the U.S.A. ($5,646 million). Total oil exports were worth 340,710 million riyals in 1980, compared with 193,300 million riyals in 1979. The oil is exported by tanker from terminals on the Gulf coast, except for a very small quantity (about 50,000 b/d) which is transported 1,200 kilometres by pipeline to Lebanese and Jordanian refineries. In 1981 Petromin completed construction of a trans-Arabian pipeline to Yanbu on the Red Sea coast. When fully operational in August 1982, the new pipeline will carry some 1.9 million b/d (about a quarter of the country's total output), mostly for export from a Red Sea tanker terminal. It will shorten the export route to Western Europe and North America by 3,500 kilometres.

INDUSTRY, GAS AND MINING

Saudi Arabia is in the throes of major industrial development financed by oil revenues under the aegis of the second and third development plans (1975–80 and 1980–85). The cornerstone of the industrialization programme is the construction of refineries and processing industries to exploit the country's oil and natural gas reserves. The major projects are being carried out as joint ventures between the state and foreign companies.

Petromin is responsible for oil refining, although the country's oldest and, so far, largest refinery at Ras Tanura is wholly-owned by Aramco. Ras Tanura processed 257 million barrels in 1980. Getty Oil and the Arabian Oil Company also run small refineries, processing about 50,000 b/d. Petromin's existing refineries are directed chiefly at the domestic market; the Jeddah refinery, which came on stream in 1968, can handle 70,000 b/d, to be expanded to 90,000 b/d, and the Riyadh refinery, in operation since 1975, had expanded production from an original 20,000 b/d to 120,000 b/d by 1981. Petromin also has a lubricating oil refinery at Jeddah, run as a joint venture with Mobil.

Petromin's refining activities are to expand greatly in the first half of the 1980s, with the construction of five new refineries as part of the Jubail/Yanbu development scheme. Four of these will be export refineries: a 250,000 b/d joint venture with Shell at Jubail; a 12,000 b/d special products refinery, also at Jubail, a joint venture with Texaco and Socal; a 250,000 b/d joint venture with Mobil at Yanbu; and a lube oil refinery, also at Yanbu, a joint venture with Ashland Oil. The fifth refinery will be 100 per cent owned by Petromin and will process 170,000 b/d for the domestic market. It will be located at Yanbu. The Yanbu refineries will get their crude supply through the trans-Arabian pipeline from the Eastern Province oilfields. Other new projects include a 350,000 b/d export refinery to be built at Rabigh, a joint venture with Petrola International, and a 250,000 b/d refinery at Juaymeh, to be built by Aramco.

The Saudi Basic Industries Corporation (SABIC), set up in 1976, is responsible for the other major industrial projects. Chief among them is the planned petrochemical development at Jubail and Yanbu, involving construction of six large-scale plants: a joint venture with Shell at Jubail to produce about two million metric tons of ethylene and related products annually; a joint venture with Mobil at Yanbu to produce 940,000 tons of ethylene and related products annually; a joint venture with a Japanese consortium to produce 600,000 tons of methanol annually at Jubail; a joint venture with two American companies, Celanese and Texas Eastern to produce 650,000 tons of methanol a year, also at Jubail; a joint venture with Exxon to produce 240,000 tons of low-density polyethylene annually; and a joint venture with Dow and with Mitsubishi (originally two separate projects) to produce together 500,000 tons of ethylene and related products annually. These plans for founding a petrochemical industry are well behind schedule but SABIC is determined to see all the planned installations come into operation in the first half of the 1980s.

Another major SABIC project is for a fertilizer plant producing 500,000 tons of urea a year, as a joint venture with the Taiwan Fertilizer Company. It should come on stream in 1983. The country's main existing fertilizer plant is at Dammam. Run by the Saudi Arabian Fertilizer Company (Safco), it produced 342,000 metric tons of urea, 46,000 metric tons of finished fertilizer and 40,000 metric tons of sulphuric acid in 1981. SABIC is also involved in expanding the iron and steel industry. Since 1978 it has run the Jeddah steel rolling plant which began operation in 1968 and produces 45,000 tons of reinforcing bars a year. The plant's capacity is being expanded to 140,000 tons. A new steel complex is to be built at Jubail in collaboration with Korf-Stahl of West Germany. The project will cost 2,000 million riyals and be completed by 1983. The plant will produce annually 800,000 tons of sponge iron and 850,000 tons of steel products.

The basis for all these ambitious heavy industry schemes is a gas-gathering project being carried out by Aramco. Natural gas will provide the raw material for the petrochemicals industry and an energy source for the steel plant. The gas-gathering scheme was initiated in 1975, and at that time it was expected to cost $5,000 million and to produce 5,500 million cubic feet a day (c.f.d.). Now estimates for the final cost of the scheme are put at around $12,000 million, although the target has been cut back to 3,500 million c.f.d. Three processing plants have been built at Berri, Shedgum and Uthmaniyah to separate out natural gas liquids (NGL) from methane, and two fractionation plants at Juaymeh on the Gulf coast and at Yanbu on the Red Sea will process the NGL into ethane, liquid petroleum gas (LPG) and condensate. Gas will be carried to Yanbu through a 1,200-kilometre trans-Arabian pipeline which came on stream in 1981. The Berri, Shedgum and Juaymeh plants had all started production by mid-1980 and the Uthmaniyah plant began operating in 1981. Apart from fuelling industrial development, the scheme should make Saudi Arabia one of the world's largest exporters of LPG at around 650,000 b/d. Aramco's refinery at Ras Tanura has been producing NGL since 1962; production in 1980 averaged 269,000 b/d.

The Government is encouraging Saudi private enterprise to develop smaller-scale industries. Industrial estates offer basic infrastructure and services at minimal charge, credit is available on easy terms, and selected products are protected by duties on imports. The building materials sector is flourishing, as are food processing and soft drinks. When the major industrial projects get underway they should stimulate secondary industries to service them and to use their output as raw materials. Between 1975 and 1978 about 70 per cent of industrial projects authorized were wholly Saudi-owned, the rest being joint ventures. As part of its policy to stimulate the Saudi private sector, the Government intends to sell off 75 per cent of SABIC's capital in 1985. This will effectively transfer projects built under SABIC's auspices to private control.

The only minerals, apart from hydrocarbons, being produced at present are limestone (for cement production), gypsum, marble, clay and salt. Substantial iron ore deposits are known to exist, as well as copper, gold, lead, zinc, silver and some uranium. The British Steel Corporation is evaluating a 350 million ton iron ore deposit in a remote part of the kingdom and other British and foreign firms are studying or prospecting for phosphorite and other minerals.

ELECTRICITY AND WATER

The Saudi electricity system has to satisfy rapidly growing urban and industrial demand, and also to provide power supply for small, widely scattered rural settlements. Until recently, generation was in the hands of a large number of small companies; there were 26, as well as Aramco, operating in the Eastern Province alone. Present policy is to create four regional grids, each operated by a single company. In 1977 the companies operating in the Eastern Province merged into a single Saudi Consolidated Electric Company (SCECO-East) managed by Aramco. A unified company for the southern region (SCECO-South) was set up in 1979. Electricity generated in major cities in 1980 totalled 17,597 million kWh, as against 5,712 million kWh in 1976. An increasing amount of electricity is now produced in association with seawater desalination; the generating capacity of desalination plants was expected to total 2,730 megawatts by 1982.

The state body with overall responsibility for the Saudi electricity system is the General Electricity Corporation, founded in 1976. The Corporation has been especially active in setting up power networks in rural areas. These networks are, where possible, to be integrated into one of the regional grids under the control of the appropriate unified company. By 1982 SCECO-South was carrying out its own rural schemes, including the largest single rural project, Tihama rural electricity supply programme, costing an estimated 4,000 million riyals.

Urban water supply has been a major challenge. The exploitation of underground sources at one time appeared the best solution, but it has encountered technical difficulties. However, aquifers of up to 1,700 metres depth are to be tapped. The largest projects are at Riyadh; the Minjur aquifer began supplying the city in 1979, and the huge Wasia aquifer is scheduled to provide 52 million gallons a day by 1983.

Desalination projects are in the hands of the Saline Water Conversion Corporation (SWCC). It expects to be supplying over 600 million gallons of fresh water per day by 1985. Jeddah already receives most of its water from that source, and massive new plants at Jubail and Al-Khobar will supply the Eastern Province. When completed in 1982, their combined output will be around 300 million gallons a day. A pipeline will carry water from the Jubail plant inland to Riyadh.

TRANSPORT

Until 1964 the only surfaced roads, besides those in the oil network, were in the Jeddah-Mecca-Medina area. Since then roads have been given priority and by May 1981 there were 21,470 kilometres of asphalted roads, 9,400 kilometres built under the second development plan. During the third plan period (1980–85), a further 6,600 kilometres of asphalted road are to be built.

The main ports are at Jeddah, Yanbu and Jizan on the Red Sea and at Dammam and Jubail on the Gulf. A programme of rapid expansion and modernization has been undertaken by the Saudi Ports Authority: in 1979 the country's major ports were handling about 66,000 metric tons of imports per day, compared with 28,000 tons in 1976, and total freight handling capacity had risen to around 40 million tons per year by 1982, well in excess of expected needs. Jeddah handles about 50 per cent of seaborne imports. As a result of a massive expansion programme, Jeddah saw its number of berths increase from 14 in 1976 to 45 by 1981. Dammam, the second largest port, has 39 berths. At Jubail work is in progress on a 16-berth commercial port, which has already begun handling freight, and an 11-berth industrial port. The industrial port alone is to cost over $1,000 million. At Yanbu the existing commercial port has grown from two to nine berths; a new industrial port is being built 20 kilometres to the south. The port of Jizan has been extensively modernized and will eventually have 12 berths.

The chief international airports are Jeddah, Dhahran and Riyadh. Although both Jeddah and Riyadh have been considerably improved in recent years, new airports are being built to serve the two cities. The new Jeddah airport, opened officially at the end of May 1981, will be the world's largest airport when completed in 1983, at a cost of over $5,000 million. The Riyadh project should cost around $4,400 million. Medin and Bisha airports have been improved and new airports have been built at Abha, Hayil, Badanah, Ta'if, Turayf, Najran, Tabouk, Jizan, Jouf, Rafah, Wajh and Al Qurayat. The Government operates the airline, Saudia, which links important Saudi cities, with regular flights to many foreign countries. The airline carried 9.5 million passengers in 1980.

The Government operates a 580-kilometre single track railway connecting the port of Dammam on the Gulf with Riyadh. Much of the track is being relaid,

SAUDI ARABIA

and a new line is to be built, linking the two cities on a shorter route. A 90-kilometre single track railway is planned between Dammam and Jubail, and the possibility of a rail link between Riyadh and Jeddah is also being considered. A line is to be built linking Jeddah with Mecca, largely to carry pilgrim traffic. Also, a Saudi-Syrian-Jordanian technical committee is studying the feasibility of reconstructing the historic Hijaz railway from Damascus to Medina.

A causeway linking Bahrain with the Saudi mainland is being built at a cost of $564 million. The Saudi Government is to foot the entire bill.

FOREIGN TRADE

The total value of the country's exports, which consist almost entirely of oil, rose from 138,242 million riyals in 1978 to 213,183 million riyals in 1979, followed by a leap to 362,886 million in 1980 and a further rise to an estimated 405,000 million riyals in 1981. The main markets for Saudi exports in 1980 were Japan (17.4 per cent), the U.S.A. (15.3 per cent), France (9.2 per cent), Thailand (6.9 per cent), the Netherlands (6.8 per cent) and Italy (6.1 per cent). Other important sources of foreign exchange are the local expenditure of Aramco and the Pilgrimage traffic.

The value of Saudi Arabia's imports increased from 69,180 million riyals in 1978 to 82,223 million riyals in 1979, 100,349 million riyals in 1980 and an estimated 119,300 million riyals in 1981. Imports include a wide range of manufactured goods, particularly machinery and transport equipment (accounting for almost 40 per cent of total import costs in 1980). Other significant imports are base metals, foodstuffs and textiles. The pattern of imports reflects the Saudi development effort and the country's poor agricultural resources. The U.S.A. has been the leading exporter to Saudi Arabia in recent years, accounting for 20.0 per cent of Saudi imports in 1980, followed by Japan (17.9 per cent), the Federal Republic of Germany (9.0 per cent), Italy (7.3 per cent) and the United Kingdom (6.4 per cent).

Saudi Arabia's current account surplus increased dramatically from 9,334 million riyals in 1973 to 81,990 million riyals in 1974, under the influence of the oil price rises. A surplus was sustained until 1977, when current receipts exceeded payments by 41,971 million riyals, but in 1978 a small deficit of 7,528 million riyals was recorded. However, with the doubling of oil prices in 1979, a surplus of 37,321 million riyals was achieved that year, followed by a record surplus of 137,746 million riyals in 1980.

FINANCE

The currency is described in the Statistical Survey. Since mid-1977, and particularly since July 1978, the Saudi Arabian Monetary Agency (SAMA) has made a series of frequent small adjustments in the exchange rate against the U.S. dollar. By May 1982 the rate was $1 = 3.425 riyals, an overall revaluation of 3 per cent since mid-1977. SAMA, established in 1952, is the central bank. Its total holdings of gold, foreign cur-

rencies and other international reserve assets reached $30,034 million at the end of 1977, This compared with $23,319 million at the end of 1975, $14,285 million at the end of 1974 and only $3,877 million at the end of 1973. At the end of 1977 Saudi reserves were surpassed only by those of West Germany. From April 1978 Saudi Arabia's reserves were redefined to exclude foreign exchange cover against the note issue, then about $5,300 million. Under the new definition, reserves at December 1978 were $19,407 million, a real fall from the previous year. During 1979 reserves dropped still further, reaching $16,756 million in October, but they have since made a sharp recovery, rising to $23,641 million by the end of 1980 and $34,422 million at the end of December 1981.

There are ten commercial banks in Saudi Arabia—two wholly Saudi and eight joint ventures. The biggest Saudi commercial bank is the National Commercial Bank and the fastest-growing the Riyad Bank, both with headqaurters in Jeddah. The banks which have been "Saudi-ized" as joint ventures with majority Saudi participation are: Bank al-Jazira (National Bank of Pakistan), Al-Bank al-Saudi al-Hollandi (Algemene Bank Nederland), Al-Bank al-Saudi al-Fransi (Banque de l'Indochine et de Suez), Saudi British Bank (British Bank of the Middle East), Arab National Bank (Arab Bank), Saudi Cairo Bank (Banque du Caire), the Saudi-American Bank (Citibank) and the Saudi Commercial United Bank (Banque du Liban et d'Outre-Mer, United Bank of Pakistan and Bank Melli Iran).

The major Saudi source of project finance is the Saudi Industrial Development Fund (SIDF), set up by the Government in 1974. It grants loans carrying only 2 per cent for up to 50 per cent of the total cost of a project (up to 80 per cent in the case of electricity projects). The SIDF is managed by Chase Manhattan Bank. The Public Investment Fund, established in 1972, finances large-scale public sector projects in commerce and industry.

Another major state financial institution to aid development is the Real Estate Development Fund (REDF), whose capital has been raised successively from 240 million riyals to 23,800 million riyals. The REDF lends interest-free for up to 70 per cent of the total cost of building homes or other types of accommodation. The Saudi Agricultural Bank, set up in 1963, offers medium- and short-term loans for farmers. It will have a larger role to play as government pressure for agricultural development increases. The Saudi Credit Bank was set up in 1973 to advance interest-free loans to low-income Saudis for purposes such as getting married or carrying out home repairs.

Saudi banks have recently become slightly more outward-looking. The most obvious example of this is the 55 per cent Saudi-owned Saudi International Bank which opened as a fully-fledged merchant bank in London in March 1976. SAMA holds 50 per cent and National Commercial Bank and Riyad Bank 2.5 per cent each. The biggest non-Saudi partner is Morgan Guaranty Trust Company, which also provides management. The other shares are held by leading Western and Japanese banks. The first wholly private

Saudi bank abroad—Al Saudi Banque—opened in Paris in the autumn of 1976. Riyad Bank has a share in the Paris-based Union de Banques Arabes et Françaises, and in the Gulf Riyad Bank in Bahrain. The NCB has small stakes in the European-Arab Holding and the Compagnie Arabe et Internationale d'Investissement, both based in Luxembourg, and in the Amman-based Arab-Jordanian Investment Bank, which opened in the spring of 1978.

INVESTMENT

SAMA is also the kingdom's investment authority, responsible for looking after the vast foreign assets, estimated at around $100,000 million at the end of 1981. Of the total of 49,464 million assets at the end of 1976, $26,900 million was reserves and $22,564 million "SAMA Investments", according to the IMF's *International Financial Statistics*. Most of this money is held in the U.S.A. and Europe. Though SAMA has been of late investing more long-term, the vast bulk of its assets are still thought to be liquid. One estimate in mid-1977 was that $17,500 million of the SAMA Investments were probably highly liquid, about $4,000 million were bonds and about $3,500 million were private placements with country or "triple-A" company borrowers. Very little official Saudi money goes into equities and almost nothing into property. Big Western banks seem to be the main beneficiaries of the vast funds at SAMA's disposal, and SAMA's investment department is advised by a small team seconded from London merchant bankers Barings and the U.S. investment bank White Weld.

AID

In 1980 foreign aid given by Saudi Arabia totalled $3,033 million, equivalent to 3.66 per cent of its gross national product, according to the OECD. This compares with $1,500 million in 1978. Most Saudi aid goes to Arab states, especially the "front-line" ones, and other Muslim states, notably Pakistan. Saudi contributions to the "front-line" states after 1967 amounted to $188 million per year; from the 1974 Rabat Arab summit $1,000 million per year. The country has generally been the biggest contributor to the various Arab funds set up to help poor Arab

and poor African states, as well as to the IMF oil facilities. In April 1981 Saudi Arabia made a $10,000 million loan to the IMF for two years. It has also lent the World Bank large sums at commercial rates. The Saudi Fund for Development, set up in 1974, makes "soft" loans to Africa, Asia and Latin America, as well as to the Arab world. The Fund disbursed $317 million in 1980.

BUDGETS

Oil revenues traditionally provide over 90 per cent of the state's budget revenue. In 1974/75 they totalled 94,190 million riyals out of 100,103 million riyals actual revenue; expenditure was only 32,038 million riyals. With the advent of the second development plan, expenditure began to catch up with income: in 1976/77 expenditure was 128,273 million riyals, only slightly behind revenue at 135,957 million riyals. For 1977/78 the budget estimates still foresaw a surplus, being set at 146,493 million riyals revenue and 111,400 million riyals outlay, but the actual figures showed a deficit (138,027 million riyals expenditure, 130,659 million riyals revenue). The following year the estimates were for a balanced budget at 130,000 million riyals, but once more expenditure crept up, despite austerity measures, to 147,400 million riyals, with revenue at 132,871 million riyals. In 1979/80 the budget was estimated to balance at 160,000 million riyals; however, the high level of oil production and the unexpected sharp rise in oil prices pushed actual revenue well beyond that figure, to around 220,000 million riyals. The 1980/81 estimates reflected this increase in revenue, with projected expenditure rising to 245,000 million riyals and projected revenue set at 261,516 million riyals. The upward trend continued in 1981/82, with revenue estimated at 340,000 million riyals and expenditure estimated at 298,000 million riyals, a projected surplus of 42,000 million riyals.

Defence and internal security normally form the largest single item in budget expenditure. In 1981/82 they accounted for 28 per cent of allocations. The proportion of total expenditure devoted to project investment, as opposed to recurring expenditure, was 71 per cent in 1980/81 and 76 per cent in 1981/82.

STATISTICAL SURVEY

AREA AND POPULATION

AREA	Census, Sept. 1974	POPULATION†			
		UN estimates (mid-year)			
		1977	1978	1979	1980
2,149,690 sq. km.*	7,012,642	7,918,000	8,259,000	8,606,000	8,960,000

* 830,000 sq. miles.
† Including Saudis living abroad (73,000 in 1974).

SAUDI ARABIA

SAUDI ARABIA-IRAQ NEUTRAL ZONE

The Najdi (Saudi Arabian) frontier with Iraq was defined in the Treaty of Mohammara in May 1922. Later a Neutral Zone of 7,044 sq. km. was established adjacent to the western tip of the Kuwait frontier. No military or permanent buildings were to be erected in the zone and the nomads of both countries were to have unimpeded access to its pastures and wells. A further agreement concerning the administration of this zone was signed between Iraq and Saudi Arabia in May 1938. In July 1975 Iraq and Saudi Arabia signed an agreement providing for an equal division of the diamond-shaped zone between the two countries, with the border following a straight line through the zone.

SAUDI ARABIA-KUWAIT PARTITIONED ZONE

A Convention signed at Uqair in December 1922 fixed the Najdi (Saudi Arabian) boundary with Kuwait. The Convention also established a Neutral Zone of 5,770 sq. km. immediately to the south of Kuwait in which Saudi Arabia and Kuwait held equal rights. The final agreement on this matter was signed in 1963. Since 1966 the Zone has been divided between the two countries and each administers its own half, in practice as an integral part of the state. However, the oil wealth of the whole Zone remains undivided and production from the on-shore oil concessions in the Partitioned Zone is shared equally between the two states' concessionaires (Aminoil and Getty).

PRINCIPAL TOWNS
(population at 1974 census)

Riyadh (royal capital)	666,840	Tabouk	74,825
Jeddah (administrative capital)	561,104	Buraidah	69,940
Makkah (Mecca)	366,801	Al-Mobarraz	54,325
Ta'if	204,857	Khamis-Mushait	49,581
Al-Madinah (Medina)	198,186	Al-Khobar	48,817
Dammam	127,844	Najran	47,501
Hufuf	101,271	Ha'il	40,502

Births and Deaths: Average annual birth rate 47.6 per 1,000 in 1970–75, 45.9 per 1,000 in 1975–80; death rate 16.9 per 1,000 in 1970–75, 14.4 per 1,000 in 1975–80 (UN estimates).

AGRICULTURE
PRINCIPAL CROPS
('000 metric tons)

	1978	1979*	1980*
Wheat . . .	120	150	150
Barley . . .	15	16	16
Millet . . .	13	10	11
Sorghum . .	152	190	170
Sesame seed . .	1	1	1
Tomatoes . .	167	167	167
Onions (dry) . .	95	95	95
Grapes . . .	56	57	57
Dates . . .	411	417	422
Citrus fruit . .	29	29	29

* FAO estimates.

Source: FAO, *Production Yearbook*.

LIVESTOCK
('000 head, year ending September)

	1978	1979*	1980*
Cattle . . .	353	370	400
Sheep . . .	2,699	4,000	4,000
Goats . . .	2,078	1,900	1,974
Asses . . .	104*	111	119
Camels . . .	156	156	156
Chickens . .	4,500	5,000	5,500

* FAO estimates.

Source: FAO, *Production Yearbook*.

LIVESTOCK PRODUCTS
(FAO estimates, '000 metric tons)

	1978	1979	1980
Beef and veal .	19	19	19
Mutton and lamb .	17	19	20
Goats' meat . .	8	9	9
Poultry meat . .	26	28	30
Other meat . .	25	25	27
Cows' milk . .	200	210	214
Sheep's milk . .	75	78	80
Goats' milk . .	56	58	61
Hen eggs . .	20.0	20.2	20.4

Source: FAO, *Production Yearbook*.

SEA FISHING
('ooo metric tons, live weight)

	1975	1976	1977	1978	1979	1980
Marine fishes	20.0	18.5	16.8	16.2	16.2	16.3
Crustaceans and molluscs .	3.0	4.8	6.6*	10.4	10.0	10.1
TOTAL CATCH . .	23.0	23.3	23.4	26.6	26.2	26.4

*FAO estimate.

Source: FAO, *Yearbook of Fishery Statistics.*

MINING*

		1974	1975	1976	1977	1978	1979
Crude petroleum .	'ooo metric tons	422,705	352,394	425,804	458,596	414,757	475,970
Natural gas . .	terajoules	21,060	21,470	22,679	23,600	23,600	25,000

* Including half the total output of the Partitioned Zone, shared with Kuwait.

Source: UN, *Yearbook of Industrial Statistics.*

1980: Crude petroleum 495.7 million metric tons; Natural gas 25,000 terajoules.

CRUDE OIL PRODUCTION BY COMPANY
(million barrels)

	TOTAL	ARAMCO	GETTY OIL	ARABIAN OIL
1938 . . .	0.5	0.5	—	—
1946 . . .	59.9	59.9	—	—
1955 . . .	356.6	352.2	4.4	—
1974 . . .	3,095.1	2,996.5	29.8	68.7
1975 . . .	2,582.5	2,491.8	31.2	59.5
1976 . . .	3,139.3	3,053.9	29.7	55.7
1977 . . .	3,358.0	3,291.2	32.0	34.8
1978 . . .	3,038.0	2,952.3	29.4	56.3
1979 . . .	3,479.2	3,376.4	30.2	72.6
1980 . . .	3,623.8	3,525.3	28.5	70.0
1981 . . .	3,586.0	3,513.2	27.2	45.6

OIL REVENUES BY SOURCE
(U.S. $ million)

	TOTAL	ARAMCO	GETTY OIL	ARABIAN OIL	OTHER COMPANIES
1939 . . .	3.2	3.2	—	—	—
1946 . . .	10.4	10.4	—	—	—
1955 . . .	340.8	338.2	2.6	—	—
1973 . . .	4,340.0	4,195.0	22.0	91.4	31.7
1974 . . .	22,573.5	2,375.0	53.3	113.6	31.6
1975 . . .	25,676.2	24,838.6	191.1	642.7	3.8
1976 . . .	30,747.5	29,937.3	247.6	559.2	3.3
1977 . . .	36,540.1	35,703.8	263.4	571.6	1.2
1978 . . .	32,233.8	31,609.0	286.6	338.2	—
1979 . . .	48,435.2	47,588.9	272.0	574.3	—
1980 . . .	84,466.4	82,716.4	469.6	1,280.4	—
1981 . . .	n.a.	99,187.0	n.a.	n.a.	n.a.

INDUSTRY

SELECTED PRODUCTS

		1977	1978	1979	1980
Fuel oil	'ooo barrels	98,280	94,794	97,997	89,003
Diesel oil	,, ,,	32,116	34,963	34,991	44,507
Gasoline and naphtha . . .	,, ,,	60,893	65,083	72,566	72,316
Liquefied petroleum gas . . .	,, ,,	57,571	64,876	79,523	74,865
Jet fuel	,, ,,	2,054	220	248	359
Kerosene	,, ,,	8,569	9,855	9,913	11,691
Asphalt, etc.	,, ,,	6,793	5,763	9,497	9,753
Cement	'ooo metric tons	1,292.5	1,790.7	2,647.6	3,202.0
Quicklime	,, ,, ,,	6.9	n.a.	n.a.	n.a.
Gypsum	,, ,, ,,	54.0	68.2	n.a.	n.a.
Electric energy*	million kWh	7,010.3	9,435.2	13,746.6	17,597.1

* Figures refer to Islamic years and cover only electricity generated in major cities.

FINANCE

100 halalah = 20 qursh = 1 Saudi riyal (SR).

Coins: 1, 5, 10, 25 and 50 halalah; 1, 2 and 4 qursh.*

Notes: 1, 5, 10, 50 and 100 riyals.

Exchange rates (May 1982): £1 sterling = 6.297 Saudi riyals; U.S. $1 = 3.425 Saudi riyals.

100 Saudi riyals = £15.88 = $29.20.

* The coins of 1, 2 and 4 qursh are being gradually withdrawn from circulation.

Note: Prior to January 1960 the prevailing exchange rate was U.S. $1 = 3.75 Saudi riyals (1 riyal = 26.67 U.S. cents). From January 1960 to August 1971 the exchange rate was $1 = 4.50 riyals (1 riyal = 22.22 U.S. cents). Between December 1971 and February 1973 the rate was $1 = 4.145 riyals (1 riyal = 24.13 U.S. cents). It was $1 = 3.730 riyals (1 riyal = 26.18 U.S. cents) from February to August 1973; and $1 = 3.55 riyals (1 riyal = 28.17 U.S. cents) from August 1973 to March 1975, when the riyal's direct link with the dollar was ended and the currency was valued in terms of the IMF Special Drawing Right (based on a weighted "basket" of currencies since July 1974), with a mid-point of 1 SDR = 4.28255 riyals. Wide fluctuations around this are allowed in order to permit a fixed rate against the U.S. dollar for extended periods of time. From August 1975 to July 1977 the rate was $1 = 3.53 riyals. The average exchange rate (riyals per U.S. dollar) was: 3.518 in 1975; 3.525 in 1977. Since July 1978 there have been frequent small adjustments in the riyal-dollar rate. The average rate (riyals per dollar) was: 3.400 in 1978; 3.361 in 1979; 3.327 in 1980; 3.383 in 1981. In terms of sterling, the exchange rate between November 1967 and June 1972 was £1 = 10.80 riyals.

BUDGET ESTIMATES

(million riyals, July 1st to June 30th)

REVENUE	1980/81	1981/82	EXPENDITURE	1980/81	1981/82
Oil royalties	58,298	84,852	Council of Ministers . . .	12,619*	13,859*
Income tax (incl. tax on oil receipts)	198,706	249,116	Municipal and rural affairs .	3,148	3,588
			Defence and aviation . .	7,685	9,683
Customs	2,037	2,542	Interior	7,456	9,729
Other items . . .	2,475	3,490	Labour and social affairs . .	2,241	2,192
			Health	3,236	4,038
			Education	13,622	16,262
			Communications . . .	1,253	1,390
			Industry, electricity and commerce . .	1,631	3,659
			Subsidies	13,142	21,066
			Projects expenditure (*see below*) .	174,737	205,925
TOTAL . . .	261,516	340,000	TOTAL (incl. others) .	245,000	298,000

* Includes foreign aid.

1982/83 Expenditure: 313,400 million riyals.

PROJECTS BUDGET
(planned expenditure in million riyals)

	1978/79	1979/80	1980/81	1981/82
Council of Ministers	4,399.4	13,964.0	18,983.7	37,208.7
Municipal and rural affairs . . .	7,966.8	9,789.8	16,597.2	22,703.5
Public works and housing . . .	5,649.4	3,022.5	5,573.8	6,308.4
Information	723.5	634.3	878.1	965.3
Civil aviation	3,912.8	6,804.6	10,644.6	11,044.5
Interior	3,330.5	4,131.9	5,507.2	7,551.1
Labour and social affairs . . .	1,452.3	2,126.5	3,491.9	2,626.0
Health	1,855.0	1,822.0	2,420.0	2,793.0
Education	5,123.1	5,771.5	7,863.3	9,869.4
Communications	7,377.0	9,811.3	14,835.5	17,760.6
Finance and national economy . .	3,309.5	7,868.3	10,638.7	13,904.9
Industry, electricity and commerce .	337.3	3,450.5*	3,027.3*	1,086.5
Agriculture and water resources . .	1,854.4	3,112.0	3,470.3	3,185.1
Public investment fund . . .	4,000.0	4,250.0	7,500.0	10,000.0
Other	50,433.0	49,379.4	63,305.8	58,918.3
Less: Earmarked expenditure . .	−18,676.3	−20,258.6	—	—
TOTAL	83,047.7	105,680.0	174,737.4	205,925.3

* Including gathering and liquefaction of gas.

FIVE-YEAR PLAN—1980–85
(proposed expenditure in million riyals)

Education	101,171.0
Health and social services . . .	42,405.7
Transport and communications . .	143,018.1
Desalination	39,602.0
Petromin	27,684.8
Saudi Basic Industries Corpn. . .	25,564.0
Electricity	52,585.2
Agriculture	7,974.5
Public Works	21,204.4
Other	320,790.3
TOTAL	782,000.0

INTERNATIONAL RESERVES*
(U.S. $ million in December each year)

	1975	1976	1977	1978	1979	1980	1981
Gold	126	125	131	207	211	204	186
IMF Special Drawing Rights .	—	—	—	—	196	271	248
Reserve position in IMF .	1,838	2,563	2,691	2,470	1,699	2,418	3,990
Foreign exchange .	21,355	24,337	27,212	16,730	17,378	20,747	27,998
TOTAL .	23,319	27,025	30,034	19,407	19,484	23,641	32,422

* From April 1978 reserves were redefined to exclude the foreign exchange cover against the note issue (then about $5,300 million).

Source: IMF, *International Financial Statistics.*

NATIONAL ACCOUNTS
(million riyals at current prices, twelve months ending June 30th)
GROSS DOMESTIC PRODUCT BY ECONOMIC ACTIVITY

	1976/77	1977/78	1978/79	1979/80*
Agriculture, Forestry, Fishing . . .	1,866	3,909	4,196	4,648
Mining and Quarrying:				
Crude petroleum and natural gas . .	128,466	126,156	131,098	241,708
Other	823	1,025	1,120	1,341
Manufacturing:				
Petroleum refining	6,221	5,908	7,442	10,276
Other	3,063	4,066	5,173	6,467
Electricity, Gas and Water	144	204	248	271
Construction	25,546	31,959	34,764	42,791
Wholesale and Retail Trade, Restaurants and Hotels	8,507	11,049	13,912	17,541
Transport, Storage and Communication . .	6,775	9,960	12,764	15,012
Finance, Insurance, Real Estate, Business Services:				
Ownership of dwellings . . .	6,924	7,632	9,663	10,962
Other	4,206	5,072	6,517	7,853
Community, Social and Personal Services .	2,609	3,293	4,155	5,261
SUB-TOTAL	195,150	210,233	231,052	364,141
Less Imputed Bank Service charge . .	−928	−1,561	−2,342	−3,279
DOMESTIC PRODUCT OF INDUSTRIES	194,222	208,672	228,710	360,852
Public Administration and Defence .	4,998	9,204	10,688	13,545
Other Government Services . . .	4,722	5,942	8,224	9,839
G.D.P. IN PRODUCERS' VALUES .	203,942	223,818	247,622	384,236
Import Duties	1,114	1,583	1,917	2,217
G.D.P. IN PURCHASERS' VALUES .	205,056	225,401	249,539	386,453

* Preliminary.

BALANCE OF PAYMENTS
(U.S. $ million)

	1974	1975	1976	1977	1978	1979	1980
Merchandise exports f.o.b.	32,665	27,294	35,632	40,351	36,993	56,521	100,716
Merchandise imports f.o.b.	−3,569	−6,004	−10,385	−14,698	−20,021	−23,530	−28,238
TRADE BALANCE	29,096	21,290	25,247	25,653	16,972	32,991	72,478
Exports of services	2,603	3,200	4,566	6,012	6,468	7,720	8,479
Imports of services	−7,070	−6,498	−11,220	−14,351	−18,909	−24,253	−33,097
BALANCE ON GOODS AND SERVICES .	24,629	17,992	18,593	17,314	4,531	16,458	47,860
Private unrequited transfers (net) . .	−518	−555	−988	−1,506	−2,845	−3,366	−4,063
Government unrequited transfers (net) .	−1,014	−3,128	−3,323	−3,901	−3,900	−3,503	−3,998
CURRENT BALANCE . . .	23,097	14,309	14,282	11,907	−2,214	9,589	39,799
Direct capital investment (net) . . .	−3,733	1,865	−397	782	556	−1,351	−3,367
Other long-term capital (net) . . .	−5,142	−11,003	−10,759	−8,286	1,223	−2,357	−24,192
Short-term capital (net)	−3,833	3,885	604	−1,706	−11,646	−5,647	−8,305
Net errors and omissions	−2	3	−2	−1	−4	—	3
TOTAL (net monetary movements) .	10,387	9,059	3,728	2,696	−12,085	234	3,938
Monetization of gold	—	−6	—	6	—	—	−9
Allocation of IMF Special Drawing Rights .	—	—	—	—	—	81	82
Valuation changes (net)	19	−19	−21	307	1,450	−236	143
CHANGES IN RESERVES . . .	10,406	9,034	3,707	3,009	−10,635	79	4,154

Source: IMF, *International Financial Statistics.*

EXTERNAL TRADE
(million riyals)

	1974	1975	1976	1977	1978	1979	1980	1981
Imports c.i.f. . .	10,149	14,823	30,691	51,662	69,180	82,223	100,350	119,300
Exports f.o.b. . .	126,223	104,412	135,154	153,209	138,242	213,183	362,886	405,000

PRINCIPAL COMMODITIES
(million riyals)

IMPORTS	1978	1979	1980	EXPORTS*	1979	1980	1981
Foodstuffs . . .	7,082	10,511	14,192	Crude petroleum	186,030	320,450	359,560
Non-metallic minerals .	2,192	2,249	3,155	Refined petroleum .	11,090	18,920	23,440
Chemical products, etc..	2,234	2,667	3,475	Others . . .	330	330	340
Wood and wooden							
articles . . .	2,058	2,332	2,597				
Textiles and clothing .	4,178	4,996	6,571				
Articles of stone,							
ceramics, glass, etc. .	3,247	2,680	3,421				
Base metals and metal							
products . . .	9,588	12,730	14,611				
Machinery (incl. electric)	19,844	22,552	24,534				
Transport equipment .	9,036	10,992	13,924				
Optical and surgical							
instruments, etc. .	2,653	2,903	3,616				
TOTAL (incl. others)	69,180	82,223	100,350	TOTAL . .	197,450	339,700	383,340

*Source: IMF, *International Financial Statistics*.

PRINCIPAL TRADING PARTNERS
(million riyals)

IMPORTS	1978	1979	1980	EXPORTS*	1978	1979	1980
Belgium . . .	1,234	1,490	1,574	Bahrain . . .	3,212	4,511	7,150
Finland . . .	827	n.a.	n.a.	Belgium . . .	3,990	7,065	13,207
France . . .	2,668	3,754	5,440	Brazil . . .	5,274	6,048	9,479
Germany, Fed. Repub..	7,467	9,024	9,112	Canada . . .	1,994	4,001	7,183
India	805	918	993	France . . .	14,776	17,856	33,525
Italy . . .	4,945	6,047	7,346	Germany, Fed. Repub..	3,779	6,022	11,029
Japan . . .	10,659	13,021	17,992	Greece . . .	180	4,578	8,129
Korea, Dem. People's				Italy . . .	9,360	17,314	22,305
Rep. . . .	1,034	n.a.	n.a.	Japan . . .	27,881	36,983	63,274
Korea, Republic .	1,105	1,598	2,408	Korea, Republic .	4,572	6,474	11,784
Kuwait . . .	359	495	391	Netherlands . .	6,018	11,807	24,754
Lebanon . . .	1,064	1,169	1,246	Philippines . .	972	1,492	2,812
Netherlands . .	3,011	2,503	3,177	Singapore . .	6,130	8,394	14,109
Pakistan . . .	322	400	509	Spain . . .	5,468	8,264	10,569
Singapore . . .	655	922	1,100	Taiwan . . .	2,498	3,287	5,961
Sweden . . .	867	n.a.	n.a.	Thailand . . .	1,076	1,730	3,462
Switzerland . . .	1,952	1,511	1,741	United Kingdom .	4,678	7,097	12,844
Taiwan . . .	1,577	1,990	2,238	U.S.A. . . .	21,771	36,753	55,866
United Kingdom .	5,093	5,841	6,504				
U.S.A. . . .	14,434	16,270	20,086				
TOTAL (incl. others)	69,180	82,223	100,350	TOTAL (incl. others)	138,242	213,183	362,886

*Figures for individual countries exclude bunker fuel.

TOURISM

Pilgrims to Mecca from abroad: 1975/76 894,573; 1976/77
719,040; 1977/78 739,319; 1978/79 830,236; 1979/80
862,520; 1980/81 812,892; 1981/82 1,943,180.

TRANSPORT
RAILWAYS

	1973	1974	1975	1976	1977
Passenger-kilometres (million) . . .	61	72	68	79	94
Freight tonne-kilometres (million) . . .	62	66	68	86	125

ROAD TRAFFIC
(motor vehicles in use)

	1975	1976	1977
Cars . . .	65,039	103,888	133,717
Taxis . .	8,514	16,515	19,244
Lorries . .	84,347	136,571	182,226
Buses . .	1,439	3,108	3,343
TOTAL .	159,339	260,082	338,530

INTERNATIONAL SEA-BORNE SHIPPING
('ooo metric tons)

	1973	1974	1975	1976
Goods loaded*	335,480	390,510	337,710	410,000
Goods unloaded	2,965†	3,582	5,779	9,259

* Provisional figures.

† Excluding livestock.

Source: UN, *Statistical Yearbook.*

CIVIL AVIATION
(total scheduled services)

	1975	1976	1977	1978
Kilometres flown ('ooo) . . .	27,500	38,900	56,100	67,000
Passengers carried ('ooo) . . .	1,836	3,268	4,705	6,268
Passenger-kilometres (million) .	1,827	3,122	4,923	6,771
Freight tonne-km. ('ooo) . . .	50,100	82,600	105,800	136,500
Mail tonne-km. ('ooo) . . .	2,000	2,600	3,700	5,500
Total tonne-km. ('ooo) . . .	217,000	366,000	552,000	750,000

Source: UN, *Statistical Yearbook.*

EDUCATION

(Academic year 1978/79)

	SCHOOLS	TEACHERS	PUPILS
Kindergarten . .	169	904	24,448
Elementary . .	5,373	46,095	862,259
Intermediate . .	1,383	16,532	245,471
Secondary . .	566	7,904	116,539
Adult . .	3,357	n.a.	142,370
Higher . .	21	551	4,877
Special . .	63	893	1,920
TOTAL (inc. others)	11,071	78,385	1,451,754

Sources (unless otherwise indicated): Kingdom of Saudi Arabia, *Statistical Yearbook*; SAMA, *Annual Report*.

THE CONSTITUTION

After Ibn Saud had finally brought the whole of present-day Saudi Arabia under his control in 1925, the territory was made into a dual kingdom.

Six years later, in 1932, the realm was unified by decree and became the Kingdom of Saudi Arabia. Saudi Arabia as a whole has in practice been developing, in recent years particularly, from monarchical towards ministerial rule. The power of the Cabinet was increased in May 1958, when several ministries were delegated to the Crown Prince. In December 1960, however, the Crown Prince resigned and King Saud assumed the Prime Ministership. In 1962, Prince Faisal resumed the Prime Ministership. In 1964 King Saud was relieved of his duties and his brother Prince Faisal was proclaimed King. King Faisal was assassinated in 1975 and succeeded by his brother Khalid.

An eight-man committee under the Chairmanship of Prince Nayef, Minister of the Interior, was formed in March 1980 to draw up a 200-article basic "system of rule", based entirely on Islamic principles. Plans were also being made for the establishment of a Consultative Council, whose 50–70 members would be nominated.

The organs of local government are the General Municipal Councils, the District Council and the tribal and village councils. A General Municipal Council is established in the towns of Mecca, Medina and Jeddah. Its members are proposed by the inhabitants and must be approved by the King. Functioning concurrently with each General Municipal Council is a General Administration Committee, which investigates ways and means of executing resolutions passed by the Council. There are also elected district councils under the presidency of local chiefs, consisting of his assistant, the principal local officials and other important persons of the district. Every village and tribe has a council composed of the sheikh, who presides, his legal advisers and two other prominent personages. These councils have power to enforce regulations.

The principal administrative divisions are as follows:

Najd: capital Riyadh. Najd is sub-divided as follows:
  1. The principality of Riyadh, to which are associated Wadi al-Dawasir, al-Aflaj, al-Hariq, al-Kharj, al-'Aridh, al-Washm and Sudair.
  2. The principality of al-Qasim, comprising 'Unaizah, Buraidah, al-Ras and their villages, and al-Mudhan-ban and its dependencies.
  3. The Northern principality (capital Hayil). This includes the tribes of Shammar, 'Anzah, al-Dhafir and Mutair, the Town of Taima in the south and some northerly towns.

Hijaz: capital Mecca. Includes the principalities of Tabouk, al-'Ula, Dhaba, al-Wajh, Amlaj, Yanbu', Medina, Jeddah, al-Lith, al-Qunfundhah, Baljarshi and Ta'if.

Asir: capital Abha. Includes Abha, Qahtan, Shahran, Rijal Alma', Rijal al-Hajr, Banu Shahr, Mahayil, Bariq, Bisha, Najran and its villages.

Eastern Province (*Al Hasa*): capital Dammam. Includes Hufuf, Al-Mobarraz, Qatif, Dhahran, Al-Khobar and Qaryat al-Jubail.

THE GOVERNMENT

HEAD OF STATE

H.M. King FAHD IBN ABDUL AZIZ

(Acceded to the throne June 13th, 1982

Crown Prince: ABDULLAH IBN ABDUL AZIZ.

COUNCIL OF MINISTERS

(June 1982)

Prime Minister: H.M. King FAHD IBN ABDUL AZIZ.

First Deputy Prime Minister and Commander of the National Guard: H.R.H. Prince ABDULLAH IBN ABDUL AZIZ.

Second Deputy Prime Minister and Minister of Defence and Aviation: H.R.H. Prince SULTAN IBN ABDUL AZIZ.

Advisers to the Minister of Defence and Aviation (with Ministerial rank): Sheikh KAMAL SINDI, Gen. OTHMAN AL-HUMAID.

Minister of Public Works and Housing: H.R.H. Prince MUTAIB IBN ABDUL AZIZ.

SAUDI ARABIA

Governor of Mecca (with Ministerial rank): H.R.H. Prince MAJED IBN ABDUL AZIZ.

Minister of the Interior: H.R.H. Prince NAYEF IBN ABDUL AZIZ.

Minister of Foreign Affairs: H.R.H. Prince SAUD AL-FAISAL.

Minister of Petroleum and Mineral Resources: Sheikh AHMED ZAKI YAMANI.

Minister of Labour and Social Affairs: Sheikh IBRAHIM IBN ABDULLAH AL-ANGARI.

Minister of Higher Education: Sheikh HASSAN IBN ABDULLAH AL-SHEIKH.

Minister of Communications: Sheikh HUSSEIN IBRAHIM AL-MANSOURI.

Minister of Finance and National Economy: MUHAMMAD ALI ABDUL-KHAIL.

Minister of Information: Dr. MUHAMMAD ABDOU YAMANI.

Minister of Industry and Power: Dr. GHAZI ABDER-RAHMAN ALGOSAIBI.

Minister of Commerce: Dr. SULAIMAN ABDUL AZIZ AL-SULAIM.

Minister of Justice: Sheikh IBRAHIM IBN MUHAMMAD IBN IBRAHIM AS-SHEIKH.

Minister of Education: Dr. ABDUL AZIZ AL-ABDULLAH AL-KHUWAITER.

Minister of Planning: Sheikh HISHAM NAZER.

Minister of Pilgrimage Affairs and Waqfs: Sheikh ABDUL WAHHAB AHMAD ABDUL WASI.

Minister of Agriculture and Water: Dr. ABDER-RAHMAN IBN ABDUL AZIZ IBN HASAN AL-SHEIKH.

Minister of Health: Dr. HUSSEIN ABDUL RAZZAK JAZAIRI.

Minister of Posts, Telegraphs and Telecommunications: Dr. ALAWI DARWISH KAYYAL.

Ministers of State: Sheikh MUHAMMAD IBRAHIM MASOUD, Dr. MUHAMMAD ABDEL LATIF MILHAM.

Adviser to the Royal Cabinet with rank of Minister: Sheikh NASSER ASH-SHITRI.

DIPLOMATIC REPRESENTATION
EMBASSIES ACCREDITED TO SAUDI ARABIA
(In Jeddah unless otherwise stated)

Afghanistan: Tariq Madina, Kilo 3, Share Al-Qadisiah; *Ambassador:* MOHAMMAD AKBAR PARWANI.

Algeria: Medina Rd., Enaikish; *Ambassador:* MOHAMMAD MUSTAFA MA'IZA.

Argentina: P.O.B. 5888; *Chargé d'affaires:* MARIO TOMÁS BEJARANO.

Australia: Villa Ruwais Quarter, P.O.B. 4876; *Ambassador:* R. D. STURKEY.

Austria: P.O.B. 767; *Ambassador:* Dr. FRANZ SCHMID.

Bahrain: Al Hamra; *Ambassador:* IBRAHIM ALI IBRAHIM.

Bangladesh: P.O.B. 6215, Kilo 3, Mecca Rd.; *Ambassador:* HUMAYUN RASHEED CHOUDHURY.

Belgium: P.O.B. 290; *Ambassador:* JACQUES MELSENS.

Brazil: P.O.B. 4479; *Ambassador:* CELSO DINIZ.

Burundi.

Cameroon: Kilo 4, Medina Rd., (Madain Al Fahd), P.O.B. 1140; *Ambassador:* Alhaji HAMMADOU ALIM.

Canada: 6th Floor, Queen's Bldg., Commercial Centre; *Ambassador:* JACQUES S. ROY.

Chad: Villa Ahmed Said Bachoul, Rou Boud; *Chargé d'affaires:* HISSÈNE ALI ISSA.

China (Taiwan): Sheikh Wadji Tahlawi Building No. 3, off Palestine Rd.; *Ambassador:* HSUEH YU-CHI.

Costa Rica: Cairo, Egypt.

Denmark: P.O.B. 5333; *Ambassador:* FRANZ HOWITZ.

Djibouti: Kilo 3, Mecca Rd.; *Ambassador:* ADAN CHEIKH HASSAN.

Egypt: (*see* Sudan).

Ethiopia: P.O.B. 495; *Chargé d'affaires a.i.:* TEKLEHAIMANOT ABAY.

Finland: P.O.B. 5382; *Ambassador:* KAI HELENIUS.

France: Sheikh Muhammad bin Abdul Wahhab St.; *Ambassador:* PIERRE ROCALVE.

Gabon: P.O.B. 5442; *Ambassador:* MOUSSAVOU GHENGA.

Gambia: P.O.B. 5458; *Ambassador:* Alhaji ALIEU E. W. F. BADJI.

Germany, Federal Republic: Medina Rd., Mr. Mustafa Ashoor Bldg.; *Ambassador:* ALFRED VESTRING.

Ghana: Medina Rd., Kilo 3; *Ambassador:* Alhaj MAHMOUD SUKA-BRAIMAH.

Greece: P.O.B. 5108; *Ambassador:* PANDELIS MENGLIDIS.

Guinea: 11 Abou Ferass Al-Handany, Roueiss; *Ambassador:* THIERNO BANIKA DIALLO.

Iceland: Stockholm, Sweden.

India: Shaikh Mohammed Ibrahim Masoud Bldg., Medina Rd.; *Ambassador:* T. T. P. ABDULLAH.

Indonesia: Khalid bin Walid St., Sharafiah, P.O.B. 10; *Ambassador:* TEUKU MUHAMMAD HADI THAJEB.

Iran: 116 Medina Rd.; *Chargé d'affaires:* E. NAHEVANDIAN.

Iraq: Medina Rd., Kilo 5, Amar ibn Yasir St.; *Ambassador:* Lt.-Gen. SHAFIQ HAMMUDI AL-DARAJI.

Ireland: Musaidiyya St., Kilo 7, Medina Rd.; *Ambassador:* EAMON O'TUATHAIL.

Italy: Ahmad Abdullah Amoudi Building, Sharafiah; *Chargé d'affaires:* Dr. RANIERI FORNARI.

Japan: P.O.B. 1260; *Ambassador:* TERUHIKO NAKAMURA.

Jordan: Kilo 4 Mecca Rd., Bin Sina St.; *Ambassador:* THARWAT TALHOUNI.

Kenya: P.O.B. 6347; *Ambassador:* NOAH OKULO.

Korea, Republic: Fateji Building, nr. the Globe, Al Muaediah; *Ambassador:* YANG SOO YOO.

Kuwait: Medina Rd., Princess Sitah Bint Saud bin Abdulaziz; *Ambassador:* SAUD MUHAMMED AL-OUSAIMI.

Lebanon: P.O.B. 987; *Ambassador:* ZAFER AL-HASAN.

Liberia: Cairo, Egypt.

Libya: Medina Road, Kilo 5; *Ambassador:* AHMED FAWZI HILAL BIN FAYID.

Malaysia: P.O.B. 593; *Ambassador:* NOOR ADLAN BIN YAHAYUDDIN

Mali: Route de Medina près d'Al Mira Bldg.; *Ambassador:* SIDI MUHAMAD YOUSSOUF DJIRE.

Malta.

Mauritania: South Madain El Fahd; *Ambassador:* MOHAMED EL HANCHI OULD MOHAMED SALEH.

Mexico: Beirut, Lebanon.

Morocco: P.O.B. 498; *Ambassador:* MUHAMMAD LARBI EL ALAMI.

Nepal: P.O.B. 7358; *Ambassador:* KEDAR PRASAD KOIRALA.

Netherlands: P.O.B. 1776; *Ambassador:* Jonkheer HUBERT VAN NISPEN.

Niger: P.O.B. 1709; *Ambassador:* OUMAROU AMADOU.

Nigeria: P.O.B. 655; *Ambassador:* Alhaji DAHIRU ARUBAKAR WAZIRI.

Norway: P.O.B. 6251; *Ambassador:* JAN ØSTERN.

Oman: P.O.B. 2271; *Ambassador:* Sheikh IBRAHIM HAMMAD AL-HARTHI.

Pakistan: P.O.B. 182; *Ambassador:* NAJMUL SAQIB KHAN.

Philippines: Kilo 5, Medina Rd., P.O.B. 4794; *Ambassador·* BENJAMIN ROMUALDEZ.

Portugal: Nova Park Hotel, Room 282; *Ambassador:* PEDRO ALVES MACHADO.

Qatar: P.O.B. 313; *Ambassador:* ABDUL-AZIZ BIN SA'AD AL-SA'AD.

Rwanda: Cairo, Egypt.

Senegal: P.O.B. 1394; *Ambassador:* MOUSTAPHA CISSÉ.

Sierra Leone: P.O.B. 7028; *Ambassador:* SULIMAN BABA TIMBO.

Singapore: P.O.B. 9296; *Chargé d'affaires:* DAMORADARAN NAIR MURUGAN.

Somalia: North Palestine Rd., Enaikish, P.O.B. 729; *Ambassador:* ABDULLAH MOHAMOUD.

Spain: P.O.B. 453; *Ambassador:* MANUEL SASSOT.

Sri Lanka: P.O.B. 9390; *Ambassador:* MOHAMMAD REYAL THASSIM.

Sudan: Mina Rd., P.O.B. 480; *Ambassador:* ABDEL-LATIF AL-DHAHAB ABDEL-LATIF (also serves Egypt's interests).

Sweden: Musa'adia, P.O.B. 2005; *Ambassador:* FREDRIK BERGENSTRÅHLE.

Switzerland: P.O.B. 1016; *Ambassador:* ANDRÉ MAILLARD.

Syria: Al Huda St., Sharafiah; *Ambassador:* ABDUL HAMID DARKAL.

Thailand: P.O.B. 2224; *Ambassador:* SUVAT SENIVONGS NA AYUTHYA.

Tunisia: Sharia Badana, Mecca Rd., Kilo 3; *Ambassador:* KACEM BOUSNINA.

Turkey: P.O.B. 70; *Ambassador:* HUSEYIN CELEM.

Uganda: P.O.B. 4838; *Chargé d'affaires:* ABUBAKAR NADDULI.

United Arab Emirates: Bin Affan St., No. 58, Sharafiah; *Ambassador:* AHMED MOHAMMAD BU-REHAIMA.

United Kingdom: P.O.B. 393; *Ambassador:* Sir JAMES CRAIG, K.C.M.G.

U.S.A.: Palestine Rd., Ruwais; *Ambassador:* RICHARD W. MURPHY.

Upper Volta: *Chargé d'affaires:* Alhaji SINLAY DJIBO.

Uruguay: North Medina Road, P.O.B. 8186; *Ambassador:* JOSÉ D. LISSIDINI.

Venezuela: Hamra Palace St.; *Ambassador:* JOSÉ ALEJANDRO SUÑE GORRIN.

Yemen Arab Republic: Mecca Rd., Kilo 4; *Ambassador:* AHMED ALI AL-MIHANI.

Yemen, People's Democratic Republic: P.O.B. 6346; *Chargé d'affaires:* AHMED AOUD HAIDRA.

Zaire: Hail St., opposite U.S. Embassy; *Relations broken off, May* 1982.

Zambia: P.O.B. 7677; *Ambassador:* MATIYA NGALANDE.

Saudi Arabia also has diplomatic relations with Grenada, Jamaica, Luxembourg, Maldives, Mauritius and New Zealand.

JUDICIAL SYSTEM

Judges are independent and governed by the rules of Islamic *Sharia*. The following courts operate:

Supreme Council of Justice: consists of eleven members and supervises work of the courts; reviews legal questions referred to it by the Minister of Justice and expresses opinions on judicial questions; reviews sentences of death, cutting and stoning.

Court of Cassation: consists of Chief Justice and an adequate number of judges; includes department for penal suits, department for personal status and department for other suits.

General (Public) Courts: consist of one or more Judges; sentences of public courts are issued by a single judge, with the exception of death, stoning and cutting, which require the decision of three judges.

Summary Courts: consist of a single judge or more; sentences are issued by a single judge.

Specialized Courts: Article 26 of the judicial system stipulates that the setting up of specialized courts is permissible by Royal Decree on a proposal from the Supreme Council of Justice.

RELIGION

Arabia is the centre of the Islamic faith and includes the holy cities of Mecca and Medina. Except in the Eastern Province, where a large number of people follow Shi'a rites, the majority of the population are of the Sunni faith. The last seventy years have seen the rise of the Wahhabi sect, who originated in the eighteenth century, but first became unified and influential under their late leader King Ibn Saud. They are now the keepers of the holy places and control the pilgrimage to Mecca.

Mecca: Birthplace of the Prophet Muhammad, seat of the Great Mosque and Shrine of Ka'ba visited by a million Muslims annually.

Medina: Burial place of Muhammad, second sacred city of Islam.

THE PRESS

Since 1964 most newspapers and periodicals have been published by press organizations administered by boards of directors with full autonomous powers, in accordance with the provisions of the Press Law. These organizations, which took over from small private firms, are privately owned by groups of individuals widely experienced in newspaper publishing and administration (*see* Publishers).

There are also a number of popular periodicals published by the Government and by the Arabian American Oil Co. and distributed free of charge. The press is subject to no legal restriction affecting freedom of expression or the coverage of news.

DAILIES

Arab News: P.O.B. 4556, Jeddah; f. 1976; English; published by Saudi Research and Marketing Company; Editor MUHAMMAD M. AL-SHIBANI.

al-Bilad: King Abdul Aziz St., Jeddah; f. 1934; Arabic; published by al-Bilad Publishing Corporation; Editor ABDULMAJID AL-SHUBUKSHI; circ. 30,000.

al-Jazirah: P.O.B. 354, Nassiriah St., Riyadh; Arabic; Dir.-Gen. SALEH AL-AJROUSH, Editor-in-Chief KHALID AL-MALEK; circ. 5,000.

al-Madina al-Munawara: Jeddah, P.O.B. 807; f. 1937; Arabic; published by al-Madina Press Establishment; Editor AHMED M. MAHMOUD; circ. 30,000.

al-Nadwah: Mecca; f. 1958; Arabic; published by Mecca Press and Information Organization; Editors HAMED MUTAWI'E, SALEH MOHAMMED JAMAL; circ. 10,000.

Okaz Newspaper: P.O.B. 1508, Jeddah; f. 1960; Arabic; Editor-in-Chief ABDULLAH AHMED AL-DARY; circ. 80,000.

al-Riyadh: P.O.B. 851, Riyadh; Arabic; published by Yamamah Press Organization; Editor TURKI A. AL-SUDARI; circ. 16,000 (Mon.-Sat.), 15,000 (Sunday).

Saudi Gazette: Saba'een Rd., P.O.B. 5576, Jeddah; f. 1975; English business daily; published by Okaz Organization; Dir.-Gen. IYAD A. MADANI; Editor SAUD S. ISLAM.

Saudi Review: P.O.B. 4288, Jeddah; f. 1966; English; daily newsletter from Saudi newspapers and broadcasting service; Publisher and Chief Editor MUHAMMAD SALAHUDDIN; Man. Dir. SHAKER AL-SANTAWI; circ. 5,000.

al-Yaum (*Today*): P.O.B. 565, Dammam; f. 1964; Dir. HAMAD AL-MUBARAK; circ. 42,000.

WEEKLIES

Akhbar al-Dhahran (*Dhahran News*): Dhahran; f. 1958; Editor 'ABD AL-AZIZ AL-ISA; circ. 1,500.

Arabian Sun: Aramco, P.O.B. 1839, Dhahran; English; published by the Arabian American Oil Co., Dhahran.

Child: P.O.B. 1508, Jeddah; f. 1976; circ. 5,000.

al-Dawa: Islamic University, Shahrah Ibn Khaldun, Riyadh; Arabic.

Hasan: Jeddah; f. 1977; children's magazine; Editor-in-Chief JACOB MUHAMMAD ISSAC; circ. 10,000.

Rabita al Alam Islami (*Journal of Muslim World League*): P.O.B. 537 and 538, Mecca: weekly and monthly in both Arabic and English; Editors MUHAMMAD MAHMOUD HAFIZ (Arabic), SAYYID HASAN MUTAHAR (English).

Saudi Business: P.O.B. 4556, Jeddah; Editor-in-Chief MUHAMMAD M. AL-SHIBANI.

Saudi Economic Survey: P.O.B. 1989, Jeddah; f. 1967; English; a weekly review of Saudi Arabian economic and business activity; Publisher S. A. ASHOOR; Managing Ed. ABDELHAKIM GHAITH.

MONTHLIES

Ahlan Wasahlan (*Welcome*): P.O.B. 620, Jeddah; flight journal by Saudi Arabian Airlines; Gen. Man. YARUB A. BALKHAIR; Editor-in-Chief MUHAMMAD SALAHUDDIN.

Al-Arab: King Faisal St., Riyadh; Editor HAMDUL JANIR.

Al-Lequ'a: P.O.B. 812, Riyadh; Editor IBRAHIM AL-ULAI AL-MAIMAN.

Al-Manhal: 44 Shahrah Arafet, P.O.B. 2925, Riyadh; literary and cultural; Arabic; Editor ABDUL QUDOOS ANSARI.

Mujalla al-Iqtisad wa al-Idara (*Journal of Economics and Administration*): Research and Development Center, King Abdulaziz University, P.O.B. 9031, Jeddah; Chief Editor Dr. MUHAMMAD M. N. QUOTAH.

Oafla-e-Zaid (*Oil Caravan*): P.O.B. 1389, Dhahran; f. 1952; published by Arabian American Oil Company.

Al-Sharkiah-Elle (*Arab Women's Magazine*): Al-Jabbul Ahalie Bldg., P.O.B. 6, Riyadh; Editor SAMIRA M. KHASHAGGI.

Al-Soqoor (*Falcons*): P.O.B. 2973, King Faisal Air Academy, Riyadh; air-force journal; cultural activities; Editor ANWAR MUHAMMAD AL-QADHEB.

Al-Tadhamon Al-Islami (*Islamic Solidarity*): Hajj Ministry, Mecca; Editor Dr. MUSTAAF ABDUL WAHID.

al-Tijarah: P.O.B. 1264, Jeddah; f. 1960; for businessmen; published by Jeddah Chamber of Commerce and Industry; Chair. Sheikh ISMAIL ABUDAWOOD; Gen. Man. WAHAB ABUZINADA; circ. 1,800.

NEWS AGENCY

Saudi Press Agency: c/o Ministry of Information, Riyadh; f. 1970; Dir.-Gen. ABDULLA HILAIL.

PUBLISHERS

al-Bilad Publishing Organization: King Abdul Aziz St., Jeddah; publishes *al-Bilad* and *Iqra'a*; Dir.-Gen. ABDULLAH DABBAGH.

Dar al-Yaum Press, Printing and Publishing Ltd.: P.O.B. 565, Dammam; f. 1964; publishes *al-Yaum*; Dir.-Gen. HAMAD AL-MUBARAK.

al-Jazirah Corporation for Press, Printing and Publishing: P.O.B. 354, Riyadh; f. 1964; 27 mems.; publishes *al-Jazirah* (daily); Dir.-Gen. SALEH AL-AJROUSH; Editor-in-Chief KHALID EL MALEK.

al-Madina Press Establishment: P.O.B. 807, Jeddah; f. 1937; publishes *al-Madina al-Munawara*; Admin. Man. A. S. AL-GHAMDI; Gen. Man. AHMED SALAH JAMJOOM.

Okaz Organization for Press and Publication: Al-Mina St., P.O.B. 1508, Jeddah; publishes *Okaz*, *Saudi Gazette* and *Child*; Gen. Man. ALI H. SHOBOKSHI.

Saudi Publishing and Distributing House: Al-Jauhara Bldg., Flats 7 and 12, Baghdadia, P.O.B. 2043, Jeddah; books in Arabic and English; Chair. MUHAMMAD SALAHUDDIN; Gen. Man. MUHAMMAD ALI AL-WAZIR.

al-Yamamah Press Establishment: Riyadh; publishes *al-Riyadh*, *al-Yamamah* and *She*; Dir.-Gen. ABDULLAH QAR'AWI.

RADIO AND TELEVISION

RADIO

Saudi Arabian Broadcasting Service: Ministry of Information, Airport Rd., Jeddah; stations at Jeddah, Riyadh, Dammam and Abha; broadcast programmes in Arabic and English; overseas service in Urdu, Indonesian, Persian, French, Somali and Swahili; Dir.-Gen. KHALID H. GHOUTH.

Aramco Radio: P.O.B. 96, Dhahran; broadcasts music and programmes in English for the entertainment of employees of Arabian-American Oil Company.

There are about 300,000 radio receivers (1980).

TELEVISION

Saudi Arabian Government Television Service: Information Ministry, P.O.B. 570, Riyadh; stations at Riyadh, Jeddah, Medina, Dammam, Qassim, Abha, Hail, Albaha, Sakaka, Al-Qurayat, Wadiadda-Wasir and Tabuk operate 8 hours daily; major stations and relay points are under construction to serve all principal towns; Dir.-Gen. MOHAMMAD AL-FHAID.

Dhahran-HZ-22-TV. Aramco TV: Arabian American Oil Co., Room 300, Administration Bldg., Dhahran; non-commercial; started 1957, since 1970 English language film-chain operation only; Man. (Residential and Recreation Services) FOUAD M. SALEH; Man. (Communicaticns) A. D. HENDRICKS.

There are about 310,000 television sets (1980).

FINANCE

BANKING

The Saudi Arabian banking system consists of: the Saudi Arabian Monetary Agency, as central note-issuing and regulatory body; twelve commercial banks (two national and ten foreign banks); and three specialist banks. There is a policy of 'Saudization' of the foreign banks.

The rising volume of oil revenues imposed a need for a central monetary authority and in 1952 the Saudi Arabian Monetary Agency (SAMA) was established in Jeddah. SAMA's functions include: bankers to the Government; stabilization of the value of the currency; administration of monetary reserves; issue of coin and notes; and regulation of banking.

(cap. = capital; p.u. = paid up; dep. = deposits; m. = million; amounts in Saudi riyals)

CENTRAL BANK

Saudi Arabian Monetary Agency (SAMA): P.O.B. 2992, Airport Rd., Riyadh; f. 1952; total assets and liabilities 26,225.7m. (Nov. 1979); Pres. and Gov. ABDUL AZIZ AL QURAISHI; Vice-Gov. HAMAD SAUD AL-SAYYARI; Controller-Gen. ABDUL WAHAB M. S. SHEIKH; publs. *Statement of Affairs* (fortnightly); *Annual Report; Statistical Summary* (twice a year); 10 brs.

NATIONAL BANKS

National Commercial Bank: P.O.B. 3555, King Abdul Aziz St., Jeddah; f. 1938; cap. and res. 2,000m. (Oct. 1981); Partners Sheikh SALEH ABDULLAH MOSA KAAKI, Sheikh ABDULAZIZ MUHAMMAD KAAKI, Sheikh SALIM BIN MAHFOOZ (Gen. Man.); 64 brs. and 3 seasonal branches for pilgrims.

Riyad Bank: P.O.B. 1047, King Abdul Aziz St., Jeddah; f. 1957; cap. p.u. and res. 1,800m.; dep. 17,874m.; total assets 34,410m. (May 1981); Chair. H.E. Sheikh ABDULLAH BIN ADWAN; Man. Dir. H.E. Sheikh ABDUL RAHMAN AL-SHEIKH; Gen. Man. Sheikh IBRAHIM M. S. SHAMS; 96 brs.

SPECIALIST BANKS

Agricultural Credit Bank: Jeddah; f. 1964; cap. 31.5m.; Dir.-Gen. IZZAT HUSNI AL-ALI.

Arab Investment Co. S.A.A.: P.O.B. 4009, Riyadh; f. 1974 by 15 Arab countries for industrial investment.

Saudi Credit Bank: Jeddah; f. 1973; provides interest-free loans for specific purposes to Saudi citizens of moderate means.

Saudi Investment Banking Corporation: P.O.B. 3533, Riyadh; f. 1977; provides medium- and long-term finance to business and individuals; foreign sponsors, particularly Chase Manhattan Bank, have provided 20 per cent of capital; Dir. and Gen. Man. RICHARD F. STACKS.

BANKS WITH FOREIGN INTERESTS

Al-Bank al-Saudi al-Fransi (*Saudi French Bank*): P.O.B. 1, Palestine Square, Al Harithy Centre, Jeddah; f. 1977; cap. 24,789m. (June 1980); Man. Dir. RAYMOND BRAVARD; Deputy Man. Dir. A. ABU AL SAMH; 17 brs.

Al-Bank al-Saudi al-Hollandi (*Saudi Dutch Bank*): P.O.B. 6677, Medina Rd., Jeddah; formerly Algemene Bank Nederland, N.V., but Saudi Arabia acquired 60 per cent participation in 1977; cap. 210m.; Chair. SAYED HUSSEIN MOHAMED ALATAS; Man. Dir. H. A. PRONK; 5 brs.

Arab National Bank Ltd.: P.O.B. 41090, Riyadh; formerly Arab Bank, Jordan, but Saudi Arabia acquired 60 per cent participation.

Bank al-Jazira: P.O.B. 6277, Jeddah; formerly National Bank of Pakistan, Jeddah, but Saudi Arabia acquired 65 per cent participation in 1976; cap. p.u. 100m., dep. 2,843m. (Dec. 1981); Chair. Sheikh ABDUL AZIZ ABDULLAH AL-SULAIMAN; Gen. Man. ATHAR HUSAIN.

Saudi American Bank (*Al-Bank al-Saudi al-Amiriki*): P.O.B. 833, Shara Matar, Riyadh; formerly Citibank, Saudi Arabia acquired 60 per cent interest in 1980; Chair. Sheikh ABDULLAH ABDUL AZIZ AL-SUDAIRY; Man. Dir. ROBERT J. BOTJER.

Saudi British Bank (*Al-Bank al-Saudi al-Biritani*): P.O.B. 9084, Riyadh; formerly Saudi branches of British Bank of the Middle East, but Saudi Arabia acquired 60 per cent interest in 1978; cap. 300m.; dep. 4,366m. (Dec. 1981); Chair. Sheikh SULIMAN SALEH OLAYAN; Man. Dir. JOHN PATON; 20 brs.

Saudi Cairo Bank: Al-Faiha Building, Medina Rd., P.O.B. 496, Jeddah; formerly Banque du Caire, but Saudi Arabia acquired 60 per cent participation; cap. p.u. 150m.; Chair. Sheikh ABDULLAH AL-DABBAGH; Man. Dir. BAHGAT S. KHALIL; 22 brs.

Saudi Commercial United Bank: P.O.B. 482, Jeddah; f. 1982 by merger of Saudi branches of Bank Melli Iran, Banque du Liban et d'Outre-Mer and United Bank Ltd. of Pakistan, with majority Saudi participation.

INSURANCE COMPANIES

Al-Alamiya Insurance Co. Ltd.: P.O.B. 2374, Jeddah; managed by Sun Alliance, London; Gen. Man. C. R. HUKE.

Credit and Commerce Insurance Co. (Saudi) Ltd.: 1001-1002 Queens Bldg., King Abdul Aziz St., P.O.B. 5248, Jeddah; Man. SYED YOUNUS.

Independent Insurance Co. of Saudi Arabia Ltd.: P.O.B. 1178, Jeddah Towers Bldg., Sharafia, Jeddah; all classes of insurance; Execs. ABDUL HAMID, JULIAN D. SHARPE.

National Insurance Co. S.A.: P.O.B. 5832, Jeddah; all classes.

Pan Arabian Insurance Co.: P.O.B. 276, El-Khereiji Bldg., Dammam; f. 1976; majority shareholder Sheikh ABDUL KARIM EL-KHEREIJI; Gen. Man. M. M. JISHI.

Red Sea Insurance Co. Ltd.: Attar Bldg., King Abdul Aziz St., Jeddah; f. 1974; Vice-Chair. and Man. Dir. AHMED ENAN; Gen. Man. MOHAMED SAID EL EZABY.

Saudi United Insurance Co. Ltd.: P.O.B. 933, Al-Khobar; f. 1976; fire, accident and marine; majority shareholding held by Ahmed Hamad Algosaibi & Bros.; Gen. Man. AHMED MUHAMMAD SABBAGH.

United Commercial Agencies Ltd. (Saudi Arabia): Medina Rd., P.O.B. 5019, Jeddah; f. 1974; Chair. GHAITH PHARAON; Man. Dir. PAUL HADDAD.

TRADE AND INDUSTRY

DEVELOPMENT

Royal Commission for Jubail and Yanbu: P.O.B. 5964, Riyadh; f. 1975; to create the basic infrastructure for new industrial cities at Jubail and Yanbu; Sec.-Gen. Dr. FAROUK MUHAMMAD AKHDAR; Dir.-Gen. for Jubail Dr. JAMIL AL-JISHI, for Yanbu Dr. YUSIF AL-TURKI.

Saudi Industrial Development Fund: P.O.B. 4143, Riyadh; f. 1974; provides interest-free loans for industrial projects with more than 25 per cent Saudi participation, particularly for expansion of electricity company; Dir.-Gen. SALEH AL-NAIM.

CHAMBERS OF COMMERCE

Chamber of Commerce and Industries: Jeddah, P.O.B. 1264; f. 1950; Pres. Sheikh ISMAIL ABUDAWOOD; Man. WAHAB ABUZINADA; publ. *Al-Tijara.*

Dammam Chamber of Commerce: P.O.B. 719, Dammam.

Mecca Chamber of Commerce and Industry: P.O.B. 1086, Al-Ghazza St., Mecca; f. 1945; Pres. SALEH MOHAMED JAMAL; Sec.-Gen. FOUAD A. HIMDY; publ. *Al Tijarah Wassina'Ah* (monthly).

Medina Chamber of Commerce: P.O.B. 443, Medina.

Riyadh Chamber of Commerce and Industry: P.O.B. 596, Riyadh; f. 1961; acts as arbitrator in business disputes, information centre; Pres. Sheikh MOHAMED A. AL-FRAIH; Sec.-Gen. SALEH TOAIMI; 12,000 mems.; publs. monthly magazine, trade directory, twice-weekly bulletin.

PETROLEUM

General Petroleum and Mineral Organization (PETROMIN): P.O.B. 757, Riyadh; f. 1962; responsible for petroleum refining, domestic marketing and distribution of petroleum products, and some exports of petroleum and LPG; after the completion of negotiations for the takeover of Aramco in September 1980, is taking steps to become Saudi National Oil Company; Gov. ABDUL HADI TAHER.

Arabian Drilling Co.: P.O.B. 932, Riyadh; f. 1964; shareholding 51 per cent, remainder French private capital; undertakes contract drilling for oil, minerals and water both inside and outside Saudi Arabia.

Arabian Geophysical and Surveying Co. (ARGAS): P.O.B. 2109, Jeddah; f. 1966; shareholding 51 per cent owned by General Petroleum and Mineral Organization (PETROMIN); remainder provided by Cie. Générale de Géophysique; geophysical exploration for oil, minerals and ground water, as well as all types of land, airborne and marine surveys; Man. Dir. FADLULLAH FAROUQ; Tech. Dir. ROBERT GALIN.

Arabian Marine Petroleum Co. (MARINCO): P.O.B. 50, Dhahran Airport; f. 1968; shareholding 51 per cent, remainder held by McDermott Co. of New Orleans, U.S.A.; undertakes marine construction work (pipelines, rigs, sea terminals, etc.).

Jeddah Oil Refinery: P.O.B. 1604, Jeddah; f. 1968; shareholding 75 per cent, remainder held by Saudi Arabian Refining Co. (SARCO); the refinery at Jeddah, Japanese-built, has a capacity of 88,000 b/d; responsible for distribution in the Western Province.

Petromin Lubricating Oil Co. (PETROLUBE): P.O.B. 1432, Jeddah; f. 1968; for the refining, processing and manufacture of lubricating oils and other related products; also distribution.

Petromin Lubricating Refinery (LUBREF): P.O.B. 1604, Jeddah; f. 1975; has initial production capacity of one million barrels of lubricating oil per year.

Petromin Marketing (PETMARK): P.O.B. 50, Dhahran Airport; f. 1967; wholly-owned by Petromin; operates the installations and facilities for the distribution of petroleum products in the Eastern, Central, Southern and Northern provinces of Saudi Arabia; Exec. Managing Dir. (Marketing Affairs) S. S. ABU AL-JADAYIL.

Petromin Services Department (PETROSERV): f. 1975; operates medical and social centres; meets health and recreational needs of personnel of Petromin and its contractors.

Petromin Tankers and Mineral Shipping Co. (PETROSHIP): P.O.B. 1600, Jeddah; f. 1968; wholly owned by Petromin; operates tanker fleet.

Riyadh Refinery: P.O.B. 3946, Riyadh; f. 1974.

Saudi Basic Industries Corporation (SABIC): P.O.B. 5101, Riyadh; f. 1976; to foster the petrochemical industry and other hydrocarbon-based industries through joint ventures with foreign partners, and market their products; Chair. Dr. GHAZI AL-GOSAIBI; Deputy Chair. and Man. Dir. Dr. ABDUL AL-ZAMIL.

FOREIGN CONCESSIONAIRES

Arabian-American Oil Co. (Aramco): Dhahran; f. 1933; holds the principal working concessions in Saudi Arabia, covering approx. 85,000 square miles; production (1981) 3,513.2 million barrels; Saudi Government in 1980 increased from 60 to 100 per cent its interest in Aramco's crude oil concession rights, facilities and production; Chair. and Chief Exec. Officer JOHN J. KELBERER; Pres. H. H. GOERNER.

Arabian Oil Co. Ltd.: P.O.B. 335, Riyadh (Head Office in Japan); f. 1958; holds concession for offshore exploitation of Saudi Arabia's half-interest in the Kuwait-Saudi Arabia Partitioned Zone; total oil production (1981) 27,946m. cubic feet; Chair. SOHEI MIZUNO; Pres. JIN MIYAZAKI.

Getty Oil Co.: P.O.B. 363, Riyadh; also office in Kuwait; f. 1928; holds concession for exploitation of Saudi Arabia's half-interest in the Saudi Arabia-Kuwait Partitioned Zone, on-shore total Zone production (1981) 54.1 million barrels.

TRANSPORT

RAILWAYS

Saudi Government Railroad Organization: P.O.B. 92, Dhahran; Pres. FAYSAL M. AL-SHEHAIL.

The Saudi Government Railroad is a single track, standard gauge line 577 km. long. In addition, the total length of spur lines and sidings is 170 km. The main line connects Dammam Port at the Arabian Gulf with Riyadh, and passes Dhahran, Abqaiq, Hufuf, Harad and al-Kharj. Plans to construct lines linking Dammam with Jubail, providing a direct link from Hufuf to Riyadh, and to restore the Hijaz railway from Medina to Damascus, were under study in 1980.

The Organization is an independent entity with a Board of Directors headed by the Minister of Communications.

ROADS

Asphalted roads link Jeddah to Mecca, Jeddah to Medina, Medina to Yanbu, Ta'if to Mecca, Riyadh to al-Kharj, and Dammam to Hufuf as well as the principal communities and certain outlying points in Aramco's area of operations. Work is proceeding on various other roads, including one which will link Medina and Riyadh. A road from Ta'if to Jizan in the south, near the Yemeni border, was officially opened in 1976. The trans-Arabian highway, linking Dammam, Riyadh, Ta'if, Mecca and Jeddah, was completed in 1967. Under the 1975–80 Plan some 9,400 km. of asphalted roads were added to the existing network. In 1980 there were 20,869 km. of tarmac roads and 22,306 km. of dirt roads. Metalled roads link all the main population centres.

National Transport Company of Saudi Arabia: P.O.B. 7280, Jeddah; specializes in inward clearance, freight forwarding, general and heavy road haulage, re-export, charter air freight and exhibitions; Man. Dir. A. D. BLACKSTOCK.

SHIPPING

Saudi Arabian Ports Authority: P.O.B. 5162, Riyadh; Pres. and Chair. Dr. FAYEZ BADR; Dir. Gen. MUHAMMAD A. BAKR.

The ports of Jeddah, Dammam, Yanbu, Jizan and Jubail, as well as a number of minor ports, are under the exclusive management of the Ports Authority.

Jeddah is the principal port and the main point of entry for pilgrims bound for Mecca. It had 43 berths by March 1981 and more are under construction. These berths have draughts ranging from 8 to 14 metres.

Dammam is the second largest port and had 39 berths by 1981. Draughts at this port range from 9 to 14 metres.

Yanbu is a busy cargo port as well as being the main port used by pilgrims bound for Medina. It has recently been extended and modernized with new docks, storage space and a special Pilgrims' Hall. The port has two berths with an additional seven under construction. The draughts range from 10 to 12 metres.

Jizan, which is the main port for the southern part of the country, comprises three berths with a draught of 10 metres and a further 10 berths with draughts of between 8 and 12 metres are under construction.

At *Jubail* there is a new deep-water port which includes 25 berths with draughts ranging from 12 to 14 metres, plus an Open Sea Tanker Terminal with four 28-metre draught berths.

In addition to the ports mentioned, there are a number of minor ports including Haql, Wejh, Umludj, Rabigh, Al Lith, Qunsudah, Farasan, Qudayma and Muwaih on the Red Sea coast and Al-Khobar, Qatif, Uqair, Ras Al-Ghar and Darin on the Arabian Gulf coast. Most of these are suitable only for small craft. Ras Mishab on the Arabian Gulf coast is operated by the Ministry of Defence and Aviation.

Nashar Saudi Lines: P.O.B. 6697, Jeddah; owners of live-stock carriers trading in Arabian Gulf, Red Sea, Mediterranean and Black Sea.

Saudi Arabian Maritime Co. (SAMARCO): P.O.B. 5746, Jeddah; tanker operations.

Saudi Lines: P.O.B. 66, Jeddah; regular cargo and passenger services between Red Sea and Indian Ocean ports; Pres. M. A. BAKHASHAB PASHA; Man. Dir. A. M. BAKHASHAB.

Saudi National Lines: P.O.B. 4181, Jeddah; regular container, Ro/Ro and general cargo service from U.S.A. to Saudi Arabia, Gulf and Red Sea ports.

CIVIL AVIATION

In April 1981 a new international airport in Jeddah, the King Abdul Aziz International Airport, was opened. It has three terminals, one of which is specifically designed to cope with the needs of the many thousands of pilgrims who visit Mecca each year. This is one of three airports being built under the auspices of the International Airports Projects of Saudi Arabia, founded in 1976. The King Khalid International Airport, at Riyadh, is due to open in 1983 and the third, the New Eastern Province Airport, is planned for the Eastern Province.

Saudia—Saudi Arabian Airlines: Saudia Bldg., P.O.B. 620, Jeddah; f. 1945; regular internal services to all major cities of Saudi Arabia; regular international services to Abu Dhabi, Aden, Algiers, Amman, Asmara, Athens, Baghdad, Bahrain, Bangkok, Beirut, Bombay, Cairo, Casablanca, Dacca, Damascus, Doha, Dubai, Frankfurt, Geneva, Istanbul, Kano, Karachi, Khartoum, Kuwait, London, Madrid, Muscat, Nairobi, New Delhi, New York, Paris, Port Sudan, Rome, Sana'a, Sharjah, Shiraz, Singapore, Teheran, Tripoli, Tunis; fleet of more than 80 aircraft including 17 Lockheed TriStar, 6 Boeing 747, 19 Boeing 737 and 6 Boeing 707; Dir.-Gen. Sheikh AHMED MATTAR; Deputy Dir.-Gen. (Admin.) M. S. BANAJA; Deputy Dir.-Gen. (Operations) T. E. BURDETTE.

Saudi Arabia is also served by the following foreign airlines: Air Algérie, Air France, Air India, Alia (Jordan), Alitalia (Italy), British Airways, China Airlines (Taiwan), Cyprus Airways, EgyptAir, Ethiopian Airlines, Gulf Air, Iberia (Spain), Iranair, Iraqi Airways, JAL (Japan), KLM (Netherlands), Korean Airlines (Republic of Korea), Kuwait Airways, Libyan Arab Airlines, Lufthansa (Federal Republic of Germany), MAS (Malaysia), MEA (Lebanon), Olympic Airways (Greece), PIA (Pakistan), Royal Air Maroc, SAS (Sweden), SIA (Singapore), Somali Airlines, Sudan Airways, Swissair, Syrian Arab Airlines, Thai International, TMA (Lebanon), Tunis Air, Turkish Airlines, Yemen Airways (Yemen Arab Republic).

TOURISM

Saudi Hotels and Resort Areas Company: P.O.B. 5500, Riyadh; Saudi Government has 22 per cent interest.

ATOMIC ENERGY

Saudi Arabia joined the International Atomic Energy Agency in January 1963. Radio isotopes are used in the oil industry and are being introduced into state-controlled agricultural schemes.

DEFENCE

Chief of the General Staff: Maj.-Gen. MUHAMMAD AS-SALAH AL-HAMMAD.

Director-General of Public Security Forces: Brig.-Gen.
ABDULLAH IBN AS-SHAIKH.

Commander of Land Forces: Maj.-Gen. ABDUL MUHSIN ALI
AL-AMRAN.

Commander of Air Force: Maj.-Gen. MUHAMMAD SABRI.

Defence Budget (1981/82): 92,500m. riyals.

Military Service: voluntary.

Total Armed Forces (July 1981): 51,700 (army 35,000;
navy 2,200; air force 14,500).

Paramilitary Forces: 30,000 National Guard and 6,500
Frontier Force and Coastguard.

EDUCATION

The educational system in Saudi Arabia resembles that
of other Arab countries. Educational institutions are run
mainly by the government. The private sector plays a
significant role at the first and second levels, but its total
contribution is quite small compared with that of the
public sector.

Pre-elementary education is provided on a small scale,
mainly in urban areas. Elementary education is of six
years' duration and the normal entrance age is 6+. The
total number of pupils in 1980/81 was 930,436, with 50,010
teachers. Intermediate education begins at 12+ and lasts
for three years. The total number of pupils in this stage for
1980/81 was 256,726, with teachers numbering 16,748.
Secondary education begins at 15+ and extends for three
years. After the first year, successful pupils branch into
science or arts groups. Total number of pupils in this stage
for 1980/81 was 100,023, with 5,962 teachers.

Industrial and commercial schools can be entered after
the completion of the intermediate stage. In 1980/81 there
were eight industrial schools, sixteen commercial schools
and one agricultural school. In addition there were one
higher technical and four higher commercial colleges
offering two-year courses. Vocational craft training institutes are maintained in six centres, providing courses in
electrical, mechanical and allied trades. Facilities exist for
the training of teachers.

There are seven universities and also the Colleges of
Education for Girls at Riyadh, Jeddah and Mecca. There
are also two Colleges of Arts for girls in Riyadh and
Damman and a Science College for girls in Dammam. A
college of social service for women has also been established
in Riyadh. Adult education is divided into two categories:
(a) to combat illiteracy; (b) follow-up. The duration of
study in each is 16 months.

Education has been allocated SR 21,294 million out of
a total of SR 245,000 million in the 1980/81 budget year.

BIBLIOGRAPHY

AL-FARSY, FOUAD. Saudi Arabia. A Case Study in Development (Kegan Paul International, Boston, 1981).

ARMSTRONG, H. C. Lord of Arabia (Beirut, 1962).

ASSAH, AHMED. Miracle of the Desert Kingdom (Johnson,
London, 1969).

ATLAS OF SAUDI ARABIA (Edward Stanford, London,
1978).

BENOIT-MÉCHIN, S. Ibn Séoud ou la naissance d'un
royaume (Albin Michel, Paris, 1955).

BROWN, E. HOAGLAND. The Saudi-Arabia-Kuwait Neutral
Zone (Beirut, 1964).

BUTLER, GRANT C. Kings and Camels: An American in
Saudi Arabia (The Devin-Adair Co., New York, 1960).

DE GAURY, GERALD. Faisal (Arthur Barker, London, 1969).

DEQUIN, HORST. Saudi Arabia's Agriculture and its
Development Possibilities (Frankfurt, 1963).

GHARAYBEH, A. Saudi Arabia (London, 1962).

HELMS, CHRISTINE MOSS. The Cohesion of Saudi Arabia
(Croom Helm, 1981).

HOBDAY, PETER. Saudi Arabia Today: An Introduction to
the Richest Oil Power (Macmillan, London, 1978).

HOLDEN, DAVID, JOHNS, RICHARD, and BUCHAN, JAMES.
The House of Saud (Sidgwick & Jackson, London,
1981).

HOWARTH, DAVID. The Desert King: Ibn Sa'ud (McGraw
Hill, New York, 1964).

LEBKICHER, ROY, RENTZ, GEORGE. and STEINCKE, MAX.
Saudi Arabia (New York, 1952).

LIPSKY, GEORGE A., and others. Saudi Arabia: Its People,
Its Society, Its Culture (New Haven, 1959).

PHILBY, H. ST. J. B. Arabia and the Wahhabis (London,
1928).

  Arabia (London, Benn. 1930).
  Arabian Jubilee (London, 1951).
  The Empty Quarter (London, 1933).
  The Land of Midian (London, 1957).
  A Pilgrim in Arabia (London, 1946).
  Saudi Arabia (London, 1955).

QUANDT, WILLAM B. Saudi Arabia in the 1980s: Foreign
Policy, Security and Oil (Brookings Institution, New
York, 1981).

SARHAN, SAMIR (Ed.). Who's Who in Saudi Arabia
(Tihama, Jeddah, and Europa, London, 2nd edn.,
1978).

TROELLER, GARY. The Birth of Saudi Arabia: Britain and
the Rise of the House of Sa'ud (London, Frank Cass,
1976).

TWITCHELL, KARL S., with the co-operation of JURJI,
EDWARD J. Saudi Arabia (Princeton, 1953).

VAN DER MEULEN, D. The Wells of Ib'n Saud (John
Murray, 1957).

WILLIAMS, K. Ibn Sa'ud: the Puritan King of Arabia
(London, Cape, 1933).

WINDER, R. BAYLY. Saudi Arabia in the Nineteenth
Century (Macmillan, London, 1965).

Spanish North Africa

GEOGRAPHY

CEUTA

The ancient port and walled city of Ceuta is situated on a rocky promontory on the North African coast overlooking the Strait of Gibraltar. It was retained by Spain as a *plaza de soberanía* when Morocco became independent in 1956 and is administered as part of Cádiz Province. The Portuguese first established a fort at Ceuta in 1415 and it was ceded to Spain by Portugal in 1668. It developed as a military and administrative centre for the former Spanish Protectorate in Morocco and now functions as a bunkering and fishing port. In 1981 its population was 70,864.

MELILLA

Melilla is situated on a small peninsula jutting out into the Mediterranean on the North African coast. It was retained by Spain as a *plaza de soberanía* when Morocco became independent in 1956 and is administered from Málaga. It was annexed by Spain in 1471 and served as a military stronghold up to the present. In 1981 it had a population of 58,773 (including the three islets separately mentioned below) and it is an active port.

PEÑÓN DE VÉLEZ, PEÑÓN DE ALHUCEMAS AND CHAFARINAS

These three rocky islets, situated respectively just west and east of Alhucemas and east of Melilla off the north coast of Morocco, are administered with Melilla. In 1981 their populations were respectively 70, 61 and 193.

HISTORY

Ceuta, Melilla and the island dependencies are known as the Plazas de Soberanía—i.e. *presidios*, or fortified enclaves, over which Spain has full sovereign rights. Children born in these dependencies, whether Christian or Muslim, are Spanish citizens and subjects. Both Ceuta and Melilla have municipal councils (*ayuntamientos*). They are administered as an integral part of Spain by an official responsible to the Ministry of the Interior. In respect of ecclesiastical and judicial affairs Ceuta is integrated with the province of Cádiz, and Melilla with the province of Málaga in Spain.

CEUTA

Ceuta is situated on the African shore opposite Gibraltar, the Strait being here about 25 km. wide. The Portuguese took Ceuta in 1415. On the union of the crowns of Spain and Portugal in 1580 Ceuta passed under Spanish rule and in 1694, when Portugal was formally separated from Spain, asked to remain under Spanish control. During the sixteenth, seventeenth and eighteenth centuries Ceuta had to endure a number of sieges at the hands of the Muslims. Ahmad Gailan, a chieftain in northern Morocco, blockaded the town in 1648–55. The Sultan of Morocco, Mulai Ismail (1672–1727), attacked Ceuta in 1674, 1680 and 1694, after which he maintained a blockade against the town until 1720. Ahmad Ali al-Rifi, a chieftain from northern Morocco, made yet another unsuccessful assault in 1732. A pact of friendship and commerce was negotiated between Spain and Morocco at Aranjuez in 1780, a peaceful agreement following in the next year over the boundaries of the Ceuta enclave. There was in 1844–45 a sharp dispute once more about the precise limits of Ceuta. Further disagreement in 1859 led to the war of 1860. Spanish forces, after an engagement at Los Castillejos, seized Tetuán in 1860. After another battle at Wadi Ras in March 1860 the conflict came to an end. A settlement was now made which enlarged the enclave of Ceuta and obliged Morocco to hand over to Spain 100 million pesetas as war indemnities. In 1874 the town became the seat of the Capitanía General de Africa.

MELILLA

Spain secured control of Melilla in 1496, the town being infeudated thereafter to the ducal house of Medina Sidonia, which was empowered to appoint the governor and seneschal with the approval of the Spanish Crown. The Rif tribesmen attacked Melilla in 1562–64. Later still, the Sultan of Morocco, Mulai Ismail (1672–1727) assaulted the town in 1687, 1696 and 1697. Sultan Muhammad b. Abdallah (1757–90) besieged Melilla in 1771 and 1774. An agreement concluded between Spain and Morocco in 1780 at Aranjuez led, however, in the following year, to a peaceful delimitation of the Melilla enclave. There was a brief period of tension in 1844 and then, in 1861, under the terms of an agreement signed at Madrid, after the Spanish-Moroccan campaign of 1860, Melilla received an extension of its boundaries. Trouble with the Rif tribesmen gave rise in 1893–94 to the so-called "War of Melilla", which ended with a settlement negotiated at Marrakesh. It was not until 1909 that Spanish forces, after a hard campaign, occupied the mountainous hinterland of Melilla between the Wadi Kert and the Wadi Muluya—a region in which, some ten miles behind Melilla, are situated the rich iron mines of Beni Bu Ifrur. In July 1921 the Rif tribes, under the command of Abd al-Krim, defeated a Spanish force near Anual and threatened Melilla itself. Only in 1926, with the final defeat of the Rif rebellion, was Spanish control restored over the Melilla region. Melilla was the first Spanish town to rise against the Government of the Popular Front on July 17th, 1936, at the beginning of the Spanish Civil War. Since 1939 both towns have been ruled as integral parts of Spain.

OTHER POSSESSIONS

The Chafarinas Islands, lying about 2½ miles off the Cabo de Agua, came under Spanish control in 1847. Peñón de Alhucemas is situated some three-quarters of a mile from the coast opposite Ajdir. It was occupied in 1673. Peñón de Vélez de la Gomera, about 50 miles farther west, came under Spanish rule in 1508, was then lost not long afterwards and reoccupied in 1564. All three possessions are, like Melilla, incorporated into the province of Málaga.

ECONOMIC SURVEY
CEUTA AND MELILLA

Ceuta and Melilla, both free ports, are in fact of little economic importance, while the other possessions, with a 1981 population of 324, mostly fishermen, are of negligible significance. The basic reason for Spanish retention of these areas is their overwhelmingly Spanish population. For instance, in the Melilla census of 1960 (the latest complete figures available), of a total population of 79,056 only 6,300 Muslims and 3,100 Jews were recorded. The 80,000 population of Ceuta was similarly composed. Ceuta's population had fallen to 64,576 by 1973, owing to the lack of economic opportunities in the town, but had risen to 70,864 by 1981. The hinterland of the two cities is small. Accordingly most of the population's food needs have to be imported, with the exception of fish which is obtained locally. Sardines and anchovies are the most important items, in an annual catch of about 16,000 tons. A large proportion of the tinned fish is sold outside Spain. More important to the economies of the cities is the port activity; most of their exports take the form of fuel supplied—at very competitive rates—to ships, most of which comes from the Spanish refinery in Tenerife. Ceuta's port is the busier but, apart from the ferries from Málaga and Almería in Spain, Melilla's port is not so frequented and its exports are correspondingly low. Ceuta exports wood, cork, foodstuffs and beverages. Industry is limited to meeting some of the everyday needs of the cities. In both cities less than two per cent of the working population are employed in agriculture. The total labour force in Ceuta in 1962 numbered 13,080 (construction 2,083, textiles 1,276, fishing 1,384 and commerce 1,768). Unemployment in both towns stood at 3,420 in December 1980. Business and port activity are sufficiently high to permit the municipalities' budgets which, by Spanish standards are high in relation to the numbers of population. More than 2.5 million tourists visit Ceuta each year, attracted by duty-free goods.

In 1980 Spain granted 1.6 million pesetas for the development of facilities in the enclaves.

STATISTICAL SURVEY
CEUTA

Area: 19 square km.

Population (March 1981, census): 70,864.

Finance: Spanish currency: 100 céntimos = 1 peseta. Exchange rates (May 1982): £1 sterling = 186.85 pesetas; U.S. $1 = 101.55 pesetas; 1,000 pesetas = £5.35 = $9.85.

External Trade: Ceuta is a duty-free port. Trade is chiefly with Spain, the Balearic and Canary Islands and Melilla.

Transport: Much of the traffic between Spain and Morocco passes through Ceuta; there are ferry services to Algeciras, Spain.

Education: (May 1981): Primary: 10,287 pupils; Secondary: 1,899 pupils.

Government: In both Ceuta and Melilla civil authority is vested in an official (Delegado del Gobierno) directly responsible to the Ministry of the Interior in Madrid. There is also a Government sub-delegate and one delegate from each of the ministries. Military authority is vested in a Commandant-General. A Mayor administers each town.

Mayor of Ceuta RICARDO MUÑOZ RODRÍGUEZ. Government Delegate in Ceuta GERARDO MARIÑAS ROMERO. Deputy elected to the Congress in Madrid FRANCISCO OLIVENCIA RUIZ. Commandant-General RICARDO RIVAS NADAL.

Religion: Most Africans are Muslims; Europeans are nearly all Catholics; there are a few Jews.

Press: Diario de Ceuta: Editora de Ceuta (EDICESA), Buenavista 1; morning; Dir. ANTONIO DE LA CRUZ AGUSTÍ.

El Faro de Ceuta: Solís 4, Ceuta; f. 1934; morning; Dir. ANTONIO LUIS FERRER PEÑA; Publr. JOAQUÍN FERRER GONZÁLEZ; circ. 5,000.

Radio: Radio Ceuta: Virgilio Oñate 1, Ceuta; commercial; owned by Sociedad Española de Radiodifusión; Dir. JOSÉ SOLERA BARCOS.

MELILLA

Area: 12.3 square km.

Population (March 1981, census): 58,773 (Melilla 58,449, Alhucemas 61, Chafarinas 193, Peñón de Vélez de la Gomera 70).

Finance: Spanish currency (*see* Ceuta).

External Trade: Melilla is a duty-free port. Most imports are from Spain but over 90 per cent of exports go to non-Spanish territories. The chief export is fish.

Transport: There is a daily ferry service to Málaga and a service to Almería. Melilla airport is served by daily flights to Málaga and Almería, operated by Iberia.

Education (1981/82): Primary 10,109 pupils; Secondary 1,092 pupils; Higher, technical and vocational 999 pupils.

Government: (*see* Ceuta above). Mayor of Melilla RAFAEL GINEL CAÑAMAQUE. Government Delegate in Melilla ENRIQUE MILLÁN LÓPEZ. Deputy elected to the Congress in Madrid José MANUEL GARCÍA-MARGALLO. Commandant-General LUIS SÁEZ LARUMBE.

Press: El Telegrama de Melilla: Ejército Español 16, Melilla; morning; Dir. JUAN SÁNCHEZ RADA.

Radio: Radio Melilla: Melilla; commercial; owned by Sociedad Española de Radiodifusión; Dir. AGUSTÍN MORICHE PÉREZ.

BIBLIOGRAPHY

AREILZA, J. MA. DE, and CASTIELLA, F. MA. Revindicaciones de España (Madrid, 1941).

BOUCHER, M. Spain in Africa (3 articles, *Africa Institute Bulletin*, May–July 1966).

HABSBOURG, OTTO D. E. Européens et Africains: L'Entente Nécessaire (Hachette, Paris, 1963).

PÉLISSIER, RENÉ. Los Territorios Españoles de Africa (Madrid, 1964).

Sudan

PHYSICAL AND SOCIAL GEOGRAPHY

J. A. Allan

THE NILE

The River Nile and its tributaries are the basis of much of the present economic activity of Sudan and of most of that currently envisaged. The river traverses diverse landscapes from the relatively humid tropical forest in the south to the arid deserts in the north. The Democratic Republic of Sudan is a huge country (2,505,813 sq. km. or 967,500 sq. miles), and the Nile waters which enter Sudan just south of Juba either evaporate or flow 3,000 km. until they reach Lake Nubia on the Egyptian border. Even those which flow down the Blue Nile traverse 2,000 km. The distances are immense and the remoteness of places on the Nile system, not to speak of those in the deserts, savannah and swamps of the rest of the country, explain much of the character of Sudan's land use. The other important factor is climate, which influences vegetation and, more important, affects the seasonal flow of the Nile tributaries.

The Blue Nile is the most important tributary, both in the volume of water which it carries (four-sevenths of the total average flow of the system) as well as in the area of irrigated land, of which it supports over 40 per cent of the present area and 70 per cent of potential irrigable land. The Blue Nile and other east-bank tributaries are sustained by monsoon rains over the Ethiopian highlands which cause the river to flood at the end of July, reach a peak in August and remain high through September and the first half of October. At Khartoum the river rises 7 metres in August. The Atbara, another seasonal east-bank tributary, provides a further one-seventh of the flow in the system, and the remaining two-sevenths come from the White Nile. The sustained flow of the White Nile arises first because its main source is Lake Victoria, which regulates the flow, and secondly because the swamps of the Sudd and Machar act as a reservoir, absorbing the irregular stream flow from the south while discharging a regular flow, much reduced by evaporation, in the north.

The River Nile is an international river system, and Sudan depends on river flows from seven other states. Sudan does not yet use all of the 18,500 million cubic metres of annual flow agreed with Egypt in 1959 as its share of the total average flow at Aswan of 84,000 million. (Egypt receives 55,500 million cubic metres while 10,000 million cubic metres are assumed to evaporate annually from Lake Nasser/Nubia). By the mid-1980s Sudan's irrigation developments will account for all its agreed share and ultimately there will be additional demands by up-stream states such as Ethiopia. Meanwhile Egypt's demand is rising and considerable water usage is planned there. For these reasons Sudan and Egypt are jointly financing the Jonglei Project, which will save 4,750 million cubic metres of water (3,850 million at Aswan) in the first phase and 4,250 million (3,440 million at Aswan) in the second. The water gained from both stages will be shared equally with Egypt. The Machar swamps will also yield water at a rate as yet undetermined but likely to be about 4,000 million cubic metres (3,240 million at Aswan).

PHYSICAL FEATURES

Sudan is generally a flat, featureless plain reflecting the proximity to the surface of the ancient, little-disturbed Basement rocks of the African continent. The Basement is overlain by the Nubian Sandstone formation in the centre and north-west of the country, and by the Umm Ruwaba formation in the south. These formations hold groundwater bodies which have, or will have, agricultural significance. No point in the country is very high above sea-level. Jebel Marra, an extinct volcano, at 3,500 metres is the highest point, while other ranges, such as the Imatong and Nuba Mountains, rise to 1,500 metres, and the Red Sea Hills to 2,000 metres. Some idea of the level character of the landscape is provided by the small amount of the fall in the Blue Nile, which starts its 2,000 km. flow through Sudan at 500 metres above sea-level at the Ethiopian border and used to flow past Wadi Halfa (now flooded) at an elevation of 156 metres. It now flows into Lake Nubia at 180 metres above sea-level. The White Nile, as it emerges from Uganda, falls some 600 metres between the border and Khartoum, a distance of 1,700 km., but falls only 17 metres in the last 700 km. from entering the southern clay plains.

CLIMATE

Average temperatures and rainfall change steadily from month to month, except where the effect of the Ethiopian highlands disturbs the east-west trend in the climatic belts in the south-east. The north of Sudan is a desert with negligible rainfalls and high average daily temperatures (summer 35°C., winter 20°C.). Low temperatures are recorded only in winter. Rainfall is convectional in origin and increases steadily south of Khartoum (200 mm. per year) until it is over 1,000 mm. per year at the southern border. Rainfall varies from year to year, especially in the north, and is seasonal. In the south it falls in the period April–October; the rainy season is progressively shorter towards the north, where it lasts only from July until August. Potential evaporation approaches 3,000 mm. per year in the north and is always over 1,400 mm. per year even in the humid south.

VEGETATION AND SOILS

The soil resources of Sudan are rich in agricultural potential. The exploitation of these resources depends on the availability of the limiting factor, water, and only a small proportion of the clay plains of central and east Sudan are currently farmed intensively. The clay plains are the result of millennia of alluvial sorting and deposition of eroded basic volcanic material from the Ethiopian highlands. Clay soils also occur in the south, being deposits of the White Nile and Sobat streams. Recent alluvium provides a basis for productive agriculture in the narrow Nile Valley north of Khartoum. Elsewhere, in the west and north the soils are sandy, with little agricultural potential, except in the dry valleys, which generally contain some soil moisture.

Vegetation is closely related to the climatic zones. From the desert in the north vegetation gradually improves through semi-arid shrub to low woodland savannah characterized by acacia and short grasses. Progressively higher rainfall towards the south promotes trees and shrubs as well as herbs, while the more reliably watered rangeland of the Bahr el Arab provides an important seasonal resource for the graziers from the poor pastures of Darfur and Kordofan. The flooded areas of the Sudd and Machar and environs support swamp vegetation and grassland. On the uplands of the southern border, rainfall is high enough to support tropical rain forest.

POPULATION

The population of Sudan was estimated at 18.4 million in 1980, rising at an annual rate of 2.75 per cent. About 71 per cent of the population live in rural areas, 18 per cent in urban and semi-urban areas and the remaining 11 per cent are nomadic. Forty-seven per cent of the population were under 15 years of age at the last census in 1973. The population is concentrated in Khartoum Province and the Central Region, where population densities were respectively 55 and 28 per sq. km. in 1973, compared with between 3.6 and 6.8 per sq. km. elsewhere. Agricultural

development in the two most populous regions created employment opportunities and this led to the doubling of these populations between 1956 and 1973, compared with rises of between zero and 50 per cent elsewhere. There are local concentrations of population in the Nuba Mountains and higher densities than average in better-farmed parts of the Southern and Darfur Regions.

The ethnic origin of the people of Sudan is mixed and the country is still subject to significant immigration by groups from Nigeria and Chad, such as the Fulani. In the south the Nuer, the Dinka and the Shilluki are the most important of the Nilotic peoples. The Arab culture and language predominate in the north, which includes the most populous provinces and the capital, Khartoum. The south is predominantly Christian and this cultural difference, added to the ethnic separateness and the extreme remoteness of the Southern Region, has been expressed in economic backwardness and a tendency to political distinctness which until recently took the form of a civil war. Juba, the main town of the extreme south, was still being supplied in 1980 from Uganda and not from the north.

The capital, Khartoum, had an estimated population of over 1 million in 1980. It is the main administrative, commercial and industrial centre of the country. As communications are very poor and since Khartoum is at least 1,000 km. distant from 80 per cent of the country, the influence which Khartoum exerts on the rest of the country is small. The relatively advanced character and general success of much of the irrigated farming on the east-central clay plains has led to a predominance of investment there and to the misguided impression that the success of the east-central plains could be transferred to other parts of the country where the resources are unfortunately much less favourable. Much of Sudan is so dry for part of each year that the only possible way to use the land and vegetation resources is by grazing, and tribes such as the Bagara traverse the plains and plateaux of Darfur and Kordofan in response to the availability of fodder.

HISTORY

Muddathir Abdel-Rahim

The geographic position of Sudan, between the Mediterranean-Middle Eastern world on the one hand and central Africa on the other, has played an important part in determining the character and politics of the country since Biblical times at least. In almost all the contacts between Sudan and the outside world Egypt has been the most important link, and, especially since the rise of Islam, the dominant one. Thus the Pharaohs, the Persians, the Greeks, the Romans, the Arabs, the Turks and the British, all those who governed or conquered Egypt in the past, have in turn found it either necessary or desirable to extend their influence, if not their power, beyond the traditional boundaries of Egypt (between the first and

second cataracts) into the lands which now constitute the Democratic Republic of Sudan. Conversely, the inhabitants of those lands, or at any rate those of them who lived in the northern parts of the country, have always had to choose between three alternative policies: domination by Egypt; independence from their neighbours; or conquest of Egypt; at one time or another each of these possibilities was actually realized. At no time, however, could either of the two countries ignore the other—a fact which, with modern Egyptian nationalists, became the justification for making the Unity of the Nile Valley for many years the *raison d'être* of Egyptian foreign policy.

ANCIENT AND MEDIEVAL

From the time of Tuthmosis I (1530–1520 B.C.) until the eighth century B.C. northern Cush (as the area as far as the Gezira was called in ancient times) was, for the most part, under the effective control of the Pharaohs. And even after the political supremacy of the Pharaohs had been completely shaken off the Cushites continued to be so thoroughly Egyptianized that, at times, they regarded themselves as the champions of true Egyptian culture.

The political mastery of the Pharaohs in Cush gradually diminished from the tenth century onwards, and by 725 B.C. the balance of power was finally turned by a series of competent Cushite leaders who established themselves as the twenty-fifth Pharaonic dynasty. The most renowned Pharaoh of this Cushite dynasty was Tirhaka (688–663 B.C.) under whose leadership the empire extended from Cush to Syria and whose wars in Syria and Judea are recorded in the Bible. Tirhaka's empire, however, did not last long; a number of setbacks led to his final defeat by the Assyrians in 666 B.C. The kingdom of Cush survived for a thousand years, during which it expanded to the south, the capital being transferred from Napata, near the fourth cataract, to Meroe, near Kaboshiya, about 160 km. north of Khartoum. But under the pressure of Nubian migrants from the south-west and the new power of Axum in the east, the Meroitic kingdom declined and there was little of its former glory left when the first Christian king of Axum raided the Nile valley in A.D. 350.

From this cataclysm emerged three Nuba kingdoms into which Christianity was introduced from Egypt under the patronage of the Empress Theodora early in the sixth century A.D.

By A.D. 639, when the Arab Muslims invaded Egypt, two Christian Nuba kingdoms occupied approximately the territory formerly covered by the Meroitic realm. With the more northerly of these the Arab invaders made a treaty which subsisted for six hundred years. Under the terms of this agreement Islam began to spread into Nubia and Arab immigration, especially after the rise in Egypt of the Bahri Mamluks around A.D. 1250, gathered momentum. As a result of the twin processes, greatly facilitated by the fact that Muslim Arab immigrants readily intermarried with the indigenous population, Nubia was gradually transferred into a largely Islamized and Arabized society. The process culminated in the collapse of the last of the Nubian Christian kingdoms in 1504 and the establishment thereafter of the Islamic Sultanate of the Funj.

The Islamic Sultanate of the Funj, otherwise known as "the Black Sultanate", was, in effect, a confederation of smaller Sultanates or tribal chieftainships, each ruled from Sinnar, the new capital city on the Blue Nile, about 270 km. south of Khartoum. The authority of the Sultan at Sinnar was recognized throughout the former lands of Cush and Nubia, including the Gezira, but was contested in Kordofan by the dynasty of Sultan Suleiman Solong, which established itself in Darfur in 1596. Largely as a result of internecine warfare and wars with the Furs in the west and the Abyssinians in the east the energies of the Funj were sapped and, by the nineteenth century, when Muhammad Ali Pasha of Egypt challenged them, their Sultanate was already in decline.

THE NINETEENTH CENTURY

Muhammad Ali had two main objectives in the Sudan: gold and slaves, both of which he needed in order to build an Egyptian-Arab empire independent of that of the Sultan in Istanbul. His ambitions in this respect were frustrated by the European powers and his dreams about gold were proved to be false. But Muhammad Ali did succeed in establishing an empire in the Nile Valley which lasted from 1821, when the last of the kings of Sinnar surrendered, until 1885 when Khartoum fell to the Mahdi. Kordofan and Darfur were subsequently added to Sinnar and, under his successors, principally Khedive Ismail, the boundaries of the empire were extended to the Great Lakes, and by 1877 the Somali coast as far as Ras Hofun was also recognized as Egyptian territory under the suzerainty of the Sultan.

Within this vast but loosely organized empire the Sudan was, at first, viewed as a province of Egypt but its administration, centred on the new capital of Khartoum, was afterwards decentralized and put under a Hakimdar (or Governor General) to whom provincial governors were responsible. And the provinces were likewise divided into smaller units which tended to follow the traditional tribal and territorial boundaries of the Funj period. The personnel of the new regime was a mixture of Circassian, Turkish, European and Armenian officers of the Ottoman-Egyptian army who were assisted, especially at the lower levels, by Sudanese sheikhs and tribal leaders.

Like its counterparts in other parts of the later Ottoman empire the Sudan administration was corrupt and far from efficient. Its difficulties, arising from the general malaise of the declining empire, were further accentuated, on the one hand by frequent and arbitrary interference from Cairo and, on the other, by the policy of rapid but poorly organized expansion which was followed by Muhammad Ali's successors, especially Khedive Ismail. Ismail furthermore was determined to abolish slavery in his own lifetime. Slavery had been part of the social system throughout the Nile Valley including the Southern Sudan. But trading rights in the newly opened South had been sold to armed adventurers, and searching for slaves was carried to extremes which were in many cases reminiscent of the barbarities of the triangular slave trade. Ismail hoped to mitigate these evils by administrative means and through the agency of European expatriates such as Sir Samuel Baker and General Charles Gordon. But the violent methods used by these men in order to abolish the slave trade alienated large sections of the population, caused considerable social and economic dislocation and to that extent weakened the government's control over the country and played into the hands of the Sudanese religious rebel Muhammad Ahmed Abdulla. In March 1881, Abdulla declared that he was the Mahdi and called upon the people to rally with him against the Turks and for the reformation of Islam. This was not, at first, taken seriously by the government. The Mahdi on the other hand showed remarkable skill in manoeuvre and organization, and under his able leadership the apparently minor rebellion was rapidly transferred into a nation-wide "jihad" which by January 1885 resulted in the fall of Khartoum. Thus began a new chapter in the history of the country during which the Sudan was governed by Sudanese; first under the Mahdi and after his death in June 1885, by the Khalifa Abdullahi whose rule lasted for more than thirteen years.

In the meantime Britain had occupied Egypt and assumed effective, but indirect, control of its government. Thus, in 1883, the Government of the Khedive, acting on what was officially described as the advice of the British Government, concluded that it could not hold the Sudan against the Mahdists and therefore decided to evacuate the country and concentrate, instead, on the development of Egypt's own resources. It was in order to execute this policy that Gordon was sent to Khartoum where he was killed when the town fell to the Mahdi. The Egyptian nationalists greatly resented this policy of evacuation which they felt was dictated by British, not Egyptian, interests.

THE CONDOMINIUM

The scramble for Africa which dominated the closing decades of the nineteenth century convinced the British Government that, in order to safeguard Britain's interests in Egypt and to ward off the Italians, the Belgians and, above all, the French from the upper reaches of the Nile, it was necessary that the Sudan be brought under British control. Since this would have brought Britain in direct conflict with the French and other European powers in central Africa, however, the British Government decided that the conquest should be done in the name of the Khedive and Egypt who, it was contended, were now in a position to reaffirm their control over what was described as Egyptian territory which had been temporarily disrupted by the Mahdist rebellion. The reconquest, as it was called, was as unpopular with the Egyptian nationalists as the policy of evacuation which had been imposed on Egypt after the fall of Khartoum to the Mahdi in 1885. In spite of opposition, the reconquest was executed by combined Egyptian and British forces under the general command of Gen. Herbert Kitchener. It took three years: from 1896 to 1898 when, on September 2nd, the last of the Mahdist forces were destroyed in the battle of Omdurman.

The Anglo-Egyptian Agreement of 1899 laid the foundations of the new regime in the Sudan. The important, but thorny question of sovereignty over the country was, however, deliberately left out of the Agreement. For, from Britain's point of view, the acceptance, as binding law, of the theory that the new regime was a restoration of the Ottoman-Egyptian regime overthrown by the Mahdi was undesirable because it would have left Britain without legal basis for its presence in the Sudan, while the alternative—

the theory that Britain was sovereign or had a share in sovereignty over the Sudan—would have aroused the hostility, not only of the Egyptians and the Sultan, but also of the French and the other European powers, and was therefore similarly undesirable. While emphasizing the claims which accrued to Britain by virtue of her participation in the reconquest, therefore, the Agreement was silent as to the juridical positions of the two conquering powers in the Sudan. This allowed Britain considerable scope for political and diplomatic manoeuvre. Thus, when the French questioned Britain's presence in the Sudan the British Government insisted that it was acting on behalf of the Khedive; when the Egyptian nationalists raised the same question they were reminded of Britain's role in the reconquest; and when they protested their inferior position in the administration of the country, though they had contributed the larger share of men and money during the reconquest and almost all the expenses of the administration, Britain maintained that this was only fair as the country was reconquered in the name of Egypt which, however, was unable to govern itself let alone the Sudan. This was perhaps illogical but from a practical point of view, it made little difference so long as Britain was in effective control of Egypt as well as the Sudan. After Egypt's independence in 1922 however, and especially after the abolition of the Caliphate, in whom sovereignty over the Sudan had theoretically resided during the Ottoman-Egyptian regime, the silence of the Agreement as to the subject of sovereignty became a source of increasing embarrassment to Britain.

The juridical dispute aside, the Agreement established in the Sudan an administration which was nominally Anglo-Egyptian but was actually a British colonial administration. Like the Ottoman-Egyptian administration it was headed by a Governor-General in whom all civil and military authority was vested. He was appointed by Khedivial decree but on the recommendation of the British Government, without whose consent he could not be dismissed. Nothing was mentioned in the Agreement about his nationality but it is not surprising that all the Governors-General of the Sudan—like the Provincial Governors and District Commissioners who assisted them—were British. The British character of the regime became more obvious after 1924, when the Egyptian troops, officers and civilians who had hitherto acted as intermediaries between the British and the Sudanese were evacuated from the Sudan following the murder in Cairo of Sir Lee Stack, the then Governor-General of the Sudan and Sirdar (i.e. C.-in-C.) of the Egyptian Army. The administration of the country was until then based on the principle of Direct Rule and was, especially before the First World War, carried out along military lines. This was necessitated by the fact that resistance to the new regime did not cease after the battle of Omdurman and risings against it occurred annually. By the end of the war, however, the process of pacification, except in the south, was completed, and the last stronghold of Mahdism was taken when, in 1916, Sultan Ali Dinar of Darfur was killed and his Sultanate made a province of the Sudan.

INDIRECT RULE

The evacuation of the Egyptians from the Sudan in 1924 was generally unpopular with the Sudanese, especially the non-Mahdists and the small but influential educated class, who sympathized with the Egyptians on grounds of common language and religion, and saw in Egypt a natural ally against the British. Demonstrations were therefore organized in order to show solidarity with the Egyptians, and a Sudanese battalion mutinied and clashed with British troops. The rising was, however, ruthlessly crushed. Relations between the Sudan Government and educated Sudanese deteriorated rapidly and a period of intense bitterness began which lasted well into the 1930s and was much aggravated by the depression and the subsequent retrenchment of salaries.

It was against this background that Indirect Rule, through the agency of tribal sheikhs and chiefs, was introduced, which soon replaced Direct Rule as the guiding principle in administration. Tribalism, which had been greatly weakened during the Mahdiyya, was revived and encouraged not only for purposes of administrative decentralization but also, and more importantly, as an alternative to bureaucratic government which necessitated the creation and employment of more and more educated Sudanese. These, because of their education, however limited, were politically more conscious than tribal leaders and therefore more difficult to control. Simultaneously with the stimulation of tribalism and tribal institutions therefore, training centres such as the military college were closed down; courses for training Sudanese administrators were discontinued; and harsh discipline which "savoured strongly of the barracks" was introduced in the Gordon College—an elementary institution which had been opened in 1902 for the training of artisans and junior officials. In general, the period from 1924 to the mid-1930s may be described as the golden age of Indirect Rule, or Native Administration; but from the point of view of education—always, under the British, closely connected with policy and administration—it was, in the words of a distinguished British scholar, "a period of utter stagnation". Economically, however, it was notable for the development of the Gezira scheme, whose cotton crops were largely responsible for the growth of the government's revenue from £S1,654,149 in 1913, when the budget was balanced for the first time since the reconquest, to over £S4 million in 1936 and nearly £S46 million in 1956. By 1982 the scheme had 2.3 million acres under irrigation and formed the basis of the country's prosperity.

The introduction of Native Administration in the Northern Sudan after 1924 was paralleled in the south, by the launching of the Government's new "Southern Policy". Until then official policy in the South was, apart from the maintenance of law and order, largely limited to the provision of various forms of assistance to Christian missionary societies which, in the words of an official annual report, worked for the proselytization of the population and "teaching these savages the elements of common sense, good behaviour, and obedience to government authority".

After the rising of 1924 which, incidentally, was led by an officer of southern (Dinka) origin, the "Southern Policy" was introduced. It had two main objectives: the prevention of the spirit of nationalism, which had already taken root in Egypt, from spreading across the Northern Sudan to the South and to other east African "possessions"; and the separation of the three southern provinces from the rest of the country with a view to their eventual assimilation by the governments of neighbouring British territories which, it was hoped, would then emerge as a great East African Federation under British control. Accordingly, Muslim and Arabic speaking people in the South, whether they were of Egyptian, northern Sudanese or west African origins, were evicted from the region while stringent systems of permits and "Closed Districts" were introduced to prevent others from entering. Southerners, on the other hand, were discouraged from visiting or seeking employment in the North, and those among them who had adopted the Muslim religion or used Arabic names, clothes or language were strongly encouraged to drop them and use, instead, Christian, English or native equivalents. Whereas education was then stagnating in the North and had so far been neglected in the South it was now enthusiastically supported by the Government—but along lines calculated to eradicate all traces of Islamic and Arabic culture, and thus gradually sever relations between the Northern and Southern provinces.

TOWARDS SELF-GOVERNMENT

As may be expected the Southern Policy, like Native Administration, was most unpopular with the nationalists who, by the mid-1930s, had recovered from the shocks they had suffered after the failure of 1924. Encouraged by the challenge which the Axis powers were then presenting to Britain and by the restoration of Egypt's position in the Sudan in 1936, itself largely the result of the changing international scene, they began to mobilize themselves and prepared to resume their offensive. The Graduates' Congress, representing the *literati* of the country, was established early in 1938. Stimulated by the war, the Atlantic Charter and the open competition of the Egyptian and Sudan Governments for their sympathy and support, the graduates, in 1942, submitted to the Government a famous Memorandum in which they demanded, *inter alia*, the abolition of the Closed Districts Ordinance; the cancellation of subventions to missionary schools and the unification of syllabuses in the North and the South; an increase in the share of the Sudanese in the administration of their country and the issue of a declaration granting the Sudan the right of self-government directly after the war. The Government refused to receive the Memorandum but nevertheless reacted by gradually transforming Native Administration into a modern system of local government and, in central government administration, by launching, in 1943, an Advisory Council for the Northern Sudan which was replaced, in 1948, by a Legislative Assembly for the Sudan as a whole. The development of local government, however, was a very slow process (the first comprehensive local government ordinance being promulgated as late as 1951); and it was in any case peripheral to the main wishes of the nationalists. The Advisory Council and the Legislative Assembly on the other hand failed to satisfy them because, among other things, they had very little power to exercise (in the case of the Council no power at all), while their composition, largely based on the principle of appointment rather than free elections, only partially reflected political opinion in the country.

Their limitations notwithstanding, the promulgation of these institutions accentuated differences within Congress and eventually split it into two rival groups. Some worried about Egypt's continued claims over the Sudan and, feeling that independence could best be achieved by co-operating with the Government, thought that Congress should participate in the Council and the Assembly however defective they were. This group, led by the Umma Party, was supported by the Mahdists, and their motto was "The Sudan for the Sudanese". Others being more distrustful of the British, felt that independence could best be achieved through co-operation with Egypt which was an Arabic-speaking and Muslim neighbouring country and, like the Sudan, despite its formal independence, a victim of British imperialism. They therefore stood for "The Unity of the Nile Valley" and, supported by the Khatmiyya, the chief rival of the Mahdists among the religious fraternities, boycotted both the Council and the Assembly.

In the meantime successive negotiations between the British and Egyptian Governments led from one deadlock to another and the unhappy schism between "the Unionists" and "the Independence Front" continued until the outbreak of the Egyptian Revolution in July 1952, The new regime promptly disowned the King and the Pasha class with whom "The Unity of the Nile Valley under the Egyptian Crown" was a basic article of political faith, and thus cleared the way for a separate settlement of the Sudan question. Neguib, Nasser and Salah Salem, all of whom had served in the Sudan and knew the Sudanese well, then staged a diplomatic coup which put the initiative in their hands.

The British had consistently justified their continued presence in the Sudan in terms of their desire to secure self-determination for the Sudanese as opposed to imposing on them a unity with Egypt which many Sudanese were prepared to resist by force of arms if necessary. Having got rid of the King the new Egyptian regime now declared that it was equally willing to grant the Sudanese the right of self-determination. On the basis of this declaration an Anglo-Egyptian Agreement was signed in 1953. This Agreement provided, among other things, for the Sudanization of the police and the civil service and the evacuation of all British and Egyptian troops in preparation for self-determination within a period of three years. Elections, held under the supervision of an international commission, resulted in the victory of the National Unionist Party (NUP). Its leader, Ismail el-Azhari, became the first Sudanese Prime Minister in January 1954 and proceeded to put the terms of the Agreement into effect. The Egyptians had

supported the NUP during the elections and it was naturally expected that Azhari would try to lead the country in the direction of union with Egypt. However, by the time the Sudanization programme was completed and the Egyptian and British troops had left the country, it was clear that he stood for independence. Several reasons led to this apparent reversal of attitude. Among these was the fact that the overwhelming majority of the NUP had looked upon solidarity with the Egyptians as a means for achieving the independence of the Sudan. Besides, the official opening of Parliament on March 1st, 1954, witnessed a violent demonstration by the Mahdists of their determination to split the country if the Government wanted to lead the Sudan along the path of unity with Egypt rather than independence. Several people were killed and the ceremony to which guests from many countries including Gen. Neguib, had been invited, was postponed. It then became obvious that independence would not only satisfy the aspirations of the Sudanese but would also save the country from civil war. One thing, however, could still frustrate the country's progress to independence: namely the mutiny of southern troops at Juba in August 1955. This was the prelude to an attempted revolt in the South in which nearly 300 northern Sudanese officials, merchants and their families were massacred. The disorders, except for some sporadic outbursts, did not spread to the other two southern provinces of Upper Nile and Bahr El Ghazal but were centred in Equatoria. Order was restored in due course but the political problem of the South which, springing from the geographic and social differences between the northern and southern provinces, had been greatly accentuated by the "Southern Policy" of the British administration, continued to present a serious challenge to the Sudanese and the unity of the Sudan. Before they could vote for independence southern members of Parliament insisted that their request for a federal form of government be given full consideration. This they were duly promised.

The Agreement had prescribed a plebiscite and other protracted procedures for self-determination. Azhari, supported by all Sudanese parties, decided to side-step these arrangements, and on December 19th, 1955, Parliament unanimously declared the Sudan an independent republic and, at the same time, resolved that a committee of five elected by Parliament exercise the powers of the Head of State in place of the Governor-General. Faced with this *fait accompli* Britain and Egypt had no choice but to recognize the Sudan's independence, which was formally celebrated on January 1st, 1956.

THE INDEPENDENT SUDAN

Since achieving independence the Sudan (renamed Sudan in 1975) has had four regimes: a civilian parliamentary regime, which lasted until November 1958; a military regime, which, under Gen. Ibrahim Abboud, continued in office until it was overthrown by a civilian coup in October 1964; a second civilian regime, which was then ushered in and lasted until May 1969 when the existing regime of Gen. Gaafar

Nimeri came to office. Successive governments under all four regimes have been faced, above all, by three major problems: that arising from the country's dependence on one cash crop, i.e. cotton; the problem of the Southern Sudan which was inherited from the British colonial regime; and the search for a permanent constitution for the country.

Throughout the greater part of the first regime the Sudan was governed by an improbable Mahdist-Khatmiyya coalition which, led by Abdalla Khalil, replaced Azhari and the non-sectarian rump of his NUP shortly after independence. During this period the Sudan established itself in the international field, joining the UN, the Arab League and, later on, the OAU. Internally, social services were expanded; the University College of Khartoum was raised to full university status; railway extensions in the Blue Nile south of Sinnar and in Darfur were completed; and the first stages of the Managil extension began operating, in July 1958, with a gross irrigable area of 80,000 hectares. But serious economic and financial problems arising from rapid expansion on the one hand and difficulty in selling cotton crops on the other began to face the country. Politically the un-natural coalition was strained by serious differences between the Mahdist Umma Party and the People's Democratic Party (PDP), the political organ of the Khatmiyya. Thus, during the Suez crisis, the PDP felt that Egypt should have been given greater support than the Prime Minister was prepared to give, while some Umma spokesmen accused the PDP of soft-ness towards, if not actual complicity with, Egypt when a minor border dispute arose between the two countries in February 1958. And whereas the Umma Party favoured a presidential form of government, with Sayyid Abdel Rahman al-Mahdi as first Presi-dent, the PDP and the Khatmiyya could not agree. A third difficulty arose from the deteriorating financial and economic situation which, having initially resulted from failure to dispose of the cotton crop of 1957, was compounded by exceptionally poor crops in 1958. With the country's reserves falling rapidly, severe and unpopular restrictions had to be imposed and, the Prime Minister felt, foreign aid had to be sought. But the PDP, already worried by what it considered was the unduly pro-western policy of Abdalla Khalil, opposed acceptance of American aid. Elections, held in February 1958, resulted in no change and the already strained coalition was returned to power. The President of the Umma Party, Sayyid Siddiq al-Mahdi, then sought an alliance with Azhari's NUP. But this was unacceptable to the Prime Minister who was the secretary of the Umma Party. Khalil—who was the Minister of Defence as well as Prime Minister and who had been an army officer—then started con-sultations with senior army officers about the possi-bility of a military coup.

ABBOUD'S MILITARY GOVERNMENT

The coup was launched on November 17th, 1958. To the people in general it came as a relief after the wrangling and differences of the parties. The two Sayyids, al-Mahdi and al-Mirghani, gave their blessing

to the regime on the understanding that the army would not stay in power longer than was necessary. Gen. Abboud assured the country that his aim was the restoration of stability and sound administration at home and the fostering of cordial relations with the outside world, particularly Egypt.

In the economic field a good start was made by following a realistic cotton sales policy which ensured the sale of both the carry-over from past seasons and the new crop. Loans from various international institutions and aid from the U.S.A., the U.S.S.R. and elsewhere were successfully negotiated. The money was used to finance such projects as the completion of the Managil extension and the construction of the Roseires Dam on the Blue Nile, and the Khashm al-Girba Dam on the Atbara. The latter was used for the purpose of irrigating an area for the resettlement of the people of Halfa whose ancient town had been submerged by waters of the High Dam at Aswan.

But discontent soon began to grow. Prompting this was the feeling that too many officers—encouraged by the absence of democratic procedures of control and accountability—had become corrupt and used public funds for private gain. The result was that when the country was again gripped by financial and economic difficulties in 1964 the public was convinced that this could not be accounted for in terms of the poor cotton crop of that year, nor in terms of over-ambitious economic development schemes; they no longer trusted the Government. A system of provincial administrations not unlike Pakistan's "Basic Democ-racies" was introduced in 1961 and this was crowned in 1962 by the creation of a central council which met for the first time in November 1963. While these arrange-ments, aimed at the training of the people in self-government, were in principle acceptable to most Sudanese, the actual working of the system—very much under the control of military personnel—not only failed to win the politically sophisticated but also alienated the civil service and professional administrators. Thus when the civil service was called to join the judiciary, university staff, workers and others in the general strike which followed the outbreak of the revolution in October 1964, the response was both complete and enthusiastic.

THE CIVILIAN COUP

The immediate cause of the revolution was the Government's heavy-handed administration in the South. This was based on the mistaken idea that the problem of the Southern Sudan was a military, not a political, problem and that it was mainly the result of the activities of the missionaries who had partici-pated in the implementation of the "Southern Policy" of the British administration. But the expulsion of missionaries in February 1964 dramatized the problem for the outside world rather than helped to solve it, while military action against both the *Anya Nya* rebels and the civilian villagers who were sometimes obliged to give them food and shelter had the effect of forcing thousands of southerners to live as refugees in neighbouring countries and convinced many that the only solution of the problem was for them to have a separate and independent state in the South. Concerned for the unity of the country, politicians, university students and others started campaigning for the view that the country could not be saved except by the removal of the military from authority and the restoration of democratic government. Orders forbidding public discussion of the southern problem and other political matters were issued but were defiantly disregarded by students. On October 21st the police, determined to break up such a discussion, opened fire on the students within the precincts of the University. One student died and the revolution was thereby set in motion. A general strike brought the country to a standstill and Gen. Abboud was forced to start negotiations with a Committee of Public Safety, to which he subsequently agreed to surrender political power. His decision was partly dictated by the fact that the army was known to be divided and that the younger officers especially were reluctant to open fire on unarmed civilian demonstrators with whom they generally sympathized.

A transitional government in which all parties including, for the first time, the Communist Party and the Muslim Brotherhood, were represented, was sworn in under Sirr al-Khatim al-Khalifa, an educationalist with a good record of service in the South, as Prime Minister. As a result of the inclusion as ministers of representatives of the communist-dominated Workers' and Tenants' Trades Unions and certain front organizations, the cabinet as a whole was dominated by the Communist Party.

After restoring the freedom of the press, raising the ban on political parties and starting a purge of the administration (which was subsequently abandoned on account of its being carried along personal and partisan lines) the new Government turned to the most important problem facing it: the problem of the Southern Sudan.

One of the first acts of the Government had been a declaration of a general amnesty in the South. On March 16th, 1965, a round table conference in which northern and southern parties participated was opened in Khartoum. It was also attended by observers from seven African countries. The northern parties proposed to set up a regional government in the South which would, among other things, have its own parliament, executive and public service commission. The southern parties which attended the conference were divided. Some wanted federation; others a separate state; while the unionists (who were not represented in the conference because the two other groups would boycott the conference if they were allowed to participate) favoured the *status quo*. The conference failed to reach a general agreement on the constitutional future of the country and the subject was then referred to a Twelve Man Committee on which all parties—except the unionists—were represented. But agreement was reached on a constructive programme of immediate action which included the repatriation of refugees and the restoration of order, freedom of religion and unrestricted missionary

activity by Sudanese nationals and the training of southerners for army, police and civil service.

Externally, the transitional Government supported national liberation movements in Southern Arabia, Congo (Kinshasa), now Zaire, and among the Eritreans in Ethiopia. But this, like the purging of the administration, was controversial and was especially disliked by the Umma Party and the NUP who, together with the Islamic Charter Front (ICF) (at the core of which was the Muslim Brotherhood), formed a front against the more left-wing PDP and the Communist Party. As a result of mounting pressure on the part of the former, elections were held in June 1965. They were boycotted by the PDP but were heavily contested by all other parties. The Umma Party won 76 seats, the NUP 53, the Communists 11 (out of the 15 seats in the graduates' constituency) and the ICF 7. For the first time tribal groups fought elections, winning 21 seats: 10 for the Beja and 11 for the Nuba of Kordofan.

COALITION GOVERNMENT AGAIN

The new Government had to be a coalition. This was formed by the Umma and the NUP with Muhammad Ahmad Mahgoub (Umma) as Prime Minister and Azhari the permanent President of the Committee of Five which collectively acted as Head of State.

To pacify the Ethiopian and Chad Governments, both of which had been provoked by the policy of the transitional Government on liberation movements in their territories, Mahgoub hastened to affirm his Government's adherence to the Accra pledges of non-interference and signed a border pact with Ethiopia in June 1966. This was followed by a number of visits to neighbouring countries to confirm the new Government's position and, at the same time, making arrangements whereby the return of Sudanese refugees from these countries would be facilitated.

Internally, the Government ran into a number of difficulties. In July 1965 there was serious rebel activity at Juba and Wau, and large numbers of southerners were killed in the course of reprisals by government troops. Subsequently there were severe difficulties in retaining southern representatives in the Government. Personal animosity between Azhari and Mahgoub led to a crisis within the coalition in October which was only solved by the mediation of the young Umma Party President, Sadiq al-Mahdi. Government policies meanwhile became increasingly right-wing, and in November 1965 the Communist Party was banned and its members unseated from the Assembly. This was contested in the courts which, in December 1966, ruled that it was illegal. But the Constituent Assembly, acting in its capacity as constitution-maker, overruled the courts' judgment. A crisis in which the judiciary and the Assembly confronted one another was thereby precipitated, but this was finally resolved in favour of the Assembly.

In the meantime a serious split was developing between the right wing of the Umma Party, led by Imam al-Hadi (Sadiq's uncle) which supported Premier Mahgoub, and the younger and more moderate elements who looked to Sadiq for more effective leadership. Sadiq, however, was reluctant to accept the Premiership not only on account of his youth (30), but also because failure (which, with the mounting financial and security problems of the country, was likely) would prejudice his political future. But events and the pressure of his supporters finally obliged him to change his mind. After a heavy defeat in a vote of censure, on July 25th, 1966, Mahgoub resigned and Sadiq was then elected Prime Minister.

Sadiq's Government was also a coalition of Umma and NUP but included, as Minister of Finance, an able expert of Khatmiyya background, Hamza Mirghani, who had been Principal Under-Secretary of the Ministry of Finance and a senior official at the World Bank. There were also two southern Ministers.

With the help of stringent controls and loans from the World Bank and IMF the economy gradually began to recover and the country's reserves of foreign currency, which had dropped to £S13 million, began to improve. Meantime the Twelve Man Committee had made considerable progress towards the settlement of the southern problem on the basis of regional government. A "Parties Conference" continued the Committee's work and, in April 1967, submitted a report in which it also recommended a regional solution. By this time the long-awaited supplementary elections in the South had been held, bringing 36 members to the Constituent Assembly of whom 10, led by William Deng, represented the Sudan African National Union (SANU), the leading Southern party. It was now possible to speed up the process of drafting the permanent constitution and the settlement of the Southern problem.

The relative success of Sadiq's Government, however, coupled with the announcement that he would stand for the Presidency under the proposed constitution, resulted in the break-up of the coalition between his wing of the Umma Party and the NUP whose leader, Azhari, like the leader of the Ansar, Imam al-Hadi, also aspired to the Presidency. Thus in May 1967, Sadiq was defeated in the Assembly and Mahgoub was once again elected Premier.

Under his leadership the new coalition of NUP and al-Hadi's branch of the Umma Party pursued a vigorous foreign policy, particularly in the Middle East after the Six Days' War. As a result the first Arab Summit Conference after the war was convened in Khartoum (August 1967) and Mahgoub, together with Iraqi and Moroccan colleagues, was subsequently entrusted with the task of finding a formula for the settlement of the Yemeni dispute. Deterioration of relations with Western powers, culminating in severance of diplomatic relations with the U.K. and the U.S.A. after the June War, was accompanied by the development of closer relations with the Eastern bloc, and the conclusion of an arms deal with the U.S.S.R. resulted in the lifting of the ban on the Sudanese Communist Party. The internal affairs of the country, particularly the already precarious financial situation, had in the meantime been somewhat neglected. The result was that when the Constituent Assembly was reconvened after the prolonged recess which followed the outbreak of hostilities in the Middle East, the opposition, under the vigorous leadership of Sadiq al-Mahdi and William Deng (who, together with the ICF, now formed the New Forces Congress), was able to defeat the Government on several occasions. This, together with the growing PDP and Communist opposition to the Draft Permanent Constitution based on Islam, regionalism and a strong executive on the presidential model, induced the Government to dissolve the Constituent Assembly on January 7th, 1968, following a mass resignation of the government members in the Assembly. Sadiq and his allies contested the constitutionality of this act in the courts. Before any judgment was pronounced, however, new elections were held in April, which were contested for the first time since 1958 by the PDP, now merged with the NUP in the new Democratic Unionist Party (DUP). This won the largest number of seats, 101, followed by Sadiq's Umma, which won 38, and al-Hadi's Umma, with 30 seats. As the DUP did not command a majority on its own, a new coalition, also with Imam al-Hadi's faction of the Umma Party, and under the leadership of Mahgoub, was formed when the Assembly was convened on May 27th.

Mahgoub's third Government, however, was unable to improve the economic and financial situation while the situation in the southern provinces continued to deteriorate. Mahgoub, moreover, fell ill and the situation was aggravated by the cabinet crisis of April-May over the reallocation of ministerial responsibilities between the Umma and DUP. The result was the bloodless coup of May 25th, 1969, when the Government was overthrown by a group of officers and civilians led by Col. (later Gen. and Field Marshal) Gaafar Mohammed Nimeri.

SUDAN UNDER NIMERI

Already the longest surviving in Sudanese history since the achievement of independence, Nimeri's regime can be said to have passed through two principal phases. During the first phase, from May 1969 until July 1971, the regime followed distinctly radical policies. This tendency—inherent in Nimeri's declared commitment to a programme of "Sudanese Socialism", which was regarded as an expression of the essential spirit of the October Revolution of 1964—was accentuated by the fact that the Communist Party and its supporters then enjoyed a uniquely dominant position in governmental and policy-making processes. A close alliance was then forged between the officially dissolved Communist Party and the new military rulers of the country, as the leaders of the more effectively banned traditional political parties and of the Tariqas (i.e. the Ansar and the Khatmiyya) were regarded as having betrayed the October Revolution of which Nimeri and his friends saw themselves as the true heirs and perpetrators. Accordingly, and in order to effectively exclude the traditional parties from the political arena, Nimeri decided to work in close co-operation with like-minded civilians—not on a personal and purely administrative basis as had been the case with Abboud—but with a view to building a permanent base of popular support on the model of the Arab Socialist Union, Egypt's one-party organization. Thus were laid the foundations of the Sudanese Socialist Union (SSU).

In the meantime Nimeri announced the formation of a predominantly civilian cabinet, some of whose members—including a number of communists who had chosen to follow his lead rather than that of their officially dissolved party—had played prominent parts in the October Revolution. At first Sayyid Babiker Awadalla, a former Chief Justice, was appointed Prime Minister and thus became the only civilian member of the Revolutionary Council. But he was subsequently replaced as Prime Minister by Gen. Nimeri who had been President of the Revolutionary Council and was subsequently elected first President of the Sudan.

Under this leadership the country was given the new name of "The Democratic Republic of the Sudan". Banks, together with a wide variety of firms and companies, were nationalized. The property of certain persons, including members of the Mahdi family, was confiscated. Several former ministers and members of traditional parties were put on trial on charges of bribery and corruption. Following an attempt on the life of Gen. Nimeri, the chief source of opposition to the regime—namely Imam al-Hadi al-Mahdi, who had for some time been gathering weapons and supporters at Aba Island on the White Nile—was crushed in March 1970.

With regard to the southern provinces in particular, the regime declared its commitment to a policy of regional administrative autonomy supported by a programme of economic development and reconstruction on socialist lines. A special Ministry for Southern Affairs was created which, under the guidance as Minister of Joseph Garang (a southern Sudanese lawyer who was a member of the Communist Party), was responsible for spelling out the details of that policy and the supervision of their implementation.

In the field of foreign affairs, one of the first decisions taken by the regime was to recognize the German Democratic Republic. This was followed by the forging of closer diplomatic and trade relations with the People's Republic of China, the U.S.S.R. and Eastern Europe. In the Middle East the regime's policy was, above all, characterized by its militant support for the Arab cause over the Palestine question and, for some time after the Libyan coup of September 1969, its association with Col. Gaddafi of Libya as well as with Nasser and the United Arab Republic (U.A.R.), now Egypt. Subsequently, Gen. Nimeri personally participated in the resolution of the Jordanian crisis and, in November 1970, it was declared that Presidents Nimeri, Sadat and Gaddafi had decided to unite the Sudan, Libya and the U.A.R. into one federal state.

This was unacceptable to the communists who, having already suffered serious internal strains resulting from differences over the question of how best to handle the new regime, now feared that they would be subjected to the same fate as their Egyptian counterparts. The growing mistrust and hostility culminated in an open bid for power by the com-

munists. This took the form of a coup which, led by Maj. Hashim al-Ata, resulted in the overthrow of Gen. Nimeri on July 19th, 1971, and the subsequent liquidation of some thirty officers who were known to favour him and his policies.

The communist coup, however, proved abortive. Its proclaimed head of state, Col. Babiker al-Nur, and his aide, Maj. Faruq Hamadalla, had been in London and while on their way back home the BOAC plane carrying them was forced down in Libya. The Libyan authorities then handed them over to Nimeri who had in the meantime regained power as a result of a popular rising which brought the newly-born communist regime to an end after only three days. A massive purge of communists followed and fourteen people were executed, including Maj. Hashim al-Ata, the two leaders back from London and Joseph Garang, who had been Minister for Southern Affairs.

The events of July 1971 ushered in the second phase of Nimeri's regime.

In so far as foreign relations are concerned, this phase has been characterized by cooler relations with the U.S.S.R. and its East European allies, matched by a gradual improvement of relations with the U.S.A. and Western European countries. This reversal of attitudes was prompted by the open encouragement which had been given by Bulgaria and the German Democratic Republic to the abortive coup of July 1971 and also by the unusually strong condemnation, by Soviet and East European governments, of the executions which followed Nimeri's return to power. Diplomatic relations, however, remained intact. In the meantime Nimeri received strong support from President Sadat of Egypt.

Commonly regarded as the nation's saviour from militant atheism, Nimeri's personal popularity rapidly soared in the wake of the abortive coup. When the first Presidential elections in Sudanese history were held in October 1971 he received almost four million votes with only 56,000 opposed. A new government was formed, the Revolutionary Command Council was dissolved and the SSU was recognized as the only legal political party in the Sudan.

The vitally important Addis Ababa Agreement between the Sudanese Government and the *Anya Nya* Southern Sudanese rebels was signed in March 1972. As a result the long standing dispute was settled on the basis of regional autonomy for the three Southern provinces. A Regional People's Assembly for the South was established at Juba with representatives in the National People's Assembly and a High Executive Council of its own. The first Head of the Executive Council was Abel Alier, a former judge, who also became a Vice-President of the Republic. The Agreement also provided for the return and rehabilitation of Southern Sudanese refugees abroad and for the integration of the former *Anya Nya* rebels into the Sudan armed forces. The ceasefire took effect on March 12th, 1972, and the process of rehabilitation and reconstruction of the region has since been gathering momentum with continued support from Khartoum and President Nimeri personally.

At the national level these developments have been matched by a gradual disengagement from the ideologically inspired postures of earlier days and the adoption, instead, of measures for the economic and social development of the country on the basis of a more pragmatic approach. Thus in January 1973, a presidential decree repealed the previous orders of expropriation and a policy of "denationalization" affecting some of the firms and companies which had previously been taken over by the state has been inaugurated. Laws intended to encourage foreign investments have also been promulgated and a strategy aimed at the marriage of Western technology and Arabian petrodollars to the vast agricultural potential of the Sudan at a time of pressing shortage of international and regional food supplies has been launched. Thus the political and economic strategies of the country—whether internally or in regard to its relations with the outside world—have been greatly transformed since 1971.

Throughout its two phases prior to 1977, however, the regime showed a consistent determination to exclude the leaders of the traditional parties and their generally right-wing supporters from the political arena. For their part these groups organized themselves into a "National Front" which operated as a largely external opposition to the regime. Supported, at different times, by such states as Libya, Iraq, Saudi Arabia and Ethiopia, the National Front made several bids to topple Nimeri by force. One of these—a standard coup attempt which was led by an army officer named Hassan Husain—took place in September 1975 but was rapidly put down and its leaders executed. In July 1976 a more sophisticated attempt—officially described as an invasion based in and financed from Libya—was made, but also came to grief and over 100 of its leaders and others accused of complicity in it were executed.

Since the prolonged stalemate—though it seriously strained the resources of both the National Front and the Government—did not bring about the results desired by either side, alternative courses of action began to be considered: not only on account of what has just been said, but also because the ideological cleavage which separated the Government and the National Front between 1969 and 1971 had been rapidly shrinking. In addition, such powers as Saudi Arabia and the U.S.A., with which the two parties to the conflict had close relations, also favoured a peaceful resolution of the dispute, for both strategic and economic reasons. As a result, protracted and partly secret negotiations were initiated, an important stage being reached in July 1977 when Sayid Sadiq al-Mahdi, who had been under sentence of death, met President Nimeri in Port Sudan. "National Reconciliation", as it was designated, gathered momentum in the course of the following months and, in consequence, the State Security Act of 1974 was abolished, large numbers of political detainees were released and many members of the National Front who had been in exile, including Sayid Sadiq al-Mahdi himself, now

returned home, some being appointed to high office, either as Ministers or in the SSU, the country's only permitted political organization. However, certain supporters both of the Government and of the National Front have shown a considerable degree of ambivalence towards reconciliation.

In an effort to meet some of the objections and reservations made by Sharif Husain al-Hindi and his Democratic Unionist faction of the National Front (which then included, for the first time, the Communist Party but neither the Ansar of Sadiq al-Mahdi nor the ICF of Dr. Hasan Turabi), a supplementary agreement, which more explicitly stressed the need for the restoration of the rule of law and respect for the independence of the judiciary, was reached and formally announced in London in April 1978. However, al-Hindi, reportedly supported by Libya and Iraq, continued to oppose the regime until his death in exile in January 1982, his argument in rejecting the reconciliation proposal being that agreements already concluded with him (and with Sadiq) had not been honoured.

In the meantime, Sadiq al-Mahdi, who had returned to Sudan and some of whose supporters still hold senior posts in the administration, showed his own dissatisfaction—especially over President Nimeri's initial support for the Camp David accord between Egypt and Israel—by resigning from the SSU and the Political Bureau in October 1978. By April 1982 disagreement between the two sides had reached such an extent that Sadiq, who had again left the country, was openly criticizing the regime in the international Arabic press, and was in turn attacked in the government-controlled media at home.

Another reason why Sadiq—as well as other sections of Sudanese, especially southern Sudanese, opinion—has been dissatisfied was Nimeri's drive, until late in 1979, for political and economic integration with Sadat's Egypt. Towards the end of 1979 and in the course of 1980, however, a number of developments induced Nimeri to change course and to move, instead, towards closer co-ordination with Saudi Arabia, the Gulf States of Qatar and the United Arab Emirates and even Iraq. One of these was the growing impression in Sudan that the Egyptian Government tended to take Sudan's support too much for granted, while the powerful Egyptian mass media sometimes distorted official Sudanese statements, which had been carefully worded to reflect Sudan's balancing act between Egypt (which had become increasingly isolated in the Arab world) and other Arab states, in order to give the impression that Sudan's position over controversial issues was much closer to Egypt's than was actually the case. Another factor making for relative estrangement between the two regimes during that period was Egypt's reported offer of Nile waters to Israel so that it may irrigate the Negev desert: a point of which President Nimeri expressed strong disapproval during his tour of the Gulf States in March 1980. A third reason for this shift has been the deteriorating economic situation (recent discoveries of petroleum in south-western Sudan notwithstanding) and, consequently, the country's need for even greater loans and grants than had already been made.

In the circumstances it is not surprising that the Sudanese ambassador to Cairo was withdrawn in December 1979 (i.e. before the Israeli ambassador's arrival there), although the embassy itself continued to function. Similar arrangements were then made with regard to the Egyptian embassy and ambassador in Khartoum. As relations with Egypt became more and more strained, relations with Libya predictably improved.

As a result of Libya's growing involvement in the Chad civil war, especially from about mid-1980 onwards, this pattern was again reversed. By March 1981 relations between Libya and Sudan had deteriorated to the extent that each was publicly calling for the other to be excluded from the Arab League, while forces and military equipment were being moved from Khartoum to the western regions of Sudan in order to ward off any possible Soviet-backed Libyan thrust from Chad. In the meantime Sudanese-Egyptian relations were rapidly improved and ambassadors restored in Cairo and Khartoum. In March 1981, moreover, the Egyptian Minister of Defence declared that any attack on Sudan would be regarded by Egypt as an attack upon itself, and President Nimeri was reportedly prepared to go as far as welcoming the establishment of U.S. military bases in Sudan. At the time of Sadat's assassination in October, there was much talk in Khartoum of an imminent Libyan attack on the country's western territories. Apart from a few ineffectual bombings, however, this proved unfounded. The assassination, although variously regarded in Sudan, as in Egypt itself, seems to have reinforced the feeling of need in the two regimes for closer mutual co-operation, as well as for more co-ordination with the U.S.A., particularly in its regional strategies for North Africa, the Gulf and the Horn of Africa. Meanwhile, relations with Ethiopia and Kenya have been greatly improved and President Nimeri was given an unusually warm reception when he visited Addis Ababa in November 1980.

Internally, the country continues to suffer the rigours of a deteriorating economy compounded by runaway inflation and, to some extent, also by the influx of refugees (numbering about half a million in 1980), mainly from Ethiopia, Uganda and Chad. Apart from the unprecedented exodus of expertise and skilled workers of all kinds, this situation has precipitated a number of strikes and demonstrations—including serious student riots which broke out in several towns in August 1979 while, in March 1981, another abortive coup took place. The appearance, also unprecedented, of a prosperous class of bureaucrats and businessmen, many of whom have accumulated wealth by doubtful means and, moreover, engaged themselves in crude forms of conspicuous consumption, has undoubtedly accentuated an already dangerous situation. In order to defuse the situation, President Nimeri has often blamed the SSU, charging its cadres with incompetence and failure to identify and protect the needs of the people whom it is supposed to lead and represent. In consequence, the First Vice-President and Secretary of the SSU, Abdul Qasim Mohammed Ibrahim, was dismissed in August 1979, his place as First Vice-President being taken by Gen. Abdel-Majid Hamid Khalil who, in September 1980, also replaced Nimeri as Secretary-General of the SSU. The membership of the Political Bureau was reduced from 27 to 17 while the number of party secretaries was cut from 15 to four. In a Cabinet reshuffle, Dr. Hasan Abdullah Turabi, leader of the ICF and ex-Dean of the Faculty of Law at the University of Khartoum, was appointed Attorney-General: a clear indication of the Government's desire that the country's laws should be brought closer to the Islamic Sharia.

Further deterioration of the economy in the course of the following months precipitated still greater discontent and, in order to qualify for IMF assistance, it was necessary to devalue the currency by 11.1 per cent and remove subsidies on some essential commodities. In November 1981, looking for a scapegoat, Nimeri dismissed his entire cabinet and declared the leadership of the SSU dissolved. However, many ministers were reinstated in the new cabinet, including Dr. Turabi and Ahmad Abdel-Rahman Mohammed as Attorney-General and Minister of the Interior respectively. As before, the Islamic elements like Turabi and Abdel-Rahman were carefully balanced by the appointment to high office of former Communist Party supporters, such as Baddredin Sulaiman as second-in-command to Nimeri in the SSU. In January 1982, when the price of sugar increased by 62 per cent, violent demonstrations broke out in a number of towns, resulting in several casualties and the closure of four universities and many schools. Thousands of urban unemployed were rounded up and despatched to the countryside. On this occasion Nimeri removed the highly respected Vice-President Khalil from all posts, along with 22 senior army officers.

Prolonged discussions about decentralization culminated in the adoption, by the Third National Congress of the SSU in January 1980, of a recommendation whereby Sudan would be divided into five regions (Northern, Eastern, Central, Kordofan and Darfur) in addition to Khartoum and the South, which would continue to enjoy a special status and administrative structure. In October 1981 the People's Assembly was dissolved, and when new elections were held in December its membership had been reduced from 366 to 151, as many of its powers had been devolved to the new regions.

In the Southern Region the February 1978 elections had resulted in the defeat of Vice-President Abel Alier and his team of regional ministers, some of whom were considered ineffective as well as corrupt. Instead a new regional government under Gen. Joseph Lagu, the former *Anya Nya* guerrilla leader, was returned to office with a number of the "old guard", such as Clement Mboro and Joseph Uduhu, holding ministerial posts. The new team, however, fell apart in the course of the year and, amid charges of corruption against him, Gen. Lagu carried out Cabinet reshuffles in January and July 1979, which were particularly remarkable in that both involved the appointment to ministerial portfolios of Abel Alier's men rather than Lagu's own followers. The ambiguity of the situation was finally removed by President Nimeri who, in February 1980, dissolved both the National and the Regional Assemblies and called upon appropriate organs to prepare for the election of new People's Assemblies instead. Lagu resigned in February and the new Regional Assembly elected Abel Alier as his replacement in May. Subsequently Lagu started to campaign for the subdivision of the Southern Region into three regions to avoid the domination of the Regional Government by one ethnic group (i.e. the Dinka). As may be expected, this view has been vigorously challenged, not only by the Dinka leaders, but also by many southerners who fear that the creation of three regional administrations in the South would weaken their collective position *vis-à-vis* the North. To promote this view, 21 politicians, including persons such as Clement Mboro and Joseph Uduhu, launched a Council for the Unity of Southern Sudan (CUSS). Since the creation of political groupings other than the SSU is illegal, all 21 were arrested. By April 1982, however, all but one of them had been released A major worry for the Government is the group's growing connections with foreign forces and organizations.

Regionalization apart, the creators of CUSS felt that Khartoum was in any case dealing unfairly with Juba. In October 1981 Abel Alier had been dismissed as President of the High Executive Council, along with his cabinet, although he remained Vice-President of the Republic. An interim cabinet under Maj.-Gen. Abdalla Rassas was appointed in their place. New elections in the South were held in June 1982, at which James Tombura, who supports the subdivision of the Southern Region, defeated Clement Mboro to become the new President of the High Executive Council.

ECONOMIC SURVEY

Susan Turner

(Based on an earlier article by JANE CARROLL)

THE MAIN CHARACTERISTICS OF THE ECONOMY

Despite 26 years of development effort, Sudan remains primarily an agricultural and pastoral country. Today, as at independence in 1956, agriculture contributes about 40 per cent of G.D.P., produces over 90 per cent of exports, and employs 80 per cent of the economically active population. The manufacturing sector is still small, contributing 9 per cent of G.D.P. in 1979/80, compared with 2 per cent in the early 1960s. Exploration for petroleum has resulted in commercially exploitable finds and this has given rise to hopes that in a few years one of the country's most crippling problems, an oil import bill which takes up 80–90 per cent of export earnings, can be solved. Sudan not only depends on agriculture, but on one main crop for its exports. In fact the share of extra-long staple cotton in the exports of Sudan can reach 70 per cent. Such dependence on one major export crop, with wide fluctuations in price and quantity exported, has caused political, as well as economic, instability. Output has fallen sharply in recent years, with cotton being replaced by food and other crops, so that in 1980 its share of exports was only 42.5 per cent, compared with 65 per cent in 1979.

With such a traditional agricultural sector, it is not surprising that Sudan has a low per caput G.N.P., at only U.S. $450 (World Bank estimate) in 1979. Sudan's G.D.P. grew at an annual rate of 4 per cent in current prices between 1961 and 1971 but, overall, economic growth has been negligible. The population was believed to have been growing annually at a rate of about 2.8 per cent but the results of the 1973 census suggested a much lower rate of increase. The 1973 census figures were subsequently revised upwards, but they have not as yet been officially released. The official estimated population in 1980 was 18,371,000 but it is widely believed that the total is about 20 million. A third population census was to start in November 1982.

The average density of population in Sudan is low and there is no population pressure on the available resources at present. Open unemployment is very insignificant. In fact, Sudan suffers from a shortage of labour, particularly during the cotton-picking season. Sudan is a large country with large unproductive areas. Unfortunately it is these vast unproductive parts which are close to the Red Sea, whereas the more productive regions are separated from the sea and from Port Sudan by distances ranging between 800 and 2,400 km. Their remoteness was a major factor in retarding economic development in the past. For the present, inadequacy of transport is one of the important bottle-necks in the economy.

Perhaps one of the most striking features of the economy has been the dominant role of the public sector in all important economic activities. Until the IMF-backed reappraisal of public sector activities in 1977, the Government owned the majority of modern capital establishments in Sudan. Its interests ranged from public utilities, to transport and communications, the non-traditional industrial sector, and domestic and export marketing. In the period 1955/56–1974/75 the Government's share in gross fixed capital formation ranged from one-half to two-thirds. Although the 1970 nationalization of commercial

SUDAN

banks and several leading commercial firms had increased the economic significance of the public sector, its actual performance was far from efficient. Public enterprise deficits averaged $50 million per year between 1975 and 1980, due largely to poor pricing policies, low productivity and inadequate management. Following the 1977 reappraisal, which highlighted these problems, the Government began moving back towards a more mixed economy. The process started with the denationalization of a number of companies, including the Bata Shoe Company and the Belgravia Dairies. In 1980 trading monopolies were removed from most of the state marketing corporations while a number of non-essential industrial companies, including sweet firms, were put up for sale.

AGRICULTURE

The availability of water is the governing factor for agriculture in Sudan. In most parts of the rainlands of Sudan drinking water for humans and animals is a crucial factor, especially before the rainy season, when land is prepared for cultivation, and after it during harvest time. However, land does not impose any constraint on the agricultural development of the country. The cultivable land is estimated to be about 84 million hectares. Only about 8 per cent of this cultivable land is being utilized in agriculture, and less than 2 million hectares are under irrigation. Half of this area is in the Gezira scheme (with its Managil extension), and the rest is irrigated by the flood waters of two small rivers in eastern Sudan, Gash and Baraka, by the flood waters of the Nile and by pumps.

Prior to the Nile Waters agreement of 1959 the distribution of water between Sudan and the U.A.R. was governed by the Nile Waters agreement of 1929, which allocated 4,000 million cubic metres to Sudan. However, with the 1959 agreement and the construction of the Roseires and Khashm el Girba dams, the water problem was temporarily solved. Sudan's entitlement to draw 18,500 million cubic metres at Aswan High Dam or the equivalent of about 20,500 million cubic metres in Sudan opened the way for considerable expansion of irrigated agriculture, although for many years less than half the annual entitlement was used. However, the development of new areas along the White and Blue Niles, the Atbara and main Nile, as well as the intensification of production in the Gezira by replacing fallow with continuous cropping of cotton, wheat, sorghum and groundnuts over 90 per cent of the area, means that Sudan is now close to drawing its complete entitlement. Construction of the Jonglei canal in Southern Sudan, as a joint Sudanese–Egyptian project, aims at conserving 4,000 million cubic metres of the 32,000 million cubic metres lost each year by evaporation from the Sudd swamp. The extra yield will be divided equally between the two countries, enabling Sudan initially to develop an extra 12,600 hectares on the west bank of the Nile. Work on the 360-km. canal started in 1978 under a $156 million contract awarded to a French consortium. With almost 100 km. completed, work is expected to end in December 1985.

One of the most important development projects of recent years is the Rahad scheme. Located on the Blue Nile, and served by the Roseires dam, Rahad is the first project in Sudan to use long-furrow irrigation on a large scale. The first 126,000 hectares were brought into cultivation in 1978 at a cost of $364 million. Finance was provided by the World Bank, the U.S.A. and Kuwait. About one-half of the irrigated area is given to medium-staple cotton, and the remainder to groundnuts and vegetables. Production is organized under a tenancy system similar to that operating in the Gezira, with management provided by the state Rahad Corporation. The second stage, now being implemented, will bring a further 210,000 hectares into production.

In spite of the significant role played by irrigation (particularly gravity irrigation) in the economic development of Sudan, the rainlands are more important. Total cropped area in Sudan—in spite of its increase in the long run—tends to fluctuate from year to year because of variations in the rainfall. The total cropped area increased from 4.3 million hectares in 1970/71 to 7.4 million hectares in 1980. The total area under irrigation was about 2 million hectares in 1980. With the exception of cotton, pulses and a proportion of groundnuts, Sudan's foodstuffs and most exported agricultural products come from the rainlands. In fact Sudan is self-sufficient in the essential foods: millet, meat, edible oils and salt.

Sudan has an animal wealth which contributes on average about 10 per cent of G.D.P. annually. It was estimated in 1980 as 18.4 million cattle, 17.8 million sheep, 12.6 million goats and 2.5 million camels. In 1980 the estimated production of milk was 1,452,000 metric tons and meat 418,000 metric tons. The share of livestock (live animals, hides and skins) in total exports increased from about 2 per cent in 1975/76 to almost 7 per cent in 1979/80. However, this percentage is not expected to increase significantly in the future because domestic consumption of meat and hides is increasing at a faster rate than production. The Government has occasionally restricted the export of animal products in order to satisfy the local market. The first commercial meat-producing project has been set up at Seleit, near Khartoum, by a firm owned by private and public Sudanese interests and by a British company, which also managed the project until October 1981. Its output will be largely for export, to Saudi Arabia and the Gulf States. A number of large-scale poultry projects are being set up near Khartoum.

Forest reserve estates, which are completely owned by the Government, cover about 1,075,000 hectares. Beside gum arabic, the other important forest products are the various types of timber which are processed by the forest department of the Ministry of Agriculture. The main consumer of forest products is the Government itself.

Sudan is rich in fish and other aquatic resources. The inland fisheries cover more than 20,000 sq. km., while marine fisheries extend for a distance of about 700 km. along the Red Sea. It is estimated that the annual total value of the output of fish and aquatic resources in Sudan is about £S10 million. Potential output of fish from the Nile is 60,000 tons annually but only about one-third of this wealth is utilized at present.

Cotton is the most important crop in Sudan from the economic point of view, being the major export, chief foreign exchange earner and main generator of income. Three main types of cotton are grown: the long-staple Barakats for the export market, with over 80 per cent of production from the Gezira; the medium-staple Akalas; and the rain-fed short staples. Akala, which can be mixed with man-made fibres, was introduced in the early 1970s to help diversify Sudan's markets in the face of falling world demand for long-staples. With the new irrigated scheme given over to its production, Akala now accounts for almost 40 per cent of production, compared with 47–50 per cent for the long-staple varieties. This change has been reflected in the direction of cotton exports. The People's Republic of China, the main customer for Akala, replaced Italy in 1977 as Sudan's main cotton partner in terms of quantity. Purchases by China now account for about one-third of all bales sold. However, Italy, as the main customer for the higher-priced Barakats, retains its lead in terms of value, accounting for 27 per cent of cotton revenue in 1981.

Cotton's share of exports normally varies between 50 and 70 per cent, but disastrous seasons in 1980 and 1981 reduced it to under 40 per cent. This fall was paralleled in cotton revenue, which fell from £S151.1 million in 1979 to £S127 million in 1980 and £S70 million in 1981. This dismal performance has been partly due to competition from synthetic fibres, but in particular it is a result of government policy in the mid-1970s to turn Sudan into the "breadbasket of the Arab World". Stress was laid on wheat and other food crops to the detriment of cotton. This neglect was most dramatically felt in yields, which were down to an average of 2 kantars per feddan in the late 1970s, and in 1981 averaged 1.5 kantars. The inevitable effect on total production, which dropped from around 900,000 bales in the early 1970s to 500,000 in 1980/81, was exaggerated by the 1975 policy decision to reduce the area under cotton in the Gezira by about one-third.

However, this policy was reversed in mid-1979 under pressure from the IMF. Renewed emphasis is being placed on cotton and other cash crops in an attempt to boost flagging export earnings. A large-scale rehabilitation programme for the irrigated sector is now under way, financed by the World Bank, the EEC, Kuwait, the ADB and the International Fund for Agricultural Development. It started in 1980 with a $76 million World Bank/EEC-financed holding programme to inject vital capital inputs into the Gezira. Its first effects were felt in the 1981/82 season when, despite a 6 per cent drop in overall cotton plantings as a result of the previous disastrous year, estimated production was up by about 30 per cent to cover 600,000 bales (each of 216.8 kg.). This reflects an increase in average yields to 3 kantars per feddan. A longer-term pro-

gramme is already under way in New Halfa, and finance for reconstruction of the Blue and White Nile pump schemes was agreed in 1981. A Kuwait-financed study for the long-term rehabilitation of the Gezira, completed in early 1982, is now being studied. Altogether, the World Bank estimates that about $1,080 million will be needed in the 1980s to rehabilitate the irrigated sector.

Sudan's main cereal crop is sorghum (durra). It is the most important staple food in Sudan and is mainly grown in the rainlands. Sudan produces about 1.5 million tons of durra annually, which is usually sufficient for domestic consumption. Excellent yields of over 2 million tons in 1981 and 1982 have encouraged the development of durra into an increasingly important export crop. Earnings were $65 million in 1981. With urbanization and social development, the consumption of bread made out of wheat flour is increasing by about 10 per cent annually. Wheat is grown mainly as a cash crop. Wheat and durra are to be phased out of the irrigated sector but groundnuts will be increased.

In 1979/80 an estimated 925,000 metric tons of unshelled groundnuts were produced, compared with 820,000 tons in 1978/79 and 1,020,000 tons the year before. Value of groundnuts and groundnut products exports in 1980 was £S24.2 million. In 1979/80 exports of shelled groundnuts totalled 595,000 metric tons.

The Kenana sugar complex, one of the world's largest, between the Blue and White Niles was officially opened in March 1981 although it had started refining a year earlier. The idea was first mooted in 1971 by Lonrho of the United Kingdom; a feasibility study was done in 1973. The project cost had originally been estimated at $180 million but in early 1981 unofficial estimates put the figure at $800–1,000 million. This huge cost over-run has been caused by delays, inflation, the unexpectedly high prices of tenders and by the fact that large loans had to be obtained on the commercial market. The Kenana Sugar Company's major shareholders are the Sudanese Government and other state interests (about 40 per cent), the Kuwait Government (the largest single shareholder, with 33 per cent), the Saudi Arabian Government (11 per cent) and the Arab Investment Company of Saudi Arabia (11.8 per cent). By February 1981 daily throughput of cane was 13,000 metric tons. Ultimate capacity is 17,000 tons per day. Output of sugar in 1981 was 112,000 tons. It was expected to rise to 175,000 tons in 1982, and to reach full production of 330,000 tons in 1983/84. Domestic consumption is 400,000 tons per year and imports costing $235 million were necessary in 1980/81. It was hoped that by 1980 Sudan would have become self-sufficient in sugar, and indeed an exporter, with four government schemes in operation with a total production capacity of 340,000 tons per year. However, none of them is working at full capacity, and their total production for 1981/82 was expected to reach only 131,000 tons. The Government is now considering the introduction of foreign management, and proposals for financing a $100 million rehabilitation programme are being studied by the World Bank and other donors.

Sudan gums have been known in trade for at least two thousand years. Gum arabic, which constituted about 10 per cent of Sudan's exports in 1969 and 5 per cent in 1973, was for many years the second export crop, until overtaken by groundnuts in 1971, and is now the fourth largest export crop, sesame being the third. It is the most important forest product and, though collected in the traditional sector, it is a purely cash crop. It is almost entirely exported, as the confectionery industry manufactures only a very small percentage of it. In the 1960s Sudan was the largest producer of gum arabic, accounting for about 92 per cent of world production in 1962–66. Its monopolistic position declined in the 1970s. In 1979 exports were worth £S18 million.

INDUSTRY

The ginning of cotton encouraged the beginning of industry in Sudan early in this century. With the expansion of cotton production the number of ginning factories have increased until the Gezira Board alone has the largest ginning enterprise under single management in the world. There are 25 spinning and textile factories. Cotton seeds are partly decorticated, while the exports of cotton seed oil and oil cakes are increasing. Groundnuts are also partly processed, with oil and cake dominating exports. Minerals (copper, iron, mica and chromite), which constitute less than 1 per cent of exports, are exported in the crudest form.

With the exception of the soap, soft drinks and oil-pressing industries, large industries manufacturing import substitutes started only after 1960. There was no government involvement in industry before 1960, but this has since increased to include the Guneid and New Halfa sugar factories, opened in the early 1960s, a tannery and five food processing plants. Following the recent shift in emphasis in favour of a more mixed economy, all except the sugar plants are being considered for sale to the private sector. What is striking about these companies, particularly the food processing industries, is that the supply of raw materials is not high enough to match the productive capacity, and therefore their weakness is not technical but agricultural.

The Khartoum-based Arab Authority for Agricultural Investment and Development has four agro-industrial ventures under construction: a dairy project, glucose production, vegetable canning and poultry, with three more planned to cover animal feed, milling and mechanized farming.

The private sector has also played an important role in the industrial development of this country. In the period 1960–69 the private sector invested £S35.9 million in industries of which £S16.1 million was Sudanese and £S19.8 foreign capital. The bulk of the investment has gone into the textile, soap, oil-pressing, footwear, soft drinks, printing, packing, flour, and knitwear industries. In the 1970s, the role of the private sector increased.

The Government has encouraged industrialization in Sudan by various means. The Approved Enterprises (Concessions) Act, 1959, gave generous concessions to infant industries. It was followed by similar acts in 1967, 1973, 1974 and 1976. The Industrial Bank, which was established in 1961, assists in the financing of private industrial enterprises with up to two-thirds of the capital required. A new Encouragement of Investment Act was introduced at the end of 1980, repealing the previous investment laws. Like its predecessors, it offers tax incentives, guaranteed repatriation of foreign capital and profits, facilitated land acquisition, customs exemption and favourable freight and electricity rates. It set up a "Secretariat-General for Investment", which took over administration of the investment regulations from several ministries and government departments, thus simplifying procedures.

A joint South Korean–Sudanese tyre factory opened near Port Sudan in 1980. It will cover all local demand, saving Sudan about $25 million per year in foreign exchange. There are three animal feed mills and some of the output is exported. There are two cement factories and two more are to be built. Sudan should then be self-sufficient in cement, although the two existing plants are running at barely half capacity, because of shortages of power and spare parts and transport problems. Demand is about 300,000 metric tons per year. The construction of a fertilizer factory south of Khartoum is now complete. Sudan has previously had to import all the fertilizers it needed.

Since 1973 international companies have shown an increasing interest in exploring for petroleum. Over 80 per cent of available concession areas are now allotted, and companies working in Sudan included Standard Oil's subsidiary, Chevron and Phillips Petroleum (both of the U.S.A.), France's Total Exploration, Texas Eastern and Union Texas. Chevron is the only one to have made any commercial finds, beginning in April 1981 with the Unity field in its south-western concession, with confirmed flows of over 10,000 barrels per day (b/d). Plans are now well advanced for construction of a 25,000 b/d refinery at Kosti. Financing for the $900 million project, which includes a 550-km. pipeline to the Unity Field, is being organized by the White Nile Petroleum Company, formed in August 1981. Shares in the company are held by Chevron and the Government (33.3 per cent each), and the IFC and Apicorp (16.7 per cent each). The oil pipeline between Port Sudan and Khartoum was completed in 1977. It is designed for the transport of motor gasoline, gas-oil and kerosene, including aviation turbine fuel. It has a capacity of 600,000 metric tons, a length of about 850 km. and a diameter of 20 cm. Chrome mining is being developed. A feasibility study into offshore minerals in the Red Sea showed considerable deposits of iron ore, zinc, copper and silver, and these are to be exploited jointly with Saudi Arabia.

FOREIGN TRADE

The value of Sudan's exports rose from £S63.4 million in 1960 to £S271.3 million in 1980, while the value of imports rose from £S63.7 million to £S788.2 million, with oil imports alone costing £S169.6 million.

The 1982/83 trade deficit is forecast at £S1,138 million. There are import restrictions and high import duties on a large number of goods, though in 1975 further categories were exempted, but export taxes are light and no licence is required for export, with the exception of goods consumed locally and in short supply.

Sudan's main exports are primary agricultural products, and since the establishment of the Gezira Scheme in 1925, cotton has dominated Sudan's exports. Between 1960 and 1971 the share of lint cotton alone ranged between 46 and 65 per cent. In 1971 the U.S.S.R. was the largest buyer of Sudan's cotton, followed closely by India, the People's Republic of China, whose share had doubled since the previous year, and the EEC. However, after the attempted coup in 1971 the U.S.S.R.'s purchases dropped to nil in 1973 when the People's Republic of China took the largest share, 51,903 tons, followed by Japan, Italy and India. China retained this position into the 1980s. With the expansion of production in the traditional sector, the relative importance of oil seeds as exports has increased and in 1981 high world prices made groundnuts the single most important export crop. The EEC is the largest buyer of Sudan's groundnuts (60 per cent). The East European countries buy about 20 per cent and the rest go to various other West European countries. Gum arabic was overtaken in importance in the 1970s. In 1978, while gum arabic formed about 7 per cent of exports, groundnuts formed 16 per cent. As a result of the Lomé Conventions which Sudan signed in 1976 and renewed in 1979, trade relations between Sudan and the EEC have been further strengthened.

The major imports are petroleum, vehicles, transport equipment, machinery, appliances and textiles, and since 1973 sugar imports have greatly increased. In 1963 Sudan produced only 61 per cent of its domestic sugar needs, but it is hoped that there will be a surplus for export at some point in the 1980s. The growth of industries which are manufacturing import substitutes has affected the pattern of imports since the mid-1960s. The imports of footwear and cigarettes are declining in relative and absolute terms.

Perhaps a more striking change has taken place in the pattern of suppliers and buyers, if the late 1960s are compared with the early 1950s. The U.K. used to be the largest seller and buyer from Sudan (30–40 per cent before independence). In 1976 only 3.5 per cent of Sudan's exports went to the U.K., and only 5.5 per cent of imports were brought from the U.K. Trade with socialist countries increased since independence until 1971 as a result of several bilateral agreements. Their share in Sudan's trade has, with the exception of the People's Republic of China, drastically declined since the attempted coup in 1971. Exports to the U.S.S.R. fell from £S18,351,000 in 1971 to £S3,000 in 1973, but rose again to £S16,484,000 in 1979. Trade with the Arab countries has been expanding in recent years and exports to them, mainly live animals and foodstuffs, have reached about 10 per cent, but imports from these countries form a smaller percentage.

While Saudi Arabia, because of oil, has become Sudan's single largest source of imports, accounting for 14 per cent of the market, the EEC as a whole supplies about 40 per cent of imports. Within this group, the United Kingdom is still the largest supplier, followed by the Federal Republic of Germany and France. The U.S.A. supplies about 8 per cent of imports. The most important customers are Italy, the People's Republic of China and Japan, with sales to the U.S.S.R. increasing again. Trade with Egypt declined in the mid-1970s, in spite of bilateral trade agreements. However, as a result of the protocol ratified in January 1977, Egypt's share of Sudan's exports has remained about the same, but Sudan's imports from Egypt declined from about 5 per cent in the early 1970s to about 2 per cent in 1979.

The Government tried to redress the chronic balance of payments deficit, which has persisted since 1956, by introducing in March 1972 an exchange tax on all transfers abroad and a subsidy paid on all receipts from abroad of about 15 per cent. This was also meant to discourage black market dealings in foreign currencies. However, despite a three-year refusal to concede to the demands of the IMF—which included devaluation—the increasingly precarious foreign exchange position made the Government agree to devalue the Sudanese pound in June 1978 from $2.87 to $2.50, in addition to raising the exchange tax from 15 per cent to 25 per cent. This effectively increased the devaluation to about 25 per cent. In May 1979 Sudan concluded an agreement with the IMF providing for a loan of 200 million SDRs (U.S.$254 million) over a period of three years. The conditions of the loan included the containment of domestic credit expansion and the encouragement of cash crop production. In September the Sudanese pound was further devalued, to $2.00, and at the same time a "parallel" rate of £S1=$1.25 was introduced for specified imports and exports. However, Sudan's continuing economic problems led to the IMF loan's being raised to SDR 427 million in November 1980. The failure of Sudan to comply with a number of conditions under the loan, notably removal of subsidies on oil, sugar and wheat, led to its being renegotiated in 1981. In October the three-year facility was replaced by a one-year credit of SDR 198 million. In return, Sudan in November devalued the pound once more, by 11.1 per cent, abolished the two-tier exchange rate system, and agreed to remove all indirect subsidies within 18 months. Petrol prices rose immediately by an average of 33 per cent, followed by sugar prices in January. Public expenditure for 1982 was cut by £S20 million.

FOREIGN AID

The Ten-Year Plan of Economic and Social Development, 1961/62–1970/71, was the country's first experience in planning, although there had been three previous attempts to develop Sudan in a systematic manner: 1946–51, 1951–56 and the Managil extension programme. In contrast to the Ten-Year Plan, the development programmes were not comprehensive, being concerned only with some projects in the public sector and depending on finance from savings of the public sector.

Out of the total investment of £S565 million, £S415.9 million was to be financed by domestic savings and £S219.7 million from foreign financial assistance.

While £S150 million of foreign aid was forecast for the period 1961/62–1970/71, £S141 million of aid in the form of grants, long-term and medium-term loans and in kind was received in the period 1960–69. However, in spite of the small difference between projected and realized foreign aid, the plan could not be properly implemented, mainly because of a shortage of domestic and foreign finance.

From the Eastern bloc, aid to Sudan from Yugoslavia has included three tanneries, a cardboard factory and 3 ships, which form part of the Sudan Shipping Line. The U.S.S.R. has provided Sudan with two grain elevators, factories for processing agricultural and dairy products, a hospital and veterinary laboratories. The change in Sudanese foreign policy, however, has since 1971 led to more aid from Western countries and from the People's Republic of China. China has built a foundry, completed the construction of a textile mill at Hassaheisa, a conference hall in Khartoum, and a section of the Khartoum-Port Sudan highway.

By early 1976 Sudan appeared to be in a favourable position to benefit from Arab aid, with close relations with most Arab states. In 1975 the Arab Fund for Economic and Social Development (AFESD) announced a ten-year plan to double G.D.P. in Sudan, and in 1975 plans were being prepared for a massive investment of $6,000 million of Arab funds in Sudan for a scheme which would produce a substantial amount of the food requirements of Arab countries by 1985. In 1960–69 Arab aid totalled about 30 per cent of the total received. In 1972 relations with Egypt and Libya deteriorated, and Sudan received aid mainly from Kuwait and Saudi Arabia. This trend continued into the 1980s, despite improved relations with Egypt after 1974, with Saudi Arabia and Kuwait remaining the main bilateral Arab aid donors, followed by Abu Dhabi. By 1980 Kuwaiti loans and project finance had totalled over 90 million Kuwaiti dinars, including aid to Sudan railways, the Rahad project, and the Sinnar and New Halfa sugar schemes. Saudi aid totalled about $300 million. The major change in Arab lending whether bilateral or from the aid agencies, has been a shift in emphasis from project finance to balance-of-payments support. Saudi Arabia is providing $150 million in 1981/82, plus $70 million in free fuel.

Aid from the United Kingdom and the U.S.A. has often been dependent on political circumstances. In 1973 the U.S.A. donated wheat worth £S3.6 million and made a loan of £S9.6 million to enable Sudan Airways to purchase two Boeings. The U.S.A. also made a contribution of £S3.9 million to the Rahad Project and in 1979 agreed to provide $100 million over five years in food aid. Direct economic aid from the U.S.A. has increased dramatically as Sudan's strategic importance has grown. Now only second to Egypt in Africa, U.S. aid for 1982 was expected to total $160 million. The United Kingdom contributed to the development of the electricity system in Juba and the Sinnar sugar refinery. It is providing large amounts of aid for power projects. Norway is to provide $4 million in general aid and financed the construction of 78 Nile barges which came into operation in 1981. Belgium is assisting with the construction of a sugar refinery at Melut. The Federal Republic of Germany has played an important role in financing the economic development of the country by contributing to the financing of the Roseires Dam, and credit from German firms helped to finance the Guneid and Khashm el Girba sugar factories.

The benefits for Sudan in aid from international organizations are considerable. EEC aid to Sudan has risen markedly, and $103–$117 million has been allocated for 1981–85 under Lomé II, compared with $93.5 million under Lomé I. It will be used to finance expansion of tea and rice projects in Southern Sudan, improvements to the rail network, and purchase of fertilizers for the agricultural rehabilitation programme. The World Bank has played a vital role in Sudan's aid projects, contributing loans of over $500 million under generous terms since 1958. The Bank has financed vital projects such as the Roseires Dam, mechanized farming, Sudan Railways extension and dieselization, the Managil Extension, and the Rahad scheme. New lending has included $65 million for the Gezira holding programme in 1980, and a total of $67 million for the White and Blue Nile pumping schemes agreed in 1981. In 1982 the Bank agreed $25 million for the second phase of Port Sudan development, and $60 million for the third highway programme.

Total external resources received in 1980 amounted to £S192 million, which was 16 per cent up on resources received in 1979. This capital inflow included £S45 million representing drawings on a $400 million loan granted by Saudi Arabia and £S116.6 million as credit from the IMF. However, the inflow of gross external resources to be used for development, amounted to only £S7.3 million, compared with £S9.5 million in 1977. Total outstanding external debts were $5,200 million in May 1982, compared with $3,436.5 million at the end of 1978. Of the 1978 debt, $1,095.5 million was to private creditors. Debt servicing during 1978 amounted to £S46.8 million against £S38.3 million in 1977. The ratio of debt servicing to export proceeds marginally increased from 13.3 per cent in 1977 to 14.3 per cent in 1978, but by 1981/82 it was expected to reach 27 per cent.

Three EEC members, the Federal Republic of Germany, the United Kingdom and the Netherlands, decided to write off their Governments' outstanding debts on Sudan in 1978 and consider them as grants. The outstanding debts amounted to $218 million, £S10.1 million and $19 million respectively. Such a generous move reduced the foreign liability of the Sudan Government by about 16 per cent in 1978. In November 1979 Sudan started negotiating for rescheduling debts with Western banks totalling about $600 million. Morgan Grenfell of the United Kingdom was appointed by the Bank of Sudan to advise it in these negotiations. A seven-year rescheduling programme was worked out in December 1981. This was followed in March 1982 by an agreement by OECD members at the Club of Paris to reschedule about $400 million in government-to-government debts due after July 1st, 1981. This was the second Club of Paris rescheduling of Sudan's debts, the first having been agreed in November 1979. Agreement was still to be reached on $440 million in outstanding trade credits.

PUBLIC FINANCE

The Sudan Government, like governments in many other underdeveloped countries, depends heavily on indirect taxes as a major source of revenue. In recent years the relative share of indirect taxes declined because of increased import restrictions, and also because of the increased revenue from direct taxes and proceeds from government agricultural enterprises. The main source of revenue from indirect taxation is import duties. Because of balance of payments deficits in recent years the Government has been trying to restrict imports of consumer goods, particularly luxuries, and those which bear the highest rates. Excise duties are growing in importance because of the growth of industries producing import substitutes. Thus, the share of excise duties in revenue from indirect taxation, 5 per cent in 1964/65, rose to 36.9 per cent in 1975/76.

The revenue from direct taxes was about 9 per cent of the total revenue of the central government in 1975/76, having been 2.7 per cent in 1963/64. The present direct taxes of Sudan are income taxes and a stamp duty.

Since the mid-1960s the Sudan Government has been finding it difficult to make all its local cash payments, whether wages and salaries or payment to contractors, on time. This seems to be the result of two main factors: underestimation of expenditure and ineffective financial control of government accounts. This problem of the illiquidity of the public sector has forced the Government to seek various ways to increase revenue and reduce expenditure, but it has not yet been solved. Deficit finance from the Bank of Sudan has been increasingly used to finance government expenditure, but this is reaching a critical limit and adding to existing inflationary pressure.

The expenditure of the central Government has been rising very fast since independence in 1956. In 1949 the total current expenditure of the central Government was £S10 million; by 1982/83 it was an estimated £S1,910 million. Besides the rise in prices and the normal expansion in government services, increased expenditure on education, national defence and the rise in wages and salaries of the employees of the public sector have accentuated the rate of increase of the total current expenditure in recent years. Revenue in the 1982/83 budget is

envisaged at £S1,343 million. The development budget is estimated at £S502 million. The majority is scheduled to go to improvements in the oil industry, and the rehabilitation of irrigated agriculture. Tighter control of the money supply continues. The budget also includes cuts in government spending, encouragement of private investment and a further shift from indirect to direct taxation.

LABOUR AND WAGES

The number of persons five years of age and over reported in the 1955/56 census as mainly engaged in economic activity was 3,800,000 out of a population of 10.2 million. In addition it was estimated, on the basis of detailed tabulations of the census returns, that 1,116,000 persons, whose main activity was not economic, took part in subsidiary economic activity. So the total number engaged to any degree in economic activity was approximately 4,916,000 or 48 per cent of the population. Sudan's labour force is overwhelmingly male. Men made up 56 per cent of the total economically active population, women 24.7 per cent, boys 14.4 per cent and girls 4.9 per cent.

Of all the males and females in the labour force 86.7 per cent were primary producers, 3.3 per cent secondary producers and 10 per cent tertiary producers. All these percentages of sex and industrial distribution of Sudan's labour force have not, it is thought, changed very much since 1955/56.

As the figures of the 1973 census have not been released officially, it is still difficult to get any reasonably accurate data beyond 1956 in order to assess the labour situation in Sudan. However, according to an ILO Employment Mission (1975), the labour force of the country, broadly defined, is estimated at 7 million persons, of whom about one million move around Sudan during any year in response to geographical disparities in employment opportunity. These are mainly migrants from western Sudan to the Gezira Scheme and to the mechanized rain-fed farming schemes in the Gedaref area, the Nuba Mountains and Kordofan. They include rural-urban as well as rural-rural migrants, but the figure excludes the movements of nomadic cattle-herding tribes in response to variations in rainfall, which amount perhaps to another million. Rural-urban labour migration in Sudan, though not yet very dramatic, is beginning to cause some concern because of its social effects as well as increasing urban unemployment.

Until about 1965 one of the country's major problems was considered to be the shortage of skilled workers. There was heavy dependence on expatriates of Greek and Armenian descent, who filled a high proportion of skilled jobs and managerial and executive posts.

However, after 1965, unemployment began to appear among skilled workers in the towns, and some economists and businessmen began to believe that the shortage of skilled workers was no longer a serious problem to the industrialization of Sudan. Sudan has

SUDAN

already started to export skilled workers, clerical staff and teachers to the Arab countries. However, the increasing "brain-drain" of high-level manpower (e.g. doctors, engineers, university lecturers, etc.) to the Arab oil-producing countries is causing concern in Sudan.

The only available figures on unemployment come from the registrations at employment exchanges in major towns. In 1967/68 31,919 were registered as unemployed. In 1974/75 registered unemployment totalled 73,881. However, it is obvious that this figure does not represent total open unemployment in Sudan. Not all the workers register themselves when they are unemployed, particularly unskilled workers. On the other hand, some workers may register more than once, while, when other workers find a job, neither they nor their employers report to the employment exchanges. Therefore, the present figures of unemployment in Sudan should be viewed with great caution.

In 1974 a new minimum wage was introduced in the private sector in stages, to become £S16.5 per month by October 1977, for enterprises which employ ten workers or more in the Khartoum and Gezira areas as well as in large towns in the other regions. However, in 1979 the minimum wage was raised to £S28 per month, while the minimum pay for unskilled workers rose to 150 piastres per day. With the increase in inflation, especially after the devaluation of the Sudanese pound in June 1978, wages and salaries rose considerably during the second half of 1978 and continued to rise in 1979. In addition, the Government introduced a job evaluation and classification scheme which was partly implemented as from January 1979. This scheme has resulted in a large increase in the cost of wages and salaries paid by the public sector and added further to inflation in Sudan. Some economists—in the absence of reliable price indices—estimated that the general price level approximately doubled between June 1978 and April 1979, because of devaluation and the job evaluation scheme. Although the main objective of the scheme is to make wages and salaries in the public sector as a whole more rational, it has increased the wage bill of the public sector by about £S100 million and created a series of strikes and discontent among employees of the public sector who are seeking to retain their acquired rights.

PLANNING AND DEVELOPMENT

The First Development Plan was a ten-year plan, 1961/62 to 1970/71. Then a Five-Year Plan (1970/71 to 1974/75) was published in 1970 and later in the year it was revised. Because of nationalization, the share of the public sector in investment increased from £S200 million to £S215 million. The private sector's share in capital investment had been fixed at £S170 million. The Plan aimed at an average annual G.D.P. growth of 7.6 per cent, with increases in industrial and agricultural output over the period of 57.4 per cent and 60.8 per cent respectively. In June 1974 it was announced that the Plan would be extended to

June 1977 and named the Amended F

To accelerate the implementation o projects earmarked in the Five-Year P which were behind schedule, the Inter Programme was formulated in December 1 was an extension of the period of the plan to 1 The programme emphasized self-sufficiency in the daily necessities of the population, but it failed to achieve its objectives. The Six-Year Plan (1977/78–1982/83) envisaged a total investment of £S2,670 million, of which £S1,570 million (59 per cent) was to be invested by the public sector and £S1,100 million (41 per cent) by the private sector. Foreign sources were to provide 53 per cent of the finance for the plan, with deficit finance providing 18 per cent and current budget surpluses representing only 6 per cent. However, the shortage of local and foreign finance and the inadequacy of the transport system (especially railways), as well as the shortage of power and cement, led to the scrapping of the Plan and its replacement by a three-year programme which aims at completing projects already started.

POWER AND TRANSPORT

The installed generating capacity of Sudan in 1977 was 112,900 kW. thermal and 19,600 kW. hydro. The total power generated in 1979 was about 900 million kWh. The number of consumers in 1976 was 68,529 residential and commercial, 558 agricultural and 844 industrial. All the main towns of Sudan are supplied with electricity and some of the small towns which lie near to the transmission lines, such as Kamlin, also enjoy this facility.

The volume of electricity used by industry was 118,353,000 kWh. in 1972, while the volume of electricity used by agriculture for pumps was 26,200,000 kWh. The electricity consumption of industry does not include that of ginning factories, the large oil mills and sugar factories. All these generate their own electricity from by-products. The grain silos at Gedaref and Port Sudan have their own generating sets.

Under what is known as the Power III electricity generating scheme, a new 60 MW steam power station is to be built at Khartoum North, a 40 MW extension is to be added to the Burri diesel station nearby and an 84 MW extension will be added to the Roseires hydroelectric station on the Blue Nile, increasing its capacity to 250 MW. The $300 million programme is being financed by the U.K., the Federal Republic of Germany and the World Bank and is expected to come into operation in 1984.

Sudan depends mainly on railways for transport. Steamers and motor transport play a secondary but increasingly important role. There are many road projects planned or under way and several trucking firms have been set up, particularly since the completion in 1980 of the Khartoum–Port Sudan highway, which runs through the Gezira and the main mechanized farming areas. The total of paved roads increased from less than 400 km. in 1979 to more than 2,000 km. by the end of 1980. Road projects include the Wad Medani-Sennar-Kosti road which, when it is finished at the end of 1982, will give the west its first all-weather road link with the centre of the country. A 582-km. road link with Kenya is being built and other roads are planned to link up with the Egyptian and Ethiopian systems.

Rail facilities, though improved, are far from adequate. Railways still account for two-thirds of freight traffic but they suffer from many problems including the fact that they are single-track and narrow gauge. They also suffer from lack of investment: the Six-Year Plan allocated only £S97.5 million to railways, compared with £S311.1 million for roads. The length of the railway network is 5,500 km. The river fleet comprises 386 low-speed old steamers of various types. River transport is mainly used between Kosti and Juba (1,435 km.) and between Dongola and Kareima (187 km.); these routes are navigable all year round. The total length of the river navigation routes is about 4,068 km., of which 1,723 km. are open all the year and the rest are seasonal. River transport between Wadi Halfa and Shellal, which lies partly on Lake Nasser, is under development at present. As far as sea transport is concerned, the government company, the Sudan Shipping Line, one of the successful public enterprises, owns 7 ships of total deadweight of 53,638 tons. After the reopening of the Suez Canal in June 1975 work began on installing new equipment at Port

Sudan, and enlarging its capacity. Congestion is still a problem. A modernization project, financed by the World Bank and the U.K. started in 1978. It will increase cargo-handling capacity to 13 million tons per year and container, roll on–roll off (ro-ro) and new deep-water berth facilities will be added. The first phase was completed in 1981, and a revised second phase began in 1982, following agreement of a $25 million World Bank credit. Proposals to redevelop Old Suakin port are being reconsidered by the EEC because of a proposed Saudi Arabian/West German port development near by, at New Suakin. Proposals for the project were the cause of the World Bank's revision of second-phase plans for Port Sudan. The proposed oil terminal has been dropped, as one is to be built at New Suakin. The communications facilities have been expanded to provide a wider geographical coverage. The telex exchange, the microwave television network and telephone automation were some of the key projects which were implemented during the last development plan. However, the telephone service in Sudan is far from satisfactory.

The government-owned Sudan Airways, formed in 1947, operates internal and international services. It connects Khartoum with twenty important Sudanese towns as well as with Europe, the Middle East and Africa. Khartoum is to have a second international airport and Juba airport is to have a new runway, terminal hall and navigational equipment, in an EEC-financed project.

STATISTICAL SURVEY

AREA AND POPULATION

AREA	Census (April 3rd, 1973)	POPULATION Mid-year Estimates			
		1973	1974	1975	1976
2,505,813 sq. km.*	14,819,271†	14,958,000	15,337,000	15,726,000	16,126,000

* 967,500 sq. miles.
† Including an estimate for nomadic tribes and an adjustment for underenumeration in the Blue Nile province.

1980 population: 18,371,000 (estimate).

PROVINCES*
(April 3rd, 1973)

	AREA (sq. miles)	POPULATION		AREA (sq. miles)	POPULATION
Bahr el Ghazal	82,530	1,387,842	Kordofan . .	146,930	2,202,977
Blue Nile .	54,880	3,804,399	Northern . .	184,200	963,609
Darfur . .	191,650	2,180,570	Red Sea . .	82,092	459,365
Equatoria .	76,495	758,412	Upper Nile .	91,190	798,813
Kassala . .	49,436	1,112,886			
Khartoum .	8,097	1,150,398	TOTAL .	967,500	14,819,271

* In February 1980 Sudan was reorganized into six regions in preparation for increased local self-government. They are: Central Region, Northern Region, Eastern Region, Kordofan Region, Darfur Region and the existing Southern Region. Khartoum is administered separately as the national capital.

PRINCIPAL TOWNS

				POPULATION (April 3rd, 1973)
Khartoum (capital).	.	.	.	333,906
Omdurman .	.	.	.	299,399
Khartoum North	.	.	.	150,989
Port Sudan .	.	.	.	132,632
Wadi Medani .	.	.	.	106,715
El Obeid .	.	.	.	90,073
Atbara .	.	.	.	66,116

Because of the flooding of the Wadi Halfa and adjacent areas by the Aswan High Dam, over 50,000 inhabitants have been resettled in Khashm el Girba, on the Atbara River.

Births and Deaths (1966): Registered births 143,052 (birth rate 10.1 per 1,000); registered deaths 13,416 (death rate 1.0 per 1,000). Birth registration is believed to be about 20 per cent complete and death registration 5 per cent complete. UN estimates put the average annual birth rate at 45.5 per 1,000 in 1970–75 and 45.8 per 1,000 in 1975–80; the average death rate is put at 20.2 per 1,000 in 1970–75 and 18.4 per 1,000 in 1975–80.

ECONOMICALLY ACTIVE POPULATION
(1973 census, provisional)

Agriculture, hunting, forestry and fishing	2,950,000
Mining and quarrying . . .	4,000
Manufacturing	179,000
Electricity, gas and water . .	45,000
Construction	87,000
Trade, restaurants and hotels . .	244,000
Transport, storage and communications .	154,000
Financing, insurance, real estate and business services	6,000
Community, social and personal services .	456,000
Activities not adequately described	315,000
TOTAL	4,442,921*

* Males 3,518,680; Females 924,241.

Mid-1980 (estimates in '000): Agriculture, etc. 4,377; Total 5,695 (*Source: FAO, Production Yearbook*).

AGRICULTURE
LAND USE
('000 hectares)

	1973	1979
Arable land*	11,958	12,345
Land under permanent crops .	42	55*
Permanent meadows and pastures*	56,000	56,000
Forests and woodlands† . .	51,960	49,250
Other land	117,640	119,950
Inland water	12,981	12,981
TOTAL . .	250,581	250,581

* FAO estimates.   † Unofficial estimates.

Source: FAO, Production Yearbook.

PRINCIPAL CROPS
('000 metric tons)

	1978	1979	1980
Wheat . . .	317	177	231
Maize . . .	45	45†	45*
Millet . . .	507	550	450*
Sorghum (Durra) .	2,017	2,408	2,200*
Rice . . .	10	7*	7*
Sugar cane* . .	1,650	1,700	1,700
Potatoes* . .	25	25	25
Sweet potatoes* .	40	41	42
Cassava (Manioc) .	103	127	122
Other roots and tubers .	115	113	113
Onions . . .	34†	35†	35*
Water melons* . .	87	89	92
Dry beans . .	3	4	4*
Dry broad beans .	20†	21†	22*
Chick-peas . .	3†	3†	3*
Other pulses . .	56	55	54
Oranges and tangerines*	46	48	51
Lemons and limes* .	37	37	38
Grapefruit* . .	55	56	57
Mangoes* . .	4	4	5
Dates* . . .	110	110	113
Bananas* . .	86	88	90
Groundnuts (in shell) .	978	980†	960*
Seed cotton . .	648†	364†	317*
Cottonseed . .	420†	230†	200*
Cotton lint . .	223	131†	114†
Sesame seed . .	214	205†	200†
Castor beans* . .	10	10	10
Tomatoes* . .	145	145	147
Pumpkins, etc.* .	58	58	59
Aubergines* . .	76	76	77
Melons* . .	10	10	10

* FAO estimates.   † Unofficial estimate.

Source: FAO, Production Yearbook.

LIVESTOCK
('000 head, year ending September)

	1978	1979	1980
Cattle . . .	15,905	17,300	18,354
Sheep . . .	17,358	17,200	17,800†
Goats . . .	12,088	12,200	12,570†
Pigs* . . .	8	8	8
Horses* . . .	20	20	20
Asses* . . .	678	680	682
Camels . . .	2,408	2,500	2,500*
Chickens* . .	25,000	26,000	27,000

* FAO estimates.   † Unofficial estimate.

Source: FAO, Production Yearbook.

LIVESTOCK PRODUCTS
('000 metric tons)

	1978	1979	1980
Beef and veal . .	190*	193	208
Mutton and lamb* .	75	81	82
Goats' meat* . .	40	42	44
Poultry meat . .	18*	20	21
Other meat* . .	68	63	63
Cows' milk* . .	900	925	940
Sheep's milk* . .	123	123	125
Goats' milk* . .	370	380	387
Butter and ghee* .	11.7	11.9	12.2
Cheese* . . .	52.1	53.3	54.7
Hen eggs . . .	29.6	31.0*	33.0*
Wool: greasy* . .	15.0	15.0	15.2
clean* . .	6.2	6.2	6.3
Cattle hides* . .	24.2	24.5	26.5
Sheep skins* . .	10.8	11.5	11.8
Goat skins* . .	7.6	8.2	8.5

* FAO estimates.

Source: FAO, Production Yearbook.

FORESTRY
ROUNDWOOD REMOVALS
('ooo cubic metres, all non-coniferous)

	1972	1973	1974	1975	1976	1977	1978
Sawlogs, veneer logs and logs for sleepers	90	60	93	30	35	41	41*
Other industrial wood* . . .	1,254	1,295	1,319	1,361	1,405	1,450	1,450
Fuel wood*	27,166	27,888	28,631	29,415	30,226	31,069	31,941
Total	28,510	29,243	30,043	30,806	31,666	32,560	33,432*

* FAO estimate.

Source: FAO, Yearbook of Forest Products.

GUM ARABIC PRODUCTION
(tons)

	1972/73	1973/74	1974/75	1975/76
Gum kashab . . .	32,418	32,410	19,697	43,030
Gum talh .	2,649	3,804	1,107	888
Total . . .	35,067	36,214	20,804	43,918

Fishing (metric tons): Total catch 27,500 (inland waters 26,000, sea 1,500) in 1979.

Source: FAO, Yearbook of Fishery Statistics.

MINING
PRODUCTION
(estimates)

		1976	1977	1978	1979
Salt (unrefined) . .	'ooo metric tons	70	92	72	91
Chromium ore* .	" " "	11.4	8.8	9.4	9.4
Magnesite (crude) .	metric tons	100	100	n.a.	n.a.
Manganese ore* .	" "	200	200	200	200
Mica	" "	550	400	1,000	1,000
Gold ore* . .	kilogrammes	9	31	31	n.a.

* Figures refer to the metal content of ores.

Source: UN, Yearbook of Industrial Statistics.

INDUSTRY
PETROLEUM PRODUCTS
(estimates, 'ooo metric tons)

	1976	1977	1978	1979
Motor spirit . . .	110	130	128	131
Aviation gasoline .	10	8	14	12
Naphtha . . .	11	15	18	12
Jet fuels . . .	50	38	26	25
Kerosene . . .	37	37	25	28
Distillate fuel oils .	325	340	505	250
Residual fuel oils .	479	506	281	310
Liquefied petroleum gas .	6	6	5	4

Source: UN, Yearbook of Industrial Statistics.

OTHER PRODUCTS

		1975	1976	1977	1978
Cement	'ooo metric tons	218	158	178	171
Wheat flour	,, ,, ,,	223	237	267	275
Sugar*	,, ,, ,,	129	114	139	138
Soap*	,, ,, ,,	38.9	43.1	50.7	48.7
Wine	'ooo hectolitres	46	46	41	39
Beer	,, ,,	96	96	88	82
Cigarettes*	million	680	690	700	710
Canned fruit and vegetables* .	'ooo metric tons	2.5	2.4	2.0	2.0
Shoes	million pairs	13.4	14.4	12.4	13.6
Woven cotton fabrics . .	million sq. metres	103	n.a.	n.a.	n.a.
Electric energy . . .	million kWh.	640	720	810	911

* Estimates.

1979: Cement 172,000 metric tons; Cigarettes 720 million; Electric energy 900 million kWh.

Source: UN, *Yearbook of Industrial Statistics.*

FINANCE

1,000 millièmes = 100 piastres = 1 Sudanese pound (£S).
Coins: 1, 2, 5 and 10 millièmes; 2, 5 and 10 piastres.
Notes: 25 and 50 piastres; £S1, £S5, £S10 and £S20.

Exchange rates (May 1982): £1 sterling = £S1.655; U.S. $1 = 900 millièmes.
£S100 = £60.44 sterling = $111.11.

Note: The Sudanese pound was introduced in April 1957, replacing (at par) the Egyptian pound, valued at U.S. $2.87156 since September 1949. This valuation was maintained in Sudan until June 1978, despite two devaluations of the U.S. dollar (in December 1971 and February 1973). The Sudanese pound was devalued to U.S. $2.50 ($1 = 400 millièmes) in June 1978 and to $2.00 ($1 = 500 millièmes) in September 1979. From September 1979 a "parallel" rate of £S1 = $1.25 was introduced for specified imports and exports. In November 1981 the two-tier system was ended and a unified rate of $1 = 900 millièmes (£S1 = $1.11) established. The exchange rate was £1 sterling = 835.78 millièmes (£S1 = £1.1965 sterling) from November 1967 to August 1971; and £1 sterling = 907.42 millièmes (£S1 = £1.102 sterling) from December 1971 to June 1972.

BUDGET*
(£S million, twelve months ending June 30th)

REVENUE		1974/75	1975/76	EXPENDITURE		1974/75	1975/76
Income tax . . .		30.9	29.1	Education		8.6	10.3
Taxes on production and consumption . . .				Public health . . .		5.2	7.2
		63.0	72.6	Other social services . .		4.9	6.2
Stamp duty and other excise duties . . .				Agriculture and forestry .		6.5	8.1
				Public works . . .		1.3	2.3
Import duties . . .		88.9	77.0	Other economic services .		20.6	23.2
Export duties . . .		10.8	19.1	Defence		39.9	43.0
Transfer fees . . .		27.5	17.6	Settlement of loans . .		27.6	40.0
Development tax . .		10.9	10.2	General administration .		147.4	160.7
Gezira Board . . .		1.8	12.6	Internal security . .		2.0	3.0
Reimbursements and interdepartmental services .		9.9	8.6				
Sugar monopoly . .		—	12.1				
TOTAL (incl. others) .		287.8	337.3	TOTAL . . .		264.0	304.4

* Figures represent consolidated cash transactions covered in the Central Budget and the Development Budget.

1978/79: revenue £S686.1m.; expenditure, recurrent £S639.1m., development £S202.9m.

1979/80: revenue £S908.4m.; expenditure, recurrent £S816.7m., development £S284.8m.

1980/81: revenue £S1,005m.; expenditure £S1,347.5m.; development £S414m.

1981/82 (estimates): revenue £S1,731m.; expenditure £S1,568m.; development £S529m.

1982/83 (estimates): revenue £S1,343m.; expenditure £S1,910m.; development £S502m.

BALANCE OF PAYMENTS
(U.S. $ million)

	1975	1976	1977	1978	1979	1980
Merchandise exports f.o.b.	411.8	588.8	658.2	563.0	514.4	689.4
Merchandise imports f.o.b.	−743.2	−625.7	−644.1	−623.9	−736.7	−1,127.4
TRADE BALANCE	−331.4	−36.9	14.1	−60.9	−222.3	−438.0
Exports of services	102.4	119.8	166.3	244.7	324.9	341.2
Imports of services	−243.0	−268.3	−274.0	−292.3	−351.3	−324.4
BALANCE ON GOODS AND SERVICES	−472.0	−185.4	−93.6	−108.5	−248.7	−421.2
Private unrequited transfers (net)	−1.2	−0.6	−0.3	1.3	9.9	209.0
Government unrequited transfers (net)	46.7	20.4	19.8	14.0	—	16.6
CURRENT BALANCE	−426.5	−165.5	−74.1	−93.2	−238.8	−195.6
Long-term capital (net)	33.0	44.4	32.2	−3.5	270.3	81.2
Short-term capital (net)	53.2	−41.0	32.4	38.9	−71.6	−111.2
Net errors and omissions	−2.1	2.4	−1.7	17.1	−80.2	−77.6
TOTAL (net monetary movements)	−342.4	−159.7	−11.2	−40.7	−120.3	−303.2
Allocation of IMF Special Drawing Rights	—	—	—	—	11.8	12.1
Valuation changes (net)	−9.2	−1.0	−10.2	−12.2	4.4	4.7
IMF Subsidy Account grants	—	0.5	1.1	1.1	1.3	1.2
Balance-of-payments loans (net)	218.5	141.8	37.3	−17.1	45.9	128.2
IMF Trust Fund loans	—	—	—	37.8	28.4	4.4
Official financing (net)	—	—	—	—	—	17.2
CHANGES IN RESERVES	−133.1	−18.4	−17.0	−31.1	−28.5	−135.4

Source: IMF, *International Financial Statistics.*

EXTERNAL TRADE
(£S million)

	1972	1973	1974	1975	1976	1977	1978	1979	1980
Imports c.i.f.*	123.1	151.8	228.4	332.9	341.4	376.5	449.5	477.3	788.2
Exports f.o.b.†	125.5	152.2	122.0	152.5	193.0	230.2	202.3	232.7	271.3

* Excluding imports of crude petroleum (£S31,120,000 in 1976).
† Excluding exports of camels (£S2,420,000 in 1971).

PRINCIPAL COMMODITIES
(£S '000)

IMPORTS	1977	1978	1979
Sugar	13,440	18,930	20,479
Tea	6,551	17,398	6,185
Coffee	1,695	5	1,598
Wheat	6,490	8,825	22,007
Textiles	28,232	37,360	26,723
Footwear	160	88	50
Sacks and jute	3,577	4,544	5,300
Fertilizers	3,370	433	5,969
Machinery	125,619	111,955	100,796
Tyres	6,509	9,657	11,173
Petroleum products	44,354	49,953	71,889
Pharmaceuticals	10,156	14,527	10,581
Iron and steel	8,327	8,750	8,759
Transport equipment	39,659	57,510	70,956
Metal manufactures	20,759	32,855	42,217

EXPORTS	1977	1978	1979
Animals	4,538	8,310	7,102
Cotton, long-staple	100,044	71,209	93,658
Cotton, others	31,518	33,723	57,602
Cottonseed	} 2,717	1,607	1,635
Cottonseed cake and meal			
Sorghum (Durra)	4,767	2,664	13,524
Groundnuts	28,803	20,725	9,956
Groundnut cake and meal	2,927	3,773	4,307
Groundnut oil	3,138	7,479	3,556
Gum arabic	13,007	13,996	18,247
Hides and skins	4,361	3,900	3,680
Sesame seed	18,258	19,182	6,278
Sesame cake and meal	2,182	1,330	1,325
Sesame oil	34	1,225	460

PRINCIPAL TRADING PARTNERS
(£S '000)

	IMPORTS			EXPORTS		
	1977	1978	1979	1977	1978	1979
Belgium	12,486	12,271	10,938	2,517	2,211	2,190
China, People's Republic .	10,288	22,349	19,623	19,597	21,032	40,748
Egypt	4,816	9,043	15,228	2,399	12,445	5,179
France	29,710	36,454	33,524	12,993	14,998	8,465
Germany, Federal Republic . .	44,311	44,126	50,900	16,842	8,813	9,578
India	17,097	21,356	10,993	20,504	7,940	785
Iraq	39,459	33,212	6,899	708	349	49
Italy	16,754	24,573	19,725	28,376	27,159	30,672
Japan	39,989	29,317	30,445	17,960	16,578	16,278
Netherlands	10,705	14,085	8,417	5,829	4,988	3,259
Poland	1,351	1,516	4,274	5,036	4,782	2,959
U.S.S.R.	1,943	839	397	7,948	6,859	16,484
United Kingdom . . .	53,065	71,705	67,772	7,375	4,992	6,315
U.S.A.	24,349	32,686	39,439	5,068	4,642	5,683
Yugoslavia	3,010	4,075	7,470	13,537	12,207	14,545
TOTAL (incl. others) . .	376,484	449,464	477,318	230,181	202,341	232,667

Source: Bank of Sudan, Khartoum.

TOURISM

	1974	1975	1976	1977
Foreign tourist arrivals . .	24,886	30,675	39,452	26,714

TRANSPORT
RAILWAY TRAFFIC
(July 1st to June 30th)

	1977/78	1978/79	1979/80
Freight ton-km. (million) . .	2,004	1,821	2,620
Passenger-km. (million) . .	1,192	1,060	1,167

Source: Railway Gazette International: *Railway Directory and Yearbook.*

ROAD TRAFFIC
(motor vehicles in use)

	1970	1971	1972
Passenger Cars . . .	27,400	30,000	29,200
Commercial Vehicles . . .	16,500	18,000	21,200

Source: UN, *Statistical Yearbook.*

INTERNATIONAL SEA-BORNE SHIPPING
(Freight traffic at Port Sudan)

	1976	1977
Goods loaded ('000 metric tons)* . .	1,070	1,200
Goods unloaded ('000 metric tons)* .	2,534	2,600

* Estimates.

Source: UN, *Statistical Yearbook.*

CIVIL AVIATION
(scheduled services)

	1975	1976	1977	1978
Kilometres flown (million) . . .	7.5	7.7	9.9	10.1
Passengers carried ('000) . . .	250	265	379	410
Passenger-km. (million) . . .	320	345	555	600
Freight ton-km. (million) . . .	7.2	7.3	10.1	10.7

Source: UN, *Statistical Yearbook.*

EDUCATION
(1979/80)

	SCHOOLS	TEACHERS	STUDENTS
Pre-Primary	905	717	45,723
Primary	5,729	41,576	1,435,127
Intermediate . . .	1,388	11,584	285,606
Secondary: Academic . .	313	3,906	130,395
Technical . .	40	680	12,702
Teacher Training . .	20	665	4,388
Tertiary . . .	15	1,385	28,985

Source: Ministry of Education, Khartoum.

Source (unless otherwise stated): Department of Statistics, H.Q. Council of Ministers, Khartoum.

THE CONSTITUTION

A Provisional Constitution was introduced by the Revolutionary Command Council in August 1971. A People's Council, including various categories of the people's working forces, was called to draft and ratify a permanent constitution. It was endorsed by the People's Assembly in April 1973 as the Permanent Constitution of Sudan.

The President

The President must be a Sudanese of at least 35 years of age. He is nominated by the Sudanese Socialist Union, is Head of State, and is responsible for maintaining the Constitution. He may appoint Vice-Presidents, a Prime Minister and Ministers who are responsible to him. He is the Supreme Commander of the People's Armed Forces and Security Forces, and the Supreme Head of the Public Service.

If satisfied that a national crisis exists, the President may declare a State of Emergency, which may entail the suspension of any or all freedoms and rights under the Permanent Constitution other than that of resort to the courts. In the event of the President's death, the First Vice-President will temporarily assume office for a period not exceeding 60 days. Following the abortive coup of September 1975, a constitutional amendment was introduced which empowers the President to take any measures and decisions he sees as "suitable".

The People's Assembly

The duration of a sitting is four years and sittings are held in public. A quorum consists of half the number of members. Amendments to the Constitution may be proposed by the President or one third of the membership of the People's Assembly. An amendment to the Constitution must have a two-thirds majority of the People's Assembly and the assent of the President. The National People's Assembly had 151 seats after the December 1981 elections. There are 68 members elected for four years by

universal adult suffrage, 70 members nominated by workers and other groups and 13 appointed by the President.

Judiciary

The State is subject to the rule of law which is the basis of government. The judiciary is an independent body directly responsible to the President and judges are appointed by the President.

Religion

Unrestricted freedom of religion is allowed and mention is specifically made of the Islamic and Christian religions.

Regional Government

Under the Regional Constitution for the Southern Sudan, the southern provinces form a single region, with its own regional executive in Juba headed by a president. The regional executive is responsible for all matters except national defence, external affairs, economic and social development, education, currency and coinage, air and inter-regional river transport, communications and tele-communications, nationality and immigration, public audit, customs and foreign trade regulations except for border trade. The Regional President is appointed by and responsible to a Regional People's Assembly. The Assembly may postpone legislation of the central Government which it considers adverse to the interests of the South, though the President is not compelled to accede to its request. The Regional Constitution can be amended only by a four-fifths majority of the central People's Assembly, where southerners are represented. The Regional People's Assembly consists of 60 members of whom 30 represent the geographical areas, 21 the people's working forces alliance and 9 the administrative units. They are elected by direct secret ballot.

Regional Assemblies in the five new regions established in 1980 were set up in 1981.

THE GOVERNMENT

HEAD OF STATE

President, Prime Minister, and Minister of Defence: Field Marshal GAAFAR MOHAMMED NIMERI (assumed power as Chairman of the Revolutionary Command Council May 25th, 1969; inaugurated as President October 12th, 1971; re-elected April 1977).

Vice-President and Minister of National Security: Gen. OMAR MOHAMMED TAYIB.

Vice-President: Lt.-Gen. JOSEPH LAGU.

CABINET

(July 1982)

Minister of Finance and Economic Planning: IBRAHIM MONEIM MANSOUR.

Minister of Education and Guidance: Dr. OSMAN SIDAHMED ISMAIL.

Minister of Health: Dr. ALI MOHAMMED FADI.

Minister of Co-operation, Trade and Supply: FAROUQ IBRAHIM AL-MAGBOUL.

Minister of Industry: MOHAMMED AL-BASHIR AL-WAGI.

Minister of Transport and Communications: KHALID HASAN ABBAS.

Minister of Construction and Public Works: BABIKR ALI AL-TAWM.

Minister of Energy and Mining: Dr. MOHAMMED SHARIF AL-TUHAMI.

Minister of Agriculture and Irrigation: Dr. OSMAN ABDEL-RAHMAN HAKIM.

Ministers in the President's Office: BAHAEDDIN MOHAMMED IDRIS, KHALID AL-KHAYR OMAR.

Minister of Internal Affairs: AHMAD ABDEL-RAHMAN MOHAMMED.

Minister of Foreign Affairs: MOHAMMED MIRGHANI MUBARAK.

Minister in the Prime Minister's Office: ABU-BAKR MOHAMMED OSMAN SALEH.

Minister of Manpower Affairs: HAYDAR MOHAMMED QABSUN.

Minister of Legal Affairs: Dr. YUSUF MIKHAIL BAKHIT.

Minister of Decentralization Affairs: SHAIKH BASHIR AL-SHAIKH.

Minister of Press Affairs: MOHAMMED MAHJOUB SULAIMAN.

Attorney-General: Dr. HASAN ABDULLAH AL-TURABI.

MINISTERS OF STATE

Ministers of State for Finance and Economic Planning: BASHIR IBRAHIM OSMAN ISHAG, Dr. ABDEL-RAHMAN ABDEL WAHHAB.

Minister of State for Irrigation: SIGHAIROUN AL-ZEIN.

Minister of State for Energy and Mining: YUSUF SULAIMAN.

Minister of State for Internal Affairs: Dr. MOHAMMED OSMAN ABU SAG.

Minister of State for Co-operation, Trade and Supply: AHMAD SALIM AHMAD.

Minister of State for Cabinet Affairs: MOHAMMED AL-HASAN AHMAD AL-HAJ.

HIGH EXECUTIVE COUNCIL FOR THE SOUTHERN REGION

President: JAMES JOSEPH TOMBURA.

Vice-President and Regional Minister of Legal Affairs: DAHOL ACHUOL.

Regional Minister of Finance and Economic Planning: OTHWAN DAK.

Regional Minister of Education and Guidance: PHILIP OBANG OYWAY.

Regional Minister of Agriculture and Natural Resources: AJO DIBI.

Regional Minister of Health and Social Welfare: NAKANWARA MANOK.

Regional Minister of Housing and Public Utilities: ARKANJO LUKWAK.

Regional Minister of Transport and Communications: SUZI MUWANE.

Regional Minister of Culture and Information: FARUQ AKASHAH.

Regional Minister of Co-operation and Rural Development: JOHN WUL.

Regional Minister of Conservation of Wildlife and Tourist Resources: HABAKUK SWORO.

Regional Minister of Public Services and Manpower: SAMUEL RENZI.

Regional Minister of Decentralized Government: CHARLES KOT KAFANI.

Regional Minister of Trade and Supply: NICOLO ABUYA.

Regional Minister of Mining and Industry: DANIEL MATHIEL.

Regional Minister of Co-operation in Khartoum: KORMIU LUKROM.

Regional Minister of High Executive Council Affairs: FRANCIS WAGU.

Adviser for Political Affairs: LASPIKU MADOMU.

Adviser for Local People's Government: WADANE BASHIR.

PEOPLE'S ASSEMBLIES

NATIONAL PEOPLE'S ASSEMBLY

The National People's Assembly has 151 members: 68 elected for four years by universal adult suffrage, 70 representatives of peasant, worker, military and professional groups and 13 appointed by the President. The Assembly was opened in May 1974. In the elections of December 1981 only candidates approved by the SSU were allowed to stand.

Speaker: IZZEDIN AS-SAYYID.

Leader: BADDREDIN SULAIMAN.

SOUTHERN REGION PEOPLE'S ASSEMBLY

The Assembly was opened in 1973. The latest elections were in June 1982. Represents the Southern Region; sits in Juba.

Chairman: MATTHEW ABOR AYANG.

Leader: ZACHARIA POL.

POLITICAL ORGANIZATION

Sudanese Socialist Union (SSU): P.O.B. 1850, Khartoum; f. 1972; only recognized political organization; Pres. Field Marshal GAAFAR MOHAMMED NIMERI; Sec.-Gen. Col. AWAD MALIK.

There are four Assistant Secretaries-General.

Political Bureau of the SSU:

All senior party committees were suspended in January 1982 and a 41-member group, chaired by President Nimeri, was set up to revitalize the party's policy-making organs.

ABEL ALIER
ZEIN EL ABDIN MOHAMMED AHMED ABDEL GADIR
KHALID HASSAN ABBAS
OMAR MOHAMMED TAYIB
EL RASHID EL TAHIR BAKR
BADDREDIN SULAIMAN
DR. AHMAD AS-SAYED HAMAD
AYN ASH-SHARIF QASIM
DR. ISMAIL HAG MUSA
DR. HASAN ABDULLAH TURABI
ABDEL-RAHMAN MOHAMMED
HAMID ALI SHASH
EL FATIH MOHAMED BASHIR BUSHARA
AHMAD IBRAHIM DERIEG
PROF. ABDULLAH HAMAD ABDULLAH
PETER GATKOUTH GUAL
HILARY LOGALI
BONA MALWAL
LT.-GEN. JOSEPH LAGU
NAFISAH AHMAD AL-AMIN

Sudanese National Front: London; coalition of exiled opposition groups; Leader (vacant).

Sudanese Progressive Front: Beirut; leftist, anti-Nimeri.

DIPLOMATIC REPRESENTATION

EMBASSIES ACCREDITED TO SUDAN
(In Khartoum unless otherwise stated)

Afghanistan: Cairo, Egypt.

Algeria: Junction El Mek Nimr St. and 67th St., P.O.B. 80; *Ambassador:* (vacant).

Australia: Cairo, Egypt.

Austria: Cairo, Egypt.

Belgium: Sharia El Mek Nimr, House No. 4, P.O.B. 969; *Ambassador:* J. M. MELSENS.

Bulgaria: El Mek Nimr St. South 7, P.O.B. 1690; *Ambassador:* IVAN MARINOV GUNINSKI.

Canada: Cairo, Egypt.

Central African Republic: Africa Rd., P.O.B. 1723; *Ambassador:* GILBERT MARIUS BANDIO.

Chad: St. 17, New Extension, P.O.B. 1514; *Ambassador:* MOULI SAID.

China, People's Republic: 69 31st St., P.O.B. 1425; *Ambassador:* SONG HANYI.

Czechoslovakia: Plot 5 Ge, House no. 39, P.O.B. 1047; *Ambassador:* LADISLAV LENGYEL.

Denmark: P.O.B. 2758; *Chargé d'affaires a.i.:* S. KUCHLER POULSEN.

Egypt: Mogram St.; *Ambassador:* AHMAD IZZAT ABDUL LATIF.

Ethiopia: 6, 11A St. 3, New Extension, P.O.B. 844; *Ambassador:* YILMA TADESSE.

Finland: Cairo, Egypt.

France: Junction 19th St. and Ali Dinar St., Block 6H East Plot 2, P.O.B. 377; *Ambassador:* ROBERT HOURCAILLOU.

German Democratic Republic: P4 (3) B2, Khartoum West, P.O.B. 1089; *Ambassador:* LOTHAR EICHELKRAUT.

Germany, Federal Republic: 53 El Baladiya Ave., Block No. 8 D.E., P.O.B. 970; *Ambassador:* FRANZ Freiherr VON MENTZINGEN.

Greece: Block 74, 31st Ave., P.O.B. 1182; *Ambassador:* Dr. DEMETRE YIANNOPOULOS.

Hungary: Block 11, Plot 12, 13th St., New Extension, P.O.B. 1033; *Ambassador:* KÁROLY HACKLER.

India: El Mek Nimr St., P.O.B. 707; *Ambassador:* S. M. S. CHADHA.

Indonesia: Cairo, Egypt.

Iran: El Baladiya Ave. (*Embassy closed June* 1982.)

Italy: 39th St., P.O.B. 793; *Ambassador:* GIULIO BILANCIONI.

Japan: House no. 24, Block 10AE, St. 3, P.O.B. 1646; *Ambassador:* TOMIZO ARIMOTO.

Jordan: 25 7th St., New Extension; *Ambassador:* NAJI ABDA AL-AZIZ.

Korea, Democratic People's Republic: 2-10 BE, 7th St., New Extension, P.O.B. 332; *Ambassador:* CHAN YOURAN.

Korea, Republic: House 2, St. 1, New Extension, P.O.B. 2414; *Ambassador:* DONG KUN KIM.

Kuwait: 9th St., New Extension; *Ambassador:* MOHAMMED SALEM EL BALHEN.

Lebanon: 60, St. 49; *Ambassador:* IBRAHIM MARDOUCHE.

Libya: Africa Rd. 50, P.O.B. 2091; *Secretary of People's Bureau:* ABDULLAH AL-AZRAQ.

Morocco: 32, 19th St.; *Ambassador:* ABDEL LATIF LAKHMIRI.

Netherlands: P.O.B. 391; *Chargé d'affaires a.i.:* F. B. A. M. VAN HAREN.

Niger: St. 1, New Extension, P.O.B. 1283; *Ambassador:* El Haj OMAROU AMADOU.

Nigeria: P.O.B. 1538; *Ambassador:* (vacant).

Norway: Cairo, Egypt.

Oman: *Ambassador:* ISA MUHAMMAD ALI.

Pakistan: House no. 6, Block 12AE, St. 3, New Extension, P.O.B. 1178; *Ambassador:* A. A. CHOWDURY.

Poland: 73 Africa Rd., P.O.B. 902; *Ambassador:* ANTONI PIERZCHALA (resident in Cairo, Egypt).

Qatar: St. 15, New Extension; *Ambassador:* (vacant).

Romania: St. 47, Plot 67, P.O.B. 1652; *Ambassador:* (vacant).

Saudi Arabia: Central St., New Extension, P.O.B. 852; *Ambassador:* HASAN ABDULLAH AL-QURASI.

Senegal: Cairo, Egypt.

Somalia: Central St., New Extension; *Ambassador:* JAALLE MOHAMED HAGI NUIR.

Spain: Street 3, New Extension, P.O.B. 2621; *Ambassador:* JOSÉ MANUEL DEL MORAL Y GRACIA SAEZ.

Sri Lanka: Cairo, Egypt.

Switzerland: New Aboulela Bldg. P.O.B. 1707; *Chargé d'affaires:* AUGUST R. DISSLER.

Syria: 3rd St., New Extension; *Chargé d'affaires a.i.:* ABDEL KARIM.

Tanzania: P.O.B. 6080; *Ambassador:* WILLIAM MBAGO.

Tunisia: Cairo, Egypt.

Turkey: 71 Africa Rd., P.O.B. 771; *Chargé d'affaires:* DARJAL BATIBAY.

Uganda: Excelsior Hotel, Room 408/410; *Ambassador:* OMAR MATARE.

U.S.S.R.: B1, A10 St., New Extension, P.O.B. 1161; *Ambassador:* VLADISLAV ZHUKOV.

United Arab Emirates: St. 3, New Extension; *Ambassador:* MOHAMED MUSBAH KHALAFAN.

United Kingdom: New Aboulela Bldg., P.O.B. 801; *Ambassador:* RICHARD ALWYNE FYJIS-WALKER.

U.S.A.: Sharia Ali Abdel-Latif; *Ambassador:* C. WILLIAM KONTOS.

Vatican: El Safeh City, Shambat, P.O.B. 623; *Apostolic Pro-Nuncio:* GIOVANNI MORETTI.

Yemen Arab Republic: St. 35, New Extension; *Ambassador:* YAHYA ABDEL RAHMAN AL-ARYAN.

Yemen, People's Democratic Republic: St. 51, New Extension; *Chargé d'affaires a.i.:* ABDEL MALIK ISMAIL.

Yugoslavia: St. 31, 79-A, Khartoum 1, P.O.B. 1180; *Ambassador:* ISNET REDZIĆ.

Zaire: Gamhouria Ave.; *Ambassador:* KUTENDAKANA PUBULU.

Sudan also has diplomatic relations with Argentina, Bahrain, Bangladesh, Brazil, Burundi, Cameroon, Chile, Cuba, Cyprus, Djibouti, Gabon, Ghana, Guinea, Iraq, the Ivory Coast, Kenya, Liberia, Malaysia, Maldives, Mali, Malta, Mauritania, Mauritius, Mozambique, Portugal, Sweden, Thailand, Togo, Viet-Nam and Zambia.

JUDICIAL SYSTEM

The administration of justice is the function of the judiciary, as a separate and independent department of state. The judiciary is formed of two divisions, the Civil Division, headed by the Chief Justice, and the Sharia (Islamic Law) Division, headed by the Grand Kadi. The general administrative supervision and control of the judiciary is vested in the Higher Judiciary Council headed by the President of the Republic. The members are the Chief Justice, who is also the President of the Supreme Court, the Grand Kadi, the Minister of Public Service and Administrative Reform, the Minister of Finance and Economics, the Attorney General, the deputies of the Chief Justice, the deputy Grand Kadi and the Dean of the Faculty of Law of the University of Khartoum. If the President does not preside, nor deputes one of the Vice-Presidents to preside, then the Chief Justice does so, as is often the case.

Civil Justice: is administered by the courts constituted under the 1976 Judiciary Act, namely the Supreme Court, Courts of Appeal and Other Courts. The Supreme Court consists of a president (the Chief Justice), his deputies, the Grand Kadi and his deputy and sufficient judges of the Supreme Court. It is the custodian of the constitution under the Permanent Constitution of Sudan of 1973. The powers and jurisdiction of the courts are defined by the Code of Civil Procedure of 1974.

Criminal Justice: is administered by the courts constituted under the 1976 Judiciary Act, namely Major

Courts and Magistrates' Courts, and their powers and jurisdiction are defined by the Criminal Procedure Code of 1974. Serious crimes are tried by Major Courts which are composed of a president and two members and have power to pass the death sentence. Major Courts are as a rule presided over by a magistrate of the First Class. There is a right of appeal against any decision or order of a Major Court and findings of guilty of murder and sentences of death or life imprisonment are subject to confirmation by the Supreme Court.

Lesser crimes are tried by Magistrates' Courts consisting of a single magistrate, or a bench of magistrates.

Local People's Courts: constituted under the 1976 Local People's Court Act to try a substantial portion of criminal and civil cases and work to some extent with the State Courts.

Chief Justice and President of the Supreme Court: KHALAFALLA EL RASHEED.

SHARIA (ISLAMIC LAW) COURTS

Justice in personal matters for the Muslim population is administered by the courts constituted under the 1976 Judiciary Act. These courts consist of panels of judges in personal matters. The religious Law of Islam is administered by these courts in matters of inheritance, marriage, divorce, family relationships and charitable trusts.

Grand Kadi: SAID AHMED EL AWAD.

Chairman of the Fatwa: SADIQ ABDEL HAY.

RELIGION

The majority of the northern Sudanese population are followers of Islam, while in the South the population is mostly either Animist or Christian. It is estimated that there are more than 9 million Muslims and over 500,000 Catholics. The Government plans to create a Sudanese National Church.

CHRISTIAN COMMUNITIES

Catholic Church:
  Roman Rite:
    Archbishop of Khartoum: P.O.B. 49, Khartoum; Most Rev. GABRIEL ZUBEIR WAKO.

    Archbishop of Juba: P.O.B. 32, Juba; Most Rev. IRENEUS WIEN DUD.

  Maronite Church: P.O.B. 244, Khartoum; Rev. Fr. YOUSEPH NEAMA.

  Greek Catholic Church: P.O.B. 766, Khartoum; Bishop PAUL ANTAKI (Egypt); Vicar ANTOINE LATIF SABBAGH (Sudan).

Coptic Orthodox Church: Bishop of Nubia, Atbara and Omdurman: Rt. Rev. BAKHOMIOS.
Bishop of Khartoum, Southern Sudan and Uganda: Rt. Rev. ANBA YOUANNIS.

Episcopal Church of the Sudan: Clergy House, P.O.B. 110, Juba; Archbishop in Sudan: The Most Rev. ELINANA JABI NGALAMU.

Evangelical Church: P.O.B. 57, Khartoum; Chair. Rev. RADI ELIAS; about 1,500 mems.; runs schools, literature centre and training centre; publ. *El Marifa*.

Greek Orthodox Church: Metropolitan of Nubia: Archbishop SINESSIOS.

Greek Evangelical Church.

Presbyterian Church: Malakal.

Sudan Council of Churches: P.O.B. 469, Khartoum; f. 1972; Gen. Sec. Rev. CLEMENT JANDA; 12 churches.

Sudan Interior Mission: P.O.B. 220, Khartoum; f. 1937; Society of International Missionaries; 30 mems.

THE PRESS

The Press was nationalized in August 1970. A General Corporation for Press, Printing and Publications was set up. The two main publishing houses are El-Ayam and El-Sahafa. These two houses publish most of the following newspapers and magazines.

DAILIES

El-Ayam: P.O.B. 363, Khartoum; f. 1953; Arabic; Chair. MAHGOUB ALI MOHAMED; Editor-in-Chief HASSAN SATTI; circ. 50–60,000.

El-Sahafa: P.O.B. 1228, Khartoum; f. 1961; Arabic; Chair. Dr. AWN EL SHARIF QASIM; Editor-in-Chief Dr. HASSAN ABDIEN; circ. 50–60,000.

PERIODICALS

El-Eza'a: P.O.B. 522, Khartoum; f. 1942; cultural affairs, particularly radio, television and theatre; Arabic; weekly; Sudan Broadcasting Service Magazine; publ. by the Government; Editor ABDULLAHI GALLAB; circ. 40,000.

El Guwat El Musallaha: f. 1969; armed forces publications, comprising a weekly newspaper and monthly magazine; Editor-in-Chief Maj. MAHMOUD GALANDER; circ. 25–30,000.

El Kibar: Arabic; monthly; publ. by Ministry of Education.

Khartoum: Arabic; monthly; publ. by the Government.

Kordofan: weekly; local events in Kordofan Province; Editor-in-Chief MUSA EL MUBARAK.

Nile Mirror: P.O.B. 126, Juba; f. 1970; English; weekly; publ. by the Government for the Southern Region; Man. Editor SIMON GAIKU.

Sudanow: P.O.B. 2651, Khartoum; f. 1976; English; monthly; political and economic affairs; publ. by the Government; Editor-in-Chief FATH EL RAHMAN MAHGOUB; circ. 15,000.

Sudan Standard: P.O.B. 15, Khartoum; English; two a week; publ. by El-Ayam Publishing and Printing House; Editor-in-Chief MEKKI AWAD EL NUR.

Youth and Sports: P.O.B. 2361, Khartoum; Arabic; publ. by the Ministry of Youth and Sports.

NEWS AGENCIES

Sudan News Agency (SUNA): P.O.B. 1506, Gamhouria Ave., Khartoum; Editor-in-Chief MUSTAFA AMIN ISMAIL.

FOREIGN BUREAUX

Middle East News Agency (MENA) (*Egypt*): Dalala Bldg., P.O.B. 740, Khartoum.

The Iraqi News Agency, the Syrian News Agency, TASS (U.S.S.R.) and Xinhua (People's Republic of China) also have bureaux in Khartoum.

PUBLISHERS

Ahmed Abdel Rahman El Tikeine: P.O.B. 299, Port Sudan.

El-Ayam Publishing and Printing House: Aboul Ela Bldg., United Nations Square, P.O.B. 363, Khartoum; f. 1953; Man. Dir. BESHIR MUHAMMAD SAID; newspapers, pamphlets and books.

El-Sahafa Publishing and Printing House: P.O.B. 1228, Khartoum; f. 1961; newspapers, pamphlets, government publications and short stories.

El-Salam Co. Ltd.: P.O.B. 944, Khartoum.

Claudios S. Fellas: P.O.B. 641, Khartoum.

Government Printer: P.O.B. 38, Khartoum; government publishing office; publications include the *Sudan Almanac*.

Khartoum University Press: P.O.B. 321, Khartoum; f.1967; academic, general and educational publishing; Man. Dir. EL-FATIH MAHGOUB.

RADIO AND TELEVISION

Sudan Broadcasting Service: P.O.B. 572, Omdurman; a government-controlled radio station which broadcasts daily in Amharic, Arabic, English, French, Somali and Tigringa; Dir. M. AWAD ALLAM.

There were an estimated 1,330,000 radio sets in 1981.

An earth satellite station operated on 36 channels at Umm Haraz has much improved Sudan's telecommunication links. A nationwide satellite network is being established with 14 earth stations in the provinces.

Sudan Television Service: P.O.B. 1094, Omdurman; f. 1962; government-owned; 35 hours of programmes per week; Dir. M. A. EL NUR.

There were an estimated 105,000 television receivers in 1981.

A microwave network to extend television transmission was begun in 1975. There is a second station at Gezira and further stations are planned at Atbarah and Port Sudan.

FINANCE

BANKING

(cap. = capital; p.u. = paid up; res. = reserves; dep. = deposits; m. = million; br. = branch; £S = Sudanese pound).

Under the Nationalization of Banks Act 1970, all banks have been nationalized and converted into limited companies controlled by the Bank of Sudan. Foreign banks were permitted to resume operations in Sudan in 1976.

CENTRAL BANK

Bank of Sudan: Sharia Gamaa, P.O.B. 313, Khartoum; f. 1960; acts as banker and financial adviser to the Government and has sole right of issue of Sudanese banknotes; cap. £S3m.; res. £S1m. (1980); Gov. MAHDI EL-FEKI; Deputy Gov. HASSAN BESHIR; 30 brs.

COMMERCIAL BANKS

Bank of Khartoum: 8 Gamhouria Ave., P.O.B. 1008, Khartoum; f. 1913; formerly Barclays Bank International; former State Bank of Foreign Trade; cap. p.u. £S3m.; dep. £S239.2m. (1980); Chair. of Board ALI HASSAN ABDALLA; Deputy Chair. and Gen. Man. SALIH MOHAMED ALI SAKRAN; 34 brs.

El Nilein Bank: Sharia el Parlaman, Sharia Khalifa, P.O.B. 466, Khartoum; f. 1965; formerly Crédit Lyonnais; authorized cap. £S5.0m.; cap. p.u. £S4.5m.; dep. £S89.1m.; Chair. SAHED BASHER IBRAHIM ISHAG; Gen. Man. MOHAMED SALIH YAHYA; 21 brs.

People's Co-operative Bank: P.O.B. 922, Khartoum; f. 1970; formerly the Misr Bank; deals with all operations and facilities of the Sudan co-operative movement; cap. p.u. £S2.3m.; dep. £S26.5m.; Chair. KARAMALLA AL-AWAD; Gen. Man. ABDEL RAHMAN SID AHMED; 10 brs. and sub-brs.

Sudan Commercial Bank: Kasr Ave., P.O.B. 1116, Khartoum; f. 1960; cap. p.u. £S2.0m.; dep. £S49.4m. (1979); Chair. MOHAMED IDRIS ABDALLA; Deputy Chair. and Gen. Man. ABDEL-GADIR MANSOUR; 9 brs. and 4 sub-brs.

Unity Bank: P.O.B. 408, Barlman Ave., Khartoum; f. 1970; formerly Juba-Omdurman Commercial Bank; cap. £S1.5m.; dep. £S180m. (1980); Chair. MAKI EL MANA.

FOREIGN BANKS

Bank of Credit and Commerce International SA (*Luxembourg*): P.O.B. 5, Khartoum; dep. £S5.0m. (July 1977); Gen. Man. ASHRAF KHAN.

Chase Manhattan Bank (*U.S.A.*): P.O.B. 2679, Khartoum.

Citibank N.A. (*U.S.A.*): P.O.B. 2743, Khartoum.

Faisal Islamic Bank (*Saudi Arabia*): P.O.B. 2415, Khartoum; cap. p.u. £S3.7m.; dep. £S35m. (May 1980); Gen. Man. E. Y. MUDAWI.

National Bank of Abu Dhabi (*United Arab Emirates*): P.O.B. 2465, Khartoum; f. 1976; dep. £S3.5m.; Gen. Man. AHMED ALABED.

DEVELOPMENT BANKS

Agricultural Bank of Sudan: P.O.B. 1363, Khartoum; f. 1957; cap. p.u. £S15m.; provides facilities for approved agricultural projects; 22 brs.

Arab-Africa Bank: P.O.B. 2721, Khartoum; Man. (vacant).

Arab Bank for Economic Development in Africa: P.O.B. 2640, Khartoum; f. 1973; cap. U.S. $738.3m.; membership comprises 18 Arab states; Pres. and Dir.-Gen. Dr. CHEDLY AYARI; Deputy Gen. Man. Dr. OMAR MOHAMED OSMAN.

Industrial Bank of Sudan: UN Square, P.O.B. 1722, Khartoum; f. 1961; cap. p.u. £S4m.; to provide technical and financial assistance for the establishment, expansion and modernization of industrial projects in the private sector and to acquire shares in industrial enterprises; Chair. and Gen. Man. HASSAN AHMED MEKKI.

Sudanese Estates Bank: El Baladiya Ave., P.O.B. 309, Khartoum; cap. £S10m.; mortgage bank to finance urban housing development in the private sector; Chair. and Man. Dir. MOHAMED MEKKI KANANI.

INSURANCE COMPANIES

African Insurance Co. (Sudan) Ltd.: El Baladiya Ave., Mohamed Hussein Bldg., P.O.B. 149, Khartoum; f. 1977; fire, accident, marine and motor; Gen. Man. ELNOMAN ELSANUSI.

Blue Nile Insurance Co. (Sudan) Ltd.: P.O.B. 2215, Khartoum; Gen. Man. MOHAMMED EL AMIN MIRGHANI.

General Insurance Co. (Sudan) Ltd.: El Mek Nimr St., P.O.B. 1555, Khartoum; Gen. Man. MOHAMMED TAWFIQ AHMED.

Islamic Insurance Co. Ltd.: Abu Sium St., P.O.B. 2776, Khartoum; all kinds.

Khartoum Insurance Co. Ltd.: P.O.B. 737, Khartoum; Gen. Man. H. MYRIALLIS.

Sudanese Insurance and Re-insurance Co. Ltd.: Sharia Jamhouriya, Nasr Sq., P.O.B. 2332, Khartoum; Gen. Man. IZZEL-DIN EL SAYED MOHAMMED.

United Insurance Co. (Sudan) Ltd.: Makkawi Bldg., Gamhouria Ave., P.O.B. 318, Khartoum; Man. Dir. HASIM EL BIREIR; Gen. Man. SEIF EL DIN YOUSIF.

TRADE AND INDUSTRY

Animal Production Corporation: P.O.B. 624, Khartoum; Gen. Man. Dr. MUSTAFA BEDAWI BASHIR.

Agricultural Research Corporation: P.O.B. 126, Wad Medani; Gen. Man. HAMID BURHAN.

Cotton Public Corporation: P.O.B. 1672, Khartoum; f. 1970; supervises all cotton marketing operations; Chair. and Gen. Man. BESHIR IBRAHIM ISHAQ; publs. *Sudan Cotton Bulletin* (monthly), *Sudan Cotton Review* (annual).

> **Alaktan Trading Co.:** P.O.B. 2067, Khartoum; Gen. Man. ABDEL RAHMAN ABDEL MONEIM.

> **National Cotton and Trade Co. Ltd.:** P.O.B. 1552, Khartoum; Gen. Man. ZIBAIR MOHAMED EL BASHIR.

> **Port Sudan Cotton Trade Co. Ltd.:** P.O.B. 590, Khartoum and P.O.B. 261, Port Sudan; Gen. Man. SAYED MOHAMED ADAM.

> **Sudan Cotton Co. Ltd.:** P.O.B. 2284, Khartoum; Gen. Man. GAAFAR SIREL KHATIM OSMAN.

Gum Arabic Company: P.O.B. 857, Khartoum; f. 1969; Chair. FUAD MOHAMMED ABU EL ELA; Gen. Man. OSMAN MOHAMMED EL HASSAN.

Industrial Production Corporation: P.O.B. 1034, Khartoum; Dir.-Gen. OSMAN TAMMAM; Deputy Chair. ABDEL LATIF WIDATALLA; incorporates:

> **Building Materials and Refractories Corporation:** P.O.B. 2241, Khartoum; Dir. MAGZOUB EL SHOUSH.

> **Food Industries Corporation:** P.O.B. 2341, Khartoum; Dir. MOHAMED EL GHALI SULIMAN.

> **Leather Industries Corporation:** P.O.B. 1639, Khartoum; Gen. Man. ALI ABDEL HAMID.

> **Oil Corporation:** P.O.B. 64, Khartoum North; Gen. Man. BUKHARI MAHMOUD BUKHARI.

> **Public Corporation for Textile Industries:** P.O.B. 765, Khartoum; f. 1975; Dir. MOHAMED SALIH MOHAMED ABDELLA.

> **Sudan Tea Co.:** P.O.B. 1219, Khartoum.

> **Sudanese Mining Corporation:** P.O.B. 1034, Khartoum; Dir. IBRAHIM MUDAWI.

> **Sugar and Distilling Industry Corporation:** P.O.B. 511, Khartoum; Man. MIRGHANI AHMED BABIKER.

Mechanized Farming Corporation: P.O.B. 2482, Khartoum; Man. Dir. AWAD EL KARIEM EL YASS.

Petroleum Public Corporation: Khartoum; f. 1976; Chair. Dr. AMIN ABU SINEINA; Gen. Man. Dr. OMER EL-SHEIKH OMER.

Public Agricultural Production Corporation: P.O.B. 538, Khartoum; Chair. and Man. Dir. ABDALLA BAYOUMO; Sec. SAAD EL DIN MOHAMMED ALI.

Public Corporation for Building and Construction: P.O.B. 2110, Khartoum; Dir. NAEIM ELDIN.

Public Corporation for Irrigation and Excavations: P.O.B. 123, Wad Medani; Gen. Sec. OSMAN EL NUR.

Public Corporation for Oil Products and Pipelines: P.O.B. 1704, Khartoum; Gen. Man. ABDEL RAHMAN SULIMAN.

Public Electricity Corporation: P.O.B. 1380, Khartoum.

Public Water Corporation: P.O.B. 1380, Khartoum.

Rahad Corporation: P.O.B. 2523, Khartoum; financed by the World Bank, Kuwait and the U.S.A.; designed to irrigate 820,000 acres and settle 70,000 people in 15,000 tenancies; Man. Dir. IBRAHIM MOHAMMED IBRAHIM.

The State Trading Corporation: P.O.B. 211, Khartoum; Chair. and Man. Dir. MUBARAK MAHGOUB LOGMAN (acting).

Automobile Corporation: P.O.B. 314, Khartoum; importer of vehicles and spare parts; Gen. Man. DAFALLA AHMED SIDDIG.

Engineering Equipment Corporation: P.O.B. 97, Khartoum; importers and distributors of agricultural, engineering and electronic equipment; Gen. Man. EZD DIN HAMID.

Silos and Storage Corporation: P.O.B. 1183, Khartoum; stores and handles agricultural products; Gen. Man. AHMED EL TAIEB HARHOOF.

Trade and Services Corporation: P.O.B. 215, Khartoum; largest importer of general merchandise and services in storage, shipping and insurance; Gen. Man. BUKHARI ABDALLA.

Sudan Gezira Board: H.Q. Barakat Wad Medani; Sales Office, P.O.B. 884, Khartoum; responsible for Sudan's main cotton producing area; the Gezira Scheme is a partnership between the Government, the tenants and the Board. The Government, which provides the land and is responsible for irrigation, receives 36 per cent of the net proceeds; the tenants, about 100,000 in 1976, receive 49 per cent. The Board receives 10 per cent, the local Government Councils in the Scheme area 2 per cent and the Social Development Fund, set up to provide social services for the inhabitants, 3 per cent. This system was to be replaced in July 1981 by a land and water charge to be paid by tenants who were to receive the work proceeds. The role of the Board would be to provide agricultural services at cost, technical supervision and execution of government agricultural policies relating to the Gezira scheme. Tenants were to continue to pay a percentage of their proceeds to the Social Development Fund. The Scheme was to retain its main objectives as an integrated socio-economic enterprise. The total possible cultivable area of the Gezira Scheme is over 5 million acres and the total area under systematic irrigation is now 2.3 million acres. In addition to cotton, groundnuts, sorghum, wheat, rice, pulses and vegetables are grown for the benefit of tenant farmers; Man. Dir. ABDEL-AZIM MOHAMMED HUSSAIN.

Sudanese Industries Association: P.O.B. 2565, Khartoum; Chair. FATHELRAHMAN EL BASHIR; Exec. Dir. A. IZZELARAB YOUSIF.

Sudan Oilseeds Co. Ltd.: P.O.B. 167, Khartoum; f. 1974; 58 per cent government-owned; exporter of oilseeds (groundnuts, sesame seeds and castor beans); Gen. Man. MOHAMMED KAILANI.

Sugar Trading Corporation: P.O.B. 1209, Omdurman; f. 1974; Gen. Man. TAHA SALIH SHARIEF.

CHAMBER OF COMMERCE

Sudan Chamber of Commerce: P.O.B. 81, Khartoum; f. 1908; Pres. SAAD ABOUL ELA; Sec.-Gen. MOHAMED HASSAN ABDALLA.

DEVELOPMENT CORPORATIONS

Sudan Development Corporation (SDC): 69 Africa Rd., P.O.B. 710, Khartoum; f. 1974 to promote and co-finance development projects with special emphasis on projects in the agricultural, agri-business, and industrial sectors, within the framework of the Government's overall development planning; cap. p.u. U.S. $200m.; Chair. and Man. Dir. MOHAMED ABDEL MAGID AHMED; Deputy Chair. and Deputy Man. Dir. MAMOUN MOHAMED EL SAYED.

Sudan Rural Development Finance Co.: Khartoum; f. 1981; SDC has 40 per cent shareholding; cap. p.u. U.S. $12.5m.; Gen. Man. HARRY DE WAAL (acting).

TRADE UNIONS

In 1971 all existing trade unions were dissolved and reconstituted according to the 1971 Trade Unions Act.

Secretary-General of Trade Unions: ABDEL MONIEM HASSAN MEDANI.

FEDERATIONS

Sudan Workers Trade Unions Federation (SWTUF): P.O.B. 2258, Khartoum; includes 38 Trade Unions of public service workers and workers of the private sector with a total membership of roughly 480,000 members; affiliated to the International Confederation of Arab Trade Unions and the Organization of African Trade Union Unity; Pres. ABDALLA NASR GINAWI; Exec. Sec. MUHIE-DIEN BAKHIET.

Agricultural Sector Workers' Trade Union: Workers' Club, Khartoum North; Pres. AWAD WIDATALLA; Sec. MOHAMMED OSMAN SALIM; 30,000 mems.

Gezira Scheme Workers' Trade Union: Barakat; Pres. IBRAHIM MOHAMMED AHMED EL SHEIKH; Sec. EL SIR ABDOON; 11,500 mems.

Health Workers' Trade Union: Khartoum Civil Hospital, Khartoum; Pres. Dr. HARITH HAMED; Sec. GAAFAR MOHAMMED SID AHMED; 25,000 mems.

Local Government Workers' Trade Union: Workers' Union, Khartoum; 25,000 mems.; Pres. ISMAIL MOHAMMED FADL; Sec. SALEM BEDRI HUMAM.

Post, Telegraph and Telephone Workers' Trade Union: Workers' Club, Khartoum; 8,463 mems.; Pres. MANSOUL EL MANNA; Sec. YASSIN ABDEL GALIL.

Public Service Workers' Trade Union: El Baladiya Ave., Khartoum; 19,800 mems.; Pres. MOHIE EDDIN BAKHEIT; Sec. ALI IDRIS EL HUSSEIN.

Railway Workers' Trade Union: Railway Workers' Club, Atbara; 32,000 mems.; Pres. MOHAMMED EL HASSAN ABDALLA; Sec. OSMAN ALI FADL.

Sudan Irrigation Workers' Trade Union: Ministry of Education, Wad Medani; 19,150 mems.; Pres. MOHAMMED HABIB; Sec. MOHAMMED AHMED.

Taxi Workers' Trade Union: Workers' Union, Khartoum; 15,000 mems.; Pres. EL RAYAN YOUSIF; Sec. EL TAYEB KHALAFALLA.

Sudanese Federation of Employees and Professionals Trade Unions: P.O.B. 2398, Khartoum; f. 1975; includes 54 Trade Unions representing 250,000 mems.; Pres. ABDALLA ALI ABDALLA; Sec.-Gen. KAMAL EL DIN MOHAMED ABDALLA.

Bank Officials' Union: Bank of Sudan, Khartoum; Pres. AHMED ABDULLAHI MOHAMED KEHIR; Sec. HASSAN MOHAMED MOHAMED ALI.

Gezira Board Officials' Union: Barakat; Pres. GALAL HAMID; Sec. OSMAN ABDEL RAHIM KHEIRAWY.

Local Government Officials' Union: Ministry of Local Government, Khartoum; Pres. SALAH IBRAHIM KHALIL; Sec. MOHAMED AWAD GABIR.

Post, Telegraph and Telephone Officials: Post Office, Khartoum; Pres. ABDEL RAHMAN EL KHIDER ALI; Sec. AWAD EL KARIM OSMAN.

Railway Officials' Union: Sudan Railways Corporation, Atbara; Pres. HASSAN HAG MUSA; Sec. EL HASSAN SIR EL KATIM.

Teachers' Union: Teachers' House, Khartoum; Pres. ABDALLA ALI ABDALLA; Sec. HASSAN IBRAHIM MARZOUG.

CO-OPERATIVE SOCIETIES

There are about 600 co-operative societies in Sudan, of which 570 are formally registered.

Central Co-operative Union: P.O.B. 2492, Khartoum; largest co-operative union operating in 15 provinces.

TRADE FAIR

Sudan Exhibitions and Fairs Corporation (Sudanexpo): P.O.B. 2366, Khartoum; Dir.-Gen. OMAR MOHAMMED SAID.

MAJOR INDUSTRIAL COMPANIES

The following are a few of the larger companies either in terms of capital investment or employment.

Aboulela Cotton Ginning Co. Ltd.: P.O.B. 121, Khartoum; cotton mills.

AGIP (Sudan) Ltd.: P.O.B. 1155, Khartoum; f. 1959; cap. £S1m.
Distribution of petroleum products.
Pres. ROSARIO DISTEFANO; Gen. Man. V. L. BELLETTI; 140 employees.

Bata (Sudan) Ltd.: P.O.B. 88, Khartoum; f. 1950; cap. £S1.7m.
Manufacturers and distributors of footwear.
Man. Dir. A. A. ALI; 1,200 employees.

The Blue Nile Brewery: P.O.B. 1408, Khartoum; f. 1954; cap. £S734,150.
Brewing, bottling and distribution of beer.
Man. Dirs. IBRAHIM ELYAS, HUSSEIN MOHAMED KEMAL, OMER EL ZEIN SAGAYROUN; 336 employees.

The Central Desert Mining Co. Ltd.: P.O.B. 20, Port Sudan; f. 1946; cap. £S150,000.
Prospecting for and mining of gold, manganese and iron ore.
Dirs. ABDELHADI AHMED BAASHER, ABU-BAKR SAID BAASHER; 274 employees.

Kenana Sugar Co. Ltd.: Khartoum; f. 1971; financed by Sudan Government and other Arab nations; 15,000 employees.
Man. Dir. OSMAN ABDULLAH AL-NAZIR.

Sudan Tobacco Co. Ltd.: P.O.B. 87, Khartoum; production of tobacco products.

TRANSPORT

RAILWAYS

Sudan Railways Corporation: P.O.B. 1812, Khartoum; P.O.B. 65, Atbara; Chair. ALI AMIR TAHA; Gen. Man. S. MOHAMED EL TAYEB.

The total length of railway in operation in 1980 was 5,500 route-kilometres. The main line runs from Wadi Halfa, on the Egyptian border, to El Obeid, via Khartoum. Lines from Atbara and Sinnar connect with Port Sudan on the coast. There are lines from Sinnar to Damazine on the Blue Nile (227 km.) and from Aradeiba to Nyala in the south-western province of Darfur (689 km.), with a 445 km. branch line from Babanousa to Wau in the former Bahr el Ghazal Province. A six-year plan to modernize the system, with French assistance, was scheduled to begin in 1977.

ROADS

National Transport Corporation: P.O.B. 723, Khartoum; Gen. Man. MOHI EL DIN HASSAN MOHAMED NUR.

Public Corporation for Roads and Bridges: P.O.B. 7565, Khartoum; f. 1976; Chair. ABDEL RAHMAN HABOUD; Dir.-Gen. ABDU MOHAMMED ABDU.

Roads in northern Sudan, other than town roads, are only cleared tracks and often impassable immediately after rain. Motor traffic on roads in the former Upper Nile Province is limited to the drier months of January–May. There are several good gravelled roads in the former Equatoria and Bahr el Ghazal Provinces which are passable all the year, but in these districts some of the minor roads become impassable after rain. Rehabilitation of communications in Southern Sudan is a major priority as the civil war completely destroyed 1,600 km. of roads and 70 bridges.

In 1977 construction of a 960-km. road linking Juba and Wau was begun with assistance from the Federal Republic of Germany. The Wad-Medani to Gedaref highway, financed by a loan from the People's Republic of China, was completed in March 1977. Over 48,000 km. of tracks are classed as "motorable", but only 2,000 km. were asphalt in 1980. A 1,190 km. tarmac road linking the capital with Port Sudan was completed during 1980.

INLAND WATERWAYS

River Transport Corporation: P.O.B. 284, North Khartoum; operates 2,500 km. of steamers on the Nile; Chair. ABDEL-RAHMAN SID AHMAD BIRAYR.

River Navigation Corporation: Khartoum; f. 1970; jointly owned by the Egyptian and Sudanese Governments; operates services between Aswan and Wadi Halfa.

The total length of navigable waterways served by passenger and freight services is 4,068 km. From the Egyptian border to Wadi Halfa and Khartoum navigation is limited by cataracts to short stretches but the White Nile from Khartoum to Juba is navigable at almost all seasons.

SHIPPING

Port Sudan, on the Red Sea, 784 km. from Khartoum, is the only seaport. There are plans to build a port at New Suakin by 1985.

Red Sea Shipping Corporation: P.O.B. 116, Khartoum; Gen. Man. OSMAN AMIN.

Sea Ports Corporation: P.O.B. 2534, Khartoum; Administrator KHALID AL-SADIG.

Sudan Shipping Line Ltd.: P.O.B. 426, Port Sudan and P.O.B. 1731, Khartoum; f. 1960; seven vessels totalling 53,638 d.w.t. operating between the Red Sea and Western Mediterranean, Northern Europe and United Kingdom; Chair. ISMAIL BAKHEIT; Gen. Man. SALAH EDDIN OMER AL AZIZ.

United African Shipping Co.: P.O.B. 339, Khartoum; Gen. Man. MOHAMED TAHA EL GINDI.

CIVIL AVIATION

The airports at Juba and Malakal in Southern Sudan are to be repaired and new airports built at Wau and Port Sudan.

Civil Aviation Department: Dir.-Gen. SIR HASSAN BESHIR.

Sudan Airways Corporation: Gamhouria Ave., P.O.B. 253, Khartoum; f. 1946; government-owned; internal services and international services to Bahrain, Egypt, Ethiopia, the Federal Republic of Germany, Greece, Italy, Kenya, Kuwait, Nigeria, Qatar, Saudi Arabia, the United Arab Emirates, the United Kingdom and the Yemen Arab Republic; fleet of 2 Boeing 737, 3 Boeing 707, 5 Fokker F-27 and 1 Twin Otter; Chair. Dr. ABDEL MAGID H. KHALIL; Gen. Man. ALI MUSA OMER.

Sudan is also served by the following foreign airlines: Aeroflot (U.S.S.R.), Air France, Alitalia, British Airways, EgyptAir, Ethiopian Airlines, Interflug (German Democratic Republic), KLM (Netherlands), Libyan Arab Airlines, Lufthansa (Federal Republic of Germany), MEA (Lebanon), SAS (Sweden), Saudia (Saudi Arabia), Swissair, Tunis Air, TWA (U.S.A.) and Yemen Airways (Yemen Arab Republic).

TOURISM

Public Corporation of Tourism and Hotels: P.O.B. 2424, Khartoum; Chair. and Dir.-Gen. MAHGOUB MOHAMED ALI.

DEFENCE

Total Armed Forces: In 1981 the armed forces totalled 71,000: army 68,000, navy 1,500, air force 1,500. There are 3,500 paramilitary forces. Military service is compulsory. Sudan has defence agreements with Egypt and receives military aid from the U.S.A.

Defence Budget: (1980) £S122.7 million.

Commander-in-Chief of the People's Armed Forces: Field Marshal GAAFAR MOHAMMED NIMERI.

EDUCATION

The Government provides free elementary education from the ages 7 to 12, intermediate from 13 to 15 and secondary from 16 to 18. In 1978 £S135.6 million was allocated for education from the national budget. Under the Six-Year Plan 1977–83, great emphasis is being placed on education.

The Plan concentrates on reducing the level of illiteracy from the 80 per cent of 1975 to 50 per cent by 1983, introduction of compulsory primary education, and technical education. The Plan involves special concentration on those involved in the industrial and agricultural sectors, the government service and housewives. It is to be linked with the development projects and resettlement schemes and the target is to reach a million people per year.

There has been a notable increase in the number of pupils in primary education, rising from 610,798 in 1969 to 1,435,127 in 1979/80. The number of teachers rose from 12,370 in 1969 to 41,576 in 1979/80. In the South, primary school enrolment in state schools increased from 53,169 in 1971/72 to 109,552 in 1979/80.

The secondary level is divided into two stages; junior secondary (intermediate) of three years' duration which is completely academic, and senior secondary (secondary) of three or four years which is of three types: academic, technical and teacher training. In the South senior secondary school enrolment increased from 909 in 1972 to 2,480 in 1976. In 1979/80 national enrolment in secondary schools totalled 143,097.

There were 15 higher education institutions in 1981. Administration was decentralized in November 1975 with the establishment of the National Council for Higher Education as a governing body to supervise and plan general policy. The University of Khartoum is under government control. The University of Cairo has a branch in Khartoum. The universities of Juba and Gezira were founded in 1975 and concentrate on rural development. There is an Islamic University at Omdurman. The Khartoum Polytechnic was formed in 1975 by the amalgamation of 13 existing technical institutes. In 1979/80 there were 4,388 students receiving training at teacher training institutes.

Projects for increasing literacy among adults have been in progress for several years.

BIBLIOGRAPHY

GENERAL

ABDEL-RAHIM, MUDDATHIR. Imperialism and Nationalism in the Sudan: A Study in Constitutional and Political Developments 1899–1956 (Oxford University Press, 1969).

ALBINO, OLIVER. The Sudan, a southern viewpoint (Oxford, 1969).

AMMAR, ABBAS, and others. The Unity of the Nile Valley, its Geographical Basis and its Manifestations in History (Cairo, 1947).

BARBOUR, K. M. The Republic of the Sudan: A Regional Geography (University of London Press, London, 1961).

BESHIR, M. O. The Southern Sudan: Background to Conflict (C. Hurst, London, 1968, Praeger, New York, 1968).

BOUSFIELD, L. Sudan Doctor (London, 1954).

BUDGE, Sir E. A. T. W. The Egyptian Sudan: Its History and Monuments (2 vols., London, 1907).
By Nile and Tigris (London, 1920).

EGYPTIAN SOCIETY OF INTERNATIONAL LAW. Documents of the Sudan 1899–1953 (Cairo, 1953).

FADL, EL S. H. Their Finest Days (Rex Collings, London, 1969).

FAWZI, S. ED DIN. The Labour Movement in the Sudan, 1946–55 (Oxford University Press, London, 1957).

GAITSKELL, ARTHUR. Gezira: A Story of Development in the Sudan (Faber, London, 1959).

HENDERSON, K. D. D. The Sudan Republic (Benn, London, 1965).

HILL, R. A Bibliography of the Anglo-Egyptian Sudan from the earliest times to 1937 (Oxford, 1939).
A Bibliographical Dictionary of the Anglo-Egyptian Sudan (new edition, Frank Cass, London, 1967).
Egypt in the Sudan 1820–1881 (Oxford University Press, London and New York, 1959).
Slatin Pasha (Oxford University Press, London, 1964, New York, 1965).
Sudan Transport: a History (London, 1965).

HODGKIN, R. A. Sudan Geography (London, 1951).

HURST, H. E. and PHILIPS, P. The Nile Basin, 7 vols. (London, 1932–38).

JACKSON, H. C. The Fighting Sudanese (London, 1954).
Sudan Days and Ways (London, 1954).

KNIGHT, R. L., and BOYNS, B. M. Agricultural Science in the Sudan (1950).

LANGLEY, M. No Woman's Country: Travels in the Anglo-Egyptian Sudan (New York, 1951).

LEBON, J. H. C. Land Use in Sudan (Geographical Publications Ltd., Bude, U.K., 1965).

NASRI, A. R. EL-. A Bibliography of the Sudan 1938–1958 (Oxford University Press, 1962).

NEWBOLD, Sir D. The Making of the Modern Sudan; the Life and Letters of Sir Douglas Newbold (London, Faber and Faber, 1953).

ODUHO, JOSEPH, and DENG, WILLIAM. The Problem of the Southern Sudan (Oxford University Press, 1963).

SANDERSON, L. P., and SANDERSON, G. N. Education, Religion and Politics in the Southern Sudan 1899–1964 (London, 1981).

SUDANESE GOVERNMENT. Ten Year Plan of Economic and Social Development 1961-62—1971-72 (Khartoum, Ministry of Finance and Economics, 1962).

TRIMINGHAM, J. S. Islam in the Sudan (London, 1949).

WATERBURY, JOHN. Hydro politics of the Nile Valley (New York, 1979).

ANTHROPOLOGY

CUNNISON, IAN. Baggara Arabs (Oxford University Press, New York, 1966).

EVANS-PRITCHARD, E. E. Kinship and Marriage among the Nuer (London, 1951).
The Nuer (London, 1940).
Witchcraft, Oracles and Magic among the Azande (London, 1937).

GRIFFITHS, V. L., and TAHA, ABDEL RAHMAN ALI. Sudan Courtesy Customs (Sudan Government, 1936).

HABER, HUGO. Das Fortleben nach dem Tode im Glauben westsudanischer Völker (Mödling, 1951).

NADEL, S. F. The Nuba: an Anthropological Study of the Hill Tribes of Kordofan (London, 1947).

PAUL, A. A History of the Beja tribes of the Sudan (Cambridge, 1954).

SELIGMAN, C. G. Pagan Tribes of the Nilotic Sudan (London, 1932).

ECONOMICS

ALI, MOHAMED ABDEL RAHMAN. *Fluctuations and Impact of Government Expenditure in the Sudan 1955–1967.* Khartoum University Press, 1974.

BESHAI, ADEL AMIN. *Export Performance and Economic Development in Sudan 1900–1967.* London, Ithaca Press, 1976.

INTERNATIONAL LABOUR OFFICE. *Growth, Employment and Equity: A Comprehensive Strategy for the Sudan.* Geneva, 1976.

MINISTRY OF NATIONAL PLANNING. *The Six-Year Plan of Economic and Social Development.* Khartoum, 1977.

NIMEIRI, SAYED. *Taxation and Economic Development: A Case Study of the Sudan.* Khartoum University Press, 1974.

SULIMAN, ALI AHMED. *Issues in the Economic Development of the Sudan.* Khartoum University Press, 1975.

HISTORY

ABBAS, MEKKI. The Sudan Question: the Dispute about the Anglo-Egyptian Condominium, 1884-1951 (London, 1952).

ARCHER, G. Personal and Historical Memoirs of an East African Administrator (London, 1963).

ARKELL, A. J. Outline History of the Sudan (London, 1938).
History of the Sudan to 1821 (2nd. ed., London, 1961).

BECHTOLD, P. K. Politics in the Sudan (London, 1978).

BOAHEN, A. ADU. Britain, the Sahara and the Western Sudan 1788-1816 (Oxford University Press, New York and London, 1964).

COLLINS, ROBERT O. The Southern Sudan 1883-1898 (Yale University Press, 1962).

COLLINS, ROBERT O. and TIGNOR, R. L. Egypt and the Sudan (Prentice, New York, 1967).

CORBYN, E. N. Survey of the Anglo-Egyptian Sudan, 1898-1944 (London, 1946).

EPRILE, CECIL. War and Peace in the Sudan 1955-1972 (David and Charles, Devon, England, 1974).

FABUNMI, L. A. The Sudan in Anglo-Egyptian Relations (Longman, London, 1965).

GRAY, RICHARD. History of the Southern Sudan 1839–89 (Oxford, 1961).

HASSAN, YUSUF FADL. The Arabs and the Sudan (Edinburgh University Press, Edinburgh, 1967).

HENDERSON, K. D. D. Survey of the Anglo-Egyptian Sudan, 1898-1944 (London, 1946).

HOLT, P. M. The Mahdist State in the Sudan: 1881–98 (Oxford University Press, 2nd edn., 1970).

A Modern History of the Sudan (Weidenfeld and Nicolson, London, 1962, Praeger, New York, 1963).

MACMICHAEL, Sir H. A. A History of the Arabs in the Sudan (2 vols., Cambridge, 1922; reprinted Frank Cass, London and Barnes & Noble, New York, 1967).

The Anglo-Egyptian Sudan (London, 1935).

The Sudan (London, 1954).

MALWAL, BONA. People and Power in Sudan (Ithaca Press, London, 1981).

ROBERTSON, Sir. J. W. R. Transition in Africa—From Direct Rule to Independence (London, 1974).

SABRY, M. Le Soudan Egyptien, 1821-98 (Cairo, 1947).

SANDERSON, G. N. England, Europe and the Upper Nile (Edinburgh University Press, Edinburgh, 1965).

SANTI, P., and HILL, R. (Eds.). The Europeans in the Sudan 1834–1878 (Oxford University Press, 1980).

SHIBEIKA, MEKKI. The Sudan in the Century 1819-1919 (Cairo, 1947).

British Policy in the Sudan: 1882–1902 (London, 1952).

The Independent Sudan: The History of a Nation (New York, 1960).

SHINNIE, MARGARET. A Short History of the Sudan up to A.D. 1500 (Khartoum, 1954).

SHINNIE, P. L. Meroe (Thames and Hudson, London, 1967).

SYLVESTER, ANTONY. Sudan under Nimeri (Bodley Head, London, 1977).

SYMES, Sir S. Tour of Duty (London, 1946).

THEOBALD A. B. The Mahdiya: A History of the Anglo-Egyptian Sudan. 1881-1899 (New York, 1951).

TONIOLO, E., and HILL, R. (Eds.). The Opening of the Nile Basin: Writings by Members of the Catholic Mission to Central Africa on the Geography and Ethnography of the Sudan 1842–1881 (Hurst, London, 1975).

WAI, D. The Southern Sudan—The Problem of National Integration (London, 1972).

The African-Arab Conflict in the Sudan (Africana Publishing Company, New York, 1981).

WARBURG, G. Islam, Nationalism and Communism in a Traditional Society—The Case of Sudan (London, 1978).

WOODWARD, PETER. Condominium and Sudanese Nationalism (London, 1979).

Syria

PHYSICAL AND SOCIAL GEOGRAPHY

W. B. Fisher

Before 1918 the term "Syria" was rather loosely applied to the whole of the territory now forming the modern States of Syria, the Lebanon, Israel and Jordan. To the Ottomans, as to the Romans, Syria stretched from the Euphrates to the Mediterranean, and from the Sinai to the hills of southern Turkey, with Palestine as a smaller province of this wider unit. Though the present Syrian Arab Republic has a much more limited extension, an echo of the past remains to colour the political thinking of a few present-day Syrians and from time to time there are references to a "Greater Syria" as a desirable but possibly remote aspiration.

The frontiers of the present-day State are largely artificial, and reflect to a considerable extent the interests and prestige of outside Powers—Britain, France, and the United States—as these existed in 1918-20. The northern frontier with Turkey is defined by a single-track railway line running along the southern edge of the foothills—probably the only case of its kind in the world; whilst eastwards and southwards boundaries are highly arbitrary, being straight lines drawn for convenience between salient points. Westwards, the frontiers are again artificial, though less crudely drawn, leaving the headwaters of the Jordan river outside Syria and following the crest of the Anti-Lebanon hills, to reach the sea north of Tripoli.

PHYSICAL FEATURES

Geographically, Syria consists of two main zones: a fairly narrow western part, made up of a complex of mountain ranges and intervening valleys; and a much larger eastern zone that is essentially a broad and open platform dropping gently towards the east and crossed diagonally by the wide Euphrates Valley.

The western zone, which contains over 80 per cent of the population of Syria, can be further subdivided as follows. In the extreme west, fronting the Mediterranean Sea, there lies an imposing ridge rising to 5,000 feet, and known as the Jebel Ansariyeh. Its western flank drops fairly gradually to the sea, giving a narrow coastal plain; but on the east it falls very sharply, almost as a wall, to a flat-bottomed valley occupied by the Orontes river, which meanders sluggishly over the flat floor, often flooding in winter, and leaving a formerly malarial marsh in summer. Farther east lie more hill ranges, opening out like a fan from the south-west, where the Anti-Lebanon range, with Mount Hermon (9,000 ft.), is the highest in Syria. Along the eastern flanks of the various ridges lie a number of shallow basins occupied by small streams that eventually dry up or form closed salt lakes. In one basin lies the city of Aleppo, once the second town of the Ottoman Empire and still close to being the largest city of Syria. In another is situated Damascus,

irrigated from five streams, and famous for its clear fountains and gardens—now the capital of the country. One remaining sub-region of western Syria is the Jebel Druse, which lies in the extreme south-west, and consists of a vast out-pouring of lava, in the form of sheets and cones. Towards the west this region is fertile, and produces good cereal crops, but eastwards the soil cover disappears, leaving a barren countryside of twisted lava and caverns, for long the refuge of outlaws, bandits, and minority groups. Because of its difficulty and isolation the Jebel Druse has tended socially and politically to go its own way, remaining aloof from the rest of the country.

The entire eastern zone is mainly steppe or open desert, except close to the banks of the river Euphrates, Tigris, and their larger tributaries, where recent irrigation projects have allowed considerable cultivation on an increasing scale. The triangularly-shaped region between the Euphrates and Tigris rivers is spoken of as the Jezireh (Arabic *Jazira*= island), but is in no way different from the remaining parts of the east.

The presence of ranks of relatively high hills aligned parallel to the coast has important climatic effects. Tempering and humid effects from the Mediterranean are restricted to a narrow western belt, and central and eastern Syria show marked continental tendencies: that is, a very hot summer with temperatures often above 100° or even 110° F., and a moderately cold winter, with frost on many nights. Very close to the Mediterranean, frost is unknown at any season, but on the hills altitude greatly reduces the average temperature, so that snow may lie on the heights from late December to April, or even May. Rainfall is fairly abundant in the west, where the height of the land tends to determine the amount received; but east of the Anti-Lebanon mountains the amount decreases considerably, producing a steppe region that quickly passes into true desert. On the extreme east, as the Zagros ranges of Persia are approached, there is once again a slight increase, but most of Syria has an annual rainfall of under ten inches.

ECONOMIC LIFE

There is a close relationship between climate and economic activities. In the west, where up to 30 or even 40 inches of rainfall occur, settled farming is possible, and the main limitation is difficult terrain; but from the Orontes Valley eastwards natural rainfall is increasingly inadequate, and irrigation becomes necessary. The narrow band of territory where annual rainfall lies between 8 and 15 inches is sometimes spoken of as the "Fertile Crescent", since it runs in an arc along the inner side of the hills from Jordan through western and northern Syria as far east as Iraq. In its normal state a steppeland covered with seasonal grass, the Fertile Crescent can often be converted by irrigation and efficient organization into a rich and productive territory. Such it was in the golden days of the Arab Caliphate; now, after centuries of decline, it is once again reviving. From the 1940s to the 1950s a marked change was seen and, thanks first to small-scale irrigation schemes and the installation of motor pumps to raise water from underground artesian sources, large areas of the former steppe are producing crops of cotton, cereals and fruit. Syria used to have a surplus of agricultural production, especially cereals, to export to Jordan and Lebanon, neither of which are self-sufficient in foodstuffs. It was expected that production would increase with the eventual doubling of Syria's irrigated area (by 640,000 hectares) as the Euphrates Dam at Tabqa develops fully. However, there have been doubts cast on the possibility of this target's being achieved; difficulties have been experienced in irrigating part of the designated area and some experts believe that perhaps 300,000 hectares may be impossible to develop according to the original plans. Over the last few years, production of cereals and cotton has declined, partly owing to lack of technical and management skills, and partly to drought. High military expenditure has also reduced available development funds.

Because of its relative openness and accessibility and its geographical situation as a "waist" between the Mediterranean and the Persian Gulf, Syria has been a land of passage, and for centuries its role was that of an intermediary, both commercial and cultural, between the Mediterranean world and the Far East. From early times until the end of the Middle Ages there was a flow of traffic east and west that raised a number of Syrian cities and ports to the

rank of international markets. Since the 1930s, following a long period of decline and eclipse resulting from the diversion of this trade to the sea, there has been a revival of activity, owing to the new elements of air transport and the construction of oil pipelines from Iraq.

In addition, Syria has been able to develop her own deposits of petroleum and phosphate; and her greatly improved political standing (as almost the successor of Egypt as the leading Arab state) has had an economic spin-off. The Syrian economy is stronger than it was, and the country is able to "balance" between the Soviet and Western political groups, though the cost of wars and internal political uncertainties have eroded some development gains. Since 1981, however, Syria has been more isolated from her Arab neighbours, and the policy of balance, both in external and internal affairs, has been less successful.

RACE AND LANGUAGE

Racially, we can distinguish many elements in the Syrian people. The nomads of the interior deserts are unusually pure specimens of the Mediterranean type, isolation having preserved them from intermixture. To the west and north there is a widely varying mosaic of other groups: the Kurds and Turkish-speaking communities of the north, and the Armenians, who form communities in the cities; groups such as the Druzes, who show some affinity to the tribes of the Persian Zagros, and many others.

As a result, there is a surprising variety of language and religion. Arabic is spoken over most of the country, but Kurdish is widely used along the northern frontier and Armenian in the cities. Aramaic, the language of Christ, survives in three villages.

HISTORY

ANCIENT HISTORY

From the earliest times, Syria has experienced successive waves of Semitic immigration—the Canaanites and Phoenicians in the third millennium B.C., the Hebrews and Aramaeans in the second, and, unceasingly, the nomad tribes infiltrating from the Arabian peninsula. This process has enabled Syria to assimilate or reject, without losing its essentially Semitic character, the alien invaders who, time and again, in the course of a long history, have established their domination over the land. Before Rome assumed control of Syria in the first century B.C., the Egyptians, the Assyrians and the Hittites, and, later, the Persians and the Macedonian Greeks had all left their mark in greater or lesser degree. Damascus is claimed to be the oldest capital city in the world, having been continuously inhabited since about 2000 B.C., and Aleppo may be even older. Under Roman rule the infiltration and settlement of nomad elements continued, almost unnoticed by historians, save when along the desert trade routes a Semitic vassal state attained a brief importance as, for example, the kingdom of Palmyra in the Syrian desert, which the Emperor Aurelian destroyed in A.D. 272 or, later still, when the Byzantines ruled in Syria, the Arab State of Ghassan, prominent throughout the sixth century A.D. as a bulwark of the Byzantine Empire against the desert tribes in the service of Sasanid Persia.

ARAB AND TURKISH RULE

When, after the death of the Prophet Muhammad in A.D. 632, the newly-created power of Islam began a career of conquest, the populations of Syria, Semitic in their language and culture and, as adherents of the Monophysite faith, ill-disposed towards the Greek-speaking Orthodox Byzantines, did little to oppose the Muslims, from whom they hoped to obtain a greater measure of freedom. The Muslims defeated the Byzantine forces at Ajnadain in July 634, seized Damascus in September 635, and, by their decisive victory on the River Yarmuk (August 636), virtually secured possession of all Syria. From 661-750 the Umayyad dynasty ruled in Syria, which, after the conquest, had been divided into four military districts or junds (Damascus, Homs, Urdun, i.e. Jordan, and Palestine). To these the Caliph Yazid I (680-83) added a fifth, Kinnasrin, for the defence of northern Syria, where in the late seventh century, the Mardaites, Christians from the Taurus, were making serious inroads under Byzantine leadership. Under Abd al-Malik (685-705) Arabic became the official language of the State, in whose administration, hitherto largely carried out by the old Byzantine bureaucracy, Syrians, Muslim as well as Christian, now had an increasing share. For Syria was now the heart of a great Empire, and the Arab Army of Syria, well trained in the ceaseless frontier warfare with Byzantium, bore the main burden of imperial rule, taking a major part in the two great Arab assaults on Byzantium in 674–8 and in 717–18.

The new regime in Syria was pre-eminently military and fiscal in character, representing the domination of a military caste of Muslim Arab warriors, who governed on the basic assumption that a large subject population, non-Muslim and non-Arab in character, would continue indefinitely to pay tribute. But this assumption was falsified by the gradual spread of Islam, a process which meant the progressive diminution of the amount of tribute paid to the State, and the consequent undermining of the fiscal system as a whole. In theory, conversion meant for the non-Arab convert (*Mawla*; in the plural, *Mawali*) full social and economic equality with the ruling caste, but in practice it was not enough to be a Muslim, one had to be an Arab as well. The discontent of the *Mawali* with their enforced inferiority expressed itself in an appeal to the universal character of Islam, an appeal which often took the form of religious heresies, and which, as it became more widespread, undermined the strength of the Arab regime.

To the ever present fiscal problems of the Arab State and the growing discontent of the *Mawali* was added a third and fatal weakness: the hostility between those Arab tribes which had arrived in Syria with or since the conquest, and those which had infiltrated there at an earlier date. The Umayyad house strove to maintain a neutral position over and above the tribal feuds; but from the moment when, under the pressure of events, the Umayyads were compelled to side with one faction to oppose the other (battle of Marj Rahit 684), their position was irretrievably compromised.

When in A.D. 750 with the accession of the Abbasid dynasty the centre of the Empire was transferred to Iraq, Syria, jealously watched because of its association with the former ruling house, became a mere province, where in the course of the next hundred years, several abortive revolts, inspired in part by the traditional loyalty to the Umayyads, failed to shake off Abbasid control. During the ninth century Syria was the object of dispute between Egypt and Baghdad. In 878 Ahmad ibn Tulun, Governor of Egypt, occupied it and, subsequently, every independent ruler of Egypt sought to maintain a hold, partial or complete, over Syria. Local dynasties, however, achieved from time to time a transitory importance, as did the Hamdanids (a Bedouin family from Northern Iraq) who, under Saif ad-Daula, ruler of Aleppo from 946–967, attained a brief ascendancy, marked internally by financial and administrative ineptitude, and externally by military campaigns against the Byzantines which did much to provoke the great Byzantine reconquest of the late tenth century. By the treaty of 997, northern Syria became Byzantine, while the rest of the country remained in the hands of the Fatimid dynasty which ruled in Egypt from 969. Fatimid control remained insecure and from about 1027 a new Arab house ruled at Aleppo—the Mirdasids, who were soon to disappear before the formidable power of the Seljuq Turks. The Seljuqs, having conquered Persia, rapidly overran Syria (Damascus fell to them in 1075) but failed to establish there a united State. As a result of dynastic quarrels, the Seljuq domination disintegrated into a number of amirates: Seljuq princes ruled at Aleppo and Damascus, a local dynasty held Tripoli and, in the south, Egypt controlled most of the littoral.

This political fragmentation greatly favoured the success of the First Crusade which, taking Antioch in 1098 and Jerusalem in 1099, proceeded to organize four feudal States at Edessa, Antioch, Tripoli and Jerusalem, but did not succeed in conquering Aleppo, Homs, Hama, and Damascus. From the death of Baldwin II of Jerusalem in 1131, the essential weakness of the crusading States began to appear. Byzantium, the Christian State of Lesser Armenia,

and the Latin principalities in Syria never united in a successful resistance to the Muslim counter-offensive which, initiated by the energetic Turkish general Zangi Atabeg of Mosul, developed rapidly in the third and fourth decades of the century. Zangi, who seized Aleppo in 1128, and the Latin State of Edessa in 1144, was succeeded in 1146 by his able son Nur ad-Din, who by his capture of Damascus in 1154 recreated in Syria a united Muslim Power. On Nur ad-Din's death in 1174, the Kurd Saladin, already master of Egypt, assumed control at Damascus and, in 1183, seized Aleppo. His victory over the Crusaders at Hattin (July 1187) destroyed the kingdom of Jerusalem. Only the partial success of the Third Crusade (1189–92) and, after his death in 1193, the disintegration of Saladin's Empire into a number of separate principalities, made it possible for the Crusaders to maintain an ever more precarious hold on the coastal areas of Syria. The emergence in Egypt of the powerful Mamluk Sultanate (1250) meant that the end was near. A series of military campaigns, led by the Sultan Baibars (1260–77) and his immediate successors, brought about the fall of Antioch (1268) and Tripoli (1289), and, with the fall of Acre in 1291, the disappearance of the crusading States in Syria.

Before the last crusading States had been reduced, the Mamluks had to encounter a determined assault by the Mongols, in the course of which Aleppo and Hama were sacked, and Damascus besieged; until, in 1260, the Mongol army of invasion was crushed at the battle of Ain-Jalut, near Nazareth. The Mongol Il-Khans of Persia made further efforts to conquer Syria in the late thirteenth century, negotiating for this purpose with the Papacy, the remaining crusader States, and Lesser Armenia. In 1280 the Mamluks defeated a Mongol army at Homs; but in 1299 were themselves beaten near the same town, a defeat which enabled the Mongols to ravage northern Syria and to take Damascus in 1300. Only in 1303, at the battle of Marj as-Suffar, south of Damascus, was this last Mongol offensive finally repelled.

The period of Mamluk rule in Syria, which endured until 1517, was on the whole one of slow decline. Warfare, periodical famine, and not least, the plague (there were four great outbreaks in the fourteenth century, and in the fifteenth century fourteen more recorded attacks of some severity) produced a state of affairs which the financial rapacity and misrule of the Mamluk governors and the devastation of Aleppo and Damascus by Timur (1400–01) served only to aggravate.

The ill-defined protectorate which the Mamluks asserted over Cilicia and considerable areas of southern Anatolia occasioned, in the late fifteenth century, a growing tension with the power of the Ottoman Turks, which broke out into inconclusive warfare in the years 1485–91. When to this tension was added the possibility of an alliance between the Mamluks and the rising power of the Safavids in Persia, the Ottoman Sultan Selim I (1512–20) was compelled to seek a decisive solution to the problem. In August 1516 the battle of Marj Dabik, north of Aleppo, gave Syria to the Ottomans, who proceeded to ensure their continued hold on the land by conquering Egypt (1517). Turkish rule, during the next three centuries, although unjustly accused of complete responsibility for a decay and stagnation which appear to have been well advanced before 1517, brought only a temporary improvement in the unhappy condition of Syria, now divided into the three provinces of Damascus, Tripoli, and Aleppo. In parts of Syria the Turkish pashas in reality administered directly only the important towns and their immediate neighbourhood; elsewhere, the older elements—Bedouin emirs, Turcoman chiefs, etc.—were left to act much as they pleased, provided the due tribute was paid. The pashas normally bought their appointment to high office and sought in their brief tenure of power to recover the money and bribes they had expended in securing it, knowing that they might, at any moment, be replaced by someone who could pay more for the post. Damascus alone had 133 pashas in 180 years. As the control of the Sultan at Constantinople became weaker, the pashas obtained greater freedom of action, until Ahmed Jazzar, Pasha of Acre, virtually ruled Syria as an independent prince (1785-1804).

The nineteenth century saw important changes. The Ottoman Sultan Mahmud II (1808-39) had promised Syria to the Pasha of Egypt, Muhammad Ali, in return for the latter's services during the Greek War of Independence. When the Sultan declined to fulfil his promise, Egyptian troops overran Syria (1831-33). Ibrahim Pasha, son of Muhammad Ali, now gave to Syria, for the first time in centuries, a centralized government strong enough to hold separatist tendencies in check and to impose a system of taxation which, if burdensome, was at least regular in its functioning. But Ibrahim's rule was not popular, for the land-owners resented his efforts to limit their social and political dominance, while the peasantry disliked the conscription, the forced labour, and the heavy taxation which he found indispensable for the maintenance of his regime. In 1840 a revolt broke out in Syria, and when the Great Powers intervened on behalf of the Sultan (at war with Egypt since 1839), Muhammad Ali was compelled to renounce his claim to rule there.

Western influence, working through trade, through the protection of religious minorities, and through the cultural and educational efforts of missions and schools, had received encouragement from Ibrahim Pasha. The French Jesuits, returning to Syria in 1831, opened schools, and in 1875 founded their University at Beirut. The American Presbyterian Mission (established at Beirut in 1820) introduced a printing press in 1834, and in 1866 founded the Syrian Protestant College, later renamed the American University of Beirut. Syria also received some benefit from the reform movement within the Ottoman Empire, which, begun by Mahmud II, and continued under his successors, took the form of a determined attempt to modernize the structure of the Empire. The semi-independent pashas of old disappeared, the administration being now entrusted to salaried officials of the central government; some effort was made to create schools and colleges on Western lines, and much was done to deprive the landowning classes of their feudal privileges, although their social and economic predominance was left unchallenged. As a result of these improvements, there was, in the late nineteenth century, a revival of Arabic literature which did much to prepare the way for the growth of Arab nationalism in the twentieth century.

MODERN HISTORY

By 1914 Arab nationalist sentiment had made some headway among the educated and professional classes, and especially among army officers. Nationalist societies like *Al-Fatat* soon made contact with Arab nationalists outside Syria—with the army officers of Iraq, with influential Syrian colonies in Egypt and America, and with the Sharif Husein of Mecca. The Husein-McMahon Correspondence (July 1915-January 1916) encouraged the Arab nationalists to hope that the end of the Great War would mean the creation of a greater Arab kingdom. This expectation was disappointed, for as a result of the Sykes-Picot Agreement, negotiated in secret between England, France, and Russia in 1916 (*see* Documents on Palestine, page 66), Syria was to become a French sphere of influence. At the end of the war, and in accordance with this agreement, a provisional French administration was established in the coastal districts of Syria, while in the interior an Arab government came into being under Amir Faisal, son of the Sharif Husein of Mecca. In March 1920 the Syrian

nationalists proclaimed an independent kingdom of Greater Syria (including the Lebanon and Palestine); but in April of the same year the San Remo Conference gave France a mandate for the whole of Syria, and in July, French troops occupied Damascus.

By 1925 the French, aware that the majority of the Muslim population resented their rule, and that only amongst the Christian Maronites of the Lebanon could they hope to find support, had carried into effect a policy based upon the religious divisions so strong in Syria. The area under mandate had been divided into four distinct units; a much enlarged Lebanon (including Beirut and Tripoli), a Syrian Republic, and the two districts of Latakia and Jebel Druse. Despite the fact that the French rule gave Syria a degree of law and order which might render possible the transition from a medieval to a more modern form of society, nationalist sentiment opposed the mandate on principle, and deplored the failure to introduce full representative institutions and the tendency to encourage separatism amongst the religious minorities. This discontent, especially strong in the Syrian Republic, became open revolt in 1925-26, during the course of which the French twice bombarded Damascus (October 1925 and May 1926).

The next ten years were marked by a hesitant and often interrupted progress towards self-government in Syria, and by French efforts to conclude a Franco-Syrian treaty. In April 1928 elections were held for a Constituent Assembly, and in August a draft Constitution was completed; but the French High Commissioner refused to accept certain articles, especially Article 2, which, declaring the Syrian territories detached from the old Ottoman Empire to be an indivisible unity, constituted a denial of the separate existence of the Jebel Druse, Latakia, and the Lebanese Republic. After repeated attempts to reach a compromise, the High Commissioner dissolved the Assembly in May 1930 and, on his own authority, issued a new Constitution for the State of Syria, much the same as that formerly proposed by the Assembly, but with those modifications which were considered indispensable to the maintenance of French control. After new elections (January 1932) negotiations were begun for a Franco-Syrian treaty, to be modelled on that concluded between England and Iraq in 1930, but no compromise could be found between the French demands and those of the nationalists who, although in a minority, wielded a dominant influence in the Chamber and whose aim was to limit both in time and in place the French military occupation, and to include in Syria the separate areas of Jebel Druse and Latakia. In 1934 the High Commissioner suspended the Chamber indefinitely. Disorders occurred early in 1936 which induced the French to send a Syrian delegation to Paris, where the new Popular Front Government showed itself more sympathetic towards Syrian aspirations than former French governments had been. In September 1936 a Franco-Syrian treaty was signed which recognised the principle of Syrian independence and stipulated that, after ratification, there should be a period of three years during which the apparatus of a fully independent State should be created. The districts of Jebel Druse and Latakia would be annexed to Syria, but would retain special administrations. Other subsidiary agreements reserved to France important military and economic rights in Syria. It seemed that Syria might now enter a period of rapid political development; but the unrest caused by the situation in Palestine, the crisis with Turkey, and the failure of France to ratify the 1936 treaty were responsible, within two years, for the breakdown of these hopes.

In 1921 Turkey had consented to the inclusion of the Sanjak of Alexandretta in the French mandated territories, on condition that it should be governed under a special regime. The Turks, alarmed by the treaty of 1936, which envisaged the emergence of a unitary Syrian State including, to all appearance, Alexandretta, now pressed for a separate agreement concerning the status of the Sanjak. After long discussion the League of Nations decided in 1937 that the Sanjak should be fully autonomous, save for its foreign and financial policies which were to be under the control of the Syrian Government. A treaty between France and Turkey guaranteed the integrity of the Sanjak, and also the Turco-Syrian frontier. Throughout 1937 there were conflicts between Turks and Arabs in the Sanjak, and in Syria a widespread and growing resentment, for it was clear that sooner or later Turkey would ask for the cession of Alexandretta. The problem came to be regarded in Syria as a test of Franco-Syrian co-operation, and when in June 1939, under the pressure of international tension, Alexandretta was finally ceded to Turkey, the cession assumed in the eyes of Syrian nationalists the character of a betrayal by France. Meanwhile, in France itself, opposition to the treaty of 1936 had grown steadily; and in December 1938 the French Government, anxious not to weaken its military position in the Near East, declared that no ratification of the treaty was to be expected.

Unrest in Syria led to open riots in 1941, as a result of which the Vichy High Commissioner, General Dentz, promised the restoration of partial self-government; while in June of the same year, when in order to combat Axis intrigues the Allies invaded Syria, General Catroux, on behalf of the Free French Government, promised independence for Syria and the end of mandatory rule. Syrian independence was formally recognized in September 1941, but the reality of power was still withheld, with the effect that nationalist agitation, inflamed by French reluctance to restore constitutional rule, and by economic difficulties due to the war, became even more pronounced. When at last elections were held once more, a nationalist government was formed, with Shukri al-Kuwatly as President of the Syrian Republic (August 1943).

Gradually all important powers and public services were transferred from French to Syrian hands; but conflict again developed over the *Troupes Spéciales*, the local Syrian and Lebanese levies which had existed throughout the mandatory period as an integral part of the French military forces in the Levant, and which, transferred to the Syrian and Lebanese Governments, would enable them to form their own armies. Strongly supported by the newly-created Arab League, Syria refused the French demand for a Franco-Syrian Treaty as the condition for the final transfer of administrative and military services which had always been the main instruments of French policy. In May 1945 disturbances broke out which ended only with British armed intervention and the evacuation of French troops and administrative personnel. The *Troupes Spéciales* were now handed over to the Syrian Government, and with the departure of British forces in April 1946 the full independence of Syria was at last achieved.

UNSTABLE INDEPENDENCE

After the attainment of independence Syria passed through a long period of instability. She was involved in a complicated economic and financial dispute with the Lebanon (1948–50) and also in various schemes for union with Iraq—schemes which tended to divide political opinion inside Syria itself and, in addition, to disrupt the unity of the Arab League. Syria, in fact, found herself aligned at this time with Egypt and Saudi Arabia against the ambitions of the Hashemite rulers of Iraq and Jordan. These rivalries, together with the profound disappointment felt at Damascus over the Arab failures in the war of 1948–49 against Israel, were the prelude to three *coups d'état* in 1949. Dislike of continued financial dependence on

France, aspirations towards a greater Syria, the resentments arising out of the unsuccessful war against the Israelis—all help to explain the unrest inside Syria.

The intervention of the army in politics was itself a cause of further tension. Opposition to the dominance of the army grew in the Syrian Chamber of Deputies to such an extent that yet another *coup d'état* was carried out in December 1951. Syria now came under the control of a military autocracy with Colonel Shishakli as head of the state. The Chamber of Deputies was dissolved in December 1951; a decree of April 1952 abolished all political parties in Syria. After the approval of a new constitution in July 1953 General Shishakli became President of Syria in August of that year. The formation of political parties was now allowed once more. Members of the parties dissolved under the decree of April 1952 proceeded, however, to boycott the elections held in October 1953, at which President Shishakli's Movement of Arab Liberation obtained a large majority in the Chamber of Deputies. Politicians hostile to the regime of President Shishakli established in November 1953 a Front of National Opposition, refusing to accept as legal the results of the October elections and declaring as their avowed aim the end of military autocracy and the restoration of democratic rule. Demonstrations at Damascus and Aleppo in December 1953 led soon to the flight of Shishakli to France. The collapse of his regime early in 1954 meant for Syria a return to the Constitution of 1950. New elections held in September 1954 brought into being a Chamber of Deputies notable for the large number of its members (81 out of 142) who might be regarded as independents grouped around leading political figures.

INFLUENCE FROM ABROAD

There was still, however, much friction in Syria between those who favoured union or at least close co-operation with Iraq and those inclined towards an effective *entente* with Egypt. In August 1955 Shukri al-Kuwatli became President of the Republic. His appointment was interpreted as an indication that pro-Egyptian influence had won the ascendancy in Syria. On October 20th, 1955, Syria made with Egypt an agreement for the creation of a joint military command with its headquarters at Damascus.

The U.S.S.R., meanwhile, in answer to the developments in the Middle East associated with the Baghdad Pact, had begun an intensive diplomatic, propaganda and economic campaign of penetration into the Arab lands. In the years 1954–56 Syria, the only Arab state where the Communist Party was legal, made a number of barter agreements with the Soviet Union and its associates in eastern Europe. A report from Cairo intimated, in February 1956, that Syria had joined Egypt in accepting arms from U.S.S.R.

At the end of October 1956 there occurred the Israeli campaign in the Sinai peninsula, an event followed, in the first days of November, by the armed intervention of Great Britain and France in the Suez Canal region. On October 30th the President of the Syrian Republic left Damascus on a visit to the Soviet Union. A state of emergency was declared in Syria. Reports from Beirut revealed on November 3rd that Syrian forces had put out of action the pipelines which carried Iraqi oil to the Mediterranean. The damage that Syrian elements had done to the pipelines earned the sharp disapproval of such Arab states as Iraq and Saudi Arabia, both of whom were now faced with a severe loss of oil revenues. The Syrian Government declared that it would not allow the repair of the pipelines until Israel had withdrawn her troops from Gaza and the Gulf of Aqaba. Not until March 1957 was it possible to restore the pipelines, Israel having in the meantime agreed to evacuate her forces from the areas in dispute.

UNION WITH EGYPT

The Syrian National Assembly, in November 1957, passed a resolution in favour of union with Egypt and the formal union of Egypt and Syria to constitute one state under the title of the United Arab Republic received the final approval of the Syrian National Assembly on February 5th, 1958. President Nasser of Egypt, on February 21st, became the first head of the combined state. A central cabinet for the U.A.R. was established in October 1958, also two regional executive councils, one for Syria and one for Egypt. A further move towards integration came in March 1960, when a single National Assembly for the whole of the U.A.R. consisting of 400 deputies from Egypt and 200 from Syria, was instituted.

Syrian dissatisfaction with the union grew over the next three years, as administration and officials of Egyptian origin came to hold influential positions in the Syrian Region, and on September 28th, 1961, there occurred in Syria a military *coup d'état* which aimed—successfully— at the separation of Syria from Egypt and at the dissolution of the United Arab Republic. Political figures representing most of the parties which existed in Syria before the establishment of the U.A.R. in 1958 met at Damascus and Aleppo on October 3rd, 1961, issuing a declaration of support for the new regime and calling for free elections to a new legislature. President Nasser now, on October 5th, recognized the *fait accompli*. Most foreign states made haste to grant formal recognition to the government at Damascus. On October 13th 1961, Syria became once more a member of the United Nations. A provisional constitution was promulgated in November and elections for a Constituent Assembly took place on December 1st, 1961.

The regime thus established in Syria rested on no sure foundation. At the end of March 1962 the Syrian Army intervened once more, bringing about the resignation of Dr. Nazim Kudsi, the President of the Republic, and also of the ministers who had taken office in December 1961. After demonstrations at Aleppo, Homs and Hama in April 1962, Dr. Kudsi was reinstated as President, but further ministerial resignations in May of that year pointed to the existence of continuing tensions within the government.

THE REVOLUTION OF 1963

A military junta, styled the National Council of the Revolutionary Command, seized control in Damascus on March 8th, 1963. In May the Baathists took measures to purge the armed forces and the administration of personnel known to favour a close alignment with Egypt. A new government, formed on May 13th and strongly Baathist in character, carried out a further purge in June and at the same time created a National Guard recruited from members of the Baath movement. These measures led the pro-Egyptian elements to attempt a *coup d'état* at Damascus on July 18th, 1963. The attempt failed, however, with a considerable loss of life. On July 27th Maj-Gen. Amin al-Hafiz, Deputy Prime Minister and Minister of the Interior, became President of the National Council of the Revolutionary Command, a position equivalent to Head of State.

BAATH SOCIALISM

The nationalization of all Arab-owned banks in 1963, and of various industrial enterprises, also the transfer of land to the peasants—all had contributed to bring about much dissatisfaction in the business world and amongst the influential landed elements. The Baath regime depended for its main support on the armed forces which, however, had been recruited in no small degree from the religious minorities in Syria, including adherents of the Shi'i (Alawi) faith—most Syrians being, in fact, of Sunni or orthodox Muslim allegiance. In general, conservative Muslims tended to oppose the Baath government under guidance of the *'ulama* and of the Muslim Brotherhood. The mass of the peasant population was thought to have some pro-Nasser sympathies; the working class (small in number) was divided between pro-Nasser and Baathist adherents; the middle and upper classes opposed the domination of al-Baath. The unease arising out of these frictions and antipathies took the form of disturbances and finally of open revolt—soon suppressed—at Hama (April 1964).

On April 25th, 1964, a provisional constitution had been promulgated, describing Syria as a democratic socialist republic forming an integral part of the Arab nation. A Presidential Council was established on May 14th, 1964, with General Hafiz as head of the state.

The as yet undeveloped petroleum and other mineral resources of Syria were nationalized in 1964, together with other industrial concerns. On January 7th, 1965, a special military court was created with sweeping powers to deal with all offences, of word or deed, against the nationalization decrees and the socialist revolution. General Hafiz denounced the *'ulama* and the Muslim Brotherhood as being involved in the resulting demonstrations. Further nationalization followed.

A National Council, almost 100 strong, was established in August 1965 with the task of preparing a new constitution which would be submitted to a public referendum. Meeting for the first time on September 1st, 1965, it created a Presidency Council, of five members, which was to exercise the powers of a head of state.

RADICAL REACTION

The tensions hitherto visible in al-Baath were, however, still active. Two groups stood ranged one against the other—on the one hand the older more experienced politicians in al-Baath, less inclined than in former years to insist on the unrestrained pursuit of the main Baathist objectives, socialism and pan-Arab union, and on the other hand the extreme left-wing elements, doctrinaire in their attitude and enjoying considerable support amongst the younger radical officers in the armed forces.

The tensions thus engendered found expression in a new *coup d'état* on February 23rd, 1966. A military junta representing the extreme radical elements in al-Baath seized power in Damascus and placed under arrest a number of personalities long identified with al-Baath and belonging to the international leadership controlling the organization throughout the Arab world—amongst them Mr. Michael Aflaq, the founder of al-Baath; General Hafiz, the chairman of the recently established Presidency Council; and Mr. Salah al-Din Bitar, the Prime Minister of the displaced administration.

ARAB-ISRAELI WAR OF 1967

The friction ever present along the frontier between Syria and Israel had flared out from time to time during recent years into violent conflict, particularly in the region of Lake Tiberias. Now, in the winter of 1966–67, the tension along the border began to assume more serious proportions. Israel, in October 1966, complained to the Security Council of the United Nations about guerilla activities from Syria across the frontier into Israeli territory. In April 1967, mortars, cannon and air force units from Syria and Israel were involved in fighting south-east of Lake Tiberias.

The continuing tension on the Syrian-Israeli frontier was now to become a major influence leading to the war which broke out on June 5th, 1967, between Israel and her Arab neighbours Egypt, Syria and Jordan. During the course of hostilities which lasted six days Israel defeated Egypt and Jordan and then, after some stubborn fighting, outflanked and overran the Syrian positions on the hills above Lake Tiberias. With the breakthrough accomplished, Israeli forces made a rapid advance and occupied the town of Quneitra about forty miles from Damascus. On June 10th Israel and Syria announced their formal acceptance of the United Nations proposal for a cease-fire, but Syria effectively boycotted the Arab summit conference held at Khartoum in August 1967 and in September the Baath party of Syria rejected all idea of a compromise with Israel. The resolution adopted by the UN Security Council in November, urging the withdrawal of the Israelis from the lands occupied by them during the June war and the ending of the belligerency which the Arab governments had up till then maintained against Israel, was rejected by Syria, which alone maintained its commitment to a reunified Palestine.

STRUGGLE FOR POWER 1968-71

The ruling Baath Party had for some years been divided into two main factions. Until October 1968 the dominant faction had been the "progressive" group led by Dr. Atassi and Dr. Makhous, the Premier and Foreign Minister respectively. This group was distinguished by its doctrinaire and Marxist-orientated public pronouncements and by the strong support it received from the U.S.S.R. It held that the creation of a strong one-party state and economy along neo-Marxist lines was of paramount importance, overriding even the need for a militant stand towards Israel and for Arab unity.

By October 1968 the government felt particularly insecure, partly owing to a feud with the new Baath régime in Iraq, and at the end of the month a new cabinet was formed including several members of the opposing "nationalist" faction. This group took less interest in ideological questions and favoured a pragmatic attitude to the economy, improved relations with Syria's Arab neighbours and full participation in the campaign against Israel, including support for the fedayeen movement. Its leader was Lt.-Gen. Hafiz al-Assad, who assumed the all-important Ministry of Defence. His critical attitude to the powerful Soviet influence on the government, seen by some "nationalists" as tantamount to colonialism in restricting Syria's freedom of action, led to a prolonged struggle with the "progressive" leadership. Cabinet reshuffles took place in March and again in May, but both Dr. Atassi and General Assad retained their positions. During the spring of 1969 a number of Communists were arrested or sent into exile, and the leader of the Syrian Communist Party, still technically an illegal organization, flew to Moscow.

General Assad attempted to take over the government in February 1969 but was forestalled by Soviet threats that if he did so all military supplies (including spares), economic and technical aid, and trade agreements would end. This would have brought about a major disruption in the national economy and the armed forces, and the "nationalists" were obliged to yield. In May General Mustafa Tlas, the Army Chief of Staff and General Assad's right-hand man, led a military delegation to Peking to buy arms. The incident indicated a new independence of Moscow. Some observers also saw this independence in the creation of a joint military command with Iraq (with whom relations improved during the spring) and Jordan. Relations with the Lebanon worsened, owing to Syria's support of the Lebanese fedayeen movement, containing many Syrian members. In the 1968–70 period this appeared to direct much of its activity towards bringing down the precarious Lebanese Government, presumably in the hope

that a more militantly anti-Israe ministry would take power.

In November 1970, following a reported *coup* attempt backed by Iraq in August, the struggle between the two factions of the Baath Party came to a head when General Assad seized power. Dr. Atassi, who was in hospital at the time, was placed under guard and a retired General, Salah Jadid, Assistant Secretary-General of the Baath Party and leader of the civilian faction, was arrested. Other members of the civilian wing were arrested or fled to the Lebanon. The coup was precipitated by attempts of Jadid and his supporters to oust Assad and Tlas from their posts. This power struggle had become acute as a result of differences over support for the Palestine guerrillas during the fighting with the Jordanian army in September. Jadid and Yusuf Zeayen, a former Prime Minister, controlled the movement of tanks from Syria into Jordan to support the Palestinian guerrillas' efforts against the Jordanian army. This, Assad and the military faction opposed. Their approach to the Palestinian problem was more akin to Nasser's and they wanted to avoid giving any provocation to Israel, because they considered the Syrian armed forces to be unready to offer adequate resistance.

ASSAD IN POWER

There was no obvious opposition to the army takeover. Ahmed Khatib became acting President and General Assad Prime Minister and Party Secretary-General. A new Regional Command of the Baath Party was formed. The old leaders were removed from their posts in a purge which stretched into the new year. Following amendments to the 1969 provisional constitution in February 1971, General Assad was elected President for a seven-year term in March. In the following month Maj.-Gen. Abdel Rahman Khlefawi became Premier and Mahmoud al-Ayoubi was appointed Vice-President. In February the first legislative body in Syria since 1966, the People's Council, was formed. Of its 173 members, 87 represented the Baath Party.

The Nasserite leanings of the new regime in foreign policy soon became apparent. Although Syria continued to reject the November 1967 UN Security Council resolution, relations with the U.A.R. and Jordan improved, and Syria's isolation in the Arab world was soon reduced. Syria's willingness to join a union with the U.A.R., Sudan and Libya almost immediately became apparent and agreement on federation with Libya and the U.A.R. was reached in April 1971, but the Federation had little effect.

After coming to power, the Assad regime increased the Syrian army's control over Saiqa. In April 1971 guerrilla operations against Israeli positions from the Syrian front were banned by the Government. Then, at the beginning of July, some guerrilla units were forced out of Syria into south Lebanon and arms destined for them and arriving from Algeria were seized by the Syrian authorities. Yet after the Jordanian Government's final onslaught on the Palestinian guerrillas in north Jordan in July Syria closed her border and in August broke off diplomatic relations when the tension had become so great that tank and artillery clashes had developed between the two armies. Egyptian mediation reduced the chances of any more serious conflict developing but diplomatic links remained severed with Jordan until October 1973. Relations with the U.S.S.R. improved during the last half of 1971 and in 1972, and in May Marshal Grechko, the Soviet Defence Minister, visited Damascus. Syria was not prepared, however, to sign a friendship treaty with the U.S.S.R. like Egypt and Iraq. On the other hand, the Syrian Government, which had been broadened in March 1972 to include representatives of parties other than the Baath like the communists, did not follow Egypt's example in July and expel its Soviet advisers.

SYRIA

In December 1972 Maj.-Gen. Khlefawi resigned from the post of Prime Minister for health reasons and a new Government was formed by Mahmoud al-Ayoubi, the Vice-President, with 16 out of 31 government portfolios going to the Baath Party. At the end of January 1973 a draft Constitution was approved by the People's Council and confirmed by a referendum in March. The Sunni Muslims were dissatisfied that the Constitution did not recognize Islam as the State religion, and as a result of their pressure an amendment was passed declaring that the President must be a Muslim. Under the Constitution freedom of belief is guaranteed, with the State respecting all religions, although the Constitution recognizes that Islamic jurisprudence was "a principal source of legislation". In 1972 a National Charter, creating a National Progressive Front, a grouping of the Baath party and its allies, came into being. In May 1973 elections were organized for the new People's Council under the aegis of the Front and 140 out of the 186 seats were won by the Progressive Front while 42 seats were won by Independents and 4 by the Opposition.

THE FOURTH ARAB-ISRAELI WAR AND ITS AFTERMATH

On the afternoon of October 6th, 1973, Egyptian and Syrian forces launched war against Israel in an effort to regain territories lost in 1967. On both the Egyptian and Syrian fronts complete surprise was achieved, giving the Arabs a strong initial advantage, much of which they subsequently lost. The course of the war is described in "The Arab-Israeli Confrontation 1967–82", pages 43–44. Although Egypt signed a disengagement agreement with Israel on January 18th, 1974, fighting continued on the Syrian front in the Golan Heights area until a disengagement agreement was signed on May 31st, after much diplomacy and travel by the U.S. Secretary of State, Dr. Henry Kissinger (see "Documents on Palestine" pages 79–80).

Syria has continued to maintain a "hard line" policy in the Middle East, especially regarding the Palestinian question, and since the 1973 war it has received vast amounts of Soviet military aid which has fully re-equipped its forces. Contact with Moscow and Eastern European states has, for most of the time, been extremely close. Syria's strong support for the PLO was vindicated in October 1974 at the Arab Summit in Rabat, Morocco, where the PLO's claim to the West Bank was recognized.

By June 1976, however, Syria was in the position of invading Lebanon to crush the Palestinians, and finding most of the remainder of the Arab world agreeing to send a peace-keeping force to Lebanon to quell the conflict.

FOREIGN AFFAIRS 1975-78

This reversal for Syria arose out of a lengthy chain of events. An improvement in relations with Jordan took place in 1975, with King Hussein visiting Damascus in April and President Assad visiting Amman in June. A joint military and political command was set up between the two countries and by the spring of 1977 their customs, electricity networks and education systems were unified. Plans were made for the eventual union of the two countries. Relations between Syria and Jordan cooled, however, after Jordan appeared to give guarded support to Sadat's peace initiative in November 1977.

The second Egyptian-Israeli disengagement agreement in Sinai, signed in September 1975, met with Syria's strong condemnation. Syria accused Egypt of going it alone, and, by agreeing to three years of peace with Israel, weakening the general Arab position and betraying the Palestinians.

Syria had shown considerable interest in the Lebanese civil war since it began in April 1975. Initially, Syria wanted to protect the position of the Palestinians in Lebanon and perhaps also further plans for a "greater Syria", sending in about 2,000 Saiqa troops in January 1976. After having secured a ceasefire Assad pledged that he would control the Palestinians in Lebanon, and the core of the PLO under Yasser Arafat began to be apprehensive that they would be dominated by Syria. By early June 1976 the fighting in Lebanon was so fierce that Syria felt obliged to intervene militarily and overtly. This time, Syria's intervention was welcomed by the Christian Right and condemned by the Palestinians and the Muslim left (and also Egypt).

A meeting of the Arab League Foreign Ministers on June 8th–9th agreed that an Arab peace-keeping force should be sent to Lebanon to effect a ceasefire. After some delay, a peace-keeping force consisting of Syrian and Libyan troops in equal proportions did arrive in Lebanon, but the fighting continued unabated until October 1976 when Arab summits at Riyadh and Cairo secured a more lasting ceasefire. A 30,000-strong Arab Deterrent Force, consisting largely of Syrian troops, was given authority by the Arab summits to maintain the peace. President Assad's prestige in Syria and the Arab world was considerably strengthened by this success. Relations with Egypt improved after a tacit understanding that Syria would end its criticism of the September 1975 Egyptian-Israeli Sinai agreement in return for Egypt's acceptance of Syria's intervention in Lebanon.

In August 1976 the Prime Minister, Mahmoud al-Ayoubi, was replaced by his predecessor, Gen. Khlefawi. He held office until March 1978, when he was succeeded by Muhammad Ali al-Halabi, previously Speaker of the People's Council.

Relations with the U.S.S.R., which had been extremely bad during most of 1976, improved after the October 1976 summits and were consolidated when Assad visited Moscow in April 1977. With Iraq, however, relations continued to be bad. Iraq shut off the flow of oil from Kirkuk to the Syrian port of Banias as a protest against Syrian intervention in Lebanon. Another Iraqi grievance was Syria's use of Euphrates water. When an attempt to assassinate the Syrian Vice-Premier and Minister of Foreign Affairs, Abdel Halim Khaddam, was made in December 1976, voices in Syria were swift to blame terrorists trained in Iraq. Relations between Syria and Egypt deteriorated again as a result of President Sadat's peace initiative in November 1977. Syria's President Assad strongly criticized the move and diplomatic relations between the two countries were broken off in December.

Syria's rift with Egypt grew even wider after Sadat and Prime Minister Begin of Israel signed the Camp David agreements (see p. 82) in the U.S.A. in September 1978. The third summit of the "Steadfastness and Confrontation Front", comprising Arab countries strongly opposed to Egypt's attempt to make a separate peace with Israel, met in Damascus in late September 1978. When the Egyptian-Israeli peace treaty was finally signed in March 1979 Syria joined most of the other Arab League member countries at a meeting in Baghdad which endorsed political and economic sanctions against Egypt.

Egypt's *rapprochement* with Israel led to a brief improvement in relations with Iraq. In October 1978 Syria and Iraq signed a National Charter for Joint Action in which the eventual intention was complete political and economic union between the two countries. Although the oil pipeline from Iraq to Banias was re-opened, the scheme for union collapsed when an internal conspiracy in Iraq in July 1979 was attributed to Syrian intrigue.

DIFFICULTIES OF THE EARLY 1980s

Although President Assad was comfortably returned for a second seven-year term of office in February 1978 (he received 99.6 per cent of the votes cast and 97 per cent of the electorate voted), there has been growing evidence of internal dissatisfaction in Syria. Important government posts are largely in the hands of Alawites, a minority Muslim sect to which Assad belongs, and since 1977 assassinations of Alawites have become an increasing problem. Some dramatic killings took place in June 1979 when more than 60 army cadets, most of them thought to be Alawites, were massacred. The slaughter was officially attributed to the Muslim Brotherhood, who have also been held responsible for subsequent killings.

President Assad's attempts to end this violence have met with little success. In January 1980 he introduced a new Cabinet under Dr. Abdul Rauf Kassem as Prime Minister, and 23 of the 37 Ministers had never before held Ministerial posts. Militias of workers, peasants and students have been set up, but have been ineffective in helping the regular authorities to curb violence. Although the Muslim Brotherhood is held responsible, and membership of it was made a capital offence on July 9th, the U.S.A., Jordan, and Iraq have all been accused of plotting violence.

By June 1981 Assad's domestic difficulties were overshadowed by his involvement in foreign affairs. During the Spring of 1980 the number of Soviet advisers in the country grew to over 4,000 and in October 1980 Syria signed a 20-year Treaty of Friendship and Co-operation with the U.S.S.R. A proposed merger between Syria and Libya, announced in September 1980, seems to have little chance of success.

On the outbreak of the Gulf War in September 1980 between Iraq and Iran, Syria supported Iran, on account of her own long-standing distrust of the rival Baath Party in Iraq. A crisis with Jordan soon developed, partly because of Syrian allegations that Muslim Brotherhood treachery was being planned from within Jordan and partly because of Jordan's support for Iraq in the Gulf War. Towards the end of 1980 Syrian and Jordanian troops faced each other across the frontier and conflict was finally averted by Saudi mediation.

Syria's biggest distraction, however, was her involvement in Lebanon. The 30,000 Syrian troops of the Arab Deterrent Force had been in Lebanon since 1976, and had been a severe drain on Syrian resources. In the summer of 1980 the Phalangist militia consolidated its position in Lebanon and came to occupy the town of Zahle in the Beka'a valley east of Beirut. Clashes developed in the Zahle area between Syrian troops and the Phalangist militia, and the Christian forces found themselves under siege in Zahle in April 1981. Syria maintained that Zahle and the Beka'a valley were vital to her security against Israel. Israeli planes made repeated sorties into Lebanon, and at the end of April Syria moved surface-to-air missiles into the Beka'a valley after two Syrian helicopters had been destroyed by Israeli planes. A prolonged international crisis developed, with the threat of war between Israel and Syria becoming serious. After Saudi and Kuwaiti mediation, however, the siege of Zahle was lifted at the end of June, and the Phalangist militia was expected to leave. The SAM missiles remained in the Beka'a valley, as the Syrians maintained that this was a separate issue.

In the following year, however, there were a number of setbacks for President Assad. In December Israel formally annexed the Golan Heights, which was a move which prompted Syria to try to obtain more arms from the U.S.S.R. A huge car bomb explosion in Damascus in November was attributed to the Muslim Brotherhood, and this was followed by further indications of incipient unrest, culminating in February 1982 in an uprising in Hama which lasted for nearly three weeks. This was eventually put down by Assad's forces, and, although it was again attributed to the Muslim Brotherhood, other opposition elements were also involved. On February 20th an opposition alliance entitled the National Alliance of the Syrian People was formed, consisting of 19 factions drawn from, among others, Baathists, Nasserites, Christians, Alawites and the Muslim Brotherhood.

These problems were completely overshadowed, however, by the Israeli invasion of Lebanon in June 1982. Israeli forces quickly reached Beirut, the Syrian missiles in the Beka'a Valley were destroyed, and the Syrian presence in Lebanon, in the guise of the Arab Deterrent Force, was rendered impotent. In early July Assad and the Syrian Foreign Minister, Abdul Halim Khaddam, held talks with King Fahd of Saudi Arabia as part of general negotiations to secure an Israeli withdrawal from Lebanon.

ECONOMIC SURVEY

Despite its proven resilience to the immense strains of war and periods of political instability, the Syrian economy today has still to be seen against a backdrop of geopolitics. As a confrontation state, a portion of whose land has been under Israeli occupation since 1967, Syria bears a heavy burden of defence expenditure which consumes up to a third of its annual budget. At the same time its position at the frontline has encouraged Syria to assume responsibility for events elsewhere in the area, resulting in 1976 in its military intervention in Lebanon. The continuing involvement in Lebanon today, combined with the threat of outright war with Israel and the unstable nature of relations with neighbouring Iraq, all affect the Syrian economy. In 1976–77, for example, Iraq decided to stop pumping oil through Syria to the Mediterranean coast, thus depriving the Government in Damacus of valuable transit revenues

and the benefits of easily accessible oil supplies at a favourable price. At the same time interruptions also occurred in the aid Syria is supposed to receive from other Arab oil states. For a period, therefore, the Government bore the cost of keeping its troops in Lebanon all alone. Financial difficulties recurred for similar reasons in 1982 when, with the Iraq-Syria pipeline closed again and Arab aid donors dissatisfied with Syria's stance on the Iraq-Iran war, the Syrian budget had to be cut by 10 per cent.

Indeed, all attempts at sustained development since Syria's independence have been disrupted by political instability. In the 1950s and 1960s frequent changes of government and alternate periods of boom and slump led to a mass exodus of capital and skills and a state of lethargy among those who stayed behind. Three years of relative calm under President Assad had just started to bring about an improvement

SYRIA

in this state of affairs when the Arab-Israeli war of October 1973 broke out, causing damage to Syria estimated at $1,800 million. Latakia port, the Banias and Tartous oil terminals and the huge Homs complex in central Syria which then housed the country's only oil refinery and generated more than 40 per cent of its power needs were virtually destroyed. The reconstruction effort needed was immense but the Government acted swiftly, bringing in economic liberalization measures to encourage investment in early 1974 and gradually, business confidence began to return, to the extent that the Third Development Plan (1971–75) ended with a flourish of unprecedented growth. This, in turn, prompted the government to reinforce investment incentives in certain sectors and to launch an ambitious Fourth Development Plan for the period 1976–80, only to find itself confronted once again with the economic repercussions of regional political problems.

In the absence of a Middle East peace settlement, Syria's best hope for economic progress lies in diversification of its sources of development finance and export revenues. This has already partly been achieved. Although, for example, the U.S. attitude to aid to Syria has been coloured by the 1980 friendship treaty with the Soviet Union, loans are still being received from the World Bank, the European Economic Community and various OPEC-backed multilateral institutions. However, exports, led by oil and cotton, still depend on the fickle world commodity markets, while the services sector, dependent on tourism and transit trade, remains extremely vulnerable to the political situation in the region.

AREA AND POPULATION

Syria covers an area of about 71,500 square miles (185,180 sq. km.), about 45 per cent of which is considered arable land. The remainder consists of bare mountain, desert and pastures suitable only for nomads. Of the total cultivable area of 8.7 million hectares little more than about 70 per cent is under cultivation. According to official statistics for mid-1980, the population (including Palestinian refugees) totalled 8,979,000. The average annual increase is estimated to be 3.8 per cent. Census totals in September 1960 and September 1970 stood at 4,565,121 and 6,304,685 respectively. Of the total population in 1973, 35.9 per cent were aged under 10 and roughly half were under the age of 15.4 years.

There has been a continuing movement from village to town, reflected in a 60 per cent increase in the urban population between 1959, when 35 per cent of the population were classified as urban, and 1969, when 40 per cent came in this category. This movement has been amply illustrated by the growth of shanty towns along the edges of the large urban centres suchs a Damascus and Aleppo. The population of Damascus and its surrounding province approximately doubled between 1959 and 1973, from over half a million to an estimated 1,456,000. By early 1979 it had grown to 2.25 million. The population of Aleppo, put at 466,026 in 1959, rose to 646,000 in 1973, the total figure for the city and its province standing at 1,522,000.

The total labour force rose from 1,524,552 in 1970 to 1,994,759 in 1977. The composition of the labour force in 1977 reflected the exodus from rural to urban areas. Of the total, agriculture, forestry, hunting and fishing employed 37.8 per cent (against 49 per cent in 1970), manufacturing and mining employed 13.7 per cent (against 12.5 per cent), trade, catering and hotels 10.2 per cent (against 9.1 per cent) and transport and communications employed 6 per cent (compared with 4 per cent in 1970).

AGRICULTURE

Agriculture has for long been a mainstay of the Syrian economy in spite of the existence of a traditionally strong trading sector and relatively successful attempts at industrialization. It accounts for roughly one-fifth of the G.D.P. and employs about half the labour force. The main areas of cultivation are a narrow strip of land along the coast from the Lebanese to the Turkish frontiers which enjoys a Mediterranean climate, is exceedingly fertile and produces fruit, olives, tobacco and cotton. East of this strip lies the northward continuation of the Lebanon range of mountains, which falls sharply on the east to the Orontes River valley whose marshes were recently reclaimed to form one of Syria's most fertile areas. In central Syria this valley joins the 100-mile wide steppe-plain which runs from the Jordanian borders northeastward towards the Euphrates valley. The plain is traditionally Syria's major agricultural area, mainly grains-producing, in which are located the main cities, Damascus, Homs, Hama and Aleppo. The importance of this plain is now being rivalled by a fourth area, the Jezira, which lies between the Euphrates in Syria and the Tigris in Iraq. Although fertile lands along the banks of the Euphrates and its tributaries had previously been cultivated, the Jezira only came into its own in the early 1950s when large-scale cotton cultivation was introduced in former pasture lands. It is now vastly increasing its output with the development of the Euphrates Dam.

One of the chief characteristics of Syria's agricultural performance, in the absence of any established large-scale irrigation system, is the violent annual fluctuation in output resulting from wide variations in rainfall. Dependence on rainfall for good harvests is nowhere more clearly shown than in the Central Bank's general indices for agricultural production, which show a swing from 156 in 1972 to 103 the following year and up again to an estimated 181 in 1977 (1970 = 100).

Agriculture's share in the G.D.P. has fallen substantially since the early 1960s. In 1962 it had contributed 32.2 per cent of G.D.P. and in 1972 25.6 per cent. In 1981 it accounted for only 19.9 per cent. Initially the decline was attributable to under-use of potential caused by the discouraging effects of the 1958 agrarian reform law on investment and the removal of the large rural landowners and urban money-lenders who had formerly provided the traditional channels of credit. The area of unused cultivable land (excluding fallow) increased from 1,892,000 hectares in 1963 to 2,825,000 hectares by

1970. Suspicion of Government intentions was gradually tempered, however, by the relaxation of the reform law and, under the post-1970 Assad administration, by a number of significant amendments. The apparent continued decline in more recent years has simply resulted from the growing comparative importance of the mining and manufacturing sector. Agriculture, forestry and fishing contributed £S10,935 million to G.D.P. in 1980 and the annual growth rate for this sector was projected at 7.8 per cent under the Fifth Five-Year Development Plan.

Extensive irrigation programmes now under way should eventually have the effect of steadying agricultural output as well as increasing it. It was with this in mind that, out of agricultural investments accounting for a sizeable 35 per cent of total investment under the Third Five-Year Plan (1971–75), the Government devoted the lion's share to the Euphrates Dam project (*see* below under Economic Development). The main task for the Fourth Development Plan, which ran from 1976 to 1980, was to put the dam's stored waters to work and to irrigate an additional 240,000 hectares of land in the Euphrates basin by the end of the decade. This area will then be expanded to 640,000 hectares in later years. Other irrigation schemes on the Yarmouk river and in the Ghab, implemented with French, and possibly later American, assistance will reclaim still more land, increasing the acreage available for such crops as cereals, sugar beet, rice and cotton.

Cotton, for long Syria's most valuable source of export earnings, ceded this distinction to petroleum in 1974. Exports of cotton have dropped both in value and volume, falling from £S836 million in 1977 to £S665.0 million in 1981. Exports of lint from the 1981 cotton crop totalled only an estimated 70,000 tons, compared with 128,000 tons in 1976/77. This drop was partly due to the expansion of the local textile industry but, even so, the government is hoping to increase revenue from cotton exports to help compensate for falling income from oil.

Although medium-staple cotton had been grown in Syria for many years, it was the high prices prevalent after the Second World War and during the Korean War that provided the greatest impetus to cotton production. The early 1950s saw the previously neglected Jezira area opened up for large-scale agriculture on a new capital intensive basis, relatively free from the traditional agricultural relations, still semi-feudal in the rest of the country. Cotton production grew from 38,000 tons in 1949 to 100,000 tons in 1950 and 220,800 tons in 1954. The area under cotton grew from 25,300 hectares in 1949 to 78,000 hectares in 1950 and 250,000 hectares in 1971/72. During the mid-1970s, when world cotton prices were low and sugar prices high, Syria, along with a number of other cotton producers, began to reduce the area under cotton in favour of sugar beet and new strains of wheat. At the start of the 1980s, however, the emphasis is on both cotton and sugar. After a cotton harvest of 322,570 tons in 1980/81 (giving 120,000 tons of lint), the crop for 1981/82 is thought to have

produced 340,000 tons for ginning, giving 130,000 tons of lint. Sugar production, meanwhile, was projected at 595,000 tons for the 1980/81 season, with a tenfold increase planned over the next five to ten years.

The textile industry, Syria's third largest industry after oil and phosphates, is undergoing expansion and local consumption of ginned cotton is expected to rise from 25 per cent of output in 1978 to 60 per cent in 1984. So far, however, cotton yarn output has suffered from the decline in annual lint production, and fell to only 25,000 tons in 1981, compared with 27,800 tons in 1977.

Syria's grain crop is also of prime importance. Wheat and barley together took up some 2,659,000 hectares in 1980, or roughly two-thirds of the total cultivated area. The combined area devoted to these crops in the period 1961–65 averaged 2,136,000 hectares. Output of both crops fluctuates considerably. In 1972 Syria produced enough grain to export 278,400 tons of wheat, worth £S84.2 million. In 1973, in contrast, there was a very poor harvest of only 593,000 tons of wheat and 102,000 tons of barley. In 1976 wheat production soared to 1,790,000 tons and in 1980 it increased still further to 2.23 million tons. Good wheat crops have also been reported since then, with the result that Syria's wheat imports in 1982 were expected to be roughly half the 195,000 tons imported in 1981.

There are a number of other actual and potential agricultural exports. The General Tobacco Organization, which exports leaf tobacco and cigarettes, processed 8,900 tons of tobacco in 1980 and this quantity was set to increase to 9,800 tons in 1981. There is also considerable room for expansion in the marketing of fruit and vegetables. The fruit crop in 1980 produced 356,000 tons of grapes, 48,000 tons of apricots and 89,000 tons of apples. Tomatoes and onions in 1980 totalled 644,000 tons and 151,000 tons respectively. A breakdown of recent trade figures, however, indicates that exports of fruit and vegetables currently represent about 4 per cent of export income.

Stockraising is another important branch of agriculture which is being developed on a large scale with finance from the World Bank and other sources. Hungary has helped to set up half a dozen poultry farms throughout the country and egg production has risen dramatically, from 650 million in 1975 to 1,335 million in 1980.

PETROLEUM

Syria was at one time thought to have no oil. The Iraq Petroleum Company group had rights throughout Syria which it abandoned in 1951 after failing to find oil in commercial quantities. Concessions granted to an independent American operator in 1955 and to a West-German led consortium in 1956 led to the discovery first of the Karachuk field in the northeastern corner of the country, then of the Suweidiya field and finally of the field at nearby Rumelan. But the oil at all three places was of low quality; that found by the Americans at Karachuk having a density of 19° API and a sulphur content of 4.5 per cent and that found by the German group at Suweidiya having a density of 25° API and 3.5 per cent sulphur content. By 1964, years before any of the three fields had begun production on a commercial basis, Syria became one of the first Arab states to discard the notion of oil concessions and nationalize its oil operations. Even at that early stage Syria's industrial planners were anxious to use the country's oil not only for export in its crude state but also as a raw material for domestic industry. For the next 10 years all exploration and exploitation was conducted solely by the state-owned General Petroleum Authority and its off-shoot, the Syrian Petroleum Company, with Soviet assistance.

Output from Suweidiya started in July 1968 and totalled one million tons the first year, of which 833,000 tons were exported. Output in 1969, when the Karachuk field went into operation, failed to reach expectations, totalling only 3.2 million tons, of which 2.3 million tons were exported. The October war in 1973 reduced production from a level of 6.3 million tons the previous year to just 5.4 million tons, recovering in 1974 to 6.2 million tons. Finally in 1976, output reached 10,039,000 tons, but dropped back to just under 8.7 million tons in 1981 and is not now expected to exceed some 7.8–7.9 million tons per year for the next few years. This is chiefly because Syria's existing fields are past their prime. Overall exports of crude oil and petroleum products totalled 6.3 million tons in 1980, dropping slightly to 6.2 million tons in 1981.

Because of the need to discover new fields, the future of the Syrian oil industry remains in doubt. Since the mid-1970s the Government has reversed its no-concessions policy and in May 1975 the first Syrian concession won by any Western company for over 15 years was awarded to a U.S. group, on production-sharing terms heavily tilted in the Government's favour and stipulating that $20 million be invested in exploration offshore. In June 1975 the Government took its new policy one stage further by offering a dozen onshore oil concessions for international bidding. Altogether 50,000 square kilometres were to be made available. The oil companies' response to the invitation was initially slow and, when the first U.S. group, Tripco, relinquished its concession in March 1976, no other company had come forward to join the search. In July 1977, however, a U.S.-Syrian consortium called Samoco took up a concession in the Deir-ez-Zor area and in December another concession in Raqqa province was taken by Shell subsidiaries, Syria Shell Petroleum Development and Pecten Syria Company. Both Shell and Samoco insisted on a larger share of eventual oil production than was agreed between the Government and Tripco. This softening of terms brought other firms on to the scene, including Challenger Oil (Chadoil) of Canada and Coastal States Gas Corporation and Chevron of the U.S.A.

Not all Syria's oil is of the poor quality found in the three original fields. The Jbeisseh field, between Hassakeh and the Iraqi border (an area in which the Iraq Petroleum Company had formerly found only

gas), was officially opened in May 1975, producing high quality oil with a gravity of 40.5° API and a 0.62 per cent sulphur content. Rompetrol of Romania has since discovered 38° API crude in its concession in the north, but not in commercial quantities. It is clear, however, that further exploration will alter the size of Syria's proven oil reserves, which were estimated in 1979 to total some 1,300 million tons, of which about 300 million tons is recoverable. Gas reserves have been revised downwards from 90,000 million to 60,000 million cubic feet.

Though Suweidiya crude is suitable for blending with lighter Algerian or Libyan crudes to produce fuel oils and the high sulphur content of the Karachuk crude makes it suitable for the production of good quality asphalt, the generally poor quality of Syrian oil, together with opposition on the part of some of the major oil companies to Syria's nationalization experiment, combined at the outset of the country's oil history to cause considerable marketing difficulties. But with the growth of sales, particularly to Greece, France, Italy and the Soviet Union, oil has become Syria's most important export. The value of oil exports, which in 1973 had amounted to £S291.2 million, soared to £S1,607.5 million in 1974 and £S5,043.6 million in 1981.

January 1975 saw the capacity of the Homs refinery restored to its former level of 2.5 million tons per year (following its virtual destruction by Israeli bombardment in October 1973) and in March 1976, with the addition of two extra distillation units installed by Czechoslovakia and Italy, this capacity doubled to 5 million tons. A second refinery, at Banias, came on stream in 1980 in trial runs and by December 1981 it had achieved full capacity of 6 million tons per year. The project, undertaken by Romania, was affected by the interruption of Iraqi oil supplies from 1976 to 1978 and its specifications had to be altered to enable it to process different grades of crude. Syria now has no plans for a third refinery, at least for the duration of the 1981–85 Plan.

Royalties for the transit of foreign crude through Syrian territory were for many years more valuable than indigenous oil production. Two pipelines carry oil from Kirkuk through Syria. One, built in 1934, leads on to a terminal at Tripoli in Lebanon. The second, completed in 1952, branches off at Homs to the Syrian terminal at Banias. A third pipeline, belonging to the Trans-Arabian Pipeline Company (Tapline) and carrying 24 million tons of Saudi Arabian crude a year to a terminal near Sidon in Lebanon, crosses about 100 miles of Syrian territory, much of which was occupied by Israel in 1967. After nationalizing the Iraq Petroleum Company in June 1972, Iraq took over payment of royalties to Syria and, after lengthy negotiations, a transit agreement was signed in January 1973 providing both for transit dues and oil supplies for Syria's own domestic use. However, the flow of oil through the Kirkuk-Banias pipeline has been interrupted more than once since then. Throughput was suspended in 1976 when negotiations between Iraq and Syria on renewing the financial clauses of the transit agreement broke down, with Iraq demanding higher oil payments (to match the

1973–74 oil price increases) and Syria seeking a proportionate increase in transit fees. For over two years Iraq refused to use the pipeline, directing its oil southwards to the Gulf and also via Turkey, through a pipeline that came on stream in 1977. The shortlived improvement in Iraqi-Syrian political relations in late 1978, combined with the world oil shortage arising from the Iranian revolution, brought a resumption of pumping from Kirkuk to Banias in 1979, but this was halted yet again in September 1980 at the start of the Iraq-Iran war. When, despite the continuation of the war, Iraq recommenced oil exports on a limited scale, the situation in the Gulf put Syria in a relatively stronger position and the Iraq-Syria pipeline came into use again in February 1981. However, Syria remained dissatisfied with the transit royalties, stating that in 1981 the pipeline cost $31 million to run but brought revenues of only $25.7 million. In April 1982, having signed an agreement to buy 8.7 million tons of oil per year from Iraq's enemy, Iran, Syria closed the Kirkuk-Banias pipeline to Iraqi oil.

INDUSTRY

A remarkable industrial boom, mainly based on textiles, occurred in Syria shortly after independence and was the main cause of the dissolution of the customs union with Lebanon in 1959, since the protectionist policies adopted by the Syrian Government to safeguard this growth came into direct conflict with Lebanon's free-trade tradition. Since then the manufacturing and mining sector has grown steadily until in 1971, for the first time, it replaced agriculture as the main generator of wealth—accounting for 19.5 per cent of the G.D.P., compared with 19.1 per cent for agriculture. The value of industrial production has risen steadily since then—the general index of industrial production (based on 1970=100) reaching 191 in 1977. The target for average annual industrial growth under the 1976–80 development plan was an ambitious 15.4 per cent, while the investment allocation for the industrial sector was £S11,289 million, representing 20.8 per cent of the total. There has been something of a change of heart since then, however, partly because of disappointing growth rates in this sector, and industry's allocation under the 1981–85 Plan fell to 16.6 per cent of the total, or £S16,899 million. The main areas of industrial development in Syria, apart from oil and gas, are phosphates, iron and steel, sugar refining, textiles and cement.

Production of phosphates started from the mines in the Palmyra area in 1972. A sudden rise in world phosphate prices in 1974 took the price of Syrian rock up to $53 per ton despite its high chlorine content and low quality. Prices and production subsequently fluctuated, but by 1980 output of phosphates had risen to 1.3 million tons with production scheduled to rise to 5 million tons per year by 1985. A $180 million Romanian-built triplesuperphosphate plant at Homs reached full production of 450,000 tons per year during 1981 and the output from this plant is combined with the annual 200,000 tons of urea from a French-built plant at Homs, completed in 1979.

The iron and steel industry, centred on Hama, comprises a 120,000-ton smelter, a rolling mill and a steel pipe plant built by firms from West Germany and Switzerland. The potential for developing Syria's own iron ore deposits, estimated at about 530 million tons, is being studied by Indian consultants. Progress in the cement industry, meanwhile, has been rather slow. Production was originally due to increase from 994,000 tons in 1975 to 6 million tons in 1980, but actual output in 1980 was slightly less than 2 million tons. Completion of a big new cement works, built with East German help at Tartous, has been delayed but is now set for 1983. This, together with other factories at Adra, Hama, Musulmiya and Aleppo, should boost overall production to 4.5 million tons per year by 1984. Syria is also establishing a sugar refining industry, geared to processing beet grown in the Euphrates basin. Refineries have been built at Raqqa, Deir-ez-Zor, Maskaneh and Salhab with finance from Abu Dhabi.

Established industries include rubber, glass and paper manufacture and the assembly of tractors, refrigerators and both black and white and colour television sets. Plans for a car assembly plant were postponed following the financial difficulties of 1976, but talks started in 1980 with a West German subsidiary of Fiat's commercial vehicles division on the construction of a $250 million commercial vehicle assembly plant. Food processing industries are also being developed.

The Euphrates Dam, with its eight 100-MW turbines, has made an important contribution to power generation in Syria, having been inaugurated in 1978. Overall output of electricity for 1981 was 4,425.1 million kWh., with production expected to rise steadily to over 7,800 million kWh. in 1985. Syria has also considered the idea of setting up a nuclear power station, since substantial amounts of uranium are thought to be associated with local phosphate deposits.

Syria's principal industries centre around the major towns, Damascus, Aleppo and Homs and the port of Latakia, and these centres, with the exception of Homs and the addition of Tartous, are also the site of Syria's free zones, set up to encourage foreign investment in the establishment of light industries, assembly plants and warehouses. The investment has not been forthcoming, however, and at the end of 1981 it was announced that the future of the free zones would be reviewed. A further industrial free zone, set up jointly with Jordan south of Deraa, may be affected by Jordan's support for Iraq in the Iraq-Iran war. The ports of Latakia and Tartous are being expanded; Tartous had a total handling capacity of 4.5 million tons in 1982, while Latakia that year handled over 3 million tons. Tartous will also have a dry dock.

EXTERNAL TRADE

Commerce has traditionally been a major occupation of Syria's towns, especially Damascus and Aleppo as they lie on the main east-west trade route. But there have been some radical changes in both the direction and the composition of Syria's trade over the years. During the mid-1960s, Syria's main suppliers were among the Eastern European bloc. In 1968 the Soviet Union and Czechoslovakia alone provided over 20 per cent of all imported goods. In 1974, though the value of their supplies had increased, these countries accounted for just under 7.2 per cent of the total. Meanwhile the value of Syria's imports over the six-year period had risen nearly fourfold, reaching £S4,571 million in 1974, and the bulk of the increase had resulted from flourishing trade ties not with the East but with Western Europe. In 1981, out of imports worth a total of £S19,781 million, countries in the European Economic Community (EEC) together provided 30 per cent. Of these, Italy led with 10 per cent, followed by West Germany with 6.7 per cent and France with 5 per cent. The U.S.A. and Japan have also achieved significant increases in the past few years. After American diplomatic relations with Syria were resumed in 1974, exports rose to £S863.9 million in 1980, accounting for 5.3 per cent of the import total that year, but dropped back to 3.8 per cent in the difficult political climate of 1981. Japan, meanwhile, improved its position, supplying 4.3 per cent of the total in 1981.

Syria's exports have increased dramatically, mainly due to oil sales. But they have nowhere near succeeded in keeping pace with imports. Exports rose by 50 per cent between 1971 and 1972, but this did not prevent the trade deficit from hitting the £S1,000 million mark one year later. Further big surges in exports were recorded in 1974, 1979 and 1980, when they increased in value by 117 per cent, 55 per cent and 30 per cent respectively. In 1981, due to poor cotton and oil sales, exports actually declined in nominal value below the level of the previous year, to the point where they covered scarcely 42 per cent of the cost of imports. A geographical analysis of Syrian trade in 1981 shows Italy to have been by far the biggest customer for Syrian goods, taking 42 per cent of the overall total. The principal EEC countries, including Italy, together accounted for 80 per cent of Syrian exports in 1981, underlying yet again the declining role played by the centrally-planned economies in Syrian trade. Following their 1980 friendship treaty, the Soviet Union and Syria have agreed to boost their bilateral trade to an overall total of 2,000 million roubles ($2,600 million) in the period 1981–85. However, this is unlikely to make much difference to trade relations with the EEC, now that these have been consolidated by a trade and aid agreement signed in 1977. Under this agreement, Syria enjoys a 100 per cent tariff cut on exports of petroleum and cotton products to the EEC and has received some $67 million in grants and low-interest loans to finance roads and other infrastructure projects.

FINANCE

The sudden increase in Syrian exports from 1972 onwards was one of the major results of a reform in the foreign exchange regulations. All exports other than cotton and crude oil were shifted to the parallel (free) market which meant a *de facto* devaluation of Syrian currency in relation to most transactions. (For details of changes in the exchange rate, *see* the Statistical Survey, following). In April 1981, in an attempt to mobilize remittances to finance private sector imports and thereby reduce pressure on the Syrian pound, the Government announced that remittances and other private sector invisible earnings would be convertible into Syrian currency at a freely floating "parallel" rate and that private businesses would be able to arrange letters of credit only through Syria's state banks.

Arab subsidies have been paid to Syria since the Khartoum summit meeting of 1967. They were reinforced at the Rabat summit of 1974, which resulted in the promise of an annual $1,000 million to Syria in its capacity as a confrontation state. The Baghdad summit of 1978 pledged to increase these subsidies to $1,800 million per year. The amount of Arab aid Syria actually received reached $690 million in 1975 but dropped to only $355 million in 1976. The amounts received in 1979 and 1980 are estimated at $1,600 million and $1,400 million respectively, but the figure for 1981 is thought to have been much lower.

State expenditure since the October 1973 war has also clearly reflected the inflow of foreign funds. The general budget soared from a total of £S6,976 million in 1974 to £S16,564 million in 1976. The events of 1976, however, caused the authorities to think again and in 1977 and 1978 overall budget expenditure increased by only about 5 per cent in absolute terms over each of the previous years. In 1979, as a result of the pledges made at the Baghdad summit, a big increase in defence spending brought the overall budget up again to £S22,600 million, half of which was set aside for development. Defence spending has remained a priority, even though in some years overall allocations have had to fall in real terms. With inflation running at an estimated 15–20 per cent annually, the 1982 consolidated budget, totalling £S33,345 million, was actually less than for the previous year. Spending on development in 1982 is to be significantly higher than in previous years, however, accounting for £S16,595 million or 50 per cent of the overall budget, compared with 45 per cent in 1981. Current defence spending, meanwhile, at £S9,705.2 million in 1982, was equivalent to 58 per cent of current expenditure.

ECONOMIC DEVELOPMENT

The most ambitious of the projects contained in the Third Five-Year Plan (1971–75) was the Euphrates Dam project, under construction since 1968. Most of the country's future industrial and agricultural development depends on this scheme, and nearly one-quarter of public investment over the plan period was earmarked for its implementation, with £S950 million allocated for the dam itself and £S643 million for land reclamation and development in the Euphrates basin. The project involved the construction of a dam 4.6 kilometres long and 60 metres high with a width of 500 metres at the bottom. The reservoir thus created, Lake Assad, has been designed to hold 12,000 million cubic metres of water, operating eight turbines and enabling the long-term irrigation of 640,000 hectares of land, some 550,000 of these by 1990. The scheme was undertaken with the help of 1,200 Soviet technicians and about £S600 million in Soviet financial assistance, under an agreement reached with the Soviet Union in April 1966. By 1977, however, only 100 Soviet experts remained on the site. In spring 1978 the entire project was formally opened, although the dam's first turbines had started to operate, ahead of schedule, in early 1974. It was estimated in 1977 that the cost of developing each hectare of land in the Euphrates basin will work out at £S20,000, making a total of up to £S14,000 million for the development of all 640,000 hectares. Despite its advantages, the dam has exacerbated friction between Syria and Iraq, which also relies on Euphrates water. Problems came to a head in 1974–75 when Turkey started to fill the reservoir behind its Keban dam on the river at the same time as Syria started to fill Lake Assad, leaving Iraq with much less water than usual. Tension on this score subsided in 1977–78, but without reaching a permanent settlement.

The Fourth Five-Year Plan started in 1976 but was interrupted by the events of that year and was reissued in 1977. It envisaged expenditure of nearly £S53,000 million, comprising £S27,000 million for projects already under way, £S17,600 million for new projects and £S8,000 million to be held in reserve. Mining and manufacturing were to take 22 per cent of the £S44,600 million earmarked for specific projects, followed by energy and fuel development (17.8 per cent) and Euphrates projects (16.6 per cent). The average annual growth rate target under the plan was 12 per cent, compared with 8.2 per cent under the previous plan. One important aspect of the plan in its original form was its emphasis on tourism, which was expected to become the country's third main source of foreign currency, after oil and cotton, by 1980. This objective was undermined by political factors, however, and although a record total of nearly 1.4 million foreign visitors arrived in Syria in 1976 with 1.29 million arriving in 1977, this was mainly a result of people fleeing the civil war in Lebanon and not an indication of future trends. The total for 1978 was down again to 1.07 million.

Like its predecessor, the Fifth Five-Year Plan (for 1981–85) is also apparently running late. An outline of the plan was issued in late 1981 but details did not become available until the following year. Its main features include a shift from industry to agriculture, an investment target of £S101,493 million (comprising £S68,705 million from the public sector, £S23,351 million from the private sector and £S9,437 million from foreign sources) and an average annual economic growth rate target of 7.7 per cent.

STATISTICAL SURVEY

AREA AND POPULATION

AREA	POPULATION†						
	Census results				Estimates (mid-year)		
	Sept. 20th, 1960	September 23rd, 1970			1978	1979	1980
		Total	Males	Females			
185,180 sq. km.*	4,565,121	6,304,685	3,233,110	3,071,575	8,328,000	8,647,000	8,979,000

* 71,498 sq. miles.   † Including Palestinian refugees, numbering 193,000 at mid-1977.

REGISTERED BIRTHS, MARRIAGES AND DEATHS

	Births	Marriages	Deaths
1977	322,357	72,530	35,860
1978	291,789	70,984	35,580
1979	304,372	70,933	35,741
1980	403,841	88,311	37,643

PRINCIPAL TOWNS

(population at 1970 census)

Damascus (capital) .	836,668*	Latakia . . . 125,716
Aleppo . . .	639,428	Deir-ez-Zor . . 66,164
Homs . . .	215,423	Hasakeh . . . 32,746
Hama . . .	137,421	

* Including suburbs, population was 923,253.

AGRICULTURE

LAND USE

('ooo hectares)

	1979	1980
Arable land	6,058	6,154
Land under permanent crops .	456	479
Permanent meadows and pastures	8,274	8,378
Forests and woodland .	459	466
Other land	3,162	2,928
Inland water . . .	109	113
TOTAL AREA .	18,518	18,518

AREA AND PRODUCTION OF PRINCIPAL CROPS

	1978 Hectares	1978 Metric tons	1979 Hectares	1979 Metric tons	1980 Hectares	1980 Metric tons
Wheat . . .	1,555,376	1,650,696	1,445,000	1,320,000	1,449,000	2,226,000
Barley . . .	1,032,565	728,695	1,102,000	395,000	1,210,000	1,587,000
Maize . . .	26,597	56,191	18,000	34,000	22,000	47,000
Millet . . .	18,573	17,288	13,000	12,000	16,000	19,000
Lentils . . .	136,116	92,375	89,000	43,000	85,000	83,000
Cotton . . .	169,114	377,246	154,000	344,000	139,000	323,000
Tobacco . . .	16,080	13,091	18,000	12,000	n.a.	n.a.
Sesame . . .	35,723	19,018	26,000	14,000	46,000	25,000
Grapes . . .	93,835	345,775	96,000	287,000	99,000	356,000
Olives . . .	234,424	303,677	241,000	196,000	249,000	392,000
Figs . . .	20,647	36,018	20,000	41,000	19,000	47,000
Apricots . . .	12,318	47,434	12,000	46,000	13,000	48,000
Apples . . .	21,015	67,302	22,000	76,000	24,000	89,000
Sugar beet . .	13,682	271,853	18,000	289,000	23,000	505,000
Pomegranates . .	5,227	28,560	6,000	36,000	6,000	32,170
Onions . . .	8,429	159,561	8,000	161,000	9,000	151,000
Tomatoes . .	30,755	501,967	28,000	457,000	35,000	644,000
Potatoes . . .	14,587	198,517	14,000	235,000	19,000	292,000

LIVESTOCK
('ooo head)

	1978	1979	1980
Cattle . .	694	760	768
Horses .	51	51	53
Camels . .	9	8	n.a.
Asses . .	236	238	242
Sheep . .	7,236	8,129	9,301
Goats . .	1,065	999	1,025
Chickens .	12,613	16,096	13,849

LIVESTOCK PRODUCTS
('ooo metric tons)

	1978	1979	1980
Beef and veal . .	18	25	n.a.
Mutton and lamb . .	59	75	} 88
Goats' meat . .	6	5*	
Poultry meat . .	33	38	n.a.
Cows' milk . .	418	452	490
Sheeps' milk . .	293	312	346
Goat's milk . .	80	73	70
Butter and ghee . .	9.9	12.4	15.8
Cheese . .	33.3	43.7	52
Hen eggs . .	49.9	61.0	n.a.
Wool: greasy . .	16.9	17.8	n.a.
clean . .	8.4	8.9	9.7

*FAO estimate.

Fishing ('ooo metric tons): Total catch 3.3 in 1976; 3.5 in 1977; 3.6 in 1978; 3.7 in 1979.

MINING

		1977	1978	1979	1980	1981
Crude petroleum . .	'ooo metric tons	9,117	8,932	8,701	8,282	8,541
Phosphate rock . . .	,, ,, ,,	425	747	1,169	1,319	1,319
Salt (unrefined) . .	,, ,, ,,	48	62	67	90	110.8
Natural gas* . . .	million cu. metres	483	536	n.a.	n.a.	n.a.

Source: OPEC, *Annual Statistical Bulletin.*

INDUSTRY
SELECTED PRODUCTS

		1978	1979	1980	1981
Cotton Yarn . . .	'ooo tons	22.7	25.9	20.5	25.2
Silk and Cotton Textiles . .	,, ,,	39.9	34.9	14.3	10.9
Woollen Fabrics . .	tons	1,403.0	1,192.0	1.3	1.2
Cement	'ooo tons	1,497.0	1,847.0	1,994.7	2,309.6
Natural Asphalt . .	,, ,,	95.0	83.0	89.0	75.6
Glass . . .	,, ,,	23.0	35.1	38.4	50.9
Soap	,, ,,	35.8	36.9	4.1	5.1
Sugar . . .	,, ,,	104.8	118.0	90.3	141.9
Margarine . . .	,, ,,	5.4	5.6	15.7	15.3
Edible Oils . . .	,, ,,	24.0	26.1	7.3	1.2
Manufactured Tobacco . .	,, ,,	8.8	9.0	9.0	9.9
Electricity . . .	million kWh.	2,702.0	3,356.0	4,082.0	4,425.1
Beer . . .	'ooo litres	6,679.0	7,759.0	1.3	8.9
Wine	,, ,,	354.0	325.0	0.1	0.2
Arak	,, ,,	1,044.0	1,573.1	1.3	0.5

FINANCE

100 piastres = 1 Syrian pound (£S).
Coins: 2½, 5, 10, 25 and 50 piastres; 1 pound.
Notes: 1, 5, 10, 25, 50, 100 and 500 pounds.

Exchange rates (May 1982): £1 sterling = £S7.216; U.S. $1 = £S3.925.
£S100 = £13.86 sterling = $25.48.

Note: The official basic exchange rate of U.S. $1 = £S2.19, established in 1949, is inoperative for all practical purposes. Prior to July 1962 the official selling rate, used for calculating the value of foreign trade, was U.S. $1 = £S3.58 (£S1 = 27.97 U.S. cents). From July 1962 to February 1973 the buying rate was $1 = £S3.80 and the selling rate was $1 = £S3.82 (£S1 = 26.18 U.S. cents). Exchange rates were adjusted frequently between February and July 1973. From July 1973 to February 1974 the buying rate was $1 = £S3.75 and the selling rate $1 = £S3.80. From February 1974 to March 1976 the buying rate was $1 = £S3.65 and the selling rate $1 = £S3.70. In April 1976 new rates of $1 = £S3.90 (buying) or £S3.95 (selling) were established. From January 1964 to July 1973 a "parallel" free market was also in operation. From early 1970 to February 1973 the free rates were $1 = £S4.30 (buying) or £S4.32 (selling). In April 1981 a two-tier market was reintroduced, with a free "parallel" rate for "invisible" earnings, including remittances from abroad. The official exchange rates were £1 sterling = £S9.12 (buying) or £S9.168 (selling) from November 1967 to August 1971; and £1 sterling = £S9.902 (buying) or £S9.954 (selling) from December 1971 to June 1972.

ORDINARY BUDGET

(£S million)

	1978	1979	1980	1981	1982
National defence	4,544.9	8,246.3	8,350.2	9,279.5	9,705.2
Cultural and social affairs .	649.8	768.0	895.5	1,248.2	1,539.9
Communications and public works .	82.9	88.3	91.9	126.7	97.9
Economic affairs and planning .	1,281.4	1,442.2	3,794.5	3,271.6	31,124.6
Administrative affairs . .	997.7	1,016.2	1,458.3	2,774.5	21,282.4
TOTAL . . .	7,556.7	11,561.0	14,590.4	16,700.5	16,750.0

CONSOLIDATED BUDGET

(£S million, incorporating both ordinary and development budgets)

	1978	1979	1980	1981	1982
Justice and Public Authorities . .	1,510.9	1,879.6	2,289.9	3,411.5	3,828.6
National Security . . .	4,573.1	8,281.5	8,414.8	9,377.8	9,778.5
Culture and Information . .	1,293.2	1,506.5	1,968.2	2,243.7	2,778.5
Social Welfare	150.3	165.8	206.9	341.8	310.9
Economy and Finance . .	1,769.4	2,077.8	4,727.2	4,104.2	4,051.1
Agriculture and Land Reclamation .	1,470.8	1,709.2	2,323.5	2,233.5	2,442.6
Industry and Mining . .	4,518.6	3,857.4	5,152.0	3,791.5	4,154.1
Public Works, Utilities and Communications	1,996.4	2,145.9	2,638.5	2,476.0	3,116.3
Other Expenditure and Revenue .	919.3	1,017.3	1,182.0	2,500.0	2,884.3
TOTAL	18,202.0	22,641.0	28,903.0	30,480.0	33,345.0

FIFTH FIVE-YEAR PLAN

(1981–85)

Total investment: £S101,493 million (agriculture £S17,200 million).

EXTERNAL TRADE

(£S million)

	1974	1975	1976	1977	1978	1979	1980	1981
Imports c.i.f. . .	4,570.9	6,235.4	9,203.3	10,496.7	9,658.8	13,066.8	16,188.1	19,781.0
Exports f.o.b. . .	2,913.9	3,440.9	4,141.3	4,199.0	4,159.5	6,453.3	8,272.7	8,253.7

COMMODITIES (£S million)

IMPORTS	1978	1979	1980	1981
Cotton textiles, other textile goods and silk . .	502.6	594.0	664.5	691.0
Mineral fuels and oils	1,268.4	3,228.5	4,196.9	6,847.3
Lime, cement and salt	147.4	344.1	378.8	320.5
Cereals	275.1	259.0	330.5	347.1
Vegetables and fruit	277.2	342.6	335.6	355.9
Machinery, apparatus and electrical materials .	689.9	851.3	827.7	975.1
Precious metals and coins	25.3	21.2	44.1	7.4
Base metals and manufactures	1,283.3	1,841.0	2,266.0	1,642.3
Vehicles	514.4	664.9	932.7	1,156.0
Chemical and pharmaceutical products . .	332.4	446.9	515.0	518.5
Preserved foods, beverages and tobacco . .	471.0	402.7	36.4	894.1
Other products	3,837.0	4,070.5	5,859.9	6,025.8

EXPORTS	1978	1979	1980	1981
Cotton (raw, yarn, textiles)	720.7	829.5	746.6	665.0
Other textile goods	179.4	254.0	301.2	404.1
Cereals	12.2	1.7	17.5	78.5
Vegetables and fruit	155.4	165.3	141.1	91.9
Preserved foods, beverages and tobacco . .	75.5	87.0	159.9	79.5
Phosphates	89.6	126.3	89.1	129.4
Crude petroleum	2,553.0	4,449.0	5,234.7	5,043.6
Other products	374.0	540.5	1,582.6	1,761.7

PRINCIPAL TRADING PARTNERS
(£S million)

IMPORTS	1978	1979	1980	1981
Austria	150.2	223.3	330.5	269.9
Belgium	225.0	291.4	286.6	512.2
China, People's Republic	215.1	214.0	223.3	318.9
France	728.7	785.9	990.4	1,013.9
German Democratic Republic	293.5	316.3	218.7	514.3
Germany, Federal Republic	1,037.5	1,163.8	1,750.0	1,319.6
Greece	159.0	171.4	251.3	308.9
Iraq	676.7	1,883.1	2,884.6	3,713.3
Italy	799.3	1,653.6	1,414.4	1,986.7
Japan	481.1	394.9	624.8	850.8
Lebanon	282.3	332.4	348.0	343.4
Netherlands	193.7	294.6	357.8	377.9
Romania	673.0	806.7	718.5	839.8
Saudi Arabia	218.2	115.5	44.5	1,524.0
Spain	283.4	309.2	544.2	491.1
U.S.S.R.	166.5	311.8	178.2	283.9
United Kingdom	336.5	443.9	537.1	430.5
U.S.A.	397.8	523.5	863.9	758.9

EXPORTS	1978	1979	1980	1981
China, People's Republic	131.0	119.9	194.4	99.2
France	399.2	1,171.1	251.9	1,136.2
Germany, Federal Republic	435.0	232.1	795.6	52.7
Greece	284.3	537.3	132.1	643.4
Iraq	1.1	229.1	116.8	5.9
Italy	348.3	1,682.5	4,576.4	3,481.2
Netherlands	377.9	207.8	123.7	33.9
Romania	92.9	373.3	933.7	810.1
Saudi Arabia	194.1	157.4	154.3	157.2
U.S.S.R.	387.3	321.9	460.9	446.2
United Kingdom	161.6	32.5	28.5	n.a.
U.S.A.	374.9	618.6	354.5	302.1

TRANSPORT

RAILWAYS

	1978	1979	1980
Passenger-km. .	360,784	421,329	381,831
Freight, 'ooo tons .	1,481	1,918	2,455

ROAD TRAFFIC

	1977	1978	1979
Passenger cars . .	69,084	65,396	66,243
Buses . . .	6,829	7,178	7,420
Lorries, trucks, etc. .	70,613	81,396	85,978
Motor-cycles . .	24,320	24,849	28,542

SHIPPING
PORT OF LATAKIA

	1975	1976	1977	1978	1979	1980
Number of steam vessels entering harbour . .	2,062	2,667	2,023	2,123	2,284	1,929
Number of sailing vessels entering harbour .	47	46	44	—	—	—
Cargo unloaded ('ooo tons) . . .	2,022	2,795	2,040	1,965	2,875	2,602
Cargo loaded ('ooo tons) . . .	150	268	367	359	322	430

CIVIL AVIATION
(Damascus Airport)

	1977		1978		1979		1980	
	Arrive	Depart	Arrive	Depart	Arrive	Depart	Arrive	Depart
Aircraft . . .	10,417	10,416	10,502	10,503	10,552	10,563	12,557	12,557
Passengers . .	435,637	453,082	531,833	563,345	515,433	557,967	559,430	655,206

TOURISM

	JORDANIANS AND LEBANESE	TOTAL VISITORS
1975	516,152	1,171,722
1976	910,249	1,389,979
1977	683,967	1,291,308
1978	657,362	1,073,828
1979	764,094	1,270,944
1980	745,856	1,228,074

Tourist Accommodation: 19,711 tourist hotel beds (1980).

EDUCATION
(1979/80)

	PUPILS		TEACHERS	
	Public Sector	Private Sector*	Public Sector	Private Sector*
Pre-School . . .	—	32,539	—	n.a.
Primary . . .	1,407,388	42,657	47,894	1,537
Preparatory . .	384,717	10,996 }	28,847	1,084
Secondary . . .	134,736	19,128 }		
Vocational . .	24,440	—	3,161	—
Teacher Training .	10,612	—	1,141	—
Universities . .	94,794	—	n.a.	—

* Excluding UNRWA schools.

Source (unless otherwise stated): Central Bureau of Statistics, Office of the Prime Minister, Damascus.

THE CONSTITUTION

A new and permanent constitution was endorsed by 97.6 per cent of the voters in a national referendum on March 12th, 1973. The 157-article constitution defines Syria as a "Socialist popular democracy" with a "pre-planned Socialist economy". Under the new constitution, Lt.-Gen. al-Assad remained President, with the power to appoint and dismiss his Vice-President, Premier and Government Ministers, and also became Commander-in-Chief of the armed forces, secretary-general of the Baath Socialist Party and President of the National Progressive Front. Legislative power is vested in the People's Council, with 195 members elected by universal adult suffrage.

THE GOVERNMENT

HEAD OF STATE

President: Lt.-Gen. HAFIZ AL-ASSAD (elected March 12th, 1971, for a seven-year term; re-elected February 8th, 1978).

CABINET

(June 1982)

Prime Minister: Dr. ABDUL-RAUF KASSEM.

Deputy Prime-Minister and Minister of Foreign Affairs: ABDUL HALIM KHADDAM.

Deputy Prime Minister in charge of Public Services: WALID HAMDUN.

Deputy Prime Minister in charge of Economic Affairs: ABDEL KADER KADDURA.

Minister of Defence: Gen. MUSTAPHA TLASS.

Minister of Information: AHMAD ISKANDER AHMAD.

Minister of the Interior: Maj.-Gen. NASIR AD-DIN NASIR.

Minister of Supply and Internal Trade: MUHAMMAD GHABBASH.

Minister of Local Administration: (vacant).

Minister of Education: MUHAMMAD NAJIB AS-SAYYID AHMAD.

Minister of Presidential Affairs: ABDUL KARIM ADI.

Minister of Higher Education: Dr. AS'AD DARGAWI.

Minister of Electricity: Eng. Dr. AHMAD UMAR YUSUF.

Minister of Culture: Dr. NAJAH AL-ATTAR.

Minister of Transport: YUNIS MUHAMMAD.

Minister of Social Affairs and Labour: YUSUF JU'AYDANI.

Minister of State for Planning Affairs: Dr. KAMAL SHARAF.

Minister of Economy and Foreign Trade: Dr. SALIM YASIN.

Minister of Oil and Natural Resources: Dr. ABDUL-JABBAR AD-DAHHAK.

Minister of Industry: MAHMUD QADDUR.

Minister of Finance: Dr. HAMDI AS-SAQQA.

Minister of State for Foreign Affairs: FARUQ AS-SHAR.

Minister of Housing and Utilities: AHMAD SALIM DARWISH.

Minister of Justice: KHALID AL-MALIKI.

Minister of Agriculture and Agrarian Reform: AMMASH JUDAY.

Minister of the Euphrates Dam: Eng. ABDUL RAHMAN MADANI.

Minister of Communications: Eng. RA'FAT AL-KURDI.

Minister of Health: Dr. GHASUB AR-RIFAI.

Minister of Public Works and Water Resources: NAYIF JARBU.

Minister of Waqfs: MUHAMMAD MUHAMMAD AL-KHATIB.

Minister of Tourism: Dr. Eng. NAWRAS AD-DAQR.

Minister of State for Cabinet Affairs: ANTOINE JUBRAN.

Ministers of State: NAYIF TA'ANI, MIKHAYIL NAQQUL, AHMAD SALIM DARWISH, Dr. DAWUD HIDU, DIB AL-MASRI, HIKMAT BAYAZID.

LEGISLATURE

MAJLIS AL-SHA'AB

Elections were held for the 195-member People's Council in November 1981. All 195 seats were won by the National Progressive Front, which fought the elections as a coalition of four parties (Baath, Arab Socialist Union, Unionist Socialist and Arab Socialist). The results gave the Baath Party at least 60 per cent of the seats. The Communist Party fought the election independently, and lost all eight seats it had held in the previous People's Council. However, it still forms part of the National Progressive Front.

Speaker: MAHMOUD AZ-ZUBI.

POLITICAL PARTIES

The National Progressive Front, headed by President Assad, was formed in March 1972 by the grouping of the five parties listed below:

Baath Arab Socialist Party: National Command, P.O.B. 849, Damascus; Arab socialist party; f. 1947; in power since 1963; supports militant Arab unity; Sec.-Gen. Pres. HAFIZ AL-ASSAD; Asst. Sec.-Gen. ABDULLAH AL-AHMAR; Regional Asst. Sec.-Gen. ZUHAYR MASA-RIQAH; publs. *al-Baath* (daily), *al-Munadel* (monthly).

Syrian Arab Socialist Union: Nasserite; Leader Dr. JAMAL ATASI; Sec.-Gen. FAUZI KAYYALI.

Unionist Socialist: Leader SAMI SOUFAN; Sec.-Gen. FAYIZ ISMAIL.

Arab Socialist Party: a breakaway socialist party; Leader ABDEL GHANI KANNOUT.

Communist Party of Syria: Sec.-Gen. KHALID BAGDASH.

DIPLOMATIC REPRESENTATION

EMBASSIES ACCREDITED TO SYRIA

(In Damascus unless otherwise stated)

Afghanistan: International Hotel, Apartment no. 256; *Chargé d'affaires:* MOHAMMAD NAZIR HOBAB.

Algeria: Raouda, Imm. Noss; *Ambassador:* ABDEL-QADER BEN-KASI.

Argentina: Raouda, Rue Ziad ben Abi Soufian; *Ambassador:* OTTO JACINTO SASSE.

Australia: 243A Farabi Street, East Villas, Dakkak Bldg., Mezzeh; *Ambassador:* D. G. WILSON.

Austria: Raouda, Chafik Mouayed St., Imm. Sabri Malki, P.O.B. 5634; *Chargé d'affaires:* KARL PAGLIARUCCI.

Bangladesh: Teheran, Iran.

Belgium: Rue Ata Ayoubi, Imm. Hachem; *Ambassador:* ERIC KOPEA.

Brazil: 76 Rue Ata Ayoubi; *Ambassador:* ANTÔNIO AMARAL DE SAMPALO.

Bulgaria: 4 Rue Chahbandar; *Ambassador:* GEORGI YANKOV.

Canada: Beirut, Lebanon.

Chad: Beirut, Lebanon.

Chile: 43 Rue Al-Rachid; *Ambassador:* MICHAEL JACOB AL-HELOU.

China, People's Republic: 83 Rue Ata Ayoubi; *Ambassador:* LOU WEIZHAO.

Colombia: Cairo, Egypt.

Cuba: 40 Rue Al-Rachid, Imm. Oustwani and Charabati; *Ambassador:* Dr. LESTER RODRÍGUEZ PÉRES.

Cyprus: *Ambassador:* GEORGE LYCOURGOS.

Czechoslovakia: Place Aboul-Alaa Al-Maari; *Ambassador:* DUŠAN ULCAK.

Denmark: Beirut, Lebanon.

Finland: Beirut, Lebanon.

France: Rue Ata Ayoubi; *Ambassador:* HENRI SERVANT.

German Democratic Republic: 60 Avenue Adnan el Malki; *Ambassador:* Dr. REINHARD ESCHERICH.

Germany, Federal Republic: 53 Rue Ibrahim Hanano (Imm. Kotob); *Ambassador:* HERIBERT WOECKEL.

Greece: 57 Rue Ata Ayoubi; *Ambassador:* CONSTANTIN GEORGIOU.

Grenada: *Ambassador:* MARIO BULLEN.

Guinea: Cairo, Egypt.

Hungary: 13 Rue Ibrahim Hanano (Imm. Roujoulé); *Ambassador:* ZOLTÁN ZSIGMOND.

India: 40/46 Ave. Al Malki, Imm. Noueilati; *Ambassador:* ASOK KUMAR RAY.

Indonesia: 19 Rue Al-Amir Ezzeddine; *Ambassador:* KARNOAN DAR MAPOTRA.

Iran: Rue Kawakbi, Imm. Oustwani; *Ambassador:* SAID ALI AKBAR MOHTACHIMI POUR.

Italy: 82 Avenue Al Mansour; *Ambassador:* ALDO PUGLIESE.

Japan: 15 Ave. Al-Jalaa; *Ambassador:* TOSHIO DADA.

Jordan: Abou Roumaneh; *Ambassador:* HUSAIN HAMMAMI.

Korea, Democratic People's Republic: Rue Fares El-Khouri-Jisr Tora; *Ambassador:* YI HONG-RYOP.

Kuwait: Rue Ibrahim Hanano; *Ambassador:* ABDUL RAZAK ABDUL KADER AL-KANDARY.

Libya: Place Al Malki, 10 Avenue Mansour; *Head of Office:* AHMAD ABDULSALAM BEN KHAYAL.

Mauritania: Ave. Al-Jala'a, Rue Karameh; *Ambassador:* MOHAMED MAHMOUD OULD WEDDADY.

Mexico: Cairo, Egypt.

Mongolia: Bucharest, Romania.

Morocco: Abou Roumaneh-Abdel Malek ben Marwan St.; *Ambassador:* DRISS BANNOUNA.

Nepal: Jeddah, Saudi Arabia.

Netherlands: Place Abou Ala'a Al-Maarri, Imm. Badr Diab; *Ambassador:* J. G. VAN DER TAS.

Nigeria: Cairo, Egypt.

Norway: Cairo, Egypt.

Oman: Amman, Jordan.

Pakistan: Avenue Al Jala'a; *Ambassador:* Maj.-Gen. SARFARAZ KHAN.

Panama: Malki, Al-Bizm St., Al-Zein Bldg., Apt. 7; *Chargé d'affaires:* LUIS CARLOS GONZÁLEZ.

Poland: Rue Georges Haddad, Imm. Chahine; *Ambassador:* BOGUSŁAW KACYNSKI.

Qatar: Abou Roumaneh, Place Madfa, Imm. Allawi No. 20; *Ambassador:* MUHAMMAD SAID AL-FAHID.

Romania: Rue Ibrahim Hanano No. 8; *Ambassador:* GRIGORE COMARTIN.

Saudi Arabia: Avenue Al Jala'a; *Chargé d'affaires:* RIAD AL-RAWAF.

Somalia: Avenue Ata Ayoubi; *Ambassador:* (vacant).

Spain: 81 Ave. Al Jala'a, Imm. Sawaf; *Ambassador:* FELIX GUILLERMO FERNÁNDEZ-SHAW.

Sudan: 76 Rue Ata Ayoubi; *Chargé d'affaires:* YOUSEF AHMAD.

Sweden: Beirut, Lebanon.

Switzerland: Malki, 31 Rue M. Kurd Ali; *Ambassador:* MAURICE JEANRENAUD.

Tanzania: Cairo, Egypt.

Trinidad and Tobago: Beirut, Lebanon.

Tunisia: Abu Rumaneh, Rue Rashid, Imm. Jabi; *Ambassador:* ABDEL-AZIZ BELTAIEF.

Turkey: 58 Avenue Ziad Bin Abou Soufian; *Ambassador:* MUSTAFA AKŞIN.

U.S.S.R.: Boustan El-Kouzbari, Rue d'Alep; *Ambassador:* VLADIMIR YUKHIN.

United Arab Emirates: Rue Raouda No. 62, Imm. Housami; *Ambassador:* KHALIFEH AHMAD A. EL-MOUBARAK.

United Kingdom: Malki; Rue Muhammad Kurd Ali; *Ambassador:* Hon. IVOR LUCAS, C.M.G.

U.S.A.: Rue Al Mansour 2; *Ambassador:* ROBERT PAGANELLI.

Uruguay: Beirut, Lebanon.

Vatican City: 82 Rue Misr, B.P. 2271 (Apostolic Nunciature): *Apostolic Pro-Nuncio:* Mgr. ANGELO PEDRONI.

Venezuela: Abou Roumaneh, Rue Nouri Pacha, Imm. Tabbah; *Ambassador:* Dr. Eugenio Omana Murillo.

Viet-Nam: 9 Avenue Malki; *Ambassador:* Vu Thanh.

Yemen Arab Republic: Abou Roumaneh, Charkassieh; *Ambassador:* Abdullah Hussain Barakat.

Yemen, People's Democratic Republic: *Ambassador:* Abdo Ali Abdul Rahman.

Yugoslavia: Ave. A. Jala'a; *Ambassador:* Jovan Peceno-vić.

Zambia: Cairo, Egypt.

Syria also has diplomatic relations with Albania, Bahrain, Burma, Djibouti, Ethiopia, Guyana, Luxembourg, Malta, Mozambique, Portugal, Senegal, Sri Lanka and Suriname.

JUDICIAL SYSTEM

High Constitutional Court: Rawda ave., Damascus; f. 1974 in accordance with the Constitution of 1973. It is the highest court in the judicial system.

Court of Cassation: Damascus; Court of appeal.

Courts of Appeal: 13 Courts of Appeal in the 13 Prefectures try all criminal cases subject to appeal, as well as all other cases within their competence by virtue of the law in force; most of them are composed of several chambers; decisions are given by three judges, one of them being the President.

Summary Courts: 227 Summary Courts try civil, commercial and penal cases within their competence; a Summary Court is constituted by one judge known as a "Judge of the Peace".

First Instance Courts: 72 First Instance Courts, constituted by one judge, deal with all cases other than those

within the competence of special tribunals. In some Prefectures are several Chambers.

Chief Justice of Syria: Jamal Naamani (President of the High Constitutional Court).

PERSONAL STATUS COURTS

For Muslims: each court consists of one judge, the "Qadi Shari'i", who deals with marriage, divorce, etc.

For Druzes: one court consisting of one judge, the "Qadi Mazhabi".

For non-Muslim Communities: for Catholics, Orthodox, Protestants, Jews.

OTHER COURTS

Courts for Minors: their constitution, officers, sessions, jurisdiction and competence are determined by a special law.

Military Court: Damascus.

RELIGION

In religion the majority of Syrians follow a form of Sunni orthodoxy. There is also a considerable number of religious minorities: Muslim Shi'ites; the Ismaili of the Salamiya district, whose spiritual head is the Aga Khan; a large number of Druzes, the Nusairis or Alawites of the Jebel Ansariyeh and the Yezidis of the Jebel Sinjar, and a minority of Christians.

MUSLIMS

Grand Mufti: Ahmad Kuftaro.

The majority of Syrians are Muslims. Most of them are Sunnites with a small number of Ismailis and Shi'ites.

CHRISTIANS

Greek Orthodox Patriarch: His Beatitude Ignatius Hazim, Patriarch of Antioch and all the Orient; P.O.B. 9, Damascus.

Greek Catholic Patriarch: H.B. Maximos V Hakim; P.O.B. 22249, Damascus, or P.O.B. 50076, Beirut, Lebanon; one million mems.; publ. *Le Lien* (monthly, in French).

Syrian Orthodox Patriarch: His Holiness Ignatius Zakka I Iwas, Patriarch of Antioch and All the East; one Catholicose, 26 Metropolitans and one Bishop; 2.5 million mems.; Bab Tooma, Damascus.

Syrian Catholic Archbishopric: P.O.B. 2129, Damascus; Archbishop of Damascus: Mgr. Eustache Joseph Mounayer.

THE PRESS

Since the coming to power of the Baath Arab Socialist Party the structure of the press has been modified according to socialist patterns. Most publications are published by organizations such as political, religious, or professional associations, trade unions, etc. and several are published by government ministries. Anyone wishing to establish a new paper or periodical must apply for a licence.

The major dailies are *al-Baath* (the organ of the party), *Tishrin* and *al-Thawrah* in Damascus, *al-Jamahir al-Arabia* in Aleppo, and *al-Fida* in Hama.

PRINCIPAL DAILIES

al-Baath (*Renaissance*): rue el Barazil, Damascus; Arabic; morning; organ of the Baath Arab Socialist Party; circ. 25,000.

Barq al-Shimal: rue Aziziyah, Aleppo; Arabic; morning; Editor Maurice Djandji; circ. 6,400.

al-Fida: rue Kuwatly, Hama; political; Arabic; morning; Publishing concession holder Osman Alouini; Editor A. Aulwani; circ. 4,000.

al-Jamahir al-Arabia: El Ouedha Printing and Publishing Organization, Aleppo; political; Arabic; Chief Editor Mortada Bakach; circ. 10,000.

al-Shabab: rue al Tawil, Aleppo; Arabic; morning; Editor Muhammad Talas; circ. 9,000.

Syria Times: Tishrin Foundation for Press and Publication, Corniche Meedan, P.O.B. 5452, Damascus; English; circ. 5,000.

al-Thawrah: El Ouedha Printing and Publishing Organization, Damascus; political; Arabic; morning; circ. 20,000.

Tishrin: Tishrin Foundation for Press and Publication, Corniche Meedan, P.O.B. 5452, Damascus; Arabic; circ. 35,000.

WEEKLIES AND FORTNIGHTLIES

al-Ajoua: Compagnie de l'Aviation Arabe Syrienne, Damascus; aviation; Arabic; fortnightly; Editor AHMAD ALLOUCHE.

Arab Press Digest: Syrian Documentation Papers, P.O.B. 2712, Damascus.

al-Esbou al-Riadi: ave. Firdoase, Tibi Bldg., Damascus; sports; Arabic; weekly; Asst. Dir. and Editor HASRAN EL BOUNNI; circ. 14,000.

al-Fursan: Damascus; political magazine; Editor Major FIFAAT ASSAD.

Hadarat al-Islam: B.P. 808, Jadet Halbouni, Jadet El Raby, Damascus; religious; Arabic; fortnightly; Publisher MOUSTAPHA ESSIBAI; Dir. AHMAD FARHAT; Editor MUHAMMAD ADIB SALEH.

Homs: Homs; literary; Arabic; weekly; Publisher and Dir. ADIB KABA; Editor PHILIPPE KABA.

Jaysh al-Shaab: P.O.B. 3320, blvd. Palestine, Damascus; f. 1946; army magazine, Arabic; weekly; published by the Political Department.

Kifah al-Oummal al-Ishtiraki: Fédération Générale des Syndicats des Ouvriers, Damascus; labour; Arabic; weekly; Published by General Federation of Trade Unions; Editor SAID EL HAMAMI.

al-Majalla al-Batriarquia: B.P. 914, Syrian Orthodox Patriarchate, Damascus; f. 1962; religious; Arabic; monthly; Dir. and Editor SAMIR ABDOH; circ. 7,000.

al-Masira: Damascus; political; weekly; published by Federation of Youth Organizations.

al-Maukef al-Riadi: El Ouehda Organization, Damascus; sports; Arabic; weekly; Published by El Ouehda Printing and Publishing Organization; circ. 5,000.

al-Nass: B.P. 926, Aleppo; f. 1953; Arabic; weekly; Publisher VICTOR KALOUS.

Nidal al-Fellahin: Fédération Générale des Laboureurs, Damascus; peasant workers; Arabic; weekly; Published by General Federation of Workers; Editor MANSOUR ABU EL HOSN.

Revue de la Presse Arabe: 67 Place Chahbandar, Damascus; f. 1948; French; twice weekly.

al-Riada: B.P. 292, near Electricity Institute, Damascus; sports; Arabic; weekly; Dir. NOUREDDINE RIAL; Publisher and Editor OURFANE UBARI.

al-Sakafa al-Isbouiya: B.P. 2570, Soukak El Sakr, Damascus; cultural; Arabic; weekly; Publisher, Dir. and Editor MADHAT AKKACHE.

al-Talia (*Vanguard*): B.P. 3031, the National Guard, Damascus; Arabic; fortnightly; Editor SOHDI KHALIL.

al-Thawrah al-Ziraia (*Agricultural Revolution Review*): Ministry of Agrarian Reform, Damascus; f. 1965; agriculture; Arabic; monthly; circ. 7,000.

al-Yanbu al-Jadid: al-Awkaf Bldg., Homs; literary; Arabic; weekly; Publisher, Dir. and Editor MAMDOU EL KOUSSEIR.

MONTHLIES

al-Dad: rue El Tital, Wakf El Moiriné Bldg., Aleppo; literary; Arabic; Dir. RIAD HALLAK; Publisher and Editor ABDALLAH YARKI HALLAK.

Ecos: P.O.B. 3320, Damascus; monthly review; Spanish.

al-Fikr al-Askaria: P.O.B. 4259, blvd. Palestine, Damascus; f. 1950; official military magazine; Editor NAKHLI KALLAS; Sec. Col. BASSAM ASKHITA.

Flash: P.O.B. 3320, Damascus; monthly review; English and French.

al-Irshad al-Zirai: Ministry of Agriculture, Damascus; agriculture; every two months.

al-Kalima: Al-Kalima Association, Aleppo; religious; Arabic; Publisher and Editor FATHALLA SAKAL.

al-Kanoun: Ministry of Justice, Damascus; juridical; Arabic.

al-Maarifa: Ministry of Culture, Damascus; f. 1962; literary; Arabic; Edited by SAFWAN KUDSI and KHALDOUN SHAMAA.

al-Majalla al-Toubilla al-Arabilla: Al-Jalla's St., Damascus; Published by Arab Medical Commission; Dir. Dr. SHAMSEDDIN EL JUNDI; Editor Dr. ADNAN TAKRITI.

Monthly Survey of Arab Economics: B.P. 2306, Damascus and B.P. 6068, Beirut; f. 1958; English and French editions; published Centre d'Etudes et de Documentation Economiques, Financières et Sociales; Dir. Dr. CHAFIC AKHRAS.

al-Mouallem al-Arabi (*The Arab Teacher*): Ministry of Education, Damascus; f. 1948; educational and cultural; Arabic.

al-Mouhandis al-Arabi: Dar Al-Mouhandisen Bldg., Azme Square, P.O.B. 2336, Damascus; published by Syrian Engineering Syndicate; scientific and cultural; Dir. Ing. GHASSAN TAYARA; Editor Eng. ADNAN IBRAHIM; bi-monthly.

al-Munadel: c/o P.O.B. 849, Damascus; magazine of Baath Arab Socialist Party.

Rissalat al-Kimia: B.P. 669, El Abid Bldg., Damascus; scientific; Arabic; Publisher, Dir. and Editor HASSAN EL SAKA.

Saut al-Forat: Deir-Ezzor; literary; Arabic; Publisher, Dir. and Editor ABDEL KADER AYACH.

al-Shourta: Directorate of Public Affairs and Moral Guidance, Damascus; juridical; Arabic.

Souriya al Arabiyya: Ministry of Information, Damascus; publicity; in four languages.

Syrie et Monde Arabe: P.O.B. 3550, Place Chahbandar, Damascus; f. 1952; economic, statistical and political survey; French and English.

al-Tamaddon al-Islami: Darwichiya, Damascus; religious; Arabic; monthly; Published by Tamaddon al-Islami Association; Dir. MUHAMMAD EL KHATIB; Editor AHMAD MAZAR EL AZMAH.

al-Yakza: Sisi St., B.P. 6677, Al Yakza Association, Aleppo; f. 1935; literary social review of charitable institution; Dir. HUSNI ABDEL-MASSIH.

QUARTERLIES

Les Archives Littéraires du Moyen Orient: Syrian Documentation Papers, P.O.B. 2712, Damascus.

Majallat Majma al-Lughah al-Arabiyyah bi-Dimashq: Arab Academy of Damascus; P.O.B. 327, Damascus; f. 1921; Islamic culture and Arabic literature, Arabic scientific and cultural terminology; circ. 2,000.

ANNUALS

Bibliography of the Middle East: Syrian Documentation Papers, P.O.B. 2712, Damascus.

General Directory of the Press and Periodicals in the Arab World: Syrian Documentation Papers, P.O.B. 2712, Damascus.

PRESS AGENCIES

Agence Arabe Syrienne d'Information: Damascus; f. 1966; supplies bulletins on Syrian news to foreign news agencies.

FOREIGN BUREAUX

Agencia EFE (*Spain*): Mazras El Malek El Adel Building, Al Mahdi Sabbagh, Damascus; Correspondent ZACHARIAS SARME.

Agenzia Nazionale Stampa Associata (ANSA) (*Italy*): P.O.B. 11997; f. 1962; Chief ADNAN KHANI.

Allgemeiner Deutscher Nachrichtendienst (ADN) (*German Democratic Republic*): P.O.B. 844, Damascus; Correspondent WILFRIED HOFFMANN.

Deutsche Presse-Agentur (dpa) (*Federal Republic of Germany*): P.O.B. 2712, Damascus; Correspondent LOUIS FARES.

Reuters: P.O.B. 3525, Ijl, Omary and Kassas Bldg., Damascus.

TASS (U.S.S.R.) also has a bureau in Damascus.

PUBLISHERS

Arab Advertising Organization: 28 Moutanabbi St., P.O.B. 2842 and 3034, Damascus; f. 1963; exclusive government establishment responsible for advertising; publishes Directory of Commerce and Industry, Damascus International Fair Guide, Daily Bulletin of Official Tenders, The Industrial Guide and The Professional Guide; Dir-Gen. HAITHAM BASHIR.

Damascus University Press: Damascus; art, geography, education, history, engineering, medicine, law, sociology, school books.

Office Arabe de Presse et de Documentation (OFA-Edition): P.O.B. 3550, Damascus; f. 1964; numerous periodicals, monographs and surveys on political and economic affairs; Dir.-Gen. SAMIR A. DARWICH. Has two affiliated branches, *OFA-Business Consulting Centre* (market surveys and services) and *OFA-Renseignements Commerciaux* (Commercial enquiries on firms and persons in Syria and Lebanon).

Syrian Documentation Papers: P.O.B. 2712, Damascus; f. 1968; publishers of *Bibliography of the Middle East* (annual), *General Directory of the Press and Periodicals in the Arab World* (annual), *Les Archives Littéraires du Moyen Orient* (quarterly), *Arab Press Digest* (weekly), and numerous publications on political, economic and social affairs and literature and legislative texts concerning Syria and the Arab world; Dir.-Gen. LOUIS FARÉS.

al-Tawjih Press: P.O.B. 3320, Palestine St., Damascus.

al-Wehda Printing and Publishing Organization (*Institut al-Ouedha pour l'impression, édition et distribution*): Damascus and Aleppo; publishes *al-Jamahir al-Arabia* and *al-Thawrah* (dailies) and *al-Maukef al-Raidi* (weekly).

Other publishers include: *Dar El-Yakaza El-Arabia Dar El-Hahda El-Arabia, Dar El-Filez, Dar El-Fatah Dubed, El-Mouassassa El-Sakafieh.*

RADIO AND TELEVISION

Directorate-General of Broadcasting and Television: Omayyad Square, Damascus; f. 1945; Dir.-Gen. FOUAD BALLAT; Eng. Dir. ANTOINE KARKOUCHE; Broadcasts Dir. KHODR OMRANE; publ. *Here is Damascus* (fortnightly).

RADIO

Director of Radio: KHODR AMRANE.

Broadcasts in Arabic, French, English, Russian, German, Spanish, Hebrew, Polish, Turkish, Bulgarian.

There were 2,230,000 receivers in use in 1978.

TELEVISION

Director of Television: MABDSALAM HIJAB.

Services started in 1960.

There were 428,585 black and white and 32,820 colour receivers in use in 1978.

FINANCE

BANKING

(cap. = capital; res. = reserves; p.u. = paid up; dep. = deposits; m. = millions; amounts in £S)

CENTRAL BANK

Central Bank of Syria: 29 Ayar Square, Damascus; f. 1956. cap. and res. 23m.; total resources 13,473m. (Sept. 1978); Gov. RIFAT AKKAD; 9 brs.

OTHER BANKS

Agricultural Bank: P.O.B. 4325, Damascus; f. 1924; Dir.-Gen. MAAN RISLAN.

Commercial Bank of Syria: P.O.B. 933, Youssef Azmeh Square, Damascus; f. 1967; 33 brs.; cap. an dres. 355m., dep. 8,544m. (1981); Pres. and Gen. Man. MAEN RASLAN.

Industrial Bank: Damascus; f. 1959; nationalized bank providing finance for industry; cap. 12.5m., dep. 304m., total investments 326m. (March 1977); 7 brs.; Chair. and Gen. Man. Dr. A. S. KANAAN.

Popular Credit Bank: Youssef Azmeh Ave., Fardoss St., P.O.B. 2841, Damascus; f. 1967; governmental bank; cap. 25m., dep. 584.1m (June 1980).

Real Estate Bank: P.O.B. 2337, Al Furat St., Damascus; f. 1966; cap. 215m.; 13 brs.; Chair. and Gen. Man. FAROUK AYYASH.

INSURANCE

Syrian General Organization for Insurance: Tajheez St., P.O.B. 2279, Damascus; f. 1953; authorized cap. 10m.; a nationalized company; operates throughout Syria, with agency in Lebanon; Chair. and Gen. Man. TAHA KATAF.

TRADE AND INDUSTRY

CHAMBERS OF COMMERCE

Damascus Chamber of Commerce: B.P. 1040, Mou'awiah St., Damascus; f. 1914; 11,000 mems.; Pres. BADREDDINE SHALLAH; Gen. Dir. MUHAMMAD THABET Gh. MAHAYNI; publ. *Economic Bulletin* (quarterly).

Aleppo Chamber of Commerce: Al-Moutanabbi Str., Aleppo; f. 1885; Pres. MUHAMMAD MAHROUSEH; Sec. EUGENE GLORE; Dir. ZEKI DAROUZI.

Hama Chamber of Commerce and Industry: Sh. Bachoura, Hama; f. 1934; Pres. ABDUL-HAMID KAMBAZ.

Homs Chamber of Commerce and Industry: Aboul-of St., P.O.B. 440, Homs; f. 1938; Pres. YUSUF AL-IKHOUAN; Dir. SELIM AL-MUSANNEF.

Latakia Chamber of Commerce: Sh. Al-Hurriyah, Latakia; Pres. JULE NASRI.

CHAMBERS OF INDUSTRY

Aleppo Chamber of Industry: Moutanabbi St., Aleppo; f. 1935; Pres. ABDEL AZIZ FANSA; 4,000 mems.

Damascus Chamber of Industry: P.O.B. 1305, Harika-Mouawiya St., Damascus; Pres. SHAFIC SOUCCAR; Dir.-Gen. ABDUL HAMID MALAKANI; publ. *Al Siniey* (Industry) (irregularly).

EMPLOYERS' ORGANIZATIONS

FEDERATIONS

Fédération Générale à Damas: Damascus; f. 1951; Dir. TALAT TAGLUBI.

Fédération de Damas: Damascus; f. 1949.

Fédération des Patrons et Industriels à Lattaquié: Latakia; f. 1953.

TRADE UNIONS

Ittihad Naqabat al-'Ummal al-'Am fi Suriya (*General Federation of Labour Unions*): Qanawat St., Damascus; f. 1948; Chair. IZZADIN NASIR; Sec. MAHMUD FAHURI.

STATE ENTERPRISES

Cotton Marketing Organization: P.O.B. 729, Aleppo; f. 1965; monopoly authority for purchase of seed cotton, ginning and sales of cotton lint; Pres. Dir.-Gen. RATEB JABER.

Syrian Petroleum Company: P.O.B. 2849, Al-Mutanabi St., Damascus; f. 1974; state agency; holds the oil concession for all Syria; exploits the Alayan, Suwadiyah, Karachuk, Rumailan and Jbeisseh oilfields; also organizes exploring, production and marketing of oil nationally; Dir. Eng. ISSA IBRAHIM YOUSSEF.

TRANSPORT

RAILWAYS

Syrian Railways: B.P. 182, Sikkethadid, Aleppo; Pres. of the Board of Administration and Gen. Man. Ing. NOFAL KASSOUHA.

The present railway system is composed of the following network:

Meydan Ekbez (Turkish frontier)–Aleppo; Cobanbey (Turkish frontier)–Aleppo; Qamishliya (Turkish frontier)–Jaroubieh (Iraq frontier); Aleppo–Homs; Koussair (Lebanese frontier)–Aleppo; Homs–Akkari (Lebanese frontier); there are 1,537 km. of normal gauge track. A line from Latakia to Kameshli (750 km.) has been completed and is operating for passenger and goods traffic. Other new lines completed include an 180-km. line from Homs to Khenefes and Palmyra, a 22-km. line from Hama to Meharden and a 42-km. line from Tartous to Akkari. A line from Homs to Damascus (204 km.) is nearing completion.

Syrian Railways: Northern Lines: 248 km.; Southern Lines: 295 km.

Hejaz Railways (narrow gauge): 301 km. in Syria; the historic railway to Medina is the subject of a reconstruction project jointly with Jordan and Saudi Arabia, but little progress has been made since the June 1967 war. Trains run from Damascus to Amman.

ROADS

Arterial roads run across the country linking the north to the south and the Mediterranean to the eastern frontier. The main arterial networks are as follows: Sidon (Lebanon)-Quneitra-Sweida-Salkhad-Jordan border; Beirut (Lebanon)-Damascus - Khan Abu Chamat - Iraq border - Baghdad; Tartous - Tell Kalakh - Homs - Palmyra; Banias - Hama - Salemie; Latakia - Aleppo - Rakka - Deir - ez - Zor - Abou Kemal·Iraq border; Tripoli (Lebanon)-Tartous-Banias-Latakia; Turkish border - Antakya; Amman (Jordan) - Dera'a - Damascus - Homs - Hama - Aleppo - Azaz (Turkish border); Kuneitra - Damascus - Palmyra - Deir-ez-Zor - Hassetche - Kamechlie.

Asphalted roads: 13,000 km., macadam roads: 1,300 km., earth roads: 6,000 km.

Projects for the construction of a further 1,600 km. of main roads are under way; the extended network is to improve links with the east of the country and with Iraq, Jordan, Lebanon and Turkey.

PIPELINES

The oil pipelines which cross Syrian territory are of great importance to the national economy, representing a considerable source of foreign exchange. Iraq halted the flow of oil through the pipeline between Kirkuk and Banias in April 1976, but it was resumed in February 1979.

Following the Iraq Government's nationalization of the Iraq Petroleum Company, the Syrian Government nationalized the IPC's pipelines, pumping stations and other installations in Syria, setting up a new company to administer them:

Syrian Company for Oil Transport (SCOT): Dir.-Gen. HANNA HADDAD.

SHIPPING

The port of Latakia is being developed and about 2,500 ships used the port in 1979; it is planned to increase the port's capacity to 5 million tons per year. A new port at Tartous is under construction.

Syrian Navigation Company: Latakia.

CIVIL AVIATION

There is an international airport at Damascus.

Syrian Arab Airlines: P.O.B. 417, Al-Jabiri St., Damascus; f. 1946, refounded 1961 after revocation of merger with Misrair forming U.A.A.; domestic services and routes to Abu Dhabi, Algiers, Athens, Baghdad, Bahrain, Benghazi, Bombay, Bucharest, Budapest, Cairo, Casablanca, Copenhagen, Delhi, Dhahran, Doha, Dubai, East Berlin, Istanbul, Jeddah, Karachi, Kuwait, Larnaca, London, Moscow, Munich, Paris, Prague, Rome, Sana'a, Sharjah, Sofia, Teheran, Tripoli and Tunis; fleet of four Caravelles, three Boeing 727 and two Boeing 747, two DC6; Chair. and Man. Dir. AHMAD H. KOUAIDER.

FOREIGN AIRLINES

The following foreign airlines serve Syria: Aeroflot (U.S.S.R.), Air France, Alitalia (Italy), Ariana Afghan Airlines, Balkan (Bulgaria), British Airways, ČSA (Czechoslovakia), EgyptAir, Interflug (German Democratic Republic), Iraqi Airways, KLM (Netherlands), Kuwait Airways, Lufthansa (Federal Republic of Germany), Malév (Hungary), Pan Am (U.S.A.), PIA (Pakistan), Qantas (Australia), SAS (Sweden), Saudia and Swissair.

TOURISM

Ministry of Tourism: Abou Firas El-Hamadani St., Damascus; f. 1972; Minister of Tourism Dr. Eng. NAWRAS AD-DAQR; Dir. of Tourist Relations IHSAN CHICHAKLI; Ministerial Adviser NADIM KANAFANI.

Middle East Tourism: P.O.B. 201, Fardoss St., Damascus; f. 1966; Pres. MOHAMED DADOUCHE; 7 brs.

DEFENCE

C.-in-C. of the Armed Forces: Lt.-Gen. HAFIZ AL-ASSAD.

Minister of Defence and Deputy C.-in-C. of the Armed Forces: Maj.-Gen. MUSTAFA TLASS.

Chief of Staff of the Armed Forces: Maj.-Gen. HIKMAT SHEHABI.

Deputy Chief of Staff: ALI ASLAN.

Air Force Commander: Maj.-Gen. SUBHI HADDAD.

Defence Budget (1981): £S9,378 million.

Military Service: 30 months (Jewish population exempted).

Total Armed Forces (July 1981): 225,500 (army 170,000, navy 2,500, air force 50,000).

Paramilitary Forces: 9,800: 8,000 Gendarmerie, 1,800 Desert Guard (Frontier Force).

The Arab Deterrent Force of approximately 30,000 in Lebanon is composed entirely of Syrian troops.

EDUCATION

Compulsory schooling lasts six years up to the age of 14, and text books are issued free in the primary sector. Both primary and secondary education are expanding rapidly, and in 1979 there were over 2 million students enrolled in schools and institutes.

Agricultural schools prepare students mainly for work in agriculture and are open to the sons of peasants. Technical schools prepare students for work in all types of factories. Higher education is provided by the Universities of Damascus, Aleppo and Latakia, and the Homs Institute of Petroleum.

The main language of instruction in schools is Arabic, but English and French are widely taught as second languages.

BIBLIOGRAPHY

ABU JABER, KAMAL S. The Arab Baath Socialist Party (Syracuse University Press, New York, 1966).

ASFOUR, EDMUND Y. Syrian Development and Monetary Policy (Harvard, 1959).

DIRECTORY OF COMMERCE AND INDUSTRY FOR THE SYRIAN ARAB REPUBLIC (Arab Advertising Organization, Damascus, 1969).

FEDDEN, ROBIN. Syria: an Historical Appreciation (London, 1946).

Syria and Lebanon (John Murray, London, 1966).

GLUBB, J. B. Syria, Lebanon, Jordan (Thames and Hudson, London, 1967).

HADDAD, J. Fifty Years of Modern Syria and Lebanon (Beirut, 1950).

HELBAOUI, YOUSSEF. La Syrie (Paris, 1956).

HITTI, PHILIP K. History of Syria; including Lebanon and Palestine (New York, 1951).

HOMET, M. L'Histoire secrète du traité franco-syrien (New Ed., Paris, 1951).

HOPWOOD, DEREK. The Russian presence in Syria and Palestine 1843–1914 (Oxford, 1969).

HOURANI, ALBERT H. Syria and Lebanon: A Political Essay (New York, 1946).

INTERNATIONAL BANK FOR RECONSTRUCTION AND DEVELOPMENT, THE. The Economic Development of Syria (Baltimore, 1955).

LLOYD-GEORGE, D. The Truth about the Peace Treaties, Vol. II (London, 1938).

LONGRIGG, S. H. Syria and Lebanon Under French Mandate (Oxford University Press, 1958).

PETRAN, TABITHA. Syria (Benn, London, 1972).

RABBATH, E. Unité Syrienne et Devenir Arabe (Paris, 1937).

RUNCIMAN, STEVEN. A History of the Crusades (London, Vol. I 1951, Vol. II 1952).

SAUVAGET, J. Les monuments historiques de Damas (Beirut, 1932).

SEALE, PATRICK. The Struggle for Syria (London, 1965).

SHARIF, A. A. Sources of Statistics in Syria (B.D.S.A., Damascus, 1964).

SPRINGETT, B. H. Secret Sects of Syria and the Lebanon (London, 1922).

STARK, FREYA. Letters from Syria (London, 1942).

THUBRON, C. A. Mirror to Damascus (Heinemann, London, 1967).

TIBAWI, A. L. Syria (London, 1962).

American Interests in Syria 1800–1901 (Oxford University Press, New York, 1966).

A Modern History of Syria (Macmillan, London, 1969).

TORREY, GORDON H. Syrian Politics and the Military (State University, Ohio, 1964).

TRITTON, A. S. The Caliphs and their Non-Muslim Subjects (London, 1930).

VAN DAM, NIKOLAOS. The Struggle for Power in Syria (Croom Helm, London, 1981).

WEULERSSE, J. Paysans de Syrie et du Proche Orient (Paris, 1946).

YAMAK, L. Z. The Syrian Social Nationalist Party (Harvard University Press, Cambridge, Mass., 1966).

ZIADEH, N. Syria and Lebanon (New York, Praeger, 1957).

Tunisia

PHYSICAL AND SOCIAL GEOGRAPHY

D. R. Harris

Tunisia is the smallest of the three countries that comprise the "Maghreb" of north Africa, but it is more cosmopolitan than either Algeria or Morocco. It forms a wedge of territory, 163,610 square kilometres in extent, between Algeria and Libya. It includes the easternmost ridges of the Atlas Mountains but most of it is low-lying and bordered by a long and sinuous Mediterranean coastline that faces both north and east. Ease of access by sea and by land from the east has favoured the penetration of foreign influences and Tunisia owes its distinct national identity and its varied cultural traditions to a succession of invading peoples: Phoenicians, Romans, Arabs, Turks and French. It was more completely Arabized than either Algeria or Morocco and remnants of the original Berber-speaking population of the Maghreb are confined, in Tunisia, to a few isolated localities in the south.

At mid-1980 the population was estimated to be 6,392,300 and the overall density was 39.1 per square kilometre. Most of the people live in the more humid, northern part of the country and at the May 1975 census about 10 per cent lived in Tunis (550,404). Situated strategically where the Sicilian Channel links the western with the central Mediterranean and close to the site of ancient Carthage, Tunis combines the functions of capital and chief port. No other town approaches Tunis in importance but on the east coast both Sousse (population 69,530 in 1975) and Sfax (population 171,297) provide modern port facilities, as does Bizerta (population 62,856) on the north coast, while some distance inland the old Arab capital and holy city of Kairouan (population 54,546) serves as a regional centre. The only other sizeable town is Djerba (population 70,217).

The principal contrasts in the physical geography of Tunisia are between a humid and relatively mountainous northern region, a semi-arid central region of low plateaux and plains and a dry Saharan region in the south. The northern region is dominated by the easternmost folds of the Atlas mountain system which form two separate chains, the Northern and High Tell, separated by the valley of the River Medjerda, the only perennially flowing river in the country. The Northern Tell, which is a continuation of the Algerian Tell Atlas, consists mainly of sandstone and extends along the north coast at heights of between 300 and 600 metres. South of the Medjerda valley the much broader Tell Atlas, which is a continuation of the Saharan Atlas of Algeria, is made up of a succession of rugged sandstone and limestone ridges. Near the Algerian frontier they reach a maximum height of 1,544 metres in Djebel Chambi, the highest point in Tunisia, but the folds die away eastward towards the Cap Bon peninsula which extends north-east to within 145 kilometres of Sicily.

South of the High Tell or Dorsale ("backbone") central Tunisia consists of an extensive platform sloping gently towards the east coast. Its western half, known as the High Steppe, is made up of alluvial basins rimmed by low, barren mountains, but eastward the mountains give way first to the Low Steppe, which is a monotonous gravel-covered plateau and ultimately to the flat coastal plain of the Sahel. Occasional watercourses cross the Steppes but they only flow after heavy rain and usually fan out and evaporate in salt flats, or sebkhas, before reaching the sea.

The central Steppes give way southward to a broad depression occupied by two great seasonal salt lakes or shotts. The largest of these, the Shott Djerid, lies at 16 metres below sea-level and is normally covered by a salt crust. It extends from close to the Mediterranean coast near Gabès almost to the Algerian frontier and is adjoined on the north-west by the Shott el Rharsa which lies at 21 metres below sea-level. South of the shotts Tunisia extends for over 320 kilometres into the Sahara. Rocky, flat-topped mountains, the Monts des Ksour, separate a flat plain known as the Djeffara, which borders the coast south of Gabès, from a sandy lowland which is partly covered by the dunes of the Great Eastern Erg.

The climate of northern Tunisia is "Mediterranean" in type with hot, dry summers followed by warm, wet winters. Average rainfall reaches 150 cm. in the Kroumirie Mountains, which is the wettest area in north Africa, but over most of the northern region it varies from 40 to 100 cm. The wetter and least accessible mountains are covered with forests in which cork oak and evergreen oak predominate, but elsewhere lower rainfall and overgrazing combine to replace forest with meagre scrub growth. South of the High Tell rainfall is reduced to between 20 and 40 cm. annually, which is insufficient for the regular cultivation of cereal crops without irrigation, and there is no continuous cover of vegetation. Large areas of the Steppes support only clumps of wiry esparto grass, which is collected and exported for paper manufacture. Southern Tunisia experiences full desert conditions. Rainfall is reduced to below 20 cm. annually and occurs only at rare intervals. Extremes of temperature and wind are characteristic and vegetation is completely absent over extensive tracts. The country supports only a sparse nomadic population except where supplies of underground water make cultivation possible, as in the famous date-producing oasis of Tozeur on the northern edge of the Shott Djerid.

HISTORY

Although the creation of the present-day independent Republic of Tunisia has been a phenomenon of the post-war period, the history of this small but important part of North Africa has displayed a certain continuity since the earliest times. From the early days of Phoenician settlement in the course of the ninth century B.C., the region has alternated between being itself a focus of political control (the Carthaginian Empire, or the period of medieval Islam, for example); and being the object of imperial aggrandizement (Rome, the Ottoman Empire, France). On top of this pattern must be superimposed the conquest of North Africa by the Arabs in the course of the seventh century A.D., which has determined the basic characteristics of Tunisia ever since.

The history of Tunisia may be said to begin with the establishment there of colonies of Phoenician settlers, and the rise of the Carthaginian Empire. Emerging, in the course of the sixth century B.C., from the mists of its legendary foundation by the semi-mythical Queen Dido, by *c.* 550 B.C. Carthage had reached a position of commercial and naval supremacy in the Mediterranean, controlling part of Sicily, and with trading colonies established as far as what is now southern Portugal. The empire reached its height in the course of the fourth century, but shortly afterwards became involved with the rising power of the Roman Republic in a bitter struggle for the hegemony of the Mediterranean. The Punic Wars (264–241; 218–201; 149–146), of which the second is memorable for Hannibal's invasion of Italy, ended in the utter destruction of Carthage as a political entity, and the incorporation of its domains within the growing empire of Rome.

After one and a half centuries of abandonment, the ancient site of Carthage was rebuilt by Augustus at the dawn of the Christian era: intensive colonization from this time onward brought to what had become the Province of Africa a new prosperity. During the first two centuries A.D. Carthage was generally accounted the second city of the Empire after Rome, but with the decline of the Empire in the west in the course of the fourth century, the great days of Roman Carthage were over. In A.D. 439 the city was lost to the Vandals, a nomadic people of Germanic origin, and became the capital of their ephemeral state, to be recovered for the Byzantine Empire in 533–34.

For the next two hundred and fifty years the history of Tunisia cannot be separated from the larger account of North Africa. Although Byzantine rule was better established in Tunisia than in the rest of the area, it was by no means secure. The tendency of the local governors to free themselves of the control of Constantinople was echoed by religious dissensions among the native population, who, largely Berber in origin, adopted various Christian heresies as tokens of their opposition to Imperial rule.

It was from another quarter, however, that the final challenge to Byzantine rule was to come. The foundation in Arabia of the power of Islam, and its rapid expansion after the death of the Prophet (632), led quickly to the Arab conquest of Egypt and Syria, and to the shattering of the precarious unity of the Byzantine Empire. The first Arab raids into North Africa soon followed (647). After a confused period, in which the Arabs, the Berbers, and the forces of Byzantium all contested for the control of North Africa, Arab control over the area was finally established (698) with the conquest of Carthage, and the foundation of the town of Tunis. Islam now spread rapidly amongst the Berbers, but did not prevent them from making further attempts to regain their independence, merely providing them with new and more convenient pretexts for revolt in the shape of new Islamic religious heresies. The greater part of the eighth century is taken up with Berber-supported Kharijite risings, manifestations of extreme left-wing Islam against the central government, and with constant revolts among the occupying Arab forces. In the last years of the Umayyad dynasty (overthrown 748–50) Tunisia escaped completely from Imperial control: the new dynasty of the Abbasids, ruling from Iraq, made strong efforts to recapture the province. Kayrawan, founded in 670 as the centre of Arab rule in the Maghreb, was retaken, but lost in 767, when a period of complete anarchy ensued. Tunisia was restored to Abbasid control in the year 800, in the person of Ibrahim ibn Aghlab. The caliph Harun al-Rashid thereupon appointed him as tributary ruler of al-Ifrikiya—corresponding more or less to the Roman Province of Africa, and to the present-day state of Tunisia.

The period of Aghlabid rule is one of great importance for the history of Tunisia. For the major part of the ninth century the country enjoyed a relatively stable and prosperous existence. Some years later Aghlabid forces began the conquest of Sicily (827–39). The middle of the ninth century was the zenith of Aghlabid rule, and was signalized by the emir Ahmed with the construction of great mosques in the major cities, and the building of an elaborate system of dams and reservoirs to supply the capital of Kayrawan. From 874 the power of the Aghlabid state began to decline; despite the virtual completion of the conquest of Sicily (878) the dynasty was finally overthrown in the course of a religious revolution from the west. Between 905 and 909 Tunisia was brought under the control of the Fatimids, adherents and fanatical propagators of the heretical doctrines of Shi'ism. Established in their new capital of Mahdiya, on the Tunisian coast, the Fatimids pursued a vigorous policy of expansion and conquest. Expeditions were sent against Egypt, and Sicily was once more ruled from North Africa, while by 933 Fatimid rule was established throughout the Maghreb. A terrible Berber revolt in 943–47 was overcome, and for the next 25 years Tunisia enjoyed a certain degree of prosperity. Fatimid power meanwhile was expanding in the east. In 969–70 the dynasty gained control of Egypt and Syria: three years later the caliph al-Muizz abandoned

Mahdiya for his new capital of Cairo, and handed over the Government of Tunisia to the Zirids, a family of Berber princes who had long supported the Fatimid regime. Under Zirid rule Tunisia enjoyed great prosperity, in which the arts and sciences, commerce and industry, all flourished, but this golden age was suddenly brought to an end in 1050 by the Zirids transferring their allegiance from Cairo to the orthodox caliph at Baghdad. Fatimid revenge was terrible. In 1051 hundreds of thousands of Hilali Arab nomads were sent against Ifrikiya from Egypt. The economy crumbled, along with the political power of the Berbers, and the country as a whole lapsed into political fragmentation. Further troubles now came from another quarter. In 1087 forces from the rising Italian city-states of Pisa and Genoa took Mahdiya, allowing the Zirids, who had held out there against the Hilali invasion, to continue as its rulers. Early in the twelfth century the Zirids renewed their loyalty to Cairo, and attempted to restore the shattered fragments of their state, but were interrupted by the Normans, who, having previously conquered Sicily and Malta, in 1148 drove the last Zirid from Mahdiya.

Norman rule in Tunisia was short-lived. By 1160 they had been ejected from their last coastal stronghold, and for the next fifty years Tunisia formed part of the empire of the caliphs of Marrakesh (the Almohads). With the thirteenth century the authority of Baghdad was briefly restored over Tunisia. In 1207 the Abbasid caliph al-Nasir set up a strong provincial government under a member of the Berber family of the Hafsids, who, having held the governorship of Tunis since 1184, were to continue as the main political force in the area until the Ottoman conquest late in the sixteenth century.

For most of the thirteenth century the Hafsids ruled over North Africa from Tripoli to central Algeria, and maintained close diplomatic and commercial relations with the trading ports and city-states of the northern shores of the Mediterranean. European interest in Tunisia had never disappeared since the temporary Norman conquest of the twelfth century: with the weakening of Hafsid rule in face of tribal and Arab unrest, Jerba came once more into Christian hands (1284–1337). In the reign of Abu'l-Abbas (1370–94) the fortunes of the dynasty once more improved, and further Christian attempts to seize coastal places were repelled. His son held off repeated Sicilian and Catalan attempts to capture Jerba, and in 1428 went on the offensive, becoming involved in operations against Malta. The last Hafsid ruler of note was Abu Amr Uthman (1435–88). Shortly after his death the Hafsid Empire began to disintegrate, and at the same time Tunisia became involved in the wider struggle between the resurgent forces of the newly-unified Spanish monarchy and the Ottoman Empire for control of the Mediterranean.

OTTOMAN RULE

With the completion of the *reconquista* in 1492, Spain turned her attentions to the conquest of Muslim North Africa. The first place in the crumbling Hafsid territories to fall under her control was Bougie, in 1510, and then Tripoli, in the same year. Ten years later the strategic place of Jerba also fell. But these events had already produced a reaction. In 1516 Algiers had come into the possession of the Turkish corsair Aruj. His brother, Khayr ed-Din Barbarossa, who had succeeded him in 1518, had in 1533 been summoned to Istanbul to act as high admiral of the Ottoman fleet. In this new capacity he drove the compliant Emir al-Hasan from Tunis (1534), and placed the town under Ottoman control. In the following year a great Spanish naval expedition re-took the town, and al-Hasan returned as the Emperor's vassal, handing over la Goleta to Spain as the price of his restoration. Further coastal strongholds subsequently passed into Spanish hands, while in 1542 al-Hassan was deposed by his son Ahmed, who, with the not disinterested help of the Turkish corsair chiefs, made a final attempt to reunite Tunisia against Spain. After a long drawn-out struggle Ahmed fell at the siege of Malta, 1565, which, together with the Spanish naval victory of Lepanto six years later, marks the climax and virtual end of their struggle with the Ottomans for control of the sea. As far as Tunisia was concerned, the sole beneficiaries of the struggle were the Ottomans. Already well established at Algiers, in 1569 the Pasha of Algiers, Uluj Ali, placed a garrison in Tunis, only to be driven out briefly (1572) in the aftermath of the Spanish victory at Lepanto. The unfortunate Hafsid was restored for the last time as nominal ruler, but in 1574 an Ottoman expedition put an end to Spanish power in Tunis, and to the Hafsid dynasty itself.

Direct Ottoman rule in Algiers lasted only seventeen years. The provincial administration set up in 1574 took its orders at first from Algiers, and later from the Porte itself, but a military revolt in 1591 reduced the power of the Pasha, the actual representative of the sultan, to a cypher, and the affairs of the state were taken over by one of the forty *deys* or high officers of the Ottoman army of occupation. By *c.* 1600 a situation had arisen analogous to that in Algiers, the *diwan*, or governing council, coming to share a pre-eminent place with the *taifa*, or guild of the corsair chiefs. By 1606 the *de facto* independence of Tunisia had been recognized. Nevertheless, for the next two and a half centuries and more, Tunisia was regarded as part of the Ottoman Empire, a convenient fiction both flattering to the government at Istanbul, and useful to the *deys* in safeguarding their rule and bolstering their reputation.

In the first half of the seventeenth century the situation of Tunis was fairly flourishing. Trade and commerce, especially with Marseilles and Livorno, prospered, while commercial relations were entered into with states as far distant as England and the Netherlands. From *c.* 1650 the power of the *deys* declined, and authority in the state gradually passed to the *beys*, originally subordinate in rank. Hammuda, *bey* from 1659 to 1663, became master of the entire country, and assured the maintenance of power in his family—the Muradids—until 1702. This was a period of decline, with tribal unrest away from Tunis, and incursions from the direction of Algiers. With the accession of Huseyn Ali Turki in 1705 a new line of *beys* brought some semblance of order to the country. The remainder of the eighteenth century passed fairly uneventfully for Tunisia, with a certain amount of quiet prosperity, despite the uncertainty of relations with Algeria, and the growing naval power of Europe in the Mediterranean.

With the aftermath of the Napoleonic Wars came the first real impact of Europe on Tunisia. The European powers, in congress at Vienna and Aachen (1815–17) forced upon the *bey* Mahmud (1814–24) the suppression of the corsairs and their piratical activities, which had provided a considerable part of the revenues of the state. The French occupied Algiers in 1830, and subsequently reduced the whole of Algeria to colonial status. The next fifty years witnessed desperate but unavailing efforts by Tunisia to avoid the same fate. Increasingly the influence of France and Britain, and later Italy, came to be manifest through the activities of their consuls. The *bey* Ahmed (1837–55) attempted to reform the army on western lines, and to liberalize the institutions of society: his efforts merely increased the financial dependence of Tunisia on France. Under Muhammad (1855–59) a proclamation of reform and equality based on the Ottoman Hatti-Sherif of 1839 was promulgated under European pressure: his successor Muhammad al-Sadik (1859–82) promulgated a Constitution (suspended 1864) which attempted to separate executive from legislative power, to codify the laws, and to guarantee the independence of the judiciary.

Nevertheless, Tunisia's position deteriorated. Increased taxes, imposed from the mid-fifties, provoked tribal rebellion, and the growing dependence on foreign loans led to foreign intervention. Annual debt charges eventually exceeded revenue and in 1869 the *bey* was obliged to accept international financial control by France, Britain and Italy. By 1881 the imminence of financial collapse decided France to intervene, especially as Britain had indicated that it would not contest French influence in Tunisia, which Germany actually encouraged. French forces invaded Tunisia in April 1881, the immediate occasion being incidents on the frontier with Algeria. They encountered no serious resistance and the *bey* was forced to accept the terms of the Treaty of Kassar Said (also known as the Treaty of Bardo) under which he remained the nominal ruler of his country while French officials took over the direction of military, financial and foreign affairs.

FRENCH PROTECTORATE

The French presence once established, French control was soon extended. In 1883 Ali IV was forced to sign the Treaty of Mersa, which formally established a French protectorate over Tunisia and brought the actual government of the country under French control. Although the office of *bey* was preserved, the real power passed to the French Resident-General. The international control commission was abolished in 1884, the currency was reformed on French lines in 1891, and the extra-territorial privileges of other Europeans were abrogated. Encouraged by large-scale grants of land, there was a considerable influx of settlers from France, and also from Italy, especially after 1900. Besides being confronted with the task of sustaining the economy, which they tackled by investment in the development of the country's resources, the French were faced with rivalry from Italy, whose ambitions in North Africa were not extinguished until the collapse of the Fascist regime in the Second World War, and with the rise of Tunisian nationalism.

Tunisian cultural and political life absorbed many French ideas but was also influenced by movements in other parts of the Islamic world. An attempt to emulate the Young Turk reformers in the Ottoman Empire was seen in the Young Tunisian movement (1908) which called for the restoration of the authority of the *bey* together with reforms on democratic lines. The achievement of independence in eastern Arab countries after the First World War, and the example of the nationalist movement in Egypt, inspired Tunisians with a greater national consciousness and in 1920 the Destour (Constitution) movement was formed under the leadership of Shaikh al-Tha'libi, one of the founders of the pre-war Young Tunisians.

The Destour called for a self-governing constitutional regime with a legislative assembly. French attempts to conciliate opinion by administrative reforms, beginning in 1920 with economic councils on which Tunisians were represented, did not satisfy the more radical elements, however, and in the face of further nationalist activity repressive measures were resorted to. Shaikh al-Tha'libi was exiled in 1923 and in 1925 the Destour movement was broken up. It revived in the years after the Depression but soon split, the old Destour leaders being accused of collaboration with France by younger members eager for political action on a broad front. In 1934, led by Habib Bourguiba, a Tunisian lawyer, these created the Néo-Destour (New Constitution) Party. The new party employed methods of widespread political agitation as a result of which Bourguiba was exiled. With the victory of the Popular Front in France in 1936 he returned to Tunisia but little was achieved in direct negotiations with the new French government, from which much had been expected in the way of reforms. The Néo-Destour was built up into a powerful organization, its influence extending into all parts of the country, and its strength was proved in a successful general strike in 1938. Widespread clashes with the police followed, martial law was proclaimed, some 200 nationalists were arrested and both the Destour and Néo-Destour parties were dissolved.

When the Second World War broke out in the following year Tunisian opinion rallied in favour of France and when Italy entered the war some 23,000 Italians in Tunisia were interned. With the fall of France Tunisia came under Vichy rule and Bizerta, Tunis and other ports were used by Germany and Italy to supply their armies in Libya. The country became a theatre of war until the defeat of the Axis forces by the Allies in 1943 brought about the eventual restoration of French authority. The *bey*, Muhammad al-Monsif, was accused of collaboration with the Axis powers and deposed; he was replaced by his cousin, Muhammad al-Amin, who reigned until Tunisia became a republic in 1957.

GROWING AUTONOMY

The virtual restoration of peace-time conditions in 1944 brought a relaxation of political restrictions and the years immediately following saw renewed agitation for political changes. French action to repress this obliged Habib Bourguiba to remove himself to Cairo in 1945 but his chief lieutenant, Salah ben Youssef, was able to remain in Tunisia. The French authorities turned their attention to political reforms and by Beylical decrees in 1945 the Council of Ministers and the Grand Council (an elected body with equal French and Tunisian representation) were reorganized, the authority of the latter being extended. These moves did not satisfy the nationalists, however, who in August 1946 at a national congress unequivocally demanded complete independence. Later in the year a ministry was formed under Muhammad Kaak which included an increased number of Tunisians (moderate leaders being appointed, the Destour and Néo-Destour having refused to participate); the French retained overriding control.

Bourguiba returned to Tunisia in 1949. In April 1950 Néo-Destour proposals were put forward for the transfer of sovereignty and executive control to Tunisian hands, under a responsible government with a Prime Minister appointed by the *bey* and an elected National Assembly which would draw up a democratic constitution. Local French interests would be protected by representation on municipal councils, and Tunisia would co-operate with France on terms of equality. These proposals were met with a reasonable response in France and a new Tunisian government was formed in August 1950, composed of an equal number of Tunisian and French ministers, with Muhammad Chenik as Chief Minister and Salah ben Youssef Minister of Justice. The object of the new Government was stated to be the restoration of Tunisian sovereignty in stages, in co-operation with France. Despite strong opposition to these developments from the European settlers (some 10 per cent of the population), who opposed all concessions to nationalist demands, further reforms were effected in September 1950 and February 1951, when French advisers to the Tunisian ministers were removed and the Resident-General's control over the Council of Ministers was diminished.

Peaceful progress towards autonomy came to a halt, however, with growing settler opposition, procrastination on the part of the French government and consequent alienation of the nationalists. Franco-Tunisian negotiations in 1951 came to nothing and Tunisian resentment erupted in strikes and demonstrations early in 1952. In February 1952 Bourguiba and other Néo-Destour leaders were arrested on the order of a new Resident-General, Jean de Hauteclocque, and a wave of violence spread throughout the country, culminating in the arrest and removal from office of the Chief Minister and the imposition of French military control.

A new government was formed under Salaheddine Baccouche, a French-inspired scheme of reforms designed to lead to eventual internal autonomy was announced in April, and a temporary easing of tension followed, although the now-proscribed Néo-Destour took their case to Cairo and the UN General Assembly. Against a background of increasing terrorism, countered by French repressive action, and in face of opposition from both the Néo-Destour and the settlers, little in the way of reform could be achieved. The *bey* at first refused to sign French reform decrees and when he yielded in December 1952 under the threat of deposition the proposals were promptly repudiated by the Néo-Destour.

Terrorist activities continued and a secret settler counter-terrorist organization, the "Red Hand", came into prominence. The situation, which approached civil war in 1953, with bands of *fellagha* active in the western highlands and around Bizerta, and terrorism and counter-terrorism in the towns, did not improve until July 1954, when the newly-formed Mendès-France government in France offered internal autonomy for Tunisia with responsibility only for defence and foreign affairs being retained by France. The French proposals were accepted and in August a new Tunisian government headed by Tahar ben Ammar, which contained moderate nationalists but also three Néo-Destour members, was formed. Negotiations with the French government began at Carthage in September 1954 and although they had reached deadlock when the Mendès-France government fell in February 1955 they were resumed in March and a final agreement was signed in Paris on June 2nd.

The agreement gave internal autonomy to Tunisia while at the same time protecting French interests and preserving the close links with France. France retained responsibility for foreign affairs, defence (including the control of frontiers) and internal security. Although it was supported by a majority of the Néo-Destour, the extremist wing, headed by the exiled Salah ben Youssef, and the old Destour and Communist elements, opposed it, as also did the settlers' organizations. An all-Tunisian cabinet was formed in September 1955 by Tahar ben Ammar, with Néo-Destour members holding six of the twelve posts.

Habib Bourguiba had returned from three years' exile in June 1955, to be followed by Salah ben Youssef in September. In October, however, ben Youssef was expelled from the party for opposition to the recent agreement and for "splitting activities". A Néo-Destour party congress at Sfax in November 1955 confirmed the expulsion and re-elected Bourguiba as party president. The congress accepted the agreement but at the same time reaffirmed that it would be satisfied only with independence and demanded the election of a constituent assembly. Clashes between "Bourguibist" and "Youssefist" factions followed and in December a conspiracy to set up a terrorist organization to prevent the implementation of the agreement was discovered. Salah ben Youssef fled to Tripoli in January 1956 and many suspected "Youssefists" were placed in detention. At the same time *fellagha* activity revived, rebel bands becoming active in the remoter parts of the country and acts of terrorism being committed against both Frenchmen and members of the Néo-Destour.

INDEPENDENCE

Against the background of these events a Tunisian delegation led by Bourguiba began independence negotiations with the French Government in Paris on February 27th, 1956. In a protocol signed on March 20th France formally recognized the independence of Tunisia and its right to exercise responsibility over foreign affairs, security and defence, and to set up a national army. A transitional period was envisaged during which French forces would gradually be withdrawn from Tunisia, including Bizerta.

Elections for a Constituent Assembly, immediately held on March 25th, resulted in all 98 seats being won by candidates of the National Front, all of whom acknowledged allegiance to the Néo-Destour. The elections were boycotted by the "Youssefist" opposition. Habib Bourguiba became Prime Minister on April 11th, leading a government in which 16 of the 17 ministers belonged to the Néo-Destour.

In the early years of independence Tunisia's relations with France were bedevilled by the question of the evacuation of French forces. A Tunisian demand for their withdrawal was rejected in July 1956 by a French government preoccupied with a deteriorating situation in Algeria. Bourguiba visited Paris in September in an attempt to promote a mediated settlement in Algeria based on French recognition of Algeria's right to independence but hopes of progress in this direction were shattered by the French kidnapping in October of five leading Algerian nationalists. Tunisia immediately severed diplomatic relations with France, anti-French riots broke out and there were clashes between French troops and Tunisian demonstrators resulting in deaths on both sides.

Moves were made early in 1957 to strengthen Tunisia's relations with her neighbours. In January a treaty of good-neighbourliness was signed with Libya and proclaimed to be a step towards establishing a "Greater Arab Maghreb", and in March, at the end of a visit by Bourguiba, a twenty-year treaty of friendship was concluded with Morocco.

The *bey*, Muhammed al-Amin, had for long been the object of criticism from Tunisian nationalist leaders who saw him as having been unwilling to participate actively in the struggle for independence and apt to rely on French support. After independence his remaining powers were whittled away and on July 25th, 1957, the Constituent Assembly decided to abolish the monarchy, proclaim Tunisia a republic and invest Bourguiba with the powers of Head of State.

RELATIONS WITH FRANCE

Although diplomatic relations with France had been resumed in January 1957, differences between the two governments in connection with the Algerian revolt soon worsened. The most serious Franco-Tunisian incident of the Algerian war occurred in February 1958 when French aircraft from Algeria attacked the Tunisian border village of Sakhiet Sidi Youssef, the scene of several clashes the previous month. The Tunisian government's reaction was to break off diplomatic relations with France, to forbid all French troop movements in Tunisia, to demand the immediate evacuation of all French bases, including Bizerta, and to take the matter before the UN Security Council. French troops were blockaded in their barracks and the extra-territorial status of Bizerta, from which French warships were banned, was abolished. In addition some 600 French civilians were expelled from the frontier area and five of the seven French consulates closed.

British and United States mediation was accepted and on April 15th it was agreed that all French troops would be evacuated and Tunisian sovereignty over Bizerta recognized; at the same time the French consulates would be reopened and the cases of the expelled French civilians examined. When further clashes between Tunisian and French forces occurred in May, a state of emergency covering the whole country was proclaimed and Tunisia again took the matter to the Security Council and also requested further arms supplies from the United States and Britain.

A new phase in Franco-Tunisian relations began with the accession to power of General de Gaulle in June 1958. An agreement was concluded on June 17th under which French troops stationed outside Bizerta were to be withdrawn during the next four months, while negotiations for a provisional agreement on Bizerta were to follow. Restrictions on French troops were removed and diplomatic relations resumed. By October the only French troops remaining in Tunisia were in Bizerta.

Further elimination of French interests had meanwhile commenced. In June the French-owned transport services and in August the electricity services of Tunis were nationalized. On November 29th President Bourguiba announced proposals for purchasing by 1960 all agricultural land in Tunisia owned by French citizens, for distribution to landless Tunisians.

POLITICAL CONSOLIDATION

With the improvement of relations with France the Tunisian government felt free to consolidate its internal position, by reforming the party structure of the Néo-Destour and by taking court proceedings against members of the former regime and "Youssefist" opponents. Prince Chadly, the eldest son of the ex-*bey*, and the former Prime Ministers, Tahar ben Ammar and Salaheddine Baccouche, were among those tried in the latter part of 1958 on charges which included the misuse of public funds and collaboration with the French authorities; sentences imposed ranged from heavy fines to imprisonment and loss of civic rights. Salah ben Youssef (*in absentia*) and 54 of his supporters were charged with plotting the death of President Bourguiba, smuggling arms from Libya, and aiming to overthrow the government; ben Youssef and several others were sentenced to death and most of the remainder received long prison sentences.

This trial reflected a widening breach between Tunisia and the United Arab Republic, from where ben Youssef had been conducting his activities. In October 1958 Tunisia had joined the Arab League, only to withdraw from a meeting of its Council ten days later after accusing the U.A.R. of attempts at domination. Diplomatic relations with the U.A.R. were severed the same month on the grounds of Egyptian complicity in the "Youssefist" attempt to assassinate President Bourguiba, and on the eve of ben Youssef's trial the President announced the capture of Egyptian officers who had secretly entered Tunisia to assist subversive elements to overthrow his government.

A further step in the establishment of a presidential system of government was taken with the promulgation on June 1st, 1959, of a new constitution for Tunisia, which provided for the election of the President for five years and permitted his re-election for three consecutive terms. The President was empowered to lay down the general policy of the state, choose the members of the government, hold supreme command of the armed forces and make all appointments to civil and military posts. The constitution also provided for the election of a National Assembly for five years and required the approval of the Assembly for the declaration of war, the conclusion of peace and the ratification of treaties. In elections which followed on November 8th President Bourguiba was unopposed and all 90 seats in the Assembly went to the Néo-Destour, their only opponents being the Communists.

THE BIZERTA CRISIS

During 1959 and 1960 Tunisian relations with France gradually improved. A trade and tariff agreement was signed on September 5th, 1959, and further agreements on technical co-operation and the transfer of French state property in Tunisia to the Tunisian government were concluded. In October 1959 President Bourguiba announced his support for President de Gaulle's offer of self-determination for Algeria, and Tunisia was subsequently able to act as intermediary between France and the Algerian rebels in moves towards a negotiated settlement.

Tunisia continued to press for the handing back of the Bizerta base and the issue came to a head on July 5th, 1961, when President Bourguiba made a formal demand for its return and repeated the claim, first put forward in 1959, to Saharan territory in Algeria adjacent to the south-western part of Tunisia. Demonstrations then took place against the continued French occupation of Bizerta. Fighting between Tunisian and French troops began around the Bizerta base and in the disputed area of the Sahara; on July 19th, 1961, diplomatic relations were again severed, and Tunisia called for a meeting of the UN Security Council. The fighting ended on July 22nd with the French in firm control of the base and town of Bizerta, over 800 Tunisians having been killed. In the south a Tunisian attempt to seize the fort of Garat el-Hamel also failed. A subsequent visit to Bizerta by the UN Secretary-General, Mr. Hammarskjöld, in an attempt to promote a settlement, was unsuccessful. A French statement on July 28th said that France wished to continue to use the base whilst a state of international tension persisted but was prepared to negotiate with Tunisia about its use during this period.

The immediate results of the Bizerta crisis were a rapprochement between Tunisia and other Arab states, a cooling of relations with the West and an improvement of relations with the Communist bloc.

The final settlement of the Bizerta dispute occupied the remainder of 1961 and much of 1962. The Algerian cease-fire in March 1962 had an immediately beneficial effect on Franco-Tunisian relations and the French base installations at Menzel Bourguiba, near Bizerta, were handed over to Tunisia on June 30th. In March 1963 agreement was reached on the transfer of some 370,000 acres of French-owned agricultural land to the Tunisian government. Other agreements, on trade and finance, were designed to reduce Tunisia's balance of payments deficit with France.

Although Algerian independence had been warmly welcomed by Tunisia the extremist doctrines of the new state conflicted with Tunisian moderation and relations quickly deteriorated. In January 1963 the Tunisian ambassador was recalled from Algiers on the grounds of alleged Algerian complicity in an unsuccessful attempt the previous month on the life of President Bourguiba in which "Youssefists" in Algeria, as well as supporters of the old Destour and army elements, were implicated. Moroccan mediation led to a conference of the Maghreb states in Rabat in February 1963 at which the Tunisians demanded the cessation of "Youssefist" activities in Algeria, and after further negotiations a frontier agreement between Tunisia and Algeria was signed in July.

EXPROPRIATION

Despite agreement with France in February 1964 on the provision of loans and credits, it was claimed that the March 1963 agreement on the transfer of French-owned land had placed too great a strain on Tunisian financial resources and had also resulted in over-exploitation of the land held by settlers, who had been given up to five years before relinquishing it. On May 11th the Tunisian National Assembly enacted legislation authorizing the expropriation of all foreign-owned lands; this affected the proprietors of some 750,000 acres. The French immediately suspended, then cancelled, all financial aid.

This nationalization of foreign-owned land was also seen as a step towards the development of socialism in the agrarian sector of the economy. The Néo-Destour's commitment to "Tunisian socialism" was emphasized in the change of the party's name to the Parti Socialiste Destourien (PSD) at the time of the presidential and general elections in November 1964, in which President Bourguiba was again elected unopposed and the PSD, the only party to present candidates, filled all 90 seats in the National Assembly. Subsequent cabinet changes included the appointment of the President's son, Habib Bourguiba, Jr., as Foreign Minister.

From 1964 onwards internal political conditions became more settled and the attention of the government was turned to the tasks of economic development. The hold of the PSD on the country was strengthened and President Bourguiba's dominating position was unchallenged. In 1966 the setting-up was announced of a Council of the Republic, consisting of members of the government and of the political bureau of the PSD, to ensure continuing stability.

FOREIGN POLICIES

Tunisia's relations with the world beyond the Arab states and Africa after 1964 tended to be influenced by the need for foreign aid, most of which was received from Western countries (particularly from the United States but also from Federal Germany) where the moderation of Tunisian policies inspired confidence. Towards the Communist world Tunisian gestures were cautious. Some economic assistance was obtained from the Soviet Union without Tunisia having shifted her non-aligned stance and, although a visit by Zhou Enlai in January 1964 was followed by the establishment of diplomatic relations between Tunisia and the People's Republic of China, President Bourguiba publicly criticized Chinese policies, including the encouragement of revolution in Africa. On African issues, Tunisia took a moderate line and inside the OAU exercised a responsible influence.

Relations with the rest of the Arab world continued to be President Bourguiba's main foreign preoccupation and here his initiatives resulted in bitter controversy. In April 1965 he openly criticized Arab League policy on Palestine and advocated a more flexible approach, with direct negotiations with Israel on the UN partition plan of 1948. This provoked severe attacks from the U.A.R. and other Arab states (excepting Morocco, Libya and Saudi Arabia), and after violent demonstrations in Cairo and Tunis both countries withdrew their ambassadors. Tunisia's refusal at the end of April to follow the example of other Arab League states in breaking off relations with Federal Germany, which had exchanged ambassadors with Israel, increased the rift. A conference of Arab heads of state at Casablanca in May at which Tunisia was not represented, categorically rejected President Bourguiba's proposal that Israel should be asked to cede territory to the Palestine refugees in return for recognition by the Arab states, and reaffirmed their determination to bring about the complete overthrow of Israel. In an open letter to those attending, President Bourguiba accused President Nasser of attempting to use the Arab League as an instrument of U.A.R. national policy and of interfering in the affairs of every Arab state; Tunisia was not prepared to take part in the debates of the Arab League in the light of this situation. In October 1966 the severance of diplomatic relations with the U.A.R. was announced.

The six-day war between Israel and the Arab states in June 1967 brought immediate reconciliation in the Arab world despite long-standing differences. Tunisian troops were dispatched to the front but the Israeli success was so swift and the cease-fire came so soon

that they were recalled before they had reached the scene of the fighting. Diplomatic relations between Tunisia and the U.A.R. were resumed and Tunisia was represented at the Arab summit meeting in Khartoum in September, which agreed not to recognize nor to negotiate with Israel.

The reconciliation between Tunisia and other Arab countries was short-lived. In May 1968, following an attack on President Bourguiba by the Syrian Prime Minister, who charged him with having betrayed the Arab struggle in Palestine, the Syrian chargé d'affaires and his staff in Tunis were accused of inciting subversive activities and expelled. The Arab League, at a meeting in Cairo on 1st September refused to hear a statement from the Tunisian delegate criticising the Arab attitude over Israel, and particularly that of the U.A.R. On 26th September the Tunisian Government announced its intention of boycotting future meetings of the League. Nevertheless, Tunisian support for the Palestinian guerrilla movement was reaffirmed.

An exchange of visits by the Foreign Ministers of Tunisia and Algeria in the spring of 1969 brought about an improved climate for negotiation on the demarcation of their common frontier and on economic matters, especially those arising from the nationalization by each country of property owned by nationals of the other. On January 6th, 1970, a treaty of Co-operation and Friendship was signed, settling all outstanding issues between the two countries. It provided notably for collaboration in the exploitation of the El Borma oil-field which straddles the Tunisia-Algeria border.

THE FALL OF AHMED BEN SALAH

Between 1964 and 1969 the chief issue in internal affairs was the drive to collectivize agriculture, carried out under the leadership of Ahmed Ben Salah, Minister of Finance and Planning. The programme was carried out in the face of massive opposition in affected areas and disagreement within the ruling party itself. In September 1969 the policy was abandoned; Ben Salah was stripped of all office, arrested, tried and sentenced to ten years' hard labour. However, he escaped from prison in February 1973 and has taken refuge in Europe, from where he has issued statements condemning President Bourguiba for acting against the people in the interests of a privileged class, and acted as the leader of the radical Popular Unity Movement (MUP), which was declared illegal in Tunisia itself.

Ben Salah was the first of several ministers to experience a sharp reversal of fortune. In November 1969 President Bourguiba appointed Bahi Ladgham to be Prime Minister but in October 1970 replaced him by Hedi Nouira. A year later the President declared that Nouira would be his successor when the time came. In March 1973 Ladgham resigned from all his political posts. Mahmoud Mestiri was the next Minister to fall into disgrace. As Minister of the Interior in 1970 and 1971, he demanded the liberalization of government. Consequently he was dismissed from the cabinet in September 1971, expelled from the party in 1972 and from the National Assembly in May 1973. When a revision of the constitution was finally proposed in March 1973 it included almost none of the measures suggested by Mestiri to modify the presidential nature of the regime. Indeed, during the next two years President Bourguiba and Prime Minister Nouira strengthened their grip on the country. In September 1974 the ninth party congress of the PSD elected Bourguiba as President-for-Life of the party and confirmed Nouira in the post of Secretary-General. Bourguiba appointed a new political bureau of 20 members, including 14 ministers, confirming a tendency to draw party and government closer together. In November Bourguiba was re-elected President of Tunisia unopposed and National Assembly elections saw all 112 PSD candidates returned, also without opposition. The new Assembly voted amendments to the constitution designating the Prime Minister as the President's successor and allowing for the appointment of a President-for-Life, a post to which the Assembly elected Bourguiba in March 1975. Further constitutional reforms in December 1975 increased presidential powers still more.

If these formal assertions of presidential authority and popularity had little substance, there could still be no doubt of Bourguiba's hold on Tunisia. Opponents of the regime received short shrift, and between 1974 and 1976 prison sentences were passed on hundreds, mostly Marxist students, for belonging to unauthorized organizations and plotting against the state.

LIBYAN MERGER

In June 1970 the President's son, Habib Bourguiba, Jr., was replaced as Foreign Minister by Mohamed Masmoudi. From that date relations with the more radical Arab states and with radical powers outside the area improved. Normal relations were resumed with the U.A.R. and Syria, and Tunisia again took up membership of the Arab League.

On January 12th, 1974, after a meeting between President Bourguiba and Colonel Gaddafi, the Libyan leader, it was announced that Tunisia and Libya were to form a union. The announcement was greeted with general surprise for, despite an improvement in relations between the two countries in previous years, President Bourguiba had always shown himself to be hostile to union. Bourguiba was to be president of the new state, with Gaddafi as his deputy. It would seem that the union agreement was managed by Mohamed Masmoudi, without the consent of the Prime Minister, Hedi Nouira, who was out of the country at the time. Nouira returned swiftly to Tunisia and Masmoudi was dismissed from his post in the Government and the party.

In the aftermath of this confused affair, relations with Libya were tense and uncomfortable. The Libyans continued to urge fulfilment of the union agreement, and in 1975 Bourguiba expressed concern at the increase of Libyan armed strength. Another bone of contention between the two countries was the delimitation of their respective sectors of the continental shelf, in which important deposits of petroleum were to be found. However, both sides agreed to submit to arbitration by the International Court of Justice in June 1977 and agreement was finally reached in February 1982. In October 1977 a joint statement was issued, saying that Tunisia and Libya had agreed to "reactivate mutual co-operation" and set up a scheme to link the electricity networks of the two countries, while experts were to discuss the possibility of other joint ventures. Relations with Algeria also improved in 1977, after Tunisia dropped its attempts at conciliation in the Sahara dispute (in which it sided with Morocco): a co-operation agreement was signed in July by the Interior Ministers of the two countries.

DOMESTIC UNREST

By 1977, with President Bourguiba in his seventies and in poor health, there was growing uncertainty over the future of the system of government which he had dominated for so long. Hedi Nouira, his designated successor, appeared to lack the powerful personality which had kept Bourguiba in command of the country, and there were signs of a succession struggle in the increasing demands for the free development of a multi-party democracy from, among others, former ministers Ahmed Ben Salah, in exile, and Mahmoud Mestiri, leader of the unofficial liberal group of Social Democrats. The arrest and trial (from June to August 1977) of 33 members of the MUP, on charges of threatening state security and defaming the President, indicated the continuing hostility of the Government to any form of organized opposition. In June Mestiri and other liberals formed a national council for the defence of public liberties (CNDLP) calling for greater political freedom; in October Mestiri, in his first meeting with President Bourguiba since his dismissal from the Government in 1971, proposed a "national pact" which would involve full acceptance by the Government of fundamental liberties such as freedom of assembly, the formation of political parties, and the publication of opposition newspapers, as stated in the Constitution. He was told that the proposed pact would not be considered in detail until the next PSD Congress in September 1979.

Meanwhile, however, a more effective political force was beginning to make itself felt. After a number of strikes by workers in 1976, a "social contract" had been drawn up early in 1977 between the Government and the General Union of Tunisian Workers (UGTT) under the leadership of Habib Achour, involving inflation-linked pay rises for the duration of the 1977–81 plan. In spite of this agreement there were further strikes in various sectors of industry towards the end of the year, demanding better pay and conditions and backed by the UGTT, which was becoming (particularly through its weekly newspaper *Ach-Chaab*) an increasingly vocal critic of government policy and an outlet for action by political dissenters in the absence of official opposition parties. As the presence of students and unemployed young people at the accompanying demonstrations suggested, the strikes reflected a sense of dissatisfaction and frustration which went beyond industrial grievances. In

December Mohamed Masmoudi, the former Foreign Minister, returned from exile in Libya and declared his support for the UGTT, thereby underlining its importance as a potential political force.

Within the Government there was disagreement as to the best way of dealing with the situation. Nouira declared that extremist infiltrators were using industrial grievances as an excuse to disrupt the country, and insisted that a forceful policy was needed to restore order. Tahar Belkhodja, the Minister of the Interior, was dismissed on December 23rd, after having suggested that the unrest should be attributed not to any one sinister cause but to social and economic problems such as a fast-increasing population and serious unemployment; only by attempting to deal with these could the crisis be averted, and rule by force would not prove to be a solution. Six other moderate members of the Cabinet resigned in sympathy, but President Bourguiba reaffirmed his support for Nouira by forming a new government in which the dissidents were replaced mainly by civil servants and technical experts, all of whom could be expected to accept Nouira's tough policy; in addition, Bourguiba brought in his son as Special Adviser.

On January 10th, 1978, Achour resigned from the political bureau and central committee of the PSD after pressure from members of the UGTT who felt that his dual role had become unacceptable. The UGTT national council called for urgent changes in the method of government and an end to the use of "intimidation" in suppressing strikes and demonstrations. On January 26th the Union finally took the drastic step of calling a general strike as a warning to the Government and in retaliation for attacks on union offices. There was rioting in Tunis and several other cities, the army was called in and at least 51 people were killed, while hundreds more were injured; a state of emergency was declared and a curfew imposed. Hundreds of demonstrators were arrested, tried and imprisoned, and Achour and other members of the UGTT executive were also taken into custody, charged with subversion. The Government accused the UGTT of a long-standing conspiracy against the state and hinted at foreign backing, presumably from Libya.

The trial of Achour and 30 other union leaders did not begin until August. The criminal court at Sousse ruled itself incompetent to try the case, which was then transferred to the State Security Court, thereby becoming overtly political. Lawyers engaged by the International Confederation of Free Trade Unions, of which Achour was Vice-President, had been expelled from the country, and there was widespread international criticism of the conduct of the trial, particularly in view of the fact that the defence lawyers were given only two weeks in which to study the enormous prosecution dossier. The trade unionists refused to answer the questions put by the prosecution, alleging that they were not being properly defended, since most of the defence lawyers had been dismissed after walking out in protest at the conduct of the trial: the defendants' silence was, however, interpreted as an admission of guilt by the PSD

newspaper, *al-Amal*. Eventually Achour was sentenced to 10 years' hard labour, and prison sentences were also passed on all but six of the other defendants. A new UGTT Secretary-General, Tijani Abid, was appointed in March 1978, and the Union expressed regret at the recent events and declared its willingness to co-operate with the Government. Although Achour was pardoned by the President in August 1979, he remained under house arrest; 263 others serving prison terms for their involvement in the riots had been pardoned in May, but it was nevertheless clear that the power of the UGTT as a source of opposition had, for the moment, been crushed.

In July 1979 the National Assembly approved an amendment to the electoral code, allowing the number of candidates in legislative elections to be twice the number of seats: in other words, voters were to have a choice for the first time, though it was still not clear whether members of parties other than the PSD would be permitted to stand. At the PSD Congress in September, the need to "open up" the party to new adherents and new ideas was emphasized, but the Prime Minister rejected the idea of a multi-party system and the "national pact" proposed two years previously by the Social Democrat group, whom he dismissed as having no programme nor precise objectives. The main opposition groups (MUP, Social Democrats and communists) declared that they would boycott the legislative elections in November, since to put forward candidates would indicate support of the present system (and would presumably not have been permitted in any case since none of the groups had official party status). At 81 per cent, the turn-out in the elections was substantially lower than on previous occasions, when it had averaged 95 per cent.

In January 1980, close to the second anniversary of the general strike and riots, there was an attack on the town of Gafsa in western Tunisia by guerrillas, originally estimated to number 300, although only 60 were later brought to trial. The Tunisian armed forces quickly regained control of the town, but 41 deaths were reported. Responsibility for the attack was claimed by a hitherto unknown group, the "Tunisian Armed Resistance", who declared that they aimed to free Tunisia from the "dictatorship" of the PSD. Although the guerrillas had apparently crossed the nearby Algerian border, the Algerian Government convincingly denied any involvement, and it was Libya which came under suspicion. The Tunisian Government said that the attackers were Tunisian migrant workers who had been trained in Libya and encouraged to make the attack in order to destabilize Bourguiba's regime: diplomatic relations with Libya were suspended. Libya expressed astonishment at these allegations and referred to the incident as a "popular uprising". Nevertheless, the attack caused international concern, particularly in France, which sent military transport aircraft to Gafsa and naval vessels to the Tunisian coast, while the U.S.A. also offered to speed up military supplies. The Gafsa attack was condemned by the more established opposition groups within Tunisia, bringing about a temporary national solidarity, although the same groups condemned the execution of 13 of the guerrillas which took place in April.

POLITICAL LIBERALIZATION

The sudden illness of Hedi Nouira in February brought renewed political uncertainty. The Minister of Education, Mohamed Mzali, was appointed as temporary government co-ordinator and in April as Prime Minister, thereby becoming Bourguiba's successor under the terms of the Constitution. Under Mzali, signs of greater political tolerance soon became apparent. The new Government which he headed included three of the ministers who had resigned in 1977 in protest at the strict measures taken against strikers, while a member of the Social Democrats' group was also included as Minister of Transport; in December Tahar Belkhodja, the former Minister of the Interior who had been dismissed in 1977, was readmitted to the Government. Most political prisoners were released in the course of the year, and in January 1981 a pardon was granted to nearly 1,000 trade union members who had been convicted of involvement in the 1978 riots. Greater tolerance was also shown towards the would-be political parties: in July 1980 permission was granted to the Social Democrats to publish two weekly periodicals, and in the following February an amnesty was given to all members of the proscribed MUP, except its leader in exile, Ahmed Ben Salah. At an extraordinary congress of the PSD in April 1981, held to discuss the 1982–86 development plan (*see* Economic Survey), President Bourguiba declared that he saw no objection to the emergence of political parties provided that they rejected violence and religious fanaticism and were not dependent "ideologically or materially" on any foreign group (which suggested that the communists and Muslim fundamentalists would not be welcome candidates). It was announced that the next parliamentary elections would probably be held early, before the end of the year. The congress elected a new party central committee of 80 representatives, some 75 per cent of whom had not previously been members of the committee.

An extraordinary congress of the UGTT was also held in April, the first since the riots of January 1978. Of the 13 members of the executive committee elected by the congress, 11 had been previous members of the committee and imprisoned in 1978. The new secretary-Taieb Baccouche, was the first non-PSD member to be elected to this post. Habib Achour was finally released in December 1981, when he was allowed to resume his position as head of the UGTT.

The process of installing a multi-party system continued with the announcement of legislative elections for November; Bourguiba promised that any participating group which gained a minimum of 5 per cent of votes cast would be officially recognized as a political party. Several tendencies refused to take part in the elections under these conditions. In July the one-party system was brought to an end with the official recognition of the Tunisian Communist Party (PCT); as a former officially recognized political party (banned since 1963), it was not required to fulfil the 5 per cent condition laid upon the other groups. In contrast to this political liberalization, 40–50 leading members of the Islamic Tendency Movement (MIT) were arrested and given prison sentences in September. The Government continued to regard this group as a dangerous influence.

Despite their threats to boycott the elections to the National Assembly, the PCT, MUP and MDS presented candidates in November, but to no avail. The result was a landslide victory for the National Front, a joint electoral pact formed by the PSD and UGTT, which gained 94.6 per cent of votes cast and won all 136 seats in the new Assembly. No other group succeeded in winning 5 per cent of the vote, and consequently none was given official recognition. Formal protests of electoral irregularities were made by the three opposition groups.

ECONOMIC SURVEY

Tunisia covers an area of 163,610 square kilometres. At the 1975 census the population was 5,572,193, with over half under 25 years old. The mid-1980 estimate was 6,392,300. The annual rate of increase in the population from 1975 to 1977 averaged 2.65 per cent. Most of the towns, and also the greater part of the rural population, are concentrated in the coastal areas. In the centre and the south, the land is infertile semi-desert, the population scattered, the standard of living very low, and the rate of growth of the population even higher than in the north.

The capital and main commercial centre is Tunis (population 550,404 in 1975) which, together with the adjacent La Goulette, is also the chief port. There are about 50,000 Europeans in Tunis, mainly French and Italians, their numbers having decreased rapidly since independence. Other towns of importance are Sfax (171,297 in 1975), which is the principal town in the south, the second port and the centre for exports of phosphates and olive oil, Djerba (70,217), Sousse (69,530), Bizerta (62,856) and Kairouan (54,546). Some 450,000 Tunisians were employed abroad in 1980, thus relieving the domestic employment situation and providing a source of foreign exchange earnings through workers' remittances from overseas. Invisible earnings from remittances were expected to total TD 115 million in 1980, about the same as in 1979.

Tunisia's development record in recent years has been fairly impressive, with per capita income reaching U.S. $850 by 1979. Total G.D.P. at factor cost in 1981 was provisionally put at TD 3,542 million by the Banque Centrale de Tunisie. Agriculture, forestry and fishing accounted for about 16 per cent of G.D.P., manufacturing 13 per cent and mining and energy 8 per cent. During the Fourth Plan period

(1973–76) G.D.P. grew at an average annual rate of 7.2 per cent at 1972 prices (about 6.2 per cent in real terms) and per capita G.D.P. grew in real terms at 4.6 per cent a year. This rate of growth was made possible by high prices for phosphates, petroleum and olive oil, up to 1975. However, the sharp decline in world demand for these export commodities, in addition to a downturn in the tourism sector and poor agricultural output, resulted in an overall slowdown in the country's economy during 1976. In 1977 it grew by 4.1 per cent. Rapidly rising prices and growing unemployment led to social unrest and a series of strikes in the autumn of 1977. In January 1978 a general strike and violent riots took place, indicating a rift between the Government and the unions.

AGRICULTURE

About two-thirds of the total area of Tunisia is suitable for farming. For agricultural purposes the country is composed of five different districts— the mountainous north, with its large fertile valleys; the north-east including the Cap Bon, where the soil is especially suitable for the cultivation of oranges and other citrus fruit; the Sahel where the olives grow; the centre with its high tablelands and pastures; and the south with oases and gardens where dates are prolific. Harvests vary considerably in size, depending on the uncertain rainfall, since cultivation is largely by dry farming and irrigation is as yet limited. The main cereal crops are wheat, barley, maize, oats and sorghum; fruit is also important— grapes, olives, dates, oranges and figs are grown for export as well as for the local market.

In good years there is a surplus of cereal for export but imports are frequently necessary and in both 1977 and 1978 cost TD 40 million. During the 1960s the agricultural sector grew at only about 1.5 per cent a year but exceptional weather conditions and improved irrigation in 1971 and 1972 resulted in excellent agricultural yields, and during the Fourth Plan period (1973–76) good weather, except in 1974, led to an average annual growth rate of 3 per cent. However, drought in the early months of 1977 caused a 7.6 per cent fall in output. Under the 1977–81 plan the agricultural sector was expected to grow by 3.5 per cent a year. The plan's objective of self-sufficiency in food, with the possibility of an exportable surplus, was not met following a drop of 1.6 per cent a year in farm production during 1977–79, the first three years. Food imports cost $438 million in 1980.

The means by which self-sufficiency should be achieved has been the cause of political conflict in the past decade. From 1960 until 1969, under the Minister of Planning, Ahmed Ben Salah, the basis of the Government's agrarian reform programme lay in the formation of collective "agricultural units". These units, consisting of 500 hectares at least, were to be operated as collectives in order to consolidate small peasant holdings and, later, to exploit land expropriated from French farmers or to be acquired eventually from owners of large or medium-sized farms. The system was controlled through credits provided by the Agricultural Bank.

By 1968 some 220 state co-operatives were in existence and several hundred more were being put together. However, opposition to the scheme was widespread. There were revelations of unsatisfactory performance, heavy debts and misappropriation of state funds. These discoveries were instrumental in the downfall and disgrace of Ben Salah, whose position was weakened by the displeasure of foreign aid donors with his agricultural policies (especially the World Bank which had previously given some support, including an $18 million loan in 1967).

Following Ben Salah's downfall farmers were given a chance to opt out of the state system which was soon dismantled. Nonetheless a law was passed providing for the eventual break-up of large private estates, to be split among individual farmers or private co-operatives. The Government has also taken a number of measures to stimulate output, including providing funds for mechanization, reducing taxes, and subsidizing fertilizers and seed purchases. In 1975 approximately half the total cultivated area of 9 million hectares was in private hands, a further 2.1 million hectares were worked by co-operative farm groups and the remainder was farmed by state or religious institutions. In April 1974 a "supervised credits scheme" was announced, whereby small and medium-sized farms could be given supervised credits on a short-term basis to improve farming methods. It was hoped that the plan would encourage the use of modern diversified crops rather than the traditional staple crops.

Grown in a belt across the northern part of the country, wheat is the most important cereal crop. The Government guarantees the price to the grower and, amongst other incentives, pays the transport costs of merchants. In 1977 Tunisia produced only 570,000 metric tons of wheat, compared with 810,000 tons in 1976, although it improved slightly over the following two years to reach 680,000 tons in 1979. This rose again in 1980 and 1981 to 870,000 and 960,000 tons respectively. The Government has encouraged the spread of the Mexican dwarf wheat and this variety now accounts for over one-tenth of output. Production of barley fluctuates according to the rainfall, and was 180,000 metric tons in 1978. It rose to 270,000 tons in 1979 and to 296,000 tons in 1980, but dropped back to 270,000 tons in 1981. Total combined production of wheat and barley in 1980 was 1.1 million metric tons.

Grapes are grown around Tunis and Bizerta. Wine production reached a peak of 1,986,000 hectolitres in 1963. By 1978 it had fallen to 424,000 hectolitres, though it reached 640,000 hectolitres in 1979 and 619,000 hectolitres in 1980. The 1980/81 harvest was expected to produce 560,000 hectolitres.

The size of olive harvests varies considerably, partly due to the two-year flowering cycle of the tree. Tunisia is usually the world's fourth largest producer of olive oil. Production reached a record 180,000 metric tons in 1975/76, fell to only 85,000 tons in 1976/77 but rose again to 136,000 tons in 1977/78. It fell again in 1978/79 to 80,000 tons. The 1980/81 total, originally projected at 180,000 tons, was expected

fifth plan, Mzali said that investment, national savings and balance-of-payments targets had been met. However, job creation was 22,000 behind the yearly target of 45,000, while G.D.P. had risen by 6.6 per cent, against the planned 7.5 per cent. The fifth plan priorities had been mining and energy, which were allocated 25 per cent of total investment, and manufacturing (23 per cent). Other priority areas were transport, housing and agriculture.

Tunisia tapped the Eurocurrency market for the first time in 1977 and obtained a $125 million loan to help finance the Miskar gas field development, a new cement plant and a new phosphate fertilizer plant. In early 1979 a $100 million loan was arranged through a consortium of international banks to finance the Tunisian section of the Algeria-Italy gas pipeline. Tunisia then stayed away from the international market until the beginning of 1981, when Compagnie Financière Immobilière et Touristique was able to raise $25 million for seven years at ½ per cent above the London interbank offered rate—a very low spread for a developing country. Banque Centrale de Tunisie officials said that total commercial borrowing in 1981 should be about $100 million. Borrowing during the sixth plan would increase sharply, they said, as aid and concessionary lines of credit taper off. Much of the new investment will be financed by joint banks being formed with Kuwait, Saudi Arabia and Algeria, and with France and Arab interests, possibly to include Iraq, Oman, Qatar and the UAE. A further development bank is to be formed by merging Banque de Développement Economique de Tunisie, Compagnie Financière Immobilière et Touristique and Société d'Investissement Arabe de Tunisie.

Increased borrowing should mean healthier prospects for Tunisia's offshore banking sector. Four offshore banking units (OBUs)—Citibank, Bank of America, National Bank of Abu Dhabi and the Paris-based Union Tunisienne de Banques—have been set up under the 1976 offshore banking law. An agreement setting up an OBU was signed with Arab African International Bank in April 1982. The main function of the OBUs is to service the offshore export manufacturing sector created in 1972. Opportunities for the OBUs have been limited by the tight margins available to Tunisia on the Eurodollar market, and by unexpectedly high revenues from oil and national savings. At least one of the OBUs has been questioning its future, but officials seem confident that future credit needs will, at worst, sustain the offshore sector at its present size.

There has been a notable change in Tunisian policy regarding foreign private investment since the fall of Ben Salah and Ladgham, who were widely reputed to favour economic policies tending towards socialism. The law of April 1972 provided a package of incentives to attract foreign and also domestic capital to set up manufacturing industries producing solely for export. By 1980 a total of about 250 export-orientated projects had been set up under the 1972 decree, employing some 25,000 people. West German, French, Belgian and Dutch firms predominate, and about 65 per cent

are in the textile sector. In 1973 a special organization, the *Agence de Promotion des Investissements* (API), was set up to centralize investment activities. Legislation was introduced in 1974 to promote investment in domestic-orientated manufacturing. In 1981 the API approved schemes valued at TD 495.5 million, 17 per cent more than in 1980. Of this, TD 419 million— roughly the same as in 1980—was for investment in production for the home market. The value of investments for export manufacturing industries rose from TD 26 million in 1980 to TD 75.5 million in 1981. Major projects were approved with the U.S. General Motors Corporation and with Peugeot and Renault of France. Industries Chimiques de Gafsa's M'dilla fertilizer complex received an investment of TD 55 million.

EXTERNAL TRADE

Tunisia has a persistent trade deficit which rose steadily during the 1960s and early 1970s. There was a deficit of TD 766.2 million in 1981, compared to TD 500.3 million in 1980 and TD 430.1 million in 1979. Exports are heavily dependent on sales of agricultural and mineral products, and thus on the success of the harvest and the condition of world mineral markets. Total exports rose to TD 1,224.8 million in 1981 from TD 891.4 million in 1980 and TD 726.7 million in 1979. Imports grew to TD 1,970.2 million in 1981 from TD 1,433.2 million in 1980 and TD 1,156.8 million in 1979.

Higher world prices for oil, phosphate rock and superphosphates meant that their value rose by 37.6 per cent, 20.9 per cent and 31.2 per cent respectively in 1980, while their volume decreased by 12.3 per cent, 18 per cent and 10.8 per cent. Phosphoric acid showed the biggest gains both in volume (up 5.6 per cent) and in value (up 63 per cent). The most disappointing performance was for olive oil exports, which fell by 50 per cent in both volume and value. Other major exports include iron ore, lead, almonds, fresh fruit, wine and light electronics.

Tunisia's main imports are machinery, crude petroleum (grades not produced locally) and petroleum products, iron and steel, sugar (raw and refined), wheat, vegetable oils and fats, electrical machinery, vehicles, timber, raw cotton and cotton yarn. In 1979 capital goods imports were worth TD 275 million and food imports rose by about 38 per cent to TD 146 million. In 1981 the biggest single increase in imports was for energy products, which rose in value by 40 per cent to TD 479 million from TD 280 million in 1980.

France is Tunisia's largest single trading partner. It supplies about 25 per cent of Tunisian imports and was followed in 1980 by Italy, West Germany, Saudi Arabia, the U.S.A. and Greece. In the same year, Greece was the most important customer for exports, followed by Italy, France, the U.S.A. and West Germany. Tunisia has a persistent trade deficit with the EEC. This fell from TD 302 million in 1978 to TD 222.8 million in 1979, then rose again to TD 343 million in 1980. EEC member countries account for around 60 per cent of Tunisia's imports and 60 per cent of its exports.

Under an agreement reached with the EEC in January 1976, the import levy on Tunisian olive oil has been abolished and tariffs on all other Tunisian agricultural products imported into EEC countries are being lowered. The agreement also covers aid to Tunisia totalling $117 million over five years, in the form of loans and grants. Nevertheless, Tunisia has been disappointed with the way in which the agreement has been implemented, and particularly with the delays in lifting the olive import restrictions. In June 1977 the EEC quota of textiles and clothing imports was reduced. This measure severely affected the Tunisian textile and clothing industries although Tunisia did not in fact fulfil its EEC quotas in 1978, as a result of a two-month strike in the industry early in 1978. Nevertheless, negotiations on this issue continued into 1979 and in March Tunisia signed an agreement, under pressure from the EEC, voluntarily to limit its textile exports to EEC countries in 1979 and 1980. In return, Tunisia wants a five-year "freeze" on its obligations to eliminate tariff barriers relating to goods imported from the EEC. Tunisia has also registered its anxiety about the possible consequences of accession to EEC membership of Greece, Spain and Portugal.

TOURISM

Between 1961 and 1972 total tourist arrivals grew at a rate of 30 per cent annually. Tourism was the nation's largest foreign currency earner from 1968 to 1976 (when it was overtaken by petroleum). The number of tourists each year has fluctuated but in 1979 totalled 1,356,000 (compared with 721,000 in 1973). Tourist receipts doubled to TD 287 million in 1981 from TD 139 million in 1977. In 1980 they totalled about TD 260 million. In recent years Algeria has replaced France as the main country of origin of tourists, followed by West Germany and the United Kingdom. There are four main centres for tourists: Hammamet, Sousse, Djerba and Tunis. A major scheme under way is the Sousse-Nord tourism project which is being financed by the Tunisian Government, the IFC and various Arab Governments,

and which will provide a total of 15,000 tourist beds in a development along two miles of coast. Another major complex is being built at Mahdia (Tunis-Nord). The *Compagnie Financière et Touristique* (COFIT) promotes and finances three types of ventures: new hotel construction; modernization of existing hotels; and other activities related to tourism such as transport, housing and real estate. The sixth plan (1982–86) will aim to add 25,000–30,000 beds to the early 1981 total of about 66,000. The number of tourists is expected to reach 2,200,000 per year by the end of the plan, compared with 1,600,000 in 1980.

FOREIGN AID

The principal sources of economic aid for Tunisia continue to be Western countries and international institutions. In recent years the U.S.A., West Germany and Saudi Arabia have been among the most important bilateral aid donors.

The World Bank Group (IBRD, IDA and IFC) has been the most important multilateral donor, providing loans and credits for investment in a variety of projects—including participation in the Société Nationale d'Investissement (SNI) and in COFIT. In 1977/78 World Bank loans to Tunisia totalled $47.5 million. In the first half of 1980 the World Bank approved loans worth more than $135 million to help to finance various projects including road construction, a gas pipeline distribution network and the modernization of ports. The European Investment Bank has lent some $27 million for the Gabès-Gafsa railway. Other loans have come from France, the United States, Kuwait and Saudi Arabia.

Tunisia's total foreign debt increased from $1,508 million in 1976 to $2,473 million at the end of 1978. The debt service ratio rose from 7.5 per cent of current receipts in 1974 to 11.5 per cent in 1978. It fell to 10.5 per cent in 1980, but was expected to rise to 11.9 per cent in 1981, and even higher during the 1982–86 plan because of increased recourse to the international money market.

STATISTICAL SURVEY

AREA AND POPULATION

AREA	CENSUS POPULATION				ESTIMATED POPULATION (mid-year)		DENSITY (per sq. km.)
	May 3rd, 1966	May 8th, 1975			1979	1980	1980
		Males	Females	Total			
163,610 sq. km.*	4,533,351†	2,811,201	2,760,992	5,572,193	6,238,200	6,392,300	39.1

* 63,170 square miles.

† Excluding adjustment for underenumeration, estimated to have been 4.0 per cent.

PRINCIPAL COMMUNES

(1975 Census)

Tunis (capital)	.	.	550,404	Sousse . . . 69,530		Gafsa . . . 42,225		
Sfax (Safaqis)	.	.	171,297	Bizerte (Bizerta) . 62,856		Gabès . . . 40,585		
Djerba	.	.	70,217	Kairouan . . . 54,546		Béja . . . 39,226		

BIRTHS, MARRIAGES AND DEATHS*

	REGISTERED LIVE BIRTHS		REGISTERED MARRIAGES		REGISTERED DEATHS	
	Number	Rate (per '000)	Number	Rate (per '000)	Number	Rate (per '000)
1974	194,600	35.6	46,672	8.5	57,555	10.5
1975	205,390	36.6	47,860	8.5	55,500	9.9
1976	208,040	36.0	42,524	7.4	50,173	8.7
1977	220,546	37.2	47,828	8.1	49,149	8.3
1978	207,342	34.1	50,226	8.3	47,270	7.8
1979	217,338	34.8	52,375	8.4	50,336	8.1
1980†	223,316	35.1	47,430	7.4	48,800	7.7

* Birth registration is reported to be at least 99 per cent complete. Death registration is estimated to be about 73 per cent complete. UN estimates for average annual death rates are: 13.3 per 1,000 in 1970–75, 11.1 per 1,000 in 1975–80.

† Provisional figures.

Source: Banque Centrale de Tunisie, quoting Institut National de la Statistique.

ECONOMICALLY ACTIVE POPULATION*

(1975 census, sample tabulation)

	MALES	FEMALES	TOTAL
Agriculture, hunting, forestry and fishing .	456,620	69,410	526,030
Mining and quarrying	26,780	430	27,210
Manufacturing	115,820	124,820	240,640
Electricity, gas and water . . .	11,160	520	11,680
Construction	139,560	1,180	140,740
Trade, restaurants and hotels . .	112,410	7,220	119,630
Transport, storage and communications . .	54,530	2,850	57,380
Financing, insurance, real estate and business services	5,800	1,910	7,710
Community, social and personal services .	169,950	47,800	217,750
Activities not adequately described .	133,920	20,100	153,930
TOTAL	1,226,550	276,150	1,502,700

* Figures refer to persons aged 15 years and over, excluding those seeking work for the first time, numbering 119,120 (males 91,760, females 27,360). In addition, the economically active population included 107,240 persons (males 65,210, females 42,030) aged 10 to 15 years. The total labour force was thus 1,729,060 (males 1,383,520, females 345,540).

Source: Institut National de la Statistique; and International Labour Office, *Year Book of Labour Statistics.*

AGRICULTURE

PRINCIPAL CROPS

('000 metric tons)

	1976	1977	1978	1979	1980	1981
Wheat	810	570	720	680	870	960
Barley	240	100	180	270	296	270
Potatoes	105	85	105	125	130	140
Olives	870	425	625	400	400	565
Tomatoes	250	320	260	280	330	380
Chillies and peppers . .	120	125	130	130	110	110
Onions	70	83	95	85	90	75
Water melons and melons . .	250	210	220	300	280	280
Grapes	101	124	65	105	136	n.a.
Dates	42	33	45	27	47	46
Sugar beet . . .	83	119	80	58	63	54
Apricots	29	28	26	21.5	26	21
Citrus fruit	163	161	220	183	160	220
Almonds	24	26	35	30	37	35
Tobacco	4.2	4.5	4.8	4.5	4.3	5.2

Source: Banque Centrale de Tunisie, quoting Ministère de l'Agriculture.

LIVESTOCK*

('000 head)

	1978	1979	1980
Horses and asses .	340.0	340.0	340.0
Cattle . . .	428.0	345.0	350.0
Camels . . .	78.0	78.0	n.a.
Sheep . . .	3,383.0	2,594.0	2,977.0
Goats . . .	664.0	489.0	559.0
Chickens . . .	22,008.3	27,390.0	n.a.

* Females only, except in the case of poultry.
Source: Banque Centrale de Tunisie.

LIVESTOCK PRODUCTS

('000 metric tons)

	1978	1979	1980
Beef and veal . .	39.0	44.1	30.9
Mutton and lamb . .	23.4	25.4	31.2
Poultry meat . .	29.0	34.5	41.5
Cows' milk . . .	176.0	221.0	253.0
Hen eggs (million) . .	510.0	630.0	732.0
Wool (greasy) . .	7.0	7.0	n.a.
Cattle hides . .	7.4	n.a.	n.a.
Sheepskins . . .	6.2	n.a.	n.a.

Source: Banque Centrale de Tunisie, quoting Ministère de l'Agriculture.

FORESTRY
ROUNDWOOD REMOVALS
('ooo cubic metres, excluding bark)

	CONIFEROUS (soft wood)			BROADLEAVED (hard wood)			TOTAL		
	1977	1978	1979	1977	1978	1979	1977	1978	1979
Sawlogs, veneer logs and logs for sleepers .	10	3	6	—	—	—	10	3	6
Pitprops (mine timber).	—	—	—	2	1	1	2	1	1
Pulpwood . . .	13	10	34	—	—	—	13	10	34
Other industrial wood .	7	5	10	60*	62*	64*	67	67	74
Fuel wood . . .	175*	180*	185*	1,646*	1,690*	1,735*	1,821*	1,870*	1,920
TOTAL . . .	205	198	235	1,708	1,753	1,800	1,913	1,951	2,035

* FAO estimate.
Source: FAO, *Yearbook of Forest Products.*

FISHING
('ooo metric tons, live weight)

	1975	1976	1977	1978	1979	1980
Total catch	45.0	49.0	53.7	54.9	57.0	61.0

Source: Banque Centrale de Tunisie, quoting Ministère de l'Agriculture (Direction de la Pêche).

MINING
('ooo metric tons)

	1975	1976	1977	1978	1979	1980
Iron Ore*	616	485	343	339	394	390
Lead Concentrates* . .	17.2	16.7	16.6	12.9	16.2	14.0
Calcium Phosphate . .	3,540	3,305	3,615	3,712	4,184	4,502
Zinc Concentrates* . .	8.8	10.0	10.6	13.4	15.8	16.9
Crude Petroleum . . .	4,609	3,710	4,304	4,944	5,537	5,627
Natural Gas (million cu. metres) .	210.5	214.0	230.1	285.9	329.9	354.7
Salt (unrefined) . . .	231	323	337	442	421	316

Source: Banque Centrale de Tunisie, quoting Institut National de la Statistique.

*Figures refer to the gross weight of ores and concentrates. The metal content (in 'ooo metric tons) was:
Iron: 326 in 1975; 269 in 1976; 180 in 1977; 185 in 1978; 212 in 1979.
Lead: 10.6 in 1975; 10.5 in 1976; 10.2 in 1977; 7.5 in 1978; 10 in 1979.
Zinc: 6.0 in 1975; 7.3 in 1976; 7.1 in 1977; 6.8 in 1978; 8.7 in 1979.

INDUSTRY

SELECTED PRODUCTS

		1977	1978	1979	1980
Superphosphates . .	'ooo metric tons	489.1	508.1	578.4	610.9
Phosphoric acid . .	„ „ „	221.4	226.7	270.0	471.6
Cement . . .	„ „ „	628.8	881.5	1,377.8	1,781.3
Lead . . .	„ „ „	19.2	16.3	17.4	19.2
Electric power . .	million kWh.	1,518	1,786	2,082	2,432
Town gas . .	'ooo cubic metres	22,128	23,640	24,263	25,056
Beer . . .	'ooo hectolitres	302.2	336.8	352.8	322.8
Cigarettes . .	millions	5,399	4,974	4,836	4,419
Wine . . .	'ooo hl.	670	424	640	619
Olive oil . .	'ooo metric tons	90	130	85	85
Semolina . .	„ „ „	287.8	322.4	316.8	325.1
Flour . . .	„ „ „	299.6	321.0	342.6	376.8
Esparto pulp . .	„ „ „	20.7	21.5	20.3	21.6
Refined sugar . .	„ „ „	40.2	54.9	57.6	61.2
Cast iron and bar iron .	„ „ „	451.1	452.3	n.a.	520.9
Lime . . .	„ „ „	337.7	426.5	463.0	484.2
Petrol . . .	„ „ „	150	159.3	162.0	150.8
Kerosene . .	„ „ „	101.2	110.4	109.0	115.1
Diesel oil . .	„ „ „	340.2	317.1	424.8	439.3
Fuel oil . . .	„ „ „	456.6	501.6	644.4	675.3

Source: Banque Centrale de Tunisie, quoting Institut National de la Statistique, Office du Vin and Office National de l'Huile.

FINANCE

1,000 millimes = 1 Tunisian dinar.

Coins: 1, 2, 5, 10, 20, 50, 100 and 500 millimes; 1 and 5 dinars.

Notes: 500 millimes; 1, 5 and 10 dinars.

Exchange rates (May 1982): £1 sterling = 1.022 dinars; U.S. $1 = 556 millimes.

100 Tunisian dinars = £97.88 = $179.95.

Note: The Tunisian dinar was introduced in November 1958, replacing the Tunisian franc (then at par with the old French franc) at the rate of 1 dinar = 1,000 francs. In August 1957 the exchange rate was fixed at $1 = 420 Tunisian francs, so the initial rate for the new currency was $1 = 420 millimes (1 dinar = $2.381). From December 1958 the relationship to French currency was 1 dinar = 1,175 old francs (11.75 new francs from January 1960). These rates remained in force until September 1964, when the dinar was devalued by 20 per cent. Between September 1964 and August 1971 the official exchange rate was $1 = 525 millimes (1 dinar = $1.905), with the dinar valued at 9.40 French francs until August 1969 and at 10.575 French francs thereafter. From December 1971 to February 1973 the par value was $1 = 483.55 millimes (1 dinar = $2.068). In terms of sterling, the exchange rate between November 1967 and June 1972 was £1 = 1.26 dinars. In February 1973 a new par value of $1 = 435.2 millimes (1 dinar = $2.298) was established but in March 1973 the French authorities ceased to maintain the franc-dollar rate within previously agreed margins. Tunisia retained its currency link with France, thus allowing its exchange rate against the dollar to vary widely from the par value. In January 1974 the Tunisian authorities announced that the franc-dinar rate would henceforth take into account the daily quotations of the Deutsche Mark in terms of francs on the Paris exchange market. The average market rates (dinars per U.S. dollar) were: 0.4772 in 1972; 0.4200 in 1973; 0.4365 in 1974; 0.4023 in 1975; 0.4288 in 1976; 0.4290 in 1977; 0.4162 in 1978; 0.4065 in 1979; 0.4050 in 1980; 0.4938 in 1981.

CURRENT BUDGET EXPENDITURE
(estimates in 'ooo dinars)

MINISTRY	1981	1982
Prime Minister's Office . . .	7,050	9,254
Plan and finance . . .	19,390	22,721
Education . . .	142,220	162,400
Defence. . . .	60,928	70,000
Public health	69,300	83,200
Interior	56,846	64,000
Agriculture	50,052	56,565
Social affairs	15,459	17,334
Youth and sports . . .	12,900	15,000
Communications and transport .	7,531	9,220
Information and cultural affairs. .	13,961	15,356
Justice	7,801	9,030
TOTAL (incl. others) .	677,800	797,000

Capital Budget ('ooo dinars): 554,000 in 1981; 645,000 in 1982.

NATIONAL ACCOUNTS
(million dinars at current prices)

ECONOMIC ACTIVITY	1978	1979	1980	1981 *
Agriculture and Forestry . . .	366.2	395.0	467.0	537.0
Fishing . . .	18.9	20.4	23.6	26.5
Crude Petroleum, Gas and Petroleum Products	146.2	238.8	330.5	390.0
Other Mining and Quarrying . .	23.6	28.4	47.2	60.0
Manufacturing . . .	255.2	315.0	388.2	465.4
Electricity and Water Supply . .	38.7	47.7	55.0	66.4
Construction and Public Works . .	181.5	210.0	230.0	263.0
Transport and Communications . .	147.8	170.1	185.2	207.3
Tourism	93.1	122.6	142.3	155.5
Other Services	561.5	639.4	745.5	840.9
GROSS DOMESTIC PRODUCT AT FACTOR COST	2,123.0	2,517.0	2,994.5	3,452.0
Indirect Taxes (net of subsidies) . .	359.0	427.0	476.5	540.0
GROSS DOMESTIC PRODUCT IN PURCHASERS' VALUES	2,482.0	2,944.0	3,471.0	3,992.0
Imports of Goods and Services . .	1,008.4	1,285.1	1,561.0	1,826.0
Less Exports of Goods and Services .	769.0	1,139.0	1,448.0	1,666.0
AVAILABLE RESOURCES . .	2,721.4	3,090.1	3,584.0	4,152.0
Government Final Consumption . .	404.3	443.6	525.5	620.0
Private Final Consumption . .	1,587.1	1,795.5	2,108.5	2,442.0
Increase in Stocks . . .	—	—15.0	25.0	25.0
Gross Fixed Capital Formation . .	730.0	866.0	925.0	1,065.0

* Provisional figures.

Source: Banque Centrale de Tunisie, quoting Ministère du Plan et des Finances.

EXTERNAL TRADE
('ooo dinars)

	1973	1974	1975	1976	1977	1978	1979	1980
Imports	286,087	488,658	572,815	656,718	782,466	899,730	1,156,768	1,427,400
Exports	178,835	397,695	345,580	338,262	398,246	468,417	726,724	904,821

PRINCIPAL COMMODITIES
('ooo dinars)

IMPORTS	1977	1978	1979	1980
Wheat and meslin (unmilled) . . .	26,946	31,249	51,342	62,795
Sugar (raw and refined) . . .	17,808	16,535	17,350	30,569
Soybean oil	2,274	8,683	23,291	16,896
Crude petroleum	43,975	31,859	79,812	126,710
Petroleum products	33,558	52,510	108,621	131,226
Pharmaceutical products . . .	15,964	14,941	20,688	24,429
Wood	18,682	19,252	22,215	32,194
Raw cotton, cotton yarn and fabrics	20,690	19,077	25,053	32,090
Plastics and products	15,164	17,868	24,003	34,542
Iron and steel	52,428	62,535	88,815	118,810
Machinery (non-electric) . . .	130,517	158,686	155,326	154,366
Electric machinery	52,268	57,807	69,578	65,670
Tractors	7,400	9,773	8,998	14,539
Road motor vehicles	12,151	17,236	24,409	1,738
Aircraft and air equipment . .	15,350	880	9,994	557
Optical and scientific equipment .	11,948	13,868	18,005	16,644
TOTAL (incl. others) . . .	782,466	899,730	1,156,768	1,427,400

EXPORTS	1977	1978	1979	1980
Fresh fruit	7,455	9,998	13,879	12,565
Olive oil	25,893	36,493	45,946	24,984
Wine	2,704	5,766	3,422	3,114
Natural phosphates	22,032	17,744	17,879	19,959
Crude petroleum	161,016	171,737	326,871	449,978
Phosphoric acid	20,699	22,809	24,783	42,766
Superphosphates	19,339	23,087	32,131	40,314
Cotton fabrics	7,648	4,868	9,394	11,242
Clothing and accessories . . .	48,047	67,836	92,769	108,039
Iron and steel	846	4,223	2,956	2,233
Refined lead	4,111	3,201	5,165	5,004
TOTAL (incl. others) . . .	398,246	468,417	726,724	904,821

Source: Banque Centrale de Tunisie, quoting Institut National de la Statistique.

PRINCIPAL TRADING PARTNERS
('ooo dinars)

Imports	1977	1978	1979	1980
Belgium/Luxembourg	18,836	27,787	27,507	38,566
Brazil	11,977	6,662	8,665	12,504
Canada	8,475	13,743	13,912	26,265
France	219,437	298,541	302,957	349,639
Germany, Federal Republic	87,895	105,237	114,338	141,970
Greece	19,539	36,363	67,173	77,512
Iraq	17,904	12,840	29,853	4,295
Italy	77,680	89,892	153,563	219,452
Netherlands	25,521	26,902	30,832	34,279
Poland	7,067	6,188	8,308	8,874
Saudi Arabia	26,471	18,920	51,177	108,161
Spain	28,603	27,648	44,342	46,615
Sweden	7,740	6,718	10,061	15,254
U.S.S.R.	5,312	6,473	8,860	11,270
United Kingdom	22,356	16,720	17,734	27,740
U.S.A.	54,331	41,626	69,060	79,770
Yugoslavia	8,302	8,384	10,141	9,352
Total (incl. others)	782,466	899,730	1,156,768	1,427,400

Exports	1977	1978	1979	1980
Algeria	9,371	6,046	12,580	15,743
Belgium/Luxembourg	14,284	15,372	21,804	26,356
Brazil	2,136	2,456	118	739
Bulgaria	1,075	682	305	2,413
Czechoslovakia	1,052	1,713	1,076	2,788
France	71,125	78,644	140,705	136,137
Germany, Federal Republic	65,093	76,827	76,323	114,413
Greece	54,246	46,906	112,884	163,907
Italy	55,266	74,287	146,713	142,603
Libya	9,949	28,079	21,125	7,432
Netherlands	17,253	19,043	31,600	39,938
Spain	1,523	1,402	2,005	3,914
Switzerland	1,749	1,477	3,110	2,258
Turkey	5,221	6,120	5,067	10,338
U.S.S.R.	1,791	1,661	1,481	2,163
United Kingdom	3,303	3,438	6,158	12,770
U.S.A.	42,310	39,617	63,331	130,112
Total (incl. others)	398,246	468,417	726,724	904,821

Source: Banque Centrale de Tunisie, quoting Institut National de la Statistique.

TRANSPORT

RAILWAYS

	1978	1979	1980
Passenger-km. (million)	692	737	862
Freight ton-km. (million)	1,373	1,479	1,711

Source: Institut National de la Statistique.

ROAD TRAFFIC
(motor vehicles in use at December 31st)

	1977	1978	1979
Private cars	110,002	115,326	120,628
Buses	3,857	4,251	4,645
Commercial vehicles	74,978	84,563	97,690
Motor cycles	10,764	10,861	11,140

SEA-BORNE SHIPPING
(freight traffic in 'ooo metric tons)

	1977	1978	1979	1980
Total goods loaded*	17,798	18,889	17,648	n.a.
La Skhirra*	13,404	14,690	13,295	n.a.
Other ports	4,394	4,199	4,353	4,608
International goods loaded* . . .	16,966	18,087	16,657	n.a.
La Skhirra*	12,971	14,623	13,185	n.a.
Other ports	3,995	3,464	3,472	3,770
Coastwise goods loaded	832	802	982	991
Total goods unloaded	6,575	6,802	7,393	8,274
International shipping	5,743	6,000	6,411	7,283
Coastwise shipping	832	802	982	991

* Including Algerian crude petroleum loaded at La Skhirra.

Source: Banque Centrale de Tunisie, quoting Office National des Ports and Institut National de la Statistique.

CIVIL AVIATION
('ooo)

	1976	1977	1978	1979
Kilometres flown . .	16,944	16,163	16,720	19,665
Passengers carried . .	1,128	1,127	1,267	1,500
Passenger-km. . .	1,499,858	1,496,135	1,670,561	2,023,381
Freight ton-km. . .	7,023	8,437	10,489	11,427
Mail ton-km. . .	791	825	838	839

1980: 1,472,000 passengers carried.

Source: Banque Centrale de Tunisie, quoting Tunis Air.

TOURISM

FOREIGN TOURIST ARRIVALS BY NATIONALITY
('ooo)

	1976	1977	1978	1979	1980
Algeria	23.5	60.4	97.8	184.1	422.5
Austria	28.9	27.9	21.6	28.6	35.7
Belgium	43.3	36.6	36.8	40.4	39.8
France	371.5	386.5	388.7	418.3	365.9
Germany, Federal Republic	139.4	151.0	172.9	250.9	307.0
Italy	50.8	53.5	59.8	68.1	68.2
Libya	10.1	39.6	60.8	23.1	4.2
Netherlands . . .	38.8	29.5	36.0	48.2	39.8
Scandinavia . . .	78.0	53.7	39.8	44.0	52.9
Switzerland . . .	39.4	37.6	35.6	37.3	38.7
United Kingdom . .	79.4	58.9	77.4	105.4	144.2
U.S.A.	13.1	12.2	11.8	11.0	9.6
TOTAL (incl. others)	977.8	1,016.0	1,141.9	1,356.0	1,602.1

Tourist Beds: (1978) 66,059; (1979) 68,843; (1980) 71,529.

Tourist Nights: (1978) 9,456,255; (1979) 12,017,016; (1980) 12,792,378.

Tourist Spending (million dinars): (1976) 126.9; (1977) 139.4; (1978) 169.7; (1979) 219.2; (1980) 259.7.

Source: Banque Centrale de Tunisie, quoting Office National du Tourisme, Tunis.

EDUCATION

	INSTITUTIONS		TEACHERS		PUPILS	
	1978/79	1979/80	1978/79	1979/80	1978/79	1979/80
Primary	2,469	2,539	25,342	26,207	994,190	1,024,537
Secondary	208	216	10,839	11,595	231,730	241,908
of which:						
Secondary Technical . .	130	147	3,130	3,345	55,613	54,233
Teacher Training . . .	7	9	128	135	2,898	3,591
University of Tunis . . .	1	1	2,090	2,236	23,339	25,602

Source: Banque Centrale de Tunisie, quoting Ministère de l'Education Nationale and Ministère de l'Enseignement Supérieur et de la Recherche Scientifique.

THE CONSTITUTION

Tunisia, which had been a French Protectorate since 1883, achieved full internal autonomy in September 1955, and was finally recognized as a fully independent sovereign State by the Protocol of Paris of March 20th, 1956, by which France abrogated the former treaties and conventions.

NATIONAL ASSEMBLY

The Constitution was proclaimed by the Constituent Assembly on June 1st, 1959. Tunisia is a free, independent and sovereign republic. Legislative power is exercised by the National Assembly which is elected (at the same time as the President) every five years by direct universal suffrage. Every citizen who has had Tunisian nationality for at least five years and who has attained twenty years of age has the vote. The National Assembly shall hold two sessions every year, each session lasting not more than three months. Additional meetings may be held at the demand of the President or of a majority of the deputies.

HEAD OF STATE

The President of the Republic is both Head of State and Head of the Executive. He must be not less than 40 years of age. There is no limit to the number of terms a President may serve. The President is also the Commander-in-Chief of the army and makes both civil and military appointments. The Government may be censured by the National Assembly, in which case the President may dismiss the Assembly and hold fresh elections. If censured by the new Assembly thus elected, the Government must resign. Should the Presidency fall vacant for any reason before the end of a President's term of office, the Prime Minister shall assume the Presidency until the end of the term.

COUNCIL OF STATE

Comprises two judicial bodies: (1) an administrative body dealing with legal disputes between individuals and State or public bodies; (2) an audit office to verify the accounts of the State and submit reports.

ECONOMIC AND SOCIAL COUNCIL

Deals with economic and social planning and studies projects submitted by the National Assembly. Members are grouped in seven categories representing various sections of the community.

THE GOVERNMENT

HEAD OF STATE

President-for-Life: HABIB BOURGUIBA (took office as President July 25th, 1957; proclaimed Life President March 18th, 1975).

THE CABINET

(June 1982)

Prime Minister: MOHAMED MZALI.

Special Adviser to the President: HABIB BOURGUIBA, Jr.

Minister Delegate to the Prime Minister in charge of Civil Service and Administrative Reform: MAZRI CHEKIR.

Minister Delegate to the Prime Minister and Director of Party: MONGI KOOLI.

Minister for Foreign Affairs: BEJI CAID ESSEBSI.

Minister of National Defence: SLAHEDDINE BALY.

Minister of Health: RACHID SFAR.

Minister of Information: TAHAR BELKHODJA.

Minister of Culture: BECHIR BEN SLAMA.

Minister of Planning and Finance: MANSOUR MOALLA.

Minister of Justice: M'HAMED CHAKER.

Minister of the Interior: IDRIS GUIGAH.

Minister of Agriculture: LASSAAD BEN OTHMAN.

Minister of Housing: MONCEF BELHAJ AMOR.

Minister of Supply: MOHAMED SAYAH.

Minister of National Economy: ABDELAZIZ LASRAM.

Minister of Education: MOHAMED FREDJ CHEDLI.

Minister of Higher Education and Scientific Research: ABDELAZIZ BEN DHIA.

Minister of Transport and Communications: SADOK BEN JOMAA.

Minister of Social Affairs: MOHAMED ENNACEUR.

Minister of Youth and Sport: MOHAMED KREIM.

LEGISLATURE
ASSEMBLÉE NATIONALE

President: MAHMOUD MESSADI.

ELECTION, NOVEMBER 1ST, 1981

1,962,127 votes (including 20,269 invalid) were cast.

	PERCENTAGE OF VOTES CAST	SEATS WON IN NATIONAL ASSEMBLY
Front National*	94.60	136
Mouvement des Démocrates Socialistes† .	3.28	0
Mouvement de l'Unité Populaire . .	0.81	0
Parti Communiste Tunisien . . .	0.78	0
Independents	0.53	0

* Joint electoral front presented by Parti Socialiste Destourien and Union Générale des Travailleurs Tunisiens.

† Only the anti-Ben Salah faction participated in the election.

POLITICAL PARTIES AND ORGANIZATIONS

Parti Socialiste Destourien—PSD: blvd. 9 Avril 1938, Tunis; f. 1934 by Habib Bourguiba, as a splinter party from the old *Destour* (Constitution) Party; moderate left-wing republican party, which achieved Tunisian independence; there is a political bureau of 20 members, and a central committee of 80 elected by the party congress; Chairman-for-Life HABIB BOURGUIBA; Sec.-Gen. MOHAMED MZALI; Head of Political Bureau MONGI KOOLI.

Parti Communiste Tunisien—PCT: Tunis; f. 1939; suspended 1963–81; Sec.-Gen. MOHAMED HARMEL.

Mouvement des Démocrates Socialistes (MDS): Tunis; in favour of a pluralist political system; participated in 1981 election but failed to win the 5 per cent of votes necessary for formal recognition as a political party; Sec.-Gen. MAHMOUD MESTIRI.

Mouvement de l'Unité Populaire (MUP): supports radical reform; split into two factions, one led by AHMED BEN SALAH, living in exile; the other led by MOHAMED BEL HADJ AMOR, failed to win the necessary 5 per cent of the votes in the 1981 election and is not officially recognized.

The **Mouvement de la Tendance Islamique** and the **Rassemblement National Arabe** were both banned in 1981.

DIPLOMATIC REPRESENTATION
EMBASSIES ACCREDITED TO TUNISIA
(In Tunis unless otherwise stated)

Albania: Algiers, Algeria.

Algeria: 18 rue de Niger; *Ambassador:* ALI KEFFI.

Argentina: Algiers, Algeria.

Australia: Algiers, Algeria.

Austria: 17 ave. de France; *Ambassador:* GEORG HOHEN-BERG.

Bangladesh: Tripoli, Libya.

Belgium: 47 rue du 1er Juin; *Ambassador:* J. BASSOM-PIERRE.

Brazil: 15 rue Es-Sayouti, El Menzah; *Ambassador:* DONATELLO GRIECO.

Bulgaria: 16 rue Moutanabbi, El Menzah; *Ambassador:* IVAN ABADJIEV.

Cameroon: Paris, France.

Canada: 2 place Virgile, Notre Dame, C.P.31, Belvédère; *Ambassador:* ARTHUR BLANCHETTE.

Central African Republic: Algiers, Algeria.

Chad: Cairo, Egypt.

China, People's Republic: 41 ave. de Lesseps; *Ambassador:* MENG YUE.

Costa Rica: Madrid, Spain.

Czechoslovakia: 98 rue de la Palestine, B.P. 680; *Ambassador:* ANDREJ PETRIČEK.

Denmark: Algiers, Algeria.

Djibouti: *Ambassador:* ALI ABDOU SULTAN.

Finland: Algiers, Algeria.

France: place de l'Indépendance; *Ambassador:* PIERRE HUNT.

Gabon: Paris, France.

German Democratic Republic: ave. d'Afrique, El Menzah; *Ambassador:* HELMUT GÜRKE.

Germany, Federal Republic: 18 rue Félicien Challaye; *Ambassador:* HANS KAHLE.

Ghana: *Ambassador:* ANTHONY W. EPHSON.

Greece: 4 rue El Jahedh, El Menzah; *Ambassador:* DIONYSIOS XENOS.

Compagnie Tunisienne de Navigation: P.O.B. 40, 5 ave. Dag Hammarskjoeld, Tunis; brs. at Bizerta, Gabès, La Skhirra, La Goulette, Sfax and Sousse; Chair. HANAFI BEN CHERIF.

Tunisian Transcontinental Transportation: 23 ave. des Etats-Unis, Tunis.

CIVIL AVIATION

There are international airports at Tunis-Carthage, Tunis-El Aouina, Djerba and Monastir. A new international airport was opened at Tozeur in January 1980.

Tunis Air (*Société Tunisienne de l'Air*): 113 ave. de la Liberté, Tunis; f. 1948; 51 per cent Government-owned; flights to Algeria, Austria, Belgium, Denmark, Egypt, France, Fed. Rep. of Germany, Italy, Kuwait, Libya, Morocco, Netherlands, Saudi Arabia, Sudan, Switzerland, Syria, U.K., United Arab Emirates and internal flights; fleet of 10 Boeing 727, 2 Boeing 737-200, 2 Boeing 737-200C; Pres. HASSOUNA MNARA.

FOREIGN AIRLINES

Aeroflot (U.S.S.R.), Air Afrique (Ivory Coast), Air Algérie, Air France, Alitalia, Austrian Airlines, Balkan (Bulgaria), British Caledonian, ČSA (Czechoslovakia), Egypt Air, Gulf Air (Bahrain), JAT (Yugoslavia), KLM (Netherlands), Libyan Arab Airlines, LOT (Poland), Lufthansa (Federal Republic of Germany), Royal Air Maroc, Sabena (Belgium), Swiss air, TWA (U.S.A.), and UTA (France) also serve Tunis.

TOURISM AND CULTURE

Office National du Tourisme Tunisien: 1 ave. Mohammed V, Tunis; f. 1958; Pres., Dir.-Gen. M'HAMED ALI BOULEYMEN.

Voyages 2000: 2 ave. de France, Tunis; f. 1964; Dir. MONCEF TRIKI; publ. *Voyages 2000*.

CULTURAL ORGANIZATIONS

Ministry of Cultural Affairs: Tunis; departments organize all national cultural events; Minister BECHIR BEN SLAMA.

Institut des Belles Lettres Arabes: 12 rue Jamaa el Haoua, 1008 Tunis BM; f. 1930; cultural centre; Dir. J. FONTAINE; publ. *IBLA* (twice yearly) and special studies.

International Cultural Centre: Hammamet; f. 1962; organizes national and international scientific and cultural conferences, and the Hammamet International Festival; provides individual study facilities for writers, musicians and painters; Dir. RACHED HAMZAOUI.

PRINCIPAL THEATRES

Théâtre Municipal de Tunis: Tunis; subsidized by the state.

Hammamet Theatre: Hammamet; open air theatre built 1963; organized by International Cultural Centre of Hammamet.

CULTURAL FESTIVALS

Carthage Festival: 22 rue Amin Raihani, El Omrane, Tunis; f. 1974; international festival of arts; held every year at the site of the ancient city and in Tunis.

Hammamet International Festival: Hammamet; annual festival, July–August; theatre, music, ballet, cinema, art; based on the open-air theatre.

Festival International de Monastir: c/o Comité Culturel Régional, Monastir; f. 1964; music, theatre, cinema, dance, etc.; Dir. AMARA SKHIRI.

DEFENCE

Estimated Defence Expenditure (1981): 104.4m. dinars.

Military Service: 1 year (selective).

Total Armed Forces (July 1981): 28,600 (army 24,000; navy 2,600; air force 2,000).

Paramilitary Forces (July 1981): 8,500 (5,000 Gendarmerie, 3,500 National Guard).

EDUCATION

Tunisia has better educational facilities than most developing countries. Approximately 80 per cent of children of school age receive an education. In 1979/80 there were 1,024,537 pupils in 2,539 primary schools and 241,908 pupils in 216 secondary schools. In 1982 an estimated 162.4 million dinars was allocated to the Ministry of Education.

Arabic only is used in the first three years of primary school, but in the higher grades French becomes progressively more important and is used almost exclusively in higher education. The University of Tunis was opened in 1959/60. It has 54 faculties and institutes. In 1980 25,602 students attended the university.

BIBLIOGRAPHY

ANTHONY, JOHN. About Tunisia (London, 1961).

ARDANT, GAVRIEL. La Tunisie d'Aujourd'hui et Demain (Paris, 1961).

ASHFORD, DOUGLAS E. Morocco-Tunisia: Politics and Planning (Syracuse University Press, 1965).

BASSET, ANDRÉ. Initiation à la Tunisie (Paris, 1950).

BOURGUIBA, HABIB. La Tunisie et la France (Paris, 1954). Hadith al-Jamaa (*Collected Broadcasts*) (Tunis, 1957).

BRUNSCHVIG, ROBERT. La Tunisie au haut Moyen Age (Cairo, 1948).

CAMBON, HENRI. Histoire de la régence de Tunisie (Paris, 1948).

DE MONTETY, HENRI. Femmes de Tunisie (Paris, 1958).

DESPOIS, JEAN. La Tunisie, ses Régions (Paris, 1959).

DUVIGNAUD, JEAN. Tunisie (Editions Rencontre, Lausanne, 1965).

DUWAJI, GHAZI. Economic Development in Tunisia (Praeger, New York, 1967).

GARAS, FELIX. Bourguiba et la Naissance d'une Nation (Paris, 1956).

GERMANN, RAIMUND E. Verwaltung und Einheitspartei in Tunisien (Europa Verlag, Zürich, 1968).

GUEN, MONCEF. La Tunisie indépendante face à son économie (Paris, 1961).

KNAPP, W. Tunisia (Thames and Hudson, London, 1972).

LAITMAN, LEON. Tunisia Today: Crisis in North Africa (New York, 1954).

LING, DWIGHT D. Tunisia, from Protectorate to Republic (Indiana University Press, 1967).

MICAUD, C. A. Tunisia, the Politics of Moderation (New York, 1964).

MOORE, C. H. Tunisia since Independence (University of California Press, Berkeley, 1965).

NERFIN, M. Entretiens avec Ahmed Ben Salah (F. Maspero, Paris, 1974).

PERROUX, F. and BARRE, R., Editors. Développement, croissance, progrès: Maroc-Tunisie (Paris, 1961).

RAYMOND, ANDRÉ. La Tunisie (Series *Que sais-je*, No. 318) (Paris, 1961).

RUDEBECK, LARS. Party and People: A Study of Political Change in Tunisia (C. Hurst, London, 1969).

RUF, WERNER KLAUS, Der Burgismus und die Aussenpolitik der unabhängigen Tunesien (Freiburg, 1969).

SYLVESTER, ANTHONY. Tunisia (Bodley Head, London, 1969).

TLATLI, SALAH-EDDINE. Tunisie nouvelle (Tunis, 1957).

ZIADEH, NICOLA A. The Origins of Tunisian Nationalism (Beirut. 1962.)

Turkey

PHYSICAL AND SOCIAL GEOGRAPHY

W. B. Fisher

Turkey is, in a remarkable sense, passage land between Europe and Asia. Nearly one-half of its 2,620 km. of land frontier is with European States—Greece, Bulgaria, and Soviet Russia; and the remainder with Iran, Iraq, and Syria. The richest and most densely populated west of Turkey looks towards the Aegean and Mediterranean Seas and is very conscious of its links with Europe; whilst in culture, racial origins, and ways of life there are frequent reminders of Turkey's geographical situation primarily as a part of Asia.

Turkey consists essentially of the large peninsula of Asia Minor, which has strongly defined natural limits: sea on three sides (the Black Sea in the north, the Aegean in the west, and the Mediterranean on the south), and high mountain ranges on the fourth (eastern) side. The small region of European Turkey, containing the cities of Istanbul (Constantinople) and Edirne (Adrianople) is on the other hand defined by a purely artificial frontier, the exact position of which has varied considerably over the last century, according to the fluctuating fortunes and prestige of Turkey herself. Another small territory, the Hatay, centred on Iskenderun (Alexandretta) and lying as an enclave in Syrian territory, was acquired as a diplomatic bargain in 1939.

PHYSICAL FEATURES

The geological structure of Turkey is extremely complicated, and rocks of almost all ages occur, from the most ancient to most recent. Broadly speaking, we may say that Turkey consists of a number of old plateau blocks, against which masses of younger rock series have been squeezed to form fold mountain ranges of varying size. As there were several of these plateau blocks, and not just one, the fold mountains run in many different directions, with considerable irregularity, and hence no simple pattern can be discerned—instead, one mountain range gives place to another abruptly, and we can pass suddenly from highland to plain or plateau.

In general outline Turkey consists of a ring of mountains enclosing a series of inland plateaus, with the highest mountains on the east, close to the U.S.S.R. and Iran. Mount Ararat, overlooking the Soviet frontier, is the highest peak in Turkey, reaching 5,165 metres, and there are neighbouring peaks almost as large. In the west the average altitude of the hills is distinctly lower, though the highest peak (Mount Erciyas or Argaeus) is over 3,900 metres. The irregular topography of Turkey has given rise to many lakes, some salt, and some fresh, and generally more numerous than elsewhere in the Middle East. The largest, Lake Van, covers nearly 4,000 sq. km. (1,100 sq. miles).

Two other features may be mentioned. Large areas of the east, and some parts of the centre of Asia Minor have been covered in sheets of lava which are often of such recent occurrence that soil has not yet been formed—consequently wide expanses are sterile and uninhabited. Secondly, in the north and west cracking and disturbance of the rocks has taken place on an enormous scale. The long, indented coast of the Aegean Sea, with its numerous oddly shaped islands and estuaries, is due to cracking in two directions, which has split the land into detached blocks of roughly rectangular shape. Often the lower parts have sunk and been

drowned by the sea. The Bosphorus and Dardanelles owe their origin to this faulting action, and the whole of the Black Sea coast is due to subsidence along a great series of fissures. Movement and adjustment along these cracks has by no means ceased, so that at the present day earthquakes are frequent in the north and west of Turkey.

Because of the presence of mountain ranges close to the coast, and the great height of the interior plateaus (varying from 800 to 2,000 metres), Turkey has special climatic conditions, characterized by great extremes of temperature and rainfall, with wide variation from one district to another. In winter conditions are severe in most areas, except for those lying close to sea-level. Temperatures of minus 30° to minus 40°C. can occur in the east, and snow lies there for as many as 120 days each year. The west has frost on most nights of December and January, and (again apart from the coastal zone) has an average winter temperature below 1°C. In summer, however, temperatures over most of Turkey exceed 30°C., with 43°C. in the south-east. There can hence be enormous seasonal variations of temperature—sometimes over 50°C., among the widest in the world.

Rainfall too is remarkably variable. Along the eastern Black Sea coast, towards the Soviet frontier, over 250 cm. fall annually; but elsewhere, amounts are very much smaller. Parts of the central plateau, being shut off by mountains from the influence of sea winds, are arid, with annual totals of under 25 cm., and expanses of salt steppe and desert are frequent. Like Iran, Turkey also has a "dead heart", and the main towns of Anatolia, including Ankara, the capital, are placed away from the centre and close to the hills, where rainfall tends to be greater.

It is necessary to emphasize the contrast that exists between the Aegean coastlands, which climatically are by far the most favoured regions of Turkey, and the rest of the country. Round the Aegean, winters are mild and fairly rainy, and the summers hot, but tempered by a persistent northerly wind, the Meltemi, or Etesian wind, which is of great value in ripening fruit, especially figs and sultana grapes.

ECONOMIC LIFE

The variety of geographical conditions within Turkey has led to uneven development, and this unevenness has been intensified by poor communications, due to the broken nature of the topography. Roads are relatively few, railways slow and often roundabout, and whole districts—sometimes even considerable towns—are accessible only by bridle track. Many rivers flow in deep gorges near their sources and either meander or are broken by cascades in their lower reaches, so that none are navigable.

Thus we find that the west of Turkey, situated close to the Aegean Sea, is by far the most densely peopled and the most intensively developed. Since 1923, however, attempts have been made to develop the Anatolian plateau and the districts in the extreme east, which, following the expulsion and massacre of the Armenians in 1914-18, for a time supported only a very scanty population. Development in the central plateau has been aided by the exploitation of several small but on the whole valuable mineral deposits, and by irrigation schemes to improve agriculture. A certain degree of industrialisation (mainly undertaken by state-sponsored and owned organisations) has also grown up, based on Turkish-produced raw materials—cotton, wool, mohair, beet-sugar, olive oil, and tobacco. The eastern districts present a more intractable problem, and development so far has been slower.

Of recent years, the considerable annual increase of population, about 2.5 per cent, has led to intensification of settlement and the bringing in of all available land for cultivation. Henceforth a principal problem for Turkey must be to improve yields from agriculture and industry. Because of the strategic importance of the country, there has been a considerable programme of road-building, largely financed by the U.S.A. In recent years absorption of Turkish labour in western Europe (chiefly the Federal Republic of Germany) provided most useful extra revenue from remittances; but with the repatriation of many of these *gastarbeiter* during the recession of the last few years, there have been problems of reabsorption (the returning workers have higher expectations) together with the need to find other sources of revenue.

Latterly, Turkey has experienced severe economic crises, compounded by political uncertainty and social instability. In 1980 there were severe shortages, due to rampant inflation and the inability to finance necessary imports. Since 1981, however, some improvement is apparent. Inflation has declined, "black market" activities are reduced, confidence is higher and export performance has improved. This has allowed the start of reform of the tax system, and a limited plan for land reform. Nevertheless, social problems (in part due to widespread unemployment, low credit-worthiness and the fact of military government) remain considerable handicaps.

RACE AND LANGUAGE

Racially, the bulk of the Turkish people show an intermixture of Mediterranean and Armenoid strains. In the western half of the country Mediterraneans and Armenoids are more or less equally represented; but further east the proportion of Armenoids steadily increases, until towards the Soviet and Iranian borders, they become almost universal. Much of south-eastern Turkey is inhabited by Kurds, a people of Indo-European descent; estimates of their number range widely, from three to over eight million. We can in addition note less important racial elements: there would seem to be small numbers of proto-Nordics in the north and west, and some authorities suggest a racial relationship between Galatia (the modern district of Ankara) and ancient Gaul. The Ottoman Turks were in the main of Turki (western Mongoloid) ancestry, but in the view of some authorities their contribution to the ethnic stocks of Turkey would seem to have been small, since they were really an invading tribal group that became an aristocracy and soon intermarried with other peoples. There are also numbers of Caucasians—particularly Circassians and Georgians—who have contributed to the racial structure of Turkey; and during 1951 a further element was added by the arrival of many thousands of Bulgarian Muslims who had been deported from their own country.

The Turkish language, which is of central Asiatic origin, is spoken over most, but by no means all of the country. This was introduced into Turkey in Seljuq times, and was written in Arabic characters, but as these are not really well adapted to the sound of Turkish, Roman (i.e. European) script has been compulsory since 1928. As well, there are a number of non-Turkish languages. Kurdish has a wide extension in the south-east, along the Syrian and Iraqi frontiers; and Caucasian dialects, quite different from either Turkish or Kurdish, occur in the north-east. Greek and Armenian were once widespread, but following the deportations of the last forty years both forms of speech are now current only in the city of Istanbul, where considerable numbers of Greeks and Armenians still live

HISTORY

ANCIENT HISTORY

The most ancient written records so far found in Asia Minor date from the beginning of the second millennium B.C. They are in Assyrian, and reveal the existence of Assyrian trading colonies in Cappadocia. These documents, together with a growing amount of archaeological evidence, show an important Copper Age culture in Central Anatolia in the third and early second millennia. Later in the second millennium the greater part of Asia Minor fell under the rule of the Hittites. This people has long been known from references in the Old Testament and other ancient texts, but its full importance was first revealed by the excavations at Boğazköy, the site of the ancient Hittite capital of Hattushash. The Hittite Empire flourished from about 1600 to about 1200 B.C., and reached its apogee in the fourteenth and thirteenth centuries, when it became one of the dominant States of the Middle East. One of the sources of Hittite strength was iron, which was first worked in Anatolia. The production of iron was for long a monopoly of the Hittite kings, but the use of iron implements eventually spread to other parts, and revolutionised agriculture, industry and war.

After the break-up of the Hittite Empire, Asia Minor was split up among a number of dynasties and peoples—Phrygians, Cimmerians, Lydians and others—about whom not very much is known. Towards the end of the Hittite period the Greeks began to invade the Aegean coast, and entered on a long struggle with the native states that is reflected in the story of the Trojan war. Greek culture spread in western Anatolia, which was gradually incorporated into the Hellenic world. A series of political changes, of which the most important are the Persian conquest in 546, the conquest of Alexander in 334, and the constitution of the Roman province of Asia in 133 B.C., did not impede the steady spread of Greek language and culture in the cities.

In A.D. 330, the Emperor Constantine inaugurated the new city of Constantinople, on the site of the old Greek trading settlement of Byzantium. This city at once became the capital of the East Roman and then of the Christian Byzantine Empire. Asia Minor was now the metropolitan province of a great Empire, and grew in wealth, prosperity and importance. Under Byzantine rule Greek Christianity, already firmly established in Roman times, spread over most of the peninsula.

SELJUQS AND OTTOMANS

At the beginning of the eleventh century a new conquest of Anatolia began—that of the Turks. The early history of the Turkish peoples is still obscure. Some references in the ancient biography of Alexander show them to have been established in Central Asia at the time of his conquests, and Turkish tribal confederacies played an important part in the invasions of Europe from late Roman times onwards. The name "Turk" first appears in historical records in the sixth century A.D., when Chinese annals speak of a powerful empire in Central Asia, founded by a steppe people called Tu-Kiu. It is from this state that the oldest surviving Turkish inscriptions have come. From the seventh century onwards the Central Asian Turks came into ever closer contact with the Islamic peoples of the Near East, from whom they adopted the Islamic faith and the Arabic script, and with them much of the complex civilisation of Islam.

From the ninth century Turks entered the service of the Caliphate in increasing numbers, and soon came to provide the bulk of its armies, its generals, and eventually its rulers.

From the tenth century whole tribes of Turks began to migrate into Persia and Iraq, and in the eleventh, under the leadership of the family of Seljuq, the Turks were able to set up a great empire comprising most of the eastern lands of the Caliphate. The Muslim armies on the Byzantine frontier had long been predominantly Turkish, and in the course of the eleventh century they began a great movement into Anatolia which resulted in the termination of Byzantine rule in most of the country and its incorporation in the Muslim Seljuq Sultanate. A Seljuq prince, Suleyman ibn Kutlumush, was sent to organize the new province, and by the end of the twelfth century his successors had built up a strong Turkish monarchy in Anatolia, with its capital in Konya (the ancient Iconium). Under the rule of the Anatolian Seljuqs, which in various forms lasted until the fourteenth century, Anatolia gradually became a Turkish land. Masses of Turkish immigrants from further east entered the country, and a Turkish, Muslim civilisation replaced Greek Christianity.

In the late thirteenth century the Sultanate of Konya fell into decay, and gradually gave way to a number of smaller principalities. One of these, in north-western Anatolia, was ruled by a certain Osman, or Othman, from whom the name Ottoman is derived. The Ottoman State soon embarked on a great movement of expansion, on the one hand in Anatolia, at the expense of its Turkish neighbours, on the other in the Balkans. Ottoman armies first crossed to Europe in the mid-fourteenth century, and by 1400 they were masters of much of the Balkan peninsula as well as of almost all Anatolia. The capital was moved first from Bursa to Edirne and then, in 1453, to Constantinople, the final conquest of which from the last Byzantine Emperor completed the process that had transformed a principality of frontier-warriors into a new great empire. Constantinople, called Istanbul by the Turks, remained the capital of the Ottoman Empire until 1922. The wave of conquest was by no means spent. For more than a century Ottoman arms continued to advance into Central Europe, while in 1516–17 Sultan Selim I destroyed the Mamluk Sultanate and incorporated Syria and Egypt into the Empire. During the reign of Sultan Suleyman I (1520–66), called the Magnificent in Europe, the Ottoman Empire was at the height of its power. In three continents the Sultan held unchallenged sway over vast territories. A skilled and highly-organised bureaucracy secured for the peoples of the Empire peace, justice and prosperity; literature, scholarship and the arts flourished; and the Ottoman armies and fleets seemed to threaten the very existence of Western Christendom.

The decay of the Empire is usually dated from after the death of Suleyman. In the West great changes were taking place. The Renaissance and the Reformation, the rapid development of science and technology, the emergence of strong, centralised nation states with constantly improving military techniques, the deflection of the main routes of international trade from the Mediterranean to the open seas, all combined to strengthen Turkey's Western adversaries while leaving her own resources unchanged or even diminished, and helped to relegate her into a backwater of cultural and economic stagnation. An imposing military façade for a while masked the internal decay that was rotting the once all-powerful Empire, but by the end of the seventeenth century the weakness of the Ottoman State was manifest. Then began the struggle of the Powers for pickings of Turkish territory and for positions of influence in the Empire. During the eighteenth century it was Austria and Russia that made the main territorial advances in the Balkans and in the Black Sea area, while England and

France were content with commercial and diplomatic privileges. In a succession of wars one province after another was lost, while internal conditions went from bad to worse. During the nineteenth century England and France began to play a more active role. British policy was generally to support the Turks against their impatient heirs. In 1854 Britain and France went to war at the side of Turkey in order to check Russian aggression, and in 1877–78 British diplomatic intervention was effective to the same end. Meanwhile the ferment of nationalist ideas had spread from the West to the subject peoples of the Empire, and one by one the Serbs, Greeks, Romanians and Bulgarians succeeded in throwing off Ottoman rule and attaining independent statehood.

More significant for Turkish history were the first stirrings of a new spirit among the Turks themselves. The first serious attempts at reform were made during the reign of Selim III (1789–1807), and during the nineteenth century a series of reforming sultans and ministers worked on a programme of reform and modernisation which, though it fell short of its avowed objectives, nevertheless transformed the face of the Ottoman Empire and began a process of change, the effects of which are still visible. In 1878 the reforming movement came to an abrupt end, and from that year until 1908 the Empire was subjected to the iron despotism of Abdul-Hamid II, who ruthlessly repressed every attempt at liberal thought and reform. In 1908 the secret opposition group known as the Young Turks seized power, and in a wave of revolutionary enthusiasm inaugurated a constitution, parliamentary government, and a whole series of liberal reforms. Unfortunately the Young Turks had little opportunity to follow up their promising start. First internal dissension, then foreign wars, combined to turn the Young Turk regime into a military dictatorship. In 1911 the Italians suddenly started a war against Turkey which ended with their gaining Libya and the Dodecanese Islands; in 1912–13 a Balkan alliance succeeded in wresting from the dying Empire most of its remaining possessions on the continent of Europe. Finally, in October 1914, Turkey entered the war on the side of the Central Powers. During the reign of Abdul-Hamid German influence had been steadily increasing in Turkey, and the process continued under the Young Turks. It was certainly helped by the growing friendship between the Western Powers and Russia, which threw the Turks into the arms of the only power that seemed ready to support them against Russian designs. German officers reorganised the Turkish Army. German businessmen and technicians extended their hold on the economic resources of the country, and German engineers and financiers began the construction of the famous Baghdad railway which was to provide direct rail communication between Germany and the Middle East.

The Turkish alliance was of immense military value to the Central Powers. The Turkish armies, still established in Syria and Palestine, were able to offer an immediate and serious threat to the Suez Canal and to the British position in Egypt. By their dogged and successful defence of the Dardanelles they prevented effective co-operation between Russia and the Western Powers. Their Balkan position assured the supremacy of the Central Powers in that important area. Their position as the greatest independent Muslim State and their prestige among Muslims elsewhere created a series of problems in the British and French Empires.

Despite their weakness and exhaustion after two previous wars, the Turks were able to wage a bitter defensive war against the Allies. At last, after two unsuccessful attempts, one on the Dardanelles and the other in Mesopotamia, a new British attack from Egypt and from India succeeded in expelling the Turks from Palestine, Syria, and most of Iraq. Defeated on all sides, cut off from their allies by the Salonica Expedition, the Turks decided to abandon the struggle, and signed an armistice at Mudros on October 30th, 1918. French, Italian and British occupation forces moved into Turkey.

For some time the victorious Powers were too busy elsewhere to attend to the affairs of Turkey, and it was not until the San Remo Conference of April 1920 that the first serious attempt was made to settle the Turkish question. Meanwhile the victors were busy quarrelling among themselves. Partly, no doubt, with the idea of forestalling Italian ambitions, the British, French, and American Governments agreed to a Greek proposal for a Greek occupation of Izmir and the surrounding country, and on May 15th, 1919, a Greek Army, under cover of allied warships, landed at Izmir. Second thoughts on the wisdom of this step appeared in the allied camp, and in October 1919 the Inter-Allied Commission in Istanbul condemned it as "unjustifiable" and as "a violation of the terms of the Armistice". The consequences of the invasion for Turkey were momentous. Now it was no longer the non-Turkish subject provinces and the Ottoman superstructure of the Turkish nation that were threatened, but the Turkish homeland itself. Moreover, the Greeks, unlike the Western Allies, showed that they intended to stay, and that they were aiming at nothing less than the incorporation of the territories they occupied into the Greek kingdom. The Turkish reaction to this danger was vigorous and immediate. The Nationalist movement, hitherto limited to a small class of intellectuals, became the mass instrument of Turkish determination to preserve the integrity and independence of the homeland. A new leader appeared to organise their victory.

THE RISE OF ATATÜRK

Mustafa Kemal, later surnamed Atatürk, was born in Salonica, then an Ottoman city, in 1880. After a promising career as a regular army officer, he achieved his first active command in Libya in 1911, and thereafter fought with distinction in the successive wars in which his country was involved. After his brilliant conduct of the defence of Gallipoli, he fought on various fronts against the Allies, and at the time of the Armistice held a command on the Syrian front. A month later he returned to Istanbul, and at once began to seek ways and means of getting to Anatolia to organise national resistance. At length he was successful, and on May 19th, 1919—four days after the Greek landing in Izmir—he arrived at Samsun, on the Black Sea coast, ostensibly in order to supervise the disbanding of the remaining Turkish forces. Instead he set to work at once on the double task of organising a national movement and raising a national army.

Meanwhile the Allied Powers were at last completing their arrangements for the obsequies of the Sick Man of Europe. After a series of conferences, a treaty was drawn up and signed by the Allied representatives and those of the Sultan's Government at Sèvres, on August 10th, 1920. The Treaty of Sèvres was very harsh—far harsher than that imposed on Germany. The Arab provinces were to be placed under British and French Mandates, to prepare them for eventual independence. In Anatolia, Armenian and Kurdish States were to be set up in the east, the south was to be divided between France and Italy, and a truncated Turkish Sultanate confined to the interior. The Straits were to be demilitarised and placed under Allied administration, with a Turkish Istanbul surrounded by Allied forces. The rest of European Turkey was to be ceded to Greece, while the Izmir district was to be under "Ottoman sovereignty and Greek administration".

This treaty was, however, never implemented. While the Allies were imposing their terms on the Sultan and his Government in Istanbul, a new Turkish State was rising in the interior of Anatolia, based on the rejection of the treaty and the principles on which it was founded. On July 23rd, 1919, Mustafa Kemal and his associates convened the first Nationalist Congress in Erzurum, and drew up a national programme. A second Congress was held in September in the same year, and attended by delegates from all over the country. An executive committee, presided over by Mustafa Kemal, was formed, and chose Ankara, then a minor provincial town, as its headquarters. Frequent meetings were held in Ankara, which soon became the effective capital of the Nationalist movement and forces. It was there that they issued the famous National Pact, the declaration that laid down the basic programme of the Kemalist movement, renouncing the Empire and the domination of the non-Turkish provinces, but demanding the total and unconditional independence of all areas inhabited by Turks. This declaration won immediate support, and on January 28th, 1920, was approved even by the legal Ottoman Parliament sitting in Istanbul. The growth of the Nationalist movement in Istanbul alarmed the Allies, and on March 16th British forces entered the Turkish part of the city and arrested and deported many Nationalist leaders. Despite this setback, followed by a new anti-Nationalist campaign on the part of the Sultan and his political and religious advisers, the Kemalists continued to advance. On March 19th, 1920, Mustafa Kemal ordered general elections, and at the end of April a National Assembly of 350 deputies met in Ankara and voted the National Pact. The Sultan and his government were declared deposed, a provisional Constitution promulgated, and a government set up with Mustafa Kemal as President.

There remained the military task of expelling the invaders. The Greco-Turkish war falls into three stages, covering roughly the campaigns of 1920, 1921 and 1922. In the first the Nationalists, hopelessly outmatched in numbers and material, were badly defeated, and the Greeks advanced far into Anatolia. Turkish resistance was, however, strong enough to impress the Allies, who, for the first time, accorded a certain limited recognition to the Nationalist Government and proclaimed their neutrality in the Greco-Turkish war. The second campaign began with Greek successes, but the Turks rallied and defeated the invaders first at İnönü—from which İsmet Pasha, who commanded the Turkish forces there, later took his surname—and then, on August 24th, 1921, in a major battle on the Sakarya River, where the Turkish forces were under the personal command of Mustafa Kemal. This victory considerably strengthened the Nationalists, who were now generally realised to be the effective Government of Turkey. The French and Italians withdrew from the areas of Anatolia assigned to them, and made terms with the new Government. The Soviets, now established on Turkey's eastern frontier, had already done so at the beginning of the year.

A period of waiting and reorganization followed, during which the morale of the Greek armies was adversely affected by political changes in Greece. In August 1922 the third and final phase of the war of independence began. The Turkish Army drove the Greeks back to the Aegean, and on September 9th reoccupied İzmir. Mustafa Kemal now prepared to cross to Thrace. To do so he had to cross the Straits, still under Allied occupation. The French and Italian contingents withdrew, and, after a menacing pause, the British followed. On October 11th an armistice was signed at Mudanya, whereby the Allied Governments agreed to the restoration of Turkish sovereignty in Eastern Thrace. In November the Sultan's Cabinet resigned, and the Sultan himself went into exile. Turkey once more had only one government, and Istanbul, the ancient seat of Empire, became a provincial city, ruled by a governor appointed from Ankara.

The peace conference opened in November 1922. After

many months of argument the treaty was finally signed on July 24th, 1923. It recognised complete and undivided Turkish sovereignty and the abolition of the last vestiges of foreign privilege. The only reservation related to the demilitarisation of the Straits, which were not to be fortified without the consent of the Powers. This consent was given at the Montreux Conference in 1936.

THE TURKISH REPUBLIC

The military task was completed, and the demands formulated in the National Pact had been embodied in an international treaty. There remained the greater task of rebuilding the ruins of long years of war and revolution—and of remedying those elements of weakness in the Turkish State and society that had brought Turkey to the verge of extinction. Mustafa Kemal saw the solution of Turkey's problems in a process of Westernisation—in the integration of Turkey, on a basis of equality, in the modern Western world. To do this it was not sufficient to borrow, as other reformers had done, the outward forms and trappings of Western civilisation. It was necessary to change the very basis of society in Turkey, and to suppress, ruthlessly if need be, the opposition that was bound to come from the entrenched forces of the old order. Between 1922 and 1938, the year of his death, Kemal carried through a series of far-reaching reforms in Turkey. These may be considered under various headings.

The first changes were political. After the deposition of Sultan Vahdeddin in November 1922, a brief experiment was made with a purely religious sovereignty, and Abdul-Mejid was proclaimed as Caliph but not Sultan. The experiment was not successful. Abdul-Mejid followed his predecessor into exile, and on October 29th, 1923, Turkey was declared a Republic, with Kemal as President. The regime of Kemal Atatürk was effectively a dictatorship—though without the violence and oppression normally associated with that word in Europe. A single party—the Republican People's Party—formed the main instrument for the enforcement of Government policy. The Constitution of April 20th, 1924, provided for an elected Parliament which was the repository of sovereign power. Executive power was to be exercised by the President and a Cabinet chosen by him.

The next object of attack was the religious hierarchy already weakened by the removal of the Sultan-Caliph. In a series of edicts the Ministry of Religious Affairs was abolished, the religious orders disbanded, religious property sequestrated, religious instruction forbidden. With the religious leaders in retreat, the attack on the old social order began. Certainly the most striking reforms were the abolition of the fez and the Arabic alphabet, and their replacement by the hat and the Latin alphabet. But these were probably less important in the long run than the abrogation of the old legal system and the introduction of new civil and criminal codes of law adapted from Europe. In 1928 Islam itself was disestablished, and the Constitution amended to make Turkey a secular State.

Not the least of the problems that faced Mustafa Kema was the economic one. Turkey needed capital. Rather than risk the independence of Turkey by inviting foreign capital in a time of weakness, Kemal adopted the principle of *Étatisme*, and made it one of the cardinal doctrines of his regime. From 1923 to 1933 the State made its main effort in railway construction, nearly doubling the length of line in that period. At the same time a start was made in establishing other industries. The major effort of industrialisation began in 1934, with the adoption of the first five-year plan —completed in 1939. While often wasteful and inefficient, State-sponsored industry was probably the only form of development possible at the time without recourse to

foreign aid. The progress achieved stood Turkey in good stead in the critical years that were to follow.

The foreign policy of the Republic was for long one of strict non-involvement in foreign disputes, and the maintenance of friendly relations with as many Powers as possible. In 1935-36, however, Turkey co-operated loyally in sanctions against Italy, and thereafter the growing threat of German and, more especially Italian, aggression led to closer links with the West. In 1938 steps were taken to strengthen economic links between Turkey and the United Kingdom. A British credit of £16 million was granted to Turkey, and a number of contracts given to British firms by Turkey.

The establishment of the Republic also put an end to the prospect of Kurdish independence offered by the Treaty of Sèvres. The Kurds were opposed to Atatürk's secularist and nationalist policies and in 1925 rose up in revolt after the abolition of the Caliphate. They were ruthlessly crushed. A more nationalist uprising in 1930 and a further revolt against the repressive actions taken by the Government were also suppressed. The Kurdish provinces remained rigorously policed, garrisons were established in larger towns and Kurdish leaders were exiled. The Kurdish language was made illegal and the Government refused to recognize any aspect of the Kurds' separate ethnic identity, calling them "mountain Turks".

The death of Kemal Atatürk in November 1938 was a great shock to Turkey. Perhaps the best testimony to the solidity of his achievement is that his regime was able to survive that shock, and the stresses and strains of the war that followed shortly after.

He was succeeded as President by İsmet İnönü, who announced his intention of maintaining and carrying on the work of his predecessor. The new President was soon called upon to guide his country through a very difficult time. As early as May 12th, 1939, a joint Anglo-Turkish declaration was issued, stating that "the British and Turkish Governments, in the event of an act of aggression leading to war in the Mediterranean area, would co-operate effectively and lend each other all the aid and assistance in their power". This prepared the way for the formal Anglo-French-Turkish Treaty of Alliance signed October 19th, 1939. It had been hoped that this Treaty would be complemented by a parallel treaty with the U.S.S.R., but the equivocal attitude of the Soviet Government, followed by the Stalin-Hitler Agreement of August 1939, made this impossible, and the Turks proceeded with the Western alliance in the face of clearly expressed Soviet disapproval. They protected themselves, however, by Protocol II of the Treaty, stipulating that nothing in the Treaty should bind them to any action likely to involve them in war with the U.S.S.R.

TURKEY DURING THE SECOND WORLD WAR

The fall of France, the hostile attitude of the Soviet Government, and the extension of German power over most of Europe, led the Turkish Government to the conclusion that nothing would be gained by provoking an almost certain German conquest. While continuing to recognize the Alliance, therefore, they invoked Protocol II as a reason for remaining neutral, and in June 1941, when German expansion in the Balkans had brought the German armies within 100 miles of Istanbul, the Turks further protected themselves by signing a friendship and trade agreement with Germany, in which, however, they stipulated that Turkey would maintain her treaty obligations to Britain.

The German attack on the U.S.S.R., and the consequent entry of that country into the Grand Alliance, brought an important change to the situation, and the Western Powers increased their pressure on Turkey to enter the war. The main consideration holding Turkey back from active participation in the war was mistrust of the U.S.S.R., and the widespread feeling that Nazi conquest and Soviet "liberation" were equally to be feared. While stopping short of actual belligerency, however, the Turks, especially after 1942, entered into closer economic and military relations with the West and aided the Allied cause in a number of ways. In August 1944 they broke off diplomatic relations with Germany, and on February 23rd, 1945, declared war on Germany in order to comply with the formalities of entry to the United Nations Conference in San Francisco.

The war years subjected Turkey to severe economic strains. These, and the dangers of armed neutrality in a world at war, resulted in the imposition of martial law, of closer police surveillance, and of a generally more authoritarian form of government. And then, between 1945 and 1950, came a further series of changes, no less remarkable than the great reforms of Atatürk. When the Charter of the United Nations came up for ratification in the Turkish Parliament in 1945, a group of members, led by Celâl Bayar, Adnan Menderes, Fuad Köprülü and Refik Koraltan, tabled a motion suggesting a series of reforms in the law and the Constitution which would effectively ensure inside Turkey those liberties to which the Turkish Government was giving its theoretical approval in the Charter. The motion was rejected by the Government, and its sponsors forced to leave the party. In November 1945, however, under pressure of a by now active and informed public opinion, President İnönü announced the end of the single-party system, and in January 1946 the opposition leaders registered the new Democratic Party. Numerous other parties followed, including the National Party (formed July 1948 and reconstituted as the Republic National Party in 1954).

TURKEY UNDER THE DEMOCRATIC PARTY

In July 1946 new elections gave the Democrat opposition 70 out of 416 seats, and there can be little doubt that completely free elections would have given them many more. During the years that followed, the breach in the dictatorship grew ever wider, and a series of changes in both law and practice ensured the growth of democratic liberties. Freedom of the Press and of association were extended, martial law ended, and, on February 15th, 1950, a new electoral law was approved, guaranteeing free and fair elections. In May 1950 a new general election was held, in which the Democrats won an overwhelming victory. Celâl Bayar became President, and a new Cabinet was formed, with Adnan Menderes as Prime Minister and Fuad Köprülü as Foreign Minister. The new regime adopted a more liberal economic policy, involving the partial abandonment of *Étatisme* and the encouragement of private enterprise, both Turkish and foreign. For a while, the stability and progress of the republic seemed to be threatened by the growing activities of groups of religious fanatics, whose programme appeared to require little less than the abrogation of all the reforms achieved by the Turkish revolution. After the attempt on the life of the liberal journalist Ahmet Emin Yalman in November 1952, the government took more vigorous action against what were called the "forces of clericalism and reaction". Many arrests were made, and in the summer of 1953 the National Party, accused of complicity in reactionary plots, was for a time outlawed and legislation was passed prohibiting the exploitation of religion for political purposes. The relations between the two main parties, after a temporary improvement in the face of the common danger of reaction, deteriorated again in the course of 1953-54, though not to such an extent as to imperil national unity. On May 2nd,

1954, in Turkey's third general election since the war, the Democrats won a resounding victory.

Encouraged by this overwhelming reaffirmation of popular support, the Government proceeded to adopt a number of measures which were criticised by the opposition as undemocratic. Both opposition parties decided to boycott the provincial council and municipal elections (September and November 1955 respectively), in which therefore the Democrats were opposed only by the very small Peasant Party and by Independents. These were able to score some successes.

In view of the smallness and weakness of the opposition parties, and the immense parliamentary majority of the Democratic Party, it was inevitable that sooner or later splits would appear within it. In October 1955 a serious crisis culminated in the dismissal or resignation from the party of nineteen deputies. These were later joined by some others and formed a new party, the Freedom Party.

Meanwhile, in September 1955, severe anti-Greek outbreaks led to the imposition of martial law in Istanbul, Izmir and Ankara, the dismissal of several senior officers and several cabinet changes. A new Cabinet, the fourth since the Democrat victory in 1950, was presented to the assembly on December 9th.

Conflict between the Government and Opposition was sharpened by the decision taken to advance the date of the general elections by more than eight months, to October 27th, 1957. The three Opposition parties—Republicans, Freedom and National Parties—first intended to present a united front, but the electoral law was changed to make this impossible. They were therefore obliged to present separate lists in each constituency, and so, although the combined votes won by Opposition candidates were slightly more than 50 per cent of the total, the Democrats again emerged triumphant, though with a diminished majority.

In the new Assembly the themes of debate continued to centre on the economic condition of the country and what the Opposition considered inroads on liberty. A Bill was passed in December 1957 amending the rules of the Assembly, and laying down a new scale of penalties for their infraction. At the same time a proposal to channel all newspaper advertisements through a single organisation was interpreted as another device for ensuring Government control over the Press. There is no doubt that its running fight with the Press contributed much to the downfall of the Menderes regime. The new regime, while not immediately sweeping away the old bans, encouraged newspaper owners and editors to draw up a "code of self-control" which was worked out with the assistance of the International Press Institute.

FOREIGN AFFAIRS 1945-60

In foreign affairs, both the People's Party and the Democrat Governments followed a firm policy of unreserved identification with the West in the cold war. Since May 1947 the United States has extended economic and military aid to Turkey on an increasing scale, and in 1950 a first indication of both the seriousness and the effectiveness of Turkish policy was given with the despatch of Turkish troops to Korea, where they fought with distinction. In August 1949 Turkey became a member of the Council of Europe, and early in 1952 acceded to full membership of the North Atlantic Treaty Organisation, in which she began to play an increasingly important part. Thereafter other arrangements were made by which Turkey accepted a role in both Balkan and Middle Eastern defence. This culminated in November 1955 in Turkey's joining the Baghdad Pact, in which the country thereafter played a major role.

In January 1957 the President of the United States announced a new programme of economic and military assistance for those countries of the area which were willing to accept it. At a further meeting held in Ankara the Muslim states belonging to the Baghdad Pact expressed their approval of this "Eisenhower Doctrine". The United States, in March 1957, made known its decision to join the military committee of the Baghdad Pact, and later in March Turkey promised to co-operate with the United States against all subversive activities in the Middle East. It was announced that financial aid would be forthcoming from Washington for the economic projects previously discussed between the members of the Baghdad Pact.

From 1958 Turkey was actively involved in settling terms for the constitution of an independent Cyprus. These were eventually agreed between Turkey, Greece, the United Kingdom and the Greek and Turkish Cypriots. Cyprus achieved independence in August 1960.

Fidelity to NATO and CENTO remained the basis of Turkey's foreign policy during the late 1950s. By the beginning of 1960, however, Turkey's relationship towards the U.S.S.R. was becoming less frigid.

THE 1960 REVOLUTION

Economic difficulties continued to be one of the main preoccupations of the Turkish Government. The development plans envisaged since 1950 had been carried forward with financial aid from the United States and from such bodies as the World Bank. These policies had been accompanied by inflationary pressures, an unfavourable trade balance, decreased imports, a shortage of foreign exchange and, since the agricultural population was in receipt of subsidies from the Government, a higher demand for consumer goods which aggravated the prevalent inflation. Social and economic unease tended to reveal itself in a drift of people from the villages to the towns, the population of centres like Ankara, Istanbul, Izmir, Bursa and Adana being considerably increased during recent years.

The influences which led to the revolution had been long at work. Hostility between the Democrats in power and the People's Party in opposition grew steadily more marked, and was sharpened towards the end of 1959 by suspicions that the Democrats were planning to hold fresh elections in the near future ahead of time. It was feared that these would, if necessary, be rigged to keep the Democrats in power indefinitely.

In May, 1959, political tension between the two main parties had already broken into violence during a political tour of Anatolia conducted by the opposition leader İsmet İnönü. The Government banned all political meetings. Blows were struck in the Grand National Assembly, and the Opposition walked out.

Much the same pattern of events ushered in the final breakdown a year later. At the beginning of April, 1960, İsmet İnönü undertook another political tour of Anatolia. At one point troops were called on to block his progress. Three of the officers involved in this incident took the strong step of resigning. The Opposition tried, but failed, to force a debate in the Assembly. On their side the Democrats set up a commission of enquiry, composed entirely of their own supporters, to investigate "the destructive and illegal activities of the P.R.P." Again the Grand National Assembly was the scene of violence, and all political activity was suspended for three months.

At this point the students took a hand. The universities had for some time been a focus of anti-government feeling, and in consequence had, like the newspapers, found their liberties attacked. On April 28th students in Istanbul demonstrated against the Menderes Government. Troops were called on to fire, and martial law was declared in Ankara and Istanbul.

As administrator of martial law, the Turkish Army found itself, contrary to its traditions, involved in politics. A group of officers decided that their intervention must be complete if Turkey was to return to Kemalist principles. In the early hours of May 27th they struck. President Bayar, Mr. Menderes, most Democratic Deputies and a number of officials and senior officers were arrested. The Government was replaced by a Committee of National Union headed by General Gürsel, a much respected senior officer who had fought with Atatürk at Gallipoli.

The coup was immediately successful and almost bloodless, though Dr. Gedik, former Minister of the Interior, committed suicide after his arrest. The accusation against the Menderes regime was that it had broken the constitution and was moving towards dictatorship. The officers insisted that they were temporary custodians of authority and would hand over to the duly constituted civilians. A temporary constitution was quickly agreed, pending the drafting of a final new one. During this interval legislative power was vested in the Committee of National Unity, and executive power in a Council of Ministers, composed of civilians as well as soldiers. On August 25th, however, ten of the eighteen Ministers were dismissed, leaving only three civilians in the Government. General Gürsel was President of Republic, Prime Minister and Minister of Defence. The courts were declared independent. Commissions were set up to inquire into the alleged misdeeds of the Menderes regime.

Although the new regime did not fail to meet political opposition, particularly among the peasants and around Izmir, a stronghold of Mr. Menderes, the main problems facing it were economic. The former regime was shown to be heavily in debt in every field. Austerity measures, including restrictions on credit, had to be put into operation and an economic planning board was set up to work out a long-term investment plan with the aid of foreign experts.

THE COMMITTEE OF NATIONAL UNITY

The Committee of National Unity, which originally consisted of 37 members, was reduced to 23 on November 13th, 1960. The 14 officers dismissed represented a group led by Colonel Turkeş, who had been pressing for the army to retain its post-revolutionary powers and to introduce radical social reforms.

This purge completed, preparations for a return to political democracy continued. A new Assembly, to act as a temporary parliament, was convened at the beginning of January 1961. It consisted of the National Unity Committee of 23, acting jointly with a House of Representatives of 271 members, both elected and nominated. In this the People's Party predominated. At the same time party politics were again legalised and a number of new parties emerged. Some of them proved short-lived, but one, the Justice Party founded by General Ragip Gümüşpala, who had been Commander of the Third Army at the time of the *coup d'état*, was destined to become formidable by attracting the support of many former adherents of the Democratic Party, which had been declared illegal.

A special committee of the Assembly framed a new constitution which had some significant changes from the 1924 version. It provided for a court to determine the constitutionality of laws, for a two-chambered legislature, and it included a reference to "social justice" as one of the aims of the State.

THE YASSIADA TRIALS

These constitutional developments took place against the background of the trial of the accused members of the Menderes regime. The trial was held on the little island of Yassiada in the Bosphorus, where the accused had been confined after arrest, and lasted from October 1960 to August 1961. The sentence of the court was pronounced on September 15th. There were fifteen death sentences, twelve of which, including that on Mr. Bayar, were commuted to life imprisonment. Adnan Menderes, Fatin Zorlu, the former Foreign Minister, and Hasan Polatkan, the former Minister of Finance, were duly hanged.

The trial inevitably absorbed the attention of the country, and there were many reminders that sympathy for the former regime and its leaders was far from dead. The most serious setback for the authorities, however, appeared in the results of the referendum on the new constitution. This was approved by 6,348,191 votes against 3,934,370, and the large minority was taken as an indication of continuing loyalty to the Democrats.

It was to electioneering that the country, still stirred by the execution of Mr. Menderes and his colleagues, turned in the autumn. The campaign, perhaps because Yassiada was ruled out as a subject for discussion, proved unexpectedly quiet. On October 15th, 1961, the elections gave the People's Party 173 seats and the Justice Party 158 seats in the National Assembly, and 36 and 70 respectively in the Senate.

These figures were a blow to the hopes of the People's Party that they would achieve an overall working majority. A coalition became necessary. The election results were also further evidence of latent support for the Democrats.

THE NEW GOVERNMENT

On October 25th, 1961, Parliament opened and the transfer of power from military to civilians was made. The revolutionaries had kept their word and a new epoch began. The next day General Gürsel, the only candidate, was elected President. But forming a government proved a much harder process. On November 10th Mr. İsmet İnönü, leader of the People's Party, was asked to form a government, and after much hesitation and strong pressure from the Army, the Justice Party agreed to join forces with its rival. A Cabinet was formed with Mr. İnönü as Prime Minister, Mr. Akıf İyidoğan, of the Justice Party, as Deputy Prime Minister, and ten more Ministers from each of the two coalition parties.

The Government remained, as Mr. İnönü said, exposed to a double fire—from those who thought the Army did too much (i.e. that civil liberties were still circumscribed) and those who thought it did too little (i.e. that it did not crush all signs of counter-revolution). The resignation of Mr. İnönü at the end of May weakened the extremists in the Justice Party, who had wanted to grant an amnesty to former supporters of Mr. Menderes. They were now face to face with the Army, the original movers of the 1960 revolution, and many of them felt it wise to moderate their demands.

By the end of June Mr. İnönü had formed a new coalition government composed of twelve Ministers from the Republican People's Party, six from the New Turkey Party, four from the Republican Peasants' Nation Party, and one Independent Minister.

The new government's programme expressed attachment to the principles of Western democracy and to the NATO alliance. It covered almost every sphere of the national life, including education, taxation, employment, and the problems of a rapidly rising birth-rate and an adverse balance of trade.

POLITICAL UNREST

The political climate during 1963 remained unsettled. In February the leading radical of the original Committee of National Unity, Colonel Turkeş, who had been in unofficial exile abroad, returned with plans to set up a new political organization. More immediately threatening to the regime were the enthusiastic crowds which greeted the temporary release of the former President, Celal Bayar, from the prison in Kayseri where he had been since his sentence. The reception appeared as a direct challenge to the revolution and was countered by violent protests, in which students and members of the armed forces participated, denouncing Mr. Bayar and his supposed supporters in the Justice Party.

In the early hours of May 21st, 1963, Ankara was the scene of yet another abortive *coup d'état*. The instigator was Colonel Aydemir, who had been responsible for the attempted revolt in February 1962. On this occasion his resort to arms, in which some of the cadets at the Military Academy were involved, was quickly suppressed. Colonel Aydemir was executed in July, 1964. One result of the attempted coup was the imposition of martial law in Ankara, Istanbul and Izmir. Originally proclaimed for one month, martial law was repeatedly prolonged.

Although the Bayar incident and Aydemir coup produced divisions inside the ranks of the Justice Party, it showed considerable successes at the local elections in November, the first to be held since 1954. These successes were mainly at the expense of the New Turkey Party and the Republican Peasants' Nation Party, Mr. İnönü's two junior partners in the coalition. They resigned from the government, and after General Gümüşpala, the leader of the Justice Party, had tried and failed to form a Ministry, the President called again on Mr. İnönü, who on December 23rd formed a minority government drawn from members of his own Republican Party and some independents. It received a vote of confidence in the Assembly.

The first months of 1964 were overshadowed by an attempt on the life of Mr. İnönü in February, and by the situation in Cyprus, where the fate of the Turkish minority created strong feeling in the mainland. Mr. İnönü's critics claimed that he had "missed the bus" by failing to intervene on the island with force when the trouble started.

RAPPROCHEMENT WITH U.S.S.R.

This, and other diplomatic efforts towards a solution, failed, and public opinion grew more irritated, not only with Greece, but also with Turkey's western allies, in particular the U.S.A. and the United Kingdom, who were accused of being lukewarm in their support for Turkey's case. In August this irritation caused a violent explosion in Izmir, when rioters wrecked the U.S. and British pavilions at the trade fair. Mr. İnönü, though moving with characteristic caution, gave a warning that the alliance with the west, the basis of Turkey's foreign policy since the war, was in danger. To reinforce his warning came several steps designed to improve relations with the U.S.S.R. When the Cyprus problem first flared up again it had appeared that the Soviet Government took the side of Greece, and the Soviet trade pavilion had also been a target for the Izmir hooligans. But feelers were out in both Moscow and Ankara, and at the end of October 1964 Mr. Erkin visited the U.S.S.R.—the first Turkish Foreign Minister to make this journey for twenty-five years. Before leaving he invoked the memory of the early days of friendship between Atatürk and Lenin, and the same precedent was made much of by his hosts, who tactfully did not try to press Turkey into premature neutralism, as they had done in the past. On Cyprus, the U.S.S.R. appeared to have moved closer to the Turkish point of view

view, the communiqué which ended Mr. Erkin's talks speaking favourably of a solution "by peaceful means on the basis of respect for the territorial integrity of Cyprus, and for the legal rights of the two national communities".

Mr. Erkin's journey was followed up in January 1965 by the visit to Ankara of a Soviet parliamentary delegation. A trade pact between the two countries followed in March. In May, Mr. Gromyko, the Soviet Foreign Minister, paid a five-day visit to Turkey, and in August, Mr. Ürgüplü, the Prime Minister, paid a return visit to the U.S.S.R.

FALL OF MR. İNÖNÜ

For all this, Cyprus continued to give the Opposition ammunition with which to harass the İnönü government. At the Senate elections in June, 1964, the Justice Party won 31 out of the 51 seats contested, thus increasing its already large majority in this House. Its success was clouded by the death of the Party's leader, General Gümüşpala. In November Mr. Süleyman Demirel, a trained engineer and a former Director General of the state water organization, was elected leader in his place, though he was without a seat in Parliament. Mr. İnönü survived more than one narrow vote of confidence, but was finally brought down on February 13th, 1965, by an adverse vote (225 to 197) in the Assembly on the Budget—the first time that the life of a Turkish government had been ended in this way. There was some speculation whether the Army would allow the Opposition to form a government: the previous November General Sunay, Chief of Staff of the Armed Forces, had warned Justice Party Deputies against criticizing the army. After a short delay, however, a coalition government was formed, made up from the four parties which had been in Opposition—the Justice Party, the New Turkish Party, the Republican Peasant's Party, and the National Party. An independent senator, Mr. Suat Ürgüplü, who had spent much of his previous career in diplomacy, headed the team as Prime Minister.

Turkey suffered a bitter blow when, in December, the General Assembly of the United Nations passed a resolution urging all states to refrain from intervention in Cyprus. This was seen as directly aimed at Turkey's aid for the Turkish minority there. The Government in Ankara denounced the resolution as being "against right, law, and international agreements".

DEMİREL CABINET

At the general election of October 11th, 1965, the Justice Party under Mr. Süleyman Demirel won an overall majority. On introducing his Justice Party Government to the Assembly, Mr. Demirel declared that the most important task would be to withstand communism "by the realization of social justice and measures of social security". Emphasis was to be put on industrialization. In spite of its working majority the Demirel Government proved hardly more successful than its predecessors in getting things done. However, elections in June 1966 for a third of the seats in the senate showed that the Justice Party was not losing popularity.

To some extent this success was attributed to the innate conservatism of the Turkish peasantry, who may have been alarmed by Mr. İnönü's statement that the People's Party was left of centre. This position was not approved by all the party—some thought it went too far, others not far enough. A convention of the party in October showed a victory for the left-wingers. Mr. Bülent

Ecevit, Minister of Labour in 1961–65, was elected general secretary of the party, with the declared intention of turning it into a party of democratic socialism. Six months later 48 senators and congressmen, led by Mr. Turhan Feyzioğlu, a former Minister, resigned from the party on the grounds that it was falling into a "dangerous leftist adventure". This was denied by Mr. Ecevit and Mr. İnönü, who supported him. They claimed that, on the contrary, their progressive policies took the wind out of other left-wing parties' sails, and so was the best barrier against communism.

In May 1967 a majority of dissidents came together to form the new Reliance Party, which proclaimed its opposition to socialism and its belief in the "spiritual values of the Turkish nation". In June Mr. Ecevit forced a fresh election of the People's Party executive, and by securing the elimination of two left-wing representatives on it he was able to emphasise that his party remained left of centre rather than left wing.

The National Party also found itself in trouble when 8 of its 31 deputies resigned. But the real threat to all parties other than the governing Justice Party was the new electoral law. This, which was finally passed in March 1968 against the protests of a united opposition, did away with the so-called "national remainder system"—a change which threatened the electoral chances of all the smaller parties but was thought to be particularly aimed at the Turkish Workers' Party, which was accused by the Government of using communist tactics.

In March 1966 President Gursel was succeeded by Senator Cevdet Sunay.

FOREIGN POLICY 1966-1969

Turkey's relations with her allies in 1966 deteriorated. The Turkish press's campaign against U.S. bases in Turkey led to a riot in Adana in March 1966. Parallel with these manifestations against Turkey's formerly most stalwart ally went an effort by the Demirel Government to make its whole foreign policy more flexible. This flexibility was symbolized by many official visits, given and received, between Turkey on the one hand, and the U.K., Romania, Bulgaria, Egypt, Yugoslavia and Morocco. One outcome of the exchanges with Arab leaders was that at the time of the June war with Israel the Turkish Government expressed its sympathy with the Arab cause.

As usual the touchstone of Turkey's foreign relations continued to be Cyprus. In 1967 this perennial problem oscillated between near settlement and near war. The military regime brought to power in Athens by the coup of April 1967 seemed ready to negotiate, but no agreement was reached.

Later in the year the situation suddenly deteriorated as a result of attacks by Greek Cypriots on the Turkish enclaves on the island on November 15th. Two days later the National Assembly voted by 432 votes to 1 to authorize the Government to send troops to foreign countries—in other words, to fight in Cyprus. There were daily Turkish flights over the island and the prospects of war seemed real. As a result of strong intervention by U.S. and UN go-betweens the worst was avoided. On December 3rd the Greeks undertook to withdraw their troops from the island and the Turks to take the necessary measures to ease tension. By February 1968 the situation had been so far restored that direct efforts to agree on a negotiated settlement for Cyprus were once again under way.

MILITARY INTERVENTION

Süleyman Demirel's Justice Party Government was faced with the growing problem of political violence from early 1968 onward. Disorders in the universities, springing from non-political educational grievances and from clashes between political extremists of the right and the left, took an increasingly violent form. Students staged anti-American riots, and in June 1969 troops had to be called in to prevent extremists disrupting examinations. The fighting between right and left factions became more serious in 1970, firearms and petrol bombs being used, and a number of political murders taking place.

Parliamentary politics also became rather confused. Elections in October 1969 produced an enlarged majority for the Justice Party, but the party soon split, a number of Mr. Demirel's right-wing opponents forming the Democratic Party. Party strengths became almost impossible to calculate, as factions and alliances formed and dissolved, and on crucial votes the support of Government and the combined Opposition parties was almost equally balanced. A new party, the National Order Party, with right-wing policies and theocratic tendencies, was formed in January 1970 by Professor Necmettin Erbakan.

Throughout 1970 and the early part of 1971, political and social unrest continued, with outbreaks of violence among students, in the trade unions and by Kurdish separatist groups. Factional bickering prevented the Government from taking effective action and on March 12th, 1971, the Chief of the General Staff and the Army, Navy and Air Force Commanders delivered a memorandum to the President. They accused the Government of allowing the country to slip into anarchy and of deviating from Atatürk's principles. They threatened that, unless "a strong and credible government" were formed at once, the armed forces would take over the administration of the State. Later that day the Demirel Cabinet resigned.

MILITARY DOMINATION OF POLITICS

A new Government was formed by Dr. Nihat Erim, with the support of both the Justice Party and the Republican People's Party (RPP). Bülent Ecevit, the RPP secretary-general, resigned from office and refused to collaborate. Dr. Erim's programme promised sweeping reforms in taxation, land ownership, education, power and industry, but the Government's attention was first directed to the suppression of political violence. The military ultimatum was followed by further bombings, kidnappings and clashes between right and left-wing students and between students and police. On April 28th, 1971, martial law was proclaimed, initially for one month, in eleven provinces, including Ankara and Istanbul.

Newspapers were suppressed, strikes were banned and large numbers of left-wingers were arrested. The National Order Party was dissolved in May 1971, the Turkish Labour Party in July. The murder of the Israeli consul-general in Istanbul by the so-called Turkish People's Liberation Army provided the military authorities with an opportunity to round up nearly one thousand suspects in Istanbul alone, including many journalists, writers and intellectuals. In September 1971, Dr. Erim introduced a number of amendments to the Constitution, limiting individual civil rights and the autonomy of universities, radio and television, placing restrictions on the press and trade unions and giving the Government powers to legislate by decree. Dr. Erim's proposal to use the new powers to introduce sweeping social and economic reforms, supported by the armed forces, was opposed by the Justice Party. A Cabinet crisis in October and December 1971 led to the formation of a new coalition Cabinet, again headed by Dr. Erim, but his proposals for taking further executive powers were opposed by the four major parliamentary parties, and in April 1972 he resigned. A Cabinet formed by Suat Ürgüplü was rejected by President Sunay, and in May a Government drawn from the Justice Party, National Reliance Party and RPP, headed by Ferit Melen, was approved. There was a swing to the left within the RPP in May; the veteran party leader İsmet İnönü resigned after 34 years as chairman, and was replaced by Bülent Ecevit. Meanwhile, the terrorist activities of the Turkish People's Liberation Army continued, and martial law was prolonged at two-month intervals.

In July 1972, dissident RPP members, opposing the dominance of the left wing led by Mr. Ecevit, formed the Republican Party. In November the RPP withdrew its support from the Melen coalition Government, but its five ministers preferred to leave the party, and stay in the Cabinet. This caused further resignations from the RPP, including that of İsmet İnönü and 25 other deputies and senators. A number of these dissidents, together with the National Reliance Party and the Republican Party joined to form the Republican Reliance Party in February 1973. The RPP, without its right wing, began actively to oppose the Melen Government, which it considered to be dominated by the armed forces, and martial law, under which, it was alleged with increasing frequency, arbitrary arrest and torture were practised. In March 1973, for the first time, the RPP voted against the prolongation of martial law, following a heated debate in which the Minister of the Interior disclosed that in the two years of martial law 1,383 persons had been sentenced by military courts, 553 acquitted, and that 179 trials were then taking place and 2,991 were in preparation.

President Sunay's term of office expired in March 1973, and the Grand National Assembly began the process of electing a new president. General Gürler resigned his post as Chief of Staff in order to stand for election, his candidature receiving the strong support of the armed forces. He was opposed by members of the Justice and Democratic Parties, while the RPP decided to abstain from voting, as a protest against the military interference in the election and the censorship of electoral news in Ankara. Despite obvious military support for General Gürler, 14 ballots failed to produce a result, and eventually the Justice Party, RPP and Republican Reliance Party agreed on a compromise candidate, Senator Fahri Korotürk, former Commander-in-Chief of the Navy, who had not belonged to any political party. He was elected President on April 6th, 1973. The following day Mr. Melen resigned, and was succeeded as Prime Minister by Naim Talû, an independent senator, who formed a Cabinet with Justice Party and Republican Reliance Party participation.

The Talû Government, although considered to be merely a caretaker administration to last until the general election, due in October 1973, brought about a number of reforms, and during its term of office the armed forces gradually withdrew from political affairs. A land reform law, distributing some 8 million acres to 500,000 peasants, was passed in June 1973, and measures were taken to prevent foreign domination of the mining and petroleum industries. A strong element within the armed forces felt that the time had come to return to a strictly military role, and that martial law had achieved its objective of crushing extremism. General Sancar, who became Chief of Staff when General Gürler resigned to make his unsuccessful attempt to become President, was opposed to military intervention in politics, and retired 196 senior officers. Many close associates of General Gürler were transferred to politically insignificant posts, and the retirement of General Batur, the Air Force Commander, removed the last of the officers who had signed the armed forces' memorandum of March 1971. Martial law was gradually lifted from the affected provinces, and came to an end in September 1973.

RECENT FOREIGN POLICY

The traditional hostility between Turkey and Greece revived following the Greek announcement in February 1974 that oil had been found in Greek territorial waters in the Aegean. This led to a dispute over the extent of national jurisdiction over the continental shelf and territorial waters, with both sides making warlike moves in Thrace and the Aegean area. Turkey began a hydrographical survey of the continental shelf in this area, claiming oil exploration rights in the eastern Aegean. The Aegean issue contributed to making a preoccupation with the possibility of a confrontation with Greece rather than the U.S.S.R. the dominating issue of Turkish foreign policy during the late 1970s. The potentially tense situation in the Aegean was overshadowed by the coup in Cyprus in July.

This coup was carried out by the Cypriot National Guard, led by officers from Greece, apparently with the support of the Greek military regime. Declaring its intention of protecting the Turkish community in Cyprus and preventing the union of Cyprus with mainland Greece, the Turkish Government proclaimed a right to intervene as a guarantor state under the Zürich agreement of 1959. On July 20th Turkish troops landed in Cyprus, and rapidly won control of the area around Kyrenia on the northern coast. The Turkish intervention in Cyprus was followed by negotiations in Geneva between Turkey, Greece and the United Kingdom. Turkey pressed for the creation of an independent federal Cypriot state, with population movements to give the Turkish community their own sector in the north. The intransigence of both Greeks and Turks, and Greece's rejection of a possible cantonal solution put forward by Turkey, led to a further successful advance by the Turkish forces in Cyprus. When a second ceasefire was called on August 16th, Turkey controlled about one-third of the total area of Cyprus.

The sector under Turkish control, all of Cyprus north of a line running from Morphou through Nicosia to Famagusta, contained more than half the livestock, citrus plantations and mineral reserves of Cyprus, with access to two major seaports. The flight of Greek Cypriot refugees from the north left the Turks a free hand to take over the administration and economy, and establish an effective partition of the island. Mr. Ecevit claimed that the Turkish military success had laid the foundation of a federal state with two autonomous administrations, allowing the Turkish Cypriot community to concentrate in the conquered area and establish their own government. On February 13th, 1975, the Turkish Cypriots unilaterally declared a "Turkish Federated State" in northern Cyprus and continued pressing for the establishment of a bi-regional federal state system in Cyprus. The State was described by the Turkish Cypriot leader, Rauf Denktaş, as the federal wing of the Republic of Cyprus, although no such Federal Republic yet existed. Greek and Turkish Foreign Ministers held talks in Rome in May 1975 on outstanding disputes between the two countries, with the future of Cyprus among the main topics. The Greek-Turkish Aegean dispute was also discussed, including the issue of who held the rights over oil exploration in the area, the equitable division of the Aegean continental shelf and the question of air space control in the area. The dispute was submitted to the International Court of Justice. In April 1978 Turkey refused to recognize the jurisdiction of the Court on this question, preferring to try to negotiate a political settlement, and in October the Court ruled that it was not competent to try the issue.

The U.S. imposed an embargo on military aid and the supply of arms to Turkey in February 1975 on the grounds that American military equipment had been used in the Turkish invasion of Cyprus in July 1974 and that Turkey had failed to make substantial progress towards resolving the Cyprus crisis. In July Turkey implemented countermeasures, including the take-over of U.S. bases in Turkey. After lengthy negotiations a new bilateral defence agreement was reached between the two countries in March 1976, but the agreement was not ratified in 1976 or 1977 due to the strength of the Greek lobby in the U.S. Congress.

In January 1978, at the beginning of his term of office, Bülent Ecevit stated that his foreign policy would be aimed at relaxation rather than tension and the exploration at the highest level of possible compromises between Greece and Turkey. A summit meeting took place at Montreux, in Switzerland, on March 9th and the progress made in personal relations between Ecevit and the Greek Prime Minister, Constantine Karamanlis, contributed to a general lessening of tension in the Aegean.

In response to a U.S. statement about the linkage of the arms embargo relaxation and U.S. arms aid, Ecevit turned to the U.S.S.R. to demonstrate that Turkey had alternatives for her national defence. In April 1978 a trade pact was agreed between the two countries and in June a friendship document was signed, which Ecevit claimed not to be in conflict with Turkey's NATO responsibilities. In response to this *rapprochement* with the U.S.S.R., the U.S. Congress lifted the arms embargo in October and four key U.S. bases in Turkey were reopened. Finally, after lengthy negotiations, a five-year defence and economic co-operation agreement was signed on March 29th, 1980. In return for economic aid to help Turkey modernize her army and fulfil her NATO obligations, the U.S. will obtain access to over twenty-five military establishments, allowing expanded surveillance of the U.S.S.R. The eagerness of the U.S. to come to an agreement grew after the Soviet invasion of Afghanistan in December 1979, which increased Turkey's strategic importance.

Some progress was achieved in the Greek-Turkish Aegean dispute in February 1980. On February 22nd Turkey revoked Notam 714 which claimed Turkish control of all air traffic over the Eastern half of the Aegean. In response, Greece revoked its civil aviation notice of 1974 which declared the Aegean unsafe and banned all flights except its own. However, the dispute flared up again in June when Turkey held its annual NATO Sea Wolf air and naval manoeuvres in the Aegean, with Greece demanding flight plans for areas which Turkey does not regard as being within Greek airspace. On July 14th Turkish Airlines resumed flights to Athens from Istanbul and Ankara.

Inter-communal talks on Cyprus, sponsored by the UN, were resumed in June 1979 but were adjourned after a week with no agreement reached. Since then little progress has been made, in spite of efforts to resume talks by the UN, and the issues appeared as intractable as ever. Turkey continued to keep an estimated 16,000 troops in Cyprus.

ECEVİT GOVERNMENT

General elections for the National Assembly and for 52 Senate seats were held on October 14th, 1973. In the National Assembly the RPP, with 185 seats, replaced the Justice Party as the largest party, but failed to win an overall majority. The RPP was believed to have won many votes from former supporters of the banned Turkish Labour Party, while the Justice Party lost support to the Democratic Party and a new organization, the

National Salvation Party (NSP). The latter, led by Professor Necmettin Erbakan, was founded in 1972 to replace his banned National Order Party, and shared its traditionalist, Islamic policies, and became the third largest party in the new National Assembly. Prime Minister Talû resigned, but then continued in office for a further three months while negotiations on the formation of a coalition government dragged on. Despite this parliamentary crisis, the armed forces remained aloof from politics. Eventually, on January 25th, 1974, a Government was formed by the RPP and NSP, with Bülent Ecevit as Prime Minister and Necmettin Erbakan as his Deputy. The Cabinet had 18 RPP members and 7 from the NSP.

The new Government, an apparently unlikely coalition of the left-of-centre RPP and the reactionary NSP, proclaimed its reforming intentions, but made concessions to the demands of its Muslim supporters which tended to deviate from Atatürk's strictly secular principles. In March 1974, Turkey was for the first time represented at an Islamic Summit Conference. The appointment of an NSP deputy as Minister of the Interior brought about a number of petty manifestations of Islamic puritanism, but the main lines of the Ecevit Government's policy seemed to be of a reforming, liberal nature, intended to remove the more excessive manifestations of the police state created during the period of military intervention. In May 1972, to mark the fiftieth anniversary of the founding of the republic, the Government amnestied 50,000 prisoners.

The land reform passed by the Talû administration came into operation in a pilot project in Urfa province, and in July the ban on opium production introduced under American pressure in 1972 was rescinded, a move which, together with the successful handling of the Cyprus question, increased Mr. Ecevit's popularity. The differences between the NSP and the RPP had been submerged during the Cyprus crisis, but once more became apparent in September. On September 16th, 1974, Mr. Ecevit announced that he had decided to resign, as the coalition was no longer viable, and to seek a stronger mandate in new elections. New elections, however, were not held immediately and President Korutürk sought to find a coalition government.

Following the resignation of the Cabinet of Bülent Ecevit on September 18th, 1974, Turkey remained for over six months without a government having parliamentary approval. Professor Sadi Irmak attempted unsuccessfully to form an interim coalition in November to prepare for new elections in 1975, but remained in office in a caretaker capacity whilst efforts were made to form a new government. Internal unrest increased during the lengthy government crisis, with serious clashes between opposing political factions and between students.

DEMİREL RETURNS TO POWER

In March 1975 Mr. Süleyman Demirel returned to power, leading a right-wing coalition, the Nationalist Front, consisting of four parties: Mr. Demirel's Justice Party (the biggest), the National Salvation Party (NSP), the Republican Reliance Party (CGP) and the neo-fascist National Action Party (NAP) founded by Colonel Alparslan Türkeş, who became a Deputy Prime Minister. Of the cabinet of 30 the Justice Party occupied 16 of the seats, the NSP eight, the CGP four, and the NAP two. The coalition did not have an overall majority in the National Assembly, but support from other parties was virtually assured. However, the precarious nature of this coalition meant that the Government had to avoid taking radical measures which would upset the co-operation between the four parties. This prevented Mr. Demirel's cabinet from tackling the pressing problems of a deteriorating economy and increasing political violence, for Erbakan refused to countenance the austerity measures demanded by the IMF while Türkeş stood in the way of a crackdown on political violence, most of which the "Grey Wolves" of the NAP were thought to have instigated. The weakness of the coalition also hampered progress towards a settlement of the Cyprus question, with Mr. Demirel having to make concessions to the militant views of the extreme right wing represented by Necmettin Erbakan's National Salvation Party. Even though Mr. Demirel's position in relation to his coalition partners was strengthened by the results of the elections to the Senate held in October 1976, when the Justice Party gained 27 of the 54 seats contested, the opposition leader, Bülent Ecevit, also increased his representation in the Upper House and the smaller parties of the coalition continued to exert pressure disproportionate to their actual strength. Between 1974 and 1977 the fortunes of the NSP fell drastically and their representation in the National Assembly was reduced from 48 to 24. Erbakan became increasingly discredited, although his deputy and chief rival, Korbut Ozal, grew in influence. At the same time the star of the NAP rose rapidly. It combines anti-Communism, Islamic values and a desire for centrally-directed free enterprise with a nationalism that would dispense with democracy. During Demirel's administration, the NAP was able to build up a system of militant cadres by placing its supporters in the police and civil service.

In spite of its difficulties, the Demirel Government continued in power in 1976 and 1977 by suspending all action over controversial issues, such as the economy, Cyprus and Greece and relations with the EEC and NATO, pending the general election scheduled for October 1977. Increasing political violence throughout Turkey and especially in the universities, between left- and right-wing groups, persuaded the authorities to bring forward the general elections to June. The political inactivity was matched by economic paralysis as it became clear that the economy was overloaded with short-term debt and banks struggled to pay foreign currency bills of payment.

Amid this financial uncertainty the election of June 1977 failed to produce the hoped-for decisive majority. While the Republican People's Party (RPP) increased its National Assembly seats to 213 out of 450, the Justice Party also increased its share from 149 to 189 seats. Bülent Ecevit, the leader of the RPP, formed a Council of Ministers but failed to agree a coalition with the smaller parties, and a week later was defeated in a vote of confidence in the Grand National Assembly. Süleyman Demirel, the leader of the Justice Party, was then invited to form a government and on August 1st a coalition came to power which gave key ministerial posts to members of Necmettin Erbakan's right-wing National Salvation Party and the National Action Party. As a result there was penetration of the university and college administrations by extreme right-wing factions and a consequent flare-up of violence on campuses. By mid-December a third of the universities were shut and 250 people had died in political violence.

The National Salvation Party contributed to the financial crisis by blocking attempts to follow IMF prescriptions for the economy, insisting on the maintenance of a 5.5 per cent growth rate and refusing to implement monetarist curbs to reduce inflation. Failure to agree on economic remedies led to the withdrawal of an IMF team on December 19th, 1977, without agreeing the necessary restructuring for the foreign debt position.

Frustration at the coalition's powerlessness led to the progressive diminution of the Justice Party's support in the Assembly between October and December 1977 as members resigned. By December 27th the coalition could muster only 214 votes and Bülent Ecevit was preparing a new coalition. Following a vote of "no confidence" in the Grand National Assembly, the Demirel government resigned on December 31st and formed a caretaker administration. On January 2nd, 1978, Bülent Ecevit formed a new government.

ECEVIT RETURNS TO POWER

After the chaos of Demirel's administration, the appointment of Ecevit as Prime Minister was greeted with great popular enthusiasm and high hopes were entertained of his promise to deal with the economic crisis and the political violence. In the economic field there was an urgent need to restore confidence by rescheduling Turkish debts, devaluing the lira and obtaining foreign finance for desperately needed arms modernization for NATO commitments. By appointing a former general, Irfan Özaydinli, to the Interior Ministry and a former police chief and Interior Minister, Necdet Uğur, to the Education Ministry, Ecevit hoped to curb the political violence that had racked the universities. Ecevit's popular support, however, was not reflected in the National Assembly. His majority rested on the defectors from the Justice Party, to 10 of whom he gave places in his Cabinet, while the number of deputies who had "crossed the floor" had resulted in a pool of about 20 independents with fickle allegiances. Radical reforms were urged on Ecevit (particularly in retrospect) but the insecure parliamentary majority, the country's economic weakness and the unwanted reputation of the RPP in the conservative rural areas as a radical party enjoined on him the necessity for caution. He began a painstaking, relentless purge of right-wing elements in the public administration in response to the cramming of their ministries by Demirel, Erbakan and Türkeş in 1975–77. He adopted an economic stabilization programme, signed a stand-by arrangement with the IMF (providing for a total of U.S. $450 million over two years) and began work on restructuring the severe short-term debt burden. He was, however, unable to secure the huge amounts of international financial assistance necessary to make the stabilization programme work and few of the targets aimed at were reached. Inflation continued at about 60–70 per cent, unemployment reached 20 per cent and, for lack of raw materials, industry was working half time. Nevertheless, Ecevit was unwilling to take further austerity measures demanded by the IMF as a condition for further aid. More seriously still, the extent of political violence went from bad to worse. Although the universities returned to normal, elsewhere more and more people were killed in acts of terrorism. Both the police force and the internal security forces (MIT) were riven by factions of left and right which made them unable to intervene. Here, too, the process of purging extremists was begun and in September Ecevit replaced the chief of security but, while the civilian tools of authority remained weak and unreformed, the maintenance of law and order depended on the armed forces and Ecevit was forced to ask the *gendarmerie* to undertake policing duties in urban areas. By December 1978 over 800 people had been killed, particularly in the eastern provinces. These new areas of violence reflected a change of tactics by the NAP, which during 1978 campaigned in Central and Eastern Anatolia, where the traditional elements of society have been least affected by modernization and which are most threatened by its arrival. Türkeş' appeal to nationalism gained him supporters, particularly in areas where Turks lived with other ethnic groups, notably the Kurds. The violence culminated in December at the south-eastern town of Karamanmaraş in the most serious outbreak of ethnic fighting since the 1920s. There the historic enmity between the orthodox Sunni majority and

the Alevi (Shi'a) minority had been exacerbated by the activities of right- and left-wing agitators. On December 21st the funeral of two members of the left-wing teachers' association, murdered the day before, was turned into a large-scale demonstration by the Alevis. The mourners were fired on by Sunni supporters of Turkeş and indiscriminate rioting erupted. After three days, over 100 people had been killed, over 1,000 injured and large parts of the Alevi quarters reduced to ruins. The MIT had failed to alert the Government to the incidents leading up to the massacre and order was not restored until the intervention of the army on the 24th.

MARTIAL LAW

The violence led to the imposition of martial law on December 26th, 1978. Although he had long been urged to take this step by Demirel, Ecevit had refused both in view of Turkey's previous experiences of martial law and to ensure the continuation of parliamentary democracy. It was imposed for two months (renewed subsequently at two-monthly intervals) in 13 provinces, all, excepting Istanbul and Ankara, in the east, although the mainly Kurdish areas of the south-east were excluded to prevent friction. Ecevit announced it was to be "martial law with a human face" and instituted a co-ordination committee to implement it comprising himself, Gen. Kenan Evren, the Chief of the General Staff, and Lt.-Gen. Sahap Yardimoğlu, the chief martial law administrator. Special military courts were established to hear cases of those arrested for martial law violations. However, even these new measures proved insufficient to curb the now endemic violence.

In April 1979 a crisis developed on the political front when six ministers, members of the group of defectors from the Justice Party, issued a public memorandum criticizing Ecevit for taking insufficient account of their views and demanding tougher measures to combat political violence, particularly of the left-wing variety, and Kurdish separatism. They also demanded a redirection of economic policies to allow more western investment and greater freedom for private enterprise. The gulf between these views and those of Ecevit's left-wing supporters in the RPP became more and more pronounced and the impossibility of reconciling the left- and right-wing elements in the coalition became clear. In response to the growth of Kurdish separatism, and alarmed by Kurdish violence in Iran, Ecevit agreed to extend martial law into six more provinces, all in the Kurdish south-east. Three RPP deputies promptly resigned, reducing the party's minority representation in the National Assembly to 211 out of 450.

As violence continued throughout the country, the authorities were forced to take the drastic measure of imposing an all-day curfew in Istanbul and Ankara on May Day to prevent riots at the traditional parades. A march planned by the more radical of the union confederations, DISK, was banned and the army ordered the arrest of its whole leadership, a severe blow to Ecevit's reputation as a champion of workers' rights and an indication of the army's increasing involvement in politics. At the General Convention of the RPP, Ecevit was re-elected Chairman unopposed, in spite of fierce criticism from right and left. By June 1979, however, the crisis in the National Assembly was serious. During the next few months Ecevit's majority gradually dwindled after a series of resignations by RPP deputies, and in the October by-elections the Justice Party achieved substantial gains. Ecevit's government resigned on October 16th. The main reason for the voters' turning against him was his failure to overcome terrorism.

On October 24th, 1979, Demirel formed a new government with the backing of the rightist NAP and the NSP, giving the government a majority of four. His cabinet was entirely made up of moderate and uncontroversial Justice Party deputies in an effort to avoid antagonizing the left-wing faction in the National Assembly and jeopardizing his slender majority. Demirel promised a tough policy on terrorism and proposed new legislation to speed up court procedure and allow wider powers for regional governors in dealing with terrorist incidents. However, the elections triggered off a wave of left-wing protest and the proposed measures gained little headway due to obstruction by the RPP, who objected to what they saw as Fascist measures.

With no improvement in the level of violence by the beginning of 1980, the military were again forced to intervene. On January 2nd the Turkish generals issued a public warning to all political parties, criticizing them for arguing and urging them to reach a consensus of opinion on anti-terrorist measures. Under threat of greater military intervention, the National Assembly immediately began to debate the government package of anti-terrorist legislation. In spite of this threat, the bill was defeated on January 15th, when the NSP voted against it, and sectarian and political killings continued at an average of ten per day. A state factory in Izmir was the scene of fighting between left-wing strikers and the army for several weeks, leading to the imposition of martial law in Izmir and Hatay on February 20th. Twenty provinces were now under martial law. At this time a number of left-wing papers were shut down, including *Politika*, and in May the Workers' Party of Turkey was dissolved by the Constitutional Court. Once again May Day processions were banned and violence broke out.

The instability of the Government was illustrated by the Grand National Assembly's inability to choose a new President after Korutürk's term expired in April 1980. This again provoked criticism from Gen. Kenan Evren, Chief of the General Staff. Neither the right nor the left was prepared to compromise on the choice of candidate and after much indecision, Ihsan Sabri Çağlayangil took office as acting President. In June the RPP tabled a censure motion intended to bring down the Government before the summer recess. It accused Demirel of allowing prices to rise and violence to continue. However, the 22 NSP deputies voted against the motion, in spite of their opposition to Demirel's pro-western pro-NATO stance, and the Government survived the motion by one vote. By August political violence had reached almost civil war proportions. Although martial law continued to be extended every two months in 20 out of the 67 provinces, clashes between right and left had caused some 2,000 deaths since the beginning of the year. Meanwhile, inflation and foreign debts continued to escalate, food and power shortages and unemployment were widespread and the political bickering continued. At the beginning of September Demirel attempted to bring forward the elections (scheduled for June 1981), which he hoped would give his party a majority and the power to deal with the country's crisis. However, this move was crushed by the opposition and the Government remained paralysed, unable to make important decisions or take vital measures.

MILITARY COUP

On September 11th, 1980, the armed forces, led by Gen. Evren, seized power in a bloodless coup, the third in 20 years. There appeared to be three main reasons for their intervention: the failure of the Government to deal with the country's political and economic chaos, the ineffectiveness of the police force, and, more immediately, the sudden resurgence of Islamic fundamentalism. This latter cause for alarm was triggered off by the rally at Konya in August, when Necmettin Erbakan and the NSP staged a march calling for restoration of the *Sheriat*, Islamic Holy Law. The leaders of the coup formed a five-man National Security Council (NSC), sworn in on September 18th. The Chairman of the NSC, Gen. Evren, became Head of State. Martial law was extended to the whole country and the Grand National Assembly was dissolved. On September 21st the NSC appointed a mainly civilian Council of Ministers, with the retired naval commander, Bülent Ulusu, as Prime Minister and Turgut Özal as Deputy Prime Minister for Economic Affairs. The new Government's chief aims were "to eradicate all seeds of terrorism" and to reduce the power of political extremists, to uphold Kemalist principles, to honour all foreign debts and existing agreements, and to return the country to democratic rule after the establishment of law and order. The Generals immediately set about putting their aims into practice. Former political leaders were detained, all suspected terrorists and political extremists were rounded up, all political activity was banned and trade union activities restricted. At the same time a tough austerity programme was introduced by Turgut Özal, Deputy Prime Minister for Economic Affairs. In October the NSC drew up a seven-point provisional constitution legitimizing the Generals' rule and providing them with unlimited powers for an indefinite period. In January 1981 the military junta announced its decision to set up a constituent assembly between August 30th and October 29th, 1981, as the first stage in the promised return to parliamentary rule.

Since the coup of September 1980, the military leaders have been systematically carrying out their campaign to eradicate all possible sources of political violence. By February 1981 the new Government claimed to have eliminated the main left-wing terrorist groups, including the powerful guerrilla organization *Dev Yol*. By May 1982, according to varying reports, between 43,000 and 100,000 suspected left- and right-wing activitists had been detained. The authorities are also taking a hard line against Kurdish nationalist organizations, as they believe that these are supported by forces in the Eastern bloc. By May 1982 there had been a number of mass trials of Kurdish activists, especially members of the PKK, the left-wing separatist Kurdish Workers' Party. In December 1980 proceedings began against 2,000 members of the left-wing Confederation of Revolutionary Trade Unions (DISK), and the trial was still going on in April 1982, causing concern in both the ICFTU and the ILO. In November 1981 a law was passed depriving the universities of their traditional administrative autonomy, and banning academics and students from political parties. In February 1982 there were 44 arrests in the biggest crackdown on left-wing intellectuals since the coup. Censorship of the press has not been officially imposed but extremist publications have been banned and the press and other media are under strict self-censorship. A number of journalists, including editors of some of the leading dailies, have been detained.

On October 15th, 1981, a Consultative Assembly was formed to draft a new constitution and to prepare the way for a return to parliamentary rule. It consists of the five members of the NSC and 160 others, 40 of whom are appointed directly by the NSC, while the remaining 120 are chosen by the NSC from candidates put forward by the governors of the 67 provinces. All former politicians are excluded and will not be allowed to stand at the next election. On October 16th all political parties were disbanded and their assets confiscated. The Constituent Assembly began work on October 23rd and the new constitution is due to be submitted to referendum in November 1982. This is expected to ban communism, fascism and religious theocracy. Elections are to be held by the spring of 1984.

The military coup in September 1980 was not condemned by Western European governments, and there is no doubt that the military leaders have had considerable success since the coup in curbing political violence and restoring law and order. However, concern has been growing in Western Europe about alleged torture in Turkey's prisons. The military rulers insist that torture is not condoned by the Government, but it was admitted in March 1982 that, since the military takeover, at least 15 terrorist suspects had died in jail after being tortured. Amnesty International's estimate in January was more than 60.

FOREIGN AFFAIRS

Turkey is recognized as a key member of NATO, both on account of its strategic position in Europe and because it is the only NATO member of the Islamic Conference. Good relations with the West remain a high priority in Turkey's foreign policy and the military leaders have repeatedly expressed their intention to apply for full membership of the EEC as soon as democracy is restored. However, relations with the West have been strained over Turkey's delay in returning to democratic rule. In December 1981 the NATO countries were divided over support

for the Turkish Government: while the U.S.A. promised to speed up aid to Turkey, EEC countries were considering the suspension of aid. In January 1982, the European Parliament voted to suspend relations with Turkey, while at the same time the Council of Europe condemned military rule, both in protest against human rights abuses and other repressive measures, the imprisonment of the former Prime Minister, Bülent Ecevit, and the delay in returning to democratic rule. In March the EEC decided to "freeze" aid to Turkey, but in May EEC countries were divided on whether to maintain the freeze.

Relations between Turkey and Greece continue to be strained, although in April 1982 the two countries agreed to relax tension. Areas of dispute include Cyprus and oil-drilling rights in, and the airspace over, the Aegean. Other aspects of Turkey's foreign policy include neutrality in the Iran/Iraq war and commitment to full rights for the Palestinians. The repeated assassinations of Turkish diplomats by Armenian terrorists have soured Turkey's relations with France and Greece in particular.

ECONOMIC SURVEY

Turkey is about 1,449 km. long and some 483 km. wide, covering an area of 779,452 sq. kilometres. The October 1975 census recorded a population of 40,347,719, and that of October 1980 showed the population to be 44,736,957, excluding over 1 million Turks working abroad, mostly in the Federal Republic of Germany. This implies an average annual growth rate between 1975 and 1980 of 2.28 per cent, compared with 2.4 per cent between 1970 and 1975. About 56 per cent of the population live in rural areas. Turkey's largest cities are the former capital of Istanbul (population 2,772,708 in 1980), the capital, Ankara (1,877,755), and the port of Izmir (757,854).

The country possesses great natural advantages: the land yields good grain and a wide variety of fruit and other products; it is rich in minerals; and it has a number of natural ports. The climate is varied and, on the whole, favourable, but communications are hindered by the mountain ranges that ring the Anatolian plateau to the north, east and south.

Gross National Product (G.N.P.) grew by an average of 7 per cent annually between 1970 and 1978. However, the rate slowed to 4 per cent in 1977 and to 3.1 per cent in 1978, when Turkey moved into a severe economic crisis.

In 1979 G.N.P. grew by only 0.7 per cent and in 1980 declined by 1.1 per cent. Growth was resumed in 1981, when G.N.P. rose by 4.4 per cent to TL 6,564,284 million. Per capita national income in 1981 was U.S. $1,099.

AGRICULTURE

Turkey relies substantially on agriculture, although its overall role is declining. More than half the labour force work on the land, but the agricultural sector in 1981 provided only 47.2 per cent of exports, whereas in 1979 it had provided 59.4 per cent. It accounts for 23.6 per cent of G.D.P. Nearby 25 million hectares, or about a third of total land

area, are under cultivation. Most of the farms are small and the average size of a family farm is only 19 acres (7.7 hectares). The country is basically self-sufficient in foodstuffs. Principal agricultural exports are cotton, tobacco, wheat, fruit and nuts. Other important crops are barley, sunflower and other oilseeds, maize, sugarbeet, potatoes, tea and olives.

During the period 1963–70, the agricultural growth rate was only 2.5 per cent per annum, mainly because of the insufficient emphasis placed on agriculture in both the First and Second Plans. However, with the introduction of land reforms and the improved utilization of land, machinery and farmer education resources, agricultural production in 1971 increased by some 30 per cent. In 1975 real growth in agriculture was 10.9 per cent, due mainly to a good wheat harvest, falling to 7.6 per cent in 1976 and to little more than 1 per cent in 1977. Agriculture grew by 2.8 per cent in 1978, by 1.8 per cent in 1979, by 3.5 per cent in 1980 and by just 0.2 per cent in 1981.

The Government is concerned to increase agricultural productivity, but tight financial policies mean that only limited project finance is available. In 1981 a mere TL 112,497 million, out of total project spending of TL 1,279,035 million, went on agriculture. However, investment in the agricultural and agro-industrial sector, both private and foreign, is increasing.

The Land and Agrarian Reform Bill of 1973 aimed at distributing 8 million acres to 500,000 peasants over a 15-year period. Many Turkish peasants own very little land and about one-tenth of all farming families have no land at all. The area covered by the Bill includes 3.5 million acres of state-owned arable land, 2.5 million acres of uncultivated state-owned land and 2 million acres of private land, which will be nationalized. A pilot project was started in Urfa province but the whole programme has been delayed, due to political uncertainty.

About half the cultivated area is devoted to cereals, the most important of which is wheat. The principal wheat-growing area is the central Anatolian plateau, but the uncertain climate causes wide fluctuations in production. Barley, rye and oats are other important crops grown on the central plateau. Maize is grown along the Black Sea coastal regions, and leguminous crops in the Izmir hinterland. Rice, normally sufficient for domestic needs, is grown in various parts of the country. Since 1977 the annual wheat harvest has stayed above the high level of 16 million tons, due to good weather and improved cultivation methods; in 1979 it reached 17.6 million tons.

Cotton has traditionally been Turkey's main export earner, growing mainly in the Izmir region and in the district round Adana, in southern Turkey. Production of cotton lint rose from under 200,000 metric tons in 1960 to a peak of 598,387 tons in 1974. Estimated output in 1980 was 483,000 tons and the forecast for 1981 is about 450,000 tons. In the 1979/80 season, 55,000 tons were exported for $97 million, compared with 49,000 tons (for $74 million) in the previous year.

Turkey produces a particularly fine type of tobacco. The three principal producing regions are the Aegean district, the Black Sea coast, and the Marmara-Thrace region. The bulk of the crop is produced in the Aegean region, where the tobacco is notable for its light golden colour and mild taste. The finest tobacco is grown on the Black Sea coast, around Samsun. Although a traditional Turkish export, its relative position as an export has been declining in recent years. Most of the tobacco exports go to buyers in the U.S.A. and East European countries. The size of the crop fluctuates considerably: in 1976 it reached a record level of 324,000 metric tons; in 1980 it was estimated at 240,000 tons. Tobacco exports were worth $395 million in 1981.

The coastal area of the Aegean, with mild winters and hot, dry summers produces the grape, fig and the olive. Dried fig exports in 1980 totalled 31,700 metric tons, earning $41.1 million. Exports of fig pulp earned a further $5 million. France is the main customer for figs. The outstanding product, however, is the sultana type of raisin, which is grown also in California and elsewhere. Turkey normally ranks second in the world as a sultana producer, but in good years becomes the largest producer in the world. The 1976 sultana harvest was only 85,000 metric tons, but improved in 1977 to an estimated 121,000 tons.

The Black Sea area, notably around the Giresun and Trabzon, produces the greatest quantity of hazel-nuts (filberts) of any region in the world; the harvest was 300,000 tons in 1979 but only 245,000 tons in 1980. Substantial amounts of walnuts and almonds are also grown.

Tea is grown at the eastern end of the Black Sea, around Rize, and in other areas. Production from State tea plantations is around 400,000–500,000 metric tons of fresh leaves per annum.

Turkey is also an important producer of oilseeds, the principal varieties grown being sunflower, cotton, sesame and linseed. It also produces olive oil, some of

which is exported. Production fluctuates, partly because of the two-year flowering cycle of the trees; it was estimated at 178,000 metric tons in 1977/78 and fell to a low of 23,000 tons in 1978/79.

Turkey was until 1972 one of the seven countries with the right to export opium under the UN Commission on Narcotic Drugs. Much opium was, however, exported illegally, particularly to the U.S.A. and Iran; partly as a result of pressure from the U.S. Government, the Turkish Government made opium cultivation illegal in 1972, but the ban was lifted in July 1974 and opium is grown in certain provinces under strict controls. Opium gum is no longer tapped from the living plant. The poppy pods (opium straw) are sold to the government, which processes them into concentrate for export as the basis for morphine and other drugs.

Sheep and cattle are raised on the grazing lands of the Anatolian plateau. Stock-raising forms an important branch of the economy. The sheep population of about 49 million (1979) is mainly of the Karaman type and is used primarily as a source of meat and milk. The bulk of the clip comprises coarse wool suitable only for carpets, blankets and poorer grades of clothing fabric, but efforts have been made in recent years to encourage breeding for wool and there are some 200,000 Merino sheep in the Bursa region.

The Angora goat produces the fine, soft wool known as mohair. Turkey is the second largest producer of mohair in the world; production averages 9,000 tons per annum.

MINERALS

Turkey has a diversity of rich mineral resources, including large quantities of bauxite, borax, chrome, copper, iron ore, manganese and sulphur. Mining and quarrying employed 115,000 workers in 1977. Minerals account for just over 5 per cent of total export earnings. About 60 per cent of all mineral output and all coal production is carried out by State enterprises. The most important state enterprise in the mining sector is Etibank, which works through its subsidiaries, Eregli Coal Mines, East Chromium Mines, Turkish Copper, Keban Lead Mines and Keçiborlu Sulphur Mines. The state enterprises increased their predominance over the private sector during the early 1960s with an investment programme backed by the Mining Investment Bank, which was set up in 1962. The policy of encouraging the private sector to play a greater part in the mining industry through the establishment of the Turkish Mining Bank Corporation (TMBC) in 1968 has failed to overcome the general reluctance on the part of private investors to view mining as a worthwhile area for long-term investment, with the result that the private sector is undercapitalized. An additional factor militating against the development of mining has been the long-held suspicion of foreign investment in mining. A Bill passed by Parliament in 1973 restricted foreign participation in mining development projects. However, this restriction was lifted in January 1980, allowing up to 49 per cent foreign participation in mining ventures.

Bituminous coal is found at and around Zonguldak on the Black Sea coast. The seams are steeply inclined, much folded, and strongly faulted. The coal is generally mined by the longwall system or a variation of it. These mines constitute the Etibank's largest operation, and the coalfield is the largest in this part of the world, including the Balkans. Most of the seams are of good coking quality, the coke being used in the steel mills at nearby Karabük. Production is about 4.8 million metric tons per year, meeting 70 per cent of domestic requirements. It is thought that coal reserves may become exhausted by the mid-1980s when Turkey will become dependent on its lignite reserves. Lignite is found in many parts of central and western Anatolia and total reserves are estimated at 5,000 million tons. In 1980 output in the public sector was 13.6 million metric tons. Seams located in western Turkey are operated by the West Lignite Mines. The other main mines are at Soma, Degirmisaz and Tuncbilçk. Newly found lignite deposits in the Afsin–Elbistan area, totalling over 300 million metric tons, are to be developed.

Practically all of Turkish iron ore comes from the Divrigi mine situated between Sivas and Erzurum in the north-east of the country and run by the Turkish Iron and Steel Corporation. The average grade of ore is from 60 to 66 per cent: reserves have been put at 28 million tons. Output of iron ore reached 3,602,000 metric tons in 1976 and 3,568,000 tons in 1978, but it fell to only 1,685,000 tons in 1979, rising again to 2,530,000 tons in 1980. Iron ore has to be imported at present but deposits at Hasan Celebi, now being studied, are expected to make domestic production sufficient for the three existing steel plants and for a fourth, planned for Sivas province.

Turkey is one of the world's largest producers of chrome. The richest deposits are in Guleman, south-eastern Turkey, in the vicinity of Iskenderun; in the area around Eskisehir, north-west Anatolia; and between Fethiye and Antalya on the Mediterranean coast. The Güleman mines, producing 25 per cent of the country's total, are operated by East Chromium Mines under Etibank. Other mines are owned and worked by private enterprise. Little chromium is used domestically and the mineral is the greatest foreign-exchange earner among mining exports. Annual output of chromite is about 700,000 tons.

Copper has been mined in Turkey since ancient times. Present-day production, conducted entirely by Etibank, comes from the Ergani Mines situated at Maden in Elâziğ, and the Morgul Copper Mine at Borçka in Çoruh province. Production of blister copper, most of which is exported to West Germany, the United Kingdom and the U.S.A., has been declining in recent years and is now about 28,000 tons per year. Known reserves of copper ore are put at 90 million tons. Studies carried out by MTA have revealed the presence of a promising copper belt along the Black Sea coast, with possible reserves of 300 million tons of medium quality ore.

Eskişehir in north-west Anatolia is the world's centre of meerschaum mining. Meerschaum, a soft, white mineral which hardens on exposure to the sun and looks like ivory, has long been used by Turkish craftsmen for pipes and cigarette-holders.

Manganese, magnesite, lead, sulphur, salt, asbestos, antimony, zinc and mercury are important mineral resources. Of these, manganese ranks first in importance. Deposits, worked by private enterprise, are found in many parts of the country, but principally near Eskişehir and in the Eregli district. Production of manganese has been around 34,000 metric tons annually in the past few years. Lead is mined at Keban, west of Elazig. Development of a new lead/zinc mine and electrolytic smelter in the Zantanti/Kayseri district is being undertaken by CINKUR, a private company 35 per cent owned by Etibank. Production of sulphur from the Keciborlu mine in Isparta province was 20,000 tons in 1977. Antimony is mined in small quantities near Balikesir and Nigde. An important new find of mercury deposits, which may amount to 440,000 tons, has been made at Sizma in Konya province. Large uranium deposits have been discovered in the Black Sea, between 1 and 2 km. below sea-level.

The Uludag (Bursa) tungsten deposits, carrying an average grade of 0.43 per cent WO_3, are among the richest in the world. Etibank and the German firm of Krupp are jointly working these deposits. Output rose from 2,600 tons of tungsten ore in 1978 to 3,400 tons in 1979. Other minerals are barytes, perlite, phosphate rock, boron minerals, cinnabar and emery (Turkey supplies more than 80 per cent of the world market for emery).

Turkey's bauxite deposits are now supplying the aluminium complex built at Seydisehir with Soviet aid. The plant's initial annual capacity was 60,000 tons of aluminium but this is to be expanded to 120,000 tons and production of alumina is expected to rise from 200,000 tons to 260,000 tons. The plant will also produce alumina for export, and semi-finished products. The reserves at Seydisehir are estimated at more than 30 million tons.

Petroleum was first struck in Turkey in 1950 and all subsequent strikes have been in the same area in the south-east of the country. It is mostly heavy-grade oil with a fairly high sulphur content. Production of crude petroleum rose from 2.4 million tons in 1966 to a peak of 3.5 million tons in 1973. In that year, domestic output satisfied about half consumption; in 1980 output was down to about 2.5 million metric tons and met only one-sixth of requirements, which total about 18 million metric tons. Iraq is the major supplier. Imports of crude oil and petroleum products in 1981 totalled $3,877 million, just $15 million more than in 1980.

Five companies produce oil: the Turkish Petroleum Corporation (TPAO), a 99 per cent state-owned Turkish company, at Garzan and Ramandag, with recently discovered deposits at Magrip, Batiraman and Kurtalan and the smaller fields at Kurtalan and Celikli; Mobil and Dorchester at Bulgrudag, Silivanka and Selmo; Shell at Kayaköy, Kurkan, Beykan and Sahaban; and Ersan, a small private Turkish company, at Kahta. Proven reserves are expected to be exhausted in 15 years. Ultimate reserves are put by TPAO at

10,000 million barrels. Exploration is continuing in the south east and in the Aegean. It is generally believed that the south-east is unpromising with regard to further reserves although a Canadian joint venture reported a find there in September 1980 and TPAO reported one in April 1981; some exploration is being carried out in the south-west. The government measures introduced in January 1980 to encourage foreign investment were partly directed at the oil firms, which previously had been reluctant to move into Turkey because of the political instability as well as the unpromising geological structures. During 1980, 23 exploration licenses were granted, of which 12 went to foreign firms. In 1981 the number increased, while work began on a major oil recovery project financed by the World Bank.

Turkey has four oil refineries: Mersin (annual capacity 4.4 million tons), Izmit (3.2 million tons), Batman (800,000 tons) and Aliaga (5 million tons, to be increased to 10 million tons with Soviet aid).

TPAO operates a 310-mile, 18-inch diameter pipeline running from the oilfields around Batman to Dörtyol on the Gulf of Iskenderun. A 980-km. oil pipeline from Kirkuk, in northern Iraq, to Turkey has a capacity of around 100,000 metric tons per day. During 1980 there was a two-month stoppage because of the Iran-Iraq war. Throughput has been at the rate of 35 million metric tons per year but in December 1980 Iraq agreed to increase this to 45–50 million tons. It also agreed to build a joint refinery and petrochemicals complex at Yumurtalik, near the pipeline's terminal, and a 460-km. pipeline from the terminal to a 100,000 barrels-per-day refinery which is being built at Kirikkale in Central Anatolia. A natural gas pipeline from Iraq may also be built. In March 1982 talks were held with Iran on the possible construction of two gas pipelines, one to serve Western Europe and the other Turkey. The closure of the pipeline from Iraq to Syria and Lebanon in April 1982 gave impetus to talks over possible expansion of the Dörtyol pipeline.

INDUSTRY

The leading role in the process of inaugurating industrialization was played by the state economic enterprises. However, by the beginning of the 1970s the private sector accounted for nearly half of industrial output and its rate of capital investment had become almost equal to public sector investment. The share of industry in the economy is increasing: whereas in 1952 industry accounted for 12 per cent of domestic product this had increased to 23.2 per cent by 1979. Manufacturing accounted for 17.5 per cent of G.D.P. in 1978. Whereas in 1962 consumer goods industries accounted for over two-thirds of industrial production, by 1972 its share had fallen to 46.5 per cent. In the same period the share of the intermediate goods industries increased from 17 to 39.4 per cent and that of capital goods from 12.9 to 14.1 per cent. Manufactured goods accounted for 28 per cent of total exports in 1979. In that year the number of workers in manufacturing industries was 1,707,000. Manufacturing grew at about 10 per cent in 1976 (compared with the Plan target of 11.7

per cent) but this growth shrank to 8 per cent in 1977 and to 3.8 per cent in 1978, as a result of a serious electricity shortage and dire lack of foreign exchange, which led to totally inadequate supplies of imported raw materials, semi-finished goods and components.

The textile and clothing industry is Turkey's largest, accounting for one-third of manufacturing employment and contributing about 20 per cent of manufacturing output. Cotton yarn is the most important export in this sector but exports of clothing are increasing steadily. In December 1981 the EEC accused Turkey of "dumping" cotton yarn and imposed a 12 per cent anti-dumping tariff.

There are three iron and steel plants. The Karabük plant, in north-west Anatolia, is run by the state-controlled Turkish Iron and Steel Corporation and has an annual capacity of 570,000 tons. The Eregli complex, in west Anatolia, produces hot and cold rolled sheets, steel strip and tinplate. Its annual capacity is 1,250,000 tons. The Iskenderun plant, with a capacity of 1.1 million tons, was built with the assistance of the Soviet Union, and its output is being doubled, also with Soviet aid. A fourth iron and steel complex was planned for Sivas but the project has been shelved for lack of finance. Turkey's total output of iron and steel products in 1978 was 3.7 million metric tons. Domestic steel needs are expected to reach 8,960,000 tons per year by 1983.

Production of cement reached a record 15.3 million metric tons in 1978 but fell back to 13.8 million tons in 1979 and to 12.9 million tons in 1980. Output recovered to 15.1 million tons in 1981. Some is exported to Syria and, increasingly, to Iraq.

Among food industries, the state-controlled sugar beet industry is the most important. Sugar production in 1981 totalled about 1.2 million tons.

The paper and board industry is dominated by the government-owned SEKA corporation which has one old-established mill at Izmir, with an annual capacity of 126,000 metric tons of paper and board, plus six mills which have been opened since 1971. Total output of paper and board was 301,000 tons in 1979. A very large paper factory is being built at Tasucu, on the south coast. A paper and cellulose factory was opened at Balikesir, in the west, in April 1981. Its eventual annual capacity is 100,000 tons of newsprint and 50,000 tons of by-products.

The motor vehicle industry was established after 1956 and by 1971 had become the largest industrial employer after the textile industry. However, it accounted for only around 5 per cent of total industrial output. Output, some of which is exported, is fragmented between 15 enterprises with resulting loss of economies of scale. The process of merging of firms (there were 22 in 1967) is expected to continue under the impact of heavier taxation. In 1979 the output was 21,500 lorries, 5,800 buses and 44,600 cars (local versions of Fiats and Renaults). However, for most of 1980/81 the industry was operating at only 25 per cent of capacity because of recession and lack of foreign exchange.

Turkey's first petrochemicals complex, situated

at Izmit, began production in 1970 of ethylene, polythene, PVC, chlorine and caustic soda. There is another petrochemicals plant at Aliaga and a third is planned at Yumurtalik. They are operated by the state-owned firm Petkim. Commercial fertilizer production has increased rapidly in recent years, reaching 6,609,000 tons in 1981. The state-owned Turkish Nitrates Corporation (TNC) has a nitrates plant at Kutahya, a triplesuperphosphates plant at Samsun and a superphosphates plant at Elazig. There are several privately-owned fertilizer plants, including triplesuperphosphates plants at Iskenderun and Yarimca. Turkey produces 75 per cent of its requirements of fertilizers and when new plants are completed it will be self-sufficient.

Other manufacturing industries include tobacco, chemicals, pharmaceuticals, construction, metal working, engineering, leather goods, glassware and ferrochrome.

Turkey's most ambitious power project, the Euphrates dam at Keban, began production in 1973. The 670 ft. high dam holds back a lake 70 miles long at the confluence of the two main branches of the Euphrates. The plant's initial capacity is 620 MW, rising to 1,240 MW.

A number of hydroelectric projects are under construction or planned. The main one is the Karakaya dam, in south-east Anatolia, at a cost of about $1,700 million. The eventual capacity will be 2,400 MW but the start-up date is some years away. A foundation stone for another major project, the Atatürk Dam, was laid in October 1981 but the project seems likely to remain stalled for some time. The Yatagan power station came on stream in 1982. In addition, several thermal power stations are being built or are planned. A 1,200-MW lignite-fired plant at Afsin-Elbistan, in the east, is much delayed but is expected to start operating in 1984; it will be the largest of its kind in the world. Other power stations are being built with Soviet, Polish and Japanese aid. Two nuclear power plants were planned, one with Soviet and the other with Swedish aid, but negotiations on both have come to a standstill.

Output of electricity in 1980 was 23,290 million kWh. Of this, 40 per cent was generated by hydropower, 25 per cent by oil and the rest by coal and lignite. There is vast untapped hydroelectric potential. Some electricity has to be imported from Bulgaria and the U.S.S.R. Installed capacity in 1979 was more than 5,000 MW.

FINANCE

The Central Bank (Merkez Bankası), the sole bank of issue, started its operations on October 3rd, 1931. It controls exchange operations and ensures the monetary requirements of certain state enterprises by the discounting of bonds issued by these establishments and guaranteed by the Treasury. Other banks are described in the Finance section on pages 845–6.

The monetary unit is the kuruş (piastre) by the law of April 1916. The Turkish lira (pound), which is, in practice, employed as the monetary unit, is made up of 100 kuruş.

The principal sources of budgetary revenue are income tax, import taxes and duties, production taxes, taxes and fees on services and revenues from State monopolies. From the beginning of 1962 agricultural incomes were taxed for the first time in recent history.

The 1982 budget covers only 10 months (March 1st–December 31st) to bring the financial year into line with the calendar year. Revenues are put at TL 1,739,759 million and expenditure at TL 1,804,759 million. Taxes are to provide 83.3 per cent of revenue, a somewhat lower proportion than in previous years. Defence spending accounts for 19 per cent of the total, but in real terms is down on 1980 allocations. Finance ministry allocations remain almost unchanged, at 47 per cent of the total, most of the ministry's funds being used for the State Economic Enterprises. Expenditure on education totals 10.5 per cent of all spending, while health receives 2.8 per cent.

Inflation, which in 1976 had been running at about 20 per cent a year, reached 100 per cent by the end of 1979 but began falling steadily in the last quarter of 1980 and was down to 36.8 per cent in 1981, according to official statistics. Unofficial estimates put the rate at around 50 per cent. It began climbing again in the first quarter of 1982, although the Government's target for the whole year was just 25 per cent. Registered unemployment rose from 8.3 per cent of the workforce in 1979 to 10.6 per cent in 1980, but the real unemployment rate is probably nearer 20 per cent.

A serious political and economic crisis came to a head in 1977, rendering Turkey virtually bankrupt. Foreign exchange transfers for all goods except strategic materials had ceased in February and many governments imposed a block on exports to Turkey, while foreign banks refused to advance any more loans. The Turkish Government introduced an austerity package in September and devalued the lira twice. It asked for IMF assistance and, after protracted negotiations, in March 1978 agreement was reached on a programme which included further devaluation of the lira by about 23 per cent overall; a limit to annual growth of 6.1 per cent; increases in deposit rates; and severe cuts in public spending. The IMF agreed to grant a $450 million credit over two years and its seal of approval on Turkey's proposed measures led foreign banks and governments to relax restrictions which they had imposed during 1977. In April six international banks set up a consortium to facilitate the re-scheduling of about $2,500 million of Turkey's foreign debts and in the same month the World Bank agreed to lend $650 million. Turkey was able to resume payment for imports in May 1978. However, the crisis continued, with Turkey still unable to service most of its debts in either 1977 or 1978. The economic targets agreed under the IMF stand-by arrangement were virtually unattainable, despite successive devaluations of the lira during 1978. The IMF refused to release the third tranche of the stand-by credit which had been due in

November and talks between the two sides were suspended the following month. In March 1979 the Government announced a new austerity package. The lira was effectively devalued by 40 per cent and a premium introduced for foreign currencies exchanged in Turkey by tourists and for the remittances of emigrant workers, to encourage them to send more of their earnings home. The measures did not produce the hoped-for signs of recovery, partly because of the lack of long-term structural reforms, and partly because, although imports were drastically pared, the cost of imported fuel continued to absorb nearly all export earnings.

After a further devaluation and new increases in prices and interest rates, Western countries and the World Bank agreed on an aid package which would involve the immediate release of about $1,450 million in extra loans and export credits.

In June 1979 the IMF agreed on a new stand-by credit totalling $315 million for one year. The agreement followed a 44 per cent devaluation of the lira announced on June 11th and new austerity measures, including further increase in the price of petrol and several other goods.

During 1979 Turkey obtained several large loans from Saudi Arabia and the Arab countries.

In January 1980 the Government introduced a new austerity package. The lira was devalued by 33 per cent. Prices of state-traded goods were raised by up to 400 per cent. Interest rates were raised and measures to promote foreign investment were announced, including lifting the ban on foreign investment in mining and oil exploration. The package attracted more foreign aid, including a $1,650 million pledge over three years from the IMF. In April 1980, OECD countries pledged aid totalling $1,160 million, of which the U.S.A. provided $295 million, the Federal Republic of Germany $246 million and the EEC as a group $100 million. The World Bank lent a total of $270 million and Saudi Arabia $250 million during the year. In July 1980 Western creditors agreed to reschedule debts totalling $3,000 million and in 1981 Turkey was seeking rescheduling of a further $2,300 million. By the end of 1981, Turkey's external debts stood at $20,457 million, of which $4,626 million had not been utilized. Long-term debts totalled $18,178 million and short-term debts were $2,279 million.

In May 1981 OECD countries pledged aid totalling $940 million, of which $350 million was from the U.S.A. The Federal Republic of Germany cut its aid from $246 million to $202 million and threatened to cut it further, urging a return to democracy. Italy pledged $115 million, Japan $110 million, France $80 million and the United Kingdom $31 million. The World Bank agreed to a further structural adjustment loan of $300 million.

Turkey's persistent trade deficit is partly offset by a net surplus on "invisible" items. Turkish workers abroad sent back remittances worth $2,490 million in 1980, while tourism generated a further $640 million. Transit trade fees were estimated at $250 million for vehicles travelling to Iraq. However, the 1981 balance of payments disclosed an overall current account deficit of $2,092 million, although this was an improvement on 1980's disastrous $2,756 million deficit. Foreign exchange reserves stood at $1,156 million in April 1982.

From 1974 to 1978 the U.S.A. imposed an arms embargo on Turkey, which contributed greatly to soaring import costs, since Turkey was obliged to finance its defence expenditure from its own resources. U.S. military aid totalled $175 million in 1978 and $202 million in 1979. The Federal Republic of Germany also provides military assistance to Turkey.

EXTERNAL TRADE

Since 1947 Turkey has had a persistent foreign trade deficit. In 1980 this deficit totalled $4,999 million, almost 65 per cent higher than in 1979. In 1981, however, it dropped to $4,230 million and the Government hopes that in 1982 it will fall further to $4,150 million. Imports are expected to total about $10,000 million and exports $5,850 million. Oil imports alone are likely to exceed $4,000 million for the third year running.

In 1979 exports of agricultural goods and livestock represented 59 per cent of the total, minerals 6 per cent and industrial and processed goods 35 per cent. Crude oil and petroleum products accounted for 34 per cent of the 1979 import bill, machinery 18 per cent, chemicals 10.3 per cent, fertilizers 7 per cent, iron and steel 7 per cent and motor vehicles 4.4 per cent.

The main exports are cotton, textiles and clothing, fruit and nuts, tobacco, livestock, cattlecake and foodstuff residues, cereals and iron, chrome, manganese and other ores. The principal imports are crude petroleum, machinery, mineral products, base metals, transport vehicles, pharmaceuticals, chemicals, vegetable products, plastic and rubber, fertilizers and textiles. In 1981 Iraq supplanted the Federal Republic of Germany as Turkey's most important single trading partner while the Middle East and North Africa became more important to Turkish traders than the EEC. It was not clear, however, whether this marked a decisive change in trading patterns or was a one-year aberration.

An association agreement with the EEC was signed in 1963, under which Turkey was granted financial aid and preferential tariff quotas. A package of minor improvements was introduced at the end of 1976 and the association agreement was revised in July 1980, offering Turkey a five-year financial aid package. Since the military coup of September 1980, aid from EEC countries has become increasingly dependent upon the restoration of democracy and human rights in Turkey. NATO countries have been divided on support for the Ankara regime: in December 1981 the United States promised to speed up aid to Turkey, while in March 1982 EEC aid worth £336 million was "frozen". Nevertheless, the Turkish Government continues to express its intention to apply for full membership of the EEC as soon as democracy has been restored.

PLANNING

During the years of the First Plan (1962–67) a real growth rate of 6.6 per cent per annum was achieved. The Second Five-Year Poan, covering the years 1968 to 1972, envisaged an annual growth rate of 7 per cent, which was almost exactly achieved. Of total investment, 22.4 per cent was allocated to manufacturing industry. The long-term target of self-sustained economic growth, i.e. independent of foreign loans, was a prominent aim of the Third Five-Plan (1973–77), which allocated almost 45 per cent of the total investment to mining and manufacturing. Priority was given to providir g a modern heavy industry base to promote export opportunities and import substitution. An annual growth rate of 7.9 per cent in G.N.P. was aimed at. However, many targets were only 60 per cent achieved and in real terms the overall growth rate was below target. The start of the Fourth Plan (1978–82) was delayed by the economic crisis of 1978 and has now been shelved.

PROSPECTS

After two years of severe economic crisis, there were signs of an upturn in the latter part of 1980, following the economic revival plan launched early in the year and the military takeover in September. G.N.P. rose by 4.3 per cent in 1981 and looked set to increase by around 5–6 per cent in 1982. Investment prospects brightened and foreign investment doubled in 1981. One sign of the improved business climate was the establishment of various foreign banking operations in Turkey. In 1981 there was an export boom, and in early 1982 a series of trade agreements signed with Iran, Syria, Iraq and other Arab states indicated a further substantial rise in exports of manufactured goods. Among measures taken by the new Government are a tax reform package, proposed reorganization of the State Economic Enterprises, freeing bank interest rates, devaluation of the lira and eliminating most government subsidies on consumer items. These measures are all aimed at controlling inflation, reducing public spending and increasing the confidence of foreign creditors, aid donors and investors.

STATISTICAL SURVEY

AREA AND POPULATION

Total Area	Thrace	Anatolia	Census Population	
			Oct. 26th, 1975	Oct. 12th, 1980
779,452 sq. km.	23,764 sq. km.	755,688 sq. km.	40,347,719	44,736,957

PRINCIPAL TOWNS
(population at 1980 census)

Ankara (capital)*	.	1,877,755	Mersin (İçel) . .	216,308
Istanbul*	.	2,772,708	Samsun . .	198,749
İzmir (Smyrna)*	.	757,854	İzmit (Kocaeli) .	190,423
Adana* .	.	574,515	Erzurum . .	190,241
Bursa .	.	445,113	Malatya . .	179,074
Gaziantep	.	374,290	Kahramanmaraş .	178,557
Konya .	.	329,139	Kirikkale . .	178,401
Eskişehir	.	309,431	Kâğrthane . .	175,540
Kayseri .	.	281,320	Antalya . .	173,501
Diyarbakir	.	235,617	Sivas . .	172,864

* Within municipal boundaries.

ECONOMICALLY ACTIVE POPULATION

('000 persons employed in October 1981)

Agriculture, hunting, forestry and fishing . . .	9,512
Mining and quarrying	128
Manufacturing	1,586
Energy, gas and water	104
Construction	583
Wholesale and retail trade	642
Transport, storage and communications . .	491
Finance, insurance and real estate . . .	213
Public and personal services (including restaurants and hotels) . . . . . . Other activities (not adequately described) . .	2,087
TOTAL	15,346

WORKERS ABROAD
('000)

	1979	1980
Australia	15	16
Austria	29	30
Belgium	23	23
France	38	38
Germany, Federal Republic .	540	591
Libya	25	38
Netherlands . . .	45	62
Switzerland . . .	18	22
TOTAL (incl. others) .	802	905

WORKERS' REMITTANCES FROM ABROAD
(U.S. $ million)

1976	1977	1978	1979	1980	1981
982.7	981.8	983.1	1,694.4	2,071.1	2,489.6

AGRICULTURE

LAND USE

	AREA ('ooo hectares)				
	1976	1977	1978	1979	1980
Area under cultivation	24,243	24,472	24,552	24,972	24,568
Market gardens and truck farms, orchards, olive groves, vineyards, etc.	3,460	3,457	3,493	3,585	3,911
Forests	20,170	20,155	20,155	20,155	20,199

Meadows and grazing lands: 26,135,000 hectares in 1967.

PRINCIPAL CROPS

	AREA ('ooo hectares)			PRODUCTION ('ooo metric tons)			
	1978	1979	1980	1978	1979	1980	1981†
Wheat . . .	9,300	9,310	9,020	16,700	17,616	16,500	17,000
Spelt . . .	46	45	41	64	69	54	40
Rye . . .	470	472	443	680	620	525	500
Barley . . .	2,600	2,762	2,800	4,750	5,219	5,300	5,900
Oats . . .	225	212	197	370	371	355	350
Maize . . .	580	588	583	1,300	1,357	1,240	1,100
Millet . . .	20	20	15	29	13	22	15
Rice (milled) . .	70	79	52	190	225	292	290
Mixed grain . .	170	155	140	211	200	183	150
Dry beans . .	100	116	114	156	165	165	165
Chick peas . .	168	206	240	205	226	275	225
Lentils . . .	177	177	191	180	184	195	200
Vetch . . .	156	149	145	120	121	114	130
Broad beans . .	31	31	30	54	52	52	55
Potatoes . . .	180	169	183	2,750	2,870	3,000	3,000
Onions (dry) . .	70	69	70	880	1,000	960	1,050
Garlic (dry) . .	13	12	13	67	75	80	75
Tomatoes . .	107	108	108	3,300	3,500	3,550	3,950
Cabbages (incl. black)	30	30	n.a.	525	586	568	585
Melons and water-melons. .	210	210	218	4,095	5,220	4,450	4,500
Aubergines (eggplants)	36	36	n.a.	610	630	650	730
Cotton (lint) . .	} 653	612	672 {	475	476	500	542
Cottonseed . .				760	762	800	830
Tobacco . . .	299	233	230	293	217	234	200
Sugar beet . .	277	270	269	8,837	8,760	6,766	11,000
Sesame seed . .	35	45	45	23	26	26	23
Sunflower seed . .	415	445	575	485	590	750	575
Olives . . .	} 81.1*	81.1*	81.3* {	1,100	430	1,350	600
Olive oil . . .				180	69	180	60
Tea (fresh leaves) .	53	54	54	449	555	476	210

* Number of trees (million).   † Estimate.

FRUIT AND NUTS
('ooo metric tons)

	1978	1979	1980	1981
Apples	1,100	1,350	1,430	1,200
Grapes . . .	3,496	3,500	3,600	3,600
Pears	270	280	330	330
Hazelnuts (filberts) .	310	300	250	350
Figs . . .	185	200	205	205
Figs (dried) . .	50	52	57	55
Walnuts . . .	130	150	122	112
Pistachios . . .	6	20	7.5	20
Almonds . . .	26	26.5	32	31
Chestnuts . . .	45	46	59	62
Oranges . . .	656	680	695	700
Lemons . . .	243	280	283	280
Mandarins . .	150	155	167	170
Peaches . . .	230	220	240	240
Plums . . .	149	140	157	150
Apricots (incl. wild) .	153	165	160	124
Cherries (incl. sour) .	141	142	156	149

LIVESTOCK
('ooo head at December)

	1978	1979	1980
Cattle . .	14,941	15,567	15,894
Buffaloes .	1,023	1,040	1,031
Sheep . .	43,942	49,026	48,630
Angora goats .	3,642	3,666	3,658
Other goats .	14,805	15,109	15,385
Horses .	812	807	794
Asses .	1,371	1,331	1,345
Pigs . .	10	13	13
Mules . .	299	315	305
Camels .	13	12	12
Chickens* .	52,121	56,233	58,584
Turkeys* .	2,590	2,705	2,865

* At October.

LIVESTOCK PRODUCTS
('ooo metric tons)

	1978	1979	1980
Beef and veal . .	173*	246*	} 242
Buffalo meat . .	19*	20*	
Mutton and lamb† .	282	285	300
Goats' meat† .	102	103	105
Pig meat† . . .	1	n.a.	1
Horse meat† . .	8	8	7
Poultry meat† . .	212	228	245
Edible offals† . .	80	89	93
Tallow† . . .	12	13	14
Cows' milk . .	3,209	3,386	3,421
Buffalo milk . .	282	297	274
Sheep milk . .	1,056	1,102	1,177
Goats' milk . .	621	626	630
Butter . . .	114.6	119.3	117
Cheese† . . .	123.4	123.6	126.5
Hen eggs . .	208.9	215.7	215.7
Honey . . .	21.6	21.7	26.1
Wool: greasy . .	56.7	59.3	60.0*
clean . .	31.7	32.6	33.0*
Cattle and buffalo hides†	34.5	45.4	47.8
Sheep skins† .	53.8	55.4	58.0
Goat skins† . .	12.8	12.9	13.1

* Unofficial figures.   † FAO estimates.

Source: FAO, *Production Yearbook* and *Monthly Bulletin of Statistics.*

FORESTRY
ROUNDWOOD REMOVALS
('ooo cubic metres, excluding bark)

	CONIFEROUS (soft wood)		BROADLEAVED (hard wood)		TOTAL	
	1978/79	1979/80	1978/79	1979/80	1978/79	1979/80
Sawlogs, veneer logs and logs for sleepers* .	4,492	4,573	1,219	1,138	5,711	5,711
Pitprops (mine timber)	553	534	86	83	639	617
Pulpwood	1,145	1,362	40	n.a.	1,185	1,362
Other industrial wood . . .	659	618	367	303	1,026	921
Fuel wood	6,731	5,819	5,811	6,438	12,542	12,257
TOTAL	13,580	12,906	7,523	7,962	21,103	20,868

* Including poles.

Source: Ministry of Forestry, Planning Dept.

SAWNWOOD PRODUCTION
('ooo cubic metres)

	1973	1974	1975	1976	1977	1978†	1979†
Coniferous sawnwood . . .	1,897	1,878	1,908	2,300	2,441	3,635	3,787
Broadleaved sawnwood . . .	550	545	552	667	707	967	925
	2,447	2,423	2,460	2,967	2,148	4,602	4,712
Railway sleepers	36*	48	38	43	44	48	52
TOTAL	2,483	2,471	2,498	3,010	3,192	4,650	4,764

* FAO estimate.   † Figures from Ministry of Forestry, Planning Dept.

Source: FAO, *Yearbook of Forest Products.*

FISHING*
('ooo metric tons, live weight)

	1977	1978	1979	1980
Inland waters	18.3	21.8	22.2	32.3
Mediterranean and Black Sea:				
Mediterranean horse mackerel .	16.7	29.4	64.1	50.0
European anchovy . . .	79.5	115.9	139.5	251.9
Other fishes . . .	49.2	76.1	121.3	90.3
TOTAL CATCH . .	163.7	243.2	347.2	424.5

* Figures cover only fishes and freshwater crustaceans.

Source: State Institute of Statistics, Prime Minister's Office.

MINING
PRODUCTION
('ooo metric tons)

	1978	1979	1980	1981
Crude petroleum . . .	2,735	2,846	2,330	2,363
Iron ore (gross weight) . . .	3,568	1,685	2,464	2,430
Chrome ore	651	554	519	519
Lignite*	9,925	10,805	13,630	14,959
Coal*	4,289	4,045	3,597	3,598
Manganese	87	34	37	12
Copper (blister)* . . .	26	22	16	27
Sulphur (pure)* . . .	19	21	23	29

* Public sector only.

INDUSTRY
SELECTED PRODUCTS

		1978	1979	1980	1981
Paper* . . .	'ooo tons	326	301	300	365
Cotton Yarn* . . .	,, ,,	37	44	41	42
Woollen Yarn* . . .	,, ,,	4.3	3.5	3.4	4.0
Cotton Fabrics* . . .	million metres	208.9	211.2	188.9	227.0
Woollen Fabrics* . .	,, ,,	6.3	6.1	5.0	5.9
Raki* . . .	'ooo litres	42,587	42,643	44,430	43,809
Beer . . .	,, ,,	202,086	211,800	n.a.	n.a.
Cigarettes . . .	'ooo tons	56	70	59	71
Pig Iron . . .	,, ,,	1,569	1,902	1,810	1,727
Steel Ingots . . .	,, ,,	1,628	1,789	1,700	1,531
Cement . . .	,, ,,	15,344	13,812	12,875	15,043
Sugar . . .	,, ,,	1,135	975	1,049	1,117
Commercial Fertilizers .	,, ,,	2,541	3,296	4,232	6,916
Sulphuric Acid (100%)* .	,, ,,	31	25	24	24
Electrolytic Copper† .	,, ,,	7.4	6.7	2.9	9.8
Aluminium Sheets .	,, ,,	2.6	1.3	0.3	1.0
Polyethylene . .	,, ,,	20.2	17.0	16.3	18
Coke* . . .	,, ,,	1,838	2,096	1,927	1,875
Motor Spirit . .	,, ,,	2,026	1,819	1,852	1,872
Kerosene . . .	,, ,,	581	442	475	297
Fuel Oils . . .	,, ,,	5,828	4,571	5,272	5,515
Hydro-electricity . .	million kWh.	9,365	10,253	11,356	12,592
Thermal Electricity .	,, ,,	12,361	12,256	11,937	12,304

* Public sector only.   † Private sector only.

FINANCE
100 kuruş = 1 Turkish lira (TL) or pound.
Coins: 1, 5, 10, 25 and 50 kuruş; 1, 2½, 5 and 10 liras.
Notes: 5, 10, 20, 50, 100, 500, 1,000 and 5,000 liras.
Exchange rates (May 1982): £1 sterling = 270.8 liras; U.S. $1 = 147.3 liras.
1,000 Turkish liras = £3.69 = $6.79.

Note: Between June 1947 and August 1960 the exchange rate was U.S. $1 = 2.80 liras (1 lira = 35.71 U.S. cents). From August 1960 to August 1970 the rate was $1 = 9.00 liras (1 lira = 11.11 U.S. cents). Between August 1970 and December 1971 the mid-point rate was $1 = 15.00 liras (1 lira = 6.67 U.S. cents), with an export (buying) rate of $1 = 14.85 liras and an import (selling) rate of $1 = 15.15 liras. From December 1971 to May 1974 the export rate was $1 = 14.00 liras (1 lira = 7.14 U.S. cents) and the import rate was $1 = 14.30 liras. Since May 1974 the rates have been adjusted frequently. The average mid-point rate (liras per U.S. $) was 13.927 in 1974; 14.442 in 1975; 16.053 in 1976; 18.002 in 1977; 24.282 in 1978; 31.078 in 1979; 76.038 in 1980; 111.219 in 1981. In terms of sterling, the exchange rate between November 1967 and August 1970 was £1 = 21.60 liras; from August 1970 to December 1971 the mid-point rate was £1 = 36.000 liras; from December 1971 to June 1972 the export rate was £1 = 36.48 liras and the import rate £1 = 37.26 liras. Since June 1972, when sterling was allowed to "float", the exchange rates have been adjusted frequently.

GENERAL BUDGET ESTIMATES
(TL million, fiscal year beginning March 1st)

REVENUE	1981	1982*	EXPENDITURE	1981	1982*
Tax revenues	1,354,800	1,449,099	Finance	737,273	835,065
Taxes on income . . .	817,240	904,099	Defence	287,633	317,700
Income tax . . .	691,200	730,021	Education	147,262	187,658
Corporation tax. .	76,040	130,000	Health and social welfare . .	55,432	50,098
Taxes on wealth . . .	16,500	24,100	Food, agriculture and livestock .	27,601	31,885
Taxes on goods . . .	188,610	191,600	Rural affairs	56,178	67,098
Taxes on services . . .	182,450	163,100	Public works . . .	26,316	38,070
Tax on banking and insurance transactions . . .	67,000	75,000	Security	36,986	57,953
			Gendarmerie	34,754	35,680
Taxes on foreign trade . .	150,000	166,200	Energy and national resources .	9,035	8,802
Other normal revenues .	89,144	146,500	Justice	24,856	28,058
Special revenues and funds .	60,000	120,041	Others	97,639	122,573
TOTAL REVENUE .	1,503,944	1,715,640	TOTAL EXPENDITURE	1,540,965	1,780,640

* The 1982 budget covers only 10 months (March 1st–December 31st), to bring the financial year into line with the calendar year.

INTERNATIONAL RESERVES
(U.S. $ million, at year end)

	1977	1978	1979	1980	1981
CENTRAL BANK:					
Gold holding	149.1	149.1	154.6	155	155
Foreign exchange	397.6	485.7	414.1	823	860
RESERVE POSITION OF THE CENTRAL BANK .	546.7	634.8	568.7	978	1,015
RESERVE HOLDINGS OF OTHER BANKS .	83.0	76.6	137.1	231	643
TOTAL RESERVES (NET) . . .	629.7	711.4	705.8	1,209	1,658

CURRENCY IN CIRCULATION
(TL million, at year end)

	1977	1978	1979	1980	1981
Currency in public circulation* . . .	62,953	93,817	141,304	217,500	296,900
Bank-notes	62,159	92,950	140,412	n.a.	n.a.
Coins	794	867	892	n.a.	n.a.
Total outstanding of bank-notes and coins .	78,764	114,616	183,800	278,600	387,399

* Outside banks.

NATIONAL ACCOUNTS
(TL million, at current prices)

	1977*	1978*	1979*	1980*	1981*
Agriculture and livestock	211,090.6	289,925.7	454,446.6	891,207.4	1,282,171.3
Forestry and logging	6,945.0	8,779.3	11,843.7	22,820.9	27,865.9
Fishing	1,718.6	2,458.3	5,290.4	11,012.7	13,615.4
Mining and quarrying	14,299.1	19,832.0	31,926.1	71,234.4	135,611.7
Manufacturing	129,706.5	232,070.5	426,454.2	870,843.5	1,317,945.0
Electricity, gas and water	14,001.0	21,488.4	33,014.6	84,635.4	127,537.9
Construction	42,095.9	63,992.0	105,831.9	213,034.2	285,216.5
Wholesale and retail trade . . .	107,004.3	165,931.1	308,196.4	642,676.1	1,010,716.8
Transport, storage and communications .	72,236.0	110,061.6	224,697.8	409,208.0	623,345.2
Financial institutions	20,237.8	25,931.4	36,955.5	71,919.9	132,539.8
Ownership of dwellings	31,631.1	51,597.4	86,750.1	191,885.3	263,603.8
Other private services	41,025.1	62,844.8	80,719.9	222,386.0	331,507.2
Government services	101,478.0	133,099.7	235,229.5	377,626.9	481,147.4
GROSS DOMESTIC PRODUCT AT FACTOR COST	793,469.0	1,188,012.2	2,041,356.7	4,080,490.7	6,032,823.9
Indirect taxes	79,455.4	102,218.5	165,279.7	279,566.0	453,483.0
Less: Subsidies	12,611.0	17,511.0	24,691.0	32,093.0	75,085.0
G.D.P. IN PURCHASERS' VALUES . .	860,313.4	1,272,719.7	2,181,945.4	4,327,963.7	6,411,221.9
Net factor income from abroad . . .	9,926.0	15,942.7	43,626.1	107,189.3	153,061.9
GROSS NATIONAL PRODUCT . . .	870,239.4	1,288,662.4	2,225,571.5	4,435,153.0	6,564,283.8

* Provisional

CONSUMER PRICE INDEX
(Ankara—1968 = 100)

	1977	1978	1979	1980	1981
Food	427.9	619.0	936.9	1,936.6	2,724.9
Clothing	430.4	661.8	1,104.5	2,265.2	3,058.3
Household Expenditures	434.6	738.5	1,199.3	2,319.2	2,786.6
Medical and Personal Care . . .	264.4	372.1	569.4	1,067.9	1,692.4
Transportation	303.2	467.6	840.4	1,796.0	2,493.4
Cultural and Recreational Expenditures	410.0	608.9	962.8	1,978.5	2,838.8
Dwelling expenditures*	191.8	293.3	439.7	1,437.0	1,785.7
ALL ITEMS	372.1	556.3	870.8	1,886.1	2,563.9

* Rent is accepted as fixed.

BALANCE OF PAYMENTS
(U.S. $ million)

	1976	1977	1978	1979	1980
Exports f.o.b.	1,960	1,754	2,287	2,266	2,910
Imports f.o.b.	−4,565	−5,082	−4,033	−4,443	−6,747
MERCHANDISE TRADE BALANCE . .	−2,605	−3,328	−1,746	−2,177	−3,837
Services (net)	−465	−1,000	−593	−655	−1,115
Transfers (net)	1,106	1,104	1,128	1,819	2,196
CURRENT BALANCE	−1,964	−3,224	−1,211	−1,013	−2,756
Long-term capital (net)	2,335	1,989	570	401	1,652
Short-term capital (net) . . .	−503	842	645	126	17
CAPITAL BALANCE	1,832	2,831	1,215	527	1,669
Net errors and omissions . . .	14	−166	−133	371	1,117
TOTAL (net monetary movements) . .	−118	−559	−129	−115	30

Source: IMF, *International Financial Statistics.*

EXTERNAL TRADE
(U.S. $ million)

	1976	1977	1978	1979	1980	1981
Imports c.i.f.	5,128.6	5,769.3	4,599.0*	5,069.5*	7,667.3*	8,933.3*
Exports f.o.b.	1,960.2	1,753.0	2,288.2	2,261.2	2,910.1	4,702.9

* Excluding grants.

PRINCIPAL COMMODITIES
(U.S. $ million)

IMPORTS	1977*	1978†	1979†	1980†	1981††‡
Machinery	1,351.3	1,015.8	1,203.3	1,150.9	1,394.8
Iron and steel	689.7	409.8	347.3	471.4	536.3
Liquid fuels	1,469.9	1,439.3	1,762.0	3,664.6	3,447.9
Medicines and dyes	443.1	378.0	419.0	595.8	739.1
Transport vehicles	572.8	450.8	283.6	230.6	225.9
Textiles and yarns	108.9	69.6	85.8	134.0	132.8
Synthetic plastic materials, natural and synthetic rubber	266.3	154.7	145.7	182.9	236.2
Fats and oils	20.6	35.0	74.6	123.7	100.5
Commercial fertilizers	214.5	283.5	356.3	394.3	244.9
Others	556.8	362.6	391.9	678.3	775.7
TOTAL	5,693.9	4,599.1	5,069.5	7,667.3	7,948.6

* Excluding grants and imports with waiver.   † Excluding grants.   ‡ January–November.

EXPORTS	1977	1978	1979	1980	1981
Agricultural products	1,041.4	1,542.8	1,343.7	1,671.7	2,219.4
Cereals, leguminous seeds	128.8	267.3	167.0	187.5	338.8
Fruits and vegetables	449.4	569.1	662.0	764.4	809.4
Hazelnuts	251.0	330.9	353.1	394.8	301.8
Sultanas	75.0	99.7	114.9	130.3	130.5
Citrus fruits	42.2	43.8	53.5	86.6	125.1
Others	81.2	94.7	140.5	152.7	252.0
Industrial crops	414.8	604.2	431.0	588.9	786.3
Tobacco	175.8	225.3	232.0	233.7	359.8
Cotton	213.6	352.9	177.0	329.9	395.0
Others	25.4	26.0	22.0	25.3	31.5
Livestock and animal products	48.4	102.2	83.7	130.9	284.9
Cattle, sheep, goats	18.9	47.3	40.1	97.7	231.5
Mohair, wool	14.6	27.9	20.4	7.6	17.2
Others	14.9	27.0	23.2	25.6	36.2
Minerals	125.8	124.1	132.6	191.0	193.3
Chrome ore	47.1	24.4	22.9	30.6	28.0
Others	78.7	99.7	109.7	160.4	165.3
Industrial products	585.8	621.3	784.9	1,047.4	2,290.2
Cotton yarn	145.7	179.6	217.8	181.2	230.6
Leather jackets and coats	39.7	28.5	28.0	30.2	54.4
Carpets and rugs	27.7	35.6	43.9	83.9	155.5
Olive oil	35.3	8.7	38.8	5.6	74.0
Others	337.4	368.9	456.4	746.5	1,775.7
TOTAL	1,753.0	2,288.2	2,261.2	2,910.1	4,702.9

PRINCIPAL TRADING PARTNERS
(U.S. $ million)

IMPORTS	1979	1980	1981	EXPORTS	1979	1980	1981*
Belgium/Luxembourg .	86	158	153	Belgium/Luxembourg .	61	56	94
France	302	377	400	France	137	164	216
Germany, Federal Republic	565	837	940	Germany, Federal Republic	495	604	643
Iran	176	803	515	Iran	12	85	234
Iraq	579	1,185	1,564	Iraq	113	135	559
Italy	468	300	372	Italy	213	218	246
Japan	222	113	206	Libya	43	60	442
Libya	208	778	789	Netherlands . .	75	205	96
Netherlands . .	84	205	166	Romania	38	71	57
Romania	235	261	372	Switzerland . .	114	125	246
Switzerland . .	250	348	533	Syria . . .	55	103	129
United Kingdom . .	221	317	434	U.S.S.R. . . .	127	169	194
U.S.A.	359	442	521	United Kingdom . .	103	105	148
				U.S.A.	104	127	223
TOTAL (incl. others)	5,070	7,667	7,949	TOTAL (incl. others)	2,261	2,910	4,048

* January to November.

TOURISM

	1977	1978	1979	1980	1981*
Number of foreign arrivals ('000) . . .	1,661	1,644	1,524	1,288	1,120
Receipts from foreign travel (million U.S. $) .	204.9	230.4	280.7	326.7	290.8
Expenditures for foreign travel (million U.S. $) .	268.5	102.6	95.1	114.7	85.2

* January to September only.

TOURISTS BY COUNTRY OF ORIGIN
('000)

COUNTRY	1976	1977	1978	1979	1980	1981*
France	124	150	141	120	87	69
Germany, Federal Republic .	197	203	218	198	155	109
Greece	38	44	54	60	59	79
Iran	50	94	137	67	109	47
Italy	74	85	88	81	63	50
Syria	35	41	52	45	38	39
United Kingdom . .	90	108	92	70	62	38
U.S.A. . . .	115	165	159	161	119	66
Yugoslavia . . .	85	76	86	103	57	36
TOTAL (incl. others)	1,676	1,661	1,644	1,524	1,288	948

* January to August only.

Tourist Accommodation (1978): 452 registered hotels, motels, boarding houses and holiday villages, with 61,316 beds.

TRANSPORT

RAILWAYS
(millions)

	1979	1980	1981*
Passenger-kilometres . .	6,802	6,011	6,150
Net ton-kilometres . .	5,814	5,167	6,020

* Estimate.

ROAD TRAFFIC
('000 motor vehicles at December 31st)

	1978	1979	1980
Passenger cars . .	597.5	658.7	711.0
Trucks . . .	285.3	309.8	327.2
Buses	85.2	91.5	96.7

SHIPPING

	1977	1978	1979	1980	1981
Number of passengers (thousands) .	1,016	897	973	861	937
Freight (thousand tons) . . .	10,495	10,767	12,690	11,381	11,296

CIVIL AVIATION
Turkish Airlines

	1979	1980	1981
Number of passengers (thousands) .	2,930	1,590	2,461
Freight (thousand tons) . . .	248	138	202

COMMUNICATIONS

	1978	1979	1980	1981*
Telephones . .	986,844	1,092,137	1,147,782	1,183,867
Radio licences .	4,274,680	4,280,000	4,282,158	4,290,688
TV licences . .	2,643,508	3,108,117	3,433,308	4,549,401

EDUCATION
(1979/80)

	INSTITUTIONS	TEACHERS	PUPILS
Primary	44,098	187,363*	5,595,356
Secondary:			
General	5,062	65,090	1,672,700
Technical and vocational .	1,718	28,644	514,923
Higher (incl. academies, teacher training and other higher technical and vocational schools, universities)	347	20,699	270,278

In the academic year 1981/82 there were 235,000 students enrolled at Turkey's 19 universities and other institutes of higher education.

Source (unless otherwise stated): Türkiye İş Bankası A.S., Economic Research Dept., Ankara.

THE CONSTITUTION

A seven-point provisional Constitution was introduced in October 1980. On October 15th, 1981, a Consultative Assembly was formed to prepare a new Constitution which will be submitted to referendum in November 1982.

THE GOVERNMENT
HEAD OF STATE
President and Chief of the General Staff: Gen. KENAN EVREN.

NATIONAL SECURITY COUNCIL
President: Gen. KENAN EVREN.
Secretary-General: Gen. NECDET ÜRUĞ.
Members: Gen. NURETTİN ERSİN.
Gen. TAHSİN ŞAHİNKAYA.
Admiral NEJAT TÜMER.

COUNCIL OF MINISTERS
(June 1982)

Prime Minister: BÜLENT ULUSU.
Deputy Prime Minister: ZEYYAD BAYKARA.
Deputy Prime Minister for Economic Affairs: TURGUT ÖZAL.
Ministers of State: MEHMET ÖZGÜNEŞ, NİMET ÖZDAŞ, İLHAN ÖZTRAK.
Minister of Justice: CEVDET MENTEŞ.
Minister of Defence: HALUK BAYÜLKEN.
Minister of Foreign Affairs: İLTER TÜRKMEN.
Minister of Finance: KAYA ERDEM.
Minister of Education: HASAN SAĞLAM.
Minister of the Interior: SELAHATTİN ÇETİNER.
Minister of Public Works: TAHSİN ÖNALP.
Minister of Trade: KEMAL CANTÜRK.

Minister of Health and Social Welfare: KAYA KILIÇTUR-GAY.
Minister of Customs and Monopolies: RECAI BATURALP.
Minister of Agriculture and Forestry: SABAHATTİN ÖZBEK.
Minister of Transport: MUSTAFA AYSAN.
Minister of Labour: TURHAN ESENER.
Minister of Industry and Technology: MEHMET TURGUT.
Minister of Energy and Natural Resources: FAHIR İLKEL.
Minister of Culture and Tourism: İHLAN EVLİYAOĞLU.
Minister of Housing and Reconstruction: ŞERİF TÜTEN.
Minister of Rural Affairs: MÜNİR GÜNEY.
Minister of Youth and Sports: VECDİ ÖZGÜL.
Minister of Social Security: SADIK ŞİDE.

CONSULTATIVE ASSEMBLY

On October 15th, 1981, a Consultative Assembly was formed to draft a new Constitution. It consists of the five members of the National Security Council (NSC), 40 members appointed directly by the NSC and 120 members chosen by the Council from candidates put forward by the governors of the 67 provinces. There is a constitution committee of 15 members. All former politicians are excluded.

Chairman of Constitution Committee: ORHAN ALDIKACTI.
Speaker: Dr. SADI IRMAK.

POLITICAL PARTIES

All activities by political parties were banned by the National Security Council on September 12th, 1980, and all political parties were dissolved on October 16th, 1981, to make way for a Consultative Assembly. Political parties which existed before that date are listed below.

Democratic Party (*Demokratik Partisi*): Ankara; f. 1970 by deputies and senators expelled from the Justice Party; nationalist and traditionalist; Leader Dr. FARUK SÜKAN; dissolved May 1980, some fmr. mems. rejoining Justice Party.

Justice Party (*Adalet Partisi*): Ankara; f. 1961; supports private enterprise within a mixed economy; Leader SÜLEYMAN DEMİREL; Sec.-Gen. NAHIT MENTESE.

Nation Party (*Millet Partisi*): Ankara; f. 1962; traditional and religious in character; Leader (vacant).

National Action Party (*Milliyetçi Hareket Partisi*): 3 Cadde 47, Bahçelievler, Ankara; f. 1969; right-wing, favours secularism, nationalism, communal progress, increased scientific activities and development; supports close co-operation between the public and private sectors; Leader ALPARSLAN TÜRKEŞ; Sec.-Gen. NECATİ GÜLTEKIN.

National Order Party (**NOP**): Ankara; f. 1969; dissolved in 1971 by the Constitutional Court for violating the Constitution; resurrected in 1979, when ABDÜLKERİM DOĞRU, NSP deputy to National Assembly, resigned from NSP and declared that he would henceforth represent National Order Party.

National Salvation Party (*Milli Selâmet Partisi*): Ankara; f. 1972; right-wing, traditionalist, Islamic; took place of National Order Party which was closed down by order of the Constitutional Court; Leader NECMETTIN ERBAKAN.

Republican People's Party (**RPP**) (*Cumhuriyet Halk Partisi*): Ankara; f. 1923 by Kemal Atatürk; favours a considerable degree of State enterprise along with continuing private enterprise. In recent years the party has moved to the left of centre; Leader (vacant); Sec.-Gen. MUSTAFA ÜSTÜNDAĞ.

Republican Reliance Party (*Cumhuriyet Guven Partisi*): Ankara; f. 1967 as the National Reliance Party by 45 members of Parliament from the Republican People's Party, who broke away as a result of the RPP's "left of centre policies"; merged with Republican Party 1973; Leader Prof. TURHAN FEYZIOĞLU.

Turkish Socialist Workers' Party (*Türkiye Sosyalist İşçi Partisi*): Ankara; f. 1974; supports nationalization of major sectors of the economy, withdrawal from NATO; Chair. AHMET KACMAZ; Sec.-Gen. YALCIN YUSUFOĞLU.

Turkish Unity Party (*Türkiye Birlik Partisi*): Ankara; f. 1966; Social democratic; Leader MUSTAFA TIMISI; publ. *Birlik* (monthly).

Workers' Party of Turkey (*Türkiye İşçi Partisi*): Çemberlitaş, Piyerloti Cad. 21/5, Istanbul; f. 1975; Pres. Mrs. BEHICE BORAN; Sec.-Gen. Dr. NIHAT SARGIN; publs. *Yürüyüs* (weekly), *Görev* (every 2 weeks), *Genç Öncü* (monthly), *Çarkbaşak* (monthly), *Yurt ve Dünya* (every 2 months); dissolved by Constitutional Court May 1980.

DIPLOMATIC REPRESENTATION

EMBASSIES AND LEGATIONS ACCREDITED TO TURKEY

(In Ankara unless otherwise stated)

Afghanistan: Cinnah Cad. 88, Çankaya; *Chargé d'affaires:* MUHAMMAD ANWER BASRAR.

Albania: Nenehatun Cad. 89, Gaziosmanpaşa; *Ambassador:* GJYLANI SHEHU.

Algeria: Şehit Ersan Cad.; *Ambassador:* MUHAMMAD KADRI.

Argentina: Iran Cad. 57/1, Çankaya; *Ambassador:* JULIO CÉSAR ETCHE GOYER.

Australia: Gaziosmanpaşa, Nenehatun Cad. 83; *Ambassador:* FRANCIS B. HALL.

Austria: Atatürk Bulvarı 189; *Ambassador:* FRANZ WUNDERBALDINGER.

Bahrain: Beirut, Lebanon.

Bangladesh: Karyağdı Sok. 18; *Ambassador:* M. C. M. MURSHED.

Barbados: London, England.

Belgium: Nenehatun Cad. 109; *Ambassador:* MARCEL KERCKOVE.

Brazil: Çankaya, Alaçam Sok. 10/2-4-5; *Chargé d'affaires:* VICTOR MANZDELLO DE MORAES.

Bulgaria: Atatürk Bulvarı 124; *Ambassador:* VLADIMIR GRANTCHAROV.

Burma: Cairo, Egypt.

Cameroon: Cairo, Egypt.

Canada: Nenehatun Cad. 75, Gaziosmanpaşa; *Ambassador:* M. BAUDOUIN.

Chad: Beirut, Lebanon.

Chile: Çankaya, Abdullah Cevdet Sok. 20/2; *Chargé d'affaires:* RAIMUNDO BARROS RAMÍREZ.

China, People's Republic: Yukarı Ayrancı 8, Durak Hoşdere Cad. 147; *Ambassador:* ZHOU JUE.

Cuba: Sofia, Bulgaria.

Czechoslovakia: Atatürk Bulvarı 245; *Ambassador:* JAN MALKOVIC.

Denmark: Kırlangıç Sok. 42, Gaziosmanpaşa; *Ambassador:* MOGENS EDSBERG.

Dominican Republic: London, England.

Egypt: Atatürk Bulvarı 126; *Ambassador:* MOHAMED W. HEGAZI.

El Salvador: Bonn, Federal Republic of Germany.

Ethiopia: Cinnah Cad. 78/1; *Ambassador:* ZEMENE KASSEGN.

Finland: Galip Dede Sok. 1/20, Farabi; *Ambassador:* ULF ERIK SLOTTE.

France: Paris Cad. 70, Kavaklıdere; *Ambassador:* FERNAND ROUILLON.

Gabon: Rome, Italy.

German Democratic Republic: Karlı Sok. 1, Gaziosmanpaşa; *Ambassador:* HEINZ SCHULZ.

Germany, Federal Republic: Atatürk Bulvarı 114; *Ambassador:* DIRCK ONCKEN.

Ghana: Rome, Italy.

Greece: Sölen Sok. 8, Çankaya; *Ambassador:* GEORGES PAPOULIAS.

Guinea: Cairo, Egypt.

Hungary: Gazi Mustafa Kemal Bulvarı 10; *Ambassador:* Dr. IVAN FOTI.

Iceland: Copenhagen, Denmark.

India: Kırlangıç Sok. No. 9, Gaziosmanpaşa; *Ambassador:* PARIMAL CHOSH.

Indonesia: Abdullah Cevdet Sok. 10, Çankaya; *Ambassador:* M. MINTAREDJA.

Iran: Tahran Cad. 10; *Chargé d'affaires:* ABULGHASSEM BJTHADI.

Iraq: Turan Emeksiz Sok. 11, Gaziosmanpaşa; *Chargé d'affaires:* FARUK A. YAHYA.

Ireland: Rome, Italy.

Israel: Farabi Sok. 43, Çankaya; *Chargé d'affaires:* LIEL AION.

Italy: Atatürk Bulvarı 118; *Ambassador:* B. ATTOİLOO.

Japan: Gaziosmanpaşa, Resit Galip Cad. 81; *Ambassador:* NOBUYASU NISHIMIYA.

Jordan: Dede Korkut Sok. 10, Çankaya; *Ambassador:* D. W. M. ALSADI.

Korea, Republic: Cinnah Cad. Alaçam Sok. 9; *Ambassador:* YOUNG PERK.

Kuwait: Kader Sok 6/3, Çankaya; *Chargé d'affaires:* ABDULRAZZAP AL-ATTAR.

Lebanon: Cinnah Cad. 11/3, Çankaya; *Ambassador:* ISSAM BEYHUM.

Libya: Ebuziya Tevfik Sok. 5, Çankaya; *Secretary of the People's Committee:* OMRAN ISSA.

Malaysia: Nenehatun Cad. 115 Gaziosmanpaşa, Çankaya; *Ambassador:* BIN HAJI MOHAMED.

Mexico: Abdullah Cevdet Sok. 20/1, Çankaya; *Ambassador:* HÉCTOR C. MANJARREZ.

Mongolia: *Ambassador:* DAGDALYN BARS.

Morocco: Atatürk Bulvarı 219/9; *Ambassador:* Dr. AHMED BENABUD.

Nepal: Islamabad, Pakistan.

Netherlands: Şehit Ersan Cad. 4, Çankaya; *Ambassador:* HUGO CARSTEN.

Niger: Cairo, Egypt.

Nigeria: Farabi Sok. 20, Çankaya; *Ambassador:* Dr. LAWRENCE A. FABUNMI.

Norway: Kelebek Sok. 20, Çankaya; *Ambassador:* PER GYLOWSEN.

Oman: Teheran, Iran.

Pakistan: Iran Cad. 37; *Ambassador:* MUFTI MOHAMMAD ABBAS.

Papua New Guinea: London, England.

Peru: Vienna, Austria.

Philippines: Teheran, Iran.

Poland: Atatürk Bulvarı 241; *Chargé d'affaires:* TADEUSZ BIEGANSKI.

Portugal: Cinnah Cad. 28/3; *Ambassador:* F. B. DE MIRANDA.

Qatar: Beirut, Lebanon.

Romania: Bükreş Sok. 4, Çankaya; *Ambassador:* VASILE PATILINET.

Saudi Arabia: Abdullah Cevdet Sok. 18, Çankaya; *Ambassador:* MOHAMMAD AL-AWADI.

Senegal: Teheran, Iran.

Somalia: Abdullah Cerdet Sok. 26/2; *Ambassador:* AL JAMMA.

Spain: Abdullah Cevdet Sok. 8, Çankaya; *Ambassador:* SANTIAGO MARTÍNEZ-CARO.

Sudan: Hosdere Cad. 198/4, Çankaya; *Ambassador:* EL-KHATIN AL-SANOUSI.

Sweden: Kâtip Çelebi Sok. 7; *Ambassador:* HENRIK LILHEGREN.

Switzerland: Atatürk Bulvari 247; *Ambassador:* DIETER CHENAUX-RÉPOND.

Syria: Çankaya, Abdullah Cevdet Sok. 7; *Ambassador:* BACHIR EL-KOTB.

Thailand: Cinnah Cad. 61, 5–6 Kavaklıdere; *Ambassador:* SOMAHIT INSINGHA.

Tunisia: Cinnah Cad. 63/6–7; *Ambassador:* ABDULKERIM GANA.

Uganda: Cairo, Egypt.

U.S.S.R.: Karyağdı Sok. 5, Çankaya; *Ambassador:* ALEXEI RODIONOV.

United Kingdom: Çankaya, Şehit Ersan Cad. 46/A; *Ambassador:* SIR PETER LAURENCE, K.C.M.G.

U.S.A.: Atatürk Bulvarı 110; *Ambassador:* ROBERT STRAUSZ-HUPE.

Vatican City: Cukurea Mahalleśı Sok. 55, Çankaya; *Apostolic Pronuncio:* Mgr. SALVATORE ASTA.

Venezuela: Abdullah Cevdet Sok. 26/1, Çankaya; *Ambassador:* HUMBERTO RUMBOS.

Yemen Arab Republic: Amman, Jordan.

Yugoslavia: Paris Cad. 47, Kavaklıdere; *Ambassador:* REDZEP DZIRA.

Zaire: Cairo, Egypt.

Zambia: Rome, Italy.

Turkey also has diplomatic relations with the Bahamas, Burundi, Cape Verde, the Central African Republic, the Comoros, the Congo, Djibouti, Equatorial Guinea, Grenada, Guinea-Bissau, Laos, Liberia, Malawi, Maldives, Mauritania, Mauritius, Rwanda, Sierra Leone, Solomon Islands, Suriname, Swaziland, Tuvalu, the United Arab Emirates, Upper Volta, Uruguay, Viet-Nam, the People's Democratic Republic of Yemen and Zimbabwe.

JUDICIAL SYSTEM

Until the foundation of the Turkish Republic, a large large part of the Turkish civil law—the laws affecting the family, inheritance, property, obligations, etc.—was based on the Koran, and this holy law was administered by special religious (Sharia) courts. The legal reform of 1926 was not only a process of secularization, but also a radical change of the legal system. The Swiss Civil Code and the Code of Obligation, the Italian Penal Code, and the Neuchâtel (Cantonal) Code of Civil Procedure were adopted and modified to fit Turkish customs and traditions.

Constitutional Court: Consists of fifteen regular and five alternate members. Reviews the constitutionality of laws passed by the Turkish Grand National Assembly. Sits as a High Council empowered to try senior members of state. The rulings of the Constitutional Court are final. Decisions of the Court are published immediately in the Official Gazette, and shall be binding on the legislative, executive, and judicial organs of the State.

Court of Cassation: The court of the last instance for reviewing the decisions and verdicts rendered by courts of law. It has original and final jurisdiction in specific cases defined by law. Members are elected by the Supreme Council of Judges.

Council of State: An administrative court of the first instance in matters not referred by law to other administrative courts, and an administrative court of the last instance in general. Hears and settles administrative disputes and expresses opinions on draft laws submitted by the Council of Ministers.

High Military Administrative Court: A military court for the judicial control of administrative acts concerning military personnel.

Military Court of Cassation: A court of the last instance to review decisions and verdicts rendered by military courts.

Court of Jurisdictional Disputes: Settles disputes among civil, administrative and military courts arising from disagreements on jurisdictional matters and verdicts.

Supreme Council of Judges: Consists of eighteen regular and five alternate members. Decides all personnel matters relating to judges.

Public Prosecutor: The law shall make provision for the tenure of public prosecutors and attorneys of the Council of State and their functions.

The Chief Prosecutor of the Republic, the Chief Attorney of the Council of State and the Chief Prosecutor of the Military Court of Cassation are subject to the provisions applicable to judges of higher courts.

Military Trial: Military trials are conducted by military and disciplinary courts. These courts are entitled to try the military offences of military personnel and those offences committed against military personnel or in military areas, or offences connected with military service and duties. Military courts may try non-military persons only for military offences prescribed by special laws.

RELIGION

ISLAM

Diyanet İşleri Reisi (*Head of Religious Affairs in Turkey*): TAYYAR ALTIKULAC.

Over 99 per cent of the Turkish people are Muslims, mostly Sunnis. Turkey is a secular state. Although Islam was stated to be the official religion in the constitution of 1924, an amendment in 1928 removed this privilege. After 1950 subsequent Governments have tried to re-establish links between religion and state affairs, but secularity has been protected, first by the revolution of 1960 and now by the recent coup.

CHRISTIAN CHURCHES

ARMENIAN ORTHODOX CHURCH

SNORK KALUSTYAN, Ermeni Patrikhanesi, Kumkapı, İstanbul.

BULGARIAN ORTHODOX CHURCH

Bulgar Ortodoks Eksarkliği, Şişli, İstanbul; Rvd. Archimandrite GANCO URUKAL.

GREEK ORTHODOX CHURCH

Archbishop of Constantinople and Ecumenical Patriarch: DIMITRIOS I, Rum Ortodox Patrikhanesi, Fener, İstanbul.

ROMAN CATHOLIC CHURCH

ARMENIAN RITE

Archbishopric of Istanbul: Sakĭzağacĭ Cad. No. 31, P.K. 183, Beyoğlu, İstanbul; f. 1830; 3 secular priests, 5 religious priests, 1 Diacre permanent, 4,100 Catholics (1981); Archbishop JEAN TCHOLAKIAN.

BYZANTINE RITE

Apostolic Exarchate of Istanbul: Beyoğlu, Hamalbaşĭ Cad. 44, İstanbul; f. 1911; 1 secular priest; Vicar delegate Rvd. THOMAS VARSAMIS, archimandrite.

Bulgarian Catholic Church: Bulgar Katolik Kilisesi, Eski Parmakkapĭ Sok. 15, Galata, İstanbul; Rvd. DIMITRI BOGDANOFF.

CHALDEAN RITE

Archbishopric of Diarbekĭr: Archevêché chaldéen, Beyoğlu, B.P. 280, Istanbul; 6 secular priests, 11,000 Catholics (1978); Archbishop PAUL KARATAS.

SYRIAN RITE

Vicariate of Mardin and Turkey: Rvd. YUSUF SAG, Patriarchal Vicar.

LATIN RITE

Metropolitan See of Izmir: Atatürk Cad. 210/6, P.K. 267, Izmir; 10 priests, 2,700 Catholics; Metropolitan DOMENICO CALOYERA, O.P.

Apostolic Vicariate of Asia Minor (attached to Archbishopric of Izmir): Apostolic Administrator Metropolitan DOMENICO CALOYERA, O.P.

Apostolic Vicariate of Istanbul: Olçek Sok. 83, Harbiye, Istanbul; f. 1742; 6 secular priests, 39 religious priests, 4,000 Catholics (1981); GAUTHIER PIERRE DUBOIS.

Mission of Trabzon: Katolik Kilisesi, P.K. 5, Samsun; 2 priests, 90 Catholics (1978); Superior Rev. P. GIUSEPPE GERMANO BERNARDINI.

JUDAISM

Jewish Community of Turkey: Chief-khakham DAVID ASSEO, Hahambasilik, Istanbul.

THE PRESS

It is almost impossible to produce a correct list of the numerous provincial newspapers, which tend to be small in circulation and rather short-lived.

Almost all Istanbul papers are also printed in Ankara and İzmir on the same day, and some in Adana. Among the most serious and influential papers are the dailies *Milliyet* and *Cumhuriyet*. The weekly *Gırgır* is noted for its political satire. The most popular dailies are the Istanbul papers *Hürriyet*, *Milliyet*, *Tercüman*, *Son Havadis*, *Günaydın* and *Cumhuriyet*; *Yeni Asir*, published in İzmir, is the best selling quality daily of the Aegean region.

PRINCIPAL DAILIES

ADANA

Cukurova: Kızılay Cad.; f. 1961; political; Proprietor ADİL İKIZ; Editor REFİK SÖLEN; circ. 1,500.

Yeni Adana: Kızılay Cad. 29; f. 1918; political; Proprietor ÇETİN REMZİ YÜREĞIR; Editor KUDDUSİ ÜSTÜN GÜVELOĞLU; circ. 2,300.

Yeni Hürsöz: Irmak Cad. 60/B, Kozan; Proprietor FEHMI KÜÇÜK.

ANKARA

Adalet: Agahefendi Sok. 8/1; f. 1962; morning; political, independent; Editor-in-Chief TURHAN DILLIGIL; Man. Editor METE BAYINDIR; monthly circ. 210,000.

Ankara Ticaret: Rüzgârlı, O.W. Han 2/6; f. 1954; commercial; Editor-in-Chief NURAY TÜZMEN; Man. Editor ABDURRAHMAN KARABAYRAKTAR; monthly circ. 100,000.

Barış: Cinnah Cad. 9/3; f. 1971; morning; political; Owner YAŞAR AYSEV; Man. Editor LEVENT YALÇIN-İSMET SOLAK; monthly circ. 120,000.

Hür Vatan: Rüzgarli Fazilet Han 4/2; f. 1981; Editor-in-Chief NIHAT KAYHAN; Man. Editor EROL ASLAN; monthly circ. 120,000.

Resmi Gazete: Başbakanlık Neşriyat, ve Müdevvenat Genel Müdürlüğü; f. 1920; official gazette.

Tasvir: Ulus Meydani Ulushan Kat 4; f. 1960; conservative; Editor-in-Chief TAHIR ZENGINGÖNÜL; Man. Editor ŞAHAP GENÇSOY; monthly circ. 140,000.

Turkish Daily News: Tunus Cad. 49/7 Kavaklıdere; f. 1961; English language; Publisher İLHAN ÇEVIK; Editor İLNUR ÇEVİK; circ. 5,600.

Turkiye Iktisat Gazetesi: Karanfil Sok. 56, Bakanlıkar; f. 1953; commercial; Editor SABAHATTIN ALPAT.

Yenigün: Rüzgârlı, Agahefendi Sok. 8/5; f. 1968; political; Owner KEMAL ÇUKURKAVAKLI; Editor-in-Chief ALEV ÇUKURKAVAKLI; monthly circ. 120,000.

Yeni Tanin: Rüzgârlı, Ucar Han, Kat 3; f. 1964; political; Proprietor BURHANETTIR GÖGÖN; Editor-in-Chief AHMET TEKEŞ.

Bursa

Bursa Hakimiyet: Ünlü Cad. Çamlıbel Işhanı 34/36; f. 1959; political; Proprietor ARMAĞAN GERÇEKSİ; Editor MEHMET VOLKON; circ. 5,867.

Haber: Kümbet Sok. 7; f. 1964; political; Editor KAZIM TAYAN; circ. 800.

Eskişehir

Milli Irade: 27 Mayis Cad., Eskişehir Pasaji 31; f. 1968; political; Proprietor ETHEM KARACA; Editor ERKUT OZGENCIL.

İstanbul

Apoyevmatini: Suriye Çarşısı 10-12, Beyoğlu; f. 1925; Greek language; Publisher Dr. Y. A. ADASOĞLU; Editor İSTEFAN PAPADOPOULOS; circ. 1,724.

Bayrak: Yerebatan Cad., Salkim Söğüt Sok. 14, Çağaloğlu; f. 1970; political; Editor MEHMET GÜNGÖR; circ. 10,000.

Bulvar: Londra Asfalti-Tercuman tesisleri; f. 1982; owner ÖMER BORNOVALI; Editor YALÇIN KAMACIOĞLU.

Cumhuriyet (*Republic*): Turkocaği Cad. 39, Çağaloğlu; f. 1924; morning; left-wing; Editors-in-Chief HASAN CEMAL, OKTAY GONENSIN; Man. Editor EMINC UŞAKLIGIL; circ. 90,000.

Dünya (*World*): Narlidere Sok. 15, Çağaloğlu; f. 1952; morning; left-wing; Editor İLYAS YEŞIL; circ. 29,500.

Ekspres: Çatalçesme Sok. 29/1, Çağaloğlu; f. 1962; evening; Editor M. KEMAL DERINKOK.

Günaydin: Alayköşkü Cad. Eryilmaz Sok. 13; f. 1960; political; Proprietor HALDUN SIMAVI; Editor RAHMI TURAN; monthly circ. 19,500,000.

Günes: Molla Feneri Sok. 3, Çağaloğlu; f. 1982; political; Owner ÖMER ÇAVUSOĞLU; Dir. Gen. GÜNERI CIVAOĞLU.

Günlük Ticaret: Çemberlitas Palas, Çemberlitas; f. 1947; political; Editor NESRİN TUNÇBİLEK; circ. 1,700.

Haber: Şeref Efendi Sok. 44, Çağaloğlu; f. 1934; Publisher DÜNDAS ENGIN; Editor HASAN KARAYAVUZ; circ. 3,300.

Hürriyet: Babıali Cad. 15-17, Çağaloğlu; f. 1948; morning; independent political; Owner EROL SİMAVI; Editor ÇETIN EMEÇ; circ. 700,000 weekdays, 800,000 Sundays.

Istanbul Postası: Çatalçesme Sok. 17, Çağaloğlu; f. 1946; commercial; Editor ŞEVKI CELIKSER; circ. 2,250.

Jamanak: İstiklâl Cad., Narmanlı Yurdu, Beyoğlu; f. 1908; Armenian; Editor SERKIS HOÇUNYAN; circ. 1,888.

Kelebek: Babıali Cad. 15-17, Çağaloğlu; f. 1972; morning; daily home magazine; Publisher EROL SİMAVI; Editor ŞADAN YOLAŞAN; circ. 90,000.

Marmara: İstiklâl Cad. Tokatlıyan iş han; f. 1941; Armenian language; Editor BEDROS ZOBYAN; circ. 1,800.

Milli Gazete: Çayhane Sok. 1, Topkapı, Çağaloğlu; f. 1973; pro-Islamic; Supports National Salvation Party; Owner and Editor-in-Chief MUSTAFA KARAHASANOĞLU; Man. Editor OSMAN TUNÇ; monthly circ. 1,500,000.

Milliyet: Nuriosmaniye Caddesi 65; f. 1950; morning; political; Editor-in-Chief TURHAN AYTUL; Man. Editor DOĞAN HEPER; monthly circ. 9,500,000.

Sabah: Divanyolu, İncili Çavuş Sok. 27, Sultanahmet; Editor MUSTAFA CERIT.

Son Havadis: Londra Asvaltı, incirli Kavşaği Çayçiçeği Sok. 1, Beşevler; f. 1961; political; Owner MUSTAFA ÖZKAN; Editor-in-Chief SELÇUK IRDEM; monthly circ. 621,854.

Tercüman: Topkapı, Tesisleri, Istanbul; f. 1961; right-wing; Man. Editor HAKKI ÖCAL; Editor UNAL SAKMAN; monthly circ. 515,000; banned October 1981.

Yeni Nesil (*New Generation*): Kazim Gürkan Cad. 6, Çağaloğlu; f. 1970 as *Yeni Asya*; political; Owner MEHMET KUTLULAR; Editor SELAHATTIN AKSAKAL; monthly circ. 450,000.

İzmir

Ege Ekonomi: 2 Beyler Sok. 49; f. 1968; commercial; Editor ABDULLAH BOZKURT; circ. 1,932.

Rapor: GOP Bulvari No. 5; f. 1979; Editor-in-Chief YAVUZ ONURSAL; Man. Editor NEŞETAN; monthly circ. 195,000.

Ticaret Gazetesi: Gazi Bulvarı 18; f. 1942; commercial and political news; Editor-in-Chief AHMET SUKUTI TÜKEL; Man. Editor ENVER AKDOĞAN; monthly circ. 95,000.

Yeni Asir: Gazi Osman Paşa Bul. 5; f. 1875; political; Owner DINÇ BILGİN; Man. Editor GÜNGÖR MENGI; monthly circ. 2,250,000.

Konya

Yeni Konya: İş Bankası Yani No. 4; f. 1945; political; Editor-in-Chief M. NACI GÜCÜYENER; Man. Editor AHMET TEZCAN; monthly circ. 70,000.

Yeni Meram: Mevlâna Cad. 13, Sağlık Pasajı; f. 1949; political; Editor-in-Chief M. YALÇIN ACHLIVAN; Man. Editor YURDANUR AL PAY; monthly circ. 39,500.

WEEKLIES

Ankara

Ekonomi ve Politika: Atatürk Bulvarı, 199/A-45, Kavaklıdere; f. 1966; economic and political; Publisher ZİYA TANSU.

Outlook: Konur Sok. 27/7 Kızılay P.K. 210; f. 1967; English language; Editor M. A. KIŞLALI.

Türkiye Ticaret Sicili: Karanfil Sok. 56, Bakanlıklar; f. 1957; commercial; Editor ISMAIL ASLAN.

Türkiye Yazıları: Selanik Cad., 7 Kızılay; literary; Proprietor-Editor AHMET SAY.

Yankı: Konur Sokak 27/7, P.K. 210, Kızılay; f. 1970; Editor MEHMET ALİ KIŞLALI.

İstanbul

Akbaba: Klodfarer Cad. 8-10, Divanyolu; f. 1923; satirical; Editor ERGIM ORLÂÇ.

Doğan Kardeş: Türbedar Sok. 22, Çağaloğlu; f. 1945; illustrated children's magazine; Editor ŞEVKET RADO; circ. 40,000.

Girgır: Alemdar Mah. 3, Cağaloğlu; satirical; Editor OĞUZ ARAL.

İstanbul Ticaret: Istanbul Chamber of Commerce, Eminönü-Unkapanı Cad.; f. 1957; commercial news; Publishers NUH KUŞÇULU, AHMET TOYDEMİR.

Pazar: Alayköskü Cad., Eryilmaz Sok., Çağaloğlu; f. 1956; illustrated; Publisher HALDUN SİMAVI.

Şalom: Bereket Han 24/5, Karaköy; f. 1948; Jewish; Publisher AVRAM LEYON.

PERIODICALS

Ankara

Adalet Dergisi: Adalet Bakanlığı; f. 1909; legal journal published by the Ministry of Justice; Editor HÜSEYIN ERGÜL; circ. 3,500.

Arayis (*Search*): Weekly political magaizne founded by Bülent Ecevit in 1981; Editor NAHIT DURU; circ. 25,000; closed down March 1981.

Azerbaycan Türk Kültür Dergisi: Vakif İş Hani 324 Anafartalar; f. 1949; literary and cultural periodical of Azerbaizhanian Turks; Editor Dr. AHMET YAŞAT.

Bayrak Dergisi: Necatibev Cad., Karakimseli Han 56; f. 1964; Publisher and Editor HAMI KARTAY.

Devlet Opera ve Balesi Genel Müdürlüğü: f. 1949; State opera and ballet; Gen. Dir. YALÇIN DAVRAN.

Devlet Tiyatrosu: Devlet Tiyatrosu Um. Md.; f. 1952; art, theatre.

Eğitim ve Bilim: Ziya Gökalp Cad. 48, Yenişehir; education and science; Editor SEYDI DINÇTÜRK.

Elektrik Muhendisligi Mecmuasi: Konur Sok, 4/3, Yenişehir; f. 1954; published by the Chamber of Turkish Electrical Engineers.

Halk Eğitimi: Milî Eğitim Bakanlığı, Halk Eğitimi Genel Müdürlüğü; f. 1966; published by a department of the Ministry of Education; educational.

Karınca: Mithat Paşa Cad. 38/A, Yenişehir; f. 1934; monthly review published by the Turkish Co-operative Society; Editor NUSRET UZGÖREN; circ. 6,000.

Maden Tetkik ve Arama Enstitüsü Dergisi: İnönü Bulvarı; f. 1935; bi-annual; publ. by Mineral Research and Exploration Institute of Turkey; English Edition *Bulletin of the Mineral Research and Exploration Institute* (bi-annual).

Mimarlık (*Architecture*): Konur Sok. 4, Kızılay; monthly; Editor AHMET SÖNMEZ.

Mühendis ve Makina: Sümer Sok. 36/1; f. 1957; engineering; monthly; Publisher Chamber of Mechanical Engineers; Dir. and Editor ISMET RİZA GEBI.

Resmi Kararlar Dergisi: Ministry of Justice, Adalet Bakanlığı; f. 1966; legal; Editor AVNI ÖZENÇ; circ. 3,500.

Türk Arkeoloji Dergisi (*General Directorate of Antiquities and Museums*): Kültür Bakanlığı, Eski Eserler ve Müzeler Genel Müdürlüğü-Cento Binasi Ulus; archaeological.

Türk Dili: Türk Dil Kurumu, Atatürk Bulvarı 217, Kavaklıdere; f. 1951; monthly; literary.

Turkey—Economic News Digest: Karanfil Sok. 56; f. 1960; Editor-inChief BEHZAT TANIR; Man. Editor SADIK BALKAN.

Türkiye Bankacılık: P.K. 121; f. 1955; commercial; Publisher MUSTAFA ATALAY.

Türkiye Bibliyografyası: Milli Kütüphane Müdürlüğü, Yenişehir; f. 1934; monthly; Turkish national bibliography; published by the Bibliographical Institute of the Turkish National Library; Dir. ORHAN DOĞAN.

Türkiye Makaleler Bibliyografyasi: Milli Kütüphane Müdürlüğü, Yenişehir; f. 1952; quarterly; f. 1952; quarterly; Turkish articles bibliography; published by the Bibliographical Institute of the Turkish National Library; Dir. IŞIN DURUÖZ.

Yeni Yayınlar, Aylık Bibliyografya Dergisi (*New Publications, Monthly Bibliographic Journal*):P.K. 440, Kızılay; f. 1956; Published by Asscn. of Univ. Library School Graduates; Dir. O. ÜSTÜN YILDIRIM; circ. 1,250.

İSTANBUL

Banka ve Ekonomik Yorumlar: Çağaloğlu, Çatalçeşme Sok. 17, Kat. 4; f. 1964; banking, economic, social and management subjects; Dir. M. KEMAL KURDAS; circ. 5,000.

Le Flambeau (*Aylik Dergi*): Pangaltı, Ölcek Sokak 82; f. 1946; 10 issues a year; published by Apostolic Vicariate of Istanbul; Gen. Man. MARCEL LINGURI.

Girgir: Istanbul; humorous cartoon magazine.

Istanbul, A Handbook for Tourists: Sişli Meydanı, 364; f. 1968; quarterly; published by Türk Turing, official travel agency of the Touring and Automobile Club of Turkey; Publisher Prof. KEMAL KUTLU; Editor ÇELIK GÜLERSOY.

İstanbul Ticaret Odası Mecmuası: İstanbul Ticaret Odası, Gümüşpala Cad., Eminönü; f. 1884; every three months; journal of the Istanbul Chamber of Commerce; Turkish and English; Editor AHMET TOYDEMIR.

Kemalizm: Bankalar Cad., Ankara H. 4; f. 1962; Publisher HÜSEYİN SAĞIROĞLU.

Kulis: Çağaloğlu Yokuşu 10/A; f. 1947; fortnightly arts magazine; Armenian; Publisher HAGOP AYVAZ.

Musiki Mecmuası: P.K. 666; f. 1948; monthly; music and musicology; Editor ETEM RUHİ ÜNGÖR.

Pirelli Mecmuası: Büyükdere Cad. 117, Gayrettepe; f. 1964; monthly; Publisher Türk Pirelli Lâstikleri A.S.; Editor NAMI ELAGÖZ; circ. 10,000.

Ruh ve Madde Dergisi: P.K. 1157; f. 1959; organ of the Metapsychic and Scientific Research Society of Turkey; Publisher ERGÜN ARIKDAL.

Sağlık Âlemi: Divanyolu Cad. Ersoy Pasajı 1, Çağaloğlu; f. 1964; health; Editor SAMIM AKAY.

Sevgi Dünyası (*World of Love*): Larmartin Cad. 26/3, Taksim; f. 1963; Publisher and Editor Dr. R. KAY-SERİLİOĞLU; circ. 5,000.

Tip Dünyasi: Ankara Cad. 31/51, Vakif İş Han, Çağaloğlu; f. 1927; monthly; organ of the Turkish Mental Health and Social Psychiatry; Editor Ord. Prof. Dr. FAHRED-DIN KERIM GÖKAY.

Türk Anglo-Amerikan ve Almaya Postasi: P.K. 192, Beyoğlu; f. 1947; commercial; Publisher KEMAL ERKAN.

Türk Folklor Araştirmalari: P.K. 46, Aksaray; f. 1949; arts and folklore; publ. by Turkish Folklore Association; Gen. Man. and Editor IHSAN HINÇER.

Turkish Trade Directory and Telex Index: Peykhane Cad. 14, Daire 1, Çemberlitas; f. 1962; annual; Publisher CIRO COSTANTE, COSTANTE BASIN AJANSI.

Türkiye Turing ve Otomobil Kurumu Belleteni: Halaskargazi Cad. 364, Şişli Meydani; f. 1930; quarterly; published by the Touring and Automobile Club of Turkey; Publisher Prof. KEMAL KUTLU; Editor ÇELIK GÜLERSOY.

Varlik: Çağaloğlu Yokuşu 40; f. 1933; monthly; literary; Editor FILIZ NAYIR.

İZMİR

İzmir Ticaret Odasi Dergisi: Atatürk Cad. 126; f. 1925; monthly; published by Chamber of Commerce of Izmir; Sec.-Gen. SULHI AREL; Man. EDIP KAÇAR.

KONYA

Çağrı Dergisi: P.K. 99; f. 1957; literary; monthly; Editor FEYZİ HALICI.

NEWS AGENCIES

Akajans: Tunus Cad. 28, Kat. 4, Bakanliklar, Ankara; Dir. YASAR GÜNGÖR.

Anatolian News Agency: Hanimeli Sok. 7, Ankara; also in Istanbul; f. 1920; Gen. Man. CEVDET TANYCLI; publ. *Weekly Economical Bulletin*.

ANKA Ajansi: Mesnitiyet Cad. No. 41/7, Ankara; Dir.-Gen. MÜSSERREF HEKIMOĞLU.

EBA Ekonomik Basin Ajansi (*Economic Press Agency*): Olgunlar Sok 2/1, Bakanliklar, Ankara; private economic news service; Publisher YAVUZ TOLUN; publs. (in English) *Newsletter* (daily review of Turkish economic and financial news), *Report* (weekly survey of Turkish public tenders and investment projects), *Briefing* (weekly evaluation of Turkish political and economic developments).

Hurriyet Haber Ajansi: Babiali Cad. 15-17 Kat 3, Çağaloğlu, Istanbul; f. 1963; Dir.-Gen. OKTAY EKSI.

İKA Haber Ajansi (*Economic and Commercial News Agency*): Atatürk Bulvarı 199/A-45, Kavaklıdere, Ankara; f. 1954; Dir. ZİYA TANSU.

Türk Haberler Ajansı (*Turkish News Agency*): Türkocağı Cad. 1/4, Çağaloğlu, Istanbul; f. 1950; 11 brs. in Turkey; Dir.-Gen. IEYLA TAUSANOĞLU.

FOREIGN BUREAUX

Agence France-Presse (AFP): Ahmet Rasim Sokak No. 23, P.K. 30, Çankaya, Ankara; Correspondent JEAN-JACQUES CAZAUX.

Agencia EFE (*Spain*): Günes Sok. 12/3, Güven Evleri Kavaklıdere, Ankara; Correspondent ERCOLE MICHELINI.

Agenzia Nazionale Stampa Associata (ANSA) (*Italy*): Gelincik Sok. 7 A/6, Kavaklıdere, Ankara; Correspondent ROMANO DAMIANI.

Associated Press (AP) (*U.S.A.*): Tunus Cad. 49-7, Kavaklıdere, Ankara; Correspondent Mrs. EMEL ANIL.

Bulgarian Telegraph Agency (BTA): Hatır Sok. 25/6, Gaziosmanpaşa, Ankara; Correspondent STEFAN SOLAKOV.

Deutsche Presse-Agentur (dpa) (*Federal Republic of Germany*): c/o ANKA Ajansı, Portakal Çiceği Sok. 63/2, Çankaya, Ankara; Correspondent RASIT GÜRDILEK.

Novinska Agencija Tanjug (*Yugoslavia*): Turan Emeksiz Sok. 12/6, Çankaya, Ankara.

Reuters (*United Kingdom*): P.K. 239, Kizilay, Ankara.

United Press International (UPI) (*U.S.A.*): Kurucesme Cad. 18-20, Arnavutkoy, İstanbul; Bureau Chief OGUZ SEREN.

AFP also has representatives in Istanbul and İzmir. AP is also represented in Istanbul. TASS (*U.S.S.R.*) and Xinhua (*People's Republic of China*) are also represented in Turkey.

PRESS ASSOCIATION

Gazeteciler Cemiyeti: Çağaloğlu, İstanbul; Pres. BURHAN FELEK; Sec. MUSTAFA YÜCEL.

PUBLISHERS

Altın Kitaplar: Çağaloğlu, Istanbul; f. 1959; fiction, non-fiction, biography, memoirs, poetry, children's books, classics, history and crime; Publisher FETHİ UL; Editor-in-Chief TURHAN BOZKURT.

Ark Ticaret Ltd. ŞTI: Ali Çetinkaya Bulv. 16/2, P.O.B. 137 Merkez, Alsancak-İzmir; f. 1962; import-export representation; imports technical books and exports all kinds of Turkish books, periodicals and newspapers; Gen. Man. ATILAN TÜMER.

Arkın Kitabevi: Ankara Cad. 60, P.K. 11, Istanbul; f. 1949; encyclopaedias, atlases, children's books, reference; Pres. and Man. RAMAZAN GÖKALP ARKIN.

Atlas Yayınevi: Nuruosmaniye Caddesi, Mengene Sokak 7-9, Istanbul; literary; Publisher RAKIM ÇALAPALA.

Başkent Yayınevi: İzmir Cad. 55/22, Ankara; literary.

Bedir Yayınevi: P.O.B. 1060, Istanbul; Islamic and Turkish books.

Cem Yayınevi: Çağaloğlu, Istanbul; f. 1964; novels, poetry, modern classics, cultural and historical books, children's books; Man. OGUZ AKKAN.

Elif Kitabevi: Sahaflar Çarşısı 4, Beyazit, Istanbul; f. 1956; all types of publications, especially historical, literary; political, drama and reference; Old Ottoman and Turkish books and periodicals; Publisher ARSLAN KAYNARDAĞ; publ. *Elif Yayınları*.

Gelişim Yayınları A.Ş.: Levent, Istanbul; encyclopaedias, reference and non-fiction; Man. ERCAN ARIKLI.

Hürriyet Yayınları: Cemal Nadir Sok. 7, Çağaloğlu, İstanbul; fiction, history, classics, poetry, general reference books; Dir. AYDIN EMEÇ.

İnkilâp Kitabevi: Ankara Cad. 95, Istanbul; general publications; export and import; Dir. NAZAR FİKRİ.

İnkılâp ve Aka Kitabevleri Kollektif Şirketi: Ankara Cad. 95, Istanbul; f. 1961; general, reference books, maps, novels, children's, educational, technical, cookery, picture books; Dirs. NAZAR FİKRİ, KARABET AKAEREN.

Kanaat Kitabevi: Ilyas Bayar Halefi, Yakup Bayar, Ankara Caddesi 133, Istanbul; f. 1896; textbooks, novels, dictionaries, posters, maps and atlases.

Kanaat Yayınları Ltd. Şti: Ankara Cad. 133/1, Istanbul; f. 1951; maps, school books; Dir. YAKUP BAYAR.

Karacan Yayinlari: Basin Sarayi, Çağaloğlu-Istanbul; f. 1980; literary books and magazines; Gen. Man. ÜLKÜ TAMER.

Kervan Yayınları: Tercüman Tesisleri Londra Asfalti Topkapi, Istanbul; literary.

Koza Yayınevi: Çağaloğlu, Ozaydin Han 6, İstanbul; non-fiction, children's books; Man. TARIK DURSUN.

Kültür Kitabevi: Ankara Cad. 62, Sirkeci, Istanbul; f. 1945; technical books, school books, language books, etc.; Dirs. İZİDOR and RENE KANT.

Neşriyat A.Ş.: Mollafenari S.1, Çağaloğlu, Istanbul; classics, children's books, novels.

Öğretim Yayınevi: Ankara Cad. 62/2, Sirkeci, Istanbul; f. 1959; English, French, German, Italian, Spanish and Dutch language courses, guides and dictionaries, phrase books for tourists; Dir. İZİDOR KANT.

Remzi Kitabevi: Ankara Caddesi 93, Istanbul; f. 1930; school textbooks, fiction, children's, science and reference books; Dir. EROL ERDURAN.

Sander Yayınevi: Kiragı Sok. 78, Osmanbey, Istanbul; Man. Dir. NECDET SANDER.

Türk Dil Kurumu: Atatürk Bulvarı 217, Kavaklıdere, Ankara; f. 1932; non-fiction.

Varlık Yayınavi: Çağaloğlu Yokuşu 40, Istanbul; f. 1946; fiction and non-fiction books; Dir. FİLİZ NAYİR.

Yazko: Aril Paşa Sok., Kurt İşhane Çağaloğlu, Istanbul; f. 1980; literary books and magazines.

Yeditepe Yayınları: P.K. 77, Çağaloğlu, Nuruosmaniye Cad., Yeni Han 21, Istanbul; publishes literature, poetry, translations, etc. and also *Yeditepe* (monthly).

PUBLISHERS' ASSOCIATION

Editörler Derneği (*Publishers' Association*): Ankara Cad. 60, Istanbul; f. 1950; Pres. RAMAZAN GÖKALP ARKIN; Sec. RAKIM ÇALAPALA.

RADIO AND TELEVISION

RADIO

Türkiye Radyo Televizyon Kurumu (T.R.T.): Nevzat Tandoğan Cad. No. 2, Kavaklıdere, Ankara; f. 1964; controls Turkish radio and television services; Dir.-Gen. MACIT AKMAN.

Home Services:

There are local radio stations in Adana, Amasya, Ankara (3), Antalya (2), Aydin-Muğla, Bursa, Çanakkale, Çukurova, Denizli, Diyarbakir, Edirne, Erzurum, Eskişehir, Gaziantep, Hakkari, Isparta-Burdur, Istanbul (3), İzmir (2), İzmit, Kayseri, Konya, Ordu-Giresun, Sivas, Samsun, Trabzon (2), Van (2) and Zonguldak.

Foreign Service (Voice of Turkey); Posta Kutusu 333, Yenişehir, Ankara.

Ankara: SW 250 kW (3). Sixteen daily short-wave transmissions in the following languages: Albanian, Arabic, Azeri, Bulgarian, Chinese, English, French, German, Greek, Hungarian, Persian, Romanian, Russian, Serbo-Croat, Turkish, Urdu; Dir. CAFER DEMIRAL.

There is also an educational radio service for schools and a station run by the Turkish State Meteorological Service. The American Forces have their own radio and television service.

In 1979 4,279,958 licensed radio receivers were in use.

TELEVISION

Türkiye Radyo Televizyon Kurumu (Ankara TV): Nevzat Tandoğan Cad. 2, Kavaklıdere, Ankara. A limited television service was set up in 1965, and regular broadcasts for Ankara began in 1968, now transmitting programmes seven days a week, averaging 50 hours a week. Head of Television Dept. TARCAN GÜNENC; Deputy Heads TEOMAN ERTAN, MEHMET TURAN AKKÜPRÜLÜLER.

In 1979 3,108,117 licensed television receivers were in use.

FINANCE

The Central Bank of the Republic of Turkey was originally founded in 1930, and constituted in its present form in 1970. The Central Bank is the bank of issue and is also responsible for the execution of monetary and credit policies, the regulation of the foreign and domestic value of the Turkish lira jointly with the Government, and the supervision of the credit system.

There are some 42 other banks functioning in Turkey. Fourteen were created by special laws to fulfil specialized services for particular industries. The Sümerbank directs the operation of a number of state-owned factories; Etibank operates primarily in the extractive industries and electric power industries; the Agricultural Bank makes loans for agriculture; the Maritime Bank operates government-owned port facilities, the merchant marine and its own fleet of ships; the Real Estate Credit Bank participates in industrial undertakings and the construction of all types of building. Other specialized banks deal with tourism, municipalities and mortgages, etc.

The largest of the private sector Turkish banks is the Türkiye İş Bankası which operates over 850 branches. The private banks borrow at medium- and long-term mainly from the State Investment Bank.

There are several other credit institutions in Turkey, including the Industrial Development Bank of Turkey, which encourages private investment in industry by acting as underwriter in the issue of share capital. The Turkiye Sınai Kalkinma Bankası was founded in 1950 with the assistance of the World Bank to stimulate industrial growth in the private sector.

There are numerous co-operative organizations, and in the rural areas there are Agricultural Sale Co-operatives and Agricultural Co-operatives. There are also a number of savings institutions.

BANKING

(cap.=capital; p.u.=paid up; auth.=authorized; dep.= deposits; res.=reserves; m.=million; brs.=branches)

(Amounts in Turkish liras, except where otherwise stated. Figures given are for December 1980, except where otherwise stated.)

STATE BANKS

Türkiye Cumhuriyet Merkez Bankası A.Ş. (*Central Bank of the Republic of Turkey*): Ulus, Ankara; f. 1930; bank of issue; cap. p.u. 25m.; res. 4,760m.; Gov. OSMAN ŞIKLAR; 21 brs.

Denizcilik Bankası T.A.O. (*Turkish Maritime Bank*): Karaköy, Istanbul; f. 1952; cap. p.u. 10,666m.; res. 2.3m.; dep. 2,844m.; Chair. and Gen. Man. VEHBİ NEJAT ÖZGECE; 21 brs.

Devlet Sanayi ve İşçi Yatırım Bankası A.Ş. (*State Industry and Workers' Investments Bank*): İzmir Caddesi 43, Kızılay, Ankara; f. 1976; cap. p.u. TL 961.3 (1981); Gen. Man. Dr. HALIT KARA.

Devlet Yatırım Bankası (*State Investment Bank*): Kızılay, Ankara; f. 1964; cap. p.u. 3,500m.; res. 3,321m.; loans to state enterprises; Chair. and Gen. Man. TARIK KIVANÇ; 1 br.

Etibank: Sıhhiye, Ankara; f. 1935; cap. p.u. 17,010m.; res. 585m.; dep. 11,100m.; Chair. and Gen. Man. Dr. ERDEMİR KARAKAŞ; 111 brs.

İller Bankası (*Municipalities Bank*): Opera, Ankara; f. 1933; cap. p.u. 2,000m.; res. 117.2m.; dep. 95m.; Chair. and Gen. Man. AYDIN EVRENKAYA; 1 br.

İstanbul Emniyet Sandığı: Cağaloğlu, Istanbul; f. 1868; res. 14.3m; dep. 2,278m.; Dir. M. ALİ AYDAŞ; 50 brs.

Sümerbank: Ulus, Ankara; f. 1933; cap. p.u. 12,990m.; res. 341m.; dep. 2,241m.; Chair. and Gen. Man. ŞÜKRÜ AKGÜNGÖR; 42 brs.

Töbank: P.O.B. 152 Ulus, Atatürk Bulvarı 163, Ankara; f. 1959; cap. p.u. 30m.; res. 196m.; dep. 10,340m.; Chair. Prof. Dr. SAİT KEMAL MİMAROĞLU; Gen. Man. TUNCAY BEYHAN; 116 brs.

Türkiye Cumhuriyeti Turizm Bankası A.Ş. (*Tourism Bank of the Republic of Turkey*): Bakanlıklar, Ankara; f. 1962; cap. 15,000m. (Dec. 1981); Chair. and Gen. Man. CAFER CANLI; 1 br.

Türkiye Cumhuriyeti Ziraat Bankası (*Agricultural Bank of the Republic of Turkey*): Ulus, Ankara; f. 1863; cap. p.u. 3,646m.; res. 1,649m.; dep. 151,786m. (Sept. 1980); Gen. Man. RAHMI ONEN; 1,057 brs.

Finance

Türkiye Emlâk Kredi Bankası A.O. (*Real Estate and Credit Bank of Turkey*): Atatürk Bulvarı 15, Ankara; f. 1926; cap. p.u. 20,000m.; dep. 50,557m. (Dec. 1981); Gen. Man. CEMAL KUIU; 287 brs.

Türkiye Halk Bankası A.Ş.: Ulus, Ankara; f. 1938; cap. p.u. 4,879.9m.; dep. 59,504.4m. (Dec. 1981); Chair. and Gen. Man. A. SAHİN ULUSOY; 603 brs.

Türkiye Vakıflar Bankası T.A.O. (*Foundation Bank of Turkey*): Kavaklıdere, Ankara; f. 1954; cap. p.u. 1,000m.; res. 185m.; dep. 57,545m.; Chair. (acting) ALİ RIZA ZORLUOĞLU; Gen. Man. A. ÇETİN ÖZKAN; 264 brs.

COMMERCIAL BANKS

Akbank T.A.S.: Meclisi Mebusan Cad. 65-69, Fındıklı, Istanbul; f. 1948; cap. p.u. 2,500m.; dep. 223,785m. (Dec. 1981); Chair. NAİM TALU; Gen. Man. HAMİT BELİG BELLİ; 602 brs.

Adanolu Bankası A.S.: Beyoğlu, Istanbul; f. 1962; auth. cap. 15,000m.; dep. 28,000m. (Dec. 1981); Chair. OSMAN KİBAR; Pres. ERHAN IŞIL; Gen. Man. EROL TOKSÖZ; 102 brs.

Bağbank (Türkiye Bağcilar Bankası) A.S.: Borsa Cad., Manısa, P.O.B. 560, Izmir; f. 1917; cap. 750m.; dep. 390,105m. (Dec. 1981); Gen. Man. DİNÇER TURGAY; 13 brs.

Caybank A.Ş.: Rize; f. 1958; cap. p.u. 2.7m.; res. 0.1m.; dep. 9.2m.; Chair. MAHMUT TOPÇU; Gen. Man. ALI RIZA TAŞPINAR; 3 brs.

Demirbank T.A.Ş.: Karaköy, Istanbul; f. 1953; cap. p.u. 20m.; res. 3.4m.; dep. 1,031m.; Chair. KAMİL GÜNDEŞ; Gen. Man. CENGIZ ESİN; 23 brs.

Egebank A.S.: İzmir; f. 1928; cap. p.u. 395m.; dep. 4,350m.; Chair. MELİH ÖZAKAT; Gen. Man. TEKİN DEĞİRMENCİ; 22 brs.

Eskişehir Bankası T.A.Ş.: Eskişehir; f. 1927; cap. p.u. 100m.; res. 3.8m.; dep. 3,477m. (Dec. 1981); Chair. MESUT EREZ; Gen. Man. YILMAZ MAZLUMOĞLU; 24 brs.

Hisarbank A.Ş.: Zincirlikuyu, Istanbul; f. 1926; cap. p.u. 500m.; res. 1.2m.; dep. 4,350m.; Chair. and Gen. Man. AHMET DEMİRER; 21 brs.

İktisat Bankası T.A.Ş.: Mecidiyeköy, Istanbul; f. 1927; cap. p.u. 100m.; res. 3.5m.; dep. 588m.; Chair. A. FUAT DAĞDEVİREN; Sec.-Gen. H. MÜNCI MERTSOY; 11 brs.

İstanbul Bankası A.S.: Istiklâl Caddesi 396-398, Müeyyet Sokak No. 1, Tünel-Istanbul; f. 1953; cap. 1,000m.; res. 24m.; dep. 36,000m. (Dec. 1981); Chair. NEVZAT ALPTÜRK; Man. Dir. ÖZER UÇURAN ÇİLLER; 96 brs.

İşçi Kredi Bankası T.A.Ş.: Kayseri; f. 1954; cap. p.u. 30m.; res. 6m.; dep. 427m.; Chair. AHMET TURAN; Gen. Man. (acting) DOĞAN ERDOĞAN; 3 brs.

Kocaeli Bankası T.A.Ş.: İzmit; f. 1927; cap. p.u. 30m.; res. 1m.; dep. 282m.; Chair. ŞAHABETTİN BENGİSU; Gen. Man. ALAEDDİN ÖZKURT; 6 brs.

Milli Aydın Bankası T.A.Ş.: Aydın; f. 1913; cap. p.u. 100m.; res. 2.2m.; dep. 712m.; Chair. GÜNERÇİN AZBAZDAR; Gen. Man. (acting) İSMET YILMAZ; 19 brs.

Ortadoğu İktisat Bankası T.A.Ş.: Sirkeci, Istanbul; f. 1929; cap. p.u. 78m.; res. 2.6m.; dep. 231m.; Chair. Prof. Dr. CEVAT SARIKAMIŞ; Gen. Man. ERTAN ÖZGÜR; 6 brs.

Pamukbank T.A.Ş.: Büyükdere Caddesi 82, Gayrettepe, Istanbul; f. 1955; nominal cap. 1,200m.; dep. 84,615m. (Dec. 1981); Chair. M. EMİN KARAMEHMET; Gen. Man. HÜSNÜ M. ÖZYEĞİN; 182 brs.

Şekerbank T.A.Ş.: Atatürk Bulvarı 55, Ankara; f. 1953; cap. p.u. 375m.; res. 34m.; dep. 7,450m.; Chair. BEHÇET OĞUR; Gen. Man. SEZAİ ŞEN; 135 brs.

Türk Dıs Ticaret Bankası A.Ş.: Harbiye, Istanbul; f. 1964; cap. p.u. 10m.; res. 111m.; dep. 1,542m.; Chair. and Gen. Man. AYETULLAH ÜSKÜDARLI; 5 brs.

Türk Ticaret Bankası A.Ş.: Bahçekapı, Istanbul; f. 1913; cap. p.u. 412m.; res. 529m.; dep. 41,807m.; Chair. and Gen. Man. BEHZAT TUNCER; 404 brs.

Türkiye Garanti Bankası A.Ş.: İstiklal Cad. Mihçıoğlu Han., Istanbul; f. 1946; cap. 2,000m.; res. 35m.; dep. 50,000m. (Dec. 1981); Chair. CAN KIRAÇ; Gen. Man. EVREN ARTAM; 297 brs.

Türkiye Imar Bankası T.A.Ş.: 29 Voyvoda Caddesi, Hacı Ali Sokak, Karaköy, Istanbul; f. 1928; cap. p.u. 402m.; res. 60m.; dep. 3,085m.; Chair. ENVER ATEŞDAĞLI; Gen. Man. EROL TÜRKER; 10 brs.

Türkiye İs Bankası A.Ş.: Kavaklıdere, Ankara; f. 1924; cap p.u. 40m.; res. 4,420m.; dep. 166,676m.; Chair. İSMAİL HAKKI BİRLER; Gen. Man. CAHİT KOCAÖMER; 861 brs.

Türkiye Tütüncüler Bankası A.Ş.: İzmir; f. 1924; cap. p.u. 29m.; res. 8m.; dep. 449m.; Chair. ALİ SÖĞÜTÇÜKLÜ; Gen. Man. ÖNDER TURANAN; 28 brs.

Uluslararası Endsütrı ve Ticaret Bankası A.Ş. (Interbank): P.O.B. 1326, Bankalar Cad. 69, Karaköy, Istanbul; f. 1888; cap. p.u. 500m.; dep. 22,311m. (Dec. 1981); Chair. BERAT AKERMAN; Man. Dir. EROL AKSOY; 14 brs.

Yapı ve Kredi Bankası A.Ş.: Istiklâl Cad., Korsan Çıkmazı No. 1, P.O.B. 250, Beyoğlu, Istanbul; f. 1944; cap. p.u. 4,906m.; res. 802m.; dep. 205,789m. (Dec. 1981); Chair. ADNAN DİNÇER; Gen. Man. HALİT SOYDAN; 591 brs.

DEVELOPMENT AND INVESTMENT BANKS

Sınai Yatırım ve Kredi Bankası A.O.: Beşiktaş, Istanbul; f. 1963; cap. p.u. 400m.; res. 71m.; Chair. CAHİT KOCAÖMER; Gen. Man. Dr. ORHAN ALTAN; 1 br.

Türkiye Sınai Kalkınma Bankası A.Ş. (*Industrial Development Bank of Turkey*): P.O.B. 17, Karaköy, Istanbul; f. 1950; cap. 3,000m.; dep. 59,641m. (Dec. 1981); Chair. BURHAN KARAGÖZ; Gen. Man. ÖZHAN EROĞUZ; 5 brs.

FOREIGN BANKS

Arap-Türk Bankası (*Arab-Turkish Bank*): Elmadağ, Istanbul; f. 1977; cap. p.u. 240m.; res. 35m.; dep. 4,376m.; Chair. ORAL ÇOBANOĞLU; Gen. Man. FARAG SHALLOUF; 1 br.

Banco di Roma: Bahçekapı, Instanbul; f. 1911; nominal cap. 1.5m.; res. 14m.; dep. 615m.; Chair. and Gen. Man. in Turkey G. ROSI; 4 brs.

Bank Mellat (*Iran*): 71 Cumhuriyet Cad., P.O.B. 5, Beyoğlu, Istanbul.

Citibank (*United States*): Branch opened in Istanbul, May 1981.

Hollantse Bank-Uni N.V.: Beyoğlu, Istanbul; f. 1921; nominal cap. 346m.; res. 4m.; dep. 226m.; Chair. and Gen. Man. in Turkey W. J. J. COZIJNSEN; 2 brs.

Osmanlı Bankası A.Ş. (*Ottoman Bank*): P.O.B. 297, Bankalar Caddesi, Karaköy, Istanbul; f. 1863; cap. p.u. 8m.; res. 432m.; dep. 24,667m. (Dec. 1981); Chair. and Gen. Man. in Turkey J. JEULIN; 113 brs.

The following foreign banks were due to open branches in Turkey in 1982: *Habib Bank* (Pakistan), *Middle East Bank* (Dubai) and *Rafidain Bank* (Iraq).

STOCK EXCHANGE

Borsa Komiserliği: Menkul Kıymetler ve Kambiyo Borsası, 4 Vakıf Han, Bahçekapı, Istanbul; f. 1873; 323 mems.; Pres. KADRİYE ŞİŞMAN; publ. *Borsa.*

INSURANCE

Güven Türk Anonim Sigorta Şirketi: Bankalar Cad., Karaköy, Istanbul; f. 1924; state-owned; Chair. and Gen. Man. A. FETHİ SOYSAL.

Sosyal Sigortalar Kurumu: Mithatpaşa Cad., Ankara; f. 1945; social insurance organization; 2,300,000 mems.; cap. and dep. 55,531.7m.; Gen. Dir. HİKMET ERİNG; publ. *Social Security Bulletin* (monthly).

PRIVATE INSURANCE

Anadolu Anonim Türk Sigorta Şirketi (*Anatolia Turkish Insurance Society*): Rıhtım Cad. 57, P.O.B. 1845, Karaköy, Istanbul; Gen. Man. BEDİİ TÜMER.

Ankara Sigorta A.Ş. (*Ankara Insurance Society*): Bankalar Cad. 80, Ankara Sigorta Hanı, Istanbul; f. 1935; Chair. MUSTAFA KEMAL SAYIL; Gen. Man. MAHMUT ÇALIŞAL.

Atlantik Sigorta A.Ş.: Bankalar Cad. 2, Kat. 4, Karaköy, Istanbul; f. 1964; fire, life, marine, accident; Chair. ALİ GÖMEC; Gen. Man. EMİN ATASAGUN.

Destek Reasurans T.A.Ş.: Cumhuriyet Cad. 6a/2, Harbiye, İstanbul; f. 1945; reinsurance; Pres. HİKMET KÜNEY; Gen. Man. TACETTİN ALİEFENDİOĞLU.

Doğan Sigorta A.Ş.: Doğan Sigorta Binası, Karaköy, Istanbul; f. 1942; fire, marine, accident; Chair. EROL SABANCI; Man. Dir. ALİ GOMEÇ.

Halk Sigorta T.A.S.: Büyükdere Cad., Halk Sigorta Merkez Hani No. 161 Zincirlikuyu, Istanbul; f. 1944; Dir. ÖMER ERÜL; Gen. Man. YÜCEL GÜNSEL.

İmtaş İttihadı Milli Türk Anonim Sigorta Şirketi (*Imtaş Insurance Company*): Büyükdere Cad. No. 132, Zincirlikuyu, Istanbul; f. 1918; Pres. MUKADDER ÖZTEKIN; Gen. Man. BÜLENT AKARCALI.

Istanbul Reinsurance Co.: Halaskargazi Cad. 309, Kat. 4, Sisli, Istanbul; Chair. HANEFİ ULUTEKIN; Gen. Man. ENGIN ASAL.

Istanbul Umum Sigorta Anonim Şirketi (*General Insurance Society of Istanbul*): Bankalar Cad. 31/33, Karaköy, Istanbul; f. 1893; Pres. ERDOĞAN DEMİRÖREN; Gen. Man. ERGÜN TÜRKER.

Milli Reasurans T.A.S.: P.O.B. 359, Sirkeci, Istanbul; f. 1929; privately owned with monopoly of re-insurance; Chair. YALCIN AHISKA; Gen. Man. CAHİT NOMER.

Şark Sigorta Anonim Şirketi: Büyükdere Cad. 145, Zincirlikuyu, Istanbul; f. 1923; Chair. HULKİ ALİSBAH; Gen. Man. CEMAL ZAGRA.

Şeker Sigorta Anonim Şirketi: Meclisi Mebusan Cad. 325, Şeker Sigorta Hanı, P.O.B. 519, Karaköy, Istanbul; Chair. ORHAN DEMIRÖZÜ; Gen. Man. (vacant).

Tam Hayat Sigorta A.Ş.: Büyükdere Cad., Tam Han, Sişli, Istanbul; general life assurance; Gen. Man. PEKER ÇUMRALI.

Tam Sigorta A.Ş.: Büyükdere Cad. 15, Tam Han, Sişli, Istanbul; all types of insurance except life; Gen. Man. GÜNER YALÇINER.

Türkiye Genel Sigorta Anonim Şirketi: 487-493 Meclisimebusan Cad., Salıpazarı, Istanbul; f. 1948; Pres. MEHMET E. KARAMEHMET; Gen. Man. ÖMER ERÜL.

TRADE AND INDUSTRY

CHAMBERS OF COMMERCE AND INDUSTRY

Union of Chambers of Commerce, Industry and Commodity Exchanges of Turkey: 149 Atatürk Bulvarı, Bakanlıklar, Ankara; f. 1952; Pres. MEHMET YAZAR; Sec.-Gen. Doç. Dr. MEHMET SAĞLAM; publs. *Turkish Economic Journal* (weekly), *Iktisadî Rapor* (annually).

There are Chambers of Commerce and Industry in all towns of the Republic. Among the most important are the following:

Adana Chamber of Commerce: Adana; f. 1894; Pres. ABDULLAH ÖNGEN; Sec.-Gen. ADNAN AKSU; 8,241 mems.; publ. *Adana Ticaret Odası Gazetesi*.

Ankara Chamber of Commerce: Şehit Teğmen Kalmaz Cad. 30; 29,113 mems.; Pres. TURGUT İLHAN; Gen. Sec. MEHMET AYDIN; publ. *Bulletin* (monthly).

Ankara Chamber of Industry: Atatürk Bul. 133/4; f. 1963; 1,471 mems.; Pres. MEHMET YAZAR; Sec.-Gen. TURGUT YURDEMİ.

Bursa Chamber of Commerce and Industry: İpek Han 5; f. 1889; 8,817 mems.; Pres. ALİ OSMAN SÖNMEZ; Sec.-Gen. ERGUN KAĞITCIBAŞİ.

Chambers of Industry for the Aegean Region: Cumhuriyet Blv. 63, İzmir; f. 1951; 3,783 mems.; Pres. ERSIN FARALYALI; Sec.-Gen. YUSUF VARDAR; publ. *Ege Bölgesi Sanayi Odası Dergisi*.

Istanbul Chamber of Commerce: Ragıp Gümüspala Cad., Eminönü, Istanbul; f. 1882; 76,472 mems.; Pres. NUH KUŞÇULU; Sec.-Gen. Prof. Dr. İSMAİL ÖZASLAN; publs. *Istanbul Ticaret Odası Mecmuasi* (bi-monthly), *Istanbul Ticaret* (weekly), *Statistical Abstract* (in English), *Exporters Directory* (trilingual).

Istanbul Chamber of Industry: Meşrutiyet Cad. 116, Tepebaşı; 5,400 mems.; Pres. NURULLAH GEZGİN;

Sec.-Gen. OKTAY GÜVEMLI; publs. *Istanbul Sanayi Odası Dergisi* (monthly).

İzmir Chamber of Commerce: Atatürk Cad. 126, İzmir, f. 1885; 11,933 mems.; Pres. MÜCAMİT BÜKTAŞ; Sec.-Gen. SULHİ AREL (acting); publ. *İzmir Ticaret Odası Dergisi* (every two months).

Mersin Chamber of Commerce and Industry: Nüzhetiye Mah. III Sok. 27; f. 1886; 3,615 mems.; Pres. MUSTAFA NİHAT SÖZMEN; Sec.-Gen. SUPLİ GÜZELOĞLU.

Samsun Chamber of Commerce and Industry: Hançerli Mah. Abbasağa Sok.; f. 1902; 3,552 mems.; Pres. MEHMET ÇEBİ; Gen. Sec. NECAT GÖKTÜRK.

EMPLOYERS' ASSOCIATION

Turkish Industrialists' and Businessmen's Association (Tüsiad): Cumhuriyet Cad., Ferah Apt. 233, Harbiye, Istanbul; f. 1971; 207 mems.; Chair. ALI KOÇMAN; Sec.-Gen. E. IHSAN ÖZOL; publs. *Görüş* (monthly economic review) and other economic reports and studies).

TRADE UNIONS

CONFEDERATIONS

DİSK (*Confederation of Progressive Trade Unions of Turkey*): Merter Sitesi, Ahmet Kutsi Tecer Cad. 12, K.5 Bayrampasa, Istanbul; c. 600,000 mems.; Pres. ABDULLAH BAŞTÜRK; Sec.-Gen. FEHMI IŞIKLAR; publs. *DISK Dergisi, DISK Ajansi*; activities suspended Sept. 1980, officials detained.

Türk-İş (Türkiye İşçi Sendikaları Konfederasyonu Genel Başkanlığı) (*Confederation of Turkish Trade Unions*): Bayındır Sok. 10, Yenişehir, Ankara; f. 1952; expelled from ICFTU, August 1981; national unions and federations with 1,800,000 mems.; Pres. İBRAHIM DENİZCİER; Sec.-Gen. SADIK ŞİDE; publs. *Turk-Iş* (monthly), *English News* (monthly).

PRINCIPAL UNIONS

Unions affiliated to Türk-İş with a membership of over 5,000.

Ağaç-İş (Türkiye Ağaç Sanayii İşçileri Sendikası) (*Wood and Lumber*): Necatibey Cad. No. 20/22-23, Yenişehir, Ankara; f. 1949; 20,882 mems.; also affiliated to IFBWW; Pres. KEMAL SARISOY; Gen. Sec. H. TAHSİN CAYLI.

Basın-İş (Türkiye Gazeteciler ve Basın Sanayii İşçileri Sendikası) (*Journalists and Press Technicians*): Necatibey Cad. 20/7, Yenişehir, Ankara; f. 1964; 15,000 mems.; Pres. HÜSEYİN DÜZGÜN; Gen. Sec. EYÜP UÇAR; publ. *Gündem* (daily).

B.İ.F. (Türkiye Belediye Hizmetelri İşçi Sendikaları Federasyonu) (*Municipal and Public Employees*): Selimpaşa Sok. No. 62, Aksaray, Istanbul; f. 1975; 20,000 mems.; Pres. HÜSEYİN PALA; Gen. Sec. FUAT ALAN.

Cimse-İş (Türkiye Çimento, Seramik ve Toprak Sanayii İşçileri Sendikası) (*Cement, Ceramic and Soil*): Necatibey Cad. 20/11-12, Yenişehir, Ankara; f. 1963; 38,816 mems.; 39 local unions; Pres. VELI EKER; Gen. Sec. MUSTAFA ULU; publ. *Çimse-Iş News* (monthly).

Deri-İş (Türkiye Deri, Debbağ, Kundura ve Saraciye Sanayii İşçileri Sendikası) (*Leather and Shoe*): Gençtürk Cad. 17, Birlik İşhanı Aksaray, Istanbul; f. 1948; 17,000 mems.; Pres. YENER KAYA; Gen. Sec. ALI ZENGIN.

Dok Gemi-İş (Türkiye Liman Dok ve Gemi Sanayii İşçileri Sendikası) (*Port, Dock and Ship Building*): Büyük Langa, Fabrika Sok. 18, Necmibey Işhanı, Kat. 3, Istanbul; f. 1947; 8,000 mems.; also affiliated to IUF; Deputy Pres. CEMAL GAVUSOĞLU; Gen. Sec. GÜNGÖR TARI.

Dyf-İş (Türkiye Demiryolları İşçi Sendikaları Federasyonu) (*Railways*): Necatibey Cad., Sezenler Sok. 5/4, Yenişehir, Ankara; f. 1952; 56,000 mems.; also affiliated to ITF; Pres. MEHMET ACIDERELI; Gen. Sec. MUHITTIN YILMAZ; publ. *Hiz* (fortnightly).

Haber-İş (Türkiye, Posta, Telegraf, Telefon, Radyo ve Television İşçileri Sendikası) (*Postal, Telegraph, Telephone, Radio and Television Workers*): Necatibey Cad., Sezenler Sok. 1/14, Yenişehir, Ankara; 15,000 mems.; Pres. ETHEM EZGÜ; Gen. Sec. MEHMET KARAGÜLMEZ.

Harb-İş (Türkiye Harb Sanayii ve Yardımcı İşkolları İşçileri Sendikası) (*Defence Industry and Allied Workers*): Inkılap Sok. 20, Kızılay, Ankara; f. 1956; 32,000 mems.; also affiliated to PSI; Pres. KENAN DURUKAN; Gen. Sec. YILMAZ ÖRNEK; publ. *Turk harb-iş* (monthly).

Hava-İş (Türkiye Sivil Havacılık Sendikası) (*Civil Aviation*): Incirli Cad., Volkan Apt. 66/1, Bakırköy, Istanbul; 6,600 mems.; Pres. İBRAHİM ÖZTÜRK; Gen. Sec. CAVIT GÜNGÖR.

Kauçuk-Iş (Türkiye Kauçuk, Lastik ve Plastik Işçileri Sendikası) (*Plastic and Tyre Workers*): Atatürk Bulvarı, Yayla Palas Apt. 114/6, Aksaray, Istanbul; 5,700 mems.; Pres. FEVZİ BAŞTÜRK; Gen. Sec. KEMAL DEMIR.

Koop-İş (Türkiye Kooperatif ve Büro İşçileri Sendikası) (*Co-operative and Office Workers*): İzmir Cad. Fevzi Çadmak Sok. 15/11-12, Yenişehir, Ankara; f. 1964; 12,000 mems.; Pres. BURHANETTIN IŞIK; Gen. Sec. KAMIL KAMIŞOĞLU.

Kristal-İş (Türkiye Şişe, Cam ve Kristal Sanayii İşçileri Sendikası) (*Glass and Crystal Industry*): Sahipmolla Cad. 24, Paşabahçe, Istanbul; f. 1965; 7,000 mems.; Pres. HASAN BASRI BABALI; Gen. Sec. AHMET KAYA.

Likat-İş (Türkiye Liman ve Kara Tahmil-Tahliye İşçileri Sendikası) (*Longshoremen*): Necatibey Cad. Sezenler Sok. 4, Kat. 5, Yenişehir, Ankara; f. 1963; 6,000 mems.; also affiliated to ITF; Pres. AHMET KURT; Gen. Sec. NESET MAZMANCI.

Maden Federasyonu (Türkiye Maden İşçileri Sendikaları Federasyonu) (*Mine Workers*): Strazburg Cad. 7, Kat. 3-5, Sıhhıye, Ankara; f. 1958; 105,000 mems.; Pres. KEMÂL ÖZER; Gen. Sec. MUSTAFA ORHAN.

Petrol-İş (Türkiye Petrol, Kimya, Azot ve Atom İşçileri Sendikası) (*Oil, Chemical and Atomic*): Yıldız Posta Cad., Evren Sitesi, D-Blok, Gayrettepe, Istanbul; f. 1950; 49,000 mems.; Pres. CEVDET SELVI; Gen. Sec. ADEM YILMAZ; publ. *Petrol-Iş* (weekly).

Sağlık-İş (Türkiye Sağlık İşçileri Sendikası) (*Health Employees*): Necatibey Cad. 23/9-10, Yenişehir, Ankara; f. 1961; 14,000 mems.; also affiliated to PSI; Pres. MUSTAFA BAŞOĞLU; Gen. Sec. ERSIN CENGIZ.

Şeker-İş (Türkiye Şeker Sanayii İşçileri Sendikası) (*Sugar Industry*): Karanfil Sok. 59, Bakanlıklar, Ankara; f. 1952; 30,000 mems.; Pres. A. YAŞAR DOĞUALP; Gen. Sec. HİKMET ALCAN; publ. *Şeker-Iş* (fortnightly).

Selüloz-İş (Türkiye Selüloz ve Mamülleri İşçileri Sendikası) (*Celluloid Industry*): Hürriyet Cad., Isılay Apt. Kat-1, Kocaeli; f. 1952; 12,000 mems.; Pres. NECATİ CANSEVER; Gen. Sec. SALİH GÜNGÖRMEZ.

Su-İş (Türkiye Baraj, Enerji, Su ve Sulama İşçileri Sendikası) (*Dam, Energy, Water and Irrigation Workers*): Büyükdere Cad. 56/1-2, Mecidiyeköy, Istanbul; f. 1950; 5,000 mems.; Pres. (vacant); Gen. Sec. NEVZAT ÖZBAY.

Tarim-İş (Türkiye Orman, Topraksu, Tarım ve Tarım Sanayii İşçileri Sendikası) (*Workers in forestry, land irrigation, agriculture and agricultural industry*): Necatibey Cad., Ankara Apt. 22/9-10-12, Yenişehir, Ankara; f. 1961; 120,000 mems.; affiliated to IFPAAW; Pres. ZEYNEL IRMAK; Gen. Sec. MAHMUT TELLİ; publ. *Agricultural News* (monthly).

Tekgida-İş (Türkiye Tütün, Müskirat Gıda ve Yardımcı İşçileri Sendikası) (*Tobacco, Drink, Food and Allied Workers' Union of Turkey*): 4 Levent Konaklar Sok., P.K. 98, Istanbul; f. 1952; 171,290 mems.; also affiliated to IUF; Pres. İBRAHİM DENİZCİER; Gen. Sec. NAZMI CEYLANDAĞ.

Teksif (Türkiye Tekstil, Örme ve Giyim Sanayii İşçileri Sendikası) (*Textile, Knitting and Clothing*): Aydoğmuş Sok. 1, Kurtuluş, Ankara; f. 1951; 120,000 mems.; also affiliated to ITGWF; Pres. ŞEVKET YILMAZ; Gen. Sec. ZEKI POLAT.

Tes-İş (Türkiye Enerji, Su ve Gaz İşçi Sendikaları) (*Energy, Water and Gas*): Meşrutiyet Cad. Karanfil Sokak 34/6, Yenişehir, Ankara; f. 1963; 53,000 mems.; Pres. ORHAN ERÇELİK; Gen. Sec. FARUK BARUT.

T.G.S. (Türkiye Gazeteciler Sendikası) (*Journalists*): Basin Sarayı, Kat. 2, Çağaloğlu, İstanbul; 6,000 mems.; Pres. NAIL GÜRELI; Gen. Sec. ALAATTIN KUTLU.

Tez-Büro-İş (Türkiye, Ticaret, Banka, Sigorta, Kooperatif, Eğitim, Tezgahtarlar ve Büro İşçileri Sendikası) (*Commercial and Clerical Employees*): Necatibey Cad. Sezenler Sok. 2/16, Sıhhıye, Ankara; f. 1962; 25,000 mems.; Pres. UĞUR BATMAZ; Gen. Sec. ŞAHIN ÜLKER.

TOREYİS (Türkiye Otel Restaurant Eğlence Yerleri İşçileri Sendikası) (*Hotel, Restaurant and Places of Entertainment*): Kuloğlu Sok., Fercioğlu Sok. 7/4, Beyoğlu-Istanbul; f. 1947; 3,000 mems.; also affiliated to IUF; Pres. SERVET SofuoğLU; Gen. Sec. CEMIL GIDER.

Tümtis (Türkiye Motorlu Taşıt İşçileri Sendikası) (*Motor Transport*): Selimpaşa Sok. 62, P.K. 292, Aksaray, İstanbul; f. 1949; 5,000 mems.; also affiliated to ITF; Pres. HÜSEYIN PALA; Gen. Sec. ABID ŞIMŞEK.

Türk Deniz Ulaş-İş (Türkiye Deniz Taşıtmacılığı İşçi Sendikaları Federasyonu) (*Seamen*): Rıhtım Cad., Çıraci Sok. 7, Tophane, İstanbul; f. 1959; 25,000 mems.; also affiliated to ITF; Pres. EMIN KUL; Gen. Sec. MUSTAFA YÖNDEM.

Türk-Metal (Türkiye Metal, Çelik, Mühimmat, Makina Metalden Mamul, Eşya ve Oto, Montaj ve Yardimoi İşçileri Sendikası) (*Auto, Metal and Allied Workers*): Gazi Mustafa Kemal Bulvarı, 40/1-2, Maltepe, Ankara; f. 1963; 55,000 mems.; Pres. MUSTAFA ÖZBEK; Gen. Sec. İBRAHIM DELIBAŞ.

Yol-İş (Türkiye Yol Yapı ve İnşaat İşçileri Sendikaları Federasyonu) (*Federation of Turkish Road Construction and Building Workers' Unions*): İzmir Cad. 22, Kat 2, Yenişehir, Ankara; f. 1963; 112,000 mems.; also affili-ated to IFBWW; Pres. MUZAFFER SARAÇ; Gen. Sec. İSMET ACAR; publ. *Yol-İş* (monthly).

Enerji-İş (Türkiye Enerji Işçi Sendikaları Federasyonu) (*Energy Workers*): Mithatpaşa Cad. 24/7, Yenişehir, Ankara; f. 1977; 15,000 mems.; Pres. NURI ŞIMŞEK; Gen. Sec. SABAHATTIN ERSOY; publ. *Enerji-İş* (month-ly).

Maden-İş (Türkiye Maden, Madeni Eşya ve Makina Sanayii İşçileri Sendikası) (*Metal, Metal Goods and Machine Industry Workers' Union of Turkey*): Barbaros Bulvarı 58, Kat 2-3-4-5, Beşiktaş, İstanbul; f. 1947; 80,000 mems.; Pres. (vacant); Gen. Sec. (vacant); publ. *Maden-İş* (fortnightly).

TRADE FAIR

İzmir Enternasyonal Fuarı (*Izmir International Fair*): Cahit Günay, Kültürpark, İzmir; f. 1929; August 20th–September 10th annually; Pres. CAHÍT GÜNAY; Dir. HAMDİ ASENA.

TRANSPORT

RAILWAYS

Türkiye Cumhuriyeti Devlet Demiryolları Isletmesi Genel Müdürlüğü—TCDD (*Turkish Republic State Railways*): Ankara; f. 1924; operates all railways and connect-ing ports of the State Railway Administration which acquired the status of a state economic enterprise in 1953; Pres. of Board and Gen. Dir. MUHTAR EROL; publ. *Demiryol* (monthly).

The total length of the railways operated within the national frontiers is 8,397 km. (1981), of which 464 km. are electrified. Five-year plans for modernizing the railway system were introduced in 1963, dieselization and elec-trification projects having since been carried out. A new direct rail link between Ankara and Istanbul, cutting the distance from 577 km. to 414 km., is expected to be com-pleted by 1995. There are direct rail links from Bulgaria to Iran and Syria.

ROADS

Bayındrılık Bakanlığı Karayolları Genel Müdürlüğü (*General Directorate of Highways*): Ankara; Dir.-Gen. TURAN EREN.

In 1982 37 km. of motorways and 83 km. of expressways were open to traffic. The total length of all roads was 60,700 km. The length of all-weather roads was 40,313 km., comprising 29,067 km. of national and 11,246 km. of pro-vincial roads. The total length of village roads is 28,617 km.

SHIPPING

Denizçilik Bankası T.A.O. (*Turkish Maritime Bank*): Genel Müdürlük, Karaköy, İstanbul; f. 1952; capital of TL 20,000m.; four maritime establishments operate passenger, cargo and ferry-boat lines on inter-city, coastal, Adriatic, Aegean and Mediterranean Sea routes; five Port Administrations offer loading, un-loading, transfer and warehousing facilities; five ship-yards and dry docks have repair and construction facilities for ships up to 60,000 tons; international con-cerns such as ship salvage and coastal security; other assets include: one hotel, 57,233 gross tons of shipping, 17 ships and 50,467 gross tons of inter-city communi-cation; 80 ferries; Dir.-Gen. Adm. (Retd.) NEJAT ÖZGECE.

D.B. Deniz Nakliyati T.A.Ş. (*D.B. Turkish Cargo Lines*): Fındıklı, Meclisi Mebusan Cad. 93-97, İstanbul; f. 1955; regular liner services between Turkey and Mediterranean, Adriatic, Red Sea, Persian Gulf, Europe, Black Sea, U.S. Atlantic and Gulf ports; Chair. Adm. (Retd.) M. RIZA AKOT; 33 dry cargo ships, 2 ro/ro, 18 bulk/ore carriers, 9 tankers.

PRIVATE COMPANIES

Türk Armatörler Birliği (*Turkish Shipowners' Association*): Ömer Abit Han K.3, Karaköy, İstanbul; f. 1972; 230 mem. shipowners; Pres. Z. KALKAVAN; Co-ordinator E. ÖZYAZICI; 2,068,120 d.w.t.

S.S. Motorlu Gemi Armatörleri Kooperatifi (*Turkish Ship-owners' Co-operative*): Ömer Abit Han K.3, Karaköy, İstanbul; f. 1960; Pres. İ. KAPTANOĞLU; Man. Dir. A. K. AZIZOĞLU; 320 vessels; 950,000 d.w.t.

Vapur Donatanları ve Acenteleri Derneği (*Turkish Ship-owners' and Shipping Agents' Association*): Mumhane Cad. Emek İşhanı K.3 No. 15, Karaköy, İstanbul; f. 1902; worldwide agency service; Pres. M. LEBLE-BİCİOĞLU; Man. Dir. C. KAPLAN.

Koçtuğ Denizçilik Işletmesi D.İ.: Bankalar Caddesi, Bozkurt-General Han Kat 5, Karaköy, P.K. 884, İstanbul; f. 1956; cargo services to and from Europe, North Africa and the U.S.A.; Pres. S. KOÇMAN, S. GÖKTUĞ; Man. Dir. M. LEBLEBİCİOĞLU; 9 cargo vessels.

Sönmez Denizçilik Şirketler Grubu: Kemeralti Cad. 24/5, Karaköy Ticaret Merkezi, Karaköy, İstanbul; Pres. H. SONMEZ; Group Man. F. ÖZDEMİR; 8 vessels; 276,368 d.w.t.

Zihni Şirketler Grubu: Rıhtım Cad. Şükür Han 28-30 K.2, Tophane, İstanbul; f. 1930; Pres. A. GÜNERİ; Man. Dir. T. EREN; 6 vessels; 232,983 d.w.t.

Cerrahoğulları Umumi Nakliyat, Vapurculuk ve Ticaret A.S.: Büyükdere Cad. 82 K.7, Gayrettepe, İstanbul; f. 1954; Pres. N. CERRAHOĞLU; Man. Dir. A. CANKAT; 4 vessels; 381,350 d.w.t.

Denizçilik Anonim Şirketi: Meclisi Mebusan Cad. 55, Fındıklı Han Kat 4, Fındıklı, Istanbul; f. 1952; tanker owners and shipbuilders, repair and dry-docking at company's shipyard in Istanbul; Pres. H. BARAN; Man. Dir. S. ÜLKÜ; 2 tankers, 2 bulk carriers; 269,890 d.w.t.

CIVIL AVIATION

There are airports for scheduled international and internal flights at Yeşilkoy (Istanbul), Esenboğa (Ankara), Adana and Dalaman (south-west), while international charter flights are handled by Antalya and Cigli (Izmir). Seventeen other airports handle internal flights only.

Türk Hava Yollari A.O. (THY) (*Turkish Airlines Inc.*): Cumhuriyet Caddesi 199-201, Harbiye, Istanbul; f. 1933; 97.35 per cent state-owned; Pres. CENGIZ SAKARYALI; Chair. ALI SAIT ÖZCIVRIL; extensive internal network and flights from Ankara and Istanbul to Abu Dhabi, Amsterdam, Athens, Baghdad, Berlin, Brussels, Cairo, Copenhagen, Geneva, Jeddah, Dhahran, Düsseldorf, Frankfurt, Hamburg, Hannover, Karachi, Cologne, Kuwait, Nicosia, London, Milan, Munich, Nürnberg, Paris, Rome, Stuttgart, Teheran, Tripoli, Vienna, Zurich; fleet of four Boeing 707, five Boeing 727, nine DC-9, two DC-10, two F-28.

Turkey is also served by the following foreign airlines: Aeroflot (U.S.S.R.), Air France, Alia (Jordan), Alitalia, Ariana (Afghanistan), Austrian Airlines, Balkan (Bulgaria), British Airways, ČSA (Czechoslovakia), Cyprus Airways, El-Al (Israel), Iran National, Iraqi Airways, JAT (Yugoslavia), KLM (Netherlands), Kuwait Airways, LOT (Poland), Lufthansa (Federal Republic of Germany), MALÉV (Hungary), MEA (Lebanon), Olympic (Greece), Pan Am (U.S.A.), PIA (Pakistan), Sabena (Belgium), Saudia, SAS (Sweden), SIA (Singapore), Swissair and TAROM (Romania).

TOURISM AND CULTURE

Ministry of Culture and Tourism: Gazi Mustafa Kemal Bulvarı 33, Ankara; Dir.-Gen. of Tourism ATALAY TÜZÜN V.; Dir.-Gen. of Information and Promotion TURGUT BOLU.

CULTURAL ORGANIZATIONS

Fine Arts General Directorate (*Güzel Sanatlar Akademisi Genel Müdürlüğü*): Education Ministry, Bakanlıklar, Ankara; Dir.-Gen. Prof. SADUN ERSIN.

PRINCIPAL THEATRES

State Theatre General Directorate (*Devlet Tiyatrosu Genel Müdürlüğü*): part of the above; runs nine playhouses; Dir.-Gen. CÜNEYT GÖKÇER.

Büyük Tiyatro (*Great Theatre*): Ankara.

Küçük Tiyatro (*Small Theatre*): Ankara.

Devlet Opera ve Balesi: Ankara; state opera and ballet; permanent classical and modern ballet company of 99 dancers; Gen. Dir. YALÇIN DAVRAN.

There are three other state theatres in Ankara, and five private companies. Istanbul has thirteen private companies.

Istanbul City Opera: Taksim, Istanbul; Dir. AYDIN GÜN.

ORCHESTRAS

Istanbul State Symphony Orchestra: Taksim, Istanbul; f. 1972; Gen. Dir. MÜKERREM BERK.; 91 mems.

Presidential Symphony Orchestra: Ankara.

ATOMIC ENERGY

Turkish Atomic Energy Commission: Prime Minister's Office, Alaçam Sokak II, Ankara; f. 1956; controls the development of peaceful uses of atomic energy; 12 mems.; Chair. Hon. M. NIMET ÖZDAŞ; Sec. Gen. EROL BARUTÇUGIL; publs. *Activity Reports, Research Reports,* etc.

There are nuclear research centres at Çekmece, near Istanbul, and at Ankara. Turkey is a member of the International Atomic Energy Agency (IAEA) and the OECD Nuclear Energy Agency (NEA).

DEFENCE

Chief of General Staff: Gen. KENAN EVREN.
Army Commander: Gen. NURETTIN ERSIN.
Navy Commander: Admiral NEJAT TÜMER.
Air Force Commander: Gen. TAHSIN ŞAHINKAYA.
Defence Budget (1981): estimated at TL 298,000 million.

Military Service: 20 months.

Total Armed Forces (1981): 569,000: army 470,000 men, with 3,500 medium tanks; navy 46,000 men, includes 14 submarines; air force 53,000 men, 303 combat aircraft.

Paramilitary Forces: 120,000 gendarmerie.

EDUCATION

When the Turkish Republic was formed, the Ministry of Education became the sole authority in educational matters, replacing the dual system of religious schools and other schools. One of the main obstacles to literacy was the Arabic script, which required years of study before proficiency could be attained. In 1928, therefore, a Turkish alphabet was introduced, using Latin characters. At the same time the literary language was simplified, and purged of some of its foreign elements. By 1980 the education budget amounted to TL 88,256 million, over 10 per cent of the state budget.

People's Schools

This change of script created a need for schools in which reading and writing in the new alphabet could be taught to adults. Temporary institutions known as "people's schools" or "national schools" were set up everywhere. During the winter months these schools gave instruction in reading and writing and other basic subjects to men and women beyond the normal school age. Between 1928 and 1935 some 2 million people received certificates of proficiency. Since then education in Turkey has made big advances, but although literacy is estimated at 65 per cent in towns, it is still much lower in the villages (30.3 per cent in 1960).

Primary Education

A compulsory school attendance law had been passed in 1913, but only under the Republic were measures taken to enforce this. Primary education is now entirely free, and co-education is the accepted basis for universal education. The number of schools has risen from 12,511 in 1950 to 44,098 in 1979, and the number of teachers from 27,144 to 187,363. In 1979/80 nearly 5.6 million children were attending primary schools.

Secondary Education

The reorganization of the system of secondary education began in the early 1920s.

Present Organization. This period of education lasts six years, and is free.

The secondary schools are divided into two stages: middle schools and *lycées*, and students who intend to proceed to higher educational institutions must pass through both stages, spending three years in the middle school and three in the *lycée*.

The middle school, although complementary to the *lycée*, is a separate unit, designed to give a definite and complete education to those students who at the end of the course will proceed directly to work. The state examination is taken by all students at the end of the third year. Graduates of a middle school are qualified either to take up

an unskilled occupation or to enter upon a vocational course at a school of a higher grade.

The *lycée* takes the student up to the age of 17 or 18 years, and those who wish to proceed to an institute of higher education must pass the state matriculation examination. The study of a modern language (English, French or German) is compulsory in middle schools and *lycées*. In addition, Latin and Greek have been taught in some *lycées* since 1940. The number of secondary schools (not including technical and vocational schools) in 1979 was 5,062 with a total of 1,672,700 students.

Adult Education. Since 1932, reading-rooms have been established in every town and many villages. They are centres of social and cultural life and provide evening classes. Their libraries, meeting-halls and recreational facilities are open to all. In the towns there are also evening trade schools which provide technical training for adults, and travelling courses are sent out to the villages.

Higher Education. Higher educational institutions in Turkey were founded, and are administered, by the State. These institutions include the universities and the higher professional schools. There are now 19 universities and 259 institutes of higher education (including teacher training colleges). Three of the universities specialize in scientific and technical subjects. The number of students enrolled at universities and other institutes of higher education was 235,000 in the academic year 1981/82.

Technical Education. The problem of technical education began to be seriously considered first in 1926; specialists were invited from Europe and America, and a plan was drawn up for perfecting the existing vocational schools and for founding new ones to meet the economic needs of each region. In 1978 there were 1,561 technical and vocational *lycées*, giving training to 469,000 students. In addition, plans were made for evening schools to train craftsmen and for the founding of teachers' technical training colleges. There are two such colleges in Ankara, one for men and one for women.

Teachers' Training. In Turkey teachers' training colleges are divided into three basic categories: two-year teacher training institutes which train teachers for primary schools, three-year teacher training institutes which train teachers for middle schools and higher teacher training schools offering a four-year course qualifying teachers for the *lycées*. Students of the higher teacher training schools take specialist subject courses in the relevant university faculty and their pedagogy courses in the higher teacher training schools. In the academic year 1974–75 there were 30,749 students enrolled in 42 teacher training colleges.

BIBLIOGRAPHY

GENERAL

ALLEN, H. E. The Turkish Transformation (Chicago, 1935).

ARMSTRONG, H. C. Grey Wolf: Mustafa Kemal: an Intimate Study of a Dictator (London, 1937).

AUBOYNEAU & FEVRET. Essai de bibliographie pour l'Empire Ottomane (Paris, 1911).

BAHRAMPOUR, FIROUZ. Turkey, Political and Social Transformation (Gaus, New York, 1967).

BEAN, G. E. Aegean Turkey (Benn, London, 1966).
Turkey's Southern Shore (Benn, London, 1968).

BERKES, NIYAZI. The Development of Secularism in Turkey (McGill University Press, Montreal, 1964).

BISBEE, ELEANOR. The New Turks (Philadelphia, 1951).
The People of Turkey (New York, 1946).

BRIDGE, ANN. The Dark Moment (New York, 1952).
The Falcon in Flight (New York, 1951).

COHN, EDWIN J. Turkish Economic, Social and Political Change (New York, Praeger, 1970).

COOKE, HEDLEY V. Challenge and Response in the Middle East: The Quest for Prosperity, 1919-1951 (New York, 1952).

Dodd, C. H. Politics and Government in Turkey (Manchester University Press, 1969).

Edgecumbe, Sir, C. N. E. Turkey in Europe (Barnes and Noble, N.Y., 1965).

Ekrem, Selma. Turkey: Old and New (New York, 1947).

Eren, Nuri. Turkey Today and Tomorrow (New York, 1964).

Frey, F. W. The Turkish Political Elite (M.I.T. Press, Cambridge, Mass., 1965).

Gökalp, Ziya. Turkish Nationalism and Western Civilisation (London, 1960).

Güntekin, Reşat Nuri (trans. Sir Wyndham Deedes). Afternoon Sun (London, 1950).

The Autobiography of a Turkish Girl (London, 1949).

Hale, William. Aspects of Modern Turkey (Bowker Publishing, Epping, 1977).

Harris, George S. The Origins of Communism in Turkey (Hoover Institution, Stanford, Calif., 1967).

Heyd, Uriel. Foundations of Turkish Nationalism: the Life and Teachings of Ziya Gökalp (Luzac and Harvill Press, London, 1950).

Language Reform in Modern Turkey (Jerusalem, 1954).

Hotham, David. The Turks (John Murray, London, 1972).

Jackh, Ernest. The Rising Crescent (New York, 1950).

Karpat, Kemal. Turkey's Politics, The Transition to a Multi-Party System (Princeton, 1959).

Kazamias, A. M. Education and the Quest for Modernity in Turkey (Allen and Unwin, London, 1967).

Kinnane, Dirk. The Kurds and Kurdistan (Oxford, 1965).

Kinross, Lord. Within the Taurus (London, 1954).
Europa Minor: Journeys in Coastal Turkey (London, 1956).
Turkey (303 photogravure illustrations, London, 1960).
Atatürk (Weidenfeld, London, 1964).

Kişlali, Ahmet Taner. Forces politiques dans la Turquie moderne (Ankara, 1967).

Koray, Enver. Türkiye Tarih Yayınları Bibliografyası 1729-1950; A Bibliography of Historical Works on Turkey (Ankara 1952).

Kürger, K. Die Türkei (Berlin, 1951).

Lamb, Harold. Suleiman the Magnificent: Sultan of the East (New York, 1951).

Lewis, Bernard. Turkey Today (London, 1940).
The Emergence of Modern Turkey (Oxford University Press, London and New York (rev. edition 1970)).

Lewis, G. L. Turkey ("Nations of the Modern World" series) (London, 1955) (3rd edn., Praeger, N.Y., 1965).

Linke, L. Allah Dethroned (London, 1937).

Lukach (Luke), Sir Harry Charles. The Old Turkey and the New (Geoffrey Bles, London, 1955).

Marfori, Terenzio. La Constituzione della Repubblica Turca (Florence, 1947).

Mellaart, James. Earliest Civilizations of the Near East (Thames and Hudson, London, 1965).
Çatal Hüyük (Thames and Hudson, London, 1967).

Moorehead, A. Gallipoli (New York, Harper, 1956).

Muntz, T. G. A. Turkey (New York, 1951).

Newman, Bernard. Turkish Crossroads (London, 1951).
Turkey and the Turks (Herbert Jenkins, London, 1968).

Orga, Irfan and Margarete. Atatürk (London, 1962).

Parker, J., and Smith, C. Modern Turkey (London, 1940).

Plate, Herbert. Das Land der Türken (Verlag Styria, Graz, Wien, Köln, 1957).

Robinson, Richard D. The First Turkish Republic (Harvard University Press, 1963).

Salter, Cedric. Introducing Turkey (Methuen, London, 1961).

Stark, Freya. Ionia (London, 1954).
Lycian Shore (London, 1951).
Riding to the Tigris (London, 1956).

Steinhaus, Kurt. Soziologie der turkischen Revolution (Frankfurt, 1969).

Szyliowicz, Joseph S. Political Change in Rural Turkey: Erdemli (Mouton, The Hague, 1966).

Toynbee, A. J. The Western Question in Greece and Turkey (Constable, London, 1923).

Toynbee, A. J., and Kirkwood, D. P. Turkey (London, 1926).
Lycian Shore (London, 1956).

Tunaya, T. Z. Atatürk, the Revolutionary Movement and Atatürkism (Baha, Istanbul, 1964).

Vali, Ferenc A. Bridge across the Bosphorus: the Foreign Policy of Turkey (Johns Hopkins Press, 1970).

Ward, Barbara. Turkey (Oxford, 1942).

Ward, Robert E., and Rustow, Oankwart A. (eds.). Political Modernizations in Japan and Turkey (Princeton University Press, 1964).

Webster, D. E. The Turkey of Atatürk: Social Progress in the Turkish Reformation (Philadelphia, 1939).

Williams, Gwyn. Turkey: A Travellers Guide and History (Faber and Faber, London, 1967).

Yalman, A. E. Turkey in my time (University of Oklahoma Press, 1956).

HISTORY

Ahmad, Feroz. The Young Turks (Oxford University Press, 1969).
The Turkish Experiment in Democracy 1950–1975 (Hurst, London, for Royal Institute of International Affairs, 1977).

Alderson, A. D. The Structure of the Ottoman Dynasty (Oxford, 1956).

Allen, W. E. D., and Muratoff, P. Caucasian Battlefields: A History of the Wars on the Turco-Caucasian Border, 1828-1921 (Cambridge, 1953).

Cahen, Claude. Pre-Ottoman Turkey (Sidgwick and Jackson, London, 1968).

Cassels, Lavender. The Struggle for the Ottoman Empire, 1717-1740 (John Murray, London, 1967).

Coles, Paul. The Ottoman Impact on Europe (Thames and Hudson, London, 1968; Brace and World, New York, 1968).

Davidson, Roderic H. Turkey (Prentice-Hall, New York, 1968).

Gurney, O. R. The Hittites (London, 1952).

Kazancigil, Ali, and Ozbudun, Ergun (Eds.). Ataturk: Founder of a Modern State (Hurst, London, 1981).

Kedourie, Elie. England and the Middle East: The Destruction of the Ottoman Empire, 1914-1921 (Cambridge, 1956).

KUSHNER, DAVID. The Rise of Turkish Nationalism (London, Frank Cass, 1980).

LANDAU, JACOB M. Pan-Turkism: A Study in Irredentism (Hurst, London, 1981).

LEWIS, BERNARD. Istanbul and the Civilization of the Ottoman Empire (University of Oklahoma Press, 1963).

LEWIS, GEOFFREY. La Turquie, le déclin de l'Empire, les réformes d'Ataturk, la République moderne (Verviers/Belgique, 1968).

LIDDELL, ROBERT. Byzantium and Istanbul (London, 1956).

LLOYD, SETON. Early Anatolia (London, 1956).

MANTRAN, ROBERT. Histoire de la Turquie (Paris, 1952).

MILLER, WILLIAM. The Ottoman Empire and its Successors, 1801-1927 (Cambridge, 1934).

OSTROGORSKY, G. History of the Byzantine State (Oxford, 1956).

PFEFFERMANN, HANS. Die Zusammenarbeit der Renaissance Päpste mit den Türken (Winterthur, 1946).

PRICE, M. PHILIPS. A History of Turkey: From Empire to Republic (London, 1956).

RAMSAUR, E. E. The Young Turks and the Revolution of 1908 (Princeton University Press, 1957).

RICE, DAVID TALBOT. Art of the Byzantine Era (Frederick A. Praeger, New York, 1963).

Byzantine Art (Penguin, London, 1962).

RICE, TAMARA TALBOT. The Seljuks (London, 1962).

RUNCIMAN, Sir STEVEN. The Fall of Constantinople, 1453 (Cambridge University Press, 1965).

SUMNER, B. H. Peter the Great and the Ottoman Empire (Oxford, 1949).

VAUGHAN, DOROTHY. Europe and the Turk: A Pattern of Alliances, 1350-1700 (Liverpool, 1954).

VERE-HODGE, EDWARD REGINALD. Turkish Foreign Policy, 1918-1948 (2nd (revised) edition, London, 1950).

WALDER, DAVID. The Chanak Affair (Hutchinson, London, 1968).

ECONOMY

HERSHLAG, Z. Y. Turkey: the Challenge of Growth (Leiden, 1968).

ISSAWI, CHARLES. The Economic History of Turkey (University of Chicago Press, 1980).

SHORTER, FREDERIC C. (ed.). Four Studies on the Economic Development of Turkey (Cass, London, 1967; Kelley, New York, 1968).

United Arab Emirates

ABU DHABI DUBAI SHARJAH RAS AL-KHAIMAH UMM AL-QUWAIN AJMAN
FUJAIRAH

GEOGRAPHY

The coastline of the seven United Arab Emirates extends for nearly 400 miles from the frontier of the Sultanate of Oman to Khor al-Odaid on the Qatar Peninsula in the Persian Gulf. The area is one of extremely shallow seas, with offshore islands and coral reefs, and often an intricate pattern of sandbanks and small gulfs as a coastline. In contrast to the Mediterranean, there is a large tide. The waters of the Gulf contain relatively abundant quantities of fish, large and small, hence fishing plays some part in local life. The climate is arid, with very high summer temperatures; and except for a few weeks in winter, air humidity is also very high. The total area of the U.A.E. has been estimated at approximately 30,000 square miles and it has a rapidly growing population, totalling 1,040,275 in 1980, concentrated in the oil boom areas of Abu Dhabi, the capital of the U.A.E., and Dubai. Many inhabitants are nomadic or settled Arabs. In the coastal towns live also many Persians, Indians, Pakistanis, Baluchis and Negros, the latter being descended from slaves carried from Africa during the course of several centuries of slave trading. The most important port is Dubai, capital of the U.A.E.'s second largest state. Its significance derives from its position on one of the rare deep creeks of the area, and it now has a very large transit trade.

HISTORY

In the early 16th century the Portuguese commercial monopoly of the Gulf area began to be challenged by other European traders eager for a share in the profits from the Eastern trade, first by the Dutch, later by the British. By the end of the century the Portuguese ascendency in the East had declined and in 1650 the Portuguese evacuated Oman losing their entire hold on the Arabian shore. Then followed a period of commercial and political rivalry between the Dutch and the British during which the initial Dutch predominance weakened and in 1766 came practically to an end, while the British were consolidating their supremacy in India.

Both European and Arab pirates were very active in the Gulf during the 17th, 18th and early 19th centuries. Lawlessness reached its height at the beginning of the 19th century when the seafaring Arab tribes were welded together and incited to pillage by Wahhabi emissaries who had established their supremacy over the whole Arabian coast of the Gulf. Attacks on British-flag vessels led to British expeditions against the pirates in 1806 and 1809 and, finally, in 1818 against the pirate headquarters at Ras al-Khaimah and other harbours along the 150 miles of "Pirate Coast". In 1820 a General Treaty of Peace for suppressing piracy and slave traffic was concluded between Great Britain and the Arab Tribes of the Gulf. Among the signatories were the principal Sheikhs of the Pirate Coast and the Sheikhs of Bahrain. A strong British squadron was stationed for some time at Ras al-Khaimah to enforce the treaty.

Many piratical acts continued to be committed and accordingly, in 1835, the Sheikhs were induced to bind themselves by a "Maritime Truce" not to engage, in any circumstances, in hostilities by sea for a period of six months (i.e. during the pearl-diving season). The advantages of this were so marked that they were easily persuaded to renew the truce and continually did so for increasing periods until, in May 1853 a Treaty of Maritime Peace in Perpetuity was concluded between all the Sheikhs of the "Trucial Coast"—as it was henceforth called—establishing a "perpetual maritime truce". It was to be watched over and enforced by the British Government, to whom the signatories were to refer any breach. The British, however, did not interfere in wars between the Sheikhs on land.

The British concern in stopping the slave trade had also led to contacts with the Trucial Coast, where the Sheikhs had been engaged in carrying slaves from Africa to India and Arabia. By agreements signed with the British in 1838–39 and 1847 the Sheikhs undertook to prohibit the carriage of slaves on board vessels belonging to them or their subjects, and consented to the detention and search of such vessels and to their confiscation in case of guilt.

Towards the end of the 19th century France, Germany and Russia showed increasing interest in the Gulf area and in 1892 Britain entered into separate but identical "exclusive" treaties with the Trucial rulers concluded on different dates, whereby the Sheikhs undertook not to cede, mortgage nor otherwise dispose of parts of their territories to anyone except the British Government, nor to enter into any relationship with a foreign government other than the British without British consent. Britain had already undertaken to protect the states from outside attack in the Perpetual Maritime Treaty of 1853.

In 1820 when the General Treaty was signed, there were only five Trucial States. In 1866, on the death of the Chief Sheikh of Sharjah, his domains were divided amongst his four sons, the separate branches of the family being established at Sharjah, Ras al-Khaimah, Dibba and Kalba.

In 1952, Kalba was incorporated into Sharjah when its ruler undertook to accept all the treaties and agreements in force between the United Kingdom and the other Trucial States. These undertakings included recognition of the right of the U.K. Government to fix state boundaries, to settle disputes between the Trucial Sheikhdoms and to render assistance to the Trucial Oman Scouts, a British-officered Arab force set up in 1952. The Ruler of Fujairah also accepted these undertakings when his state was recognized as independent in 1952.

In 1952 on British advice a Trucial Council was established at which all seven rulers met at least twice a year under the chairmanship of the Political Agent in Dubai. It was formed with the object of inducing the rulers to adopt a common policy in administrative matters and in the hope that an eventual federation of the states would ensue.

The advent of commercial production of oil in mid-1962 gave Abu Dhabi a great opportunity for development. The deposition of the Ruler, Sheikh Shakhbut, in 1966 removed a major obstacle to implementing this opportunity, and the history of this sheikhdom since then is a classic example of a society being transformed almost overnight by the acquisition of immense wealth. Dubai has also benefited greatly from the oil boom.

In June 1965 Sheikh Saqr of Sharjah was deposed. In spite of an appeal to the UN Secretary-General, supported by Iraq and the United Arab Republic, the accession of his cousin, Sheikh Khalid, passed off without incident. There was an unsuccessful attempt on the Sheikh's life in July 1970.

After June 1966 Britain gradually built a substantial military base at Sharjah, with the object of replacing Aden as the major base in the Middle East; by July 1968 the force of 3,000 men was also larger than Bahrain's and Sharjah had become the principal base in the Gulf but the forces were withdrawn from the area by the end of 1971. The Trucial Oman Scouts, a force of some 1,600 men officered and paid for by Britain and based in Sharjah, were proposed as the nucleus of a federal security force after British withdrawal in 1971, but some states, notably Abu Dhabi, were already creating their own defence forces.

It was feared that friction might be aroused by disputes over the ill-defined state borders; those between Qatar, Abu Dhabi and Dubai were settled early in 1970, the settlement being disputed by Saudi Arabia, whose claimed territory overlapped that of Abu Dhabi to a considerable extent. In July 1970 King Faisal requested that a plebiscite be held in the Buraimi district now ruled by Abu Dhabi. In the autumn of 1974 a border agreement was signed with Saudi Arabia on the Liwa oases, whereupon Saudi

Arabia recognized the U.A.E. and Ambassadors were exchanged. Further down the Gulf, offshore rights also caused trouble. Rival claims over the island of Abu Musa were made by both Sharjah and Iran when petroleum exploration began in 1970, but in 1971 an agreement was reached to split the profits from any oil production on the island.

The original proposals for the formation of a federation on the departure of British influence included Bahrain and Qatar, as well as the seven Trucial States, but negotiations on the participation of the larger and more developed states eventually broke down in 1971, and they opted for separate independence. On December 1st, 1971, Britain terminated all existing treaties with the Trucial States. The following day Abu Dhabi, Dubai, Sharjah, Umm al-Quwain, Ajman and Fujairah formed the United Arab Emirates and a treaty of friendship was made with Britain.

Ras al-Khaimah refused to join the Union until February 1972, when it had become clear that neither Britain nor any Arab government was prepared to take action on Iran's seizure of the two Tumb islands in the Gulf belonging to the sheikhdom. In December 1971 the U.A.E. became a member of both the Arab League and the United Nations.

In January 1972 the Ruler of Sharjah, Sheikh Khalid, was killed by rebels led by his cousin, Sheikh Saqr, who had been deposed as Ruler in 1965. The rebels were captured, and Sheikh Sultan succeeded his brother as Ruler. Sheikh Sultan soon confirmed that he would rule according to the relatively liberal principles of his brother and retain Sharjah's membership of the U.A.E.

Although the U.A.E. remained one of the most conservative Arab states, it gave considerable support to the Arab cause in the October War of 1973 and participated in the oil cut-backs and boycotts associated with it. It was the first state to operate a total ban on oil exports to the U.S.A.

In December 1973 the separate Abu Dhabi Government was disbanded and, in a cabinet reshuffle, some of its members became federal ministers. Most notably the Abu Dhabi oil minister, Mani Said al-Otaiba, became the first federal oil minister. The government reorganization involved a considerable extension of central authority and was a further step towards integration of the seven sheikhdoms. Abu Dhabi was using its economic power to encourage its partners to accept a greater degree of unity, although some seemed reluctant to abandon more of their personal authority. In May 1975, at a session of the Supreme Council, the seven Emirs gave their consent in principle to further steps for centralization. In November 1975 Sharjah merged the Sharjah National Guard with the Union Defence Force, and also handed control of its broadcasting station to the Federal Ministry of Communications, its police to the Ministry of the Interior and its courts to the Ministry of Justice. The Sharjah flag was abolished in favour of the federal tricolour. Fujairah immediately did the same, and Abu Dhabi gave up its flag.

The merger of the main defence forces (the Union Defence Force, the Abu Dhabi Defence Force and the Dubai Defence Force) was finally agreed upon in early May 1976, when General Sheikh Khalifa bin Zayed al-Nahayan, the Crown Prince of Abu Dhabi, was made Deputy Supreme Commander (Sheikh Zayed became Supreme Commander). In November 1976 Article 142 of the provisional constitution was amended so that the right to levy armed forces and acquire weapons was placed exclusively in the hands of the Federal Government.

During 1976 Sheikh Zayed had shown such impatience about the speed at which the Emirates were achieving centralization that he threatened not to stand for a second term as President of the U.A.E., beginning in November 1976. In the event, he was re-elected unanimously after the Supreme Council had granted the Federal Government greater control over defence, intelligence services, immigration, public security and border control. A cabinet reshuffle followed in January 1977 in which the Ministers were said to be chosen on the principle of individual merit rather than representation of the seven Emirates. The new 40-member Federal National Council, which was inaugurated on March 1st, 1977, showed the same spirit of re-invigoration, as only seven members of the first five-year session (1971–76) were included.

During 1978, however, it seemed that the unity of the Federal Defence Force was under strain. A dispute arose in February 1978, when Sheikh Zayed appointed his second son, Sheikh Sultan, as Commander-in-Chief of the Armed Forces. Sheikh Rashid of Dubai claimed that he was not consulted. Thereafter the forces of Dubai and Ras al-Khaimah refused to accept orders from the Federal Commander, and Dubai independently ordered a number of British tanks.

The United Arab Emirates attempted to play a mediatory role in the divisions in the Arab world which followed President Sadat of Egypt's peace initiative in visiting Israel in November 1977. The U.A.E. supported the decision to ostracize Egypt, taken at the Baghdad summit in November 1978, and subsequently reduced investment in and aid to Egypt.

Mounting pressure from within the Emirates for a more united federation in 1978 led to the setting up of a joint Cabinet-Federal National Council committee to discuss methods of achieving this. Events in Iran in 1979 and the resultant security threat prompted a full meeting of the Council of Ministers and the Federal National Council in February. The outcome of this was a 10-point memorandum advocating the abolition of all internal borders, the unification of defence forces and the merging of revenues in a federal budget, which was subsequently submitted to the Supreme Council.

Despite their widespread support in the Emirates, these proposals aggravated the long-standing rivalry between Abu Dhabi, the financial mainstay of the federation, and Dubai, increasingly critical of the centralized federal government in recent years. Dubai announced that it rejected the memorandum completely and, together with Ras al-Khaimah, boycotted a Supreme Council meeting in March.

It was thought that the deadlock had been broken for the time being when Sheikh Rashid, ruler of Dubai, became Prime Minister of the federal government in July 1979. A new cabinet was formed, preserving a similar balance of power between the Emirates as before. Ras al-Khaimah has integrated its defence force with the federal force, and both Abu Dhabi and Dubai have pledged to contribute 50 per cent of their oil revenues to the federal budget, but Dubai's forces are still in practice a separate army. Further attempts at integration include the construction of national roads and installation of telecommunications, and the central planning and financing of health, education and agriculture. In November 1981 Sheikh Rashid was re-elected Prime Minister by the Supreme Council, and Sheikh Zayed was re-elected President.

The foreign policy of the U.A.E. is motivated chiefly by its support for Arab unity, especially in the Palestinian cause, and the country is a founder member of the Co-operation Council for the Arab States of the Gulf, established in March 1981 to work towards economic, social and political integration in the Gulf (*see* p. 177). There is also an individual territorial dispute: in 1980 and 1981 the U.A.E. restated its claim to the three Gulf islands of Abu Musa, Greater Tumb and Lesser Tumb, formerly owned by Sharjah and Ras al-Khaimah but occupied since 1970 by Iran.

ECONOMIC SURVEY

INTRODUCTION

Prior to the discovery of oil, the economy of the seven sheikhdoms, or emirates, that formed the Trucial States was based on pearling, fishing, trade and a limited amount of agriculture. In the nineteenth century piracy, as defined by the Western powers that came into contact with the area, also formed an important source of income for the coastal tribes. Since 1958, when oil was first struck off Abu Dhabi, and in particular since June 1962, when the first oil was exported, the economy of the area has undergone dramatic change. The pace of this change, though, increased appreciably following independence from

Britain in 1971, leading to the creation of the federal state of the United Arab Emirates (U.A.E.), and the OPEC price rises of 1973/74.

The U.A.E. covers approximately 77,700 sq. km., most of which is either sand desert or *sabkha*, salt flats. At the March 1968 census its population was 179,126. The pace of its rapid economic change can be seen in the dramatic increase in population during the 1970s, reaching 655,937 in 1975 and 1,040,275 at the December 1980 census. The marked inequality in the sex ratio, with 69 per cent of the population being male in 1980, indicates the large amount of immigration that has been necessary to sustain the country's economic growth. In 1982 it was estimated by the Planning Ministry that non-nationals accounted for 90 per cent of the work-force, and it seems likely that only about 25 per cent of the total population consists of indigenous citizens. The country has the world's highest level of G.N.P. per caput, estimated by the World Bank at $23,410 in 1979, and the economy continues to expand rapidly, with a growth rate of 21.6 per cent in 1980.

Despite the progress in the U.A.E. towards political integration, there is little co-ordination in economic policies. Abu Dhabi's wealth tends to overshadow the other emirates, but at the same time it is the main factor that holds the seven emirates together. Apart from the difference between Abu Dhabi and Dubai over participation in the oil industry, the two main emirates do not appear to co-operate on building up their various industries. The main instrument of development policy is the federal budget, which is essentially concerned with the implementation of federal infrastructure policy. Individual emirates also draw up separate budgets for municipal expenditure and local projects. The constitution provides for all services such as health and education to come under federal control. Abu Dhabi is the moving force behind the federal budget, contributing more than 90 per cent of the revenue, although both Abu Dhabi and Dubai have pledged 50 per cent of their oil revenues in the future to the federal budget.

PETROLEUM AND GAS

The economy of the U.A.E. is dominated by petroleum. In January 1980 oil reserves were estimated at 35,972.6 million barrels, and in 1979 668.2 million barrels of crude oil were produced, giving a reserves-to-production ratio of 44 years. Current government policy aims at conservation through a reduction in oil exports. However, the world oil glut has severely reduced the country's oil income, and budget prospects in the early 1980s look less promising than they have done for several years. Between 1971 and 1980 total oil receipts increased by approximately 25 times their original value, and, particularly between 1973 and 1976, the economy expanded very rapidly. In this period, public sector spending grew at an annual rate of 72 per cent. The second half of the 1970s, though, saw a period of entrenchment.

Abu Dhabi currently produces about 80 per cent of the U.A.E.'s total oil production, Dubai 18 per cent, and Sharjah 2 per cent. Oil production expanded rapidly from 14,200 barrels per day (b/d) in the first year of production, 1962, to average 1,059,000 b/d in 1971. Output then nearly doubled to 1,998,700 b/d in 1977 before falling to around 1,830,000 b/d in 1978 and 1979. In 1980 production averaged 1,354,065 b/d and in 1981 it fell a further 16 per cent to 1,133,743 b/d, a figure lower than that of any year since 1971. Gas reserves in 1980 were estimated at 588,300 million cubic metres. In terms of pricing, the U.A.E. has played a generally moderate role in OPEC. In January 1979 the price of its marker crude, Murban light, was raised from $13.26 to $14.10 per barrel. After the June 1979 OPEC meeting which set the OPEC ceiling at $23.50, Murban crude was priced at $21.56 per barrel. In December 1979 Murban crude rose to $27.56 per barrel, and during 1980 the upward pressure on prices continued, so that at the beginning of 1981 it had reached $36.56 per barrel. At the end of 1981 the U.A.E. agreed to the unified OPEC price of $34 per barrel for màrker crude.

Abu Dhabi

The first company to obtain an oil concession in Abu Dhabi was the Trucial Coast Development Oil Company, which was granted a concession over the entire territory in 1939. In 1962 the consortium was renamed the Abu Dhabi Petroleum Company (ADPC), and during the 1960s it gradually relinquished much of its concession. Prior to 1973 the major companies in the consortium were BP, Shell, Compagnie Française des Pétroles (CFP), the Near East Development Corporation, and Participations and Explorations Corporation. Under an agreement made on December 20th, 1972, the Abu Dhabi National Oil Company (ADNOC), which had been founded in 1971, acquired a 25 per cent share from January 1st, 1973, and in a further agreement signed on September 2nd, 1974, ADNOC's participation was increased to 60 per cent, back-dated to January 1st, 1974. ADNOC also has a monopoly over oil distribution and is responsible for all oil installations and oil-based industries in the emirate. The second largest oil company in Abu Dhabi, founded in 1954, is Abu Dhabi Marine Areas Ltd. (ADMA), which in 1971 was a consortium of BP and CFP. In December 1972 BP sold 45 per cent of its shares to the Japan Oil Development Company (JODCO) and in the same month the Abu Dhabi Government, in the form of ADNOC, acquired a 25 per cent share, rising to a 60 per cent share in 1974. In 1977 ADNOC and ADMA agreed to establish a new company, ADMA–OPCO (with the same shareholders as ADMA), for offshore work, and in 1978 the Abu Dhabi Company for Onshore Oil Operations (ADCO) was formed from ADPC for onshore work. These two companies produced 93 per cent of Abu Dhabi's oil in 1979, and the remaining four companies in the emirate, the Abu Dhabi Oil Company Ltd., the Total Abu al-Bukoosh Company, the Al-Bunduq Company Ltd., and Amerada Hess produce about 7 per cent. The main onshore oilfields are the Bu Hasa and Asab fields, while the main offshore ones are the Umm Shaif and Lower Zakum fields.

Developments in 1981 included the granting of a 35-year concession offshore to the West German company Deminex, and the beginning of work by the Umm Addalkh Development Company, set up in 1978 by ADNOC and JODCO, on the three offshore fields of Delma, Satah and Jamain.

The Government has continually planned to develop its downstream production, and its first refinery, at Umm al-Nar, came on stream in 1976 with a capacity of 15,000 b/d. A second refinery, at Ruwais, was begun in 1978 and test production began in June 1981. The initial capacity of the Ruwais refinery, to be reached in 1983, is 120,000 b/d, and it was planned to expand this to 300,000 b/d by 1984. In

1981, however, reduced demand led to the postponement of this planned increase for up to 18 months. In 1982 work is also due to begin on a second refinery at Umm al-Nar. During the 1970s there were several plans for the development of petrochemical industries in the emirate, but the only one to come to fruition has been the fertilizer complex at Ruwais, to be known as the Abu Dhabi Fertilizer Company, which is held two-thirds by ADNOC and one-third by CFP. When completed in the mid-1980s, it will produce 1,000 tons per day of ammonia, and 1,500 tons per day of urea.

In January 1981 ADNOC announced that it would spend $38,000 million in the next five years on increased oil and gas exploration, and on expanding Abu Dhabi's petrochemical industries. In October a new 1,561 sq. km. offshore concession was granted to Attock Oil for 35 years, and in the same month Deminex started exploration in its concession. By 1985 the emirate plans to expand its crude oil production to 3 million b/d.

During the early 1970s much gas was flared off, but in 1977 the LNG plant at Das Island started recovering offshore associated gas and soon afterwards plans were set in motion for a scheme to collect onshore gas. This scheme, known as GASCO, was due to begin production in 1981. The natural gas field discovered in the Khuff formation offshore is thought to be one of the largest in the world, and in 1981 a new gas field was found underlying the offshore Zakum oilfield.

Abu Dhabi's income from the hydrocarbon sector rose from $750 million in 1973 to about $4,500 million in 1974. Income rose to $6,780 million in 1978 and to $9,580 million in 1979.

Abu Dhabi's oil is exported through two main terminals. The Jebel Dhanna terminal was completed in 1963. Additional installations, finished in 1974, increased the export capacity of ADPC's Murban oil to 1,280,000 b/d. ADMA–OPCO's Umm Shaif and Zakum oil is exported through the Das terminal. Two smaller terminals exist at Abu al-Bukoosh and Mubarraz. At the beginning of 1980 ADNOC and JODCO began work on a new terminal, to cost $750 million, on Delma Island.

Dubai

Dubai is the second largest oil producer in the U.A.E. In 1963 Conoco took over the earlier oil concession, held from 1937 to 1961 by Iraq Petroleum Company, and formed the Dubai Petroleum Company (DPC), concentrating on offshore production. In 1954 CFP and Hispanoil had obtained an onshore concession, and formed Dubai Marine Areas Ltd. (DUMA). In 1963 DPC acquired a 50 per cent share in DUMA's concession and then released some of its shares to other companies, so that by the late 1960s CFP, Hispanoil, Continental Oil, Texaco, Sun Oil and Wintershall all had shares in DUMA–DPC's concession. In 1973 it seems that the Government of Dubai acquired a 25 per cent share in participation in DUMA–DPC, which was increased to 60 per cent in 1974. Nevertheless, the former concessionnaire

companies continued to operate under the same conditions until in 1979 the Government decided to buy back 50 per cent of the production to market it directly.

Although oil was first discovered in Dubai in 1966, production did not begin until 1969. In 1970 12,496,140 barrels were produced and production continued to rise until 1978, when output was 132,256,290 barrels, an average of 362,346 b/d. This level fell slightly to 354,293 b/d in 1979 and similar levels were maintained in 1980 and 1981. Output is mainly from the two offshore fields of Fateh and South-west Fateh, but some oil is also lifted from the Rashid and Falah offshore fields. In 1980 Dubai's proven recoverable oil reserves were estimated at 1,400 million barrels, which, at present rates, could be exhausted by 1990.

During the 1970s Dubai's natural gas was flared off, but in 1980 the Dubai National Gas Treatment Plant (Dugas), costing $400 million, came on stream. Dubai's gas reserves are estimated at 1,500,000 million cubic feet, and the Dugas plant at Jebel Ali has a treatment capacity of 100 million cubic feet per day. The plant can also produce 11,000 b/d of propane, 7,000 b/d of butane and 7,000 b/d of condensate. Most of this production is shipped to Japan.

Sharjah

Oil production began in Sharjah in 1974 from the Mubarak field at the rate of 60,000 b/d, and it has brought in revenues of around Dh 20 million per year since then, apart from in 1975 and 1976, when the value of exports rose to about Dh 30 million each year. Four consortia were responsible for oil exploration and production in the 1970s: Crescent Petroleum Company, Foreman Exploration, Reserve Oil and Gas and Amoco, which took over its concession in 1976. At the end of 1980, however, Amoco announced a major new onshore oil and gas find. Exports of crude oil from this Sajaa field are due to start in June 1982 at a rate of 25,000 b/d, rising to 80,000 b/d in 1983. Output from the first two gas wells is projected at 50 million cubic feet per day of gas and 5,000 b/d of condensate from Sajaa 1, and 22 million cubic feet per day of gas and 2,000 b/d of condensate from Sajaa 2. Export revenues from these fields are expected to reduce greatly Sharjah's international debt, which is in the region of $600–$1,000 million.

Ajman, Fujairah, Ras al-Khaimah, and Umm al-Quwain

Of the remaining emirates, Ras al-Khaimah appears to have the largest oil and gas reserves. Offshore discoveries made in 1976 and 1977 proved not to be commercially exploitable, but Gulf Oil made new discoveries off the west coast in 1981. Also in 1981 an onshore concession was granted to a consortium of Amoco and Gulf Oil, and seismic tests have suggested the possibility of a hydrocarbon-bearing structure in this concession. Umm al-Quwain's first well was "spudded" in 1981, and exploration continues there, as it does in Ajman and Fujairah. The Federal Government plans increased exploration in the northern emirates during the next five years, and in 1981 a plan for a 100,000 b/d refinery was announced for Fujairah.

INDUSTRY

Since the U.A.E. was formed in 1971, the diversification of the economy away from oil has been a clearly stated government policy. The development of an integrated infrastructure and extensive construction work took place in the 1970s, and this early industrial development was manned largely by immigrant labour. It is estimated that in 1975 the labour force of the U.A.E. was 296,516 (286,555 males and 9,961 females), of whom about 85 per cent were non-nationals. In the mid-1970s non-Arab Asians accounted for about 70 per cent of all work permit visa applications, and it seems that perhaps 60 per cent of the present work force are in this category. Recent anxiety over increasing crime rates, with Abu Dhabi's Planning Department blaming these on the large number of Asian workers and unemployment, has led the U.A.E. to seek labour arrangements with other Arab countries. Thus in March 1981 Tunisia signed an agreement with Abu Dhabi for the provision of labour, and a similar agreement with Morocco was signed at the end of the year.

The industrial structure of the individual emirates varies largely according to their oil revenues. Thus Dubai, with its long tradition of entrepôt trading and relatively small oil reserves, has developed non-oil industry to the greatest extent, whereas Abu Dhabi has tended to build up its hydrocarbon downstream production.

The Ministry of Electricity and Water is responsible for 11 power stations at Umm al-Quwain, Falaj al-Mualla, Dhaid, Masfut, Manama, Uzun, Masafi, Fujairah, Qidfa and Dibba. Production at these plants rose 29 per cent in the first six months of 1980 to 124,304 MW. On the east coast a 33-kV overhead transmission system has been installed and a number of small contracts in 1980 were issued to link up the remainder of the power supply system in this area. In Dubai power is generated by the locally-owned Dubai Electricity Company, and in 1980 a steam power station at Jebel Ali was inaugurated with 60 MW generators. Planned generating capacity at Dubai is to increase from 712 MW in June 1980 to 1082 MW by 1984. Ras al-Khaimah, Sharjah and Abu Dhabi emirates are also responsible for their own power. To cope with increasing demand, Abu Dhabi's Umm al-Nar power station's capacity is to be raised to 1,040 MW by 1984, and Sadiyat Island is to have a new power and desalination plant, to be opened in 1985, with a capacity of 300 MW. One of the U.A.E.'s main projects over the next four years is the construction of the Taweelah power and desalination complex on the Abu Dhabi-Dubai border. Site work began in January 1982 and, when completed it will have a capacity of 2,000 MW and 175 million gallons of water per day.

The lack of water resources has led to much investment in the provision of fresh water, and by 1985 there should be 22 desalination plants in the U.A.E. In 1982 annual water demand was estimated at 565 million cubic metres, of which agriculture used 410 million cubic metres. Examples of projects planned are a desalination plant in Fujairah, producing 2 million gallons per day and planned to be in operation in 1983, and a reverse osmosis desalination plant, with a capacity of 3.6 million gallons per day, proposed for Ajman.

Abu Dhabi

Most of Abu Dhabi's heavy industry is centred on the Jebel Dhanna-Ruwais industrial zone, 250 km. to the west of Abu Dhabi city, which was officially opened by Sheikh Zayed in March 1982. This is mostly oil-related, with the oil refinery at Ruwais and the planned fertilizer plant forming the central projects (*see* Petroleum and gas). An iron and steel plant has been under study for a number of years, but is not yet at the planning stage. It is intended that a new industrial city, with a population of 80,000, will eventually be built at Ruwais.

In 1979 the General Industries Corporation was set up to co-ordinate non-oil development, and by early 1981 it was involved in a paper bag factory, a brick works, a concrete block factory, a steel-rolling mill, and an animal feed plant, all of which had begun production in the preceding two years. Light industry is concentrated in the al-Musalah area, just over the bridges joining Abu Dhabi island to the mainland. At the beginning of 1982 a new contractor classification scheme came into operation in Abu Dhabi, leading to the creation of six categories of contractors. This is aimed at preventing unqualified contractors from making unrealistic bids for new contracts.

Dubai

Dubai has taken the lead in developing non-oil industry, and this has been centred on Jebel Ali port and industrial area, 30 km. to the west of Dubai city. The decision to build a new deep-sea port was taken in August 1976, and by mid-1981 there were 15 km. of quays. The port will eventually have 74 berths, and in 1981 it was used by 1,091 ships, compared with 484 in 1980. The first major plant to come into operation was the Dubai Aluminium Company (DUBAL) smelter, which came on stream at the end of 1979. It was built at a cost of $800 million, and has an installed capacity of 135,000 metric tons of aluminium ingots per year. During 1980 it was producing approximately 1,000 tons per week and in 1981 it produced 106,000 tons, of which 77,347 tons went to Japan. DUBAL is powered by five 100-MW gas turbines, driven by fuel from the neighbouring Dubai Gas Liquefaction (DUGAS) plant. This came on stream in 1980 at a cost of $400 million. In 1979 a third industrial plant, DUCAB (a cable manufacturer owned by the Dubai government and BICC of Britain), came into production. The largest dry dock in the world, capable of accommodating a 1 million-ton oil tanker, has also been built, but by 1981 this had not yet found an operator. As a result, Sheikh Rashid has offered it to OAPEC. In May 1980, in an effort to promote Dubai's industrial development, Sheikh Rashid decreed that Jebel Ali should be a free trade zone. A second, light, industrial area has also been built up around the extended Port Rashid in Dubai itself.

The Northern Emirates

Industrial development in the remaining emirates has been based largely on the construction industry and port expansion. Port Khaled, in Sharjah town, has been developed as a container port, as has Khor Fakkan on the east coast. In Sharjah there are a lubricating oil plant, a rope factory, the Sharjah Oxygen Company, a factory making plastic pipes and a cement plant producing 700 tons per day. In March 1981 the Gulf Industries Complex in Sharjah's industrial zone was finally opened, producing furniture and household utensils. In the future it plans further factories for glassware and carpets. In April 1982 the Gulf Company for Agricultural Development's fodder factory at Mina Khaled was officially opened. Costing $11.5 million, it will store and bag up to 13 different types of animal feed, making the U.A.E. virtually self-sufficient.

Ras al-Khaimah has developed a valuable export business in aggregate (stones used in making concrete) from the Hajar Mountains. In 1980 it saw the opening of the first explosives factory in the Gulf, and early in 1981 a pharmaceutical factory was also opened. The emirate has a cement factory, an asphalt company and a lime kiln, and in 1981 a new company, the Ras al-Khaimah Company for White Cement, was set up to build the Gulf's first white cement factory at Khor Khuwair. This joint Kuwaiti-U.A.E. venture is due to come on stream in 1984, producing 300,000 tons of white cement per year.

At the end of 1980 the Government of Fujairah established a Department of Industry and Economy to organize industrial development. To date Fujairah has factories producing marble, tiles, concrete blocks, tyres and shoes, and in 1981 a cement plant was opened at Dibba. In February 1982 Fujairah's $4.9 million rockwool (asbestos) factory started operations, with an annual capacity of 5,000 tons, and it is planned to open a new ceramics factory in June. A Portland Cement works with a capacity of 500,000 metric tons per year built by Voest-Alpine of Austria, is also to open in Fujairah in 1982, as is the new port which will eventually have 11 berths. Umm al-Quwain has also concentrated on construction, and the newly formed Umm al-Quwain Cement Industries Company plans to build a cement works producing 1 million tons per year to add to the one already in existence. Ajman, the smallest emirate, has a dry dock and a ship repair yard which began operating in 1976.

AGRICULTURE

Since the establishment of an agricultural experimental station at Digdagga (Ras al-Khaimah) in 1955, agriculture in the U.A.E. has undergone a major transformation. Traditionally, agriculture was based on nomadic pastoralism, in association with some oasis cultivation at Liwa, Dhaid, Al Ain, Falaj al-Mualla and on the east coast. This cultivation was totally dominated by dates. Although dates still predominate, the production of vegetables has increased dramatically, to the extent that the Minister of Agriculture reported at the end of 1981 that the U.A.E. was self-sufficient in vegetables. While for the month of December that may have been true, it is clear that, for the year as a whole, the U.A.E. still has to import well over 70 per cent of its food requirements, including vegetables.

It is estimated that the total area under agricultural holdings increased from 125,691 dunums in 1973 to 233,560 dunums in 1979. Over this period, the area planted with vegetables increased from 23,800 to 42,860 dunums, and the area of fruit trees from 50,000 to 102,622 dunums. In 1979 the value of vegetable production was Dh 169.7 million. Most agriculture takes place on the gravel plains on either side of the Hajar Mountains, at Al Ain or at Liwa. This expansion has been implemented through the creation of a widespread government extension service, which in 1979 maintained four District Centres, 21 Agricultural Extension Centres, and seven Experimental Nurseries. In general, agricultural inputs are provided to farmers at half their real cost, with the Government subsidizing fertilizers, seeds and pesticides at 50 per cent of cost. A Central Laboratory for the Ministry of Agriculture and Fisheries was officially opened near Al Ain in April 1982.

There are also a number of large-scale agricultural enterprises in the U.A.E. Thus in 1981 there were three private dairy farms, namely the Arab Company for Animal Production in Ras al-Khaimah at Digdagga, the Emirates Livestock and Agricultural Products Ltd. in Umm al-Quwain, and a third at Al Ain. There are also four poultry farms, a French-sponsored fresh vegetable concern at Al Ain, and a government wheat project on 600 hectares at Al Oha, near Al Ain. Experiments in hydroponics are also being undertaken on Sadiyat Island.

The Government is concerned to increase agricultural production and recent budget allocations have been higher than the 1 per cent allocated to agriculture in the 1970s. However, the increased cultivation of vegetables, and in particular the extensive forestry programme, have led to severe problems with the water tables. Between 1976 and 1977 850 new wells were dug by government teams, and it seems likely that at least this number were also dug privately. The consequent fall in the water table has been dramatic, especially near the coast. Thus in 1980 the water table in Ras al-Khaimah fell by 3.37 metres. In places this has led to increased salinity of soil and water. As a result, several farms are now going out of production. The Government has attempted to alleviate the problem through the construction of catchment dams, such as those at Wadi Ham and Wadi Bih, and it is also allocating much desalinated water for agricultural purposes. This, however, represents a costly investment.

An interesting new agricultural departure was announced in June 1980, when the Emirates Sheep and Livestock Farm took over 10,000 acres at Jhimpir, in Pakistan, to breed animals for export to the U.A.E.

TRADE AND TRANSPORT

During the 1970s the U.A.E.'s oil revenues enabled the emirates to retain a healthy overall balance of trade. Government figures indicate that exports rose from Dh 6,444.5 million in 1973 to Dh 37,661 million in 1978, during which time imports rose from Dh 3,279 million to Dh 18,103.6 million, giving an increase in the trade surplus from Dh 3,165.5 million to Dh 19,557 million. Over this period, crude oil exports fell slightly in importance from 96.2 per cent of all exports to 95 per cent. The biggest import items are basic manufactures, machinery and transport equipment, food and live animals. The leading purchasers of crude oil from Abu Dhabi are Japan, the U.S.A., France and the Netherlands. All of Sharjah's oil exports go to the U.S.A. The leading suppliers of imports into Abu Dhabi and Dubai are Japan, the United Kingdom, the U.S.A. and the Federal Republic of Germany. The healthy trade balance is reflected in the growing foreign assets of the U.A.E. ($10,000 million in 1979), even though only part of the individual emirates' foreign exchange reserves is deposited with the Central Bank.

In 1980 there was an upsurge in the U.A.E.'s imports, and Dubai's imports rose by 17 per cent over the 1979 figure. Exports for 1980 for the U.A.E. as a whole rose to Dh 81,000 million, with imports at Dh 32,400 million, and in 1981 exports had fallen to about Dh 78,000 million, while imports rose to Dh 35,600 million. This rise in imports has been partly due to the Gulf War, during which the U.A.E. ports have handled large amounts of goods for Iran. Recent falls in oil production are likely to lead to a relative decline in the country's trade surplus. One way in which trade has been allocated has been through the designation of trade free zones, as at Jebel Ali, and in 1982 or early 1983 Port Zayed is also due to be established as such. From April 1982 customs duty in Dubai and Sharjah has been lowered from 3 per cent to 1 per cent, to bring it in line with Abu Dhabi.

The modern internal transport system of the U.A.E. was largely developed in the late 1960s and 1970s, when main roads were constructed to link all the major cities. One of the characteristics of the country's economy over recent years has been the expansion in the number of major airports. Abu Dhabi international airport was opened in 1968 and expanded during the 1970s. Due to congestion, a New Abu Dhabi International Airport (NADIA) was planned in the 1970s and it should open early in 1982 at an estimated cost of Dh 1,500 million. Dubai's international airport is the busiest in the region, and during 1980 the number of airlines with scheduled services rose to 36, serving 95 destinations. The third international airport in the country is at Sharjah but, opening in 1977, it had difficulties in attracting traffic, owing to the proximity of Dubai. Nevertheless, it also expanded its turnover in 1980 and attracted the civil airline of the People's Republic of China, which chose Sharjah as its only staging point in the Lower Gulf. Ras al-Khaimah has the fourth international airport, and it too has had problems in attracting traffic. A further new international airport is planned for Al Ain but this is unlikely to be operational before 1984.

The latest development in the field of transport is the possibility of a rail link joining Dubai to the other U.A.E. cities. Transmark, a subsidiary of British Rail, was consulted in 1981 over the possible development of such a link. The Government of Abu Dhabi has already agreed to a railway joining Abu Dhabi island with NADIA.

BANKING AND FINANCE

The unit of currency in the U.A.E. is the dirham (Dh), which was created in 1973 to replace the Bahraini dinar and the Qater/Dubai riyal, formerly used in the emirates. The dirham is linked officially to the IMF's Special Drawing Right but in practice to the U.S. dollar. In 1979 and 1980 the Currency Board revalued the dirham by small amounts (up to one per cent) against the dollar in order to try to curb capital outflows from the country (there are no exchange controls), which were attracted by generally higher interest rates in the U.S.A., the United Kingdom and elsewhere. The revaluations were also designed to ease the tightness of liquidity in the domestic money market caused by the capital outflows.

Discussions on a common currency were held by Bahrain, Kuwait, the U.A.E. and Qatar in 1975 and 1976, but the idea was eventually abandoned because of the divergent interests and central banking practices of the four states. During 1980, however, financial links with other countries in the Gulf were strengthened through the agreement between the U.A.E., Kuwait, Qatar and Libya to set up a new international insurance company. The U.A.E. was also one of a number of Arab states to agree to contribute to a fund designed to iron out economic and social differences between Arab countries.

A central monetary institution, the U.A.E. Currency Board, was established in May 1973, but inter-emirate rivalry prevented it from being given full central banking powers. This has led to a rapid multiplication of banks in the country. The U.A.E. has 53 commercial banks, foreign and domestic, with 350 branches. There are also five "restricted licence" banks and several representative offices, investment/merchant banking operations and money changers. The Currency Board, managed mainly by expatriates, was able to bring only a little order into the banking free-for-all. A moratorium on the opening of new banks was imposed in 1975, but was lifted temporarily in May 1976 (as a result of what appear to have been political pressures) to allow five more banks (four Arab and one British) to operate. The moratorium was then re-imposed, but with the let-out for international banks of restricted licences, which allow all operations except domestic retail banking. Twelve such restricted licences were issued in 1976, but only five such banks have opened. In December 1980 the U.A.E. Central Bank replaced the old Currency Board, and the rulers of Abu Dhabi and Dubai agreed to place one-half of their national revenues with the new institution. In April 1981 the moratorium was lifted again but in May the Governor of the Central Bank announced that no foreign banks would be granted new branch licences. In July 1981 the Central Bank became more aggressive and told all foreign banks that they had until 1984 to reduce their operations to eight branches each. This would lead to the closure of 89 branches by nine foreign banks. In June 1981 the Government had announced that it was setting up an industrial bank, with an initial capital of Dh 200 million and the Government holding a 51 per cent stake in it. Early in 1982 the Central Bank again intervened to keep a high level of liquidity in the country by imposing a 30 per cent interest-free reserve requirement on dirham loans placed outside the U.A.E. for less than one year. This replaced the former 15 per cent charge imposed in May 1981 for loans up to three months.

Inflation and the growth of bank credit have both been reduced since 1980. Between 1974 and 1977 inflation in the U.A.E. was running at about 25 per cent, but by 1981 this was down to 15 per cent. Likewise, the growth in bank credits has fallen from 21 per cent in 1978 to 14 per cent in 1980. Money supply has also been rising more slowly. In the three years to December 1976 currency in circulation rose by 387 per cent and overall domestic liquidity by 782 per cent. Money supply, however, rose by only 11 per cent in 1978 and 16 per cent in 1979.

In many economic matters, the individual emirates continue to pursue their own separate ways, although they do not publish detailed budgets. Abu Dhabi and Dubai are the only two emirates which provide funds for the federal budget, with Abu Dhabi providing the bulk of these. Federal expenditure is divided into current expenditure, development expenditure and expenditure for investment. Recent expenditure forecasts in the federal budget have been as follows: Dh 10,500 million in 1978, Dh 10,100 million in 1979, Dh 14,069 million in 1980, Dh 26,232 million in 1981 and Dh 22,559 million in 1982. Actual expenditure in the late 1970s was much higher than the budgeted figure, being Dh 27,500 million in 1978, Dh 31,000 million in 1979 and Dh 38,000 million in 1980. The recent reduction in the federal budget reflects the Government's attempts to curb inflation. In 1982 the draft budget envisages expenditure of Dh 22,559 million and revenue of Dh 20,276 million, with a budget deficit of Dh 2,283 million. This is believed to be the U.A.E.'s first deficit budget, and reflects the fall in oil prices and production. In the 1982 draft budget the education ministry is to get Dh 194 million (down from Dh 433 million in 1981), agriculture Dh 25 million, communications Dh 290 million, electricity and water Dh 500 million, and health Dh 145 million. In 1980 defence took about 28 per cent of the federal budget, and in 1982 it is expected to take approximately 50 per cent. In view of the falling revenue from oil, and also to reduce smoking, the government introduced its first tax, a 30 per cent tax on cigarettes, in 1981.

In contrast to the federal budget, the Abu Dhabi budget for 1982 is 17.5 per cent higher than that of 1981. Of the projected expenditure of Dh 11,571 million, Dh 7,000 million is to be spent on Abu Dhabi's development projects.

DEVELOPMENT PLANNING

Until 1981 development expenditure in the U.A.E. came from the annual federal budget, and there has been no attempt at detailed long-term integrated economic planning, although Abu Dhabi did have a loose development plan for 1977–79. Despite this lack of overall planning, major achievements in the fields of health and education have been achieved within the emirates. Thus in 1972/73 there were only 24,508 male and 15,605 female students in the country as a whole, whereas in 1979/80 the figures had increased to 67,596 male and 54,423 female students, and a university had been established in 1977/78 at Al Ain for higher education. In 1980/81 950 students were admitted to the university, and there are currently plans to build a 14 sq. km. campus city at Al Ain to house the university.

The end of the 1970s saw a great increase in health facilities in the country, with the number of hospital beds available rising from 1,750 in 1979 to 3,500 in April 1981. This increase was partly brought about through the completion of two major new hospitals at Al Ain. In 1981 Abu Dhabi city had three main hospitals, and Dubai four. The other emirates all have at least one hospital each.

The first Five-Year Plan was meant to have been implemented in 1981, to run until 1985, but by the beginning of 1982 full details of its allocations had not been disclosed. Overall expenditure is estimated to be Dh 16,000 million for the five years, with Abu Dhabi receiving 21 per cent, Fujairah 12.5 per cent, Sharhaj 10.8 per cent, Ras al-Khaimah 9.4 per cent, Umm al-Quwain 7.7 per cent, Dubai 5.3 per cent, and Ajman 4.4 per cent. The Plan predicts an overall increase of 20 per cent in the country's G.D.P. up to 1985, and it is estimated that Dh 1,200 million will be spent in subsidies and loans to farmers and fishermen by the Ministry of Agriculture and Fisheries. In the field of education, the U.A.E. plans to build a further 379 schools by 1985, bringing the total to 762. Of the Dh 16,000 million to be spent in the Plan, Dh 3,500 million is for investment projects and Dh 8,400 million for schemes already under construction, but it is uncertain how the remainder is specifically to be spent.

The U.A.E., however, has not only been concerned with its own development, and Abu Dhabi, through its Fund for Arab Economic Development (ADFAED), has been a major source of international aid. External assistance in the form of grants, "soft" loans and participations averaged $1,100 million per year in the period 1974–78; in 1979 it was almost $1,500 million. ADFAED was set up in 1971 with a capital of $120 million; its commitments up to the end of 1980 totalled $800 million. In 1982, though, due to falling oil revenue, the U.A.E. is more than halving its foreign aid budget.

STATISTICAL SURVEY

AREA AND POPULATION

	AREA (sq. km.)	POPULATION* (Census, Dec. 1980)	DENSITY (per sq. km.)
Abu Dhabi . . .	67,350	449,000	6.7
Dubai . . .	3,900	278,000	71.3
Sharjah . . .	2,600	159,000	61.2
Ras al-Khaimah . .	1,700	73,700	43.4
Ajman . . .	250	36,100	144.4
Fujairah . . .	1,150	32,200	28.0
Umm al-Quwain . .	750	12,300	16.4
TOTAL . .	77,700†	1,040,275‡	13.4

* Figures for individual emirates are rounded to the nearest 100.
† 30,000 sq. miles.
‡ Comprising 717,475 males and 322,800 females.

Capital: Abu Dhabi (estimated population 250,000 in 1978).

SEA FISHING

('000 metric tons)

	1972	1973	1974	1975	1976
Total catch (live weight) . .	43.0	43.0	68.0	68.0	64.4

1977-80: Annual catch as in 1976.

Source: FAO, *Yearbook of Fishery Statistics.*

MINING

		1974	1975	1976	1977	1978	1979
Crude petroleum . . .	'000 metric tons	81,441	82,058	95,265	97,555	89,605	89,832*
Natural gas* . . .	terajoules	36,463	30,940	34,252	54,858	92,324	84,268

* Provisional.

1980: Crude petroleum 84.2 million metric tons.

863

PRODUCTION OF CRUDE PETROLEUM
(million barrels)

	1976	1977	1978	1979	1980
Abu Dhabi . . .	580.5	602.8	527.8	533.3	494.6
Dubai . . .	114.8	116.4	132.2	129.3	127.7
Sharjah . . .	13.5	10.3	8.1	5.0	3.8
TOTAL . .	708.9	729.5	668.1	667.6	626.1

PRODUCTION OF LIQUEFIED GAS*
('ooo metric tons)

	1978	1979	1980
Liquefied natural gas . .	1,257.4	1,378.8	2,032.4
Liquefied petroleum gas . .	429.6	603.5	755.2
of which: Propane . .	207.0	291.2	355.9
Butane . .	154.3	211.8	271.8
Pentane . .	68.4	100.4	137.5

* Figures refer to Abu Dhabi only.

Sources: Middle East Economic Digest, Special Report, December 1979;
U.A.E. Currency Board, *Statistical Supplement*, September 1980; and
Central Bank of the U.A.E., *Bulletin*, June 1981.

INDUSTRY
(gross value of manufacturing production,
million dirhams)

	1977	1978*
Food	364.1	468.5
Spinning, weaving and leather .	284.7	313.5
Wood and wood furniture . .	208.2	232.2
Printing, paper and paper products	134.4	148.6
Chemicals and petroleum products .	657.2	1,209.5
Non-metallic mineral products .	758.2	955.9
Basic metal products and engineering	702.4	767.9
Miscellaneous . . .	138.3	135.4
TOTAL . . .	3,247.5	4,231.5

* Provisional.

Source: Ministry of Planning, *Statistical Survey* 1978/79.

ELECTRICITY
(million kWh., Abu Dhabi)

	1972	1973	1974	1975	1976	1977	1978	1979*
Estimated production .	477	692	896	1,335	1,942	2,863	3,759	4,340

* Provisional.

Source: UN, *Yearbook of Industrial Statistics*.

FINANCE

100 fils = 1 U.A.E. dirham.
Coins: 1, 5, 10, 25 and 50 fils; 1 dirham.
Notes: 1, 5, 10, 50 and 100 dirhams.
Exchange rates (May 1982): £1 sterling = 6.749 dirhams; U.S. $1 = 3.671 dirhams.
100 U.A.E. dirhams = £14.82 = $27.24.

Note: Before June 1966 the currency used by the states of Trucial Oman (now the United Arab Emirates) was the Persian Gulf Indian rupee, valued at 1s. 6d. sterling (£1 = 13.33 rupees). When the Indian rupee was devalued in June 1966, Abu Dhabi adopted the Bahrain dinar (of 1,000 fils) while the other states used Saudi Arabian currency prior to the introduction of the Qatar/Dubai riyal (at par with the old rupee) in September 1966. The Bahrain dinar, equal to 10 old rupees, was valued at U.S. $2.10 ($1 = 476.19 fils) until August 1971; at $2.28 ($1 = 438.60 fils) from December 1971 to February 1973; and at $2.533 ($1 = 394.74 fils) from February 1973. The Q/D riyal, also used in Qatar, was valued at 21 U.S. cents ($1 = 4.762 riyals) until August 1971; at 22.8 U.S. cents ($1 = 4.386 riyals) from December 1971 to February 1973; and at 25.33 U.S. cents ($1 = 3.947 riyals) from February 1973. Between November 1967 and June 1972 the Bahrain dinar was valued at 17s. 6d. sterling (87½ new pence) and the Q/D riyal at 1s. 9d. (8.75 new pence), the exchange rates being £1 = 1.143 dinars = 11.43 riyals. In May 1973 the U.A.E. adopted a common currency, the dirham, which was at par with the Q/D riyal (renamed the Qatar riyal) and thus valued at 25.33 U.S. cents. The market exchange rate has been frequently adjusted. It corresponded to the original par value ($1 = 3.947 dirhams) from January to November 1976 and was $1 = 3.898 dirhams from February 1977 to January 1978. The rate was $1 = 3.978 dirhams from January to September 1978; and $1 = 3.838 dirhams from October 1978 to June 1979. After further frequent adjustments, the rate was $1 = 3.688 dirhams between July and November 1980. A new rate of $1 = 3.671 dirhams was introduced in November 1980. The average rates (dirhams per dollar) were: 3.996 in 1973; 3.959 in 1974; 3.961 in 1975; 3.953 in 1976; 3.903 in 1977; 3.871 in 1978; 3.816 in 1979; 3.707 in 1980.

FEDERAL BUDGET EXPENDITURE
(million U.A.E. dirhams)

	1979	1980	1981*
CURRENT BUDGET			
State†	71.1	73.7	211.5
Finance and industry	30.6	38.5	60.9
Economy and trade	8.1	9.4	12.7
Interior, justice and defence	4,511.7	7,659.9	9,342.0
Housing and public works	38.5	43.1	54.0
Communications	60.1	64.1	83.3
Health	667.0	867.3	1,266.3
Agriculture and Fisheries	55.4	83.2	86.8
Education and youth	864.0	993.0	1,210.7
Petroleum	16.9	15.6	22.4
Electricity and water	156.4	273.9	383.0
TOTAL (including others)	7,362.4	12,260.8	21,278.5
DEVELOPMENT BUDGET			
Interior, justice and defence	79.0	63.1	310.5
Electricity and water	51.5	131.4	310.4
Housing	82.3	130.0	216.9
Communications	93.4	203.3	377.2
Health	79.6	82.1	261.5
Agriculture	45.9	54.5	195.8
Education and youth	148.2	237.5	432.7
TOTAL (including others)	598.4	935.9	2,555.7
EQUITY PARTICIPATION	449.0	1,975.2	2,298.2
TOTAL EXPENDITURE	8,459.8	15,171.9	26,132.4

* Forecasts.

† Includes Council of Ministers and National Federal Council.

Revenue (million dirhams): 8,686.2 in 1979; 23,235.0 in 1980.

1982: Budget: revenue 20,275.6 million dirhams, expenditure 22,559.5 million dirhams.

DEVELOPMENT PLAN
(1981–85)
Total investment: 171,100 million dirhams.

EXTERNAL TRADE

(million U.A.E. dirhams)

	1975	1976	1977	1978	1979	1980	1981
Imports c.i.f.* . . .	10,571	13,150	19,703	20,765	26,527	32,425	n.a.
Exports f.o.b.† . . .	27,609	34,328	37,612	35,327	52,023	76,884	73,555

Exports of crude petroleum (million dirhams): 27,006 in 1975; 33,123 in 1976; 36,138 in 1977; 33,528 in 1978; 49,078 in 1979; 72,125 in 1980; 68,796 in 1981.

* Figures refer to Abu Dhabi, Dubai and Sharjah only. Data exclude inter-emirate trade, transit trade and imports of gold and silver.

† *Source:* IMF, *International Financial Statistics.*

COMMODITY GROUPS

(million U.A.E. dirhams)

	IMPORTS*			NATIONAL EXPORTS†			RE-EXPORTS†		
	1978‡	1979‡	1980	1978	1979	1980	1978	1979‡	1980
Food and live animals . .	1,902.0	2,570.9	3,251.2	1.0	4.2	18.8	313.8	602.7	800.1
Beverages and tobacco . .	374.8	717.3	637.9	—	—	12.3	108.9	134.6	108.2
Crude materials (inedible) except fuels . . .	289.0	321.9	552.0	7.6	5.1	24.9	64.2	72.3	128.9
Mineral fuels, lubricants, etc.	778.3	2,711.8	3,703.7	—	—	411.0	15.8	31.5	392.9
Animal and vegetable oils and fats	58.7	73.9	106.8	—	—	—	1.5	2.3	18.1
Chemicals	895.2	1,170.0	1,506.9	—	—	17.9	46.6	73.2	156.6
Basic manufactures . .	4,888.9	6,033.9	6,865.0	99.4	229.1	459.1	343.3	420.3	593.7
Machinery and transport equipment . . .	9,123.1	9,797.2	11,646.0	7.2	—	6.4	488.6	829.9	992.8
Miscellaneous manufactured articles	2,289.4	2,988.4	3,895.7	—	—	2.6	388.5	531.6	575.2
Other commodities and transactions . . .	191.3	196.2	259.6	—	—	0.1	19.3	8.0	21.3
TOTAL . . .	20,790.7	26,581.6	32,424.8	115.2	238.4	953.1	1,790.5	2,706.3	3,787.9

* Abu Dhabi, Dubai and Sharjah.

† Abu Dhabi and Dubai. Figures exclude petroleum.

‡ Including transit trade through Abu Dhabi (million dirhams): Imports 25.3 in 1978, 54.4 in 1979; Re-exports 216.3 in 1979.

Source: Central Bank of the U.A.E. *Bulletin,* June 1981.

PRINCIPAL TRADING PARTNERS
(million U.A.E. dirhams)

IMPORTS*	1978	1979	1980
Australia	236.1	285.5	520.7
Bahrain	198.2	1,733.1	1,926.9
China, People's Rep.	299.6	423.5	502.7
France	970.4	1,384.2	1,913.0
Germany, Fed. Rep.	2,170.5	2,148.5	1,847.8
Hong Kong	305.1	532.6	511.3
India	614.9	711.7	754.7
Italy	780.4	1,120.5	1,515.2
Japan	3,813.5	4,406.5	5,513.3
Korea, Republic	271.5	453.9	735.5
Netherlands	978.8	613.4	813.6
Singapore	386.6	717.9	966.6
Taiwan	281.2	464.6	575.8
United Kingdom	3,701.3	4,170.4	4,549.4
U.S.A.	2,504.4	3,453.5	4,292.3
TOTAL (incl. others)	20,844.7	26,642.4	32,589.1

EXPORTS†	1978	1979‡	1980
Bahrain	35.7	103.6	126.9
Iran	595.3	910.5	1,341.4
Iraq	15.3	39.7	147.5
Kuwait	71.6	97.3	138.3
Oman	25.8	44.1	395.4
Pakistan	37.8	47.7	140.2
Qatar	260.6	300.3	368.5
Saudia Arabia	503.6	800.3	851.4
Yemen Arab Repub.	225.8	370.5	171.9
TOTAL (incl. others)	1,905.7	2,944.7	4,740.9

† Figures refer to Abu Dhabi and Dubai only, including re-exports but excluding petroleum.
‡ Including transit trade through Abu Dhabi totalling 216.3 million dirhams.

* Figures refer to Abu Dhabi, Dubai and Sharjah only, including transit trade through Abu Dhabi and Dubai.

Source: Central Bank of the U.A.E. *Bulletin,* June 1981.

TRANSPORT
INTERNATIONAL SEA-BORNE SHIPPING
(estimated freight traffic in 'ooo metric tons)

	1972	1973	1974	1975	1976	1977
Goods loaded	58,900	74,833	82,891	81,626	95,600	97,115
Crude petroleum	58,297	73,668	81,691	80,376	95,447	96,835
Other cargo	603	1,165	1,200	1,250	153	280
Goods unloaded	840	900	1,020	1,250	1,500	n.a.

Source: United Nations, *Statistical Yearbook.*

COMMUNICATIONS
The number of telephones in use in the United Arab Emirates as a whole was 165,000 in 1981.

EDUCATION
United Arab Emirates

	1977/78	1978/79	1979/80	1980/81
Schools	279	297	322	362
Students	97,274	108,427	124,019	141,424
Teachers	7,443	8,255	9,611	10,991

Source: Ministry of Education, *Annual Report.*

THE CONSTITUTION

A provisional constitution for the U.A.E. was set up in December 1971. This laid the foundation for the federal structure of the Union of the seven sheikhdoms, previously known as the Trucial States.

The highest federal authority is the Supreme Council which comprises the rulers of the seven Emirates. It elects a president and vice-president from among its members. The president appoints a prime minister and a cabinet. The legislature is the Federal National Council, a consultative assembly comprising 40 members appointed by the emirates for a two-year term.

In July 1975 a committee was appointed to draft a permanent federal constitution, but the National Council decided in 1976 to extend the provisional constitution for five years. The provisional constitution was extended for another five years in December 1981. In November 1976, however, the Supreme Council amended Article 142 of the provisional constitution so that the right to levy armed forces was placed exclusively in the hands of the federal government.

THE GOVERNMENT

HEAD OF STATE

President: Sheikh ZAYED BIN SULTAN AL-NAHAYAN (Ruler of Abu Dhabi).

Vice-President: Sheikh RASHID BIN SAID AL-MAKTUM (Ruler of Dubai).

SUPREME COUNCIL OF RULERS

(with each ruler's date of accession)

Ruler of Sharjah: Sheikh SULTAN BIN MUHAMMAD AL-QASIMI (1972).

Ruler of Ras al-Khaimah: Sheikh SAQR BIN MUHAMMAD AL-QASIMI (1948).

Ruler of Umm al-Quwain: Sheikh RASHID BIN AHMAD AL-MU'ALLA (1981).

Ruler of Ajman: Sheikh HUMAID BIN RASHID AL-NUAMI (1981).

Ruler of Dubai: Sheikh RASHID BIN SAID AL-MAKTUM (1958).

Ruler of Abu Dhabi: Sheikh ZAYED BIN SULTAN AL-NAHAYAN (1966).

Ruler of Fujairah: Sheikh HAMAD BIN MUHAMMAD AL-SHARQI (1974).

COUNCIL OF MINISTERS

(June 1982)

Prime Minister: Sheikh RASHID BIN SAID AL-MAKTUM.

Deputy Prime Minister: Sheikh MAKTUM BIN RASHID AL-MAKTUM.

Deputy Prime Minister: Sheikh HAMDAN BIN MUHAMMAD AL-NAHAYAN.

Minister of the Interior: Sheikh MUBARAK BIN MUHAMMAD AL-NAHAYAN.

Minister of Finance and Industry: Sheikh HAMDAN BIN RASHID AL-MAKTUM.

Minister of Defence: Sheikh MUHAMMAD BIN RASHID AL-MAKTUM.

Minister of Economy and Trade: Sheikh SULTAN BIN AHMED AL-MUALLA.

Minister of Information and Culture: Sheikh AHMED BIN HAMED.

Minister of Communications: AHMED SAID AL-MULLA.

Minister of Public Works and Housing: MUHAMMAD KHALIFA AL-KINDI.

Minister of Education and Youth Affairs: SAID SALMAN.

Minister of Petroleum and Mineral Resources: MANI SAID AL-OTEIBA.

Minister of Electricity and Water: HAMAD BIN NASIR AL-UWAIS.

Minister of Justice, Islamic Affairs and Endowments: MUHAMMAD ABDEL AR-RAHMAN AL-BAKR.

Minister of Health: HAMAD ABD AR-RAHMAN AL-MIDFA.

Minister of Labour and Social Affairs: SAIF AL-JARWAN.

Minister of Planning: SAID GHOBASH.

Minister of Agriculture and Fisheries: SAID AR-RUQBANI.

Minister of State for Internal Affairs: HAMOUDA BIN ALI DHARIRI.

Minister of State for Foreign Affairs and Acting Minister of Foreign Affairs: RASHID BIN ABDULLAH AL-NUAIMI.

Minister of State for Cabinet Affairs: SAID AL-GHAITH.

Minister of State for Supreme Council Affairs: Sheikh ABDEL-AZIZ BIN HUMAID AL-QASIMI.

Minister of State without Portfolio: Sheikh AHMED BIN SULTAN AL-QASIMI.

LEGISLATURE

FEDERAL NATIONAL COUNCIL

Formed under the provisions of the temporary constitution, it is composed of 40 members from the various Emirates (8 each from Abu Dhabi and Dubai, 6 each from Sharjah and Ras al-Khaimah, and 4 each from Ajman, Fujairah and Umm al-Quwain). Each Emirate appoints its own representatives separately. The Council studies laws proposed by the Council of Ministers and can reject them or suggest amendments. The second five-year session of the Federal National Council was inaugurated in Abu Dhabi on March 1st, 1977.

Speaker: TARYAM OMRAN TARYAM (Sharjah).

Deputy Speaker: HAMAD BOU SHIHAB.

DIPLOMATIC REPRESENTATION

EMBASSIES ACCREDITED TO THE UNITED ARAB EMIRATES

(In Abu Dhabi unless otherwise stated)

Afghanistan: Baghdad, Iraq.

Algeria: P.O.B. 3070; *Ambassador:* HASHIMI QADDOURI.

Australia: P.O.B. 559; *Consul-General:* ROBERT MCAUSLAN.

Austria: P.O.B. 3095; *Chargé d'affaires:* Dr. PETER SINGER.

Bangladesh: P.O.B. 2504; *Ambassador:* MAHBUB AL-HUQ.

Belgium: P.O.B. 3686; *Ambassador:* JACQUES HOUARD.

Brazil: P.O.B. 3027; *Chargé d'affaires:* (vacant).

Canada: Kuwait City, Kuwait.

Denmark: P.O.B. 6666; *Minister Counsellor:* ERIK W. SVENNINGSEN.

Egypt: P.O.B. 4026; *Ambassador:* (vacant).

Finland: Jeddah, Saudi Arabia.

France: P.O.B. 4014; *Ambassador:* JEAN HONNORET.

Gabon: P.O.B. 2653; *Ambassador:* AHMAD NDIMAL.

Germany, Federal Republic: P.O.B. 2591; *Ambassador:* Dr. EBERHARD KUHNT.

Greece: Kuwait City, Kuwait.

India: P.O.B. 4090; *Ambassador:* LALITENDU MANSINGH.

Indonesia: P.O.B. 7256; *Chargé d'affaires:* ABDUL LATIF MUHAMMAD TAMAN.

Iran: P.O.B. 4080; *Ambassador:* (vacant).

Iraq: P.O.B. 4030; *Ambassador:* SAAD ABDUL MAJID AL-FAISAL.

Ireland: Jeddah, Saudi Arabia.

Italy: P.O.B. 6752; *Ambassador:* ANTONIO NAPOLITANO.

Japan: P.O.B. 2430; *Ambassador:* NOBORU NAKAHIRA.

Jordan: P.O.B. 4024; *Ambassador:* AMER SHAMOUT.

Korea, Republic: Abu Dhabi; *Ambassador:* PHILIP CHOY.

Kuwait: P.O.B. 926; *Ambassador:* QASIM OMAR AL-YAGOUT.

Lebanon: P.O.B. 4023; *Ambassador:* MAHMOUD HAMMOUD.

Libya: P.O.B. 2091; *Secretary of People's Committee:* ALI MAHMUD MARIA.

Malaysia: Kuwait City, Kuwait.

Mauritania: P.O.B. 2714; *Ambassador:* ABDALLA YOUSEF AL-GHAZALI.

Mexico: Beirut, Lebanon.

Morocco: P.O.B. 4066; *Ambassador:* ABDUL AZIZ AL-MATAWI AL-MASHKURI.

Nepal: Jeddah, Saudi Arabia.

Netherlands: P.O.B. 6560; *Chargé d'affaires:* D. J. J. VAN LOTTUM.

Niger: Khartoum, Sudan.

Norway: Jeddah, Saudi Arabia.

Pakistan: P.O.B. 846; *Ambassador:* AMIR GULISTAN JANJUA.

Philippines: P.O.B. 3215; *Chargé d'affaires:* ALBERTO ENCOMIENDA.

Qatar: P.O.B. 3503; *Chargé d'affaires:* IBRAHIM A. H. NIMAH.

Saudi Arabia: P.O.B. 4057; *Ambassador:* SALIH SULAIMAN AL FAWZAN.

Senegal: Jeddah, Saudi Arabia.

Somalia: P.O.B. 4155; *Ambassador:* ABDULLAH HAJ ABDUL RAHMAN.

Spain: P.O.B. 6474; *Ambassador:* FAUSTO NAVARRO IZQUIERDO.

Sri Lanka: P.O.B. 6534; *Chargé d'affaires:* R. P. E. JAYASINGHE.

Sudan: P.O.B. 4027; *Ambassador:* Dr. ABDUL LATIF ABDUL HUMAID IBRAHIM.

Sweden: Kuwait City, Kuwait.

Switzerland: P.O.B. 6116; *Commercial Counsellor:* WILLY FRIES.

Syria: P.O.B. 4011; *Ambassador:* MUHAMMAD KABOUR.

Tanzania: Cairo, Egypt.

Thailand: Jeddah, Saudi Arabia.

Tunisia: P.O.B. 4166; *Ambassador:* MOHSEN FRINI.

Turkey: P.O.B. 3204; *Ambassador:* METIN KUSTAOGLU.

United Kingdom: P.O.B. 248; *Ambassador:* HAROLD BERNERS WALKER, C.M.G.

U.S.A.: P.O.B. 4009; *Ambassador:* (vacant).

Venezuela: Kuwait City, Kuwait.

Yemen Arab Republic: P.O.B. 2095; *Ambassador:* AHMAD HUSSEIN AL-MARUNI.

Zaire: P.O.B. 2592; *(relations broken off, May 1982).*

The U.A.E. also has diplomatic relations with Chile, Ecuador, Honduras, Kenya, Maldives, Mauritius, Nigeria and Oman.

JUDICIAL SYSTEM

The 95th article of the provisional constitution of 1971 provided for the setting up of a Union Supreme Court and Union Primary Tribunals.

The Union has exclusive legislative and executive jurisdiction over all matters that are concerned with the strengthening of the federation such as foreign affairs, defence and Union armed forces, security, finance, communications, traffic control, education, currency, measures, standards and weights, matters relating to nationality and emigration, Union information, etc.

President Sheikh Zayed signed the law establishing the new federal courts on June 9th, 1978. The new law effectively transferred local judicial authorities into the jurisdiction of the federal system.

Primary tribunals in Abu Dhabi, Sharjah, Ajman and Fujairah are now primary federal tribunals and primary tribunals in other towns in those Emirates have become circuits of the primary federal tribunals.

The primary federal tribunal may sit in any of the capitals of the four Emirates and have jurisdiction on all administrative disputes between the Union and individuals, whether the Union is plaintiff or defendant. Civil disputes between Union and individuals will be heard by primary federal tribunals in the defendant's place of normal residence.

The new law requires that all judges take a constitutional oath before the Minister of Justice and Islamic Affairs and that the courts apply the rules of Sharia (Islamic religious laws) and that no judgment contradicts Sharia. All employees of the old judiciaries will be transferred to the federal authority without loss of salary or seniority.

Chief Sharia Justice: AHMED ABDUL AZIZ AL-MUBARAK.

RELIGION

Most of the inhabitants are Muslims of the Sunni sect. About 20 per cent of the Muslims are Shi'ites.

THE PRESS

The Ministry of Information has placed a moratorium on new titles.

ABU DHABI

Abu Dhabi Chamber of Commerce Review: P.O.B. 662, Abu Dhabi; monthly; Arabic, some articles in English.

al-Dhafra: P.O.B. 4288, Abu Dhabi; independent; published by Dar al-Wahdah; Arabic; weekly.

Emirates News: P.O.B. 3627, Abu Dhabi; published by al-Ittihad Press and Publishing Corporation; daily; English; Man. Editor MUHAMMAD OMER ELKHIDIR.

Gulf News: P.O.B. 6519, Dubai; an A. W. Galadari enterprise; daily; English; two weekly supplements, *Junior News* (Monday), *Al Jum'a* (weekend); Editor SHAHID NAYEEM; circ. 23,000.

Hiya: P.O.B. 2488, Abu Dhabi; published by Dar al-Wahdah; Arabic weekly for women.

al-Ittihad (*Unity*): P.O.B. 17, Abu Dhabi; f. 1972; daily; Editor-in-Chief KHALED MUHAMMAD AHMAD.

Recorder: P.O.B. 2310, Abu Dhabi; daily news bulletin; English.

U.A.E. and Abu Dhabi Official Gazette: P.O.B. 899, Abu Dhabi; Arabic.

U.A.E. Press Service Daily News: P.O.B. 2035, Abu Dhabi; daily; English; Editor RASHID AL-MAZROUI.

al-Wahdah: P.O.B. 2488, Abu Dhabi; f. 1973; independent; daily; Man. Editor RASHID AWEIDHA; Gen. Man. KHALIFA AL-MASHWI.

DUBAI

Akhbar Dubai: Department of Information, Dubai Municipality, P.O.B. 1420, Dubai; f. 1965; weekly; Arabic.

al-Bayan: Dubai; owned by Sheikh Rashid; daily; Arabic.

Dubai External Trade Statistics: P.O.B. 516, Dubai; monthly, English; yearly, Arabic and English.

Dubai Official Gazette: P.O.B. 516, Dubai; Arabic; quarterly or as necessary.

Gulf Mirror: P.O.B. 874, Dubai; branch office of the Gulf weekly newspaper; English; circ. 16,000.

Khaleej Times: P.O.B. 11243; Dubai; a Galadhari enterprise; English; daily; Exec. Editor S. M. AHMED; Editor J. E. COLLIER; circ. 40,000.

Recorder: P.O.B. 1579, Dubai; P.O.B. 597, Sharjah; daily news bulletin; English.

Trade and Industry: P.O.B. 1457; f. 1975; published by Dubai Chamber of Commerce and Industry; Arabic and English; monthly; circ. 7,500.

RAS AL-KHAIMAH

Ras al-Khaimah: P.O.B. 87, Ras al-Khaimah; Chamber of Commerce magazine; quarterly; Arabic and English.

Ras al-Khaimah Magazine: P.O.B. 200, Ras al-Khaimah; monthly; Arabic; Chief Editor AHMED AL-TADMORI.

SHARJAH

al-Khalij: P.O.B. 30, Sharjah; political, independent; daily; Arabic; Dir.-Gen. and Editor-in-Chief RASHID OMRAN TARYAM; circ. 56,000.

al Tijarah: Sharjah; monthly; Arabic/English, published by Sharjah Chamber of Commerce and Industry.

NEWS AGENCY

Emirates News Agency (WAM): Abu Dhabi; f. 1977; operated by the Ministry of Information; Dir. IBRAHIM AL ABIB.

FOREIGN BUREAUX

Agenzia Nazionale Stampa Associata (ANSA) (*Italy*): P.O.B. 3790, Abu Dhabi; Correspondent RAWI A. ABEIDOH.

Reuters (*U.K.*): P.O.B. 5010, Deira, Dubai.

RADIO AND TELEVISION

United Arab Emirates Radio: P.O.B. 63, Abu Dhabi; f. 1969; stations in Abu Dhabi, Dubai, Umm al-Quwain and Ras al-Khaimah all broadcasting in Arabic over wide area; Abu Dhabi also broadcasts in English, French and Urdu, Dubai in English and Ras al-Khaimah in Urdu. There is colour TV in Abu Dhabi, Dubai and Ras al-Khaimah. The television stations take advertisements. Dubai Radio and the FM station in Abu Dhabi (Capital Radio) also take advertisements; estimated radio receivers 200,000 (1980), TV receivers 100,000 (1980).

Abu Dhabi Television: P.O.B. 637, Abu Dhabi.

Dubai Radio and Colour Television: P.O.B. 1695, Dubai; Dir.-Gen. ABDUL GHAFFOUR SAYYED IBRAHIM; Controller of Dubai Radio HASSAN AHMED.

FINANCE

(cap.=capital; p.u.=paid up; dep.=deposits; Dh.= dirhams; m.=million)

BANKING

The moratorium on new banks, originally introduced in 1975, was relaxed in April 1981, but in May it was announced that no foreign banks would be granted new branch licences.

United Arab Emirates Central Bank: P.O.B. 854, Abu Dhabi; f. 1973; acts as issuing authority for local currency; superseded UAE Currency Board December 1980; authorized cap. 300m. dirhams; Chair. of Board Sheikh SUROUR BIN MUHAMMAD AL-NAHAYAN; Gov. ABDUL MALIK AL-HAMR.

United Arab Emirates Bankers' Association: P.O.B. 2734, Abu Dhabi.

PRINCIPAL BANKS

Al Ahli Bank: P.O.B. 1719, Dubai; Man. K. RAFLA.

Arab Bank for Investment and Foreign Trade: P.O.B. 2484, Abu Dhabi; cap. p.u. Dh. 60m.; Man. B. E. NOUIOUA.

Bank of the Arab Coast: P.O.B. 342, Ras al-Khaimah; f. 1975; cap. Dh. 100m.; Chair. Sheikh OMAR BIN ABDULLAH AL-QASIMI; Chief Exec. LEN FORSYTH.

Bank of Oman Ltd.: P.O.B. 1250, Deira, Dubai; f. 1967; cap. p.u. 243m. dirhams (Dec. 1981); 22 brs. in U.A.E., 12 brs. overseas; Gen. Man. ABDULLAH AL-GHURAIR.

Bank of Sharjah: P.O.B. 1394, Sharjah; f. 1973; cap. and dep. 455m. dirhams (Dec. 1981); Chair. MUBARAK ABDUL AZIZ AL-HASSAWI; Gen. Man. RACHID NACEUR.

Commercial Bank of Dubai Ltd.: P.O.B. 1709, Dubai; f. 1969; cap. p.u. Dh. 200m. (Dec. 1981); brs. in Dubai (4), Abu Dhabi (1), Sharjah (1), Ras al-Khaimah (1); Gen. Man. R. W. ROBERTSON.

Commercial Development Bank of Sharjah: Sharjah.

Dubai Bank: P.O.B. 2545, Deira, Dubai; f. 1970; control is held by local interests, but Swiss, French and American banks are also participating; p.u. cap. 100m. dirhams; Chair. ABDUL RAHIM BIN IBRAHIM GALADARI; Gen. Man. G. J. CRUDEN.

Dubai Islamic Bank: P.O.B. 1080, Deira, Dubai; Chair., Bd. of Dirs. S. A. LOOTAH.

Emirates Commercial Bank: P.O.B. 939, Abu Dhabi; cap. p.u. Dh. 42m.; dep. Dh. 1,068m. (1981); Gen. Man. J. C. HENDRY; brs. in Dubai, Al Ain and Ruwais.

Emirates National Bank: P.O.B. 26, Deira, Dubai; f. 1977; cap. p.u. Dh. 34m. (Nov. 1980); Chair. and Man. Dir. MAJED AHMED AL-GHURAIR; Chief Exec. R. NARAYANAN.

Federal Commercial Bank Ltd.: P.O.B. 2934, Abu Dhabi; Gen. Man. M. A. HARDCASTLE.

First Gulf Bank: P.O.B. 414, Ajman; formerly Ajman Arab Bank; cap. p.u. Dh. 120m.; brs. in Abu Dhabi and Sharjah.

Investment Bank for Trade and Finance: P.O.B. 2875, Abu Dhabi; P.O.B. 1885, Sharjah; Man. A. H. KANAAN.

Khalij Commercial Bank: P.O.B. 2629, Abu Dhabi; f. 1975; Chair. ABDULLAH DARWISH; Gen. Man. D. H. ALEXANDER.

National Bank of Abu Dhabi: P.O.B. 4, Abu Dhabi; f. 1968; cap. p.u. Dh. 600m.; total assets Dh. 22,700m. (Dec.

1981). Chair. H.E. AHMED KHALIFA AL-SUWEIDI; Chief Exec. ASSAAD SAMAAN ASSAAD.

National Bank of Dubai: P.O.B. 777, Dubai; f. 1963; brs. in Abu Dhabi and Umm al-Quwain; cap. p.u. Dh. 273.7m.; Man. Dir. ABDULLA MUHAMMAD SALEH; Gen. Man. A. A. H. PHIMISTER.

National Bank of Ras al-Khaimah: P.O.B. 5300, Ras al-Khaimah; P.O.B. 1531, Deira, Dubai; f. 1977; cap. p.u. Dh. 25m. (Nov. 1980); Gen. Man. D. R. E. MURRAY.

National Bank of Sharjah: P.O.B. 4, Sharjah; cap. p.u. Dh. 75m.; dep. Dh. 983m. (Dec. 1981); Chair. Shaikh AHMED BIN SULTAN AL-QASIMI; Chief Exec. IAIN W. McNAB.

Union Bank of the Middle East: P.O.B. 2923, Dubai; f. 1977; cap. Dh. 1,000m.; cap. p.u. Dh. 241.5m.; dep. Dh. 1,971.0m. (Dec. 1981); Gen. Man. A. HEWITT.

United Arab Bank: P.O.B. 3562, Abu Dhabi; brs. in Sharjah, Dubai, Deira-Dubai and Ras al-Khaimah; Gen. Man. DENIS HEBRAUD.

FOREIGN BANKS

Algemene Bank Nederland N.V. (*Netherlands*): Faraj Bin Hamoodah Bldg., Sheikh Hamdan St., P.O.B. 2720, Abu Dhabi; Man. J. W. S. DE FABER; P.O.B. 2567, Deira, Dubai; P.O.B. 1971, Sharjah; Man. W. A. E. J. LEMSTRA (Dubai and Sharjah).

Al-Nilein Bank: P.O.B. 6013, Abu Dhabi.

Amsterdam-Rotterdam Bank N.V. (*Netherlands*): P.O.B. 2941, Dubai.

Arab Bank (*Jordan*): P.O.B. 875, Abu Dhabi; P.O.B. 1650, Dubai; P.O.B. 130, Sharjah; P.O.B. 20, Ras al-Khaimah; Ajman; Man. G. BAKRI.

Arab-African International Bank (*Egypt*): P.O.B. 1049, Dubai; P.O.B. 928, Abu Dhabi; Chair. and Man. Dir. EBRAHIM AL-EBRAHIM; Deputy Chair. and Man. Dir. MOHAMED ABDEL MUTTELEB SABEK.

Bank of Baroda (*India*): P.O.B. 2303, Abu Dhabi; also branches in Deira (Dubai), Sharjah, Ras al-Khaimah, Fujairah and Umm al-Quwain.

Bank of Credit and Commerce International SA and Overseas: Middle East Regional Office: P.O.B. 2622, Abu Dhabi; 11 brs. in Abu Dhabi, 9 brs. in Dubai, 4 in Sharjah and one each in Ajman, Umm al-Quwain, Ras al-Khaimah and Fujairah; Gen. Man. SALEEM SIDDIQI.

Bank Melli Iran: P.O.B. 2656, Abu Dhabi; P.O.B. 1894, Dubai; P.O.B. 459, Sharjah; P.O.B. 248, Fujairah; P.O.B. 1888, Al-Ain; P.O.B. 448, Ajman; Man. S. A. TAMERI.

Bank Saderat Iran: P.O.B. 700, Abu Dhabi; P.O.B. 4182, Dubai; also Sharjah, Ajman, Ras al-Khaimah and Fujairah; Man. M. SHARAZI.

Banque de l'Indochine et de Suez (*France*): P.O.B. 4005, Dubai.

Banque de Paris et des Pays-Bas (*France*): P.O.B. 2742, Abu Dhabi; P.O.B. 1944, Dubai; Gen. Man. (Abu Dhabi) G. TABET; Man. (Dubai) A. ADM.

Banque du Caire (*Egypt*): P.O.B. 533, Abu Dhabi; P.O.B. 1502, Dubai; P.O.B. 254, Sharjah; P.O.B. 618, Ras al-Khaimah; Gen. Man. AHMED ABDEL HAMID.

Banque du Liban et d'outre mer (*Lebanon*): P.O.B. 4370, Dubai; f. 1951; Chair. and Pres. Dr. NAAMAN AZHARI; U.A.E. Man. HENRI CHADAREVIAN.

Banque Libanaise pour le Commerce (*France*): P.O.B. 4207, Dubai; P.O.B. 854, Sharjah; P.O.B. 3771, Abu Dhabi; P.O.B. 771, Ras al-Khaimah.

Barclays Bank International (*U.K.*): P.O.B. 2734, Abu Dhabi; P.O.B. 1891, Dubai; P.O.B. 1953, Sharjah; Man. K. G. STIRZAKER.

British Bank of the Middle East (*Hong Kong*): brs. in Dubai, Sharjah, Khorfakan, Ras al-Khaimah, Abu Dhabi, Fujairah, Kalba, Jebel Ali, Al Ain, Jebel Dhana, Das Island, Hisn Dibba, Muhullab Dibba, Ajman and Umm al-Quwain; Man. J. C. DUNCAN.

Chartered Bank (*U.K.*): P.O.B. 240, Abu Dhabi; P.O.B. 999 and 1125, Dubai; P.O.B. 5, Sharjah; P.O.B. 1240, Al Ain; Man. K. S. WESTON.

Citibank (*U.S.A.*): P.O.B. 749, Dubai; P.O.B. 346, Sharjah; P.O.B. 999, Abu Dhabi; P.O.B. 294, Ras al-Khaimah; P.O.B. 1430, Al Ain; Man. S. CRABTREE.

Distributors Co-operative Credit Bank of Iran: P.O.B. 888, Abu Dhabi; Man. N. C. CHAUAN.

First National Bank of Chicago (*U.S.A.*): P.O.B. 1655, Dubai; P.O.B. 1278, Sharjah; Asst. Vice-Pres. and Man. ANDREW G. TRYPANIS; P.O.B. 2747, Abu Dhabi; Asst. Vice-Pres. and Man. WILLIAM J. CUTHBERT.

Grindlays Bank Ltd. (*U.K.*): P.O.B. 241, Abu Dhabi; P.O.B. 225, Ras al-Khaimah; P.O.B. 357, Sharjah; P.O.B. 4166, Dubai; P.O.B. 1100, Al Ain; P.O.B. 452, Ajman; P.O.B. 92, Fujairah; P.O.B. 490, Umm al-Quwain and 4 other brs. in United Arab Emirates; Man. P. J. W. LEWIS-JONES.

Habib Bank AG Zürich (*Switzerland*): P.O.B. 2681, Abu Dhabi; P.O.B. 1166, Sharjah; P.O.B. 3306, Dubai; P.O.B. 168, Ajman; P.O.B. 181, Umm al-Quwain; P.O.B. 767, Ras al-Khaimah; Man. R. A. CHOWDHRY.

Habib Bank Ltd. (*Pakistan*): P.O.B. 888, Dubai; P.O.B. 897, Abu Dhabi; f. 1941; 17 other brs. in United Arab Emirates; Man. W. RAZA.

Janata Bank (*Bangladesh*): P.O.B. 2630, Abu Dhabi; P.O.B. 3342, Dubai; Man. ALI KABIR.

Lloyds Bank International (*U.K.*): P.O.B. 3766, Dubai; Man. R. C. SEAMER.

Rafidain Bank (*Iraq*): P.O.B. 2727, Abu Dhabi; Man. H. A. HAFIDH.

Royal Bank of Canada: P.O.B. 3614, Dubai; Man. V. T. TUDBALL.

Toronto Dominion Bank (*Canada*): P.O.B. 2664, Abu Dhabi; P.O.B. 2294, Dubai.

United Bank (*Pakistan*): P.O.B. 1000, Dubai; P.O.B. 237, Abu Dhabi; 17 other brs. in U.A.E.; Man. AHMED RAZA.

There are also 5 Banks operating on restricted licences and 12 banks which have representative offices.

INSURANCE

Abu Dhabi National Insurance Co.: ADNIC Bldg., Sh. Khalifa St., P.O.B. 839, Abu Dhabi; f. 1973; cap. 30m. dirhams subscribed 25 per cent by the Government of Abu Dhabi and 75 per cent by United Arab Emirates nationals; Gen. Man. WASEF SALIM JABSHEH.

Al Ahlia Insurance Co.: P.O.B. 128, Ras al-Khaimah; f. 1977; cap. 2.9m.; Gen. Man. DESMOND REYNOLDS, A.C.I.I.

Al Ain Ahlia Insurance Co.: P.O.B. 3077, Abu Dhabi; f. 1975; cap. 15m. dirhams; Chair. HAMIL AL-GAITH; Gen. Man. JAMIL HAJJAR; brs. in Dubai and Al Ain.

Dubai Insurance Co.: P.O.B. 3027, Dubai; f. 1970; Chair. MAJID AL FUTTAIM; Gen. Man. FAROUK HUWAIDI.

Sharjah Insurance and Reinsurance Co.: P.O.B. 792, Sharjah; f. 1970; cap. 100m. dirhams.

Union Insurance Co.: Head Office: P.O.B. 460, Umm al-Quwain; P.O.B. 4623, Dubai; P.O.B. 3196, Abu Dhabi.

CHAMBERS OF COMMERCE

Federation of Chambers of Commerce and Industry: P.O.B. 3014, Abu Dhabi.

Abu Dhabi Chamber of Commerce and Industries: P.O.B. 662, Abu Dhabi; f. 1969; 5,000 mems.; Pres. SAEED BIN AHMED AL-OTAIBA; publ. monthly magazine in Arabic.

Ajman Chamber of Commerce and Industry: P.O.B. 662, Ajman; Pres. HAMAD MOHAMED ABU SHAHAB.

Dubai Chamber of Commerce and Industry: Ben Yass St., P.O.B. 1457, Dubai; f. 1965; 8,600 mems.; Pres. SAEED JUMA AL-NABOODAH; Dir.-Gen. NIZAR SARDAST; publ. *Trade and Industry*.

Ras al-Khaimah Chamber of Commerce, Industry and Agriculture: P.O.B. 87, Ras al-Khaimah; f. 1967; 4,000 mems.; Chair. ALI ABDULLA MUSABEH; Dir. ZAKI SAQR; publ. quarterly magazine in Arabic.

Sharjah Chamber of Commerce and Industry: P.O.B. 580, Sharjah; f. 1970; Pres. ABDUL AZIZ BIN MOHAMED AL-QASIMI; Dir.-Gen. ABDUL RAZAK AL-HAJIRI; publ. *Al-Tijara*.

Umm al-Quwain Chamber of Commerce and Industry: P.O.B. 436, Umm al-Quwain.

DEVELOPMENT

Federal Ministry of Planning: P.O.B. 2847, Abu Dhabi; Under-Sec. AHMED MANSOUR.

United Arab Emirates Development Bank: P.O.B. 2449, Abu Dhabi; f. 1974; participates in development of real estate, agriculture, fishery, livestock and light industries; cap. p.u. Dh. 500m.; Gen. Man. MOHAMED SALEM AL-MELEHY.

Abu Dhabi Fund for Arab Economic Development (ADFAED): P.O.B. 814; f. 1971; purpose is to offer economic aid to other Arab States and other developing countries in support of their development; capital limited at inception to Dh. 500 million paid by Abu Dhabi Government; in June 1974 capital was raised to Dh. 2,000 million; Man. Dir. NASSER M. AL-NOWAIS.

Abu Dhabi Planning Department: P.O.B. 12, Abu Dhabi; supervises Abu Dhabi's Development Programme; Chair. Sheikh SAIF BIN MUHAMMAD AL-NAHAYAN; Under-Sec. H. E. HASSAN MOUSA AL-QAMZI.

Abu Dhabi Development Finance Corpn.: P.O.B. 30, Abu Dhabi; purpose is to provide finance to the private sector.

Abu Dhabi Investment Authority (ADIA): P.O.B. 3600, Abu Dhabi; f. 1976.

TRADE AND INDUSTRY

PRINCIPAL PETROLEUM CONCESSIONS

In September 1974 the Government of Abu Dhab acquired a 60 per cent interest in ADPC and ADMA, and early in 1975 an increase of this interest to 100 per cent was under consideration. In the Spring of 1975 Abu Dhabi withdrew from pressing for 100 per cent interest, but in July 1975 it was announced that Dubai had successfully concluded a 100 per cent participation with the companies represented offshore and onshore in Dubai.

Ministry of Petroleum and Mineral Resources: P.O.B. 59, Abu Dhabi; Minister MANI SAID AL-OTEIBA.

ABU DHABI

Abu Dhabi Company for Onshore Oil Operations (ADCO): P.O.B. 270, Abu Dhabi; name changed from Abu Dhabi Petroleum Co. Ltd. (ADPC) in February 1979; share- holders are ADNOC (60 per cent), British Petroleum, Shell and Compagnie Française des Pétroles (9.5 per cent each), Exxon and Mobil (4.75 per cent each) and Partex (2 per cent); production (1980): 267,336,146 barrels; Chair. Sheikh TAHNOUN BIN MOHAMED AL-NAHAYAN; Gen. Man. G. K. TAYLOR.

Abu Dhabi Marine Operating Company (ADMA-OPCO): P.O.B. 303, Abu Dhabi; operates a concession 60 per cent owned by the Abu Dhabi National Oil Co. and 40 per cent by Abu Dhabi Marine Areas Ltd., Britannic House, Moor Lane, London, EC2Y 9BU, England (BP-Japan Oil Development Co. Ltd. 26⅔ per cent; Compagnie Française des Pétroles 13⅓ per cent). The concession lies in the Abu Dhabi offshore area and currently produces oil from Zakum and Umm Shaif fields. ADMA-OPCO was created in 1977 as an operator for the concession which between September 1974 and October 1977 was operated by ADMA Ltd. in its role as an interim operator. The new company is owned by the shareholders of the concession in the same proportion of ownership. ADMA-OPCO also operates the Bunduq field on behalf of the Bunduq Company; production (1980): 184,633,098 barrels (24,432,892.6 metric tons); Gen. Man. Dr. A. J. HORAN.

Abu Dhabi Gas Liquefaction Company (ADGLC): P.O.B. 3500, Abu Dhabi; owned by Abu Dhabi National Oil Co., 51 per cent; the British Petroleum Co., 16⅓ per cent; Compagnie Française des Pétroles, 8⅓ per cent; Mitsui and Co., 22$\frac{4}{10}$ per cent; Mitsui Liquefied Gas Co., 2$\frac{9}{20}$ per cent. The LNG plant on Das Island, which cost about $500 million, was commissioned in 1977. The plant uses natural gas produced in association with oil from offshore fields and has a design capacity of approximately 2.2 million tons of LNG per year and 800,000 tons of LPG per year. The liquefied gas is sold to the Tokyo Electric Power Co., Japan; Gen. Man. Dr. D. G. B. HORNE.

Abu Dhabi National Oil Company (ADNOC): P.O.B. 898, Abu Dhabi; f. 1971; state company; deals in all phases of oil industry; inaugurated its own refinery on Umm Al-Nar island, May 1976; Ruwais Refinery was commissioned in 1981; holds 60 per cent participation in operations of ADMA-OPCO and ADCO, and 50 per cent of ZADCO and UDECO; has 100 per cent control of Abu Dhabi National Oil Company for Distribution (ADNOC-FOD), Abu Dhabi National Tankers Co. (ADNATCO), National Drilling Co. (NDC) and interests in numerous other companies; Chair. Sheikh TAHNOUN BIN MOHAMED AL-NAHYAN; Gen. Man. MAHMOUD HAMRA KROUHA.

Abu Dhabi Oil Company (Japan) (ADOCO): Abu Dhabi; consortium of Japanese oil companies including Maruzen, Daikyo and Nihon Kogyo; holds offshore concession, extended by 1,582.5 sq. km. in 1979; export of oil from Mubarraz Island terminal began in June 1973; production 7,905,927 barrels (1978).

Bunduq Oil Co.: revenues are shared equally between Abu Dhabi and Qatar; owners: BP 33.3 per cent, CFP 33.3 per cent, Japanese interests 33.3 per cent.

Total Abu al-Bukhoosh: P.O.B. 4058, Abu Dhabi; owned by Compagnie Française des Pétroles, operator of Abu al-Bukhoosh field; began production from the Abu al-Bukhoosh offshore field in July 1974; average production of 66,000 b/d in 1980; Partners in the field are Amerada Hess, Ker McGee and Charter Ltd.

DUBAI

Department of the Ruler's Affairs and Petroleum Affairs: P.O.B. 207, Dubai; government supervisory body; Dir. MAHDI AL-TAJIR.

Dubai Petroleum Company: P.O.B. 2222, Dubai; holds offshore concession which began production in 1969; average production rate (1980): 349,274 b/d, (1981): 358,598 b/d.

Sedco-Houston Oil Group: Dubai; holds onshore concession of over 1 million acres as well as the offshore concession formerly held by Texas Pacific Oil.

SHARJAH

Concessions are owned by the Buttes Group, the Crescent Group (25.7 per cent owned by Buttes) and Amoco and Forman Explorations.

TRANSPORT

ROADS

Roads are rapidly being developed in the United Arab Emirates, and Abu Dhabi and Dubai are linked by a good road which is dual carriageway for most of its length. This road forms part of a west coast route from Shaam, at the U.A.E. border with the northern enclave of Oman, through Dubai and Abu Dhabi to Tarif. An east coast route links Dibba with Muscat. Other roads include the Abu Dhabi-Al Ain highway and roads linking the northern Emirates. An underwater tunnel links Dubai Town and Deira by dual carriageway and pedestrian subway.

SHIPPING

Dubai has been the main commercial centre in the Gulf for many years. In 1968 work was begun on a new artificial deep-water port to supplement the traditional harbour. Port Rashid had been expanded to 37 berths by 1980. Abu Dhabi has also become an important port since the opening of the first section of its artificial harbour, Port Zayed. Eventually it is planned to create 17 deep-water berths and extensive storage facilities. There are smaller ports in Sharjah and Ras al-Khaimah. Work on a dry-dock scheme for Dubai was completed in 1979. It possesses two docks capable of handling 500,000-ton tankers, seven repair berths and a third dock able to accommodate 1,000,000-ton tankers. By 1981 the port of Jebel Ali, Dubai, contained 66 berths. Five deep-water berths were completed at Port Saqr, Ras al-Khaimah in 1979. Current modernization of Port Khalid in Sharjah will double its berth capacity.

United Arab Shipping Co. (SAG): Kuwait; f. 1976; shareholders are Kuwait, U.A.E., Saudi Arabia, Bahrain, Qatar and Iraq; Chair. EID ABDULLAH YUSUF (Bahrain); Chief Exec. ABDULAZIZ HUSSEIN SALAAT.

CIVIL AVIATION

There are international airports at Dubai, Abu Dhabi and Ras al-Khaimah, and a smaller one at Sharjah, which forms part of SHARJAHPORT, which links air, sea and overland transportation services. Abu Dhabi's new Nadia international airport opened for commercial use in January 1982, and a new airport at Al Ain is scheduled for 1983.

Gulf Air Dubai: Sheikh Alsabah Bldg., Al-Mhkhtoum St., P.O.B. 4410, Deira; daily service to Abu Dhabi, Bahrain, Bombay, Doha, Karachi, Kuwait, London and Muscat; six times weekly to Bombay; four times weekly to Cairo; twice weekly to Colombo, Delhi and Larnaca; and once a week to Amman and Paris.

Air Intergulf: P.O.B. 3360, Sharjah; charter airline.

Aeroflot (U.S.S.R.), Air Djibouti, Air France, Air India, Air Malta, Air Tanzania, Alia (Jordan), Alitalia (Italy), Alyemda (Yemen P.D.R.), Bangladesh Biman, British Caledonian, British Airways, Cathay Pacific (Hong Kong), ČSA (Czechoslovakia), Cyprus Airways, EgyptAir, Ethiopian Airlines, Garuda (Indonesia), Gulf Air (Bahrain), Iran Air, Iraqi Airways, Japan Airlines, KLM (Netherlands), Kuwait Airways, LOT (Poland), Lufthansa (Federal Repub. of Germany), MAS (Malaysia), Middle East Airlines (Lebanon), Olympic (Greece), PIA (Pakistan), Sabena (Belgium), Saudia, SIA (Singapore), Sudan Airways, Swissair, Syrian Arab Airlines, Tarom (Romania), TMA (Lebanon), Tunis Air, Uganda Airlines and Yemen Airways (Yemen Arab Republic) serve Dubai and Abu Dhabi, while Gulf Air, Air Lanka, Syrian Arab Airways and Yemen Airways (Yemen Arab Republic) serve Sharjah. Ras al-Khaimah is served only by Kuwait Airways.

TOURISM AND CULTURE

Ministry of Information and Culture: P.O.B. 17, Abu Dhabi.

Ministry of Information and Culture: P.O.B. 67, Dubai.

Ministry of Information and Culture: P.O.B. 55, Sharjah.

Dubai Information Department: P.O.B. 1420, Dubai (local government); Dir. OMAR DEESI.

Ras al-Khaimah Information and Tourism Department: P.O.B. 200, Ras al-Khaimah (local government); Dir. AHMED TADMORI.

DEFENCE

Chief of Staff of Federal Armed Forces: Brig.-Gen. MUHAMMAD SA'ID AL-BADI.

The Union Defence Force and the armed forces of the various Emirates were formally merged in May 1976, although difficulties have since been experienced (*see* History). Military service is voluntary.

Total armed forces (July 1981): 42,500 (army 40,000; navy 1,000; air force 1,500).

Defence Budget (1980): 4,500 million dirhams.

EDUCATION

The U.A.E. is engaged in an expansion of education which is seen as a unifying force for the future of the federation. In 1971 there were about 28,000 pupils in the U.A.E., and by 1981 the number had increased to 141,424. There are primary and secondary schools in all the states and further education in technical fields is available in the more advanced areas. Teachers from other Arab countries, most notably Kuwait, Egypt and Jordan, supplement the U.A.E.'s inadequate native teaching staff. Many students receive higher education abroad. A university opened at Al Ain in Abu Dhabi in the autumn of 1977 with 300 students; the number of students reached nearly 1,800 by 1980 and it is planned to raise the total to 4,000 or 5,000 during the 1980s.

BIBLIOGRAPHY

ABDULLAH, M. MORSY. The Modern History of the United Arab Emirates (Croom Helm, London, 1978).

ALBAHARNA, H. M. The Legal Status of the Arabian Gulf States (Manchester University Press, May 1969).

BUSCH, B. C. Britain and the Persian Gulf 1894–1914 (University of California Press, 1967).

DANIELS, JOHN. Abu Dhabi: A Portrait (Longman, London, 1974).

FENELON, K. G. The United Arab Emirates: an Economic and Social Survey (Longman, London, 1973).

HAWLEY, DONALD FREDERICK. Courtesies in the Trucial States (1965).

The Trucial States (George Allen and Unwin, London, 1971).

MINISTRY OF INFORMATION AND CULTURE. United Arab Emirates: A Record of Achievement, 1979–81 (Abu Dhabi, 1981).

HAY, Sir RUPERT. The Persian Gulf States (Middle East Institute, Washington, 1959).

MANN, CLARENCE. Abu Dhabi: Birth of an Oil Sheikhdom (Khayats, Beirut, 1964).

MARLOWE, JOHN. The Persian Gulf in the 20th Century (Cresset Press, London, 1962).

MILES, S. B. The Countries and Tribes of the Persian Gulf (3rd edition, Cass, London, 1966).

OTEIBA, MANI SAID AL-. Petroleum and the Economy of the United Arab Emirates (Croom Helm, London, 1977).

SADIQ, MUHAMMAD T., and SNAVELY, WILLIAM P. Bahrain, Qatar and the United Arab Emirates: Colonial Past, Present Problems, and Future Prospects (Heath, Lexington, Mass., 1972).

ZAHLAN, ROSEMARIE SAID. The Origins of the United Arab Emirates (Macmillan, London, 1978).

Yemen Arab Republic

GEOGRAPHY

The Yemen Arab Republic lies at the south-west corner of the Arabian peninsula and comprises two well-defined areas—the highlands inland, and the coastal strip along the Red Sea. The climate of the highlands is considered the best in all Arabia since it experiences a régime rather like that of East Africa, with a warm temperate and rainy summer, and a cool, moderately dry winter with occasional frost and some snow. As stated below (see Yemen P.D.R.), these conditions are thought to be produced by an upper air current that brings very moist air from the Atlantic, giving rise to a minor monsoonal effect of heavy summer rainfall. As much as 35 inches of rain may fall annually on the higher parts of the interior, with 15–20 inches over much of the plateau; but the coast receives under 5 inches generally, and in the form often of irregular downpours. There is therefore the phenomenon of streams and even rivers flowing perennially in the highlands, but failing to reach the coast.

Because of this climatic gradation, from desert to temperate conditions, the Yemen has a similar gradation of crops and vegetation. The highest parts appear as "African", with scattered trees and grassland. Crops of coffee, qat, cereals and vegetables are grown, whilst lower down, "Mediterranean" fruits appear, with millet and, where irrigation water is available, bananas. Finally, near the coast, the date palm becomes the only tree.

The area of the Yemen is approximately 75,000 square miles and its population (including nationals abroad) was estimated at 8.6 million in 1980. The capital is Sana'a (on the d'El Jehal plateau, altitude 7,260 ft.).

HISTORY

In classical times the Yemen formed part of the south-eastern area of Arabia Felix. One of the best-known kingdoms in that region was that of Sheba, which lasted from 950 to 115 B.C. From then until the sixth century A.D. Arabia Felix was ruled by the Himyarite dynasty, from whom the modern Imams claim descent. In A.D. 525 the Ethiopians conquered the Himyarite Kingdom, and they in turn were overthrown by a Persian invasion in 575. During the seventh century the country nominally accepted Islam and the Sunnis of the Shafi'i rite established their power in the Tihama (the coastal region), and the Zaidis, a moderate branch of the Shia, held the highlands.

During the ninth century the Zaidi Imam Yahya al-Hadi ila'l-Haqq founded the Rassid dynasty of the Yemen, which has survived, with some interruptions, to modern times.

In 1517 the Yemen was conquered by the Ottoman Turks, but their power was continually contested by other European powers, and their authority was not great. Fierce tribal and religious warfare led the Turks to establish in 1872 a full occupation of the country under a Turkish Vali. This occupation lasted until the Mudros armistice of 1918, but in 1911 the Imam Yahya had led a full-scale revolt which secured a treaty confirming Turkish suzerainty, but dividing administrative control between the Imam in the highlands and the Turks in the Tihama and on the coast.

During the First World War the Imam had supported the Turks, and the British had therefore supported Idrisi invaders from the small state of the Asir to the north of the Yemen. A succession dispute broke out in the Asir in 1923 in the course of which Imam Yahya of the Yemen had occupied the port of Hodeida and the coastal areas. By the Treaty of Mecca in October 1926 the Sheikh of the Asir was placed formally under the protection of Ibn Sa'ud; this position, however, was never enthusiastically accepted by the Imam, who continued to bait the new king of Arabia and also to encroach on the British-protected territory of the Aden Protectorate. In these activities he seemed to have had the support of Italy, with whom he signed a treaty of friendship in 1926; and a Soviet trade delegation made a brief appearance in the country at this time. In 1930 following on a dispute over his Hijaz borders he encouraged the Sheikh of the Asir to revolt against Ibn Sa'ud; the latter attempted to settle the dispute by peaceful means, and negotiations dragged on until 1934. In April of that year, however, Ibn Sa'ud decided on more drastic action; marching on the Yemen, he drove the Yemeni troops out of Hodeida, and in a bloodless campaign of a month forced them back into Sana'a. The peace treaty of Ta'if allotted Tihama and Najran to Ibn Sa'ud but otherwise left the boundaries of the Yemen undisturbed —a policy of moderation that won him considerable prestige. At the same time Britain formally recognized the independence of the Yemen by treaty, and ended for a time a long series of frontier disputes.

The despotic and conservative Imam Yahya continued to rule until February 1948, when an attempted coup d'état by Sayyid Abdullah al-Wazzir resulted in his murder; his eldest son, Saif al-Islam Ahmad, however, succeeded to the throne and drove out the insurgent. Since then the Yemen has been co-operating in international affairs; in January 1951 a start was made on the development of the country with British, American and French technical aid, and at the same time full diplomatic relations were established for the first time with foreign powers, including Britain, the U.S.A. and Egypt.

In the winter of 1953 Yemen, with Arab support, began pressing before the United Nations her claims to Aden and the territories of the Aden Protectorate, and throughout the summer of 1954, and again in 1955, there was a series of frontier incidents.

In April 1955 an attempted coup d'état against the Imam Ahmad was defeated, and the royal conspirators executed; but one consequence may have been the Imam's decision in August of that year to set up a formal cabinet. During 1956 relations were established with the Soviet Union and a military pact was concluded with Egypt, Saudi Arabia and Syria.

The frontier dispute between Britain and the Yemen was continued late in December 1956 and in 1957, when Yemeni tribesmen were reported to have attacked villages in the Aden Protectorate. The Crown Prince visited London for talks in November 1957, but hostilities flared up again in the spring of 1958 and the political committee of the Arab League denounced the actions of Great Britain in the Aden territories. Two bomb incidents in Aden itself led to the enforcement in May 1958 of a temporary state of emergency. Unsuccessful talks to settle the dispute were held in July 1958 and May 1959. (For a fuller account of the border dispute see the chapter on Yemen P.D.R.)

A Yemeni delegation, headed by the Crown Prince, visited Cairo in February 1958 for negotiations which led to a federal union between the United Arab Republic and the Yemen, established by an agreement signed in Damascus on March 8th. The new union was named the United Arab States, and was to have a unified defence and foreign policy, and later a Customs union and common currency. Few practical steps were taken to that end and although, in November 1961, the Yemen renewed the agreement for a further three years, the Federation was formally dissolved by the United Arab Republic in December 1961.

In May 1959 disorders followed the departure of the Imam Ahmad to Europe and the Crown Prince Muhammad al-Badr introduced various reforms, including the innovation of a Representative Council. This policy was reversed on the return of the Imam in August.

CIVIL WAR 1962—1969

In March 1961 there was an unsuccessful attempt to assassinate the Imam, who was wounded in the shoulder. The Imam died in September 1962, and was briefly succeeded by his son Muhammad Badr. But a week later a revolt broke out, led by Colonel Abdullah Sallal, supported by troops from the U.A.R. The new Imam fled into the hills after a series of attempts to regain the capital, and Republican forces gained control of most of the country. The Republic was soon recognized by the U.S.S.R. and the United States, and early in 1963 was admitted to the United Nations. Britain, however, continued to give recognition to the Royalist régime, and stated on a number of occasions that she would only recognize the Republic when U.A.R. forces were withdrawn. Fighting continued until 1969 and was particularly severe in the winter of 1963–64 and much of 1968. An Observer Mission dispatched by the United Nations found that an agreement for simultaneous withdrawal of U.A.R. troops and Saudi Arabian military supplies had not been implemented by either side. The Mission operated from July 1963 to September 1964.

The rapprochement between U.A.R. and Saudi Arabia in February 1964 suggested that a solution would not be long delayed, and recognition by Jordan of the Republican régime was a further important step towards complete acceptance of the Revolution and its consequences. Britain, nevertheless, maintained her stand in support of the Royalists.

In May 1964 a new Republican Government was announced under the terms of a new Constitution published in April. The Prime Minister, Hamud Al Jaifi, soon displayed his command of the situation, which was emphasised by the frequent absences of the President for medical treatment in Cairo and Europe. In a policy statement in June a programme of school, hospital and road building was announced, and in July an agreement was signed in Cairo to establish a U.A.R./Yemen co-ordinating council and a joint military command; 90 per cent of the expenses of these ventures would be provided by Egypt, which had already sent an estimated 40,000 troops into the country in support of the Republicans.

In September the UN military observers left the country, while at the same time Sallal was attending the Arab Summit Conference in Alexandria. Following this meeting

President Nasser and King Faisal discussed the Yemen situation, and this led in November to a meeting at Erkwit in the Sudan, at which republican and royalist delegations agreed to a cease-fire and the convening of a national congress. Differences over procedure forced the postponement of this, and in December the royalists resumed the offensive. During January the Imam al-Badr proclaimed a constitutional charter. This military and political offensive led to dissensions in the republican cabinet, culminating in the fall of Hamud Al Jaifi in January 1965, and his replacement by Lieut.-Gen. Hassan Al-Amri with a mandate to stiffen the war effort. In April, however, Lieut.-Gen. Amri resigned, and was replaced by the moderate Muhammad Ahmad Noman, who embarked on a policy of conciliation. The long postponed National Congress met in May in the village of Khamer, though without the participation of the royalists, and on May 9 the text was published of an interim constitution, setting up a supreme Consultative Assembly with power to make laws, remove members of the Republican Council, and nominate the President. Despite the energetic efforts of Mr. Noman to achieve a peace settlement, it was not long before his sympathy for the Baathist cause ran him into opposition from the Egyptian authorities, who retained a measure of financial control over the Yemen. In July Noman resigned and after a few days of uncertainty President Sallal announced a new cabinet headed by Lieut.-Gen. Amri. The return to prominence of the military, pro-Egyptian element coincided with a number of important Royalist advances, and relations between the U.A.R. and Saudi Arabia worsened dangerously as each accused the other once again of complicity in the civil war.

THE SEARCH FOR A SETTLEMENT

In late summer events took a more hopeful turn when President Nasser and King Faisal concluded an agreement at Jeddah to bring the war to an end and to establish, within fifteen months, a Yemeni government free from outside interference. The agreement stipulated that a cease-fire was to be declared immediately; Saudi Arabia was to stop supplying arms to the Royalist forces; an interim government of moderate politicians, excluding both the Imam al-Badr and President Sallal, was to be set up within three months; after which the Egyptian forces, numbering about 50,000, were to be withdrawn during the ten-month period ending September 23rd, 1966. By November 23rd, 1966, a plebiscite would be held to enable the Yemenis to choose the political form they wished their state to assume.

Although the immediate effects of the Jeddah agreement were hopeful, including the establishment of a more representative Presidency Council for the Republic, and of a U.A.R./Saudi Arabian Peace Committee, the good intentions of the participants to the agreement were soon eroded. In November 1965 a conference of Republican and Royalist envoys meeting at Haradh reached deadlock over the next steps to be taken, and through 1966 the implementation of the agreement seemed less and less likely as relations between Egypt and Saudi Arabia deteriorated. Egyptian troop numbers in the Yemen, far from being reduced, were built up; despite a further U.A.R./Saudi meeting in August in Beirut, chaired by Kuwait, a solution seemed no nearer. Worse still, in September 1966 friction between Lt.-Gen. Amri and President Sallal came into the open when the latter returned to Sana'a. A large delegation, led personally by the Premier, then flew to Cairo to demand complete independence from U.A.R. for the Yemen régime, and the permanent removal of the President. The U.A.R. response to this was to arrest the members of the delegation, and Sallal himself assumed the duties of the premiership. This was followed by a drastic purge of the republican armed forces and administration, and a wave of riots, trials and executions. The dissident republican elements took refuge in the mountains to the north of Sana'a.

During the latter months of 1966 republican and royalist operations began to escalate. Egyptian aircraft were in action, and on several occasions air raids were made on the Saudi Arabian towns of Jizan and Najran. In January allegations were made of the use of poison gas, a charge denied by the U.A.R.

Meanwhile there was considerable diplomatic activity. In January Sallal formed the Popular Revolutionary Union at a meeting attended by Makkawi (*see* Yemen P.D.R.). Outside Yemen, a Union of Popular Forces was formed, led by Ibrahim al-Wazir, who visited Riyad and Geneva calling for an Islamic State of Yemen, the withdrawal of Egyptian troops, and the ending of Saudi Arabian aid.

THE EGYPTIAN WITHDRAWAL

Early in August 1967, on the occasion of the meeting of Foreign Ministers at Khartoum to prepare an agenda for an Arab summit conference, the U.A.R. delegate announced that the Egyptian Government was once again prepared to put into effect the agreement drawn up with King Faisal of Saudi Arabia at Jeddah in August 1965. The supervision of the withdrawal of troops would be entrusted to a committee of three Arab states. According to Radio Sana'a, a principal factor influencing this change of heart by the Egyptians was the British decision on a definite date for the withdrawal of troops from Aden, in January 1968.

On August 31st an agreement on these terms was finally reached by King Faisal and President Nasser at the Arab leaders' conference at Khartoum. Egyptian troops were to be withdrawn within three months; a plebiscite to determine the political future of the Yemen was to be held within a further six months; President Sallal was to lead a transitional government; the whole agreement to be carried out under the supervision of representatives of three independent Arab states, Iraq, Morocco and Sudan. Although President Sallal immediately protested against the peace plan, his opposition did not prove an obstacle.

The Egyptian army, with an estimated strength of up to 80,000 men, had effectively colonized the Republican-held sector of the Yemen, and was in general neither popular nor well regarded for its military prowess. Thus its withdrawal, which was completed by January 1968, was not altogether unwelcome although it naturally encouraged the Royalist forces to become bolder. It also led to the deposition of President Sallal in November, carried out while he was on an official visit to Iraq, and the institution of a three-man Presidency Council headed initially by Abdul Rahman al-Iriani. In December 1967 General Hassan Al-Amri, a militant republican, replaced the moderate Muhammad Noman on the Council; shortly afterwards he also became Prime Minister, again replacing a more moderate man. The National Liberation Front, the left-wing force that had come to power in the newly independent territory of Southern Yemen, also came to possess considerable influence in the Yemen at this time.

The Royalist army continued to make progress early in 1968, and for some time the Republican capital of Sana'a was virtually besieged. Its defendants claimed that the Imam was still receiving generous aid from Saudi Arabia, while much of their own equipment had been taken by the Egyptians. By April the pressure on Sana'a had relaxed somewhat; a left-wing plot to overthrow the Al-Amri government was unsuccessful. In June the Royalist leader, Imam Muhammad al-Badr, was deposed by his followers in favour of his son (his cousin according to some accounts), Muhammad bin Hussein.

THE END OF THE CIVIL WAR

During the 1968–69 period it became evident that the Royalist military effort was in decline after its major offensive following the Egyptian withdrawal. By the summer of 1969 the leading members of the Royalist camp were all in exile, and their followers had apparently accepted the Sana'a government. The principal cause of this swift collapse appeared to be a feud within the royal family following the deposition of the Imam. The Saudi Arabian Government's confidence in the Royalists, already weakened by their failure to capture Sana'a, thus diminished further; eventually the Saudis ceased their financial and military assistance on which the Royalists had depended. Since the Republicans were apparently in receipt of substantial arms supplies from other Arab countries and the U.S.S.R. their success was assured.

Nevertheless, there was a short-lived revival of military activity in the north-east during the winter of 1969–70. Rebel tribesmen, said to be opposed to rule from Sana'a rather than positive supporters of the Imam, surrounded the town of Saada for some weeks. This development, plus the massive economic problems faced by the government, led to the resignation of the Prime Minister, Abdallah Kurshoumi, in February 1970, only six months after he had succeeded General Al-Amri. Muhsin Al-Aini, the Ambassador in Moscow, was then appointed Prime Minister.

In March 1970 the Premier and the Foreign Minister met Saudi Arabian officials privately during the Islamic Foreign Ministers Conference at Jeddah. Although no formal announcement of the outcome was made, it appeared that an informal peace settlement was agreed upon. As a result, the leading Royalists, apart from the Imam and the royal family itself, returned to Sana'a in May 1970 and were offered a number of posts in the administration.

The government was said to be anxious to open relations with the Western countries which had recognized the Royalist régime; in July 1969 diplomatic relations with Federal Germany were restored at a time when several Arab states followed an opposite policy in recognizing the G.D.R. (East Germany). One result was a generous offer of economic and financial aid from Bonn. In July 1970 Saudi Arabia formally opened diplomatic relations with the republic, followed by Britain and France.

In December 1970 a new constitution was promulgated, providing for a Consultative Council to replace the National Assembly. Elections were held in February and March 1971.

In July 1971 there were rumours of an attempt by senior army officers to overthrow the Government, and several officers were dismissed. In September the Prime Minister, Lt.-Gen. Hassan al-Amri, went into exile (until 1975) after reportedly murdering a man in his office. Tension between Sana'a and Aden increased in the first half of 1972 as supporters of FLOSY and the South Arabian League, opponents of the Aden Government, gathered on the borders between the two states.

Serious fighting broke out on the border in September, but an Arab League mission was able to mediate and a ceasefire became effective in October. A peace agreement and an agreement on eventual unification of the two Yemens were signed in Cairo on October 28th. Further details were discussed in Tripoli (Libya) in November by the Presidents of the two Yemens, and it was agreed that the people of Yemen would establish a single state, to be known as the Yemen Republic, with Sana'a as its capital,

Islam as the State religion and Arabic as the official language. Committees were set up to discuss details of the unification. In January 1973 it appeared that certain obstacles had arisen in the progress towards union, but in February a new political organization, the Yemeni Union, was formed in Sana'a in anticipation of the forthcoming union. At the end of May fighting again broke out on the border between the two Yemens, and on May 30th, Sheikh Muhammad al-Othman, a member of the three-man Presidential Council, was assassinated by unknown gunmen. Although this incident temporarily soured relations between the two Yemens, it was announced in June that talks on unity would continue.

In December 1972 Mohsin al-Aini resigned as Prime Minister and a new government was later formed under Abdullah al-Hajari. The Government of Abdullah al-Hajari had to contend with a great deal of violence, particularly in the south of the country, and in September 1973 President Iriani and President Salem Rubayi Ali of South Yemen met in Sana'a and decided to extend the one year period originally decided upon for the unification of their two countries, and to concentrate on suppressing terrorism and sabotage.

A new Government under Hassan Makki took office in March 1974, pledged to continue the policies of the former Prime Minister, Abdullah al-Hajari, and in particular to work for unification with South Yemen. On June 13th, however, a bloodless *coup* took place in which a seven-man military junta, under the leadership of pro-Saudi Colonel Ibrahim al-Hamadi, suspended the Constitution and Consultative Council and dissolved the armed forces high command and the Yemeni National Union. Colonel Hamadi later stated that the *coup* had been necessary to remedy economic and administrative chaos. The former President, Qadi Abdul Rahman al-Iriani, later left for Damascus. A provisional constitution was issued on June 19th and on June 21st a new Government was formed under Mohsin al-Aini. The policy of the new Government was stated to include openness to all Arab States, support for non-alignment and adherence to the Arab League Charter and the UN Charter. The goal of ultimate unity with South Yemen was to be preserved.

In January 1975 Mohsin al-Aini was relieved of his post of Prime Minister and replaced by the former Chairman of the central bank, Abdel-Aziz Abdel-Ghani. Although it was hoped that a return to constitutional government would be made in June 1975 (after one year of military rule), Col. Hamadi merely announced in May 1975 that he would nominate a commission to supervise the election of a Popular Assembly which would in turn amend the constitution. In October 1975 Col. Hamadi issued a decree proroguing the Constituent Assembly and calling for new elections to be held under the supervision of the supreme electoral committee, but no date was fixed for the elections.

During 1975 there were signs that the Yemen Arab Republic was drawing closer to Saudi Arabia and the U.S.A. In August, King Khaled of Saudi Arabia gave 810 million Saudi riyals to the Yemen as budget and development project support, and in April 1976 a plan was announced whereby Saudi Arabia would bear the expense of re-equipping sections of the Yemeni army with U.S. weapons. In contrast to this, President Hamadi had declared, in August 1975, that his relations with the Soviet Union were "frozen" and that the Yemen Arab Republic had turned down offers of help with arms from the Soviet Union.

Eventual union of the two Yemens appeared to have been brought slightly nearer in February 1977 when the two Heads of State met at Qaataba, near the border with South Yemen, and established a joint council consisting of their respective Ministers of Foreign Affairs, Economy, Trade and Planning. The Council decided to meet for discussion every six months, alternately in Sana'a and Aden. A joint economic, trade and planning sub-committee was also set up.

In April 1977 Qadi Abdullah al-Hajari, Prime Minister between December 1972 and February 1974, was assassinated in London. He had been a minister under the Imam and had been slow to transfer his allegiance to the republican government. As Prime Minister he had also forged close links with Saudi Arabia, and had never been enthusiastic about effecting the union of the two Yemens.

In July 1977 Hamadi had to face a rebellion of the northern tribes, mainly supporters of the former Imamate. In October Hamadi was assassinated in Sana'a, and there has since been much speculation about who was responsible. Another member of the Military Command Council, Lt.-Col. Ahmed ibn Hussein al-Ghashmi, took over as Chairman. Although he survived an assassination attempt within two weeks of taking over as Chairman, he placated some of the dissident elements in the Yemen for a while by doubling the pay of the army and giving every soldier a daily ration of the narcotic qat. At the same time he became increasingly dependent on Saudi Arabia for aid, and was apparently unwilling to promote the long-awaited unification with South Yemen, although regular discussions continued.

Towards the end of May 1978 there were reports of a rebellion against President al-Ghashmi, led by Major Abdulla Abdel Alem, in the south of the country. Major Alem had been one of the members of al-Ghashmi's Presidential Council, and after the rebellion fled to South Yemen. At the end of June President al-Ghashmi was assassinated. The Yemen Arab Republic claimed that the assassination was engineered by South Yemen, and suspected that Major Alem had been instrumental. A suitcase carried by a South Yemen envoy contained a bomb which exploded and killed both President al-Ghashmi and the envoy. Whatever was the truth of the matter, the affair had repercussions in South Yemen, where President Salem Rubayi Ali was ousted and executed, and fighting broke out on the frontier between the two countries in July 1978 (*see* Yemen P.D.R., History).

In spite of the insecurity and assassinations, the Yemen Arab Republic made some advance towards a more democratic form of government. In February 1978 the Command Council appointed a Constituent People's Assembly of 99 members for a term of between two and three years, whose task was to propose the form of the Presidency, to review the Constitution and prepare the way for eventual elections. In April the Assembly elected Col. al-Ghashmi to be President of the Republic. The Command Council was then dissolved. The Assembly survived al-Ghashmi's assassination in June 1978, and, together with the Council of Ministers, it set up a four-man Presidential Council, with Qadi Abdul Karim al-Arshi (also Speaker of the Constituent Assembly) as its Chairman. The main task of the Presidential Council was to maintain power until the election of a new President. Lt.-Col. Ali Abdullah Saleh was elected President on July 17th, 1978.

President Saleh survived an assassination attempt in September 1978 and an attempted coup by senior military officers in October, thought to have external backing. Suspicion of South Yemeni involvement in both these events put increased strain on the relations between North and South Yemen. Between October 1978 and January 1979 the North Yemen Government repeatedly accused South Yemen of territorial violations and sabotage. Sporadic border clashes during these months escalated into open warfare during February and March 1979. The North Yemen opposition group, the National Democratic Front, carried out disruptive action in cities of the North and claimed to have captured several towns which it refused to relinquish. A mediation team from Syria, Jordan and Iraq arranged a ceasefire on March 2nd but, when this failed to hold and the fighting worsened, the Arab League intervened to enforce its implementation and supervise withdrawals from occupied territory in the second half of March.

At a meeting arranged by the Arab League in Kuwait on March 29th the Heads of State of North and South Yemen agreed that the only permanent way of settling the countries' differences was by unification, and they pledged their commitment to this in a peace treaty. Meetings of the Joint Constitutional Committee and Heads of State have since taken place. The signing of a 20-year Treaty of Friendship and Co-operation between the U.S.S.R. and South Yemen in October 1979 was considered by some as a threat to future Yemeni unity, but in May 1980 both countries agreed to establish joint economic projects and to co-ordinate their development plans as a step towards unification. A meeting of the Joint Military Committee, held in Sana'a in May 1981, announced that it had achieved "complete agreement and success". Renewed trouble from the National Democratic Front (NDF), however, was reported in the triangle formed by Hodeida, Taiz and Sana'a in April 1981. Guerrilla activity in the south of the country continued throughout 1981 and into 1982. In April 1982 it was reported that the town of Juban had fallen to the NDF. Although it was acknowledged that the

NDF were being backed by South Yemen, plans for the union of the two countries continued to be pursued. A co-operation agreement was signed with Aden in December 1981, and in January 1982, it was announced that the two countries had agreed on a 136-article draft constitution which was to be submitted to a referendum in each country.

The Yemen Arab Republic has in fact moved closer to the U.S.S.R. After buying U.S. arms worth £160 million in March 1979, the Sana'a Government concluded an arms deal with Moscow in November 1979, and abstained in early 1980 from the UN General Assembly condemnation of the Soviet invasion of Afghanistan. Although the Sana'a Government has relied on both the U.S.S.R. and U.S.A. for arms, finance has continued to come from Saudi Arabia, both in the form of aid and in the form of remittances from the 600,000 North Yemenis who work in Saudi Arabia.

President Saleh has taken several steps to make the North Yemen Government more democratic. In May 1979 he appointed a 15-member Consultative Council and expanded the membership of the Constituent People's Assembly to 159. In May 1980 he formed a Committee for National Consultation to prepare for a General People's Congress. The Committee is chaired by Hussain Abdullah al-Maqdami and has 51 other members. In October 1980 Dr. Abdul Karim al-Iryani replaced Abdel-Aziz Abdel-Ghani as Prime Minister in a government reshuffle aimed at bringing in new blood to further the five-year development plan and strive towards genuine Yemeni unity.

ECONOMIC SURVEY

A census carried out in 1980 gave the population of the Yemen Arab Republic as 8,556,974 (including nationals abroad), probably about equal to the total native population of the whole of the rest of the Arabian peninsula. The country has traditionally been able to support such a population because of its relatively high rainfall and fertile soil, permitting dense subsistence agriculture in favourable areas.

In recent years, however, the North Yemen economy has been transformed, not through internal developments, but as a result of the sudden rush of oil wealth in neighbouring Saudi Arabia. The census estimated that 1,395,123 Yemenis were working abroad, mostly as temporary immigrant labour in Saudia Arabia and other Gulf states. Even if this figure is exaggerated—an independent estimate in 1981 gave a figure of around 500,000 North Yemenis working abroad—the emigration of such a large part of the adult work-force represents a serious drain on the labour resources available to the economy. As a consequence, agriculture has declined and attempts to develop industry have been checked. Although aware of the problems posed by labour shortages, the Government cannot afford to stem the tide of emigration since the workers' remittances, worth $971 million in 1981, are an essential source of foreign currency without which the country's huge trade deficit could not be sustained—exports at present cover around one per cent of imports by value.

The Government's development effort has been

channelled into a Three-Year Plan (1974–76) and two Five-Year Plans (1977–81 and 1982–86). Planned allocations were 936 million riyals under the first plan and a much more ambitious 16,500 million riyals under the second. There was no possibility of North Yemen's generating capital sums of this size domestically, so massive foreign investment was called for, calculated at 75 per cent of financing for the Three-Year Plan and 42 per cent for the first Five-Year Plan. Projected investment for the second Five-Year Plan (1982–86) is 28,900 million riyals. About 45 per cent of this is expected to come from foreign aid, with almost $200 million per year from Saudi Arabia and $100 million per year from Kuwait. Most other investment should come from the Yemeni private sector. G.D.P. is planned to grow by 7.0 per cent annually under the second Five-Year Plan, compared with 6.2 per cent annual growth achieved under the previous Plan.

The country's backwardness clearly shows in the priority accorded under the Plans to the provision of basic electricity and water supplies for the main towns, developing a transport and telecommunications network, and providing simple health and education facilities. Agricultural development, especially through irrigation schemes, is another priority, with 4,430 million riyals allocated for the second Five-Year Plan period. Only a small degree of industrial development has so far been achieved, though manufacturing output is projected to rise by 12 per cent annually from 1982 to 1986.

AGRICULTURE

Yemen contains some of the most fertile land in the Arabian Peninsula, both in the highlands, where agriculture has always been extensively practised, and in the dry coastal plain of the Tihama. Total cultivated area, according to estimates made in 1977 by the UN Economic Commission for Western Asia, amounts to 1,500,000 hectares, equivalent to 8 per cent of Yemen's area. Of this cultivated land, 85 per cent is irrigated solely by rainwater. Yemen's best-known crop is coffee, grown mainly in the hills behind the Tihama, although it is cultivated in various degrees all over the country. It used to be Yemen's largest foreign exchange earner, but the amount of land devoted to it has decreased, partly because of fluctuation in demand on the world market, partly because the farmers found the narcotic, qat, to be a more profitable crop. In 1972 the Government announced measures to limit the cultivation and consumption of qat, but production of the narcotic has recovered from this setback. The increase in consumer spending in the second half of the 1970s especially favoured qat production for the local market as against coffee production for export.

Yemen's major cereal crop is sorghum (durra), grown at any altitude up to 9,000 feet. The harvest of sorghum and millet was estimated at 686,000 metric tons in 1980. Other cereals are wheat, barley and maize. Total cereal production in 1980 was 891,000 tons. Although a comparatively large area is allocated to cereals, the yield is poor and Yemen relies on imports of staple foods. Floods as well as drought can cause loss of output. The Government is planning a grain distribution system involving the building of silos at Hodeida and setting up flour mills and bakeries, but attempts to increase cereal production under the Five-Year Plan have largely failed.

The highland areas also produce many fruits and vegetables, citrus fruits, apricots, peaches, grapes, tomatoes and potatoes being the main crops; but others, such as cauliflowers, lettuces, peas, cucumbers and water melons are being introduced at the instigation of the Ministry of Agriculture.

The hot Tihama plain produces dates, and tobacco and cotton plantations have been established there to form the basis for local industries. Cotton in particular assumed some importance as a cash crop; in 1973/74 total cotton and cottonseed exports were worth 35.2 million riyals. However, after 1974/75 cotton production fell sharply, from 27,238 tons to 9,200 tons in 1976/77, while the area planted with cotton fell from 39,493 hectares to 13,233 hectares. Exports have since virtually ceased. This decline appears to have been due to the low prices maintained by the Government, a shortage of agricultural credit facilities, lack of improved seeds and adverse weather conditions.

Because droughts are so frequent, Yemen's major concern is to achieve efficient irrigation systems and water storage schemes and to utilize the ground water which exists in the Tihama.

Development of the Tihama region is the pivot of the Yemen's agricultural policy. A Tihama Development Authority has been set up and finance is being provided by the United Nations, the International Development Association (IDA), the Kuwait Fund for Arab Economic Development (KFAED), the International Fund for Agricultural Development (IFAD) and other sources. The most important project at present being undertaken by the Development Authority is the $85 million Wadi Mawr scheme to improve 25,000 hectares of farm land, due for completion by 1984. It is estimated that total spending on the Tihama plain could reach $1,000 million during the second Five-Year Plan period. Output of cotton, vegetables, cereals and oilseeds is expected to increase substantially, and livestock farming should expand.

Another major project is the $210 million Marib dam and irrigation scheme, which is being financed by the Abu Dhabi Fund for Arab Economic Development (ADFAED). When completed the scheme will provide perennial irrigation for 6,000 hectares of sorghum and wheat, and 5,000 hectares of intermittent irrigation. The UN is financing a pilot project for the development of a sugar cane industry and an agricultural advisory centre near Taiz. An Agricultural Credit Bank has been set up with a $3.4 million grant from the Government. In 1979 the IDA approved a $10 million credit for secondary education, aimed mainly at agricultural training, and a training school at Surdud is planned.

Yemen is also receiving agricultural aid from the Netherlands, China, Japan and other Arab states. In 1976 a Livestock Development Corporation (LDC) was set up with total credit facilities of $32 million—of which $17 million emanated from foreign sources. The LDC will establish eight 50-cow dairy farms, a livestock fattening farm, a poultry unit and a feedmill, construct three urban slaughterhouses and about 154 municipal retail market stalls, improve production of hides and skins, aid animal health services and ensure supervised credit to some 900 traditional sector landowners, smallholder livestock and poultry owners and irrigated fodder crop producers. At the same time, a livestock and range improvement centre will be established with a village range development programme under which 1,250 hectares of suitable land will be improved for grazing. A group of Dutch and West German firms plans to set up a chicken farm to provide 37 million eggs and 1,550 tons of broiler meat per year. Efforts are also to be made to exploit the country's fish resources. The annual catch, in the region of 17,000 tons in 1980, could be increased to 28,500 tons, it is estimated, with proper investment.

INDUSTRY AND MINING

It is calculated that industry accounts for only 5 per cent of Yemen's Gross Domestic Product and employs less than 4 per cent of the labour force. With a few exceptions, the existing and projected new industries are mainly based on the traditional occupations such as textiles, leather work, basketry, jewellery and glass-making, and, where possible, local raw materials. The Government's aim is to become self-sufficient in food processing, clothing and construction industries, that is, those sectors which could be made independent of imported raw materials. There is a state-owned spinning and weaving factory at Sana'a, established under an agreement of 1958 between Yemen and China, and completed in 1967. The plant, the Sana'a Textile Factory, employs 1,500 workers, many of them women. China is continuing to make aid available for the textile industry, with plans to set up a mill in Hodeida. The Bajil textile factory, set up by French and Syrian interests in the 1950s, encountered financial difficulties and never went into production. A United Nations report of 1968 recommended its urgent rehabilitation and repair, and a Dutch firm conducted a study. Modernization was proposed under the Three-Year Plan (1973/74 to 1975/76). In addition, there are two cotton-cleaning plants in Hodeida, and one in Zebid, and a cotton seed oil and cake plant in Hodeida; these are privately owned. The textile industry is clearly the most promising line of industrial development in Yemen. The Yemen Cotton Company, owned 51 per cent by the Government, 30 per cent by the Yemeni Bank for Reconstruction and Development and 19 per cent by private interests, provides the plants with raw cotton, over which it has monopoly rights.

Other industries include soft drinks factories, a cigarette plant at Hodeida, built with Italian aid, an oxygen plant, originally set up by the U.S.S.R. and now state-operated, and a plant making aluminium products. A plastics plant outside Taiz, built in 1973, produces mattresses, plastic tubes and plasticized paper. The IFC granted a $3 million loan in 1978 for a dairy and fruit juice plant in Hodeida. The Yemeni Company for Industrial Development was formed to develop light industry, particularly in Sana'a, Taiz and Hodeida. Denmark lent the Yemen 37 million riyals in 1978 to set up light industries, in 1980 a Maltese firm agreed to participate in a soap and detergents plant in Sana'a and in 1982 a West German firm announced that it was setting up a bottle factory, but industrialization is progressing very slowly, even with the increased aid which has been made available.

The Soviet-built cement factory at Bajil, which uses local limestone deposits, is one of the more successful ventures. Its current output is only 62,000 tons per year, however. Although it should eventually achieve an output of 250,000 tons per year, this has to be seen against Yemen's rapidly growing needs. Estimates of cement imports in 1977 ranged from 500,000 tons to 800,000 tons. The Five-Year Development Plan (1976/77 to 1980/81) envisaged the construction of two new plants, the first at Omran and the second at Taiz, each capable of an annual output of 500,000 tons, and a ready-mix concrete plant to be sited near Sana'a.

The rock salt factory at Salif, managed by the Ministry of Economy, utilizes local salt deposits, estimated to contain at least 25 million tons. Until 1975, the salt, which is of high quality, was nearly all exported to Japan. The Salt Company had invested about $400,000 to raise production to 500,000 tons per year and the KFAED provided loans to extend bulk-loading facilities at Salif port. A further KFAED loan of KD 1.2 million was given to exploit the deposits further and to raise production to 1 million tons per year by 1974. In 1975, however, Japanese customers ceased imports of salt, claiming that it contained impurities. The Government was understandably concerned in view of the large investments in the industry and the amount of goods imported from Japan.

During 1977 the planned expansion of salt mining facilities begun under the Three-Year Plan was completed. With design capacity of 1 million tons per year, Salif is likely to be profitable in the long term due to fairly high salt purity, proximity to deep water and low-cost open pit mining. The Yemen Salt Mining Corporation is now seeking new market outlets. The U.S.S.R., Bangladesh and North Korea are among countries to have accepted shipments, but full capacity working at Salif may have to await the completion of new chloralkali plants in other Middle East countries.

The salt at Salif is the only mineral at present exploited in Yemen on any scale. There are also salt deposits at Maarib in the east and at Qumah, near Salif. A mineral resources survey has been started by the U.S. Agency for International Development (AID). Other minerals known to exist in Yemen are: coal, copper (at Hamoura, near Taiz), iron, sulphur, lead, zinc, silver, gold and uranium. The exploitation of copper deposits at Hamoura is being studied by KFAED experts. Talks are being held with South Yemen on the working of copper deposits in the Beida area. A marble quarry and factory should start production during the Second Five-Year Plan period (1982–86).

The Yemen Petroleum Company, a joint venture between the Government and the YBRD, has the monopoly of imports, storage and distribution of oil products.

In 1970 a joint company, the Yemen Oil and Mineral Industrial Company, was formed by the Yemeni Government with the Algerian state-owned oil concern, SONATRACH. It was announced in 1972 that oil had been found in the Tihama but in the same year the company had to be dissolved because of lack of capital. The Government made it known that it would welcome foreign firms who wished to prospect for oil. In January 1974 an agreement was signed with Shell (Hamburg) to prospect for oil in the northern territorial waters, the company also having the right to refine any oil found. The agreement was extended in 1976 to cover part of the southern offshore area. Yemen Shell Explorations (YSE), formed in 1976 and registered in West Germany, drilled two deep wells, one offshore and one in the northern Tihama, but both without success. American, Japanese and Brazilian companies also have offshore concessions and the Government is optimistic about the prospects of finding oil. Toyo Menka Kaisha of Japan has a 2,500 sq. km. concession off the southern coast. Exploration costs have been shared with Santa Fe International of the U.S.A. The Brazilian company Petrobras began exploration in 1982. A refinery is now being built at Hodeida, where Mobil International Petroleum Corporation and Yemen Oil and Mineral Resources are set up to a lube oil blending plant. This plant will supply the domestic market. Another is proposed for Salif.

COMMUNICATIONS

It is only since the revolution in 1962 that Yemen has established regular links with the outside world, and that good roads have been built connecting the main towns. Road construction now has high priority in development plans. Reasonable tarred roads connect Sana'a with Hodeida, Sana'a with Mocha via Taiz, and Hodeida with Taiz. The Sana'a-Hodeida road, completed in 1962, was built by Chinese engineers and is a spectacular achievement. The Sana'a-Taiz-Mocha road was built with American aid. A road north through Saada to the Saudi border was completed in 1982. Work is also in progress on a road eastwards from Sana'a to Marib and a road from Dhamar to Raada and Baida on the South Yemen border across difficult mountain terrain. The repair and maintenance of existing roads is proving a problem, since neither the equipment nor the personnel is available locally. Altogether there were estimated in 1981 to be about 15,600 km. of roads, of which only 1,400 km. were asphalted. In addition there are a number of gravel feeder roads under construction. These are of great importance for the transport of agricultural produce which otherwise cannot reach centres of distribution. More asphalting is being done, especially around Sana'a and a number of hard-surfaced roads are planned, notably the Amran–Hajja road.

Improvement in the roads system is reflected in the increasing imports of motor vehicles, both commercial and private.

There are three ports in Yemen: Hodeida, Mocha and Salif, of which the most important is Hodeida, where a new harbour was completed in 1962 by the U.S.S.R. Mocha cannot be used by ships of any size at present. With the expansion of salt mining at Salif, the harbour is being rebuilt to enable it to take ships of up to 5,000 tons and a bulk petrol plant is also planned. Since Hodeida suffers badly from silting, there are tentative plans to develop Salif into the country's main port, but these are very much in the future. In the meantime, the Yemen Port Corporation obtained finance totalling $6 million in May 1977 from the International Development Association to develop the port of Hodeida. The envisaged project involves construction of a deep-sea berth, restoration of existing berth facilities, dredging and the installation of new equipment. The project also involves the improvement of existing port facilities at Mocha, which will be provided with 10 more berths. Hodeida is one of the world's most congested ports, with waiting times of up to six months for unloading.

There are airports at Sana'a, Hodeida and Taiz and smaller airstrips in other towns. Sana'a airport, built by the U.S.S.R. and equipped by West Germany, is capable of taking large aircraft, and both Hodeida and Taiz can take international flights. Facilities for air travel are poor by international standards.

Work began in late 1976 on the expansion of Sana'a airport to proper international standards. This work is being primarily Saudi Arabian financed. The Iraq Development Fund is providing a $15 million loan to be used mainly for the construction of an international airport at Hodeida. A contract for the work has been awarded to Costain International and Amay Road-stone Construction of the U.K. In May 1977 a Yemeni-Saudi Arabian airline company was established to take over the national airline, Yemen Airways. The joint company has a capital of $30 million, of which 51 per cent has been subscribed by the Yemeni Government and the remaining 49 per cent is subscribed by Saudi Arabia. The company will also be involved in developing airport facilities in the Yemen. The Yemen Airways fleet was expanded in 1979 with the purchase of Canadian aircraft.

Much work is now being done on providing Yemen with a telecommunications system, one of the Development Plan priorities. The three main towns, Sana'a, Taiz and Hodeida are linked by a 600 km. telephone line, built by East German experts, and are also connected to a number of other towns where telephone exchanges are in operation: Bajil, Ibb, Dhamar, Yerim, Manakha, Zebid, Beit-el-Faqih and Hais. East Germany also helped to found a Communications College at Sana'a. A six-channel microwave scatter system linking Sana'a and Taiz is being implemented by the United Nations and Sana'a is linked via Aden with the rest of the world. There are radio transmitters at Sana'a and Taiz and various small wireless communications posts scattered throughout the country. Work has started on a television network to operate from Sana'a. There were some 14,000 telephone lines at the end of 1976 and work has begun on an automatic system. In 1980 work was started on a network to connect remote villages with the main system. An earth satellite station was completed in October 1976 by Cable and Wireless (U.K.) and Nippon Electric of Japan. Sited at Ghuraff, near Sana'a, and costing close to $1 million, it is linked to the INTELSAT (International Telecommunications Satellite Organization) system and can provide over 100 channels. As a further development, Cable and Wireless has proposed an internal microwave system.

FOREIGN TRADE

Yemen's trade is characterized by an ever-increasing level of imports and negligible exports. In the second half of the 1970s, exports covered only between 0.5 per cent and 1.5 per cent of the value of imports. In 1978/79 exports totalled 28.5 million riyals, compared with imports worth 5,080.4 million riyals. The figures for 1979/80 were, exports 92.8 million riyals, imports 7,705.3 million riyals. These official estimates of imports are almost certainly well below the real figures, since large quantities of goods are smuggled into the country to avoid the high import duties.

Until 1977 the major exports were coffee and cotton. In 1976/77 cotton accounted for 24.9 million riyals and coffee for 10.2 million riyals out of total exports of 51.3 million riyals. By 1979/80, however, there were no recorded cotton exports and coffee exports were worth only 4.4 million riyals out of a total 92.8 million riyals. The largest single export item in that year was biscuits (12.7 million riyals). Other exports include hides and skins, salt, sweets and artisanal products.

Officially recorded imports more than doubled between 1976/77, when they totalled 3,035.3 million riyals, and 1979/80, when the total was 7,705.3 million riyals. The failure of Yemen's agriculture led to a rise in imports of food and live animals from 868.4 million riyals in 1976/77 to 1,894.6 million riyals in 1979/80, while the influx of capital goods for development projects under the Five-Year Plan pushed up imports of machinery and transport equipment from 965.7 million riyals to 2,474.5 million riyals over the same period. However, the largest percentage increase between 1976/77 and 1979/80 was in imports of basic manufactured goods (668.2 million riyals to 1,780.5 million riyals), as money earned in Saudi Arabia was spent on a flood of foreign consumer goods.

By far the major supplier is Saudi Arabia, providing goods worth 1,535.9 million riyals in 1979/80, a figure which would be considerably higher if smuggled items could be taken into account. Other major suppliers are Japan (862.1 million riyals in 1979/80), France, the United Kingdom, the Federal Republic of Germany and the People's Republic of China.

FINANCE AND FOREIGN AID

Yemen benefits from a considerable inflow of foreign aid which, coupled with remittances from Yemenis living abroad, has compensated for the poor performance of the domestic productive sectors. These flows have resulted, however, in a rise in liquidity which, with increasing government expenditure, has led in turn to inflation, a sharp rise in imports and the depreciation of the Yemeni riyal.

Yemen has a very large budgetary deficit. In the 1982/83 budget expenditure was set at 8,470 million riyals and revenue at 5,280 million riyals, leaving a projected deficit of 3,190 million riyals. Saudi Arabia has consistently made available budgetary aid to Yemen, with a figure of $102.9 million having been agreed for 1981/82. This was apart from other Saudi development aid, estimated at a further $181.5 million for the year.

Much practical aid in the fields of health, education and social welfare has flowed into Yemen, particularly from China, the Soviet Union, the World Health Organization and UNICEF. China, in particular, has supplied technical manpower in a number of sectors, including 177 medical workers in 1980 and a number of "agro-technicians". These however, are not always part of an aid package, and must be paid for separately. The Arab states appear to be increasingly ready to co-operate with Yemen in providing both financial and practical assistance. Kuwait and Saudi Arabia and, more recently, the United Arab Emirates, have provided schools, hospitals and clinics and many other Arab countries have sent teachers to Yemen. Qatar has provided aid for schools, hospitals and roads, and radio and television staff training. In 1974 Iraq announced aid for education, health and transport projects and is helping with the Hodeida port improvements. In 1977 Kuwait announced that it aimed to invest about 2,000 million riyals ($441 million) in joint-venture development projects in the private and public sectors, to be carried out under the Yemen's Five-Year Development Plan (1976/77 to 1980/81), but by February 1981 Kuwaiti investment under the plan had reached only the more modest figure of $127.7 million. Arab aid is supporting major infrastructural projects, such as the building of Hodeida international airport, the Taiz water supply and sewerage project, and road building schemes.

Yemen relies heavily on teachers recruited from Egypt to staff its schools. In 1979 Yemen requested another 1,340 teachers, in addition to about 2,700 already working there. Other Arab countries also make their contribution and Saudi Arabia has already spent $10.3 million on education projects in Yemen.

Before 1975 the Government of Yemen had relied rather more on aid from the Eastern bloc countries and had secured arms supplies mainly from the Soviet Union. Since then, however, arms have been purchased increasingly from the U.S.A., with finance provided by Saudi Arabia, although Saudia Arabia threatened in 1980 to withdraw aid for American weapons if Yemen continued to accept military training aid from the Soviet Union.

Although the U.S.S.R. is still a major aid donor, increasing amounts of aid are being provided by Western sources, in particular the Netherlands, West Germany and the U.S.A. In 1981 it was estimated that West Germany was providing around $20 million per year, and the Netherlands and the U.S.A. around $13 million each annually. The World Bank is an important source of loans through the IDA, and UN agencies provide much technical assistance, especially the UNDP. Yemen's total outstanding debt on loans from all foreign sources was estimated at 2,764.8 million riyals in September 1980.

Increased aid is an important factor in the country's economic planning and has played a part in the Yemen's dramatically improved financial position. However, the main factor here has been the flow of remittances from Yemenis working abroad. According to official 1980 estimates, there are 1.4 million Yemenis working in Saudi Arabia and the Gulf countries and they remitted $971 million in 1981. In 1980 Yemen's trade deficit was $1,672 million and its deficit on goods and services together was $1,693 million. However, this was partly offset by net private transfers of $1,070 million and net official transfers, including aid, of $146 million, so that the current account was actually in deficit by $478 million. In addition, there was a net capital inflow of $277 million. The trade deficit is likely to rise owing to the rapid import growth brought about by development projects' need for capital goods and by increased demand from the populace for consumer goods. Foreign remittances will continue while there is a demand for Yemeni labour in the Gulf States and Saudi Arabia. Saudi Arabia has, in the past, been particularly generous with credits, largely from a desire to protect its frontier.

As a result, the country's international reserves rose from $126.9 million at the end of 1973 to $1,459.4 million at the end of 1978, although they had fallen back to $961.6 million by the end of 1981.

Other relevant indicators are the latest figures for currency in circulation outside the banking system and money supply. Currency in circulation (outside banks) rose rapidly from 465.5 million riyals at the

end of 1973 to 1,080.5 million riyals at the end of 1975, 4,963 million riyals by the end of 1978 and 7,439 million riyals at the end of 1981. Similar growth marked the money supply (currency in circulation plus demand deposits at commercial banks), which rose from 540.9 million riyals at the end of 1973 to 5,716.3 million riyals at the end of 1978 and 8,330.9 million riyals at the end of 1981, with a very strong expansion in demand deposits from 91.5 million riyals at the beginning of 1975 to 824.2 million riyals at the end of 1981. This monetary expansion has been accompanied by strong inflationary pressures. Unofficial estimates put the annual rate of inflation as high as 40 per cent.

STATISTICAL SURVEY

AREA AND POPULATION

Area	Total (1980)	Sana'a (capital) (1980)	Taiz (1980)	Hodeida (1980)
200,000 sq. km.	8,556,974*	277,817	119,572	126,386

* Of whom 1,395,123 lived abroad.

AGRICULTURE
PRINCIPAL CROPS
('000 metric tons)

	1978	1979	1980*
Wheat . . .	44	58	54
Barley . . .	50	54	56
Maize . . .	89	94	95
Sorghum . . .	641	686	686
Potatoes . . .	107	116	116
Pulses . . .	77	79	80
Vegetables . . .	226	230	230
Grapes . . .	45	49	11
Coffee (green) . . .	4	4	4
Tobacco (leaves) . . .	5	6	6
Cotton (lint) . . .	1	2*	2

* FAO estimates.

Source: FAO, *Production Yearbook.*

LIVESTOCK
(FAO estimates, 'ooo head, year ending September)

	1978	1979	1980
Horses . . .	3	3	3
Asses . . .	700	716	730
Cattle . . .	840	950	950
Camels . . .	105	106	106
Sheep . . .	3,120	3,150	3,200
Goats . . .	7,280	7,800	7,300
Poultry . . .	3,287	3,350	3,386

Source: FAO, *Production Yearbook.*

LIVESTOCK PRODUCTS
(FAO estimates, 'ooo metric tons)

	1978	1979	1980
Beef and veal . .	12	13	14
Mutton and lamb .	13	13	13
Goats' meat . .	38	38	41
Poultry meat . .	1	1	1
Cows' milk . .	64	64	64
Sheep's milk . .	52	52	54
Goats' milk . .	135	135	135
Cheese . . .	17.2	17.2	17.3
Butter . . .	3.9	3.9	4.0
Hen eggs . .	10.4	10.5	10.7
Cattle hides . .	1.8	2.0	2.2
Sheep skins . .	2.1	2.2	2.2
Goat skins . .	6.2	6.4	6.7

Source: FAO, *Production Yearbook.*

SEA FISHING
('ooo metric tons, live weight)

	1975	1976	1977	1978	1979	1980
Total catch . . .	14.6	16.5	17.5	19.3	19.3*	17.0

* FAO estimate.

Source: FAO, *Yearbook of Fishery Statistics.*

INDUSTRY
SELECTED PRODUCTS
(year ending June 30th)

		1973/74	1974/75	1975/76
Cotton textiles . . .	million yards	11.1	10.1	8.4
Electricity . . .	million kWh.	25.8	31.6	34.3
Aluminium products . .	tons	200.0	200.0	200.0
Paints	'ooo gallons	48.0	54.0	60.0
Mineral drinks . . .	million bottles	27.2	27.5	27.8
Cement . . .	hundred tons	50.0	55.0	63.0

Source: Central Bank of Yemen.

FINANCE

100 fils = 1 Yemeni riyal.
Coins: 1, 5, 10, 25 and 50 fils.
Notes: 1, 5, 10, 20, 50 and 100 riyals.
Exchange rates (May 1982): £1 sterling = 8.39 Yemeni riyals; U.S. $1 = 4.56 Yemeni riyals.
100 Yemeni riyals = £11.92 = $21.92.

Note: The Yemeni riyal was introduced in 1964, with an initial value of 6s. 8d. sterling (£1 = 3.00 riyals) or 93.33 U.S. cents (U.S. $1 = 1.071 riyals). Thereafter, the authorities allowed the currency to depreciate on the free market while applying a system of multiple official exchange rates. By 1970 the free rate was $1 = 5.50 riyals (£1 = 13.20 riyals). In June 1971 multiple practices were eliminated, leaving a single rate which held fairly stable at $1 = 5.00 riyals until February 1973, since when the Central Bank has set a selling rate of $1 = 4.50 riyals. The mid-point rate was $1 = 4.575 riyals until April 1975, since when it has been $1 = 4.5625 riyals. Before 1975 the riyal was divided into 40 buqsha, rather than 100 fils. Notes of 10 and 20 buqsha have been withdrawn from circulation but coins of ½, 1 and 2 buqsha are still in use.

BUDGET
('000 riyals, year ending June 30th)

			REVENUE	EXPENDITURE
1978/79	.	.	2,193,375	3,177,090
1979/80			3,013,000	4,384,000
1980/81			4,435,230	6,804,120
1981/82			5,280,000	8,470,000

Source: Ministry of Treasury and Central Bank of Yemen.

DEVELOPMENT PLAN, 1982–86
(proposed fixed capital investment in million riyals)

Agriculture	4,430
Mining	905
Manufacturing	3,510
Electricity and water . . .	2,040
Construction . . .	640
Trade, restaurants and hotels . .	2,870
Transport and communications . .	4,640
Finance . . .	100
Dwellings and real estate services .	3,745
Government services . . .	4,250
Other services	270
TOTAL . . .	27,400

EXTERNAL TRADE
(million riyals, year ending June 30th)

	1972/73	1973/74	1974/75	1975/76	1976/77	1977/78	1978/79	1979/80
Imports c.i.f. . . .	410.7	745.0	981.0	1,706.9	3,035.3	3,938.7	5,080.4	7,705.3
Exports f.o.b. . . .	25.3	55.4	53.0	50.1	51.3	33.4	28.5	92.8

PRINCIPAL COMMODITIES
(million riyals)

IMPORTS c.i.f.	1976/77	1977/78	1978/79	1979/80
Food and live animals . . .	868.4	981.6	1,304.8	1,894.6
Beverages and tobacco . . .	49.0	85.5	110.5	114.6
Crude materials (inedible) except fuels	12.7	19.8	15.9	35.3
Mineral fuels, lubricants, etc. . .	58.9	108.0	139.4	369.5
Animal and vegetable oils and fats .	11.2	28.4	52.2	42.5
Chemicals	155.3	223.1	302.0	473.6
Basic manufactures . . .	668.2	975.2	1,270.3	1,780.5
Machinery and transport equipment .	965.7	1,155.2	1,581.4	2,474.5
Miscellaneous manufactured articles .	243.0	359.7	313.3	465.9
Unspecified items	2.9	36.4	10.5	54.3
TOTAL . . .	3,035.3	3,938.7	5,080.4	7,705.3

EXPORTS f.o.b.	1976/77	1977/78	1978/79	1979/80
Biscuits	3.2	4.1	8.5	12.7
Coffee	10.2	0.9	2.2	4.4
Cotton	24.9	—	—	—
Hides and skins . . .	6.1	5.2	4.7	5.7
TOTAL (incl. others) .	51.3	33.4	28.5	92.8

PRINCIPAL TRADING PARTNERS
(million riyals)

IMPORTS c.i.f.	1977/78	1978/79	1979/80
Australia . . .	158.7	43.8	250.6
China, People's Repub. .	133.0	182.0	427.9
France . . .	224.5	456.4	645.1
Germany, Fed. Repub. .	233.9	242.9	467.5
Greece . . .	40.0	96.3	295.3
India . . .	184.5	171.6	229.5
Italy . . .	205.3	299.1	410.4
Japan . . .	449.2	509.8	862.1
Korea, Republic .	8.7	75.4	152.2
Kuwait . .	27.9	45.8	109.2
Netherlands .	152.0	204.3	331.4
Saudi Arabia .	620.1	1,238.4	1,535.9
United Kingdom .	194.7	377.7	489.6
U.S.A. . . .	43.9	140.8	136.2
TOTAL (incl. others) .	3,938.7	5,080.4	7,705.3

EXPORTS f.o.b.	1975/76	1976/77	1977/78
China, People's Repub. .	24.6	24.9	0.0
Djibouti . . .	0.5	0.8	2.9
Italy . . .	8.7	6.0	2.9
Saudi Arabia . .	4.6	4.5	5.0
Yemen, People's Dem. Repub. . . .	8.4	12.6	20.1
TOTAL (incl. others) .	50.1	51.3	33.4

Source: Central Bank of Yemen.

TRANSPORT
ROAD TRAFFIC 1973
Private cars 2,288, motor cycles 6,063, taxis 3,329, trucks 6,957.

SHIPPING

	VESSELS ENTERING HODEIDA PORT	TONNAGE UNLOADED
1972 . . .	506	506,991
1973 . . .	520	530,943

CIVIL AVIATION
(Yemen Airways)

	PASSENGERS CARRIED	FREIGHT (tons)
1972	48,600	567
1973	43,400	431

EDUCATION
(1976/77)

	PUPILS		
	Male	Female	Total
Primary	191,258	30,224	221,482
Intermediate	15,249	2,427	17,676
Higher Secondary (General) . .	6,485	712	7,197
Higher Secondary (Commercial) .	212	—	212
Higher Secondary (Trades) . .	291	—	291
Primary Teacher Training . .	626	486	1,112
Secondary Teacher Training . .	363	175	538

Source (except where otherwise stated): Yemen Arab Republic Central Planning Organization.

PROVISIONAL CONSTITUTION
(Published June 19th, 1974)

In the name of the people, the Chairman of the Command Council, having taken cognizance of Command Council Proclamation No. 1 for 1974, Command Council Proclamation No. 4 for 1974 suspending the Constitution, and Command Council Proclamation No. 5 for 1974 increasing the membership of the Command Council, and desiring to consolidate the bases of authority during the transitional period and to regulate the rights and duties of all employees in a manner conducive to fruitful production to raise the country to the level which we all hope it will attain, we announce in the name of the people that during the transitional period the country will be governed in accordance with the following rules:

Chapter One: General Principles: the State:

Article 1: Yemen is an Arab, Islamic, and independent state enjoying full sovereignty. Its system is republican. The Yemeni people are a part of the Arab nation.

Article 2: The people are the source of all authority.

Article 3: Islam is the state religion and Arabic the official state language.

Article 4: The Islamic Sharia is the source of all laws.

Article 5: Yemen is an indivisible whole and its defence is the sacred duty of all citizens.

Chapter Two: Rights and Duties:

Article 6: Yemenis have equal rights and general duties.

Article 7: Personal freedom is guaranteed in accordance with the provisions of the law.

Article 8: There shall be no crime and no penalty except as laid down by law and there shall be no penalty for acts except those committed after the promulgation of the law (applying to them).

Article 9: Homes are inviolate: it is therefore inadmissible to enter them except in such instances as prescribed by the law.

Article 10: The confiscation of funds is prohibited, except within the confines of the law.

Article 11: No person's property shall be expropriated except in the public interest, in the instances prescribed by the law, and with just compensation to the person.

Article 12: The citizens have the right to express their thoughts by means of speech, writing, or voting within the confines of the law.

Article 13: Places of worship and learning have immunity which cannot be violated except in instances required by security needs and as prescribed by the law.

Chapter Three: The System of Government:

Article 14: The Chairman of the Command Council shall assume the function of general sovereignty, particularly in taking the measures he deems necessary to protect the revolution and the republican régime.

Article 15: The Command Council shall assume the functions of the legislative and executive authorities of the state. It shall also have the power to lay down general policy and define its general framework.

Article 16: The Government is the executive and administrative body responsible for carrying out the state's general policy as laid down by the Command Council.

Article 17: The judiciary is independent, and there shall be no authority over it except for the law. Its verdicts shall be handed down and executed in accordance with the principles of the Sharia.

Chapter Four: Concluding Rules:

Article 18: All the rules determined by the laws, bylaws and decisions prior to the issuance of this constitutional declaration shall remain in force unless they conflict with the rules of this declaration or unless they are amended or revoked.

Article 19: During the transitional period action shall be taken to restore constitutional and democratic life on sound bases in view of the need to provide the Yemeni people with a dignified life and a bright future.

Article 20: This constitutional declaration shall come into force from the date of its issuance and it shall be published in the Official Gazette.

In February 1978 a 99-member Constituent People's Assembly was appointed by the Command Council to (i) propose the form of the presidency; (ii) amend the constitution, (iii) carry out various functions related to the eventual holding of parliamentary elections; (iv) review and give recommendations on the budget, domestic and foreign affairs, draft laws, etc. In April the Command Council was dissolved. In May 1979 the Constituent People's Assembly was increased to 159 members and a 15-member Consultative Council was set up. In May 1980 a 52-member Committee for National Consultation was set up to prepare for a General People's Congress. In October 1981 a government resolution called for the setting up of the Congress, and it was later announced that the Congress will comprise 1,000 people, 700 of whom will be elected.

THE GOVERNMENT
HEAD OF STATE
President: Col. ALI ABDULLAH SALEH (took office July 18th, 1978).
Vice-Presidents: Qadi ABDUL KARIM AL-ARASHI, Dr. ABDEL-AZIZ ABDEL-GHANI.

CABINET
(June 1982)

Prime Minister: Dr. ABDUL KARIM AL-IRYANI.

Deputy Prime Minister for Economic Affairs: Dr. HASSAN MUHAMMAD MAKKI.

Deputy Prime Minister for Internal Affairs: Lt.-Col. MUJAHID YAHYA ABU SHUWARIB.

Minister of Public Works: Eng. ABDULLAH HUSSAIN AL-KURSHUMI.

Legal Adviser and Minister of State: HUSSAIN ALI AL-HUBAISHI.

Minister of Electricity, Water and Sewerage: Eng. MUHAMMAD AHMED JUNAID.

Minister of Foreign Affairs: ALI LUTF AL-THAWR.

Minister of State for People's Constituent Assembly Affairs: AHMED MUHAMMAD AL-SHAJANI.

Minister of Awqaf (Waqfs): Qadi ALI BIN ALI AL-SAMMAN.

Minister of Local Government: Lt.-Col. LUTFI HUSAYN AL-KILABI.

Minister of Social, Labour and Youth Affairs: AHMED SALEH AL-ROUEINI.

Minister of Agriculture and Fishery Resources: Dr. AHMED AL-HAMDANI.

Minister for Civil Service and Administrative Correction: ISMAIL AHMED AL-WAZIR.

Minister of Education and Instruction: Dr. AHMED ABDUL AL-MALIK AL-ASBAHI.

Minister of Communications and Transport: Eng. AHMED MUHAMMAD AL-ANISI.

Minister of Economy: MUHAMMAD HIZAM AL-SHOHATI.

Minister of Justice: MUHSIN MUHAMMAD AL-OLAFI.

Minister of Information and Culture: HASSAN AHMED AL-LAWZI.

Minister of Municipalities and Housing: MUHAMMAD HUSAYN JAGHMAN.

Minister of Finance: Dr. MUHAMMAD YAHYA AL-ADI.

Minister of State and Head of Oil and Mineral Wealth Foundation: ALI ABDURRAHMAN AL-BAHR.

Minister of State and Secretary General of the Higher Council of Youth and Sports: AHMED MUHAMMAD LUQMAN.

Minister of Supply and Trade: Dr. HUSAIN ABDUL KHALIQ AL-JALLAL.

Minister of the Interior: Lt.-Col. ALI MUHAMMAD ATHRIB.

Minister of Development and President of Central Planning Organization: FUAD QUAID MUHAMMAD.

Minister of Health: Dr. MUHAMMAD AHMED AL-KABAB.

CONSTITUENT PEOPLE'S ASSEMBLY

Speaker: Qadi ABDUL KARIM AL-ARASHI.

Originally composed of 99 members, the Constituent People's Assembly was increased to 159 members in May 1979. The new members were named by Presidential decree. At the same time a 15-member Consultative Council was set up. Preparations are being made for a General People's Congress (*see* Provisional Constitution).

DIPLOMATIC REPRESENTATION
EMBASSIES ACCREDITED TO THE YEMEN ARAB REPUBLIC
(In Sana'a unless otherwise stated)

Albania: Cairo, Egypt.

Algeria: Ali Abdul Moghni St.; *Ambassador:* MOHAMMED SABBAGH.

Australia: Jeddah, Saudi Arabia.

Austria: Jeddah, Saudi Arabia.

Belgium: Jeddah, Saudi Arabia.

Bulgaria: Cairo, Egypt.

Canada: Jeddah, Saudi Arabia.

China, People's Republic: Zubairy St.; *Ambassador:* TETUNG HAN JUO.

Czechoslovakia: Gamal Abdul Naser St.; *Chargé d'affaires:* EDUARD BRUNCLIK.

Denmark: Jeddah, Saudi Arabia.

Ethiopia: Zubairy St.; *Ambassador:* (vacant).

Finland: Jeddah, Saudi Arabia.

France: Gamal Abdul Naser St.; *Ambassador:* LUC BALDIT.

German Democratic Republic: 26 September St.; *Ambassador:* WERNER KEMPE.

Germany, Federal Republic: Republican Palace St.; *Ambassador:* Dr. WOLF-DIETRICH SCHILLING.

Greece: Jeddah, Saudi Arabia.

Hungary: Cairo, Egypt.

India: Zubairy St.; *Ambassador:* D. P. PASRICHA.

Iran: *Ambassador:* (vacant).

Iraq: Ali Zubiri St.; *Ambassador:* ABDUL WADDAD YUSSIF AL-JADOUA.

Italy: 65 Gamal Abdul Naser St.; *Ambassador:* FRANCESCO PULCINI.

Japan: Tareeq Al-Darie, Safaye Al-Garbiya; *Ambassador:* TOSHIO SAIKI.

Jordan: Hadda Rd.; *Ambassador:* (vacant).

Kenya: Addis Ababa, Ethiopia.

Korea, Democratic People's Republic: Zubairy St.; *Ambassador:* CHOE UK-MYONG.

Kuwait: Hadda Rd.; *Ambassador:* TALAK YAKOUB AL-GHOUSSAYIN.

Lebanon: Zira'a St.; *Chargé d'affaires:* ADIB ALAM UDDIN.

Libya: Zubairy St.; *Chairman of People's Committee:* ABDUL RAHMAN MUHAMMAD ATTIG.

Morocco: Jeddah, Saudi Arabia.

Netherlands: House of Abdullah Safaar, nr. Old Radio Station, P.O.B. 463; *Chargé d'affaires:* C. J. VAN TOOREN.

Norway: Jeddah, Saudi Arabia.

Oman: Hadda Rd.; *Ambassador:* ABDULLAH SA'ID RASHID AL-BALUCH.

Pakistan: Ring Road, P.O.B. 2848; *Ambassador:* (vacant).

Poland: Cairo, Egypt.

Qatar: Jeddah, Saudi Arabia.

Romania: Khartoum, Sudan.

Saudi Arabia: Arman Bldg., Hadda Rd.; *Ambassador:* TARRAD AL-HARITHI.

Somalia: Wadi Dahr St.; *Ambassador:* ABDUL NOOR AHMED MAHMOUD.

Spain: Jeddah, Saudi Arabia.

Sudan: Hadda Rd., P.O.B. 517; *Ambassador:* ABDULLAH ALI JABER.

Sweden: Jeddah, Saudi Arabia.

Switzerland: Jeddah, Saudi Arabia.

Syria: Zubairy St.; *Ambassador:* ASSAF HASSOUN.

Tunisia: Jeddah, Saudi Arabia.

Turkey: Jeddah, Saudi Arabia.

U.S.S.R.: 26 September St.; *Ambassador:* OLEG G. PERESSIPKINE.

United Arab Emirates: Hadda Rd.; *Ambassador:* SAIF SA'IID SAA'ID.

United Kingdom: 23/25 Qasr Al Jumhuri St., P.O.B. 1287; *Ambassador:* JULIAN WALKER, C.M.G., M.B.E.

U.S.A.: Beit Al-Halali; *Ambassador:* DAVID E. ZWEIFEL.

Viet-Nam: Cairo, Egypt.

Yugoslavia: Kuwait City, Kuwait.

The Yemen Arab Republic also has diplomatic relations with Cuba, Djibouti, Luxembourg, Mali, Malta, Mexico, Nigeria, Portugal and Uganda.

JUDICIAL SYSTEM

President of the State Security Court: Qadi GHALIB ABDULLA RAJEH (political cases).

Public Prosecutor: Lt.-Col. MUHAMMAD KHAMIS.

Attorney General: Lt.-Col. MUHSIN MUHAMMAD AL-ULUFI.

Sharia Court: Sana'a; deals with cases related to Islamic law.

Disciplinary Court: prosecution office for maladministration and misappropriation of public funds; Chair. MUHAMMAD ABDO NUMAN.

THE PRESS

DAILIES

Al Gumhuryyah (*The Republic*): Information Office, Taiz; Arabic; government-owned.

Al Thawra (*The Revolution*): Ministry of Information, Sana'a; Arabic; government-owned.

WEEKLY AND OTHER

Al Bilad: P.O.B. 1438, Sana'a; Arabic; weekly; inclined to right.

Mareb: Dar Al-Qalam, Taiz; Arabic; weekly; supports Nasserite ideas.

As-Sabah: P.O.B. 599, Hodeida; Arabic; weekly; reformist.

As-Salam: P.O.B. 181, Sana'a; f. 1948; Arabic; weekly; political, economic and general essays; circ. 7,000; Editor ABDULLA ASSAKAL.

Sana'a: P.O.B. 193, Sana'a; Arabic; fortnightly; inclined to left.

Al Shab: Al-Andalus Bookshop, Sana'a; Arabic; weekly; slightly left-inclined.

Al-Ta'wn: Al Ta'wn Building, Jubairi St., Sana'a; Arabic; weekly; supports co-operative societies.

Al-Yemen: Sana'a; Arabic; fortnightly; inclined to right.

NEWS AGENCY

Saba News Agency: Sana'a; f. 1970; Dir. HASSAN AL-ULUFI.

RADIO AND TELEVISION

Radio Hodeida: Hodeida; government-controlled local radio; broadcasts in Arabic, 4 hours daily.

Radio Sana'a: Sana'a; government-controlled station, broadcasts in Arabic, 15 hours daily; Dir.-Gen. ABDUL RAHMAN AL-MUTARIB.

Radio Taiz: Taiz; government-controlled station; broadcasts in Arabic, 4 hours daily.

There are 250,000 receiving sets.

A television station opened in September 1975 and a national TV network was achieved in March 1980.

FINANCE

BANKING

(cap. = capital; p.u. = paid up; m. = million; br. = branch; amounts in riyals)

Central Bank of Yemen: P.O.B. 59, Sana'a; f. 1971; cap. p.u. 10m.; Gov. and Chair. ABDULLA SANABANI; Gen. Man. ALI ALI AL-NUSEIF.

Yemen Bank for Reconstruction and Development: P.O.B. 541, Sana'a; f. 1962; cap. 100m.; consolidated bank; 24 brs.; Chair. MUHAMMAD A. ALWAJIH; Gen. Man. ABDULAZIZ Y. ALMAKTARI.

Bank of Credit and Commerce International S.A. (*Luxembourg*): P.O.B. 160, Sana'a.

Arab Bank Ltd.: P.O.B. 68, Amman, Jordan; Tahrir (Liberation) Square, Sana'a; br. in Hodeida.

Banque de l'Indochine et de Suez: Sana'a.

British Bank of the Middle East (*Hong Kong*): P.O.B. 2932, Hodeida; Man. G. JOHN; P.O.B. 4886, Taiz: Man. M. W. MALCOLM.

Citibank (*U.S.A.*): P.O.B. 2133, Sana'a.

Habib Bank Ltd. (*Pakistan*): P.O.B. 3927, Al-Akhwa Hotel Bldg.; Man. and Asst. Vice-Pres. S. M. NASIM.

Housing Credit Bank: P.O.B. 638, Sana'a; Chair. AHMAD JABER AFIF.

International Bank of Yemen: Sana'a; f. 1980.

Rafidain Bank (*Iraq*): Sana'a.

United Bank of Pakistan: Ali Abdul Mugni St., Sana'a.

INSURANCE

Yemen General Insurance Co. S.A.Y.: Asia Hotel Bldg., Sana'a St., P.O.B. 3952, Hodeida; all classes of insurance; brs. in Taiz and Sana'a; Gen. Man. MUHAMMAD WAHID EL DIN ASSAF.

TRADE AND INDUSTRY

CHAMBERS OF COMMERCE

Sana'a Chamber of Commerce: Bab El-Yemen, P.O.B. 195, Sana'a.

Taiz Chamber of Commerce: 26th September St., P.O.B. 1029, Taiz.

Yemen Chamber of Commerce: Azzoubairi St., P.O.B. 3370, Hodeida.

Ibb also has a Chamber of Commerce.

NATIONALIZED ORGANIZATIONS

General Cotton Organization: Sana'a.

Hodeida Electricity and Water Company: P.O.B. 3363, Hodeida; affiliate of Yemen Bank for Reconstruction and Development.

National Tobacco and Matches Co.: P.O.B. 3571, Hodeida; f. 1964; monopoly importing and sales organization for tobacco and matches; cigarette manufacture and tobacco growing; Chair. A. A. NAGI.

Yemen Company for Foreign Trade: Hodeida.

Yemen Oil and Mineral Resources Corporation (YOMINCO): P.O.B. 81, Sana'a; sole petroleum and lube oil supplier; Minister of State and Chair. of Bd. ALI ABDURRAHMAN AL-BAHR; Gen. Man. ADEL KHORSHEED.

Yemen Printing and Publishing Co.: P.O.B. 1081, Sana'a; f. 1970; publishes ten newspapers (including two government newspapers); Chair. AHMAD MUHAMMAD HADI.

TRANSPORT

ROADS

There are about 1,650 km. of main roads, of which about 600 km. are asphalted and the rest gravelled. Highways run from Hodeida to Sana'a, and from Moka to Taiz, Ibb and Sana'a. A highway from Sana'a to Saada was opened in May 1977.

SHIPPING

Hodeida is a Red Sea port of some importance, and the Yemen Navigation Company runs passenger and cargo services to many parts of the Middle East and Africa.

Adafar Yemenite Line: Hodeida.

Hodeida Shipping and Transport Co.: P.O.B. 3337, Hodeida.

Middle East Shipping Co.: P.O.B. 3700, Hodeida; brs. in Mocha and Saleef.

CIVIL AVIATION

There are three international airports—Al Rahaba at Sana'a, Al Ganad at Taiz and Hodeida Airport.

Yemen Airways: Zubairy St., Sana'a; internal services and external services to Abu Dhabi, Aden, Cairo, Damascus, Dhahran, Djibouti, Doha, Jeddah, Khartoum, Kuwait, London and Sharjah; supervised by a ministerial committee headed by the Minister of Communications; Chair. and Pres. MUHAMMAD AL-HAIMI; Gen. Man. RIDA HAKEM; fleet of 2 DC-6, 1 Boeing 737-15, 3 DC-3.

The following airlines also serve the Yemen Arab Republic: Aeroflot (U.S.S.R.), Air Djibouti, Air France, Air India, Alyemda (People's Democratic Republic of Yemen), Ethiopian Airlines, Kuwait Airways, Saudia (Saudi Arabia), Somali Airlines and Syrian Arab Airlines, in addition to charter flights by various carriers.

TOURISM

Yemen Tourism Co.: Sana'a; Chair. ABDUL HADI AL-HAMADANI.

DEFENCE

Commander-in-Chief of the Armed Forces: Lt.-Col. ABDEL-AZIZ BARTI.

Defence Budget: 970.2 million riyals (1981).

Military Service: 3 years.

Armed Forces: In July 1981 the forces totalled 32,100: army 30,000, navy 600, air force 1,500; paramilitary forces: 20,000 tribal levies.

EDUCATION

The development of a modern educational system in the Yemen Arab Republic gained impetus after the 1962 revolution. However, the implementation of extensive educational reform was delayed by the civil war which extended until 1967. It is estimated that between 1970 and 1975 the proportion of children aged 6 to 11 years who were enrolled at primary schools increased from 10 to 25 per cent. In 1975 only about 3 per cent of children aged 12 to 17 attended secondary schools. The latest statistics on the number of pupils can be found in the Statistical Survey. The University of Sana'a had 2,760 pupils in the 1976/77 academic year.

In addition to military colleges, more specific institutions are being established under the Educational Development Project, especially in the field of vocational training.

BIBLIOGRAPHY

ANSALDI, C. Il Yemen nella storia e nella leggenda (Rome, 1933).

ATTAR, MOHAMED SAID EL-. Le sous-développement Economique et Social du Yémen (Editions Tiers-Monde, Algiers, 1966).

BALSAN, FRANÇOIS. Inquiétant Yémen (Paris, 1961).

BETHMANN, E. W. Yemen on the Threshold (American Friends of the Middle East, Washington, 1960).

COLONIAL OFFICE. Aden and the Yemen (H.M.S.O., London, 1960).

DEUTSCH, ROBERT. Der Yemen (Vienna, 1914).

DOE, BRIAN. Southern Arabia (Thames and Hudson. London, 1972).

FAROUGHY, A. Introducing Yemen (New York, 1947).

FAYEIN, CLAUDE. A French Doctor in the Yemen (Robert Hale, London, 1957).

HELFRITZ, H. The Yemen: A Secret Journey (Allen and Unwin, London, 1958).

HEYWORTH-DUNNE, G. E. Al-Yemen: Social, Political and Economic Survey (Cairo, 1952).

INGRAMS, HAROLD. The Yemen; Imams, Rulers and Revolutions (London, 1963).

MACRO, ERIC. Bibliography of the Yemen, with Notes on Mocha (University of Miami Press, 1959).

Yemen and the Western World since 1571 (C. Hurst, London, and Praeger, New York, 1968).

O'BALLANCE, EDGAR. The War in the Yemen (Faber, London, 1971).

PAWELKE, GUNTHER. Der Yemen: Das Verbotene Land (Econ. Verlag., Düsseldorf, 1959).

PETERSON, J. E. Yemen, the Search for a Modern State (Croom Helm, London, 1981).

ROUAUD, ALAIN. Le Yémen (Editions Complexe, Brussels, 1979).

SCHMIDT, DANA ADAMS. Yemen, the Unknown War (Bodley Head, London, 1968).

SCOTT, H. In the High Yemen (Murray, London, 1942).

U.S.G.P.O. Geology of the Arabian Peninsula: Yemen (Washington, 1967).

WENNER, MANFRED W. Yemen: a selected Bibliography of Literature since 1960 (Library of Congress Legislative Reference Service, Washington, D.C., 1965).

Modern Yemen, 1918-1966 (Johns Hopkins Press, Baltimore, U.S.A., 1967).

People's Democratic Republic of Yemen

(Southern Yemen)

PHYSICAL AND SOCIAL GEOGRAPHY

W. B. Fisher

On November 30th, 1967, the People's Republic of Southern Yemen came into existence, formed from the former British Colony and Protectorate of Aden (75 sq. miles and 111,000 sq. miles respectively), together with the islands of Perim (5 sq. miles) and Kamaran (22 sq. miles). Socotra (1,400 sq. miles) elected to join the new state. The Kuria Muria group of islands were returned to Muscat by Britain but the new Republican government revoked this decision. In November 1970 the name of the Republic was changed to the "People's Democratic Republic of Yemen". The capital is Aden. The state is divided into six governorates formed from Aden and the 20 states of the old South Arabian Protectorate. The Republic lies at the southern end of the Arabian peninsula, approximately between longitude 43° and 56°E., with Perim Island a few miles due west, in the strait marking the southern extremity of the Red Sea; Kamaran Island some 200 miles north of Perim; Socotra and the Kuria Muria groups in the extreme east, the former at the entrance to the Gulf of Aden, the latter near the coast of Oman. The Republic has frontiers with the Yemen Arab Republic, Saudi Arabia, and Oman, but none of these frontiers is fully delimited, and in some instances they are disputed. Atlases still show considerable variation in the precise boundaries of all four territories, or sometimes do not indicate them at all.

Physically, the Republic comprises the broken and dislocated southern edge of the great plateau of Arabia. This is an immense mass of ancient granites, once forming part of Africa, and covered in many places by shallow, generally horizontal layers of younger sedimentary rocks. The whole plateau has undergone downwarping in the east and elevation in the west, so that the highest land (over 10,000 ft.) occurs in the extreme west, near the Red Sea, with a gradual decline to the lowest parts (under 1,000 ft.) in the extreme east. The whole of the southern and western coasts of the Republic were formed by a series of enormous fractures, which produced a flat but very narrow coastal plain, rising steeply to the hill country a short distance inland. Percolation of molten magma along the fracture-lines has given rise to a number of volcanic craters, now extinct, and one of these, partly eroded and occupied by the sea, forms the site of Aden port.

An important topographic feature is the Wadi Hadhramaut, an imposing valley running parallel to the coast at 100–150 miles distance inland. In its upper and middle parts, this valley is broad, and occupied by a seasonal torrent; in its lower (eastern) part it narrows considerably, making a sudden turn south-eastwards and reaching the sea. This lower part is largely uninhabited, but the upper parts, where alluvial soil and intermittent flood water are available, are occupied by a farming population.

The details of climate in the Republic are simple to state, but extremely difficult to explain. Rainfall is everywhere scanty, but relatively more abundant on the highlands and in the west. Thus Aden itself has 5 in. of rain annually, entirely in winter (December-March), whilst in the lowlands of the extreme east, it may rain only once in five or ten years. In the highlands a few miles north of Aden, falls of up to 30 in. occur, for the most part during summer, and this rainfall also gradually declines eastwards, giving 15–20 in. in the highlands of Dhofar. Ultimately, to the north and east, rainfall diminishes to almost nil, as the edges of the Arabian Desert are reached. This unusual situation of a reversal in climatic conditions over a few miles is thought to be the result of two streams of air; an upper one, damp and unstable in summer, and originating in the equatorial regions of East Africa; and a lower current, generally drier and related to conditions prevailing over the rest of the Middle East. In this way the low lying coastal areas have a maximum of rainfall in winter, and the hills of both the Yemens a maximum in summer. Temperatures are everywhere high, particularly on the coastal plain, which has a southern aspect: mean figures of 76°F. (Jan.) to 89° (June) occur at Aden town, but maxima of over 100° are common.

Except on the higher parts, which have a light covering of thorn scrub (including dwarf trees which exude a sap from which incense and myrrh are derived), and the restricted patches of cultivated land, the territory of the Republic is devoid of vegetation. Cultivation is limited to small level patches of good soil on flat terraces alongside the river beds, on the floor and sides of the Wadi Hadhramaut, or where irrigation from wells and cisterns can be practised. The most productive areas are: Lahej, close to Aden town; two districts near Mukalla (about 300 miles east of Aden), and parts of the middle Hadhramaut. Irrigation from cisterns hollowed out of the rock has long been practised, and Aden town has a famous system of this kind, dating back many centuries.

The country must rely heavily on foreign subvention for any development. Less than 2 per cent of the territory is cultivable; the chief industrial activity is refining of imported oil at Aden, with a plant running much below capacity—though there is hope of exploiting offshore oil; and there are few native raw materials.

HISTORY

ADEN COLONY

When the Portuguese first rounded the Cape of Good Hope (1497–98), Aden was a port of some commercial importance, acting as a rendezvous for ships bound from India to the Red Sea and at the same time enjoying an active local trade with the Persian Gulf and the coast of East Africa. In 1513 the Portuguese, under Albuquerque, tried to capture the town, though without success. The Ottoman Turks, in their endeavour to deny the Portuguese access to the Red Sea, seized Aden in 1538, but their hold on the Yemen proved to be precarious. There was a serious revolt against the Ottoman régime in 1547–51 and a still more dangerous rebellion in 1566–70. When in the course of the seventeenth century the Ottoman state fell into decline, the authority of the Sultan over this distant region became little more than nominal, effective power in the Yemen passing now into the hands of local chieftains, the most notable of whom, after 1735, was the Sultan of Lahej. The discovery of the Cape route to India had greatly diminished the prosperity of Aden as a commercial entrepôt, but with the Napoleonic campaign in Egypt in 1798, Aden assumed strategic importance in Britain's plan of containment. In 1799 Britain occupied the island of Perim. Shortage of water compelled a withdrawal to the mainland where friendly relations were established with the Sultan of Lahej with whom later in 1902 a commercial treaty was concluded. However, the need to possess a base in these waters under the British flag doubled with the coming of the steamship. Negotiations began for the purchase of the island of Socotra, which in 1834 was temporarily occupied by the East India Company; they might have succeeded had not the relations with the Sultan suddenly deteriorated in 1837 following the plunder near Aden of a wrecked Indian vessel flying the British flag. The incident was followed by the despatch by the East India Company of a British force from Bombay, under the command of Captain Haines of the Indian navy, which, on January 16th, 1839, captured Aden. By the peace treaty, the Sultan was guaranteed an annual sum of 6,000 dollars and Aden became part of the British Empire, administered by the government of Bombay. The Sultan did not finally abandon his efforts to regain Aden until 1857 when permanent peace was established with Britain. Perim Island was ceded in the same year. The Kuria Muria Islands had already been acquired in 1854 from the Sultan of Oman. With the opening of the Suez Canal and the revival of the Red Sea route, Aden, which had been a free port since 1853, increased in importance. In the twentieth century, with the gradual replacement of coal by oil, Aden, closely linked to the Persian Gulf area, enhanced its historic position as a fuelling station. Aden's strategic value is also based on plentiful supplies of fresh drinking water from the artesian wells at Shaikh Othman.

In 1932, the administration of Aden passed to the Governor-General of India in Council; in April 1937,

it was vested in a separately appointed governor, who was also commander-in-chief, and who was assisted by an Executive Council. Crown Colony status had in fact been granted two years previously by the Government of India Act 1935. A Legislative Council for Aden, granted in 1944, was inaugurated in 1947. In 1955 the Aden Colony (Amendment) Order came into force, providing for an elected element in the Council; the first elections were held in December of the same year. Further constitutional changes were made in 1959. On January 4th, 1959, voting took place for the choice of 12 elected members of the Legislative Council. Nine Arabs, 2 Somalis and 1 Indian were elected to the Council. Large numbers of the Arab population boycotted the election.

On January 16th, 1961, Sir Charles Johnston, the Governor of Aden, announced to the Legislative Council of Aden that the (then) Colonial Secretary, Mr. Macleod, had approved a ministerial system of government for Aden and that members of the Executive Council in charge of administrative departments would soon assume ministerial status. The Governor also spoke of a possible closer association with the West Aden Protectorate and in particular with the Federation of Arab Emirates of the South. The Federation was renamed the Federation of South Arabia in April 1962. On November 30th, 1967, Aden and the Protectorate of South Arabia achieved independence under the name of the People's Republic of Southern Yemen.

SOUTH ARABIAN PROTECTORATE

Behind Aden and stretching some 600 miles along the coast is the territory of 20 former states whose rulers, between 1882 and 1914, entered into protective treaty relations with the British Government and acknowledged the authority of the Governor of Aden as Governor of the Protectorate. Many of the States later entered into closer treaty relations, and, while retaining independent control in the internal affairs of their respective territories, the rulers accepted the advice on administration offered by British Agents and Political Officers appointed by the Governor. Britain guaranteed protection to the States and they agreed not to cede territory to foreign powers.

EASTERN PROTECTORATE STATES

Formerly named the Eastern Aden Protectorate, the region covered by the States comprised the Hadhramaut (consisting of the Qu'aiti State of Shihr and Mukalla, and the Kathiri State of Sai'un), the Mahra Sultanate of Qishn and Socotra, the Wahidi Sultanates of Balhaf and Bir'ali, and the Sheikhdoms of Irqa and Haura. At July 1st, 1966, the total population of the area was estimated at 326,000. The Qu'aiti Sultan first concluded a protectorate treaty with Britain in 1888. In 1918 following an agreement between the Qu'aiti and the Kathiri Sultans, the latter accepted the protectorate treaty as extending to his State. Both Sultans agreed by further treaties, signed in 1937 and 1939, to accept the advice of a British Agent in all matters except those concerning the religion and custom of Islam. The British Agent for the Eastern Protectorate States was stationed at Mukalla in the territory of the premier chief, the Qu'aiti Sultan of Shihr and Mukalla. Both he and the Kathiri Sultan were constitutional rulers and were assisted by State Councils. Close co-operation existed between the two states in constitutional and in economic matters.

In 1949 an advisory treaty was concluded with the Wahidi Sultan of Balhaf. The Mahra Sultan of Qishn and Socotra signed a treaty of protection with Britain in 1866 and by it the Island of Socotra and the Abd Alkuri and Brothers Islands came within the protectorate.

WESTERN PROTECTORATE STATES

The former Western Protectorate comprised 17 states. Population at July 1st, 1966, was estimated at 570,000. Five of the States, in 1944 and 1945, agreed by advisory treaties with Britain to accept the advice of the Governor of Aden on administrative affairs— the Fadhli, the Lower 'Aulaqi and the Lower Yafa'i Sultans, the Sherif of Beihan and the Amir of Dhala. In 1952 similar treaties were signed by the Upper 'Aulaqi Sheikh and the 'Audhali Sultan; and a joint advisory and protectorate treaty was accepted by the newly elected Sultan of Lahej. The British Political Officers and the Arab Assistant Political Officers for the Western Protectorate States were under the supervision of the Assistant High Commissioner whose headquarters were in Al Ittihad, the Federal capital.

The British authorities, in 1954 and again in 1956, had discussed a plan of federation with local rulers in the West Aden Protectorate. On February 11th, 1959, the rulers of six (out of 17) states in the Western Protectorate signed a Federal Constitution and also a Treaty of Friendship and Protection with Great Britain. The British Government promised financial and military aid which would assist the Federation (embracing 'Audhali, Lower Yafa'i, Fadhli, Dhala, Beihan and Upper 'Aulaqi) to become eventually an independent state. The members of the Federation bound themselves not to enter into foreign relations of whatsoever kind without the approval of Great Britain. Lahej joined the Federation in October 1959, and Lower 'Aulaqi, 'Aqrabi and Dathina in February 1960. The Wahidi States of Balhaf and Bir Ali in the Eastern Aden Protectorate joined in 1962. Aden Colony became a member in January 1963, and Haushabi and Shaib joined in April. In 1965 there were three further accessions: the 'Alawi and Muflahi Sheikhdoms, and the Upper 'Aulaqi Sultanate. The new Federal capital was Al Ittihad near Bir Ahmed.

The U.K. met the cost of defence, including the R.A.F. and Protectorate levy establishments. Beside the security forces maintained by the U.K. Government there were tribal guards in the Western States partially supported by the States, and the Mukalla Regular Army maintained by the Qu'aiti State.

At the end of November 1961 the British Government handed over control of the Aden Protectorate

Levies to the Federation of Arab Emirates of the South. The Levies—which would be henceforth the Army of the Federation—had been formed in 1928 to protect Aden on the landward side and to provide garrisons for the Red Sea islands of Perim and Kamaran. An Arab force trained and commanded by British officers, the Levies consisted in 1961 of five infantry battalions, an armoured car squadron, and various signals and administrative units. The Levies came under the control of the Sultan of Lahej, who was Minister of Defence to the Federation, but command of the force still rested in the hands of a British officer as hitherto; for operational purposes the Levies were at the disposal of the G.O.C. Land Forces, Middle East.

ADEN AND THE YEMEN

Relations between the Protectorate and the neighbouring State of the Yemen were at all times delicate. Frequent encroachments led to the demarcation of frontiers which were accepted in a convention signed with the Ottoman government in March 1914. During the first World War, the Turkish troops from Yemen occupied the greater part of the Protectorate, and though in 1919 most of the chiefs resumed their treaty relations with Britain, the Imam of Sana'a, who exercised the principal religious authority in Yemen, being the most powerful of the Chieftains, maintained his claim to the entire territories. He sought to enforce it by occupying the Amiri district including the Radhfan tribes and parts of Haushabi, Sha'ibi and Upper Yafa'i territory, and the Audhali plateau. He also occupied territory not then within the Protectorate, the district of the Beidha Sultan. Britain continually repelled the Imam's advance and in 1928 he was compelled to withdraw from most of the Amiri territory. The Anglo-Yemenite treaty of peace and friendship was signed in February 1934, and was to be valid for 40 years; the two powers agreed to respect the *status quo,* and to negotiate for the classification of frontiers; Britain recognized the independence of the Yemen and the Imam agreed to evacuate the remainder of the Amiri district. In 1950 they agreed further to set up a frontier commission and to exchange diplomatic missions. In 1953 Yemen pressed her claims to the territories of the Aden Protectorate before the United Nations, and in subsequent years there was a series of border incidents. In December 1956 both tribesmen and Yemeni forces were reported to have raided villages in the Protectorate and made invasions into Western Aden. Similar incidents of varying degrees of importance continued until 1959. During this period there was a substantial flow of arms and technicians into the Yemen from the U.S.S.R. and its allies, and in March 1958 a formal union with the U.A.R. was announced. Britain sent troop reinforcements and R.A.F. units to repel these attacks, and in 1958 it established a separate military command in Aden. On two occasions the Yemen brought the dispute before the United Nations on the grounds that the U.K. was committing acts of aggression against her territory.

Incidents along the ill-defined frontier between Aden and the Yemen became less numerous in 1959, and relations improved in 1960.

In August 1962 the Yemen denounced the agreements reached at the London conference (discussed below), and reiterated its claim to the Aden territories. The revolution which broke out in the Yemen on September 27th, 1962, led to the establishment of a Republic of the Yemen. Colonel Sallal, the leader of the revolution, stated at this time that the new régime did not intend to press a claim to the Aden territories and hoped indeed for friendship with Britain. The U.S.S.R. and the U.A.R. recognized the republican régime almost immediately, and the United States followed suit in December, but Britain refused recognition. The new Yemen government frequently accused Britain of giving assistance to the Royalist resistance during the winter of 1962–63; the British legation at Taiz was closed, there were several minor conflicts in the border area, and another Yemen protest was made at the UN.

British and Federal forces carried out extensive military operations against dissident border tribesmen in 1964 and 1965; officials claimed these measures were necessary mainly because of unrest created by Yemeni agents. Direct clashes with Yemeni forces also occurred; the situation remained complex owing to the continuing presence of Royalist forces in the area. In 1964 Britain proposed that UN observers should patrol the border areas; the republican government, however, would not accept this, claiming that no frontier was necessary as Aden and the Federation all belonged by right to the Yemen. This attitude did not help relations during the independence negotiations or with the new Southern Yemen government.

CONSTITUTIONAL DEVELOPMENTS

In August 1960 Sir Charles Johnston became Governor of Aden in succession to Sir William Luce. The new Governor announced to the Legislative Council of the Aden Colony in January 1961 that a ministerial system was to be introduced into Aden. Sir Charles Johnston also noted that efforts were in progress to promote constitutional development within Aden and in particular to bring about a closer association between the West Aden Protectorate and the Federation of Arab Emirates of the South.

A constitutional conference, which included five Ministers from Aden and five from the Federation, met in London (July–August 1962) under the chairmanship of Mr. Duncan Sandys, the Colonial Secretary. The Aden Trade Union Congress and its political wing, the People's Socialist Party (both counted much on the support of Yemenis who worked in Aden and aimed at the ultimate union of the Yemen, Aden, the Federation and the other territories of the West Aden Protectorate) denounced the conference held in London. On July 23rd, 1962, they called a strike to protest against the composition of the existing Legislative Council of Aden and to demand a general election and the establishment of an autonomous government in Aden before further progress should be made towards union with the Federation of Arab Emirates.

The discussions undertaken in August 1962 led to a White Paper recommending the incorporation of Aden into the Federation as a constituent state. It specified that Britain would retain sovereignty over Aden and responsibility for its defence and internal security. These proposals were the principal features of a draft treaty between Britain and the Federation (re-named the Federation of South Arabia); Perim and the Kuria Muria islands, although administered by the governor of Aden, were to be excluded.

There was considerable opposition in Aden to incorporation into the Federation. Several political parties opposed the move, and strikes and demonstrations directed against it occurred throughout 1962. Serious riots coincided with the Aden Legislative Council's passing of the draft treaty in September. Nevertheless, Britain and the Federation duly signed the agreement in January 1963 and Aden formally became a member of the Federation later that month.

ADEN'S INCORPORATION IN THE FEDERATION

Aden's new government consisted of a nine-member Council of Ministers, all Adenis except for the British Attorney-General. Since its principal economic support remained British forces expenditure it could hardly expect to escape the suspicions of the radical Arab nationalist movements. In May 1963 representatives of the United Nations Committee on decolonization visited Yemen but were not allowed into Aden or the Federation. In July they issued a report which claimed that most of the population disliked "the repressive laws and police methods" of the government; it accused Britain of attempting to prolong its control whilst most South Arabians wanted union with the Yemen. Britain, of course, rejected the report. In the meantime two more states—the Haushabi Sultanate and the Shaibi Sheikdom—had joined the Federation, now 14 strong; on April 1st all customs barriers were abolished within the Federation, Aden remaining a free port.

In December 1963 an attempt to assassinate the High Commissioner in Aden killed two people and injured over fifty; a state of emergency was declared and large numbers of political activists were detained. Although no charges were made, several weeks elapsed before many activists were released, and much opinion in Aden and beyond clearly thought this police treatment was too harsh.

MOVES TOWARDS INDEPENDENCE

In June 1964 a constitutional conference was held in London and an agreement was signed whereby the Federation of South Arabia, inclusive of Aden, would become independent not later than 1968. Further discussions took place in London in August 1965, but the talks failed, and violence in Aden increased. It was estimated that between December 1963 and May 1966 60 people had been killed and 350 injured in Aden alone as a result of terrorism, one-third of the casualties being British. Meanwhile, in March 1965, Mr. Abd al-Qawi Makkawi became Chief Minister of Aden. However, in September 1965 the Aden Council of Ministers was dismissed, and the Colony's constitution suspended, because of mounting terrorism and the Council's failure either to condemn the terrorists or take any action against them.

POLITICAL REALIGNMENTS

The political scene in South Arabia, as viewed from the side of the nationalist elements, presented at this time an appearance of increasing confusion. The People's Socialist Party, led by Mr. Abdallah al-Asnag, had merged, in May 1965, with the Committee for the Liberation of Occupied South Yemen and with the South Arabian League to form the Organization for the Liberation of the Occupied South. A further development took place in January 1966, when the Organization for the Liberation of the Occupied South united with the National Front for the Liberation of the Occupied South, an extremist group operating from the Yemen with Egyptian support and responsible for the campaign of terrorism in Aden. Out of this new fusion of interests came the Front for the Liberation of Occupied South Yemen (FLOSY), in which political figures like Mr. Makkawi and Mr. al-Asnag now began to assume positions of prominence. The South Arabian League, however, declined to accept the prospect of complete absorption in a united nationalist movement and resumed its former independence. Over against these various nationalist forces stood the "traditionalist" elements, embodied in the sheikhdoms and sultanates of the South Arabia Federation (and also of the East Aden Protectorate).

Of great importance too, as a factor influencing the affairs of South Arabia was the situation in the Yemen, itself divided between tribesmen loyal to the old Imamate and supported by Saudi Arabia, and the republican régime maintained and controlled by Egypt—a situation, in short, which reflected in itself the confrontation of Egypt and Saudi Arabia for a dominant voice in the affairs of Arabia as a whole.

THE DEFENCE QUESTION

In February 1966 the British Government issued a White Paper on Defence, outlining future defence cuts, which declared that, when Aden became independent in 1968, all British forces would be withdrawn and concentrated at Bahrain in the Persian Gulf; it also made known that the British Government did not propose to enter into defence agreements with the newly independent state of South Arabia.

This announcement gave grounds for alarm to the sheikhdoms and sultanates embraced within the Federation that the National Guard of the Federation might be confronted in the future with a Yemen able to call on large numbers of Egyptian troops. The federal authorities sent a delegation to London, hoping to persuade the British Government to at least assist with the rapid strengthening of the federal forces and with the provision of equipment. In June the British Government offered to contribute as much as £5,500,000 towards the capital cost of expanding and re-equipping the armed forces of the Federation. It

also declared its readiness to continue its contribution (about £5,000,000) to the federal budget each year and to increase, to the extent of some £2,500,000, its share (hitherto about £4,600,000) in the maintenance of the federal troops. This aid was to continue for three years after independence, provided that no radical change occurred in the political situation of an independent South Arabia. The British Government still declined, however, to undertake the defence of South Arabia after it had won independence.

The extreme nationalist organizations had long advocated the acceptance in full of the UN resolutions passed in December 1963. Now, in May 1966, the Federal Government of South Arabia made known its readiness at last to take the resolutions as a basis for future action.

THE UN MISSION

In June 1966 the UN Committee on Colonialism urged that a United Nations Mission be sent to South Arabia to advise on the best means of giving effect to the UN resolutions of 1963 and 1965: resolutions which envisaged the granting of independence to South Arabia, the withdrawal of British forces, the return of political leaders in exile or in detention and the holding of elections under international supervision. In August 1966 the British Government declared that it welcomed the appointment of such a mission, but it insisted that it could not abandon its responsibilities for the maintenance of good order in South Arabia and that it was bound to observe the agreements which it had made with the local states existing in the area.

PREPARATIONS FOR INDEPENDENCE

In April 1967 Lord Shackleton, Minister without Portfolio, was sent to South Arabia to assist the High Commissioner in examining the possibilities for the establishment of a "caretaker" régime representing all the interested elements in South Arabia. The nationalist organizations continued, however, to reject all appeals for co-operation with the British and the federal authorities.

On June 20th, 1967, the British Government made known the measures that it intended to bring into effect. The date of independence was to be January 9th, 1968. To check the growing violence in South Arabia it was proposed to suspend trial by jury in respect of terrorist activities. On the other hand, the ban on the NLF was to be removed and consideration given to the possible release of some detainees. The British Government also declared that it would be willing to accept a draft constitution which the federal régime was now circulating to its member states. This constitution would prepare the ground for eventual elections on a basis of universal adult suffrage and for the establishment, as soon as circumstances allowed, of an administration representative of all the political elements in South Arabia. Regarding the problem of the uncommitted states in the East Aden Protectorate, Great Britain favoured their union with the Federation of South Arabia.

During July 1967 Britain continued her efforts to establish in Aden and the associated territories a broad-based provisional administration which should hold office until the moment of independence in January 1968. To facilitate the achievement of this aim the Federal Government consented to invite one of its own members, Mr. Bayumi, to form an interim administration with the aid, if possible, of FLOSY and the NLF. These nationalist organizations remained adamant, however, in their refusal to recognize the federal régime, which, in their view, reflected in its structure pre-eminently the interests of the local sultans. Mr. Bayumi's endeavour to gain the co-operation of the nationalist groups ended in failure and on July 27th the federal authorities relieved him of his appointment as Prime Minister designate.

Meanwhile, in South Arabia itself, during August to October 1967 the authority of the sultans crumbled rapidly before the advancing tide of nationalism. The swift advance of the NLF was due, not least of all, to the alignment on its side of a large measure of support amongst the local tribes against their traditional rulers, and also to the determination of the federal armed forces to maintain a neutral attitude. During September and October the NLF also moved into the territories of the Eastern Aden Protectorate, the sultanates of Qaiti, Kathiri and Mahra now passing under its influence. The High Commissioner announced on September 5th that Britain was now prepared to recognize the nationalist forces in general as representative of the local populations and would be willing to enter into negotiations with them.

THE CLASH BETWEEN NATIONALISTS

The collapse of the federal regime left the main nationalist organizations face to face. There had been discussions between them, under Egyptian auspices, at Cairo and in the Yemen, but without much sign of ultimate agreement. Now, the notable success of the NLF had done much to diminish the prospect before the Front for the Liberation of the Occupied South Yemen. This latter organization was under the disadvantage that it operated largely under Egyptian guidance and not in South Arabia itself, but from the Yemen. Its chief support in Aden had come from the numerous Yemeni elements formerly working there. Of adverse effect, too, was the fact that its leaders, Abdallah al-Asnag and Abd al-Qawi Makkawi, had been working from the Yemen as exiles during the past two years. The imminence of an Egyptian withdrawal from the Yemen also contributed to a decline in its influence.

With the federal structure now in ruins, the immediate question was whether or not the two main nationalist groups could be brought into mutual co-operation. Conflict soon broke out, however, between them, and fierce fighting developed in the northern suburbs of Aden during September. The South Arabian Army was able to enforce a brief ceasefire, and the rival organizations met in Cairo in October, but without any agreement. Fresh fighting then began, FLOSY being finally defeated when the Army high command joined forces with the NLF.

The latter then insisted that Britain should regard it as the sole valid representative of the people of South Arabia—a course of action which the authorities in London agreed to take on November 11th, 1967. On November 14th it was announced at Aden that Qahtan al-Shaabi, one of the founders of the NLF, would lead a delegation to Geneva to hold discussions with the representatives of Britain.

The evacuation of British troops from Aden had begun earlier on August 25th, 1967. As the situation unfolded itself in Aden, the British Government resolved to hasten the withdrawal of its forces and to advance the independence of South Arabia from January 9th, 1968, to a date if possible in the second half of November 1967. On November 27th, after the British troops had made over large areas of Aden to the armed forces of South Arabia, the NLF proclaimed the creation of the People's Republic of Southern Yemen. At Geneva, Qahtan al-Shaabi announced on November 28th that agreement had been reached with Great Britain over the cession of Aden and its associated territories. The last British troops in Aden were withdrawn on November 29th, 1967. Qahtan al-Shaabi, with the approval of the NLF, was appointed the first President of the Republic on November 30th. Unlike most former British dependencies, Southern Yemen did not join the Commonwealth.

[*Note:* Since Southern Yemen's independence the neighbouring Yemen Arab Republic has been sometimes referred to as "North Yemen".]

INDEPENDENCE

The withdrawal of the British troops meant a serious loss of revenue to the new Republic. To maintain the armed forces inherited from the era of British control would impose on the Republic a large expenditure. Moreover, the closure of the Suez Canal had brought about a great falling off in the entrepôt trade of Aden and in the bunkering of ships. The continuance, in the immediate future, of financial aid from Britain was therefore of prime importance to the new regime in Aden. During the negotiations in Geneva between Britain and the NLF in November 1967 the British representatives agreed to make available financial aid to South Arabia for a period of six months (December 1st, 1967, to May 31st, 1968) at a rate amounting to about £2 million per month, but subsequent British aid was rejected.

There was disagreement also between Southern Yemen and Britain over the Kuria Muria Islands. These islands, about 40 miles from the south coast of Arabia and 200 miles east of the border between Southern Yemen and the Sultanate of Muscat and Oman, had been handed over to Britain in 1954 and, though administered subsequently from Aden, had not been included formally within the Aden Protectorate. On November 30th, 1967, Britain had made known to the United Nations her intention to restore the Kuria Muria Islands to the Sultan of Muscat—a decision which gave rise to much bitterness amongst the members of the new government in Aden, which continued to claim these islands and also Perim and Kamaran.

INTERNAL DISSENSION

The administration of President al-Shaabi had to meet other serious difficulties also. In the first months of 1968 it had carried out a series of "purges" in the armed forces and the police of Southern Yemen. Discontent amongst the armed forces increased after the annual conference of the NLF convened at Zinjibar, east of Aden, in March 1968. The more extreme elements in the NLF were reported to have put forward at the conference resolutions designed to force the Government of Southern Yemen further to the left—amongst them resolutions calling for the appointment of political commissars to all army units, for the strengthening of the NLF militia and for the creation of "popular guards". A demand was also made, it would seem, at this conference, for the establishment of popular councils in all six of the governorates of Southern Yemen—these provincial councils having the right to elect a supreme council which would control the affairs of the new Republic. There was in March 1968 a real danger of conflict between the moderate and the extreme elements in the NLF. On March 20th the army intervened to bring about the dismissal of several ministers identified with the more radical section of the Front. The extremists indeed had been taking matters into their own hands in the eastern areas of the Republic. Here the radical elements had established popular councils of their own choice, ignoring the governors appointed from the central regime, ousting members of the armed forces and the police, and seizing the oil installations at Mukalla. The tensions thus generated showed no sign of a rapid abatement, and on May 15th, 1968, there was a short-lived rebellion in the region of Jaar, Abyan and Shuqra.

Another more serious uprising occurred at the end of July 1968, when two groups of armed rebels cut roads in the Radfan and Aulaqi districts north and east of Aden. The leaders of this rebellion were named as Colonel Abdullah Saleh al Aulaqi ("Colonel Sabaa"), formerly the NLF commander of security forces, and Brig. Nasser Buraik al Aulaqi, who until independence had been commander of the South Arabian Army. These risings were quickly crushed by NLF forces. Both FLOSY and the rival exiled political organization, the South Arabian League, claimed credit for this threat to the Government of President al-Shaabi. Although several members of the FLOSY High Command were captured during the campaign, the economic difficulties of the country continued to act as a serious threat to the stability of the new régime. These difficulties enforced drastic cuts in government expenditure during the summer of 1968.

NEIGHBOURING HOSTILITY

Relations with neighbouring states continued to be poor, and the government blamed all unrest within the country on elements operating from these states. FLOSY, operating from Yemen and now without its Egyptian support, the deposed sheikhs and sultans from the Federation (now mostly in Saudi Arabia), and the Sultan of Muscat and Oman with his British

advisers were claimed to be the most important of these. There were reports of large supplies of Soviet military equipment reaching Aden, some of which were displayed in military parades; units of the Soviet fleet visited Aden more and more frequently, while there were fewer visits by British or other Western naval vessels.

In June 1969 President al-Shaabi resigned following a reported power struggle; Salem Rubayi Ali, a former commando leader who had gone into semi-exile in the provinces after a dispute with the leadership, came to power as Chairman of a new five-man Presidential committee, and a new cabinet was formed which included several other exiles. The new regime was seen as even more left-wing and pro-Soviet than its predecessor.

In November 1969 the government announced the nationalization of 36 foreign firms, including shipping, insurance and commercial companies, but excluding the BP oil refinery at Little Aden.

In November 1970 a new Constitution was promulgated, changing the name of the country to the People's Democratic Republic of Yemen, with a view to possible Yemeni unity. However, relations with the other Yemen and with other neighbouring states failed to improve, and during 1972 the People's Democratic Republic seemed threatened on all sides. Omani forces attacked frontier posts of the Aden Government in its drive against the rebels in its Dhofar province. These were grouped under the Popular Front for the Liberation of Oman (PFLO) and were supported by the Aden Government. Forces of FLOSY and the South Arabian League were also reported to be gathering on the Yemeni borders. Saudi Arabia, as well as the Yemen Arab Republic, gives refuge to dissidents from the People's Democratic Republic, mainly because of the Aden Government's ideology.

In March 1974 the Arab League Foreign Ministers, meeting in Tunis, set up a conciliation commission in an attempt to end the long-standing conflict between the People's Democratic Republic and Oman over the support given by the Yemen P.D.R. Government to PFLO rebels in Oman.

POSSIBLE YEMENI UNITY

Serious fighting broke out on the border with the Yemen Arab Republic in September 1972, but an Arab League mission was able to mediate and a ceasefire became effective in October. A peace agreement on eventual unification of the two Yemens was signed in Cairo on October 28th. Further details were discussed in Tripoli (Libya) in November by the Presidents of the two Yemens, and it was agreed that the people of the Yemen would establish a single state, to be known as the Yemeni Republic, with Sana'a as its capital, Islam as the state religion and Arabic as the official language. Committees were set up to discuss details of the unification. Prospects for unity fluctuated, and by September 1973 the chances of union had become more remote, and the one-year period originally decided upon for unification was extended for another year. The subsequent coup in the Yemen Arab Republic in June 1974, when a pro-Saudi military junta gained control, made the union seem even more unrealistic. Subsequent events seemed to confirm this opinion, although the inter-Yemeni joint economic and financial committee continued to hold meetings. In the spring of 1975, however, the North Yemen Government accused Southern Yemen of "acts of sabotage" over the frontier.

The possibility of a fresh direction in foreign affairs opened up in March 1976, when the Yemen P.D.R. and Saudi Arabia established diplomatic relations. Saudi Arabia hitherto had not recognized Southern Yemen since its achievement of independence in 1967. The two sides declared that they wanted to normalize their relations in order "to guarantee the security and stability of the Arab peninsula and to serve the interests of the Arab nations while excluding foreign intervention". On the next day a ceasefire was announced between the Yemen P.D.R. and Oman, and although the fighting has virtually ceased, an uneasy peace exists.

INTERNAL TENSIONS

President Rubayi Ali had been inclining towards Peking in policy since his visit to China in 1970. He was at the same time, however, prepared to accept aid from Saudi Arabia and the West (hence the establishment of diplomatic relations with Saudi Arabia in March 1976). In contrast, Abdul Fattah Ismail, who had become Secretary-General of the NLF in 1971, favoured a much more pro-Soviet policy, and a rift grew up between them. In June 1975 the Vanguard (ex-Baathist) and the People's Democratic Union (Communist) parties were absorbed by the NLF to form the United Political Organization – National Front (UPONF), of which Abdul Fattah Ismail became Secretary-General. It was no secret that Abdul Fattah Ismail wanted to transform the National Front into a far more radical Vanguard Party during the first half of 1978, a move about which President Rubayi Ali was unenthusiastic.

The assassination of President al-Ghashmi of North Yemen on June 24th, 1978, provided the impetus which toppled President Rubayi Ali two days later. It was reported that al-Ghashmi was killed by a bomb in a suitcase carried by an envoy from South Yemen. Whether this was instigated by President Rubayi Ali, or, as seems more likely, was arranged by other forces in South Yemen to discredit President Rubayi Ali, the fact remains that Rubayi Ali was ousted and later executed. Heavy fighting ensued between troops loyal to Ali and the ruling party militias which continued even after the new President took power. The Prime Minister, Ali Nasser Muhammad, became interim Head of State, but there was no doubt that the power of Abdul Fattah Ismail had, for a time, been made more secure, and that South Yemen had moved further into the Soviet camp. At an emergency session of the Arab League, held on July 2nd, 1978, the 16 Arab countries present voted unanimously for an economic and political boycott of South Yemen. The "steadfastness" States, i.e. those

(of which South Yemen is one) which disagreed most strongly with President Sadat's peace initiative in visiting Israel, stayed away from the meeting. Quite apart from the question of whether South Yemen was responsible for al-Ghashmi's death, the more conservative Arab countries were concerned about South Yemen's growing links with the U.S.S.R., and the threat this posed to the situation in the Horn of Africa, where South Yemen had already been backing Ethiopia against Eritrean rebels and Somalia.

In July 1978 relations with the Yemen Arab Republic again reached crisis point, with South Yemen accusing its neighbour of invading its northern territory. Each subsequently accused the other of military build-ups along the border but the menace of outright war eventually subsided.

Abdul Fattah Ismail managed to hold on to his powerful position when the three parties within the National Front reorganized themselves into the Yemen Socialist Party in October. At the first session of the elected 111-member Supreme People's Council in December, Ismail was elected Chairman of the Presidium which was to replace the Presidential Council, and thus became Head of State. Extensive Cabinet changes took place in August 1979.

At the beginning of 1979 fierce fighting broke out between government forces and troops of the opposition movement, the United Front for South Yemen. At the same time there were reports of armed clashes between the followers of Prime Minister Muhammad and President Ismail and, simultaneously, between Ismail's supporters and supporters of the Defence Minister and, in another instance, those of the Minister of the Interior. In early February the airport at Beihan was reportedly under siege from rebels who had mutinied and joined the United Front Forces.

The continuing border skirmishes with the Yemen Arab Republic escalated into full-scale warfare in February and March. After one unsuccessful ceasefire, truce talks arranged by the Arab League ended, surprisingly, in a firm Unity agreement (see Yemen Arab Republic History). Practical realization of this unity seemed little closer by June 1982, even though pro-unity announcements were frequently made, and the two countries even agreed on a 136-article Constitution in January 1982, although it was to be submitted to a referendum in each of the two countries.

A change of leadership in South Yemen in April 1980 did not appear to weaken the desire for eventual unity. Abdul Fattah Ismail was replaced by the Prime Minister, Ali Nasser Muhammad, as Head of State and Secretary-General of the Yemen Socialist Party. A 20-year Treaty of Friendship between South Yemen and the U.S.S.R., signed in November 1979, seemed to strengthen the position of Abdul Fattah Ismail, but some reports speculated that Ismail was replaced because Moscow had lost confidence in him.

Under Ali Nasser Muhammad, South Yemen still remains staunchly pro-Soviet, although at the end of June 1980 Ali Nasser Muhammad visited Saudi Arabia at the invitation of King Khalid. This is in accord with theories that Ali Nasser Muhammad would like to cease relying solely on the U.S.S.R. and wants to end South Yemen's isolation from the Arab world. Ali Nasser Muhammad's rise also represents the consolidation of power of the faction who were born in South Yemen. Abdul Fattah Ismail was born in what is now the Yemen Arab Republic. Ali Nasser Muhammad's position was consolidated in October 1980 when his posts were confirmed at an Extraordinary Meeting of the Yemen Socialist Party.

During the spring of 1981 it was thought that Soviet influence in the country had increased, and in May 1981 Brig. Ali Ahmad Nasser Antar was removed from his post as Minister of Defence because, it was thought, he refused to take orders from Soviet advisers. He was later given the post of First Deputy Chairman of the Council of Ministers and Minister of Local Administration, a post which removed him from his power base with the army. In April 1982 the South Yemen Government signed an economic protocol with the U.S.S.R., by which the U.S.S.R. would help in construction work.

ECONOMIC SURVEY

The People's Democratic Republic of Yemen (PDRY) consists of the former British colony of Aden and the former Eastern and Western Aden Protectorates. The country covers about 130,000 sq. miles and the population was estimated to be 2,030,000 at mid-1981. The population has been growing at an average annual rate of almost 3 per cent since 1970. Lacking petroleum deposits, the country's average income is among the lowest in the Arab world but is believed to be rapidly increasing. According to tentative estimates by the World Bank, G.N.P. per caput was $370 in 1979. The most important town is Aden, with a population of 264,326 in 1973, followed by Mukalla in the east, with a population of about 50,000. The Governorates vary greatly in size and have changed their names and boundaries several times for administrative or political reasons. It was announced in 1980 that the Governorates (with their capitals) would be: Aden (Aden); Tuban (Hawtah); Abyan (Zinjibar); Shibwah (Ataq); Hadhramaut (Mukalla); Ghaydah (Ghaydah). The Governorates' finances and administration are centrally controlled, although the provincial councils are responsible for planning and finance on a local level.

Most of the population is concentrated in the west and one of the Government's most difficult tasks since independence has been to unite the various regions politically, administratively and economically. Whether political and economic union with the Yemen Arab Republic will be possible or successful is open to question. Little has so far resulted from efforts to achieve either political unification or economic co-operation.

Under British rule, the country was sustained by the position of Aden on the main shipping route to Europe from the Far East, India and East Africa via Suez. The British Petroleum refinery, completed in 1954, was the focus of industry and trade. In addition, the British troops stationed in Aden and the many foreign visitors who came ashore from ships calling at the port provided a market for services and luxury goods which encouraged local merchants and entrepreneurs and brought plenty of foreign exchange into Aden. This prosperity was, in the main, confined to the then Aden Colony where there was a boom in construction work between 1955 and 1965. The

British Government was more concerned with maintaining the Aden base and the port installations than with developing the hinterland although certain agricultural areas were developed during this period. The Abyan district, where development started in 1947, became one of the major cotton-producing areas and a similar scheme was carried out in Lahej in the 1960s. In the Hadhramaut, where there are fertile valleys in an otherwise barren area, the Governments of the states of Quaiti and Kathiri financed irrigation schemes and agricultural developments.

The closure of the Suez Canal in 1967 and the withdrawal of British troops in the same year, put an end to the Republic's commercial prosperity. Furthermore, British aid and military expenditure, which amounted to about £11 million in 1960, increasing to £36 million by 1967, and had more than covered the visible trade deficit, was discontinued after withdrawal, making it impossible for the Government to cover the budget deficit. In such a situation the Republic had no choice but to turn to other countries for sources of finance and technical aid to assist it in the transition from a service economy to one based on agriculture and manufacturing. The favourable terms offered by the Communist countries, coupled with a seeming lack of interest on the part of the West, made it inevitable that the Aden Government should turn to the Eastern bloc.

In November 1969 a decree was issued nationalizing all important foreign assets in the Republic, with the exception of the BP refinery, which was not taken over until 1977. This development, although a logical one in view of the regime's socialist leanings, nevertheless tended to frighten off firms which might otherwise have risked some investment, and made the Republic more than ever dependent on the Soviet Union, China and East Germany.

The Three-Year Development Plan (1971-74), although limited by shortage of funds, aimed at the creation, firstly, of a communications network, secondly the expansion of agricultural production and, thirdly, the establishment of small-scale light industries, based on locally produced raw materials. Some progress was made, notably in telecommunications, and it was estimated that about 80 per cent of the total allocation was invested.

The Five-Year Plan (1974–79) began in April 1974. Total capital investment in the Plan was set at 92 million dinars, preliminary allocations of 144 million dinars having been rejected as too ambitious, but this figure was later reduced to 75 million dinars. In the event, however, actual investment over the Plan period was estimated by the IMF at 39 million dinars per year. Special attention was paid to the development of fisheries and the oil industry. The Plan was drawn up with assistance from Soviet experts and most Eastern bloc countries and China promised extensive aid for projects.

The Second Five Year Plan (1979–83) was allocated 370 million dinars, or about 74 million dinars per year. Again the priority was increased productivity in manufacturing, fisheries and agriculture. In 1980, however, this Plan was abandoned and a revised Plan (1981–1985) was introduced. It had become clear that the targets set for increased productivity were unrealistic. The new Plan gives priority to making the best use of existing industries—the Aden oil refinery, the cement and salt industries and fisheries. Agricultural expansion is hampered by lack of water, and a number of studies, some already under way, for irrigation and water supply projects are included in the Plan. Projected investment under the revised Plan is 415 million dinars.

The main income is expected to come from increases in foreign aid, remittances from expatriates and increased traffic through Aden port. The Government is possibly justified in its faith in increased foreign remittances, which now amount to about $700 million per year, at least in the short term. These must still be channelled into development investment rather than personal expenditure. There are doubts about the level of foreign aid that can be obtained unless the Government is prepared to modify its political stance and seek aid from more varied sources. Aden port has not shown the regeneration expected after the re-opening of the Suez Canal. Uncertainties regarding sources of income thus contributed greatly to the revision of the Plan.

A study carried out by the World Bank proposed alternative strategies based on either a continuation of existing policies, in which case G.N.P. would be expected to increase by 5 per cent per year up to 1982, or increased liberalization of the economy to produce a growth rate of 9.7 per cent per year. In 1980 the Government carried out liberalization measures, chiefly aimed at helping farmers, fishermen and merchants. These measures were reinforced by the Law to Encourage Investment, introduced in February 1982. This law sought to induce Yemenis working abroad to invest their money in productive enterprises in South Yemen, by offering extensive tax concessions and guarantees against nationalization.

AGRICULTURE

The area of arable land in South Yemen is estimated at 405,000 hectares, only 1.4 per cent of the total land area, and a mere 121,000 hectares is actually under cultivation. The most intensively cultivated areas are Abyan, east of Aden, and Lahej, north of Aden. The river valleys of the Hadhramaut area are also fertile and relatively well-developed. The Kuwait Fund for Arab Economic Development (KFAED) financed a pre-investment study of the Abyan delta and in May 1974 agreed to lend 4.2 million Kuwaiti dinars to help finance land reclamation and irrigation in the area. Bulgaria is also aiding the project. The Abyan Dam project began in 1974 and is now completed. The IDA has provided loans worth $7 million to develop agriculture in the Hadhramaut and $8 million for agricultural development in Wadi Beihan. The Government is giving priority to several agricultural projects and an Agricultural Fund provides economic assistance to farmers. Considerable foreign assistance (mainly from the Eastern bloc, Arab and UN sources and the Kuwait Fund) continues to be given in the form of finance and technical aid projects, such as irrigation development and the introduction of new farming methods and equipment.

Cotton is produced mainly in Lahej and Abyan. The government-controlled Abyan Board supervises the whole process of growing and marketing and has its own ginnery at El Kad. Cotton is also produced in other areas and the Cotton Producers' Associations were the most flourishing co-operatives in the country. The area under cotton has been declining, in spite of cash incentives offered to growers, with an estimated 12,000 hectares devoted to cotton in 1980, as against 14,000 hectares in 1971. Two more ginneries are planned, as well as a cottonseed oil factory at Maalla.

The Republic is able, on the whole, to meet local demand for most vegetables but imports onions, potatoes and fruit. The main fruits and vegetables grown are tomatoes, carrots, salad vegetables, bananas and melons. Bananas in particular are produced in quantity and the Food and Agriculture Organization has recommended an expansion of banana-growing, provided export markets can be found. In 1980 the banana crop was estimated at 22,000 metric tons.

Wheat is grown mainly in the Hadhramaut and Beihan but is not enough for the country's needs. The balance is imported mainly from Australia. Other cereals produced include barley, millet and sorghum. Cereal production was estimated at 117,000 metric tons in 1980, a slight improvement over previous years. Tobacco is grown in the coastal areas, mainly in the Ghail Ba Wazir area. Livestock production has remained fairly static for the last ten years and considerable numbers of sheep and goats have to be imported to satisfy local meat demand.

The resources available at present are not sufficient to finance agricultural development schemes over the whole country and efforts are being concentrated in the Lahej, Abyan, Beihan and Hadhramaut areas. In the east, the developments most likely to take place are the expansion of tobacco growing and the development of the fishing industry, with Mukalla as its centre. In recent years agricultural production has been severely disrupted by weather conditions. Because of drought in 1976 and 1977, recourse to food aid was necessary. In 1977 the UN World Food Programme gave $5 million in aid for drought victims and $4.5 million for a school meals programme while Japan provided rice aid of over $800,000 equivalent.

FISHERIES

The Arabian Sea fishing grounds are the Republic's greatest potential source of wealth. Most of the 10,000 fishermen fish only in territorial waters, their equipment is often poor and efficient marketing of the catch is impossible with the present state of communications. In 1979, however, co-operatives were permitted to sell 40 per cent of their catch direct to the market at a significantly higher price than that paid by the National Fish Marketing Corporation. The main species caught are the Indian oil-sardine, Indian mackerels and cuttlefishes. Cuttlefishes are important to the export market, while there is much potential for increased sales of mackerels and tuna to the domestic market. Since 1973 exports of fish have taken a very encouraging turn and several foreign countries are involved in developing the industry. The total catch rose from 36,813 metric tons in 1975 to 64,143 tons in 1976, slumped to 48,053 tons in 1978, but recovered to 75,393 tons in 1980.

The national fishing fleet has 16 deep-sea fishing boats provided by the U.S.S.R., Japan and China. Local fishermen, who are organized into 13 co-operatives, operate smaller coastal vessels while independent fishermen fish in one-man boats. A Soviet-Yemeni company and two Japanese companies are currently fishing in Yemeni waters. On the processing side there are two fish canning factories, at Mukalla and Shukra, a fishmeal factory (with another due to go into production) and a fish freezing plant at Mukalla. Soviet contractors are at work on the development of Hedjuff fishing port, to be completed by 1985. A project, financed by Libya, to develop a two-berth general cargo and fishing harbour at Mukalla is now underway. According to UN and Soviet sources, fishing provides the main hope for developing an export-based industry in the country. Exports of fish and fish products are estimated to be worth about 20 million per year.

INDUSTRY

The BP refinery, which accounted for over 80 per cent of the country's total industrial output, was taken over in Spring 1977 by the Aden Refinery Company, a partnership between the Yemeni National Petroleum Company and the Saudi Arabian state oil company, Petromin. The refinery, which was built by BP in 1954 with a capacity of some 8 million tons per year, was badly affected by the closure of the Suez Canal in June 1967. In recent years it had been running at only about one-half of its capacity. BP is believed to have been glad to dispose of it, because it was not an economic proposition. Compensation will be paid at book value, with BP's 40 expatriate employees at the refinery being retained under a management, technical and marketing services contract. In April 1979 BP turned bunkering facilities over to the Government. The bunkering operation had a turnover of only 100,000 tons, compared with 2.5 million tons in 1967. The refinery is to be expanded under the revised Second Five Year Plan to produce light-grade products. The terminal will be dredged to take tankers of up to 500,000 tons.

The future of the Aden oil refinery, the PDRY's only large industrial complex, is of paramount importance to the country's economic development. Its relative decline is highlighted by recent trade figures. Between 1970 and 1973 the export of petroleum products in value terms fell from 45 million dinars to 28.4 million dinars, the latter representing 72 per cent of a much reduced total export bill of 39.4 million dinars, compared with 63 per cent of exports totalling 49.7 million dinars in 1967. Imports of crude petroleum for the refinery fell from 33.3 million dinars (44.6 per cent of total imports valued f.o.b.) to 23.7 million dinars in 1973, representing 44.3 per cent of an almost equally reduced import total. With the large increase in petroleum prices, product exports appeared to soar—but only in value terms—in 1974, standing at 78.7 million dinars or 94 per cent of total exports, while imports of crude petroleum, costing 73.3 million dinars, represented 58.6 per cent of the total import bill in the same year. There was an obvious fall in any terms in 1975, when exports of petroleum products stood at only 59.9 million dinars (93 per cent of total exports) and the necessary crude imports at only 44.2 million dinars (45.9 per cent of total imports). Subsequently exports of petroleum products fell still further to 50.9 million dinars in 1976 and 46.5 million dinars in 1977. Crude imports were 76.1 million dinars in 1976 and 58.6 million dinars in 1977.

The Government intends to give priority to oil prospecting and, to this end, has offered very favourable terms to oil companies. Exploration agreements were first signed with East German and Soviet firms, and Western participation was also welcomed; a Canadian firm was awarded a concession in 1975. A joint Yemeni/Algerian company did some prospecting in the Hadhramaut but went into liquidation in 1976. In 1977 Agip, the refining and distribution subsidiary of the Italian state agency ENI, signed an offshore oil exploration agreement, and Siebens Oil and Gas began drilling in the Samaha offshore concession. In June 1979 ENI signed a long-term agreement for the exploration and production of petroleum and natural gas in two more zones, one on-shore and one offshore, covering 15,000 sq. km. An American firm, Hunt Oil, is also interested in exploration, and the Brazilian company Braspetro was awarded an offshore concession in 1982.

Saudi Arabia has agreed to finance the construction of an oil terminal on the Hadhramaut coast, connected by pipeline to the Saudi Arabian oilfields.

Industrial developments are planned to take the form of agro-industries. The Three-Year Development Plan envisaged the establishment of a textile industry based on local cotton; fruit and vegetable processing and canning plants; a cigarette factory; fish-canning plants and a tanning industry. This last would be particularly suitable since skins are at present exported in the raw state and there is much wastage.

Some progress has been made, with China building a textile factory and a cigarette factory going into operation in 1973. The Chinese-built textile mill, opened in 1975, has a capacity of 7.2 million metres of cloth per year. The factory is, however, running into maintenance difficulties because of its reliance on Chinese-manufactured spare parts. An agreement signed in 1980 with Czechoslovakia provides for expansion of the mill to make polyester fabrics.

Existing industries (in Aden) are: the manufacture of cement blocks, tiles and bricks; salt production; soft drinks bottling and dairy plants. In the western Governorates there are also cotton ginneries, flour mills and seed-crushing plants. The fishing industry (see above) centres on Mukalla. Consultants are working at the possibility of a $75 million cement plant, to be located in Abyan, possibly using the extensive limestone deposits reported to exist to the east of Aden. A feasibility study is being carried out by the U.S.S.R. to evaluate limestone and clay deposits. The German Democratic Republic is helping with the establishment of factories making flour, biscuits, vegetable oil and animal fodder. A tomato purée factory, capable of producing 1,500 tons per year, started operating in 1976. An agricultural implements factory set up in 1976 is being expanded.

Known mineral resources are few but the country has not yet been fully explored. Prospecting for copper and other minerals started at the end of 1975. Experts from several countries have conducted surveys. A British firm—Hunting Surveys—won a $1.5 million contract in 1976 to carry out a mineral survey in a 1,300 sq. km. area to the south-west of Mukalla. Copper deposits have already been reported, and beach sands have been investigated. The first phase of this work was completed in late 1977 and a second phase contract has been awarded, worth $1.8 million, with finance from the ADFAED. Prospects for a commercially viable mineral deposit still seem very doubtful although surveys in Wadi Ghabar and the Eastern Governorates indicate the presence of a number of minerals, including copper, lead, zinc and molybdenum.

All mineral and raw material sources in the country were declared publicly-owned in August 1973.

TRANSPORT AND COMMUNICATIONS

Several international airlines visit Khormaksar airport (formerly an RAF base), which has been extended and improved with Soviet assistance. Another airport is planned at Riyan; the KFAED is providing half the cost of $27 million. The Democratic Yemen Airlines Company provides an air link with Yemen and other neighbouring countries. The company has had significant commercial success. Aden port handles nearly all the Republic's trade, as well as some of that of the Yemen Arab Republic. Transit trade to Yemen, however, has declined owing to the development of the port of Hodeida. The free port of Aden attracted a large volume of traffic and all the commercial activities associated with a large port flourished, providing comfortable livings for the

Adeni merchants but contributing little to the development of the other sectors of the economy. The disadvantages of a free port in the changed situation after 1967, not least the hindrance to industrial development caused by the lack of protective tariffs, led the Government, after much deliberation, to remove Aden's free port status, although there is still a free zone for transit trade.

In view of the disastrous effect of Aden's stagnation on a precarious economy, the Government viewed the re-opening of the Suez Canal in June 1975 with a satisfaction verging on jubilation. Plans for the port include dredging, improvement of mooring and repair facilities; expansion of the duty-free shopping zone and the construction of tourist facilities. The scheme is being financed by the World Bank, the Arab Fund for Economic and Social Development and Libya. As it turned out, the increase in traffic fell short of expectations. It was reported in early 1976 that only 150 ships per month were now calling at the port compared with 100 per month before the canal was re-opened. There had been optimistic forecasts that up to 500 ships per month would use the port once the Suez Canal link was re-opened. There was some further recovery in activity during 1977, and in October a 15 per cent surcharge was introduced. Cargo traffic increases when Hodeida or Jeddah is congested, but the fuel bunkering activity is only a fraction of pre-1967 levels and Aden has also lost the passenger transit trade. By 1980 the port was handling about 200 ships per month, still less than a third of its capacity.

Aden is an important cable communications centre. The Soviets have built a radio station in Aden, and the Greeks another station in Mukalla. In March 1978 the U.K. firm Cable and Wireless was nationalized by the Yemen Telecommunications Corporation (YTC), which plans to replace existing equipment with a satellite system.

There are good roads round Aden and motorable tracks throughout the western area. A new road has been built, with massive Chinese aid, between Aden and Mukalla. A 92-km. road from Naqubah to Nisab is being built with finance from the IDA, KFAED and the OPEC Development Fund. Some 22,400 vehicles were in use in the country in 1976, including over 11,900 private cars and 10,500 commercial vehicles.

FOREIGN TRADE

The trade deficit continued to grow up to 1969. Government austerity measures and the lack of foreign exchange reduced imports in 1970 by over £7 million but exports continued at much the same level. In 1971 and 1972 both imports and exports declined but the value of imports, particularly of oil products, rose steeply after 1973 as a result of increased oil prices and general inflation. The Government was forced to call on the International Monetary Fund's oil facility. The trade balance deteriorated further up to 1978, when a fall in imports to 109.6 million dinars and a rise in exports to 76.4 million dinars left a smaller deficit than in previous years, at 33.2 million dinars. In 1979 imports rose to 121.3 million dinars, but exports also increased to 85.8 million dinars. The main commodities exported (excluding petroleum products) are cotton, hides and skins, dried fish, rice and coffee. The chief imports (excluding petroleum) are clothing, foodstuffs and livestock. The drop in petroleum trade was particularly significant, as it made reduction of activity at the refinery inevitable, with consequent repercussions on the whole fragile economy. In 1966, bunkering made up a third of total exports, but by 1970 this proportion had fallen to less than 7 per cent. Petroleum products are now chiefly exported to markets in Africa and Asia rather than Europe.

FINANCE AND FOREIGN AID

The Republic has had difficulty in maintaining financial stability since independence. In December 1966 international reserves amounted to $62.4 million. By the end of 1970 they were $59.3 million. In the same period, the budget deficit grew from 100,000 dinars to over 4 million dinars. This deficit was substantially cut in 1971, largely because more foreign grants were obtained, but expenditure still had to be held down with adverse effects on development. The situation was considered to be so serious in 1972 that the salaries of many government employees were cut by anything from 15 to 50 per cent and restrictions were placed on foreign travel. By the end of 1973 the situation was a little better and international reserves were $76.0 million. In 1975 the International Monetary Fund agreed to the purchase of SDR 7.25 million to help with balance of payments problems and general inflation. The overall payments deficit in 1974 was $24 million but the Government's measures, combined with the IMF aid, were having their effect by 1976 and the economy was being brought under control. At the end of 1975 reserves (excluding gold) had fallen to $54.0 million, including drawings of $27.7 million on IMF facilities, but by the end of 1976 reserves had recovered to $81.5 million, with IMF drawings having increased to $42.8 million. The situation continued to improve in subsequent years. At the end of 1979 reserves were $209.7 million, with IMF drawings at $24.0 million. By the end of 1981 reserves had risen to $254.5 million, while IMF drawings were only $4.4 million. Development expenditure for 1981 was set at 114 million dinars ($338 million), compared with 91 million dinars for the previous year. Total projected budget expenditure for 1980 was 194 million dinars.

In the absence of recent trade figures, it must be assumed that the increase in net reserves reflects foreign aid flows resulting in part from the general *détente* with neighbouring Middle Eastern countries. The IMF, to which the country is now heavily committed, is continuing to watch over the economy. A study team sent by the IMF in 1978/79 recommended a move away from strict leftist policies towards a restimulation of the private sector. In 1980, in response to this pressure, the Government introduced measures to stimulate private enterprise and the free market economy. Remittances from expatriate workers have become such an important factor in the

economy that in 1982 the Government offered expatriates tax concessions and guarantees against nationalization if they would invest in South Yemen. Remittances are estimated at around $700 million per year.

The abrupt cessation of British aid to the Republic after the withdrawal of troops in November 1967 caused a crisis which enabled the communist bloc to step into the breach. The Soviet Union, under an agreement of February 1969, which included aid specifically for fisheries, undertook to provide technical aid and experts for a number of development projects. A separate agreement, signed in August 1969, covered aid for agriculture and irrigation. The first agreement was extended in February 1970 to include aid in kind worth 5.5 million roubles and, most important of all, a low-interest loan of 7 million roubles repayable over 12 years. This loan was significant in that actual financial aid was offered rather than aid in the form of goods or technical assistance. The U.S.S.R. was reported to have offered a further loan of 18 million roubles in 1976. Five hospitals, including a children's hospital and a maternity home, are being built with Soviet aid. The U.S.S.R. is also considering the finance of several projects included in the Second Five-Year Plan, notably a power station for Aden and further modernization of the port. In 1979 a loan of 24 million roubles was made for development projects, which included mineral surveys and agricultural development. Soviet contractors are engaged in the Hedjuff fishing port project and the building of Hiswa power station. South Yemen has also benefited from infrastructural work carried out by the U.S.S.R. in connection with its military facilities in the country.

The German Democratic Republic agreed to a loan of $22 million in October 1969 and China granted a $18 million loan in 1970, both part of large aid and trade "package deals". Both covered a wide range of projects, including, in the case of the German Democratic Republic, the construction of telephone facilities and the establishment of light industries; and, in the case of China, help with the road-building programme. Most of the communist bloc countries have offered aid to the Republic, particularly for communications projects such as the Aden television station built with Czech aid. Large development loans were obtained in 1979 from Bulgaria and Czechoslovakia, while China lent a further $12.5 million for the purchase of industrial goods.

The richer Arab states are also a major source of aid. In the early 1970s their contribution was on a fairly small scale, although Kuwait provided 4.2 million Kuwaiti dinars for agricultural development in the Abyan delta, Algeria granted $4 million worth of development aid, Libya agreed a loan of 5.8 million dinars, and Iraq gave a $5 million interest-free loan in 1974 and a further $10 million loan the following year. In 1975 the Government launched a diplomatic offensive to improve relations with the rich Gulf states. A grant of $5 million was forthcoming from Kuwait, the United Arab Emirates agreed to finance a minerals survey, and the Abu Dhabi Fund for Arab

Economic Development granted aid for the fishing industry. Since then, aid from Arab countries has sharply increased, despite occasional contretemps, especially with Saudi Arabia. In 1977, in addition to aid mentioned in previous sections, Kuwait agreed to provide $13.5 million for hospital building, the Saudi Fund for Development offered $20 million equivalent for electricity projects and also agreed on assistance for a housing scheme in Al Mansoura. The $28 million Wadi Hadhramaut electricity scheme, for which bids were invited in 1978/79, is being financed by Kuwait, Saudi Arabia, Libya and the World Bank. Libya is also involved in financing the Mukalla harbour development and the Aden sewerage project. Iraq pledged further development aid in 1979. Algeria and Abu Dhabi have agreed to finance the Al-Mansoura power station project, to be completed by 1983, and KFAED and the OPEC Fund for International Development have both committed $10.5 million for road building. The Islamic Development Bank, of which South Yemen became a member in 1977, loaned $5.5 million

for the Aden Water Supply scheme in 1981 and $12 million to finance oil imports in 1982.

The Republic's relations with the West have deteriorated not only because of the British refusal to continue aid, but as a result of the *rapprochement* with the Eastern bloc countries. The main sources of aid, other than the socialist countries and the Arab states, have been the United Nations and the World Bank. The IDA has provided funds for road building, agriculture and rural development, as well as over $10 million for education and training schemes. One of the country's main difficulties is lack of trained manpower, manifested in the shortage of staff to run statistical departments and to collect information on the economy. The manpower does exist—the number of civil servants almost doubled between 1973 and 1977—but most of the trained people are abroad where the rewards are greater. There are serious labour shortages also in the manual trades such as repair work and construction. A number of countries have offered training schemes for Yemenis to study abroad

STATISTICAL SURVEY

AREA AND POPULATION

(Census of May 14th, 1973)

	GOVERNORATES							TOTAL
	First	Second	Third	Fourth	Fifth	Sixth	Thamoud	
Population ('000) .	291	273	311	162	451	61	41	1,590
Area (sq. miles) .	2,695	4,929	8,297	28,536	32,991	25,618	27,000	130,066*

* 336,869 sq. km.

Estimated Population ('000 at mid-year): 1,797 in 1977; 1,853 in 1978; 1,910 in 1979; 1,969 in 1980; 2,030 in 1981.

Capital: Aden (population 264,326 in 1973).

The Governorates were re-organized in March 1980 and reduced to six.

EMPLOYMENT

(1976)

TOTAL	AGRICULTURE AND FISHING	MINING AND QUARRYING	MANUFACTURING	CONSTRUCTION	ELECTRICITY, GAS AND WATER	COMMERCE	TRANSPORT	SERVICES	MISCELLANEOUS
370,655	182,065	2,232	15,824	16,797	3,145	27,955	14,575	87,220	20,842

AGRICULTURE
PRINCIPAL CROPS
(FAO estimates)

	AREA ('ooo hectares)			PRODUCTION ('ooo tons)		
	1978*	1979*	1980	1978*	1979*	1980
Millet	40	45	45	65	70	73
Wheat	15	15	15	18	25	25
Barley	2	2	2	2	2	2
Sesame seed . . .	5	5	5	4	4	4
Cottonseed . . .	} 12	12	12	{ 9	9	8
Cotton (lint) . . .				4	4	4

* Unofficial estimates.

Source: FAO, *Production Yearbook.*

LIVESTOCK
(FAO estimates, year ending September)

	1978	1979	1980
Cattle . .	100,000	110,000	120,000
Sheep . .	870,000	970,000	980,000
Goats . .	1,180,000	1,300,000	1,350,000
Asses . .	160,000	160,000	165,000
Camels . .	100,000	100,000	100,000

Source: FAO, *Production Yearbook.*

LIVESTOCK PRODUCTS
(FAO estimates, metric tons)

	1977	1978	1979	1980
Mutton and lamb . .	6,000	6,000	6,000	6,000
Goats' meat . .	5,000	5,000	5,000	5,000
Cows' milk . .	7,000	7,000	7,000	7,000
Sheep's milk . .	11,000	11,000	12,000	12,000
Goats' milk . .	24,000	24,000	25,000	25,000
Hen eggs . .	1,500	1,600	1,600	1,700

Source: FAO, *Production Yearbook.*

FISHING
('ooo metric tons, live weight)

	1975	1976	1977	1978	1979	1980
Marine fishes	31.0	48.6	48.5	43.1	42.6	65.8
Cuttlefishes	5.8	15.5	15.5	5.0	9.0	9.6
TOTAL CATCH . . .	36.8	64.1	64.0	48.1	51.6	75.4

Source: FAO, *Yearbook of Fishery Statistics.*

MINING
('ooo metric tons)

	1974	1975	19,6	1977*	1978*	1979*
Salt (unrefined)	75	75	75	75	75	75

* Estimate.

INDUSTRY
SELECTED PRODUCTS

		1976†	1977†	1978†	1979†
Salted, dried or smoked fish . . .	metric tons	1,100	1,100	1,100	n.a.
Motor spirit (Petrol)	'ooo metric tons	84	209	210	224
Kerosene	,, ,, ,,	100	100	140	410
Jet fuel	,, ,, ,,	261	160	160	160
Distillate fuel oils	,, ,, ,,	297	374	404	410
Residual fuel oil	,, ,, ,,	819	956	923	950
Electric energy*	million kWh.	223	233	242	245

* Figures refer to Aden only.   † Estimates.

Source: United Nations, *Yearbook of Industrial Statistics.*

FINANCE
1,000 fils = 1 Yemeni dinar (YD).

Coins: 1, 2½, 5, 25 and 50 fils.

Notes: 250 and 500 fils; 1, 5 and 10 dinars.

Exchange rates (May 1982): £1 sterling = 635.0 fils; U.S. $1 = 345.4 fils.

100 Yemeni dinars = £157.48 = $289.52.

Note: Before independence (November 30th, 1967) the currency unit was the South Arabian dinar (SA dinar), introduced in April 1965 with a value of £1 sterling, then worth U.S. $2.80. On November 18th, 1967, the pound and dinar were both devalued to $2.40 ($1 = 416.67 fils). Following independence the SA dinar was replaced by the Southern Yemen dinar (called the Yemeni dinar since 1971), with the same value. The exchange rate (1 dinar = $2.40) remained in force until August 1971. Between December 1971 and February 1973 the rate was 1 dinar = $2.6057 ($1 = 383.77 fils). The present dollar valuation has been effective since February 1973. The dinar was at par with the pound sterling until the latter was allowed to "float" in June 1972.

BUDGET
('ooo dinars, April 1st to March 31st)

REVENUE	1971/72	1972/73	1973/74*	EXPENDITURE	1971/72	1972/73	1973/74*
Taxes on personal income	1,050	1,078	1,221	General administration .	1,152	1,886	2,693
Taxes on corporate income . .	2,712	1,388	1,952	Defence and security† .	9,184	9,798	10,444
Other taxes . .	195	132	134	Public works and communications .	1,146	1,041	1,076
Import duties . .	5,869	4,406	5,143	Economic services .	1,886	1,154	1,550
Excise duties . .	872	1,269	2,170	Education . . .	2,615	2,711	3,836
Stamp duties . .	405	378	432	Health . . .	1,013	996	1,152
Other indirect taxes .	423	387	526	Agriculture . . .	417	417	491
Non-tax revenue . .	3,550	2,100	3,763	Pensions . . .	287	376	276
Other receipts . .	910	908	—	Local authorities . .	389	365	458
				Other services . .	2,646	2,937	756
TOTAL . .	15,986	12,046	15,341	TOTAL . .	20,735	21,681	22,732

* Estimates.   † Including expenditure of the Ministry of the Interior.

Source: United Nations, *Statistical Yearbook.*

1974/75 ('ooo dinars): Revenue 18,130; Expenditure 27,450.   **1978/79** ('ooo dinars): Revenue 46,510; Expenditure 61,400.
1975/76 ('ooo dinars): Revenue 13,860; Expenditure 25,550.   **1979/80** ('ooo dinars): Revenue 54,210; Expenditure 76,160.
1976/77 ('ooo dinars): Revenue 25,710; Expenditure 39,150.   **1980/81** ('ooo dinars): Revenue 86,020; Expenditure 96,020.
1977/78 ('ooo dinars): Revenue 34,890; Expenditure 47,370.

Revised Five-Year Plan (1980-85): Total proposed expenditure 425 million dinars.

COST OF LIVING
(Consumer Price Index for Aden.   Base: 1970 = 100)

	1971	1972	1973	1974	1975	1976	1977
Food . . .	107.5	112.3	139.6	171.7	184.9	189.6	191.5
Fuel and light . . .	102.0	108.0	111.0	156.0	202.0	207.0	216.0
Clothing . . .	100.9	123.9	131.2	216.5	283.5	320.2	356.9
Rent . . .	100.0	90.0	75.0	75.0	75.0	75.0	75.0
ALL ITEMS . .	105.7	110.5	128.6	159.0	178.1	184.8	194.3

Source: International Labour Office, *Year Book of Labour Statistics.*

BALANCE OF PAYMENTS
(U.S. $ million)

	1975	1976	1977	1978	1979	1980
Merchandise exports f.o.b. . . .	19.7	44.3	46.9	39.4	38.8	59.6
Merchandise imports f.o.b. . . .	−171.1	−257.4	−344.2	−367.1	−387.1	−598.1
TRADE BALANCE. . . .	−151.4	−213.1	−297.3	−327.7	−348.3	−538.5
Exports of services . . .	35.6	47.5	51.5	61.4	79.0	112.9
Imports of services . . .	−37.3	−50.1	−72.7	−75.3	−98.7	−142.7
BALANCE ON GOODS AND SERVICES .	−153.1	−215.7	−318.5	−341.6	−368.0	−568.3
Private unrequited transfers (net) .	58.8	119.3	187.3	254.8	311.5	347.1
Government unrequited transfers (net)	10.1	46.3	55.0	40.2	24.9	84.0
CURRENT BALANCE . . .	−84.2	−50.1	−76.2	−46.6	−31.6	−137.2
Long-term capital (net) . . .	31.3	57.9	66.4	82.6	52.1	78.9
Short-term capital (net) . . .	9.6	26.1	−24.0	−11.6	−35.3	24.6
Net errors and omissions . .	16.2	−20.5	46.8	42.5	35.9	71.4
TOTAL (net monetary movements) .	−27.2	13.5	13.1	66.9	21.1	37.8
Allocation of IMF Special Drawing Rights .	—	—	—	—	5.5	5.6
Valuation changes (net) . . .	−1.9	−1.2	2.5	13.1	5.3	−10.9
IMF Subsidy Account grants . .	—	0.2	0.7	0.7	0.7	0.7
IMF Trust Fund loans . .	—	—	3.6	11.1	11.4	9.6
CHANGES IN RESERVES . .	−29.1	12.5	19.9	91.8	44.0	42.8

Source: IMF, *International Financial Statistics.*

EXTERNAL TRADE
(million dinars)

	1974	1975	1976	1977	1978	1979	1980
Imports c.i.f. . .	144.6	111.5	142.4	187.9	198.7	319.4	527.4
Exports f.o.b. . .	78.7	59.3	61.2	62.4	66.7	161.4	269.0

Source: IMF, *International Financial Statistics.*

PRINCIPAL COMMODITIES
('000 dinars)

	IMPORTS*			EXPORTS*		
	1975	1976	1977	1975	1976	1977
Food and live animals	21,940	22,235	28,450	2,592	5,640	7,527
of which: Wheat and wheat flour	3,606	5,398	6,051	3	—	—
Rice	4,673	3,072	3,315	—	—	—
Refined sugar	4,757	2,349	2,882	—	—	—
Fresh fish	—	—	—	1,472	3,907	5,844
Coffee	—	—	—	669	1,170	1,209
Beverages and tobacco	955	1,242	1,312	65	112	183
Crude materials (inedible) except fuels	1,970	2,531	2,928	1,021	4,301	1,963
of which: Cotton lint and seed	—	—	—	472	3,565	1,263
Petroleum products	11,641	21,189	22,082	24	5,262	5,807
Animal and vegetable oils and fats	683	730	1,222	6	34	8
Chemicals	2,785	3,221	3,488	24	28	4
Basic manufactures	10,602	11,368	15,182	75	39	18
Machinery and transport equipment	10,316	20,103	42,231	21	6	230
Miscellaneous manufactured articles	1,198	2,393	4,434	59	70	30
TOTAL (inc. others)	62,144	85,107	121,329	3,906	15,496	15,773

* Excluding imports and exports of foreign-owned companies. Total imports of crude petroleum (in million dinars) were: 44.2 in 1975; 76.1 in 1976; 58.6 in 1977. Total exports of petroleum products (in million dinars) were: 55.4 in 1975; 51.0 in 1976; 52.5 in 1977; 59.2 in 1978; 152.8 in 1979; 255.4 in 1980.

Source: Middle East Economic Digest, September 28th, 1979.

PRINCIPAL TRADING PARTNERS
('000 dinars)

IMPORTS*	1976	1977	1978	EXPORTS*	1976	1977	1978†
Australia	3,149	5,734	6,434	China, People's Republic.	473	2	773
China, People's Republic.	4,374	2,976	8,693	Djibouti	507	99	129
Germany, Fed. Republic.	1,724	2,579	5,109	France	286	145	696
Iraq	3,979	8,931	5,728	Germany, Fed. Republic.	790	111	82
Italy	1,782	9,010	3,806	Italy	1,211	659	686
Japan	9,390	21,166	12,940	Japan	3,593	6,017	1,688
Kuwait	11,331	11,621	11,521	Saudi Arabia	202	341	633
Netherlands	3,321	6,350	10,952	Singapore	1,079	628	223
Singapore	1,657	3,469	4,306	Sri Lanka	907	30	47
Thailand	2,154	3,025	7,273	Sudan	3	587	—
U.S.S.R.	3,503	6,023	6,040	Yemen Arab Republic.	5,117	5,279	809
United Kingdom	10,853	13,682	16,364				
TOTAL (incl. others)	85,106	121,447	122,768	TOTAL (incl. others).	14,498	15,769	7,635

* Excluding petroleum (other than trade of the Yemen Kuwait Terminal Company) and exports by foreign-owned companies.

† Excluding exports by the Yemen Kuwait Terminal Company (5,093,000 dinars).

Source: Middle East Economic Digest, June 6th, 1980.

TRANSPORT
ROAD TRAFFIC
(motor vehicles registered)

	1973	1974	1975	1976
Passenger cars	10,600	10,700	11,600	11,900
Commercial vehicles . . .	7,900	8,100	9,900	10,500

INTERNATIONAL SEA-BORNE SHIPPING
PORT OF ADEN

	1966	1969	1973	1976	1977
Number of ships	6,246	1,568	1,320	2,336	2,605
Displacement ('ooo net reg. tons) .	31,425	8,089	5,565	9,944	10,738
Transit passengers	146,000	2,519	—	—	—
Dry cargo imported ('ooo metric tons) .	647	406	312	387	618
Dry cargo exported ,, ,, ,,	184	99	65	80	79
Oil imports . . . . ,, ,,	8,072	6,068	3,342	1,779	1,811
Oil exports . . . . ,, ,,	3,985	5,584	2,724	1,311	1,294
Oil bunkers . ,, ,, ,,	3,486	387	388	638	658

Source: Middle East Economic Digest, September 28th, 1979.

CIVIL AVIATION
(1975)

AIRCRAFT MOVEMENTS	PASSENGERS			FREIGHT (kilos)	
	Arrivals	Departures	Transit	Inward	Outward
6,376	91,051	85,432	22,829	1,019,044	863,258

EDUCATION
NUMBER OF SCHOOLS
(1974/75)

Primary schools	1,036
Intermediate schools	105
Secondary schools	19
Teachers' colleges for males . .	2
Teachers' colleges for females . .	1
Technical institutes . . .	1

Source (except where otherwise stated): Central Statistical Office, Central Planning Commission, Aden.

THE CONSTITUTION

Before the 1970 constitution was drawn up existing ordinances and regulations remained in force, with Presidential authority replacing the powers of the British and Federal Governments. The National Front general command, which had 41 members, formed the interim legislative authority. The country is divided into eight (later six) administrative Governorates. The two-year term of office granted to the National Front expired on November 30th, 1969, and was formally renewed for another year. Following the adoption of the new constitution on November 30th, 1970, a Provisional Supreme People's Council of 101 selected members took over legislative powers.

Amendments to the Constitution allowing for the formation of the Yemen Socialist Party were approved by the Supreme People's Council in October 1978. General elections took place in December 1978 for a 111-member Council which subsequently elected a Presidium, whose Chairman became Head of State. In March 1979 a constitutional commission from both the People's Democratic Republic of Yemen and the Yemen Arab Republic was appointed to draw up a Constitution for a unified state. A 136-article Constitution was produced which has yet (June 1982) to be submitted to a referendum in each country.

THE GOVERNMENT

HEAD OF STATE

President: ALI NASSER MUHAMMAD (appointed April 21st, 1980, and confirmed by the Supreme People's Council April 27th 1980).

PRESIDIUM OF THE SUPREME PEOPLE'S COUNCIL

(elected May 16th, 1982)

Chairman: ALI NASSER MUHAMMAD.
Secretary-General: MUTLAQ ABDULLAH HASAN.
Members: SAID SALEH SALEM, SULTAN MUHAMMAD AD-DOSH, AIDA ALI SAID, ALI AHMAD NASSER AS-SALAMI, FARES SALEM AHMAD, Dr. MUHAMMAD AWAD AS-SA'ADI, TAHA ALI SALIH, RASHID ABU BAKR AL-MIHDHAR.

COUNCIL OF MINISTERS

(June 1982)

Prime Minister: ALI NASSER MUHAMMAD.
First Deputy Prime Minister and Minister of Local Administration: ALI AHMAD NASSER ANTAR.
Deputy Prime Minister and Minister of Fish Resources: ANIS HASAN YAHYA.
Deputy Prime Minister: ALI ABDUL RAZZAQ BA DIB.
Minister of Defence: Brig. SALIH MUSLIH QASIM.
Chairman of People's Security Committee: MAHDI ABDULLAH SA'ID.
Minister of Foreign Affairs: SALIM SALIH MUHAMMAD.
Minister of Interior: Col. MUHAMMAD ABDULLAH AL-BATANI.
Minister of State for Cabinet Affairs: ABDULLAH AHMAD GHANIM.
Minister of Health: Dr. ABDULLAH AHMAD BIKAYR.
Minister of Construction: HAYDAR ABU BAKR AL-ATTAS.

Minister of Finance: MAHMUD SAI'D MAHDI.
Minister of Labour and Civil Service: NASR NASIR ALI.
Minister of Culture and Tourism: RASHID MUHAMMAD THABIT.
Minister of Education: HASAN AHMAD AS-SALLAMI.
Minister of Communications: ABDULLAH MUHAMMAD AZIZ.
Minister of Agriculture and Agrarian Reform: MUHAMMAD SULAYMAN NASIR.
Minister of Industry: ABDUL QADIR BA JAMMAL.
Minister of Justice and Waqfs: KHALID FADL MANSUR.
Minister of Trade and Supply: AHMAD UBAYD AL-FADLI.
Minister of Planning: Dr. FARAJ BIN GHANIM.
Minister of Housing: AHMAD MUHAMMAD AL-QA'TABI.
Chairman of State Committee for Information: MUHAMMAD ABDUL QAWI.

LEGISLATURE

SUPREME PEOPLE'S COUNCIL

Consists of 111 members, elected December 1978.
Chairman of Presidium: ALI NASSER MUHAMMAD.
Secretary-General: MUTLAQ ABDULLAH HASAN.

POLITICAL PARTY

Yemen Socialist Party: Aden; f. October 1978 as successor to United Political Organization—National Front (UPO-NF); Marxist-Leninist "Vanguard" party based on "scientific socialism"; has Political Bureau (5 mems. and 2 candidate mems. *see* below), Executive Cttee. (8 mems. and 3 candidate mems.), Secretariat (5 mems.), Appeals Cttee. (6 mems.), Information Cttee. (10 mems.) and Central Cttee. (47 mems. and 11 candidate mems.); Chair. ABDUL FATTAH ISMAIL.

POLITICAL BUREAU

Secretary-General: ALI NASSER MUHAMMAD.
ALI AHMAD NASSER ANTAR.
ABU BAKR ABDUL RAZZAQ BA DIB.
SALIH MUNASSAR AS-SIYAYLI.
ABDUL GHANI ABDUL QADIR.
ALI SHAYI HADI (Candidate member).
Dr. ABDULLAH AHMAD AL-KHAMIRJ (Candidate member).

DIPLOMATIC REPRESENTATION

EMBASSIES ACCREDITED TO THE PEOPLE'S DEMOCRATIC REPUBLIC OF YEMEN

(In Aden unless otherwise stated)

Albania: *Ambassador:* SULEJMAN TOMCINI.
Algeria: Sana'a, Yemen Arab Republic.
Bangladesh: Baghdad, Iraq.
Belgium: Cairo, Egypt.
Bulgaria: Khormaksar; *Ambassador:* ATANAS SAMSAREV.
Canada: Jeddah, Saudi Arabia.
China, People's Republic: 145 Andalus Gardens, Khormaksar; *Ambassador:* TANG YONG.
Cuba: 36 Socotra Rd., Khormaksar; *Ambassador:* ULISES ESTRADA LASCALLE.
Czechoslovakia: Qasem Hilal St., Khormaksar; *Ambassador:* I. VOLES.
Denmark: Jeddah, Saudi Arabia.
Ethiopia: Abdulla Assaidi St., Ma'alla; *Ambassador:* HUSAYN ISMAIL HUSAYN.
France: Sayhut St., Khormaksar; *Ambassador:* C. JEANTELOT.

German Democratic Republic: Khormaksar; *Ambassador:* RAINER NEUMANN.

Germany Federal Republic: 49 Abyan Beach Rd., Khormaksar; *Chargé d'affaires:* K.-G. SCHON.

Guinea: Addis Ababa, Ethiopia.

Hungary: Tumnah St.; *Ambassador:* L. BENCZEKOVITS.

India: Premjee Chambers, Tawahi; *Ambassador:* MUHAMMAD ALI KANGA.

Iraq: Miswat St., Khormaksar; *Ambassador:* TAHA AZIZ HUSSEIN.

Italy: Tawahi; *Ambassador:* M. PETROCELLI.

Japan: Crescent Hotel, Steamer Point; *Ambassador:* TOSHIO YAMAZAKI.

Jordan: Sana'a, Yemen Arab Republic.

Korea, Democratic People's Republic: Khormaksar; *Ambassador:* KIM UNG.

Kuwait: Sana'a, Yemen Arab Republic.

Lebanon: Sana'a, Yemen Arab Republic.

Libya: Airport Rd., Khormaksar (People's Bureau); *Secretary:* SALIM MUHAMMAD HUSSAIN.

Mongolia: Cairo, Egypt.

Netherlands: Cairo, Egypt.

Pakistan: 34 Kassim Hilal, Khormaksar; *Chargé d'affaires:* M. NAZIRUDDIN.

Poland: Cairo, Egypt.

Romania: Abyan Beach Rd., Plot No. 106, Khormaksar; *Chargé d'affaires:* (vacant).

Saudi Arabia: *Chargé d'affaires:* A. R. ALTHEMY.

Somalia: Britannic Court, Dolphin Square, Ma'alla; *Ambassador:* MUHAMMAD JAMA ELMI.

Spain: Addis Ababa, Ethiopia.

Sudan: Tawahi; *Chargé d'affaires:* S. A. SALEH.

Sweden: Addis Ababa, Ethiopia.

Switzerland: Addis Ababa, Ethiopia.

Syria: Sana'a, Yemen Arab Republic.

Tanzania: Addis Ababa, Ethiopia.

Uganda: Addis Ababa, Ethiopia.

U.S.S.R.: Abyan Beach Rd., Khormaksar; *Ambassador:* VLADISLAV ZHUKOV.

United Kingdom: 28 Shara Ho Chi Minh, Khormaksar; *Chargé d'affaires a.i.:* M. T. McKERNAN.

Viet-Nam: 110 Awadh Al-Saaidy St., Khormaksar; *Ambassador:* LEE QUANG KHAI.

Yugoslavia: Mogadishu, Somalia.

Zambia: Cairo, Egypt.

The People's Democratic Republic of Yemen also has diplomatic relations with Afghanistan, Angola, Austria, Djibouti, Greece, Grenada, Guyana, Iran, Jamaica, Kampuchea, Kenya, Malta, Mexico, Nicaragua, the Philippines, Senegal, Seychelles and Turkey.

JUDICIAL SYSTEM

The administration of justice is entrusted to the Supreme Court and Magistrates' Courts. In the former Protectorate States Muslim law and local common law (Urfi) are also applied.

President of the Supreme Court: NAJIB SHAMIRI.

RELIGION

The majority of the population are Muslim but there are small Christian and Hindu communities.

THE PRESS

DAILY

14 October: P.O.B. 4227, Aden; not published on Saturdays; f. 1968; Editorial Dir. FURUQ MUSTAFA RIFAT; Chief Editor AHMAD ABDUL RAHMAN BIKR.; circ. 20,000.

WEEKLIES

Ar-Rayah (*The Banner*): Aden; f. 1980.

Al-Thawri: P.O.B. 4227, Aden; published on Saturday; mouthpiece of Central Committee of the Yemen Socialist Party; Chair. ZAKI BARAKAT.

Qadaya al-Asr (*Issues of the Age*): Aden; f. 1981; publ. by Central Committee of Yemen Socialist Party.

MONTHLY

Al-Thaqafa al-Jadida: P.O.B. 1187, Aden; f. Aug. 1970; a cultural monthly review issued by the Ministry of Culture and Tourism; Arabic; circ. 3,000.

NEWS AGENCIES

Aden News Agency (ANA): P.O.B. 1207, Tawahi, Aden; f. 1970; government-owned; Dir.-Gen. NAJIB MUHAMMAD IBRAHIM.

FOREIGN BUREAU

Agentstvo Pechati Novosti (APN) (*U.S.S.R.*): Aden; Correspondent NIKOLAI Y. LEVCHENKO.

PUBLISHER

14 October Corporation for Printing, Publishing, Distribution and Advertising: Aden; is under control of State Committee for Information; Chair. and Gen. Man. SALIH AHMAD SALAH.

RADIO AND TELEVISION

State Radio and TV Commission: Aden; f. 1979; Chair. HASAN AHMAD AS-SALLAMI; is under control of State Committee for Information.

RADIO

Democratic Yemen Broadcasting Service: P.O.B. 1264, Aden; transmits 100 hours a week in Arabic; Dir.-Gen. for Broadcasting: JAMAL AL-KHATIB; there are about 150,000 receivers in the country.

TELEVISION

Democratic Yemen Broadcasting Service: P.O.B. 1264, Aden; programmes for four hours daily, mainly in Arabic; other series in English and French. Dir.-Gen. UMAR ABDUL-AZIZ MUHAMMAD. There are about 25,000 receivers.

FINANCE

CENTRAL BANK

Bank of Yemen: P.O.B. 452, Aden; replaced Yemeni Currency Authority 1972; cap. p.u. 500,000 YD; Governor SALIM MUHAMMAD AL-ASHWALI; publ. *Annual Report.*

COMMERCIAL BANK

National Bank of Yemen: P.O.B. 5, Crater, Aden; f. 1969 by nationalizing and amalgamating the local branches of the seven foreign banks in Aden; cap. p.u. 1.25 million YD; total resources 85.4 million YD (December 1978); Gen. Man. Ayoob Nazir A. Wahed; 21 brs.

INSURANCE

All foreign insurance interests were nationalized in November 1969.

National Insurance and Re-insurance Co.: P.O.B. 456, Aden; Lloyd's Agents.

TRADE AND INDUSTRY

National Chamber of Commerce and Industry: P.O.B. 473, Crater; 4,000 mems.; Pres. Abdelrehman al-Sailani; Sec. Monasar Bazara; Gen. Man. Abdulla Salem Khader.

National Company for Foreign Trade: Crater, Aden; f. 1969; incorporates main foreign trading businesses, and arranges their supply to the National Company for Home Trade; Gen. Man. Hussein Abu Bakr.

National Company for Home Trade: Crater, Aden; f. 1969; marketing of cars, electrical goods, agricultural machinery, building materials and general consumer goods; incorporates the main foreign trading businesses which were nationalized in 1970; Gen. Man. Abdul Rahman al-Sailawi.

TRADE UNION

General Confederation of Workers of the People's Democratic Republic of Yemen: P.O.B. 1162, Ma'alla, Aden; f. 1956; affiliated to WFTU and ICFTU; 35,000 mems.; Pres. Sultan Muhammad ad-Dosh; Gen. Sec. Abdul Razak Shaif; publ. *Sout A Omal* weekly; circ. approx. 4,500.

CO-OPERATIVES AND MARKETING

There are 65 co-operative societies, mostly for agricultural products; the movement was founded in 1965 and is now the responsibility of the Ministry for Agriculture and Agrarian Reform.

STATE ENTERPRISE

Yemeni National Oil Co: P.O.B. 5050, Aden; sole petroleum concessionaire, importer and distributor of oil products in the country; Gen. Man. Taha Ahmed al-Ahdel.

TRANSPORT

ROADS

Yemen Land Transport Company: Aden; f. 1980; incorporates former Yemen Bus Company and all other local public transport; Chair. Abdul Jalil Tahir Badr.

Aden has 140 miles (225 km.) of roads, of which 127 miles (204 km.) have bituminous surfacing. There are 6,382 miles (10,270 km.) of rough tracks passable for motor traffic in the hinterland, of which 716 miles (1,152 km.) have bituminous surfacing.

SHIPPING

Yemen Maritime Lines Company: P.O.B. 1228, Steamer Point, Aden; founded 1970 following nationalization and amalgamation of foreign shipping companies; freight and passenger services; branch in Mukalla,

agents at Berbera (Somalia) and Mocha and Hodeida (Yemen Arab Republic); Aden Coasters, an affiliate, provides services for trans-shipment via Aden Free Zone to the Red Sea ports, East Africa and Bombay; Gen. Man. Ahmad Salih as-Sallam.

Yemen Ports Department: Aden; f. 1888; state administrative body; Dir.-Gen. Abdulla Muhammad Aziz. Aden Main Harbour has 20 first-class berths. In addition there is ample room to accommodate vessels of light draught at anchor in the 18-foot dredged area. There is also 800 feet of cargo wharf accommodating vessels of 300 feet length and 18 feet draught. Aden Oil Harbour accommodates four tankers of 57,000 tons and up to 40 feet draught.

CIVIL AVIATION

Alyemda (*Democratic Yemen Airlines*): P.O.B. 6006, Alyemda Bldg., Khormaksar, Aden; f. 1971 as wholly owned Corporation by the Government; passenger and cargo services to Abu Dhabi, Addis Ababa, Djibouti, Jeddah, Kuwait, Mogadishu, Sharjah, Nairobi and Bombay; fleet: one Boeing 707-320C, one 720B, three Dash 7, five DC-3; Gen. Man. Saeed Nagi Sinan.

Other companies operating services include the following: Aeroflot (U.S.S.R.), Air Djibouti, Air India, Ethiopian Airways, Kuwait Airways, MEA (Lebanon), Saudia, Somali Airlines, Yemen Airways (Yemen Arab Republic).

Aden Civil Airport is at Khormaksar, 7 miles (11 km.) from the Port. It was established in 1952, and is operated by the Civil Aviation Department.

DEFENCE

Commander of the General Staff: Abdullah Ali Nasr.

Commander of Militia National Command: Salih Ahmad al-Bakhti.

Commander of Air Force: Abdullah Ali Alaywah.

Commander of Naval Forces: Ahmad Abdullah Muhammad.

Defence Expenditure: 43.9 million dinars (1980).

Total Armed Forces: (July 1981) 24,300: army 22,000, navy 1,000, air force 1,300.

EDUCATION

The educational system consists of four years of Primary, three years of Intermediate and four to six years of Secondary schooling. There are 225 Government Primary Schools, 29 Intermediate Schools and 6 Secondary Schools, and a Technical Institute at Ma'alla, Aden, with a branch at Little Aden. Other higher education is received abroad.

In addition there are 12 Government-Aided and 5 Private Primary Schools, and 10 Grant-Aided and 4 Private Intermediate Schools. Teacher-Training Centres provide over 200 places for men and women trainees while adult education is provided by evening classes.

BIBLIOGRAPHY

Brinton, J. Y. Aden and the Federation of South Arabia (American Soc. of Int. Law, Washington, 1964).

Central Office of Information. Aden and South Arabia (London, H.M.S.O., 1965).

COLONIAL OFFICE. Accession of Aden to the Federation of South Arabia (London, H.M.S.O., 1962).

COLONIAL OFFICE. Treaty of Friendship and Protection between the United Kingdom and the Federation of South Arabia (London, H.M.S.O., 1964).

FEDERATION OF SOUTH ARABIA. Conference on Constitutional Problems of South Arabia (H.M.S.O., 1964).

GAVIN, R. J. Aden 1839–1967 (Hurst, London, 1973).

GEHRKE, Dr. ULRICH. Südarabien, Südarabische Föderation oder Süd-Jemen? (*Orient* Magazine, German Near and Middle East Association, Hamburg, 1967).

HARDING, H. LANKESTER. Archaeology in the Aden Protectorate (London, H.M.S.O., 1964).

HICKINBOTHAM, Sir TOM. Aden (London, Constable, 1959).

INGRAMS, DOREEN. A Survey of the Social and Economic Conditions of the Aden Protectorate (London).

INGRAMS, W. H. A Report on the Social, Economic and Political Conditions of the Hadhramaut, Aden Protectorate (London, 1936).

JOHNSTON, CHARLES. The View from Steamer Point (London, Collins, 1964).

KING, GILLIAN. Imperial Outpost–Aden (New York, Oxford University Press, 1964).

KOUR, Z. H. The History of Aden, 1839-1972 (London, Frank Cass, 1980).

LITTLE, TOM. South Arabia (London, Pall Mall Press, 1968).

MAWER, JUNE KNOX. The Sultans Came to Tea (Murray, London, 1961).

PAGET, JULIAN. Last Post: Aden 1964–67 (Faber and Faber, London, 1969).

QAT COMMISSION OF INQUIRY. Report (Aden, 1958).

TREVASKIS, Sir KENNEDY. Shades of Amber, A South Arabian Episode (London, Hutchinson, 1967).

VAN DER MEULEN, DANIEL. Hadramaut: Some of Its Mysteries Unveiled (Leiden, 1932, reprinted 1964).

WATERFIELD, GORDON. Sultans of Aden (Murray, London, 1968).

PART FOUR

Other Reference Material

A

Abbas, Ferhat; Algerian politician; b. 24 Aug. 1899, Taker, Constantine; ed. Algiers Univ.

Formerly a chemist at Sétif; Leader of *Association des Etudiants musulmans* 26-31; took part in org. of the Algeria People's Union 38; published "Manifesto of the Algerian People" 43; founded Amis du Manifeste et de la Liberté (A.M.L.) 44; under detention May 45-March 46; took part in the formation of the Union Démocratique du Manifeste Algérien (U.D.M.A.) 46; elected rep. to French Constitutional Assembly 46, later mem. of French Union Assembly; elected to Algerian Assembly 48 and 54; Leader of U.D.M.A. 46-56; joined Nat. Liberation Front (FLN) 55; mem. FLN del. to Eleventh Gen. Assembly of UN 57; Prime Minister of Provisional Government of the Algerian Republic (GPRA) in Tunisia 58-61; Pres. of the Chamber of Algeria 62-63; detained July 64-June 65.
Publs. *Le jeune algérien* 31, *La nuit coloniale* 62.
2 rue Arago, Algiers, Algeria.

Abboud, Gen. Ibrahim; Sudanese officer and politician; b. 1900; ed. Gordon Memorial Coll., Khartoum and Military Coll., Khartoum.

Entered Sudan Defence Force; served 39-45 war with Sudanese contingent, British Army in Eritrea, Ethiopia and Libya; Dep. C.-in-C. Sudanese Army 54, C.-in-C. 56-64; Pres. Supreme Military Council, Prime Minister and Minister of Defence 58-64.
Suakin, Sudan.

Abdalla, Ismail-Sabri, PH.D.; Egyptian economist; b. 25 Dec. 1924, Malawi; ed. Abdin and Khedive Ismail schools, Cairo and Paris Univs.

Lecturer, Alexandria Univ. 51-54, Cairo Univ. 54-56; Econ. Adviser, Econ. Devt. Org. 57-59; Chief Editor *Dar Al-Maarif* Publishing House 65-69; Dir.-Gen. Inst. of Nat. Planning 69-71, Chair. of Board 72-, Dir.-Gen. May 75-; Deputy Minister of Planning 71, Minister of State for Planning 72-74, Minister 74-75; Deputy Chair. of Board, Soc. Egyptienne d'Econ. politique, de statistique et de législation 72-; mem. Gov. Council Soc. for Int. Devt. 76-, Vice-Pres. 79-; founding mem. and now Chair. Third World Forum; fmr. mem. Board now Chair. Council for the Devt. of Econ. and Social Research in Africa; mem. UN Cttee. for Devt. Planning and Special Adviser to Exec. Dir. of UN Environment Programme for co-ordination of the Mediterranean Blue Plan; Co-ordinator UN Univ. Project: Arab Alternative Future; mem. Exec. Cttee. Int. Foundation for Devt. Alternatives.
Publs. *Economie et Structure Economique* 52, *Lectures in Economics* (Arabic) 54, *The Organization of the Public Sector* (Arabic) 69, *Confrontation with Israel* (Arabic) 69, *Political Papers* (Arabic) 72; *Towards a New Economic World Order* (in Arabic) 76; various articles in Arabic, English and French.
Third World Forum, P.O. Box 43, Orman, Cairo; Home: 6 Ibn Malek Street, Guizeh, Egypt.

Abdalla, Sayed Abdel Rahman, M.B.A.; Sudanese politician and diplomatist; b. 1933, Abu Hamad; ed. Khartoum Univ. Coll. and School of Admin. and New York Univ.

Joined Ministry of Interior, Sub-Mamour 56; Inspector, Tokar district, later of Kassala Province; joined Halfa People's Settlement Comm. 59; Dir. Inst. of Public Admin. 63-65; Dir. UN African Admin. Training and Research Inst., Morocco 65; Dir. Nat. Inst. of Public Admin., UN, Libya; fmr. Chair. Sudan Public Service Council, Kenana Sugar Project, Sudan; fmr. mem. Sudan Supreme Judicial Council of Sudan Comm. of resettlement of population made homeless by the Aswan Dam; Deputy Minister of Local Govt. Aug. 71; Minister of Public Service and Admin. Reform 71-77, of Industry and Mining 77, of Communications 77-78, of Transport 78; Deputy Dir. and Officer-incharge, Div. of Devt. Admin., UN Dept. of Tech. Cooperation, New York 79-80; mem. Exec. Bureau, Sudanese Socialist Union, Asst. Sec.-Gen. 78-79; Perm. Rep. of Sudan to UN 80-.
Permanent Mission of Sudan to the United Nations, 210 East 49th Street, New York, N.Y. 10017, U.S.A.

Abdel-Ghani, Abdul-Aziz, M.A.(ECON.); Yemeni economist and politician; b. 4 July 1939, Haifan, Yemen Arab Repub.; ed. Colorado Coll. and Colorado Univ.

Minister of Health 67-68, of Economy 68-69, 70-71; Chair. Technical Office, Board of Planning 69-70; Gov. Central Bank of Yemen 71-75; Prime Minister 75-80; mem. Presidential Council; Second Vice-Pres.; Vice-Chair. Cttee. for second Five-Year Plan April 81-.
P.O. Box 38, Sana'a, Yemen Arab Republic.

Abdelghani, Col. Mohamed Ben Ahmed; Algerian army officer and politician; b. 18 March 1927, Ghazouet, Oran region; primary and secondary educ. in Algiers.

Joined nationalist movement, Parti du Peuple Algérien 43; arrested and imprisoned 45-46; joined Nat. Liberation Front (FLN) at start of war for nat. independence 54; Commdr. of First Mil. Region (Algiers) 62-65, Fourth Mil. Region (Ouargla) 65-67, Mil. Region of Constantine 67-74; promoted Col. 69; mem. Revolutionary Council 65-79, Political Cttee. of FLN Jan. 79-June 80, June 81-; Minister of the Interior 74-79; Prime Minister March 79-.
Office du Premier Ministre, Palais du Gouvernement, Algiers, Algeria.

Abdel Meguid, Abdel Razzaq, PH.D.(ECONS.); Egyptian politician; b. 4 May 1931, Alexandria; ed. Faculty of Commerce, Alexandria Univ., Univs. of Birmingham and Oxford.

Director of Regional Planning, Aswan Governorate 60-62; Visiting Prof., Texas Univ. 62; Dir. Research Dept., Bank of Alexandria 63; Chief Expert, Ministry of Planning; Minister of Planning April-Oct. 77, 78-80; Deputy Dir., then Dir. Foreign Investment Authority; Asst. Sec.-Gen. UN, Developing Countries Div. Dec. 77; Deputy Prime Minister for the Economy May 80-Jan. 82.
Publs. numerous books on the social and economic aspects of the Egyptian governorates, on economic planning and development and banking in the Middle East.
Council of Ministers, Cairo, Egypt.

Abdel Meguid, Ahmed Esmat, PH.D.; Egyptian diplomatist; b. 22 March 1923, Alexandria; ed. Faculty of Law, Alexandria Univ. and Univ. of Paris.

Attaché and Sec. Egyptian Embassy, London 50-54; Ministry of Foreign Affairs, Head of British Desk 54-56, Asst. Dir. Legal Dept. 61-63, Head, Cultural and Technical Assistance Dept. 67-68; Counsellor, Perm. Mission to European Office of UN, Geneva 57-61; Minister Counsellor, Egyptian Embassy, Paris 63-67; Official Spokesman of Govt. and Head Information Dept. 68-69; Amb. to France 69-70; Minister of State for Cabinet Affairs 70-72; Perm. Rep. to UN 72-; Chair. Cairo Preparatory Conf. for Geneva Peace Conf. 77; mem. Int. Law Asscn., took part in UN confs. on the Law of the Sea 59, on Consular Relations 63 and on the Law of Treaties 69; Ordre National de Mérite, France 67; Grand Croix 71; 1st Class Decoration, Egypt 70.
Publs. *Comparative Study of Prize Courts* 51, articles in *Revue Egyptienne de Droit International.*
Permanent Mission of Egypt to the UN, 36 East 67th Street, New York, N.Y. 10021, U.S.A.

Abdel-Rahman, Ibrahim Helmi, PH.D.; Egyptian international official and politician; b. 5 Jan. 1919; ed. Univs. of Cairo, London, Edinburgh, Cambridge and Leiden.
Lecturer in Astronomy and Astrophysics, later Asst. Prof. Cairo Univ. 42-54; Sec.-Gen. Council of Ministers 54-58; Dir. Egyptian Atomic Energy Comm. 54-59; mem. and Sec.-Gen. Nat. Science Council 56-58; mem. Nat. Planning Comm. 57-60; Dir. Inst. of Nat. Planning 60-63; UN Commr. for Industrial Devt. 63-66; Exec. Dir. UN Industrial Devt. Org. (UNIDO) 67-74; Senior Adviser to the Prime Minister 75; Minister of Nat. Planning and Admin. Reform 75-76; Adviser to the Prime Minister for Planning and Econ. Affairs March 76-; mem. Egyptian Acad. of Science and Institut d'Egypte.
Council of Ministers, Cairo, Egypt.

Abdessalam, Belaid; Algerian politician; b. July 1928, Dehemcha.
Former Hon. Pres. Union Générale des Etudiants Musulmans Algériens; Instructor Front de Libération Nat. (FLN) school, Oujda; in Cabinet of M. Abdelhamid Mehri, Tunisia 60; Political Adviser in Cabinet of M. Ben Khedda 61; in charge of Economic Affairs, FLN Provisional Exec. 62; Pres., Dir.-Gen. SONATRACH 64-65; Minister of Industry and Energy 65-77, of Light Industry 77-79; Chair. FLN Cttee. on Economic Affairs March 79-81; Chair. Council Org. of Arab Petroleum Exporting Countries (OAPEC) 74.
Front de Libération Nationale, place Emir Abdelkader, Algiers, Algeria.

Abdul-Khail, Muhammad Ali, B.A.; Saudi Arabian government official and financial executive; b. 1935, Buraida; ed. Cairo Univ.
Began career as Asst. Dir. of Office of Minister of Communications 56, later Dir.; Dir.-Gen. of Inst. of Public Admin. 61-64; Deputy Minister of Finance and Nat. Econ. 64-70, Vice-Minister 70-71, Minister of State for Finance and Nat. Econ. 71-75, Minister 75-; Chair. of Board, Saudi Int. Bank, London, Public Investments Fund, Inst. of Public Admin., Saudi Industrial Devt. Fund, Saudi Fund for Devt.; Chair. Board of Govs. Islamic Devt. Bank; mem. Supreme Consultative Council of Petroleum and Minerals, Supreme Cttee. for Admin. Reform, Royal Comm. on Jubail and Yanbu Industrial Estates; mem. Board, Saudia-Saudi Arabian Airlines Corpn., Petroleum and Minerals Corpn. (PETROMIN), Council of Civil Service; decorations from Belgium, Egypt, France, Niger, Pakistan, Saudi Arabia, Sudan, Luxembourg, Indonesia, Spain, Zaire, Fed. Repub. of Germany, Togo, Repub. of China.
Ministry of Finance and National Economy, Riyadh, Saudi Arabia.

Abdullah as Sheikh, Sheikh Hassan; Saudi Arabian politician; b. 1932; ed. Shariah Coll., Mecca and Al Azhar Univ., Cairo.
Former mem. Judicial Supervisory Cttee.; Vice-Pres. Judicial Supervisory Cttee.; Minister of Educ. and Health 62, later of Educ., of Higher Educ. 75-81; Chief Dir. Council of Arts, Sciences and Literature 62-; Chancellor Univ. of King Abdelaziz, Univ. of Riyadh, Islamic Univ. of Imam Muhammad ibn Saud, Islamic Univ. at Medina -81; Chair. Board of Trustees, Univ. of Petroleum and Minerals -81; Dir. Muhammad ibn Saud, Islamic Univ. at Medina -81; Dir. Archaeological Dept.
Publs. *Duwarna Fi Al-Kufah* (Our Turn in the Struggle), *Brave Ideas, Dignity of The Individual in Islam.*
c/o Ministry of Higher Education, Riyadh, Saudi Arabia.

Abdullah ibn Abdulaziz ibn Abdelrahman el Faisal el Saud, H.R.H. Prince; Saudi Arabian Prince and army officer; b. Aug. 1921; brother of H.M. King Fahd (*q.v.*). Commander of Saudi Arabian Nat. Guard 62-; Second

Deputy Prime Minister 75-82, First Deputy Prime Minister June 82-; became Crown Prince 82.
c/o National Guard, Riyadh, Saudi Arabia.

Abu Dhabi, Ruler of (*see* Nahayan, H.H. Sheikh Zayed bin Sultan al-).

Abu Ghazalah, Lieut.-Gen. Muhammad Abdul-Karim, B.COMM., M.SC.; Egyptian army officer and politician; b. 1 Jan. 1930, Delengat Behera; ed. Cairo Univ., Stalin and Cairo Mil. Acads. and American War Coll.
Fought in Palestine War 48, Suez War 56, June 67 and Oct. 73 Wars; rank of Major 58, Col. 66, Major-Gen. 74, Lieut.-Gen. May 80; Commdr. artillery brigade and div. 69-71, Chief of Staff artillery corps 74; Dir. Mil. Intelligence and Reconnaissance 74-76; Mil. Attaché, Washington, D.C. 76-80; Chief of Staff Egyptian Armed Forces 80-81; Minister of Defence and War Prodn. and C.-in-C. of the Armed Forces 81-; numerous military medals.
Publs. *Soviet Military Strategy, History of the Art of War* (5 vols.), *The Guns Opened Fire at Noon* (*October War*), *Mathematics and Warfare* and numerous books on military affairs.
Ministry of Defence, P.O. Box 78, Heliopolis, Cairo, Egypt.

Abushadi, Mohamed Mahmoud, PH.D., B.COM., A.C.I.P.; Egyptian banker; b. 15 Aug. 1913, Fayoum; ed. Cairo Univ., Chartered Inst. of Patent Agents, and American Univ., Washington, D.C., U.S.A.
Controller-Gen. Insurance Dept., Ministry of Finance 49-52; Dir.-Gen. Govt. Insurance and Provident Funds 53; Chair. and Man. Dir. Development and Popular Housing Co. 54-55; Sub.-Gov. Nat. Bank of Egypt 55-60, Man. Dir. 61-67, Chair. 67-70; Chair. Social Insurance Org. 56-57; Chair. and Man. Dir. Cairo Insurance Co. 56-57; Man. Dir. Cairo Bank 56-57; Chair. Union de Banques Arabes et Françaises, Paris 70-, UBAF Bank Ltd., London 72-; Pres. Int. Bankers' Asscn. 76-; Order of the Repub., Second Class, Order of Merit, First Class.
Publs. *The Art of Central Banking and its Application in Egypt* 52, *Central Banking in Egypt* 52, *Will New York attract Arab Capital?* 74, *The Experience of Arab-French Banks* 74, *Oil Funds: the search for supplementary recycling mechanisms* 75, *The Role of Finance in Promoting Arab European Business Cooperation* 76.
Union de Banques Arabes et Françaises, 190 avenue Charles-de-Gaulle, 92523 Neuilly sur Seine; Home: 52 avenue Foch, 75016 Paris, France.

Abu Taleb, Sufi Hassan, D.EN.DROIT; Egyptian professor and politician; b. 27 Jan. 1925, Fayoum; ed. Cairo Univ. Law School, Faculty of Law, Paris and Rome Univs.
Professor of Law Cairo Univ. 52-58, Chair. History and Philosophy of Law Dept. 58-65; Legal Adviser, Univ. of Assiut (Asyut) 65, Univ. of Cairo 67; joined Arab Socialist Union 62, Sec.-Gen. 64; lecturer in law, Beirut Arab Univ. 70-72; Prof. of Law, Cairo Univ. 72, appointed Vice-Pres. 73, Pres. 75-Nov. 78; elected mem. for Fayoum, People's Assembly Oct. 76; joined Arab Socialist Party Nov. 76; a founder of Nat. Democratic Party 78; mem. Higher Ministerial Cttee. for Egyptian-Sudanese Political and Economic Fed.; elected Speaker, People's Assembly Nov. 78-; mem. Bd. of Dirs., Islamic Studies Inst., Cairo, Conf. on Islamic Educ., Mecca (Makkah); has lectured at several American Univs.
Publs. *Arab Society* 65, *Studies in Arab Nationalism, The Legal Status of Women in the Arab Countries* (in French) and many others.
Officer of the Speaker, The People's Assembly, Cairo, Egypt.

Abuzeid, Salah; Jordanian diplomatist and former politician; b. 21 April 1925, Irbid; ed. Law Coll. of Syrian Univ., Damascus and Syracuse Univ., U.S.A.

Government Official 50-58; Dir. Amman Radio Station 58-59; Asst. Dir.-Gen. Hashemite Broadcasting Service 59-62, Dir.-Gen. of Hashemite Broadcasting Service and Chief of Nat. Guidance 62-64; Minister of Information 64-65, 67, of Culture and Information 67-68; Amb. to U.K. 69; Minister of Culture and Information 69-70; Special Adviser to H.M. The King 70-72; Minister of Foreign Affairs 72-73; mem. Senate, Head of Foreign Relations Cttee. 74-76; Adviser to H.M. The King 76; Amb. to United Kingdom 76-78; sentenced to three years' imprisonment for misuse of funds 79; sentence later reduced to six months; numerous decorations.
Publ. *Al Hussein bin Talal* 58.
c/o Ministry of Foreign Affairs, Amman, Jordan.

Achour, Habib; Tunisian trade union leader and politician; b. 1913.
Joined Néo-Destour party 34; founded Union Générale Tunisienne de Travail (UGTT) with Farhat Hached 46; arrested for inciting strikes 47, 52; elected Sec.-Gen. UGTT 63-66; mem. Political Bureau, Parti Socialiste Destourien (PSD) 47-66; imprisoned March-Sept. 66; elected mem. Nat. Assembly 69; readmitted to Political Bureau 70 (-Jan. 78) and re-elected Sec.-Gen. UGTT 70 (-March 78); sentenced to 10 years' hard labour following severe anti-government rioting Jan. 78, later pardoned but remained under house arrest 79; pardoned and released Nov. 81; appointed Pres. UGTT 81.
Union Générale Tunisienne du Travail, 29 Place M'Hamed Ali, Tunis, Tunisia.

Adams, Michael Evelyn, M.A.; British writer; b. 31 May 1920; ed. Sedbergh School and Christ Church, Oxford.
Commonwealth Fund Fellowship in U.S.A. 54-55; Middle East Corresp. *The Guardian* 56-62; Asst. to Dir. Voluntary Service Overseas 64-67; Dir. of Information, Council for the Advancement of Arab-British Understanding (CAABU) 68-78; Editor-in-Chief *Middle East International*.
Publs. *Suez and After* 58, *Umbria* 64, *Voluntary Service Overseas* 68, *Chaos or Rebirth* 68, *Handbook to the Middle East* (Editor) 71, *Publish it Not . . .* (with Christopher Mayhew) 75.
Middle East International, 21 Collingham Road, London, SW5 ONU, England.

Adams, Robert McCormick, A.M., PH.D.; American anthropologist and archaeologist; b. 23 July 1926; ed. Univ. of Chicago.
Archaeological field work at Jarmo, Iraq 50-51; joined staff of Univ. of Chicago 54, Dir. Oriental Inst. 62-68, 81- Prof. of Anthropology 63-, Harold H. Swift Distinguished Service Prof. 75-, Dean, Div. of Social Science 70-74, 79-80; Field studies of irrigation and settlement patterns in central and southern Iraq 56-58, 60, 67, 68-69, 73-75, Iran 60-61; excavations in Iran 63, Syria 70, Saudi Arabia 76; Chair. Assembly of Behavioral and Social Sciences, Nat. Research Council 73-76, American Oriental Soc.; Vice-Chair. Cttee. on Science and Public Policy, Nat. Acad. of Sciences 77-81, Chair. (acting) 80-81; Fellow, American Acad. of Arts and Sciences, American Anthropological Asscn., American Asscn. for the Advancement of Science; mem. German Archaeological Inst., Nat. Acad. of Science, Middle East Studies Asscn., American Philosophical Soc.; Assoc. mem. Iraqi Academy; Trustee, Nat. Opinion Research Center 70-, Nat. Humanities Center 76-, Russell Sage Foundation 78-.
Publs. *City Invincible: a Symposium of Urbanization and Cultural Development in the Ancient Near East* (co-editor with C. H. Kraeling) 60, *Land Behind Baghdad: a History of Settlement on the Diyala Plains* 65, *The Evolution of Urban Society: Early Mesopotamia and Pre-hispanic Mexico* 66, *The Uruk Countryside* (with H. J. Nissen) 72, *Corners of a Foreign Field* (co-editor with C. S. Schelling) 79,

Heartland of Cities: Surveys of Ancient Settlement and Land Use on the Central Floodplain of the Euphrates 81.
The Oriental Institute, 1155 East 58th Street, Chicago, Illinois 60637; and 5805 South Dorchester Avenue, Chicago, Illinois 60637, U.S.A.

Adasani, Mahmoud, B.SC.; Kuwaiti engineer; b. 31 Jan. 1934; ed. Kuwait, American Univ., Beirut and Univ. of Southern California.
Assistant petroleum engineer, Kuwait Oil Co (KOC) 58-60, petroleum engineer 60, Dir. KOC 60-; Technical Asst., Gen. Oil Affairs Dept., Ministry of Finance and Oil 60-63; Dir. of Technical Affairs 63-66, Asst. Under-Sec. for Oil Affairs 66-75; Under-Sec., Ministry of Oil June 75-; Man. Dir. Salwa Construction Co.; Dir. Kuwait Metal Pipeline Co. 70-79; Kuwait Rep., Bureau of the Org. of Arab Petroleum Exporting Countries (OAPEC) Jan. 75- (Chair. 78); Chair. Petroleum Resources Conservation Board 76-; OPEC Gov. for Kuwait; mem. American Inst. Mechanical Engineers, Kuwait Soc. Engineers.
Publs. *Oil of Kuwait, The Greater Burgan Field, North Kuwait Oil Fields.*
Ministry of Oil, P.O. Box 5077, Kuwait.

Adasani, Muhammad Youssef al-; Kuwaiti politician.
Head, Kuwait Municipality 55; elected to Nat. Assembly 67; Amb. to Saudi Arabia 67-70, to Lebanon 70; Minister of Planning 76-80; Minister of Public Works April 80-Jan. 81; elected to revived Nat. Assembly Feb. 81, elected Speaker March 81.
National Assembly, Kuwait City, Kuwait.

Adib, Albert; Lebanese editor; b. 1 July 1908, Mexico.
Editor many magazines, Cairo 27-30, Beirut 30-38; Pres. Acad. of Oriental Music, Beirut 33-38; Gen. Dir. Radio-Levant Broadcasting Station, Beirut 38-43; Editor and proprietor *Al-Adib* review, Beirut 42-; mem. various acads. and foreign cultural insts.; Knight, Order of Cedar.
Publ. *Liman* (poems) 52.
P.O. Box 11-878, Beirut, Lebanon.

Adni, Daniel; Israeli concert pianist; b. 6 Dec. 1951, Haifa; ed. High Schools in Haifa and Tel-Aviv, Conservatoire of Music in Paris.
First Recital in Haifa 63; professional debut, London 70; New York debut 76; has played at most musical centres of the world incl. U.K., Fed. Repub. of Germany, Israel; U.S.A., Japan, South Africa, Switzerland, Norway, Netherlands, Romania; made over 12 records for EMI-His Master's Voice; First Prize, Paris Conservatoire; First Prize, Young Concert Artists' Auditions, New York.
c/o Ibbs and Tillett, 450-452 Edgware Road, London, W2 1EG, England.

Afghanistan, former King of (*see* Mohammed Zahir Shah).

Aga Khan, Prince Sadruddin; Iranian UN official, b. 1933, Paris, France; ed. Harvard Univ. and Harvard Univ. Graduate School for Arts and Sciences.
UNESCO Consultant for Afro-Asian Projects 58; Head of Mission and Adviser to UN High Commr. for Refugees 59-60; UNESCO Special Consultant to Dir.-Gen. 61; Exec. Sec. Int. Action Cttee. for Preservation of Nubian Monuments 61; UN Dep. High Commr. for Refugees 62-65, High Commr. 66-67; Consultant to Sec.-Gen. of UN 78; Publr. *The Paris Review*; Founder and Sec. Harvard Islamic Asscn.; Pres. Council on Islamic Affairs, New York; mem. Inst. of Differing Civilizations, Brussels, World Wildlife Fund; Founding mem. and Pres. Groupe de Bellerive; numerous awards and decorations including Commdr. Légion d'Honneur, Dag Hammerskjold Hon. Medal 79.
Publ. *International Protection of Refugees.*
Chateau de Bellerive, 1245 Collonge-Bellerive, Geneva, Switzerland.

Ahmad, Maj.-Gen. Mohammed al-Baqir; Sudanese army officer and politician; b. 1927, El Sofi; ed. Commercial Secondary School, Khartoum, Military Coll. and Cairo Univ. Commissioned 50; Chief of Staff, Southern Command 58; Mil. Gov. Upper Nile Province 59; Mil. Attaché, London 66-67; Dir. of Training and Chief of Staff, Southern Command 68; Commdr. Mil. Coll. 68-69; Under-Sec. Ministry of Defence 69; First Deputy Chief of Staff of Armed Forces 69-70, Chief of Staff 70-71; Minister of Interior 71-73, Jan.-Aug. 75; First Vice-Pres. of Sudan 72-77; mem. Exec. Bureau, Sudanese Socialist Union, Council, Univ. of Khartoum 70-71; del. to several int. confs.; several decorations.
Executive Bureau, Sudanese Socialist Union, P.O. Box 1850, Khartoum, Sudan.

Ahmad, Othman Ibrahim al-, M.B.A.; Saudi Arabian civil servant; b. 12 Dec. 1942, Saudi Arabia.
Expert, Inst. of Public Admin. 68-71, Dir.-Gen. Bd. of Employment and Examination, Civil Service Bureau 71-76, Asst. Vice-Pres., Gen. Bureau, Civil Service 76-78, Vice-Pres. 78-81; Asst. Sec.-Gen. for Organizational Affairs, League of Arab States 81-.
Publs. *Employment Policy in Saudi Arabia* 71, *Workforce in the Government Sector and Employment Problems* 75, *Methods of Assessment of the Needs for Government Employment* 77, *Problems and Policies in Planning Government Employment* 79.
League of Arab States, Avenue Khéreddine Pacha, Tunis, Tunisia; P.O. Box 1222, Riyadh, Saudi Arabia.

Aini, Mohsin A. al; Yemeni diplomatist and politician; b. 1932; ed. Cairo Univ. and Univ. of Paris.
Schoolteacher, Aden 58-60; Int. Confederation of Arab Trade Unions 60-62; Minister of Foreign Affairs, Yemeni Republic Sept.-Dec. 62; Perm. Rep. to UN Dec. 62-65, 65-66, 67-69; Amb. to U.S.A. 63-65, 65-66; Foreign Minister May-July 65; Prime Minister Nov. 67; Personal Rep. of Chair. Republican Council 67; Amb. to U.S.S.R. 68-70; Prime Minister and Foreign Minister Feb. 70-Feb. 71; Amb. to France July-Sept. 71; Prime Minister, Minister of Foreign Affairs 71-72, June 74-June 75; Amb. to U.K. 73-74, to France 75-76; Perm. Rep. to UN 79-81; Amb. to Fed. Repub. of Germany 81-.
Embassy of the Yemen Arab Republic, 5300 Bonn 2, Kraterstrasse, 7 Federal Republic of Germany.

Aktuğ, Savlet K.; Turkish diplomatist; b. 14 March 1926, Afyon; ed. Galatasaray Lycée, Istanbul, Faculty of Law, Univ. of Ankara.
Editor, Anatolian News Agency 45-49; Commentator, Ankara Radio; Dir. of Information Dept., Office of the Dir.-Gen. of the Press, Ankara; Deputy Dir.-Gen. Anatolian News Agency; served in the Ministry of Foreign Affairs 52-, in Amman, in Berne (First Sec.); Chargé d'Affaires and Counsellor, Turkish Embassy, Rio de Janeiro 63-69; Deputy Dir.-Gen. of Dept. of Information; Chef de Cabinet to the Minister of Foreign Affairs; Turkish Consul-Gen. (Ministerial rank), London 71-76; Amb. to Tunisia 76-79; Deputy Sec.-Gen. for Information, Spokesman of Ministry of Foreign Affairs 80; Amb. to Czechoslovakia 81-; several foreign decorations.
Embassy of Turkey, Pevnostni 3, Střešovice, Prague 6, Czechoslovakia.

Akturk, Yildirim, B.SC.; Turkish administrator; b. 1941, Izmit; ed. Univ. of Liverpool, England, Harvard Business School.
Engaged in research at Univ. of London and a research centre; Head, Incentives Dept., and special research expert, State Planning Org.; joined state electricity co. TESTAS 76, Head, Admin. Board -80; Head, State Planning Org. 80-.
State Planning Organization, Ankara, Turkey.

Al-Azzawi, Hikmet (*see* Azzawi, Hikmat al-).

Alhegelan, Sheikh Faisal Abdul Aziz; Saudi Arabian diplomatist; b. 7 Oct. 1929, Riyadh; ed. Faculty of Law, Fouad Univ., Cairo.
Ministry of Foreign Affairs 52-54; served Embassy in Washington, D.C. 54-58; Chief of Protocol in Ministry 58-60; Political Adviser to H.M. King Sa'ud 60-61; Amb. to Spain 61-68, to Venezuela and Argentina 68-75, to Denmark 75-76, to U.K. 76-79, to U.S.A. June 79-; Order of King Abdulaziz; Gran Cruz, Order of Isabela la Católica (Spain), Gran Cordon, Orden del Libertador (Venezuela); Grande Oficial, Orden Riobranco (Brazil).
Embassy of Saudi Arabia, 1520 18th Street, N.W., Washington, D.C. 20036, U.S.A.

Ali, Ahmad Mohamed, PH.D.; Saudi Arabian administrator; b. 13 April 1934, Medina Munawwara; ed. Medina Munawwara, Cairo Univ., Univ. of Michigan, State Univ. of New York at Albany.
Vice-Chancellor, King Abdul Aziz Univ., Jeddah 67-72; Deputy Minister for Technical Affairs, Ministry of Educ. 72-75, Pres. Islamic Devt. Bank Sept. 75-.
Islamic Development Bank, P.O. Box 5925, Jeddah, Saudi Arabia.

Ali, Lieut-Gen. Kamal Hassan; Egyptian army officer and politician; b. 18 Sept. 1921, Abdin, Cairo; ed. secondary school, Mil. Acad., British Armoured School, Staff Coll., Festrel Acad., U.S.S.R., Nasser Higher Mil. Acad.
Career in Army from graduation at Mil. Acad. 42; promoted Lieut. 42, First Lieut. 46, Capt. 48; Senior Instructor, Armour School 53; Major 54; Staff Officer, 2nd Armoured Operational Group 56; Lieut.-Col. 57; Commdr. 70th Brigade 60; Instructor, Staff Coll. 61; Brigadier 65, Commdr. 2nd Armoured Brigade 66; Chief of Staff, 21st Armoured Div. 68, Commdr. 69; Chief of Operational Branch, Operations Dept. 70; Major-Gen. and Chief of Staff of Armoured Corps 71, Dir. 72; Asst. Minister of War 75; Chief of Gen. Intelligence 75; Minister of Defence and Mil. Production, C.-in-C. of Armed Forces, Lieut.-Gen. 78-80; Deputy Prime Minister and Minister of Foreign Affairs May 80-; Liberation Order 52, Memorial Order 58; many ribbons and medals.
Ministry of Foreign Affairs, Cairo, Egypt.

Ali, Salah Omar al-; Iraqi diplomatist; b. 1 July 1937; ed. Al-Mustansiriyah Univ., Baghdad.
Member of Revolutionary Command Council 68-70; Editor-in-Chief of *Al-Thawra* newspaper 69; Minister for Information March-July 70; Amb. to Sweden 72-76, to Spain 76-78; Perm. Rep. to the UN 78-81; fmr. mem. leadership of Arab Baath Socialist Party.
Ministry of Foreign Affairs, Baghdad, Karradat Mariam, Iraq.

Alier, Abel, LL.B., LL.M.; Sudanese politician; b. 1933, Bor District, Upper Nile Province (now Jonglei Province); ed. Univs. of Khartoum, London, Yale.
Former advocate; District Judge in El Obeid, Wad Medani and Khartoum until 65; participant in Round Table Conf. and mem. Twelve Man Cttee. to study the Southern problem 65-66; mem. Constitution Comms. 66-67, 68; fmr. mem. Law Reform Comm.; mem. Board of Dirs., Industrial Planning Corpn. 68-69; mem. Nat. Scholarship Board 68-69; Minister of Housing May-Oct. 69; Minister of Supply and Internal Trade Oct. 69-July 70; Minister of Works June 70-July 71; Minister for Southern Affairs Aug. 71-April 72; Vice-Pres. 71-78; Pres. High Exec. Council for the Southern Region 72-78, May 80-Oct. 81; Chair. Nat. Council for Devt. of Jonglei Canal Area 77-, Tech. Cttee. to establish Regional System of Govt. in Sudan; mem.

Political Bureau, Sudanese Socialist Union -82; Hon. LL.D. (Khartoum) 78; Most Honoured Son of the Sudan Medal.
Ministry of Foreign Affairs, Khartoum, Sudan.

Al-Jamali, Asim (*see* Jamali, Asim al-).

Allegro, John Marco; British philologist and archaeologist; b. 17 Feb. 1923; ed. Wallington County Grammar School and Univ. of Manchester.
Royal Navy 41-46; Manchester Univ. 47-52; research in Hebrew dialects, Magdalen Coll., Oxford 52-53; British rep. on Int. Editing Team for Dead Sea Scrolls, Jerusalem 53-; Lecturer in Comparative Semitic Philology and Hebrew, Univ. of Manchester 54-62, in Old Testament and Intertestamental Studies 62-70; Adviser to Jordanian Govt. on Dead Sea Scrolls 61-; Trustee and Hon. Sec. Dead Sea Scrolls Fund 62-70.
Publs. *The Dead Sea Scrolls* 56, 64, *The People of the Dead Sea Scrolls* 59, *The Treasure of the Copper Scroll* 60, 64, *Search in the Desert* 64, *The Shapira Affair* 65, *Discoveries in the Judaean Desert* (Vol. 5) 68, *The Sacred Mushroom and the Cross* 70, *The End of a Road* 70, *The Chosen People* 71, *Lost Gods* 77, *The Dead Sea Scrolls and the Christian Myth* 79, *All Manner of Men* 82.
5 Ballahane Close, Port Erin, Isle of Man.

Almanqour, Sheikh Nasir Hamad, G.C.V.O., B.A.; Saudi Arabian diplomatist; b. 1927, Riyadh; ed. Cairo Univ.
Attaché, Foreign Ministry 52; Rep. of Ministry of Educ. Najd Province, Dir. of Educ. in Najd 54, Asst. Dir.-Gen. of Educ. 55, Dir.-Gen. 56, Dir.-Gen., Ministry of Educ. 57; Dir. Riyadh Univ. 58; Minister of State for Cabinet Affairs and Minister of Labour and Social Affairs 59; Amb. to Japan 64, to Sweden 68, to Spain 73-80, to U.K. Dec. 80-, to Ireland 82-; mem. Supreme Council Manuscripts Inst., Cairo, Diplomatic Inst., Jeddah; King Abdulaziz Order (Second Class); Gran Cruz, Orden del Mérito Civil (Spain), Grand Cordon, Order of Brilliant Star (Republic of China).
Embassy of Saudi Arabia, 30 Belgrave Square, London, SW1X 8QB, England.

Aloni, Shulamit, LL.M.; Israeli lawyer and politician; b. 1928, Tel Aviv; ed. Teachers' Seminary, Hebrew Univ; Editor radio programmes on legal matters and civil rights; Columnist *Ydiot Achoronot* (daily); mem. 6th Knesset (Parl.) for Mapai 65-69; Chair. Consumers' Council 66-70. founder and Pres. Citizens Rights Movement 73-; mem. 8th Knesset 73-77, 9th Knesset June 77-; Minister without Portfolio 74-75.
Publs. *The Citizen and His State* 58, (7th edn. 74), *The Rights of Children in Israel* 61, *The Arrangement—From a Halachi State to a State of Law* 70.
The Knesset, Jerusalem; Home: Kfar Shmariahu, Israel.

Alpert, Carl; Israeli journalist and university official; b. 12 May 1913; ed. Boston Univ., U.S.A.
Editor *The New Palestine* 40-47; Nat. Pres. American Young Judaea 40-41; Nat. Dir. Educ. Dept. Zionist Org. of America 47-52; emigrated to Israel 52; Dir. Public Relations Dept., Technion Israel Inst. of Technology 52-68; Exec. Vice-Chair. Technion Board of Govs. 62-; Nat. Pres. Asscn. of Americans and Canadians in Israel 57-59; author int. syndicated weekly column in 42 newspapers.
Technion Israel Institute of Technology, Technion City, Haifa, Israel.

Al-Saffar, Salman Mohamed (*see* Saffar, Salman Mohamed al-).

Alwan, Hamia; Iraqi politician and former journalist; b. 1930, Babylon Governorate; ed. American Univ. in Beirut.
Served Ministry of Finance for several years; arrested several times for political activity; Editor-in-Chief and

Publisher *Al-Shaab* newspaper; served in State Org. of Commerce; Dir.-Gen. of Information 68; Minister of State for Presidential Affairs 68; Minister of Culture and Information 69, of Youth 70; Head of Iraqi-German Friendship Asscn. 72; Minister of Information 72; Head of Exec. Bureau, Gen. Fed. of Iraqi Youth 74; Minister of State 74-76; Head of Bureau of Vice-Chair. of Revolutionary Command Council with rank of Minister 76-77; Minister of State for Foreign Affairs Jan. 77-.
Ministry of Foreign Affairs, Karradat Mariam, Baghdad, Iraq.

Amin, Mahmoud, M.SC., PH.D.; Egyptian petroleum geologist; b. 30 April 1920, Cairo; ed. Cairo Univ., London Univ.
Deputy Gen. Man. of Exploration and Production, Egyptian Petroleum Corpn. 58-68; Chair. Western Desert Petroleum Corpn. 68-75; Asst. Sec.-Gen. OAPEC 75-79; Petroleum consultant 79-.
Publs. *Economics of Petroleum Resources*, about 52 scientific papers in geology and petroleum, about 100 articles on petroleum.
20 Mohamed Hassan Street, Heliopolis, Cairo; Home: 391 Horyia Street, Apartment 802, Alexandria, Egypt.

Amin, Mostafa, M.A.; Egyptian journalist; b. 21 Feb. 1914, Cairo; ed. American Univ. of Cairo and Georgetown Univ., U.S.A.
Began his career publishing or writing for magazines, incl. *El Raghaeb, Rose el Youssef* 28; Deputy Chief Editor *Akher Saa* weekly magazine 34, Editor-in-Chief 38; City Editor *Al Ahram* daily 39-44, Diplomatic Editor 40; Editor-in-Chief *Al Isnain* weekly 41-44; founder *Akhbar el Yom* weekly newspaper and publishing house, jointly with his brother Ali Amin 44; mem. House of Reps. 44; purchased *Akher Saa* weekly magazine 46; founded *Akher Lahza, El Guil* 51, weekly magazines; arrested 26 times for editorial policies during 51; co-founded *Al-Akhbar* daily 52; published *Al Mokhtar* for Reader's Digest 56-67; Vice-Chair. Press Board 60, dismissed by Pres. Gamal Abdul Nasser 60; Chair. of Board, Dar al Hilal Publishers 61; Chair. of Board, Akhbar el Yom Publishers 62-64, Editorial Man. 64-65; arrested 65, sentenced to life imprisonment 66, reprieved by Pres. Anwar Sadat 74; Editor-in-Chief *Akhbar el Yom* 74-76; staff writer 76-.
Publs. *Laughing America* 43, *First Year in Prison*.
Dar Akhbar el Yom, 6 Sharia al-Safaha, Cairo, Egypt.

Amin, Samir, D.ECON.; Egyptian economist; b. 4 Sept. 1931, Cairo; ed. Univ. of Paris.
Senior Economist, Econ. Devt. Org., Cairo 57-60; Technical Adviser for Planning to Govt. of Mali 60-63; Prof. of Econs., Univs. of Poitiers, Paris and Dakar; Dir. UN African Inst. for Econ. Devt. and Planning 70-.
Publs. *Trois expériences africaines de développement, Mali, Guinée, Ghana* 65, *L'Economie du Maghreb* (2 vols.) 67, *Le développement du capitalisme en Côte d'Ivoire* 68, *Le monde des affaires sénégalaises* 68, *Maghreb in the Modern World* 70, *L'Accumulation à l'échelle mondiale* 70, *L'Afrique de l'Ouest bloquée* 71, *Le développement inégal* 73, *The Arab Nation* 78, *Class and Nation* 80.
African Institute for Economic Development and Planning, rue 18 Juin, B.P. 3186, Dakar, Senegal.

Amouzegar, Jamshid, B.C.E., M.S., PH.D., Iranian politician; b. 25 June 1923; ed. Univs. of Teheran, Cornell, Washington.
United Nations Expert, Mission to Iran 51; Chief, Engineering Dept. 52-55; Deputy Minister of Health 55-58; Minister of Labour 58-59, of Agriculture 59-60; Consulting Engineer 60-64; Minister of Health 64-65, of Finance 65-74, of Employment 74, of Interior 74-76; Minister of State 76-77; Prime Minister 77-78; Sec.-Gen. Nat. Resurgence Party 76-77, Jan.-Aug. 78; Chair. Int. Civil Service Advisory

Board of UN; Pres. Org. of Petroleum Exporting Countries (OPEC) 74.
Kakh Avenue, Teheran, Iran.

Amri, Gen. Hassan al-; Yemeni politician.
Took part in the Revolution against the Imamate 62; Minister of Transport Sept.-Oct. 62, of Communications Oct. 62-April 63; mem. Council of the Revolutionary Command 62-63; Vice-President of Yemen 63-66; mem. Political Bureau 63-66; Prime Minister Jan.-April 65, July 65-Sept. 66; C.-in-C. Yemen Armed Forces 67-71; mem. Presidential Council and Prime Minister April-July 69, Aug.-Sept. 71; in exile in Lebanon until Jan. 75; returned to Yemen A.R. Jan. 75.

Amuzegar, Jahangir, PH.D.; Iranian economist and politician; b. 13 Jan. 1920; ed. Univs. of Teheran, Washington and California.
Teaching Asst., Univ. of California, Los Angeles 51-53; Lecturer, Whittier Coll. 53, Univ. of Michigan 53-55; Asst. Prof. Pomona Coll., Claremont, California 55-56; Asst. Prof. Michigan State Univ., E. Lansing, Mich. 56-58; Assoc. Prof. Occidental Coll. and Univ. of Calif., Los Angeles 58-60; Brookings Research Prof. 60-61; Lecturer, Univ. of Maryland 63-73; Adjunct Prof. American Univ. 75-; Econ. Adviser, Plan Org., Govt. of Iran 56-57; Minister of Commerce, Iran 61-62; mem. Council of Money and Credit 61-62, High Econ. Council 61-62; mem. Board of Dirs. Bank Melli Iran 61-62; Chair. Board, Foreign Trade Co. (Iranian Govt. Org.) 61-62; Minister of Finance 62; Chair. High Council of Nat. Iranian Oil Co. 62; Chief of Iranian Econ. Mission, Washington, D.C. 63-73; Amb.-at-Large 63-78; Exec. Dir. Int. Monetary Fund, Washington, D.C. 73-79, Consultant 79-.
Publs. *Technical Assistance in Theory and Practice: The Case of Iran* 66, *Iran: Economic Development under Dualistic Conditions* 71, *Energy Policies of the World: Iran* 75, *Iran: An Economic Profile* 77, *Comparative Economics* 81.
c/o International Monetary Fund, 700 19th Street, N.W., Washington, D.C. 20431, U.S.A.

Anderson, Sir (James) Norman (Dalrymple), O.B.E., Q.C., M.A., LL.D., D.D., F.B.A.; British educationalist; b. 29 Sept. 1908; ed. St. Lawrence Coll., Trinity Coll., Cambridge.
Missionary, Egypt Gen. Mission 32-40; Capt. Libyan Arab Force 40-41; Major (Political Officer for Sanusi Affairs) 41; Lieut.-Col. (Sec. for Arab Affairs, Civil Affairs Branch, G.H.Q., M.E. 43, Political Sec. 43); Col. (Chief Sec., Civil Affairs Branch) 44-46; lectured on Islamic Law in Cambridge 47-50; Lecturer in Islamic Law, School of Oriental and African Studies, Univ. of London 47; Reader in Oriental Laws, Univ. of London 51-53; Prof. of Oriental Laws, Univ. of London 53-75; Head of Dept. of Law, School of Oriental and African Studies 53-71; Lecturer in Mohammedan Law, Council of Legal Educ. 53-71; Visiting Prof., Princeton Univ. and New York Univ. Law School 58, Harvard Law School 66; Chair. U.K. National Comm. of Comparative Law 57-59; Dir. Inst. of Advanced Legal Studies, Univ. of London 59-76; Dean, Faculty of Laws, Univ. of London 65-69; Pres. Soc. of Public Teachers of Law 68-69; Chair. House of Laity, Gen. Synod of Church of England 70-79; mem. Panel of Advisory Jurists to Northern Nigerian Govt. 58, 62; Vice-Pres. Int. African Law Asscn.; mem. Int. Cttee. of Comparative Law 63-67; Hon. Fellow, School of Oriental and African Studies 77; Libyan Order of Independence, Class II 59.
Publs. *The World's Religions* (Gen. Editor) 50, *Islamic Law in Africa* 54, *Islamic Law in the Modern World* 59, *Changing Law in Developing Countries* (Editor) 63, *Family Law in Asia and Africa* (Editor) 68, *Into the World: The need and limits of Christian involvement* 68, *Christianity: the Witness of History* 69, *Christianity and Comparative Religion* 70, *Morality, Law and Grace* 72, *A Lawyer among the Theo-*

logians 73, *Law Reform in the Muslim World* 76, *Issues of Life and Death* 76, *Liberty, Law and Justice* 78, *The Mystery of the Incarnation* 78, *The Law of God and the Love of God* 80, *God's Word for God's World* 81; contributions on Islamic Law, etc., to various learned journals.
9 Larchfield, Gough Way, Cambridge, England.

Ansari, Dr. Hooshang, M.A.; Iranian politician; b. 1928; ed. England, U.S.A. and Japan.
Successively Special Reporter of Int. News Service and Int. News Photos; Press Attaché of Publication and Propaganda Dept. in Japan; Commercial Attaché in Japan, Econ. Attaché, Tokyo; Chief, Supervisory Comm. of Public Supplies, mem. High Council on Iranian Aviation; Technical Under-Sec., Ministry of Commerce; Special Ambassador in African countries; Amb. to Pakistan and Ceylon 65-66; Minister of Information 66-67; Amb. to U.S.A. 67-69; Minister of Economy 69-Nov. 77, concurrently of Finance 74-Nov. 77; Chair. of Board and Gen. Man. Dir. Nat. Iranian Oil Co. (N.I.O.C.) 77-79.
Teheran, Iran.

Anwar, Mohamed Samih; Egyptian diplomatist; b. 10 Dec. 1924, Cairo; ed. Univ. of Cairo.
Ministry of Justice 46-54; First Sec. Ministry of Foreign Affairs 54; served Embassies in U.S.S.R. 57-62, U.K. 63-65; Amb. to Kuwait 66-68; Under-Sec. Ministry of Foreign Affairs 68-70; Amb. to Iran 71-74; Minister of State for Foreign Affairs 74-75; Amb. to U.K. 75-79, to U.S.S.R. 80-81; Order of the Repub. 2nd Class 58, Order of Merit 1st Class 68, Order of Homayoun First Class (Iran) 74, Order of the Flag (Yugoslavia) 70.
Ministry of Foreign Affairs, Cairo, Egypt.

Arafat, Yasser (*pseudonym* of Mohammed Abed Ar'ouf Arafat al-Qudwa al-Husseini); Palestinian resistance leader; b. Dec. 1929, Jerusalem; ed. Cairo Univ.
Leader Gaza Youth section *al-Faoutowa* Palestinian guerrilla org., Sec. to its leader Abdul Qader al-Husseini 46; joined League of Palestinian Students 44; mem. Exec. Cttee. 50, Pres. 52-56; formed, with others, Al Fatah movt. 56; engineer in Egypt 56, Kuwait 57-65; Founder mem. of Palestine Nat. Liberation Movement (Al Fatah) 59, Pres. Exec. Cttee. June 68-; Chair. Exec. Cttee. Palestine Liberation Org. Feb. 69-, Pres. Cen. Cttee., Head Political Dept. 73-; Gen. Commdr. Palestinian Revolutionary Forces; addressed UN Gen. Assembly Nov. 74; Joliot-Curie Gold Medal, World Peace Council Sept. 75.
Palestine Liberation Organization, Colombani Street, Off Sadat Street, Dr. Raji Nasr Building, Ras Beirut, Lebanon.

Arashi, Qadi Abdul Karim al-; Yemeni politician.
Former Minister for Local Govt. and the Treasury; Speaker of the Constituent People's Assembly Feb. 78-; Chair. Provisional Presidential Council June-July 78; Vice-Pres. Yemen Arab Republic July 78-.
Constituent People's Assembly, Sana'a, Yemen Arab Republic.

Aref, Lt.-Gen. Abdul-Rahman Mohammed (brother of late Pres. Abdul Salam Aref); Iraqi army officer and politician; b. 1916; ed. Baghdad Military Acad.
Joined Army 36; took part in July 58 Revolution, Chief of Gen. Staff Armoured Corps Dept. 58-61; Commdr. 5th Div. 63; assisted in overthrow of Gen. Kassem 63; mem. Regency Council 65; Asst. Chief of Staff Iraqi Armed Forces 63-64; Acting Chief of Staff 64, Chief of Staff 64-68; Pres. of Iraq 66-68; also Prime Minister May-July 67.

Arens, Moshe, M.K.; Israeli professor and diplomatist; b. 7 Dec. 1925, Lithuania; ed. Massachusetts and California Insts. of Technology, U.S.A.
Associate Prof. of Aeronautical Engineering, Technion (Israel Inst. of Technology), Haifa; Deputy Dir. Israel Aircraft Industries, Lod; Amb. to U.S.A. 82-; elected to Knesset, mem. Knesset Finance Cttee. 73; Israel Defence

Prize 71; Assoc. Fellow, American Inst. of Aeronautics and Astronautics.
Publs. several books on propulsion and flight mechanics.
Embassy of Israel, 3514 International Drive, N.W., Washington, D.C. 20008, U.S.A.; Home: 49 Hagderot, Savyon, Israel.

Argov, Shlomo, M.SC.(ECON.) Israeli diplomatist; b. 14 Dec. 1929, Jerusalem; ed. Georgetown Univ., Washington D.C., London School of Econs.
National Mil. Service 47-50; Prin. Asst., Tech. Services Div., Prime Minister's Office, Jerusalem then to Dir.-Gen., Prime Minister's Office 55-59; Consul-Gen. of Israel, Lagos 59-60; Counsellor, Embassy of Israel, Accra 60-61; Consul, New York 61-64; Deputy Dir. U.S. Div., Ministry for Foreign Affairs 65-68, Asst. Dir.-Gen. (Dir. of Israel Information Services) 74-77; Minister, Embassy of Israel, Washington D.C. 68-71; Amb. to Mexico 71-74, to the Netherlands 77-79, to the U.K. Sept. 79-, wounded in assassination attempt June 82.
Embassy of Israel, 2 Palace Green, London, W8 4QB, England.

Ariburun, Gen. Tekin; Turkish politician; b. 1905, Istip, Yugoslavia; ed. Kulei and Konya Mil. Schools, Harbiye (Mil.) Coll. and War Acad.
Staff Officer in Turkish Air Force; served as first Turkish Air Attaché in Germany, U.S.A. and first Turkish Commanding Gen. NATO Defence Coll., Paris; promoted to rank of Brig.-Gen. 50, Gen. 59; Commdr. Turkish Air Force 59-60, retd.; Senator for Istanbul 64-80; Speaker of Senate 70-77; Candidate for Presidency 73; Justice Party.
c/o Cumhuriyet Senatosu, Ankara, Turkey.

Aridor, Yoram, M.JUR.; Israeli politician; b. 24 Oct. 1933, Tel-Aviv; ed. Hebrew Univ. of Jerusalem.
Member Knesset 69-, Chair. Knesset Cttee. for Interior and Environmental Affairs 75-77, Chair. Sub-Cttee. for Constitutional Law 75-77, mem. Cttee. for Legislation and Justice 69-81; Deputy Minister in the Prime Minister's Office 77-81, Minister of Finance Jan. 81-, of Communications Jan.-July 81; Chair. Herut (Freedom) Movt. in Histadrut (Gen. Fed. of Labour) 72-77, mem. Central Cttee. Herut Movt. 61-, Chair. Secretariat 79-.
Ministry of Finance, Jerusalem, Israel.

Asaad, Kamal el, L. EN D.; Lebanese politician; b. 1929; ed. Law Faculty, Beirut and Univ. de Paris.
Practising lawyer; Deputy 53-; Mayor of Marjéyoun; Minister of Education 61-64; Pres. Chamber of Deputies 64-65, 72-; Minister of Water Resources and Health 66; mem. Nat. Dialogue Cttee. Sept. 75.
Hazmieh, Imm. Haddad, Beirut, Lebanon.

Ashtal, Abdalla Saleh, M.A.; Yemeni diplomatist; b. 5 Oct. 1940; ed. Menelik II Secondary School, Addis Ababa, Ethiopia, American Univ. of Beirut, Lebanon, New York Univ.
Assistant Dir. of Sana'a Branch, Yemeni Bank for Reconstruction and Devt. 66-67; mem. Supreme People's Council, 5th Province 67-68; Editor *Ash-avara* (weekly) 67-68; mem. Exec. Cttee. of Gen. Command, Nat. Liberation Front 68-72; Political Adviser, Perm. Mission to UN 70, Senior Counsellor 72-73, Perm. Rep. 73-; concurrently non-resident Amb. to Canada Oct. 74- and to Mexico Nov. 75-.
Permanent Mission of People's Democratic Republic of Yemen to the United Nations, 413 East 51st Street, New York, N.Y. 10022, U.S.A.

Asiltürk, Oğuzhan; Turkish politician; b. 1935, Malatya; ed. Tech. Univ. of Istanbul.
Served Dept. of Highways and State Irrigation Admin.; later set up own engineering firm; Provincial Chair. Nat. Order Party, Ankara; mem. for Ankara, Nat. Assembly;

Sec.-Gen. Nat. Salvation Party (NSP) (all political activity suppressed Sept. 80-); Minister of Interior 74-77, of Industry and Technology July-Dec. 77.
National Salvation Party, Ankara, Turkey.

Assad, Lt.-Gen. Hafiz al-; Syrian army officer and politician; b. 6 Oct. 1930, Qardaha, Lattakia.
Minister of Defence and Commdr. of Air Force Feb. 66-Nov. 70; Prime Minister Nov. 70-April 71; Sec.-Gen. Baath Party 71-; Pres. of Syria March 71-; mem. Pres. Council, Fed. of Arab Repubs. 71-; Pres. Nat. Progressive Front 72-; Commdr. in Chief of Armed Forces 73-; Dr. h.c. (Damascus) 72.
Office of the President, Damascus, Syria.

Atassi, Nureddin, M.D.; Syrian politician; b. 1929; ed. Damascus Univ.
Minister of the Interior Aug. 63; Deputy Prime Minister Oct. 64; mem. Syrian Presidential Council May 64-Dec. 65; Pres. of Syria 66-70, also Prime Minister 68-70; Sec.-Gen. Syrian Baath Party 66-Oct. 70; in exile in Libya.

Atherton, Alfred Leroy, B.SC., M.A.; American diplomatist; b. 22 Nov. 1921, Pittsburgh; ed. Harvard Univ.
Joined Foreign Service 47; Second Sec., U.S. Embassy, Syria 53-56; Consul, Aleppo, Syria 57-58, Calcutta, India 62-65; Int. Relations Officer, Bureau of Near Eastern and S. Asian Affairs, State Dept. 59-61, Deputy Dir. 65-66, Country Dir. (Iraq, Jordan, Lebanon, Syria) 66-67, (Israel and Arab-Israeli Affairs) 67-70, Deputy Asst. Sec. of State 70-74, Asst. Sec. of State 74-78; Amb. at Large with Special Responsibility for Middle East Peace Negotiations 78-79; Amb. to Egypt May 79-.
American Embassy, 5 America El Latinia Street, Cairo, Egypt.

Atiqi, Abdel-Rahman Salem al-; Kuwaiti diplomatist and politician; b. 5 April 1928; ed. High School, Kuwait.
Secretary-General, Police Dept., Kuwait 49-59; Dir.-Gen. Health Dept. 59-61; Del. to UN 60-61, to WHO, Geneva 61, to UN Gen. Assembly 61; Amb. to U.S.A. 62-63; Under-Sec. Ministry of Foreign Affairs 63-67; Minister of Finance and Oil Affairs 67-75, of Finance 75-81; Chair. Kuwait Fund for Arab Econ. Devt. 77-80, The Public Inst. for Social Security 77-; Gov. for Kuwait, Islamic Devt. Bank; Adviser to the Amir with rank of Minister Aug. 81-.
Council of Ministers, Kuwait City, Kuwait.

Atrash, Muhammad al-, M.A., PH.D.; Syrian international official; b. 13 Nov. 1934, Tartous; ed. American Univ., Beirut, Lebanon, American Univ., Washington, D.C., U.S.A., London School of Econs.
Joined Cen. Bank of Syria 63, Research Dept. 63, Head of Credit Dept. 66-70; Alt. Exec. Dir. IMF 70-73; Deputy Gov. Cen. Bank of Syria 74; Exec. Dir. IBRD 74-76, IMF 76-78; del. to Second Cttee. of UN Gen. Assembly, to UNCTAD and other int. econ. confs. 63-70; part-time Lecturer, Univ. of Damascus 63-70; mem. Deputies of IMF Interim Cttee. of the Board of Governors on Reform of Int. Monetary System 72-74; Assoc. mem. IMF Interim Cttee. 74-76, *ex officio* mem. 76-78; Minister of Economy and Foreign Trade 80-Dec. 81.
Publs. articles in *Al-Abhath* (Quarterly of the American Univ. of Beirut) 63, 64, 66.
Ministry of Foreign Affairs, Damascus, Syria.

Attar, Mohammed Said al-; Yemeni economist; b. 26 Nov. 1927; ed. Ecole Pratique des Hautes Etudes à la Sorbonne, Inst. d'Etudes du Développement Econ. et Social (I.E.D.E.S.), Univ. de Paris.
Research I.E.D.E.S. 60-62; Dir.-Gen. Yemen Bank for Reconstruction and Devt. 62-65, Pres. 68-71; Minister of Econ. 65, 67-68; Pres. Econ. Comm. 65-66; Pres. Board, Yemen Bank and Econ. High Comm. 66-68; Minister of

Foreign Affairs 67-69; Vice-Pres. High Cttee. for Planning; mem. Int. Asscn. of Sociology; Perm. Rep. to UN 69-71, 73-74; Deputy Premier for Financial Affairs, Minister of Econ. 71; Exec. Sec. UN Econ. Comm. for Western Asia (ECWA) 74-; Special Adviser to govt. on the economic plan 81-.
Publs. *L'industrie du gant en France* 61, *L'épicerie à Paris* 61, *Etude sur la croissance économique de l'Afrique Occidentale* 62, *Le marché industriel et les projets de l'Arabie Séoudite* 62, *Le sous-développement économique et social du Yemen (Perspectives de la Révolution Yemenite)* 64, Arabic edn. 65.
Economic Commission for Western Asia (ECWA), B.P. 4656, Beirut, Lebanon.

Attiga, Ali Ahmed, B.SC., M.SC., PH.D.; Libyan economist; b. Oct. 1931, Misurata; ed. Univ. of Wisconsin and Univ. of California, U.S.A.
Assistant Econ. Adviser, Nat. Bank of Libya 59-60, Dir. of Research 60-64; Under-Sec. Ministry of Planning and Devt. 64-66, Dir. Econ. Research Div. 66-68; Minister of Planning and Devt. 68-69, concurrently of the Economy 69; Gen. Man. Libya Insurance Co. 70-73, Chair. 73; Chair. Nat. Investment Co. 71-73, Libya Hotel and Tourism Co. 71-73; Chair. and Gen. Man. Nat. Drilling Co.; Sec.-Gen. Org. of Arab Petroleum Exporting Countries (OAPEC) 73-82; mem. Board of Dirs., Arab Reinsurance Co., Beirut. Publ. *The Impact of Oil on the Libyan Economy 1956–1969* 74.
National Drilling Company, Tripoli, Libya.

Avidom (Mahler-Kalkstein), Menahem, B.A.; Israeli composer; b. 6 Jan. 1908; ed. American Univ. Beirut, and in Paris.
Lecturer on theory of music, Hebrew Conservatoire of Music, Tel-Aviv 36-, and Music Teachers' Training Coll. Tel-Aviv 45-; Sec.-Gen. Israel Philharmonic Orchestra 46-; Vice-Pres. Board of Dirs. Acum Ltd. (Composers and Authors Asscn.), Dir.-Gen. 56-; Dir. Arts Dept. Jerusalem Convention Centre 52; Art Adviser, Govt. Tourist Centre, Ministry of Commerce and Industry 54-; Pres. League of Composers 58; mem. Nat. Arts Council 62; Israel State Prize 61, Tel-Aviv Municipality Prize 48, 56; Israel Philharmonic Prize 53; Authors' and Composers' Asscn. Prize 62.
Compositions include: *A Folk Symphony* 47, *Symphony No. 2 David* 48, *Mediterranean Sinfonietta* 51, 2 Piano Sonatinas 49, *Concertino* for violinist Jascha Heifetz, *Concertino* for cellist Gregor Piatigorsky 51, *Alexandra Hashmonaith* (opera in 3 acts) 52, *Jubilee Suite, Triptyque Symphonique, In Every Generation* (opera) 55, *The Crook* (opera in 2 acts) 65, *B-A-C-H Suite* for chamber orchestra, *Sinfonietta* 66, *Twelve Changing Preludes* for piano 68, *Symphonie Variée* for chamber orchestra 69, *The Farewell* (opera in 1 act) 70, concerto for strings and flute, music for strings, symphonies 3, 4, 5, 6 and 7, psalms and cantatas, septet for woodwind, piano and percussion, string quartet No. 2, quartet for brass instruments, *The Pearl and The Coral* (ballet) 72, *Spring* overture for symphony orchestra 73, *Six Inventions for Piano in Homage and on the name of Arthur Rubinstein* 73, *Passacaglia for Piano* 73, *Yemenite Wedding Suite* 74, *Piece on the name of SCHoEnBerG for Piano* 74, *The Emperor's New Clothes* (one-act comic opera) 75; *Twelve Hills* cantata 76, *Five Psalms* 76, *Leachar* cantata 76, *Jodephat's cave* dramatic scene 77, *Once Upon a Time* (5 short tales for piano) 78, *The End of King Og* (children's opera) 78, *Movements for Strings* 79, *The First Sin* (opera in four scenes) 79, *Elegie, At Rachel's Tomb, The Voice of Rovina* (3 vocal compositions) 80, *Sinfonia Brevis* (Symphony No. 10) 81, *Monothema* (sonatina for string quartet) 82.
30 Semadar Street, Ramat-Gan, Israel.

Avineri, Shlomo; Israeli professor of political science and diplomatist; b. 20 Aug. 1933, Bielsko, Poland; ed.

Shalva Secondary School, Tel-Aviv, Hebrew Univ. Jerusalem and London School of Econs.
Professor of Political Science, Hebrew Univ. Jerusalem 71-, Dir. Eshkol Research Inst. 71-74, Dean of Faculty of Social Sciences 74-76; Dir.-Gen. Ministry of Foreign Affairs 77; visiting appointments at Yale Univ. 66-67, Wesleyan Univ., Middletown, Conn. 71-72, Research School of Social Sciences, Australian Nat. Univ. 72, Cornell Univ. 73, Univ. of Calif., San Diego 79; Fellow Woodrow Wilson Center, Washington, D.C. 81; mem. Presidium of Exec. Council, World Zionist Org. 78-; British Council Scholarship 61; Rubin Prize in the Social Sciences 68, Peretz Naphtali Prize in Econ. and Social Sciences 77, Present Tense Award for social and political analysis 81.
Publs. *The Social and Political Thought of Karl Marx* 68, *Karl Marx on Colonialism and Modernization* 68, *Israel and the Palestinians* 71, *Marx Socialism* 72, *Hegel's Theory of the Modern State* 73, *Varieties of Marxism* 77, *The Making of Modern Zionism* 81.
Department of Political Science, The Hebrew University, Jerusalem; Home: 50 Harlap Street, Jerusalem, Israel.

Avni, Tzvi; Israeli composer; b. 2 Sept. 1927, Germany. Arrived in Israel as a child; studied with Abel Ehrlich, Paul Ben-Haim and Mordecai Seter, Tel-Aviv Acad. of Music, with Aaron Copland and Lukas Foss at Tanglewood, Mass., and electronic music at Columbia Univ.
Compositions include: *Songs for Soprano and Orchestra* 57, *Woodwind Quintet* 59, *Prayer* for string orchestra 61, *Summer Strings* for string quartet 62, *Chaconne for Harp* 62, *Capriccio* for orchestra 63, *Vocalise* (electronic music) 64, *Two Pieces for Four Clarinets* 65, *Meditations on a Drama* for chamber orchestra 66 (ACUM Prize), *Collage* for Mezzo Soprano, Fl., Perc. and electronic tape 67, *Yerushalayim Shel Ma'ala* for mixed choir and orchestra 68, *Churban Habayit* for mixed choir and orchestra 68, *Five Pantomimes* for eight players 68, *Akeda* for chamber groups and narrator 69, *String Quartet No. 2* (Liberson Prize 69), *Requiem for Sounds* (ballet music), *Ein Dor* (ballet music) 70, *Holiday Metaphors* for symphony orchestra 70 (Engel Prize 73), *All the King's Women* (ballet music) 71, *By the Waters of Babylon* (prelude for small orchestra) 71, *Michtam* for David's harp and string quartet 75, *Two Psalms* for oboe and string quartet 75, *Al Harachamim* for choir 73, *Frames* (ballet music) 74, *On this Cape of Death* for orchestra 74, *Retrospection* for cello, percussion and tape 75, *Four Songs* for voice and piano 75, *He and She* (ballet music) 76, *Leda and the Swan* for soprano and clarinet 76, *Three Madrigals* for mixed choir 77, *Genesis Reconsidered* (ballet music) 78, *Piano Sonata No. 2, Epitaph* 79, *Beyond the Curtain* for piano quartet 79, *Programme Music 1980* for symphony orchestra.
Office: Rubin Academy of Music, 7 Smolenskin Street, Jerusalem; Home: 7 Zangwill Street, Tel-Aviv, Israel.

Awadi, Dr. Abdul Rahman al-; Kuwaiti politician; b. c. 1936; ed. American Univ. of Beirut, Univ. of Aberdeen, Harvard Univ.
Resident, then Registrar, Medical Dept., Sabah Hospital 63-69, Asst. Head 69-71; Asst. Under-Sec. of State and Dir. of Preventive Medical Services, Ministry of Public Health 71-75; Minister of Health 75-; Chair. Exec. Board, Council of Arab Ministers of Health Dec. 76-; Pres. 33rd Assembly, WHO.
Ministry of Health, Kuwait City, Kuwait.

Ayari, Chedly, L. EN D.; Tunisian economist and politician; b. 24 Aug. 1933.
Head of Admin., Tunisian Banking Soc. 58-59; Asst., Faculty of Law and Political and Econ. Sciences, Univ. of Tunis 59-60, Dean 65-67; Econ. Adviser, Perm. Mission to UN 60-64; Exec. Dir. Int. Bank for Reconstruction and Devt. (IBRD), Int. Devt. Asscn. (IDA), Int. Finance Corpn. (IFC) 64-65; Dir. CERES (Centre d'Etudes et de

Recherches Economiques et Sociales) 67-69; Sec. of State in charge of the Nat. Plan 69-70; Minister of Educ., Youth and Sport 70-71; Amb. to Belgium and Luxembourg Feb.-March 72; Minister of the Nat. Economy March 72-74, of Planning 74-75; Chair. of Board, Pres. and Gen. Man. Arab Bank for Econ. Devt. in Africa March 75-; Pres. UN Industrial Cttee. 62; del. to UN Confs. on Commerce and Devt. 62, 64; Grand Cordon, Order of the Repub. Publs. Numerous articles in economic journals.
Arab Bank for Economic Development in Africa, Baladia Road, P.O. Box 2640, Khartoum, Sudan; and Gammarth, La Marsa, Tunis, Tunisia.

Ayyoubi, Mahmoud al-; Syrian politician; b. 1932.
Former Dir.-Gen. for Admin. Affairs, Euphrates Dept.; Minister of Educ. 69-71, and Deputy Prime Minister 70-71; Vice-Pres. of Syria 71-75; Prime Minister 72-76; mem. Baath Party Regional Command 71-75, Jan. 80-.
c/o Baath Party, Damascus, Syria.

Azzawi, Hikmat al-, B.A.COMM.; Iraqi politician; b. 1934, Diyalah; ed. Coll. of Commerce and Econs., Baghdad Univ.
Reserve Lieutenant 57-58; Supt. Cen. Bank of Iraq 58-63, First Supt. 63; Auditor, Dir. of Stores and Warehouses, Dir. of Marketing, State Co. for Electrical Instruments and Equipment 66-68; Dir.-Gen., Chair. Govt. Purchasing Board 68; Chair. General Trade Establishment 69; Under-Sec. Ministry of Econ. 69; mem. Board of Dirs. Cen. Bank of Iraq 69; Minister of Econ. 72-76, of Foreign Trade 75-77; Minister of State without Portfolio 77; mem. Baath Arab Socialist Party 53-, mem. of Leadership of Baghdad Branch 65, Deputy Sec. Baghdad Branch 71, mem. Regional (Iraqi) Command Jan. 77-; Chief Ed. *Al-Iktisad* (Economist) magazine, Baghdad.
Baghdad, Iraq.

B

Badran, Mudar, B.A.; Jordanian politician and civil servant; b. 1934, Jerash; ed. Univ. of Damascus, Syria.
Lieutenant and Legal Consultant, Jordanian armed forces 57, Capt. and Legal Adviser to the Armed Forces Treasury 62; Asst. Chief, Jordanian Foreign Intelligence 65; Deputy Chief of Gen. Intelligence 66, Chief 68; Retd. Maj.-Gen. 70; Chief Chamberlain of the Royal Court 70, Sec.-Gen.; Nat. Security Adviser to King Hussein 71; Minister in the Royal Court 72; Deputy Head, Exec. Office of Occupied Territories Affairs 72-73; Minister of Educ. 73-74; Chief of the Royal Court 74-76; Prime Minister and Minister of Defence 76-79, Aug. 80-, also Minister of Foreign Affairs 76-79; fmr. Exec. Council of Arab Nat. Union.
Office of the Prime Minister, Amman, Jordan.

Bahar, Abdul Aziz Ahmed al-, B.A.ECONS.; Kuwaiti businessman; b. 1929; ed. American Univ. Beirut.
Director-General of Housing Dept., Ministry of Finance 56-61, of Kuwait Fund for Arab Econ. Devt. 61-62; Chair. Kuwait Nat. Industries 63-65, Kuwait Insurance Co. 65-67, Kuwait Foreign Trading Contracting and Investment Co. 65-73; Dir. Rifbank 67-74; Chair. Commercial Bank of Kuwait 65-78, Arab European Financial Management Co., Kuwait; Dir. United Bank of Kuwait Ltd., London 75-78; Deputy Chair. Commercial Bank of Dubai 70-78; Dir. Arab Trust Co. 75-78; Chair. Kuwait Investment Co. 81-; mem. Board of Dirs. Bank of Bahrain and Kuwait 81-; Hon. Consul Repub. of Costa Rica; mem. Int. Banking Asscn., Advisory Cttee. to American Coll in Switzerland
P.O. Box Safat 460, Kuwait.

Bahnini, Hadj M'Hammed, L. EN D., L. ÈS L.; Moroccan politician; b. 1914, Fez; ed. Lycée Gouraud (now "Lycée Hassan II"), Rabat.
Sec. Royal Palace; Magistrate, Haut Tribunal Chérifien; Instructor, College Impérial and Private Tutor to H.R.H. Crown Prince Moulay El Hassan, Prince Moulay Abdallah,

Princess Lalla Aïcha and Princess Lalla Malika; Dir. of the Imperial Cabinet 50-61; Del. Judge, Meknès 51; Exiled Dec. 52-July 54; Sec.-Gen. of the Cabinet 55-72; Minister of Justice 58-60; Minister of Admin. Affairs 65-70; Minister of Nat. Defence 70-71; Minister of Justice 71; Vice-Premier and Minister of Justice April-Nov. 72; Minister of State for Culture 74-81.
Office of the Minister of State, Ministry of Culture, Rabat, Morocco.

Bahrain, Ruler of (*see* Khalifa, Sheikh Isa bin Sulman al-).

Bakdash, Khalid; Syrian politician; b. 1912; ed. Damascus Inst. of Law.
Member of Parl. 54-58; Sec.-Gen. Syrian Communist Party 54-; self-imposed exile in East Europe 58-66; returned to Syria April 66; mem. Cen. Cttee. Syrian Nat. Progressive Front 72-.
Ave. Akrad, Damascus, Syria.

Bakhtiar, Shapour; Iranian lawyer and politician; b. 1916; ed. in Paris and Beirut.
Supporter of Nat. Front opposition to Govt. of Shah Mohammad Reza Pahlavi; Deputy Minister during Nat. Front Govt. of Dr. Muhammad Musaddiq 51-53; imprisoned several times during reign of Shah; Deputy Leader of Nat. Front -79; Chair. Regency Council and Prime Minister Jan.-Feb. 79; resigned after return of Ayatollah Ruhollah Khomeini (q.v.) Feb. 79.
Paris, France.

Bakr, Field Marshal Ahmed Hassan al-; Iraqi army officer and politician; b. 1914; ed. Military Academy.
Army career 36-58; Commdr. First Infantry Brigade 57; forced to retire from Iraq Army 58; Prime Minister of Iraq Feb. 63 and Nov. 63; Vice-Pres. of Iraq Nov. 63-Jan. 64; Amb. Jan.-Sept. 64; President of Iraq, Prime Minister and C.-in-C. of Armed Forces July 68-July 79; Chair. Revolutionary Command Council July 68-July 79; Minister of Defence 73-77; promoted to rank of Field Marshal 69.
Baghdad, Iraq.

Bakr, El Rashid el Tahir; Sudanese politician; b. 1930, Karkoj; ed. Univ. of Khartoum.
Former advocate; imprisoned for opposition to the regime of Gen. Ibrahim Abboud (q.v.) 58-64; Minister of Animal Resources and Justice 65; Amb. to Libya 72-74; apptd. mem. Political Bureau, Sudanese Socialist Union (SSU) and Sec. Farmers' Union in the SSU 72; Asst. Sec.-Gen. Sectoral Orgs., SSU 74; Speaker, People's Nat. Assembly 74-76, May 80-81; Second Vice-Pres. of Sudan 76-80; Prime Minister 76-77, Minister of Foreign Affairs 77-80; Chair. OAU Council of Ministers 78-79.
People's National Assembly, Khartoum, Sudan.

Balafrej, Ahmed; Moroccan politician; b. 1908; ed. Univs. of Paris and Cairo.
Secretary-General of Istiqlal (Independence) Party 44; later exiled by French, returned to Morocco 55; Minister of Foreign Affairs 55-58; Prime Minister May-Dec. 58; Ambassador-at-Large 60-61; Dep. Prime Minister June 61; Minister of Foreign Affairs 61-Nov. 63; Personal Rep. of King with rank of Minister 63-June 72.
c/o The Royal Palace, Rabat, Morocco.

Baly, Slaheddine, L. EN D.; Tunisian politician; b. 29 July 1926, Tunis; ed. Tunisia and France.
Inspector of Finance 49; Officer in Army 57; Public Prosecutor, Permanent Mil. Tribunal 57-66; Head of Office of Sec. of State for Nat. Defence 66-71; Sec.-Gen., Ministry of Defence 71; Perm. Sec., Nat. Defence Council 71-73; Minister of Justice 73-80, of Nat. Defence April 80-; mem. Central Cttee. Parti Socialiste Destourien 74-; Municipal Councillor, Tunis 72; Mayor Sidi Bou Saïd 75; Pres. Asscn. d'Amitié Tunisie-Italie 78-; Sec.-Gen. Tunisian

Olympic Cttee. 60-; Grand Cordon, Ordre de l'Indépendance, Ordre de la République and foreign decorations.
Ministry of Defence, Tunis, Tunisia.

Bani-Sadr, Abolhasan; Iranian politician; b. 1933, Hamadan, W. Iran; ed. Sorbonne and Teheran Univs.
Supporter of Dr. Muhammad Musaddiq (Prime Minister of Iran 51-53); joined underground anti-Shah movement 53; imprisoned after riots over Shah's land reforms 63; in exile in Paris 63-79; taught at the Sorbonne; close associate of the Ayatollah Ruhollah Khomeini (*q.v.*), and returned to Iran after overthrow of Shah; Minister of Econ. and Financial Affairs 79-80; mem. Supervisory Bd. of Cen. Bank of Iran 79; Acting Foreign Minister Nov. 79 (dismissed); Pres. Islamic Repub. of Iran Feb. 80-June 81 (dismissed); mem. Revolutionary Council 79-81, Pres. 80-81; C.-in-C. of Armed Forces 80-81 (dismissed); went underground, then fled to France July 81, subsequently formed the National Council of Resistance to oppose the Govt. in alliance with Massoud Rajavi, Leader of Mujaheddin Khalq, Abdel-Rahman Ghassemlov, Leader of the Democratic Party of Kurdistan, the Nat. Democratic Front and other resistance groups Chair. 81-.
Publs. *The Economics of Divine Unity, Oil and Violence*, and numerous articles and pamphlets on economics and politics.

Barakat, Lt.-Col. Abdullah Hosain; Yemeni politician; b. 26 Jan. 1934, Sana'a; ed. Mil. Coll., Sana'a, Police Coll., Cairo, Ain Shams Univ. and Cairo Univ.
Director of Police, Security and Passports, Taiz 61, of Public Security 62-64; Deputy, Ministry of Interior 64; Minister of Agriculture 65, of Interior 67-71; Amb. to Sudan 71, to Algeria and Tunisia 72-74; Minister of Social Affairs, Labour and Youth 74; Deputy Prime Minister for Interior Affairs 75; Amb. to Syria April 81-.
Embassy of the Yemen Arab Republic, Abou Roumaneh, Charkassieh, Damascus, Syria.

Barakat, Gamal Eddin, LL.B., B.LITT.; Egyptian diplomatist; b. 18 Feb. 1921, Cairo; ed. Helwan Secondary School, Cairo Univ., Hague Acad. of Int. Law, Oriel Coll. Oxford.
Third Sec., Egyptian Embassy, London 50-52; with Political Dept., Ministry of Foreign Affairs 53-55; Secretariat, Anglo-Egyptian Treaty negotiations 54; Consul-Gen., Aleppo, Syria 55-58; Counsellor, Washington, D.C. 58-60; Head of In-Service Training Dept., Ministry of Foreign Affairs 61-63; mem. OAU Experts Cttee., Addis Ababa 63-64; Amb. to Uganda 64-68, also to Burundi 68, to Finland 68-73; Asst. to the President's Adviser on Nat. Security 73-74; Head of Cultural Relations and Tech. Co-operation Dept., Ministry of Foreign Affairs 75; Amb. to Iraq Jan. 76-77; Dir. Diplomatic Inst., Ministry of Foreign Affairs 79-; Order of the Repub. 54, 64, Order of Merit (Egypt) 58, 73, Order of Merit (Syria) 58, Order of the Lion (Finland) 73.
Publs. *Status of Aliens in Egypt* 49, *Diplomatic Terminology* (in English and Arabic) 61.
55 Hegaz Street, Heliopolis, Cairo, Egypt.

Barakat, Ghaleb, B.B.A.; Jordanian civil servant; b. 20 Sept. 1927, Jaffa; ed. American Univ. Beirut.
Teacher, Nat. Coll., Tripoli 49-50, Teachers' Coll., Tripoli 50-52, Asst. Dir. 51-52; Chief Clerk and Press Attaché, Jordan Tourist Dept. 52-54; Tourist and Press Attaché, Royal Jordan Embassy, Rome 54-60; Dir. of Tourism 60-; Pres. Arab Int. Tourist Union 64, 70; Dir.-Gen. Tourism Authority 60-67, Under Sec. Ministry of Tourism and Antiquities, Dir. Gen. 68, Dir.-Gen. Tourism Authority 68-72, Minister of Tourism and Antiquities and Chair. Tourism Authority 72-79, concurrently of Transport 72; Chair. Board of Dirs., Hotels and Resthouses Corpn. 67-79; Lecturer, Faculty of Econ. and Commerce, Univ. of Jordan 67-79; Chair. Middle East Travel Comm., World Tourism

Org. 79, WTO Envoy on tourism sectoral support mission to the Middle East 80; Perm. Rep. of Jordan to UN, Geneva 80-; Chair. Group of 77, Geneva Jan.-March 82; Jordanian, Belgian, Mexican, Romanian and Vatican decorations.
P.O. Box 9064, Amman, Jordan.

Baramki, Dimitri Constantine, B.A., PH.D.; Jordanian archaeologist; b. 1909; ed. St. George's School, American Univ. of Beirut, Univ. of London.
Teacher, Jerusalem 25-26; Student Inspector of Antiquities, Palestine 27-28, Inspector 29; Senior Archaeological Officer 45; Archaeological Adviser and Librarian, American School of Oriental Research, Jerusalem 49-51; Curator of Museums 51-75; Asst. Prof. of Ancient History American Univ. of Beirut 51-53, Assoc. Prof. 53, Prof. 58-75; Distinguished Prof. Lebanese Univ. 75-80; UNESCO Expert in Prehistoric Archaeology, accred. to Libya 64-65, excavated numerous sites in Palestine; Prof. Emer. American Univ. of Beirut.
Publs. Numerous articles in the Quarterly of the Dept. of Antiquities, Palestine and in other publications.
American University of Beirut, Beirut, Lebanon.

Barenboim, Daniel; Israeli concert pianist and conductor; b. 15 Nov. 1942, Buenos Aires, Argentina; studied piano with his father and other musical subjects with Nadia Boulanger, Edwin Fischer and Igor Markevitch.
Debut in Buenos Aires at age of seven; played Bach D Minor Concerto with orchestra at Salzburg Mozarteum at age of nine; has played in Europe regularly 54-; yearly tours of U.S.A. 57-; has toured Japan, Australia and S. America; has played with or conducted New Philharmonia Orchestra, London Symphony Orchestra, New York Philharmonic, Philadelphia Orchestra, Israel Philharmonic, Vienna Philharmonic, Berlin Philharmonic, etc.; frequently tours with English Chamber Orchestra and with them records for E.M.I. (projects include complete Mozart Piano Concertos and late Symphonies); other recording projects include complete Beethoven Sonatas and Beethoven Concertos (with New Philharmonia Orchestra conducted by Klemperer); has appeared in series of Master-classes on B.B.C. television; presented Festival of Summer Music on South Bank, London, 68, 69; leading role in Brighton Festival 67-; appears regularly at Edinburgh Festival; conductor, Edinburgh Festival Opera 73; Musical Dir. Orchestre de Paris 75-.
c/o Harold Holt Ltd., 31 Sinclair Rd., London, W14 0NS, England.

Barkovsky, Anatoly; Soviet diplomatist; b. 1921, Moscow; ed. Diplomatic Acad.
Attaché, Third Sec., Second Sec., First Sec., U.S.S.R. Embassy, Egypt 52-57, Counsellor 59-61; Consul-Gen., Syria 61; Amb. to Syria 61-68, to Cyprus 71-73, to Iraq 74-82.
Ministry of Foreign Affairs, Moscow, U.S.S.R.

Bar-Lev, Lieut.-Gen. Haim; Israeli officer and politician; b. 1924, Austria; ed. Mikhwe Israel Agricultural School, Columbia Univ. School of Econs. and Admin., U.S.A.
Joined Palmach Units 42; Platoon Commdr., Beith-Ha'Arava 44; Commdr. D Co., Yesreel 45-46; Commdr. Palmach N.C.P.'s course and C.O. Eight Regt., Negev Brigade 47, Operations Officer 48; Commdr. Armoured Units 48; Instructor and later Commdr., Bn. Commdrs. course 49-52; Chief of Staff, Northern Command 52-53; C.O. Givati Brigade 54-55; Dir. G.H.Q. Training Div. 56; Commdr. Armoured Brigade during Sinai campaign; Commdr. Armoured Corps 65-71; made study tour of armoured corps of Western European countries and U.S.A. 61; visited U.S. army installations and the armies of the Philippines, Japan, Thailand and S. Viet-Nam; Dir. Gen. Staff, Operations Branch 64-66; Deputy Chief of Staff,

Israel Defence Forces 67, Chief of Staff 68-72; Minister of Commerce and Industry 72-June 77; elected to Knesset June 77; Sec.-Gen. Israel Labour Party Aug. 78-.
Neve Magen, Israel.

Batu, Hamit, LL.B.; Turkish diplomatist; b. 1919; ed. Univ. of Lyon.
Ministry of Foreign Affairs 44-; Sec. to Dept. of Econ. Affairs; Sec. to Directorate of Int. Orgs. and Confs. 47; Sec., London 47-51; Head of Section, Cabinet of Minister of Foreign Affairs 51-54, Private Sec. to the Minister 54-56; First Counsellor, London 56-57, Oslo 57-59, Moscow 59-61; Gen. Dir., Dept. of Cultural Rels. and European Council Affairs 61-66; Amb. to Afghanistan 66-71, to Finland 71-74; Gen. Dir. of Political Planning and Research 74-76; Asst. Sec.-Gen. to Minister of Foreign Affairs, in charge of politico-military affairs 76-77; Amb. to France 78-80, to Italy Dec. 80-.
Embassy of Turkey, 28 Via Palestro, 00185 Rome, Italy.

Baykara, Zeyyad; Turkish economist, financier and politician; b. 8 July 1918, Kemaliye; ed. Faculty of Political Sciences, Ankara Univ.
Administrative posts including Dir.-Gen. State Treasury, Under.-Sec. Prime Minister's Office and Ministry of Finance; Minister of State 72-73; Deputy Prime Minister 74-75; Minister of Justice April-June 77; mem. Senate; Minister of State and Deputy Prime Minister Sept. 80-.
Office of the Deputy Prime Minister, Devlet Bakanlığı, Bakanlıklar, Ankara, Turkey.

Bayramoğlu, Fuat; Turkish diplomatist; b. 23 March 1912, Ankara; ed. School of Political Sciences (Mülkiye), Istanbul and Univ. of Liège.
Entered Diplomatic Service 39; mem. Gen. Directorate of Press and Publication Cttee. 43; Head of Secretariat Prime Minister's Office 44-46; Chair. Press Dept. Cttee. 46; Dir. in Foreign Ministry 48; Consul, Cyprus 49; Consul-Gen., Jerusalem 51-53; Dir.-Gen. Consular and Claims Dept., Ministry of Foreign Affairs, Ankara 53-57; Amb. to Norway 57-59, to Iraq 59-60, to Iran 60-62, to Italy 62-63; Sec.-Gen. Ministry of Foreign Affairs 63-64; Amb. to Belgium 64-67, to Italy 67-69, to U.S.S.R. 69-71; Chair. Inspection Corps, Ministry of Foreign Affairs 71-72; Sec.-Gen. to the Pres. of Turkey 72-77; Homayoun Order of Iran 62, Grand Croix de Mérite Civil (Spain) 63, Gran Croce all' Ordine al merito della Repubblica (Italy) 69, Presidential and Ministry of Foreign Affairs Distinguished Service awards 73; Gold Medal of Iqbal Birth Centenary (Pakistan) 79; Silver and Gold Medals from seven int. philatelic exhbns.
Publ. *Rubaiat* book of poems; several legal and sociological articles; *Rubailer* (book of quatrains) 74, revised and enlarged edn. 76; *Turk Cam Sanati ve Beykoz İşleri* (Turkish Glass Art) 74, *Turkish Glass Art and Beykoz Ware* 76, some firmans with illuminations and with the Sultan's signatures (in English) 76, (in French) 79.
Kandilli, Vaniköy Cad. No. 60, Istanbul, Turkey.

Bayülken, Ümit Halûk; Turkish diplomatist; b. July 1921; ed. Lycée of Haydar Paşa, Istanbul, Ankara Univ.
Joined Ministry of Foreign Affairs 44, Vice-Consul, Frankfurt 47, First Sec., Bonn 50; Dir. Middle East Section 51-53; Political Adviser to UN Del. 53-59; mem. Turkish Del. to Cyprus Joint Cttee., London 59-60; Dir.-Gen. Policy Planning Group, Ministry of Foreign Affairs 60-63, appointed Minister Plenipotentiary; Asst. Sec.-Gen. for Political Affairs 63-64; Sec.-Gen. Ministry of Foreign Affairs 64-66; Amb. to U.K. 66-69; Perm. Rep. to UN 69-71; Minister of Foreign Affairs 71-74; Sec.-Gen. CENTO 75-77; Sec.-Gen. of the Presidency 77-80; Senator July 80-; Minister of Defence July 80-; Head of several overseas dels. since 52, Order Isabel la Catolica (Spain), German Grand Cross of Merit, Hon. G.C.V.O. (U.K.) 67, Star of the

First Order (Jordan) 72, (Tunisia) 73, (Egypt) 73, Sitara-i-Pakistan 70, Sirdar-i-Ali (Afghanistan) 72.
Publs. several papers on minorities, Cyprus and foreign policy.
Ministry of Defence, Milli Savunma Bakanlığı, Ankara, Turkey.

Bazargan, Mehdi; Iranian politician, businessman and university professor; b. 1905; ed. Univ. of the Sorbonne.
Assistant Prof., Teheran Univ., then Prof., then Dean; fmr. Man. Dir. Nat. Oil Co. of Iran; Founder mem. and Leader Nehzat Azardi (Freedom of Iran Movement) 61; arrested for anti-Govt. activities 62; Man. Dir. Yad Construction Co.; Founder mem. Iranian Cttee. for the Defence of Liberty and Human Rights Dec. 77; appointed Prime Minister by Ayatollah Khomeini (*q.v.*) Feb.-Nov. 79.
Publs. booklets on Islam and modern civilization.
c/o Office of the Prime Minister, Qajar Palace, Teheran, Iran.

Bedjaoui, Mohammed, LL.D.; Algerian politician; b. 21 Sept. 1929, Sidi-Bel-Abbès; ed. Univ. of Grenoble and Institut d'Etudes Politiques, Grenoble.
Junior Lawyer, Court of Appeal, Grenoble 51-53; research worker at Centre National de la Recherche Scientifique (C.N.R.S.), Paris 56-58; Legal Counsellor of the Arab League in Geneva 59-62; Legal Counsellor Provisional Republican Govt. of Algeria in Exile 58-61; Exec. Sec. to Pres. of Nat. Constituent Assembly 62; mem. Del. to UN 57, 62, 77, 78, Dels. to confs. of OAU and Non-Aligned Countries; Sec.-Gen. Council of Ministers, Algiers 62-64; Pres. Soc. Nat. des chemins de fer algériens (S.N.C.F.A.) 64; Dean of the Faculty of Law. Algiers Univ. 64-65; Minister of Justice and Keeper of the Seals 64-70; mem. Comm. on Int. Law, UN 65-(81), special reporter 65-70; Amb. to France 70-79; Perm. Rep. to UNESCO 71-79; Head Dels. to UN Conf. on Succession of States in Respect of Treaties 77 and Conf. on the Law of the Sea 76-80; Perm. Rep. to UN 79-82; co-Pres. UN Comm. of Inquiry (Iran) 80; Vice-Pres. UN Council for Namibia 79-82; Chair. Group of 77, Geneva 81-82; mem. Int. Court of Justice, The Hague March 82-; Chair. Cttee. on the Drafting of an Int. Convention against the Recruitment, Use, Financing and Training of Mercenaries; Assoc. Inst. of Int. Law; mem. French Soc. of Int. Law; Carnegie Endowment for Int. Peace 56; Ordre du Mérite Alaouite, Morocco; Order of the Repub., Egypt; Commdr. Légion d'honneur.
Publs. *International Civil Service* 56, *Fonction publique internationale et influences nationales* 58, *La révolution algérienne et le droit* 61, *Succession d'états* 70, *Non-alignement et droit international* 76, *Terra nullius, droits historiques et autodétermination* 78, *Pour un nouvel ordre économique international* 78, numerous legal articles.
International Court of Justice, Peace Palace, 2517 KJ, The Hague, Netherlands; Home: 39 rue des Pins, Hydra, Algiers, Algeria.

Begin, Menachem Wolfovitch, M.JUR.; Israeli politician; b. 16 Aug. 1913, Brest-Litovsk, Poland (now U.S.S.R.); ed. Warsaw Univ.
Active in Jewish Youth Movement "Betar"; Chair. "Betar" in Czechoslovakia 36, in Poland 39; confined in Siberian labour camp by Moscow Comm. of N.K.V.D. 40-42; came with Polish army to Palestine 42; C.-in-C. Irgun Zvi Leumi 43-48, leading revolt against British rule in Palestine; mem. Knesset (Israel Parl.); Leader of the Opposition in Knesset 48-67, 69-77; Minister without Portfolio 67-69; Founder and Chair. Herut (Freedom Movement); joint Chair. of Likud Bloc 73-; Prime Minister June 77-, also acting Minister of Defence 80-81; Hon. D.Litt. (Yeshiva Univ. N.Y.) 78; Nobel Prize for Peace (shared with the late Pres. Sadat) 78.
Publs. *The Revolt; personal memoirs of the Commander of*

Irgun Zvi Leumi 49, *The White Nights, Behmatret* 78.
Office of the Prime Minister, Jerusalem; and 1 Rosenbaum Street, Tel-Aviv, Israel.

Belkhodja, Tahar; Tunisian politician and former agricultural engineer; b. 3 June 1931, Mahdia.
Active mem. Néo-Destour (now called Parti Socialiste Destour) 47-, now mem. Central Cttee.; Agricultural Eng. 56; Sec.-Gen. Union Gén. des Etudiants Tunisiens 57-59; Officer of Néo-Destour Political Bureau for Students 59; Pres. Confed. of North African Students 59; Pres. Int. Asscn. of Students of Agriculture 58; Chef de Cabinet to Sec. of State for Foreign Affairs 60; Minister Plenipotentiary, Chargé d'Affaires in Paris 61; Amb. to Guinea, Ivory Coast, Mali, Mauritania, Senegal 61-66; Chef de Cabinet to Sec. of State for Plan and Nat. Econ. 66; Head of Nat. Security 67; Amb. to Senegal 69, to Spain 70; Sec. of State, Ministry of Agriculture 70; Minister of Youth and Sports 70; Amb. to Vatican City 71, also Perm. Rep. to Geneva 71; Minister of the Interior 73-77; Amb. to Fed. Repub. of Germany 80-81; Grand Cordon, Order of Independence; Grand Cordon, Order of the Repub. of Tunisia; several foreign decorations.
c/o Embassy of Tunisia, 5300 Bonn 2, Godesberger Allee 103, Federal Republic of Germany.

Ben Abbes, Youssef, M.D.; Moroccan diplomatist and former politician; b. 15 Aug. 1921, Rabat; ed. Marrakesh, Medical Coll. of Algiers and Paris.
Joined Public Health Service 49, Dir. several hospitals, then Insp. of Health; Minister of Health 58-61, of Health and Educ. 61-62, of Educ., Youth and Sport 62-65; Mayor of Marrakesh and Pres. Provincial Council; Senator for Marrakesh; Amb. to U.A.R. 65-66, to Italy 67-69, to Algeria 69-70; Minister of Foreign Affairs Oct. 70-71; Amb. to Spain 71-72, to France and UNESCO Sept. 72- (also accred. to the Vatican 76-); Commdr., Ordre nat. du Trone, Ordre nat. du Mérite; other orders and decorations.
Embassy of Morocco, rue Le Tasse 3, Paris 16e, France.

Benabdallah, Abdel-Aziz; Moroccan professor; b. 28 Nov. 1923; ed. Univ. of Algiers.
General Dir. for the Conservation and Registry of Land Properties 57; Dir. of Higher Educ. for Scientific Research 58-61; Dir. of Nat. Arabization Centre 61-68; Dir.-Gen. Bureau of Co-ordination of Arabization in the Arab World, Arab League, Rabat 69-; Prof., Faculty of Arts, Mohamed V Univ., Rabat and also Dar-el-Hadith Inst., al-Qarawiyine Univ., Fez.; Editor *Al-Qods* magazine; mem. Iraqi Acad., Royal Moroccan Acad., Indian Acad., Jordanian Acad.
Publs. in Arabic: *Philosophy and Morality in Ibn El Khatib* 49, *Aspects of Maghreb Civilization* (2 edns., third entitled *Gifts of Maghreb Cilivization), History of Medicine* 59, *History of Morocco* (2 vols.), *Geography of Morocco* (3 edns.), about 30 specialized dictionaries, *Dictionary of Native Arabic and Foreign Words used in Moroccan Dialects, with a Comparative Study of Dialects of the Arab World, Evolution of Thought and Language, Classical Arabic and Moroccan Dialects, Catalogue of Moroccan Commentators and Readers of the Koran, Arabization and the Future of the Arabic Language;* in French: *Les Grands Courants de la Civilisation du Maghreb* 58, *l'Art Maghrebin* 62, *Clarté sur l'Islam ou l'Islam dans ses sources* (2 edns.), *Vérité sur le Sahara, La Pensée Islamique et le Monde Moderne.*
Bureau de coordination de l'arabisation, 8 rue Angola, Rabat, Morocco.

Ben Abdallah, Moncef, L. ÈS SC.; Tunisian economist; b. 21 Oct. 1946, Tunis; ed. Ecole Centrale, Paris.
Engineer, Chief of Prodn., Soc. Tunisienne d'Electricité et du Gaz 72-75; Chargé de mission, Office of Minister of Nat. Econ. 75-76; Deputy Dir. state petroleum co. (ETAP) 78-79; Dir. of Industry, Ministry of Industry, Mines and

Energy 79; Chef de Cabinet, Ministry of Nat. Econ. 80; Pres.-Dir.-Gen. Agence de Promotion des Investissements Oct. 80-; Commdr. Order of the Republic.
Agence de Promotion des Investissements, 7 Rue du Royaume de l'Arabie Saoudite, Tunis, Tunisia.

Ben Ammar, Hassib; Tunisian professor and politician; b. 11 April 1924; ed. Coll. Sadiki, Tunis and Faculty of Sciences, Paris.
Active mem. of Destour groups abroad 42-52; mem. Destour Fed., Tunis 54; Sec.-Gen. of the Econ. and Social Board 59; Sec.-Gen. of Destour Youth Movt. 60; Mayor of Tunis 63-65, Gov. 65-69; Amb. to Italy 69; Minister of Defence 70-71; mem. Cen. Cttee., Destour Socialist Party (DSP) 64; mem. Political Bureau DSP, Chair. 69-70, Supreme Cttee. DSP 70, Council of Nat. Defence 71; Editor *Ar-Rai* and *Démocratie* newspapers, organs of the Mouvement des Démocrates Socialistes; Grand Cordon, Order of Independence, Grand Cordon, Order of the Repub.
c/o Parti Socialiste Destourien, boulevard 9 avril 1938, Tunis, Tunisia.

Ben Bella, Mohammed; Algerian politician; b. 1916.
Warrant Officer in Moroccan regiment during Second World War (decorated); Chief O.S. rebel military group in Algeria 47; imprisoned 49-52 (escaped); directed Algerian nat. movement from exile in Libya 52-56; arrested Oct. 56; held in France 59-62; Vice-Premier, Algerian Nationalist Provisional Govt., Tunis 62; Leader, Algerian Political Bureau, Algeria 62; Premier of Algeria Sept. 62-June 65, President of Algeria Sept. 63-June 65, concurrently Minister of Interior Dec. 64-June 65; overthrown by mil. coup and imprisoned 65; under house arrest 65-79; restricted residence, Msila 79-80; freed 81; Chair. Int. Islamic Comm. for Human Rights, London 82-; Lenin Peace Prize 64.
Paris, France.

Bendjedid, Col. Chadli (*see* Chadli, Col. Bendjedid).

Benhamouda, Boualem; Algerian politician.
Minister of Ex-Combattants 65-70, of Justice 70-80, of Public Works 77-80, of the Interior Jan. 80-; mem. Political Bureau of Nat. Liberation Front (FLN); Chair. FLN Cttee. on Education, Training and Culture 79-80; Minister of Finance Jan. 82-.
Ministry of Finance, Algiers, Algeria.

Benhima, Mohamed, M.D.; Moroccan physician and politician; b. 25 June 1924; ed. Faculté de Médecine de Nancy, France.
Chief Medical Officer, Had Court District 54-56; Chief of Cen. Service for Urban and Rural Hygiene 56-57; Head of Personal Office of Minister of Public Health 57-60; Sec.-Gen., Ministry of Public Health Jan.-June 60; Gov. of Provinces of Agadir and Tarfaya 60-61; Minister of Public Works 61-62, 63-65, of Commerce, Industry, Mines, Handicrafts and Merchant Marine 62-63, of Nat. Educ. 65-67; Prime Minister 67-69; Minister of Agriculture and Agrarian Reform 69, of Public Health 69-72, of the Interior 72-73; Minister of State for Co-operation and Training 73-77, for the Interior 77-79; decorations from Govts. of Belgium, France, Morocco, Sweden, Ethiopia, Tunisia, Liberia and Egypt.
Km. 5,500, Route des Zaërs, Rabat, Morocco.

Benjenk, Munir P., B.SC. (ECON.); Turkish public servant; b. 1924; ed. English Lycée and Robert Coll., Istanbul and London School of Economics.
Worked with B.B.C., Reading, U.K. 49-51; served with Turkish Army in Korea 51-52; with OEEC (now OECD), Paris 53-63; mem. Perm. Mission to Washington, D.C. of OEEC 55-57; Dir. Sardinian Village Devt. Project 59-60; Asst. Dir. Devt. Dept., OECD 62-63; with Int. Bank for Reconstruction and Devt. 63-; Head of Econ. Advisory

Mission, Algeria 64, Head of N. Africa Div. 65-67, Deputy Dir. Middle East and N. Africa Dept. 67-68, Europe, Middle East and N. Africa Dept. 68-69, Dir. 70-72, Vice-Pres. Europe, Middle East and N. Africa 72-75, 76-80, for External Relations 80-; Visiting Fellow, St. Antony's Coll., Oxford 75-76; Ordine al Merito della Repubblica Italiana, Order of the Cedars of Lebanon 73.
1308 28th Street, N.W., Washington, D.C. 20007; and International Bank for Reconstruction and Development, 1818 H Street, N.W., Washington, D.C. 20433, U.S.A.

Ben Salah, Ahmed, D.D'ETAT; Tunisian politician; b. 13 Jan. 1926; ed. Collège Sadiki, Tunis and Univ. of Paris.
Teacher, Lycée de Sousse 48-51; Del. Tunisian Trade Union Movement at Int. Confederation of Trade Unions, Brussels 51-54; Sec.-Gen. Union Générale Tunisienne du Travail 53-56; Minister of Public Health and Social Affairs 58-60, for the Plan and Finance 61-64, for the Plan and Nat. Economy 64-69, for Educ. Sept. 69-70; Asst. Sec.-Gen. Destour Socialist Party 64-70; imprisoned 70, escaped Feb. 73; Sec.-Gen. Mouvement de l'Unité Populaire (M.U.P.); living in exile in Europe.
c/o Socialist International, 88A St. John's Wood High Street, London, NW8 7SJ, England.

Benslimane, Abdelkader, B.A.; Moroccan politician; b. 22 Feb. 1932, Rommani; ed. Toulouse Univ., France.
Joined Ministry of Finance 57, Head of Admin. Div. 57-59, Head of Budget Dept. and Censor at Central Bank 61-63; Minister, Embassy to France 61-63; Dir.-Gen. Bureau d'Etudes et de Participations Industrielles 63-66; Del. to Maghreb Perm. Consultative Cttee. 66-72, Vice-Pres. 65-72; Amb. to Benelux and EEC Feb.-Nov. 72; Minister of Trade, Industry, Mines and Merchant Marine 72-74, of Finance 74-77; Chair. and Gen. Man. Banque Nat. pour le Développement Economique Jan. 78-; Gov. Arab Fund for Econ. and Social Devt., Arab Bank for Econ. Devt. in Africa, Islamic Devt. Bank, African Devt. Bank, African Devt. Fund.
B.P. 407, Place des Alaouites, Rabat, Morocco.

Ben Yahya, Prince Abdul Rahman; Yemeni politician.
Deputy Prime Minister until 67; Prime Minister 67-68; mem. Imamate Council 67-68; in exile 68-; royalist.

Berenblum, Isaac, M.D., M.SC.; Israeli pathologist and experimental biologist; b. 26 Aug. 1903; ed. Bristol Grammar School and Leeds Univ.
Riley-Smith Research Fellow, Dept. Experimental Pathology and Cancer Research, Leeds Univ. Medical School 29-36; Beit Memorial Research Fellow, Dunn School of Pathology, Oxford Univ. 36-40; Departmental and Univ. Demonstrator in Pathology, Oxford Univ. 40-48; in charge of Oxford Univ. Research Centre of British Empire Cancer Campaign 40-48; Special Research Fellow, Nat. Cancer Inst., Bethesda, Md., U.S.A. 48-50; Head of Dept. of Experimental Biology, The Weizmann Inst. of Science, Rehovot, Israel 50-71; Visiting Prof. of Oncology, Hebrew Univ., Jerusalem 50-56; mem. Israel Research Council 52-57; Jack Cotton Prof. of Cancer Research, The Weizmann Inst. of Science, Rehovot, Israel 62-71, Emer. Prof. 71-; Hon. Life Mem. New York Acad. of Sciences, World Acad. of Sciences, American Asscn. of Cancer Research, Israel Acad. of Sciences and Humanities; Weizmann Prize of Municipality of Tel-Aviv-Yaffo 59; Rothschild Prize for Biology 66; Israel Prize 74; Bertner Award for Cancer Research, Texas 78; Alfred P. Sloan, Jr. Prize, General Motors Cancer Foundation 80.
Publs. *Science versus Cancer* 46, *Man Against Cancer* 52, *Cancer Research Today* 67, *Carcinogenesis as a Biological Problem* 74.
33 Ruppin Street, Rehovot, Israel.

Berger, Morroe, PH.D.; American educator and writer; b. 25 June 1917; ed. Columbia Univ., New York.

Assistant Prof., Princeton Univ. 52-58, Assoc. Prof. 58-61, Prof. of Sociology 62-; Dir. Program in Near Eastern Studies, Princeton Univ. 62-68, 73-77; mem., Chair. Joint Cttee. of Near and Middle East, of American Council of Learned Socs. and Social Science Research Council 62-69; Consultant to U.S. Office of Educ. 65-68; mem. Governing Boards, American Research Center, Egypt (Pres. 74-78), American Research Inst., Turkey 64-67; Pres. Middle East Studies Asscn. 67; Chair. Council on Int. and Regional Studies, Princeton Univ. 68-77, Chair. Dept. of Sociology 71-74.
Publs. *Equality by Statute* 52, 67, *Bureaucracy and Society in Modern Egypt* 57, *The Arab World Today* 62, *Madame de Staël on Politics, Literature and National Character* 64, *Islam in Egypt Today* 70, *Real and Imagined Worlds: The Novel and Social Science* 77; Editor *New Metropolis in the Arab World* 63; Translator and Adapter (with others) *The Recited Koran, A History of the First Recorded Version* 75; numerous articles in learned journals and contributions to encyclopaedias.
Jones Hall, Princeton University, Princeton, New Jersey 08540, U.S.A.

Berk, Mükerrem; Turkish musician; b. 1917; ed. Istanbul Conservatoire.
Joined Presidential Symphony Orchestra 37, Principal Flute and Woodwind leader 41-68, Admin. Dir. 60-68; Gen. Dir. State Opera and Ballet 69-74; Dir. Istanbul State Symphony Orchestra and Izmir State Symphony Orchestra 74-; many tours in U.S.A., United Kingdom, W. Europe, Scandinavia, Middle East, India, Pakistan and U.S.S.R.
Istanbul Devlet Senfoni Orkestrasi Atatürk Kültür Merkezi, Taksim, Istanbul; Home: Molla Bayiri Sok. no. 32/4, Fındıklı-Istanbul, Turkey.

Berkol, Faruk N., LL.D.; Turkish diplomatist; b. 9 Sept. 1917, Istanbul; ed. Univs. of Istanbul and Paris and School of Political Science, Paris.
Joined Ministry of Foreign Affairs 41; First Sec., Washington, D.C. 45-50; Counsellor, later Chargé d'Affaires, London 52-56; Chef de Cabinet to Pres. of Turkey 56-60; Amb. to Tunisia 62-67, to Belgium 67-72; UN Under-Sec. Gen., UN Disaster Relief Co-ordinator 72-; mem. Mexican Acad. of Int. Law; decorations from Afghanistan, Belgium, Fed. Repub. of Germany, France, Italy, Liberia, Libya, Luxembourg, Spain and Tunisia.
Publs. *Le Statut juridique actuel des portes maritimes orientales de la Méditerranée* 40, and books and articles in Turkish and French on the Balkan *entente* and Turkish economic expansion.
Office of the United Nations Disaster Relief Co-ordinator, Palais des Nations, 1211 Geneva 10, Switzerland.

Berman, Yitzhack; Israeli politician and lawyer; b. 1913, Russia; ed. Teacher Training Coll., Jerusalem, Univ. Coll., London and Inner Temple, London.
Settled in Palestine 21; served in British Army 42-45; mem. Command, Irgun Zevayi Leumi, later Major, Israeli Defence Force 48-50; Gen. Man. Willis Overland & Kaizer Assembly Plant, Haifa 50-54; private law practice, Tel Aviv 54-80; mem. Cen. Cttee. Liberal Party 68-; mem. Knesset 77-, Speaker March 80-81.
c/o The Knesset, Jerusalem 91 999, Israel.

Bertini, Gary; Israeli conductor; b. 1 May 1927, Bessarabia; U.S.S.R.; ed. Israel, Univ. of Paris, Conservatorio Verdi, Milan, Conservatoire Nat. Paris and studies under Arthur Honegger.
Founder RINAT Chamber Choir 55; Founder Jeunesses Musicales d'Israel; teacher of conducting at Rubin Acad. of Music; Artistic Dir. and Conductor Israel Chamber Orchestra; Principal Guest Conductor Scottish Nat. Orchestra; Regular Guest Conductor Hamburg State Opera, Paris Opera, Scottish Opera, BBC, Israel Philharmonic Orchestra and Jerusalem Philharmonic Orchestra; Prof.

Tel-Aviv Univ.; Founder, Israel Chamber Orchestra; Artistic Adviser Israel Festival; has conducted many orchestras in Israel and abroad, often performing contemporary Israeli music; composer of symphonic and chamber music, ballets, incidental music to more than 40 plays, and music for films and radio.
5 Basel Street, Tel-Aviv, Israel.

Bilgic, Mehmet Saadettin, M.D.; Turkish surgeon and politician; b. 1921, Isparta; ed. Konya Lycée, Univ. of Istanbul.
Member of Nat. Assembly 61-80; mem. Nat. Exec., Justice Party 62-70, 76-, Deputy Leader 62-64, Leader June-Nov. 64; Minister of Communications 67-69, of National Defence Aug.-Oct. 77; mem. Nat. Exec. and Deputy Leader, Democratic Party 70-75; Deputy Leader and Head Nat. Party Org. of Justice Party 76-78; Head Nat. Org. of Justice Party 79- (all political activity suspended Sept. 80-).
Adalet Partisi, Genel Mertezi, Selânik Caddesi, Kızılay, Ankara, Turkey.

Binder, Leonard; American university professor; b. 20 Aug. 1927; ed. Boston Latin School, Harvard Coll., Harvard Univ., Princeton Univ. and Oxford Univ.
Assistant Prof. Univ. Calif., Los Angeles 56-61; Assoc. Prof. and Prof. Univ. of Chicago 61-77, Chair. Dept. of Political Science 64-67. Chair. Cttee, on Near Eastern Studies 63-65; mem. New Nations Cttee. 61-; Fellow, Center for Advanced Studies in the Behavioral Sciences 67-68; Field Research in Pakistan 54-55, in Iran 58-59, in Egypt 60-61, in Lebanon 64, in Tunisia 64, 65, 66, 69; Chair. Research and Training Cttee., Middle East Studies Asscn.; Pres. Middle East Studies Asscn. 73-74; Dir. Middle East Center, Univ. of Chicago 73-76; Co-Dir. Islam and Social Change Project 76-77.
Publs. *Religion and Politics in Pakistan* 60, *Iran: Political Development in a Changing Society* 61, *The Ideological Revolution in the Middle East* 64, Editor, *Politics in the Lebanon* 65, Co-author, *Crises and Sequences in Political Development* 72, Editor, *The Study of the Middle East* 76, *In a Moment of Enthusiasm; Political Power and the Second Stratum in Egypt* 78 also numerous articles in periodicals.
5512 South Harper Avenue, Chicago, Illinois 60637, U.S.A.

Birincioglu, Ahmet Ihsan; Turkish politician; b. 1923, Trabzon; ed. Faculty of Law, Istanbul Univ.
Worked as a lawyer; Justice Party Deputy; Senator for Trabzon 75; fmr. Minister of Customs and Monopoly; Minister of Defence Nov. 79-Sept. 80.
c/o Ministry of Foreign Affairs, Dişişleri Bakanlığı, Müdafaa Cad., Bakanlıklar, Ankara, Turkey.

Bishara, Abdulla Yacoub; Kuwaiti diplomatist; b. 1936; ed. Cairo Univ., Balliol Coll., Oxford, St. John's Univ. New York.
Second Sec., Kuwait Embassy, Tunisia 63-64; Dir. Office of Minister of Foreign Affairs, Kuwait 64-71; Perm. Rep. to UN 71-81, concurrently Amb. to Argentina; del. to numerous int. confs.; Foreign Affairs adviser to Prime Minister 81; Sec.-Gen. Gulf Co-operation Council May 81-.
Gulf Co-operation Council Secretariat, Riyadh, Saudi Arabia.

Bitat, Rabah; Algerian politician; b. 19 Dec. 1925, Constantine Region.
Joined Parti du Peuple Algérien 40, Mouvement pour le Triomphe des Libertés démocratiques 47; participated in formation of Organisation spéciale 48; wanted, sentenced *in absentia* to 10 years; participated in foundation of Comité révolutionnaire d'Unité et d'Action 54, later of Front de Libération Nationale and Armée de Libération Nationale; arrested March 55, held in France till 62;

hunger strike, granted political status 60, after being appointed Minister of State in Provisional Revolutionary Govt. of Algerian Repub. 58; mem. Conseil National de la Révolution Algérienne 56; mem. Political Bureau, in charge of Party Org. 62-63; Deputy Premier 62-63, Third Deputy Premier 63; in exile in France 63-65; Minister of State 65-66; Minister of State in charge of Transport 66-77; Pres. Nat. People's Assembly March 77-; acting Pres. of Algeria Dec. 78-Feb. 79.
Assemblée nationale populaire, Algiers, Algeria.

Blum, Yehuda Z., M.JUR., PH.D.; Israeli professor and diplomatist; b. 2 Oct. 1931, Bratislava, Czechoslovakia; ed. elementary schools in Bratislava and Budapest, Secondary school in Jerusalem, Hebrew Univ. Jerusalem, Univ. of London, England.
Worked as Law Clerk 55-56; Asst. to Judge Advocate Gen., Israel Defence Forces 56-59; Asst. Legal Adviser, Ministry of Foreign Affairs 62-65; Lecturer, Faculty of Law, Hebrew Univ. of Jerusalem 65-68, Senior Lecturer 68-72, Prof. 72-; UNESCO Fellow, Univ. of Sydney, Australia and UN Secretariat's Legal Dept., New York 68; Senior Research Scholar, Univ. of Michigan 69; Visiting Prof., School of Law, Univ. of Texas 71, New York 75-76; Perm. Rep. to the UN 78-; Arlozoroff Prize 62, Nordau Prize 78.
Publs. *Historic Titles in International Law* 65, *Secure Boundaries and Middle East Peace* 71, *The Juridical Status of Jerusalem* 74.
Permanent Mission of Israel to the United Nations, 800 Second Avenue, New York, N.Y. 10017, U.S.A.

Bouabid, Maati, L. EN D.; Moroccan lawyer and politician; b. 11 Nov. 1927, Casablanca; ed. Lycée Lyautey, Casablanca, Univ. of Bordeaux, France.
In practice as Barrister, Casablanca 53-56; Public Prosecutor, Tangier 56-57; Attorney-Gen. Court of Appeal 57-58; Minister of Labour and Social Affairs 58-60, of Justice 77-81; Prime Minister March 79-; fmr. Pres. of Municipal Council of Casablanca; fmr. mem. Union Nat. des Forces Populaires; Medal of the Green March.
Présidence du Conseil de Gouvernement, Rabat, Morocco.

Boucetta, M'Hamed, L. EN D.; Moroccan politician; b. 1925, Marrakesh; ed. Ecole Sidi Mohamed, Lycée Moulay Idriss, Fez, Univ. of Paris, France, Inst. des Etudes Supérieures, Paris.
Worked as lawyer in Casablanca; joined Istiqlal Party, Dir. *Al-Istiqlal* (party newspaper) 55, mem. Political Bureau 56, Exec. Cttee. 63-, Sec.-Gen. 74-; Sec. of State for Foreign Affairs 56; Minister of Justice 61-63; Minister of State without Portfolio March-Oct. 77, for Foreign Affairs Oct. 77- (renamed Minister of Foreign Affairs and Co-operation Nov. 81).
Ministère des Affaires Etrangères et de la Coopération, Rabat, Morocco.

Bourguiba, Habib Ben Ali; Tunisian politician; b. 3 Aug. 1902; ed. Collège Sadiki, Lycée Carnot, Univ. of Paris, Ecole Libre des Sciences Politiques.
Active in politics and journalism since 28; mem. Destour Party 21, broke away and formed Néo-Destour Party (outlawed by the French) 34; imprisoned by the French 34-36 and 38-43; escaped to Middle East 45, travelled to promote Tunisian independence 45-49, world tour 51 during Tunisian negotiations with French Govt.; arrested 52, placed under surveillance at Tabarka (Jan.), imprisoned at Remada (March), in solitary confinement, Ile de la Galite (May) until 54; released 54, under surveillance in France 54-55, during negotiations; returned to Tunisia following Franco-Tunisian Agreements 55; Pres. Tunisian Nat. Assembly, Prime Minister, Pres. of the Council, 56-59, 59-, concurrently Minister of Foreign Affairs and Defence 56-59; Pres. of Repub. July 57-, Life Pres. March

75-; Pres. Destour Socialist Party, Life Pres. 74-; Ordre du Sang, Ordre de la confiance en diamants.
Publs. *Le Destour et la France* 37, *La Tunisie et la France* 54.
Présidence de la République, Tunis, Tunisia.

Bourguiba, Habib, Jr., L. ès D. (s. of Pres. Habib Bourguiba, *q.v.*); Tunisian diplomatist and politician; b. 9 April 1927; ed. College Sadiki, Lycée Carnot de Dijon, Faculté de Droit, Paris and Grenoble Univs.
Collaborated in nat. liberation movement, especially 51-54; lawyer in training, Tunis 54-56; Counsellor, Tunisian Embassy, Washington 56-57; Ambassador to Italy 57-58, to France 58-61, to U.S.A. 61-63, concurrently to Canada and Mexico; Sec.-Gen. to Presidency of the Repub. 64; Asst. Sec.-Gen. Destour Socialist Party 64-69; mem. Nat. Assembly 64-; Sec. of State for Foreign Affairs 64-69, Minister of Foreign Affairs 69-70, of Justice June-Nov. 70; Special Adviser to the Pres. Dec. 77-; Pres. and Dir.-Gen. Banque de Développement Economique de Tunisie 71-; Grand Cordon de l'Ordre de l'Indépendance de la République Tunisienne, Grand Officier, Légion d'Honneur (France), many foreign decorations.
Villa Al Mahroussa, Avenue Salammbo, Tunis, Tunisia.

Boustany, Elie J., LIC. EN DROIT; Lebanese lawyer and diplomatist; b. 20 Aug. 1918; ed. Univ. of Saint-Joseph, Beirut.
Chef de Bureau, Office of Pres. of the Repub. 42, Head of Youth Dept. 43; Sec. Lebanese Embassy, Paris 44-45; Head of Legis., Ministry of Justice 47; Counsellor, Lebanese Embassy, Rome 56-58, 62-64, Madrid 58-60, London 60-62; Head Litigation Dept., Ministry of Foreign Affairs 64-66; Amb. to Senegal 66-71, concurrently accred. to Mali, Guinea, The Gambia; Dir. Int. Relations, Ministry of Foreign Affairs 71; Amb. to People's Repub. of China May 72-; Officer Order of Merit of the Repub. (Italy) 58, Commdr. Order of Civil Merit (Spain) 60, Grand Officer Nat. Order (Senegal) 71.
Publs. *Les codes libanais annotés et traduits* (7 vols.), *Recueil des traités* (2 vols.), *Législation libanaise* 1954-56;. contribs. to Lebanese magazines and periodicals.
Lebanese Embassy, 51 Tung Liu Chieh, San Li Tun, Peking, People's Republic of China; and Ministry of Foreign Affairs, Beirut, Lebanon.

Boustany, Fouad Ephrem, DR.-ès-LETTRES; Lebanese scholar; b. 15 Aug. 1906; ed. Deir-el-Kamar Coll. and Univ. St. Joseph, Beirut.
Teacher in Arab Literature, Islamic Insts. and History of Arab Civilization, Institut des Lettres Orientales 33-; Dir. Ecole Normale 42-53; Prof. of Near Eastern History and Civilizations, Inst. des Sciences Politiques 45-55; Prof. of Arab Literature, Islamic Philosophy and Arab History, Acad. Libanaise des Beaux-Arts 47-53; Rector Univ. Libanaise 53-70; Sec.-Gen. Lebanese Nat. Comm. for UNESCO 48-55, Int. Comm. for Translation of Classic Works 49-, Acad. Libanaise; Dr. h.c. Univs. of Lyon 57, Austin, Texas 58, Georgetown, Washington, D.C. 58; decorations from: Lebanon, France, Vatican, Spain, Italy, Iran, Tunisia, Morocco and Senegal.
Publs. *Au temps de l'Emir* 26, *Ar-Rawae* (critical studies) 27, *Pourquoi* 30, *Histoire du Liban sous les Chéhab* of Amir Haïdar Chéhab (with Dr. A. Rustem) 33-35, *Bagdad, capitale des lettres abbassides* 34, *Le rôle des chrétiens dans l'établissement de la dynastie Omayyade* 38, *Le style orale chez les Arabes préislamiques* 41, *Al-Magani al Haditah* (5 vols.) 46-50, *Cinq jours à travers la Syrie* 50, *Les dits desmois* 73, *Le Problème du Liban* 78, *Encyclopedia Arabica* (12 vols.) 56-78.
Université Libanaise, Bir Hassan, Beirut, Lebanon.

Boutaleb, Abdelhadi; Moroccan politician; b. 23 Dec. 1923, Fez; ed. Al Qarawiyin Univ., Fez.
Professor of Arabic History and Literature, and Tutor

to Prince Moulay Hassan and Prince Moulay Abdallah; Founder-mem. Democratic Party of Independence 44-51; campaigned, through the Party, for Moroccan independence, and for this purpose attended UN Session, Paris 51, and Negotiating Conf. at Aix-les-Bains 54-56; Minister of Labour and Social Questions in Bekkai Govt. 56; Chief Editor of journal *Al Rayal Am* 56-61; Amb. to Syria Feb. 62; Sec. of State, Ministry of Information Nov. 62, Ministry of Information, Youth and Sports Jan. 63; Minister of Information, Youth and Sports June 63; Interim Minister in Charge of Mauritania and Sahara Nov. 63; Minister of Justice 64-67, of Nat. Educ. and Fine Arts 67; Minister of State 68; Minister of Foreign Affairs 69-70; Pres. of Parl. 70-71; Amb. to U.S.A. Jan. 75-77; Prof. of Constitutional Law and Political Insts., Mohamed V Univ., Rabat; Adviser to King Hassan II (*q.v.*) 77-78; Minister of State in charge of Information Oct. 78; Tutor to Crown Prince Sidi Mohamed 78-; decorations from Morocco, France, Spain, Italy, Tunisia and Egypt include Commdr. of the Throne of Morocco, Grand Cordon of the Repub. of Egypt and Commdr. du Mérite Sportif, France.
Publs. Many cultural and literary works.
c/o Ministry of Information, Rabat, Morocco.

Bouteflika, Abdelaziz; Algerian politician; b. 2 March 1937, Oujda; ed. Morocco.
Major, Nat. Liberation Army (ALN) and Sec. of Gen. Staff; Minister of Sports and Tourism 62-63, of Foreign Affairs 63-79; Adviser to the Pres. 79-80; Head of del. to UN 63-79; mem. FLN Political Bureau 64-81, of Revolutionary Council 65-79; led negotiations with France 63-66, for nationalization of hydrocarbons 71; leader of dels. to many confs. of Arab League, OAU 68, Group of 77 67, Non-aligned countries 73, 29th Session of UN Gen. Assembly 74, Preparatory Conf. to Summit Meeting of OPEC 75, 7th Special Session of UN Gen. Assembly 75; Leader of del. to Conf. on Int. Econ. Cooperation, Paris 75-76.
Front de Libération Nationale, place Emir Abdelkader, Algiers, Algeria.

Boutros-Ghali, Boutros, LL.B., PH.D.; Egyptian politician and international civil servant; b. 14 Nov. 1922, Cairo; ed. Cairo and Paris Univs.
Former Prof. of Int. Law and Head, Dept. of Political Sciences, Cairo Univ.; fmr. mem. Cen. Cttee. Arab Socialist Union; Pres. Centre of Political and Strategic Studies, Al-Ahram; Minister of State for Foreign Affairs Oct. 77-; Vice-Pres. Egyptian Soc. of Int. Law; fmr. mem. Cttee. on Application of Conventions and Recommendations of Int. Labour Org.; fmr. mem. Int. Comm. of Jurists, Geneva and Council and Exec. Cttee. of Int. Inst. of Human Rights, Strasbourg.
Publs. *Contribution à l'étude des ententes régionales* 49, *Cours de diplomatie et de droit diplomatique et consulaire* 51, *Le principe d'égalité des états et les organisations internationales* 61, *Foreign Policies in World Change* 63, *l'Organisation de l'unité africaine* 69, *La Ligue des états arabes* 71, *Les conflits des frontières en Afrique* 73.
2 avenue El Nil, Giza, Cairo, Egypt.

Bozbeyli, Ferruh; Turkish lawyer and politician; b. 21 Jan. 1927, Pazarcık, Maras Prov.; ed. Univ. of Istanbul.
Practised law until 65; mem. Parl. (Justice Party—JP) 61-70; Vice-Pres. JP Parl. Group 61-62; Deputy Speaker Nat. Assembly 62-65; Speaker 65-70; founded Democratic Party (DP) 70, Leader 70-79; Candidate for Presidency 73.
Publs. seven works.
Democratic Party, Ankara, Turkey.

Bozer, Prof. Dr. Ali Husrev; Turkish jurist; b. 28 July 1925, Ankara; ed. Ankara Univ. and Neuchâtel Univ. Switzerland and Harvard Law School.
Assistant judge, Ankara 51; Asst., Faculty of Law,

Ankara Univ. 52-60, Agrégé 55-60, Head of Dept. 61-, Prof. of Commercial Law 65-; lawyer at bar, Ankara 52-; Dir. Inst. de Recherche sur le Droit commercial et bancaire 60-; Judge, European Court of Human Rights 74-; mem. Admin. Council, Radio-TV de Turquie 68-71, Vice-Pres. 71-73.

Publs. *Les Droits d'Administration et de Jouissance des Père et Mère sur les Biens de l'Enfant, Nantissement Commercial, Aperçu général sur le Droit des Assurances Sociales en Droit turc, Droit commercial pour les Employés de Banques, Papiers valeurs pour les Employés de Banques;* monographs and articles in several reviews in Turkish and French.

Ahmet Rasim sok. 35/5, Çankaya, Ankara, Turkey.

Brahimi, Lakhdar; Algerian diplomatist; b. 1934; ed. Medersa Algiers, Institut des Sciences Politiques, Algiers, and Ecole des Sciences Politiques, Paris.
Perm. Rep. of F.L.N. and later of Provisional Govt. of Algeria in South East Asia 56-61; Gen. Secretariat Ministry of External Affairs 61-63; Amb. to U.A.R. and Sudan 63-70; Perm. Rep. to Arab League 63-70; Amb. to U.K. 71-79; mem. Cen. Cttee. of F.L.N. 79-.
c/o Ministry of Foreign Affairs, 6 rue Claud Bernard, El Mouradia, Algiers, Algeria.

Bruno, Michael, PH.D.; Israeli professor; b. 30 July 1932, Hamburg, Germany; ed. Reali School, Haifa, King's Coll., Cambridge, and Stanford Univ., U.S.A.
Senior Economist, Bank of Israel 57-61, Deputy Dir. 61-63, Joint Dir. Research Dept. 64-65; on staff, Hebrew Univ. of Jerusalem 63-, Prof. of Econs. 70-; Dir. of Research, Maurice Falk Inst. for Econ. Research in Israel 72-75; Economic Policy Adviser to Ministry of Finance 75-76; Pres. Israel Economic Asscn. 77-79; Visiting Prof. of Econs., Harvard Univ. and M.I.T. 65-67, 70-71, 76-77; mem. Israel Acad. of Sciences and Humanities; Fellow, Econometric Soc.; Rothschild Prize in Social Science 74.
Publs. articles in economic journals.
Department of Economics, Hebrew University of Jerusalem, Mount Scopus, Jerusalem; Home: 15 Hovevei Zion Street, Jerusalem, Israel.

Bualy, Nassir Seif El (*see* El Bualy).

Burg, Yosef, DR. PHIL.; Israeli politician; b. 31 Jan. 1909, Dresden, Germany; ed. Univs. of Berlin and Leipzig, Pedagogical Inst., Leipzig, Rabbinical Seminary Berlin, and Hebrew Univ. of Jerusalem.
Directorate, Palestine Office, Berlin 36; Nat. Exec. Mizrachi; Zionist Gen. Council 38-51; mem. Exec. Hapoel Hamizrachi 44-; Deputy Speaker First Knesset (Israeli Parl.) 49-51; Minister of Health, Govt. of Israel 51-52; Minister of Posts and Telegraphs 52-58; Minister of Social Welfare 59-70, of the Interior 70-76, of Welfare July-Nov. 75; Minister of the Interior and the Police June 77, of Religious Affairs Aug. 81-; Chair. Ministerial Autonomy Negotiations Cttee. 79; Nat. Religious Party.
6 Ben Maimon Street, Jerusalem, Israel.

Burgan, Salih Khalil, M.D.; Jordanian politician; b. 1918; ed. American Univ. of Beirut.
Physician, Transjordan Frontier Forces 43-46, Dir. of Arab Physicians, T.F.F. 46-48; Private Physician, Zerka 48-63; M.P. 61-63; Minister of Health April 63-July 64, of Social Affairs and Labour Feb. 66, Sept. 66, 67-69, of Public Health Sept. 66-Aug. 67, of Social Labour, Home, Municipal and Rural Affairs April 67-69; mem. of Senate 63-69; Regional Dir. ILO Beirut 69-75, Asst. Dir.-Gen. ILO June 75-; Al Kawkab Medal (1st Grade); Grand Knight of the Holy Sepulchre.
Case Postale 500, CH-1211 Geneva 22, Switzerland.

Burns, Norman, M.A.; American economist and educationalist; b. 14 Nov. 1905; ed. Wittenberg Univ., Ohio, Yale Univ. and Univ. of Montpellier, France.

Assistant Prof. of Econs. American Univ. of Beirut 29-32; U.S. Govt. Service as foreign trade economist, U.S. Tariff Comm., Dir. Foreign Service Inst. of State Dept., Dep. Dir. for Near East and South Asia, Int. Co-operation admin., Econ. Adviser, UN Relief and Works Agency, Beirut, Dir. United States operations missions, Amman 34-61; Pres. American Univ. of Beirut 61-65; Vice-Pres. Musa Alami Foundation of Jericho, Washington D.C.; mem. Board of Govs. Middle East Inst., Washington 67-; Hon. LL.D. (Wittenberg Univ.); Commdr. Order of Cedar of Lebanon 65.
Publs. *The Tariff of Syria 33, Government Budgets of Middle East Countries* (Editor) 56, *Planning Economic Development in the Arab World 59, Education in the Middle East 65, The Challenge of Education in the Developing Countries 73, The Energy Crisis and U.S. Middle East Policy 73.*
3813 North 37th Street, Arlington, Va. 22207, U.S.A.

Butros, Fouad; Lebanese lawyer and politician; b. 1918; ed. Coll. des Frères, Beirut and Univ. of Lyon.
Judge, Civil and Mixed Commercial Court, Beirut 43-46; Judge Mil. Tribunal 45-46; Court Lawyer 47-; Govt. Lawyer 51-57; Minister of Nat. Educ. and of the Plan 59-60; mem. Chamber of Deputies (now Nat. Assembly) 60-, Deputy Speaker 60-61; Minister of Justice 61-64; Vice-Pres. of the Council, Minister of Educ. and Defence 66, Minister of Foreign Affairs and of Tourism Feb.-Oct. 68; Deputy Prime Minister, Minister of Foreign Affairs Dec. 76-, of Defence 76-78; numerous decorations and honours.
Office of the Deputy Prime Minister, Beirut; Home: Sursock Street, Fouad Butros Building, Beirut, Lebanon.

C

Çağatay, Mustafa; Cypriot politician; b. 1937, Limassol; ed. Nicosia Turkish Lycée.
Started law practice in Limassol 63; elected Deputy for Limassol, Turkish Communal Chamber 70, mem. for Kyrenia, Legislative Assembly, "Turkish Federated State of Cyprus" 76; Minister of Finance 76, of Labour, Social Security and Health May-Dec. 78; Prime Minister Dec. 78- (acting Dec. 81-Feb. 82); mem. Turkish Cypriot Cttee., Turkish and Greek Cypriot Talks on Humanitarian issues 74; mem. Nat. Unity Party.
Office of the Prime Minister, "Turkish Federated State of Cyprus" (Kibris), Lefkoşa (Nicosia), Mersin 10, Turkey.

Çağlayangil, Ihsan Sabri; Turkish politician; b. 1908; ed. Faculty of Law, Univ. of Istanbul.
Formerly with Ministry of Interior; Gov. of Yozgat, then of Antalya 48-53, of Çannakale 53-54, of Sivas 54, of Bursa 54-60; Senator for Bursa 61-80; Minister of Labour Feb.-Oct. 65, of Foreign Affairs 65-71; Pres. Senate Foreign Affairs Cttee. 72-75; Minister of Foreign Affairs 75-June 77, July-Dec. 77; Chair. Senate of the Republic Nov. 79-Sept. 80; Acting Pres. of Turkey April-Sept. 80; Justice Party.
Şehit Ersan Caddesi 30/15, Çankaya, Ankara, Turkey.

Cahen, Claude Louis Alfred, D. ès L.; French university professor (retd.); b. 1909; ed. Sorbonne, Ecole des Langues Orientales, Ecole Normale Supérieure, Paris.
Lecturer, Ecole des Langues Orientales, Paris 37-54; Prof., Faculty of Letters, Univ. of Strasbourg 45-59, Sorbonne, Paris 59-79; Pres. Société Asiatique; Dir. *Journal of the Economic and Social History of the Orient*, Centre d'Etudes de l'Orient Contemporain; mem. Acad. des Inscriptions et de Belles-Lettres, Inst. de France 73; Schlumberger Prize 45.
Publs. *La Syrie du Nord au temps des Croisades 40, Le régime féodal de l'Italie normande 40, Pre-Ottoman Turkey 68, Der Islam (Fischer Weltgeschichte) 68,* French edn.

L'Islam 70, *Makhzumiyyat* 77, *Les Peuples Musulmans dans l'histoire médiévale* 77, various studies in Turkish history, Islamic economic and social history, and history of the Crusades.
62 avenue Carnot, Savigny s. Orge 91 600, France.

Callaghan, Maj.-Gen. William; Irish army officer.
Commander Irish Battalion, UN forces, Congo 61; three tours with UN troops, Cyprus; acting Chief of Staff UN Truce Supervisory Org., Israeli-Syrian border 78; Commdr. United Nations Interim Force in Lebanon (UNIFIL) 81-.
UNIFIL Headquarters, Naqoura, Lebanon.

Celik, Vedat, B.A.; Cypriot politician; b. 6 May 1935' Tera; ed. English School, Cyprus and Univ. of Wales, Cardiff.
Civil Service 53-60, Admin. Officer, Turkish Educ. Dept. 59-60; Asst. Sec., Ministry of Interior 60-61; First Sec. and Counsellor, Ankara 61-68; Liaison Officer to UNFICYP 68-73; Under-Sec. to Pres. Turkish Communal Chamber 69-73; Minister of Commerce, Industry and Tourism 73-75; Turkish Cypriot Rep. to UN 74-78; mem. for Kyrenia, Legislative Assembly of "Turkish Federated State of Cyprus (TFSC)" 76-; Deputy Prime Minister, Minister of Defence and Foreign Affairs, "TFSC" 76-78, Minister of Tourism and Information 78.
Publs. various papers on constitutional and political aspects of the Cyprus problem.
Kumsal, Lefkoşa (Nicosia), Mersin 10, Turkey.

Chadirji, Rifat Kamil, DIP.ARCH.; Iraqi architect; b. 6 Dec. 1926, Baghdad; ed. Hammersmith School of Arts and Crafts, London.
Founder, Senior Partner and Dir. Iraq Consult 52-; Section Head, Baghdad Building Dept., Waqaf Org. 54-57; Dir.-Gen. Housing, Ministry of Finance 58-59, Head Planning Cttee. Ministry of Housing 59-63; returned to full-time private practice with Iraq Consult 63-78; appointed Counsellor to Mayoralty of Baghdad 80; mem. Mayor's Council 58-61; mem. Iraqi Tourist Board 70-75; works include Cabinet Ministers' building, U.A.E. 76, Nat. Theatre, Abu Dhabi, U.A.E. 77, Al-Ain Public Library, U.A.E. 78; exhibitions in Iraq, Sudan, Ghana, Turkey, Greece, Lebanon, Jordan, England, Kuwait, Austria and the U.A.E.; First Prize for Council of Ministers' building, Baghdad 75, First Prize New Theatre Abu Dhabi 77, First Prize Council of Ministers, Abu Dhabi 78.
7 Khansa Street, Adhamiyah, Baghdad, Iraq.

Chadli, Col. Bendjedid; Algerian army officer and politician; b. 14 April 1929.
Served in French Army before start of Algerian war for nat. independence 54; joined Maquisards guerrilla forces 55; Commdr. 13th Battalion, Army of Nat. Liberation 60, mem. Gen. Staff 61; Commdr. of Constantine Mil. Region, East Algeria 63, of Second Mil. Region (Oran) 64-79; mem. Revolutionary Council 65; Acting Minister of Defence and Chief of Staff Nov. 78-Jan. 79; Sec.-Gen. Nat. Liberation Front Jan. 79-; Pres. of Algeria and Minister of Defence Feb. 79-.
Office du Président, Palais du Gouvernement, Algiers, Algeria.

Chaker, Abdelmajid; Tunisian politician and diplomatist.
Secretary of State for Agriculture 62-64, for Information 64-66; Amb. to Algeria 66-70, to Yugoslavia 70-73, to Sweden 73-79, to Spain 79-; mem. Néo Destour, later Socialist Destour Party, Dir. until Nov. 64, mem. Bureau Politique Nov. 64-71, mem. Cen. Cttee. 71-.
Tunisian Embassy, Plaza Alonso Martínez 3, Madrid 4, Spain.

Chaker, M'hamed; Tunisian politician; b. 31 Dec. 1930, Sfax; ed. Sfax and Univ. of Paris.
Govt. Admin. President's Office 57-58; Asst. Controller

of Public Spending 58-64; Dir. of Public Service 64-68; mem. Nat. Cttee. for Reform of Public Service and Admin. Structures 68-69; Dir. of Regional Admin., Secretariat of State for the Interior 69-72; Dir.-Gen. Tunisian Agency for Technical Co-operation 72-79; Dir. Ecole Nat. d'Administration Jan.-Nov. 79; Sec. of State responsible to the Prime Minister for Admin. Reform 79-80; Minister of Justice April 80-; mem. Central Cttee. Parti Socialiste Destourien 71-; Officier, Ordre de l'Indépendance, Ordre de la Republique.
Ministry of Justice, Tunis, Tunisia.

Chamoun, Camille, LL.D.; Lebanese lawyer; b. 3 April 1900; ed. Coll. des Frères and Law School, Beirut.
Qualified as lawyer 24; mem. Parl. 34-; Minister of Finance 38; Minister of Interior 43-44; Minister to Allied Governments in London 44; Head of Del. to Int. Civil Aviation Conf., Chicago 44, UNESCO Conf. and UN Preparatory Comm. 45; Del. to UN Gen. Assembly, London and N.Y. 46; Lebanese rep. Interim Comm., UN 48; Pres. Lebanese Republic 52-58; leader Liberal Nationalist Party 58-; Minister of Interior, of Post Office and Telecommunications, of Hydraulic and Electrical Resources May 75-Dec. 76, of Foreign Affairs June-Dec. 76, of Defence Sept.-Dec. 76; mem. Nat. Dialogue Cttee. Sept. 75.
Home: Saadyat, Lebanon.

Chatti, Habib; Tunisian diplomatist and politician; b. 1916; ed. Sadik Coll., Tunis.
Journalist 37-52, Editor *Ez-Zohra* 43-50, *Es-Sabah* 50-52; imprisoned 52, 53; Head, Press Cabinet of Pres. of Council 54-55, Head, Information Service 55; mem. Nat. Council, Néo-Destour Party 55; Dir. *Al Amal* 56; Vice-Pres. Constituent Nat. Assembly 56; Ambassador to Lebanon and Iraq 57-59, to Turkey and Iran 59-62, to U.K. 62-64, to Morocco 64-70, to Algeria 70-72; Dir. of the Presidential Cabinet 72-74; Minister of Foreign Affairs 74-77; mem. Cen. Cttee. Destour Socialist Party 74-; Deputy to Nat. Assembly 74-; Sec.-Gen. Org. of the Islamic Conf. 80-; Grand Cordon Ordre de la Répub. Tunisienne, several foreign decorations.
Organization of the Islamic Conference, Secretariat-General, Kilo 6, Mecca Road, P.O. Box 178, Jeddah, Saudi Arabia.

Chaufournier, Roger Amedée, LL.D.; French international official; b. 23 Jan. 1924; ed. Ecole des Hautes Etudes Commerciales, Univ. of Paris, Faculties of Arts and Law, Univ. of Uppsala, Sweden, Univ. of Illinois, U.S.A.
Economist, World Bank 52-56, Special Rep. to Peru 65-60, Division Chief, Latin American Dept. 60-63, Division Chief, Europe 63-64, Deputy Dir. Western Hemisphere Dept. 64-68, Dir., Western Africa Dept. 68-72, Regional Vice-Pres., Western Africa 72-79, Regional Vice-Pres., Europe, Middle East and North Africa 79-; Fellow, Swedish Inst. 48-49; Fulbright Fellow 49-50; Fellow, Inst. of Int. Educ.
World Bank, 1818 H Street, N.W., Washington, D.C. 20433; 1 Pettit Court, Potomac, Maryland 20854, U.S.A.

Chelli, Tijani; Tunisian politician; b. 23 March 1931, Nabeul; ed. Collège Sadiki, Tunis, Ecole Polytechnique, Paris and Ecole Nat. des Ponts et Chaussées, Paris.
Engineer, Ministry of Public Works, Kef 59-60; Deputy Chief Engineer of Roads and Bridges 60; Dir. of Transport 61; Dir. of Sea and Air Transport 62; Pres. Dir.-Gen. Société Nationale des Chemins de Fer Tunisiens 65-67; Dir. of Industry, Dept. of Planning and Nat. Economy 67-69; Pres. Dir.-Gen. Industries Chimiques Maghrébines (ICM) Jan.-Nov. 69; Minister of Public Works 69-70, of the Economy 70-72; Pres., Dir.-Gen. Investment Promotion and Industrial Land Agency 73-75, Investment Promotion Agency 76-80; Chair. Econ. and Social Council

76-79; Grand Cordon, Order of the Republic; Grand Croix, Order of Merit (Fed. Repub. of Germany).
Ministère d'Equipement, Cité Jardins, Tunis, Tunisia.

Christofides, Andreas N., M.A.; Cypriot broadcasting official; b. 20 Aug. 1937; ed. Pancyprian Gymnasium, Nicosia, Athens Univ. and Columbia Univ., New York.
Teacher at Pancyprian Gymnasium 58-63; Dir. of Radio Programmes of Cyprus Broadcasting Corpn. 64-67; Dir.-Gen. of Cyprus Broadcasting Corpn. 67-; fmr. Chair. Cyprus State Theatre Org.; mem. Admin. Council European Broadcasting Union; first Nat. Award Prize for *Points of View I, II and III, Conversations of the Night.* Publs. include: Essays: *Letters from New York* 65, *Points of View I* 66, *Points of View II* 69, *Introduction to Propaganda* 66, *Love Songs from Cyprus* 64, *An Anthology of Poetry from Cyprus* (with K. Montis) 69, *An Anthology of Short Stories* (with P. Ioannides) 71, *Points of View III;* Poems: *A Strange Illustration* 69, *Analytical Propositions* 70, *Conversations of the Night.*
Cyprus Broadcasting Corporation, P.O. Box 4824, Nicosia, Cyprus.

Christophides, Ioannis; Cypriot politician; b. 21 Jan. 1924, Nicosia; ed. Pancyprian Gymnasium, Nicosia, Gray's Inn Law School, London.
Barrister-at-Law; joined family banking and insurance firms 48, Chief Exec. 54-72; Chair. of several private cos. 54-72; Chair. Cyprus Telecommunications Authority 66-72; Vice-Chair. Commonwealth Telecommunications Board 70-72; Minister of Foreign Affairs 72-74, 75-78; Pres. Nicosia Branch, Cyprus Red Cross 64-72.
25 El. Venizelos Street, Nicosia, Cyprus.

Clerides, Glavkos John, B.A., LL.B.; Cypriot lawyer and politician; b. 1919; ed. Pancyprian Gymnasium, Nicosia, Univ. Tutorial Coll., London, King's Coll., London Univ., Gray's Inn, London.
Served with R.A.F. 39-45; shot down and taken prisoner 42-45 (mentioned in despatches); practised law in Cyprus 51-60; Head of Greek Cypriot Del., Constitutional Comm. 59-60; first Minister of Justice of the Republic 59-60; mem. House of Representatives 60-, Pres. of the House 60-76; Acting Pres. of Repub. 60-76, Temporary Pres. July-Dec. 74; Head of Greek Cypriot Del. to London Conf. 64; Rep. to Consultative Assembly of the Council of Europe; mem. Political Cttee. and Standing Cttee.; Rep. Greek Cypriots in UN sponsored talks 68-76; Chair. Democratic Rally 76-; Gold Medal Order of the Holy Sepulchre.
56 Metochio Street, Nicosia, Cyprus.

Cluverius, Wat Tyler, IV, B.S., M.A.; American diplomatist; b. 4 Dec. 1934; Arlington, Mass.; ed. Northwestern Univ., Indiana Univ.
Officer, U.S. Navy 57-62; Third Sec. and Vice-Consul, Embassy in Jeddah 67-69; Second Sec., Tel Aviv 69-72; Deputy Dir., Office of Israeli and Arab-Israeli Affairs, U.S. Dept. of State 73-76; Amb. to Bahrain 76-78; Dir. Office of Lebanon, Jordan, Syria and Iraq, Bureau of Near Eastern Affairs, Dept. of State 78-; U.S. Dept. of State Meritorious Honor Award 69.
Bureau of Near Eastern and South Asian Studies, Department of State, 2201 C Street, N.W., Washington, D.C. 20520, U.S.A.

Cohn, Haim H.; Israeli lawyer; b. 11 March 1911; ed. Univs. of Munich, Hamburg and Frankfurt-am-Main, Germany, Hebrew Univ. of Jerusalem, and Govt. Law School, Jerusalem.
Admitted to Bar of Palestine 37; Sec. Legal Council, Jewish Agency for Palestine, Jerusalem 47; State Attorney, Ministry of Justice, Hakirya 48, Dir.-Gen. 49; Attorney-Gen. Govt. of Israel 50; Minister of Justice and Acting Attorney-Gen. 52; Attorney-Gen. 52-60; Justice, Supreme Court of Israel 60-81; Deputy Pres 70-81; mem. Perm. Court

of Arbitration, The Hague 62-, UN Comm. on Human Rights 65-67; Deputy Chair. Council of Higher Educ., Israel 58-71; mem. Board of Govs., Int. Inst. of Human Rights, Strasbourg; mem. Exec. Council Asscn. Internationale de Droit Pénal, Paris; Deputy Pres. Board of Govs. Hebrew Univ. of Jerusalem; Visiting Prof. of Law, Univ. of Tel-Aviv; mem. Int. Comm. of Jurists, Geneva 73-; Pres. Israel Soc. of Criminology 75-; Pres. Int. Asscn. of Jewish Lawyers and Jurists 75-; Hon. LL.D. (John Jay College of Criminal Justice, City Univ. of New York) 80, (Aberdeen, Georgetown Univ.) 81, Hon. D.Litt (Hebrew Union Coll., Cincinnati) 82, Hon. D.Sc. (Weizmann Inst. of Science, Rehovot) 82.
Publs. *The Foreign Laws of Marriage and Divorce* (English) 37, *Glaube und Glaubensfreiheit* (German) 67, *The Trial and Death of Jesus* (Hebrew) 68, English edn. 71, *Jewish Law in Ancient and Modern Israel* 72.
36 Tchernihovsky Street, Jerusalem, Israel.

Craig, Sir (Albert) James (Macqueen), K.C.M.G., M.A.; British diplomatist; b. 13 July 1924, Liverpool; ed. Liverpool Inst. High School, Queen's Coll., Oxford, Magdalen Coll., Oxford.
Lecturer in Arabic, Durham Univ. 48; Principal Instructor, Middle East Centre for Arab Studies 55; Foreign Office 58; H.M. Political Agent in Dubai, Trucial States 61; First Sec., Embassy in Beirut 64; Counsellor, Jeddah 67; Fellow, St. Antony's Coll., Oxford 70; Head, Near East and North Africa Dept., Foreign and Commonwealth Office 71; Deputy High Commr. in Malaysia 75; Amb. to Syria 76-79, to Saudi Arabia 79-.
British Embassy, Jeddah, Saudi Arabia; c/o Outward Bag Room (Jeddah), Foreign and Commonwealth Office, London, S.W.1, England.

D

Daccak, Nassouh, L. EN D.; Syrian financial administrator; b. 1916, Damascus; ed. Damascus Univ.
Head Dept. of Foreign Trade, Ministry of Econ. 47-50; Dir. of Trade, Ministry of Econ. 50-51, Dir. of Econ. Affairs 51-59; Chair. Board of Dirs., Gen. Man. Industrial Bank 59-62; Gen. Sec. Ministry of Labour and Social Affairs 62-63; Chair. Board of Credit and Money 71-78; Gov. Cen. Bank of Syria 71-78; Alt. Gov. IMF, Arab Fund for Social and Econ. Devt.; mem. Board of Dirs., European Arab Bank.
c/o Central Bank of Syria, 29 Ayar Square, Damascus, Syria.

de Garang, (Enok) Mading; Sudanese politican; b. 1 Jan. 1934, Kongor; ed. Malek, Atar Intermediate School, Rumbek Secondary School, Manchester Coll. of Science and Technology, England, London Univ. Inst. of Educ.
Member of Southern Nationalist Movement 56-; co-founder Sudan African Nat. Union, Manchester, U.K. 63; Ed. *Voice of Southern Sudan*, Manchester, U.K. 63; Man. Spearhead Press, Malakal 63; Ed. *Light* 63-65; Asst. Production Man., Haile Selassie Printing Press, Ethiopia 65-67; studied then taught at Africa Lit. Centre, Kitwe, Zambia 67-69; co-founder, later Dir., Southern Sudan Asscn., London; Ed. *Grass Curtain*, London 70-72; External Spokesman, South Sudan Liberation Movement 70-March 72; mem. High Exec. Council for Southern Region, Minister for Information, Culture, Youth and Sports, Tourism and Wildlife, Social Services April 72-73, for Rural Devt. and Co-operatives 73-75, for Information and Culture 75-77, Youth and Sports July 75-76; mem. People's Regional Assembly for Bor; mem. Cen. Cttee. Sudanese Socialist Union; First Class Medal (Two Niles) for Peace.
Home: Kongor District, Jonglei Province, Sudan.

Demirel, Süleyman; Turkish hydraulic engineer and politician; b. 1924, Islâmköy, Isparta Prov.; ed. High School, Afyon and Istanbul Technical Univ.

Qualified engineer; worked in U.S.A. 49-51, 54-55; with Dir.-Gen. Electrical Studies, Ankara 50-52; in charge of building various hydro-electric schemes 52-54; Head of Dept. of Dams 54; Dir.-Gen. of Water Control 54-55; first Eisenhower Fellow for Study in U.S.A. 54; Dir. State Hydraulics Admin. 55-60; private practice including Consultant to Morrison-Knudsen, and lecturer Middle East Technical Univ. 61-65; Pres. Justice Party 64- (political activity banned Sept. 80-); Deputy Prime Minister Feb.-Oct. 65; Prime Minister 65-71, 75-June 77, July-Dec. 77, Nov. 79-Sept. 80; internal exile Sept.-Oct. 80, freed Oct. 80.

Denktaş, Rauf; Cypriot lawyer; b. 27 Jan. 1924; ed. English School, Nicosia, and Lincoln's Inn, London.

Interpreter, Court Clerk, Teacher until 43; called to Bar, Lincoln's Inn 47; mem. Consultative Assembly under Colonial Govt. of Cyprus 48, also mem. Turkish Affairs Cttee. 48-49; Junior Crown Counsel, Attorney-Gen.'s Office 49-53, Crown Counsel 53-56; Solicitor-Gen. 56-57; Chair. Fed. of Turkish Cypriot Asscns. 57-60; mem. Turkish Cypriot del. to Conf. on Independence of Cyprus, London 59; rep. to Conf. on Mil. aspects of Treaty of Establishment 59; Head of Turkish Cypriot del. to Constitutional Cttee. 59-60; Pres. Turkish Communal Chamber 60-63, 68-73; Head of del. to Conf. on Cyprus, London 63; also attended UN Security Council 64; prohibited from returning by Greek Cypriot authorities 64; in exile in Turkey 64-67; detained after secretly returning to Cyprus 67; in exile in Turkey 67-68; Vice-Pres. Turkish Cypriot Admin. 68-73, Pres. 73-75; Turkish Cypriot Spokesman in intercommunal talks 68-76; Vice-Pres. of Cyprus 73-; Pres. "Turkish Federated State of Cyprus" (Kibris) 75-.

Publs. *Secrets of Happiness* (1st edn. 43, 2nd edn. 73), *Hell Without Fire* 44, *A Handbook of Criminal Cases* 55, *Five Minutes to Twelve* 66, *The AKRITAS Plan* 72, *A Short Discourse on Cyprus* 72, *The Cyprus Problem* 73.

Office of the President, "Turkish Federated State of Cyprus" (Kibris), Lefkoşa (Nicosia), via Mersin 10, Turkey.

Dimechkié, Nadim, G.C.V.O., M.A.; Lebanese diplomatist; b. 5 Dec. 1919; ed. American Univ. of Beirut.

Director-General Ministry of Nat. Economy 43-44; Lebanese del. Joint Supply Board for Syria and Lebanon 42-44; Counsellor, Lebanese Embassy, London 44-49; Consul-Gen., Ottawa 50; Dir. Econ. and Social Dept., Ministry of Foreign Affairs 51-52; Chargé d'Affaires, Cairo 52, Minister 53-55; Minister to Switzerland 55-57; Amb. to U.S.A. 58-62; Dir. Econ. Affairs, Ministry of Foreign Affairs 62-66; Amb. to U.K. 66-78; Doyen of the Diplomatic Corps in U.K. 77-78; Special Adviser on Foreign Affairs to Minister of Foreign Affairs and Prime Minister 79; Lebanese Order of Cedars, Syrian Order of Merit, Tunisian Order of Merit, Greek Order of Phoenix, Egyptian Order of Ismail, etc.

Ministry of Foreign Affairs, Beirut, Lebanon.

Dimitrios I (Dimitrios Papadopoulos); Greek Orthodox Archbishop of Constantinople and Ecumenical Patriarch; b. 8 Sept. 1914, Istanbul; ed. Theological School of Halki, Heybeliada-Istanbul.

Ordained Deacon 37; Ordained Priest 42; Preacher in Edessa, Greece 37-38; Preacher, Parish of Feriköy-Istanbul 39-45; Priest of Orthodox Community, Teheran 45-50; Head Priest, Feriköy 50-64; Bishop of Elaia, Auxiliary Bishop of the Patriarch Athenagoras in Istanbul 64-72; Metropolitan of Imvros and Tenedos 72; Archbishop of Constantinople and Ecumenical Patriarch 72-.

Rum Ortodoks Patrikhanesi, Fener, Istanbul, Turkey.

Dimitriou, Nicos George, F.C.I.S.; Cypriot merchant banker, industrialist and diplomatist; b. 16 July 1920; ed. Larnaca Commercial Lyceum, Greek Gymnasium, Athens, and Maiden Erlegh Private School, Reading, England.

Manager and Sec. N. J. Dimitriou Ltd., Merchant Bankers 52-62, Man. Dir. 62-; Man. Dir. Larnaca Oil Works Ltd. 63-; dir. several Cyprus companies; Dir. Bank of Cyprus Ltd. 60-62; Chair. Cyprus Chamber of Commerce 60-63; Pres. Chamber of Commerce and Industry, Larnaca 63-68, Pezoporicos Club, Larnaca 57-68; Pres. Cyprus Soc. of Inc. Secretaries 68; Consul-Gen. of Denmark 61; mem. Council Cyprus Chamber of Commerce and Industry 63-68; Chair. Cyprus Devt. Corpn. Ltd. 66-68; Minister of Commerce and Industry 68-70; Chair. Electricity Authority of Cyprus 70-73, Advisory Board Nat. and Grindlays Bank Ltd. 70-73; Amb. to U.S.A. 74-79, also High Commr. in Canada 74-79; Dir. Bank of Cyprus (Holdings) Ltd. 79-; Commdr. Order of Cedar of Lebanon; Commdr. Order of Dannebrog.

Publ. *Chambers of Commerce—their Objects and Aims.*

Artemis Avenue 39, Larnaca, Cyprus.

Dinitz, Simcha, M.S.; Israeli diplomatist; b. 23 June 1929; ed. Univ. of Cincinnati and School of Foreign Service and Graduate School, Georgetown Univ.

Director, Office of the Dir.-Gen., Ministry of Foreign Affairs 61-63; Political Sec. to Minister of Foreign Affairs 63-66; Minister, Embassy of Israel, Rome 66-68, Washington 68-69; Political Adviser to the Prime Minister 69, later Dir.-Gen. Office of the Prime Minister; Amb. to U.S.A. 73-78; Vice-Pres., Hebrew Univ. of Jerusalem March 79-; Chair. The Leonard Davies Inst. of Int. Relations, Hebrew Univ.; mem. Israeli del. to the UN 63, 64, 65.

Publ. *The Legal Aspect of the Egyptian Blockade of the Suez Canal* (Georgetown Law Journal) 56.

40 Nayot, Jerusalem, Israel.

Doğramaci, Ihsan, M.D.; Turkish pediatrician and educator; b. 3 April 1915; ed. Istanbul, Harvard, Washington Univs.

Associate Prof. of Pediatrics, Ankara Univ. 49-54, Prof. of Child Health and Head of Dept. 55-63, Dir. Inst. of Child Health, Ankara 58-63; Prof. of Pediatrics and Head of Dept. Hacettepe Faculty of Medicine 63-, Dean of Faculty June 63-Nov. 63; Pres. Ankara Univ. 63-65; Pres. Hacettepe Science Centre, Ankara 65-67; Pres. Hacettepe Children's Medical Centre 75-81; mem. UNICEF Exec. Board 60-75, Chair. 68-70; Chair. Board of Trustees, Middle East Technical Univ. 65-67; Pres. Hacettepe Univ. 67-75, now Hon. Rector; Pres. Int. Pediatric Asscn. 68-77, Exec. Dir. 77-; mem. Standing Cttee. Standing Conf. of Rectors and Vice-Chancellors of the European Univs. 69-; Pres. Council of Rectors of Turkish Univs. 75-81; mem. Board Int. Children's Centre (Paris) 70-; mem. WHO Global Advisory Cttee. on Medical Research 79-; Pres. Turkish and Int. Children's Centre 80-, Higher Educl. Council of Turkey 81-; Corresp. mem. Acad. Nat. de Médecine, France 73-, Deutsche Akad. der Naturforscher, Leopoldina 76; hon. mem. several foreign pediatrics socs.; Hon. LL.D. (Nebraska and Glasgow Univs.), Dr. h.c. (Nice Univ.), Hon. D.Sc. (Baghdad and Anatolian Univs.); Nat. Award for Distinguished Service (Scientific and Technical Research) 78; Officier Légion d'Honneur 78, Officer, Order of Duarte, Sanchez y Mella (Dominican Repub.), First Rank Commdr. of the Order of the Lion (Finland), Léon Bernard Foundation Prize 81; Editor *The Turkish Journal of Pediatrics, Bulletin of the International Pediatric Association*, Consulting Editor *Journal of Clinical Computing.*

Publs. *Annenn Kitabi* (Mother's Handbook on Child Care) 10 edns. 52-80, *Premature Baby Care* 54, *Porphyrias in Childhood* 64, *Care of Mother and Child* 67, various monographs and articles on child health and pediatric topics; consulting Ed. *Clinical Pediatrics* (Philadelphia).

Turkish and International Children's Centre, P.K. 2 Maltepe, Ankara, Turkey.

Driss, Rachid; Tunisian journalist and diplomatist; b. 27 Jan. 1917; ed. Sadiki Coll., Tunis.
Joined Néo-Destour Party 34; journalist exiled in Cairo, and with President Bourguiba founder mem. Bureau du Maghreb Arabe 46-52; returned to Tunisia 55; Editor *El Amal;* Deputy, Constitutional Assembly 56; Sec. of State Post Office and Communications 57-64, mem. Nat. Assembly 59-, Political Bureau Destour Socialist Party 58-; Amb. to the U.S.A. and Mexico 64-70; Perm. Rep. to UN 70-76; Pres. Econ. and Social Council 71; Grand Cordon de l'Ordre de l'Indépendance de la République Tunisienne and foreign decorations.
Publs. *From Bab Souika to Manhattan* (in Arabic) 80, *A l'aube, la lanterne* 81, *Memories from the Maghreb Arab Bureau in Cairo* (in Arabic) 81.
rue St. Cyprien 2016, Carthage, Tunisia.

Duaij, Ahmad Ali al-, B.A.; Kuwaiti company director; b. 25 Dec. 1937; ed. Shuwaikh Secondary School, Kuwait, Reading Technical Coll., Keele Univ. and St. Antony's Coll., Oxford, England.
Joined Ministry of Foreign Affairs 62; joined Planning Board as Sec. 62, Sec.-Gen. 63, Dir.-Gen. with rank of Perm. Under-Sec. 64-75; Chair. and Man. Dir. Kuwait Real Estate Investment Consortium 75-.
Publs. Regular articles in Kuwait, Lebanese and British Press.
Kuwait Real Estate Investment Consortium (K.S.C.), P.O. Box 23411, Kuwait.

Dubai, Ruler of (see Maktum, H.H. Sheikh Rashid bin Said al-).

Dultzin, Leib (Leon Aryeh); Israeli business executive; b. 31 March 1913, Minsk, Russia.
Lived in Mexico 28-56, Israel 65-; mem. of the executive, Jewish Agency. Treas. 68-78, Chair. 78-; Minister without Portfolio, Govt. of Israel 70-73; Gov. Pal Land Devt. Co. Ltd., Bank Leumi le-Israel; Dir. Rassco Ltd., Yakhim Hakal Co. Ltd., Otzar Hataasiya; mem. World Directorate, Keren Hayesod; mem. of numerous Zionist orgs.
Publs. *The Economic Role of the Middle Class, The Middle Classes and their Role in the Productive Absorption of New Immigrants.*
The Jewish Agency, P.O. Box 92, Jerusalem; Home: 11 Mapu Street, Tel-Aviv, Israel.

Dupont-Sommer, André Louis; French Semiticist; b. 23 Dec. 1900; ed. Univ. of Paris.
Secretary, Collège de France 34-40; Dir. of Studies, School of Higher Studies 38-; Prof., Univ. of Paris 45-63; Pres. of Inst. of Semitic Studies, Univ. of Paris 52-; Prof. Collège de France 63-71, Hon. Prof. 72; mem. Institut de France 61-; Secrétaire Perpétuel de l'Académie des Inscriptions et Belles-Lettres 68-; Foreign mem. Accad. dei Lincei (Rome); Corresp. mem. Austrian Acad. of Sciences; Officier Légion d'Honneur; Commandeur des Palmes académiques.
Publs. *La Doctrine gnostique de la lettre wâw d'après une lamelle araméenne inédite* 46, *Les Araméens* 49, *Les inscriptions araméennes de Sfiré* 48, *Aperçus préliminaires sur les manuscrits de la mer Morte* 50, *Nouveaux aperçus sur les manuscrits de la mer Morte* 53, *Les Ecrits esséniens découverts près de la mer Morte* 59, 60, 64, 80, and others.
Palais Mazarin, 25 quai de Conti, Paris 6e, France.

Duval, H.E. Cardinal Léon-Etienne; Algerian (b. French) ecclesiastic; b. 9 Nov. 1903, Chênex, France; ed. Petit Séminaire, Roche-sur-Foron, Grand Séminaire Annecy, Séminaire français Rome and Pontifica Universitas Gregoriana.
Ordained priest 26; Prof. Grand Séminaire Annecy 30-42; Vicar-Gen. and Dir. of works, Diocese of Annecy 42-46; consecrated Bishop of Constantine and Hippo 46; Arch-

bishop of Algiers 54-; created Cardinal 65; took Algerian nationality 65; Officier Légion d'Honneur.
Publs. *Paroles de Paix* 55, *Messages de Paix 1955-1962* 62, *Laïcs, prêtres, religieux dans l'Eglise selon Vatican II* 67.
Archbishop's House, 13 rue Khelifa-Boukhalfa, Algiers, Algeria.

E

Eban, Abba, M.A.; Israeli politician; b. (as Aubrey Solomon) 2 Feb. 1915, South Africa; ed. Queens' Coll., Cambridge.
Liaison Officer of Allied H.Q. with the Jewish population in Jerusalem 40; Chief Instructor at the Middle East Arab Centre in Jerusalem; entered service of Jewish Agency 46; Liaison Officer with UN Special Comm. on Palestine 47; Rep. of Provisional Govt. to UN 48, Perm. Rep. with rank of Minister 49; Amb. to U.S.A. 50-59; Minister without Portfolio 59-60; Minister of Educ. and Culture 60-63; Deputy Prime Minister June 63-66; Minister of Foreign Affairs 66-74; mem. of Knesset 74-; Guest Prof. Columbia Univ. 74, Haifa Univ. 75, Inst. for Advanced Study, Princeton Univ. 78; Pres. Weizmann Inst. of Science 58-66; Hon. L.H.D., Hon. Ph.D., Hon. Dr. New York, Maryland, Boston, Chicago, Cincinnati Univs.; foreign mem. American Acad. of Arts and Sciences 60.
Publs. *Maze of Justice* 46, *Social and Cultural Problems in the Middle East* 47, *The Toynbee Heresy* 55, *Voice of Israel* 57, *Tide of Nationalism* 59, *Chaim Weizmann: A Collective Biography* 62, *Israel in the World* 66, *My People* 68, *My Country* 73, *An Autobiography* 77.
The Knesset, Jerusalem, Israel.

Ecevit, Bülent, B.A.; Turkish journalist and politician, b. 28 May 1925, Istanbul; ed. Robert Coll., Ankara; London and Harvard Univ.
Government official 44-50; Turkish Press Attaché's Office, London 46-50; Foreign News Editor, Man. Editor later Political Dir. *Ulus* (Ankara) 50-61, Political Columnist, *Ulus* 56-61; M.P. (Republican People's Party) 57-60, 61-80; mem. Constituent Assembly 61; Minister of Labour 61-65; Political Columnist *Milliyet* 65; Sec.-Gen. Republican People's Party 66-71, Chair. 72-80 (resigned when political activity banned Sept. 80-); Prime Minister Jan.-Nov. 74, June-July 77, 78-79; internal exile Sept.-Oct. 80, freed Oct. 80; journalist *Arayis* 81; imprisoned for publicly criticizing the dissolution of political parties by the military government Dec. 81-Feb. 82; detained for allegedly making political statements to the foreign press April 82, sentenced to three months' imprisonment July 82.
Publs. *Ortanin Solu* (Left of Centre) 66, *Bu Düzen Değismelidir* (The System Must Change) 68, *Atatürk ve Devrimcilik* (Atatürk and Revolution) 70, *Sohbet* (conversations), *Demokratik Sol* (Democratic Left) 74, *Diş Politika* (Foreign Policy) 75, *Işçi-Köylü Elele* (Workers and Peasants Together) 76, *Siirler* (Poems) 76, *Sömürü Düzeninde Yeni Asama* (A New Stage in the Exploitative System) 80; Translations into Turkish: *Gitanjali* (R. Tagore) 41, *Straybirds* (R. Tagore) 43, *Cocktail Party* (T. S. Eliot) 63.
Or-an Şehri, Ankara, Turkey.

Echiguer, Mohammed Haddou (see Shiguer, Mohamed Haddou).

Eddé, Raymond, L. en D.; Lebanese lawyer and politician b. 1913; ed. Univ. Saint Joseph, Beirut.
Member of Parl. 53-57-60-65-68-72; Leader, Nat. Bloc Party 49-; Minister of Interior, of Public Works, of Social Affairs, and of Posts, Telegraphs and Telephones 58-59; Candidate for Presidency 58, May 76; Minister of Public Works, Agriculture, Planning, Water and Power 68-72; mem. Nat. Dialogue Cttee. Sept. 75; self-imposed exile in Paris since 76.

Publs. *Loi sur les Immeubles de Luxe, Loi sur le Secret Bancaire, Loi sur le compte joint.*
c/o Assemblée Nationale, Place de l'Etoile, Beirut, Lebanon.

Egerton, Stephen Loftus, C.M.G.; British diplomatist; b. 21 July 1932; ed. Eton and Trinity Coll., Cambridge.
Officer, British Army 52-53; entered Foreign (later Diplomatic) Service 56; Middle East Centre for Arab Studies, Shemlan, Lebanon 57; Pol. Officer, British Embassy, Kuwait 58-61; Private Sec. to Parliamentary Under-Sec., Foreign Office 61-63; First Sec., Baghdad 63-67; First Sec., Perm. Mission of U.K. to UN 67-70; Asst. Head, Arabian and Near East Depts., Foreign and Commonwealth Office (FCO) 70-72; Counsellor, Tripoli 72-73; Head of Energy Dept., FCO 73-77; Consul-Gen., Rio de Janeiro 77-80; Amb. to Iraq Sept. 80-.
British Embassy, Sharia Salah Ud Din, Karkh, Baghdad, Iraq; and Foreign and Commonwealth Office, King Charles Street, London S.W.1, England.

Ehrlich, Simcha; Israeli industrialist and politician; b. 15 Dec. 1915, Poland; ed. high school and econ. studies.
Industrialist; mem. Tel-Aviv Municipality Council 55-69; mem. Knesset 69-; fmr. Deputy Mayor and Head of Lighting and Water Dept. of Sanitation Dept. of Bureau of Municipal Corpn.; fmr. Nat. Sec. of Liberal Party; mem. Exec. Cttee., Gattal; mem. of Knesset Finance Cttee. and Sub-cttee. for Defence Budget; Minister of Finance 77-79, a Deputy Prime Minister 79-, Minister of Agriculture 81-; Chair. Habimah Co.; mem. Publicity Cttee. for Israel Opera; Likud.
Ministry of Agriculture, Jerusalem, Israel.

Eilts, Hermann Frederick, PH.D., LL.D., L.H.D.; American diplomatist; b. 23 March 1922, Germany; ed. Ursinus Coll., Johns Hopkins Univ. School of Advanced Int. Studies, Univ. of Pennsylvania Nat. War Coll.
Counsellor and Deputy Chief of Mission, American Embassy, Libya 64-65; Amb. to Saudi Arabia 65-70; Diplomatic Adviser U.S. Army War Coll. 70-73; Amb. to Egypt 73-79; retd. from foreign service June 79; Prof. of Middle Eastern Affairs, Boston Univ. 79-; Arthur S. Flemming Distinguished Govt. Service Award 58; U.S. Army Decoration for Distinguished Civilian Service 73, Dept. of State Distinguished Service Award 79, Joseph C. Wilson Award for achievement in international affairs 80.
Boston University, 745 Commonwealth Avenue, Boston, Massachusetts 02215, U.S.A.

Eisenstadt, Shmuel N., M.A., PH.D.; Israeli professor of sociology; b. 10 Sept. 1923, Warsaw, Poland; ed. Hebrew Univ., Jerusalem and London School of Economics.
Chairman, Dept. of Sociology, Hebrew Univ., Jerusalem 51-68, Prof. of Sociology 59-, Dean, Faculty of Social Sciences 66-68; Fellow Center for Advanced Studies in the Behavioral Sciences, Stanford Univ. 55-56; Visiting Prof., Univ. of Oslo 58, Univ. of Chicago 60, Harvard Univ. 66, 68-69; Carnegie Visiting Prof., Mass. Inst. of Technology 62-63; Chair. Council on Community Devt., Israel 62-66, Israeli Sociological Soc. 69-72; Visiting Prof., Univ. of Michigan 70, Univ. of Chicago 70, Univ. of Zurich 75, Harvard Univ. 75-80; Simon Visiting Prof., Univ. of Manchester 77; Visiting Prof. Univ. of Vienna 80, Univ. of Bern 80; Hon Research Fellow Australian Nat. Univ. 77; mem. Advisory Board *International Encyclopedia of the Social Sciences*; Fellow, Netherlands Inst. of Advanced Studies 73; mem. Israel Acad. of Sciences and Humanities, Int. Sociological Soc., American Sociological Asscn.; Foreign Hon. mem. American Acad. of Arts and Sciences, American Philosophical Soc.; Hon. Fellow, London School of Econs.; McIver Award, American Sociological Asscn, Rothschild Prize in Social Sciences, Israel Prize in Social Sciences.
Publs. *The Absorption of Immigrants* 54, *Political Sociology* (editor) 55, *From Generation to Generation* 56, *Essays on Sociological Aspects of Economical and Political Development* 61, *The Political Systems of Empires* 63, *Essays on Comparative Institutions* 65, *Modernization, Protest and Change* 66, *Israeli Society* 68, *The Protestant Ethic and Modernization* 68, *Political Sociology of Modernization* (in Japanese) 68, *Comparative Perceptives on Social Change* (editor) 68, *Charisma and Institution Building: Selections from Max Weber* (editor) 68, *Ensayos sobre el Cambio Social y la Modernización* (Spanish) 69, *Modernização e Mudança Social* (Portuguese) 69, *Political Sociology* (editor) 71, *Social Stratification and Differentiation* 71, *Tradition, Change and Modernity* 73, *The Form of Sociology: Paradigms and Crisis* (with M. Curelaru) 76, *Revolution and the Transformation of Societies* 78, *Political Clientilism, Patronage and Development* (co-editor with R. Lemarchand) 81.
The Hebrew University, Jerusalem; Home: Rechov Radak 30, Jerusalem, Israel.

Eitan, Lieut.-Gen. Rafael; Israeli army officer; b. 1929; ed. Tel-Aviv and Haifa Univs.
Fought with Palmach, Jerusalem and Katamon 46; Commdr., Paratroop company, Sinai campaign 56; Commdr. Paratroop Brigade, Six-Day War 67, in Jordan Rift 67-68; Div. Commdr., Golan Heights, Yom Kippur War 73; Major-Gen. 73; Gen. and Commdr., Northern Region Command 74-77; Chief of Gen. Staff, G Branch 77-78; Chief of Staff of Israel Defence Forces April 78-; commendation for service in Kunhila Battle 55, decorations of Independence War, Sinai campaign, Six-Day War and Yom Kippur War.
Office of the General Staff, Israel Defence Forces, 9 Itamar Ben-Ari Street, Tel-Aviv; Moshav Tel Adashim, Tel-Aviv, Israel.

Elath, Eliahu, PH.D.; Israeli diplomatist; b. 30 July 1903; ed. Hebrew Univ. of Jerusalem and American Univ. of Beirut.
Jewish Agency 34; Jewish Agency observer to San Francisco Conf. 45; Head of Jewish Agency's Political Office in Washington, D.C.; Israeli Amb. to U.S.A. 48-50; Minister to U.K. 50-52, Amb. 52-59; Adviser, Ministry of Foreign Affairs 59-60; Pres. Hebrew Univ., Jerusalem 61-67; Vice-Pres. Jewish Colonization Asscn.; Pres. Israel Oriental Soc.; Chair. Afro-Asian Inst., Tel-Aviv; Hon. Chair. Truman Inst. for Peace, Hebrew Univ., Jerusalem; Hon. Ph.D.
Publs. *Bedouin, their Life and Manners* 34, *Trans-Jordan* 35, *Israel and Her Neighbours* 57, *The Political Struggle for the inclusion of Elath in the Jewish State* 67, *San Francisco Diary* 71, *British Routes to India* 71, *Zionism and the Arabs* 74, *The Struggle for Statehood* 80.
17 Bialik Street, Beth Hakerem, Jerusalem, Israel.

El Bualy, Nassir Seif, B.A.ECON.; Omani diplomatist; b. 9 Jan. 1925, Dar es Salaam, Tanzania.
Assistant Dir. of Information, Zanzibar 56-60, Asst. Principal Sec. 60-65; Asst. Dir. Mwananchi Group of Cos., Dar es Salaam 65-68; Senior Admin., Dept. of Finance, United Arab Emirates 69-70; Dir. of Social Affairs and Acting Dir. of Information, Oman 71, Dir.-Gen. of Information and Tourism 72-73; Chargé d'Affaires, Omani Embassy in London Feb.-June 73, Amb. 73-80; Head of Asian and Australian Affairs, Ministry of Foreign Affairs; appointed to Consultative Assembly 81-.
Ministry of Foreign Affairs, Muscat, Oman.

El Goulli, Slaheddine, D.EN DROIT.; Tunisian diplomatist and economist; b. 22 June 1919, Sousse; ed. Collège de Sousse, Collège de Sainte Barbe and Université de Paris.
Tunisian Bar 47; in private industry 49-56; active in Tunisian Nat. Liberation Movement, Europe 47-56; Gen. Consul, Marseilles 56-57; Counsellor, Washington 58, Minister, Washington 59-61; Alt. Exec. Dir. World Bank

61; Amb. to Belgium, also accred. to Netherlands and Luxembourg 62, concurrently Perm. Rep. to EEC; Perm. Rep. to UN 69; Amb. to U.S.A. 69-73, concurrently to Mexico 70-73, to Venezuela 72-73; Special Diplomatic Adviser to Foreign Minister 74-76; Amb. to Netherlands 76-78; Adviser, Foreign Ministry 79; Chair. Philips Electronics (Tunisia) 80-; Grand Cordon de l'Ordre de la République Tunisienne 66, also decorations from Belgium, Netherlands and Luxembourg.
2 rue des roses, La Marsa, Tunisia.

Eliraz, Israel, M.A.; Israeli writer, playwright and teacher; b. 24 March 1936, Jerusalem; ed. Hebrew Univ., Jerusalem, Tel-Aviv Univ., Sorbonne, Paris.
Plays produced in Israel, Paris, London, New York, Belgium and Germany; libretti commissioned and performed by Hamburgische Staatsoper 71, Israeli Festival 73, Bayerische Staatsoper 76; Teacher in Jerusalem; Lecturer, Hebrew Univ.; awarded two first prizes by Nat. Council for Culture and Art, Israel.
Publs. novels: *Tin Swings, Last Birds, Golden Summer, A Voyage;* plays: *Far from the Sea—Far from the Summer, The Bear, The Banana, Round Trip, Three Women in Yellow, The Persian Protocoles;* libretti: *Ashmedai, Massada 967, The Temptation, Elsa-Homage, The Fire and the Mountains, The Journey;* choreographies: *M.A.S.A.D.A. 77, Little Savage Square 77, Wings (Hanna Senesh)* 79.
6 Jabotinsky Street, Jerusalem, Israel.

Elmandjra, Mahdi, PH.D.; Moroccan international official; b. 13 March 1933; ed. Lycée Lyautey, Casablanca, Putney School, Vermont, U.S.A., Cornell Univ., London School of Economics and Univ. de Paris.
Head of Confs., Law Faculty, Univ. of Rabat 57-58; Adviser Ministry of Foreign Affairs, and to Moroccan Del. to UN 58-59; Dir.-Gen. Radiodiffusion Télévision Marocaine 59-60; Chief of African Div., Office of Relations with mem. States, UNESCO 61-63; Dir. Exec. Office of Dir.-Gen. of UNESCO 63-66; Asst. Dir.-Gen. of UNESCO for Social Sciences, Human Sciences and Culture 66-69; Visiting Fellow, Centre for Int. Studies, London School of Econs. and Political Sciences 70; Asst. Dir-Gen. of UNESCO for Pre-Programming 71-75, Special Adviser to the Dir.-Gen. 75-76; Prof. Univ. Mohamed V, Rabat 77-; Co-ordinator, African Conf. of Govt. Experts on Tech. Cooperation between developing countries (UNDP) 79-80. Pres. World Future Studies Fed., Moroccan Asscn. for Future Studies; Vice-Pres. Morocco-Japan Asscn.; mem. Acad. of the Kingdom of Morocco, Soc. for Int. Devt., World Acad. of Art and Science, Futuribles, Pugwash Movement, Arab Thought Forum; Chevalier, Ordre des Arts et Lettres (France).
Publ. *The United Nations System: An Analysis* 73; co-author *No Limits to Learning* (report to Club of Rome, translated into 12 languages) 79, *Prix de la Vie Economique* 81.
B.P. 53, Rabat, Morocco.

Erbakan, Necmettin; Turkish politician; b. 1926, Sinop; ed. Inst. of Mechanics, Technical Univ. of Istanbul and Technische Universität, Aachen, Federal Republic of Germany.
Assistant Lecturer Inst. of Mechanics, Technical Univ. of Istanbul 48-51; Engineer, Firma Deutz 51-54; Prof. Technical Univ. of Istanbul 54-66; Chair. Industrial Dept., Turkish Asscn. of Chambers of Commerce 66-68, Chair. of Asscn. 68; mem. Nat. Assembly 69-80; f. Nat. Order Party 70 (disbanded 71); Chair. Salvation Party Oct. 72- (political activity banned Sept. 80-); Deputy Prime Minister Jan.-Sept. 74, April 75-June 77, July-Dec. 77; Minister of State Jan.-Sept. 74; internal exile Sept.-Oct. 80; on trial April 81; detained Oct. 80-July 81.
National Salvation Party, Ankara, Turkey.

Erdem, Kaya; Turkish government official; b. 1928, Safranbolu; ed. Acad. of Commercial and Econ. Sciences. Worked for State Sugar Co., rising to Dir. of Accounting 51-61; joined Ministry of Finance 61, Dir.-Gen. State Treasury, Ministry of Finance; Financial Counsellor, Turkish Embassy, London, Dir.-Gen. Social Security Org.; Sec.-Gen. State Treasury; Minister of Finance Sept. 80-.
Ministry of Finance, Maliye Bakanlığı, Ulus, Ankara, Turkey.

Erkmen, Hayrettin, D.ECON.S.; Turkish economist and politician; b. 1915, Giresun; ed. Ankara School of Political Sciences, Geneva School of Econs. and Lausanne School of Law.
Reporter, Board of Financial Research, Ministry of Finance 48; Asst. Prof. of Econs., Univ. of Istanbul 49; Minister of Labour 53-55, 57-58, of Commerce 58-60, of Reconstruction (acting) 59-60, of Foreign Affairs 79-80; mem. Nat. Assembly (Dem. Party) before 60; mem. Senate (Justice Party) 75-80; arrested after mil. coup 60, found guilty on corruption charges 61.
Publ. *La participation des salariés à la gestion de l'entreprise* 48.
c/o Ministry of Foreign Affairs, Dışişleri Bakanlığı, Müdafaa Cad. Bakanlıklar, Ankara, Turkey.

Erkmen, Nizamettin; Turkish politician; b. 1919, Giresun.
Director of Legal Affairs, Samsun; mem. Nat. Assembly for Giresun 61-80; Sec.-Gen. Justice Party until 74; Minister of State, Deputy Prime Minister 73-74; Justice Party.
Dr. Mediha Eldem Sok. 73/14, Ankara, Turkey.

Ersin, Gen. Nurettin; Turkish army officer; b. 1918, Gelibolu; ed. Army Military Acad. and Staff Coll.
Commander, Turkish Peace Force, Cyprus 74; promoted to full Gen. 74; Commdr. First Army 77; Commdr. Turkish Army (Ground Forces) 78-.
c/o Ministry of National Defence, Milli Savunma Bakanlığı, Bakanlıklar, Ankara, Turkey.

Ertekün, Mehmet Necati Münir, O.B.E., Q.C., M.A.; Cypriot judge; b. 7 Dec. 1923, Nicosia; ed. Froebel School, Kyrenia, Brentwood School, Essex, St. John's Coll. Cambridge, Gray's Inn, London.
McMahon Law Studentship, St. John's Coll., Cambridge 46; Crown Counsel, Tanganyika (now Tanzania) 48-53; Solicitor-Gen., Cyprus 53-60; Turkish Judge, Supreme Constitutional Court of Cyprus 60; Pres. Supreme Court of Turkish Cypriot Admin. 67-75, of "Turkish Federated State of Cyprus (TFSC)" 75-78; Constitutional and Legal Adviser to Pres. of TFSC (became TFSK 81) 79-; Legal Adviser to Turkish Cypriot del. to Mixed Constitutional Comm. on Cyprus 59-60; mem. Turkish Cypriot del. to Second Geneva Conf. on Cyprus Aug. 74; Pres. Supreme Council of Judicature of "TFSC" 75-78, of Supreme Electoral Comm. 76-78; mem. Supreme Council of Public Prosecutors 76-78.
Publs. *Inter-Communal Talks and the Cyprus Problem* 77, *In Search of a Negotiated Cyprus Settlement* 81.
3 Müfit Güleroğlu Street, Lefkoşa, Mersin 10, Turkey.

Esenbel, Melih; Turkish diplomatist; b. 15 March 1915, Istanbul; ed. Galatasaray Lycée, Faculty of Law, Istanbul.
Ministry of Foreign Affairs 36, Third Sec., Private Cabinet of Sec.-Gen., Later in Second Political Dept.; Second Sec., Paris and First Sec. of Protocol Dept. of Ministry of Foreign Affairs 44; First Sec., later Counsellor, Washington, D.C. 45-52; Dir.-Gen. Dept. of Int. Econ. Affairs 52; del. to UN Gen. Assembly 52, 53; Asst. Sec.-Gen. for Econ. Affairs

and Sec.-Gen. of Int. Co-operation Admin. 54-56; participated in negotiations for Baghdad Pact 55; Sec.-Gen. Ministry of Foreign Affairs 57-59, participated in Zürich and London Confs. on independence of Cyprus 59; Amb. to U.S.A. 60; Senior Adviser, Ministry of Foreign Affairs 60-63; Amb. to Japan 63-66, to U.S.A. 67-74; Minister of Foreign Affairs 74-75; Amb. to U.S.A. 75-79; Chevalier, Légion d'Honneur (France) 41, Cross of Order of Isabel la Católica (Spain) 56, Gran Cruz del Mérito Civil (Spain) 59, Cavaliere di Gran Croce (Italy) 57, Order of the Sacred Treasure (Japan) 58, Grand Cordon Order of the Brilliant Star (Repub. of China) 58, Knight, Grand Cross, Royal Order of the Phoenix (Greece) 59, Sardar Ali (Afghanistan) 58, Grand Cross (Fed. Repub. of Germany) 54.
Gelincik S. 8/17 Guvenevler, Ankara, Turkey.

Essaafi, M'hamed; Tunisian diplomatist; b. 26 May 1930; ed. Collège Sadiki and Univ. of Paris.
Secretariat of Foreign Affairs, Tunis 56; Tunisian Embassy, London 56-57; First Sec., Washington 57-60; Dir. of American Dept., Secr. of Foreign Affairs, Tunis 60-62, American Dept. and Int. Conf. Dept. 62-64; Amb. to U.K. 64-69; Sec.-Gen. Foreign Affairs, Tunis 69-70; Amb. to U.S.S.R. 70-74, to Federal Repub. of Germany 74-76; Sec.-Gen. Ministry of Foreign Affairs 76-78; Amb. to Belgium, Luxembourg and the EEC 78-80; Perm. Rep. of Tunisia to UN 80-81; Grand Officier de l'Ordre de la République Tunisienne.
Tunis, Tunisia.

Essebsi, Beji Caid; Tunisian politician.
Former Minister of Interior, of Defence 69-70; expelled from ruling Parti Socialiste Destourien (PSD) for protesting at lack of democracy in Tunisia 72; became prominent mem. Mouvement des Démocrates Socialistes (MDS), unofficial opposition movt., rejoined PSD at invitation of Pres. Bourguiba March 80, mem. *Errai* group; Minister Delegate to Prime Minister Dec. 80-April 81; Minister of Foreign Affairs April 81-.
Ministry of Foreign Affairs, Tunis, Tunisia.

Etemadi, Noor Ahmad; Afghan diplomatist; b. 22 Feb. 1921, Kandahar; ed. Istiqlal Lycée, Kabul, and Kabul Univ.
Joined Ministry of Foreign Affairs 46, Asst. Chief of Protocol, Dir. for Econ. Relations, Dir.-Gen. for Political Affairs 57; diplomatic posts in London and Washington; Deputy Minister of Foreign Affairs 63; Amb. to Pakistan 64; Minister of Foreign Affairs 65-71, Prime Minister 67-71; Amb. to Italy 72-73, to U.S.S.R. 73-74, 75-76, to Pakistan 76-78; arrested June 78.
Kabul, Afghanistan.

Evenari, Michael; Israeli botanist; b. 9 Oct. 1904; ed. Univ. of Frankfurt, Germany.
Staff of Botany Dept., Univ. of Frankfurt 27-28, German Univ., Prague 28-31; Staff of Technische Hochschule, Darmstadt 31-33, Lecturer 33; External Teacher, Hebrew Univ., Jerusalem 34-37, Instructor 37-44, Lecturer 44, Chair. Dept. of Botany 45-, Prof. 51-; Vice-Pres. Hebrew Univ., Jerusalem 53-59; Fellow Linnean Soc.; Hon. Fellow American Botanical Soc.; mem. German Acad. of Science; Major Research on ancient desert agriculture and its modern application and studies in germination, physiology and ecology of desert plants; Hon. Ph.D. (Technical Univ., Darmstadt).
Publ. *The Negev—The Challenge of a Desert* 71.
Department of Botany, Hebrew University of Jerusalem, Bitanim, Jerusalem 91904, Israel.

Evren, Gen. Kenan; Turkish army officer; b. 1918, Alaşehir; ed. Military Acad., Artillery School and Staff Coll.
Artillery Officer 38; served in Korea; promoted to Gen. 64; Commdr. 1st Army Corps.; Chief of Staff of Commdr.

of the Land Forces, then Deputy Chief of Staff of the Armed Forces; promoted to full Gen. 74; Commdr. Fourth Army (Aegean Army), Izmir 76; Chief of the Land Forces 77; Chief of Staff of the Armed Forces 78-; Head, Turkish mil. del. to U.S.S.R. 75; led coup deposing civilian govt. Sept. 80; Head of State and Chair. Nat. Security Council Sept. 80-.
The Presidency, Ankara, Turkey.

Evron, Ephraim; Israeli diplomatist; b. 1920, Haifa; ed. Reali Secondary School, Haifa, Hebrew Univ. of Jerusalem.
Served in British Army 41-46; in Israeli Foreign Service 49-56, 61-; Political Sec. to Minister of Foreign Affairs 49-51; Chief of Bureau, Office of the Prime Minister 51-52, Ministry of Defence 54-55; worked in the Histadrut (Gen. Fed. of Labour) 56-61; Counsellor, Embassy of Israel to the U.K. 61-63, Minister 63-65; Minister at Embassy to U.S.A. 65-68; Amb. to Sweden 68-69, to Canada 69-71; Asst. Dir.-Gen. of Ministry of Foreign Affairs 72-73, Deputy Dir.-Gen. 73-77, Dir.-Gen. 77-78; Amb. to U.S.A. Jan. 79-82.
Ministry of Foreign Affairs, Jerusalem, Israel.

Eytan, Walter, M.A.; Israeli public official; b. 24 July 1910; ed. St. Paul's School, London and Queen's Coll. Oxford.
Lecturer in German, Queen's Coll., Oxford 34-46; Principal, Public Service Coll., Jerusalem 46-48; Dir.-Gen., Ministry for Foreign Affairs, Israel 48-59; Ambassador to France 60-70; Political Adviser to Minister of Foreign Affairs 70-72; Chair. Israel Broadcasting Authority 72-78; Commdr. Légion d'Honneur 76.
Publ. *The First Ten Years* 58.
18 Balfour Street, 92 102 Jerusalem, Israel.

F

Fahd ibn Abdul Aziz; King of Saudi Arabia; b. 1922.
Minister of Educ. 53, of the Interior 62-Oct. 75; Second Deputy Prime Minister 68-75, First Deputy Prime Minister 75-82; became Crown Prince 75; acceded to throne on the death of his brother June 82; Prime Minister June 82-.
Royal Palace, Riyadh, Saudi Arabia.

Fahmy, Ismail; Egyptian diplomatist and politician; b. 2 Oct. 1922; ed. Cairo Univ.
Entered diplomatic service 46; Vice-Consul, Egyptian Consulate, Paris 47-49; mem. Perm. Mission to UN 49-57, Counsellor 57; advised and led numerous dels. from United Arab Republic and Egypt to UN Gen. Assembly and Confs., 49-71, rep. on Boards and Cttees of several int. orgs.; Perm. Rep. and Gov. for Egypt (later United Arab Repub.) IAEA 57-60, Vice-Pres. Board of Govs. 59-60, Vice-Chair. Second Conf. of IAEA 57; Dir. Dept. of Int. Orgs. and Confs., Ministry of Foreign Affairs 64-68; Amb. to Austria 68-71; Under-Sec. of State for Foreign Affairs 71-73; Minister of Tourism April-Oct. 73, of Foreign Affairs 73-77; Vice-Pres. Council of Ministers 75-77; mem. Higher Council for Nuclear Energy 75-77.
22 Saraya El Gezira Zamalek, Cairo, Egypt.

Fahmy, Col.-Gen. Mohamed Ali; Egyptian armed forces officer; b. 11 Oct. 1920, Cairo; ed. Secondary School, Engineering Faculty of Cairo Univ., Mil. Acad., Staff Coll., Air Defence Acad. in Kalinin, U.S.S.R.
Served in Second World War 39, Palestine War 48; Instructor, Senior Officers' Studies Inst. 52-53; Army Operations Dept. 52-58; served in Suez War 56; Commdr. 2nd Light A/A Regt. 58, 14th A/A Regt. 58-59, 64th A/A Regt. 59-61, 6th Artillery Group 61-63; Chief of Staff, 5th Artillery Div. 63-66, Commdr. 66-68; took part in mil. operations 67; Air Defence Chief of Staff 68-69; C.-in-C.

Air Defence Forces 69-75; served in October War 73; C.-in-C. Armed Forces 75-78; Mil. Adviser to the Pres. Oct. 78-; rank of Maj.-Gen. 65, Lt.-Gen. 73, Col.-Gen. (4-star Gen.) 79; Order of Liberation 52, Memorial Order of Founding of U.A.R. 58; Mil. Star 71; Star of Honour (PLO) 74; Yugoslav Star with Gold Belt, First Class 74; Order of King Abdul-Aziz, First Class (Saudi Arabia) 74; numerous ribbons and medals.
Publs. Two books on the Palestinian Campaign, *Germany, a Threat to Peace*, *Germany between East and West* (in two parts), book on African unity, book on African nationalism, *The Fourth Service: The History of the Egyptian Air Defence Force*.
c/o Ministry of War, Cairo, Egypt.

Faisal, Prince Mohammed Saud al- (*see* Saud al-Faisal).

Farhat, Abdallah; Tunisian politician; b. 28 Aug. 1914, Ouerdenine; ed. Ecole Supérieure de langue Arabe, Tunis. Member Parti Néo-Destour 34-; Dir. Féd. Nat. des P.T.T.; Dir. Féd. Gén. des Fonctionnaires, Treas.-Gen. Union Gén. des Travailleurs Tunisiens 48-56; mem. 2nd Political Bureau 52, 55-; Vice-Pres. Constituent Assembly 56-59; Deputy Nat. Assembly 59-; Dir. Cabinet of the Pres. 56-62, 70-71, 71-72; Pres. and Dir.-Gen. Soc. Nat. d'Investissement 63-64; Sec. of State for Post and Tele-communications (P.T.T.) 64-69; Sec. of State for Agriculture Sept.-Nov. 69, Minister for Agriculture 69-71, for Nat. Defence 72-74, for Public Works Jan.-Sept. 74, for Transport and Communications Sept. 74-June 76, of Nat. Defence 76-80; Grand Cordon Ordre de l'Indépendence, Ordre de la République; many foreign decorations.
Ministère de la Défence, Tunis, Tunisia.

Faris, Mustapha, DIPL.ING.; Moroccan engineer, politician and banker; b. 17 Dec. 1933; ed. Ecole Nat. des Ponts et Chaussées, Paris.
Government Civil Engineer, Dept. of Public Works 56-61; Dir. of Supply, Nat. Irrigation Office 61-65; Dir.-Gen. of Hydraulic Engineering 65-69; Sec. of State for Planning attached to Prime Minister's Office 69-71; Minister of Finance 71-72; Pres., Dir.-Gen. Banque Nationale pour le Développement Economique 72-77; fmr. Vice-Pres. Int. Comm. on Large Dams; Gov. IBRD (World Bank), African Devt. Bank; Ordre du Trône.
c/o Banque Nationale pour le Développment Economique, B.P. 407, place des Alaouites, Rabat, Morocco.

Fasi, Mohammed El: Moroccan educationist; b. 2 Sept. 1908; ed. Al Qarawiyin Univ., Fez, Univ. de Paris à la Sorbonne and Ecole des langues orientales, Paris.
Teacher, Inst. des Hautes Etudes Marocaines 35-40; Head Arab manuscript section, Bibliothèque Gén., Rabat 40; Tutor to Prince Moulay Hassan 41-44, 47-52; Rector Al Qarawiyin Univ. 42-44, 47-52; Vice-Pres. Conseil des Uléma 42-; Founder-mem. Istiqlal Party 44; under restriction 44-47, 52-54; Minister of Nat. Educ. 55-58; Rector of the Univ. of Morocco 58; Pres. Moroccan Del. to Gen. Conf. of UNESCO 56, 58, 60, 64, Vice-Pres. 62; Pres. Co-ordination Centre for Nat. Comms. of UNESCO in Arab countries; leader of numerous UNESCO Confs. in the Arab World, Pres. Exec. Board of UNESCO 64; Pres. Conseil d'Admin. Asscn. des Univs. Partiellement ou Entièrement de Langue Francaise (AUPELF) 66; Pres. Conseil Exec., Asscn. des Univs. Africains 67; Minister for Cultural Affairs and Original Educ. 68; Pres. Conseil Exec., Asscn. des Univs. Islamiques 69; mem. Exec. Board and Special Cttee., UNESCO Nov. 78-; Tutor to the Crown Prince and the Royal Princesses 72-; mem. Acad. of Arabic Language, Cairo 58, Acad. of Iraq, Académie royale marocaine 80; Dr. h.c. Univ. of Bridgeport 65, Lagos 68, Jakarta 68.
Publs. Numerous works including *L'évolution politique et*

culturelle au Maroc 58, *La Formation des Cadres au Maroc 60*, *Chants anciens des femmes de Fès 67*.
avenue des Muriers, route de Zaërs, Rabat, Morocco.

Fattal, Dia Allah El-, L. EN D.; Syrian diplomatist; b. 1927; ed. Syrian Univ., Damascus, School of Int. Service, American Univ., Washington, D.C.
With Legation to the Holy See, Rome 52-57; Second Sec. Addis Ababa 58-61; Second, then First Sec., Washington, D.C. 62-65, Chargé d'affaires 65-67; Counsellor Mission to UN New York 67-72; Amb. to Holy See, Rome 75-81; Perm. Rep. to UN, Geneva -81; Perm. Rep. to UN, New York 81-.
Permanent Mission of Syria to the United Nations, 150 East 58th Street, Room 1500, New York, N.Y. 10022, U.S.A.

Feinberg, Nathan, DR.IUR.UTR.; Israeli emeritus professor of international law; b. 6 June 1895; ed. Univ. of Zürich and Graduate Inst. of Int. Studies, Geneva.
Head of Dept., Ministry of Jewish Affairs, Lithuania 19-21; Sec. Cttee. of Jewish Dels., Paris 22-24; law practice in Palestine 24-27 and 34-45; Lecturer, Univ. of Geneva 31-33; Lecturer, Hebrew Univ., Jerusalem 45-49, Assoc. Prof. 49-52, Prof. of Int. Law and Relations 52-66, Dean of Faculty of Law 49-51, Prof. Emer. 65-; Lectured at Acad. of Int. Law, The Hague 32, 37, 52; mem. Perm. Court of Arbitration; mem. Inst. of Int. Law; Fellow of the Int. Inst. of Arts and Letters; Dr. h.c. and mem. Board of Governors, Hebrew Univ.
Publs. *La Question des Minorités à la Conférence de la Paix de 1919-1920 et L'Action Juive en Faveur de la Protection Internationale des Minorités 29*, *La Juridiction de la Cour Permanente de Justice Internationale dans le Système des Mandats 30*, *La Juridiction de la Cour Permanente de Justice dans le Système de la Protection Internationale des Minorités 31*, *La Pétition en Droit International 33*, *Some Problems of the Palestine Mandate 36*, *L'Admission de Nouveaux Membres à la Société des Nations et à l'Organisation des Nations Unies 52*, *The Jewish Struggle Against Hitler in the League of Nations (Bernheim Petition)* (Hebrew) *57*, *The Legality of a "State of War" after the Cessation of Hostilities 61*, *Palestine under the Mandate and the State of Israel: Problems of International Law* (Hebrew) *63*, *The Jewish League of Nations Societies* (Hebrew) *67*, *The Arab-Israel Conflict in International Law 70*, *On an Arab Jurist's Approach to Zionism and the State of Israel 71*, *Studies in International Law, with special Reference to the Arab-Israel Conflict 79*, *Essays on Jewish Issues of Our Time* (Hebrew) *80*, etc.; co-editor: *The Jewish Year Book of International Law 49*; Editor *Studies in Public International Law in Memory of Sir Hersch Lauterpacht* (in Hebrew) *62*.
6 Ben Labrat Street, Jerusalem 92307, Israel.

Fernea, Robert Alan, PH.D.; American anthropologist; b. 25 Jan. 1932; ed. Reed Coll., Portland, Oregon, and Univ. of Chicago.
Assistant, Assoc. Prof. of Anthropology, American Univ. in Cairo 59-65, Social Research Center, American Univ. in Cairo 61-65; Dir. Nubian Ethnological Survey 61-65; Visiting Lecturer, Univ. of Alexandria 63, 64; Consultant, Ford Foundation in U.A.R. 63-65; Post-doctoral Fellow, Harvard Univ. 65-66; Prof. of Anthropology, Univ. of Texas at Austin 66-, Dir. Middle East Center 66-73; mem. Board of Governors, American Research Center in Egypt Inc. 78-; Fellow, American Anthropological Asscn., Founding Fellow, Middle East Studies Asscn. of N. America; Univ. of Chicago Fellow 54, Nat. Science Foundation Fellowship 56, 57, Danforth Fellow 54-59, Faculty Fulbright-Hays Fellow (Afghanistan) 67, (Morocco) 71-72, French Cultural Exchange Fellow (Paris) 77, Fellow American Research Center in Egypt 80-81.
Publs. *Symposium on Contemporary Egyptian Nubia 67*,

Shaykh and Effendi 70, *Nubians in Egypt: Peaceful People* 73, and numerous anthropological articles.
University of Texas at Austin, Department of Anthropology, Burdine Hall, Room 370, Austin, Texas 78712, U.S.A.

Feyzioğlu, Turhan, LL.D.; Turkish lawyer, political scientist and politician; b. 19 Jan. 1922; ed. Galatasaray Lycée, Istanbul Univ. and Ecole Nat. d'Administration, Paris.
Assistant Prof. Ankara Political Science School 45-47, Assoc. Prof. 47-54; Research, Nuffield Coll., Oxford 54; Co-editor *Forum* 54-58; Prof. Ankara Univ. 55; Dean, Political Science School, Ankara 56; M.P. 57, 61, 65-80; mem. Nat. Exec. Cttee. Republican People's Party 57-61; Pres. Middle East Technical Univ. 60; mem. Constituent Assembly 60; Minister of Education 60; Minister of State 61; Deputy Prime Minister 62-63; mem. Turkish High Planning Council 61-63, Asst. Sec.-Gen. Republican People's Party 64, Vice-Pres. Parl. Group 65-66; founded Nat. Reliance Party (now Republican Reliance Party) 67, Pres. 67- (political activity banned Sept. 80-); mem. Consultative Assembly (now Parliamentary Assembly), Council of Europe 64-66, 72-75, Vice-Pres. 74-75; Deputy Prime Minister 75-June 77, Deputy Prime Minister and Minister of State Jan.-Sept. 78; constitutional adviser to the Pres. "Turkish Federated State of Cyprus" March 82-.
Publs. *Administration Law* 47, *Judicial Review of Unconstitutional Laws* 51, *Les Partis Politiques en Turquie* 53, *The Reforms of the French Higher Civil Service* 55, *Democracy and Dictatorship* 57, *The Communist Danger* 69, *In the Service of the Nation* 75, Atatürk's Rational and Scientific Approach to the Modernization of Turkey 81, Kemal Atatürk, Leader de la Libération Nationale et du Développement dans la Paix 82.
Farabi sok., 9/3, Çankaya, Ankara, Turkey.

Filali, Abdel Aziz, LL.D.; Moroccan judge and administrator; b. 10 June 1924; ed. Lycée Gouraud, Rabat, Lycée Lyautey, Casablanca, Ecole Nat. d'Org. Economique et Sociale, Paris and Grenoble Univ., France and Inst. des Hautes Etudes, Rabat.
Practised at the Bar, Casablanca 51-55; First Pres. Int. Tribunal of Tangier, Court of Appeal Tangier and Court of Appeal Rabat 55-; Lecturer Inst. des Hautes Etudes Marocaines, Ecole Marocaine d'Administration, then Asst. Dir. Ecole Marocaine; Pres. Centre Africain de Formation et de Recherche Administratives pour le Développement (C.A.F.R.A.D.), Tangier 64-; mem. Comm. for Arabization of Code of Civil Procedure 63, Comm. for Arabization of Code of Obligations and Contracts 64; Pres. Comm. for Arabization of Code of Commercial Law 65; designated Conciliator and Arbitrator, Int. Centre for Settlement of Investment Disputes, Washington, D.C., U.S.A.; Arbitrator Franco-Arab Chamber of Commerce 76-; Dr. h.c. Univ. of Grenoble.
Publs. *Marriage in Moroccan Law* (in Arabic), *Notes Judiciaires* (in French).
angle boulevard Alexandre 1er and boulevard de la Grande Ceinture, Quartier Europa, Casablanca, Morocco.

Filali, Abdellatif; Moroccan diplomatist; b. 26 Jan. 1928, Fez; ed. Coll. Moulay Idriss, Lycée Mixte, Fez, Univ. of Paris.
Joined Ministry of Foreign Affairs, rank of Amb. 57; Perm. Rep. to the UN 58-59; Chief of Royal Cabinet 59-60; Chargé d'affaires, Embassy to France 60-61; Amb. to Belgium, the Netherlands and Luxembourg 62-63, to People's Repub. of China 65-67, to Algeria 67-68, to Spain 69-71 and 74-78; Minister of Higher Educ. 68-69, of Foreign Affairs 71-72; Perm. Rep. to the UN 78-80; Amb. to U.K. 80-March 81.
c/o Ministry of Foreign Affairs, Rabat, Morocco.

Fisher, William Bayne, B.A., DR. DE L'UNIV. (Paris); British geographer; b. 24 Sept. 1916; ed. Univ. of Manchester and Univs. of Louvain, Caen and Paris.
Research Fellow 37-40; served in Royal Air Force 40-46, commissioned 41, O.C. R.A.F. Liaison Unit, Syria and Lebanon 44-45; Lecturer, Univ. of Manchester 46; Senior Lecturer, Dept. of Geography, Aberdeen Univ. 47-53; Reader and Head of Dept. of Geography, Univ. of Durham 54-56, Prof. 56-81, Dir. Inst. of Middle Eastern and Islamic Studies 62-65, Principal Graduate Coll. 65-81; Consultant H.M. Govt., Govt. of Libya and Harvard Univ., U.S.A.; Leader Univ. Expedition to Libya 51; Visiting Prof. Univ. of Louvain, Belgium 78, Prof. Emer. 81.
Publs. *The Middle East—a Physical, Social and Regional Geography* 50, 78, *Spain* (with H. Bowen-Jones) 57, *Malta* (with H. Bowen-Jones and J. C. Dewdney), Editor Vol. I *The Cambridge History of Iran* (Land and People) 68, *Populations of the Middle East and North Africa* (with J. I. Clarke) 72, *Resources, Environment and the Future* 82, General Editor *University of Durham Commemorative Volumes* 82-.
Department of Geography, Science Laboratories, South Road, Durham DH1 3LE; and 42 South Street, Durham, DH1 4QP, England.

Fitouri, Mohamed, L. EN D.; Tunisian politician; b. 4 April 1925, Kairouan; ed. Lycée Carnot, Tunis, Inst. des Hautes Etudes, Tunis and Faculté de Droit, Paris.
Called to the Bar 52; mem. Council, Nat. Asscn. of Lawyers 60; Advocate, Court of Cassation 62; mem. Econ. and Social Council 63; City Counsellor, Tunis 69; Deputy to Nat. Assembly Nov. 69-; Minister of Justice 70-71, of Finance 71-77, of Foreign Affairs 77-80; mem. Political Bureau of Parti Socialiste Destourien 74; Grand Cordon, Ordre de la République, Ordre de l'Indépendance.
17 rue Slaheddine El Ayoubi, Tunis, Tunisia.

Franjiya, Sulaiman; Lebanese politician; b. 15 June 1910, Zgharta; ed. coll. at Zgharta, near Beirut.
Elected to Parl. as Independent mem. 60 and 64; Minister of Posts, Telegraphs and Telephones and Minister of Agriculture 60-61; Minister of the Interior 68; Minister of Justice, Minister of Econ., Minister of Public Works, Minister of Nat. Econ. 69-70; head, trade del. to negotiate Soviet-Lebanese trade and payments agreement; Pres. of Lebanon 70-76.
Beirut, Lebanon.

Frei, Ephraim Heinrich, D.PHIL.; Israeli physicist; b. 2 March 1912, Vienna, Austria; ed. Vienna Univ. and Hebrew Univ. of Jerusalem.
Broadcasting Engineer, British Army and attached to British Embassy, Athens 42-46; Head Electronics Section Scientific Dept., Ministry of Defence, Israel 48-50; with Weizmann Inst. of Science 53-, Prof. and Head Dept. of Electronics 61-77, Prof. Emer. 77-; mem. Inst. for Advanced Study, Princeton, N.J. 50; Int. Research Fellow. Stanford Research Inst., Calif. 60; Scientific Dir. and Chair. of Board Yeda Research and Devt. Co. 75-80; mem. Board, Miles-Yeda Ltd. 75-80; Chair. Combined Conf. of 12th Int. Conf. on Medical and Biological Engineering and 5th Conf. on Medical Physics; Chair. I.E.E.E. Comm. on Magnetics in Life Sciences 73-79, Fellow, I.E.E.E. 67, Life Fellow 82; Life mem. Magnetics Soc. 80; Hon. mem. Israel Soc. of Medical and Biological Engineering 81; Weizmann Prize 57.
Publs. scientific papers on electronics and physics.
Weizmann Institute, Rehovot, Israel.

Freiha, Said; Lebanese newspaper proprietor; b. 1903.
Chairman Board Dar Assayad S.A.L. which publishes *Assayad* (weekly) 43-, *Achabaka* (weekly) 56-, *Al-Anwar* (daily) 59-.
Dar Assayad, Hamzieh, P.O.B. 1038, Beirut, Lebanon.

Frye, Richard Nelson, PH.D.; American orientalist; b. 10 Jan. 1920; ed. Univ. of Ill., Harvard Univ., and School of Oriental and African Studies, London.

Junior Fellow, Harvard 46-49; visiting scholar, Univ. of Teheran 51-52; Aga Khan Prof. of Iranian, Harvard 57-; Visiting Prof., Oriental Seminary, Frankfurt Univ. 58-59; Hamburg Univ. 68-69; assoc. Editor *Bulletin Asia Institute* and *Indo-Iranica;* Dir. Asia Inst. of Pahlavi Univ., Shiraz 69-74; co-founder Nat. Asscn. of Armenian Studies 60; Hon. mem. German Archaeological Inst.

Publs. *Notes on the early coinage of Transoxiana* 49, *History of the Nation of the Archers* 52, *Narshakhi, The History of Bukhara* 54, *Iran* 56, *The Heritage of Persia* 62, *The Histories of Nishapur* 65, *Bukhara, the Medieval Achievement* 65, *Corpus Iranian Inscriptions* 68, 71, *Qasr-i Abu Nasr Excavations* 73, *The Golden Age of Persia* 75; Editor: *Bulletin Asia Institute* (monographs), *Cambridge History of Iran Vol. IV.*

546 Widener Library, Cambridge 38, Mass., U.S.A.

G

Gaddafi, Col. Muammar Muhamed Abdulsalam Abu Miniar; Libyan army officer and politician; b. 1942, Serte; ed. Sebha, Misurata, Military Acad., Benghazi, Benghazi Univ.

Served with Libyan Army 65-; took leading part in coup to depose King Idris Sept. 69; promoted to Col. 69; Chair. Revolutionary Council and C.-in-C. of Armed Forces of Libya 69-77; Prime Minister 70-72; Minister of Defence 70-77; mem. Pres. Council, Fed. Arab Repubs. 71-; rank of Maj.-Gen. Jan. 76, still keeping the title of Col.; Revolutionary Leader of Socialist People's Libyan Arab Jamahiriya March 77-; Sec.-Gen. of Gen. Secretariat of Gen. People's Congress 77-79.

Publs. *The Green Book* (3 vols.), *Military Strategy and Mobilisation, The Story of the Revolution.*

Revolution Leader's Bureau, Tripoli, Libya.

Gafny, Arnon, M.A.; Israeli economist and banker; b. 1932, Tel-Aviv; ed. Bard Coll., N.Y., U.S.A. and Hebrew Univ., Jerusalem.

Falk Inst. for Econ. Research 54-56; Asst. to Financial Adviser to Chief of Staff, Israel Defence Forces 57-59; Chief Asst., Budgets Dept., Ministry of Finance 59-61; Head, Econ. and Commercial Dept. of Ports Authority 61; Dir. Ashdod Port 61-70; Dir. of Budgets, Ministry of Finance 70-75, Dir.-Gen. Ministry of Finance 75-76; Gov. Bank of Israel 76-82.

c/o Bank of Israel, Mizpeh Building, 29 Jaffa Road, Jerusalem, P.O. Box 780, Israel.

Galadari, Abdel-Wahab Bin-Ibrahim; United Arab Emirates business executive; b. 1938, Dubai; ed. American Univ., Beirut.

Clerk with British Bank of the Middle East, then admin. post with Dubai Electrical Co.; founded re-export business with brothers Abdel-Rahim and Abdel-Latif 60, real estate co. *c.*62; Dir. Nat. Bank of Dubai 65-69; left family business 76; formed Union Bank of the Middle East 77 (now Chair.); Chair. A. W. Galadari Holdings (including Galadari Finance Co., A. W. Galadari Construction, Abdel Wahab Galadari Commodities and *Gulf News*) and over 20 associated cos.; Proprietor Hyatt Regency and Galadari Galleria hotels.

A. W. Galadari Group of Companies, P.O. Box 22, Dubai, United Arab Emirates.

Gamassi, Gen. Muhammad Abdul Ghani al-; Egyptian army officer and government official; b. 9 Sept. 1921, al-Batanoun, Menoufia Governorate; ed. Mil. Acad., Staff Coll., Nasser Higher Mil. Acad.

Assistant Dir. of Mobilization Dept. 54-55; Commdr. 5th

Reconnaissance Regt. 55-57; Staff Officer, Armoured Corps 57-59; Commdr. 2nd Armoured Brigade 59-61; Commdr. Armour School 61-66; Chief, Army Operational Branch 66-67; Chief of Staff, Eastern Mil. Zone Sept. 67-68; Deputy Dir. Reconnaissance and Intelligence Dept. 68-70; Commdr. Operational Group, Syrian Front 70-71; Chief, Armed Forces Training Dept. 71-72; Chief of Operations Dept. and Deputy Chief of Staff of Armed Forces 72-73; Chief of Staff of Armed Forces 73-74; Minister of War and War Production, and C.-in-C. of Armed Forces 74-78, also a Deputy Prime Minister 75-78; Mil. Adviser to the Pres. 78; Order of Liberation 52, Memorial Order of Founding of U.A.R. 58, Star of Honour 73, Star of Honour (PLO) 74, Knight, Order of Mil. Honour (Syria) 74, Order of Courage (Libya) 74, Order of the Two Niles, First Class (Sudan) 74, Order of King Abdel Aziz, First Class (Saudi Arabia) 74, Order of Homayoun, First Class (Iran) 75; numerous ribbons and medals.

Cairo, Egypt.

Gazit, Mordechai, M.A.; Israeli diplomatist; b. 5 Sept. 1922; ed. Hebrew Univ., Jerusalem.

Minister, Embassy of Israel to U.S.A. 60-65; Asst. Dir.-Gen. Ministry of Foreign Affairs 65-67; Deputy Dir.-Gen. Ministry of Immigrant Absorption 69-70; Asst. Dir.-Gen. Ministry of Foreign Affairs 70-72, Dir.-Gen. 72-73; Dir.-Gen., Political Adviser Prime Minister's Office 73-75; Head of Israeli del. at Geneva talks with Egyptians 75; Amb. to France 75-79; Int. Fellowship, Brandeis Univ., Waltham, Massachusetts 80; Fellow, Center of Int. Affairs, Harvard 81; Senior Research Fellow, Truman Inst., Davis Inst. for Int. Relations, Hebrew Univ., Shiloah Center for Middle Eastern and African Studies, Tel-Aviv Univ.

7 Diskin Street, Kiryat Wolfson, Jerusalem 92473, Israel.

Gazit, Maj.-Gen. Shlomo; Israeli army officer; b. 1926, Turkey; ed. Tel-Aviv Coll., Tel-Aviv Univ.

Joined Palmach 44, successively served in 8th Co., Sixth Regt., and as Co. Commdr. Harel Brigade; Editor *Maarachot* (Army monthly) 49-51; Regimental Commdrs.' course 51; Dir. Office of the Deputy Chief of Staff until 53; Dir. Chief of Staff's Office 53-54; Deputy Battalion Commdr. G'Vati Brigade 55; Liaison Officer with French Army Del., Sinai Campaign 56; Asst. to Mil. Attaché, France 57; Instructor Israeli Defence Forces Staff and Command Coll. 58-59; with Gen. Staff 60-61; Deputy Commdr. Golani Brigade 62; co-founder and Instructor, Nat. Defence Coll., Jerusalem 63; served in senior posts, Intelligence Branch, Gen. Staff 64-67; Dir. Dept. of Mil. Govt. 67; Co-ordinator of Administered Areas, Ministry of Defence 67-74; Rank of Maj.-Gen. 73; Dir. of Mil. Intelligence, Israeli Defence Forces 74-79; on academic vacation Sept. 79, Fellow Center for Int. Affairs, Harvard Univ.

Israeli Defence Forces, General Staff, 9 Itamar Ben-Avi Street, Tel-Aviv, Israel.

Gemayel, Bachir, LL.B.; (son of Pierre Gemayel, *q.v.*); Lebanese army officer; b. 10 Nov. 1947; ed. Jamhour Secondary School, St. Joseph's Univ., Beirut, and Southwestern Univ., Texas.

Law practice; mem. Kataeb Party (*Phalanges Libanaises*); Pres. Achrafieh Sector, Commdr. Mil. Council, Kataeb; C.-in-C. of United Lebanese Forces (an amalgamation of Phalangist and Liberal Party militias) May 79-; defeated rival militia of Dany Chamoun (Liberal Party) July 80.

Kataeb Military Council Headquarters, Medawar, Achrafieh, Lebanon.

Gemayel, Sheikh Pierre; Lebanese politician; b. 6 Nov. 1905; ed. Univ. St. Joseph, Beirut and Cochin Hospital, Paris.

Trained as a pharmacist; founded Parti Démocrate Social Libanais—Les Phalanges (Kataeb Party) 36, leader 37-; imprisoned 37, 43; organized general strike 43; established the first Labour Code 44; Leader of the oppo-

sition movt. 58; Deputy for Beirut 60; Minister of Public Works 60, of Finance 60-61, of Communications 60, of Public Health 60, 61, of Nat. Educ. 60 and Agriculture 60; Minister of Public Works May 61-Feb. 64; Minister of the Interior 66-67; mem. Nat. Dialogue Cttee. Sept. 75; Lebanese, Polish and Egyptian decorations.
al-Kata'eb, P.O.B. 992, Place Charles Hélou, Beirut; Home: rue de l'Université St. Joseph, Beirut, Lebanon.

Ghaffari, Abolghassem, DR. SC. MATH., PH.D.; Iranian mathematician; b. 1909, Teheran; ed. Darolfonoun School and Univs. of Nancy, Paris, London and Oxford, England. Associate Prof., Teheran Univ. 37-42, Prof. of Mathematics 42-; Mathematics Research Asst. King's Coll., London 47-48; Research Fellow, Harvard 50-51, Research Assoc., Princeton 51-52; mem. Inst. for Advanced Study, Princeton 51-52; Senior Mathematician, Nat. Bureau of Standards, Washington, D.C. 56-57; aeronautical research scientist 57-64; Professorial Lecturer, American Univ., Washington, D.C. 58-62; aerospace scientist, Goddard Space Flight Center, Greenbelt, Md. 64-; Visiting Prof. of Mathematics, Arya-Mehr Univ. of Technology, Teheran 74-75; has lectured at Univs. of Harvard, Maryland, Princeton and Columbia and at Massachusetts Inst. of Technology; mem. American, French and British Mathematical Societies; Fellow Washington Acad. of Sciences, New York Acad. of Sciences, American Asscn. for the Advancement of Science; mem. Iranian Higher Council of Education 54-58; Iranian Del. to 5th Pakistan Science Conf. Lahore 53, to Int. Congresses of Mathematicians, Cambridge, Mass. 50, Amsterdam 54, Edinburgh 58, Stockholm 62, NASA Del. to Int. Congress of Mathematics, Moscow 66, Nice, France 70, Vancouver, Canada 74; mem. Iranian Comm. for UNESCO 54; mem. American Astronomical Soc.; Orders of Homayoun and of Danesh (first class) and of Sepass (first class); U.S. Special Apollo Achievement Award and Presidential Award of Apollo II Commemorative Certificate.
Publs. *Sur l'Equation Fonctionelle de Chapman-Kolmogoroff* 36, *The Hodograph Method in Gas Dynamics* 50, about 60 research articles on Differential Equations in the Large, Brownian Motion, Transonic and Supersonic Flows, Lunar Flight Optimization, Astrodynamics and General Relativity.
5420 Goldsboro Road, Bethesda, Md. 20817, U.S.A.

Ghaidan, Gen. Saadoun; Iraqi army officer and politician; b. 1930; ed. secondary educ. in Aana and Military Coll., Baghdad.
Commissioned 2nd Lieut. 53; Commdr. of Khalid bin Al-Waleed Tank Bn. 63, participated in Ramadan Revolution 63; Commdr. Republican Palace Tank Bn., taking part in overthrow of Govt. in July 68; became Gen. Commdr. of Repub. Bodyguard Forces and mem. Revolutionary Command Council 68; Gen. Commdr. of Forces in Baghdad 69; Minister of the Interior 70-74, of Transport and Communications 74-June 82; Deputy Prime Minister July 79-June 82; numerous medals.
Ministry of Transport and Communications, Baghdad, Iraq.

Ghanem, Mohamed Hafez, PH.D.; Egyptian lawyer and government official; b. 28 Sept. 1925; ed. Cairo Univ. and Univ. de Paris.
Lecturer, Faculty of Law, Alexandria Univ. 49; Prof. of Public Int. Law and Vice-Dean, Faculty of Law, Ain Shams Univ. 60-68; Minister of Tourism 68-69, of Educ. 69-71; Sec.-Gen. Arab Socialist Union 73; Deputy Premier and Minister of Higher Educ. April 75-76, Deputy Premier and Minister responsible for Social Devt. and Services 76-77; Head of Ministerial Cttee. for Local Govt. 76-; Deputy Prime Minister, Minister for Sudan and for Council Affairs 77-78; Attorney, Legal and Econ. Consultant 78-; Prof. of Public Int Law, Ain Shams Univ. 78-;

Pres. Egyptian Soc. of Int. Law; mem. Arbitration Conciliation and Mediation Comm. of Org. of African Unity (OAU) 66-71; mem. Legal Consultative Comm. for Afro-Asian Countries 58-65; State Prize for best publ. in field of Int. Law and Political Science 60.
Publs. *Public International Law* (Arabic) 64, *International Organization* 67, *International Responsibility* 72.
26 Mahmoud Bassiouny, Cairo (Office); 3 Sharia El Bergass, Garden City, Cairo, Egypt.

Gherab, Mohamed Habib; Tunisian UN official.
Former Amb. to Spain; Special Adviser to Tunisian Sec. of State for Foreign Affairs 67-69; mem. del. to XXIII session of UN Gen. Assembly; Asst. Sec.-Gen. of UN and Dir. of Personnel 69-79; Sec.-Gen., UN Conf. on New and Renewable Sources of Energy March 79-.
UN Secretariat, New York, N.Y., U.S.A.

Ghissassi, Abdellatif; Moroccan politician; b. 19 Nov. 1937, Taza; ed. Lycée Moulay Idriss, Fez, Lycée Lyautey, Casablanca, Ecole Nat. des Ponts et Chausées, Paris, Ecole Nat. de l'Aviation Civile, Paris.
Teacher, Ecole Mohammedia d'Ingénieurs 62-72; Dir. Ministry of Public Works 62-68, Gen. Sec. 68-72, Minister 72-74; Dir. Soc. Marocaine des Industries de Raffinage 73-74; Minister of Commerce, Mines, Industry and Merchant Marine 74-77, of Finance 77-79, of Agriculture and Agrarian Reform 79-82; Officier, Ordre du Mérite 72; Commdr. Ordre Nat. du Mérite (France) 75, Ordre du Mérite (Mauritania) 77.
4 rue Abou Iblane, Rabat, Morocco (Home).

Ghorbal, Ashraf, PH.D.; Egyptian diplomatist; ed. Cairo Univ. and Harvard, Mass., U.S.A.
Joined Egyptian Del. to UN 49; Head Egyptian Interests Section, Indian Embassy, Washington 68-73; Press Adviser to the Pres. Feb.-Nov. 73; Amb. to U.S.A. Nov. 73-.
Embassy of Egypt, 2310 Decatur Place, N.W., Washington, D.C. 20008, U.S.A.

Ghotbzadeh, Sadeq; Iranian politician; b. 1936.
Joint Leader student branch of national resistance movement after 53; imprisoned twice for political activities; entered U.S.A. 58, forced to leave 62; engaged in further anti-Shah activities; joined Ayatollah Khomeini (*q.v.*) in Paris 78; mem. Revolutionary Council 79; Dir. Radio and Television Feb.-Nov. 79; Minister of Foreign Affairs Nov. 79-June 80; under house arrest June 81-, arrested April 82 and put on trial for plotting to kill Ayatollah Khomeini and seize power.
c/o Ministry of Foreign Affairs, Teheran, Iran.

Ghoussein, Talat al-; Kuwaiti diplomatist; b. 1924; ed. American Univ. of Cairo.
Foreign News Editor *As-Shaab* (Jaffa, Palestine) 46-47; Controller, Arab Nat. Bank Ltd., Jaffa, Palestine 47-48; Editor Foreign News and Dir. of English Section, Broadcasting Station of Jordan 48-49; Dir. Press and Public Information, Ministry of Foreign Affairs, Yemen 49-53; Sec.-Gen. Development Board, Kuwait 53-60; Dep. Private Sec. to Amir of Kuwait 60-61; Minister-Counsellor, Kuwait Embassy, Washington 62-63, Amb. to U.S.A. 63-70, concurrently to Canada 65-70; Amb. to Morocco 70-71, to Japan 71-78, also accred. to Australia, Indonesia and Malaysia; Amb. to Yemen Arab Republic 78-81; rejoined Foreign Ministry staff in Kuwait Sept. 81-.
c/o Ministry of Foreign Affairs, Kuwait City, Kuwait.

Ghozali, Sid Ahmed; Algerian petroleum executive; b. 31 March 1937, Marnia; ed. Ecole des Ponts et Chaussées, Paris.
Formerly Dir. of Energy, Ministry of Industry and Energy; Adviser, Ministry of the Economy 64; Under-Sec., Ministry of Public Works 64-65; Pres., Dir.-Gen. Société nationale de transports et de commercialisation des hydrocarbures (SONATRACH) 66-79; Minister of Water

Affairs 79; mem. Org. technique de mise en valeur des richesses du sous-sol saharien 62-.
SONATRACH, 80 Avenue Ahmed Ghermoul, Algiers, Algeria.

Glubb, Lieut.-Gen. Sir John Bagot, K.C.B., C.M.G., D.S.O., O.B.E., M.C.; British officer; b. 16 April 1897; ed. Cheltenham and Royal Military Acad. Woolwich.
2nd Lieut. Royal Engineers 15, served France; served Iraq 20; Admin. Inspector Iraq Govt. 26; Officer Commdg. Desert Area (Transjordan) 30; Officer Commdg. Arab Legion, Transjordan (now Jordan) 38-56.
Publs. *Story of the Arab Legion* 48, *A Soldier with the Arabs* 57, *Britain and the Arabs* 59, *War in the Desert* 60, *The Great Arab Conquests* 63, *The Empire of the Arabs* 63, *The Course of Empire* 65, *The Lost Centuries* 67, *Syria, Lebanon, Jordan* 67, *A Short History of the Arab Peoples* 69, *The Life and Times of Muhammad* 70, *Peace in the Holy Land* 71, *Soldiers of Fortune* 73, *The Way of Love* 74, *Haroon al Raschid and the Great Abbasids* 76, *Into Battle: a Soldier's Diary of the Great War* 77, *Arabian Adventures* 78, *A Purpose for Living* 80, *The Changing Scenes of Life: An Autobiography* 81.
West Wood St. Dunstan, Mayfield, Sussex, England.

Gobbi, Hugo Juan, LL.D., LL.M.; Argentine diplomatist; b. 27 Aug. 1928, Charata, Chaco; ed. Univs. of La Plata and Buenos Aires.
Worked in Foreign Service in Brazil, Chile and Org. of American States (OAS) 55-65; Head of UN, South American and Legal Depts., Foreign Ministry 61-66; Alternate Rep. of Argentina to the UN 66-67; Vice-Chair. 6th Cttee. UN Gen. Assembly 68; Amb. to Egypt (also accred. to Sudan and Ethiopia) 69-72, to Czechoslovakia 73-76; Private Legal Practice in Buenos Aires 76-80; Special Rep. of UN Sec.-Gen. in Cyprus, UN Under-Sec.-Gen. 80-; Argentine Del. to Inter-American Council of Jurists 59; mem. Argentine Del. to 21st, 22nd and 23rd sessions of UN Gen. Assembly, on boundaries of Chile 60, on Argentina-Paraguay River Navigation Cttee. 64; Head Del. to UN Conf. on Representation of States in their Relations with Int. Organizations; mem. Inter-American Juridical Cttee. 58-65; decorations from Spain, Brazil, Peru, Bolivia, Paraguay and Egypt.
Publs. *Admission and Exclusion of Members in the Organization of American States* 66, *Legalism, Pragmatism and Error in Argentinian Foreign Policy* 79.
UNFICYP, P.O. Box 1642, Nicosia, Cyprus; Home: Sargento Cabral 881, 44° J, Buenos Aires, Argentina.

Gölcüklü, Ahmet Feyyaz: Turkish judge and academic; b. 4 Oct. 1926, Mugla; ed. Univ. of Istanbul and Univ. of Neuchâtel, Switzerland.
Assistant Professor, Faculty of Political Sciences, Univ. of Ankara, Assoc. Prof. 58, Prof. 65-, Dir. School of Journalism and Broadcasting 69 and 72, Dean Faculty of Political Sciences 73-76; Judge, European Court of Human Rights 77-; mem. Constituent Assembly 81.
Publs. *Examination of the Accused Person in Penal Matters* 52, *Personal Liberty of the Accused in Criminal Procedure* 58, *A Research on Juvenile Delinquency in Turkey* 63, *Turkish Penal System* 65, *Mass Communication Law* 73.
Pilot Sokak 8/4, Çankaya, Ankara, Turkey.

Goldmann, Nahum; Israeli (fmrly. American) Zionist leader; b. 10 July 1895, Wisznewo, Lithuania; ed. Heidelberg, Berlin and Marburg Univs.
Editor and Publisher German Hebrew Encyclopedia Judaica 22-34; mem. Zionist Political Comm. 27; Act. Chair. Zionist Action Cttee. 33; escaped from Germany 34; Rep. of Jewish Agency to L. of N.; in U.S. 41; Rep. Jewish Agency for Palestine in U.S.A. during Second World War; Pres. World Jewish Congress 51-77 (mem. 34-), World Zionist Org. 56-68 (mem. 34-), Conf. on Jewish Claims against

Germany, Memorial Foundation for Jewish Culture; Chair. Cttee. on Jewish Claims against Austria 50-.
Publs. *N. G. Autobiography: 60 Years of Jewish Life* 69, *Où va Israel* 75, *Le Paradoxe Juif* 77, *Community of Fate* 77.
Rashba 9, Jerusalem, Israel; 12 avenue Montaigne, Paris, France.

Goldstein, Rabbi Israel, M.A., D.D., D.H.L., LITT.H.D., LL.D., PH.D.; American Rabbi; b. 18 June 1896; ed. Univ. of Pennsylvania, Jewish Theological Seminary of America and Columbia Univ.
Rabbi Congregation B'nai Jeshurun N.Y.C. 18-60, Rabbi Emeritus 61-; Pres. Jewish Conciliation Board of America 29-68 (now Hon. Pres.), Jewish Nat. Fund of America 33-43 (now Hon. Pres.); Pres. Synagogue Council of America 42-44, Zionist Organization of America 44-46; Chair. World Confed. of Gen. Zionists 46-72 (now Hon. Pres.); United Palestine Appeal 47-49; Co-Chair. United Jewish Appeal 47-49; Treas. Jewish Agency 47-49; Pres. Amidar Israel Nat. Housing Co. for Immigrants 48-49; mem. World Jewish Congress Exec. 48-, and Chair. of its Western Hemisphere Exec. 50-60, Hon. Vice-Pres. 59-; Pres. American Jewish Congress 51-58; now Hon. Pres.; Pres. World Hebrew Union; mem. Jewish Agency for Palestine Exec. 48-72; World Chair. Keren Hayesod-United Israel Appeal 61-71; mem. Board of Govs. Hebrew Univ. of Jerusalem, Weizmann Inst. of Science, Univ. of Haifa; Founder Brandeis Univ. 46; Chair. Jerusalem Artists' House 67-70; Chair in Zionism at Hebrew Univ. of Jerusalem, Synagogue of Hebrew Univ. of Jerusalem; Chair in Practical Theology, Jewish Theological Seminary of America; Hon. Pres. Asscn. of Americans and Canadians in Israel; Hon. doctorates from Brandeis Univ., New York Univ., Univ. of Pennsylvania, Hebrew Univ. of Jerusalem.
Publs. *A Century of Judaism in New York* 30, *Towards a Solution* 40, *Mourner's Devotions* 41, *Brandeis University* 51, *American Jewry Comes of Age* 55, *Transition Years* 62, *Israel at Home and Abroad* 73, *Jewish Justice and Conciliation* 81.
12 Pinsker Street, Jerusalem, Israel.

Goren, Maj.-Gen. Shlomo; Israeli Rabbi; b. 1917, Poland; ed. Hebrew Univ., High Theological Seminar, Jerusalem.
In Israel 25-; co-founder Kfar Hassidim; Chief Chaplain, Israel Defence Forces 48-71; Chief Rabbi of Tel-Aviv (elected June 68); Ashkenazi Chief Rabbi of Israel Oct. 72-; Rabbi Kook Prize, State of Israel Prize.
Publs. *Nezer Hakodesh* (on Maimonides), *Shaarei Tahara, Talmud Yerushalmi Meforash, Torath Ha Moadim, Piskei Hilchoth Tzavah Hagrah Vehavushalmi, Responsa: Mashiv Milchama;* works on religion in military life, prayers for soldiers, etc.
Chief Rabbinate, Hechal Shlomo, Jerusalem; Private Office: 35 Shaul Hamelech Boulevard, Tel-Aviv, Israel.

Goulli, Slaheddine El (see El Goulli).

Graham, Sir John Alexander Noble, Bart., K.C.M.G.; British diplomatist; b. 15 July 1926, Calcutta; ed. Eton Coll., Trinity Coll. Cambridge.
Served in the Army 44-47; joined Diplomatic Service 50; Principal private Sec. to Foreign Sec. 69-72; Minister, Head of Chancery, British Embassy to U.S.A. 72-74, Amb. to Iraq 74-77, to Iran 79-80; Deputy Under-Sec.; FCO 77-78, 80-81; Perm. Rep. to NATO 82-.
North Atlantic Treaty Organization, 1110 Brussels, Belgium.

Gümrükçüoğlu, Rahmi Kamil, B.SC., M.A.; Turkish diplomatist; b. 18 May 1927, Balçic, Romania; ed. Haydar Pasha Coll. Istanbul, Ankara Univ. and Graduate School, Harvard Univ.

Joined Ministry of Foreign Affairs 49; Second Sec., London 52, First Sec. 58; Head of Foreign Int. Econ. Relations Dept., Ministry of Foreign Affairs 58-60; Counsellor, Cairo 60-63; Deputy Dir.-Gen. Dept. of Int. Econ. Affairs, Ministry of Foreign Affairs 63-65, Head of Special Bureau for Econ. Co-operation with U.S.S.R. 65-67, Dir.-Gen. Dept. of Int. Econ. Affairs 67-71; Amb. to Council of Europe 71-75, mem. Governing Board, European Resettlement Fund 71-75; Amb. to Iran 75-78; Deputy Sec.-Gen. for Econ. Affairs, Ministry of Foreign Affairs 78-; Amb. to U.K. 81-; rep. in many bilateral and multilateral talks; negotiated over 100 int. agreements on financial, econ., tech. and industrial matters.
Publs. articles and studies on foreign investment in Turkey, econ. integration among developing countries, econ. devt. in U.S.S.R. 58, 64, 65, 66.
c/o Ministry of Foreign Affairs, Dişişleri Bakanliği, Müdafaa Cad., Bakanlıklar, Ankara, Turkey.

Gur, Lieut.-Gen. Mordechai; Israeli army officer; b. 5 May 1930; ed. Hebrew Univ.
Served in Haganah; Co. Commdr. during Independence War; Deputy Commdr. Paratroop Corps 57; Instructor, Command and Staff Coll. 58; C.O. Golani Brigade 61-63; Chief of Operations 64-65; in charge of Command and Staff Coll. 65-66; Staff and Command 66-67; C.O. Paratroop Brigade during Six-Day War 67; mem. Israeli Del. to UN Emergency Session 67; C.O. Israeli Forces in Gaza and N. Sinai, Northern Command 67-72; Mil. Attaché, Washington 72-73; C.O. Northern Command during Yom Kippur War Oct. 73; Chief Mil. Negotiator at Geneva Peace Conf. Dec. 73; Chief of Staff 74-78; joined Koor Industries as Head of Koor Mechanics 78-; Pres. Friends of Ben-Gurion Univ., Sde-Boker Complex.
Publs. 3 children's books, 3 books on military history.
c/o Ministry of Defence, Tel-Aviv, Israel.

Gurney, Oliver Robert, M.A., D.PHIL.; British assyriologist; b. 28 Jan. 1911; ed. Eton Coll. and New Coll. Oxford.
Army Service 39-45; Shillito Reader in Assyriology, Oxford Univ. 45-, Prof. 65-, Emeritus Prof. 78; Fellow of British Acad. 59-, Magdalen Coll. Oxford 63-; Editor *Anatolian Studies* 59-.
Publs. *The Geography of the Hittite Empire* (with J. Garstang) 59, *The Hittites* 52, 75, *The Sultantepe Tablets I and II* (with J. J. Finkelstein and P. Hulin) 57, 64, *Ur Excavations—Texts VII* 74, I, *Sumerian Literary Texts* (with S. N. Kramer) 76, *Some Aspects of Hittite Religion* (The Schweich Lectures 76) 77.
Bayworth Corner, Boars Hill, Oxford, England.

H

Habash, George, M.D.; Palestinian nationalist leader; b. 1925, Lydda, Palestine; ed. American University of Beirut.
Member Youth of Avengeance 48; formed soc. of progressive students 55 which later became Arab Nationalists' Movement; practised as doctor 50s; leader of Popular Front for the Liberation of Palestine Nov. 67- (introduced Marxist-Leninist thought to the Palestinian cause); Leader of Arab Nationalists' Movement.
c/o Palestine Liberation Organization, Colombani Street, Off Sadat Street, Dr. Raji Nasr Building, Ras Beirut, Lebanon.

Habashi, Wadie; Sudanese agricultural economist and politician; b. 14 Aug. 1917, Merwi; ed. Univ. of Khartoum and Oxford Univ.
Worked on the Al Aalyab, Burgaeg and White Nile devt. schemes; Agricultural Insp. for Khartoum Province and later for Merwi, Dongla and Halfa; Technical Adviser to the Minister of Agriculture; Asst. Dir. for Planning and

Devt., Dept. of Agriculture, Dir. 55-66; Rep. of Sudan to FAO Conf. 56, to Int. Tobacco Conf., Rhodesia 63; Chair. Admin. Council of El Gash Scheme Comm.; Dir. Production Section, Equatoria Schemes Comm.; Head, Advisory Comm. for Agricultural Research; mem. Gezira Scheme Admin. Council; mem. Studies Comm., Faculty of Agriculture, Univ. of Khartoum; with FAO 66-71, Dir. FAO-ECA Joint Agricultural Div., Addis Ababa; with IBRD and Kuwait Fund for Arab Econ. Devt. 71; Minister of Agriculture 71-73, of Agriculture, Food and Natural Resources 73-74; Pres. Nat. Council for Research July 74-, OAU Scientific Council for Africa May 75-.
c/o OAU Scientific, Technical and Research Commission, Nigerian Ports Authority Building, P.M.B. 2359, Marina, Lagos, Nigeria.

Habib, Philip Charles, B.S., PH.D.; American diplomatist; b. 25 Feb. 1920, New York; ed. Univ. of Idaho and Univ. of California at Berkeley.
Served U.S. Army, rank of Capt. 42-46; entered Foreign Service 49; Third Sec., U.S. Embassy, Canada 49-51; Second Sec., New Zealand 52-54; research specialist, Dept. of State 55-57; Consulate-Gen., Trinidad 58-60; Foreign Affairs Officer, Dept. of State 60-61; Counsellor for Pol. Affairs, U.S. Embassy, Republic of Korea 62-65, Repub. of Viet-Nam 65-67; rank of Minister 66-67, Amb. 69-71; Deputy Asst. Sec. of State for East Asian and Pacific Affairs 64-75; Under-Sec. of State for Pol. Affairs 76-78; Diplomat-in-residence, Stanford Univ. 78-79; retired from Foreign Service 79; Senior Adviser to Sec. of State 79-; United States Special Envoy to the Middle East (Lebanon conflict) April 81-.
Department of State, Washington, D.C. 20250, U.S.A.; Home: 1606 Courtland Rd., Belmont, California 94002, U.S.A.

Haddad, Sulaiman Ahmed al-; Kuwaiti banker and politician; b. 1930; ed. Kuwait Aazamieh Secondary School, and Cairo Univ.
Secretary of Educ. Council of Kuwait; fmr. Financial Asst., Ministry of Educ. and mem. Constituent Assembly for formation of Kuwaiti Constitution; mem. National Assembly 63-; fmr. Chair. and Man. Dir. Arab African Bank; Chair. ARTOC Bank Ltd., Int. Resources and Finance Bank, Arab Investment Co. in Asia and Kuwait; mem. Board, Arab African Bank, Cairo; Deputy Chair. and Man. Dir. ARTOC (S.A.K.).
Arab African Bank, 44 Abdel Khalek Sarwat Street, Cairo, Egypt; ARTOC, El Sour Street, Arab Gulf Building, P.O. Box 23074, Safat, Kuwait.

Hadjioannou, Kyriacos, F.R.A.I., PH.D.; Cypriot teacher and diplomatist; b. 1909; ed. Famagusta Gymnasium, Athens Univ. and Oxford Univ.
Greek Master, Kyrenia Gymnasium 32-35, Famagusta 36-45; Principal, Famagusta Gymnasium 46-48, 57-60, 63-69; Amb. to U.A.R. 60-63; Lecturer, Teachers' Training Coll., Morphou 48-53; Principal, Morphou Gymnasium 53-57; Pres. United Nat. Solid Front 57-59; Founder and Pres. Philological and Scientific Soc. of Famagusta 60-61, 64-; Fellow, Royal Anthropological Inst. of Great Britain and Ireland 46-; Grand Cordon of the Repub. (Egypt); prizes: D. Marangos (EFSA) 73, Athens Acad. 76, Hellenic Cultural Soc. of Cyprus 77, Gold Medal of Merit of Int. Asscns. of Lions Clubs 79, Hon. Citizenship and Gold Medal of Limassol 79.
Publs. *The Loan-words of Medieval and Modern Greek Cypriot Dialect* 36, *Cypriot Fables* 48, *Literary Texts of the Medieval and Modern Greek Cypriot Dialect with Introductions and Commentaries* 61, *Ta en Diaspora* 69, *Diplomacy and machinations in the Courts of the Lusignan Kings of Cyprus* 70, *Ta en Diaspora B* 79, *Ancient Cyprus in Greek Sources:* Vol. I, *Legendary Traditions, History and Ethnology from Prehistoric Times to the Year 395 A.D.* 71,

Vol. II, *Mythology and Religion, Geography and Geology* 73, Vol. III, Part I, *Letters, Sciences, Arts and Crafts from Homeric Times to the Year 395 A.D.* 75, Vol. III, Part II, *Cyprian Glosses* 77, Vol. IV, Parts I and II, *Supplements from the Greek Inscriptions and the Latin Texts with Prolegomena and Notes* 80, and articles in Greek, German English, French and Belgian journals.
McFadden Street 12, Limassol, Cyprus.

Hafez, Maj.-Gen. Amin el; Syrian army officer and politician; b. 1911.
Former Military Attaché in Argentina; took part in the revolution of March 1963; Dep. Prime Minister, Mil. Gov. of Syria and Minister of Interior March-Aug. 63; Minister of Defence and Army Chief of Staff July-Aug. 63; C.-in-C. of Armed Forces July 63-64; Pres. of Revolutionary Council July 63-May 64; Pres. Presidency Council May 64-Feb. 66; Prime Minister Nov. 63-May 64, Oct. 64-Sept. 65; sentenced to death *in absentia* Aug. 71; living in exile.

Haithem, Muhammad Ali; Yemeni politician; b. 1940, Dathina, Southern Arabia.
Formerly school teacher; Minister of Interior 67; mem. Presidential Council of S. Yemen 69-71; Chair. Council of Ministers 69-70; mem. Nat. Front Gen. Command.
Now living in Cairo, Egypt.

Hakim, George (*see* Maximos V Hakim).

Hakim, Tawfiq al-, B.A.; Egyptian novelist and playwright; b. 9 Oct. 1898, Alexandria; ed. Muhammad Ali Secondary School, Cairo, Law School, The Egyptian Univ., Cairo, Collège des Lois, Sorbonne, Paris.
Director-General Nat. Library 51-56; Under-Sec. Higher Council of Arts, Letters and Social Sciences 56-59, 60-; Perm. Rep. of U.A.R. at UNESCO 59-60; Dir. *Al Ahram* newspaper; mem. Cairo Arabic Language Acad. 54-; State Prize for Literature; State Prize for Merit; Republican Chain; Hon. Dr. (Egyptian Acad. of Arts).
Publs. novels: *The Soul's Return* 33, *A Rural Deputy's Diary* 37; plays: *The Cavemen* 33, *Shahrazad* 34, *Pigmalyun* 42, *Solomon the Wise* 43, *Rejuvenation* 50, *Journey into the Future* 57, *Praksa* 60, *The Sultan's Dilemma* 60, *The Tree Climber* 62, *Food for Every Mouth* 63, *Fate of a Cockroach* 66.
c/o Al Ahram, Shalia Lal-Galaa, Cairo, Egypt.

Halabi, Mohammed Ali el-; Syrian politician; b. 1937, Damascus; ed. Teachers Training School and Damascus Univ.
Teacher 54-62; mem. Regional Command of Baath Party, Damascus; Mayor of Damascus; mem. Arab Fed. Assembly; Speaker of People's Council 73-78; Prime Minister 78-80; Pres. Arab Parl. Union 74-76.
c/o Office of the Prime Minister, Damascus, Syria.

Halefoğlu, Vahit M., K.C.V.O., M.A.; Turkish diplomatist; b. 1919; ed. Antakya Coll. and Univ. of Ankara.
Turkish Foreign Service 43-, served Vienna, Moscow, Ministry of Foreign Affairs, London 46-59; Dir.-Gen. First Political Dept., Ministry of Foreign Affairs 59-62; Amb. to Lebanon 62-65, concurrently accred. to Kuwait 64-65; Amb. to U.S.S.R. 65-66; to the Netherlands 66-70; Deputy Sec.-Gen. for Political Affairs, Ministry of Foreign Affairs 70-72; Amb. to Fed. Repub. of Germany 72-; Lebanese, Finnish, British, Greek, Italian, German and Spanish decorations.
Embassy of Turkey, Utestrasse 47, Bonn-Bad Godesberg, Federal Republic of Germany.

Halkin, Shimon, B A., M.A., D.H.L.; American Hebrew scholar and author; b. 30 Oct. 1899, Dovsk, Russia; ed. N.Y. City Coll., Chicago, New York and Columbia Univs.
Instructor in Hebrew and Hebrew Literature, Hebrew Union College School for Teachers, N.Y. 24-32; Teacher, Geulah High School, Tel-Aviv 32-39; Lecturer in Bible,

Jewish, Sociology and Modern Hebrew Literature, Chicago Coll. of Jewish Studies 40-43; Prof. of Hebrew and Hebrew Literature, Jewish Inst. of Religion, New York City 43-49; Assoc. Prof. of Hebrew Literature, Hebrew Univ. of Jerusalem 49-56, Prof. and Head of Dept. 56-68; Visiting Prof., Univ. of Calif. 54-55, Jewish Theological Seminary, N.Y. 65-66; Emer., Hebrew Univ. of Jerusalem 69; mem. Acad. of Hebrew Language; Pres. Israel PEN Club; Tchernichovsky Prize for translation of Whitman 53, of Seferis 77; Bialik Prize for Literature 68, State of Israel Prize for Literature 75.
Publs. *Yehiel Ha-Hagri* (novel) 28, *An Ethical Philosophy of Life* 28, *Hebrew Literature in Palestine* 42, *Arai va-Keva* 42, *Al Mashber* 45, *Al Ha-Iy* (collected poems) 43, *Modern Hebrew Literature: Trends and Values* 51, *La Littérature Hebraïque Moderne* 57, *Ma'avar Yabok* (collected poems) 65, *Literatura Hebrea Moderna* 68, *Collected Literary Essays and Studies* (3 vols., Hebrew) 71, *Adrift, Collected Short Stories* 73, *Collected Poems* 76, and numerous others; translations of Shakespeare, Maeterlinck, Whitman, Shelley, Jack London, Seferis, etc.
Redak Street, Jerusalem, Israel.

Hamad, Abdlatif Yousef al-; Kuwaiti economist and banker.
Director-General Kuwait Fund for Arab Econ. Devt. 63-81, Chair. 81-; Dir. Kuwait Investment Co. -81; Chair. Prefabricated Buildings Co. of Kuwait; Chair. United Bank of Kuwait Ltd., London -81; Chair. Middle East Int. Fund; Dir. American Express Int. Fund -81; Exec. Dir. Arab Fund for Econ. and Social Devt. -81; fmr. Chair. Cie. Arabe et Int. d'Investissement; Dir. Scandinavian Securities Corpn. 77-81; Trustee Kuwait Inst. of Econ. and Social Planning in the Middle East, Inst. of Palestine Studies, Univ. of Jordan; mem. Perm. Cttee. for Aid to the Arabian Gulf and Yemen; Minister of Finance and Planning March 81-; IMF Gov. for Kuwait 81-.
Ministry of Finance, P.O. Box Safat 9, Kuwait.

Hammadi, Sadoon; Iraqi economist and politician; b. 22 June 1930, Karbala; ed. in Beirut, Lebanon and U.S.A.
Professor of Econs., Univ. of Baghdad 57; Deputy Head of Econ. Research, Nat. Bank of Libya, Tripoli 61-62; Minister of Agrarian Reform 63; Econ. Adviser to Presidential Council, Govt. of Syria 64; Econ. Expert, UN Planning Inst., Syria 65-68; Pres. Iraq Nat. Oil Co. (INOC) 68; Minister of Oil and Minerals 68-74, of Foreign Affairs 74-.
Publs. *Towards a Socialist Agrarian Reform in Iraq* 64, *Views About Arab Revolution* 69, *Memoirs and Views on Oil Matters* 80.
Ministry of Foreign Affairs, Baghdad, Karradat Mariam, Iraq.

Hare, Raymond Arthur, A.B.; American diplomatist; b. 3 April 1901; ed. Grinnell Coll.
Instructor, Robert Coll., Constantinople 24-27; Exec. Sec. American Chamber of Commerce for Levant 26-27; Clerk, later Vice-Consul, U.S. Consulate-Gen., Constantinople 27-28; Language Officer, Paris 29, also Vice-Consul 31; Sec. in Diplomatic Service and Vice-Consul, Cairo 31, Beirut 32; Third Sec. and Vice-Consul, Teheran 33, Consul 35; Second Sec. Cairo 39, also at Jeddah 40-44, also Consul, Cairo 40; Second Sec., later First Sec. and Consul, London 44; Dept. of State 46; Nat. War Coll. 46-47; Chief, Div. of S. Asian Affairs 47; Deputy Dir. Office of Near East and African Affairs 48; Deputy Asst. Sec. State for Near East, S. Asian and African Affairs Oct. 49; Amb. to Saudi Arabia and Minister to Yemen 50-53; Amb. to Lebanon 53-54; Dir.-Gen. U.S. Foreign Service 54-56; Amb. to Egypt 56-58, to United Arab Republic 58-59, also Minister to Yemen 59; Dep. Under-Sec. of State for Political Affairs 60-61; Amb. to Turkey 61-65; Asst. Sec. of State

for Near Eastern and South Asian Affairs 65-66; Pres. Middle East Inst. 66-69, Nat. Chair. 69-76, Emeritus 76- Middle East Institute, 1761 N. Street, N.W., Washington, D.C. 20036; 3214 39th Street, N.W., Washington, D.C. 20016, U.S.A.

Hariri, Rafik; Saudi Arabian (b. Lebanese) business executive; b. 1945, Sidon, Lebanon.
Emigrated to Saudi Arabia 65; teacher, then clerk, engineering co.; set up Civil Construction Establishment (Ciconest) building co. 70, joined with Oger Enterprises to form Saudi Oger 78; acquired entire Oger co. Feb. 79; has carried out several major hotel, hospital, factory, palace and govt. office contracts in Saudi Arabia and Lebanon (through subsidiary Oger Liban) including the Sunrise City administrative complex, Dammam, Saudi Arabia 81.
Saudi Oger, Riyadh, Saudi Arabia.

Harkavy, Rabbi Zvi (Hirsh Gershon), B.A., M.A., TH.D.; Israeli (b. Russian) author and bibliographer; b. 1 Feb. 1908; ed. Inst. in U.S.S.R., Jerusalem Teachers' Seminary, Haifa Technion, Hebrew Univ. of Jerusalem, Petach Tikva Yeshiva, C.S.R.A.
Leader in Zionist underground in U.S.S.R.; repatriated to Palestine 26; Commdr. in Hagana 26-47; schoolmaster and lecturer Jerusalem Teachers' Seminaries 30-; Dir. Eretz Yisrael Publishing House 35-; Chaplain in Israeli Army 48-49; Dir. Dept. of Refugees in Ministry of War Casualties and later Editor of Ministry of Religious Affairs *Monthly* 49-53; Dir. Central Rabbinical Library of Israel 53-68; Editor *Hasefer* 54-; participated in world congresses; Visiting Prof. Yeshiva Univ., N.Y. 59; lectured at U.S.S.R. Acad. of Sciences, Leningrad 62; initiator of Religious Univ. (Bar-Ian) in Israel; one of the founders of the Religious Academics and Authors Orgs. and fmr. Chair.; Leader, Hapoel Hamizrachi, "Great Israel" Movement; an Editor of the *General Encyclopaedia* and of many periodicals and books; Komemiut, Hamishmar, Haganah, Ale, Hagana-Yerushalayim and Etziony Medals. Publs. Biographies (Ed.): *Rambam, Rabbi Shmuel Strashun, Rabbi Mates Strashun, Rabbi I. M. Pines, Professor Simcha Assaf, A. E. Harkavy, Rabbi Reuven Katz—Chief Rabbi of Petach Tikva, The Family Maskil L'eytan, The Family Harkavy;* Essays: *Jews of Salonica, The Jewish Community of Ekaterinoslav; Scepticism of Pascal; The Man, The Plant, The Animal, Inorganic Nature; The Secret of Happy Marriage, Sexual Hygiene from the Religious and Scientific Viewpoint; Shomrei Hagachelet—Responsa of Soviet Rabbis* 66, *My Father's Home* 68, *Autobibliography* 71, *Ein Roe* 72; *Book of Ekaterinoslav-Dnepropetrovsk* 73, *The Works of A. E. Harkavy* (20 vols.), *A Fragment of Anan's Sefer Hamiswot, from the Yevpatoria manuscript* 75; also 1,400 articles and papers on Rabbinics, bibliography, theology, philosophy, archaeology, philology, history and Dead Sea Scrolls.
P.O. Box 7031, 7 Haran Street, Jerusalem 91070, Israel.

Harman, Avraham, B.A.; Israeli diplomatist; b. 1914; ed. Oxford Univ.
Moved to Palestine 38; held posts in Jewish Agency 38-48; Deputy Dir. Govt. Information Bureau 48-49; Consul-Gen. Montreal 49-50; Dir. Israel Information Office, N.Y. 50-53; Consul-Gen. Washington, D.C. 53-55; Ministry of Foreign Affairs 55-56; Exec. Jewish Agency 56-59; Amb. to the U.S.A. 59-68; Pres. Hebrew Univ. 68-.
The Hebrew University, Mount Scopus, Jerusalem, Israel.

Hart, Parker T.; American business consultant; b. 28 Sept. 1910; ed. Dartmouth Coll., Harvard Univ., Institut Universitaire de Hautes Etudes Internationales, Geneva, and School of Foreign Service, Georgetown Univ.
Translator, Dept. of State 37-38; Foreign Service Officer 38-69, served Vienna, Pará (Brazil), Cairo, Jeddah, Dhahran

38-47; Dept. of State 47-49; Consul-Gen. Dhahran 49-51; Nat. War Coll. 51-52; Dir. Office of Near Eastern Affairs, Dept. of State 52-55; Dep. Chief of Mission and Counsellor, Cairo 55-58; Consul-Gen. and Minister, Damascus 58; Dep. Asst. Sec. of State, Near East and South Asia Affairs 58-61; Amb. to Saudi Arabia 61-65, concurrently Minister to Kingdom of Yemen 61-62 and Amb. to Kuwait 62-63; Amb. to Turkey 65-68; Asst. Sec. of State for Near Eastern and South Asian Affairs 68-69; Dir. Foreign Service Inst. 69; Pres. Middle East Inst., Washington, D.C. 69-73; Consultant, Bechtel Corpn.; mem. Emer. Board of Govs., Middle East Inst., Washington, D.C.; Emer. mem. Board of Trustees, American Univ. Beirut; mem. of Visiting Cttee. in Near Eastern Languages and Civilizations Harvard Univ.; mem. Int. Advisory Cttee., American Security Bank; Co-Pres. American-Turkish Soc.; mem. Royal Soc. for Asian Affairs, Washington Inst. of Foreign Affairs, Council on Foreign Relations.
4705 Berkeley Terrace, N.W., Washington, D.C. 20007, U.S.A.

Hasani, Ali Nasir Muhammad (*see* Muhammad, Ali Nasser).

Haseeb, Khair El-Din, PH.D.; Iraqi economist and statistician; b. 1 Aug. 1929, Iraq; ed. Baghdad Univ. and London School of Econs., Cambridge Univ., England.
Civil service 47-54; Head of Research and Statistics Dept., Iraqi Petroleum Co. 59-60; Lecturer, Baghdad Univ. 60-61, Assoc. Prof. 65-71, Prof. of Econs. 71-74; Dir.-Gen. Iraqi Fed. of Industries 60-63; Chair. Centre for Devt. and Industrial Mgt. 63, Social Security Org. 63-65; Gov. and Chair. Cen. Bank of Iraq 63-65; Pres. Gen. Org. for Banks 64-65; Acting Pres. Econ. Org. 64-65; Gov. for Iraq, IMF 63-65; Alt. Gov. for Iraq, IBRD 63-65; Dir. Iraq Nat. Oil Co. 67-68; Chief of Natural Resources and Science and Technology Div., UN-ECWA, Beirut 74-; Dir. Gen. Centre for Arab Unity Studies, Beirut 81-.
Publs. *The National Income of Iraq, 1953-1961* 64, *Sources of Arab Economic Thought in Iraq 1900-1971* 73, *Workers' Participation in Management in Arab Countries* 71, and several articles in English and Arabic.
Centre for Arab Unity Studies, P.O. Box 113-6001, Beirut, Lebanon.

Hashim, Jawad M., PH.D.; Iraqi politician; b. 10 Feb. 1938; ed. London School of Econs. and Political Science, Univ. of London.
Professor of Statistics, Univ. of Baghdad 67; Dir.-Gen. Cen. Statistical Org. 68; Minister of Planning 68-71, 72-74; mem. Planning Board and Econ. Office, Revolutionary Command Council 74; Pres. Arab Monetary Fund (AMF) 77-82, Arab Fund for Economic and Social Devt. (AFESD) 77-82; Chair. ECWA May 75; mem. Group 30, Study Group on Energy and the World Economy.
Publs. *Capital Formation in Iraq 1957-1970, National Income—Its Methods of Estimation, The Evaluation of Economic Growth in Iraq 1950-1970*, and eighteen articles, c/o Arab Monetary Fund, P.O. Box 2818, Abu Dhabi, United Arab Emirates.

Hassan II, King of Morocco; 17th Sovereign of the Alouite dynasty; b. 9 July 1929; ed. Bordeaux Univ.
Son of Mohammed V; invested as Crown Prince Moulay Hassan 57; C.-in-C. and Chief of Staff of Royal Moroccan Army 57; personally directed rescue operations at Agadir earthquake disaster 60; Minister of Defence May 60-June 61; Vice-Premier May 60-Feb. 61; Prime Minister Feb. 61- Nov. 63, June 65-67; succeeded to throne on death of his father, 26 Feb. 1961; Minister of Defence. Commdr.-in-Chief of the Army Aug. 71-; Chair. Org. of African Unity 72-73.
Publ. *The Challenge* (memoirs) 79.
Royal Palace, Rabat, Morocco.

Hassan ibn Talal, B.A.; Crown Prince of Jordan; b. 20 March 1947, Amman; ed. Harrow School, England, Christ Church, Oxford Univ.

Brother of H.R.H. Hussein ibn Talal, King of Jordan (*q.v.*), and heir to the throne; Acting Regent during absence of King Hussein; Ombudsman for Nat. Devt. 71-; Founder of Royal Scientific Soc. of Jordan 70, the Arab Thought Forum; Hon. Gen. of Jordanian Army; Guest Speaker Int. Labour Conf., Geneva 77 and other fora.

Publs. *The Palestine Question* 64, *Study on Jerusalem* 79, *Palestinian Self-Determination* 81, articles on economic and political issues.

Office of the Crown Prince, The Royal Palace, Amman, Jordan.

Hassan, Abdullah el-, DIP.ARTS; Sudanese diplomatist and politician; b. 1925; ed. Gordon Secondary School, Khartoum Univ. Coll.

District Officer and Commissioner 49-56; Consul Gen. to Uganda 56-58; Head Political Section, Ministry of Foreign Affairs 58-60; Amb. to Ghana 60-64; Dir. Gen. Ministry of Information 65; Amb. to France 65-67, to Ethiopia 67-69; Under-Sec. Ministry of Foreign Affairs 69-70; Amb. to U.S.S.R. 71, to U.K. 72; Minister of Rural Devt. 72-73, of Interior 73-75; Sec. Gen. to the Presidency 75-; mem. Political Bureau, Sudanese Socialist Union 72-77; Sec.-Gen. Sudanese Nat. Council for Friendship, Solidarity and Peace; mem. numerous dels.; Order of the Republic, First Class, numerous foreign decorations.

Office of the Cabinet, Khartoum, Sudan.

Hassan, Ahmad Y. al-, D.I.C., PH.D.; Syrian engineer and professor; b. 25 June 1925, Palestine; ed. Govt. Arab Coll., Jerusalem, Univ. of Cairo, Imperial Coll., London, Univ. Coll., London.

Professor of Mechanical Engineering, Aleppo Univ. 54-, Chair. Mechanical Engineering Dept. 63-67, Dean, Faculty of Eng. 64-67; Minister of Petroleum, Electricity and Industrial Projects 67-70; Pres. Aleppo Univ. 73-79; Dir. and Research Worker, Inst. for the History of Arab Science; Founder and Editor *Journal for the History of Arabic Science*; Visiting Prof. Univ. College London 80-; Chevalier, Légion d'Honneur.

Publs. *Theory of Machines* 64, *Machine Design* 65, *Power Stations* 66, *Taq-al-Din and Arab Mechanical Engineering* 67; co-author, paper in *Proceedings of Royal Soc. of London* 64, *Al Jazari's Compendium of the Mechanical Arts, Banu Musa's Book of Ingenious Machines*.

Institute for the History of Arabic Science, University of Aleppo, Aleppo; Home: P.O.B. 467, Aleppo, Syria.

Hassan, Cleto (*see* Rial, Cleto Hassan).

Hassan Rial, Cleto (*see* Rial, Cleto Hassan).

Hatem, Mohammed Abdel Kader, M.SC., PH.D.; Egyptian politician; b. 1918, Alexandria; ed. Military Acad., Univs. of London and Cairo.

Member, Nat. Assembly 57; Adviser to the Presidency, subsequently Deputy Minister for Presidential Affairs 57; Minister of State responsible for broadcasting and television 59; Minister for Culture, Nat. Guidance and Tourism 62; Deputy Prime Minister for Cultural Affairs and Nat. Guidance 65; Deputy Prime Minister and Minister for Culture and Information 71-74; Chair. of Board *Al-Ahram* 74; Asst. to Pres. of the Repub. and Supervisor-Gen. of Specialized Nat. Council 74-; elected mem. for People's Assembly 79; mem. Gen. Secr. Arab Socialist Union; hon. doctorates from two French Univs. and from Democratic People's Repub. of Korea.

Specialized National Councils, Arab Socialist Union Building, Corniche el-Nil, Cairo, Egypt.

Hawari Ahmed, Mahmoud el-; Egyptian journalist; b.12 April 1921; ed. Polytechnic School, Cairo.

Director, Arab Information Center Press Office, New York 55-58; Man. Editor Middle East News Agency, Cairo 58-65, Chair. of Board 65-74; Dir. Magazine Dept., Nat. Publishing House 65-67; Chair. Nat. Distributing Co. 67; Publishing Man. Al-Katib Al-Arabi Publishing House 67-69; Adviser, Editing and Publishing Org. 69-71; Dir.-Gen. Egyptian Book Org. 71-72; Under-Sec. of State, Ministry of Information Feb. 76-; Gold Cross, Order of King George I of Greece 60.

Isis Building, Garden City, Cairo, Egypt.

Haydar, Mohammad Haydar; Syrian politician; b. 1931; ed. secondary schools, Lattakia, Damascus Univ.

Teacher Lattakia, Hama 51-60; with Ministry of Agrarian Reform 60-63; Dir. Alghab Establishment, Hama 63; Dir. Agrarian Reform, Damascus, Daraa, Alsuweidaa 64; Dir. Legal and Administrative Affairs Ministry of Agric. and Agrarian Reform 65; Gov. Alhasakeh 66; teacher Damascus 68; mem. Command Damascus branch of Baath Arab Socialist Party (BASP) 68, temporary Regional Command BASP 70; mem. Regional and National Commands BASP and mem. Central Command Progressive Nat. Front of Syria -73; Minister of Agric. and Agrarian Reform -73; Deputy Prime Minister for Economic Affairs 73-76; mem. Nat. Command BASP, Nat. Progressive Front 80-.

Foreign Relations Bureau, Baath Arab Socialist Party, Damascus, Syria.

Hayek, His Beatitude Ignace Antoine, D.PHIL., D. ÈS SC., Syriac ecclesiastic; b. 14 Sept. 1910; ed. Séminaire Patriarcal, Charfé, Lebanon, Pontifical Coll. of Propaganda Fide, Rome, and Oriental Pontifical Inst., Rome.

Ordained priest 33; successively or concurrently Dir. of School, Curate and Vicar-Gen., Aleppo; Archbishop of Aleppo 59-68; Syriac Patriarch Antioch 68-.

Patriarcat Syriaque Catholique d'Antioche, rue de Damas, B.P. 116/5087, Beirut, Lebanon.

Hazim, Mgr. Ignace; Syrian ecclesiastic; b. 1921, Mharde; ed. l'Institut Saint-Serge, Paris.

Director of a secondary theological inst, Beirut; Rector of Theological Inst., Antioch; elected Bishop of Latakia 66, took up post 70; Greek Orthodox Patriarch of Antioch and All the East 79-; Pres. Middle East Ecumenical Council; mem. Central Cttee. Ecumenical Council of Geneva.

Publs. *La Résurrection et l'homme d'aujourd'hui* and in Arabic: *I Believe, The Telling of Your Word Enlightens, The Church in the Middle East* (translation of the work by Père Corbon), *God's Design* (translation of the work by Suzanne de Dietrich).

P.O. Box 9, Damascus, Syria.

Hedda, Ali; Tunisian diplomatist; b. 30 Oct. 1930, Sousse; ed. Inst. des Sciences Politiques, Paris.

Attaché, Washington, D.C. 56; Sec. Ministry of Foreign Affairs 57; with Secr. of State for Planning and Nat. Econ., Central Bank 58-66; Minister, Rome 66; Amb. to Senegal 70-72, also accred. to Mali, Mauritania, Guinea, Liberia, Sierra Leone and The Gambia; Dir. Int. Co-operation, Ministry of Foreign Affairs 72; Dir. Cabinet of the Prime Minister 73; Amb. to U.S.A. Nov. 73-81, concurrently to Mexico and Venezuela 74-81; Grand Officer, Ordre de la République Tunisienne, Officier, Ordre de l'Indépendance, Tunisia, Order of the Republic, Italy.

Ministry of Foreign Affairs, Tunis, Tunisia.

Hegazy, Abdel Aziz, D.PHIL.; Egyptian economist and politician; b. 3 Jan. 1923; ed. Fuad Univ., Cairo, Birmingham Univ., England.

Dean, Faculty of Commerce, Ain Shams Univ. 66-68; mem. Nat. Assembly 69-75; Minister of the Treasury 68-73; Deputy Prime Minister, Minister of Finance, Econ. and Foreign Trade 73-74; First Deputy Prime Minister April-Sept. 74, Prime Minister 74-75; now teaching and working

as a management consultant and Certified Accountant in Cairo, Jeddah and Beirut.
Cairo, Egypt.

Hegelan, Sheikh Faisal Abdul Aziz al- (*See* Alhegelan).

Heikal, Mohammed Hasanein; Egyptian journalist; b. 1923.
Reporter Akher Saa Magazine 44; Editor *Al-Akhbar* 56-57; Editor-in-Chief *Al-Ahram* daily newspaper 57-74; ordered to resign Oct. 75; Editor and Chair. Establishment Board 60-74; mem. Central Cttee. Arab Socialist Union 68; Minister of Nat. Guidance 70; arrested Sept. 81, released by Pres. Mubarak Nov. 81.
Publs. *Nahnou wa America* 67, *Nasser: The Cairo Documents* 72, *The Road to Ramadan* 75, *Sphinx and Commissar* 79, *The Return of the Ayatollah* 81.
Cairo, Egypt.

Hélou, Charles; Lebanese lawyer, journalist and politician; b. 1911; ed. St. Joseph (Jesuit) Univ. and Ecole Française de Droit, Beirut.
Barrister at Court of Appeal and Cassation Beirut 36; founded newspaper *L'Eclair du Nord* at Aleppo Syria 32; founded *Le Jour* Beirut 34; was Political Dir. of the latter until apptd. Lebanese Minister to the Vatican 47; fmr. Pres. Cercle de la Jeunesse Catholique Beirut; fmr. Sec.-Gen. Catholic Action of Lebanon; Minister of Justice and Health Sept. 54-May 55; Minister of Education Feb.-Sept. 64; President of Lebanon 64-70; Minister of State July-Aug. 79; Pres. Asscn. des Parlementaires de Langue Française 73-.
Kaslik, Jounieh, Lebanon.

Herzog, Gen. Chaim, LL.B.; Israeli lawyer, military expert and diplomatist; b. 17 Sept. 1918, Belfast, N. Ireland; ed. Wesley Coll., Dublin, London and Cambridge Univs., Lincoln's Inn, London, Israeli Bar, Jerusalem.
Went to Palestine 35; served in British Army, World War II; rank of Maj.; Dir. Intelligence, Israeli Defence Forces 48-50; Defence Attaché, Washington, D.C., and Ottawa 50-54; Field Commands 54-59; Dir. Mil. Intelligence 59-62; Gen. 61; Man. G.U.S. Industries 62-72; Gov. West Bank of the Jordan 67; Senior Partner, Herzog, Fox and Neeman 72-; Perm. Rep. to UN 75-78; mem. Leadership Bureau, Israel Labour Party; mem. Knesset 81-; prominent broadcaster; Hon. Doctorate (Yeshiva Univ., N.Y., Jewish Theological Seminary, N.Y., Bar Ilan Univ., Israel); Hon. K.B.E. 70.
Publs. *Israel's Finest Hour* (Hebrew and English) 67, *Days of Awe* (Hebrew) 73, Editor *Judaism, Law and Ethics* 74, *The War of Atonement* 75, *Who Stands Accused?* 78, co-author *Battles of the Bible* 78, *The Arab-Israeli Wars* 82 and numerous articles in foreign journals.
25 Ibn Gvirol Street, Tel-Aviv, Israel.

Hilal, Ahmed Izzedin, B.SC.; Egyptian engineer and politician; b. 5 Dec. 1924, Alexandria; ed. Univ. of Cairo.
Chemical Engineer, Suez Refinery, Anglo-Egyptian Oil Fields Co. 46-62, Refinery Man. 62; Operations Man. Egyptian Gen. Petroleum Corpn. (EGPC) 63, Deputy Gen. Man. EGPC 64-68, Gen. Man. 68-71, Chair. and Man. Dir. 71-73; Minister of Petroleum 73-, also of Industry and Mining Nov. 77-Oct. 78; Deputy Prime Minister for Production May 80-.
Ministry of Petroleum, 2 Latin America Street, Garden City, Cairo, Egypt.

Hillel, Shlomo; Israeli politician; b. 23 April 1923, Baghdad, Iraq; ed. Herzliah School, Tel-Aviv, Hebrew Univ., Jerusalem.
Settled in Palestine 30s; mem. 2nd, 3rd Knessets (Parl.) 53-59; Amb. to Guinea 59-61, to Ivory Coast 61-63, concurrently to Dahomey (now Benin), Upper Volta and Niger; mem. Perm. Mission to UN 64-67; Asst. Dir.-Gen. Ministry of Foreign Affairs in charge of Middle East Affairs 67-69; Minister of Police 69-June 77; Co-ordinator of

Political Contracts with the Arab leadership in the Administered Territories 70; mem. 9th Knesset; Minister for the Interior June-Oct. 74; Chair. Ministerial Cttee. for Social Welfare 74-77; Chair. Sephardi Fed. 76-; Commdr. Nat. Order of the Repubs. of the Ivory Coast, Upper Volta, Dahomey.
The Knesset, Jerusalem, Israel.

Hindawi, Thaugan el-, ED.M.; Jordanian politician; b. 18 Feb. 1927; ed. Arab Coll., Jerusalem, Univ. of Cairo, Univ. of Maryland, U.S.A.
Principal, Teachers' Training Coll., Bet Hannina, Jerusalem 56-60; Supervisor of Educ. 60-63; Cultural Attaché, Cairo 64; Under-Sec. Ministry of Information 64-65; Minister of Information 65, of Educ. 65-70; Amb. to Kuwait 71-73; Minister of State for Prime Minister's Affairs 73; Minister of Finance 73-74, of Educ. 74-76; Amb. to Egypt 77-79; many decorations from Jordan, Tunisia, France, Fed. Repub. of Germany and Malaysia.
Publ. *Palestinian Issue* (textbook).
c/o Ministry of Foreign Affairs, Amman, Jordan.

Horowitz, Yigael; Israeli politician; b. 1918, Degania.
Former mem. Labour Party; joined *Rafi* faction in 60s; formed State List party (since 73 part of *Likud* front), later called *Laam*; Minister of Commerce, Industry and Tourism 77-78, of Finance Nov. 79-Jan. 81.
c/o Ministry of Finance, Hakinya, Ruppin Street, Jerusalem, Israel.

Hoss, Selim al-, PH.D.; Lebanese politician, banker and professor of economics, b. 20 Dec. 1929, Beirut; ed. American Univ. of Beirut, Indiana Univ.
Accountant, Beirut 52-54; corresp. at Beirut Chamber of Commerce 54-55; Instructor, later Assoc. Prof. American Univ. Beirut 55-67; Financial Adviser to Kuwait Fund for Arab Econ. Devt. 64-66; with Bank of Lebanon 66; Chair. Banking Control Comm. 67-73; Chair. and Gen. Man. Nat. Bank for Industrial and Tourist Devt. 73-76; Prime Minister 76-80, remaining as Prime Minister in caretaker capacity July-Oct. 80; also Minister of the Economy and Trade, and Minister of Information Dec. 76-July 79; Chair. CAII June 81-.
Publs. *The Development of Lebanon's Financial Markets* 74, *Nafiza Ala Al Mustakbal* (Window on the Future) 81.
B.A.I.I. Centre Géfinor, Bloc B, Apartment 1401, 14th Floor, P.O. Box 11-9692, Beirut and Doha, Na'meh, Beirut, Lebanon.

Howard, Harry Nicholas, A.B., M.A., PH.D.; American consultant on international affairs; b. 19 Feb. 1902; ed. Univs. of Missouri and California.
Gregory Fellow in History Univ. of Missouri 26-27; Research Asst. in Modern European History Univ. of California 28-29; Asst. Prof. History, Univ. of Oklahoma 29-30; Associate Prof. History, Miami Univ. 30-37, Prof. 40-42; Lecturer Contemporary Problems, Univ. of Cincinnati 37-42; served Dept. of State as Head, East European Unit 42-44; mem. U.S. Del. UN Conf. on Int. Orgs. 45, Chief, Near East Branch Research Div. 45-47, Adviser Div. of Greek, Turkish and Iranian Affairs 47-49, UN Adviser, Dept. of State, Bureau of Near East, S. Asian and African Affairs 49-56; Acting U.S. Rep. Advisory Comm. UNRWA, Beirut 56-61; Special Asst. to Dir. of UNRWA 62-63; Adviser U.S. Del. UN Balkan Comm. 47-50; Prof. of Middle East Studies, School of Int. Service, American Univ., Washington, D.C. 63-68, Adjunct Prof. 68-69; Chair. Middle East Program, Foreign Service Inst., Dept. of State 66, 71-72; Faculty Adviser FSI 66-67; Reserve Consultant, Dept. of State 67-68; Assoc. Editor *Middle East Journal* 63-68; mem. Board of Govs. Middle East Inst. 63-79, Emeritus 79-; Nat. Council, Americans for Middle East Understanding; Consultant Middle East, Cincinatti Council on World Affairs 68-69; mem. Board Dirs. ANERA 68-79; Lecturer, Middle East, U.S. Army

War Coll., Pa. 70-72, Visiting Prof. Missouri, Indiana, Calif. (Berkeley), Columbia and Colorado Univs.; Order of the Phoenix (Greece).
Publs. *The Partition of Turkey, A Diplomatic History 1913-1923* 31, *Military Government in the Panama Canal Zone* 31 (with Prof. R. Kerner), *The Balkan Conferences and the Balkan Entente* 30-35, *A Study in the Recent History of the Balkan and Near Eastern People* 36, *The Problem of the Turkish Straits* 47, *The United Nations and the Problem of Greece* 47, *The General Assembly and the Problem of Greece* 48, *Yugoslavia* (co-author) 49, *Soviet Power and Policy* (co-author) 55, *The King-Crane Commission* 63, *Turkey, The Straits and U.S. Policy* 74.
6508 Greentree Road, Bradley Hills Grove, Bethesda, Md. 20817, U.S.A.

Humaidan, Dr. Abdul Ali al-; United Arab Emirates diplomatist; b. 20 Sept. 1931, Bahrain; ed. Univs. of Baghdad and Paris.
Deputy Rep. of Kuwait to UNESCO 67-69; Prof. of Political Science, Univ. of Kuwait 69-70; Legal Adviser to the Abu Dhabi Govt. 71-72; Perm. Rep. of the United Arab Emirates to UN 72-81; Chargé d'affaires a.i. in Oman 81.
Ministry of Foreign Affairs, P.O. Box 1, Abu Dhabi, United Arab Emirates.

Hussain, Abdul Aziz; Kuwaiti politician; b. 1921; ed. Teachers' Higher Inst., Cairo and Univ. of London.
Head, Kuwait Cultural Bureau, Cairo 45-50; Gen. Dir. of Education, Kuwait 52-61; Ambassador to Egypt 61-62; Minister of State for Cabinet Affairs 63-65, 71-.
Publ. *Arab Community in Kuwait* 60.
Ministry of State for Cabinet Affairs, Kuwait.

Hussain, Saddam, LL.B.; Iraqi politician; b. 28 April 1937, Tikrit; ed. Al-Karkh (Gaghdad) and Al-Qasr al-Aini (Cairo) secondary schools, Cairo Univ. and al-Mustanseriya Univ. Baghdad.
Joined Arab Baath Socialist Party 57; sentenced to death for attempted execution of Gen. Kassem 59; in Egypt 62, joined Baath Party, Cairo; returned to Iraq 63; mem. 4th Regional Congress and 6th Nat. Congress, Baath Party 63, mem. Regional Leadership 63, mem. 7th Nat. Congress, Syria 64; arrested for plotting overthrow of Pres. Aref Oct. 64; mem. Nat. Leadership, Baath Party 65, 66-, Deputy Sec. Regional Leadership 65-79, Sec. July 79-; played prominent role in Revolution of July 68; Vice-Pres. Revolutionary Command Council Nov. 69-July 79, Pres. July 79-; rank of Gen. Jan. 76; Order of Rafidain, 1st Class, Jan. 76.
Publ. *One Trench or Two.*
Revolutionary Command Council, Baghdad, Iraq.

Hussein, Hamzah Abbas, B.A.(ECONS.); Kuwaiti central banker; b. 1 Oct. 1934, Kuwait; ed. American Univ. of Beirut.
Government official 59; Admin. Asst., Civil Service Comm. 59-60; attended several postgraduate courses on money and banking 60-62; Sec. and Currency Officer, Kuwait Currency Board 63-68; Deputy Gov. Cen. Bank of Kuwait 68-73, Gov. 73-; Chair. of Board, Banking Studies Centre of Kuwait 70-.
Central Bank of Kuwait, P.O. Box 526, Kuwait.

Hussein ibn Talal, King of Jordan; b. 14 Nov. 1935; ed. Victoria Coll., Alexandria, Egypt and Harrow School and Royal Mil. Acad. Sandhurst, England.
Succeeded his father August 11th, 1952; came to power May 2nd, 1953; married 55, Princess Dina, daughter of Abdel-Hamid Aoun of Saudi Arabia; daughter Princess Alia, b. 56 (marriage dissolved); married 61, Antoinette Gardiner (assumed name of Muna el Hussein); sons, Prince Abdullah, b. 62, Prince Feisal, b. 63; twin daughters, Princess Zein, Princess Aisha, b. 68 (marriage dissolved);

married 72, Alia Toukan (died Feb. 77), daughter of Baha'uddin Toukan; daughter Princess Haya, b. 74; son Prince Ali, b. 75; married 78, Elizabeth Halaby (assumed name of Noor El-Hussein); sons Prince Hamzeh, b. 80, Prince Hashem, b. 81; Order of Al-Nahda, of Al-Kawkab, of Al-Istiqlal Medal, and many other decorations.
Publs. *Uneasy Lies the Head* 62, *My War with Israel* 67.
Royal Palace, Amman, Jordan.

I

Ibrahim, Major Abul Gasim Mohammed; Sudanese army officer and politician; b. 1937, Omdurman; ed. Khartoum Secondary School and Military Coll.
Commissioned 61; mem. Revolutionary Council 69; Minister of Local Govt. 69; Asst. Prime Minister for Services July 70; Minister of Interior Nov. 70; Minister of Health 71-74, and of Social Welfare 73-74, of Agriculture, Food and Natural Resources 74-76; Deputy Sec.-Gen. Sudanese Socialist Union (SSU), Sec.-Gen. Aug. 76-79; Commr. for Khartoum Province Aug. 76-79; First Vice-Pres. of Sudan Aug. 77-79; reportedly left Sudan for Saudi Arabia Aug. 79.

Ibrahim, Wing Commdr. Hassan; Egyptian businessman and fmr. politician; b. 1917; ed. Egyptian Mil. Coll. and Egyptian Air Force Coll.
Served Egyptian Air Force 39-52; mem. Revolutionary Council 52-56; Minister for Presidency and for Production 54-56; Chair. Economic Development Organization 57-59; Pres. El Nasr Company (pencil and graphite production) 58-61, Paints and Chemicals Industries 59-61; mem. Presidential Council 62-64; Vice-Pres. of U.A.R. 64-65; business exec. 66-; Pres. Middle East Financing and Consultation Co., Egyptian Catering and Contracting Co., Egyptian Granite Co.; Nile Collar of Egypt; various orders and decorations from Syria, Yugoslavia, Cameroon, Niger, Yemen, Bulgaria, Poland, Lebanon, G.D.R., Morocco, Malaysia, Libya.
10 Abdel-Rahman Fahmy Street, Garden City, Cairo; Home: 6 Khartoum Street, Heliopolis, Cairo, Egypt.

Ibrahim, Izzat; Iraqi politician; b. 1942, al-Dour; ed. secondary schools.
Editor *Voice of the Peasant* 68, Head, Supreme Cttee. for People's Work 68-70; Minister of Agrarian Reform 70-74; Vice-Chair. Supreme Agric. Council 70-71, Chair. 71; Minister of Agriculture 73-74; Minister of Interior 74-79; mem. Revolution Command Council, Deputy Chair. July 79-; Asst. Sec. Regional Command of Arab Baath Socialist Party July 79-.
Revolution Command Council, Baghdad, Iraq.

Ibrahim, Sid Moulay Abdullah; Moroccan politician; b. 1918; ed. Ben Youssef Univ., Marrakesh and the Sorbonne, Paris.
Mem. Istiqlal (Independence) Party 44-59; mem. Editorial Cttee. *Al Alam* (Istiqlal organ) 50-52; imprisoned for political reasons 52-54; Sec. of State for Information and Tourism, First Moroccan Nat. Govt. 55-56; Minister of Labour and Social Affairs 56-57; Prime Minister and Minister of Foreign Affairs Dec. 58-May 60; leader Union National des Forces Populaires 59-72, suspended from party 72.
c/o Union National des Forces Populaires, B.P. 747, Casablanca, Morocco.

Idris I (Sayyid Muhammad Idris as-Sanusi); former King of Libya; b. 13 March 1890.
Son of Sayyid Muhammad al-Mahdi; succeeded his uncle, Sayyid Ahmed Sherif as-Sanusi, in charge of affairs of the Senusiya Order 16; became Amir of Cyrenaica; proclaimed King of Libya 2 Dec. 50; ascended the throne 24 Dec.

51; deposed by military coup Sept. 69; sentenced to death *in absentia* 71; granted Egyptian nationality April 74.

Imady, Dr. Mohammed; Syrian economist and planner; b. 1 Dec. 1930, Damascus; ed. Damascus Secondary School, Damascus Univ. and New York Univ.
Deputy Minister of Planning 68-72, Minister 72; Minister of Economy and Foreign Trade 72-79; Pres. Arab Econ. Soc. 74-75, Syrian Econ. Soc. 76; Pres. Arab Fund for Econ. and Social Devt. June 79-, Dir.-Gen. and Chair. 81-; Chair. Board of Govs. IMF, IBRD 75-76; Gov. for Syria, IMF, Islamic Devt. Bank; Founders Day Award (New York Univ.).
Publ. *Economic Development and Planning* (textbook in Arabic for Damascus Univ.) 68, revised 69, 71.
Arab Fund for Economic and Social Development, P.O. Box 21923, Kuwait City, Kuwait; Home: Tijara, Korneish Bazeih, The New Way, Damascus, Syria.

Ioannides, Georghios X.; Cypriot lawyer and politician; b. 1924, Ktima, Paphos; ed. Greek Gymnasium, Paphos. Clerk, Civil Service 41-45; studied law, Middle Temple, London, and called to Bar 47; lawyer, Paphos 48-70; mem. House of Reps. (Patriotic Front Group) 60-70; Minister of Justice 70-72, of the Interior and Defence 72-74, of Justice and Health 76-78; Minister to the Presidency 78-80.
c/o The Presidency, Nicosia, Cyprus.

Iriani, Abdul Karim al-, PH.D. ECONS.; Yemeni economist and politician; b. Djibla, Southern Province, Yemen Arab Republic; ed. univ. in U.S.A.
Member of Board of Directors, Yemen Bank of Reconstruction and Development July 73-; Minister of State for Socio-Economic Devt. March-June 74; Central Planning Office; Minister of Devt. 76-77, of Education and Rector Sana'a Univ. 76-78; Chief Planner, Devt. Office 77-79; Chair. Central Planning Office 79-80; Minister of Agriculture March-July 79; Prime Minister Oct. 80-.
P.O. Box 38, Sana'a, Yemen Arab Republic.

Irmak, Sadi; Turkish professor and politician; b. 15 May 1904, Seydişehir, Konya; ed. Konya, Univs. of Istanbul and Berlin.
Teacher, Gazi Educ. Inst.; Chief Medical Officer, Ankara; Lecturer in Physiology, Istanbul Univ. 32, Prof. 40; mem. Parl. for Konya 43-50; Minister of Labour 45-47; Faculty of Medicine, Munich Univ. 50-52; Senator 74-80; Prime Minister Nov. 74-March 75; Pres. Istanbul Univ. Inst. of Research on Atatürk's Reforms; Republican People's Party; Pres. Constituent Assembly 81-.
Kazim Orbayc 14, Istanbul-Chichli, Turkey.

Iryani, Sheikh Qadi Abd al Rahman al-; Yemeni religious and political leader; b. 18 July 1917.
Member of Revolutionary Council 62-74; Minister of Justice 62-63; Vice-Pres. Exec. Council Oct. 63-Feb. 64; mem. Political Bureau 64-74; mem. Presidency Council 65-74, Chair. 69-74 (deposed by mil. coup); Chair. Peace Cttee. set up after Khamer Peace Talks May 65; leader of Zaidi (Shi'a) sect; exiled, Libya and Syria; invited to return Sept. 81, returned Oct.
Sana'a, Yemen Arab Republic.

Isa bin Sulman al-Khalifa (*see* Khalifa, Sheikh Isa bin Sulman al-).

Işik, Hasan Esat; Turkish diplomatist and politician; b. 1916, Istanbul; ed. Lycée of Galatasaray, Faculty of Law, Univ. of Ankara.
Ministry of Foreign Affairs 40-; Consulate-Gen., Paris 45-49; Head of Section, Dept. of Commerce and Econ. Affairs, and Dept. of Int. Econ. Relations 49-52; mem. del. to UN Office, Geneva 52-54; Dir.-Gen. of Dept. of Commerce and Commercial Agreements, Ministry of Foreign Affairs 54-57; Asst. for Econ. Affairs to Sec.-Gen.

of Ministry of Foreign Affairs, Sec.-Gen. Econ. Co-operation Int. Org. 57-62; Amb. to Belgium, led negotiations for Asscn. with EEC 62-64, to U.S.S.R. 64-65, 66-68; Minister of Foreign Affairs 65; Amb. to France 68-73; mem. Nat. Assembly 73; Minister of Defence 74, June-July 77, 78-79; Republican People's Party (RPP).
c/o Ministry of National Defence, Milli Savunma Bakanliği, Bakanliklar, Ankara, Turkey.

Ismail, Abdul Fattah; Yemeni politician; b. 28 July 1939; ed. Tawani Nat. School, Aden Tech. School in Little Aden.
Engaged on technical staff of British Petroleum Co. 57; joined Nat. Liberation Front (NLF) 59; in charge of NLF mil. and political activities in Aden 64; mem. NLF Exec. Cttee. 65; Minister of Culture and Nat. Guidance and of Yemen Unity Affairs 67; Sec.-Gen. Nat. Front 69-75, United Political Org.-the Nat. Front (UPONF) 75-78; mem. Presidential Council 69-78; Pres., Chair. Revolutionary Council 78-80; Chair. Presidium, Supreme People's Council 78-80; Sec.-Gen. Yemen Socialist Party 78-80, Chair. 80-; Chair. Yemeni Council for Peace and Solidarity in the People's Democratic Repub. of Yemen; mem. Presidium of Afro-Asian People's Solidarity Org. (AAPSO) and of World Peace Council; Dr. h.c. (Moscow Univ.) Aug. 76; Order of 14th October Revolution 80.
Yemen Socialist Party, Aden, People's Democratic Republic of Yemen.

Ismail, Ahmed Sultan, B.SC.; Egyptian engineer and politician; b. 14 April 1923, Port Said; ed. Cairo Univ.
Worked as shift engineer, maintenance engineer at various power stations 45-64; mem. Exec. Board Electrical Projects Corpn. 64-; Nat. Defence Coll. 67; Gov. Menufia Prov. 68-71; Minister of Power 71-76; Deputy Premier for Production and Minister for Electric Power and Energy 76-78; Consulting Engineer 78-; Order of Repub., First Class.
43 Ahmed Abdel Aziz Street, Dokki, Cairo, Egypt.

Issawi, Charles Philip, M.A.; American economist; b. 1916; ed. Victoria Coll. Alexandria and Magdalen Coll. Oxford.
Secretary to Under-Sec. of State, Ministry of Finance, Cairo 37-38; Head of Research Section, Nat. Bank of Egypt, Cairo 38-43; Adjunct Prof. American Univ. of Beirut 43-47; UN Secretariat Economic Affairs Officer 48-55; Visiting Lecturer, Harvard Univ. 50, Johns Hopkins 67, Princeton Univ. 74; Prof. Columbia Univ. 51-75, Princeton Univ. 75-; Pres. Middle East Studies Asscn. of N. America 73.
Publs. *Egypt: an Economic and Social Analysis* 47, *An Arab Philosophy of History* 50, *Egypt at Mid-Century* 54, *Mushkilat Qaumia* 59, *The Economics of Middle East Oil* (co-author) 62, *Egypt in Revolution* 63, *The Economic History of the Middle East 1800-1914* 66, *The Economic History of Iran 1800-1914* 71, *Oil, the Middle East and the World* 72, *Issawi's Laws of Social Motion* 73, *The Economic History of Turkey* 80, *The Arab World's Legacy* 81, *The Economic History of the Middle East and North Africa* 82.
Princeton University, Princeton, N.J. 08540, U.S.A.

Izziddin, Ibrahim, B.A.; Jordanian diplomatist; b. 3 Dec. 1934; Beirut, Lebanon; ed. American Univ. of Beirut.
Served in Ministry of Communications, Prime Minister's Office, and Press Section of Ministry of Foreign Affairs 55-58; Deputy Dir. Book Publishers, Beirut 58-65; Dir. of Foreign Press, Ministry of Information 65-68, Under-Sec. 71-75; Press Sec. to H.R.H. King Hussein (*q.v.*) 68-70; Dir. Public Relations for Alia (Royal Jordanian Airlines) 70-71; Amb. to Switzerland 75-77, to Fed. Repub. of Germany 77-78, to U.K. 78-; Order of Istiqlal, Second Class, Cedar of Lebanon.
Embassy of the Hashemite Kingdom of Jordan, 6 Upper Phillimore Gardens, London, W8 7HB, England.

J

Jaber al-Ahmed al-Jaber al-Sabah (*see* Sabah, Jaber al-Ahmed al-Jaber al-).

Jaber al-Ali al-Salem al-Sabah (*see* Sabah, Jaber al-Ali al-Salem al-).

Jabre, Jamil Louis; Lebanese writer; b. 1924; ed. Univ. Saint-Joseph, Beirut.
Director of *Al-Hikmal* Revue; Cultural Counsellor for dailies *Al Jaryda* and *L'Orient* and United Unions for Employees and Workers; Founder-mem. Lebanese P.E.N. Club, Amis du Livre, Club du Roman, Club de la Jeunesse Vivante.
Publs. include: *Fever, After the Storm, Agony* (3 vols.), *May Ziadé, Amine Rihani, Gébrane Khalil Gébrane, Tagore, May: Authoress, Jahiz and the Society of His Times, Views on Contemporary American Literature* (essays), *Dream of Nemrod.*
Secteur Chalhoub, Immeuble Nassim Audi, Zalka, Beirut, Lebanon.

Jacovides, Andreas Jacovou, M.A., LL.B.; Cypriot diplomatist; b. 19 Dec. 1936, Nicosia; ed. St. John's Coll., Cambridge, Middle Temple, London.
Called to the bar 60; First Sec., then Counsellor, Perm. Mission of Cyprus to the UN 60-65; Dir. Second, then First Political Div., Ministry of Foreign Affairs, also Chief Asst. to Foreign Minister 65-69; Minister, Dep. Perm. Rep. to UN 69-76, Amb., Dep. Perm. Rep. 76-79; High Commr. in Barbados, Trinidad and Tobago and Guyana 72-82, in Jamaica 73-82, in the Bahamas 75-82, in Canada 79-82; Amb. to U.S.A. 79-82, Amb. Designate to Brazil 79-82, to Ecuador 79-82; mem. UN Int. Law Comm. 81-(86) Henry Fellow, Harvard Univ. Law School 59-60 Dr. h.c. Mount Vernon Coll., U.S.A. 81 mem. American Soc. of Int. Law; Life mem. Cambridge Union Soc.; Knight Commdr. Order of the Phoenix.
Ministry of Foreign Affairs, Nicosia, Cyprus.

Jaffar, Khalid Mohammed; Kuwaiti diplomatist; b. 12 Aug. 1922; ed. Mubarakia School, Kuwait.
Teacher, Kuwait 40-42; Treasurer-Gen., Kuwait Municipality 42-45; Kuwait Oil Co., rose to Supt. of Public Relations 42-61; Lord Chamberlain to His Highness The Amir of Kuwait 61-62; Amb., Ministry of Foreign Affairs, Kuwait May-Dec. 62, concurrently Head of Press and Culture Div., Ministry of Foreign Affairs; mem. Delegation to UN before admission of Kuwait as a mem. 62; deputized for Under-Sec. of State at the Ministry of Foreign Affairs 62-63; Amb. to U.K. 63-65, to Lebanon 65-70, concurrently to France 65-66, to Turkey 67-70; Amb. to Turkey 70-72, concurrently to Bulgaria, Greece 71-72; Dir. of Protocol, Ministry of Foreign Affairs 72-75; Amb. to U.S.A. 75-80; Dir. Pol. Dept., Ministry of Foreign Affairs Jan. 82-; Ordre du Mérite National (France), Grand Cordon de l'Ordre des Cèdres (Lebanon), Order of St. Gregory the Great (Holy See), Orden Francisco de Miranda (Venezuela).
Ministry of Foreign Affairs, Kuwait City, Kuwait.

Jaidah, Ali Mohammed, M.SC.; Qatari international official; b. 24 Sept. 1941, Doha; ed. London Univ.
Head of Econs. Div. in Dept. of Petroleum Affairs, Ministry of Finance and Petroleum 66-71, Dir. of Petroleum Affairs in Dept. of Petroleum Affairs 71-76; mem. Exec. Office of OAPEC; Gov. for OPEC of Qatar until Dec. 76; Sec.-Gen. OPEC 77-79; Dir.-Gen. and mem. Board of Dirs., Qatar Gen. Petroleum Corpn. (QGPC) 79-; Head of dels. to OPEC, OAPEC and other petroleum confs.; Silver Medallion of Federal Austria.
QGPC, P.O. Box 3122, Doha, Qatar.

Jalal, Mahsoun B., PH.D.ECON.; Saudi Arabian international official; b. 26 June 1936; ed. Cairo Univ., Rutgers Univ., U.S.A., Univ. of California, U.S.A.

Professor, Chair. Dept. of Econs., Riyadh Univ. 67-75; Consultant to various Govt. agencies 67-75; formed the Consulting Centre (first Saudi econ. and management consultancy firm); Vice-Chair., Man. Dir. Saudi Fund for Devt. 75-79; mem. Civil Service Council 75-; Dir. Saudi Int. Bank, London 75-, Chair., Nassau 79-; Dir. Saudi Basic Industries Corpn.; Chair. Saudi Investment Banking Corpn., Board of Govs. OPEC Fund 79-, Saudi Tunisian Devt. Investment Co. 81, and several investment cos.; Trustee Arab League Org. for Educ., Culture and Science; Exec. Dir. IMF 78-81; Golden Star (First Class) Taiwan 78, Tanda Mahputera (Indonesia) 78, L'Insigne de Chevalier de l'Ordre National (Mali) 78.
Publs. *Principles of Economics*, other books and articles on econ. devt. and econ. theory.
P.O. Box 4587, Riyadh, Saudi Arabia 7; 1432 Lady Bird Drive, McLean, Va. 22101, U.S.A. (Home).

Jalloud, Major Abdul Salam Ahmed; Libyan politician; b. 15 Dec. 1944; ed. Secondary School, Sebha, Mil. Acad., Benghazi.
Joined underground movement formed by Gaddafi early 1960s; assigned to Army Engineering Corps; headed military operation to take control of Tripoli in 1969 coup; member, Revolutionary Command Council 69-77; Vice-Pres., Minister of the Interior and Local Govt., promoted to Major and made mem. of Defence Council 70, later Deputy Prime Minister for Production 70-71, Minister of Industry and the Econ. and Acting Minister of the Treasury 70-72; Prime Minister 72-77; Asst. Sec.-Gen. General Secretariat of the General People's Congress 77-79.
c/o General Secretariat of the General People's Congress, Tripoli, Libya.

Jamal, Jasim Yousif; Qatari diplomatist; b. 17 Sept. 1940; ed. Northeast Mo. State Univ., Kirksville, Mo., U.S.A. and Univ. of New York.
Ministry of Educ., Dir. Admin. Affairs 58-63, Cultural Adviser, U.S.A. 63-68; Dir. of Cultural Affairs 68-72; Perm. Rep. to UN 72-; non-resident Amb. to Canada, Brazil and Argentina.
Permanent Mission of Qatar to the United Nations, 747 Third Avenue, 22nd Floor, New York, N.Y. 10017, U.S.A.

Jamali, Asim al-; Omani politician; b. 15 Jan. 1935, Muscat; ed. Univ. of Karachi Medical Coll., Univ. of London.
Medical Officer of Health, Dubai 60-63; at London School of Hygiene and Tropical Medicine 64-65; Health Adviser to Trucial States Council, Dubai 65-70; Minister of Health, Oman 70-74, Minister without Portfolio and Special Rep. of the Sultan 74-76; Minister of Land Affairs and Municipalities 76-79, of Public Works May 79-; Chair. Bank of Oman and the Gulf 80-; Renaissance Medal 74, Medal of the First Order.
Ministry of Public Works, Muscat, Oman.

Jamjoom, Ahmed Salah, B.COM.; Saudi Arabian businessman and politician; b. 1925, Jeddah; ed. Fouad Univ. Cairo and Harvard Law School.
Joined Arab Bank, Jeddah 50; Minister of State and mem. Council of Ministers 58-59; Supervisor of Economic Dept. 59-60; Minister of Commerce 60; Minister of Trade and Industry 61-62; Dir. and Partner, Mohd. Nour Salah Jamjoom & Bros. 62-; Dir. Jamjoom Vehicles and Equipment and Jamjoom Construction; Gen. Man. Madina Press. Org.
Publs. *An Approach to an Integrated Economic Development* 60, *Economics of Mecca* 67.
Mohamed Nour Salah Jamjoom and Brothers, Riyadh, and P.O. Box 1247, Jeddah, Saudi Arabia.

Jarring, Gunnar, PH.D.; Swedish diplomatist; b. 12 Oct. 1907; ed. Lund Univ.
Associate Prof. Turkic Languages Lund Univ. 33-40;

Attaché Ankara 40-41; Chief Section B Teheran 41; Chargé d'Affaires a.i. Teheran and Baghdad 45, Addis Ababa 46-48; Minister to India 48-51, concurrently to Ceylon 50-51, to Persia, Iraq and Pakistan 51-52; Dir. Political Div. Ministry of Foreign Affairs 53-56; Perm. Rep. to UN 56-58; rep. on Security Council 57-58; Amb. to U.S.A. 58-64, to U.S.S.R. 64-73, and to Mongolia 65-73; Special Rep. of Sec.-Gen. of UN on Middle East situation Nov. 67-; Grand Cross, Order of the North Star.
Publs. *Studien zu einer osttürkischen Lautlehre* 33, *The Contest of the Fruits—An Eastern Turki Allegory* 36, *The Uzbek Dialect of Qilich, Russian Turkestan* 37, *Uzbek Texts from Afghan Turkestan* 38, *The Distribution of Turk Tribes in Afghanistan* 39, *Materials for the Knowledge of Eastern Turkestan* (Vols. I-IV) 47-51, *An Eastern Turki-English Dialect Dictionary* 64, *Literary Texts from Kashghar* 80.
Karlavägen 85, S-114 59 Stockholm, Sweden.

Jordan, King of **(**see Hussein ibn Talal**).**

Joukhdar, Mohammed Saleh, B.A., M.A.; Saudi Arabian economist and politician; b. 1932; ed. Univs. of California and Southern California.
Economic Consultant to Directorate-Gen. of Petroleum and Minerals, Saudi Arabia 58; Govt. Rep. Supervisory Cttee. for Expenditure and Purchasing, Arabian Oil Co. 61, Dir. 61-66; Sec.-Gen. Org. of Petroleum Exporting Countries (OPEC) 67-68; Deputy Minister of Petroleum and Mineral Resources 69; Deputy Gov. for Oil Affairs, PETROMIN 70-73; Amb. in Charge of Petroleum and Econ. Desk, Ministry of Foreign Affairs 73-74; on leave of absence as petroleum consultant 74-; mem. American Soc. of Economists.
Ministry of Petroleum and Mineral Resources, P.O. Box 247, Riyadh, Saudi Arabia.

Juffali, Ahmed; Saudi Arabian businessman; b. 15 Oct. 1924; ed. Saudi Arabia and United Kingdom.
Managing Dir., E. A. Juffali & Bros. 45-; mem. Board of Dirs. Saudi Electric Co. 52-; Man. Dir. Saudi Cement Co. 58, Medina Electric Co. 58-; Hon. Danish Consul-Gen. 59-; Chair. Nat. Insurance Co. SA (Luxembourg) 74, Nat. Automobile Industry Co. Ltd. 76, Arabian Metal Industries Ltd. 75, Fluor Arabia Ltd. 76, Arabia Electric Ltd. 76, Saudi Building Systems Ltd. 76, Pool Arabia Ltd. 76, MARCO 76, Beck Arabia 76, Orient Transport Co. 77, Saudi Steel Products Co. 78, Saudi Refrigerators Manufacturing Co. 80, Saudi Ericsson Communications Ltd. 80, Saudi Airconditioning Manufacturing Co. 80, Saudi Tractor Manufacturing Co. 80, Saudi Business Machines Ltd. 80; Founder and Board mem. Al-Bank Al-Saudi Al-Hollandi 75; Man. Dir. Saudi-Bahraini Cement Co. 75; mem. Saudi German Econ. Co-operation Cttee. 76, Wells Fargo Bank International Advisory Council 77; mem. U.S.-Saudi Arabian Joint Comm. on Econ. Co-operation -80, Chase International Advisory Cttee. -80; Hon. Kt. 1st Class (Denmark) 74.
E. A. Juffali & Bros., King Abdul Aziz Street, P.O. Box 1049, Jeddah, Saudi Arabia.

K

Kaddafi, Col. Muammar al- (see Gaddafi).

Kaddori, Fakhri Yasin, DR.RER.POL.; Iraqi economist; b. 28 Aug. 1932; ed. Adhamiya Intermediate School and Central Secondary School, Baghdad, Coll. of Commerce and Econs. (Univ. of Baghdad), State Univ. of Iowa, Cologne Univ., Int. Marketing Inst. (Harvard Univ.).
Director of Internal Trade, Ministry of the Economy 64-68; Minister of the Economy 68-71, mem. Planning Board 68-; mem. Bureau of Econ. Affairs, Revolutionary Command Council 71-73, Chair. 73-76, Acting Chair. 76-; Gov. Central Bank of Iraq 76-78; Sec.-Gen. Arab Econ. Unity Council, Cairo 78-82; Pres. Exec. Cttee. for Profes-

sional and Popular Orgs. in Iraq 75-77; Chair. Iraqi Economist Asscn. 72-74, 77-.
Arab Economic Unity Council, P.O. Box 925100, Ashmeisani, Alhusein Quarter, Amman, Jordan; Home: 20 Aisha El-Taymouria Street, Garden City, Cairo, Egypt.

Kaissouni, Abdel Moneim, B.COM., B.SC., PH.D.; Egyptian financial administrator and politician; b. 1916; ed. Univ. of Cairo and London School of Economics.
With Barclays Bank, England 42-43; Lecturer and Asst. Prof. of Econs., Univ. of Cairo 44-46; Dir. Middle East Dept. IMF, Washington, and later Chief Technical Rep. in Middle East 46-50; with Nat. Bank of Egypt 50-54; Minister of Finance, Econ. and Deputy Prime Minister 54-66, 68; Chair. Arab Int. Bank 71-76, 78; Deputy Prime Minister for Econ. and Financial Affairs Nov. 76-May 78, also Minister of Planning Oct. 77-May 78; Economic Adviser to Minister of Finance Jan. 82-; Chair. European Arab Holding, Luxembourg 72; mem. Higher Econ. Council, Egypt 74; Chair. IMF and IBRD annual meetings 55; Pres. Cairo Conf. on Devt. 62; Pres. UN Conf. on Trade and Devt. 64; Grand Cordon of the Repub. (Egypt).
c/o 35 Abdel Khalek Sarwat Street, Cairo, Egypt.

Kamel, Muhammad Ibrahim; Egyptian diplomatist and politician; b. 1923; graduated in law.
Second Sec., London 50, served successively in Mexico, Kinshasa, Bonn and Montreal; Amb. to Fed. Rep. of Germany 73-77; Minister of Foreign Affairs 77-78; Amb. Extraordinary, Ministry of Foreign Affairs Nov. 78-; Chief Exec. and co-founder Dar al-Maal al-Islami Bank 81.
c/o Ministry of Foreign Affairs, Cairo, Egypt and Dar al-Maal al-Islami Bank, P.O. Box 7667, Airport Road, opposite Central Hospital, Abu Dhabi, United Arab Emirates.

Karageorghis, Vassos, PH.D., F.S.A., F.R.S.A.; Cypriot archaeologist; b. 29 April 1929, Trikomo; ed. Pancyprian Gymnasium, Nicosia, Univ. Coll. and Inst. of Archaeology, London Univ.
Assistant Curator, Cyprus Museum 52-60, Curator 60-63, Acting Dir., Dept. of Antiquities, Cyprus 63-64, Dir. 64-; mem. Gov. Body, Cyprus Research Centre; Fellow, Soc. of Antiquaries, London, Univ. Coll. London; Corresp. Fellow, British Acad.; Foreign Fellow, Accademia dei Lincei, Rome; Corresp. mem. Archaeological Soc., Athens, Acad. of Athens, Austrian Acad. of Sciences; mem. German Archaeological Inst., Berlin, Royal Soc. for Humanistic Studies, Lund, Royal Swedish Acad.; Dr. h.c. (Univs. of Lyon, Göteborg, Athens, Birmingham, Toulouse); Commonwealth Prize 78; Chevalier de l'Ordre de la Légion d'Honneur; Order of Merit, First Class (Fed. Repub. of Germany).
Publs. *Treasures in the Cyprus Museum* 62, *Nouveaux Documents pour l'Etude du Bronze Récent à Chypre* 64, *Corpus Vasorum Antiquorum I* 63, and *II* 65, *Sculptures from Salamis I* 64, *II* 66, *Excavations in the Necropolis of Salamis I* 67, *II* 70, *III* 73, *IV* 78, *Cyprus* (Archaelogia Mundi) 68, *Salamis-New Aspects of Antiquity* 69, *Altägäis und Altkypros* (with H.-G. Buchholz) 71, and *Cypriot Antiquities in the Pierides Collection, Larnaca* 73, *Excavations at Kition I: The Tombs* 74, *The Civilization of Prehistoric Cyprus* 75, *Alaas, a Protogeometric Necropolis in Cyprus* 75, *La Céramique Chypriote de Style figuré* (with J. des Gagniers) 76, *Vases et Figurines de l'Age du Bronze à Chypre* (with J. des Gagniers) 76, *Kition, Mycenaean and Phoenician discoveries in Cyprus* 76, *Hala Sultan Tekké I, Excavations 1897-1971* (with P. Åström and D. M. Bailey) 76, *Fouilles de Kition II, Objets Egyptiens et Egyptisants* (with G. Clerc, E. Lagarce and J. Leclant) 76, *Fouilles de Kition III, Inscriptions Phéniciennes* (with M.-G. Guzzo Amadasi), *Kition IV, The non-Cypriot pottery* (with others) 81, *Cypriot Antiquities in the Medelhausmuseet*, Stockholm (with C.-G. Styrenius and M.-G. Winbladh) 77, *Memoirs*

vol. II 77, *Two Cypriot Sanctuaries of the end of the Cypro-Archaic period* 77, *The goddess with uplifted arms in Cyprus* 77 and articles in German, American, English and French journals.
Cyprus Museum, P.O. Box 2024, Nicosia; Home: 12 Kastorias Street, Nicosia, Cyprus.

Karami, Rashid Abdul Hamid; Lebanese politician; b. 1921; ed. Fuad I Univ., Cairo.
Minister of Nat. Economy and Social Affairs 54-55; Prime Minister and Minister of the Interior Sept. 55-March 56; Prime Minister Sept. 58-May 60; Minister of Finance, Economy, Defence and Information Oct. 58-Oct. 59, of Finance and Defence Oct. 59-May 60; Prime Minister and Minister of Finance Oct. 61-April 64; Prime Minister 65-66, 66-67, 67-68, 69-70, May 75-Dec. 76; Minister of Defence May 75-Sept. 76, of Finance and Information May 75-Dec. 76; mem. Nat. Dialogue Cttee. Sept. 75; Leader Parliamentary Democratic Front 78-.
Rue Karm Ellé, Beirut, Lebanon.

Karim-Lamrani, Mohammed; Moroccan government official; b. 1 May 1919, Fez.
Economic adviser to H.M. the King of Morocco; Dir. Gen. Office Chérifien des Phosphates 67-; Chair. Crédit du Maroc; Minister of Finance 71; Prime Minister 71-72.
Direction Générale, OCP, Angle Route d'El Jadida et Boulevard de la Grande Ceinture, Casablanca, Morocco.

Karmal, Babrak; Afghan politician and diplomatist; b. 1929; ed. Kabul Univ.
Detained for 5 years for political activities in 1950s; in Ministry of Planning 57-65; mem. of Parl. 65-73; f. Khalq political party 65, Leader breakaway Parcham party 67-77; after merger in 77 of Khalq and Parcham parties to form People's Democratic Party of Afghanistan (PDPA) Deputy Leader 77-78; Editor underground newspaper *Parcham*; Deputy Prime Minister and Vice-Pres. of Revolutionary Council April-July 78; Amb. to Czechoslovakia (also accred. to Hungary) 78-79; returned to Afghanistan after Soviet invasion Dec. 79; Prime Minister of Afghanistan Dec. 79-June 81; Pres. of the Revolutionary Council, Gen. Sec. of PDPA Cen. Cttee. and mem. of Politburo Dec. 79-; C.-in-C. of the Armed Forces Dec. 79-.
Office of the President, Revolutionary Council, Da Khalkoo Koor, Kabul, Afghanistan.

Kassem, Dr. Abdul-Rauf al-, D.ARCH.; Syrian politician; b. 1932, Damascus; ed. Damascus Univ. School of Arts, Istanbul and Geneva Univs.
Teacher of architecture, School of Fine Arts Damascus, Dean 64-70, Head, Architecture Dept., School of Civil Engineering Damascus Univ. 70-77, Rector 77-79; concurrently engineer 64-77; Gov. of Damascus 79-80; elected mem. Baath party Regional Command Dec. 79, Central Command of Progressive Nat. Front April 80; Prime Minister Jan. 80-; mem. Higher Council for Town Planning 68-; mem. Nat. Union of Architects' Perm. Comm. on Town Planning 75-; Hon. Prof. Geneva Univ. 75-.
Office of the Prime Minister, Damascus, Syria.

Katzir, Ephraim, M.SC., PH.D.; Israeli scientist, teacher and administrator; b. (as Ephraim Katchalski) 16 May 1916, Kiev, Russia; ed. Hebrew Univ., Jerusalem.
Head of Dept. of Biophysics, Weizmann Inst. of Science 51-73, Prof. 78-; Chief Scientist, Ministry of Defence 66-68; Pres. of Israel 73-78; Prof. Tel-Aviv Univ. 78-; Visiting Prof., Hebrew Univ. 53-61; Guest Scientist, Harvard Univ. 57-59; Senior Foreign Scientist Fellowship, Univ. of California, Los Angeles 64; Chair. Weizmann Inst. Cttee. for Katzir Centre; mem. Israel Acad. of Sciences and Humanities, Nat. Acad. of Sciences, U.S.A., American Acad. of Arts and Sciences (Foreign Hon. mem.), Leopol-

dina Acad. of Science, German Democratic Repub., American Soc. of Biological Chemists (Hon.), Ciba Foundation, Int. Union of Biochemistry and many other orgs.; Foreign mem. Royal Society, London; mem. Editorial Board, *Biopolymers*, series on *Applied Biochemistry and Bioengineering* and *Advances in Experimental Medicine and Biology*; Hon. Ph.D. (Brandeis, Michigan, Harvard, Northwestern and Hebrew Univs., Polytechnic Inst. of New York, Hebrew Union Coll., Jerusalem, Weizmann Inst. of Sciences, McGill Univ., Montreal, Eidgenössische Technische Hochschule, Zürich, Thomas Jefferson Univ., Pa., Oxford); Tchernikhovsky Prize 48, Weizmann Prize 50, Israel Prize Natural Science 59, Rothschild Prize Natural Sciences 61; Linderstrøm-Lang Gold Medal 69, Hans Krebs Medal 72.
Publs. numerous papers and articles on polyamino acids, polymers, structure and function of living cells, and enzyme engineering.
Weizmann Institute of Science, P.O. Box 26, Rehovot, Israel.

Kayla, Ziya; Turkish economist; b. 28 Dec. 1912; ed. School of Political Sciences, Istanbul.
Ministry of Finance 34-63, Asst. Inspector, Inspector and Chief Inspector of Finance 34-60; Deputy Minister of Finance 60-63; Chair. Board of Dirs. and Dir.-Gen. Central Bank of Turkey 63-66; Alternate Gov. IBRD 61-66; Pres. Banks' Asscn. of Turkey 63-66; Sec.-Gen. Comm. of Regulation of Bank Credits 63-66, Head of Foreign Investment Encouragement Cttee. 63-66; mem. Board of Controllers of the Prime Ministry 66-70; Chair. Türkiye Vakiflar Bankasi 71-76, Central Bank of Turkey 78-80; mem. Higher Educ. Council 81-.
Publs. *Emission Movements in Turkey* 67, *Treasury and Central Bank's Relations* 70, *Knowledge of the Economic Situation* 78, *Central Bank's Operations* 81.
Mesnevi sokak 8/8, Ankara, Turkey.

Kayra, Cahit; Turkish civil servant and diplomatist; b. 13 March 1917; ed. Univ. of Ankara.
Inspector of Finance 42-50; Counsellor, Gen. Dir. of Finance 50-55; private financial adviser 55-59; Head of Foreign Trade Dept., Ministry of Trade 59-60; Head of Turkish Perm. Del. to Gen. Agreement on Tariffs and Trade (GATT) 60-63; Deputy Under-Sec. of State to Min. of Finance 63-64; Head of Turkish Del. to OECD 64-67; Head of Research Dept., Ministry of Finance 67-73; Minister of Energy and Natural Resources 74; mem. Gen. Admin. Board of the Republican People's Party 77, Nat. Assembly for Ankara; mem. Board, Türkiye İş Bankası.
Publs. *Middle Eastern Oil* 53, *A Guide to the Turkish System of Taxation* 57, *Import Policy in Turkey* 63, *A Rational Customs Policy* 69, *Foreign Financing Techniques* 70, *Free Trade of Gold in Turkey* 71, *Balance of Payments of Turkey* 72.
Cumhuriyet Halk Partisi (Republican People's Party), Ankara, Turkey.

Kedourie, Elie, B.SC.(ECON.); British professor of politics and editor.
Assistant Lecturer, then Lecturer in Politics and Public Admin., London School of Economics 53-60; Reader in Political Studies with special reference to the Middle East, London Univ. 61-65; Prof. of Politics, London Univ. 65-; Editor *Middle Eastern Studies* 64-; Fellow, British Acad. 75-, Netherlands Inst. for Advanced Study 80-81.
Publs. *England and the Middle East: the Destruction of the Ottoman Empire* 56, *Nationalism* 60, *Afghani and Abduh* 66, *The Chatham House Version* 70, *Nationalism in Asia and Africa* 71, *Arabic Political Memoirs and Other Studies* 74, *In the Anglo-Arab Labyrinth* 76, *The Middle Eastern Economy* (Ed.) 78, *The Jewish World* (Ed.) 79, *Islam in the Modern World and Other Studies* 80, *Towards a Modern*

Iran (Ed. with Sylvia G. Haim) 80, *Modern Egypt* (ed. with Sylvia G. Haim) 80.
London School of Economics, Houghton Street, Aldwych, London, W.C.1, England.

Kelani, Haissam; Syrian diplomatist; b. 6 Aug. 1926, Hamah; ed. Mil. Coll., Air Gen. Staff Coll., Paris and High Mil. Air Acad., Paris.
General Pilot 61-62; Amb. to Algeria 62-63, to Morocco 65-67; Sec.-Gen. Ministry of Foreign Affairs 67-69; Amb. to the German Democratic Repub. 69-72; Perm. Rep. to UN 72-76; Dir. Dept. of Int. Organizations, Ministry of Foreign Affairs; mem. Expert, Human Rights Cttee. 77-80; Hon. Dr. Contemporary History; Hon. Ph.D. (Leipzig) 73; twelve medals. Publs. ten books, many articles in Arab reviews.
c/o Ministry of Foreign Affairs, Damascus, Syria.

Kellou, Mohamed; Algerian lawyer and diplomatist; b. 27 March 1931, Mansoura; ed. Univs. of Algiers and Montpellier.
Lawyer, Algiers; fmr. Vice-Pres. Union Générale des Etudiants Musulmans Algériens (U.G.E.M.A.) (in charge of Foreign Affairs); Front de Libération Nationale (F.L.N.) Rep. in U.K. 57-61; Chief of Provisional Govt. of Algeria Diplomatic Mission to Pakistan 61-62; Chief of Africa-Asia-Latin America Div., Ministry of Foreign Affairs, Republic of Algeria 62-63; Amb. to U.K. 63-64, to Czechoslovakia 64-70, concurrently to Hungary 65-70, to Poland 66-70, to Argentina, Chile, Uruguay, Bolivia and Peru 70-75, to People's Repub. of China 75-77, to Fed. Repub. of Germany Nov. 79-; mem. People's Nat. Assembly Feb. 77, Chair. Foreign Affairs Cttee. March 77.
Embassy of Algeria, Rheinallee 32, 5300 Bonn 2, Federal Republic of Germany.

Kemal, Yaşar; Turkish writer and journalist; b. 1923; self-educated.
Novels transl. into English: *Memed, My Hawk* 61, *The Wind from the Plain* 63, *Anatolian Tales* 68, *They Burn the Thistles* 73, *Iron Earth Copper Sky* 74, *The Legend of Ararat* 75, *The Legend of the Thousand Bulls* 76, *The Undying Grass* 77, *The Lords of Akchasez* (Part I), *Murder in the Ironsmiths Market* 79, *The Saga of a Seagull* 81; novels, short stories, plays and essays in Turkish; books translated into several languages.
P.K. 14, Basinköy, Istanbul, Turkey.

Khaddam, Abdel Halim; Syrian politician.
Minister of the Economy and Foreign Trade 69-70; Deputy Prime Minister and Minister of Foreign Affairs Nov. 70-; mem. Regional Command, Baath Party May 71-.
Ministry of Foreign Affairs, Damascus, Syria.

Khalid, Mansour, LL.D.; Sudanese diplomatist and lawyer; b. 13 Dec. 1931, Sudan; ed. Univs. of Khartoum, Pennsylvania, Algeria and Paris.
Began his career as an attorney, Khartoum 57-59; Legal officer, UN, N.Y. 62-63; Deputy UN resident rep., Algeria 64-65; Bureau of Relations with Member States, UNESCO. Paris 65-69; Visiting Prof. of Int. Law, Univ. of Colorado 68; Minister of Youth and Social Affairs, Sudan 69-71; Chair. of Del. of Sudan to UN Gen. Assembly 70, 72, 73, 74, Special Consultant and Personal Rep. of UNESCO Dir.-Gen. for UNWRA fund-raising mission 70; Perm. Rep. to UN for Sudan 71, Pres. Security Council 72; Minister of Foreign Affairs 71-75, Feb.-Sept. 77, of Educ. 75-July 76; Asst. to the Pres. for Co-ordination and Foreign Affairs 76, for Co-ordination 77; mem. Exec. Bureau of Sudanese Socialist Union; dismissed from political posts July 78, Chair. OAU Ministerial Cttee. on Impact of Petroleum Price Increases on Africa and Afro-Arab Econ. Co-op. 73-75; Fellow, Woodrow Wilson Center, Smithsonian Inst., Washington, D.C. 79-80; Financial and Investment Consultant 80-; Special Consultant and Personal Rep. of

Exec. Dir. of UNEP 81-; Visiting Prof. of Devt. Studies, Univ. of Khartoum 81.
Publs. *Private Law in Sudan* 70, *The Nile Basin, Present and Future* 71, *Solution of the Southern Problem and its African Implications* 72, *The Decision-Making Process in Foreign Policy* 73, *The Sudan Experiment with Unity* 73, *A Dialogue with the Sudanese Intellectuals.*
P.O. Box 3029, Khartoum, Sudan; 9 Jubilee Place, London, S.W.3, England.

Khalifa, Sheikh Hamed bin Isa al-; Heir Apparent to H.H. Emir of Bahrain; b. 28 Jan. 1950; ed. Secondary School, Manama, Applegarth Coll., Godalming, Mons Officer Cadet School, Aldershot, England, and U.S. Army Command and Gen. Staff Coll., Fort Leavenworth, Kansas, U.S.A.
Founder, Commdr. Bahrain Defence Force, Head Defence Dept., Govt. of Bahrain 68-; mem. State Admin. Council 70-71; Minister of Defence 71-; Deputy Pres. Family Council of Al-Khalifa 74-; Pres. Bahrain High Council for Youth and Sports 75-, Bahrain Equestrian and Horse Racing Asscn. 77-; awarded many foreign decorations.
Private Office of the Heir Apparent, Court of the Amir, Rifa'a Palace, Manama, Bahrain.

Khalifa, H.H. Sheikh Isa bin Sulman al-; Ruler of the State of Bahrain; b. 3 July 1933.
Appointed heir-apparent by his father, H.H. Sheikh Sulman bin Hamad al-Khalifah 58; succeeded as Ruler on the death of his father Nov. 61; took title of Amir Aug. 71; Chair. Supreme Oil Council; Hon. K.C.M.G.
Rifa'a Palace, Manama, Bahrain.

Khalifa, Shekh Khalifa bin Sulman al-; Bahrain politician; b. 1935.
Son of the late Sheikh Sulman and brother of the ruler, Sheikh Isa; Dir. of Finance and Pres. of Electricity Board 61; Pres. Council of Admin. 66-70; Pres. State Council 70-73, Prime Minister 73-; Chair. Bahrain Monetary Agency.
Council of Ministers, Manama, Bahrain.

Khalifa bin Hamad al-Thani, Sheikh (*see* Thani, Sheikh Khalifa bin Hamad al-).

Khalil, Gen. Abdel-Majid; Sudanese army officer and politician.
Formerly Maj.-Gen. and Deputy Chief of Staff; promoted to Lt.-Gen. July 78; Chief of Staff 78-79; promoted to Gen. May 79; Minister of Defence and C.-in-C. of People's Armed Forces May 79-Jan. 82, also First Vice-Pres. of Sudan Aug. 79-Jan. 82; Sec.-Gen. Sudanese Socialist Union Sept. 80-Jan. 82 (removed from all posts Jan. 82).
Ministry of Defence, Khartoum, Sudan.

Khalil, Mohamed Kamal El-Din; Egyptian diplomatist.
Lecturer in Int. and Public Law 41-56; Dir. of Research Dept., U.A.R. Ministry of Foreign Affairs 56-60; Minister Plenipotentiary, London 60-61; Dir. North American Dept. U.A.R. Ministry of Foreign Affairs 61-64; Amb. to Jordan 64-66, to Sudan 66-71; Under-Sec. of State for Foreign Affairs Sept. 71-74; Amb. to Belgium 74-79, also to EEC; Amb. to France 79-.
Publ. *The Arab States and the Arab League* (2 vols.) 62.
Embassy of the Arab Republic of Egypt, 56 Avenue d'Iena, Paris 16e, France.

Khalil, Mustafa, M.SC., D.PHIL.; Egyptian engineer, politician and banker; b. 1920; ed. Univ. of Cairo, Illinois Univ., U.S.A.
Served in Egyptian State Railways 41-47, 51-52; Training with Chicago-Milwaukee Railways (U.S.A.) 47; Lecturer in Railways and Highway Engineering, Ain Shams Univ., Cairo 52; Tech. Consultant to Transport Cttee., Perm. Council for Nat. Production 55; Minister of Communication and Transport 56-64, of Industry, Mineral Resources and Electricity 65-66; Deputy Prime Minister 64-65;

resigned from Cabinet 66; Head of Broadcasting Corpn. 70; Sec.-Gen. Central Cttee., Arab Socialist Union 70-76; Prime Minister 78-80, also Minister of Foreign Affairs 79-80; Deputy Chair. Nat. Democratic Party May 80-; Chair. Arab Int. Bank, Cairo 80-.
Arab International Bank, 35 Abdel Khalek Sarwat Street, Cairo, Egypt.

Khamenei, Hojatoleslam Seyyed Ali; Iranian religious leader and politician; b. 15 July 1939, Meshed, Khorassan; ed. Navab School and Qom.
Studied under Ayatollah Khomeini 59; fought in uprising 63; founded clandestine resistance org. 63; returned to Meshed 65; imprisoned six times 65-79; a founder of the Clergy Asscn. 78; exiled to Iranshahr, then Jiroft 79; mem. Revolutionary Council until its dissolution 79, former Rep. of Revolutionary Council to Defence Ministry; personal rep. of Ayatollah Khomeini to Supreme Defence Council; Superintendent of the Guardian Corps of the Islamic Revolution; Deputy to Majlis (consultative assembly); Friday Prayer Leader, Teheran 80-; Sec.-Gen. and mem. Central Cttee., Islamic Republican Party Sept. 80-; Pres. of Iran Oct. 81-; survived assassination attempt June 81.
Publs. *The Future of Islamic Territory* 67, *Muslims in the Indian Liberation Movement, The Complete Outline of Islamic Thought in the Quran, Patience, The Depth of Daily Prayer, A Correct Understanding of Islam, Imam Sadiq's Life, Teachings from Nahjul Balagah, Collection of Lectures on Imamate and Our Position;* Translations: *A Critique of Western Civilization, Reconciliation* (by Iman Hassam).
Office of the President, Teheran, Iran.

Khane, Abd-El Rahman, M.D.; Algerian politician, administrator and physician; b. 6 March 1931, Collo; ed. Univ. of Algiers.
Served as officer in Nat. Liberation Army until Algerian independence 62; Sec. of State provisional govt. (GPRA) 58-60; Gen. Controller Nat. Liberation Front 60-61; Head of Finance Dept. GPRA 61-62; Pres. Algerian-French tech. org. for exploiting wealth of Sahara sub-soil 62-65; Pres. Electricité et Gaz d'Algérie July-Oct. 64; mem. Board Dirs. Nat. Petroleum Research and Exploitation Co. 65-66; Minister of Public Works and Pres. Algerian-French Industrial Co-operation Org. 66-70; Physician, Cardiology Dept., Univ. Hospital of Algiers 70-73; Sec.-Gen. OPEC 73-74; Exec. Dir. UNIDO Jan. 75-.
UNIDO, Vienna International Centre, P.O. Box 400, A-1400 Vienna, Austria; 42 Chemin B. Brahimi, El Biar, Algiers, Algeria.

Khani, Abdallah Fikri El-, LL.D.; Syrian politician, diplomatist and judge; b. 1925, Damascus; ed. Syrian Univ., Damascus, St. Joseph's Univ., Beirut, and American Univ., Beirut.
Law practice 47-49; various functions including Sec.-Gen. in Presidency of Repub. 49-59; Lecturer, School of Law, Syrian Univ. 54-58; Minister Counsellor, then Minister Plenipotentiary, Madrid, Brussels, Ankara, London and Paris 59-69; Perm. Rep. to UNESCO 66-69; Sec.-Gen. Ministry of Foreign Affairs 69-72; Head of del. to UN Gen. Assembly and Security Council 70; Chair. Syrian del. to Syro-Lebanese Perm. Comm. 69-72; Minister of Tourism 72-76; Sec.-Gen., then Deputy Minister for Foreign Affairs 76-77; Amb. to India and Amb. designate to Afghanistan 78-81; mem: and Vice-Chair. (79) UN Sub.-Comm. on Prevention of Discrimination and Protection of Minorities 78-80; mem. Int. Court of Justice, The Hague Jan. 81-; Bronze Medal from Pope Paul VI and Syrian, Egyptian, Jordanian, Indonesian and Argentinian decorations.
International Court of Justice, Peace Palace, Carnegie-plein, 2517 KJ, The Hague, Netherlands.

Khatib, Ahmed al-; Syrian politician; b. 1931, Salkhad, Jabal al-Arab region.
Formerly Head, Syrian Teachers Asscn.; mem. Presidential Council Sept. 65-Feb. 66; Pres. of Syria Nov. 70-Feb. 71; Chair. People's Council Feb.-Dec. 71; Prime Minister and Chair. of Federal Ministerial Council, Fed. of Arab Repubs. 71-75; mem. Baath Party, elected to Leadership Cttee. May 71.
People's Council, Damascus, Syria.

Khayata, Abdul Wahab Ismail, PH.D.(ECONS.); Syrian economist; b. 24 Feb. 1924, Aleppo; ed. Ecole Française de Droit, Beirut, London School of Econs., Univ. of Louvain, Belgium.
Lecturer, then Prof. of Econs. and Financial Analysis 56-68; with Central Bank of Syria, rising to Deputy Gov. 53-63; Under-Sec., Ministry of Planning 63-68; Financial Adviser, UN, Beirut 69-71, 73-74; Deputy Dir. for Europe and the Middle East, UNDP, New York 71-73; Gen. Man. FRAB Bank International, Paris 74-78; Pres. and Deputy Chair. Cen. Bank of Oman 78-.
Publs. textbooks on planning, economics and finance and papers on finance in the Middle East and international economic co-operation.
Central Bank of Oman, P.O. Box 4161, Ruwi, Oman.

Khayyal, Abdullah al; Saudi Arabian diplomatist and politician; b. 1913; ed. Cairo Univ.
Private Sec. to Minister of Foreign Affairs, H.R.H. Prince Faisal 32; Dir.-Gen. of Schools, Eastern Saudi Arabia and Dir. A.H.S.A. Central School 41; Second Sec. Saudi Arabian Legation, Baghdad 43; First Sec. and Chargé d'Affaires 45; Minister to Iraq 47-55; Perm. Del. to UN 55-57; Ambassador to U.S.A. 55-63, concurrently Minister to Mexico 56-60, Ambassador 60-63; Pres. Islamic Center, Washington, D.C. 55-68; Dir. of Public Works 64; later Amb. to United Arab Emirates; Amb. to Austria Oct. 77-; Chair. Board of Trustees, Vienna Islamic Centre.
Saudi Arabian Embassy, Formanegasse 38, A-1190 Vienna, Austria.

Khelil, Ismail, D. EN D.; Tunisian diplomatist and international official; b. 7 Nov. 1932, Gafsa; ed. Sadiki Coll., Tunis, Grenoble Univ., France.
United States Division Foreign Affairs Secretariat 57; Sec. Tunisian Embassy, Rome and Rep. to FAO 57-60; Counsellor, later Minister Plenipotentiary Tunisian Embassy, Washington, D.C. 60-64; Alternative Exec. Dir. for Tunisia, IBRD (World Bank) 62-64; Amb. and Dir. Int. Co-operation Ministry of Foreign Affairs 64-69; Sec.-Gen. Ministry of Foreign Affairs 67-69; Amb. to U.K. 69-72, to Belgium and Luxembourg and Rep. to European Communities 72-78; Dir.-Gen. Int. Co-operation Ministry of Foreign Affairs 78-79; Pres. Dir.-Gen. Tunis Air 79-80; Exec. Dir. IBRD Nov. 81-; Commdr. Ordre de la République; Officier Ordre de l'Indépendance de Tunisie and decorations from 11 other countries.
IBRD, Suite E-1107, 1818 H Street, N.W., Washington, D.C. 20433; Home: 5407 Uppingham Street, Chevy Chase, Md. 20015, U.S.A.

Khene, Abderrahman (*see* Khane, Abd-El Rahman).

Khlefawi, Gen. Abdel Rahman; Syrian army officer and politician; b. 1927, Damascus; ed. schools in Damascus, Military School, Homs.
Representative of Syria, Joint Arab Command, Cairo 64-67; Head, Armoured Forces Admin., Damascus 67-68; Head, Officers' Board, Ministry of Defence 68-70; Minister of the Interior Nov. 70-April 71; Prime Minister 71-72, 76-78; mem. Regional Command, Baath Party.
Damascus, Syria.

Kholi, Hassan Sabri el-; Egyptian diplomatist: b. 25 Feb. 1922, Tanta; ed. Univ. of Cairo, Mil. and Staff Colls.
Fought in Palestine War 48; Prof., Senior Officer Studies

Inst.; opened Infantry School, Syria 57; Dir. Office for Palestine at the Presidency, Office for Public Affairs; Personal Rep. of the Pres. 64-75; has represented Egypt at UN, Arab League and Arab Summit Confs.; UNICEF Rep. in Arab Countries 75-76; Chief Mediator of Arab League in Lebanon crisis 76-77; Pres. Egyptian Soc. for the Mentally Handicapped, Asscn. for Welfare of the Disabled and Handicapped; numerous foreign decorations.
Publs. *The Palestine Case, Sinai, The Policy of Imperialism and Zionism towards Palestine during the First Half of the Twentieth Century*, and several research papers on Palestine.
50 Khalifa Mamoun Street, Cairo, Egypt.

Khomeini, Ayatollah Ruhollah; Iranian religious leader; b. 17 May 1900, Khomein; ed. in Khomein and at theological school, Qom.
Religious teacher in theological school, Qom; arrested in Qom after riots over Shah's land reforms June-Aug. 63; in exile, Turkey 64-65, Najaf, Iraq 65-78, Neauphle-le-Château, France Oct. 78-Feb. 79; from France acted as leader in revolution which toppled Shah Mohammad Reza Pahlavi with aim of creating Islamic Repub.; returned to Iran Feb. 79; appointed Mehdi Bazargan (*q.v.*) as Prime Minister; returned to the theological seminary, Qom, but continued as leader of Islamic movement March 79-; under new constitution, became Velayat Faghih (religious leader) 80-.
Publs. *The Government of Theologians* (lectures while in exile), numerous religious and political books and tracts.
Madresseh Faizieh, Qom; Home: 61 Kuche Yakhchal Ghazi, Qom, Iran.

Khoury, Sheikh Maitre Michel Bechara al-. LL.B.; Lebanese businessman and politician; b. 24 Nov. 1926; ed. Univ. St. Joseph, Beirut, Paris Univ. Faculté de Droit, Inst. d' Etudes Politiques and Coll. de France.
Political section, Ministry of Foreign Affairs 46-49; Lebanese Bar 48, law practice -53; Contributor to *Le Jour* daily 44-47, then Assoc. Ed.; Dir.-Gen. Ets. Derwiche Youssef Haddad 53-; mem. Board Nat. Council of Tourism 62-66, Pres. 64-72; Minister of Defence and of Guidance, Information and Tourism Dec. 65-April 66; Minister of Planning and Tourism 67-68; Leader Destour Party 73-; Personal Rep. of Pres. Sarkis on missions abroad 77; Gov. Lebanese Central Bank 78-; Commdr. Order of Merit (Brazil), Gran Cruz, Orden del Mérito Civil (Spain) and other decorations.
rue Michel Chiha, Kantari, Beirut, Lebanon.

Kidron, Abraham, B.A.; Israeli diplomatist; b. 19 Nov. 1919; ed. Hebrew Univ. of Jerusalem.
Joined Ministry of Foreign Affairs, Jerusalem 49-50; Attaché, Rome Embassy 50-52; Ministry of Foreign Affairs, Jerusalem 53-54; Consul, Cyprus 54-56; First Sec. (Press) London Embassy 57-59; Head of Research Dept. and Spokesman, Ministry of Foreign Affairs 59-63; Minister, Israel Legation, Yugoslavia 63-65; Amb. to Philippines 65-67; Asst. Dir.-Gen. Ministry of Foreign Affairs, Jerusalem 69-71, Deputy Dir.-Gen. 72-73, Dir.-Gen. 73-76; Amb. to Netherlands 76-77, to U.K. 77-79, to Australia 79-.
Embassy of Israel, 6 Turrana Street, Yarralumla, A.C.T. 2600, Australia.

Kikhia, Mansur Rashid; Libyan diplomatist; b. 1 Dec. 1931, Benghazi; ed. Faculty of Law, Univ. of Cairo and Paris.
Joined Diplomatic Service 57; Asst. in Nationality and Consular Affairs Section, Ministry of Foreign Affairs 57, Head, Treaties and Int. Confs. Section 58-60, 62-65; Second Sec. for Consular and Cultural Affairs, Libyan Embassy to France 60-62; Chargé d'Affaires, France Jan.-Aug. 62, Algeria Feb.-Aug. 63; Consul-Gen., Geneva 65-67; mem. Del. of Libya to UN 61, 66-70, Chair. 70, 72, 75, 76,

Vice-Chair. 77-78, Rep. on Security Council 76-77; Under-Sec. Ministry of Unity and Foreign Affairs 69-72; Perm. Rep. to UN Feb.-July 72; Minister of Foreign Affairs July 72-73; private law practice, Tripoli 73-75; Perm. Rep. to UN Aug. 75-80, concurrently Amb. to Canada March 79-80; Vice-Pres. UN Gen. Assembly 78; Chair. Libyan Del. to 3rd UN Conf. on Law of the Sea 76-78, Preparatory Comm. for special session on disarmament 77-78, *ad hoc* Comm. on drafting of Int. Convention against taking of hostages 77; Chair. UN Security Council Sanctions Comm. 77, UN Advisory Cttee. on Int. Year for Disabled Persons 79; Vice-Chair. Del. of Libya to UN 77-79.
Foreign Affairs Secretariat, Tripoli, Libya.

Kırca, Ali Coşkun, LL.D.; Turkish diplomatist; b. 1927, Istanbul; ed. Galatasaray Lycée, Istanbul, Law School, Istanbul Univ.
With Ministry of Foreign Affairs, Third Sec., then Second Sec., NATO 50-56; Lecturer in Pol. Science, Ankara Univ. 56-61; mem. Constituent Assembly 61; mem. for Istanbul, Nat. Assembly 61-69; Minister, Ministry of Foreign Affairs 69; UN Office, Geneva 70; Perm. Rep. of Turkey to NATO 76-78, to UN 80-; Senior Adviser, Ministry of Foreign Affairs 78-80.
Permanent Mission of Turkey to the United Nations, 821 United Nations Plaza, 11th Floor, New York, N.Y. 10017, U.S.A.

Kirk, George Eden, M.A.; American (b. British) author; b. 1911; ed. Cambridge, and Schools of Archaeology Athens and Jerusalem.
Epigraphist with Colt expedition, Palestine 35-38; Staff Officer (Int.) at G.H.Q. Middle East Forces 40-45; Instructor, Middle East Centre for Arab studies 45-47; M.E. specialist Royal Inst. of International Affairs 47-52; Assoc. Prof. Int. Relations, American Univ. of Beirut 53-57; Lecturer, Harvard Univ. Center for Middle Eastern Studies 57-66; Prof. of History, Univ. of Mass. 66-79, Dir. of Graduate Studies in History 70-73.
Publs. *A Short History of the Middle East* 48 (definitive edn. 64), *The Middle East in the War* 52, *The Middle East, 1945-50* 55, *Contemporary Arab Politics* 61; contributed to: *The Military in the Middle East* (ed. Sydney N. Fisher) 63, *Forces of Change in the Middle East* (ed. Maurice M. Roumani) 71, *Propaganda and Communication in World History* (ed. Harold D. Lasswell *et al.*) 79.
32 Cosby Ave., Amherst, Mass. 01002, U.S.A.

Kishtmand, Sultan Ali; Afghan politician.
Minister of Planning April-August 78; arrested Aug. 78, death sentence commuted to 15 years' imprisonment Oct. 79, released after overthrow of Pres. Amin Dec. 79; mem. Politburo of Central Cttee. of People's Democratic Party of Afghanistan (PDPA), mem. Presidium Dec. 79-; Deputy Prime Minister Dec. 79-June 81, Minister of Planning Dec. 79-; Prime Minister June 81-; Pres. State Planning Cttee. June 81-.
Office of the Prime Minister, c/o Revolutionary Council, Da Khalkoo Koor, Kabul, Afghanistan.

Kisim, Marwan al-, PH.D.; Jordanian politician; b. 12 May, 1938, Amman; ed. Eastern Michigan, Columbia and Georgetown Univs., U.S.A.
Joined Ministry of Foreign Affairs 62; Consul-Gen., New York 64-65; Deputy Dir. of Protocol 66; Political Officer, Jordanian Embassy, Beirut 67-68, U.S.A. 68-72; Sec. to Crown Prince Hassan (*q.v.*) 72-75; Dir.-Gen. Royal Hashemite Court 75-76; Minister of State 76; Minister of Supply 77-79; Minister of State for Foreign Affairs 79-80, Minister of Foreign Affairs July 80-; Jordanian, Syrian, Mexican, Lebanese, Chinese and Italian decorations.
Ministry of Foreign Affairs, Amman, Jordan.

Kittani, Ismat T., B.ECON.; Iraqi United Nations official; b. 5 April 1929, Amadiya; ed. Knox Coll., Galesburg, Ill., Yale Univ.

High School teacher, Iraq; joined Foreign Ministry 52; Attaché, Cairo 54-57; mem. Iraqi mission to UN 57. Acting Perm. Rep. 58-59; mem. Gov. Board ILO 59; alt. mem. Exec. Board WHO 61; Perm. Rep. to European Office of UN 61-64; Chief, Specialized Agencies and Admin. Cttee. of Co-ordination Affairs, Dept. of Econ. and Social Affairs, UN Secr. 64; Sec. Econ. and Social Council 65-67; Principal Officer, later Dir. Exec. Office of Sec.-Gen. of UN 67-69; Deputy to Asst. Sec.-Gen. for Inter-Agency Affairs 69-70; Asst. Sec.-Gen. for Inter-Agency Affairs 71-73; Exec. Asst. to UN Sec.-Gen. 73-75; Dir.-Gen. Dept. of Int. Orgs. and Confs., Ministry of Foreign Affairs 75-; fmr. del. of Iraq to various int. comms. and confs.; Rapporteur-Gen. 5th Non-Aligned Summit Conf., Sri Lanka 76, Chair. Pol. Cttee. 6th Non-Aligned Summit Conf., Cuba 79; Under Sec. Min. of Foreign Affairs 80-; Pres. Second Review Conf. Treaty on the Non-Proliferation of Nuclear Weapons, Geneva 80; Pres. UN Gen. Assembly 81-82.
Ministry of Foreign Affairs, Karradat Mariam, Baghdad, Iraq.

Klibi, Chédli, D.LITT.; Tunisian politician and international official; b. 6 Sept. 1925, Tunis; ed. Sadiki Coll., Univ. of Tunis, Sorbonne, Paris.
Journalist 51-57, working successively for *As Sabah, An Nadwa, Sawt el Amal;* Prof. of Arabic, Lycée Carnot 57-58; Lecturer, Inst. des Hautes Etudes, Univ. of Tunis; Gen. Man. Tunisian Radio and Television 58-61; Sec. of State for Information and Cultural Affairs 61-64, for Cultural Affairs Nov. 64, for Guidance and Cultural Affairs 66-69; mem. Central Cttee., Parti Socialiste Destourien (PSD) Jan. 68-; Mayor of Carthage 63-; Minister of Cultural Affairs and Information 69-73; Head of Departmental Staff of Pres. 74-76; Minister of Cultural Affairs 76-78, of Information Sept. 78; mem. Political Bureau PSD June 79-; Sec.-Gen. of League of Arab States June 79-; mem. Arab Language Acad., Cairo 70; Grand Cordon Order of the Repub.; Grand Cordon, Order of Independence.
Publs. *The Arabs facing the Palestinian Problem, On Islam and Modernity, Culture is a Challenge of Civilisation,* and numerous articles.
Secretariat General, League of Arab States, Avenue Khéreddine Pasha, Tunis, Tunisia.

Koç, Vehbi; Turkish businessman; b. 1901.
Opened first grocery shop in Ankara 17; formed Koç Trading Corpn. 37, General Elektrik Türk 49, and many other companies; assoc. with numerous major firms in U.S.A. and Europe; Chair. Koç Holding Corpn. 64-; manufactured Turkey's first passenger car (Anadol) 66, second (Murat, under licence from Fiat) 71; Founded Vehbi Koç Foundation 69, Turkish Educ. Foundation 69; Order of Merit (Fed. Repub. of Germany) 74.
Publ. *My Life Story* (in Turkish) 73.
Koç Holding Corporation, Fındıklı, Ankara, Turkey.

Koçman, Ali, M.SC.; Turkish business executive; b. 1943, Turkey; ed. lycée and Acad. of Economic and Commercial Sciences, Istanbul.
Spent two years in the shipping industry in U.K. and U.S.A.; Gen. Man. Koç shipping, automotive, food, import and export ccs.; Pres. CONTURCON Int. Shipping Conf. 77-; Turkish del. to numerous int. confs. and Head economic dels. to U.S.A., U.K. and Japan 80-; Pres. Turkish Businessmen's and Industrialists' Asscn. (TUSIAD) Nov. 80-; mem. Board of Dirs. Turkish Employee Confed.
Koç Holding Corporation, Fındıklı, Ankara, Turkey.

Kollek, Theodore (Teddy); Israeli politician; b. 1911; ed. Vienna.
Went to Palestine 34; mem. Kibbutz Ein-Gev. 37; with Zionist Youth groups in Europe and U.K. 38-40; Political Dept., Jewish Agency 42-47; Liaison with Jewish Under-

ground in Europe 42-45; mem. Haganah mission to U.S.A. 47-48; Minister Plenipotentiary, Washington 51-52; Dir.-Gen. Prime Minister's Office, including Dept. for Applied Civilian Scientific Research, Bureau of Statistics, Govt. Press and Information Office, the devt. of broadcasting services, est. Israel Govt. Tourist Office, 52-64; Chair. Govt. Tourist Corpn. 56-65; Chair. Israel 10th Anniversary Celebrations; Mayor of Jerusalem 65-; Head of Nuclear Desalination of Water Project 64-66; Chair. Board of Governors, Israel Museum 65-; Hon. doctorate (Hebrew Univ., Jerusalem) 77; Rothschild Medal and Bublick Prize 75.
Publs. (with Moshe Pearlman) *Jerusalem: Sacred City of Mankind* 68, *Pilgrims to the Holy Land* 70, (with Amos Kollek) *For Jerusalem* (autobiography), and numerous articles.
Municipality of Jerusalem, Jerusalem; Home: 6 Rashba Street, Jerusalem, Israel.

Konuk, Nejat; Cypriot lawyer, politician and writer; b. 1928, Nicosia; ed. Turkish Lycée, Cyprus and Law Faculty of Ankara Univ.
Began career as Legal Adviser in Turkish Civil Service; Sec.-Gen. and Acting Dir.-Gen. of Turkish Communal Chamber; Under-Sec. to Rauf Denktash (*q.v.*, Deputy Pres. of Turkish Cypriot Admin.) 68-69; Minister of Justice and Internal Affairs, Turkish Cypriot Admin. 69-75; mem. for Nicosia, Turkish Cypriot Legislative Assembly 70-; Minister of Interior, Turkish Cypriot Admin. 73-74; founder mem. Nat. Unity Party 75, Party Leader 76-78; Prime Minister "Turkish Federated State of Cyprus" July 76-Feb. 78; Leader, Democratic People's Party (DPP) 79-82; Pres. Legislative Assembly July-Dec. 81, March 82-; resigned from DPP Feb. 82.
Publs. essays on literature, various papers on Cyprus, political articles 53-77.
Kumsal, Lefkoşa (Nicosia), Mersin 10, Turkey.

Kooli, Mongi, L.EN.D.; Tunisian politician; b. 15 March 1930, Ksar Hellal; ed. Sadiki Coll., Univ. of Paris.
Head, Dept. for Economic and Social Improvement, Parti Socialiste Destourien (PSD) 60-64, Asst. Dir. for External Relations, PSD; Governor of Jendouba, then of Bizerte 64-69; Amb. to Spain 69-74; Sec. of State to Minister of Foreign Affairs 74-76; Minister for Public Health 76-77; Minister responsible to the Prime Minister April 80-; mem. Political Bureau PSD 76-, Head April 80-; Deputy for Monastir 74-79; Vice-Pres. Town Council of Tunis 73-; Grand Cordon, Ordre de l'Indépendance, Grand Officier, Ordre de la République.
Office of the Head of the Political Bureau, Parti Socialiste Destourien, boulevard 9 avril 1938, Tunis, Tunisia.

Korutürk, Admiral Fahri S.; Turkish naval officer and fmr. Head of State; b. 12 Aug. 1903, Istanbul; ed. Naval Acad. and Naval War Coll.
Joined Navy 20; Naval Attaché, Berlin 35, Rome 36, Berlin and Stockholm 42-43; Naval Adviser to Turkish del., Montreux Conf.; Commdr. Naval War Acad. 45-46; Commdr. Submarine Fleet 53; Chief of Intelligence, General Staff, Armed Forces 54; Commdr. of Sea-going Fleet 55-56; C.-in-C. Straits Area 56-57, Admiral 57; C.-in-C. of Navy and Commdr. of Allied Forces, Black Sea 57-60; Amb. to U.S.S.R. 60-64; mem. Defence Cttee. of the Senate 68; Head Presidential Senate Group 71-73; Pres. of Turkey 73-80; Senator for life April 80-.
Cumhuriyet Senatosu, Türkiye Büyüt Millet Meclisi, Ankara, Turkey.

Kotaite, Assad, LL.D.; Lebanese lawyer and aviation official; b. 6 Nov. 1924; ed. French Univ. of Beirut, Univ. of Paris, Inst. des Hautes Etudes Internationales, Paris and Acad. of Int. Law, The Hague.
Practising barrister 48-49; Head, Legal Services, Int. Agreements and External Relations, Dir. of Civil Aviation,

Ministry of Public Works and Transport 53-56; Rep. to Int. Civil Aviation Org. (ICAO) 56-70, Sec.-Gen. 70-76, Pres. ICAO Council Aug. 76-; mem. UN Transport and Communications Comm. 57-79; Chair. 59; Chair. Air Transport Cttee., ICAO 59-62, 65-68; Medal Al Mérito and Diploma of Ibero-American Inst. of Aeronautical and Space Law; Golden Medal of Merit (Lebanon), Award of Air Law Soc. (Brazil), Gran Cruz del Mérito Aeronáutico (Spain), Orden Francisco de Miranda (Venezuela), Comendador y Gran Oficial del Mérito Aeronáutico (Brazil), Gran Cruz del Mérito Aeronáutico (Colombia).
International Civil Aviation Organization, 1000 Sherbrooke Street West, Montreal, P.Q. H3A 2R2, Canada.

Kudsi, Nazem el, PH.D.; Syrian former Head of State; b. 1906; ed. American Coll., Beirut, Damascus Univ. and Univ. of Geneva.
Barrister in Aleppo 30; Dep. for Aleppo 36, 47, 55; Minister Plenipotentiary, Washington 44-45; Prime Minister and Minister for Foreign Affairs 50; Pres. Council of Ministers 54-57; Leader, Populist Party; held no political office during United Arab Republic régime 58-61; Pres. of the Syrian Arab Republic 61-63, retired 63.
Aleppo, Syria.

Kuwait, H.H. The Ruler of (see Sabah, Amir Jaber al-Ahmed al-Jaber al-).

Kyprianou, Spyros; Cypriot politician; b. 28 Oct. 1932, Limassol; ed. City of London Coll. and Gray's Inn.
Founded Nat. Union of Cypriot Students in U.K. (EFEKA), Pres. 52-54; Sec. in London to Archbishop Makarios 52-54, London Sec. of Ethnarchy of Cyprus 54-56, 57-59; also journalist 52-56; rep. of Ethnarchy of Cyprus, New York 56-57; mem. Cttee. Nat. Democratic Front for Reconstruction (EDMA, later Patriotic Front) 59; Greek Cypriot rep. at Athens conf. for drafting of agreement on the application of the Tripartite Alliance (Cyprus-Greece-Turkey); Minister of Justice 16-22 Aug. 60, of Foreign Affairs 60-72; leader of del. to UN Gen. Assembly 64-71, 74; Pres. Cttee. of Foreign Mins. of Council of Europe April-Dec. 67; law practice 72-76; Pres. House of Reps. 76-77; President of Cyprus Aug. 77-; Grand Cross, Order of George I (Greece) 62, Grand Cross (Fed. Repub. of Germany) 62, Grand Star of the Repub. (United Arab Repub. now, Egypt) 61, Grand Cross, Order of Boyaca (Colombia) 66, Grand Cross, Order of Merit (Chile) 66, Ecclesiastical decoration, Order of St. Aikaterini of Sinai 66, Grand Silver Cross (Austria) 73, Star of Socialist Republic of Romania 79, Grand Cross of the Holy Sepulchre 81 and decorations from Syria, Czechoslovakia, German Democratic Republic, Yugoslavia, Nepal, Bulgaria and Hungary.
Presidential Palace, Nicosia, Cyprus.

L

Labidi, Abdelwahab; Tunisian financier; b. 22 April 1929, Kef; ed. Coll. Sidiki, Tunis, Inst. des Hautes Etudes, Tunis, Faculty of Law, Univ. of Paris.
Former Gen. Man. Banque de Tunisie; Insp.-Gen. Banque Nat. Agricole de Tunisie; Man. Soc. Tunisienne de Banque; Man. Dir. Nat. Devt. Bank of Niger 64-69; Vice-Pres. African Devt. Bank 69-70, Pres. 70-76; Pres. African Devt. Fund 73-76; Chair. Sifida (Geneva) 73-77; Adviser to Scandinavian Bank Ltd. (London) 77-; mem. Exec. Cttee. Club de Dakar, Governing Council of Soc. for Int. Devt.
62 bis rue de Latour, 75016 Paris, France.

Ladgham, Bahi; Tunisian politician; b. 10 Jan. 1913, Tunis.
Joined Dept. of Interior 33, subsequently moved to Finance Dept.; formed Bureau tunisien de la libération

nationale, New York 50; mem. Political Bureau Parti Socialiste Destourien (PSD) (Néo-Destour Party -64) 55-71; Sec. of State for the Presidency and Sec. of State for Defence 56-69; Prime Minister of Tunisia 69-70; Chair. Arab Cttee. supervising the ceasefire between Jordanian Govt. and the Palestinian guerrillas in Jordan 70-71; fmr. personal rep. of Pres. Bourguiba; fmr. Sec.-Gen. Parti Socialiste Destourien.
Parti Socialiste Destourien, boulevard 9 avril 1938, Tunis, Tunisia.

Lalla Aicha, H.R.H. Princess; Moroccan diplomatist; b. 1930.
Eldest daughter of late King Mohammed V; Ambassador to United Kingdom 65-69, to Italy 69-71; Pres. Moroccan Red Crescent; Grand Cordon of Order of the Throne.
c/o Ministry of Foreign Affairs, Rabat, Morocco.

Lamrani, Mohammed Karim (see Karim-Lamrani, Mohammed).

Landau, Moshe, LL.B.; Israeli judge; b. 1912, Danzig, Germany (now Gdańsk, Poland); ed. London Univ.
Arrived in Palestine 33; called to Palestine Bar 37, Magistrate of Haifa 40, District Court Judge, Haifa 48, Justice Supreme Court, Jerusalem 53-, Deputy Pres. 76-80, Pres. 80-.
The Supreme Court, Jerusalem, Israel.

Laraki, Moulay Ahmed, M.D.; Moroccan physician and diplomatist; b. 15 Oct. 1931, Casablanca; ed. Univ. of Paris.
With Ministry of Foreign Affairs 56-57; Perm. Rep. to UN 57-58; Head of Hospital Services, Casablanca 56-61; Ambassador to Spain 61-65, to U.S.A., concurrently accred. to Mexico, Canada and Venezuela 65-67; Minister of Foreign Affairs 67-69; Prime Minister 69-71; Minister of State for Foreign Affairs 74-77.
Ministry of Foreign Affairs, Rabat, Morocco.

Lasram, Abdelaziz, L. EN D.; Tunisian politician; b. 25 March 1928, Tunis; ed. Univ. of Paris, Ecole Nat. d'Administration de Paris.
Embassy Sec. to Secretariat for Foreign Affairs 57-59; Head of Dept. of Planning 59-60; Councillor, Tunisian Embassy, Moscow 60-61; Deputy Dir. and Head Commerce Dept., Secretariat of Planning and Finance 61-65; Minister, Tunisian Embassy, Paris 65-70; Dir. of Int. Co-operation, Ministry of Foreign Affairs 70-71, Sec.-Gen. 71; Pres. and Dir.-Gen. Banque Nat. de Tunisie 72-74; Minister of Nat. Economy 74-77, April 80-; Dir.-Gen. Société d'Assurances Maghrebia 77-80; mem. Parti Socialiste Destourien; Grand Cordon, Ordre de la République.
Ministry of National Economy, Tunis, Tunisia.

Levinson, Jacob; Israeli banker; b. 1932; ed. Hebrew Univ., Jerusalem.
Member Kibbutz Rosh Hanikra 49-61; fmr. Sec. Hatnu'ah Hame'uhedet (United Youth Movement); fmr. Head Econ. Dept., Hevrat Ovdim (Gen. Co-operative Asscn. of Labour); now Chair. Board of Dirs., Bank Hapoalim B.M.; mem. Board of Man., Hevrat Ovdim; mem. Advisory Board, Bank of Israel.
Publs. numerous articles in econ. and general books and periodicals.
Bank Hapoalim B.M., 50 Rothschild Boulevard, Tel-Aviv, Israel.

Levy, David; Israeli politician; b. 1938, Morocco.
Emigrated to Israel 57; construction worker; joined Histadrut; elected to Knesset, representing Herut (Freedom) group of Gahal 69- (subsequently of Likud Bloc); Likud cand. for Sec.-Gen. of Histadrut 77, 81; now Chair. Likud group in Histadrut; Minister of Immigrant Absorption June 77-Jan. 78, of Construction and Housing Jan. 78-; Deputy Prime Minister Aug. 81-.
Ministry of Construction and Housing, Jerusalem, Israel.

Lewis, Bernard, B.A., PH.D., F.B.A., F.R.HIST.S.; British university professor; b. 31 May 1916; ed. Univs. of London and Paris.
Lecturer in Islamic History, School of Oriental Studies, Univ. of London 38; served R.A.C. and Intelligence Corps 40-41; attached to Foreign Office 41-45; Prof. of History of the Near and Middle East, Univ. of London 49-74; Cleveland E. Dodge Prof. of Near Eastern Studies, Princeton Univ. 74-, Long-term mem. School of Social Science, Inst. for Advanced Study 74-; Visiting Prof. of History, Univ. of California at Los Angeles 55-56, Columbia Univ. 60, Indiana Univ. 63, Princeton Univ. 64, Inst. for Advanced Study 69; mem. American Philosophical Soc.; Corresp. Fellow Inst. d'Egypte, Cairo; hon. mem. Turkish Historical Soc.
Publs. *The Origins of Isma'ilism* 40, *Turkey Today* 40, *British Contributions to Arabic Studies* 41, *Handbook of Diplomatic and Political Arabic* 47, *Land of Enchanters* (Editor) 48, *The Arabs in History* 50 (revised edns. 58, 64, 66, 70), *Notes and Documents from the Turkish Archives* 52, *The Kingly Crown* 61, *The Emergence of Modern Turkey* 61 (revised edn. 68), *Historians of the Middle East* (ed. with P. M. Holt) 62, 64, *Istanbul and the Civilization of the Ottoman Empire* 63, 68, *The Middle East and the West* 64, 68, *The Assassins* 67, *Race and Colour in Islam* 71, Co-editor *Encyclopaedia of Islam* 56-, *Cambridge History of Islam* 70, *Islam in History: Ideas, Men and Events in the Middle East* 73; *Islam from the Prophet Muhammad to the Capture of Constantinople* (2 vols.) 74, *History Remembered, Recovered, Invented* 75, *The World of Islam* (U.K. title, published in U.S.A. as *Islam and the Arab World*) (Editor) 76, *Population and Revenue in the Towns of Palestine in the Sixteenth Century* (with A. Cohen) 78, *The Muslim Discovery of Europe* 82.
110 Jones Hall, Princeton University, Princeton, N.J. 08540, U.S.A.

Lewis, Samuel Winfield, B.A.; American diplomatist; b. 1 Oct. 1930, Houston; ed. Yale and Johns Hopkins Univs.
Executive Asst., American Trucking Asscn., Washington 53-54; entered Foreign Service 54; with Consulate, Naples 54-55; Consul, Florence 55-59; Officer-in-Charge Italian Affairs, Dept. of State 59-61; Special Asst. to Under-Sec. of State 61-63; Dep. Asst. Dir. U.S. AID Mission to Brazil 64-66; Deputy Dir. Office for Brazil Affairs, Dept. of State 67-68; senior staff mem. for Latin American Affairs, Nat. Security Council, White House 68-69; Special Asst. for Policy Planning, Bureau of Inter-American Affairs 69, to Dir. Gen. Foreign Service 69-71; Deputy Chief of Mission and Counsellor, U.S. Embassy, Kabul 71-74; Deputy Dir. Policy Planning Staff, Dept. of State 74-75, Asst. Sec. of State for Int. Organization 75-77; Amb. to Israel 77-; mem. Council on Foreign Relations; Visiting Fellow, Princeton Univ. 63-64; William A. Jump Award 67; Meritorious Honor Award (Dept. of State, AID) 67; Distinguished Honor Award 77.
Embassy of the United States, 71 Rehov Hayarkon, Tel-Aviv, Israel.

Linowitz, Sol Myron, LL.D., J.D.; American lawyer and diplomatist; b. 7 Dec. 1913, Trenton, N.J.; ed. Hamilton Coll., Cornell Univ.
Admitted to New York Bar 38; partner in law firm 46-; Chair. Board Xerox Corpn. 58-66, Xerox Int. 66; U.S. Rep. to Org. of American States 66-69; Co-negotiator Panama Canal Treaties 77; Chair. Presidential Comm. on World Hunger 79; Amb. at Large for Middle East Negotiations 79-81.
Publ. *This Troubled Urban World.*
1 Farragut Square S., Washington, D.C. 20006; Home: 2325 Wyoming Avenue N.W., Washington, D.C. 20008, U.S.A.

Lloyd, Seton, C.B.E., M.A., F.B.A., F.S.A., A.R.I.B.A.; British archaeologist; b. 30 May 1902; ed. Uppingham and Architectural Asscn.
Assistant to Sir Edwin Lutyens, P.R.A. 27-28; excavated for Egypt Exploration Society, Egypt 29-30, for Oriental Inst., Univ. of Chicago in Iraq 30-37, for Univ. of Liverpool in Turkey 37-39; Technical Adviser, Govt. of Iraq, Directorate-Gen. of Antiquities 39-49; Dir. British Inst. of Archaeology in Ankara 49-61, Hon. Sec. 64-74, Pres. 74-; Prof. of Western Asiatic Archaeology, Univ. of London 62-69, Emer. Prof. 69-; Pres. British School of Archaeology in Iraq 78-; Hon. M.A. (Edinburgh); Lawrence of Arabia Medal (Royal Soc. for Asian Affairs) 71, Gertrude Bell Memorial Medal (British School of Archaeology in Iraq) 78; Certificate of Merit, Turkey 73.
Publs. *Mesopotamia* 34, *Sennacherib's Aqueduct at Jerwan* 35, *The Gimilsin Temple* 40, *Presargonid Temples* 42, *Ruined Cities of Iraq* 42, *Twin Rivers* 43, *Foundations in the Dust* 48, *Early Anatolia* 56, *Alanya-Ala'iyya* 58, *Art of the Ancient Near East, Beycesultan* 62, *Mounds of the Near East* 63, *Highland Peoples of Early Anatolia* 67, *The Archaeology of Mesopotamia* 78.
Woolstone Lodge, Faringdon, Oxon., England.

Logali, Hilary Nyigilo Paul; Sudanese politician; b. 1931, Juba, Equatoria Province; ed. Khartoum Univ., Yale Univ.
Official with Ministry of Finance and Econs. 57-64; Minister of Works and Natural Resources 65, of Communications 65; Sec.-Gen. Southern Front Party 65-67, Vice-Pres. of Party 67-69; Minister of Labour and Co-operation 67-69; political detention without trial 69-70; Man. Dir. Bata Nationalized Corpn. 70-71, Watania Distillery Corpn. 71; Commr. for Equatoria Province with Ministerial rank 71-72; Minister of Finance and Econ. Planning in Southern Regional Govt., Juba 72-75; Speaker, Regional People's Assembly 75-78; mem. Cen. Cttee. and Political Bureau of Sudanese Socialist Union (SSU) 72-77; mem. for Juba Territorial Constituency in People's Regional Assembly 73-78; Asst. Sec.-Gen. SSU 76-, Head of Southern Regional Secretariat 76-77, mem. Exec. Bureau, SSU Cen. Cttee. 77-82; Regional Minister of Admin. and Police, High Exec. Council for Southern Region 80-81; Chair. Univ. of Juba; Order of the Two Niles, First Class; Order of the Constitution; Order of the Repub., First Class.
Executive Bureau of the Sudanese Socialist Union, P.O. Box 1850, Khartoum, Sudan.

Loutfy, Aly, PH.D.; Egyptian professor of economics and government minister; b. 6 Oct. 1935, Cairo; ed. Ain Shams and Louzan Univs.
Joined staff, Faculty of Commerce Ain Shams Univ. 57, latterly Prof. and Chair. Dept. of Econs.; Prof. High Inst. of Co-operative and Admin. Studies; Part-time Prof. Inst. of Arab Research and Studies, Cairo; mem. Bd. of Dirs. Bank of Alexandria 77-78, Legislation, Political Science and Econ. Asscn. 77, Delta Sugar Co. 78; Minister of Finance Oct. 79-May 80; Head, Board of Dirs. Financial and Economic Consultative Center, Cairo 81; Ideal Prof. Award, Egyptian Univs. 74, Gold Mercury Int. Award 79.
Publs. *Economic Evolution, Economic Development, Economic Planning, Studies in Mathematical Economy and Econometrics, Financing Problems in Under-Developed Countries, Industrialization Problems in Under-Developed Countries;* 25 research papers in economics in Arabic, French and English.
128 El-Tahrir Street, Dokki, Giza, Egypt.

Lozi, Ahmad Abdel Kareem Al-; Jordanian politician; b. 1925, Jubeiha, nr. Amman; ed. Teachers' Training Coll., Baghdad, Iraq.
Teacher, 50-53; Asst. to Chief of Royal Protocol 53-56; Head of Ceremonies, Ministry of Foreign Affairs 57; mem. Parl. 61-62, 62-63; Asst. to Chief of Royal Court

63-64; Minister of State, Prime Minister's Office 64-65; mem. Senate 65; Minister of the Interior for Municipal and Rural Affairs 67; mem. Senate 67; Minister of Finance 70-71; Prime Minister 71-73; Pres. Nat. Consultative Council 78-80; Chief of Royal Hashemite Court 79-80; various Jordanian and foreign decorations.
National Consultative Council, Amman, Jordan.

Lucas, Hon. Ivor Thomas Mark, C.M.G., M.A.; British diplomatist; b. 25 July 1927, Southampton; ed. St. Edward's School and Trinity Coll., Oxford.
Royal Artillery 45-48; joined diplomatic service 51; Head Middle East Dept., Foreign and Commonwealth Office 75-79; Amb. to Oman 79-81, to Syria Jan. 82-.
British Embassy, rue Muhammad Kurd Ali, Malki, Damascus, Syria.

M

Maarouf, Taha Muhyiddin (*see* Maruf, Taha Muhyiddin).

Mabrouk, Ezzidin Al-, LL.B., LL.M.; Libyan politician; b. 28 May 1932; ed. Cairo Univ. and Univ. Coll., London.
Public Prosecutor, Tripoli 56; subsequently Judge, Summary Court, Tripoli, Pres. Tripoli Court and Counsellor of Supreme Appeal Court; Senior Legal Adviser, Org. of Petroleum Exporting Countries (OPEC); Minister of Petroleum, Libya 70-77; Sec. for Petroleum, Gen. Peoples' Cttee. 77-80; Chair. OAPEC 79.
c/o Office of the Secretary for Petroleum, P.O. Box 256, Tripoli, Libya.

Macki, Ahmed al-Nabi; Omani diplomatist; b. 17 Dec. 1939, Muscat; ed. Cairo and Paris.
Member, Oman Del. to UNESCO 69-70; Dir. of Offices of Prime Minister and Minister of Foreign Affairs 70-71; First Perm. Rep. of Oman to UN 71-72; Under-Sec. Ministry of Foreign Affairs 72-73; Perm. Rep. to UN 73-75, Amb. to U.S.A. 73-77, Non-Resident Amb. to Canada 74-77, to Argentina 75-77; Amb. to France Oct. 77-, Non-Resident Amb. to Belgium Nov. 78-, to Spain Dec. 78-; Perm. Del. to UNESCO Nov. 77-; Head of Mission to EEC March 80-.
Ambassade d'Oman, 67 avenue Kléber, 75116 Paris, France.

Maghour, Kamal Hassan; Libyan diplomatist and politician; ed. Cairo Univ. Law School.
Legal Adviser to the oil industry in Libya 70; has represented Libya at Int. Court of Justice, The Hague; Amb. to UN 72-76, to France 76-78, to People's Repub. of China 78-81; Head Petroleum Secretariat March 82-.
Petroleum Secretariat, P.O. Box 256, Tripoli, Libya.

Maguid, Yahya Abdel, C.ENG., A.M.I.C.E.; Sudanese politician; b. 7 Oct. 1925, Omdurman; ed. Gordon Memorial Coll. and Imperial Coll., London.
Received practical training in construction of irrigation projects with British companies specializing in this field; held various posts in Ministry of Irrigation, rising to Under-Sec. Sept. 69; part-time lecturer, Univ. of Khartoum; Minister of Irrigation and Hydro-electric Power 71; Minister of State for Irrigation, Agriculture, Food and Natural Resources 71-74; Minister of Irrigation and Hydro-electric Power 75-80; Sec.-Gen. UN Water Conf. June 76-March 77; mem. Int. Comm. for Hydraulic Law.
Ministry of Irrigation and Hydro-electric Power, P.O. Box 878, Khartoum, Sudan.

Mahdi, Dr. Sadiq al- (since 1978 known as **Sadiq Abdul Rahman**); Sudanese politician (great-grandson of Imam Abdul Rahman al-Mahdi); b. 1936; ed. Comboni Coll., and St. John's Coll., Khartoum and Oxford Univ.
Leader, Umma Mahdist Party 61 and leader United Nat. Front; Deputy to Constituent Assembly 66; Prime Minister

66-67; arrested on a charge of high treason 69; under house arrest in Egypt 70-71; returned to Sudan and arrested Dec. 71; released May 73, left Sudan 73, formed a National Front of opposition forces; organized an abortive coup with Sherif al-Hindi 76, sentenced to death *in absentia* 76; pardoned and returned to Sudan Sept. 77; mem. Cen. Cttee. Sudanese Socialist Union March-Oct. 78, Politburo Aug.-Oct. 78; led a mediation mission in U.S. hostages in Iran crisis Jan. 80.
Publ. *Problems of the South Sudan.*
Ministry of Information and Culture, P.O. Box 291, Khartoum, Sudan.

Mahdi al Tajir, Mohamed; United Arab Emirates administrator; b. 26 Dec. 1931, Bahrain; ed. Bahrain Govt. School and Preston Grammar School, Lancs., England.
Department of Port and Customs, Govt. of Bahrain, Dir. 55-63; Dir. Dept. of His Highness the Ruler's Affairs and Petroleum Affairs March 63-; Dir. Nat. Bank of Dubai Ltd. 63-; Dir. Dubai Petroleum Co. April 63-; Dir. Dubai Nat. Air Travel Agency Jan. 66-; Dir. Qatar-Dubai Currency Board Oct. 65-73, United Arab Emirates Currency Board 73; Chair. South Eastern Dubai Drilling Co. April 68-; Amb. of the United Arab Emirates to U.K. 72-, also accred. to France 72-77; Dir. Dubai Dry Dock Co. 73-; Hon. Citizen of State of Texas, U.S.A. 63.
Department of H.H. The Ruler's Affairs and Petroleum Affairs, P.O. Box 207, Dubai; and Embassy of the United Arab Emirates, 30 Prince's Gate, London, S.W.7, England.

Mahfuz, Nagib; Egyptian author; b. 11 Dec. 1911, Cairo; ed. Univ. of Cairo.
Civil servant 34-; successively with Univ. of Cairo, Ministry of Waqfs, Dept. of Arts and Censorship Board; fmr. Dir.-Gen., now Adviser, Cinema Org. of Egypt; State Prize for 1st vol. *Bain al-Kasrain* 57.
Publs. novels: *Khan al Khalili* 46, *Midaq Alley* 47, *The Castle of Desire* (Vol. I) 56, *Between the Two Castles* (Vol. II) 57, *The Sugar Bowl* (Vol. III) 57 (trilogy *Bain al-Kasrain*), *Children of Our Alley* 59, The Thief and the Dogs 61, *Quails in Autumn* 62, *The Road* 64, *The Beggar* 65, *Gossip by the Nile* 66, *Miramar* 67; short story collections: *The Whisper of Madness* 38, *God's World* 63, *At the Sign of the Black Cat* 69, *Under the Umbrella* 69, *A Story Without Beginning or End* 71; *Mirrors* (contemporary history) 72.
c/o Cinema Organization, TV Building, Maspero Street, Cairo, Egypt.

Mahgoub, Mohammed Ahmed; Sudanese lawyer and politician; b. 1908; ed. Gordon Coll. and Khartoum School of Law.
Qualified as an architect and lawyer; practising lawyer; mem. Legislative Assembly 48-54; accompanied Umma Party Del. to Lake Success 47; mem. Constitution Amendment Comm.; non-party candidate in Gen. Election 54; Leader of the Opposition 54-56; Minister of Foreign Affairs 56-58; practising solicitor 58-64; Minister of Foreign Affairs 64-Feb. 65; Prime Minister 65-66; Prime Minister and Minister of Foreign Affairs 67-68; Prime Minister and Minister of Defence 68-69.
Publs. *Democracy on Trial*, and several vols. of poetry (in Arabic).
60c Prince's Gate, Exhibition Road, London, S.W.7, England.

Mahroug, Smail; Algerian economist; b. 21 Oct. 1926, Bougaa; ed. Univ. of Paris.
In Morocco 53-62, active in Front de Libération Nationale (FLN), also Dir. of Planning, Moroccan Govt.; returned to Algeria, Chef de Cabinet of Head of Econ. Affairs, Provisional Govt. 62; Econ. Counsellor to Pres. 63-70; Dir.-Gen. Caisse Algérienne de Développement 63-65; Dir.-Gen. Ministry of Finance 65-66; Minister of Finance 70-Feb. 76;

Chair. Union Méditerranéenne de Banques 76-; Chair. Group of 24, IMF 74.
Union Méditerranéenne de Banques, 50 rue de Lisbonne, 75008 Paris, France.

Makki, Mohammed Hassan, D.ECON.; Yemeni politician and diplomatist; b. 22 Dec. 1933; ed. Univs. of Bologna and Rome.
Adviser, Ministry of Econ. 60-62, Deputy Minister 62, Minister 63-64; Chair. Yemen Bank for Reconstruction and Devt. 62-63; Minister of Foreign Affairs 64, 66, 67-68, of Communications 65; Adviser to the Prime Minister 65-66; Amb. to Italy 68-70, to Fed. Repub. of Germany 70-72; Deputy Prime Minister 72-74, Prime Minister March-June 74; Deputy Prime Minister for Econ. Affairs June-Dec. 74, Oct. 80-; Perm. Rep. to UN 74-76, Amb. to U.S.A. and Canada 75-76.
Ministry of Foreign Affairs, Sana'a, Yemen Arab Republic.

Maktum, H.H. Sheikh Rashid bin Said al-; Ruler of Dubai; b. 1914; ed. privately.
Succeeded his father, Said bin Maktum, as 4th Sheikh 58; Vice-Pres. United Arab Emirates (UAE) Dec. 71-; Prime Minister May 79-.
Royal Palace, Dubai, United Arab Emirates.

Malek, Reda; Algerian diplomatist; b. 1931; ed. Univs. of Algiers and Paris.
Director of weekly *El Moudjahid*, Tunis 57-61; mem. F.L.N. Del. to Evian talks 61; Amb. to Yugoslavia 63-65, to France 65-70, to U.S.S.R. 70-77; Minister of Information and Culture 77-79. Amb. to U.S.A. 79-
Embassy of Algeria, 2118 Kalorama Road, N.W., Washington, D.C. 20008, U.S.A.

Malik, Charles Habib, M.A., PH.D.; Lebanese philosopher, educationist and diplomatist; b. 1906, Bterram, Al-Koura; ed. American Univ. of Beirut, and Harvard and Freiburg Univs.
Instructor, Maths. and Physics, American Univ., Beirut 27-29; with *Al Hilal* Publ. House, Cairo 29-30; with Rockefeller Found. Exped., Cairo 30-32; Asst. in Philosophy, Harvard 36-37; Instructor in Philosophy, American Univ., Beirut 37-39; Adjunct-Prof. 39-43, Assoc. Prof. 43-45, Head of Dept. 39-45, on leave 45-55, Dean of Graduate Studies and Prof. of Philosophy 55-60, Distinguished Prof. of Philosophy 62-76, Emer. Prof. 76-; E. K. Hall Visiting Prof., Dartmouth Coll. 60; Visiting Prof. Harvard Summer School 60; University Prof. American Univ., Washington 61-62; Minister of Lebanon to U.S.A. 45-53, to Cuba 46-55; Minister designate to Venezuela 47-48; Amb. to U.S.A. 53-55; Lebanese del. UN Conf. and Signatory UN Charter 45; mem. and Chair. Lebanese del. to UN 45-58; Pres. 13th Gen. Assembly UN 58-59; del. to Bandung Conf. 55; Minister for Foreign Affairs 56-58, for Nat. Education and Fine Arts 56-57; mem. of Parl. 57-60; Pres. Economic and Social Council 48; Chair. Human Rights Comm. 51, 52; Chair. Lebanese del. for Peace Treaty with Japan 51; Pres. Security Council 53, 54; Grand First Magistrate of the Holy Orthodox Church; Dir. Woodrow Wilson Foundation 61-63; Pres. World Council of Christian Educ. 67-71; Vice-Pres. United Bible Societies 66-72; Jacques Maritain Dist. Prof. of Moral and Political Philosophy, Catholic Univ., Washington 81-; Pascal Lecturer Waterloo Univ., Canada 81; Fellow, Inst. for Advanced Religious Studies at the Univ. of Notre Dame, Indiana 69; Hon. Pres. World Lebanese Cultural Union; Hon. Life mem. American Bible Soc.; mem. Société européenne de Culture; Fellow, American Asscn. for Advancement of Science, American Geog. Soc.; mem. American Philos. Asscn., American Philos. Soc., American Acad. of Arts and Sciences, Acad. of Human Rights, etc.; founding mem. Lebanese Acad.; numerous awards and decorations.
Publs. *War and Peace* 50, *Problems of Asia* 51, *Problem of Coexistence* 55, *Christ and Crisis* 62, *Man in the Struggle*

for Peace 63, *God and Man in Contemporary Christian Thought* 71, *God and Man in Contemporary Islamic Thought* 72, *The Wonder of Being* 73, *Almuqaddimah* 77; numerous other published works and articles.
American University, Beirut, Lebanon; and Harvard Club, 27 West 44th Street, New York, U.S.A.

Malikyar, Abdullah; Afghan diplomatist; b. 1909; ed. Isteklal Coll., Kabul, and Franco-Persian Coll., Teheran.
Secretary and Gen. Dir. Prime Minister's Office 31-35; Head, Govt. Purchasing Office, Europe 36-40; Vice-Pres. Central Bank and Deputy Minister of Commerce 41-42. Gov. of Herat 42-47, 51-52; Minister of Communications 48-50; Pres. Hillmand Valley Authority Projects 53-62; Minister of Commerce 55-57, of Finance 57-64, Deputy Prime Minister 63-64; Amb. to U.K. 64-67, to U.S.A. 67-71, concurrently to Argentina, Brazil, Canada, Chile and Mexico, to Iran 77-78; Sardar Ali Reshteen Decoration.
c/o Ministry of Foreign Affairs, Kabul, Afghanistan.

Mammeri, Mouloud; Algerian writer; b. 28 Dec. 1917; ed. Rabat, Algiers and Paris.
Former Dir. of Anthropological, Prehistoric and Ethnological Research Centre, Algiers; Prix des quatre jurys for *La colline oubliée* 53.
Publs. Novels: in French *La colline oubliée* 52, *Le Sommeil du juste* 55, *L'opium et le bâton* 65, *La Traversée* 82; Plays: *Le Foehn* 67, *Le Banquet* 74; *Les isefra de Si Mohand* (collection of oral poems in Berber), *Poèmes kabyles anciens, Tajerrumt n aziýt* (Berber grammar) 76, *Machaho* (*Contes berberes de Kabylie*) 80, *Tellemchaho* (*Contes berbères de Kabylie*).
82 rue Laperlier, El-Biar, Algiers, Algeria.

Mandelbaum, Moshe Y., PH.D.; Israeli economist and banker; b. 3 March 1933, Jerusalem; ed. Mizrahi Teachers' Coll., Jerusalem, Hebrew Univ., Jerusalem, and Vanderbilt Univ., Tennessee.
Price Commissioner and Deputy Dir.-Gen. Ministry of Commerce and Industry 71-74; Dir.-Gen. 74-77; Vice-Chair. Industrial Devt. Bank of Israel 78-81; Chair. Israel Foreign Trade Risk Insurance Corpn., Diamond Inst., Public Price Cttee.; mem. Jerusalem Town Council; Deputy Gov. Bank of Israel 81-82, Gov. Jan. 82-; Senior Lecturer, Dept. of Econs., Bar-Ilan Univ.
Publs. numerous papers on banking, business and economics.
Bank of Israel, P.O. Box 780, Jerusalem, Israel.

Manqour, Nasir Hamad al- (*see* Almanqour).

Marei, Sayed Ahmed; Egyptian agriculturist and politician; b. 26 Aug. 1913; ed. Faculty of Agriculture, Cairo Univ.
Worked on his father's farm after graduation; subsequently with import-export, pharmaceutical, seed, and fertilizer companies; mem. Egyptian House of Commons 44; Del. mem. Higher Cttee. for Agrarian Reform 52-; Chair. of Board, Agricultural Co-operative Credit Bank 55-56; initiated "Supervised Credit System"; Minister of State for Agrarian Reform 56-57; Minister of Agriculture and Agrarian Reform 57-58; Central Minister for Agricultural and Agrarian Reform in the U.A.R. 58-61; Dep. Speaker; Nat. Assembly and Man. Dir. Bank Misr, Cairo 62-67, Minister of Agriculture and Agrarian Reform 67-70; Deputy Premier for Agriculture and Irrigation 72-73; First Sec. Arab Socialist Union (ASU) 72-73; Personal Asst. to Pres. Sadat 73; Sec.-Gen. UN World Food Conf. Rome 74; Pres. UN World Food Council 75-77; Speaker, People's Assembly 75-78; Asst. to Pres. Oct. 78-.
Publs. *Agrarian Reform in Egypt* 57, *U.A.R. Agriculture Enters a New Age* 60, *Food Production in Developing Countries* 68, *Agriculture in Egypt*.
9 Sh. Shagaret El Dorr, Zamalek, Cairo, Egypt.

Maruf, Taha Muhyiddin, LL.B.; Iraqi politician and diplomatist; b. 1924, Sulaimaniyah; ed. Coll. of Law, Univ. of Baghdad.
Worked as lawyer; joined Diplomatic Service 49; Minister of State 68-70; Minister of Works and Housing 68; Amb. to Italy, concurrently non-resident Amb. to Malta and Albania 70-74; Vice-Pres. of Iraq April 74-; mem. Higher Cttee. of Nat. Progressive Front 75-; Chair. African Affairs Bureau of Revolutionary Command Council 76-.
Office of the Vice-President of the Republic, National Assembly Building, Baghdad, Iraq.

Mashhour, Mashhour Ahmed; Egyptian engineer and politician; b. April 1918; ed. Faculty of Eng., Cairo Univ., Staff Officers' Coll.
Ministry of Transport 41; Army Eng. 42; eng. studies in Corps of Engs., British Army 43-44; tech. studies in Corps of Engs., U.S. Army; Officer, Corps of Engs., Egyptian Army; Lecturer, U.A.R. Acad. of War 48-52; Dir. of Transit, Suez Canal Authority 56; Del. Chair. of Canaltex Co. and mem. Board of Dirs. of Timsah Ship Building Co., Ismailia; Chair. and Man. Dir. Suez Canal Authority 65-; Sec. for Governorate of Ismailia, Arab Socialist Union 65-71, mem. People's Assembly 76-; mem. Nat. Council of Production; Gold Mercury Int. Award 79; Repub. Medal (3rd Class); Mil. Service Medal (1st Class); Liberation Medal; Palestine Medal; Order of Merit (1st Class); Commdr. Légion d'honneur (France); Order of Polonia Restituta; Mono-Grand Officier (Togo).
Suez Canal Authority, Ismailia, Egypt.

Masmoudi, Mohamed, LL.B.; Tunisian politician; b. 29 May 1922; ed. Tunis and Univ. of Paris.
Member of Tunisian Nationalist Movement 34-, Néo-Destour Party 40-; Minister of State in Govt. negotiating Tunisian independence 53-55; Minister of the Economy 55-56; Amb. to France 57-58, 65-70; Minister of Information 58-61; Sec.-Gen. Destour Socialist Party 69-74; Minister of Foreign Affairs 70-74; assoc. with *Action*, later renamed *Afrique Action*; in exile 74-77; returned to Tunisia 77; under house arrest Dec. 77-, released 81.
Publ. *Les Arabes dans la tempête* 77.
La Manouba, Tunis, Tunisia.

Mavrommatis, Andreas; Cypriot lawyer; b. 1932, Larnaca; ed. Greek Gymnasium, Limassol, and Lincoln's Inn, London.
Called to Bar 54; practised law, Cyprus 54-58; Magistrate, Paphos 58-60; District Judge 60; District Judge, Nicosia 64-70; Minister of Labour and Social Insurance 70-72; Special Legal Adviser to Ministry of Foreign Affairs 72-; Head Cyprus Del. to European Conf. on Security and Co-operation; Perm. Rep. to UN Office in Geneva 75-79, in New York Jan. 79-; Dir.-Gen. Ministry of Foreign Affairs; Vice-Pres. ECOSOC, Pres. 80; Chief Negotiator, intercommunal talks on Cyprus 82-.
Publ. *A List of Treaties of the Republic of Cyprus in Force on 1.1.1973* 74.
Permanent Mission of Cyprus at the United Nations, 820 Second Avenue, New York, N.Y. 10017, U.S.A.; 10 Plato Street, Nicosia 116, Cyprus.

Maximos V Hakim, (fmrly. **Archbishop George S. Hakim**), D.D.; Lebanese ecclesiastic; b. 18 May 1908, Tanta, Egypt; ed. St. Louis School, Tanta, Holy Family Jesuit School, Cairo and St. Anne Seminary, Jerusalem.
Teacher Patriarchal School, Beirut 30-31; Rector and Principal Patriarchal School, Cairo 31-43; Archbishop of Acre, Haifa, Nazareth and all Galilee 43-67; elected Patriarch of Antioch and all the East, Alexandria and Jerusalem Nov. 67; founded *Le Lien*, (French) Cairo 36, *Ar-Rabita* (Arabic) Haifa 43; Commdr. Légion d'Honneur; Dr. h.c. (Laval Univ. Canada, Algiers Univ. and many U.S. univs.).

Publ. *Pages d'Evangile lues en Galilée* (transl. into English, Dutch and Spanish) 54.
Greek Catholic Patriarchate, P.O. Box 50076, Beirut, Lebanon; P.O. Box 22249, Damascus, Syria; Daher 16, Cairo, Egypt.

Mazidi, Feisal, B.ECON.; Kuwaiti economist; b. 2 May 1933; ed. Kuwait and Univ. Coll. of N. Staffordshire, Keele, England.
Appointed to Dept. of Finance and Economy 59; Dir. State Chlorine and Salt Board; Dir. Kuwait Oil Co. Ltd. 60; Econ. Asst. to Minister of Finance and Economy 60; Chair. Econ. and Industrial Cttee. 61; Dir. Kuwait Fund for Econ. Development of Arab Countries 62; mem. Kuwait Univ. Higher Council 62-64; Chair. and Man. Dir. Kuwait Chemical Fertilizer Co. 64-71; Chair. Govt. Oil Concession Cttee. 63-65, Govt. Refinery Cttee. 64-66, Kuwait Maritime Mercantile Co. 65-70; Dir. Petrochemical Industries Co. 63-71, Kuwait United Fisheries Co. 71-76; Pres. Kuwait Associated Consultants 71-; Chair. Kuwait Resources Engineering and Management International (KUREMI) 76-78; mem. Kuwait Econs. Soc.; Arab League Prize for paper on Natural Gas 63.
Publs. *Natural Gas in Kuwait and its Utilization* 63, *Kuwait as a Base for Petrochemicals* 65, *International Investments* 79.
Kuwait Associated Consultants, P.O. Box 5443, Kuwait.

Meguid, Abdel Razzaq Abdel (see Abdel Meguid, Abdel Razzaq).

Meguid, Ahmet Esmat Abdel (see Abdel Meguid, Ahmet Esmat).

Melen, Ferit; Turkish politician; b. 1906, Van; ed. School of Political Science, Univ. of Ankara.
District Officer, Local Admin. 31-33; Auditor, Ministry of Finance 33-43, Dir.-Gen. of Incomes 43-50; Deputy for Van (Repub. People's Party) 50-64; Minister of Finance 62-65; Senator for Van 64-67; mem. Council of Europe 66-67; participated in formation of Nat. Reliance Party (now part of Republican Reliance Party) 67, later Deputy Leader; Minister of Nat. Defence 71-72, 75-77; Prime Minister 72-73.
Republican Reliance Party, Ankara, Turkey.

Mellink, Machteld Johanna, PH.D.; Netherlands archaeologist; b. 26 Oct. 1917; ed. Amsterdam and Utrecht Univs.
Field Asst. Tarsus excavations 47-49; Asst. Prof. of Classical Archæology Bryn Mawr Coll. 49-53, Assoc. Prof., Chair. Dept. of Classical and Near Eastern Archæology 53-62, Prof. 62-; staff mem. Gordion excavations organized by Pennsylvania Univ. Museum 50-, during which the putative tomb of King Midas was discovered 57; field dir. excavations at Karataş-Semayük in Lycia 63-, excavations of painted tombs in Elmali district 70-; Chair. Gordion Publs. Cttee. 76-; Pres. Archaeological Inst. of U.S.A. 81-.
Publs. *Hyakinthos* 43, *A Hittite Cemetery at Gordion* 56; *Archaeology in Asia Minor* (reports in *American Journal of Archaeology*) 55-, editor *Dark Ages and Nomads c. 1000 B.C.*, *Frühe Stufen der Kunst* (with J. Filip) 74.
Department of Classical and Near Eastern Archaeology, Bryn Mawr College, Bryn Mawr, Pa. 19010, U.S.A.

Memmi, Albert; Tunisian writer; b. 15 Dec. 1920; ed. Lycée Carnot, Tunis, Univ. of Algiers and Univ. de Paris.
Teacher of Philosophy in Tunis 55; Dir. Psychological Centre, Tunis 56; Researcher, Centre national de la recherche scientifique, Paris 59-; Asst. Prof. Ecole pratique des hautes études 59-66, Prof. 66-70; Prof. Univ. of Paris 70-, Dir. Dept. of Social Sciences 73; Vice-Pres. PEN Club 76; Prix Fénéon 54, Prix de Carthage, Prix Simba 78; Chevalier, Légion d'honneur; Commdr. Ordre de Nichan Iftikhar; Officier, Palmes Académiques; Syndic des Ecrivains de langue française 81; mem. Acad. des Sciences d'Outremer 75.

Publs. include: *The Pillar of Salt* 53, *Strangers* 55, *Anthologie des écrivains nord-africains* 55, *Colonizer, Colonized* 57, *Portrait of a Jew* 62, *Le français et le racisme* 65, *The Liberation of the Jew* 66, *The Dominated Man* 68, *Le Scorpion* 69, *Jews and Arabs* 74, *Entretien* 75, *La terre intérieure* 76, *Le désert* 77, *La dépendance* 79, *Le racisme* 82.
5 rue Saint Merri, Paris 4e, France.

Mentes, Cevdet; Turkish judge and politician; b. 1915; Bitlis; ed. Istanbul Univ.
Former public prosecutor and judge; mem. Supreme Court of Appeal 58-, Pres. 72-; Minister of Justice Sept. 80-.
Ministry of Justice, Adalet Bakanlığı, Bakanlıklar, Ankara, Turkey.

Merillon, Jean-Marie; French diplomatist; b. 12 Feb. 1926; ed. Ecole Nat. d'Administration.
Served at Ministry of Foreign Affairs 52-68; Amb. to Jordan 68-73, to Repub. of Viet-Nam 73-75, to Greece 75-77, to Algeria 79-; Dir. for Political Affairs 77-79.
Ambassade de France, rue Larbi Alik, Hydra, Algiers, Algeria.

Merlin, Samuel; Israeli author and director of political studies; b. 17 Jan. 1910; ed. Lycée, Kishineff, Univ. of Paris.
Secretary-General World Exec., Zionist Revisionist and New Zionist Org. 34-38; Editor-in-Chief Yiddish daily *Di Tat*, Warsaw, Poland 38-39; Sec.-Gen. Hebrew Cttee. for Nat. Liberation 40-48; mem. First Knesset 48-51; Pres. Israel Press Ltd. 50-57; Dir. of Political Studies, Inst. for Mediterranean Affairs, N.Y. 57-; Lecturer, Middle East Studies, Fairleigh Dickinson Univ., N.J. 71-; Hon. mem. of Abu Gosh village near Jerusalem.
Publs. *The Palestine Refugee Problem* 58, *United States Policy in the Middle East* 60, *The Ascent of Man* (Co-Author) 63, *The Cyprus Dilemma* (Editor) 67, *The Big Powers and the Present Crisis in the Middle East* 68, *The Search for Peace in the Middle East* 69, *Guerre et Paix au Moyen Orient* 70.
Institute for Mediterranean Affairs, 428 East 83rd Street, New York, N.Y. 10028, U.S.A.

Meshel, Yeruham; Israeli trade unionist; b. 24 Nov. 1912, Pinsk, Russia.
Immigrated to Palestine 33; Sec. Metal Workers' Union, Tel-Aviv, mem. Tel-Aviv Labour Council Exec. 45; mem. Trade Union Centre of Histadrut Exec. Cttee., Chair. Industrial Workers' Div. 50-60, mem. Central Exec. Bureau 60-, Chair. Trade Union Centre 61, Deputy Sec.-Gen. Histadrut 64-74, Head of Histadrut Social Security Centre and Arab Workers' Dept., Acting Sec.-Gen. Histadrut 73, Sec.-Gen. 74-; Vice-Pres. ICFTU and Asian Regional Org. (ARO) of ICFTU 75-; mem. Central Cttee. and Bureau, Israel Labour Party; rep. to numerous int. labour confs.
Histadrut, 93 Arlosorof Street, Tel-Aviv, Israel.

Messadi, Prof. Mahmoud; Tunisian educationist and politician; b. 28 Jan. 1911, Tazarka; ed. Coll. Sadiki and Lycée Carnot, Tunis, Univ. of Paris.
Professor Lycée Carnot 36-38, Coll. Sadiki 38-48; Asst. Prof. Centre d'Etudes Islamiques, Univ. of Paris 48-52, Inst. des Hautes Etudes de Paris 48-55; Head Dept. of Secondary Educ., Tunis 55-58; Insp.-Gen. of Public Educ. 58-; Sec. of State for Nat. Educ. Youth and Sports 58-68; Minister of State 69-70; Minister of Cultural Affairs 73-Dec. 76; Deputy, Nat. Assembly; Pres. Nat. Assembly Nov. 81-; mem. Cen. Cttee. Destour Socialist Party; Grand Cordon Ordre de l'Indépendance, Ordre de la République.
Publs. *Essoud* (The Dam), *Haddatha Abou Houraira*, *Maouled en-Nassian* (Birth of Oblivion).
c/o Ministère des Affaires Culturelles, Place du Gouvernement, Tunis, Tunisia.

Mestiri, Mahmoud; Tunisian diplomatist; b. 25 Dec. 1929; ed. Inst. d'Etudes Politiques, Univ. de Lyons.
Served in several Tunisian Dels. to UN; Alt. Rep. to UN 58, 59; Head of Tunisian special Diplomatic Mission to Congo (Léopoldville) 60; Asst. to Personal Rep. of UN Sec.-Gen. to Govt. of Belgium 61; Deputy Perm. Rep. of Tunisia to UN 62-65; Sec.-Gen. for Foreign Affairs, Tunis 65-67; Perm. Rep. to UN 67-69; Chair. UN Special Cttee. on the Situation with Regard to Implementation of Declaration on the Granting of Independence to Colonial Countries and Peoples 68; Amb. to Belgium Sept. 69, to Luxembourg Oct. 69, to EEC Nov. 69, to Fed. Repub. of Germany 71-73, to U.S.S.R. 73-74, to Poland 74-76, to UN 76-80.
c/o Ministry of Foreign Affairs, Tunis, Tunisia.

Meulen, Daniel van der (*see* van der Meulen, Daniel).

Mili, Mohamed Ezzedine; Tunisian civil servant; b. 4 Dec. 1917; ed. Ecole Normale Supérieure de Saint-Cloud and Ecole Nationale Supérieure des Télécommunications, Paris.
Telecommunications Engineer, Ministry of Posts 47-56; Dir.-Gen. of Telecommunications 57-65; Vice-Pres. Plan for Africa, Int. Telecommunication Union (ITU) 60-64; Pres. Admin. Council 64, Pres. Plan for Africa ITU 64-65, Vice-Sec.-Gen. ITU 65-66, Sec.-Gen. 66-; Commdr. Ordre de la République (Tunisia), Commdr. Order of Vasa (Sweden), Officier Ordre de l'Indépendance (Tunisia), Gran Cruz de la Orden de Duarte, Sánchez y Mella con Placa de Plata (Dominican Repub.), Honor al Mérito Medal (Paraguay), Grand Star of the Order of Merit of Telecommunications (Spain), Commdr. of the Order of Leopold (Belgium), Officier, Légion d'honneur; Philip Reis Medal (Fed. Repub. of Germany); Diploma of Honour (Int. Council of Archives) 78.
International Telecommunication Union, Place des Nations, 1211 Geneva 20; Home: 5 route de Mon Idée, 1226 Thônex, Switzerland.

Minin, Viktor; Soviet diplomatist; b. 1926, Moscow.
Joined Ministry of Foreign Affairs 48; Counsellor, U.S.S.R. Embassy, Turkey 65-68; Amb. to Laos 68-72; Dept. Dir. Ministry of Foreign Affairs 72-78; Amb. to Guinea 78-82, to Iraq 82-.
Embassy of the U.S.S.R., Mansour Street 4, Daoudi 140, Baghdad, Iraq.

Moalla, Mansour, L. EN D., L. ÈS L., LL.D.; Tunisian economist; b. 1 May 1930, Sfax; ed. Inst. des Etudes Politiques, Ecole Nat. d'Administration, Paris.
Inspecteur des Finances 56; Technical Adviser, Ministry of Finance 57-58; Dir.-Gen. Banque Centrale de Tunisie 58-61; Dir. of Admin., Office of the Pres. 61-63, 68-69; Dir. Ecole Nat. d'Administration (ENA) 63-69; Under-Sec. of State, Ministry of Commerce and Industry 67-68; Sec. of State (then Minister) for Posts, Telegraphs and Telecommunications (PTT) 69-70; Deputy Minister in charge of the Nat. Plan 70-71, Minister for Planning 71-75; Pres., Dir.-Gen. Banque Int. Arabe de Tunisie 75-, Tunisian Insurance Group 75-76; Minister of Planning and Finance April 80-; mem. Cen. Cttee. Destour Socialist Party 71-, mem. Political Bureau 71-74; Grand Cordon, Order of the Repub., Order of Independence.
Ministry of Planning and Finance, Tunis; 32 avenue de la République, Carthage, Tunisia.

Moberly, John Campbell, C.M.G.; British diplomatist; b. 27 May 1925, Exmouth, Devon; ed. Winchester Coll. and Magdalen Coll., Oxford.
War service in Royal Navy 43-47; entered Foreign (later Diplomatic) Service 50; service at Foreign Office and in Bahrain and Kuwait 50-59; British Political Agent in Doha, Qatar 59-62; First Sec., Athens 62-66; with FCO 66-68; Canadian Nat. Defence Coll., Kingston, Ont. 68-69;

Counsellor, Washington, D.C. 69-73; Dir. Middle East Centre for Arab Studies, Shemlan, Lebanon 73-75; Amb. to Jordan 75-79; Asst. Under-Sec. of State, FCO 79-.
35 Pymers Mead, Croxted Road, West Dulwich, London, S.E.21; and The Cedars, Temple Sowerby, Penrith, Cumbria, England.

Moberly, Patrick Hamilton, C.M.G., M.A.; British diplomatist; b. 2 Sept. 1928; ed. Winchester Coll., Trinity Coll., Oxford.
Entered Foreign (later Diplomatic) Service 51; British Embassy, Baghdad 53-57, Prague 57-59; service at Foreign Office 59-62; British Embassy, Dakar 62-64; with Ministry of Defence 64-66; Foreign Office 67-69; British High Commission, Ottawa 69-70; British Embassy, Tel-Aviv 70-74; Foreign Office 74-81, Asst. Under-Sec. of State, FCO 76-81; Amb. to Israel 81-.
British Embassy, 192 Renov Hayarkon, Tel-Aviv, Israel; and Foreign and Commonwealth Office, King Charles Street, London, S.W.1, England.

Moday, Yitzhak; Israeli politician; b. 1926, Tel-Aviv; ed. Geulah High School, Tel-Aviv, Technion Univ., Haifa, Univ. of London and Hebrew Univ. of Jerusalem.
Served in Palestine Police Force 43; served in Israeli armed forces (Lieut.-Col.) 48-50; Mil. Attaché, London 51-53; Mil. Commdr., Gaza, Six-Day War 67; chemical factory construction and industrial co. admin. 51-73; Minister of Energy, Infrastructure and Communications 78-81, Minister without Portfolio 81-; Pres. Israel-America Chamber of Commerce; Likud Party.
Cabinet Office, Jerusalem, Israel.

Mohammed Zahir Shah; fmr. King of Afghanistan; b .15 Oct. 1914; ed. Habibia High School, Istiqlal Coll. (both in Kabul), Lucée Janson-de-Sailly and Univ. of Montpellier, France.
Graduated with highest honours; attended Infantry Officers' School, Kabul 32; married Lady Homira, Nov. 4th 1931; children, Princess Bilqis, Prince Ahmad Shah Khan, Princess Maryam, Prince Mohammed Nadir Khan, Prince Shah Mahmoud Khan, Prince Mohammed Daoud Jan, Prince Mirvis Jan; Asst. Minister in Ministry of Nat. Defence 32-33; acting Minister of Educ. 33; crowned King Nov. 8th, 33, deposed July 73; abdicated Aug. 73.

Mohieddin, Dr. (Ahmed) Fuad; Egyptian politician; b. 1926.
Former Governor of Alexandria; Minister of State for Local Govt. and People's Organizations 73-74; Minister of Health 74-76, of People's Assembly Affairs 76-79; Chair. Foreign Affairs Cttee. of People's Assembly -80; Deputy Prime Minister for Cabinet Affairs and Local Government and Minister of State for Al-Azhar Affairs 80-82; Prime Minister and Minister of Al-Azhar Affairs Jan. 82-.
Office of the Prime Minister, Cairo, Egypt.

Mohieddin, Zakaria; Egyptian army officer and politician; b. May 1918; ed. Mil. Coll. and Staff Officers' Coll., Cairo.
Former lecturer Mil. Coll. and Staff Officers' Coll. and Dir.-Gen. Intelligence; Minister of the Interior 53-58; Minister of the Interior U.A.R. 58-62, Vice-Pres. U.A.R. and Chair. Aswan Dam Cttee. 61-62; mem. Nat. Defence Cttee. 62-69, Presidency Council 62-64; mem. Exec. Cttee. Arab Socialist Union 64-69; Deputy Prime Minister 64-65, June 67-68; Prime Minister and Minister of the Interior 65-66.
52 El-Thawra Street, Dokki, Cairo, Egypt.

Moini, Amir-Ghassem; Iranian mechanical engineer and politician; b. June 1925; ed. Teheran Univ.
Ministry of Labour and Social Affairs 47-; Teheran Labour Dept.; Deputy Head Inspection Office; Acting Head of Fars Prov. Labour Dept., later Head; Deputy Head

Teheran Branch of Workers' Social Insurance Org.; Deputy Dir.-Gen. Employment Services, later Dir.-Gen.; Sec.-Gen. Graduate Guidance Org.; Technical Under-Sec., Ministry of Labour and Social Affairs; mem. Board of Dirs. Social Insurance Org.; Acting Sec.-Gen. Iran Novin Party 71; Minister of Labour and Social Services 73-76, of the Interior 76-77; Homayoun Order, First Class.
c/o Ministry of the Interior, Teheran, Iran.

Montazeri, Ayatollah Hussein Ali; Iranian religious leader; b. *c.* 1923, Najafabad, Isfahan; ed. Isfahan Theological School.
Teacher of science and philosophy, Theological School, Qom; arrested after riots over Shah's land reform 63; visited Ayatollah Khomeini in Iraq 64; arrested several times and exiled to rural parts of Iran 64-74; imprisoned 74-78; Leading Ayatollah of Teheran 79-80; returned to Qom Feb. 80.
Faizeyeh Theological Seminary, Qom, Iran.

Moqaddem, Sadok; Tunisian diplomatist and parliamentarian; b. 1914; ed. Lycée Carnot, Tunis, Faculty of Sciences, Montpellier and Faculty of Medicine, Paris.
Physician, Tunis; mem. Néo-Destour 34-, mem. Political Bureau 52-; Sec. of State for Justice 54-55, for Public Health 55-56; mem. to Constituent Ass. 56-59, mem. Nat. Assembly 59-; Ambassador to Egypt 56-57; Sec. of State for Foreign Affairs 57-62; Ambassador to France 62-64; Pres. Nat. Assembly 64-69, 69-81; Chair. Destour Socialist Party 70; Grand Cordon of Nat. Order of Independence, Grand Cordon, Nat. Order of the Repub.; several foreign decorations.
c/o National Assembly, Palais du Bardo, Tunis, Tunisia.

Morocco, King of (*see* Hassan II).

Mostofi, Khosrow, M.A., PH.D.; Iranian professor; b. 8 July 1921; ed. Univs. of Teheran and Utah.
Instructor in Political Science, Portland State Univ. 58-59, Asst. Prof. 59-60, Univ. of Utah 60-65; Acting Dir. Inst. of Int. Studies, Univ. of Utah 62-63; Assoc. Prof., Univ. of Utah 65-70, Prof. 70-; Acting Chair. Dept. of Political Science 67; Dir. Middle East Center, Univ. of Utah 67-; Fulbright-Hays Fellow, Turkey and Iran 65-66; Board mem. American Inst. of Iranian Studies 68, CASA 73-; Co-Dir. American Center for Iranian Studies in Teheran 70; mem. N.D.F.L. Panel of Consultants, U.S.O.E. 68-70, 76, American Asscn. of Univ. Profs., American Acad. of Political Sciences, Western Political Science Asscn.
Publs. *Suez Dispute: A Case Study of a Treaty* 57, *Aspects of Nationalism: The Sociology of Colonial Revolt* 64, *Parsee Nameh: A Persian Reader in 8 Vols.* Vol. I, II 63, 4th edn. Vol. I 69, *Iran* in *Encyclopaedia Britannica* 74, *Idries Shah* in *Studies in Art and Literature of the Near East* 74.
Room 19, Middle East Center, University of Utah, Salt Lake City, Utah 84112; Home: 2481 East 13th South Street, Salt Lake City, Utah 84108, U.S.A.

Moulay Hassan Ben El Mehdi, H.R.H. Prince (Cousin of King Hassan II); Moroccan diplomatist; b. 14 Aug. 1912.
Caliph Northern Zone of Morocco 25; Amb. to Great Britain 57-64, to Italy 64-67; Pres. of Admin. Council, Nat. Bank for Econ. Devt. 65-67; Gov. Banque du Maroc 69-; decorations include, Ouissam Alaoui, Charles I Medal, Great Military Ouissam, Great Medal of Portugal, Great Dominican Medal, Great Naval Medal, Great Mahdaoui Medal, Great Houssni Medal.
Banque du Maroc, 277 avenue Mohammed V, Rabat, Morocco.

Mounayer, H.E. Eustache Joseph, D. en. L.; Syrian ecclesiastic; b. 6 June 1925; ed. Seminary of Benedictine Fathers, Jerusalem, Patriarchal Seminary, Charfé, Lebanon and Pontifical Univ. of Latran, Rome.
Ordained priest 49; Sec. of Archbishop of Damascus 54-58,

concurrently Sec. of Apostolic Nunzio, Pres. ecclesiastic court: Sec. of Cardinal Tappouni 59-71; consecrated bishop 71; Patriarchal Auxiliary Bishop 71-78; Archbishop of Damascus 78-; Dir. *Al-Karma* (review in Arabic).
Publs. *Les Synodes Syriens Jacobites* (in French), *Le Schihim* (in Arabic).
Syrian Catholic Archbishopric, P.O. Box 2129, Damascus, Syria.

Moussalli, Paul Michel Négib, LIC. en D.; Lebanese lawyer and United Nations official; b. 9 April 1932; ed. Lycée français de garçons, Beirut, Faculty of Law, Beirut, Univ. of Lyons, France, Max Planck Inst. für Ausländisches Öffentliches Recht und Völkerrecht, Heidelberg, Germany, and Graduate Inst. of Int. Studies, Geneva, Switzerland.
Legal Adviser, Office of UN High Commr. for Refugees (UNHCR), Geneva 61-62; UNHCR Rep. for Tunisia 62; UNHCR Rep. at Tripartite Repatriation Comm. (Algerian refugees) 62; UNHCR Rep. for Algeria 62-63; UNHCR Legal Adviser, Geneva (questions relating to refugees in Africa and Asia) 63-66; UNHCR Regional Rep. for Africa 66-70; Acting Dir. of Admin. and Management, UNHCR, Geneva 71-74, Dir. 75-78; Dir. Legal Dept. responsible for int. protection of refugees 79-.
Office of United Nations High Commissioner for Refugees, Palais des Nations, Geneva, Switzerland.

Moussavi, Hussein; Iranian politician; b. 1942, Iran; ed. National Univ., Teheran.
Joined Islamic Soc. at univ. in Teheran and active in Islamic Socs. since; imprisoned briefly for opposition to the Shah 73; a founder mem. Islamic Republican Party (IRP) 79; appointed Chief Ed. IRP newspaper *Islamic Republic* 79; Foreign Minister Aug.-Oct. 81; elected Prime Minister by Majlis (consultative assembly) Oct. 81-.
Office of the Prime Minister, Teheran, Iran.

Mubarak, Lt.-Gen. (Muhammad) Hosni; Egyptian air force officer and politician; b. 4 May 1928, Minuffya Governorate; ed. Military and Air Acads., Cairo.
Instructor, Air Acad. 52-59; Commdr. air squadron, later jet fighter brigade 59-64, Commdr. Egyptian bomber squadron, Yemen Civil War 62; studied at Frunze Mil. Acad., U.S.S.R. Feb. 64-April 65; Commdr. various air bases 65-67, Dir.-Gen. Air Acad. 67-69; Chief of Staff, Air Force 69, C.-in-C. 72-75; promoted to Lt.-Gen. 73; Vice-Pres. of Repub. April 75-Oct. 81; Dir.-Gen. Egyptian Arms Procurement Agency April 75-; mem. Higher Council for Nuclear Energy 75-; Vice-Pres. Nat. Democratic Party 78-80, Sec.-Gen. Sept. 81-; Pres. and C.-in-C. Armed Forces Oct. 81-; Chair. Nat. Democratic Party Jan. 82-.
Office of the President, Abdeen, Cairo, Egypt.

Müezzinoğlu, Ziya; Turkish civil servant and diplomatist; b. 5 May 1919; ed. Ankara Univ.
Inspector of Finance, Turkish Ministry of Finance 42-53; Adviser to Treasury, Ministry of Finance 53-59; Dir.-Gen. of Treasury 59-60; Dir.-Gen. of Treasury and Sec.-Gen. Org. for Int. Econ. Co-operation in Turkey 60; mem. Constituent Assembly 60; Chair. Interministerial Cttee. for Foreign Econ. Relations 62; Sec. of State of State Planning Org. 62-64; Amb. to Fed. Repub. of Germany 64-67; Amb., Perm. Del. to EEC 67-72; Minister of Finance 72-73, 78-79, of Trade June-July 77; mem. Nat. Security Council; mem. Senate and Foreign Relations Cttee. 75; Republican People's Party.
Cankaya, Oran Sitesi 58/6, Ankara, Turkey.

Muhammad, Ali Nasser; Yemeni politician; b. 1939, Dathina Rural District.
Active mem. of Nat. Liberation Front (NLF) 63-67; Gov. of the Islands 67, of Second Province 68; mem. Nat. Front Gen. Command 68; Minister of Local Govt. 69, later of Defence; mem. Front Exec. Cttee. 70; mem. Presidential Council of People's Democratic Repub. of Yemen 71-78,

Chair. June-Dec. 78; Chair. Council of Ministers (Prime Minister) 71-, Pres. April 80-; mem. Supreme People's Council 71-, Chair. Presidium April 80-; mem. Political Bureau of Nat. Front 72-75, of United Political Org.-Nat. Front 75-78, of Yemen Socialist Party Oct. 78-, Sec.-Gen. April 80-; Minister of Educ. 74-75 of Finance Dec. 78-Aug. 79.
Supreme People's Council, Aden, People's Democratic Republic of Yemen.

Mzali, Mohamed, LIC. EN. PHIL.; Tunisian politician; b. 23 Dec. 1925, Monastir; ed. Sadiki Coll., Univ. of Paris. Teacher at Coll. Sadiki, Lycée Alaoui and Univ. of Zitouna 50-56; Founder and Chief Ed. *El-Fikr* magazine 55-; Secretary of State for Education 56-58; Deputy Nat. Assembly 59-; Dir. of Youth and Sports, President's Secretariat 59-64; Dir.-Gen. Radiodiffusion Télévision Tunisienne (RTT) 64-68; Sec. of State for Nat. Defence 68-69; Minister of Youth and Sports 69-70, of Education 69-70, 71-73, 76-80; Minister of Health 73-76; Prime Minister April 80-; Mem. Parti Socialiste Destourien (PSD) 47-, mem. Cen. Cttee. 64, Political Bureau 64-70, 74-, Sec.-Gen. April 80-; Municipal Councillor, Tunis 60, 63; First Vice-Pres. Tunis Town Council 60-63, Pres. Culture, Youth and Sports Comm. 60-66; Pres. Ariana Town Council 59-72; Founder *El Fikr* 55; Pres. Union des Ecrivains Tunisiens 70-; Pres. Tunisian Olympic Cttee. 62-; First Vice-Pres. Int. Olympic Cttee. 76-; Pres. Int. Cttee. Jeux Méditerranéens 79-; mem. Arab Language Acad., Cairo 75-, Damascus 80-; Foreign Assoc. mem. French Sports Acad. 78-; Grand Cordon, Ordre de l'Indépendance, Ordre de la République, Médaille de Mérite Sportif.
Publs. *La Démocratie* 55, *Recueil d'Editoriaux d'El Fikr* 69, *Prises de positions* 73, *Etudes* 75, *Points de Vue* 75, *Les Chemins de la Pensée* 79.
Office of the Secretary-General, Parti Socialiste Destourien, boulevard 9 avril 1938, Tunis, Tunisia.

N

Nabulsi, M. Said, M.A., PH.D.; Jordanian banker; b. 1928, Palestine; ed. Univ. of Damascus, Syria, Univ. of California at Berkeley, Georgetown Univ., Washington, D.C. Secretary-General, Central Bank of Syria 64-67; Head of Research, Central Bank of Jordan 68-72, Gov. and Chair. of Board. 73-; Minister of Nat. Econ. 72-73; Gov. Int. Monetary Fund, Arab Monetary Fund; mem. Board of Trustees, Univ. of Jordan, Yarmouk Univ.
Publs. numerous articles, research papers in economic journals.
Central Bank of Jordan, P.O. Box 37, Amman; Home: Shmeisani, Amman, Jordan.

Nabulsi, Omar, L. en D., M.A.; Jordanian lawyer and politician; b. 1 April 1936, Nablus; ed. Cairo, Ain Shams and London Univs.
Legal Adviser, Sasco Petroleum Co., Libya 59-61; Legal and Political Attaché, Arab League 61-69; Asst. Dir., Royal Court of Jordan 69-70; Minister of Nat. Economy 70-72; Amb., Ministry of Foreign Affairs 72; Amb. to U.K. 72-73; Minister of Agriculture and Nat. Econ. 73-Jan. 75; Legal and Econ. Adviser to Arab Fund for Econ. and Social Devt. 75-77; Lawyer and Consultant in Corporate and Business Legal Affairs 77, 80-; Minister of Reconstruction, Devt. and Labour 80; Order of Al-Kawkab (First Class).
Publs. several articles in legal journals.
P.O. Box 35116, Amman, Jordan.

Naguib, Ibrahim; Egyptian architect and politician; b. 24 June 1911; ed. Royal School of Engineering, Giza. Chartered Structural Engineer, London 35; Architect State Bldg. Dept., Ministry of Public Works 31, Head Technical

Dept. 44-52, Insp. N. Cairo Zone 52-55; Del. Lecturer, Alexandria Univ. 46-50, Ain Shams Univ. 54-62; Controller of Municipal and Village Affairs, Cairo Governorate 55-57; Dir.-Gen. of Technical Research and Inspection, Ministry of Municipal and Village Affairs 57-60; Deputy Minister of Housing and Public Utilities 62-67; mem. Cen. Cttee. Arab Socialist Union 68-72, Gen. Secr. 72-74; mem. People's Assembly, Vice-Chair. Services Cttee. 69-71; Minister of Tourism 71-72, of Tourism and Civil Aviation 74-77; Chair. Cttee. of Int. Experts in charge of project for salvaging Temples on Philae Island, Aswan, Cttee. for Urban Reconstruction; Pres. Afro-Asian Housing Org. 63-67; mem. Board, Egyptian Soc. of Engineers; mem. Inst. of Structural Engineers, London; Hon. Pres. Soc. of Architects; has participated in numerous int. scientific confs.
Publs. *Architectural Drawing* 40, *Buildings of Nubia* 45, *Code of Practice for Structural Engineering* 46, *Foundations of Buildings in Egypt and the Sudan* 51, *Village Buildings and the Farmer's House* 53, *The Nature of Soil, and Foundations in the City of Cairo* 59, *Housing in Developing Countries* 68, *Trends in Architecture in the Arab Countries* 69.
Cairo, Egypt.

Naguib, Gen. Mohammed (*see* Neguib, Gen. Mohamed).

Nahayan, H.H. Sheikh Zayed bin Sultan al-; President of the United Arab Emirates and Ruler of Abu Dhabi; b. 1918.
Governor of Eastern Province of Abu Dhabi 46-66; deposed his brother Sheikh Shakhbut and succeeded to Sheikhdom 66; Pres. Fed. of Arabian Emirates 69-71; Pres. United Arab Emirates (U.A.E.) 71-.
Amiri Palace, Abu Dhabi, United Arab Emirates.

Nakib, Ahmed Abdul Wahab Al-; Kuwaiti diplomatist; b. 30 July 1933, Kuwait; ed. Adam State Coll., Colorado, U.S.A.
First Sec., Kuwait Embassy, London 62-63; Counsellor, first Perm. Mission of Kuwait to UN 63-66; Consul-Gen., Nairobi, Kenya 66-67; Amb. to Pakistan 67-70, to U.K. 71-75, also accred. to Denmark, Norway and Sweden 71-75; Chair. and Man. Dir. Kuwait Projects Co. 75-.
Kuwait Projects Co., P.O. Box 23982, Safat, Kuwait.

Nan Nguema, Marc Saturnin, PH.D.; Gabonese economist and oil executive; b. 13 April 1934; ed. Paris Univ., Ecole Nationale d'Administration, Paris.
Civil servant, Paris 60-63; Dir. Economic Affairs Dept., Government of Gabon 63; Econ. Affairs Officer UN Dept. of Econ. and Social Affairs (research and policies) New York 64-65, to UNCTAD 65-68; Perm. Rep. of Gabon to UN, Geneva 68; Sec.-Gen. and Deputy Gen. Man. Elf Gabon 76-81, Econ. and Financial Exec. Elf Aquitaine Paris Nov. 70-; Adviser to Exec. Dir. IMF 72-75; Rep. of Gabon to OPEC Econ. Comm. Board 75-76; Sec.-Gen. OPEC July 81-.
OPEC, Obere Donaustrasse 93, 1020 Vienna, Austria.

Nashashibi, Nasser Eddin; Jordanian (b. Palestine) editor and diplomatist; b. 1924; ed. Arab Coll., Jerusalem and American Univ. Beirut.
Arab Office, Jerusalem 45-47; Chief Chamberlain, Amman 51; Dir.-Gen. Hashemite Broadcasting 52; Roving Editor *Akhbar El Yom*, Cairo; Chief Editor *Al Gomhouria*, Cairo 59-65; Roving Rep. of the Arab League June 65-67; Roving Dip. Editor *Al-Ahram*, Cairo; now freelance writer and journalist in Europe and Middle East; Jordanian Independence Star, 1st degree.
Publs. *Steps in Britain* (Arabic) 48, *What Happened in the Middle East* 58, *Short Political Stories* 59, *Return Ticket to Palestine* 60, *Some Sand* 62, *An Arab in China* (Arabic and English) 64, *Roving Ambassador* 70, *The Ink is Black* 71, *No Camel No Sand* 76, *I Am the Middle East* 77, *Do You Know My Love Called Jerusalem?* 82.

55 avenue de Champel, Geneva, Switzerland; and 26 Lowndes Street, London, England.

Nasir, Mohammed, B.SC., M.A., ED.D.; Iraqi educator and diplomatist; b. 1911; ed. Teacher Training Coll., Baghdad, American Univ., Beirut and Columbia Univ., New York.
Schoolteacher 31-32; Prof. of Educ. and Dean of Coll. of Educ., Baghdad Univ. 41-45, 55-63; Cultural Attaché and Perm. Rep. of Iraq to Arab League Cultural Comm. 45-48; Cultural Attaché, Washington 48-54; Alternate Del. to UN 5th Gen. Assembly; Pres. Teachers Union of Iraq 63-64; mem. Council, Univ. of Baghdad 63-64; Minister of Educ. 64; Ambassador to U.S.S.R. 65-66; Minister of Culture and Nat. Orientation 66; Prof. of Educational Admin., and fmr. Chair. Coll. of Educ. Kuwait Univ. 67-77.
Publs. include many school books in Arabic, *Arabic Readings* (2 vols., joint author) 40, *Civic Education* (joint author) 40, *Guide to Higher Education in the U.S.A.* 57, *Readings in Educational Thought*, Vol. I 73, *Arabic-Islamic Educational Thought* 77.
College of Education, Kuwait University, P.O. Box 8063, Salmia, Kuwait and 46/95 University Community, Baghdad, Iraq.

Nasr, Asad Yusuf, M.SC.; Lebanese airline executive; b. 11 Sept. 1927, Haifa; ed. American Univ. of Beirut and Cambridge Univ.
Instructor in Mathematics and Statistics, American Univ. of Beirut 50-55; Expert at Ministry of Nat. Econ. 50-52; Manager for Gen. Planning and Economics, Middle East Airlines (MEA) 55-63, Exec. Vice-Pres. 63-65, Gen. Man. 65-76, Man. Dir. 76-77, Man. Dir. and Deputy Chair. 77, Chair. of the Board and Pres. Dec. 77-May 82; Airline Tech. Man. Award, Air Transport World 75; Gold Labour Medal (Lebanon) 75; Gold Medal, Asscn. of Engineers Graduates of Esib 78; Commdr. Nat. Order of Chad 73, Officer Nat. Order of Lebanon 74, Order of Repub. of Egypt 74, Légion d'honneur 75.
Publ. *The Asna Formula: A New Concept* 78.
Home: 87 Mexico Street, Beirut, Lebanon.

Navon, Yitzhak; Israeli politician; b. 9 April 1921, Jerusalem; ed. Hebrew Univ. of Jerusalem.
Director, Hagana Arabic Dept., Jerusalem 46-49; Second Sec., Israel Legation in Uruguay and Argentina 49-51; Political Sec. to Foreign Minister 51-52; Head of Bureau of Prime Minister 52-63; Head Dept. of Culture, Ministry of Educ. and Culture 63-65; mem. Knesset 65-78, fmr. Deputy Speaker; fmr. Chair. Knesset Defence and Foreign Affairs Cttee.; Chair. World Zionist Council 73-78; Pres. of Israel May 78-; mem. Mapai Party 51-65, Rafi 65-68, Labour Alignment 68-78; Yediot Ahronot's Kinor David prize.
Publs. *Hollekh Birkida* 44, *Romancero Sephardi* (collection of songs) 68, *Bustan Sephardi* (play), *Six Days and Seven Gates* 76.
Office of the President, Jerusalem, Israel.

Nebenzahl, Itzhak Ernst, DR.IUR.; Israeli public official; b. 24 Oct. 1907; ed. Univs. of Frankfurt and Freiburg.
Settled in Palestine 33; Dir. Jerusalem Econ. Corpn. 47-61, Jerusalem Devt. Dept., Jewish Agency 48-50, Bank Leumi le-Israel Ltd. 56-61; Hon. Consul-Gen. of Sweden 52-62; Chair. Post Office Bank 54-61, of Advisory Cttee. and Council, Bank of Israel 57-62; State Comptroller of Israel 61, re-elected 66, 71, 76-81; Pres. Fifth Int. Congress of Int. Org. of Supreme Audit Insts. (INTOSAI) 65, Chair. 65-68, now mem. Gov. Board; Public Complaints Commr. (Ombudsman) 71-81; Vice-Chair. Int. Ombudsman Steering Cttee. 77-; host of 2nd Int. Ombudsman Conf., Jerusalem 80; Pres. Jerusalem Coll. of Technology 82-; Chair. Government Comm. on Organization of Fuel Supply and Market; mem. Board Leo Balck Zusl; fmr. mem. Petroleum Board, Anti-Trust Council ,and several govt. inquiry cttees., including inquiry into Yom Kippur war; Partner,

Hollander Concern (Stockholm, New York, London, Buenos Aires, Paris, Tokyo, etc.), Chair. Board of Dirs. 47-61; Prof. Ordinarius Emeritus, Faculty of Law, Frankfurt Univ.; Chevalier (1st Class), Royal Swedish Order of Vasa 57.
Jerusalem College of Technology, P.O. Box 16031, Jerusalem 91-160; Home: 9 Batei Mahse Street, Old City, Jerusalem, Israel.

Ne'eman, Yuval, B.SC., DIP. ING., D.E.M., D.I.C., PH.D.; Israeli soldier and scientist; b. 14 May 1925; ed. Herzlia High School, Tel-Aviv, Israel Inst. of Technology, Haifa, Ecole Supérieure de Guerre, Paris, and London Univ.
Hydrodynamics Design Engineer 45; in Hagana 46; Captain, Israeli Defence Forces (Infantry) 48, Major 49, Lieut.-Col. 50, Col. 55; Defence Attaché, London 58-60; joined Israel Atomic Energy Establishments 60, Scientific Dir., Soreq Research Establishment 61-63; Head, Physics Dept., Tel-Aviv Univ. 62-, Prof. of Physics 64-; Research Fellow, Calif. Inst. of Technology 63, Visiting Prof. of Physics 64-65; Vice-Rector and Vice-Pres., Tel-Aviv Univ. 65-66, Pres. 71-75; Senior Adviser and Chief Scientist, Ministry of Defence 75-76; Dir. Inst. of Advanced Studies; Wolfson Chair Extraordinary of Theoretical Physics, Tel-Aviv Univ. 77; Chair. Steering Cttee. Project on Waterway between the Mediterranean and the Dead Sea 78-; mem. Israel Atomic Energy Comm. 66-, Israel Nat. Acad. of Sciences 66-; known mainly for his co-discovery of Unitary Symmetry (The Eightfold Way) 61; Foreign Hon. mem., American Acad. of Arts and Sciences 70; Foreign Assoc. Nat. Acad. of Sciences, U.S.A. 72; Hon. Life mem. New York Acad. of Sciences 73; Hon. D.Sc.; Weizmann Prize for the Sciences 66; Rothschild Prize 68, Israel Prize for Exact Sciences 69; Albert Einstein Medal and Prize (U.S.A.) 70.
Publs. *The Eightfold Way* (with M. Gell-Mann) 64, *Algebraic Theory of Particle Physics* 67, *The Past Decade in Particle Theory* (with E. C. G. Sudarshan) 73; about 150 articles on physics, astrophysics and philosophy of science.
Department of Physics and Astronomy, Tel-Aviv University, Tel-Aviv, Israel.

Neguib, Gen. Mohamed; Egyptian army officer; b. 1901, Khartoum, Sudan; ed. Sudan Schools, Gordon Coll., Khartoum, Royal Mil. Acad. and Egyptian Univ., Cairo.
Commissioned in infantry 17; served in Gen. Staff, Adjutant-Gen. and Q.M.-Gens'. departments during Second World War; Sub-Governor of Sinai and Governor of Red Sea Provinces in Frontier Corps; Col. Commdg. 2nd Machine Gun Bn.; Brig., 2nd in commd. of Egyptian troops in Palestine and commdg. successively 1st, 2nd, 3rd, 4th and 10th Inf. Bdes. during hostilities with Israel 48; Dir.-Gen. Frontier Corps 50, Dir.-Gen. Infantry 51, C.-in-C. Egyptian Army July 52; Prime Minister, Minister for War and Marine, C.-in-C. of the Army and Military Gov. of Egypt 52-53; Pres. of the Repub. of Egypt 53-54.
Cairo, Egypt.

Nemery, Field Marshal Gaafar (see Nimeri).

Nimatallah, Yusuf A., PH.D.(ECONS.); Saudi Arabian economist; b. 1936; ed. American Univ., Beirut and Univ. of Massachusetts.
With Banque de l'Indochine 52-57; Teaching Asst. in Econs., Univ. of Mass. 63-65; Prof. Monetary and Int. Econs., Univ. of Riyadh 65- (on leave 73-); Adviser to Minister of Finance on Money and Banking, Oil Finance and Planning 67-73; Adviser to Sultan of Oman on Oil, Finance, Money and Banking; Deputy Chair. and Pres. Central Bank of Oman 75-78; Deputy Chair. UBAF Arab American Bank, New York 76-78; Alt. Exec. Dir. IMF 79-81, Exec. Dir. 81-.
International Monetary Fund, 700 19th Street, N.W., Washington, D.C. 20431, U.S.A.

Nimeri, Field Marshal Gaafar Mohammed al-; Sudanese army officer and political leader; b. 1 Jan. 1930, Omdurman; ed. Hantaib Secondary School, Medani, Sudan Military Coll.
Former Commdr. Khartoum garrison; campaigns against rebels in Southern Sudan; placed under arrest on suspicion of plotting to overthrow the Government; led successful mil. coup May 69; promoted from Col. to Maj.-Gen. May 69, to Field Marshal May 79; Chair. Revolutionary Command Council (R.C.C.) 69-71; C.-in-C. of Armed Forces 69-73; Minister of Defence May-June 69, 72-73, 74-76, 78-79; Prime Minister Oct. 69-Aug. 76, Sept. 77-; Minister of Foreign Affairs 70-71, of Planning 71-72, of Finance Sept. 77-March 78, of Agriculture and Irrigation 81-; Pres. of Sudan Oct. 71-; Supreme Commdr. of Armed Forces 76-; Pres. Political Bureau, Sudanese Socialist Union 71-, Sec.-Gen. 71-76, Pres. Aug. 79-; Pres. of OAU 78-79.
Office of the President, Khartoum, Sudan.

Nimir, Ibrahim Mohamed Aly, B.A., F.I.B.; Sudanese banker; b. 1922; ed. Gordon Memorial Coll. and Univ. of Wales.
Governor and Chair. Bank of Sudan 72-80; Chair. Savings and Investment Council 73; mem. Ministerial Council for Nat. Econ. 73-74, Khartoum Univ. Council 74-, Islamic Univ. Council 74-, Board of Dirs. Sudanese Devt. Corpn. 74-; Alt. Gov. for Sudan, Int. Monetary Fund 72-.
c/o Bank of Sudan, Sharia Gamaa, Khartoum, P.O. Box 313, Sudan.

Nissim, Moshe, LL.D.; Israeli politician; b. 1935, Jerusalem; ed. Hebrew Univ. of Jerusalem.
Elected to Knesset 59- (as rep. of Union of Gen. Zionists 59, subsequently as rep. of Gahal faction of the Liberal Party, then of the Likud Bloc); has served on Defence, Foreign Affairs, Constitution, Law and Justice, Labour and Housing Cttees. of the Knesset; Co-Chair. Likud group 75-79; Chair. Exec. Cttee., Likud Feb. 78-; Minister without Portfolio Jan. 78-Aug. 80; Minister of Justice Aug. 80-.
Ministry of Justice, Jerusalem, Isarel.

Nofal, Sayed, DR. ARTS; Egyptian international civil servant; b. 1910; ed. Cairo Univ.
Head of Literary Dept. *Al Sivassa* 35-38; Teacher, Cairo Univ. 38; later Dir. of Technical Secr., Ministry of Educ. and Ministry of Social Affairs; later Dir. of Legislative Dept., Upper House of Egyptian Parl.; later Dir. Political Dept., League of Arab States, Asst. Sec.-Gen. 60-79.
Publs. include *Poetry of Nature in Arabic and Western Literature* 44, *Egypt in the United Nations* 47, *The Egyptian Parliament in a Quarter of a Century* 51, *The Political Status of the Emirates of the Arab Gulf and Southern Arabia* 59, *A Comparative Study of the Arab League's, United Nations and American States Organisation's Systems* 60, *Ben-Gurion's Version of History* 62, *The Arab-Israeli Conflict* 62, *Arab Unity* 64, *Arab Nationalism* 65, *Arab Socialism* 66, *The Record of Israel* 66, *Joint Arab Action Book I* 68, *Book II* 71, *The Arab Gulf or The Eastern Borders of the Arab Homeland* 69, *An Introduction to Israeli Foreign Policy* 72, *The Relationship between the United Nations and the Arab League* 75, *The International Function of the Arab League* 75, *The Future of Joint Arab Action* 77.
9 Khan Younis Street, Madinet al Mohandesseen, Dokki, Cairo, Egypt.

Nouira, Hedi; Tunisian politician; b. 6 April 1911, Monastir; ed. High School, Sousse, and Paris.
Secretary of Gen. Confed. of Tunisian Workers 38; in detention 38-43; Sec.-Gen. of Parti Socialiste Destourien 42-54, 69-80; Minister of Commerce 54-55; Minister of Finance 55-58; Founder and Dir. of Central Bank of

Tunisia 58-70; Minister of the Economy 70; Prime Minister 70-80.
c/o Premier Ministère, La Kasbah, Tunis, Tunisia.

Nowar, Ma'an Abu; Jordanian diplomatist; b. 26 July 1928, Amman; ed. London Univ.
Joined Jordanian Arab Army 43, Commdr. Infantry Brigade 56-63; Counsellor, Jordanian Embassy, London 63; Dir. Jordan Civil Defence 64-67, Jordan Public Security 67-69; Asst. Chief of Staff for Gen. Affairs 69-72; Minister of Culture and Information 72, of Public Works 80, of Youth, Culture, Tourism and Antiquities 80-; Amb. to U.K. 73-76; Mayor of Amman 76; Jordanian Star (1st Class) and Spanish, Syrian and Lebanese war decorations. Publs. *The Battle of Karameh, In the Path of Jerusalem, 40 Armoured Brigade, The State in War and Peace, Military History—H.M. King Talal.*
Ministry of Public Works, Amman, Jordan.

Numairy, Field Marshal Gaafar (*see* Nimeri).

Nuseibeh, Hazem Zaki, M.A., PH.D.; Jordanian politician; ed. Rawda Coll., Jerusalem, Victoria Coll., Alexandria, American Univ. of Beirut, Law School, Jerusalem, Woodrow Wilson School of Public and Int. Affairs and Princeton Univ.
Under-Secretary, Ministry of Nat. Econ. 57-59; Pres. Jordan Devt. Board 59-61; Minister of Foreign Affairs 62-63, 65-66; Minister of Royal Court 63-65; Prof. of Int. Affairs, Jordan Univ. 66-67; Minister of Reconstruction and Devt. 67-69; Amb. to Egypt 69-71, to Turkey 71-73, to Italy 73-75, also accred. to Austria and Switzerland; Perm. Rep. to UN 76-.
Publs. *Ideas of Arab Nationalism* 56, *Palestine and the United Nations* 81.
Jordanian Mission to the United Nations, 866 United Nations Plaza, Room 550-552, New York, N.Y. 10017, U.S.A.

O

Obaid, Fikri Makram, M.A.; Egyptian politician; b. 29 Feb. 1916, Hermidat, nr. Qenna; ed. Univ. of Cairo Law School.
Law School Rep. on Higher Cttee., Cairo Univ. Student Union 32; joined private law firm 37-50; Lawyer, Court of Cassation, and own law practice 50; Sec.-Gen. Heliopolis Branch, Liberation Rally 53; mem. nat. congress, Nat. Union 56; appointed to People's Assembly Oct. 76; joined Socialist Liberal Party 76, then Vice-Chair.; appointed Sec.-Gen. at foundation of Nat. Democratic Party July 78; mem. Political Bureau, Nat. Democratic Party; Deputy Prime Minister in charge of People's Assembly Affairs Oct. 78-, also of Consultative Council Affairs Sept. 80-; elected to People's Assembly June 79-.
Office of the Deputy Prime Minister, People's Assembly Building, Cairo, Egypt.

Obeidi, Abdul Ati El-, M.SC.; Libyan politician; b. 10 Oct. 1939; ed. Libyan Univ., Manchester Univ., England.
Lecturer, Libyan Univ. 67-70; Acting Minister of Foreign Affairs 70; Minister of Labour 70-77, of Civil Service 74-77; Chair. Gen. Popular Cttee. 77-79; Sec.-Gen. Gen. People's Congress 79-81; Sec. Bureau for External Relations 80-; decorations from Tunisia, The Philippines and Malaysia.
Bureau for External Relations, Tripoli; Home: P.O. Box 2256, Benghazi, Libya.

Okasha, Sarwat Mahmoud Fahmy, D. ÈS L.; Egyptian diplomatist, politician and banker; b. 18 Feb. 1921; ed. Military Coll. and Cairo Univ.
Cavalry officer 39; took part in Palestine war 48-49; Mil. Attaché, Berne 53-54, Paris and Madrid 54-56; Attaché in Presidency of Republic 56-57; U.A.R. Ambassador to Italy 57-58; Minister of Culture and Nat. Guidance and

Pres. of Supreme Council for Literature. Art and Social Sciences 58-62; Chair. Board of Dirs. of Nat. Bank of Egypt 62; mem. UNESCO Exec. Board 62; **mem. Nat. Assembly and Pres. Foreign Affairs Comm. 64-66; Deputy Prime Minister, Minister of Culture 66-68; Minister of Culture 68-71;** Asst. to the Pres. 71-June 72; Pres. of Supreme Council for Literature, Art and Social Sciences; Pres. Egypt-France Ass'n. 65-; Visiting Prof. Coll. de France 73; Corresp. Fellowship, British Acad. 75; led campaign in co-operation with UNESCO to save temples of Abu Simbel and Philae of Nubia; numerous awards incl. UNESCO Gold Medal 70.
Publs. 36 works (incl. translations) since 42, *History of Art* (6 vols.), *The Muslim Painter and the Divine* 79.
Villa 34, St. 14, Maadi, Cairo, Egypt.

Ökün, Gündüz; Turkish university professor and politician; b. 1936.
Former Dean, Faculty of Political Sciences, Univ. of Ankara; Minister of Foreign Affairs June-July 77, 78-79; Republican People's Party.
c/o Republican People's Party, Ankara, Turkey.

Olçay, Osman; Turkish diplomatist; b. 17 Jan. 1924; ed. St. Joseph French Coll., Istanbul, and Faculty of Political Science, Univ. of Ankara.
Joined Ministry of Foreign Affairs, Turkey 45; Lieut., Turkish Army 46; Foreign Ministry 47; Vice-Consul, London 48-50, Second Sec., London 50-52; Chief of Section, Dept. of Econ. Affairs, Ministry of Foreign Affairs 52-54; First Sec. NATO, Paris 54, Counsellor and Deputy Perm. Rep. 58-59; Asst. Dir.-Gen. NATO Dept., Min. of Foreign Affairs, Ankara 59-60, Dir.-Gen. 60-63, Asst. Sec.-Gen. 63-64; Amb. to Finland 64-66, to India and Ceylon 66-68; Deputy Sec.-Gen. of NATO, Brussels 69-71; Minister of Foreign Affairs March-Dec. 71; Perm. Rep. to UN 72-75, to NATO Aug. 78-.
Turkish Delegation to NATO, Boulevard Léopold III, 1110 Brussels, Belgium.

Oman, Sultan of (*see* Qaboos bin Said).

Omran, Adnan; Syrian diplomatist; b. 9 Aug. 1934, Syria; ed. Univ. of Damascus, Moscow, U.S.S.R. and Columbia Univ., U.S.A.
Ministry of Foreign Affairs 62-63; mem. Perm. Mission to UN 63-66; First Sec., Moscow 66-68; Consul-Gen., Embassy in Berlin, German Dem. Repub. 68-70; Dir. Int. Org. and Conf. Dept., Ministry of Foreign Affairs 70-71, Palestine Dept. 71-72, Special Bureau Dept. 72-74, concurrently mem. Del. to UN 70-73; Amb. to U.K. and Sweden 74-80; Asst. Sec.-Gen. for Political Affairs, League of Arab States Oct. 80-.
League of Arab States, Khairaldin Basha Street, Tunis, Tunisia.

Onan, Umit Suleyman; Cypriot barrister and politician; b. 1928, Nicosia; ed. Turkish Lycée, Cyprus, Lincoln's Inn, London.
Member of Nicosia Municipal Council 53-58, of Cyprus House of Reps. 60; Cyprus Rep. at Consultative Assembly of Council of Europe 61; Turkish Cypriot Rep. to Tripartite Liaison Cttee. 63; mem. Turkish Cypriot Legislative Assembly 73, Deputy Leader 73-75; Turkish Cypriot Chief Negotiator at Intercommunal Talks 76-.
Office of the Chief Negotiator, Lefkoşa (Nicosia), Mersin 10, Turkey.

Örek, Osman Nuri; Cypriot lawyer and politician; b. 1925; ed. Turkish Lycée, Nicosia, Univ. of Istanbul and Middle Temple, London.
Founder-mem. Cyprus Turkish Asscn., London; Sec.-Gen. Cyprus Turkish Nat. Union Party 55-60; Deputy Chair. High Council of Ecvaf 56-60; rep. Turkish Cypriot Community at London Conf. 59 and subsequent Joint Cttee.; Minister of Defence 59; mem. Exec. Council of Turkish

Cypriot Provisional Admin. for Defence 67-74, concurrently for Internal Affairs 67-70, and External Affairs 67-72; mem. Exec. Council of Autonomous Turkish Cypriot Admin. for Vice-Presidency and Defence 74-75; Vice-Pres. "Turkish Federated State of Cyprus" (TFSC) 75-76; Minister of Defence 75-76; Pres. TFSC Legislative Assembly 76-78; Prime Minister April-Dec. 78; Leader, Nat. Unity Party 78; Founder-mem. Democratic People's Party 79.
Law Office of Osman N. Örek and Associates, Müftü Raci Street, Ontaş Building Nos. 1 and 2, Lefkoşa, Mersin 10, Turkey; Home: 10 Ismail Beyoglu Street, Lefkoşa, Mersin 10, Turkey.

Ortiz, René Genaro; Ecuadorian chemical and industrial engineer, economist and administrator; b. 31 Dec. 1941, Quito; ed. Nat. Polytechnic School, Quito, Univ. of Miami, Tufts Univ. and Harvard Univ.
Marketing Head of Ecuadorian State Petroleum Corpn. (CEPE) 73-75, Asst. Consultant for CEPE Gen. Man. 75-78; Chief Adviser to Minister of Natural and Energy Resources and Chief Co-ordinator of Petroleum Policy Advisory Bd., 75-78; mem. OPEC Econ. Comm. Bd. 75-78, of Bd. of Govs. 75-78, Sec.-Gen. of OPEC 79-81; Head del. to Bd. of Latin American Energy Org. 76-78; mem. Oxford Energy Club 78-; Hon. Citizen, Cape Canaveral, of Brebad County, Fla.; Exec. of Year, Ecuador 77.
Publs. *Programmed Instruction for Management Training Centre in Ecuador* 73, *Project Management with PERT and CPM* 78.
c/o OPEC, Obere Donaustrasse 93, 1020 Vienna, Austria.

Osman, Ahmed, LL.D.; Moroccan diplomatist and politician; b. 3 Jan. 1930, Oujda; m. Princess Lallah Nezha (sister of King Hassan II, q.v.); ed. Royal High School, Rabat, Univ. of Rabat and Univ. of Bordeaux, France.
Member of Royal Cabinet (judicial matters) 56; joined Ministry of Foreign Affairs 57; Sec.-Gen. Ministry of Nat. Defence 59-61; Amb. to Fed. Repub. of Germany 61-62; Under Sec.-of-State for Industry and Mines 63-64; Pres. and Gen. Man. Moroccan Navigation Co. 64-67; Ambassador to U.S.A., Canada and Mexico 67-70; Minister of Admin. Affairs 70-71; Dir. of Royal Cabinet 71-72; Prime Minister 72-79; Head Nat. Defence Council March 79-; Parliamentary Rep. for Oujda 77-; Leader of Nat. Independent Group in Chamber of Reps., Leader of Independent Liberals Dec. 80-; participated in UN sessions 57, 58, 60, 61, Conf. on Maritime Law 58, Conf. of the League of Arab States 61; Leader of Moroccan Dels. to various Int. Confs.
National Defence Council, Rabat, Morocco.

Osman, Osman Ahmed, B.SC.; Egyptian civil engineer; b. 6 April 1917; ed. Cairo Univ.
Founded Civil engineering co. 41; Chair. The Arab Contractors (Osman Ahmed Osman & Co.) 49-73 (now Hon. Life Pres.), and of its assoc. companies, Saudi Enterprises, Kuwaiti Engineering Co., The Libyan Co. for Contracting and Devt.; Minister of Reconstruction 73-74, of Housing and Reconstruction 74-76; mem. for Ismailia, People's Assembly Oct. 76-; mem. National Democratic Party, Chair. NDP Cttee. for Popular Devt.; Deputy Prime Minister for Popular Devt. Feb.-May 81; Chair. Syndicate of Engineers March 79-; Chair. Ismaili Football Club; Head Agricultural Projects Complex for Food Security; Hon. LL.D. (Ricker Coll. of the North East) 76; Repub. Medal (1st Class), Russian Hero of Labour Medal; Nile Medal (1st Class) 80.
Chief works undertaken include: (in Egypt) Aswan High Dam, Suez Canal deepening and widening, Port Said Shipyard, Cairo Int. Airport, High Dam Electric Power Transmission Lines, Guiza Bridge and Ramses Bridge over the Nile, Suez Canal restoration, Suez Canal area devt. programme, western coast devt. programme; (in Saudi Arabia) Dhahran Airport, Riyadh Mil. Coll., Dammam Mil. Barracks; (in Kuwait) Municipality Centre, Kuwait drainage system; (in Libya) Benghazi drainage system, Benghazi Stadium; (in Iraq) Kirkuk area Feeder Canal; (in Jordan) Khaled Ibn El-Walid Dam and Tunnels (Yarmouk River); (in Sudan) 200 bedroom First Class Hotel.
Publ. *The High Dam* (lecture) 66, *My Experience* 81.
People's Assembly, Cairo, Egypt.

Otaiba, Mana Said al-, M.SC.; United Arab Emirates economist; b. 15 May 1946; ed. Univ. of Baghdad.
Chairman of Board, Abu Dhabi Nat. Oil Co.; mem. Abu Dhabi Planning Board; Pres. Dept. of Petroleum, Minerals and Industry; Chair. of Board, Abu Dhabi Gas Liquefaction Co.; Minister of Petroleum and Industry (Abu Dhabi) 72-73, of Petroleum and Mineral Resources (U.A.E. Fed. Govt.) 73-79, of Petroleum and Natural Resources June 79-; Pres. OPEC 79, OAPEC 80; mem. Board of all seven oil cos. in Abu Dhabi; has travelled on State visits, etc. throughout Arab countries. W. Europe, U.S., Canada.
Publs. *The Abu Dhabi Planning Board, The Economy of Abu Dhabi, Organization of the Petroleum Exporting Countries, Petroleum and the Economy of the United Arab Emirates.*
Ministry of Petroleum, P.O. Box 59, Al Batin Area, Abu Dhabi, United Arab Emirates.

Othman, Khalil Issa, M.SC.(ECON); Jordanian international official; b. Nov. 1937, Jerusalem; ed. Bethlehem High School, American Univ., Cairo, Univ. of London.
Attaché, Ministry of Foreign Affairs, Amman 62; Third Sec., Jordanian Embassy, London 62-64; Lecturer, Faculty of Islamic Law, Amman 67; First Sec. Perm. Mission of Jordan to the UN 68-71; UN Official, Area Officer Lebanon and Syria, UNDP 71-73; Regional Project Officer UNDP, New York 73-75; UNDP Liaison Officer with ECWA and Deputy Resident Rep. Beirut and Amman 75-77; Resident Rep. UNDP, Kuwait 77-.
United Nations Development Programme, P.O. Box 2993, Safat, Kuwait.

Othman as-Said, Muhammad; Libyan politician; b. Oct. 1922; ed. Sanusi religious institutions, Fezzan.
Head of Religious Court for Admin. Region of Brak 45; organized Libyan Nationalist Activity in Fezzan 47; imprisoned by French 48-50; Leader Fezzan Del. to Libyan Independence Comm. 50; mem. Constituent Assembly 50; mem. Advisory Comm. to UN in Libya 50; Minister of Health, Libya 51, later Minister of Public Health until 58; Deputy to Constituent Assembly 58; Minister for Econ. Affairs 60; Prime Minister 60-March 63; Deputy 64; private business 64-; numerous decorations.
Geraba Street 6, Tripoli, Libya.

Özal, Turgut, M.SC.; Turkish economist and government official; b. 1927, Malatya; ed. Univ. of Istanbul.
Worked for Gen. Directorate, Electrical Survey Administration on projects for hydroelectric dams of Hirfanli, Kemer and Demirkopru, also Asst. to Gen. Dir.; Postgraduate work in U.S.A. 52-53; mem. Scientific Advisory Board, Ministry of Defence 60-61; Teacher, Middle East Technical Univ.; Special Technical Advisor to the Prime Minister; Under Sec., State Planning Organization 67-71; Consultant of Special Projects, World Bank 71-73; Man. Dir. various industrial organizations 73-79; Head, Turkish Asscn. of Working Industries (MESS) May-Dec. 79; Under-Sec. to Prime Minister and Acting Under-Sec., State Planning Org. 79-80; Deputy Prime Minister for Econ. Affairs Sept. 80-; IMF Gov. for Turkey Oct. 80-; fmr. Head Economic Comm. Council, Money and Credit Council, RCD Coordination Council, Tourism Coordination Council, Mining Expansion Projects Council, Fresh Fruit and Vegetables Export Promotion Council, EEC Coordination Council.
Office of the Deputy Prime Minister for Economic Affairs, Ankara, Turkey.

Özbek, Dr. Sabahattin; Turkish agronomist and politician; b. 1915, Erzincan; ed. Secondary School, Istanbul, Faculty of Agriculture, Univ. of Ankara.
Lecturer, Faculty of Agriculture, Univ. of Ankara 38, Asst. Prof. 41, Prof. 53, Dean 55-57, 65-68; Visiting Prof. Univs. of Michigan and Calif. 50-51, 57-58; Minister of Nat. Educ. 72-73, of Communications 73-74, of Agriculture and Forestry Sept. 80-; founded Atatürk Univ., Erzurum, later Co-Founder Faculty of Agriculture, Adana; Chair. Agricultural Cttee. for the preparation of First Five-Year Devt. Plan; mem. Turkish Atomic Energy Comm.; Prize of Professional Honour, Union of Agricultural Engineers; Independent.
Publs. 35 books in Turkish and foreign languages.
Ministry of Agriculture and Forestry, Taram ve Orman Bakanlığı, Ankara, Turkey.

Özdaş, Mehmet Nimet, DR.ING.; Turkish professor of mechanical engineering; b. 26 March 1921, Istanbul; ed. Technical Univ. of Istanbul, Imperial Coll., London and London Univ.
Dozent, Technical Univ. of Istanbul 52, Prof. 61-73, Dir. Computation Centre 62-64; Visiting Prof. Case Inst. of Technology 58-59; Sec.-Gen. Scientific and Technical Research Council 64-67, mem. Science Board 68-71; Rep. to CENTO Science Council 65, to NATO Science Cttee. 66-73; Dir. Marmara Scientific and Industrial Research Inst. 69-73; Asst. Sec.-Gen. for Scientific and Environmental Affairs, NATO Sept. 73-79; Prof. of Automatic Control, Istanbul Technical Univ. 79-.
Publs. about 20 articles in English in scientific periodicals, many articles in Turkish and five books.
Istanbul Technical University ITÜ, Gümüşsuyu, Istanbul, Turkey.

P

Pachachi, Adnan al-, PH.D.; Iraqi diplomatist; b. 14 May 1923; ed. American Univ. of Beirut and Georgetown Univ., Washington, D.C.
Joined Foreign Service 44, served Washington, Alexandria; Dir.-Gen. of Political Affairs, Council of Ministers 57-58; Dir.-Gen. Ministry of Foreign Affairs 58-59; Perm. Rep. of Iraq to UN 59-65; Minister of State Dec. 65-66; Minister of Foreign Affairs 66-67; Perm. Rep. to UN 67-69; Minister of State, Govt. of Abu Dhabi, United Arab Emirates (UAE) 71-74; Personal Rep. of Pres. of the UAE and mem. Abu Dhabi Exec. Council 74-.
c/o Manhal Palace, Abu Dhabi, United Arab Emirates.

Paganelli, Robert Peter, B.A.; American diplomatist; b. 3 Nov. 1931, New York; ed. Hamilton Coll., Clinton and Harvard Univ., U.S.A.
Air Force 51-54; joined Foreign Service 58; Attaché, U.S. Embassy, Beirut 60-61, Second Sec. 63-65; Vice-Consul and Third Sec., Basra and Baghdad 61-63; Second Sec. and Political Officer, Damascus 65-67, Amman 67-68; assigned to Washington, D.C. 68-71; First Sec. and Political Officer, Rome 71-74; Amb. to Qatar 74-77; mem. Exec. Seminar on Nat. and Int. Affairs, Dept. of State 77-78; Dir. Office of Western European Affairs 78-79; Minister-Counsellor and Deputy Chief of Mission, Rome 79-81; Amb. to Syria 81-; Woodrow Wilson Fellow 57-58; Meritorious Honor Award (Dept. of State) 66, 74.
American Embassy, rue al-Mansour 2, Damascus, Syria.

Pahlbod, Mehrdad, B.SC.; Iranian politician; b. Teheran; ed. Univ. of Teheran and in France.
Former Deputy Prime Minister and Sec. of State for Fine Arts; Minister of Culture and Arts 64-79; mem. Political Bureau, Rastakhiz Party.
Teheran, Iran.

Panayides, Tasos Christou, M.A.; Cypriot diplomatist; b. 9 April 1934, Ktima, Paphos; ed. Paphos Gymnasium,

Teachers' Training Coll., Univ. of London, Univ. of Indiana (U.S.A.).
Instructor 54-59; First Sec. to the Pres. 60-68; Dir. of Office of the Pres. 69; Amb. to Fed. Repub. of Germany, also accred. to Switzerland, Austria and IAEA; High Commr. in the U.K. Feb. 79- also accred. to Denmark, Malta, Norway, Sweden, Iceland; Grand Order of the Fed. Repub. of Germany, Grand Cross in Gold with Stars and Sash of Repub. of Austria.
Cyprus High Commission, 93 Park Street, London, W1Y 4ET; 5 Cheyne Walk, London, S.W.3, England.

Papadopoulos, Tassos; Cypriot lawyer and politician; b. 1934; ed. Pancyprian Gymnasium, Nicosia, King's Coll., London, and Gray's Inn, London.
Law practice, Nicosia 55-59; fmr. mem. EOKA; mem. Constitutional Comm. drafting Cyprus Constitution 59-60; Minister of Interior *a.i.* 59-60; Minister of Labour and Social Insurance 60-70; Acting Minister of Agriculture 64-66, Minister of Health 60-70; M.P., Deputy Pres. House of Reps. July 70-; practising lawyer; Rep. of Greek Cypriot Community at Intercommunal Talks June 76-July 78.
Chanteclair Building, Apt. 105-205, Nicosia, Cyprus.

Papaioannou, Ezekias; Cypriot journalist; b. 8 Oct. 1908; ed. American Acad., Larnaca, Cyprus.
Secretary-General, Progressive Party of the Working People (Anorthotikon Komma Ergazomenou Laou— AKEL) 49-; Deputy of AKEL, House of Reps. 60-; mem. Foreign Affairs Cttee., House of Reps. 60-, Chair. Communications and Works Cttee. 70-.
AKEL, 10 Akamantos Street, P.O. Box 1827, Nicosia; and 8 Doiranis Street, Nicosia, Cyprus.

Parker, Richard B., M.S.; American diplomatist; b. 3 July 1923, Philippines; ed. Kansas State Univ. and Princeton Univ.
Woodrow Wilson Fellow, Princeton Univ.; Second Sec., Amman 55-56; Dept. of State 57-61; First Sec., Beirut 61-64; Political Counsellor, Cairo 65-67; Country Dir. for U.A.R., Dept. of State 67-70; Minister Counsellor, Rabat 70-74; Amb. to Algeria 74-77, to Lebanon 77-78, to Morocco 78-79; Faculty Adviser, Air Univ., Maxwell Air Force Base 79-; retired from foreign service 80; Diplomat-in-residence, Univ. of Virginia 80-; Editor *Middle East Journal* 81-.
Publ. *Practical Guide to Islamic Monuments of Cairo* 74, *Practical Guide to Islamic Monuments of Morocco.*
1761 N Street, N.W., Washington, D.C. 20036, U.S.A.

Patinkin, Don, PH.D.; Israeli economist; b. 8 Jan. 1922; ed. Univ. of Chicago.
Assistant Prof. of Economics, Univ. of Chicago 47-48; Research Assoc., Cowles Comm. for Economic Research 47-48; Assoc. Prof. of Economics, Univ. of Ill. 48-49; Lecturer, The Eliezer Kaplan School of Economics and Social Sciences, Hebrew Univ. 49, Assoc. Prof. of Econs. 52, Prof. 57; Dir. of Research, Maurice Falk Inst. for Economic Research, in Israel 56-72; Pres. Econometric Soc. 74; mem. Israel Acad. of Sciences and Humanities 63; Foreign Hon. mem. American Acad. of Arts and Sciences, Hon. mem. American Econ. Asscn; Rothschild Prize 59, Israel Prize 70; Hon. D. Hum.Litt (Univ. of Chicago) 76.
Publs. *Money, Interest and Prices: An Integration of Monetary and Value Theory* 56 (2nd edn. 65), *The Israel Economy: The First Decade* 59, *Studies in Monetary Economics* 72, *Keynes' Monetary Thought: a Study of its Development* 76, *Keynes, Cambridge and The General Theory* (co-editor) 77, *Essays On and In the Chicago Tradition* 80, *Anticipations of the General Theory? and other essays on Keynes* 82.
Chovevei Zion 5, Talbieh, Jerusalem 92225, Israel.

Patsalides, Andreas, B.SC.ECONS.; Cypriot politician; b. 23 Sept. 1922; ed. Greek Gymnasium, Limassol, School of

Econs. and Political Science, London and Harvard Univ., Mass.

Various posts in Public Service; Dir.-Gen. Planning Bureau then Economic Planning Comm. 59-68; Minister of Finance 68-79; Gov. Bank of Cyprus Nov. 79-.

Bank of Cyprus Ltd., P.O. Box 1472, 86, 88, 90 Phaneromeni Street, Nicosia, Cyprus.

Pazhwak, Abdurrahman; Afghan diplomatist; b. 7 March 1919.

Has been successively mem. Historical Section of Afghan Acad.; Dir. Foreign Publications Section of Afghan Press Dept.; Editor daily *Islah* and acting Dir.-Gen. of Bakhtar News Agency; Pres. Pashto-Tolana; Dir.-Gen. Publs. Section, Afghan Press Dept.; Press and Cultural Attaché, Afghan Embassy, London; mem. of Section of Information Dept. of ILO; Press and Cultural Attaché, Afghan Embassy, Washington; Dir. Section for East Asia and Dir. a.i., Section for UN, and Int. Confs., Afghan Ministry for Foreign Affairs; Dir.-Gen. Political Affairs in Ministry of Foreign Affairs 56; Perm. Rep. to UN 58-73; Amb. to Fed. Repub. of Germany 73, to India 73-77, to U.K. 77-78; Pres. UN Human Rights Comm. 63, 21st Session of UN Gen. Assembly 66, 5th Special Session 66 and of Emergency Session of Gen. Assembly on Middle East 66; Special Envoy to Fourth Summit of Non-Aligned Countries, Algiers 73, to Summit of Islamic Conf., Lahore 74; Special Envoy to Pres. of Bangladesh; arrested after April 78 revolution, released Dec. 79, flew to Delhi for medical attention March 82 and announced intention to set up a govt.-in-exile to unite all political groups resisting Soviet occupation.

Publs. *Aryana or Ancient Afghanistan, Pakhtunistan* (both in English), *Tales of the People* 58 (in Persian), and many other works.

Delhi, India.

Peres, Shimon; Israeli politician; b. 15 Aug. 1923, Poland; ed. New York Univ., Harvard Univ.

Immigrated to Palestine 34; fmr. Sec. Hano'ar Ha'oved Movt.; mem. Haganah Movt. 47; Head of Israel Naval Service, Ministry of Defence 48; Head of Defence Mission in U.S.A. 50; Deputy Dir.-Gen. of Ministry of Defence 52-53, Dir.-Gen. 53-59, Deputy Minister of Defence 59-65; mem. Knesset -59; mem. Mapai Party 59-65, founder mem. and Sec.-Gen. Rafi Party 65, mem. Labour Party after merger 68; Minister for Econ. Devt. in the Administered Areas and for Immigrant Absorption 69-70, of Transport and Communications 70-74, of Information March-June 74, of Defence 74-77; Acting Prime Minister April-May 77; elected Leader of Labour Party June 77.

Publs. *The Next Phase* 65, *David's Sling* 70, *Tomorrow is Now* 78, *With These Men* 78 and numerous political articles in Israeli and foreign publications.

Israel Labour Party, P.O. Box 3263, Tel-Aviv, Israel.

Perlman, Itzhak; Israeli violinist; b. 31 Aug. 1945, Tel-Aviv; ed. Tel-Aviv Acad. of Music, Juilliard School, U.S.A.

Gave recitals on radio at the age of 10; went to U.S.A. 58; studied with Ivan Galamian and Dorothy De Lay; first recital at Carnegie Hall 63; has played with major American orchestras 64-; has toured Europe regularly and played with major European orchestras 66-; debut in U.K. with London Symphony Orchestra 68; appearances at Israel Festival, South Bank Summer Concerts, London 68, 69.

c/o Harold Holt Ltd., 31 Sinclair Road, London, W14 0NS, England.

Perowne, Stewart Henry, O.B.E., K.ST.J., M.A., F.S.A.; British orientalist and historian; b. 17 June 1901; ed. Haileybury Coll., Corpus Christi Coll. Cambridge, and Harvard Univ.

English Lecturer, Govt. Arab Coll. Jerusalem 27-30; Asst. Sec. Palestine Govt. 30-32, Asst. District Commr. 32-34; Asst. Sec. Malta 34-37; Political Officer, Aden 37; Arabic

Programme Organizer, B.B.C. 38; Information Officer, Aden 39-41; Public Relations Attaché, British Embassy, Baghdad 41-44, Oriental Counsellor 44-47; Colonial Sec. Barbados 47-50; Acting Gov. March-Oct. 49; Adviser, Ministry of Interior, Cyrenaica 50-51; Adviser on Arab Affairs, U.K. Del. UN Gen. Assembly 51; discovered ancient Aziris 51; Hon. Asst. Jerusalem Diocesan Refugee Organization 52; designed and supervised seven Arab refugee villages 52-56; Faculty mem. "College Year in Athens" 65-66; Hon. Fellow Corpus Christi Coll., Cambridge 81.

Publs. *The One Remains* 54, *Herod the Great* 56, *The Later Herods* 58, *Hadrian* 60, *Caesars and Saints* 62, *The Pilgrim's Companion in Jerusalem and Bethlehem* 63, *The Pilgrim's Companion in Roman Rome* 63, *The Pilgrim's Companion in Athens* 65, *Jerusalem* 65, *The End of the Roman World* 66, *Death of the Roman Republic* 68, *Roman Mythology* 69, *The Siege within the Walls* 70, *Rome* 71, *The Journeys of Saint Paul* 73, *The Caesars' Wives: above Suspicion?* 74, *The Archaeology of Greece and the Aegean* 74, *Holy Places of Christendom* 76.

44 Arminger Road, London, W12 7BB, England.

Petrides, Frixos L.; Cypriot teacher and politician; b. 1915, Nicosia; ed. Pancyprian Gymnasium and Univ. of Athens.

In Athens during Second World War; teacher, Pancyprian Gymnasium after Second World War; Chair. Pancyprian Asscn. 47-60; Headmaster, Pancyprian Gymnasium 60; Chair. of Board, Cyprus Broadcasting Corpn. 60-70; Minister of Educ. 70-72; Chair. Cyprus Tourism Org. 72-.

Cyprus Tourism Organization, P.O. Box 4535, Nicosia, Cyprus.

Pharaon, Ghaith Rashad, PH.D., M.B.A.; Saudi Arabian business executive; b. 7 Sept. 1940, Riyadh; ed. Stanford Univ., Harvard Univ.

Founder Saudi Arabia Research and Devt. Corpn. (Redec) 65, now Chair. of Board and Dir.-Gen.; Chair. Board Saudi Arabian Parsons Ltd., Saudi Automotive Industries Ltd., Redec Daelim Ltd., Interstal, Saudi Chemical Processors Ltd., Arabian Maritime Co., Saudi Inland Transport, United Commercial Agencies, etc.; Vice-Chair. Jezirah Bank Ltd., Saudi Light Industries Ltd., Arabian Chemical Industries Ltd.; mem. Board Okaz Publications, Tihama; Commendatore (Italy); King Abdul Aziz Award.

P.O. Box 1935, Jeddah; Home: Ghaith Pharaon Residence, Ruwais, Jeddah, Saudi Arabia.

Polyakov, Vladimir Porfiriyevich, PH.D.; Soviet diplomatist; b. 1931; ed. Inst. of Oriental Studies, Moscow.

Diplomatic Service 56-; Counsellor, Syria 61-65; various posts in Ministry of Foreign Affairs 65-67; Counsellor-Minister, Egypt 68-71; Amb. to People's Democratic Repub. of Yemen 72-74, to Egypt May 74- (expelled Sept. 81.)

Embassy of the U.S.S.R., 95 Sh. El Giza (Giza), Cairo, Egypt.

Pritchard, James Bennett, A.B., B.D., PH.D., S.T.D., D.D., L.H.D. American orientalist; b. 4 Oct. 1909; ed. Asbury; Coll., Drew Univ., Univ. of Pa.

Professor of Old Testament Literature, Crozer Theological Seminary 42-54; Annual Prof. American School of Oriental Research, Jerusalem 50-51; Visiting Prof. 56-57, 61-62; Prof. Old Testament Literature Church Divinity School of the Pacific 54-62; Prof. Religious Thought, Univ. of Pa. and Curator of Biblical Archaeology Univ. Museum 62-78, Assoc. Dir. 67-76, Dir. 76-77; Visiting Prof. of Archaeology, American Univ. of Beirut 67, Trustee 70-; mem. American Oriental Soc., Archaeological Inst. of America (Pres. 73-74), Soc. for Biblical Literature; Editor *Journal of the American Oriental Soc.* 52-54.

Publs. *Palestinian Figures* 43, *Ancient Near Eastern Texts* 50, *The Ancient Near East in Pictures* 54, *Archaeology and* the Old Testament 58, Gibeon, Where the Sun Stood Still 62, The Ancient Near East: Supplementary Texts and Pictures 69, The Ancient Near East Vol. II 75, Recovering Sarepta 78. University Museum, 33rd and Spruce Streets, Philadelphia Pa. 19104 U.S.A.

Q

Qaboos bin Said; Sultan of Oman; b. 18 Nov. 1940; ed. by British tutors and at Royal Military Coll., Sandhurst. In Britain 58-66; served in British Army and studied local government; returned to Salalah 66; deposed his father Said bin Taimur 70; Sultan July 70-, also Minister of Foreign Affairs, Defence and Finance.
The Palace, Muscat, Sultanate of Oman.

Qaddafi, Col. Muammar al- (see Gaddafi, Muammar al-).

Qaissi, Fawzi al- (see Kaissi, Fawzi al-).

Qatar, Amir of (see Thani, Sheikh Khalifa bin Hamad al-).

Qotbzadeh, Sadeq (see Ghotbzadeh, Sadeq).

Quandt, William B., PH.D.; American educationist and administrator; b. 1941; ed. Stanford Univ., Massachusetts Inst. of Tech.
Served with RAND Corpn., California 68-72; with National Security Council Staff, Middle East Office 72-74, 77-79; Assoc. Prof. of Political Science, Univ. of Pennsylvania 74-76; Senior Fellow Foreign Policy Program, Brookings Institution.
Publs. Revolution and Political Leadership: Algeria 54-68, 69, The Politics of Palestinian Nationalism (Co-author), Decade of Decisions: American Policy towards the Arab-Israeli Conflict 67-76, Saudi Arabia in the 1980s; Foreign Policy, Security, Oil.
The Brookings Institution, 1775 Massachusetts Avenue, Washington, D.C. 20036, U.S.A.

Quddus, Ihsan Abdal (son of the late Rose al-Yussuf, famous actress and writer); Egyptian writer; b. 1 Jan. 1919; ed. Univ. of Cairo.
Practised law 42; joined magazine Rose al-Yussuf 42, imprisoned for attack on govt. 45, released and became Chief Editor, again imprisoned 50, 51; first novel publ. 54; Editor Akhbar al-Yom until 74; writer for Al-Ahram May 74-.
Publs. include I am Free 54, Do not Turn out the Sun (two vols.) 60, Nothing Matters 63.
c/o Al-Ahram, Galaa Street, Cairo, Egypt.

Quraishi, Abdul Aziz al-, M.B.A., F.I.B.A.; Saudi Arabian government official; b. 1930, Hail; ed. Univ. of Southern California, U.S.A.
General Man. State Railways 61-68; Pres. Gen. Personnel Bureau 68-74; Minister of State 71-74; Pres. and Gov. Saudi Arabian Monetary Agency 74-; Gov. Int. Monetary Fund, Arab Monetary Fund; Alt. Gov. for Saudi Arabia Islamic Devt. Bank; mem. Board of Dirs., Supreme Council for Petroleum and Mineral Affairs, Gen. Petroleum and Mineral Org., Public Investment Fund, Pension Fund.
Saudi Arabian Monetary Agency, P.O.Box 2992, Riyadh; Home: Saudi Arabian Monetary Agency Staff Compound, Malaz, Riyadh, Saudi Arabia.

R

Rabin, Maj.-Gen. Yitzhak; Israeli army officer and politician; b. 1 March 1922, Jerusalem; ed. Kadoorie Agricultural School, Kfar Tabor, and Staff Coll., England.
Palmach commands 43-48, including War of Independence; represented Israel Defence Forces (I.D.F.) at Rhodes armistice negotiations; fmr. Head of Training Dept.,

I.D.F.; C.-in-C. Northern Command 56-59; Head, Manpower Branch 59-60; Deputy Chief of Staff and Head, Gen. Staff Branch 60-64, Chief of Staff I.D.F. 64-68; Amb. to U.S.A. 68-73; mem. Knesset Jan. 74-; Minister of Labour March-April 74; Prime Minister 74-June 77, also Minister of Communications 74-75; Leader Labour Party 74-April 77; Hon. Doctorates, Jerusalem Univ. 67, Dropsie Coll. 68, Brandeis Univ. 68, Yeshiva Univ. 68, Coll. of Jewish Studies, Chicago 69, Univ. of Miami 70, Hebrew Union Coll., Boston 71.
c/o The Knesset, Jerusalem, Israel.

Rafael, Gideon; Israeli diplomatist; b. Germany 5 March 1913; ed. Univ. of Berlin.
Emigrated 34; mem. Kibbutz 34-43; active in Haganah and war services 39-42; Jewish Agency, Political Dept. 43; in charge of preparation of Jewish case for Jewish Agency, Political Dept., Nuremberg War Crimes Trial 45-46; mem. of Jewish Agency Comm. to Anglo-American Comm. of Enquiry 46, and of Jewish Agency mission to UN Special Comm. for Palestine 47; mem. Israel Permanent Del. to UN 51-52; alternate rep. to UN 53; rep. at UN Gen. Assemblies 47-66; Counsellor in charge of Middle East and UN Affairs, Ministry for Foreign Affairs 53-57; Amb. to Belgium and Luxembourg 57-60, to the European Econ. Community 59; Deputy Dir.-Gen. Ministry of Foreign Affairs 60; Head of Israel Del. Int. Conf. Law of the Sea, Geneva 60; Deputy Dir.-Gen. Ministry for Foreign Affairs 60-65; Perm. Rep. to UN, Geneva 65-66; Special Amb. and Adviser to Foreign Minister May 66-67; Perm. Rep. of Israel to UN 67; Dir.-Gen. Ministry of Foreign Affairs 67-71; Senior Political Adviser to Minister of Foreign Affairs 72-73; Amb. to U.K. 73-77, concurrently non-Resident Amb. to Ireland 75-77; Head of Del. to UNCTAD III 72.
Kiryath Yovel, Jerusalem, Israel.

Rahal, Abdellatif; Algerian diplomatist; b. 1922.
Professor of mathematics; Govt. service 62; Dir.-Gen. Presidential Cabinet 63; first Algerian Amb. to France 64; then posts in Ministry of Foreign Affairs; Sec.-Gen. Ministry of Foreign Affairs until 70; Perm. Rep. to UN 70-77; Minister of Higher Educ. and Scientific Research 77-79.
c/o Ministry of Higher Education and Scientific Research, 1 rue Attard Bachir, Algiers, Algeria.

Raphael, Farid Elie; Lebanese banker and government official; b. 27 Oct. 1933, Dlebta, Kesrouan; ed. Univ. of St. Joseph, Beirut, Univ. of Lyons, France.
Joined Compagnie Algérienne de Crédit et de Banque, Beirut 56, Asst. Man. 65, Gen. Man. 67, mem. Board 67-; Founded Banque Libano Française SAL, Paris 67, Gen. Man. 71-; mem. Board 73-, Chair. and Gen. Man. 79-; founded Banque Libano Française (France) S.A. 76, Vice-Chair. and Gen. Man.; Minister of Justice, Finance, Posts, Telephones and Telecommunications 76-79.
Banque Libano Française SAL., P.O.Box II 808, Beirut, Lebanon; Home. Baroody Building, Hazmieh, Lebanon.

Rasheed, Khalafalla el, LL.B., LL.M.; Sudanese judge; b. 15 Feb. 1930, Merowe District; ed. Hantub Secondary School, Univ. Coll. of Khartoum, Cambridge and London Univs.
Joined Sudan Judiciary 55; District Judge (Second Grade) 56, First Grade 60; in practice as advocate 56-57; recalled to Judiciary 57; transferred to Attorney-Gen.'s Dept. 62; Advocate Gen. 67-72; Pres. Supreme Court (Chief Justice) 72-; Order of King Abdul Aziz, Third Class, Order of El Nilein, First Class, Order of Algamhuria, First Class.
Publs. The Law and the Citizen (pamphlet) 67, various newspaper articles on legal topics.
Law Courts, P.O. Box 763, Khartoum, Sudan.

Rashid bin Said al-Maktum (*see* Maktum, Rashid bin Said al-).

Rateb, Mrs. Aisha, PH.D.; Egyptian politician; ed. Faculty of Law, Cairo Univ.
Junior Lecturer, Faculty of Law, Cairo Univ., Prof. of Int. Law; Minister of Social Affairs 71-76, of Social Affairs and Insurance 76-77; Amb. Extraordinary, Ministry of Foreign Affairs Nov. 78-; Chair. Int. Law Cttee. 73-.
c/o Ministry of Foreign Affairs, Cairo, Egypt.

Rawi, Saad Abdul Baki al-, PH.D.; Iraqi educator; b. 15 June 1930, Anah; ed. American Univ., Beirut, Univ. of Illinois and Stanford Univ., U.S.A.
Professor of Biochem., Baghdad Univ. 59-68, Vice-Pres. 68, Pres. 71-74; Pres. Basrah Univ. 69; Minister of Educ. 69; UNESCO Research Scholarship, Warsaw Univ. 62-63, Nat. Science Foundation Scholarship for Research at Oregon State Univ. 66; Dir. UNESCO Regional Office for Science and Technology in the Arab States 77-; taken part in numerous int. confs. on educ.; mem. Iraqi Chem. Soc., Arab Students Org. in U.S.A.; Exec. mem. Iraqi Teachers Syndicate.
Publs. *The Relationship of Secondary Education to Higher Education* 71, *The Development of Higher Education and its Objectives in Iraq* 72 and articles on biochemistry in scientific journals.
UNESCO Regional Office for Science and Technology, 8 Abdel Rahman Fahmy Street, Garden City, Cairo, Egypt.

Rayes, Ghazi al-; Kuwaiti diplomatist; b. 23 Aug. 1935; ed. Cairo Univ.
Third Sec., Ministry of Foreign Affairs 62; Kuwaiti Embassy, Washington and Beirut 65-67; Chair. Int. Affairs Section, Ministry of Foreign Affairs 67-70; Counsellor, Kuwaiti Embassy, Beirut 70-73; Amb. to Bahrain 74-80, to United Kingdom Dec. 80-.
Embassy of Kuwait, 46 Queen's Gate, London S.W.7, England.

Razzek, Brig. Aref Abdel; Iraqi politician; b. 1914; ed. Military Acad.
Entered Air Force 36; became Commdr. Habbaniya base; Minister of Agriculture Nov. 63-Dec. 63; Commdr. of Air Forces Dec. 63-July 65; Prime Minister and Acting Minister of Defence Sept. 65; Abortive *coup d'état* Sept. 65, June 66; imprisoned June 66.
Baghdad, Iraq.

Rebeyrol, Philippe; French diplomatist; b. 14 June 1917, Paris; ed. Lycée Louis-le-Grand, Paris, Ecole Normale Supérieure, Univ. de la Sorbonne.
Professor, Inst. Français, Barcelona 42-45; Head of Inst. de Hautes Etudes, Bucharest 46-49; Counsellor for Cultural Affairs, French Embassy to Egypt 51-55; Chargé d'affaires, Algeria 62-68; Amb. to Cameroon 68-71; Dir. Amb. to Tunisia 74-80, to Greece 80-82; Officier, Légion d'Honneur; Commdr., Ordre Nat. de Mérite.
Publs. Articles on the history of Art.
34 rue de Grenelle, Paris 7e, France.

Recanati, Daniel; Israeli banker; b. 26 Oct. 1921, Greece.
Chairman and Man. Dir. IDB Bankholding Corpn. Ltd.; Chair. and Man. Dir. Israel Discount Bank Ltd.; Chair. Board of Dirs. Barclays Discount Bank Ltd., Discount Bank Investment Corpn. Ltd.; dir. of several cos.
Israel Discount Bank, 27-31 Yehuda Halevy Street, Tel-Aviv, Israel.

Remez, Brig.-Gen. Aharon; Israeli air force officer and diplomatist; b. 8 May 1919; ed. Herzliah Grammar School, Tel-Aviv, Harvard School of Business Administration, U.S.A., and Woodrow Wilson School of Public and International Affairs, Princeton, U.S.A.
Agricultural training in Kibbutz, Givat Haim 37-39; Emissary to Zionist Youth Movement, U.S.A. 39-41; Royal Air Force 42-47; mem. Kibbutz Kfar Blum 47-; Dir.

of Planning and Operations, later Chief of Staff, Israel Air Force 48; Commdr.-in-Chief Israel Air Force 48-51; Head, Ministry of Defence Purchasing Mission, U.S.A. 51-53; Aviation Adviser to Minister of Defence 53-54; mem. Board of Dirs. Solel Boneh Ltd., Exec. Dir. Koor Industries Ltd. 54-59; mem. Knesset 56-57; Admin. Dir. Weizmann Inst. of Science, Rehovot 59-60; Dir. Int. Co-operation Dept., Ministry for Foreign Affairs 60-64, Adviser on Int. Co-operation to Minister for Foreign Affairs 64-65; Consultant to OECD 64-65; Chair. Nat. Aviation Council 63-65; Amb. to U.K. 65-70; Dir.-Gen. Israel Ports Authority 70-; Chair. Israel Airports Authority.
Israel Ports Authority, Maya Building, 74 Petah Tiqva Road, P.O. Box 20121, Tel-Aviv; Home: 8 San Martin Street, Jerusalem, Israel.

Riad, Mahmoud; Egyptian diplomatist; b. 8 Jan. 1917; ed. Military Acad. and General Staff Coll.
Egyptian Rep. to Mixed Armistice Comm. 49-52; Dir. Dept. of Arab Affairs, Ministry of Foreign Affairs 54-55; Ambassador to Syria 55-58; President's Counsellor on Foreign Affairs 58-62; Chair. Del. to UN Econ. Comm. for Africa 61; Ambassador and Perm. Rep. to UN 62-64; Minister of Foreign Affairs 64-72, Deputy Premier 71-72; Pres. Adviser Jan.-June 72; Sec.-Gen. League of Arab States 72-79.
Publ. *The Struggle for Peace in the Middle East* 81.
c/o Ministry of Foreign Affairs, Cairo, Egypt.

Riad, Mahmoud Mohammed, PH.D.; Egyptian electrical and electronic engineer; b. 4 June 1918, Cairo; ed. Cairo Univ., Imperial Coll., London Univ.
Assistant Prof. of Telecommunications, Alexandria Univ. 43-56; Head Eng. Dept., Atomic Energy Org. 56-57; Dir.-Gen. Telecommunications Org. 57-64; Sec.-Gen. Arab Telecommunications Union 58-79; Minister of Communications 64-65; Chair. Electricity Corpn. 65-66, Electrical and Electronic Industries Corpn. 66-68; Prof. of Electronics, Kuwait Univ. 68-71; Minister of Transport and Communications 71-April 75; Fellow, American Inst. of Electrical and Electronic Engineers, Inst. of Electrical Engineers, England.
Publs. various papers on science and engineering in technical journals.
c/o Arab Telecommunications Union, 83 Ramses Street, Cairo; and Ministry of Transport and Communications, Cairo, Egypt.

Rial, Cleto Hassan, B.SC., M.A.; Sudanese administrator; b. 1 Sept. 1935, Wau, Bahr El Ghazal; ed. Comboni Coll., Khartoum, Xavier Univ., Ohio, Univ. of Notre Dame, Indiana, Inst. of Social Studies, The Hague, Royal Inst. of Public Admin., London.
Executive Officer, Ministry of Local Govt. 58-59; Schoolmaster, Comboni Coll., Khartoum 59-60; Finance Insp. Ministry of Finance and Econs. 62-63; Lecturer Inst. of Public Admin. 63-72; Sec.-Gen. High Exec. Council for the Southern Region 72-; Sudanese Rep. at Conf. on African Devt. held by Massachusetts Inst. of Tech. at Athens 63; participated in Seminar on Nat. Govt. Admin., Tokyo 76; toured African countries consulting Southern Sudanese leaders in exile 69-71; mem. Second Order of the Nile.
Publ. *Methods and Techniques of Community Development Programmes* 66.
Secretariat General, P.O. Box 17, Juba, Sudan.

Rifa'i, Abdul Munem; Jordanian diplomatist and politician; b. 1917; ed. American Univ. of Beirut.
In service of King Abdullah 38; Chief Sec. of Govt. 40; Asst. Chief of Royal Court 41-42; Consul-Gen. in Cairo, Lebanon and Syria 43-44; Del. to Treaty Conf. with Great Britain 46; Under-Sec. of Foreign Affairs 47; Minister to Iran and Pakistan 49; Amb. to United States and Perm. Rep. to UN 53-57, to Lebanon 57, to Great Britain 58;

Chief of Nat. Guidance 59; Perm. Rep. to UN 59-66; Amb. to U.A.R. 66, 67-68; Minister of Foreign Affairs 68-69; Prime Minister March-Aug. 69; Deputy Prime Minister, Minister of Foreign Affairs and Senator 69-70; Prime Minister June 70-71; Personal Rep. to H.M. King Hussein 72-73; Perm. Rep. to Arab League 73; Amb. to Egypt Sept.-Dec. 73; Special Adviser to H.M. King Hussein on Int. Affairs Dec. 73-74, mem. Senate 74-; numerous decorations.
The Senate, Amman, Jordan.

Rifa'i, Zaid al-, M.A.; Jordanian diplomatist; b. 27 Nov. 1936, Amman (son of fmr. Prime Minister Samir Rifa'i and nephew of Abdul Munem Rifa'i, *q.v.*); ed. Victoria Coll., Cairo, and Harvard and Columbia Univs.
Joined diplomatic service 57; served at embassies in Cairo, Beirut and London and at the Perm. Mission of Jordan at UN; Chief of Royal Protocol 65; Sec.-Gen. of Royal Court and Private Sec. to H.M. King Hussein 67; Chief of Royal Court 69-70; Amb. to U.K. 70-72; Political Adviser to H.M. King Hussein 72-73; Prime Minister May 73-July 76; Minister of Foreign Affairs and Defence 73-76.
Amman, Jordan.

Rivlin, Moshe; Israeli administrator; b. 1925, Jerusalem; ed. Teacher's Seminary, Graduate Alumna Inst. for Jewish Studies, Mizrachi Teachers' Coll. and Hebrew Univ., Jerusalem.
Joined Haganah 40; Head, Council of Youth Movts., Jerusalem 44-46; served as Maj.-Gen. in Israeli Army 48; Consul, New York 52-58; Dir. Information Dept., The Jewish Agency 58-60, Sec.-Gen. 60-66, Dir.-Gen. and Head of Admin. and Public Relations Dept. 66-71; Dir.-Gen. of reconstituted Jewish Agency 71-77; Chair. Board of Dirs. of Keren Kayemeth Le Israel 77-; Assoc. mem. Exec., World Zionist Org. 71, Chair. Haganah veterans in Israel; mem. Boards of Govs. of Ben-Gurion Univ., Coll. for Public Admin., Jewish Telegraphic Agency; mem. Exec. Cttee. of Yad Ben-Zvi, Council of Yad Ben-Gurion, Boards of Dirs. of *Jerusalem Post*, El Al and the Hebrew Univ.
Keren Kayemeth Le Israel, P.O. Box 283, Jerusalem; 1 Keren Kayemeth Street, Jerusalem, Israel.

Rolandis, Nicos, BAR.-AT-LAW; Cypriot lawyer and politician; b. 10 Dec. 1934, Limassol; ed. Pancyprian Gymnasium, Nicosia, and Middle Temple, London.
Practised Law; Partner then Chair. and Man. Dir. of several industrial and commercial companies; joint founder of the Democratic Camp, (now the Democratic Party); Minister of Foreign Affairs March 78-.
Ministry of Foreign Affairs, Nicosia, Cyprus.

Rosenne, Meir, PH.D.; Israeli diplomatist; b. 19 Feb. 1931, Jassy, Romania; ed. Inst. d'Etudes Politiques, Paris, Faculté de Droit, Paris and Inst. des Hautes Etudes Internationales.
Served Consulate-Gen. of Israel, Paris 53-57; E. European Desk, Ministry of Foreign Affairs 57-61; Consul, New York, Del. to UN Gen. Assembly, Human Rights Comm. 61-67; Ministry of Foreign Affairs 67-69; Co-ordinator and Dir. of Foreign Relations, Atomic Energy Comm. 69-71; Legal Adviser, Ministry of Foreign Affairs 71-79; mem. del. of Israel to Geneva Peace Conf. 73, negotiations with Egypt 74, with Syria 74, with U.S.A. and Egypt 75, Camp David 78 and Washington talks 79; Amb. to France 79-.
Embassy of Israel, 3 rue Rabelais, 75008 Paris, France.

Rosenne, Shabtai, LL.B., PH.D.; Israeli lawyer and diplomatist; b. 24 Nov. 1917; ed. London Univ. and Hebrew Univ. of Jerusalem.
Advocate (Israel), Political Dept., Jewish Agency for Palestine 46-48; Legal Adviser, Ministry of Foreign Affairs 48-66; Deputy Perm. Rep. to UN 67-71; Perm. Rep. to UN (Geneva) 71-74; Ministry of Foreign Affairs 74-; mem. Del. to UN Gen. Assemblies 48-81, Vice-Chair.

Legal Cttee. 60; mem. Del. to Armistice Negotiations with Egypt, Jordan, Lebanon and Syria 49; mem. Del. to UN Conf. on Law of the Sea, Chair. 73, 78-82; Chair. Del. to UN Conf. on Law of Treaties 68, 69, mem. other UN confs.; Govt. Rep. before Int. Court of Justice in several cases; mem. Int. Law Comm. 62-71, UN Comm. on Human Rights 68-70; Assoc. and mem. Inst. of Int. Law 63-; Rapporteur, Termination and Modification of Treaties 65; Visiting Prof. Bar-Ilan Univ. 76-; Hon. mem. American Soc. of Int. Law 76; Israel Prize 60, Certificate of Merit, American Soc. of Int. Law 68.
Publs. *International Court of Justice* 57, *The Time Factor in Jurisdiction of the International Court of Justice* 60, *The Law and Practice of the International Court* (2 vols.) 65, *The Law of Treaties: Guide to the Vienna Convention* 70, *The World Court: What It Is And How It Works* 73, *Documents on the International Court of Justice 1974* 79, *The 1978 Rules of the International Court of Justice: A Commentary* 82; and numerous articles, mainly on law.
Ministry of Foreign Affairs, Hakiriya, Romema, Jerusalem, 99250 Israel.

Rouillon, Fernand; French diplomatist; b. 11 Dec. 1920, Condrieu (Rhône); ed. Tivoli Coll., School of Political Sciences, Bordeaux Univ.
With Ministry of Foreign Affairs 44-; Dept. of Econ. Affairs 44-47; Tunis, London (NATO) and Ottawa 47-56; Dept. of Eastern Europe 56-58, of Cultural Affairs 58-60; Rabat, New York (UN), and Athens 60-70; Asst. Dir. Dept. of Middle East 70-75; Amb. to Syria 75-82, to Turkey Jan. 82-; Officier, Légion d'Honneur; Officier, Ordre National du Mérite.
French Embassy, rue du Paris, Ankara, Turkey.

Runciman, The Hon. Sir Steven (James Cochran Stevenson), Kt., M.A., F.B.A.; British historian; b. 7 July 1903; ed. Eton Coll. and Trinity Coll., Cambridge.
Fellow Trinity Coll., Cambridge 27-38; Lecturer Cambridge Univ. 31-38; Press Attaché, British Legation, Sofia 40-41; Prof. of Byzantine Studies, Istanbul Univ. 42-45; Rep. of British Council, Greece 45-47; Chair. Anglo-Hellenic League 51-67; Trustee, British Museum 60-67; Pres. British Inst. of Archaeology at Ankara 61-75; Fellow, British Acad. 57; Hon. Fellow, Trinity Coll., Cambridge 65; Hon. Litt.D. (Cambridge, London, Chicago, Durham, St. Andrews, Oxford, Birmingham), Hon. LL.D. (Glasgow), Hon. D.Phil. (Thessalonika), Hon. D.D. (Wabash, U.S.A.).
Publs. *The Emperor Romanus Lecapenus* 29, *The First Bulgarian Empire* 30, *Byzantine Civilization* 33, *The Medieval Manichee* 47, *History of the Crusades* (3 vols.) 51-54, *The Eastern Schism* 55, *The Sicilian Vespers* 58, *The White Rajahs* 60, *The Fall of Constantinople 1453* 65, *The Great Church in Captivity* 68, *The Last Byzantine Renaissance* 70, *The Orthodox Churches and the Secular State* 71, *Byzantine Style and Civilization* 75, *The Byzantine Theocracy* 77, *Mistra* 80.
Elshieshields, Lockerbie, Dumfriesshire, Scotland.

S

Saad al-Abdullah al-Salem al-Sabah, Sheikh (*see* Sabah, Sheikh Saad al-Abdullah al Salem al-).

Saba, Elias, B.LITT.; Lebanese economist and politician; b. 1932, Lebanon; ed. American Univ. of Beirut and Univ. of Oxford.
Economic Adviser to Ministry of Finance and Petroleum, Kuwait and Kuwait Fund for Arab Econ. Devt. 61-62; Chair. Dept. of Econs., American Univ. of Beirut 63-67; Assoc. Prof. of Econs., American Univ. of Beirut 67-69; Deputy Prime Minister of the Lebanon, Minister of Finance and Minister of Defence 70-72; Econ. and Financial Adviser to Pres. 72-73; Chair. and Gen. Man. St. Charles City Centre, S.A.L. 74-; Chair. and Chief Exec.

The Associates S.A.R.L. 81-; mem. Nat. Dialogue Cttee. Sept. 75; mem. Governing Board, Int. Inst. of Human Rights.
Publ. *Postwar Developments in the Foreign Exchange Systems of Lebanon and Syria 62.*
Biarritz Building, P.O. Box 9500, Beirut, Lebanon.

Saba, Hanna, D. en D.; Egyptian jurist and diplomatist; b. 23 July 1909; ed. Coll. of Jesuit Fathers, Cairo, Faculté de Droit, Paris, and Ecole Libre des Sciences Politiques, Paris.
Adviser to Legal Department, Egyptian Govt. 33-42; Ministry of Foreign Affairs, Cairo 42, Counsellor 46, Minister 52; Dir. of Treaties Div., UN Secr. 46-50; Juridical Adviser, UNESCO 50-67; Asst. Dir.-Gen. of UNESCO 67-71; Alt. Chair. UNESCO Appeal Board 73; Vice-Chair. Asscn. of French and Arab Jurists, Arbitration Council of Franco-Arab Chamber of Commerce, Paris; mem. Governing Board, Int. Inst. of Human Rights; Grand Officer of Merit, Egypt; Officer of the Nile; Grand Cross of Merit, Order of Malta.
Publs. *L'Islam et la nationalité 32, L'évolution dans la technique des traités, Les droits économiques et sociaux dans le projet de pacte des droits de l'homme, Les ententes et accords régionaux dans la Charte des Nations Unies* (Course at Acad. of Int. Law, The Hague 52), *L'Activité quasi-législative des institutions spécialisées des Nations Unies* (Course at Acad. of Int. Law, The Hague 64).
3 boulevard de la Saussaye, Neuilly (Hauts de Seine) 92.200, France.

Sabah, Sheikh Ali Khalifa al-, M.SC.; Kuwaiti politician; b. 22 Oct. 1945; ed. Victoria Coll., Cairo, Univs. of San Francisco and London.
Head, Economics Dept., Ministry of Finance and Oil 68-73; Asst. Under-Sec., Ministry of Finance and Oil 73-75; Under-Sec., Ministry of Finance 75-78; Chair. Int. Gulf Bank 76-78; Pres. OPEC, Chair. Dollar Cttee. 78; Minister of Oil Feb. 78-; Chair. Board of Dirs. Kuwait Petroleum Corpn. Jan. 80-.
Ministry of Oil, Kuwait City, Kuwait.

Sabah, H.H. Sheikh Jaber al-Ahmed al-Jaber al-; Amir of Kuwait; b. 1928; ed. Almubarakiyyah School and privately.
Governor, Ahmedi and Oil Areas 49-59; Pres. Dept. of Finance and Econ. 59; Minister of Finance and Econ. 62, of Finance and Industry 63; Minister of Finance and Industry and Minister of Commerce 65; Prime Minister 65-77; Nominated Heir-Apparent 66; Amir of Kuwait Jan. 78-.
Office of H.H. the Amir, Amiri Diwan, Seif Palace, Kuwait.

Sabah, Sheikh Jaber al-Ali al-Salem al-; Kuwaiti politician; b. 1928.
President of Dept. of Electricity, Water and Gas 52-63; mem. High Exec. Cttee. to organize establishments and depts. 54; mem. Defence High Council; Minister of Information 64-71, 75-81; Deputy Prime Minister 75-81; Chair. Kuwait Int. Petroleum Investment Co. (KIPIC) Jan. 81-.
c/o Council of Ministers, Kuwait City, Kuwait.

Sabah, Sheikh Saad al-Abdullah al-Salem al-; Kuwaiti politician.
Deputy Pres., Police and Public Security Dept. until 61; Minister of the Interior 61-65; Minister of the Interior and Defence 65-78; Head of Ministerial Cttee. on Labour Problems 75-78; Crown Prince Jan. 78-; Prime Minister Feb. 78-.
Office of the Prime Minister, Kuwait City, Kuwait.

Sabah, Sheikh Sabah al-Ahmed al-Jabir al-; Kuwaiit politician; b. 1929; ed. Mubarakiyyah National School, Kuwait and privately.
Member Supreme Cttee. 56-61; Head of Dept. of Social Affairs and Dept. of Printing, Press and Publications 61;

Minister of Guidance of News 63; Minister of Foreign Affairs 63-, acting Minister of Oil 65-67; Minister of Oil Affairs 67; acting Minister of the Interior 78; Deputy Prime Minister Feb. 78-; acting Minister of Information March 81-.
Ministry of Foreign Affairs, Kuwait.

Sabah, H.H. Sheikh Salem al-Sabah al- (son of late Sheikh Sabah al-Salem al-Sabah, Amir of Kuwait); Kuwaiti diplomatist; b. 18 June 1937; ed. Secondary School, Kuwait, Gray's Inn, London, and Christ Church, Oxford.
Joined Foreign Service 62; Head of Legal (later Political) Dept. Ministry of Foreign Affairs; Amb. to the U.K. 65-70, to U.S.A. 70-75, also accred. to Canada; Minister of Social Affairs and Labour 75-78, of Defence 78-.
Ministry of Defence, Kuwait.

Sabah, Sheikh Saud Nasir al-; Kuwaiti diplomatist; b. 3 Oct. 1944, Kuwait.
Barrister-at-Law, Gray's Inn; Legal Dept., Ministry of Foreign Affairs; Rep. to Sixth Cttee., UN Gen. Assembly 69-74, to Seabed Cttee. 69-73; Vice-Chair. del. to Conf. on Law of the Sea 74-75; rep. of del. to Conf. on Law of Treaties 69; Amb. to U.K., also accred. to Denmark, Norway and Sweden 75-80, to U.S.A. 81-.
Embassy of Kuwait, 2940 Tilden Street, N.W., Washington, D.C. 20008. U.S.A.

Saber, Mohieddin, PH.D.; Sudanese international official and former politician; b. 1919, Dalgo, Sudan; ed. Cairo Univ., Bordeaux Univ., France, Sorbonne, Paris.
Director, Ministry of Social Affairs 54; Lecturer in Anthropology, Cairo Univ. in Khartoum 56-59; Editor-in-Chief *El Esteglal* and *Sout El Sudan,* daily papers 55; Man. *El Zaman* daily paper 57-59; UNESCO Expert and Head of Social Sciences Dept., Arab States Training Centre for Community Devt., Sirs el Layyan, Menoufia, Egypt 59-68; mem. Constituent Assembly of Sudan 68-69; Minister of Educ. 69-72; Dir. Arab Literacy and Adult Educ. Org. (ARLO) 73-75; Dir.-Gen. Arab League Educational, Cultural and Scientific Org. (ALECSO) 75-; Perm. mem. Afro-Asian Writers' Asscn.; Loyal Son of the Sudan Order 71, Order of the Repub. (Egypt) 70, Nat. Order (Chad) 70.
Publs. *Cultural Change and Community Development 62, Researches in Community Development Programmes 63, Local Government and Community Development in Developing Countries 63, Nomad and Nomadism—Concepts and Approaches* (with Dr. Lewis Meleka) 66, *Adult Education in the Sudan 69, The New Educational System in the Sudan 70, Studies on Issues Related to Development and Adult Education 75, Adult Education as Science* (co-author) 75; numerous studies and papers.
Arab League Educational, Cultural and Scientific Organization, 109 Tahrir Street, Dokki, Cairo, Egypt.

Sabri, Wing Cdr. Ali; Egyptian air force officer and politician; b. 30 Aug. 1920; ed. Military Acad. and Air Force Acad.
Fought in Palestine War 48; Minister for Presidential Affairs, Egypt 57-58, U.A.R. 58-62; Pres. Exec. Council 62-64, Prime Minister 64-65; Vice-Pres. of Repub. Oct. 65-67; Sec.-Gen. Arab Socialist Union Oct. 65-67, 68-Sept. 69; Deputy Prime Minister 67 and Minister of Local Govt. 67-Oct. 67; Resident Minister for Suez Canal Zone Oct. 67-68; Vice-Pres. of Repub. 70-71; on trial for treason Aug. 71, sentenced to life imprisonment Dec. 71, released May 81.
Cairo, Egypt.

Sadiq Abdul Rahman (see Mahdi, Sadiq al-).

Saffar, Salman Mohamed al-, PH.D.; Bahrain diplomatist; b. 1931, Bahrain; ed. Baghdad Univ., Iraq and Sorbonne, Paris.
Primary school teacher, Bahrain 49-54, Secondary school

teacher 59-60; with Ministry of Foreign Affairs, Bahrain; Perm. Rep. to UN Sept. 71-.
Permanent Mission of Bahrain to United Nations, 747 Third Avenue, 19th Floor, New York, N.Y. 10017, U.S.A.

Sagar, Abdul Aziz al-Hamad al; Kuwaiti businessman and politician; b. 1913; ed. Secondary School, Bombay.
Member Municipality Board 52-55, Devt. Board 52-55; Chair. Kuwait Chamber of Commerce 59-, Nat. Bank of Kuwait 59-65; Jt. Council 61-62; Chair. Kuwait Oil Tanker Co. 61-64, 65-; mem. Constituent Assembly 63-, Speaker 63-65; Minister of Health 63; Chair. Red Crescent Soc. 66-; Vice-Chair. then Chair. FRAB Bank Int., Paris April 82-.
Kuwait Chamber of Commerce, P.O. Box 775, Ali Salem Street, Kuwait City, Kuwait.

Sahnoun, Hadj Mohamed, M.A.; Algerian diplomatist; b. 8 April 1931; ed. Lycée of Constantine, Univ. de Paris à la Sorbonne and New York Univ.
Director of African, Asian and Latin American Affairs, Ministry of Foreign Affairs 62-63, of Political Affairs 64; Del. to UN Gen. Assembly 62-63, 64-65; Asst. Sec.-Gen. Org. of African Unity (OAU) 64-73, Arab League 74; Amb. to Fed. Repub. of Germany 75-79, to France Oct. 79-.
Publ. *Economic and Social Aspects of the Algerian Revolution 62.*
c/o Algerian Embassy, 18 rue Hamelin, Paris 16e, France; and Ministry of Foreign Affairs, 6 rue Claude Bernard, El Mouradia, Algiers, Algeria.

Said, Edward W., M.A., PH.D.; American university professor; b. Nov. 1935, Jerusalem; ed. Victoria Coll., Cairo, Mt. Hermon School, Massachusetts, Princeton and Harvard Univs.
Instructor in English, Columbia Univ. 63-65, Asst. Prof. of English and Comparative Literature 67-69, Prof. 69-74, Parr Prof. 74-; Visiting Prof. of Comparative Literature, Harvard Univ. 74, of Humanities, Johns Hopkins Univ. 79; Editor, *Arab Studies Quarterly*; Chair. Board of Trustees, Inst. of Arab Studies; mem. Palestine Nat. Council, Council on Foreign Relations, New York, Acad. of Literary Studies, PEN Club, New York; Fellow, Center for Advanced Study in Behavioral Science, Stanford 75-76; Senior Fellow School of Criticism and Theory, Northwestern Univ.; Bowdoin Prize, Harvard Univ.; Lionel Trilling Award 76.
Publs. *Joseph Conrad and the Fiction of Autobiography, Beginnings: Intention and Method, Orientalism, The Question of Palestine, Literature and Society, Criticism between Culture and System, Covering Islam 81.*
419 Hamilton Hall, Columbia University, New York, N.Y. 10027, U.S.A.

Said, Faisal bin Ali al-; Omani politician; b. 1927, Muscat.
Attached to Ministry of Foreign Affairs, Muscat 53-57; lived abroad 57-70; Perm. Under-Sec. Ministry of Educ. 70-72; Minister of Econ. Affairs 72; Perm. Rep. to UN 72-73; Minister of Educ. 73-76, of Nat. Heritage 76-, of Culture 79-.
Ministry of National Heritage and Culture, Muscat, Oman.

Saif al-Islam, al-Hassan ben Yahya, H.H.; Yemeni politician.
Crown Prince of the Yemen 62-; Prime Minister 62-67; Head of Mil. Council 67; in exile 68-.

Saif al-Islam, Mohamed al-Badr, H.R.H.; Prince of the Yemen; b. 1927; ed. Coll. for Higher Education, Sana'a.
Son of King of the Yemen; Minister for Foreign Affairs 55-61, and Minister of Defence and C.-in-C. 55-62; succeeded to Imamate on the death of his father, Imam Ahmed Sept. 62; left Taiz following Republican *coup d'état* Sept. 62, leading Royalist resistance 62-68; replaced by Imamate Council May 68; in exile 68-.

Saif al-Islam, Mohammed ben Hussein; Yemeni politician; b. 1938.
Former diplomatic rep. to Fed. Germany; Vice-Pres. Imamate Council 67-May 68, Pres. of Council May 68; Commdr. of Royalist Armed Forces 67-68; in exile 68-.

Salah, Abdullah A.; Jordanian diplomatist; b. 31 Dec. 1922; ed. Bishop Gobat's School, Jerusalem, and American Univ. of Beirut.
Field Educ. Officer, United Nations Relief and Works Agency (UNRWA), Jordan 52-62; Ambassador to Kuwait 62-63, to India 63-64, to France 64-66, 67-70; Minister of Foreign Affairs 66-67, 70-72; Amb. to U.S.A. 73-80, also accred. to Mexico; several decorations.
Ministry of Foreign Affairs, Amman, Jordan.

Salam, Saeb; Lebanese politician; b. 1905; ed. American Univ. of Beirut, London School of Econs.
Elected Provisional Head Lebanese Govt. 43; deputy 43-47, 51; Minister of Interior 46, 60-61; Minister Foreign Affairs 46; Prime Minister 52, 53, 60-61, concurrently Minister of Defence 61; pioneer Lebanese civil aviation 45; Pres. Middle East Airlines Co., Beirut 45-56; Pres. Nat. Fats & Oil Co. Ltd., Beirut; Prime Minister 70-73; Pres. Makassed Philanthropic Islamic Asscn. 58-; mem. Nat. Dialogue Cttee. Sept. 75.
Rue Moussaitbé, B.P. 206, Beirut, Lebanon.

Saleh, Lt.-Col. Ali Abdullah; Yemeni army officer and politician; b. *c.* 1942.
Participated in coup 74 which brought Lt.-Col. al Hamdi to power; Security Chief, Taiz Province 77-78; mem. Provisional Presidential Council, Deputy C.-in-C. of Armed Forces June-July 78; Pres. of Yemen Arab Repub. and C.-in-C. of Armed Forces July 78-.
Office of the President, Sana'a, Yemen Arab Republic.

Salem, Gen. Mamdouh Muhammad; Egyptian police officer, administrator and politician; b. 1918, Alexandria; ed. Police Acad.
Police Commdr., Alexandria 64-68; Gov. of Assiyut 68-70, of Alexandria 70-71; Deputy Prime Minister, Minister of the Interior 71-75, Prime Minister 75-78, also Minister of Interior Feb.-Oct. 77; Asst. to the Pres. Oct. 78-; Leader Arab Socialist Party 75-78; mem. Higher Council for Nuclear Energy 75.
Office of the President, Cairo, Egypt.

Salim, Dr. Khalil, ED.D.; Jordanian politician and economist; b. 1921, El-Husn; ed. American Univ. Beirut, Univ. of London, Columbia Univ., U.S.A.
Teacher in secondary schools 41-49; Insp. of Educ. 59-56; Dir. of Cultural Affairs 52-55; Asst. Under-Sec. of Educ. 55-62; Minister of Social Welfare and Minister of State, Prime Minister's Office 62, Minister of Nat. Economy 62-63; Gov. Central Bank of Jordan 63-73; Pres. Nat. Planning Council 73-74; Amb. to France, non-resident Amb. to Belgium 75-78, also to EEC 77-78; mem. Nat. Consultative Council and Chair. NCC Fiscal and Admin. Cttee. 78-; Pres. Authority for Tourism and Antiquities 62-63; Chair. Co-operative Union 65-68, Public Insurance Corpn. 71-73, Inst ,of Banking Studies 71-73, Nat. Cttee. for Population 73-74, Cttee. for Environment 73-74; Deputy Chair. Royal Scientific Soc. 70-73, Alia Airline 71-74; mem. Exec. Board UNESCO 76-; Gov. IMF, IBRD 63-74; Chair. and Gen. Man. Arab Finance Corpn. (Jordan) 79-; mem. M'uta Univ. Board of Trustees, Supreme Educl. Council 80-; Sec. Gen. Arab Thought Forum 81; Al-Istiqlal Medal, Second Class 59, Al-Kawkab Medal, First Class 62, Al-Nahdah Medal, First Class 73.
Publs. *Reorganization of Educational Administration in Jordan* 60 and books on mathematics, teaching, educ. admin. in Jordan, articles, lectures and broadcasts.
Arab Finance Corporation, P.O. Box 35104, Amman, Jordan.

Sallal, Marshal Abdullah; Yemeni army officer and politician; b. 1917; ed. in Iraq.
Returned to Yemen from Iraq 39; imprisoned 39; army service 40-48, 55-; imprisoned 48-55; Gov. of Hodeida 59-62; Chief of Staff to Imam Mohammed Sept. 62; led coup against the Imam and proclaimed a Repub. Sept. 62; Pres. of the Revolutionary Council and C.-in-C. of Republican forces during civil war 62-67; Prime Minister 62-64, 66-67, concurrently Minister of Foreign Affairs 63-64.
Cairo, Egypt.

Sallam, Mohamed Abdulaziz, B.A.; Yemeni diplomatist; b. 15 Dec. 1933, Taiz; ed. secondary school in Helwan, Egypt, Stockbridge School, Mass. and Temple Univ., Philadelphia, Pa., U.S.A.
Engaged in private sector 60-61; Instructor, Belguis Coll. 61-62; Dir.-Gen. Ministry of Public Health 62-63; Minister and Chargé d'Affaires, Embassy in Baghdad 63-64; Deputy Minister of Foreign Affairs 64-65; Chair. Board, Yemen Drug Co. 65-66; Minister of Foreign Affairs 66-67; Dir.-Gen. Office of the Prime Minister 70-71; Amb. in Ministry of Foreign Affairs 71-73; Minister with rank of Amb., Embassy in London 73-74; Amb., Deputy Perm. Rep. to UN 74-76, Perm. Rep. 76-78; leader of dels. to various int. confs. incl. UN Gen. Assembly 65, Fifth Emerengcy Special Session, Fourth Summit Conf. of Arab League 67.
c/o Ministry of Foreign Affairs, Sana'a, Yemen Arab Republic.

Salman, Salah, M.D., F.A.C.S.; Lebanese physician and government official; b. 24 Jan. 1936, Beirut; ed. American Univ. Beirut School of Medicine, Johns Hopkins Univ. School of Medicine, U.S.A.
Minister of Public Health March-June 72; Assoc. Prof. and Chair. of Dept. of Otolaryngology, American Univ. of Beirut 74-; Minister of Interior, Housing and Co-operatives 76-79; Penrose Award, Faculties of Medical Sciences 61.
Publs. 19 papers in int. and local medical journals in otolaryngology and allied subjects.
American University of Beirut; Home: Lyon Street, Najjar Building, Beirut, Lebanon.

Salzman, Pnina; Israeli pianist; b. 1923; ed. Ecole Normale de Musique and Conservatoire National de Musique, Paris.
Gave first concert in Paris at age of twelve; since then has given concerts in five continents; travels all over the world every year, playing with most of the major orchestras; over 300 concerts with Israeli orchestras.
20 Dubnov St., Tel-Aviv, Israel.

Samiy, Abdol Hossein, M.D.; Iranian physician and minister; b. 20 June 1930, Iran; ed. Stanford Univ., Univ. of Calif., Los Angeles and Cornell Univ.
Assistant in Medicine, Cornell Univ. 56-57, Fellow in Physiology 57-58; Asst. in Medicine and later Research Fellow, Harvard Medical School 58-60; Deputy Minister of Health, Iran 62-64: Dir. Firowzgar Medical Centre 64, Pars Hosp. 69-73; Minister of Science and Higher Educ. 74-77; Chancellor, Reza Shah Kabir Univ. 75-78; fmr. Pres. Imperial Medical Center of Iran; Prof. of Medicine, Cornell Univ. Medical Coll.; fmr. Vice-Chair. Imperial Iranian Acad. of Sciences; Borden Award for Medical Research, Larken Award for Medical Research.
Publs. 16 medical papers; Co-editor: *International Textbook of Medicine* 76.
Avenue Jaleh-Avenue Iran No. 5, Teheran, Iran.

Sanbar, Moshe, M.A.(ECON.); Israeli banker and economist; b. 29 March 1926, Kecskemét, Hungary; ed. Univ. of Budapest and Hebrew Univ., Jerusalem.
Emigrated to Israel 48; Project Dir., Israel Inst. of Applied Social Research and later Deputy Dir. 51-58; Lecturer in Statistics, Hebrew Univ., Jerusalem 57-61; Dir. Research Dept., Deputy Dir. Internal State Revenue

Div., Ministry of Finance 58-63, Dir. of Budgets 63-68; Econ. Adviser to Ministry of Finance 63-68; Deputy Chair. and later Chair., Industrial Devt. Bank of Israel 68-71; Chief Econ. Adviser to Minister of Finance 69-71; Acting Deputy Minister of Commerce and Industry 70-71; Gov. Bank of Israel 71-76; Chair. of Board, Electrochemical Industries (Frutarom) Ltd. 76; Chair. Econ. Devt. and Refugee Rehabilitation Trust, Board of Dirs. Habimah Nat. Theatre; Pres. Israel Asscn. of Graduates in the Social Sciences and Humanities; Chair. Board of Trustees of Coll. of Admin.; Hon. Pres. World Fed. of Hungarian Jews.
Publs. *My Longest Year* (Yad Vashem Prize) 66; many articles and research studies on economic subjects.
44 Pincas Street, Tel-Aviv, Israel.

Sancar, Gen. Semih; Turkish army officer; b. 1911, Erzurum; ed. Artillery School, War Acad.
Served in Turkish Army as Commdr. of Artillery Battery and Battalion, Asst. Commdr. Army Corps Artillery, Dept. Chief, Branch Section Dir. in Land Forces and Gen. Staff H.Q.; then Instructor War Acad.; Dir. of Personnel, Dir. of Operations Turkish Gen. Staff; promoted to rank of Gen. 69; Commdr. of Gendarmerie 69; Commdr. 2nd Army; Commdr. Turkish Land Forces 72-73; Chief of Gen. Staff 73-78.
c/o General Staff Headquarters, Ankara, Turkey.

Sanjabi, Karim, L. EN D.; Iranian lawyer and politician; b. 1904; ed. Political Science School, Teheran, Univ. of Teheran, Univ. of the Sorbonne, Paris.
Entered Ministry of Education 34, Ministry of Finance 39; Prof. of Law; arrested by British during Second World War, banned from Kermanshah during War; founding mem. Mihan movement, then Iran Party, 43-44; supporter of Musaddiq during Nat. Front Govt., Minister of Educ. May-Dec. 51; arrested after fall of Musaddiq Govt. 53; resumed political activities 60, mem. Cen. Cttee. of Nat. Front; founder mem. Iranian Cttee. for Defence of Liberty and Human Rights Dec. 77; Minister of Foreign Affairs Feb.-April 79.
c/o Ministry of Foreign Affairs, Teheran, Iran.

Sanusi, H.R.H. Prince Hassan Rida; Former Crown Prince of Libya; b. 1934.
Son of H.M. King Idris I; became Crown Prince on death of his Great Uncle, Ahmed Sherif as-Sanusi, Dec. 50; in exile 69-.

Saouma, Edouard; Lebanese agricultural engineer and international official; b. 6 Nov. 1926, Beirut; ed. St. Joseph's Univ. School of Eng., Beirut, Ecole Nat. Supérieure d'Agronomie, Montpellier, France.
Director, Tel Amara Agricultural School 52-53, Nat. Centre for Farm Mechanization 54-55; Sec.-Gen. Nat. Fed. of Lebanese Agronomists 55; Dir.-Gen. Nat. Inst. for Agricultural Research 57-62; mem. Governing Board, Nat. Grains Office 60-62; Deputy Regional Rep. for Asia and Far East, FAO 62-65, Dir. Land and Water Devt. Div. 65-75, Dir.-Gen. of FAO 76-; Minister of Agric., Fisheries and Forestry Oct.-Nov. 70; Corresp. mem. Accademia Nazionale di Agricultura (Italy); Dr. h.c. (Universidad Nacional Agraria, Peru, Agriculture Univ. La Molina, Peru, Univ. of Seoul, Repub. of Korea, Univs. of Uruguay, Indonesia, Warsaw, Philippines, Punjab and Pakistan); Order of the Cedar (Lebanon), Said Akl Prize (Lebanon); Chevalier du Mérite Agricole (France), Grand Croix Ordre National (Chad, Ghana and Upper Volta); Grand Cruz al Mérito Agrícola (Spain); Knight Commdr. Order of Merit (Greece); Orden del Mérito Agrícola (Colombia), Gran Oficial del Orden de Vasco Nuñez de Balboa (Panama).
Publs. technical publs. in agriculture.
Food and Agriculture Organization of the United Nations, Via delle Terme di Caracalla, 00100 Rome, Italy.

Sarkis, Elias, L. EN D.; Lebanese banker and politician; b. 20 July 1924; ed. Université Saint Joseph, Beirut.
Former Magistrate, Cour des Comptes; Pres. Management Cttee. of Intra Bank 67; fmr. Dir.-Gen. Cabinet of Presidency; Gov. Bank of Lebanon 68-76; Pres. of Lebanon Sept. 76-; Pres. Comm. Supérieure des Banques; Medal of Independence, First Class, Jordan.
Présidence de la République, Palais de Baabda, Beirut, Lebanon; Home: Mar Takla, Lebanon.

Saud al-Faisal, H.R.H. Prince Mohammed, B.A.(ECONS.); Saudi Arabian diplomatist; b. Riyadh; *s.* of late King Faisal; ed. Princeton Univ., U.S.A.
Former Deputy Minister of Petroleum and Mineral Resources; Minister of State for Foreign Affairs March-Oct. 75, Minister of Foreign Affairs Oct. 75-; leader del. to UN Gen. Assembly 76; Special Envoy of H.M. King Khaled in diplomatic efforts to resolve Algerian-Moroccan conflict over Western Sahara, and the civil war in Lebanon; mem. Saudi Arabian del. to Arab restricted Summit, Riyadh, Oct. 76, and to full Summit Conf. of Arab League, Oct. 76; Founding mem. King Faisal's Int. Charity Soc.; Chair. Islamic Investment Co., Faisal Islamic Bank of Sudan 77-, Faisal Islamic Bank of Egypt 77-; co-founder Dar al-Maal al-Islami Bank 81; Pres. Int. Asscn. of Islamic Banks.
Ministry of Foreign Affairs, Jeddah, Saudi Arabia.

Saudi Arabia, Royal Family of (*see* under first names, as Fahd, King).

Savidor, Menahem; Israeli politician and administrator; b. 20 Aug. 1918, U.S.S.R.; ed. Univs. of Vilno (now Vilnius) and Paris.
Director-General, Citrus Products Export Board 68-77; Gen. Man. Israeli Railways 54-65; leader of the opposition, Tel-Aviv Municipal Council 69-74; mem. Knesset 77-, elected Speaker July 81; Nat. Chair. Maccabi Sport Movt. in Israel 68-75; Chair. Lord Kagan Foundation for Soviet Immigrants 70-, Kalman Ginsburg Foundation for Orphans of Warriors and Children of War Invalids 76-, Philharmonia Choir, Tel-Aviv 77-; Chair. Israeli-French Parliamentary Asscn., Israel-France Chamber of Commerce; Chevalier Légion d'honneur, Officier de la Couronne Belge.
The Knesset, Jerusalem, Israel.

Sayah, Mohamed; Tunisian politician; b. 31 Dec. 1933; ed. Sadikia, Sfax, and Training School for Higher Education, Tunis.
Joined Néo-Destour Party 49; mem. Gen. Union of Tunisian Students 52-62, mem. Exec. Bureau 57-62, Sec.-Gen. 60-62; Asst. Dir. Néo-Destour Party and Chief Editor *L'Action* 62-64, Gen. Sec. of Destourian Youth, Gen. Sec. of Tunisian Youth 63-64; mem. High Comm. DSP 70-; Deputy Nat. Assembly 64-; Minister of Information 69-70; Perm. Rep. to UN, Geneva 70; Minister Public Works and Housing 71-73, of Youth and Sports 73; Minister at the Prime Minister's Office 73-80; Minister of Supply 81-; mem. Central Cttee., then mem. Political Bureau and Dir. Destour Socialist Party 64.
Publs. Several books on the history of the National Tunisian Movement.
Ministry of Supply, Tunis, Tunisia.

Schaeffer-Forrer, Claude Frédéric Armand, M.A.; French archaeologist; b. 6 March 1898; ed. Strasbourg, Oxford and Paris Univs.
Curator Prehistoric, Roman and Early Medieval Museum, Palais Rohan, Strasbourg 21-32; Curator Coins and Medals Dept. Strasbourg Univ. 26-32; Curator French Nat. Museums 33-54; Dir. of Research at Nat. Centre of Scientific Research, Paris 46-54; Vice-Pres. Comm. des Fouilles, Direction Générale des Relations Culturelles, Ministry of Foreign Affairs; mem. French Inst. 53; Hon. Prof. Collège de France 74; Dir. expedition Ras Shamra, Syria 29- (discovered Canaanite alphabetic cuneiform records); Cyprus 32, 34, 35, 46, 47, 49-, Malatya, Turkey 46, 47, 48, 50; mem. Archaeological Cttee. Ministry of Education; Hon. Fellow St. John's Coll. Oxford; mem. Nat. Society of Antiquaries, France; corresp. mem. Belgian Royal Acad., Danish Royal Acad.; corresp. Fellow of British Acad.; Hon. Fellow Royal Anthropological Inst. of Great Britain and Ireland, etc.; hon. mem. Deutsche Morgenländische Gesellschaft; served as Capt. Corvette with Fighting French Naval Forces 40-45; D.Litt. h.c. (Oxon.), D.C.L. h.c. (Glasgow), Hon. F.S.A.; Gold Medal, Soc. of Antriesiqua 58, Scientific and Philological Soc., Famagusta, Cyprus 65, Hon. Citizen of Latakia (Syria), Famagusta (Cyprus).
Publs. *Haches néolithiques* 24, *Tertres funéraires préhistoriques dans la forêt de Haguenau* (2 vols.) 26, 30, *Missions en Chypre* 36, *Ugaritica I* 39, *Cuneiform Texts of Ras Shamra-Ugarit* 39, *Stratigraphie comparée et Chronologie de l'Asie occidentale* 48, *Ugaritica II* 49, *Enkomi-Alasia* 52, *Ugaritica III* 56, *Ugaritica IV* 62, *Ugaritica V* 65, *Ugaritica VI* 69, *Alasia I* 72, *Ugaritica VII* 78, *Palais Royal d'Ugarit VII* 80.
Le Castel Blanc, 16 rue Turgot, St. Germain-en-Laye 78100; and l'Escale, B.P. 16, La Croix-Valmer (83), France.

Schocken, Gershom; Israeli editor and publisher; b. Sept. 1912; ed. Univ. of Heidelberg and London School of Economics.
Joined staff of *Haaretz* (daily newspaper) 37, publisher and editor 39-; Dir. Schocken Publishing House Ltd.; mem. Knesset (Parl.) 55-59.
Haaretz Building, 21 Salman Schocken Street, P.O. Box 233, Tel-Aviv, Israel.

Sela, Michael (Salomonowicz), M.SC., PH.D.; Israeli chemist and immunologist; b. 6 March 1924, Tomaszow, Poland; ed. Hebrew Univ., Jerusalem and Geneva Univ.
Joined Weizmann Inst. of Science 50; W. Garfield Weston Prof. of Immunology; Head of Dept. of Chem. Immunology 62-75; Dean of Faculty of Biology 70-73; mem. Board of Govs. 70-; Vice-Pres. 70-71, Pres. Weizmann Inst. of Science 75-; Visiting Scientist Nat. Insts. of Health (NIH), U.S.A. 56-57, 60-61, Univ. of Calif., Berkeley 67-68; Fogarty Scholar-in-Residence, Fogarty Int. Centre, U.S.A. 73-74; mem. WHO Expert Advisory Panel on Immunology 62-; mem. Int. Cell Research Org. 65-; mem. Council, Int. Union of Pure and Applied Biophysics 72-78; Chair. Board of Advisors of Basle Inst. of Immunology 74-79, Council of European Molecular Biology Org. 75-; mem. Board of Trustees Int. Fed. Insts. for Advanced Studies 76-, Exec. Cttee. 82-; Pres. Int. Union of Immunological socs. 77-80; mem. Scientific and Technical Advisory Comm., UNDP/World Bank/WHO Special Programme for Research and Training in Tropical Diseases 79-, WHO Advisory Comm. on Medical Research 79-; mem. Scientific Council, Int. Inst. of Cellular and Molecular Pathology, Brussels 80-, Council Paul Ehrlich Foundation, Frankfurt 80-; mem. Israel Acad. of Sciences and Humanities 71, Pontifical Acad. of Sciences 75; Hon. mem. American Soc. of Biological Chemists 68, Scandinavian Soc. for Immunology 71, Harvey Soc. 72, American Soc. of Immunologists 73, Société Française d'Immunologie 79; Foreign mem. Max-Planck Soc., Freiburg 67; Foreign Hon. mem. American Acad. of Arts and Sciences 71; Foreign Assoc. Nat. Acad. of Sciences, U.S.A. 76; serves many editorial boards, incl. *European Journal of Immunology, Critical Views of Biochemistry, Immunological Communications*; Israel Prize in Natural Sciences 59, Otto Warburg Medal of German Soc. of Biological Chem. 68, Rothschild Prize in Chem. 68, Emil von Behring Prize of Phillipps Univ. 73, NIH Lectureship 73, Gairdner Foundation Int. Award 80.
Publs. over 500 in immunology, biochem. and molecular biology.
Weizmann Institute of Science, Rehovot, Israel.

Senoussi, Ahmad (*see* Snoussi, Ahmed).

Senoussi, Badreddine, LL.M., M.H.; Moroccan politician; b. 30 March 1933, Fez; ed. Univ. of Bordeaux, Chamber of Commerce, Paris.
Adviser, "Haut Tribunal Chérifien", Rabat 56; Civil Service Admin., Ministry of State 57; Sec.-Gen. Nat. Tobacco Co. 58; Head, Royal Cabinet 63; Under-Sec. of State for Commerce and Industry 64, for Admin. Affairs 65; Minister of Post Office and Telecommunications 66, of Youth, Sports and Social Affairs 70-71; Amb. to U.S.A. 71-74, to Iran 75-76, to U.K. 76-80; awarded many foreign decorations.
Ministère des Affaires Etrangères, Rabat, Morocco.

Sezgin, Ismet; Turkish politician; b. 1928, Aydin; ed. Higher School of Econs. and Commerce.
Worked in banking; Mayor of Aydin 55; Justice Party Deputy 61; Minister of Youth and Sports 69-71, of Finance Nov. 79-Sept. 80.
c/o Ministry of Finance, Maliye Bakanliği, Ulus, Ankara, Turkey.

Shadli Bin-Jeddid (*see* Chadli, Col. Bendjedid).

Shafei, Col. Hussein; Egyptian army officer and politician; b. 1918; ed. Mil. Coll., Cairo.
Commissioned as 2nd Lieut. 38; took part in Palestine hostilities 48; graduated from Staff Officers' Coll. 53 and apptd. Officer-in-Charge Cavalry Corps; Minister of War and Marine April-Sept. 54, of Social Affairs Sept. 54-58; Minister of Labour and Social Affairs, U.A.R. 58-61; Vice-Pres. and Minister of Social Affairs and Waqfs 61-62; mem. Presidency Council 62-64; Vice-Pres. of U.A.R. (Egypt) 64-67, 70-75; Deputy Prime Minister and Minister of Waqfs 67-71.
6 Sharai Wizaret, El Ziraä Dokki, Giza, Egypt.

Shah, Idries; professor and author; b. 16 June 1924, Simla, India; ed. private and traditional Middle Eastern schools.
Studied in Middle East, Europe and S. America; Dir. of Studies, Inst. for Cultural Research 66-; Visiting Prof. Univ. of Geneva 72-73, Univ. of Calif. 76, 77, New York Univ. Graduate School, New Jersey Inst. for Advanced Int. Studies; Adviser, Middle Eastern Authorities, Int. Center for Educ. Advancement (ICEA) 77-; Contributor to VI World Congress of Psychiatry 77; author of numerous works on philosophy; Patron Cambridge Poetry Festival 75; Fellow, Royal Econ. Soc., Royal Soc. of Arts; Life mem. British Asscn., The National Trust; mem. PEN, Club of Rome; Life Gov. Royal Hosp. and Home for Incurables; Gov. Royal Humane Soc.; Consultant Nuclear Protection Advisory Group (NuPAG) 80-; Prof. h.c. (Univ. of La Plata) 74; Int. Community Service Award 73; six first prizes during UNESCO World Book Year 73; Gold Medal, Services to Poetry 75; Distinguished Contribution to Human Thought Award 75; subject of BBC documentary film 69, of vol. of collected papers in honour of Idries Shah 74; Lord of the Manor of Newmarket 77.
Publs. *Oriental Magic* 56, *Secret Lore of Magic* 57, *Destination Mecca* 57, *The Sufis* 64, *Special Problems* 66, *Exploits of Nasruddin* 66, *Tales of the Dervishes* 67, *The Pleasantries* 68, *The Way of the Sufi* 68, *Reflections* 68, *Caravan of Dreams* 68, *Wisdom of the Idiots* 69, *The Dermis Probe* 69, *The Book of the Book* 69, *Thinkers of the East* 70, *The Magic Monastery* 72, *The Subtleties of the Inimitable Mulla Nasruddin* 73, *The Elephant in the Dark* 74, *Learning How to Learn* 78, *Beginning to Begin* 78, *Special Illumination* 78, *A Veiled Gazelle* 78, *The Hundred Tales of Wisdom* 78, *A Perfumed Scorpion* 79, *World Tales* 79, *Seeker After Truth* 82, Contributor; *Oxford Companion to the Mind;* Advisory Editor, *Human Nature Journal;* articles in specialist journals and reviews in the field of education.
c/o Jonathan Cape Ltd., 30 Bedford Square, London, WC1B 3EL, England.

Shakhbut bin Sultan bin Zaid, H.H. Sheikh; former Ruler of Abu Dhabi; b. 1905.
Succeeded to Sheikdom 28, deposed Aug. 66; sons Zaid b. 30, Sultan b. 36.
Manama, Bahrain.

Shamgar, Meir; Israeli lawyer; b. 1925, Danzig; ed. Govt. law classes, and London Univ.
Settled in Palestine 39; detained by British Admin. for underground activities, deported to East Africa 44-48; Col. in Israeli Army 48-68; Mil. Advocate-Gen. 61-68; Attorney-Gen. 68-75; Justice, Supreme Court of Israel July 75-; Chair. Advisory Council, Inst. of Criminology, Tel-Aviv Univ.; fmr. Law Lecturer, Hebrew Univ., Jerusalem, Tel-Aviv; mem. Israel Bar Council 61-68; mem. of Council, Int. Soc. of Mil. Law and Law of War.
Publs. various legal essays in Israeli and foreign journals.
Supreme Court of Israel, Jerusalem, Israel.

Shamir, Moshe; Israeli writer; b. 15 Sept. 1921; ed. Tel-Aviv Herzliya Gymnasium.
Former mem. Kibbutz Mishmar Haemek; in Haganah underground units 47-48; Capt. in Israel Army 48; Lit. Ed. *Maariv;* mem. Hebrew Acad.; mem. Knesset 77-81; Ussiskin Prize 48, Brenner Prize 53, Bialik Prize 55, Neumann Literary Award, New York Univ. 81.
Publs. (novels) *He Walked in the Fields, Under the Sun, With his own Hands, King of Flesh and Blood, David's Stranger, Naked You Are, The Border, A Dove from an Alien Cote* 73; (plays) *He Walked in the Fields, The War of the Sons of Light, The Heir,* and others.
3 Rosanis, Tel-Aviv, Israel.

Shamir, Yitzhak; Israeli politician; b. 1915, Poland; ed. Hebrew Secondary School, Białystok, Warsaw Univ. and Hebrew Univ., Jerusalem.
Mem. Irgun Zvai Leumi (Jewish Mil. Org.) 37, then a founder and leader of Lohamei Herut Yisrael (Stern Gang) 40-41; arrested by British Mandatory Authority 41, 46 (exiled to Eritrea); given political asylum in France, returned to Israel 48; retd. from political activity until 55; Sr. post Civil Service 55-65; Man. Dir. several business concerns 65-; mem. Herut Movt. 70, mem. Exec. Cttee. and Dir. Immigration Dept., later Org. Dept. 70-75, Chair. Exec. Cttee. 75-; elected to 8th Knesset, Herut Party 73, Speaker 77-80; Minister of Foreign Affairs March 80-.
Ministry of Foreign Affairs, Jerusalem, Israel.

Sharif, Omar (Michel Shalhoub); Egyptian actor; b. 10 April 1932, Cairo; ed. Victoria Coll., Cairo.
Salesman, lumber-import firm; made first film *The Blazing Sun* 53; starred in 24 Egyptian films and two French co-production films during following five years; commenced int. film career with *Lawrence of Arabia.*
Films include: *Lawrence of Arabia, The Fall of the Roman Empire, Behold a Pale Horse, Ghengis Khan, The Yellow Rolls Royce, Doctor Zhivago, Night of the Generals, Mackenna's Gold, Funny Girl, Cinderella—Italian Style, Mayerling, The Appointment, Che, The Last Valley, The Horsemen, The Burglars, The Mysterious Island, The Tamarind Seed, Juggernaut, Funny Lady, Ace up My Sleeve, Crime and Passion, Ashanti, Bloodline.*
Publ. *The Eternal Male* (autobiog.) 78.
c/o William Morris Agency (U.K.) Ltd., 147 Wardour Street, London, W.1, England.

Sharif-Emami, Jaffar, G.C.M.G.; Iranian engineer and politician; b. 8 Sept. 1910, Teheran; ed. Secondary School, Teheran, German Central Railway School and Borås Technical School, Sweden.
Joined Iranian State Railways 31, Technical Deputy Gen. Dir. 42-46, Gen. Dir. 50-51; Chair. and Man. Dir. Independent Irrigation Corpn. 46-50; Under-Sec. of State to Ministry of Roads and Communications, Minister of Roads and Communications 50-51; mem. High Council, Plan Org. 51-52, Man. Dir. and Chair. High Council, Plan Org. 53-54;

Senator from Teheran 55-57, 63-79, Pres. of Senate 63-79; Minister of Industry and Mines 57-60; Prime Minister Aug. 60-May 61, Aug.-Nov. 78; Deputy Custodian Pahlavi Foundation 62-79, mem. Board of Trustees 66; Chair. Industrial and Mining Devt. Bank 63-79; Pres. Iranian Asscn. of World Federalists 63-79; Pres. Iranian Engineers Asscn. 66-79; Pres. Third Constituent Assembly 67; Pres. of 22nd Int. Conf. of the Red Cross 73; Pres. Int. Bankers Asscn. 75; mem. American Soc. of Civil Engineers 46- (Life mem. 79-), Board of Dirs. Royal Org. of Social Services 62-79, Board of Trustees, Pahlavi Univ. 62-79, Nat. Univ. Teheran 62, Aria Mehr Tech. Univ., Teheran 65-79, Queen Pahlavi's Foundation; mem. Red Lion and Sun 63, Vice-Pres. 63, Deputy Chair. 66-79; mem. of Board of Founders of Soc. for Preservation of Nat. Monuments 66; Dr. h.c. Seoul Univ. 78; Iranian decorations: Order of Homayoun, First Grade, Order of Taj, First Class, and nine others; foreign decorations incl. Grosses Kreuz Verdienstorden (Germany), Grand Croix de la Légion d'Honneur (France), Order of Rising Sun, First Class (Japan), Order of St. Michael and St. George (U.K.) and 25 others.
425 E. 58th Street, New York, N.Y. 10022, U.S.A.

Sharifi, Ahmad-Hushang, PH.D.; Iranian educationist, b. 1925, Teheran; ed. France.
With Iranian Consulate, Paris; mem. Perm. Del. to UNESCO; French Language Translator, Teheran Univ. 57, Finance Teacher 58, Lecturer in Political Science 60, Prof. of Political Science 66; Financial and Admin. Adviser to Ministry of Educ. 64, Under-Sec. of Educ. 64; Principal, Teachers Training Coll. 68; Chancellor Nat. Univ., Teheran 73, Rector 76; Minister of Educ. 74-76; fmr. mem. Iran Novin Party.
National University of Iran, Evin, Teheran, Iran.

Sharon, Major-Gen. Ariel; Israeli army officer and politician; b. 1928.
Active in Hagana since early youth; Instructor, Jewish Police units 47; Platoon Commdr. Alexandroni Brigade; Regimental Intelligence Officer 48; Co. Commdr. 49; Commdr. Brigade Reconnaissance Unit 49-50; Intelligence Officer, Cen. Command and Northern Command 50-52; studies at Hebrew Univ. 52-53; in charge of Unit 101, on numerous reprisal operations until 57; studies Staff Coll., Camberley, U.K. 57-58; Training Commdr., Gen. Staff 58; Commdr. Infantry School 58-69; Commdr. Armoured Brigade 62; Head of Staff, Northern Command 64; law studies, Tel-Aviv Univ. 66; Head Brigade Group during Six-Day War 67; resigned from Army July 73; recalled as Commdr. Cen. Section of Sinai Front during Yom Kippur War Oct. 73, forged bridgehead across Suez Canal; with others formed Likud Front Sept. 73; mem. Knesset (Parl.) 73-74, 77-; joined army reserves Dec 74; Adviser to Prime Minister 75-77; Minister of Agriculture 77-81, of Defence Aug. 81-.
Ministry of Defence, Jerusalem, Israel.

Shazly, Lt.-Gen. Saad Mohamed al Hosseiny el-, M.POL.SC.; Egyptian army officer; b. 1 April 1922, Cairo; ed. Khedive Ismail Secondary School, Cairo, Cairo Univ., Mil. Coll., and in U.S.S.R.
Officer of the Guards 43-48; Platoon Commdr. Arab-Israeli War 48; Commdr. of Parachute School 54-56; Commdr. of Parachute Battalion 56-58; Commdr. United Arab Repub. Contingent, UN, Congo 60-61; Defence Attaché, London 61-63; Brig. Commdr. in Yemen Civil War 65-66; Commdr. Shazly Group, Egyptian-Israeli War 67; Commdr. of Special Forces 67-69; Commdr. Red Sea District 70-71; Chief of Staff of Egyptian Armed Forces 71-73; Amb. to U.K. 74-75, to Portugal 75-78; founded Egyptian Nat. Front March 80, Sec.-Gen. 80-; Founder and Chief Ed. *Al Gabha* magazine Aug. 80-; holder of 23 decorations including Order of the Repub., 1st Class, Etoile d'Honneur,

Médaille Mil. du Courage, Médaille du Congo, Knight Syrian Honour Star, Palestinian Honour Star.
Publs. *How an Infantry Division Can Cross a Water Barrier* 73, *Fonética Arabe Com Letras Portuguesas* 78, *Kuraanunn Kariim* 78, *Memoires of the 73 War* 79, *The Arab-Israeli Conflicts in the Past and in the Future* (to be published 82).
P.O.Box 778, Alger-Gare, Algeria.

Shebani, Dr. Omar, M.A., PH.D.; Libyan educationist; b. 1930; ed. Cairo, Ain-Shams Univs. and Boston, George Washington Univs., U.S.A.
Assistant Dir. Teachers' Coll., Univ. of Libya (now Univ. of Garyounis) 65; Dir. of Youth Dept. 68, Asst. Prof., Pres. 70-76, Vice-Chancellor 76-.
c/o General Administration, University of Garyounis, P.O. Box 1308, Benghazi, Libya.

Shenouda III, Anba, B.A., B.D.; Egyptian ecclesiastic; b. 3 Aug. 1923.
Former Prof. of Theology and Patrology, Coptic Orthodox Theological School, Cairo; Pope of Alexandria and Patriarch of The See of St. Mark in all Africa and the Near East 71; removed from post by Pres. Sadat and banished to desert monastery Wadi Natroun Sept. 81.
St. Mark's Patriarchate, Anba Ruiess Building, Ramses Street, Abbasiya, Cairo, Egypt.

Shiguer, Mohamed Haddou; Moroccan politician; b. 1932; ed. Mohammed V Univ.
Taught for 12 years; mem. Nat. Assembly; Minister of Post and Telecommunications 64-66, of Agriculture 66-67, of the Royal Cabinet 67, of Defence 67-68, of Primary Educ. 68-72, of Nat. Educ. 72-73, of the Interior 73-77, of Co-operation and Professional Training 77-78, of Relations with Parliament 78-81.
c/o Ministry of Relations with Parliament, Rabat, Morocco.

Shihata, Ibrahim F. I., L. EN D., S.J.D.; Egyptian jurist, development financier and administrator; b. 19 Aug. 1937; ed. Cairo Univ., Harvard Univ., U.S.A.
Member of the Council of State of Egypt 57-60; Lecturer, Faculty of Law, Ain Shams Univ. 64-66, Assoc. Prof. 70-72; Legal Adviser to Kuwait Fund for Arab Econ. Devt. 66-70, Gen. Counsel 72-76; also adviser and consultant to Arab Govts. and Int. Orgs. 65-; Dir.-Gen. OPEC Fund for Int. Devt. 76-; mem. Exec. Board, Int. Fund for Agricultural Devt. 77-, Oxford Energy Club, North-South Round Table; Trustee Georgetown Univ. Center of Int. and Foreign Trade Law, Centre of Research for the New Int. Econ. Order, Oxford.
Publs. Eleven books and more than sixty essays on different aspects of international law and finance.
OPEC Fund for Int. Devt., P.O. Box 995, Vienna 1011, Austria.

Shukry, Ibrahim; Egyptian politician; b. 22 Sept. 1916.
Joined Misr al-Fatat (Young Egypt) party 35; shot in Cairo strike 35; managed family estate, Sharbeen; Sec.-Gen. Misr al-Fatat 46; elected Vice-Pres., then Pres. Socialist Party (formerly Misr al-Fatat) 47-53; mem. for Kahaliyya, People's Assembly 49-52; imprisoned for opposing the monarchy 52, released after revolution 52; returned to estate; joined Arab Socialist Union on its formation 62, elected to Exec. Cttee. 64; re-elected mem. for Kahaliyya 64-68; Pres. Farmers' Union and Sec. Professional Asscn. 65-66; Gov. Wadi al-Gadeed 68-76; elected to People's Assembly 76; Minister of Agric. and Agrarian Reform Feb. 77-May 78, of Land Improvement May-Oct. 78; Chair. new Socialist Labour Party and Man Ed. *Al-Sha'b* (party newspaper) Oct. 78-; Leader of the Opposition, People's Assembly 79-.
Socialist Labour Party, People's Assembly Street, Cairo, Egypt.

Sidarouss, H.E. Cardinal Stephanos I; Egyptian ecclesiastic; b. 1904; ed. Jesuits' Coll. Cairo, Univ. de Paris, Faculté de Droit, and Ecole Libre des Sciences Politiques. Barrister, Egypt 26-32; Vincentian Priest 39-; Prof. Seminaries at Evreux, Dax and Beauvais (France); Rector Coptic Catholic Seminary, Tahta 46, Tanta 47-53, Maadi 53-58; Auxiliary Bishop to the Patriarch of Alexandria 47-58, Patriarch 58-; created Cardinal 65.
34 Ibn Sandar Street, Koubbeh Bridge, Cairo, Egypt.

Sidi-Baba, Dey Ould; Moroccan diplomatist and politician; b. 1921, Atar, Mauritania.
Counsellor, Ministry of Foreign Affairs, Morocco 58, Head of African Div. 59; mem. Moroccan Dels. to UN Gen. Assembly 59-64; Acting Perm. Rep. of Morocco to UN 63-65, Perm. Rep. 65-67; Minister of Royal Cabinet 67-; Amb. to Saudi Arabia 71-72; Dir. Royal Cabinet 72-73; Minister of Educ. 73-74, of Waqfs and Islamic Affairs 74-77; Pres. Chamber of Reps. 77-; mem. Nat. Defence Council March 79-; Commandeur du Trône Alaouite; Niger Grand Order of Merit; Officer of Libyan Order of Independence; Commdr. of Syrian Order of Merit.
Chamber of Representatives, Rabat, Morocco.

Sidky, Aziz, B.ENG., M.A., PH.D.; Egyptian politician; b. 1 July 1920; ed. Cairo Univ., Univ. of Oregon and Harvard Univ.
Minister of Industry 56-63; Deputy Prime Minister for Industry and Mineral Wealth 64-65; Adviser for Production Affairs to Pres. of U.A.R. 66-67; Minister of Industry, Petroleum and Mineral Wealth 68-71; Deputy Prime Minister 71-72, Prime Minister 72-73; Personal Asst. to Pres. Sadat 73-75; has attended many int. confs. on industrial affairs.
c/o The Presidency, Cairo, Egypt.

Siilasvuo, Lieut.-Gen. Ensio; Finnish army officer; b. 1 Jan. 1922, Helsinki; ed. Lycée of Oulu, Finnish Mil. Acad., Finnish Command and Staff Coll.
Platoon Commdr., Infantry Co. Commdr. and Chief of Staff, Infantry Regiment 11 41-44; Company Commdr., Infantry Regiment 1 45-50; attended Command and Staff Coll. 51-52; various staff appointments in mil. districts of N. Finland 53-57; Commdr. Finnish Contingent, UN Emergency Force 57; Mil. Observer, UN Observation Group in Lebanon 58; Finnish Defence Attaché in Warsaw 59-61; Staff Officer Third Div. 62-64; Commdr. Finnish Contingent, UN Force in Cyprus 64-65; Instructor, Nat. Defence Coll. 65-67; Chief, Foreign Dept. GHQ 67; Senior Staff Officer, UN Truce Supervision Org. in Palestine 67-70; Chief of Staff, UN Truce Supervision Org. in Palestine 70-73; Commdr. UN Emergency Force 73-75; Chief Co-ordinator of UN Peace-keeping Missions in the Middle East 75-80, retired from UN service 80; Grand Cross Order of the Lion of Finland 1st Class; Finnish Cross of Freedom 3rd and 4th Class; Knight of the Order of the White Rose of Finland.
Castreninkatu 6A18, 00530 Helsinki 53, Finland.

Siklar, Osman; Turkish banker; b. 1929; ed. Acad. of Econ. and Commercial Sciences, Istanbul.
Foreign Exchange Dept., Central Bank 54-59; trained at Société Générale, Paris 60-61; Deputy Rep. Central Bank of Turkey, Zürich 62-64, Gen. Man. Foreign Exchange Dept., Turkey 65-75, Vice-Gov. 76-78; retired from Central Bank, then Chair. several export cos.; mem. Bd. Anadolu Bankasl bank, Istanbul; returned to Central Bank as Gov. Jan. 81-.
Central Bank of Turkey, Bankalar Cad. 48, Ankara, Turkey.

Simavi, Haldûn; Turkish journalist; b. 1925; ed. Kabataş Lisesi, Istanbul.
Publisher and Gen. Man. of daily newspapers *Günaydin, Saklambac,* weekly mags. *Tarkan, Kara Murat, Girgir;*

fırt, and monthly publications *Er Dehorasyon, Gagdaş Bilim, Turkish Treasures, Tekshil* and trimestrial *Vizon,* co-owner Istanbul daily newspaper *Hürriyet.*
Veb Ofset, Ileri Matbaacılık A.S. Cağaloğlu, Istanbul, Turkey.

Simon, Akiba Ernst, PH.D.; Israeli educationist; b. 15 March 1899; ed. Univs. of Berlin and Heidelberg.
Editor (with Martin Buber) *Der Jude* 23-24; Lecturer in Jewish subjects, Frankfurt-am-Main 22-28; taught at various schools in Germany and Palestine 28; Assoc. Dir. of Jewish Adult Education Centre of Germany 33-34; Lecturer Hebrew Univ. of Jerusalem 38-50, Assoc. Prof. of Educ. 50-55, Prof. 55-68, Prof. Emer. 68-; Visiting Prof. of Educ., Jewish Theological Seminary of America, N.Y. 47-48, 62; Visiting Prof. of Educ. at Univ. of Judaism, L.A., Calif. 56-57; mem. Research Board Leo Baeck Inst. of Jews from Germany; mem. Board Religious Youth Village; co-Editor Pedagogical Encyclopaedia, 5 vols. (Hebrew); Israeli State Prize for Educ. 67; Buber-Rosenzweig Medal 69; Prize of the City of Jerusalem; Dr. Theol. h.c., Dr. of Jewish Letters h.c.
Publs. *Ranke und Hegel* 29, *Das Werturteil im Geschichtsunterricht* 31, *Bialik* 35, *Educational Meaning of Socratic Irony* (Hebrew) 49, *Pioneers of Social Education—Pestalozzi and Korczak* (Hebrew), *The Teaching of Pestalozzi* 53, 61 (Hebrew), *Jewish Adult Education in Nazi Germany as Spiritual Resistance, Franz Rosenzweig's Position in the History of Jewish Education* (Hebrew), *Freud the Jew* (Hebrew, German and English), *Martin Buber and the Faith of Judaism* (Hebrew), *Martin Buber and German Jewry* (English) 58, *Aims of Secondary Education in Israel* (Hebrew) 61, *Brücken* (Collected Essays—German) 65, *M. Buber's Correspondence* (3 vols.) (German, with G. Schaeder), 72-75, *Buber's Political Philosophy and Practice* (Hebrew) 73, Autobiography in *Pedagogics in Autobiographies* (German) 75, *Martin Buber's Lebendige Erbe* (German and Hebrew) 78, *Entscheidung zum Judentum* (Decision for Judaism, Collected Essays) 80.
35 Ben Maimon Avenue, Jerusalem, Israel.

Sindi, Sheikh Kamil; Saudi Arabian airline executive; b. 3 Jan. 1932, Mecca.
Joined Saudi Arabian Airlines and Civil Aviation Org. 47; in charge of Operations and Maintenance Dept. 47; Sec. to Dir.-Gen. until 60; Dir.-Gen. of Civil Aviation 61-66; Dir-Gen. Saudi Arabian Airlines (SAUDIA) 67-79; Pres. Arab Air Carriers Organisation (AACO) 71-; mem. Exec. Cttee. IATA 74-; Asst. Minister of Defence and for Civil Aviation Affairs 79-; Chevalier de l'Order d'Orange Nassau.
c/o Ministry of Defence and Aviation, Jeddah, Saudi Arabia.

Slaoui, Driss; Moroccan politician and banker; b. 12 Dec. 926, Fez; ed. Univs. of Grenoble and Paris, France.
Director-General Sûreté Nationale, Casablanca 56-58; Sec. of State for Interior, then for Commerce and Industry; Minister of Commerce and Industry 59-61; Dir. of Royal Cabinet March 62; Minister of Public Works 62-63, of Finance 63-64, of Nat. Economy and Agriculture Nov. 63-64; Gov. Banque du Maroc (Central Bank) 64-68; Minister of Justice 68-69; Dir.-Gen. Royal Cabinet 69-71; Perm. Rep. to UN 74-76; Counsellor to King Hassan Oct. 77-; Pres. Dir.-Gen. Société Nat. d'Investissement 78-80; Rep. to Int. Court of Justice in Western Sahara case June-July 75.
c/o Ministry of Foreign Affairs, Rabat, Morocco.

Slim, Taieb; Tunisian politician and diplomatist; b. 1914; ed. Tunis Lycée and Univ. of Paris.
Member Néo-Destour Party, detained 41-43; Arab Maghreb Bureau, Cairo 46-49; Head, Tunisian Office, Cairo 49, established Tunisian offices, New Delhi, Jakarta,

Karachi; Head, Foreign Affairs, Presidency of Council of Ministers 55-56; Ambassador to U.K. 56-62, also accredited to Denmark, Norway and Sweden 60-62; Perm. Rep. to UN 62-67, concurrently Amb. to Canada; Minister, Personal Rep. of the Pres. 67-70; mem. Nat. Assembly 69; Amb. to Morocco 70-71; Minister of State 71-72; Amb., Perm. Rep. to UN, Geneva 73-74; Amb. to Canada 74-76; Minister of State 76-77; Perm. Rep. of Tunisia to UN 81-; mem. Political Bureau Destour Socialist Party 71-74.
Permanent Mission of Tunisia to the United Nations, 40 East 71st Street, New York, N.Y. 10021, U.S.A.

Smith, Wilfred Cantwell, M.A., PH.D., D.D., LL.D., LITT.D., L.H.D.; Canadian university professor; b. 21 July 1916; ed. Upper Canada Coll., Univ. of Grenoble, Univ. of Madrid, American Univ. Cairo, Univ. of Toronto, Cambridge and Princeton Univs.
Served as rep. among Muslims of the Canadian Overseas Missions Council, chiefly in Lahore 40-49; Lecturer in Indian and Islamic History, Univ. of the Punjab, Lahore 41-45; Prof. of Comparative Religion 49-63, and Dir. Inst. of Islamic Studies, McGill Univ. 51-63; Prof. of World Religions and Dir. Center for the Study of World Religions, Harvard Univ. 64-73, also Visiting Prof. of History of Religion 74-78, McCulloch Prof. of Religion, Dalhousie Univ. 73-78; Prof. of Comparative History of Religion, Chair. The Study of Religion, Harvard Univ. 78-; Pres. American Soc. for the Study of Religion 66-69; Pres. Middle East Studies Asscn. of North America 77-78, Canadian Theological Soc. 79-80, Pres.-Elect American Acad. of Religion 81-82; Fellow, Royal Soc. of Canada (Pres. Humanities and Social Science Section 72-73), American Acad. of Arts and Sciences; Chauveau Medal, Royal Soc. of Canada 74.
Publs. *Modern Islam in India* 43 (revised edns. 47, 65, 78), *Islam in Modern History* 57, 77 (Arabic trans. 75), *Meaning and End of Religion* 63, 78, *Faith of Other Men* 63, *Modernisation of a Traditional Society* 66, *Questions of Religious Truth* 67, *Belief and History* 77, *Faith and Belief* 79, *Towards a World Theology* 81, *On Outstanding Islam* 81. 1581 Massachusetts Avenue, Cambridge, Massachusetts, U.S.A.

Snoussi, Ahmed, LL.D.; Moroccan diplomatist; b. 22 April 1929; ed. Lycées at Meknes and Casablanca, Schools of Law and Political Sciences, Paris.
In Nationalist Movement; cabinet attaché to Minister of State in negotiations with France 56; Head, Press Div. Ministry of External Affairs 56; Sec.-Gen. Conf. on status of Tangiers; Moroccan Del. to UNESCO Conf. and UN; Dir.-Gen. Information; mem. Tech. Co-op. Mission to Congo and King's special envoy to Congo 58-59; UN Conciliation Mission to Congo 61; Sec.-Gen. Ministry of Information, Tourism Handicrafts and Fine Arts 61-65; Ambassador to Nigeria and Cameroon 65-67; Minister of Information 67-71; Amb. to Tunisia 71-73, to Algeria 73-75, to Mauritania 78-80; mem. Moroccan Del. to UN 75-77; Editor numerous magazines, including *Maroc* (Ministry of External Affairs) and *Maroc Documents* (Ministry of Information); Officer Order of the Throne of Morocco, Cross of Courage and Endurance (Mission to Congo), decorations from Jordan and Yugoslavia.
Embassy of the Kingdom of Morocco, Nouakchott, Mauritania.

Solh, Rashid; Lebanese lawyer and politician; b. 1926, Beirut; ed. Coll. des Frères des Ecoles Chrétiennes, Coll. Al Makassed, Faculty of Law, Beirut.
Successively Judge, Pres. of the Labour Arbitration Council, Examining Magistrate, Attorney-Gen. of the Charéi Tribunal; Independent mem. Chamber of Deputies for Beirut 64, 72; Prime Minister Oct. 74-May 75.
Chambre des Députés, Place de l'Etoile, Beirut, Lebanon.

Solh, Takieddine; Lebanese politician and diplomatist; b. 1909; ed. American Univ. of Beirut, and Univ. Saint Joseph, Beirut.
Former Civil Servant; fmr. Counsellor, Embassy to United Arab Repub., and to the Arab League; Prof. of Arabic, Lycée français 35-43; mem. of Parl. 57, 64; Pres. Foreign Affairs Comm. 64-; Minister of the Interior 65; Prime Minister, Minister of Finance 73-74; appointed Prime Minister July 80 (unable to form govt.).
Beirut, Lebanon.

Soliman, Mohammed Sidki; Egyptian army officer and politician; b. 1919; ed. Fuad I Univ., Cairo.
Colonel in U.A.R. Army -62; Minister for the High Dam Sept. 62-Sept. 66; Prime Minister 66-67; Deputy Prime Minister, Minister of Industry and Power 67-70; Pres. Soviet-Egyptian Friendship Soc.; Order of Lenin.
Cairo, Egypt.

Soteriades, Antis; Cypriot lawyer and diplomatist; b. 10 Sept. 1924; ed. London Univ. and Gray's Inn, London.
In legal practice, Nicosia 51-56; detained on suspicion of assisting EOKA 56; escaped and became EOKA leader for Kyrenia district; mem. Exec., Edma Party May 59; High Commr. to U.K. Oct. 60-66; Amb. to United Arab Repub. (now Egypt) 66-78, concurrently to Lebanon 67-78, to Syria 67-78, to Iraq 73-78; Amb. to Yugoslavia 79-, concurrently to Algeria and Sudan; Knight of Order of St. Gregory the Great (Vatican) 63.
Embassy of Cyprus, Diplomatska Kolonija 9, Belgrade, Yugoslavia.

Soulioti, Stella; Cypriot lawyer and politician; b. 1920; ed. Limassol, Victoria Girls' Coll., Alexandria, St. James' Secretarial Coll., London and Gray's Inn, London.
Worked in Cyprus Govt. Public Information Office; in W.A.A.F. Middle East in Second World War; qualified as barrister after war; joined family practice; Minister of Justice Aug. 60-70, concurrently Minister of Health 64-66; Law Commr. 71-; Co-ordinator for Foreign Aid to Cyprus Refugees Aug. 74-; Adviser on Intercommunal Talks for Solution of Cyprus Problem 76-; Chair. Cyprus Overseas Relief Fund 77; Pres. Cyprus Red Cross Soc.; Chair. Scholarship Board; Vice-Pres. Cyprus Anti-Cancer Soc.; Hon. LL.D. (Nottingham Univ.) 72.
P.O. Box 4102, Nicosia, Cyprus.

Spain, James W., M.A., PH.D.; American diplomatist; b. 22 July 1926, Chicago; ed. Univ. of Chicago, Columbia Univ.
Consultant to Sec. of the Army, Tokyo 49-50; Cultural Officer, Dept. of State, Karachi, Pakistan 51-53; Research Fellow, Ford Foundation 53-55; Research Lecturer, Columbia Univ. 55-63; mem. Policy Planning Staff, Dept. of State 63-64; Dir. Office of Research and Analysis for Near East-South Asian Affairs 64-66; Country Dir. for Pakistan and Afghanistan 66-69; Chargé d'affaires, Islamabad 69; Consul-Gen., Istanbul 70-72; Deputy Chief of Mission, Ankara 72-74; Diplomat in Residence, Florida State Univ., Tallahassee 74-75, Amb. to Tanzania 75-79, to Turkey 80-81.
Publs. *The Way of the Pathans* 62, *The Pathan Borderland* 63.
c/o Department of State, Washington, D.C. 20520, U.S.A.

Spuler, Bertold, DR. PHIL.; German university professor; b. 5 Dec. 1911; ed. Univs. of Heidelberg, Munich, Hamburg and Breslau.
Collaborator Soc. for Silesian History 34-35; Asst. Dept. of East European History, Univ. of Berlin and Co-editor *Jahrbücher für Geschichte Osteuropas* 35-37; Asst. Dept. of Near Eastern Studies, Univ. of Göttingen 37-38; Dozent, Univ. of Göttingen 38-42; Full Prof. Univ. of Munich 42, Göttingen 45, Hamburg 48-80; Ed. *Handbuch der*

Orientalistik 49-, _Der Islam_ 49-; Hon. Dr. Theol. (Berne); Hon. Dr. ès Lettres (Bordeaux).

Publs. include _Die europäische Diplomatie in Konstantinopel bis 1739_ 35, _Die Minderheitenschulen der europäischen Türkei von der Reformzeit bis zum Weltkriege_ 36, _Die Mongolen in Iran: Politik, Verwaltung und Kultur der Ilchanzeit 1220-1350_ 39, 3rd edn., 68, _Die Goldene Horde, Die Mongolen in Russland, 1223-1302_ 43, 2nd edn. 65, _Die Gegenwartslage der Ostkirchen in ihrer staatlichen und volklichen Umwelt_ 48, 2nd edn. 69, _Geschichte der islamischen Länder im Überblick I: Chalifenzeit II: Mongolenzeit_ 52-53, _Iran in frühislamischer Zeit: Politik, Kultur, Verwaltung und öffentliches Leben 633-1055_ 52, _Regenten und Regierungen der Welt_ 53, 2nd edn. (with additions) 66, 72, _Wissenschaftl. Forschungsbericht: Der Vordere Orient in islamischer Zeit_ 54, _The Age of the Caliphs_ 60, 2nd edn. 68, _The Age of the Mongols_ 60, 2nd edn. 68, _Geschichte der morgenländischen Kirchen_ 61, _Les Mongols et l'Europe_ (English edn. 71) 61, _Wüstenfeld-Mahlersche Vergleichungstabellen der muslimischen, iranischen und orient-christlichen Zeitrechnung_, 3rd edn. 61, _Innerasien seit dem Aufkommen der Türken_ 65, _Geschichte des Mongolen nach Zeugnissen des 13 u. 14 Jahrhunderts_ (English edn. 71) 68, _Die historische und geographische Literatur Irans_ 68, _Der Islam: Saeculum-Weltgeschichte III-VII_ 66-72, _Kulturgeschichte des Islams (Östlicher Teil)_ 71, _Die Kunst des Islam_ (with J. Sourdel-Thomine) 73, _Gessammelte Aufsätze_ 80, _Die Orthodoxen Kirchen_ (85 articles in _Int. Kirchl. Zeitschrift_, Bern) 39-81, _Studien zur Geschichte und Kultur des Vorderen Orients_ 81. Mittelweg 90, Hamburg 13, Federal Republic of Germany.

Stark, Dame Freya Madeline, D.B.E.; British explorer and writer; b. 31 Jan. 1893; ed. School of Oriental Studies and privately.
Travelled in Middle East and Iran 27-39 and in South Arabia 34-35, 37-38; joined Ministry of Information Sept. 39, sent to Aden 39, Cairo 40, Baghdad as attaché to Embassy 41, U.S.A. and Canada 44; Hon. LL.D. (Glasgow Univ.) 52, Hon. D.Litt. (Durham) 70; C.B.E. 53; recipient of the Founders' Medal (Royal Geographical Soc.), of Mungo Park Medal (Royal Scottish Geographical Soc.), Richard Burton Memorial Medal (Royal Asiatic Soc.), and of Sir Percy Sykes Medal (Royal Central Asian Soc.); Sister Commdr., Order of St. John of Jerusalem.
Publs. _The Valley of the Assassins_ 34, _The Southern Gates of Arabia_ 36, _Baghdad Sketches_ 37, _Seen in the Hadhramaut_ 38, _A Winter in Arabia_ 40, _Letters from Syria_, 42, _East is West_ 45, _Perseus in the Wind_ 48, _Traveller's Prelude_ 50, _Beyond Euphrates_ 51, _Winter in Arabia_ 52, _Ionia_ 54, _The Lycian Shore_ 56, _Alexander's Path_ 58, _Riding to the Tigris_ 59, _Dust in the Lion's Paw_ 61, _The Journey's Echo_ (an anthology) 63, _Rome on the Euphrates_ 66, _The Zodiac Arch, Time, Movement and Space in Landscape_ 69, _The Minaret of Djam_ 70, _Turkey, Sketch of Turkish History_ 71, _Selected Letters_ Vols. I-V 74, 75, 76, 77, 78, _A Peak in Darien_ 76.
Asolo, Treviso, Italy; and c/o John Murray, 50 Albermarle Street, London, W.1, England.

Steel, Sir David Edward Charles, Kt., D.S.O., M.C., B.A.; British company director; b. 29 Nov. 1916; ed. Rugby School and Univ. Coll., Oxford.
Officer, Q.R. Lancers, in France, the Middle East, N. Africa and Italy 40-45; Admitted as solicitor 48, worked for Linklaters and Paines 48-50; Legal Dept., British Petroleum Co. Ltd. 50-56, N.Y. 58, Pres. B.P. (N. America) Ltd. 59-61, Regional Co-ordinator, Western Hemisphere, B.P. Co. Ltd. 61-62; Man. Dir. Kuwait Oil Co. Ltd. 62-65, Dir. 65; Man. Dir. B.P. Co. Ltd. 65-72, Deputy Chair. 72-75, Chair. 75-81; Chair. B.P. Oil 76-77; Dir. Bank of England 78-; mem. Board of Trustees, _The Economist_ 79-. Chair. The Wellcome Trust 82-; Deputy Chair. Governing Body Rugby School 82-.

The Wellcome Trust, 183 Euston Rd., London NW1 2BP, England.

Stephani, Christakis, B.COMM., F.C.A.; Cypriot banker; b. 28 Sept. 1926, Cyprus; ed. London School of Econs. and Political Science.
Accountant-General of the Repub. of Cyprus 60-65; Gov. Cen. Bank of Cyprus 65-.
Central Bank of Cyprus, P.O. Box 5529, 36 Metochiou Street, Nicosia, Cyprus.

Stirling, Sir Alexander John Dickson, K.B.E., C.M.G.; British diplomatist; b. 10 Oct. 1926, Rawalpindi, India (now Pakistan); ed. Edinburgh Acad. and Lincoln Coll., Oxford.
Royal Air Force 45-48; Foreign Office 51; Middle East Centre for Arabic Studies 52; British Embassy, Cairo 52, Foreign Office 56, British Embassy, Baghdad 59, Amman 62, Santiago 65, Foreign Office 67; Political Agent, Bahrain 69, Amb. to Bahrain 71; Counsellor, British Embassy, Beirut 72; Royal Coll. of Defence Studies 76; Amb. to Iraq 77-80, to Tunisia 80-.
British Embassy, 5 Place de la Victoire, Tunis, Tunisia; and Foreign and Commonwealth Office, King Charles Street, London, S.W.1, England.

Strausz-Hupe, Robert, A.M., PH.D.; American diplomatist; b. 25 March 1903, Vienna, Austria; ed. Univ. of Pennsylvania.
Engaged in investment banking 27-37; Assoc. Ed., _Current History_ 39-41; Assoc. Prof. of Political Science, Univ. of Pa. 46-52, Prof. 52-; Dir. Foreign Policy Research Inst. 55-69; Amb. to Ceylon and Repub. of Maldives 70-72, to Belgium 72-74, to Sweden 74-75, to Turkey July 81-; Perm. Rep. to North Atlantic Council 76-77; fmr. Dir. Atlantic Council of U.S.A.; Diplomat-in-Residence Foreign Policy Research Inst., Philadelphia 77-; Guest Prof. Geschwister Scholl Inst. Ludwig-Maximilians Univ., Munich 78-79; mem. Council on Foreign Relations, American Political Science Asscn.; F.R.G.S., Fellow, Bd. of Visitors Nat. Defence Univ. 77-78; Distinguished Public Service Medal (U.S. Dept. of Defense), Marilla Ricker Award (U.S. Dept. of State) 75, and other awards.
Publs. _The Russian-German Riddle_ 40, _Axis-America_ 41, _Geopolitics_ 42, _The Balance of Tomorrow_ 45, _International Relations_ 50, _The Zone of Indifference_ 52, _Power and Community_ 56, _Protracted Conflict_ (co-author) 59, _A Forward Strategy for America_ 61 (co-author), _Building the Atlantic World_ (co-author) 63, _In My Time_ 67, _Dilemmas Facing the Nation_ 79; over 40 articles on int. affairs.
United States Embassy, Atatürk Bulvarı 110, Ankara, Turkey.

Stylianou, Petros Savva; Cypriot educationalist, writer and politician; b. 8 June 1933, Kythrea; ed. Pancyprian Gymnasium and Univ. of Athens and Salonika.
Served with Panhellenic Cttee. of the Cyprus Struggle (PEKA) and Nat. Union of Cypriot Univ. Students (EFEK), Pres. EFEK 53-54; Co-founder Dauntless Leaders of the Cypriot Fighters Org. (KARI) joined liberatiog movement 55, detained 55, escaped; leader Nat. Strikinn Group; arrested 56 and sentenced to 15 years imprisonment; transferred to English prison, repatriated 59; mem. Central Cttee. United Democratic Reconstruction Front (EDMA) 59; Deputy Sec.-Gen. Cyprus Labour Confederation (SEK) 59, Sec.-Gen. 60-62; founded Cyprus Democratic Labour Fed. (DEOK) 62, Sec.-Gen. 62-74, now Hon. Pres.; mem. House of Reps. 60-70, Sec. of House 60-62; Dir. _Ergatika Chronika_ (Labour Annals) 60; Man. Editor _Ergatiki Foni_ (Voice of the Working Class) 60-62; Man. Editor DEOK Newspaper _Ergatikos_ (Workers' Struggle) 62-63; Man. Editor _Allagi_ (Change) 63; mem. Co-ordination Cttee. of 28 associated vocational and scientific orgs. 64-66; Gen. Sec. Cypriot Arab Friendship Asscn. 64-66; mem. Cyprus Afro-Asian Solidarity Cttee. 64-66; Vice-Pres.

Cyprus-G.D.R. Friendship Asscn. 64-68; Pres. Pancyprian Org. for the Disabled 66-; founder Pancyprian Olive Produce Org. 67; Man. Dir. *Kypriakos Logos* (Scientific Cypriot) 69-; Dir. *Anapericon Vema* magazine (The Step of the Disabled) 70-; founder and Pres. Free Kythrea Asscn. 75; Dir. daily newspaper *Ta Nea* (The News) 70; also founder and Dir. *Oikogenia kai Sholion* (Family and School) magazine 70; Pres. Nicosia Fed. of Parents, Pancyprian Confed. of Parents' Cttees. 69-73; Pres. Council of Cyprus Historical Museum and Archives 74-, Pancyprian Cttee. for Enclaved Greek Population 74-; Cyprus Nat. Sec. of Int. Fed. for Rehabilitation of the Disabled 74-; founder and Pres. Political Cttee. for the Cyprus Struggle (PEKA) 76-; mem. Int. Org. of Archives 76-; mem. Exec. Cttee. of World Org. for the Rehabilitation of the Disabled 76-; Pres. Co-ordination Cttee. for the Cyprus Struggle (SEKA) 76-; Dir. Nat. Struggle Museum 79-; Under-Minister of the Interior Sept. 80-; silver medal of Cape Andrew's Monastery 73; gold medal of the Pancyprian Cttee. for the Enclaved Greek Population 76; Hon. parchment of the Soc. of Greek Writers (Athens) 78; First Cyprus Govt. Prize for Narrative 78, 79.

Publs. *The Kyrenia Castle* 66, *The Epic of Central Prisons* 67, *Hours of Resurrection* 67, *Problems on Education* 68, *The National, Scientific and Cultural Necessity for the Creation of a National University in Cyprus* 69, *Sean Macstiofain, Leader of the IRA and Adorer of Hellenism* 73, *Saint Demetrianos—Bishop of Chytri-Cyprus* 73, *Historical Data relating to the Ethnarchical Role of the Cyprus Church* 73, *Achievements and Targets in the Rehabilitation of the Disabled* 73, *Laographicon Minologion* 73, *Peri to vasilion ton Chytron* 74, *Oi tris ftochoi Agioi tis Kythreas* 75, *To xerizoma* 75, *The Cyprus Revolution of 1606 under the leadership of Petros Avendanios* 75, *Black Book I* 75, *Black Book II, III, IV, V* 76, *Yi mou odinis yi* 76, *To Ponemeno tragoudi tis Riomiosynis* 78, *Turkish Massacres in Smyrna in 1922* 79, *The Lepers of Cyprus* 79, documents of Cypriot guerrillas detained under British administration, *Disechta chronia, An* 79, *aei Paides* 82.
10 Kimon Street, Engomi, Nicosia, Cyprus.

Sudeari, Abdel-Muhsin M. el-, B.SC.; Saudi Arabian agronomist; b. 1936, Riyadh; ed. Colorado and Arizona Univs., U.S.A.
Assignments with Ministry of Agric. and Water 62-72; Amb. to FAO 72; Head numerous dels. to int. confs. 72-75; elected Chair. Preparatory Cttee. for Establishment of Int. Fund for Agricultural Devt. (IFAD) 75; elected Pres. IFAD Dec. 77, Chair. Exec. Board IFAD 77-; several awards.
International Fund for Agricultural Development, 107 Via del Serafico, 00142 Rome, Italy.

Sullivan, William Healy; American diplomatist; b. 12 Oct. 1922; ed. Brown Univ. and Fletcher School of Law and Diplomacy.
United States Navy 43-46; Foreign Service 47-, served Bangkok 47-49, Calcutta 49-50, Tokyo 50-52, Rome 52-55, The Hague 55-58; Officer-in-Charge, Burma Affairs, Dept. of State 58-59; Foreign Affairs Officer 59; UN Adviser, Bureau of Far Eastern Affairs 60-63; Special Asst. to Under-Sec. for Political Affairs 63-64; Amb. to Laos 64-69; Deputy Asst. Sec. of State for E. Asia (with special responsibility for Viet-Nam); Amb. to the Philippines 73-77, to Iran 77-79; Pres. American Assembly 79-.
American Assembly, Columbia University, New York, N.Y. 10027, U.S.A.

Sultan ibn Abdul Aziz, H.R.H. Prince; Saudi Arabian politician; b. 1924; brother of H.M. King Fahd (*q.v.*).
Minister of Agric. 53, of Communications 55-62, of Defence 62-; Second Deputy Prime Minister June 82-.
Ministry of Defence, Jeddah, Saudi Arabia.

T

Taha, Mohammed Fathi; Egyptian meteorologist; b, 15 Jan. 1914, Cairo; ed. Cairo Univ. and Imperial Coll. of Science and Technology, London.
Under-Secretary of State and Chair. Board of Dirs. Egyptian Meteorological Authority 53-75; Meteorological Counsellor to Ministry of Civil Aviation 76-; Vice-Pres. IAF 65; mem. WMO Exec. Cttee. 55, Second Vice-Pres. 59-63, Pres. 71-79; Pres. Perm. Meteorological Cttee., Arab League 71-77; Chair. Nat. Cttee. on Geodesy and Geophysics 65-75; mem. High Comm. on Outer Space Research for Peaceful Uses, Nat. Comm. for Int. Council of Scientific Unions and many other cttees. dealing with scientific research in Egypt.
Egyptian Meteorological Authority, Koubry El-Quobba P.O., Cairo, Egypt.

Taher, Abdulhady H., PH.D.; Saudi Arabian government official; b. 1930; ed. Ain Shams Univ. Cairo and California Univ.
Entered Saudi Arabian Govt. service 55; Dir.-Gen. Ministry of Petroleum and Mineral Resources 60; Gov.-Gen. Petroleum and Mineral Org. (PETROMIN) 62-; Pres. 82-; Man. Dir. Saudi Arabian Fertilizers Co. (SAFCO) 66-76, Jeddah Oil Refinery 70-; Chair. Arab Maritime Petroleum Transport Co. -81; Trustee Coll. of Petroleum and Minerals, Dhahran; Dir. Saudi Arabian Railroads, Arabian American Oil Co. (ARAMCO); Hon. mem. American Petroleum Engineers' Asscn.
Publs. *Income Determination in the International Petroleum Industry* 66, *Saudi Arabia's Economic Development and Petroleum Strategies* 70, *Energy—A Global Outlook* 81.
PETROMIN, P.O.B. 757, Riyadh, Saudi Arabia.

Takla, Philippe; Lebanese politician; b. 1915; ed. Univ. Law School, Beirut.
Law practice, Beirut 35-45; M.P. 45, 47; Minister of Nat. Economy and Communication 45-46, 48-49; Minister of Foreign Affairs 49, 61-64, 64-65; Gov. Bank of Lebanon 64-66, 66-67; Minister of Foreign Affairs and of Justice 66; Perm. Rep. to UN 67-68; Amb. to France 68-71; Minister of Foreign Affairs 74-76, also of Educ. and Planning 75-76; mem. Nat. Dialogue Cttee. Sept. 75.
Rue Maarad, Beirut, Lebanon.

Takriti, Saddam Hussain (*see* Hussain, Saddam).

Tal, Josef; Israeli composer; b. 1910, Poland; ed. Berlin State Acad. of Music.
Went to Israel 34; taught piano and composition at Jerusalem Acad. of Music 37, Dir. 48-52; Head, Dept. of Musicology, Hebrew Univ., Jerusalem 66-72; Dir. Israel Centre for Electronic Music 61-; has appeared with Israel Philharmonic Orchestra and others as pianist and conductor; concert tours of Europe, U.S.A., Far East; UNESCO Scholarship for research in electronic music.
Works include: *Saul at Ein Dor* 57, *Amnon and Tamar* 61, *Ashmedai* 69, *Manada* 73, *Temptation* 76 (operas), Symphony No. 1 53, No. 2 60, No. 3 79, *Concerto for Harpsichord and Electronics* 64, *Double Concerto* (for violin and violoncello) 70, other cantatas, quintets, music for ballet and several books on the theory of music.
Department of Musicology, Hebrew University, Jerusalem; Home: 3 Dvora Haneviyah Street, Jerusalem, Israel.

Talal ibn Abdul Aziz, Amir; Saudi Arabian Prince; b. 1930; brother of H.M. King Fahd (*q.v.*); ed. secondary school.
Minister of Communications 53-54; Amb. to France 55-56; Minister of Finance and Nat. Econ. 61; Vice-Chair. Planning Council; Chair. Supreme Comm. on Mecca Holy Buildings and Facilities; Hon. Sec.-Gen. UN and Special Envoy to UNICEF April 80-; Chair. UNDP for the Gulf Arab States 81-.
Cairo, Egypt.

Taleb-Ibrahimi, Ahmed, M.D.; Algerian doctor and politician; b. 5 Jan. 1932; ed. Univ. of Paris.
Son of Sheikh Bachir Ibrahimi, spiritual leader of Islam in Algeria; Dir. Jeune Musulman 52-54, Union Générale des Etudiants Musulmans Algériens 55-56, French Fed. of the FLN 56-57; imprisoned in France 57-62, in Algeria 64-65; Doctor, Hôpital Mustapha, Algiers 62-64; Minister of Nat. Educ. 65-70; mem. UNESCO Exec. Board; Minister of Information and Culture 70-77; mem. FLN Political Bureau -81; Minister and Adviser to the Pres. 77-82, Minister of Foreign Affairs May 82-.
Publs. *Contribution à l'histoire de la médecine arabe au Maghreb* 63, *Lettres de Prison* 66, *De la décolonisation à la révolution culturelle* 73.
Ministry of Foreign Affairs, 6 rue Claude Bernard, El Mouradia, Algiers, Algeria.

Talhouni, Bahjat, LL.B.; Jordanian politician; b. 1913, Ma'an; ed. Damascus Univ.
Lawyer 36-38; Judge, Kerak 38-52; Pres. Court of Appeals 52-53; Minister of Interior 53, of Justice 53-54; Chief Royal Cabinet 54-60, 63-64, June-Aug. 69, 73-74; Prime Minister 60-62, 64-65, 67-70, concurrently Minister of Foreign Affairs 67-68, of Defence 68-69, of Interior April-Sept. 68; mem. Senate 62-, Pres. of Senate Dec. 74-; Personal Rep. of H.M. King Hussein 67-69; mem. Consultative Council 67; Pres. Cttee. for Preparation of Civil Law 71.
Parliament Buildings, P.O. Box 72, Amman, Jordan.

Talib, Maj.-Gen. Naji; Iraqi soldier and politician; b. 1917; ed. Iraqi Staff Coll. and Sandhurst, England.
Military Attaché, London 54-55; Commdr. Basra Garrison 57-58; Minister of Social Affairs 58-59; lived abroad 59-62; Minister of Industry 63-64; mem. U.A.R.-Iraq Joint Presidency Council 64-65; Minister of Foreign Affairs 64-65; Prime Minister and Minister of Petroleum Affairs 66-May 67.
Baghdad, Iraq.

Talû, Naim; Turkish banker and politician; b. 22 July 1919; ed. Faculty of Economics, Istanbul Univ.
Joined Türkiye Cumhuriyet Merkez Bankası (Central Bank of Repub. of Turkey) 46, Chief 52, Asst. Dir. of Ankara Branch 55-58, Dir. of Exchange Dept. 58-62, Asst. Gen. Dir. 62-66, Acting Pres. and Gen. Dir. 66-67, Pres. and Gen. Dir. 67-70, Gov. 70-71; Chair. Foreign Investment Encouragement Cttee. 67-68; Chair. Banks' Asscn. of Turkey 67-71; Sec.-Gen. Cttee. for Regulation of Bank Credits 67-70; Minister of Commerce 71-73; Prime Minister 73-74; mem. Senate 72-76; Chair. and Man. Dir. Akbank TAŞ 75-76; Chair. Akbank TAŞ, Akçimento Ticaret A.Ş., Olmuk Mukavva San. ve Tic. A.Ş. April 76-; mem. Ankara Educ. Foundation, Soc. for Protection of Children in Turkey.
Akbank TAŞ, Meclisi Mebusan Cad. 65-69, Fındıklı, Istanbul, Turkey.

Tariki, Abdallah; Saudi Arabian oil executive; b. 19 March 1919; ed. Univs. of Cairo and Texas.
Studied at Univ. of Texas and worked as trainee with Texaco Inc. in W. Texas and California 45-49; Dir. Oil Supervision Office, Eastern Province, Saudi Arabia (under Ministry of Finance) 49-55; Dir.-Gen. of Oil and Mineral Affairs (Saudi Arabia) 55-60; Minister of Oil and Mineral Resources 60-62; Dir. Arabian American Oil Co. 59-62; Leader Saudi Arabian Del. at Arab Oil Congresses 59, 60; Independent Petroleum Consultant 62-; Pres. Arab Petroleum Consultants; co-founder of OPEC; publisher of monthly petroleum magazine *Naft El-Arab*; adviser to Egyptian, Algerian and Kuwaiti Govts. on oil matters.
KAC Building, Floor 10, Appartment 3, Sharie Hilali, Kuwait; Home: P. O. Box 22699, Kuwait City, Kuwait.

Tartakower, Arie, DR. IUR., D.RER.POL.; Israeli (b. Polish) university professor; b. 24 Sept. 1897; ed. Univ. of Vienna.

Co-founder Zionist Labour Movement and Chair. Zionist Labour Party, Poland 22-39; Lecturer, Inst. of Jewish Sciences, Warsaw 32-39; Dir. Dept. of Relief and Rehabilitation of World Jewish Congress (U.S.A.) 39-46; fmr. Prof., Lecturer and Head, Dept. of Sociology of the Jews, Hebrew Univ., Jerusalem; Hon. Vice-Pres. World Jewish Congress; mem. Gen. Council World Zionist Org.; mem. World Secr. Zionist Labour Movement; Co-founder and fmr. Pres. Israel Asscn. for UN; Chair. World Asscn. for Hebrew Language and Culture; Ruppin Award, Municipality of Haifa 60, Bareli Award, Jewish Labor Confederation of Israel 62, Ben Zvi Award, Govt. of Israel 72.
Publs. include: *History of the Jewish Labour Movement, Jewish Emigration and Jewish Policy of Migration, The Jewish Refugee, Jewish Wanderings in the World, The Wandering Man, The Jewish Society, History of Jewish Colonization* (2 vols.), *The Tribes of Israel* (3 vols.), *The Role of Revolution in Jewish History* (vol. I) 74.
1 Ben Yehuda Road, Jerusalem; Home: 45a King George Street, Jerusalem, Israel.

Taryam, Omran Taryam; United Arab Emirates politician; b. Sharjah; ed. Cairo Univ.
Chairman Omani Students Union while studying in Cairo *c.* 52, took part in many demonstrations against colonialism and imperialism, arrested in Egypt on suspicion A being Baathist; returned to the Gulf, set up newspaper of organ of Arab nationalism, Kuwait, later set up as *Khaleej* newspaper, Sharjah; Speaker Fed. Nat. Council Oct. 76-.
Federal National Council, P.O. Box 836, Abu Dhabi, United Arab Emirates.

Tawfik Abdel Fattah, Zakaria; Egyptian cotton executive and politician; b. 18 Aug. 1920; ed. Cairo Univ.
With Bank Misr; then Commercial Attaché, Brussels, Madrid 48-57; Dir.-Gen. Exchange Control Office 61; Under-Sec. for Cotton Affairs, Ministry of Econ. 61-65; Chair. Gen. Cotton Org. High Cttee. for Cotton 65-75; Minister of Commerce and Supply 75-78; Chair. Gen. Union of Chambers of Commerce 71-75; Pres. Afro-Asian Org. for Econ. Co-operation (AFRASEC) 72; now Chair. Suez Canal Bank; mem. Econ. Researches Council, Acad. of Scientific Research; awards from Italy, France, Greece, Belgium and Spain.
Suez Canal Bank, 11 Sabry Abu Alam, Cairo, Egypt.

Tekoah, Yosef; Israeli diplomatist; b. 4 March 1925; ed. Université L'Aurore, China, and Harvard Univ.
Instructor in Int. Relations, Harvard Univ. 47-48; Deputy Legal Adviser, Ministry of Foreign Affairs 49-53; Dir. Armistice Affairs, and Head Israel Dels. to Armistice Comms. with Egypt, Jordan, Syria and Lebanon 53-58; Deputy Perm. Rep. to UN 58, Acting Perm. Rep. 59-60; Amb. to Brazil 60-62, to U.S.S.R. 62-65; Asst. Dir.-Gen Ministry of Foreign Affairs 66-68; Perm. Rep. to UN 68-75;. Pres. Ben Gurion Univ., Beersheva 75-80, Chancellor 81-. Publ. *In the Face of Nations: Israel's Struggle for Peace* 76. c/o Ben Gurion University of the Negev, P.O. Box 653, Beersheva 84120, Israel.

Thani, Sheikh Abdul-Aziz bin Khalifa al-, B.S.; Qatar politician; b. 12 Dec. 1948, Doha; ed. Indiana North and George Washington Univs., U.S.A.
Deputy Minister of Finance and Petroleum June-Dec. 72; Minister of Finance and Petroleum 72-; Chair. Board of Dirs. Qatar Nat. Bank 72-, Qatar Nat. Petroleum Co. (became Gen. Petroleum Corpn. 74) 73-; Chair. Joint Management Cttee., QPC and Shell Qatar 73-; Gov. for Qatar, Int. Monetary Fund and World Bank 72-, also of Islamic Devt. Bank; Chair. State of Qatar Investment Board 72-; Rep. to numerous confs. of OPEC,

OAPEC, UN, IMF, IBRD, Islamic Summit, Non-aligned confs., etc.
Ministry of Finance and Petroleum, P.O. Box 3322, Doha, Qatar.

Thani, Sheikh Khalifa bin Hamad al-; Amir of Qatar; b. 1932, Doha.
Heir-Apparent 48; served as Chief of Security Forces, Chief of Civil Courts; Deputy Ruler of Qatar 60-72, Minister of Educ. 60-70, of Finance and Petroleum Affairs Sept. 71-Feb. 72; Prime Minister Sept. 71-; Chair. Investment Board for State Reserves 72; deposed his cousin Sheikh Ahmad and took office as Amir of Qatar Feb. 72.
The Royal Palace, Doha, Qatar.

Thesiger, Wilfred, C.B.E., D.S.O., M.A.; British traveller; b. 3 Jan. 1910; ed. Eton and Magdalen Coll., Oxford.
Explored Danakil country of Abyssinia 33-34; Sudan Political Service, Darfur and Upper Nile Provinces 35-39; served in Ethiopia, Syria and Western Desert with Sudan Defence Force and Special Air Service, Second World War; explored the Empty Quarter of Arabia 45-50; lived with the Madan in the Marshes of Southern Iraq 50-58; awarded Back Grant, Royal Geographical Soc. 36, Founders Medal 48; Lawrence of Arabia Medal, Royal Central Asian Soc. 55; David Livingstone Medal, Royal Scottish Geographical Soc. 61, Royal Soc. of Literature Award 64, Burton Memorial Medal, Royal Asiatic Soc. 66; Hon. D.Litt. (Leicester) 68.
Publs. *Arabian Sands* 58, *The Marsh Arabs* 64, *Desert, Marsh and Mountain: The World of a Nomad* 79.
15 Shelley Court, Tite Street, London, S.W.3, England.

Tjeknavorian, Loris Zare; Iranian (of Armenian parentage) composer and conductor; b. 13 Oct. 1937; ed. Vienna Acad. of Music, Salzburg Mozarteum.
Worked in U.S.A. until 70; fmr. Teaching Fellow, Univ. of Michigan; fmr. Composer-in-Residence, Concordia Coll., Minnesota; returned to Iran 70; Composer-in-Residence, Ministry of Culture and Fine Arts; Principal Conductor, Teheran Opera 72-79; Composer-in-Residence, American Armenian Int. Coll., La Verne, California 80-; Chair. Board of Trustees, Inst. of Armenian Music, London; fmr. mem. Board of Trustees, Shahbanou Farah Foundation, Teheran; Order of Homayoun; several int. tours as a conductor with many of the world's major orchestras.
Works include: *Requiem for the Massacred* 75, *Simorgh* (ballet music), *Lake Van Suite, Erebouni* for 12 strings 78, *Life of Christ, Symphony* 80, *Credo Symphony, Liturgical Mass, Suite for Flute*, a piano concerto, several operas, and more than 35 film scores.
c/o Basil Douglas Limited, 8 St. George's Terrace, London, NW1 8XJ, England.

Tlass, Lieut.-Gen. Mustapha el-; Syrian army officer and politician; b. 11 May 1932, Rastan City, Mouhafazat Homs; ed. Mil. and Law Colls.
Active mem. Baath Arab Socialist Party 47-, Sec. of Rastan Section 51; Sports teacher, Al-Kraya School, Mouhafazat al-Soueda 50-52; attended Mil. Coll. 52-54; deputed to Egyptian army 59-61; Insp. Ministry of Supply 62; mem. Free Officers' Movement 62-63, detained 62-63; Commdr. Tank Bn. and Chief of Cen. Region of Nat. Security Court 63; Chief of Staff, 5th Armoured Brigade 64-66; mem. Regional Command, Regional Congress of Baath Arab Socialist Party 65, 68, 69, 75, 80, of Politbureau 69-, of Nat. Council of Revolution 65-; participated in movement of 23 Feb., promoted to Commdr. of Cen. Region and of 5th Armoured Brigade; rank of Maj.-Gen. Feb. 68-, Chief of Staff of Armed Forces Feb. 68-70, First Deputy Minister of Defence Feb. 68-72; participated in correctional movement installing Pres. Hafez Al-Assad Nov. 70; First Deputy C.-in-C. Armed Forces 70-72, Deputy C.-in-C. 72, now C.-in-C.; mem. People's Council 71-; Minister of Defence 72-; Deputy Chief of Joint

Supreme Mil. Council of Syrian and Egyptian Armed Forces 73; Pres. Armed Forces Party 77; mem. Syrian-Egyptian Supreme Political Leadership 77; rank of Lieut.-Gen. 78; 28 orders and medals; doctorate from Supreme Inst. for Mil. Studies, U.S.S.R. 80.
Publs. *Guerrilla War, Military Studies, An Introduction to Zionist Strategy, The Arab Prophet and Technique of War, The Armoured Brigade as an Advanced Guard, Bitter Memories in the Military Prison of Mezzah, The Fourth War between Arabs and Israel, The Second Chapter of the October Liberation War, Selections of Arab Poetry, The Steadfastness Front in confrontation with Camp David, The Algerian Revolution, Art of Soviet War, American Policy under the Carter regime, The Technological Revolution and Development of the Armed Forces.*
Ministry of Defence, Damascus, Syria.

Tombazos, George; Cypriot politician; b. 2 Feb. 1919; ed. Pancyprian Gymnasium, Dentists' School of Athens.
Worked as dentist at Morphou 50-66; M.P. for Nicosia 60-66; Minister of Agriculture and Natural Resources 66-70; Head, Central Information Service 70-75; Minister of Communications and Works 75-78, of Agriculture and Natural Resources 78-80; Minister of Health Sept. 80.
Ministry of Health, Nicosia, Cyprus.

Toumazis, Panayotis, M.SC.ENG.; Cypriot civil engineer and company director; b. 1912, Famagusta; ed. Greek secondary school (Gymnasium), Famagusta and Nat. Tech. Univ. (Metsovion), Athens.
Municipal Engineer, Famagusta; private practice as consultant eng.; Founder and Pres. of Pan. and Dion. Toumazis, Consultancy, PANTOUMAZIS Co. Ltd., ATLAS-PANTOU Co. Ltd., ATLAS KATASKEVE Ltd. (building and civil engineering construction firms); Pres. Famagusta Devt. Corpn., Famagusta Fed. of Trade and Industry, Architects' and Civil Eng. Council of Registration; mem. Civil Eng. and Architects' Asscn.; mem. House of Reps. 60-70; Minister of Natural Resources and Agriculture 70-72; Vice-Pres. Cyprus Port Org. 75-.
8 Yiangos Tornaritis Street, Limassol, Cyprus.

Triantafyllides, Michalakis Antoniou; Cypriot judge; b. 12 May 1927, Nicosia; ed. Gray's Inn, London.
Practised as a lawyer in Cyprus 48-60, serving for three years as Sec. of Human Rights Cttee. of Bar; mem. Greek Cypriot del. to Joint Constitutional Comm. which drafted Cyprus Constitution 59-60; Greek Cypriot Judge, Supreme Constitutional Court 60-, now Pres.; mem. European Comm. of Human Rights 63-.
Supreme Constitutional Court of Cyprus, Nicosia, Cyprus.

Tsur, Yaakov; Israeli diplomatist; b. 18 Oct. 1906; ed. Hebrew Coll. Jerusalem, Univ. of Florence and Sorbonne.
Member staff daily newspaper *Haaretz*, Tel-Aviv 29; Dir. French Dept. and later Co-Dir. Propaganda Dept. Jewish Nat. Fund, Jerusalem 30; special Zionist missions, Belgium, Greece, France 34-35; Bulgaria and Greece 40; Dir. Publicity Dept. Jewish Agency Recruiting Council 42; Liaison officer with G.H.Q. British Troops in Egypt 43-45; Head, del. to Greece 45; Pres. Israeli Army Recruiting Cttee. Jerusalem 48; Minister to Argentina 49-53, Uruguay 49-53, Chile 50-53 and Paraguay 50-53; Amb. to France 53-59; Dir.-Gen. Foreign Office 59; Chair. Zionist Gen. Council 61-68; Chair. Jewish Nat. Fund 60-76.
Publs. *Shaharit shel Etmol* (autobiography) 66, French trans.—*Prière du Matin* 67 (English ed. *Sunrise in Zion*), *An Ambassador's Diary in Paris* 68, *La Révolte Juive* (Italian, Spanish and Russian trans.) 70, *Portrait of the Diaspora* 75, *The Saga of Zionism* (in French, English and Spanish) 77.
c/o P.O. Box 283, Jerusalem, Israel.

Tueni, Ghassan, M.A.; Lebanese newspaper editor and politician; b. 1926; ed. Harvard Univ.
Publisher and Editor-in-Chief, *An-Nahar* (daily newspaper) and *An-Nahar Arabe et International* (weekly, published in Paris); Deputy Prime Minister, Minister of Educ. and Information 70-71; fmr. Parl. Deputy; arrested and detained Dec. 73; Minister for Social Affairs and Labour, for Tourism, for Industry and Oil 75-76; Perm. Rep. to UN 77-; mem. Nat. Dialogue Cttee. Sept. 75.
Permanent Mission of Lebanon to the United Nations, 866 United Nations Plaza, Room 531-533, New York, N.Y. 10017, U.S.A.

Turabi, Hassan A., LL.B., LL.M., D. EN D.; Sudanese lawyer and politician; b. 1 Feb. 1932, Kassala; ed. Univs. of Khartoum, London and Paris.
Lecturer, Faculty of Law, Univ. of Khartoum 57, Dean 64-65; mem. Constituent Assembly 65-68, Advisory Comm. for the Constitution 66-68; Sec.-Gen. Islamic Charter Front 65-69; Constitutional expert, United Arab Emirates 68-69; in political detention for most of 69-77; mem. Politburo and Cen. Cttee., Sudanese Socialist Union 78-, Asst. Sec.-Gen. for Information and External Relations 78-80; Attorney-General 79-; dismissed Oct. 81, reinstated Nov. 81; Order of the Repub. (First Class).
Publs. Articles on constitutional questions 65-69, *Prayer 71*, *Faith in the Life of Man 74*, *The Status of Women 75* (books in Arabic).
P.O. Box 1515, Khartoum, Sudan.

Türkmen, İlter; Turkish diplomatist; b. 1927, Istanbul; ed. Galatasaray Lycée, Istanbul, Faculty of Political Sciences, Ankara.
Joined Ministry of Foreign Affairs 50; served in dels. to UN and NATO; Counsellor, Turkish Embassy, Egypt, and U.S.A. 61-64; Dir.-Gen. of Policy Planning Dept., Ministry of Foreign Affairs 64, Asst. Sec.-Gen. for Political Affairs 67, Amb. to Greece 68, to U.S.S.R. 72; Perm. Rep. to UN 75-78; Special Asst. to UN Sec.-Gen. on refugee problems; Sec.-Gen., Min. of Foreign Affairs Aug.-Sept. 80, Minister of Foreign Affairs Sept. 80-.
Ministry of Foreign Affairs, Dişişleri Bakanliği, Müdafaa Cad., Bakanlıklar, Ankara, Turkey.

U

Ucuzal, Omer; Turkish politician; b. 1922, Malatya; ed. Faculty of Law, Ankara Univ.
Served as prosecutor and judge in civil service; Justice Party Senator 64; mem. Speakership Council of the Senate; Chair. Justice Party; Minister of Justice Nov. 79-Sept. 80.
c/o Ministry of Justice, Adalet Bakanliği, Bakanlıklar, Ankara, Turkey.

Ulusu, Vice-Adm. Bülent; Turkish naval officer and politician; b. 1923, Istanbul; ed. Naval Acad.
Various command posts in navy; rank of Rear-Admiral 67, Vice-Admiral 70; fmr. Commdr. of War Fleet; Commdr. of Turkish Naval Forces -80; fmr. Under-Sec., Ministry of Defence; Prime Minister of Turkey Sept. 80-.
Office of the Prime Minister, Başbakanlık, Bakanlıklar, Ankara, Turkey.

Umri, Gen. Hassan (*see* Amri, Gen. H.).

Urwick, Alan Bedford, C.M.G., M.A.; British diplomatist; b. 2 May 1930, London; ed. Dragon School, Rugby, New Coll. Oxford.
Joined Foreign Service 52; served in Embassies in Belgium 54-56, U.S.S.R. 58-59, Iraq 60-61, Jordan 65-67, U.S.A. 67-70, Egypt 71-73; seconded to Cabinet Office as Asst. Sec., Cen. Policy Review Staff 73-75; Head of Near East and North Africa Dept., Foreign and Commonwealth

Office 75-76; Minister, British Embassy in Madrid 77-79; Amb. to Jordan 79-.
British Embassy, Third Circle, Jebel Amman, P.O. Box 87, Amman, Jordan; c/o Foreign and Commonwealth Office, King Charles Street, London, S.W.1.

Uzan, Aharon; Israeli agriculturist; b. Tunisia.
Emigrated to Israel 49; co-founder, settler, Moshav Ghilat, in Negev 49, Sec., later Head of supply network; mem. Knesset (Parl.) 65-69; Deputy Minister of Agriculture 66-69; Gen. Sec. Tnuat Hamoshavim 70-74; Minister of Communications March-June 74, of Agriculture 74-June 77, also of Communications 75-77; Labour Party.
Labour Party of Israel, P.O. Box 3263, Tel-Aviv, Israel.

V

van der Meulen, Daniel; Netherlands author and explorer; b. 1894; ed. Arnhem, and Univ. of Leyden.
Dutch East India Civil Service 15-23, 32-41, 45-48; Neths. Consul, Jeddah 26-31; Minister to Saudi Arabia 41-45; Adviser to Lieut. Gov.-Gen. van Mook, Java 45-48; organizer and leader Arabic broadcasts, Neths. World Radio, Hilversum 48-51; exploration of S.W. Arabia 31, 39, 43, 52, 58-59, 62-63, 64, 67, 71, 72, 75; hon. mem. Netherlands Royal Geographical Soc.; Patron's Medal, Royal Geographical Soc., London 47; Officer, Order of Orange Nassau (Netherlands).
Publs. *Hadhramaut, Some of its Mysteries Unveiled 32*, *Aden to The Hadhramaut* in English 47, Swedish and German, *Onbekend Arabië 51*, *Ontwakend Arabië 53*, *The Life Story of King Ibn Saud of Saudi Arabia* (in Indonesian, Dutch and English) 52, revised edn. 57, re-titled *The Wells of Ibn Saud*, *Faces in Shem 61*, *Ik Stond Erbij 64*, *Verdwijnend Arabië*, *Mijn Weg Naar Arabië en de Islam, Hoort Gy de donder niet 77*, *Don't You Hear the Thunder?*, *A Dutchman's Life Story* (English version of autobiography) 82.
9 Flierderweg, Gorssel, Netherlands.

Vassiliou, Simos G., B.SC.(ECON.), F.I.S.; Cypriot economist; b. 11 Jan. 1919, Cyprus; ed. Nicosia Agricultural Coll., Univ. of London, Harvard Univ., U.S.A.
Produce Inspector, Dept. of Agric. 35-40; Customs and Excise Officer 40-54; Statistics and Research Officer, Labour Dept. 54-55; Asst. Government Statistician Financial Sec.'s Office 55-57, Government Statistician 57-62; Economic Affairs Officer, UN 62-64, Head of Technical Co-operation Section 64-65, Officer-in-Charge, Devt. Planning Advisory Services 65-69, Asst Dir. 69-77, Dir. 77-80, Interregional Adviser on Devt. Planning 80-81; Minister of Finance April 82-,
Publ. *The Economy of Cyprus* (with A. J. Mayer) 63.
Ministry of Finance, Nicosia; Home: 7 Chalcedon Street, Nicosia 133, Cyprus.

Velayati, Dr. Ali Akbar; Iranian politician; b. 1945, Teheran; ed. Teheran Univ.
Joined Nat. Front (of Mossadegh) 61; a founder of the Islamic Asscn. of Faculty of Medicine, Teheran Univ. 63; underground political activities in support of Ayatollah Khomeini -79; proposed for Prime Minister by Ayatollah Khomeini Oct. 81 (candidature rejected by the Majlis); Minister of Foreign Affairs Dec. 81-.
Ministry of Foreign Affairs, Teheran, Iran.

Veniamin, Christodoulos; Cypriot lawyer and government official; b. 15 Sept. 1922, Kato Moni; ed. Nicosia Samuel School, Middle Temple.
Joined Govt. service 42; joined Admin. Cadre 49; Exec. Officer for resettlement 51-54; Asst. Sec. in Depts. of Local Govt. and Admin., Personnel, Finance, Commerce and Industry, Social Services, Communications and Works, Agriculture and Natural Resources 55-59; Asst. District Commr. Larnaca 59; Head of Admin., Limassol District

60-68; Dir.-Gen. Ministry of Foreign Affairs 68-74; Minister of Interior and Defence 75-; Grand Cross of Honour with Star and Shoulderband (Fed. Repub. of Germany); Grand Officer, Order of Merit (Italy); Order of the Cedar (Lebanon).
Ministry of the Interior, Nicosia, Cyprus.

W

Watanyar, Col. Muhammad Aslam; Afghan politician and army officer.
Supporter of coup which overthrew Pres. Daoud April 78; Deputy Prime Minister and Minister of the Interior April 78-March 79; Minister of Defence 79-80; Chief of Staff of the Army March-April 79.
Ministry of Defence, Kabul, Afghanistan.

Wazzan, Chafic al-, LL.B.; Lebanese politician; b. 1925, Beirut; ed. al-Makassed Coll., St. Joseph's Univ., Beirut.
Law Practice 47-; Deputy for Beirut, Nat. Assembly 68; Minister of Justice Jan.-Oct. 69; Pres. Higher Islamic Council 63-, Lebanese Muslim Congress; fmr. mem. Presidium *al-Hayat al-Wataniya* party; Prime Minister Oct. 80-.; tendered resignation June 82.
Office du Président du Conseil des Ministres, Place de l'Etoile, Beirut, Lebanon.

Weitz, Raanan, PH.D.; Israeli rural development planner; b. 27 July 1913; ed. Hebrew Gymnasia, Jerusalem Hebrew Univ. and Univ. of Florence.
Rural Settlement Dept., Jewish Agency 37-, fmr. Village Instructor, now Head of Dept.; service with Intelligence Corps, British 8th Army, Second World War; fmr. mem. Haganah; mem. Exec., Zionist Org. 63-; Chair. Nat. and Univ. Inst. of Agriculture 60-66; Head, Settlement Study Centre 63-; Prof. of Rural Devt. Planning, Univ. of Haifa 73-78, of Rural Devt. Theory, Bar Ilan Univ. 78-.
Publs. *Agriculture and Rural Development in Israel: Projection and Planning* 63, *Rural Planning in Developing Countries* (Editor) 65, *Agricultural Development—Planning and Implementation* 68, *From Peasant to Farmer: A Revolutionary Strategy for Development* 71, *Rural Development in a Changing World* (Editor) 71, *Urbanization and the Developing Countries, Report on the Sixth Rehovot Conference* (Editor) 73, *Employment and Income Generation in New Settlement Projects* 78, *Integrated Rural Development: The Rehovot Approach* 79, *Growth, Values and Development Planning—A General Theory for Developing Countries.*
Zionist Organization, P.O. Box 92, Jerusalem; Home: Moshav Ora, Harei-Yehuda, Harei-Yehuda Mobile P.O., Israel.

Weizman, Ezer; Israeli politician and air force officer (retd.); b. 15 June 1924; ed. Hareali School, Haifa and R.A.F. Staff Coll.
Officer, Israel Air Force 48-66 and fmr. Commanding Officer, I.A.F.; Chief General Staff Branch 66-69; Minister of Transport 69-70; Chair. Exec. Cttee. Herut Party 71, expelled Nov. 80, joined Movt. for State Renewal 81; Minister of Defence 77-80.
28 Hageffen Street, Ramat, Hasheram, Israel.

West, John Carl, B.A., LL.B.; American lawyer, politician and diplomatist; b. 27 Aug. 1922, Camden, South Carolina; ed. The Citadel, Univ. of South Carolina.
Admitted to S. Carolina Bar 48; partner in West, Holland Furman and Cooper (law firm) 47-70; mem. S. Carolina Senate 54-66; Lieut.-Gov. of S. Carolina 66-70, Gov. 71-75; partner in West, Cooper, Bowen, Beard and Smoot 75-77; Amb. to Saudi Arabia 77-81; Distinguished Prof. of Middle East Studies Univ. of South Carolina 81; now law practice, Hilton Head, South Carolina; mem. American Legion, Kershaw County Chamber of Commerce, Board of Trustees, Southern Center for Int. Studies; Democrat;

Army Commendation Medal, Knight Commdr., Order of Merit (Federal Repub. of Germany).
P.O. Drawer 13, Hilton Head Island, South Carolina 29938, U.S.A.

Wilton, Sir (Arthur) John, K.C.M.G., K.C.V.O., M.C., M.A.; British diplomatist (retd.); b. 21 Oct. 1921, London; ed. Wanstead High School and St. John's Coll., Oxford.
Open Scholarship 41; Commissioned Royal Ulster Rifles 42, served with Irish Brigade in N. Africa, Italy and Austria 43-46 (mentioned in despatches 45); H.M. Diplomatic Service 47-49; served Lebanon, Egypt, Gulf Sheikhdoms, Romania, Aden, Yugoslavia; Dir. Middle East Centre for Arab Studies 60-65; Amb. to Kuwait 70-74; Asst. Under-Sec., FCO 74-76; Amb. to Saudi Arabia 76-79; Dir. London House for Overseas Graduates 79-; Chair. Arab British Centre 81-.
London House, Mecklenburgh Square, London, WCIN 2AB, England.

Winder, Richard Bayly, A.M., PH.D.; American university professor; b. 11 Sept. 1920, Greensboro, North Carolina; ed. Haverford Coll., Princeton Univ.
With American Field Service 42-45, mentioned in despatches (U.K.); mem. Staff, American Univ. Beirut (Lebanon) 47-49; Instructor, Princeton Univ., New Jersey 47, later Assoc. Prof., later Asst. Dean of Coll.; Prof. of History and Near Eastern Languages and Literature, New York Univ. 66-, Chair. Dept. of Near Eastern Languages and Literature, Washington Square Coll. 66-68, Acting Dean of Coll. 68-69, Dean 69-71, Dean of Faculty of Arts and Sciences 70-77, Dir. Center for Near Eastern Studies 66-; Chair. Grants Comm., American Research Center in Egypt 71-74, mem. Exec. Comm. and Board of Govs.; mem. Board of Dirs. Amideast; Trustee, American Univ. of Cairo; Chair. East-West Group Ltd.; mem. American History Asscn., Royal Asiatic Soc. (U.K.), Middle East Inst., American Oriental Soc., Royal Central Asian Soc. (Hon. Sec. U.S.A.), Middle East Studies Asscn., (Dir. 66-71, Pres. 68-69); decorated with Purple Heart.
Publs. *An Introduction to Modern Arabic* (with F. J. Ziadeh) 57, *The World of Islam; Studies in Honour of Philip K. Hitti* (Ed., with J. Kritzeck) 60, *Current Problems in North Africa* (Ed.) 60, *Saudi Arabia in the Nineteenth Century* 65, *Near Eastern Round Table 1967–68* (Ed.) 69; also some translations.
Department of Near Eastern Languages, New York University, New York, N.Y. 10003, U.S.A.

Wise, George Schneiweis; American university professor; b. 1906, Poland; ed. Columbia Univ.
Associate Dir. Bureau for Applied Social Research, Columbia Univ. 49-52, Lecturer in Sociology 50-52; Visiting Prof., Univ. of Mexico 56; Chair. Board of Govs. Hebrew Univ. 53-62, Jewish Telegraph Agency 51-55; Pres. Tel-Aviv Univ. 63-71, Chancellor (for life) 71-; Trustee Mount Sinai Medical Center, Miami 77-.
Tel-Aviv University, Ramat-Aviv, Tel-Aviv, Israel; Home: 5401 Collins Avenue, Miami Beach, Fla. 33140, U.S.A.

Wright, Patrick Richard Henry, C.M.G., M.A.; British diplomatist; b. 28 June 1931, Reading; ed. Marlborough Coll., Merton Coll., Oxford.
Joined Foreign Office 55; Middle East Centre for Arabic Studies, Shemlan 56; Second Sec., Beirut 58-60; British Embassy, Washington 60-65; Private Sec. to Perm. Under-Sec., Foreign Office 65-67; First Sec., Cairo 67-70; Deputy Political Resident, Bahrain 70-72; Head Middle East Dept., Foreign Office 72-74; Private Sec. (Overseas Affairs) to the Prime Minister 74-77; Amb. to Luxembourg 77-79, to Syria 79-81; Deputy Under-Sec., Foreign Office 82-; Postmaster, Merton Coll., Oxford 51.
c/o Foreign and Commonwealth Office, King Charles Street, London, S.W.I.

Y

Yaacobi, Gad, M.SC.; Israeli politician; b. 18 Jan. 1935, Moshav Kfar Vitkin; ed. Tel-Aviv Univ., School of Law and Econs.
Member Moshavim Movt. 60-67; Asst. to Minister of Agriculture, Head of Agriculture and Settlement Planning and Devt. Centre 60-66; mem. Cen. Cttee. Histadrut, Labour Union, Rafi Faction 66-; Chair. Econ. Council Rafi Faction 66-67; mem. Cen. Cttee., Secr. Labour Party; Asst. to Sec. Labour Party 66-70; mem. Parl. (Knesset) 69-, Parl. Finance Cttee. 69-70, Parl. Defence and Foreign Affairs Cttee. 74, Deputy Minister of Transport 70-74, Minister June 74-June 77; Chair. of Cttee. for Econ. Affairs of the Knesset June 77-.
Publs. *The Quality of Power* 71, *The Freedom to Choose* 75 and many articles on economics and politics.
13 Shirtei Israel Street, Ramat Hasharon, Israel.

Yadin (formerly Sukenik), **Lt.-Gen. Yigael,** M.A., PH.D.; Israeli soldier, archaeologist and politician; b. 21 March 1917, Jerusalem; ed. Hebrew Univ., Jerusalem.
Chief of Gen. Staff Branch, Haganah H.Q. 47; Chief of Operations, Gen. Staff, Israel Defence Forces 48; Chief of Gen. Staff Branch 49, Chief of Staff 49-52; Archaeological Research Fellow, Hebrew Univ. 53-54, Lecturer in Archaeology 55-59, Assoc. Prof. 59-63, Prof. 63-; Dir. Excavations at Hazor 55-58, 69, Bar Kochba 60-61, Megiddo 60, 66-67, 70-71, Masada 63-65; Leader Democratic Movt. for Change 76-78, Democratic Movt. 78- (disbanded 81); Deputy Prime Minister 77-81, acting Minister of Defence 80; mem. Israel Acad. of Sciences and Humanities; corresp. mem. British and French Acads.
Publs. *The Scroll of the War of the Sons of Light against the Sons of Darkness* 55, *The Message of the Scrolls* 57, *Hazor I: The First Season of Excavations*, *Hazor II: Second Season*, *Hazor III-IV: Third Season*, *A Genesis Apocryphon* (with N. Avigad) 56, *Warfare in Biblical Lands* 63, *Finds in a cave in the Judaean Desert* 63, *Masada: First Season of Excavations* 65, *The Ben-Sirah Scroll from Masada* 65, *Masada: Herod's Fort and the Zealots' Last Stand* 66, *Philacteries from Qumran* 69, *Bar-Kochba* 71, *Hazor* (Schweich Lectures) 72, *Hazor* 75, *The Temple Scrolls* 77.
47 Ramban Road, Jerusalem, Israel.

Yadlin, Aharon; Israeli politician; b. 17 April 1926; ed. Hebrew Univ.
Co-founder Kibbutz Hatzerim; fmr. mem. Presidium, Israel Scouts Movement; mem. Knesset (Parl.) 59-; Deputy Minister of Educ. and Culture 64-72; Gen. Sec. Israel Labour Party 72-75; Minister of Educ. and Culture 74-77; Chair. Educational and Cultural Cttee. of the Knesset 77-79, Beit Berl Coll. of Educ., Scientific Advisory Council, Ben Gurion Research Inst. and Archives, Beersheva Theatre.
Publs. *Understanding the Social System* 57, *The Aim and the Movement* (on Socialism) 69, articles on sociology, education and youth.
Kibbutz Hatzerim, Mobile Post, Hanegev, Israel.

Yafi, Mohamed Selim El- (*see* El-Yafi, Mohamed Selim).

Yahia, General Tahir; Iraqi army officer and politician; b. 1915; ed. primary school, Tikrit, secondary school, Baghdad, Teachers' Training Coll. and Military Coll.
Former teacher, Mamounia School, Baghdad; mem. Nat. Movement 41; Commdr., Armoured Cars' Battalion, Palestine War 48; mem. Military Court, Habaniya 48; mem. Free Officers' Group 58, later Dir.-Gen. of Police; Chief of Staff, Iraqi Army Feb.-Nov. 63; Prime Minister 63-65; Deputy Prime Minister 67; Prime Minister and acting Minister of the Interior 67-68; Al-Khidma Medal, Al-Chaja Medal, Al-Rafidain Medal.
Baghdad, Iraq.

Yahyawi, Muhammad Saleh; Algerian politician; b. 1932, Barika.
Worked as a teacher before start of Algerian war for nat. independence; joined Maquisards 56; promoted Capt., then Commdt. 62-64; elected to Cen. Cttee. of Nat. Liberation Front (FLN) 64, Revolutionary Council July 65; Regional Mil. Commdr. 65; Head Mil. Acad. at Cherchill 69-77; Exec. Sec. of FLN Oct. 77-.
Front de libération nationale, place Emir Abdelkader, Algiers, Algeria.

Yamani, Sheikh Ahmed Zaki; Saudi Arabian politician; b. 1930, Mecca; ed. Cairo Univ., New York Univ. and Harvard Univ.
Saudi Arabian Govt. service; private law practice; Legal Adviser to Council of Ministers 58-60; Minister of State 60-62; mem. Council of Ministers 60-; Minister of Petroleum and Mineral Resources 62-; Dir. Arabian American Oil Co. 62-; Chair. Board of Dirs. Gen. Petroleum and Mineral Org. (PETROMIN) 63-, Coll. of Petroleum and Minerals, Dhahran 63-; Chair., Board of Dirs. Saudi Arabian Fertilizer Co. (SAFCO) 66-; Sec. Gen. Org. of Arab Petroleum Exporting Countries (OAPEC) 68-69, Chair. 74-75; mem. several int. law asscns.
Publ. *Islamic Law and Contemporary Issues.*
Ministry of Petroleum and Mineral Resources, Riyadh, Saudi Arabia.

Yariv, Maj.-Gen. Aharon; Israeli army officer and politician; b. 1920, Moscow, U.S.S.R.; ed. French Staff Coll.
Emigrated to Palestine 35; Capt. British Army 41-46; Haganah 46-47; various posts with Northern Command and General Staff, Israel Defence Forces (IDF) 48-50, Operations Div., General Staff 51; Founder and Commandant IDF Command and Staff Coll. 52-56; Mil. Attaché, Washington and Ottawa 57-60; joined Mil. Intelligence 61, Dir. until 72; Special Adviser to the Prime Minister 72-73; mem. Knesset 74-77; Minister of Transport March-June 74, of Information June 74-Jan. 75; Head, Center of Strategic Studies, Tel-Aviv Univ.
c/o Tel-Aviv University, Tel-Aviv, Israel.

Yassin, Aziz Ahmed, PH.D., D.I.C., B.SC.; Egyptian consulting engineer; b. 13 Aug. 1918; ed. Abbassia Secondary School, Cairo Univ., and Imperial Coll., London.
Ministry of Housing and Public Utilities, rising to Under-Sec. of State 39-59; Dir.-Gen., Vice-Chair. Building Research Centre 54-59, Chair., Pres. Tourah Portland Cement Co., Alexandria Portland Cement Co. 59-63; mem. Board of Dirs. Helwan Portland Cement Co., Sudan Portland Cement Co. 59-63; Chair. Egyptian Cement Cos. Marketing Board 59-63; Chair., Pres. Egyptian Gen. Org. for Housing and Public Building Contracting Cos. 63-65; Minister of Tourism and Antiquities 65-67, of Housing and Construction 66-68; mem. Board of Aswan High Dam Authority 66-68; External Prof. of Soil Mechanics, Cairo Univ. 51-, of Civil Engineering, Ain Shams Univ.; mem. Building Research and Technology Council, Egyptian Acad. of Science and Technology 72-; Sec.-Gen. Federation of Arab Engineers (FAE) 75; mem. several other scientific civil engineering and building orgs.; Order of the Repub. 1st Class, Order of the Banner (Hungary), Commdr.'s Cross with Star of Order of Resurrection of Poland.
Publs. *Model Studies on the Bearing Capacity of Piles* 51, *Bearing Capacity of Deep Foundations in Clay Soils, Testing Sand Dry Samples with the Tri-axial Apparatus* 53, *Bearing Capacity of Piles* 53, *The Industry of Building Materials in Egypt* 57.
4 Waheeb Doas Street, Maadi, Cairo, Egypt.

Yazdi, Dr. Ibrahim; Iranian politician; b. c. 1933.
Studied and worked as physician in U.S.A. for sixteen years; close associate of Ayatollah Khomeini (*q.v.*) during exile in Neauphle-le-Château, France Oct. 78-Feb. 79;

Deputy Prime Minister with responsibility for Revolutionary Affairs Feb.-April 79; Minister of Foreign Affairs April-Nov. 79; Dir. *Kayhan* May 80-.
Kayhan, Ferdowsi Avenue, Teheran, Iran.

Yazıcı, Bedi, M.SC.; Turkish business executive; b. 1917; ed. Robert Coll., Columbia Univ.
Fire and Marine Man. Nat. Reinsurance Co. 43-48; Prof. of Insurance, Business School of Istanbul 45-50; Man. Dir. The Credit Bank of Turkey 62-63, Porcelain Industries Inc. of Istanbul 62-63; Pres. The Gen. Insurance Co. of Turkey 48-63, Istanbul Chamber of Commerce 60-63; mem. Insurance Board, Ministry of Commerce 44-64; Chair. and Man. Dir. TAM Insurance Co. 64-74; TAM Life Insurance Co. 66-74; Chair. and Man. Dir. AKSIGORTA Insurance Co. 74-; fmr. Deputy Chair. and Man. Dir. DOGAN Insurance Co.; Trustee, Robert Coll. 64-70.
Aksu Han, Karakoy, Istanbul, Turkey.

Yazıcı, Bülent, M.S.; Turkish banker; b. 3 Feb. 1911; ed. Robert Coll., Istanbul, and Columbia Univ.
Ministry of Finance 34-38; Insp. 38-45; Financial Counsellor, Turkish Embassy, Washington 45-49; Dep. Gen. Dir. Dept. of the Treasury 49-50; Dep. Gen. Man. Industrial Development Bank of Turkey 50-60; Dir. and Gen. Man. Türkiye İs Bankası A.S. 60-67; Chair. American-Turkish Foreign Trade Bank 64-67, Union of Chambers of Commerce, Industry and Exchanges of Turkey 60-62; Vice-Chair. Asscn. of Banks of Turkey 60-67; Chair. Industrial Devt. Bank of Turkey 60-69, Man. Dir. 69-71; Dir. Tam Hayat Sigorta A.S. 67-; Advisory Dir. Unilever-İş Ticerat ve Sanayi, Sti 68-; Chair. and Man. Dir. Akbank TAŞ 71-75; Chair. Akcimento A.Ş., Cimsa A.Ş., Turkish Management Educ. Foundation; Commodore, Deniz Klubu.
36 Devriye Sok., Moda, Kadıköy, Istanbul, Turkey.

Yeganeh, Mohammed, M.A.; Iranian economist; b. 5 May 1923; ed. Teheran Univ., Columbia Univ., New York.
Economic Affairs Officer, UN Middle East Studies Section 49-58; UNDP Adviser to Govt. of Tunisia 58-59; Head UN Industrial Section 59-64; Deputy Minister for Econ. Affairs 64-69; Minister of Devt. and Housing 69-70; Special Econ. Adviser to Prime Minister 70-71; Alt. Exec. Dir. for Middle East, Int. Bank for Reconstruction and Devt. 71-72; Exec. Dir. Int. Monetary Fund 72-73; Gov. Cen. Bank of Iran 73-76; Minister of State 76-77, in charge of Budget and Plan 77-78; Minister of Econ. Affairs and Finance 77-78; fmr. Chair. OPEC Special Fund Vienna; Homayoun Medal 66, First Degree 77, Devt. Medal 67.
Publs. *Suspension of Penalties* 46, *Foreign Trade and Commercial Policies of Iran* 50, *Investments in the Petroleum Industry of the Middle East* 52, *Perspectives décennales des développements économiques en Tunisie* 60, *Economics of the Middle Eastern Oil* (with Charles Issawa, *q.v.*) 62, *Reflections on the Teheran Oil Agreement* 71, *Possibilities for Co-operation among Developing Countries in Development Utilization of Natural Gas* 71.
Teheran, Iran.

Yemen, Former King of the (*see* Saif al-Islam, Mohamed Al-Badr, H.M. The Imam).

Yoseph, Ovadya; Israeli Rabbi; b. Baghdad, Iraq.
Member, Sephardi Rabbinical Court 45; Chief of Rabbinical Court of Appeals and Deputy Chief Rabbi of Egypt (Cairo) 47; mem. regional Rabbinical Court of Petach Tiqva 51, Jerusalem 58; mem. Grand Court of Appeals, Jerusalem 65; Pres. of Great Metivta, Jerusalem; Pres. "Yeshivat Thora Ve-horaa", Tel-Aviv; mem. Management "Yeshivat Porath" Jerusalem; Pres. Cttee. of Building Fund for Yeshivat "Porath Yoseph" in the Old City; Chief Rabbi and Chief of Rabbinical Court of Tel-Aviv May 68-; Sephardi Chief Rabbi of Israel Oct. 72-; Rabbi Kook Prize, Rabbi Uziel Prize.

Publs. *Yobia Omer*, several vols. of Responsa, *Hazon Ovadia*.
Chief Rabbinate, 51 Hamelech David Boulevard, Tel-Aviv, Israel.

Younes Gabir, Brig. Abu-Bakr; Libyan army officer; b. Nov. 1942, Zella; ed. locally, Mil. Coll., Tripoli, English Language Centre, Tripoli.
Promoted Lieut. Aug. 67; participated in coup of Sept. 69 which overthrew King Idris (*q.v.*); mem. Revolution Command Council 69-77, Gen. Secretariat of Gen. People's Congress 77-78; Commdr.-in-Chief of Armed Forces.
General Headquarters of the Armed Forces, Tripoli, Libya.

Z

Zadok, Haim; Israeli lawyer and politician; b. 2 Oct. 1913, Poland; ed. Rawa Ruska, Poland, Warsaw Univ. and Jerusalem Law School.
Immigrated 35; took up private practice as lawyer 45; with Haganah and Jewish Settlement Police until 48; Major in Reserve I.D.F., War of Independence; Deputy Attorney-Gen. 49-52; in private law practice 52-65, 67-74, 78-; Lecturer, Tel-Aviv Univ. 53-61; mem. Knesset 59-78; mem. Advisory Council, Bank of Israel; Chair. Income Tax Reform Cttee.; Israel Del. to Council of Europe 61-65; Minister of Commerce and Industry May 65-66, concurrently Minister of Devt. May 65-66; Chair. Knesset Foreign Affairs and Defence Cttee. 70-74, mem. Constitutional, Legal and Judicial Cttee. until 74; Minister of Justice 74-77, of Religious Affairs June-Nov. 74 and Jan.-June 77; Lecturer, Hebrew Univ. 78-80; Chair. Exec. Cttee. Hebrew Univ., Jerusalem 69-74; Labour Party.
31 Hamitnadev Street, Afeka, Tel-Aviv, Israel.

Zahedi, Ardeshir, B.SC.; Iranian diplomatist; b. 17 Oct. 1928; ed. in Teheran, American Univ. of Beirut and State Univ. of Utah (U.S.A.).
Treasurer, Iran-American Comm. 50-52; Civil Adjutant to H.I.M. Shahanshah Aryamehr 54-79; Amb. to U.S.A. 60-62, to U.K. 62-67, to Mexico 73-76, to U.S.A. 73-79; Minister of Foreign Affairs 67-71; sentenced to death (*in absentia*) by Islamic Revolutionary Court; Hon. LL.D. (Utah State Univ.) 60, (Chungang Univ., Seoul) 69, (East Texas Univ.) 73, (Kent State Univ.) 74, (St. Louis Univ.) 75; numerous decorations from 24 countries including Crown with Grand Cordon, Order of Taj, First Class 75.

Zahir, Abdul; Afghan politician; b. 1909, Lagham; ed. Habibia High School, Kabul and Columbia and Johns Hopkins Univs., U.S.A.
Practised medicine in U.S.A. before returning to Kabul 43; Chief Doctor, Municipal Hospital, Kabul 43-50; Deputy Minister of Health 50-55, Minister 55-58; Amb. to Pakistan 58-61; Chair. House of the People 61-64, 65-69; Deputy Prime Minister and Minister of Health 64-65; Amb. to Italy 69-71; Prime Minister 71-72.
Kabul, Afghanistan.

Zalzalah, Abdul Hassan, PH.D.; Iraqi economist and regional official; b. 28 Dec. 1927, Amarah; ed. Coll. of Law, Baghdad, Indiana Coll.
Deputy Gov., later Gov. Central Bank of Iraq; former Amb. to Iran; former Minister of Industry, Planning, acting Minister of Finance; Vice-Chair. Asscn. of Iraqi economists; Asst. Sec.-Gen. for Econ. Affairs, League of Arab States 79-.
General Secretariat, Arab League, Khairaldin Basha Street, Tunis, Tunisia.

Zayed bin Sultan al-Nahayan, H.H. Sheikh (*see* Nahayan, H.H. Sheikh Zayed bin Sultan al-).

Zayyat, Mohamed Hassan el-, M.A., D.PHIL.; Egyptian diplomatist; b. 14 Feb. 1915; ed. Cairo and Oxford Univs.
Lecturer and Asst. Prof. Alexandria Univ. 42-50; Cultural

Attaché, Egyptian Embassy, Washington, D.C. 50-54, First Sec. and Counsellor 54; Counsellor, Egyptian Embassy, Teheran 55-57, Minister 57; Del. of Egypt on UN Advisory Council for Somaliland 57-60, Special Envoy and Ambassador of U.A.R. in Somaliland 60; Head of Dept. of Arab Affairs and Perm. Del. of U.A.R. to Arab League 60-62; Alt. Perm. Rep. of U.A.R. to UN 62-65; Ambassador to India, concurrently accred. to Nepal 64-66; Under-Sec. of State for Foreign Affairs 65-67; Deputy Minister, Chair. U.A.R. State Information Service and Govt. Spokesman 67-69; Perm. Rep. to UN 69-72; Minister of State for Information 72, of Foreign Affairs 72-73; Adviser to the Pres. 73-75; Contributor to several Arabic newspapers; decorations from Egypt, Somalia, Tunisia, Mauritania, Chad, Lebanon, Iran, Thailand, Belgium, Italy, Poland and Senegal.
7 Hasan Sabry Street, Zamalek, Cairo, Egypt.

Zeayen, Dr. Yusuf; Syrian politician; b. 1931; ed. Damascus Univ. and osteopathy study in the U.K.
Minister of Agrarian Reform Nov. 63-May 64; Ambassador-designate to U.K. Aug. 64; mem. Syrian Presidential Council 64; mem. Nat. Revolutionary Council 65; Prime Minister Sept.-Dec. 65, 66-68; Baath Party.
c/o The Baath Party, Damascus, Syrian Arab Republic.

Zeevy, Maj.-Gen. Rechavam; Israeli officer and government official; b. 20 June 1926, Jerusalem.
Service in Palmach 44-48; Intelligence Officer 48-49; Operations Officer 49; Battalion Commdr. 50-53; Staff Officer G.H.Q. 53-55; Chief of Staff, Southern Command 55-57; Chief of Org. Dept., G.H.Q. 57-59; U.S. Army Command and Gen. Staff Coll. 59-60; Chief of Staff Cen. Command 60-64; Asst. Chief of Operations, G.H.Q. 64-68; G.C.O. Cen. Command 68-73; Asst. Chief of Staff and Chief of Operations 73-74; Intelligence and Special Matters Adviser to the Prime Minister 74-77; Chair. Board Museum Haaretz, Tel-Aviv Dec. 81-.
Publs. several articles on the History of the Holy Land.
Home: Ramat-Hasharon, Israel.

Zentar, Mehdi M'rani; Moroccan diplomatist; b. 6 Sept. 1925, Meknes; ed. lycée de Meknès, Faculté de Droit, Univ. de Paris.
Chef de Cabinet Moroccan Minister of State responsible for independence negotiations with France and Spain 56; Dir. of Gen. Admin. with rank of Minister Plenipotentiary Ministry of Foreign Affairs 56-58, Dir. African Div. 58; Dir. Nat. Tourist Office 58; Consul-Gen., Paris 59, Legal Adviser to Ministry of Foreign Affairs 60-61; Dir. of Political Affairs (with rank of Amb.) 61-63; Head Moroccan del. to Constitutional Conf. of OAU 62; Amb. to Yugoslavia 64-66, to U.A.R. (now Egypt) 66-70, to Italy (also accred. to Greece) 74-78; Perm. Rep. to UN 71-74, 81-.
Permanent Mission of Morocco to the United Nations, 1 Dag Hammarskjöld Plaza, 245 East 47th Street, 28th Floor, New York, N.Y. 10017, U.S.A.

Ziartides, Andreas; Cypriot trade unionist; b. 1919; ed. Pancyprian Gymnasium, Nicosia.
Trade unionist 37-; mem. Pancyprian Trade Union Cttee. 41, Gen. Sec. 43-47; Gen. Sec. Pancyprian Fed. of Labour 47-; mem. Central Cttee. Cyprus Working People's Progressive Party (AKEL); mem. House of Reps. Cyprus 60-; mem. Exec. Cttee. World Fed. of Trade Unions (WFTU), Vice-Pres. 82-.
Pancyprian Federation of Labour, 31-35 Archemou Street, Nicosia, Cyprus.

Ziv-Av, Itzhak; Israeli administrative official; b. 4 June 1907; ed. Inst. of Pedagogy, Smolensk.
Farmer, Magdiel, Sharon Valley, Palestine 26-; Man. Editor *Haboker* 35-48; Dir. Public Relations Div., Ministry of Defence and Gen. H.Q., Israel Defence Forces 48-52; Dir.-Gen. Israel Farmers' Fed. 52-75, Chair. Council 75-; mem. Exec. Cttee. Int. Fed. of Agricultural Producers (IFAP) 75-; Chair. Exec. Cttee., Co-ordinating Bureau, Israeli Econ. Orgs. 67-; Chair. Land Developing Authority 76-; Editor *Farmers of Israel* (periodical) 62-; mem. Board of Dirs. Jewish Nat. Fund; mem. Council, State Land Authority.
Publs. *The Unknown Land, I seek my Brethren, The Price of Freedom, Forever Ours, From Frontier to Frontier, A World to Live In, Another World, There is a Land,* and poetry for children.
Israel Farmers' Federation, P.O. Box 209, Tel-Aviv; Home: Narkissiun Avenue 20, Ramat-Gan, Israel.

Zukerman, Pinchas; Israeli violinist; b. 16 July 1948, Israel; ed. Israel Conservatory, Acad. of Music, Tel-Aviv, Juilliard School of Music, New York.
Studied with Ivan Galamian; debut in New York with New York Philharmonic 69, in U.K. at Brighton Festival 69; concert and recital performances throughout U.S.A. and Europe; directs, tours and plays with English Chamber Orchestra; has performed at Spoleto, Pablo Casals and Edinburgh Festivals; Dir. South Bank Summer Music 78-; Musical Dir. St. Paul's Chamber Orchestra; Leventritt Award 67.
c/o Harold Holt Ltd., 31 Sinclair Road, London, W14 0NS, England.

Zurayk, Constantine Kaysar, M.A., PH.D.; Lebanese educationist; b. 18 April 1909; ed. American Univ. of Beirut, Univ. of Chicago and Princeton Univ.
Assistant Prof. of History, American Univ. of Beirut 30-42, Assoc. Prof. 42-45; First Counsellor, Syrian Legation, Washington 45-46; Syrian Minister to U.S.A. 46-47; Vice-Pres. and Prof. of History, American Univ. of Beirut 47-49; Rector, Syrian Univ. Damascus 49-52; Vice-Pres. American Univ. of Beirut 52-54, Acting Pres. 54-57; Distinguished Prof. of History, American Univ. of Beirut 56-76, Emeritus 76-; mem. Syrian Del. to UN Gen. Assembly and Alternate Rep. of Syria on Security Council 46-47; mem. Exec. Board UNESCO 50-54; Pres. Int. Asscn. of Univs. 65-70, Hon. Pres. 70-; mem. Int. Comm. for Scientific and Cultural History of Mankind; Corresp. mem. Iraq Acad., Arab Acad., Damascus; Hon. mem. American Historical Asscn.; Chair. Inst. for Palestine Studies 65-; Order of Merit, Distinguished Class (Syria), Educ. Medal, First Class (Lebanon); Commdr. Order of the Cedar (Lebanon).
Publs. *Al-Wa'y al Qawmi* (National Consciousness); *Ma'na al-Nakbah* (The Meaning of the Disaster); *Ayyu Ghadin* (Whither Tomorrow); *Nahnu wa-al-Tarikh* (Facing History); *Hadha al-'Asr al-Mutafajjir* (This Explosive Age); *Fi Ma'rakat al-Hadarah* (In the Battle for Culture); *Ma'na al-Nakbah Mujaddadan* (The Meaning of the Disaster Again), *More than Conquerors, Nahnu wa-al-Mustqbal* (Facing the Future); Editor, Ismai'l Beg Chol's *Al-Yazidiyyah qadiman wa hadithan* (Yazidis past and present), *Ibn al-Furat's History* Vols. VII-IX (partly with Najla Izzeddin); Editor and translator Miskawayh's *Tahdhib al-Akhlaq* (The Refinement of Character).
American University of Beirut, Beirut, Lebanon.

Calendars, Time Reckoning and Weights and Measures

Muslim Calendar

The Muslim era dates from July 16th, A.D. 622, which was the beginning of the Arab year in which the *Hijra*, Muhammad's flight from Mecca to Medina, took place. The Muslim or Hijra Calendar is lunar, each year having 354 or 355 days, the extra day being intercalated eleven times every thirty years. Accordingly the beginning of the Hijra year occurs earlier in the Gregorian Calendar by a few days each year. The Muslim year 1403 A.H. begins on October 19th, 1982.

The year is divided into the following months:

1.	Muharram	30 days	7.	Rajab	30 days
2.	Safar	29 ,,	8.	Shaaban	29 ,,
3.	Rabia I	30 ,,	9.	Ramadan	30 ,,
4.	Rabia II	29 ,,	10.	Shawwal	29 ,,
5.	Jumada I	30 ,,	11.	Dhu'l-Qa'da	30 ,,
6.	Jumada II	29 ,,	12.	Dhu'l-Hijja	29 or 30 days

The Hijra Calendar is used for religious purposes throughout the Islamic world and is the official calendar in Saudi Arabia and the Yemen. In most Arab countries it is used side by side with the Gregorian Calendar for official purposes, but in Turkey and Egypt the Gregorian Calendar has replaced it.

PRINCIPAL MUSLIM FESTIVALS

New Year: 1st Muharram. The first ten days of the year are regarded as holy, especially the tenth.

Ashoura: 10th Muharram. Celebrates the first meeting of Adam and Eve after leaving Paradise, also the ending of the Flood and the death of Husain, grandson of Muhammad. The feast is celebrated with fairs and processions.

Mouloud (*Birth of Muhammad*): 12th Rabia I.

Leilat al Meiraj (*Ascension of Muhammad*): 27th Rajab.

Ramadan (*Month of Fasting*).

Id ul Fitr or **Id ul Saghir** or **Küçük Bayram** (*The Small Feast*): Three days beginning 1st Shawwal. This celebration follows the constraint of the Ramadan fast.

Id ul Adha or **Id al Kabir** or **Büyük Bayram** (*The Great Feast, Feast of the Sacrifice*): Four days beginning on 10th Dhu'l-Hijja. The principal Muslim festival, commemorating Abraham's sacrifice and coinciding with the pilgrimage to Mecca. Celebrated by the sacrifice of a sheep, by feasting and by donations to the poor.

Hijra Year	1401		1402		1403	
New Year . . .	Nov. 9th,	1980	Oct. 30th,	1981	Oct. 19th,	1982
Ashoura . . .	Nov. 18th,	,,	Nov. 8th,	,,	Oct. 28th,	,,
Mouloud . . .	Jan. 18th,	1981	Jan. 8th,	1982	Dec. 28th,	,,
Leilat al Meiraj . .	May 31st,	,,	May 21st,	,,	May 10th,	1983
Ramadan begins .	July 3rd,	,,	June 23rd,	,,	June 12th,	,,
Id ul Fitr . . .	Aug. 2nd,	,,	July 23rd,	,,	July 12th,	,,
Id ul Adha . . .	Oct. 9th,	,,	Sept. 29th,	,,	Sept. 18th,	,,

Note: Local determinations may vary by one day from those given here.

Iranian Calendar

The Iranian Calendar, introduced in 1925, was based on the Hijra Calendar, adapted to the solar year. Iranian New Year (*Nowruz*) occurs at the vernal equinox, which usually falls on March 21st Gregorian. In Iran it was decided to base the calendar on the coronation of Cyrus the Great, in place of the Hijra, from 1976, and the year beginning March 21st, 1976, became 2535. During 1978, however, it was decided to revert to the Hijra Calendar. The year 1360 began on March 21st, 1982.

The Iranian year is divided into the following months:

1.	Favardine	31 days	7.	Mehr	30 days
2.	Ordibehecht	31 ,,	8.	Aban	30 ,,
3.	Khordad	31 ,,	9.	Azar	30 ,,
4.	Tir	31 ,,	10.	Dey	30 ,,
5.	Mordad	31 ,,	11.	Bahman	30 ,,
6.	Chariver	31 ,,	12.	Esfand	29 or 30 days

The Iranian Calendar is used for all purposes in Iran and Afghanistan, except the determining of Islamic religious festivals, for which the lunar Hijra Calendar is used.

Hebrew Calendar

The Hebrew Calendar is solar with respect to the year but lunar with respect to the months. The normal year has 353–355 days in twelve lunar months, but seven times in each nineteen years an extra month of 30 days (*Adar II*) is intercalated after the normal month of Adar to adjust the calendar to the solar year. New Year (*Rosh Hashanah*) usually falls in September of the Gregorian Calendar, but the day varies considerably. The year 5742 began on September 29th, 1981, and 5743 starts on September 18th, 1982.

The months are as follows:

1.	Tishri	30 days	7.	Nisan	30 days
2.	Marcheshvan	29 or 30 days	8.	Iyyar	29 ,,
3.	Kislev	29 or 30 ,,	9.	Sivan	30 ,,
4.	Tebeth	29 days	10.	Tammuz	29 ,,
5.	Shebat	30 ,,	11.	Ab	30 ,,
6.	Adar	29 ,,	12.	Ellul	29 ,,
	(Adar II)	30 ,,			

The Hebrew Calendar is used to determine the dates of Jewish religious festivals only.

Standard Time

The table shows zones of standard time, relative to Greenwich Mean Time (G.M.T.). Many of the individual countries adopt daylight saving time at certain times of year.

Traditional Arabic time is still widely used by the local population in Saudi Arabia except in most of the Eastern Province. This system is based upon the local time of sunset when timepieces are all set to 12.

G.M.T.	1 Hour Ahead	2 Hours Ahead	3 Hours Ahead	3½ Hours Ahead	4 Hours Ahead	4½ Hours Ahead
Algeria Morocco Spanish North Africa	Tunisia	Cyprus Egypt Israel Jordan Lebanon Libya Sudan Syria Turkey	Bahrain Iraq Kuwait Yemen, P.D.R.	Iran	Oman Qatar United Arab Emirates	Afghanistan

Note: Saudi Arabia and the Yemen Arab Republic use solar time.

Weights and Measures

Principal weights and units of measurement in common use as alternatives to the Metric and Imperial systems.

WEIGHT

Unit	Country	Metric Equivalent	Imperial Equivalent
Charak	Afghanistan	1·764 kg.	3·89 lb.
Hogga	Iraq	1·27 kg.	2·8 lb.
Kharwar	Afghanistan	564·528 kg.	1,246·2 lb.
Khord	Afghanistan	110·28 grammes	3·89 oz.
Maund	Yemen, P.D.R. / Saudi Arabia	37·29 kg.	82·28 lb.
Qintar (Kantar) or Buhar	Cyprus / Egypt and Sudan	228·614 kg. / 44·928 kg.	504 lb. / 99·05 lb.
Ratl or Rotl	Saudi Arabia / Egypt	0·449 kg.	0·99 lb.
Seer	Afghanistan	7·058 kg.	15·58 lb.
Uqqa or Oke	Cyprus / Egypt	1·27 kg. / 1·245 kg.	2·8 lb. / 2·751 lb.
Yeni Okka	Turkey	1 kg.	2·205 lb.

LENGTH

Unit	Country	Metric Equivalent	Imperial Equivalent
Busa	Saudi Arabia / Sudan	2·54 cm.	1 in.
Dirraa, Dra or Pic	Cyprus	60·96 cm.	2 ft.
Gereh-gaz-sha	Afghanistan	6·6 cm.	2·6 in.
Kadam or Qadam	Sudan	30·48 cm.	1 ft.

CAPACITY

Unit	Country	Metric Equivalent	Imperial Equivalent
Ardabb or Ardeb.	Saudi Arabia Sudan Egypt	198·024 litres	43·56 gallons
Kadah	Sudan Egypt	2·063 litres	3·63 pints
Keila.	Cyprus	36·368 litres	8 gallons
	Sudan Egypt	16·502 litres	3·63 gallons
Ratel .	Sudan	0·568 litre	1 pint

AREA

Unit	Country	Metric Equivalent	Imperial Equivalent
Donum or Dunum	Cyprus	1,335·8 sq. metres	0·33 acre
	Iraq	2,500 sq. metres	0·62 acre
	Israel Jordan	1,000 sq. metres	0·2471 acre
	Syria Turkey	919·04 sq. metres	0·2272 acre
Feddan	Saudi Arabia Sudan Egypt	4,201 sq. metres	1·038 acres
Yeni Donum	Turkey	10,000 sq. metres (1 hectare)	2·471 acres

METRIC TO IMPERIAL CONVERSIONS

Metric Units	Imperial Units	To Convert Metric into Imperial Units Multiply by :	To Convert Imperial into Metric Units Multiply by :
Weight			
Gramme	Ounce (Avoirdupois)	0·035274	28·3495
Kilogramme (kg.)	Pound (lb.)	2·204622	0·453592
Metric ton ('000 kg.)	Short ton (2,000 lb.)	1·102311	0·907185
	Long ton (2,240 lb.)	0·984207	1·016047
	(The short ton is in general use in the U.S.A., while the long ton is normally used in Britain and the Commonwealth.)		
Length			
Centimetre	Inch	0·3937008	2·54
Metre	Yard (=3 feet)	1·09361	0·9144
Kilometre	Mile	0·62137	1·609344
Volume			
Cubic metre	Cubic foot	35·315	0·0283
	Cubic yard	1·30795	0·764555
Capacity			
Litre	Gallon (=8 pints)	0·219969	4·54609
	Gallon (U.S.)	0·264172	3·78541
Area			
Square metre	Square yard	1·19599	0·836127
Hectare	Acre	2·47105	0·404686
Square kilometre	Square mile	0·386102	2·589988

SELECT BIBLIOGRAPHIES

BOOKS ON THE MIDDLE EAST

(See also Bibliographies at end of Chapters in Part II)

ABDEL MALEK, A. La Pensée Politique Arab Contemporaine (Editions du Seuil, Paris, 1970).

ABIR, MORDECHAI. Oil, Power and Politics: Conflict in Arabia, The Red Sea and The Gulf (Frank Cass, London, 1974).

ABU JABER, KAMEL S. The Arab Baath Socialist Party (Syracuse University Press, New York, 1966).

ABU-LUGHOD, IBRAHIM (ed.). The Transformation of Palestine: Essays on the Development of the Arab-Israeli Conflict (Northwestern University Press, Evanston, Ill., 1971).

ADAMS, MICHAEL (ed.). The Middle East: A Handbook (Anthony Blond, London, 1971).

ADAMS, MICHAEL and MAYHEW, CHRISTOPHER. Publish it Not . . . the Middle East Cover-up (Longman, London, 1975).

AJAMI, FOUAD. The Arab Predicament (Cambridge University Press, 1981).

ALDERSON, A. D. The Structure of the Ottoman Dynasty (New York, Oxford University Press, 1956).

ALLEN, RICHARD. Imperialism and Nationalism in the Fertile Crescent: Sources and Prospects of the Arab-Israeli Conflict (Oxford University Press, London, 1975).

ANTONIUS, GEORGE. The Arab Awakening. 4th edition (Beirut, 1961).

ARBERRY, A. J. (ed.). Religion in the Middle East—Volume I Judaism and Christianity, Volume II Islam and General Summary (Cambridge University Press, 1969).

ASHTOR, E. A Social and Economic History of the Near East in the Middle Ages (Collins, London, 1976).

ASKARI, HOSSEIN, and CUMMINGS, JOHN THOMAS. Middle East Economies in the 1970s (Praeger, New York, 1976).

ASTOR, DAVID, AND YORKE, VALERIE. Peace in the Middle East: Superpowers and Security Guarantees (Transworld Publishers—Corgi Books, 1978).

ATIYAH, EDWARD. The Arabs (Baltimore, 1955).

ATLAS OF THE ARAB WORLD AND THE MIDDLE EAST (Macmillan, London, 1960).

BAER, GABRIEL. Population and Society in the Arab East (Routledge, London, 1964).

BASTER, JAMES. The Introduction of Western Economic Institutions into the Middle East (Royal Inst. of Int. Affairs and O.U.P., 1960).

BELL, J. BOWYER. The Long War, Israel and the Arabs since 1946 (Englewood Cliffs, 1969).

BERQUE, JACQUES. L'Islam au Défi (Gallimard, Paris, 1980).

BERQUE, JACQUES and CHARNAY, J.-P. Normes et Valeurs dans l'Islam Contemporaine (Payot, Paris, 1966).

BETHELL, NICHOLAS. The Palestine Triangle (André Deutsch, London, 1979).

BETHMANN, ERICH W. A Selected Basic Bibliography on the Middle East (American Friends of the Middle East, Washington, 1964).

BIDWELL'S GUIDES TO GOVERNMENT MINISTERS, Vol. II, The Arab World 1900-1972. Compiled and edited by Robin Bidwell (Frank Cass, London, 1973).

BINDER, LEONARD. The Ideological Revolution in the Middle East (New York, 1964).

BROCKELMANN, C. History of the Islamic Peoples (New York and London, 1947-48).

BULL, General ODD. War and Peace in the Middle East: the Experience and Views of a UN Observer (London, Leo Cooper, 1976).

BULLARD, Sir R. Britain and the Middle East from the earliest times to 1952 (London, 1952).

BULLOCH, JOHN. The Making of a War: The Middle East from 1967-1973 (Longman, London, 1974).

CARRÉ, OLIVIER. L'Idéologie Palestinienne de Résistance (Armand Colin, Paris, 1972).

CARRÈRE D'ENCAUSSE, HÉLÈNE. La Politique Soviétique au Moyen-Orient, 1955-1975 (Presses de la Fondation Nationale des Sciences Politiques, Paris, 1976).

CATTAN, HENRY. Palestine and International Law: The Legal aspects of the Arab-Israeli Conflict (Longman, London, 1973).

CATTAN, J. Evolution of Oil Concessions in the Middle East and North Africa (Oceana, Dobbs Ferry, New York, 1967).
The Question of Jerusalem (London, 1980).

CHALIAND, GÉRARD. People Without a Country: The Kurds and Kurdistan (Zed Press, 1980).

CHOMSKY, NOAM. Peace in the Middle East?: Reflections on Justice and Nationhood (Collins, 1976).

CLARKE, JOHN I., and FISHER, W. B. (Ed.). Populations of the Middle East and North Africa (University of London Press, 1972).

COHEN, MICHAEL J. Palestine: Retreat from the Mandate (Elek Books, London, 1978).

COOK, M. A. (ed.). Studies in the Economic History of the Middle East (Oxford University Press, 1970).

COOLEY, JOHN K. Green March, Black September: The Story of the Palestinian Arabs (Frank Cass, London, 1973).

COON, C. S. Caravan: the Story of the Middle East (New York, 1951, and London, 1952).
The Impact of the West on Social Institutions (New York, 1952).

COSTELLO, V. F. Urbanisation in the Middle East (Cambridge University Press, 1977).

DANIEL, NORMAN. Islam and the West (Edinburgh University Press, revised edition 1963).
Islam, Europe and Empire (Edinburgh University Press, 1964).

DE VORE, RONALD M. (ed.). The Arab-Israeli Conflict: A Historical, Political, Social and Military Bibliography (Clio Press, Oxford, 1977).

DIMBLEBY, JONATHAN, and McMULLIN, DONALD. The Palestinians (Quartet, London, 1970).

DUPUY, TREVOR N. Elusive Victory: The Arab-Israeli Wars 1947-1974 (MacDonald and Jane's, London, 1979).

ENCYCLOPAEDIA OF ISLAM, THE. 4 vols. and supplement (Leiden, 1913–38).

ETTINGHAUSEN, RICHARD. Books and Periodicals in Western Languages dealing with the Near and Middle East (Washington, Middle East Institute, 1952).

FIELD, HENRY. Bibliography on Southwestern Asia: VII, A Seventh Compilation (University of Miami, 1962).

FIELD, MICHAEL. $100,000,000 a Day—Inside the World of Middle East Money (Sidgwick and Jackson, London, 1975).

FISHER, S. N. Social Forces in the Middle East (Cornell University Press, Ithaca, N.Y., 3rd edition, 1977).
The Middle East: A History (Alfred Knopf, New York, revised edition, 1978).

FISHER, W. B. The Middle East—a Physical, Social and Regional Geography (London, 7th edition, 1978).

FRYE, R. N. (ed.). The Near East and the Great Powers (Harvard University Press, Cambridge, Mass., 1951, and Oxford University Press, London, New York, and Toronto, 1952).

EL-GHONEMY, MOHAMMED RIAD (ed.). Land Policy in the Near East (Rome, 1967).

GIBB, H. A. R. Mohammedanism (London, 1949).
Modern Trends in Islam (Chicago, 1947).
Studies on the Civilisation of Islam (London, 1962).

GIBB, H. A. R., and BOWEN, HAROLD. Islamic Society and the West (2 vols., London, 1950, 1957).

GILBERT, MARTIN. The Arab-Israeli Conflict: Its History in Maps (Weidenfeld and Nicolson, London, 1974).

GILMOUR, DAVID. The Dispossessed: The Ordeal of the Palestinians 1917–80 (Sidgwick & Jackson, London, 1980).

GLUBB, Lt.-Gen. Sir JOHN. A Short History of the Arab Peoples (Hodder and Stoughton, London, 1969).

GOLAN, GALIA. The Soviet Union and the Middle East Crisis (Cambridge University Press, 1977).

GOMAA, AHMED M. The Foundation of the League of Arab States (Longman, London, 1977).

GRANT, D. (ed.). The Islamic Near East (University of Toronto Press, 1960).

GRUNDWALD, K., and RONALL, J. O. Industrialisation in the Middle East (Council for Middle East Affairs, New York, 1960).

GRUNEBAUM, GUSTAVE E. VON (ed.). Unity and Variety in Muslim Civilisation (Chicago, 1955).
Islam: Essays on the Nature and Growth of a Cultural Tradition (London, Routledge and Kegan Paul, 1961).
Modern Islam: the Search for Cultural Identity (London, 1962).

HALPERN, MANFRED. The Politics of Social Change in the Middle East and North Africa (Princeton University Press, N.Y., 1963).

HARTSHORN, J. E. Oil Companies and Governments (Faber, London, 1962).

HASSAN BIN TALAL, CROWN PRINCE OF JORDAN. A Study on Jerusalem (Longman, London, 1980).

HATEM, M. ABDEL-KADER. Information and the Arab Cause (Longman, London, 1974).

HAYES, J. R. (Editor). The Genius of Arab Civilisation (London, Phaidon, 1976).

HAZARD. Atlas of Islamic History (Oxford University Press, 1951).

HERSHLAG, Z. Y. Introduction to the Modern Economic History of the Middle East (E. J. Brill, Leiden, 1964).

HERZOG, Maj.-Gen. CHAIM. The War of Atonement (London, Weidenfeld and Nicolson, 1975).
The Arab-Israeli Wars (London, Arms and Armour Press, 1982).

HIGGINS, ROSALYN. United Nations Peacekeeping 1946–67: Documents and Commentary, Volume I The Middle East (Oxford University Press, 1969).

HIRO, DILIP. Inside the Middle East (Routledge and Kegan Paul, London, 1981).

HIRST, DAVID. Oil and Public Opinion in the Middle East (Praeger, New York, 1966).
The Gun and the Olive Branch: the Roots of Violence in the Middle East (Faber, London, 1977).

HIRSZOWICZ, LUKASZ. The Third Reich and the Arab East (Routledge and Kegan Paul, London, 1966).

HITTI, PHILIP K. History of the Arabs (London, 1940, 10th edn., 1970).
A Short History of the Near East (New York, 1966).
Makers of Arab History (Macmillan, London, 1968).
Islam. A Way of Life (Oxford University Press, London, 1971).

HOARE, IAN, and TAYAR, GRAHAM (eds.). The Arabs. A handbook on the politics and economics of the contemporary Arab world (B.B.C. Publications, London, 1971).

HODGKIN, E. C. The Arabs (Modern World Series, Oxford University Press, 1966).

HOLT, P. M. Studies in the History of the Near East (Cass, London, 1973).

HOLT, P. M., LAMBTON, A. K. S., LEWIS, B. (eds.). The Cambridge History of Islam. Vol. I The Central Islamic Lands (Cambridge University Press, 1970); Vol. II The Further Islamic Lands, Islamic Society and Civilization (Cambridge University Press, 1971).

HOURANI, A. H. Minorities in the Arab World (London, 1947).
A Vision of History (Beirut, 1961).
Arabic Thought in the Liberal Age 1798-1939 (Oxford Univ. Press, 1962).
Europe and the Middle East (Macmillan, 1980).
The Emergence of the Modern Middle East (Macmillan, 1981).

HUDSON, MICHAEL C. Arab Politics: The Search for Legitimacy (Yale University Press, New Haven and London, 1977/78).

HUREWITZ, J. C. Unity and Disunity in the Middle East (New York, Carnegie Endowment for International Peace, 1952).
Middle East Dilemmas (New York, 1953).
Diplomacy in the Near and Middle East (Vol. I, 1535-1914; Vol. II, 1914-56; Van Nostrand, 1956).
Soviet-American Rivalry in the Middle East (ed.) (Pall Mall Press, London, and Praeger, New York, 1969).
Middle East Politics: The Military Dimension (Pall Mall Press, London, 1969).

AL-HUSAY, KHALDUN S. Three Reformers; A Study in Modern Arab Political Thought (Khayats, Beirut, 1966).

HUSSEIN, MAHMOUD. Les Arabes au présent (Seuil, Paris, 1974).

INTERNATIONAL INSTITUTE FOR STRATEGIC STUDIES. Sources of Conflict in the Middle East (Adelphi Papers, International Institute for Strategic Studies, London, 1966).

IONIDES, MICHAEL. Divide and Lose: the Arab Revolt 1955-58 (Bles, London, 1960).

IRWIN, I. J. Islam in the Modern National State (Cambridge University Press, Cambridge, 1965).

ISSAWI, CHARLES (ed.). The Economic History of the Middle East, 1800–1914 (University of Chicago Press, 1966).

ISSAWI, CHARLES, and YEGANEH, MOHAMMED. The Economics of Middle Eastern Oil (Faber, London, 1963).

IZZARD, MOLLY. The Gulf (John Murray, London, 1979).

JANIN, R. Les Eglises orientales et les Rites orientaux (Paris, 1926).

JANSEN, G. H. Non-Alignment and the Afro-Asian States (Praeger, New York, 1966).
Militant Islam (Pan Books, London, 1979).

JONES, DAVID. The Arab World (Hilary House, New York, 1967).

KARPAT, KEMAL H. Political and Social Thought in the Contemporary Middle East (Pall Mall Press, London, 1968).

KEDOURIE, ELIE. England and the Middle East (London, 1956).
The Chatham House Version and other Middle-Eastern Studies (Weidenfeld and Nicolson, London, 1970).
Arabic Political Memoirs and Other Studies (Frank Cass, London, 1974).
In the Anglo-Arab Labyrinth (1976).
Islam in the Modern World and Other Studies (Mansell, London, 1980).
Towards a Modern Iran (1980).

KELLY, J. B. Eastern Arabian Frontiers (Faber, London, 1963).
Arabia, the Gulf and the West: A Critical View of the Arabs and their Oil Policy (Weidenfeld and Nicolson, London 1980).

KERR, MALCOLM. The Arab Cold War 1958–1964 (Oxford University Press, 1965).

KHADOURI, M. Political Trends in the Arab World (Johns Hopkins Press, Baltimore, 1970).

KHADOURI, M., and LIEVESNY, H. J. (eds.). Law in the Middle East, Vol. I (Washington, 1955).

KHALIL, MUHAMMAD. The Arab States and the Arab League (historical documents) (Khayat's, Beirut).

KHOURI, FRED J. The Arab-Israeli Dilemma (Syracuse/New York, 1968).

KINGSBURY, R. C., and POUNDS, N. J. G. An Atlas of Middle Eastern Affairs (New York, 1963).

KIRK, GEORGE E. The Middle East in the War (London, 1953).
A Short History of the Middle East: from the Rise of Islam to Modern Times (New York, 1955).
Contemporary Arab Politics (Methuen, London, 1961).

KUMAR, RAVINDER. India and the Persian Gulf Region (London, 1965).

KURZMAN, DAN. Genesis 1948: The First Arab/Israeli War (Vallentine, Mitchell, London, 1972).

KUTSCHERA, CHRIS. Le Mouvement national Kurde (Flammarion, Paris, 1979).

LALL, ARTHUR. The UN and the Middle East Crisis (New York/London, 1968).

LAQUEUR, W. Z. Communism and Nationalism in the Middle East (London and New York, 1957).
A History of Zionism (Weidenfeld and Nicolson, London, 1972).
The Struggle for the Middle East: The Soviet Union and the Middle East 1958-68 (Routledge and Kegan Paul, London, 1969).
Confrontation: The Middle-East War and World Politics (Wildwood, London, 1974).

(ed.) The Middle East in Transition (Routledge and Kegan Paul, London, 1958).
(ed.) The Israel-Arab Reader (New York/Toronto/London, 1969).

LAWRENCE, T. E. The Seven Pillars of Wisdom (London, 1935).

LEIDEN, CARL (ed.). The conflict of traditionalism and modernism in the Muslim Middle East (Austin, Texas, 1969).

LENCZOWSKI, GEORGE. The Middle East in World Affairs (Ithaca, N.Y., Cornell University Press, 1956).
Oil and State in the Middle East (Cornell Univ. Press, 1960).

LEWIS, B. The Arabs in History (London, 1950 and 1954).
The Middle East and the West (London, 1964).
Race and Colour in Islam (London, 1971).
Islam in History (London, 1973).
Islam to 1453 (London, 1974).

LIPPMAN, THOMAS W. Understanding Islam: An Introduction to the Moslem World (New American Library, New York, 1982).

LLOYD, SELWYN. Suez 1956: A Personal Account (Jonathan Cape, London, 1978).

LONGRIGG, S. H. Oil in the Middle East (London, 1954, 3rd edn., London, 1968).
The Middle East: a Social Geography (London, 2nd rev. edn., 1970).

MACDONALD, ROBERT W. The League of Arab States (Princeton University Press, Princeton, 1965).

MANNIN, ETHEL. A Lance for the Arabs (London, 1963).

MANSFIELD, PETER. The Ottoman Empire and Its Successors (Macmillan, London, 1973).
(ed.). The Middle East: A Political and Economic Survey, 5th edition (Oxford U.P., London, 1980).
The Arabs (London, Allen Lane, 1976).

MICHAELIS, ALFRED. Wirtschaftliche Entwicklungsprobleme des Mittleren Ostens (Kiel, 1960).

MIKDASHI, ZUHAYR. The Community of Oil Exporting Countries (George Allen and Unwin, London, 1972).

MIQUEL, ANDRÉ. Islam et sa civilisation (Paris, 1968).

MONROE, ELIZABETH. Britain's Moment in the Middle East 1914–71 (London, Chatto and Windus, new Edition 1981).

MOORE, JOHN MORTON. The Arab-Israeli Conflict (3 vols. Readings and Documents, Princeton, 1976).

MOSLEY, LEONARD. Power Play: The Tumultuous World of Middle East Oil 1890–1973 (Weidenfeld and Nicolson, London, 1973).

NASR, SEYYED HOSSEIN. Science and Civilization in Islam (Harvard, 1968).

NEVAKIVI, JUKKA. Britain, France and the Arab Middle East 1914–20 (Athlone Press, University of London, 1969).

NUTTING, ANTHONY. The Arabs (Hollis and Carter, London, 1965).
No End of a Lesson, The Story of Suez (Constable, London, 1967).

O'BALLANCE, EDGAR. The Third Arab-Israeli War (Faber and Faber, London, 1972).

OWEN, ROGER. The Middle East in the World Economy 1800–1914 (Methuen, London, 1980).

OXFORD REGIONAL ECONOMIC ATLAS. The Middle East and North Africa (Oxford University Press, 1960).

PEARSON, J. D. (ed.). Index Islamicus (Cambridge, 1967).

PENNAR, JAAN. The U.S.S.R. and the Arabs: The Ideological Dimension (Hurst, London, 1973).

PLAYFAIR, IAN S. O. The Mediterranean and the Middle East (History of the Second World War, H.M.S.O., London, 1966).

POLIAK, A. N. Feudalism in Egypt, Syria, Palestine, and the Lebanon, 1250–1900 (London, Luzac, for the Royal Asiatic Society, 1939).

POLK, W. R. The United States and the Arab World (Harvard University Press, 1965, rev. edn. 1970).
(ed. with CHAMBERS, R. L.) Beginnings of Modernization in the Middle East: the Nineteenth Century (University of Chicago Press, 1969).
The Elusive Peace: The Middle East in the Twentieth Century (Frank Cass, London, 1980).

PORATH, Y. The Emergence of the Palestinian Arab National Movement 1918–1929 (Frank Cass, London, 1974).

PROCTOR, J. HARRIS (ed.). Islam and International Relations (Pall Mall Press, London, 1965).

QUBAIN, FAHIM I. Education and Science in the Arab World (Johns Hopkins Press, Baltimore, 1967).

RIKHYE, Maj.-Gen. I. J. The Sinai Blunder (Frank Cass, London, 1980).

RIVLIN, B., and SZYLIOWICZ, J. S. (eds.). The Contemporary Middle East—Tradition and Innovation (Random House, New York, 1965).

ROBERTS, D. S. Islam: A Concise Introduction (Harper & Row, New York, 1982).

RODINSON, MAXIME. Islam and Capitalism (France, 1965, England 1974).
La Fascination de l'Islam (Maspero, Paris, 1980).
The Arabs (Croom Helm, London, 1981).

RO'I, YA'ACOV. The Limits of Power: Soviet Policy in the Middle East (Croom Helm, London, 1978).

RONART, STEPHAN and NANDY. Concise Encyclopaedia of Arabic Civilization (Amsterdam, 1966).

RONDOT, PIERRE. The Destiny of the Middle East (Chatto & Windus, London, 1960).
L'Islam (Prismes, Paris, 1965).

ROUHANI, FUAD. A History of OPEC (Pall Mall Press, London, 1972).

SACHAR, HOWARD M. Europe Leaves the Middle East 1936–1954 (Allen Lane, London, 1973).

SAID, EDWARD W. The Question of Palestine (Routledge, London, 1979).
Covering Islam (Routledge, London, 1982).

SAUVAGET, J. Introduction à l'histoire de l'orient musulman (Paris, 1943) (2nd edn. re-cast by C. CAHEN, Univ of Calif. Press, 1965).

SAVORY, R. M. Introduction to Islamic Civilization (Cambridge University Press, 1976).

SAYIGH, YUSIF. The Determinants of Arab Economic Development (Croom Helm, London, 1977).

SEARIGHT, SARAH. The British in the Middle East (Weidenfeld and Nicolson, London, 1969).

SHABAN, M. A. The Abbasid Revolution (Cambridge University Press, 1970).
Islamic History A.D. 600–750 (A.H. 132) A New Interpretation (Cambridge University Press, 1971).

SHARABI, H. B. Governments and Politics of the Middle East in the Twentieth Century (Van Nostrand, New York, 1962).
Nationalism and Revolution in the Arab World (Van Nostrand, New York, 1966).
Palestine and Israel: The Lethal Dilemma (Pegasus Press, N.Y., 1969).

SID-AHMED, MUHAMMAD. After the Guns Fell Silent (Croom Helm, London, 1976).

SMITH, W. CANTWELL. Islam and Modern History (Toronto, 1957).

SOUTHERN, R. W. Western Views of Islam in the Middle Ages (Oxford, 1957).

SPECTOR, IVAR. The Soviet Union and the Muslim World (Seattle, University of Washington Press, 1956).

STARK, FREYA. Dust in the Lion's Paw (London and New York, 1961).

STEVENS, GEORGINA G. (ed.). The United States and the Middle East (Prentice Hall, N.J., 1964).

STEWART, DESMOND. The Middle East: Temple of Janus (Hamish Hamilton, London, 1972).

STOCKING, G. W. Middle East Oil. A Study in Political and Economic Controversy (Vanderbilt University Press, Nashville, 1970).

SUMNER, B. H. Tsardom and Imperialism in the Far East and Middle East (London, Oxford University Press, 1940).

THAYER, P. W. (ed.). Tensions in the Middle East (Baltimore, 1958).

THOMAS, D. WINTON (ed.). Archaeology and Old Testament Study (Oxford University Press, 1967).

THOMAS, L. V., and FRYE, R. N. The United States and Turkey and Iran (Cambridge, Mass., 1951).

TREVELYAN, HUMPHREY (Lord). The Middle East in Revolution (Macmillan, London, 1970).

TRIMINGHAM, J. SPENCER. The Sufi Orders in Islam (Clarendon Press, Oxford, 1971).

TUGENDHAT, C. Oil: The Biggest Business (Eyre and Spottiswoode, London, 1968).

VATIKIOTIS, P. J. Conflict in the Middle East (George Allen and Unwin, London, 1971).

WADSMAN, P., and TEISSEDRE, R.-F. Nos Politiciens face au Conflit Israélo Arabe (Paris, 1969).

WAINES, DAVID. The Unholy War (Medina Press, Wilmette, 1971).

WALKER, CHRISTOPHER J. Armenia: The Survival of a Nation (Croom Helm, London, 1980).

WARRINER, DOREEN. Land and Poverty in the Middle East (London, 1948).
Land Reform and Development in the Middle East: Study of Egypt, Syria and Iraq (London, 1962).

WATT, W. MONTGOMERY. Muhammad at Mecca (Clarendon Press, Oxford, 1953).
Muhammad at Medina (Clarendon Press, Oxford, 1956).
Muhammad, Prophet and Statesman (Oxford University Press, 1961).
Muslim Intellectual—Al Ghazari (Edinburgh University Press, 1962).
Islamic Philosophy and Theology (Edinburgh University Press, 1963).
Islamic Political Thought: The Basic Concepts (Edinburgh University Press, 1968).

WILSON, RODNEY. Trade and Investment in the Middle East (Macmillan Press, 1977).

WOOLFSON, MARION. Prophets in Babylon: Jews in the Arab World (Faber, London, 1980).

YALE, WILLIAM. The Near East (University of Michigan Press, Ann Arbor, 1968).

ZEINE, Z. N. The Struggle for Arab Independence (Beirut, 1960).

BOOKS ON NORTH AFRICA
(See also Bibliographies at end of Chapters in Part III)

ABUN-NASR, JAMIL M. A History of the Maghrib (Cambridge University Press, 1972).

ALLAL EL-FASSI. The Independence Movements in Arab North Africa, trans. H. Z. Nuseibeh (Washington, 1954).

AMIN, SAMIR. L'Economie du Maghreb (2 vols., Editions du Minuit, Paris, 1966).
The Maghreb in the Modern World (Penguin Books, London, 1971).

BARBOUR, NEVILLE, Editor. A Survey of North West Africa (The Maghreb) (Royal Institute of International Affairs, Oxford University Press, 1959).

BERQUE, JACQUES. Le Maghreb entre Deux Guerres (2nd edn., Editions du Seuil, Paris, 1967).

BRACE, R. M. Morocco, Algeria, Tunisia (Prentice-Hall, Englewood Cliffs, N.J., 1964).

BROWN, LEON CARL (ed.). State and Society in Independent North Africa (Middle East Institute, Washington, 1966).

CAPOT-REY, R. Le Sahara Français (Paris, 1953).

CENTRE D'ETUDES DES RELATIONS INTERNATIONALES. Le Maghreb et la Communauté Economique Européenne (Editions F.N.S.P., Paris, 1965).

CENTRE DE RECHERCHES SUR L'AFRIQUE MÉDITERRANÉENNE D'AIX EN PROVENCE. L'Annuaire de l'Afrique du Nord (Centre Nationale de la recherche scientifique, Paris, annually).

CHARBONNEAU, J. Editor. Le Sahara Français (Cahiers Charles de Foucauld, No. 38, Paris, 1955).

DUCLOS, J., LECA, J., and DUVIGNAUD, J. Les Nationalismes Maghrébins (Centre d'Etudes des Relations Internationales, Paris, 1966).

ECONOMIC COMMISSION FOR AFRICA. Main Problems of Economic Co-operation in North Africa (Tangier, 1966).

FURLONGE, Sir GEOFFREY. The Lands of Barbary (Murray, London, 1966).

GALLAGHER, C. F. The U.S. and North Africa (Cambridge, Mass., 1964).

GARDI, RENÉ. Sahara, Monographie einer grossen Wüste (Kummerley and Frey, Berne, 1967).

GAUTIER, E. F. Le Passé de l'Afrique du Nord (Paris, 1937).

GERMIDIS, DIMITRI, with the help of DELAPIERRE, MICHEL. Le Maghreb, la France et l'enjeu technologique (Editions Cujas, Paris, 1976).

GORDON, D. C. North Africa's French Legacy 1954–62 (Harvard, 1962).

HAHN, LORNA. North Africa: from Nationalism to Nationhood (Washington, 1960).

HERMASSI, ELBAKI. Leadership and National Development in North Africa (University of California Press, 1973).

HESELTINE, N. From Libyan Sands to Chad (Leiden, 1960).

JULIEN, CH.-A. Histoire de l'Afrique du Nord (2nd Edition, 2 Vols., Paris 1951-52).
L'Afrique du Nord en Marche (Paris, 1953).
History of North Africa: From the Arab Conquest to 1830. Revised by R. Le Tourneau. Ed. C. C. Stewart (Routledge and Kegan Paul, London, 1970).

KHALDOUN, IBN. History of the Berbers. Translated into French by Slane (4 vols., Algiers, 1852-56).

KNAPP, WILFRID. North West Africa: A Political and Economic Survey (Oxford University Press, 3rd edition 1977).

LE TOURNEAU, ROGER. Evolution Politique de l'Afrique du Nord Musulmane (Paris, 1962).

LEVI-PROVENÇAL, E. Islam d'Occident (Etudes d'Histoire Médiévale, Paris, 1948).

LISKA, G. The Greater Maghreb: From Independence to Unity? (Center of Foreign Policy Research, Washington, 1963).

MARÇAIS, G. La Berberie Musulmane et l'Orient au Moyen Age (Paris, 1946).

MOORE, C. H. Politics in North Africa (Little, Brown, Boston, 1970).

MORTIMER, EDWARD. France and the Africans, 1944–1960 (Faber, London, 1969).

MUZIKÁR, JOSEPH. Les perspectives de l'intégration des pays maghrébins et leur attitude vis-à-vis du Marché Commun (Nancy, 1968).

NICKERSON, JANE S. Short History of North Africa (New York, 1961).

PARRINDER, GEOFFREY. Religion in Africa (Pall Mall Press, London, 1970).

POLK, WILLIAM R. (ed.). Developmental Revolution: North Africa, Middle East, South Asia (Middle East Institute, Washington, 1963).

RAVEN, SUSAN. Rome in Africa (Evans Brothers, London, 1970).

ROBANA, ABDERRAHMA. The Prospects for an Economic Community in North Africa (Pall Mall, London, 1973).

SAHLI, MOHAMED CHERIF. Décoloniser l'Histoire; introduction à l'histoire du Maghreb (Maspero, Paris, 1965).

SCHRAMM, JOSEF. Die Westsahara (Paunonia-Verlag, Freilassing, 1969).

STEEL, R. (ed.). North Africa (Wilson, New York, 1967).

TOYNBEE, Sir ARNOLD. Between Niger and Nile (Oxford University Press, 1965).

TRIMINGHAM, J. S., The Influence of Islam upon Africa (Longmans, London, and Librairie du Liban, Beirut, 1968).

TUTSCH, HANS E. Nordafrika in Gärung (Frankfurt, 1961). From Ankara to Marrakesh (New York, 1962).

UNESCO. Arid Zone Research, Vol. XIX: Nomades et Nomadisme au Sahara (UNESCO, 1963).

UNIONS, LABOUR AND INDUSTRIAL RELATIONS IN AFRICA; AN ANNOTATED BIBLIOGRAPHY. Cornell Research Papers in International Relations, 4 (Cornell University Press, New York, 1965).

WARREN, CLINE, and SANTMYER, C. Agriculture of Northern Africa (U.S. Dept. of Agriculture, Washington, 1965).

ZARTMAN, I. W. Government and Politics in North Africa (New York, 1964).
(ed.) Man, State and Society in the Contemporary Maghrib (Pall Mall, London, 1973).

SELECT BIBLIOGRAPHY (PERIODICALS)

ACTA ORIENTALIA ACADEMIAE SCIENTIARUM HUNGARICAE. H-1363 Budapest, P.O.B. 24, Hungary; f. 1950; three times a year; text in English, French, German or Russian; Editor F. TÖKEI.

ACTA ORIENTALIA. Publ. Munksgaard, Nørre Søgade 35, DK 1370 Copenhagen K, Denmark, by the Oriental Societies of Denmark, Norway, and Sweden; history, language, archaeology and religions of the Near and Far East; one issue a year; Editor Prof. SØREN EGEROD; Editorial Sec. Mrs. LISE SODE-MOGENSEN, Scandinavian Institute of Asian Studies, Kejsergade 2, DK 1155 Copenhagen K, Denmark.

AFRICA CONTEMPORARY RECORD. Africana Publishing Co., Holmes & Meier Publishers Inc., IUB Building, 30 Irving Place, New York, N.Y. 10003, U.S.A.; annual survey and documents.

AFRICA GUIDE. World of Information, 21 Gold St., Saffron Walden, Essex, CB10 1EJ, England; annually; Editor ENVER CARIM.

AFRICA QUARTERLY. Indian Centre for Africa, Indian Council for Cultural Relations, Azad Bhavan, Indraprastha Estate, New Delhi, India; f. 1961; Editor A. R. BASU; circ. 500.

AFRICA RESEARCH BULLETINS. Africa Research Ltd., 18 Lower North St., Exeter, EX4 3EN, Devon, England; f. 1964; monthly bulletins on (a) political and (b) economic subjects.

L'AFRIQUE ET L'ASIE MODERNES, 13 rue du Four, 75006 Paris, France; f. 1948; political, economic and social review; quarterly.

AGRIBUSINESS IN THE MIDDLE EAST AND NORTH AFRICA. Chase World Information Corporation, One World Trade Center, Suite 4627, New York, N.Y. 10048, U.S.A.; publs. *Saudi Arabia, Iran, Egypt, Sudan*.

AL-ABHATH. Publ. American University of Beirut, Beirut, Lebanon; f. 1948; Editor IHSAN ABBAS; annual on Middle East studies.

ALAM ATTIJARAT (*The World of Business*). Johnston International Publishing Corpn. (New York), Beirut; Arabic; business; 10 issues a year; Editor NADIM MAKDISI.

AL-IKTISSAD AL-ARABI (*Arab Business*). 66–69 Great Queen St., Carlton House, London, W.C.2, England; f. 1975; monthly; Editor MUSTAPHA KARKOUTI.

AL-TIJARA AL-ARABIYA AL-INKLEEZYA (*Anglo-Arab Trade*). Sahara Publications, 91–93 King St., London, W.6; Arabic; quarterly.

ANATOLIAN STUDIES. c/o British Academy, Burlington House, Piccadilly, London, W1V 0NS, England; f. 1949; annual of the British Inst. of Archaeology at Ankara; Editor Prof. O. R. GURNEY.

ANATOLICA. Netherlands Historical and Archaeological Institute at Istanbul, Istiklâl Caddesi 393, Istanbul-Beyoğlu, Turkey; f. 1967; annual; Editors: HANDAN ALKIM, C. NIJLAND, E. J. VAN DONZEL, SEMRA ÖGEL, J. J. ROODENBERG.

ANNALES ARCHÉOLOGIQUES ARABES SYRIENNES. Direction Générale des Antiquités et des Musées, University St., Damascus, Syria; f. 1951; archaeological and historical review; yearly; Dir.-Gen. Dr. AFIF BAHNASSI.

ANNUAIRE DE L'AFRIQUE DU NORD. Edited by the Centre de Recherches et d'Etudes sur les Sociétés Mediterranéennes, 3 blvd. Pasteur, Aix-en-Provence; published by the Centre National de la Recherche Scienti-fique, 15 quai Anatole France, 75700 Paris, France; Dir. Prof. FLORY, France; f. 1962; year book contains special studies on current affairs, chronologies, chronicles, documentation and bibliographies.

ANNUAL SURVEY OF AFRICAN LAW. Rex Collings Ltd., 6 Paddington St., London W1.

THE ARAB ECONOMIST. Centre for Economic, Financial and Social Research and Documentation SAL, Gefinor Tower, Clemenceau Street, Bloc B—P.O.B. 11–6068, Beirut, Lebanon; f. 1969; Chair. Dr. CHAFIC AKHRAS; monthly; circ. 7,300.

ARAB MONTH. 14–16 Duke's Rd., London, WC1H 9AD; f. 1978; current affairs, business, arts; Editor LOGAN GOURLEY.

ARAB OIL AND GAS. Arab Petroleum and Gas Research Centre, 7 avenue Ingres, 75781 Paris, France; petroleum and gas; English; twice monthly.

ARAB OIL AND GAS DIRECTORY. Arab Petroleum and Gas Research Centre, 7 avenue Ingres, 75781 Paris, France; annually.

ARABICA. c/o Institut d'études arabes et islamiques, 13 rue de Santeuil, 75231 Paris Cedex 05, France; Editor M. ARKOUN; 3 a year.

ARAMTEK MIDEAST REVIEW. Aramtek Corporation, 122 East 42nd St., Suite 3703, New York, N.Y. 10017; f. 1976; business news and features; U.S.A. Editor-in-Chief M. HANDAL; Man. Editor B. F. OTTAVIANI.

ARCHIV FÜR ORIENTFORSCHUNG. c/o Institut für Orientalistik der Universität Wien, Universitätsstrasse 7/V, A-1010 Vienna I, Austria; f. 1923; yearly; Editors HANS HIRSCH, HERMANN HUNGER.

ARMENIAN REVIEW. Armenian Research Foundation, 212 Stuart St., Boston, Mass. 02116, U.S.A.; f. 1948; Editor JAMES H. TASHJIAN; quarterly.

ASIAN AFFAIRS. Royal Society for Asian Affairs, 42 Devonshire St., London, W.1, England; f. 1901; three times per year.

ASIAN AND AFRICAN STUDIES. Israel Oriental Society, The Institute of Middle Eastern Studies, Haifa University, Haifa, Israel; f. 1965; Editor GABRIEL R. WARBURG; 3 a year.

L'ASIE NOUVELLE. 94 rue St. Lazare, 75442 Paris Cédex 09, France; weekly and special issues; Dir. ANDRÉ ROUX.

ASIEN-BIBLIOGRAPHIE. Asien Bücherei, Postfach 1120, D-3590 Bad Wildungen, German Federal Republic; quarterly.

BELLETEN. Türk Tarih Kurumu, Kizilay Sokak no. 1, Ankara, Turkey; f. 1937; history and archaeology of Turkey and the Near East; quarterly; Editor ULUĞ IĞDEMIR.

BIBLIOTHECA ORIENTALIS. Published by Netherlands Institute for the Near East, Noordeindsplein 4A-6A, Leiden, Netherlands; f. 1943; edited by E. VAN DONZEL, M. N. VAN LOON, H. J. A. DE MEULENAERE, M. J. MULDER, C. NIJLAND, M. STOL; bi-monthly.

BRITISH SOCIETY FOR MIDDLE EASTERN STUDIES BULLETIN. Department of Islamic & Middle Eastern Studies, The Muir Institute (University of Edinburgh), 7–8 Buccleuch Place, Edinburgh, EH8 9LW; published at Middle East Centre, St. Antony's College, 68 Woodstock Rd., Oxford, OX2 6JF; Editor Prof. J. D. LATHAM; twice a year.

BULLETIN OF THE SCHOOL OF ORIENTAL AND AFRICAN STUDIES. School of Oriental and African Studies, University of London, London, WC1E 7HP, England; three issues annually.

BULLETIN OF SUDANESE STUDIES. P.O.B. 321, Khartoum; Arabic; published by Sudan Research Unit, University of Khartoum; f. 1968; bi-annual; Editor AWN AL-SHARIF QASIM.

LES CAHIERS DE TUNISIE. Published by Faculté des Lettres et Sciences Humaines de Tunis, 94 Blvd. de 9 Avril 1938, B.P. 1128, Tunis; f. 1953; covers research in humanities; quarterly; Dir. MOHAMED TALBI; Editor-in-Chief BÉCHIR TLILI.

CHUTO TSUHO (The Middle East News). The Middle East Institute of Japan, 15 Mori Bldg., 8-10 Toranomon 2-chome, Minato-ku, Tokyo, Japan; f. 1958; Editor Y. NAKAYAMA; bi-monthly.

LE COMMERCE DU LEVANT. Kantari St., SFAH Building, Beirut, Lebanon; two editions (bi-weekly and monthly).

COMUNITÁ MEDITERRANEA. Lungotevere Flaminio 34, Rome; law and political science relating to Mediterranean countries; Pres. E. BUSSI.

CRESCENT INTERNATIONAL. 338 Hollyberry Trail, Willowdale, Ontario, Canada M2H 2P6; f. 1980; deals with Islamic movement throughout the world; twice per month.

DEUTSCHE MORGENLÄNDISCHE GESELLSCHAFT; ZEITSCHRIFT. Deutsche Morgenländische Gesellschaft, Seminar für Sprachen und Kulturen Nordafrikas, Otto-Behaghel-Str. 10, D-6300 Giessen, Federal Republic of Germany; f. 1847; covers the history, languages and literature of the Orient; bi-annual.

DEVELOPING BUSINESS IN THE MIDDLE EAST AND NORTH AFRICA. Chase World Information Corporation, One World Trade Center, New York, N.Y. 10048, U.S.A.; publs. *Saudi Arabia, Egypt, Iran, Iraq, Algeria, The Gulf States.*

DEVELOPING ECONOMIES, THE. Institute of Developing Economies, 42 Ichigaya Hommura-cho, Shinjuku-ku, Tokyo 162, Japan; f. 1962; English, quarterly.

L'ECONOMISTE ARABE. Centre d'Etudes et de Documentation Economiques, Financières et Sociales, S.A.L., B.P. 6068, Beirut, Lebanon; monthly; Pres. Dr. CHAFIC AKHRAS, Dir.-Gen. Dr. SABBAH AL HAJ.

EUROPE OUTREMER. 6 rue de Bassano, Paris 16e, France; f. 1923; economic and political material on French-speaking states of Africa; monthly.

FRANCE-PAYS ARABES. Published by L'Association de Solidarité Franco-Arabe, 12-14 rue Augereau, 75007 Paris, France; f. 1968; politics, economics and culture of the Arab world; monthly; Dir. LUCIEN BITTERLIN.

FREE PALESTINE. P.O.B. 492, London, SW19 4PJ; f. 1968; monthly; Editor AZIZ YAFI.

GULF GUIDE AND DIARY. World of Information, 21 Gold St., Saffron Walden, Essex, CB10 1EJ; events in Kuwait, Bahrain, Qatar, Saudi Arabia, the United Arab Emirates, Iraq, Oman, the Yemen Arab Republic and the People's Democratic Republic of Yemen; Editor ENVER CARIM; annual.

HAMIZRAH HEHADASH. Israel Oriental Society. The Hebrew University, Jerusalem, Israel; f. 1949; Hebrew with English summary; Middle Eastern, Asian and African affairs; quarterly; Editor AHARON LAYISH.

HESPERIS-TAMUDA. Faculté des Lettres et des Sciences Humaines, Université Mohammed V, 3 rue Ibn Batouta, Rabat, Morocco; f. 1921; history, archaeology, civilization of Maghreb and Western Islam, special reference to bibliography.

HUNA LONDON (BBC Arabic Radio Times). BBC Arabic Service, P.O.B. 76, Bush House, Strand, London, WC2B 4PH; f. 1960; circ. throughout the Arab world; monthly; Editor DOUGLAS S. S. EVANS; Advtg. Consultant LESLIE KNIGHT, O.B.E.

IBLA. Institut des Belles Lettres Arabes, 12 rue Jamâa el Haoua, 1008 Tunis BM, Tunisia; f. 1937; twice a year.

INDO-IRANIAN JOURNAL. D. Reidel Publishing Co., P.O.B. 17, 3300 AA Dordrecht, Netherlands; f. 1957; quarterly; Editors J. W. DE JONG, F. B. J. KUIPER and M. WITZEL.

INTERNATIONAL CRUDE OIL AND PRODUCT PRICES. Middle East Petroleum and Economic Publications, P.O.B. 4940, Nicosia, Cyprus; f. 1971 (in Beirut); six-monthly review and analysis of crude oil and product price trends in world markets; Publisher FUAD W. ITAYIM.

INTERNATIONAL JOURNAL OF MIDDLE EAST STUDIES, Cambridge University Press, The Edinburgh Bldg.. Shaftesbury Rd., Cambridge CB2 2RU, England; Journal of the Middle East Studies Association of North America and the British Society for Middle Eastern Studies; first issue Jan. 1970; four times per year.

IRANISTISCHE MITTEILUNGEN. Antigone-Verlag, 3559 Allendorf an der Eder, P.O.B. 1147, Federal Republic of Germany; f. 1967; Editor HELMHART KANUS-CREDÉ.

IRAQ. British School of Archaeology in Iraq, 31–34 Gordon Square, London, WC1H 0PY, England; f. 1932; semi-annually.

DER ISLAM. D2 Hamburg 13, Rothenbaumchaussee 36, Federal Republic of Germany; 2 issues a year.

ISLAMIC QUARTERLY. The Islamic Cultural Centre, 146 Park Rd., London, N.W.8, England; f. 1954; quarterly; Editor Dr. M. A. ZAKI BADAWI.

ISRAEL AND PALESTINE. P.O.B. 130–10, 75463 Paris Cedex 10, France; f. 1971; monthly; Editor MAXIM GHILAN; also publishes a monthly monitoring report on the Palestinians under Israeli rule (Bamerkhav), in English and Hebrew.

IZVESTIA AKADEMII NAUK-OTEDELENIE LITERATURY I YAZYKA. Soviet Academy of Sciences, Moscow, U.S.S.R.; bi-monthly.

JEUNE AFRIQUE. Groupe J. A. 51 av. des Ternes, Paris 17e, France; f. 1960; Publisher BECHIR BEN YAHMED; weekly.

JEUNE AFRIQUE ECONOMIE. Groupe J. A. 51 av. des Ternes, Paris 17e, France; f. 1981; Publisher BECHIR BEN YAHMED; monthly.

JOURNAL OF AFRICAN LAW. School of Oriental and African Studies, University of London, London, WC1E 7HP; two issues annually.

JOURNAL OF THE AMERICAN ORIENTAL SOCIETY. American Oriental Society, 329 Sterling Memorial Library, New Haven, Conn. 06520, U.S.A.; f. 1842; Biblical studies, Ancient Near East, South and Southeast Asia, Islamic Near East, and Far East; quarterly.

JOURNAL ASIATIQUE. Journal de la Société Asiatique, 3 rue Mazarine, 75006 Paris, France; f. 1822; Dir. D. GIMARET; covers all phases of Oriental research; quarterly.

JOURNAL OF INDIAN PHILOSOPHY. D. Reidel Publishing Co., P.O.B. 17, 3300 AA Dordrecht, Netherlands; f. 1970; quarterly; Editor BIMAL K. MATILAL.

JOURNAL INSTITUTE OF MUSLIM MINORITY AFFAIRS. King Abdulaziz University, P.O.B. 1540, Jeddah, Saudi Arabia; two a year; Man. Editor Dr. SYED Z. ABEDIN.

JOURNAL OF NEAR EASTERN STUDIES. Oriental Institute, University of Chicago, 1155 East 58th St., Chicago, Ill. 60637, U.S.A.; devoted to the Ancient and Medieval Near and Middle East, archaeology, languages, history, Islam; Editor R. BIGGS.

JOURNAL OF PALESTINE STUDIES. P.O.B. 11-7164, Beirut, Lebanon; f. 1971; published jointly by Inst. for Palestine Studies and Kuwait Univ.; Palestinian affairs and the Arab-Israeli conflict; Editor HISHAM SHARABI; circ. 6,000.

MAGHREB-MACHREK (*Monde Arabe*). Fondation Nationale des Sciences Politiques, Centre de l'Orient contemporain et Direction de la Documentation, La Documentation Française, 29–31 quai Voltaire, 75340 Paris Cedex 07, France; f. 1964; quarterly.

THE MAGHREB REVIEW. 96 Marchmont St., London, WC1N 1AG; f. 1976; every two months; North African affairs; Editor MOHAMED BEN MADANI.

MAGHREB-SÉLECTION. Ediafric - La Documentation Africaine, 57 ave. d'Iéna, 75783 Paris Cedex 16, France; weekly; French.

M.E.N. WEEKLY. Middle East News Agency, 4 Sharia el Sherifein, Cairo, Egypt; f. 1962; weekly news bulletin.

THE MIDDLE EAST. 63 Long Acre, London, WC2E 9JH, England; f. 1974; political, economic and cultural monthly; Editor NADIA HIJAB.

MIDDLE EAST BUSINESS YEARBOOK, 69 Great Queen St., London, W.C.2; Editor GRAHAM BENTON.

MIDDLE EAST CONTEMPORARY SURVEY. Holmes & Meier, IUB Building, 30 Irving Place, New York 10003, U.S.A.; annual publication describing and analysing events in the Middle East during the year under survey.

MIDDLE EAST ECONOMIC DIGEST. MEED Ltd., 21 John St., London, WC1N 2BP, England; f. 1957; weekly report on economic developments; Chair. PETER KILNER; Publisher JONATHAN WALLACE; Editor RICHARD PURDY.

MIDDLE EAST ECONOMIC SURVEY. Middle East Research and Publishing Centre, P.O.B. 4940, Nicosia, Cyprus; f. 1957 (in Beirut); weekly review of petroleum and economic news; Editor and Publisher FUAD W. ITAYIM.

MIDDLE EAST INTERNATIONAL. 21 Collingham Rd., London, SW5 0NU; f. 1971; fortnightly; political and economic developments, book reviews; Editor MICHAEL WALL.

THE MIDDLE EAST JOURNAL. Middle East Institute, 1761 N St., N.W., Washington, D.C. 20036, U.S.A.; journal in English devoted to the study of the modern Near East; f. 1947; quarterly; Editor RICHARD B. PARKER; circ. 4,600.

MIDDLE EAST PERSPECTIVE. 850 Seventh Ave., New York, N.Y. 10019, U.S.A.; monthly newsletter of Jewish affairs; Editor Dr. ALFRED LILIENTHAL.

MIDDLE EAST REVIEW. World of Information, 21 Gold St., Saffron Walden, Essex, CB10 1EJ, England; annual; Editor ENVER CARIM.

MIDDLE EAST STUDIES ASSOCIATION BULLETIN. Department of Oriental Studies, University of Arizona, Tucson, Ariz. 85721, U.S.A.; twice yearly.

THE MIDDLE EAST YEARBOOK. 63 Long Acre, London, WC2E 9JH, England; f. 1980; annual; Editor PAMELA ANN SMITH.

MIDDLE EASTERN STUDIES. Frank Cass & Co. Ltd., Gainsborough House, 11 Gainsborough Rd., London, E11 1RS; England; f. 1964; Editor ELIE KEDOURIE; four times yearly.

MIDEAST MARKETS. Bracken House, Cannon St., London. EC4P 4BY; fortnightly newsletter; Editor SIMON HENDERSON.

MIDEAST REPORT. 60 East 42nd Street, Suite 1433, New York, N.Y. 10017, U.S.A.; political analysis, oil and finance and business intelligence.

MOYEN-ORIENT ECONOMIQUE. Ediafric - La Documentation Africaine, 57 ave. d'Iéna, 75783 Paris Cedex 16, France; f. 1978; twice monthly; economic information about the Middle East.

THE MUSLIM WORLD. 77 Sherman St., Hartford, Conn, 06105, U.S.A.; f. 1911; Islamic studies in general and Muslim-Christian relations in past and present; quarterly; Editors WILLEM A. BIJLEFELD, WADI' Z. HADDAD and YVONNE Y. HADDAD.

NARODY ASII I AFRIKI (Istoriya, Ekonomika, Kultura). Akad. Nauk S.S.S.R., ul. Zhdanova, 12, Moscow, U.S.S.R.; f. 1955; bi-monthly.

NEAR EAST REPORT. 444 N. Capitol St., N.W., Washington, D.C. 20001, U.S.A.; f. 1957; analyses U.S. policy in the Near East; circ. 40,000; weekly; Editor MOSHE DECTER.

NEW OUTLOOK. 2 Karl Netter Street, Tel-Aviv 65202, Israel; f. 1957; Israeli and Middle Eastern Affairs; dedicated to Jewish-Arab rapprochement; monthly; circ. 10,000; Editor SIMHA FLAPAN.

OEL (Zeitschrift für die Mineralölwirtschaft). 2 Hamburg 13, Alsterkamp 20, Federal Republic of Germany; f. 1963; monthly.

OIL AND GAS JOURNAL. Penn Well Publishing Co., 1421 S. Sheridan, Tulsa, Oklahoma 74101, U.S.A.; f. 1902; petroleum industry and business weekly; Publisher JOHN FORD; Editor GENE T. KINNEY.

ORIENT. German Orient Institute, 2 Hamburg 13, Mittelweg 150, Federal Republic of Germany; f. 1960; current affairs articles in German, English and French; Documents, Book Reviews and Bibliographies; quarterly; Editor Dr. UDO STEINBACH.

ORIENTE MODERNO. Istituto per l'Oriente, via A. Caroncini 19, 00197 Rome, Italy; f. 1921; chronicle of events, articles, book reviews; monthly.

PALESTINE AFFAIRS. P.O.B. 1691, Beirut, Lebanon; studies of Palestine problem; f. 1971; monthly in Arabic; Editor BILAL EL-HASSAN.

PERSICA. Netherlands-Iranian Society; c/o NINO, Noordeindsplein 4A-6A, 2311 AH Leiden, Netherlands; f. 1963; annual; Editors E. DURING CASPERS, J. DE BRUIJN, Prof. Dr. P. H. L. EGGERMONT, W. FLOOR, K. KREMER and C. NIJLAND.

PETROLEUM ECONOMIST. 107 Charterhouse St., London, EC1M 6AA, England; f. 1934; monthly, in English and Japanese editions; English circ. 7,086; Editor BRYAN COOPER.

PETROLEUM TIMES. IPC Business Press Ltd., Quadrant House, Sutton, Surrey, SM25AS, England; f. 1899; monthly.

PETROLEUM TIMES PRICE REPORT. IPC Business Press Ltd., Quadrant House, Sutton, Surrey, SM2 5AS, England; twice monthly.

POLITICA INTERNAZIONALE. Via del Tritone 62B, 00187 Rome, Italy; published by Istituto per le relazioni tra Italia e i Paesi dell' Africa, America Latina e Medio Oriente; monthly Italian edition; twice-yearly English edition.

REVUE D'ASSYRIOLOGIE ET D'ARCHEOLOGIE ORIENTALE. Presses Universitaires de France, 12 rue Jean-de-Beauvais, 75005 Paris, France; f. 1923; 2 a year; Dirs. ANDRÉ PARROT, PAUL GARELLI.

LA REVUE BIBLIOGRAPHIQUE DU MOYEN ORIENT. Publisher L. FARÈS, B.P. 2712, Damascus, Syria.

REVUE DES ETUDES ISLAMIQUES. Librairie Orientaliste Paul Geuthner S.A., 12 rue Vavin, 75006 Paris, France; f. 1927; Editors H. LAOUST and D. SOURDEL.

RIVISTA DEGLI STUDI ORIENTALI. Scuola Orientale, Facoltà di Lettere, University of Rome, Rome, Italy; quarterly; Publisher GIOVANNI BARDI.

ROCZNIK ORIENTALISTYCZNY. Grójecka 17, 02-021 Warsaw, Poland; f. 1915; Editor-in-Chief EDWARD TRYJARSKI; Sec. JANUSZ DANECKI; semi-annual.

ROYAL ASIATIC SOCIETY OF GREAT BRITAIN AND IRELAND JOURNAL. 56 Queen Anne Street, London, W1M 9LA, England; f. 1823; covers all aspects of Oriental research.

AL-SINA'A (Industry). Iraqi Federation of Industries, P.O.B. 5665, South Gate, Baghdad, Iraq; f. 1977 by merger of *Al-Sinai* and *Alam Al Sina'a*; articles in Arabic and English; bi-monthly.

STUDIA ISLAMICA, G. P. Maisonneuve et Larose, 15 rue Victor-Cousin, 75005 Paris, France; bi-annual.

STUDIES IN ISLAM. Indian Institute of Islamic Studies, Panchkuin Rd., New Delhi 110001, India; quarterly; f. 1964.

SUDANOW. P.O.B. 2651, Khartoum, Sudan; f. 1976; monthly; political, economic and cultural; circ. 15,000; Editor FATH EL RAHMAN MAHJOUB.

SUMER. Directorate-General of Antiquities, Baghdad, Iraq; archaeological; bi-annual.

TÜRK KÜLTÜRÜ ARAŞTIRMALARI. T. K. Araştırma Enstitüsü, P.K. 14, Çankaya, Ankara, Turkey; f. 1964; scholarly articles in Turkish; bi-annual; Editor Dr. ŞÜKRÜ ELÇIN.

TURKOLOGISCHER ANZEIGER. Oriental Institute of the University of Vienna; A-1010 Wien I, Universitäts-strasse 7/V, Austria; annual.

U.S.S.R. AND THIRD WORLD. Central Asian Research Centre, 8 Wakley St., London, EC1V 7LT, England; surveys development of Soviet and Chinese policies in the Middle East, Asia, Africa, Latin America and the Caribbean; six issues per year.

WELT DES ISLAMS, DIE. Publ. E. J. Brill, Oude Rijn 33a, Leiden, Netherlands; f. 1913; contains articles in German, English and French on the contemporary Muslim world; Editor Prof. Dr. O. SPIES, University of Bonn.

WIENER ZEITSCHRIFT FÜR DIE KUNDE DES MORGEN-LANDES. Oriental Institute of the University of Vienna, A-1010 Wien I, Universitätsstrasse 7/V, Austria; f. 1887; annually.

Research Institutes

Associations and Institutes Studying the Middle East and North Africa.

(*See also* Regional Organizations—Education in Part I)

AFGHANISTAN

Anjumani Tarikh (*Historical Society*): Kabul; f. 1931; to study and promote international knowledge of the history of Afghanistan; Head AHMAD ALI MOTAMEDI; publs. *Aryana* (quarterly, in Pashtu and Dari) and *Afghanistan* (English and French, quarterly).

The Asia Foundation: P.O.B. 257, Kabul; f. 1955; assists local institutions and organizations concerned with education and socio-economic development; Representative JOEL W. SCARBOROUGH.

British Institute of Afghan Studies: P.O.B. 3052, Kabul; f. 1972; supports research relating to history, antiquities, archaeology, languages, literature, art, culture, customs and natural history of Afghanistan; Dir. R. H. PINDER WILSON; publs. *Annual Report, Afghan Studies* (annually).

ALGERIA

Institut d'Etudes Arabes: Université d'Alger, 2 rue Didouche Mourad, Algiers.

Institut d'Etudes Orientales: Université d'Alger, 2 rue Didouche Mourad, Algiers; publ. *Annales*.

AUSTRALIA AND NEW ZEALAND

Australian Middle East Studies Association: Footscray Institute of Technology, P.O.B. 64, Footscray, Victoria 3011; Political Science Department, University of Canterbury, Christchurch, New Zealand; f. 1981; Co-ordinators Dr. I. H. HERRMAN, Dr. R. MACINTYRE; publs. *AMESA Bulletin* (monthly survey of international literature), *AMESA Occasional Publications*.

Programme in Middle East Studies: University of Western Australia, Nedlands, Western Australia 6009; f. 1975 to promote, encourage and facilitate teaching, research and the dissemination of information on the Middle East; Dir. Prof. R. GABBAY.

AUSTRIA

Afro-Asiatisches Institut in Wien: A-1090 Vienna, Türkenstrasse 3; f. 1959; seminars and language courses and other cultural exchange between African and Asian students in Vienna; Gen. Sec. GERHARD BITTNER; Pres. Bishop Dr. A. WAGNER; publ. *Treffpunkte* (quarterly).

Institut für Orientalistik der Universität Wien: A-1010 Vienna, Universitätsstrasse 7/V; f. 1886; library of 20,000 vols.; Dir. Prof. Dr. ANDREAS TIETZE; publ. *Wiener Zeitschrift für die Kunde des Morgenlandes* (annual), *Turkologischer Anzeiger* (annual), *Archiv für Orientforschung* (annual).

BELGIUM

Centre pour l'Etude des Problèmes du Monde Musulman Contemporain: 44 ave. Jeanne, 1050 Brussels; f. 1957; publs. *Correspondance d'Orient-Etudes* and collections *Correspondance d'Orient* and *Le monde musulman contemporain—Initiations*.

Centrum voor Onderzoek van het Arabisch en de Cultuur van de Arabische Landen (COACAL) (*Center for Research on Arabic and the Culture of the Arab Countries*) (*CRACAC*): 5 St.-Pieterspein, B-9000 Ghent; f. 1975; non-profit organization; Dir. Prof. Dr. M. PLANCKE; Sec. Prof. L. DE MEYER; publ. monographs.

Departement Oriëntalistiek: Faculteit van de Wijsbegeerte en Letteren, Katholieke Universiteit te Leuven,

Blijde Inkomststraat 21, B3000 Leuven; f. 1936; Pres. Prof. E. LIPIŃSKI; 25 mems.; publs. *Orientalia Lovaniensia Analecta, Orientalia Lovaniensia Periodica, Bibliothèque du Muséon* (1929-68), *Orientalia et Biblica Lovaniensia* (1957–68).

Fondation Egyptologique Reine Elisabeth: Parc du Cinquantenaire, 10, B1040 Brussels; f. 1923 to encourage Egyptian studies; 1,450 mems.; library of 90,000 vols.; Pres. M. E. DE BONVOISIN; Dir. M. J. BINGEN and H. DE MEULENAERE; publs. *Chronique d'Egypte, Bibliotheca Aegyptiaca, Papyrologica Bruxellensia, Bibliographie Papyrologique sur fiches, Monumenta Aegyptiaca, Rites égyptiens, Papyri Bruxellenses Graecae, Monographies Reine Elisabeth*.

CZECHOSLOVAKIA

Department of Oriental Studies of the Slovak Academy of Sciences: Slovak Academy of Sciences, Klemensova 19, 884 16 Bratislava; f. 1960; 11 mems.; Pres. Dr. I. DOLEZAL; Vice-Dir. Dr. V. KRUPA; publ. *Asian and African Studies* (annual).

Oriental Institute: 11837 Prague 1, Lázeňská 4; f. 1922; Head of Inst. J. CESAR, D.SC.; publs. *Archív Orientální* (quarterly), *Nový Orient* (monthly).

DENMARK

Orientalsk Samfund (*Orientalist Association*): Institute of Iranian Studies, Kejsergade 2, 1155 Copenhagen K; f. 1915 to undertake the study and further the understanding of Oriental cultures and civilizations; 50 mems.; Pres. Prof. SØREN EGEROD; Sec. Prof. J. P. ASMUSSEN; publ. *Acta Orientalia* (annually).

EGYPT

Academy of the Arabic Language: 26 Sharia Taha Hussein, Giza; f. 1932; Pres. Dr. IBRAHIM MADKOUR; Sec. Dr. MAHDI ALLAM; publs. *Review* (twice yearly), books on reviving Arabic heritage, lexicons and directories of scientific and technical terms.

American Research Center in Egypt Inc.: 2 Midan Kasr el Doubara, Cairo, and International Affairs Bldg., Columbia Univ., New York, N.Y. 10027; f. 1948 by American universities to promote research by U.S. and Canadian scholars in all phases of Egyptian civilization, including archaeology, art history, humanities and social sciences; grants and fellowships available; 27 institutional mems. and 700 individual mems.; Pres. KLAUS BAER; Vice-Pres. CHARLES E. BUTTERWORTH; Cairo Dir. ROBERT J. WENKE; Exec. Dir. PAUL E. WALKER; publs. *Journal* (annual), *Newsletter* (quarterly).

Deutsches Archäologisches Institut (*German Institute of Archaeology*): 22 Sharia Gezira al Wusta, Zamalek, Cairo; Dir. Prof. Dr. WERNER KAISER.

Institut Dominicain d'Etudes Orientales: Priory of the Dominican Fathers, 1 Sharia Masna al-Tarabish, Abbasiyah, Cairo; f. 1953; Dir. Père G. C. ANAWATI; publ. *Mélanges* (yearly).

Institut d'Egypte: 13 Sharia Sheikh Rihane, Cairo; f. 1798; studies literary, artistic and scientific questions relating to Egypt and neighbouring countries; Pres. Dr. SILEMAN HAZIEN; Sec. Gen. P. GHALIOUNGU; publs. *Bulletin* (annual), *Mémoires* (irregular).

Institut Français d'Archéologie Orientale: 37 rue El-Cheikh Aly Youssef, Mounira, Cairo; f. 1880; excavations, research and publications; library of 60,000 vols.; Dir. Mme PAULE POSENER-KRIEGER; publs. _Bulletin_, _Annales Islamologiques_.

Netherlands Institute for Archaeology and Arabic Studies: 1 Sharia Dr. Mahmoud Azmi, Zamalek, P.O.B. 1271, Cairo; f. 1971; Dir. Dr. R. PETERS; publs. in the field of Arabic Studies.

Société Archéologique d'Alexandrie: 6 Sharia Mahmoud Moukhtar, Alexandria; f. 1893; 150 mems.; Pres. A. M. SADEK; Sec.-Gen. and Editor D. A. DAOUD; Treas. M. F. MANSOUR; publs. _Bulletins_, _Mémoires_, _Monuments de l'Egypte Gréco-Romaine_, _Cahiers_, _Publications Spéciales_, Archaeological and Historical Studies.

Société Egyptienne d'Economie Politique, de Statistique et de Législation: 16 ave Ramses, B.P. 732, Cairo; f. 1909; 1,550 mems.; Pres. Dr. GAMAL EL OTEIFI; Sec.-Gen. Dr. MAHMOUD HAFEZ GHANEM; Tech.-Secs. Dr. FATHI EL MASSAFAWI and Dr. SAKR AHMED SAKR; publ. _Revue_ (quarterly in Arabic, French and English).

Society for Coptic Archaeology: 222 Avenue Ramses, Cairo; f. 1934; 370 mems.; library of 11,500 vols.; Pres. MIRRIT BOUTROS GHALI; Treas. Dr. BOUTROS BOUTROS GHALI; Dir. of Studies Dr. L. S. B. MacCOULL; publs. _Bulletin_ (annual), _Fouilles_, _Bibliothéque d'Art et d'Archéologie_, _Textes et Documents_, etc.

FINLAND

Suomen Itämainen Seura (_Finnish Oriental Society_): Fabianinkatu 24 A, 00100 Helsinki, 10; f. 1917; 150 mems.; Pres. Prof. JUSSI ARO; Sec. Dr. T. HARVIAINEN; publ. _Studia Orientalia_.

FRANCE

Centre d'Etudes de l'Orient Contemporain: 13 rue de Santeuil, 75231 Paris Cedex 05; f. 1943; collaborates with la Documentation française and runs course on contemporary Arab World; Dir. H. MAMMERI.

Centre de Hautes Etudes sur l'Afrique et l'Asie Modernes: 13 rue du Four, 75006 Paris; f. 1936; Dir. G. R. MALECOT; publs. _L'Afrique et L'Asie Modernes_ (quarterly), _Cahiers de l'Afrique et l'Asie_ (irregular), _Langues et dialectes d'Outre-Mer_ (irregular), _Recherches et documents du CHEAM_ (irregular), _Cahiers du CHEAM_ (irregular).

Fondation Nationale des Sciences Politiques: 27 rue Saint-Guillaume, Paris 7e; f. 1945; Administrator M. GENTOT; Centre d'Etudes et de Recherches Internationales, Dir. G. HERMET; Arab World section has research team of 9 mems.; publs. include _Maghreb-Machrek_ (quarterly).

Institut d'Etudes Arabes et Islamiques: Université de la Sorbonne Nouvelle (Paris III), 13 rue de Santeuil, 75231 Paris Cedex 05; Dir. M. ARKOUN.

Institut d'Etudes Iraniennes: Université de la Sorbonne Nouvelle, 13 rue de Santeuil, 75231 Paris Cedex 05; f. 1947; Dir. GILBERT LAZARD; publs. _Travaux_, _Studia Iranica_ (journal), _Abstracta Iranica_ (annual bibliography).

Institut d'Etudes Sémitiques: Institut d'Etudes Sémitiques, 11 place Marcelin-Berthelot, 75231 Paris Cedex 05; f. 1930; Pres. A. DUPONT-SOMMER; publ. _Semitica_.

Institut d'Etudes Turques de l'Université de la Sorbonne Nouvelle—Paris III: 13 rue de Santeuil, 75231 Paris Cedex 05; Dir. LOUIS BAZIN.

Institut du Monde Arabe: 28 _bis_ rue de Bourgogne, 75007 Paris; f. 1980; Pres. PHILIPPE ARDANT; Sec.-Gen. BOUTROS DIB.

Institut National des Langues et Civilisations Orientales: 2 rue de Lille, Paris 7e; attached to Univ. de la Sorbonne Nouvelle Paris III; f. 1795; faculties of languages and civilizations of West Asia and Africa; the Far East, India and Oceania; Eastern Europe; library of 600,000 vols. and 2,000 MSS.; over 8,000 students, 90 teachers, 170 lecturers; Pres. H. DE LA BASTIDE; Sec. Mme J. FIATTE; publs. various Oriental studies.

Institut de Papyrologie: Université de Paris-Sorbonne, 1 rue Victor-Cousin, Paris 5e; Dir. JEAN SCHERER.

Société Asiatique: 3 rue Mazarine, 75006 Paris; f. 1822; 700 mems.; library of 80,000 vols.; Pres. CLAUDE CAHEN; Vice-Pres. J. FILLIOZAT, A. CAQUOT; Secs. L. BAZIN, Y. HERVOUET, M. SOYMIE; publs. _Journal Asiatique_ (quarterly), _Cahiers de la Société Asiatique_.

FEDERAL REPUBLIC OF GERMANY

Altorientalisches Seminar der Freien Universität Berlin: D-1000 Berlin 33, Bitterstr. 8–12; f. 1950.

Arbeitsgemeinschaft Vorderer Orient (AGVO): 2000 Hamburg 13, Mittelweg 150; consists of German research orgs. into politics, science and commerce of the Middle East; 36 mem. insts.; Sec. Dr. UDO STEINBACH.

Deutsche Morgenländische Gesellschaft: 1000 Berlin 30, Postfach 1407; Sec. Dr. DIETER GEORGE; f. 1845; publs. _Zeitschrift_ (semi-annual), _Abhandlungen für die Kunde des Morgenlandes_, _Bibliotheca Islamica_, _Wörterbuch der Klassischen Arabischen Sprache_, _Beiruter Texte und Studien_, _Verzeichnis der orientalischen Handschriften in Deutschland_, etc.

Deutsches Orient-Institut: 2000 Hamburg 13, Mittelweg 150; f. 1960 from the Nah-und Mittelostverein e.V.; since 1965 has been affil. to Deutsches Übersee-Institut; devoted to research in politics, science and commerce of Near and Middle East; Dir. Dr. UDO STEINBACH; publs. _Orient_ (quarterly), _Mitteilungen_ (irregular).

Internationale Gesellschaft fuer Orientforschung: Mertonstrasse 17-25, Frankfurt/Main; f. 1948; 400 mems.; Pres. Prof. R. SELLHEIM; publ. _Oriens_ (annual).

Nah- und Mittelost Verein e.V. (_German Near and Middle East Association_): D2 Hamburg 13, Mittelweg 151; f. 1934; 600 mems.; Chair. HANS-OTTO THIERBACH; Gen. Sec. R.-E. FRHR. v. LÜTTWITZ.

Seminar für Orientalische Sprachen: Adenauerallee 102, 53 Bonn; institute attached to the University of Bonn; Dir. Prof. Dr. J. KREINER; Middle East Dept. Dir. Prof. Dr. T. NAGEL.

INDIA

Asiatic Society of Bombay: Town Hall, Bombay 400 023; f. 1804; 1,498 mems.; to investigate and encourage Sciences, Arts and Literature in relation to Asia; maintains Central Library of the State of Maharashtra; volumes 207–416 up to 31st March 1980; 2,300 MSS. and 5,000 old coins; Pres. SOLI J. SORABJEE; Hon. Sec. Mrs. BANSARI K. SHETH; in 1973 the society established the Dr. P. V. Kane Research Inst. to promote, encourage and facilitate research in Oriental studies; publs. annual _Journal_, reports, critical annotated texts of rare Sanskrit and Pali MSS.

Indian Institute of Islamic Studies: Panchkuin Rd., New Delhi 110001 and Tughlaqabad, New Delhi, 110062; f. 1963; library of 50,000 vols. and 2,400 MSS; Pres. HAKEEM ABDUL HAMEED; Dir. S. A. ALI; publ. _Studies in Islam_ (quarterly), _Islamic and Comparative Law Quarterly_, _Bulletin of Comparative Religion_ (quarterly), _Newsletter_ (quarterly).

Iran League: Navsari Bldg. (2nd floor), Dr. Dadabhoy Navroji Rd., Fort, Bombay 400 001; f. 1922; 300 mems.; Pres. Sir JAMSETJEE JEEJEEBHOY, Bart.; Sec. D. C. LELINWALLA; publs. *The Iran League Quarterly Newsletter* and translations and commentaries in modern Persian of Avesta texts.

IRAN

The Asia Institute: University of Shiraz; Dir. Dr. Y. M NAWABI; publs. *Bulletin, Monographs.*

British Institute of Persian Studies: Kucheh Alvand, Khiaban Dr. Ali Shariati, Gholhak, P.O.B. 2617, Teheran; f. 1961; cultural institute, with emphasis on history and archaeology; 850 individual mems.; Hon. Sec. S. J. WHITWELL, C.M.G., M.C.; publ. *Iran* (annual).

IRAQ

British School of Archaeology in Iraq: 31-34 Gordon Sq., London, WC1H oPY; British Archaeological Expedition to Iraq, Baghdad; Dir. M. D. ROAF.

Deutsches Archäologisches Institut: 71B/11 Hurriya Square, Karrada, Baghdad.

Instituto Hispano-Arabe de Cultura: Al-Maghreb St., P.O.B. 2256, Alwiyya; f. 1958; Dir. JUAN M. CASADO.

Iraq Academy: Waziriyah, Baghdad; f. 1947 to maintain the Arabic language to undertake research into Arabic history, Islamic heritage and the history of Iraq, and to encourage research in the modern arts and sciences; Pres. Dr. SALEH A. AL-ALI; Sec.-Gen. Dr. NOORI H. AL-QISSI; publ. *Bulletin of the Iraq Academy* (bi-annual.)

ISRAEL

Academy of the Hebrew Language: P.O.B. 3449, Jerusalem 91 034; f. 1953; study and development of the Hebrew language and compilation of an historical dictionary; Pres. Prof. Z. BEN-HAYYIM; publs. *Zikhronot, Leshonenu* (quarterly), *Leshonenu La'am*, monographs and dictionaries.

W. F. Albright Institute of Archaeological Research in Jerusalem: 26 Salah ed-Din, P.O.B. 19096, Jerusalem; f. 1900 by American Schools of Oriental Research; research in Syro-Palestinian archaeology, Biblical studies, Near Eastern history and languages; sponsors excavations; Pres. JOSEPH CALLAWAY; Dir. S. GITIN.

The Ben-Zvi Institute: P.O.B. 7504, Jerusalem; f. 1948; sponsors research in the history and culture of Jewish communities in the East; library of MSS. and printed books; Chair. Prof. AMNON COHEN; publ. *Sefunot* (annual), *Pe'amin* (quarterly), monographs and reports.

British School of Archaeology in Jerusalem: P.O.B. 19283, Jerusalem; f. 1920; archaeological research and excavation; hostel and library; Chair. Rev. Prof. P. R. ACKROYD, M.A., M.TH., PH.D., D.D.; Dir. Canon J. WILKINSON, M.A., S.T.D., F.S.A.; publ. *Levant.*

Couvent Saint Etienne des Pères Dominicains, Ecole Biblique et Archéologique Française: P.O.B. 19053, Jerusalem; f. 1890; research, Biblical and Oriental studies, exploration and excavation in Palestine; Dir. FRANÇOIS REFOULÉ, O.P.; library of 60,000 vols.; publs. *Revue Biblique, Etudes Bibliques, Etudes Palestiniennes et Orientales, Cahiers de la Revue Biblique, Bible de Jérusalem.*

Historical Society of Israel: P.O.B. 4179, Jerusalem; f. 1925 to promote the study of Jewish history and general history; 1,000 mems.; Pres. Prof. M. STERN; publ. *Zion* (quarterly).

Institute of Asian and African Studies: Hebrew University of Jerusalem, Jerusalem; f. 1926; studies of medieval and modern languages, culture and history of Middle East, Asia and Africa; Chair. Prof. SHAUL SHAKED; publs. *Max Schloessinger Memorial Series, Jerusalem Studies in Arabic and Islam*, Translation series.

Institute of Holy Land Studies: P.O.B. 1276 Mt. Zion, Jerusalem 901012; f. 1959; Christian study centre, grad. and undergrad.; Pres. Dr. GEORGE GIACUMAKIS.

Israel Exploration Society: 3 Shemuel ha-Nagid St., P.O.B. 7041, Jerusalem 91070; f. 1913; excavations and historical research, congresses and lectures; 4,000 mems.; Chair. Prof. A. BIRAN; Hon. Pres. Prof. B. MAZAR; Hon. Sec. J AVIRAM; publs. *Eretz Yisrael* (Hebrew annual, with English summaries), *Qadmoniot* (Hebrew quarterly), *Israel Exploration Journal* (English quarterly), various books on archaeology (in Hebrew and English).

Israel Oriental Society: The Hebrew University, Jerusalem; f. 1949; lectures and symposia to study all aspects of contemporary Middle Eastern, Asian and African affairs; Pres. ABBA EBAN; publs. *Hamizvah Hehadash* (Hebrew quarterly), *Oriental Notes and Studies* (1951–71), *Asian and African Studies* (three a year).

Orientalisches Institut der Görres-Gesellschaft: Schmidt-Schule, P.O.B. 19424, Jerusalem; historical and archaeological studies.

Pontifical Biblical Institute: 3 Paul Emile Botta St., P.O.B. 497, Jerusalem 91004; f. 1927; study of Biblical languages and Biblical archaeology, history, topography; in conjunction with Hebrew University of Jerusalem; seminar for post-graduate students, student tours; Dir. Rev. WILLIAM DALTON, S.J.

Shiloah Center for Middle Eastern and African Studies: Tel-Aviv University, Ramat Aviv, P.O.B. 39012; f. 1959; Head Prof. ITAMAR RABINOVICH; Dir. ELIE REKHISS; publs. *Middle East Record* (annual), *Middle East Contemporary Survey* (annual), also monographs studies and occasional papers.

The Harry S. Truman Research Institute for the Advancement of Peace: The Hebrew University of Jerusalem, Mount Scopus, Jerusalem 91905; f. 1966; conducts and sponsors social science and historical research, organizes conferences and publishes works on the Middle East, Asia and Africa; Academic Dir. Prof. HAROLD Z. SCHIFFRIN; Exec. Dir. Dr. YITZHAK SHICHOR.

Wilfrid Israel House for Oriental Art and Studies: Kibbutz Hazorea, Post Hazorea 30060; f. 1947; opened 1951 in memory of late Wilfrid Israel; a cultural centre for reference, study and art exhbns.; houses Wilfrid Israel collection of Near and Far Eastern art and cultural materials; local archaeological exhibits from neolithic to Byzantine times; science and art library; Dir. Dr. M. MERON; Sec. and Curator for Far and Middle Eastern Art Dr. U. R. BAER; Curator for Archaeology E. MEIRHOF.

ITALY

Istituto di Studi del Vicino Oriente: Università degli Studi, Citta Universitarià, Rome; Dir. Prof. M. LIVERANI.

Istituto Italiano per il Medio ed Estremo Oriente (ISMEO): Palazzo Brancaccio, via Merulana 248, Rome; f. 1933; Pres. Prof. GHERHADO GNOLI; publs. *East and West* (quarterly), *Rome Oriental Series, Nuovo Ramusio*, Archaeological Reports and Memoirs.

Istituto Italo-Africano: via Ulisse Aldrovandi 16, Rome; Pres. Prof. TULLIA CARETTONI; Sec.-Gen. Amb. Dott. LUIGI GASBARRI.

Istituto per le relazione tra l'Italia e i paesi dell'Africa, America Latina e Medio Oriente: Via del Tritone 62B, Rome; f. 1971; publ. *Politica Internazionale* (monthly Italian edition, twice yearly English edition).

JAPAN

Ajia Keizai Kenkyusho (*Institute of Developing Economies*):
42 Ichigaya-Hommura-cho, Shinjuku-ku, Tokyo 162;
f. 1958; 269 mems.; Chair. MIYOHEI SHINOHARA; Pres.
HISATOSHI MORISAKI; library of 190,000 vols.; publs.
Ajia Keizai (Japanese, monthly), *The Developing
Economies* (English, quarterly), occasional papers in
English.

Chuto Chosakai (*Middle East Institute of Japan*): 15 Mori
Bldg., 8-10 Toranomon 2-chome, Minato-ku, Tokyo;
f. 1956; Chair. YOSHIHIRO NAKAYAMA; publs. *Chuto
Tsuho* (Middle East News—bi-monthly), *Chuto Nenkan*
(Yearbook of Middle East and North Africa), *Chuto
Seiji Keizai News* (Political and Economic News of the
Middle East) (twice a month).

Nippon Orient Gakka i (*Society for Near Eastern Studies in
Japan*): Tokyo Tenrikyokan. 9, 1-chome, Kanda
Nishiki-cho, Chiyoda-ku, Tokyo 101; f. 1954; 715
mems.; Pres. Dr. ATSUUJI ASHIKAGA; publs. *Oriento*
(Japanese, twice-yearly), *Orient* (European languages
annual).

LEBANON

**Centre d'Etudes et de Recherches sur le Moyen-Orient
Contemporain (CERMOC):** Rue de Damas, B.P. 2691,
Beirut; f. 1977; 12 research fellows; university research and documentation institution; library specializes in human and social sciences concerning the
Middle East; Dir. ANDRÉ BOURGEY.; publs. 10 books
on contemporary Middle East.

Centre de Documentation Economique sur le Proche-Orient:
Faculté de Sciences Economiques et de gestion des
entreprises, Université Saint-Joseph, B.P. 293, Beirut,
f. 1971; selection and analysis of documents and publs.
on the economy of Middle East Arab countries and oil
economy; Dir. Miss KATIA SALAMEH.

**Centre for Economic, Financial and Social Research and
Documentation SAL:** Gefinor Centre, Bloc B 500–502
Clemenceau St., P.O.B. 11-6668, Beirut; f. 1958; Chair.
Dr. CHAFIC AKHRAS; Dir.-Gen. Dr. SABBAH AL HAJ.

Institut de Recherches d'Economie Appliquée: Faculté de
Sciences Economiques et de gestion des entreprises,
Université Saint Joseph, B.P. 293, Beirut; f. 1963;
economic studies of the Lebanon and other countries of
the Middle East; Dir. Prof. ALEXANDRE CHAIBAN;
publ. *Proche-Orient, études économiques* (quarterly).

Institut Français d'Archéologie du Proche Orient: rue du
Proche-Orient, B.P. 11-1424, Beirut; f. 1946; library of
26,000 vols. (Bibliothèque Henri Seyrig); Dir. ERNEST
WILL; publs. *Syria, Revue d'Art et d'Archéologie* (annual),
Bibliothèque Archéologique et Historique.

P.L.O. Research Centre: P.O.B. 1691, Beirut; f. 1965;
studies Palestine problem; publs. irregular monographs,
books, essays, a monthly and a chronology in Arabic
(occasional works in English).

THE NETHERLANDS

Assyriologisch Instituut der Rijksuniversiteit: Rijksuniversiteit Leiden, Noordeindsplein 4A, 2311 AH Leiden;
Dir. K. R. VEENHOF.

Netherlands Institute for the Middle East (*Midden Oosten
Instituut*): Kettingstraat 2, P.O.B. 10, The Hague;
f. 1949; publ. *Bulletin* (Press Digest, for members only).

Netherlands Institute for the Near East (*Nederlands
Instituut voor het Nabije Oosten*): Noordeindsplein
4A-6A, Leiden; Dir. Dr. E. VAN DONZEL; library of
25,000 vols. and 300 periodicals; Publs. *Bibliographia
Antiqua, Anatolica, Studia Francisci Scholten Memoriae*

*dicata, Scholae de Buck, Publications de l'Institut
historique et archéologique néerlandais de Stamboul,
Bibliotheca Orientalis, Tabulae de Liagre Böhl, Studia
de Laigre Böhl.*

PAKISTAN

Institute of Islamic Culture: Club Rd., Lahore; f. 1950;
Dir. Prof. M. SAEED SHEIKH; Hon. Publication Adviser
and Sec. M. ASHRAF DARR; publs. *Al-Ma'arif* (monthly),
about 200 publications on Islamic subjects in English
and Urdu.

Islamic Research Institute: P.O.B. 1035, Islamabad; f.
1960; Dir. Dr. A. J. HALEPOTA.

R.C.D. Cultural Institute: 366, F6/1, St. 44, Islamabad;
Dir. Prof. S. Q. FATIMI.

POLAND

Polskie Towarzystwo Orientalistyczne (*Polish Oriental
Society*): ul. Sniadeckich 8, IV piętro, p. 15, 00-656
Warsaw; f. 1922; 300 mems.; Pres. STANISŁAW KAŁUŻ-
YŃSKI, MIKOŁAJ MELANOWICZ, ALEKSANDER DUBIŃSKI,
WŁODZIMIERZ ZAJĄCZKOWSKI; Sec. LESZEK CYRZYK;
publ. *Przegląd Orientalistyczny* (quarterly).

Zakład Archeologii Śródziemnomorskiej (*Research Centre
for Mediterranean Archaeology*): Palac Kultury i
Nauki, Room 1909, Warsaw; f. 1956; research in-
stitute of Academy of Sciences; documentation and
publication of Polish excavations in the Middle East
and antiquities in Polish museums; Assistant Profs.
Dr. KAROL MYŚLIWIEC, Dr. ZSOLT KISS; publs.
*Travaux du Centre d'Archéologie Méditerranéenne,
Palmyre, Faras, Etudes et Travaux, Deir el Bahari, Nea
Paphos, Alexandrie, Corpus Vasorum Antiquorum,
Corpus Signorum Imperii Romani.*

PORTUGAL

Instituto David Lopes de Língua Arabe e Cultura Islâmica:
Faculdade de Letras, Cidade Universitária, 1600
Lisbon; f. 1968; library; 2 teachers; specializes in
Arabic and Islamic studies.

SPAIN

Asociación Española de Orientalistas: Juan XXIII 5,
Madrid 3; f. 1965; publs. *Boletín* (annual), etc.

Egyptian Institute of Islamic Studies: Francisco de Asis
Méndez Casariego 1, Madrid 2; affiliated to Ministry
of Higher Education, Cairo; f. 1950; Dir. Dr. SALAH
FADL; publs. *Magazine of the Egyptian Institute* and
other educational books.

**Instituto "Benito Arias Montano" de Estudios Hebraicos
Sefardies y Oriente Próximo** (*Institute of Hebrew,
Sephardic and Near East Studies*): Duque de Medinaceli
4, Madrid 14; f. 1940; branch in Barcelona; 18 mems.
Dir. JOSÉ LUIS LACAVE RIAÑO; Sec. PILAR ARANGÜENA
PERNAS; publ. *Sefarad* (quarterly) and books.

SWEDEN

Nordiska Afrikainstitutet (*Scandinavian Institute of African
Studies*): P.O.B. 2126, S-75002, Uppsala; research and
documentation centre, organizes seminars and publishes wide range of books and pamphlets, also news-
letters in Swedish and English; library of 26,000 vols.;
Dir. Dr. M. STAHL; publs. *Annual Seminar Proceedings,
Research Reports, Africana, Newsletter.*

SWITZERLAND

Centre d'Etude du Proche-Orient Ancien: Université de
Genève, 3 place de l'Universitaire, 1211 Geneva 4;
Dir. YVES CHRISTE.

Schweizerische Gesellschaft für Asienkunde: Ostasiatisches Seminar der Universität Zürich, Mühlegasse 21, 8001 Zurich; publ. *Asiatische Studien / Etudes Asiatiques* (bi-annual), *Schweizer Asiatische Studien* (Monographien und Studienhefte).

SYRIA

Institut Français d'Etudes Arabes: B.P. 344. Damascus; f. 1922; library of 40,000 vols., 354 periodicals; Dir. GEORGES BOHAS; Scient. Sec. JEAN-PAUL PASCUAL; 18 scholars; publs. *Bulletin d'Etudes Orientales* (annually, 30 vols. published), monographs, translations and Arabic texts (105 vols. published).

Near East Foundation: B.P. 427, Damascus.

TUNISIA

Institut des Belles Lettres Arabes: 12 rue Jamâa el Haoua, 1008 Tunis BM; f. 1930; cultural centre; Dir. J. FONTAINE; publs. *IBLA* (twice yearly) and special studies.

TURKEY

British Institute of Archaeology at Ankara: Tahran Caddesi 24, Kavaklidere, Ankara; f. 1948; archaeological research and excavation; Dir. D. H. FRENCH; publs. *Anatolian Studies* (annual), *Occasional Publications*.

Centri di Studi Italiani in Turchia: Dr. Mediha Eldem Sokak 68, Yenişehir, Ankara; Dir. Prof. GIUSEPPE MANICA; Mesrutiyet Caddesi 161, Istanbul; Dir. Prof. ADELIA RISPOLI; Ataturk Caddesi, 280, Izmir; Comm. NICOLA DELPINO.

Deutsches Archäologisches Institut: Sira Selvi 123, Taksim, Istanbul; Dir. Prof. Dr.-Ing. W. MÜLLER-WIENER; publs. *Istanbuler Mitteilungen* (annual), *Istanbuler Forschungen, Beihefte zu Istanbuler Mitteilungen*.

Institut Français d'Etudes Anatoliennes: Palais de France, Beyoğlu, P.K. 280, Istanbul; f. 1930; library of *c.* 6,000 vols.; Dir. GEORGES LE RIDER.

Netherlands Historical and Archaeological Institute: Istiklâl Caddesi 393, Beyoğlu, Istanbul; f. 1958; library of 12,000 vols.; Dir. Dr. J. J. ROODENBERG; publs. *Publications de l'Institut Historique et Archéologique Néerlandais de Stamboul, Anatolica*.

Österreichisches Kulturinstitut Istanbul: Belvedere Apt. 101/2, Tesvikiye, P.K. 6, Istanbul; Dir. Prof. Dr. J. E. KASPER.

Regional Cultural Institute: University of Istanbul, Faculty of Letters; Dir. Prof. SENCER TONGUÇ.

Turk Dil Kurumu (*Turkish Linguistic Society*): 217 Atatürk Bulevar, Ankara; f. 1932; 539 mems.; library of 25,000 vols.; Pres. Prof. Dr. SERAFETTIN TURAN; Sec.-Gen. CAHIT KULEBI; publs. *Türk Dili* (monthly), *Türk Dili Arastirmalari-Belletin* (annual).

Türk Kültürünü Araştırma Enstitüsü (*Institute for the Study of Turkish Culture*): P.K. 14, Çankaya, Ankara; f. 1961; scholarly research into all aspects of Turkish culture; Dir. Prof. Dr. AHMET TEMİR; publs. *Türk Kültürü* (monthly), *Cultura Turcica* (semi-annual), *Türk Kültürü Araştırmaları* (semi-annual).

Turk Tarih Kurumu (*Turkish Historical Society*): Kizilay Sok. 1, Ankara; f. 1931; 41 mems.; library of 150,000 vols.; Pres. Ord. Prof. ENVER ZIYA KARAL; Gen. Dir. ULUĞ İĞDEMİR; publs. *Belleten* (quarterly), *Belgeler* (twice a year).

Türkiyat Enstitüsü (*Institute of Turcology*): University of Istanbul, Bayezit, Istanbul; f. 1924; research into Turkish language, literature, history and culture; library of 20,000 vols.; Dir. Dr. M. CAVID BAYSUN.

U.S.S.R.

Institute of Oriental Studies, U.S.S.R. Academy of Sciences: Armyansky per. 2, Moscow; attached to Dept. of History.

Institute of Oriental Studies of the Academy of Sciences of the Armenian S.S.R.: Ul. Abovyana 15, Yerevan 1, Armenian S.S.R.; Dir. G. K. SARKISYAN.

Institute of Oriental Studies of the Academy of Sciences of the Georgian S.S.R.: Ul. Tskhakaya 10, Tbilisi, Georgian S.S.R.; Dir. G. V. TSERETELI.

Institute of Peoples of the Near and Middle East of the Academy of the Azerbaijan S.S.R.: Prospekt Narimanova 31, Baku, Azerbaijan S.S.R.; f. 1958; Dir. Z. M. BUNIYATOR.

Section of Oriental Studies and Calligraphy of the Academy of Sciences of the Tadzhik S.S.R.: Ul. Parvin 8, Dushanbe, Tadzhik S.S.R.: Dir. A. M. MIRZOEV.

UNITED KINGDOM

Anglo-Arab Association, The: 21 Collingham Rd., London, SW5 0NU; non-political; Chair. Sir RICHARD BEAUMONT, K.C.M.G., O.B.E.; Exec. Dir. D. R. COLLARD, O.B.E.

Arab Research Centre: 4th Floor, 1-2 Hanover St., London, W1R 9WB; f. 1969; research into problems and issues concerning the Arab world; library of 1,000 vols.; commissions writing of special papers; holds international symposia (one or two a year); Chair. ABDEL MAJID FARID; Man. ALIA ARNALL; publ. *Arab Paper* (10 a year).

Centre for Arab Gulf Studies: University of Exeter, Thornlea, New North Road, Exeter, EX4 4JZ; Dir. Dr. M. A. SHABAN.

Centre for Middle Eastern and Islamic Studies: University of Durham, South End House, South Rd., Durham City, DH1 3TG; f. 1962; encourages, develops and co-ordinates activities in a number of university depts. in field of Middle Eastern and Islamic studies; organizes seminars, lectures and conferences; Documentation unit f. 1970 to monitor economic, social and political devts. in the region; Dir. J. D. NORTON.

Council for the Advancement of Arab-British Understanding (CAABU): The Arab-British Centre, 21 Collingham Rd., London, SW5 0NU; f. 1967.

Egypt Exploration Society: 3 Doughty Mews, London, WC1N 2PG; f. 1882; library of 4,500 vols.; Sec. SHIRLEY K. STRONG; publs. *Excavation Memoirs, Archaeological Survey, Graeco-Roman Memoirs, Journal of Egyptian Archaeology, Texts from Excavations*, etc.

Islamic Cultural Centre (and London Central Mosque): 146 Park Rd., London, N.W.8; f. 1944 to spread Islamic culture in Great Britain; library of 10,000 vols., mostly Arabic; Dr. M. A. ZAKI BADAWI; publ. *Islamic Quarterly*.

Maghreb Studies Association: c/o The Secretary, Mr. Keith Sutton, Department of Geography, University of Manchester, Oxford Rd., Manchester, M13 9PL; f. 1981; independent; to promote the study of and interest in the Maghreb; organizes lectures, and conferences; issues occasional publications and co-operates with the periodical *The Maghreb Review* (q.v.); Chair. Prof. ERNEST GELLNER.

Middle East Association: Bury House, 33 Bury St., London, SW1Y 6AX; f. 1961; an asscn. for firms actively promoting U.K. trade with 21 Arab countries, plus Afghanistan, Ethiopia, Iran and Turkey; 450 mems.; Dir.-Gen. E. F. GIVEN, C.M.G., C.V.O.; Sec. C. W. NORTH, M.B.E.

Middle East Centre: Faculty of Oriental Studies, Sidgwick Ave., Cambridge CB3 9DA; Dir. Prof. R. B. SERJEANT, PH.D.; Sec. R. L. BIDWELL, PH.D.; publ. *Arabian Studies* (annual).

Middle East Centre: St. Antony's College, 68 Woodstock Rd., Oxford, OX2 6JF; f. 1958; Dir. Dr. MUSTAFA M. BADAWI; library of 29,000 vols. and archive of private papers and photographs; publs. St. Antony's Middle East monographs.

Muslim Institute for Research and Planning: 6 Endsleigh St., London, WC1H 0DS; f. 1974; research programmes, academic and current affairs seminars; library of 6,000 vols.; 450 mems.; Dir. Dr. KALIM SIDDIQUI.

Palestine Exploration Fund: 2 Hinde Mews, London, W.1. f. 1865; 900 subscribers; Pres. The Archbishop of Canterbury; Sec. Mrs. G. WEBSTER, M.A.; publ; *Palestine Exploration Quarterly.*

Royal Asiatic Society of Great Britain and Ireland: 56 Queen Anne St., London, W1M 9LA; f. 1823 for the study of the history, sociology, institutions, customs, languages and art of Asia; approx. 900 mems.; approx. 700 subscribing libraries; library of 100,000 vols. and 1,500 MSS; branches in various Asian cities; Pres. Prof. Sir CYRIL PHILIPS; Sec. Miss E. V. GIBSON; publs. *Journal* and monographs.

Royal Society for Asian Affairs: 42 Devonshire St., London, W.1; f. 1901; 1,400 mems. with past or present knowledge of the Middle East, Central Asia or the Far East; library of about 5,000 vols.; Pres. Lord GREENHILL of HARROW, G.C.M.G., O.B.E.; Chair. Sir ARTHUR DE LA MARE, K.C.M.G., K.C.V.O.; Sec. Miss M. FITZSIMONS; publ. *Journal* (3 times a year).

School of African and Asian Studies: University of Sussex, Falmer, Brighton, Sussex BN1 9QN; Dean PRAMIT CHAUDHURI, B.A., M.SC. (CANTAB).

School of Oriental and African Studies, University of London: Malet St., London, WC1E 7HP; f. 1916; library of over 480,000 vols. and 2,600 MSS.; Dir. Prof. C. D. COWAN.

UNITED STATES OF AMERICA

America-Mideast Educational & Training Services, Inc. (AMIDEAST): 1717 Massachusetts Ave., N.W., Washington, D.C. 20036; f. 1951; a private, non-profit organization for furthering communication and understanding between the peoples of the Middle East and N. Africa and the people of the U.S.A. through educational and international programmes; offices in Washington, D.C. and Egypt, Jordan, Lebanon, Morocco, Tunisia, Yemen, West Bank/Gaza and Syria; Pres. ORIN D. PARKER; publ. *Human Resource Developments* (quarterly).

American Oriental Society: 329 Sterling Memorial Library, Yale Station, New Haven, Conn. 06520; f. 1842; 1,650 mems.; library of 19,560 vols.; Pres. RICHARD MATHER; Sec. STANLEY INSLER; publs. *Journal* (quarterly), monograph series, essay series and offprint series.

American Schools of Oriental Research: 4243 Spruce St., Philadelphia, Pa. 19104; f. 1900; approx. 2,000 mems.; support activities of independent archaeological institutions abroad: The Albright Institute of Archaeological Research, Jerusalem, Israel, the American Center of Oriental Research in Amman, Jordan, and the Cyprus American Archaeological Research Institute in Nicosia, Cyprus; Pres. JAMES A. SAUER; publs. *Biblical Archaeologist* (quarterly), *Bulletin* (quarterly), *Journal of Cuneiform Studies* (quarterly), *Annual.*

Centre for Contemporary Arab Studies: Georgetown University, Washington, D.C.; f. 1975; Chair. Dr. JOHN RUEDY; Dir. Dr. MICHAEL C. HUDSON; publs. on social economic, political, cultural and development aspects of Arab World.

Center for Middle Eastern Studies: University of Chicago, 5848 S. University Ave., Chicago, Ill. 60637; f. 1966; research into medieval and modern cultures of the Middle East from Morocco to Pakistan; Dir. RICHARD L. CHAMBERS.

Center for Middle Eastern Studies: Harvard University, 1737 Cambridge St., Cambridge, Mass. 02138; research on Middle Eastern subjects, primarily modern.

Center for Middle Eastern Studies: The University of Texas at Austin, Tex. 78712; f. 1960; linguistic and social studies of Middle East languages and cultures; Dir. Dr. M. A. JAZAYERY; publs. two monograph series on 19th and 20th century Middle East.

Center for Near East and North African Studies: University of Michigan, 144 Lane Hall, Ann Arbor, Mich. 48109; f. 1961; research into the ancient, medieval and modern cultures of the Near East and North Africa, Near Eastern languages and literature; library of over 160,000 vols.; Dir. Dr. ERNEST T. ABDEL-MASSIH.

Gustave E. von Grunebaum Center for Near Eastern Studies: University of California, Los Angeles, 405 Hilgard Ave., Los Angeles, Calif. 90024; f. 1957; social sciences, culture and language studies of the Near East since the rise of Islam; a growing programme of Ancient Near Eastern Studies; library of over 100,000 vols. and outstanding MSS. collection in Arabic, Armenian, Hebrew, Persian and Turkish; Dir. SPEROS VRYONIS, Jr.

Hairenik Association, Inc.: 212 Stuart St., Boston, Mass. 02216; f. 1899; Man. Editor Dr. KEVORK DONOYAN; publs. *Armenian Review, The Armenian Weekly, Hairenik Daily;* circ. 8,000.

Hoover Institution on War, Revolution and Peace: Stanford University, Stanford, Calif. 94305; f. 1919; contains important collection of materials on Middle East and North Africa; Dir. W. G. CAMPBELL; publs. about twenty books each year, plus six-volume survey of the Institution's library.

The Iran Foundation, Inc.: Empire State Bldg., New York, N.Y. 10001; project assistance relating to the advancement of health and education in Iran and other culturally related areas.

Institute for Mediterranean Affairs: 428 East 83 St., New York, N.Y. 10028; established under charter of the University of the State of New York to evolve a better understanding of the historical background and contemporary political and socio-economic problems of the nations and regions that border on the Mediterranean Sea, with special reference to the Middle East and North Africa; 350 mems.; Pres. Ambassador SEYMOUR M. FINGER; Chair. Prof. N. S. FATEMI; Vice-Chair. Prof. A. P. LERNER; Dir. SAMUEL MERLIN.

Israel Institute: Yeshiva University, Amsterdam Ave. and 185th St., New York, N.Y. 10033; f. 1954; research into modern Israel and her cultural and political problems, Jewish history and culture; publs. *Sura, Talpioth.*

Joint Committee on the Near and Middle East: c/o Social Science Research Council, 605 Third Avenue, New York, N.Y. 10016; the Committee is co-sponsored by the American Council of Learned Societies and administers for U.S. and Canadian citizens, a programme of grants for research by individual scholars in the social sciences and humanities, a programme of dissertation research fellowships as well as research conferences and seminars.

Middle East Center: University of Utah, Salt Lake City, Utah 84112; f. 1960; co-ordinates programme in Middle East languages and area studies in 12 academic departments; B.A., M.A. and Ph.D. in Middle East Studies with area of concentration in Arabic, Hebrew, Persian, Turkish, anthropology, history and political science; annual summer programme for Utah educators in the Middle East, research and exchange agreements with several universities; research fellowships for pre-doctoral and post-doctoral work in Egypt, Pakistan and several other countries in the region through membership of international study organizations; library of 116,000 vols.; Dir. Dr. KHOSROW MOSTOFI.

Middle East Institute: 1761 N St., N.W., Washington, D.C. 20036; f. 1946; exists to develop and maintain facilities for research, publication and dissemination of information, with a view to developing in the United States a more thorough understanding of the countries of the Middle East; the Institute holds an annual conference on Middle East affairs, an annual seminar on business in the Middle East and a continuing series of language classes, colloquia and lectures; library 15,000 vols.; 1,800 mems.; Pres. Hon. L. DEAN BROWN; Sec. STEVEN R. DORR; Dir. of Publs. Hon. RICHARD B. PARKER; publs. _Middle East Journal_ (quarterly) and occasional books.

Middle East Institute: Columbia University, 1113 International Affairs Bldg., New York, N.Y. 10027; f. 1954; a graduate training programme on the modern Middle East for students seeking professional careers as regional specialists, research into problems of economics, government, law, and international relations of the Middle East countries, and their languages and history; library of more than 150,000 vols. in Middle East vernaculars and equally rich in Western languages including Russian; Dir. Prof. J. C. HUREWITZ; publs. _Publications in Near and Middle East studies_ (completed), _Modern Middle East Series_ (irregular).

Middle East Studies Association of North America: Department of Oriental Studies, University of Arizona, Tucson, Ariz. 85721; f. 1966 to promote high standards of scholarship and instruction in Middle East studies, to facilitate communication among scholars through meetings and publications, and to foster co-operation among persons and organizations concerned with the scholarly study of the Middle East since the rise of Islam; 1,500 mems.; Pres. (1982) I. WILLIAM ZARTMAN; Pres. Elect (1982) RICHARD ANTOUN; Exec.-Sec. MICHAEL BONINE; publs. _International Journal of Middle East Studies_ (quarterly), _Bulletin_ (twice a year), _Newsletter_ (triannually), etc.

Middle East Studies Centre: Portland State Univ., Portland, Ore. 97207; f. 1965; Middle East language and area studies, emphasizing Arabic and Hebrew languages, history, political science, geography, anthropology and sociology; Dir. CHARLES M. WHITE.

Near East Foundation: 29 Broadway, Suite 1125, New York, N.Y. 10006, U.S.A.; f. 1930. Aims: to conduct educational programmes and agricultural projects in order to improve standards of living in underdeveloped areas of Asia and Africa, primarily the Near East; Hon. Chair. CLEVELAND E. DODGE; Vice-Chair. J. B. SUNDERLAND; Pres. JOHN M. SUTTON; Exec. Dir. JAMES C. MOOMAW; publs. _Annual Report_, newspaper (semi-annually).

Near Eastern Languages and Literatures, Department of: Indiana University, Bloomington, Indiana 47405; courses in Arabic and Hebrew languages and literature both modern and classical, history, political science and religions of the area are taught through other Departments; Chair. VICTOR DANNER.

Oriental Institute: 1155 East 58th St., Chicago, Ill. 60637; f. 1919; principally concerned with cultures and languages of the ancient Near East; extensive museum; affiliated to the University of Chicago; Dir. ROBERT McC. ADAMS.

Program in Near Eastern Studies: Princeton University, Jones Hall, Princeton, N.J. 08544; f. 1947; research in all aspects of the modern Near East; library of 300,000 vols.; Dir. L. CARL BROWN; publs. _Princeton Studies on the Near East_ (irregular), _Princeton Near East Papers_ (irregular).

Semitic Museum: Harvard University, 6 Divinity Ave., Cambridge, Mass. 02138; f. 1889; sponsors exploration and research in Western Asia; contains collection of exhibits from ancient Near East, including collection of 19th century photographs; open by appointment; Curator Dr. CARNEY E. S. GAVIN; Dir. F. M. CROSS.

VATICAN CITY

Pontificium Institutum Orientale (_Pontifical Oriental Institute_): 7 Piazza Santa Maria Maggiore, 00185-Rome; f. 1917; library of 150,000 vols.; Rector Rev. PETER-HANS KOLVENBACH, S.J.; Sec. Rev. J. ŘEZÁČ, S.J.; publs. _Orientalia Christiana Periodica, Orientalia Christiana Analecta, Concilium Florentinum_ (_Documenta et Scriptores_), _Anaphorae Syriacae_.